GRANGER'S
INDEX TO POETRY

SUPPLEMENT TO THE FIFTH EDITION

1960–1965

GRANGER'S
INDEX TO POETRY

SUPPLEMENT TO THE FIFTH EDITION

INDEXING ANTHOLOGIES PUBLISHED
FROM JULY 1, 1960 TO DECEMBER 31, 1965

EDITED BY WILLIAM F. BERNHARDT
AND KATHRYN W. SEWNY

 COLUMBIA UNIVERSITY PRESS

MORNINGSIDE HEIGHTS NEW YORK 1967

PREFACE

This Supplement to the Fifth Edition of GRANGER'S INDEX TO POETRY indexes 97 anthologies. One of these—*The Case for Poetry* (CaFP)—is the second edition of a work that was indexed in the 1955 Supplement but was omitted from the Fifth Edition. Another anthology—*The Golden Treasury of the Best Songs and Lyrical Poems in the English Language,* with a fifth book selected by John Press (GTBS-P)—is a new version of Palgrave's original *Golden Treasury . . .* (GTBS). Later editions of other anthologies indexed in the Fifth Edition have not been indexed again in the Supplement in order to avoid unnecessary repetition. Instead, it is planned to incorporate such volumes into the next complete edition of GRANGER'S INDEX.

In addition to the new anthologies indexed here, two volumes—*Ballads and Sea Songs from Nova Scotia* (BSNS) and *Ballads and Songs from Ohio* (BSO)—are reprints of earlier editions that have not previously been indexed in GRANGER'S.

The Supplement follows the arrangement and style of the Fifth Edition with the exception of one change in the SUBJECT INDEX. Inasmuch as the subject of a poem is often the same as its title (for example, as with a poem entitled "Spring"), listings of poems with the same title as the subject have been omitted from the SUBJECT INDEX. In such cases a cross-reference refers the reader to the same word in the TITLE AND FIRST LINE INDEX for additional poems about the subject.

Last, but not least, the editors wish to thank the following persons for their services in compiling the Supplement: Robert Chase, Darlene Finkel, Kenneth Haydock, Sarah Maguire, and Kathy Solomon.

W. F. B.
K. W. S.

November, 1966

CONTENTS

EXPLANATORY NOTES

The TITLE AND FIRST LINE INDEX is the principal index and must be used in connection with both the AUTHOR INDEX and the SUBJECT INDEX.

In the TITLE AND FIRST LINE INDEX initial capitals in the important words of the titles distinguish titles from first lines. Symbols are listed after both titles and first lines. However, more complete information as to translators, acts and scenes, abridgments, and variant titles is given in the title entries.

When the title and first line of a poem are the same, only the title entry has been indexed. When they are so nearly the same as to be adjacent, again only the title has been indexed, with the first line added in quotation marks and in parentheses to the title entry.

In the arrangement of the title entries, indention is important. Single indention indicates a selection from the work named above; double indention with parentheses indicates a variant title.

Because the Mother Goose rhymes are so much better known by first lines than by the artificial and varying titles given to them in various collections, only their first lines have been included in the TITLE AND FIRST LINE INDEX.

In such titles as "Ode," "Poem," "Song," "Sonnet," too frequent to be distinctive, the first line is added to the title given in the anthology (for example, Ode: "How sleep the brave who sink to rest"). The title is then alphabeted by first line under "Ode," "Poem," etc.

Titles and first lines beginning with "O" and "Oh" have been filed, as in previous editions, as if all were spelled "O," and are alphabeted according to the words which follow.

"Mac," "Mc," and "M'" are filed as if all were spelled "Mac."

Arabic and Chinese names in the AUTHOR INDEX are filed as if written in one word (for example, "Ben Hazm" comes after "Benét" and before "Benjamin" and "Li Ho" comes after "Lieberman" and before "Liliencron"). Old-style Japanese names are handled in the same way as Chinese names (that is, as if written in one word), while modern Japanese names are usually inverted in the Western manner for filing purposes. Japanese names in the AUTHOR INDEX are filed in agreement with this practice.

A KEY TO SYMBOLS is provided, with dates and editions added after titles of anthologies.

ABBREVIATIONS

abr.	abridged	*N.T.*	New Testament
ad.	adapted	*O.T.*	Old Testament
add.	additional	*orig.*	original
arr.	arranged	*pant.*	pantomime
at.	attributed	*par.*	paraphrase
Bk.	book	*pr.*	prose
br.	brief	*prol.*	prologue
c.	copyright	*pseud.*	pseudonym
ch.	chapter	Pt.	part
comp.	compiled *or* compiler	*rev.*	revised
comps.	compilers	sc.	scene
cond.	condensed	Sec.	section
diff.	different	*sel.*	selection
Eng.	English	*sels.*	selections
fr.	from	*sl.*	slightly
frag.	fragment	*st.*	stanza
incl.	included *or* including	*sts.*	stanzas
introd.	introduction *or* introductory	*tr.*	translator, translation,
ll.	lines		*or* translated
Mid.	Middle	*trs.*	translators *or* translations
misc.	miscellaneous	*var.*	various
mod.	modernized *or* modern	*vers.*	version *or* versions
	wr.	wrong *or* wrongly		

KEY TO SYMBOLS

ACV   Anthology of Commonwealth Verse, An. *Margaret J. O'Donnell, ed.* (c.1963)   Blackie & Son Limited

AGP   Anthology of German Poetry through the 19th Century; in English Translations with the German Originals. *Alexander Gode and Frederick Ungar, eds.* (c.1964)   Frederick Ungar Publishing Co.

AmLP   American Lyric Poems; from Colonial Times to the Present. *Elder Olson, ed.* (c.1964)   Appleton-Century-Crofts

AmNP   American Negro Poetry. *Arna Bontemps, ed.* (c.1963)   Hill and Wang

AmPC   American Poems; a Contemporary Collection. *Jascha Kessler, ed.* (c.1964)   Southern Illinois University Press

AnML   Anthology of Medieval Lyrics, An. *Angel Flores, ed.* (c.1962)   The Modern Library

AnMoPo   Anthology of Modern Poetry (Hutchinson English Texts). *John Wain, ed.* (c.1963)   Hutchinson & Co., Ltd.

AnSP   Anthology of Spanish Poetry from Garcilaso to García Lorca, An, in English Translation with Spanish Originals. *Angel Flores, ed.* (1961)   Doubleday & Company, Inc.

AP   American Poetry. *Gay Wilson Allen, Walter B. Rideout, and James K. Robinson, eds.* (c.1965)   Harper & Row

BBGG   Beastly Boys and Ghastly Girls. *William Cole, ed.* (c.1964)   The World Publishing Company

BFSS   Ballads and Folk Songs of the Southwest; More than 600 Titles, Melodies, and Texts Collected in Oklahoma. *Ethel Moore and Chauncey O. Moore, comps.* (c.1964)   University of Oklahoma Press

BiCB   Birthday Candles Burning Bright; a Treasury of Birthday Poetry. *Sara Brewton and John E. Brewton, eds.* (c.1960)   The Macmillan Company

BoC   Book of Comfort, A; an Anthology. *Elizabeth Goudge, ed.* (c.1964)   Coward-McCann

BoLP   Book of Love Poems, A. *William Cole, ed.* (c.1965)   The Viking Press

BSNS   Ballads and Sea Songs from Nova Scotia. *W. Roy Mackenzie, comp.* (1963; reprinted in facsimile from the original edition of 1928)   Folklore Associates, Inc.

BSO　　　　Ballads and Songs from Ohio. *Mary O. Eddy, comp.* (1964; reprinted in facsimile from the original edition of 1939) Folklore Associates, Inc.

BuBa　　　　Bundle of Ballads, A. *Ruth Manning-Sanders, comp.* (c.1959) J. B. Lippincott Company

CABA　　　　College Anthology of British and American Verse, The. *A. Kent Hieatt and William Park, eds.* (1964) Allyn and Bacon, Inc.

CABL　　　　Collins Albatross Book of Longer Poems; English and American Poetry from the Fourteenth Century to the Present Day. *Edwin Morgan, ed.* (c.1963) William Collins Sons & Company

CaFP　　　　Case for Poetry, The; a Critical Anthology. *Frederick L. Gwynn, Ralph W. Condee, and Arthur O. Lewis, Jr., eds.* (2d ed., c.1965) Prentice-Hall, Inc.

CBEP　　　　Cassell Book of English Poetry, The. *James Reeves, ed.* (c.1965) Harper & Row

CoFP　　　　Contemporary French Poetry; Fourteen Witnesses of Man's Fate. *Alexander Aspel and Donald Justice, eds.* (c.1965) The University of Michigan Press

CoIP　　　　Contemporary Italian Poetry; an Anthology. *Carlo L. Golino, ed.* (1962) University of California Press

CoPo　　　　Controversy of Poets, A; an Anthology of Contemporary American Poetry. *Paris Leary and Robert Kelly, eds.* (c.1965) Doubleday & Company, Inc.

CTC　　　　Confucius to Cummings; an Anthology of Poetry. *Ezra Pound and Marcella Spann, eds.* (c.1964) New Directions

DaDu　　　　Dawn and Dusk; Poems of Our Time. *Charles Causley, ed.* (1963) Franklin Watts, Inc.

DiPo　　　　Dimensions of Poetry, The; a Critical Anthology. *James E. Miller, Jr., and Bernice Slote, eds.* (c.1962) Dodd, Mead & Company

DTC　　　　Dylan Thomas's Choice; an Anthology of Verse Spoken by Dylan Thomas. *Ralph Maud and Aneirin Talfan Davies, eds.* (c.1963) New Directions

EaLo　　　　Earth Is the Lord's, The; Poems of the Spirit. *Helen Plotz, comp.* (c.1965) Thomas Y. Crowell Company

EiCP　　　　Eighteenth-Century Poetry. *Patricia Meyer Spacks, ed.* (c.1964) Prentice-Hall, Inc.

ELP　　　　English Lyric Poems, 1500–1900. *C. Day Lewis, ed.* (c.1961) Appleton-Century-Crofts, Inc.

EnPE　　　　English Poetry of the Mid and Late Eighteenth Century; an Historical Anthology. *Ricardo Quintana and Alvin Whitley, eds.* (1963) Alfred A. Knopf

EnRePo English Renaissance Poetry; a Collection of Shorter Poems from Skelton to Jonson. *John Williams, ed.* (c.1963) Doubleday & Company, Inc.

ErPo Erotic Poetry; the Lyrics, Ballads, Idyls, and Epics of Love— Classical to Contemporary. *William Cole, ed.* (1963) Random House

EvOK Everybody Ought to Know. *Ogden Nash, ed.* (c.1961) J. B. Lippincott Company

FaBV Family Book of Verse, The. *Lewis Gannett, ed.* (c.1961) Harper & Row

FaPL Famous Poems and the Little-known Stories behind Them. *Ralph L. Woods, ed.* (c.1961) Hawthorn Books, Inc.

FISC Fire and Sleet and Candlelight. *August Derleth, ed.* (1961) Arkham House

FoBA Fourteen British & American Poets. *Rowland L. Collins, ed.* (c.1964) The Macmillan Company

GoJo Golden Journey, The; Poems for Young People. *Louise Bogan and William Jay Smith, comps.* (c.1965) Reilly & Lee

GTBS-P Golden Treasury of the Best Songs & Lyrical Poems in the English Language, The. *Francis Turner Palgrave, comp. With a fifth book selected by John Press.* (c.1964) Oxford University Press

HaSV Harrap Book of Sea Verse, The. *Ronald Hope, ed.* (1960) Published in cooperation with the Seafarers' Education Service by George G. Harrap & Co., Ltd.

ILP Introduction to Literature: Poems. *Lynn Altenbernd and Leslie L. Lewis, eds.* (c.1963) The Macmillan Company

LiPo Lincoln and the Poets. *William W. Betts, Jr., ed.* (c.1965) University of Pittsburgh Press

LOW Lean Out of the Window; an Anthology of Modern Poetry. *Sara Hannum and Gwendolyn E. Reed, comps.* (1965) Atheneum

LV Lyric Verse. *Edwin Rakow, ed.* (c.1962) The Odyssey Press

MeEL⁻ Medieval English Lyrics; a Critical Anthology. *R. T. Davies, ed.* (1964) Northwestern University Press

MeP Meditative Poem, The; an Anthology of Seventeenth-Century Verse. *Louis L. Martz, ed.* (1963) Doubleday & Company, Inc.

MGP Modern German Poetry, 1910–1960; an Anthology with Verse Translations. *Michael Hamburger and Christopher Middleton, eds.* (c.1962) Grove Press, Inc.

MMA Men Who March Away; Poems of the First World War. *I.M. Parsons, ed.* (c.1965) The Viking Press

MoBS Modern Ballads and Story Poems. *Charles Causley, ed.*

(1965)   Franklin Watts, Inc. English edition, published in 1964 by Brockhampton Press Ltd., had title Rising Early

MoLP   Modern Love Poems. *D. J. Klemer, ed.* (c.1961) Doubleday & Company, Inc.

MoRP   Modern Religious Poems; a Contemporary Anthology. *Jacob Trapp, ed.* (c.1964) Harper & Row

MP   Modern Poets, The; an American-British Anthology. *John Malcolm Brinnin and Bill Read, eds.* (c.1963) McGraw-Hill Book Company

NePoEA-2   New Poets of England and America; Second Selection. *Donald Hall and Robert Pack, eds.* (c.1962) The World Publishing Company

NNP   New Negro Poets: U.S.A. *Langston Hughes, ed.* (c.1964) Indiana University Press

OBCV   Oxford Book of Canadian Verse in English and French, The. *A. J. M. Smith, ed.* (1960) Oxford University Press

OBNC   Oxford Book of Nineteenth-Century English Verse, The. *John Hayward, ed.* (c.1964) Oxford University Press

OnMSP   100 More Story Poems. *Elinor Parker, comp.* (c.1960) Thomas Y. Crowell Company

OnP   100 Poems. *A. J. M. Smith, ed.* (c.1965) Charles Scribner's Sons

OPP   Of Poetry and Power; Poems Occasioned by the Presidency and by the Death of John F. Kennedy. *Erwin A. Glikes and Paul Schwaber, eds.* (c.1964) Basic Books, Inc.

Par   Parodies; an Anthology from Chaucer to Beerbohm—and After. *Dwight Macdonald, ed.* (c.1960) The Modern Library

PoAu 1-2   Poetry in Australia. Vols. I-II. Vol. I: From the Ballads to Brennan. *T. Inglis Moore, comp.* Vol. II: Modern Australian Verse. *Douglas Stewart, comp.* (1965) University of California Press

PoCH   Poet's Choice. *Paul Engle and Joseph Langland, eds.* (1962) The Dial Press

PoDB   Poems of Doubt and Belief; an Anthology of Modern Religious Poetry. *Tom F. Driver and Robert Pack, eds.* (c.1964) The Macmillan Company

PoIE   Poetry in English. *Warren Taylor and Donald Hall, eds.* (c.1963) The Macmillan Company

PoLF   Poems That Live Forever. *Hazel Felleman, ed.* (1965) Doubleday & Company, Inc.

PoNC   Poets of North Carolina. *Richard Walser, ed.* (1963) Garrett & Massie, Inc.

PoPl   Poetry for Pleasure; the Hallmark Book of Poetry. (c.1960) Doubleday & Company, Inc.

PoPo   Poems and Poets. *David Aloian, ed.* (c.1965) Webster Division, McGraw-Hill Book Company

PoSa   Poetry Sampler, A. *Donald Hall, ed.* (c.1962) Franklin Watts, Inc.

PoSC   Poems for Seasons and Celebrations. *William Cole, ed.* (c.1961) The World Publishing Company

PP   Poems on Poetry; the Mirror's Garland. *Robert Wallace and James G. Taaffe, eds.* (1965) E. P. Dutton & Co., Inc.

PtTo   Poets of Today; a New American Anthology. *Walter Lowenfels, ed.* (c.1964) International Publishers

RBL   Renaissance and Baroque Lyrics; an Anthology of Translations from the Italian, French, and Spanish. *Harold Martin Priest, ed.* (c.1962) Northwestern University Press

RePo   Reading of Poetry, The. *William D. Sheldon, Nellie Lyons, and Polly Rouault, eds.* (c.1963) Allyn and Bacon, Inc.

RoGo   Roofs of Gold; Poems to Read Aloud. *Padraic Colum, ed.* (c.1964) The Macmillan Company

SD   Sprints and Distances; Sports in Poetry and the Poetry in Sport. *Lillian Morrison, comp.* (c.1965) Thomas Y. Crowell Company

SeCP   Seventeenth Century Poetry; the Schools of Donne and Jonson. *Hugh Kenner, ed.* (c.1964) Holt, Rinehart and Winston, Inc.

SGR   Songs of the Gold Rush, The. *Richard A. Dwyer and Richard E. Lingenfelter, eds.* (1964) University of California Press

SiGo   Singing and the Gold, The; Poems Translated from World Literature. *Elinor Parker, comp.* (c.1962) Thomas Y. Crowell Company

SIV   Stories in Verse. *Max T. Hohn, ed.* (c.1961) The Odyssey Press

SoPo   Sound of Poetry, The. *Mary C. Austin and Queenie B. Mills, eds.* (c.1963) Allyn and Bacon, Inc.

STF   Speaker's Treasury of 400 Quotable Poems, The. *Croft M. Pentz, comp.* (c.1963) Zondervan Publishing House

StP   Studying Poetry; a Critical Anthology of English and American Poems. *Karl Kroeber and John O. Lyons, eds.* (c.1965) Harper & Row

ThGo   Thread of Gold, A; an Anthology of Poetry. *Eleanor Graham, comp.* (c.1964) The Bodley Head

ThLM   This Land Is Mine; an Anthology of American Verse. *Al Hine, ed.* (c.1965) J. B. Lippincott Company

ToPo   Today's Poets; American and British Poetry since the 1930's. *Chad Walsh, ed.* (c.1964) Charles Scribner's Sons

TRV   Treasury of Religious Verse, The. *Donald T. Kauffman, comp.* (c.1962) Fleming H. Revell Company

TwGP   Twenty German Poets; a Bilingual Collection. *Walter Kauf-
        mann, ed.* (c.1962) The Modern Library
UnTE   Uninhibited Treasury of Erotic Poetry, An. *Louis Untermeyer,
        ed.* (1963) The Dial Press
VaPo   Variety of Poetry, The; an Anthology. *Edward A. Bloom,
        Charles H. Philbrick, Elmer M. Blistein, eds.* (c.1964) The
        Odyssey Press
VP   Victorian Poetry; Ten Major Poets. *Robert Bernard Martin,
        ed.* (c.1964) Random House
WaPE   Wayside Poems of the Early Eighteenth Century. *Edmund
        Blunden and Bernard Mellor, eds.* (1964) Hong Kong Uni-
        versity Press (U.S. agent: Oxford University Press)
WePo   Wealth of Poetry, A; Selected for the Young in Heart. *Winifred
        Hindley, ed., with the assistance of John Betjeman.* (c.1963)
        Basil Blackwell
WiR   Wind and the Rain, The; an Anthology of Poems for Young Peo-
        ple. *John Hollander and Harold Bloom, eds.* (c.1961)
        Doubleday & Company, Inc.

TITLE AND FIRST LINE INDEX

A. A violent order is disorder. Connoisseur of Chaos. Wallace Stevens. CABA
A. B. C. of Devotion, An. *Unknown.* MeEL
A celuy que pluys eyme en mounde. To the One I Love Most. *Unknown.* MeEL
A Deux. William Wood. BoLP
A 11. Louis Zukofsky. CoPo
A is for Alex. Line-up for Yesterday. Ogden Nash. SD
A is our army so true and so brave. The Alphabet. *Unknown.* BFSS
A! Mercy, Fortune. *Unknown.* MeEL
A Perigord pres del muralh. Bertrans de Born, *tr. fr. Provençal by* Ezra Pound. CTC
A Terre. Wilfred Owen. MMA
A was once an apple-pie. A Nonsense Alphabet. Edward Lear. SoPo
Aa went te Blaydon Races, 'twas on the ninth o' June. Blaydon Races. *Unknown.* ELP
Abandoned is the house. Murder House. Elizabeth J. Coatsworth. FiSC
Abasis. Christopher Middleton. *Fr.* Herman Moon's Hourbook. NePoEA-2
Abbot of Inisfalen, The. William Allingham. OnMSP
Abbreviated serpent among crystal rocks. The Capture of Larache. Luis de Góngora. AnSP
   Love in Fantastic Triumph. CBEP
Abdolonymus the Sidonian. Jones Very. AP
Abel. Demetrios Capetanakis. GTBS-P
Abenámar. *Unknown, tr. fr. Spanish by* William M. Davis. AnML
Abide with Me. Henry Francis Lyte. FaPL
Abiding. A. B. Simpson. STF
Abnegation. Martial, *tr. fr. Latin by* Thomas Moore. UnTE
Abnormal Is Not Courage, The. Jack Gilbert. PtTo
Aboard a train three thousand miles. The Hand. Irving Feldman. AmPC
Aboriginal Mother's Lament, An. Charles Harpur. ACV
Abou Ben Adhem. Leigh Hunt. FaBV; PoPo; SIV; TRV
   (Abu Ben Adhem.) BoC
About a brutal murder. The Bear River Murder. *Unknown.* BSNS
About suffering they were never wrong. Musée des Beaux Arts. W. H. Auden. CABA; CaFP; DiPo; GTBS; MP; PoIE; PoSa; StP
About the Cool Water. Kenneth Rexroth. ErPo
About the little chambers of my heart. Gone. Mary Elizabeth Coleridge. OBNC
About the Shark, phlegmatical one. The Maldive Shark. Herman Melville. AP; CBEP
About this lady many fruitful trees. The Lady with the Unicorn. Vernon Watkins. MP
About to marry and invest. The Dorking Thigh. William Plomer. WePo
About Two Kings I'll Write Half-a-Poem. Bertran de Born, *tr. fr. Provençal by* James J. Wilhelm. AnML
About you/ For some time. Mixed Emotions. Vernon Ward. PoNC
Above and below the ship, this blue. Becalmed. John Blight. PoAu-2
Above finespun, unruffled sheets. Lovebirds. William Jay Smith. ErPo
Above the beach, the vineyard. The Flower. Robert Penn Warren. PoPl
Above the Dock. T. E. Hulme. GTBS-P; WePo
Above the Fresh Ruffles of the Surf. Hart Crane. Voyages, I. AP; CABA; CABL; HaSV; PoIE
Above the Hills of Time. Thomas Tiplady. TRV
Above the quiet dock in midnight. Above the Dock. T. E. Hulme. GTBS-P; WePo
Above the voiceful windings of a river. At the Grave of Henry Vaughan. Siegfried Sassoon. EaLo; GTBS-P
Above the wary waiting world. Christmas Song. Bliss Carman. PoSC
Abracadabra, and here I am. Lament for the Frontiers of the Empire. Jack Lindeman. PtTo
Abraham. Edwin Muir. MoRP
Abraham Davenport. Whittier. SIV
Abraham Lincoln. Stephen Vincent Benét. LiPo; PoSC
Abraham Lincoln. Bryant. PoPo
   (Death of Lincoln, The.) AP; LiPo

Abraham Lincoln. Edmund Clarence Stedman. LiPo
Abraham Lincoln; an Horatian Ode. Richard Henry Stoddard. LiPo
Abraham Lincoln Walks at Midnight. Vachel Lindsay. AmLP; FaBV; LiPo; MoRP; PoPl; PoPo; RePo; ThLM
Abraham's Knife. George Garrett. PoFl
Abraham's Madness. Bink Noll. ToPo
Absalom and Achitophel, Pt. I. Dryden. CABL
   George Villiers, Duke of Buckingham, *sel.* PoSa
Absence. Matthew Arnold. Switzerland, VI. CBEP; VP
Absence. Guido Gozzano, *tr. fr. Italian by* Carlo L. Golino. CoIP
Absence. Pierre Louÿs, *tr. fr. French by* Horace M. Brown. *Fr.* The Songs of Bilitis. UnTE
Absence. "Gabriela Mistral," *tr. fr. Spanish by* Kate Flores. AnSP
Absence. Shakespeare. *See* Sonnets, LVII.
Absence, hear thou my protestation. Present in Absence. *Unknown.* GTBS-P
Absence, the noble truce. Caelica, XLV. Fulke Greville. EnRePo
Absences. Philip Larkin. PoCh
Absent, The. Edwin Muir. MoRP
Absent from thee I languish still. A Song. Earl of Rochester. ELP
Absolution. Siegried Sassoon. MMA
Absorbed in One Fond Thought That Makes Me Run. Petrarch, *tr. fr. Italian by* Dwight Durling. Sonnets to Laura: To Laura in Life, CXXXVI. AnML
Abt Vogler. Robert Browning. DiPo; VP
Abu Ben Adhem. Leigh Hunt. *See* Abou Ben Adhem.
Abundance. Conrad Ferdinand Meyer, *tr. fr. German by* Helen Sebba. AGP
Academic. Theodore Roethke. StP
Accept this garland and this girl together. Double Gift. *Unknown.* UnTE
Accept, thou shrine of my dead saint. The Exequy. Henry King. CABA; CaFP; SeCP
Acceptance. Robert Frost. MoRP
According to eternal laws. Walter Savage Landor. EiCP
Accountability. Paul Laurence Dunbar. PoLF
Accusation, The. James Wright. AmPC
Achilles and the King. John Logan. AmPC
Achilles' Revenge. Homer, *tr. fr. Greek by* Bryant. *Fr.* The Iliad, XXII. SIV
Achtung. Sappho, *tr. fr. Greek by* Thomas Hardy. CTC
Acis and Galatea, *sels.* John Gay.
   Love in Her Eyes. ELP
   O Ruddier than the Cherry. ELP
Acme and Septimius. Catullus, *tr. fr. Latin by* Abraham Cowley. UnTE
Acquainted with the Night. Robert Frost. AP; DiPo; FoBA; MP; PoIE; PoLF; PoSa
Acrobat. Rachel Field. *Fr.* A Circus Garland. SoPo
Across the ages they come thundering. Say This of Horses. Minnie Hite Moody. PoLF
Across the bristled and sallow fields. The Hawk. Raymond Knister. OBCV
Across the dim frozen fields of night. Night Train. Robert Francis. LOW
Across the empty garden-beds. The Sailing of the *Sword.* William Morris. ILP
Across the fields of yesterday. Sometimes. Thomas S. Jones, Jr. TRV
Across the greening lawn. A Northern Spring. Gene Baro. NePoEA-2
Across the open countryside. The Unsettled Motorcyclist's Vision of His Death. Thom Gunn. NePoEA-2
Across the Sea. William Allingham. HaSV
Across the seas of Wonderland to Mogadore we plodded. Forty Singing Seamen. Alfred Noyes. OnMSP
Across the stony ridges. Ballad of the Drover. Henry Lawson. PoAu-1
Across the Straits. Rosemary Dobson. PoAu-2
Across the tapestry-lands of the Middle Ages. The Witches. Leah Bodine Drake. FiSC
Across the void's indifferent flood. Speculations. O. B. Hardison, Jr. PoNC
Across the years he could recall. The Secret Heart. Robert P. Tristram Coffin. PoSC
Act of Love. Vernon Scannell. ErPo

Act II. Katherine Davis. PoP1
Acteon. Ovid, *tr. fr. Latin by* Arthur Golding. *Fr.* Metamorphoses, III. CTC
Actor, The. James Sexton Layton. PoNC
Actress, The. Dorothy Parker. PoPo
Acts of Youth, The. John Wieners. CoPo
Adam. Philip Booth. MoLP
Adam. Anthony Hecht. CoPo
Adam. Rainer Maria Rilke, *tr. fr. German by* M. D. Herter Norton. MoRP
Adam and Eve, *sels.* Karl Shapiro.
  Recognition of Eve, The. ToPo
  Sickness of Adam, The. AP
Adam Bell, Clym of the Clough, and William of Cloudesley. *Unknown.* BuBa
Adam Birkett took his gun. Birkett's Eagle. Dorothy S. Howard. MoBS
Adam is a pupil of mine. Athlete. Don Maynard. PoAu-2
Adam Lay Ibounden [*or* I-bowndyn *or* Y-bounden *or* Yboundin]. *Unknown.* CBEP; CTC; ILP; PoIE; ThGo
  (Adam Lay in Bondage.) MeEL
"Adam, my child, my son." Adam. Anthony Hecht. CoPo
Adam on His Way Home. Robert Pack. ErPo; PoDB
Adam—the First Kiss. Hal Porter. ACV
Adam to Lilith. Christopher Brennan. *Fr.* Lilith. PoAu-1
Adam's Curse. W. B. Yeats. DiPo; PP
Adam's first wife had soft lips but no soul. Lilith. X. J. Kennedy. UnTE
Adam's Footprint. Vassar Miller. ToPo
Adam's Offering. Friedrich Hebbel, *tr. fr. German by* Lyn Goetze Snyder. AGP
Addict. Mabel MacDonald Carver. FiSC
Address to a Mummy, *sl. abr.* Horace Smith. RoGo
Address to My Infant Daughter. Wordsworth. EvOK; Par
Address to My Soul. Elinor Wylie. AmLP; MoRP
Address to the Deil. Burns. EiCP; enPE
Address to the Soul Occasioned by a Rain, An. Edward Taylor. AP
Address to the Unco Guid, or the Rigidly Righteous. Burns. EnPE
Addressed to Haydon. Keats. CBEP; OBNC
Adepts, The. Lawrence Durrell. ErPo
Adieu, adieu! my native shore. Childe Harold's Farewell to England. Byron. *Fr.* Childe Harold's Pilgrimage. PoP1
Adieu, Farewell, Earth's Bliss. Thomas Nashe. *Fr.* Summer's Last Will and Testament. CaFP; ELP; PoIE; PoSa
  (In Time of Pestilence 1593.) CBEP; DTC
  (In Time of Plague.) EnRePo
  (Litany in Time of Plague, A.) CABA
  (Song.) DiPo; StP
Adieu, me lovely Nancy. Fragments of Irish Songs. *Unknown.* BSO
Adieu the woods and waters' side. Lines on Leaving a Scene in Bavaria. Thomas Campbell. OBNC
Adieu to the graves where my fathers now rest! The Wyandotte's Farewell Song. *Unknown.* BSO
Adjuration. Frank Belknap Long. FiSC
Adjuration. Charles Enoch Wheeler. AmNP
Adlestrop. Edward Thomas. GoJo
Admiral Benbow. *Unknown.* CBEP
Admiral Kelly gave orders on the first of May. Kelly the Pirate (B *vers.*). *Unknown.* BSNS
Admission. Henry Vaughan. MeP
Admonition for Spring. L. A. MacKay. OBCV
Admonition to a Traveller. Wordsworth. GTBS-P
Adolescence. P. K. Page. OBCV
Adolescent. "Vincenzo Cardarelli," *tr. fr. Italian by* Cosimo Corsano. CoIP
Adolphus Elfinstone. Gelett Burgess. BBGG
Adon 'Olam. *Unknown, tr. fr. Hebrew by* F. De Sola Mendes. EaLo
Adonais. Shelley. CABA; FaPL; PoIE, *much abr.;* StP
  Sels.
  Elegy on the Death of John Keats, An. OBNC
  "He has outsoared the shadow of our night." BoC; PoSa
Adone, L', *sel.* Giambattista Marino, *tr. fr. Italian by* Philip Ayres.
  Proem, The. To Love. RBL
Adonis. Hilda Doolittle ("H. D."). AP; PoP1
Adoration. Mme Guyon. *See* By Thy Life I Live
Adriatic. Robert Conquest. PP
Adulescentia, *sel.* Robert Fitzgerald.
  "Miraculously, through prayer to Saint Anthony." SD
Adult Lullaby, An. *Unknown.* MeEL
Adulterers and customers of whores. Womanisers. John Press. ErPo
Advantages of Learning, The. Martial, *tr. fr. Latin by* Kenneth Rexroth. ErPo
Advantages of living with two cultures, The. Bonne Entente. F. R. Scott. OBCV
Advent Meditation. Alice Meynell. MoRP
Adventurers, The. John Thompson. PoAu-2
Adventures. Arthur Kramer. BiCB

Adventures of Isabel. Ogden Nash. OnMSP
Adversaries. Louis Johnson. ACV
Advice from a Nightwatchman. Ian Healy. Poems from the Coalfields, II. PoAu-2
Advice to a Fair Wanton. Ovid, *tr. fr. Latin by* Christopher Marlowe. *Fr.* Amores. UnTE
Advice to a Prophet. Richard Wilbur. AnMoPo; CoPo; MoRP; MP; ToPo
Advice to a Raven in Russia December, 1812. Joel Barlow. AmLP
Advice to Bachelors. *Unknown, tr. fr. German by* Louis Untermeyer. UnTE
Advice to Country Girls. *Unknown, tr. fr. German by* Louis Untermeyer. UnTE
Ae Fond Kiss. Burns. CABA; ELP; WePo
Ae weet forenicht i the yow-trummle. The Watergaw. "Hugh MacDiarmid." PoIE
Aelf-scin, the Shining Scimmer the Gleam, the Shining, The. Michael McClure. CoPo
Aella, *sel.* Thomas Chatterton.
  Minstrel's Song. DiPo
  (My Love Is Dead.) WiR
Aeneas at Washington. Allen Tate. AP
Aeneid, The, *sels.* Vergil, *tr. fr. Latin.*
  Batalis and the Man, *fr.* I, *tr. by* Gawin Douglas. CTC
  Boat Race, The, *fr.* V, *tr. by* Rolfe Humphries. SD
  Boxing Match, The, *fr.* V, *tr. by* Rolfe Humphries. SD
Aeolian Harp, The. Herman Melville. AP
Aeolus. Rolfe Humphries. RePo
Aeroplane. Mary McBride Green. SoPo
Aesop, *sel.* Sir John Vanbrugh.
  In the Sprightly Month of May. UnTE
Aetatis suae fifty-two. The Progress of Marriage. Swift. EiCP
Aether. Allen Ginsberg. CoPo
Affection and Desire. Sir Walter Ralegh. *See* Conceit Begotten by the Eyes.
Affliction ("Broken in pieces all asunder"). George Herbert. MeP
Affliction ("When first thou didst entice to thee my heart"). George Herbert. CABA; MeP; SeCP
Affliction is a stormy deep. Submission in Affliction. *Unknown.* STF
Affliction of Margaret, The. Wordsworth. GTBS-P
Afforestation. E. A. Wodehouse. SD
Afráh ("Afráh laves her garments in the waters"). Judah Halevi, *tr. fr. Hebrew by* William M. Davis. AnML
Afraid. Walter de la Mare. ThGo
Africa Speaks. Michael Dei-Anang. ACV
Africa, you were once just a name to me. The Continent That Lies within Us. Abioseh Nicol. ACV
African Affair, The. Bruce McM. Wright. AmNP
African blues. Notes for a Speech. LeRoi Jones. CoPo
African Christmas. John Press. DaDu
African Dance. Langston Hughes. RePo
African Heaven. Frank Parkes. ACV
After, *sel.* Lizette Woodworth Reese.
  Daily Round. ThGo
After a Dutch Master. Conrad Ferdinand Meyer, *tr. fr. German by* Daniel Coogan. AGP
After a fearful maze where doubt. Chimera. Barbara Howes. MP
After a Journey. Thomas Hardy. DTC; ELP; GTBS-P; OBNC
After a Line by John Peale Bishop. Donald Justice. PoCh
After Apple-picking. Robert Frost. AP; CaFP; DiPo; FoBA; RoGo; StP
After Blenheim. Robert Southey. *See* Battle of Blenheim, The.
After Dark Vapours. Keats. CBEP
  (Sonnet: "After dark vapours have oppress'd our plains.") OBNC
After Death. Christina Rossetti. VP
After Dilettante Concetti. Henry Duff Traill. Par
After each other they speak, but neither speaks with the other. Philosophical Conversation. Schiller. TwGP
After, each, word, he, places, a, comma. "Poet." William Jay Smith. RePo
After eleven years and a couple of children. Adversaries. Louis Johnson. ACV
After Ever Happily; or, The Princess and the Woodcutter. Ian Serraillier. BoLP
After-Glow, The. Mathilde Blind. OBNC
After Goliath. Kingsley Amis. NePoEA-2; PoCh
After great pain, a formal feeling comes. Emily Dickinson. AP; CABA; FoBA; PoIE
After hot loveless nights, when cold winds stream. The Sisters. Roy Campbell. ErPo
After Hours. Robert Mezey. AmPC; ToPo
After I got religion and steadied down. "Butch" Weldy. Edgar Lee Masters. *Fr.* Spoon River Anthology. PoPo
After it became obvious that the strange rain would never stop. Tentative Description of a Dinner [Given] to Promote the

Impeachment of President Eisenhower. Lawrence Ferlinghetti. CoPo; PtTo
After Johnson's Dance. Charles H. Souter. PoAu-1
After Long Silence. W. B. Yeats. AnMoPo; DiPo; FoBA; PoPl
After many scornes like these. What Hee Suffered. Ben Jonson. Fr. A Celebration of Charis. SeCP
After Margrave died, nothing. History of a Literary Movement. Howard Nemerov. PP
After Our Wedding Day. Heine, tr. fr. German by Walter Kaufmann. TwGP
After Reading Certain Books. Mary Elizabeth Coleridge. EaLo
After St. Augustine. Mary Elizabeth Coleridge. TRV
After Shakespeare. Alex Comfort. ErPo
After she/ had complained about. The Proposition. Paul Blackburn. ErPo
After Sunday Dinner We Uncles Snooze. John Ciardi. ToPo
After Sunset. Grace Hazard Conkling. MoRP
After the Accident. Henri Michaux, tr. fr. French by Dori Katz. CoFP
After the blast of lightning from the east. The End. Wilfred Owen. MMA
After the brief bivouac of Sunday. The Stenographers. P. K. Page. OBCV
After the cloud embankments. Reconnaissance. Arna Bontemps. AmNP
After the Dark. Emola Chamberlain. STF
After the Dazzle of Day. Walt Whitman. FoBA
After the First Nocturnal Visit. Leopold von Goeckingk, tr. fr. German by George C. Schoolfield. AGP
After the first powerful plain manifesto. The Express. Stephen Spender. GoJo; MP; PoPl; RoGo; VaPo
After the Flood Went Down, God Said. Genesis, VIII: 22, IX: 12, Bible, O.T. ThGo
After the Funeral. Dylan Thomas. DiPo; PoIE; ToPo
After the heaped piles and the cornsheaves waiting. Harvest and Consecration. Elizabeth Jennings. NePoEA-2
After the long wake, when many were drunk. Attitudes. Richard Eberhart. ToPo
After the Pangs [of a Desperate Lover]. Dryden. Fr. An Evening's Love, II, i. ELP; StP; UnTE
(Love's Fancy.) ErPo
After the planes unloaded, we fell down. The Dead in Europe. Robert Lowell. DTC; ToPo
After the Pleasure Party. Herman Melville. AP
After the red leaf and the gold have gone. A Spell before Winter. Howard Nemerov. ToPo
After the Sea-Ship. Walt Whitman. CBEP; HaSV
After the Second Flood. Wilhelm Lehmann, tr. fr. German by Babette Deutsch. MGP
After the shot the driven feathers rock. Rainbow. Robert Huff. NePoEA-2
After the Storm. Henry Vaughan. See Bird, The.
After the Surprising Conversions. Robert Lowell. AP; CABA
After the tiff there was silence, till. The Lovers. W. R. Rodgers. WePo
After the Visit. Thomas Hardy. OBNC
After the wind. The Blizzard Ape. Kenneth Pitchford. CoPo
After these years of lectures heard. To a Friend, on Her Examination for the Doctorate in English. J. V. Cunningham. EiCP
After those first days. Death of a Bird. Jon Silkin. DaDu
After Tsui-tao. "Klabund," tr. fr. German by Walter Kaufmann. TwGP
After Two Years. Richard Aldington. PoPl
After Work. John Oxenham. TRV
After You, Madam. Alex Comfort. ErPo; UnTE
Aftermath. Longfellow. AP
Afternoon./ Teacher and nun. Street Scene. Robert Mezey. ToPo
Afternoon dark increases with the clock, The. Late Tutorial. Vincent Buckley. PoAu-1
Afternoon falls, The. The Water Wheel. Antonio Machado. AnSP
Afternoon for a Small Boy. Bink Noll. ToPo
Afternoon is dark and not with rain, The. The Breaking of the Day. Peter Davison. CoPo
Afternoon late summer, in a room, An. At My Grandmother's. David Malouf. PoAu-2
Afternoon lies glazed upon the wall, The. Glass Poem. Karl Shapiro. PoIE
Afternoon on a Hill. Edna St. Vincent Millay. SoPo
After-Thought. Wordsworth. The River Duddon, XXXIV. OBNC
Afterward. Erich Fried, tr. fr. German by Christopher Middleton. MGP
Afterwards. Thomas Hardy. AnMoPo; CBEP; GTBS-P; OBNC; PoIE
Afterwards, sel. Gertrude Stein.
"I like to have a home life in the house." LOW

Afton Water. Burns. ILP; PoIE
(Sweet Afton.) CABA
Again and again I kiss thy gates at departing. Roma. Rutilius. CTC
Again and then again . . . the year is born. New Year's Day. Robert Lowell. CABA
Again at Christmas did we weave. In Memoriam A. H. H., LXXVIII. Tennyson. VP
Again, dear Earth, on flying feet. Homeward Song. Olive Tilford Dargan. PoNC
Again I see my bliss at hand. Meeting [or The Lake]. Matthew Arnold. Switzerland, I. CBEP; ELP; VP
Again rejoicing Nature sees. Composed in Spring. Burns. CBEP
Again the day. If the Stars Should Fall. Samuel Allen. NNP
Again the veld revives. Namaqualand after Rain. William Plomer. ACV
Againe. Robert Herrick. SeCP
Against an elm a sheep was tied. Fable V: The Wild Boar and the Ram. John Gay. EiCP
Against Consummation. Petronius Arbiter. See Doing a Filthy Pleasure Is.
Against Fruition. Sir John Suckling. ErPo
Against Idleness and Mischief. Isaac Watts. See Little Busy Bee.
Against Love. Sir John Denham. CBEP
Against Modesty in Love. Matthew Prior. ErPo
Against Seasons. Robert Mezey. AmPC
Against the Age. Louis Simpson. NePoEA-2
Against the Barons' Enemies. Unknown. MeEL
Against the burly air I strode. Genesis. Geoffrey Hill. ACV
Against the clear intensity of dawn. Budding Spring. Jack Lindsay. PoAu-1
Against the day of sorrow. Trifle. Georgia Douglas Johnson. AmNP
Against the False Magicians. Thomas McGrath. PP
Against the moon now eldritch-thin. Sorceress. Gertrude Claytor. FiSC
Against Them Who Lay Unchastity to the Sex of Women. William Habington. Fr. Castara, II. SeCP
Against Women. Juvenal, tr. fr. Latin by Dryden. Fr. Satires. UnTE
Against Women. Unknown. MeEL
Agamemnon, sel. Aeschylus, tr. fr. Greek by Dallam Simpson. Signal Fire, The. CTC
Age. Friedrich Hölderlin, tr. fr. German by Willard R. Trask. AGP
Age. Sir Thomas More. Fr. The Pageants of Thomas More. EnRePo
Age. R. S. Thomas. ToPo
Age. At. to Edward Tuck and to H. S. Fritsch. See How Old Are You?
Age after age and all alone. The Wandering Moon. James Reeves. RePo
Age and Youth. Unknown, tr. fr. German by Louis Untermeyer. UnTE
Age demanded an image, The. Ezra Pound. Fr. Hugh Selwyn Mauberley. PoIE
Age is a quality of mind. How Old Are You? [or Age]. At. to Edward Tuck and to H. S. Fritsch. BiCB; PoLF
Age of Gold. Pietro Metastasio, tr. fr. Italian by Ezra Pound. CTC
Aged Lover Renounceth Love, The. Thomas, Lord Vaux. EnRePo
Aged man, that mowes these fields. A Dialogue betwixt Time and a Pilgrime. Aurelian Townsend. SeCP
Aged Mother, Mary, even though—when that thing. Complaint. Ted Hughes. PoDB
Ageing Athlete, The. Neil Weiss. SD
Ageless. Unknown, tr. fr. Greek by Louis Untermeyer. UnTE
Ages and Ages Returning at Intervals. Walt Whitman. AP
Aghadoe. John Todhunter. BoLP
Agincourt. Michael Drayton. CBEP
(Ballad of Agincourt, The.) EnRePo
Agitation of the air, An. End of Summer. Stanley Kunitz. AmLP
Aglaura, sels. Sir John Suckling.
No, No, Fair Heretic. CBEP
(Song: "No, no, fair heretic, it needs must be.") CABA; PoIE
Why So Pale and Wan? BoLP; CaFP; CBEP; DiPo; ELP; EvOK; FaBV
(Encouragements to a Lover.) GTBS-P
(Song: "Why so pale and wan, fond lover?") CABA; PoIE; PoPl; SeCP
Agonie, The. George Herbert. MeP
(Philosophers Have Measured Mountains.) TRV
Ah, Are You Digging on My Grave? Thomas Hardy. ILP; PoPo; VP
Ah Ben!/ Say how, or when. An Ode for Ben Jonson. Robert Herrick. DiPo; PoSa; SeCP
Ah, broken is the golden bowl!—the spirit flown forever. Lenore. Poe. AP

Ah, Chloris! could I now but sit. Child and Maiden. Sir Charles Sedley. *Fr.* The Mulberry Garden, III, ii. GTBS-P

Ah, Christ, I love you rings to the wild sky. Sonnets at Christmas, II. Allen Tate. AP; PoDB

Ah could we wake in mercy's name. Song for an Allegorical Play. John Ciardi. PoCh

Ah! County Guy, the hour is nigh. A Serenade. Sir Walter Scott. *Fr.* Quentin Durward. GTBS-P

Ah, did you once see Shelley plain. Memorabilia. Robert Browning. ACV; CABA; ILP; OBNC; PP

Ah! fair face gone from sight. Lionel Johnson. *Fr.* In Memory. OBNC

Ah for one hour of youthful joy! The Old Man Dreams. Oliver Wendell Holmes. PoLF

Ah, for the month of May, of May. The Prisoner. *Unknown.* AnML

Ah, God, Who Made Her Good to See. Charles d'Orléans, tr. fr. French by James Edward Tobin. AnML

Ah! he is fled! The British Church. Henry Vaughan. MeP

Ah! How I Fear, Milady, Lest I Die. Guillaume de Machaut, tr. fr. French by Norman R. Shapiro. AnML

Ah How I Like to See Great Power Pass. Bertran de Born, tr. fr. Provençal by James J. Wilhelm. AnML

Ah How Sweet It Is to Love. Dryden. *Fr.* Tyrannic Love. PoIE

Ah, I remember well—and how can I. Early Love [or First Flame]. Samuel Daniel. *Fr.* Hymen's Triumph. BoLP; ErPo

Ah, little road, all whirry in the breeze. The Road. Helene Johnson. AmNP

Ah Love! could you and I with Him conspire. Omar Khayyám, tr. by Edward Fitzgerald. *Fr.* The Rubáiyat. PoPl

Ah Me, Alas! Am I So Very Base. Cino da Pistoia, tr. fr. Italian by Daniel J. Donno. AnML

Ah me! full sorely is my heart forlorn. The Schoolmistress. William Shenstone. EnPE

Ah Me Poor Wretch, Who Loved a Falcon. *Unknown, tr. fr. Italian by Sonia Raiziss and Alfredo de Palchi.* AnML

Ah Me, Shall I No Longer See. Heinrich von Morungen, tr. fr. German by J. B. Leishman. AnML

Ah me the hand upon the body. Legerdemain. Kenneth Mackenzie. PoAu-2

Ah me! those old familiar bounds. Ode on a Distant Prospect of Clapham Academy. Thomas Hood. CBEP

Ah, Mingo Revulgo, Mingo! The Barbs of Mingo Revulgo. *Unknown.* AnML

Ah Moon, You Shine Too Long. Christine de Pisan, tr. fr. French by Muriel Kittel. AnML

Ah, my Anthea! Must my heart still break? What Shame Forbids to Speak. Robert Herrick. UnTE

Ah, my Clio! every day. To Clio. John Dyer. WaPE

Ah my dear angry Lord. Bitter-Sweet. George Herbert. FoBA

Ah my Perilla! do'st thou grieve to see. To Perilla. Robert Herrick. SeCP

Ah! on Thanksgiving Day, when from East and from West. The Pumpkin. *Unknown.* PoSC

Ah! Posthumus! Our yeares hence flye. His Age. Robert Herrick. SeCP

Ah, Poverties, Wincings, and Sulky Retreats. Walt Whitman. CBEP

Ah, see the fair chivalry come, the companions of Christ! Te Martyrum Candidatus. Lionel Johnson. BoC

Ah! Sun-Flower. Blake. *Fr.* Songs of Experience. CABA; CBEP; DiPo; ELP; FoBA; OBNC

Ah, take these lips away; no more. Deadly Kisses. Pierre de Ronsard. RBL

Ah, That I Were Far Away. Arthur Hugh Clough. *Fr.* Amours de Voyage. OBNC

Ah! the May was grand this mornin'! The Song of the Thrush. T. A. Daly. LV

Ah, through the open door. Spring Morning. D. H. Lawrence. BoLP

Ah, wasteful woman, she that may. Unthrift. Coventry Patmore. *Fr.* The Angel in the House. FaPL

Ah, Waves, I Come to See. Martin Códax, tr. fr. Portuguese by William M. Davis. AnML

Ah, well, I abandon you, cherrywood smokestack. The Artist. Kenneth Koch. AmPC

Ah, well! In the great Empire of all. Anne Peters. *Fr.* Kevin O'Culihain, Zorro Tio of the Andes, Exile. PtTo

Ah what avails the sceptred race. Rose Aylmer. Walter Savage Landor. CABA; CBEP; ELP; FaPL; ILP; OBNC; RoGo

"Ah, what can ail thee, knight-at-arms [or wretched wight]." *See* "O what can ail thee, knight-at-arms."

Ah, What of Life! Does No One Answer Me? Francisco de Quevedo, tr. fr. Spanish by William M. Davis. AnSP

Ah! who can tell how hard it is to climb. James Beattie. *Fr.* The Minstrel; or, The Progress of Genius. EnPE

Ah, with the Grape my fading Life provide. Omar Khayyám, tr. by Edward Fitzgerald. *Fr.* The Rubáiyát. GTBS-P

Ah! woe is me, condemned to bear. For One in Doubt. Charles Wesley. Three Hymns, 3. WaPE

Ah, Woe to Me Alas, for Love Has Bound. Cino da Pistoia, tr. fr. Italian by Daniel J. Donno. AnML

Ah, Yes, I Wrote the "Purple Cow." Gelett Burgess. PoPl

Ah, you should see Cynddylan on a tractor. Cynddylan on a Tractor [in Spring]. R. S. Thomas. PoCh

Ah, your dewy pinions swinging. Goethe, tr. fr. German by Aurelia G. Scott. AGP

Aha! A guest. Morgiana Dances. William Rose Benét. SIV

Ahoy and ahoy, birds. Wings and Wheels. Nancy Byrd Turner. SoPo

Aids to Composition. Robert Conquest. PP

Ailing Fountain, The. "Aldo Palazzeschi," tr. fr. Italian by Carlo L. Golino. CoIP

Ails a Human Heart. Mechthild von Magdeburg, tr. fr. German by R. G. L. Barrett. AnML

Aim Was Song, The. Robert Frost. PP

Air. Jacques Dupin, tr. fr. French by William Brown. CoFP

Air. W. S. Merwin. AmPC; CoPo

Air: Sentir avec ardeur. Marie-Françoise-Catherine de Beauveau, Marquise de Boufflers, tr. fr. French by Ezra Pound. CTC

Air and Angels. John Donne, CBEP; EnRePo (Aire and Angels.) SeCP

Air by Sammartini, An. Louis Dudek. OBCV

Air comes in tickly. Sneezing. Marie Louise Allen. SoPo

Air grows calm and clear, The. Ode to Francisco Salinas. Luis de León. AnSP

Air is like a butterfly, The. Easter. Joyce Kilmer. SoPo

Air is mild, not quite. A Sleep. Larry Eigner. CoPo

Air is thick with nerves and smoke, The: pens tremble in sweating hands. University Examinations in Egypt. D. J. Enright. MP

Air Plant, The. Hart Crane. PoIE

Air Shaft. Ian Healy. Poems from the Coalfields, I. PoAu-2

Air sings of marble by the soothing sea, The. The Temple by the Sea. Geoffrey Dutton. ACV

Air Tunnel, Monticello. Bink Noll. ToPo

Aircraft, Landing. Colin Thiele. ACV

Aire and Angels. John Donne. *See* Air and Angels.

Airman Who Flew over Shakespeare's England, The. Hyam Plutzik. PoPl

Airplane taxis down the field, The. Taking Off. *Unknown.* SoPo

Airs of Pei, sel. Confucius, tr. fr. Chinese by Ezra Pound. *Fr.* The Classic Anthology.

Efficient Wife's Complaint, The. CTC

Airs! that wander and murmur round. The Siesta. *Unknown.* SiGo

Airstrip in Essex, An. Donald Hall. PoCh

Airy Tomb, The. R. S. Thomas. ToPo

Aishah-Schechinah. Robert Stephen Hawker. OBNC

Al Aaraaf. Poe. AP
  To Science. Prologue. CBEP
  (Sonnet: To Science.) ILP

Aladdin. James Russell Lowell. RoGo

Aladdin Throws Away His Lamp. Elias Lieberman. LV

Alan. Raymond Roseliep. FiSC

Alarm and time clock still intrude too early. And on This Shore. M. Carl Holman. AmNP

Alarm clocks tick in a thousand furnished rooms, The. North Infinity Street. Conrad Aiken. AP

Alas, Alack. Walter de la Mare. EvOK

Alas! alas! the while. A Night with a Holy-Water Clerk. *Unknown.* MeEL

Alas! count your days: the days which have gone. Jean de Sponde. *Fr.* Sonnets de la Mort. RBL

Alas! deceite that in truste is nowe. Trust Only Yourself. *Unknown.* MeEL

Alas How Long ("Alas how long shall I and my maidenhead lie"). *Unknown.* ErPo

Alas, how pleasant are their dayes. The Unfortunate Lover. Andrew Marvell. MeP

Alas, how soon the hours are over. Plays. Walter Savage Landor.

Alas! If I Had Married. *Unknown, tr. fr. Catalan by William M. Davis.* AnML

Alas, my hart will brek in three. Fearful Death. *Unknown.* MeEL

Alas, my love! ye do me wrong. Greensleeves. *Unknown.* UnTE

Alas! noble Prince Leopold, he is dead. The Death of Prince Leopold. William McGonagall. EvOK

Alas our day is forst to flie by night. The Flight into Egypt. Robert Southwell. MeP

Alas our good Kaspar is dead. Kaspar Is Dead. Hans Arp. MGP

Alas! Poor Queen. Marion Angus. ACV

Alas, So All Things Now. Earl of Surrey, after Petrarch. EnRePo

Alas! that liquid look, that lovely face! Petrarch, tr. by Joseph Auslander. Sonnets to Laura: To Laura in Death, I. RBL

Alas! the lovely face, the eyes that save. Petrarch, *tr. by* Maria Armi. Sonnets to Laura: To Laura in Death, I. RBL

Alas! they had been friends in youth. The Scars Remaining. Samuel Taylor Coleridge. *Fr.* Christabel. OBNC

Alas 'tis true I have gone here and there. Sonnets, CX. Shakespeare. CBEP

Alas! 'tis very sad to hear. Walter Savage Landor. GTBS-P

Alas! too well we know our loss. Concerning Them That Are Asleep. R. W. Raymond. STF

Alas, Ugly Lady, You Complained. Joan de Guilhade, *tr. fr. Portuguese* by William M. Davis. AnML

Alas! what shul we freres do. A Friar Complains. *Unknown.* MeEL

Alas, whereto have vanished all my years! Walther von der Vogelweide, *tr. fr. German by* Janet Alison Livermore. AGP

Alaska. Joaquin Miller. ThLM

Alastor; or, The Spirit of Solitude. Shelley. CABL

Alba ("Creeper grows over thorn"). Confucius, *tr. fr. Chinese by* Ezra Pound. *Fr.* The Classic Anthology: Songs of T'ang. CTC

Alba ("When the nightingale to his mate"). Ezra Pound. *Fr.* Langue d'Oc. PoIE

Alba. Derek Walcott. GoJo

Alba after Six Years. Christopher Middleton. NePoEA-2

Albeit the Venice girls get praise. Ballade of the Women of Paris. Villon. UnTE

Alchemist, The. Robert Kelly. CoPo

Alex, perhaps a colour of which neither of us had dreamt. Letter to Alex Comfort. Dannie Abse. MP

Alexander and Campaspe, *sel.* John Lyly.
Cupid and Campaspe. GTBS-P; ILP
(Cupid and My Campaspe.) CABA

Alexander, that good magistrate without frontiers. Juan Lorenzo. *Fr.* The Book of Alexander. AnML

Alexander's Feast; or, The Power of Music. Dryden. GTBS-P; StP; WiR

Alexandria. Lawrence Durrell. ToPo

Alfred, a Masque, *sel.* James Thomson *and* David Mallet.
Rule, Britannia, *fr.* II, v. Thomson. EiCP; GTBS-P

Alfred Lord Tennyson ("Alfred was a ninny"). Reed Whittemore. PP

Algonkian Burial. Alfred Goldsworthy Bailey. OBCV

Alice. Charles Cotton. *Fr.* Resolution in Four Sonnets . . . Concerning Four Rural Sisters. UnTE

Alice Brand. Sir Walter Scott. *Fr.* The Lady of the Lake. OnMSP

"Alice, dear, what ails you." A Frosty Night. Robert Graves. MoBS

Alice, for whom my love is deep. Proof Positive. Deems Taylor. UnTE

Alice is tall and upright as a pine. Alice. Charles Cotton. *Fr.* Resolution in Four Sonnets . . . Concerning Four Rural Sisters. UnTE

Alice's Adventures in Wonderland, *sels.* "Lewis Carroll."
"Beautiful soup, so rich and green," *fr. ch.* 10. Par
Evidence Read at the Trial of the Knave of Hearts, *fr. ch.* 12. GTBS-P
Father William, *fr. ch.* 5. BiCB; FaPL; GoJo; PoLF; RePo
(" 'You are old, Father William,' the young man said.") Par
How Doth the Little Crocodile, *fr. ch.* 2. Par; SoPo
Lobster Quadrille, The, *fr. ch.* 10. Par
"Speak roughly to your little boy," *fr. ch.* 6. Par
(Duchess' Lullaby, The.) BBGG
"Twinkle, twinkle, little bat!" *fr. ch.* 7. Par
Voice of the Lobster, The, *fr. ch.* 10. EvOK
(" 'T is the voice of the Lobster; I heard him declare.") Par

Alien. Donald Jeffrey Hayes. AmNP

Alike. Dorothy Aldis. RePo

Alike from love and marriage hurry. Advice to Bachelors. *Unknown.* UnTE

Alison. *Unknown.* See Alisoun.

Alison Gross. *Unknown.* BuBa

Alisoun. *Unknown.* CTC
(Alison.) MeEL

Aliter. Confucius, *tr. fr. Chinese by* Ezra Pound. *Fr.* The Classic Anthology: Songs of Ch'en. CTC

All, All of a Piece [Throughout]. Dryden. *Fr.* The Secular Masque. CBEP; ELP

All along the backwater. Duck's [*or* Ducks'] Ditty. Kenneth Grahame. *Fr.* The Wind in the Willows. GoJo; SoPo

All around the Town, *sels.* Phyllis McGinley. SoPo
B's the Bus.
C Is for the Circus.
P's the Proud Policeman.

All beauty calls you to me and you seem. From the Sea. Sara Teasdale. MoLP

All but Blind. Walter de la Mare. WePo

All Christmas night upon the shelf. The Mouse. Hugh McCrae. PoAu-1

All day beneath the hurtling shells. The Dancers. W. W. Gibson. MMA

All day beside the shattered tank he'd lain. Reconciliation. C. Day Lewis. MP

All day I follow. The Plowman. Raymond Knister. OBCV

All Day It Has Rained. Alun Lewis. GTBS-P; WePo

All day long I have been working. Madonna of the Evening Flowers. Amy Lowell. AmLP

All day my sheep have mingled with yours. Shepherdess. Norman Cameron. *Fr.* Three Love Poems. GTBS-P

All day rain fell. Ode on Contemplating Clapham Junction. Christopher Middleton. *Fr.* Herman Moon's Hourbook. NePoEA-2

All day she hurried to get through. Mis' Smith. Albert Bigelow Paine. PoLF

All day she sits behind a bright brass rail. The Travel Bureau. Ruth Comfort Mitchell. LV

All day the great guns barked and roared. Molly Pitcher. Laura E. Richards. ThLM

All day the sand, like golden chains. Scot in the Desert. Laurie Lee. ToPo

All day they loitered by the resting ships. The *Wanderer*. John Masefield. CABL

All Dressed Up for Easter. Aileen Fisher. RePo

All-embracing, The. Frederick W. Faber. TRV

All fixed: early arrival at the flat. Nothing to Fear. Kingsley Amis. ErPo

All Fools' Day. *Unknown.* SoPo

All for Love. Byron. GTBS-P; PoPo

All for Love, *sels.* Dryden.
Epilogue: "Poets, like disputants, when reasons fail." DiPo
Prologue: "What flocks of critics hover here to-day." DiPo

All for Love. *Unknown, tr. fr. German by* Louis Untermeyer. UnTE

All glass may yet be whole. The Scarred Girl. James Dickey. ToPo

"All hands alive! We're goin' about!" Hen Overboard. Robert P. Tristram Coffin. RePo

All horizons are round. Fragment III. Helmut Heissenbüttel. MGP

All human things are subject to decay. MacFlecknoe. Dryden. CABA; CABL; DiPo; PoIE; PP; StP

All I can give you is broken-face gargoyles. Broken-Face Gargoyles. Carl Sandburg. ILP

All in All. Tennyson. *See* In Love, If Love Be Love.

All in Green Went My Love Riding. E. E. Cummings. AmLP; FaBV; GoJo; SD; VaPo

All in the April Morning. Katharine Tynan. ThGo

All in the Downs the fleet was moor'd [*or* moored]. Black-eyed Susan. John Gay. GTBS-P; RoGo

All in the Morning. *Unknown.* BiCB

All is best, though we oft doubt. Milton. *Fr.* Samson Agonistes. BoC

All is still/ Under the Pines. Under the Pines. Arthur S. Bourinot. OBCV

All is the same still. Earth and heaven locked in. Emily Brontë. C. Day Lewis. GTBS-P

All Is Vanity. Ecclesiastes, I: 14-15, III: 19, Bible, *O.T.* TRV

All Is Vanity. Andreas Gryphius, *tr. fr. German by* George C. Schoolfield. AGP

All judgment of this infinity. Maurice Scève. *Fr.* Délie. RBL

All kings and their favourites [*or* favorites]. The Anniversary [*or* Anniversarie]. John Donne. CBEP; DiPo; MeP; OnP; SeCP

All kings are hollow. The Cool, Cool Country. John Shaw Neilson. PoAu-1

All-knowing Lamp. *Unknown, tr. fr. Greek by* Louis Untermeyer. UnTE

All love at first, like generous wine. Love. Samuel Butler. CBEP

All men are wormes: but this no man. In silke. On Court-Worme. Ben Jonson. SeCP

All men,—the preacher saith,—whate'er or whence. Frederick Goddard Tuckerman. *Fr.* Sonnets. PoIE

All my emprises have been fill'd with Thee. Walt Whitman. *Fr.* Prayer of Columbus. TRV

All my favourite characters have been. Mythology. Lawrence Durrell. DTC

All my past life is mine no more. Love and Life. Earl of Rochester. ELP

All My Pretty Ones. Anne Sexton. CoPo

"All My Pretty Ones? Did You Say All?" Bink Noll. ToPo

All my senses, like beacon's flame. Caelica, LVI. Fulke Greville. EnRePo

All nature has a feeling: woods, fields, brooks. Eternity of Nature. John Clare. StP

All Nature seems at work. Slugs leave their lair. Work without Hope. Samuel Taylor Coleridge. CABA; ILP

All night a noise of leaping fish. The Fisher. Roderic Quinn. PoAu-1

All Night by the Rose. *Unknown.* CBEP
(Rose's Scent, The.) WiR
All night I lie awake and hear. Remembering. "Michael Lewis." *Fr.* Cherry Blossoms. UnTE
All other joys of life he strove to warm. George Meredith. Modern Love, IV. VP
All over America railroads ride through roses. Landscape as Metal and Flowers. Winfield Townley Scott. GoJo
All over the earth are roads. Alone. Hermann Hesse. TwGP
All passes. Art alone. Austin Dobson, *after* Théophile Gautier. *Fr.* Ars Victrix. CTC
All poppies or lips of women. The Word Comes Down. Pierre Reverdy. CoFP
All right, Robert Frost. CABA
All right: and with that wry acceptance you follow the cowtrack. The Dogwood. Robert Penn Warren. *Fr.* Dark Woods. PoDB
All right, I was Welsh. Does it matter? A Welsh Testament. R. S. Thomas. ToPo
All Saints' Day, *sel.* Margherita Guidacci, *tr. fr. Italian by* Carlo L. Golino.
"Often I have thought: is this." CoIP
All saints revile her, and all sober men. The White Goddess. Robert Graves. PoIE
All Souls. Liboria E. Romano. FiSC
All-Souls' Day. Siegfried Sassoon. MoRP
All such proclivities are tabulated. The Quiet Glades of Eden. Robert Graves. ErPo
All swells against me, tempts me, and assails. Jean de Sponde. *Fr.* Sonnets de la Mort. RBL
All That Comes to Be. "Klabund," *tr. fr. German by* Walter Kaufmann. TwGP
All That Glisters Is Not Gold. Shakespeare. *Fr.* The Merchant of Venice, II, vii. CTC
All that I am to Earth belongs. William Baylebridge. *Fr.* Life's Testament. PoAu-1
All that I do is clumsy and ill timed. The Doppelganger. Daryl Hine. OBCV
All that I know. My Star. Robert Browning. EvOK
All that is left. The Little Trumpet. Corrado Govoni. CoIP
All That Matters. Edgar A. Guest. LV
All that remains for me. Envoi. Arthur Symons. UnTE
All That Was Mortal. Sara Teasdale. MoRP
All that we see, about, abroad. On the Universality and Other Attributes of the God of Nature. Philip Freneau. AP
All that you do should be right, but that ought to be sufficient. Political Doctrine. Schiller. TwGP
All That's Past. Walter de la Mare. GoJo; StP
All the actors (and the actresses) ended the same day. The Big Theater. André Pieyre de Mandiargues. CoFP
All the animals in my poems go into the ark. Prologue. Jon Silkin. PoDB
All the bells of heaven may ring. A Child's Laughter. Swinburne. PoLF
All the breath and the bloom of the year in the bag of one bee. Summum Bonum. Robert Browning. BoLP
All the Flowers of the Spring. John Webster. *Fr.* The Devil's Law Case. CBEP; ELP
(Speech by Romelio.) PoIE
All the Hills and Vales Along. Charles Hamilton Sorley. MMA
All the long forenoon, the loitering of insects. The Forenoon. Christopher Middleton. *Fr.* Herman Moon's Hourbook. NePoEA-2
All the night in woe. The Little Girl Found. Blake. *Fr.* Songs of Experience. CBEP; DiPo
All the others translate: the painter sketches. The Composer. W. H. Auden. PoPo
All the paths of the Lord are lovingkindness and truth. *Fr.* Psalm XXV, Bible, *O.T.* BoC
All the people in my poems walk into the dark. Epilogue. Jon Silkin. PoDB
All the Scenes of Nature Quicken. Christopher Smart. ELP
All the Way My Saviour Leads Me. Fanny J. Crosby. STF
All the wide air was trawled for cloud. L'Ile du Levant: The Nudist Colony. Barbara Howes. PoCh
All the woods are now in flower. The Wooing. *Unknown.* UnTE
All the World's a Stage. Shakespeare. *Fr.* As You Like It, II, vii. DiPo; PoLF; PoSa
(Seven Ages of Man, The.) PoPo
All their lives in a box! What generations. The Silkworms. Douglas Stewart. AnMoPo; PoAu-2
All Things Bright and Beautiful. Mrs. C. F. Alexander. ThGo
All things take arms against you. The bad weather. The Broken Glass. Umberto Saba. CoIP
All things that pass. Passing and Glassing. Christina Rossetti. OBNC
All Those Hymnings up to God. Abbie Huston Evans. MoRP
All those who knew you are dispersed or dead. Sestina for Khasan Israelov. John Wain. *Fr.* Wildtrack. ToPo
All thoughts, all passions, all delights. Love. Samuel Taylor Coleridge. GTBS-P

All through that summer at ease we lay. The Castle. Edwin Muir. AnMoPo
All through the garden I went and went. The Butterbean Tent. Elizabeth Madox Roberts. GoJo
All through the night the happy sheep. The Happy Sheep. Wilfrid Thorley. SoPo
All Too Much I Long to See. Adam de la Halle, *tr. fr. French by* Irma Brandeis. AnML
All travellers at first incline. Stella's Birthday. Swift. ILP
All Turns into Yesterday. *Unknown.* MeEL
All visible, visibly. Runner. W. H. Auden. SD
All was as it was when I went in. Apopemptic Hymn. Dorothy Auchterlonie. PoAu-2
All who have loved, be sure of this from me. Richard Watson Dixon. *Fr.* Love's Consolation. OBNC
All windows open, moths. Three Part Invention. Paul Blackburn. CoPo
All Winter I Lay Alone until a Lady Brought Me Solace. Der Burggrave von Regensburg, *tr. fr. German by* Ruth Yorck *and* Kenward Elmslie. AnML
All women born are so perverse. Triolet. Robert Bridges. LV
All women love dance in a dying light. They Sing, They Sing. Theodore Roethke. *Fr.* The Dying Man. PoDB
All ye poets of the age. Namby-Pamby. Henry Carey. Par
All ye that passe by this holy place. A Second Epitaph. *Unknown.* MeEL
All you on emigration bent. The Settler's Lament. *Unknown.* PoAu-1
All you that are enamored of my name. Demos. E. A. Robinson. AP
Alle that beth of herte trewe. The Death of King Edward I. *Unknown.* MeEL
Allegory of the Brevity of Things Human. Luis de Góngora, *tr. fr. Spanish by* Roy Campbell. AnSP
Alleluia! Alleluia! Let the Holy Anthem Rise. *Unknown.* PoSC
Allie ("Allie, call the birds in"). Robert Graves. DaDu; GoJo; LOW
All's over, then: does truth sound bitter. The Lost Mistress. Robert Browning. CBEP; OBNC
All's Well. Whittier. CBEP
Alma; or, The Progress of the Mind, *sel.* Matthew Prior.
"Matthew met Richard; when or where." EiCP
Alma Venus, *sel.* Bernard O'Dowd.
"Door of existence, beacon of our haze." PoAu-1
Almighty Judge, how shall poore wretches brook. Judgement. George Herbert. MeP; SeCP
Almighty and all present Power. A Sergeant's Prayer. Hugh Brodie. LV
Almighty God, Fader of Hevene. A Prayer to the Trinity. *Unknown.* MeEL
Almighty God, Who Made the Noble State. Alain Chartier, *tr. fr. French by* James Edward Tobin. AnML
Almond Blossom in Wartime. Stephen Spender. ACV
Almost a Madrigal. Salvatore Quasimodo, *tr. fr. Italian by* Allen Mandelbaum. CoIP
Almost-tropic night crept through my door, The. Vampire. Walter H. Kerr. FiSC
Almost yesterday, those gentle ladies stole. The Lost Ingredient. Anne Sexton. CoPo
Alone. Hermann Hesse, *tr. fr. German by* Walter Kaufmann. TwGP
Alone. Poe. PoSa
Alone. Siegfried Sassoon. WePo
Alone Am I, Alone I Wish to Be. Christine de Pisan, *tr. fr. French by* Muriel Kittel. AnML
Alone and ever weary with dark care. Petrarch. Sonnets to Laura: To Laura in Life, XXVIII. RBL
Alone in Martyrdom I Have Been Left. Christine de Pisan, *tr. fr. French by* Muriel Kittel. AnML
Alone in the hot sun. The Song-Maker. Kingsley Fairbridge. ACV
Alone in the night. Stars. Sara Teasdale. MoRP; PoPo
Alone Lord God, in Whom our trust and peace. Out of the Deep Have I Called unto Thee, O Lord. Christina Rossetti. VP
Alone on Lykaion since man hath been. Mt. Lykaion. Trumbull Stickney. AmLP
Alone, remote, nor witting where I went. The Altar. E. A. Robinson. PoDB
Alone the pallid cuckoo now. Pallid Cuckoo. David Campbell. PoAu-2
Alone Walking. *Unknown.* CBEP
(Wishing My Death.) MeEL
Along a river-side, I know not where. The Washers of the Shroud. James Russell Lowell. AP
Along the black. Night Ride. Sir Herbert Read. BoLP; WePo
Along the Field as We Came By. A. E. Housman. A Shropshire Lad, XXVI. UnTE
Along the garden terrace, under which. Modern Love, XXXVII. George Meredith. VP
Along the line of smoky hills. Indian Summer. Wilfred Campbell. OBCV; PoP1

Along the River Shore. Joan Zorro, *tr. fr. Portuguese by* William M. Davis. AnML
Along the river's side did Cynthia stray. Cynthia Sporting. Giambattista Marino. RBL
Along the roadside, like the flowers of gold. Prelude. Whittier. *Fr.* Among the Hills. AP
Along the serried coast the Southerly raves. Sea-Grief. Dowell O'Reilly. PoAu-1
Along the wind-swept platform, pinched and white. Morning Express. Siegfried Sassoon. WePo
Alons au bois le may cueillir. Charles d'Orléans, *tr. fr. French by* W. E. Henley. SiGo
Aloof upon the day's immeasured dome. The Black Vulture. George Sterling. AmLP
Alphabet, The. James Reaney. ACV
Alphabet, The. Karl Shapiro. MoRP
Alphabet, The, *with music. Unknown.* BFSS
Alphabet noodles. Baby Toodles. Joseph S. Newman. BBGG
Alphabet of Famous Goops, An, *sel.* Gelett Burgess.
    "Bohunkus would take off his hat, and bow and smile, and things like that." BBGG
Alphonso of Castile. Emerson. AP
Alpine Spirit's Song. Thomas Lovell Beddoes. OBNC
Alpine View. Melville Cane. PoPl
Alpine Winter, The. Antoine-Girard de Saint-Amant, *tr. fr. French by* Rose E. Burckhardt. RBL
Already blushes in thy cheek. Nemesis. Emerson. PoIE
Already the moon has shown me two crescents. Maurice Scève. *Fr. Délie.* RBL
Als I me rode this endre day. The Singing Maid. *Unknown.* MeEL
Also the beautiful dies.—Its spell binds all men and immortals. Nenia. Schiller. AGP
Also Ulysses once—that other war. Kilroy. Peter Viereck. ThLM
Altar, The. George Herbert. FoBA; MeP; PoSa; SeCP; VaPo
Altar, The. E. A. Robinson. PoDB
Altarwise by Owl-Light. Dylan Thomas. ToPo
Although a lumberman 'tis clear. Paddy the Beaver. Thornton Burgess. RePo
Although confused with details and a dunce. To a History Professor. *Unknown.* UnTE
Although I can see him still. The Fisherman. W. B. Yeats. SD
Although I shelter from the rain. The Lamentation of the Old Pensioner. W. B. Yeats. PoPo
Although the night is damp. The Firefly Lights His Lamp. *Unknown.* SoPo
Alumnus Football. Grantland Rice. PoLF
Alun Mabon's Song. John Ceiriog Hughes. WePo
Alvargonzález, being single. The House of Alvargonzález. Antonio Machado. AnSP
Always she loved the sound of bells. Joan of Arc. Hugh McCrae. PoAu-1
Always the same, when on a fated night. The Onset. Robert Frost. AP
Always too eager for the future, we. Next, Please. Philip Larkin. EiCP; PoIE
Always we have believed. Disguises. Elizabeth Jennings. NePoEA-2
Am Driven Mad. Allen Polite. NNP
Am I a stone, and not a sheep. Good Friday. Christina Rossetti. TRV; VP
Am I, Am I, Am I Fair? Eustache Deschamps, *tr. fr. French by* Muriel Kittel. AnML
Am I emptied, Lord, of self? Heartsearch. Evelyn K. Gibson. STF
Am I failing? For no longer can I cast. Modern Love, XXIX. George Meredith. CABA; FaPL; VP
Am I indeed as wretched as I seem? Goethe. *Fr.* Torquato Tasso, V, v. TwGP
Am I My Neighbor's Keeper? Richard Eberhart. ToPo
Am I sober now or drunk? After the First Nocturnal Visit. Leopold von Goeckingk. AGP
Am *I* the bullet. Cause & Effect. May Swenson. OPP
Am I thy gold? Or purse, Lord, for thy wealth. Meditation Six [*or* Another Meditation at the Same Time]. Edward Taylor. *Fr.* Preparatory Meditations, First Series. AmLP; AP; MeP
Amanda, *with music. Unknown.* BFSS
Amanda's Complaint. Philip Freneau. AP
Amarante, L'. Jean Ogier de Gombauld, *tr. fr. French by* Harold M. Priest. *Fr.* Guirlande de Julie. RBL
Amarantha sweet and fair[e]. To Amarantha [That She Would Dishevell Her Haire]. Richard Lovelace. SeCP; UnTE
Amateur Flute, The. *Unknown.* Par
Amazement fills my heart to-night. Thanksgiving. Robert Nichols. MMA
Ambition. "Joachim Ringelnatz," *tr. fr. German by* Christopher Middleton. MGP
Ambition is the young man's sinecure. Of Motion. O. B. Hardison, Jr. PoNC

Ambuscade. Hugh McCrae. PoAu-1
Ambushed by Angels. Gustav Davidson. FiSC
Amends to the Tailors and Soutars. William Dunbar. CBEP
America. Samuel Francis Smith. PoLF
America for Me. Henry van Dyke. RePo
America the Beautiful. Katharine Lee Bates. EaLo; FaBV; FaPL; LV
American Change. Allen Ginsberg. CABL
American Flag, The. Joseph Rodman Drake. AmLP
American Gothic. Samuel Allen. *See* To Satch.
American Letter: For Gerald Murphy. Archibald MacLeish. ILP
American now mind my song. John Chinaman's Appeal. Mart Taylor. SGR
American Poetry. Louis Simpson. PP
American Primitive. William Jay Smith. MP; PoPl
Ametas and Thestylis Making Hay-Ropes. Andrew Marvell. SeCP
Amid my bale I bathe in bliss. A Strange Passion of a Lover. George Gascoigne. EnRePo
Amid the Din of Earthly Strife. Henry Warburton Hawkes. TRV
Amid the stony slapping of the waves. Barnacle Geese. Charles Higham. PoAu-2
Amidst thy sacred effigies. The Emancipation Group. Whittier. LiPo
Aminta, *sel.* Tasso, *tr. fr. Italian by* Leigh Hunt.
    Golden Age, The. RBL
Amo Amas. John O'Keefe. BoLP
Among a people who doubted. Zechariah. Earl Marlatt. MoRP
Among our young lass[i]es is [*or* there's] Muirland Meg. Muirland Meg [*or* She'll Do It]. Burns. ErPo; UnTE
Among School Children. W. B. Yeats. CABA; CaFP; DiPo; FoBA; GTBS-P; ILP; PoIE
Among Shallows. Leonard Clark. HaSV
Among Sweet Tones in Forest Bowers. Ulrich von Lichtenstein, *tr. fr. German by* Kenneth Oliver. AnML
Among the first and farthest! Elk and deer. John Day, Frontiersman. Yvor Winters. PoSa
Among the first to go are always a few. Only the Beards Are Different. Bruce Dawe. PoAu-2
Among the Hills, *sel.* Whittier.
    Prelude: "Along the roadside, like the flowers of gold." AP
Among the pines that overlook. Ohio. *Unknown.* BSO
Among the plastic flowers one honest one. The Woolworth Philodendron. Stephen Sandy. CoPo
Among the smoke and fog of a December afternoon. Portrait of a Lady. T. S. Eliot. MP
Among those joys, 'tis one at eve to sail. Sailing upon the River. George Crabbe. *Fr.* The Borough. OBNC
Among Those Killed in the Dawn Raid Was a Man Aged a Hundred. Dylan Thomas. AnMoPo
Among those who promised us our honors. Palermo, Mother's Day, 1943. William Belvin. PoPl
Among twenty snowy mountains. Thirteen Ways of Looking at a Blackbird. Wallace Stevens. AP; CABA; DiPo; PoSa
Amor Aeternalis. Clark Ashton Smith. FiSC
Amor Dei. *Unknown.* BoC
Amor Mysticus. Sister Marcela de Carpio de San Felix, *tr. fr. Spanish by* John Hay. RBL
Amores, *sels.* Ovid, *tr. fr. Latin by* Christopher Marlowe.
    Advice to a Fair Wanton. UnTE
    Apology for Loose Behavior. UnTE
    In Summer's Heat. UnTE
    Possessive Lover, The. UnTE
    Shameful Impotence. ErPo
    (Impotent Lover, The.) UnTE
Amoretti, *sels.* Spenser.
    VIII. "More than most fair, full of the living fire." CABA
    XIX. "The merry cuckow, messenger of spring." ILP
    XXV. "How long shall this like dying life endure." EnRePo
    XXVI. "Sweet is the Rose, but growes upon a brere." ILP
    XXVIII. "The laurel leaf, which you this day do wear." CABA
    XXX. "My love is like to ice, and I to fire." ErPo
    XXXIV. "Like [*or* Lyke] as a ship that through the ocean wide [*or* wyde]." DiPo; ILP; PoIE
    XXXVII. "What guile is this, that those her golden tresses." StP
    XLIV. "When those renowned noble peers of Greece." CABA
    LIII. "The panther knowing that his spotted hide." EnRePo
    LV. "So soft as I her beauty do behold." PoIE
    LVII. "Sweet warrior when shall I have peace with you?" StP
    LVIII. "Weak is the assurance that weak flesh reposeth." (By Her That Is Most Assured to Her Self.) EnRePo
    LXVII. "Like [*or* Lyke] as a huntsman after weary chase." EnRePo; ILP; PoIE; PoSa
    LXVIII. "Most glorious Lord of life, that on this day." BoC; CABA; EnRePo
    (Easter Morning.) TRV

Amoretti, *sels.* (*continued*)
LXX. "Fresh Spring, the herald of love's mighty king." CABA; StP
LXXV. "One day I wrote her name upon the strand." CABA; CBEP; ILP; StP
LXXXVIII. "Since I have lacked the comfort of that light." EnRePo
Amoris Exsul: In the Bay. Arthur Symons. OBNC
Amorist, The. *Unknown, tr. fr. Greek by* Louis Untermeyer. UnTE
Amorous Dialogue between the Mistris and Her Aprentice, An. *Unknown.* UnTE
Amorous Silvy, The. *Unknown.* UnTE
Amorous Thorn, An. Franco Sacchetti, *tr. fr. Italian by* Daniel J. Donno. AnML
Amours, Les, *sel.* Joachim du Bellay, *tr. fr. French by* George Wyndham.
On His Deafness, XXVI. RBL
Amours de Marie, *sels.* Pierre de Ronsard, *tr. fr. French.* RBL
His Lady's Death, *tr. by* Andrew Lang.
His Lady's Tomb, *tr. by* Andrew Lang.
"Marie, arise, my indolent sweet saint!" *tr. by* Curtis Hidden Page.
To His Young Mistress, *tr. by* Andrew Lang.
Amours de Voyage, *sels.* Arthur Hugh Clough.
Ah, That I Were Far Away, Canto III, *introd.* OBNC
Juxtaposition, Canto III, vi. OBNC
Spirit from Perfecter Ages, A, Canto II, *introd.* OBNC
"There are two different kinds, I believe, of human attraction," Canto II, xi. GTBS-P
"Tibur is beautiful, too, and the orchard slopes, and the Anio," Canto III, xi. GTBS-P
(So Not Seeing I Sung.) OBNC
Ye Ancient Divine Ones, Canto I, x. OBNC
Ampara. Federico García Lorca, *tr. fr. Spanish by* Rachel Benson *and* Robert O'Brien. AnSP
Amphitryon, *sel.* Dryden.
Hourly I Die. UnTE
Ample make this bed. Emily Dickinson. AP; FoBA
Amy Margaret. William Allingham. BiCB
Amyntas Led Me to a Grove. Aphra Behn. *Fr.* The Dutch Lover. ErPo
(Willing Mistress, The.) UnTE
Anabasis, *sel.* "St.-J. Perse," *tr. fr. French by* T. S. Eliot.
Song: Under the Bronze Leaves. PoPl
Ana(Mary Army)gram. George Herbert. CABA
Anatomie of the World, An. John Donne. *See* First Anniversary, The.
Ancestors. Robert Graves. AnMoPo
Ancestors of Isaac Pye, The. Ballad of Cap'n Pye. Robert P. Tristram Coffin. SIV
Ancient Chinese Map of the World. Wieland Schmied, *tr. fr. German by* Christopher Middleton. MGP
Ancient Historian. Chris Wallace-Crabbe. PoAu-2
Ancient Music. Ezra Pound. Par
Ancient Person, for whom I. A Song of a Young Lady to Her Ancient Lover. Earl of Rochester. ErPo
Ancient poets and their learned rhymes, The. An Answer to Some Verses Made in His Praise. Sir John Suckling. PP
Ancient pond, The. Haiku. Basho. CaFP
Ancient story I'll tell you anon, An. King John and the Abbot of Canterbury. *Unknown.* SIV
Ancient Thought, The. Watson Kerr. TRV
Ancient to Ancients, An. Thomas Hardy. GTBS-P
Ancient Virgin, An. George Crabbe. *Fr.* The Parish Register. OBNC
Ancient, winged god, who didst first draw breath. Tasso, *tr. fr. Italian by* Lorna de' Lucchi. RBL
Ancient Winter. Salvatore Quasimodo, *tr. fr. Italian by* Allen Mandelbaum. CoIP
And a ah-la-dee. Little Mathey Grove. *Unknown.* BFSS
"And after all," she says, "and after all." Concerning the Economic Independence of Women. John V. A. Weaver. SIV
"And all her silken flanks with garlands drest." Vlamertinghe: Passing the Chateau. Edmund Blunden. MMA
And all is well, tho' faith and form. In Memoriam A. H. H., CXXVII. Tennyson. VP
. . . and all the sails hang limp. Comes Fog and Mist. William Hart-Smith. *Fr.* Christopher Columbus. PoAu-2
And all the streets lie snug there, clean and regular. Morning. Alfred Lichtenstein. MGP
And all the time the waves, the waves, the waves. John Betjeman. *Fr.* Beside the Seaside. HaSV
And all things are of God. God Was in Christ. Second Corinthians, Bible, *N.T.* TRV
And Angling, Too. Byron. *Fr.* Don Juan. SD
And are ye sure the news is true? The Sailor's Wife. William Julius Mickle. GTBS-P; HaSV
And art thou grieved, sweet and sacred Dove. Grieve Not the Holy Spirit, &c. George Herbert. MeP
And art Thou mine, my dearest Lord? On the Sacrament. Elizabeth Rowe. Three Hymns, 2. WaPE

And boys, be in nothing so moderate as in love of man. Robinson Jeffers. *Fr.* Shine, Perishing Republic. TRV
And call the vales, and bid them hither cast. Milton. *Fr.* Lycidas. WePo
And Can the Physician? *Unknown.* ELP
And children grow up slowly with deep eyes. Ballad of Outer Life. Hugo von Hofmannsthal. TwGP
And Death Shall Have No Dominion. Dylan Thomas. ACV; EaLo; MoRP; PoDB; PoIE; ToPo; WePo
And Did Those Feet in Ancient Time. Blake. *Fr.* Milton. CABA; CaFP; CBEP; FaBV; PoSa
(Jerusalem.) EaLo; EvOK
(Preface.) ILP; PoIE
(Prelude.) OBNC
And do they so? have they a Sense. Rom. Cap. 8. Ver. 19. Henry Vaughan. MeP
And dragging their shining skins. Deeply Gone. Jon Silkin. FiSC
And Every Sky Was Blue and Rain. Ralph Hodgson. *Fr.* To Deck a Woman, II. LOW
And Fall Shall Sit in Judgment. Audre Lorde. NNP
And God said . . . I do set my bow in the cloud. The Rainbow. Genesis, Bible, *O.T.* BoC
And God stepped out on space. The Creation. James Weldon Johnson. FaBV; PoPl; SIV; WePo
And Hate,/ Fear's ugliest child. Fragment from Nothing. Elizabeth J. Coatsworth. LV
And have we done with War at last? Two Fusiliers. Robert Graves. MMA
And he said, A certain man had two sons. St. Luke, Bible, *N.T.* BoC
And here face down beneath the sun. You, Andrew Marvell. Archibald MacLeish. AmLP; AP; CaFP; FaBV; MP; PoIE; StP; VaPo
And here's the happy, bounding flea. The Flea. Roland Young. PoPl
And how much of this. The Death of Nick Charles. LeRoi Jones. CoPo
And I bowed my body and beheld all about. William Langland. *Fr.* The Vision of Piers Plowman. CTC
And I have come upon this place. L'An Trentiesme de Mon Eage. Archibald MacLeish. AmLP
And I have learned how diving's done. Fantasia. Dorothy Livesay. OBCV
And I said to the man who stood at the gate of the year. M. Louise Haskins. *Fr.* The Gate of the Year. TRV; WePo
And, I said, you can take your rich aunts and uncles. The Day I Kicked a Bankroll Out the Window. Charles Bukowski. PtTo
And I shall depart. And the birds will remain. The Definitive Journey. Juan Ramón Jiménez. AnSP
And I took her down by the river. The Faithless Wife. Federico García Lorca. AnSP; ErPo
And I Turned from the Inner Heart. Jon Silkin. PoDB
And if. Tangere. Theodore Enslin. CoPo
And if he ever should come back. The Last Words. Maurice Maeterlinck. PoPl
And if I say I love you, what of that? Another Song. Marion Strobel. MoLP
And If Some Place I Have a Home. Neidhart von Reuental, *tr. fr. German by* Margaret F. Richey. AnML
And in September, O what keen delight! September. Folgore da San Geminiano. *Fr.* Sonnets of the Months. SD
And is the great cause lost beyond recall? Faith. Ada Cambridge. PoAu-1
And Is There Care in Heaven? Spenser. *Fr.* The Faerie Queene, II, 8. OnP
(Guardian Angels of Men.) BoC
And is this—Yarrow!—This the stream. Yarrow Visited. Wordsworth. GTBS-P
And just by crossing the short sea. Channel Crossing. George Barker. ACV; GTBS-P; ToPo
And Lightly, Like the Flowers. Pierre de Ronsard, *tr. fr. French by* W. E. Henley. RBL
And, lo! leading a blessed host comes one. Lincoln. Harriet Monroe. LiPo
And man is a spirit. Louis MacNeice. *Fr.* Holes in the Sky. TRV
And me happiest when I compose poems. The Birth of Tragedy. Irving Layton. OBCV
And nature, the old nurse, took. The Manuscripts of God. Longfellow. TRV
And near me on the grass lies Glanvil's book. Matthew Arnold. *Fr.* The Scholar Gipsy. ACV
And "No" she answered to his plea. Ballad of the Huntsman. Selma Robinson. SIV
And now all nature seem'd in love. On a Banck as I Sate a Fishing. Sir Henry Wotton. SeCP
And now. An attempt. Behold the Lilies of the Field. Anthony Hecht. CoPo; NePoEA-2
And now both bands in close embraces met. Heaps on Heaps. Matthew Concanen. *Fr.* A Match at Football. SD
And Now in Age I Bud Again. George Herbert. CBEP
And now Love sang; but his was such a song. Willowwood, 2. Dante Gabriel Rossetti. *Fr.* The House of Life. VP

"And now," said the Governor, gazing abroad on the piled-up store. The First Thanksgiving Day. Margaret Junkin Preston. SIV; ThLM

And now she cleans her teeth into the lake. Camping Out. William Empson. ToPo

And now the green household is dark. In the Tree House at Night. James Dickey. ToPo

And now the rain again. The Rain and the Rainbow. Leo Fredericks. ACV

"And now to God the Father," he ends. In Church. Thomas Hardy. *Fr.* Satires of Circumstance. DiPo; DTC; PoDB; VaPo; VP

And now where're he strayes. Richard Crashaw. *Fr.* Saint Mary Magdalene. Par

And now you're ready who while she was here. Epigram. J. V. Cunningham. ErPo

And on This Shore. M. Carl Holman. AmNP

And one morning while in the woods I stumbled suddenly upon the thing. Between the World and Me. Richard Wright. AmNP

And one of the malefactors which were hanged railed on him. St. Luke, Bible, *N.T.* BoC

And Paris be it or Helen dying. A Fragment on Death. Villon. CTC

And Polly being drowsy she hung down her head. Polly Oliver. *Unknown.* BSNS

And preparing a net. Wave. Barbara Guest. AmPC

And rustling flowers for some third party waited. Their Lonely Betters. W. H. Auden. LOW

And Ruth said, Intreat me not to leave. Ruth, Bible, *O.T.* PoPl

And seeing the multitudes, he went up. St. Matthew, Bible, *N.T.* PoPl

And Shall Trelawny Die? Robert Stephen Hawker. *See* Song of the Western Men, The.

And she, being old, fed from a mashed plate. Old Woman. Iain Crichton Smith. NePoEA-2

And she gave birth to a strong healthy boy. Baobab. Hans Arp. MGP

And she said. Ritratto. Ezra Pound. PP

And She Washed His Feet with Her Tears, and Wiped Them with the Hairs of Her Head. Sir Edward Sherburne, *after the Italian of* Giambattista Marino. CBEP; RBL

And silence. The End of Man Is His Beauty. LeRoi Jones. AmNP

And so depart into dark. Homage to Ezra Pound. Gilbert Highet. Par

And so I somehow-nohow played. Robert Browning. *Fr.* Fifine at the Fair. Par

And so, in that dark chamber, marble was the floor. San Francesco, at Night. Yves Bonnefoy. CoFP

And So Men Say, I Love Thee! Derwent Coleridge. CBEP

And so one sees all living matter perish. Sonnet VII. Louise Labé. RBL

And So Should You. *Unknown.* STF

And so the day drops by; the horizon draws. Frederick Goddard Tuckerman. *Fr.* Sonnets. PoIE

And so we two came where the rest have come. The Question. F. T. Prince. GTBS-P

And so you found that poor room dull. Appearances. Robert Browning. CBEP

"And something that . . . that is theirs—no longer ours." The Dispossessed. John Berryman. AP; PoCh

And still we stood and stared far down. "Therefore Is the Name of It Called Babel." Sir Osbert Sitwell. MMA

And Suddenly It's Evening. Salvatore Quasimodo, *tr. fr. Italian by* Allen Mandelbaum. CoIP

And suddenly the flowing night stands still. Burning Bush. Louis Untermeyer. MoLP

And the angel spoke and made an effort. Joseph's Suspicion. Rainer Maria Rilke. MoRP

And the curtains, the lamp. True to a Dream. Donald Petersen. NePoEA-2

And the first grey of morning fill'd the east. Sohrab and Rustum. Matthew Arnold. CABL; VP

And the Green Grass Grew All Around, *with music. Unknown.* BFSS

And the Horns of Summer Fell Silent. Georg Heym, *tr. fr. German by* Michael Hamburger. MGP

And the Lord Was Not in the Whirlwind. Louis MacNeice. *Fr.* Visitations, VII. EaLo

And the many days and the many nights that I lay as one barren. A Canticle to the Christ in the Holy Eucharist. Brother Antoninus. ToPo

And the mist: and the rain in the west: and the wind steady. The Omelet of A. MacLeish. Edmund Wilson. Par

And the Old Women Gathered. Mari Evans. NNP

And the Pear Trees Shiver. Jocelyn Macy Sloan. FiSC

And then I pressed the shell. The Shell. James Stephens. HaSV; LV

And then I wakened up in such a fright. Midnight. James Stephens. DTC

And Then the Sun. Pradip Sen. ACV

And then went down to the ship. Canto I. Ezra Pound. AP; PoIE

"And There Was a Great Calm." Thomas Hardy. MoRP

And There Was Mary Magdalene and the Other Mary, Sitting Over against the Sepulchre. W. R. Rodgers. WePo

And there were in the same country shepherds [*or* shepherds in the same country] abiding in the field. Christmas Eve [*or* The Angels of Bethlehem *or* The First Christmas]. St. Luke, Bible, *N.T.* BiCB; BoC; SoPo

And they both lived happily ever after. After Ever Happily; *or,* The Princess and the Woodcutter. Ian Serraillier. BoLP

And they had fixed the wedding day. Wordsworth. *Fr.* The Thorn. EvOK

And this digester, this digester of food. Poem. Conrad Aiken. *Fr.* Time in the Rock. VaPo

And this freedom will be the freedom of all. A Free Nation. Edwin Markham. TRV

And this is now their home. H. H. Dugmore. *Fr.* A Reminiscence of 1820. ACV

And this July—its nakedness burned out. Tansy for August. Theodore Enslin. CoPo

And this reft house is that the which he built. On a Ruined House in a Romantic Country. Samuel Taylor Coleridge. Par

And thou art dead, as young and fair. Elegy on Thyrza. Byron. GTBS-P

And thou hast walked about (how strange a story!). Address to a Mummy. Horace Smith. RoGo

And thus continuing, she said. Wordsworth. *Fr.* The Sailor's Mother. Par

And Thus He Spoke. John A. Stone. SGR

And Thus in Nineveh. Ezra Pound. PP

And walked across Potomac into Thebes. Effigy. Georgia Lee McElhaney. CoPo

And was it good for you this time? The Love-making: His and Hers. Eve Merriam. UnTE

And was the day of my delight. In Memoriam A. H. H., XXIV. Tennyson. VP

And we marched against them there in the next spring. Archibald MacLeish. *Fr.* Conquistador. ThLM

And what is love? It is a doll dress'd [*or* dressed] up. Modern Love. Keats. CBEP; OBNC

And what is so rare as a day in June. June. James Russell Lowell. *Fr.* The Vision of Sir Launfal. AmLP; FaBV; FaPL

"And When He Had Scourged Jesus, He Delivered Him to Be Crucified." W. R. Rodgers. WePo

And when he was twelve years old, they went up after the custom of the feast. St. Luke, Bible, *N.T.* BoC

And when I heard their voices on the stair. The Betrayal. Josephine W. Johnson. MoRP

And when she strides. Jacqueline. "Will Inman." OPP

And while my visitor prattled. Secret Thoughts. Christopher Morley. *Fr.* Translations from the Chinese. EvOK

And Who Has Seen a Fair Alluring Face. George Peele. ErPo

And who shall say. Magic. Thomas Wolfe. PoPl

And who shall separate the dust. Common Dust. Georgia Douglas Johnson. AmNP

And why to me this, thou lame Lord of fire. An Execration upon Vulcan. Ben Jonson. SeCP

And will tomorrow come? And if it comes. The Humming Stair. Joseph Payne Brennan. FiSC

"And will you cut a stone for him." The Stone. W. W. Gibson. PoPo; SIV

And Wilt Thou Leave Me Thus? Sir Thomas Wyatt. CBEP; EnRePo; PoIE

(Lover's Appeal, The.) GTBS-P

And with great fear I inhabit the middle of the night. The Acts of Youth. John Wieners. CoPo

And yet this great wink of eternity. Voyages, II. Hart Crane. AmLP; DTC; PoDB; PoIE; VaPo

And You as Well Must Die, Beloved Dust. Edna St. Vincent Millay. PoLF

And you believed that I would do it so? Broken Monologue. "Michael Lewis." UnTE

Andante, ma Non Assai. Rufinus, *tr. fr. Greek by* Dudley Fitts. ErPo

Andre. Gwendolyn Brooks. RePo

Andrea del Sarto. Robert Browning. CABA; CTC; DiPo; StP; VP

Andrew Bardeen, *with music. Unknown.* BFSS

(Andrew Batan, *with music.*) BSO

Andrew Lammie. *Unknown.* BSNS

Andrew Rykman's Prayer, *sel.* Whittier. "If there be some weaker one." TRV

Andy's Gone with Cattle. Henry Lawson. PoAu-1

Ane doolie sessoun to ane cairfull dyte. The Testament of Cresseid. Robert Henryson. CABL

Anear the centre of that northern crest. James Thomson. *Fr.* The City of Dreadful Night. GTBS-P

Anecdote of the Jar. Wallace Stevens. AP; CaFP; PoIE; SIV; VP

Anecdotes of the Late War, *sel.* Charles Olson. "That (like the man sd) Booth." LiPo

Angel in the House, The, *sels.* Coventry Patmore.
Honor and Desert, II, iv, 1. FaPL
Love at Large. StP
Rainbow, The, II, iii, 2. GTBS-P
Revelation, The, I, viii, 2. GTBS-P; OBNC
Tribute, The, I, iv, 2. FaPL; OBNC
Unthrift, I, iii, 3. FaPL
Angel living near the moon, An. To Dick, on His Sixth
Birthday. Sara Teasdale. BiCB
Angel, robed in spotless white, An. Dawn. Paul Laurence
Dunbar. AmNP; PoLF
Angel told Mary, An. A Christmas Carol. Harry Behn.
BiCB
Angel Unawares, An. *Unknown.* TRV
Angelo Orders His Dinner. Bayard Taylor. Par
Angels are stooping, The. A Cradle Song. W. B. Yeats.
PoPl
Angels Came a-Mustering, The. *Unknown, tr. fr. Hebrew by*
Israel Zangwill. EaLo
Angels from the long ago. The Light Now Shineth. *Un-*
known. STF
Angels of Bethlehem, The. St. Luke, Bible, *N.T. See* Christ-
mas Eve.
Angels walking under the palm trees. A Little Carol of the
Virgin. Lope de Vega. AnSP
Angel, where you soar. A Prayer. Alfred Noyes. PoPl
Angelus inquit pastoribus. Now the Most High Is Born.
James Ryman. MeEL
Anger. Robert Creeley. CoPo
Anger in its time and place. Charles *and* Mary Lamb. ThGo
Anglais Mort à Florence. Wallace Stevens. AP
Angler's Song, The, *sel.* William Basse.
"As inward love breeds outward talk." SD
Angora anger who art in heaven. Lyric. Gil Orlovitz. ToPo
Angry threat of silence, ever present, The. Woman Telephon-
ing. Joseph Joel Keith. FiSC
Anguish of the earth absolves our eyes, The. Absolution.
Siegfried Sassoon. MMA
Anguish'd Doubt Broods over Eden, The. Christopher Brennan.
Fr. Lilith. PoAu-1
Angus McGregor. Lew Sarett. SIV
Animal Crackers. Christopher Morley. SoPo
Animal Fair, The. *Unknown.* SoPo
Animal Store, The. Rachel Field. SoPo
Animals, The. Edwin Muir. AnMoPo; PoDB
Animals. Walt Whitman. Song of Myself, XXXII. PoPl
(Beasts, The.) CBEP
("I think I could turn and live with animals, they are so
placid and self-contained.") BoC
Animals are silent in the hold, The. Noah's Song. Evan
Jones. PoAu-2
Ann, Ann!/ Come! quick as you can! Alas, Alack. Walter
de la Mare. EvOK
Ann and the Fairy Song. Walter de la Mare. *Fr.* A Child's
Day. FaBV
Ann Rutledge. Edgar Lee Masters. *See* Anne Rutledge.
Anna. Burns. UnTE
(Gowden Locks of Anna, The.) CBEP
Annabel Lee. Poe. AP; BoLP; DiPo; FaPL; OnMSP; PoPl;
PoPo; RoGo; SIV
Annan Water. *Unknown.* BuBa
Anne Rutledge. Edgar Lee Masters. *Fr.* Spoon River Anthol-
ogy. AmLP; ILP; LiPo; PoPl; PoSC; ThLM
(Ann Rutledge.) PoSa
Annie Died the Other Day. E. E. Cummings. ErPo
Annie Laurie. William Douglas. FaBV
Annie of Lochroyan. *Unknown.* BuBa
Annihilation of Nothing, The. Thom Gunn. NePoEA-2
Anniversary [*or* Anniversarie], The. John Donne. CBEP;
DiPo; MeP; OnP; SeCP
Anniversary. Richmond Lattimore. PoCh
Anniversary. R. S. Thomas. ToPo
Anniversary. John Wain. MP; NePoEA-2; ToPo
Anniversary in September. Beatrice Curtis Brown. BiCB
Announced by all the trumpets of the sky. The Snow-Storm.
Emerson. AP; DiPo; LV; PoLF; PoPo; StP; VaPo;
WiR
Annunciation. John Donne. MeP
Annunciation. Ruth Gilbert. *Fr.* The Blossom of the
Branches. ACV
Annunciation, The. W. S. Merwin. AP
Annunciation, The. *Unknown.* MeEL
Annunciations. Geoffrey Hill. NePoEA-2
Anonymous as cherubs. Two Voices in a Meadow. Richard
Wilbur. CaFP
Anonymous Drawing. Donald Justice. NePoEA-2
Another. Abraham Cowley, *after the Greek of* Anacreon.
SeCP
Another. Richard Lovelace. SeCP
Another and the Same. Samuel Rogers. *Fr.* Human Life.
OBNC
Another armored animal—scale. The Pangolin. Marianne
Moore. AP

Another Birthday. Ben Jonson. WiR
Another epic! Who inflicts again. Byron. *Fr.* English Bards
and Scotch Reviewers. EiCP
Another Grace for a Child. Robert Herrick. CABA; CaFP;
GoJo
(Child's Grace, A.) EaLo
("Here a little child I stand.") ThGo
Another hill town. Hotel Paradiso e Commerciale. John
Malcolm Brinnin. MP; PoCh
Another. In Defence of Their Inconstancie. Ben Jonson.
SeCP
Another Ladyes Exception Present at the Hearing. Ben Jonson.
Fr. A Celebration of Charis. SeCP
Another man has fled to Habana, Jorge. Shadows for the Sun.
Carl Yeargens. PtTo
Another Meditation at the Same Time. Edward Taylor. *See*
Meditation Six.
Another Ode to the North-East Wind. *Unknown.* Par
Another on the University Carrier. Milton. CABA
Another Poem on Nietzsche. Stefan George, *tr. fr. German by*
Walter Kaufmann. TwGP
Another September. Thomas Kinsella. PoCh
Another Song. Donald Justice. NePoEA-2
Another Song. Marion Strobel. MoLP
Another Spring. Christina Rossetti. VP
Another to the Same. Horace, *tr. fr. Latin by* William
Browne. Odes, I, 5. WiR
Another Year ("Another year is dawning"). Frances Ridley
Havergal. STF
Another Year ("Another year has now been born"). Oswald
J. Smith. STF
Answer, The. Robinson Jeffers. MoRP
Answer to Some Verses Made in His Praise, An. Sir John
Suckling. PP
Answer you, Sirs? Do I understand aright? Giuseppe Capon-
sacchi. Robert Browning. *Fr.* The Ring and the Book. VP
Answered Prayer, The. Annie Johnson Flint. STF
Answering a Letter from a Younger Poet. Brewster Ghiselin.
PoCh
Answers, The. Robert Clairmont. SoPo
Answers. Elizabeth Jennings. PoDB
Ant, The ("The ant, a prodigy of strength"). Richard Armour.
PoPo
Ant, The ("The ant has made himself illustrious"). Ogden
Nash. FaBV
Ant-ology. Christian Morgenstern, *tr. fr. German by* R. C. F.
Hull. MGP
Ant on the tablecloth, An. Departmental. Robert Frost. DiPo
Ant Sun, The. Christopher Middleton. *Fr.* Herman Moon's
Hourbook. NePoEA-2
Anthem for Doomed Youth. Wilfred Owen. EvOK; GTBS-P;
PoPo
Antichrist. Edwin Muir. EaLo
Anticipation. Emily Brontë. OBNC
Anticipation. Lord De Tabley. ELP
Antigone, *sel.* Sophocles, *tr. fr. Greek by* F. L. Lucas.
What a Piece of Work Is a Man. SiGo
Antigonish. Hughes Mearns. *See* Little Man Who Wasn't
There, The.
Antiplatonick, The. John Cleveland. SeCP
Antique Harvesters. John Crowe Ransom. AP
Antique Shop. Carl Carmer. RePo
Antiquity of Freedom, The. Bryant. AP
Antiwarwoman. Curtis Zahn. PtTo
Antonin Artaud. René Char, *tr. fr. French by* David Lunde.
CoFP
Antonio. Laura E. Richards. SoPo
Antonio Torres Heredia. Arrest of Antoñito el Camborio.
Federico García Lorca. AnSP
Antony and Cleopatra, *sel.* Shakespeare.
Cleopatra: The Barge She Sat In, *fr.* II, ii. DiPo
Antony's Oration. Shakespeare. *Fr.* Julius Caesar, III, ii.
PoPl
Ant's a Centaur, The. Ezra Pound. *Fr.* Pisan Cantos. PoSa
Ants are walking under the ground, The. The People. Eliza-
beth Madox Roberts. GoJo; SoPo
Anvil of God's Word, The. *Unknown.* STF
Any Human to Another. Countee Cullen. MoRP
Any Man to His Secretary. Hilary Corke. ErPo
Any Wife to Any Husband. Robert Browning. OBNC
Anyone Lived in a Pretty How Town. E. E. Cummings. AP;
CABA; CaFP; DiPo; EvOK; ILP; MP; PoSa
Anyway, the old man said, and winked at the barmaid. Yes
Please Gentlemen. A. R. D. Fairburn. ACV
Anzac Cove. Leon Gellert. PoAu-1
Ape, The. Roland Young. PoPl
Apeneck Sweeney spreads his knees. Sweeney among the
Nightingales. T. S. Eliot. AP; CABA; CaFP; DiPo;
FoBA; ILP
Apennine. Pier Paolo Pasolini, *tr. fr. Italian by* William F.
Weaver. CoIP
Apes yawn and adore their fleas in the sun. The Jaguar. Ted
Hughes. PoPl; ToPo

Aphrodite Pandemos. *Unknown, tr. fr. Greek by* Louis Unter-
meyer. UnTE
Apis! the men you boxed with, grateful that you. The World's
Worst Boxer. Lucilius. SD
Apocalypse. Edith Lovejoy Pierce. MoRP
Apollo and Daphne. Giambattista Marino, *tr. fr. Italian
by* Philip Ayres. RBL
Apollo and Daphne. W. R. Rodgers. ErPo
Apologia pro Vita Sua. Samuel Taylor Coleridge. PP
Apologie for the Precedent Hymnes on Teresa, An. Richard
Crashaw. MeP
Apology. Paul Bartlett. PoNC
Apology, The. Emerson. AP
Apology, An: "Of Heaven or Hell I have no power to sing."
William Morris. *Fr.* The Earthly Paradise. OBNC;
PoIE
Apology for Bad Dreams. Robinson Jeffers. AP; ILP
Apology for Loose Behavior. Ovid, *tr. fr. Latin by* Christopher
Marlowe. *Fr.* Amores. UnTE
Apology for Understatement. John Wain. NePoEA-2; ToPo
Apology for Youth. Sister Mary Madeleva. PoPl
Apopemptic Hymn. Dorothy Auchterlonie. PoAu-2
Apostles of the hidden sun. The Last Supper. Oscar Wil-
liams. MoRP
Apparel of green woods and meadows gay. On Revisiting
Cintra after the Death of Catarina. Luís de Camões.
RBL
Apparently with no surprise. Emily Dickinson. AP; CABA;
CaFP; ILP
Apparition, The. John Donne. CABA; CBEP; EnRePo;
SeCP
Apparition of His Mistresse Calling Him to Elizium, The.
Robert Herrick. SeCP
Apparition of these faces in the crowd, The. In a Station of
the Metro. Ezra Pound. CABA; CaFP; PoIE; VaPo
Apparitions. Thomas Curtis Clark. TRV
Apparitions Are Not Singular Occurrences. Diane Wakoski.
CoPo
Appeal to the Phoenix. Louis Untermeyer. UnTE
Appearances. Robert Browning. CBEP
Applause flutters onto the open air. A Snapshot for Miss
Bricka Who Lost in the Semi-final Round of the Pennsyl-
vania Lawn Tennis Tournament at Haverford, July, 1960.
Robert Wallace. SD
Apple blossom is crystal white. Brown Bear's Honey Song.
Kathryn Jackson. RePo
Apple Gathering, An. Christina Rossetti. BoLP; OBNC
Apple Offering. *Unknown, tr. fr. Greek by* Louis Untermeyer.
UnTE
Apple-Tree, The. Brian Vrepont. PoAu-2
Apple trees are made to sing in. The Comfortable Apple Trees.
Grace Taber Hallock. RePo
Apples. Laurie Lee. WePo
(Autumn Apples.) BoC
Apples and Water. Robert Graves. DaDu; PoIE
Appoggiatura. Donald Jeffrey Hayes. AmNP
Approaches. George Macdonald. TRV
Après-midi d'un faune, L', *sel.* Stéphane Mallarmé, *tr. fr.
French by* Aldous Huxley.
"Proud of my music, let me often make." ErPo
April. Sara Teasdale. PoSC; SoPo
April. Eunice Tietjens. SoPo
April. Sir William Watson. FaBV
(Song: "April, April.") PoSC
April again, and its message unvaried, the same old impromptu.
The Burden of Junk. John Classco. OBCV
April, April. April [or Song]. Sir William Watson. FaBV;
PoSC
April Day: Binsey. Michael Hamburger. DaDu
April Fool. Elizabeth J. Coatsworth. RePo
April Fool. Eleanor Hammond. SoPo
April Fool. Hal Summers. DaDu
April Fools' Day. Marnie Pomeroy. PoSC
April Inventory. W. D. Snodgrass. AP; CABA; MP; PoPl
April is the cruellest month, breeding. The Waste Land. T. S.
Eliot. AP; CABA
April Rise. Laurie Lee. BoC
April Snow, The. Jones Very. AP
April's Amazing Meaning. George Dillon. AmLP; BoLP
Ara Mara Amara. "Aldo Palazzeschi," *tr. fr. Italian by* Carlo
L. Golino. CoIP
Arabian Nights Entertainments. *Unknown. See* Thousand
and One Nights, The.
Arachnida, Female. Aletha Humphreys. FiSC
Aran. Rudolf Hagelstange, *tr. fr. German by* Michael Ham-
burger. MGP
Arawata Bill. Denis Glover. ACV
Arbor Day Tree, An. *Unknown.* RePo
Arbor Vitae. Coventry Patmore. The Unknown Eros, II, iii.
OBNC
Arcades, *sel.* Milton.
Nymphs and Shepherds [Dance No More]. CBEP; ELP
Arcadia, *sels.* Sir Philip Sidney.

My True Love Hath My Heart. CBEP; DiPo; ILP
(Ditty, A: "My true-love hath my heart, and I have his.")
GTBS-P
(My True Love.) WePo
Sestina. StP
What Tongue Can Her Perfections Tell. EnRePo
When Two Suns Do Appear. EnRePo
Archaic Torso of Apollo. Rainer Maria Rilke, *tr. fr. German
by* Walter Kaufmann. TwGP
Archer, The. A. J. M. Smith. OBCV
Archer is awake, The! Peace on Earth. William Carlos
Williams. LOW
Archie of Cawfield. *Unknown.* BuBa
Archimedes and the Student. Schiller, *tr. fr. German by*
Walter Kaufmann. TwGP
Archy and Mehitabel, *sels.* Don Marquis.
Archy Confesses. EvOK
Hen and the Oriole, The. EvOK
Prudence. LV
Archy Does His Part, *sel.* Don Marquis.
Fate Is Unfair. EvOK
Archys Life of Mehitabel, *sel.* Don Marquis.
Mehitabel Tries Marriage. WePo
Arcturus is his other name. Emily Dickinson. FaBV
Ardent lover cannot find, The. The Disappointed Wife. Hetty
Wright. WaPE
Are All the Children In? *Unknown.* STF
Are God and Nature then at strife. Tennyson. *Fr.* In Memo-
riam A. H. H., LV. TRV
Are the desolate, dark weeks. These. William Carlos Wil-
liams. AP
Are They Shadows That We See? Samuel Daniel. *Fr.*
Tethys' Festival. PoIE
Are We Thankful ("Are we being fair, I wonder")? *Un-
known.* STF
Are You a Marsupial? John Becker. RePo
Are you an active member. Do You Just Belong? *Unknown.*
STF
"Are you awake, Gemelli." Star-Talk. Robert Graves. GoJo
Are You Born? Muriel Rukeyser. MoRP
"Are you looking for someone, you who come pattering."
Thoughts of Thomas Hardy. Edmund Blunden. PoCh
Are You looking for us? We are here. The 151st Psalm. Karl
Shapiro. EaLo
Are you so weary? Come to the window. Wind in the Grass.
Mark Van Doren. FaBV
Are you standing at Wit's-End Corner. Wit's-End Corner.
Unknown. STF
Arethusa. Shelley. WiR
Argument of His Book, The. Robert Herrick. PoIE; SeCP
Aria. Delmore Schwartz. ErPo
Aridity. "Michael Field." BoC; TRV
Aridity. C. S. Lewis. BoC
Ariel. David Campbell. PoAu-2
Ariel to Miranda:—Take. To a Lady with a Guitar. Shelley.
GTBS-P
Ariel's Dirge. Shakespeare. *See* Full Fathom Five.
Ariel's Song. Shakespeare. *See* Come unto These Yellow
Sands.
"Arise, arise, ye seven brethren." The Seven Brethren. *Un-
known.* BSNS
Arise, Fond Lover, Who Sleeps on Chilly Mornings. Nuño
Fernández de Turneol, *tr. fr. Portuguese by* William M.
Davis. AnML
Aristotle to Phyllis. John Hollander. PoCh
Arithmetic ("Arithmetic is where numbers fly like pigeons").
Carl Sandburg. RePo
Arizona Boys and Girls, *with music. Unknown.* BFSS
Ark, The. Irving Feldman. AmPC
Ark, The. Eugenio Montale, *tr. fr. Italian by* Carlo L. Golino.
CoIP
Armada, The, *sel.* Macaulay. *Fr.* Lays of Ancient Rome.
"Night sank upon the dusky beach, and on the purple sea."
OBNC
Armistice Day. John Freeman. MMA
Armand! I lose my vital heat. François Maynard, *tr. fr.
French by* Henry Carrington. RBL
Armor of Mars, The. Pause. Rosa Zagnoni Marinoni. FiSC
Armorial. Ralph Gustafson. ACV
Armour's Undermining Modesty. Marianne Moore. AP
Arms and the Boy. Wilfred Owen. PoPo
Arms reversed and banners craped. A Dirge for McPherson.
Herman Melville. AP
Army Corps on the March, An. Walt Whitman. PoLF
Arnold, warm with God. The Last Warmth of Arnold. Greg-
ory Corso. CoPo
Arno's Vale. Charles Sackville. WaPE
Around the images of thirty years. The Municipal Gallery
Revisited. W. B. Yeats. GTBS-P
Around the Corner. Charles Hanson Towne. PoLF
A-Roving. *Unknown.* UnTE
Arrange the scene with only a shade of difference. An In-
cident. Douglas Le Pan. ACV

Arras. P. K. Page. OBCV
Arrest of Antoñito el Camborio. Federico García Lorca, tr. fr. Spanish by Robert O'Brien. AnSP
Arrest of Oscar Wilde at the Cadogan Hotel, The. John Betjeman. DTC
Arrival at the Waldorf. Wallace Stevens. PP
Arrival of the Greenhorn, The. John A. Stone. RePo; SGR, with music.
Arrival of the San Francisco, with music. Isaac W. Baker. SGR
Arrivals and Departures. Melvin Walker La Follette. CoPo
Arrow and the Song, The. Longfellow. LV; PoPl
Arrow Flying Past, An. Gustavo Adolfo Bécquer, tr. fr. Spanish by J. M. Cohen. AnSP; SiGo
Arrow rides upon the sky, An. Love Song. Samuel Allen. NNP
Arrows of Love. Chauras, tr. fr. Sanskrit by E. Powys Mathers. SiGo
Arrow's quick indeed, swift swirls away the air, An. Concerning Time. Christian Friedrich Hunold. AGP
Ars Poetica. X. J. Kennedy. ErPo; PP
Ars Poetica. Archibald MacLeish. AP; CaFP; DiPo; PoPl; PoPo; PP; VaPo
Ars Poetica about Ultimates. Tram Combs. MP
Ars Victrix, sel. Austin Dobson, after Théophile Gautier.
"All passes. Art alone." CTC
Arsenal at Springfield, The. Longfellow. AP
Art. Herman Melville. AP; PoIE
Art of Love, The, sels. Ovid, tr. fr. Latin by Dryden.
"In Cupid's school whoe'er would take degree." UnTE
"Kiss if you can: Resistance if she make." ErPo
Art of Poetry, The. Nicolas Boileau-Despréaux. See Art poétique, L'.
Art of Poetry, The. Yves Bonnefoy, tr. fr. French by Vincent Stewart. CoFP
Art of Poetry, An. James McAuley. ACV
Art of the Sonnet, sels. Gil Orlovitz. ToPo
"Bowed negress, who aghast but the light."
"If I could rise and see my father young."
"Such folly of margins that may retaliate."
Art poétique, L', sel. Nicolas Boileau-Despréaux, tr. fr. French by Sir William Soames and John Dryden.
"Rash author, 'tis a vain presumptuous crime." PP
Art Thou Gone in Haste? Unknown. ELP
Art thou gone so far. Ode: The Spirit Wooed. Richard Watson Dixon. OBNC
Art thou pale for weariness. To the Moon. Shelley. GTBS; RePo
Art Thou Poor? Thomas Dekker and others. Fr. The Pleasant Comedy of Patient Grissell, I, i. CBEP
(Happy Heart, The.) GTBS-P
"Artemidora! Gods invisible." The Death of Artemidora. Walter Savage Landor. Fr. Pericles and Aspasia. OBNC
Artemis. Peter Davison. ErPo
Artemis. Dulcie Deamer. PoAu-1
Artichoke, The. Ibn al-Talla, tr. fr. Arabic by William M. Davis. AnML
Artist, The. Kenneth Koch. AmPC
Artist and His Work, The. Michelangelo, tr. fr. Italian by John Addington Symonds. RBL
Artist as Cuckold, The. Unknown, tr. fr. Greek by Louis Untermeyer. UnTE
Artist on Penmaenmawr, The. Charles Tennyson-Turner. OBNC
Artist, who underneath the table. On a Spider. Edward Littleton. WaPE
Arundel Tomb, An. Philip Larkin. NePoEA-2
As a beauty I am not a star. My Face. Anthony Euwer. PoLF
As a child [or As a Black Child I was a dreamer]. Four Sheets to the Wind and a One-Way Ticket to France, 1933. Conrad Kent Rivers. AmNP; NNP
As a child holds a pet. Port Bou. Stephen Spender. MP
As a dare-gale skylark scanted in a dull cage. The Caged Skylark. Gerard Manley Hopkins. VP
As a fond mother, when the day is o'er. Nature. Longfellow. AP; PoLF; TRV
As a friend to the children commend me the Yak. The Yak. Hilaire Belloc. FaBV
As a maid was walking in her garden. The Single Sailor (A vers.). Unknown. BSNS
As a naked man I go. In Waste Places. James Stephens. CaFP
As a Plane Tree by the Water. Robert Lowell. AP; DTC; PoDB; VaPo
As a Possible Lover. LeRoi Jones. AmNP
As a shy deer that hurtles into sunlight. For Simone Weil. Sister M. Thérèse. MoRP
As a sloop with a sweep of immaculate wing on her delicate spine. Buick. Karl Shapiro. CoFP; PoIE
As a twig trembles, which a bird. She Came and Went. James Russell Lowell. FaPL
As a water lily only blooms. Hope's Forecast. Ethel Romig Fuller. RePo

As a white candle. The Old Woman. Joseph Campbell. ACV
As a young stag the thicket passed [or past]. Fable XIII: The Tame Stag. John Gay. CBEP; EICP
As Adam Early in the Morning. Walt Whitman. AP
As after noon, one summer's day. Cupid Mistaken. Matthew Prior. EiCP
As Ah walked oot, yah Sunday morn. Bleeberrying. Jonathan Denwood. MoBS
As an audacious knight. Of a Bee. Tasso. RBL
As at noon Dulcina rested. Come to Me Soon. Sir Walter Ralegh. UnTE
As beautiful as the hands. For Miriam. Kenneth Patchen. ToPo
As beautiful Kitty one morning was tripping. Kitty of Coleraine. Unknown. SIV
As Birds Are Fitted to the Boughs. Louis Simpson. BoLP
As blossoms white, bricks quiver in light. Manhattan Skyline. Eugene M. Kayden. LV
As children bring their broken toys. Reproof. Unknown. STF
As Cloris [or Chloris] full of harmless thoughts. A Song. Earl of Rochester. ErPo; UnTE
As Cloe came into the room t'other day. A [or The] Lover's Anger. Matthew Prior. ErPo; UnTE
As day did darken on the dewless grass. The Wind at the Door. William Barnes. CBEP; ELP; GTBS-P
As difference blends into identity. In Identity. Josephine Miles. OPP
As doctors give physic by way of prevention. For My Own Monument. Matthew Prior. EiCP
As Dolly and her favorite swain. The Unfortunate Reminder. William Pattison. UnTE
As down in Cupid's garden for pleasure I did walk. The Prentice Boy. Unknown. BSNS
As due by many titles I resign. John Donne. Holy Sonnets, II. MeP
As far as most of what you call people, my darling, are. Suburban Homecoming. John Ciardi. ToPo
As fire, unfound are pole approaches pole. William Baylebridge. Fr. Love Redeemed. PoAu-1
As from an ancestral oak. Similes for Two Political Characters of 1819. Shelley. CBEP
As gay for you to take your father's ax. To a Young Wretch. Robert Frost. PoDB
As God claps hands of time and space. Chant. Oscar Williams. MoRP
As he climbs down our hill, my kestrel rises. Esyllt. Glyn Jones. DTC
As he trudged along to school. The Story of Johnny Head-in-Air. Heinrich Hoffmann. BBGG
As Hermes once stoole to his feathers light. A Dream after Reading Dante's Episode of Paolo and Francesca [or On a Dream]. Keats. CBEP; DiPo
As Holy Kirke makes mind. The Nativity. Unknown. MeEL
As I beheld a winters evening air. Another. Richard Lovelace. SeCP
As I came down Talbingo Hill. Bullocky Bill. Unknown. PoAu-1
As I came home the other night. The Drunken Fool. Unknown. BFSS
As I came o'er the Cairney Mount. My Bonnie Highland Laddie. Burns. UnTE
As I came over Windy Gap. Running to Paradise. W. B. Yeats. LOW
As I came to the edge of the woods. Come In. Robert Frost. DiPo; FaBV; FoBA; PoIE; WePo
As I drive to the junction of lane and highway. At Castle Boterel. Thomas Hardy. DTC; GTBS-P; OBNC; PoSa
As I fell—from mind-perch precarious. This Here Is Hell. Samuel M. Bradley. FiSC
As I hear it, now when there is company. Grandmother and Grandson. W. S. Merwin. NePoEA-2
As in hoary [or hoarie] winter's night stood shivering in the snow. The Burning Babe. Robert Southwell. CABA; CBEP; ILP; MeP; PoIE; StP
As I lay asleep in Italy. The Mask of Anarchy. Shelley. CABL
As I lay upon a night. Jesus Reassures His Mother. Unknown. MeEL
As I lie here in the sun. Jonah. Randall Jarrell. MoRP
As I listened from a beach-chair in the shade. Their Lonely Betters. W. H. Auden. GoJo
As I mused by the hearthside. At Home, Alone with the Cat. Walter de la Mare. BoC
As I once came from Toggingham. Tottingham Frolic. Unknown. UnTE
As I passed by a river side. The Crow and the Crane. Unknown. BuBa
As I returned from London. Johnny German. Unknown. BFSS
As I rode over to tavern barry. The Dying Cowboy (A vers.). Unknown. BSO
As I Roved Out. Unknown. DTC
As I sail o'er life's wide ocean. The Pilot. Unknown. STF

As I sailed by the churchyard. Serenade to a Cornish Fox. Charles Causley. HaSV

As I Sat at the Café. Arthur Hugh Clough. *Also in* Dipsychus. ELP; WePo, *st.* 1 (Spectator ab Extra, 3 *sts.*) GTBS-P

As I Sat on a Sunny Bank. *Unknown.* PoPo

As I sat under a sycamore tree. I Saw Three Ships. *Unknown.* HaSV

As I sd to my/ friend. I Know a Man. Robert Creeley. AmPC; CoPo

As I sit in twilight late alone by the flickering oak-flame. A Twilight Song. Walt Whitman. FoBA

As I stood at the door. In the College of Surgeons. James Stephens. LOW

As I walked down by the river side. Lost Willie. *Unknown.* BSO

As I walked down to Louisville some pleasure for to find. The Lily of the West (B *vers.*). *Unknown.* BSO

As I Walked in the Woods. *Unknown.* UnTE

As I walked out of St. James's Hospital. The Bad Girl's Lament. *Unknown.* BFSS

As I walked out of Tom Sherman's barroom. The Cowboy's Lament. *Unknown.* BFSS

As I walked out on a fine summer's evening. Waterloo. *Unknown.* BSNS

As I Walked Out One Evening. W. H. Auden. DiPo; MP; PoSa

As I walked out one evening down by a river clear. Reilly's Farewell. *Unknown.* BSNS

As I walked out one evening down by the river side/ I overheard a damsel. The Banks of Claudie. *Unknown.* BSNS

As I walked out one evening down by the river side,/ Along the banks of sweet Dundee. The *Lady of the Lake*. *Unknown.* BSNS

As I walked out one evening fair. The Dark-eyed Sailor. *Unknown.* BSNS

As I walked out one May morning,/ One May morning so early. I'm Seventeen Come Sunday. *Unknown.* UnTE

As I walked out one May morning/ To see if the leaves had come. John of Hazelgreen (B *vers.*). *Unknown.* BFSS

As I walked out one midsummer's morning. The Banks of Sweet Primroses. *Unknown.* ELP

As I walked out one morning/ All in the month of May. The Banks of Claudy. *Unknown.* BSO

As I walked out one morning/ All for to take the air. Johnny German. *Unknown.* BSNS

As I walked out one morning early. John Riley. *Unknown.* BSO

As I walked out one morning fair all in the month of June. The Dawning of the Day. *Unknown.* BSNS

As I walked out one morning for pleasure. Whoopee High Ogie. *Unknown.* BFSS

As I walked out one morning in May. Who Will Shoe Your Feet? *Unknown.* BFSS

As I walked over London bridge. Georgie. *Unknown.* BFSS

As I wandered on the beach. The Great Blue Heron. Carolyn Kizer. NePoEA-2

As I wandered the forest. The Wild Flower's Song. Blake. CBEP

As I was a-hoeing, a-hoeing my lands. The Six Badgers. Robert Graves. GoJo

As I was a walking down a London street. The Gypsy's Wedding Day. *Unknown.* BSO

As I was a walking, I cannot tell where. Narcissus, Come Kiss Us! *Unknown.* ErPo

As I was a-walking mine alone. Archie of Cawfield. *Unknown.* BuBa

As I was a-walking the other day. The Shoemaker. *Unknown.* SoPo

As I was a-walking the streets of Laredo. Cowboy's Lament. *Unknown.* ThLM

As I was fishing off Pondy Point. Jim Desterland. Hyam Plutzik. FiSC

As I was going down Treak Street. Micky Thumps. *Unknown.* WePo

As I was going to my father's house. The Cruel Mother [*or* Two Little Babes]. *Unknown.* BFSS

As I was going to St. Ives. Riddle. Mother Goose. SoPo

As I was going up the stair. The Little Man Who Wasn't There [*or* Antigonish]. Hughes Mearns. LV; PoLF; SoPo

As I was out walking for pleasure one day. The Indian Mohee. *Unknown.* BFSS

As I was reading the book of nature. The Book of Nature. Richard Eberhart. PoDB

As I was sailing down the coast. The High Barbaree. Laura E. Richards. SoPo

As I was sitting in my chair. The Perfect Reactionary. Hughes Mearns. LV

As I was traveling toward the city of satisfactions. The City of Satisfactions. Daniel Hoffman. CoPo

As I was waiting for the bus. Sight Unseen. Kingsley Amis. ErPo; NePoEA-2

As I was walkin' the jungle round, a-killing of tigers an' time. Ballad. Guy Wetmore Carryl. Par

As I was walking. Kore. Robert Creeley. CoPo

As I was walking all alone [*or* alane]. The Twa [*or* Two] Corbies. *Unknown.* BuBa; CBEP; ELP; GTBS-P; ILP; OnP; StP

As I was walking all alone,/ Between a water and a wa. The Wee Wee Man. *Unknown.* ELP

As I was walking home just now, from seeing. The Departure from Hydra. Kenneth Koch. AmPC

As I was walking mine alone. The Little Wee Man. *Unknown.* BuBa

As I was walking one midsummer morning. O Dear O. *Unknown.* ErPo

As I was walking one morning in spring. I Shall Be Married on Monday Morning. *Unknown.* ErPo

As I was walking out one morning, I met a buxom lass. Buxom Lass. *Unknown.* ErPo

As I went a walking by yon far distant shore. The Indian Lass. *Unknown.* BSNS

As I went a walking one evening in June. The Chippewa Stream. *Unknown.* BSNS

As I went a walking one evening in June. The Lass of Mohee. *Unknown.* BSNS

As I went a walking one evening of late. The Pride of Glencoe. *Unknown.* BSNS

As I went down the hill along the wall. Meeting and Passing. Robert Frost. FoBA

As I went down the village street. Village Christmas. Margaret Widdemer. RePo

As I went down to Darbytown. The Darby Ram. *Unknown.* BSO

As I went down to Dymchurch Wall. In Romney Marsh. John Davidson. HaSV

As I went forth one May morning, fol de rol, &c. Carrion Crow. *Unknown.* BSNS

As I went on Yol Day. Jankin, the Clerical Seducer. *Unknown.* MeEL

As I went out a Crow. The Last Word of a Bluebird. Robert Frost. GoJo; ThGo

As I went Out on Christmas Day. *Unknown.* CBEP

As I went up the Brandy Hill. Brandy Hill. *Unknown.* CBEP

As I went walking down the street I met big Dixie Brown. Dixie Brown. *Unknown.* BSNS

As if from heaven so you now me greet. Lilacs. Christian Wagner. AGP

As if he listened. Silence: something far. Buddha. Rainer Maria Rilke. TwGP

As if it were. Merritt Parkway. Denise Levertov. ToPo

As imperceptibly as grief. Emily Dickinson. AP; DiPo; FoBA

As in a Rose-Jar. Thomas S. Jones, Jr. PoLF

As in the gardens, all through May, the rose. His Lady's Tomb. Pierre de Ronsard. *Fr.* Amours de Marie. RBL

As inward love breeds outward talk. William Basse. *Fr.* The Angler's Song. SD

As it fell. The Camellia. Basho. RePo

As it fell one holy-day. Little Musgrave and [the] Lady Barnard. *Unknown.* CABL; ErPo

As it fell out on a holy day,/ The drops of rain did fall. The Bitter Withy. *Unknown.* PoIE

As it fell out on a holy-day,/ And upon a holy-tide-a. John Dory. *Unknown.* BuBa

As it fell out upon a day. Dives and Lazarus. *Unknown.* ELP

As it fell upon a day. The Nightingale. Richard Barnfield. *Fr.* The Passionate Pilgrim. GTBS-P

As Jimmy and his own true love went walking out one day. Jimmy and His Own True Love. *Unknown.* BSNS

As Johnson and the young Coldwell. Johnson and Coldwell. *Unknown.* BSNS

As Johnson and the young Colonel. Johnson and the Colonel. *Unknown.* BSNS

As Joseph knocked upon his door. No Room. Dorothy Conant Stroud. STF

As Joseph was a-walking. The Cherry Tree Carol. *Unknown.* ThGo

As Jupiter's all-seeing eye. Fable IV: The Eagle, and the Assembly of Animals. John Gay. EiCP

As Kaethe Kollwitz knew. Death Swoops. Kenneth Pitchford. CoPo

As Kingfishers Catch Fire. Gerard Manley Hopkins. DiPo; EaLo; MoRP; VP

As life runs on, the road grows strange. Sixty-eighth Birthday. James Russell Lowell. StP

As Lilies White, More Crimson than the Rose. Guillaume de Machaut, *tr. fr.* French by Dwight Durling. AnML

As little children fear a spectral shade. His Scorn of Life and Consolation for Death. Jean-Baptiste Chassignet. RBL

As long as I live. Me. Walter de la Mare. BiCB; ThGo

As long as you allowed her complete liberty. The Incentive. Martial. UnTE

As loving hind that (hartless) wants her deer. A Letter to Her Husband, Absent upon Publick Employment. Anne Bradstreet. CBEP

As many, Mother, are your moods and forms. Bernard O'Dowd. *Fr.* The Bush. PoAu-1

As Margaret was in her pretty bouree. William and Margaret. *Unknown.* BSNS

As nature leaves whatever lives to face. A Dedication of 1924. Rainer Maria Rilke. TwGP

As Ocean Holds the Globe. Feodor Tyutchev, *tr. fr. Russian by* Babette Deutsch. SiGo

As often as not, on fair days, there is time. That Dying. Alastair Reid. OPP

As on Serena's Panting Breast. *Unknown.* UnTE

As on the day that gave you to the earth. Primeval Words: Orphic. Goethe. TwGP

As once grave Pluto drove his royal wheels. Proserpine's Ragout. Mary Leapor. WaPE

As once, if not with light regard. Ode on the Poetical Character. William Collins. EiCP; EnPE; StP

As one of the curious gatherers. Party Line. Joseph Joel Keith. FiSC

As one that for a weary space has lain. The Odyssey. Andrew Lang. OBNC; PoLF

As one who, long in thickets and in brakes. The Garden. William Cowper. *Fr.* The Task. EnPE

As over the swelling ocean's tide. On the Banishment of Cicero. Philip Wharton. WaPE

As Rochefoucault [*or* Rochefaucauld] his maxims drew. Verses on [*or* On] the Death of Dr. Swift. Swift. CABL; EiCP

As Salt Resolved in the Ocean. Rumi, *tr. fr. Persian by* A. J. Arberry. SiGo

As ships, becalmed at eve, that lay. Qua Cursum Ventus. Arthur Hugh Clough. HaSV; PoIE

As silent as a mirror is believed. Legend. Hart Crane. CABA

As slow our ship her foamy track. The Journey Onwards. Thomas Moore. GTBS-P

As some brave admiral, in former war. The Maimed Debauchee. Earl of Rochester. CABA; CBEP

As some fond virgin, whom her mother's care. Epistle to Miss Blount [*or* To a Young Lady on Her Leaving Town after the Coronation]. Pope. CaFP; DiPo; OnP; WePo

As sometimes in a dead man's face. In Memoriam A. H. H., LXXIV. Tennyson. VP

As soon as I withdraw to take my rest. Sonnet IX. Louise Labé. RBL

As soon as night comes my demon springs up out of the ground. Magdalene. Boris Pasternak. MoRP

As sure as we have a fatherland. Fellow-Citizens. Verner von Heidenstam. PoPl

As Sylvia in her garden strayed. Sylvia and the Bee. Mary Leapor. WaPE

As the April fool came over the hill. April Fool. Hal Summers. DaDu

As the bow unto the cord is. Longfellow. *Fr.* The Song of Hiawatha. TRV

As the Breeze That Cools the Blood. Gustavo Adolfo Bécquer, *tr. fr. Spanish by* Edward F. Gahan. AnSP

As the cat/ climbed over. Poem. William Carlos Williams. CABA; LOW

As the fair sun touches the earth each day. To The Virgin. Rutebeuf. AnML

As the First Snow Fell. Leopold von Goeckingk, *tr. fr. German by* George C. Schoolfield. AGP

As the gods began one world, and man another. Snakecharmer. Sylvia Plath. NePoEA-2; PP

As the hart panteth after the water brooks. Psalm XLII, Bible, *O.T.* BoC; TRV

As the holly groweth green. The Holly. Henry VIII, King of England. CTC

As the moon sinks on the mountain-edge. Far beyond Us. *Unknown.* SiGo

As the poem drifts under the cry of the sea. Adriatic. Robert Conquest. PP

As the proud horse with costly trappings gay. William Falconer. *Fr.* The Shipwreck. HaSV

As the rain falls. Rain. William Carlos Williams. AP

As the sin that was sweet in the sinning. The Poets at Tea, 3. Barry Pain. Par

As the sweet sweat of roses in a still. The Comparison. John Donne. ErPo

As the Team's Head-Brass. Edward Thomas. GTBS-P; MMA

As the wise men of old brought gifts. The Gift. William Carlos Williams. MoRP; PoPl

As there, along the elmy hedge, I go. Troubles of the Day. William Barnes. GTBS-P

As Thomas was cudgelled one day by his wife. Epigram. Swift. WePo

As though an aged person were to wear. Elegy for the Monastery Barn. Thomas Merton. CoPo

As thro' the Land at Eve We Went. Tennyson. *Fr.* The Princess. FoBA

As Thy Days So Shall Thy Strength Be. "George Klingle." TRV

As time one day by me did pass. Henry Vaughan. MeP

As to that poet (if so great a one as he). A Letter from the Country to a Friend in Town. John Oldham. PP

As to the lanes I took my way. Summer Morning. Jean Ingelow. ThGo

As travellours when the twilight's come. The Pilgrimage. Henry Vaughan. MeP

As Turpin was a riding across the moor. Dick Turpin and the Lawyer. *Unknown.* BSNS

As virtuous men pass mildly away. A Valediction: Forbidding Mourning. John Donne. CABA; CaFP; DiPo; EnRePo; FaPL; FoBA; ILP; MeP; PoIE; SeCP; VaPo

As We Are So Wonderfully Done with Each Other. Kenneth Patchen. ErPo

As we get older we do not get any younger. Chard Whitlow. Henry Reed. DTC; Par

As We Were a-Sailing. *Unknown.* BSNS

As, when a beauteous nymph decays. Stella's Birthday. Swift. PP

As, when a lofty pile is raised. To Stella. Swift. EiCP

As when a man, that sails in a balloon. The Balloon. Tennyson. RoGo

As when a stone is dropped in water, the harmonies of the universe. Buddha. Theodore Holmes. CoPo

As when desire, long darkling, dawns, and first. Bridal Birth. Dante Gabriel Rossetti. *Fr.* The House of Life. VP

". . . As When Emotion Too Far Exceeds Its Cause." G. C. Oden. AmNP

As when one sets himself, Lady, to raise. To Vittoria Colonna. Michelangelo. RBL

As William walking with his wife was seen. A Fair Exchange. La Fontaine. UnTE

As You Are, My Friend. Vernon Ward. PoNC

As You Came from the Holy Land. *Unknown, sometimes at.* to Sir Walter Ralegh. PoSa

(Walsinghame.) CBEP

"As you go down to yonder town." The Elfin Knight (B *vers.*). *Unknown.* BSO

"As you go down to yondos town." Rosemary and Thyme. *Unknown.* BFSS

"As you go into yonders town." The Cambric Shirt (A *vers.*). *Unknown.* BFSS

As you lay in sleep. Cartography. Louise Bogan. PoPl

As You Leave the Room. Wallace Stevens. AP

As You Like It, *sels.* Shakespeare.

All the World's a Stage, *fr.* II, vii. DiPo; PoLF; PoSa (Seven Ages of Man, The.) PoPo

Blow, Blow, Thou Winter Wind, *fr.* II, vii. CBEP; DiPo; ELP; EnRePo; GTBS-P; ILP; PoIE; PoPo; WePo; WiR (Song: "Blow, blow, thou winter wind.") CTC

"Come apace, good Audrey. I will fetch up your goats, Audrey," *fr.* III, iii. PP

It Was a Lover and His Lass, *fr.* V, iii. CBEP; ELP; GTBS-P; UnTE (Song: "It was a lover and his lass.") CTC

Song: "If the scorn of your bright eyne," *fr.* IV, iii. CTC

Song: "What shall he have that kill'd the deer?" *fr.* IV, ii. CTC

Under the Greenwood Tree, *fr.* II, v. CBEP; ELP; EnRePo; GTBS-P; WiR (Song: "Under the greenwood tree.") CTC

Why Should This a Desert Be, *fr.* III, ii. CTC

As you must strain the heart, strain your souls and strive. After Tsui-tao. "Klabund." TwGP

As you need, a white bear leisurely. To the Reader. Denise Levertov. CoPo

As You Say; an Anti-Poem. Karl Shapiro. *Fr.* The Bourgeois Poet. CaFP

("As you say (not without sadness), poets don't see, they feel.") PP

As Zillah on a certain day. Zillah (A *vers.*). *Unknown.* BSNS

Ascension-Day. Henry Vaughan. MeP

Ascension-Hymn. Henry Vaughan. MeP

Ascent. Wendell Berry. AP

Ascension. John Donne. MeP

Ascetic, The. Victor J. Daley. PoAu-1

Ase I me rod this ender day. The Five Joys of Mary. *Unknown.* MeEL

Ash Wednesday. T. S. Eliot. ACV; AP

Ash Wednesday. Alfred Lichtenstein, *tr. fr. German by* Michael Hamburger. MGP

Ashes ("Ashes/ of dead things") Umberto Saba, *tr. fr. Italian by* Thomas G. Bergin. CoIP

Ashtabula Disaster, The. Julia Moore. EvOK

Asides from the Clowns, *sel.* Jules Laforgue, *tr. fr. French by* William Jay Smith.

"My clear-cut heart, my tender soul." PoPl

Asides on the Oboe. Wallace Stevens. AP

Ask, and it shall be given you; seek, and ye shall find. St. Matthew, VII: 7, 8, Bible, *N.T.* BoC

Ask Me No More. Thomas Carew. *See* Song, A: "Ask me no more where Jove bestows."

Ask Me No More. Tennyson. *Fr.* The Princess. FoBA; UnTE
("Ask me no more: the moon may draw the sea.") OBNC
Ask me no more where Jove bestows. A Song [*or* Ask Me No More]. Thomas Carew. CABA; ELP; PoIE; SeCP
Ask not the cause, why sullen spring. Song to a Fair Young Lady Going Out of the Town in the Spring. Dryden. CABA; PoIE
Ask Not to Know This Man. Ben Jonson. CABA
(Little Shrub Growing By, A.) CBEP; EnRePo
Ask Not Ungainly. Horace, *tr. fr. Latin by* Ezra Pound. Odes, I, 2. CTC
Ask nothing more of me, sweet. Oblation. Swinburne. BoLP
Ask the dead. They Know. Ryah Tumarkin Goodman. FiSC
Asking for It. Siegfried Sassoon. MoRP
Asleep. Wilfred Owen. MMA; WePo
Asleep, My Love? Shakespeare. *Fr.* A Midsummer Night's Dream, V, i. CTC
Asolando, *sel.* Robert Browning.
Epilogue: "At the midnight in the silence of the sleep-time." FaBV; OBNC; PoIE
Asphodel, That Greeny Flower, *sel.* William Carlos Williams.
"Of asphodel, that greeny flower." PP
Ass, The. Edwin Allan. PoPI
Assassination, The. Marvin Solomon. OPP
Assassination of John F. Kennedy, The. Gwendolyn Brooks. OPP
Assassination of the President, The. November 25, 1963. Thomas Whitbread. OPP
Assassinations 1963, The. Stuart McCarrell. PtTo
Asses, *sel.* Padraic Colum.
"I know where I'd get." LOW
Assimilation. Irving Feldman. AmPC
Assyrian came down like the wolf on the fold, The. The Destruction of Sennacherib. Byron. DiPo; EvOK; OnMSP; PoIE; PoLF; SIV
Astonished poplars hide. Paysage Moralisé. John Hollander. ErPo
Astronomers predict his sun is dying. Protagonist. Edith Henrich. MoRP
Astrophel. Spenser. StP
Astrophel and Stella, *sels.* Sir Philip Sidney.
Sonnets.
I. "Loving in truth, and fain in verse my love to show." CABA; CBEP; ILP; PoIE; PP
VII. "When nature made her chief work, Stella's eyes." CABA
XV. "You that do search for every purling spring." ILP
XXI. "Your words, my friend, right healthful caustics, blame." CABA
XXVIII. "You that with allegory's curious frame." ILP
XXXI. "With how sad steps, O Moon, thou climbst the skies." CaFP; DiPo; EnRePo; ILP; PoIE; StP
XXXV. "What may words say, or what may words not say." CABA
XXXIX. "Come sleep! O sleep, the certain knot of peace." CABA; CBEP; EnRePo; PoIE; StP
(Sleep.) FaPL
XLI. "Having this day my horse, my hand, my lance." EnRePo; ILP
LXIV. "No more, my Dear, no more these counsels try." FaPL
LXXI. "Who will in fairest book of Nature know." CABA
LXXIV. "I never drank of Aganippe well." CABA; EnRePo
LXXVI. "She comes, and straight there-with her shining orbs do move." CABA
LXXXIV. "Highway, since you my chief Parnassus be." EnRePo; ILP
XCIX. "When far-spent night persuades each mortal eye." CABA
CIX. "Thou blind man's mark, thou fool's self-chosen snare." *Sometimes considered part of* Astrophel and Stella; *also in* Certain Sonnets. CABA; EnRePo; ErPo; PoSa; VaPo
CX. "Leave me, O love, which reachest but to dust." *Sometimes considered part of* Astrophel and Stella; *also in* Certain Sonnets. CABA; DiPo; EnRePo; OnP; PoSa
Songs.
Fourth Song: "Only joy! now here you are." EnRePo; FaPL; UnTE
Tenth Song: "O dear life, when shall it be?" EnRePo
Eleventh Song: "Who is it that this dark night." EnRePo
At a bygone Western country fair. At a Country Fair. Thomas Hardy. VP
At a Calvary near the Ancre. Wilfred Owen. MoRP
At a Child's Baptism. Vassar Miller. GoJo
At a Country Fair. Thomas Hardy. VP
At a Cowboy Dance. James Barton Adams [*wr.,* John Burton Adams]. RePo
At a Solemn Music [*or* Musick]. Milton. GTBS-P; MeP; OnP
At a Solemn Musick. Delmore Schwartz. MoRP
At a springe wel under a thorn. The Spring under a Thorn. *Unknown.* MeEL
At a Time. Ray Mathew. PoAu-2

At a Vacation Exercise in the College, Part Latin, Part English, *sel.* Milton.
"Hail native Language, that by sinews weak." PP
At a Window. Carl Sandburg. MoLP
At an Inn. Thomas Hardy. VP
At Bannockburn the English lay. Bannockburn. Burns. PoPo
At Birth. Anthony Thwaite. NePoEA-2
At Bungendore. James McAuley. PoAu-2
At Casterbridge Fair, *sel.* Thomas Hardy.
Former Beauties, II. OBNC
At Castle Boterel. Thomas Hardy. DTC; GTBS-P; OBNC; PoSa
At counters where I eat my lunch. Marble-Top. E. B. White. LV
At court I met it, in clothes brave enough. On Some-thing, That Walkes Some-where. Ben Jonson. SeCP
At Dawn. Arthur Symons. OBNC
At dawn of day I saw a man. The Drunkard's Doom. *Unknown.* BSO
At dawn she lay with her profile at that angle. Daybreak. Stephen Spender. MoLP
At Dawn the Virgin Is Born. Lope de Vega, *tr. fr. Spanish by* W. S. Merwin. AnSP
At Daybreak. Helen Hoyt. BiCB
At daybreak Don Alonso rises with the sun. Moriana's Poison. *Unknown.* AnML
At Dieppe: Rain on the Down. Arthur Symons. OBNC
At dinner, she is hostess, I am host. Modern Love, XVII. George Meredith. ILP; VP
At Dirty Dick's and Sloppy Joe's. Song of the Master and Boatswain. W. H. Auden. *Fr.* The Sea and the Mirror. DTC; HaSV
At Dunwich. Anthony Thwaite. MoBS
At Ease. Walter de la Mare. GTBS-P
At Eutaw Springs the valiant died. To the Memory of the Brave Americans. Philip Freneau. AP; PoLF
At evening, sitting on this terrace. Bat. D. H. Lawrence. GTBS-P
At evening when the lamp is lit. The Land of Story-Books. Robert Louis Stevenson. FaPL
At every proper christening. To Patricia on Her Christening Day. Edith Ballinger Price. BiCB
At every step he heard the devil's moan. Borderline. R. H. Grenville. FiSC
At every stroke his brazen fins do take. The Whale. John Donne. PoSa
At first, he wondered why he should be spared. The Madman. Constance Urdang. PoPI
At first I hoped she would accept a dime. Femme Fatale. Vincent Starrett. FiSC
At first I prayed for Light. Prayer—Answer. Ednah D. Cheney. STF
At first I said: "I will not have, I think." Birthday. Elaine V. Emans. BiCB
At first I thought a pest. Armour's Undermining Modesty. Marianne Moore. AP
At first I would not reply, and my shame showed upon my cheeks. Remorse. Pierre Louÿs. *Fr.* The Songs of Bilitis. UnTE
At first it was too hot, and then too wet. Uncle Bing. Vincent Starrett. LV
At Flores in the Azores Sir Richard Grenville lay. The *Revenge:* A Ballad of the Fleet. Tennyson. FoBA; OnMSP
At four o'clock. Roosters. Elizabeth Bishop. AmLP
At Galway Races. W. B. Yeats. SD
At Grass. Philip Larkin. DaDu; SD
At Gull Lake: August, 1810. Duncan Campbell Scott. OBCV
At half-past six A.M. the sun. Beside the Sea. George Johnston. ACV
At half-past three a single bird. Emily Dickinson. AmLP; AP
At Home, Alone with the Cat. Walter de la Mare. BoC
At Home, Alone with the Dog. Harold Monro. BoC
At Home in Heaven. Robert Southwell. MeP
At home, in my flannel gown, like a bear to its floe. 90 North. Randall Jarrell. AP; ILP
At its margin. Ode to Arnold Schoenberg. Charles Tomlinson. NePoEA-2
At Last. Whittier. AP
(To Paths Unknown.) TRV
At last, as far as I could cast my eyes. The Spanish Galleons Seen by an Aztec. Dryden. *Fr.* The Indian Emperor. HaSV
At last I put off love. He Abjures Love. Thomas Hardy. OBNC
At last we parley: we so strangely dumb. Modern Love, XLVI. George Meredith. VP
At last you do not find—you have—the dark. In Time of Darkness. Raymond Roseliep. FiSC
At last you yielded up the album, which. Lines on a Young Lady's Photograph Album. Philip Larkin. ToPo
At least—to pray—is left—is left. Emily Dickinson. AP
At length arrived, your book I take. On Receiving a Copy of Mr. Austin Dobson's "Old World Idylls." James Russell Lowell. AP

At length, my friends, the feast of life is o'er. On the Death of an Epicure. Richard Graves. CBEP

At length their long kiss severed, with sweet smart. Nuptial Sleep. Dante Gabriel Rossetti. *Fr.* The House of Life. VP

At Little Virgil's Window. Edwin Markham. TRV

At low tide like this how sheer the water is. The Bight. Elizabeth Bishop. PoSa

At Majority. Adrienne Rich. NePoEA-2

At Matsushima. Shiki, *tr. fr. Japanese by* Harold G. Henderson. SiGo

At Melville's Tomb. Hart Crane. AmLP; AP; PoIE

At midnight, in the month of June. The Sleeper. Poe. AP; CBEP

At moost mischief. My Lute and I. Sir Thomas Wyatt. MeEL

At My Father's Grave. "Hugh MacDiarmid." GTBS-P; PoIE

At My Grandmother's. David Malouf. PoAu-2

At My Mother's Knee. *Unknown.* STF

At night, by the fire. Domination of Black. Wallace Stevens. AP; ILP

At night I dreamt I was back in Ch'ang-an. Dreaming That I Went with Li and Yü to Visit Yüan Chen. Po Chü-i. SiGo

At night I hug my pillow. The Mistress of Bernal Francés. *Unknown.* AnML

At night the ticking of the clock. The Clock. Jean Jaszi. SoPo

At nightfall they carried the stranger dead into the house. Wayfaring. Georg Trakl. MGP

At nine in the morning there passed a church. Faintheart in a Railway Train. Thomas Hardy. CTC

At noon the sun puffed up, outsize. Idyll. Francis Webb. PoAu-2

At once, from hence, my lines and I depart. To Mr. T. W. John Donne. PP

At Only That Moment. Alan Ross. ErPo

At Peace. Rumi, *tr. fr. Persian by* A. J. Arberry. SiGo

At Perigord near to the wall. A Perigord pres del muralh. Bertrans de Born. CTC

At Set of Sun. "George Eliot." PoPl; TRV

At seventeen I spent cold cash. Hearthside Story. X. J. Kennedy. CoPo

At six o'clock we were waiting for coffee. A Miracle for Breakfast. Elizabeth Bishop. StP

At sixteen she was a potential celebrity. Clara. Ezra Pound. DTC

At sunset, when the night-dews fall. The Snail. James Reeves. RePo

At Tea. Thomas Hardy. Satires of Circumstance, I. VaPo

At the Aquarium. Max Eastman. LV; PoPo

At the Ascension. Luis de León, *tr. fr. Spanish by* James Edward Tobin. AnSP

At the Bottom of the Well. Louis Untermeyer. GoJo

At the bridge of late. Venice. Nietzsche. TwGP

At the Brooklyn Docks. Dorothy Gilbert. OPP

At the corner of Wood Street, when daylight appears. The Reverie of Poor Susan. Wordsworth. CBEP; GTBS-P; WiR

At the Cross. *Unknown.* STF

At the Draper's. Thomas Hardy. Satires of Circumstance, XII. VaPo

At the end of a long-walled garden. The Cottage Hospital. John Betjeman. GTBS-P

At the end of the garden walk. The Cold Green Element. Irving Layton. OBCV

At the end of the third act, poetry gutters down. After Shakespeare. Alex Comfort. ErPo

At the End of Things, *sel.* Arthur Edward Waite. "Cast away fear." TRV

At the equinox when the earth was veiled in a late rain. Continent's End. Robinson Jeffers. FaBV

At the Executed Murderer's Grave. James Wright. AmPC

At the first sound the golden sun arises from the deep. Enitharmon Revives with Los. Blake. *Fr.* Vala; or, The Four Zoas. OBNC

At the foot of the slope. Ara Mara Amara. "Aldo Palazzeschi." CoIP

At the foot of your dry well. Reunion. W. S. Merwin. AmPC

At the Fountain by the Gateway. Wilhelm Müller, *tr. fr. German by* Francis Owen. AGP

At the Gate of Heaven. Conrad Ferdinand Meyer, *tr. fr. German by* D. G. Wright. AGP

At the ghetto end. Bedford Avenue. Art Berger. PtTo

At the Grave of Henry Vaughan. Siegfried Sassoon. EaLo; GTBS-P

At the Grave of My Father. Matthias Claudius, *tr. fr. German by* Dorothea M. Singer. AGP

At the Great Wall of China. Edmund Blunden. GTBS-P

At the head of Weal Water, about twelve at noon. The North Country Collier. *Unknown.* HaSV

At the heart of the cyclone tearing the sky. The Place of Peace. Edwin Markham. TRV

At the Keyhole. Walter de la Mare. DTC

At the large foot of a fair hollow tree. The Country Mouse. Abraham Cowley. SeCP

At the last, tenderly. The Last Invocation. Walt Whitman. FoBA; TRV

At the long tables of time. The Jugs. Paul Celan. MGP

At the Mid Hour of Night. Thomas Moore. OBNC ("At the mid hour of night, when stars are weeping, I fly.") GTBS-P

At the midnight in the silence of the sleep-time. Epilogue. Robert Browning. *Fr.* Asolando. FaBV; OBNC; PoIE

At the Nadir. Gerta Kennedy. PoPl

At the New Year. Kenneth Patchen. ToPo

At the next vacancy for God, if I am elected. In Place of a Curse. John Ciardi. CaFP; ToPo

At the Ocean's Verge. Ralph Gustafson. OBCV

At the Place of the Sea. Annie Johnson Flint. STF

At the Poem Society a black-haired man stands up to say. Fresh Air. Kenneth Koch. PP

At the road's end glimmer the station lights. Fetching the Wounded. Laurence Binyon. MMA

At the Roman Baths, Bath. Edward Lucie-Smith. NePoEA-2

At the round earth's imagin'd [*or* imagined] corners, blow. Holy Sonnets, VII. John Donne. CABA; CBEP; DiPo; EaLo; EnRePo; FoBA; ILP; MeP; PoIE; SeCP; StP; VaPo

At the seashore I came upon a golden shell. Seashell. Rubén Darío. AnSP

At the Setting of the Sun. *Unknown.* CBEP

At the Slackening of the Tide. James Wright. AmPC; CABA

At the start, god made the sun. Songs of Creation. Heine. TwGP

At the Tennis Clinic. I. L. Martin. SD

At the time it seemed unimportant: he was lying. The Day. Roy Fuller. ToPo

At the time of Matines, Lord thu were itake. The Hours of the Passion. *Unknown.* MeEL

At the top of the world, where fields of snow. Mrs. Santa Claus' Christmas Present. Alice S. Morris. PoSC

At the training depot that first morning. The Misfit—1939–1945. C. Day Lewis. StP

At the Wedding March. Gerard Manley Hopkins. FoBA

At the Winter Solstice. Daniel G. Hoffman. StP

At the Worst, *sel.* Israel Zangwill. "Evil is here? That's work for us to do." TRV

At Thirty Years. Heinz Piontek, *tr. fr. German by* Michael Hamburger. MGP

At three in the morning. Pointed Boots. Christopher Middleton. *Fr.* Herman Moon's Hourbook. MGP

At twenty thousand feet—the earth below was overcast. Long Lines. Paul Goodman. OPP

At two A.M. a thing, jumping out of a manhole. News Report. David Ignatow. ErPo

At Viscount Nelson's lavish funeral. 1805. Robert Graves. EvOK

At War. Russell Atkins. AmNP

At Woodlawn I heard the dead cry. The Lost Son. Theodore Roethke. AP

Atalanta in Calydon, *sels.* Swinburne.
  Before the Beginning of Years. ACV; VP
  (Chorus: "Before the beginning of years.") TRV
  (Chorus from "Atalanta.") CBEP
  Chorus: "When the hounds of spring are on winter's traces." CTC; EvOK; GTBS-P; ILP; PoIE; PoSa
  (Hounds of Spring, The.) FaBV
  (When the Hounds of Spring.) VP

Atavism. Elinor Wylie. FiSC

Athirst in spirit, through the gloom. The Prophet. Pushkin. EaLo

Athlete. Don Maynard. PoAu-2

Athletes. Walker Gibson. SD

Athletic Employment. *Unknown.* SD

Athwart a bull, the sun. Myths. Wieland Schmied. MGP

Athwart the sky a lowly sigh. London. John Davidson. OBNC; StP

Atlantic is a stormy moat, and the Mediterranean. The Eye. Robinson Jeffers. AmLP; AP; PoPo

Atlantis. W. H. Auden. PoPl

Atlantis. Stanton A. Coblentz. FiSC

Atlantis. Hart Crane. *Fr.* The Bridge. AmLP

Atlas, The, *sels.* Kenneth Slessor. PoAu-2
  Dutch Seacoast.
  King of Cuckooz, The.
  Mermaids.
  Post-Roads.

Atmosphere Is Incandescent, The. Rosalía de Castro, *tr. fr. Spanish by* Edwin Morgan. AnSP

Attend church? Of course we do. Attending Church. *Unknown.* STF

Attend, young friends, while I relate. Maria Bewell. *Unknown.* BSO

Attending Church. *Unknown.* STF
Attentive eyes, fantastic heed. A Poet. Thomas Hardy. VP
Attic, The. Henri Coulette. NePoEA-2; PoP1
Atticus. Pope. *Fr.* Epistle to Dr. Arbuthnot. PoSa
Attitudes. Richard Eberhart. ToPo
Attraction. *Unknown.* STF
Au Beau Milieu. Frank Borden Hanes. PoNC
Au bon vieulx temps. Clément Marot, *tr. fr. French by* George Wyndham. RBL
Au Jardin des Plantes. John Wain. NePoEA-2
Au Tombeau de Mon Père. Ronald McCuaig. PoAu-2
Aubade. William Empson. ToPo
Aubade. Edith Sitwell. WePo
Aubade: Dick, the Donkey-Boy. Sir Osbert Sitwell. DaDu
Auburn. Paul Verlaine, *tr. fr. French by* Lawrence M. Bensky. ErPo
Aucassin and Nicolette, *sel. Unknown, tr. fr. French by* Andrew Lang.
Who Would List. CTC
Auctioneer of parting, The. Emily Dickinson. AP
Audience pricks an intellectual ear, The. Concert-Interpretation. Siegfried Sassoon. CBEP
Auguries of Innocence. Blake. CABA; CABL; DiPo; FaBV; ILP; OBNC; OnP; RePo, 4 *ll.*
  ("To see a world in a grain of sand.") TRV, 4 *ll.*
  Sels.
  "God appears, and God is Light." TRV
  Many Birds. ThGo
August. Brother Antoninus. ToPo
August. Folgore da San Geminiano, *tr. fr. Italian by* Dante Gabriel Rossetti. *Fr.* Sonnets of the Months. CTC
August. Swinburne. WiR
August-Advertisement. Theodor Storm, *tr. fr. German by* Frances Sturmer-Robb. AGP
August Hail. J. V. Cunningham. PoIE; PoSa
August Night. May Swenson. MoLP
August Saturday Night on the Negro Street. Karl Shapiro. ToPo
Augustus was a chubby lad. The Story of Augustus, Who Would Not Have Any Soup. Heinrich Hoffman. BBGG; GoJo
Auld Lang Syne. Burns. EiCP; EnPE; PoLF
Auld Reikie. Robert Fergusson. CABL
Auld Robin Gray. Lady Anne Lindsay. GTBS-P
Auld wife sat her ivied door, The. Ballad. Charles Stuart Calverley. Par; WiR
Aunt Cora. Kenneth Pitchford. CoPo
Aunt Eliza. Harry Graham. LV
Aunt Ella. Guy Owen. PoNC
Aunt Helen. T. S. Eliot. FoBA; PoSa
Aunt Jane ("Aunt Jane, of whom I dreamed"). Alden A. Nowlan. FiSC
Aunt Mary ("Aunt Mary died of eating twelve red peppers"). John Ciardi. PoDB
Aunt Matilda. Barbara Euphan Todd. BoC
Aura amara, L'. Arnaut Daniel, *tr. fr. Provençal by* Ezra Pound. CTC
Aureng-Zebe, *sel.* Dryden.
  Prologue: "Our author, by experience, finds it true." CBEP; PP
Aurora, *sel.* Earl of Stirling.
  To Aurora, Sonnet XXXIII. GTBS-P
Aurora Leigh, *sel.* Elizabeth Barrett Browning.
  "Earth's crammed with heaven." TRV
Aus einer Kindheit. Kenneth Koch. AmPC
Auspex. James Russell Lowell. AmLP; AP
Austerity is not asperity. At the Winter Solstice. Daniel G. Hoffman. StP
Austerity of Poetry. Matthew Arnold. VP
Australasia, *sel.* William Charles Wentworth.
  "Land of my birth! though now, alas! no more." PoAu-1
Australia. A. D. Hope. ACV
Australia. Bernard O'Dowd. PoAu-1
Australia and the Amazon. John A. Stone. SGR
Australian, The. Arthur H. Adams. PoAu-1
Australian Symphony, An. George Essex Evans. ACV
Australia's on the Wallaby. *Unknown.* PoAu-1
Austrian Army, An. Alaric A. Watts. PoPo
Autet e bas. Arnaut Daniel, *tr. fr. Provençal by* Ezra Pound. CTC
Authentic, The! I said. Denise Levertov. *Fr.* Matins. PtTo
Authentic, The! Shadows of it. Matins. Denise Levertov. CoPo; ToPo
Author to Her Book, The. Anne Bradstreet. AP
  (Author and Her Book, The.) StP
Author to His Wife, of a Woman's Eloquence, The. Sir John Harington. ErPo
Author's Epitaph, Made by Himselfe, The. Sir Walter Ralegh.
  See Even Such Is Time.
Author's favourite pipe am I, An. The Pipe. Sir John Squire. PoP1
Auto Wreck. Karl Shapiro. AmLP; ILP; PoP1; PoPo
Autobiographical Fragment. Kingsley Amis. DaDu; NePoEA-2

Autobiography, An. Ernest P. Rhys. ACV
Autocrat of the Breakfast Table, The, *sel.* Oliver Wendell Holmes.
  Chambered Nautilus, The. AmLP; AP; DiPo; HaSV; LV; PoLF
  ("Build thee more stately mansions, O my soul," *last st.*) TRV
Automobile Mechanics. Dorothy Baruch. SoPo
Autumn. Roy Campbell. AnMoPo; GTBS-P
Autumn. "Vincenzo Cardarelli," *tr. fr. Italian by* Cosimo Corsano. CoIP
Autumn. Emily Dickinson. PoP1
Autumn. T. E. Hulme. LOW
Autumn. "Gabriela Mistral," *tr. fr. Spanish by* Muriel Kittel. AnSP
Autumn. Rainer Maria Rilke, *tr. fr. German.* PoPo, *tr. by* M. D. Herter Norton; SiGo, *tr. by* Jessie Lemont
Autumn. William Jay Smith. RePo
Autumn. *Unknown, tr. fr. Irish by* Frank O'Connor. PoSC
Autumn. Humbert Wolfe. PoLF
Autumn again, the leopardlike and burning. Howard Sergeant. *Fr.* The Leaves of Europe. ToPo
Autumn Apples. Laurie Lee. *See* Apples.
Autumn, cloud blades on the horizon. Clear after Rain. Tu Fu. PoP1
Autumn Dawn. Antonio Machado, *tr. fr. Spanish by* Jean Rogers Longland. PoP1
Autumn Garden. Dino Campana, *tr. fr. Italian by* Carlo L. Golino. CoIP
Autumn Hath All the Summer's Fruitful Treasure. Thomas Nashe. *Fr.* Summer's Last Will and Testament. EnRePo
Autumn Idleness. Dante Gabriel Rossetti. *Fr.* The House of Life, LXIX. ILP
Autumn is over the long leaves that love us. The Falling of the Leaves. W. B. Yeats. PoPo
Autumn Morning. Frances Frost. RePo
Autumn, my Alan, is a spectre. Alan. Raymond Roseliep. FiSC
Autumn Rain. Aileen Fisher. RePo
Autumn Song. Noel Harry Brettell. ACV
Autumn Song, An. Edward Dowden. ACV
Autumn Storm, The. Basho, *tr. fr. Japanese by* Harold G. Henderson. RePo
Autumn Tints. Mathilde Blind. LV
Autumn upon us was rushing, The. Ravings. Thomas Hood, the Younger. Par
Autumn Verses. Rubén Darío, *tr. fr. Spanish by* Kate Flores. AnSP
Autumn. We already felt it coming. Autumn. "Vincenzo Cardarelli." CoIP
Autumnal. Rubén Darío, *tr. fr. Spanish by* Anita Volland. AnSP
Autumnal. Ernest Dowson. OBNC
Autumnal. Rolfe Humphries. MoRP
Autumnal Equinox on Mediterranean Beach. Robert Penn Warren. VaPo
Autumnal Evening, An. "Fiona Macleod." PoSC
Autumnal Ode. Aubrey Thomas De Vere. OBNC
Autumnal Spring Song. Vassar Miller. PoSa
Autumn's good, a cosy season. Autumn. *Unknown.* PoSC
Autumnus. Joshua Sylvester. StP
Avarice. George Herbert. FoBA
Ave atque Vale. Swinburne. OBNC; StP; VP
Ave Maria. Hart Crane. *Fr.* The Bridge. PoDB
Ave Maris Stella. *Unknown.* CTC
Avenge, O Lord, thy slaughtered saints, whose bones. On the Late Massacre in Piedmont [*or* Piemont]. Milton. CABA; CBEP; DiPo; FoBA; GTBS-P; PoIE; StP
Avenue Bearing the Initial of Christ into the New World, The. Galway Kinnell. CoPo; NePoEA-2; PoDB
Avery Anameer. Joseph Payne Brennan. FiSC
Avoid the reeking herd. The Eagle and the Mole. Elinor Wylie. PoPo
Avondale Mine Disaster, The. *Unknown.* ThLM
Awake. Mary Elizabeth Coleridge. OBNC
Awake, Aeolian lyre, awake. The Progress of Poesy. Thomas Gray. CBEP; EiCP; EnPe; GTBS-P; PP
Awake, Awake! Thomas Campion. ELP
Awake, awake, my lyre! A Supplication. Abraham Cowley. GTBS-P
Awake, awake! thou heavy sprite. Awake, Awake! Thomas Campion. ELP
Awake, Awake to Love and Work. G. A. Studdert-Kennedy. TRV
Awake! for Morning in the bowl of Night. Rubáiyát of Omar Khayyám. *Tr. by* Edward Fitzgerald. ILP; SiGo. *See also* Wake! for the Sun, who scattered into flight.
Awake, glad heart! get up, and sing. Christs Nativity. Henry Vaughan. MeP
Awake, my heart, to be loved, awake, awake! Robert Bridges. GTBS-P
Awake sad heart, whom sorrow ever drowns. The Dawning. George Herbert. MeP

Award. Ray Durem. NNP; PtTo
Aware Aware. Tram Combs. MP
Away. James Whitcomb Riley. TRV
Away above a Harborful. Lawrence Ferlinghetti. ErPo
Away, away in the Northland. A Legend of the Northland. Phoebe Cary. OnMSP
Away despair; my gracious Lord doth heare. The Bag. George Herbert. MeP; SeCP
Away in a Manger. Martin Luther. *See* Cradle Hymn.
Away! the moor is dark beneath the moon. Stanzas—April, 1814. Shelley. OBNC
Away Up on the Yuba, *with music.* John A. Stone. SGR
Away with Funeral Music. Robert Louis Stevenson. WePo
Away with silks, away with lawn. Clothes Do but Cheat and Cozen Us. Robert Herrick. ErPo
Away with that tradition of wretched glory. The Technique of Love. Jascha Kessler. AmPC
Away with These Self-loving Lads. Fulke Greville. Caelica, LII. EnRePo
  (Of His Cynthia.) ELP
Away with You! Begone! Begone! Charles d'Orléans, *tr. fr. French by* Dwight Durling. AnML
Awful Responsibility, An. Keith Preston. PoP1
Awful shadow of some unseen power, The. Hymn to Intellectual Beauty. Shelley. ILP; OBNC
AWOL. George Bratt. PtTo
Axe angles, An/ from my neighbor's ashcan. Junk. Richard Wilbur. CaFP; LV
Axe-Helve, The. Robert Frost. CABL
Axe in the Wood, The. Clifford Dyment. ACV
Ay, tear her tattered ensign down! Old Ironsides. Oliver Wendell Holmes. AmLP; AP; FaPL; LV; PoP1; ThLM
"Aye! I am a poet and upon my tomb." And Thus in Nineveh. Ezra Pound. PP
Aye, up at the feast, by Melhill's brow. Melhill Feast. William Barnes. CBEP; OBNC
Azalea, The. Coventry Patmore. ELP
Aziola, The. Shelley. CBEP
Aztec sacrifice, An. Le Musée Imaginaire. Charles Tomlinson. NePoEA-2

B

B Negative. X. J. Kennedy. NePoEA-2
Baa, Baa, Black Sheep. Mother Goose. SoPo
Bab-Lock-Hythe. Laurence Binyon. SD; WePo
Babe is cold, The. Candle and Star. Elizabeth J. Coatsworth. BiCB
Babiaantje, The. F. T. Prince. ACV
Babushka. Edith M. Thomas. OnMSP
Baby. George Macdonald. BiCB; TRV
Baby cat is soft an sweet, A. Cats. Marchette Chute. SoPo
Baby Christ, when He was born, The. The Birthday of the Lord. Mary Jane Carr. BiCB
Baby is born[or borne], us bliss [or blis] to bring, A. Dear Son, Leave Thy Weeping [or Jesus Comforts His Mother]. *Unknown.* CTC; MeEL
Baby new to earth and sky, The. In Memoriam A. H. H., XLV. Tennyson. VP
Baby-Sitter Blues. Edith Earnshaw. PoNC
Baby Toodles. Joseph S. Newman. BBGG
Babylon. Laura Benét. FiSC
Babylon ("Babylon that was beautiful is Nothing now"). Siegfried Sassoon. MoRP
Babylon. *Unknown.* CBEP; SIV
Babylon, Babylon, Babylon the Great. Vachel Lindsay. LiPo
Baby's Debut, The. James Smith. Par
Baby's Name, The. Tudor Jenks. BiCB
Bacchae, *sel.* Euripides, *tr. fr. Greek by* Gilbert Murray. Where Shall Wisdom Be Found? SiGo
Bacchanal. Irving Layton. OBCV
Bacchus. Emerson. AP
Bacchus. William Empson. PoCh
Bacchus in Tuscany, *sels.* Francesco Redi, *tr. fr. Italian.* RBL
  "If the grape's kindly juice," *tr. by* Lorna de' Lucchi.
  "Talk of Chocolate!" *tr. by* Leigh Hunt.
Back and side go bare, go bare. Drinking Song. At. to William Stevenson *and to* John Still. *Fr.* Gammer Gurton's Needle. WiR
Back from the kill. Contest. Florence Victor. SD
Back from the Paved Way. Robert D. Fitzgerald. PoAu-2
Back from the trebly crimsoned field. Wanted—a Man. Edmund Clarence Stedman. LiPo
Back Lane. R. D. Murphy. PoAu-2
Back of the loaf is the snowy flour. "Give Us This Day Our Daily Bread." Maltbie D. Babcock. TRV
Back of your neck, more base than stone, The. Jacques Dupin. *Fr.* Fits and Starts. CoFP

Back out of all this now too much for us. Directive. Robert Frost. AP; CABA; DiPo; OnP; PoDB
Backwater Pond: The Canoeists. W. S. Merwin. PoP1
Bad Children, The. Carl Bode. ToPo
Bad Girl's Lament, The. *Unknown.* BSNS
Bad I am, but yet thy child. Gerard Manley Hopkins. BoC
Bad Joke, A. Martial, *tr. fr. Latin by* Louis Untermeyer. UnTE
Bad Kittens, The. Elizabeth J. Coatsworth. RePo
Bad Morning, A. Bertolt Brecht, *tr. fr. German by* Michael Hamburger. MGP
Bad Season Makes the Poet Sad, The. Robert Herrick. CABA
Badger. John Clare. CBEP; WiR
Bag, The. George Herbert. MeP; SeCP
Bagpipe Music. Louis MacNeice. GTBS-P; ILP; PoSa
Bailada: "Let's dance now, all of us, all of us, oh my maidens." Airas Núñez, *tr. fr. Portuguese by* Seth G. Thornton. SiGo
  (Let the Three of Us Now Dance, Oh Friends, *tr. by* Laurence A. Sharpe.) AnML
Bailiff's Daughter of Islington, The. *Unknown.* BFSS, *with music;* PoPo; RePo
Bait [or Baite], The. John Donne. CABA; DiPo; ErPo; ILP; SD; StP
Balaam. John Keble. OBNC
Balade de Bon Conseyl. Chaucer. PoIE
  (Truth.) CBEP
  (Truth Shall Set You Free.) MeEL
Bald heads forgetful of their sins. The Scholars. W. B. Yeats. CaFP; FoBA
Balder, *sel.* Sydney Dobell.
  Chanted Calendar, A. BoC
Ball and the Club, The. Forbes Lindsay. SD
Ball of fire shoots through the tamarack, A. The Scarlet Tanager. Joel Benton. AmLP
Ball will bounce, but less and less, A. Juggler. Richard Wilbur. PoIE
Ballad, A: "As I was walkin' the jungle round, a-killin' of tigers an' time." Guy Wetmore Carryl. Par
Ballad: "Auld wife sat at her ivied door, The." Charles Stuart Calverley. Par; WiR
Ballad: "He went by with another." "Gabriela Mistral," *tr. fr. Spanish by* Muriel Kittel. AnSP
Ballad: "My lady was found mutilated." Leonard Cohen. OBCV
Ballad: "Oh come, my joy, my soldier boy." Henry Treece. DaDu
Ballad: "O! shairly ye hae seen my love." William Soutar. WePo
Ballad: O What Is That Sound? W. H. Auden. *See* O What Is That Sound Which So Thrills the Ear?
Ballad: "Of all the girls that e'er were seen." John Gay. ErPo
Ballad, A: "'Twas when the seas were roaring." John Gay. *Fr.* The What D'Ye Call It. StP
Ballad for Fat Margot. Villon, *tr. fr. French by* Muriel Kittel. AnML
  (Ballade of Villon and Fat Margot, *tr. by* John Payne.) UnTE
Ballad in "G," A. Eugene Fitch Ware. PoLF
Ballad in Praise of Seafaring Men, An. *Unknown.* HaSV
Ballad of a Mine, A. Robin Skelton. MoBS
Ballad of a Nun, A. John Davidson. OnMSP
Ballad of Agincourt, The. Michael Drayton. *See* Agincourt.
Ballad of All [the] Trades, A. *Unknown.* ErPo; UnTE
Ballad of Banners (1944), The. John Lehmann. MoBS
Ballad of Billy Rose, The. Leslie Norris. MoBS
Ballad of Cap'n Pye. Robert P. Tristram Coffin. SIV
Ballad of China, A. Laura E. Richards. RePo
Ballad of Dead Ladies, The. Villon, *tr. fr. French by* Dante Gabriel Rossetti. CTC
  (Ballad of the Ladies of Olden Times, *tr. by* Ellen Willis.) AnML
  (Snows of Yester-Year, The, *tr. by* Dante Gabriel Rossetti.) WiR
Ballad of Despair, A. Wade Wellman. FiSC
Ballad of Dreamland, A. Swinburne. ILP
Ballad of East and West, The. Kipling. FaBV; PoPo; SIV
  "Oh, East is East, and West is West," *sel.* TRV
Ballad of Father Gilligan, The. W. B. Yeats. EaLo; PoPo; SIV; WePo
Ballad of Flérida. Gil Vicente, *tr. fr. Spanish by* Beatrice Gilman Proske. RBL
Ballad of Hell, A. John Davidson. ACV; StP
Ballad of John Silver, A. John Masefield. EvOK
Ballad of Juliana. *Unknown, tr. fr. Spanish by* Edwin Honig. AnML
Ballad of Ladies' Love, Number Two. Villon. *See* Ballade of Ladies' Love.
Ballad of Marjorie, A. Dora Sigerson Shorter. SIV
Ballad of Outer Life. Hugo von Hofmannsthal, *tr. fr. German by* Walter Kaufmann. TWGP
Ballad of Queensland (Sam Holt), A. G. H. Gibson. PoAu-1

Ballad of Reading Gaol, The. Oscar Wilde. FaPL *Sels.*
  Capital Punishment. WePo
  "He did not wear his scarlet coat." OBNC
  "In Reading gaol by Reading town." PoPl
Ballad of Red Fox, The. Melvin Walker La Follette. LOW
Ballad of Remembrance, A. Robert Hayden. AmNP
Ballad of Sir John Franklin, A. George Henry Boker. OnMSP
Ballad of Sir Patrick Spens, The. *Unknown. See* Sir Patrick Spens.
Ballad of the Boll Weevil, The. *Unknown.* ThLM
Ballad of the Boston Tea-Party, A. Oliver Wendell Holmes. ThLM
Ballad of the Cool Fountain. *Unknown, tr. fr. Spanish by* Edwin Honig. AnML
Ballad of the Despairing Husband. Robert Creeley. AmPC; ToPo
Ballad of the Double Bed. Eve Merriam. UnTE
Ballad of the Drover. Henry Lawson. PoAu-1
Ballad of the Epiphany. Charles Dalmon. OnMSP
Ballad of the Fair Melisenda. *Unknown, tr. fr. Spanish by* Edwin Honig. AnML
Ballad of the Flood. Edwin Muir. MoBS
Ballad of the Golden Bowl. Sara Henderson Hay. OnMSP
Ballad of the Good Lord Nelson, A. Lawrence Durrell. ErPo
Ballad of the Goodly Fere. Ezra Pound. MoBS; PoSa
Ballad of the Huntsman. Selma Robinson. SIV
Ballad of the Ladies of Olden Times. Villon. *See* Ballad of Dead Ladies, The.
Ballad of the Mulberry Road, A. Ezra Pound. LOW
Ballad of the Oysterman, The. Oliver Wendell Holmes. AP; SIV
Ballad of the Tempest. James Thomas Fields. PoLF
Ballad of the Trial of Sodom. Vernon Watkins. MoRP
Ballad of the Two Tapsters. Vernon Watkins. MoBS
Ballad of the Unmiraculous Miracle. Vassar Miller. ToPo
Ballad of Trees and the Master, A. Sidney Lanier. AP; PoLF; TRV
Ballad of Two Kings. Grant Code. FiSC
Ballad to Queen Elizabeth, A. Austin Dobson. HaSV
Ballad to the Tune of "The Cut-Purse," A. Swift. PP
Ballad upon a Wedding, A. Sir John Suckling. CABA; CABL; CBEP; Par; UnTE
  (Ballade, A.: Upon a Wedding.) SeCP
Ballade: To a Fish of the Brooke. John Wolcot. CBEP
Ballade, A: Upon a Wedding. Sir John Suckling. *See* Ballad upon a Wedding, A.
Ballade against Woman Inconstant, A. Chaucer. CABA
Ballade-Catalogue of Lovely Things, A. Richard Le Gallienne. LV
Ballade of Ladies' Love. Villon, *tr. fr. French by* John Payne. UnTE
  (Ballad of Ladies' Love, Number Two.) ErPo
Ballade of Lawn Tennis, A. Franklin P. Adams. SD
Ballade of Lost Objects. Phyllis McGinley. PoCh
Ballade of the Fair Helm-Maker. Villon, *tr. fr. French by* John Payne. UnTE
  (Belle Heaulmiere to the Daughters of Joy, *tr. by* Anthony Bonner.) AnML
Ballade of the Women of Paris. Villon, *tr. fr. French by* Swinburne. UnTE
Ballade of Villon and Fat Margot. Villon. *See* Ballad for Fat Margot.
Ballade to Rosamund. Chaucer. *See* To Rosamund.
Ballata: "I found myself one day all, all alone." Angelo Poliziano, *tr. fr. Italian by* John Addington Symonds. RBL
Ballata V: "Light do I see within my Lady's eyes." Guido Cavalcanti, *tr. fr. Italian by* Ezra Pound. CTC
Ballet of the Fifth Year, The. Delmore Schwartz. MP
Balloon, The. Tennyson. RoGo
Balloon Man, The. Rose Fyleman. SoPo
Balloon Man. Jessica N. North. SoPo
Balm of the world, come, quiet night! The Hermit. Josef von Eichendorff. AGP
Balmy breezes are aloft, The. Hope in Springtime. Ludwig Uhland. AGP
Bañalbufar, a Brazier, Relativity, Cloud Formations & the Kindness & Relentlessness of Time, All Seen through a Window While Keeping the Feet Warm at the Same Time As. Paul Blackburn. CoPo
Banana. Charles G. Bell. ErPo
Banana-stuffed, the ape behind the brain. After Sunday Dinner We Uncles Snooze. John Ciardi. ToPo
Bananas ripe and green, and gingerroot. The Tropics in New York. Claude McKay. AmNP
Band Marches, The. Detlev von Liliencron, *tr. fr. German by* Calvin S. Brown. AGP
Band Music. John Fuller. NePoEA-2
Bandog, The. Walter de la Mare. EvOK
Bang Bang Bang/ Said the nails in the Ark. The History of the Flood. John Heath-Stubbs. MoBS
Bangkok. F. R. Scott. OBCV

Bangum Rode the Riverside, *with music. Unknown.* BFSS
Bankrupt. Cortlandt W. Sayres. PoLF
Bank o' Doon, The. Burns. *See* Ye Banks and Braes.
Banks of Brandywine, The. *Unknown.* BSNS
Banks of Claudie [*or* Claudy], The. *Unknown.* BSNS; BSO, *with music*
Banks of Newfoundland, The. *Unknown.* BSNS
Banks of Sweet Dundee, The. *Unknown.* BSNS; BSO
Banks of Sweet Primroses, The. *Unknown.* ELP
Banks of the Condamine, The. *Unknown.* PoAu-1
Banks of the Nile, The. *Unknown. See* William and Nancy.
Banks of Wye, The, *sels.* Robert Bloomfield. OBNC
  Coracle Fishers, The.
  Meandering Wye.
Banks which crumble bejeweled. The Trout. René Char. *Fr.* Four Fascinators. CoFP
Bannockburn. Burns. PoPo
Banquet, The. George Herbert. MeP
Baobab. Hans Arp, *tr. fr. German by* Christopher Middleton. MGP
Bar, The. *Unknown.* STF
Bar Not the Door. Thomas Campion. UnTE
Bar-Room Matins. Louise MacNeice. EaLo
Bar to heaven, a door to hell, A. The Bar. *Unknown.* STF
Bar was black with blistered age, The. Ghost-Town Saloon: Winter. Joseph Payne Brennan. FiSC
Barbara Allen [*or* Allan]. *Unknown.* BFSS, *with music;* BSNS; BSO, *with music;* CABA; CBEP; DiPo; SIV, *with music*
  (Barbara Ellen.) BSNS; BSO, *with music* (A *and* B *vers.*)
  (Barbary Ellen, *with music.*) BSNS
  (Bonny Barbara Allen, D *and* F *vers.;* E *vers., with music.*) BSO
Barbara Frietchie. Whittier. AP; CTC; FaBV; FaPL; PoLF; PoSC; ThLM
Barbary Ellen. *Unknown. See* Barbara Allen.
Barb'd blossom of the guarded gorse. A Song of Winter. Emily Davis Pfeiffer. ACV
Barber, The. Moses Browne. WaPE
Barber, Barber ("Barber, barber, shave a pig"). *Unknown.* EvOK
Barber snips and snips, The. Barber's Clippers. Dorothy Baruch. SoPo
Barberry-Bush, The. Jones Very. AP
Barber's, The. Walter de la Mare. GoJo; SoPo
Barber's art, no trivial whim, The. The Barber. Moses Browne. WePE
Barber's Clippers. Dorothy Baruch. SoPo
Barbs of Mingo Revulgo, The. *Unknown, tr. fr. Spanish by* William M. Davis. AnML
Bard, The. Blake. *See* Hear the Voice of the Bard.
Bard, The. Thomas Gray. EiCP; EnPE; GTBS-P; StP
  "Fair laughs the morn, and soft the zephyr blows," *sel.* HaSV
Bard, The. James Shirley. ErPo
Bard who is singing of Wollombi Jim, The. Jim the Splitter. Henry Kendall. PoAu-1
Bards, The. Walter de la Mare. DTC
Bards, The. Robert Graves. DTC
Bards of passion and of mirth. Ode on the Poets. Keats. GTBS-P
Bare Arms of Trees, The. John Tagliabue. LV
Bare mud, slippery, wet and brown. Highway to Nowhere. Grant Code. FiSC
Barefoot Boy, The. Whittier. PoLF
  "Blessings on thee, little man," *sel.* PoPl
Barefoot I went and made no sound. The Viper. Ruth Pitter. DaDu
Barely a twelvemonth after. The Horses. Edwin Muir. ACV; PoIE; PoSa
Barge she sat in, like a burnished throne, The. Cleopatra: The Barge She Sat In. Shakespeare. *Fr.* Antony and Cleopatra, II, ii. DiPo
Barine, the Incorrigible. Horace, *tr. fr. Latin by* Louis Untermeyer. Odes, II, 8. UnTE
Bark leaps love-fraught from the land, The; the sea. The Thousand Islands. Charles Sangster. *Fr.* The St. Lawrence and the Saguenay. OBCV
Bark smells like pineapple: Jeffries. Foxtail Pine. Gary Snyder. CoPo
Barks the melancholy dog. Wakeful in the Township. Elizabeth Riddell. PoAu-2
Barn, The. Elizabeth J. Coatsworth. BiCB; SoPo
Barnacle Geese. Charles Higham. PoAu-2
Barney and Katie, *with music. Unknown.* BSO
Barney O'Hea. Samuel Lover. SIV
Barney O'Lean, *with music. Unknown.* BSO
Baroness Mu Impeded in Her Wish to Help Famine Victims in Wei. Confucius, *tr. fr. Chinese by* Ezra Pound. *Fr.* The Classic Anthology: Yung Wind. CTC
Baroque Gravure, A. Thomas Merton. CoPo
Baroque-handled and sharp. The Compasses. George Mac-Beth. NePoEA-2

Baroque Wall-Fountain in the Villa Sciarra, A. Richard Wilbur. MP; PoCh; ToPo
Barrel-Organ, The. Alfred Noyes. FaBV; LV
Barren Spring. Dante Gabriel Rossetti. The House of Life, LXXXIII. OBNC; VaPo
Barrier stone has rolled away, The. Easter. Edwin L. Sabin. PoSC
Barter. Marie Blake. PoPl
Barter. Sara Teasdale. FaBV; LV
Bartholdi Statue, The. Whittier. ThLM
Bartholomew. Norman Gale. BiCB
Bartleme Fair. George Alexander Stevens. ELP
Base Details. Siegfried Sassoon. MMA
Base Stealer, The. Robert Francis. GoJo; SD
Baseball Note. Franklin P. Adams. SD
Baseball's Sad Lexicon. Franklin P. Adams. SD
Basia, sels. Johannes Secundus, tr. fr. Latin by John Nott. Insatiate, The. UnTE
  Neaera's Kisses.
Bastard's Lot, The. Richard Savage. CBEP
Bat. D. H. Lawrence. GTBS-P
Bat, The. Ruth Pitter. DaDu;WePo
Bat, The. Theodore Roethke. GoJo
Batalis and the Man, The. Vergil, tr. fr. Latin by Gawin Douglas. Fr. The Aeneid, I. CTC
Bathed Is My Blood. Oliver La Grone. NNP
Bathing Girl, A. Johannes V. Jensen, tr. fr. Danish by Charles Wharton Stork. PoPl
Bathing herself, a girl with silver feet. The Young Bather. Unknown. UnTE
Batter my heart, three-person'd [or personed] God; for you. Holy Sonnets, XIV. John Donne. CABA; CaFP; CBEP; DiPo; EaLo; EnRePo; FoBA; ILP; MeP; OnP; PoIE; SeCP; StP; VaPo
Batter'd wreck'd old man, A. Prayer of Columbus. Walt Whitman. LV
Battered roof where stars went tripping, A. The Sleepers. F. W. Harvey. MMA
Batteries Out of Ammunition. Kipling. Fr. Epitaphs of the War. MMA
Battery grides and jingles, The. The Day's March. Robert Nichols. MMA
Battery Moving Up to a New Position from Rest Camp: Dawn. Robert Nichols. MMA
Battle, The. Ben Said al-Magribi, tr. fr. Arabic by Lysander Kemp. AnML
Battle: Hit. W. W. Gibson. PoPo
Battle Hymn of the Republic. Julia Ward Howe. AmLP; EaLo; FaPL; ThLM
  (Mine Eyes Have Seen the Glory.) TRV
Battle Hymn of the Spanish Rebellion. L. A. MacKay. OBCV
Battle of Blenheim, The. Robert Southey. FaBV; OBNC; PoLF; PoPo; PoSa; SIV; StP
  (After Blenheim.) GTBS-P; TRV
Battle of Fredericksburg, The. Unknown. BSNS
Battle of New Orleans, The. Thomas Dunn English. ThLM
Battle of Otterburn, The. Unknown. OnMSP
Battle of the Baltic, The. Thomas Campbell. CBEP; GTBS-P; HaSV; RoGo
Battle rent a cobweb diamond-strung. Range-finding. Robert Frost. AmLP; CABA
Battle Within, The. Christina Rossetti. TRV
Battlefield. Richard Aldington. MMA
Battle-Field, The. Bryant. PoLF
  "Truth, crushed to earth, shall rise again," sel. TRV
Battlefield. August Stramm, tr. fr. German by Michael Hamburger. MGP
Baucis and Philemon. Swift. EiCP
Baudelaire. Delmore Schwartz. MP
Bavarian Gentians. D. H. Lawrence. DiPo; GoJo; GTBS-P; PoIE; PoSa
Bawl of a steer, The. The Cowboy's Life. At. to James Barton Adams. SoPo
Bay of Biscay, The. Andrew Cherry. HaSV
Bay was anchor, sky, The. Offshore. Philip Booth. SD
Baying Hounds, The. Mary Gilmore. PoAu-1
Be. "Will Inman." PoNC
Be assured, the Dragon is not dead. Vanity. Robert Graves. GTBS-P
Be aware. Squanderings. Witter Bynner. MoLP
Be Careful What You Say. Joseph Kronthal. STF
Be extra careful by this door. The Whisperer. Mark Van Doren. UnTE
Be Friendly. Walter E. Isenhour. STF
Be Gallant, Mannerlie and Pure of Heart. Jean Froissart, tr. fr. French by Jacques LeClercq. AnML
Be in me as the eternal moods. Δωρια (Doria). Ezra Pound. AnMoPo; PoIE
Be kind and tender to the Frog. The Frog. Hilaire Belloc. FaBV; GoJo; RePo
Be kind, good sir, and I'll lift my sark. Confucius. Fr. The Classic Anthology: Songs of Cheng. CTC

Be Like the Bird. Victor Hugo, tr. fr. French. SoPo
Be mute, this autumn; gather in the world. In March. Philip Martin. PoAu-2
Be natural. The Name. Robert Creeley. CoPo; ToPo
Be near me when my light is low. In Memoriam A. H. H., L. Tennyson. ELP; FoBA; VP
Be neither song, nor game, nor feast. Ring Out, Wild Bells. Tennyson. Fr. In Memoriam A. H. H. WiR
Be not so desolate. Promise. "Æ." BoC
Be Quiet, Sir! Unknown. ErPo
  (Cautious Struggle, The.) UnTE
Be real, show organs, show blood, Oh let me. Oh Ease Oh Body-Strain Oh Love Oh Ease Me Not! Wound-Bore. Michael McClure. CoPo
Be sad, be cool, be kind. The Long Shadow of Lincoln. Carl Sandburg. LiPo
Be silent, secret, and conceal. Silentium. Feodor Tyutchev. PoPl; SiGo
Be Still. Betsy W. Kline. STF
Be Still, My Heart. Unknown. STF
Be Still, My Soul. Archilochus, tr. fr. Greek by C. M. Bowra. SiGo
Be Still, My Soul. Katharina von Schlegel, tr. fr. German by Jane L. Borthwick. TRV
Be still, my soul, be still; the arms you bear are brittle. A Shropshire Lad, XLVIII. A. E. Housman. OBNC
Be still, my soul: the Lord is on thy side. Be Still, My Soul. Katharina von Schlegel. TRV
Be Still My Soul, Weary of Pleasure. Camillo Sbarbaro, tr. fr. Italian by Carlo L. Golino. CoIP
Be Still. The Hanging Gardens Were a Dream. Trumbull Stickney. AmLP
Be Strong. Maltbie Davenport Babcock. LV
Be swift, dear heart, in saying. Kindness. Unknown. STF
Be Thankful. Mark Bullock. STF
Be the mistress of my choice. What Kind of Mistress He Would Have. Robert Herrick UnTE
Be True. Horatius Bonar. TRV
Be True to Your Condition in Life. John Audelay. MeEL
Be ware, squire, yeoman and page. Service Is No Heritage. Unknown. CBEP
Be Wise, and Fly Not. Thomas Campion. UnTE
Be with me, Beauty, for the fire is dying. On Growing Old. John Masefield. MoRP; PoLF
Be with me, Luis de San Angel, now. Ave Maria. Hart Crane. Fr. The Bridge. PoDB
Be with us, Lord, at eventide. Grace at Evening. Edwin McNeill Poteat. TRV
Beach Burial. Kenneth Slessor. PoAu-2
Beach Head, The. Thom Gunn. ToPo
Beach House. Mary Rita Hurley. PoPl
Bead Mat, The. Walter de la Mare. CBEP
Beagles. W. R. Rodgers. SD
Beale Street, Memphis. Thurmond Snyder. NNP
Bear down lightly. To Destiny. Unknown. EaLo
Bear on the Delhi Road, The. Earle Birney. PoCh
Bear River Murder, The. Unknown. BSNS
Bear sleeps in the cellar hole, A, where pine needles. New Hampshire. Donald Hall. NePoEA-2
Bear that breathes the northern blast, The. Upon a Wasp Chilled with Cold. Edward Taylor. CBEP
Bear untamable and wild, A. Infant Innocence. A. E. Housman. PoPo
Bearded Oaks. Robert Penn Warren. MP; VaPo
Bearer of Evil Things, The. Robert Frost. CBEP
Bearing their birds and gardens on their hats. L'Après Midi d'une Fille aux Cheveau de Lin. Ronald McCuaig. PoAu-2
Beast, The. Theodore Roethke. AmLP
Beast with Chrome Teeth, The. Thurmond Snyder. NNP
Beasts. Paul Engle. PoCh
Beasts, The. Walt Whitman. See Animals.
Beasts ("Beasts in their major freedom") Richard Wilbur. MP; ToPo
Beat! Beat! Drums! Walt Whitman. AP; FaBV; FoBA; LV; PoLF
Beat Child, The. Chuck Stoddard. LV
Beatific Vision, The. G. K. Chesterton. MoRP
Beating Heart, The. Heine, tr. fr. German by Louis Untermeyer. UnTE
Beau, The. Unknown. WaPE
Beaucourt Revisited. A. P. Herbert. MMA
Beauteous, Yea Beauteous More than These. Christopher Smart. Fr. A Song to David. EaLo
Beautiful and happy girl, A. Memories. Whittier. AP
Beautiful as the flying legend of some leopard. Judith of Bethulia. John Crowe Ransom. DTC
Beautiful Changes, The. Richard Wilbur. ILP
Beautiful Childhood. Gottfried Benn, tr. fr. German by Walter Kaufmann. Fr. Morgue. TwGP
Beautiful landscape! I could look on thee. On a Beautiful Landscape. William Bowles. PoPo

Beautiful must be the mountain whence ye come. Nightingales. Robert Bridges. OBNC; PoPl

Beautiful Railway Bridge of the Silv'ry Tay. The Tay Bridge Disaster. William McGonagall. EvOK

Beautiful soup, so rich and green. "Lewis Carroll." *Fr.* Alice's Adventures in Wonderland. Par

Beautiful star in heav'n so bright. Star of the Evening. James M. Sayles. Par

Beautiful, through clear skies newly blue. Spring Landscape. Melvin Walker La Follette. NePoEA-2

Beautiful Young Nymph Going to Bed, A. Swift. EiCP; UnTE

Beautifully Janet slept. Janet Waking. John Crowe Ransom. AmLP; PoIE; PoPo

Beautifully, now, they walk among these new. Six Nuns in the Snow. Phyllis McGinley. LV

Beauty. Basho, *tr. fr. Japanese by* Harold G. Henderson. SoPo

Beauty. Corrado Govoni, *tr. fr. Italian by* Carlo L. Golino. CoIP

Beauty, a Silver Dew. *Unknown.* CBEP

Beauty and Terror. Lesbia Harford. PoAu-1

Beauty and the Artist. Michelangelo, *tr. fr. Italian by* John Addington Symonds. RBL

Beauty and youth, with manners sweet, and friends. On the Grave of a Young Cavalry Officer Killed in the Valley of Virginia. Herman Melville. AP

Beauty Clear and Fair. John Fletcher. *Fr.* The Elder Brother. CBEP

Beauty depends on simplicity. The Inner Man. Plato. PoPl

Beauty does not walk through lovely days. Beauty and Terror. Lesbia Harford. PoAu-1

Beauty Imposes. John Shaw Neilson. PoAu-1

Beauty in woman; the high will's decree. He Compares All Things with His Lady, and Finds Them Wanting. Guido Cavalcanti. SiGo

Beauty Is Most at Twilight's Close. Pär Lagerkvist, *tr. fr. Swedish by* G. Kenneth Laycock. PoPl; SiGo

Beauty is not caused it is. Emily Dickinson. PoPo

Beauty is something more than a sky, a bird, a field. Something More. Thad Stem, Jr. PoNC

Beauty like hers is genius. Not the call. Genius in Beauty. Dante Gabriel Rossetti. *Fr.* The House of Life. VP

Beauty of Job's Daughters, The. Jay Macpherson. ACV; PoCh

Beauty of manhole covers, The—what of that? Manhole Covers. Karl Shapiro. GoJo

Beauty of Woman of Noble Heart. Guido Cavalcanti, *tr. fr. Italian by* Maurice Valency. AnML

Beauty Sat Bathing. Anthony Munday. *Fr.* Primaleon of Greece. CBEP; UnTE
(Colin.) GTBS-P

Beauty Self. *Unknown.* UnTE
("My love in her attire doth show her wit.") GTBS-P

Beauty, Since You So Much Desire. Thomas Campion. ErPo
(Place of Cupid's Fire, The.) UnTE

Beauty, Sweet Love. Samuel Daniel. To Delia, XLII. EnRePo

Beauty! thou art a wanderer on the earth. Behold, O Aspasia! I Send You Verses. Walter Savage Landor. *Fr.* Pericles and Aspasia. OBNC

Beauty's Pageant. Dante Gabriel Rossetti. The House of Life, XVII. VP

Beauty's Transitoriness. Christian Hoffmann von Hoffmannswaldau, *tr. fr. German by* George C. Schoolfield. AGP

Beaver Pond. Anne Marriott. ACV

Becalmed. John Blight. PoAu-2

Becalmed in old Back Bay's dead water sulk. George Starbuck. Poems from a First Year in Boston, IV. PoDB

Because, forsooth, you're young and fair. To His Young Mistress. Anacreon. UnTE

Because He Liked to Be at Home. Kenneth Patchen. ToPo

Because he was a butcher and thereby. Reuben Bright. E. A. Robinson. PoPo; StP

Because He Was Tempted. *Unknown.* STF

Because I believe in the community of little children. The Massacre of the Innocents. William Jay Smith. EaLo

Because I could not stop for death. Emily Dickinson. AmLP; AP; CABA; CaFP; CBEP; DiPo; FoBA; ILP; MoRP; OnP; PoIE; PoPo
(Chariot.) TRV

Because I do not hope to turn again. Ash Wednesday. T. S. Eliot. ACV; AP

Because I feel that, in the Heavens above. To My Mother. Poe. AP; PoPo

Because I had loved so deeply. Compensation. Paul Laurence Dunbar. AmNP

Because I Liked You. A. E. Housman. More Poems, XXXI. WePo
("Because I liked you better.") VP

Because I love and serve a whore *sans glose.* Ballade of Villon and Fat Margot. Villon. UnTE

Because I was content with these poor fields. Musketaquid. Emerson. AP

Because, just then, I'd nothing else to do. World's End. G. K. Chettur. ACV

Because My Hands Hear the Flowers Thinking. Kenneth Patchen. ToPo

Because of its profusion, some profess. Lèse Majesté. Paul Bartlett. PoNC

Because our talk was of the cloud-control. Secret Parting. Dante Gabriel Rossetti. *Fr.* The House of Life. VP

Because the ground-creature looked so sad. The Little Green Blackbird. Kenneth Patchen. PoCh

Because you have thrown off your prelate lord. On the New Forcers of Conscience under the Long Parliament. Milton. CABA; StP

Because you love me I have much achieved. Encouraged. Paul Laurence Dunbar. TRV

Because You Prayed. "C. B. B." STF

Because your voice was at my side. Chamber Music, XVII. James Joyce. WePo

Becoming a Dad. Edgar A. Guest. PoLF

Bed, The. Robert Creeley. StP

Bed in Summer. Robert Louis Stevenson. GoJo; LV; PoPl

Bed without a Woman, A. Raymond Souster. ErPo

Bedford Avenue. Art Berger. PtTo

Bedlam Hills. Vivian Smith. PoAu-2

Bedouin Song. Bayard Taylor. BoLP

Beds are made close to a wall flat. Saturday Morning. Richard Howard. ErPo

Bedtime. Elizabeth J. Coatsworth. ThGo

Bedtime. Eleanor Farjeon. SoPo

Bedtime Story. George MacBeth. NePoEA-2

Bedtime Story for My Son. Peter Redgrove. NePoEA-2

Bedtime Tales. Joseph Joel Keith. FiSC

Bee and the Petunia, The. Katherine Hoskins. ErPo

Bee, he has white honey, The. Dulce Ridentem. Stephen Vincent Benét. LOW

Beech and Oak. Thomas Love Peacock. CBEP

Beech Leaves. James Reeves. RePo

Beeg Irish cop dat walk hees beat. Two 'Mericana Men. T. A. Daly. SIV

Beehould a cluster to itt selfe a vine. Sonnet. William Alabaster. MeP

Beeny Cliff. Thomas Hardy. OBNC

Bees build in the crevices, The. The Stare's Nest by My Window. W. B. Yeats. GTBS-P

Beetle loves his unpretending track, The. Wordsworth. *Fr.* Liberty. Par

Beetles,/ noisy bumble bees. Come Visit My Garden. Tom Dent. NNP

Before Harvest. Robert Fitzgerald. PoPl

Before He formed a star. His Plan. *Unknown.* STF

Before I woke, the customed thews. Male Torso. Christopher Middleton. NePoEA-2

Before man came to blow it right. The Aim Was Song. Robert Frost. PP

Before me, where a raven croaks. Ode. Théophile de Viau. RBL

Before our lives divide for ever. The Triumph of Time. Swinburne. VP

Before she has her floor swept. Portrait by a Neighbor. Edna St. Vincent Millay. LOW

Before Sunset. Swinburne. StP

Before the Barn-Door Crowing. John Gay. *Fr.* The Beggar's Opera. CBEP
(Song.) ErPo

Before the Beginning of Years. Swinburne. *Fr.* Atalanta in Calydon. ACV; VP
(Chorus from "Atalanta.") CBEP; TRV

Before the cathedral in grandeur rose. How the Great Guest Came. Edwin Markham. SIV

Before the falling summer sun. Musings. William Barnes. OBNC

Before the glare o' dawn I rise. The Shearer's Wife. Louis Esson. PoAu-1

Before the Harvest. "Martin Greif," *tr. fr. German by* Clark Stillman. AGP

Before the Paling of the Stars. Christina Rossetti. CBEP
(Christmas Carol, A.) BiCB

Before the prim old mirror. Hair-dressing. Louis Untermeyer. UnTE

Before the Roman came to Rye or out to Severn strode. The Rolling English Road. G. K. Chesterton. EvOK

Before the Sabbath. David Ignatow. OPP

Before the sixth day of the next new year. On the Cards and Dice. Sir Walter Ralegh. EnRePo

Before the solemn, bronze Saint Gaudens made. An Ode in Time of Hesitation. William Vaughn Moody. AP

Before the Statue of Ilaria del Caretto. Salvatore Quasimodo, *tr. fr. Italian by* Allen Mandelbaum. CoIP

Before the sun was scuttled. Blue Ridge Parkway. H. A. Sieber. PoNC

Before the World Was Made. W. B. Yeats. GTBS-P
Before Thy Throne. William Boyd Carpenter. TRV
Before we light the tribal fires again. Since We Are Property. Lilith Lorraine. FiSC
Before you bid, for Christmas' sake. For Them. Eleanor Farjeon. ThGo
Before you love. A Proverb. *Unknown.* BoLP
Beggar in dirt. Dervish. Georgia Lee McElhaney. CoPo
Beggar Maid, The. Tennyson. OnMSP
Beggar man came over the lea, A. The Jolly Beggar. *Unknown.* BFSS.
Beggar to the graveyard hied, A. Poverty. *Unknown. Fr.* The Panchatantra. SIV
Beggar's Opera, The, *sels.* John Gay.
  Before the Barn-Door Crowing. CBEP
  (Song: "Before the barn-door crowing.") ErPo
  Highwaymen, The. WiR
  If the Heart of a Man. CBEP; ELP
  Through All the Employments of Life, *fr.* I, i. StP
  Were I Laid on Greenland's Coast. CBEP
  Youth's the Season. WiR
Beggar's Serenade. John Heath-Stubbs. ErPo
Begging. Henry Vaughan. MeP
Begging Another, on Colour of Mending the Former. Ben Jonson. *Fr.* A Celebration of Charis. SeCP
  (Begging Another Kiss.) StP
  (For Love's Sake.) UnTE
Begin the Day with God. *Unknown.* TRV
  (Rules for Daily Life.) STF
Beginning My Studies. Walt Whitman. CBEP
Beginning of Day, The. Euripides, *tr. fr. Greek.* SiGo
Beginning of fall. The End of Summer. Basho. RePo
Begotten by the meeting of rock with rock. Sea Holly. Conrad Aiken. AP
Begracde with Glory, glorified with Grace. Meditation. 1 Cor. 3. 21.22. All Things Are Yours. Edward Taylor. *Fr.* Preparatory Meditations, First Series. MeP
Behind him lay the gray Azores. Columbus. Joaquin Miller. PoPo; SIV; ThLM
Behind me—dips eternity. Emily Dickinson. AP
Behind shut doors, in shadowy quarantine. The First Time. Karl Shapiro. ErPo
Behind the house the upland falls. After the Pleasure Party. Herman Melville. AP
Behind the wall of St. John's in the city. The Garden at St. John's. May Swenson. PoPl
Behind the wild bird's throat. Wood-Thrush. John Hall Wheelock. PoDB
Behold a silly, tender babe. New Prince, New Pomp. Robert Southwell. ELP; MeP
Behold, bless ye the Lord. Psalm CXXXIV, Bible, *O.T.* TRV
Behold, from the land of the farther suns. The Black Riders, XXIX. Stephen Crane. AP
Behold her, single in the field. The Solitary Reaper [*or* The Reaper]. Wordsworth. CABA; CaFP; CBEP; DiPo; FoBA; GTBS-P; ILP; OBNC; OnP; PoIE; PoSa; RoGo; StP
Behold how good and how pleasant it is. Psalm CXXXIII, Bible, *O.T.* TRV
Behold, my fair, where'er we rove. The Winter's Walk. Samuel Johnson. CBEP; EiCP
Behold, O Aspasia! I Send You Verses. Walter Savage Landor. *Fr.* Pericles and Aspasia. OBNC
Behold once more with serious labor here. To the Reader. Samuel Daniel. PP
Behold the apples' rounded worlds. Apples [*or* Autumn Apples]. Laurie Lee. BoC; WePo
Behold the hippopotamus! The Hippopotamus. Ogden Nash. FaBV
Behold the Lilies of the Field. Anthony Hecht. CoPo; NePoEA-2
Behold the Lovely Maid! Solomon ibn Gabirol, *tr. fr. Hebrew by* William M. Davis. AnML
Behold the Man! *Unknown.* STF
Behold the rocky wall. The Two Streams. Oliver Wendell Holmes. AP
Behold the Sea, *sel.* Aaron Kurtz, *tr. fr. Yiddish.* "They got you last night." PtTo
Behold the works of William Morris. Rondel. *Unknown.* Par
Behold these woods, and mark, my sweet. A Pastoral Courtship. Earl of Rochester. UnTE
Behold this fleeting world, how all things fade. An Epitaph of the Death of Nicholas Grimald. Barnabe Googe. EnRePo
Behold this needle: when the Arctic stone. A Compass Needle. Francis Quarles. CBEP
Behold thy darling, which thy lustfull care. Francis Quarles. *Fr.* Emblems. MeP
Behold yon' hill, how it is swell'd with pride. Describes the Place Where Cynthia Is Sporting Herself Girolamo Petri. RBL

Beholde me, I pray thee, with all thine whole reson. Wofully Araide. *Unknown.* MeEL
Beholde the father, is his daughters sonne. The Nativitie of Christ. Robert Southwell. MeP
Beholders, The. James Dickey. AP
Being a Christian. *Unknown.* STF
Being at last on our way. Departure. William Hart-Smith. *Fr.* Christopher Columbus. PoAu-2
Being Gypsy. Barbara Young. SoPo
Being Here. Walter Bauer, *tr. fr. German by* Christopher Middleton. MGP
Being in his resting place. A Dog Sleeping on my Feet. James Dickey. PP
Being now three or four years more than sixty. The World's Wonders. Robinson Jeffers. PoDB
Being set on the idea. Atlantis. W. H. Auden. PoPl
Being so young he feels the weight of history. The Conscript. Louis MacNeice. AnMoPo
Being Twins. Kathryn Jackson. BiCB
Being without quality. Vox Humana. Thom Gunn. NePoEA-2
Being your slave, what should I do but tend. Sonnets, LVII. Shakespeare. BoLP; GTBS-P
Bel m'es quan lo vens m'alena. Arnaut Daniel, *tr. fr. Provençal by* Harriet Waters Preston. SiGo
Belgravia. Barbara Guest. AmPC
Belief. A. R. Ammons. OPP
Belief and Unbelief. Robert Browning. *Fr.* Bishop Blougram's Apology. FaBV
Belief in Plan of Thee. Walt Whitman. TRV
Believe me, I say to the gentleman with the pince-nez. In the Library. Elizabeth Brewster. OBCV
Believe me, I understand your refusal. Letter to Pasternak. Ralph Pomeroy. CoPo
Believe Me, If All Those Endearing Young Charms. Thomas Moore. CBEP; ELP; FaBV; OBNC; PoPl
Believe the Bible. A. B. Simpson. STF
Believer he and unbeliever both. Epitaph. Robert Francis. PoIE
Belinda lived in a little white house. The Tale of Custard the [*or* the Custard] Dragon. Ogden Nash. PoPl; WePo
Belisarius. Longfellow. WiR
Bell-Birds. Henry Kendall. PoAu-1
Bell-bottomed Trousers. *Unknown.* UnTE
Bell, my silver tongued bell. Theme. Carl Spitteler. PoPl
Bell-rope that gathers God at dawn, The. The Broken Tower. Hart Crane. AP; PoIE; VaPo
Bell Speech. Richard Wilbur. AP; CABA
Bell struck one, and shook the silent tower, The. Fair Elenor. Blake. FoBA
Bell Tower. Léonie Adams. AmLP; PoPl
Bella was young and Bella was fair. Unhappy Bella. *Unknown.* ErPo
Belle Heaulmiere to the Daughters of Joy, The. Villon. *See* Ballade of the Fair Helm-Maker.
Bellerophon, *sel.* Euripides, *tr. fr. Greek by* John Addington Symonds.
  There Are No Gods. EaLo
Belles of the eighties were soft, The. Reflections Outside of a Gymnasium. Phyllis McGinley. SD
Bellman, The. Robert Herrick. CBEP
Bellman's Song, The. *Unknown.* DiPo
Bells, The. Rosalía de Castro, *tr. fr. Spanish by* Edwin Morgan. AnSP
Bells, The. Poe. FaPL; PoLF; PoPo
  "Hear the mellow wedding bells," *sel.* PoPl
Bells are booming down the bohreens. Ireland with Emily. John Betjeman. GTBS-P
Bells are tolling, The. Tolling Bells. Lady Kasa. SiGo
Bells chime clear, The. The Christening. Walter de la Mare. BiCB
Bells for John Whiteside's [Whitesides, *wr.*] Daughter. John Crowe Ransom. AmLP; AP; CaFP; DTC; ILP; PoIE; PoPo; StP; VaPo
Bells of Heaven, The. Ralph Hodgson. EaLo; GoJo; PoIE; PoSa
Bells of London, The. *Unknown.* EvOK
Bells of Shandon, The. Francis Sylvester Mahony. RoGo
Bells of waiting Advent ring, The. Christmas. John Betjeman. BoC; WePo
Belongings, The. Theodore Enslin. CoPo
Beloved, let us love: love is God. Love Is God. Horatius Bonar. TRV
Beloved, may your sleep be sound. Lullaby. W. B. Yeats. AnMoPo
Beloved, there is nothing I can say. A Cold Wind Blows. Zoe Kincaid Brockman. PoNC
Beloved, thou hast brought me many flowers. Sonnets from the Portuguese, XLIV. Elizabeth Barrett Browning. ILP; OBNC
Below the Brow I Bear Your Lovely Countenance. Jordi de Sant Jordi, *tr. fr. Catalan by* William M. Davis. AnML

Below the hall. The Pine-Trees in the Courtyard. Po Chü-i. SiGo
Below the thunders of the upper deep. The Kraken. Tennyson. CABA; CaFP; FoBA; OBNC; VaPo; WiR
Below there rests the knight. Epitaph. Cervantes. *Fr.* Don Quixote. RBL
Belshazzar had a letter. Emily Dickinson. CBEP; MoRP
Belsnickel. Arthur Guiterman. BBGG
Ben Battle was a soldier bold. Faithless Nelly [*or* Nellie] Gray. Thomas Hood. SIV; WePo
Ben Hall was out on the Lachlan side. The Death of Ben Hall. Will H. Ogilvie. PoAu-1
Bend back thy bow, O Archer, till the string. The Archer. A. J. M. Smith. OBCV
Bend low again, night of summer stars. Summer Stars. Carl Sandburg. LOW; RePo
Beneath a Cool Shade. Aphra Behn. UnTE
Beneath a Myrtle Shade. Dryden. *Fr.* The Conquest of Granada. UnTE
　(Song of the Zambra Dance.) ErPo
Beneath a withered bush the serpent waits. The Serpent Waits. Joseph Payne Brennan. FiSC
Beneath the sagging roof. Ezra Pound. *Fr.* Hugh Selwyn Mauberley. PoIE
Beneath these fruit-tree boughs that shed. The Green Linnet. Wordsworth. CBEP; GTBS-P
Beneath these poppies buried deep. Epitaph on Robert Southey. Thomas Moore. PP
Beneath these shades, beside yon winding stream. On Visiting the Graves of Hawthorne and Thoreau. Jones Very. AP
Beneath this slab. Lather as You Go. Ogden Nash. WePo
Beneath this stone lies young John Calf. Epitaph on Jean Veau. Clément Marot. RBL
Benedicite, what dreamed I this night? What Dreamed I? *Unknown.* CBEP
Benediction. Donald Jeffrey Hayes. AmNP
Benediction. Stanley Kunitz. AnMoPo; MoRP
Bent double, like old beggars under sacks. Dulce et Decorum Est. Wilfred Owen. CBEP; FaBV; MMA; PoIE
Beppo. Byron. CABL
Bereft. Robert Frost. FaPL; FoBA; PoDB
Berg, The. Herman Melville. AP; CBEP
Berlin Crisis. Florence Victor. OPP
Bermudas. Andrew Marvell. CABA; CBEP; HaSV; ILP; MeP; SeCP; ThLM
　(Song of the Emigrants in Bermuda.) GTBS-P
Bert Schultz. Colin Thiele. PoAu-2
Bertran de Born. Ludwig Uhland, *tr. fr. German by* Walter Kaufmann. TwGP
Bertrand de Born. Heine, *tr. fr. German by* Walter Kaufmann. TwGP
Beshrew that heart that makes my heart to groan. Sonnets, CXXXIII. Shakespeare. CBEP
Beside me she sat, hand hooked and hovering. An Egyptian Passage. Theodore Weiss. CoPo
Beside his heavy-shouldered team. Bullocky. Judith Wright. PoAu-2
Beside that tent and under guard. Geronimo. Ernest McGaffey. ThLM
Beside the dark sand and the winged foam. Poem by the Clock Tower, Sumner. James K. Baxter. ACV
Beside the idle summer sea. Rondel. W. E. Henley. OBNC
Beside the mountain roads, the men. Blue Smoke. Frances Frost. RePo
Beside the pool where shadows flit. The Fool of Love. *Unknown.* UnTE
Beside the pounding cataracts. The City of the End of Things. Archibald Lampman. OBCV
Beside the Sea. George Johnston. ACV
Beside the Seaside, *sel.* John Betjeman.
　"And all the time the waves, the waves, the waves." HaSV
Beside the slew the poplars play. A Prairie Water Colour. Duncan Campbell Scott. OBCV
Beside the ungathered rice he lay. The Slave's Dream. Longfellow. WePo
Beside yon straggling fence that skirts the way. The Village Schoolmaster. Goldsmith. *Fr.* The Deserted Village. PoSa
Beside you. Nightsong. Philip Booth. MoLP
Besse Bunting. *Unknown.* MeEL
Bessie Bell and Mary Gray, *with music. Unknown.* BFSS
Bessie of Ballington Brae. *Unknown.* BSNS
Best and brightest, come away. The Invitation. Shelley. GTBS-P
Best Choice, The. *Unknown.* STF
Best for Me, The. *Unknown.* STF
Best for Us, The. Olive H. Burnett. STF
Best Game the Fairies Play, The. Rose Fyleman. SoPo
Best Memory Course, The. *Unknown.* STF
Best of artists hath no thought to show, The. The Lover and the Sculptor. Michelangelo. RBL
Best Old Feller in the World, The (A *vers., with music*). *Unknown.* BFSS

Best Spiders for soup, The. Cobwebbery. Jonathan Williams. PoNC
Best thing in the world, but I better be quick about it, The. Biotherm. Frank O'Hara. CoPo
Best Treasure, The. John J. Moment. TRV
Bestiary. A. M. Klein. OBCV
Bête Humaine. Francis Brett Young. SIV
Beth has some mittens. Richer. Aileen Fisher. BiCB
Bethlehem of Judea. *Unknown.* BiCB
Bethsabe's Song. George Peele. *Fr.* David and Bethsabe. CBEP; EnRePo
Betrayal. Hester H. Cholmondeley. TRV
Betrayal, The. Josephine W. Johnson. MoRP
Betsey Evans. *Unknown.* BSO
Betsy Baker. *Unknown.* BSNS
Betsy Jane's Sixth Birthday. Alfred Noyes. BiCB
Better Answer, A. Matthew Prior. ELP
Better Bargain, The. Congreve. UnTE
Better never trouble Trouble. Trouble. David Keppel. PoLF
Better Resurrection, A. Christina Rossetti. VP
Better than flowers. William Carlos Williams. *Fr.* Paterson. MoLP
Better to see your cheek grown hollow. Madman's Song. Elinor Wylie. LOW
Betty at the Party. *Unknown.* BiCB
Between Botallack and the light. A Ballad of a Mine. Robin Skelton. MoBS
Between Cellini's Perseus and the Sabine Rape. More Nudes for Florence. Harold Witt. ErPo
Between Chicago and St. Paul. Mel Weisburd. PtTo
Between extremities. Vacillation. W. B. Yeats. PoDB
Between me and the moving world's. Presence. John Moffit. MoRP
Between me and the sunset, like a dome. The Man against the Sky. E. A. Robinson. AP
Between the dark and the daylight. The Children's Hour. Longfellow. FaBV; FaPL; PoLF; PoPl
Between the exhilaration of Beginning. The Middle-Time. Lona M. Fowler. TRV
Between the first pangs and the last of love. This Little Vigil. Charles G. Bell. MoLP
Between the Karim Shahir. Rochelle Owens. CoPo
Between the midnight and the morn. The Secret Muse. Roy Campbell. BoC
Between the wheeze of her torpor and the wind of her falling. Faintly and from Far Away. Vassar Miller. CoPo
Between the World and Me. Richard Wright. AmNP
Between town and the. The Quarry Pool. Denise Levertov. ToPo
Between trains, on this day of snow. At the Roman Baths, Bath. Edward Lucie-Smith. NePoEA-2
Between Two Prisoners. James Dickey. AP
Betwene [*or* Bitwene] Mersh and Averil. Alison. *Unknown.* CTC; MeEL
Betwixt and Between. Hugh Lofting. BiCB
Betwixt twelve hours and eleven. Amends to the Tailors and Soutars. William Dunbar. CBEP
Bewar, squier, yeman, and page. A Warning to Those Who Serve Lords. *Unknown.* MeEL
Bewick Finzer. E. A. Robinson. AP
Bewildered with the broken tongue. Words in Time. Archibald MacLeish. PoCh
Bewilderment at the Entrance of the Fat Boy into Eden, A. Daryl Hine. OBCV
Beyond all this, the wish to be alone. Wants. Philip Larkin. GTBS-P
Beyond antiseptic white. Semi-Private. Mabel MacDonald Carver. FiSC
Beyond any doubt (and you can add "peradventure," too). Little Saucers, Big Saucers. Thad Stem, Jr. PoNC
Beyond Barriers. William J. Pomeroy. PtTo
Beyond I wander. "Novalis." *Fr.* Hymns to the Night, IV. TwGP
Beyond Kerguelen. Henry Kendall. PoAu-1
Beyond Possession. Elizabeth Jennings. BoC
Beyond surprise, my ribs start up from the ground. The Defeated. W. S. Merwin. AmPC
Beyond the Chagres. James Stanley Gilbert. PoLF
Beyond the field where crows cawed at a hawk. Two Lives and Others. Winfield Townley Scott. PoPl
Beyond the Horizon. Oskar Loerke, *tr. fr. German by* Christopher Middleton. MGP
Beyond the hour we counted rain that fell. Old Countryside. Louise Bogan. AmLP
Beyond the Hunting Woods. Donald Justice. PoPl
Beyond the image of the willow. The Importance of Poetry, or the Coming Forth from Eternity into Time. Hyam Plutzik. PP
Beyond the Last Lamp. Thomas Hardy. OBNC
Beyond the low marsh-meadows and the beach. The Pines and the Sea. Christopher Pearse Cranch. AmLP; ILP
Beyond the shadow of the ship. Samuel Taylor Coleridge. *Fr.* The Rime of the Ancient Mariner. BoC

Beyond the Sphere Which Turns Most Distant. Dante, *tr. fr. Italian by* Maurice Valency. *Fr.* La Vita Nuova. AnML
("Beyond the sphere which spreads to widest space," *tr. by* Dante Gabriel Rossetti.) CTC
Beyond the thickets of my self. Nightmare. Joseph Payne Brennan. FiSC
Beyond the turning sea's far foam. At War. Russell Atkins. AmNP
Beyond the Veil. Henry Vaughan. *See* They Are All Gone into the World of Light.
Beyond the window's tracery. The Woman at the Window. Donald Wandrei. FiSC
Bianca. Arthur Symons. UnTE
Bianca among the Nightingales. Elizabeth Barrett Browning. GTBS-P
Bible, The. Sir Walter Scott. *Fr.* The Monastery. TRV
Bible, The. Dorothy Conant Stroud. STF
Bicycalamity. Edmund W. Peters. SD
Bid me not speak, bid me be still. Mignon. Goethe. TwGP
Bid me to live, and I will live. To Anthea, Who May Command Him Anything. Robert Herrick. BoC; CBEP; GTBS-P; SeCP
Bide a Wee! John Oxenham. TRV
Biftek aux Champignons. Henry Augustin Beers. AmLP
Big Clock, The. *Unknown.* SoPo
Big Crash Out West. Peter Viereck. PoPl
Big Rock Candy Mountain, The. *Unknown.* WePo
Big Steamers. Kipling. Par
Big strong work horses working every day. Work Horses. Edith Newlin Chase. SoPo
Big Tent under the Roof, The. Ogden Nash. RePo
Big Theater, The. André Pieyre de Mandiargues, *tr. fr. French by* Charles P. Wright, Jr. CoFP
Big Turtle, A. *Unknown.* SoPo
Big Wind. Theodore Roethke. GoJo
Big yellow trolley lumbers along. There Are So Many Ways of Going Places. Leslie Thompson. SoPo
Bigger the box the more it holds, The. Boxes and Bags. Carl Sandburg. RePo
Biggest Killing, The. Edward Dorn. CoPo
Bight, The. Elizabeth Bishop. PoSa
Biglow Papers, The, *sels.* James Russell Lowell.
1st Series, No. III.
What Mr. Robinson Thinks. LV
2d Series, Introduction.
Courtin', The. SIV
2d Series, No. VI.
Sunthin' in the Pastoral Line. AP
(Spring.) FaBV
Bilitis. Pierre Louÿs, *tr. fr French by* Horace B. Brown. *Fr.* The Songs of Bilitis. UnTE
Bill. J. L. Salzburg. BiCB
Bill Jones had been the shining star upon his college team. Alumnus Football. Grantland Rice. PoLF
Bill the Weaver. *Unknown.* BSNS
Bill the Whaler. Will Lawson. PoAu-1
Billows swell, the winds are high, The. Temptation. William Cowper. EiCP
Billy Boy (A *vers., with music; B, C, D, and E vers.*). *Unknown.* BSO
Billy Budd, *sel.* Herman Melville.
Billy in the Darbies. CBEP
Billy Holiday,/—Lady—Day. Walt Delegall. *Fr.* Elegy for a Lady. PtTo
Billy, in one of his nice new sashes. Tender-heartedness. Harry Graham. WePo
Billy in the Darbies. Herman Melville. *Fr.* Billy Budd. CBEP
Billy O'Rourke. *Unknown.* BSO
Billy the Kid. Jack Spicer. CoPo
Billy the Kid. *Unknown.* ThLM
Binker ("Binker—what I call him—is a secret of my own"). A. A. Milne. PoPl
Binnorie. *Unknown. See* Two Sisters, The.
Binsey Poplars (Felled 1879). Gerard Manley Hopkins. AnMoPo; ELP; PoPo; VP
Biography for Traman, *sel.* Winfield Townley Scott.
"Let us record/ The evenings when we were innocents of twenty." ErPo
Biotherm. Frank O'Hara. CoPo
Birches. Robert Frost. DiPo; FaBV; FoBA; ILP; LV; PoIE; PoLF; PoPl; StP
Bird, The. Louis Simpson. NePoEA-2
Bird, The. Rabindranath Tagore. The Gardener, LXVII. PoPl; SiGo
Bird, The. Henry Vaughan. MeP
(After the Storm.) BoC
(To a Bird after a Storm.) TRV
Bird Came down the walk, A. Emily Dickinson. AmLP; AP; CABA; DiPo; FoBA; GoJo; PoLF; PoPo; SoPo
Bird Causeways, The. Oskar Loerke, *tr. fr. German by* Christopher Middleton. MGP

Bird Fancier, The. James Kirkup. PoPo
Bird is lost, The. Yardbird's Skull. Owen Dodson. AmNP
Bird is my neighbour, a whimsical fellow and dim, The. The Crane Is My Neighbour. John Shaw Neilson. PoAu-1
Bird shadows mounting. Larry Eigner. CoPo
Bird-shaped island, with secretive bird-voices. New Guinea. James McAuley. PoAu-2
Bird spades the soil, The. Lightning Victory. René Char. CoFP
Bird you caught me, with blue feathers, The. Letter: The Japanese, to Her Husband at War. William Walsh. PoPl
Birdcatcher, The. Ralph Hodgson. PoIE
Birdie with a yellow bill, A. Time to Get Up. Robert Louis Stevenson. ThGo
Birdies, can there be any doubt. November. James Reaney. *Fr.* A Suit of Nettles. OBCV
Birds. Robinson Jeffers. AP
Birds. "Llywelyn." PoAu-2
Birds and Bees. *Unknown, tr. fr. German by* Louis Untermeyer. UnTE
Birds are gone to bed, the cows are still, The. Hares at Play. John Clare. CBEP
Birds Are in the Air at Ease. Francisco de Quevedo, *tr. fr. Spanish by* William M. Davis. AnSP
Birds are of passage now. Words for the Raker of Leaves. Léonie Adams. PoCh
Birds are our angels—out of heaven. Birds. "Llywelyn." PoAu-2
Birds far-off and open in the evening. The Gentle Hill. Salvatore Quasimodo. PoPl
Birds in the air. Mary's Song. Eleanor Farjeon. ThGo
Birds in the Garden. *Unknown.* ThGo
Bird's Nest, The. John Drinkwater. EvOK; SoPo
Birds of Killingworth, The. Longfellow. *Fr.* Tales of a Wayside Inn. OnMSP
Birds of Paradise, The. John Peale Bishop. GoJo
Birds of Paradise. Christina Rossetti. VP
Birds of the Air, The. Hollis Freeman. STF
Birds stayed not their singing. Armistice Day. John Freeman. MMA
Birdwatchers of America. Anthony Hecht. CoPo
Birkett's Eagle. Dorothy S. Howard. MoBS
Birks of Aberfeldy, The. Burns. CTC
Birmingham. Louis MacNeice. ILP
Birth. Olive Tilford Dargan. PoNC
Birth, The. Rosemary Dobson. PoAu-2
Birth-Bond, The. Dante Gabriel Rossetti. The House of Life, XV. VP
Birth of Christ. Rainer Maria Rilke, *tr. fr. German by* M. D. Herter Norton. MoRP
Birth of Mary. Rainer Maria Rilke, *tr. fr. German by* M. D. Herter Norton. MoRP
Birth of Robin Hood, The. *Unknown.* BuBa
Birth of Saint Patrick, The. Samuel Lover. PoSC
Birth of the Squire, The. John Gay. EiCP
Birth of Tragedy, The. Irving Layton. OBCV
Birthday. Elaine V. Emans. BiCB
Birthday, A. Rachel Field. BiCB
Birthday, A. Christina Rossetti. BoLP; FaPL; VP; WiR
Birthday, birthday; little boy has a birthday. Birthday Gifts. Louise Binder Scott and J. J. Thompson. BiCB
Birthday Bus, The. Mary Ann Hoberman. BiCB
Birthday Cake, The. Victoria Chase. BiCB
Birthday Cake. Ivy O. Eastwick. BiCB
Birthday Cake. Aileen Fisher. BiCB
Birthday-Cake Glockenspiel, The. Elizabeth Henley. BiCB
Birthday Candles. Louise Binder Scott and J. J. Thompson. BiCB
Birthday candles, shine your brightest. Six Birthday Candles Shining. Mary Jane Carr. BiCB
Birthday Child, The. Rose Fyleman. BiCB
Birthday Garden. Ivy O. Eastwick. BiCB
Birthday Gift. Ethel Barnett de Vito. BiCB
Birthday Gifts. Herbert Asquith. BiCB
Birthday Gifts. Louise Binder Scott and J. J. Thompson. BiCB
Birthday Morning. Jean Ingelow. *See* Seven Times One.
Birthday of the Lord, The. Mary Jane Carr. BiCB
Birthday Rhyme. *Unknown.* BiCB
Birthdays. Marchette Chute. BiCB
Birthdays. Mother Goose. *See* Monday's Child Is Fair of Face.
Birthdays? yes, in a general way. Sincere Flattery of R. B. J. K. Stephen. Par
Birthplace. James Larkin Pearson. PoNC
Bishop Blougram's Apology. Robert Browning. OBNC
Sels.
Belief and Unbelief. FaBV
"When the fight begins within himself." TRV
Bishop of Atlanta, The: Ray Charles. Horace Julian Bond AmNP
Bishop Orders His Tomb at Saint Praxed's Church, The. Robert Browning. CABA; CaFP; DiPo; ILP; OnP; PoIE; VaPo; VP

Bishop sat in lordly state and purple cap sublime, The. Tang-malangaloo. P. J. Hartigan. PoAu-1
Bishop seduces the world with his voice, The. The Bishop of Atlanta: Ray Charles. Horace Julian Bond. AmNP
Bit of the Book, A. Margaret E. Sangster. TRV
"Bite deep and wide, O Axe, the tree." Isabella Valancy Crawford. *Fr.* Malcolm's Katie. OBCV
Bits of Straw. John Clare. WiR
Bitter air, The. L'aura amara. Arnaut Daniel. CTC
Bitter king in anger to be gone, A. Like an Old Proud King in a Parable. A. J. M. Smith. OBCV
Bitter-sweet. George Herbert. FoBA
Bitter Withy, The. *Unknown.* PoIE
Bitumen flanges of this living track. Reflection after Empire. James Boyer May. PtTo
Bitwene Mersh and Averil. *See* Betwene Mersh and Averil.
Bivouac of the Dead, The. Theodore O'Hara. FaPL
Bivouac on a Mountain Side. Walt Whitman. AP; PoLF
Black and Gold. Nancy Byrd Turner. SoPo
Black and white. Things to Learn About. John Becker. RePo
Black & white glare blink in the inky Air Force night, The. Journals Nov. 22, '63. Allen Ginsberg. OPP
Black Are the Stars. Raymond Roseliep. FiSC
Black-burnin' shame is your garb, quo' they. The Scarlet Woman. "Hugh MacDiarmid." ACV
Black cat yawns, The. Cat. Mary Britton Miller. SoPo
Black Crispus Attucks taught. Dark Symphony. Melvin B. Tolson. AmNP
Black Diamond. Nikolay Gumilyov, *tr. fr. Russian by* Babette Deutsch. SiGo
Black Eggs. Hans Arp, *tr. fr. German by* Christopher Middleton. MGP
Black Finger, The. Angelina W. Grimké. AmNP
Black fool, why winter here? These frozen skies. Advice to a Raven in Russia December, 1812. Joel Barlow. AmLP
Black grows the southern sky, betokening rain. Sudden Shower. John Clare. CBEP; PoSC
Black Is a Soul. Joseph White. PtTo
Black is what the prisons are. The African Affair. Bruch McM. Wright. AmNP
Black Jackets. Thom Gunn. MP
Black Man Talks of Reaping, A. Arna Bontemps. AmNP
Black Marigolds, *much abr.* Bilhana, *formerly at. to* Chauras, *tr. fr. Sanskrit by* E. Powys Mathers. ErPo
I Love Long Black Eyes, *sel.* SiGo
Black milk of daybreak we drink it at nightfall. Fugue of Death. Paul Celan. MGP
Black November Turkey, A. Richard Wilbur. AmLP
Black Patch on Lucasta's Face, A. Richard Lovelace. SeCP
Black Riders, The, *sels.* Stephen Crane.
  "Behold, from the land of the farther suns," XXIX. AP
  "Black riders came from the sea," I. AP
  Blade [*or* Blades] of Grass, The ("In heaven/ Some little blades of grass"), XVIII. AP; PoPl; PoPo
  "God fashioned the ship of the world carefully," VI. AP
  "God in wrath, A," XIX. AP
  "God lay dead in heaven," LXVII. AP
  "I looked here," VIII. AP
  "I saw a man pursuing the horizon," XXIV. AP
  "I stood musing in a black world," XLIX. AP
  "I stood upon a high place," IX. AP; PoPo
  "I stood upon a highway," XXXIV. AP
  "If I should cast off this tattered coat," LXVI. AP
  "In the desert," III. AP
  "It was wrong to do this," said the angel," LIV. AP
  "Livid lightnings flashed in the clouds, The," XXXIX. AP
  "Love walked alone," XLI. AP
  Man Saw a Ball of Gold in the Sky, A, XXXV. EvOK; PoPl; PoPo
  "Man went before a strange God, A," LI. AP
  "Many red devils ran from my heart," XLVI. AP
  "Many workmen," XXXI. PoPo
  "Places among the stars," XXIII. AP
  "Should the wide world roll away," X. AP
  "There was, before me," XXI. AP
  "There was crimson clash of war," XIV. AP
  "Truth," said a traveller," XXVIII. AP
  "Upon the road of my life," LX. AP
  "Well then, I hate Thee, unrighteous picture," XII. AP
Black Riders came from the sea. The Black Riders, I. Stephen Crane. AP
Black Rook in Rainy Weather. Sylvia Plath. MP; NePoEA-2; PoDB; PP
Black-smocked smiths, smattered with smoke. *See* Swart smeked smithes, smatered with smoke.
Black Spirit. Tom Poots. FiSC
Black swallows swooping or gliding. The Skaters. John Gould Fletcher. SD
Black Tambourine. Hart Crane. AP; CBEP
Black velvet where a shining diamond. Black Diamond. Nikolay Gumilyov. SiGo
Black Vulture, The. George Sterling. AmLP

Black Water and Bright Air. Constance Carrier. SD
Black: you are Black Hell, its dark portals. Colors. Luigi Bartolini. CoIP
Blackbird, The; or, Logan's Lament, *with music. Unknown.* BSO
Blackbird, The. Humbert Wolfe. GoJo; RePo
Blackbird by Belfast Lough, The. *Unknown, tr. fr. Irish by* Frank O'Connor. SiGo
Blackbird is singing on Michigan's shore, The. The Blackbird; or, Logan's Lament. BSO
Blackbird Singing, A. R. S. Thomas. BoC; WePo
Blackbird Suddenly, A. Joseph Auslander. RePo
Blackened and bleeding, helpless, panting, prone. Chicago. Bret Harte. ThLM
Black-eyed Susan. John Gay. GTBS-P; RoGo
Blackjack Davy, The, *with music. Unknown.* BFSS
Blacksmiths. *Unknown.* CABA; WiR
  (Smoke-blackened Smiths.) MeEL
Blacksmith's Daughter, The. Heinz Piontek, *tr. fr. German by* Michael Hamburger. MGP
Blade [*or* Blades] of Grass, The. Stephen Crane. The Black Riders, XVIII. AP; PoPl; PoPo
Blaeberry Courtship, The (A *and* B *vers.*). *Unknown.* BSNS
Blame Not My Lute. Sir Thomas Wyatt. EnRePo
Blanche is/ And navy the tree full of holes. Song in a Winter Night. Bink Noll. ToPo
Blank book, beginning of a day. Eighth Poem. Giovanni Papini. CoIP
Blanket Street. Inez Hogan. BiCB
Blasted with sighs and surrounded with tears. Twicknam [*or* Twickenham] Garden[s]. John Donne. CBEP; DiPo; SeCP
Blaydon Races. *Unknown.* ELP
Bleeberrying. Jonathan Denwood. MoBS
Blennerhassett's Island. Thomas Buchanan Read. ThLM
Bless love and hope. Full many a withered year. Love and Hope. Dante Gabriel Rossetti. *Fr.* The House of Life. VP
Bless This House. *Unknown.* TRV
Blessed be that lady bright. A Cause for Wonder. *Unknown.* MeEL
Blessed, blessed/ Oh blessed. Thomas McGrath. *Fr.* Letter to an Imaginary Friend. PtTo
Blessed Damozel, The. Dante Gabriel Rossetti. DiPo; ILP; OBNC; OnP; PoIE; VP
Blessed is every one that feareth the Lord. Psalm CXXVIII, Bible, *O.T.* TRV
Blessed Mary, moder virginal. A Short Prayer to Mary. *Unknown.* MeEL
Blessed Nearness. Mary Bullock. STF
Blessed whom, ere he was born, the gods for their favors had chosen. The Gifts of Fortune. Schiller. AGP
Blessed with a joy that only she. The Gift of God. E. A. Robinson. AP
Blessed Yearning. Goethe. *See* Blissful Longing.
Blessing, A. Numbers, VI:24-26, Bible, *O.T.* ThGo
Blessing, A [*or* The]. James Wright. AmPC; StP
Blessing and Honor. Horatius Bonar. TRV
Blessing on one hand of women! The Hand That Rocks the Cradle Is the Hand That Rules the World. William Ross Wallace. PoLF
Blessings of Surrender, The. Mary J. Helphingtine. STF
Blessings on all the kids who improve the signs in the subways. Graffiti. Edward Field. CoPo
Blessings on thee, little man. The Barefoot Boy. Whittier. PoLF; PoPl
Blest are your North parts, for all this long time. To Mr. I. L. John Donne. SeCP
Blest be the God of love. Even-Song. George Herbert. MeP
Blest be the year, the month, the hour, the day. Petrarch. *Fr.* Sonnets to Laura: To Laura in Life. RBL
Blest Leaf! whose aromatic gales dispense. Isaac Hawkins Browne. *Fr.* A Pipe of Tobacco. Par
Blest Order, which in power dost so excell. The Priesthood. George Herbert. MeP
Blest pair of Sirens, pledges of Heavn's [*or* Heavn's] joy. At a Solemn Music [*or* Musick]. Milton. GTBS-P; MeP; OnP
Blight. Emerson. AP
"Blighters." Siegfried Sassoon. MMA
Blind, The. Erich Fried, *tr. fr. German by* Christopher Middleton. MGP
Blind Beggar's Daughter of Bednall Green, The. *Unknown.* BSO
Blind Boy, The. Colley Cibber. GTBS-P; RoGo
Blind but Happy. Fanny Crosby. TRV
Blind Girl. W. S. Merwin. NePoEA-2
Blind lamentation in the wind, moon-days of winter. South Wind. Georg Trakl. MGP
Blind Love. Shakespeare. *See* Sonnets, CXLVIII.
Blind Man. Michael Hamburger. NePoEA-2
Blind man, A. I can stare at him. A Solitude. Denise Levertov. NePoEA-2

Blind-Man's Buff. Blake. WiR
Blind Man's Regret, The, *with music. Unknown.* BFSS
Blind Men and the Elephant, The. John Godfrey Saxe. OnMSP
Blinded Bird, The. Thomas Hardy. EaLo; VP
Blinded Soldier to His Love, The. Alfred Noyes. PoPl
Blindest buzzard that I know, The. A Sketch. Christina Rossetti. GTBS-P
Blissful Longing. Goethe, *tr. fr. German by* Albert Bloch. AGP
  (Blessed Yearning, *tr. by* Walter Kaufmann.) TwGP
Blithe and bonny country lass, A. Coridon's Song. Thomas Lodge. *Fr.* Rosalynde. UnTE
Blithe Mask, The. Dollett Fuguet. TRV
Blizzard Ape, The. Kenneth Pitchford. CoPo
Block City. Robert Louis Stevenson. SoPo
Block Party. Eve Merriam. PtTo
Block the cannon; let no trumpets sound. Sunset Horn. Myron O'Higgins. AmNP
Blond cowl terse as a blunt threat to injure, The. Love among the Manichees. William Dickey. PoCh
Blood from the shoulder drips from couch to floor. On the Triumph of Judith. Lope de Vega. AnSP
Blood thudded in my ears. I scuffed. First Confession. X. J. Kennedy. NePoEA-2
Bloody and a sudden end, A. John Kinsella's Lament for Mrs. Mary Moore. W. B. Yeats. DTC
Bloody, and stained, and with mothers' cries. The Innocents. Jay Macpherson. OBCV
Bloody Mary's venomous flames can curl. The Martyrdom of Bishop Farrar. Ted Hughes. PoDB
Bloody Sire, The. Robinson Jeffers. VaPo
Bloom of beauty! early flower. Ode to the Hon. Miss Carteret. Ambrose Philips. WaPE
Blooming Nelly. Burns. UnTE
Blossom, The. Blake. *Fr.* Songs of Innocence. CBEP; FoBA; GoJo
Blossom[e], The. John Donne. FoBA; SeCP
Blossom of the Branches, The, *sels.* Ruth Gilbert. ACV
  Annunciation.
  Nativity.
  Quickening, The.
Blossoms and Storm. Sadaiye, *tr. fr. Japanese by* Harold G. Henderson. SiGo
Blossoms of babies. Handfuls. Carl Sandburg. AP
Blot in the 'Scutcheon, A, *sel.* Robert Browning.
  "There's a woman like a dew-drop, she's so purer than the purest." UnTE
Blotting Paper. Thad Stem, Jr. PoNC
Blow! blow! The winds are so hoarse they cannot blow! Storm at Sea. Sir William Davenant. RoGo
Blow, Blow, Thou Winter Wind. Shakespeare. *Fr.* As You Like It, II, vii. CBEP; DiPo; ELP; EnRePo; GTBS-P; ILP; PoIE; PoPo; WePo; WiR
  (Song.) CTC
Blow, Boys, Blow! *Unknown.* BSNS
Blow, Bugle, Blow. Tennyson. *See* Splendor Falls on Castle Walls, The.
Blow Me Eyes! Wallace Irwin. BoLP
Blow, northerne wind. Love for a Beautiful Lady. *Unknown.* MeEL
Blow out, you bugles, over the rich Dead! The Dead. Rupert Brooke. *Fr.* 1914. FaPL
Blow the Man Down (A *and* B *vers., with music*). *Unknown.* BSNS
Blow, Wind, Blow. Mother Goose. SoPo
Blown in the morning, thou shalt fade ere noon. The Rose of Life. Luis de Góngora. RBL
Blown Newspaper, A. "Will Inman." PoNC
Blows the wind today, and the sun and the rain are flying. To S. R. Crockett. Robert Louis Stevenson. OBNC
Blue and the Gray, The, *abr.* Francis Miles Finch. ThLM
Blue as the glass once blown by lips at Tyre. Among Shallows. Leonard Clark. HaSV
Blue Battalions, The. Stephen Crane. AP
Blue Bird, The. Mary Elizabeth Coleridge. WePo
Blue drifted the sea; the waters of the sun. The Sea. Herman Gorter. SiGo
Blue-Fly, The. Robert Graves. ILP
Blue Girls. John Crowe Ransom. PoPo; PoSa
Blue Heron, The. Theodore Goodridge Roberts. OBCV
Blue jay scuffling in the bushes follows, The. On the Move. Thom Gunn. AnMoPo; MP; NePoEA-2; ToPo
Blue Moles. Sylvia Plath. NePoEA-2
Blue mountains to the north of the walls. Taking Leave of a Friend. Li Po, *tr. by* Ezra Pound. AnMoPo
Blue on White. Elizabeth J. Coatsworth. RePo
Blue Ridge Parkway. H. A. Sieber. PoNC
Blue robe on their shoulders, A. The Seven Fiddlers. Sebastian Evans. OnMSP
Blue Sleigh. Winfield Townley Scott. MP
Blue Smoke. Frances Frost. RePo
Bluebeard's Wife. Daryl Hine. ACV
Bluejay, fly to my windowsill. Invitation. Harry Behn. SoPo

Blues/ Never climb a hill. Get Up, Blues. James A. Emanuel. AmNP
Blues and Bitterness. Lerone Bennett. NNP
Blues Ballad. Kenneth Pitchford. *Fr.* Good for Nothing Man. CoPo
Blurt, Master Constable, *sel.* Thomas Middleton.
  "Love is like a lamb, and love is like a lion." BoLP
Blush of dawn! Song before the Battle. Friedrich Hauff. AGP
Blushing rose and purple flower, The. A Song of Pleasure. Phillip Massinger. *Fr.* The Picture. UnTE
Blythe was your comin. For My Newborn Son. Sydney Goodsir Smith. ACV
Boar, The. Robert Kelly. CoPo
Boarder, The. Louis Simpson. PoPl
Boar's Head Carol, The. *Unknown.* MeEL
Boastful Husbandman. *Unknown, tr. fr. German by* Louis Untermeyer. UnTE
Boat, The. Robert Kelly. CoPo
Boat, The. Robert Pack. NePoEA-2
Boat, a Boat, A. *Unknown.* CBEP
Boat Race, The. Vergil, *tr. fr. Latin by* Rolfe Humphries. *Fr.* The Aeneid, V. SD
Boatman, The. Jay Macpherson. OBCV
Boatman he can dance and sing, The. Dance the Boatman. *Unknown.* ThLM
Boats. Rowena Bennett. SoPo
Boats as Van Gogh painted them, The. Les Saintes-Maries-de-la-Mer. Alan Ross. DaDu
Boats sail on the rivers. The Rainbow. Christina Rossetti. *Fr.* Sing-Song. SoPo
Bob Southey! You're a poet—Poet-laureate. Dedication. Byron. *Fr.* Don Juan. CTC; ILP
Bobby Blue. John Drinkwater. SoPo
Bodhisattva Undoes Hell, A. Jerome Rothenberg. CoPo
Body and the dreams of the lady, The. Air. Jacques Dupin. CoFP
Body, long oppressed, The. This Corruptible. Elinor Wylie. MoRP
Body of, The. Epitaph. Benjamin Franklin. TRV
Body Politic, The. Donald Hall. MP
Body's Beauty. Dante Gabriel Rossetti. The House of Life, LXXVII. ILP
Bohemians, The. Ivor Gurney. MMA
Bohunkus would take off his hat, and bow and smile, and things like that. Gelett Burgess. *Fr.* An Alphabet of Famous Goops. BBGG
Boisterous Poem about Poetry, A, *sel.* John Wain.
  "I have a notion that the world is round." PP
Bold Dighton (A *vers.*). *Unknown.* BSNS
  (*Tiger* and the *Lion,* The, B *vers.*) BSNS
Bold Knight and the Gruesome Dragon, The. Wilhelm Busch, *tr. fr. German by* Francis Owen. AGP
Bold Lanty was in love, you see, with lively Rosie Carey. Lanty Leary. Samuel Lover. BoLP
Bold Privateer, The. *Unknown.* BSO
Bold Rangers, *with music. Unknown.* BFSS
Boldness in Love. Thomas Carew. ErPo; UnTE
Boll Weevil, De, *with music. Unknown.* SIV
Bolt and bar the shutter. Mad as the Mist and Snow. W. B. Yeats. AnMoPo
Bombardment. Richard Aldington. MMA
Bombardment. D. H. Lawrence. MMA
Bombay Arrival. Laurie Lee. ToPo
Bon Mot, A. *Unknown.* ErPo
"Bon soir, ma chérie." Comrades in Arms: Conversation Piece. *Unknown.* ErPo
Bond-slave to Christ, and in my bonds rejoicing. Paul John Oxenham. TRV
Bone Thoughts on a Dry Day. George Starbuck. MP
Bones, The. W. S. Merwin. NePoEA-2
Bonne Entente. F. R. Scott. OBCV
Bonnie Banks of Fordie, The. *Unknown.* BuBa
Bonnie Black Bess, *with music. Unknown.* BFSS
Bonnie Blue Flag, The. Annie Chambers Ketchum. ThLM
Bonnie Dundee, *abr.* Sir Walter Scott. *Fr.* The Doom of Devorgoil. Par
Bonnie George Campbell. *Unknown.* ELP; PoPo
  (Bonnie James Campbell.) BFSS, *with music;* CBEP
Bonnie lassie, will ye go. The Birks of Aberfeldy. Burns. CTC
Bonnie Lesley. Burns. CTC; GTBS-P; PoIE
  (Saw Ye Bonny Lesley?) CBEP
Bonniest lass that ye meet neist, The. For A' That an' A' That. Burns. UnTE
Bonny Barbara Allen. *Unknown. See* Barbara Allen.
Bonny Broom, The, *with music. Unknown.* BFSS
Bonny Bunch of Roses, The, *with music. Unknown.* BSNS
  (Bonny Bunch of Roses O, The, *diff. vers.*) BSNS
Bonny Earl of Murray [*or* o' Moray], The. *Unknown.* BuBa; CBEP; ELP
Bonny heir, the well-favoured heir, The. The Heir of Linne. *Unknown.* BuBa
Bonny House of Airlie, The. *Unknown.* BuBa

(Lady Ogalbie, *with music*.) BFSS
Bonny Kilmeny gaed up the glen. Kilmeny. James Hogg. *Fr.* The Queen's Wake. CABL
Bonny Scotland. *Unknown. See* Paisley Officer, The.
Book, The. Winfred Ernest Garrison. TRV
Book, A. Hannah More. PoSC
Book of Alexander, The, *sel.* Juan Lorenzo, *tr. fr. Spanish by* William M. Davis.
"Alexander, that good magistrate without frontiers." AnML
Book of Kells, The. Howard Nemerov. CoPo
Book of Merlin, The. Jack Spicer. CoPo
Book of Nature, The. Richard Eberhart. PoDB
Book of Percival, The. Jack Spicer. CoPo
Book of the Dead, *sels. Unknown, tr. fr. Egyptian by* Robert Hillyer.
Dead Man Ariseth and Singeth a Hymn to the Sun, The. SiGo
He Is like the Lotus. EaLo
Book of the World, The. Giambattista Marino, *tr. fr. Italian by* William Drummond of Hawthornden. RBL
(Lessons of Nature, The.) GTBS-P
Book of Thel, The. Blake. FoBA; OBNC
Thel's Motto, *sel.* DiPo
Book of True Love, The, *sels.* Juan Ruiz, Archpriest of Hita, *tr. fr. Spanish.* AnML
Don Pitas Payas, *tr. by* William M. Davis.
Easter Day, *tr. by* James Edward Tobin.
Encounter of the Archpriest with Ferrand García, *tr. by* Edwin Honig.
Hill Song, *tr. by* William M. Davis.
Of the Characteristics of Small Women, *tr. by* William M. Davis.
"When you're together with her, and you have a good excuse," *tr. by* Hubert Creekmore. ErPo
Book of verses underneath the bough, A. Omar Khayyám, *tr. by* Edward Fitzgerald. *Fr.* The Rubáiyát. DiPo
Book Our Mothers Read, The. Whittier. TRV
Bookmark. St. Theresa of Avila. *See* St. Teresa's Book-Mark.
Book-Worms, The. Burns. LV
Boom! Howard Nemerov. MP; PoDB
Boon Nature to the woman bows. The Tribute. Coventry Patmore. *Fr.* The Angel in the House. FaPL; OBNC
Boot and Saddle ("Boot, saddle, to horse, and away!"). Robert Browning. PoPo
Booth led boldly with his big bass drum. General William Booth Enters into Heaven. Vachel Lindsay. AmLP; BoC; ILP
Borderline. R. H. Grenville. FiSC
Border Line. Langston Hughes. PoCh
Bores hed in hondes I bring, The. The Boar's Head Carol. *Unknown.* MeEL
Borgia, thou once were almost too august. On Seeing a Hair of Lucretia Borgia. Walter Savage Landor. CABA
Born by a whim. Signature. Dorothy Livesay. OBCV
Born during flight, circled by sword and fire. Epitaph for Mariana, His Brother Paul's Little Daughter. Andreas Gryphius. AGP
Born I was of a girl of twenty. My Life, My Death. Hans Egon Holthusen. MGP
Born in a trance; we wake, observe, inquire. Another and the Same. Samuel Rogers. OBNC
Born in my mouth, the naked beast leaned out. A Warning to My Love. David Wagoner. NePoEA-2
Born in the garret, in the kitchen bred. A Sketch from Private Life. Byron. OBNC
Born, nurtured, wedded, prized, within the pale. La Fayette. Dolley Madison. ThLM
Born of the sorrowful of heart. For Paul Laurence Dunbar. Countee Cullen. Four Epitaphs, 3. AmNP
Born of the union of Chaos and Time. Erda. Vera Bishop Konrick. FiSC
Borough, The, *sels.* George Crabbe.
"'Describe the Borough'—though our idle Tribe," Letter I. CABL
Peter Grimes, Letter XXII. EnPE; OBNC; WePo
Sailing upon the River, *fr.* Letter IX. OBNC
Schools, Letter XXIV. CTC
Slum Dwelling, A, *fr.* Letter XVIII. OBNC
Vicar, The, *fr.* Letter III. OBNC
Winter Views Serene, *fr.* Letter IX. OBNC
Borrowed wings on his ankles. Perseus. Louis MacNeice. StP
Bosnia. November. And the mountain roads. Sarajevo. Lawrence Durrell. GTBS-P
Boss I have seen Mehitabel the cat. Mehitabel Tries Marriage. Don Marquis. *Fr.* Archys Life of Mehitabel. WePo
Boston Bugler, *with music. Unknown.* BSO
Boston Charlie. Walt Kelly. GoJo
Boston Hymn. Emerson. TRV
Boston. Lord God, the ocean never to windward. Poems from a First Year in Boston. George Starbuck. NePoEA-2
Botany Bay. *Unknown.* PoAu-1
Both my eyes, my dearest, close. Theodor Storm, *tr. fr. German by* D. G. Wright. AGP

Bottles are empty, the breakfast was good, The. The Morning After. ErPo; UnTE
Bottom's Song. Shakespeare. *Fr.* A Midsummer Night's Dream, III, i. CTC
Bouncing Ball. Sara Ruth Watson. SoPo
Bound No'th Blues. Langston Hughes. AmNP
Bound to a boy's swift feet, hard blades of steel. River Skater. Winifred Welles. SD
Bound to my heart as Ixion to the wheel. Dirge for the New Sunrise. Edith Sitwell. *Fr.* Three Poems of the Atomic Age. ACV; EaLo; MoRP
Bound to the Caucasus of my suffering. Maurice Scève. *Fr.* Délie. RBL
Bourgeois' hat flies off his pointed head, The. End of the World. "Jakob van Hoddis." MGP
Bourgeois Poet, The, *sels.* Karl Shapiro.
"As you say (not without sadness), poets don't see, they feel." PP
(As You Say; an Anti-Poem.) CaFP
"Bourgeois poet closes the door of his study and lights his pipe, The." PP
Bourne, The. Christina Rossetti. ELP; OBNC
Bout with Burning. Vassar Miller. ToPo
Bow down my soul in worship very low. St. Isaac's Church, Petrograd. Claude McKay. AmNP
Bow Lamkin, *with music. Unknown.* BFSS
Bowed by the weight of centuries he leans. The Man with the Hoe. Edwin Markham. AmLP; EaLo; FaPL; PoPo; TRV
Bowed negress, who aghast but the light. Gil Orlovitz. *Fr.* Art of the Sonnet. ToPo
Bowl of October, A. Helen Bevington. PoNC; RePo
Box upon Her Head, The. *Unknown.* BSNS
Boxer. Joseph P. Clancy. SD
Boxer's Face, The. Lucilius, *tr. fr. Greek by* Humbert Wolfe. SD
Boxes and Bags. Carl Sandburg. RePo
Boxing Match, The. Vergil, *tr. fr. Latin by* Rolfe Humphries. *Fr.* The Aeneid. SD
Boy and the Flute, The. Björnstjerne Björnson, *tr. fr. Norwegian by* Sir Edmund Gosse. PoPl
Boy and the Mantle, The. *Unknown.* UnTE
Boy! bring an ounce of Freeman's best. Isaac Hawkins Brown. *Fr.* A Pipe of Tobacco. Par
Boy climbed up into the tree, The. The Rescue. Hal Summers. DaDu
Boy in the Barn, The. Sir Herbert Read. DaDu
Boy on the Back of a Wagon. Thad Stem, Jr. PoNC
Boy, the giant beauty. Instruction in the Art. Philip Booth. SD
Boy Who Laughed at Santa Claus, The. Ogden Nash. BBGG
Boy with a Cart, The, *sel.* Christopher Fry.
Rain. BoC
Boy with His Hair Cut Short. Muriel Rukeyser. MP; PoPl; RoGo
Boys and girls who live in books, The. Adventures. Arthur Kramer. BiCB
Boys, by Girls Held in Their Thighs. John Peale Bishop. ErPo
Boy's Day. Ruth Evelyn Henderson. BiCB
Boys flying kites haul in their white-winged birds. Words. *Unknown.* PoLF
Boys in October. Irving Layton. OBCV
Boys in sporadic but tenacious droves. The Horse Chestnut Tree. Richard Eberhart. CaFP; PoDB; PoPl; PoPo; ToPo
Boys like puppets dangling. Spring Is a Looping-free Time. Martin Robbins. SD
Boys' Names. Eleanor Farjeon. BiCB
Boys of Wexford, The. *Unknown.* ELP
Boy's Song, A. James Hogg. WiR
Boy's Summer Song, A. Paul Laurence Dunbar. RePo
Bracelet, The. Tristan l'Hermite, *tr. fr. French by* Thomas Stanley. RBL
Bracelet of Grass, The. William Vaughn Moody. AP
Brackish reach of shoal off Madaket, A. The Quaker Graveyard in Nantucket. Robert Lowell. AmLP; AnMoPo; AP; CABL; PoIE; ToPo
Braddock's Fate, with an Incitement to Revenge. Stephen Tilden. ThLM
Braes o' Yarrow, The (A *and* B *vers., with music*). *Unknown.* BFSS
Braes of Yarrow, The. John Logan. GTBS-P
Brahma. Emerson. AmLP; AP; CBEP; DiPo; EaLo; PoIE; PoPo
Brain forgets, but the blood will remember, The. The Dark Chamber. Louis Untermeyer. MoLP
Brain is wider than the sky, The. Emily Dickinson. CaFP
Brain, the blood, the busy thews, The. William Baylebridge. *Fr.* Life's Testament. PoAu-1
Brain, within it's groove, The. Emily Dickinson. AP; DiPo
Brainstorm. Howard Nemerov. ToPo
Bramble Briar [*or* Brier], The, *with music. Unknown.* BFSS; BSO

Brandy Hill. *Unknown.* CBEP
Brash and bare and whistling cold. Song of January. Gerta Kennedy. PoPl
Brave Donahue. *At. to* Jack Donahue. PoAu-1
Brave flowers, that I could gallant it like you. A Contemplation upon Flowers. Henry King. CBEP; ELP; SeCP; StP
Brave infant of Saguntum, clear[e]. A Pindaric Ode [*or* To the Immortall Memorie, and Friendship of That Noble Paire, Sir Lucius Cary, and Sir H. Morison]. Ben Jonson. SeCP; StP
Brave Wolfe. *Unknown.* ThLM
  (Quebec, *sl. diff.*) BSNS
Brawling of a sparrow in the eaves, The. The Sorrow of Love. W. B. Yeats. FoBA
Bread. Nancy Keesing. PoAu-2
Bread. R. S. Thomas. BoC
Bread, The/ popping out of hot ovens. We Are Gathered Together. Estelle Gershgoren. PtTo
Bread and Milk. Christina Rossetti. *Fr.* Sing-Song. CBEP
Bread of Life, The. Mary A. Lathbury. *See* Break Thou the Bread of Life.
Bread the Holy. Elizabeth J. Coatsworth. MoRP
Break, Break, Break. Tennyson. CABA; DiPo; FaBV; FoBA; GoJo; GTBS-P; HaSV; ILP; LV; OBNC; PoPl; PoSa
Break not my loneliness, O Wanderer! The Dove's Loneliness. George Darley. OBNC
Break of Day. John Clare. CBEP
Break [*or* Breake] of Day. John Donne. CABA; EnRePo; ErPo
Break of Day. John Shaw Neilson. PoAu-1
Break of Day in the Trenches. Isaac Rosenberg. GTBS-P; MMA
Break Thou the Bread of Life. Mary A. Lathbury. TRV
  (Bread of Life, The.) StP
Breakfast in a Bowling Alley in Utica, New York. Adrienne Rich. CoPo
Breakfast with Gerard Manley Hopkins. Anthony Brode. Par
Breaking. J. Alex. Allan. PoAu-2
Breaking a line of pines, a wide white gate. Alan Mulgan. *Fr.* Golden Wedding. ACV
Breaking from under that thy cloudy Vail. Upon Combing Her Hair. Lord Herbert of Cherbury. StP
Breaking of the Day, The. Peter Davison. CoPo
Breaking through the sandy soil. Personal Letter to the Ephesians. Carl Bode. ToPo
Breaking waves dashed high, The. The Landing of the Pilgrim Fathers. Felicia Dorothea Hemans. FaBV; FaPL; ThLM
Breath of Air, A. James Wright. PoPl
Breath on a Piece of Broken Glass. Wolfdietrich Schnurre, *tr. fr. German by* Michael Hamburger. MGP
Breathe not, hid Heart: cease silently. To an Unborn Pauper Child. Thomas Hardy. AnMoPo; GTBS-P
Breathes There a Man. Samuel Hoffenstein. PoPl
Breathes There the Man. Sir Walter Scott. *Fr.* The Lay of the Last Minstrel. LV
  (Patriot, The.) OBNC
  (Patriotism.) TRV
Breathing something German at the end. The Gift to Be Simple. Howard Moss. MoRP; MP
Breathless, we flung us on the windy hill. The Hill. Rupert Brooke. BoLP; MoLP; WePo
Brébeuf and His Brethren, *sels.* E. J. Pratt.
  Martyrdom of Brébeuf and Lalemant, 16 March 1649, The. OBCV
  "Three miles from town to town over the snow." ACV
Bredon Hill. A. E. Housman. A Shropshire Lad, XXI. VP
Breed of Athletes, The. Euripides, *tr. fr. Greek by* Moses Hadas. SD
Breed of vermin lies, A. The Character Assassins. Gottfried Keller. AGP
Breeze is sharp, the sky is hard and blue, The. Sonnets, Part II, XIV. Frederick Goddard Tuckerman. AP
Breeze of the sea breathe soft upon these names. Tower Hill Memorial. Anthony Michael Morrison. HaSV
Breeze Tells Me, Loved One, The. Antonio Machado, *tr. fr. Spanish by* James Duffy. AnSP
Breezes went steadily thro' the tall pines, The. Nathan Hale. *Unknown.* SIV
Brennan on the Moor. *Unknown.* BSNS
Brererton Omen, The, *sel.* Felicia Dorothea Hemans.
  "Yes! I have seen the ancient oak." CTC
Breton Afternoon. Ernest Dowson. OBNC
Brevities. Siegfried Sassoon. PoLF
Brew your potion, mix your spell. Comrade in Arms. T. Inglis Moore. PoAu-2
Brewer's Coachman, The. William Taylor. WaPE
Brewer's Man, The. L. A. G. Strong. DTC
Brewing of Soma, The, *sel.* Whittier.
  Dear Lord and Father of Mankind. TRV
Bridal Birth. Dante Gabriel Rossetti. The House of Life, II. VP

Bridal Song. Beaumont *and* Fletcher. *See* Hold Back Thy Hours.
Bridal Song. Fletcher *and* Shakespeare. *Fr.* The Two Noble Kinsmen, I, i. CBEP
Bride loved old words, and found her pleasure marred. Five Epigrams. J. V. Cunningham. UnTE
Bride of Corinth, The. Goethe, *tr. fr. German by* Helen Kurz Roberts. AGP
Bride of Lammermoor, The, *sel.* Sir Walter Scott.
  Look Not Thou, *fr. ch.* 3. CBEP
Bride, white of hair, is stooped over her cane, The. To Have and Too Old. Richard Armour. LV
Bridge, The, *sels.* Hart Crane.
  Atlantis. AmLP
  Ave Maria. PoDB
  Powhatan's Daughter.
    River, The. AP
    Van Winkle. FaBV
  Three Songs.
    National Winter Garden. ErPo
  To Brooklyn Bridge. AP; CABA; DiPo; ILP; PoDB; PoIE; PoPl; ThLM
  Tunnel, The. AP
Bridge, The. Longfellow. FaPL
Bridge Builder, The. Will Allen Dromgoole. TRV
  (Building the Bridge for Him.) STF
Bridge of Sighs, The. Thomas Hood. GTBS-P
Bridge, The, says: Come across, try me; see how good I am. Potomac Town in February. Carl Sandburg. EvOK
Bridges. Rhoda W. Bacmeister. SoPo
Brief Biography. Marguerite George. FiSC
Brigade Must Not Know, Sir, The. *Unknown.* ThLM
Bright as Venus' golden star. The Insatiate. Johannes Secundus. *Fr.* Basia. UnTE
Bright Babe! whose awfull Beauties make. A Hymne for the Epiphanie. Sung as by the Three Kings. Richard Crashaw. MeP
Bright captures, wing-shimmers, facts. Spider. Richmond Lattimore. PP
Bright clasp of her whole hand around my finger. To My Daughter. Stephen Spender. BoC
Bright-haired Spirit! Golden Brow! Onward to Far Ida. George Darley. *Fr.* Nepenthe. OBNC
Bright is the ring of words. Robert Louis Stevenson. *Fr.* Songs of Travel. OBNC
Bright shadows of true rest! some shoots of blisse. Son-Dayes. Henry Vaughan. SeCP
Bright Sirius! that when Orion pales. The Star Sirius. George Meredith. VP
Bright spark, shot from a brighter place. The Starre. George Herbert. MeP
Bright Star! Would I Were Steadfast as Thou Art. Keats. CABA; FoBA; GTBS-P; ILP; OnP; PoIE; PoPo
  (Bright Star.) DiPo; FaPL
  (Sonnet.) FaBV; OBNC
Brigid, the daughter of Duffy, she wasn't like other young things. St. Brigid. Denis A. McCarthy. SIV
Brindabella. Douglas Stewart. PoAu-2
Bring Back. Anne Ridler. ACV
Bring every child. Christmas Songs. Gerta Kennedy. PoPl
Bring me the sunset in a cup. Emily Dickinson. AP; FoBA
Bring me wine, but wine which never grew. Bacchus. Emerson. AP
Bring that red mouth of yours. Madrigal de Verano. Federico García Lorca. ErPo
Bring Us in Good Ale. *Unknown.* MeEL
Bringing Him Up. Lord Dunsany. BBGG
Brisk Girl, The. *Unknown.* UnTE
Brisk young lover came a-courting me, A. Died of Love. *Unknown.* CBEP
British Church, The. George Herbert. MeP
British Grenadiers, The. *Unknown.* CBEP
Brittish Church, The. Henry Vaughan. MeP
Brittle beauty that nature made so frail. The Frailty and Hurtfulness of Beauty. Earl of Surrey. VaPo
Broad-backed hippopotamus, The. The Hippopotamus. T. S. Eliot. PoDB; PoPl; PoSa
Broad shadows fall. On all the mountain side. A Sunset at Les Eboulements. Archibald Lampman. OBCV
Brobinyak has dragon eyes, The. What You Will Learn about the Brobinyak. John Ciardi. EvOK
Broken altar, Lord, thy servant rears, A. The Altar. George Herbert. FoBA; MeP; PoSa; SeCP; VaPo
Broken Appointment, A. Thomas Hardy. CBEP; DTC
Broken Bowl, The. Jones Very. MeP
Broken-down Digger, The. *Unknown.* PoAu-1
Broken-down Squatter, The. *Unknown.* PoAu-1
Broken-Face Gargoyles. Carl Sandburg. ILP
Broken Faith. Giambattista Marino, *tr. fr. Italian by* Harold M. Priest. RBL
Broken Glass, The. Umberto Saba, *tr. fr. Italian by* Thomas G. Bergin. CoIP
Broken Heart, The. John Donne. DiPo; ILP

Broken Heart, The, *sels.* John Ford.
  Can You Paint a Thought? *fr.* III, ii. CBEP
  Oh, No More, No More! *fr.* IV, iii. ELP
Broken in pieces all asunder. Affliction. George Herbert. MeP.
Broken is the tall column and the green laurel. Petrarch. *Fr.*
  Sonnets to Laura: To Laura in Death. RBL
Broken Monologue. "Michael Lewis," *fr. the German.* UnTE
Broken Music. Dante Gabriel Rossetti. The House of Life,
  XLVII. VP
Broken pillar of the wing jags from the clotted shoulder, The.
  Hurt Hawks. Robinson Jeffers. AP; DiPo; PoPo
Broken snow should leave the traces, The. The Snow. Robert
  Creeley. AP
Broken the column and the green bay tree. Petrarch. *Fr.*
  Sonnets to Laura: To Laura in Death. RBL
Broken Tower, The. Hart Crane. AP; PoIE; VaPo
Broncho That Would Not Be Broken, The. Vachel Lindsay.
  RoGo
Bronze. Derek Walcott. ToPo
Brook, The. Tennyson. FaBV; GoJo
Brook in February, The. Sir Charles G. D. Roberts. OBCV
Brook of the Heart, The. Emily Dickinson. *See* Have you got
  a brook in your little heart?
Brooklyn Heights. John Wain. ToPo
Brooms. Dorothy Aldis. SoPo
Brother and Sister. "Lewis Carroll." BBGG
Brother Fire. Louis MacNeice. AnMoPo
Brother Green, *with music. Unknown.* BFSS
  (Song of Brother Green, The, *with music.*) BSO
Brother Jonathan's Lament for Sister Caroline. Oliver Wendell
  Holmes. ThLM
Brother, Lift Your Flag with Mine. Josephine Daskam Bacon.
  PoSC
Brother men, who after us still live. Villon's Epitaph. Villon.
  AnML
Brother, sing your country's anthem. Brother, Lift Your Flag
  with Mine. Josephine Daskam Bacon. PoSC
Brother to the firefly. Morning Light the Dew-Drier. Effie Lee
  Newsome. AmNP
Brother, you who have the light, tell me where mine is.
  Melancholy. Rubén Darío. AnSP
Brothers. Solomon Edwards. NNP
Brothers, The. Amy Groesbeck. FiSC
Brothers. Gerard Manley Hopkins. FoBA
Brothers, The. Edwin Muir. GTBS-P
Brown Adam. *Unknown.* BuBa
Brown and furry. The Caterpillar. Christina Rossetti. *Fr.*
  Sing-Song. GoJo; SoPo
Brown Bear, The. Mary Austin. PoSC
Brown Bear's Honey Song. Kathryn Jackson. RePo
Brown bunny sits inside his burrow. The Rabbit. Edith King.
  SoPo
Brown enormous odor he lived by, The. The Prodigal. Eliza-
  beth Bishop. MP
Brown Girl, The. *Unknown.* ELP
Brown girl she has houses and lands, The. Lord Thomas and
  Fair Annet (D vers.). *Unknown.* BSO
Brown Is My Love. *Unknown.* CBEP
  (Song Set by Nicholas Yonge.) CTC
Brown Jug, The. Francis Fawkes. CBEP
Brown lived at such a lofty farm. Brown's Descent; or, The
  Willy-Nilly Slide. Robert Frost. EvOK; StP
Brown of Ossawatomie. Whittier. ThLM
Brown Penny. W. B. Yeats. BoLP; ELP
Brown River, Smile. Jean Toomer. AmNP
Brown, sad-coloured hillside, where the soil, A. The Sower.
  Sir Charles G. D. Roberts. OBCV
Brown's Descent; or, The Willy-Nilly Slide. Robert Frost.
  EvOK; StP
Bruised Titans, The. Keats. *Fr.* Hyperion; a Fragment.
  OBNC
Bruisers of England, the men of tremendous renown, The. The
  Fancy. William Rose Benét. SD
Brute hawk wings pump the livid air. Hawk. Guy Owen.
  PoNC
Bryant. James Russell Lowell. *Fr.* A Fable for Critics. AP
B's the Bus. Phyllis McGinley. *Fr.* All around the Town.
  SoPo
Bubble, The. Kenneth Hopkins. DaDu
Bubbles ("Bubble, Bubble, light and airy"). George H. Shorey.
  PoPl
Bubbling brook doth leap when I come by, The. Nature. Jones
  Very. AP
Buck Duke and Mamma. Eleanor Ross Taylor. PoNC
Buck Fever. Bert Cooksley. SIV
Buck in the Snow, The. Edna St. Vincent Millay. AmLP
Buckle the spur and belt again. Lofty Lane. Edwin Gerard.
  PoAu-1
Bucolic Eclogues, *sel.* Ethel Anderson.
  Waking, Child, While You Slept. PoAu-2
Buddha. Theodore Holmes. CoPo
Buddha. Rainer Maria Rilke, *tr. fr. German by* Walter Kauf-
  mann. TwGP

Buddha in the Glory. Rainer Maria Rilke, *tr. fr. German by*
  Walter Kaufmann. TwGP
Budding Spring. Jack Lindsay. PoAu-1
Budging the sluggard ripples of the Somme. Hospital Barge at
  Cérisy. Wilfred Owen. CBEP
Buds of April dare not yet unfold, The. Like an April Day.
  Johan Sebastian C. Wellhaven. SiGo
Buffalo, The. Herbert Price. ACV
Buffalo Bill's. E. E. Cummings. CABA
Buffalo Creek. J. Le Gay Brereton. PoAu-1
Buffalo Skinners, The. *Unknown.* BFSS, *with music;* ThLM
Bugle sounds the measured call to prayers, The. Sunday: New
  Guinea. Karl Shapiro. PoPl
Bugler boy from barrack, A (it is over the hill). The Bugler's
  First Communion. Gerard Manley Hopkins. VP
Bugler sent a call of high romance, The. The Last Post.
  Robert Graves. MMA
Bugler's First Communion, The. Gerard Manley Hopkins.
  VP
Buick. Karl Shapiro. CaFP; PoIE
Build a little fence of trust. Today. Mary Frances Butts.
  TRV
"Build me straight, O worthy Master." Longfellow. *Fr.* The
  Building of the Ship. HaSV
Build thee more stately mansions, O my soul. Oliver Wendell
  Holmes. *Fr.* The Chambered Nautilus. TRV
Builder of Houses, The. Jane Cooper. AmPC
Builders. Purd E. Deitz. TRV
Builder's Lesson, A. John Boyle O'Reilly. PoLF
Building of Sand. Grant Code. FiSC
Building of Solomon's Temple, The, *with music. Unknown.*
  BSNS
Building of the Ship, The, *sel.* Longfellow.
  "Build me straight, O worthy Master!" HaSV
Building the Bridge for Him. William Allen Dromgoole. *See*
  Bridge Builder, The.
Bulkeley, Hunt, Willard, Hosmer, Meriam, Flint. Hamatreya.
  Emerson. AP
Bull, The. René Char, *tr. fr. French by* Richard G. Stern.
  Four Fascinators, I. CoFP
Bull, The. William Carlos Williams. MP
Bull, The. Judith Wright. PoAu-2
Bull Calf, The. Irving Layton. OBCV
Bull Morgan McCarthy. *Unknown.* BSNS
Bulletin. Chana Faerstein. OPP
Bullets blot out the Life-Time smile. Instead of an Elegy.
  G. S. Fraser. OPP
Bullfrog. Ted Hughes. DaDu
Bullock bellied in a green marsh. Laggandoan, Harris.
  Norman MacCaig. AnMoPo
Bullocky. Judith Wright. PoAu-2
Bullocky Bill. *Unknown.* PoAu-1
Bully, The. Earl of Rochester. CBEP
Bulosan Now. Alvaro Cardona-Hine. PtTo
Bumpy Was Dead and Lay in His Grave. *Unknown.* BSO
Bunch of Grapes, The. George Herbert. MeP
Bunch of the boys were whooping it up in the Malamute saloon,
  A. The Shooting of Dan McGrew. Robert W. Service.
  PoLF
Bunch of Wild Flowers. Luke Zilles. RePo
Bunches of Grapes. Walter de la Mare. GoJo
Bung Yer Eye. Stewart Edward White. RePo
Bunthorne's Song. W. S. Gilbert. *Fr.* Patience. VaPo
Bunyip and the Whistling Kettle, The. John Manifold.
  PoAu-2
Burden of Junk, The. John Glassco. OBCV
Burgeis, thou haste so blowen atte the cole. Too Much Sex.
  Unknown. MeEL
Burial. Mark Van Doren. MoBS
Burial of Sir John Moore at [or after] Corunna, The. Charles
  Wolfe. CBEP; FaPL; GTBS-P; RoGo
Burial of Terror, The. Carl Bode. ToPo
Buried Child. *fr.* Dorothy Wellesley. *Fr.* Deserted House.
  DTC
Buried Life, The. Matthew Arnold. VP
Burke and Wills. Ken Barratt. PoAu-2
Burn Ovid with the rest. Lovers will find. Penal Law. Austin
  Clarke. GTBS-P
Burn stilly, thou; and come with me. To a Candle. Walter
  de la Mare. ELP
Burncombe Hollow. William Barnes. OBNC
Burning Babe, The. Robert Southwell. CAPA; CBEP; ILP;
  MeP; PoIE; StP
Burning Bush, The. Norman Nicholson. EaLo
Burning Bush. Louis Untermeyer. MoLP
Burning Bush, The. Henry van Dyke. TRV
Burning eye, The. The Skeptic. Loring Williams. FiSC
Burning of Books, The. Bertolt Brecht, *tr. fr. German by*
  H. R. Hays. PoPl
Burning of the Leaves, The. Laurence Binyon. DTC;
  GTBS-P
Burning the Christmas Greens. William Carlos Williams.
  AP; CABL

Burnished, burned-out, still burning as the year. The Public Garden. Robert Lowell. AP
Burnt Norton. T. S. Eliot. *Fr.* Four Quartets. CABL
Bursting Leaves, Flowers Opening. Wolfram von Eschenbach, *tr. fr. German by* Gillian Barker *and* Kenneth Gee. AnML
Bury Me Not on the Chickamauga, *with music. Unknown.* BFSS
Bury Me Not on the Lone Prairie. *Unknown. See* Dying Cowboy, The ("Oh, bury me not . . .").
"Bury me," the bishop said. St. Swithin. Daniel Henderson. SIV
Bush, The, *sel.* Bernard O'Dowd.
    "As many, Mother, are your moods and forms." PoAu-1
Bush Christening, A. A. B. Paterson. PoAu-1
Bush-Fiddle, The. Judith Green. PoAu-2
Bush on Mount Venus, The. Donald Finkel. CoPo
Bush that has most briers and bitter fruit, The. The Barberry-Bush. Jones Very. AP
Bushed. Earle Birney. OBCV
Bushman's Song, A. A. B. Paterson. PoAu-1
Bushrangers, The. Edward Harrington. PoAu-1
Busie old foole, unruly Sunne. *See* Busy old fool, unruly Sun.
Business. Arthur Guiterman. LV
Business Girls. John Betjeman. WePo
Business of the lambing ewes would make me, The. Eagles over the Lambing Paddock. Ernest G. Moll. PoAu-2
Bustle in a house, The. Emily Dickinson. AmLP; AP; CBEP; DiPo; FaBV; StP
    (Morning after Death, The.) MoRP; PoLF
Busts and Bosoms Have I Known. *Unknown.* ErPo
Busy Carpenters. James S. Tippett. SoPo
Busy, curious, thirsty fly. On a Fly Drinking Out of His Cup [or The Fly]. William Oldys. CBEP; LV
Busy [or Busie] old fool, unruly Sun. The Sun Rising. John Donne. CABA; CBEP; DiPo; EnRePo; ILP; PoIE; SeCP; UnTE; VaPo
But as they left the dark'ning heath. Sir Walter Scott. *Fr.* Marmion. ELP
But Bacchus was not so content: he quyght forsooke their land. King Midas. Ovid. *Fr.* Metamorphoses. CTC
But be contented: when that fell arrest. Sonnets, LXXIV. Shakespeare. CBEP
But do not let us quarrel any more. Andrea del Sarto. Robert Browning. CABA; CTC; DiPo; StP; VP
But for the steady wash of rain. No Country You Remember. Robert Mezey. AmPC; ToPo
But give them me, the mouth, the eyes, the brow! Orpheus and Eurydice. Robert Browning. CTC
But God's Own Descent. Robert Frost. *Fr.* Kitty Hawk. EaLo; MoRP
But hark! What hubbub now is this that comes. Charles Harpur. *Fr.* The Temple of Infamy. PoAu-1
But how many moons be in the year? Robin Hood and the Curtal Friar. *Unknown.* BuBa
But how shall we this union well express? The Soul and the Body. Sir John Davies. *Fr.* Nosce Teipsum. CTC
But I Am Growing Old and Indolent. Robinson Jeffers. AP
But I Do Not Need Kindness. Gregory Corso. CoPo
But I have sinuous shells, of pearly hue. The Shells. Walter Savage Landor. HaSV
But I want you to understand. The Gardener at Thirty. Jascha Kessler. AmPC
But I *was* dead, an hour or more. Escape. Robert Graves. ILP
But in the crowding darkness not a word did they say. The Old Marrieds. Gwendolyn Brooks. AmNP
But in the darkest hour of night. Only a Beauty, Only a Power. John Masefield. MoRP
But in the last days it shall come to pass. Neither Shall They Learn War Any More. Micah, Bible, O. T. TRV
But Is There No Flower, Perfume or Violet? Eustache Deschamps, *tr. fr. French by* Muriel Kittel. AnML
But, knowing now that they would have her speak. The Defence of Guenevere. William Morris. StP
But let applause be dealt in all we may. The Vicar. George Crabbe. *Fr.* The Borough. OBNC
But lo, what think you; suddenly. A Moon Rainbow. Robert Browning. BoC
But love, first learnèd in a lady's eyes. Shakespeare. *Fr.* Love's Labour's Lost. PP
But most by numbers judge a poet's song. Pope. *Fr.* An Essay on Criticism. PP
But poets are name-proud craftsmen; Greeks and Jews. Karl Shapiro. *Fr.* Essay on Rime. PP
But still the thunder of Los peals loud, and thus the thunders cry. Blake. *Fr.* Jerusalem. PoIE
But That Is Another Story. Donald Justice. NePoEA-2
"But that was nothing to what things came out." Welsh Incident. Robert Graves. BoC; WePo
But That Was Yesterday. Aileen Fisher. SoPo
But that which most I wonder at, which most. Innocence. Thomas Traherne. MeP

But there is one, they say. He Walks at Peace. *Unknown. Fr.* Tao Teh King. TRV
But unto him came swift calamity. Sonnets, Part II, IX. Frederick Goddard Tuckerman. AP
But What's in the Larder? Tennyson. ThGo
But where began the change; and what's my crime? Modern Love, X. George Meredith. VP
But yet how unrelentingly you swelled. Moon. Yvan Goll. MGP
But yet one thought has often stayed by me. Harriet Eleanor Hamilton King. *Fr.* The Sermon in the Hospital. BoC
But you were wrong that desolate dusk. For Thomas Hardy. Jane Cooper. AmPC
"Butch" Weldy. Edgar Lee Masters. *Fr.* Spoon River Anthology. PoPo
Butcher Boy, The (A *and* B *vers., with music*). *Unknown.* BSNS
    (Butcher's Boy, The, B *vers., with music.*) BSO
    (Jersey City, A *vers., with music.*) BSO
Butterbean Tent, The. Elizabeth Madox Roberts. GoJo
Buttercup, the cow, had a new baby calf. The New Baby Calf. Edith Newlin Chase. SoPo
Butterflies. Alfred Noyes. BoC
Butterfly, The. Margaret Avison. OBCV
Butterfly, The. Gray Burr. CoPo
Butterfly, The. Kikaku, *tr. fr. Japanese by* Harold G. Henderson. SoPo
Butterfly. William Jay Smith. GoJo; RePo
Butterfly, The. Spenser. *Fr.* Muiopotmos. BoC
Butterfly, a cabbage-white, The. Flying Crooked. Robert Graves. MP
Butterfly and the Caterpillar, The ("A butterfly, one summer morn"). Joseph Lauren. OnMSP
Butterfly was once a worm, A. Concerning Wings. Zoe Kincaid Brockman. PoNC
Buttons. Walter de la Mare. DTC
Buxom Lass. *Unknown.* ErPo
Buzz-saw snarled and rattled in the yard, The. "Out, Out—." Robert Frost. CABA; ILP; PoIE; PoPo; SIV
By a Bank of Pinks and Lilies. *Unknown.* ErPo
By a route obscure and lonely. Dream-Land. Poe. AmLP; AP; CBEP
By and by. Epitaph on a Waiter. David McCord. PoPo
By Blue Ontario's Shore, *sel.* Walt Whitman.
    "I swear I begin to see the meaning of these things." PoIE
By bluster, graft, and doing people down. A Tribute to the Founder. Kingsley Amis. NePoEA-2
By channels of coolness the echoes are calling. Bell-Birds. Henry Kendall. PoAu-1
By Cool Siloam's Shady Rill. Reginald Heber. ELP
By dark severance the apparition head. Painted Head. John Crowe Ransom. AP; PoIE
By Day and by Night. W. S. Merwin. AmPC
By day she woos me, soft, exceeding fair. The World. Christina Rossetti. VP
By day the bat is cousin to the mouse. The Bat. Theodore Roethke. GoJo
By day, the returning terror of swifts, the scream. Flight. Laurence Whistler. DaDu
By day the river's throat was bare of adornments. Night Fiesta on the River. Qadi ben Lubbal. AnML
By day the skyscraper looms in the smoke and sun and has a soul. Skyscraper. Carl Sandburg. PoPl
By far/ The naughtiest. Extremely Naughty Children. Elizabeth Godley. BBGG
By Gentle Love. *Unknown.* TRV
By God I hate to grow old. Covent Garden Market. Carl Bode. *Fr.* London Sonnets. ToPo
By God, My Lords, Let Us Lift the Veil. Ferrán Sánchez Calavera, *tr. fr. Spanish by* William M. Davis. AnML
By Her Aunt's Grave. Thomas Hardy. Satires of Circumstance, III. PoPo; VaPo
By her that is most assured to her self. Amoretti, LVIII. Spenser. EnRePo
By Him. Ben Jonson. TRV
By his commandment he maketh the snow to fall apace. Snow. Ecclesiasticus, Bible, Apocrypha. BoC
By Lea's dear banks, where joined in play. Musing by a River. Moses Browne. WaPE
By Master Saville who, conceivably, from the accuracy of the drawing. *The River Map* and We're Done. Charles Olson. CoPo
By miracles exceeding power of man. Crucifying. John Donne. MeP
By Moonlight. May Sarton. MoLP
By Moonlight. *Unknown, tr. fr. French by* Louis Untermeyer. UnTE
By Night. Philip Jerome Cleveland. TRV
By night we linger'd on the lawn. In Memoriam A. H. H., XCV. Tennyson. OBNC; VP
By none but me can the tale be told. Dante Gabriel Rossetti. *Fr.* The White Ship. HaSV

By our first strange and fatal[1] interview. Elegy [or Elegie] XVI: On His Mistress. John Donne. Elegies, XVI. CABL; FoBA; SeCP

By reason of despair we set forth behind you. The Murder of Moses. Karl Shapiro. EaLo

By rocks and twigs and garter snakes. Elsie's House. Stanley McNail. FiSC

By rose and verdant valley. Earth-born. Robert E. Howard. FiSC

By Saint Mary, my lady. To Mistress Isabel[1]. Pennell. John Skelton. *Fr.* The Garlande of Laurell. CBEP; PoIE; StP

By Saturday I said you would be better on Sunday. The Operation. Robert Creeley. ToPo

By sloth on sorrow fathered. Lollocks. Robert Graves. DTC; EvOK

By the Bivouac's Fitful Flame. Walt Whitman. AP; LV

By the borders of the ocean. The Bonny Bunch of Roses (B *vers.*). *Unknown.* BSNS

By the city dead-house by the gate. The City Dead-House. Walt Whitman. FoBA

By the dangers of the ocean. The Bonny Bunch of Roses O. *Unknown.* BSNS

By the Deep Sea. Byron. *Fr.* Childe Harold's Pilgrimage. OBNC

("Oh! that the desert were my dwelling-place.") ILP

By the Earth's Corpse. Thomas Hardy. PoDB

By the Exeter River. Donald Hall. MoBS

By the Fire. Elizabeth J. Coatsworth. RePo

By the Firelight. L. A. G. Strong. DaDu

By the Flat Cup. Horace, *tr. fr. Latin by* Ezra Pound. *Fr.* Odes. CTC

By the flow of the inland river. The Blue and the Gray. Francis Miles Finch. ThLM

By the glim of a midwinterish early morning. Son and Father. C. Day Lewis. EaLo

By the Hoof of the Wild Goat. Kipling. *Fr.* Plain Tales from the Hills. OBNC

By the Lightning We Lost Our Sight. *Unknown.* BSNS

By the morning hours. The Morning Hours. *Unknown.* PoPl

By the North Gate, the wind blows full of sand. Lament of the Frontier Guard. Li Po. AP

By the old Moulmein Pagoda, lookin' eastward to the sea. Mandalay. Kipling. FaBV

By the rivers of Babylon, there we sat down, yea, we wept, when we remembered Zion. Psalm CXXXVII, Bible, *O. T.* CaFP

By the road to the contagious hospital. Spring and All. William Carlos Williams. AP; CABA; PoIE; PoSa; VaPo

By the rude bridge that arched the flood. Concord Hymn [or Hymn]. Emerson. AP; FaPL; LV; OnP; PoIE; PoPl; ThLM

By the Sea. Richard Watson Dixon. OBNC

By the Sea. John Hollander. AmPC

By the Sea. Christina Rossetti. HaSV

By the Sea. Wordsworth. *See* It Is a Beauteous Evening.

By the sea, by the waste, nocturnal sea. Questions. Heine. HaSV

By the shores of Gitche Gumee. Hiawatha's Childhood. Longfellow. *Fr.* The Song of Hiawatha. RePo

By the side of a green stagnate pool. A Pastoral. G. A. Stevens. ErPo

By the Statue of King Charles at Charing Cross. Lionel Johnson. BoC; OBNC; RoGo

By the Sweat of My Brow I Toiled. *Unknown, tr. fr. French by* Daisy Aldan. AnML

By the time he's suited. Cold Fact. Dick Emmons. PoPl

By the time you swear you're his. Unfortunate Coincidence. Dorothy Parker. PoPl; PoPo

By the waters of Babylon. Memento. Rudolf Hagelstange. MGP

By the wayside, three crows sat on a cross. Adam on His Way Home. Robert Pack. ErPo; PoDB

By the Wood. Robert Nichols. MMA

By this he knew she wept with waking eyes. Modern Love, I. George Meredith. ILP; StP; VP

By this, Leander, being near the land. Christopher Marlowe. *Fr.* Hero and Leander. ErPo

By this low fire I often sit to woo. Sonnets, Part I, XXV. Frederick Goddard Tuckerman. AP

By This to Remember. Barry Spacks. OPP

By Thy Life I Live. Mme Jeanne Marie Guyon. TRV (Adoration). STF

By Water's Edge Sing Sisters Three. *Unknown, tr. fr. French by* Norman R. Shapiro. AnML

By Way of Preface. Edward Lear. *See* How Pleasant to Know Mr. Lear

By what strange prescience he plucks the green. The Well-Finder. Harold Vinal. FiSC

By what word's power, the key of paths untrod. Heart's Hope. Dante Gabriel Rossetti. *Fr.* The House of Life. VP

By yon castle wa', at the close of the day. There'll Never Be Peace. Burns. CBEP

By your unnumbered charities. Hospital for Defectives. Thomas Blackburn. GTBS-P

Bye, Baby Bunting. Mother Goose. SoPo

Byrnies, The. Thom Gunn. NePoEA-2

Byron, *sel.* Joaquin Miller.

In Men Whom Men Condemn as Ill. PoLF

Byron Recollected at Bologna. Samuel Rogers. *Fr.* Italy. OBNC

Byzantium. W. B. Yeats. CABA; DiPo; FoBA; ILP; PoIE; StP; VaPo

C

C Is for the Circus. Phyllis McGinley. *Fr.* All around the Town. SoPo

Cabbage, onions, green tomatoes. Miss Sallie's Chowchow. Edith Earnshaw. PoNC

Cable Hymn, The. Whittier. ThLM

Cables entangling her. She Is Far from the Land. Thomas Hood. DTC; WiR

Cachalot, The, *sel.* E. J. Pratt.

"Thousand years now had his breed, A." OBCV

Caelia's fair, the charming toast. On a Painted Lady. William Pattison. WaPE

Caelica, *sels.* Fulke Greville.

"Absence, the noble truce," XLV. EnRePo

"All my senses, like beacon's flame," LVI. EnRePo

"Away with these self-loving lads," LII. EnRePo

(Of His Cynthia.) ELP

"Caelica, I overnight was finely used," XXXVIII. EnRePo

"Cupid, thou naughty boy, when thou wert loathed," XII. EnRePo

"Down [or Downe] in the depth of mine iniquity," XCIX. EnRePo; PoIE

"Earth, The, with thunder torn, with fire blasted," LXXXVI. EnRePo

"Eternal Truth, almighty, infinite," XCVII. EnRePo

"Faction that ever dwells," XXIX. EnRePo

"Farewell, sweet boy; complain not of my truth," LXXXIV. EnRePo

"Fie, foolish Earth, think you the heaven wants glory," XVI. EnRePo

"I, with whose colors Myra dressed her head," XXII. EnRePo

(Myra.) CBEP

"In night, when colors all to black are cast," C. EnRePo

"Man, dream no more of curious mysteries," LXXXVIII. EnRePo

"Nurse-life wheat, within his green husk growing, The," XL. EnRePo

"Sion lies waste, and thy Jerusalem," CIX. EnRePo

"When all this all doth pass from age to age," LXIX. EnRePo

"When as man's life, the light of human lust," LXXXVII. PoIE

"World, that all contains, is ever moving, The," VII. EnRePo

"Wrapped up, O Lord, in man's degeneration," XCVIII. EnRePo

"You little stars that live in skies," IV. CBEP

"You that seek what life is in death," LXXXII. EnRePo

Café Tableau. May Swenson. Erpo

Caffer Commando, The, *sel* Thomas Pringle.

"Hark! heard ye the signals of triumph afar?" ACV

Caged in old woods, whose reverend echoes wake. Captivity. Samuel Rogers. OBNC

Caged Skylark, The. Gerard Manley Hopkins. VP

Cain Shall Not Slay Abel Today on Our Good Ground. Malcolm Lowry. OBCV

Cake. Miriam Clark Potter. BiCB

Calf-Path, The. Sam Walter Foss. PoLF

Caliban in the Coal Mines. Louis Untermeyer. PoPl; PoPo; TRV; WePo

Caliban upon Setebos; or, Natural Theology in the Island. Robert Browning. VP

Calico Pie. Edward Lear. CBEP; SoPo

California, *with music. Unknown.* BSO

California as It Is and Was, *with music.* John A. Stone. SGR

California Ball, *with music.* John A. Stone. SGR

California Bank Robbers, *with music.* John A. Stone. SGR

California Bloomer, *with music.* John A. Stone. SGR

California Humbugs, *with music.* Mart Taylor. SGR

California Legislature. John A. Stone. SGR

California over the Left. "Jack the Grumbler." SGR

California people are determined if they find, The. California Bank Robbers. John A. Stone. SGR

California Stage Company, *with music.* John A. Stone. SGR

Caligula. Robert Lowell. CoPo

Call, The. James Dickey. *See* Owl King, The.

Call for the Robin Redbreast [and the Wren]. John Webster. *Fr.* The White Devil. CaFP; CBEP; StP
(Cornelia's Song.) PoIE
(Land Dirge, A.) GTBS-P

Call Him the Lover and call me the Bride. The Song the Body Dreamed in the Spirit's Mad Behest. Brother Antoninus. ErPo

Call is for belief, The. The Fundament Is Shifted. Abbie Huston Evans. MoRP

Call it neither love nor spring madness. Without Name. Pauli Murray. AmNP

Call it not vain—they do not err. The Minstrel Responds to Flattery. Sir Walter Scott. *Fr.* The Lay of the Last Minstrel. OBNC

Call the roller of big cigars. The Emperor of Ice-Cream. Wallace Stevens. AmLP; AP; CABA; CaFP; PoIE; PoSa

Call to Conflict. *Unknown.* STF

Call to Youth. Horace, *tr. fr. Latin by* Hugh Vibart Mac-Naghten. Odes, III, 2. SiGo

Called a star's orbit to pursue. Star Morals. Nietzsche. TwGP

Called Away. Richard Le Gallienne. SoPo

Caller Herrin'. Lady Nairne. HaSV

Calling the Cows Home. Jean Ingelow. *Fr.* The High Tide on the Coast of Lincolnshire (1571). ThGo

Calling to mind since first my love begun. Idea, LI. Michael Drayton. EnRePo

Callst thou me friend? What rhetorick is this? Meditation. Cant. 5.1. Eate Oh Friendes and Drink Yea Drink Abundantly Oh Beloved. Edward Taylor. *Fr.* Preparatory Meditations, Second Series. MeP

Calm, The. John Donne. CABL; StP

Calm after Storm. Frank Yerby. AmNP

Calm as that second summer which precedes. Charleston. Henry Timrod. AmLP; AP

Calm is the landscape when the storm has passed. Peace in the Welsh Hills. Vernon Watkins. GTBS-P

Calm is the morn without a sound. In Memoriam A. H. H., XI. Tennyson. ELP; FoBA; OBNC; OnP; VP

Calm of heaven rests upon my heart, The. Blessed Nearness. Mary Bullock. STF

Calm Soul of All Things. Matthew Arnold. *Fr.* Lines Written in Kensington Gardens. TRV

Calm [or Calme] was the day, and through the trembling air [or ayre]. Prothalamion. Spenser. CABA; CaFP; EnRePo; GTBS-P; OnP; PoIE; StP; VaPo

Calm Was the Even. Dryden. *Fr.* An Evening's Love, IV, i. DiPo

Calm Winter Sleep. Hilary Corke. MP

Calvary. E. A. Robinson. PoDB; PoPo

Calyx of the oboe breaks, The. Music. Conrad Aiken. AP

Cambric Shirt, The. *Unknown. See* Elfin Knight, The.

Cambridge Ladies [Who Live in Furnished Souls], The. E. E. Cummings. *Fr.* Sonnets—Realities. CBEP; PoSa

Camden Magpie. Hugh McCrae. PoAu-1

Came the relief. "What, sentry, ho!" Relieving Guard. Bret Harte. RoGo

Came to lakes; came to dead water. A Field of Light. Theodore Roethke. MP; ToPo

Camel, The. Ogden Nash. SoPo

Camel, at the close of day, The. And So Should You. *Unknown.* STF

Camel has a single hump, The. The Camel. Ogden Nash. SoPo

Camellia, The. Basho, *tr fr. Japanese by* Harold G. Henderson. RePo

Camel's Hump, The. Kipling. *Fr.* Just-so Stories. EvOK

Camerados. Bayard Taylor. Par.

Camp. Patrick Anderson. OBCV

Camp Fire. Beatrice Marion Bromley. ACV

Camp Hymn, The. Mary S. Edgar. TRV

Camp in the Prussian Forest, A. Randall Jarrell. AP

Camp within the West, The. Roderic Quinn. PoAu-1

Camping Out. William Empson. ToPo

Camptown. John Ciardi. ThLM

Campus on the Hill, The. W. D. Snodgrass. AP; MP; ToPo

Can a bell ring in the heart. When Death Came April Twelve 1945. Carl Sandburg. AP

Can I forget that winter night. A Leap-Year Episode. *At. to* Eugene Field. BoLP

Can I not sing but "Hoy." Jolly Wat. *Unknown.* BuBa

Can I see another's woe. On Another's Sorrow. Blake. *Fr.* Songs of Innocence. CBEP; FaBV

Can it be possible no words shall welcome. Comforting Lines. *Unknown.* STF

Can it be right to give what I can give? Sonnets from the Portuguese, IX. Elizabeth Barrett Browning. CTC

Can there be a moon in heaven to-night. Isabelle. James Hogg. Par

Can we not force from widowed [or widdowed] poetry. An Elegy [or Elegie] upon the Death of Doctor Donne, Dean of Paul's [or the Dean of St. Paul's, Dr. John Donne]. Thomas Carew. CABA; PP; SeCP; StP

Can ye [or you] play me Duncan Gray. Duncan Gray [or the Thrusting of It]. Burns. ErPo; UnTE

Can you make me a cambric shirt. Lovers' Tasks. *Unknown.* CBEP

Can You Paint a Thought? John Ford. *Fr.* The Broken Heart. CBEP

"Can you throw a stone, or can you toss a ball?" The Twa Brothers (B *vers*). *Unknown.* BSO

Canadian Authors Meet, The. F. R. Scott. ACV; OBCV

Canadian Boat Song, The. *Unknown, at to.* John Galt. CBEP; OBNC

Canadian Herd-Boy, The. Susanna Moodie. OBCV

Canaries were his hobby. The Glass Blower. James Scully. MP

"Canary-birds feed on sugar and seed." The Plaint of the Camel. Charles Edward Carryl. EvOK; SoPo

Canberra in April. J. R. Rowland. PoAu-2

Cancer Cells, The. Richard Eberhart. AnMoPo; ToPo

Candle, A. Sir John Suckling. ErPo

Candle and Book. Nina Willis Walter. TRV

Candle and Star. Elizabeth J. Coatsworth. BiCB

Candle Burning in the Night, A. Susan B. Warner. ThGo

Candle Indoors, The. Gerard Manley Hopkins. AnMoPo; DiPo

Candles splutter, The; and the kettle hums. The Still Small Voice. A. M. Klein. OBCV

Canoe. Patrick Anderson. SD

Canoe, The. Isabella Valancy Crawford. OBCV

"O love, art thou a silver fish?" *sel.* ACV

Canoe Speaks, The, *sel.* Robert Louis Stevenson.

"On the great streams the ships may go." SD

Canoe-Trip. Douglas Le Pan. OBCV

Canonization, The. John Donne. CABA; CaFP; CBEP; DiPo; EnRePo; FoBA; PoIE; SeCP; StP; UnTE; VaPo

Canst thou not minister to a mind diseas'd. Shakespeare. *Fr.* Macbeth. TRV

Cant. W. H. Davies. MoRP

Canterbury Tales, The, *sels.* Chaucer.
Prologue. CaFP, *much abr.*; CTC, *much abr.*; DiPo, 18 *ll.*; ILP; OnP, *abr.*; PoIE, *abr.*
Miller, The, *mod. vers. by* Nevill Coghill. WePo
"Parson of a country town was he, The," *mod. vers. by* H. C. Leonard. TRV
Shipman, The. HaSV
Squire, The, *mod. vers. by* Nevill Coghill. WePo
Ten of Chaucer's People, *mod. vers. by* Nevill Coghill. PoSa
Wife of Bath, The, *mod. vers. by* Nevill Coghill. WePo
Franklin's Prologue and Tale, The. CABL
Merchant's Tale, The, *abr., mod. vers. by* Frank Ernest Hill. UnTE
Nun's Priest's Tale, The. CABL; StP
Pardoner's Prologue and Tale, The. CABL
(Pardoner's Tale, The.) PoIE
Reeve's Tale, The, *mod. vers. by* Frank Ernest Hill. UnTE
Sir Thopas. Par
Prologue to Sir Thopas. Par

Canticle. Wendell Berry. AP

Canticle. James McAuley. PoAu-2

Canticle of Darkness. Wilfred Watson. ACV

Canticle of the Creatures, The. St. Francis of Assisi. *See* Canticle of the Sun.

Canticle of the Sun. St. Francis of Assisi, *tr. fr. Italian.* BoC
(Canticle of the Creatures, The, *tr. by* William M. Davis.) AnML
(Cantico del Sole, *tr. by* Ezra Pound.) CTC
(Song of the Creatures, The, *tr. by* Matthew Arnold.) SiGo

Canticle to the Christ in the Holy Eucharist, A. Brother Antoninus. ToPo

Canticle to the Waterbirds, A. Brother Antoninus. StP

Cantico del Sole. St. Francis of Assisi. *See* Canticle of the Sun.

Cantiga: "Grace and beauty has the maid." Gil Vicente. *See* Song: "Grace and beauty has the maid."

Canto I: "And then went down to the ship." Ezra Pound. AP; PoIE

Canto II: "Hang it all, Robert Browning." Ezra Pound. AP

Canto XLV: "With Usura/ With usura hath no man a house of good stone." Ezra Pound. AnMoPo; PoIE

Canzone: "Clear, fresh, and dulcet streams." Petrarch, *tr. fr. Italian by* Leigh Hunt. Sonnets to Laura: To Laura in Life, Canzone XIV. RBL

Canzone: Donna Mi Priegha. Guido Cavalcanti, *tr fr. Italian by* Ezra Pound. CTC
(Lady Begs Me, A, *tr. by* Joseph Tusiani.) AnML

Canzone: "Into a little close of mine I went." Lorenzo de' Medici, *tr. fr. Italian by* John Addington Symonds. RBL
Canzone: "O my own Italy! though words are vain." Petrarch, *tr. fr. Italian by* Lady Dacre. RBL
Canzone: Of the Gentle Heart. Guido Guinicelli, *tr. fr. Italian by* Dante Gabriel Rossetti. CTC
(Gentle Heart, The, *tr. by* Daniel J. Donno.) AnML
Cap and Bells, The. W. B. Yeats. OnMSP
Cape Ann. T. S. Eliot. *Fr.* Landscapes. DaDu; EvOK; GoJo
Capital I gave a party. Confusions of the Alphabet. John Wain. DaDu
Capital Punishment. Oscar Wilde. *Fr.* The Ballad of Reading Gaol. WePo
Capital ship for an ocean trip, A. A Nautical Ballad. Charles Edward Carryl. RePo
Capital Square. Patrick Anderson. OBCV
Capitolo VIII. Ariosto, *tr. fr. Italian.* RBL
Captain Arthur Phillip and the Birds. Lex Banning. PoAu-2
Captain bold from Halifax who dwelt in country quarters, A. Unfortunate Miss Bailey. *Unknown.* DTC
Captain Carpenter. John Crowe Ransom. AP; MP; PoIE; PoSa; StP
Captain Glen. *Unknown.* BSNS
Captain Kelly Lets His Daughter Go to Be a Nun. Thomas Butler Feeney. PoPl
Captain Kidd. Stephen Vincent Benét. ThLM
Captain of the *Oberon*, The. Francis Webb. *Fr.* A Drum for Ben Boyd. ACV
Captain of the Years. Arthur R. Macdougall, Jr. TRV
Captain, or Colonel, or Knight in arms. When the Assault Was Intended to the City. Milton. GTBS-P; RoGo
Captain Reece. W. S. Gilbert. EvOK
Captain Robert Kidd. *Unknown.* BSNS
Captain Stood on the Carronade, The. Frederick Marryat. *Fr.* Snarleyvow; or, The Dog Fiend. HaSV; RePo
Captains of Small Farms, The. Robert P. Tristram Coffin. RePo
Captive. Marion Strobel. ErPo
Captivity. Samuel Rogers. OBNC
Capture of Larache, The. Luis de Góngora, *tr. fr. Spanish by* Frances Fletcher. AnSP
Capturing Elephants. Franz Baermann Steiner, *tr. fr. German by* Christopher Middleton. MGP
Caput apri refero. The Boar's Head Carol. *Unknown.* MeEL
Car Journey. Albert Ehrenstein, *tr. fr. German by* Christopher Middleton. MGP
Carcosa. Lin Carter. FiSC
Cardinal. Zoe Kincaid Brockman. PoNC
Cardinal, A. W. D. Snodgrass. PP
Care and heavy thought weigh me down. Estat ai en greu cossirier. Beatriz de Dia. ErPo
Care-Charmer Sleep [Son of the Sable Night]. Samuel Daniel. To Delia, LI. CaFP; CBEP; EnRePo (XLV); GTBS-P; PoIE (LIV); VaPo
Care-charming Sleep. John Fletcher. *Fr.* The Tragedy of Valentinian, V, ii. ELP
Careful Angler, The. Robert Louis Stevenson. SD
Careful man I ought to be, A. Service Supreme. *Unknown.* STF
Careful observers may foretel[l] the hour. A Description of a City Shower. Swift. CABL; CBEP; EiCP; PoIE; VaPo
Careless for an instant I closed my child's fingers in the jamb. Fingers in the Door. David Holbrook. NePoEA-2
Careless Love. *Unknown.* BFSS, *with music;* UnTE
Careless seems the great Avenger; history's pages but record. James Russell Lowell. *Fr.* The Present Crisis. TRV
Careless Willie. *Unknown.* BBGG
Carentan O Carentan. Louis Simpson. MoBS
Cargoes. John Masefield. DiPo; FaBV; ILP; PoPo; RoGo; WePo
Carl Hamblin. Edgar Lee Masters. *Fr.* Spoon River Anthology. ILP
Carmina. Robert Mezey. ToPo
Carmina Burana, *sel. Unknown, tr. fr. Latin by* Helen Waddell.
"O Spring the long-desired." SiGo
Carnival Songs, *sel.* Lorenzo de' Medici, *tr. fr. Italian by* Richard Aldington.
Triumph of Bacchus and Ariadne. CTC
Carol: "Deep in the fading leaves of night." W. R. Rodgers. DTC
Carol: "Here's a wreath of Christmas holly." Charles Edward Eaton. PoNC
Carol: "I sing of a maiden." *Unknown. See* I Sing of a Maiden.
Carol: "I was a lover of turkey and holly." Anne Wilkinson. OBCV
Carol: "There was a Boy bedded in bracken." John Short. DTC
Carol for Children, A. Ogden Nash. EaLo
Carol of Agincourt, A. *Unknown.* MeEL
Carol of St. George, A. *Unknown.* MeEL

Carol of the Bird, The. Walt Whitman. *See* Death Carol.
Carol with Variations. Phyllis McGinley. PoPo
Carolina Wrens. Edith Earnshaw. PoNC
Caroline, II: To the Evening Star. Thomas Campbell. *See* To the Evening Star.
Caroline of Edinburgh [*or* Edinboro *or* Edinborough] Town. *Unknown.* BFSS, *with music;* BSNS; BSO
Carousel, The. G. G. Oden. AmNP
Carpe Diem. Antoine de Baïf, *tr. fr. French by* Henry Carrington. RBL
Carpe Diem. Pierre de Ronsard, *tr. fr. French by* Curtis Hidden Page. RBL
Carpe Diem. Shakespeare. *See* O Mistress Mine.
Carpenter, The. George Macdonald. TRV
Carpenter of Galilee, The. Hilda W. Smith. TRV
Carpenter's Son, The. A. E. Housman. A Shropshire Lad, XLVIII. VaPo
Carrefour. Amy Lowell. MoLP
Carriage from Sweden, A. Marianne Moore. MP
Carrion. Harold Monro. Youth in Arms, IV. MMA
Carrion Comfort. Gerard Manley Hopkins. BoC; CABA; FoBA; PoDB; PoIE; VaPo
(Sonnet: "Not, I'll not, carrion comfort, Despair, not feast on thee.") OBNC
Carrion Crow, The. Thomas Lovell Beddoes. *See* Old Adam.
Carrion Crow, The. *Unknown. See* Tailor and the Crow, The.
Carrot has a green fringed top, A. Vegetables. Rachel Field. SoPo
Carry me back to old Virginny. Old Virginny. James A. Bland. FaBV
Carrying a bunch of marigolds. A Negro Woman. William Carlos Williams. PoIE
Carthon, *sel.* James Macpherson.
"King of Morven," Carthon said, "I fall in the midst of my course." EnPE
Cartography. Louise Bogan. PoPl
Cartography. Joel Oppenheimer. CoPo
Carts of the Wee Blind Lass, The. Kenneth Patchen. ToPo
Caryatid. Gottfried Benn, *tr. fr. German by* Michael Hamburger. MGP
Case History. Lilith Lorraine. FiSC
Casey at the Bat. Ernest Lawrence Thayer. PoPl; SD; SIV
Casey Jones. *Unknown, arr. by* T. Lawrence Seibert; PoPo; ThLM
Casey's Revenge. James Wilson. OnMSP
Caspar Hauser Song. Georg Trakl, *tr. fr. German by* David Luke. MGP
Cassandra. Robinson Jeffers. VaPo
Cassandra Southwick. Whittier. PoIE
Cassel (Carps at Wilhelmstrasse 15). "Joachim Ringelnatz," *tr. fr. German by* Christopher Middleton. MGP
Cast all your cares on God; that anchor holds. Tennyson. *Fr.* Enoch Arden. TRV
Cast aside dull books and thought. Invitation to the Dance. *Unknown.* UnTE
Cast away fear. Arthur Edward Waite. *Fr.* At the End of Things. TRV
Castara, *sels.* William Habington.
Against Them Who Lay Unchastity to the Sex of Women, *fr.* II. SeCP
To Castara: Upon Beautie, *fr.* II. SeCP
To Roses in the Bosom[e] of Castara, *fr.* I. SeCP; UnTE
Castara, see that dust, the sportive wind. To Castara: Upon Beautie. William Habington. *Fr.* Castara, *fr.* I. SeCP
Castaway, The. William Cowper. CABA; CBEP; EiCP; ELP; EnPE; PoSa
Castile. Miguel de Unamuno, *tr. fr. Spanish by* Eleanor L. Turnbull. PoPl
Casting All Your Care upon Him. *Unknown.* STF
Castle, The. Edwin Muir. AnMoPo
Castle of Chillon, The. Byron. *See* Prisoner of Chillon, The.
Castle of Indolence, The, *sel.* James Thomson.
"O mortal man, who livest here by toil." EiCP
Casual Gold. Maud E. Uschold. SoPo
Casualty. Robert Nichols. MMA
Cat. Dorothy Baruch. SoPo
Cat, The. Baudelaire, *tr. fr. French by* Roy Campbell. PoPl
Cat, The. Oliver Herford. FaBV
Cat. Mary Britton Miller. SoPo
Cat and I. Fight. Jean Jaszi. RePo
Cat and Mouse. Ted Hughes. EaLo
Cat and the Fish, The. Thomas Gray. *See* Ode on the Death of a Favorite Cat.
Cat and the Moon, The. W. B. Yeats. GoJo; LOW; RoGo; WePo
Cat Asks Mouse Out. Stevie Smith. DaDu
Cat on Couch. Barbara Howes. PoSa
Cat runs races with her tail, The. Signs of Winter. John Clare. PoSC; WiR
Cat went here and there, The. The Cat and the Moon. W. B. Yeats. GoJo; LOW; RoGo; WePo
Cat! who has[t] pass'd thy grand climacteric. To a Cat [*or* To Mrs. Reynolds's Cat]. Keats. BoC; DiPo

Catalpa Tree ("Catalpa, in you a song, a cache"). Miriam Waddington. OBCV
Catch. Robert Francis. PP
Caterpillar, The. Christina Rossetti. *Fr.* Sing-Song. GoJo; SoPo
Cathemerinon, *sels.* Prudentius, *tr. fr. Latin by* Helen Waddell. SiGo
  "Earth is sweet with roses, The."
  "Take him, earth, for cherishing."
Cats. Marchette Chute. SoPo
Cats. Theodor Däubler, *tr. fr. German by* Christopher Middleton. MGP
Cats. Eleanor Farjeon. ThGo
Cat's Conscience, A. *Unknown.* PoLF
Cat's Eye. Paul Engle. LV
Cats sleep/ Anywhere. Cats. Eleanor Farjeon. ThGo
Cattle. *Unknown.* SoPo
Catullus de Lesbia. Swift. CBEP
Catullus, *tr. fr. Latin by* Louis Untermeyer. UnTE
Catullus to Lesbia. James Reeves. ErPo
Catullus, you're a fool. I said. Catullus Talks to Himself. Catullus. UnTE
Caucasus, The ("The Caucasus lay vast in light"). Boris Pasternak, *tr. fr. Russian by* Eugene M. Kayden. PoPl
Caught in the exhaustion of an endless loneliness. Creation. V. N. Bhushan. ACV
Caught in the glib catcher's net. Sockeye Salmon. Ronald Hambleton. OBCV
Caught without wife and mother, child. Getting Drunk with Daughter. Robert Huff. NePoEA-2
Cauld blaws the wind frae east to west. Up in the Morning Early. Burns. PoSC
Cause & Effect. May Swenson. OPP
Cause for Wonder, A. *Unknown.* MeEL
"Cause of loving God is God alone, The." The One Thing Needful. Vassar Miller. PoCh
Caution. *Unknown, tr. fr. German by* Louis Untermeyer. UnTE
Caution to Poets, A. Matthew Arnold. CBEP
Cautionary Tale, A. Anne Wilkinson. OBCV
Cautious Struggle, The. *Unknown. See* Be Quiet, Sir!
Cavalry Crossing a Ford. Walt Whitman. AP; CABA; CBEP; PoPl; PoPo; RePo; StP
Cawsand Bay. *Unknown.* HaSV
Cean Dubh Deelish. *Unknown. See* Dear Dark Head.
Cedar Grove, The. *Unknown.* BSNS
Ceiling of his bedroom, The. Cartography. Joel Oppenheimer. CoPo
Celebrate the season of the death/ of the city. The Kimono. Don Gordon. PtTo
Celebrated Return. Clarence Major. AmNP
Celebration. Leonard Cohen. ErPo
Celebration. Robert Sward. *Fr.* Five Poems for J. F. K. OPP
Celebration of Charis in Ten Lyrick Peeces, A. Ben Jonson. SeCP
  Sels.
  Begging Another Kiss. StP
  (For Love's Sake.) UnTE
  His Excuse for Loving. EnRePo
  How He Saw Her. EnRePo
  So White, So Soft, So Sweet. UnTE
  Triumph of Charis, The. CABA; CBEP; ELP; OnP
  (Her Triumph.) CaFP; CTC
Celery. Ogden Nash. LV; RePo; WePo
Celestial Surgeon, The. Robert Louis Stevenson. BoC; TRV
Celia Bleeding, to the Surgeon. Thomas Carew. SeCP
Celle Qui Meurt. Nancy Westlake. PtTo
Cenotaph, The. Charlotte Mew. MMA
Centaur, The. May Swenson. MP
Centenarian's Story, The. Walt Whitman. CTC
Center of all centers, core of cores. Buddha in the Glory. Rainer Maria Rilke. TwGP
Centipede along the threshold crept, The. The Haunted House. Thomas Hood. WiR
Centipede Was Happy Quite, A. Mrs. Edward Craster. SoPo
  (Puzzled Centipede, The.) RePo
Central America, painted so fine, The. Loss of the *Central America*. John A. Stone. SGR
Centuries Are His, The. Georgia Moore Eberling. TRV
Cerelle. Margaret Bell Houston. SIV
Ceremonies for Candlemas Eve. Robert Herrick. ILP
Ceremony. Richard Wilbur. PP
Ceremony after a Fire Raid. Dylan Thomas. PoDB
Ceremony for Birth and Naming. Ridgely Torrence. MoRP
Ceremony must be found, The. Speaking of Poetry. John Peale Bishop. PP
Certain Mercies. Robert Graves. GTBS-P
Certain people would not clean their buttons. The Bohemians. Ivor Gurney. MMA
Certain poets/ have written good poems. On the Poet's Leer. David Ray. NePoEA-2

Certain Presbyterian pair, A. The Presbyterian Wedding. *Unknown.* ErPo
Certain True Woords Spoken Concerning One Benet Corbett after Her Death. Richard Corbet. SeCP
Cervantes. E. C. Bentley. EvOK
Cerylas, jesting, called his pretty jade. Hors d'Oeuvre. Deems Taylor. UnTE
Challenge. Samuel Hazo. SD
Challenge, The. Longfellow. AP
Challenge, The. *Unknown, tr fr. Spanish by* Louis Untermeyer. UnTE
Challenger, The. Donald Wandrei. FiSC
Chamber Music, *sels.* James Joyce.
  "Because your voice was at my side," XVII. WePo
  "Gentle lady, do not sing," XXVIII. MoLP
  Goldenhair, V. RePo
  ("Lean out of the window.") BoLP; LOW
  "In the dark pine-wood," XX. BoLP
  My Love Is in a Light Attire, VII. LOW; StP
  "O, it was out by Donnycarney," XXXI. WePo
  Strings in the Earth and Air, I. LOW
Chamber over the Gate, The. Longfellow. AP
Chambered Nautilus, The. Oliver Wendell Holmes. *Fr.* The Autocrat of the Breakfast Table, *ch.* 4. AmLP; AP; DiPo; HaSV; LV; PoLF
  "Build thee more stately mansions, O my soul," *sel.* TRV
Chambermaid's Second Song, The. W. B. Yeats. ErPo
Chameleon, The. E. H. W. Meyerstein. AnMoPo
Chances, The. Wilfred Owen. MMA
Chancing upon the Devil in the doorway. Rosemary Dobson. *Fr.* The Devil and the Angel. ACV
Change, The. Abraham Cowley. SeCP
Change. Raymond Knister. OBCV
Changed, *sel.* George Abbe.
  "I saw a man turned into money." PtTo
Changes. "Owen Meredith." PoLF
Changing the Wheel. Bertolt Brecht, *tr. fr. German by* Michael Hamburger. MGP
Channel Crossing. George Barker. ACV; GTBS-P; ToPo
Channel Firing. Thomas Hardy. CABA; ILP; PoIE; StP; VP
Channel Passage, A. Rupert Brooke. HaSV
Channel Rhyme, A. Cicely Fox Smith. HaSV
Channel U.S.A.—Live. Adrien Stoutenburg. OPP; ThLM
Chanson Innocente ("In just-spring"). E. E. Cummings. *See* In Just-Spring.
Chanson Innocente ("Little tree"). E. E. Cummings. *See* Little Tree.
Chant. Oscar Williams. MoRP
Chant for All the People on Earth. Leslie Woolf Hedley. PtTo
Chant you loud of punishments. Three Poems, 2. Stephen Crane. AP
Chanted Calendar, A. Sydney Dobell. *Fr.* Balder. BoC
Chanticleer. John Farrar. SoPo
Chanticleer. Margaret Irvin. PoAu-2
Chanting the Square Deific. Walt Whitman. PoIE
Chapel Deacon. R. S. Thomas. ACV; ToPo
Chaplinesque. Hart Crane. AP
Character Assassins, The. Gottfried Keller, *tr. fr. German by* Harold Lenz. AGP
Character of a Happy Life, The. Sir Henry Wotton. FaPL; GTBS-P; PoIE; PoPo
Character of Holland, The. Andrew Marvell. CABL
Chard Whitlow. Henry Reed. DTC; Par
Charge, The. Denise Levertov. NePoEA-2
Charge of the Light Brigade, The. Tennyson. FaBV; PoPl
Charing Cross. *Unknown.* CBEP
Chariot, The. Emily Dickinson. *See* Because I could not stop for death.
Chariot Race, The. Vergil, *tr. fr. Latin by* Smith Palmer Bovie. *Fr.* Georgics. SD
Charis guesse, and doe not misse. Clayming a Second Kisse by Desert. Ben Jonson. *Fr.* A Celebration of Charis. SeCP
Charis one day in discourse. Urging Her of a. Promise. Ben Jonson. *Fr.* A Celebration of Charis. SeCP
Charitas Nimia; or, The Deare Bargain. Richard Crashaw. MeP
Charles Augustus Anderson, *with music. Unknown.* BSNS
Charles Guiteau. *Unknown.* BFSS, *with music;* BSO
  (Garfield's Murder.) ThLM
Charles the First, *sel.* Shelley.
  Widow Bird [Sate Mourning for Her Love], A. CBEP; ELP; WePo
  (Song, A.) OBNC
  ("Widow bird sate mourning for her love, A.") GTBS-P
Charles used to watch Naomi, taking heart. Laboratory Poem. James Merrill. MP; NePoEA-2
Charleston. Henry Timrod. AmLP; AP
Charleston Garden, A. Henry Bellamann. PoLF
Charm against the Toothache, A. John Heath-Stubbs. DaDu; MP
Charm for Going a-Hunting. Mary Austin. RePo

Charm me asleep. and melt me so. To Musique, to Becalme His Fever. Robert Herrick. GoJo

Charming bearded singer! Make the beast's tune. Fidelio. Michael McClure. PtTo

Charming Oysters I cry. Oysters. Swift. ErPo

Chartless. Emily Dickinson. *See* I never saw a moor.

Chaste Arabian Bird, The. Earl of Rochester. ErPo

Chaste Florimel. Matthew Prior. ErPo

Chasten your fears, I have not been destroyed. Sonnet VI. Mark Van Doren. MoLP

Chatter of a death-demon from a tree-top, The. War Is Kind, XIX. Stephen Crane. AP

Chaucer. Longfellow. AmLP; AP; CBEP; DiPo; PP

Check. James Stephens. LOW

Cheer up, ye young men all, let nothing fright you. Brave Wolfe. *Unknown.* ThLM

Cheerful Welcome, A. *Unknown.* MeEL

Chequer-Board of mingled Light and Shade, A? Life's Chequer-Board. John Oxenham. TRV

Cher Maitre:/ Neither my explication. A Letter to Wilbur Frohock. Daniel Hoffman. CoPo

Cherry. Gene Baro. ErPo

Cherry Blossoms, *sels.* "Michael Lewis," *after the Chinese.* UnTE

    Cursing and Blessing.

    Leaving.

    Living and Dying.

    Longing.

    Remembering.

Cherry-ripe. Thomas Campion. *See* There Is a Garden in Her Face.

Cherry [*or* Cherrie]-ripe. Robert Herrick. ELP; SeCP

Cherry Robbers. D. H. Lawrence. PoIE

Cherry-Tree Carol, The. *Unknown.* CBEP; DiPo; ELP; OnMSP; ThGo; VaPo

    (Joseph Was an Old Man. *with music.*) BFSS

Chesapeake and the Shannon, The ("The *Chesapeake* so bold"), *with music. Unknown.* BSNS

Chesapeake and the Shannon, The (" 'Twas of the *Shannon* frigate"). *Unknown.* BSNS

Chestnut casts his flambeaux, and the flowers, The. Last Poems, IX. A. E. Housman. VP

Chestnut Roasters, The. Joseph Payne Brennan. FiSC

Chevy Chase. *Unknown.* BFSS; Buba

Chez-Nous. A. G. Austin. PoAu-2

Chiaroscuro. Carole Bergé. ErPo

Chicago. Bret Harte. ThLM

Chicago. Carl Sandburg. AP; FaBV; PoIE; PoPl

Chicago *Defender* Sends a Man to Little Rock, Fall, 1957, The. Gwendolyn Brooks. AmNP

Chief defect of Henry King, The. Henry King. Hilaire Belloc. BBGG; DTC

Chief of organic numbers! On Seeing a Lock of Milton's Hair. Keats. PP

Chiefs of State marched up the hill, The. Alpine View. Melville Cane. PoPl

Chieftain to the Highlands bound, A. Lord Ullin's Daughter. Thomas Campbell. GTBS-P; RoGo

Child, The. Donald Hall. NePoEA-2

Child, The. Reginald Massey. ACV

Child, The. Ivor Popham. EaLo

Child. Carl Sandburg. TRV

Child and Maiden. Sir Charles Sedley. *Fr.* The Mulberry Garden, III. ii. GTBS-P

Child and the Shadow, The. Elizabeth Jennings. NePoEA-2

Child came to a pool in the heart of a thicket, The. The Pool. Leah Bodine Drake. FiSC

Child Crying. Anthony Thwaite. NePoEA-2

Child! do not throw this book about. Dedication on the Gift of a Book to a Child. Hilaire Belloc. ThGo

Child Dying, The. Edwin Muir. GTBS-P

Child Harold, *sel.* John Clare.

    Stanzas: "How beautiful this hill of fern swells on!" OBNC

Child Ill, A. John Betjeman. DTC

Child Is Born, A. *Unknown.* STF

Child is holy and most wise, The. The Child. Ivor Popham. EaLo

Child of my winter, born. Heart's Needle. W. D. Snodgrass. AmPC; CoPo

Child of Peace, The. Selma Lagerlof, *tr. fr. Swedish by* Charles Wharton Stork. PoPl

Child on Top of a Greenhouse. Theodore Roethke. LOW; PoPl; StP; WePo

Child riding the stormy mane of noon, A. Are You Born? Muriel Rukeyser. MoRP

Child should always say what's true, A. The Whole Duty of Children. Robert Louis Stevenson. EvOK; ThGo

Child skipping jump on the quay at the Mill, A. Poor Old Horse. David Holbrook. NePoEA-2

Child, the current of your breath is six days long. Unknown Girl in the Maternity Ward. Anne Sexton. CoPo

Child! Three-times blessed child! In what afflicted ages. Concerning the Birth of Christ, 1657. Andreas Gryphius. AGP

Child Wife. Joseph Joel Keith. FiSC

Childbirth. Ted Hughes. ToPo

Childe Harold's Pilgrimage, *sels.* Byron.

    Childe Harold's Farewell to England, *fr.* I. PoPl

    Dedication: To Ianthe. OBNC

    Eve of Waterloo, The, *fr.* III. FaBV; OBNC

    "Fair Greece! sad relic of departed Worth!" *fr.* II. ILP

    Fatal Spell, The, *fr.* IV. OBNC

    Lake Leman, *fr.* III. OBNC

    "Oh! that the desert were my dwelling-place," *fr.* IV. ILP (By the Deep Sea.) OBNC

    Ocean, The, *fr.* IV. ("There is a pleasure in the pathless woods.") HaSV; PoIE

    "Stop!—for thy tread is on an Empire's dust!" *fr.* III. ILP

"Childe Roland to the Dark Tower Came." Robert Browning. VP

Childhood. Sir Thomas More. *Fr.* The Pageants of Thomas More. EnRePo

Childhood. Ned O'Gorman. PoPl

Childhood, *sel.* Arthur Rimbaud, *tr. fr. French by* Louise Varèse. *Fr.* Illuminations.

    "I am the saint at prayer on the terrace," IV. PoPl

Childhood. Georg Trakl, *tr. fr. German by* Christopher Middleton. MGP

Childhood and School-Time. Wordsworth. *Fr.* The Prelude, I. OBNC

    ("Fair seed-time had my soul, and I grew up.") OnP

Childhood is when the mouth tastes earth. Childhood. Ned O'Gorman. PoPl

Childhood's Trials. Mrs. C. F. Alexander. ThGo

Childless Woman in Heaven, The. Katharine Tynan. BoC

Children are dumb to say how hot the day is. The Cool Web. Robert Graves. GTBS-P

Children are frightening. The Journey to Golotha. K. Raghavendra Rao. ACV

Children, behold the Chimpanzee. The Chimpanzee. Oliver Herford. FaBV

Children born of fairy stock. I'd Love to Be a Fairy's Child. Robert Graves. BiCB; SoPo

Children celebrate a failure and a treason, The. Fifth of November. K. W. Gransden. DaDu

Children, if you dare to think. Warning to Children. Robert Graves. PoIE

Children in the Market-Place. Henry van Dyke. TRV

Children look down upon the morning-grey. C. Day Lewis. BoC

Children of a Future Age. Blake. CBEP

Children of Light. Robert Lowell. AP; PoPl; ToPo

Children of light, The—mongoloid. The Bad Children. Carl Bode. ToPo

Children of the Poor, The, *sel.* Gwendolyn Brooks.

    "What shall I give my children? who are poor." PoCh

Children of the Wind. Carl Sandburg. WePo

Children picking up our bones. A Postcard from the Volcano. Wallace Stevens. AP

Children she had missed, The. The Childless Woman in Heaven. Katharine Tynan. BoC

Children sing in far Japan, The. Singing. Robert Louis Stevenson. ThGo

Children When They're Very Sweet. John Ciardi. BBGG

Children Won't Do What They Ought. Walther von der Vogelweide, *tr. fr. German by* Ruth Yorck *and* Kenward Elmslie. AnML

Children, you are very little. Good and Bad Children. Robert Louis Stevenson. BBGG; ThGo

Children's Crusade 1939. Bertolt Brecht, *tr. fr. German by* Michael Hamburger. MoBS

Children's Don't, A, *sel.* Harry Graham.

    "Don't tell Papa his nose is red." BBGG

Children's Hour, The. Longfellow. FaBV; FaPL; PoLF; PoPl

Children's Song. R. S.Thomas. BoC

Children's voices in the orchard. New Hampshire. T. S. Eliot. Landscapes, I. GTBS-P; LOW; PoSa

Child's Carol. Eleanor Farjeon. RePo

Child's Christmas Song, A. T. A. Daly. BiCB

Child's Day, A, *sel.* Walter de la Mare.

    Ann and the Fairy Song. FaBV

Child's Grace, A. Robert Herrick. *See* Another Grace for a Child.

Child's Laughter, A. Swinburne. BiCB; PoLF

Child's Power of Wonder, The. P. K. Saha. ACV

Child's Thought of God, A. Elizabeth Barrett Browning. TRV

Child's Thought of Harvest, A. "Susan Coolidge." PoSC

Chiliasm. Richard Eberhart. EaLo

Chime of the Sea, The. Dante Gabriel Rossetti. *See* Sea Limits, The.

Chimera, The. Dino Campana, *tr. fr. Italian by* Carlo L. Golino. CoIP

Chimera. Barbara Howes. MP

Chimes. Dante Gabriel Rossetti. OBNC
Chimney Sweeper, The ("A little black thing among the snow"). Blake. *Fr.* Songs of Experience. CABA; CBEP; EnPE; FoBA; PoIE
Chimney Sweeper, The ("When my mother died I was very young"). Blake. *Fr.* Songs of Innocence. CaFP; CBEP; DiPo; EnPE; FoBA; ILP; PoIE
Chimpanzee, The. Oliver Herford. FaBV
Chinese Ballad. William Empson. ToPo
Chinese Poem Written in B.C. 718, A ("The K'e still ripples to its banks"). *Unknown, tr. fr. Chinese.* WePo
Chinese Poem Written B.C. 1121, A ("White clouds are in the sky"). *Unknown, tr. fr. Chinese.* WePo
Chipmunk. Marie de L. Welch. RePo
Chipmunks jump, and. Valentine. Donald Hall. BoLP
Chippewa Stream, The, *with music. Unknown.* BSNS
Chivalry. "Æ." MoRP
"Chkk! chkk!" hopper-grass. Confucius. *Fr.* The Classic Anthology: Shao and the South. CTC
Chloe. *Unknown.* UnTE
Chloe found Amyntas lying. Rondelay [*or* Kiss Me, Dear]. Dryden. DiPo; UnTE
Chloe, the contours of your bust. To Chloe. Earnest Albert Hooton. UnTE
Chloe's a nymph in flowery grove. Chloe. *Unknown.* UnTE
Chloride of Lime and Charcoal. Louis Zukofsky. CoPo
Chloris' Eyes and Breasts ("Chloris! on thine eyes I gaz'd"). Giambattista Marino, *tr. fr. Italian by* Sir Edward Sherburne. RBL
Choice, The. Hilary Corke. MP
Choice. Angela Morgan. PoLF
Choice, The. Dorothy Parker. BoLP
Choice, The. Dante Gabriel Rossetti. The House of Life, LXXIII. GTBS-P
Choicest gifts at christenings, The. Gifts. Hazel Harper Harris. BiCB
Choir of spirits on a cloud, A. William Baylebridge. *Fr.* Life's Testament. PoAu-1
Choirmaster's Burial, The. Thomas Hardy. DTC
Choose. Verna Bishop. STF
Choose Something like a Star. Robert Frost. PoCh
Choose the darkest part o' the grove. A Spell. Dryden. *Fr.* Oedipus. WiR
Choose to be changed. Oh, experience the rapture of fire. Sonnets to Orpheus, II, 12. Rainer Maria Rilke. TwGP
Choose you this day whom you will serve. Choose. Verna Bishop. STF
Choosing a Mast. Roy Campbell. BoC; HaSV
Choosing Shoes. ffrida Wolfe. SoPo
Chop-Cherry. Robert Herrick. CBEP; UnTE
Chopping Fire-Wood. Robert Pack. NePoEA-2
Chorale: "Often had I found her fair." A. D. Hope. ErPo; UnTE
Choric Song: "There is sweet music here that softer falls." Tennyson. *Fr.* The Lotos-Eaters. OBNC
(There Is Sweet Music Here.) FaBV
"Hateful is the dark-blue sky," 1 *st.* HaSV
Choristers, The. Bliss Carman. ACV
Chorus: "Before the beginning of years." Swinburne. *See* Before the Beginning of Years.
Chorus: "Doom is dark and deeper than any sea-dingle." W. H. Auden. GTBS-P
Chorus: "Let us give ourselves to pleasure." Juan del Encina, *tr. fr. Spanish by* Beatrice Gilman Proske. RBL
Chorus: "Son of Man, behold with thine eyes, and hear with thine ears." T. S. Eliot. *Fr.* The Rock. PoDB
Chorus: "When love has passed its limits." Euripides, *tr. fr. Greek by* Frederic Prokosch. *Fr.* Medea. SiGo
Chorus: "When the hounds of spring are on winter's traces." Swinburne. *Fr.* Atalanta in Calydon. CTC; EvOK; GTBS-P; ILP; PoIE; PoSa
(Hounds of Spring, The.) FaBV
(When the Hounds of Spring.) VP
Chorus: "You have seen the house built, you have seen it adorned." T. S. Eliot. *Fr.* The Rock. PoDB
Chorus from "Atalanta." Swinburne. *See* Before the Beginning of Years.
Chorus of the Dead, The. Conrad Ferdinand Meyer, *tr. fr. German by* Meno Spann. AGP
Choruses Descriptive of Dido's States of Mind. Giuseppe Ungaretti, *tr. fr. Italian by* Lowry Nelson, Jr. *Fr.* The Promised Land. CoIP
Chou and the South, *sel.* Confucius, *tr. fr. Chinese by* Ezra Pound. *Fr.* The Classic Anthology.
"In the South be drooping trees." CTC
Chough, The ("The chough, said a dictionary"). James Reaney. OBCV
Christ. Theodore Holmes. CoPo
Christ, The. John Oxenham. TRV
Christ Alone. Shel Helsley. STF
Christ Alone. Theodore Monod. STF
Christ Calls Man Home. *Unknown.* MeEL
Christ! Christ! Christ! That the World. Kenneth Patchen. ToPo

Christ Church Bells. Henry Aldrich. CBEP
Christ Climbed Down. Lawrence Ferlinghetti. MoRP
Christ comes to mind and comes across the mind. Burns Singer. *Fr.* Sonnets for a Dying Man. NePoEA-2
Christ Complains to Sinners. *Unknown.* MeEL
Christ for Everything ("Christ for life, and Christ for living"). R. A. Belsham. STF
Christ God's red shadow hangs upon the wall. Christmas in Black Rock. Robert Lowell. ToPo
Christ has no hands but our hands. The World's Bible. Annie Johnson Flint. STF; TRV
Christ! I am Christ's! and let the name suffice you. Frederic W. H. Myers. *Fr.* Saint Paul. TRV
Christ in the Clay-Pit. Jack Clemo. GTBS-P
Christ in the Hospital. Roy Campbell. BoC
Christ in You. *Unknown.* STF
Christ Is Coming. W. Macomber. STF
Christ maketh to man a fair present. Love Unlike Love. *Unknown.* MeEL
Christ, My Beloved. William Baldwin. ELP
Christ, My Salvation ("Christ, my Lord, is my salvation"). Eva Gray. STF
Christ of his gentleness. In the Wilderness. Robert Graves. BoC
Christ of the Andes, The. Edwin Markham. SIV
Christ Our Lord. George Herbert. *See* Love ("Love bade me welcome, yet my soul drew back").
Christ Speaks. Gerard Manley Hopkins. *See* To Him Who Ever Thought with Love of Me.
Christ the dew in the clod. Johnny Appleseed's Hymn to the Sun. Vachel Lindsay. MoRP
Christ the Lord is risen today. Easter Hymn. Charles Wesley. TRV
Christ, Whose Glory Fills the Skies. Charles Wesley. ELP
Christ will prove the true attraction. Attraction. *Unknown.* STF
Christ with me, Christ before me, Christ behind me. Phyllis Garlick. *Fr.* St. Patrick. TRV
Christabel, *sel.* Samuel Taylor Coleridge.
Scars Remaining, The. OBNC
Christening, The. Walter de la Mare. BiCB
Christening, The. A. A. Milne. BiCB
Christening-Day Wishes for My God-Child, Grace Lane Berkley II. Robert P. Tristram Coffin. BiCB
Christian, seek not yet repose. Watch and Pray. Charlotte Elliott. STF
Christian Soldier, The, *sel.* G. A. Studdert-Kennedy.
"Peace does not mean the end of all our striving." TRV
Christians Reply to the Philosopher, The, *sel.* Sir William Davenant.
Life and Death. BoC
Christmas. John Betjeman. BoC; WePo
Christmas. Mary Mapes Dodge. BiCB
Christmas. Mother Goose. SoPo
Christmas Antiphones, *sel.* Swinburne.
"Thou whose birth on earth." TRV
Christmas at Babbitt's. Henry Hallam Tweedy. TRV
Christmas at Freelands. James Stephens. ILP
Christmas at Sea. Robert Louis Stevenson. FaBV; HaSV
Christmas Bells. Longfellow. *See* I Heard the Bells on Christmas Day.
Christmas Birthday. Grace Ellen Glaubitz. BiCB
Christmas cakes. Birthday Cake. Ivy O. Eastwick. BiCB
Christmas Candle, The. Kate Louise Brown. SoPo
Christmas Carol, A: "Angel told Mary, An." Harry Behn. BiCB
Christmas Carol, A: "Before the paling of the stars." Christina Rossetti. *See* Before the Paling of the Stars.
Christmas Carol, A: "Everywhere, everywhere, Christmas tonight!" Phillips Brooks. SoPo
Christmas Carol, A: "God bless the master of this house." *Unknown.* RePo
Christmas Carol, A: "Holly wreath that now, The." Fred Cogswell. ACV
Christmas Carol, A: "In the bleak mid-winter." Christina Rossetti.
(In the Bleak Mid-Winter.) BoC; TRV, abr.
(What Can I Give Him? abr.) ThGo
"What can I give Him?" *st.* 5. BiCB
Christmas Carol, A: "Star that shone on Bethlehem, shine on London city." Gilbert Thomas. MoRP
Christmas Caroll, A, Sung to the King in the Presence at White-Hall. Robert Herrick. GoJo
Christmas Childhood, A, *sel.* Patrick Kavanagh.
"My father played the melodion." DTC
Christmas Comes. Earle Birney. ACV
Christmas comes but once a year. Christmas. Mother Goose. SoPo
Christmas Cradlesong, A. Lope de Vega, *tr. fr. Spanish by* George Ticknor. PoPl
Christmas Dawn. Fleur Adcock. ACV
Christmas Day. Andrew Young. DaDu
Christmas Eve. St. Luke, II: 8-14, Bible, *N.T.* BiCB
(Angels of Bethlehem, The, II: 8-16.) BoC
(First Christmas, The, II: 8-16.) SoPo

Christmas Eve. Zoe Kincaid Brockman. PoNC
Christmas Eve. C. Day Lewis. EaLo
Christmas Eve. *Unknown.* TRV
Christmas Eve, and twelve of the clock. The Oxen. Thomas Hardy. CaFP; MoRP; PoDB; PoIE; PoSa; VP
Christmas Eve Legend. Frances Frost. BiCB
Christmas Eve under Hooker's Statue. Robert Lowell. AP; PoDB; ThLM
Christmas Folk-Song, A. Lizette Woodworth Reese. OnMSP; ThGo
Christmas Hymn, A. Richard Wilbur. CoPo; MoRP
Christmas in Black Rock. Robert Lowell. ToPo
Christmas in the Heart. *Unknown.* RePo
Christmas Is Coming. *Unknown.* SoPo
Christmas is in the air. Five Days Old. Francis Webb. PoAu-2
Christmas Is Remembering. Elsie Binns. BiCB
Christmas Lullaby for a New-born Child. Yvonne Gregory. AmNP
Christmas Morning. Elizabeth Madox Roberts. PoSC; RePo
Christmas Mourning. Vassar Miller. CoPo
Christmas 1945. Al Hine. ThLM
Christmas 1942. Eric Irvin. PoAu-2
Christmas Pageant. Margaret Fishback. PoSC
Christmas Sermon, A, *sel.* Robert Louis Stevenson. To Be Honest, to Be Kind. PoLF
Christmas Song. Bliss Carman. PoSC
Christmas Songs. Gerta Kennedy. PoPl
Christmas Sonnet, A. E. A. Robinson. EaLo; PoDB
Christmas twigs crispen and needles rattle, The. New Year's Poem. Margaret Avison. OBCV
Christmas was in the air and all was well. Karma. E. A. Robinson. AP; ILP
"Christo et Ecclesiae" 1700. Oliver Wendell Holmes. *Fr.* Two Sonnets: Harvard. AP
Christo Smarrito. Giambattista Marino, *tr. fr. Italian by* Sir Edward Sherburne. RBL
Christofero had a mind. The Great Discovery. Eleanor Farjeon. PoSC
Christopher Columbus. Stephen Vincent Benét. RePo
Christopher Columbus, *sels.* William Hart-Smith. PoAu-2
   Cipangu.
   Comes Fog and Mist.
   Departure.
   Space.
   Waterspout, The.
Christopher Robin goes. Hoppity. A. A. Milne. FaBV
Christ's Bondservant. George Matheson. STF; TRV
Christs Nativity. Henry Vaughan. MeP
Christs Returne out of Egypt. Robert Southwell. MeP
Christs Sleeping Friends. Robert Southwell. MeP
Christ's Tear Breaks My Heart. *Unknown.* MeEL
Christ's Victory and Triumph, *sel.* Giles Fletcher. He Is a Path. TRV
Chronos, Chronos, mend thy pace. The Secular Masque. Dryden. DiPo
"Chuff! chuff! chuff! An' a mountainbluff. A Song of Panama. Damon Runyon. ThLM
Chugachimute I Love the Name. Rochelle Owens. CoPo
Chunky together, the marchers blacken their way. May Day Demonstrators. Maurice Lindsay. ACV
Church, The. Edwin Muir. MoRP
Church Bell—Winter Time. Thad Stem, Jr. PoNC
Church do seem a touching sight, The. In Church. William Barnes. WePo
Church Going. Philip Larkin. AnMoPo; GTBS-P; ILP; MP; PoDB; PoIE; ToPo
Church in the Heart, The. Morris Abel Beer. TRV
"Church is dead, The," said brother Brown. The Pastor's Friend. *Unknown.* STF
Church-Lock and Key. George Herbert. MeP
Church-Monuments. George Herbert. CABA; FoBA; MeP; PoIE
Church-Musick. George Herbert. MeP
Church of the Holy Innocents, Dunedin. "Robin Hyde." ACV
Church Porch, The, *sels.* George Herbert.
   "Let vain or busy thoughts have there no part." TRV
   "Thou, whose sweet youth and early hopes inhance." MeP
Church Windows, The. George Herbert. *See* Windows, The.
Churches, lord, all the dark churches, The. Crag Jack's Apostasy. Ted Hughes. EaLo
Church's one foundation, The. Battle Hymn of the Spanish Rebellion. L. A. MacKay. OBCV
Churchyard leans to the sea with its dead, The. The Old Churchyard of Bonchurch. Philip Bourke Marston. OBNC
Churchyard on the Sands, The. Lord De Tabley. OBNC
Churl in spirit, up or down, The. In Memoriam A. H. H., CXI. Tennyson. VP
Cicada, The. H. M. Green. PoAu-1
Cicada-Shell. Basho, *tr. fr. Japanese.* SoPo
Cinderella. Cynthia Pickard. PoPl

Cinema, at the Lighthouse. Henri Coulette. *Fr.* The War of the Secret Agents. NePoEA-2
Cipangu. William Hart-Smith. *Fr.* Christopher Columbus. PoAu-2
Circlet, The. The Numbers. Joel Oppenheimer. CoPo
Circling months begin this day, The. The New Year's Gift to Phyllis. Matthew Prior. CBEP
Circumcision of Our Lord, The. *Unknown, tr. fr. French by* Daisy Aldan. AnML
Circumstance. Shelley. CBEP
Circus, The. Elizabeth Madox Roberts. SoPo
Circus Animals' Desertion, The. W. B. Yeats. DiPo; PoIE; PP
Circus Garland, A, *sels.* Rachel Field. SoPo
   Acrobat.
   Elephant, The.
   Girl on the Milk-white Horse, The.
   Next Day.
   Parade.
   Performing Seal, The.
Circus of battleships carrying heavy laughter, A. Celebrated Return. Clarence Major. AmNP
Circus Parade, The. Olive Beaupré Miller. SoPo
Citation and Examination of William Shakespeare, The, *sel.* Walter Savage Landor. Maid's Lament, The. OBNC
Cities and Thrones and Powers. Kipling. *Fr.* Puck of Pook's Hill. GoJo; OBNC
Citizen, The. Vilma Howard. NNP
Citizens in the Round. Robert P. Tristram Coffin. RePo
City Considered as a Tulip Tree, The. Carl Bode. *Fr.* London Sonnets. ToPo
City Council, *with music.* David G. Robinson. SGR
City Dead-House, The. Walt Whitman. FoBA
City has streets, The. City Streets and Country Roads. Eleanor Farjeon. SoPo
City in the Sea, The. Poe. AmLP; AP; CBEP; HaSV; ILP; PoIE
City, The: Midnight. Bruce Dawe. PoAu-2
City of Dreadful Night, The, *abr.* James Thomson. OBNC
   Sels.
   "Anear the centre of that northern crest," XVI. GTBS-P
   "He stood alone within the spacious square," IV. WiR
City of God. Samuel Johnson. TRV
City of Golf, The. Robert Fuller Murray. SD
City of Satisfactions, The. Daniel Hoffman. CoPo
City of the dead is zoned, The. Part-Time Tenant. Edna Meudt. FiSC
City of the End of Things, The. Archibald Lampman. OBCV
City Rain. Paul Bartlett. PoNC
City Rain. Rachel Field. SoPo
City shuffles through the snow, the whirling snow, and I, indifferent, The. Dead of Winter. Anthony Towne. StP
City Streets and Country Roads. Eleanor Farjeon. SoPo
City Trees. Edna St. Vincent Millay. RePo
City's steeple-towers remove away, The. On Leaving Bruges. Dante Gabriel Rossetti. CBEP
Civilities. Thomas Whitbread. SD
Civilized, crying how to be human again: this will tell you how. Signpost. Robinson Jeffers. PoPo
Clack your beaks you cormorants and kittiwakes. A Canticle to the Waterbirds. Brother Antoninus. StP
Clancy of the Overflow. A. B. Paterson. PoAu-1
Clap, clap the double nightcap on! William Gifford. Walter Savage Landor. GTBS-P
Clara. Ezra Pound. DTC
Clarel, *sel.* Herman Melville.
   Epilogue: "If Luther's day expand to Darwin's year." AP
Clarified into present. The Exchanges II. Robert Kelly. CoPo
Clash of arms which shook the Persian state, The. Abdolonymus the Sidonian. Jones Very. AP
Class Dismissed. *Unknown, tr. fr. Greek by* Louis Untermeyer. UnTE
Class Distinction. Schiller, *tr. fr. German by* Walter Kaufmann. TwGP
Classic Anthology, The, *sels.* Confucius, *tr. fr. Chinese by* Ezra Pound. CTC
   Airs of Pei, *sel.*
   Efficient Wife's Complaint, The.
   Chou and the South, *sel.*
   "In the South be drooping trees."
   Deer Sing, *sel.*
   Fraternitas.
   Shao and the South, *sels.*
   " 'Chkk! chkk!' hopper-grass."
   "Three stars, five stars rise over the hill."
   Songs of Ch'en, *sels.*
   Aliter.
   "Marsh bank, lotus rank."
   Songs of Cheng, *sels.*
   "Be kind, good sir, and I'll lift my sark."
   "Hep-Cat Chung, 'ware my town."
   "In chariot like an hibiscus flower at his side."

Classic Anthology, The, *sels.* (*continued*)
  "So he won't talk to me when we meet?"
  Songs of T'ang, *sel.*
    Alba.
  Wei Wind, *sel.*
    Pedlar.
  Yung Wind, *sels.*
    Baroness Mu Impeded in Her Wish to Help Famine Victims in Wei.
    Sans Equity and sans Poise.
Classic landscapes of dreams are not, The. The Snowfall. Donald Justice. NePoEA-2
Classic Waits for Me, A. E. B. White. Par
Claw-free love, when I was. Roc's Brood. Samuel M. Bradley. FiSC
Clayming a Second Kisse by Desert. Ben Jonson. *Fr.* A Celebration of Charis. SeCP
Clean Curtains. Carl Sandburg. LV
Clean Gentleman, The. George Abbe. FiSC
Cleaning Up. Edward Dyson. PoAu-1
Cleanly rush of the mountain air, The. The Dead Knight. John Masefield. GTBS-P
Clear and high, a mountain. The Hike. Neil Weiss. SD
Clear after Rain. Tu Fu, *tr. fr. Chinese by* Kenneth Rexroth. PoP1
Clear cool note of the cuckoo which has ousted the legitimate nest-holder, The. Sincere Flattery of W. W. (Americanus). J. K. Stephen. Par
Clear, fresh, and dulcet streams. Canzone. Petrarch. Sonnets to Laura: To Laura in Life, Canzone XIV. RBL
Clear Honor of the Liquid Element. Luis de Góngora, *tr. fr. Spanish by* Longfellow. RBL
  (Pride of the Fourth and Liquid Element, *tr. by* J. M. Cohen.) AnSP
Clear, placid Leman! thy contrasted lake. Lake Leman. Byron. *Fr.* Childe Harold's Pilgrimage. OBNC
Clear was the course of the cold floods. *Unknown. Fr.* The Destruction of Troy. HaSV
Clear water in a brilliant bowl. The Poems of Our Climate. Wallace Stevens. MP; PP
Clearing, The. LeRoi Jones. CoPo
Clearing at Dawn. Li T'ai-po, *tr. fr. Chinese by* Arthur Waley. SiGo
Cleo on the Section Gang. The Park. Robin Blaser. CoPo
Cleobulus' Epitaph. Simonides, *tr. fr. Greek by* Richmond Lattimore. PoP1
Cleon. Robert Browning. StP; VP
Cleopatra: The Barge She Sat In. Shakespeare. *Fr.* Antony and Cleopatra, II, ii. DiPo
Cleric Courts His Lady, A. *Unknown.* MeEL
Clerimont's Song. Ben Jonson. *See* Still to Be Neat.
Clerk Colven. *Unknown.* BuBa
Clerk Saunders. *Unknown.* CBEP; OnP
Clerk Ther Was of Cauntebrigge Also, A. W. W. Skeat. Par
Clerks, The. E. A. Robinson. CABA
Click Go the Shears, Boys. *Unknown.* PoAu-1
Clickety-clack. Song of the Train. David McCord. SoPo
Cliff Klingenhagen. E. A. Robinson. AP; CaFP
Cliffs that rise a thousand feet. Sailing Homeward. Chan Fang-sheng. SiGo
Clifton Grove, *sel.* Henry Kirke White.
  "Lo! in the West, fast fades the ling'ring light." OBNC
Climb. Winifred Welles. BiCB
Climb to Virtue, The. Simonides, *tr. fr. Greek by* C. M. Bowra. SiGo
Climbing in Glencoe. Andrew Young. SD
Climbing the beanstalk of your mind, I reach. High Kingdom. Howard Sergeant. ToPo
Clipper Ships and Captains. Stephen Vincent Benét. RePo
Clippity clop, clippity clop. The Milkman. Jane W. Krows. SoPo
Clock, The. Jean Jaszi. SoPo
Clock-a-Clay. John Clare. CBEP; OBNC
Clock stopped, A. Emily Dickinson. AP; CABA
Clod and the Pebble, The. Blake. *Fr.* Songs of Experience. CABA; CBEP; FaBV; OBNC
Clof, clop, clok. The Ailing Fountain. "Aldo Palazzeschi." CoIP
Clootie. *Unknown.* BuBa
Clorinda and Damon. Andrew Marvell. SeCP
Close eyes, bow head. *Unknown.* ThGo
Close, Mortal Eyes. Ruth Pitter. BoC
Close softly thine arms about me like a girdle. Endearments. Pierre Louÿs. *Fr.* The Songs of Bilitis. UnTE
Close to Me. "Gabriela Mistral," *tr. fr. Spanish by* Langston Hughes. PoP1
Close-wrapped in living thought I stand. All-Souls' Day. Siegfried Sassoon. MoRP
Close Your Eyes! Arna Bontemps. AmNP
Closing Cadence. John Moffit. MoRP
Closing of the Rodeo, The. William Jay Smith. MP; RePo; SD
Closing Time. James Michie. NePoEA-2

Clote, The. William Barnes. ELP
Clothes. Frances Frost. RePo
Clothes Do but Cheat and Cozen Us. Robert Herrick. ErPo
Cloud, The. Shelley. CBEP; PoIE; RePo
Cloud and Flame. John Berryman. AP
Cloud and Wind. Dante Gabriel Rossetti. The House of Life, XLIV. VP
Cloud-backed heron will not move, The. The Heron. Vernon Watkins. GTBS-P; MP
Cloud-capp'd towers, the gorgeous palaces, The. Shakespeare. *Fr.* The Tempest, IV, i. PoP1
Cloud moved close, A. The bulk of the wind shifted. The Visitant. Theodore Roethke. PoIE
Cloud of dust on the long, white road, A. The Teams. Henry Lawson. PoAu-1
Cloud only goes, A. Clouds. Jean Jaszi. RePo
Cloud-puffball, torn tufts, tossed pillows. That Nature Is a Heraclitean Fire and of the Comfort of the Resurrection. Gerard Manley Hopkins. CABA; DiPo; GTBS-P
Clouded Morning, The. Jones Very. AP
Clouds. Dorothy Aldis. SoPo
Clouds. Rupert Brooke. BoC
Clouds. Jean Jaszi. RePo
Clouds. Shakespeare. *Fr.* The Tempest, IV, i. BoC
Clouds. *Unknown.* SoPo
Clouds on the mountain. On a Mountain Road. Wu Ch'ing-jen. SiGo
Clouds, which rise with thunder, slake, The. All's Well. Whittier. CBEP
Clover-burr was two feet high, and the billabongs were full, The. Irish Lords. Charles H. Souter. PoAu-1
Clover for Breakfast. Frances Frost. RePo
Clown, The. Mary Catherine Rose. SoPo
Clowns. Louis MacNeice. DaDu
Clowns in a garish air. On panicky pedals. The Necromancers. John Frederick Nims. PoCh
Clown's Song, The. Shakespeare. *Fr.* Twelfth Night. *See* Come Away, Come Away, Death.
Clustering rainbow-grapes. Balloon Man. Jessica N. North. SoPo
Coachman's Yarn, The. E. J. Brady. PoAu-1
Coal for Mike. Bertolt Brecht, *tr. fr. German by* H. R. Hays. PoP1
Coarse/ jocosity. Archy Confesses. Don Marquis. *Fr.* Archy and Mehitabel. EvOK
Cobb Would Have Caught It. Robert Fitzgerald. MP; SD
Cobbler, The. Eleanor Alletta Chaffee. SoPo
Cobwebbery. Jonathan Williams. PoNC
Cock Again, The. Kikaku, *tr. fr. Japanese by* Harold G. Henderson. SoPo
Cock and the Bull, The. Charles Stuart Calverley. Par
Cock Crow. Edward Thomas. GTBS-P
Cock-crowing. Henry Vaughan. MeP
Cock is crowing, The. The Merry Month of March [*or* Written in March]. Wordsworth. EvOK; GoJo; SoPo
Cockies of Bungaree. *Unknown.* PoAu-1
Cockles and Mussels. *Unknown.* ELP
Cocks crow. What They Do. Eleanor Farjeon. ThGo
Cocoon. David McCord. PoPo
Cocooning, The. Frédéric Mistral, *tr. fr. Provençal by* Harriet Waters Preston. *Fr.* Mirèio. PoP1
Cocteau's *Opium*: 1. Donald Finkel. CoPo
Cocteau's *Opium*: 2. Donald Finkel. CoPo
Coffee-cups cool on the Vicar's harmonium. A Game of Consequences. Paul Dehn. ErPo
Coffee-House Lecture, A. Robert Mezey. CABA
Coin, The. Sara Teasdale. LV; RePo
Coin from Bir el Abbas. Peter Huchel, *tr. fr. German by* Christopher Middleton. MGP
Coins and Coffins under My Bed. Diane Wakoski. CoPo
Cold Are the Crabs. Edward Lear. GoJo
Cold as the breath of winds that blow. Lucasta's World. Richard Lovelace. SeCP
"Cold coming we had of it, A." Journey of the Magi. T. S. Eliot. BoC; CaFP; DiPo; DTC; EaLo; FoBA; ILP; MoRP; MP; PoIE; PoPo; PoSa; WePo
Cold Divinities, The. James Wright. AmPC
Cold eyelids that hide like a jewel. Dolores. Swinburne. VP
Cold Fact. Dick Emmons. PoP1
Cold Green Element, The. Irving Layton. OBCV
Cold Heaven, The. W. B. Yeats. CTC; GTBS-P
Cold in the earth—and the deep snow piled above thee. Remembrance. Emily Brontë. OBNC; PoIE
Cold Iron. Kipling. OnMSP
Cold Logic. Barney Hutchinson. SD
Cold Spring, A. Elizabeth Bishop. MP; StP
Cold Wind Blows, A. Zoe Kincaid Brockman. PoNC
Coldest day in all the year, The. The Smithfield Market Fire. Fred Dallas. WePo
Coldly, sadly descends. Rugby Chapel—November, 1857. Matthew Arnold. CBEP; VP
Cole, that unwearied prince of Colchester. Variations of an Air: After Lord Tennyson. G. K. Chesterton. Par

Cole Younger, *with music. Unknown.* BFSS
Colin. Anthony Munday. *See* Beauty Sat Bathing.
Colin Clout's Come Home Again. Spenser. CABL
  "So to the sea we came; the sea? that is," *sel.* HaSV
Coliseum, The. Poe. AP
Collages and Compositions. Richmond Lattimore. PP
Collar, The. George Herbert. CABA; CaFP; CBEP; EaLo;
  FaPL; FoBA; ILP; MeP; OnP; PoIE; SeCP; StP
Collar-Bone of a Hare, The. W. B. Yeats. AnMoPo
Collector, The. Raymond Souster. ErPo; OBCV
Collier, The. Vernon Watkins. DaDu; DTC
Colloquy in Black Rock. Robert Lowell. AP; PoDB
Colly, My Cow. *Unknown.* EvOK
Colombine. Hugh McCrae. PoAu-1
Colonel B. Afforestation. E. A. Wodehouse. SD
Colonial Set. Alfred Goldsworthy Bailey. OBCV
Colonist in His Garden, A. William Pember Reeves. ACV
Color. Melville Cane. RePo
Color. Christina Rossetti. *Fr.* Sing-Song. SoPo
  (What Is Pink?) GoJo
Color—caste—denomination. Emily Dickinson. EaLo
Color of Cold, The. André Pieyre de Mandiargues, *tr. fr.*
  French by Donald Justice. CoFP
Color of stone when leaves are yellow, The. Autumn. Wil-
  liam Jay Smith. RePo
Color of walls of scratches of cracks of brightness. The
  Aelf-scin, the Shining Scimmer the Gleam, the Shining.
  Michael McClure. CoPo
Colors. Luigi Bartolini, *tr. fr. Italian by* Carlo L. Golino.
  CoIP
Colors we depend on are, The. The Love Bit. Joel Oppen-
  heimer. CoPo
Colossians III:3: Our Life Is Hid with Christ in God. George
  Herbert. FoBA
Colossus, The. Sylvia Plath. MP; NePoEA-2
Colours of the setting sun, The. The Sliprails and the Spur.
  Henry Lawson. PoAu-1
Columbiad, The, *sel.* Joel Barlow.
  One Centred System. AP
Columbine, The. Jones Very. AP
Columbus. Arthur Hugh Clough. PoSC
Columbus. Joaquin Miller. PoPo; SIV; ThLM
Columbus looks towards the New World. Space. William
  Hart-Smith. *Fr.* Christopher Columbus. PoAu-2
Com home againe! Christ Calls Man Home. *Unknown.*
  MeEL
Combe, The ("The combe was ever dark, ancient and dark").
  Edward Thomas. GTBS-P; PoIE
Combination XI. Helmut Heissenbüttel, *tr. fr. German by*
  Christopher Middleton. MGP
Come again to the place. After the Visit. Thomas Hardy.
  OBNC
Come, all of you bold rangers. Bold Rangers. *Unknown.*
  BFSS
Come all old maids that are squeamish. Eurynome. Jay
  Macpherson. OBCV
Come all who desire to hear of a jest. The Foolish Miller.
  Unknown. UnTE
Come all ye brave Americans and unto me give ear. Major
  André. *Unknown.* BFSS
Come all ye human countrymen, with pity lend an ear.
  Charles Augustus Anderson. *Unknown.* BSNS
Come all ye jolly tarsmen, come listen to my song. Kelly the
  Pirate (A *vers.*). *Unknown.* BSNS
Come all ye men and maidens and listen to my song. The
  Maid of the Mountain Brow. *Unknown.* BSNS
Come all ye merry huntsmen. The Ranger (A *vers.*). *Un-
  known.* BSO
Come, all ye merry sportsmen. The Ranger (B *vers.*). *Un-
  known.* BSO
Come all ye rounders if you want to hear. *See* Come all you
  rounders . . .
Come, All Ye Roving Rangers, *with music. Unknown.* BSO
Come, all ye seamen bold. Admiral Benbow. *Unknown.* CBEP
Come all ye sons of Brittany. Braddock's Fate, with an
  Incitement to Revenge. Stephen Tilden. ThLM
Come all ye tender-hearted people. Garfield's Murder. *Un-
  known.* ThLM
Come, all ye young and foolish lads. The Shrewd Maiden.
  Unknown. BSO
Come, all ye young hunters that follow the gun. Polly Band.
  Unknown. BSO
Come all you aged people, I pray you lend an ear. When the
  Battle It Was Won. *Unknown.* BSNS
Come, all you belles and beaux. Courting in the Kitchen.
  Unknown. BSNS
Come, all you bold Americans, I pray you now draw near.
  Major Andrews' Execution. *Unknown.* BSNS
Come all you bold heroes that plough the rough main. Bold
  Dighton (A *vers.*). *Unknown.* BSNS
Come all you bold seamen that ploughs the rough main. The
  Tiger and the *Lion. Unknown.* BSNS
Come, all you bold shanty boys. The Jam at [*or* on] Gerry's
  Rock[s]. *Unknown.* BFSS; BSNS

Come, all you brave gallants, and listen a while. Robin Hood
  and the Butcher. *Unknown.* BuBa
Come all you brisk and lively lads, come listen unto me. The
  Plains of Waterloo (A *vers.*). *Unknown.* BSNS
Come all you Britons, I pray give ear. The Heights of Alma.
  Unknown. BSNS
Come all you Californians, I pray open wide your ears. Cross-
  ing the Plains. John A. Stone. SGR
Come, All You Fair Maidens ("Come, all you fair and tender
  ladies"), *with music. Unknown.* BFSS
Come all you gallant bushrangers and outlaws of disdain.
  Jack Donahue. *Unknown.* BSNS
Come, all you good people, wherever you be. A Song on the
  Death of Colonel Crafford. *Unknown.* BSO
Come, all you jolly buffalo skinners, and listen to my song.
  The Buffalo Skinners. *Unknown.* BFSS; ThLM
Come all you jolly sailors bold. The Rocks of Scilly. *Un-
  known.* BSNS
Come all you jolly travellers that's out of work, just mind.
  Cockies of Bungaree. *Unknown.* PoAu-1
Come all you jovial sailors bold. Jolly Sailors Bold. *Un-
  known.* BSNS
Come all you lads bound over the deep, I hope you will attend.
  By the Lightning We Lost Our Sight. *Unknown.* BSNS
Come, all you little Runabouts. A Tract for Autos. Arthur
  Guiterman. RePo
Come, all you Mississippi girls, and listen to my noise.
  Mississippi Girls. *Unknown.* BFSS
Come all you old, both great and small, attend unto my fame.
  My Father's Servant Boy. *Unknown.* BSNS
Come all you old men all. Quebec. *Unknown.* BSNS
Come all you people far and near. The Rose of Britain's Isle.
  Unknown. BSNS
Come, all you [*or* ye] rounders, if you want to hear. Casey
  Jones. *Unknown.* FaBV, *arr. by* T. Lawrence Seibert;
  PoPo; ThLM
Come, all you tender Christians. Charles Guiteau; or, The
  Murder of James A. Garfield. *Unknown.* BFSS; BSO
Come, all you Texas Rangers. The Texas Rangers. *Unknown.*
  BFSS
Come all you true-born shanty boys, wherever you may be.
  Geary's Rock. *Unknown.* SIV
Come all you true Irish boys, please listen to me. Morrissey
  and the Black. *Unknown.* BSNS
Come all you young fellows that carry a gun. At the Setting
  of the Sun. *Unknown.* CBEP
Come all you young people and listen to my song. The Young
  Man Who Wouldn't Plow Corn. *Unknown.* BFSS
Come, all you young people, I pray you draw near. Arizona
  Boys and Girls. *Unknown.* BFSS
Come, all young men and maidens, attend unto my rhyme.
  Caroline of Edinburgh [*or* Edinboro *or* Edinborough]
  Town. *Unknown.* BFSS; BSNS; BSO
Come, all young men, I will tell you now. The Lazy Man.
  Unknown. BSO
Come, all young men, pay strict attention. True Lover. *Un-
  known.* BSO
Come along, boys, and listen to my tale. The Old Chisholm
  Trail. *Unknown.* BFSS
Come and sit down and I'll sing you a ditty. The Lady's Fan.
  Unknown. BSNS
Come apace, good Audrey. I will fetch up your goats, Audrey.
  Shakespeare. *Fr.* As You Like It. PP
Come away. Dooms-Day. George Herbert. SeCP
Come Away, Come Away, Death. Shakespeare. *Fr.* Twelfth
  Night, II, iv. CBEP; FoBA; ILP
  (Clown's Song, The.) CTC
  (Come Away Death.) DiPo; ELP
  (Dirge of Love.) GTBS-P; VaPo
  (Feste's Song.) ELP
Come Away, Come, Sweet Love. *Unknown.* EnRePo
  (To His Love.) ELP
Come Away Death. Shakespeare. *See* Come Away, Come
  Away, Death.
"Come back at dead of night and speak to me." The Two
  Societies. John Hall Wheelock. PoCh
Come back before the birds are flown. The Recall. James
  Russell Lowell. AP
Come back to me, who wait and watch for you. Monna Inno-
  minata, I. Christina Rossetti. VP
Come, Bewitcher! *Unknown, tr. fr. Spanish by* William M.
  Davis. AnML
Come, brothers! rally for the right! The Bonnie Blue Flag.
  Annie Chambers Ketchum. ThLM
Come, Chloe, and Give Me Sweet Kisses. Charles Hanbury
  Williams. UnTE
Come, come, what doe I here? Henry Vaughan. MeP
Come dally me, darling, dally me with kisses. Psyche to Cupid:
  Her Ditty. James Broughton. ErPo
Come, dear children, let us away. The Forsaken Merman.
  Matthew Arnold. CBEP; HaSV; VP
Come, Death, I'd have a word with thee. Motley. Walter de
  la Mare. MMA

Come, Death—My Lady Is Dead.   Charles d'Orléans(?).
MeEL
Come down, dear love, be quick. A Lover's Words. Vernon
Watkins. DTC
Come down, O Christ and help me! reach thy hand. E Tene-
bris. Oscar Wilde. CABA
Come Down, O Maid [from Yonder Mountain Height].
Tennyson. Fr. The Princess, Pt. VII. CABA; CaFP;
CBEP; DiPo; FoBA; GTBS-P; OBNC
Come, fill the Cup, and in the fire of Spring. Omar Khayyám,
tr. by Edward Fitzgerald. Fr. The Rubáiyát. FaBV; LV
Come, Follow Me. Thomas Campion. EnRePo
Come, freighted heart, within this port. Lovemusic. Carolyn
Kizer. ErPo
Come from a distant country. At Birth. Anthony Thwaite.
NePoEA-2
Come, gentle Spring—ethereal mildness come. Spring. James
Thomson. Fr. The Seasons. EiCP
Come, gentlemen all, and listen a while. Robin Hood and the
Bishop of Hereford. Unknown. BuBa; SIV
Come Green Again. Winfield Townley Scott. PoPl
Come . . . have do with dillying. Shrine to What Should Be.
Mari Evans. NNP
Come hither all sweet maidens soberly. On an Engraved Gem
of Leander. Keats. CBEP
Come hither, Evan Cameron! The Execution of Montrose.
William Edmonstoune Aytoun. OnMSP
Come Hither, My Dear One. John Clare. BoLP; ELP
Come Hither, You That Love. John Fletcher. ELP
Come, Holy Ghost, our souls inspire. John Cosins, ad. fr.
Latin. BoC
Come Hymen come, for here to thee we bring. Wedding Hymn.
Luis de Góngora. Fr. The Solitudes. AnSP; RBL
Come In. Robert Frost. DiPo; FaBV; FoBA; PoIE; WePo
"Come in an' sit ye down," old Gruda said. Second Sight.
H. S. Neill. FiSC
Come into Animal Presence. Denise Levertov. AP
Come into the Garden, Maud. Tennyson. Fr. Maud. BoLP;
CBEP; FaBV; PoIE
Come, January, I Give You These Treats. Folgore da San
Geminiano, tr. fr. Italian by Joy Gould. Fr. Sonnets of the
Months. AnML
Come, John sit thee down, I have somewhat to say. An
Amorous Dialogue between the Mistris and Her Aprentice.
Unknown. UnTE
Come, ladies and gentlemen, listen to my song. Down on
Roberts' Farm. Claude Reeves. ThLM
Come lasses and lads. May-Pole Dance. Unknown. WePo
Come leave the loathed stage. Ode to Himselfe. Ben Jonson.
SeCP
Come! let us draw the curtains. Autumn. Humbert Wolfe.
PoLF
Come, let us join our friends above. The Ever-living Church.
Charles Wesley. STF
Come, let us pity those who are better off than we are. The
Garret. Ezra Pound. PoPl
Come, let us plant the apple tree. Bryant. Fr. The Planting
of the Apple Tree. PoSC
Come, Let Us Sing, with music. Unknown. BFSS
Come, Let Us Taste Delight. Charles d'Orléans, tr. fr. French
by Muriel Kittel. AnML
Come, listen all unto my song. How Cyrus Laid the Cable.
John Godfrey Saxe. SIV
Come listen, come listen, young people all. Little Golden.
Unknown. BSO
Come listen, good people, to accommodate. The Silk Merchant's
Daughter. Unknown. BFSS
Come, listen to a ranger, you kindhearted stranger. The Dis-
heartened Ranger. Unknown. BFSS
Come listen to me, you gallants so free. Robin Hood and Alan
a Dale. Unknown. BuBa
Come, Little Babe. Nicholas Breton. PoIE
"Come, little cottage girl, you seem." The Poets at Tea, 6.
Barry Pain. Par
Come, little Drummer Boy, lay down your knapsack here. The
Soldiers' Friend. George Canning and John Hookham
Frere. Par
Come live and be merry. Laughing Song. Blake. Fr. Songs
of Innocence. SoPo
Come, Live with Me and Be My Love. C. Day Lewis. ILP;
StP
Come live with me and be my love. The Bait[e]. John Donne.
CABA; DiPo; ErPo; ILP; SD; StP
Come live with me, and be my love. The Passionate Shepherd
to His Love. Christopher Marlowe. BoLP; CABA;
CaFP; CBEP; CTC; DiPo; ELP; GTBS-P; ILP; OnP;
PoIE; PoLF; PoPo; PoSa; StP; UnTE; WePo
Come live with me and be my wife. A Modern Romance. Paul
Engle. PoPl
Come lovely and soothing death. Death Carol [or The Carol of
the Bird]. Walt Whitman. Fr. When Lilacs Last in the
Dooryard Bloom'd. LV; MoRP

Come, Madam, come, all rest my powers defy [or defie]. To
His Mistress Going to Bed [or Elegy XIX: Going to Bed].
John Donne. Fr. Elegies. EnRePo; ErPo; FoBA; SeCP;
UnTE
Come Mamina. Umamina. B. W. Vilikazi. SiGo
Come, Muse, migrate from Greece and Ionia. Walt Whitman.
Fr. Song of the Exposition. PP
Come, My Celia. Ben Jonson. Fr. Volpone. CABA; FaBV
("Come, my Celia, let us prove.") EnRePo
(Song to Celia.) ErPo; SeCP
(To Celia.) UnTE
Come, my fine cat, against my loving heart. The Cat. Baude-
laire. PoPl
Come, my friends. Tennyson. Fr. Ulysses. TRV
Come, my songs, let us express our baser passions. Further
Instructions. Ezra Pound. MP
Come Night, Come Romeo. Shakespeare. Fr. Romeo and
Juliet, III, ii. BoLP
Come not the earliest petal here, but only. Quiet. Marjorie
Pickthall. OBCV
Come not, when I am dead. Go By. Tennyson. OBNC
Come now behold. The Glory of and Grace in the Church Set
Out. Edward Taylor. Fr. Gods Determinations. AP
Come, now, my friends, come lend attention. The Green Fields
and Meadows (A vers.). Unknown. BSO
Come now, you who carry. A Coffee-House Lecture. Robert
Mezey. CABA
Come, O world's comfort, silent night. The Hermit. Joseph
von Eichendorff. TwGP
Come o'er the hills, and pass unto the wold. A Winter Hymn
—to the Snow. Ebenezer Jones. OBNC
Come On In. Unknown. SD
Come Out, Come Out, Ye Souls That Serve. Christopher
Brennan. Fr. The Wanderer. PoAu-1
Come out for a while and look from the outside in. Christmas
Eve. C. Day Lewis. EaLo
Come out o' door, 'tis Spring! 'tis May. May. William
Barnes. PoSC
"Come out with me!" cried the little red sled. The Little Red
Sled. Jocelyn Bush. SoPo
Come rede me, dame, come tell me, dame. Nine Inch Will
Please a Lady. Burns. ErPo
Come, rouse up, ye bold-hearted Whigs of Kentucky. Old
Tippecanoe. Unknown. ThLM
Come, Sable Night. Unknown. EnRePo
Come sapless blossom, creep not stil on earth. The Sap. Henry
Vaughan. MeP
Come, set thee down by these cool streams. Then Lose in Time
Thy Maidenhead. Unknown. ErPo
Come, Shepherds, Come. John Fletcher. Fr. The Faithful
Shepherdess, I, iii. ErPo
Come sit aneath this pinetree, whose lofty tressèd crown.
Country Music. Plato. SiGo
Come, Sleep ("Come, Sleep, and with thy sweet deceiving").
Beaumont and Fletcher. Fr. The Woman-Hater, III, i.
ELP
Come sleep! O sleep, the certain knot of peace. Astrophel and
Stella, XXXIX. Sir Philip Sidney. CABA; CBEP;
EnRePo; FaPL; PoIE; StP
Come slowly, Eden. Emily Dickinson. UnTE
Come, sons of summer, by whose toil[e]. The Hock-Cart; or,
Harvest Home. Robert Herrick. SeCP; StP
Come, Spirit of Thy Holy Love. My Heart's Desire. Un-
known. STF
Come, Stumpy, old man, we must shift while we can. The
Broken-down Squatter. Unknown. PoAu-1
Come then, and like two Doves with silv'rie wings. The
Apparition of His Mistresse Calling Him to Elizium.
Robert Herrick. SeCP
Come to me broken dreams and all. The Still Voice of Harlem.
Conrad Kent Rivers. NNP
Come to me in my dreams, and then. Longing. Matthew
Arnold. Faded Leaves, V. CBEP; PoLF; VP
Come to me in the silence of the night. Echo. Christina
Rossetti. ELP; OBNC; VP
Come to Me Soon. Sir Walter Ralegh. UnTE
Come to our well-run desert. W. H. Auden. Fr. For The
Time Being. TRV
Come to the judgment, golden threads. The Judgment of the
May. Richard Watson Dixon. OBNC
Come to your heaven you heavenly quires. New Heaven, New
Warre. Robert Southwell. MeP
Come unto Me ("Come unto Me, said Jesus"). Flora Osgood.
STF
Come unto Me (" 'Come unto Me,' said One below"). John
Stuart. STF
Come unto These Yellow Sands. Shakespeare. Fr. The
Tempest, I, ii. CBEP; PoIE
(Ariel's Song.) CTC; GoJo
Come Up from the Fields Father. Walt Whitman. PoPo
Come Visit My Garden. Tom Dent. NNP
Come, we shepherds, whose blest sight. In the Holy Nativity

of Our Lord God, a Hymn Sung as by the Shepherds [*or* An Hymne of the Nativity]. Richard Crashaw. CABA; MeP

Come, when no graver cares employ. To the Rev. F. D. Maurice. Tennyson. GTBS-P

"Come, wife," said good old Farmer Gray. The Little Dog under the Wagon. *Unknown.* PoLF

Come with bird's voices when the light grows dim. The Holy Spirit. Evelyn Underhill. BoC

Come with rain, O loud Southwester! To the Thawing Wind. Robert Frost. LOW

Come, Woeful Orpheus. *Unknown.* EnRePo

Come, worthy Greek, Ulysses, come. Ulysses and the Siren. Samuel Daniel. CABA; EnRePo; HaSV; StP

Come, ye fair, ambrosial flowers. A Nosegay for Laura. Francis Fawkes. WaPE

Come ye hither all, whose taste. The Invitation. George Herbert. MeP

Come, You Pretty False-eyed Wanton. Thomas Campion. ELP; StP

Comes a cry from Cuban water. Cuba Libre. Joaquin Miller. ThLM

Comes a dun in the morning and raps at my door. The Poet and the Dun. William Shenstone. PP

Comes Easter, Ah, without Him. *Unknown, tr. fr. Spanish by* William M. Davis. AnML

Comes Fog and Mist. William Hart-Smith. *Fr.* Christopher Columbus. PoAu-2

Comes the time. Algonkian Burial. Alfred Goldsworthy Bailey. OBCV

Comes the time when it's later. A Wicker Basket. Robert Creeley. AmPC; ToPo

Comes to knock and knock again. Galileo Galilei. William Jay Smith. PoCh

Comfort. Elizabeth Barrett Browning. TRV

Comfort but a queer companion, A. Woman. *Unknown.* UnTE

Comfort for the Sleepless. H. C. Bradby. BoC

Comfort me with stars, not apples. Star Drill. T. Inglis Moore. PoAu-2

Comfort When Work Seems Difficult. Isaiah, XLI: 6-7, 9-10, Bible, *O.T.* BoC

Comfort Ye, Comfort Ye My People. Isaiah, XL: 1-11, Bible, *O.T.* EaLo

Comfortable Apple Trees, The. Grace Taber Hallock. RePo

Comforted. Amy Carmichael. TRV

Comforting Lines. *Unknown.* STF

Comin' thro' the Rye. Burns. UnTE

Coming, The. Anthony Delius. ACV

Coming and the Appearing, The. *Unknown.* STF

Coming around the Horn, *with music.* John A. Stone. SGR

Coming Child, The. Richard Crashaw. TRV

Coming down the mountain in the twilight. Where the Hay-fields Were. Archibald MacLeish. LOW

Coming Forth by Day of Osiris Jones, The, *sel.* Conrad Aiken. Nursery, The. LOW

Coming Home. Rolfe Humphries. MoRP

Coming Homeward Out of Spain. Barnabe Googe. EnRePo

Coming into the store at first angry. The Man Who Finds That His Son Has Become a Thief. Raymond Souster. OBCV

Coming late, as always. The Poem. W. S. Merwin. PP

Coming of Good Luck, The. Robert Herrick. CBEP

Coming of Spring, The. Nora Perry. SoPo

Coming of Wisdom with Time, The. W. B. Yeats. DiPo

Coming up England by a different line. I Remember, I Remember. Philip Larkin. AnMoPo

Comings and Goings, *sels.* Jean Follain, *tr. fr. French by* Dori Katz. CoFP
"Should the stroller absentmindedly kick."
"Sound of the wind revives former days, The."

Commemorative of a Naval Victory. Herman Melville. AP

Commission. Ezra Pound. MP

Commissioner bet me a pony, The—I won. Songs of the Squatters. Robert Lowe. PoAu-1

Common Bill (A *vers., with music*). *Unknown.* BSO

Common Dust. Georgia Douglas Johnson. AmNP

Common Ground, A, *sel.* Denise Levertov.
"Not 'common speech.'" PP

Common speech, The, is, spend and God will send. Gascoigne's Memories, III. George Gascoigne. EnRePo

Commotion of these waves, however strong, cannot disturb. Louis Dudek. *Fr.* Europe. OBCV

Communal. Mary Fullerton. PoAu-1

Communique, I, *sel.* John William Corrington.
"Life at the peak of the Radiant Days." PtTo

Companion Fear is at my side. The News. "Sec." TRV

Companion me. Closing Cadence. John Moffit. MoRP

Companions. Margaret Widdemer. FiSC

Companions were we in the grove and glen! Sonnets, Part II, VIII. Frederick Goddard Tuckerman. AP

Companionship. Maltbie D. Babcock. STF

Company of boatmen I'll have you to know, A. Jacket So Blue; or, A Company of Boatmen. *Unknown.* BFSS

Comparison, The. John Donne. ErPo

Comparison. Mary Ann Hoberman. BiCB

Comparison, A. *Unknown.* STF

Compass Needle, A. Francis Quarles. CBEP

Compasses, The. George MacBeth. NePoEA-2

Compassionate Fool, The. Norman Cameron. CBEP; GTBS-P

Compatience perses, reuth and marcy stoundes. The Passion of Jesus. *Unknown.* MeEL

Compelled to Love. Walter Stone. ErPo

Compensation. Paul Laurence Dunbar. AmNP

Compensation. Emerson. AP

Complacencies of the peignoir, and late. Sunday Morning. Wallace Stevens. AmLP; AP; CABA; CABL; CaFP; OnP; PoDB; PoIE; StP

Complacent Cliff-Dweller, The. Margaret Fishback. PoLF

Complains, Being Hind'red the Sight of His Nymph. Girolamo Preti, *tr. fr. Italian by* Philip Ayres. RBL

Complaint. Joseph Bennett. StP

Complaint. Ted Hughes. PoDB

Complaint. Rainer Maria Rilke, *tr. fr. German by* Michael Hamburger. MGP

Complaint, A. Wordsworth. CBEP

Complaint, The; or, Night Thoughts on Life, Death and Immortality, *sel.* Edward Young.
"Tired Nature's sweet restorer, balmy Sleep!" Night I. EnPE

Complaint of a Lover Rebuked. Petrarch, *tr. by the Earl of* Surrey. *See* Love That Liveth and Reigneth in My Thought.

Complaint of Rosamond, The, *sel.* Samuel Daniel.
Lonely Beauty. CTC

Complaint of the Absence of Her Lover Being upon the Sea. Earl of Surrey. ELP

Complaint of the Fair Armouress [*or* Armoress], The. Villon, *tr. fr. French by* Swinburne. CTC; UnTE
(Lament of the Lovely Helmet-Dealer, *tr. by* Hubert Creekmore.) ErPo
(Old Woman Laments the Days of Her Youth, The, *tr. by* Muriel Kittel.) AnML

Complaint of the Morpethshire Farmer, The. Basil Bunting. CTC

Complaint of the Weavers. Chrétien de Troyes, *tr. fr. French by* Daisy Aldan. *Fr.* Yvain. AnML

Complaint of Troilus, The. Chaucer. *Fr.* Troilus and Criseyde, V. DiPo

Complaint That His Ladie after She Knew of His Love Kept Her Face Alway Hidden from Him. Earl of Surrey. PoIE

Complaint to His Purse. Chaucer. CABA
(Compleynt of Chaucer to His Purse, The.) PoIE
(Song to His Purse for the King, A.) MeEL

Compleat Swimmer, The. Charles Edward Eaton. PoNC

Composed at Neidpath Castle, the Property of Lord Queensberry 1803. Wordsworth. GTBS-P

Composed at thirty, my funeral oration: Here lies. A Funeral Oration. David Wright. MP

Composed in Spring. Burns. CBEP

Composed in the Tower before his execution. "More Light! More Light!" Anthony Hecht. NePoEA-2

Composed upon Westminster Bridge, September 3, 1802. Wordsworth. CABA; CaFP; CBEP; DiPo; FaBV; FoBA; ILP; OBNC; PoIE; PoLF; PoPl; PoPo; VaPo; WePo
(Upon Westminster Bridge.) GTBS-P; PoSa; StP

Composed While under Arrest. Mikhail Yuryevich Lermontov, *tr. fr. Russian by* Max Eastman. SiGo

Composer, The. W. H. Auden. PoPo

Composition of Pat Young, The. Pat Young. Kenneth Mackenzie. PoAu-2

Computation, The. John Donne. DiPo

Comrade in Arms. T. Inglis Moore. PoAu-2

Comrades in Arms: Conversation Piece. *Unknown.* ErPo

Comrades, leave me here a little, while as yet 'tis early morn. Locksley Hall. Tennyson. CABA; CABL; DiPo

Comrades of risk and rigour long ago. Prisoners. F. W. Harvey. MMA

Comus, *sels.* Milton.
Sabrina Fair. CBEP; ELP
Sweet Echo, Sweetest Nymph. ELP
(Echo.) CBEP

Conceit Begotten by the Eyes. Sir Walter Ralegh. EnRePo
(Affection and Desire.) CBEP

Conceived to be seeing. Lynceus the Warden. Goethe. AGP

Concerning Mme. Robert. Deems Taylor, *tr. fr. French.* UnTE

Concerning the Birth of Christ, 1657. Andreas Gryphius, *tr. fr. German by* George C. Schoolfield. AGP

Concerning the Economic Independence of Women. John V. A. Weaver. SIV

Concerning the Nature of Love. Lucretius, *tr. fr. Latin by* Dryden. *Fr.* De Rerum Natura. ErPo

Concerning Them That Are Asleep. R. W. Raymond. STF

Concerning Time. Christian Friedrich Hunold, *tr. fr. German by* George C. Schoolfield. AGP

Concerning Unnatural Nature: An Inverted Form. Hollis Summers. ErPo
Concerning Wings. Zoe Kincaid Brockman. PoNC
Concert-Interpretation. Siegfried Sassoon. CBEP
Concert Party. Siegfried Sassoon. MMA
Concert Scene. John Logan. NePoEA-2
Concluding Chorus: "Though he believe it, no man is strong." W. H. Auden. *Fr.* Paid on Both Sides. AnMoPo
Conclusion, The. Sir Walter Ralegh. *See* Even Such Is Time.
Conclusion: "It was a Summer's night, a close warm night." Wordsworth. *Fr.* The Prelude. OBNC
Conclusion: "Now have I brought a woork too end which neither Joves fierce wrath." Ovid, *tr. fr. Latin* by Arthur Golding. *Fr.* Metamorphoses, XV. CTC
Conclusive Voyage, The. Juan Ramón Jiménez, *tr. fr. Spanish* by H. R. Hays. PoPl
(Definitive Journey, The, *tr. by* Angel Flores. AnSP
Concord Hymn. Emerson. AP; FaPL; LV; OnP; PoIE; ThLM
(Hymn Sung at the Completion of the Concord Monument April 19, 1836.) PoPl
Condemned to hope's delusive mine. On the Death of Dr. [or Mr.] Robert Levet [a Practiser in Physic]. Samuel Johnson. CBEP; EiCP; VaPo
Condors. Padraic Colum. GoJo
Coney Island of the Mind, A, *sels.* Lawrence Ferlinghetti. ToPo
"Constantly risking absurdity."
"Dove sta amore."
Funny Fantasies Are Never so Real as Oldstyle. ErPo
"In Golden Gate Park that day."
Confession. George Herbert. FoBA; MeP
Confession. Ralph Pomeroy. CoPo
Confession in Brief, A. Mathurin Régnier, *tr. fr. French* by Wilfrid Thorley. RBL
Confession of a Stolen Kiss. Charles d'Orléans. *See* My Ghostly Father.
Confessional, The. *Unknown, tr. fr. Latin* by Louis Untermeyer. UnTE
Confessions. Robert Browning. ELP; GTBS-P
Confessor, The. G. G. Belli, *tr. fr. Italian* by Harold Norse. ErPo
Confirmation, The. Edwin Muir. WePo
Confirmation, The. Karl Shapiro. ErPo
Conflict of Convictions, The. Herman Melville. AP
Confusion. Christopher Hervey. Par
Confusions of the Alphabet. John Wain. DaDu
Congo, The. Vachel Lindsay. FaPL
In the Congo, *sel.* WePo
Conjecture for a Short Mechanic. Alan Planz. PtTo
Conjuror, The. E. V. Lucas. BiCB
Connecticut Elm, The. Emma Swan. PoPl
Connoisseur of Chaos. Wallace Stevens. CABA
Conon in Exile. Lawrence Durrell. ToPo
Conquered Banner, The. Abram Joseph Ryan. FaPL
Conqueror Worm, The. Poe. AP
Conquest. Georgia Douglas Johnson. AmNP
Conquest of Granada, The, *sels.* Dryden.
Beneath a Myrtle Shade, *fr.* Pt. I, Act III, sc. i. UnTE
(Song of the Zambra Dance.) ErPo
Wherever I Am, *fr.* Pt. I, Act IV, sc. ii. DiPo
Conquistador. Georgia Lee McElhaney. CoPo
Conquistador, *sel.* Archibald MacLeish.
"And we marched against them there in the next spring." ThLM
Conscience. George Herbert. MeP
Conscience. Giambattista Marino, *tr. fr. Italian* by Sir Edward Sherburne. RBL
Conscious. Wilfred Owen. MMA
Conscript, The. Louis MacNeice. AnMoPo
Consecration. *Unknown.* TRV
Consecration of the House. W. S. Fairbridge. PoAu-2
Consider. Christina Rossetti. TRV
Consider a new habit—classical. Arras. P. K. Page. OBCV
Consider the mysterious salt. In Time like Air. May Sarton. MoLP
Consider the sea's listless chime. The Sea Limits [or The Chime of the Sea]. Dante Gabriel Rossetti. BoC; HaSV
Consider This and in Our Time. W. H. Auden. AnMoPo
Considering the Snail. Thom Gunn. MP; NePoEA-2
Consistently his courage fought. Postscript. Vernon Watkins. OPP
Consolation, A. Shakespeare. *See* Sonnets, XXIX.
Consolation. Theodor Storm, *tr. fr. German* by D. G. Wright. AGP
Consolation. *Unknown.* STF
Consolation-Aria. Johann Christian Günther, *tr. fr. German* by George C. Schoolfield. AGP
Consolation of Philosophy, *sel.* Boethius, *tr. fr. Latin* by Elizabeth I, Queen of England.
Happy Too Much. CTC
Consolation to M. Du Périer. François de Malherbe, *tr. fr. French* by Henry Carrington. RBL

Conspiracy, The. Guy Owen. PoNC
Constancies. *Unknown, tr. fr. German* by Louis Untermeyer. UnTE
Constancy of a Lover, The. George Gascoigne. EnRePo
Constant Farmer's Son, The. *Unknown.* BSNS
Constant Lover, The. Sir John Suckling. *See* Out Upon It.
Constant One, The. George Dillon. AmLP
Constantly risking absurdity. Lawrence Ferlinghetti. *Fr.* A Coney Island of the Mind. ToPo
Constellation like day, A; the horizon behind it by lights and flares fingered and shrouded. Nocturnal Landscape. Anton Schnack. MGP
Constructed many thousand years ago. The Bird Causeways. Oskar Loerke. MGP
Consummate Happiness. Wordsworth. *Fr.* The Prelude. OBNC
Consummation. *Unknown, tr. fr. Greek* by Louis Untermeyer. UnTE
Contagious Hospital, The. William Carlos Williams. *See* Spring and All.
Contemplate all this work of Time. In Memoriam A. H. H., CXVIII. Tennyson. VP
Contemplating the sky. Tranquil Night. Luis de León. AnSP
Contemplation, *sel.* Francis Thompson.
"Nature one hour appears a thing unsexed." OBNC
Contemplation upon Flowers, A. Henry King. CBEP; ELP; SeCP; StP
Contemplations. Anne Bradstreet. AP
"When I behold the heavens as in their prime," *sel.* AmLP
Contemplative, The. Sister M. Thérèse. MoRP
Contempt of the World. *Unknown.* MeEL
Contend in a sea which the land partly encloses. The Yachts. William Carlos Williams. AP; ILP; OnP; VaPo
Contention of Ajax and Ulysses, The, *sel.* James Shirley.
Glories of Our Blood and State, The. CBEP; ILP
(Death the Leveller.) GTBS-P
Contentment. Oliver Wendell Holmes. AP
Contentment in Poverty. Issa, *tr. fr. Japanese* by Harold G. Henderson. RePo
Contest. Florence Victor. SD
Continent That Lies within Us, The. Abioseh Nicol. ACV
Continent's End. Robinson Jeffers. FaBV
Continuaunce/ Of remembraunce. A Lover Left Alone. *Unknown.* MeEL
Contract. LeRoi Jones. PtTo
Contrapuntalist, A—/ composer of chorales. Melchoir Vulpius. Marianne Moore. AP
Contrary Boy, The. Gaston V. Drake. BBGG
Contrast. Eileen Duggan. ACV
Contravention. René Char, *tr. fr. French* by David Lunde. CoFP
Contrite Heart, The. William Cowper. EiCP
Convent at Fahr, The. Albin Zollinger, *tr. fr. German* by Christopher Middleton. MGP
Conventicle. Gerrit Lansing. CoPo
Convergence of the Twain, The. Thomas Hardy. ILP; OnP; VP
Conversation in Avila. Phyllis McGinley. EaLo; PoPo
Conversation in the Mountains. Li Po, *tr. fr. Chinese.* SiGo
Conversation of Prayer, The. Dylan Thomas. GTBS-P
Conversation Piece. Arthur Freeman. ErPo
Conversational. *Unknown.* BoLP
Conversations. Guido Gozzano, *tr. fr. Italian* by Carlo L. Golino. CoIP
Conversations in Courtship, *sel. Unknown, tr. fr. Egyptian into Italian* by Boris de Rachewiltz, *tr. into English* by Ezra Pound.
"Darling, you only, there is no duplicate." CTC
Conversion. Frances Angermayer. PoLF
Convict of Clonmel, The. *Unknown, tr. fr. Irish* by J. J. Callanan. SD
Convict's Lament on the Death of Captain Logan, A. *Unknown.* PoAu-1
Coo, coo, coo! Country Rhyme. *Unknown.* ThGo
Cool and violent night, The. Impressions. O. B. Hardison, Jr. PoNC
Cool as a cucumber. Lily McQueen. Sara Jackson. BoLP
Cool, Cool Country, The. John Shaw Neilson. PoAu-1
Cool small evening shrunk to a dog bark and the clank of a bucket, A. Encounter. Ted Hughes. ToPo
Cool Tombs. Carl Sandburg. AP; PoLF; PoPo
Cool waters tumble, singing as they go. A Garden. Sappho. SiGo
Cool Web, The. Robert Graves. GTBS-P
Coole Park and Ballylee, 1931. W. B. Yeats. GTBS-P
Coolness. Onitsura, *tr. fr. Japanese* by Harold G. Henderson. SiGo
Coolness in Summer. Ryusui, *tr. fr. Japanese* by Harold G. Henderson. RePo
Coon explains it. Evolution. Rochelle Owens. CoPo
Cooper. James Russell Lowell. *Fr.* A Fable for Critics. AP
Cooper's Hill. Sir John Denham. SeCP

Cop slumps alertly on his motorcycle, The. Corner. Ralph Pomeroy. CoPo
Copper-green Phillip. Captain Arthur Phillip and the Birds. Lex Banning. PoAu-2
Copperfaces, The ("The copperfaces, the red men, handed us tobacco"). Carl Sandburg. *Fr.* The People, Yes. RePo
Copperhead. Charles Edward Eaton. PoNC
Cor Cordium. Swinburne. VP
Coracle Fishers, The. Robert Bloomfield. *Fr.* The Banks of Wye. OBNC
Coral-colored yew-berries. Autumn Tints. Mathilde Blind. LV
Coral Grove, The. James Gates Percival. AmLP
Coridon's Song. Thomas Lodge. *Fr.* Rosalynde. UnTE
Corinna in Vendome. Pierre de Ronsard, *tr. fr. French by* Robert Mezey. ErPo
Corinna, pride of Drury-Lane. A Beautiful Young Nymph Going to Bed. Swift. EiCP; UnTE
Corinna to Tanagra. Walter Savage Landor. *Fr.* Pericles and Aspasia. OBNC
Corinna's Going a-Maying. Robert Herrick. CABA; CBEP; DiPo; PoIE; SeCP
Corn. Sidney Lanier. AP
Corn-grinding Song. *Tr. fr. Zuni Indian by* Natalie Curtis. RePo
Corn Must Be Sown. Thomas Carlyle. ThGo
Corn Rigs Are Bonny [*or* Bonnie]. Burns. CBEP; ErPo (Rigs o' Barley, The.) UnTE
Cornelia's Song. John Webster. *See* Call for the Robin Redbreast.
Corner, The. Walter de la Mare. BiCB
Corner. Ralph Pomeroy. CoPo
Corner of the Field, The. Frances Cornford. BoLP
Cornfield, The. Elizabeth Madox Roberts. GoJo
Coromandel Fishers, The. Sarojini Naidu. RePo
Coronach. Sir Walter Scott. *Fr.* The Lady of the Lake, III. GTBS-P; WiR
Coronation Day at Melrose. Peter Bladen. PoAu-2
Coronet, The. Andrew Marvell. MeP; PP
Corposant. Peter Redgrove. NePoEA-2
Corpse-Plant, The. Adrienne Rich. CoPo
Corpus Christi Carol, The. *Unknown.* See Lully, Lullay.
Correlated Greatness. Francis Thompson. *Fr.* The Heart. GTBS-P
Corrib: An Emblem. Donald Davie. PoCh
Corridor, The. Thom Gunn. ToPo
Corroded flat as hills allow. Bedlam Hills. Vivian Smith. PoAu-2
Corruption. Henry Vaughan. MeP; SeCP
Corsair, The, *sel.* Byron. Sunset over the Ægean. OBNC
Cortège. Jerome G. Rothenberg. OPP
Cosmic Fabric, The. Yakov Polonsky, *tr. fr. Russian by* Avrahm Yarmolinsky *and* Cecil Cowdery. EaLo
Cosmos Shows His Power, The. Manuel González Prada, *tr. fr. Spanish by* William M. Davis. AnSP
Cost, The. Flora L. Osgood. STF
Cosy fire is bright and gay, The. The Poets at Tea, 4. Barry Pain. Par
Cottage Hospital, The. John Betjeman. GTBS-P
Cotter's Saturday Night, The. Burns. EiCP
Cotton blouse you wear, your mother said, The. McDonogh Day in New Orleans. Marcus B. Christian. AmNP
Cotton Mather. Stephen Vincent Benét. ThLM
Could I have said while he was here. In Memoriam A. H. H., LXXXI. Tennyson. VP
Could I take me to some cavern for mine hiding. O for the Wings of a Dove. Euripides. *Fr.* Hippolytus. SiGo
Could It Have Been a Shadow? Monica Shannon. SoPo
Could Juno's self more sovereign presence wear. Venus Victrix. Dante Gabriel Rossetti. *Fr.* The House of Life. VP
Could mortal lip divine. Emily Dickinson. DiPo
Could these faint numbers glow with equal fire. To the Fair Unknown. William Taylor. WaPE
Could We. *Unknown.* STF
Could we but draw back the curtains. If Only We Understood. *Unknown.* STF
Could we but see men as they are! A Window in the Breast. *Unknown.* SiGo
Could we forget the widow'd hour. In Memoriam A. H. H., XL. Tennyson. VP
Could we only see the goodness. Could We. *Unknown.* STF
Could You Do That? Burns. UnTE
Could You Spare Some Time for Jesus? Lester Knickman. STF
Couldn't Stand the Press. Mart Taylor. SGR
Counsel to Girls. Robert Herrick. *See* To the Virgins, to Make Much of Time.
Count Arnaldos. *Unknown, tr. fr. Spanish by* William M. Davis. AnML
Count William's Escapade. Guillaume de Poitiers. *See* Under the Sun I Ride Along.

Count your blessings. *Unknown.* ThGo
Counter-Attack. Siegfried Sassoon. SIV
Counters. Elizabeth J. Coatsworth. SoPo
Counting. Fenton Johnson. AmNP
Counting. Carl Sandburg. MoLP
Counting on Flowers. John Ciardi. PP
Counting-out Rhyme. Edna St. Vincent Millay. GoJo
Counting Sheep. Aileen Fisher. SoPo
Counting the Beats. Robert Graves. DTC; ELP; GTBS-P; PoIE
Country Bachelor's Complaint, The. Luis de Góngora, *tr. fr. Spanish by* Edward Churton. RBL
Country Clergy, The. R. S. Thomas. GTBS-P; PoIE
Country Club Sunday. Phyllis McGinley. PoPo
Country Lad, The. Nicholas Breton. *Fr.* The Passionate Shepherd. CBEP (Pastoral: "Who can live in heart so glad.") ELP
Country lad and bonny lass, A. Have-at a Venture. *Unknown.* ErPo
Country Lane. Margaret Stanion Darling. FiSC
Country Letter. John Clare. CBEP
Country Life, A: To His Brother, M. Tho: Herrick. Robert Herrick. SeCP
Country Lovers, The. *Unknown.* UnTE
Country Mouse, The. Abraham Cowley, *after* Horace. SeCP
Country Music. Plato, *tr. fr. Greek by* Robert Bridges. SiGo
Country of a Thousand Years of Peace, The. James Merrill. PoCh
Country Rhyme. *Unknown.* ThGo
Country Saga, A. Sam Ragan. PoNC
Country Summer. Léonie Adams. GoJo
Country Towns. Kenneth Slessor. PoAu-2
Countryman's Wooing, A. Theocritus, *tr. fr. Latin by* Charles Stuart Calverley. Idylls, XXVII. ErPo
Countryside Sleeps, Trembling, The. Juan Ramón Jiménez, *tr. fr. Spanish by* Eloise Roach. AnSP
County Ball, The, *sel.* Winthrop Mackworth Praed. County Member, The. OBNC
Couple, The. Joel Oppenheimer. CoPo
"Courage!" he said, and pointed toward the land. The Lotos-Eaters. Tennyson. DiPo; FoBA; OnMSP; OnP; PoIE; VP
Courage my Soul, now learn to wield. A Dialogue, between the Resolved Soul, and Created Pleasure. Andrew Marvell. MeP; SeCP
Courage, my Soul! now to the silent wood. Peace. Bhartrihari. SiGo
Couronne Impériale, La. Claude de Malleville, *tr. fr. French by* Judith McDowell. *Fr.* Guirlande de Julie. RBL
Course of a Particular, The. Wallace Stevens. PoIE
Court and Country Love. *Unknown.* UnTE
Courtesies of good-morning and good-evening. On Dwelling. Robert Graves. CBEP
Courtesy. Hilaire Belloc. BoC
Courthouse Bell. Thad Stem, Jr. PoNC
Courtin', The. James Russell Lowell. *Fr.* The Biglow Papers, 2d series, Introduction. SIV
Courting in the Kitchen, *with music. Unknown.* BSNS
Courtship of the Yonghy-Bonghy-Bo, The. Edward Lear. EvOK; OnMSP; WiR
Cousin Emily and the Night Visitor. Kendrick Smithyman. ACV
Cousin Florence. Richard Eberhart. ToPo
Cousin Nancy. T. S. Eliot. FoBA; PoSa
Couth/ Sooth/ (befo de Wa). 3 Sit-Ins Agin. Jonathan Williams. PoNC
Covent Garden Market. Carl Bode. *Fr.* London Sonnets. ToPo
Coventry Carol. *Unknown.* ELP; MeEL
Cover your heavens, Jove. Prometheus. Goethe. TwGP
Covering the Subject. Richard Armour. RePo
Covey of cotton-dressed, apple-breasted girls, A. Wax. Winfield Townley Scott. ErPo
Cow, The. Bernard O'Dowd. PoAu-1
Cow, The. Robert Louis Stevenson. SoPo
Cow Dance. Bruce Beaver. PoAu-2
Cow in Apple Time, The. Robert Frost. CABA; PoLF
Cowboy, The. *Unknown. See* Cowboy's Lament, The.
Cowboy Song. Charles Causley. PoSa
Cowboy's Dream, The, *with music. Unknown.* BFSS
Cowboy's Lament, The. *Unknown.* BFSS, *with music;* ThLM (Cowboy, The.) BSO (Dying Cowboy, The.) BSNS; BSO (A *and* C *vers.*)
Cowboy's Life, The. *At. to* James Barton Adams. SoPo
Cowboy's Return, The, *with music. Unknown.* BFSS
Cows. James Reeves. PoSC
Cows! Cows! With ears like mouths of telephones. Band Music. John Fuller. NePoEA-2
Coxswain's Line, The. H. E. Cressman. RePo
Coy Lass Dress'd Up in Her Best, The. *Unknown.* ErPo
Coy nature (which remain'd, though aged grown). Abraham Cowley. *Fr.* Ode upon Dr. Harvey. Par
Crab-Apple. Ethel Talbot. BiCB

Crabbèd Age and Youth. Shakespeare. The Passionate Pilgrim, XII. UnTE
(Madrigal, A: "Crabbed age and youth.") GTBS-P
Crabbing. Norman Levine. OBCV
Cradle and the Cross, The. A. S. Reitz. STF
Cradle and Throne. *Unknown.* STF
Cradle Hymn. Martin Luther, *tr. fr. German.* BiCB
(Away in a Manger.) ThGo
Cradle Hymn. Isaac Watts. SoPo
(Cradle Song.) ThGo
Cradle Song, A: "Angels are stooping, The." W. B. Yeats. PoPl
Cradle Song: "Hush, honey, hush." Sir Herbert Read. DaDu
Cradle Song: "Hush! my dear, lie still and slumber." Isaac Watts. *See* Cradle Hymn.
Cradle Song: "O my deir hert, young Jesus sweit." *Unknown.* EaLo
Cradle Song: "Sleep, my darling, sleep." Louis MacNeice. PoPl
Cradle Song: "Sleep, sleep, beauty bright." Blake. PoLF; PoPl
(Sleep! Sleep! Beauty Bright.) CBEP
Cradle Song, A: "Sweet dreams form a shade." Blake. *Fr.* Songs of Innocence. CBEP
Cradle Song of the Elephants. Adriano del Valle, *tr. fr. Spanish by* Alida Malkus. RePo
Crag Jack's Apostasy. Ted Hughes. EaLo
Crane Is My Neighbour, The. John Shaw Neilson. PoAu-1
Cranes, The. Po Chü-i, *tr. fr. Chinese by* Arthur Waley. SiGo
Craving of Samuel Rouse for clearance to create, The. The Slave and the Iron Lace. Margaret Danner. AmNP
Crawl Blues. Vincent McHugh. ErPo
Crazy Jane and Jack the Journeyman. W. B. Yeats. FoBA
Crazy Jane on God. W. B. Yeats. FoBA; PoDB
Crazy Jane Talks with the Bishop. W. B. Yeats. CABA; DiPo; ErPo; FoBA; ILP
Crazy World, The. William Gay. PoAu-1
Created, The. Jones Very. PoIE
Created for whose sake? The praying. Don't Sit under the Apple Tree with Anyone Else but Me. Robert Pack. CoPo
Created purely from glass the saint stands. In Piam Memoriam. Geoffrey Hill. NePoEA-2
Creation. V. N. Bhushan. ACV
Creation, The. James Weldon Johnson. FaBV; PoPl; SIV; WePo
Up from the Bed of the River, *sel.* EaLo
Creator of night and of birth, The. Special Starlight. Carl Sandburg. MoRP
Creature was a changeling child, The. Stranger Bride. Jocelyn Macy Sloan. FiSC
Crécy and Agadir, the siege at Acre. Celle Qui Meurt. Nancy Westlake. PtTo
Credences of Summer. Wallace Stevens. AP
Credibility. John Ciardi. ToPo
Credit. *Unknown.* STF
Creditor, The. Louis MacNeice. EaLo
Credo. Robinson Jeffers. PoPl
Credo. E. A. Robinson. AP; ILP
Credo. Jonathan Williams. PoNC
Creed, A. Edwin Markham. PoPl
Creed, A. John Masefield. MoRP
Creed, A. *Unknown.* STF
(My Daily Creed.) TRV
Creek, The. W. W. E. Ross. OBCV
Creek of the Four Graves, The, *sel.* Charles Harpur.
"Settler in the olden times went forth, A." PoAu-1
Creep into thy narrow bed. The Last Word. Matthew Arnold. CABA; OBNC; PoSa
Creeper grows over thorn. Alba. Confucius. *Fr.* The Classic Anthology: Songs of T'ang. CTC
Cremation of Sam McGee, The. Robert W. Service. PoLF; SIV
Crepe Myrtle. Charles Edward Eaton. PoNC
Cresophontes, *sel.* Euripides, *tr. fr. Greek by* Moses Hadas. Prayer to Peace. PoPl
Cresseid's Complaint against Fortune. Robert Henryson. *Fr.* The Testament of Cresseid. MeEL
Crew Cut. David McCord. SD
Crib, The. Christopher Morley. BiCB
Cricket, The. Vincent Bourne, *tr. fr. Latin by* William Cowper. PoLF
Cricket in the garden is awake, The. A Little Night Music. Felix Stefanile. FiSC
Cricket Triolet, A. Coulson Kernahan. WePo
Crime and Punishment. James Sexton Layton. PoNC
Crime Was in Granada, The. Antonio Machado, *tr. fr. Spanish by* Kate Flores. AnSP
Crinolines and Bloomers. *Unknown.* ThLM
Crisis. Thad Stem, Jr. PoNC
Critic, The. John Farrar. SoPo
Critic of the days of yore, The. Narcissus and Some Tadpoles. Victor J. Daley. PoAu-1

Critics. George Crabbe. PP
Critics, The. Lawrence Durrell. ToPo
Croak of a raven hoar, The. Mammon Marriage. George Macdonald. CBEP
Crocodile, The. *Unknown.* CBEP
Crocus, The. Walter Crane. SoPo
Cromwell, Our Chief of Men. Milton. CABA
Cronie Is Dead, *with music. Unknown.* BFSS
Crooked heels. The Cobbler. Eleanor Alletta Chaffee. SoPo
Crooked paths, The. The Goat Paths. James Stephens. GoJo; PoDB
Crooked Sixpence, The. Mother Goose. *See* There Was a Crooked Man.
Croppy Boy, The. William B. McBurney. SIV
Croppy Boy, The. *Unknown.* CBEP
Cross. *See also* Crosse.
Cross. Langston Hughes. AmNP; PoLF
Cross, The. Shelley. BoC
Cross, The. Allen Tate. AP; PoDB
Cross and the Tomb, The. Annie Johnson Flint. STF
Cross of Snow, The. Longfellow. AP; FaPL
Cross Patch. Mother Goose. EvOK
Cross Ties. X. J. Kennedy. CoPo
Crosse. *See also* Cross.
Crosse, The. George Herbert. MeP
Crosse of Jesu Christ be ever oure spede. An A. B. C. of Devotion. *Unknown.* MeEL
Crossing. Philip Booth. LV
Crossing, The. Philippe Jaccottet, *tr. fr. French by* Donald Justice. CoFP
Crossing alone the nighted ferry. More Poems, XXIII. A. E. Housman. GTBS-P
Crossing Brooklyn Ferry. Walt Whitman. AP; CABA; CABL; DiPo; PoIE
Crossing the Bar. Tennyson. CABA; DiPo; FaBV; FaPL; FoBA; HaSV; ILP; LV; OBNC; PoLF; PoPo; TRV; VP
Crossing the Plains. Joaquin Miller. AmLP
Crossing the Plains, *with music.* John A. Stone. SGR
Crossing the River. *Unknown, tr. fr. Chinese by* Arthur Waley. SiGo
Crotchet Castle, *sel.* Thomas Love Peacock.
Priest and the Mulberry-Tree, The. OnMSP
Crouched on the pavement, close by Belgrave Square. West London. Matthew Arnold. PoPo
Crow, The. John Clare. WePo
Crow and the Crane, The. *Unknown.* BuBa
Crowded Out. Florence White Willett. STF
Crowd's Acclaim, The. Friedrich Hölderlin. *See* Men's Applause.
Crow's harsh dissyllables, A. A Valediction. Melvin Walker La Follette. CoPo
Crucified to the World. *Unknown.* MeEL
Crucifix. Elder Olson. MoRP
Crucifixion. Mrs. Roy L. Peifer. STF
Crucifixion, The. *Unknown.* MeEL
Crucifying. John Donne. MeP
Cruel Mother, The, *with music. Unknown.* BFSS (B *vers.*); BSO
(Two Little Babes, A *vers., with music.*) BFSS
Cruel Naughty Boy, The. *Unknown.* BBGG
Cruelty has a human heart. A Divine Image. Blake. OBNC; PoIE
Cruise of the *Monitor,* The. George Henry Boker. ThLM
Crumbling is not an instant's act. Emily Dickinson. AP; DiPo
Crumbs. Walter de la Mare. SoPo
Crust of bread and a corner to sleep in, A. Life. Paul Laurence Dunbar. AmNP
Crustaceans. Roy Fuller. ToPo
Cry of the guitar, The. The Guitar. Federico García Lorca. AnSP
Cry to Mary, A. St. Godric. MeEL
Crystal, The *sel.* Sidney Lanier.
"Oh, what amiss may I forgive in Thee." TRV
Crystal Cabinet, The. Blake. DiPo; OBNC
Crystal Moment. Robert P. Tristram Coffin. LV
Cuba Libre. Joaquin Miller. ThLM
Cubes. Mary Fullerton. PoAu-1
Cuckoo, The. *Unknown.* CBEP
Cuckoo, bubbling your green words across half Berkshire. Hearing the Cuckoo. John Heath-Stubbs. DaDu
Cuckoo's double note, The. Wiltshire Downs. Andrew Young. GTBS-P
Cuddie, for shame hold up thy heavy head. October Eclogue. Spenser. *Fr.* The Shepheardes Calender. PP
Cudgelled but Contented Cuckold, The. La Fontaine. UnTE
Culbin Sands. Andrew Young. GTBS-P
Culprit, The. A. E. Housman. Last Poems, XIV. VP
Cultural Presupposition, The. W. H. Auden. CABA
Cupboard, The. Walter de la Mare. SoPo
Cupid and Campaspe. John Lyly. *Fr.* Alexander and Campaspe. GTBS-P; ILP
(Cupid and My Campaspe.) CABA

Cupid and Death, *sel.* James Shirley.
  Victorious Men of Earth. CBEP
  (Last Conqueror, The.) GTBS-P
Cupid and My Campaspe. John Lyly. *See* Cupid and Campaspe.
Cupid, beware, there'll come a day. Warning to Cupid. *Unknown.* UnTE
Cupid, dumb idol, peevish saint of love. Idea, XXVI. Michael Drayton. EnRePo
Cupid Mistaken. Matthew Prior. EiCP
Cupid, thou naughty boy, when thou wert loathed. Caelica, XII. Fulke Greville. EnRePo
Cupids Call. James Shirley. ErPo
Cupid's Pastime. Francis Davison. UnTE
Cups without Wine Are Lowly. Judah Halevi, *tr. fr. Hebrew by* William M. Davis. AnML
Curate's Kindness, The. Thomas Hardy. ILP; VP
Curbstones are to balance on. What They Are For. Dorothy Aldis. SoPo
Curé in his windy gown, The. Saint Francis. John Peale Bishop. EaLo
Cure me with quietness. For Sleep or Death. Ruth Pitter. WePo
Curfew Must Not Ring Tonight. Rose Hartwick Thorpe. SIV
Curfew tolls the knell of parting day, The. Elegy Written in a Country Churchyard. Thomas Gray. CABA; CABL; CaFP; CBEP; DiPo; EiCP; EnPE; FaPL; GTBS-P; ILP; OnP; PoIE; PoLF; PoPo; PoSa; StP
Curiosity. Harry Behn. SoPo
Curious knot God made in Paradise, A. Upon Wedlock and Death of Children. Edward Taylor. AP
Curled in his fist, though nothing's there. Flogged Child. Joseph Joel Keith. FiSC
Curly Locks. Mother Goose. SoPo
Curse, The. John Donne. CBEP
Curse God and Die, You Said to Me. Archibald MacLeish. *Fr.* J. B. EaLo
Curse of Kehama, The. *sels.* Robert Southey. OBNC
  Kehama's Curse.
  Love Indestructible.
Curse on the Cat, A. John Skelton. *Fr.* Phyllyp Sparowe. EvOK
Cursing and Blessing. "Michael Lewis," *after the Chinese.* *Fr.* Cherry Blossoms. UnTE
Curtain rises on Act II, The. Act II. Katherine Davis. PoPl
Curtains were half drawn, the floor was swept, The. After Death. Christina Rossetti. VP
"Cusha! Cusha! Cusha!" calling. Calling the Cows Home. Jean Ingelow. *Fr.* The High Tide on the Coast of Lincolnshire (1571). ThGo
Custer's Last Charge. Frederick Whittaker. OnMSP; PoLF; ThLM
Custer's Last Fierce Charge, *with music. Unknown.* BFSS
  (Last Fierce Charge, The.) BSO
Customs-House, The. Eugenio Montale, *tr. fr. Italian by* Carlo L. Golino. CoIP
Cut down that timber! Bells, too many and strong. The Planster's Vision. John Betjeman. PoPl
Cut out/ the insides. Hegel. LeRoi Jones. CoPo
Cuttings, Later. Theodore Roethke. AP; PoIE
Cutty Wren, The. *Unknown.* CBEP; WiR
Cycle. Gottfried Benn, *tr. fr. German by* Walter Kaufmann. *Fr.* Morgue. TwGP
Cycle, The. Theodore Roethke. ToPo
Cyclops. Ovid, *tr. fr. Latin by* Arthur Golding. *Fr.* Metamorphoses, XIII. CTC
Cymbals crash, The. A Victory Dance. Alfred Noyes. PoLF
Cymbeline, *sels.* Shakespeare.
  Fear No More the Heat o' the Sun, *fr.* IV, ii. CABA; CBEP; FoBA; ILP
  (Fear No More.) DiPo; ELP; EnRePo; PoIE; PoSa; RoGo
  (Fidele.) BoC; GTBS-P; PoPo
  (Fidele's Dirge.) WePo
  (Song: "Fear no more the heat o' th' sun.") CTC; VaPo
  Hark, Hark! the Lark, *fr.* II, iii. CBEP; DiPo; EnRePo; FaBV; FoBA; ILP; PoIE
Cynara. Ernest Dowson. *See* Non Sum Qualis Eram Bonae sub Regno Cynarae.
Cynddylan on a Tractor [in Spring]. R. S. Thomas. BoC; DaDu
Cynthia Sporting. Giambattista Marino, *tr. fr. Italian by* Philip Ayres. RBL
Cynthia's Revels, *sels.* Ben Jonson.
  Kiss, The, *fr.* IV, iii. UnTE
  "Queen and huntress, chaste and fair," *fr.* V, vi. ILP
  (Hymn to Diana.) EnRePo; GTBS-P; SeCP; WiR
  (Queen and Huntress.) CABA; CBEP
  "Slow, slow, fresh fount, keep time with my salt tears," *fr.* I, ii. ILP
  (Echo's Song.) PoIE

  (Slow, Slow, Fresh Fount.) ELP
  (Song: "Slow, slow, fresh mount, keep time with my salt tears.") EnRePo; SeCP
Cypress stood up like a church, The. Bianca among the Nightingales. Elizabeth Barrett Browning. GTBS-P
Cyriack, this three years' day these eyes, though clear. To [Mr.] Cyriack Skinner, upon His Blindness. Milton. DiPo; FoBA; PoIE
Cyriack, whose grandsire, on the royal bench. To Cyriack Skinner. Milton. GTBS-P

D

Da spreeng ees com'; but oh, da joy. Da Leetla Boy. T. A. Daly. SIV
Dabbling in the Dew. *Unknown.* UnTE
Daddy Fell into the Pond. Alfred Noyes. RePo
Daddy had a little boy. Does Daddy Go? *Unknown.* STF
Dad's Greatest Job. *Unknown.* STF
Daedalus. Ovid, *tr. fr. Latin by* Ezra Pound. *Fr.* Metamorphoses, VIII. CTC
Daemon Lover, The. *See* Demon Lover, The.
Daffadowndilly. Mother Goose. SoPo
Daffodils. *Unknown, tr. fr. Japanese.* SoPo
Daffodils, The. Wordsworth. *See* I Wandered Lonely as a Cloud.
Dahlias. Padraic Colum. GoJo
Daily dawns another day. Inscription for the Ceiling of a Bedroom. Dorothy Parker. LV
Daily Grind, The. Fenton Johnson. AmNP
Daily Round. Lizette Woodworth Reese. *Fr.* After. ThGo
Daily the yellow sun comes over the hill. The Sun. Georg Trakl. MGP
Dainty Sweet Bird. *Unknown.* EnRePo
Daisies. Andrew Young. GoJo
Daisy, The. Tennyson. OBNC
Daisy. Francis Thompson. FaBV; OBNC
Daley's Dorg Wattle. W. T. Goodge. PoAu-1
Dalfin, a Target for Your Bow. Peirol *and* Dalfin d'Alvernhe, *tr. fr. Provençal by* Thomas G. Bergin. AnML
Dalliance of the Eagles, The. Walt Whitman. CABA
Dame Jane a sprightly nun and gay. The Penitent Nun. John Lockman. ErPo; UnTE
Damelias' Song to His Diaphenia. At. to Henry Constable *and* to Henry Chettle. *See* Diaphenia.
Damn it all! all this our South stinks peace. Sestina: Altaforte. Ezra Pound. CaFP; PoIE; StP
Damnation of Vancouver, *sel.* Earle Birney.
  Speech of the Salish Chief. OBCV
Damned ship lurched and slithered, The. Quiet and quick. A Channel Passage. Rupert Brooke. HaSV
Damon come drive thy flocks this way. Clorinda and Damon. Andrew Marvell. SeCP
Dampe, The. John Donne. SeCP
Damsel Possessed of Great Beauty, A, *with music. Unknown.* BSO
Dan Bartholmew's Dolorous Discourses. George Gascoigne. EnRePo
Dan Dunder. John Ciardi. BBGG
Dan Pope first in vogue. The Lass of Isleworth Mill. Richard Wooddeson. WaPE
Dance, The. LeRoi Jones. CoPo
Dance, The. William Carlos Williams. GoJo
Dance Called David, The. Theodore Weiss. CoPo
Dance Figure. Ezra Pound. AnMoPo
Dance of the Abakweta. Margaret Danner. Far from Africa, 2. AmNP; NNP
Dance the Boatman. *Unknown.* ThLM
Dancer dances, The. The dance. Suffering. Jacques Auditberti. CoFP
Dancers, The. W. W. Gibson. MMA
Dancers, The. Roland E. Robinson. ACV
Dancing Ploughmen, The. M. K. Joseph. ACV
Dancing Seal, The. W. W. Gibson. OnMSP
Dancing with such salacious gestures. Familiarity Breeds Indifference. Martial. UnTE
Dandelions. Marchette Chute. BiCB
Dandoo, *with music. Unknown.* BFSS
Danger is silent in the bloodless square. Capital Square. Patrick Anderson. OBCV
Danger of loss eternal. Michelangelo, *tr. fr. Italian by* Joseph Tusiani. RBL
Dangerous Establishment. Erich Kästner, *tr. fr. German by* Michael Hamburger. MGP
Dangers of Foot-ball, The. John Gay. *Fr.* Trivia; or, The Art of Walking the Streets of London. SD
Daniel. Vachel Lindsay. *See* Daniel Jazz, The.
Daniel at Breakfast. Phyllis McGinley. LV
Daniel Boone. Stephen Vincent Benét. PoPl

Daniel Boone stepped up to a window. Frontier. Josephine Miles. OPP

Daniel Jazz, The. Vachel Lindsay. CBEP (Daniel.) WePo

Daniel Webster's Horses. Elizabeth J. Coatsworth. FiSC

Dankwerts, scholarship boy from the slums. Our Supervisors Will Do That for Us! David Holbrook. NePoEA-2

Danny Deever. Kipling. CaFP; DiPo; GTBS-P; PoLF; PoPo; VaPo

Danny Murphy. James Stephens. RoGo

Danny's Wooing. David McKee Wright. PoAu-1

Danse Macabre. Antonia Y. Schwab. FiSC

Dante. Michelangelo, tr. fr. Italian by Longfellow. RBL

Dante and Beatrice in the Earthly Paradise. Dante, tr. fr. Italian by Dorothy Sayers. Fr. Divina Commedia: Purgatorio. BoC

Dante attained the purgatorial hill. The Vigil. Theodore Roethke. Fr. Four for Sir John Davies. PoDB

Dante's Angels. Dante, tr. fr. Italian by Dorothy Sayers. Fr. Divina Commedia: Purgatorio. BoC

Dante's Heaven. Dante, tr. fr. Italian by Dorothy Sayers. Fr. Divina Commedia: Paradiso. BoC

Danube to the Severn gave, The. In Memoriam A. H. H., XIX. Tennyson. FoBA; GTBS-P; VP

Daphne. Bliss Carman. OBCV

Dappled sky, a world of meadows, A. Jean Ingelow. Fr. Divided. OBNC

Darby Ram, The. Unknown. BSO

Darest Thou Now O Soul. Walt Whitman. AmLP; TRV

Darius Green and His Flying-Machine. John Townsend Trowbridge. PoLF

Darius the Mede was a king and a wonder. The Daniel Jazz [or Daniel]. Vachel Lindsay. CBEP; WePo

Dark accurate plunger down the successive knell. The Subway. Allen Tate. AP

Dark and the Fair, The. Stanley Kunitz. PoCh

Dark Angel, The. Lionel Johnson. GTBS-P

Dark blue of early autumn, The. Sleep Impression. Carl Sandburg. RePo

Dark brain. Poem to the Man on My Fire Escape. Diane Wakoski. CoPo

Dark brown is the river. Where Go the Boats? Robert Louis Stevenson. GoJo; SoPo

Dark bull quartered in my eye, The. Jerome Rothenberg. Fr. Three Landscapes. CoPo

Dark Chamber, The. Louis Untermeyer. MoLP

Dark creeping Ivy, with thy berries brown. To the Ivy. John Clare. CBEP

Dark day, A. The rain in Washington, the little feet of death. The Assassinations 1963. Stuart McCarrell. PtTo

Dark eyed/ O woman of my dreams. Dance Figure. Ezra Pound. AnMoPo

Dark-eyed Gentleman, The. Thomas Hardy. PoIE

Dark-eyed Sailor, The. Unknown. BSNS

Dark Eyes at Forest Hills. I. L. Martin. SD

Dark Glass, The. Dante Gabriel Rossetti. The House of Life, XXXIV. VP

Dark, gray receding tide uncovers, The. By the Sea. John Hollander. AmPC

Dark green truck on the cement platform, The. Train Window. Robert Finch. OBCV

Dark Hills, The. E. A. Robinson. AP; GoJo; ILP; PoIE; PoSa

Dark Hotel. Alfred Dorn. FiSC

Dark house, by which once more I stand. In Memoriam A. H. H., VII. Tennyson. DiPo; FoBA; GTBS-P; OBNC; PoIE; PoSa; VP

Dark house, dark lonely grave. The Grave. T. Gwynn Jones. SiGo

Dark House in Autumn. Conrad Pendleton. FiSC

Dark in a Corner of the Room. Gustavo Adolfo Bécquer, tr. fr. Spanish by Kate Flores. AnSP

Dark is kind and cozy, The. God's Dark. John Martin. PoLF

Dark Night of the Soul, The. St. John of the Cross, tr. fr. Spanish. ErPo, tr. by E. Allison Peers; RBL, tr. by David Lewis
(Obscure Night of the Soul, The, tr. by Arthur Symons.) BoC
(One Dismal Night, tr. by Kate Flores.) AnSP

Dark Rosaleen, sels. David McKee Wright. PoAu-1
"My Love is the voice of a song," IX.
"On a shining silver morning long ago," I.

Dark Symphony. Melvin B. Tolson. AmNP

Dark Testament. Pauli Murray. AmNP

Dark was the sky, and not one friendly star. Death. Philip Freneau. Fr. The House of Night. AP

Dark water, underground. The Cycle. Theodore Roethke. ToPo

Dark Women. Ted Hughes. ToPo

Dark Woods, sel. Robert Penn Warren.
Dogwood, The, II. PoDB

Dark Yuggoth. Lin Carter. FiSC

Darkling Swallows Will Come Again, The. Gustavo Adolfo Bécquer, tr. fr. Spanish by Kate Flores. AnSP

Darkling Thrush, The. Thomas Hardy. CaFP; DiPo; EvOK; ILP; OBNC; OnP; PoDB; PoIE; PoSa; RoGo; StP; VP

Darkness. Byron. ILP

Darkness crumbles away, The. Break of Day in the Trenches. Isaac Rosenberg. GTBS-P; MMA

Darkness has called to darkness, and disgrace. As a Plane Tree by the Water. Robert Lowell. AP; DTC; PoDB; VaPo

Darkness: the rain sluiced down; the mire was deep. The Redeemer. Siegfried Sassoon. MMA

Darkness wears off, and, dawning into light. The Figures on the Frieze. Alastair Reid. ErPo

Darling, each morning a blooded rose. Corinna in Vendome. Pierre de Ronsard. ErPo

Darling, If You Only Knew. Edward Newman Horn. ErPo

Darling of God and Men, beneath the gliding stars. Lucretius. Fr. De Rerum Natura. PoPl

Darling, you only, there is no duplicate. Unknown. Fr. Conversations in Courtship. CTC

Das Liebesleben. Thom Gunn. ErPo

Datur Hora Quieti. Sir Walter Scott. Fr. The Doom of Devorgoil, I. GTBS-P

Daughter of earth and water, her bounty. The Artichoke. Ibn al-Talla. AnML

Daughter of Jove, relentless power. Hymn to Adversity. Thomas Gray. GTBS-P; StP

Daughter to that good Earl, once President. To the Lady Margaret Ley. Milton. GTBS-P

Daughters, daughters, do ye grieve? Thammuz. William Vaughn Moody. AP

Daughters of the Seraphim led round their sunny flocks, The. The Book of Thel. Blake. FoBA; OBNC

Daughters of Time, the hypocritic Days. Days. Emerson. AP; CaFP; CBEP; ILP; PoIE; PoPo

Davenport Gap. Jonathan Williams. OPP

David. Michelangelo, tr. fr. Italian by Harold M. Priest. RBL

David and Bethsabe, sel. George Peele.
Bethsabe's Song, fr. sc. i. CBEP; EnRePo

David Garrick. Goldsmith. Fr. Retaliation. CBEP

David with the sling. David. Michelangelo. RBL

David's Song. Robert Browning. Fr. Saul. FaBV

Davy came trippling o'er the hills. The Blackjack Davy. Unknown. BFSS

Davy Crockett in his woodman dress. Lament for the Alamo. Arthur Guiterman. RePo

Davy, the Dicer. Sir Thomas More. DiPo

Dawn. Paul Laurence Dunbar. AmNP; PoLF

Dawn, The. Sahl ben Malik, tr. fr. Arabic by Lysander Kemp. AnML

Dawn. Frederick George Scott. PoPl

Dawn. Frank Dempster Sherman. TRV

Dawn. Tasso, tr. fr. Italian by Harold M. Priest. RBL

Dawn. Unknown, tr. fr. Greek by Louis Untermeyer. UnTE

Dawn. William Carlos Williams. LV; PoPl

Dawn! And I fled. Morning Window. Olive Tilford Dargan. PoNC

Dawn Boy's Song. Unknown, tr. fr. Navaho Indian by Washington Matthews. FaBV

Dawn breaking as I woke. Alba. Derek Walcott. GoJo

Dawn Brings with It, The. Juan Ramón Jiménez, tr. fr. Spanish by James Wright. AnSP

Dawn cried out: the brutal voice of a bird. In All These Acts. Brother Antoninus. ToPo

Dawn is here. Now I must go. Leaving. "Michael Lewis." Fr. Cherry Blossoms. UnTE

Dawn is not distant, The. Longfellow. Fr. Tales of a Wayside Inn: The Saga of King Olaf. TRV

Dawn of a bright June morning. Mass of Love. Unknown. PoPl

Dawn songs in the dews of young orange trees. In England's Green & (a Garland and a Clyster). Jonathan Williams. CoPo

Dawning, The. George Herbert. MeP

Dawning of morn, the day-light's sinking, The. Thee, Thee, Only Thee. Thomas Moore. OBNC

Dawning of the Day, The, with music. Unknown. BSNS

Dawn's precise pronouncement waits, The. The Edge of Day. Laurie Lee. ToPo

Day, The. Roy Fuller. ToPo

Day, The. Edwin Muir. PoDB

Day, The. Theodore Spencer. PoPo

Day and Night. Baldoon Dhingra. ACV

Day and Night. Lady Anne Lindsay. ThGo

Day and Night. Eugenio Montale, tr. fr. Italian by Carlo L. Golino. CoIP

Day and night I wander widely. God. Gamaliel Bradford. TRV

Day began with water music, The. September Winds. Helen Bevington. PoNC

Day-Breakers, The. Arna Bontemps. AmNP

Day by Day ("Day by day, oh Master, make me"). A. G. Fisher. STF
Day by Day (" 'Day by day,' the promise reads"). Stephen F. Winward. TRV
Day dawns with scent of must and rain, The. Mirror in February. Thomas Kinsella. GTBS-P
Day had fled, the moon arose, The. George Gordon McCrae. *Fr.* Mamba the Bright-eyed. PoAu-1
Day I Kicked a Bankroll Out the Window, The. Charles Bukowski. PtTo
Day in Autumn, A. R. S. Thomas. WePo
Day in Spring, A. "Jake Falstaff." BoC
Day is a golden grain of corn. Day and Night. Baldoon Dhingra. ACV
Day is again begun. Unrest. Richard Watson Dixon. OBNC
Day is cold, and dark, and dreary, The. The Rainy Day. Longfellow. PoLF; PoPl
Day Is Done, The. Longfellow. LV; PoPl
Day is done, gone the sun. God Is Nigh. *Unknown.* TRV
Day Is Dying in the West. Mary A. Lathbury. TRV
Day of Love, A. Dante Gabriel Rossetti. The House of Life, XVI. VP
Day on Which I Took the Cross, The. Reinmar von Hagenau, *tr. fr. German by* Margaret F. Richey. AnML
Day recedes in white, The. A Still Day. Joseph Cherwinski. RePo
Day Returns, The. Robert Louis Stevenson. TRV
Day she came, the trees and bushes slept, The. The Visit. Robert Mezey. AmPC
Day That I Have Loved. Rupert Brooke. PoLF
Day the bridge club met with me, The. Just a Breeze! Edith Earnshaw. PoNC
Day, The—the Way. John Oxenham. TRV
Day was a year at first, The. The Day. Theodore Spencer. PoPo
Day was hot, The. The forests were on fire. The Monkey. Vladislav Khodasevich. PoPo
Day was spent, the moon shone bright, The. The Garden Gate. *Unknown.* BSO
Day when Charmus ran with five, The. A Mighty Runner. E. A. Robinson. SD
Daybreak. Longfellow. PoLF
Daybreak. Stephen Spender. MoLP
Daydreamers. Norma L. Davis. PoAu-2
Dayley Island. Frederick Seidel. CoPo
Days. Karle Wilson Baker. RePo
Days. Emerson. AP; CaFP; CBEP; ILP; PoIE; PoPo
Days are gone, The. Older Grown. Kate Greenaway. BiCB
Day's End. Lesbia Harford. PoAu-1
Day's grown old, the fainting sun, The. Evening. Charles Cotton. WiR
Day's March, The. Robert Nichols. MMA
Days of '49, The, *with music.* Charley Rhodes. SGR
Days shorten, the south blows wide for showers now, The. Salmon-fishing. Robinson Jeffers. SD
Dazzled, how the brown moth flutters. Where More Is Meant. Christopher Morley. RePo
Dazzled [*or* Dazel'd] thus with height of place. Upon the Sudden Restraint of the Earl of Somerset, Falling from Favour. Sir Henry Wotton. ELP; SeCP
De Amore. Ernest Dowson. OBNC
De Anima. Howard Nemerov. ToPo
De Consolatione Philosophiae. Boethius. *See* Consolation of Philosophy.
"De Gustibus." Robert Browning. VP
De Profundis. Dorothy Parker. ErPo
De Profundis. Christina Rossetti. VP
De Profundis, *sel.* Tennyson.
"Out of the deep, my child, out of the deep," I. ILP
De Rerum Natura, *sels.* Lucretius, *tr. fr. Latin.*
"Darling of God and Men, beneath the gliding stars," *fr.* I, *tr. by* Basil Bunting. PoPl
Nature of Love, The, *fr.* IV. *tr. by* Dryden. UnTE
Concerning the Nature of Love, *shorter sel.* ErPo
What Has This Bugbear Death, *fr.* III, *tr. by* Dryden. CTC
De Roberval, *sel.* John Hunter-Duvar.
La Belle Sauvage. OBCV
Deacon's Masterpiece, The; or, The Wonderful "One-Hoss Shay." Oliver Wendell Holmes. AP; PoIE; PoLF
Dead, The ("Blow out, you bugles, over the rich Dead"). Rupert Brooke. 1914, III. FaPL
Dead, The ("These hearts were woven"). Rupert Brooke. 1914, IV. MMA
Dead. Lionel Johnson. OBNC
Dead, The. C. Day Lewis. MP
Dead, The. Jones Very. AP
Dead and Gone. Anthony Thwaite. DaDu
Dead and the Living One, The. Thomas Hardy. MMA
Dead are born from the dark again, The. Reversions. Alfred Dorn. FiSC
Dead Boy. John Crowe Ransom. MP
Dead in Europe, The. Robert Lowell. DTC; ToPo
Dead in the Villages. Alfonso Gatto, *tr. fr. Italian by* John A. Scott. CoIP

Dead! Is it possible? He, the bold rider. Custer's Last Charge. Frederick Whittaker. OnMSP; PoLF; ThLM
Dead Knight, The. John Masefield. GTBS-P
Dead Man Ariseth and Singeth a Hymn to the Sun, The. *Unknown, tr. fr. Egyptian by* Robert Hillyer. *Fr.* Book of the Dead. SiGo
Dead Man's Dump. Isaac Rosenberg. CABL; GTBS-P; MMA
Dead Mole, A. Andrew Young. GTBS-P
Dead of Winter. Anthony Towne. StP
Dead pomp sneering underground. Stanzas on a Visit to Long-leat House in Wiltshire, October 1953. George Barker. ToPo
Dead President, The. Edward Rowland Sill. LiPo
Dead shalt thou lie; and nought. Achtung. Sappho. CTC
Dead woman lay in her first night's grave, The. The Dead and the Living One. Thomas Hardy. MMA
Deadly Kisses. Pierre de Ronsard, *tr. fr. French by* Andrew Lang. RBL
Deaf Woman's Courtship, The. *Unknown. See* Old Woman, Old Woman.
Dear Ann, wherever you are. For Ann Scott-Moncrieff. Edwin Muir. GTBS-P
Dear Aunt Ella, who warred with dirt. Aunt Ella. Guy Owen. PoNC
Dear Bill,/ When I search the past for you. A Letter to William Carlos Williams. Kenneth Rexroth. PP
Dear boy, you will not hear me speak. Pangloss's Song: A Comic-Opera Lyric. Richard Wilbur. AP
Dear brother Robin, this comes from us all. Country Letter. John Clare. CBEP
"Dear brother, when you go home to-night." Yonder School. *Unknown.* BFSS
Dear Cloe, how blubbered is that pretty face? A Better Answer. Matthew Prior. ELP
Dear common flower, that grow'st beside the way. To the Dandelion. James Russell Lowell. AP
Dear, damned, distracted town, farewell! A Farewell to London. Pope. CBEP
Dear Dark Head. *Unknown, tr. fr. Modern Irish by* Sir Samuel Ferguson. BoLP; SiGo; UnTE
(Cean Dubh Deelish.) ACV
Dear friend, far off, my lost desire. In Memoriam A. H. H., CXXIX. Tennyson. VP
Dear friend! whose holy, ever-living lines. The Match. Henry Vaughan. MeP
Dear friends, come listen to the tale. The Wreck of the *Atlantic. Unknown.* BSNS
Dear Geese, whose haunt is where weak waters flow. Sonnet. Luis de Góngora. RBL
Dear George,/ At last the blowfly's buzz retreats. Letter to a Friend. John Thompson. PoAu-2
Dear God, another day is done. An Evening Prayer. *Unknown.* STF
Dear God,/ give us a flood of water. The Prayer of the Little Ducks Who Went into the Ark. Carmen Bernos de Gasztold. ThGo
Dear God, my little boy of three. A Father's Prayer. *Unknown.* STF
Dear God, the standards of the knights. The Battle. Ben Said al-Magribi. AnML
Dear Grandmamma, with what we give. Grandmamma's Birthday. Hilaire Belloc. PoPl
Dear, If You Change. *Unknown.* CBEP; EnRePo
Dear is sleep; better to be stone now. To Night. Michelangelo. RBL
Dear little, pretty, favourite ore. On a Halfpenny which a Young Lady Gave a Beggar, and which the Author Redeemed for Half-a-Crown. Henry Fielding. CBEP
"Dear little tree that we plant today." An Arbor Day Tree. *Unknown.* RePo
Dear Lizbie Browne. To Lizbie Browne. Thomas Hardy. DTC; ELP
Dear Lord and Father of Mankind. Whittier. *Fr.* The Brewing of Soma. TRV
Dear Lord—before I take my place. A Driver's Prayer. *Unknown.* STF
Dear Lord, for all in pain. For All in Pain. Amy Carmichael. TRV
Dear Lord's best interpreters, The. In Earthen Vessels. Whittier. TRV
Dear Master, In Whose Life I See. John Hunter. TRV
Dear Mr. Editor: I wish to say. A Grievance. J. K. Stephen. Par
Dear mother, dear mother, the Church is cold. The Little Vagabond. Blake. CBEP
Dear night! this world's defeat. Night. Henry Vaughan. BoC
Dear Old Dad. Eva Gilbert Shaver. STF
Dear, on a day of dumb rain. Rain. Howard Moss. ErPo
Dear reliques of a dislodg'd soul, whose lack. Death's Lecture at the Funeral of a Young Gentleman. Richard Crashaw. SeCP

Dear Reynolds! as last night I lay in bed. Epistle to John Hamilton Reynolds. Keats. OBNC

Dear Smith, the sleest, paukie thief. Epistle to James Smith. Burns. CABL

Dear Son, Leave Thy Weeping. *Unknown.* CTC
(Jesus Comforts His Mother.) MeEL

Dear soul be strong! Richard Crashaw. *Fr.* On a Prayer Book Sent to Mrs. M. R. ErPo

Dear Tom, this brown jug that now foams with mild ale. The Brown Jug. Francis Fawkes. CBEP

Deare friend sit down, and bear awhile this shade. The Palm-Tree. Henry Vaughan. MeP

Deare love, for nothing lesse than thee. The Dreame. John Donne. SeCP

Dearest Love of God, I Pray Thee, Evermore Enfold My Soul. Mechthild von Magdeburg, tr. fr. German by R. G. L. Barrett. AnML

Death. Emily Brontë. OBNC

Death. John Clare. GTBS-P

Death. John Donne. See Death, Be Not Proud.

Death. Philip Freneau. *Fr.* The House of Night. AP

Death. George Herbert. MeP; PoIE; SeCP

Death. Friedrich Hölderlin, tr. fr. German by Lyn Goetze Snyder. AGP

Death. Walter Savage Landor. FaBV
("Death stands above me, whispering low.") OBNC

Death. Sir Thomas More. *Fr.* The Pageants of Thomas More. EnRePo

Death. Shelley. DiPo

Death. William Walsh. CBEP

Death, and darkness get you packing. Easter Hymn. Henry Vaughan. MeP

Death and the Maiden. Matthias Claudius, tr. fr. German by Dorothea M. Singer. AGP

Death, Be Not Proud. John Donne. Holy Sonnets, X. CBEP; FaBV; PoSa; StP; TRV
(Death.) BoC
("Death, be not proud, though some have called thee.") CABA; CaFP; DiPo; EnRePo; FoBA; ILP; MeP; OnP; PoIE; PoPo; SeCP

Death Bed. *See* Deathbed.

Death before Killing, A. Gray Burr. OPP

Death by Water. Hans Carl Artmann, tr. fr. German by Eva Hesse. MGP

Death by Water. T. S. Eliot. *Fr.* The Waste Land. DaDu; HaSV

Death Cannot Sour the Sweetness of Her Face. Petrarch, tr. fr. Italian by Morris Bishop. Sonnets to Laura: To Laura in Death, LXXXI. AnML

Death Carol. Walt Whitman. *Fr.* When Lilacs Last in the Dooryard Bloom'd. MoRP
(Carol of the Bird, The.) LV

Death execrable! Malady, Death and Resurrection of Saint Lazarus. *Unknown.* AnML

Death from Cancer. Robert Lowell. In Memory of Arthur Winslow, I. MP; PoSa
("This Easter, Arthur Winslow, less than dead.") AP

Death in Leamington. John Betjeman. ACV; PoPl

Death-in-Love. Dante Gabriel Rossetti. The House of Life, XLVIII. VP

Death in the Desert, A, *sels.* Robert Browning.
"For life, with all it yields of joy and woe." TRV
Old Whom God Loves, The. BoC

Death Is a Little Thing. George Abbe. FiSC

Death is here and death is there. Death. Shelley. DiPo

Death is the supple suitor. Emily Dickinson. StP

Death Mask of a Fisherman. George Bruce. ACV

Death, my lifes Mistress, and the soveraign Queen. To His Mistress for Her True Picture. Lord Herbert of Cherbury. SeCP

Death of a Bird. Jon Silkin. DaDu

Death of a Peasant. R. S. Thomas. PoIE

Death of a Son. Jon Silkin. GTBS-P

Death of a Toad, The. Richard Wilbur. AP; CABA; CaFP; VaPo

Death of a Whale. John Blight. PoAu-2

Death of an Aircraft. Charles Causley. MoBS

Death of Antoñito el Camborio. Federico García Lorca, tr. fr. Spanish by Robert O'Brien. AnSP

Death of Artemidora, The. Walter Savage Landor. *Fr.* Pericles and Aspasia. OBNC

Death of Ben Hall, The. Will H. Ogilvie. PoAu-1

Death of Jefferson, The. Hezekiah Butterworth. ThLM

Death of King Edward I, The. *Unknown.* MeEL

Death of Lincoln, The. Bryant. *See* Abraham Lincoln.

Death of Little Boys. Allen Tate. MP

Death of Nearchus, The. Alan Ansen. OPP

Death of Nick Charles, The. LeRoi Jones. CoPo

Death of Our Ladie, The. Robert Southwell. MeP

Death of Peter Esson, The. George Mackay Brown. NePoEA-2

Death of Prince Leopold, The. William McGonagall. EvOK

Death of Robert, Earl of Huntingdon, *sel.* Anthony Munday and Henry Chettle.

Dirge for Robin Hood. CBEP
(Dirge: "Weep, weep, ye woodmen, wail.") CTC
(Robin Hood's Funeral.) WiR

Death of Robin Hood, The. *Unknown.* BuBa

Death of Santa Claus, The. Vincent Starrett. FiSC

Death of Sir Nihil, book the nth. Tywater. Richard Wilbur. PoSa

Death of the Ball Turret Gunner, The. Randall Jarrell. AP; CaFP; ILP; PoPl; PoPo

Death of the Bird, The. A. D. Hope. PoAu-2

Death of the Flowers, The. Bryant. PoLF

Death of the Hired Man, The. Robert Frost. FoBA
Home, *sel.* TRV

Death of the Old Year, The, *sel.* Tennyson.
"Full knee-deep lies the winter snow." PoSC

Death of Venus, The. Robert Creeley. AmPC; StP

Death of Vitellozzo Vitelli, The. Irving Feldman. MP

Death on a Live Wire. Michael Baldwin. MoBS

Death, poker-faced and wearing livery. Dark Hotel. Alfred Dorn. FiSC

Death Song, A. Paul Laurence Dunbar. PoLF

Death Song. Robert Stephen Hawker. OBNC

Death stands above me, whispering low. Death. Walter Savage Landor. FaBV; OBNC

Death Swoops. Kenneth Pitchford. CoPo

Death, that struck when I was most confiding. Death. Emily Brontë. OBNC

Death the Leveller. James Shirley. *See* Glories of Our Blood and State.

Death, thou wast once an uncouth hideous thing. Death. George Herbert. MeP; PoIE; SeCP

Death-Wake, The; or, Lunacy, *sel.* Thomas Stoddart. Mirthful Lunacy. OBNC

Death, when you come to me, tread with a footstep. So Might It Be. John Galsworthy. PoLF

Death Bed, The. Thomas Hood. GTBS-P; OBNC
(We Watch'd Her Breathing.) ELP

Death-Bed. A. L. Rowse. WePo

Death-Bed, The. Siegfried Sassoon. MMA

Deaths at Paragon, Indiana, The. John Woods. CoPo

Death's Jest Book, *sels.* Thomas Lovell Beddoes.
Dirge: "If thou wilt ease thine heart," *fr.* II, ii. OBNC
Dirge: "Swallow leaves her nest, The," *fr.* I, iv. CBEP
(Voice from the Waters, A.) OBNC
Dirge: "We do lie beneath the grass," *fr.* V, iv. OBNC; WiR
(We Do Lie beneath the Grass.) ELP
"Fair and bright assembly, A: never strode," *fr.* II, iii. CTC
L'Envoi: "Who findeth comfort in the stars and flowers. OBNC
Old Adam, *fr.* V, iv. ELP
(Carrion Crow, The.) WiR
(Wolfram's Song.) CBEP
Song: "We have bathed, where none have seen us," *fr.* IV, iii. OBNC
Song by Isbrand ("Squats on a toad-stool"), *fr.* III, iii. OBNC

Death's Lecture at the Funeral of a Young Gentleman. Richard Crashaw. SeCP

Debate, A. Gaucelm Faidit, Uc de la Bacalaria, *and* Savaric de Mauleon, tr. fr. Provençal by Paul Blackburn. AnML

Debate with the Rabbi. Howard Nemerov. PoPl

Deborah danced, when she was two. Experience. Aline Kilmer. BiCB

Debt, The. Paul Laurence Dunbar. AmNP; TRV

Decade, A. Amy Lowell. BoLP; PoPl

Decades behind me. A Right-of-Way, 1865. William Plomer. DTC

Decameron, The, *sel.* Boccaccio, tr. fr. Italian by Lorna de' Lucchi.
Ballata: "I am young and fain to sing." RBL

Decay. George Herbert. MeP; SeCP

Deceiver Time. Luis de Góngora, tr. fr. Spanish by James Edward Tobin. AnSP

December, my dear, on the road to Nijmegen. The Road to Nijmegen. Earle Birney. OBCV

Dec. '63. Robert Sward. *Fr.* Five Poems for J. F. K. OPP

December Stillness. Siegfried Sassoon. MoRP

December 3. Vittorio Sereni, tr. fr. Italian by Carlo L. Golino. CoIP

Deceptions. Philip Larkin. CABA; ErPo; GTBS-P

Deck us all with Boston Charlie. Boston Charlie. Walt Kelly. GoJo

Declaration at Forty. Judson Crews. UnTE

Decline. Georg Trakl, tr. fr. German by Michael Hamburger. MGP
(Untergang, tr. by Walter Kaufmann.) TwGP

Decline and Fall of a Roman Umpire. Ogden Nash. SD

Decoration Day. Longfellow. PoSC

Dedication: "Bob Southey! You're a poet—Poet-laureate." Byron. *Fr.* Don Juan. CTC; ILP

Dedication, The: "Lord, my first fruits present themselves to thee." George Herbert. MeP

Dedication, The: "My God, thou that didst dye for me." Henry Vaughan. MeP
Dedication: "These to His memory—since he held them dear." Tennyson. *Fr.* Idylls of the King. CABA
Dedication, A: "They are rhymes rudely strung with intent less." Adam Lindsay Gordon. PoAu-1
Dedication: To Ianthe. Byron. *Fr.* Childe Harold's Pilgrimage. OBNC
Dedication: To Leigh Hunt, Esq. Keats. FoBA; OBNC
Dedication: To the Count of Niebla. Luis de Góngora, *tr. fr. Spanish* by Frances Fletcher. *Fr.* Fable of Polyphemus and Galatea. AnSP
Dedication of 1924, A. Rainer Maria Rilke, *tr. fr. German* by Walter Kaufmann. TwGP
Dedication on the Gift of a Book to a Child. Hilaire Belloc. ThGo
Dedication to Christina G. Rossetti. Swinburne. StP
Dedicatory Ode, *sel.* Hilaire Belloc.
They Say That in the Unchanging Place. PoLF
Deep and soft and far off over country. Before Harvest. Robert Fitzgerald. PoPl
Deep black against the dying glow. An Autumnal Evening. "Fiona Macleod." PoSC
Deep, deep in yonder valley. Flo-Ella. *Unknown.* BSO
Deep down the Blackman's Mind. R. E. G. Armattoe. ACV
Deep in Love. *Unknown.* CBEP
Deep in my soul there roared the crashing thunder. Calm after Storm. Frank Yerby. AmNP
Deep in the brown bosom. Bangkok. F. R. Scott. OBCV
Deep in the cool, dark wood. Undertone. Dorothy Quick. FiSC
Deep in the fading leaves of night. Carol. W. R. Rodgers. DTC
Deep in the shady sadness of a vale. Saturn. Keats. *Fr.* Hyperion; a Fragment. OBNC
Deep in the wave is a coral grove. The Coral Grove. James Gates Percival. AmLP
Deep on the convent-roof the snows. St. Agnes' Eve. Tennyson. ILP
Deep sea, whose thundering waves in tumult roar. To Don Juan de Austria. Fernando de Herrera. RBL
Deep Song. Antonio Machado, *tr. fr. Spanish* by John Crow. AnSP
Deep Summer, after Midnight. Thad Stem, Jr. PoNC
Deep-sworn Vow, A. W. B. Yeats. FoBA; PoPo
Deeply Gone. Jon Silkin. FiSC
Deeply repentant of my sinful ways. Gaspara Stampa, *tr. fr. Italian* by Lorna de' Lucchi. RBL
Deer Hunt. Sam Ragan. PoNC
Deer Sing, *sel.* Confucius, *tr. fr. Chinese* by Ezra Pound. *Fr.* The Classic Anthology. Fraternitas. CTC
Defeat may serve as well as victory. Victory in Defeat. Edwin Markham. PoLF; PoPl
Defeated, The. W. S. Merwin. AmPC
Defence of Guenevere, The. William Morris. StP
Defence of the Alamo, The. Joaquin Miller. OnMSP
Defiant Song, A. Kay Johnson. PtTo
Definition. May Sarton. MoLP
Definition of Love, The. Andrew Marvell. CBEP; DiPo; PoIE; SeCP; StP; VaPo
Definitive Journey, The. Juan Ramón Jiménez. *See* Conclusive Voyage, The.
Deformed Mistress, The. Sir John Suckling. ErPo
Deftly, admiral, cast your fly. Song. W. H. Auden. GTBS-P
Degenerate Douglas! O the unworthy lord! Composed at Neidpath Castle, the Property of Lord Queensberry 1803. Wordsworth. GTBS-P
Deigne at my hands this crown of prayer and praise. La Corona. John Donne. MeP
Dejection; an Ode. Samuel Taylor Coleridge. CABA; CBEP; OBNC; PoIE; StP
Delay Has Danger, *sel.* George Crabbe. *Fr.* Tales of the Hall.
Sad Lover, The. OBNC
Delgadina. *Unknown, tr. fr. Spanish* by Lysander Kemp. AnML
Delia. Samuel Daniel. *See* To Delia.
Delicate corner shot, The. Civilities. Thomas Whitbread. SD
Delicate fabric of bird song, A. May Day. Sara Teasdale. PoSC
Delicate young Negro stands, A. Anonymous Drawing. Donald Justice. NePoEA-2
Delicious Beauty. John Marston. UnTE
Délie, *sels.* Maurice Scève, *tr. fr. French.* RBL
"All judgment of this infinity," *tr.* by Harold M. Priest.
"Already the moon has shown me two crescents," *tr.* by Wallace Fowlie.
"Bound to the Caucasus of my suffering," *tr.* by Wallace Fowlie.
"Happiness of our happiness enflaming desire, The," *tr.* by Wallace Fowlie.
"I by myself, she in another's arms," *tr.* by Ida Fasel.

"If it is Love, why then does he kill me," *tr.* by Wallace Fowlie.
"If with her hand my fatal enemy," *tr.* by Wallace Fowlie.
"In the April of my age I was living free," *tr.* by Ida Fasel.
"Indolence of soft feathers, The," *tr.* by Wallace Fowlie.
"Lady, you are the body, and I am your shadow," *tr.* by Wallace Fowlie.
"Let silence or speech be permitted each one," *tr.* by Wallace Fowlie.
"Like Hecate you will make me wander," *tr. unknown.*
"Longer than a Platonic century," *tr.* by Wallace Fowlie.
"O years, O months, weeks, days and hours," *tr.* by Wallace Fowlie.
"Some delight in telling stories," *tr.* by Wallace Fowlie.
"White dawn had hardly finished, The," *tr.* by Wallace Fowlie.
Delight in Disorder. Robert Herrick. CABA; CBEP; ErPo; FaBV; ILP; PoIE; PoSa; PP; SeCP; StP; VaPo ("Sweet disorder in the dress, A.") GTBS-P
Delight it is in youth and May. More Poems, XVIII. A. E. Housman. VP
Delightful would it be to me to be in Uchd Ailiun. Hymn of St. Colum. *Unknown.* HaSV
Delights of the bottle and charms of old wine, The. Love and Wine. Thomas Shadwell. UnTE
Deliver Me. Amy Carmichael. STF
Deliver me, O beloved, from this evil. Lotuses. Witter Bynner. MoLP
Delivering Children. David Holbrook. NePoEA-2
Delphic and Theban and Corinthian. Four Legs, Three Legs, Two Legs. William Empson. ToPo
Demagogue, The. Phyllis McGinley. *Fr.* Epitaphs for Three Prominent Persons. LV
Demon Lover, The. *Unknown.* BuBa; CABA; PoPo (Daemon Lover, The.) CBEP
Demos. E. A. Robinson. AP
Denial, A. Elizabeth Barrett Browning. OBNC
Deniall. George Herbert. MeP
Denied, she screamed in rage, and ran away. You Can't Be Wise. Paul Engle. PoPl
Denise: A Letter Never Sent. Henri Coulette. *Fr.* The War of the Secret Agents. NePoEA-2
Dentist, The. Rose Fyleman. SoPo
Dentist drilled for two-and-one-half hours, The. Berlin Crisis. Florence Victor. OPP
Denuded Is the Earth. Antonio Machado, *tr. fr. Spanish* by Edward F. Gahan. AnSP
Denunciation. Wolfdietrich Schnurre, *tr. fr. German* by Michael Hamburger. MGP
Deo gracias, Anglia. A Carol of Agincourt. *Unknown.* MeEL
Deor's Lament. *Unknown, tr. fr. Anglo-Saxon.* LV (Deor, *tr.* by Burton Raffel.) CaFP
Departed friend, I do not come. Exequy: To Peter Allt. Kildare Dobbs. OBCV
Departed—to the judgment. Emily Dickinson. CABA
Departmental. Robert Frost. DiPo
Departure. William Hart-Smith. *Fr.* Christopher Columbus. PoAu-2
Departure. Coventry Patmore. The Unknown Eros, I, viii. FaPL; OBNC
Departure, The, an Elegy. Henry King. SeCP
Departure from Hydra, The. Kenneth Koch. AmPC
Departure in the Dark. C. Day Lewis. MP
"Deponent further sayeth The Bella J." Robert Hayden. *Fr.* Middle Passage. PtTo
Deposition by John Wilmot, A. Vincent McHugh. ErPo
Deprived of root, and branch and rind. A Maypole. Swift. CBEP
Derelict. Young E. Allison. OnMSP
"Dermont, you look so healthy now." The Drunkard's Dream. *Unknown.* BSO
Dervish. Georgia Lee McElhaney. CoPo
Descend, Beautiful Sun. Friedrich Hölderlin, *tr. fr. German* by Philip Allan Friedman. AGP
Descending. Robert Pack. NePoEA-2
Descent, The. William Carlos Williams. PoCh
Descent of Odin, The. Thomas Gray. EiCP
"Describe the Borough"—though our idle tribe. Letter I. George Crabbe. *Fr.* The Borough. CABL
Describes Rationally the Irrational Effects of Love. Sister Juana Inés de la Cruz, *tr. fr. Spanish* by Samuel Beckett. AnSP
Describes the Place Where Cynthia Is Sporting Herself. Girolamo Preti, *tr. fr. Italian* by Philip Ayres. RBL
Description, A. Lord Herbert of Cherbury. SeCP
Description of a City Shower, A. Swift. CABL; CBEP; EiCP; PoIE; VaPo
Description of a View. William Empson. ACV
Description of Beauty, A, *sel.* Samuel Daniel.
Enjoy Thy April Now. ELP; StP
Description of His Ugly Lady, A. Thomas Hoccleve. MeEL
Description of London, A. John Banks. WaPE

Description of Love, A. Sir Walter Ralegh. CBEP; ELP; UnTE
(Now What Is Love.) PoLF
Description of Maidenhead, A. Earl of Rochester. UnTE
Description of Sir Geoffrey Chaucer, The. Robert Greene. Fr. Greene's Vision. CTC
(Sir Geoffrey Chaucer.) WePo
Description of Spring. Earl of Surrey, after Petrarch. ILP; StP
(Soote Season, The.) EnRePo
(Spring.) PoIE
Description of the Morning, A. Swift. CABA; CaFP; EiCP; ILP; PoIE; StP
Desert Claypan. Frederick T. Macartney. PoAu-2
Desert, I'll call this castle which you were. True Name. Yves Bonnefoy. CoFP
Desert moves out on half the horizon, The. The Supper after the Last. Galway Kinnell. PoCh
Desert Places. Robert Frost. AP; CABA; DiPo; FoBA; PoIE; PoPo
Deserted Buildings under Shefford Mountain. John Glassco. OBCV
Deserted Farm. Guy Owen. PoNC
Deserted House. Sam Ragan. PoNC
Deserted House, sel. Dorothy Wellesley.
Buried Child, The. DTC
Deserted Village, The. Goldsmith. EnPE; ILP
Sels.
"Ill fares the land, to hastening ills a prey." TRV
"Near yonder copse, where once the garden smiled." TRV
Parson, The. WePo
Village Schoolmaster, The. PoSa
Desideria. Wordsworth. See Surprised by Joy.
Design. Robert Frost. AmLP; AP; CABA; CaFP; ILP; PoDB; PoIE; PoPo
Design for a Bowl. Anacreon, tr. fr. Greek by Thomas Moore. UnTE
Desire. Pierre Louÿs, tr. fr. French by Horace M. Brown. Fr. The Songs of Bilitis. UnTE
Desire for your bright hands. Ancient Winter. Salvatore Quasimodo. CoIP
Desire has never, through this maze's green. On an Old Castle-Park. Ferdinand von Saar. AGP
Desire that all men have is all my love. Love and Marriage. Ray Mathew. PoAu-2
Desiree,/ I find it most bitter that you. Denise: A Letter Never Sent. Henri Coulette. Fr. The War of the Secret Agents. NePoEA-2
Desolate. Sydney Dobell. CBEP; OBNC
Desolate and lone. Lost. Carl Sandburg. PoPl; PoPo; RePo
Desolation of the Poor Sentimental Poet. Sergio Corazzini, tr. fr. Italian by Ronald Farrar. CoIP
Despair. W. S. Merwin. AmPC
Despair Herself Regards Me as Her Son. Cecco Angiolieri, tr. fr. Italian by Daniel J. Donno. AnML
Despair is given me. Where Fled. John Wieners. CoPo
Despair, that seeking for the Ding-an-sich. Preludes for Memnon, V. Conrad Aiken. PoDB
Despairing Embrace, The. Pierre Louÿs, tr. fr. French by Horace M. Brown. Fr. The Songs of Bilitis. UnTE
Despairing Lover, The. William Walsh. BoLP; ELP; WePo
Despise the World. Unknown. MeEL
Despite and Still. Robert Graves. CBEP
Despite the drums we were ready to go. The Mountaineers. Dannie Abse. PP
Desponding Phyllis was endued. Phyllis. Swift. EiCP
Destined, while living, to sustain. An Epitaph on Herself. Hetty Wright. WaPE
Destiny. Sir Edwin Arnold. PoLF
Destiny. Matthew Arnold. VP
Destruction of Bulfinch's House, The. Stephen Sandy. CoPo
Destruction of Sennacherib, The. Byron. DiPo; EvOK; OnMSP; PoIE; PoLF; SIV
Destruction of Troy, The, sel. Unknown.
"Clear was the course of the cold floods." HaSV
Detail from an Annunciation by Crivelli. Rosemary Dobson. PoAu-2
Detail. Luke Zilles. RePo
Deuce, a roast of scraggy quails, a bit, The. Francesco Berni, tr. fr. Italian by Lorna de' Lucchi. RBL
Deutsches Reich. Schiller, tr. fr. German by Walter Kaufmann. TwGP
Development of Idiotcy, A. Ebenezer Jones. OBNC
Deviator, The. Bertram Warr. OBCV
Devil, The. Unknown. STF
Devil and the Angel, The, sels. Rosemary Dobson.
"Chancing upon the Devil in the doorway," I. ACV
Methuselah, VI. PoAu-2
Devil and the Governor, The, sel. William Forster.
"In New South Wales, as I plainly see." PoAu-1
Devil daddied Cerberus, lamented of his progeny. Hybris, Nemesis, One, Two, Three. Alicia Ostriker. StP
Devil Doll. Lisa Grenelle. FiSC
Devil's Advice to Story-Tellers, The. Robert Graves. CBEP

Devil's Law Case, The, sel. John Webster.
All the Flowers of the Spring. CBEP; ELP
(Speech by Romelio.) PoIE
Devil's Nine Questions, The. Unknown. BFSS
Devil's Song, The. Unknown. BSNS
Devouring Time, blunt thou the lion's paw. Sonnets, XIX. Shakespeare. CBEP; DiPo; FoBA
Devout Man Prays to His Relations, The. William Herebert. MeEL
Devout Prayer of the Passion, A. Unknown. MeEL
Dew Sat on Julia's Hair. Robert Herrick. ELP
Dew, the rain and moonlight, The. A Net to Snare the Moonlight. Vachel Lindsay. PoLF
Dewdrops hang from leaf and stem. May Thirtieth. Unknown. PoSC
Dey had a gread big pahty down to Tom's de othah night. The Party. Paul Laurence Dunbar. AmNP
Dial Tone, The. Howard Nemerov. ToPo
Dialect Quatrain. Marcus B. Christian. AmNP
Dialogue, A. John Dowland. HaSV
Dialogue. Howard Nemerov. PoPl
Dialogue between the Lovelorn Sir Hugh and Certain Ladies of Venice, A. Thomas Deloney. UnTE
Dialogue between the Resolved Soul, and Created Pleasure, A. Andrew Marvell. MeP; SeCP
Dialogue between the Soul and Body, A. Andrew Marvell. MeP; SeCP
Dialogue between Thyrsis and Dorinda, A. Andrew Marvell. SeCP
Dialogue betwixt Time and a Pilgrime, A. Aurelian Townsend. SeCP
Dialogue in Praise of the Owl and the Cuckoo. Shakespeare. See When Daisies Pied.
Dialogue of Self and Soul, A. W. B. Yeats. CABA; PoDB
"Living man is blind and drinks his drop, A," sel. DTC
Dialogue on the Headland. Robert Graves. ACV
Dialogue with a Door. Catullus, tr. fr. Latin by John Nott. UnTE
Diamond Ring, The. Unknown. See Zillah.
Diana, with music. Unknown. BSO
Diane de Poitiers, Josephine and Pompadour. Mother Goose Rhyme. Kenneth Rexroth. ErPo
Diaphenia. At. to Henry Constable and to Henry Chettle. CBEP; GTBS-P
(Damelias' Song to His Diaphenia.) ELP
Diary of a Church Mouse. John Betjeman. BoC
Dick and Will. Elizabeth Madox Roberts. BiCB
Dick Johnson Reel, The. "Jake Falstaff." EvOK
Dick Straightup. Ted Hughes. ToPo
Dick Turpin and the Lawyer. Unknown. BSNS
Dick Turpin's Ride. Unknown. BSNS
Dictum: For a Masque of Deluge. W. S. Merwin. AP
Did a blowing cherry blossom drift in? At Daybreak. Helen Hoyt. BiCB
Did all the lets and bars appear. The March into Virginia. Herman Melville. AP; PoIE
Did I love thee? I only did desire. Rondo. George Moore. UnTE
Did it yell. Cicada-Shell. Basho. SoPo
Did Not. Thomas Moore. ErPo
Did Sabine grace adorn my living line. Wordsworth. Fr. An Evening Walk. EiCP
"Did she take your hat, Billy Boy, charming Billy?" Billy Boy (E vers.). Unknown. BSO
Did the harebell loose her girdle. Emily Dickinson. FaBV
Did you ever see a wild goose floating on the ocean? The Wild Goose. Unknown. BSNS
Did you ever sit and ponder, sit and wonder, sit and think. Life's a Funny Proposition after All. George M. Cohan. PoLF
Did you ever think how queer? A Birthday. Rachel Field. BiCB
Did you never hear tell of pretty Polly Brannigan. Fragments of Irish Songs. Unknown. BSO
Did you hear of the curate who mounted his mare. The Priest and the Mulberry-Tree. Thomas Love Peacock. Fr. Crotchet Castle. OnMSP
Did you think of us this morning. Who Prayed? Unknown. STF
Dido ("Dido was the Carthage Queen"). Thomas Campion. CBEP
Didyma. Unknown, tr fr Greek by Louis Untermeyer. UnTE
Didymus. Louis MacNeice. EaLo
Died of Love. Unknown. CBEP
Dietrich Bonhoeffer, Awaiting Execution in a Concentration Camp, Prays for His Fellow Prisoners. Dietrich Bonhoeffer, tr. fr. German. BoC
Difference, The. Eleanor A. Chaffee. BiCB
Difference, The. Benjamin Franklin. PoPo
Difference, The. Guido Gozzano, tr. fr. Italian by Carlo L. Golino. CoIP
Difference, The ("Drop an unkind word or careless"). Unknown. STF
Difference, The (" 'Twixt optimist and pessimist"). Unknown. LV

Difficult Combination, The. Schiller, *tr. fr. German by* Walter Kaufmann. TwGP
Digging for China. Richard Wilbur. GoJo; LOW; MP
Digging It Out. John Hollander. AmPC
Dignity of Labor, The. Robert Bersohn. PoPl
Dilation. "Will Inman." PoNC
"Dim grows your face, and in my ears." A Colonist in His Garden. William Pember Reeves. ACV
Dim script on the yellow sheets of pioneer diaries, The. Missouri Rhapsody. James Daugherty. RePo
Dim sea glints chill, The. The white sun is shy. The Sign-Post. Edward Thomas. PoIE
Ding Dong. A. C. Hilton. Par
Ding, Dong, Bell. Mother Goose. SoPo
Ding dong, ding dong. Ding Dong. A. C. Hilton. Par
Dink's Song. *Unknown.* ErPo
Dinosaur, The. Carl S. Junge. SoPo
Dinosaurs are not all dead, The. Steam Shovel. Charles Malam. PoPo
Diodorus Siculus. *Unknown.* ErPo
Dionysus. Irving Layton. ErPo
Dip down upon the northern shore. In Memoriam A. H. H., LXXXIII. Tennyson. VP
Dipsychus, *sels.* Arthur Hugh Clough.
　As I sat at the Café, *fr.* Pt. II, sc. ii, *also in* Spectator ab Extra. ELP; WePo, *st.* 1
　(Spectator ab Extra, 3 *sts.*) GTBS-P
　There Is No God, *fr.* Pt. I, sc. v. FaPL
　"Yet I could think, indeed, the perfect call," *fr.* Pt. II, sc. v. OBNC
Dirce. Walter Savage Landor. *Fr.* Pericles and Aspasia. CBEP; CTC; OBNC; StP
Direct Song. Eve Merriam. UnTE
Direct This Day. Thomas Ken. TRV
Directions. Onitsura, *tr. fr. Japanese by* Harold G. Henderson. SoPo
Directive. Robert Frost. AP; CABA; DiPo; OnP; PoDB
Dirge, A: "Hark, now everything is still." John Webster. *Fr.* The Duchess of Malfi. CBEP
Dirge: "If thou wilt cease thine heart." Thomas Lovell Beddoes. *Fr.* Death's Jest Book. OBNC
Dirge, A: "Naiad, hid beneath the bank." William Johnson Cory. OBNC
Dirge: "1-2-3 was the number he played but today the number came 3-2-1." Kenneth Fearing. CaFP; PoIE; PoSa; ThLM
Dirge, A: "Rough wind, that moanest loud." Shelley. CABA; DiPo; LV; WiR
Dirge: "Swallow leaves her nest, The." Thomas Lovell Beddoes. *Fr.* Death's Jest Book, I, iv. CBEP
　(Voice from the Waters, A.) OBNC
Dirge: "We do lie beneath the grass." Thomas Lovell Beddoes. *Fr.* Death's Jest Book, V, iv. OBNC; WiR
　(We Do Lie beneath the Grass.) ELP
Dirge: "Weep, weep, ye woodmen, wail." Anthony Munday *and* Henry Chettle. *See* Dirge for Robin Hood.
Dirge: "What longer need hath she of loveliness." Sarojini Naidu. ACV
Dirge for a Bad Boy. E. V. Rieu. BBGG
Dirge for McPherson, A. Herman Melville. AP
Dirge for Robin Hood. Anthony Munday *and* Henry Chettle. *Fr.* Death of Robert, Earl of Huntingdon. CBEP
　(Dirge: "Weep, weep, ye woodmen, wail.") CTC
　(Robin Hood's Funeral.) WiR
Dirge for the New Sunrise. Edith Sitwell. *Fr.* Three Poems of the Atomic Age. ACV; EaLo; MoRP
Dirge in "Cymbeline." William Collins. *See* Song from Shakespeare's "Cymbeline," A.
Dirge in Woods. George Meredith. OBNC; VP; WiR
Dirge of Love. Shakespeare. *See* Come Away, Come Away, Death.
Dirge without Music. Edna St. Vincent Millay. LV; MoRP
Dirigible, The. Ralph W. Bergengren. SoPo
Dirty Word, The. Karl Shapiro. PoCh
Disabled. Wilfred Owen. MMA
Disappointed Wife, The. Hetty Wright. WaPE
Disappointment, The. Earl of Rochester. UnTE
Disappointment ("Disappointment—His appointment"). Edith Lillian Young. TRV
Discerning the Lord's Body. Carrie Judd Montgomery. STF
Discipleship. C. O. Bales. STF
Discipline. George Herbert. PoLF
Discord in Childhood. D. H. Lawrence. CBEP
Discordants. Conrad Aiken. BoLP
　Music I Heard, *sel.* PoPo
Discouraged. Lucille Stanaback. STF
Discouragement's mold, the first cobweb of despair. The Invaders. Jocelyn Macy Sloan. FiSC
Discoveries. Vernon Watkins. PoIE
Discovery, The. J. C. Squire. PoSC
Discreet householder exclaims on the grandsire, A. Old Man Playing with Children. John Crowe Ransom. AnMoPo
Discretion. *Unknown.* CBEP
Disdain Me Not. Sir Thomas Wyatt. EnRePo

Disdain Returned. Thomas Carew. LV, 2 *sts.*; PoIE, 3 *sts.*
　(He That Loves a Rosy Cheek.) FaBV, 2 *sts.*
　(True Beauty, The.) GTBS-P 2 *sts.*; PoPo, 2 *sts.*
Disguises. Elizabeth Jennings. NePoEA-2
Disheartened Ranger, The, *with music. Unknown.* BFSS
Dishonest Miller, The (B *vers., with music*). *Unknown.* BSO
Dishonor. Edwin Denby. ErPo
Disillusionment of Ten o'Clock. Wallace Stevens. LOW; PoIE; PoPo; PoSa
Disinherited, The, *sel.* Mary Gilmore.
　"Sudden autumn winds, like hounds, The." PoAu-1
Dismantled Ship, The. Walt Whitman. CABA; CBEP
Dismissing bees and bookmen from. Professor Nocturnal. Raymond Roseliep. FiSC
Dispersion, The. Heinz Piontek, *tr. fr. German by* Christopher Middleton. MGP
Dispossessed, The. John Berryman. AP; PoCh
Dispute of Charlot and the Barber, The. Rutebeuf, *tr. fr. French by* William M. Davis. AnML
Dispute of Elena and Maria. *Unknown, tr. fr. Spanish by* William M. Davis. AnML
Dissolution, The. John Donne. ILP
Dissolving, the coals shift. Rain swaddles us. The Ruin. Charles Tomlinson. NePoEA-2
Distance. Robert Creeley. CoPo
Distance in Your Touch, The. "Will Inman." PoNC
Distant as the Duchess of Savoy. *Unknown.* MeEL
Distant Drum, The. Calvin C. Hernton. NNP
Distant evening peaceful with the sound of bells, The. Grass and Milk. Alfonso Gatto. CoIP
Distracted with care. The Despairing Lover. William Walsh. BoLP; ELP; WePo
Distraction. Henry Vaughan. SeCP
Distraction is the panacea, Sir! Modern Love, XXVII. George Meredith. VP
Dithyramb in Retrospect. Peter Hopegood. PoAu-2
Ditty, A: "My true-love hath my heart, and I have his." Sir Philip Sidney. *See* My True Love Hath My Heart.
Diver, The. Leonard E. Nathan. ErPo
Diver, The. Theobald Purcell-Buret. HaSV
Diver, The. W. W. E. Ross. OBCV
Divers are like insertions, incisions, when they fall. The Compleat Swimmer. Charles Edward Eaton. PoNC
Diversely passioned is the lover's heart. The Eleventh Property. Sir Thomas More. *Fr.* The Twelve Properties or Conditions of a Lover. EnRePo
Diverting History of John Gilpin, The. William Cowper. EiCP; RoGo; WePo
　(John Gilpin.) CABL
Dives and Lazarus. *Unknown.* ELP
Divided, *sel.* Jean Ingelow.
　"Dappled sky, a world of meadows, A." OBNC
Divina Commedia, *sels.* Dante, *tr. fr. Italian.*
　Paradiso.
　　Dante's Heaven, *fr.* I, *tr. by* Dorothy Sayers. BoC
　　"I raised my eyes aloft, and I beheld," 4 *ll.* TRV
　Purgatorio.
　　Dante and Beatrice in the Earthly Paradise, *fr.* XXVIII, *tr. by* Dorothy Sayers. BoC
　　Dante's Angels, *fr.* VIII, *tr. by* Dorothy Sayers. BoC
Divina Commedia (*poems introductory to* Longfellow's *tr. of the* Divine Comedy, I-VI). VP
　(Sonnets on the Divina Commedia.) ILP
　　How Strange the Sculptures, II. DiPo
Divination by a Cat. Anthony Hecht. StP
Divine Comedy, The. Dante. *See* Divina Commedia.
Divine Image, A ("Cruelty has a human heart"). Blake. OBNC; PoIE
Divine Image, The ("To Mercy, Pity, Peace, and Love"). Blake. *Fr.* Songs of Innocence. CBEP; EnPE; OBNC; PoIE; TRV
Divine Office of the Kitchen, The. Cecily Hallack. PoLF. *See also* Lord of All Pots and Pans and Things.
Divine Oracles, tell me when. In Acknowledgment of the Praises of European Writers. Sister Juana Inés de la Cruz. AnSP
Divine Paradox, The. *Unknown.* PoIE
　(Wit Wonders.) MeEL
Divine Poems, *sels.* José Garcia Villa.
　"Sir, I commend to you the spirit," XLV. MoRP
　"Within the city of my death," LXXIV. MoRP
Divine Ship Sails the Divine Sea for You, The. Walt Whitman. MoRP
Divinely Superfluous Beauty. Robinson Jeffers. MoLP; PoPL
Division, The. Thomas Hardy. VP
Division of Parts, The. Anne Sexton. NePoEA-2
Dixie Brown. *Unknown.* BSNS
Dixie's Green Shore, *with music. Unknown.* BFSS
Dixie's Isle. *Unknown.* BSNS
Dizain to Clément Marot. Marguerite de Navarre, *tr. fr. French by* Wilfrid Thorley. RBL
Dmitri of Carpathos. Lawrence Durrell. AnMoPo
Do' a-stan'in' on a jar, fiah a-shinin' thoo. Howdy, Honey, Howdy! Paul Laurence Dunbar. PoLF

Do [*or* Doe] but consider this small dust. The Hour-Glass [*or* Houre-Glasse]. Ben Jonson. CBEP; EnRePo; SeCP
Do I love you? The question might be well. In Consolation. Vassar Miller. ToPo
Do I Not Deal with Angels. Kenneth Patchen. ToPo
Do I Really Pray? John Burton. STF
Do It Now. *Unknown.* STF
Do it, then. If you do. It. Richmond Lattimore. PP
Do not ask me, charming Phillis. By the Bank of Pinks and Lilies. *Unknown.* ErPo
Do not conceive that I shall here recount. A Virgin Declares Her Beauties. Francesco da Barberini. ErPo
Do not despair. For Johnny. John Pudney. WePo
Do not enforce the tired wolf. Prelude to an Evening. John Crowe Ransom. AP; ILP; PoCh
Do not enquire from the centurion nodding. The Silver Age. Thom Gunn. ToPo
Do Not Fear. John Fletcher. *Fr.* The Faithful Shepherdess, III, i. CBEP
Do not fear, my love; no danger. Precaution. Heine. UnTE
Do not fear to put thy feet. Do Not Fear. John Fletcher. *Fr.* The Faithful Shepherdess. CBEP
Do Not Go Gentle into That Good Night. Dylan Thomas. ACV; AnMoPo; CABA; DiPo; FaPL; MP; PoSa; ToPo; WePo
Do Not, Oh Do Not Prize. *Unknown.* CBEP
Do not press my hands. Intimate. "Gabriela Mistral." AnSP
Do not rub the notched coin clean. Coin from Bir el Abbas. Peter Huchel. MGP
Do not rumple my Top-Knot. The Coy Lass Dress'd Up in Her Best. *Unknown.* ErPo
Do Not Speak to Me, Count. *Unknown, tr. fr. Spanish by* James Duffy. AnML
Do not spend your time in fretting. When Things Go Wrong. *Unknown.* STF
Do not stifle me with the strange scent. Alien. Donald Jeffrey Hayes. AmNP
"Do not take a bath in Jordan." Scotch Rhapsody. Edith Sitwell. MP
Do not weep, maiden, for war is kind. War Is Kind, I. Stephen Crane. AP; DiPo; PoLF; PoPo; StP; ThLM
Do Something. *Unknown.* STF
Do They Miss Me at Home? A Parody, *with music.* Mart Taylor. SGR
Do we indeed desire the dead. In Memoriam A. H. H., LI. Tennyson. VP
Do We Not Hear Thy Footfall? Amy Carmichael. TRV
Do you ask me what I think of. What I Think of Hiawatha. J. W. Morris. Par
Do You Ask What the Birds Say? Samuel Taylor Coleridge. ThGo
Do You Fear the Wind? Hamlin Garland. PoPl
Do You Just Belong? *Unknown.* STF
Do You Know What the Hedgehog Said? "Spervogel," *tr. fr. German by* Ruth Yorck *and* Kenward Elmslie. AnML
Do you love me? *Unknown.* PoSC
Do You Not Father Me. Dylan Thomas. ToPo
"Do you not hear the Aziola cry." The Aziola. Shelley. CBEP
Do you remember? To James. Frank Horne. BiCB; LV
Do you remember an Inn? Tarantella. Hilaire Belloc. WePo
Do you remember me? or are you proud? Walter Savage Landor. *Fr.* Ianthe. OBNC
Do you remember, passer-by, the path. James Garber. Edgar Lee Masters. *Fr.* Spoon River Anthology. ILP
Do You Remember That Night? *Unknown, tr. fr. Gaelic by* Eugene O'Curry. BoLP
Do you remember that you wanted to be a Marguerite Gautier? Marguerite. Rubén Dario. AnSP
Do you remember the meadow-field. The Meadow-Field. Charles Sangster. *Fr.* Pleasant Memories. OBCV
Do you suppose it's really really true. Run, Kitty, Run! Jimmy Garthwaite. BBGG
Do you think we skip. The Zobo Bird. Frank A. Collymore. GoJo
Do your days seem long, your pleasures few. He Cares. Owen C. Salway. STF
Doctor Faustus. Geoffrey Hill. NePoEA-2
Dr. Faustus, *sels.* Christopher Marlowe.
  Face of Helen, The. FaBV
  "That I might have unto my paramour." FaPL
Dr. Fell and Points West. Ogden Nash. RePo
Doctor fingers my bruise. The Passing Out. Philip Levine. AmPC
Dr. Newman with the crooked pince-nez. Grotesque. Robert Graves. DTC
Doctor punched my vein, The. Scyros. Karl Shapiro. ILP
Dr. Unlikely, we love you so. Horror Movie. Howard Moss. NePoEA-2
Doctors' Row. Conrad Aiken. AP; PoPl
Doctrinal Point. William Empson. ToPo
Doe but consider this small dust. *See* Do but consider this small dust.
Does Daddy Go? *Unknown.* STF
Does It Matter? Siegfried Sassoon. PoPo

Does the eagle know what is in the pit? Thel's Motto. Blake. *Fr.* The Book of Thel. DiPo
Does the road wind up-hill all the way? Up-Hill. Christina Rossetti. FaPL; OBNC; VP; WiR
Dog, The. Oliver Herford. FaBV
Dog. William Jay Smith. GoJo
Dog and Gun. *Unknown. See* Jolly Farmer, The.
Dog and the Cat, The. Grace Taber Hallock. RePo
Dog called Sesamè slewed out, The. Stray Dog, near Ecully, Valley of the Rhône. Margaret Avison. OBCV
Dog emerges from the flies, A. Nino, the Wonder Dog. Roy Fuller. PoPo
Dog in a Car. David McCord. RePo
Dog loved its churlish life, The. Lupercalia. Ted Hughes. ToPo
Dog Sleeping on My Feet, A. James Dickey. PP
Dog trots freely in the street, The. Lawrence Ferlinghetti. *Fr.* Oral Messages. ToPo
Dog will often steal a bone, A. A Cat's Conscience. *Unknown.* PoLF
Dog yelped, skunk let fly, The. Larry Eigner. CoPo
Dogma. Babette Deutsch. MoLP
Dogs. Frances Cornford. *Fr.* Feri's Dream. ThGo
Dogs are quite a bit like people. Dog. William Jay Smith. GoJo
Dogwood, The. Robert Penn Warren. Dark Woods, II. PoDB
Doing a Filthy Pleasure Is [and Short]. Petronius Arbiter, *tr. fr. Latin by* Ben Jonson. CABA; ErPo
  (Against Consummation.) UnTE
Doll in the doll-maker's house, A. The Dolls. W. B. Yeats. StP
Doll Song. "Lewis Carroll." SoPo
Dollar and a Half a Day, A. *Unknown.* BSNS
Dollar I Gave, A. *Unknown.* STF
Dolls, The. John Ciardi. ToPo
Dolls, The. W. B. Yeats. StP
Dolor. Theodore Roethke. AP; CABA; ILP; PoIE; PoSa
Dolor Oogo. Sir Arthur Quiller-Couch. HaSV
Dolores. Swinburne. VP
  "We shift and bedeck and bedrape us," *sel.* UnTE
Dome of Sunday, The. Karl Shapiro. AP
Domestic: Climax. Merrill Moore. ErPo
Domination of Black. Wallace Stevens. AP; ILP
Dominic Has a Doll. E. E. Cummings. PoPl
Dominion of Australia, The. Brunton Stephens. PoAu-1
Don Juan, *sels.* Byron.
  And Angling, Too, *fr.* XIII. SD
  Dedication: "Bob Southey! You're a poet—Poet-laureate." CTC; ILP
  Fragment: "I would to heaven that I were so much clay," *on the back of the poet's MS of* I. CTC; ILP
  Haidée and Don Juan, *fr.* II. OBNC
  "In her first passion woman loves her lover," *fr.* I. ErPo; UnTE
  Isles of Greece, The, *fr.* III. CBEP; PoIE; RoGo
  My Days of Love Are Over, *fr.* I. OBNC
  "'Twas midnight—Donna Julia was in bed," *fr.* I. UnTE
Don Pitas Payas. Juan Ruiz, Archpriest of Hita, *tr. fr. Spanish by* William M. Davis. *Fr.* The Book of True Love. AnML
Don Quixote, *sels.* Cervantes, *tr. fr. Spanish by* Samuel Putnam. RBL
  Epitaph: "Below there rests the knight."
  Epitaph: "Here Dulcinea doth lie."
  "Love's mariner am I."
  "Oh, could my 'was' an 'is' become."
  "O thou above who in thy bed."
  "Ye trees and shrubs, each plant."
Don Quixote in England, *sel.* Henry Fielding.
  Hunting Song, *fr.* II. StP
Donald Munro. *Unknown.* BSNS
Donall Oge: Grief of a Girl's Heart. *Unknown, tr. fr. Modern Irish by* Lady Gregory. BoLP
Done is a battell on the dragon blak! A Hymn of the Resurrection. William Dunbar. MeEL
Done to death by slanderous tongues. Epitaph. Shakespeare. *Fr.* Much Ado about Nothing. CTC
Dong with a Luminous Nose, The. Edward Lear. CBEP; FaBV; WiR
Donkey, The. G. K. Chesterton. BoC; FaBV; LV; PoLF; PoPo
Donkey, The. P. R. Kaikini. ACV
Donkey, The. *Unknown.* BiCB
Donkey. Mark Van Doren. EaLo
Donne, the delight of Phoebus, and each Muse. To John Donne. Ben Jonson. StP
Don't. *Unknown.* STF
Don't ask where is Wisdom be sought as ecstatic music. The Undertaking. Gerrit Lansing. CoPo
Don't be sad, goldeyed toad. The Polish Reaper. Peter Huchel. MGP
Don't blush, dear sir, your flame to own. To a Gentleman in Love with a Negro Woman. Sneyd Davies. WaPE
Don't boast your unbelief in woods! A Warning to Skeptics. Leah Bodine Drake. FiSC

Don't Dare Be Larger than a Sparrow's Head. Christine Lavant, *tr. fr. German by* Nora Wydenbruck. MGP
Don't get discouraged when you hear. Don't. *Unknown.* STF
Don't get the wrong idea. Eyewitness. Rodney Hall. PoAu-2
Don't knock any nails in the wall. Thoughts on the Length of Exile. Bertolt Brecht. MGP
Don't Quit. *Unknown.* STF
Don't read odes, boy, timetables. For a Senior College Textbook. Hans Magnus Enzensberger. MGP
Don't scream at me you God damn' wops. Kennedy Ucciso. Richard F. Hugo. OPP
Don't Shake the Bottle, Shake Your Mother-in-Law. Phyllis McGinley. LV
Don't Sit under the Apple Tree with Anyone Else but Me. Robert Pack. CoPo
Don't Tell Me. *Unknown.* STF
Don't tell Papa his nose is red. Harry Graham. *Fr.* A Children's Don't. BBGG
Don't waste your time in longing. Shine Just Where You Are. *Unknown.* STF
Don't worry, it will come! You're drawing near. Sonnet. Phillipe Jaccottet. CoFP
Don't you remember sweet Betsy from Pike. Sweet Betsy from Pike. *Unknown.* BFSS
Dooley Is a Traitor. James Michie. NePoEA-2
Doom. Rubén Darío, *tr. fr. Spanish by* Kate Flores. AnSP
Doom is dark and deeper than any sea-dingle. Chorus. W. H. Auden. GTBS-P
Doom of Devorgoil, The, *sels.* Sir Walter Scott.
Bonnie Dundee, *abr., fr.* II, ii. Par
Datur Hora Quieti, I. GTBS-P
Doomed Man, The. Joseph Addison Alexander. TRV
Dooms-Day. George Herbert. SeCP
Door, The. Robert Creeley. ToPo
Door is on the latch tonight, The. Christmas Eve. *Unknown.* TRV
Door of existence, beacon of our haze. Bernard O'Dowd. *Fr.* Alma Venus. PoAu-1
Door still swinging to, and girls revive, The. A Dream of Fair Women. Kingsley Amis. MP
Doors. Carl Sandburg. LOW
Doors were cedar, The. Four Preludes on Playthings of the Wind, II. Carl Sandburg. AmLP
Doors, where my heart was used to beat. In Memoriam A. H. H., CXIX. Tennyson. DiPo; OBNC; VP
Doppelganger, The. Daryl Hine. OBCV
Dora Markus. Eugenio Montale, *tr. fr. Italian by* Carlo L. Golino. CoIP
Dorchester Giant, The. Oliver Wendell Holmes. OnMSP
Δωρια (Doria). Ezra Pound. AnMoPo; PoIE
Doric. Angelos Sikelianos, *tr. fr. Greek by* Edmund Keeley *and* Philip Sherrard. ErPo
Dorking Thigh, The. William Plomer. WePo
Dorothy Q. Oliver Wendell Holmes. AP
Dosser in Springtime, The. Douglas Stewart. ErPo
Dost see how unregarded now. Sonnet. Sir John Suckling. ELP
Dost thou look back on what hath been. In Memoriam A. H. H., LXIV. Tennyson. VP
Dost thou remember ever, for my sake. Mathilde Blind. *Fr.* Love in Exile. OBNC
Dot is five and Jack is ten. A Puzzling Example. Virginia Sarah Benjamin. BiCB
. . . Doth most humbly show it. The Humble Petition of Poor Ben to the Best of Monarchs, Masters, Men, King Charles. Ben Jonson. PP
Doth not wisdom cry? and understanding put forth her voice? Proverbs, Bible, *O.T.* BoC
Doth some one say that there be gods above? There Are No Gods. Euripides. *Fr.* Bellerophon. EaLo
Doth then the world go thus, doth all thus move? William Drummond of Hawthornden. GTBS-P
Doting father once there was, A. Piano Practice. Ian Serraillier. BBGG
Double Duty. W. E. Farbstein. PoPl
Double flower we are, A. A Waltz in the Afternoon. Beth Bentley. BoLP
Double Gift. *Unknown, tr. fr. Greek by* Louis Untermeyer. UnTE
Double Monologue. Adrienne Rich. NePoEA-2
Double Play, The. Robert Wallace. PP; SD
Double Tree, The. Winfield Townley Scott. PoPl
Doubt of Future Foes, The. Elizabeth I, Queen of England. CTC
Douglas Tragedy, The. *Unknown.* PoPo
Dove. The. T. S. Eliot. *Fr.* Four Quartets: Little Gidding. BoC
Dove-colored, the shadows melt and mingle. Twilight. Feodor Tyutchev. SiGo
Dove descending breaks the air, The. The Dove. T. S. Eliot. *Fr.* Four Quartets. BoC
Dove sta amore. Lawrence Ferlinghetti. *Fr.* A Coney Island of the Mind. ToPo
Dove that remained outside, outside the dovecote. Rainer Maria Rilke, *tr. fr. German by* Walter Kaufmann. TwGP

Dover Beach. Matthew Arnold. BoLP; CABA; CaFP; CBEP; DiPo; DTC; EaLo; FaBV; FaPL; GTBS-P; HaSV; ILP; LV; OBNC; OnP; PoIE; PoPl; PoPo; PoSa; StP; TRV; VaPo; VP
"Sea is calm to-night, The," *sel.* WePo
Dover Bitch, The. Anthony Hecht. NePoEA-2; PP
Dove's Loneliness, The. George Darley. OBNC
Down/ Down into the fathomless depths. Black Is a Soul. Joseph White. PtTo
Down a Sunny Easter Meadow. Nancy Byrd Turner. SoPo
Down Beyond the Hillside. *Unknown.* BSO
Down by the church-way walk, and where the brook. An Ancient Virgin. George Crabbe. *Fr.* The Parish Register. OBNC
Down by the Salley Gardens. W. B. Yeats. BoLP; CTC; FoBA
Down! Down! Eleanor Farjeon. SoPo
Down every passage of the cloister hung. Upon the Death of George Santayana. Anthony Hecht. AmLP; CoPo
Down from his post in the tower. Across the Straits. Rosemary Dobson. PoAu-2
Down in a Garden. *Unknown.* CBEP
(Riddle, The.) UnTE
Down in Dallas. X. J. Kennedy. CoPo; OPP
Down in old England there lived three brothers. The Pirates. *Unknown.* BSO
Down in Skytown, *with music. Unknown.* BSO
Down [or Downe] in the depth of mine iniquity. Caelica, XCIX. Fulke Greville. EnRePo; PoIE
Down in the Hollow. Aileen Fisher. SoPo
Down in the lowlands a poor boy did wander. The Fisherman's Boy. *Unknown.* BSO
Down in the Meadows. *Unknown.* CBEP
Down in the meadows fresh and gay. Deep in Love. *Unknown.* CBEP
Down in the meadows the other day. Down in the Meadows. *Unknown.* CBEP
Down in the rushes beside the pool. The Frogs' Singing-School. E. T. Carbell. SoPo
Down in the South, by the waste without sail on it. Beyond Kerguelen. Henry Kendall. PoAu-1
Down in yon garden sweet and gay. Willy Drowned in Yarrow. *Unknown.* GTSB-P
Down near the end of a wandering lane. A Rhyme of the Dream-Maker Man. William Allen White. PoLF
Down on Roberts' Farm. Claude Reeves. ThLM
Down on the beach when the tide is out. Treasures. Mary Dixon Thayer. SoPo
Down the blue night the unending columns press. Clouds. Rupert Brooke. BoC
Down the carved hills the bison come. Gates of the Rockies. James Daugherty. RePo
Down the Glimmering Staircase. Siegfried Sassoon. *Fr.* Vigils. PoLF
Down the lane by the Butts in the headlights. Delivering Children. David Holbrook. NePoEA-2
Down the Rain Falls. Elizabeth J. Coatsworth. SoPo
Down through the spheres that chant the Name of One. The Path of the Stars. Thomas S. Jones, Jr. MoRP
Down, Wanton, Down. Robert Graves. ErPo
Down with the rosemary and bays. Ceremonies for Candlemas Eve. Robert Herrick. ILP
Down, you mongrel, Death! The Poet and His Book. Edna St. Vincent Millay. AmLP
Downe to the King's most bright-kept baths they went. Homer. *Fr.* The Odyssey. CTC
Downgoing. Gustav Davidson. FiSC
Downhill I came, hungry, and yet not starved. The Owl. Edward Thomas. DTC; GTBS-P; PoIE; PoSa
Down-Pullers, The. Walter E. Isenhour. STF
Downtown-Boy Uptown. David Henderson. NNP
Downward through the evening twilight. Hiawatha's Childhood. Longfellow. *Fr.* The Song of Hiawatha. FaBV
Dowsabel. Michael Drayton. *Fr.* The Shepherd's Garland. UnTE
Dozens of girls would storm up. Embraceable You. Ira Gershwin. BoLP
Draft Horse, The. Robert Frost. CaFP
Dragonfly, The. Chisoku, *tr. fr. Japanese by* Harold G. Henderson. SoPo
Drake's Drum ("Drake he's in his hammock, an' a thousand miles away"). Sir Henry Newbolt. HaSV; WePo
Dramatic Fragment. Trumbull Stickney. CBEP
Draw me nere. The Magician and the Baron's Daughter. *Unknown.* MeEL
Draw near, dear friends, and hear from me. McAfee's Confession. *Unknown.* BSO
Drawer, The. George MacBeth. NePoEA-2
Dream, A. Matthew Arnold. GTBS-P
Dream, A. Blake. *Fr.* Songs of Innocence. CBEP
Dream. Witter Bynner. MoLP
Dream, The. Byron. CABL
Dream. Solomon Edwards. NNP
Dream, A. Keats. *Fr.* The Fall of Hyperion. OBNC
Dream, A, after Reading Dante's Episode of Paolo and Francesca. Keats. DiPo

Dream, A, after Reading Dante's Episode (*continued*) (On a Dream.) CBEP
Dream and the Blood, The. Louis Untermeyer. UnTE
Dream-Daemon, The. Lin Carter. FiSC
Dream Girl. Carl Sandburg. MoLP
Dream Is Not Enough, The. Zoe Kincaid Brockman. PoNC
Dream-Land. Poe. AmLP; AP; CBEP
Dream Land. Christina Rossetti. VP
Dream of a Baseball Star. Gregory Corso. SD
Dream of Death, A. W. B. Yeats. FoBA
Dream of dolorous women stole my sleep, A. Vampire Bride. Felix Stefanile. FiSC
Dream of Fair Women, A. Kingsley Amis. MP
Dream of Governors, A. Louis Simpson. PoSa
Dream of Horses, A. Ted Hughes. NePoEA-2
Dream of Surreal Science, A. Sri Aurobindo Ghose. ACV
Dream of the Unknown, A. Shelley. GTBS-P
Dream-Pedlary. Thomas Lovell Beddoes. CBEP; OBNC; WiR
Dream-Song. Walter de la Mare. RePo
Dream, A—'tis but a dream, our being. Johann Gottfried Herder, *tr. fr. German by* Alexander Gode. AGP
Dream Variation [*or* Variations]. Langston Hughes. AmNP; PoPl
Dream within a Dream, A. Poe. AP; CBEP
Dreame, The. John Donne. SeCP
Dreamer, The. Christian Morgenstern, *tr. fr. German by* R. C. F. Hull. MGP
Dreamer of Dreams. William Herbert Carruth. PoLF
Dreaming Lake, The. Julius Mosen, *tr. fr. German by* Anne Jennings. AGP
Dreaming That I Went with Li and Yü to Visit Yüan Chen. Po Chü-i, *tr. fr. Chinese by* Arthur Waley. SiGo
Dreaming when dawn's left hand was in the sky. Omar Khayyám, *tr. by* Edward Fitzgerald. *Fr.* The Rubáiyát. PoSa
Dreams. Victor J. Daley. PoAu-1
Dreams. Langston Hughes. LV
Dreams. Poe. CBEP
Dreams fled away, this country bedroom, raw. Another September. Thomas Kinsella. PoCh
Dream's my burden, leaden frost my foe, A. Oskar Loerke. *Fr.* The Stone Path. MGP
Dreams of the Sea. W. H. Davies. HaSV
Dreary Change, The. Sir Walter Scott. OBNC
Dred of deth, sorow of sin. In His Utter Wretchedness. John Audelay. MeEL
Dredged out of that night were the eyes. The Art of Poetry. Yves Bonnefoy. CoFP
Dress your gold locks, make soft your azure eyes. Sonnet. Philippe Desportes. RBL
Dressed up in my melancholy. Song. M. Carl Holman. AmNP
Dressing. Henry Vaughan. MeP
Drifter off Tarentum, A. Kipling. *Fr.* Epitaphs of the War. MMA
Drifting smoke is gone, today, The. Fourth of July. S. S. Gardons. AmPC
Drink to me only with thine eyes. To Celia [*or* Song]. Ben Jonson. CABA; CBEP; DiPo; ELP; EnRePo; FaBV; GTBS-P; ILP; LV; PoIE; PoLF; PoPl; PoPo; PoSa; SeCP
Drink with Something in It, A. Ogden Nash. PoPl
Drinking. Abraham Cowley, *after the Greek of* Anacreon. CABA; PoSa; SeCP; StP
(On Drinking.) WePo
(Thirsty Earth, The.) WiR
Drinking Song. *At. to* William Stevenson *and to* John Still. *Fr.* Gammer Gurton's Needle. WiR
Drive the pilings deep! Beach House. Mary Rita Hurley. PoPl
Driver's Prayer, A. *Unknown.* STF
Droning a drowsy syncopated tune. The Weary Blues. Langston Hughes. FaBV
Droop under doves' wings silent, breathing shapes. The Night Nurse Goes Her Round. John Gray. OBNC
Drop a stitch, drop a stitch. Forecast. Sydney King Russell. FiSC
Drop an unkind word or careless. The Difference. *Unknown.* STF
Drop, drop, slow tears. A Hymn [*or* A Litany]. Phineas Fletcher. BoC; CBEP
Drop Me the Seed. John Masefield. MoRP
Dropping back with the ball ripe in my palm. The Passer. George Abbe. SD
Drought. Frederick E. Laight. OBCV
Drought, *sel.* Francis Carey Slater.
"Sky is a blue, coiled serpent, The." ACV
Droving Man. Thea Astley. PoAu-2
Drowning Poet, The. James Merrill. PP
Drowning with Others. James Dickey. CoPo
Drowsy Herodotus holds him there, The. Ancient Historian. Chris Wallace-Crabbe. PoAu-2
Drowsy Sleeper, The. *Unknown. See* Who Is at My Bedroom Window?

Drug Addict, The. Miriam Waddington. *Fr.* Three Prison Portraits. ACV
Drug Store. Karl Shapiro. ILP; MP
Drug Store. John V. A. Weaver. ThLM
Druggist, The. Larry Rubin. FiSC
Drum, The. John Scott. CBEP
Drum for Ben Boyd, A, *sels.* Francis Webb.
Captain of the *Oberon*, The. ACV
Papuan Shepherd, A. PoAu-2
Drum on your drums, batter on your banjos. Jazz Fantasia. Carl Sandburg. LV; WePo
Drummer Boy of Waterloo, The ("When battle roused each warlike charm"), *with music. Unknown.* BFSS
(Waterloo, A *vers., with music.*) BSO
Drummer Boy of Waterloo, The ("With wringing hands and aching breast"), C *vers., with music. Unknown.* BSO
Drummer Hodge. Thomas Hardy. AnMoPo; GTBS-P; ILP; VP
"Drums and fifes are a beating, The." Dixie's Isle. *Unknown.* BSNS
Drums, drums, I too am dead. November 25, 1963. William Butler. OPP
Drums gather and humble us beyond escape. Belief. A. R. Ammons. OPP
Drums have entered my heart, The. Cortège. Jerome G. Rothenberg. OPP
Drunk in the Furnace, The. W. S. Merwin. MP; NePoEA-2
Drunkard, The. Philip Levine. NePoEA-2
Drunkard's Doom, The, *with music. Unknown.* BSO
Drunkard's Dream, The, *with music. Unknown.* BSO
Drunken Fisherman, The. Robert Lowell. AP
Drunken Fool, The, *with music. Unknown.* BFSS
Drunken Lover. Owen Dodson. AmNP
Dry leaves fall, as if from far away, The. Autumn. Rainer Maria Rilke. PoPo
Dry Loaf. Wallace Stevens. AnMoPo
Dry Salvages, The. T. S. Eliot. *Fr.* Four Quartets. CABA
"River is within us, the sea is all about us, The," *sel.* HaSV
Dry vine leaves burn in an angle of the wall. The Thousand Things. Christopher Middleton. NePoEA-2
Du Perier, must thy grief eternal be? Consolation to M. Du Périer. François de Malherbe. RBL
Dual Site, The. Michael Hamburger. MP; NePoEA-2
Dublin. Louis MacNeice. ACV
Dublin Bay, *with music. Unknown.* BFSS
Duchess of Malfi, The, *sel.* John Webster.
Dirge, A: "Hark, now everything is still," *fr.* IV, ii. CBEP
Duck-chasing. Galway Kinnell. MP
Ducks. Frederick William Harvey. BoC
Ducks at Dawn. James S. Tippett. SoPo
Duck's Ditty. Kenneth Grahame. *Fr.* The Wind in the Willows. GoJo
(Ducks' Ditty.) SoPo
Duel, The. Eugene Field. OnMSP; PoLF; PoPl; SoPo
Duenna, The, *sel.* Sheridan.
Song: "If a daughter you have, she's the plague of your life," *fr.* I, iii. LV
Duino Elegies, The, *sel.* Rainer Maria Rilke, *tr. fr. German by* Walter Kaufmann.
Elegy IX: "Why, if the span of existence may be completed." TwGP
Duke of Gordon's Daughter, The ("The Duke of Gordon had three daughters"). *Unknown.* BuBa
Duke of Merchant's daughter walked out one summer's day, The. Six Questions. *Unknown.* BSNS
Dulce et Decorum Est. Wilfred Owen. CBEP; FaBV; MMA; PoIE
Dulce Ridentem. Stephen Vincent Benét. LOW
Dull as I was, to think that a Court Fly. A Black Patch on Lucasta's Face. Richard Lovelace. SeCP
Dull to myself, and almost dead to these. The Bad Season Makes the Poet Sad. Robert Herrick. CABA
Dulled by the news, all day I kept behind. Elegy for the New Year. Jack Marshall. OPP
Dulnesse. George Herbert. MeP
Dumb Dick. Leslie A. Fiedler. ErPo
Dumb Maid, The, *with music. Unknown.* BFSS
Duncan Campbell. *Unknown.* BSNS
Duncan Gray ("Can ye play me Duncan Gray"). Burns. ErPo
(Thrusting of It, The.) UnTE
Duncan Gray ("Duncan Gray cam here to woo"). Burns. GTBS-P
Dunkirk. Robert Nathan. SIV
Duns Scotus. Thomas Merton. CoPo
Duns Scotus's Oxford. Gerard Manley Hopkins. GTBS-P; PoIE; VP
Duplicity of Women, The. John Lydgate. MeEL
Dürer would have seen a reason for living. The Steeple-Jack. Marianne Moore. AmLP; AP; ILP
During a Bombardment by V-Weapons. Roy Fuller. ToPo
During the Bath. Giambattista Marino, *tr. fr. Italian by* Frank Warnke. RBL
During Wind and Rain. Thomas Hardy. ELP; GTBS-P; PoIE; PoSa

Dusk in the Domain. Dorothea Mackellar. PoAu-1
Dusk of Horses, The. James Dickey. AP; ToPo
Dusk sifted into my breathless room, The. Deep Song. Antonio Machado. AnSP
Dusky night rides down the sky, The. Hunting Song. Henry Fielding. *Fr.* Don Quixote in England. StP
Dust. Randolph Stow. PoAu-2
Dust and clay. Ascension-Hymn. Henry Vaughan. MeP
Dust in a cloud, blinding weather. Apples and Water. Robert Graves. DaDu; PoIE
Dust in this room, The. Old Room. Erich Fried. MGP
Dust is such a pleasant thing. In Praise of Dust. Rachel Field. RePo
Dust of Snow. Robert Frost. WePo
Dutch Lover, The, *sel.* Aphra Behn.
　Amyntas Led Me to a Grove. ErPo
　(Willing Mistress, The.) UnTE
Dutch Lullaby, A. Eugene Field. *See* Wynken, Blynken, and Nod.
Dutch Proverb, A. Matthew Prior. LV
Dutch Seacoast. Kenneth Slessor. *Fr.* The Atlas. PoAu-2
Dutchess' Lullaby, The. "Lewis Carroll." *Fr.* Alice's Adventures in Wonderland. BBGG
　("Speak roughly to your little boy.") Par
Dwarf of Disintegration. Oscar Williams. PoCh
D'ye ken John Peel with his coat so gray. John Peel. John Woodcock Graves. SD
Dying. Giuseppe Ungaretti, *tr. fr. Italian by* Lowry Nelson, Jr. CoIP
Dying Californian, The, *with music. Unknown.* BFSS; BSO
Dying Child, The. John Clare. CBEP
Dying Cowboy, The (*diff. versions*). *Unknown. See* Cowboy's Lament, The.
Dying Cowboy, The ("Oh bury me not on the lone prairie"). *Unknown.* BFSS (A *vers., with music.*)
　(Bury Me Not on the Lone Prairie.) FaBV
Dying Eagle, The. E. J. Pratt. ACV
Dying Eusebio's Address to the Cross, The. Pedro Calderón de la Barca, *tr. fr. Spanish by* D. F. McCarthy. RBL
Dying firelight slides along the quirt, A. The End of the Weekend. Anthony Hecht. NePoEA-2
Dying Man, The, *sels.* Theodore Roethke.
　Exulting, The. PoDB
　They Sing, They Sing. PoDB
Dying Man in His Garden, The. George Sewell. GTBS-P
Dying Speech of an Old Philosopher. Walter Savage Landor. *See* I Strove with None.
Dying Stockman, The. *Unknown.* PoAu-1
Dying Swan, The. Tennyson. WiR
Dynasts, The, *sel.* Thomas Hardy.
　Night of Trafalgar, The, *fr.* Pt. I, Act V, sc. vii. HaSV
Dysynni Valley, The. Theodore Holmes. CoPo

E

E Tenebris. Oscar Wilde. CABA
'E was sittin' on a door-step. The Road to Vagabondia. Dana Burnet. PoLF
E. P. Ode pour l'Election de Son Sepulchre. Ezra Pound. *Fr.* Hugh Selwyn Mauberley. PoIE; PP
　("For three years, out of key with his time.") AP; CABA; ILP
Each alone on the heart of the earth. And Suddenly It's Evening. Salvatore Quasimodo. CoIP
Each and All. Emerson. AP; ILP; PoIE
Each care-worn face is but a book. The Strangers. Jones Very. CBEP
Each day she woke with sullen eyes. The Witch. Stanley McNail. FiSC
Each hour until we meet is as a bird. Winged Hours. Dante Gabriel Rossetti. The House of Life, XXV. VP
Each in His Own Tongue. William Herbert Carruth. TRV
Each instant of his life a task, he never rests. The Poet. James Kirkup. PP
Each man must suffer his fate. The Spirit of Poetry Speaks. Richard Eberhart. OPP
Each man owes his country. Dalton Trumbo. *Fr.* For a Convict's Wife. PtTo
Each Morning. LeRoi Jones. Hymn for Lanie Poo, Sec. 4. NNP
Each morning I lift my blind to stare. Urban Roses. Ted Isaac. PoPl
Each of us like you. Adonis. Hilda Doolittle ("H. D."). AP; PoPl
Each on his own strict line we move. Too Late. Matthew Arnold. Faded Leaves, II. VP
Each one shall sit at table with his own cup and spoon. A Practical Program for Monks. Thomas Merton. CoPo
Each pale Christ stirring underground. Words for a Resurrection. Leo Kennedy. OBCV

Each time his will abdicated. Possession. Lynne Lawner. ErPo
Each time I return to Johannesburg it is summer. David Wright. *Fr.* Seven South African Poems. ACV
Eager he look'd. Another train of years. One Centred System. Joel Barlow. *Fr.* The Columbiad. AP
"Eager to search, in and throughout its ways." Dante and Beatrice in the Earthly Paradise. Dante. *Fr.* Divina Commedia: Purgatorio. BoC
Eagerly/ Like a woman hurrying to her lover. Four Glimpses of Night. Frank Marshall Davis. AmNP
Eagle, The. Tennyson. CaFP; CBEP; DiPo; GoJo; GTBS-P; OnP; PoIE; PoPo; StP; VaPo; WePo; WiR
Eagle, The. Andrew Young. WePo
Eagle and the Mole, The. Elinor Wylie. PoPo
Eagle for an Emperor. Falconry. Anne Wilkinson. OBCV
Eagle That Is Forgotten, The. Vachel Lindsay. MoRP
Eagles and lions, kings of birds and beasts. Of Seals and Arms. John Taylor. CBEP
Eagles over the Lambing Paddock. Ernest G. Moll. PoAu-2
Eagle's shadow runs across the plain. Zebra. "Isak Dinesen." GoJo
Ear-Maker and the Mould-Mender, The. La Fontaine. UnTE
Earl Brand (B *and* C *vers.*). *Unknown.* BSO
　(Soldier, A, A *vers., with music.*) BSO
Earl March look'd on his dying child. The Maid of Neidpath. Thomas Campbell. GTBS-P
Earl Mar's Daughter. *Unknown.* BuBa
Early Astir. Sir Herbert Read. DaDu
Early Dawn. Hilaire Belloc. ThGo
Early dew woos the half-opened flowers, An. Haroun's Favorite Song. *Unknown. Fr.* The Thousand and One Nights. SiGo
Early, early I walked in the city. Early Astir. Sir Herbert Read. DaDu
Early in One Spring, *with music. Unknown.* BFSS
Early in the Morning. Louis Simpson. PoIE; PoSa
Early Indians were our first poets, The. Lake Winnipesaukee. Olive Driver. RePo
Early Love. Samuel Daniel. *Fr.* Hymen's Triumph. ErPo
　(First Flame.) BoLP
Early Morning Feed. Peter Redgrove. BoC
Early one morning as I went out to plow. Farmer Jones's Wife. *Unknown.* BFSS
Early Rising. John Godfrey Saxe. PoLF
Early sun on Beaulieu water. Youth and Age on Beaulieu River, Hants. John Betjeman. MP
Early Supper. Barbara Howes. GoJo; PoPl
Early thou goest forth, to put to rout. To a "Tenting" Boy. Charles Tennyson-Turner. OBNC
Early Unfinished Sketch. Austin Clarke. ErPo
Earnest, earthless, equal attuneable. Spelt from Sibyl's Leaves. Gerard Manley Hopkins. PoDB; VP
Earth. Bryant. AP
Earth. Oliver Herford. LV
Earth. John Hall Wheelock. MoRP
Earth and Death, The. Cesare Pavese, *tr. fr. Italian by* Norman T. Di Giovanni. CoIP
Earth and I Gave You Turquoise. N. Scott Momaday. PoPl
Earth and Sea. Pushkin, *tr. fr. Russian by* Sir Cecil Kisch. SiGo
Earth and Sky. Euripides, *tr. fr. Greek by* C. M. Bowra. EaLo
Earth and Sky. Eleanor Farjeon. PoSC
Earth does not understand her child. The Return. Edna St. Vincent Millay. PoPl
Earth draws her breath so gently, heaven bends. The Marriage of Earth and Heaven. Jay Macpherson. OBCV
Earth gave Thee a cradle, O Christ, and a cross. Cradle and Throne. *Unknown.* STF
Earth has not anything to show more fair. Composed upon Westminster Bridge, September 3, 1802. Wordsworth. CABA; CaFP; CBEP; DiPo; FaBV; FoBA; GTBS-P; ILP; OBNC; PoIE; PoLF; PoPl; PoPo; PoSa; StP; VaPo; WePo
Earth Is Enough. Edwin Markham. TRV
Earth Is sweet with roses, The. Prudentius. *Fr.* Cathemerinon. SiGo
Earth Is the Lord's, The. Psalms, XXIV, Bible, *O.T.* EaLo ("Earth is the Lord's and the fulness thereof, The.") SiGo
Earth Late Choked with Showers, The. Thomas Lodge. *Fr.* Scillaes Metamorphosis. PoSa
Earth, like a Girl, Sipped the Rains, The. Judah Halevi, *tr. fr. Hebrew by* William M. Davis. AnML
Earth, ocean, air, beloved brotherhood! Alastor; or, The Spirit of Solitude. Shelley. CABL
Earth out of Earth. *Unknown.* CBEP; MeEL
Earth raised up her head. Earth's Answer. Blake. *Fr.* Songs of Experience. CBEP; EnPE
Earth rolls on through empty space, its journey's never done, The. The Ramble-eer. *Unknown.* PoAu-1
Earth Trembles Waiting. Blanche Shoemaker Wagstaff. PoLF
Earth, The, with thunder torn, with fire blasted. Fulke Greville. Caelica, LXXXVI. EnRePo

Earth-Born. Robert E. Howard. FiSC
Earthen Jugs. "Gabriela Mistral," *tr. fr. Spanish by* Kate Flores. AnSP
Earthly nurse she sits and sings, An. The Great Silkie of Sule Skerrie. *Unknown.* BuBa
Earthly Paradise, The, *sels.* William Morris.
  Apology, An: "Of Heaven or Hell I have no power to sing." OBNC; PoIE
  October. OBNC
  Road of Life, The. OBNC
Earthly props are useless. Props. John Oxenham. TRV
Earth's Answer. Blake. *Fr.* Songs of Experience. CBEP; EnPE
Earth's crammed with heaven. Elizabeth Barrett Browning. *Fr.* Aurora Leigh. TRV
Earth's Night. William Allingham. TRV
Earthy Anecdote. Wallace Stevens. GoJo
Easiest Way, The. *Unknown, tr. fr. Greek by* Louis Untermeyer. UnTE
East Anglian Bathe. John Betjeman. SD
East Anglian Seas and Shores, *sel.* George Crabbe.
  "Turn to the watery world! But who to thee." HaSV
East is yellow as a daffodil, The. Sunrise. Lizette Woodworth Reese. LV
Eastbourne. Eugenio Montale, *tr. fr. Italian by* Carlo L. Golino. CoIP
Easter ("I got me flowers"). George Herbert. TRV
  ("I got me flowers to strew thy way.") BoC
Easter ("Rise heart; thy Lord is risen"). George Herbert. MeP
Easter. Joyce Kilmer. SoPo
Easter. Edwin L. Sabin. PoSC
Easter Day. Christina Rossetti. VP
Easter Day. Juan Ruiz, Archpriest of Hita, *tr. fr. Spanish by* James Edward Tobin. *Fr.* The Book of True Love. AnML
Easter-Day. Henry Vaughan. MeP
Easter, Day of Christ Eternal. Maurice Moore. STF
Easter duck and Easter chick. Some Things That Easter Brings. Elsie Parrish. SoPo
Easter Hymn. A. E. Housman. More Poems, I. CABA; CaFP; EaLo; ILP
Easter Hymn. Michael Thwaites. MoRP
Easter Hymn. Henry Vaughan. MeP
Easter Hymn. Charles Wesley. TRV
Easter Island. Frederick George Scott. OBCV
Easter Morning. Spenser. See Amoretti, LXVIII.
Easter 1916. W. B. Yeats. AnMoPo; CABA; DiPo; FoBA; PoIE
  "Too long a sacrifice," *sel.* PoPo
Easter Song, An. "Susan Coolidge." TRV
Easter Song. Kenneth Leslie. MoRP
Easter Wings. George Herbert. CABA; MeP; PP; SeCP; StP; VaPo
  "Lord, who createdst man in wealth and store," *sel.* PoSa
Eastertide. Carl Bode. *Fr.* The Sacred Seasons. PoPo
Eastward I Stand, Mercies I Beg. *Unknown, tr. fr. Anglo-Saxon by* Sarah Plotz. EaLo
Easy Decision, An. Kenneth Patchen. LOW; ToPo
Easy is the triolet. Triolet. W. E. Henley. LV
Ebb and Flow, The. Edward Taylor. AP
Ebb slips from the rock, the sunken, The. Night. Robinson Jeffers. AP
Ebb Tide, The. Robert Southey. OBNC
Ecce Homo. Nietzsche, *tr. fr. German by* Walter Kaufmann. TwGP
Ecce Puer. James Joyce. PoIE; PoPl; StP
Ecchoing Green, The. Blake. See Echoing Green, The.
Ecclesiastes, *sels.* Bible, *O.T.*
  All Is Vanity, I: 14-15, III: 19. TRV
  "To every thing there is a season, and a time," III: 1-8, PoPl
Ecclesiastes. Joseph Langland. PoPl
Ecclesiastical Sketches, *sel.* Wordsworth.
  Inside of King's College Chapel, Cambridge. OBNC
  (Within King's College Chapel, Cambridge.) GTBS-P
Ecclesiasticus, *sels.* Bible, Apocrypha. BoC
  "He was as the morning star in the midst of a cloud, and as the moon at the full," L: 6-12.
  Let Us Now Praise Famous Men, XLIV: 1-15, XXXVIII: 26-39.
  "Look upon the rainbow, and praise him that made it," XLIII: 12-13.
  "My son, if thou come to serve the Lord, prepare thy soul for temptation," II: 1-13.
  Snow, XLIII: 14-16, 18-24.
  Sun, Moon and Stars, XLIII: 1-11.
Echo. Milton. See Sweet Echo, Sweetest Nymph.
Echo. Thomas Moore. ELP
  (Echoes.) CBEP; GTBS-P
Echo. Christina Rossetti. ELP; OBNC; VP
Echo of song I heard you sing, An. Lost Voice on This Hill.

Echoes. Walter de la Mare. RePo
Echoes. W. E. Henley. *Poems indexed separately by titles and first lines.*
Echoes. Thomas Moore. See Echo.
Echoing [*or* Ecchoing] Green, The. Blake. *Fr.* Songs of Innocence. CaFP; CBEP; DiPo; PoSC; WiR
Echo's Song. Ben Jonson. See Slow, Slow, Fresh Fount.
Eclipse, An. Pindar, *tr. fr. Greek by* C. M. Bowra. SiGo
Eclogue for Christmas, An. Louis MacNeice. AnMoPo
Eclogue I, *sel.* Garcilaso de la Vega, *tr. fr. Spanish by* Edwin Morgan.
  "O waters running pure and crystal clear." AnSP
Eclogues, *sels.* Vergil, *tr. fr. Latin.*
  Eighth Pastoral of Virgil, The, *tr. by* Dryden. EiCP
  "For thee, little boy, will the earth pour forth gifts," *fr.* IV, *tr. by* James Laughlin. PoPl
Economical Poet, The. Christian Morgenstern, *tr. fr. German by* Walter Kaufmann. TwGP
Ecstasy, The. John Donne. CABA; DiPo; EnRePo; FoBA; OnP; PoIE; StP; UnTE
  (Extasie, The.) MeP; SeCP
  (Extasy, The.) CBEP
Ecstasy. Arthur Symons. UnTE
Ecstasy Dream Grace, *sel.* Johannes R. Becher, *tr. fr. German by* Christopher Middleton.
  If I Roared. MGP
Ecstatic bird songs pound. Dawn. William Carlos Williams. LV; PoPl
Eden. Milton. *Fr.* Paradise Lost, IV. DiPo
Eden. Thomas Traherne. MeP
Edgar A. Guest Considers "The Good Old Woman Who Lived in a Shoe" and the Good Old Truths Simultaneously. Louis Untermeyer. PoPl
Edgar Allan Poe. Robert H. Barlow. FiSC
Edgar Guest. Oscar Williams. PP
Edge of Day, The. Laurie Lee. ToPo
Edi be thu, Hevene Quene. In Praise of Mary. *Unknown.* MeEL
Edmund Pollard. Edgar Lee Masters. *Fr.* Spoon River Anthology. ErPo
Education of Nature, The. Wordsworth. See Three Years She Grew in Sun and Shower.
Edward. *Unknown.* BSO; CABA; CaFP; CBEP; ELP; ILP; PoIE; StP
  (Edward, Edward!) BuBa; OnP; PoPo; PoSa; SIV
Edward the Third had seven sons. The Ballad of Banners (1944). John Lehmann. MoBS
Eel, The. Eugenio Montale, *tr. fr Italian by* Carlo L. Golino. CoIP
Eel, The. Ogden Nash. FaBV
E'er I begin, I must premise. Fable II: The Vulture, the Sparrow, and Other Birds. John Gay. EiCP
Effect of Snow, The, *sel.* Robert Finch.
  "I have seen the snow like a mirage impending," III. ACV
Efficient Wife's Complaint, The. Confucius, *tr. fr. Chinese by* Ezra Pound. *Fr.* The Classic Anthology: Airs of Pei. CTC
Effigy. Georgia Lee McElhaney. CoPo
Effort at Speech between Two People. Muriel Rukeyser. MP
Effortlessly Democratic Santa Fe Trail. Martha Baird. PoPl
Egan O Rahilly. *Unknown, tr. fr. Irish by* James Stephens. CBEP
Egg-and-Dart. Robert Finch. OBCV
Egg and the Machine, The. Robert Frost. CABA
Ego. Philip Booth. MP
Ego. Norman MacCaig. GTBS-P
Egoism. W. Craddle. LV
Egrets. Judith Wright. GoJo
Egyptian Passage, An. Theodore Weiss. CoPo
Eheu! Rubén Darío, *tr. fr. Spanish by* Anita Volland. AnSP
Eight-Cylinder Man. Florence Ripley Mastin. LV; PoPo
824: The Love and Life of Women. Night Café. Gottfried Benn. MGP
Eight Oars and a Coxswain ("Eight oars compel"). Arthur Guiterman. SD
Eight o'Clock. A. E. Housman. Last Poems, XV. CABA; PoIE; WePo
Eight Sandbars on the Takano River. Gary Snyder. CoPo
1805. Robert Graves. EvOK
Eighteenth day of June, my boys, The. Wellington and Waterloo. *Unknown.* BSNS
Eighth Air Force. Randall Jarrell. ILP; PoCh
8th May 1945. Franz Baermann Steiner, *tr. fr. German by* Michael Hamburger. MGP
Eighth Pastoral of Virgil, The. Vergil, *tr. fr. Latin by* Dryden. *Fr.* Eclogues. EiCP
Eighth Poem. Giovanni Papini, *tr. fr. Italian by* Carlo L. Golino. CoIP
Either she was foul, or her attire was bad. Shameful Impotence [*or* The Impotent Lover]. Ovid. Amores, III, vii. ErPo; UnTE
El Camino Verde. Paul Blackburn. CoPo

Elbows in wine-slops, news of the ocean isles. Cipangu. William Hart-Smith. *Fr.* Christopher Columbus. PoAu-2
Elder Brother, The, *sel.* John Fletcher.
  Beauty Clear and Fair, *fr.* III, v. CBEP
"Elder father, though thine eyes." The Holy of Holies. G. K. Chesterton. MoRP; TRV
Elder Tree. Conrad Aiken. AP
Elders at Their Services Begin, The. J. V. Cunningham. StP
Eldorado. Poe. AP; PoPo; RePo; SIV; WiR
Elected Silence. sing to me. The Habit of Perfection. Gerard Manley Hopkins. FoBA; ILP; PoIE; VP
Election, The. Robert Pack. CoPo
Electric car jerks, The. In the Tube. Richard Aldington. WePo
Elegiac Stanzas. Wordsworth. CABL; OBNC
  (Nature and the Poet.) GTBS-P
Elegie, An: "Let me be what I am, as Virgil cold." Ben Jonson. SeCP
Elegie VII: "Natures lay ideot, I taught thee to love." John Donne. *Fr.* Elegies. SeCP
Elegie XVI: On His Mistris. John Donne. *See* Elegy XVI: On His Mistress.
Elegie IV: Perfume, The. John Donne. *Fr.* Elegies. SeCP
Elegie XIX: To His Mistris Going to Bed. John Donne. *See* To His Mistress Going to Bed.
Elegie Made by Mr. Aurelian Townshend in Remembrance of the Ladie Venetia Digby, An. Aurelian Townshend. SeCP
Elegie on the Lady Jane Pawlet, Marchion: of Winton, An. Ben Jonson. SeCP
Elegie upon the Death of the Deane of Pauls, Dr. John Donne, An. Thomas Carew. *See* Elegy upon the Death of Doctor Donne, Dean of Paul's, An.
Elegies, *sels.* John Donne.
  Elegy IX: Autumnal, The. DiPo
  Elegy V: His Picture. EnRePo
    (His Picture.) CBEP
  Elegy X: "Image of her whom I love, more than she." MeP
  Elegie VII: "Natures lay Ideot, I taught thee to love." SeCP
  Elegie XVI: On His Mistris. SeCP
    (Elegy XVI: On His Mistress.) CABL
    (Elegy on His Mistress.) FoBA
  Elegie IV: Perfume, The. SeCP
  Elegie XIX: To His Mistris Going to Bed. SeCP
    (To His Mistris [*or* Mistress] Going to Bed.) ErPo; UnTE
    (Elegy XIX: Going to Bed.) EnRePo
    (Elegy to His Mistress Going to Bed.) FoBA
Elegies, *sels.* Eugène Guillevic, *tr. fr.* French *by* Tod Perry *and* Maurice O'Meara. CoFP
  "Happy are they."
  "He probably held too tight."
  "Noon is the outsider."
  "There are some who must."
Elegy IX: Autumnal, The. John Donne. *Fr.* Elegies. DiPo
Elegy, An: "Friend, whose unnatural early death." David Gascoyne. MP
Elegy XIX: Going to Bed. John Donne. *See* To His Mistress Going to Bed.
Elegy V: His Picture. John Donne. *See* His Picture.
Elegy: "I know but will not tell." Alan Dugan. AP
Elegy X: "Image of her whom I love, more then she." John Donne. *Fr.* Elegies. MeP
Elegy: "Let them bury your big eyes." Edna St. Vincent Millay. AmLP
Elegy, The: "Madam, no more! The time has come to eat." A. D. Hope. ErPo
Elegy: "My father was born with a spade in his hand and traded it." John Ciardi. ToPo
Elegy: "My prime of youth is but a frost of cares." Chidiock Tichborne. PoSa
  (His Elegy.) PoIE
  (Lines before Execution.) CBEP
Elegy: "O snatch'd away in beauty's bloom!" Byron. GTBS-P
Elegy XVI: On His Mistress. John Donne. *Fr.* Elegies. CABL
  (Elegie XVI: On His Mistress.) SeCP
  (Elegy on His Mistress.) FoBA
Elegy, An: "Since you must go, and I must bid farewell." Ben Jonson. EnRePo
Elegy, An: "Though beauty be the mark of praise." Ben Jonson. EnRePo
Elegy: "Whenever we touched, I thought of the Lying-in Hospital." Robert Layzer. PoPl
Elegy IX: "Why, if the span of existence may be completed." Rainer Maria Rilke, *tr. fr.* German *by* Walter Kaufmann. *Fr.* The Duino Elegies. TwGP
Elegy for a Dead Soldier. Karl Shapiro. AP; FaPL; ThLM, *much abr.;* ToPo
Elegy for a Lady, *sel.* Walt Delegall.
  "Billy Holiday,/—Lady—Day." PtTO
Elegy for a Nature Poet. Howard Nemerov. PP
Elegy for Helen Trent. Paris Leary. CoPo
Elegy for Jane. Theodore Roethke. AP; CaFP; MP; PoPo
Elegy for J. F. K. W. H. Auden. OPP
Elegy for Lucy Lloyd. Llewelyn Goch, *tr. fr* Welsh *by* Ernest Rhys. SiGo
Elegy for Minor Poets. Louis MacNeice. PP
Elegy for the Monastery Barn. Thomas Merton. CoPo
Elegy for the New Year. Jack Marshall. OPP
Elegy in a Country Churchyard. G. K. Chesterton. EvOK; MMA
Elegy Just in Case. John Ciardi. MP
Elegy on a Lap Dog, An. John Gay. DiPo
Elegy on an Australian Schoolboy, *sel.* Zora Cross.
  "O brother in the restless rest of God!" PoAu-1
Elegy on His Mistress. John Donne. *See* Elegy XVI: On His Mistress.
Elegy on Shakespeare. William Basse. CBEP
Elegy on That Glory of Her Sex, Mrs. Mary Blaize, An. Goldsmith. CBEP
Elegy on the Death of a Mad Dog. Goldsmith. *Fr.* The Vicar of Wakefield, *ch.* 17. CBEP; PoPo; PoSa; RoGo
Elegy on the Death of John Keats, An. Shelley. *Fr.* Adonais. OBNC
Elegy on the Death of Sidney. Sir Edward Dyer. EnRePo
Elegy on the Lady Marckham. John Donne. FoBA
Elegy on Thyrza. Byron. GTBS-P
Elegy to His Mistress. Ovid. *See* In Summer's Heat.
Elegy to His Mistress Going to Bed. John Donne. *See* To His Mistress Going to Bed.
Elegy to the Memory of an Unfortunate Lady. Pope. CBEP; OnP
Elegy upon the Death of Doctor Donne, Dean of Paul's, An. Thomas Carew. PP; StP
  (Elegie upon the Death of the Deane of Pauls, Dr. John Donne, An.) SeCP
  (Elegy upon the Death of the Dean of St. Paul's, Dr. John Donne, An.) CABA
Elegy Written in a Country Churchyard. Thomas Gray. CABA; CABL; CaFP; CBEP; DiPo; EiCp; EnPE; FaPL; GTBS; ILP; OnP; PoIE; PoLF; PoPo; PoSA; StP
Elementary School Classroom in a Slum, An. Stephen Spender. ILP; MP
Elements, The. W. H. Davies. RePo
Elephant, The. Herbert Asquith. SoPo
Elephant, The. Hilaire Belloc. SoPo
Elephant, The. Rachel Field. *Fr.* A Circus Garland. SoPo
Elephant, The. A. E. Housman. FaBV; PoPo
Elephant always carries his trunk, The. The Elephant's Trunk. Alice Wilkins. SoPo
Elephant Is an Odd Affair, An. Zhenya Gay. RePo
Elephant Is Slow to Mate, The. D. H. Lawrence. PoPl
Elephant's Trunk, The. Alice Wilkins. SoPo
Elephants walking. Holding Hands. Lenore M. Link. SoPo
Eletelephony. Laura E. Richards. GoJo; SoPo
Elevation. Franz Werfel, *tr. fr.* German *by* Christopher Middleton. MGP
Elevator Man Adheres to Form, The. Margaret Danner. PtTo
Eleventh Commandment, The, *sel.* John Holmes.
  "When Moses came down from the mountain and the cloud." MoRP
Eleventh Hour, The. Francis St. Vincent Morris. WePo
Eleventh Property, The. Sir Thomas More. *Fr.* The Twelve Properties or Conditions of a Lover. EnRePo
Elf and the Dormouse, The. Oliver Herford. OnMSP; SoPo
Elf-King, The. Goethe. *See* Erlking, The.
Elf-light, owl-light. Dusk in the Domain. Dorothea Mackellar. PoAu-1
Elfin Knight, The. *Unknown.* BSO (B *vers., with music*); BuBa
  (Cambric Shirt, The, A, B, *and* C *vers., with music.*) BFSS
  (Rosemary and Thyme, *with music.*) BFSS (D *vers.*); BSO (A *vers.*)
Elfin Wife, The. "Jake Falstaff." BoC
Elixer, The. George Herbert. MeP
  ("Teach me, my God and King.") ThGo
Elizabeth of Bohemia. Sir Henry Wotton. CBEP; GTBS-P
  (On His Mistris, the Queen of Bohemia.) SeCP
  (To His Mistress, the Queen of Bohemia.) ELP
Ella, fell a/ Maple tree. Picnic. Hugh Lofting. GoJo
Ellen the Fair. *Unknown.* BSNS
Elms are proud. Bedtime. Elizabeth J. Coatsworth. ToGo
Elsie Marley. *Unknown.* BBGG
Elsie's House. Stanley McNail. FiSC
Elusive Shadow of My Substance, Stay. Sister Juana Inés de la Cruz, *tr. fr. Spanish by* Kate Flores. AnSP
Elysium is as far as to. Emily Dickinson. CABA; DiPo; FaPL; PoIE
Emancipation Group, The. Whittier. LiPo
Emancipation of George-Hector (*a Colored Turtle*), The. Mari E. Evans. AmNP

Embankment, The. T. E. Hulme. GTBS-P
Embarrassed Judge. *Unknown, tr. fr. Greek by* Louis Untermeyer. UnTE
Embarrassing Episode of Little Miss Muffet, The. Guy Wetmore Carryl. OnMSP; RePo
Embattled towers, the level lilied moat, The. The Fishers. Ruth Pitter. BoC
Embers of the day are red, The. Evensong. Robert Louis Stevenson. TRV
Emblem of England's ancient faith. To an Oak Tree. Sir Walter Scott. *Fr.* Waverley. OBNC
Emblems, *sels.* Francis Quarles. MeP
"Behold thy darling, which thy lustfull care," V, 8.
"How shall my tongue expresse that hallow'd fire," V, 11.
"My soule is like a bird; my flesh, the cage," V, 10.
"World's a floore, whose swelling heapes retaine, The," II, 7.
Embraceable You. Ira Gershwin. BoLP
Emerald cages a jungle, The. Prologue for a Bestiary. Ronald Perry. NePoEA-2
Emeralds are singing on the grasses, The. How Many Heavens. Edith Sitwell. MoRP
Emergency Maker, The. David Wagoner. NePoEA-2
Emerson. James Russell Lowell. *Fr.* A Fable for Critics. AP
("There comes Emerson first.") PP
Emigrant, The, *sel.* Alexander McLachlan.
Song: "Old England is eaten by knaves." OBCV
Emigrant, The, *sel.* Standish O'Grady.
Winter in Lower Canada. OBCV
Emigrant from Pike, *with music.* John A. Stone. SGR
Emily Brontë. C. Day Lewis. GTBS-P
Emily Carr. Wilfred Watson. OBCV
Emily Geiger. *Unknown.* PoLF
Emmy. Arthur Symons. OBNC
Empedocles on Etna, *sel.* Matthew Arnold.
"Far, far from here." GTBS-P
Emperor, The. Tu Fu, *tr. fr. Chinese by* E. Powys Mathers. SIV
Emperor and Turk, I wot. Carpe Diem. Antoine de Baïf. RBL
Emperor of Ice-Cream, The. Wallace Stevens. AmLP; AP; CABA; CaFP; PoIE; PoSa
Emperors of the Island. Dannie Abse. DaDu
Empire Finals at Verona, The, *sel.* Jonathan C. Williams. "In a twinkling/ of a flash-boom." PtTo
Empire State, *sel.* Olga Cabral.
"I am a prisoner of bones." PtTo
Employment ("He that is weary, let him sit"). George Herbert. SeCP
Empress, The. Diane Wakoski. CoPo
Empty carousel in a deserted park, The. The Carousel. G. C. Oden. AmNP
Empty House. Elizabeth J. Coatsworth. FiSC
Empty House. Stephen Spender. WePo
Empty of life I live, and wait. Lines Born of the Fire of Love for God. St. Theresa of Avila. RBL
Empty of stars still. Fancy Fishing. James L. Weil. FiSC
Emus. Mary Fullerton. PoAu-1
En las Internas Entrañas. St. Theresa of Avila, *tr. fr. Spanish by* Father Benedict Zimmerman. RBL
En Route. Duncan Campbell Scott. OBCV
Encased in mud, and breathing valley steam. The Buffalo. Herbert Price. ACV
Enchanted Knight, The. Edwin Muir. DaDu
Enchanted Lyre, The. George Darley. OBNC
Enchanted Shirt, The. John Hay. RePo
Enchantment, The. Theocritus, *tr. fr. Greek by* Thomas Creech. *Fr.* Idylls. CTC
Encinctured with a twine of leaves. A Fragment. Samuel Taylor Coleridge. OBNC
Encounter. Ted Hughes. ToPo
Encounter. August Stramm, *tr. fr. German by* Michael Hamburger. MGP
Encounter of the Archpriest with Ferrand García. Juan Ruiz, Archpriest of Hita, *tr. fr. Spanish by* Edwin Honig. *Fr.* The Book of True Love. AnML
Encouraged. Paul Laurence Dunbar. TRV
Encouragements to a Lover. Sir John Suckling. *See* Why So Pale and Wan?
End, The. A. A. Milne. *See* When I Was One.
End, The. Wilfred Owen. MMA
End of Another Home Holiday. D. H. Lawrence. DTC
End of February. Bañalbufar, a Brazier, Relativity, Cloud Formations & the Kindness & Relentlessness of Time, All Seen through a Window While Keeping the Feet Warm at the Same Time As. Paul Blackburn. CoPo
End of Man Is His Beauty, The. LeRoi Jones. AmNP
End of Summer, The. Basho, *tr. fr. Japanese by* Harold G. Henderson. RePo
End of Summer. Stanley Kunitz. AmLP
End of the Day, The. Robert Creeley. AmPC
End of the Season on a Stormy Day—Oban. Iain Crichton Smith. NePoEA-2

End of the Weekend, The. Anthony Hecht. NePoEA-2
End of the World. "Jakob van Hoddis," *tr. fr. German by* Christopher Middleton. MGP
End of the World, The. Archibald MacLeish. AP; CaFP; ILP; PoIE; PoPo; PoSa; StP
End of the Year, The. Su T'ung-po, *tr. fr. Chinese by* Kenneth Rexroth. PoPl
Endearments. Pierre Louÿs, *tr. fr. French by* Horace M. Brown. *Fr.* The Songs of Bilitis. UnTE
Endless cycle of idea and action. T. S. Eliot. *Fr.* The Rock. TRV
Endless the darkly-printed tombstones rise. Edgar Allan Poe. Robert H. Barlow. FiSC
Endure what life God gives and ask no longer span. Sophocles. *Fr.* Oedipus at Colonus. DTC
Endymion, *sels.* Keats.
"O sovereign power of love! O grief! O balm!" *fr.* II. OBNC
"Thing of beauty is a joy for ever, A," *fr.* I. BoC; CTC; FaBV; ILP; OBNC; PoPl; TRV
Enemy of Life, The. Sir Thomas Wyatt. CBEP
Enfors we us with all our might. A Carol of St. George. *Unknown.* MeEL
Engine. James S. Tippett. SoPo
Engineer, The. A. A. Milne. RePo
Engineers. Jimmy Garthwaite. SoPo
England. *Unknown.* CBEP
England and Switzerland 1802. Wordsworth. GTBS-P
England! awake! awake! awake! Prelude to Ch. IV. Blake. *Fr.* Jerusalem. OBNC
England his heart; his corpse the waters have. Epitaph on Drake. Richard Barnfield. HaSV
England in 1819. Shelley. CABA; StP
(Sonnet: England in 1819.) CBEP
England, My England. W. E. Henley. PoLF
English A. John Ciardi. ToPo
English Are Frosty, The. Alice Duer Miller. *Fr.* The White Cliffs. PoLF
English Bards and Scotch Reviewers, *sels.* Byron.
"Another epic! Who inflicts again." EiCP
"Next comes the dull disciple of thy school." PP
William Lisle Bowles.
Engraved on the Collar of a Dog, Which I Gave to His Royal Highness. Pope. CABA; CBEP; StP
(Epigram: Engraved on the Collar of a Dog Which I Gave to His Royal Highness.) DiPo
(Epigram: "I am His Highness' dog at Kew.") LV
Enigma. Hugh McCrae. PoAu-1
Enigma. Katherine Reeves. FiSC
Enigma for Christmas Shoppers. Phyllis McGinley. PoPl
Enigmatic moon has at long last died, The. Stevedore. Leslie M. Collins. AmNP
Enion Replies from the Caverns of the Grave. Blake. *Fr.* Vala; or, The Four Zoas. OBNC
Enitharmon Revives with Los. Blake. *Fr.* Vala; or, The Four Zoas. OBNC
Enjoy Thy April Now. Samuel Daniel. *Fr.* A Description of Beauty. ELP; StP
Enjoyment, The. Antoine-Girard de Saint-Amant, *tr. fr. French by* Thomas Stanley. RBL
Enjoyment, The. *Unknown.* ErPo
Enoch Arden, *sel.* Tennyson.
"Cast all your cares on God; that anchor holds." TRV
Enormous fortress loomed black and grim, An. Crime and Punishment. James Sexton Layton. PoNC
Enosis. Christopher Pearse Cranch. *See* Gnosis.
Enough is not enough! Glory to Autumn! Abundance. Conrad Ferdinand Meyer. AGP
Enough Not One. Benjamin Franklin. TRV
"Enough," she said. But the dust still rained around her. Dust. Randolph Stow. PoAu-2
Enquiring fields, courtesies, The. Pastoral. Allen Tate. AP
Enter No (Silence Is the Blood Whose Flesh). E. E. Cummings. AP
Enter the chilly no-man's land of about. The Ghost's Leave-taking. Sylvia Plath. NePoEA-2
Enter the dream-house, brothers and sisters, leaving. Newsreel. C. Day Lewis. ILP
Enter these enchanted woods. The Woods of Westermain. George Meredith. VP
Enterprise. Nissim Ezekiel. ACV
Enthroned above the world although he sit. Immanence. Richard Hovey. TRV
Enthusiast, The; or, The Lover of Nature. Joseph Warton. EnPE
Entire, more than entire have we been devastated! Tears of the Fatherland. Andreas Gryphius. ACP
Entrance and exit wounds are silvered clean. Recalling War. Robert Graves. AnMoPo; MMA
Entreat Me Not to Leave Thee. Ruth, I: 16-17, Bible, *O.T.* TRV
Enviable Isles, The. Herman Melville. AmLP
Envied by us all. Maple Leaves. Shiko. SiGo; SoPo
Envoi "All that remains for me." Arthur Symons. UnTE

Envoi: "Fly, white butterflies, out to sea." Swinburne. GoJo
Envoi (1919). Ezra Pound. *Fr.* Hugh Selwyn Mauberley. CaFP; CTC; PoIE
Ephesians, *sel.* Bible, *N.T.*
  "Wherefore I ask that ye faint not at my tribulations for you," III: 13-21. BoC
Epic of Gilgamesh. *Unknown. See* Gilgamesh.
Epicoene; or, The Silent Woman, *sel.* Ben Jonson.
  Still to Be Neat, *fr.* I, i, *tr. fr. the Latin of* Jean Bonnefons. CABA; CBEP; PoSa; StP
  (Clerimont's Song.) PoIE; SeCP; VaPo
  (Song: "Still to be neat, still to be dressed.") EnRePo
  ("Still to be neat, still to be dressed.") ILP
Epicure, The. Abraham Cowley, *after the Greek of* Anacreon. SeCP
Epigram: "And now you're ready who while she was here." J. V. Cunningham. ErPo
Epigram: "As Thomas was cudgelled one day by his wife." Swift. WePo
Epigram: Burnt Ship, A. John Donne. DiPo
Epigram: Engraved on the Collar of a Dog Which I Gave to His Royal Highness. Pope. *See* Engraved on the Collar of a Dog . . .
Epigram: "Face that should content me wonders well, A." Sir Thomas Wyatt. CTC
Epigram, An: "Gil's history appears to me." Matthew Green. StP
Epigram: "How many drag the marriage chain." Royall Tyler. StP
Epigram: "I am His Highness' dog at Kew." Pope. *See* Engraved on the Collar of a Dog . . .
Epigram: "Isn't it." Alfred Kreymborg. BoLP
Epigram: "No wonder that Oxford and Cambridge profound." *Unknown.* WaPE
Epigram: "On parent knees, a naked new-born child." Sir William Jones. PoPl
Epigram: "You ask me how Contempt who claims to sleep." J. V. Cunningham. *See* You Ask Me How Contempt Who Claims to Sleep.
Epigram on Handel and Bononcini. Byron. CBEP
Epigram on Two Ladies. Sophia Burrell. ErPo
Epigramme: "Some four years ago I made Phillis an offer." Philippe Desportes, *tr. fr. French by* Charles Cotton. RBL
Epigrams on Priapus. *Unknown.* ErPo
Epigraph: "I give you the end of a golden string." Blake. *Fr.* Jerusalem, *ch.* 4. OBNC
Epilogue: "All the people in my poems walk into the dark." Jon Silkin. PoDB
Epilogue: "At the midnight in the silence of the sleep-time." Robert Browning. *Fr.* Asolando. FaBV; OBNC; PoIE
Epilogue: Author to Reader. Henri Coulette. *Fr.* The War of the Secret Agents. NePoEA-2
Epilogue: "If Luther's day expand to Darwin's year." Herman Melville. *Fr.* Clarel. AP
Epilogue: "Now my charms are all o'erthrown." Shakespeare. *Fr.* The Tempest, V, i. CTC
Epilogue: "Poets, like disputants, when reasons fail." Dryden. *Fr.* All for Love. DiPo
Epilogue: "There's something in a stupid ass." Byron. Par
Epilogue: "Thus far, with rough and all-unable pen." Shakespeare. *Fr.* King Henry V. CTC
Epilogue: "Truly, my Satan, thou art but a dunce." Blake. *Fr.* The Gates of Paradise. CABA; OBNC
Epilogue: "When that I was and a little tiny boy." Shakespeare. *See* When That I Was.
Epipsychidion, *sels.* Shelley.
  "Ship is floating in the harbour now, A." HaSV
  "True Love in this differs from gold and clay." OBNC
Epistemological Rag, The. Gray Burr. CoPo
Epistle, An: "First, last and always dearest, closest, best." A. D. Hope. PoAu-2
Epistle I: "Meeting a monster of mourning wherever I go." George Barker. PoIE
Epistle III: "Pult'ney, methinks you blame my breach of word." John Gay. EiCP
Epistle, An, Containing the Strange Medical Experience of Karshish, the Arab Physician. Robert Browning. CABL; VP
  "So, the All-Great, were the All-Loving too," *sel.* TRV
Epistle to Dr. Arbuthnot. Pope. CABA; CABL; PoIE *Sels.*
  Atticus. PoSa
  "Pains, reading, study, are their just pretense." PP
Epistle to Henry Wriothesley, Earl of Southampton. Samuel Daniel. EnRePo
Epistle to James Smith. Burns. CABL
Epistle to John Hamilton Reynolds. Keats. OBNC
Epistle to John Lapraik, an Old Scottish Bard. Burns. EnPE
  "I am nae poet, in a sense," *sel.* PP
Epistle to Miss Blount. Pope. CaFP; DiPo
  (To a Young Lady on Her Leaving [the] Town after the Coronation.) OnP; WePo
Epistle to the Reader. Walker Gibson. PP

Epistrophe. LeRoi Jones. NNP
Epitaph: "Believer he and unbeliever both." Robert Francis. PoIE
Epitaph: "Body of, The." Benjamin Franklin. TRV
Epitaph: "Done to death by slanderous tongues." Shakespeare. *Fr.* Much Ado about Nothing, V iii. CTC
Epitaph: "Even such is Time, which takes in trust." Sir Walter Ralegh. *See* Even Such Is Time.
Epitaph: "Here lies Michael of the small bone." Lawrence Durrell. AnMoPo
Epitaph, An: "Here lieth under this marble ston." *Unknown.* MeEL
Epitaph: "I lived my life from day to day." Mathurin Régnier, *tr. fr. French by* Ida Fasel. RBL
Epitaph, An: "Interred beneath this marble stone." Matthew Prior. EiCP; PoIE
Epitaph, An: "O mortal folk, you may behold and see." Stephen Hawes. CBEP
Epitaph, An: On Elizabeth Chute. Ben Jonson. EnRePo
Epitaph: "Poem in the rock and, The." R. S. Thomas. WePo
Epitaph: "Say he was sad, for there was none to love him." Robert Nathan. MoLP
Epitaph: "Time and the World, whose magnitude and weight." Robert Southey. OBNC
Epitaph: Time, Which Does All Creatures. François Maynard, *tr. fr. French by* Henry Carrington. RBL
Epitaph: "Warm summer sun shine kindly here." Robert Richardson. PoLF
Epitaph: "When I shall be without regret." J. V. Cunningham. PoCh
Epitaph. Cæcil. Boulstr. Lord Herbert of Cherbury. SeCP
Epitaph for a Cat. Margaret E. Bruner. PoLF
Epitaph for a Godly Man's Tomb, An. Robert Wild. CBEP
Epitaph for a Horseman. Michael Hamburger. NePoEA-2
Epitaph for Chaeroneia. Aristotle, *tr. fr. Greek by* C. R. Kennedy. SiGo
Epitaph for Mariana, His Brother Paul's Little Daughter. Andreas Gryphius, *tr. fr. German by* Gertrude C. Schwebell. AGP
Epitaph for the Poet. George Barker. PoIE
Epitaph, Found Somewhere in Space. Hugh Wilgus Ramsaur. TRV
Epitaph in Form of a Ballad, The. Villon, *tr. fr. French by* Swinburne. CTC
  (Villon's Epitaph, *tr. by* Muriel Kittel.) AnML
Epitaph in Sirmio. David Morton. PoLF
Epitaph of Sir Thomas Gravener Knight, An. Sir Thomas Wyatt. EnRePo
Epitaph of the Death of Nicholas Grimald, An. Barnabe Googe. EnRePo
Epitaph on a Bombing Victim. Roy Fuller. ToPo
Epitaph on a Dentist. *Unknown.* LV
Epitaph on a Pessimist. Thomas Hardy. PoIE; VP
Epitaph on a Waiter. David McCord. PoPo
Epitaph on a Worthy Clergyman. Benjamin Franklin. TRV
Epitaph on an Army of Mercenaries. A. E. Housman. Last Poems, XXXVII. MMA; PoIE; StP
Epitaph on Clere, An. Earl of Surrey. CBEP
Epitaph on Drake. Richard Barnfield. HaSV
Epitaph on Elizabeth, L. H. Ben Jonson. CABA; ELP; EnRePo; PoIE; SeCP
Epitaph on Herself, An. Hetty Wright. WaPE
Epitaph on His Grandfather, An. Thomas Shipman. CBEP
Epitaph on Jean Veau. Clément Marot, *tr. fr. French by* Henry Carrington. RBL
Epitaph on Johnson. William Cowper. EiCP
Epitaph on Rabelais. Pierre de Ronsard, *tr. fr. French by* R. N. Currey. RBL
Epitaph on Robert Southey. Thomas Moore. PP
Epitaph on S. P. [Salomon *or* Salathiel Pavy], a Child of Q. El. [Queen Elizabeth's] Chapel [*or* Chappel], An. Ben Jonson. CABA; EnRePo; PoSa; SeCP; VaPo
Epitaph on Sir Albert Morton's Wife. Sir Henry Wotton. *See* Upon the Death of Sir Albert Morton's Wife.
Epitaph on the Countess Dowager of Pembroke. William Browne. *See* On the Countess Dowager of Pembroke.
Epitaph on the Earl of Leicester. Sir Walter Ralegh. EnRePo
Epitaph on the Lady Mary Villers, An. Thomas Carew. SeCP
Epitaph on the Marchioness of Winchester, An. Milton. FoBA
Epitaph to the Four Husbands of Miss Ivy Saunders. *Unknown.* WePo
Epitaph upon a Young Married Couple Dead and Buried Together, An. Richard Crashaw. ELP; ILP; SeCP
Epitaph upon the Celebrated Claudy Philips, Musician Who Died Very Poor, An. Samuel Johnson. CBEP
Epitaphs for Three Prominent Persons. Phyllis McGinley. LV
Epitaphs of the War, 1914-18, *sels.* Kipling. MMA
  Batteries Out of Ammunition.
  Drifter off Tarentum, A.
  Refined Man, The.
Epithalamion. Spenser. CaBL; EnRePo; ILP
Epithalamion Made at Lincolnes Inne. John Donne. SeCP

Epithalamium. Leo Kennedy. OBCV
Epithalamium, *sel.* Johannes Secundus, *tr. fr. Latin by* George Ogle.
   Wedding Night, The. UnTE
Epode. Ben Jonson. SeCP
Equal Troth. Dante Gabriel Rossetti. The House of Life, XXXII. VP
Equals. Louis Untermeyer. UnTE
Equilibrists, The. John Crowe Ransom. AP; CaFP
Equinoctial cypress speaks, The. Ivory. Mario Luzi. CoIP
Erasers are such handy things. Mistakes. George W. Swarberg. STF
Erda. Vera Bishop Konrick. FiSC
Ere on my bed my limbs, I lay. The Pains of Sleep. Samuel Taylor Coleridge. CBEP; OBNC
Ere the steamer bore him Eastward, Sleary was engaged to marry. The Post That Fitted. Kipling. OnMSP
Ere-while of musick, and ethereal mirth. The Passion. Milton. MeP
Erie Canal, The. *Unknown.* RePo
Erige Cor Tuum ad Me in Caelum. Hilda Doolittle ("H. D."). AP
Erin's Lovely Home. *Unknown.* BSNS
Erith. *Unknown.* CBEP
Erlington. *Unknown.* BuBa
Erlking, The. Goethe, *tr. fr. German by* Sir Walter Scott. SIV
   (Elf-King, The, *tr. unknown.*) PoPo
Eρωσ (Eros). Robert Bridges. ILP; PoIE.
Eros, pray discard your bow. Plea to Eros. *Unknown.* UnTE
Eros Turanros. E. A. Robinson. AmLP; AP; ILP; PoIE
Erosion. James Larkin Pearson. PoNC
Erthe oute of erthe is wonderly wroghte. Earth out of Earth. *Unknown.* MeEL
Escalade. Arthur Symons. UnTE
Escapade, The. David Ignatow. PP
Escape, An. Abu Nuwas, *tr. fr. Arabic by* E. Powys Mathers. ErPo
Escape. Robert Graves. ILP
Escape. Elinor Wylie. RePo
Escape me?/ Never. Life in a Love. Robert Browning. OBNC
Especially When the October Wind. Dylan Thomas. CABA; DiPo; ToPo
Essay on Criticism, An. Pope. CABA
   Sels.
   "But most by numbers judge a poet's song," *fr.* Pt. II. PP
   "First follow Nature, and your judgment frame," *fr.* Pt. I. PP
   Little Learning Is a Dangerous Thing, A, *fr.* Pt. II. PoLF
   "Of all the causes which conspire to blind," Pt. II. ILP; PoIE
   "Sound must seem an echo to the sense, The," *fr.* Pt. II. PoPo
   " 'Tis hard to say, if greater want of skill," *fr.* Pt. I. PP
Essay on Deity. Elder Olson. MoRP
   "Know then thyself, presume not God to scan," *fr.* Epistle II. CaFP; DiPo; PoIE; PoSa; TRV
   "Lo, the poor Indian! whose untutored mind," *fr.* Epistle I. PoIE
   Vice, *fr.* Epistle II. PoPl
Essay on Rime, *sels.* Karl Shapiro. PP
   "But poets are name-proud craftsmen; Greeks and Jews."
   "There is a general idiom to all rime."
Essential oils are wrung. Emily Dickinson. AP; CBEP
Estat ai en greu cossirier. Beatriz de Dia, *tr. fr. Provençal by* Paul Blackburn. ErPo
Esterina, your twenty years threaten you. Falsetto. Eugenio Montale. CoIP
Esther, *sel.* Wilfrid Scawen Blunt.
   "He who has once been happy is for aye." OBNC
Esthétique du Mal. Wallace Stevens. PoDB
Estuary is wide, The. Off Saguenay. A. G. Bailey. ACV
Esyllt. Glyn Jones. DTC
Et Cetera. Earl of Rochester. UnTE
Eternal, The. Esaias Tegnér, *tr. fr. Swedish by* Charles Wharton Stork. TRV
Eternal Christmas. Elizabeth Stuart Phelps. TRV
Eternal Goodness, The, *sel.* Whittier.
   "I see the wrong that round me lies." TRV
Eternal Life. Henry More. TRV
Eternal Reward, Eternal Pain. Sir Thomas More. *Fr.* The Twelve Weapons of Spiritual Battle. EnRePo
Eternal Spirit of the chainless Mind! Sonnet on Chillon [or On the Castle of Chillon]. Byron. The Prisoner of Chillon, *introd. sonnet.* CABL; GTBS-P; ILP; PoPl; PoPo
Eternal Truth, almighty, infinite. Caelica, XCVII. Fulke Greville. EnRePo
Eternity. Blake. DiPo; OBNC; PoIE
Eternity. Sir Thomas More. *Fr.* The Pageants of Thomas More. EnRePo
Eternity at Lourmarin. René Char, *tr. fr. French by* Paul Engle. CoFP

Eternity is like unto a ring. Time and Eternity. Bunyan. WiR
Eternity of Nature. John Clare. StP
Eternity to Come. Johann von Rist, *tr. fr. German by* Robert Kramer. AGP
Eternity's Low Voice. Mark Van Doren. EaLo
Ethelstan, *sel.* George Darley.
   Runilda's Chant. HaSV
Ethereal minstrel! pilgrim of the sky! To the Skylark. Wordsworth. GTBS-P
Eton Boating Song. William Johnson Cory. ELP
Etta Moten's Attic. Margaret Danner. Far from Africa: Four Poems, 4. AmNP
Euclid. Vachel Lindsay. PoPo
Euclid Alone. Edna St. Vincent Millay. FaBV
Eulalie. Poe. EvOK; Par
Euphrosyne. Matthew Arnold. VP
Europa. William Plomer. MoBS
Europe. John Ashbery. CoPo
Europe, *sels.* Louis Dudek. OBCV
   "Commotion of these waves, however strong, cannot disturb, The," XIX.
   "Sea retains such images, The," XCV.
Eurydice, The—it concerned thee, O Lord. The Loss of the *Eurydice.* Gerard Manley Hopkins. FoBA; VP
Eurynome. Jay Macpherson. OBCV
Evanthe's niplets are like sard. Niplets. *Unknown.* ErPo
Eve. David Gascoyne. GTBS-P
Eve. Ralph Hodgson. EvOK; OnMSP; WePo
Eve. Rainer Maria Rilke, *tr. fr. German by* M. D. Herter Norton. MoRP
Eve. Christina Rossetti. GTBS-P
Eve in Reflection. Jay Macpherson. OBCV
Eve of Christmas, The. James Kirkup. DaDu
Eve of St. Agnes, The. Keats. CABA; CABL; CaFP; DiPo; FoBA; ILP; OBNC; PoIE; PoLF; StP
Eve of Waterloo, The. Byron. *Fr.* Childe Harold's Pilgrimage. FaBV; OBNC
Eve-Song. Mary Gilmore. PoAu-1
Eve, with her basket, was. Eve. Ralph Hodgson. EvOK; OnMSP; WePo
Even a floating feather in the air can trace. Day and Night. Eugenio Montale. CoIP
Even as a child, of sorrow that we give. Pride of Youth. Dante Gabriel Rossetti. The House of Life, XXIV. OBNC; VP
Even as a king may sometimes seize a glass. A Woman's Fate. Rainer Maria Rilke. TwGP
Even as a lover, dreaming, unaware. Sonnets, Part II, XIII. Frederick Goddard Tuckerman. AP
Even as I wandered the tropic jungle of fever. Shub-Ad. Robert H. Barlow. FiSC
Even as the moon grows queenlier in mid-space. Gracious Moonlight. Dante Gabriel Rossetti. The House of Life, XX. VP
Even, I think, when you're bathing. A Bathing Girl. Johannes V. Jensen. PoPl
Even if stonebreakers do not want. Car Journey. Albert Ehrenstein. MGP
Even in the Darkness. Helene Mullins. MoRP
Even infinity has epochs and hierarchies of days. A Posture for Next Year. H. A. Sieber. PoNC
Even now/ I love long black eyes that caress like silk. I Love Long Black Eyes. Bilhana, *formerly at. to* Chauras. *Fr.* Black Marigolds. SiGo
Even now/ My thought is all of this gold-tinted king's daughter. Black Marigolds. Bilhana, *formerly at. to* Chauras. ErPo
Even on clear nights, lead the most supple children. The Great Bear. John Hollander. MP; NePoEA-2
Even So. Dante Gabriel Rossetti. OBNC
Even so deep in the jungle they were not safe. The Garden of Ships. Douglas Stewart. PoAu-2
Even so distant, I can taste the grief. Deceptions. Philip Larkin. CABA; ErPo; GTBS-P
Even-Song. George Herbert. MeP
Even Such Is Time. Sir Walter Ralegh. EnRePo; OnP
   (Author's Epitaph, Made by Himselfe, The.) BoC
   (Conclusion, The.) EvOK; FaPL
   (Epitaph: "Even such is Time, which takes in trust.") CTC; TRV
   (Sir Walter Raleigh the Night before His Death.) PoPo
   (Verses.) PoIE
   (Written on the Night before His Execution.) WePo
Even though it's raining. Others. Harry Behn. SoPo
Even when your friend, the radio, is still; even when her. X Minus X. Kenneth Fearing. AmLP
Evening. Charles Cotton. WiR
Evening. Andreas Gryphius, *tr. fr. German by* George C. Schoolfield. AGP
Evening. Hugh McCrae. PoAu-1
Evening. Charles Sangster. ACV
Evening. Schiller, *tr. fr. German by* Walter Kaufmann. TwGP

Evening. Edith Sitwell. MoBS
Evening. Robert Wallace. PoPo
Evening at Sea, An. John Press. HaSV
Evening Beauty. Vincent Voiture, *tr. fr. French by* William Frederic Giese. RBL
Evening, blue, voluptuous, of June, The. The Walk on the Beach. John Gould Fletcher. BoLP; MoLP
Evening comes early, and soon discovers. Master's in the Garden Again. John Crowe Ransom. AP
Evening falls soon in the hills across the river. The White Eagle. Nan McDonald. PoAu-2
Evening Fancy. Friedrich Hölderlin, *tr. fr. German by* W. Edward Brown. AGP
Evening Gleam, The. James Devaney. PoAu-1
Evening has brought its. Witnesses. W. S. Merwin. AmPC
Evening in the Sanitarium. Louise Bogan. MP
"Evening is red on the island of Palau." Palau. Gottfried Benn. MGP
Evening Landscape. Pol de Mont, *tr. fr. Flemish by* Jethro Bithell. SiGo
Evening light accompanied by all the dead, The. Weep—Those Whose Eyes Are Dry Shall Weep. Alfonso Gatto. CoIP
Evening of Gavinana. "Vincenzo Cardarelli," *tr. fr. Italian by* Cosimo Corsano. CoIP
Evening Party. Piero Jahier, *tr. fr. Italian by* Carlo L. Golino. CoIP
Evening: Ponte al Mare, Pisa. Shelley. CBEP
Evening Prayer. Amelia Josephine Burr. SIV
Evening Prayer, An. *Unknown.* STF
Evening Song. Gottfried Keller, *tr. fr. German by* D. G. Wright. AGP
Evening Song. Sidney Lanier. AP; FaPL
Evening Song. Philip von Zesen, *tr. fr. German by* George C. Schoolfield. AGP
Evening Star. George Barker. ErPo; PoCh
Evening Star, The. Amy Carmichael. TRV
Evening Star. Poe. AP
Evening Star, enemy of lovers, why. Evening Star. George Barker. ErPo; PoCh
Evening Walk, An, *sel.* Wordsworth.
"Did Sabine grace adorn my living line." EiCP
Evening-Watch, The. Henry Vaughan. MeP
Evening Wind, The. Bryant. AP
Evening's Love, An, *sels.* Dryden.
After the Pangs [of a Desperate Lover], *fr.* II, i. ELP; StP; UnTE
(Love's Fancy.) ErPo
Calm Was the Even, *fr.* IV, i. DiPo
You Charmed Me Not, *fr.* II, i. DiPo
Evenings of Certain Lives, The. Gottfried Benn, *tr. fr. German by* Christopher Middleton. MGP
Evensong. Robert Louis Stevenson. TRV
Evensong. George Tankervil. TRV
Ever-fixed Mark, An. Kingsley Amis. ErPo
Ever let the Fancy roam! The Realm of Fancy. Keats. GTBS-P
Ever-living Church, The. Charles Wesley. STF
Ever On. *Unknown.* STF
Ever since I've been living far out. The Tree. Rainer Brambach. MGP
Everest of Tears. Wolfgang Weyrauch, *tr. fr. German by* Michael Hamburger. MGP
Evergreen shadow and the pale magnolia, The. Souls Lake. Robert Fitzgerald. MP
Everlasting Mercy, The, *sels.* John Masefield.
"I did not think, I did not strive." BoC; TRV
"O Christ who holds the open gate." TRV
Everlasting universe of things, The. Mont Blanc. Shelley. PP
Every branch big with it. Snow in the Suburbs. Thomas Hardy. GoJo; VP; WePo
Every Day. Ingeborg Bachmann, *tr. fr. German by* Christopher Middleton. MGP
Every day is a fresh beginning. New Every Morning. *Unknown.* STF
Every day is Judgment Day. Judgment Day. John Oxenham. TRV
Every day thou might lere. Remember the Day of Judgment. *Unknown.* MeEL
Every morning lean thine arms awhile. Begin the Day with God. *Unknown.* TRV
Every Morning When I Wake. Dylan Thomas. *Fr.* Under Milk Wood. LOW
Every night I sleep. In the Trench. Leon Gellert. PoAu-1
Every night my prayers I say. System. Robert Louis Stevenson. LV
Every Time I Climb a Tree. David McCord. SoPo
Every time the bucks went clattering. Earthy Anecdote. Wallace Stevens. GoJo
Every valley drinks. Winter Rain. Christina Rossetti. WiR
Every woman of true royalty owns. The Secret Land. Robert Graves. BoC
Everyone grumbled. The sky was grey. Daddy Fell into the Pond. Alfred Noyes. RePo

Everyone knows he's blind as a bat. The Umpire. Walker Gibson. SD
Everyone grows younger; my thinning hair. Figures of Authority. Edward Watkins. StP
Everyone Sang ("Everyone suddenly burst out singing"). Siegfried Sassoon. FaBV; GTBS-P; LOW; PoPl; PoSC; RePo
"Everything in the Air Is a Bird." Barbara Guest. AmPC
Everything is black and gold. Black and Gold. Nancy Byrd Turner. SoPo
Everything is sexual at the beach. Concerning Unnatural Nature: An Inverted Form. Hollis Summers. ErPo
Everything is stopped. Stopped. Allen Polite. NNP
Everything Is Swept Away by the Brief Year. Francisco de Quevedo, *tr. fr. Spanish by* Kate Flores. AnSP
Everything you own, Robert. Concerning Mme. Robert. Deems Taylor. UnTE
Everything's been different. The Birthday Child. Rose Fyleman. BiCB
Everywhere, everywhere, Christmas tonight. A Christmas Carol. Phillips Brooks. SoPo
Everywhere, everywhere, following me. Camerados. Bayard Taylor. Par
Eve's Speech to Adam. Milton. *Fr. Paradise Lost,* IV. DiPo
Eve's Temptation and Fall. Milton. *Fr. Paradise Lost,* IX. DiPo
Evidence, The. Hebrews, XI: 1, Bible, *N.T.* TRV
Evidence Read at the Trial of the Knave of Hearts. "Lewis Carroll." *Fr. Alice's Adventures in Wonderland.* GTBS-P
Evil Days. Boris Pasternak, *tr. fr. Russian by* Bernard Guilbert Guerney. MoRP
Evil Eye, The. John Ciardi. MoBS
Evil has no home. Evil Is Homeless. D. H. Lawrence. MoRP
Evil is here? That's work for us to do. Israel Zangwill. *Fr.* At the Worst. TRV
Evil Is Homeless. D. H. Lawrence. MoRP
Evocation. Herman Stowell King. FiSC
Evolution. Rochelle Owens. CoPo
Evolution. John Banister Tabb. PoPl
Ex Nihilo. David Gascoyne. GTBS-P
Ex Ore Infantium. Francis Thompson. *See* Little Jesus.
Example, The. W. H. Davies. LV
Exceeding Great Army, An. Ethan Ayer. FiSC
Excelente Balade of Charitie, An. Thomas Chatterton. EnPE; StP
Excelsior. Longfellow. OnMSP
Except ourselves, we have no other prayer. Without Ceremony. Vassar Miller. CoPo
Except the Lord build the house. Psalm CXXVIII, Bible, *O.T.* TRV
Excesses of God, The. Robinson Jeffers. MoRP
Exchanges II, The. Robert Kelly. CoPo
Excursion, The. Tu Fu, *tr. fr. Chinese by* Amy Lowell *and* Florence Ayscough. SD
Excursion, The, *sel.* Wordsworth.
Wanderer Recalls the Past, The, *fr.* I. OBNC
Excuse of Absence, An. Thomas Carew. SeCP
Execration upon Vulcan, An. Ben Jonson. SeCP
Execution of Montrose, The. William Edmondstoune. Aytoun. OnMSP
Exequy, The. Henry King. CABA; CaFP; SeCP
Exequy: To Peter Allt. Kildare Dobbs. OBCV
Exercise Book. Paul Dehn. WePo
Exert thy voice, sweet harbinger of spring! To the Nightingale. Countess of Winchilsea. PoIE
Exeunt. Richard Wilbur. PoLF
Exile's Letter. Li Po, *tr. fr. Chinese by* Ezra Pound. CTC
Exile's Return, The. Robert Lowell. AP
Exit. John Gould Fletcher. PoPo
Exit from Eden. Milton. *Fr. Paradise Lost,* XII. DiPo
Exit the ribald clown. Colombine. Hugh McCrae. PoAu-1
Exodus for Oregon. Joaquin Miller. FaPL
Expansive puppets percolate self-unction. The Canadian Authors Meet. F. R. Scott. ACV; OBCV
Expense of spirit in a waste of shame, The. Sonnets, CXXIX. Shakespeare. CABA; CaFP; CBEP; DiPo; EnRePo; ErPo; FoBA; OnP; PoIE; StP; VaPo
Experience. Lesbia Harford. PoAu-1
Experience. Aline Kilmer. BiCB
Experience. Dorothy Parker. BoLP; PoPl
Expiration, The. John Donne. CBEP; SeCP
Explanation of the Grasshopper, An. Vachel Lindsay. SoPo
Explanations of Love. Carl Sandburg. MoLP
Explanatory Epistle, An. John Banks. WaPE
Exploration. Daniel Hoffman. CoPo
Explorations. Louis MacNeice. ILP
Expostulation, An. Isaac Bickerstaffe. BoLP
Expostulation and Reply. Wordsworth. CBEP
Exposure. Wilfred Owen. MMA
Express, The. Stephen Spender. GoJo; MP; PoPl; RoGo; VaPo

Express train gropes and thrusts its way through darkness, The. On Crossing the Rhine Bridge at Cologne by Night. Ernst Stadler. MGP

Extasie, The. Abraham Cowley. SeCP

Extasy [or Extasie], The. John Donne. *See* Ecstasy, The.

Extempore Effusion upon the Death of James Hogg. Wordsworth. CBEP

Extended Invitation. Jesse Stuart. FiSC

Extensions, *sel.* Jean Follain, *tr. fr. French by* Dori Katz. "From being aware of all this beauty." CoFP

Extremely Naughty Children. Elizabeth Godley. BBGG

Exultation is the going. Emily Dickinson. AP; CABA; CBEP

Exulting, The. Theodore Roethke. *Fr.* The Dying Man. PoDB

Eye, The. Robinson Jeffers. AmLP; AP; PoPo

Eye can hardly pick them out, The. At Grass. Philip Larkin. DaDu; SD

Eye luminous, The. The Offender. Denise Levertov. NePoEA-2

Eye of Humility, The. Kay Smith. OBCV

Eye You See Isn't, The. Antonio Machado, *tr. fr. Spanish by* William M. Davis. AnSP

Eyeless labourer in the night, The. Woman to Man. Judith Wright. PoAu-2

Eyelids meet, The. He'll catch a little nap. In the Smoking-Car. Richard Wilbur. ToPo

Eyes and Tears. Andrew Marvell. MeP

Eyes are lying again, posing, The. Self-Portrait. Robert Pack. CoPo

Eyes of clear serenity. Madrigal. Gutierre de Cetina. AnSP

Eyes open to a cry of pulleys, The. Love Calls Us to the Things of This World. Richard Wilbur. PoDB; ToPo

Eyes, side-to-side. Directions. Onitsura. SoPo

Eyes That Drew from Me Such Fervent Praise, The. Petrarch, *tr. fr. Italian by* Edwin Morgan. Sonnets to Laura: To Laura in Death, XXIV. AnML

("Eyes, the face, the limbs of heavenly mould, The," *tr. by* Lady Dacre. RBL

Eyes, ye treasured windows of my sight. Evening Song. Gottfried Keller. AGP

Eyewitness. Rodney Hall. PoAu-2

F

Fable IV: Eagle, and the Assembly of Animals, The. John Gay. EiCP

Fable X: Elephant and the Bookseller, The. John Gay. EiCP

Fable L: Hare and Many Friends, The. John Gay. EiCP

Fable VII: Lion, the Fox, and the Geese, The. John Gay. EiCP

Fable: "Mountain and the squirrel, The." Emerson. FaBV; OnMSP; PoPl; PoPo; TRV; VaPo

(Mountain and the Squirrel, The.) GoJo

Fable XX: Old Hen and the Cock, The. John Gay. EiCP

Fable XIII: Plutus, Cupid, and Time. John Gay. EiCP

Fable: Poet and His Patron, The. Edward Moore. WaPE

Fable XLV: Poet and the Rose, The. John Gay. EiCP

Fable XIII: Tame Stag, The. John Gay. EiCP

(Tame Stag, The.) CBEP

Fable II: Vulture, the Sparrow, and Other Birds, The. John Gay. EiCP

Fable V: Wild Boar and the Ram, The. John Gay. EiCP

Fable for Blackboard. George Starbuck. CaFP

Fable for Critics, A, *sels.* James Russell Lowell. AP
Bryant.
Cooper.
Emerson.
("There comes Emerson first, whose rich words, every one.") PP
Hawthorne.
Lowell.
Poe and Longfellow.
Whittier.

Fable of Polyphemus and Galatea, *sels.* Luis de Góngora, *tr. fr. Spanish by* Frances Fletcher. AnSP
Dedication: To the Count of Niebla.
Polyphemus' Love Song.

Fable of the Magnet and the Churn, The. W. S. Gilbert. *Fr.* Patience. OnMSP; RePo

Fabulla, sweet virgin, you have learned your lesson too well. The Too Literal Pupil. Martial. UnTE

Façade, *sels.* Edith Sitwell.
Hornpipe. GTBS-P
Madame [or Madam] Mouse Trots. DaDu; LOW

Face, A. Robert Browning. CTC

Face, A. Marianne Moore. PoCh

Face, The. Edwin Muir. GTBS-P

Face it—you must—and do not turn away. Autumnal. Rolfe Humphries. MoRP

Face of all the world is changed, I think, The. Sonnets from the Portuguese, VII. Elizabeth Barrett Browning. CTC

Face of Helen, The. Christopher Marlowe. *Fr.* Dr. Faustus. FaBV

Face of Poverty. Lucy Smith. NNP

Face of the Fisherman, The. Walter Höllerer, *tr fr. German by* Michael Hamburger. MGP

Face of the Waters, The. Robert D. Fitzgerald. PoAu-2

Face that should content me wonders well, A. Epigram. Sir Thomas Wyatt. CTC

Face to the wall and behind him. The Wall. Louis MacNeice. PoIE

Faces from a Bestiary. X. J. Kennedy. NePoEA-2

Faction, that ever dwells. Caelica, XXIX. Fulke Greville. EnRePo

Factory Windows Are Always Broken. Vachel Lindsay. PoIE; PoPo

Facts have no eyes. One must. Observation of Facts. Charles Tomlinson. NePoEA-2

Fade in the sound of summer music. Notes for a Movie Script. M. Carl Holman. AmNP

Fade, then—die, depart, and come no more. *Fr.* Priapus and the Pool. Conrad Aiken. AmLP

Faded Leaves. Matthew Arnold. VP
Sels.
Longing, V. CBEP; PoLF
River, The, I. CBEP

Faded Pictures. William Vaughn Moody. AP

Fads and Fancies. Edith Earnshaw. PoNC

Faerie Queene, The, *sel.* Robin Blaser.
"Okay a nightingale." CoPo

Faerie Queene, The, *sels.* Spenser.
And Is There Care in Heaven? *fr.* II, 8. OnP
(Guardian Angels of Men.) BoC
Port after Stormy Seas, *fr.* I, 9. HaSV
Tale of Calidore, The, VI, 9. StP

Fain Would I Change That Note. Unknown, at. to Tobias Hume. CBEP; ELP

Fain Would I Live in Safest Freedom. August, Graf von Platen, *tr. fr. German by* Edwin Morgan. SiGo

Fain Would I Wed a Fair Young Man. Thomas Campion. UnTE

Fain would I wish that my heart cannot will. Heart-Coldness. Michelangelo. RBL

Faint Heart. Rufinus, *tr. fr. Greek by* F. A. Wright. ErPo

Faintheart in a Railway Train. Thomas Hardy. CTC

Faintly and from Far Away. Vassar Miller. CoPo

Fair and bright assembly, A: never strode. Thomas Lovell Beddoes. *Fr.* Death's Jest Book. CTC

Fair, and Soft, and Gay, and Young. Robert Gould. UnTE

Fair Annet's Song. Elinor Wylie. AmLP

Fair as the night, when all the astral fires. Love Sonnets, VIII. Charles Harpur. PoAu-2

Fair Aye Sits at Her Cruel Lady's Feet. Unknown, *tr. fr. French by* Jacques LeClercq. AnML

Fair Charlotte. Unknown. BFSS, *with music;* BSO (A vers., with music; C vers.)

Fair Cloris in a pig-stye lay. A Song to Cloris. Earl of Rochester. ErPo

Fair daffodils [or Faire daffodils], we weep to see. To Daffodils [or Daffodills]. Robert Herrick. CBEP; ELP; EvOK; GoJo; GTBS-P; OnP; PoIE; PoPo; SeCP; WePo

Fair Elenor. Blake. FoBA

Fair Ellen one morn from her cottage had strayed. Ellen the Fair. Unknown. BSNS

Fair Exchange, A. La Fontaine. UnTE

Fair Fannie Moore, *with music.* Unknown. BFSS

Fair flower of fifteen springs, that still. To His Young Mistress. Pierre de Ronsard. *Fr.* Amours de Marie. RBL

Fair Flower of Northumberland, The. Unknown. BuBa

Fair flower, that dost so comely grow. The Wild Honey Suckle. Philip Freneau. AmLP; AP; CBEP; PoLF

Fair Greece! sad relic of departed worth! Byron. *Fr.* Childe Harold's Pilgrimage, II. ILP

Fair Helen. Unknown. *See* Helen of Kir[k]connell.

Fair Iris I love and hourly I die. Hourly I Die. Dryden. *Fr.* Amphitryon. UnTE

Fair is my love, and cruel as she's fair. To Delia, VI. Samuel Daniel. EnRePo

Fair is my love that feeds among the lilies. Fair Is My Love [or Sonnet]. Bartholomew Griffin. *Fr.* Fidessa, More Chaste than Kind. CBEP; ErPo

Fair Lady of the Plains, The, *with music.* Unknown. BFSS

Fair laughs the morn, and soft the zephyr blows. Thomas Gray. *Fr.* The Bard. HaSV

Fair Lunacy! I see thee, with a crown. Mirthful Lunacy. Thomas Stoddart. *Fr.* The Death-Wake; or, Lunacy. OBNC

Fair maid sat in her bower-door, A. Young John. Unknown. BuBa

Fair maiden, white and red. A Voice from the Well. George Peele. *Fr.* The Old Wives' Tale. CBEP

Fair Margaret and Sweet William (A vers., with music). Unknown. BFSS

(Lady Margaret and Sweet William, *with music.*) BSO
(Sweet William and Lady Marget, B *vers., with music.*)
BFSS
Fair Naiads of the river, that reside. Sonnet. Garcilaso de la
Vega. RBL
Fair now is the springtide, now earth lies beholding. The Mes-
sage of the March Wind. William Morris. OBNC; WiR
Fair Now to Behold the Outgreening. Bernart de Ventadorn,
tr. fr. Provençal by Thomas G. Bergin. AnML
Fair [*or* Faire] pledges of a fruitful[l] tree. To Blossoms.
Robert Herrick. GTBS-P; SeCP
Fair Rohtraut. Eduard Möricke, *tr. fr. German by* Isabel S.
MacInnes. AGP
Fair seed-time had my soul, and I grew up. Childhood and
School-Time. Wordsworth. *Fr.* The Prelude. OBNC; OnP
Fair ship, that from the Italian shore. In Memoriam A. H. H.,
IX. Tennyson. VP
Fair Singer, The. Andrew Marvell. CBEP
Fair Sou-Chong-Tee, by a shimmering brook. Story of the
Flowery Kingdom. James Branch Cabell. OnMSP
Fair stood the wind for France. Agincourt [*or* The Ballad of
Agincourt]. Michael Drayton. CBEP; EnRePo
Fair Sylvia, cease to blame my youth. Song. Francis Atter-
bury. WaPE
Fair Virtue, the Mistress of Philarete, *sel.* George Wither.
Shall I, Wasting in Despair, *also given in* Fidelia. BoLP;
PoIE
(Manly Heart, The.) FaBV; GTBS-P
Fair white hind with golden horns, A. Petrarch. *Fr.* Sonnets
to Laura: To Laura in Life. RBL
Fair would I have a pretty thing. A Pretty Thing. *Unknown.*
UnTE
Fair Young Miss, The, *with music. Unknown.* BFSS
(Lover's Lament, A, *sl. diff. vers., with music.*) BSO
Fair Young Wife, The. Helen Adam. FiSC
Faire daffadills, we weep to see. *See* Fair daffodils, we weep
to see.
Faire pledges of a fruitful tree. *See* Fair pledges of a fruitful
tree.
Faire soule, how long shall veyles thy graces shroud? A Home
in Heaven. Robert Southwell. MeP
Fairest between Lincoln and Lindsey. *Unknown. See* When
the Nightingale Sings.
Fairest day that ever yet has shone. The Lost. Jones Very.
PoIE
Fairest Isle. Dryden. *Fr.* King Arthur, V, i. CBEP
Fairest Lord Jesus. *Unknown.* TRV
Fairies, The. William Allingham. CBEP; EvOK; FaBV;
OnMSP; RoGo
Fairies. Rose Fyleman. SoPo
Fairies dance the livelong night, The. In the Moonlight. Nor-
reys Jephson O'Conor. SoPo
Fairies' Farewell, The. Richard Corbet. CBEP
(Farewell to the Fairies.) EvOK
(Proper New Ballad, A, Intituled The Faeryes Farewell;
or, God-A-Mercy Will.) SeCP
Fairy Artist, The. Nellie M. Garabrant. PoPL
Fairy Ship, The. "Gabriel Setoun." PoPL
Fairy Story. Barbara Euphan Todd. BoC
Fairy Tale, A. Kenneth Mackenzie. PoAu-2
Fairy Thorn, The. Sir Samuel Ferguson. OnMSP
Fairy Voyage, A. *Unknown.* SoPo
Fairy Went a-Marketing, A. Rose Fyleman. SoPo
Fairy Wood, The. Arthur Symons. BoC
Fairy's Life, A. Shakespeare. *See* Where the Bee Sucks.
Fairy's Reply to Saturn, The. Thomas Hood. *Fr.* The Plea of
the Midsummer Fairies. OBNC
Faith. Ada Cambridge. PoAu-1
Faith. Elizabeth York Case, *wr. at. to* Edward Bulwer-Lytton.
TRV
Faith. Victor J. Daley. PoAu-1
Faith. Margaret E. Sangster. TRV
Faith. John Banister Tabb. TRV
Faith. Whittier. TRV
Faith. Ella Wheeler Wilcox. TRV
Faith is a fine invention. Emily Dickinson. CBEP; DiPo;
FaBV
Faith of Abraham Lincoln, The. Abraham Lincoln, *arr. by* Carl
Sandburg. TRV
Faith shuts her eyes. Faith. Victor J. Daley. PoAu-1
Faithful, The. Jane Cooper. AmPC; NePoEA-2
Faithful Few, The. Chester E. Shuler. STF
Faithful Shepherdess, The, *sels.* John Fletcher.
Come, Shepherds, Come, *fr.* I, iii. ErPo
Do Not Fear, *fr.* III, i. CBEP
River God, The, *fr.* III, i. BoC
Faithless. Louis Lavater. PoAu-1
Faithless. *Unknown, tr. fr. Greek by* Louis Untermeyer.
UnTE
"Faithless again!" I cry, and she replies. Infatuated. *Un-
known.* UnTE
Faithless Nellie [*or* Nelly] Gray. Thomas Hood. SIV; WePo
Faithless Wife, The. Federico García Lorca, *tr. fr. Spanish by*
Robert O'Brien. AnSP; ErPo

Fakir upon his bed of nails, The. Glad World. Robert D.
Fitzgerald. ACV
Falcon, The. "The Knight of Kürenberg," *tr. fr. German by*
Ruth Yorck *and* Kenward Elmslie. AnML
("I reared me a falcon longer than one year," *tr. by* Alex-
ander Gode.) AGP
Falcon, The. *Unknown. See* Lully, Lullay.
Falcon, The. Elinor Wylie. LOW
Falconry. Anne Wilkinson. OBCV
Fall. Friedrich Hölderlin, *tr. fr. German by* Hedwig Hellmann.
AGP
Fall, The. Walter Kaufmann. OPP
Fall, The. Earl of Rochester. UnTE
Fall gently and still, good corn. Corn Must Be Sown. Thomas
Carlyle. ThGo
Fall in Corrales. Richard Wilbur. CoPo; VaPo
Fall, Leaves, Fall. Emily Brontë. ELP; FaBV
Fall of Hyperion, The, *sel.* Keats.
Dream, A. OBNC
Fall of the Leaf, The. Henry David Thoreau. AP
Fall which twisted love to lust, The. In Praise of Music in
Time of Pestilence. Daryl Hine. OBCV
Fallen Angels (nine times the space that measures day and
night"). Milton. *Fr.* Paradise Lost, I. DiPo
Falling Asleep. Siegfried Sassoon. ILP
Falling Asleep over the Aeneid. Robert Lowell. AP; ToPo
Falling flower, The. Haiku. Moritake. CaFP
Falling of the Leaves, The. W. B. Yeats. PoPo
Falling Snow. *Unknown.* SoPo
Falling Star, The. Sara Teasdale. SoPo
False bards the sacred fire pervert. The Indignation of Talie-
sin. Thomas Love Peacock. CBEP
False Country of the Zoo. Jean Garrigue. MP
False dawns. Hiawatha. Stephen Sandy. CoPo
False Gods. Walter de la Mare. EaLo
False Knight on [*or* upon] the Road, The. *Unknown.* BuBa;
CBEP
(Fause Knicht on the Road, The.) BFSS
False Lambkin, *with music. Unknown.* BSO
False life! a foil and no more, when. Quickness. Henry
Vaughan. BoC; ELP; SeCP
False Love. Sir Walter Ralegh. CBEP
False Lover, The. *Unknown. See* Willie Taylor.
False! or Inconstancy. Congreve *See* False Though She Be.
False Poets and True. Thomas Hood. PP
False Sir John a-wooing came. May Colvin. *Unknown.* BuBa
False Though She Be [to Me]. Congreve. CBEP;WePo
(False! or Inconstancy.) BoLP
False world, good-night: since thou hast brought. To the
World: A Farewell for a Gentlewoman, Virtuous and No-
ble. Ben Jonson. EnRePo; SeCP
Falsetto. Eugenio Montale, *tr. fr. Italian by* Carlo L. Golino.
CoIP
Fame. Robert Browning. PP
Fame. Sir Thomas More. *Fr.* The Pageants of Thomas More.
EnRePo.
Fame. John Banister Tabb. AmLP
Fame and Friendship. Austin Dobson. PoPo
Fame I am called, marvel you nothing. Fame. Sir Thomas
More. *Fr.* The Pageants of Thomas More. EnRePo
Fame is a food that dead men eat. Fame and Friendship.
Austin Dobson. PoPo
Fame, like a wayward girl, will still be coy. On Fame. Keats.
CABA; CBEP
Fames pillar here, at last, we set. The Pillar of Fame. Robert
Herrick. SeCP
Familiar Friends. James S. Tippett. SoPo
Familiar, year by year, to the creaking wain. The Sower.
Laurence Binyon. MMA
Familiarity Breeds Indifference. Martial, *tr. fr. Latin by* Louis
Untermeyer. UnTE
Familie, The. George Herbert. MeP
Families, when a child is born. On the Birth of His Son. Su
Tung-p'o. TRV
Family. *Unknown.* STF
Family Altar, The. Georgia B. Adams. STF
Family Bible, *sels.* Eleanor Ross Taylor.
Granddaughter. PoNC
Uncle. PoNC
Family is a little book, The. Family. *Unknown.* STF
Famous painter, jealous of his wife, A. The Superfluous Sad-
dle. La Fontaine. UnTE
Fancy, The. William Rose Benét. SD
Fancy, and I, last evening walked. To Amoret Gone from Him.
Henry Vaughan. CBEP
Fancy Dress. Dorothea Mackellar. PoAu-1
Fancy, Farewell. Sir Edward Dyer. EnRePo
Fancy Fishing. James L. Weil. FiSC
Fancy (quoth he), farewell, whose badge I long did bear. The
Green Knight's Farewell to Fancy. George Gascoigne.
EnRePo
Fanny, *sel.* Fitz-Greene Halleck.
"Fanny was younger once than she is now." CTC
Fantasia. Dorothy Livesay. OBCV

Fantasy on the Resurrection. Vassar Miller. PoDB; ToPo

Far above us where a jay. Morning on the Lièvre. Archibald Lampman. SD

Far away. Threnody. Thomas Lovell Beddoes. StP

Far Away and Long Ago. Rubén Darío, *tr. fr. Spanish by* Denise Levertov. AnSP

Far away under us, they are mowing on the green steps. The Beholders. James Dickey. AP

Far beyond Us. *Unknown, tr. fr. Japanese by* Ishii *and* Obata. SiGo

Far Bugles. Olive Tilford Dargan. PoNC

Far Cry from Africa, A. Derek Walcott. ToPo

"Far enough down is China," somebody said. Digging for China. Richard Wilbur. GoJo; LOW; MP

Far far from gusty waves, these children's faces. An Elementary School Classroom in a Slum. Stephen Spender. ILP; MP

Far, far from here. Matthew Arnold. *Fr.* Empedocles on Etna. GTBS-P

Far Field, The. Theodore Roethke. ToPo

Far from Africa: Four Poems. Margaret Danner. AmNP
   Dance of the Abakweta, 2. AmNP; NNP
   Etta Moten's Attic, 4. AmNP
   Garnishing the Aviary, 1. AmNP; NNP
   Visit of the Professor of Aesthetics, The, 3. AmNP; NNP

Far from the court's ambitious noise. The Enjoyment. Antoine-Girard de Saint-Amant. RBL

Far from You and Close to Care. Marqués de Santillana, *tr. fr. Spanish by* Frances Fletcher. AnML

Far in the country of Arden. Dowsabel. Michael Drayton. *Fr.* The Shepherd's Garland. UnTE

Far in the grim Northwest beyond the lines. Temagami. Archibald Lampman. OBCV

Far off, above the plain the summer dries. Second Air Force. Randall Jarrell. AP

Far on the desert ridges. Wind-Song. *Tr. by* Natalie Curtis. RePo

Far out in the wilds of Oregon. The Nonpareil's Grave. M. J. McMahon. SD

Far sail shimmers, white and lonely, A. A Sail. Mikhail Lermontov. PoPl

Far spread, below. The Story of Vinland. Sidney Lanier. *Fr.* Psalm of the West. ThLM

Far Trumpets Blowing. Louis F. Benson. TRV

Faradiddle Dyno. *Unknown.* CBEP

Fare not abroad, O Soul, to win. Quo Vadis? Myles Connolly. TRV

Fare Thee Well. Byron. FaPL; OBNC

Fare Well. Walter de la Mare. GTBS-P

Fare Ye Well, Inniskillen, *with music. Unknown.* BSO

Fare ye well and adieu to the old Spanish ladies! Spanish Ladies. *Unknown.* BSNS

Fare you well, green fields. A Prisoner for Life. *Unknown.* BFSS

Farewel, too little and too lately known. *See* Farewell, too little and too lately known.

Farewele! Advent, Christmas is come. Farewell! Advent. James Ryman. MeEL

Farewell, A: "Go fetche to me a pint o' wine." Burns. GTBS-P

Farewell, A: "My fairest child, I have no song to give you." Charles Kingsley. LV

Farewell, A: "My horse's feet beside the lake." Matthew Arnold. Switzerland, III. VP

Farewell: "Now, good night, my friends so dear." Heinrich Albert, *tr. fr. German by* Martin Zwart. AGP

Farewell, A: "With all my will, but much against my heart." Coventry Patmore. The Unknown Eros, I, xvi. GTBS-P; OBNC

Farewell! Advent. James Ryman. MeEL

Farewell, dear babe, my heart's too much content! In Memory of My Dear Grandchild Elizabeth Bradstreet, Who Deceased August, 1665, Being a Year and a Half Old. Anne Bradstreet. AP

Farewell, dear scenes, for ever closed to me. Lines Written on a Window-Shutter at Weston. William Cowper. EiCP

Farewell false love, the oracle of lies. False Love. Sir Walter Ralegh. CBEP

Farewell—farewell to thee, Araby's daughter! The Peri's Lament for Hinda. Thomas Moore. *Fr.* Lalla Rookh. OBNC

Farewell happy fields. Satan's Speech. Milton. *Fr.* Paradise Lost, I. DiPo

Farewell! I goe to sleep; but when. The Evening-Watch. Henry Vaughan. MeP

Farewell, incomparable element. Hymn to Earth. Elinor Wylie. AmLP

Farewell, Love, and all thy laws for ever! A Renouncing of Love. Sir Thomas Wyatt. StP

Farewell, merry maidens, to song, and to laugh. Song of the Shetland Fishers. Sir Walter Scott. HaSV

Farewell, old California, I'm going far away. Australia and the Amazon. John A. Stone. SGR

Farewell, rewards and fairies. The Fairies' Farewell [*or* Farewell to the Fairies *or* A Proper New Ballad]. CBEP; EvOK; SeCP

"Farewell, Romance!" the Cave-men said. The King. Kipling. CABA

Farewell, sweet boy; complain not of my truth. Caelica, LXXXIV. Fulke Greville. EnRePo

Farewell, sweetest country; out of my heart, you roses. London. Manmohan Ghose. ACV

Farewell, This World. MeEL

Farewell! thou art too dear for my possessing. Sonnets, LXXXVII. Shakespeare. FoBA; GTBS-P; StP

Farewell, thou child of my right hand, and joy. On My First Son. Ben Jonson. CABA; CaFP; DiPo; EnRePo; PoIE; SeCP

Farewell, thou fertile soil that Brutus first out found. Going towards Spain. Barnabe Googe. EiCP

Farewell, Thou Minstrel Harp. Sir Walter Scott. *See* Harp of the North.

Farewell thou thing, time-past so knowne. so deare. His Farewell to Sack. Robert Herrick. SeCP

Farewell to Arms, A. George Peele. *See* His Golden Locks.

Farewell to Barn and Stack and Tree. A. E. Housman. A Shropshire Lad, VIII. PoIE; PoPo

Farewell to Folly, *sel.* Robert Greene.
   Maesia's Song. CTC

Farewell to London, A. Pope. CBEP

Farewell to old England for ever. Botany Bay. *Unknown.* PoAu-1

Farewell to the Court. Sir Walter Ralegh. CBEP; EnRePo

Farewell to the Fairies. Richard Corbet. *See* Fairies' Farewell, The.

Farewell to Van Gogh. Charles Tomlinson. GTBS-P

Farewell to Winnipeg. Roy Daniells. OBCV

Farewell [*or* Farewel] too little and too lately known. To the Memory of Mr. Oldham. Dryden. CABA; CaFP; DiPo; OnP; PoIE; PP; StP; VaPo

Farewell, Ungrateful Traitor. Dryden. *Fr.* The Spanish Friar, V, i. CBEP; ELP

Farewell you everlasting hills! I'm cast. Mans Fall, and Recovery. Henry Vaughan. MeP

Far-fetched with tales of other worlds and ways. Home from Abroad. Laurie Lee. ToPo

Farm Boy after Summer. Robert Francis. PoIE; PoSa

Farm Child. R. S. Thomas. DaDu; WePo

Farm near Norman's Lane, The. Mary Finnin. PoAu-2

Farm on the Great Plains, The. William Stafford. PoCh

Farmer. Liberty Hyde Bailey. RePo

Farmer, The. Fredegond Shove. MMA

Farmer Jones's Wife, *with music. Unknown.* BFSS

Farmer Remembers the Somme, The. Vance Palmer. PoAu-1

Farmer Went Trotting, A. *Unknown.* EvOK

Farmer, you were young once. Age. R. S. Thomas. ToPo

Farmer's Boy, The. *sel.* Robert Bloomfield.
   Moonlight . . . Scattered Clouds. OBNC

Farmer's Bride, The. Charlotte Mew. ErPo

Farmer's Concern, The. Bertolt Brecht, *tr. fr. German by* Michael Hamburger. MGP

Farmer's Daughter, The, *with music. Unknown.* BFSS

Farmer's goose, who in the stubble. The. The Progress of Poetry. Swift. CABA; CBEP; EiCP

Farmer's Wife, The. Anne Sexton. NePoEA-2

Farmhand Tom, with his apple and turnip face, The. Tom. Sir Osbert Sitwell. DaDu

Farmyard, The, *with music. Unknown.* BFSS
   (Farmyard Song, A, *arr. by* Maria Hastings.) SoPo

Farragut. William Tuckey Meredith. ThLM

Farther he went the farther home grew, The. For the Grave of Daniel Boone. William Stafford. PoPl

Farther [*or* Further] in summer than the birds. Emily Dickinson. AP; PoSa

Fast. John Tagliabue. SD

Fast Ball. Jonathan Williams. PoNC

Faster, Earth, Faster. Juan Ramón Jiménez, *tr. fr. Spanish by* Eloise Roach. AnSP

Faster, faster/ O Circe, Goddess. The Strayed Reveller. Matthew Arnold. VP

Fat black bucks in a wine-barrel room. The Congo. Vachel Lindsay. FaPL; WePo

Fat green frog sits by the pond. Grandfather Frog. Louise Seaman Bechtel. RePo

Fat man thought, The. The Galoshes. Alfred Lichtenstein. MGP

Fatal Acquaintance, A (A *and* B *vers.*). *Unknown.* BSO

Fatal Sisters, The. Thomas Gray, *after the Icelandic.* EiCP; EnPE

Fatal Snowstorm, The. *Unknown.* BSNS

Fatal Spell, The. Byron. *Fr.* Childe Harold's Pilgrimage. OBNC

Fate Is Unfair. Don Marquis. *Fr.* Archy Does His Part. EvOK

Fate of a Broom, The—an Anticipation. Thomas Love Peacock. CBEP

Father, The. Donald Finkel. CoPo
Father. Robert Pack. CoPo
Father. Mildred Weston. PoSC
Father and Son. F. R. Higgins. ACV; BoC
Father and Son. Stanley Kunitz. MP
Father calls me William, sister calls me Will. Jest 'fore Christmas. Eugene Field. FaBV; PoLF
Father, chancing to chastise. Self-Sacrifice. Harry Graham. BBGG
Father, come home. Gather These Bones. Lewis Turco. FiSC
Father darts out on the stairs, The. Early Morning Feed. Peter Redgrove. BoC
Father! father! where are you going? Little Boy Lost. Blake. *Fr.* Songs of Innocence. CBEP
"Father Francisco! Father Francisco!" The Confessional. *Unknown.* UnTE
Father has a workshop. The Workshop. Aileen Fisher. SoPo
Father heard his children scream. The Stern Parent. Harry Graham. BBGG
Father, How Wide Thy Glories Shine. Charles Wesley. TRV
Father, I scarcely dare to pray. A Last Prayer. Helen Hunt Jackson. TRV
Father in Heaven, after Each Lost Day. Petrarch, *tr. fr. Italian by* Bernard Bergonzi. Sonnets to Laura: To Laura in Life, XLVIII. AnML
Father in heaven, make me wise. A Father Speaks. *Unknown.* STF
Father, in Thy mysterious presence kneeling. Prayer for Strength. Samuel Johnson. TRV
Father, in Thy starry tent. Rest in Peace. Wilfred J. Funk. PoLF
Father Malloy. Edgar Lee Masters. *Fr.* Spoon River Anthology. PoPo
Father of all! in every [*or* ev'ry] age. The Universal Prayer. Pope. PoIE; VaPo
Father of lights! what Sunnie seed. Cock-crowing. Henry Vaughan. MeP
Father, part of his double interest. Holy Sonnets, XVI. John Donne. MeP
Father said, "Call him Anthony." Naming the Baby. May Richstone. BiCB
Father said that maybe. Tummy Ache. Aileen Fisher. SoPo
Father . . . —Say the *confiteor.*—I said it. The Confessor. G. G. Belli. ErPo
Father Speaks, A. *Unknown.* STF
Father, Teach Me. Walter M. Lee. STF
Father, this year's jinx rides us apart. All My Pretty Ones. Anne Sexton. CoPo
Father! thy wonders do not singly stand. The Spirit-Land. Jones Very. AmLP
Father to the Man. John Knight. EaLo
Father, we thank Thee for the night. A Prayer. *Unknown.* SoPo
Father William. "Lewis Carroll." *Fr.* Alice's Adventures in Wonderland. BiCB; FaPL; GoJo; PoLF; RePo
("'You are old, Father William,' the young man said.") Par
Fatherland, The. James Russell Lowell. PoPl
Father's Business, The. Edwin Markham. TRV
Father's Gold, The. *Unknown.* STF
Father's Notes of Woe, A. Sir Walter Scott. *Fr.* The Lay of the Last Minstrel. OBNC
Father's Prayer, A. *Unknown.* STF
Father's Story. Elizabeth Madox Roberts. PoSC
Fatima. Tennyson. UnTE
Fault, The. Edward Lucie-Smith. NePoEA-2
Fause Knicht on the Road, The. *Unknown. See* False Knight on the Road, The.
Faust, *sel.* Goethe, *tr. fr. German by* John Anster.
Lose This Day Loitering. PoLF
(Prologue: "Lose this day loitering, 'twill be the same story.") TRV
Faustine, *abr.* Swinburne. UnTE
Faustus. Christopher Marlowe. *See* Dr. Faustus.
Fe, Fi, Fo, Fum. *Unknown.* EvOK
Fear death?—to feel the fog in my throat. Prospice. Robert Browning. CBEP; DiPo; FaBV; FaPL; ILP; PoIE; PoLF; TRV
Fear No More the Heat o' the Sun. Shakespeare. *Fr.* Cymbeline, IV, ii. CABA; CBEP; DiPo; ELP; EnRePo FoBA; ILP; PoIE; PoSa; RoGo
(Fidele.) BoC; GTBS-P; PoPo
(Fidele's Dirge.) WePo
(Song.) CTC; VaPo
Fear Not. J. Bullock. STF
Fear Not, Dear Love. Thomas Carew. UnTE
(Secresie Protested.) SeCP
Fear not the despots raging. Song under Shadow. William Rose Benét. MoRP
Fear of Death Confounds Me, The. William Dunbar. *See* Lament for the Makaris.
Fear of God, The. Robert Frost. MoRP
Feare not (deare Love) that I'le reveale. Secresie Protested. Thomas Carew. SeCP

Fearful Death. *Unknown.* MeEL
Fearful the chamber's quiet; the veiled windows. A Development of Idiotcy. Ebenezer Jones. OBNC
Fears in Solitude, *sel.* Samuel Taylor Coleridge.
"On the green sheep-track, up the heathy hill." OBNC
Feast, The. David Wagoner. NePoEA-2
Feast of Saint Andrew the Apostle. Carl Bode. *Fr. The Sacred Seasons.* ToPo.
Feather or Fur. John Becker. RePo
Feathered Faith. *Unknown.* STF
Feathers of the willow, The. Song. Richard Watson Dixon. CBEP; GTBS-P; OBNC
Feathers up fast, and steeples; then in clods. The Fountain. Donald Davie. GTBS-P
Featherstone's Doom. Robert Stephen Hawker. OBNC
Features of the Sky. Pierre Reverdy, *tr. fr. French by* Joseph de Roche. CoFP
February. John Clare. *Fr.* The Shepherd's Calendar. OBNC
February Birthday. Nancy Byrd Turner. BiCB
February brings despair. At the Nadir. Gerta Kennedy. PoPl
February Moon. Wilhelm Lehmann, *tr. fr. German by* Michael Hamburger. MGP
February, 1924. Rainer Maria Rilke, *tr. fr. German by* Walter Kaufmann. TwGP
February Twilight. Sara Teasdale. SoPo
Feed. Raymond Knister. OBCV
Feeling Her End Would Come with Summer's End. Rosalía de Castro, *tr. fr. Spanish by* Kate Flores. AnSP
Feeling it with me. Walking on Water. James Dickey. NePoEA-2
Feet in the Fire, The. Conrad Ferdinand Meyer, *tr. fr. German by* Walter Kaufmann. TwGP
Feet of the rats, The. Four Preludes on Playthings of the Wind, IV. Carl Sandburg. AmLP
Felicia Ropps. Gelett Burgess. BBGG
Felix Randal. Gerard Manley Hopkins. AnMoPo; CaFP; DiPo; FoBA; GTBS-P; OBNC; RoGo; StP; VP
Feller isn't thinkin' mean, A. Out Fishin'. Edgar A. Guest. PoLF
Fellow came to dine with me, A. Reviewer. Goethe. TwGP
Fellow-Citizens. Verner von Heidenstam, *tr. fr. Swedish by* Charles Wharton Stork. PoPl
Fellow That Looks like Me, The. *Unknown.* BSNS
Fellows up in Personnel, The. The Perforated Spirit. Morris Bishop. PoPo
Female Warrior, The. *Unknown.* BSO
Femina contra Mundum. G. K. Chesterton. MoRP
Femme Fatale. Vincent Starrett. FiSC
Fence-walker, balancer, your devil-may-care. Divination by a Cat. Anthony Hecht. StP
Fenian Song, The. *Unknown.* BSNS
Feri's Dream. Frances Cornford. BoC
Dogs, *st.* 1. ThGo
Fern Hill. Dylan Thomas. CABA; DiPo; EvOK; FaBV; GoJo; GTBS-P; MP; PoLF; PoPl; RoGo; ToPo; WePo
(Under the Apple Boughs.) BoC
Ferry Me across the Water. Christina Rossetti. *Fr.* Sing-Song. GoJo
(Ferryman, The.) SoPo
Ferry Ride. Selma Robinson. LV
Ferry-Boats. James S. Tippett. SoPo
Ferryman, The. Christina Rossetti. *See* Ferry Me across the Water.
Fertile Muck, The. Irving Layton. OBCV
Feste Burg ist unser Gott, Ein. Martin Luther. *See* Mighty Fortress Is Our Lord, A.
Feste's Final Song. Shakespeare. *See* When That I Was.
Feste's Song. Shakespeare. *See* Come Away, Come Away, Death.
Festubert: The Old German Line. Edmund Blunden. MMA
Fetching the Wounded. Laurence Binyon. MMA
Fever, A. John Donne. DiPo
Few leaves stay for a while on the trees, A. The Last Leaf. Harry Behn. RePo
Few miles from, A. Chugachimute I Love the Name. Rochelle Owens. CoPo
Few Signs, A. Grantland Rice. LV
Fiddler, A. Walter de la Mare. LOW
Fiddler of Dooney, The. W. B. Yeats. DiPo; PoPo
Fidele. Shakespeare. *Fr.* Cymbeline. *See* Fear No More the Heat o' the Sun.
Fidele and Fortunio, *sel.* Anthony Munday.
Fidele's Song. CBEP
Fidele's Dirge. Shakespeare. *See* Fear No More the Heat o' the Sun.
Fidele's Song. Anthony Munday. *Fr.* Fidele and Fortunio. CBEP
Fidelia, *sel.* George Wither.
Shall I, Wasting in Despair, *also given in* Fair Virtue. BoLP; PoIE
(Manly Heart, The.) FaBV; GTBS-P
Fidelio. Michael McClure. PtTo

Fidessa, More Chaste than Kind, *sel.* Bartholomew Griffin. Fair Is My Love, XXXVII. CBEP
(Sonnet: "Fair is my Love that feeds among the lilies.") ErPo
Fie, foolish Earth, think you the heaven wants glory. Caelica, XVI. Fulke Greville. EnRePo
Fie upon hearts that burn with mutual fire. Against Fruition. Sir John Suckling. ErPo
Field-Glasses. Andrew Young. CBEP; GTBS-P
Field of Autumn. Laurie Lee. ToPo
Field of Light, A. Theodore Roethke. MP; ToPo
Field of Long Grass. A. J. M. Smith. BoLP
Field of Plunder. Charles Humboldt. PtTo
Field of wheat is of such beauty, The. Beauty. Corrado Govoni. CoIP
Fields are chill, the sparse rain has stopped, The. Clearing at Dawn. Li T'ai-po. SiGo
Fields are spread like tablecloths, The. The Moon. Elizabeth J. Coatsworth. RePo
Fields from Islington to Marybone, The. Prelude to Chapter II. Blake. *Fr.* Jerusalem. OBNC
Fierce and brooding holocaust of faith, The. Two Poems on the Catholic Bavarians. Edgar Bowers. PoCh
Fierce luster of sun on sea, the gulls. The Purse—Seine. Paul Blackburn. CoPo
Fierce musical cries of a couple of sparrowhawks hunting on the headland, The. The Birds. Robinson Jeffers. AP
Fife Tune. John Manifold. GoJo
Fifine at the Fair, *sel.* Robert Browning.
"And so I somehow-nohow played." Par
Fifteen churches lie here. At Dunwich. Anthony Thwaite. MoBS
Fifteen men on the dead man's chest. Derelict. Young E. Allison. OnMSP
Fifth Birthday Gift. Marjorie Lederer. BiCB
Fifth of November. K. W. Gransden. DaDu
Fifth Sense, The. Patricia Beer. MoBS
Fifty Acres. James Larkin Pearson. PoNC
Fifty years and three. Our Happy Home. *Unknown.* ThGo
Fig-tree, a falling woolshed, a filled-in well, A. Mullabinda. David Rowbotham. PoAu-2
Fight. Jean Jaszi. RePo
Fighting South of the Ramparts. *Unknown, tr. fr. Chinese by* Arthur Waley. SiGo
Figmental mannequin, Turk's-head for the trap. To the Eternal Feminine. Tristan Corbière. ErPo
Figs from Thistles. Edna St. Vincent Millay. *See* First Fig.
Figures of Authority. Edward Watkins. StP
Figures on the Frieze, The. Alastair Reid. ErPo
File into yellow candle light, fair choristers of King's. Sunday Morning, King's Cambridge. John Betjeman. BoC; EaLo
Fill, kind misses, fill the bowl. Heat. Anacreon. UnTE
Fill the Bowl, Butler! *Unknown.* MeEL
Fill the bowl with rosie wine. The Epicure. Abraham Cowley. SeCP
Filled with yellow pears. Half of Life. Friedrich Hölderlin. AGP
Final Hunger, The. Vassar Miller. ToPo
Final Procession. Audrey McGaffin. OPP
Final Soliloquy of the Interior Paramour. Wallace Stevens. PoIE
Final Word, The. Dom Moraes. NePoEA-2
Finale. Paul Bartlett. PoNC
Finale: Presto. Peter Davison. CoPo
Finally a Valentine. Louis Zukofsky. OPP
Finally, from your house there is no view. Water Island. Howard Moss. MP; NePoEA-2
Finally stays no more away. Consolation-Aria. Johann Christian Günther. AGP
Finches, The. Thomas W. Shapcott. PoAu-2
Find Out Moonshine. Helen Bevington. PoNC
Finding is the first act. Emily Dickinson. AP; CABA
Fine Clay. Winifred Shaw. PoAu-1
Fine delight that fathers thought, The; the strong. To R. B. Gerard Manley Hopkins. CBEP; GTBS-P
Fine Flowers in the Valley. *Unknown.* CBEP
Fine Knacks for Ladies. *Unknown.* CBEP; EnRePo
(Pedlar, A.) WiR
Fine old wine and a fair young wife, A. Age and Youth. *Unknown.* UnTE
Fingers in the Door. David Holbrook. NePoEA-2
Finis. Waring Cuney. AmNP
Finnigan's Wake, *with music. Unknown.* BSO
Fir Tree, A. Heine, *tr. fr. German by* Walter Kaufmann. TwGP
("Fir tree standing lonely, A," *tr. by* Margaret R. Richter.) AGP
Fire, The. Charles G. Bell. MoLP
Fire. M. V. Woodgate. BoC
Fire and Ice. Robert Frost. CABA; CaFP; DiPo; FoBA; ILP; PoDB; PoPl; PoPo; WePo
Fire at Alexandria, The. Theodore Weiss. CoPo
Fire at Murdering Hut. Judith Wright. ACV

Fire gave the match a body. The Match. Francis Ponge. CoFP
Fire had come to these woods one day. Hidden Scars. Sam Ragan. PoNC
Fire in the Heavens, and Fire along the Hills. Christopher Brennan. *Fr.* The Quest of Silence. PoAu-1
Fire-mist and a planet, A. Each in His Own Tongue. William Herbert Carruth. TRV
Fire of Drift-Wood, The. Longfellow. AP
Fire of Love, The. Charles Sackville. UnTE
Fire on the Hearth. Rowena Bennett. RePo
Fire Place, The. E. W. Mandel. OBCV
Fire Seven Times Tried This, The. Shakespeare. *Fr.* The Merchant of Venice, II, ix. CTC
Fire that dances. Features of the Sky. Pierre Reverdy. CoFP
Fire was slow kindling, The—it was damp wood. The Fire. Charles G. Bell. MoLP
Fire, water, woman are man's ruin. A Dutch Proverb. Matthew Prior. LV
Fireballs and thunder augment the wailing wind. The Ides of March. Roy Fuller. PoCh
Firedrake sejant on a field of sard, A. Prenatal Fantasy. Walter H. Kerr. FiSC
Fireflies. Aileen Fisher. SoPo
Fireflies, The, *sel.* Charles Mair.
"How dreamy-dark it is!" OBCV
Fireflies/ Play hide-and-seek in the tall grass. Phosphorescence. Melville Cane. RePo
Firefly, The. Issa, *tr. fr. Japanese by* Harold G. Henderson. RePo
Firefly, The. Ogden Nash. PoPo
Firefly. Elizabeth Madox Roberts. GoJo
Firefly Lights His Lamp, The. *Unknown, tr. fr. Japanese.* SoPo
Firefly's flame, The. The Firefly. Ogden Nash. PoPo
Fireworks. James Reeves. PoSC
Fireworks of inclement weather, The. News from Amiata. Eugenio Montale. CoIP
Firm in the good brown earth. Planting a Tree. Nancy Byrd Turner. RePo
First/ it's not heat prostration. Woman par Excellence. Rochelle Owens. CoPo
First Anniversary, The: An Anatomie of the World. John Donne. MeP
First, April, she with mellow showers. The Four Sweet Months. Robert Herrick. WiR
First Autumn, The. Marshall Schacht. MoRP
First-born. Marion Buchman. PtTo
First came the primrose. A Chanted Calendar. Sydney Dobell. *Fr.* Balder. BoC
First came the special issues of the magazines. We Who Do Not Grieve in Silence. Oscar Mandel. OPP
First Christmas, The. St. Luke, Bible, *N.T. See* Christmas Eve.
First Christmas Night of All. Nancy Byrd Turner. BiCB
First cold showers pour, The. The Monkey's Raincoat. Basho. SoPo
First Confession, X. J. Kennedy. NePoEA-2
First Confession, A. W. B. Yeats. FoBA
First Corinthians, *sel.* Bible, *N.T.*
Love, XIII. TRV
First Cycle of Love Poems, *sel.* George Barker.
"My joy, my jockey, my Gabriel," V. DaDu; ErPo
First Daddy/ Then Mama. Life Cycle in the Delta. George Huston Bass. PtTo
1st Dance—Making Things New—6 February 1964. Jackson MacLow. CoPo
First day it rained we were glad, The. Flood. Irving Feldman. MP
First day of Christmas, The. The Twelve Days of Christmas. *Unknown.* LV
First day of Yole have we in mind, The. Sing We Yule. *Unknown.* MeEL
First Fig. Edna St. Vincent Millay. PoLF
(Figs from Thistles.) FaBV
First Flame. Samuel Daniel. *See* Early Love.
First follow Nature, and your judgment frame. Pope. *Fr.* An Essay on Criticism. PP
First I looked on, after a long time far from home. American Change. Allen Ginsberg. CABL
First in the North. The black sea-tangle beaches. The Mythical Journey. Edwin Muir. ILP
First it was a pretty flower, dressed in pink and white. Riddle. Christina Rossetti. SoPo
First It Was Singing. Jon Silkin. PoDB
First, last and always dearest, closest, best. An Epistle. A. D. Hope. PoAu-2
First Lesson. Philip Booth. MP; SD
First Love. Laurie Lee. ToPo
First Man on Venus. Robert Watson. PoNC
First Meditation. Theodore Roethke. *Fr.* Meditations of an Old Woman. AP

("On love's worst ugly day.") PoDB
First month of his absence, The. Song. Alun Lewis. DTC
First of April, some do say, The. All Fool's Day. *Unknown.* SoPo
First of May, The. Barbara Guest. AmPC
First of the first. The Old Pope Is Comforted by the Thought of the Young Pompilia. Robert Browning. *Fr.* The Ring and the Book. BoC
First Property, The ("The first point is to love but one alone.") Sir Thomas More. *Fr.* The Twelve Properties or Conditions of a Lover. EnRePo
First Reader. Paris Leary. CoPo
First September day was blue and warm, The. The Artist on Penmaenmawr. Charles Tennyson-Turner. OBNC
First shot out of that sling, The. After Goliath. Kingsley Amis. NePoEA-2; PoCh
First Snow. Marie Louise Allen. SoPo
First Snow in Alsace. Richard Wilbur. AP
First Snowfall. Giosuè Carducci. *See* Snowfall.
First Snow-fall, The, *sel.* James Russell Lowell.
"Snow had begun in the gloaming, The." PoSC
First Song. Galway Kinnell. GoJo; MP
First Spring Day, The. Christina Rossetti. WiR
First Thanksgiving Day, The. Margaret Junkin Preston. SIV; ThLM
First Thanksgiving of All. Nancy Byrd Turner. RePo
First that came in was scarlet red, The. Lord Vanover. *Unknown.* BSO
First Time, The. Karl Shapiro. ErPo
First time he kissed me, he but only kissed. Sonnets from the Portuguese, XXXVIII. Elizabeth Barrett Browning. CTC; ILP
First time I saw little Weevil he was on the western plain. The Ballad of the Boll Weevil. *Unknown.* ThLM
First to Throw a Stone. *Unknown.* STF
First Winter's Day. Dorothy Aldis. SoPo
Firstborn Land, The. Ingeborg Bachmann, *tr. fr. German by* Christopher Middleton. MGP
Firstë stock, father of gentilesse. Gentilesse. Chaucer. CBEP
Fish, The. Elizabeth Bishop. GoJo; LV; PoPl; PoPo
Fish, The. Rupert Brooke. BoC
Fish, The. Ralph Gustafson. OBCV
Fish. William Jay Smith. RePo
Fish and the Man, The. Leigh Hunt. *See* Fish, the Man, and the Spirit, The.
Fish Answers, A. Leigh Hunt. *See* Fish, the Man, and the Spirit, The.
Fish (fly-replete, in depth of June). Heaven. Rupert Brooke. ILP
Fish has laid her succulent eggs. Vicissitudes of the Creator. Archibald MacLeish. VaPo
Fish Sonata, The. Winfield Townley Scott. MP
Fish, the Man, and the Spirit, The, *sel.* Leigh Hunt.
"You strange, astonished-looking, angle-faced." HaSV
  (Fish and the Man, The.) RoGo
  (Fish Answers, A.) BoC
  (To a Fish.) BoC
Fisher, The. Roderic Quinn. PoAu-1
Fisher, The. William Renton. WePo
Fisherman, The. Douglas Stewart. ACV
Fisherman, The. W. B. Yeats. SD
Fisherman's Boy, The. *Unknown.* BSO
Fisherman's Girl, The. *Unknown.* BSO
Fishers, The. Ruth Pitter. BoC
Fishes and the Poet's Hands, The. Frank Yerby. AmNP
Fishing. Dorothy Wellesley. BoC
Fishing. Wordsworth. *Fr.* The Prelude. SD
Fishing Season. Val Vallis. PoAu-2
Fit of Rhyme [*or* Rime] against Rhyme, A. Ben Jonson. PP; SeCP
Fit of Something against Something, A. Alan Ansen. PP
Fits and Starts, *sel.* Jacques Dupin, *tr. fr. French by* James Stephens *and* Wai-lim Yip.
"Back of your neck, more base than stone, The." CoFP
Five Bells. Kenneth Slessor. PoAu-2
Five Days Old. Francis Webb. PoAu-2
Five Epigrams. J. V. Cunningham. UnTE
Five Hours, (and who can do it less in?). The Lady's Dressing Room. Swift. ErPo
Five-in-June. Lysbeth Boyd Borie. BiCB
Five Joys of Mary, The. *Unknown.* MeEL
Five little monkeys. The Monkeys and the Crocodile. Laura E. Richards. SoPo
Five minutes, five minutes more, please. Bedtime. Eleanor Farjeon. SoPo
Five Poems for J. F. K. Robert Sward. OPP
Five Students, The. Thomas Hardy. GTBS-P
Five summer days, five summer nights. The Blue-Fly. Robert Graves. ILP
Five Visions of Captain Cook, *sel.* Kenneth Slessor.
"Flowers turned to stone! Not all the botany." PoAu-2
Five Voyages of Arnor, The. George Mackay Brown. NePoEA-2

Five years have past; five summers, with the length. Lines Composed [*or* Written] a Few Miles above Tintern Abbey. Wordsworth. CABA; CABL; CaFP; DiPo; FaPL; FoBA; ILP; OBNC; PoIE; StP
Five Years Old. Marie Louise Allen. BiCB
Five Years Old. Lysbeth Boyd Borie. BiCB
Flag, The. Shelley Silverstein. PoSC
Flag Goes By, The. Henry Holcomb Bennett. LV; RePo
Flagmakers, The. J. M. Murphy. PtTo
Flags. Gwendolyn Brooks. AmNP
Flame azalea, mayapple, maple, thornapple, A. The Flower-Hunter in the Fields. Jonathan Williams. PoNC
Flame-flower, Day-torch, Mauna Loa. Lines to a Nasturtium (a Lover Muses). Anne Spencer. AmNP
Flame-Heart. Claude McKay. AmNP
Flame of God. Amy Carmichael. *See* Deliver Me.
Flaming Heart, The. Richard Crashaw. MeP
Flannan Isle. W. W. Gibson. HaSV; SIV; WePo
Flapper. D. H. Lawrence. BoLP
Flash Jack from Gundagai. *Unknown.* PoAu-1
Flat One, A. W. D. Snodgrass. AmPC; AP; NePoEA-2; PoCh
Flavius, If Your Girl Friend. Catullus, *tr. fr. Latin by* Horace Gregory. ErPo
Flaws cling to flesh as dews cling to a rose. Fantasy on the Resurrection. Vassar Miller. PoDB; ToPo
Fle fro the pres and dwelle with sothefastnesse. *See* Flee from the prees . . .
Flea, The. John Donne. CABA; CBEP; FoBA; SeCP
Flea, The. Roland Young. PoPl
Fled are those times, when, in harmonious strains. George Crabbe. *Fr.* The Village. PoSa
Flee from [*or* Fle fro] the prees [*or* pres *or* press] and dwell[e] with sothefastness [*or* soothfastness]. Balade de Bon Conseyl [*or* Truth *or* Truth Shall Set You Free]. Chaucer. CBEP; MeEL; PoIE
Flesh. Mary Fullerton. PoAu-1
Flesh, and cars, tar, dug holes beneath stone. Contract. LeRoi Jones. PtTo
Flesh and the Spirit, The. Anne Bradstreet. AP
Flight, The. Sara Teasdale. BoLP
Flight. Harold Vinal. FiSC
Flight. Laurence Whistler. DaDu
Flight into Egypt, The. Robert Southwell. MeP
Flight of Love, The. Shelley. *See* Lines: "When the lamp is shattered."
Flight of pigeons over the ploughed fields. Pigeons. Günter Eich. MGP
Flight of the Roller-Coaster. Raymond Souster. ACV
Flo was fond of Ebenezer. The Tides of Love. T. A. Daly. PoPl
Floated in the cove. The Boat. Robert Kelly. CoPo
Floating, face up, on the open. Queer's Song. Richard Howard. *Fr.* Gaiety. ErPo
Floating Old Man, The. Edward Lear. WiR
Flock of sheep that leisurely pass by, A. To Sleep. Wordsworth. GTBS-P
Flo-Ella. *Unknown.* BSO
Flogged Child. Joseph Joel Keith. FiSC
Flood. Irving Feldman. MP
Flood-tide below me! I see you face to face! Crossing Brooklyn Ferry. Walt Whitman. AP; CABA; CABL; DiPo; PoIE
Flood was down in the Wilga swamps, three feet over the mud, The. How the Fire Queen Crossed the Swamp. Will H. Ogilvie. PoAu-1
Flora MacDonald and the King, *with music. Unknown.* BFSS
Flora's Flower. *Unknown, tr. fr. Latin by* John Addington Symonds. UnTE
Floret Silva Undique. *Unknown, tr. fr. German by* Elizabeth Closs. AnML
Florida. Elizabeth Bishop. MP
Flow Forth, Abundant Tears. *Unknown.* EnRePo
Flow gently, sweet Afton! among thy green braes. Afton Water [*or* Sweet Afton]. Burns. CABA; ILP; PoIE
Flow Not So Fast. *Unknown.* EnRePo
Flow on forever, in thy glorious robe. Niagara. Lydia Huntley Sigourney. AmLP
Flower, The. George Herbert. BoC; ELP; MeP; SeCP
Flower, The. Robert Penn Warren. PoPl
Flower-Cart Man, The. Rachel Field. SoPo
Flower-fed Buffaloes, The. Vachel Lindsay. GoJo; PoIE; PoSa; RePo
Flower Given to My Daughter, A. James Joyce. PoPl
Flower-Hunter in the Fields, The. Jonathan Williams. PoNC
Flower in the Crannied Wall. Tennyson. DiPo; FaBV; PoIE; PoPl; PoPo; TRV
Flower of This Purple Dye. Shakespeare. *Fr.* A Midsummer Night's Dream, III, ii. CTC
Flower that smiles to-day, The. Mutability. Shelley. OBNC; PoPo
Flower was offer'd to me, A. My Pretty Rose-Tree. Blake. *Fr.* Songs of Experience. FoBA

Flower, which of Adon's blood. The Rose. Tasso. RBL
Flowering almond tree. Almond Blossom in Wartime. Stephen Spender. ACV
Flowering Currant. Patrick MacDonogh. ErPo
Flowers by the Sea. William Carlos Williams. AmLP; GoJo
Flowers every night. At Peace. Rumi. SiGo
Flowers I pass have eyes that look at me, The. Man in Harmony with Nature. Jones Very. AP
Flowers in a Garden. Christopher Smart. ThGo
Flowers in a Meadow, The. Frances Cornford. ThGo
Flowers in the Valley. Unknown. OnMSP
Flowers left thick at nightfall in the wood. In Memoriam: Easter 1915. Edward Thomas. GTBS-P; PoIE
Flowers lift their open mouths in the dark, The. The Storm. Ben Suhayd. AnML
Flower's Name, The. Robert Browning. Garden Fancies, I. ACV; CTC
Flowers of Darkness. Frank Marshall Davis. AmNP
Flowers of the willow-herb are wool. Seed-Time. George Meredith. VP
Flowers shall hang upon the palls. Death. John Clare. GTBS-P
Flowers there are, partaking. Tapers. Frances Angevine Gray. FiSC
Flowers turned to stone! Not all the botany. Kenneth Slessor. Fr. Five Visions of Captain Cook. PoAu-2
Flowers upon the rosemary spray, The. The Rosemary Spray. Luis de Góngora. RBL
Flush or Faunus. Elizabeth Barrett Browning. BoC
Flush with the pond the lurid furnace burned. The Steam Threshing-Machine. Charles Tennyson-Turner. OBNC
Flushing Meadows, 1939. Daniel Hoffman. CoPo
Flute-Players, The. Jean-Joseph Rabéarivelo, tr. fr. French by Dorothy Blair. SiGo
Flute Song. Unknown, tr. fr. Greek by T. F. Higham. SiGo
Fluttering swarm, A. Blossoms and Storm. Sadaiye. SiGo
Fly, The. Blake. Fr. Songs of Experience. CBEP; DiPo; PoSa
Fly, The. Walter de la Mare. LV
Fly, The. Francisco de Quevedo y Villegas, tr. fr. Spanish by Philip Ayres. RBL
Fly, The. William Oldys. See On a Fly Drinking Out of His Cup.
Fly Caught in a Cobweb, A. Richard Lovelace. SeCP
Fly, envious Time, till thou run out thy race. On Time. Milton. BoC; CABA; DiPo; MeP; PoPo; StP; TRV
Fly-fishing. John Gay. Fr. Rural Sports. SD
Fly, white butterflies, out to sea. Envoi. Swinburne. GoJo
"Fly with me then to all's and the world's end." The World's End. William Empson. ToPo
Flying above California. Thom Gunn. ToPo
Flying arrow hardly was aware, The. Deceiver Time. Luis de Góngora. AnSP
Flying Bum, The: 1944. William Plomer. DTC
Flying Cloud, The. Unknown. BSNS
Flying Crooked. Robert Graves. MP
Flying Fish, The, II. John Gray. OBNC
Flying Tailor, The. James Hogg. Par
Flying word from here and there, A. The Master. E. A. Robinson. LiPo
Fo' a yeah or mo' on this roof I'se layed. The Signal Fire. Aeschylus. Fr. Agamemnon. CTC
Focus of eyes, focus of arrows. Sebastian. Gene Baro. PoDB
Foes to our race! if ever ye have known. Critics. George Crabbe. BoC
Fog. Carl Sandburg. AP; FaBV; PoPl; PoPo; SoPo
Fog had made a twilight on the water, The. From This the Strength. Fred Lape. SIV
Fog Land. Ingeborg Bachmann, tr. fr. German by Michael Hamburger. MGP
Foggy Dew, The. Unknown. ELP; UnTE (2 vers.) (Foggy, Foggy Dew.) DTC
Foil, The. George Herbert. FoBA
Folks ain't got no right to censuah othah folks about dey habits. Accountability. Paul Laurence Dunbar. PoLF
Folks at home half the time are thinkin' about dirt, The. Soap, the Oppressor. Burges Johnson. PoLF
Folks Need a Lot of Loving. Strickland Gillilan. TRV
Follow a shadow [or shaddow], it still flies you. Song: That Women Are but Men's Shadows. Ben Jonson. CBEP; PoIE; SeCP
Follow back from the gull's bright arc and the osprey's plunge. Water Ouzel. William H. Matchett. PoCh
Follow Jesus. Unknown. STF
Follow, poet, follow right. W. H. Auden. Fr. In Memory of W. B. Yeats. TRV
Follow the Leader. Harry Behn. SoPo
Follow Thy Fair Sun. Thomas Campion. CBEP; ELP; EnRePo
Follow Your Saint. Thomas Campion. CBEP; EnRePo; VaPo
Following the Sun. Jascha Kessler. AmPC
Folly you may lead to fall. To Nietzsche. Christian Morgenstern. TwGP

Fond credos, wooden ecstasies! The Stranger. Adrienne Rich. CoPo
Fond man, that canst beleeve her blood. Celia Bleeding, to the Surgeon. Thomas Carew. SeCP
Fool—/ Killer lurks between the branches of every tree. The Book of Percival. Jack Spicer. CoPo
Fool of Love, The. Unknown, tr. fr. Russian by Louis Untermeyer. UnTE
Foolish man who boasts that he is able, The. Boastful Husbandman. Unknown. UnTE
Foolish Miller, The. Unknown. UnTE
Foolish Proverb. Unknown, tr. fr. Greek by Louis Untermeyer. UnTE
Foolish rhythm turns in my idle head, A. A Tune. Arthur Symons. BoLP; OBNC
Fools of '49, The. John A. Stone. SGR
Fool's Prayer, The. Edward Rowland Sill. OnMSP; PoLF
Fool's Preferment, A, sel. Thomas D'Urfey. I'll Sail upon the Dog-Star. CBEP
Football. Walt Mason. SD
Football Song. Sir Walter Scott. SD
Footnote to Lord Acton. Cynthia Ozick. OPP
Footprints now on bread or cake. To a Child with Eyes. Mark Van Doren. LOW
Footsteps of a hundred years, The. The Founders of Ohio. William Henry Venable. ThLM
Footwear. May Justus. SoPo
For a Birthday. Elaine V. Emans. BiCB
For a Christening. Vernon Watkins. MoRP
For a Convict's Wife, sel. Dalton Trumbo. "Each man owes his country." PtTo
For a Dead Lady. E. A. Robinson. AmLP; AP; VaPo
For a God that would smile like a child. Without More Weight. Giuseppe Ungaretti. PoPl
For a good decade. The Drunk in the Furnace. W. S. Merwin. MP; NePoEA-2
For a Lady I Know. Countee Cullen. Four Epitaphs, 4. AmNP
(Lady I Know, A.) TRV
For a maiden sweetness, and for strength of men. John Oxenham. Fr. A Little Te Deum of the Commonplace. TRV
For a man that is almost blind. Mock Medicine. Unknown. MeEL
For a Poetry Reading to Which No One Came. Larry Rubin. FiSC
For a Senior College Textbook. Hans Magnus Enzensberger, tr. fr. German by Eva Hesse. MGP
For a shape, and a bloom, and an air, and a mien. Song. Edward Moore. WaPE
For A' That and A' That, parody. Shirley Brooks. Par
For A' That an' [or and] A' That. Burns. CABA; ILP; LV; UnTE
(Is There for Honest Poverty.) EiCP
(Man's a Man for A' That, A.) EnPE; PoPo
For a Very Old Man, on the Death of His Wife. Jane Cooper. NePoEA-2
For a War Memorial. G. K. Chesterton. MMA
For a Wedding Performed on Thanksgiving in the Week of President Kennedy's Death. George T. Wright. OPP
For All in Pain. Amy Carmichael. TRV
For All Sorts and Conditions. Norman Nicholson. EaLo
For all Thy ministries. John Oxenham. Fr. A Little Te Deum of the Commonplace. TRV
For all true words that have been spoken. Thanksgiving. Margaret E. Sangster. TRV
For an Age of Plastics. Plymouth. Donald Davie. NePoEA-2
For an Epitaph at Fiesole. Walter Savage Landor. OBNC
For Ann Scott-Moncrieff. Edwin Muir. GTBS-P
For Anne. Leonard Cohen. BoLP; PoCh
For Anne Gregory. W. B. Yeats. DiPo; DTC; PoSa
For Annie. Poe. AP
For April I Give You the Countryside. Folgore da San Geminiano, tr. fr. Italian by Joy Gould. Fr. Sonnets of the Months. AnML
For Arvia. E. A. Robinson. BiCB
For August, be your dwelling thirty towers. August. Folgore da San Geminiano. Fr. Sonnets of the Months. CTC
For Autumn. Eleanor Farjeon. ThGo
For City Spring. Stephen Vincent Benét. PoPl
For Danny whistling slowly. Feed. Raymond Knister. OBCV
For dedy liif, my livy deth I wite. Come, Death—My Lady Is Dead. Charles of Orleans(?). MeEL
For E. McC. Ezra Pound. SD
For each one body that i' th' earth is sown. The Resurrection Possible and Probable. Robert Herrick. ILP
For Echo is the soul of the voice exerting itself in hollow places. The Instruments. Christopher Smart. WiR
For England when, with favouring gale. The Leadsman's Song. Unknown. HaSV
For Eros II. Audrey Wurdemann. MoLP
For Ever, Fortune, Wilt Thou Prove. James Thomson. CBEP; GTBS-P

For every bird there is this last migration. The Death of the Bird. A. D. Hope. PoAu-2

For Every Evil. *Unknown.* EvOK

For every hour that thou wilt spare me now. Love's Usury. John Donne. FoBA

For Every Man. Max I. Reich. STF

For every sip the Hen says grace. Grace. Walter de la Mare. ThGo

For eyes he waves greentipped. Slug in Woods. Earle Birney. OBCV

For February Twelfth. Muriel M. Gessner. RePo

For flowers that bloom about our feet. Thanksgiving. Emerson. SoPo

For Fran. Philip Levine. PoCh

For from my cradle you must know that I. Michael Drayton. *Fr.* To My Most Dearly Loved Friend, Henry Reynolds, Esq. PP

For God While Sleeping. Anne Sexton. CABA; NePoEA-2; PoDB

For God's sake [*or* Godsake] hold your tongue and let me love. The Canonization. John Donne. CABA; CaFP; CBEP; DiPo; EnRePo; FoBA; PoIE; SeCP; StP; UnTE; VaPo

For grazing innocence a salad. Poets in Africa. Roy Campbell. ACV

For He laid the foundations of the earth. Praise the Lord, O My Soul! *Fr.* Psalm CIV, Bible, *O.T.* ThGo

For Her Love I Cark and Care. *Unknown.* CBEP

For Her Sake. Alastair Reid. PoPl

"For here you drownded six king's daughters." My Pretty Colinn. *Unknown.* BSO

For him, it seems, everything was molten. Court-ladies flow in gentle streams. The Laughing Hyena, by Hokusai. D. J. Enright. MP

For his mind, I doe not care. Another Ladyes Exception Present at the Hearing. Ben Jonson. *Fr.* A Celebration of Charis. SeCP

For his mother's sake he took the brown girl home. Lord Thomas and Fair Annet (C *vers.*). *Unknown.* BSO

For Hurdy-Gurdy. Sergio Corazzini, *tr. fr. Italian by* Ronald Farrar. CoIP

For I am not without authority in my jeopardy. Christopher Smart. *Fr.* Jubilate Agno. EiCP

For I Dipped into the Future. Tennyson. *Fr.* Locksley Hall. PoLF
("For I dipt into the future, far as human eye could see.") TRV

For I Will Consider My Cat Jeoffry. Christopher Smart. *Fr.* Jubilate Agno. CTC; EiCP
(My Cat Jeoffry.) PoSa; WiR

For in and out, above, about, below. Omar Khayyám, *tr. by* Edward Fitzgerald. *Fr.* The Rubáiyát. TRV

For Instruction. Vassar Miller. ToPo

For Jan. John Wieners. CoPo

For Jane Kane, Whom We Knew in Our Young Marriages. Bink Noll. ToPo

For Jim, Easter Eve. Anne Spencer. AmNP

For John F. Kennedy His Inauguration. Robert Frost. OPP

For John Keats, Apostle of Beauty. Countee Cullen. Four Epitaphs, 2. AmNP

For John Kennedy, Jr. Raymond Roseliep. OPP

For John Kennedy of Harvard. Edward Pols. OPP

For Johnny. John Pudney. WePo

For life, with all it yields of joy and woe. Robert Browning. *Fr.* A Death in the Desert. TRV

For lo to the sea that fleets about the land. Sir John Davies. *Fr.* Orchestra. HaSV

For, lo, the winter is past. The Winter Is Past. The Song of Solomon, Bible, *O.T.* SoPo

For love of lovely words, and for the sake. Skerryvore. Robert Louis Stevenson. ILP

For Lover Man, and All the Other Young Men Who Failed to Return from World War II. Mance Williams. NNP

For love's sake, kiss[e] me once again[e]. Begging Another, on Colour of Mending the Former [*or* Begging Another Kiss]. Ben Jonson. *Fr.* A Celebration of Charis. SeCP; StP; UnTE

For many unsuccessful years. Against Modesty in Love. Matthew Prior. ErPo

For Maria at Four. John Becker. BiCB

For Mary. Kenneth Rexroth. PoPl

For me, for me, two horses wait. The Wizard's Funeral. R. W. Dixon. ELP

For me who go. Parting. Buson. SiGo

For Miriam. Kenneth Patchen. ToPo

For Mr. X I've Only Mischief. Joan de Guilhade, *tr. fr. Portuguese by* William M. Davis. AnML

For morning sun and evening dew. Thanksgiving. Arthur Ketchum. STF

For Music. Byron. *See* There Be None of Beauty's Daughters.

For My Contemporaries. J. V. Cunningham. PoSa; PP

For My Daughter. W. B. Yeats. *Fr.* Prayer for My Daughter. MoRP

For My Dead Brother. Alvah Bessie. PtTo

For My Grandmother. Countee Cullen. Four Epitaphs, 1. AmNP

For My Newborn Son. Sydney Goodsir Smith. ACV

For My Own Monument. Matthew Prior. EiCP

For my part, I'le not meddle with the cause. Homer. *Fr.* The Odyssey. CTC

For My People. Margaret Walker. AmNP; MoRP

For my unborn son. Two Poems, II. Robert J. Abrams. NNP

For Nature daily through her grand design. Sonnets, Part I, XXVI. Frederick Goddard Tuckerman. AP

. . . For nature then/ (The coarser pleasures of my boyish days). Wordsworth. *Fr.* Lines Written a Few Miles above Tintern Abbey. ACV

For Now. W. S. Merwin. CoPo

For Once, Then, Something. Robert Frost. AP

For One in Doubt. Charles Wesley. Three Hymns, 3. WaPE

For one long term, or e'er her trial came. Inscription: For the Door of the Cell in NewGate Where Mrs. Brownrigg, the 'Prentice-Cide, Was Confined Previous to Her Execution. George Canning *and* John Hookham Frere. Par

For Paul Laurence Dunbar. Countee Cullen. Four Epitaphs, 3. AmNP

For right is right, since God is God. Right Is Right. Frederick W. Faber. TRV

For Robert Frost, *sel.* Galway Kinnell.
"I saw you once on the TV." PP

For Saturday. Christopher Smart. *Fr.* Hymns for the Amusement of Children. EiCP
(Hymn for Saturday.) EiCP

"For shame!" cries Cypris as she sees. Indignant Protest. *Unknown.* UnTE

For shame, for shame, Oxonians all! Written at Oxford: On Stealing the Body of a Girl for Dissection. *Unknown.* StP

For shame, thou everlasting wooer. The Antiplatonick. John Cleveland. SeCP

For Simone Weil. Sister M. Thérèse. MoRP

For Sleep or Death. Ruth Pitter. WePo

For Strength. Rabindranath Tagore. *Fr.* Gitanjali. MoRP

For the Barbers. Joel Oppenheimer. CoPo

For the Bicentenary of Isaac Watts. Norman Nicholson. EaLo

For the Book of Love. Jules Laforgue, *tr. fr. French by* Jethro Bithell. ErPo

For the dim regions whence my fathers come. Outcast. Claude McKay. AmNP

For the doubling of flowers is the improvement of the gard'ner's talent. Christopher Smart. *Fr.* Jubilate Agno. EiCP

For the Earth God. *Unknown, tr. fr. Dahomean song by* Frances Herskovits. EaLo

For the Fallen. Laurence Binyon. WePo

For the first twenty years, since yesterday. The Computation. John Donne. DiPo

For the gladness here where the sun is shining at evening. Carl Sandburg. *Fr.* Our Prayer of Thanks. TRV

For the Grave of Daniel Boone. William Stafford. PoPl

For the Marriage of Faustus and Helen. Hart Crane. AP

For the New Railway Station in Rome. Richard Wilbur. PoDB

For the One Who Would Take Man's Life in His Hands. Delmore Schwartz. ThLM

For the Sake of Somebody. Burns. WePo

For the second shot. The Zen Archer. James Kirkup. EaLo

For the Time Being; a Christmas Oratorio, *sels.* W. H. Auden.
"Come to our well-run desert." TRV
He Is the Way. EaLo
Powers and Times Are Not Gods. MoRP

For the Union Dead. Robert Lowell. MP

For the whole world before thee is as a little grain of the balance. Wisdom of Solomon, Bible, Apocrypha. BoC

For thee, little boy, will the earth pour forth gifts. Vergil. *Fr.* Eclogues. PoPl

For Them. Eleanor Farjeon. ThGo

For them the sun shines ever in full might. Life after Death. Pindar. EaLo

For they who fashion songs must live too close to pain. Weltschmerz. Frank Yerby. AmNP

For This Is Wisdom. "Laurence Hope." *Fr.* The Teak Forest. PoLF

For Thomas Hardy. Jane Cooper. AmPC

For those my unbaptized rhymes. His Prayer for Absolution. Robert Herrick. TRV

For Though the Caves Were Rabbited. Henry David Thoreau. VaPo

For thoughts that curve like winging birds. I Yield Thee Praise. Philip Jerome Cleveland. TRV

For three years, out of key with his time. E.P. Ode pour l'Election de Son Sepulchre. Ezra Pound. *Fr.* Hugh Selwyn Mauberley. AP; CABA; ILP; PoIE; PP

For Two Children. René Char, *tr. fr. French by* Paul Engle. CoFP

For Vicki at Seven. Sydney King Russell. BiCB
For weeks and weeks the autumn world stood still. How One Winter Came in the Lake Region. Wilfred Campbell. OBCV
For whatever is let go. May Song. Wendell Berry. AP
For whom so many travails? for yourself? whose breath. Jean de Sponde. *Fr.* Sonnets de la Mort. RBL
For whom the possessed sea littered, on both shores. Requiem for the Plantagenet Kings. Geoffrey Hill. AnMoPo
For wisdom, which is the worker of all things, taught me. Wisdom. Wisdom of Solomon, Bible, Apocrypha. BoC
For You. Carl Sandburg. MoRP
For you who are seeking to serve with your best. In His Service. Clarence E. Clar. STF
Forbearance. Della Adams Leitner. STF
Force That through the Green Fuse Drives the Flower, The. Dylan Thomas. AnMoPo; CABA; CBEP; DiPo; ILP; PoIE; ToPo
Ford Madox Ford. Robert Lowell. MP; PoCh
Fore Thought. May Sarton. MoLP
Foreboding. Grant Code. FiSC
Foreboding, The. Robert Graves. ELP; StP
Forecast. Sydney King Russell. FiSC
Foreign Affairs. Stanley Kunitz. AnMoPo
Foreign Children. Robert Louis Stevenson. GoJo
Foreign Summer. W. S. Merwin. AmPC
Foreigner Comes to Earth on Boston Common, A. Horace Gregory. EaLo
Forenoon, The. Christopher Middleton. *Fr.* Herman Moon's Hourbook. NePoEA-2
Forenoon and afternoon and night. Life. Edward Rowland Sill. TRV
Forerunners, The. George Herbert. MeP
Foreseen for so many years: these evils this monstrous. May–June 1940. Robinson Jeffers. StP
Forest, The. Dorothy Quick. FiSC
Forest Fire. Edna Davis Romig. SIV
"Forest folk," The. Strawberries Mit Cream. Rochelle Owens. CoPo
Forest Hymn, A. Bryant. AP
Forest Leaves in Autumn, *sel.* John Keble.
  "Red o'er the forest glows the setting sun." OBNC
Forest Shapes. Donald Wandrei. FiSC
Forest's afire, The! October's Song. Eleanor Farjeon. PoSC
Forget. *Unknown.* STF
Forget each kindness that you do as soon as you have done it. The Best Memory Course. *Unknown.* STF
Forget It. *Unknown.* PoLF
Forget Not Yet. Sir Thomas Wyatt. CBEP; EnRePo; PoIE (Supplication, A.) GTBS-P
Forget the old year's sorrows, forget its lonely days. Forget. *Unknown.* STF
Forgetting God. J. E. Harvey. STF
Forgive Me, Sire. Norman Cameron. GTBS-P
Forgive me that I pitch your praise too low. Apology for Understatement. John Wain. NePoEA-2; ToPo
Forgive Me When I Whine. *Unknown.* STF
Forgive, O Lord, My Little Jokes on Thee. Robert Frost. EaLo
"Forgive them, for they know not what they do!" Abraham Lincoln. Edmund Clarence Stedman. LiPo
Forgive Us, O Lord. T. S. Eliot. *Fr.* Murder in the Cathedral. EaLo
Forgiven. A. A. Milne. SoPo
Forgiveness. Elizabeth Sewell. EaLo
Forgotten City, The. William Carlos Williams. PoPl
Forgotten Man, The. Edwin Markham. PoLF
Form of Adaptation, A. Robert Creeley. AmPC
Form of awe he was—and yet it seemed, A. Satan. Michael Madhusudan Dutt. ACV
Form of Epitaph, A. Laurence Whistler. GTBS-P
Form of Women, A. Robert Creeley. AmPC
Formal Elegy. John Berryman. OPP
Former Barn Lot. Mark Van Doren. FaBV; LOW; PoPl
Former Beauties. Thomas Hardy. *Fr.* At Casterbridge Fair. OBNC
Forms, *sel.* Theodore Enslin.
  "Things being what they are do not imply necessity." CoPo
Forsaken Bride, The. *Unknown. See* O Waly, Waly.
Forsaken Garden, A. Swinburne. CBEP; GTBS-P; OBNC; StP; VaPo; VP
Forsaken Merman, The. Matthew Arnold. CBEP; VP
  "Come, dear children, let us away," *sel.* HaSV
Fortress, The. Anne Sexton. ToPo
Forty Singing Seamen. Alfred Noyes. OnMSP
Forward lay sunlight silver on the sea. The Waterspout. William Hart-Smith. *Fr.* Christopher Columbus. PoAu-2
Forward Youth that would appear, The. An Horatian Ode upon Cromwell's Return from Ireland. Andrew Marvell. CABL; GTBS-P; SeCP
Foundation of Faith. John Drinkwater. MoRP
Foundation waits, The (will rise). A Weekday. Larry Eigner. CoPo

Foundations. Henry van Dyke. TRV
Founders of Ohio, The. William Henry Venable. ThLM
Fount, The. Rubén Darío, *tr. fr. Spanish by* William M. Davis. AnSP
Fountain, The. Donald Davie. GTBS-P
Fountain. Elizabeth Jennings. BoC; PoCh
Fountain, The. Giambattista Marino, *tr. fr. Italian by* Sir Edward Sherburne. RBL
Fountain, The. Wordsworth. GTBS-P
Fountain, coolest fountain. Ballad of the Cool Fountain. *Unknown.* AnML
Fountain flows, but where the bowl, The. The Broken Bowl. Jones Very. AP
Fountains mingle with the river, The. Love's Philosophy. Shelley. BoLP; FaBV; GTBS-P; PoIE; UnTE; WePo
Four. Elise Gibbs. BiCB
Four Ages of Man, The. W. B. Yeats. MoRP
Four and Eight. ffrida Wolfe. BiCB
Four and twentieth Day of May, The. The Swimming Lady: or, A Wanton Discovery. *Unknown.* ErPo; UnTE
Four-and-twenty nobles rode to the King's hall. Glenlogie. *Unknown.* BuBa
Four be the things I am wiser to know. Inventory. Dorothy Parker. PoPo
Four bright candles. Cake. Miriam Clark Potter. BiCB
Four Calls, The. Lydia Hadley. STF
Four card-players: an ikon of the saint. Dmitri of Carpathos. Lawrence Durrell. AnMoPo
Four Corners to My Bed. *Unknown. See* White Paternoster, The.
Four Days in November. Marjorie Mir. OPP
Four days the earth was rent and torn. Bombardment. Richard Aldington. MMA
Four Ducks on a Pond. William Allingham. WePo
Four Epitaphs. Countee Cullen.
  For a Lady I Know, 4. AmNP
  (Lady I Know, A.) TRV
  For John Keats, Apostle of Beauty, 2. AmNP
  For My Grandmother, 1. AmNP
  For Paul Laurence Dunbar, 3. AmNP
Four Fascinators. René Char, *tr. fr. French by* Richard G. Stern. CoFP
  Bull, The.
  Lark, The.
  Serpent, The.
  Trout, The.
Four for Sir John Davies. Theodore Roethke. AP
  Vigil, The, *sel.* PoDB
Four Glimpses of Night. Frank Marshall Davis. AmNP
Four horsemen rode out from the heart of the range. The Bushrangers. Edward Harrington. PoAu-1
400-Meter Freestyle. Maxine W. Kumin. SD
Four is too big for his breeches. Four. Elise Gibbs. BiCB
Four Legs, Three Legs, Two Legs. William Empson. ToPo
Four Little Foxes. Lew Sarett. LV; PoSC; RePo
Four Marys, The, *with music. Unknown.* BFSS
Four o'clock strikes. Out of School. Hal Summers. DaDu
Four pointes, my will, or I hence departe. A Last Will and Testament. *Unknown.* MeEL
Four Preludes on Playthings of the Wind. Carl Sandburg. AmLP; AP
Four Psalms. Bertolt Brecht, *tr. fr. German by* Christopher Middleton. MGP
Four Quartets, *sels.* T. S. Eliot.
  Burnt Norton. CABL
  Dry Salvages, The. CABA
    "River is within us, the sea is all about us, The." HaSV
  Little Gidding. GTBS-P; PoIE
  Dove, The. BoC
Four Quartz Crystal Clocks. Marianne Moore. MP
Four Questions Addressed to His Excellency the Prime Minister. James P. Vaughn. AmNP
Four seasons fill the measure of the year. The Human Seasons. Keats. GTBS-P; PoPo; WiR
Four Sheets to the Wind and a One-Way Ticket to France, 1933. Conrad Kent Rivers. AmNP; NNP
Four small nouns I put to pasture. Green Man. Lawrence Durrell. AnMoPo
4 sniffs & I'm high. Aether. Allen Ginsberg. CoPo
Four Sweet Months, The. Robert Herrick. WiR
Four Things ("Four things in any land must dwell"). *Unknown.* TRV
Four Things ("Four things a man must learn to do"). Henry van Dyke. LV; PoLF; TRV
Four III. E. E. Cummings. WePo
Four trees—upon a solitary acre. Emily Dickinson. AP
Four years old when the blackberries come! Hal's Birthday. Lucy Larcom. BiCB
Fourth Napoleon, *sel.* J. A. R. McKellar.
  Love in a Cottage. PoAu-2
Fourth of July. S. S. Gardons. AmPC
Fourth Song: "Only joy, now here you are." Sir Philip Sidney. *See* Only Joy, Now Here You Are.

Fowls in the Frith. *Unknown.* CBEP
(I Live in Great Sorrow.) MeEL
Fox and the cat, as they travell'd one day, The. The Virtuous
Fox and the Self-righteous Cat. John Cunningham.
OnMSP
Fox-coloured Pheasant Enjoyed His Peace, The. Peter Levi.
DaDu
Fox he came lolloping, lolloping, The. Hunting Song. Donald
Finkel. MoBS
Fox Walked Out, The (A *and* B *vers., with music*). *Un-
known.* BFSS
Foxglove by the cottage door, The. Four and Eight. ffrida
Wolfe. BiCB
Foxgloves. Ted Hughes. LOW
Foxtail Pine. Gary Snyder. CoPo
Fower oufant wivies stude. The Wee May o' Caledon. Lewis
Spence. ACV
Fra Bank to Bank. Mark Alexander Boyd. PoIE
Fra Lippo Lippi. Robert Browning. CABL; CTC; VP
Fragment III: "All horizons are round." Helmut Heissen-
büttel, *tr. fr. German by* Christopher Middleton. MGP
Fragment, A: "Encinctured with a twine of leaves." Samuel
Taylor Coleridge. OBNC
Fragment, A: "I cannot find my way to Nazareth." Yvor
Winters. PoIE
Fragment, A: "I walked along a stream for pureness rare."
Christopher Marlowe. CTC
Fragment: "I would to heaven that I were so much clay."
Byron. *Fr.* Don Juan. CTC; ILP
Fragment: "There is a river clear and fair." Catherine Fan-
shawe. Par
Fragment: "Walk with thy fellow-creatures: note the hush."
Henry Vaughan. TRV
Fragment from Nothing. Elizabeth J. Coatsworth. LV
Fragment of a Greek Tragedy. A. E. Housman. Par
Fragment on Death, A. Villon, *tr. fr. French by* Swinburne.
CTC
Fragments from Italy, *sel.* John Ciardi.
"Nona Domenica Garnaro sits in the sun." ToPo
Fragments on the Poet and the Poetic Gift, *sel.* Emerson.
"If bright the sun, he tarries." PP
Fragoletta. Swinburne. UnTE
Fragonard. Ogden Nash. RePo
Frail Hands. Lucia Trent. FiSC
Frail Life! in which, through mists of human breath. Life and
Death. Sir William Davenant. *Fr.* The Christians Reply
to the Philosopher. BoC
Frail the white rose and frail are. A Flower Given to My
Daughter. James Joyce. PoPl
Frailty and Hurtfulness of Beauty, The. Earl of Surrey. VaPo
France; an Ode. Samuel Taylor Coleridge. StP
Francis Beaumont's Letter from the Country to Jonson. Ben
Jonson. SeCP
Frank Courtship, The, *sel.* George Crabbe.
Jonas Kindred's Household. OBNC
Frank Fidd, *with music. Unknown.* BSNS
Frankie and Johnny (A *vers., with music*). *Unknown.* BSO
(Frankie, B *vers., with music*). BSO
(Frankie Lee, C *vers., with music*). BSO
Frankie she's a good girl. Frankie. *Unknown.* BSO
Franklin's Prologue and Tale, The. Chaucer. *Fr.* The Canter-
bury Tales. CABL
"Frater Ave atque Vale." Tennyson. FoBA; GTBS-P
Fraternitas. Confucius, *tr. fr. Chinese by* Ezra Pound. *Fr.*
The Classic Anthology: Deer Sing. CTC
Fraud, a forger, and informer, too, A. A Bad Joke. Martial.
UnTE
Fred Apollus at Fava's. Nicholas Moore. ErPo
"Fred, where is north?" West-running Brook. Robert Frost.
AP; DiPo
Frederick Douglass. Robert Hayden. AmNP
Free evening fades, outside the windows fastened with deco-
rative iron grilles, The. Evening in the Sanitarium.
Louise Bogan. MP
Free Nation, A. Edwin Markham. TRV
Freedom and Love. Thomas Campbell. GTBS-P
Freight Train, The. Rowena Bennett. RePo
French bus halts on the Plateau of Antiques, The. A Visit to
Van Gogh. Charles Causley. PoCh
French Lisette; a Ballad of Maida Vale. William Plomer.
ErPo
Frescoes that crumble, marbles bullet-scarred. The Fault.
Edward Lucie-Smith. NePoEA-2
Fresh Air. Kenneth Koch. PP
Fresh Cheese and Cream. Robert Herrick. UnTE
Fresh clad from heaven in robes of white. In My Own Album.
Charles Lamb. CBEP
Fresh from the dewy hill, the merry year. Song. Blake.
FoBA
Fresh Newborn Rose. Guido Cavalcanti, *tr. fr. Italian by*
James J. Wilhelm. AnML
Fresh Paint. Boris Pasternak, *tr. fr. Russian by* Babette
Deutsch. PoPl

Fresh Spring, the herald of love's mighty king. Amoretti,
LXX. Spenser. CABA; StP
Friar, The. Thomas Love Peacock. *Fr.* Maid Marian. SD
Friar and the Fair Maid, The. *Unknown.* UnTE
Friday came and the circus was there. The Circus. Elizabeth
Madox Roberts. SoPo
Friar Complains, A. *Unknown.* MeEL
Friars' Enormities. *Unknown.* MeEL
Friday; or, The Dirge. John Gay. *Fr.* The Shepherd's Week.
EiCP
Friend Bernard de Ventadorn. Bernart de Ventadorn, *tr. fr.
Provençal by* James J. Wilhelm. AnML
Friend, I Can't Deny. Joan de Guilhade, *tr. fr. Portuguese by*
William M. Davis. AnML
Friend, I have lost the way. The Way. Edwin Muir. LOW
Friend of Humanity and the Knife-Grinder, The. George
Canning *and* John Hookham Frere. Par
Friend or Two, A. Wilbur D. Nesbit. PoLF
Friend Who Just Stands By, The. B. Y. Williams. PoLF
Friend, whose unnatural early death. An Elegy. David
Gascoyne. MP
Friendless and faint, with martyred steps and slow. Calvary.
E. A. Robinson. PoDB; PoPo
Friendly Beasts, The. *Unknown.* BiCB; OnMSP; PoSC;
SoPo
Friendly cow all red and white, The. The Cow. Robert Louis
Stevenson. SoPo
Friends Beyond. Thomas Hardy. GTBS-P
Friends, our lives are lost in rhyme. The Orgy. Antoine-
Girard de Saint-Amant. RBL
Friends, Romans, countrymen, lend me your ears. Antony's
Oration. Shakespeare. *Fr.* Julius Caesar. PoPl
Friendship, like love, is but a name. Fable L: The Hare and
Many Friends. John Gay. EiCP
Frightful Basilisk, Most Poisonous, The. Giacomo da Lentino,
tr. fr. Italian by Daniel J. Donno. AnML
Frog, The. Hilaire Belloc. FaBV; GoJo; RePo;
Frog and the Mouse, The. *Unknown.* BSO (C, D, *and* E
vers.); WiR
(Frog Song, The, B *vers., with music*.) BSO
(Froggy Went a-Courting, *with music*.) BFSS
(Mr. Frog Went a-Courting, A *vers., with music*.) BSO
Frog He Would a-Wooing Go, A. *Unknown.* BSNS, *with
music;* OnMSP
Frog under you, A. The Wife. Denise Levertov. ErPo
Frog went walking one fine day, A. The Frog and the Mouse.
Unknown. WiR
Froggy Went a-Courting. *Unknown. See* Frog and the Mouse,
The.
Frogs jump. Jump or Jingle. Evelyn Beyer. SoPo
Frogs' Singing-School, The. E. T. Carbell. SoPo
Frolicsome Farmer, The. *Unknown.* UnTE
From a city window, 'way up high. Motor Cars. Rowena
Bennett. SoPo
From a Foreign Land. Roy Fuller. OPP
From a granite rib of rock off Viareggio. Off Viareggio.
Kenneth Pitchford. CoPo
From a Hint in the Minor Poets. Samuel Wesley. CBEP
From a land of milk and honey. Weeping and Singing. César
Tiempo. MoRP
From a magician's midnight sleeve. Late Air. Elizabeth
Bishop. PoPl
From a poverty-shadowed life. Imagined Happiness. Erik
Axel Karlfeldt. PoPl
From a Woman to a Greedy Lover. Norman Cameron. *Fr.*
Three Love Poems. GTBS-P
From a wreck of tree in the wash of night. Speak with the
Sun. David Campbell. ACV
From All That Dwell below the Skies. Isaac Watts. TRV
From all the rest I single out you, having a message for you.
To One Shortly to Die. Walt Whitman. CBEP
From almost naught to almost all I flee. On the Calculus.
J. V. Cunningham. PoIE
From an Old Maid. Vassar Miller. ToPo
From art, from nature, from the schools. In Memoriam A. H.
H., XLIX. Tennyson. VP
From being aware of all this beauty. Jean Follain. *Fr.* Ex-
tensions. CoFP
From bill to breast a snake. Swan. Edward Lowbury.
GTBS-P
From childhood's hour I have not been. Alone. Poe. PoSa
From Citron-Bower. Hilda Doolittle ("H. D."). AP
From Country to Town. Hartley Coleridge. CBEP
From days of youth I remember sailing. Ulysses. Umberto
Saba. CoIP
From Eastertide to Eastertide. A Ballad of a Nun. John
Davidson. OnMSP
From fairest creatures we desire increase. Sonnets, I. Shake-
speare. CTC
From Far Shores, from Kingdoms. Gottfried Benn, *tr. fr.
German by* Christopher Middleton. MGP
From fear to fear, successively betrayed. Reflection from
Rochester. William Empson. ToPo

From friendly bells of a white bell-tower. Towns. Corrado Govoni. CoIP
From ghoulies and ghosties. Ghoulies and Ghosties [or Litany for Halloween]. *Unknown.* PoSC; SoPo
From Gloucester Out. Edward Dorn. CoPo
From gods of other men, fastidious heart. False Gods. Walter de la Mare. EaLo
From going always over bars his glance. The Panther. Rainer Maria Rilke. PoPl
From harmony, from heavenly harmony. Song for Saint Cecilia's Day. Dryden. CABA; CBEP; DiPo; GTBS-P; ILP; OnP; PoIE
From her bed's high and odoriferous roome. Homer. *Fr.* The Odyssey. CTC
From here through tunnelled gloom the track. The Railway Junction. Walter de la Mare. CBEP
From immaculate construction to half death. The Man from the Top of the Mind. David Wagoner. NePoEA-2
From low to high doth dissolution climb. Mutability. Wordsworth. CABA; FoBA; StP
From merciless invaders. The Spanish Armada. John Still. HaSV
From my mother's sleep I fell into the State. The Death of the Ball Turret Gunner. Randall Jarrell. AP; CaFP; ILP; PoPl; PoPo
From My Window. Mary Elizabeth Coleridge. OBNC
From noise and bustle far away. Betsy Baker. *Unknown.* BSNS
From noise of scare-fires rest ye free. The Bellman. Robert Herrick. CBEP
From Nothing Strange. Gustav Davidson. FiSC
From now on kill America out of your mind. Millions Are Learning How. James Agee. PoPl
From Oberon in fairyland. The Mad-Merry Pranks of Robin Good-Fellow. *Unknown.* CBEP
From one Word are all things, and this one all things speak. Thomas à Kempis, *tr. fr. Latin.* BoC
From out the dark, where blurs the buildings' height. City Rain. Paul Bartlett. PoNC
From Pent-up Aching Rivers. Walt Whitman. AP; CABA
From plains that real to southward, dim. Heat. Archibald Lampman. OBCV
From pleasure of the bed. The Chambermaid's Second Song. W. B. Yeats. ErPo
From plum-tree and cherry. Flowering Currant. Patrick MacDonogh. ErPo
From prayer that asks that I may be. Deliver Me [or Flame of God]. Amy Carmichael. STF
From shadowy stratas of his mind. Intuition. R. H. Grenville. FiSC
From Soil Somehow the Poet's Word. Kenneth Leslie. OBCV
From Spiralling Ecstatically This. E. E. Cummings. PoDB
From stainless steel basins of water. The Operation. W. D. Snodgrass. StP; ToPo
From Stirling Castle we had seen. Yarrow Unvisited. Wordsworth. GTBS-P
From the Alembic. H. A. Sieber. PoNC
From the Arabic; an Imitation. Shelley. CBEP
From the Ballad of Two-Gun Freddy. Walter R. Brooks. SoPo
From the Cadenced Roar of the Waves. Rosalía de Castro, *tr. fr. Spanish by* Kate Flores. AnSP
From the dark mood's control. The Recovery. Edmund Blunden. CBEP
From the dead hand I take the bow he wielded. Funeral Hymn. *Unknown.* SiGo
From the depth of the dreamy decline of the dawn through a notable nimbus of nebulous noonshine. Nephelidia. Swinburne. Par; VP
From the desert I come to thee. Bedouin Song. Bayard Taylor. BoLP
From the first cry. First It Was Singing. Jon Silkin. PoDB
From the first shock of leaves their alliance. Park Poem. Paul Blackburn. CoPo
From the forests and highlands. Hymn of Pan. Shelley. PoIE
From the Fortress of Upper Bergamo. Salvatore Quasimodo, *tr. fr. Italian by* Allen Mandelbaum. CoIP
From the geyser ventilators. Business Girls. John Betjeman. WePo
From the Greek Anthology. Crinagoras, *tr. fr. Greek by* Kenneth Rexroth. SD
From the Gulf. Will H. Ogilvie. PoAu-1
From the hag and hungry goblin. Tom o' Bedlam's Song [or Roaring Mad Tom]. *Unknown.* CBEP; EvOK; PoSa; StP; WiR
From the heart of a flower. Leave It to Me Blues. Joel Oppenheimer. CoPo
From the Highest Camp. Thom Gunn. MP
From the hodge porridge. The Farmer's Wife. Anne Sexton. NePoEA-2
From the island aquamarine. Index (8). Gil Orlovitz. ToPo
From the mantle of night. Tasso, *tr. fr. Italian by* Lorna de' Lucchi. RBL

From the night storm sad wakes the winter day. November Morning. Edmund Blunden. WePo
From the sad eaves the drip-drop of the rain. Desolate. Sydney Dobell. CBEP; OBNC
From the Sea. Sara Teasdale. MoLP
From the ship's deck I saw. Voyage to Montevideo. Dino Campana. CoIP
From the skylight up high. The Skylight. Dino Campana. CoIP
From the tattered banana tree after months of waiting. Banana. Charles G. Bell. ErPo
From the thin slats of the Venetian blinds. Underwood. Howard Moss. MP; NePoEA-2; PP
From the top of a bridge. The River Is a Piece of Sky. John Ciardi. PoPl; SoPo
From the White Day to Take Me. Francisco de Quevedo, *tr. fr. Spanish by* Kate Flores. AnSP
From Thee to Thee. Solomon Ibn Gabirol, *tr. fr. Hebrew by* Israel Abrahams. EaLo
From this far, late-come country that still keeps. Gordon Childe. David Martin. PoAu-2
From this high quarried ledge I see. The Mountain over Aberdare. Alun Lewis. ACV
From this hospital bed. The Injury. William Carlos Williams. AP
From This the Strength. Fred Lape. SIV
From this valley they say you are going. The Red River Valley. *Unknown.* BFSS
From Thought to Thought, from Mountain Peak to Mountain. Petrarch, *tr. fr. Italian by* Morris Bishop. Sonnets to Laura: To Laura in Life, Canzone XVII. AnML
From thy fair face I learn, O my loved lord. Love Lifts to God. Michelangelo. RBL
From troubles of the world. Ducks. Frederick William Harvey. BoC
From what I am, to be what I am not. Return. Vassar Miller. ToPo
From where I sit, I see the stars. Midnight. Archibald Lampman. OBCV
From Wynyard's Gap the livelong day. A Trampwoman's Tragedy. Thomas Hardy. OBNC
From yonder wood, mark blue-eyed Eve proceed. Progress of Evening. Walter Savage Landor. OBNC
From you I have been absent in the spring. Sonnets, XCVIII. Shakespeare. BoC; DiPo
From you, Ianthe, little troubles pass. Walter Savage Landor. *Fr.* Ianthe. OBNC
Frontier. Josephine Miles. OPP
Frost and snow, frost and snow. Ariel. David Campbell. PoAu-2
Frost at Midnight. Samuel Taylor Coleridge. BoC; CABA; CABL; CBEP; ILP; OBNC; PoIE; StP; VaPo
Frost flowers on the window glass. A Valentine. Eleanor Hammond. RePo
Frost-locked all the winter. Spring. Christina Rossetti. OBNC
Frost Pane, The. David McCord. RePo
Frost performs its secret ministry, The. Frost at Midnight. Samuel Taylor Coleridge. BoC; CABA; CABL; CBEP; ILP; OBNC; PoIE; StP; VaPo
Frostbite. Conrad Aiken. PoPo
Frosted over with cold flakes. First Winter's Day. Dorothy Aldis. SoPo
Frosty Night, A. Robert Graves. MoBS
Frugal snail, with forecast of repose, The. The Housekeeper. Vincent Bourne. PoLF
Fruit and Greens. Umberto Saba, *tr. fr. Italian by* Thomas G. Bergin. CoIP
Fruit of the Flower. Countee Cullen. PoLF
Fugitive Slaves, The. Jones Very. AP
Fugue of Death. Paul Celan, *tr. fr. German by* Christopher Middleton. MGP
Fulfillment. Vassar Miller. NePoEA-2
Full-berried the elderbush: tranquility childhood lived. Childhood. Georg Trakl. MGP
Full faith I have she holds that rarest gift. Modern Love, XXXII. George Meredith. VP
Full Fathom Five [Thy Father Lies]. Shakespeare. *Fr.* The Tempest, I, ii. CABA; CaFP; CBEP; DiPo; ELP; FoBA; ILP; PoIE
(Ariel's Dirge.) EvOK; GoJo
(Sea Dirge, A.) GTBS-P; HaSV
(Song.) OnP
Full flowering moon! In your light. The Gods of Greece. Heine. TwGP
Full knee-deep lies the winter snow. Tennyson. *Fr.* The Death of the Old Year. PoSC
Full many a fiend did haunt this house of rest. An Imitation of Spenser. John Armstrong. WaPE
Full many a glorious morning have I seen. Sonnets, XXXIII. Shakespeare. CBEP; FoBA; ILP
Full Moon: New Guinea. Karl Shapiro. PoPo
Full of her long white arms and milky skin. The Equilibrists. John Crowe Ranson. AP; CaFP

Full sea rolls and thunders, The. W. E. Henley. *Fr.* Echoes. HaSV
Full Well I Know How to Speak of Love. Raimbaut d'Aurenga, *tr. fr. Provençal by* Maurice Valency. AnML
Fundament Is Shifted, The. Abbie Huston Evans. MoRP
Funeral, [*or* Funerall], The. John Donne. CABA; CBEP; DiPo; EnRePo; MeP; SeCP
Funeral Home, The. Robert Mezey. AmPC
Funeral Hymn. *Unknown. tr. fr. Sanskrit by* Arthur A. Macdonell. SiGo
Funeral Oration, A. David Wright. MP
Funeral Oration for a Mouse. Alan Dugan. AP
Funeral Rites of the Rose, The. Robert Herrick. CABA; PoSa
Funny Fantasies Are Never So Real as Oldstyle. Lawrence Ferlinghetti. *Fr.* A Coney Island of the Mind. ErPo
Funny, how Felicia Ropps. Felicia Ropps. Gelett Burgess. BBGG
Funny Old Man and His Wife, The. *Unknown.* SoPo
Furl that banner, for 'tis weary. The Conquered Banner. Abram Joseph Ryan. FaPL
Furnace is of stone and clay, A. The Fire Place. E. W. Mandel. OBCV
Furnished Lives. Jon Silkin. NcPoEA-2; PoDB
Furniture of a Woman's Mind, The. Swift. CaFP; PoIE
Furry Bear. A. A. Milne. SoPo
Further Fables for Our Times, *sel.* James Thurber. Morals. FaBV
Further in summer than the birds. Emily Dickinson. *See* Farther in summer than the birds.
Further Instructions. Ezra Pound. MP
Further than this we may not know. Foundation of Faith. John Drinkwater. MoRP
Fury of Aerial Bombardment, The. Richard Eberhart. AnMoPo, ILP; MP; PoIE; PoPo; ToPo
Futile to chide the stinging shower. Perspectives. Dudley Randall. AmNP
Futility. Wilfred Owen. CBEP; GTBS-P; MMA
Future, The. George Frederick Cameron. OBCV
Future holds hidden, The. Symbolum. Goethe. AGP
Fuzzy Wuzzy, Creepy Crawly. Lillian Schulz Vanada. SoPo

G

GI. Raymond Roseliep. FiSC
Gabriel, fram Hevene King. The Annunciation. *Unknown.* MeEL
Gabriel John. *Unknown.* CBEP
Gaiety, *sel.* Richard Howard.
    Queer's Song. ErPo
Gaiety of three winds is a game of green, The. White Goat, White Ram. W. S. Merwin. PoDB
Gaily bedight. Eldorado. Poe. AP; PoPo; RePo; SIV; WiR
Galante Garden, I. Juan Ramón Jiménez, *tr. fr. Spanish by* H. R. Hays. PoPl
Galileo Galilei. William Jay Smith. PoCh
Gallant Welsh, of all degrees, The. The Welsh. E. V. Lucas. LV
Gallantly within the Ring. John Hamilton Reynolds. SD
Gallent Tree, The. *Unknown. See* Maid Freed from the Gallows, The.
Galleys of Spain. *Unknown, tr. fr. Spanish by* Sir John Bowring. RBL
Gallop of Fire, A. Marie E. J. Pitt. PoAu-1
Galoshes. Rhoda W. Bacmeister. SoPo
Galoshes, The. Alfred Lichtenstein, *tr. fr. German by* Michael Hamburger. MGP
Galway Races. *Unknown.* SD
Gambler, The ("A gambler's life I do admire"), *with music.* John A. Stone. SGR
Game of Consequences, A. Paul Dehn. ErPo
Game of Dice, A. *Unknown, tr. fr. Greek by* Louis Untermeyer. UnTE
Game of Glass, A. Alastair Reid. PoCh
Game was ended, and the noise, The. Football. Walt Mason. SD
Gamesters All. Du Bose Heyward. SIV
Gammer Gurton's Needle, *sel. At. to* William Stevenson *and to* John Still.
    Drinking Song. WiR
Ganga. Thomas Blackburn. MoBS
Gangrene. Philip Levine. AmPC
Ganymed. Goethe, *tr. fr. German by* W. Edward Brown. AGP
    (Ganymede, *tr. by* Walter Kaufmann.) TwGP
Garden, The. William Cowper. *Fr.* The Task. EnPE
Garden, The. Andrew Marvell. CABA; CABL; CaFP; CBEP; DiPo; MeP; OnP; PoIE; PoLF; PoSa; SeCP; StP; VaPo
    (Thoughts in a Garden.) GTBS-P

(Thoughts in a Summer Garden.) BoC
Garden, The. Ezra Pound. CABA; MP; PoIE
Garden, A. Sappho, *tr. fr. Greek by* T. F. Higham. SiGo
Garden, The. Joshua Sylvester. CBEP
Garden, The. Jones Very. AP
Garden, The. William Carlos Williams. PoDB
Garden at St. John's, The. May Swenson. PoP1
Garden by the Sea, A. William Morris. OBNC
Garden Fancies, *sels.* Robert Browning.
    I. The Flower's Name ACV; CTC
    I. Sibrandus Schafnaburgensis. CTC
Garden flew round with the angel, The. The Pleasures of Merely Circulating. Wallace Stevens. LOW
Garden Gate, The. *Unknown.* BSO
Garden in Chicago, A. Karl Shapiro. PoIE
Garden is a lovesome thing, God wot, A! My Garden. Thomas Edward Brown. FaBV; PoLF; TRV
Garden of Bamboos, The. E. Powys Mathers, *tr. fr. street song of Annam.* BoLP
Garden of Gethsemane. Boris Pasternak, *tr. fr. Russian by* Bernard Guilbert Guerney. MoRP
Garden of Love, The. Blake. *Fr.* Songs of Experience. CABA; CBEP; DiPo; FaBV; FoBA; PoIE; StP; VaPo
Garden of Olives, The. Rainer Maria Rilke, *tr. fr. German by* M. D. Herter Norton. MoRP
Garden of Proserpine, The. Swinburne. DiPo; FaBV; OBNC; OnP; PoIE; PoP1; VP
Garden of Shadow, The. Ernest Dowson. OBNC
Garden of Ships, The. Douglas Stewart. PoAu-2
Garden Party, The. Hilaire Belloc. DTC
Garden Puzzle. Gray Burr. CoPo
Garden Seat, The. Thomas Hardy. GoJo
Garden Song, A. Austin Dobson. OBNC
Gardener, The. Eduard Möricke, *tr. fr. German by* Ernst Rose. AGP
Gardener, The, *sel.* Rabindranath Tagore.
    Bird, The, LXVII. PoP1; SiGo
Gardener, The. *Unknown.* CBEP
Gardener at Thirty, The. Jascha Kessler. AmPC
Gardener stands in his bower door, The. The Gardener. *Unknown.* CBEP
Gardener, Tobias Baird, A. The Headless Gardener. Ian Serraillier. BoC
Gardener's Song, The. "Lewis Carroll." *Fr.* Sylvie and Bruno. EvOK
    (Mad Gardener's Song, The.) WiR
Gardens No Emblems. Donald Davie. NePoEA-2
Garfield's Murder. *Unknown. See* Charles Guiteau.
Garlande of Laurell, The, *sels.* John Skelton.
    To Mistress Isabel[l] Pennell. CBEP; PoIE; StP
    To Mistress Margaret Hussey. CBEP; DiPo; GoJo; PoIE; PoSa
    To Mistress Margaret Tilney. MeEL
    To Mistress Margery Wentworth. CBEP; EnRePo
Garnishing the Aviary. Margaret Danner. Far from Africa, 1. AmNP; NNP
Garret, The. Ezra Pound. PoP1
Garrulous old man who once had owned, The. Under the Casuarina. Elizabeth Riddell. PoAu-2
Gas was on in the Institute, The. A Shropshire Lad. John Betjeman. MoBS
Gascoigne's Good Morrow. George Gascoigne. EnRePo
Gascoigne's Lullaby. George Gascoigne. PoIE
    (Lullaby of a Lover, The.) EnRePo
Gascoigne's Memories, *sels.* George Gascoigne. EnRePo
    "Common speech, The, is, spend and God will send," III.
    "In haste, post haste," IV.
    "Vain excess of flattering fortune's gifts, The," II.
Gascoigne's Praise of His Mistress. George Gascoigne. EnRePo
Gascoigne's Woodmanship. George Gascoigne. EnRePo
Gascon Punished, The ("A Gascon, being heard one day to swear"). La Fontaine. UnTE
Gaspard Tragedy, The, *with music. Unknown.* BSNS
Gasping and bent. The Slave. Hans Werner Cohn. MGP
Gate of the Year, The, *sel.* M. Louise Haskins.
    "And I said to the man who stood at the gate of the year," *sel.* TRV; WePo
Gates of Paradise, The, *sel.* Blake.
    Epilogue: "Truly, my Satan, thou art but a dunce." CABA; OBNC
Gates of the Rockies. James Daugherty. RePo
Gates of the Year, The. John Mervin Hull. STF
Gateway, The. A. D. Hope. ErPo; UnTE
Gather These Bones. Lewis Turco. FiSC
Gather Ye Rosebuds While Ye May. Robert Herrick. *See* To the Virgins, to Make Much of Time.
Gathering, The. E. J. Pratt. *Fr.* Towards the Last Spike. OBCV
Gathering, The. Sir Walter Scott. *Fr.* The Lady of the Lake. OBNC
Gathering Leaves. Robert Frost. LOW; RePo
Gathering Song of Donald the Black. Sir Walter Scott. GTBS-P

Gaucelm, three plays of love. A Debate. Gaucelm Faidit, Uc de la Bacalaria, *and* Savaric de Mauleon. AnML
Gaunt man, Abraham Lincoln, woke one morning, The. Stephen Vincent Benét. *Fr.* John Brown's Body. LiPo
Gay Florimel, of generous birth. A Song. *Unknown.* WaPE
Gay, gay, gay, gay. Remember the Day of Judgment. *Unknown.* MeEL
Gay go up and gay go down. The Bells of London. *Unknown.* EvOK
Gay Goshawk, The. *Unknown.* BuBa; CABL
Gay hussars, The—I love them all. Song of the Vivandière. Heine. UnTE
Gay Spanish Maid, The. *Unknown.* BSNS
Gaze Not on Swans. Henry Noel. ELP
Gaze not on thy beauty's pride. Good Counsel to a Young Maid. Thomas Carew. CBEP
Geary's Rock. *Unknown. See* Jam on Gerry's Rocks, The.
Gebir, *sel.* Walter Savage Landor.
     Shepherd and the Nymph, The. OBNC
Gem of the crimson-colour'd even. To the Evening Star [*or* Caroline, II]. Thomas Campbell. GTBS-P; OBNC; TRV
General, The. Siegfried Sassoon. FaBV; MMA
General came in a new tin hat, The. Pershing at the Front. Arthur Guiterman. SIV
General Store. Rachel Field. SoPo
General, That Tank. Bertolt Brecht, *tr. fr. German by* Christopher Middleton. MGP
General William Booth Enters [into] Heaven. Vachel Lindsay. AmLP; BoC; ILP
Generations. Robert Clark. PoAu-2
Generous Years, The. Stephen Spender. PoCh
Genesis, *sels.* Bible, O.T.
     After the Flood Went Down, God Said, VIII: 22, IX: 12. ThGo
     Rainbow, The, IX: 12-16. BoC
Genesis. Geoffrey Hill. ACV
Genius in Beauty. Dante Gabriel Rossetti. The House of Life, XVIII. VP
Genteel in personage. The Maid's Husband. Henry Carey. Two Songs, 2. WaPE
Gentian. "Klabund," *tr. fr. German by* Christopher Middleton. MGP
Gentilesse. Chaucer. CBEP
Gentill butler, bell ami. Fill the Bowl, Butler! *Unknown.* MeEL
Gentle Breeze with a Whispered Cry, The. Gustavo Adolfo Bécquer, *tr. fr. Spanish by* Alice Jane McVan. AnSP
Gentle Heart, The. Guido Guinicelli. *See* Canzone: Of the Gentle Heart.
Gentle Hill, The. Salvatore Quasimodo, *tr. fr. Italian by* Allen Mandelbaum. PoPl
Gentle Knight/ Now Give Me a Kiss. *Unknown, tr. fr. Spanish by* William M. Davis. AnML
Gentle Lady, do not sing. James Joyce. *Fr.* Chamber Music. MoLP
Gentle Name. Selma Robinson. BiCB; LV
Gentleman in Oils. Harold Vinal. FiSC
Gentleman with polished hair, A. The Clean Gentleman. George Abbe. FiSC
Gently Dip. George Peele. *Fr.* The Old Wives' Tale. ELP
Gently I stir a white feather fan. In the Mountains on a Summer Day. Li Po. SD
Gently, Johnny My Jingalo. *Unknown.* UnTE
Geography. Kenneth Koch. AmPC
George Collins, *with music. Unknown.* BFSS
George Crabbe. E. A. Robinson. AP; PP
Georg Grosz. Else Lasker-Schüler, *tr. fr. German by* Christopher Middleton. MGP
George-Hector. The Emancipation of George-Hector (a Colored Turtle). Mari E. Evans. AmNP
George Jones. *Unknown.* BSNS
George lives in an apartment and. Radiator Lions. Dorothy Aldis. SoPo
George Riley. *Unknown.* BSO
George Villiers, Duke of Buckingham. Dryden. *Fr.* Absalom and Achitophel. PoSa
George Washington ("George Washington is tops with me"). Shelley Silverstein. PoSC
George Washington ("George Washington, the farmer"). James S. Tippett. RePo
Georgia Dusk. Jean Toomer. AmNP
Georgics, *sels.* Vergil, *tr. fr. Latin.*
     Chariot Race, The, *fr.* III, *tr. by* Smith Palmer Bovie. SD
     "What makes a plenteous harvest, when to turn," *fr.* I, *tr. by* Dryden. EiCP
Georgie, *with music. Unknown.* BFSS
Georgie Allen ("Georgie's mother came to him"), *with music. Unknown.* BFSS
Geranium, The. Sheridan. ErPo; UnTE
Germany? But where is it? I cannot find such a country. Deutsches Reich. Schiller. TwGP
German National Character. Schiller, *tr. fr. German by* Walter Kaufmann. TwGP
Geronimo. Ernest McGaffey. ThLM

Gerontion. T. S. Eliot. AnMoPo; AP; CABA; CABL; DiPo; FoBA; GTBS-P; ILP; OnP; PoIE; StP
Gerry's Rocks. *Unknown. See* Jam on Gerry's Rocks, The.
Gertrude and Gulielma, sister-twins. Sonnets, Part II, XV. Frederick Goddard Tuckerman. AP
Get it right or let it alone. Morals. James Thurber. *Fr.* Further Fables for Our Time. FaBV
"Get on, you hounds, get on." Ballad of Juliana. *Unknown.* AnML
Get Somebody Else. Paul Laurence Dunbar. TRV
Get Up and Bar the Door. *Unknown.* BFSS, *with music;* OnMSP; PoIE; VaPo
Get Up, Blues. James A. Emanuel. AmNP
Get up, get up for shame, the blooming morn. Corinna's Going a-Maying. Robert Herrick. CABA; CBEP; DiPo; PoIE; SeCP
"Get up, get up, Lord Douglas," she cried. Lord William and Lord Douglas. *Unknown.* BFSS
"Get up, get up, pretty Polly," he says. Pretty Polly. *Unknown.* UnTE
"Get up, our Anna dear, from the weary spinning wheel." The Fairy Thorn. Sir Samuel Ferguson. OnMSP
Get You Gone. Sir Charles Sedley. ELP
Gethsemane. W. B. Tappan. STF
Gettin' Born. Anthony Euwer. PoPl
Getting Drunk with Daughter. Robert Huff. NePoEA-2
Ghazel of Absence, A. Gerrit Lansing. CoPo
Ghetto-born, depression-bred. The Ark. Irving Feldman. AmPC
Ghost, The. Walter de la Mare. ELP
Ghost. R. H. Grenville. FiSC
Ghost, The. James Wright. FiSC
Ghost in Birmingham, The. Ishmael Reed. PtTo
Ghost Lake's a dark lake, a deep lake and cold. The Skater of Ghost Lake. William Rose Benét. PoPo; SIV
Ghost of a mouldy larder is one thing, A; whiskery bread. Corposant. Peter Redgrove. NePoEA-2
Ghost of the Buffaloes, The. Vachel Lindsay. *See* Ghosts of the Buffaloes, The.
Ghost, that loved a lady fair, A. The Phantom-Wooer. Thomas Lovell Beddoes. WiR
Ghost to Come. Margaret Widdemer. FiSC
Ghost-Town Saloon: Winter. Joseph Payne Brennan. FiSC
Ghostly Father, The. Peter Redgrove. MoBS; NePoEA-2
Ghostly Reaper. Harold Vinal. FiSC
Ghosts. Winifred Adams Burr. FiSC
Ghosts. Elizabeth Jennings. NePoEA-2
Ghosts. Alastair Reid. FiSC
Ghost's Lament, The. *Unknown.* BuBa
Ghost's Leavetaking, The. Sylvia Plath. NePoEA-2
Ghosts of the Buffaloes, The. Vachel Lindsay. LV
     (Ghost of the Buffaloes, The.) RePo
Ghoulies and Ghosties. *Unknown.* PoSC
     (Litany for Halloween.) SoPo
Ghosts' Stories. Alastair Reid. NePoEA-2
Giant firefly, A. The Firefly. Issa. RePo
Giantess. Baudelaire, *tr. fr. French by* Karl Shapiro. ErPo
Gib and gibbet, these shall be my signs. The Hanged Thing. Walter H. Kerr. FiSC
Gie the Lass Her Fairin'. Burns. ErPo
Gift, The. John Ciardi. MP
Gift, The. William Carlos Williams. MoRP; PoPl
Gift of God, The. E. A. Robinson. AP
Gift of God, A. *Unknown.* STF
Gift Outright, The. Robert Frost. AmLP; AP; OPP; PoIE; PoPo; RePo
Gift to Be Simple, The. Howard Moss. MoRP; MP
Gifts. Hazel Harper Harris. BiCB
Gifts of Fortune, The. Schiller, *tr. fr. German by* Alexander Gode. AGP
Gifts of God, The. George Herbert. *See* Pulley, The.
Giles Corey. *Unknown.* ThLM
Gilgamesh, *sel. Unknown, tr. fr. Babylonian tablets by* William Ellery Leonard.
     Seduction of Engadu. ErPo
Gil's history appears to me. An Epigram. Matthew Green. StP
Gimboling. Isabella Gardner. ErPo
Gin a body meet a body. Rigid Body Sings. James Clerk-Maxwell. Par
Gin the Goodwife Stint. Basil Bunting. CTC
Ginevra. Samuel Rogers. PoLF
Gingham dog and the calico cat, The. The Duel. Eugene Field. OnMSP; PoLF; PoPl; SoPo
Gipsies. *See also* Gypsies.
Gipsies came to our good lord's gate, The. Johnie Faa. *Unknown.* BuBa
Giraffe, The. Geoffrey Dearmer. WePo
Girl, A. Edwin Denby. BoLP
Girl. Dom Moraes. NePoEA-2
Girl, A. Ezra Pound. BoLP
Girl hustles her islands of pure flesh, The. For Jan. John Wieners. CoPo
Girl in a Library, A. Randall Jarrell. PoNC

Girl in a Window, A. James Wright. ErPo
Girl in the sand, The. Nude Kneeling in Sand. John Logan. ErPo
Girl in the tea shop, The. The Tea Shop. Ezra Pound. WePo
Girl is twirling a parasol, A. Snapshot. John Fuller. NePoEA-2
Girl on the Milk-white Horse, The. Rachel Field. *Fr.* A Circus Garland. SoPo
Girl to Soldier on Leave. Isaac Rosenberg. MMA
Girl Walking. Charles G. Bell. ErPo
Girl Who Was Drowned at Onslow, The. *Unknown.* BSNS
Girl with Guitar. O. B. Hardison, Jr. PoNC
Girls, The/ of golden summers whirl. Siasconset Song. Philip Booth. CaFP; StP
Girls' Names. Eleanor Farjeon. BiCB
Girls scream. School's Out. W. H. Davies. BoC
Girt in dark growths, yet glimmering with one star. Sleepless Dreams. Dante Gabriel Rossetti. The House of Life, XXXIX. VP
Girtonian Funeral, A. *Unknown.* Par
Gisli, the Chieftain, *sel.* Isabella Valancy Crawford. Song of the Arrow, The. OBCV
Git yer little sage hens ready. At a Cowboy Dance. James Barton Adams [*wr.,* John Burton Adams]. RePo
Gita Govinda, *sel.* Jayadeva, *tr. fr. Sanskrit by* George Keyt. "Sandal and garment of yellow and lotus garlands upon his body of blue." ErPo
Gitanjali, *sels.* Rabindranath Tagore.
  For Strength ("This is my prayer to Thee"), XXXVI. MoRP
  I Have Got My Leave, XCIII. BoC
  If It Is Not My Portion, LXXIX. BoC
  Let This Be My Parting Word, XCVI. MoRP
  Song-Offering, A, LVII. SiGo
Giuseppe Caponsacchi. Robert Browning. The Ring and the Book, VI. VP
Give All to Love. Emerson. AP; PoLF; PoPo
Give him the darkest inch your shelf allows. George Crabbe. E. A. Robinson. AP; PP
Give me a Girle (if one I needs must meet). Women. William Cartwright. ErPo
Give Me a Kiss. *Unknown.* UnTE
Give me a man that is not dull. His Desire. Robert Herrick. CABA
Give me black souls. African Heaven. Frank Parkes. ACV
Give me hunger. At a Window. Carl Sandburg. MoLP
Give me kisses! Do not stay. To Lesbia. John Godfrey Saxe. UnTE
Give Me More Love. Thomas Carew. UnTE
  (Mediocrity in Love Rejected.) VaPo
Give me, my love, that billing kiss. The Kiss. Thomas Moore. BoLP
Give me my scallop-shell of quiet. The Passionate Man's Pilgrimage [*or* His Pilgrimage]. Sir Walter Ralegh. CABA; CBEP; DTC; EnRePo; FaPL; ILP; PoIE; TRV; WePo
Give me that man, that dares bestride. His Cavalier. Robert Herrick. GoJo
Give me the priest these graces shall possess. The Priest of Christ. Thomas Ken. TRV
"Give me the salt spray in my face." What the Red-haired Bo'sun Said. Charles H. Souter. PoAu-1
Give me to be Thy child, and learn for ever at Thy knee. Amor Dei. *Unknown.* BoC
Give me truths. Blight. Emerson. AP
Give me your hand old Revolutionary. The Centenarian's Story. Walt Whitman. CTC
Give money me, take friendship whoso list. Of Money. Barnabe Googe. EnRePo
Give My Heart a Song. Anna M. Gilleland. STF
Give Place, Ye Lovers. Earl of Surrey. EnRePo
Give to imagination some pure light. Modern Love, XXXVIII. George Meredith. VP
Give to me the life I love. The Vagabond. Robert Louis Stevenson. PoPo
Give to the Winds Thy Fears. Paul Gerhardt, *tr. fr. German by* John Wesley. PoPo
Give unto the Lord, O ye mighty, give unto the Lord glory and strength. The Twenty-fourth Psalm [*wr.*]. Psalm XXIX, Bible, *O. T.* PoPo
Give us a good digestion, Lord. A Prayer. *Unknown.* STF
Give us a virile Christ for these rough days. A Virile Christ. Rex Boundy. TRV
Give us a wrack or two, Good Lard. The Wreckers' Prayer. Theodore Goodridge Roberts. OBCV
Give Us Sober Men. Walter E. Isenhour. STF
"Give Us This Day Our Daily Bread." Maltbie D. Babcock. TRV
Give Way. Donald Finkel. NePoEA-2
Given, not lent. Unto Us a Son Is Given. Alice Meynell. MoRP
Giver of Life, The. *Unknown, tr. fr. Dahomean song by* Frances Herskovits. EaLo

Giving and Taking. James Kirkup. EaLo
Glad and blithe mote ye be. A Hymn of the Incarnation. *Unknown.* MeEL
Glad that I live, am I. The Sun and the Rain. Lizette Woodworth Reese. ThGo
Glad World. Robert D. Fitzgerald. ACV
Glance, The. George Herbert. MeP
Glance at the Album, A. Gray Burr. CoPo
Glass. Robert Francis. PP
Glass Blower, The. James Scully. MP
Glass Falling. Louis MacNeice. DaDu
Glass Houses. E. A. Robinson. MoRP
Glass is going down, The. The Sun. Glass Falling. Louis MacNeice. DaDu
Glass of Beer, A. James Stephens. CBEP; DTC
  (Righteous Anger.) PoPl
Glass of Water, The. Wallace Stevens. AP; CABA
Glass Poem. Karl Shapiro. PoIE
Glasses, The. Christian Morgenstern, *tr. fr. German by* Walter Kaufmann. TwGP
Gleam of the camp fires of emigrant trains, The. The Land We Adore. SGR
Gleaming sign in Mystic, Connecticut, A. Summer Excursion: Signs and Portents. Helen Bevington. PoNC
Glenlogie. *Unknown.* BuBa
Glitter of Pebbles. Dom Moraes. ACV
Glittering roofs are still with frost, The; each worn. A January Morning. Archibald Lampman. ACV; OBCV
Gloire de Dijon. D. H. Lawrence. ELP; ErPo
Glooms of the live-oaks, beautiful-braided and woven. The Marshes of Glynn. Sidney Lanier. AP; PoIE
Glories of Our Blood and State, The. James Shirley. *Fr.* The Contention of Ajax and Ulysses. CBEP; ILP (Death the Leveller.) GTBS-P
Glory and loveliness have passed away. Dedication: To Leigh Hunt, Esq. Keats. FoBA; OBNC
Glory be to God for dappled things. Pied Beauty. Gerard Manley Hopkins. CABA; CaFP; DiPo; EaLo; FoBA; GoJo; GTBS-P; ILP; MoRP; OBNC; PoDB; PoPl; PoPo; StP; TRV; VP; WePo
Glory Hallelujah! or, John Brown's Body. *Unknown.* ThLM
Glory of and Grace in the Church Set Out, The. Edward Taylor. *Fr.* Gods Determinations. AP
"Glory of Him who moves all things soe'er, The." Dante's Heaven. Dante. *Fr.* Divina Commedia: Paradiso. BoC
Glory of Nature, The. Frederick Tennyson. OBNC
Glory of Women. Siegfried Sassoon. MMA
Gloucester Moors. William Vaughn Moody. AP; FaPL
Glove, The. Robert Browning. MeP
Glove and the Lions, The. Leigh Hunt. SIV; StP
Glycine's Song. Samuel Taylor Coleridge. PoPl
  (Song: "Sunny shaft did I behold, A.") PoSC
Gnarled Riverina Gum-Tree, A. Ernest G. Moll. PoAu-2
Gnat, The. Joseph Beaumont. CBEP
Gnat, be my messenger, and fly. To a Gnat. *Unknown.* UnTE
Gnome, The. Harry Behn. SoPo
Gnosis. Christopher Pearse Cranch. ILP
  (Enosis.) PoIE
  (Stanza from an Early Poem.) AmLP
Go and ask Robin to bring the girls over. Vision by Sweetwater. John Crowe Ransom. AP
Go and Catch a Falling Star. John Donne. *See* Song: "Go and catch a falling star."
"Go away from my window, you'll waken my father." The Drowsy Sleeper (C *vers.*). *Unknown.* BSO
Go back, dark blood, to the springs from which you came. The Dream and the Blood. Louis Untermeyer. UnTE
"Go, build to me a little boat." Sweet William (D *vers.*). *Unknown.* BSO
Go By. Tennyson. OBNC
Go count the stars! Counting. Fenton Johnson. AmNP
Go Down Death (a Funeral Sermon). James Weldon Johnson. AmNP; TRV
Go Down, Moses. *Unknown.* EaLo
Go, dumb-born book. Envoi (1919). Ezra Pound. *Fr.* Hugh Selwyn Mauberley. CaFP; CTC; PoIE
Go fetch to me a pint o' wine. A Farewell. Burns. GTBS-P
Go, for they call you, Shepherd, from the hill. The Scholar Gipsy. Matthew Arnold. CABA; ILP; OBNC; VP
Go from me. Yet I feel that I shall stand. Sonnets from the Portuguese, VI. Elizabeth Barrett Browning. DiPo
Go, Grieving Rimes of Mine, to That Hard Stone. Petrarch, *tr. fr. Italian by* Morris Bishop. Sonnets to Laura: To Laura in Death, LX. AnML
Go! Heart, Hurt with Adversity. *Unknown.* MeEL
Go! little bill, and command me hertely. She Saw Me in Church. *Unknown.* MeEL
Go! little bill, and do me recommende. A Love Letter. *Unknown.* MeEL
Go, little quair. L'Envoy: To His Book. John Skelton. EnRePo
Go Little Ring. *Unknown.* CBEP
Go look in yonder cottage, all deserted and alone. Fair Fannie Moore. *Unknown.* BFSS

Go, lovely boy! to yonder tower. Verses Written during the War, 1756-1763. Thomas Osbert Mordaunt. CBEP

Go, Lovely Rose. Edmund Waller. CaFP; CBEP; CTC; GTBS-P; ILP; OnP; PoSa; StP (Song.) CABA; ELP; GoJo; PoIE; SeCP

Go, loving woodbine, clip with lovely grace. On a Pair of Garters. Sir John Davies. CBEP

Go, my songs, seek your praise from the young and from the intolerant. Ité. Ezra Pound. PP

Go, my songs, to the lonely and the unsatisfied. Commission. Ezra Pound. MP

Go, Nightly Cares. Unknown. EnRePo

Go out, good ships, across the tide. Ships. Nancy Byrd Turner. SoPo

Go out in this dear summertide. Paul Gerhardt, tr. fr. German by George C. Schoolfield. AGP

Go Out, Worm, with Nine Little Worms. Unknown, tr. fr. German by Ruth Yorck and Kenward Elmslie. Fr. Magic Spells. AnML

Go patter to lubbers and swabs, d'ye see. Poor Jack. Charles Dibdin. HaSV

Go! piteous hart, rased with dedly wo. Unfriendly Fortune. John Skelton. MeEL

Go prettie child and beare this Flower. To His Saviour, a Child; a Present, by a Child. Robert Herrick. SeCP

Go roll a prairie up like cloth. The Merry Miner. Constance Rourke. RePo

Go, Rose. John Gay. CBEP

Go, Sad Complaint. Charles d'Orléans(?). MeEL

Go sad or sweet or riotous with beer. The Old Women. George Mackay Brown. NePoEA-2

Go, Silly Worm. Joshua Sylvester. CBEP

Go, Songs. Francis Thompson. FaBV

Go, soul, the body's guest. The Lie. Sir Walter Ralegh. CBEP; CTC; EnRePo; OnP; PoIE

Go Take the World. Jay Macpherson. OBCV

Go through the gates with closed eyes. Close Your Eyes! Arna Bontemps. AmNP

"Go to jail. Go directly to jail. Do not pass go. Do not collect $200.00." The Book of Merlin. Jack Spicer. CoPo

Go to Saint Pether, with music. Unknown. BSO

Go to the western gate, Luke Havergal. Luke Havergal. E. A. Robinson. AP; CaFP; ILP; PoDB; PoIE

"Go way, go way," says she, "young man." The Six Questions. Unknown. BFSS

Go when the morning shineth. Secret Prayer. John Cross Belle. STF

Go Where Glory Waits Thee. Thomas Moore. OBNC

Goat, The. Umberto Saba, tr. fr. Italian by Thomas G. Bergin. CoIP

Goat, The. Unknown. PoLF

Goat Paths, The. James Stephens. GoJo; PoDB

Goblin lives in the chimney place, A. Fire on the Hearth. Rowena Bennett. RePo

Goblin Market. Christina Rossetti. VP

God. Gamaliel Bradford. TRV

God. James Larkin Pearson. PoNC

God and the Bayadeer, The. Goethe, tr. fr. German by Alexander Gode. AGP

God and the Holy Ghost. D. H. Lawrence. MoRP

God and yet a man, A. The Divine Paradox [or Wit Wonders]. Unknown. MeEL; PoIE

God appears, and God is Light. Blake. Fr. Auguries of Innocence. TRV

God approached dissolves into the air, The. Doctrinal Point. William Empson. ToPo

God banish from your house. Benediction. Stanley Kunitz. AnMoPo; MoRP

God Be in My Head. Unknown. Fr. Sarum Primer. BoC; EaLo; TRV

God be praised. Working with God. "George Eliot." Fr. Stradivarius. TRV

God bless my little kitchen. A Kitchen Prayer. M. Petersen. STF

"God bless the man who first invented sleep!" Early Rising. John Godfrey Saxe. PoLF

God bless the master of this house. Christmas Carol. Unknown. RePo

God breathe a blessing on. Bestiary. A. M. Klein. OBCV

God broke the years to hours and days. As Thy Days So Shall Thy Strength Be. "George Klingle." TRV

God came to Abram. Ballad of the Trial of Sodom. Vernon Watkins. MoRP

God can do it, A. But how can one follow. Sonnets to Orpheus, I, 3. Rainer Maria Rilke. TwGP

God Does Do Such Wonderful Things. Angela Morgan. TRV

God Doeth All Things Well. Unknown. STF

God fashioned the ship of the world carefully. The Black Riders, VI. Stephen Crane. AP

God-forgotten. Thomas Hardy. VP

God gave one little talent to his keeping. One-Talent Man. James Larkin Pearson. PoNC

God, give me sympathy and sense. A Prayer. Margaret Bailey. TRV

God, Give Us Men! Josiah Gilbert Holland. LV (Wanted.) TRV

God give you faith this coming year! Invocation for the New Year. Margaret D. Armstrong. STF

God gives to you another year. The New Year. Unknown. STF

God gives us joy that we might give. Life's Joy. Unknown. STF

God grant me privacy. Morning Prayer. Nissim Ezekiel. ACV

God guard me from those thoughts men think. A Prayer for Old Age. W. B. Yeats. AnMoPo

God has His best things for the few. His Best. Unknown. STF

God has His times: No power of man. On Time with God. C. D. Nutter. STF

God has no end of material. Little Things. Unknown. STF

God hath not promised. What God Hath Promised. Annie Johnson Flint. STF; TRV

God hath two wings, which he doth ever move. Mercy and Love. Robert Herrick. PoPo

God, How I Hate You. Arthur Graeme West. MMA

God! how they plague his life, the three damned sisters. The Little Brother. James Reeves. DTC

God I had forgotten how. New York—Albany. Lawrence Ferlinghetti. PoCh

God! I will pack, and take a train. The Old Vicarage, Grantchester. Rupert Brooke. WePo

God, if this were enough. If This Were Faith. Robert Louis Stevenson. Fr. Songs of Travel. OBNC

God in Whom We Trust, The. Unknown. STF

God in wrath, A. The Black Riders, XIX. Stephen Crane. AP

God is a proposition. Third Enemy Speaks. C. Day Lewis. Fr. The Magnetic Mountain. EaLo

God Is at the Anvil. Lew Sarett. TRV

God is coming! Apocalypse. Edith Lovejoy Pierce. MoRP

God Is in Every Tomorrow. Unknown. STF

God, Is, Like, Scissors. José Garcia Villa. EaLo

God Is Nigh. Unknown. TRV

God is our refuge and strength. Psalm XLVI, Bible, O.T. TRV

God is the Old Repair Man. The Old Repair Man. Fenton Johnson. AmNP

God Is There. Walter E. Isenhour. STF

God Is with Me. Oswald J. Smith. STF

God knew what lay before us. The Best for Us. Olive H. Burnett. STF

God knows, not I, the reason why. Faith. Margaret E. Sangster. TRV

God Knows the Answer. F. B. Whitney. STF

God Knows What He's About. Unknown. STF

God lay dead in heaven. The Black Riders, LXVII. Stephen Crane. AP

God Leads the Way. Cleanthes, tr. fr. Greek by C. C. Martindale. EaLo

God love you now, if no one else will ever. Ode for the American Dead in Korea. Thomas McGrath. PoPl

God made a little gentian. Emily Dickinson. FaBV

God Makes a Path. Roger Williams. TRV

God makes sech nights, all white an' still. The Courtin'. James Russell Lowell. Fr. The Biglow Papers. SIV

God Moves in a Mysterious Way. William Cowper. See Light Shining Out of Darkness.

God of Abraham, God of Isaac, God of Jacob. Fire. M. V. Woodgate. BoC

God of Comfort, The. Unknown. STF

God of Galaxies, The. Mark Van Doren. MoRP

God of Our Fathers. Daniel Crane Roberts. LV

God of our fathers, known of old. Recessional. Kipling. CABA; FaBV; OBNC; TRV

God of our fathers, Whose almighty hand. God of Our Fathers. Daniel Crane Roberts. LV

God of the Earth, the Sky, the Sea. Samuel Longfellow. TRV

God of the Meridian. Keats. StP

God Our Father, sel. Frederick William Faber. There's a Wideness in God's Mercy. ThGo, abr.; TRV (All-embracing, The, sl. diff.) TRV

God Pity Him. Unknown. STF

God prosper long our noble king. Chevy Chase. Unknown. BFSS

God rest you, merry Innocents. A Carol for Children. Ogden Nash. EaLo

"God save the King" the trumpets sound. Eastbourne. Eugenio Montale. CoIP

God save the Rights of Man! Ode. Philip Freneau. AP

God Send Us Men, sel. F. J. Gillman. "God send us men with hearts ablaze." TRV

God send us wit to banish far. Peace in the World. John Galsworthy. PoLF

God strengthen me to bear myself. The Battle Within. Christina Rossetti. TRV

God Suffices. St. Theresa of Avila. See St. Teresa's Book-Mark.

God the Architect. Harry Kemp. TRV
God, though this life is but a wraith. Prayer. Louis Unter-
    meyer. LV
God, to get the clay that stayed me. William Baylebridge. *Fr.*
    Life's Testament. PoAu-1
God Was in Christ. Second Corinthians, V: 18-21, Bible, *N.T.*
    TRV
God, we don't like to complain. Caliban in the Coal Mines.
    Louis Untermeyer. PoPl; PoPo; TRV; WePo
God who created me. Prayer. Henry Charles Beeching. SD
God, who touchest earth with beauty. The Camp Hymn. Mary
    S. Edgar. TRV
God with honor hang your head. At the Wedding March.
    Gerard Manley Hopkins. FoBA
God would come, the god would go, The. Man Is God's Nature.
    Richard Eberhart. EaLo; MoRP
Goddess, The. Thom Gunn. ToPo
Goddess, The. Denise Levertov. AP; PoCh
Goddis sonne is borne. A Cause for Wonder. *Unknown.* MeEL
Gode sire, pray ich thee. I Am from Ireland. *Unknown.*
    MeEL
Godfrey Gordon Gustavus Gore. William Brighty Rands.
    BBGG
Go-d'ling, *with music. Unknown.* BFSS
Godly Girzie. Burns. ErPo; UnTE
Godmother. Phyllis B. Morden. SoPo
Godolphin Horne. Hilaire Belloc. DTC
Gods and Goddesses, Those Great, The. Christine de Pisan,
    tr. fr. French by Dwight Durling. AnML
God's angry man, His crotchety scholar. The Thunderer.
    Phyllis McGinley. EaLo
God's body is all space. Essay on Deity. Elder Olson. MoRP
God's Call. *Unknown.* STF
God's Dark. John Martin. PoLF
Gods Determinations Touching His Elect, *sels.* Edward Taylor.
    Glory of and Grace in the Church Set Out, The. AP
    Joy of Church Fellowship Rightly Attended, The. AP;
        CBEP
    Preface, The: "Infinity, when all things it beheld." AmLP;
        AP; ILP
God's Education. Thomas Hardy. MoRP
God's Eye Is on the Sparrow. Bertha Meyer. STF
God's Funeral. Thomas Hardy. PoDB
God's Garden. Richard Burton. TRV
God's Grandeur. Gerard Manley Hopkins. BoC; CABA;
    CaFP; DiPo; FoBA; ILP; MoRP; OBNC; PoDB; PoIE;
    PoPo; StP; VP
Gods Have Heard My Vows, The. *Unknown.* EnRePo
God's Ideal Mother. Cora M. Pinkham. STF
God's Judgment on a Wicked Bishop. Robert Southey.
    OnMSP
God's Key. *Unknown.* STF
Gods of fortune had quit my abode, The. Bonnie Black Bess.
    Unknown. BFSS
Gods of Greece, The. Heine, *tr. fr. German by* Walter Kauf-
    mann. TwGP
Gods of the Dana, The. Leah Bodine Drake. FiSC
God's Pay. *Unknown.* STF
God's Presence Makes My Heaven. Oswald J. Smith. STF
God's Residence. Emily Dickinson. TRV
God's Saints. Henry Vaughan. TRV
    ("God's Saints are shining lights.") ThGo
God's Thanks to Job. Robert Frost. *Fr.* A Masque of Reason.
    MoRP
God's Treasure. "A. M. N." STF
God's Will Is Best ("God's will is better than our will").
    Thelma Curtis. STF
God's Word. John Clifford. TRV
God's World. Edna St. Vincent Millay. FaBV; LV; MoRP;
    PoPl; PoSC; RePo
Goe happy rose, and enterwove. To the Rose. Robert Herrick.
    SeCP
Goethe in Weimar sleeps, and Greece. Memorial Verses.
    Matthew Arnold. CABA; PP
Goethe said that 'twixt embraces. Not Lotte. Katherine
    Hoskins. ErPo
Gog. Ted Hughes. AnMoPo
Goin' down the road, Lawd. Bound No'th Blues. Langston
    Hughes. AmNP
Going, The. Thomas Hardy. ELP; FaPL; StP
Going. Robert Kelly. CoPo
Going. Philip Larkin. ToPo
Going Back Again. "Owen Meredith." EvOK
Going home by lamplight across Boston Common. A Revivalist
    in Boston. Adrienne Cecile Rich. EaLo
Going Home with Jesus. Walter E. Isenhour. STF
Going to him! Happy letter! Emily Dickinson. DiPo
Going to Sleep in the Country. Howard Moss. PoCh; StP
Going Too Far. Mildred Howells. OnMSP
Going towards Spain. Barnabe Googe. EnRePo
Gold and all this werdis win. Crucified to the World. *Un-
    known.* MeEL
Gold as an infant's humming dream. Long Summer. Laurie
    Lee. ToPo

Gold-colored skin of my Lebanese friends, The. A Trip to
    Four or Five Towns. John Logan. AmPC
Gold-headed Finn has ridden away. The Last Pagan Mourns
    for Dark Rosaleen. Joseph Payne Brennan. FiSC
Gold-headed rose for bees to sup. The Flowers in a Meadow.
    Frances Cornford. ThGo
"Gold is for the mistress—silver for the maid." Cold Iron.
    Kipling. OnMSP
Gold Lake and Gold Bluff. John A. Stone. SGR
Gold locks, and black locks. The Barber's. Walter de la Mare.
    GoJo; SoPo
Gold moons. Scissors and Paste. Zoe Kincaid Brockman. *Fr.*
    Three Cinquains. PoNC
Gold of heaven, The. Love. Tom Dent. NNP
Gold-tinted Dragon, The. Karla Kuskin. SoPo
Golden Age, The. Tasso, *tr. fr. Italian by* Leigh Hunt. RBL
Golden Bird, The. Rex Ingamells. PoAu-2
Golden Bough. Elinor Wylie. LV
Golden crocus reaches up, The. The Crocus. Walter Crane.
    SoPo
Golden eagle swooped out of the sky, The. Salmon Drowns
    Eagle. Malcolm Lowry. OBCV
Golden eve is all astir, The. Theme. James Stephens. ACV
Golden Glove, The, *with music. Unknown.* BSNS
Golden Gullies of the Palmer, The. *Unknown.* PoAu-1
Golden Hour, The. Thomas Moore. *Fr.* Lalla Rookh. OBNC
Golden Journey to Samarkand, The, *sel.* James Elroy Flecker.
    Prologue: "We who with songs beguile your pilgrimage." GoJo
Golden light has presently, The. Evening Song. Philip von
    Zesen. AGP
Golden Mean, The. Horace, *tr. fr. Latin by* Margaret M. Fitz-
    gerald. Odes, II, 10. SiGo
Golden-rod is yellow, The. *See* Goldenrod is yellow, The.
Golden Rule, The. James Wells. STF
Golden Slumbers. Thomas Dekker, *and others. Fr.* The Pleas-
    ant Comedy of Patient Grissell. ELP
Golden sun that brings the day, The. In Praise of the Sun.
    "A. W." CTC
Golden Spurs, The. *Unknown, tr. fr. Greek by* Louis Unter-
    meyer. UnTE
Golden stars in thousands shimmer. The Stars. Robert
    Hamerling. AGP
Golden strand that weaves through tapestry, A. The Father's
    Gold. *Unknown.* STF
Golden Vanity, The. *Unknown.* CBEP; ELP; HaSV; WiR
Golden Wedding, *sel.* Alan Mulgan.
    "Breaking a line of pines, a wide white gate." ACV
Golden-winged, silver-winged. Birds of Paradise. Christina
    Rossetti. VP
Golden Wings. William Morris. OBNC
Goldenhair. James Joyce. *See* Lean Out of the Window.
Goldenrod [*or* Golden-rod] is yellow, The. September. Helen
    Hunt Jackson. GoJo; PoLF
Goldyn Targe, The, *sel.* William Dunbar.
    "O reverend Chaucere, rose of rethoris all." PP
Golf Links [Lie So Near the Mill], The. Sarah N. Cleghorn.
    PoLF; PoPl; PoPo
Golfers. Irving Layton. SD
Golgotha. John Hall Wheelock. MoRP
Golgotha Is a Mountain. Arna Bontemps. AmNP
Gondoliers, The, *sel.* W. S. Gilbert.
    Grand Inquisitor's Song, The. OnMSP
Gone. Mary Elizabeth Coleridge. OBNC
Gone. Walter de la Mare. GoJo
Gone, The. Jesse Stuart. FiSC
Gone, I say, and walk from church. The Truth the Dead
    Know. Anne Sexton. NePoEA-2; ToPo
Gone in the Wind. James Clarence Mangan. CBEP
Gone is the city, gone the day. The Right Kind of People.
    Edwin Markham. PoPo; SIV
Gone were but the Winter. Spring Quiet. Christina Rossetti.
    GTBS-P; ThGo
Gone while your tastes were keen to you. For E. McC. Ezra
    Pound. SD
"Goneys an' gullies an' all o' the birds o' the sea." Sea-
    Change. John Masefield. HaSV
Good aged Bale, that with thy hoary hairs. To Doctor Bale.
    Barnabe Googe. EnRePo
Good and Bad Children. Robert Louis Stevenson. BBGG;
    ThGo
Good and great God, can I not think of Thee. To Heaven.
    Ben Jonson. EnRePo; PoIE; SeCP
Good and great God! How should I fear. No Coming to God
    without Christ. Robert Herrick. TRV
Good are attracted by Men's perceptions, The. Motto to the
    Songs of Innocence and of Experience. Blake. FoBA
Good Bishop Valentine. Eleanor Farjeon. PoSC
Good-bye. Emerson. FaPL
Good-bye by er Howdy-do. James Whitcomb Riley. CTC
Good-bye, good-bye to Summer! Robin Redbreast. William
    Allingham. WePo
Good-Bye My Fancy! Walt Whitman. AP
Good-by, old Paint, I'm leaving Cheyenne. Old Paint. *Un-
    known.* BFSS

Good-bye, proud world! I'm going home. Good-bye. Emerson. FaPL
Goodbye the Office. Richard Lyons. PtTo
Goodbye to the Aegean. On the Athenian Dead at Ecbatana. Plato. PoPl
Good Christians all, both great and small, I pray you lend an ear. The Avondale Mine Disaster. *Unknown.* ThLM
Good Counsel to a Young Maid. Thomas Carew. CBEP; ErPo
Good day, good day. In Honour of Christmas. *Unknown.* MeEL
Good day, Sire Christemasse our king. In Honour of Christmas. *Unknown.* MeEL
Good father, I have sent for you because. The Merry Little Maid and Wicked Little Monk. *Unknown.* ErPo
Good for Nothing Man, *sels.* Kenneth Pitchford.
  Blues Ballad. CoPo
  Jacqueline Gray. CoPo
  Onion Skin, The. CoPo
  Pickup in Tony's Hashhouse. CoPo; ErPo
  Young Buck's Sunday Blues. CoPo
Good Friday. George Herbert. FoBA
Good Friday, *sel.* John Masefield.
  "Wild duck, stringing through the sky, The." BoC
  (Madman's Song, The.) ACV
Good Friday. Christina Rossetti. TRV; VP
Good Friday. *Unknown.* BoC
Good Friday, 1613. Riding Westward. John Donne. DiPo; EnRePo; FoBA; MeP; PoIE; SeCP; StP
Good Friday was the day. The Martyr. Herman Melville. LiPo; PoIE
Good girls are down from the Bronx, The. Greenwich Village Saturday Night. Irving Feldman. AmPC
Good God, What a Night That Was. Petronius Arbiter, *tr. fr. Latin by* Kenneth Rexroth. ErPo
Good grey [*or* gray] guardians of art, The. Museum Piece. Richard Wilbur. PoIE; PoPl
Good intent of God became the Christ, The. The Christ. John Oxenham. TRV
Good king had three daughters, The. Delgadina. *Unknown.* AnML
Good King Wenceslas. *Unknown, tr. fr. Latin by* John Mason Neale. OnMSP
Good Lady. A Negro Peddler's Song. Fenton Johnson. AmNP
Good Little Girl, The. A. A. Milne. BBGG
Good Lord Nelson had a swollen gland, The. A Ballad of the Good Lord Nelson. Lawrence Durrell. ErPo
Good Man in Hell, The. Edwin Muir. MoRP
Good Master and Mistress. *Unknown.* EvOK
"Good men and true! in this house who dwell." The Croppy Boy. William B. McBurney. SIV
Good Morning. Muriel Sipe. SoPo
"Good-morning; good-morning!" the General said. The General. Siegfried Sassoon. FaBV; MMA
Good morning, Life—and all. A Greeting. W. H. Davies. MoRP
"Good morning, pretty Polly, we have met in good time." Pretty Polly. *Unknown.* BSO
Good morning to you, Lord of the world! Invocation. Levi Isaac of Berditshev. EaLo
Good Morrow, The. John Donne. CABA; CBEP; DiPo; EnRePo; FaBV; PoIE; SeCP; StP; UnTE
"Good morrow, little rose-bush!" The Sweet, Red Rose. Mary Mapes Dodge. BiCB
Good morrow to the day so fair. The Mad Maid's Song. Robert Herrick. WiR
Good news. It seems he loved them after all. A Song about Major Eatherly. John Wain. CABL; ToPo
Good news to tell! The Corner. Walter de la Mare. BiCB
Good Night! Eleanor Farjeon. ThGo
Good Night! Thomas Hood. SoPo
Good Night! Victor Hugo, *tr. fr. French.* SoPo
Good Night! John Banister Tabb. ThGo
Good-night! Good night! Good Night. Victor Hugo. SoPo
Good-night to the Season. Winthrop Mackworth Praed. OBNC
Good of the Chaplain to enter Lone Bay. Billy in the Darbies. Herman Melville. *Fr.* Billy Budd. CBEP
Good Old Days of '50, '1, and '2, The. J. Riley Mains. SGR
Good old pope does nothing now but eat, The. Pope Clement's Illness. Francesco Berni. RBL
Good people all, give ear, I pray. Kirtle Gaol. *Unknown.* BSNS
Good people all, of every sort. Elegy on the Death of a Mad Dog. Goldsmith. *Fr.* The Vicar of Wakefield. CBEP; PoPo; PoSa; RoGo
Good people all, with one accord. An Elegy on That Glory of Her Sex, Mrs. Mary Blaize. Goldsmith. AmML
Good rain knows when to fall, The. The Rain at Night. Tu Fu. SiGo
Good reason thou allow. Of the Clock and the Cock. George Turberville. EnRePo
Good Rich Man, The. G. K. Chesterton. DTC

Good Shepherd, have You skipped away to leave. At the Ascension. Luis de León. AnSP
Good Sportsmanship. Richard Armour. LV
Good Susan, Be as Secret as You Can. *Unknown.* ErPo
Good Sword and a trusty hand, A. The Song of the Western Men [*or* And Shall Trelawny Die?]. Robert Stephen Hawker. CBEP; EvOK; OBNC; RoGo
Good Taste. Christopher Logue. DaDu
Good Thanksgiving, A. "Marian Douglas." PoLF
Good Thing Is, We Know, The. Antonio Machado, *tr. fr. Spanish by* William M. Davis. AnSP
Good Tidings of Great Joy! Mrs. C. F. Alexander. ThGo
Good was the girl Eulalia. The Sequence of Saint Eulalia. *Unknown.* AnML
Goodness gracious sakes alive! Tardiness. Gelett Burgess. BBGG
Goody Blake and Harry Gill, *sel.* Wordsworth.
  "Oh! what's the matter? what's the matter?" Par
Goody O'Grumpity. Carol Ryrie Brink. RePo
Goole Captain, The. Leonard Clark. DaDu
Goops they lick their fingers, The. Table Manners. Gelett Burgess. BBGG
Goose Fish, The. Howard Nemerov. CaFP
Goose that laid the golden egg, The. Ars Poetica. X. J. Kennedy. ErPo; PP
Gordian Knot, The. *Unknown.* UnTE
Gordon Childe. David Martin. PoAu-2
Gorilla lay on his back, The. Au Jardin des Plantes. John Wain. NePoEA-2
Gospel According to You, The. *Unknown.* STF
Gospel of Labor, The. Henry van Dyke. TRV
Gothic looks solemn, The. On Oxford. Keats. Par
Gourd-Heads, The. William D. Barney. FiSC
Gowden Locks of Anna, The. Burns. *See* Anna.
Goya. Conrad Aiken. AmLP
Grace. Walter de la Mare. ThGo
Grace, A. Thomas Tiplady. TRV
Grace Ananne [*or* GraceAnAnne]. Lysbeth Boyd Borie. BiCB; RePo
Grace and beauty has the maid. Song [*or* Cantiga]. Gil Vicente. RBL; SiGo
Grace before Sleep. Sara Teasdale. MoRP
Grace at Evening. Edwin McNeill Poteat. TRV
Graceful and sure with youth, the skaters glide. The Skaters. John Williams. SD
Graceful as acorus [*or* lotus flower. Aliter. Confucius. *Fr.* The Classic Anthology: Songs of Ch'en. CTC
Gracious Moonlight. Dante Gabriel Rossetti. The House of Life, XX. VP
Graeme and Bewick. *Unknown.* CBEP
Graffiti. Edward Field. CoPo
Grammarian's Funeral, A. Robert Browning. DiPo; VP
Grand Finale. Sara King Carleton. FiSC
Grand Inquisitor's Song, The. W. S. Gilbert. *Fr.* The Gondoliers. OnMSP
Grand Old Duke of York, The. Mother Goose. SoPo
Granddaughter. Eleanor Ross Taylor. *Fr.* Family Bible. PoNC
Grandfather Frog. Louise Seaman Bechtel. RePo
Grandfather Watts's Private Fourth. H. C. Bunner. PoSC
Grandfather's Ghost. Joseph Payne Brennan. FiSC
Grandmamma's Birthday. Hilaire Belloc. PoPl
Grandma's Song. *Unknown. See* Little Johnny Green.
Grandmother and Grandson. W. S. Merwin. NePoEA-2
Grandmother's mother: her age, I guess. Dorothy Q. Oliver Wendell Holmes. AP
Grandmother's Visit. William Wise. RePo
Grandparents. Robert Lowell. ToPo
Granite. Rainer Brambach, *tr. fr. German by* Christopher Middleton. MGP
Grant, Lord, that through the printed page. Call to Conflict. *Unknown.* STF
Grape is ripened, tilled the field, The. Quiet. Giuseppe Ungaretti. PoPl
Grapes. Pushkin, *tr. fr. Russian by* Babette Deutsch. SiGo
Grapes are ripe, the frost is near, The. Pastoral X. Robert Hillyer. LOW
Grass. Carl Sandburg. FaBV; PoLF; PoPl; PoPo
Grass and Milk. Alfonso Gatto, *tr. fr. Italian by* John A. Scott. CoIP
Grass is short and newly yellow-green, The. Return to Lane's Island. William H. Matchett. PoPl
Grass is very green, my friend, The. A Unison. William Carlos Williams. PoIE
Grass of levity. Mortality. *Unknown.* CBEP
Grass so little has to do, The. Emily Dickinson. RePo
Grasshopper, The. Abraham Cowley. WiR
Grasshopper, grasshopper, hop-o-the grasses. Grasshopper Hop-o-the Grasses. Grace Taber Hallock. RePo
Grasshopper Green. *Unknown.* SoPo
Grasshopper Hop-o-the Grasses. Grace Taber Hallock. RePo
Grasshopper, the grasshopper, The. An Explanation of the Grasshopper. Vachel Lindsay. SoPo

Grasshopper, your tiny song. Earth. John Hall Wheelock. MoRP
Gratiana Dancing and Singing. Richard Lovelace. CBEP
Gratitude. William Cornish. See Pleasure It Is.
Gratitude. Christopher Smart. Fr. Hymns for the Amusement of Children. EiCP
Grave, The, sel. Robert Blair. "Whilst some affect the sun and some the shade." EnPE
Grave, The. T. Gwynn Jones, tr. fr. Welsh by Ernest Rhys. SiGo
Grave, A. Marianne Moore. CABA; PoIE
Grave wise man that had a great rich lady, A. Of an Heroical Answer of a Great Roman Lady to Her Husband. Sir John Harington. ErPo
Gravely she goes about her little duties. The Elfin Wife. "Jake Falstaff." BoC
Graves by the river must have melted in, The. An Exceeding Great Army. Ethan Ayer. FiSC
Graveyard, The. Jane Cooper. NePoEA-2
Gray. See also Grey.
Gray Horizons. Sam Ragan. PoNC
Gray is the sea; the shore is gray. The Town. Theodor Storm. AGP
Gray sea and the long black land, The. See Grey sea . . .
Gray Squirrel, The. Humbert Wolfe. GoJo
Gray Whales are going south: I see their fountains, The. Ocean. Robinson Jeffers. AP
Great Adventurer, The. Unknown. See Love Will Find Out the Way.
Great are the Fallen of Thermopylae. The Greek Dead at Thermopylae. Simonides. SiGo
Great Auk's Ghost, The. Ralph Hodgson. PoPl
Great Bear, The. John Hollander. MP; NePoEA-2
Great Blue Heron, The. Carolyn Kizer. NePoEA-2
Great brass bell of austerity, Sousa. Edward Dorn. CoPo
Great cathedral stood silent and calm, The. The Actor. James Sexton Layton. PoNC
Great Chinese Dragon, The. Lawrence Ferlinghetti. ToPo
Great Churches. Unknown. STF
Great Discovery, The. Eleanor Farjeon. PoSC
Great Farm. Philip Booth. PoPl
Great God, I Ask Thee for No Meaner Pelf. Henry David Thoreau. AP
(My Prayer.) PoPl
Great God of Hope, how green Thy trees. Hope. Amy Carmichael. TRV
Great God Pan, The. Elizabeth Barrett Browning. See Musical Instrument, The.
Great-Grandmother, The. Robert Graves. DTC
Great Hunt, The. Carl Sandburg. MoLP
Great Is My Envy of You, Earth, in Your Greed. Petrarch, tr. fr. Italian by Edwin Morgan. Sonnets to Laura: To Laura in Death, XXXII. AnML
Great Lover, The. Rupert Brooke. WePo
Great Magicians, The. C. Day Lewis. EaLo
Great Panjandrum [Himself], The. Samuel Foote. Par; PoLF
Great Silkie of Sule Skerrie, The. Unknown. BuBa
Great Sled-Makers, The. Kenneth Patchen. ToPo
Great spirits now on earth are sojourning. Addressed to Haydon. Keats. OBNC
Great Sun, flame of Christ. Jean de la Ceppède. Fr. Théorèmes Spirituels. RBL
Great Things. Thomas Hardy. GTBS-P
Great Time, A. W. H. Davies. WePo
Great Wave, The: Hokusai. Donald Finkel. PoPl
Great Waves Breaking with a Roar. Gustavo Adolfo Bécquer, tr. fr. Spanish by John Haines. EnSP
Great wind blowing, raging sea, A. Comforted. Amy Carmichael. TRV
Great Zeus, beset by love and lechery. Matter of Taste. Unknown. UnTE
Greater Love. Wilfred Owen. ACV; GTBS-P
Greatest City, The. Walt Whitman. RePo
Greatest imposition that the public ever saw, The. Humbug Steamship Companies. John A. Stone. SGR
Greatest poem ever known, The. To a Child. Christopher Morley. BiCB
Greatest Show on Earth. Felicia Lamport. LV
Greedy little sparrow. Birds in the Garden. Unknown. ThGo
Greek Dead at Thermopylae, The. Simonides, tr. fr. Greek by T. F. Higham. SiGo
Greeks were wrong who said our eyes have rays, The. Lamarck Elaborated. Richard Wilbur. AP
Green and Pleasant Land, A. John Peale Bishop. PoPl
Green are the woods where the lovers wander. Green Woods. Elizabeth J. Coatsworth. FiSC
Green Autumn Stubble, The. Unknown, tr. fr. Irish by Patrick Browne. SiGo
Green be the turf above thee. On the Death of Joseph Rodman Drake. Fitz-Greene Halleck. AmLP; FaPL
Green Beds (B and C vers., with music). Unknown. BSNS
(Green Bed, The.) BSO

(Liverpool Landlady, The, A vers.) BSNS
Green catalpa tree has turned, The. April Inventory. W. D. Snodgrass. AP; CABA; MP; PoPl
Green Door, The. Leah Bodine Drake. BiCB
Green Dryad's Plea, The. Thomas Hood. Fr. The Plea of the Midsummer Fairies. OBNC
Green embellishment of human life. Hope. Sister Juana Inés de la Cruz. AnSP
Green Fields and Meadows, The (A vers., with music). Unknown. BSO
Green goods, fruit, the colors of the fairest. Fruit and Greens. Umberto Saba. CoIP
Green, Green Is El Aghir. Norman Cameron. MoBS
Green Grow the Lilacs, with music. Unknown. BFSS
Green Grow the Rashes. Burns. CABA; CTC; EnPE; ErPo; PoIE
(Green Grow the Rashes, O.) EiCP; UnTE
Green Grows the Laurel (A vers., with music). Unknown. BFSS
Green. I want you green. Somnambulist Ballad. Federico García Lorca. AnSP
Green is the plane-tree in the square. A London Plane-Tree. Amy Levy. WePo
Green Knight's Farewell to Fancy, The. George Gascoigne. EnRePo
Green Leaf, The. Louis Zukofsky. CoPo
Green level of lily leaves, A. To Paint a Water Lily. Ted Hughes. PP
Green light floods the city square, The. Sunken Evening. Laurie Lee. ToPo
Green Linnet, The. Wordsworth. CBEP; GTBS-P
Green little vaulter in the sunny grass. To the Grasshopper and the Cricket. Leigh Hunt. OBNC
Green Man. Lawrence Durrell. AnMoPo
Green Melody. Andreas Okopenko, tr. fr. German by Christopher Middleton. MGP
Green Mossy Banks of the Lea, The, with music. Unknown. BSNS
Green Mountain Boys, The. Bryant. PoPl
Green Place, A. William Jay Smith. RePo
Green River. Bryant. AP
Green road lies this way, The. El Camino Verde. Paul Blackburn. CoPo
Green rushes with red shoots. Plucking the Rushes. Unknown. SiGo
Green rustlings, more than regal charities. Royal Palm. Hart Crane. AP; PoIE
Green-shadowed people sit, or walk in rings. Spring. Philip Larkin. ACV
Green Shepherd, The. Louis Simpson. MP
Green Snake, when I hung you round my neck. To the Snake. Denise Levertov. NePoEA-2; PoIE; ToPo
Green stands a fir tree, who. Think of It, My Soul. Eduard Möricke. AGP
Green Stream, A. Wang Wei, tr. fr. Chinese by Witter Bynner and Kiang Kang-hu. SD
Green Woods. Elizabeth J. Coatsworth. FiSC
Green-yellow is the light. Love Is a Bullet. Frank Borden Hanes. PoNC
Greene's Vision, sel. Robert Greene.
Description of Sir Geoffrey Chaucer, The. CTC
(Sir Geoffrey Chaucer.) WePo
Greenland Fishery, The. Unknown. HaSV
Greensleeves. Unknown. CBEP; PoIE; UnTE
Greenwich Village Saturday Night. Irving Feldman. AmPC
Greenwood Siding, The, with music. Unknown. BSNS
Greeting, A. W. H. Davies. MoRP
Greeting. Unknown. ThGo
Gregory Griggs. Laura E. Richards. SoPo
Grene groweth the holy. Love Ever Green. King Henry VIII(?). MeEL
Grevus is my sorrow. Unkindness Has Killed Me. Unknown. MeEL
Grey. See also Gray.
Grey as a guinea-fowl is the rain. Kitchen Song. Edith Sitwell. DaDu
Grey brick upon brick. Dublin. Louis MacNeice. ACV
Grey Cock, The. Unknown. ELP
Grey day left the dusk in doubt, The. Winter Night. Robert Fitzgerald. PoPl
Grey horse, Death, in profile bears the young Titus, The. The Polish Rider. Derek Walcott. ToPo
Grey [or Gray] sea and the long black land, The. Meeting at Night. Robert Browning. BoLP; CaFP; CBEP; DiPo; ELP; FaBV; HaSV; OBNC; PoPl; PoPo; WePo
Grey winter hath gone, like a wearisome guest. September in Australia. Henry Kendall. PoAu-1
Grey woods within whose silent shade. The Ocean Wood. Lord De Tabley. CBEP
Grief. Elizabeth Barrett Browning. CBEP; OBNC; PoLF; StP
Griesly Wife, The. John Manifold. MoBS
Grievance, A. J. K. Stephen. Par

Grieve Not the Holy Spirit, &c. George Herbert. MeP
Grieve not too much, my Albius, since Glycera is no longer. It Always Happens. Horace. Odes, I, 33. UnTE
"Grill me some bones," said the Cobbler. At the Keyhole. Walter de la Mare. DTC
Grim and Gloomy. James Reeves. RePo
Grim Cotton Mather. Cotton Mather. Stephen Vincent Benét. ThLM
Grim messenger of God. Malachi. Earl Marlatt. MoRP
Grizzly Bear. Mary Austin. GoJo; SoPo
Grizzly Bear is huge and wild. Infant Innocence. A. E. Housman. DTC; LV
Groggy fighter on his knees, The. Athletes. Walker Gibson. SD
Groping along the tunnel, step by step. The Rear-Guard. Siegfried Sassoon. ACV
Gross sun squats above, The. Song. Dom Moraes. NePoEA-2
Grotesque ("Dr. Newman with the crooked pince-nez"). Robert Graves. DTC
Grotesque ("Sir John addressed the Snake-god in his temple"). Robert Graves. DTC
Grotesque Love-Letter, A. Unknown. MeEL
Groundhog, The. Richard Eberhart. AmLP; CABA; DTC; ILP; PoIE; PoSa; StP; ToPo
Ground Hog Day. Marnie Pomeroy. PoSC
Group of jolly cowboys, A. When the Work's All Done This Fall. Unknown. BFSS
Groves of Blarney, The. Richard Alfred Millikin. CBEP
Groves were God's first temples, The. A Forest Hymn. Bryant. AP
Grow old along with me! Rabbi Ben Ezra. Robert Browning. BiCB; FaBV; OBNC; PoPl; TRV; VP
Grow Weary if you will, let me be sad. Lesbia. Richard Aldington. PoLF
Growing. Frances Frost. BiCB
Growing Old. Rose Henderson. BiCB
Growing Old. Unknown, tr. fr. Irish by Frank O'Connor. ErPo
Growing old but not retiring. Ever On. Unknown. STF
Growing Smiles. Unknown. PoLF
Growing Up. Harry Behn. BiCB; SoPo
Growing Up. Arthur Guiterman. BiCB
Growing Up. A. A. Milne. BiCB; ThGo
Growing Up. Unknown. BiCB
Growing Up. Edna Kingsley Wallace. BiCB
Growltiger's Last Stand. T. S. Eliot. RoGo
Growth of Sym, The. C. J. Dennis. ACV
Gr-r-r—there go, my heart's abhorrence! Soliloquy of the Spanish Cloister. Robert Browning. CABA; CaFP; DiPo; ILP; PoIE; VP
Gryll Grange, sel. Thomas Love Peacock. Love and Age. OBNC
Guard of Honor. Robert Hazel. OPP
Guard Thy Tongue. Alice M. Barr. STF
Guardian Angels of Men. Spenser. See And Is There Care in Heaven?
Guardian Angels of the Creatures. Blake. See Night.
Guardians, The. Geoffrey Hill. NePoEA-2
Gude Lord Graeme is to Carlisle gane. Graeme and Bewick. Unknown. CBEP
Guest, The. Wendell Berry. AP
Guest, The. Unknown. BoC; EaLo
(Guests.) EvOK
(Preparations.) CBEP; WePo
Guest Room. Olive Tilford Dargan. PoNC
Guests. Unknown. See Guest, The.
Guests, The. Louis Zukofsky. CoPo
Guide, O Christ, this little hand. Unknown. ThGo
Guido, I should wish that you, Lapo and I. To Guido Cavalcanti. Dante. AnML
Guidwife when your guidman's from home. Could You Do That? Burns. UnTE
Guilty. Marguerite Wilkinson. TRV
Guinevere, sel. Tennyson. Fr. Idylls of the King. "I made them lay their hands in mine and swear." TRV
Guirlande de Julie, sels. Tr. fr. French. RBL
Amarante, L'. Jean Ogier de Gombauld, tr. by Harold M. Priest.
Couronne Impériale, La. Claude de Malleville, tr. by Judith McDowell.
Madrigal: "Receive, oh Nymph adorable." Charles de Sainte-Maure, Duc de Montausier, tr. by Harold M. Priest.
Narcisse, Le. Charles de Sainte-Maure, Duc de Montausier, tr. by Harold M. Priest.
Violette, La. Jean Desmarets de Saint-Sorlin, tr. by Judith McDowell.
Guiseppe, da barber, ess greata for mash. Mia Carlotta. Thomas Daly. WePo
Guitar, The. Federico García Lorca, tr. fr. Spanish by Rachel Benson and Robert O'Brien. AnSP
Guitar Lament for a Mountain Boy. Carl De Suze. CaFP
Gull Lake set in the rolling prairie. At Gull Lake: August, 1810. Duncan Campbell Scott. OBCV

Gull rides on the ripples of a dream, A. A Walk in Late Summer. Theodore Roethke. PoDB
Gull, up close, A. Seagulls. John Updike. StP
Gulliver. Kenneth Slessor. ACV
Gulls spiral high above. Dayley Island. Frederick Seidel. CoPo
Gun explodes them, The. The Sprinters. Lee Murchison. SD
Gun full swing the swimmer catapults and cracks, The. 400-Meter Freestyle. Maxine W. Kumin. SD
Gunga Din. Kipling. FaPL; OnMSP; PoPl; PoPo; WePo
Guppy, The. Ogden Nash. WePo
Gusts of Winter Are Gone, The. Meleager, tr. fr. Greek by L. P. Chamberlayne. SiGo
Guvener B. is a sensible man. What Mr. Robinson Thinks. James Russell Lowell. Fr. The Biglow Papers. LV
Gwalia Deserta, sel. Idris Davies. "O what can you give me?" DTC
Gypsies. See also Gipsies.
Gypsies. John Clare. CBEP
Gypsies in the Wood. Unknown. DTC
Gypsies three I found one day. The Three Gypsies. Nikolaus Lenau. AGP
Gypsy, a gypsy, A. Being Gypsy. Barbara Young. SoPo
Gypsy Davy. Unknown. See Gypsy Laddie, The.
Gypsy Jane. William Brighty Rands. SoPo
Gypsy Laddie, The (A vers., with music). Unknown. BSO (Gypsy Davy, B vers., with music.) BSO
Gypsy's Wedding Day, The, with music. Unknown. BSO
Gypsy's Window, The. Denise Levertov. ToPo
Gyres, The. W. B. Yeats. GTBS-P

H

H-Bomb Evening Down, An. H. A. Sieber. PoNC
H. Communion, The. George Herbert. MeP
H.M.S. Glory at Sydney. Charles Causley. HaSV
H.M.S. Pinafore, sel. W. S. Gilbert. When I Was a Lad. PoPo
(Ruler of the Queen's Navee, The.) DiPo
H. Scriptures, The. George Herbert. MeP
H. Scriptures. Henry Vaughan. MeP
H——, thou return'st from Thames, whose naiads long. An Ode on the Popular Superstitions of the Highlands of Scotland. William Collins. EiCP
Ha! are there wood-ghosts in this solitude. La Belle Sauvage. John Hunter-Duvar. Fr. De Roberval. OBCV
Ha ha! ha ha! this world doth pass. Faradiddle Dyno. Unknown. CBEP
Ha' we lost the goodliest fere o' all. Ballad of the Goodly Fere. Ezra Pound. MoBS; PoSA
Ha! wh'are [or where] ye gaun, ye crowlan [or crowlin'] ferlie! To a Louse, on Seeing One on a Lady's Bonnet at Church. Burns. ILP; OnP; PoPo
Habana. Julian Bond. NNP
Habit of Perfection, The. Gerard Manley Hopkins. FoBA; ILP; PoIE; VP
Habits of the Hippopotamus. Arthur Guiterman. FaBV; RePo
"Had he and I but met." The Man He Killed. Thomas Hardy. ILP; LV; PoIE; PoPl; PoPo; VP
Had I but plenty of money, money enough and to spare. Up at a Villa—Down in the City. Robert Browning. CBEP; GTBS-P
Had I the Choice. Walt Whitman. PP
Had not each distant good. 22nd November, 1963. George Dekker. OPP
Had she come all the way for this. The Haystack in the Floods. William Morris. CABA; ILP; OBNC; StP
Had to be/ she would come. Bulosan Now. Alvaro Cardona-Hine. PtTo
Had we but world enough, and time. To His Coy Mistress. Andrew Marvell. CABA; CaFP; CBEP; DiPo; ELP; ErPo; FaBV; ILP; MeP; OnP; PoIE; PoLF; PoPl; PoSa; SeCP; StP; UnTE; VaPo
Hadn't heard of the atom bomb. The Seals in Penobscot Bay. Daniel Hoffman. MP
Hadn't I been. Distance. Robert Creeley. CoPo
Hadst thou not simplicity. how should. Birth of Christ. Rainer Maria Rilke. MoRP
Hag, The. Robert Herrick. PoSC; WiR
Hagen's Dying Song. Felix Dahn, tr. fr. German by Walter Kaufmann. TwGP
Haidée and Don Juan. Byron. Fr. Don Juan. OBNC
Haiku: "Ancient pond, The." Basho, tr. fr. Japanese by Donald Keene. CaFP
(Old Pond, The, tr. unknown.) SoPo
Haiku: "Falling flower, The." Moritake, tr. fr. Japanese by Babette Deutsch. CaFP

Haiku: "I wonder in what fields today." Chiyo, *tr. fr. Japanese by* Curtis Hidden Page. CaFP
Haiku: "World of dew, The." Issa, *tr. fr. Japanese by* Donald Keene. CaFP
Hail, door, to husband and to father dear. Dialogue with a Door. Catullus. UnTE
Hail, Holy Light. Milton. *Fr.* Paradise Lost, III. OnP ("Hail, holy light, offspring of Heaven first-born.") PoIE
Hail! King I thee call. A Lyric from a Play. *Unknown.* MeEL
Hail! meek-eyed maiden, clad in sober grey. Ode to Evening. Joseph Warton. WaPE
Hail native Language, that by sinews weak. Milton. *Fr.* At a Vacation Exercise in the College, Part Latin, Part English. PP
Hail [*or* Haile], sister springs. The Weeper. Richard Crashaw. MeP; SeCP
Hail, Sympathy! thy soft idea brings. William Lisle Bowles. Byron. *Fr.* English Bards and Scotch Reviewers. OBNC
Hail to thee, blithe spirit! To a Skylark. Shelley. DiPo; FaBV; GTBS-P; OBNC; OnP; PoIE; PoLF; RoGo; VaPo
Hail to thy living light. Ode to Morning. William Mason. WaPE
Haile gracefull morning of eternall Daye. Sonnet. William Alabaster. MeP
Haile! sterne superne. Haile! in eterne. A Hymn to Mary. William Dunbar. MeEL
Haill! Quene of Heven and steren of blis. A Little Hymn to Mary. *Unknown.* MeEL
Hair. Remy de Gourmont, *tr. fr. French by* Jethro Bithell. ErPo
Hair-dressing. Louis Untermeyer. UnTE
Hair long, cheekbones high. Three Dreams. James Michie. NePoEA-2
Hair, My Pretty Hair. Joan Zorro, *tr. fr. Portuguese by* William M. Davis. AnML
Hair Ribbons. *Unknown.* BiCB
Haircut. Karl Shapiro. MP
Hairless and worse than leathery, the skin. Corrib: An Emblem. Donald Davie. PoCh
Hairy Dog, The. Herbert Asquith. SoPo
Half a league, half a league. The Charge of the Light Brigade. Tennyson. FaBV; PoPl
Half close your eyelids, loosen your hair. He Thinks of Those Who Have Spoken Evil of His Beloved. W. B. Yeats. CTC
Half-heard. Christopher Koch. PoAu-2
Half-moons of her calves eclipse, The. Notes on a Girl. Peter Kane Dufault. ErPo
Half of Life. Friedrich Hölderlin, *tr. fr. German.* AGP, *tr. by* Willard R. Trask *and* Alexander Gode; TwGP, *tr. by* Walter Kaufmann
Half of my life is gone, and I have let. Mezzo Cammin. Longfellow. CBEP; ILP
Half of your book is to an index grown. Half Your Book. Swift. StP
Half past nine—high time for supper. In Praise of Cocoa, Cupid's Nightcap. Stanley J. Sharpless. ErPo
Half the time they munched the grass, and all the time they lay. Cows. James Reeves. PoSC
Half Your Book. Swift. StP
Hallelujah; a Sestina. Robert Francis. PoCh
Hallowe'en. Harry Behn. PoSC; RePo
Halloween. Marnie Pomeroy. PoSC
Halloween: A Poem for Children. Robert Watson. PoNC
Hallowe'en Indignation Meeting. Margaret Fishback. PoSC
Hal's Birthday. Lucy Larcom. BiCB
Halted against the shade of a last hill. Spring Offensive. Wilfred Owen. GTBS-P
Hamatreya. Emerson. AP
Hamelin Town's in Brunswick. The Pied Piper of Hamelin. Robert Browning. SIV
Hamlet, *sels.* Shakespeare.
  Ophelia's Song ("Tomorrow is Saint Valentine's day"), *fr.* V, v. UnTE
  [Po]nius' Advice to Laertes, *fr.* I, iii. PoPl
  [ra]gged Pyrrhus, he whose sable arm, The," *fr.* II, 2. Par
  Be, or Not to Be, *fr.* III, i. DiPo
  'To be, or not to be: that is the question.") PoPl; PoSa
[...]er, The. Carl Sandburg. PoPo
[...]er and Anvil. Samuel Valentine Cole. PoLF
[...]ered to the serenity of copper. Bronze. Derek Walcott. [...]Po
[...]ers, The. Ralph Hodgson. GoJo; PoIE
[...] The. Irving Feldman. AmPC
[...]and Foot, The. Jones Very. AmLP; AP
[...] at Callow Hill Farm, The. Charles Tomlinson. [...]PoEA-2
[...]Mirror, A. Walt Whitman. CBEP
[...]of Lincoln, The. Edmund Clarence Stedman. LiPo
[...]of the copper boy pours tea. Café Tableau. May Swen-[...]. ErPo

Hand That Held It, The. W. G. Elmslie. TRV
Hand That Rocks the Cradle Is the Hand That Rules the World, The. William Ross Wallace. PoLF
Hand That Signed the Paper, The. Dylan Thomas. MoRP
Handful of old men walking down the village street, A. Memorial Day. Theodosia Garrison. PoSC
Handfuls. Carl Sandburg. AP
Handiwork of God, The. *Unknown.* TRV
Hands. Louis Untermeyer. MoLP
Hands and Eyes. Louis MacNeice. PoDB
Hands must touch and handle many things, The. The New Man. Jones Very. AP
Hands of Christ, The. His Hands. John Richard Moreland. TRV
Hands of God, The. D. H. Lawrence. MoRP
Handy Spandy. Mother Goose. SoPo
Hang it all, Robert Browning. Canto II. Ezra Pound. AP
Hang on! Cling on! No matter what they say. Keep Your Grit. *Unknown.* STF
Hang thee, vile North Easter. Another Ode to the North-East Wind. *Unknown.* Par
Hang up those dull, and envious fooles. Another. In Defence of Their Inconstancie. Ben Jonson. SeCP
Hanged Thing, The. Walter H. Kerr. FiSC
Hanging, The. J. E. H. MacDonald. OBCV
Hanging from the beam. The Portent. Herman Melville. AP; CaFP; CBEP; WiR
Hangman Tree, The, *with music. Unknown.* BFSS
Hangtown Gals, *with music.* John A. Stone. SGR
Hannah Armstrong. Edgar Lee Masters. *Fr.* Spoon River Anthology. LiPo
Hannah was a lady. The Lady of the Tomahawk. Robert P. Tristram Coffin. SIV
Hans Christian Andersen in Central Park. Hy Sobiloff. PoPl
Hap. Thomas Hardy. CABA; EaLo; PoDB
Hap which Paris had as due for his desert, The. Gascoigne's Praise of His Mistress. George Gascoigne. EnRePo
Happie is he, that from all businesse cleere. The Praises of a Countrie Life. Ben Jonson. SeCP
Happiness. Walter E. Isenhour. STF
Happiness. A. A. Milne. BoC
Happiness. Umberto Saba, *tr. fr. Italian by* Thomas G. Bergin. CoIP
Happiness of a Flea, The. Tasso, *tr. fr. Italian by* William Drummond of Hawthornden. RBL
Happiness of our happiness enflaming desire, The. Maurice Scève. *Fr.* Délie. RBL
Happy and Contented in Your Hut. Francisco de Quevedo, *tr. fr. Spanish by* William M. Davis. AnSP
Happy are men who yet before they are killed. Insensibility. Wilfred Owen. MMA; StP
Happy are they. Eugene Guillevic. *Fr.* Elegies. CoFP
Happy child facing the road. Dead in the Villages. Alfonso Gatto. CoIP
Happy have we met. Old Toast. *Unknown.* WePo
Happy Heart, The. Thomas Dekker. See Art Thou Poor?
Happy Hen, The. James Agee. ErPo
Happy Hours That Hurry Away. Gutierre de Cetina, *tr. fr. Spanish by* Kate Flores. AnSP
Happy insect, what can be. The Grasshopper. Abraham Cowley. WiR
Happy Insensibility. Keats. See In a Drear-nighted December.
Happy lover who has come, A. In Memoriam A. H. H., VIII. Tennyson. VP
Happy Miner, The. John A. Stone. SGR
Happy New Year! Happy New Year! *Unknown.* PoSC
Happy Night, The. John Sheffield, Duke of Buckingham and Normanby. UnTE
Happy Sheep, The. Wilfred Thorley. SoPo
Happy the hare at morning, for she cannot read. The Cultural Presupposition. W. H. Auden. CABA
Happy the man, and happy he alone. Horace, *par. by* Dryden. *Fr.* Odes, III, 29. SiGo
Happy the man who, safe on shore. The Hurricane. Philip Freneau. AP
Happy the man, who void of cares and strife. The Splendid Shilling. John Philips. Par
Happy the man, whose wish and care. Ode on Solitude [*or* The Quiet Life *or* Solitude]. Pope. CBEP; DiPo; GTBS-P; OnP; PoIE; PoPl; PoPo
Happy the tree, that scarcely feels. Doom. Rubén Darío. AnSP
Happy those early days [*or* dayes], when I. The Retreat [*or* Retreate]. Henry Vaughan. BoC; CABA; CBEP; GTBS-P; MeP; PoIE; SeCP; StP
Happy Too Much. Boethius, *tr. fr. Latin by* Elizabeth I, Queen of England. *Fr.* Consolation of Philosophy. CTC
Happy Warrior, The. Sir Herbert Read. MMA
Happy who like Ulysses, or that lord. Heureux qui, comme Ulysse, a fait un beau voyage. Joachim du Bellay. *Fr.* Regrets. RBL
Happy youth, that shalt possesse. To My Cousin (C. R.) Marrying My Lady (A.). Thomas Carew. SeCP
Harald, the Agnostic Ale-loving Old Shepherd Enemy of the

Harald (*continued*)
Whisky-drinking Ploughmen and Harvesters, Walks over the Sabbath Hill to the Shearing. George Mackay Brown. NePoEA-2

Harbingers. Basho, *tr. fr. Japanese by* Harold G. Henderson. PoPl; RePo

Harbingers are come, The. See, see their mark. The Fore-runners. George Herbert. MeP

Harbor, The. Carl Sandburg. PoPl

Harbor wears a look of space, The. Little Steamboat. Oscar Williams. PoPl

Hard as hurdle arms, with a broth of goldfish flue. Harry Ploughman. Gerard Manley Hopkins. VP

Hard by the Wildbrooks I met Mary. Meeting Mary. Eleanor Farjeon. BiCB

Hard coming we had of it, A. The Poets. David Wevill. PP

Hard Lines. Tom Robinson. BiCB

Hard Rain's a-Gonna Fall. Bob Dylan. PtTo

Hard to exert the tuneful voice. The Shrimp. Moses Browne. WaPE

Hardly thinking of years, but sensing their flow, again. Notes for an Autobiography. Charles Edward Eaton. PoNC

Hares at Play. John Clare. CBEP

Hares on the Mountain. *Unknown.* CBEP; ErPo; UnTE

Hark, ah, the nightingale. Philomela. Matthew Arnold. ILP; PoIE; VP

Hark, all you ladies that do sleep! In the Dark What the Day Doth Forbid. Thomas Campion. UnTE

Hark Back. Richard Eberhart. ToPo

Hark, Hark! the Lark. Shakespeare. *Fr.* Cymbeline, II, iii. CBEP; DiPo; EnRePo; FaBV; FoBA; PoIE
("Hark, hark! the lark at heaven's gate sings.") ILP

Hark! heard ye the signals of triumph afar? Thomas Pringle. *Fr.* The Caffer Commando. ACV

Hark, my Flora! Love doth call us. A Song of Dalliance. William Cartwright. ErPo

Hark, now everything is still. A Dirge. John Webster. *Fr.* The Duchess of Malfi. CBEP

Hark, once more the flute's complaining. Serenade. Clemens Brentano. AGP

Hark! she is call'd, the parting houre is come. On the Assumption. Richard Crashaw. MeP

Hark! the cock proclaims the morning. St. Matthias. Christopher Smart. *Fr.* Hymns and Spiritual Songs. EiCP

Hark to the whimper of the sea-gull. The Sea-Gull. Ogden Nash. PoPo

Hark! Young Democracy from sleep. Bernard O'Dowd. *Fr.* Young Democracy. PoAu-1

Harken how the flute complains. Serenade. Clemens Brentano. SiGo

Harlequin of Dreams, The. Sidney Lanier. AP

Harlot's Catch. Robert Nichols. ErPo

Harlot's House, The. Oscar Wilde. StP

Haroun's Favorite Song. *Unknown, tr. fr. Arabic by* E. Powys Mathers. *Fr.* The Thousand and One Nights. SiGo

Harp of the North. Sir Walter Scott. The Lady of the Lake: Prologue. ILP
(Farewell, Thou Minstrel Harp.) OBNC

Harp Player's Song, The. Goethe, *tr. fr. German by* Walter Kaufmann. *Fr.* Wilhelm Meister. TwGP
(Song of the Harp-Player, *tr. by* Herman Salinger.) AGP

Harp Song of the Dane Women. Kipling. *Fr.* Puck of Pook's Hill. OBNC

Harp That Once through Tara's Halls, The. Thomas Moore. OBNC; PoLF; RoGo

Harper, The. Thomas Campbell. CBEP

Harried we were, and spent. The Waradgery Tribe. Mary Gilmore. PoAu-1

Harrow-on-the-Hill. John Betjeman. DaDu

Harrowing of Hell, The. William Langland, *mod. by* Nevill Coghill. *Fr.* The Vision of Piers Plowman. BoC

Harry Pearce. David Campbell. PoAu-2

Harry Ploughman. Gerard Manley Hopkins. VP

Hart and Hare. *Unknown.* CBEP

Hart Crane. Robert Creeley. AP

Hart he loves the high wood, The. Hart and Hare. *Unknown.* CBEP

Harvest and Consecration. Elizabeth Jennings. NePoEA-2

Harvest Moon, The. Longfellow. AP

Harvest Moon. Ryota, *tr. fr. Japanese by* Harold G. Henderson. RePo

Harvest of the Sea, The. *Unknown, tr. fr. Manx by* William Henry Gill. HaSV

Has anybody seen my Mopser? The Bandog. Walter de la Mare. EvOK

Has someone seen Christ in you today? Christ in You. *Unknown.* STF

Hassan, *sels.* James Elroy Flecker.
"Thy dawn, O Master of the world, thy dawn," *fr.* II, ii. WePo
War Song of the Saracens, *fr.* III, iii. FaBV

Hast Never Come to Thee an Hour. Walt Whitman. CBEP

Hast thou not known? hast thou not heard, that the everlasting God. They That Wait Upon the Lord. Isaiah, Bible, *O.T.* BoC; TRV

Hast thou then survived. Address to My Infant Daughter. Wordsworth. EvOK; Par

Haste thee, Nymph, and bring with thee. Mirth, with Thee I Mean to Live. Milton. *Fr.* L'Allegro. FaBV

Haste to the Wedding. Alex Comfort. ErPo

Hasty is the flight of birds. Woe, all that was ever ready to soar. 8th May 1945. Franz Baermann Steiner. MGP

Hasty-Pudding, The. Joel Barlow. AP

Hate Whom Ye List. Sir Thomas Wyatt. EnRePo

Hateful is the dark-blue sky. Tennyson. *Fr.* The Lotos-Eaters: Choric Song. HaSV

Hath woman then no rights, presumptuous Paine? The Rights of Women. William Cowper. CBEP

Hatred. Gwendolyn B. Bennett. AmNP

Hats off!/ Along the street there comes. The Flag Goes By. Henry Holcomb Bennett. LV; RePo

Hatters, The. Nan McDonald. PoAu-2

Haughty Snail-King, The. Vachel Lindsay. LOW

Haunted House, The. Thomas Hood. WePo; WiR

Haunted Palace, The. Poe. AmLP; AP; WiR

Have-at a Venture. *Unknown.* ErPo

Have Courage, My Boy, to Say, No. *Unknown.* STF

Have Faith in God. Joe Budzynski. STF

Have I a wife? Bedam I have! The Brewer's Man. L. A. G. Strong. DTC

Have I Done My Best for Jesus? Edwin Young. STF

Have I Found Her. *Unknown.* EnRePo

Have Mercy, Love! Give Ear. Guittone d'Arezzo, *tr. fr. Italian by* Maurice Valency. AnML

Have pity on us, Power just and severe. Prayer. John Hall Wheelock. EaLo

Have We Not Seen Thy Shining Garments Hem. Amy Carmichael. TRV

Have ye beheld (with much delight). Upon the Nipples of Julia's Breast. Robert Herrick. ErPo; UnTE

Have you any room for Jesus. Room for Jesus. Barbara H. Staples. STF

"Have you been to your dinner, Jimmy Random, my son." Jimmy Random, My Son. *Unknown.* BFSS

Have you come to the Red Sea place in your life. At the Place of the Sea. Annie Johnson Flint. STF

Have you committed all to God? Our Times Are in His Hands. Mary D. Freeze. STF

Have you ever heard of the Sugar-Plum Tree? The Sugar-Plum Tree. Eugene Field. SoPo

Have you ever tried to get along. The Other Person's Place. Donald H. Hover. STF

Have you got a brook in your little heart? Emily Dickinson. FaBV
(Brook of the Heart, The.) BoLP

Have you had your tonsils out? The New Neighbor. Rose Fyleman. SoPo

Have you heard of the dreadful fate. The Ashtabula Disaster. Julia Moore. EvOK

Have you heard of the quaint people. Strawberries in November. John Shaw Neilson. PoAu-1

Have you heard of the wonderful one-hoss shay. The Deacon's Masterpiece; or, The Wonderful "One-Hoss Shay." Oliver Wendell Holmes. AP; PoIE; PoLF

Have you heard the Master's call? The Master's Call. Oswald J. Smith. STF

Have you not fallen asleep to strong men's rowing. The Rowers. Laura Benét. FiSC

Have you not in a chimney seen. A Description of Maidenhead. Earl of Rochester. UnTE

Have you not noted, in some family. The Birth-Bond. Dante Gabriel Rossetti. The House of Life, XV. VP

Have you not read. Despite and Still. Robert Graves. CBEP

Have you not seen them fighting for the lead. The Chariot Race. Vergil. *Fr.* Georgics. SD

Have you observed the wench in the street. The Wench in the Street. *Unknown.* CBEP

Have you seen but a bright lily grow. So White, So Soft, So Sweet. Ben Jonson. *Fr.* A Celebration of Charis. UnTE

Have You Watched the Fairies? Rose Fyleman. SoPo

Haven. Donald Jeffrey Hayes. AmNP

Having banged the piano too hard. The Fish Sonata. Winfield Townley Scott. MP

Having been tenant long to a rich Lord. Redemption. George Herbert. CABA; EaLo; PoSa; SeCP

Having Climbed to the Topmost Peak of the Incense-Burner Mountain. Po Chü-i, *tr. fr. Chinese by* Arthur Waley. SD

Having interr'd her infant-birth. An Ode upon a Question Moved, Whether Love Should Continue for Ever? Lord Herbert of Cherbury. SeCP

Having this day my horse, my hand, my lance. Astrophel and Stella, XLI. Sir Philip Sidney. EnRePo; ILP

Having used every subterfuge. A Renewal. James Merrill. PoPl

Hawicks' Crossing. Jane Stuart. FiSC
Hawk, The. Raymond Knister. OBCV
Hawk. Guy Owen. PoNC
Hawk in the Rain, The. Ted Hughes. ACV; ToPo
Hawk Roosting. Ted Hughes. GTBS-P; MP; NePoEA-2
Hawk with heavy-lidded eyes, The. The Last Summer. Vivian Smith. PoAu-2
Hawking. Michael Drayton. *Fr.* Polyolbion. SD
Hawthorne. James Russell Lowell. *Fr.* A Fable for Critics. AP
Hawthorn Hedge, The. Judith Wright. PoAu-2
Hawthorne—May 23, 1864. Longfellow. CBEP
Hayfield. Aileen Fisher. RePo
Hay! hay! by this day. The Scholar Complains. *Unknown.* MeEL
Hayfoot; strawfoot; the illiterate seasons. Wessex Guidebook. Louis MacNeice. PoIE
Haying. Ethel Romig Fuller. SIV
Haymakers, Rakers. Thomas Dekker *and* John Ford. *Fr.* The Sun's Darling. ELP
Haystack, The. Andrew Young. DaDu
Haystack in the Floods, The. William Morris. CABA; ILP; OBNC; StP
Haze. Buson, *tr. fr. Japanese by* Harold G. Henderson. RePo
Haze. Henry David Thoreau. PoPl
  (Woof of the Sun, Ethereal Gauze.) AP
He Abjures Love. Thomas Hardy. OBNC
He always comes on market days. The Balloon Man. Rose Fyleman. SoPo
He and his, unwashed all winter. The Native. W. S. Merwin. NePoEA-2
He and She. Eugene Fitch Ware. PoLF
He ate and drank the precious Words. Emily Dickinson. AP; RePo
He bare him up, he bare him down. The Corpus Christi Carol. *Unknown.* MeEL
He bites upon the mouth her mouth has cut. Adam—the First Kiss. Hal Porter. ACV
He brought a team from Inversnaid. The Man from Inversnaid. Robert Fuller Murray. SD
He built no temple, yet the farthest sea. The Man Christ. Therese Lindsey. TRV
He burst from bed. Boy's Day. Ruth Evelyn Henderson. BiCB
He by no means flies straight at petunia. The Bee and the Petunia. Katherine Hoskins. ErPo
He came bringing us a milkpail full. Buck Duke and Mamma. Eleanor Ross Taylor. PoNC
He came in silvern armor, trimmed with black. Sonnet I. Gwendolyn B. Bennett. AmNP
He came to me last night, as if there had never. The Druggist. Larry Rubin. FiSC
He came to my desk with quivering lip. The New Leaf. *Unknown.* STF
He came to the desert of London town. William Blake. James Thomson. CBEP
He came unlook'd for, undesir'd. Song. Sara Coleridge. CBEP
He can hear the owl's flight in daylight. Blind Man. Michael Hamburger. NePoEA-2
He Cares. Owen C. Salway. STF
He carried her out into the sleigh. Fair Charlotte (C *vers.*). *Unknown.* BSO
He clasps the crag with crooked hands. The Eagle. Tennyson. CaFP; CBEP; DiPo; GoJo; GTBS-P; OnP; PoIE; PoPo; StP; VaPo; WePo; WiR
He climbed up the peak. High Brow. Robert Fitch. SD
He comes with western winds, with evening's wandering airs. Emily Brontë. *Fr.* The Prisoner. BoC; ELP
He Comforts Himself. Christopher Morley. *Fr.* Translations from the Chinese. EvOK
He Compares All Things with His Lady, and Finds Them Wanting. Guido Cavalcanti, *tr. fr. Italian by* Dante Gabriel Rossetti. SiGo
He Could Have Found His Way. Kathleen Dalziel. PoAu-1
He could not breathe in a crowded place. The Pioneer. William B. Ruggles. SIV
He could not die when trees were green. The Dying Child. John Clare. PoPl
He courted her many a long winter night. Lady Isabel and the Elf Knight (E *vers.*). *Unknown.* BSO
He crouches, and buries his face on his knees. The Last of His Tribe. Henry Kendall. PoAu-1
He did not come to woo U Nu. Just Dropped In. William Cole. GoJo; PoPl
He did not fear his enemies. The Statesman. Phyllis McGinley. *Fr.* Epitaphs for Three Prominent Persons. LV
He did not wear his scarlet coat. The Ballad of Reading Gaol. Oscar Wilde. FaPL; OBNC
He didn't want to do it with skill. Lion & Honeycomb. Howard Nemerov. PP
He died for me, my Saviour, He. It Was for Me. Eva Gray. STF

"He died," saith the cross, "my very name." The Cross and the Tomb. Annie Johnson Flint. STF
He dines alone surrounded by reflections. Witch Doctor. Robert Hayden. AmNP
He disappeared in the dead of winter. In Memory of W. B. Yeats. W. H. Auden. ACV; CABA; PoIE; PP; StP
He does not lead me year by year. Step by Step. Barbara C. Ryberg. STF
He Doeth All Things Well. Anne Brontë. TRV
He dreamed of lovely women as he slept. Undergraduate. Merrill Moore. ErPo
He dressed himself in the finest of clothes. Lord Thomas and Fair Ellen. *Unknown.* BSO
He drew a circle that shut me out. Outwitted. Edwin Markham. LV; PoPo; TRV
He drowsed and was aware of silence heaped. The Death-Bed. Siegfried Sassoon. MMA
He dwelt within the hills beyond the town. Apology. Paul Bartlett. PoNC
He entered the shop. Birthday Gift. Ethel Barnett de Vito. BiCB
He enters, and mute on the edge of a chair. In the Study. Thomas Hardy. *Fr.* Satires of Circumstance. PoPo
He feared the dark, his parents knew. On the Staircase. Wade Wellman. FiSC
He Fears His Good Fortune. Thomas Hardy. VP
He fears the tiger standing in his way. The Drunkard. Philip Levine. NePoEA-2
He Fell among Thieves. Sir Henry Newbolt. OnMSP
He felt the wild beast in him betweenwhiles. Modern Love, IX. George Meredith. VP
He first deceased; before a little tried. Upon the Death of [or Epitaph on] Sir Albert Morton's Wife. Sir Henry Wotton. CBEP; SeCP; WePo
He followed her up, he followed her down. Pretty Polly. *Unknown.* BFSS
He found her by the ocean's moaning verge. Modern Love, XLIX. George Meredith. VP
He frightens us. Death. Friedrich Hölderlin. AGP
He from the wind-bitten North with ship and companions descended. A Drifter off Tarentum. Kipling. *Fr.* Epitaphs of the War. MMA
He Gave Himself for Me. *Unknown.* STF
He gave the solid rail a hateful kick. The Egg and the Machine. Robert Frost. CABA
He Gave Up Golf. Edith Earnshaw. PoNC
He gave us all a good-bye cheerily. Messmates. Sir Henry Newbolt. HaSV
He gazed at her with his whole soul. Dark Eyes at Forest Hills. I. L. Martin. SD
He gives to me His wondrous grace. This Blessed Christ of Calvary. *Unknown.* STF
He Giveth More [Grace]. Annie Johnson Flint. STF; TRV
He grew where waves ride nine feet high. In Memoriam Roy Campbell. R. N. Currey. ACV
He grinds the clover at its root. Eight-Cylinder Man. Florence Ripley Mastin. LV; PoPo
He grins a little as they drive him by. Dog in a Car. David McCord. RePo
He had awaited me. A Meeting. Daniel Hoffman. CoPo
He had been stuttering, by the edge. Hart Crane. Robert Creeley. AP
He had fought for the wrong causes. Suicide. Louis MacNeice. DTC
He had grown quieter now. "The Prophet." Sam Ragan. PoNC
He had his son with him, a fine young Squire. The Squire. Chaucer. *Fr.* The Canterbury Tales. WePo
He had no pact with time: his mind was ever. Toward Avernus. Harold Vinal. FiSC
He Had Served Eighty Masters. Lesbia Harford. PoAu-1
He hangs between his wings outspread. The Eagle. Andrew Young. WePo
He has fashioned the stars and the moons to the music. Imagery. Harindranth Chattopadhyaya. ACV
He Has Not Sung Who's Made No Sound. Jaufré Rudel, *tr. fr. Provençal by* Harvey Birenbaum. AnML
He has outsoared the shadow of our night. Shelley. *Fr.* Adonais. BoC; PoSa
He heard, and dreamed the night-wind on. Muse-haunted. Hugh McCrae. PoAu-1
He held the lamp of Truth that day. The Hand That Held It. W. G. Elmslie. TRV
He hides his heart. Sightings I. Jerome Rothenberg. CoPo
He invented a rainbow but lightning struck it. Bushed. Earle Birney. OBCV
He is a man who thinks. Shh! The Professor Is Sleeping. John Morris. CABA
He Is a Path. Giles Fletcher. *Fr.* Christ's Victory and Triumph. TRV
He is always standing there. My Policeman. Rose Fyleman. SoPo

He Is Coming. Gladys M. Gearhart. STF
He is dead, the beautiful youth. Killed at the Ford. Long-fellow. AP
He is gone before thee, carrying His cross, and He died for thee. The Royal Way of the Holy Cross. Thomas à Kempis. BoC
He is gone on the mountain. Coronach. Sir Walter Scott. *Fr.* The Lady of the Lake. GTBS-P; WiR
He Is like the Lotus. *Unknown, tr. fr. Egyptian by* Robert Hillyer. *Fr.* Book of the Dead. EaLo
He Is Not Dead. Sir Thomas Wyatt. CBEP
He is not dead nor liveth. The Buried Child. Dorothy Wellesley. *Fr.* Deserted House. DTC
He is not the wise man, who comes. The Imbecile. Donald Finkel. NePoEA-2
He is quick, thinking in clear images. In Broken Images. Robert Graves. PoIE
He is running like a wasp. Pole Vault. Shiro Murano. SD
He is so small, he does not know. Six Weeks Old. Chris-topher Morley. BiCB
He is stark mad, whoever says. The Broken Heart. John Donne. DiPo; ILP
He is that fallen lance that lies as hurled. A Soldier. Robert Frost. ILP; PoPo; ThLM
He Is the Way. W. H. Auden. *Fr.* For the Time Being; a Christmas Oratorio. EaLo
He jests at scars that never felt a wound. Shakespeare. *Fr.* Romeo and Juliet, II, ii. BoC
He knew he had the place alone. School Days. Thad Stem, Jr. PoNC
He Knoweth Not That the Dead Are Thine. Mary Elizabeth Coleridge. OBNC
He knows, He loves, He cares. The Best Choice. *Unknown.* STF
He Knows the Way. *Unknown.* STF
He knows when shadows come my way. Because He Was Tempted. *Unknown.* STF
He lay, and those who watched him were amazed. The Sprig of Lime. Robert Nichols. GTBS-P
He left his pants upon a chair. The Mistake. Theodore Roethke. UnTE
He left me exposed on a hill of woman, my mother. Oedipus at San Francisco. Donald Finkel. CoPo
He Lived amidst th' Untrodden Ways. Hartley Coleridge. Par
 (Imitation of Wordsworth, An.) CBEP
He lives among a dog. The Child. Donald Hall. NePoEA-2
He Lives! He Lives to Bless! Dorothy Conant Stroud. STF
He loved the brook's soft sound. The Peasant Poet. John Clare. OBNC
He Loves and He Rides Away. Sydney Dobell. OBNC
He lying spilt like water from a bowl. Poem. Alison Boodson. ErPo
He makes himself comfortable. 1st Dance—Making Things New—6 February 1964. Jackson MacLow. CoPo
He makes sweet music who, in serious lines. Sir John Beau-mont. *Fr.* To His Late Majesty, Concerning the True Form of English Poetry. PP
He Maketh No Mistake. A. M. Overton. STF
He-man, the sea-man, The. Pickup in Tony's Hashhouse. Kenneth Pitchford. *Fr.* Good for Nothing Man. CoPo; ErPo
He Met Her at the Green Horse. Peter Levi. NePoEA-2
He must not laugh at his own wheeze. The Humorist. Keith Preston. EvOK
He never knew what made him feel so sure. The Shape of Fear. Sydney King Russell. FiSC
He never spoke a word to me. Simon the Cyrenian Speaks. Countee Cullen. AmNP
He Never Will Forget. "M. G. H." STF
He, of his gentleness. In the Wilderness. Robert Graves. EaLo
He often would ask us. The Choirmaster's Burial. Thomas Hardy. DTC
He Ought to Know! *with music.* John A. Stone. SGR
He passed beyond the utmost realm of stars. The Challenger. Donald Wandrei. FiSC
He past; a soul of nobler tone. In Memoriam A. H. H., LX. Tennyson. VP
He paused on the sill of a door ajar. The Newcomer's Wife. Thomas Hardy. VP
He played by the river when he was young. Washington. Nancy Byrd Turner. SoPo
He prayeth best, who loveth best. Samuel Taylor Coleridge. *Fr.* The Rime of the Ancient Mariner. TRV
He prayeth well who loveth well. Samuel Taylor Coleridge. *Fr.* The Rime of the Ancient Mariner. ThGo
He preached upon "breadth" till it argued him narrow. Emily Dickinson. AP; CABA
He probably held too tight. Eugène Guillevic. *Fr.* Elegies. CoFP
He ran the course and as he ran he grew. Innocence. Thom Gunn. NePoEA-2; ToPo

He Remembers Forgotten Beauty. W. B. Yeats. CTC
He Renounceth All the Effects of Love. Thomas, Lord Vaux. EnRePo
He replied to his own question, and with the unmannered. A Meditation on John Constable. Charles Tomlinson. NePoEA-2
He rises and begins to round. The Lark Ascending. George Meredith. CABL; WiR
He riseth up early in the morning. The Mighty Hunter. Mrs. J. B. Worley. PoLF
He rose at dawn and, fired with hope. The Sailor Boy. Tenny-son. HaSV
He said, "Do not point your gun." A Parting Shot. C. Day Lewis. DaDu
He sang of God—the mighty source. Christopher Smart. *Fr.* A Song to David. TRV
He sat alone upon an ash-heap by. Love. Nicholas Moore. ErPo
He sat in a wheeled chair, waiting for dark. Disabled. Wilfred Owen. MMA
He sat upon the deck. Longfellow. *Fr.* Sir Humphrey Gilbert. HaSV
He saw beneath the bughouse wall. Solo for Bent Spoon. Donald Finkel. NePoEA-2
He saw her from the bottom of the stairs. Home Burial. Robert Frost. AP; StP
He sent us letters, which we read. The Summer Story. John Lehmann. MP
He sipped at a weak hock and seltzer. The Arrest of Oscar Wilde at the Cadogan Hotel. John Betjeman. DTC
He sort/ of embodied. The Young President: March 1964. John Tagliabue. OPP
He spake, and drew the keen-edged sword that hung. Achilles' Revenge. Homer. *Fr.* The Iliad. SIV
He spoke of poetry: his lips had shrunk. The Pure Poet. Roy Fuller. ToPo
He stands in rags upon the heaving prow. Jonah. Thomas Blackburn. DaDu
He stood alone within the spacious square. James Thomson. *Fr.* The City of Dreadful Night. WiR
He stood, and heard the steeple. Eight o'Clock. A. E. Hous-man. Last Poems, XV. CABA; PoIE; WePo
He stood in the pulpit. The Pastor. William C. Summers. STF
He struggled to kiss her. She struggled the same. An Original Love-Story. *Unknown.* BoLP
He swings down like the flourish of a pen. Skier. Robert Francis. SD
He talked, and as he talked. The Story-Teller. Mark Van Doren. LOW
He tasted love with half his mind. In Memoriam A. H. H., XC. Tennyson. VP
He tells you when you've got on too much lipstick. The Perfect Husband. Ogden Nash. LV
He That Is Down. Bunyan. *See* Shepherd Boy's Song, The.
He that is weary, let him sit. Employment. George Herbert. SeCP
He that lies at the stock. Rock, Ball, Fiddle. *Unknown.* CBEP
He That Loves. Sir Philip Sidney. ErPo
He That Loves a Rosy Cheek. Thomas Carew. *See* Disdain Returned.
He that loves and fears to try. He That Loves. Sir Philip Sidney. ErPo
He that will be a lover in every wise. Three Things Jeame Lacks. *Unknown.* MeEL
He that will court a wench that is coy. Song. *Unknown.* ErPo
He Thinks of His Past Greatness When a Part of the Constel-lations of Heaven. W. B. Yeats. DTC
He Thinks of Those Who Have Spoken Evil of His Beloved. W. B. Yeats. CTC
He thought he kept the universe alone. The Most of It. Rob-ert Frost. CABA; CaFP; PoIE; PoSa
He thought he saw an Elephant. The [Mad] Gardener's Song. "Lewis Carroll." *Fr.* Sylvie and Bruno. EvOK; WiR
He thought, in his great weariness, to mount. Nightmare. R. H. Grenville. FiSC
He told himself and he told his wife. The Riddle. Ralph Hodgson. PoPl
He took Miss Mouse upon his knee. The Frog and the Mouse (E *vers.*). *Unknown.* BSO
He travels after a winter sun. Tilly. James Joyce. PoIE
He truly adored the sun, as crimson it sank from the hill-top. Caspar Hauser Song. Georg Trakl. MGP
He turned his field into a meeting-place. W. H. Auden. *Fr.* In Time of War. PoPl
He usually managed to be there when. Because He Liked to Be at Home. Kenneth Patchen. ToPo
He walked through the woods. The Walk. W. W. Eustace Ross. SD
He Walks at Peace. *Unknown, tr. fr. Chinese. Fr.* Tao Teh King. TRV

He walks, the enchanter, on his sea of glass. Antichrist. Edwin Muir. EaLo
He walks where clean lakes lie. The Contemplative. Sister M. Thérèse. MoRP
He wanders over the wild countryside. The Donkey. P. R. Kaikini. ACV
He was a fellow brown of hue. The Seaman. *Unknown.* HaSV
He was a high born gentleman. Gypsy Davy. *Unknown.* BSO
He was as loyal as them all—and more. Peeping Tom. Francis Hope. ErPo
He was as old as old could be. Danny Murphy. James Stephens. RoGo
He was as the morning star in the midst of a cloud, and as the moon at the full. Ecclesiasticus, Bible, Apocrypha. BoC
He was at Naples writing letters home. Esthétique du Mal. Wallace Stevens. PoDB
He was born in Deutschland, as you would suspect. The Progress of Faust. Karl Shapiro. DiPo; MP
He was found by the Bureau of Statistics to be. The Unknown Citizen. W. H. Auden. CABA; MoRP; PoPo
He was going to be all that a mortal should be—tomorrow. Do It Now. *Unknown.* STF
He Was Not Willing. Lucy R. Meyer. STF
He was now alone. The lovers had wandered across. Poet and Goldsmith. Vernon Watkins. PoCh
He was protuberant behind, before. Johnson on Pope. David Ferry. PP
He was the Word that spake it. The Sacrament. John Donne. TRV
He was the youngest son of a strange brood. Otto. Theodore Roethke. ToPo
He wasn't handsome or young or even clever, but oh. On Don Juan del Norte, Not Don Juan Tenorio del Sur. Alan Dugan. ErPo
He went by with another. Ballad. "Gabriela Mistral." AnSP
He went out at dusk. Deserted House. Sam Ragan. PoNC
He went so blithely on the way. The Blithe Mask. Dollett Fuguet. TRV
He went up under the gray foliage. The Garden of Olives. Rainer Maria Rilke. MoRP
He Who Asks a Wolf to Dine Soon Has Cause to Wail. "Spervogel," *tr. fr. German by* Ruth Yorck *and* Kenward Elmslie. AnML
He who bends to himself a joy. Eternity. Blake. DiPo; OBNC; PoIE
He who did most, shall bear most; the strongest shall stand the most weak. Robert Browning. *Fr.* Saul. TRV
He who died on Calvary. A Thought. Margaret E. Sangster. TRV
He who has a thousand friends has not a friend to spare. Make Friends. Ali Ben Abu Taleb. TRV
He who has once been happy for aye. Wilfrid Scawen Blunt. *Fr.* Esther. OBNC
He who hath never warred with misery. Epistle to Henry Wriothesley, Earl of Southampton. Samuel Daniel. EnRePo
He who hung on Calvary's tree. Wondrous Son of God. Berniece Goertz. STF
He who of Rankine sang, lies stiff and deid. On the Author. Burns. CBEP
He, who once was my brother, is dead by his own hand. Justice Is Reason Enough. Diane Wakoski. CoPo
He who ordained, when first the world began. Light and Darkness. Michelangelo. RBL
He Who Scrubs a Raven White. Hans Rosenplüt, *tr. fr. German by* Ruth Yorck *and* Kenward Elmslie. AnML
He Who Weeps Goes Not Alone. Rosalia de Castro, *tr. fr. Spanish by* Kate Flores. AnSP
He Whom a Dream Hath Possessed. Shaemas O'Sheel. TRV
He Will Make the Grade. Edith Earnshaw. PoNC
He Will Praise His Lady. Guido Guinicelli, *tr. fr. Italian by* Dante Gabriel Rossetti. SiGo
He with body waged a fight. The Four Ages of Man. W. B. Yeats. MoRP
He wooed me sweet and he wooed me strong. Waltz. Ruth Forbes Sherry. FiSC
He Would Not Stay for Me. A. E. Housman. WePo
Head Byzantine, The, or from/ Fayyum. Resting Figure. Denise Levertov. ToPo
Head, my Lord, an honourable piece, An. Meditation. Col. 1.18. He Is the Head of the Body. Edward Taylor. *Fr.* Preparatory Meditations, Second Series. MeP
Head next to mine but turned aside, you lie. Sonnet: Head Next to Mine. Carl Bode. ToPo
Head That Once Was Crowned with Thorns, The. Thomas Kelly. TRV
Head thrusts in as for the view, A. All Revelation. Robert Frost. CABA
Headless Gardener, The. Ian Serraillier. BoC
Heads of strong old age are beautiful, The. Promise of Peace. Robinson Jeffers. AP

Heads round the table disagree, The. The Trial. Dannie Abse. ACV
Heal us, Emmanuel, here we are. Jehovah-Rophi. William Cowper. EiCP
Healing the Wound. Heine, *tr. fr. German by* Louis Untermeyer. UnTE
Health, A. Edward Coote Pinkney. FaPL
Health enough to make work a pleasure. A Wish for the New Year. Phillips Brooks. STF
Health! I seek thee;—dost thou love. Robert Bloomfield. *Fr.* Shooter's Hill. OBNC
Heaps on Heaps. Matthew Concanen. *Fr.* A Match at Football. SD
Hear, d'you hear? One blast. Witching Hour. Norma Farber. FiSC
Hear! Hear! Lilian's Song. George Darley. OBNC
Hear me [*or* Heare mee], O God! A Hymn [*or* Hymne] to God the Father. Ben Jonson. EnRePo; SeCP
Hear the carols. Know It Is Christmas. Lois Snelling. BiCB
Hear the fluter with his flute. The Amateur Flute. *Unknown.* Par
Hear the mellow wedding bells. Poe. *Fr.* The Bells. PoPl
Hear the sledges with the bells. The Bells. Poe. FaPL; PoLF; PoPo
Hear the Voice of the Bard. Blake. *Fr.* Songs of Experience. CBEP; ELP
  (Bard, The.) TRV
  (Introduction.) EnPE
Hear us, O Lord, from Heaven, Thy dwelling place. The Harvest of the Sea. *Unknown.* HaSV
Hear what Claudius suffered: When his wife knew he was asleep. Juvenal. *Fr.* Satires, VI. ErPo
Hear, Ye Ladies. John Fletcher. *Fr.* The Tragedy of Valentinian. ELP
  (Power of Love, The.) UnTE
Hear ye virgins, and I'll teach. To Virgins. Robert Herrick. UnTE
Heare mee, O God! *See* Hear me, O God!
Hearing how tourists, dazed with reverence. Terrible Beauty. Kingsley Amis. ErPo; NePoEA-2
Hearing one saga, we enact the next. Remembering the Thirties. Donald Davie. PP
Hearing our voices raised. Looking On. Anthony Thwaite. NePoEA-2
Hearing Russian Spoken. Donald Davie. GTBS-P; NePoEA-2
Hearing the Cuckoo. John Heath-Stubbs. DaDu
Hearken, thou craggy ocean pyramid. To Ailsa Rock. Keats. HaSV; OBNC
Hearken to me, gentlemen. King Estmere. *Unknown.* BuBa
Hearse Song, The. *Unknown.* DTC
Heart, The, *sel.* Francis Thompson.
  Correlated Greatness. GTBS-P
Heart, The. Georg Trakl, *tr. fr. German by* Michael Hamburger. MGP
Heart-affluence in discursive talk. In Memoriam A. H. H., CIX. Tennyson. VP
Heart and Mind. Edith Sitwell. MP
Heart asks pleasure first, The. Emily Dickinson. AP; CBEP; PoIE; PoSa
Heart-Coldness. Michelangelo, *tr. fr. Italian by* John Addington Symonds. RBL
Heart, my heart, with griefs confounded whence you no deliv'rance find. Be Still, My Soul. Archilochus. SiGo
Heart of a Woman, The. Georgie Douglas Johnson. PoLF
Heart of flaming sulphur, flesh of tow, A. Beauty and the Artist. Michelangelo. RBL
Heart of Midlothian, The, *sel.* Sir Walter Scott.
  Proud Maisie, *fr. ch.* 38. CBEP; ILP; PoPo; StP
  (Madge Wildfire Sings.) OBNC
  (Pride of Youth, The.) GTBS-P
Heart of the city, The. The Market. Gary Snyder. *Fr.* Mts. & Rivers. CoPo
Heart Path. Vernon Ward. PoNC
Heart-summoned. Jesse Stuart. FiSC
Heart That Weeps, A. Oswald J. Smith. STF
Heart to Praise Thee, A. George Herbert. TRV
Heart was ever a hunting thing, The. Old Hunter. Guy Owen. PoNC
Hearthside Story. X. J. Kennedy. CoPo
Hearts are pumping, The—feel!—the air. Air Shaft. Ian Healy. Poems from the Coalfields, I. PoAu-2
Heart's Compass. Dante Gabriel Rossetti. The House of Life, XXVII. VP
Heart's Content. *Unknown.* PoLF
Heart's Haven. Dante Gabriel Rossetti. The House of Life, XXII. VP
Heart's Hope. Dante Gabriel Rossetti. The House of Life, V. VP
Heart's Needle. W. D. Snodgrass. AmPC, *abr.;* CoPo
  "Winter again and it is snowing," V. AP
Heartsearch. Evelyn K. Gibson. STF
Heat. Anacreon, *tr. fr. Greek by* Abraham Cowley. UnTE

Heat. Hilda Doolittle ("H. D."). AP; PoIE; PoPo
Heat. Archibald Lampman. OBCV
Heat. Kenneth Mackenzie. PoAu-2
Heather, The. Steen Steensen Blicher, tr. fr. Danish by Charles Wharton Stork. SiGo
Heaven. Rupert Brooke. ILP
Heaven. Digby Mackworth Dolben. BoC
Heaven. George Herbert. MeP; SeCP
Heaven ("Heaven is closed"). Unknown, par. fr. German by Louis Untermeyer. UnTE
Heaven ("Think of—/ Stepping on shore"). Unknown. PoLF
Heaven above is softer blue. Possession. Unknown. TRV
Heaven has different signs to me. Emily Dickinson. PoIE
Heaven-Haven. Gerard Manley Hopkins. CaFP; DiPo; FoBA; ILP; OBNC; PoSa; VP; WePo
(I Have Desired to Go.) HaSV
Heaven is closed, proclaims the preacher. Heaven. Unknown. UnTE
Heaven is in my hand, and I. A Blackbird Suddenly. Joseph Auslander. RePo
Heaven of Animals, The. James Dickey. AP; ToPo
Heavenborn Helen, Sparta's queen. Troy Town. Dante Gabriel Rossetti. VP
"Heavenly Father"—take to thee. Emily Dickinson. PoIE
Heavenly Grass. Tennessee Williams. PoPl
Heavenly King, Glorious God of Light. Giraut de Bornelh, tr. fr. Provençal by Norman R. Shapiro. AnML
Heavenly Tree Grows Downward, The. Gerrit Lansing. CoPo
Heavens declare the glory of God, The. Psalm XIX, Bible, O.T. TRV
Heaviest of Flowers, the Head. Philip Larkin. ToPo
Heaving roses of the hedge are stirred, The. Winter Will Follow. Richard Watson Dixon. GTBS-P
Heavy Bear Who Goes with Me, The. Delmore Schwartz. AmLP; MP
Heavy hours are almost past, The. Song. George Lyttelton. WaPE
Hebrews, sel. Bible, N.T.
Evidence, The, XI: 1. TRV
He'd had enough of lying in the furze. The Ghostly Father. Peter Redgrove. MoBS; NePoEA-2
He'd have given me rolling lands. The Choice. Dorothy Parker. BoLP
He'd have the best, and that was none too good. The Very Rich Man. Dorothy Parker. PoPo
He'd play, after the bawdy songs and blues. When de Saints Go Ma'chin' Home. Sterling A. Brown. AmNP
Hedgehog. Anthony Thwaite. DaDu
Hegel. LeRoi Jones. CoPo
Heigh-ho on a Winter Afternoon. Donald Davie. NePoEA-2
Heigh-ho, what shall a shepheard doe. James Shirley. Fr. The Triumph of Beautie Song. ErPo
Heigh-o, weigh-o. Unknown. ThGo
"Heigho," yawned one day King Francis. The Glove. Robert Browning. StP
Height of the Ridiculous, The. Oliver Wendell Holmes. PoPl
Heights of Alma, The. Unknown. BSNS
Heimdall. Harold Vinal. FiSC
Heir of Linne, The. Unknown. BuBa
Heirloom. A. M. Klein. OBCV
Hélas. Oscar Wilde. UnTE
Helen of Kir[k]connell. Unknown. CBEP; ELP; ILP
(Fair Helen.) GTBS-P; WePo
Helen, thy beauty is to me. To Helen. Poe. AP; BoLP; CABA; CaFP; CBEP; FaBV; FaPL; ILP; OnP; PoIE; PoLF; PoPo; StP; VaPo
Helen Was Just Slipped into Bed. Matthew Prior. EiCP
(Reasonable Affliction, A.) StP
Helian. Georg Trakl, tr. fr. German by Christopher Middleton. MGP
Hell of a Day, A. Tim Reynolds. PtTo
Hellas, sel. Shelley.
World's Great Age Begins Anew, The. PoIE
Hellenics, The, sel. Walter Savage Landor.
Ternissa. OBNC
(On Ternissa's Death.) ELP
Help me! help me! now I call. To His Mistresses. Robert Herrick. ErPo; SeCP; UnTE
Help Us to Live. John Keble. TRV
Helping Hand, A. Georgia B. Adams. STF
Hem and Haw. Bliss Carman. PoPo
Hemmed-in Males. William Carlos Williams. PoSa
Hen and the Oriole, The. Don Marquis. Fr. Archy and Mehitabel. EvOK
Hen Overboard. Robert P. Tristram Coffin. RePo
Hence, all you vain delights. Melancholy. John Fletcher and [at.] Thomas Middleton. Fr. The Nice Valour. GTBS-P
Hence, loathed Melancholy. L'Allegro. Milton. CABA; CBEP; FoBA; GTBS-P; ILP
Hence, vain deluding Joys. Il Penseroso. Milton. CABA; CBEP; EiCP; FoBA; GTBS-P; ILP
"Henceforth I learn, that to obey is best." Exit from Eden. Milton. Fr. Paradise Lost. DiPo

Henry and Mary. Robert Graves. DaDu; GoJo; LOW
Henry VIII. Shakespeare and probably John Fletcher. See King Henry VIII.
Henry V. Shakespeare. See King Henry V.
Henry James. Robert Louis Stevenson. OBNC
Henry King. Hilaire Belloc. BBGG; DTC
Henry Martyn. Unknown. CBEP; BSNS, with music
Henry, My Son. Unknown. See Lord Randal.
Henry the Eighth. Shakespeare and probably John Fletcher. See King Henry VIII.
Henry the Fifth. Shakespeare. See King Henry V.
Henry was a young king. Henry and Mary. Robert Graves. DaDu; GoJo; LOW
Hens, The. Elizabeth Madox Roberts. GoJo; SoPo
Hep-Cat Chung, 'ware my town. Confucius. Fr. The Classic Anthology: Songs of Cheng. CTC
Her, a Statue. Thomas Stoddart. OBNC
Her arms across her breast she laid. The Beggar Maid. Tennyson. OnMSP
Her body is not so white as. Queen-Ann's-Lace. William Carlos Williams. AP
Her breast is cold; her hands how faint and wan! Virtue. Walter de la Mare. MMA
Her Careful Distinct Sex Whose Sharp Lips Comb. E. E. Cummings. ErPo
Her cheeks are hot, her cheeks are white. Bianca. Arthur Symons. UnTE
Her cheeks were white, her eyes were wild. The Sea. W. H. Davies. HaSV
Her Eyes. John Crowe Ransom. PoPl
Her eyes are homes of silent prayer. In Memoriam A. H. H., XXXII. Tennyson. VP
Her eyes long hollowed out to pits of shadow. The Worshiper. Vassar Miller. NePoEA-2
Her eyes the glow-worm lend thee. The Night Piece, to Julia. Robert Herrick. ELP; FaPL; ILP; PoIE; SeCP; UnTE; VaPo
Her father loved me: oft invited me. Othello and Desdemona. Shakespeare. Fr. Othello, I, iii. BoC
Her Favorites. Mattie Lee Hausgen. PoPl
Her Gifts. Dante Gabriel Rossetti. The House of Life, XXXI. VP
Her hair of silver fine, bristling doth part. Portrait. Francesco Berni. RBL
Her hair upgathered thus behind the neck. Doric. Angelos Sikelianos. ErPo
Her hand which touched my hand she moved away. On a Hand. Hilaire Belloc. BoLP
Her Irish maids could never spoon out mush. Mary Winslow. Robert Lowell. ILP
Her Kind. Anne Sexton. MP; ToPo
Her Letter. Bret Harte. PoLF
Her life is in the marble! yet a fall. Her, a Statue. Thomas Stoddart. OBNC
Her love is like an island. My Mother's Love. Unknown. STF
Her Man Described by Her Owne Dicatmen. Ben Jonson. Fr. A Celebration of Charis. SeCP
Her mother when she was young. Kemp Owyne [or Oweyne]. Unknown. BuBa; CBEP
Her mother watched her closely, yet one day. The Surprise. Unknown. UnTE
Her name, cut clear upon this marble cross. The Actress. Dorothy Parker. PoPo
Her name, Melissa, means she is a bee. Melissa. Unknown. UnTE
Her name was Dilliki Dolliki Dinah. A Ballad of China. Laura E. Richards. RePo
Her Nativity. Robert Southwell. MeP
Her patience is infinite. The Problems of a Writing Teacher. David Ray. NePoEA-2
Her Reply. Sir Walter Ralegh. See Nymph's Reply to the Shepherd, The.
Her Street Is Dark. Antonio Machado, tr. fr. Spanish by John Crow. AnSP
Her Strong Enchantments Failing. A. E. Housman. Last Poems, III. CBEP
Her Triumph. Ben Jonson. See Triumph of Charis, The.
Her voice did quiver as we parted. On Fanny Godwin. Shelley. OBNC
Her world is all aware. She reads. For Her Sake. Alastair Reid. PoPl
Her wraithful turnings and her soft answers head/ Me off. Soft Answers. Robert Bagg. UnTE
Heraclitus. William Johnson Cory, par. fr. the Greek of Callimachus. CBEP; OBNC; SiGo; WePo
Herbs and Simples. Martha Keller. FiSC
Herd-Boy's Song, The. Chen Shan-min, tr. fr. Chinese by E. D. Edwards. SiGo
Herding Lambs. Ruth Pitter. DaDu
Here. R. S. Thomas. GTBS-P
Here a little child I stand. Another Grace for a Child [or A Child's Grace]. Robert Herrick. CABA; CaFP; EaLo; GoJo; ThGo

Here, a sheer hulk, lies poor Tom Bowling. Tom Bowling. Charles Dibdin. CBEP

Here, above. The Man-Moth. Elizabeth Bishop. PoCh

Here all is sunny, and when the truant gull. Skerryvore: The Parallel. Robert Louis Stevenson. ILP

Here alone in the night between wind and water. Companions. Margaret Widdemer. FiSC

Here am I now cast down. Ex Nihilo. David Gascoyne. GTBS-P

Here am I, this carrot eating. In Common. Gene Derwood. PoPl

Here among long-discarded cassocks. Diary of a Church Mouse. John Betjeman. BoC

Here and near as the hands of the sea. The Inland Sea. Howard Sergeant. ToPo

Here and Now. Catherine Cater. AmNP

Here are no signs of festival. African Christmas. John Press. DaDu

Here are old trees, tall oaks, and gnarléd pines. The Antiquity of Freedom. Bryant. AP

Here, at the beginning of the new season. Meditation on the BMT. Paul Blackburn. CoPo

Here at the Vespasian-Carlton, it's just one. Boom! Howard Nemerov. MP; PoDB

Here beside dwelleth. The Magician and the Baron's Daughter. Unknown. MeEL

Here, beside the Latin sea. Eheu! Rubén Darío. AnSP

Here by the moorway you returned. Your Last Drive. Thomas Hardy. OBNC

Here, by the shore, a carven figure shows. The Living Statue. Unknown. UnTE

Here by the windy docks I stand alone. Octaves, XXIII. E. A. Robinson. ILP

Here, by this crumbling wall. Butterflies. Alfred Noyes. BoC

Here, Caelia, for thy sake I part. To the Mutable Fair. Edmund Waller. SeCP

Here comes a girl so damned shapely. Girl Walking. Charles G. Bell. ErPo

Here comes the elephant. The Elephant. Herbert Asquith. SoPo

Here comes the evening and the rains cease. Evening of Gavinana. "Vincenzo Cardarelli." CoIP

Here Dead Lie We. A. E. Housman. More Poems, XXXVI. PoLF

Here Dulcinea doth lie. Epitaph. Cervantes. Fr. Don Quixote. RBL

Here envying and lies. On Leaving Prison. Luis de León. AnSP

Here even experts can. Ragout Fin de Siècle. Erich Kästner. ErPo; TwGP

Here helms and swords are made of chalices. On Rome in the Pontificate of Julius II. Michelangelo. RBL

Here I Am. Ann Morrissett. BoLP

Here I am, an old man in a dry month. Gerontion. T. S. Eliot. AnMoPo; AP; CABA; CABL; DiPo; FoBA; GTBS-P; ILP; OnP; PoIE; StP

Here I Lie. Marguerite George. FiSC

Here in a distant place I hold my tongue. Egan O Rahilly. Tr. by James Stephens. CBEP

Here, in a field. In a Field. Robert Pack. NePoEA-2

Here in foreign land this rose. To Her Far Away. Nikolaus Lenau. AGP

Here, in my rude log cabin. The Battle of New Orleans. Thomas Dunn English. ThLM

Here in the midnight, where the dark mainland and island. Night Hymns on Lake Nipigon. Duncan Campbell Scott. OBCV

Here in the mountains the moon I love. The Moon in the Mountains. Chen Shan-min. SiGo

Here in the newspaper, the wreck of the East Bound. It's Here in the. Russell Atkins. AmNP

Here in the pine shade is the nest of night. Night and the Pines. Duncan Campbell Scott. OBCV

Here in their health and youth they're sitting down. Schoolgirl on Speech-Day in the Open Air. Iain Crichton Smith. NePoEA-2

Here, in this little Bay. Magna Est Veritas. Coventry Patmore. Fr. The Unknown Eros. GTBS-P; OBNC

Here, in this sequestered close. A Garden Song. Austin Dobson. OBNC

Here in this shabby house at dead of night. Foreboding. Grant Code. FiSC

Here is a place that is no place. Madhouse. Calvin C. Hernton. NNP

Here is a room with heavy-footed chairs. The Nature of an Action. Thom Gunn. ACV

Here Is a Toast That I Want to Drink. Walter Lathrop. PoLF

Here is an apple. Like your little breast. Apple Offering. Unknown. UnTE

Here is the ancient floor. The Self-unseeing. Thomas Hardy. OBNC; VP

Here is the Dog. Since time began. The Dog. Oliver Herford. FaBV

Here is the grackle, people. Fable for Blackboard. George Starbuck. CaFP

Here is the place; right over the hill. Telling the Bees. Whittier. AP; PoIE

Here is this silver crucifix, to recall. Crucifix. Elder Olson. MoRP

Here Is Wisdom. James Larkin Pearson. PoNC

Here Jack and Tom are paired with Moll and Meg. Modern Love, XVIII. George Meredith. VP

Here Johnson lies—a sage, by all allowed. Epitaph on Johnson. William Cowper. EiCP

Here lapped in hallowed slumber Saon lies. Saon of Acanthus. Callimachus. TRV

Here lay a fair fat land. Culbin Sands. Andrew Young. GTBS-P

Here lie Ciardi's pearly bones. Elegy Just in Case. John Ciardi. MP

Here lie my husbands One Two Three. Epitaph to the Four Husbands of Miss Ivy Saunders. Unknown. WePo

Here lies a clerk who half his life had spent. The Volunteer. Herbert Asquith. MMA

Here lies a great and mighty king. On Charles II. Earl of Rochester. PoSa

Here Lies a Lady. John Crowe Ransom. EvOK; VaPo

Here lies a piece of Christ; a star in dust. An Epitaph for a Godly Man's Tomb. Robert Wild. CBEP

Here lies a poor woman who was always tired. On a Tired Housewife. Unknown. EvOK; WePo

Here lies an aged corpse, which late. An Epitaph on His Grandfather. Thomas Shipman. CBEP

Here lies, but seven years old, our little maid. Afraid. Walter de la Mare. ThGo

Here lies David Garrick, describe me who can. David Garrick. Goldsmith. Fr. Retaliation. CBEP

Here lies Michael of the small bone. Epitaph. Lawrence Durrell. AnMoPo

Here lies old Hobson, Death hath broke his girt. On the University Carrier. Milton. FoBA

Here lies resting, out of breath. Little Elegy. X. J. Kennedy. CaFP; GoJo

Here lies the noble warrior that never blunted sword. Epitaph on the Earl of Leicester. Sir Walter Ralegh. EnRePo

Here lies the poet, deaf and dumb. Lines for a Dead Poet. David Ferry. PP

Here lies [or lyes], to each her parent's ruth. On My First Daughter. Ben Jonson. EnRePo; SeCP

Here lies what's left. On Leslie Moore. Unknown. LV

Here lieth one who did most truly prove. Another on the University Carrier. Milton. CABA

Here lieth under this marble ston. An Epitaph. Unknown. MeEL

Here must wee rest; and where else should wee rest? A Serious and a Curious Night-Meditation. Thomas Traherne. SeCP

Here Nature holds as in a hollowed hand. The Skylark's Nest. R. H. Long. PoAu-1

Here often, when a child I lay reclined. Lines. Tennyson. CABA; StP

Here on the mountain pass. On the Mountain Pass. Matsuo Basho. SiGo

Here, or not many feet from hence. Certain True Woords Spoken Concerning One Benet Corbett after Her Death. Richard Corbet. SeCP

Here she lies, a pretty bud. Upon a Child That Died. Robert Herrick. StP

Here she was wont to go, and here! and here! Ben Jonson. Fr. The Sad Shepherd. ILP

Here sit a shepherd and a shepherdess. The Green Shepherd. Louis Simpson. MP

Here sparrows build upon the trees. My Early Home. John Clare. PoLF

Here take my picture; though I bid farewell. His Picture [or Elegy V]. John Donne. Elegies, V. CBEP; EnRePo

Here the Frailest Leaves of Me. Walt Whitman. AP

"Here the hangman stops his cart." The Carpenter's Son. A. E. Housman. A Shropshire Lad, XLVII. VaPo

Here the jack-hammer jabs into the ocean. Colloquy in Black Rock. Robert Lowell. AP; PoDB

Here the young lover, on his elbow raised. The Corner of the Field. Frances Cornford. BoLP

Here they all come to die. The Country of a Thousand Years of Peace. James Merrill. PoCh

Here they are. The soft eyes open. The Heaven of Animals. James Dickey. AP; ToPo

Here this row is disintegrated wombs. Man and Woman Walk through the Cancer Ward. Gottfried Benn. TwGP

Here we bring new water. A New Year Carol. Unknown. PoSC

Here we come again, again, and here we come again! Child's Carol. Eleanor Farjeon. RePo

Here we come a-wassailing. The Wassail Song. Unknown. PoSC

Here we come gathering nuts an' may. Nuts an' May. Unknown. EvOK

Here we dance Looby Loo. Looby Loo. *Unknown.* SoPo
Here we halt our march, and pitch our tent. The Green Mountain Boys. Bryant. PoPl
Here where deer cross over at dark. The Conspiracy. Guy Owen. PoNC
Here, where the breath of the scented-gorse floats through the sun-stained air. Breton Afternoon. Ernest Dowson. OBNC
Here where the dead lie hidden. Hide-and-Seek. Robert Francis. PoIE; PoSa
Here, where the taut wave hangs. Life's Circumnavigators. W. R. Rodgers. GTBS-P
Here where the wind is always north-north-east. New England. E. A. Robinson. CABA; VaPo
Here, where the world is quiet. The Garden of Proserpine. Swinburne. DiPo; FaBV; OBNC; OnP; PoIE; PoPl; VP
Here where we are, wrapped in the afternoon. Obligations. Jane Cooper. AmPC; NePoEA-2
Here you see old Tom Moore. The Days of '49. Charley Rhodes. SGR
Heredity. Thomas Hardy. CBEP; CTC
Here's a body—there's a bed. Good Night. Thomas Hood. SoPo
Here's a little mouse and. Four III. E. E. Cummings. WePo
Here's a mellow cup of tea, golden tea! The Poets at Tea, 7. Barry Pain. Par
Here's a summer, heavy and hard. Elegy for Lucy Lloyd. Llewelyn Goch. SiGo
Here's a wreath of Christmas holly. Carol. Charles Edward Eaton. PoNC
Here's an example from/ A butterfly. The Example. W. H. Davies. LV
"Here's Cooper, who's written six volumes to show." Cooper. James Russell Lowell. *Fr.* A Fable for Critics. AP
Here's shade and comfort by this towering tree. Christmas 1942. Eric Irvin. PoAu-2
Here's the garden she walked across. The Flower's Name. Robert Browning. *Fr.* Garden Fancies. ACV; CTC
Here's the mail, sort it quick. A Sure Sign. Nancy Byrd Turner. SoPo
Here's the tender coming. The Press-Gang. *Unknown.* HaSV
Here's to the Maiden. Sheridan. *Fr.* The School for Scandal. CBEP; ELP
Here's to the man who invented stairs. Stairs. Oliver Herford. RePo
Here's to the Red of it! A Toast to the Flag. John Daly. PoLF
Hereto I come to view a voiceless ghost. After a Journey. Thomas Hardy. DTC; ELP; GTBS-P; OBNC
Heritage. Gwendolyn B. Bennett. AmNP
Heritage. Countee Cullen. AmNP
   What Is Africa to Me? sel. FaBV
Heritage. Kathleen Merrick. HaSV
Herman Moon's Hourbook, sels. Christopher Middleton. NePoEA-2
   Abasis.
   Ant Sun, The.
   Forenoon, The.
   Ode on Contemplating Clapham Junction.
   Pointed Boots.
   Waterloo Bridge.
Hermit, The. Joseph von Eichendorff, *tr. fr. German.* AGP, *tr. by Meno Spann; TwGP, tr. by Walter Kaufmann*
Hermit's Song, The. *Unknown, tr. fr. Irish by Frank O'Connor.* SiGo
Hermogenes's Song. Ben Jonson. *Fr.* The Poetaster. PoIE
Hero, The. Geoffrey Drake. HaSV
Hero and Leander. Christopher Marlowe (First *and* Second Sestiads), *completed by* George Chapman. CABA (First *and* Second Sestiads)
   Sels.
   "By this, Leander, being near the land," *fr.* Second Sestiad. ErPo
   "She stay'd not for her robes, but straight arose," *fr.* Second Sestiad. UnTE
Hero Leaves His Ship, The. Barbara Guest. AmPC
Heroes paused upon the plain, The. The Byrnies. Thom Gunn. NePoEA-2
Heron, The. Vernon Watkins. GTBS-P; MP
Hers was a small room. Paneled in Pine. Marguerite George. FiSC
Hertha. Swinburne. VP
Hervé Riel. Robert Browning. OnMSP
He's awfully nosy, that puppy of mine. Puppy. Edith Earnshaw. PoNC
He's bought a bed and a table too. Mary Ann. Joseph Tabrar. BoLP
He's Coming. Mark Van Doren. FaBV
He's gone, and all our plans. To His Love. Ivor Gurney. MMA
He's the Man for Me, *with music.* John A. Stone. SGR
Hesitant we stand by a sled at the top of the hill. Winter Lovers. Robert Watson. PoNC

Hesperia. Swinburne. OBNC
Hesperus. John Clare. GTBS-P
Hester. Charles Lamb. GTBS-P
Heureux qui, comme Ulysse, a fait un beau voyage. Joachim du Bellay, *tr. fr. French by* G. K. Chesterton. *Fr.* Regrets. RBL
Hey, all you children. The Lord's Name Be Praised! *Unknown.* ThGo
Hey, Diddle, Diddle. Mother Goose. SoPo
Hey! now, now, now. Welcome! Our Messiah. *Unknown.* MeEL
Hey! the little postman. The Postman. Laura E. Richards. SoPo
Hey, you swelled-up turkey feller! November's Come. Joseph C. Lincoln. RePo
hHahh!/ Hew the main stem (hHahh!). Tree Will Mow Thickets. "Will Inman." PoNC
Hiawatha. Stephen Sandy. CoPo
Hiawatha's Childhood. Lonfellow. *Fr.* The Song of Hiawatha. FaBV; RePo
Hibakusha. Eileen Egan. PtTo
Hickory, Dickory, Dock. Mother Goose. PoPl; SoPo
Hicks's Farewell, *with music. Unknown.* BFSS
Hid by the august foliage and fruit. To a Chameleon. Marianne Moore. PoPl
Hidden in wonder and snow, or sudden with summer. Laurentian Shield. F. R. Scott. OBCV
Hidden Scars. Sam Ragan. PoNC
Hide, Absolon. Chaucer. CBEP
   (Lady without Paragon, A.) MeEL
Hide-and-Seek. Robert Francis. PoIE; PoSa
Hide not thy love and myne shal bee. Pure Simple Love. Aurelian Townsend. SeCP
Hide of a leopard and hide of a deer. The Giraffe. Geoffrey Dearmer. WePo
Hiding. Dorothy Aldis. SoPo
Hiding tuft, a green-barked yew-tree, A. The Hermit's Song. *Unknown.* SiGo
Hie upon Hielands. *See* High upon Highlands.
Hierusalem. *Unknown. See* Jerusalem, My Happy Home.
Higgledy, Piggledy. Mother Goose. SoPo
High/ in your room. The Belongings. Theodore Enslin. CoPo
High and proud on the barnyard fence. Chanticleer. John Farrar. SoPo
High Barbaree, The. Laura E. Richards. SoPo
High Bridge above the Tagus River at Toledo, The. William Carlos Williams. CTC
High Brow. Robert Fitch. SD
High cockalorum diddledum! Direct Song. Eve Merriam. UnTE
High Diver. Robert Francis. SD
High Flight. John Gillespie Magee, Jr. LV; TRV
High Germany. *Unknown.* CBEP
High grace, the dower of Queens; and therewithal. Her Gifts. Dante Gabriel Rossetti. The House of Life, XXXI. VP
High Kingdom. Howard Sergeant. ToPo
High on a mountain's highest ridge. Wordsworth. *Fr.* The Thorn. Par
High on the southern wall the clock. The Nursery. Conrad Aiken. *Fr.* The Coming Forth by Day of Osiris Jones. LOW
High overhead. Looking Up at Airplanes, Always. Rolfe Humphries. RePo
High Place. André Pieyre de Mandiargues, *tr. fr. French by* Donald Justice. CoFP
High Place at Marib, The. Grant Code. FiSC
High Summer. Jascha Kessler. AmPC
High Tide on the Cost of Lincolnshire, The (1571). Jean Ingelow. OnMSP
   Calling the Cows Home, sel. ThGo
High-toned Old Christian Woman, A. Wallace Stevens. AP
High up in the courts of heaven today. A Little Dog-Angel. Norah M. Holland. PoLF
High up on the craggy mountain. Bertran de Born. Ludwig Uhland. TwGP
High upon Highlands [*or* Hie upon Hielands]. Bonnie George [*or* James] Campbell. *Unknown.* CBEP; ELP; PoPo
High Waves That Ride the Sea. Raimbaut de Vaqueiras, *tr. fr. Provençal by* William M. Davis. AnML
High wisdom holds my wisdom less. In Memoriam A. H. H., CXII. Tennyson. VP
High-yellow of my heart, with breasts like tangerines. The Peasant Declares His Love. Emile Roumer. ErPo
Higher Calling, The. W. M. Czamanske. STF
Higher Pantheism, The. Tennyson. TRV; VP
Higher Pantheism in a Nutshell, The. Swinburne. Par; VP
Higher than a house. Riddle. Mother Goose. SoPo
Highest, The. Schiller, *tr. fr. German by* Walter Kaufmann. TwGP
Highland Mary. Burns. *See* Ye Banks and Braes.
Highly beloved and intimate was he. Ten of Chaucer's People: A Greedy Friar. Chaucer. *Fr.* The Canterbury Tales. PoSa
Highmindedness, a jealousy for good. Addressed to Haydon. Keats. CBEP

Highroad's barren scar, A. Autumn Dawn. Antonio Machado. PoPl
Highway, since you my chief Parnassus be. Astrophel and Stella, LXXXIV. Sir Philip Sidney. EnRePo; ILP
Highway to Nowhere. Grant Code. FiSC
Highwayman, The. Alfred Noyes. BoLP; FaBV; PoLF; PoPo; SIV
Highwaymen, The. John Gay. Fr. The Beggar's Opera. WiR
Hike, The. Neil Weiss. SD
Hill, The. Rupert Brooke. BoLP; MoLP; WePo
Hill, The. Edgar Lee Masters. Fr. Spoon River Anthology. AmLP
Hill above the Mine, The. Malcolm Cowley. PoPl
Hill-billy, hill-billy come to buy. Pedlar. Confucius. Fr. The Classic Anthology: Wei Wind. CTC
Hill Farmer Speaks, The. R. S. Thomas. GTBS-P
Hill full, a hole full, A. Riddle. Mother Goose. SoPo
Hill Song. Juan Ruiz, Archpriest of Hita, tr. fr. Spanish by William M. Davis. Fr. The Book of True Love. AnML
Hill Song of La Zarzuela. Unknown, tr. fr. Spanish by William M. Davis. AnML
Hill Wife, The. Robert Frost. FoBA
Hillcrest. E. A. Robinson. AP; PoIE
Hills, The. Rachel Field. RePo
Hills. Arthur Guiterman. RePo
Hills and rivers of the lowland country, The. A Protest in the Sixth Year of Ch'ien Fu. Ts'ao Sung. FaBV
Hills hover in their snow-shawls, The. Birth. Olive Tilford Dargan. PoNC
Hillside. Alexander Craig. PoAu-2
Hillside Thaw, A. Robert Frost. DiPo; StP
Him Evermore I Behold. Longfellow. TRV
Hippety Hop to the Barber Shop. Mother Goose. SoPo
Hippocrene. Amy Lowell. MoLP
Hippolytus, sel. Euripides, tr. fr. Greek by Gilbert Murray. O for the Wings of a Dove. SiGo
Hippopotamus, The. Hilaire Belloc. PoPl
Hippopotamus, The. T. S. Eliot. PoDB; PoPl; PoSa
Hippopotamus, The. Ogden Nash. FaBV
Hippopotamus is strong, The. Habits of the Hippopotamus. Arthur Guiterman. FaBV; RePo
Hir bowgy cheekes been as softe as clay. A Description of His Ugly Lady. Thomas Hoccleve. MeEL
Hiroshima. Murray Noss. PoPo
His Age. Robert Herrick. SeCP
His age drawn out behind him to be watched. Old Man. Elizabeth Jennings. NePoEA-2
His are the generous days that balance. The Generous Years. Stephen Spender. PoCh
His arm—a wonder and an admiration. The Wrestler. Stefan George. LV
His art is eccentricity, his aim. Pitcher. Robert Francis CaFP; PP; SD
His Being Was in Her Alone. Sir Philip Sidney. ELP
His Best. Unknown. STF
His blood on my arm is warm as a bird. Prayer for Messiah. Leonard Cohen. OBCV
His body is of lizard size. The Chameleon. E. H. W. Meyerstein. AnMoPo
His bridle hung around the post. Horse. Elizabeth Madox Roberts. RePo
His brother said that pain was what he knew. Traction. Howard Moss. OPP
His car was worth a thousand pounds and more. One Poet Visits Another. W. H. Davies. DTC
His Cavalier. Robert Herrick. GoJo
His Creed. Robert Herrick. ILP; WePo
His delicate fingers, moving among the roses. The Utopia of Lord Mayor Howard. Randolph Stow. PoAu-2
His Desire. Robert Herrick. CABA
His Discourse with Cupid. Ben Jonson. Fr. A Celebration of Charis. SeCP
His Elegy. Chidiock Tichborne. See Elegy: "My prime of youth is but a frost of cares."
His Excuse for Loving. Ben Jonson. Fr. A Celebration of Charis. EnRePo; SeCP
His eyes are big and soft and bright. Young Flash the Deer. Thornton Burgess. RePo
His eyes are quickened so with grief. Lost Love. Robert Graves. ILP
His eyes can be quite old and stern. Father. Mildred Weston. PoSC
His Fare-well to Sack. Robert Herrick. SeCP
His father gave him a box of truisms. The Truisms. Louis MacNeice. PoIE
His fingers wake, and flutter; up the bed. Conscious. Wilfred Owen. MMA
His friends went off and left Him dead. The Resurrection. Jonathan Brooks. AmNP
His glance, worn by the passing of the bars. The Panther. Rainer Maria Rilke. TwGP
His Golden Locks [Time Hath to Silver Turned]. George Peele. Fr. Polyhymnia. EnRePo; PoIE; PoSa
(Farewell to Arms, A.) BoC
(Old Knight, The.) CBEP

(Sonnet, A.) ELP
His Grace! impossible! what, dead. A Satirical Elegy on the Death of a Late Famous General, 1722 Swift. CABA; StP
His graceful swag blocks catch the eye. The Destruction of Bulfinch's House. Stephen Sandy. CoPo
His Grange, or Private Wealth. Robert Herrick. GoJo
His Hands. John Richard Moreland. TRV
His hands worked ceaselessly at the coverlet. Testament. Sister M. Thérèse. MoRP
His hearing left him twenty years ago. Old Farmer Alone. Robert P. Tristram Coffin. MoLP
His heart was in his garden; but his brain. Sonnets, Part II, VII. Frederick Goddard Tuckerman. AP
His hottest love and most delight. The Happy Hen. James Agee. ErPo
His house was never short of bake-meat pies. Ten of Chaucer's People: A Gluttonous Rich Man. Chaucer. Fr. The Canterbury Tales. PoSa
His knapsack on his shoulder slung. The Soldier of Waterloo. Unknown. BSO
His Lady's Death. Pierre de Ronsard, tr. fr. French by Andrew Lang. Fr. Amours de Marie. RBL
His Lady's Tomb. Pierre de Ronsard, tr. fr. French by Andrew Lang. Fr. Amours de Marie. RBL
His Life Is Ours. Dorothy Conant Stroud. STF
His Litany to the Holy Spirit. Robert Herrick. DTC; ELP; PoLF
His malice was a pimple down his good. Three around the Old Gentleman. John Berryman. AP
His mother's fondness wrought his father's frown. Jacob and the Angel. Brother Antoninus. MoRP
His Mother's Service to Our Lady. Villon, tr. fr. French by Dante Gabriel Rossetti. CTC
His Mother's Wedding Ring. George Crabbe. See His Wife's Wedding Ring.
His naked skin clothed in the torrid mist. The Serf. Roy Campbell. GTBS-P
His name/ was Mohammed Sheab. In Memoriam. Giuseppe Ungaretti. CoIP
His Name at the Top. Unknown. STF
His name, they told me afterwards, was Able. In Memory of My Uncle Timothy. Alastair Reid. NePoEA-2
His name was Heimdall and it was a name. Heimdall. Harold Vinal. FiSC
His nose is short and scrubby. My Dog. Marchette Chute. SoPo
His pads furring the scarp's rime. The Snow-Leopard. Randall Jarrell. MP
His paper propped against the electric toaster. Daniel at Breakfast. Phyllis McGinley. LV
His Picture. John Donne. Fr. Elegies. CBEP
(Elegy V: His Picture.) EnRePo
His Pilgrimage. Sir Walter Ralegh. See Passionate Man's Pilgrimage, The.
His Plan. Unknown. STF
His Plan for Me. Martha Snell Nicholson. STF
His Poetrie His Pillar. Robert Herrick. SeCP
His Poverty. Rutebeuf, tr. fr. French by James Edward Tobin. AnML
His Prayer for Absolution. Robert Herrick. TRV
His Prayer to Ben Jonson. Robert Herrick. ILP; PoSa; PP
His Presence. Dale Schulz. STF
His Repentance. Rutebeuf, tr. fr. French by Norman R. Shapiro. AnML
His Scorn of Life and Consolation for Death. Jean-Baptiste Chassignet, tr. fr. French by John R. Galt. RBL
His Shield. Marianne Moore. DTC
His son meant something that he couldn't name. A Spring Night. Robert Beloof. PoPo
His stature was not very tall. The Description of Sir Geoffrey Chaucer. Robert Greene. Fr. Greene's Vision. CTC; WePo
His trousers are torn, rolled up to the knee. The Teacher Sees a Boy. Margaret Morningstar. STF
His Wife's Wedding Ring. George Crabbe. CBEP
(His Mother's Wedding Ring.) OBNC
His wild heart beats with painful sobs. The Happy Warrior. Sir Herbert Read. MMA
History. Emerson. AmLP
History. Robin Skelton. OPP
History of a Literary Movement. Howard Nemerov. PP
History of the Flood, The. John Heath-Stubbs. MoBS
History of the World as Pictures, The. Nancy Sullivan. CoPo
Hither thou com'st: the busy wind all night. The Bird [or To a Bird after a Storm or After the Storm]. Henry Vaughan. BoC; MeP; TRV
Hither where tangled thickets of the acacia. The Babiaantje. F. T. Prince. ACV
Hits and Runs. Carl Sandburg. SD
Ho! Cupid calls, come Lovers, come. Cupids Call. James Shirley. ErPo
Ho! for California! with music. Jesse Hutchinson. SGR
Ho, for taxis green or blue. Taxis. Rachel Field. SoPo
Ho, for the Pirate Don Durk of Dowdee. The Pirate Don Durk of Dowdee. Mildred Plew Merryman. SoPo

Ho! Ho! The fine fellow. Camden Magpie. Hugh McCrae. PoAu-1

Ho! Persephone brings flowers, to them. The Old Men. Irving Feldman. MP

Hoarded Grapes. *Unknown, tr. fr. Greek by* Louis Untermeyer. UnTE

Hobbes clearly proves that every creature. Swift. *Fr.* On Poetry; a Rhapsody. PP

Hock-Cart, The; or, Harvest Home. Robert Herrick. SeCP; Stp

Hog Butcher for the World. Chicago. Carl Sandburg. AP; FaBV; PoIE; PoPl

Hohenlinden. Thomas Campbell. CBEP; GTBS-P; OBNC; OnMSP; RoGo; WePo

Hokku: "Persimmon, The, lo!" Chiyo, *tr. fr. Japanese by* Curtis Hidden Page, LV

Hokku Poems. Richard Wright. AmNP

Hold Back Thy Hours [Dark Night]. Beaumont *and* Fletcher. *Fr.* The Maid's Tragedy, I, ii. ILP; UnTE
(Bridal Song: "Hold back thy hours, dark Night, till we have done.") ErPo

Hold fast to dreams. Dreams. Langston Hughes. LV

Hold Fast Your Dreams. Louise Driscoll. BiCB; SoPo

Hold hard, Ned! Lift me down once more, and lay me in the shade. The Sick Stockrider. Adam Lindsay Gordon. ACV; PoAu-1

Hold her softly, not for long. At a Child's Baptism. Vassar Miller. GoJo

Hold it up sternly—see this it sends back, (who is it, is it you?). A Hand-Mirror. Walt Whitman. CBEP

Hold Thou My Hands. William Canton. ThGo

Hölderlin. Delmore Schwartz. MoRP

Holdfast, The. George Herbert. FoBA

Holding a beggar's child. Meditation. Toyohiko Kagawa. TRV

Holding Hands. Lenore M. Link. SoPo

Holes in the Sky, sel. Louis MacNeice.
"And man is a spirit." TRV

Holiday. Adrienne Cecile Rich. MoLP

Holland, that scarce deserves the name of land. The Character of Holland. Andrew Marvell. CABL

Hollow eyes of shock remain, The. Two Years Later. John Wieners. CoPo

Hollow heads turn toward the picket fence. 250 Willow Lane. Joseph Joel Keith. FiSC

Hollow Men, The. T. S. Eliot. AP; DiPo; FoBA; OnP; PoPl

Holly, The. Henry VIII, King of England. CTC

Holly against Ivy. *Unknown.* MeEL

Holly and Ivy ("Holly and ivy made a great party"). *Unknown.* CBEP

Holly and the Ivy, The ("The holly and the ivy/ When they are both full grown"). *Unknown.* ELP

Holly and Ivy ("Holy stond in the hall"). *Unknown. See* Nay, Ivy, Nay.

Holly standeth [*or* Holly stond] in the hall fair to behold. Nay, Ivy, Nay [*or* Holly and Ivy]. *Unknown.* CBEP; MeEL

Holly wreath that now, The. A Christmas Carol. Fred Cogswell. ACV

Holy angels and blest. A Christmas Cradlesong. Lope de Vega. PoPl

Holy bereth beris. Holly against Ivy. *Unknown.* MeEL

Holy Communion, The. Henry Vaughan. MeP

Holy Earth, The, sel. John Hall Wheelock.
In the Immense Cathedral. MoRP

Holy Fair, The. Burns. EiCP

Holy, holy, holy Lord unnamed. Sonnet. William Alabaster. MeP

Holy Innocents, The. Robert Lowell. PoDB; ToPo

Holy of Holies, The. G. K. Chesterton. MoRP; TRV

Holy Sonnets, sels. John Donne.
"As due by many titles I resigne," II. MeP
"At the round earth's imagin'd corners, blow," VII. CABA; CBEP; DiPo; EaLo; EnRePo; FoBA; ILP; MeP; PoIE; SeCP; StP; VaPo
"Batter my heart, three personed God; for you," XIV. CABA; CaFP; CBEP; DiPo; EaLo; EnRePo; FoBA; ILP; MeP; OnP; PoIE; SeCP; StP; VaPo
"Death, be not proud, though some have called thee," X. CABA; CaFP; CBEP; DiPo; EnRePo; FaBV; FoBA; ILP; MeP; OnP; PoIE; PoPo; PoSa; SeCP; StP; TRV
(Death.) BoC
"Father, part of his double interest," XVI. MeP
"I am a little world made cunningly," V. CABA; EnRePo; FoBA; MeP; SeCP; StP
"If faithful soules be alike glorifi'd," VIII. MeP
"If poisonous [*or* poysonous] mineral[l]s, and if that tree," IX. CABA; EnRePo; FoBA; PoIE; MeP; SeCP
"O might those sighes and teares returne againe," III. MeP
"Oh my blacke soule! now thou art summoned," IV. MeP
"Oh, to vex me, contraryes meet in one," XIX. MeP
"Show me, dear Christ, thy spouse so bright and clear," XVIII. ILP; MeP
"Since she whom I lov'd hath paid her last debt," XVII. FoBA; MeP

"Spit in my face you Jews, and pierce my side," XI. FoBa; MeP

"This is my playes last scene, here heavens appoint," VI. MeP; SeCP

"Thou hast made me; and shall thy work decay?" I. EnRePo; MeP; SeCP

"What if this present were the worlds last night?" XIII. MeP; OnP

"Why are we by all creatures waited on?" XII. CABA; MeP

"Wilt thou love God, as he thee! then digest," XV. MeP

Holy Spirit, The. Evelyn Underhill. BoC

Holy Spirit, Lead Me. *Unknown.* STF

Holy stond in the hall. *See* Holly standeth in the hall fair to behold.

"Holy Supper is kept, indeed, The." James Russell Lowell. *Fr.* The Vision of Sir Launfal. TRV

Holy Thursday ("'Twas on a Holy Thursday"). Blake. *Fr.* Songs of Experience. EnPe; ILP; PoIE; StP

Holy Thursday ("'Twas on a Holy Thursday"). Blake. *Fr.* Songs of Innocence. BoC; CBEP; DiPo; EnPE; FoBA; PoIE; StP

Holy Willie's Prayer. Burns. EnPE; VaPo

Homage to Charles Laughton. Gil Orlovitz. ToPo

Homage to Diana. Sir Walter Ralegh. WiR

Homage to Ezra Pound. Gilbert Highet. Par

Homage to Sextus Propertius, sels. Ezra Pound.
"Me happy, night, night full of brightness." ErPo
"Shades of Callimachus, Coan ghosts of Philetas." AnMoPo; PP

Homage to thee, O Ra, at thy tremendous rising! The Dead Man Ariseth and Singeth a Hymn to the Sun. *Unknown. Fr.* Book of the Dead. SiGo

Home. Robert Frost. *Fr.* The Death of the Hired Man. TRV

Home. Verner von Heidenstam, *tr. fr. Swedish by* Charles Wharton Stork. PoPl

Home. W. E. Henley. PoLF

Home. Martha Snell Nicholson. STF

Home, The. Rabindranath Tagore. GoJo

Home. Henry van Dyke. STF

Home again? Spendthrift. I. A. Richards. PoPl

Home at Last. G. K. Chesterton. TRV

Home Burial. Robert Frost. AP; StP

Home came our goodman [*or* this good old man]. Our Goodman. *Unknown.* BSO; UnTE

Home from Abroad. Laurie Lee. ToPo

Home from Guatemala, back at the Waldorf. Arrival at the Waldorf. Wallace Stevens. PP

Home is the place where, when you have to go there. Home. Robert Frost. *Fr.* The Death of the Hired Man. TRV

Home Leave. Barbara Howes. MP

Home Prayer, A. *Unknown. See* Lord of all Pots and Pans and Things.

Home, Sweet Home. John Howard Payne. FaPL; LV

Home They Brought Her Warrior Dead. Tennyson. *Fr.* The Princess. FoBA

Home, thou return'st from Thames, whose Naiads long. An Ode on the Popular Superstitions of the Highlands of Scotland. William Collins. EnPE

Home Thoughts. Carl Sandburg. MoLP

Home-Thoughts, from Abroad. Robert Browning. CBEP; DiPo; FaBV; ILP; PoIE; LV; OBNC; PoLF; PoPo; VP

Home-Thoughts from France. Isaac Rosenberg. MMA

Home-Thoughts, from the Sea. Robert Browning. CaFP; CBEP; HaSV; ILP

Home Town. W. D. Snodgrass. ToPo

Hometown, how will it look then? Return. Bertolt Brecht. MGP

Home Truths from Abroad. *Unknown.* Par

Homer in a Garden. James Larkin Pearson. PoNC

Homesick? and yet your country walks. To Henry Vaughan. A. J. M. Smith. OBCV

Homesick Blues. Langston Hughes. PoPl

Home-Sickness. Justinus Kerner, *tr. fr. German by* James Clarence Mangan. SiGo

Homeward Song. Olive Tilford Dargan. PoNC

Honest John and William Relief. John A. Stone. SGR

Honest Miner, An, *with music.* John A. Stone. SGR

Honest William, an easy and good-natured fellow. The Brewer's Coachman. William Taylor. WaPE

Honey/ When de man. Sister Lou. Sterling A. Brown. AmNP

Honey & Water. Medieval Christ Speaks on a Spanish Sculpture of Himself. Rochelle Owens. CoPo

Honey Bee, The. Don Marquis. PoPl; PoPo

Honey Dew Falls from the Tree. John Clare. PoIE

Honey-flowers to the honey-comb. Chimes. Dante Gabriel Rossetti. OBNC

Honey from silkworms who can gather. Lines to a Critic. Shelley. CBEP

Honeysuckle, The. Dante Gabriel Rossetti. CBEP

Honolulu and Back. John Logan. AmPC

Honor and Desert. Coventry Patmore. The Angel in the House, II, iv, l. FaPL

Honor is flashed off exploit, so we say. St. Alphonsus Rodriguez. Gerard Manley Hopkins. PoIE

Honor to Celery. Hans Magnus Enzensberger, *tr. fr. German by* Christopher Middleton. MGP

Honourable Entertainment Given to the Queen's Majesty in Progress at Elvetham, 1591, The, *sel.* Nicholas Breton. In the Merry Month of May. PoSa
(Phillida and Coridon.) UnTE

Honours that the people give always, The. The Thespians at Thermopylae. Norman Cameron. · GTBS-P

Hooded reptile, in his guile, The. The Serpent. Joseph Langland. MP

Hoopoe. George Darley. *Fr.* Nepenthe. OBNC

Hop-poles stand in cones, The. The Midnight Skaters. Edmund Blunden. GoJo; GTBS-P; WePo

Hope. Amy Carmichael. TRV

Hope. Sir Richard Fanshawe. CBEP

Hope. Sister Juana Inés de la Cruz, *tr. fr. Spanish by* Kate Flores. AnSP

Hope. Anna Blake Mezquida. TRV

Hope in Springtime. Ludwig Uhland, *tr. fr. German by* Martin Zwart. AGP

Hope is a crushed stalk. Dark Testament. Pauli Murray. AmNP

Hope is a subtle glutton. Emily Dickinson. DiPo

Hope is the thing with feathers. Emily Dickinson. CBEP; DiPo; FoBA

Hope of Our Hearts. Sir Edward Denny. STF

Hope Overtaken. Dante Gabriel Rossetti. The House of Life, XLII. VP

Hope's Forecast. Ethel Romig Fuller. RePo

Hoppity. A. A. Milne. FaBV

Hoppity Toads. Aileen Fisher. RePo

Horae Canonicae, *sels.* W. H. Auden. PoDB
Prime.
Sext.

Horatian Ode upon Cromwell's Return from Ireland, An. Andrew Marvell. CABL; GTBS-P; SeCP

Horatius. Macaulay. *Fr.* Lays of Ancient Rome. PoLF

Horn, The. James Reaney. OBCV

Hornpipe. Edith Sitwell. *Fr.* Façade. GTBS-P

Horologe, The. Clark Ashton Smith. FiSC

Horoscope. J. V. Cunningham. PoIE

Horror Movie. Howard Moss. NePoEA-2

Hors d'Oeuvre. Deems Taylor, *tr. fr. French.* UnTE

Horse. Elizabeth Madox Roberts. RePo

Horse & Rider. Wey Robinson. SD

Horse breaks glass, A. Horses. Myra Von Riedemann. OBCV

Horse Chestnut Tree, The. Richard Eberhart. CaFP; PoDB; PoPl; PoPo; ToPo

Horse is foaming, The. Like dogs brown. Ride. "Klabund." TwGP

Horse Thief, The. William Rose Benét. OnMSP

Horseman, The. Walter de la Mare. GoJo; SoPo

Horsemen, The. Gene Baro. NePoEA-2

Horsepower crops Araby for pasture. Mordent for a Melody. Margaret Avison. ACV

Horses. Richard Armour. PoPl

Horses. Louis MacNeice. DaDu

Horses, The. Edwin Muir. ACV; PoIE; PoSa

Horses. Myra Von Riedemann. OBCV

Horses and Men in the Rain. Carl Sandburg. PoLF

Horses of the Sea, The. Christina Rossetti. *Fr.* Sing-Song. GoJo

Horses on the Camargue. Roy Campbell. BoC; DaDu; GTBS-P

Horses, the pigs, The. Familiar Friends. James S. Tippett. SoPo

Horses were ready, the rails were down, The. Where the Pelican Builds. Mary Hannay Foott. PoAu-1

Hospice of the Word. Brother Antoninus. ToPo

Hospital, A. Alfred Noyes. PoPl

Hospital Barge at Cérisy. Wilfred Owen. CBEP

Hospital for Defectives. Thomas Blackburn. GTBS-P

Hospital Waiting-Room, The. W. H. Davies. CBEP

Hospital Window, The. James Dickey. CoPo

Hot-Cross Buns. Mother Goose. SoPo

Hot Night on Water Street ("Hot midsummer night"). Louis Simpson. MP

Hot sun, cool fire, tempered with sweet air. Bethsabe's Song. George Peele. *Fr.* David and Bethsabe. CBEP; EnRePo

Hot-Weather Song, A. Don Marquis. RePo

Hotel de l'Univers et Portugal. James Merrill. NePoEA-2

Hotel Paradiso e Commerciale. John Malcolm Brinnin. MP; PoCh

Hound of Heaven, The. Francis Thompson. FaBV; FaPL; ILP; PoIE; TRV
Our God Finds Us, *sel.* BoC

Hounded Lovers, The. William Carlos Williams. MoLP

Hounds of Spring, The. Swinburne. *See* Chorus: "When the hounds of spring are on winter's traces."

Hour after Hour, Day after Day. Rosalia de Castro, *tr. fr. Spanish by* Muriel Kittel. AnSP

Hour after hour the cards were fairly shuffled. Whist. Eugene Fitch Ware. PoLF

Hour before the Day, An. Eduard Möricke, *tr. fr. German by* Gerd Gillhoff. AGP

Hour-Glass, The. Ben Jonson. CBEP; EnRePo; SeCP

Hour of Death, The. Felicia Hemans. OBNC

Hour of Prayer, The. Georgia. B. Adams. STF

Hour of Prayer, The. Charlotte Elliott. STF

Hour told by the owl and the moon, The. Lament for Better or Worse. Gene Baro. FiSC; NePoEA-2

Hour which might have been yet might not be, The. Stillborn Love. Dante Gabriel Rossetti. The House of Life, LV. VP

Hourly I Die. Dryden. *Fr.* Amphitryon. UnTE

Hours before dawn we were woken by the quake. Aubade. William Empson. ToPo

Hours of Idleness. Byron. *See* Tear, The.

Hours of the Passion, The. *Unknown.* MeEL

House. Robert Browning. DiPo; PP

House, The. Robert Creeley. CoPo

House and Grounds, A. Leigh Hunt. CBEP

House and Home. Victor Hugo, *tr. fr. French.* TRV

House and Land. Allen Curnow. ACV

House and Shutter. Lewis Turco. PoPl

House by the Side of the Road, The. Sam Walter Foss. LV; TRV

House Carpenter, The. *Unknown. See* James Harris.

House had gone to bring again, The. The Need of Being Versed in Country Things. Robert Frost. PoSa

House is built of logs and stone, A. House and Home. Victor Hugo. TRV

House is crammed, The: tier beyond tier they grin. "Blighters." Siegfried Sassoon. MMA

House of Alvargonzálcz, Thc. Antonio Machado, *tr. fr. Spanish by* Denise Levertov. AnSP

House of Cards, The. Christina Rossetti. *Fr.* Sing-Song. PoPl

House of Christmas, The. G. K. Chesterton. MoRP

House of Falling Leaves We Entered in, The. William Stanley Braithwaite. *Fr.* The House of Falling Leaves. PoLF

House of Fire. Theodore Weiss. CoPo

House of Life. Dorothy Quick. FiSC

House of Life, The, *sels.* Dante Gabriel Rossetti.
Autumn Idleness, LXIX. ILP
Barren Spring, LXXXIII. OBNC; VaPo
Beauty's Pageant, XVII. VP
Birth-Bond, The, XV. VP
Body's Beauty, LXXVIII. ILP
Bridal Birth, II. VP
Broken Music, XLVII. VP
Choice, The, LXXIII. GTBS-P
Cloud and Wind, XLIV. VP
Dark Glass, The, XXXIV. VP
Day of Love, A, XVI. VP
Death-in-Love, XLVIII. VP
Equal Troth, XXXII. VP
Genius in Beauty, XVIII. VP
Gracious Moonlight, XX. VP
Heart's Compass, XXVII. VP
Heart's Haven, XXII. VP
Heart's Hope, V. VP
Her Gifts, XXXI. VP
Hope Overtaken, XLII. VP
Kiss, The, VI. VP
Lamp's Shrine, The, XXXV. VP
Last Fire, XXX. VP
Life-in-Love, XXXVI. VP
Love and Hope, XLIII. VP
Love Enthroned, I. OBNC; VP
Love-Letter, The, XI. VP
Love-Moon, The, XXXVII. VP
Love-Sweetness, XXI. VP
Lovers' Walk, The, XII. VP
Love's Baubles, XXIII. VP
Love's Fatality, LIV. VP
Love's Last Gift, LIX. VP
Love's Lovers, VIII. VP
Love's Testament, III. VP
Lovesight, IV. GTBS-P; OBNC; VP
Mid-Rapture, XXVI. VP
Moonstar, The, XXIX. VP
Morrow's Message, The, XXXVIII. VP
Nuptial Sleep, VI (A). VP
Parted Love, XLVI. VP
Passion and Worship, IX. VP
Portrait, The, X. VP
Pride of Youth, XXIV. OBNC; VP
Secret Parting, XLV. VP
Severed Selves, XL. VP
Silent Noon, XIX. ILP; OBNC; VP
Sleepless Dreams, XXXIX. VP
Sonnet, The ("A sonnet is a moment's monument"), *introd.* ILP; PP; StP; VP

House of Life, The, *sels.* (*continued*)
Soul-Light, XXVIII. VP
Stillborn Love, LV. VP
Superscription, A, XCVII. CBEP; GTBS-P; OBNC
Supreme Surrender, VII. VP
Through Death to Love, XLI. VP
True Woman: Her Heaven, LVIII. VP
True Woman: Her Love, LVII. VP
True Woman: Herself, LVI. VP
Venus Victrix, XXXIII. VP
What Smouldering Senses, VI. UnTE
Willowwood, XLIX-LII. VP
Winged Hours, XXV. VP
Without Her, LIII. CBEP; OBNC; VP
Youth's Antiphony, XIII. VP
Youth's Spring-Tribute, XIV. VP
House of Night, The, *sel.* Philip Freneau.
Death. AP
House of the Mouse, The. Lucy Sprague Mitchell. SoPo
House of Yesterday. Walter Shedlofsky. FiSC
House on Maple Hill, The. Stanley McNail. FiSC
House on the Hill, The. E. A. Robinson. GoJo; LV; PoSa
House that Jack Built, The. *Unknown.* SoPo
House-Top, The. Herman Melville. AP
House was lonely, all dark and bare, The. House of Life. Dorothy Quick. FiSC
House was shaken by a rising wind, The. Brainstorm. Howard Nemerov. ToPo
House, you are done. Consecration of the House. W. S. Fairbridge. PoAu-2
Housed in each other's arms. Song for a Marriage. Vassar Miller. ToPo
Housekeeper, The. Vincent Bourne, *tr. fr. Latin by* Charles Lamb. PoLF
Housemates. Odell Shepard. MoRP
Houses ("Houses are faces"). Aileen Fisher. SoPo
Houses are haunted, The. Disillusionment of Ten o'Clock. Wallace Stevens. LOW; PoIE; PoPo; PoSa
Houses, churches, mixed together. A Description of London. John Banks. WaPE
Houses of men are on fire, The. The Seventh Hell: Of Smoke, Where Fire-Raisers Try in Vain to Escape from a Shower of Hot Sand Falling from a Cloud. Jerome Rothenberg. CoPo
Housewife, The. Catherine Cate Coblentz. TRV
Housewifery. Edward Taylor. DiPo; ILP; StP
(Huswifery.) AP; EaLo; FaBV
How? *Unknown.* STF
How am I to withhold my soul. Love Song. Rainer Maria Rilke. SiGo
How amiable are thy tabernacles, O Lord of hosts! Psalm LXXXIV, Bible, *O.T.* TRV
How Annandale Went Out. E. A. Robinson. AP; ILP
How Beastly the Bourgeois Is. D. H. Lawrence. PoIE
How beauteous is the bond. The Peau de Chagrin of State Street. Oliver Wendell Holmes. AP
How beautiful was, that one bright day. Hawthorne—May 23 1863. Longfellow. CBEP
How beautiful the earth is still. Anticipation. Emily Brontë. OBNC
How beautiful this hill of fern swells on! Stanzas. John Clare. *Fr.* Child Harold. OBNC
How blessed was the created state. The Fall. Earl of Rochester. UnTE
How bright on the blue. The Kite. Harry Behn. RePo
How! butler, how! Fill the Bowl, Butler. *Unknown.* MeEL
How calm, how beautiful, comes on. The Golden Hour. Thomas Moore. *Fr.* Lalla Rookh. OBNC
How Can I Keep From Singing? *sel.* Robert Lowry. "What though my joys and comforts die?" TRV
How Can I Keep My Maidenhead. Burns. ErPo; UnTE
How can I tell them what it was I saw. Lincoln's Dream. Ridgely Torrence. LiPo
How can I, that girl standing there. Politics. W. B. Yeats. FoBA; PoPo; StP
How Can Man Die Better. Tyrtaeus, *tr. fr. Greek by* T. F. Higham. SiGo
How can our minds and bodies be. Grace before Sleep. Sara Teasdale. MoRP
How can that be, lady, which all men learn. The Artist and His Work. Michelangelo. RBL
How can the tree but waste and wither away. No Pleasure without Some Pain. Thomas, Lord Vaux. EnRePo
How Can You? Maxine Stevens. STF
How changed is here each spot man makes or fills! Thyrsis. Matthew Arnold. ILP; OBNC; StP; VP
How charming is this little spot. To Mrs. Boteler. Mary Chandler. WaPE
How cold are thy baths, Apollo! Jugurtha. Longfellow. AP
How cool the breeze. Coolness. Onitsura. SiGo
How cool the cattle seem. Cattle. *Unknown.* SoPo
How could I keep my soul so that it might. Love Song. Rainer Maria Rilke. TwGP

How could I know. The Dance Called David. Theodore Weiss. CoPo
How could you dream mere body's eloquence. A Prophecy. Christopher Levenson. ErPo
How Cyrus Laid the Cable. John Godfrey Saxe. SIV
How dare one say it? The Unexpressed. Walt Whitman. PP
How dear to my heart are the scenes of my childhood. The Old Oaken Bucket. Samuel Woodworth. LV
How Death Comes. *Unknown.* MeEL
How deep is his duplicity who in a flash. High Diver. Robert Francis. SD
How delicious is the winning. Freedom and Love. Thomas Campbell. GTBS-P
How delightful, at sunset, to loosen the boat! The Excursion. Tu Fu. SD
How did the party go in Portman Square? Juliet. Hilaire Belloc. BoLP; WePo
"How did you know her?" Story from Russian Author. Peter Redgrove. NePoEA-2
How do I love thee? Let me count the ways. Sonnets from the Portuguese, XLIII. Elizabeth Barrett Browning. BoC; BoLP; CTC; FaBV; FaPL; ILP; LV; PoLF; PoPl; PoPo; TRV
How do you like to go up in a swing. The Swing. Robert Louis Stevenson. GoJo; LV; SoPo
How Do You Live? *Unknown.* STF
"How does the water." How the Waters Come Down at Lodore. Robert Southey. PoPo
How doth the little busy bee. Little Busy Bee [*or* Against Idleness and Mischief]. Isaac Watts. Par; SoPo
How Doth the Little Crocodile. "Lewis Carroll." *Fr.* Alice's Adventures in Wonderland. Par; SoPo
How dreamy-dark it is! Charles Mair. *Fr.* The Fireflies. OBCV
How Easily Men's Cheeks Are Hot. Verner von Heidenstam, *tr. fr. Swedish by* Charles Wharton Stork. PoPl
How fair is youth that flies so fast! Then be happy, ye who may. Triumph of Bacchus and Ariadne. Lorenzo de' Medici. *Fr.* Carnival Songs. CTC
How Far? Vassar Miller. CoPo
How fares it with the happy dead? In Memoriam A. H. H., XLIV. Tennyson. VP
How fell sage Helen? through a swain like thee. A Countryman's Wooing. Theocritus. *Fr.* Idylls. ErPo
How fresh, O Lord, how sweet and clean. The Flower. George Herbert. BoC; ELP; MeP; SeCP
How Gentle God's Commands. Philip Doddridge. TRV
How Gray the Rain. Elizabeth J. Coatsworth. SoPo
How green the green at Salem is. The Burial of Terror. Carl Bode. ToPo
How happier is that flea. The Happiness of a Flea. Tasso. RBL
How happy is he born and taught. The Character of a Happy Life. Sir Henry Wotton. FaPL; GTBS-P; PoIE; PoPo
How hard is my fortune. The Convict of Clonmel. *Unknown,* *tr. by* J. J. Callanan. SD
How He Saw Her. Ben Jonson. *Fr.* A Celebration of Charis. EnRePo; SeCP
How I Brought the Good News from Aix to Ghent (*or* Vice Versa). R. J. Yeatman *and* W. C. Sellar. OnMSP
How I wish I Was Single Again, *with music. Unknown.* BSO
How in Heaven's name did Columbus get over. Columbus. Arthur Hugh Clough. PoSC
How in morning splendor. Ganymede. Goethe. TwGP
How is man parcell'd out? how ev'ry hour. The Tempest. Henry Vaughan. MeP
How It Strikes a Contemporary. Robert Browning. CABL; CTC; GTBS-P; PP
How large that thrush looks on the bare thorn-tree. Winter. Dante Gabriel Rossetti. CBEP
How large unto the tiny fly. The Fly. Walter de la Mare. LV
How like a winter hath my absence been. Sonnets, XCVII. Shakespeare. CABA; CBEP; DiPo; EnRePo; GTBS-P; VaPo
How like an angel came I down! Wonder. Thomas Traherne. CBEP; MeP; PoIE; SeCP; StP
How like the breath of love the rustling breeze. The Moon in September. Kashiprosad Ghose. ACV
How long ago she planted the hawthorn hedge. The Hawthorn Hedge. Judith Wright. PoAu-2
How long I pleaded I can never guess. Long Pursuit. *Unknown.* UnTE
How long shall I pine for love? Pining for Love. Francis Beaumont. BoLP
How long shall this like dying life endure. Amoretti, XXV. Spenser. EnRePo
How Long This Night Is. *Unknown.* MeEL
How long until the war's end sets you free? Longing. "Michael Lewis." *Fr.* Cherry Blossoms. UnTE

How love came to an end, I do not know. Love's Ending. Paul Bartlett. PoNC

How lovely are these swans. The Swans. Andrew Young. WePo

How lovely the elder brother's. Brothers. Gerard Manley Hopkins. FoBA

How low when angels fall their black descent. The Promise in Disturbance. George Meredith. Modern Love: Prologue. VP

How many a father have I seen. In Memoriam A. H. H., LIII. Tennyson. VP

How many a thing which we cast to the ground. Modern Love, XLI. George Meredith. VP

How many a time have I. Byron. *Fr.* The Two Foscari. HaSV

How many dawns, chill from his rippling rest. To Brooklyn Bridge. Hart Crane. *Fr.* The Bridge. AP; CABA; DiPo; ILP; PoDB; PoIE; PoPl; ThLM

How many dear companions who enlivened for us. Remembrance. Vasily Zhukovsky. SiGo

How many drag the marriage chain. Epigram. Royall Tyler. StP

How Many Foolish Things. Michael Drayton. *See* How Many Paltry, Foolish, Painted Things.

How Many Heavens. Edith Sitwell. MoRP

How many humble hearts have dipped. To a Post-Office Inkwell. Christopher Morley. PoLF

How many miles to Babylon. *Unknown.* CBEP

How Many Miles to Mylor? A. L. Rowse. DaDu

How many of the body's health complain. Soul-Sickness. Jones Very. AP

How Many Paltry, Foolish, Painted Things. Michael Drayton. Idea, VI. EnRePo
(How Many Foolish Things.) CBEP

How many suns have blazed and died within. Musings of an Insomniac. Edith Ogutsch. FiSC

How many thousands never heard the name. Samuel Daniel. *Fr.* Musophilus. PP

How Many Times? Thomas Lovell Beddoes. *Fr.* Torrismond. ELP

How many times these low feet staggered. Emily Dickinson. AP; CABA

How McDougal Topped the Score. Thomas E. Spencer. PoAu-1

How most unworthy, echoing in mine ears. Sonnets, Part II, XII. Frederick Goddard Tuckerman. AP

How much living have you done? The Poet Speaks. Georgia Douglas Johnson. AmNP

How much more. The Process. Robert Kelly. CoPo

How nice to be a local swan. Sitting Pretty. Margaret Fishback. PoLF

How oft am I for rhyme to seek? Swift. *Fr.* To Dr. Delany. PP

How oft, when thou, my music, music play'st. Sonnets, CXXVIII. Shakespeare. ILP

How Old Are You? *At. to* Edward Tuck *and to* H. S. Fritsch. PoLF
(Age.) BiCB

How Old Brown Took Harper's Ferry. Edmund Clarence Stedman. OnMSP

How Old Is My Heart. Christopher Brennan. *Fr.* The Wanderer. PoAu-1

How Old Is Pilar? Manuel González Prada, *tr. fr. Spanish by* William M. Davis. AnSP

"How old is she, Billy, Billy, Billy Boy." Billy Boy (C vers.) *Unknown.* BSO

How old is thirty-six, about? Prattle. John Ciardi. BiCB

How One Winter Came in the Lake Region. Wilfred Campbell. OBCV

How peaceable it seems for lonely men. The Crow. John Clare. WePo

How placid, how divinely sweet. Meandering Wye. Robert Bloomfield. *Fr.* The Banks of Wye. OBNC

How Pleasant to Know Mr. Lear. Edward Lear. CBEP
(By Way of Preface.) GTBS-P; PoSa

How pleased within my native bowers. The Landskip. William Shenstone. CBEP

How pure at heart and sound in head. In Memoriam A. H. H., XCIV. Tennyson. VP

How pure, how beautiful, how fine. Reflections Dental. Phyllis McGinley. LV

How rich, O Lord! how fresh thy visits are! Unprofitablenes. Henry Vaughan. MeP

How Samson Bore Away the Gates of Gaza. Vachel Lindsay. MoRP

How say you? Let us, O my dove. Robert Browning. *Fr.* Two in the Campagna. BoLP

"How shall I a habit break?" A Builder's Lesson. John Boyle O'Reilly. PoLF

How shall I array my love? The Question. Frederick Goddard Tuckerman. AP

How shall I speak of doom, and ours in special. Tales from a Family Album. Donald Justice. NePoEA-2

How shall my tongue expresse that hallow'd fire. Francis Quarles. *Fr.* Emblems. MeP

How shall the wine be drunk, or the woman known? A Voice from under the Table. Richard Wilbur. ToPo

How shall we praise the magnificence of the dead. Tetélestai. Conrad Aiken. PoDB

How should I love my best? Madrigal. Lord Herbert of Cherbury. SeCP

How should I praise thee, Lord! how should my rymes. The Temper. George Herbert. MeP

How shril are silent tears? when sin got head. Admission. Henry Vaughan. MeP

How silent lurks this perfect anarchist. Arachnida, Female. Aletha Humphreys. FiSC

How Sleep the Brave. William Collins. CBEP
(Ode: "How sleep the brave who sink to rest.") EiCP; ELP
(Ode: Written in the Beginning of the Year 1746.) EnPE
(Ode Written in MDCCXLVI.) GTBS-P

How slowly moves the snail, that builds. Wild Oats. W. H. Davies. ACV

"How smooth's your brow, my lady Elspat!" Lady Elspat. *Unknown.* BuBa

How soon doth man decay! Mortification. George Herbert. FoBA; MeP; SeCP

How Soon Hath Time [the Subtle Thief of Youth]. Milton. CABA; FoBA; OnP
(On Being Arrived at the Age of Twenty-three.) PoIE
(On His Having Arrived at the Age of Twenty-three.) DiPo
(Sonnet.) MeP; TRV

How startling to find the portraits of the gods. Mythological Sonnets, XVI. Roy Fuller. ErPo

How still. Sea Calm. Langston Hughes. LOW

How still, how happy! These are words. Emily Brontë. OBNC

How still it is here in the woods. Solitude. Archibald Lampman. CBEP; OBCV

How still the day is, and the air how bright! By the Wood. Robert Nichols. MMA

How straight it flew, how long it flew. Seaside Golf. John Betjeman. PoPl; SD

How strange it seems! These Hebrews in their graves. The Jewish Cemetery at Newport. Longfellow. AP

How Strange Love Is, in Every State of Consciousness. Delmore Schwartz. MuLP

How strange the sculptures that adorn these towers! Divina Commedia, II. Longfellow. AP; DiPo; ILP

How subtle-secret is your smile! Oscar Wilde. *Fr.* The Sphinx. UnTE

How sweet and lovely dost thou make the shame. Sonnets, CXV. Shakespeare. CBEP

How Sweet I Roamed. Blake. *See* Song: "How sweet I roamed from field to field."

How sweet is the shepherd's sweet lot. The Shepherd. Blake. *Fr.* Songs of Innocence. CBEP

How sweet it is, at first approach of morn. Oliver Goldsmith, the Younger. *Fr.* The Rising Village. OBCV

How sweet the answer echo makes. Echo [*or* Echoes]. Thomas Moore. CBEP; ELP; GTBS-P

How sweet the moonlight sleeps upon this bank! Shakespeare. *Fr.* The Merchant of Venice, V, i. BoC

How sweet the name of Jesus sounds. The Name of Jesus. John Newton. STF

How sweetly doth My Master sound! My Master! The Odour. George Herbert. MeP

How tenderly the evening creeps between. Evening. Hugh McCrae. PoAu-1

How terrifying it is in the night, the convex face of the black land! Four Psalms, I. Bertolt Brecht. MGP

How the Fire Queen Crossed the Swamp. Will H. Ogilvie. PoAu-1

How the Flowers Grow. "Gabriel Setoun." SoPo

How the Great Guest Came. Edwin Markham. SIV

How the Helpmate of Blue-Beard Made Free with a Door. Guy Wetmore Carryl. SIV

How the red road stretched before us, mile on mile. Independence. Nancy Cato. PoAu-2

How the Waters Come Down at Lodore. Robert Southey. PoPo

How They Bite. *Unknown.* SD

How They Brought the Good News from Ghent to Aix. Robert Browning. PoPo; RoGo; SIV; WePo

How they ring their bells, these priests! How pressing they make it. Goethe. *Fr.* Venetian Epigrams. TwGP

How time reverses. For My Contemporaries. J. V. Cunningham. PoSa; PP

How to keep—is there any any, is there none such. The Leaden Echo and the Golden Echo. Gerard Manley Hopkins. DTC; GTBS-P; OBNC; PoDB; VP

How to speak of it. Verba in Memoriam. Barbara Guest. OPP

How to Tell the Top of a Hill. John Ciardi. SoPo

How to Tell the Wild Animals. Carolyn Wells. RePo

How to Treat Elves. Morris Bishop. PoPl

How to win her. A Serious Poem. Ernest Walsh. ErPo

How tranquil is man's life. The Life Withdrawn. Luis de León. AnSP

How unpleasant to Meet Mr. Eliot! Lines for Cuscuscaraway and Mirza Murad Ali Beg. T. S. Eliot. PoPl

How vainly men themselves amaze. The Garden [or Thoughts in a Summer Garden]. Andrew Marvell. BoC; CABA; CABL; CaFP; CBEP; DiPo; GTBS-P; MeP; OnP; PoIE; PoLF; PoSa; SeCP; StP; VaPo

How We Heard the Name. Alan Dugan. CaFP

How well her name an Army doth present. Ana(Mary Army)gram. George Herbert. CABA

"How will he hear the bell at school?" Mutterings over the Crib of a Deaf Child. James Wright. PoPl; StP

How wisely Nature did decree. Eyes and Tears. Andrew Marvell. MeP

How would you like bright dreams today. In an Editor's Office. Zoe Kincaid Brockman. PoNC

How you burn about me. Ganymed. Goethe. AGP

Howdy, Honey, Howdy! Paul Laurence Dunbar. PoLF

Howe'er, 'tis well, that while mankind. To the Honorable Charles Montague, Esq. Matthew Prior. EiCP

Howl, sel. Allen Ginsberg.
    "What sphinx of cement and aluminum bashed open their skulls," II. PoCh

"How's your father?" came the whisper. Conversational. Unknown. BoLP

Hubbard oh Hubbard, you've served me wrong. How I Wish I Was Single Again. Unknown. BSO

Hucksters haggle in the mart, The. For a War Memorial. G. K. Chesterton. MMA

Hugest mammal in the land, The. Ant-ology. Christian Morgenstern. MGP

Hugh Selwyn Mauberley (Life and Contacts). Ezra Pound. AP; CABA
    Sels.
    "Age demanded an image, The," II. PoIE
    "Beneath the sagging roof," X. PoIE
    Envoi (1919). CaFP; CTC; PoIE
    E. P. Ode pour l'Election de Son Sepulcre, I. PoIE; PP
    ("For three years, out of key with his time.") ILP (I-V)
    "There died a myriad," V. PoIE
    "These fought in any case," IV. PoIE; PoSa; ThLM

Hughley Steeple. A. E. Housman. A Shropshire Lad, LXI. VP

Human Abstract, The. Blake. *Fr.* Songs of Experience. DiPo

Human Instinct, A. Christopher Morley. *Fr.* Translations from the Chinese. EvOK

Human Life. Matthew Arnold. VP

Human Life, *sels.* Samuel Rogers.
    Another and the Same. OBNC
    Man's Going Hence. OBNC

Human Misery. Andreas Gryphius, *tr. fr. German* by George C. Schoolfield. AGP

Human Seasons, The. Keats. GTBS-P; PoPo; WiR

Human Things. Howard Nemerov. StP; ToPo

Humble Petition of Poor Ben to the Best of Monarchs, Masters, Men, King Charles, The. Ben Jonson. PP

Humble Service. Lillian G. Heard. STF

Humble we must be, if to Heaven we go. Humility. Robert Herrick. WePo

Humbly Showeth./ That I went to warm myself in Lady Betty's Chamber. To Their Excellencies the Lords Justices of Ireland, the Humble Petition of Frances Harris. Swift. ILP; Par

Humbug Steamship Companies, *with music.* John A. Stone. SGR

Humility. Robert Herrick. WePo

Humming Stair, The. Joseph Payne Brennan. FiSC

Humorist, The. Keith Preston. EvOK

Humpty Dumpty. Unknown. CaFP

Humpty Dumpty's Song. "Lewis Carroll." *Fr.* Through the Looking Glass. GTBS-P; OnMSP

Hunchback in the Park, The. Dylan Thomas. AnMoPo; DiPo; MP; PoIE; ToPo

Hunchback on the corner, with gum and shoelaces, The. Pursuit. Robert Penn Warren. MP

Hundred mares, all white, A! their manes. The Mares of the Camargue. Frédéric Mistral. *Fr.* Mirèio. PoPl

Hundred slag piles north of us, A. Two Poems about President Harding, II. James Wright. AmPC

Hundred-sunned Phenix. George Darley. *See* Phoenix, The.

Hunger and Rain. Sam Ragan. PoNC

Hunger was loneliness, betrayed. Bread. R. S. Thomas. BoC

Hungering on the gray plain of its birth. A Lion Named Passion. John Hollander. NePoEA-2

Hungry Waves, The. Dorothy Aldis. RePo

Hunter, The. Ogden Nash. EvOK; SD

Hunter Trials. John Betjeman. DaDu

Hunting. Gary Snyder. CoPo

Hunting after Gold. John A. Stone. SGR

Hunting of Cupid, The, *sel.* George Peele.
    What Thing Is Love. ELP; EnRePo; UnTE

Hunting of the Snark, The. "Lewis Carroll." OBNC; OnMSP

Hunting Song. Henry Fielding. *Fr.* Don Quixote in England, II. StP

Hunting Song. Donald Finkel. MoBS

Hunting Song. Sir Walter Scott. EvOK; GTBS-P; SD; WiR

Hurdle of water, and O these waters are cold, A. Formal Elegy. John Berryman. OPP

Hurl down the nerve-gnarled body hurtling head. The Final Hunger. Vassar Miller. ToPo

Hurrah for Greer County, *with music.* Unknown. BFSS

Hurrah for the Lachlan. The Shearer's Song. Unknown. PoAu-1

Hurrahing in Harvest. Gerard Manley Hopkins. BoC; CBEP; PoIE; VP

Hurricane, The. Hart Crane. AP

Hurricane, The. Philip Freneau. AP

Hurry to bless the hands that play. The Players Ask for a Blessing on the Psalteries and on Themselves. W. B. Yeats. PoDB

Hurry Tomorrow. Ivy O. Eastwick. BiCB

Hurt Hawks. Robinson Jeffers. AP; DiPo; PoPo

Hurt No Living Thing. Christina Rossetti. *Fr.* Sing-Song. SoPo; ThGo

Hurt was the nation with a mighty wound. Lincoln. Paul Laurence Dunbar. LiPo

Husband to a Wife, A. Robert Louis Stevenson. *See* My Wife.

Husbands and Wives ("Husbands would never go whoring"). Unknown, *tr. fr. Greek* by Louis Untermeyer. UnTE

Hush, honey, hush. Cradle Song. Sir Herbert Read. DaDu

Hush, lullay. Lullaby. Léonie Adams. AmLP

Hush! my dear, lie still and slumber. Cradle Hymn [or Cradle Song]. Isaac Watts. SoPo; ThGo

Hush, new baby, bob-cats creep. Lullaby for Peregrine. Robert P. Tristram Coffin. RePo

Hush! not a whisper! Oars, be still! The Coracle Fishers. Robert Bloomfield. *Fr.* The Banks of Wye. OBNC

Hush'd Be the Camps To-Day. Walt Whitman. LiPo

Hushed to inaudible sound the deepening rain. The Lyre-Bird. Roland Robinson. PoAu-2

Huswifery. Edward Taylor. *See* Housewifery.

Hut, The. Ruth Pitter. DaDu

Hut in the bush of bark or rusty tin, The. The Hatters. Nan McDonald. PoAu-2

Hyacinths to Feed Thy Soul. Sadi, *tr. fr. Persian.* *Fr.* The Gulistan. TRV

Hybris, Nemesis, One, Two, Three. Alicia Ostriker. StP

Hymeneall Dialogue, An. Thomas Carew. SeCP

Hymen's Triumph, *sels.* Samuel Daniel.
    Early Love. ErPo
    (First Flame.) BoLP
    Love Is a Sickness. CBEP; ELP; PoIE

Hymn, A: "Drop, drop, slow tears." Phineas Fletcher. CBEP
    (Litany, A.) BoC

Hymn: "Lord, by whose breath all souls and seeds are living." Andrew Young. EaLo

Hymn, A: "Loving Shepherd of thy sheep." Jane E. Leeson. ThGo

Hymn: "O dream, digestion of my soul!" "Jakob van Hoddis," *tr. fr. German* by Christopher Middleton. MGP

Hymn: "When storms arise." Paul Laurence Dunbar. TRV

Hymn: "Words of hymns abruptly plod, The." Louise Townsend Nicholl. EaLo

Hymn, A, after Reading "Lead, Kindly Light." Paul Laurence Dunbar. TRV

Hymn for Lanie Poo, *sel.* LeRoi Jones.
    Each Morning, *Sec. 4.* NNP

Hymn for Saturday. Christopher Smart. *See* For Saturday.

Hymn of Joy. Henry van Dyke. TRV

Hymn of Labor. Henry van Dyke. TRV

Hymn of Pan. Shelley. PoIE

Hymn of St. Colum. Unknown, *tr. fr. Irish.* HaSV

Hymn of the Incarnation, A. Unknown. MeEL

Hymn of the Resurrection, A. William Dunbar. MeEL

Hymn of the Sea, A. Bryant. HaSV

Hymn on the Seasons, A. James Thomson. *Fr.* The Seasons. EiCP

Hymn Sung at the Completion of the Concord Monument April 19, 1836. Emerson. *See* Concord Hymn.

Hymn to Adversity. Thomas Gray. GTBS-P; StP

Hymn [or Hymne] to Christ, at the Author's Last Going into Germany, A. John Donne. DiPo; EnRePo; FoBA; MeP

Hymn to Colour. George Meredith. OBNC

Hymn to Diana. Ben Jonson. *See* Queen and Huntress.
Hymn to Earth. Elinor Wylie. AmLP
Hymn [*or* Hymne] to God My God, in My Sickness[e]. John Donne. BoC; CABA; DiPo; DTC; EnRePo; MeP; PoIE; SeCP
Hymn [*or* Hymne] to God the Father, A. John Donne. BoC; CaFP; DiPo; EaLo; EnRePo; FoBA; PoIE; PoPo; SeCP (To Christ.) MeP
Hymn [*or* Hymne] to God the Father, A. Ben Jonson. EnRePo; SeCP
Hymn to Intellectual Beauty. Shelley. ILP; OBNC
Hymn to Jesus, A. Richard of Caistre. MeEL
Hymn to Mary, A. William Dunbar. MeEL
Hymn to Mary, A. *Unknown.* MeEL
Hymn to Poverty, A. Edward Moore. WaPE
Hymn to Proserpine. Swinburne. OBNC; VP
Hymn to St. Teresa. Richard Crashaw. CABL
(In Memory of the Vertuous and Learned Lady Madre de Teresa That Sought an Early Martyrdome.) MeP
Hymn to the Cross, A. *Unknown.* MeEL
Hymn to the Morning, An. Mary Leapor. WaPE
Hymn to the Night. Longfellow. AmLP; AP
Hymn to the Spirit of Nature. Shelley. GTBS-P
Hymn Written after Jeremiah Preached to Me in a Dream. Owen Dodson. AmNP
Hymne for the Epiphanie, A. Sung as by the Three Kings. Richard Crashaw. MeP
Hymne of the Nativity, Sung as by the Shepheards, An. Richard Crashaw. *See* In the Holy Nativity of Our Lord God, a Hymn Sung as by the Shepherds.
Hymne to Christ, at the Authors Last Going into Germany, A. John Donne. *See* Hymn to Christ . . .
Hymne to God My God, in My Sicknesse. John Donne. *See* Hymn to God My God, in My Sickness.
Hymne to God the Father, A. John Donne. *See* Hymn to God the Father, A.
Hymne to God the Father, A. Ben Jonson. *See* Hymn to God the Father, A.
Hymns and Spiritual Songs, *sels.* Christopher Smart. EiCP
Nativity of Our Lord and Savior Jesus Christ, The.
St. Mark.
St. Matthias.
Hymns for the Amusement of Children, *sels.* Christopher Smart. EiCP
For Saturday.
(Hymn for Saturday.) CBEP
Gratitude.
Long-Suffering of God.
Mirth.
Hymns to the Night, *sels.* "Novalis," *tr. fr. German by* Walter Kaufmann. TwGP
"Beyond I wander," *fr.* IV.
"Must morning always come again?" *fr.* II.
Hynd Etin. *Unknown.* BuBa
Hynd Horn. *Unknown.* BuBa
Hyperion; a Fragment, *sels.* Keats. OBNC
Bruised Titans, The, *fr.* II.
Saturn, *fr.* I.
Hyperion's Song of Fate. Friedrich Hölderlin, *tr. fr. German by* Philip Allan Friedman. AGP
Hypsithilla, ask me over. An Invitation to an Invitation. Catullus. ErPo
Hyssop. Walter de la Mare. BoC

I

I. Karl Wolfskehl, *tr. fr. German by* Christopher Middleton. MGP
I/ have arrived. Status Symbol. Mari Evans. PtTo
I;/ Thou. The Little Poem of Life. John Oxenham. TRV
I admire the driven, those who rise from choice. Cinema, at the Lighthouse. Henri Coulette. *Fr.* The War of the Secret Agents. NePoEA-2
I admit the briar. A First Confession. W. B. Yeats. FoBA
I advocate a semi-revolution. A Semi-Revolution. Robert Frost. FoBA
I ain't afeard uv snakes, or toads, or bugs, or worms, or mice. Seein' Things. Eugene Field. LV
I Ain't No Candidate. James Larkin Pearson. PoNC
I Almost Did—Very Nigh—Had Not God Stopped the Lie. Elizabeth Turner. ThGo
I, Alphonso, live and learn. Alphonso of Castile. Emerson. AP
I always feel sorry. Hoppity Toads. Aileen Fisher. RePo
I always hope Father is going to play. Newspaper. Aileen Fisher. SoPo
I always struggled for things beyond my reach. Like the Prime Mover. Mehdi Ali Seljouk. ACV
I always was afraid of Soame's Pond. Atavism. Elinor Wylie. FiSC

I Am. John Clare. CBEP; GTBS-P; OBNC; PoIE; PoPl; PoSa
I am a boatman by my trade. Jack Williams. *Unknown.* BSNS; BSO
I am a bold fellow. The Young Dandelion. Dinah Maria Mulock Craik. RePo
I am a broken-hearted milkman, in grief I'm arrayed. Polly Perkins. *Unknown.* BoLP; DTC; ELP
I am a copper wire slung in the air. Under a Telephone Pole. Carl Sandburg. PoPo
I Am a Creature. Giuseppe Ungaretti, *tr. fr. Italian by* Lowry Nelson, Jr. CoIP
I am a gay young lassie and I love my Jimmy well. The Lovely Banks of Boyne. BSNS
I am a gentleman in a dustcoat trying. Piazza Piece. John Crowe Ransom. AP; CBEP; ErPo; PoSa
I am a happy miner, I love to sing and dance. The Happy Miner. John A. Stone. SGR
I am a jolly shanty boy. Bung Yer Eye. Stewart Edward White. RePo
I am a jolly young fellow. The Jolly Driver. *Unknown.* UnTE
I am a lean bird, and sinewy. The Vulture. Israel Kafu Hoh. ACV
I Am a Little Church (No Great Cathedral). E. E. Cummings. MoRP
(Number 77.) LV
I am a little world made cunningly. Holy Sonnets, V. John Donne. CABA; EnRePo; FoBA; MeP; SeCP; StP
I am a man now. Here. R. S. Thomas. GTBS-P
I am a man with no ambitions. The Advantages of Learning. Martial. ErPo
I am a monster. History. Robin Skelton. OPP
I am a native of the land of Erin. A Convict's Lament on the Death of Captain Logan. *Unknown.* PoAu-1
I Am a Parcel of Vain Strivings Tied. Henry David Thoreau. AP
I am a part of all that I have met. Tennyson. *Fr.* Ulysses. TRV
I am a prisoner of bones. Olga Cabral. *Fr.* Empire State. PtTo
I am a seaman. The Sailor's Tragedy. *Unknown.* BSNS
I am a soul in the world: in. The Invention of Comics. LeRoi Jones. AmNP
I am a tree of time, a swaying shadow. Tree of Time. K. D. Sethna. ACV
I am a very little girl. Little Phillis. Kate Greenaway. BiCB
I am a wounded man. Pity. Giuseppe Ungaretti. CoIP
I am a young girl. Young Girl: Annam. Padraic Colum. LOW
I am a young jolly brisk sailor. Tarpauling Jacket. *Unknown.* DTC
I am Aeolus, who keep. Aeolus. Rolfe Humphries. RePo
I Am Alone ("I am alive to loneliness"). V. Bhanot. ACV
I Am an American. Elias Lieberman. PoLF
I Am an Enemy to Trickery and Pride. Peire Cardenal, *tr. fr. Provençal by* Harvey Birenbaum. AnML
I am an old bachelor, early and early. The Old Bachelor. *Unknown.* BSNS
I am an old man now. Ossian. Joseph Payne Brennan. FiSC
I am anxious after praise. Egoism. W. Craddle. LV
I am approaching. Past dry. Loot. Thom Gunn. ErPo; NePoEA-2
I Am Ardent, I Am Brunette. Gustavo Adolfo Bécquer, *tr. fr. Spanish by* Kate Flores. AnSP
"I am as brown as brown can be." The Brown Girl. *Unknown.* ELP
I Am as I Am. Sir Thomas Wyatt. CBEP
I am as light as any roe. Women Are Worthy. *Unknown.* MeEL
I am called Childhood. In play is all my mind. Childhood. Sir Thomas More. *Fr.* The Pageants of Thomas More. EnRePo
I am confident. More Truth and Light. John Robinson. TRV
"I am," cried Apollo—when Daphne he wooed. To Apollo Making Love. Thomas Tickell. WaPE
I am custodian of close things. When Senses Fled. John Woods. CoPo
I Am Dark and Fair to See. *Unknown.* UnTE
I am driven mad with the printed word. Am Driven Mad. Allen Polite. NNP
I am fevered with the sunset. The Sea Gypsy. Richard Hovey. RePo
I am four monkeys. The Tree. Alfred Kreymborg. PoPl
I Am François, to My Dismay. Villon, *tr. fr. French by* Harvey Birenbaum. AnML
I Am from Ireland. *Unknown.* *See* I Am of Ireland.
I am glad daylong for the gift of song. Rhapsody. William Stanley Braithwaite. AmNP
I am going far away, far away unto the home. The Miner's Farewell. Mart Taylor. SGR
I am going home with Jesus. Going Home with Jesus. Walter E. Isenhour. STF
I am his Highness' dog at Kew. Engraved on the Collar of a

I bought me a Parrot in Trinidad. Parrot. William Jay Smith. RePo
I brake to see the vacant field, the sky above the wall. André du Bouchet. *Fr.* White Motor. CoFP
I break my bread. There are the great gold fields. Bread the Holy. Elizabeth J. Coatsworth. MoRP
I bring fresh showers for the thirsting flowers. The Cloud. Shelley. CBEP; PoIe; RePo
I bring you with reverent hands. A Poet to His Beloved. W. B. Yeats. MoLP
I built a chimney for a comrade old. Two at a Fireside. Edwin Markham. TRV
I built a snare one day and sought to capture. Trap. Walter H. Kerr. FiSC
I Built My Hut. T'ao Ch'ien, tr. fr. *Chinese by* Arthur Waley. SiGo
I built my soul a lordly pleasure-house. The Palace of Art. Tennyson. VP
I Buried the Year. W. Luff. STF
I buried you deeper last night. To a Persistent Phantom. Frank Horne. AmNP
I burn, yet am I cold; I am a-cold, yet burn. Barnabe Barnes. *Fr.* Parthenophil and Parthenophe. PoIE
I burne, and cruell you, in vaine. Song: To My Mistris, I Burning in Love. Thomas Carew. SeCP
I by myself, she in another's arms. Maurice Scève. *Fr.* Délie. RBP
I call her my Krishna flower. Krishnakali. Rabindranath Tagore. ACV
I came across her browsing on a slope. Cow Dance. Bruce Beaver. PoAu-2
I came from far for thee. "This Do in Remembrance of Me." *Unknown.* STF
I came from Salem City. Oh California. John Nichols. SGR
I came out singing. To Come Out Singing. Jon Silkin. PoDB
I came to a great door. The Beast. Theodore Roethke. AmLP
I Came to a Valley in the Wilderness. Garcilaso de la Vega, tr. fr. *Spanish by* Edwin Morgan. AnSP
I came to Jesus. George White. STF
I came to the town to see my lady. Sally Brown (B *vers.*). *Unknown.* BSNS
I came to the well-loved house. Frail Hands. Lucia Trent. FiSC
I came upon them by a strip of sea. The Net Menders. Brian Vrepont. PoAu-2
I Can Climb Our Apple Tree. Jessie Orton Jones. RePo
I can close my eyes and see Him. The Last Day. Lola Derosier. STF
I can love both fair and brown. The Indifferent. John Donne. CABA; DiPo; UnTE
I Can neither Hold You nor Let You Go. Sister Juana Inés de la Cruz, tr. fr. *Spanish by* Kate Flores. AnSP
I can not do it alone. Jesus and I. Dan Crawford. TRV
I can remember our sorrow, I can remember our laughter. Memory. Helen Hoyt. PoLF
I can sing of myself a true song, of my voyages telling. The Seafarer. *Unknown.* HaSV
I cannot but believe, though you were dead. Nurse. Frances Cornford. LV
I cannot, but God can. Not I, but God. Annie Johnson Flint. STF
I cannot find my way: there is no star. Credo. E. A. Robinson. AP; ILP
I cannot find my way to Nazareth. A Fragment. Yvor Winters. PoIE
I cannot give you the Metropolitan Tower. Parting Gift. Elinor Wylie. LOW
I cannot hear thy voice with others' ears. To the Canary Bird. Jones Very. AP
I cannot live nor die. The Ghost. James Wright. FiSC
I cannot live with you. Emily Dickinson. AP; CBEP; DiPo; FaPL; PoIE
I cannot love thee as I ought. In Memorial A. H. H., LII. Tennyson. VP
I cannot ope mine eyes. Mattens. George Herbert. MeP
I cannot say, and I will not say. Away. James Whitcomb Riley. TRV
I cannot see the features right. In Memoriam A. H. H., LXX. Tennyson. VP
I cannot sleep or take the air. A Snowy Day. Dafydd ap Gwilym. SiGo
I cannot spare water or wine. Mithridates. Emerson. AP
I cannot speak to crowds. This I Can Do. H. T. Lefevre. STF
I cannot take these poor. Said the Innkeeper. Myles Connolly. TRV
I cannot tell their wonder nor make known. John Masefield. *Fr.* Ships. HaSV
I cannot tell who loves the Skeleton. La Bella Bona Roba. Richard Lovelace. SeCP
I cannot tell you how it was. May. Christina Rossetti. VP
I cannot tell you now. The Great Hunt. Carl Sandburg. MoLP
I cannot turn from Jesus. I Turn to Jesus. Oswald J. Smith. STF
"I can't come in, Lady Margie," he said. Young Hunting (C *vers.*). *Unknown.* BFSS
I can't remember where I'd been. The Green Door. Leah Bodine Drake. BiCB
I Care Not for These Ladies. Thomas Campion. CABA; ErPo (When We Court and Kiss.) UnTE
"I carry my death within me." My Death. A. J. M. Smith. OBCV
I caught a tremendous fish. The Fish. Elizabeth Bishop. GoJo; LV; PoP1; PoPo
I caught this morning morning's minion. The Windhover. Gerard Manley Hopkins. AnMoPo; BoC; CABA; CaFP; DiPo; EaLo; FoBA; GTBS-P; ILP; OBNC; OnP; PoDB; PoIE; PoP1; StP; VaPo; VP
I celebrate myself. Song of Myself. Walt Whitman. AP; PoIE; PP
I chanced upon an early walk to spy. The Orchard and the Heath. George Meredith. OBNC
I charm thy life. Kehama's Curse. Robert Southey. *Fr.* The Curse of Kehama. OBNC
I claim the right of knowing whom I serve. Manhood. Oliver Wendell Holmes. *Fr.* Wind-Clouds and Star-Drifts. AP
I climb the hill: from end to end. In Memoriam A. H. H., C. Tennyson. FoBA; VP
I climbed up on the merry-go-round. Merry-go-round. Dorothy Baruch. SoPo
I cling to this mangled tree. Rivers. Giuseppe Ungaretti. CoIP
I Close Her Eyes. Heine, tr. fr. *German by* Louis Untermeyer. UnTE
I closed another chapter. My Book of Life. Frances Humphrey. STF
I come back to the geography of it. Letter 27. Charles Olson. CoPo
I come from haunts of coot and hern. The Brook. Tennyson. FaBV; GoJo
I come from Salem County. Cowboy Song. Charles Causley. PoSa
I come more softly than a bird. Mary Austin. *Fr.* Rhyming Riddles. SoPo
I Could Give All to Time. Robert Frost. MoRP
I could have painted pictures like that youth's. Pictor Ignotus. Robert Browning. CTC
I could love her with a love so warm. The World Is a Mighty Ogre. Fenton Johnson. AmNP
I could love thee till I die. The Platonic Lady. Earl of Rochester. UnTE
I could not keep love down. The Power of Love. *Unknown.* *Fr.* The Thousand and One Nights. SiGo
I could resign that eye of blue. Abnegation. Martial. UnTE
I couldn't hold no office job. I Ain't No Candidate. James Larkin Pearson. PoNC
I couldn't touch a stop and turn a screw. Thirty Bob a Week. John Davidson. CABL; OBNC
I crept through the house like a ghost. Spectre. Sydney King Russell. FiSC
I cry my matches at Charing Cross. Charing Cross. *Unknown.* CBEP
I Cry to You as I Pass Your Windows. Christopher Brennan. *Fr.* The Wanderer. PoAu-1
I cry your mercy—pity—love!—aye, love! To Fanny. Keats. UnTE
I Curse the Hour, the Moment and the Day. Guillaume de Machaut, tr. fr. *French by* Jacques LeClercq. AnML
I cut the stuff. A Spin. Jonathan Williams. PoNC
I Danced before I Had Two Feet. Max Dunn. PoAu-2
I deemed thy garments, O my Hope, were grey. Hope Overtaken. Dante Gabriel Rossetti. The House of Life, XLII. VP
I did not cry at all. Song of the Captured Woman. James Devaney. PoAu-1
I did not know you then. The Blinded Soldier to His Love. Alfred Noyes. PoP1
I did not lose my heart in summer's even. More Poems, XXXVII. A. E. Housman. VP
I did not see the iris move. A Matter of Life and Death. Anne Ridler. MoLP; MP
I did not think, I did not strive. John Masefield. *Fr.* The Everlasting Mercy. BoC; TRV
I did not think that I should find them there. The Clerks. E. A. Robinson. CABA
I did not want to be old Mr. Uncle Dog: The Poet at 9. Robert Sward. CoPo
I did not want to die. I wanted you. Sacco Writes to His Son. Alun Lewis. DTC
I didn't get much sleep last night. Underwear. Lawrence Ferlinghetti. CoPo
I died for Beauty—but was scarce. Emily Dickinson. AP; DiPo; FoBA; ILP; PoPo

I dig in the soft earth all. The Negatives. Philip Levine. NePoEA-2

I do/ dig Everything Swinging. Credo. Jonathan Williams. PoNC

I do believe that die I must. His Creed. Robert Herrick. ILP; WePo

I Do Confess Thou Art Sae Fair. Burns. CBEP

I do confess thou'rt smooth and fair. To His Forsaken Mistress. *At. to* Sir Robert Ayton. ErPo

I do not always know what lies before me. God Doeth All Things Well. *Unknown.* STF

I do not ask. A Preacher's Prayer. *Unknown.* STF

I do not believe this room. A Game of Glass. Alastair Reid. PoCh

I do not count the day. What the Grecian Earns. Kenneth Patchen. ToPo

I do not count the hours I spend. Waldeinsamkeit. Emerson. AP

I do not have the voice to praise you, great brother. Antonin Artaud. René Char. CoFP

I do not know much about gods; but I think that the river. The Dry Salvages. T. S. Eliot. *Fr.* Four Quartets. CABA

I do not know what next may come. The Best for Me. *Unknown.* STF

I do not know where to begin. His Poverty. Rutebeuf. AnML

I do not know why. It is not only. The Double Tree. Winfield Townley Scott. PoP1

I Do Not Love Thee. Caroline Norton. WePo

I do not love to wed. The Poet Loves a Mistress but Not to Marry. Robert Herrick. ErPo

I do not say this. "Your Need Is Greater than Mine." Theodore Enslin. CoPo

I do not think a prudent one. Prudence. Don Marquis. *Fr.* Archy and Mehitabel. LV

I do not think the ending can be right. But That Is Another Story. Donald Justice. NePoEA-2

I do not understand the world, father. On the Subject of Poetry. W. S. Merwin. PP

I do not want a gaping crowd. When I Am Dead. James Edward Wilson. PoLF

I do not want to turn away. Two Poems, I. Robert J. Abrams. NNP

I doe but name thee Pembroke, and I find. To William Earle of Pembroke. Ben Jonson. SeCP

I don't believe in 'ristercrats. My Sort o' Man. Paul Laurence Dunbar. AmNP

I don't know any more what it used to be. A Girl. Edwin Denby. BoLP

I don't mind eels. The Eel. Ogden Nash. FaBV

I dote the baple buds are swellig. Kerchoo! Margaret Fishback. PoSC

I doubt he even bothers to suspect this world. Boy on the Back of a Wagon. Thad Stem, Jr. PoNC

I doubt not God is good, well-meaning, kind. Yet Do I Marvel. Countee Cullen AmNP

I dreaded that first robin so. Emily Dickinson. AP; CBEP

I Dream a World. Langston Hughes. AmNP

I dream of Jeanie with the light brown hair. Jeanie with the Light Brown Hair. Stephen Foster. FaPL; LV

I dream of journeys repeatedly. The Far Field. Theodore Roethke. ToPo

I dream of the rainbow. Winter War. "Klabund." TwGP

I dream of you, to wake: would that I might. Monna Innominata, III. Christina Rossetti. VP

I Dream'd in a Dream. Walt Whitman. AP

I dream'd that as I wander'd by the way. A Dream of the Unknown. Shelley. GTBS-P

I dream'd that I walk'd in Italy. Going Back Again. "Owen Meredith." EvOK

I dream'd there would be Spring no more. In Memoriam A. H. H., LXIX. Tennyson. VP

I dream'd this mortal part of mine. The Vine. Robert Herrick. ErPo; UnTE

I dreamed a dream the other night, when everything was still. Prospecting Dream. John A. Stone. SGR

I dreamed all my fortitude screamed. Letter across Doubt and Distance. M. Carl Holman. AmNP

I dreamed I saw that ancient Irish Queen. Chivalry. "Æ." MoRP

I Dreamed My Love. *Unknown.* UnTE

I dreamed Ted Williams. Dream of a Baseball Star. Gregory Corso. SD

I dreamed that one had died in a strange place. A Dream of Death. W. B. Yeats. FoBA

I dreamed the Fairies wanted me. Crab-Apple. Ethel Talbot. BiCB

I dreamed [or dream'd] we both were in a bed. The Vision [to Electra]. Robert Herrick. SeCP; UnTE

I dreamt her sensual proportions. The Death of Venus. Robert Creeley. AmPC; StP

I dreamt I came to heaven's gate. At the Gate of Heaven. Conrad Ferdinand Meyer. AGP

I dreamt the other night I was in Heaven. Assimilation. Irving Feldman. AmPC

I dressed my father in his little clothes. The Boat. Robert Pack. NePoEA-2

I drove up to the graveyard, which. The Soul Longs to Return Whence It Came. Richard Eberhart. ToPo

I drown in the drumming ploughland, I drag up. The Hawk in the Rain. Ted Hughes. ACV; ToPo

I Dwell in Deep Anxiety. Beatritz de Dia, tr. fr. Provençal by Harvey Birenbaum. AnML

I dwell in Possibility. Emily Dickinson. AP; PP

I dwelt alone. Eulalie. Poe. EvOK; Par

I Eat My Peas with Honey. *Unknown.* EvOK (Peas.) RePo

I enter, and I see thee in the gloom. Sonnets on the Divina Commedia, III. Longfellow. AP; ILP

I Entered Where I Did Not Know. St. John of the Cross, tr. fr. Spanish by Willis Barnstone. AnSP (Verses Written upon an Ecstasy of High Contemplation, tr. by E. Allison Peers.) RBL

I envy not in any moods.) In Memorial A. H. H., XXVII. Tennyson. OBNC; VP

I explain the silvered passing of a ship at night. War Is Kind, VI. Stephen Crane. AP

I fasted for some forty days on bread and buttermilk. The Pilgrim. W. B. Yeats. PoSa

I father'd me brogues and spit on me stick. Billy O'Rourke. *Unknown.* BSO

I fear the headless man. The Lover's Ghost. Louis Simpson. FiSC

I fear thy kisses, gentle maiden. Shelley. GTBS-P

I Feed a Flame Within. Dryden. *Fr.* Secret Love. PoIE

I feel so exceedingly lazy. A Hot-Weather Song. Don Marquis. RePo

I felt a cleaving in my mind. Emily Dickinson. DiPo

I felt a funeral, in my brain. Emily Dickinson. AP; CABA; DiPo; FoBA

I Felt like Slapping Him. Edith Earnshaw. PoNC

I felt the lurch and halt of her heart. Lightning. D. H. Lawrence. UnTE

I fill this cup to one made up of loveliness alone. A Health. Edward Coote Pinkney. FaPL

I find it normal, passing these great frontiers. Manchouli. William Empson. AnMoPo

I Find No Peace. Petrarch, tr. fr. Italian by Sir Thomas Wyatt. Sonnets to Laura: To Laura in Life, CIV. DiPo; PoIE ("I find no peace, and all my war is done.") RBL (I Find No Peace, yet Am Not Armed for War, tr. by Maurice Valency.) AnML

I fled Him, down the nights and down the days. The Hound of Heaven. Francis Thompson. FaBV; FaPL; ILP; PoIE; TRV

I Flung Up My Arm Half from Sleep. Tram Combs. MP

I followed once a fleet and mighty serpent. A Subterranean City. Thomas Lovell Beddoes. StP

I forgot my Lord in the summertime. Forgetting God. J. E. Harvey. STF

I found a dimpled spider, fat and white. Design. Robert Frost. AmLP; AP; CABA; CaFP; ILP; PoDB; PoIE; PoPo

I found a little beetle, so that Beetle was his name. Forgiven. A. A. Milne. SoPo

I Found God. Mary Afton Thacker. TRV

I found him drowned on the rock that night. Sea Dirge. Tom Scott. ACV; HaSV

I found myself one day all, all alone. Ballata. Angelo Poliziano. RBL

I found ten kinds of wild flowers growing. Late October. Sara Teasdale. PoSC

I found them there today. Mementos, II. W. D. Snodgrass. AmPC; NePoEA-2

I Found without a Guard. Albrecht von Johansdorf, tr. fr. German by Gillian Barker and Kenneth Gee. AnML

I found your Horace with the writing in it. On First Looking into Loeb's Horace. Lawrence Durrell. ToPo

I Gave My Love a Gay Gold Ring, *with music. Unknown.* BFSS

I gave myself to him. Emily Dickinson. CBEP; FaBV; FaPL; FoBA

I Gaze upon Her Light Crisp-curling Hair. Fazio degli Uberti, tr. fr. Italian by Dwight Durling. AnML

I gaze, where August's sunbeam falls. Newark Abbey. Thomas Love Peacock. OBNC

I Gazed upon My Country's Walls. Francisco de Quevedo, tr. fr. Spanish by Kate Flores. AnSP

I gently touched her hand: she gave. I Pressed Her Rebel Lips. *Unknown.* ErPo

I give my word on it. There is no way. Still and All. Burns Singer. NePoEA-2

I give the praise to Christ alone. Flowers in a Garden. Christopher Smart. ThGo

I give you now Professor Twist. The Purist. Ogden Nash. GoJo

I give you the end of a golden string. Epigraph. Blake. *Fr.* Jerusalem. OBNC

I go downhill some days to a little room. Oldest Cemetery. Mark Van Doren. FiSC

I go out like a ghost. Home Town. W. D. Snodgrass. ToPo

I got a valentine from Timmy. Valentine. Shelley Silverstein. PoSC

I got me flowers to strew Thy way. Easter. George Herbert. BoC; TRV

I got up on Thursday morning. Johnny Dile. *Unknown.* BSO

I grant thou wert not married to my Muse. Sonnets, LXXXII. Shakespeare. CBEP

I green in the meadow of the young village. Green Melody. Andreas Okopenko. MGP

I Grew Up in a Village. *Unknown, tr. fr. Spanish by* William M. Davis. AnML

I grow old under an intensity. Mirror. James Merrill. NePoEA-2

I guess there is a garden named. The Mirror Perilous. Alan Dugan. MP

I guess today. John Plans. Dorothy Mason Pierce. BiCB

I ha' seen them 'mid the clouds on the heather. The White Stag. Ezra Pound. LOW

I had a beginning but shall have no end. Stone Angel. Anne Ridler. EaLo

I had [*or* bought me] a cat and the cat pleased me. The Farmyard [*or* A Farmyard Song]. *Unknown.* BFSS; SoPo

I had a dog and his name was Blue. Old Blue. *Unknown.* SD

I had a dream last night, I dreamed. Andre. Gwendolyn Brooks. RePo

I had a dream the other night. Rainbow Willow. *Unknown.* BFSS

I had a dream, which was not all a dream. Darkness. Byron. ILP

I had a father. The Blacksmith's Daughter. Heinz Piontek. MGP

I had a feeling in my neck. Mumps. Elizabeth Madox Roberts. SoPo

I had a little bird. The Orphan's Song. Sydney Dobell. ELP; OBNC

I had a little dog, and my dog was very small. Feri's Dream [*or* Dogs]. Frances Cornford. BoC; ThGo

I Had a Little Husband. *Unknown.* EvOK

I Had a Little Nut Tree. Mother Goose. CBEP; *2 sts.* (Nut Tree, The.) SoPo, *3 sts.*

I Had a Little Pony. Mother Goose. SoPo

I had a lovely bottle, bottle-blue. One Man's Goose; or, Poetry Redefined. George Starbuck. PP

I had a silver penny. Nursery Rhyme of Innocence and Experience. Charles Causley. DaDu; GoJo; WePo

"I had a true love, but she left me." The Quaker's Wooing. *Unknown.* BSO

I had expected something quite different. Between Chicago and St. Paul. Mel Weisburd. PtTo

I had finished my dinner. An Easy Decision. Kenneth Patchen. LOW; ToPo

I had four brothers over the sea. Perrie, Merrie, Dixi, Domini [*or* Perry Merry Dictum Dominee]. *Unknown.* BFSS; BSO

I had never before held death, pale and polished, in my hands. The Captain of the *Oberon.* Francis Webb. *Fr.* A Drum for Ben Boyd. ACV

I had no time to hate, because. No Time to Hate. Emily Dickinson. PoLF

I had not minded—walls. Emily Dickinson. CABA

I had over-prepared the event. Villanelle: The Psychological Hour. Ezra Pound. CTC

I had returned from dreaming. Dream. Witter Bynner. MoLP

I had the nicest Christmas list. His Name at the Top. *Unknown.* STF

I had thought of putting an/ altar. Prayer. Isabella M. Brown. NNP

I had walked life's way with an easy tread. I Met the Master. *Unknown.* PoLF; STF

I had written him a letter which I had, for want of better. Clancy of the Overflow. A. B. Paterson. PoAu-1

I Hae a Wife o' My Ain. Burns. EiCP

I hailed the bus and I went for a ride. Ferry Ride. Selma Robinson. LV

I hardly suppose I know anybody who wouldn't rather be a success than a failure. Kindly Unhitch That Star, Buddy. Ogden Nash. PoPl

I hate and love. Why? You may ask but. Odi et Amo. Catullus, *tr. by* Ezra Pound. CTC

I hate, and yet I love thee too. To Lesbia. Catullus, *tr. by* Abraham Cowley. PoPl

"I hate successful people," you declare. What's Hard. Laurence Lerner. NePoEA-2

I hate that drum's discordant sound. The Drum. John Scott. CBEP

I hate the dreadful hollow behind the little wood. Maud. Tennyson. VP

I hate the man who builds his name. Fable XLV: The Poet and the Rose. John Gay. EiCP

I hate the money-lending avarice. Sonnet. Joachim du Bellay. *Fr.* Regrets. RBL

I hate those potent madmen, who keep all. John Crowne. BoC

I Hate to See You Clad. Paul Verlaine, *tr. fr. French by* Louis Untermeyer. UnTE

I hate to spend the night. Thanks Just the Same. *Unknown.* PoLF

I have a dog. Notice. David McCord. SoPo

I have a friend so kind and true. My Friend. Marjorie Lorene Buster. STF

I have a funny Airedale dog. My Airedale Dog. W. L. Mason. SoPo

I Have a Gentle Cock. *Unknown.* CBEP (I Have a Noble Cock.) MeEL

I have a little bed. My Bed. Lucy Sprague Mitchell. SoPo

I have a little home amidst the city's din. The Complacent Cliff-Dweller. Margaret Fishback. PoLF

I have a little pussy. Little Gray Pussy. *Unknown.* SoPo

I have a little shadow that goes in and out with me. My Shadow. Robert Louis Stevenson. FaBV; SoPo

I have a little valentine. My Valentine. Kitty Parsons. SoPo

I Have a New Garden. *Unknown.* MeEL

I Have a Noble Cock. *Unknown. See* I Have a Gentle Cock.

I have a notion that the world is round. John Wain. *Fr.* A Boisterous Poem about Poetry. PP

I have a picture in my room in which. Intaglio. Henri Coulette. PoCh

I Have a Rendezvous with Death. Alan Seeger. FaBV; FaPL; LV; PoPl; ThLM

I have a room where into no one enters. Memory. Christina Rossetti. OBNC

I have a smiling face, she said. The Mask. Elizabeth Barrett Browning. CBEP; OBNC

I have a suit of new clothes in this happy new year. When I Think of the Hungry People. O-Shi-O. TRV

I have a vague remembrance. The Challenge. Longfellow. AP

I Have a Young Sister. *Unknown.* MeEL; PoIE

I have abjured the flesh, and I. Two against One. *Unknown.* UnTE

I have an understanding with the hills. After Sunset. Grace Hazard Conkling. MoRP

I Have Been a Forester. *Unknown.* CBEP

I have been busy writing a terribly critical. Notes on a Certain Terribly Critical Piece. Reed Whittemore. PP

I have been dreaming all a summer day. Dreams. Victor J. Daley. PoAu-1

I have been here before. Sudden Light [*or* Song IV: Sudden Light]. Dante Gabriel Rossetti. CBEP; CTC; ELP; OBNC; PoLF

I have been in love, and in debt, and in drink. The Mad Lover. Alexander Brome. CBEP

I have been in the woods alone. In the Woods Alone. *Unknown.* SiGo

I have been in this bar. The Man Who Married Magdalene: Variation on a Theme by Louis Simpson. Anthony Hecht. CoPo

I have been one acquainted with the night. Acquainted with the Night. Robert Frost. AP; DiPo; FoBA; MP; PoIE; PoLF; PoSa

I have been through the valley of weeping. The God of Comfort. *Unknown.* STF

I have been walking today. Furnished Lives. Jon Silkin. NePoEA-2; PoDB

I have been warned. It is more than thirty years since I wrote. But I Am Growing Old and Indolent. Robinson Jeffers. AP

I have been wondering. A Letter. Anthony Hecht. StP

I have been young, and now am not too old. Report on Experience. Edmund Blunden. CBEP; GTBS-P

I have begun to die. The Sentry. Alun Lewis. DTC

I have breakfast, dinner, tea. *Unknown.* ThGo

I have built for you a rain palace. The Rain Palace. Yvan Goll. MGP

I have buried her under a stone. The Stationmaster's Lament. Jerome Rothenberg. CoPo

I have but one story. Summer Is Gone. *Unknown.* PoPl

I have carried for five years. The Return. Jon Silkin. NePoEA-2

I have come back again. The Return of the Native. Harley Matthews. PoAu-2

I have come far enough. A Form of Women. Robert Creeley. AmPC

I have come on the River of Yellow Flowers. A Green Stream. Wang Wei. SD

I have come to the borders of sleep. Lights Out. Edward Thomas. MMA

I have consider'd it; and find. The Resolve. Henry Vaughan. MeP

I have consider'd it, and finde. The Reprisall. George Herbert. MeP

I Have Desired to Go. Gerard Manley Hopkins. *See* Heaven-Haven.

I have done one braver thing. The Undertaking. John Donne. CBEP

I have drunk ale from the Country of the Young. He Thinks of His Past Greatness When a Part of the Constellations of Heaven. W. B. Yeats. DTC

I have eaten/ the plums. This Is Just to Say. William Carlos Williams. AnMoPo; GoJo; PoIE

I have eaten all my words. The Lost Language. Irving Feldman. AmPC

I have entreated care to cut the thread. Dan Bartholmew's Dolorous Discourses. George Gascoigne. EnRePo

I have followed you model. Ode to a Model. Vladimir Nabokov. PoPl

I have forgotten you as one forgets at dawning. Words. Helen Morgan Brooks. NNP

I have gone out, a possessed witch. Her Kind. Anne Sexton. MP; ToPo

I Have Got My Leave. Rabindranath Tagore. Fr. Gitanjali. BoC

I have grown past hate and bitterness. Nationality. Mary Gilmore. PoAu-1

I have grown tired of sorrow and human tears. The Fairy Wood. Arthur Symons. BoC

I have had playmates, I have had companions. The Old Familiar Faces. Charles Lamb. CBEP; GTBS-P; PoPl; PoSa

I have heard how in Ohio. Coal for Mike. Bertolt Brecht. PoPl

I have heard nothing. Annunciation. Ruth Gilbert. Fr. The Blossom of the Branches. ACV

I have heard talk of bold Robin Hood. Robin Hood and the Two Priests. Unknown. BuBa

I have heard that hysterical women say. Lapis Lazuli. W. B. Yeats. AnMoPo; DTC; FoBA; ILP; PoIE; PP

"I have heard the sunset song of the birches." War Is Kind, VII. Stephen Crane. AP

I have humped my bluey in all the States. My Old Black Billy. Edward Harrington. PoAu-1

I have in my house. My House. Jane W. Krows. SoPo

I have just arrived across the Plains. Emigrant from Pike. John A. Stone. SGR

I have just come down from my father. The Hospital Window. James Dickey. CoPo

"I have just come from the salt, salt sea." James Harris (B vers.). Unknown. BSO

I have just seen a beautiful thing. The Black Finger. Angelina W. Grimké. AmNP

I have known love and hate and work and fight. To a Photographer. Berton Braley. LV

I have known nights rain-washed and crystal-clear. Wisdom. Frank Yerby. AmNP

I have known one bound to a bed by wrist and ankle. The Choice. Hilary Corke. MP

I have known the inexorable sadness of pencils. Dolor. Theodore Roethke. AP; CABA; ILP; PoIE; PoSa

I have known the strange nurses of Kindness. But I Do Not Need Kindness. Gregory Corso. CoPo

I have learned. Wordsworth. Fr. Tintern Abbey. TRV

I have learned the wondrous secret. Abiding. A. B. Simpson. STF

I have led her home, my love, my only friend. Tennyson. Fr. Maud. ELP

I have lived enough, having seen one thing, that love hath an end. Hymn to Proserpine. Swinburne. OBNC; VP

I Have Loved England. Alice Duer Miller. Fr. The White Cliffs. PoLF

I Have Loved Flowers. Robert Bridges. GoJo

I have loved so many violent loves. Declaration at Forty. Judson Crews. UnTE

I Have Made a Sirventes in Which No Word Is Missing. Bertran de Born, tr. fr. Provençal by Paul Blackburn. AnML

I have made, too, one of the most delicate, dainty similes. George Villiers, Duke of Buckingham. Fr. The Rehearsal. Par

I have met them at close of day. Easter 1916. W. B. Yeats. AnMoPo; CABA; DiPo; FoBA; PoIE

I have mislaid the torment and the fear. Success. William Empson. ToPo

I have no Brother,—they who meet me now. Thy Brother's Blood. Jones Very. AP

I Have No Liking for One Who in All Things Is Not. Jordi de Sant Jordi, tr. fr. Catalan by William M. Davis. AnML

"I have no name." Infant Joy. Blake. Fr. Songs of Innocence. BiCB; CBEP; FoBA; GoJo; PoLF

I have no wings, but yet I fly. Mary Austin. Fr. Rhyming Riddles. SoPo

I have no wit, no words, no tears. A Better Resurrection. Christina Rossetti. VP

I have not been as Joshua when he fought. Three Helpers in Battle. Mary Elizabeth Coleridge. EaLo

I have not needed you for thirteen years. Father. Robert Pack. CoPo

I have put on my trappings for the evening. Evening Party. Piero Jahier. CoIP

I have said that the soul is not more than the body. I Hear and Behold God in Every Object. Walt Whitman. MoRP

I have seen. The Hammer. Carl Sandburg. PoPo

I have seen a gum-tree. Flesh. Mary Fullerton. PoAu-1

I have seen all the works that are done under the sun. All Is Vanity. Ecclesiastes, Bible, O.T. TRV

I have seen, O desolate one, the voice has its tower. Bell Tower. Léonie Adams. AmLP; PoPl

I have seen old ships sail like swans asleep. The Old Ships. James Elroy Flecker. EvOK; HaSV; RoGo

I have seen tall chimneys without smoke. Drought. Frederick E. Laight. OBCV

I have seen the Birds of Paradise. The Birds of Paradise. John Peale Bishop. GoJo

I have seen the snow like a mirage impending. The Effect of Snow, III. Robert Finch. ACV

I have seen your feet gilded by morning. Metamorphoses of M. John Peale Bishop. ErPo

I Have Set My Heart on Serving God. Giacomo da Lentino, tr. fr. Italian by Maurice Valency. AnML

I have sinned; I have betrayed the innocent blood. Dorothy L. Sayers. Fr. The Just Vengeance. BoC

I have so many faults myself. What I See in Me. Unknown. STF

I have sometimes thought how it would have been. World I Have Not Made. Elizabeth Jennings. ACV

I Have Sought Long. Sir Thomas Wyatt. EnRePo

I Have Sought Thee Daily. Solomon Ibn Gabirol, tr. fr. Hebrew by Israel Zangwill. SiGo

I have sown beside all waters in my day. A Black Man Talks of Reaping. Arna Bontemps. AmNP

I have spoken with a goat. The Goat. Umberto Saba. CoIP

I have sung, to deceive the evil-sounding clock of time. Jean Cocteau. Fr. Plain Song. PoPl

I have sunk to the cold weary depths of despair! Mourning. Josephine Van Passan. STF

I have thee, thou hast me. Unknown, tr. fr. German by Alexander Gode. AGP

I Have These Many Evenings Watched for My Beloved. Wolfram von Eschenbach, tr. fr. German by Charles E. Passage. Fr. Titurel. AnML

I have tied my humpback behind my mother. Homage to Charles Laughton. Gil Orlovitz. ToPo

I Have to Have it. Dorothy Aldis. SoPo

I have told you in another poem, whether you've read it or not. My Burial Place. Robinson Jeffers. AP

I have tossed hours upon the tides of fever. Bout with Burning. Vassar Miller. ToPo

I have twelve oxen that be fair and brown. Twelve Oxen. Unknown. RePo

I have two friends. The Twins. Kathryn Jackson. BiCB

I have wished a bird would fly away. A Minor Bird. Robert Frost. LOW

I have within me such a dream of pain. Vision of a Past Warrior. Peter La Farge. PtTo

I have worshipped in churches and chapels. At My Mother's Knee. Unknown. STF

I have yielded utterly. On the Words "Dilectus Meus Mihi." St. Theresa of Avila. RBL

I, having loved ever since I was a child a few things, never having wavered. Modern Declaration. Edna St. Vincent Millay. MoLP

I Hear America Singing. Walt Whitman. FaBV; FoBA; PoPl; PoPo; PoSC

I hear and Behold God in Every Object. Walt Whitman. MoRP

I Hear It Was Charged against Me. Walt Whitman. PoPo

I hear leaves drinking Rain. The Rain. W. H. Davies. LV

I hear the engine pounding. The Ways of Trains. Elizabeth J. Coatsworth. SoPo

I hear the man downstairs slapping the hell out of his stupid wife again. The .38. Ted Joans. NNP

I hear the night hanging down in white holes. Masterindex: 23. Gil Orlovitz. ToPo

I hear the noise about thy keel. In Memoriam A. H. H., X. Tennyson. VP

I hear the voice of the bells. My New Year Prayer. Unknown. STF

I hear things crying in the world. The Assassination of John F. Kennedy. Gwendolyn Brooks. OPP

I heard a bird at dawn. The Rivals. James Stephens. PoPl

I Heard a Bird Sing. Oliver Herford. PoLF; SoPo

I heard a fly buzz when I died. Emily Dickinson. AmLP; AP; CABA; DiPo; FoBA; ILP; PoIE

I heard a horseman. The Horseman. Walter de la Mare. GoJo; SoPo

I Heard a Linnet Courting. Robert Bridges. PoPo

I heard a mouse. The Mouse. Elizabeth J. Coatsworth. SoPo

I heard a Noise. Unknown. EnRePo

I heard a thousand blended notes. Lines Written in Early Spring [or Written in Early Spring]. Wordsworth. ACV; CBEP; GTBS-P; ILP; PoLF; PoPo; StP; TRV

I heard a voice that cried, "Make way for those who died!" The March. J. C. Squire. PoSC

I Heard a Young Man Saying. Julia Fields. NNP

I Heard an Angel Singing. Blake. CBEP
I Heard Christ Sing. "Hugh MacDiarmid." ACV
I heard it told. The Lay of Hildebrand. *Unknown.* AnML
I heard no sound of wild feet. Enigma. Katherine Reeves. FiSC
I heard no sound where I stood. The Sleeping House. Tennyson. *Fr.* Maud. OBNC
I heard of gold at Sutter's Mill. When I Went Off to Prospect. John A. Stone. SGR
I Heard the Bells on Christmas Day. Longfellow. PoSC (Christmas Bells.) RePo; TRV
I heard the old, old men say. The Old Men Admiring Themselves in the Water. W. B. Yeats. GoJo
I heard the sighing of the reeds. In Ireland: By the Pool at the Third Rosses. Arthur Symons. OBNC
I heard the singing of a thrush. Country Lane. Margaret Stanion Darling. FiSC
I heard the sparrows shouting "Eat, eat." In the Night Fields. W. S. Merwin. AP; PoCh
I heard the trailing garments of the Night. Hymn to the Night. Longfellow. AmLP; AP
I heard the wild geese flying. Wild Geese. Elinor Chipp. RePo
I Heard You Solemn-Sweet Pipes of the Organ. Walt Whitman. CBEP
I Held a Lamb. Kim Worthington. SoPo
I held it truth, with him who sings. In Memoriam A. H. H., I. Tennyson. DiPo; FoBA; OBNC; VP
I hid my heart in a nest of roses. A Ballad of Dreamland. Swinburne. ILP
I Hid My Love When Young. John Clare. *See* Secret Love.
I hoe and I plow. Farmer. Liberty Hyde. Bailey. RePo
I hoed and trenched and weeded. A. E. Housman. A Shropshire Lad, LXIII. PoPo
I hold Helvellyn in my fingers, here. Thomas Gray in Patterdale. Norman Nicholson. ACV
I hold him wise and well y-taught. Discretion. *Unknown.* CBEP
I hold that when a person dies. A Creed. John Masefield. MoRP
I hoped that with the brave and strong. He Doeth All Things Well. Anne Brontë TRV
I hung my verses in the wind. The Test. Emerson. PP
"I, if I perish, perish"—Esther spake. Monna Innominata, VIII. Christina Rossetti. VP
I imagine the midnight moment's forest. The Thought-Fox. Ted Hughes. NePoEA-2
I in My Bed of Thistles. Rosalía de Castro, *tr. fr. Spanish by* Edwin Morgan. AnSP
I joy, deare Mother, when I view. The British Church. George Herbert. MeP
I Keep Three Wishes Ready. Annette Wynne. SoPo
I kenning through astronomy divine. Meditation Eight. Edward Taylor. *Fr.* Preparatory Meditations, First Series. AP; StP
I kept my answers small and kept them near. Answers. Elizabeth Jennings. PoDB
I killed them, but they would not die. The Immortals. Isaac Rosenberg. MMA
I kind of like the playful porpoise. The Porpoise. Ogden Nash. RePo
I kissed a kiss in youth. Scintilla. William Stanley Braithwaite. AmNP
I kissed my darling at the zoo. The Prodigy. A. P. Herbert. EvOK
I kissed you in the dead of dark. The Accusation. James Wright. AmPC
I Knew a Boy with Hair like Gold. Melvin Walker La Follette. NePoEA-2
I knew a most superior camper. The Bunyip and the Whistling Kettle. John Manifold. PoAu-2
I knew a simple soldier boy. Suicide in the Trenches. Siegfried Sassoon. MMA
I Knew a Woman [Lovely in Her Bones]. Theodore Roethke. CABA; ErPo; MP; PoIE; StP; ToPo; UnTE
I knew an old lady. Antique Shop. Carl Carmer. RePo
I knew this Master Host would hold me in. Extended Invitation. Jesse Stuart. FiSC
I knew you forever and you were always old. Some Foreign Letters. Anne Sexton. PoCh; ToPo
I Know. Verda Group. STF
I know a bank whereon the wild thyme blows. A Violet Bank. Shakespeare. *Fr.* A Midsummer Night's Dream, II, i. RePo
I know a little cupboard. The Cupboard. Walter de la Mare. SoPo
I know a little garden-close. A Garden by the Sea. William Morris. OBNC
I Know a Man. Robert Creeley. AmPC; CoPo
I know a moon door in the Forbidden City. Moon Door. Mary Kennedy. BoLP
I know a place all fennel-green and fine. A Green Place. William Jay Smith. RePo
I know a place, in the ivy on a tree. The Bird's Nest. John Drinkwater. EvOK; SoPo

I know a wasted place high in the Alps. Two Poems on the Catholic Bavarians. Edgar Bowers. PoCh
I know, although when looks meet. Crazy Jane and Jack the Journeyman. W. B. Yeats. FoBA
I know an old house, grey with years. Opening Door. Winifred Adams Burr. FiSC
I know but will not tell. Elegy. Alan Dugan. AP
I Know Full Well the Water's Flowing Power. St. John of the Cross, *tr. fr. Spanish by* James Edward Tobin. AnSP
I Know He Is Real. *Unknown.* STF
I know him, February's thrush. The Thrush in February. George Meredith. OBNC
I know him now, not now to know demanding. Nunc Scio, Quid Sit Amor. L. A. MacKay. OBCV
I know I have a lot of faults. Let Me Look at Me. Bessie June Martin. STF
I know I need not wait nor run to meet you, yet. Be. "Will Inman." PoNC
I know it is my sinne, which locks thine eares. Church-Lock and Key. George Herbert. MeP
I know lots of men who are in love and lots of men who are married. I Never Even Suggested It. Ogden Nash. PoLF
I know not by what methods rare. Prayer. *Unknown.* STF
I know not how that Bethlehem's Babe. Our Christ. Harry Webb Farrington. STF; TRV
I know not if among rocks. The Chimera. Dino Campana. CoIP
I know not if from uncreated spheres. Michelangelo, *tr. fr. Italian by* George Santayana. RBL
I Know Not What I Seek Eternally. Rosalía de Castro, *tr. fr. Spanish by* Muriel Kittel. AnSP; SiGo
I know not what my health will be. I Know. Verda Group. STF
I know not what shall befall me: God hangs a mist o'er my eyes. Mary Gardiner Brainard. *Fr.* Not Knowing. TRV
I know not when this tiresome man. The Sundowner. John Shaw Neilson. PoAu-1
I know not where my steps may lead. He Knows the Way. *Unknown.* STF
I know not why I yearn for thee again. Dreams of the Sea. W. H. Davies. IIaSV
I know, Sister, that solitude. To a Severe Nun. Thomas Merton. CoPo
I know some lonely houses off the road. Emily Dickinson. CBEP; FoBA
I know that face! Daphne. Bliss Carman. OBCV
I know that He exists. Emily Dickinson. ILP
I know that he is ten years old. The Difference. Eleanor A. Chaffee. BiCB
I know that I shall meet my fate. An Irish Airman Foresees His Death. W. B. Yeats. AnMoPo; CABA; FoBA; GoJo; GTBS-P; ILP; MMA; PoPl; PoPo
I know that this was Life—the track. In Memoriam A. H. H., XXV. Tennyson. VP
I know the mind that feels indeed the fire. William Cowper. *Fr.* Table Talk. PP
I know the thing that's most uncommon. On a Certain Lady at Court. Pope. CBEP
I know the wayes of learning; both the head. The Pearl. George Herbert. MeP; SeCP
I know there are some fools that care. The Deformed Mistress. Sir John Suckling. ErPo
I know two women. The Wife. Robert Creeley. AmPC; AP; ToPo
I know what the caged bird feels, alas! Sympathy. Paul Laurence Dunbar. CoPo
"I know where I'd get." Padraic Colum. *Fr.* Asses. LOW
I Know Where I'm Going. *Unknown.* ELP
I knowed a man, which he lived in Jones. Thar's More in the Man than Thar Is in the Land. Sidney Lanier. AP
I Laid Me Down upon a Bank. Blake. CBEP
I lately lost a preposition. The Naughty Preposition. Morris Bishop. LV
I Lately Vowed. John Oldmixon. ErPo
I Lay Awake, Wandering in That Limbo. Gustavo Adolfo Bécquer, *tr. fr. Spanish by* John Haines. AnSP
I lay down with my love and there was song. Armorial. Ralph Gustafson. ACV
I leaned out of window, I smelt the white clover. Seven Times Three—Love. Jean Ingelow. *Fr.* Songs of Seven. PoLF
I leant upon a coppice gate. The Darkling Thrush. Thomas Hardy. CaFP; DiPo; EvOK; ILP; OBNC; OnP; PoDB; PoIE; PoSa; RoGo; StP; VP
I learn, as the years roll onward. Life's Lessons. *Unknown.* PoLF; STF
I leave mortality, and things below. The Extasie. Abraham Cowley. SeCP
I leave thy praises unexpress'd. In Memoriam A. H. H., LXXV. Tennyson. VP
I leave you in your garden. To Yvor Winters, 1955. Thom Gunn. GTBS-P
I lie here on the hill of spring. In Spring. Eduard Mörike. SiGo
I lie sleepless in the half light. Peace, like a Lamb. Leonard Clark. WePo

I lift mine eyes, and all the windows blaze. Sonnets on the Divina Commedia, V. Longfellow. AP; ILP

I lift my heart to Thee, O God. Thankful Heart. F. W. Davis. STF

I lift the Lord on high. Père Lalemant. Marjorie Pickthall. OBCV

I like a church; I like a cowl. The Problem. Emerson. AP

I like a look of agony. Emily Dickinson. AP; CBEP

I Like Gayety and Horsing Around. The Monk of Montaudun, tr. fr. Provençal by Paul Blackburn. AnML

I Like My Body When It Is with Your. E. E. Cummings. Fr. Sonnets—Actualities. ErPo; UnTE

I like not tears in tune, nor do I prize. On the Memory of Mr. Edward King, Drown'd in the Irish Seas. John Cleveland. SeCP

I like the fall. The Mist and All. Dixie Willson. SoPo

I like the hinting of the hare. The Old Squire. Wilfrid Scawen Blunt. SD

I like to find. Pleasures. Denise Levertov. AP

I like to have a home life in the house. Gertrude Stein. Fr. Afterwards. LOW

I like to look for bridges. Bridges. Rhoda W. Bacmeister. SoPo

I Like to Quote. Mitchell D. Follansbee. PoPl

I like to see it lap the miles. Emily Dickinson. AmLP; AP; CABA; CaFP; DiPo; FoBA; RePo
(Railway Train, The.) FaBV
(Train, The.) CBEP; PoPo

I like to see the wind. Hayfield. Aileen Fisher. RePo

I live all alone, and I am a young girl. The Garden of Bamboos. Tr. by E. Powys Mathers. BoLP

I Live and Do Not Live in Myself. St. John of the Cross, tr. fr. Spanish by Stephan Stepanchev. AnSP

I Live in Great Sorrow. Unknown. See Fowls in the Frith.

I live invisible (in my whole sky). Too Bright a Day. Norman MacCaig. GTBS-P

I lived my life from day to day. Epitaph. Mathurin Régnier. RBL

I loathe that I did love. The Aged Lover Renounceth Love. Thomas, Lord Vaux. EnRePo

I loitered weeping with my bride for gladness. James Agee. Fr. Lyrics. PoPl

I long for you. Everest of Tears. Wolfgang Weyrauch. MP

I long to be the wanton breeze. Lovesick. Unknown. UnTE

I long to talk with some old lover's ghost. Love's Deity [or Deitie]. John Donne. DiPo; EnRePo; FoBA; ILP; SeCP

I Look into My Glass. Thomas Hardy. CABA; CBEP

I looked for that which is not, nor can be. A Pause of Thought. Christina Rossetti. OBNC

I looked here. The Black Riders, VIII. Stephen Crane. AP

I looked in the first glass. The Three Mirrors. Edwin Muir. PoIE

I looked into my heart to write. Summer Song I. George Barker. ToPo

I Looked Up from My Writing. Thomas Hardy. MMA

I lost a World—the other day! Emily Dickinson. DiPo

I Lost the Love of Heaven. John Clare. CBEP; ELP
(Vision, A.) GTBS-P; PoIE

I Love a Flower. Thomas Phillipps(?). MeEL

I love at early morn, from new-mown swath. Summer Images. John Clare. CBEP

I love daffodils. Spring Song. Hilda Conkling. PoSC

I Love Him Who Loves Me, Otherwise None. Charles d'Orléans, tr. fr. French by Muriel Kittel. AnML

"I love, I love, and whom love ye?" I Love a Flower. Thomas Phillipps(?). MeEL

I Love Little Pussy. Jane Taylor. SoPo

I Love Long Black Eyes. Bilhana, formerly at. to Chauras, tr. fr. Sanskrit by E. Powys Mathers. Fr. Black Marigolds. SiGo

I love my God, but with no love of mine. By Thy Life I Live [or Adoration]. Mme Guyon. STF; TRV

I Love My Jean. Burns. See Of A' the Airts.

I love my life, but not too well. Love Song. Harriet Monroe. AmLP

I love Octopussy, his arms are so long. The Octopussycat. Kenyon Cox. SoPo

I love old gardens best. A Charleston Garden. Henry Bellamann. PoLF

I love the church that Jesus bought. Not on Sunday Night. Unknown. STF

I love the old melodious lays. Proem. Whittier. AP

I love the secret place of prayer. The Secret Place of Prayer. Georgia B. Adams. STF

I love thee, but love be free. Love in Reason. Luis de Góngora. RBL

I love thee not, Sabidius. To Sabidius. Martial. DiPo

I love thee when thy swelling buds appear. The Tree. Jones Very. PoSC

I love them, I listen to them. The Bells. Rosalía de Castro. AnSP

I love this white and slender body. The White and Slender Body. Heine. UnTE

I love Thy Word, O God. The Word of God. J. Harold Gwynne. STF

I love to peep out on a summer's morn. Summer Morning. John Clare. CBEP; PoSC

I love to rise in a summer morn. The Schoolboy. Blake. Fr. Songs of Experience. CBEP

I love to see, when leaves depart. Autumn. Roy Campbell. AnMoPo; GTBS-P

I love you. Love. Unknown. TRV

"I love you"/ That's the word she used. That's All She Wrote. H. A. Sieber. PoNC

I love you first because your face is fair. V-Letter. Karl Shapiro. AP; MoLP; ThLM

I love you, great new Titan! Soldier: Twentieth Century. Isaac Rosenberg. MMA

"I love you, sweet: how can you ever learn." Youth's Antiphony. Dante Gabriel Rossetti. The House of Life, XIII. VP

I love you—Titan lover. Girl to Soldier on Leave. Isaac Rosenberg. MMA

I Love You . . . Why Do You Hate Me? Rosalía de Castro, tr. fr. Spanish by Edwin Morgan. AnSP

I Loved a Lass. George Wither. UnTE

I loved him not; and yet, now he is gone. The Maid's Lament. Walter Savage Landor. Fr. The Citation and Examination of William Shakespeare. OBNC

I loved you first: but afterwards your love. Monna Innominata, IV. Christina Rossetti. VP

I loved you in the lone streets of the city. Dino Campana. Fr. Two Lyrics for S. A. CoIP

I Loved You Once. Pushkin, tr. fr. Russian by Dudley Randall. AmNP

I, Lysidus, equestrian, offer these. The Golden Spurs. Unknown. UnTE

I M J F K. Ruth Landshoff Yorck. OPP

I. M. Margaritae Sorori. W. E. Henley. See Margaritae Sorori.

I made a loaf of bread. The White Bird. Roy McFadden. ACV

I made a posy [or posie] while the day ran by. Life. George Herbert. CBEP; FoBA; MeP; SeCP

I made believe fly. Make Believe. Harry Behn. RePo

I made my fire of little sticks. Little Sticks. Eric Rolls. PoAu-2

I made my shroud but no one knows. See I make my shroud but no one knows.

I made them lay their hands in mine and swear. Guinevere. Tennyson. Fr. Idylls of the King. TRV

I made up my mind in early day. The Mexico Trail. Unknown. BFSS

I make a pact with you, Walt Whitman. A Pact. Ezra Pound. CBEP; PoPl

I make man's ancient food. Bread. Nancy Keesing. PoAu-2

I make [made, wr.] my shroud but no one knows. Song. Adelaide Crapsey. AmLP; LV

I marked all kindred Powers the heart finds fair. Love Enthroned. Dante Gabriel Rossetti. The House of Life, I. OBNC; VP

I married me a wife in the month of June. Risselty Rosselty. Unknown. DiPo

I may be dead to-morrow, uncaressed. For the Book of Love. Jules Laforgue. ErPo

I May, I Might, I Must. Marianne Moore. PoPo; RePo

I may never be as clever as my neighbor down the street. Dad's Greatest Job. Unknown. STF

I may not touch the hand I saw. A Separation. William Johnson Cory. OBNC

I meant not to defend the scapes of any. Apology for Loose Behavior. Ovid. Fr. Amores. UnTE

I meant to do my work today. Called Away. Richard Le Gallienne. SoPo

I meet you in an evil time. An Eclogue for Christmas. Louis MacNeice. AnMoPo

I met a little Elf-man, once. The Little Elf [or Elfman]. John Kendrick Bangs. BiCB; SoPo

I met a man as I went walking. Puppy and I. A. A. Milne. SoPo

I met a ragged man. The Song. Theodore Roethke. AP

I met a sad girl in our town. Poem. Keith Sinclair. ACV

I met a traveler [or traveller] from an antique land. Ozymandias [of Egypt]. Shelley. CABA; CaFP; CBEP; DiPo; GTBS-P; ILP; LV; OBNC; OnP; PoIE; PoLF; PoPo; PoSa; RoGo; StP

I met an elf-man in the woods. How to Treat Elves. Morris Bishop. PoPl

I met God in the morning. The Secret. Ralph Spaulding Cushman. STF; TRV

I met the Bishop on the road. Crazy Jane Talks with the Bishop. W. B. Yeats. CABA; DiPo; ErPo; FoBA; ILP

I Met the Master. Unknown. PoLF; STF

I mind as 'ow the night afore that show. The Chances. Wilfred Owen. MMA

I missed him when the sun began to bend. Lost and Found. George Macdonald. TRV

I Mix in Life. Samuel Taylor Coleridge. CBEP

I mourn unhappy days that are no more. Petrarch. *Fr.* Sonnets to Laura: To Laura in Death. RBL
I Much Dislike, I Dare Avow It. The Monk of Montaudun, *tr. fr. Provençal by* Maurice Valency. AnML
I Murder Hate by Field or Flood. Burns. CBEP
I must be dreaming through the days. Experience. Lesbia Harford. PoAu-1
I must be flattered. The imperious. Modern Love, XXVIII. George Meredith. VP
"I must be going, no longer staying." The Grey Cock. *Unknown.* ELP
I must depart, but like to his last breath. Parted Souls. Lord Herbert of Cherbury. SeCP
I must go down to the seas again, to the lonely sea and the sky. Sea-Fever. John Masefield. FaBV; HaSV; PoLF; PoPl; PoPo; RePo
I Must Go Walk the Wood[s]. *Unknown.* CBEP; MeEL (Wood So Wild, The.) WiR
I must have passed the crest a while ago. The Long Hill. Sara Teasdale. LV; PoPl
I must not say that thou wast true. Euphrosyne. Matthew Arnold. VP
I must not think of thee; and, tired yet strong. Renouncement. Alice Meynell. BoLP; OBNC
I must remember. Shelley Silverstein. PoSC
I myself saw furious with blood. Aeneas at Washington. Allen Tate. AP
I need a little stick when I. I Have to Have It. Dorothy Aldis. SoPo
I need a strength to keep me true. My Need. *Unknown.* STF
I Need No Sky. Witter Bynner. EaLo
I Need Not Go. Thomas Hardy. DTC
I need not shout my faith. Thrice eloquent. Silence. Charles Hanson Towne. TRV
I Ne'er Was Struck. John Clare. ELP
I never cut my neighbor's throat. Guilty. Marguerite Wilkinson. TRV
I never drank of Aganippe well. Astrophel and Stella, LXXIV. Sir Philip Sidney. CABA; EnRePo
I Never Even Suggested It. Ogden Nash. PoLF
I never have seen the snow so white. Christmas Birthday. Grace Ellen Glaubitz. BiCB
I never hear the word "escape." Emily Dickinson. FoBA
I Never Knew. Glenn E. Wagoner. STF
I never knew a kangaroo. Pockets. Rowena Bennett. RePo
I never knew what real peace meant. I Never Knew. Glenn E. Wagoner. STF
I never like the fellow's plan. The Down-Pullers. Walter E. Isenhour. STF
I never lost as much but twice. Emily Dickinson. AP
I never loved your plains! Hills. Arthur Guiterman. RePo
I never quite saw fairy-folk. Very Nearly. Queenie Scott-Hopper. SoPo
I never saw a moor. Emily Dickinson. AP; CBEP; DiPo; EvOK; FoBA; PoPo
(Chartless.) PoLF; PoPl; TRV
I never saw a Purple Cow. The Purple Cow. Gelett Burgess. PoLF; PoPl; SoPo
I Never Saw the Field. Neidhart von Reuental, *tr. fr. German by* Margaret F. Richey. AnML
I never sawe my Layde laye apart. Complaint That His Ladie after She Knew of His Love Kept Her Face Alway Hidden from Him. Earl of Surrey. PoIE
I Never Shall Love the Snow Again. Robert Bridges. FaBV
I never wander where the bord'ring reeds. Fly-fishing. John Gay. *Fr.* Rural Sports. SD
I never went to Mamble. Mamble. John Drinkwater. WePo
I, now at Carthage. He, shot dead at Rome. Vale from Carthage. Peter Viereck. PoPo
I now think Love is rather deaf than blind. My Picture Left in Scotland. Ben Jonson. EnRePo; SeCP
I nursed it in my bosom while it lived. Memory. Christina Rossetti. OBNC
I often have to wonder. Snoring. Aileen Fisher. SoPo
I often have wondered how women love men. Green Grows the Laurel. *Unknown.* BFSS
I often in the evening meet with birds. Black Spirit. Tom Poots. FiSC
I often say my prayers. Do I Really Pray? John Burton. STF
I often see a puffy toad. The Proud Toad. Grace Taber Hallock. RePo
I often sit and wish that I. A Kite. *Unknown.* SoPo
I Often Think of Writing Home, *with music.* John A. Stone. SGR
I often wander on the beach. The Old Swimmer. Christopher Morley. LV; SD
I often wish I were King. If I Were King. A. A. Milne. RePo
I often wonder as the fairy-story. The Lucky Marriage. Thomas Blackburn. GTBS-P
I once had a sweet little doll, dears. The Lost Doll. Charles Kingsley. *Fr.* The Water Babies. SoPo
I Once Was a Maid. Burns. *Fr.* The Jolly Beggars. UnTE

I once wrote a letter as follows. The Invoice. Robert Creeley. AmPC
I only knew one poet in my life. How It Strikes a Contemporary. Robert Browning. CABL; CTC; GTBS-P; PP
I Ought to Weep. *Unknown.* MeEL
I own John Graydon's place. John Graydon. Wilson MacDonald. ACV
I pace the sounding sea-beach and behold. Milton. Longfellow. AmLP; AP; StP
I paced alone on the road across the field. The Home. Rabindranath Tagore. GoJo
I paid a man at Martinmas. The Plowman. Burns. UnTE
I Pass in Silence. John Clare. BoLP
I past beside the reverend walls. In Memoriam A. H. H., LXXXVII. Tennyson. VP
I paused last eve beside the blacksmith's door. God's Word. John Clifford. TRV
I peeled bits of straw and I got switches too. Bits of Straw. John Clare. WiR
I pitched my day's leazings in Crimmercrock Lane. The Dark-eyed Gentleman. Thomas Hardy. PoIE
I pitied one whose tattered dress. The Vesture of the Soul. "Æ." ACV
I placed a jar in Tennessee. Anecdote of the Jar. Wallace Stevens. AP; CaFP; PoIE; VaPo
"I play for Seasons; not Eternities." Modern Love, XIII. George Meredith. OBNC; PoIE; VP
I Played on the Grass with Mary. Ernest Walsh. ErPo
I played with you 'mid cowslips blowing. Love and Age. Thomas Love Peacock. *Fr.* Gryll Grange. OBNC
I plucked a honeysuckle where. The Honeysuckle. Dante Gabriel Rossetti. CBEP
I plucked pink blossoms from mine apple-tree. An Apple Gathering. Christina Rossetti. BoLP; OBNC
I, Pluto. Tilottama Daswani. ACV
I pray the prayer the Easterners do. Salaam Alaikum. *Unknown.* PoLF
I Pray Thee Leave. Michael Drayton. *See* To His Coy Love.
I pray you, let us roam no more. Thomas Moore. *Fr.* Odes to Nea. OBNC
I prayed for strength, and then I lost awhile. The Answered Prayer. Annie Johnson Flint. STF
I preached as never sure to preach again. Richard Baxter. *Fr.* Love Breathing Thanks and Praise. TRV
I Pressed Her Rebel Lips. *Unknown.* ErPo
I proclaim Thee great and wonderful. Psalm. Murilo Mendes. MoRP
I promise you by the harsh funeral. Burns Singer. *Fr.* Sonnets for a Dying Man. NePoEA-2
I Pursue a Form. Rubén Darío, *tr. fr. Spanish by* Doreen Bell. AnSP
I Put an End to Singing. Peire Vidal, *tr. fr. Provençal by* William M. Davis. AnML
I put my hand upon her toe. Gentley, Johnny My Jingalo. *Unknown.* UnTE
I Put My Hat upon My Head. Samuel Johnson. StP
I question not God's means or ways. God Knows the Answer. F. B. Whitney. STF
I raised a falcon for more than a year. The Falcon. "The Knight of Kürenberg." AnML
I raised my eyes aloft, and I beheld. Dante. *Fr.* Divina Commedia: Paradiso. TRV
I ran all night along the river. Rhyme from the Confino. Luigi Bartolini. CoIP
I ran for a catch. A Cricket Triolet. Coulson Kernahan. WePo
I reached that waterhole, its mud designed. The Dancers. Roland E. Robinson. ACV
I read an impatient man. To a Western Bard Still a Whoop and a Holler Away from English Poetry. William Meredith. PP
I read in Dante how that hornèd light. S.S. *Lusitania.* Matthew Arnold. CBEP
I read it in the Gita. Au Beau Milieu. Frank Borden Hanes. PoNC
I reared me a falcon longer than one year. "The Knight of Kürenberg," *tr. fr. German by* Alexander Gode. AGP
I reckon—when I count at all. Emily Dickinson. PP
I Refuse to Be a Nun. *Unknown, tr. fr. Spanish by* James Duffy. AnML
I remember a dug-out in the backyard as children. Reflections upon a Recurrent Suggestion by Civil Defense Authorities That I Build a Bombshelter in My Backyard. Reed Whittemore. PoCh
I remember a house where all were good. In the Valley of the Elwy. Gerard Manley Hopkins. PoIE
I Remember, I Remember. Thomas Hood. CBEP; ELP; FaBV; ILP; StP
(Past and Present.) GTBS-P; TRV
I Remember, I Remember. Philip Larkin. AnMoPo
I remember, I remember, when once I used to mine. California as It Is and Was. John A. Stone. SGR
I remember the Chillicothe ball players. Hits and Runs. Carl Sandburg. SD
I remember the neckcurls, limp and damp as tendrils. Elegy for Jane. Theodore Roethke. AP; CaFP; MP; PoPo

I remember your dream, born of the hawkless hills. Conjecture for a Short Mechanic. Alan Planz. PtTo
I remembered Sulayma when the passion. In Battle. Abu-l-Hasan ben al-Qabturnuh. AnML
I rise in the dawn, and I kneel and blow. The Song of the Old Mother. W. B. Yeats. LOW; PoPo
I said "I see." The Blind. Erich Fried. MGP
I said I splendidly loved you; it's not true. Sonnet. Rupert Brooke. CBEP
I said in my heart, "I am sick of four walls and a ceiling." Richard Hovey. *Fr.* Spring. RePo
I said, "Let me walk in the fields." Obedience. George Macdonald. TRV
I said—Then, dearest, since 't is so. The Last Ride Together. Robert Browning. VP
I Said, This Misery Must End. Christopher Brennan. *Fr.* Pauca Mea. PoAu-1
I said to her, darling, I said. Vivamus, Mea Lesbia. Catullus, *tr. by* Frank O. Copley. StP
I Said to Love. Thomas Hardy. VP
I said to myself almost in prayer. A Trial Run. Robert Frost. WePo
I Said to the Leaf. Carleton Drewry. MoRP
I said to the man who stood at the gate of the year. *See* And I said to the man . . .
I sang the songs of red ripped-up vengeance. The Poet and War. Albert Ehrenstein. MGP
I sat before my glass one day. The Other Side of a Mirror. Mary Elizabeth Coleridge. CBEP
I sat beside the red stock route. Harry Pearce. David Campbell. PoAu-2
I Sat Cross-legged upon a Stone. Walther von der Vogelweide, *tr. fr. German by* Gillian Barker *and* Kenneth Gee. AnML
I sat here this morning, detached, summoning up, I think. The Deviator. Bertram Warr. OBCV
I sat with Love upon a woodside well. Willowwood, 1. Dante Gabriel Rossetti. The House of Life, XLIX. VP
I saw/ Your hands on my lips like blind needles. Pirouette. Audre Lorde. NNP
I saw a boy with eager eye. The Two Boys. Mary Lamb. CBEP
I Saw a Chapel All of Gold. Blake. CABA; CBEP
I Saw a Cherry weep, and why? The Weeping Cherry. Robert Herrick. WePo
I saw a donkey. The Donkey. *Unknown.* BiCB
I saw a fair maiden. A Lullaby of the Nativity. *Unknown.* MeEL
I saw a famous man eating soup. Soup. Carl Sandburg. RePo
I saw a fly within a bead. A Trapped Fly. Robert Herrick. WiR
I saw a gnome. The Gnome. Harry Behn. SoPo
I saw a man pursuing the horizon. The Black Riders, XXIV. Stephen Crane. AP
I saw a man raking leaves. Man Raking Leaves. Thad Stem, Jr. PoNC
I saw a man turned into money. George Abbe. *Fr.* Changed. PtTo
I Saw a Peacock. *Unknown.* CBEP
I saw a proud, mysterious cat. The Mysterious Cat. Vachel Lindsay. GoJo; SoPo
I saw a querulous old man, the tobacconist of Eighth Street. The Tobacconist of Eighth Street. Richard Eberhart. ToPo
I Saw a Ship a-Sailing. Mother Goose. SoPo
I saw a ship a-sailing. The Fairy Ship. "Gabriel Setoun." PoPl
I saw a ship a-sailing, a-sailing, a-sailing. An Old Song Resung. John Masefield. EvOK
I saw a ship of martial build. The Berg. Herman Melville. AP; CBEP
I saw a silvery creature scurrying. Riddle #29: The Moon and the Sun. *Unknown.* CaFP; GoJo
I saw a slowly-stepping train. God's Funeral. Thomas Hardy. PoDB
I Saw a Stable. Mary Elizabeth Coleridge. TRV
I saw a star slide down the sky. The Falling Star. Sara Teasdale. SoPo
I saw a staring virgin stand. Two Songs from a Play, I. W. B. Yeats. *Fr.* The Resurrection. CABA; FoBA; ILP; PoDB; PoIE
I saw a thing, and stopped to wonder. The Pine Bough. Richard Aldridge. PoSC
I saw a worm, with many a fold. Psyche. Jones Very. AP
I saw a young snake glide. Snake. Theodore Roethke. AnMoPo; PoPl
I saw an aged beggar in my walk. The Old Cumberland Beggar. Wordsworth. CABL
"I saw an elephant walking down the road." April Fool. Elizabeth J. Coatsworth. RePo
I saw an old man with a long white beard. Building of Sand. Grant Code. FiSC
I saw autumn today . . . incipiently, on the sunset. Walter Benton. *Fr.* This Is My Beloved. UnTE

I saw between a shadow and a bough. The Ungathered Apples. James Wright. ErPo
I saw by looking in his eyes. The Wandering Jew. E. A. Robinson. PoDB
I saw dawn creep across the sky. A Summer Morning. Rachel Field. SoPo
I Saw Eternity. Louise Bogan. StP
I saw eternity the other night. The World. Henry Vaughan. CABA; CBEP; DiPo; FaBV; FaPL; ILP; MeP; OnP; PoIE; SeCP; StP
I saw fair[e] Chloris [*or* Cloris] walk[e] alone. On Chloris [*or* a Gentlewoman] Walking in the Snow[e]. William Strode. BoC; ELP
I saw from the Beach. Thomas Moore. HaSV; OBNC
I saw God! Do you doubt it? What Tomas Said in a Pub. James Stephens. ILP
I Saw God Wash the World. William L. Stidger. TRV
I saw highland maidens dancing. When Don Luis Was in Cuenca. Luis de Góngora. RBL
I saw him at a funeral in town. Perennial Mourner. Sydney King Russell. FiSC
I saw him forging link by link his chain. The Slave. Jones Very. AP
I saw him once before. The Last Leaf. Oliver Wendell Holmes. AmLP; AP; CaFP; PoIE; PoLF; PoPo
I saw him steal the light away. God's Education. Thomas Hardy. MoRP
I saw his searching eyes at all the bars. The Man I Met. Joseph Payne Brennan. FiSC
I Saw in Louisiana a Live-Oak Growing. Walt Whitman. AP; CBEP; FoBA
I saw in the East a sign, a sign. Blues Ballad. Kenneth Pitchford. *Fr.* Good for Nothing Man. CoPo
I Saw My Lady Weep. *Unknown.* CBEP; ELP
I Saw My Life as Whitest Flame. Christopher Brennan. *Fr.* Towards the Source. PoAu-1
I saw myself leaving. Reflections. Carl Gardner. NNP
I saw no infant. First-born. Marion Buchman. PtTo
I saw no way—the heavens were stitched. Emily Dickinson. AP
I saw old Autumn in the misty morn. Ode: Autumn. Thomas Hood. ILP; OBNC
I Saw One Hanging. *Unknown.* STF
I saw only the edge. A Glance at the Album. Gray Burr. CoPo
I saw that country in a dream. Wilderness Theme. Ian Mudie. PoAu-2
I saw the best minds of my generation. Squeal. Louis Simpson. Par
I saw the lovely arch. The Rainbow. Walter de la Mare. SoPo
I saw the ramparts of my native land. Sonnet: Death Warnings. Francisco de Quevedo y Villegas. RBL
I saw the sky descending, black and white. Where the Rainbow Ends. Robert Lowell. AP
I saw the spectre of a king. Ballad of Two Kings. Grant Code. FiSC
I saw the spiders marching through the air. Mr. Edwards and the Spider. Robert Lowell. AP; CABA; ILP; MP; ToPo
I saw the spires of Oxford. The Spires of Oxford. Winifred M. Letts. PoLF
I saw the spot where our first parents dwelt. The Garden. Jones Very. AP
I saw the sunlit vale, and the pastoral fairy-tale. The Sunlit Vale. Edmund Blunden. CBEP
I saw the two starlings. The Manoeuvre. William Carlos Williams. LOW
I Saw the Wind Today. Padraic Colum. Reminiscence, II. GoJo; LOW
(Wind, The.) RoGo
I Saw Three Ships. *Unknown.* HaSV; RePo
I saw where in the shroud did lurk. On an Infant Dying as Soon as Born. Charles Lamb. GTBS-P
I saw with open eyes. Stupidity Street. Ralph Hodgson. LOW
I saw you once on the TV. Galway Kinnell. *Fr.* For Robert Frost. PP
I saw you toss the kites on high. The Wind. Robert Louis Stevenson. SoPo
I saw your twenty-day blue eyes. For Two Children. René Char. CoFP
I say the pulpit (in the sober use). William Cowper. *Fr.* The Task. TRV
I Say to the Mountain. Zoe Kincaid Brockman. PoNC
I scarce believe [*or* beleeve] my love to be so pure. Love's Growth. John Donne. FoBA; MeP
I scooped up the moon. The Moon. Ryuho. SoPo
I scooped up the moon's footprints but. Because My Hands Hear the Flowers Thinking. Kenneth Patchen. ToPo
I see a farmer walking by himself. The Farmer. Fredegond Shove. MMA
I see around me here. The Wanderer Recalls the Past. Wordsworth. *Fr.* The Excursion. OBNC
I see before me now a traveling army halting. Bivouac on a Mountain Side. Walt Whitman. AP; PoLF

I see black dragons mount the sky. Shapes and Signs. James Clarence Mangan. ACV
I See God. *Unknown.* STF
I see her dancing in the square. Danse Macabre. Antonia Y. Schwab. FiSC
I See His Blood upon the Rose. Joseph Mary Plunkett. MoRP; PoLF; TRV
I see now, not far away, the savage pit. Recognition of Death. Joseph Payne Brennan. FiSC
I see that there it is on the beach. Memorial Service for the Invasion Beach Where the Vacation in the Flesh Is Over. Alan Dugan. MP
I see that wreath which doth the wearer arm. To My Dead Friend Ben: Johnson. Henry King. SeCP
I see the February moon lie down. February Moon. Wilhelm Lehmann. MGP
I see the four-fold man, the humanity in deadly sleep. Blake. *Fr.* Jerusalem. PoIE
I see the golden hunter go. Bliss Carman. *Fr.* Songs of the Sea-Children. OBCV
I see the map of summer, lying still. Movies for the Home. Howard Moss. NePoEA-2
I See the Moon. *Unknown.* SoPo
I see the use; and know my blood [or bloud]. The Storm. Henry Vaughan. CBEP; MeP
I see the wrong that round me lies. Whittier. *Fr.* The Eternal Goodness. TRV
I see the young bride move among. George Barker. *Fr.* The True Confession of George Barker. ErPo
I see them,—crowd on crowd they walk the earth. The Dead. Jones Very. AP
I see them working in old rectories. The Country Clergy. R. S. Thomas. GTBS-P; PoIE
I see you did not try to save. Passing the Graveyard. Andrew Young. DTC
I see you in her bed. The Lovemaker. Robert Mezey. CABA; NePoEA-2
I Seek to Make My Speech a Yawp as Bitter. Dante, tr. fr. *Italian by* Leslie A. Fiedler. AnML
I seem to hear lamenting. The Old Woman Laments the Days of Her Youth. Villon. AnML
I send you here a sort of allegory. To ——: With the Following Poem. Tennyson. *Fr.* The Palace of Art. VP
I send you here a wreath of blossoms blown. Roses. Pierre de Ronsard. RBL
I send you perfume fresh as dew. Perfume. *Unknown.* UnTE
I serve a mistress whiter than the snow. Fidele's Song. Anthony Munday. *Fr.* Fidele and Fortunio. CBEP
I set my heart to sing of leaves. Anticipation. Lord De Tabley. ELP
I shall be capricious, I shall have a whim. A Man's Woman. Mary Carolyn Davies. PoLF
I Shall Be Loved as Quiet Things. Karle Wilson Baker. MoLP
I Shall Be Married on Monday Morning. *Unknown.* ErPo
I shall go as my father went. The Tenancy. Mary Gilmore. PoAu-1
I shall go away. And the birds will still be there. The Conclusive Voyage. Juan Ramón Jiménez. PoPl
I shall hate you. Hatred. Gwendolyn B. Bennett. AmNP
I shall just put away this hoarded bottle. Addict. Mabel MacDonald Carver. FiSC
I shall never get you put together entirely. The Colossus. Sylvia Plath. MP; NePoEA-2
I shall not be myself, death. Zenith. Juan Ramón Jiménez. AnSP
I Shall Not Care. Sara Teasdale. PoPl
"I Shall Not Die for Thee." Padraic Colum. CTC
I shall not miss the roses, fading. Grapes. Pushkin. SiGo
I shall not see thee. Dare I say. In Memoriam A. H. H., XCIII. Tennyson. VP
I shall not wonder more, then. Change. Raymond Knister. OBCV
I shall rot here with those whom in their day. In Death Divided. Thomas Hardy. DTC
I shall say, Lord, "Is it music, is it morning." Resurgam. Marjorie Pickthall. OBCV
I shall say what inordinat love is. Inordinate Love. *Unknown.* MeEL
I shall wear laughter on my lips. Hope. Anna Blake Mezquida. TRV
I shipped on a vessel the other day. Rio Grande (C *vers.*). *Unknown.* BSNS
I shoot the Hippopotamus. The Hippopotamus. Hilaire Belloc. PoPl
I shot a golf ball into the air. The Ball and the Club. Forbes Lindsay. SD
I shot an arrow into the air. The Arrow and the Song. Longfellow. LV; PoPl
I shot an otter because I had a gun. The Shooting. Robert Pack. CoPo
I shot my friend to save my country's life. The Body Politic. Donald Hall. MP

I should have been delighted there to hear. The Cold Divinities. James Wright. AmPC
I should have seen the sign: "Fresh paint." Fresh Paint. Boris Pasternak. PoPl
"I should like to buy you a birthday present," said Billy to Betsy Jane. Betsy Jane's Sixth Birthday. Alfred Noyes. BiCB
I should pray but my soul is stopt. At the Ocean's Verge. Ralph Gustafson. OBCV
I sieze the sphery harp. I strike the strings. Enitharmon Revives with Los. Blake. *Fr.* Vala; or, The Four Zoas. OBNC
I sike when I singe. The Crucifixion. *Unknown.* MeEL
I sing her worth and praises hy. A Description. Lord Herbert of Cherbury. SeCP
I Sing of a Maiden. *Unknown.* BuBa; CABA; CBEP; ELP; MeEL; PoIE
(Carol: "I sing of a maiden.") BoC
I sing of autumn and the falling fruit. Ship of Death. D. H. Lawrence. DTC
I sing of brooks, of blossoms, birds, and bowers. The Argument of His Book. Robert Herrick. PoIE; SeCP
I Sing of Olaf [Glad and Big]. E. E. Cummings. PoIE; StP
I sing of Tony Caesar, a big league arbiter of unimpeachable repute. Decline and Fall of a Roman Umpire. Ogden Nash. SD
I Sing the Body Electric. Walt Whitman. CTC *Sels.*
"O my body! I dare not desert the likes of you in other men and women, nor the likes of the parts of you." ErPo
"This is the female form." ErPo
I Sing the Mighty Power of God. Isaac Watts. TRV
I sing the Name which none can say. On the Name of Jesus. Richard Crashaw. MeP
I sing the Praise of honored wars. Soldier's Song. Tobias Hume. WiR
I sing the sofa. I, who lately sang. The Sofa. William Cowper. *Fr.* The Task. EiCP
I sing to him that rests below. In Memoriam A. H. H., XXI. Tennyson. VP
I, singularly moved. Winter. Coventry Patmore. The Unknown Eros, I, iii. OBNC
I Sit and Look Out. Walt Whitman. CABA; CBEP ("I sit and look out upon all the sorrows of the world.") TRV
I sit in a roadside diner. September 1, 1965. Paris Leary. CoPo
I sit in one of the dives. September 1, 1939. W. H. Auden. OnP
I sit in the top of the wood, my eyes closed. Hawk Roosting. Ted Hughes. GTBS-P; MP; NePoEA-2
I sit on the roadside bank. Changing the Wheel. Bertolt Brecht. MGP
I sit within my room, and joy to find. The Presence. Jones Very. PoIE
I slouch in bed. Two Hangovers. James Wright. AmPC
I smile sometimes, although my grief be great. The Passion of a Lover. George Gascoigne. EnRePo
I somersault just like a clown. Somersault. Dorothy Aldis. SoPo
I sometimes hold it half a sin. In Memoriam A. H. H., V. Tennyson. VP
I Sometimes Think. R. P. Lister. LV
I sometimes think I'd rather crow. To Be or Not to Be. *Unknown.* WePo
I sorrow for youth—ah, not for its wildness (would that were dead!). Christopher Brennan. *Fr.* The Wanderer. ACV
I sought a theme and sought for it in vain. The Circus Animals' Desertion. W. B. Yeats. DiPo; PoIE; PP
I sought Him in a great cathedral, dim. Search. Anne Marriott. TRV
I sought immortality. The Crib. Christopher Morley. BiCB
I Sought My Soul. *Unknown.* TRV
I Sought the Lord. *Unknown.* TRV
I Sought with Eager Hand. Allan Dowling. ErPo
I Sought You. John Hall Wheelock. BoLP
I Sowed the Seeds of Love. *Unknown.* ELP
(Seeds of Love, The.) CBEP; WiR
I span and Eve span. Eve-Song. Mary Gilmore. PoAu-1
I Speak Not, I Trace Not, I Breathe Not Thy Name. Byron. FaPL
I speak of that great house. Beyond the Hunting Woods. Donald Justice. PoPl
I speak of that lady I heard last night. The Lady's Complaint. John Heath-Stubbs. MP
I speak this poem now with grave and level voice. Immortal Autumn. Archibald MacLeish. AP
I spent a night turning in bed. The Whip. Robert Creeley. ToPo
I spent a week in Washington. I Felt like Slapping Him. Edith Earnshaw. PoNC
I spent the day in a heavenly way. Katharine. Heine. UnTE

I spied a very small brown duck. Duck-chasing. Galway Kinnell. MP
I splash—I flop. The Lesson. Jane W. Krows. SoPo
I spoke a word. Influence. John Oxenham. STF
I spot the hills. Theme in Yellow. Carl Sandburg. RePo
I sprang to the rollocks and Jorrocks and me. How I Brought the Good News from Aix to Ghent (or Vice Versa). R. J. Yeatman *and* W. C. Sellar. OnMSP
I sprang to the stirrup, and Joris, and he. How They Brought the Good News from Ghent to Aix. Robert Browning. PoPo; RoGo; SIV; WePo
I Stand Corrected. Margaret Fishback. PoPl
I stand up here where storm winds blow. The Lad of the Mountain. Ludwig Uhland. AGP
I started early, took my dog. Emily Dickinson. CBEP; DiPo
I stayed the night for shelter at a farm. The Witch of Coös. Robert Frost. *Fr.* Two Witches. AP; DiPo
I stepped from plank to plank. Emily Dickinson. AP
I stepped on the black winter seeds. Seeds. Thurmond Snyder. NNP
I stole forth dimly in the dripping pause. Moon Compasses. Robert Frost. DiPo
I stole the prince and I brought him here. The Grand Inquisitor's Song. W. S. Gilbert. *Fr.* The Gondoliers. OnMSP
I stood above the sown and generous sea. The Morality of Poetry. James Wright. PP
I stood aside to let the cows. Man and Cows. Andrew Young. DaDu
"I stood at the back of the shop, my dear." At the Draper's. Thomas Hardy. *Fr.* Satires of Circumstance. VaPo
I stood beside a hill. February Twilight. Sara Teasdale. SoPo
I stood musing in a black world. The Black Riders, XLIX. Stephen Crane. AP
I Stood on a Battlement the Late Eve Darkened. Der von Kürenberg, *tr. fr. German by* Margaret F. Richey. AnML
I stood on the bridge at midnight. The Bridge. Longfellow. FaPL
I stood one day beside a blacksmith's door. The Anvil of God's Word. *Unknown.* STF
I Stood upon a High Place. Stephen Crane. The Black Riders, IX. AP; PoPo
I stood upon a highway. The Black Riders, XXXIV. Stephen Crane. AP
I Stood upon a Star. Sara Teasdale. RePo
I stood where Love in brimming armfuls bore. Love's Baubles. Dante Gabriel Rossetti. The House of Life, XXIII. VP
I stopped to watch a man strike at the trunk. The Axe in the Wood. Clifford Dyment. ACV
I stretched my mind until I stood. I Stood upon a Star. Sara Teasdale. RePo
I Stroll. Peter Redgrove. NePoEA-2
I strolled along the Garfield avenue. A Second Birthday. Albert Kayper-Mensah. ACV
I Strove with None. Walter Savage Landor. *Fr.* The Last Fruit off an Old Tree. PoIE; PoPo; PoSa
(Dying Speech of an Old Philosopher.) FaPL; GTBS-P
("I strove with none, for none was worth my strife.") OBNC
I struck the board, and cried [*or* cry'd], No more. The Collar. George Herbert. CABA; CaFP; CBEP; EaLo; FaPL; FoBA; ILP; MeP; OnP; PoIE; SeCP; StP
I studied my tables over and over, and backward and forward, too. A Mortifying Mistake. Anna Maria Pratt. RePo
I summon to the winding ancient stair. A Dialogue of Self and Soul. W. B. Yeats. CABA; PoDB
I suppose you have heard all the talkin'. Joaquin the Horse-Thief. John A. Stone. SGR
I supposed I knew my Bible. Read the Bible Through. Amos R. Wells. STF
I swear I begin to see the meaning of these things. Walt Whitman. *Fr.* By Blue Ontario's Shore. PoIE
I swear my eyes won't see the light. Encounter of the Archpriest with Ferrand García. Juan Ruiz, Archpriest of Hita. *Fr.* The Book of True Love. AnML
I swim in darkness, swim. Arrivals and Departures. Melvin Walker La Follette. CoPo
I Take 'Em and Like 'Em. Margaret Fishback. PoPl
I take it he doesn't think at all. The Pike. John Bruce. SD
I take the twist-about, empty street. The Rendezvous. Bernard Spencer. GTBS-P
I take thee now to be no other. Adam. Philip Booth. MoLP
I talk to the birds as they sing i' the morn. I Pass in Silence. John Clare. BoLP
I taste a liquor never brewed. Emily Dickinson. AP; CABA; DiPo; FaBV; FoBA
(Little Tippler, The.) EvOK
I tell thee, Dick, where I have been. A Ballad [*or* Ballade] upon a Wedding. Sir John Suckling. CABA; CABL; CBEP; Par; SeCP; UnTE
I tell you, hopeless grief is passionless. Grief. Elizabeth Barrett Browning. CBEP; OBNC; PoLF; StP

I tell you, Lesbia, life is love. Catullus to Lesbia. James Reeves. ErPo
I tell you there is nothing there at all. The Unexplored. Burnham Eaton. FiSC
I Thank You God for Most This Amazing. E. E. Cummings. EaLo; PoDB
(I Thank You God.) MoRP
I that in health was [*or* heill wes] and gladnes[s]. Lament for the Makaris [*or* The Fear of Death Confounds Me]. William Dunbar. CBEP; MeEL; PoIE; PP
I thee advise. To One That Had Little Wit. George Turberville. EnRePo
I think and think again:—What thinks the goose? The Difference. Guido Gozzano. CoIP
I Think Continually of Those Who Were Truly Great. Stephen Spender. CaFP; EaLo; MoRP; PoIE; PoPl
(I Think Continually of Those.) DiPo; PoSa; PP
(Truly Great, The.) BoC
I think I could turn and live with animals, they are so placid and self-contained. Animals [*or* The Beasts]. Walt Whitman. Song of Myself, XXXII. BoC; CBEP; PoPl
I think I remembered this moorland. We Have Been Here Before. Morris Bishop. EvOK
"I think I'm going to die," I tried to say. Finale: Presto. Peter Davison. CoPo
I think it better that in times like these. On Being Asked for a War Poem. W. B. Yeats. PP
I think little Louie will turn out a crook. Psychological Prediction. Virginia Brasier. BBGG
I think mice. Mice. Rose Fyleman. EvOK; SoPo
I think of all the things at school. Johnny's History Lesson. Nixon Waterman. PoLF
I think of the tribes: the women prized for fatness. The Tribes. Roy Fuller. ToPo
I think of the unknowing art my watching made. Voyeur. John Edward Hardy. ErPo
I think of thee when from the ocean glimmer. My Love Is Near. Goethe, *tr. by* Francis Owen. AGP
I think of you when the sun's glorious shimmer shines from the sea. Nearness of Her Lover. Goethe, *tr. by* Walter Kaufmann. TwGP
I think oft times as night draws nigh. Are All the Children In? *Unknown.* STF
I think she sleeps: it must be sleep, when low. Modern Love, XV. George Meredith. VP
I think that I am drawing to an end. The Poets at Tea, 2. Barry Pain. Par
I think that I shall never make. In a Garden. Donald C. Babcock. LV
I think that I shall never see. Song of the Open Road. Ogden Nash. PoPo
I think that I shall never see. Trees. Joyce Kilmer. PoPo
I think that I shall never ski. Winter Trees. Conrad Diekmann. SD
I think that look of Christ might seem to say. The Meaning of the Look. Elizabeth Barrett Browning. TRV
I Think That Love Will Come My Way. Reinmar von Hagenau, *tr. fr. German by* Gillian Barker *and* Kenneth Gee. AnML
I think the dead are tender. Shall we kiss? She. Theodore Roethke. BoLP; ErPo
I think the gentle soul of him. Ilicet. Theodosia Garrison. PoLF
I think when Judas' mother heard. Judas Iscariot. Countee Cullen. PoLF
I thought I heard a knock on the door. Rispetti: On the Death of a Child. Paul Heyse. PoPl
I thought I heard the captain say. Leave Her, Johnny. *Unknown.* HaSV
I thought I saw an angel flying low. Nocturne at Bethesda. Arna Bontemps. AmNP
I thought Love lived in the hot sunshine. Where to Seek Love. Blake. *Fr.* William Bond. TRV
I thought of happiness, how it is woven. The Work of Happiness. May Sarton. MoRP
I thought of the mariners of Solomon. The Peacock of Java. William Jay Smith. RePo
I thought of Thee, my partner and my guide. After-Thought. Wordsworth. *Fr.* The River Duddon. OBNC
I thought once how Theocritus had sung. Elizabeth Barrett Browning. Sonnets from the Portuguese, I. OBNC
I thought they'd be strangers aroun' me. The Curate's Kindness. Thomas Hardy. ILP; VP
"I thought you loved me." "No, it was only fun." In the Orchard. Muriel Stuart. ErPo
I threatened to observe the strict decree. The Holdfast. George Herbert. FoBA
I to My Perils. A. E. Housman. CaFP
I told the Sun that I was glad. The Sun. John Drinkwater. SoPo
I, Too. Langston Hughes. AmNP
(I, Too, Sing America.) PoLF
I, too, dislike it; there are things that are important beyond all

this fiddle. Poetry. Marianne Moore. AP; CABA; ILP; PoIE; PoPo; PoSa; PP; StP

I too have suffer'd; yet I know. Urania. Matthew Arnold. VP

I too my shovel, pick and pan. Striking a Lead. John A. Stone. SGR

I, Too, Sing America. Langston Hughes. *See* I, Too.

I Took a Bow and Arrow. John Ciardi. EvOK

I took a piece of plastic clay. Sculpture. *Unknown.* PoLF

I took a walk through woods and snow. Deserted Farm. Guy Owen. PoNC

I took money and bought flowering trees. Planting Flowers on the Eastern Embankment. Po Chü-i. SiGo

I took my heart in my hand. Twice. Christina Rossetti. OBNC

I took my oath I would inquire. The Inquest. W. H. Davies. CBEP; DTC; GTBS-P

I took my power in my hand. Emily Dickinson. FoBA

I took the crazy short-cut to the bay. Swimmers. Louis Untermeyer. SIV

I touch you all over. Love's Eschatology. Vassar Miller. ToPo

I touch you in the night, whose gift was you. The Science of the Night. Stanley Kunitz. MP; UnTE

I towered far, and lo! I stood within. God-forgotten. Thomas Hardy. VP

I travel through thin jails of rain. Patrol. Ralph Pomeroy. CoPo

I Traveled [*or* Travelled] among Unknown Men. Wordsworth. *Fr.* Lucy. CBEP; FaBV; GTBS-P; ILP; OBNC

I travell'd on, seeing the hill, where lay. The Pilgrimage. George Herbert. MeP

I travel'd thro' a land of men. The Mental Traveller. Blake. DiPo

I trust I have not wasted breath. In Memoriam A. H. H., CXX. Tennyson. VP

I Turn to Jesus. Oswald J. Smith. STF

I turned an ancient poet's book. Home. Henry van Dyke. STF

I twist your arm. A Deux. William Wood. BoLP

I upon the first creation. Gratitude. Christopher Smart. *Fr.* Hymns for the Amusement of Children. EiCP

I used to curse the wind and rain. Cursing and Blessing. "Michael Lewis." *Fr.* Cherry Blossoms. UnTE

I used to have the fairest fatherland. Heine, *tr. fr. German by* Alexander Gode. AGP

I used to scratch medals, when I was a lad. Ambition. "Joachim Ringelnatz." MGP

I used to see her in the door. Paul. James Wright. PoPl

I used to wonder. Border Line. Langston Hughes. PoCh

I Vecchi. Ezra Pound. PoIE

I vex my heart with fancies dim. In Memoriam A. H. H., XLII. Tennyson. VP

I wage not any feud with Death. In Memoriam A. H. H., LXXXII. Tennyson. VP

I wait for his foot fall. Earth Trembles Waiting. Blanche Shoemaker Wagstaff. PoLF

I Wake and Feel the Fell of Dark [Not Day]. Gerard Manley Hopkins. DiPo; FoBA; GTBS-P; ILP; PoDB; PoIE; StP; VP

I wake late and leave. A Cardinal. W. D. Snodgrass. PP

I wake to sleep, and take my waking slow. The Waking. Theodore Roethke. AP; MP; PoPl; ToPo

I wakened on my hot, hard bed. The Watch. Frances Cornford. DTC

I Wakened to a Calling. Delmore Schwartz. PoPl

I walk beside the prisoners to the road. A Camp in the Prussian Forest. Randall Jarrell. AP

I walk [*or* walked] down the garden-paths. Patterns. Amy Lowell. BoLP; OnMSP

I walk, reunited with fire, in the uncertain paper blending. André du Bouchet. *Fr.* White Motor. CoFP

I walk through the long schoolroom questioning. Among School Children. W. B. Yeats. CABA; CaFP; DiPo; FoBA; GTBS-P; ILP; PoIE

I walked along a stream for pureness rare. A Fragment. Christopher Marlowe. CTC

I walked in the lonesome evening. Across the Sea. William Allingham. HaSV

I walked one day on a lonely road. No Greater Love. *Unknown.* STF

I Walked Out to the Graveyard to See the Dead. Richard Eberhart. PoIE

I Walked the Other Day. Henry Vaughan. BoC ("I walkt the other day to spend my hour"). MeP

I walked, when love was gone. A Breath of Air. James Wright. PoPl

I wander thro' [*or* through] each charter'd [*or* chartered] street. London. Blake. *Fr.* Songs of Experience. CABA; CaFP; CBEP; DiPo; EnPE; FoBA; ILP; OBNC; OnP; PoIE; PoSa; StP

I wander through the silent night. Nocturne. Joseph von Eichendorff. SiGo

I Wandered Lonely as a Cloud. Wordsworth. CABA; CaFP; DiPo; FoBA; ILP; LV; PoPl; PoIE; PoPo; RoGo (Daffodils, The.) FaBV; GoJo; GTBS-P; OBNC; OnP; PoSa; WePo

I wandered to the village, Tom. Twenty Years Ago. *Unknown.* BFSS

I wandered up to Beaucourt; I took the river track. Beaucourt Revisited. A. P. Herbert. MMA

I wane and weary: come, thou swifter One. To the Daemon Sublimity. Clark Ashton Smith. FiSC

I Want a Pasture. Rachel Field. RePo

I want nothing but your fire-side now. At Home, Alone with the Dog. Harold Monro. BoC

I want—this whole revolting brew. Last Letter. Hans Egon Holthusen. MGP

I want to be still as a quiet hill. Be Still. Betsy W. Kline. STF

I Want to Die While You Love Me. Georgia Douglas Johnson. AmNP

I want to see the slim palm trees. Heritage. Gwendolyn B. Bennett. AmNP

I want to write a book of chaste and simple verse. Landscape. Baudelaire. SiGo

I wanted a rifle for Christmas. Presents. Marchette Chute. EvOK

I wanted the gold, and I sought it. The Spell of the Yukon. Robert W. Service. PoPl

I wanted to harness and go. Baroness Mu Impeded in Her Wish to Help Famine Victims in Wei. Confucius. *Fr.* The Classic Anthology: Yung Wind. CTC

I warned the parents, you know. Father to the Man. John Knight. EaLo

I was a boy when I heard three red words. Threes. Carl Sandburg. PoLF

I was a lover of turkey and holly. Carol. Anne Wilkinson. OBCV

I was a stricken deer, that left the herd. In His Mental Illness, William Cowper Finds He Is Not Alone. William Cowper. BoC

I was a warrior's weapon, once. Riddle #14: A Horn. *Unknown.* DiPo

I was a young maid truly. The Sandgate Girl's Lamentation. *Unknown.* ELP

I was always a lover of ladies' hands! Your Hands. Ernest Dowson. UnTE

I was angry with my friend. A Poison Tree. Blake. *Fr.* Songs of Experience. CABA; CaFP; CBEP; DiPo; FoBA; VaPo

I was apprenticed as a callow lad. The Stone. Walter H. Kerr. FiSC

I was aware that it was May. Guillaume de Lorris. *Fr.* Romance of the Rose. AnML

I was born in Boston, boys. Boston Bugler. *Unknown.* BSO

I was brought up in Sheffield, both low and high degree. The Sheffield Apprentice. *Unknown.* BFSS

I was but sixteen summers old. Phidile. Matthias Claudius. AGP

I was carried to a font. Dithyramb in Retrospect. Peter Hopegood. PoAu-2

I was confused; I cannot promise more. Sonnet XIV. Mark Van Doren. MoLP

I was glad when they said unto me. Psalm CXII, Bible, *O.T.* TRV

I was going, Mother, to Villa Real. Hill Song of La Zarzuela. *Unknown.* AnML

I was going to make a boat. But That Was Yesterday. Aileen Fisher. SoPo

I was not sorrowful, I could not weep. Spleen. Ernest Dowson. CBEP

I was of delicate mind. I stepped aside for my needs. The Refined Man. Kipling. *Fr.* Epitaphs of the War. MMA

I was one with woods; my body, the Earth. Brajendranath Seal. *Fr.* The Quest Eternal. ACV

I was the patriarch of the shining land. John Sutter. Yvor Winters. PoPl; PoSa

"I was inching, Mother, of that poor old horse." Reserved. Walter de la Mare. GTBS-P

I was thy neighbour once, thou rugged Pile! Elegiac Stanzas [*or* Nature and the Poet]. Wordsworth. CABL; GTBS-P; OBNC

I was wrong, quite wrong. Soliloquy 2. Richard Aldington. MMA

I was young/ when I foreswore. A Deposition by John Wilmot. Vincent McHugh. ErPo

I watch her fingers where they prance. Enigma. Hugh McCrae. PoAu-2

I watched the Captains. Captain of the Years. Arthur R. Macdougall, Jr. TRV

I watched the new moon fly. The Golden Bird. Rex Ingamells. PoAu-2

I watched them tearing a building down. Which Are You? *Unknown.* PoLF

I weep for Adonais—he is dead. Adonais. Shelley. CABA; FaPL; PoIE; StP

I well remember those old times. Old Forty-nine. Mart Taylor. SGR

I went across the pasture lot. The Cornfield. Elizabeth Madox Roberts. GoJo

I Went in Quest of Measure. Macías O Namorado, *tr. fr. Portuguese by* William M. Davis. AnML

I went into a public-'ouse to get a pint o' beer. Tommy. Kipling. CABA; FaBV

I went into the fields, but you were there. You. John Masefield. MoRP

I went into the woods, I was alone. Red Dust. Wolfgang Weyrauch. MGP

I went on Friday afternoons. Au Tombeau de Mon Père. Ronald McCuaig. PoAu-2

I went out to the hazel wood. The Song of Wandering Aengus. W. B. Yeats. BoLP; DiPo; GoJo; LOW; PoSa

I went to heaven. Emily Dickinson. FaBV

I went to her who loveth me no more. Song. Arthur O'Shaughnessy. OBNC

I went to seek for Christ. The Search. James Russell Lowell. TRV

I went to the animal fair. The Animal Fair. *Unknown.* SoPo

I Went to the City. Kenneth Patchen. PoPl

I went to the dances at Chandlerville. Lucinda Matlock. Edgar Lee Masters. *Fr.* Spoon River Anthology. FaBV; ILP; PoPo

I Went to the Fair at Bonlaghy, *with music. Unknown.* BSO

I went to the Garden of Love. The Garden of Love. Blake. *Fr.* Songs of Experience. CABA; CBEP; DiPo; FaBV; FoBA; PoIE; StP; VaPo

I went to turn the grass once after one. The Tuft of Flowers. Robert Frost. AP; CBEP; PoPo

I whispered, "I am too young." Brown Penny. W. B. Yeats. BoLP; ELP

I who ere while the happy Garden sung. Paradise Regained. Milton. CABL

I whom thou seest with horyloge in hand. Time. Sir Thomas More. *Fr.* The Pageants of Thomas More. EnRePo

I will arise and go now, and go to Innisfree. The Lake Isle of Innisfree. W. B. Yeats. BoC; DiPo; FaBV; FaPL; FoBA; ILP; PoPl; PoPo; RoGo

I will be a lion. Wild Beasts. Evaleen Stein. SoPo

I will be the gladdest thing. Afternoon on a Hill. Edna St. Vincent Millay. SoPo

I Will Bow and Be Simple. *Unknown.* EaLo

I will endow you with a false glow. Miserere. William Pillin. PtTo

I Will Enjoy Thee Now. Thomas Carew. *See* Rapture, A.

I will exchange a city for a sunset. Barter. Marie Blake. PoPl

I Will Give My Love an Apple. *Unknown.* CBEP

I will go back to the great sweet mother. Swinburne. *Fr.* The Triumph of Time. FaPL

I will go out and hear the strain. Macquarie Place. Robert D. Fitzgerald. PoAu-2

I will go with the first air of morning. Fishing. Dorothy Wellesley. BoC

I will have an image. Larry Eigner. CoPo

"I will have to my supper a chicken without a bone." An Old Man's Courtship. *Unknown.* BFSS

I will lift up mine eyes unto the hills. Psalm CXXI, Bible, O.T. CBEP; LV; TRV

I will make you brooches and toys for your delight. Romance. Robert Louis Stevenson. BoLP; PoSC

I Will No Longer Serve You. Christine de Pisan, *tr. fr. French by* Muriel Kittel. AnML

I will not doubt, though all my ships at sea. Faith. Ella Wheeler Wilcox. TRV

I Will Not Let Thee Go. Robert Bridges. OBNC

I Will Not Pick Verbena. *Unknown, tr. fr. Spanish by* James Duffy. AnML

I will not say to you, "This is the Way; walk in it." To My Son. *Unknown.* PoLF

I will not shut me from my kind. In Memoriam A. H. H., CVIII. Tennyson. VP

I Will Praise the Lord at All Times. William Cowper. EiCP

I Will Sing and So Relieve. Guiot de Dijon, *tr. fr. French by* Patricia Terry. AnML

I will sing, if ye will hearken. The Laird o' Logie. *Unknown.* CBEP

I will teach you my townspeople. Tract. William Carlos Williams. AnMoPo; AP; CABL; ILP; MP; StP

I will tell you of a fellow. Woman's Resolution. *Unknown.* BSO

I wish I could remember that first day. Monna Innominata, II. Christina Rossetti. VP

I wish I could tell it—how wondrous is He. I Know He Is Real. *Unknown.* STF

I wish I had a great big ball. Bouncing Ball. Sara Ruth Watson. SoPo

I wish I had a man - any man. Chiaroscuro. Carole Bergé. ErPo

I wish I lived in a caravan. The Peddler's Caravan. William Brighty Rands. SoPo

I Wish I Was Single Again. *Unknown. See* When I Was Single.

I wish I were where Helen lies. Helen of Kir[k]connell [*or* Fair Helen]. *Unknown.* CBEP; ELP; GTBS-P; ILP; WePo

I wish my tongue were a quiver the size of a huge cask. L. A. MacKay. *Fr.* The Ill-tempered Lover. OBCV

I wish no rich-refined Arabian gold. Parthenope. Barnabe Barnes. *Fr.* Parthenophil and Parthenophe. CBEP

I wish that Easter eggs would do. If Easter Eggs Would Hatch. Douglas Malloch. SoPo

I Wish That My Room Had a Floor. Gelett Burgess. LV; RePo

I wish you all that pen and ink. Thanksgiving Wishes. Arthur Guiterman. PoSC

I, with Whose Colors. Fulke Greville. Caelica, XXII. EnRePo

(Myra.) CBEP

I woke to a shout: "I am Alpha and Omega!" Gog. Ted Hughes. AnMoPo

I woke up with foreboding, and despair. Comfort for the Sleepless. H. C. Bradby. BoC

I wold fain be a clarke. The Scholar Complains. *Unknown.* MeEL

I wolde witen of sum wis wight. The World an Illusion. *Unknown.* MeEL

I Wonder as I Wander. *Unknown, arr. by* John Jacob Niles. EaLo

I wonder, by my troth, what thou and I. The Good-Morrow. John Donne. CABA; CBEP; DiPo; EnRePo; FaBV; PoIE; SeCP; StP; UnTE

I wonder do you feel today. Two in the Campagna. Robert Browning. ELP; GTBS-P; OBNC

I wonder, have I giv'n my best to Jesus. Have I Done My Best for Jesus? Edwin Young. STF

I wonder if Christ had a little black dog. The Little Black Dog. Elizabeth Gardener Reynolds. PoLF

I wonder if the elephant. Pete at the Zoo. Gwendolyn Brooks. LOW

I wonder if the engine. Engine. James S. Tippett. SoPo

I wonder if the old cow died or not. The Question. W. W. Gibson. MMA

I wonder if the sap is stirring yet. The First Spring Day. Christina Rossetti. WiR

I wonder if there's anywhere. Teddy's Wonderings. John Kendrick Bangs. BiCB

I wonder if this new reality is going to destroy me. The Hero Leaves His Ship. Barbara Guest. AmPC

I wonder in what fields today. Haiku. Chiyo. CaFP

I wonder, James, through the whole history. To His Friend ———. Henry Vaughan. PP

I wonder the way ghosts come to be . . . . Do you think there will be a ghost. Ghost to Come. Margaret Widdemer. FiSC

I worshipped, when my veins were fresh. William Baylebridge. *Fr.* Life's Testament. PoAu-1

I wot full well that beauty cannot last. To His Friend. George Turberville. CTC

I would be dismal with all the fine pearls of the crown of a king. To a Blue Flower. John Shaw Neilson. PoAu-1

I would be His if He were anywhere. If He Were Anywhere. Cecil Hemley. PoDB

I Would Be True. Howard Arnold Walter. TRV

(My Creed.) PoLF

I would follow Jesus. Follow Jesus. *Unknown.* STF

I would have gone; God bade me stay. Weary in Well-doing. Christina Rossetti. VP

I would I had thrust my hands of flesh. Edmund Pollard. Edgar Lee Masters. *Fr.* Spoon River Anthology. ErPo

I would I were beneath a tree. Three Woulds. *Unknown.* LV

I would kiss the whole length of the rich black locks that grace thy neck. The Kiss. Pierre Louÿs. *Fr.* The Songs of Bilitis. UnTE

I Would Like to Be—a Bee. Dorothy W. Baruch. BiCB

I would like to dive. The Diver. W. W. E. Ross. OBCV

I would make a list against the evil days. A Ballade-Catalogue of Lovely Things. Richard Le Gallienne. LV

I Would Not Ask. Grace E. Troy. STF

I would not meek in dire rebuttal. Pride and Hesitation. Cerise Farallon. UnTE

I would not wish to sit. Between Two Prisoners. James Dickey. AP

I would rather have one little rose. Kindness during Life. *Unknown.* STF

I would set all things whatsoever front to back. Wyndham Lewis. *Fr.* One-Way Song. CTC

I would take words. To Hold in a Poem. A. J. M. Smith. ACV

I would to heaven that I were so much clay. Fragment. Byron. *Fr.* Don Juan. CTC; ILP

I Wouldn't Have an Old Man. *Unknown.* BSO
I wrote him a letter asking him for old times' sake. Hannah Armstrong. Edgar Lee Masters. *Fr.* Spoon River Anthology. LiPo
I wrote some lines once on a time. The Height of the Ridiculous. Oliver Wendell Holmes. PoPl
I years had been from home. Emily Dickinson. CBEP; DiPo
I Yield Thee Praise. Philip Jerome Cleveland. TRV
I yield unto the conquering hand of age. To Louis XIII. François de Malherbe. RBL
I you assure. To Mistress Margaret Tilney. John Skelton. *Fr.* The Garlande of Laurell. MeEL
Iago Prytherch his name, though, be it allowed. A Peasant. R. S. Thomas. ToPo
Ianthe, *sels.* Walter Savage Landor.
   "Do you remember me? or are you proud?" OBNC
   "From you, Ianthe, little troubles pass." OBNC
   "Ianthe! you resolve to cross the sea!" OBNC
   "My hopes retire; my wishes as before." OBNC
   "Past ruin'd [*or* ruined] Ilion Helen lives." CBEP; CTC; ELP; OBNC; PoIE; PoSa
   "Remain, ah not in youth alone." OBNC
   "Well I remember how you smiled." CBEP; OBNC
Ianthe! you resolve to cross the sea! Walter Savage Landor. *Fr.* Ianthe. OBNC
Ibant Obscurae. Thomas Edward Brown. OBNC
Ibycus. John Heath-Stubbs. PoCh
Icarus. Gottfried Benn, *tr. fr. German by* Michael Hamburger. MGP
Icarus. Ronald Bottrall. GTBS-P
Ice. Sir Charles G. D. Roberts. OBCV
Ice. Stephen Spender. GTBS-P
Ice and Fire. Giambattista Marino, *tr. fr. Italian by* Sir Edward Sherburne. RBL
Ice and Fires Contend with My Child. Lope de Vega, *tr. fr. Spanish by* W. S. Merwin. AnSP
Ice built, ice bound, and ice bounded. Alaska. Joaquin Miller. ThLM
Ice-Cream Man, The. Rachel Field. SoPo
Ice-Skaters. Elder Olson. SD
Ice tinkled in glasses. Blues and Bitterness. Lerone Bennett. NNP
Iceberg, The. W. S. Merwin. PoIE
Ich am of Irlaunde. I Am from Ireland. *Unknown.* MeEL
"Ich wünscht', ich wäre ein Vöglein." The Bird. Louis Simpson. NePoEA-2
Ichabod. Whittier. AP; CBEP; LV
Icicle finger of death, aimed, The. Digging It Out. John Hollander. AmPC
Icos. Charles Tomlinson. GTBS-P
I'd Have You, Quoth He. *Unknown.* ErPo
I'd like to be a dentist with a plate upon the door. The Dentist. Rose Fyleman. SoPo
I'd Like to Be a Lighthouse. Rachel Field. SoPo
I'd like to cut the preaching short. Of the Characteristics of Small Women. Juan Ruiz, Archpriest of Hita. AnML
I'd Love to Be a Fairy's Child. Robert Graves. BiCB; SoPo
I'd rather have the thought of you. Choice. Angela Morgan. PoLF
I'd rather see a sermon than to hear it any day. How Do You Live? *Unknown.* STF
Idea, *sels.* Michael Drayton.
   "Calling to mind since first my love begun," LI. EnRePo
   "Cupid, dumb idol, peevish saint of love," XXVI. EnRePo
   "How many paltry, foolish, painted things," VI. EnRePo
   (How Many Foolish Things.) CBEP
   "Like an adventurous seafarer am I," I. HaSV
   "Since there's no help, come, let us kiss and part," LXI. BoLP; CABA; CaFP; CBEP; DiPo; EnRePo; FaPL; ILP; PoIE; PoSa; WePo
   (Love's Farewell.) GTBS-P
   "Stay, speedy time; behold, before thou pass," XVII. EnRePo
   "Three sorts of serpents do resemble thee," XXX. EnRePo
To the Reader of These Sonnets, *introd. sonnet.* EnRePo
Idea for a sonnet came, The. They Roasted Me Instead. Edith Earnshaw. PoNC
Idea of Order at Key West, The. Wallace Stevens. AmLP; AP; ILP; PoIE; PP
Ideal Age for a Man, The. Monica Shannon. BiCB
Ideal Beauty. Fernando de Herrera, *tr. fr. Spanish by* Longfellow. RBL
Ideal Passion, *sel.* George Edward Woodberry.
   Immortal Love. PoPo
Ides of March, The. Roy Fuller. PoCh
Idle dayseye, the laborious wheel, The. O. Richard Wilbur. StP
Idle poet, here and there, An. The Revelation. Coventry Patmore. *Fr.* The Angel in the House. GTBS-P; OBNC
Idly she yawned, and threw her heavy hair. Sonnet. George Moore. ErPo
Idolatry. Arna Bontemps. AmNP
Idyll. Francis Webb. PoAu-2

Idyllic Scene, An. Luis de Góngora, *tr. fr. Spanish by* Edward Meryon Wilson. *Fr.* The Solitudes. RBL
Idylls, *sels.* Theocritus, *tr. fr.* Greek.
   Countryman's Wooing, The, XXVII, *tr. by* Charles Stuart Calverley. ErPo
   Enchantment, The, II, *tr. by* Thomas Creech. CTC
Idylls of the King, *sels.* Tennyson.
   Dedication: "These to His Memory—since he held them dear." CABA
   Guinevere.
      "I made them lay their hands in mine and swear." TRV
   Lancelot and Elaine.
      Song of Love and Death, The. OBNC
   Merlin and Vivien.
      In Love, if Love Be Love. CABA
      (Vivien's Song.) OBNC
   Passing of Arthur, The. OBNC
If. Mortimer Collins. Par
If. Kipling. FaPL; LV; WePo
If/ ice shall melt. If Ice. W. W. E. Ross. OBCV
If a daughter you have, she's the plague of your life. Song. Sheridan. *Fr.* The Duenna. LV
If a good man were ever housed in Hell. The Good Man in Hell. Edwin Muir. MoRP
If a man who turnips cries. The Turnip Seller. Samuel Johnson. EvOK
If a rowdy meet a rowdy. The Rowdy. John A. Stone. SGR
If after kirk ye bide a wee. An Angel Unawares. *Unknown.* TRV
If All the Grief and Sorrow, the Strife. Bertran de Born, *tr. fr. Provençal by* James J. Wilhelm. AnML
If All the Seas Were One Sea. *Unknown.* SoPo
If all the ships I have at sea. My Ships. Ella Wheeler Wilcox. PoLF
If all the world and love were young. The Nymph's Reply to the Shepherd [*or* Her Reply]. Sir Walter Ralegh. CABA; CaFP; CBEP; DiPo; CTC; ILP; PoPo; PoSa; StP
If All the World Was Apple Pie. *Unknown.* SoPo
If All the World Were Paper. *Unknown.* CBEP
   (Interrogativa Cantilena.) DiPo
If all those pretty maidens were as hares on the mountain. Hares on the Mountain. *Unknown.* CBEP
If, antique hateful bird. The Raven. Adrienne Rich. NePoEA-2
If any flower that here is grown. Inscription in a Garden. George Gascoigne. CBEP
If any God should say. Rebirth. Kipling. OBNC
If any have a stone to shy. The Pebble. Elinor Wylie. MoRP
If any mourn us in the workshop, say. Batteries Out of Ammunition. Kipling. *Fr.* Epitaphs of the War. MMA
If any vague desire should rise. In Memoriam A. H. H., LXXX. Tennyson. VP
If any vision should reveal. In Memoriam A. H. H., XCII. Tennyson. VP
If anyone has fun. Notes on a Track Meet. David McCord. SD
If anyone long for a musical song. 'Tis but a Wanton Trick. *Unknown.* UnTE
If apples were pears. To My Valentine. *Unknown.* SoPo
If as the windes and waters here below. The Storm. George Herbert. MeP
If aught [*or* ought] of oaten stop, or pastoral song. Ode to Evening [*or* To Evening]. William Collins. CABA; CaFP; CBEP; EiCP; EnPE; GTBS-P; OnP; StP
If Bethlehem were here today. Christmas Morning. Elizabeth Madox Roberts. PoSC; RePo
If blossoms could blossom. To Be Sung. Peter Viereck. FaBV
If bright the sun, he tarries. Emerson. *Fr.* Fragments on the Poet and the Poetic Gift. PP
If but One Year. *Unknown.* STF
If but some vengeful god would call to me. Hap. Thomas Hardy. CABA; EaLo; PoDB
If but your creditors, the which you chyde. Dizain to Clément Marot. Marguerite de Navarre. RBL
If by Dull Rhymes Our English Must be Chained. Keats. PP
   (On the Sonnet.) CABA; ILP
If Candlemas Day be dry and fair. *Unknown.* PoSC
If Candlemas Day be fair and bright. *Unknown.* PoSC
If Christ Were Here To-Night. Margaret E. Sangster. TRV
If Crossed with All Mishaps. William Drummond of Hawthornden. CBEP
If death is what he seeks in life he fails. The Malefic Surgeon. Gerrit Lansing. CoPo
If doughty deeds my lady please. Robert Graham. GTBS-P
If dreams, as ancient sages hold. To a Young Lady That Told Me My Fortune in the Cards. Thomas Catesby Paget. WaPE
If Easter Be Not True. Henry H. Barstow. TRV
If Easter Eggs Would Hatch. Douglas Malloch. SoPo

If ever a garden was a Gethsemane. For Jim, Easter Eve. Anne Spencer. AmNP
If ever at Saint Peter's gate. The Plea. John Drinkwater. MoRP
If ever chance or choice thy footsteps lead. The Flying Tailor. James Hogg. Par
If ever happiness hath lodg'd with man. Consummate Happiness. Wordsworth. *Fr.* The Prelude. OBNC
If ever I render back your heart. Song for a Slight Voice. Louise Bogan. AmLP
If ever I saw blessing in the air. April Rise. Laurie Lee. BoC
If ever there is something nice. Five Years Old. Lysbeth Boyd Borie. BiCB
If ever there lived a Yankee lad. Darius Green and His Flying-Machine. John Townsend Trowbridge. PoLF
If ever two were one, then surely we. To My Dear and Loving Husband. Anne Bradstreet. AP; CBEP; PoLF
If ever you should go by chance. How to Tell the Wild Animals. Carolyn Wells. RePo
If external action is effete. The Past Is the Present. Marianne Moore. PP
If faithfull soules be alike glorifi'd. Holy Sonnets, VIII. John Donne. MeP
If Frequently to Mass. Christine de Pisan. *See* If I'm in Church More Often Now.
If from the public way you turn your steps. Michael. Wordsworth. DiPo
If girls were as charming after the fact as before it. Andante, ma Non Assai. Rufinus. ErPo
If God ever had intended. Man Has No Smokestack. *Unknown.* STF
If God has been good enough to give you a poet. Let Them Alone. Robinson Jeffers. AP
If grief for grief can touch thee. Emily Brontë. OBNC
If he had not taken her to the forest. The Forest. Dorothy Quick. FiSC
If he is held in love. Joyful Prophecy. Vassar Miller. CoPo
If He Were Anywhere. Cecil Hemley. PoDB
If heaven were to do again. The Peaceful Shepherd. Robert Frost. MoRP
If her forehead was not snow. Lope de Vega, *tr. fr. Spanish* by Elisha Kane. RBL
If her neck is. Parallel Texts. Robert Kelly. CoPo
If here and now be but a timely span. Here and Now. Catherine Cater. AmNP
If I/ Were a bee. I Would Like to Be—a Bee. Dorothy W. Baruch. BiCB
If I can bear your love like a lamp before me. The Lamp. Sara Teasdale. MoLP
If I can stop one heart from breaking. Emily Dickinson. PoLF; TRV
If I Could Only Live at the Pitch That Is Near Madness. Richard Eberhart. PoPl; ToPo
If I could rise and see my father young. Gil Orlovitz. *Fr.* Art of the Sonnet. ToPo
If I could trust mine own self with your fate. Monna Innominata, XIII. Christina Rossetti. VP
If I dare pray for one. A Prayer. Vernon Watkins. MoRP; PoPl
If I dont bring you. The Couple. Joel Oppenheimer. CoPo
If I freely may discover. Hermogenes's Song. Ben Jonson. *Fr.* The Poetaster. PoIE
If I Go Not, Pray Not, Give Not. *Unknown.* STF
If I Had a Firecracker. Shelley Silverstein. PoSC
If I had a hundred dollars to spend. The Animal Store. Rachel Field. SoPo
If I had a spoon. Clouds. Dorothy Aldis. SoPo
If I had but one year to live. If but One Year. *Unknown.* STF
If I had lightly given at the first. A Lodging for the Night. Elinor Wylie. ErPo
If I had trained a gull I'd send it off to Boothbay Harbor. A Ghazel of Absence. Gerrit Lansing. CoPo
If I had wings like Noah's dove. Dink's Song. *Unknown.* ErPo
If I have erred or run a course unfit. To the Right Worthy Knight Sir Fulke Greville. Samuel Daniel. EnRePo
If I have faltered more or less. The Celestial Surgeon. Robert Louis Stevenson. BoC; TRV
If I Have Made, My Lady. E. E. Cummings. FaBV
"If I hold my breath and do not speak." Ganga. Thomas Blackburn. MoBS
If I kiss Anthea's breast. Love Perfumes All Parts. Robert Herrick. UnTE
If Is, like Solomon. O to Be a Dragon. Marianne Moore. CTC; PoPl
"If I live yet, it is for good, more love." The Old Whom God Loves. Robert Browning. *Fr.* A Death in the Desert. BoC
If I love and serve my beauty with good heart. Ballad for Fat Margot. Villon. AnML
If I make the lashes dark. Before the World Was Made. W. B. Yeats. GTBS-P

If I may not reflect and fashion poems. Goethe. *Fr.* Torquato Tasso. TwGP
If I Might Live to See the Day. Friedrich von Hausen, *tr. fr. German by* Margaret F. Richey. AnML
If I might see another Spring. Another Spring. Christina Rossetti. VP
If I Must Feel Your Wrath Eternally. Guillaume de Machaut, *tr. fr. French by* Norman R. Shapiro. AnML
If I must go, let it be easy, slow. Improvisation on an Old Theme. Dorothy Livesay. ACV
If I must of my senses lose. Prayer. Theodore Roethke. MP
If I Roared. Johannes R. Becher, *tr. fr. German by* Christopher Middleton. *Fr.* Ecstasy Dream Grace. MGP
If I Saw One Who Could Say He Was Come from Her. Albrecht von Johansdorf, *tr. fr. German by* Margaret F. Richey. AnML
If I should cast off this tattered coat. The Black Riders, LXVI. Stephen Crane. AP
If I should die and leave you here a while. Turn Again to Life. Mary Lee Hall. PoLF
If I should die, think only this of me. The Soldier. 1914, V. BoC; FaBV; FaPL; LV; PoLF; PoP1; PoPo
If I Should Die To-Night. Ben King. PoLF
If I Should Ever by Chance. Edward Thomas. GoJo
If I should ever need to reach your heart. Understanding. Pauline E. Soroka. PoLF
If I should go away. Post-script for Gweno. Alun Lewis. GTBS-P; WePo
If I should pamphleteer twenty years against royalists. To the Ghost of John Milton. Carl Sandburg. PP
If I should touch her she would shriek and weeping. Secretary. Ted Hughes. ErPo; ToPo
If I shouldn't be alive. Emily Dickinson. DiPo
If I think myself. The Insidious Dr. Fu Man Chu. LeRoi Jones. CoPo
If I was up on yonder hill. My True Love Has Gone to France. *Unknown.* BSO
If I were a bear. Furry Bear. A. A. Milne. SoPo
If I were a cripple. As You Are, My Friend. Vernon Ward. PoNC
If I Were a Pilgrim Child. Rowena Bennett. RePo
If I were fierce, and bald, and short of breath. Base Details. Siegfried Sassoon. MMA
If I Were Fire, I'd Burn the World Away. Cecco Angiolieri, *tr. fr. Italian by* Daniel J. Donno. AnML
If I were hanged on the highest hill. Mother o' Mine. Kipling. TRV
If I were just a fairy small. A Fairy Voyage. *Unknown.* SoPo
If I Were King, *sel.* Justin Huntly M'Carthy.
  If I Were King ("If I were king—ah, love, if I were king"), *introd. poem, par. fr. the French of* Villon. LV; PoLF
If I Were King. A. A. Milne. RePo
If I were king—ah, love, if I were king. Justin Huntly M'Carthy. *Fr.* If I Were King. LV; PoLF
If I were John and John were Me. A Thought. A. A. Milne. ThGo
If Ice. W. W. E. Ross. OBCV
If I'm in Church More Often Now. Christine de Pisan, *tr. fr. French by* Dwight Durling. AnML
  (If Frequently to Mass, *tr. by* J. G. Legge.) PoP1
If, in an odd angle of the hutment. Eighth Air Force. Randall Jarrell. ILP; PoCh
If in some far-off, future day. Epitaph for a Cat. Margaret E. Bruner. PoLF
If in that Syrian garden, ages slain. Easter Hymn. A. E. Housman. CABA; CaFP; EaLo; ILP
If, in the mind of God or book of fate. The Day. Edwin Muir. PoDB
If, in the silent mind of One all-pure. In Utrumque Paratus. Matthew Arnold. OBNC
If, in thy second state sublime. In Memoriam A. H. H., LXI. Tennyson. VP
If it form one landscape that we the inconstant ones. In Praise of Limestone. W. H. Auden. CABA; PoIE
If it is love, why then does he kill me. Maurice Scève. *Fr.* Délie. RBL
If It Is Not My Portion. Rabindranath Tagore. *Fr.* Gitanjali. BoC
If my dear love were but the child of state. Sonnets, CXXIV. Shakespeare. FoBA
If it should come to this. A Prospect of Death. Andrew Young. DTC
If it so happens. No Escape. Lilith Lorraine. FiSC
If it were less beautiful. A Song for Beauty. P. Lal. ACV
If it were not for the voice. Nakatsukasa. *Fr.* Shui Shu. SiGo
If it were only still! Pastoral. Edna St. Vincent Millay. RePo
If It Were Spring. Leonard Cohen. ACV
If it's true that Nature can. Epitaph on Rabelais. Pierre de Ronsard. RBL

If Jesus Came to Your House. *Unknown.* STF

If Jesus Christ is a man. The Song of a Heathen. Richard Watson Gilder. TRV

If Lazarus (says the great Pascal). Middle Passage. O. B. Hardison, Jr. PoNC

If Life Survives These Years of Bitter Woe. Petrarch, *tr. fr. Italian by* Maurice Valency. Sonnets to Laura: To Laura in Life, XI. AnML

If Life were never bitter. If. Mortimer Collins. Par

If life's pleasures cheer thee. Our Rock. Francis Scott Key. STF

If little mice have birthdays. Birthday Cake. Aileen Fisher. BiCB

If love, for love of long time had. Love Continual. John Heywood. CBEP

If love were what the rose is. A Match. Swinburne. ELP

If Luther's day expand to Darwin's year. Epilogue. Herman Melville. *Fr.* Clarel. AP

If meadow-grass can turn to milk. Fairy Story. Barbara Euphan Todd. BoC

If men may credit give to true reported fames. In Praise of a Gentlewoman. George Gascoigne. EnRePo

If Mercy Were a Friend to My Desires. Guido Cavalcanti, *tr. fr. Italian by* Daniel J. Donno. AnML

If Michael, leader of God's host. The Rose of Peace. W. B. Yeats. PoDB

If my baby have a squint. By the Firelight. L. A. G. Strong. DaDu

If my bark sink. Emily Dickinson. TRV

If, My Darling. Philip Larkin. ToPo

If my rough hammer gives a human face. Michelangelo, *tr. fr. Italian by* Joseph Tusiani. RBL

If Nancy Hanks. Nancy Hanks. Rosemary Benét. FaBV; LiPo; PoPl; RePo

If Nature say to you. The Daily Grind. Fenton Johnson. AmNP

If neither brass nor marble can withstand. The Power of Time. Swift. CBEP

If no love is, O God, what fele I so? Petrarch. *Fr.* Sonnets to Laura: To Laura in Life. RBL

If No One Ever Marries Me. Laurence Alma-Tadema. BiCB

If none but you in the world today. The Gospel According to You. *Unknown.* STF

If of thy mortal goods thou are bereft. Hyacinths to Feed Thy Soul. Sadi. *Fr.* The Gulistan. TRV

If one could have that little head of hers. A Face. Robert Browning. CTC

If one disdain me, then I fly. Song of the Inconstant Hylas. Honoré d'Urfé. RBL

If one should bring me this report. In Memoriam A. H. H., XIV. Tennyson. VP

If only I'd quit fooling round with rhyme. Epistle to the Reader. Walker Gibson. PP

If only once for every perjured oath. Barine the Incorrigible. Horace. Odes, II, 8. UnTE

If only once the chariot of the Morn. The Glory of Nature. Frederick Tennyson. OBNC

If Only We Understood. *Unknown.* STF

If ought of oaten stop, or pastoral song. *See* If aught of oaten stop, or pastoral song.

If people ask me. Politeness. A. A. Milne. PoPl

If poisonous minerals [*or* poysonous mineralls], and if that tree. Holy Sonnets, IX. John Donne. CABA; EnRePo; FoBA; MeP; PoIE; SeCP

If radio's slim fingers can pluck a melody. Proof. Ethel Romig Fuller. TRV

If She Be Made of White and Red. Shakespeare. *Fr.* Love's Labour's Lost, I, ii. CTC

If sleep and death be truly one. In Memoriam A. H. H., XLIII. Tennyson. FoBA; OBNC; VP

If someone asks you. Mitchell Donian. PoSC

If suddenly blackness crawled. Cat's Eye. Paul Engle. LV

If the day looks kinder gloomy. Just Keep on Keepin' On. *Unknown.* STF

If the deep night is haunted, it is I. Rendezvous. Robert Hillyer. MoLP

If the drink that satisfied. Poem. R. A. K. Mason. ACV

If the dull substance of my flesh were thought. Sonnets, XLIV. Shakespeare. CBEP

If the golden-crested wren. A Child's Laughter. Swinburne. BiCB

If the grape's kindly juice. Francesco Redi. *Fr.* Bacchus in Tuscany. RBL

If the Heart of a Man. John Gay. *Fr.* The Begger's Opera. CBEP; ELP

If the quick spirits in your eye. Song: Perswasions to Enjoy. Thomas Carew. SeCP

If the red slayer think he slays. Brahma. Emerson. AmLP; AP; CBEP; DiPo; EaLo; PoIE; PoPo

If the scorn of your bright eyne. Song. Shakespeare. *Fr.* As You Like It, IV, iii. CTC

If the Stars Should Fall. Samuel Allen. NNP

If the Tomb Is Not Oblivion. Manuel González Prada, *tr. fr. Spanish by* William M. Davis. AnSP

If the World Were Mine. *Unknown, tr. fr. German by* Ruth Yorck *and* Kenward Elmslie. AnML

If there be any one can take my place. Monna Innominata, XII. Christina Rossetti. VP

If there be some weaker one. Whittier. *Fr.* Andrew Rykman's Prayer. TRV

If There Be Sorrow. Mari Evans. NNP

If there exists a hell—the case is clear. To Sir Toby. Philip Freneau. AP

If there were dreams to sell. Dream-Pedlary. Thomas Lovell Beddoes. CBEP; OBNC; WiR

If there's a fox, he said, I'll whistle the beggar. Mahony's Mountain. Douglas Stewart. PoAu-2

If there's one who often falters. First to Throw a Stone. *Unknown.* STF

If these brief lays, of Sorrow born. In Memoriam A.H.H., XLVIII. Tennyson. VP

If this country were a sea (that is solid rock). Pennines in April. Ted Hughes. WePo

If This Insensate Rage. Conon de Béthune, *tr. fr. French by* Patricia Terry. AnML

If this life-saving rock should fail. On Middleton Edge. Andrew Young. SD

If this little world to-night. Earth. Oliver Herford. LV

If this our little life is but a day. A Sonnet to Heavenly Beauty. Joachim du Bellay. *Fr.* L'Olive. CTC; RBL

If This Were Faith. Robert Louis Stevenson. *Fr.* Songs of Travel. OBNC

If this worlds friends might see but once. The Seed Growing Secretly. Henry Vaughan. MeP

If thou art sleeping, maiden. Song. Gil Vicente. RBL; SiGo

If thou dislik'st the piece thou light'st on first. To the Soure Reader. Robert Herrick. SeCP

If thou must love me, let it be for naught. Sonnets from the Portuguese, XIV. Elizabeth Barrett Browning. BoLP; CTC; OBNC; PoPo

If thou of fortune be bereft. Not by Bread Alone. James Terry White. PoLF

If thou serve a lord of prise. A Warning to Those Who Serve Lords. *Unknown.* MeEL

If thou shouldst ever come by choice or chance. Ginevra. Samuel Rogers. PoLF

If thou survive my well-contented day. Sonnets, XXXII. Shakespeare, CBEP; GTBS-P; PP

If thou wilt ease thine heart. Dirge. Thomas Lovell Beddoes. *Fr.* Death's Jest Book. OBNC

If Thou Wilt Mighty Be. Sir Thomas Wyatt. EnRePo

If thou wouldst make me speak, Lord, give me speech. The Preacher's Prayer. George Macdonald. TRV

If thou would'st view fair Melrose aright. Sir William of Deloraine at the Wizard's Tomb. Sir Walter Scott. *Fr.* The Lay of the Last Minstrel. OBNC

If to be absent were to love. To Lucasta, [on] Going beyond the Seas. Richard Lovelace. GTBS-P; HaSV; ILP; SeCP

If to demands of others I agree. Resolving Doubts. William Dickey. ErPo

If to grow old in Heaven is to grow young. True Woman: Her Heaven. Dante Gabriel Rossetti. The House of Life, LVIII. VP

If We Break Faith. Joseph Auslander. TRV

If we could see below. The Foil. George Herbert. FoBA

If we had lived on that long-gone day. Crucifixion. Mrs. Roy L. Peifer. STF

If we had won the war with waving. The Other Possibility. Erich Kästner. TwGP

If We Must Die. Claude McKay. AmNP; FaBV

If what heals can bless. Come Green Again. Winfield Townley Scott. PoPl

If whatever is, is right. Pope. Manuel González Prada. AnSP

If when the wind blows. Daniel Webster's Horses. Elizabeth J. Coatsworth. FiSC

If with her hand my fatal enemy. Maurice Scève. *Fr.* Délie. RBL

If women could be fair, and yet not fond. A Renunciation. Edward de Vere, Earl of Oxford. GTBS-P

If yet I have not all thy love. Lovers Infinitenesse. John Donne. MeP; SeCP

If you, agree, agree to be indifferent. The St. Petersburg Paradox. O. B. Hardison, Jr. PoNC

If you are merry sing away. Mirth. Christopher Smart. *Fr.* Hymns for the Amusement of Children. EiCP

If You Are No Longer. Vittorio Sereni, *tr. fr. Italian by* Carlo L. Golino. CoIP

If You Came. Ruth Pitter. DaDu

If you can keep your head when all about you. If. Kipling. FaPL; LV; WePo

If you can make life brighter. Humble Service. Lillian G. Heard. STF

If you cannot speak like angels. Something You Can Do. *Unknown.* STF

If you ever, ever, ever meet a grizzly bear. Grizzly Bear. Mary Austin. GoJo; SoPo

If you ever get there. Going. Robert Kelly. CoPo
If You Go to Bathe, Juanica. *Unknown, tr. fr. Spanish by* James Duffy. AnML
If you happen to walk out. The Fenian Song. *Unknown.* BSNS
If You Leave at Daybreak. Lope de Vega, *tr. fr. Spanish by* Kate Flores. AnSP
If you love God, take your mirror between your hands and look. Song. Mahmud Djellaladin Pasha. ErPo
If you never do anything for anyone else. The Immoral Proposition. Robert Creeley. ToPo
If You Never Talked with Fairies. Elsie Melchert Fowler. BiCB
If you press a stone with your finger. Natural Law. Babette Deutsch. MoLP
If you promise me a rose. Promise Me a Rose. Bob Merrill. BoLP
If you see a package. Secrets. Elsie Melchert Fowler. BiCB
If you see a tall fellow ahead of the crowd. Forget It. *Unknown.* PoLF
If you shortened many a road and put a halo. Raftery's Dialogue with the Whiskey. Padraic Fallon. DTC
If You Should Meet a Crocodile. *Unknown.* SoPo
If you should rise from Nowhere up to Somewhere. The Fear of God. Robert Frost. MoRP
If you sit down at set of sun. At Set of Sun. "George Eliot." PoPl; TRV
If you spin me around until I'm so dizzy. Six of Cups. Diane Wakoski. CoPo
If you, that have grown old, were the first dead. The New Faces. W. B. Yeats. GTBS-P
If you think you are beaten, you are. The Man Who Thinks He Can. Walter D. Wintle. PoLF
If You Trap the Moment. Blake. DiPo
If You Truly Want Me. *Unknown, tr. fr. Spanish by* William M. Davis. AnML
If you wander far enough. Oh No. Robert Creeley. AmPC
If you want a great revival. Pray, Christian, Pray! *Unknown.* STF
If you want to work in the kind of a church. It's You. L. A. McDonald. STF
If you were coming in the fall. Emily Dickinson. AP; DiPo; FaPL
If you were to ask me why I dwell among green mountains. Conversation in the Mountains. Li Po. SiGo
"If you will answer these questions for me." The Devil's Nine Questions. *Unknown.* BFSS
If you will tell me why the fen. I May, I Might, I Must. Marianne Moore. PoPo; RePo
If you would know yourself, regard what others are doing. The Key. Schiller. TwGP
If your brother has a burden. A Helping Hand. Georgia B. Adams. STF
If you're anxious for to shine in the high aesthetic line as a man of culture rare. Bunthorne's Song. W. S. Gilbert. *Fr.* Patience. VaPo
If You're the Man You Ought to Be. Walter E. Isenhour. STF
If You've Never. Elsie M. Fowler. SoPo
Ignorance of Death. William Empson. ToPo
Ignorant two, we glide. On Minding One's Own Business. James Wright. PoPl
Il Penseroso. Milton. CABA; CBEP; EiCP; FoBA; GTBS-P; ILP
Ile gaze no more on her bewitching face. Song: Murdring Beautie. Thomas Carew. SeCP
Iliad, The, *sels.* Homer, *tr. fr.* Greek.
  Achilles' Revenge, *fr.* XXII, *tr. by* Bryant. SIV
  "Meanwhile Achilles, plung'd," *fr.* I, *tr. by* the Earl of Derby. PoPl
  Night Encampment outside Troy, *fr.* VIII, *tr. by* Tennyson. RoGo
Ilicet. Theodosia Garrison. PoLF
I'll build a house of arrogance. Haven. Donald Jeffrey Hayes. AmNP
I'll buy a horse for my young son. The Solitary Horseman. Guy Owen. PoNC
I'll Come to Thee. Robert Herrick. UnTE
Ill days and dolorous nights and years accurst. The Incubus of Time. Clark Ashton Smith. FiSC
Ill fares the land, to hastening ills a prey. Goldsmith. *Fr.* The Deserted Village. TRV
"I'll give to you a paper of pins,/ And that's the way my love begins." A Paper of Pins. *Unknown.* BFSS; BSO
"I'll give to you a paper of pins/ If that's the way true love begins." The Keys of Heaven (C *vers.*). *Unknown.* BSO
"I'll give to you a paper of pins,/ If you will tell me how true love begins." The Keys of Heaven (B *vers.*). *Unknown.* BSO
I'll go where You want me to go, dear Lord. Think It Over. *Unknown.* STF
I'll kick your walls to bits, I'll die scratching a tunnel. Gulliver. Kenneth Slessor. ACV
Ill Luck. Baudelaire, *tr. fr. French by* Roy Campbell. PoPl

I'll Make Some Verses Just for Fun. William IX, Count of Poitiers, *tr. fr. Provençal by* Thomas G. Bergin. AnML
I'll never be a nun, I trow. Nightingale Weather. Andrew Lang. ACV
I'll Never Love Thee More. James Graham, Marquess of Montrose. CBEP
I'll not allow the birchtree. Alun Mabon's Song. John Ceiriog Hughes. WePo
I'll not be silent, though you put your finger. Francisco de Quevedo. *Fr.* Satiric and Censorious Epistle. AnSP
I'll not forget the warm blue night when my bold girl. A Thing Remembered. *Unknown.* ErPo
I'll range around the shady bowers. Love for Love's Sake. Henry Carey. WaPE
I'll Sail upon the Dog-Star. Thomas D'Urfey. *Fr.* A Fool's Preferment. CBEP
I'll sing you a song, though it may be a sad one. Sioux Indians. *Unknown.* BFSS
I'll sing you a true song of Billy the Kid. Billy the Kid. *Unknown.* ThLM
I'll talk no more. Young Africa's Resolve. Dennis Osadebay. ACV
I'll tell thee everything I can. "Lewis Carroll." *Fr.* Through the Looking-Glass. Par
I'll tell you. I'll Tell You in My Own Way. Marcabru. AnML
I'll tell you a story, I'll not keep you long. The Liverpool Landlady. *Unknown.* BSNS
I'll tell you a tale of my love and I. The Shepherd and the Milkmaid. *Unknown.* UnTE
I'll tell you how the sun rose. Emily Dickinson. AP; FaBV; ILP; RePo
I'll Tell you in My Own Way. Marcabru, *tr. fr. Provençal by* Paul Blackburn. AnML
I'll tell you of a fellow. Common Bill (A *vers.*). *Unknown.* BSO
Ill-tempered Lover, The, *sel.* L. A. MacKay.
  "I wish my tongue were a quiver the size of a huge cask." OBCV
I'll Twine White Violets. Meleager, *tr. fr. Greek by* Goldwin Smith. SiGo
I'll write a poem, then sink to dreams. Count William's Escapade. Guillaume de Poitiers. ErPo
Illa iuventus, that is so nise. Fearful Death. *Unknown.* MeEL
Illic Jacet. A. E. Housman. Last Poems, IV. VP
Ills I sorrow at, The. Any Human to Another. Countee Cullen. MoRP
Illuminations, *sel.* Arthur Rimbaud, *tr. fr. French by* Louise Varèse.
  Childhood ("I am the saint at prayer on the terrace"), IV. PoPl
Illustration, The. To a Steam Roller. Marianne Moore. PP
Illustrious Ancestors. Denise Levertov. ToPo
Illyria's hair fell down. The Oracular Portcullis. James Reaney. ErPo
I'm a lean dog, a keen dog, a wild dog, and lone. Lone Dog. Irene Rutherford McLeod. LV
I'm a peevish old man with a penny-whistle. Beggar's Serenade. John Heath-Stubbs. ErPo
I'm a strange contradiction; I'm new and I'm old. A Book. Hannah More. PoSC
I'm a Tight Little Irishman, *with music. Unknown.* BSO
I'm Bound for the Rio Grande. *Unknown. See* Rio Grande.
I'm far frae my hame, an' I'm weary aftenwhiles. My Ain Countree. Mary Demarest. TRV
I'm fonder of carats than carrots. I Take 'Em and Like 'Em. Margaret Fishback. PoPl
I'm Glad My Birthday Comes in May! Ivy O. Eastwick. BiCB
I'm Glad the Sky Is Painted Blue. *Unknown.* SoPo
I'm going home to stop awhile. Then Hurrah for Home! John A. Stone. SGR
I'm going out to clean the pasture spring. The Pasture. Robert Frost. AmLP; BoC; DiPo; GoJo; PoPl; SoPo; WePo
I'm going to roll up. Jack's Blues. Robert Creeley. ToPo
I'm going to try and suit. That's the Way to Talk It. Mart Taylor. SGR
I'm growing very big and tall. Growing Up. Edna Kingsley Wallace. BiCB
I'm hiding, I'm hiding. Hiding. Dorothy Aldis. SoPo
I'm jilted, forsaken, outwitted. The Jilted Nymph. Thomas Campbell. BoLP
I'm just a poor wayfaring stranger. Poor Wayfaring Stranger. *Unknown.* BFSS
I'm longing for the forest. Home. Verner von Heidenstam. PoPl
I'm looking rather seedy now while holding down my claim. Little Old Sod Shanty. *Unknown.* BFSS
I'm mining in a dry ravine. The Sensible Miner. John A. Stone. SGR
I'm nobody! Who are you? Emily Dickinson. CBEP; DiPo; PoPl
"I'm old." Old Botany Bay. Mary Gilmore. PoAu-1
I'm only a little sparrow. The Sparrow's Song. *Unknown.* STF

I'm Owre Young to Marry Yet. Burns. UnTE
I'm persistent as the pink locust. The Pink Locust. William Carlos Williams. PP
I'm picking my mother a present. Dandelions. Marchette Chute. BiCB
I'm Pleased When Gaudy Eastertime. Bertran de Born, *tr. fr. Provençal by* William M. Davis. AnML
(War Song, A, *2 sts., tr. by* Ezra Pound.) CTC
I'm pretty old. Five-in-June. Lysbeth Boyd Borie. BiCB
I'm really a very unfortunate man. The Unfortunate Man. *Unknown.* BFSS
I'm Sad and Lonely Here, *with music.* John A. Stone. SGR
I'm seven years old. Middle-aged Child. Inez Hogan. BiCB
I'm Seventeen Come Sunday. *Unknown.* UnTE
I'm sitting alone by the fire. Her Letter. Bret Harte. PoLF
I'm Smith of Stoke, aged sixty-odd. Epitaph on a Pessimist. Thomas Hardy. PoIE; VP
I'm something I have never been. Something Very Elegant. Aileen Fisher. BiCB
I'm sorry for the old wharves. The Old Wharves. Rachel Field. SoPo
I'm Thankful That My Life Doth Not Deceive. Henry David Thoreau. VaPo
I'm the gardener long ago. Lawn-Mower. Dorothy Baruch. SoPo
I'm the Police Cop Man, I Am. Margaret Morrison. SoPo
"I'm the sort of girl." Nausicäa. Irving Layton. ErPo
I'm three years old and like to wear. Hair Ribbons. *Unknown.* BiCB
I'm travellin' down the Castlereagh, and I'm a station-hand. A Bushman's Song. A. B. Paterson. PoAu-1
I'm wearing awa', Jean. The Land o' the Leal. Lady Nairne. GTBS-P
Image, The. Roy Fuller. GTBS-P; ToPo
Image, The. Sylvia Townsend Warner. SIV
Image from D'Orleans. Ezra Pound. LOW
Image of her whom I love, more then she. Elegy X. John Donne. MeP
Imagery. Harindranth Chattopadhyaya. ACV
Imaginary good, or true. On Fame. John Banks. WaPE
Imagination, How Impaired and Restored. Wordsworth. *Fr.* The Prelude, XII. OBNC
Imagine it, a Sophocles complete. The Fire at Alexandria. Theodore Weiss. CoPo
Imagine that any mind ever *thought* a red geranium! Red Geranium and Godly Mignonette. D. H. Lawrence. GTBS-P
Imagine this beast of the frozen Northeast. The Love Life (and Death) of a Moose. Richard Armour. LV
Imagine what Mrs. Haessler would say. Dance of the Abakweta. Margaret Danner. Far from Africa: Four Poems, 2. AmNP
Imagined Happiness. Erik Axel Karlfeldt, *tr. fr. Swedish by* Charles Wharton Stork. PoPI
Imbecile, The. Donald Finkel. NePoEA-2
Imitation of Chaucer. Pope. Par
Imitation of Joy. Salvatore Quasimodo, *tr. fr. Italian by* Allen Mandelbaum. CoIP
Imitation of Spenser, An. John Armstrong. WaPE
Imitation of Wordsworth, An. Hartley Coleridge. *See* He Lived amidst th' Untrodden Ways.
Immanence. Richard Hovey. TRV
Immeasurable haze. To the Holy Spirit. Yvor Winters. PoIE
Immense Hour. Juan Ramón Jiménez, *tr. fr. Spanish by* Edward F. Gahan. AnSP; SiGo
Immensitie cloystered in thy deare wombe. Nativitie. John Donne. MeP
Immoral Proposition, The. Robert Creeley. ToPo
Immorality, An. Ezra Pound. GoJo; PoPI; PoSa
Immortal Autumn. Archibald MacLeish. AP
Immortal is an ample word. Emily Dickinson. FoBA
Immortal Love. George Edward Woodberry. *Fr.* Ideal Passion. PoPo
Immortal Love, forever full. Our Master. Whittier. TRV
Immortal love, too high for my possessing. Immortal Love. George Edward Woodberry. *Fr.* Ideal Passion. PoPo
Immortal Part, The. A. E. Housman. A Shropshire Lad, XLIII. StP
Immortal Spirit, The. Stephen Spender. MoRP
Immortal spirit hath no bars, The. Dawn. Frederick George Scott. PoPI
Immortal Spirit is that single ghost, The. The Immortal Spirit. Stephen Spender. MoRP
Immortality. Schiller, *tr. fr. German by* Walter Kaufmann. TwGP
Immortall Heat, O let thy greater flame. Love. George Herbert. MeP
Immortall Love, authour of this great frame. Love. George Herbert. MeP
Immortals, The. Isaac Rosenberg. MMA
Immured in time as bees in amber were. Beyond Barriers. William J. Pomeroy. PtTo
Impatiently she tampered with the locks. Bluebeard's Wife. Daryl Hine. ACV
Impenitent, we meet again. To Philip Levine, on the Day of Atonement. Robert Mezey. AmPC

Imperfect Enjoyment, The. Earl of Rochester. ErPo; UnTE
Imperial Adam. A. D. Hope. ErPo; UnTE
Impetuous Resolve, An. James Whitcomb Riley. BiCB
Importance of Poetry, or the Coming Forth from Eternity into Time, The. Hyam Plutzik. PP
Important Statement. Patrick Kavanagh. PoCh
Importune Me No More. Elizabeth I, Queen of England. *See* When I Was Fair and Young.
Impossible Fact, The. Christian Morgenstern, *tr. fr. German by* Walter Kaufmann. TwGP
Impossible to Trust Women. *Unknown.* MeEL
Impotent Lover, The. Ovid. *See* Shameful Impotence.
Impression du Matin. Oscar Wilde. CABA
Impressions. O. B. Hardison, Jr. PoNC
Imprisoned, The. Robert Fitzgerald. MP
Impromptu. Francis Atterbury. WaPE
Impromptu. Thomas Gray. EiCP
(On Lord Holland's Seat near M——e, Kent.) CABA
Improvisation on an Old Theme. Dorothy Livesay. ACV
Improvisations: Light and Snow, *sel.* Conrad Aiken.
"This girl gave her heart to me." BoLP
In a Bath Teashop. John Betjeman. BoC
In a Boat. D. H. Lawrence. BoLP
In a cavern, in a cañon. Oh My Darling Clementine. Percy Montrose. SGR
In a certain crypt-like courtroom. When Nobody Prays. Merl A. Clapper. STF
In a coign of the cliff between lowland and highland. A Forsaken Garden. Swinburne. CBEP; GTBS-P; OBNC; StP; VaPo; VP
In a cool curving world he lies. The Fish. Rupert Brooke. BoC
In a Corner of Eden. Peter Levi. NePoEA-2
In a Country Church. R. S. Thomas. ToPo
In a Crumbling. Kenneth Patchen. ToPo
In a dark, silent, shady grove. Et Cetera. Earl of Rochester. UnTE
In a Dark Time. Theodore Roethke. EaLo; ToPo
In a dream last night. Iron. Bertolt Brecht. MGP
In a Drear-nighted December. Keats. CBEP; ELP
(Happy Insensibility.) GTBS-P
(Stanzas.) OBNC
In a far-away northern country in the placid pastoral region. The Ox-Tamer. Walt Whitman. CBEP
In a Field. Robert Pack. NePoEA-2
In a frosty sunset. Winter in East Anglia. Edmund Blunden. WePo
In a Garden. Donald C. Babcock. LV
In a garden of shining sea-weed. The Sea Princess. Katharine Pyle. SoPo
In a garden shady this holy lady. Song for St. Cecilia's Day. W. H. Auden. MP
In a Girl's Album. Cedric Dover. WePo
In a Glass-Window for Inconstancy. Lord Herbert of Cherbury. SeCP
In a glorious garden grene. The Lily-white Rose. *Unknown.* MeEL
In a Gondola, *sel.* Robert Browning.
"Moth's kiss, first, The." UnTE
In a goodly night, as in my bede I laye. Waking Alone. *Unknown.* MeEL
In a gorge titanic. Ula Masondo's Dream. William Plomer. MoBS
In a green place lanced through. The Blue Heron. Theodore Goodridge Roberts. OBCV
In a high wind. Hands and Eyes. Louis MacNeice PoDB
In a hole of the heel of an old brown stocking. Stocking Fairy. Winifred Welles. SoPo
In a Poem. Robert Frost. PP
In a Prominent Bar in Secaucus [One Day]. X. J. Kennedy. PoCh; UnTE
In a Railway Compartment. John Fuller. NePoEA-2
In a shelter one night, when death was taking the air. In the Shelter. C. Day Lewis. BoC
In a Shoreham Garden. Laurence Lerner. NePoEA-2
In a small bitterness of wind. Young Argonauts. Sheila Wingfield. SD
In a snug little court as I stood t'other day. The Pleasing Constraint. Aristaenetus. ErPo
In a solitude of the sea. The Convergence of the Twain. Thomas Hardy. ILP; OnP; VP
In a Spring Still Not Written Of. Robert Wallace. PP
In a stable of boats I lie still. The Lifeguard. James Dickey. CoPo
In a Station of the Metro. Ezra Pound. CABA; CaFP; PoIE; VaPo
In a summer cottage. Nightmare. Anne Marx. FiSC
In a tabernacle of a toure. Quia Amore Langueo. *Unknown.* MeEL
In a tree at the edge of the clearing. On Falling Asleep to Birdsong. William Meredith. PoCh
In a twinkling/ of a flash-boom. Jonathan C. Williams. *Fr.* The Empire Finals at Verona. PtTo
In a valley of this restless mind. Quia Amore Langueo. *Unknown.* CBEP

In a white gully among fungus red. Native Born. Eve Langley. PoAu-2
In a Wine Cellar. Victor J. Daley. PoAu-1
In a Wood. Thomas Hardy. *Fr.* The Woodlanders. OBNC; PoPl
In a wood they call the Rouge Bouquet. Rouge Bouquet. Joyce Kilmer. PoPl
In After Time. Richard Eberhart. MoRP
In all the parish not a dame dared stir. Ten of Chaucer's People: The Wife of Bath. Chaucer. *Fr.* The Canterbury Tales. PoSa
In All These Acts. Brother Antoninus. ToPo
In all this cool. Coolness in Summer. Ryusui. RePo
In all this world of visible images. Ceremony for Birth and Naming. Ridgely Torrence. MoRP
"In America," began. The Student. Marianne Moore. MP
In Amsterdam there dwelt a maid. The Maid of Amsterdam. *Unknown.* HaSV
In an Age of Fops and Toys. Emerson. Voluntaries, III. PoLF; PoPo
"So nigh is grandeur to our dust," *last 4 ll. of* III. TRV
In an Arbour Green. Robert Weever. ELP
(In Youth Is Pleasure.) CBEP
In an Editor's Office. Zoe Kincaid Brockman. PoNC
In an envelope marked. Personal. Langston Hughes. AmNP
In an Iridescent Time. Ruth Stone. PoPl
In an obscure night. Dark Night of the Soul. St. John of the Cross. RBL
In an Orchard a Little Fountain Flows. *Unknown, tr. fr. French by* Patricia Terry. AnML
In an Orchard, under the Leaves of a Hawthorn. *Unknown, tr. fr. Provençal by* Maurice Valency. AnML
In an upper room at midnight. The Love Feast. W. H. Auden. ErPo
In Acknowledgment of the Praises of European Writers. Sister Juana Inés de la Cruz, *tr. fr. Spanish by* Constance Urdang. AnSP
In all the good Greek of Plato. Survey of Literature. John Crowe Ransom. MP
In ancient times, as story tells. Baucis and Philemon. Swift. EiCP
In anguish we uplift. War Song. John Davidson. OBNC
In any medium except that of verse. Wyndham Lewis. *Fr.* One-Way Song. PP
In Aprell and in May. Besse Bunting. *Unknown.* MeEL
In April around Easter the Streams Grow Clear. Marcabru, *tr. fr. Provençal by* Paul Blackburn. AnML
In April, when raining is sunlight. Great Farm. Philip Booth. PoPl
In Arlington Cemetery. Stanley Koehler. OPP
In autumn down the beechwood path. Beech Leaves. James Reeves. RePo
In Baltimore there lived a boy. The Boy Who Laughed at Santa Claus. Ogden Nash. BBGG
In Battle. Abu-l-Hasan ben al-Qabturnuh, *tr. fr. Arabic by* Lysander Kemp. AnML
In bed we laugh, in bed we cry. Translation of Lines by Benserade. Samuel Johnson. CABA
In Bertram's Garden. Donald Justice. ErPo
In bonny Scotland blithe and gay. Bonny Scotland. *Unknown.* BSNS
In borrows boots which don't fit. Small Game. Philip Levine. AmPC
In breaking of belief in human good. Litany of the Lost. Siegfried Sassoon. MoRP
In Breughel's great picture, The Kermess. The Dance. William Carlos Williams. GoJo
In Broken Images. Robert Graves. PoIE
In Cabined Ships at Sea. Walt Whitman. HaSV
In Cawsand Bay lying, with the Blue Peter flying. Cawsand Bay. *Unknown.* HaSV
In certain minds the strength wells. The Rich Interior Life. Richard Eberhart. MoRP
In chariot like an hibiscus flower at his side. Confucius. *Fr.* The Classic Anthology: Songs of Cheng. CTC
In Charlotte Town where I was born. Barbara Ellen. *Unknown.* BSNS
In Christ ("In Christ there is no East or West"). John Oxenham. *See* No East or West.
In Church. William Barnes. WePo
In Church. Thomas Hardy. Satires of Circumstance, II. DiPo; DTC; PoDB; VaPo; VP
In college once I climbed the tree. Sickle Pears. Owen Dodson. AmNP
In comes the captain's daughter, the captain of the yeos. The Boys of Wexford. *Unknown.* ELP
In Commendation of Music. William Strode. ELP
In Common. Gene Derwood. PoPl
In Consolation. Vassar Miller. ToPo
In Cumberland city as you shall all hear. Jimmy and Diana. *Unknown.* BSO
In Cumberland City I've often heard say. Diana. *Unknown.* BSO
In Cupid's school whoe'er would take degree. Ovid. *Fr.* The Art of Love. UnTE

In darkest hours, in nights so drear. With Thee. Cora M. Pinkham. STF
In Darkness and Aridity. Psalms, CXXX, Bible, *O.T.* BoC
In de dead of night I sometimes. The Old Cabin. Paul Laurence Dunbar. PoLF
In Death Divided. Thomas Hardy. DTC
In Defense of Felons. Robert Mezey. ToPo
In desert wastes there stands a tree. The Tree in the Desert. Friedrich Hebbel. AGP
In desolation, here a lost world lies. Epitaph, Found Somewhere in Space. Hugh Wilgus Ramsaur. TRV
In Dispraise of Poetry. Jack Gilbert. PP
In Distrust of Merits. Marianne Moore. AP; EaLo
In dog-days plowmen quit their toil. The Swimmer. John Crowe Ransom. SD
In dreams the Daemon comes, upon the hour. The Dream-Daemon. Lin Carter. FiSC
In Dreamy Swoon. George Darley. *Fr.* Nepenthe. OBNC
In Dublin city where I did dwell. The Butcher Boy (B vers.). *Unknown.* BSNS
In Dublin's fair city, where the girls are so pretty. Cockles and Mussels. *Unknown.* ELP
In Earthen Vessels. Whittier. TRV
In Ego with Us All. John Ciardi. ToPo
In eighteen hundred fifty, when Gold Lake was in its prime. Gold Lake and Gold Bluff. John A. Stone. SGR
In England's Green & (a Garland and a Clyster). Jonathan Williams. CoPo
In every church, in every clime. The Faithful Few. Chester E. Shuler. STF
In every feature noble pride. Bertrand de Born. Heine. TwGP
In every place ye may well see. What Women Are Not. *Unknown.* MeEL
In every seed to breathe the flower. Faith. John Banister Tabb. TRV
In Every Thing Give Thanks. *Unknown.* STF
In Exile. Blanche Edith Baughan. ACV
In faith, I do not love thee with mine eyes. Sonnets, CXLI. Shakespeare. CBEP
In Faith Methinks It Is No Right. Sir Thomas Wyatt. CBEP
In fear of the gods let. Song of the Parcae. Goethe. AGP
In February there are days. When. Dorothy Aldis. RePo
In February when few gusty flakes. Ground Hog Day. Marnie Pomeroy. PoSC
In five-score summers! All new eyes. 1967. Thomas Hardy. VP
In Flanders Fields. John McCrae. FaBV; LV; OBCV; PoPl; PoPo
In Flaundres whilom was a compaignye. The Pardoner's Tale. Chaucer. *Fr.* The Canterbury Tales. PoIE
In form and feature, face and limb. The Twins. Henry S. Leigh. BiCB; PoPl
In Front of the Landscape. Thomas Hardy. OBNC
In front of the horse's rump bright as a lantern. Sleighride. Patrick Anderson. OBCV
In futurity/ I prophetic see. The Little Girl Lost. Blake. *Fr.* Songs of Experience. DiPo
In Gaspard of late a young damsel did dwell. The Gaspard Tragedy. *Unknown.* BSNS
In gayer hours, when high my fancy run. The Bastard's Lot. Richard Savage. CBEP
In Going to My Naked Bed. Richard Edwards. CBEP
In Golden Gate Park that day. Lawrence Ferlinghetti. *Fr.* A Coney Island of the Mind. ToPo
In Good Old Colony Times, *with music. Unknown.* BFSS
In good old times, which means, you know. Verses Intended to Go with a Posset Dish to My Dear Little Goddaughter, 1882. James Russell Lowell. AP
In good plain French your words devoutly rise. Rondeau: In Good Plain French. Vincent Voiture. RBL
In Greencastle, Indiana, a fair young maiden dwelled. A Fatal Acquaintance (A vers.). *Unknown.* BSO
In Greencastle lived a maiden. A Fatal Acquaintance (B vers.). *Unknown.* BSO
In Hardin County, 1809. Lulu E. Thompson. PoSC
In Hardwood Groves. Robert Frost. AmLP
In Harmony with Nature. Matthew Arnold. PoIE
In haste, post haste, when first my wandering mind. Gascoigne's Memories, IV. George Gascoigne. EnRePo
In heaven/ Some little blades of grass. The Blade of Grass. Stephen Crane. The Black Riders, XVIII. AP; PoPl; PoPo
In Heaven a spirit doth dwell. Israfel. Poe. AP; PoPo
In Heaven soaring up, I drop an eare. The Joy of Church Fellowship Rightly Attended. Edward Taylor. *Fr.* Gods Determinations. AP; CBEP
In her fair cheeks two pits do lie. A Song. Thomas Carew. UnTE
In her first passion woman loves her lover. Byron. *Fr.* Don Juan. ErPo; UnTE
In her lone cottage on the downs. Miss Thompson Goes Shopping. Martin Armstrong. WePo
In Him. Annie Johnson Flint. TRV

In his chamber, weak and dying. A Strike among the Poets. *Unknown.* PP
In his face the trace of Europe. The Face of the Fisherman. Walter Höllerer. MGP
In his father's face flying. Icarus. Ronald Bottrall. GTBS-P
In his grandmother's garden was a cake with seven candles. Seven Times One Are Seven. Robert Hillyer. BiCB
In His hands I leave tomorrow. Tomorrow. Della Adams Leitner. STF
In His Mental Illness, William Cowper Finds He Is Not Alone. William Cowper. BoC
In his own image the Creator made. On Man. Walter Savage Landor. OBNC
In his sea lit. The Double Play. Robert Wallace. PP; SD
In His Service. Clarence E. Clar. STF
In His Utter Wretchedness. John Audelay. MeEL
In history we read of a freemason king. The Building of Solomon's Temple. *Unknown.* BSNS
In Hoc Signo. Godfrey Fox Bradby. TRV
In Honour of Christmas. *Unknown.* MeEL
In Hospital: Poona (I). Alun Lewis. DTC
In Hospital: Poona (II). Alun Lewis. DTC
In Hotels Public and Private. Ralph Pomeroy. CoPo
In Identity. Josephine Miles. OPP
In Imitation of the Tenth Satire of Juvenal. Samuel Johnson. *Fr.* The Vanity of Human Wishes. PoIE
In India there lived a noble lord. Lord Bakeman. *Unknown.* BSNS
In Ireland: By the Pool at the Third Rosses. Arthur Symons. OBNC
In Islington for the moment I reside. Important Statement. Patrick Kavanagh. PoCh
In Jersey City where I did dwell. The Butcher's Boy [*or* Jersey City]. *Unknown.* BSO
In July you fish my voice from the ponds. Four Psalms, III. Bertolt Brecht. MGP
In June, amid the golden fields. The Groundhog. Richard Eberhart. AmLP; CABA; DTC; ILP; PoIE; PoSa; StP; ToPo
In Just-Spring. E. E. Cummings. FaBV; RePo
(Chanson Innocente.) AmLP
In Labyrinths. Frank Borden Hanes. PoNC
In late autumn sun. Four Days in November. Marjorie Mir. OPP
In late summer the wild geese. August Hail. J. V. Cunningham. PoIE; PoSa
In Lincolnshire, a village full of tongues. On Looking at Stubb's Anatomy of the Horse. Edward Lucie-Smith. NePoEA-2
In Lisbon by the Sea. Joan Zorro, *tr. fr. Portuguese by* William M. Davis. AnML
In Little Rock the people bear. The Chicago *Defender* Sends a Man to Little Rock, Fall, 1957. Gwendolyn Brooks. AmNP
In London city there did dwell. The Farmer's Daughter. *Unknown.* BFSS
In London City where I once did dwell. Barbara Allen. *Unknown.* SIV
In London, September, 1802. Wordsworth. PoPo
(London, MDCCCII.) GTBS-P
In London there lived a pretty fair maid. The Constant Farmer's Son. *Unknown.* BSNS
In London town where I did dwell. The Butcher Boy (A *vers.*). *Unknown.* BSNS
In London was young Beichan born. Young Beichan and Susie Pye. *Unknown.* OnMSP
In Love, If Love Be Love. Tennyson. *Fr.* Idylls of the King: Merlin and Vivien. CABA
(All in All.) TRV
(Vivien's Song.) OBNC
In love they wore themselves in a green embrace. Adolescence. P. K. Page. OBCV
In many places here and. Fate Is Unfair. Don Marquis. *Fr.* Archy Does His Part. EvOK
In March. Philip Martin. PoAu-2
In March, for You a Gift of Fish I Boast. Folgore da San Geminiano, *tr. fr. Italian by* Joy Gould. *Fr.* Sonnets of the Months. AnML
In Marion, the honey-locust trees are falling. Two Poems about President Harding, I. James Wright. AmPC
In May, when sea-winds pierced our solitudes. The Rhodora. Emerson. AmLP; AP; FaBV; ILP; PoIE; TRV
In Medias Res. William Stafford. StP
In Memoriam. "Max Adeler." *See* Willie.
In Memoriam. Giuseppe Ungaretti, *tr. fr. Italian by* Lowry Nelson, Jr. CoIP
In Memoriam I: Elizabeth at Twenty. Richard Weber. ErPo
In Memoriam II: Elizabeth in Italy. Richard Weber. ErPo
In Memoriam A. H. H. Tennyson. ILP, *much abr.*; VP
Sels.
"Are God and Nature then at strife," *fr.* LV. TRV
"Be near me when my light is low," L. ELP; FoBA
"By night we linger'd on the lawn," XCV. OBNC
"Calm is the morn without a sound," XI. ELP; FoBA; OBNC; OnP

"Danube to the Severn gave, The," XIX. FoBA; GTBS-P
"Dark House, by which once more I stand," VII. DiPo; FoBA; GTBS-P; OBNC; PoIE; PoSa
"Doors, where my heart was used to beat," CXIX. DiPo; OBNC
"I climb the hill: from end to end," C. FoBA
"I envy not in any moods," XXVII. OBNC
"I held it truth, with him who sings," I. DiPo; FoBA; OBNC
"If sleep and death be truly one," XLIII. FoBA; OBNC
"Is it, then, regret for buried time," CXVI. FoBA
"Love is and was my Lord and King," CXXVI. OBNC
"Man, that with me trod, The," *fr.* Epilogue. TRV
"Now fades the last long streak of snow," CXV. BoC; GTBS-P; OBNC; PoSa
"O living will that shalt endure," CXXXI. DiPo; FoBA
"Oh yet we trust that somehow good," LIV. DiPo; EaLo; FaPL; OBNC; PoIE; TRV
"Old warder of these buried bones," XXXIX. FoBA
"Old Yew, which graspest at the stones," II. ELP; FoBA; GTBS-P; OBNC
"Our little systems have their day," *fr.* Proem. TRV
"Perplext in faith, but pure in deeds," *fr.* XCVI. TRV
"Ring out, wild bells, to the wild sky," CVI. DiPo; FaPL; FoBA; PoIE; TRV; WiR, *fr.* CV *and* CVI
"Risest thou thus, dim dawn, again," LXXII. OBNC
"So careful of the type?' but no," LVI. DiPo; OBNC
"Strong Son of God, immortal Love," Proem. FaPL; PoIE; TRV
(Strong Son of God.) EaLo
"There rolls the deep where grew the tree," CXXIII. FoBA
"Thy voice is on the rolling air," CXXX. DiPo; FaPL; TRV
"Till now the doubtful dusk reveal'd," *fr.* XCV. GTBS-P
"Time draws near the birth of Christ, The," XXVIII. FoBA
"Time draws near the birth of Christ, The," CIV. FoBA
"To-night the winds begin to rise," XV. GTBS-P; OBNC; PoSa
"Unwatch'd the garden bough shall sway," CI. ELP; GTBS-P; OBNC; OnP
"What hope is here for modern rhyme," LXXVII. PP
"When rosy plumelets tuft the larch," XCI. OBNC
"Wish, that of the living whole, The," LV. DiPo; OBNC
"Witch-elms that counterchange the floor," LXXXIX. OBNC
"You say, but with no touch of scorn," XCVI. FoBA
"Yule-clog sparkled keen with frost, The," *fr.* LXXVIII. TRV
In Memoriam; Easter 1915. Edward Thomas. GTBS-P; PoIE
In Memoriam; Ingvald Bjorndal and His Comrade. Malcolm Lowry. OBCV
In Memoriam Paul Eluard. Paul Celan, *tr. fr. German by* Michael Hamburger. MGP
In Memoriam Roy Campbell. R. N. Currey. ACV
In Memoriam S. C. W., v.c. Charles Sorley. MMA
In Memory, *sel.* Lionel Johnson.
"Ah! fair face gone from sight," II. OBNC
In Memory of Abraham Lincoln. Oliver Wendell Holmes. LiPo
In Memory of Arthur Winslow. Robert Lowell. AP
Death from Cancer, *sel.* MP; PoSa
In Memory of Eva Gore-Booth and Con Markiewicz. W. B. Yeats. CABA
In Memory of Jane Fraser. Geoffrey Hill. DaDu
In Memory of Major Robert Gregory. W. B. Yeats. DiPo
In Memory of My Dear Grandchild Elizabeth Bradstreet, Who Deceased August, 1665, Being a Year and a Half Old. Anne Bradstreet. AP
In Memory of My Uncle Timothy. Alastair Reid. NePoEA-2
In Memory of the Vertuous and ·Learned Lady Madre de Teresa That Sought an Early Martyrdome. Richard Crashaw. *See* Hymn to St. Teresa.
In Memory of Two Sons. Russell Stellwagon. STF
In Memory of W. B. Yeats. W. H. Auden. ACV; CABA; PoIE; PP; StP
Sels.
"Follow, poet, follow right." TRV
"In the nightmare of the dark." TRV
In Men Whom Men Condemn as Ill. Joaquin Miller. *Fr.* Byron. PoLF
In Merioneth, over the sad moor. Dead. Lionel Johnson. OBNC
In merry Scotland, in merry Scotland. Henry Martyn. *Unknown.* CBEP
In Mill o' Tiftie there lived a man. Andrew Lammie. *Unknown.* BSNS
In Mississippi cold lilies. Telegram. William J. Margolis. PtTo
In Moses' hand 'twas but a rod. What Is That in Thine Hand? Eva Gray. STF
In Mourning. Abu-l-Hasan al Husri, *tr. fr. Arabic by* Lysander Kemp. AnML
In moving-slow he has no peer. The Sloth. Theodore Roethke. PoPo
In my cave lives a solitary rat. Chez-Nous. A. G. Austin. PoAu-2

In my childhood rumours ran. Mermaid, Dragon, Fiend. Robert Graves. AnMoPo
In My Craft or Sullen Art. Dylan Thomas. AnMoPo; CaFP; DiPo; GTBS-P; ILP; PoSa; PP
In my dark hermitage, aloof. Stormcock in Elder. Ruth Pitter. BoC
In My Dream I Saw a Woman. Friedrich von Hausen, tr. fr. German by Margaret F. Richey. AnML
In my ear their words are ringing. The Last Goodbye. John A. Stone. SGR
In My New Clothing. Basho, tr. fr. Japanese. SoPo
In My Own Album. Charles Lamb. CBEP
In My Place. Esther Archibald. STF
In Nakedness. Marnie Pomeroy. ErPo
In need of time, I thought that I. New Technique. Richard Armour. PoPo
In Nets of Golden Wires. Unknown. EnRePo
In New South Wales, as I plainly see. William Forster. Fr. The Devil and the Governor. PoAu-1
In night, when colors all to black are cast. Caelica, C. Fulke Greville. EnRePo
In 1945, when the keepers cried kaput. The Gift. John Ciardi. MP
In nineteen-thirty-four I spent July. 1934. Donald Hall. PoPl
In No Strange Land. Francis Thompson. See Kingdom of God, The.
In No Way Can a Prisoner Reveal. Richard the Lion-hearted, tr. fr. French by Patricia Terry. AnML
In November. Archibald Lampman. OBCV
In November, in the days to remember the dead. St. Malachy. Thomas Merton. CoPo
In October, Figuring Up Your Share. Folgore da San Geminiano, tr. fr. Italian by Joy Gould. Fr. Sonnets of the Months. AnML
In Oklahoma. Life Is Motion. Wallace Stevens. AmLP; SD
In old good days a mode of loving reigned. Aux bon vieulx temps. Clément Marot. RBL
In one moment. Dino Campana. Fr. Two Lyrics for S. A. CoIP
In Orange, tree-plague has struck the mile-long groves, greased. Orange County Plague: Scenes. Laurence Lieberman. CoPo
In order to remove us. Song XVIII. Alfonso X, King of Castile and Leon. AnML
In our country, in our country. The Merry Hay-Makers; or, Pleasant Pastime between the Young-Men and Maids, in the Pleasant Meadows. Unknown. ErPo
In our old shipwrecked days there was an hour. Modern Love, XVI. George Meredith. VP
In Oxford town the faggots they piled. Latimer's Light. Unknown. TRV
"In Paris, at the Louvre, there have I seen." Modern Love, XXXIII. George Meredith. VP
In part these nightly terrors to dispel. Moonlight . . . Scattered Clouds. Robert Bloomfield. Fr. The Farmer's Boy. OBNC
In "pastures green"? Not always; sometimes He. On the Twenty-third Psalm. Unknown. TRV
In Paths Untrodden. Walt Whitman. AP
In Piam Memoriam. Geoffrey Hill. NePoEA-2
In pious times, e'r priest-craft did begin. Absalom and Achitophel, Pt. I. Dryden. CABL
In pity for man's darkening thought. Two Songs from a Play. II. W. B. Yeats. Fr. The Resurrection. CABA; FoBA; ILP; PoDB; PoIE
In Place of a Curse. John Ciardi. CaFP; ToPo
In placid hours well-pleased we dream. Art. Herman Melville. AP; PoIE
In Plymouth Town there lived a maid. A-Roving. Unknown. UnTE
In Portly town there lived a merchant. The Bramble Brier. Unknown. BSO
In Praise of a Gentlewoman. George Gascoigne. EnRePo
In Praise of Cocoa, Cupid's Nightcap. Stanley J. Sharpless. ErPo
In Praise of Dust. Rachel Field. RePo
In Praise of Ivy. Unknown. EnRePo
In Praise of Limestone. W. H. Auden. CABA; PoIE
In Praise of Mary. Unknown. MeEL
In Praise of Music in Time of Pestilence. Daryl Hine. OBCV
In Praise of Neptune. Thomas Campion. CBEP; WiR
In Praise of the Sun. "A. W." CTC
In Prison. William Morris. CBEP
In Procession. Robert Graves. MP
In rain or shine; in heat or snow. Pushcart Row. Rachel Field. SoPo
In Rainy-gloomy Weather. John Davies of Hereford. CBEP
In Reading gaol by Reading town. Oscar Wilde. Fr. The Ballad of Reading Gaol. PoPl
In rigorous hours, when down the iron lane. Winter. Robert Louis Stevenson. ACV; WePo
In Romney Marsh. John Davidson. HaSV

In sad despair I wandered, my heart was filled with woe. The Fellow That Looks like Me. Unknown. BSNS
In Salem seasick spindrift drifts or skips. Salem. Robert Lowell. CABA; PoPo; ToPo
In Santa Maria del Popolo. Thom Gunn. GTBS-P; NePoEA-2; PoIE
In Scarlet town, where I was born. Barbara Allan [or Bonny Barbara Allen]. Unknown. BFSS; BSO (C and D vers.); DiPo
In School Days. Whittier. PoPl; SIV
In search of what and where, behind whose tombs. The Line of Life. James Sexton Layton. PoNC
In secreit place, this hindir nicht. The Man of Valour to His Fair Lady. William Dunbar. MeEL
In secret place where once I stood. The Flesh and the Spirit. Anne Bradstreet. AP
In seventeen hundred and ninety-four. The Greenland Fishery. Unknown. HaSV
In shades we live, in shades we die. Amanda's Complaint. Philip Freneau. AP
In shards the sylvan vases lie. The Ravaged Villa. Herman Melville. AP; CTC
In short, all men betray us women. Jean de Meun. Fr. The Romance of the Rose. AnML
In Siberia's wastes. Siberia. James Clarence Mangan. RoGo
In silent night, when rest I took. Some Verses upon the Burning of Our House, July 10th, 1666. Anne Bradstreet. AP
In smoky outhouses of the court of love. In the Queen's Room. Norman Cameron. Fr. Three Love Poems. GTBS-P
In some unused lagoon, some nameless bay. The Dismantled Ship. Walt Whitman. CABA; CBEP
In speaking of a person's faults. Be Careful What You Say. Joseph Kronthal. STF
In spite of all the learned have said. The Indian Burying Ground. Philip Freneau. AP; CBEP; PoIE; PoLF; PoPl; StP; ThLM
In spite of all the solemn-hearted fools. The Joy of Love. Allan Dowling. ErPo
In spite of cold and chills. Daffodils. Unknown. SoPo
In spite of her sniffle. The Sniffle. Ogden Nash. RePo; WePo
In spite of purple sky, moonless. The Night Refuses a Dreamer. Grant Code. FiSC
In Spite of Sorrow. Adoniram Judson. TRV
In Spring. Eduard Mörike, tr. fr. German by Vernon Watkins. SiGo
In Spring in Warm Weather. Dorothy Aldis. BiCB
In Springfield mountains there did dwell. Springfield Mountain (C vers.). Unknown. BSO
In stature, the Manlet was dwarfish. The Manlet. "Lewis Carroll." Par
In Story-town where I did live. Barbara Ellen (A vers.). Unknown. BSO
In summer when the hills are blond. January. Geoffrey Dutton. PoAu-2
In summer when the woods be bright. Robin Hood and Guy of Gisborne. Unknown. BuBa
In Summer's Heat. Ovid, tr. fr. Latin by Christopher Marlowe. Fr. Amores, I. UnTE
(Elegy to His Mistress.) ErPo
In summer's mellow midnight. The Night-Wind. Emily Brontë. PoSa; RoGo
In summertime on Bredon. Bredon Hill. A. E. Housman. A Shropshire Lad, XXI. VP
In sunburnt parks where Sundays lie. Cobb Would Have Caught It. Robert Fitzgerald. MP; SD
In Sweet Communion. John Newton. TRV
In tender youth a red, red rose didst seem. To Lucrezia d'Este. Tasso. RBL
In Tenebris, sel. Thomas Hardy.
"Wintertime nighs," I. PoDB
In that ancient beechwood alongside the Ouse. The Treasure. Sydney Middleton Clarke. HaSV
In that building, long and low. The Ropewalk. Longfellow. AP
In that final rage I saw my hair turn white. Metamorphosis. Eli Mandel. ACV
In that November off Tehuantepec. Sea Surface Full of Clouds. Wallace Stevens. AP
In that rest made green by window shades. Afternoon for a Small Boy. Bink Noll. ToPo
In that so sudden summer storm they tried. Summer Storm. Louis Simpson. ErPo
In the Age of Gold. Children of a Future Age. Blake. CBEP
In the American dream it is customarily deleted. The Bush on Mount Venus. Donald Finkel. CoPo
In the April of my age I was living free. Maurice Scève. Fr. Délie. RBL
In the Barnyard. Dorothy Aldis. RePo
In the Bazaars of Hyderabad. Sarojini Naidu. RePo
In the Beginning. Daniel G. Hoffman. PP
In the Beginning. Dylan Thomas. MoRP
In the beginning, at every step, he turned. The Sickness of Adam. Karl Shapiro. Fr. Adam and Eve. AP

In the Beginning Was the. Lee Murchison. SD
In the beginning was the three-pointed star. In the Beginning. Dylan Thomas. MoRP
In the beginning was the Word, and the Word was with God, and the Word was God. St. John, Bible, *N.T.* BoC
In the Beginninging. William D. Barney. FiSC
In the Bleak Mid-Winter. Christina Rossetti. *See* Christmas Carol, A: "In the bleak mid-winter."
In the blossom-land Japan. An Old Song. "Yehoash." SiGo
In the blue hubbub of the same-through-wealth sky. Geography. Kenneth Koch. AmPC
In the Book of My Thought. Charles d'Orléans, tr. fr. French by Muriel Kittel. AnML
In the breeze a humming tune. July. Theodor Storm. AGP
In the burgeoning age of Arnaut when for God and man to be. A Fit of Something against Something. Alan Ansen. PP
In the castle of my soul. Walter Rauschenbusch. *Fr.* The Postern Gate. TRV
In the Churchyard. Eleanor Ross Taylor. PoNC
In the Churchyard at Cambridge. Longfellow. AP
In the Cities. D. H. Lawrence. WePo
In the City. Humbert Wolfe. BoC
In the city of memorials. In Arlington Cemetery. Stanley Koehler. OPP
In the Clear Cold. Sergei Yesenin, tr. fr. *Russian by* Babette Deutsch. SiGo
In the close covert of a grove. The Geranium. Sheridan. ErPo; UnTE
In the College of Surgeons. James Stephens. LOW
In the Congo. Vachel Lindsay. *Fr.* The Congo. WePo
In the courtyard grows a rare tree. A Rare Tree. *Unknown. Fr.* Nineteen Han Poems. SiGo
In the cowslip pips I lie. Clock-a-Clay. John Clare. CBEP; OBNC
In the daisied lap of summer. The Season's Lovers. Miriam Waddington. OBCV
In the dark night where none could ever spy. Wasted Night. *Unknown.* UnTE
In the Dark None Dainty. Robert Herrick. CBEP
In the dark pine-wood. James Joyce. *Fr.* Chamber Music. BoLP
In the Dark What the Day Doth Forbid. Thomas Campion. UnTE
In the dawn of breaking day. With Him. Julia E. Martin. STF
In the Days of Rin-Tin-Tin. Daniel Hoffman. CoPo
In the Days When the Cattle Ran. Hamlin Garland. RePo
In the dead park a bench sprawls drunkenly. End of the Season on a Stormy Day—Oban. Iain Crichton Smith. NePoEA-2
In the deep kingdom under ground. Under Ground. James Reeves. RePo
In the Deep Museum. Anne Sexton. ToPo
In the desert. The Black Riders, III. Stephen Crane. AP
In the deserted moon-blanch'd street. A Summer Night. Matthew Arnold. CBEP; VP
In the downhill of life, when I find I'm declining. Tomorrow. John Collins. GTBS-P
In the dream, in the charmed dream we are flying. The Eye of Humility. Kay Smith. OBCV
In the drifting rain the cows in the yard are as black. Milking before Dawn. Ruth Dallas. ACV
In the drinking-well. Aunt Eliza. Harry Graham. LV
In the Dying of Daylight. Walter de la Mare. ACV
In the early mornings. May Song. Lope de Vega. AnSP
In the environs of the funeral home. The Funeral Home. Robert Mezey. AmPC
In the evening, just before. For Mary. Kenneth Rexroth. PoPl
In the evening we came back. A Light Left On. May Sarton. MoLP
In the Fair Times of New-born Spring. William IX, Count of Poitiers, tr. fr. *Provençal by* Thomas G. Bergin. AnML
In the family drinking well. Sister Nell. *Unknown.* BBGG
In the far corner. The Blackbird. Humbert Wolfe. GoJo; RePo
In the Fashion. A. A. Milne. RePo
In the first year of the last disgrace. News of the World II. George Barker. DTC
In the fleece of your flesh. The Moment before Conception. Eve Merriam. UnTE
In the Garden at Swainston. Tennyson. OBNC
In the Garden of the Lord. Helen Keller. LV; TRV
In the glow of early morning. Christ Is Coming. W. Macomber. STF
In the good old colony times. The Three Rogues (B *vers.*). *Unknown.* BSO
In the Gorge. W. S. Merwin. AmPC
In the Grass. Annette von Droste-Hülshoff, tr. fr. *German by* S. G. Flygt. AGP
In the Green Grass. Pero Meogo, tr. fr. *Portuguese by* William M. Davis. AnML
In the green light of water, like the day. The Swans. Edith Sitwell. ACV

In the greenest of our valleys. The Haunted Palace. Poe. AmLP; AP; WiR
In the grey wastes of dread. Horses on the Camargue. Roy Campbell. BoC; DaDu; GTBS-P
In the Half Light of Holding and Giving. John Wieners. CoPo
In the Headlights. Charles Edward Eaton. PoNC
In the Heart of a Seed. Kate L. Brown. RePo
In the Heart of Contemplation. C. Day Lewis. MP
In the Highlands. Robert Louis Stevenson. ACV; FaBV
In the Highlands of Scotland there lived a young man. The Blaeberry Courtship (B *vers.*). *Unknown.* BSNS
In the Holy Nativity of Our Lord God, a Hymn Sung as by the Shepherds. Richard Crashaw. CABA
(Hymne of the Nativity, Sung as by the Shepheards, An.) MeP
Shepherd's Hymn, The, *sel.* BoC
In the hot valley of the never was. The Last Campaign. Geoffrey Lehmann. PoAu-2
In the hour of my distress. His Litany to the Holy Spirit. Robert Herrick. DTC; ELP; PoLF
In the house I have a cat. The Dog and the Cat. Grace Taber Hallock. RePo
In the Immense Cathedral. John Hall Wheelock. *Fr.* The Holy Earth. MoRP
In the inn they had no room. Easter, Day of Christ Eternal. Maurice Moore. STF
In the Interstices. Ruth Stone. ErPo
In the Isle of Dogs. John Davidson. OBNC
In the kitchen of the old house, late. In the Old House. Donald Hall. NePoEA-2
In the Library. Elizabeth Brewster. OBCV
In the light beneath the leafage. A Shot in the Park. William Plomer. MP
In the lonely hours of the spirit. Helian. Georg Trakl. MGP
In the lonesome latter years. The Promissory Note. Bayard Taylor. Par
In the long, sleepless watches of the night. The Cross of Snow. Longfellow. AP; FaPL
In the lower lands of day. Before Sunset. Swinburne. StP
In the Lupanar at Pompeii. James Dickey. ToPo
In the Margin of the Text. Gene Frumkin. PtTo
In the May evening. The Old Ones. Frances Bellerby. DaDu
In the Merry Month of May. Nicholas Breton. *Fr.* The Honourable Entertainment Given to the Queen's Majesty in Progress at Elvetham, 1591. PoSa
(Phillida and Coridon.) UnTE
In the mid-city, under an oiled sky. A Garden in Chicago. Karl Shapiro. PoIE
In the moment of his glory. Lincoln Slain. Edwin Markham. LiPo
In the month of June the grass grows high. Reading the Book of Hills and Seas. T'ao Ch'ien. SiGo
In the Moonlight. Norreys Jephson O'Conor. SoPo
In the Moonlight. Kenneth Patchen. ToPo
"In the moonlight evening." By Moonlight. *Unknown.* UnTE
In the moral world, too, there's nobility. Common natures. Class Distinction. Schiller. TwGP
In the morning. A. E. Housman. WePo
In the morning air, the freighter *Havskar*. At the Brooklyn Docks. Dorothy Gilbert. OPP
In the morning, in the dark. The Night Hunt. Thomas MacDonagh. RoGo
In the morning, in the morning. In the Morning. A. E. Housman. WePo
In the mountains. The Guests. Louis Zukofsky. CoPo
In the Mountains on a Summer Day. Li Po, tr. fr. *Chinese by* Arthur Waley. SD
In the mustardseed sun. Poem on His Birthday. Dylan Thomas. DiPo
In the Naked Bed, in Plato's Cave. Delmore Schwartz. ILP; PoDB
In the nativity of time. Love Made in the First Age. Richard Lovelace. SeCP
In the Night. Elizabeth Jennings. MP
In the night. War Is Kind, XVIII. Stephen Crane. AP
In the Night Fields. W. S. Merwin. AP; PoCh
In the nightmare of the dark. W. H. Auden. *Fr.* In Memory of W. B. Yeats. TRV
In the old age black was not counted fair. Sonnets, CXXVII. Shakespeare. CBEP; DiPo
In the old days (a custom laid aside). Abraham Davenport. Whittier. SIV
In the old days with married women's stockings. The Libertine. Louis MacNeice. DTC
In the Old House. Donald Hall. NePoEA-2
In the olive darkness of the sally-trees. The Bull. Judith Wright. PoAu-2
In the Orchard. James Stephens. LOW; RoGo
In the Orchard. Muriel Stuart. ErPo
In the Orchard. *Unknown, tr. fr. Provençal by* Swinburne. UnTE

In the orchestra the fixed stars. Round Dance, & Canticle. Robert Kelly. CoPo
In the pages of the past. Africa Speaks. Michael Dei-Anang. ACV
In the pale summertime, when far above you. Of Swimming in Lakes and Rivers. Bertolt Brecht. SD
In the park I saw a stranger. Interrupted Romance. Unknown. UnTE
In the Person of Woman Kind. Ben Jonson. SeCP
In the pure soul, although it sing or pray. Eternal Christmas. Elizabeth Stuart Phelps. TRV
In the purple light, heavy with redwood, the slopes drop seaward. Apology for Bad Dreams. Robinson Jeffers. AP; ILP
In the Queen's Room. Norman Cameron. Fr. Three Love Poems. GTBS-P
In the queer light, in twilight. The Young Man in April. Rupert Brooke. BoLP
In the Redwood Forest. Ralph Pomeroy. CoPo
In the reproof of chance. Shakespeare. Fr. Troilus and Cressida. HaSV
In the sea wave tosses side by side with wave. Muhammad Iqbal. Fr. An Invocation. ACV
In the season of Spring is the season of growing. In the Spring. Ibycus. SiGo
In the Seraglio. David R. Slavitt. ErPo
In the Servants' Quarters. Thomas Hardy. MoRP
In the shadow of Old South Church the turn of spring is. A Foreigner Comes to Earth on Boston Common. Horace Gregory. EaLo
In the shape of this night, in the still fall of snow, Father. At the New Year. Kenneth Patchen. ToPo
In the Shelter. C. Day Lewis. BoC
In the shop they've been put. Cassel (Carps at Wilhelmstrasse 15). "Joachim Ringelnatz." MGP
In the silence that prolongs the span. Black Jackets. Thom Gunn. MP
In the Sistina ("In the Sistina's twilit vaulted land"). Conrad Ferdinand Meyer, tr. fr. German by Walter Kaufmann. TwGP
In the Smoking-Car. Richard Wilbur. ToPo
In the soft dark night. Fireflies. Aileen Fisher. SoPo
In the sorrow and the terror of the nations. The Mother. Nettie Palmer. PoAu-1
In the South be drooping trees. Confucius. Fr. The Classic Anthology: Chou and the South. CTC
In the Sprightly Month of May. Sir John Vanbrugh. Fr. Aesop. UnTE
In the Spring. Ibycus, tr. fr. Greek by Walter Headlam. SiGo
In the Spring. Meleager, tr. fr. Greek by Andrew Lang. SiGo
In the spring, in the morning. Herding Lambs. Ruth Pitter. DaDu
In the spring of the year, in the spring of the year. The Spring and the Fall. Edna St. Vincent Millay. BoLP
In the Stoneworks. John Ciardi. PoDB
In the Study. Thomas Hardy. Fr. Satires of Circumstance. PoPo
In the summer palace the fireflies have lost their way. Ninth Moon. Li Ho. SiGo
In the sweet shire of Cardigan. Simon Lee the Old Huntsman. Wordsworth. GTBS-P
In the sweet sunny south there was peace and content. The Sunny South. Unknown. BSNS
In the third month, a sudden flow of blood. The Vow. Anthony Hecht. PoCh
In the time of old sin without sadness. Variations of an Air: After Swinburne. G. K. Chesterton. Par
In the time of wild roses. Bab-Lock-Hythe. Laurence Binyon. SD; WePo
In the time when swan and swan. Waratah. Roland Robinson. PoAu-1
In the town of Waxford I used to live and dwell. The Waxford Girl. Unknown. BSO
In the town up river. Song of the Rice Bargees. Bertolt Brecht. MGP
In the Tree House at Night. James Dickey. ToPo
In the Trench. Leon Gellert. PoAu-1
In the Trenches. Richard Aldington. MMA
In the Tube. Richard Aldington. WePo
In the Valley of the Elwy. Gerard Manley Hopkins. PoIE
In the vegetarian guest-house. The Flying Bum: 1944. William Plomer. DTC
In the ventless room. Hospice of the Word. Brother Antoninus. ToPo
In the village churchyard she lies. In the Churchyard at Cambridge. Longfellow. AP
In the village of the dead. Hunting. Gary Snyder. CoPo
In the White Giant's Thigh. Dylan Thomas. ToPo
In the wild October night-time, when the wind raved round the land. The Night of Trafalgar. Thomas Hardy. Fr. The Dynasts. HaSV

In the Wilderness. Robert Graves. BoC; EaLo
In the winter, in the winter. The Organ Grinders' Garden. Mildred Plew Merryman. SoPo
In the winter time we go. White Fields. James Stephens. PoSC; SoPo
In the Woods. Frederick George Scott. ACV
In the Woods Alone. Unknown, tr. fr. Latin by Helen Waddell. SiGo
In the wracks of Walsingham. Lament for Walsingham. Unknown. CBEP
In the year that king Uzziah died, I saw also the Lord. Isaiah's Angels. Isaiah, Bible, O.T. BoC
In these days of indigestion. Some Little Bug. Roy Atwell. PoLF
In these Fair Vales. Wordsworth. CBEP
In Thine Arms. Oliver Wendell Holmes. TRV
In Thine Own Heart. "Angelus Silesius," tr. fr. German. TRV
In 'thirty-nine, in Poland. Children's Crusade 1939. Bertolt Brecht. MoBS
In this brown husk a dale of hawthorn dreams. Seeds. Muriel Stuart. BoC
In this country the lightning makes stone spring up and grow. The Mineral Kingdom. Jacques Dupin. CoFP
In this fair stranger's eyes of grey. Absence. Matthew Arnold. Switzerland, VI. CBEP; VP
In this glass palace are flowers in golden baskets. The Lovers. Conrad Aiken. AP
In this green month when resurrected flowers. Memorial Wreath. Dudley Randall. NNP
In This Hour. Josephine W. Johnson. MoRP
In This Strange House. Carleton Drewry. MoRP
In this the hour of new reckonings! This Hour. Oliver La Grone. NNP
In this unpeopled shady valley. To Corinna. Théophile de Viau. RBL
In this world, the Isle of Dreams. The White Island. Robert Herrick. WiR
In This World's Raging Sea. William Drummond of Hawthornden. CBEP
In those sad words I took farewell. In Memoriam A. H. H., LVIII. Tennyson. VP
In thronged procession gliding slow. The Logs. Sir Charles G. D. Roberts. ACV
In Time like Air. May Sarton. MoLP
In Time like Glass. W. J. Turner. ILP
In Time of Crisis. Raymond Patterson. PtTo
In Time of Daffodils. E. E. Cummings. PoDB
In Time of Darkness. Raymond Roseliep. FiSC
In Time of Pestilence 1593. Thomas Nashe. See Adieu, Farewell, Earth's Bliss.
In Time of Plague. Thomas Nashe. See Adieu, Farewell, Earth's Bliss.
In Time of Silver Rain. Langston Hughes. SoPo
In Time of "The Breaking of Nations." Thomas Hardy. CaFP; ILP; MMA; MoRP; PoPo; PoSa; VP
In Time of War, sel. W. H. Auden. PoPl
"He turned his field into a meeting-place." In time of yore when shepherds dwelt. Olden Love-making. Nicholas Breton. DiPo
In time the strong and stately turrets fall. Licia, XXVIII. Giles Fletcher. ILP
Time's concatenation and/ Carnal conventicle. Mortmain. Robert Penn Warren. PoCh
In times of old, when time was young. Vanbrug's House. Swift. PP
In tottering row, like shadows, silently. By the Sea. Richard Watson Dixon. OBNC
In Town. David McKee Wright. ACV
In towns like ours where fifty years are just. The Yellow Cat. Leslie Nelson Jennings. FiSC
In unexperienc'd infancy. Shadows in the Water. Thomas Traherne. SeCP
In Utrumque Paratus. Matthew Arnold. OBNC
In vain to me the smiling mornings shine. Sonnet on the Death of [Mr.] Richard West. Thomas Gray. EiCP; EnPE; StP
In vain with mimic skill my pencil tries. On an Unsuccessful Attempt to Draw Lord Boyle's Picture. Elizabeth Rowe. WaPE
In vaine faire sorceresse, thy eyes speake charmes. To a Wanton. William Habington. SeCP
In Virgine [or Virgyne] the sweltry [or sweltrie] sun 'gan sheene. An Excelente Balade of Charitie. Thomas Chatterton. EnPE; StP
In Vitam Humanam. Francis Bacon. See Life.
In Waste Places. James Stephens. CaFP
In Westminster Abbey. John Betjeman. CaFP; ILP
In what order or what degree. Be True to Your Condition in Life. John Audelay. MeEL
In What Region, in What Part of the World? Gutierre de Cetina, tr. fr. Spanish by Kate Flores. AnSP
In what torn[e] ship soever I embark[e]. A Hymn [or

Hymne] to Christ, at the Author's Last Going into Germany. John Donne. DiPo; EnRePo; FoBA; MeP

In where the smoke runs black against the snow. Spring Offensive, 1941. Maurice Biggs. PoAu-2

In Whose Will Is Our Peace? J. V. Cunningham. PoIE

In Winter. Zoe Kincaid Brockman. *Fr.* Three Cinquains. PoNC

In winter I get up at night. Bed in Summer. Robert Louis Stevenson. GoJo; LV; PoPl

In winter in my room. Emily Dickinson. AP; ErPo

In winter my loved one retires. Fog Land. Ingeborg Bachmann. MGP

In winter, when it's cold out. Baseball Note. Franklin P. Adams. SD

In winter when people pay a call. Visitors. Harry Behn. SoPo

In winter, when the fields are white. Humpty Dumpty's Song. "Lewis Carroll." *Fr.* Through the Looking-Glass. GTBS-P; OnMSP

In wonderment I walk to music pouring. Undersong. Mark Van Doren. PoCh

In Wonted Walks. Sir Philip Sidney. CABA

In Xanadu did Kubla Khan. Kubla Khan. Samuel Taylor Coleridge. BoC; CABA; CaFP; CBEP; DiPo; ELP; FaBV; FaPL; GoJo; ILP; OBNC; OnP; PoIE; PoPl; PP; RoGo; StP

In yonder grave a Druid lies. Ode on the Death of Mr. Thomson. William Collins. CBEP; FiCP

In yonder isle beyond Argyle. Sir Neil and Glengyle. *Unknown.* BSNS

In Your Arrogance. Lynne Lawner. ErPo

In your daily round of duties. The Golden Rule. James Wells. STF

In your next letter I wish you'd say. Letter to N.Y. Elizabeth Bishop. MP

In your silk robe I hate to see you clad. I Hate to See You Clad. Paul Verlaine. UnTE

In youth, gay scenes attract our eyes. The Vanity of Existence. Philip Freneau. AP

In youth I served my time. Retirement. *Unknown.* ErPo

In Youth Is Pleasure. Robert Wever. *See* In an Arbour Green.

In zummer, leäte at evenen tide. The Rwose in the Dark. William Barnes. CBEP

Inauguration Day: January 1953. Robert Lowell. ToPo

Inbound. Burnham Eaton. FiSC

Inca had three arrows in his hand, The. The Inca's Arrows. Manuel González Prada. AnSP

Incarnate Devil. Dylan Thomas. ToPo

Incarnate One, The. Edwin Muir. PoDB; PoIE

Inca's Arrows, The. Manuel González Prada, *tr. fr. Spanish by* Kate Flores. AnSP

Incense. Vachel Lindsay. MoRP

Incentive, The. Martial, *tr. fr. Latin by* Louis Untermeyer. UnTE

Incident, An. Douglas Le Pan. ACV

Incident of the French Camp, An. Robert Browning. PoPo; RoGo

Incidents in Playfair House. Nicholas Moore. ErPo

Inclusions. Elizabeth Barrett Browning. UnTE

Incomparable Light, The. Richard Eberhart. MoRP

Inconsistent. Mark Van Doren. BoLP

Incubus of Time, The. Clark Ashton Smith. FiSC

Independence. Nancy Cato. PoAu-2

Independence Bell. *Unknown.* SIV

Independence Day. William Jay Smith. MP

Independent, The. Phyllis McGinley. *Fr.* Epitaphs for Three Prominent Persons. LV

Indestructible, The, *sel.* George Hitchcock. "Manila! City of wounds!" PtTo

Indestructible, The. To Goethe. Nietzsche. TwGP

Index (8). Gil Orlovitz. ToPo

Indian Burying Ground, The. Philip Freneau. AP; CBEP; PoIE; PoLF; PoPl; StP; ThLM

Indian Children. Annette Wynne. SoPo

Indian Emperor, The, *sel.* Dryden. Spanish Galleons Seen by an Aztec, The, *fr.* I. ii. HaSV

Indian Mohee, The. *with music. Unknown.* BFSS (Indian Lass, The. *diff. vers.*). BSNS (Lass of Mohee, The.) BSNS

Indian Names. Lydia Huntley Sigourney. PoLF; RePo

Indian Prayer. Chief Joseph Strongwolf. TRV

Indian Queen, The, *sel.* Sir Robert Howard *and* John Dryden. Poor Mortals. PoIE

Indian Reservation: Caughnawaga. A. M. Klein. OBCV

Indian Serenade. Shelley. BoLP; FaPL; PoPl; UnTE (Lines to an Indian Air.) GTBS-P

Indian Summer. Wilfred Campbell. OBCV; PoPl

Indian Summer Day on the Prairie, An. Vachel Lindsay. SoPo

Indiana: no blustering summit or coarse gorge. Midwest. John Frederick Nims. PoPl

Indians. John Fandel. RePo

Indications and tally of time, The. Walt Whitman. *Fr.* Song of the Answerer. PP

Indifference. G. A. Studdert-Kennedy. TRV

Indifferent, The. John Donne. CABA; DiPo; UnTE

Indignant Protest. *Unknown, tr. fr. Greek by* Louis Untermeyer. UnTE

Indignation of Taliesin, The. Thomas Love Peacock. CBEP

Indolence of soft feathers, The. Maurice Scève. *Fr.* Délie. RBL

Indolent wind on the prairie. Prairie Wind. Duncan Campbell Scott. ACV

Ineffertile Lea, The. Hans Arp, *tr. fr. German by* Christopher Middleton. MGP

Infant Innocence. A. E. Housman. DTC; LV; PoPo

Infant Joy. Blake. *Fr.* Songs of Innocence. BiCB; CBEP; FoBA; GoJo; PoLF

Infant Sorrow. Blake. *Fr.* Songs of Experience. CBEP; DiPo; FoBA; OBNC

Infatuated. *Unknown, tr. fr. Greek by* Louis Untermeyer. UnTE

Infinite, The. Giacomo Leopardi, *tr. fr. Italian by* Kenneth Rexroth. SiGo

Infinite consanguinity it bears. Hart Crane. *Fr.* Voyages. PoIE

Infinite power essenciall, The. Mary, Queen of Heaven. *Unknown.* MeEL

Infinity, when all things it beheld. The Preface. Edward Taylor. *Fr.* Gods Determinations. AmLP; AP; ILP

Influence. John Oxenham. STF

Ingoldsby Legends, The, *sel.* "Thomas Ingoldsby." Jackdaw of Rheims, The. OnMSP

Ingratefull Beauty Threatned. Thomas Carew. SeCP

Inherited Estate, The. Thom Gunn. ToPo

Inhuman Henry; or, Cruelty to Fabulous Animals. A. E. Housman. BBGG

Initial. Arthur Boyars. NePoEA-2

Injury, The. William Carlos Williams. AP

Inland Sea, The. Howard Sergeant. ToPo

Inner Man, The. Plato, *tr. fr. Greek.* PoPl

Inner Temple Masque, The, *sel.* William Browne. Siren's Song, The. HaSV

Inner Vision, The. Wordsworth. GTBS-P

Innocence. Thom Gunn. NePoEA-2; ToPo

Innocence. Thomas Traherne. MeP

Innocent country girl going to town, An. Advice to Country Girls. *Unknown.* UnTE

Innocents, The. Jay Macpherson. OBCV

Innocent's Song. Charles Causley. DaDu; GTBS-P

Innumerable Christ, The. "Hugh MacDiarmid." EaLo

Inordinate Love. *Unknown.* MeEL

Inquest, The. W. H. Davies. CBEP; DTC; GTBS-P

Insatiableness. Thomas Traherne. VaPo

Insatiate, The. Johannes Secundus, *tr. fr. Latin by* John Nott. *Fr.* Basia. UnTE

Inscription: "Ye powers unseen, to whom the bards of Greece." Mark Akenside. CBEP

Inscription for an Old Bed. William Morris. WiR

Inscription for the Ceiling of a Bedroom. Dorothy Parker. LV

Inscription: For the Door of the Cell in Newgate Where Mrs. Brownrigg, the 'Prentice-Cide, Was Confined Previous to Her Execution. George Canning *and* John Hookham Frere. Par

Inscription for the Entrance to a Wood. Bryant. AmLP; AP; ILP

Inscription in a Garden. George Gascoigne. CBEP

Inscription on a Chemise. *Unknown, tr. fr. Arabic by* E. Powys Mathers. *Fr.* The Thousand and One Nights. ErPo

Inscriptions on Greek tombstones intrigued him. Ronald Wyn. Robert Bagg. MP

Insensibility. Wilfred Owen. MMA; StP

Inside of King's College Chapel, Cambridge. Wordsworth. *Fr.* Ecclesiastical Sketches. OBNC (Within King's College Chapel, Cambridge.) GTBS-P

Inside that figure rides opaque malice. The Picador Bit. Bink Noll. ToPo

Insidious Dr. Fu Man Chu, The. LeRoi Jones. CoPo

Inspector of stairs is on the stairs, The. The. Walk-up. W. S. Merwin. CoPo

Inspiration. Mary Fullerton. PoAu-1

Inspiration. Henry David Thoreau. AP

Instance, An. Alastair Reid. PP

Instantaneous ("Instantaneously!"). Vivian Ayers. NNP

Instead of an Elegy. G. S. Fraser. OPP

Instead of being sad and hurt. Forbearance. Della Adams. Leitner. STF

Instead of swinging from a beam. Avery Anameer. Joseph Payne Brennan. FiSC

Instruction in the Art. Philip Booth. SD

Instruments, The. Dryden. *Fr.* Song for St. Cecilia's Day. PoPo

Instruments, The. Christopher Smart. WiR

Insufficient Vengeance. Martial, *tr. fr. Latin by* Louis Untermeyer. UnTE

Intaglio. Henri Coulette. PoCh
Integer Vitae. Thomas Campion. *See* Man of Life Upright, The.
Intercessor, An. *Unknown.* STF
Interests of a black man in a cellar, The. Black Tambourine. Hart Crane. AP; CBEP
Interior. Padraic Colum. ACV
Interior. Phillippe Jaccottet, *tr. fr. French by* David Pryce-Jones. CoFP
Interlude. Walter Savage Landor. GTBS-P
Interlude: The Casement. Christopher Brennan. PoAu-1
Internal Cerberus! whose griping fangs. Conscience. Giambattista Marino. RBL
International Hymn. George Huntington. PoLF
Interpreters, The. D. J. Enright. PP
Interred beneath this marble stone. An Epitaph. Matthew Prior. EiCP; PoIE
Interrogativa Cantilena. *Unknown. See* If All the World Were Paper.
Interrogative. Sister M. Thérèse. MoRP
Interrupted Romance. *Unknown, tr. fr. Russian by* Louis Untermeyer. UnTE
Interview near Florence, An. Samuel Rogers. *Fr.* Italy. OBNC
Intimate. "Gabriela Mistral," *tr. fr. Spanish by* Kate Flores. AnSP
Intimate Party in Guadalajara, Dec. 1963. Anthony Ostroff. OPP
Intimations of Sublimity. Wordsworth. *Fr.* The Prelude. OBNC
Into a little close of mine I went. Canzone. Lorenzo de' Medici. RBL
Into Battle. Julian Grenfell. MMA
Into Her Eyes a Tear Crept. Gustavo Adolfo Bécquer, *tr. fr. Spanish by* Kate Flores. AnSP
Into My Heart. A. E. Housman. A Shropshire Lad, XL. GoJo; PoPo
("Into my heart an air that kills.") EvOK
Into my heart's treasury. The Coin. Sara Teasdale. LV; RePo
Into the big-flaked sugar-snow. Maple Feast. Frances Frost. RePo
Into the Hearth They Are Tossing Logs. Manuel González Prada, *tr. fr. Spanish by* Kate Flores. AnSP
Into the shadow Kunai-mai-pa Mo. Kunai-mai-pa Mo. Ethel Anderson. PoAu-2
Into the temple the gaunt old saint strode, by the Spirit led. The Light in the Temple. William Rose Benét. MoRP
Into the Twilight. W. B. Yeats. PoPo
Into the woods my Master went. A Ballad of Trees and the Master. Sidney Lanier. AP; PoLF; TRV
Into these loves, who but for passion looks. To the Reader of These Sonnets. Michael Drayton. *Fr.* Idea. EnRePo
Introduction: "Hear the voice of the Bard!" Blake. *See* Hear the Voice of the Bard.
Introduction: "Piping down the valleys wild." Blake. *See* Piping down the Valleys Wild.
Intruder, The. Carolyn Kizer. NePoEA-2
Intuition. R. H. Grenville. FiSC
Inundation, The. Howard Sergeant. *Fr.* The Leaves of Europe. ToPo
Invaders, The. Jocelyn Macy Sloan. FiSC
Invariably when wine redeems the sight. The Wine Menagerie. Hart Crane. AP
Inventing funny games for two active three-year-olds. Baby-Sitter Blues. Edith Earnshaw. PoNC
Invention of Comics, The. LeRoi Jones. AmNP
Inventor's Wife, The. Mrs. E. T. Corbett. PoLF
Inventory, The. Burns. CABL
Inventory. Dorothy Parker. PoPo
Inversnaid. Gerard Manley Hopkins. CABA; FoBA; GTBS-P; PoIE
Investment, The. Robert Frost. LV
Investor's Soliloquy. Kenneth Ward. LV
Invictus. W. E. Henley. Echoes, IV. FaBV; FaPl; LV; PoIE; PoPl; PoPo
("Out of the night that covers me.") OBNC
Invisible Atoms of the Air, The. Gustavo Adolfo Bécquer, *tr. fr. Spanish by* Kate Flores. AnSP
(Rima, *tr. by* Harold Morland.) SiGo
Invisible Painter. Alfred Dorn. FiSC
Invitation. Harry Behn. SoPo
Invitation, The. Tom Buchan. ACV
Invitation, The. George Herbert. MeP
Invitation, The. Shelley. GTBS-P
Invitation to a Mistress. *Unknown, tr. fr. Latin by* George F. Whicher. UnTE
Invitation to an Invitation, An. Catullus, *tr. fr. Latin by* Gardner E. Lewis. ErPo
Invitation to the Dance. *Unknown, tr. fr. Latin by* John Addington Symonds. UnTE
Invitation to the Voyage. Baudelaire, *tr. fr. French by* Richard Wilbur. SiGo

Invitation to Youth. *Unknown, tr. fr. Latin by* John Addington Symonds. UnTE
Invite to Eternity, An. John Clare. OBNC
Inviting a Friend to Supper. Ben Jonson. EnRePo; SeCP
Invocation: "Good morning to you, Lord of the world!" Levi Isaac of Berditshev, *tr. fr. Hebrew by* Olga Marx. EaLo
Invocation, An: "In the sea wave tosses side by side with wave," *sel.* Muhammad Iqbal. ACV
Invocation: "Let me be buried in the rain." Helene Johnson. AmNP
Invocation: "O Sleep! I bring thee this long-cellared wine." Phillippe Desportes, *tr. fr. French by* William Frederic Giese. RBL
Invocation: "O world watched over by the cold moon and the mindless stars." Carleton Drewry. MoRP
Invocation: "Of man's first disobedience, and the fruit." Milton. *Fr.* Paradise Lost, I. DiPo
Invocation: "Perfection ever rising to perfection." *Unknown, tr. fr. Sotho by* G. H. Franz. SiGo
Invocation: "Rarely, rarely, comest thou." Shelley. *See* Rarely, Rarely Comest Thou.
Invocation, An: "To God, the everlasting, who abides," *sel.* John Addington Symonds.
"O God, unknown, invisible, secure." TRV
Invocation for the New Year. Margaret D. Armstrong. STF
Invoice, The. Robert Creeley. AmPC
Inward Morning, The. Henry David Thoreau. AP
I'r hen Iaith a'i Chanedon. Walter Dowding. ACV
Ireland ("Ireland never was contented"). Walter Savage Landor. GTBS-P
Ireland with Emily. John Betjeman. GTBS-P
Iris, lilac, lily, milk. Lalique. Hal Porter. PoAu-2
Irish Airman Foresees His Death, An. W. B. Yeats. AnMoPo; CABA; FoBA; GoJo; GTBS-P; ILP; MMA; PoPl; PoPo
Irish Lords. Charles H. Souter. PoAu-1
Iron. Bertolt Brecht, *tr. fr. German by* Michael Hamburger. MGP
Iron-Wind Dances. Lew Sarett. *Fr.* Thunderstorms. LV
Irradiations, *sel.* John Gould Fletcher.
"O seeded grass, you army of little men." PoPo
Irresponsive silence of the land, The. The Thread of Life. Christina Rossetti. OBNC
Irritable Song. Russell Atkins. AmNP
Is a caterpillar ticklish? Only My Opinion. Monica Shannon. SoPo
Is an enchanted thing. The Mind Is an Enchanting Thing. Marianne Moore. AP
"Is anybody there?" said the Traveller. *See* "Is there anybody, there?" said the Traveller.
Is dead. Is dead. How all. Bulletin. Chana Faerstein. OPP
Is 5, *sel.* E. E. Cummings.
"My sweet old etcetera." CABA; PoPl
Is it because that lad is dead. Vision. Frank Sidgwick. MMA
Is it illusion? or does there a spirit from perfecter ages. A Spirit from Perfecter Ages. Arthur Hugh Clough. *Fr.* Amours de Voyage. OBNC
Is it not by his high superfluousness we know/ Our God? The Excesses of God. Robinson Jeffers. MoRP
Is It Not Sure? *Unknown.* CBEP
Is It Possible? Sir Thomas Wyatt. CBEP; ELP; EnRePo
Is it so far from thee. The Chamber over the Gate. Longfellow. AP
It is the hour? We leave this resting place. The Wayfarers. Rupert Brooke. MoLP
Is it, then, regret for buried time. In Memoriam A. H. H., CXVI. Tennyson. FoBA; VP
Is less like that of a bean. The Manner of a Poet's Germination. José Garcia Villa. PP
Is Love a Boy? *Unknown.* EnRePo
Is Memory most of miseries miserable. Memory. Dante Gabriel Rossetti. CBEP
Is My Team Ploughing [*or* Plowing]. A. E. Housman. A Shropshire Lad, XXVII. ILP; PoPo; PoSa; VP; WePo
Is not only my heart, full of fairer life. Men's Applause. Friedrich Hölderlin, *tr. by* Walter Kaufmann. TwGP
Is not my heart hallowed and filled with truer life. The Crowd's Acclaim. Friedrich Hölderlin, *tr. by* Martin Zwart. AGP
Is she not come? The messenger was sure. Tristram and Iseult. Matthew Arnold. VP
"Is Sin, then, fair?" The Sting of Death. Frederick George Scott. OBCV
Is something like the rest. The Politics of Rich Painters. LeRoi Jones. CoPo
Is that dance slowing in the mind of man. Four for Sir John Davies. Theodore Roethke. AP
Is the basketball coach a homosexual lemon manufacturer? Aus einer Kindheit. Kenneth Koch. AmPC
Is there a cause why we should wake the dead? The Yew-Tree. Vernon Watkins. EaLo
Is there a great green commonwealth of Thought. Sonnet. John Masefield. ILP
"Is there anybody, there?" said the Traveller. The Listeners.

Walter de la Mare. CaFP; ILP; OnMSP; OnP; PoPl; PoPo; RePo; SIV
Is there anyone here who has a desire. Poor Diggings. Mart Taylor. SGR
Is there anything else that is better worth. Nothing Better. *Unknown.* STF
Is There for Honest Poverty. Burns. *See* For A' That an' A' That.
Is there some problem in your life to solve. God's Key. *Unknown.* STF
Is this a fast, to keep. To Keep a True Lent. Robert Herrick. TRV
Is this a holy thing to see. Holy Thursday. Blake. *Fr.* Songs of Experience. EnPE; ILP; PoIE; StP
Is this dancing sunlight. Symphony. Frank Horne. AmNP
"Is this Henry, my own true love." Love Henry. *Unknown.* BFSS
Is this to live?—to cower and stand aside. The Eleventh Hour. Francis St. Vincent Morris. TRV
Is your place a small place? Your Place. John Oxenham. TRV
Isabel met an enormous bear. Adventures of Isabel. Ogden Nash. OnMSP
Isabelle. James Hogg. Par
Isaiah, *sels.* Bible, *O.T.*
  Comfort When Work Seems Difficult, XLI: 6-7, 9-10. BoC
  Comfort Ye, Comfort Ye My People, XL: 1-11. EaLo
  Isaiah's Angels, VI: 1-8. BoC
  Perfect Peace, XXVI: 3. TRV
  They That Wait upon the Lord, XL: 28-31. TRV
  ("Hast thou not known? hast thou not heard, that the everlasting God," XL: 28-31, XLIX: 13-16.) BoC
Isaiah of Souillac, The. W. S. Merwin. PoDB
Isaiah, the country-boy, marched against the jazz. Babylon, Babylon, Babylon the Great. Vachel Lindsay. LiPo
Isaiah's Angels. Isaiah, VI: 1-8, Bible, *O.T.* BoC
Island, The. Edwin Muir. PoIE
Island, The. Giuseppe Ungaretti, *tr. fr. Italian by* Lowry Nelson, Jr. CoIP
Island Galaxy, An. John Ciardi. ToPo
Islands. Ralph Pomeroy. CoPo
Islands all around. At Matsushima. Shiki. SiGo
Islands are islands though in the steady sea. Islands. Ralph Pomeroy. CoPo
Isles of Greece, The. Byron. *Fr.* Don Juan, III. CBEP; RoGo
  ("Isles of Greece, the isles of Greece, The.") PoIE
Isles of Greece, The. Demetrios Capetanakis. GTBS-P
Isn't it. Epigram. Alfred Kreymborg. BoLP
Isn't she soft and still? Captive. Marion Strobel. ErPo
"Isn't the violet a dear little flower? And the daisy, too." The Lay Preacher Ponders. Idris Davies. ACV
Isolation: To Marguerite. Matthew Arnold. Switzerland, IV. VP
  (To Marguerite.) CBEP
Israfel. Poe. AP; PoPo
It. Richmond Lattimore. PP
It Always Happens. Horace, *tr. fr. Latin by* Thomas Charles Baring. Odes, I, 33. UnTE
It baffles the foreigner like an idiom. Drug Store. Karl Shapiro. ILP; MP
It Bids Pretty Fair. Robert Frost. CaFP
It brims in the white cistern; flows. A Meditation upon the Toothache. Laurence Lerner. NePoEA-2
It chanced his lips did meet her forehead cool. Modern Love, VI. George Meredith. VP
It chanced of late a shepherd swain. Cupid's Pastime. Francis Davison. UnTE
It Couldn't Be Done. *Unknown.* STF
It dropped so low in my regard. Emily Dickinson. CABA; PoPl
It ended, and the morrow brought the task. Modern Love, II. George Meredith. ILP; VP
It falls, the peony. The Red Peony. Buson. RePo
It fell about the Lammas tide. The Battle of Otterburn. *Unknown.* OnMSP
It fell about the Martinmas day/ When the green leaves were falling. Barbara Allan. *Unknown.* BSNS
It fell about the Martinmas time/ And a gay time it was then. Get Up and Bar the Door. *Unknown.* BFSS; OnMSP; PoIE; VaPo
It fell in the ancient periods. Uriel. Emerson. AP
It fell on a day and a bonny summer day. The Bonny House of Airlie [*or* Lady Ogalbie]. *Unknown.* BFSS; BuBa
It Fell on a Summer's Day. Thomas Campion. ErPo; UnTE
It flows through old hushed Aegypt and its sands. The Nile. Leigh Hunt. OBNC
It fortifies my soul to know. "With Whom Is No Variableness, neither Shadow of Turning." Arthur Hugh Clough. TRV
It Goes against My Interest to Confess It. Gustavo Adolfo Bécquer, *tr. fr. Spanish by* Doreen Bell. AnSP
It Happened. Efua Sutherland. ACV
It happened on a Sunday. Camp. Patrick Anderson. OBCV

It happened to be on the first of May. The Old *Ramillies.* *Unknown.* BSNS
It has all. From Gloucester Out. Edward Dorn. CoPo
It has been hours in these rooms. E. W. Mandel. *Fr.* Minotaur Poems. OBCV
It has been rumored that there are. Adjuration. Frank Belknap Long. FiSC
It has happened before. Four Preludes on Playthings of the Wind, III. Carl Sandburg. AmLP
It Has Thrust Its Talons through the Morning Clouds. Wolfram von Eschenbach, *tr. fr. German by* Charles E. Passage. AnML
It is/ yet almost. "Everything in the Air Is a Bird." Barbara Guest. AmPC
It is a Beauteous Evening [Calm and Free]. Wordsworth. CABA; CBEP; DiPo; FaPL; FoBA; HaSV; ILP; PoIE; PoLF; PoPo
  (By the Sea.) GTBS-P; TRV
It is a beauteous morning, calm and free. Country Club Sunday. Phyllis McGinley. PoPo
It is a cold courage. Marigold. Louise Townsend Nicholl. RePo
It is a fearful thing to fall into the hands of the living God. The Hands of God. D. H. Lawrence. MoRP
"It is a foolish thing," said I. Tolerance. Thomas Hardy. MoRP
It is a good plan, and began with childhood. Monologue of a Deaf Man. David Wright. MP
It is a lost road into the air. An Airstrip in Essex. Donald Hall. PoCh
It is a most exciting thing. The New Garden. Reginald Arkell. RePo
It is a new America. Brown River, Smile. Jean Toomer. AmNP
It is a solemn evening, golden-clear. The After-Glow. Mathilde Blind. OBNC
It is a strange, miraculous thing. Enigma for Christmas Shoppers. Phyllis McGinley. PoPl
It is a sultry day; the sun has drunk. Summer Wind. Bryant. AP
It is a winter's tale. A Winter's Tale. Dylan Thomas. OnP
It is all a rhythm. The Rhythm. Robert Creeley. CoPo
It is all falling away, the days fall faster now. Descending. Robert Pack. NePoEA-2
It is always so: the declining. Returning from Harvest. Vernon Watkins. StP
It is always the women who are the Watchers. And There Was Mary Magdalene and the Other Mary, Sitting Over against the Sepulchre. W. R. Rodgers. WePo
It is [*or* was] an ancient Mariner. The Rime of the Ancient Mariner. Samuel Taylor Coleridge. CABA; CABL; CaFP; CBEP; DiPo; FaBV; FaPL; ILP; OBNC; PoSa; RoGo; SIV; StP; VaPo; WePo
It is an honorable Thought. Emily Dickinson. AP
It is an illusion that we were ever alive. The Rock. Wallace Stevens. AP
It is because the sea is blue. The Great Wave: Hokusai. Donald Finkel. PoPl
It is Christmas in the mansion. Christmas in the Heart. *Unknown.* RePo
It is dangerous for a woman to defy the gods. Letter to My Sister. Anne Spencer. AmNP
It is done! Laus Deo! Whittier. AP
It is easier to be angry than to pity. Humbert Wolfe. *Fr.* The Uncelestial City. AP
It is equal to living in a tragic land. Dry Loaf. Wallace Stevens. AnMoPo
It is evening. Senlin says, and in the evening. Conrad Aiken. *Fr.* Senlin; a Biography. LOW.
It is far to Assisi. The Garden. William Carlos Williams. PoDB
It is Finished. John Hall Wheelock. MoRP
It is hard for those who have never known persecution. Why Should Men Love the Church? T. S. Eliot. *Fr.* The Rock. MoRP
It is hard going to the door. The Door. Robert Creeley. ToPo
"It Is I, Be Not Afraid." A. B. Simpson. STF
It is in captivity. The Bull. William Carlos Williams. MP
It Is in Winter That We Dream of Spring. Robert Burns Wilson. AmLP
It is late afternoon. Out of my study window. Out of My Window. Reed Whittemore. PoPl
It is late last night the dog was speaking of you. Donall Oge: Grief of a Girl's Heart. *Unknown.* BoLP
It is myself. To a Dog Injured in the Street. William Carlos Williams. PP
It is necessary to wait until the boss's eyes are on you. Notes from a Slave Ship. Edward Field. PP
It is no longer necessary to sleep. A Man Walking and Singing. Wendell Berry. AP
It is no vulgar nature I have wived. Modern Love, XXXV. George Meredith. VP

It is not bad. Let them play. The Bloody Sire. Robinson Jeffers. VaPo
It is not Beauty I demand. The Loveliness of Love [or A Song]. George Darley. GTBS-P; OBNC
It is not Beauty I've discovered here. The Crossing. Philippe Jaccottet. CoFP
It is not death, that sometime in a sigh. Sonnet. Thomas Hood. OBNC
It is not four years ago. Proffered Love Rejected [or The Rejected Offer]. Sir John Suckling. ErPo; UnTE
It Is Not Growing like a Tree. Ben Jonson. Fr. A Pindaric Ode. CABA; DiPo; LV; PoIE
(Noble Nature, The.) GTBS-P; PoPo
(Short Measures.) WePo
It is not in the books. The Three Movements. Donald Hall. NePoEA-2
It is not its air but our own awe. The Iceberg. W. S. Merwin. PoIE
It is not life upon Thy gifts to live. Life. Jones Very. AP
It Is Not Only the Dead. Frank Belknap Long. FiSC
It Is Not the Sea. Guy Owen. PoNC
It is not the still weight. The Jungle. William Carlos Williams. CABA
It is not to be thought of that the Flood. Sonnet. Wordsworth. ACV
It is plain now what you are. Your head has dropped. Carrion. Harold Monro. Fr. Youth in Arms. MMA
It is portentous, and a thing of state. Abraham Lincoln Walks at Midnight. Vachel Lindsay. AmLP; FaBV; LiPo; MoRP; PoPl; PoPo; RePo; ThLM
It is queer to think that many people. The Man with the Rake. Christopher Morley. Fr. Translations from the Chinese. EvOK
It Is Raining. Lucy Sprague Mitchell. SoPo
It is so many ages now since He. Our Father. Roberta Teale Swartz. MoRP
It is the association after all. A Way of Looking. Elizabeth Jennings. PP
It is the best, erely and late. Be True to Your Condition in Life. John Audelay. MeEL
"It is the blood of the little gray hound." Edward. Unknown. BSO
It is the day when he was born. In Memoriam A. H. H., CVII. Tennyson. VP
It Is the Evening Hour; the Rapid Sky. Petrarch, tr. fr. Italian by Morris Bishop. AnML
It is the Harvest Moon! On gilded vanes. The Harvest Moon. Longfellow. AP
It is the miller's daughter. The Miller's Daughter. Tennyson. CBEP; UnTE
It is the pain, it is the pain, endures. Villanelle. William Empson. PoIE
It is the picnic with Ruth in the spring. The Picnic. John Logan. BoLP; NePoEA-2
It is the same if I lie on the left or the right side. Love Poem. Karl Krolow. MGP
It is the sea's edge lubbers love. Sailing, Sailing. Gray Burr. CoPo
It is the season of the sweet wild rose. Modern Love, XLV. George Meredith. VP
It is the snow-gum silently. The Snow-Gum. Douglas Stewart. PoAu-2
It is the thirty-first of March. Peter Bell. John Hamilton Reynolds. OBNC; Par
It is the white Plum Tree. 'Tis the White Plum Tree. John Shaw Neilson. PoAu-1
It is this deep blankness is the real thing strange. Let It Go. William Empson. PoIE
It Is Time. Ted Joans. NNP
It is time to be old. Terminus. Emerson. AP; PoLF
It is time to explain myself—let us stand up. Walt Whitman. Fr. Song of Myself. DiPo
It Is Too Late! Longfellow. Fr. Morituri Salutamus. PoLF
It is Ulysses that approaches from the east. The World as Meditation. Wallace Stevens. AP
It is very nice to think. Robert Louis Stevenson. ThGo
It is what he does not know. On a Squirrel Crossing the Road in Autumn, in New England. Richard Eberhart. PoCh
It Is Worthless to Write a Line. Bernart de Ventadorn, tr. fr. Provençal by Paul Blackburn. AnML
It Isn't the Cough. Unknown. LV
It isn't the thing you do. The Sin of Omission. Margaret E. Sangster. TRV
It keeps eternal whisperings around. On the Sea. Keats. CABA; DiPo; FoBA
It little profits that an idle king. Ulysses. Tennyson. CABA; CaFP; CBEP; DiPo; FoBA; ILP; PoIE; PoPo; PoSa; StP; VaPo; VP
It makes a man feel happy. Three Sweethearts. Heine. UnTE
It makes no difference abroad. Emily Dickinson. AP; DiPo
It May Be. Max Jacob, tr. fr. French by Wallace Fowlie. PoPl
It May Be Good. Sir Thomas Wyatt. EnRePo
It May Be Like This. Lilith Lorraine. FiSC

It may be that a strange dream. It May Be. Max Jacob. PoPl
It May Not Always Be So. E. E. Cummings. Sonnets—Unrealities, I. FaBV; MoLP
It might be lonelier. Emily Dickinson. FoBA
It must be right sometimes to entertain. Love's Justification. Michelangelo. RBL
It must have been one o'clock at night. To Remain. C. P. Cavafy. ErPo
It once might have been, once only. Youth and Art. Robert Browning. CTC
It rained/ Upon the tall windows. The Lime Avenue. Sacheverell Sitwell. LOW
It rained a mist, it rained a mist. The Jews' Daughter. Unknown. BFSS
It rains, it mists, it rains, it mists. The Jew's Garden. Unknown. BSO
It really gives me heartfelt pain. Maria Jane. Alfred Scott-Gatty. BBGG
It Really Happened. Elizabeth Henley. BiCB
It rose before us on the starboard bow. The Wave. Andrew Charles Wehner. HaSV
It seemed that out of the battle I escaped. Strange Meeting. Wilfred Owen. AnMoPo; DTC; FaPL; GTBS-P; ILP; MMA; PoIE
It seemed to me when I saw her. The Torn Nightgown. Joel Oppenheimer. CoPo
It seems a day. Nutting. Wordsworth. CBEP
"It seems a shame." The Last Flower. John Travers Moore. PoSC
It seems a stage. The Gypsy's Window. Denise Levertov. ToPo
It seems I have no tears left. They should have fallen. Tears. Edward Thomas. CBEP; GTBS-P
It seems that I hear that beauty who. Lament of the Lovely Helmet-Dealer. Villon. ErPo
It seems there are only reptiles in the hold. The Oars of the Galley. Ali ben Hariq. AnML
It seems wrong that out of this bird. A Blackbird Singing. R. S. Thomas. BoC; WePo
It semes white and is red. The Sacrament of the Altar. Unknown. MeEL
It sifts from leaden sieves. Emily Dickinson. DiPo; RePo
(Snow, The.) PoPl
It slouched at the window changing. Nekros. Richard O'Connell. OPP
It started as a pilgrimage. Enterprise. Nissim Ezekiel. ACV
It takes a heap o' children to make a home that's true. Edgar A. Guest Considers "The Good Old Woman Who Lived in a Shoe" and the Good Old Truths Simultaneously. Louis Untermeyer. PoPl
It takes a long time to hear what the sands. The Bones. W. S. Merwin. NePoEA-2
It was a chilly winter's night. A Winter Night. William Barnes. OBNC
It was a deliberate moment, and O. W. H. Rodgers. Fr. Resurrection—an Easter Sequence. ACV
It was a dismal and a fearful night. On the Death of Mr. William Hervey. Abraham Cowley. CBEP; SeCP
It was a falling castle, full of drafts. For a Poetry Reading to Which No One Came. Larry Rubin. FiSC
It was a kind and northern face. Praise for an Urn. Hart Crane. AP
It was a knight in Scotland born. The Fair Flower of Northumberland. Unknown. BuBa
It was a lady of the North she lov'd a gentleman. The Jovial Tinker. Unknown. UnTE
It was a little captive cat. The Singing Cat. Stevie Smith. BoC; DaDu
It Was a Lover and His Lass. Shakespeare. Fr. As You Like It, V, iii. CBEP; ELP; GTBS-P; UnTE
(Song.) CTC
It was a night of early spring. Wisdom. Sara Teasdale. AmLP
It was a place that I had known before. Carcosa. Lin Carter. FiSC
It was a puritanical lad. Two Puritans. Unknown. UnTE
It was a summer [or summer's] evening. The Battle of Blenheim [or After Blenheim]. Robert Southey. FaBV; GTBS-P; OBNC; PoLF; PoPo; PoSa; SIV; StP; TRV
It was a Summer's night, a close warm night. Conclusion. Wordsworth. Fr. The Prelude. OBNC
It was a tall young oysterman lived by the riverside. The Ballad of the Oysterman. Oliver Wendell Holmes. AP; SIV
It was a wondrous realm beguiled. Alfred Domett. Fr. Ranolf and Amohia. ACV
It was all in the month of June. Barbara Ellen (B vers.). Unknown. BSO
It was all on a hollow day. Little Matty Groves. Unknown. BFSS
It was an ancient Mariner. See It is an ancient Mariner.
It was an old, old, old, old lady. One, Two, Three! H. C. Bunner. PoLF

It was as if Gauguin. Etta Moten's Attic. Margaret Danner. Far from Africa: Four Poems, 4. AmNP
It was as white as the morning star at dawn. The White Horse. Abu Salt Umayya. AnML
It was cause for laughter of a special brand. The Fish. Ralph Gustafson. OBCV
It was dark till the dust of battle covered. The Spear. Abu Zakariyya. AnML
It was down in the country a poor girl was weeping. The Fisherman's Girl. *Unknown.* BSO
It was early, early in one spring. Early in One Spring. *Unknown.* BFSS
It was early, early in the spring. The Croppy Boy. *Unknown.* CBEP
It Was for Me. Eva Gray. STF
It was in a pleasant time. Earl Mar's Daughter. *Unknown.* BuBa
It was in and about the Martinmas time. Barbara Allan. *Unknown.* CABA
It was in October, a favorite season. Elegy for a Nature Poet. Howard Nemerov. PP
It was in the town of Waterford. Waterford Town. *Unknown.* BSNS
It Was in Vegas. J. V. Cunningham. UnTE
It was just before Custer's last fierce charge. Custer's Last Fierce Charge. *Unknown.* BFSS
It was just before that last great charge. The Battle of Fredericksburg. *Unknown.* BSNS
It was just before the last fierce charge. The Last Fierce Charge. *Unknown.* BSO
It was laughing time, and the tall Giraffe. Laughing Time. William Jay Smith. SoPo
It was like something done in fever, when nothing fits. Walter Benton. *Fr.* This Is My Beloved. UnTE
It was many and many a year ago. Annabel Lee. Poe. AP; BoLP; DiPo; FaPL; OnMSP; PoPl; PoPo; RoGo; SIV
It Was My Choice. Sir Thomas Wyatt. EnRePo
It was my thirtieth year to heaven. Poem in October. Dylan Thomas. AnMoPo; BoC; CaFP; DaDu; DiPo; PoIE; PoPl; StP; ToPo; WePo
It was noon when the company marched to the railroad-station. Stephen Vincent Benét. *Fr.* John Brown's Body. ThLM
It was not death, for I stood up. Emily Dickinson. CABA; CBEP
It Was Not in the Winter. Thomas Hood. ELP
It was not like your great and gracious ways. Departure. Coventry Patmore. The Unknown Eros, I, viii. FaPL; OBNC
It was not night, not even when the·darkness came. The Annunciation. W. S. Merwin. AP
It was of a sea captain that followed the sea. The Sea Captain (A *vers.*). *Unknown.* BSNS
It was on a Sunday morn. The Three Butchers. *Unknown.* BFSS
It was on a Wednesday night, the moon was shining bright. Jesse James. *Unknown.* PoPo; WiR
It was on Christmas Day. All in the Morning. *Unknown.* BiCB
It was on one morning early. The Pretty Little Girl. *Unknown.* BSO
It was on September the eighteenth day. McLellan's Son. *Unknown.* BSNS
It was one afternoon when I was young. The Tale the Hermit Told. Alastair Reid. NePoEA-2
It was only a kindly smile he gave. Little Things. *Unknown.* STF
It was only two fields away from the house. In Memoriam I: Elizabeth at Twenty. Richard Weber. ErPo
It was quite a day at Melrose. All the folks had come to town there. Coronation Day at Melrose. Peter Bladen. PoAu-2
It was six men of Indostan. The Blind Men and the Elephant. John Godfrey Saxe. OnMSP
It was so cold the skyline seemed to splinter. Contrast. Eileen Duggan. ACV
It was something you did not know. An Air by Sammartini. Louis Dudek. OBCV
It was strange. O strange. A Green and Pleasant Land. John Peale Bishop. PoPl
It was such a bright morning. A Day in Spring. "Jake Falstaff." BoC
It was the cooling hour, just when the rounded. Haidée and Don Juan. Byron. *Fr.* Don Juan. OBNC
It was the day that the sun's rays. Petrarch. *Fr.* Sonnets to Laura: To Laura in Life. RBL
It was the evening before the night. The Eve of Christmas. James Kirkup. DaDu
It was the flowery season of the year. Luis de Góngora. *Fr.* The Solitudes. AnSP; RBL
It was the man from Ironbark who struck the Sydney town. The Man from Ironbark. A. B. Paterson. PoAu-1
It was the month of April. Ballad of Flérida. Gil Vicente. RBL
It was the morning of that blessèd day. Petrarch. *Fr.* Sonnets to Laura: To Laura in Life. RBL
It was the night before the famous day. The Death of Santa Claus. Vincent Starrett. FiSC

It was the schooner *Hesperus*. The Wreck of the *Hesperus*. Longfellow. FaPL; SIV
It was the season, when through all the land. The Birds of Killingworth. Longfellow. *Fr.* Tales of a Wayside Inn. OnMSP
It was the time of year. A Prehistoric Camp. Andrew Young. CBEP
It was the time when lilies blow. Lady Clare. Tennyson. OnMSP
It was the very month of May. Barbary Ellen. *Unknown.* BSNS
It was there, again. Nightmare in Morganza. Joseph Joel Keith. FiSC
It was, they say, the left hand struck him down. November 22, 1963. Robert M. Chute. OPP
It was this way. Rumoresque Senum Severiorum. Marcus Argentarius. ErPo
It was this way in times gone past. Too Bad! Wilhelm Busch. AGP
It was three slim does and a ten-tined buck in the bracken lay. The Revenge of Hamish. Sidney Lanier. AP; SIV
It was through a mucous membrane, a kind of mouth. Lion, Leopard, Lady. Douglas Le Pan. OBCV
It was Tiny's habit. Sketches of Harlem. David Henderson. NNP
It was too dark in the chimney corner to see. Cinderella. Cynthia Pickard. PoPl
It was upon a Lammas night. Corn Rigs Are Bonny [*or* The Rigs o' Barley]. Burns. CBEP; ErPo; UnTE
It was water I was trying to think of all the time. Appoggiatura. Donald Jeffrey Hayes. AmNP
It was where the wooden pier. Dora Markus. Eugenio Montale. CoIP
It was wintertime. Star of the Nativity. Boris Pasternak. PoPl
It was worth the while of a boy to live. In the Days When the Cattle Ran. Hamlin Garland. RePo
"It was wrong to do this," said the angel. The Black Riders, LIV. Stephen Crane. AP
It wasn't our battalion, but we lay alongside it. Sergeant-Major Money. Robert Graves. MMA
It were as if the heavens. Moon-Night. Joseph von Eichendorff. SiGo
It wes upon a Scere Thorsday that oure Lord aros. Judas Sells His Lord. *Unknown.* MeEL
It will be with us always through our lives. The Quiet Flower. Josephine W. Johnson. MoRP
It will not always be like this. A Day in Autumn. R. S. Thomas. WePo
It will not stay! The robe so pearly white. The April Snow. Jones Very. AP
Italian Extravaganza. Gregory Corso. CoPo
Italy, *sels.* Samuel Rogers.
    Byron Recollected at Bologna. OBNC
    Interview near Florence, An. OBNC
Italy, O thou to whom belong. To Italy. Vincenzo da Filicaia. RBL
Ité. Ezra Pound. PP
It'll Be a Long Time Again before My Friends. Peire Vidal, *tr. fr. Provençal by* Paul Blackburn. AnML
It's a dark and dreary season. Triolet on a Dark Day. Margaret Fishback. PoSC
It's a debatable land. The winds are variable. Report from the Carolinas. Helen Bevington. PoNC
It's a great deal better to lose than win. After Reading Certain Books. Mary Elizabeth Coleridge. EaLo
It's a strange courage. El Hombre. William Carlos Williams. CABA
"It's a sunny pleasant anchorage, is Kingdom Come." Port of Many Ships. John Masefield. HaSV
It's a very odd thing. Miss T. Walter de la Mare. GoJo; SoPo
It's a warm wind, the west wind, full of birds' cries. The West Wind. John Masefield. PoPl
It's all aboard for outer space. Space Travel. Jane W. Krows. SoPo
It's all too swift; it's over all too soon. A Plea for Postponement. Petronius. UnTE
It's all very well to dream of a dove that saves. Birdwatchers of America. Anthony Hecht. CoPo
It's American frigate from Baltimore came. Paul Jones (A *vers.*). *Unknown.* BSNS
It's awf'lly bad luck on Diana. Hunter Trials. John Betjeman. DaDu
It's being tried in Fugee in South America. Morrissey and the Russian. *Unknown.* BSNS
It's dark in this wood, soft mocker. Praise to the End! Theodore Roethke. ToPo
It's easy to talk of the patience of Job. Humph! Job hed nothin' to try him! The Inventor's Wife. Mrs. E. T. Corbett. PoLF
Its former green is blue and thin. The Garden Seat. Thomas Hardy. GoJo
It's four long years since I reached this land. The Lousy Miner. John A. Stone. SGR

It's funny how a little thing. Reminder. *Unknown.* STF

It's funny how often they say to me, "Jane?" The Good Little Girl. A. A. Milne. BBGG

"It's going to rain," said Noah. His friend laughed. Noah. Hermann Hagedorn. MoRP

It's hard to be locked up in prison. The Prisoner's Song. *Unknown.* BSNS

It's Here in the. Russell Atkins. AmNP

It's in Your Face. *Unknown.* PoLF

It's I've got a ship in the north country. The Golden Vanity. *Unknown.* ELP

It's Jamie rose on a May morning. James o' Broodies. *Unknown.* BFSS

It's jolly/ Odd what pops into. E. E. Cummings. ThLM

It's Lamkin was a mason good. Lamkin. *Unknown.* CBEP

It's never night when you die. The Bull. René Char. *Fr.* Four Fascinators. CoFP

It's no go the merrygoround, it's no go the rickshaw. Bagpipe Music. Louis MacNeice. GTBS-P; ILP; PoSa

"It's not I," said the cat. Who Is Tapping at My Window. A. G. Deming. SoPo

It's not quite all merely to be hungry. Hunger and Rain. Sam Ragan. PoNC

It's not so much the things without. Happiness. Walter E. Isenhour. STF

It's of a bonny shepherdess. The Sailor and the Shepherdess. *Unknown.* BSNS

It's of a farmer who lived in York. The Devil's Song. *Unknown.* BSNS

It's of a handsome young lady gay. The Diamond Ring. *Unknown.* BSNS

It's of a highway robber a story I will tell. Brennan on the Moor. *Unknown.* BSNS

It's of a noble steamer, the *Cedar Grove* by name. The *Cedar Grove. Unknown.* BSNS

It's of a rich lady in England did dwell. The Lost Lady Found. *Unknown.* BSNS

It's of a rich merchant in London did dwell. The Box upon Her Head. *Unknown.* BSNS

It's of a Saturday evening as we made up the plan. Johnny Doyle. *Unknown.* BSNS

It's of a tailor who was cutting out a coat. The Tailor and the Crow (A *vers.*). *Unknown.* BSNS

It's over, it's over! Taking Down the Tree. Aileen Fisher. RePo

It's Pleasant to Think. Elizabeth J. Coatsworth. RePo

Its quick soft silver bell beating, beating. Auto Wreck. Karl Shapiro. AmLP; ILP; PoPl; PoPo

It's raining today and I'm reading about pharmacies in Paris. Les Réalités. Barbara Guest. AmPC

It's such a static reference; looking. Epistrophe. LeRoi Jones. NNP

It's the Same the Whole World Over. *Unknown. See* She Was Poor but She Was Honest.

It's the wave of the sea in my blood, and I'll nere be free. Sea Fret. Teresa Hooley. HaSV

It's there you'll see confectioners with sugar sticks and dainties. Galway Races. *Unknown.* SD

It's whisky here and whisky there. Whisky Johnny (B *vers.*). *Unknown.* BSNS

It's Wonderful. Walter E. Isenhour. STF

It's wonderful dogs they're breeding now. Tim, an Irish Terrier. Winifred M. Letts. BoC

It's wonderful, so wonderful. It's Wonderful. Walter E. Isenhour. STF

It's You. L. A. McDonald. STF

Itylus. Swinburne. StP; VP

I've a friend, over the sea. Time's Revenges. Robert Browning. VP

I've a pal called Billy Peg-Leg, with one leg a wood leg. Peg-Leg's Fiddle. Bill Adams. RePo

I've always thought Polonius a dry. Lines to His Son on Reaching Adolescence. John Logan. NePoEA-2

I've buried Troy, I've conquered Rome. On Stage, off Stage. Robert Watson. PoNC

I've come this far to freedom. Midway. Naomi Long Madgett. NNP

"I've giv'n up golf forever, Wife." He Gave Up Golf. Edith Earnshaw. PoNC

I've got a mule, her name is Sal. The Erie Canal. *Unknown.* RePo

I've Got a New Book from My Grandfather Hyde. Leroy Jackson. RePo

I've got shoes with grown up laces. Growing Up. A. A. Milne. BiCB; ThGo

I've grown a goitre by dwelling in this den. On the Painting of the Sistine Chapel. Michelangelo. RBL

I've guests tonight in my house. Guest Room. Olive Tilford Dargan. PoNC

I've had you on my mind a thousand years. God's Thanks to Job. Robert Frost. *Fr.* A Masque of Reason. MoRP

I've heard, I've heard. Margaret Woods. BoC

I've heard them lilting at our ewe-milking. Lament for Flodden. Jane Elliot. GTBS-P; WePo

I've just come down from the mines. The Miner's Lament, III. David G. Robinson. SGR

"I've just come from a place." The Little Duck. Joso. SoPo

I've just got [in] across the plains. The Arrival of the Greenhorn. John A. Stone. RePo; SGR

I've known ere now an interfering branch. The Axe-Helve. Robert Frost. CABL

I've known rivers. The Negro Speaks of Rivers. Langston Hughes. AmNP

I've never been to London. Fifty Acres. James Larkin Pearson. PoNC

I've seen a dying eye. Emily Dickinson. FoBA; PoLF

I've shore at Burrabogie, and I've shore at Toganmain. Flash Jack from Gundagai. *Unknown.* PoAu-1

I've traveled the mountains all over. He's the Man for Me. John A. Stone. SGR

I've tried in vain, day after day. The Promise. Mary E. Fowler. STF

I've walked along with Jesus. His Presence. Dale Schulz. STF

I've watched the clouds by day and night. Watching Clouds. John Farrar. SoPo

I've worked on the Nine-Mile, likewise on the River. The Broken-down Digger. *Unknown.* PoAu-1

Ivory. Mario Luzi, *tr. fr. Italian by* Carlo L. Golino. CoIP

Ivory Bed, The. Winfield Townley Scott. ErPo

Ivory, Coral, Gold, The. William Drummond of Hawthornden. ELP

Ivory Gate, The, *sel.* Thomas Lovell Beddoes. Mighty Thoughts of an Old World, The. GoJo

Ivry. Macaulay. FaBV

Ivy, chefe of trees it is. In Praise of Ivy. *Unknown.* MeEL

Ivy o'er the mouldering wall, The. The Sun-Dial. Thomas Love Peacock. *Fr.* Melincourt. OBNC

Ixions of the slow wheel of the day. Christ in the Hospital. Roy Campbell. BoC

J

J. B., *sel.* Archibald MacLeish. Curse God and Die, You Said to Me. EaLo

J. F. K. Ralph Gordon. OPP

Jabberwocky. "Lewis Carroll." *Fr.* Through the Looking-Glass. CABA; CaFP; CBEP; DiPo; FaBV; GoJo; LV; PoIE; PoPl; PoPo; VaPo

Jack and His Father. John Heywood. DiPo

Jack and Jill. Mother Goose. SoPo

Jack Be Nimble. Mother Goose. SoPo

Jack Denver died on Talbragar when Christmas Eve began. Talbragar. Henry Lawson. PoAu-1

Jack Donahue, *with music. Unknown.* BSNS

Jack Ellyat Heard the Guns. Stephen Vincent Benét. *Fr.* John Brown's Body. PoLF

Jack Frost. Helen Bayley Davis. SoPo

Jack Monroe. *Unknown. See* Jack, the Sailor.

Jack o'Lantern. Anna Chandler Ayre. SoPo

Jackolanterns. Rainer Maria Rilke, *tr. fr. German by* Christopher Middleton. MGP

Jack (quoth his father) how shall I ease take? Jack and His Father. John Heywood. DiPo

Jack Sheppard. *Unknown.* BSNS

Jack, the jolly ploughboy, was ploughing up his land. The Jolly Ploughboy. *Unknown.* BSNS

Jack, the Sailor (A *vers., with music*). *Unknown.* BSO
(Jack Monroe, D *vers., with music.*) BFSS
(Jack Went a-Sailing, B *vers.*) BSO
(Jackie Frazier, *with music.*) BFSS
(Wealthy Merchant, The, C *vers., with music.*) BSO

Jack Williams. *Unknown.* BSNS; BSO

Jackdaw of Rheims, The. "Thomas Ingoldsby." *Fr.* The Ingoldsby Legends. OnMSP

Jacket So Blue; or, A Company of Boatmen, *with music. Unknown.* BFSS

Jackie Frazier. *Unknown. See* Jack, the Sailor.

Jacko the Skunk, in black and white. The Skunk. Alfred Noyes. RePo

Jack's Blues. Robert Creeley. ToPo

Jacob and the Angel. Brother Antoninus. MoRP

Jacobite's Epitaph, A. Macaulay. OBNC

Jacob's Ladder, The. Denise Levertov. CaFP; CoPo; ToPo

Jacqueline. "Will Inman." OPP

Jacqueline Gray. Kenneth Pitchford. *Fr.* Good for Nothing Man. CoPo

Jaguar, The. Ted Hughes. PoPl; ToPo

Jam on Gerry's Rocks, The (A *vers.*). *Unknown.* BSNS
(Geary's Rock, *with music.*) SIV
(Gerry's Rocks, B *vers.*) BSNS
(Jam at Gerry's Rock, The, *with music.*) BFSS

James Bird. *Unknown.* BFSS, *with music;* BSO (A *vers., with music;* B *vers.*)

James Garber. Edgar Lee Masters. *Fr.* Spoon River Anthology. ILP
James Harris (B, C, *and* E *vers., with music;* D *vers.*). *Unknown.* BSO
(House Carpenter, The, *with music.*) BFSS; BSO (A *vers.*)
James Honeyman. W. H. Auden. MoBS
James Munks's Confession. *Unknown.* BSO
James o'Broodies, *with music. Unknown.* BFSS
James Rigg. James Hogg. Par
Jane, Do Be Careful. Irene Page. BBGG
Jane, Jane. Aubade. Edith Sitwell. WePo
Jane looks down at her organdy skirt. In Bertram's Garden. Donald Justice. ErPo
Jane's Marriage ("Jane went to Paradise"). Kipling. BoC
Janet Waking. John Crowe Ransom. AmLP; PoIE; PoPo
Janie on the Moor (A *and* B *vers.*). *Unknown.* BSNS
Janitor's Boy, The. Nathalia Crane. PoLF
Jankin, the Clerical Seducer. *Unknown.* MeEL
January. Elizabeth J. Coatsworth. PoSC
January. Geoffrey Dutton. PoAu-2
January. James Reaney. *Fr.* A Suit of Nettles. OBCV
January brings the snow. The Months. Sara Coleridge. RePo
January cold desolate. The Months. Christina Rossetti. *Fr.* Sing-Song. LV
January 1. Marnie Pomeroy. PoSC
January Morning, A. Archibald Lampman. ACV; OBCV
January Night. Rafael Alberto Arrieta, tr. *fr. Spanish by* Muna Lee. SiGo
January sky is deep and calm, The. Reason for Not Writing Orthodox Nature Poetry. John Wain. MP; PP; ToPo
Japan That Sank under the Sea. Satoru Sato. PoPl
Jason. Anthony Hecht. CoPo
Jason and Medea. Alun Lewis. CBEP
Jazz Fantasia. Carl Sandburg. LV; WePo
Jazz of This Hotel, The. Vachel Lindsay. PoPl
Jazz Poem. Carl Wendell Hines, Jr. PtTo
(Two Jazz Poems.) AmNP
Jazzonia. Langston Hughes. AmNP
Jealous Lover, The. *Unknown.* BSO
Jealous Wife, The. Vernon Scannell. ErPo
Jealousy. Mary Elizabeth Coleridge. OBNC
Jealousy. Sir William Davenant. *Fr.* The Siege of Rhodes. BoLP
Jean. Burns. *See* Of A' the Airts.
Jeanie with the Light Brown Hair. Stephen Foster. FaPL; LV
Jehovah-Rophi. William Cowper. EiCP
Jelly Jake and Butter Bill. Leroy F. Jackson. BBGG
Jemima. *Unknown. See* There Was a Little Girl.
Jemima is my name. Mima. Walter de la Mare. BiCB
Jenny. Dante Gabriel Rossetti. VP
Jenny Kiss'd [*or* Kissed] Me. Leigh Hunt. BiCB; LV; PoPl
(Rondeau: "Jenny kissed me when we met.") FaBV; WePo
Jenny kiss'd me in a dream. "Such Stuff as Dreams." Franklin P. Adams. LV
"Jenny Kiss'd Me When We Met." Paul Dehn. LV
Jenny Wren. *Unknown.* EvOK
Jeremy's Secrets ("Jeremy's six, so his sisters say"). Barbara E. Todd. BiCB
Jersey City. *Unknown. See* Butcher Boy, The.
Jerusalem, *sels.* Blake.
"But still the thunder of Los peals loud, and thus the thunders cry," *fr. ch.* 4. PoIE
Epigraph: "I give you the end of a golden string," *fr. prologue to ch.* 4. OBNC
"I see the four-fold man, the humanity in deadly sleep," *fr. ch.* 1. PoIE
Male & Female Loves in Beulah. OBNC
Prelude: "England! awake! awake! awake!" *fr. prologue to ch.* 4. OBNC
Prelude: "Fields from Islington to Marybone, The," *fr. prologue to ch.* 2. OBNC
Jerusalem. Blake *Fr.* Milton. *See* And Did Those Feet in Ancient Time.
Jerusalem, My Happy Home. *Unknown, at to* "F. B. P.," *after the Latin* Urbs Beata Hierusalem. CBEP
(Hierusalem.) CTC
Jerusalem Street and Paradise Square. Closing Time. James Michie. NePoEA-2
Jesse James. William Rose Benét. SIV; ThLM
Jesse James. *Unknown.* PoPo; WiR; BFSS, *diff. vers., with music*
Jesse James was a man who killed many a man. Jesse James. *Unknown.* BFSS
Jesse James was a two-gun man. Jesse James. William Rose Benét. SIV; ThLM
Jest 'fore Christmas. Eugene Field. FaBV; PoLF
Jester in the Trench. Leon Gellert. PoAu-1
Jester walked in the garden, The. The Cap and Bells. W. B. Yeats. OnMSP
Jesu Christ, my lemmon swete. Jesus, My Sweet Lover. *Unknown.* MeEL

Jesu! for thy mercy endelesse [*or* for thy wondes fife]. Jesu! Send Us Peace. *Unknown.* MeEL
Jesu! I now begin. *Unknown.* BoC
Jesu, Lorde, that madest me. A Hymn to Jesus. Richard of Caistre. MeEL
Jesu, Lord, welcom thou be. A Prayer to the Sacrament of the Altar. *Unknown.* MeEL
Jesu, no more! It is full tide. Upon the Bleeding Crucifix. Richard Crashaw. SeCP
Jesu! Send Us Peace. *Unknown.* MeEL
Jesu, that hast me dere iboght. A Devout Prayer of the Passion. *Unknown.* MeEL
Jesu thie love within mee is soe maine. Sonnet. William Alabaster. MeP
Jesus, almighty King of Blis. The Nativity. *Unknown.* MeEL
Jesus and His Mother. Thom Gunn. AnMoPo; CaFP; EaLo
Jesus and I. Dan Crawford. TRV
Jesus Bids Man Remember. *Unknown.* MeEL
Jesus bids us shine with a clear, pure light. A Candle Burning in the Night. Susan B. Warner. ThGo
Jesus Christ, I Pray with All My Might. Christine Lavant, *tr. fr. German by* Nora Wydenbruck. MGP
Jesus Christ, who brought good news. Subversive. William Rose Benét. MoRP
Jesus Comforts His Mother. *Unknown. See* Dear Son, Leave Thy Weeping.
Jesus Contrasts Man and Himself ("Jesus doth him bimene"). *Unknown.* McEL
Jesus, Estrella, Esperanza, Mercy. Middle Passage. Robert Hayden. AmNP
Jesus, my Lord, when I look upon Thee. Thy Nail-pierced Hands. Kathryn Bowsher. STF
Jesus Never Fails. Walter E. Isenhour. STF
Jesus never will forget me. He Never Will Forget. "M. G. H." STF
Jesus our brother, kind [*or* strong] and good. The Friendly Beasts. *Unknown.* BiCB; OnMSP; PoSC; SoPo
Jesus Reassures His Mother. *Unknown.* MeEL
Jesus Reproaches His People. *Unknown.* MeEL
Jesus Return. Henry van Dyke. TRV
Jesus, teach me how to be. The Housewife. Catherine Cate Coblentz. TRV
Jesus, tender shepherd, hear me. Mary L. Duncan. ThGo
Jesus, Thou divine Companion. Hymn of Labor. Henry van Dyke. TRV
Jesus to Those Who Pass By. *Unknown.* MeEL
Jesus, Thy life is mine! A Prayer. *Unknown.* STF
Jesus woundes so wide. The Wells of Jesus Wounds. *Unknown.* MeEL
Jew. Karl Shapiro. ToPo
Jew to Jesus, The. Florence Kiper Frank. TRV
Jewelled mine of the pomegranate, whose hexagons of honey. The. The Pomegranate. Louis Dudek. OBCV
Jewels, The. Baudelaire, *tr. fr. French by* Paul Blackburn. ErPo
Jewish Cemetery at Newport, The. Longfellow. AP
Jewish king now walks at large and sound, The. Zaph Describes the Haunts of Malzah. Charles Heavysege. *Fr.* Saul. OBCV
Jew's Daughter, The, *with music. Unknown.* BFSS
(Jew's Garden, The, *with music.*) BSO
Jezebel Jones smelled really punk. The Tale of the Skunk and Poor Jez. John Becker. RePo
Jig. C. Day Lewis. WePo
Jig for Sackbuts. Dominic Bevan Wyndham Lewis. ErPo
Jilted Nymph, The. Thomas Campbell. BoLP
Jim. Hilaire Belloc. *See* Jim, Who Ran Away from His Nurse, and Was Eaten by a Lion.
Jim at the Corner. Eleanor Farjeon. SoPo
Jim Bludso, of the *Prairie Belle*. John Hay. PoPo
Jim Desterland. Hyam Plutzik. FiSC
Jim Jones. *Unknown.* PoAu-1
Jim the Splitter. Henry Kendall. PoAu-1
Jim was a Sailor. Jim at the Corner. Eleanor Farjeon. SoPo
Jim, Who Ran Away from His Nurse, and Was Eaten by a Lion. Hilaire Belloc. EvOK
(Jim.) BBGG
Jiminy Jiminy Jukebox! Wheatcakes! Crumbs! Mole. William Jay Smith. RePo
Jimmy and Diana. *Unknown.* BSO
Jimmy and His Own True Love. *Unknown.* BSNS
Jimmy Randal. *Unknown. See* Lord Randal.
Jimmy Random, My Son. *Unknown. See* Lord Randal.
Jinny the Just. Matthew Prior. CABL
Jippy and Jimmy. Laura E. Richards. SoPo
Jittery Jim. William Jay Smith. BBGG
Joan of Arc. Hugh McCrae. PoAu-1
Joan to Her Lady. *Unknown.* UnTE
Joan's Door. Eleanor Farjeon. BiCB
Joaquin the Horse-Thief. John A. Stone. SGR
Job. Elizabeth Sewell. EaLo

Job, sel. Bible, O.T.
  My Soul Is Weary of My Life, X: 1-22. EaLo
Job That's Crying to Be Done, The. Kipling. TRV
Jock o' [or of] Hazeldean. Sir Walter Scott. GTBS-P; ILP; PoPo; StP
Jock o' Hazeldean. Unknown. See John of Hazelgreen.
Joe Bowers, with music. Unknown, at. to John Woodward. BFSS; SGR
Joe Green Joe Green O how are you doing today? An Old Inmate. Kenneth Mackenzie. PoAu-2
Jog On, Jog On. Shakespeare. Fr. The Winter's Tale, IV, ii. CBEP
Johannes Milton, Senex. Robert Bridges. PoPl
John Anderson, My Jo. Burns. CABA; CaFP; CBEP; EiCP; EnPE; ErPo; FaBV; GTBS-P; PoIE; PoPo; PoSa; UnTE
John Bolo's Acting Grim. Dinis, King of Portugal, tr. fr. Portuguese by William M. Davis. AnML
John Brown in Kansas settled, like a steadfast Yankee farmer. How Old Brown Took Harper's Ferry. Edmund Clarence Stedman. OnMSP
John Brown of Ossawatomie spake on his dying day. Brown of Ossawatomie. Whittier. ThLM
John Brown's Body, sels. Stephen Vincent Benét.
  "Gaunt man, Abraham Lincoln, woke one morning, The." LiPo
  "It was noon when the company marched to the railroad-station." ThLM
  Jack Ellyat Heard the Guns. PoLF
  Off to the War. SIV
  There Was a Girl I Used to Go With. LOW
  Three Elements. EaLo
John Brown's body lies a-mouldering in the grave. Glory Hallelujah! or, John Brown's Body. Unknown. ThLM
John Chinaman. Unknown. SGR
John Chinaman, My Jo, with music. J. W. Conner. SGR
John Chinaman's Appeal. Mart Taylor. SGR
John Coltrane—an Impartial Review. Alfred B. Spellman. NNP
John courts Perrette, but all in vain. To Promise Is One Thing, to Perform Is Another. La Fontaine. UnTE
John Day, Frontiersman. Yvor Winters. PoSa
John Dory. Unknown. BuBa
John Funston (A and B vers., with music). Unknown. BSO
John Gilpin. William Cowper. See Diverting History of John Gilpin, The.
John Graydon. Wilson MacDonald. ACV
John Grumlie. Allan Cunningham. PoLF
John had. Happiness. A. A. Milne. BoC
John Henry. Unknown. ThLM; PoPo, longer vers.
John is the tallest—he's ever so high. Comparison. Mary Ann Hoberman. BiCB
John James Audubon. Stephen Vincent Benét. ThLM
John Kinsella's Lament for Mrs. Mary Moore. W. B. Yeats. DTC
John Milton said the world is a starry rain. A Willing Suspension. John Holmes. PoCh
John of Hazelgreen (B vers., with music). Unknown. BFSS
  (Jock o'Hazeldean, A vers., with music.) BFSS
John Otto. W. S. Merwin. AP
John Peel. John Woodcock Graves. SD
John Plans. Dorothy Mason Pierce. BiCB
John Quincy Adams. Stephen Vincent Benét. PoPl
John Riley. Unknown. BSO
John Sutter. Yvor Winters. PoPl; PoSa
John warns me of nostalgia. Not Wholly Lost. Raymond Souster. OBCV
John Winter. Laurence Binyon. HaSV
Johnie [or Johnnie] Armstrong. Unknown. PoPo; SIV; VaPo
Johnie Faa. Unknown. See Wraggle Taggle Gipsies, The.
Johnnie Crack and Flossie Snail. Dylan Thomas. Fr. Under Milk Wood. DaDu; GoJo; LOW
Johnnie Sands. Unknown, at. to John Sinclair and to J. Simmonds. BSO
  (She Loved Her Husband Dearly, with music.) BFSS
Johnny and the Highwayman, with music. Unknown. BFSS
Johnny Appleseed's Hymn to the Sun. Vachel Lindsay. MoRP
Johnny bought the youngest a gay gold ring. The Two Little Sisters. Unknown. BSO
Johnny Doyle. Unknown. BSNS
  (Johnny Dile, with music.) BSO
Johnny Fife and Johnny's Wife. Mildred Plew Merryman. SoPo
Johnny German. Unknown. BFSS, with music; BSNS
Johnny, I Hardly Knew Ye. Unknown. ELP
Johnny O Dutchman, with music. Unknown. BFSS
Johnny Went to Church One Day. Unknown. BBGG
Johnny's been on sea, Johnny's been on shore. Young Johnny. Unknown. BFSS
Johnny's History Lesson. Nixon Waterman. PoLF
John's manners at the table. The Visitor. Katharine Pyle. BBGG
Johnson and Coldwell. Unknown. BSNS

Johnson and the Colonel, with music. Unknown. BSNS
Johnson on Pope. David Ferry. PP
Jolly Beggar, The, with music. Unknown. BFSS
Jolly Beggars, The. Burns. EiCP
  I Once Was a Maid, sel. UnTE
Jolly boating weather. Eton Boating Song. William Johnson Cory. ELP
Jolly Boatman. Unknown. BSO
Jolly Driver, The. Unknown. UnTE
Jolly Farmer, The, with music. Unknown. BFSS
  (Dog and Gun, A and B vers.) BSO
Jolly old clown, The. The Clown. Mary Catherine Rose. SoPo
Jolly Ploughboy, The. Unknown. BSNS
Jolly Sailors Bold. Unknown. BSNS
Jolly Wat. Unknown. BuBa
Jonah. Thomas Blackburn. DaDu
Jonah. Randall Jarrell. MoRP
Jonas Kindred's Household. George Crabbe. Fr. The Frank Courtship. OBNC
Jonathan Bing. Beatrice Curtis Brown. OnMSP; SoPo
Jonathan Gentry, sel. Mark Van Doren.
  Tom's Sleeping Song, fr. III. LOW
Jonathan Moulton lost his wife. The Two Wives. Daniel Henderson. SIV
Jordan ("When first my lines [or verse]"). George Herbert. MeP; PP; SeCP; VaPo
Jordan ("Who sayes [or says] that fictions"). George Herbert. CABA; PP; SeCP; VaPo
Jorge Hernandez, architect. Intimate Party in Guadalajara, Dec. 1963. Anthony Ostroff. OPP
Joseph and Mary, with music. Unknown. BFSS
Joseph Rodman Drake. Fitz-Greene Halleck. See On the Death of Joseph Rodman Drake.
Joseph Was an Old Man. Unknown. See Cherry-Tree Carol, The.
Joseph's Suspicion. Rainer Maria Rilke, tr. fr. German by M. D. Herter Norton. MoRP
Journals Nov. 22, '63. Allen Ginsberg. OPP
Journey into Misery. Yvan Goll, tr. fr. German by Christopher Middleton. MGP
Journey of the Magi. T. S. Eliot. BoC; CABA; CaFP; DiPo; DTC; EaLo; FoBA; ILP; MoRP; MP; PoIE; PoPo; PoSa; WePo
Journey Onwards, The. Thomas Moore. GTBS-P
Journey to Golgotha, The. K. Raghavendra Rao. ACV
Journeyman Tailor, The, with music. Unknown. BFSS
Journeyman's Song, The. Wilhelm Müller, tr. fr. German by Francis Owen. AGP
Jovial Tinker, The. Unknown. UnTE
Joy and Peace in Believing. William Cowper. TRV
Joy, great joy, was the message. Joy to the World. Unknown. STF
Joy, I did lock thee up: but some bad man. The Bunch of Grapes. George Herbert. MeP
Joy in the rising of our Orient starre. Her Nativity. Robert Southwell. MeP
Joy, joy to mortals! The rejoicing fires. Love's Triumph. Ben Jonson. EnRePo
Joy of Church Fellowship Rightly Attended, The. Edward Taylor. Fr. Gods Determinations. AP; CBEP
Joy of Love, The. Allan Dowling. ErPo
Joy of My Life. Henry Vaughan. BoC
Joy to the World. Unknown. STF
Joyful, joyful, we adore Thee. Hymn of Love. Henry van Dyke. TRV
Joyful Prophecy. Vassar Miller. CoPo
Joyful Traveller, The. Joseph von Eichendorff, tr. fr. German by Stewart H. Benedict. AGP
Jubilate Agno, sels. Christopher Smart.
  "For I am not without authority in my jeopardy." EiCP
  For I Will Consider My Cat Jeoffry. CTC; EiCP
  (My Cat Jeoffrey.) PoSa; WiR
  "For the doubling of flowers is the improvement of the gard'ner's talent." EiCP
  "Rejoice in God, O ye tongues; give the glory to the Lord, and the Lamb." EiCP
Jubilate not when you judge that no rack is required. Rainer Maria Rilke. Fr. Sonnets to Orpheus, II, 9. TwGP
Judas. Georg Heym, tr. fr. German by Christopher Middleton. MGP
Judas Iscariot. Countee Cullen. PoLF
Judas Sells His Lord. Unknown. MeEL
Judeebug's Country. Joe Johnson. PtTo
Judge enforcing the obsolete law, The. W. H. Auden. Fr. On This Island. TRV
Judgement. George Herbert. MeP; SeCP
Judgment of the May, The. Richard Watson Dixon. OBNC
Judges, Judges. Gene Baro. NePoEA-2
Judging Distances. Henry Reed. Lessons of the War, II. GTBS-P
Judgment Day. John Oxenham. TRV
Judith of Bethulia. John Crowe Ransom. DTC
Juggler. Richard Wilbur. PoIE

Juggling Jerry. George Meredith. VP
Jugs, The. Paul Celan, *tr. fr. German by* Christopher Middleton. MGP
Jugurtha. Longfellow. AP
Juice glass throbs against his lips, The. A Negro Judge. Frederick Seidel. CoPo
Juke box has a big square face, The. King Juke. Kenneth Fearing. PoPo
Julia was careless, and withal. Upon Julia's Fall. Robert Herrick. UnTE
Juliana. *Unknown, tr. fr. Latin by* George F. Whicher. BoLP
Julie, I pledge thee this Narcissus fair. Le Narcisse. Charles de Saint-Maure, Duc de Montausier. *Fr.* Guirlande de Julie. RBL
Juliet. Hilaire Belloc. BoLP; WePo
Julius Caesar, *sels.* Shakespeare.
  Antony's Oration, *fr.* III, ii. PoPl
  There Is a Tide, *fr.* IV, ii. PoPl
    ("There is a tide in the affairs of men.") TRV
July. Theodor Storm, *tr. fr. German by* Alexander Gode. AGP
July. Lyudmila Tatyanicheva, *tr. fr. Russian by* Babette Deutsch. SiGo
Jumblies, The. Edward Lear. EvOK; GoJo; OnMSP; SoPo; WiR
Jump or Jingle. Evelyn Beyer. SoPo
"Jump up behind me and away we will ride." Pretty Molly. *Unknown.* BFSS
June ("Over his keys the musing organist"). James Russell Lowell. *Fr.* The Vision of Sir Launfal. PoLF
June ("What is so rare"). James Russell Lowell. *Fr.* The Vision of Sir Launfal. FaBV
    ("And what is so rare as a day in June.") AmLP; FaPL
June-bug roosted under a leaf, The. A Night in June. James Larkin Pearson. PoNC
June Light. Richard Wilbur. CaFP
June Morning. Hugh McCrae. PoAu-1
Jungle, The. William Carlos Williams. CABA
Juniper Tree, The. Wilfred Watson. BoLP
Junk. Richard Wilbur. CaFP; LV
Just a Breeze! Edith Earnshaw. PoNC
Just a Mile Beyond. Aileen Fisher. RePo
Just a Smack at Auden. William Empson. ToPo
Just a solitude. Little Air. Stéphane Mallarmé. PoPl
Just after Noon with Fierce Shears. Tram Combs. MP
Just and Unjust. Lord Bowen. PoPl
Just as a silkworm with much selfless pain. Michelangelo, *tr. fr. Italian by* Joseph Tusiani. RBL
Just as an empty form. Michelangelo, *tr. fr. Italian by* Joseph Tusiani. RBL
Just as I used to say. Lawrence Ferlinghetti. *Fr.* Pictures of the Gone World. ToPo
Just as my fingers on these keys. Peter Quince at the Clavier. Wallace Stevens. AP; CABA; ILP; MP; VaPo
Just at the self-same beat of Time's wide wings. The Bruised Titans. Keats. *Fr.* Hyperion; a Fragment. OBNC
Just before bed. The Mother's Tale. Eleanor Farjeon. BiCB
Just Dropped In. William Cole. GoJo; PoPl
Just for a handful of silver he left us. The Lost Leader. Robert Browning. FaPL
Just for Today. Sybil F. Partridge. TRV
Just Keep on Keepin' On. *Unknown.* STF
Just now the lilac is in bloom. The Old Vicarage, Grantchester. Rupert Brooke. FaBV
Just off the highway to Rochester, Minnesota. A Blessing. James Wright. AmPC; StP
Just lost, when I was saved! Emily Dickinson. AP
Just-so Stories, *sel.* Kipling.
  Camel's Hump, The. EvOK
"Just the place for a Snark!" the Bellman cried. The Hunting of the Snark. "Lewis Carroll." OBNC; OnMSP
Just to Be Glad. Merlin G. Miller. STF
Just Vengeance, The, *sel.* Dorothy Sayers.
  "I have sinned; I have betrayed the innocent blood." BoC
Justice Is Reason Enough. Diane Wakoski. CoPo
Justice of Men! I Go in Search of You. Rosalía de Castro, *tr. fr. Spanish by* Edwin Morgan. AnSP
Juxtaposition. Arthur Hugh Clough. *Fr.* Amours de Voyage. OBNC

K

Kaddish. Allen Ginsberg. AmPC
"O Russian faced, woman on the grass," *sel.* PtTo
Kafka in England. Franz Baermann Steiner, *tr. fr. German by* Michael Hamburger. MGP
Kangaroo, The. *Unknown.* SoPo
Kangaroo by Nightfall. Noel Macainsh. PoAu-2
Kangaroo has a heavy tail, The. Tails. Rowena Bennett. RePo

Kant and His Interpreters. Schiller, *tr. fr. German by* Walter Kaufmann. TwGP
Karma. E. A. Robinson. AP; ILP
Karolin's Song. Ben Jonson. *See* Though I Am Young.
Karshish, the picker-up of learning's crumbs. An Epistle Containing the Strange Medical Experience of Karshish, the Arab Physician. Robert Browning. CABL; VP
Kaspar Is Dead. Hans Arp, *tr. fr. German by* Christopher Middleton. MGP
Kate and Her Horns. *Unknown.* BSNS
Katharine. Heine, *tr. fr. German by* Louis Untermeyer. UnTE
Katherine Johnstone. *Unknown.* BuBa
Kath'rine Jaffrey, *with music. Unknown.* BFSS
Katzenjammer Kids, The. James Reaney. OBCV
Kayak, The. *Unknown.* RePo
K'e still ripples to its banks, The. A Chinese Poem Written in B.C. 718. *Unknown.* WePo
Keats. Longfellow. AP
Keen, Fitful Gusts Are Whispering Here and There. Keats. CABA
Keep a Poem in Your Pocket. Beatrice Schenk de Regniers. SoPo
Keep Darkness. Leslie Nelson Jennings. FiSC
Keep love a-boiling; keep soup in the pot. Recipe. *Unknown.* UnTE
Keep Sweet. *Unknown.* STF
Keep Your Grit. *Unknown.* STF
Keeping Victory. Walter E. Isenhour. STF
Kehama's Curse. Robert Southey. *Fr.* The Curse of Kehama. OBNC
Keine Lazarovitch. Irving Layton. ACV
Kelly the Pirate (A, B, *and* C *vers., with music*). *Unknown.* BSNS
Kemp Oweyne [*or* Owyne]. *Unknown.* BuBa; CBEP
Kennedy Poem. Neil Myers. OPP
Kennedy Ucciso. Richard F. Hugo. OPP
Kentucky Belle. Constance Fenimore Woolson. SIV
Kentucky water, clear springs: a boy fleeing. The Swimmers. Allen Tate. AP
Kerchoo! Margaret Fishback. PoSC
Kettle descants in a cozy drone, The. At Tea. Thomas Hardy. *Fr.* Satires of Circumstance. VaPo
Kevin O'Culihain, Zorro Tio of the Andes, Exile, *sel.* Anne Peters.
  "Ah, well! In the great Empire of all." PtTo
Key, The. Schiller, *tr. fr. German by* Walter Kaufmann. TwGP
Key of the Kingdom, The. *Unknown.* CBEP
Keys of Heaven, The (B *and* C *vers., with music*; D *vers.*). *Unknown.* BSO
  (Paper of Pins, A.) BFSS, *with music*; BSO (A *vers.*)
Kibbutz Sabbath. Levi Ben Amittai, *tr. fr. Hebrew by* Simon Halkin. EaLo
Kick a Little Stone. Dorothy Aldis. SoPo
Kickoff. In the Beginning Was the. Lee Murchison. SD
Kid Has Gone to the Colors, The. W. M. Herschell. PoLF
Kid Stuff. Frank Horne. AmNP
Kilcash. *Unknown, tr. fr. Irish by* Frank O'Connor. WePo
Killed at the Ford. Longfellow. AP
Killer, The. Richard Eberhart. OPP
Killers are killed, their violent rinds, The. Lunch on Omaha Beach. Bink Noll. StP; ToPo
Killing, The. Edwin Muir. ACV; MoRP; PoPl
Kilmeny. James Hogg. *Fr.* The Queen's Wake. CABL
Kilroy. Peter Viereck. ThLM
Kimono, The. Don Gordon. PtTo
Kind and True. Aurelian Townsend. CBEP
Kind Are Her Answers. Thomas Campion. ELP
Kind friends, if you will listen, a story I will tell. The Sherman Cyclone. *Unknown.* BFSS
Kind of Libation, A. James L. Weil. OPP
Kind of like a stormy day, take it all together. A Rainy Day. Joseph C. Lincoln. RePo
Kind pity [*or* Kinde pitty] chokes my spleen[e]; brave scorn forbids. Satire [*or* Satyre] III: On Religion. John Donne. *Fr.* Satires. CABA; CABL; MeP; SeCP
Kind solace in a dying hour! Tamerlane. Poe. AP
Kinde pitty chokes my spleene; brave scorn forbids. *See* Kind pity chokes my spleen . . .
Kindly Unhitch That Star, Buddy. Ogden Nash. PoPl
Kindly watcher by my bed, lift no voice in prayer. Music. George DuMaurier. CBEP
Kindness. Sylvia Plath. BoC
Kindness. *Unknown.* STF
Kindness during Life. *Unknown.* STF
Kindness to Animals. Laura E. Richards. SoPo
Kindness to Animals. *Unknown.* SoPo
King, The. Kipling. CABA
King Arthur, *sel.* Dryden.
  Fairest Isle, *fr.* V, i. CBEP
King Arthur, growing very tired indeed. Salad: After Tennyson. Mortimer Collins. Par
King David. Heine, *tr. fr. German by* Walter Kaufmann. TwGP

King Estmere. *Unknown.* BuBa
King Francis was a hearty king, and loved a royal sport. The Glove and the Lions. Leigh Hunt. SIV; StP
King George raised his jewelled pen. The Means Massacre. Robert P. Tristram Coffin. SIV
King-heart. Seed of a lofty. Mausoleum. Rainer Maria Rilke. MGP
King Henry V, *sels.* Shakespeare.
Epilogue: "Thus far, with rough and all-unable pen." CTC
Once More unto the Breach, *fr.* III, i. FaBV; PoSa
King Henry VIII, *sel.* Shakespeare *and probably* John Fletcher. Orpheus with His Lute, *fr.* III, i, *song by* Fletcher, *also at. to* Shakespeare. CBEP; EnRePo; FoBA
King John and the Abbot of Canterbury. *Unknown.* SIV
King Juke. Kenneth Fearing. PoPo
King Midas. Ovid. *tr. fr. Latin by* Arthur Golding. *Fr.* Metamorphoses, XI. CTC
King Midas Has Asses' Ears. Donald Finkel. NePoEA-2
King might miss the guiding star, A. Far Trumpets Blowing. Louis F. Benson. TRV
King of Comforts! King of life! Praise. Henry Vaughan. MeP
King of Cuckooz, The. Kenneth Slessor. *Fr.* The Atlas. PoAu-2
King of glorie, King of peace,/ With the one make warre to cease. L'Envoy. George Herbert. MeP
King of glorie, King of peace,/ I will love thee. Praise. George Herbert. MeP
King of hell came singing, The. Lucifer. Maxwell Anderson. MoRP
King of love my Shepherd is, The. The Lord Is My Shepherd. Sir H. W. Baker. ThGo
King of mercy, King of love. Begging. Henry Vaughan. MeP
"King of Morven," Carthon said, "I fall in the midst of my course." James Macpherson. *Fr.* Carthon. EnPE
King Orpheo. *Unknown.* BuBa
King Paladin plunged on his moon-coloured mare. Mad Marjory. Hugh McCrae. PoAu-1
King Phillip had vaunted his claims. A Ballad to Queen Elizabeth. Austin Dobson. HaSV
King Richard II, *sels.* Shakespeare.
Let's Talk of Graves, *fr.* III, ii. DiPo
This Blessed Plot . . . This England, *fr.* II, i. FaBV
King Richard III, *sel.* Shakespeare.
"Methought I saw a thousand fearful wrecks," *fr.* I, iv. HaSV
King sits in Dunfermline town [*or* Dumferling toune], The. Sir Patrick Spens [*or* Spence]. *Unknown.* BuBa; CABA; CABL; CaFP; CBEP; DiPo; ELP; GoJo; HaSV; ILP; OnP; PoIE; PoPo; PoSa; RoGo; SIV; StP
King was on his throne, The. The Vision of Belshazzar. Byron. OnMSP; RoGo
King was sick, The. His cheek was red. The Enchanted Shirt. John Hay. RePo
King William and King James. *Unknown. See* William of Orange; or, The Battle of Boyne.
Kingdom of God, The. Francis Thompson. CaFP; EaLo; GTBS-P; PoIE; TRV
Kingdoms fall in sequence, like the waves on the shore, The. The Sparrow's Skull. Ruth Pitter. EaLo
Kingdoms of the Earth go by, The. In Hoc Signo. Godfrey Fox Bradby. TRV
Kingly were his rags, his uniform. The Drug Addict. Miriam Waddington. *Fr.* Three Prison Portraits. ACV
King's College Chapel. Charles Causley. BoC
Kings from the East, The. Heine, *tr. fr. German into Scottish by* Alexander Gray. ACV
King's Highway, The. John Masefield. TRV
King's X. Hollis Summers. StP
Kirby with Muckby-cum-Sparrowby-cum Spinx. A Lincolnshire Tale. John Betjeman. FiSC
Kirtle Gaol, *with music. Unknown.* BSNS
Kiss, The. Austin Dobson. LV
Kiss, The. Ben Jonson. *Fr.* Cynthia's Revels. UnTE
Kiss, The. Pierre Louÿs, *tr. fr. French by* Horace M. Brown. *Fr.* The Songs of Bilitis. UnTE
Kiss, The. Thomas Moore. BoLP
Kiss, The. Dante Gabriel Rossetti. The House of Life, VI. VP
(What Smouldering Senses.) UnTE
Kiss, The. Siegfried Sassoon. MMA
Kiss, The. George Wither. UnTE
Kiss and the Cup, The. *Unknown, tr. fr. Greek by* Louis Untermeyer. UnTE
Kiss, if you can: Resistance if she make. Ovid. *Fr.* Art of Love. ErPo
Kiss, lovely Celia, and be kind. Love's Courtship. Thomas Carew. UnTE
Kiss Me, Dear. Dryden. *See* Rondelay: "Chloe found Amyntas lying."
Kiss Me, Sweet. Ben Jonson, *after the Latin of* Catullus. UnTE
(To Celia.) EnRePo

(To the Same.) SeCP
"Kiss me there where pride is glistening." Aria. Delmore Schwartz. ErPo
Kiss of death by water or desire, The. Sailor. P. K. Page. ACV
Kiss, A. She is gone. Disappearing. Absence. Guido Gozzano. CoIP
Kiss'd Yestreen. *Unknown.* ErPo
Kisses Make Men Loath to Go. *Unknown.* UnTE
Kissin'. *Unknown.* BoLP
(Kissing's No Sin.) UnTE
Kissing the Dancer. Robert Sward. CoPo
Kissing's No Sin. *Unknown. See* Kissin'.
Kit Carson's Ride. Joaquin Miller. SIV
Kit Hath Lost Her Key. *Unknown.* UnTE
Kitchen Prayer, A. M. Petersen. STF
Kitchen Song. Edith Sitwell. DaDu
Kite, The. Harry Behn. RePo
Kite, A. *Unknown.* SoPo
Kite Is a Victim, A. Leonard Cohen. SD
Kite Poem. James Merrill. MP
Kitty Hawk, *sel.* Robert Frost.
But God's Own Descent. EaLo; MoRP
Kitty of Coleraine. *Unknown.* SIV
Klingling, boomboom, and chingdada. The Band Marches. Detlev von Liliencron. AGP
Klondike, The. E. A. Robinson. ThLM
Knave's a knave, A. The True Tar. Henry Carey. Two Songs, I. WaPE
Knee Lunes. Robert Kelly. CoPo
Knight and a Lady Bride, A, *with music. Unknown.* BFSS
Knight from the world's end, The. A Dream of Governors. Louis Simpson. PoSa
Knight Stained from Battle, The. William Herebert. MeEL
Knight Was with His Lady Fondly Lying, A. Gaucelm Faidit, *tr. fr. Provençal by* Norman R. Shapiro. AnML
Knight without a name, The. *Unknown.* WiR
Knight's Tomb, The. Samuel Taylor Coleridge. CBEP
Knob and hump upon this tree. A Gnarled Riverina Gum-Tree. Ernest G. Moll. PoAu-2
Know Celia, (since thou art so proud). Ingratefull Beauty Threatned. Thomas Carew. SeCP
Know It Is Christmas. Lois Snelling. BiCB
Know the world by heart. Theory of Poetry. Archibald Mac-Leish. AP
Know Then Thyself. Pope. *Fr.* An Essay on Man, Epistle II. DiPo, 18 *ll.*
("Know then thyself, presume not God to scan.") CaFP, 18 *ll.*; PoIE, *longer sel.*; PoSa, 18 *ll.*; TRV, 18 *ll.*
Know you faire on what you looke. On Mr. George Herberts Booke Intituled the Temple of Sacred Poems, Sent to a Gentle-woman. Richard Crashaw. MeP
Knowest thou the land where bloom the lemon trees. Mignon. Goethe, *tr. by* James Elroy Flecker. *Fr.* Wilhelm Meister. SiGo
Knowing what's possible, one knows. Empty House. Elizabeth J. Coatsworth. FiSC
Knowledge of Light, The. Henry Rago. PoCh
Know'st thou the land where the fair citron blows. Mignon. Goethe, *tr. by* Edgar A. Bowring. *Fr.* Wilhelm Meister. PoPl
Kokin Shu, *sel. Tr. fr. Japanese by* Arthur Waley.
"My love/ Is like the grasses." Ono no Yoshiki. SiGo
Ko-Ko's Song. W. S. Gilbert. *Fr.* The Mikado. LV
Kore. Robert Creeley. CoPo
Korea. Harland Ristau. PtTo
Korf reads much, and he is quick. The Glasses. Christian Morgenstern. TwGP
Korosta Katzina Song. *Unknown, tr. fr. Hopi Indian by* Natalie Curtis. SiGo
Kraken, The. Tennyson. CABA; CaFP; FoBA; OBNC; VaPo; WiR
Krishnakali. Rabindranath Tagore. ACV
Ku-Klux. Madison Cawein. ThLM
Kubla Khan; or, A Vision in a Dream. Samuel Taylor Coleridge. BoC; CABA; CaFP; CBEP; DiPo; ELP; FaBV; FaPL; GoJo; ILP; OBNC; OnP; PoIE; PoPl; PP; RoGo; StP
Kunai-mai-pa Mo. Ethel Anderson. PoAu-2
Kupris bears trophies away. Sophocles. *Fr.* Women of Trachis. CTC
Kurdish Shepherds. Alan Ross. DaDu
Kyrie, so kyrie. Jankin, the Clerical Seducer. *Unknown.* MeEL

L

La Bella Bona Roba. Richard Lovelace. SeCP
La Bella Donna della Mia Mente. Oscar Wilde. UnTE
La Belle Dame sans Merci. Keats. CABA; CBEP; DiPo;

ELP; FoBA; GoJo; GTBS-P; ILP; OBNC; OnP; PoIE; PoPo; PoSa; StP; VaPo; WePo
La Belle Sauvage. John Hunter-Duvar. *Fr.* De Roberval. OBCV
La Condition Botanique. Anthony Hecht. MP
La Corona. John Donne. MeP
La Fayette. Dolley Madison. ThLM
La Figlia Che Piange. T. S. Eliot. PoIE
La Tour du Sorcier. Sir Osbert Sitwell. DaDu
Labor Day. Marnie Pomeroy. PoSC
Labor Not in Vain. *Unknown.* STF
Labor raises honest sweat. The Dignity of Labor. Robert Bersohn. PoPl
Labor Room. Gottfried Benn, *tr. fr. German by* Walter Kaufmann. TwGP
Labor sweet that I sustained in thee, The. To the Translation of Palingenius. Barnabe Googe. EnRePo
Laboratory, The. Robert Browning. SIV
Laboratory Poem. James Merrill. MP; NePoEA-2
Labourer, A. R. S. Thomas. ToPo
Labyrinth, The. Edwin Muir. PoIE
Lack of Steadfastness. Chaucer. CBEP
(Lack of Stedfastnesse.) ILP
Lad of the Mountain, The. Ludwig Uhland, *tr. fr. German by* Francis Owen. AGP
Ladd I the dance a midsomer day. A Night with a Holy-Water Clerk. *Unknown.* MeEL
Ladder, The. Gene Baro. NePoEA-2
Ladies' Aid, The. *Unknown.* PoLF
Ladies I do here present you. A Present to a Lady. *Unknown.* ErPo
Ladies I Like Well Dressed. Pere March, *tr. fr. Catalan by* William M. Davis. AnML
Ladies, who of my lord would fain be told. Gaspara Stampa, *tr. fr. Italian by* Lorna de' Lucchi. RBL
Ladies You See Time Flieth. *Unknown.* EnRePo
Lads in their hundreds to Ludlow come in for the fair, The. A Shropshire Lad, XXIII. A. E. Housman. VP
Lady, a lady, a lady of late, A. Earl Brand (C *vers.*). *Unknown.* BSO
Lady and the Bear, The. Theodore Roethke. GoJo
Lady asks me, A. Canzone: Donna Mi Priegha. Guido Cavalcanti. CTC
Lady at the Watchman's Song Perceived, A. Wolfram von Eschenbach, *tr. fr. German by* Charles E. Passage. AnML
Lady Begs Me, A. Guido Cavalcanti. *See* Canzone: Donna Mi Priegha.
Lady came to a bear by a stream, A. The Lady and the Bear. Theodore Roethke. GoJo
Lady Clare. Tennyson. OnMSP
Lady Comes to an Inn, A. Elizabeth J. Coatsworth. SIV
Lady Elspat. *Unknown.* BuBa
Lady Flower, *with music. Unknown.* BFSS
Lady! helpe, Jesu! mercy. In His Utter Wretchedness. John Audelay. MeEL
Lady I Know, A. Countee Cullen. *See* For a Lady I Know.
Lady, I thank thee for thy loveliness. The Moonstar. Dante Gabriel Rossetti. The House of Life, XXIX. VP
Lady, I trust it is not to do harm. A Volume of Chopin. James Picot. PoAu-2
Lady Isabel and the Elf-Knight (*diff. versions*). *Unknown.* BSNS (A *and* B *vers.*); BSO (A *vers., with music;* E *vers.*); SIV
(Little Golden, B *vers.*) BSO
(My Pretty Colinn, D *vers., with music.*) BSO
(Ocean Wave, The, C *vers.*) BSO
(Pretty Polly, *with music.*) BFSS (B *vers.*); BSNS (C *vers.*)
(Sweet William, A *vers., with music.*) BFSS
Lady Lost. John Crowe Ransom. PoSa
Lady, lovely lady. Vain and Careless. Robert Graves. DaDu; LOW
Lady Margaret and Sweet William. *Unknown. See* Fair Margaret and Sweet William.
Lady of Heaven and earth, and therewithal. His Mother's Service to Our Lady. Villon. CTC
Lady of Shalott, The. Tennyson. CABL; DiPo; SIV; VP; WePo; WiR
Lady of the Lake, The, *sels.* Sir Walter Scott.
Alice Brand, *fr.* IV. OnMSP
Coronach, *fr.* III. GTBS-P; WiR
Harp of the North. Prologue. ILP
(Farewell, Thou Minstrel Harp.) OBNC
Gathering, The, *fr.* III. OBNC
Song: "Soldier, rest! thy warfare o'er," *fr.* I. OBNC
Lady of the Lake, The. *Unknown.* BSNS
Lady of the Manor, The. George Crabbe. *Fr.* The Parish Register. OBNC
Lady of the Tomahawk, The. Robert P. Tristram Coffin. SIV
Lady Ogalbie. *Unknown. See* Bonny House of Airlie, The.
Lady Stood Alone, A. Dietmar von Aist, *tr. fr. German by* Margaret F. Richey. AnML
Lady, sweet, now do not frown. Joan to Her Lady. *Unknown.* UnTE

Lady, That in the Prime of Earliest Youth. Milton. FoBA
Lady Thinks She Is Thirty, A. Ogden Nash. PoPl
Lady took exception to assertions, The. Salems of Oppression. Joseph Joel Keith. FiSC
Lady who lived in Uganda, A. The Panda. William Jay Smith. RePo
Lady Who Offers Her Looking-Glass to Venus, The. Matthew Prior. CBEP
Lady who stands on my long writing table. Leaving Ithaca. W. D. Snodgrass. AmPC
Lady, why doth love torment you? Love's Torment. *Unknown.* UnTE
Lady, Wilt Thou Heal My Smart? Heinrich von Morungen, *tr. fr. German by* Herman Salinger. AnML
Lady with the Unicorn, The. Vernon Watkins. MP
Lady without Paragon, A. Chaucer. *See* Hide, Absolon.
Lady World, You Tell the Devil. Walther von der Vogelweide, *tr. fr. German by* Gillian Barker *and* Kenneth Gee. AnML
Lady, you are the body, and I am your shadow. Maurice Scève. *Fr. Délie.* RBL
Lady, your art or wit could ne'er devise. To a Lady Who Sent Me a Copy of Verses at My Going to Bed. Henry King. PP
Ladybird, Ladybird. Mother Goose. CBEP; SoPo
(To the Lady-Bird.) PoPl
Lady's Complaint, The. John Heath-Stubbs. MP
Lady's Dressing Room, The. Swift. ErPo
Lady's Fan, The, *with music. Unknown.* BSNS
Lady's-Maid's Song, The. John Hollander. ErPo
(Lady's-Maid Song, The.) MP
Laggandoan, Harris. Norman MacCaig. AnMoPo
Laid in My Quiet Bed. Earl of Surrey. EnRePo
Laird o' Logie, The. *Unknown.* CBEP
Lais Now Old. *Unknown.* EnRePo
Lak of Stedfastnesse. Chaucer. *See* Lack of Steadfastness.
Lake, The. Matthew Arnold. *See* Meeting.
Lake, in dark-blue reverie, The. The Dreaming Lake. Julius Mosen. OBCV
Lake is sharp along the shore, The. Lakeshore. F. R. Scott. OBCV
Lake Isle, The. Ezra Pound. CABA
Lake Isle of Innisfree, The. W. B. Yeats. BoC; DiPo; FaBV; FaPL; FoBA; ILP; PoPl; PoPo; RoGo
Lake lay blue below the hill, The. The Blue Bird. Mary Elizabeth Coleridge. WePo
Lake Leman. Byron. *Fr.* Childe Harold's Pilgrimage. OBNC
Lake Winnipesaukee. Olive Driver. RePo
Lakeshore. F. R. Scott. OBCV
Lalique. Hal Porter. PoAu-2
Lalla Rookh, *sels.* Thomas Moore. OBNC
Golden Hour, The.
Peri's Lament for Hinda, The, *fr.* The Fire-Worshippers.
L'Allegro. Milton. CABA; CBEP; FoBA; GTBS-P; ILP
Mirth, with Thee I Mean to Live, *sel.* FaBV
Lama, The. Ogden Nash. RePo
Lamarck Elaborated. Richard Wilbur. AP
Lamb, The. Blake. *Fr.* Songs of Innocence. CABA; CaFP; CBEP; DiPo; EaLo; EnPE; FoBA; GoJo; ILP; PoIE; PoPl; PoPo; TRV; VaPo
Lamb of God, Thy faithful promise. The Coming and the Appearing. *Unknown.* STF
Lament: "Listen, children:/ Your father is dead." Edna St. Vincent Millay. PoPl; PoPo
Lament: "Oh, everything is far." Rainer Maria Rilke, *tr. fr. German by* C. F. MacIntyre. PoPl
Lament, A: "O World! O Life! O Time!" Shelley. GTBS-P; PoPo
Lament: "Sleep and death, the dusky eagles." Georg Trakl, *tr. fr. German by* Michael Hamburger. MGP
(Lament: "Sleep and death, the gloomy eagles," *tr. by* Walter Kaufmann.) TwGP
Lament, A: "We who are left, how shall we look again." W. W. Gibson. MMA
Lament: "When I was a windy boy and a bit." Dylan Thomas. ErPo
Lament for Better or Worse. Gene Baro. FiSC; NePoEA-2
Lament for Culloden. Burns. CBEP; GTBS-P
Lament for Flodden. Jane Elliot. GTBS-P; WePo
Lament for Glasgerion. Elinor Wylie. AmLP
Lament for the Alamo. Arthur Guiterman. RePo
Lament for the Frontiers of the Empire. Jack Lindeman. PtTo
Lament for the Love of Heroes, The. Wolfram von Eschenbach, *tr. fr. German by* Gillian Barker *and* Kenneth Gee. AnML
Lament for the Makaris [*or* Makers]. William Dunbar. CBEP; PP
(Fear of Death Confounds Me, The.) MeEL
(Lament for the Makaris, Quhen He Wes Seik.) PoIE
Lament for Tintoretta. William Collins. Three Fragments, 3. WaPE
Lament for Walsingham. *Unknown.* CBEP

Lament in Autumn. Harold Stewart. PoAu-2
Lament of a Border Widow, *with music. Unknown.* BFSS
Lament of a Man for His Son. *Unknown, tr. fr. Paiute Indian by* Mary Austin. LV
Lament of the Frontier Guard. Li Po, *tr. fr. Chinese by* Ezra Pound. AP
Lament of the Lovely Helmet-Dealer. Villon. *See* Complaint of the Fair Armouress, The.
Lament of the Virgin. Gonzalo de Berceo, *tr. fr. Spanish by* Beatrice P. Patt. AnML
Lamentable Case, A. Sir Charles Hanbury Williams. ErPo; UnTE; WaPE
Lamentation of Enion, The. Blake. *Fr.* Vala; or, The Four Zoas. OBNC
Lamentation of the Old Pensioner, The. W. B. Yeats. PoPo
Lamia. Keats. CABL
Lamkin. *Unknown.* CBEP
Lamp, The. Sara Teasdale. MoLP
Lampe, The. Henry Vaughan. MeP
Lamps burn all the night. The Fifth Sense. Patricia Beer. MoBS
Lamps inside the house, The. 2000 A.D. Beverly Connelly. FiSC
Lamp's Shrine, The. Dante Gabriel Rossetti. The House of Life, XXXV. VP
L'An Trentiesme de Mon Eage. Archibald MacLeish. AmLP
Lancelot and Elaine, *sel.* Tennyson. *Fr.* Idylls of the King. Song of Love and Death, The. OBNC
Land, The. Kipling. OnMSP
Land Dirge, A. John Webster. *See* Call for the Robin Redbreast.
Land I Came thro' Last, The. Christopher Brennan. *Fr.* The Wanderer. PoAu-1
Land lies in water; it is shadowed green. The Map. Elizabeth Bishop. RePo
Land o' the Leal, The. Lady Nairne. GTBS-P
Land of Counterpane, The. Robert Louis Stevenson. EvOK; ILP; PoPl; SoPo
Land of my birth! though now, alas! no more. William Charles Wentworth. *Fr.* Australasia. PoAu-1
Land of Story-Books, The. Robert Louis Stevenson. FaPL
Land of the Never-ending Heart. Kenneth Patchen. ToPo
Land, that, from the rule of kings, The. The Bartholdi Statue. Whittier. ThLM
Land was ours before we were the land's, The. The Gift Outright. Robert Frost. AmLP; AP; OPP; PoIE; PoPo; RePo
Land We Adore, The, *with music. Unknown.* SGR
Landing of the British Settlers of 1820, The, *sel.* Alex Wilmot. "North, south, east, west, the settlers scatter wide." ACV
Landing of the Pilgrim Fathers, The. Felicia Dorothea Hemans. FaBV; FaPL; ThLM
Landscape. Baudelaire, *tr. fr. French by* George Dillon. SiGo
Landscape as Metal and Flowers. Winfield Townley Scott. GoJo
Landscape before Easter. Werner Zemp, *tr. fr. German by* Christopher Middleton. MGP
Landscape, Deer Season. Barbara Howes. GoJo
Landscape near a Steel Mill. Herschel Horn. PtTo
Landscape near an Aerodrome, The. Stephen Spender. StP
Landscape, suspended from our loins, The. Aircraft, Landing. Colin Thiele. ACV
Landscape, The (the landscape!) again: Gloucester. The Librarian. Charles Olson. CoPo
Landscape with Figures. Theodore Enslin. CoPo
Landscapes, *sels.* T. S. Eliot.
  Cape Ann, V. DaDu; EvOK; GoJo
  New Hampshire, I. GTBS-P; LOW; PoSa
  Virginia, II. PoSa
Landskip, The. William Shenstone. CBEP
Landsman, The. Moschus, *tr. fr. Greek by* Shelley. SiGo
Language, The. Robert Creeley. CoPo
Language has not the power to speak what love indites. John Clare. OBNC
Langue d'Oc, *sel.* Ezra Pound.
  Alba. PoIE
Lanky head of a she in the inn over there, The. A Glass of Beer [or Righteous Anger]. James Stephens. CBEP; DTC; PoPl
Lanthorn is to keep the candle light, The. Bunyan. ThGo
Lanty Leary. Samuel Lover. BoLP
Lapis Lazuli. W. B. Yeats. AnMoPo; DTC; FoBA; ILP; PoIE; PP
L'Après Midi d'une Fille aux Cheveux de Lin. Ronald McCuaig. PoAu-2
Larger, gentler slopes of its mouth opening upon the ocean, The. The Dysynni Valley. Theodore Holmes. CoPo
Lariat snaps, The; the cowboy rolls. The Closing of the Rodeo. William Jay Smith. SD
Lark, The. René Char, *tr. fr. French by* Richard G. Stern. Four Fascinators, IV. CoFP
Lark, The. Bernart de Ventadorn. *See* When I See the Skylark Winging.
Lark Ascending, The. George Meredith. CABL; WiR

Lark he rises early, The. Break of Day. John Clare. CBEP
Lark's Song, The. Blake. *Fr.* Milton, II. WiR (Vision of the Lamentation of Beulah over Ololon, A.) OBNC
Larry McGee. *Unknown.* BSNS
Lars Porsena of Clusium. Horatius. Macaulay. *Fr.* Lays of Ancient Rome. PoLF
L'Art pour l'Art. Christian Morgenstern, *tr. fr. German by* Walter Kaufmann. TwGP
Las' night you hear da op'ra? Da Wheestlin' Barber. T. A. Daly. SIV
Lascivious shivers. Early bloom. As if. Subway Train. Gottfried Benn. MGP
Lass and the Friar, The. Burns, *sometimes at. to the* Earl of Rochester. UnTE
Lass of Isleworth Mill, The. Richard Wooddeson. WaPE
Lass of Mohee, The. *Unknown. See* Indian Mohee, The.
Lass That Made the Bed for Me, The. Burns. UnTE
Lassitude. Paul Verlaine, *tr. fr. French by* Lawrence M. Bensky. ErPo
Last and greatest herald of Heaven's King, The. Saint John the Baptist. William Drummond of Hawthornden. CBEP; EaLo; GTBS-P
Last Buccaneer, The. Charles Kingsley. HaSV (Old Buccaneer, The.) EvOK
Last Campaign, The. Geoffrey Lehmann. PoAu-2
Last Chance, The. Andrew Lang. SD
Last Chantey, The. Kipling. HaSV
Last Charge, The. BSO
Last cinder of sky and first ardor of day. The Lark. René Char. *Fr.* Four Fascinators. CoFP
Last Confession, A. W. B. Yeats. ELP; ErPo; FoBA
Last Conqueror, The. James Shirley. *See* Victorious Men of Earth.
Last Day, The. Lola Derosier. STF
Last Defile, The. Amy Carmichael. TRV
Last evening when I went to bed. Our Birthday. Marion Edey. BiCB
Last Fierce Charge, The. *Unknown. See* Custer's Last Fierce Charge.
Last Fire. Dante Gabriel Rossetti. The House of Life, XXX. VP
Last Flower, The. John Travers Moore. PoSC
Last Fruit off an Old Tree, The, *sel.* Walter Savage Landor. I Strove with None. PoIE; PoPo; PoSa
  (Dying Speech of an Old Philosopher.) FaPL; GTBS-P ("I strove with none, for none was worth my strife.") OBNC
Last Good-bye, The. John A. Stone. SGR
Last Invocation, The. Walt Whitman. FoBA; TRV
Last Leaf, The. Harry Behn. RePo
Last Leaf, The. Oliver Wendell Holmes. AmLP; AP; CaFP; PoIE; PoLF; PoPo
Last Letter. Hans Egon Holthusen, *tr. fr. German by* Marianne Leibholz. MGP
Last Lines. Emily Brontë. BoC; CBEP; FaPL (No Coward Soul Is Mine.) EaLo; OBNC; PoIE "Though earth and man were gone," *sel.* TRV
Last Meeting. Gwen Harwood. PoAu-2
Last night, ah, yesternight, betwixt her lips and mine. Non Sum Qualis Eram Bonae sub Regno Cynarae [or Cynara]. Ernest Dowson. BoLP; CABA; FaPL; GTBS-P; OBNC; PoPl; UnTE
Last night as I lay on the prairie. The Cowboy's Dream. *Unknown.* BFSS
Last night at black midnight I woke with a cry. The Ghosts of the Buffaloes. Vachel Lindsay. LV; RePo
Last night I did not fight for sleep. In Hospital: Poona (I). Alun Lewis. DTC
"Last night I dreamed a ghastly dream." Ballad of the Flood. Edwin Muir. MoBS
Last night I heard a *rat-tat-too.* Rain Riders. Clinton Scollard. SoPo
Last night I took a journey. Traveling on My Knees. Sandra Goodwin. STF
Last night I watched my brothers play. The Brothers. Edwin Muir. GTBS-P
Last night in the open shippen. Christmas Day. Andrew Young. DaDu
Last night knives flashed. LeChien cried. The Wolves. Galway Kinnell. NePoEA-2
Last night my little boy confessed to me. Two Prayers. Andrew Gillies. TRV
Last Night of November, The. *Unknown.* BSO
Last night that she lived, The. Emily Dickinson. CBEP; DiPo; FoBA; ILP
Last night while I was dreaming. *Unknown, tr. fr. German by* D. G. Wright. AGP
Last night while we were fast asleep. New Year's Day. Rachel Field. SoPo
Last of His Tribe, The. Henry Kendall. PoAu-1
Last Pagan Mourns for Dark Rosaleen, The. Joseph Payne Brennan. FiSC
Last Post, The. Robert Graves. MMA

Last Prayer, A. Helen Hunt Jackson. TRV
Last Ride Together, The. Robert Browning. VP
Last Ride Together, The. J. K. Stephen. Par
Last Saturday night me wife she died. Fragments of Irish Songs. *Unknown.* BSO
Last sea-thing dredged by sailor Time from Space. Australia. Bernard O'Dowd. PoAu-1
Last, since a pinch of dust may quench the eyes. Lilith on the Fate of Man. Christopher Brennan. *Fr.* Lilith. PoAu-1
Last Summer, The. Vivian Smith. PoAu-2
Last Supper, The. Ranier Maria Rilke, *tr. fr. German by* M. D. Herter Norton. MoRP
Last Supper, The. Oscar Williams. MoRP
Last time I saw Donald Armstrong, The. The Performance. James Dickey. NePoEA-2
Last Warehouse, The. May Miller. PtTo
Last Warmth of Arnold, The. Gregory Corso. CoPo
Last Will and Testament, A. *Unknown.* MeEL
Last Will of the Drunk. Myra Von Riedemann. OBCV
Last Word, The. Matthew Arnold. CABA; OBNC; PoSa
Last Word of a Bluebird, The. Robert Frost. GoJo; ThGo
Last Words, The. Maurice Maeterlinck, *tr. fr. French by* Frederick York Powell. PoPl
Last year's Christmas Eve at five. Legend, Not Quite House-broken. Erich Kästner. TwGP
Lat no man booste of conning nor vertu. Transient as a Rose. John Lydgate. MeEL
Late Air. Elizabeth Bishop. PoPl
Late as last summer. Thou Didst Say Me. Miriam Wadding-ton. OBCV
Late-flowering Lust. John Betjeman. ErPo
Late lark twitters from the quiet skies, A. Margaritae Sorori [*or* Some Late Lark Singing]. W. E. Henley. CBEP; OBNC; PoPo; PoSa; TRV
Late last night I slew my wife. Necessity. Harry Graham. WePo
Late October. Sara Teasdale. PoSC
Late September sun fills the room with light. Death-Bed. A. L. Rowse. WePo
Late Snow. Issa, *tr. fr. Japanese by* Harold G. Henderson. RePo
Late Snow & Lumber Strike of the Summer of Fifty-four, The. Gary Snyder. PtTo
Late that mad Monday evening. Madness One Monday Eve-ning. Julia Fields. NNP
Late Tutorial. Vincent Buckley. PoAu-2
Late Winter. James McAuley. PoAu-2
Lately, Alas, I Knew a Gentle Boy. Henry David Thoreau. AP
Lately, I've become accustomed to the way. Preface to a Twenty Volume Suicide Note. LeRoi Jones. AmNP; NNP
Lately Our Poets. Walter Savage Landor. CABA ("Lately our poets loiter'd in green lanes.") GTBS-P
Latest Decalogue, The. Arthur Hugh Clough. CABA; CaFP; CBEP; GTBS-P; ILP; OBNC; PoIE; TRV; VaPo
Lather as You Go. Ogden Nash. WePo
Latimer's Light. *Unknown.* TRV
Laugh and Be Merry. John Masefield. PoPl
Laugh, and the world laughs with you. Solitude. Ella Wheeler Wilcox. PoLF
Laugh, Be Jolly. A. E. Housman. *See* Think No More, Lad.
Laughing god born of a startling answer, The. Bacchus. Wil-liam Empson. PoCh
Laughing Hyena, by Hokusai, The. D. J. Enright. MP
Laughing, she flashes down the shifting tides of green. Water Sprite. Donald Wandrei. FiSC
Laughing Song. Blake. *Fr.* Songs of Innocence. CBEP; DiPo; GoJo; PoSC; SoPo
Laughing Time. William Jay Smith. SoPo
Laughing youngsters, The. Spring Song. Federico García Lorca. AnSP
Laughter of children brings. Early Supper. Barbara Howes. GoJo; PoPl
Laura Sleeping. Charles Cotton. ELP
Laureate, The. William Aytoun. Par
Laurel leaf, which you this day do wear, The. Amoretti, XXVIII. Spenser. CABA
Laurentian Shield. F. R. Scott. OBCV
L'Aurore Grelottante. Peter Levi. NePoEA-2
Laus Deo! Whittier. AP
Laustic, The. Marie de France, *tr. fr. French by* Charles E. Passage. AnML
Lavender's blue, diddle diddle. The Country Lovers. *Un-known.* UnTE
Law against Lovers, The, *sel.* Sir William Davenant. Wake All the Dead. CBEP; ELP
Law in the Country of the Cats. Ted Hughes. ToPo
Law like Love. W. H. Auden. CaFP
Law makes long spokes of the short stakes of men. Legal Fiction. William Empson. ToPo
Law of Death, The. John Hay. SIV
Law, say the gardeners, is the sun. Law like Love. W. H. Auden. CaFP

Lawlands o' Holland, The. *Unknown.* HaSV
Lawn as white as driven snow. The Pedlar. Shakespeare. *Fr.* The Winter's Tale, IV, iii. WiR
Lawn-Mower. Dorothy Baruch. SoPo
Lawrence, of Virtuous Father Virtuous Son. Milton. CABA (To Mr. Lawrence.) DiPo; GTBS-P
Lawyer's Invocation to Spring, The. Henry Howard Brownell. PoLF
Lay a garland on my hearse. John Fletcher. *Fr.* The Maid's Tragedy. ILP
Lay. me down beneaf de willers in de grass. A Death Song. Paul Laurence Dunbar. PoLF
Lay me in the woodbox. Last Will of the Drunk. Myra Von Riedemann. OBCV
Lay me on an anvil, O God. Prayers of Steel. Carl Sandburg. AP
Lay of Hildebrand, The. *Unknown, tr. fr. German by* Her-man Salinger. AnML
Lay of the Last Minstrel, The, *sels.* Sir Walter Scott. Breathes There the Man, *fr.* VI. LV
  (Patriot, The.) OBNC
  (Patriotism.) TRV
Father's Notes of Woe, A, *fr.* IV. OBNC
Minstrel Responds to Flattery, The, *fr.* V. OBNC
Rosabelle, *fr.* VI. GTBS-P
Sir William of Deloraine at the Wizard's Tomb, *fr.* II. OBNC
Lay Preacher Ponders, The. Idris Davies. ACV
Lay these words into the dead man's grave. In Memoriam Paul Eluard. Paul Celan. MGP
Lay this laurel on the one. Emily Dickinson. AP
Lay up nearer, brother, nearer. The Dying Californian. *Un-known.* BFSS; BSO
Lay Your Sleeping Head, My Love. W. H. Auden. VaPo
Laying the Dust. Denise Levertov. ToPo
Lays of Ancient Rome, *sels.* Macaulay.
Armada, The, *sel.*
  "Night sank upon the dusky beach, and on the purple sea." OBNC
Horatius. PoLF
Lazy laughing languid Jenny. Jenny. Dante Gabriel Rossetti. VP
Lazy Lou. Mary Mapes Dodge. BBGG
Lazy Man, The. *Unknown.* BSO
Lazy Mary, Will You Get Up? Maud, *and* Miska Petersham. RePo
Lazybones. Robert P. Tristram Coffin. SIV
Le Monocle de Mon Oncle. Wallace Stevens. AP
Le Musée Imaginaire. Charles Tomlinson. NePoEA-2
Le saltimbanque is coming with. Song for Zarathustra. Law-rence Durrell. ToPo
Lead gently, Lord, and slow. A Hymn after Reading "Lead, Kindly Light." Paul Laurence Dunbar. TRV
Lead, Kindly Light. Cardinal Newman. *See* Pillar of the Cloud, The.
Lead me, O God, and thou my Destiny. God Leads the Way. Cleanthes. EaLo
Leaden Echo and the Golden Echo, The. Gerard Manley Hopkins. DTC; GTBS-P; OBNC; PoDB; VP
Leaden-eyed, The. Vachel Lindsay. MoRP; PoPo
Leaders of the Crowd, The. W. B. Yeats. PoPo
Leadsman's Song, The. *Unknown.* HaSV
Leaf after Leaf. Walter Savage Landor. TRV
Leaf Fall. Heinrich Leuthold, *tr. fr. German by* D. G. Wright. AGP
Leaf-Makers, The. Harold Stewart. PoAu-2
Lean back, and get some minutes' peace. Faustine. Swinburne. UnTE
Lean Out of the Window. James Joyce. Chamber Music, V. BoLP; LOW
  (Goldenhair.) RePo
Leap-Year Episode, A. *At.* to Eugene Field. BoLP
Learn, flowers, from me, what parts we play. Allegory of the Brevity of Things Human. Luis de Góngora. AnSP
Learn if you must, but do not come to me. Glass Houses. E. A. Robinson. MoRP
Learned and a happy ignorance, A. Eden. Thomas Traherne. MeP
Leave go my hands, let me catch breath and see. In the Orchard. *Unknown.* UnTE
Leave Her, Johnny. *Unknown.* HaSV
Leave It to Me Blues. Joel Oppenheimer. CoPo
Leave Me, O Love. Sir Philip Sidney. *Sometimes considered Sonnet CX of* Astrophel and Stella; *also in* Certain Sonnets. CABA; DiPo; EnRePo; OnP; PoSa
Leave me, world, just let me go! Seclusion. Eduard Möricke. AGP
Leave off, good Beroe, now. To an Old Gentlewoman Who Painted Her Face. George Turberville. EnRePo
Leave stone behind, rise higher! Burst. Caryatid. Gottfried Benn. MGP
Leave-taking. A. Swinburne. OBNC; PoLF
Leave the flattering libraries, the graceful Eastern towns. Guard of Honor. Robert Hazel. OPP

Leave the How with Jesus. How? *Unknown.* STF
Leave the uproar! At a leap. Nature and Life. George Meredith. PoIE; VP
Leave to the street its glare and race. Shadowed. Burnham Eaton. FiSC
Leaves. Sara Teasdale. PoP1
Leaves are born, The; the organ man. Six in June. Mary Carolyn Davies. BiCB
Leaves before the Wind. May Sarton. MoLP
Leaves Do Not Mind at All, The. Annette Wynne. SoPo
Leaves fall, fall as from far, The. Autumn. Rainer Maria Rilke. SiGo
Leaves have their time to fall. The Hour of Death. Felicia Dorothea Hemans. OBNC
Leaves of Europe, The, *sels.* Howard Sergeant. ToPo
 "Autumn again, the leopardlike and burning."
 Inundation, The.
 Man Meeting Himself.
Leaves of the summer, lovely summer's pride. Sonnet: Leaves. William Barnes. OBNC
Leaves, though little time they have to live, The. October Maples, Portland. Richard Wilbur. CoPo
Leaves would have been mere leaves. Invisible Painter. Alfred Dorn. FiSC
Leaving. "Michael Lewis," *after the Chinese. Fr.* Cherry Blossoms. UnTE
Leaving Ithaca. W. D. Snodgrass. AmPC
Leaving the House of a Friend. Basho, *tr. fr. Japanese by* Harold G. Henderson. RePo
Lecture upon the Shadow, A. John Donne. CABA; CaFP; DiPo; EnRePo; FoBA; SeCP
Leda. Rubén Darío, *tr. fr. Spanish by* Doreen Bell. AnSP
Leda. Rainer Maria Rilke, *tr. fr. German by* Walter Kaufmann. TwGP
Leda and the Swan. W. B. Yeats. CABA; CaFP; DiPo; ErPo; FoBA; GTBS-P; ILP; OnP; PoIE; StP; VaPo
Leetla Boy, Da. T. A. Daly. SIV
Leetla Giorgio Washeenton. T. A. Daly. PoSC
Leezie Lindsay, *with music. Unknown.* BFSS
Left leg flung out, head cocked to the right. Poet. Karl Shapiro. ToPo
Legacie, The. John Donne. SeCP
Legacy: My South. Dudley Randall. NNP
Legal Fiction. William Empson. ToPo
Legend. Hart Crane. CABA
Legend. John Hall Wheelock. MoLP
Legend has sunk it where the shoreless foam. Atlantis. Stanton A. Coblentz. FiSC
Legend, Not Quite Housebroken. Erich Kästner, *tr. fr. German by* Walter Kaufmann. TwGP
Legend of Ramapo Mountain. Jennie M. Palen. FiSC
Legend of the Bewitched Nunnery. Max Herrmann-Neisse, *tr. fr. German by* Babette Deutsch *and* Avrahm Yarmolinsky. MGP
Legend of the Hills. Lilith Lorraine. FiSC
Legend of the Northland, A. Phoebe Cary. OnMSP
Legendary Abraham. The Succession. Edwin Muir. PoDB
Legerdemain. Kenneth Mackenzie. PoAu-2
Legree's big house was white and green. Simon Legree—a Negro Sermon. Vachel Lindsay. SIV
Legs, The. Robert Graves. PoSa
Legs being uneven, The. The Letter. Paul Blackburn. CoPo
Legs of the elk punctured the snow's crust, The. To Christ Our Lord. Galway Kinnell. MP
Leichhardt in Theatre, *sel.* Francis Webb.
 Room, The. PoAu-2
Leila. George Hill. AmLP
Leisure. W. H. Davies. LV; RePo; WePo
Lemming, The/ Leaves wear. October. H. A. Sieber. PoNC
Lemuel's Blessing. W. S. Merwin. CoPo
Lend a Hand. Edward Everett Hale. TRV
Lenore. Gottfried August Bürger, *tr. fr. German by* Francis Owen. AGP
Lenore. Poe. AGP
Lenore awoke when skies were red. Lenore. Gottfried August Bürger. AGP
Lenox Avenue Mural. Langston Hughes. AmNP
Lens. Anne Wilkinson. OBCV
Lent. W. R. Rodgers. DTC
Lent Lily, The. A. E. Housman. A Shropshire Lad, XXIX. PoSC
Lenten Is Come with Love to Toune. *Unknown.* MeEL
 (Spring Has Come to Town with Love.) CABA
L'Envoi: "O love triumphant over guilt and sin." Frederic L. Knowles. TRV
L'Envoi: "When earth's last picture is painted and the tubes are twisted and dried." Kipling. PoP1; TRV
L'Envoi: "Who findeth comfort in the stars and flowers." Thomas Lovell Beddoes. *Fr.* Death's Jest Book. OBNC
L'Envoy: "King of glorie, King of peace." George Herbert. MeP
L'Envoy: To His Book. John Skelton. EnRePo
Leo Frank and Mary Phagan. *Unknown.* BSO
Leona Wise, *with music. Unknown.* BSO

Lepanto. G. K. Chesterton. FaBV
Leprechaun—the omadhaun!—that lives in County Clare, The. Of Certain Irish Fairies. Arthur Guiterman. PoLF
Les Halles d'Ypres. Edmund Blunden. MMA
Les Réalités. Barbara Guest. AmPC
Les Saintes-Maries-de-la-Mer. Alan Ross. DaDu
Les Silhouettes. Oscar Wilde. HaSV
Lesbia. Richard Aldington. PoLF
Lesbia forever on me rails. Catullus de Lesbia. Swift. CBEP
Lèse Majesté. Paul Bartlett. PoNC
Less passionate the long war throws. The Long War. Laurie Lee. ToPo
Less said the better. Missing. John Pudney. WePo
Less than two hours it took the Iroquois. The Martyrdom of Brébeuf and Lalemant, 16 March 1649. E. J. Pratt. *Fr.* Brébeuf and His Brethren. OBCV
Lesser griefs that may be said, The. In Memoriam A. H. H., XX. Tennyson. VP
Lesson, The. Jane W. Krows. SoPo
Lesson, A. Wordsworth. GTBS-P
 (Small Celandine, The.) FoBA
Lesson in Detachment, A. Vassar Miller. NePoEA-2
Lessons of Nature, The. Giambattista Marino. *See* Book of the World, The.
Lessons of the War, *sels.* Henry Reed.
 Judging Distances, II. GTBS-P
 Naming of Parts, I. CaFP; DTC; GoJo; ILP; MP; PoP1; StP; WePo
Lest men suspect your tale to be untrue. The Devil's Advice to Story-Tellers. Robert Graves. CBEP
Lest you should think that verse shall die. The Poet. Pope. CBEP
Lester Young. Ted Joans. AmNP
Let all the world in every corner sing. George Herbert. ThGo
Let America Be America Again. Langston Hughes. PtTo
Let Be at Last. Ernest Dowson. PoSa
Let come what will, let come what may! Consolation. Theodor Storm. AGP
Let Dogs Delight. Isaac Watts. ThGo
Let dull and ignorant pretenders art condemn. John Oldham. *Fr.* Upon the Works of Ben Jonson. PP
Let every Roman boy be taught to know. Call to Youth. Horace. Odes, III, 2. SiGo
Let forrain nations of their language boast. The Sonne. George Herbert. SeCP
Let happy throats be mute. Threnody. Donald Jeffrey Hayes. AmNP
Let Her Give Her Hand. *Unknown.* BoLP; ELP
Let her rest. One of the Sidhe. Mary Kennedy. FiSC
Let him kiss me with the kisses of his mouth. The Song of Songs. Song of Solomon, Bible, *O.T.* UnTE
Let it disturb no more at first. Fountain. Elizabeth Jennings. BoC; PoCh
Let It Go. William Empson. PoIE
Let it not your wonder move. His Excuse for Loving. Ben Jonson. *Fr.* A Celebration of Charis. EnRePo; SeCP
Let it rain! The Engineer. A. A. Milne. RePo
Let man's soul be a sphere, and then, in this. Good Friday, 1613. Riding Westward. John Donne. DiPo; EnRePo; FoBA; MeP; PoIE; SeCP; StP
Let me be a little kinder. A Creed [*or* My Daily Creed]. *Unknown.* STF; TRV
Let me be buried in the rain. Invocation. Helene Johnson. AmNP
Let me be what I am, as Virgil cold. An Elegie. Ben Jonson. SeCP
Let me but do my work from day to day. Work. Henry van Dyke. TRV
Let me confess that we two must be twain. Sonnets, XXXVI. Shakespeare. CBEP
Let me decease within thine arms, my Dear. Pierre de Ronsard, *tr. fr. French by* George Wyndham. RBL
Let me die in the spring. Transmigration. Seth D. Cudjoe. ACV
Let me discern by living faith. Discerning the Lord's Body. Carrie Judd Montgomery. STF
Let Me Enjoy (Minor Key). Thomas Hardy. FaBV; MoRP
Let Me Go Warm. Luis de Góngora, *tr. fr. Spanish by* Longfellow. RBL
Let me go where'er I will. Music. Emerson. FaBV
Let Me Look at Me. Bessie June Martin. STF
Let me no more despise. A Song in Humility. Carleton Drewry. MoRP
Let me not to the marriage of true minds. Sonnets, CXVI [*or* True Love]. Shakespeare. BoC; CABA; CaFP; CBEP; DiPo; EnRePo; FaBV; FoBA; GTBS-P; ILP; LV; OnP; PoIE; PoP1; PoPo; PoSa; TRV; WePo
Let me pour forth. A Valediction: Of Weeping. John Donne. CABA; CBEP; SeCP
Let me pour upon the mind. Remember the Source. Richard Eberhart. MoRP
Let me remember on this day. Others. *Unknown.* STF
Let me take this other glove off. In Westminster Abbey. John Betjeman. CaFP; ILP

Let me tell you the story of how I began. Song: Lift Boy. Robert Graves. DTC

Let Mine Eyes See Thee. St. Theresa of Avila, *tr. fr. Spanish* by Arthur Symons. RBL

Let no man cum into this hall. Now Is the Time of Christmas. *Unknown.* MeEL

Let no man see my girl. Inconsistent. Mark Van Doren. BoLP

Let no one mourn his mount, upholstered bone. Epitaph for a Horseman. Michael Hamburger. NePoEA-2

Let not our town be large, remembering. On the Building of Springfield. Vachel Lindsay. MoRP

Let Not Us. *Unknown.* CBEP

Let not young souls be smothered out before. The Leaden-eyed. Vachel Lindsay. MoRP; PoPo

Let nothing affright you. God Suffices. St. Theresa of Avila, *tr. by* Mildred E. Johnson. RBL

Let nothing disturb thee/ Let nothing dismay thee. St. Teresa's Book-Mark. St. Theresa of Avila, *tr. by* E. Allison Peers. BoC

Let nothing disturb thee,/ Nothing affright thee. St. Teresa's Bookmark [*or* Lines Written in Her Breviary]. St. Theresa of Avila, *tr. by* Longfellow. CTC; EaLo; SiGo; TRV

Let observation with extensive view. The Vanity of Human Wishes; the Tenth Satire of Juvenal, Imitated. Samuel Johnson. CABA; EiCP; EnPE; VaPo

Let others sing of Mars, and of his train. The Proem: To Love. Giambattista Marino. *Fr.* L'Adone. RBL

Let schoolmasters puzzle their brain. The Three Pigeons. Goldsmith. *Fr.* She Stoops to Conquer. ELP

Let silence or speech be permitted each one. Maurice Scève. *Fr. Délie.* RBL

Let the bells of Easter toll. Easter Song. Kenneth Leslie. MoRP

Let the bird of loudest lay. The Phoenix and the Turtle. Shakespeare. CABA; CBEP; EnRePo; StP

Let the boy try along this bayonet-blade. Arms and the Boy. Wilfred Owen. PoPo

Let the drowsy soul awake! Stanzas on the Death of His Father. Jorge Manrique. AnML

Let the foul scene proceed. The Marionettes. Walter de la Mare. MMA

Let the knowing speak. Adjuration. Charles Enoch Wheeler. AmNP

Let the musicians begin. At a Solemn Musick. Delmore Schwartz. MoRP

Let the robed kings march in the mind. A Letter from a Friend. John Morris. CABA

Let the snake wait under. A Sort of a Song. William Carlos Williams. PoIE; PP

Let the Three of Us Now Dance, Oh Friends. Airas Núñez. *See* Bailada: "Let's dance now, all of us, all of us, oh my maidens."

Let Them Alone. Robinson Jeffers. AP

Let them bestow on every earth a limb. On Himself, on Hearing What Was His Sentence. James Graham, Marquess of Montrose. CBEP

Let them bury your big eyes. Elegy. Edna St. Vincent Millay. AmLP

Let them lie,—their day is over. Refrigerium. Frederick Goddard Tuckerman. AP

Let them say to my Lover. Amor Mysticus. Sister Marcela de Carpio de San Felix. RBL

Let There Be Law. Mark Van Doren. MoRP

Let things touch your mind. Details. Luke Zilles. RePo

Let This Be My Parting Word. Rabindranath Tagore. *Fr.* Gitanjali. MoRP

Let those who are in favour with their stars. Sonnets, XXV. Shakespeare. CBEP

Let thy soul walk slowly in thee. Silence. Samuel Miller Hageman. TRV

Let us be like a bird for a moment perched. Wings. Victor Hugo. TRV

Let us begin and carry up this corpse. A Grammarian's Funeral. Robert Browning. DiPo; VP

Let us begin and portion out these sweets. A Girtonian Funeral. *Unknown.* Par

Let us give ourselves to pleasure. Chorus. Juan del Encina. RBL

Let Us Go Down, the Long Dead Night Is Done. Christopher Brennan. *Fr.* Towards the Source. PoAu-1

Let us go hence, my songs; she will not hear. A Leave-taking. Swinburne. OBNC; PoLF

Let us go then, you and I. The Love Song of J. Alfred Prufrock. T. S. Eliot. AP; CABA; CaFP; CBEP; DiPo; FoBA; ILP; MP; PoIE

Let Us Keep Christmas. Grace Noll Crowell. TRV

Let us move the stone gentleman to the toadstool wood. The Stone Gentleman. James Reeves. DaDu

Let us not look upon. Prayer. Witter Bynner. EaLo

"Let us not speak, for the love we bear one another." In a Bath Teashop. John Betjeman. BoC

Let Us Now Praise Famous Men. Ecclesiasticus, XLIV: 1-15, Bible, Apocrypha. BoC

Let us record/ The evenings when we were innocents of twenty. Winfield Townley Scott. *Fr.* Biography for Traman. ErPo

Let us section his nude body. The Probes. Michael Goldman. OPP

Let us sing and all be gay. Nuns' Drinking Song. *Unknown.* AnML

Let us sit by the hissing steam radiator a winter's day, grey wind. Horses and Men in the Rain. Carl Sandburg. PoLF

Let us take the road. The Highwaymen. John Gay. *Fr.* The Beggar's Opera. WiR

Let us walk in the white snow. Velvet Shoes. Elinor Wylie. GoJo; PoPl; SoPo

Let Us with a Gladsome Mind. Milton. TRV

Let vain or busy thoughts have there no part. George Herbert. *Fr.* The Church Porch. TRV

Let Your Pastor Know. *Unknown.* STF

Let your song be delicate. Song Be Delicate. John Shaw Neilson. PoAu-1

Lethe. Hilda Doolittle ("H. D."). AmLP

Let's contend no more, Love. A Woman's Last Word. Robert Browning. CBEP; UnTE

Let's Dance, Let's Dance, Us Pretties. Joan Zorro, *tr. fr. Portuguese by* William M. Davis. AnML

Let's dance now, all of us, all of us, oh my maidens. Bailada. Airas Núñez. SiGo

Let's go play in the sun. Out. Nathaniel Burt. MoLP

Let's smile and be kind—life is so short. Life Is So Short. Margaret S. Hall. STF

Let's Talk of Graves. Shakespeare. King Richard II, *fr.* III, ii. DiPo

Letter, The. Paul Blackburn. CoPo

Letter, A. Anthony Hecht. StP

Letter across Doubt and Distance. M. Carl Holman. AmNP

Letter for Melville 1951. Charles Olson. CoPo

Letter from a Friend, A. John Morris. CABA

Letter from Brooklyn, A. Derek Walcott. ToPo

"Letter from my love today, A!" A Ballad of Hell. John Davidson. ACV; StP

Letter from the Country to a Friend in Town, A. John Oldham. PP

Letter: The Japanese, to Her Husband at War. William Walsh. PoPl

Letter to a Friend. John Thompson. PoAu-2

Letter to Alex Comfort. Dannie Abse. MP

Letter to an Imaginary Friend, *sel.* Thomas McGrath. "Blessed, blessed/ Oh blessed." PtTo

Letter to Her Husband, Absent upon Publick Employment, A. Anne Bradstreet. CBEP

Letter to My Mother. Salvatore Quasimodo, *tr. fr. Italian by* Allen Mandelbaum. CoIP

Letter to My Sister. Anne Spencer. AmNP

Letter to N.Y. Elizabeth Bishop. MP

Letter to Pasternak. Ralph Pomeroy. CoPo

Letter to the Countess of Denbigh, A. Richard Crashaw. SeCP

Letter to the Honorable Lady Miss Margaret-Cavendish-Holles-Harley, A. Matthew Prior. EiCP

Letter to the President, *sel.* Walter Lowenfels. "What weather of shelters." PtTo

Letter to Wilbur Frohock, A. Daniel Hoffman. CoPo

Letter to William Carlos Williams, A. Kenneth Rexroth. PP

Letter 27. Charles Olson. CoPo

Letter Written on a Ferry Crossing Long Island Sound. Anne Sexton. MP

Letters of the Jews as strict as flames, The. The Alphabet. Karl Shapiro. MoRP

Letty's Globe. Charles Tennyson Turner. CBEP

Levedy, ic thonke thee. Thanks and a Plea to Mary. *Unknown.* MeEL

Leveling his pole like some quixotic lance. Challenge. Samuel Hazo. SD

Leves Amores. Arthur Symons. UnTE

Leviathan; a Poem in Four Movements. Kenneth Pitchford. CoPo

Lewis and Clark. Stephen Vincent Benét. RePo

Liberal nature did dispense. Woman's Arms. Anacreon. UnTE

Libertine, The. Louis MacNeice. DTC

Liberty, *sel.* Wordsworth. "Beetle loves his unpretending track, The." Par

Librarian, The. Charles Olson. CoPo

Library Is on Fire, The. René Char, *tr. fr. French by* Ralph Freedman, Donald Justice, *and* Paulène Aspel. CoFP

Lichen. Mary Fullerton. PoAu-1

Licht Nichts, The. Violet Jacob. ACV

Licia, *sel.* Giles Fletcher. "In time the strong and stately turrets fall," XXVIII. ILP

Lido, The. Edmund Wilson. ErPo

Lie, The. Sir Walter Ralegh. CBEP; CTC; EnRePo; OnP; PoIE

Lie back, daughter, let your head. First Lesson. Philip Booth. MP; SD

"Lie still, my newly married wife." The Griesly Wife. John Manifold. MoBS
Life. Francis Bacon. GTBS-P
  (In Vitam Humanam.) PoIE
Life. Anna Letitia Barbauld. TRV
  ("Life! I know not what thou art.") GTBS-P
Life. Paul Laurence Dunbar. AmNP
Life. George Herbert. CBEP; FoBA; MeP; SeCP
Life. Edward Rowland Sill. TRV
Life. Jones Very. AP
Life after Death. Pindar, *tr. fr. Greek by* Walter Headlam. EaLo
Life and Death. Sir William Davenant. *Fr.* The Christians Reply to the Philosopher. BoC
Life and Death of Jason, The, *sel.* William Morris. Song of the Argonauts. HaSV
Life and Love. Whittier. TRV
Life at the peak of the Radiant Days. John William Corrington. *Fr.* Communique, I. PtTo
Life by the Cabin Fire, A, *with music.* John A. Stone. SGR
Life Cycle in the Delta. George Huston Bass. PtTo
Life has loveliness to sell. Barter. Sara Teasdale. FaBV; LV
Life hurries on, a frantic refugee. Petrarch. *Fr.* Sonnets to Laura: To Laura in Death. RBL
Life! I know not what thou art. Life. Anna Letitia Barbauld. GTBS-P; TRV
Life in a Love. Robert Browning. OBNC
Life in California, *with music.* David G. Robinson. SGR
Life-in-Love. Dante Gabriel Rossetti. The House of Life, XXXVI. VP
Life is inadequate, but there are many real. Independence Day. William Jay Smith. MP
Life Is Motion. Wallace Stevens. AmLP; SD
Life is our quest. The Way of Life. Joseph V. B. Danquah. ACV
Life Is So Short. Margaret S. Hall. STF
Life-Lesson, A. James Whitcomb Riley. PoLF
Life may be given in many ways. James Russell Lowell. *Fr.* Ode Recited at the Harvard Commemoration. LiPo
Life of Life! Thy lips enkindle. Hymn to the Spirit of Nature. Shelley. GTBS-P
Life of Sabbaths here beneath, A! Thomas Traherne. *Fr.* The Third Century. MeP
Life of the Blessed, The. Luis de León, *tr. fr. Spanish by* Bryant. RBL
Life (priest and poet say) is but a dream. Lines to a Dragon Fly. Walter Savage Landor. OBNC
Life that is free as the bandits' of old, A. Brave Donahue. *At. to* Jack Donahue. PoAu-1
Life was a narrow lobby, dark. For the Bicentenary of Isaac Watts. Norman Nicholson. EaLo
Life Withdrawn, The. Luis de León, *tr. fr. Spanish by* Edwin Morgan. AnSP
Life without Passion, The. Shakespeare. *See* Sonnets, XCIV.
Lifeguard, The. James Dickey. CoPo
Life's a Funny Proposition after All. George M. Cohan. PoLF
Life's Chequer-Board. John Oxenham. TRV
Life's Circumnavigators. W. R. Rodgers. GTBS-P
Life's Joy. *Unknown.* STF
Life's Lessons. *Unknown.* PoLF; STF
Life's Little Things. *Unknown.* STF
Life's Testament, *sels.* William Baylebridge. PoAu-1
  "All that I am to Earth belongs," XI.
  "Brain, the blood, the busy thews, The," II.
  "Choir of spirits on a cloud, A," XVII.
  "God, to get the clay that stayed me," XIII.
  "I worshipped, when my veins were fresh," VI.
  "This miracle in me I scan," VIII.
Lift Every Voice and Sing. James Weldon Johnson. FaBV
Lift not the painted veil which those who live. Sonnet. Shelley. OBNC
Lift up your eyes on high. Erige Cor Tuum ad Me in Caelum. Hilda Doolittle ("H. D."). AP
"Lift up your hartes and be glad." A Cheerful Welcome. *Unknown.* MeEL
Lift your arms to the stars. John Hall Wheelock. BoLP
Lifted by the teaching of a Master. Peter. Earl Marlatt. MoRP
Lifting my eyes from Hesiod's book. Class Dismissed. *Unknown.* UnTE
Light. Hermann Hagedorn. MoRP
Light and Darkness. Michaelangelo, *tr. fr. Italian by* John Addington Symonds. RBL
Light and Glory of the World, The, *sel.* William Cowper. "Spirit breathes upon the world, The." TRV
Light and Love, Hope and Faith. Eva Gray. STF
Light beyond compare is the light I saw, The. The Incomparable Light. Richard Eberhart. MoRP
Light Breaks Where No Sun Shines. Dylan Thomas. AnMoPo; ErPo
Light do I see within my Lady's eyes. Ballata V. Guido Cavalcanti. CTC

Light drunkenly reels into shadow. Wet Windy Night on a Pavement. A. S. J. Tessimond. WePo
Light exists in spring, A. Emily Dickinson. StP
Light flows our war of mocking words, and yet. The Buried Life. Matthew Arnold. VP
Light had gone out from his vanquished eyes, A. The Dying Eagle. E. J. Pratt. ACV
Light in the Temple, The. William Rose Benét. MoRP
Light is made to shine in darkness. Light and Love, Hope and Faith. Eva Gray. STF
Light Left On, A. May Sarton. MoLP
Light Listened. Theodore Roethke. ToPo; UnTE
Light, my light, the world-filling light, the eye-kissing light. A Song-Offering. Rabindranath Tagore. *Fr.* Gitanjali. SiGo
Light Now Shineth, The. *Unknown.* STF
Light of evening, Lissadell, The. In Memory of Eva Gore-Booth and Con Markiewicz. W. B. Yeats. CABA
Light of Other Days, The. Thomas Moore. *See* Oft in the Stilly Night.
Light of the eyes in the house of the crow, The. Lost Month. W. S. Merwin. AmPC
Light Shining Out of Darkness. William Cowper. EaLo; EiCP; EnPE; FaPL; PoIE; TRV; VaPo
  (God Moves in a Mysterious Way.) CBEP; ELP
  (Mysterious Way, The.) VP
Light, that out of the west looked back once more. Night Thoughts in Age. John Hall Wheelock. PoDB
Light the first light of evening, as in a room. Final Soliloquy of the Interior Paramour. Wallace Stevens. PoIE
Light this day, light of joy! I say he who is sad. The Circumcision of Our Lord. *Unknown.* AnML
Light wake early in this house. Various Wakings. Vincent Buckley. PoAu-2
Light-winged Smoke, Icarian Bird. Henry David Thoreau. *See* Smoke.
"Light you down, light you down." Young Hunting (B *vers.*). *Unknown.* BFSS
Lighthearted William. William Carlos Williams. LOW; PoSa
Lighting a spill late in the afternoon. A Winter Talent. Donald Davie. NePoEA-2
Lightless, unholy, eldritch thing. The Bat. Ruth Pitter. DaDu; WePo
Lightly stepped a yellow star. Emily Dickinson. AP
Lightning. Witter Bynner. MoLP
Lightning. D. H. Lawrence. UnTE
Lightning flash, A. Summer Night. Shiki. SiGo
Lightning is a yellow fork, The. Emily Dickinson. LV
Lightning is local. Local Light. Millen Brand. PtTo
Lightning! Lightning! Lightning! Without thunder! Flushing Meadows, 1939. Daniel Hoffman. CoPo
Lightning Victory. René Char, *tr. fr. French by* Dori Katz and Donald Justice. CoFP
Lightning writhes wildly. In the gaunt light a tower. The Feet in the Fire. Conrad Ferdinand Meyer. TwGP
Lights of a hundred cities are fed by its midnight power, The. The River of Stars. Alfred Noyes. OnMSP
Lights of people shandle holiness. Land of the Never-ending Heart. Kenneth Patchen. ToPo
Lights Out. Edward Thomas. MMA
Liguria. "Vincenzo Cardarelli," *tr. fr. Italian by* Cosimo Corsano. CoIP
Like a deaf man meshed in his endless silence. Poem. John Wain. PoCh
Like a fleet thief, this sparrow has. House and Shutter. Lewis Turco. PoP1
Like a gaunt, scraggly pine. Lincoln. John Gould Fletcher. LiPo
Like a huge python, winding round and round. Our Casuarina Tree. Toru Dutt. ACV
Like a painting it is set before one. The View from the Window. R. S. Thomas. BoC
Like a private eye she searches. The Jealous Wife. Vernon Scannell. ErPo
Like a river that's begun. Love Poem to Helen. René Guy Cadou. CoFP
Like a skein of loose silk blown against a wall. The Garden. Ezra Pound. CABA; MP; PoIE
Like a small gray. The Gray Squirrel. Humbert Wolfe. GoJo
Like a white wall whereon forever breaks. Octaves, XVIII. E. A. Robinson. ILP
Like an adventurous seafarer am I. Idea, I. Michael Drayton. HaSV
Like an April Day. Johan Sebastian C. Wellhaven, *tr. fr. Norwegian by* Charles Wharton Stork. SiGo
Like an hart, the live-long day. The Relief on Easter Eve. Thomas Pestel. CBEP
Like an Old Proud King in a Parable. A. J. M. Smith. OBCV
Like any grey old-timer droving dreams. The Town. David Rowbotham. PoAu-2
Like [*or Lyke*] as a huntsman after weary chase [*or chace*]. Amoretti, LXVII. Spenser. EnRePo; ILP; PoIE; PoSa

Like [or Lyke] as a ship, that through the ocean wide. Amoretti, XXXIV. Spenser. DiPo; ILP; PoIE
Like as the Damask Rose You See. Unknown. CBEP
Like as the hart, that lifteth up his ears. He Renounceth All the Effects of Love. Thomas, Lord Vaux. EnRePo
Like as the waves make towards the pebbled shore. Sonnets, LX. Shakespeare. CBEP; EnRePo; GTBS-P
Like as, to make our appetites more keen. Sonnets, CXVIII. Shakespeare. CABA; CBEP
Like Barbarossa's beard bright with oil. Boys in October. Irving Layton. OBCV
Like children in the market-place. Children in the Market-Place. Henry van Dyke. TRV
Like Flowers We Spring. Unknown. CBEP
Like gript stick. The Sermon. Richard Hughes. BoC
Like Hecate you will make me wander. Maurice Scève. Fr. Délie. RBL
Like Jonah in the green belly of the whale. Emily Carr. Wilfred Watson. OBCV
Like labour-laden moonclouds faint to flee. Through Death to Love. Dante Gabriel Rossetti. The House of Life, XLI. VP
"Like men riding." Nelly Trim. Sylvia Townsend Warner. ErPo
Like one who'in her third widdowhood doth professe. To Mr. Rowland Woodward. John Donne. MeP
Like plump green floor plans. Rotation. Julian Bond. NNP
Like rain it sounded till it curved. Emily Dickinson. LV
Like Sieur Montaigne's distinction. Golfers. Irving Layton. SD
Like snooker balls thrown on the table's faded green. A Poet's Progress. Michael Hamburger. PP
Like so many other young men in those troubled. For Lover Man, and All the Other Young Men Who Failed to Return from World War II. Mance Williams. NNP
Like souls that balance joy and pain. Sir Launcelot and Queen Guinevere. Tennyson. ACV
Like the Idalian queen. Madrigal. William Drummond of Hawthornden. ELP
Like the Prime Mover. Mehdi Ali Seljouk. ACV
Like the sweet apple which reddens upon the topmost bough. A Young Bride. Sappho. SiGo
Like this rock/ of San Michele. I Am a Creature. Giuseppe Ungaretti. CoIP
Like This Together. Adrienne Rich. CoPo
Like to a monarch who in triumph takes. As the First Snow Fell. Leopold von Goeckingk. AGP
Like to the clear in highest sphere. Rosaline [or Rosalind]. Thomas Lodge. Fr. Rosalynde; or, Euphues' Golden Legacy. GTBS-P; PoIE; UnTE
Like to the Falling of a Star. Henry King. See Sic Vita.
Like to These Unmeasurable Mountains. Jacopo Sannazaro, tr. fr. Italian by Sir Thomas Wyatt. CABA
Like truthless dreams so are my joys expired. Farewell to the Court. Sir Walter Ralegh. CBEP; EnRePo
Likeness, A. Robert Browning. CTC
Likeness has made them animal and shy. The Twins. Karl Shapiro. PoSa
Lila, sel. Goethe, tr. fr. German by Walter Kaufmann. "Scared hesitation." TwGP
Lilacs. Christian Wagner, tr. fr. German by Dorothea M. Singer. AGP
Lilacs shall bloom for Walt Whitman. Memories of Whitman and Lincoln. James Oppenheim. LiPo
L'Ile du Levant: The Nudist Colony. Barbara Howes. PoCh
Lilian's Song. George Darley. OBNC
Lilies lie in my lady's bower, The. The Poets at Tea, 8. Barry Pain. Par
Lilith, sels. Christopher Brennan. PoAu-1
Adam to Lilith.
Anguish'd Doubt Broods over Eden, The.
Lilith on the Fate of Man.
Lilith. X. J. Kennedy. UnTE
Lilith on the Fate of Man. Christopher Brennan. Fr. Lilith. PoAu-1
Lilly, The. Blake. Fr. Songs of Experience. FoBA
Lilly and the Rose, The. Unknown. See Maidens Came, The.
Lilly in a Christal, The. Robert Herrick. SeCP
Lily and the Rose may be, The. La Couronne Impériale. Claude de Malleville. Fr. Guirlande de Julie. RBL
Lily McQueen. Sara Jackson. BoLP
Lily of the West, The. Unknown. BFSS, with music; BSO (A vers., with music; B vers.)
Lily-white Rose, The. Unknown. MeEL
Lime Avenue, The. Sacheverell Sitwell. LOW
Limerick: "There was a young girl of Asturias." Unknown. BBGG
Limerick: "There was a young lady from Del." Unknown. LV
Limerick: "There was a young lady named Bright." Unknown. LV
Limerick: "There was a young lady of Firle." Edward Lear. RePo

Limerick: "There was a young lady of Niger." Unknown, at. to Cosmo Monkhouse. See There Was a Young Lady of Niger.
Limerick: "There was a young lady of Oakham." Unknown. BBGG
Limerick: "There was a young lady whose chin." Edward Lear. See There Was a Young Lady Whose Chin.
Limerick: "There was a young lady whose eyes." Edward Lear. GoJo
Limerick: "There was a young lady whose nose." Edward Lear. RePo
Limerick: "There was a young man from Japan." Unknown. LV
Limerick, A: "There was a young man from Trinity." Unknown. LV
Limerick: "There was an enchanting young bride." Unknown. LV
Limerick: "There was an old lady of Chertsey." Edward Lear. RePo
Limerick: "There was an old man in a tree." Edward Lear. See There Was an Old Man in a Tree.
Limerick: "There was an old man of Antigua." Unknown. LV
Limerick: "There was an old man of Corfu." Edward Lear. RePo
Limerick: "There was an old man of Hong Kong." Edward Lear. RePo
Limerick: "There was an old man of Ibream." Edward Lear. RePo
Limerick: "There was an old man of the Dee." Edward Lear. RePo
Limerick: "There was an old man of The Hague." Edward Lear. EvOK
Limerick: "There was an old man of Thermopylae." Edward Lear. EvOK
Limerick: "There was an old man who said: 'How.'" Edward Lear. EvOK
Limerick: "There was an old man who said, 'Hush!'" Edward Lear. GoJo
Limerick: "There was an old man, who when little." Edward Lear. RePo
Limerick: "There was an old man with a beard." Edward Lear. See There Was an Old Man With a Beard.
Limerick: "There was an old man with a gong." Edward Lear. GoJo
Limerick: "There was an old person of Diss." Edward Lear. GoJo
Limerick, A: "There was an old person of Fratton." Unknown. LV
Limerick: "There was an old person of Hurst." Edward Lear. RePo
Limerick: "There was an old person of Ickley." Edward Lear. EvOK
Limerick: "There was an old person of Minety." Edward Lear. RePo
Limerick: "There was an old person of Stroud." Edward Lear. RePo
Limerick: "There was an old person of Ware." Edward Lear. See There Was an Old Person of Ware.
Limerick: "There was once a young lady of Ryde." Unknown. EvOK
Limitations of Human Art. William Collins. Three Fragments, 2. WaPE
Lincoln. Paul Laurence Dunbar. LiPo
Lincoln. John Gould Fletcher. LiPo
Lincoln. Harriet Monroe. LiPo
Lincoln. James Whitcomb Riley. LiPo
Lincoln?/ He was a mystery in smoke and flags. Carl Sandburg. Fr. The People, Yes. LiPo
Lincoln is not dead. He lives. Lincoln Triumphant. Edwin Markham. LiPo
Lincoln Slain. Edwin Markham. LiPo
Lincoln—the Boy. James Whitcomb Riley. LiPo
Lincoln, the Man of the People. Edwin Markham. LiPo
Lincoln Triumphant. Edwin Markham. LiPo
Lincoln was a long man. Abraham Lincoln. Stephen Vincent Benét. LiPo; PoSC
Lincoln's Dream. Ridgely Torrence. LiPo
Lincolnshire Poacher, The. Unknown. OnMSP; SD (Poacher, The.) WiR
Lincolnshire Tale, A. John Betjeman. FiSC
Linden Tree, The. Dietmar von Aist. See On the Linden Overhead a Bird Was Caroling Its Lay.
Line in long array where they wind betwixt green islands, A. Cavalry Crossing a Ford. Walt Whitman. AP; CABA; CBEP; PoPl; PoPo; RePo; StP
Line of Life, The. James Sexton Layton. PoNC
Line-up for Yesterday. Ogden Nash. SD
Liner She's a Lady, The. Kipling. FaBV
Lines: "Here often, when a child I lay reclined." Tennyson. CABA; StP
Lines: "Though all the Fates should prove unkind." Henry David Thoreau. See Though All the Fates Should Prove Unkind.

Lines: "When the lamp is shattered." Shelley. ILP; OBNC; VaPo
(Flight of Love, The.) GTBS-P; PoLF
(When the Lamp Is Shattered.) CBEP
Lines before Execution. Chidiock Tichborne. *See* Elegy: "My prime of youth is but a frost of cares."
Lines Born of the Fire of Love for God. St. Theresa of Avila, *tr. fr. Spanish by* Shirley White Johnston. RBL
Lines Composed a Few Miles above Tintern Abbey, on Revisiting the Banks of the Wye during a Tour, July 13, 1798. Wordsworth. CABA; CaFP; DiPo; FaPL; FoBA; ILP; OBNC; PoIE; StP
(Lines Written a Few Miles above Tintern Abbey.) CABL Sels.
". . . For nature then/ (The coarser pleasures of my boyish days)." ACV
"I have learned."
(Tintern Abbey.) TRV
Lines for a Dead Poet. David Ferry. PP
Lines for a President. Robert Watson. OPP
Lines for Cuscuscaraway and Mirza Murad Ali Beg. T. S. Eliot. PoPl
Lines from a Sampler. *Unknown.* ThGo
Lines from Catullus. Sir Walter Ralegh. EnRePo
Lines on a Young Lady's Photograph Album. Philip Larkin. ToPo
Lines on Leaving a Scene in Bavaria. Thomas Campbell. OBNC
Lines on the Mermaid Tavern. Keats. DiPo; ILP; PP
(Mermaid Tavern, The.) GTBS-P
Lines Supposed to Have Been Addressed to Fanny Brawne. Keats. BoLP; OBNC
(This Living Hand.) CABA
Lines to a Critic. Shelley. CBEP
Lines to a Dragon Fly. Walter Savage Landor. OBNC
Lines to a Movement in Mozart's E-Flat Symphony. Thomas Hardy. BoLP; ELP
Lines to a Nasturtium (a Lover Muses). Anne Spencer. AmNP
Lines to an Indian Air. Shelley. *See* Indian Serenade.
Lines to Garcia Lorca. LeRoi Jones. NNP
Lines to His Son on Reaching Adolescence. John Logan. NePoEA-2
Lines, Written a Few Miles above Tintern Abbey. Wordsworth. *See* Lines Composed a Few Miles above Tintern Abbey.
Lines Written in Early Spring. Wordsworth. ACV; CBEP; PoLF; PoPo; StP
(Written in Early Spring.) GTBS-P; ILP; TRV
Lines Written in Her Breviary. St. Theresa of Avila. *See* St. Teresa's Book-Mark.
Lines Written in Kensington Gardens, *sel.* Matthew Arnold. Calm Soul of All Things. TRV
Lines Written Nov. 22, 23—1963. Gregory Corso. OPP
Lines Written on a Window-Shutter at Weston. William Cowper. EiCP
Link, The. Robert Lowth. WaPE
Links are chance, the chain is fate, The. Mathematics of Love. Michael Hamburger. NePoEA-2
Linnet in the rocky dells, The. Song. Emily Brontë. OBNC
Linnet who had lost her way, A. Tennebris Interlucentem. James Elroy Flecker. CBEP
Lion. Mary Fullerton. PoAu-1
Lion, The. Vachel Lindsay. RePo
Lion & Honeycomb. Howard Nemerov. PP
Lion and the Mouse, The. Jeffreys Taylor. OnMSP; RePo
Lion and the Unicorn, The. *Unknown.* EvOK
Lion has a tail and a very fine tail, A. In the Fashion. A. A. Milne. RePo
Lion is a kingly beast, The. The Lion. Vachel Lindsay. RePo
Lion, Leopard, Lady. Douglas Le Pan. OBCV
Lion Named Passion, A. John Hollander. NePoEA-2
Lion of my sun, my fiery joy. The Psalm of St. Priapus. James Broughton. ErPo
Lion of Winter, The. Shakespeare. *See* Now the Hungry Lion Roars.
Lion sleeps with open eyes, The. Faces from a Bestiary. X. J. Kennedy. NePoEA-2
Lion, tired with state affairs, A. Fable VII: The Lion, the Fox, and the Geese. John Gay. EiCP
Lion with the heat oppressed, A. The Lion and the Mouse. Jeffreys Taylor. OnMSP; RePo
Lip. J. V. Cunningham. ErPo
Lip and the Heart, The. John Quincy Adams. AmLP
Lip was a man who used his head. Lip. J. V. Cunningham. ErPo
Liquor and Love. The World Narrowed to a Point. William Carlos Williams. MoLP
List the harp in window wailing. The Aeolian Harp. Herman Melville. AP
Listen, children: Your father is dead. Lament. Edna St. Vincent Millay. PoPl; PoPo

Listen here, Joe. Without Benefit of Declaration. Langston Hughes. AmNP
Listen, I will tell thee what is done in the caverns of the grave. Enion Replies from the Caverns of the Grave. Blake. *Fr.* Vala; or, The Four Zoas. OBNC
Listen, lass, if you would be. Caution. *Unknown.* UnTE
Listen, my children, and you shall hear. Paul Revere's Ride. Longfellow. *Fr.* Tales of a Wayside Inn. CaFP; FaBV; RePo; SIV; ThLM
Listen, my friends:—our neighbor is ill! "Jesse Thoor." *Fr.* Speeches and Invocations. MGP
"Listen, now, verse should be as natural." Poetry for Supper. R. S. Thomas. ToPo
Listen now, whoever you may be. To the Faithful. Marcos Ana. BoC
Listen: Put on Morning. W. S. Graham. MP
Listen: the ancient voices hail us from the farther shore. Mayflower. Conrad Aiken. MP
Listen, the hay-bells tinkle as the cart. The Holy Innocents. Robert Lowell. PoDB; ToPo
Listen to me, as when ye heard our father. The Canadian Boat Song. *Unknown, at. to* John Galt. CBEP; OBNC
Listen to the cicada's burning drone. The Cicada. H. M. Green. PoAu-1
Listen to the Exhortation of the Dawn. The Salutation of the Dawn. *Unknown.* PoLF
Listen to the listen to the. Tele-News Blues. Peter Dufault. LV
Listen to the People: Independence Day, 1941, *sel.* Stephen Vincent Benét.
"This is Independence Day." PoSC
Listen . . ./ With faint dry sound. November Night. Adelaide Crapsey. WePo
Listeners, The. Walter de la Mare. CaFP; ILP; OnMSP; OnP; PoPl; PoPo; RePo; SIV
Listening. Amy Lowell. PoPo
Listeth, lordes, in good entent. Sir Thopas. Chaucer. *Fr.* The Canterbury Tales. Par
Litany, A: "Drop, drop, slow tears." Phineas Fletcher. *See* Hymn, A: "Drop, drop, slow tears."
Litany, A: "Ring out your bells." Sir Philip Sidney. *See* Ring Out Your Bells.
Litany for Halloween. *Unknown.* *See* Ghoulies and Ghosties.
Litany in Time of Plague, A. Thomas Nashe. *See* Adieu, Farewell, Earth's Bliss.
Litany of the Dark People, The. Countee Cullen. EaLo; MoRP
Litany of the Heroes, *sels.* Vachel Lindsay.
"Would I might rouse the Lincoln in you all." LiPo; PoSC
"Would I might wake St. Francis in you all." MoRP
Litany of the Lost. Siegfried Sassoon. MoRP
Little Air. Stéphane Mallarmé, *tr. fr. French by* Roger Fry. PoPl
Little Alexander's dead. Obituary. "Max Adeler." DTC
Little and Great. Charles Mackay. PoLF
Little Beach Bird, The. Richard Henry Dana. AmLP
Little Billee. Thackeray. HaSV
Little Bird, The. Walter de la Mare. BiCB
Little Bird, A. Aileen Fisher. SoPo
Little Black Boy, The. Blake. *Fr.* Songs of Innocence. BoC; CABA; CaFP; CBEP; DiPo; EnPE; FoBA; ILP; OBNC; PoIE
Little Black Dog, The. Elizabeth Gardner Reynolds. PoLF
Little black thing among the snow, A. The Chimney Sweeper. Blake. *Fr.* Songs of Experience. CABA; CBEP; EnPE; FoBA; PoIE
Little Blue Ribbons. Austin Dobson. BiCB
Little Bo-Peep. Mother Goose. SoPo
Little Boy Blue. Eugene Field. PoLF
Little Boy Blue. Mother Goose. SoPo
Little Boy Found, The. Blake. *Fr.* Songs of Innocence. CBEP
Little Boy Lost ("Father! father! where are you going?"). Blake. *Fr.* Songs of Innocence. CBEP
Little Boy Lost, A ("Nought loves another as itself"). Blake. *Fr.* Songs of Experience. CBEP; PoIE
"Little Boy Lost, A." Jerome Rothenberg. CoPo
Little boy lost in the lonely fen. The Little Boy Found. Blake. *Fr.* Songs of Innocence. CBEP
Little boy of heavenly birth, A. Out of Bounds. John Banister Tabb. TRV
Little boy wandering alone in the night, A. The Boy in the Barn. Sir Herbert Read. DaDu
Little boys and little maidens. Little Catkins. Aleksandr Blok. EaLo
Little Brother. Aileen Fisher. BiCB
Little Brother, The. James Reeves. DTC
Little brown baby-bird, lapped in your nest. Lullaby of the Iroquois. Pauline Johnson. ACV
Little brown boy. Helene Johnson. AmNP
Little Busy Bee. Isaac Watts. SoPo
(Against Idleness and Mischief.) Par
Little cares that fretted me, The. Out in the Fields with God. *Unknown.* TRV

Little Carol of the Virgin, A.   Lope de Vega, *tr. fr. Spanish by* Denise Levertov.   AnSP
Little caterpillar creeps, The.   Cocoon.   David McCord.   PoPo
Little Catkins.   Aleksandr Blok, *tr. fr. Russian by* Babette Deutsch.   EaLo
Little Charlie Chipmunk.   Helen C. LeCron.   SoPo
Little charm of placid mien.   To Miss Georgiana.   Ambrose Philips.   WaPE
Little child, A.   Bethlehem of Judea.   *Unknown.*   BiCB
Little children, never give.   Kindness to Animals.   *Unknown.*   SoPo
Little colt-broncho, loaned to the farm, A.   The Broncho That Would Not Be Broken.   Vachel Lindsay.   RoGo
Little colts caper and kick up their heels.   In Spring in Warm Weather.   Dorothy Aldis.   BiCB
Little cousin is dead, by foul subtraction, The.   Dead Boy.   John Crowe Ransom.   MP
Little Creature, The.   Walter de la Mare.   EvOK
Little Dog-Angel, A.   Norah M. Holland.   PoLF
Little Dog under the Wagon, The.   *Unknown.*   PoLF
Little Duck, The.   Joso, *tr. fr. Japanese by* Harold G. Henderson.   SoPo
Little Elegy.   X. J. Kennedy.   CaFP; GoJo
Little Elegy.   Elinor Wylie.   LOW
Little elephant was crying, The.   Cradle Song of the Elephants. Adriano del Valle.   RePo
Little Elf, The.   John Kendrick Bangs.   BiCB
   (Little Elfman, The.)   SoPo
Little Fable.   Roy Fuller.   DaDu
Little fairy snowflakes.   Santa Claus.   *Unknown.*   SoPo
Little Family, The, *with music. Unknown.*   BFSS; BSO
Little Fighting Chance, The.   *Unknown.*   BSNS
Little fish that in the stream doth fleet, The.   To Alexander Neville.   Barnabe Googe.   EnRePo
Little fly,/ Thy summer's play.   The Fly.   Blake.   *Fr. Songs of Experience.*   CBEP; DiPo; PoSa
Little freckled lad with a cheerful grin.   What in the World! Edith Earnshaw.   PoNC
Little Gidding.   T. S. Eliot.   *Fr.* Four Quartets.   CTBS-P; PoIE
Little Giffen.   Francis Orr Ticknor.   FaPL
Little Girl, The.   Nicholas Moore.   ErPo
Little girl all in her garden, A.   The Cowboy's Return.   *Unknown.*   BFSS
Little Girl Found, The.   Blake.   *Fr.* Songs of Experience. CBEP; DiPo
Little Girl Lost, The.   Blake.   *Fr.* Songs of Experience.   DiPo
Little girls.   Day's End.   Lesbia Harford.   PoAu-1
Little girls that live next door, The.   Grace Ananne [*or* GraceAnAnne].   Lysbeth Boyd Borie.   BiCB; RePo
Little girls, through the blowing leaves.   Through the Blowing Leaves.   Glenn Ward Dresbach.   BoC
Little Golden.   *Unknown. See* Lady Isabel and the Elf-Knight.
Little Gray Pussy.   *Unknown.*   SoPo
Little Green Blackbird, The.   Kenneth Patchen.   PoCh
Little Green Orchard, The.   Walter de la Mare.   EvOK
Little hope, a lot of faith, A.   Worry.   George W. Swarberg.   STF
Little House, The.   Pierre Louÿs, *tr. fr. French by* Horace M. Brown.   *Fr.* The Songs of Bilitis.   UnTE
Little Hymn to Mary, A.   *Unknown.*   MeEL
Little I ask; my wants are few.   Contentment.   Oliver Wendell Holmes.   AP
Little Indian, Sioux or Crow.   Foreign Children.   Robert Louis Stevenson.   GoJo
Little inmate, full of mirth.   The Cricket.   Vincent Bourne.   PoLF
Little Jack Frost.   *Unknown.*   SoPo
Little Jack Horner.   Mother Goose.   SoPo
Little Jack Horner/ Sits in a corner.   Frederick Winsor.   *Fr.* The Space Child's Mother Goose.   LV
Little Jesus.   Francis Thompson.   TRV
   (Ex Ore Infantium.)   FaBV
Little Jesus, came to town, The.   A Christmas Folk-Song. Lizette Woodworth Reese.   OnMSP; ThGo
Little Jesus, wast Thou shy?   Little Jesus [*or* Ex Ore Infantium].   Francis Thompson.   FaBV; TRV
Little John Bottlejohn.   Laura E. Richards.   RePo
Little Johnny Green, *with music. Unknown.*   BSNS
   (Grandma's Song, *with music.*)   BSO
Little Lad.   *Unknown.*   BiCB
Little lamb, who made thee?   The Lamb.   Blake.   *Fr.* Songs of Innocence.   CABA; CaFP; CBEP; DiPo; EaLo; EnPE; FoBA; GoJo; ILP; PoIE; PoPl; PoPo; TRV; VaPo
Little Land, The.   Robert Louis Stevenson.   SoPo
Little Learning Is a Dangerous Thing, A.   Pope.   *Fr.* An Essay on Criticism.   PoLF
Little less returned for him each spring, A.   Anglais Mort à Florence.   Wallace Stevens.   AP
Little light is going by, A.   Firefly.   Elizabeth Madox Roberts. GoJo
Little Lucy Lavender.   Lucy Lavender.   Ivy O. Eastwick.   BiCB
Little madness in the spring, A.   Emily Dickinson.   AP

Little Maid, The.   *Unknown.*   BSO
Little Man Who Wasn't There, The.   Hughes Mearns.   LV; SoPo
   (Antigonish.)   PoLF
Little marsh-plant, yellow green, A.   The Sundew.   Swinburne.   ELP; OBNC; WePo
Little Mary Pickford.   Leo Frank and Mary Phagan.   *Unknown.*   BSO
Little Matha [*or* Mathey *or* Matty] Grove [*or* Groves].   *See* Little Musgrave and Lady Barnard.
Little Miss Muffet.   Mother Goose.   SoPo
Little Miss Muffet discovered a tuffet.   The Embarrassing Episode of Little Miss Muffet.   Guy Wetmore Carryl.   OnMSP; RePo
Little moths are creeping, The.   Interior.   Padraic Colum.   ACV
Little mouse in gray velvet.   Mouse.   Hilda Conkling.   SoPo
Little Musgrave and Lady Barnard.   *Unknown.*   CABL; ErPo
   (Little Matha Grove, A, B, C, D, *and* E *vers., with music.*) BSNS
   (Little Mathey Grove, A *vers., with music.*)   BFSS
   (Little Matty Groves, B *vers., with music.*)   BFSS
Little Nancy Etticoat.   Riddle.   Mother Goose.   SoPo
Little new neighbor, have you come to be.   Welcome.   Rose Waldo.   SoPo
Little Night Music, A.   Felix Stefanile.   FiSC
Little noises of the house, The.   During a Bombardment by V-Weapons.   Roy Fuller.   ToPo
Little old man came in from plow, The.   Dandoo.   *Unknown.*   BFSS
Little old man came over the sea, A.   Old Taffyham.   *Unknown.*   BSO
Little Old Sod Shanty, *with music. Unknown.*   BFSS
Little onward lend thy guiding hand, A.   Samson Agonistes. Milton.   ILP
Little Orphant Annie.   James Whitcomb Riley.   BBGG
Little Phillis.   Kate Greenaway.   BiCB
Little Piggy.   Thomas Hood.   SoPo
Little Poem of Life, The.   John Oxenham.   TRV
Little Prince Carl he stole away.   What the Lord High Chamberlain Said.   Virginia Woodward Cloud.   BBGG
Little Prince of long ago, A.   Sons of the Kings.   Joan Agnew.   BiCB
Little Rain.   Elizabeth Madox Roberts.   SoPo
Little Red Sled, The.   Jocelyn Bush.   SoPo
Little saint best fits a little shrine, A.   A Ternarie of Littles, upon a Pipkin of Jellie Sent to a Lady.   Robert Herrick.   GoJo
Little Satellite.   Jane W. Krows.   SoPo
Little Saucers, Big Saucers.   Thad Stem, Jr.   PoNC
Little sharp vexations, The.   Our Burden Bearer.   Phillips Brooks.   TRV
Little Shrub Growing By, A.   Ben Jonson.   *See* Ask Not to Know This Man.
Little Song in Assisi, A.   George Barker.   ToPo
Little soul, like a cloud, like a feather.   To His Soul.   Hadrian.   PoPl
Little sound, A.   Many a Mickle.   Walter de la Mare.   FaBV
Little sparrows, The.   Pastoral.   William Carlos Williams.   MP
Little Steamboat.   Oscar Williams.   PoPl
Little Sticks.   Eric Rolls.   PoAu-2
Little taper set tonight.   The Christmas Candle.   Kate Louise Brown.   SoPo
Little Te Deum of the Commonplace, A, *sels.* John Oxenham.
   "For all Thy ministries."   TRV
   "For maiden sweetness, and for strength of men."   TRV
Little Things.   James Stephens.   EaLo; GoJo; WePo
Little Things ("God has no end of material").   *Unknown.*   STF
Little Things ("It was only a kindly smile he gave").   *Unknown.*   STF
Little things, that run, and quail.   Little Things.   James Stephens.   EaLo; GoJo; WePo
Little thinks, in the field, yon red-cloaked clown.   Each and All. Emerson.   AP; ILP; PoIE
Little think'st thou, poor[e] flower.   The Blossom[e].   John Donne.   FoBA; SeCP
Little Thomas.   F. Gwynne Evans.   BBGG
Little Tippler, The.   Emily Dickinson.   *See* I taste a liquor never brewed.
Little Tom Dogget.   Colly, My Cow.   *Unknown.*   EvOK
Little toy dog is covered with dust.   Little Boy Blue.   Eugene Field.   PoLF
Little Tree.   E. E. Cummings.   LOW; RoGo
   (Chanson Innocente.)   PoSC
Little Trotty Wagtail.   John Clare.   CBEP
Little Trumpet, The.   Corrado Govoni, *tr. fr. Italian by* Carlo L. Golino.   CoIP
Little Tumescence, A.   Jonathan Williams.   ErPo
Little Turtle, The.   Vachel Lindsay.   GoJo; SoPo
Little Vagabond, The.   Blake.   CBEP
Little Valley in Spring, The.   Onitsura, *tr. fr. Japanese by* Harold G. Henderson.   SiGo

Little Venetian square, The. Sandro Penna, *tr. fr. Italian by* Carlo L. Golino. CoIP
Little Wee Man, The. *Unknown. See* Wee Wee Man, The.
Little while, a little while, A. Emily Brontë. OBNC
Little Whistler, The. Frances Frost. SoPo
Little white horses are out on the sea. White Horses. Winifred Howard. SoPo
Little wind, blow on the hill-top. Little Wind. Kate Greenaway. GoJo
Little Word, A. *Unknown.* STF
Little Work, A. George Du Maurier. *Fr. Trilby.* PoLF
Little wrists. So That Even a Lover. Louis Zukofsky. CoPo
Liu Ch'e. Ezra Pound. AP
Live all thy sweet life thro'. A Summer Wish. Christina Rossetti. OBNC
Live Blindly. Trumbull Stickney. AmLP
Live so that you tempt not the sea relentless. The Golden Mean. Horace. Odes, II, 10. SiGo
Live thy Life. The Oak. Tennyson. PoPl
Liverpool Girls. *Unknown.* HaSV
Liverpool Landlady, The. *Unknown. See* Green Beds.
Lives in winter. Riddle. Mother Goose. SoPo
Livid lightnings flashed in the clouds, The. The Black Riders, XXXIX. Stephen Crane. AP
Living and Dying. "Michael Lewis," *after the Chinese. Fr.* Cherry Blossoms. UnTE
Living and Dying. Manuel González Prada, *tr. fr. Spanish by* Kate Flores. AnSP
Living man is blind and drinks his drop, A. W. B. Yeats. *Fr.* A Dialogue of Self and Soul. DTC
Living? Our Supervisors Will Do That for Us! David Holbrook. NePoEA-2
Living Statue, The. *Unknown, tr. fr. Greek by* Louis Untermeyer. UnTE
Living Temple, The. Oliver Wendell Holmes. AP
Lizards and Snakes. Anthony Hecht. CoPo
Llama, The. Hilaire Belloc. EvOK
Lo, as a careful housewife runs to catch. Sonnets, CXLIII. Shakespeare. CBEP
Lo, as a dove when up she springs. In Memoriam A. H. H., XII. Tennyson. VP
Lo! Death has reared himself a throne. The City in the Sea. Poe. AmLP; AP; CBEP; HaSV; ILP; PoIE
Lo, I have opened unto you the wide gates of my being. Psalm to My Beloved. Eunice Tietjens. BoLP; ErPo
Lo! in Corruption's lumber room. The Fate of a Broom—an Anticipation. Thomas Love Peacock. CBEP
Lo! in the mute, mind wilderness. The Unicorn. George Darley. *Fr.* Nepenthe. OBNC
Lo! in the West, fast fades the ling'ring light. Henry Kirke White. *Fr.* Clifton Grove. OBNC
Lo, Lord, Thou ridest! The Hurricane. Hart Crane. AP
Lo! 't is a gala night. The Conqueror Worm. Poe. AP
Lo, the poor Indian! whose untutored mind. Pope. *Fr.* An Essay on Man, Epistle I. PoIE
Lo, the winter is past. The Time of the Singing of Birds. The Song of Solomon, Bible, O.T. ThGo
Lo, thus, as prostrate, "in the dust I write." James Thomson. *Fr.* The City of Dreadful Night. OBNC
Lo, upon the carpet, where. Tamerlane. Victor J. Daley. PoAu-1
Lo, Victress on the Peaks. Walt Whitman. PoIE
Lo! where the four mimosas blend their shade. For an Epitaph at Fiesole. Walter Savage Landor. OBNC
Lo! where the rosy-bosomed Hours. Ode on the Spring. Thomas Gray. EiCP; GTBS-P
"Loaded with benefits daily." Mercies and Blessings. *Unknown.* STF
Lobbed ball plops, then dribbles to the cup, The. Ford Madox Ford. Robert Lowell. MP; PoCh
Lobster Quadrille, The. "Lewis Carroll." *Fr.* Alice's Adventures in Wonderland. Par
Local Light. Millen Brand. PtTo
Local Places. Howard Moss. NePoEA-2
Locate I/ love you. The Language. Robert Creeley. CoPo
Lochinvar. Sir Walter Scott. *Fr.* Marmion, V. EvOK; FaBV; OBNC; PoPo; RoGo; SIV
Lochmabyn Harper, The. *Unknown.* BuBa
Locksley Hall. Tennyson. CABA; CABL; DiPo
For I Dipped into the Future, *sel.* PoLF
("For I dipt into the future, far as human eye could see.") TRV
Locust, The. *Tr. fr. Zuni Indian by* Frank Cushing. RePo
Lodged. Robert Frost. RePo
Lodging for the Night, A. Elinor Wylie. ErPo
Loe here a little volume but great booke. An Ode Which Was Prefixed to a Prayer Booke Given to a Young Gentlewoman. Richard Crashaw. MeP
Lofty Lane. Edwin Gerard. PoAu-1
Logical Song, A. *Unknown.* ErPo
Logs, The. Sir Charles G. D. Roberts. ACV
Lollay, lollay, little child, why wepestou so sore? An Adult Lullaby. *Unknown.* MeEL
Lollocks. Robert Graves. DTC; EvOK
Lolly Trudom, *with music. Unknown.* BFSS

Lollypops, The. Cordia Thomas. SoPo
Lombardy Bell. Clemente Rèbora, *tr. fr. Italian by* Carlo L. Golino. CoIP
London. Blake. *Fr.* Songs of Experience. CABA; CaFP; CBEP; DiPo; EnPE; FoBA; ILP; OBNC; OnP; PoIE; PoSa; StP
London. John Davidson. OBNC; StP
London. Manmohan Ghose. ACV
London; a Poem in Imitation of the Third Satire of Juvenal. Samuel Johnson. EiCP; EnPE
London, 1802 ("Milton! thou should'st be living . . ."). Wordsworth. CABA; DiPo; FaBV; FoBA; ILP; OBNC; PoIE; PoPo; StP
(Same, The.) GTBS-P
London, MDCCCII ("O friend! I know not which way I must look"). Wordsworth. *See* In London, September, 1802.
London is painted round them: burly railings. Street Performers, 1851. Terence Tiller. AnMoPo; GTBS-P
London Plane-Tree, A. Amy Levy. WePo
London Prentice, The. *Unknown.* UnTE
London Snow. Robert Bridges. GTBS-P; OBNC; PoIE; PoSa; StP; WePo; WiR
London Sonnets, *sels.* Carl Bode. ToPo
City Considered as a Tulip Tree, The.
Covent Garden Market.
Who Calls the English Cold?
London Train. Paul Dehn. LV
Lone crow caws from the tall dead gum, The. Sheaf-Tosser. Eric Rolls. PoAu-1
Lone Dog. Irene Rutherford McLeod. LV
Lone Gentleman. "Pablo Neruda," *tr. fr. Spanish by* Clayton Eshleman. ErPo
Lone, lone and lone I stand. The Myall in Prison. Mary Gilmore. PoAu-1
Lone, phallic, A—let's get. Tour de Force. Peter Kane Dufault. ErPo
Lone Star Trail, The, *with music. Unknown.* BFSS
Lone watch of the moon over mountains old, The. Mortality. James Devaney. PoAu-1
Loneliest One, The. Nietzsche, *tr. fr. German by* Walter Kaufmann. TwGP
Loneliness. Hashin, *tr. fr. Japanese by* Harold G. Henderson. PoPl; SiGo
(No Sky at All.) SoPo
Lonely Beauty. Samuel Daniel. *Fr.* The Complaint of Rosamond. CTC
Lonely I lay in the heather-soft hollow. The Heather. Steen Steensen Blicher. SiGo
Lonely Louisa, *with music. Unknown.* BSO
Lonely Lover. Robert P. Tristram Coffin. MoLP
Lonely molar of a whore, The. Cycle. Gottfried Benn. *Fr.* Morgue. TwGP
Lonely music arose and bid, A. Wrack. Irving Feldman. AmPC
Lonely Scarecrow, The. James Kirkup. DaDu
Lonely season in lonely lands, when fled, The. November. Robert Bridges. OBNC
Lonely Street, The. William Carlos Williams. MP
Lonely Valley. *Unknown.* BSO
Long ago, I tucked away. Old Closet. Selma Robinson. LV
Long ago to Thee I gave. *Unknown.* BoC
Long autumn rain. An Autumn Song. Edward Dowden. ACV
Long canoe, The. Lullaby. Robert Hillyer. LOW
Long-expected one and twenty. A Short Song of Congratulation. Samuel Johnson. CABA; EiCP; ELP; StP
Long grass searches the wind, The. Shearing Grass. Peter Redgrove. NePoEA-2
Long-haired Yak has long black hair, The. Yak. William Jay Smith. RePo
Long Harbour, The. Mary Ursula Bethell. ACV
Long he attained it by looking. Turning-Point. Rainer Maria Rilke. MGP
Long, hideously long the plodding was. Babylon. Laura Benét. FiSC
Long Hill, The. Sara Teasdale. LV; PoPl
Long-legged Fly. W. B. Yeats. AnMoPo; CaFP; PoIE
Long life and success to a true Irish bawd. The Wedding of Ballyporeen. *Unknown.* BSNS
Long life to old Whalan of Waitin' a While. Whalan of Waitin' a While. J. W. Gordon. PoAu-1
Long Lines. Paul Goodman. OPP
Long, Long Ago. *Unknown.* PoSC
Long long ago on Calvary. Victory. *Unknown.* STF
Long ago when the world was a wild place. Bedtime Story. George MacBeth. NePoEA-2
Long Love that in My Thought Doth Harbor, The. Petrarch, *tr. fr. Italian by* Sir Thomas Wyatt. Sonnets to Laura: To Laura in Life, CIX. CABA
(Long Love, The.) ILP
(Lover for Shamefastness Hideth His Desire within His Faithful Heart, The.) StP
Long night succeeds thy little day. Margaret Love Peacock for Her Tombstone, 1826. Thomas Love Peacock. OBNC
Long over, what's on the tree. To Her Body, against Time. Robert Kelly. CoPo

Long Pursuit. *Unknown, tr. fr. Greek by* Louis Untermeyer. UnTE
Long River, The. Donald Hall. NePoEA-2
Long-rolling, The. The Main-Deep. James Stephens. HaSV; PoPo
Long Shadow of Lincoln, The. Carl Sandburg. LiPo
Long Small Room, The. Edward Thomas. PoIE
Long-Suffering of God. Christopher Smart. *Fr.* Hymns for the Amusement of Children. EiCP
Long Summer. Laurie Lee. ToPo
Long Time a Child. Hartley Coleridge. CBEP (Sonnet: "Long time a child, and still a child when years.") OBNC
Long, Too Long America. Walt Whitman. FoBA
Long Trail, The. Kipling. FaBV
Long War, The. Laurie Lee. ToPo
Long war had ended, The. The Next War. Sir Osbert Sitwell. MMA
Long was I, Lady Luck, your serving-man. Davy, the Dicer. Sir Thomas More. DiPo
Long whip lingers, The. Horses. Louis MacNeice. DaDu
Longer than a Platonic century. Maurice Scève. *Fr. Délie.* RBL
Longing. Matthew Arnold. Faded Leaves, V. CBEP; PoLF; VP
Longing. George Herbert. MeP
Longing. "Michael Lewis," *after the Chinese. Fr.* Cherry Blossoms. UnTE
Looby Loo. *Unknown.* SoPo
Look, The. Elizabeth Barrett Browning. TRV
Look, The. Sara Teasdale. BoLP; WePo
Look at him there in his stovepipe hat. American Primitive. William Jay Smith. MP; PoPl
Look at Jonah embarking from Joppa, deterred by. Tom Fool at Jamaica. Marianne Moore. AP
Look at me. Here I Am. Ann Morrissett. BoLP
Look at the eyes look from my tail. Peacock and Nightingale. Robert Finch. OBCV
Look at the fish! Fish. William Jay Smith. RePo
Look at the stars! look, look up at the skies! The Starlight [*or* Starlit] Night. Gerard Manley Hopkins. BoC; DiPo; GTBS-P; VP
Look at this village boy, his head is stuffed. Farm Child. R. S. Thomas. DaDu; WePo
Look away now from the high lonesome hills. Admonition for Spring. L. A. MacKay. OBCV
Look back with longing eyes and know that I will follow. The Flight. Sara Teasdale. BoLP
Look down; be still. Wonga Vine. Judith Wright. PoAu-2
Look Down Fair Moon. Walt Whitman. FoBA
Look down the lone green valley. Lonely Valley. *Unknown.* BSO
Look down the long valley and there stands a mountain. Too Anxious for Rivers. Robert Frost. CBEP
Look, Edwin! Edna St. Vincent Millay. GoJo
Look forth and tell me what they do. Hammer and Anvil. Samuel Valentine Cole. PoLF
Look God, I have never spoken to You. Conversion. Frances Angermayer. PoLF
Look, How Beautiful. Robinson Jeffers. MoRP
Look how her close defences laddered now. Apollo and Daphne. W. R. Rodgers. ErPo
Look how the golden children. New Leaves. Juan Ramón Jiménez. PoPl
Look how the lark soars upward and is gone. False Poets and True. Thomas Hood. PP
Look in my face; my name is Might-have-been. A Superscription. Dante Gabriel Rossetti. The House of Life, XCVII. CBEP; GTBS-P; OBNC
Look in this cast, and know the hand. The Hand of Lincoln. Edmund Clarence Stedman. LiPo
Look in thy glass, and tell the face thou viewest. Sonnets, III. Shakespeare. CABA; EnRePo
Look! Look at me! Tree Birthdays. Mary Carolyn Davies. BiCB
Look Not Thou. Sir Walter Scott. *Fr.* The Bride of Lammermoor. CBEP
Look now, at this February street in April. A Street in April. Louis Dudek. OBCV
Look off, dear Love, across the sallow sands. Evening Song. Sidney Lanier. AP; FaPL
Look Out Below! Charles R. Thatcher. PoAu-1
Look out how you use proud words. Primer Lesson. Carl Sandburg. PoPl; RePo
Look out! Look out! You've spilt the ink. April Fools' Day. Marnie Pomeroy. PoSC
Look out upon the stars, my love. A Serenade. Edward Coote Pinkney. AmLP
Look, stranger, on this island now. Seascape. W. H. Auden. GTBS-P
"Look, there's a robin." Little Brother. Aileen Fisher. BiCB
Look to the Leaf. *Unknown, tr. fr. German by* Louis Untermeyer. UnTE
Look upon the rainbow, and praise him that made it. Ecclesiasticus, Bible, Apocrypha. BoC

Look, we don't give a hoot if Zippo-Fasteners have gone to war. Memorial to the Great Big Beautiful Self-sacrificing Advertisers. Frederick Ebright. ThLM
Look you, Gil, at dawn. Mingo's Discourse. Juan del Encina. RBL
"Look!" you said. "Look!" Two Egrets. John Ciardi. PoPl
Looke Home. Robert Southwell. MeP
Looke well about, ye that lovers be. Against Women. *Unknown.* MeEL
Looking at the Moon and Thinking of One Far Away. Chang Chiu-ling, *tr. fr. Chinese by* Witter Bynner. SiGo
Looking away from my sin and my shame. That's Faith. S. N. Leitner. STF
Looking by chance in at the open window. The Foreboding. Robert Graves. ELP; StP
Looking-Glass, The. Kipling. EvOK
Looking-Glass River. Robert Louis Stevenson. LV
Looking On. Anthony Thwaite. NePoEA-2
Looking Up at Airplanes, Always. Rolfe Humphries. RePo
Loose to the breeze her golden tresses flow'd. Petrarch. *Fr.* Sonnets to Laura: To Laura in Life. RBL
Loot. Thom Gunn. ErPo; NePoEA-2
Lord Alcohol. Thomas Lovell Beddoes. WiR
Lord, art thou at the table head above. The Reflexion. Edward Taylor. *Fr.* Preparatory Meditations, First Series. AP
Lord, art Thou wrapped in cloud. The Evening Star. Amy Carmichael. TRV
Lord Bakeman. *Unknown. See* Young Beichan and Susie Pye.
Lord Bateman. *Unknown. See* Young Beichan and Susie Pye.
Lord, behold our family here assembled. A Prayer for the Household. Robert Louis Stevenson. TRV
Lord bless thee and keep thee, The. A Blessing. Numbers, Bible, *O.T.* ThGo
Lord, by whose breath all souls and seeds are living. Hymn. Andrew Young. EaLo
Lord, can a crumb of earth [*or* dust] the earth outweigh. Prologue. Edward Taylor. AmLP; AP; MeP
Lord Christ, My Darling Is So Dear. C. Hansen-Bay. ThGo
Lord Finchley. Hilaire Belloc. DTC
Lord, for to-morrow and its needs. Just for Today. Sybil F. Partridge. TRV
Lord God whose mercy guards the virgin jungle. Asking for It. Siegfried Sassoon. MoRP
Lord had a job for me, The. Get Somebody Else. Paul Laurence Dunbar. TRV
Lord hath builded for Himself, The. The Unknown God. Henry Francis Lyte. TRV
Lord, how can man preach thy eternal word? The [Church] Windows. George Herbert. CABA; CBEP; ILP; MeP; SeCP
Lord, How Shall I Me Complain. *Unknown.* CBEP
Lord, I am like the mistletoe. To God. Robert Herrick. TRV
Lord, I my vows to Thee renew. Direct This Day. Thomas Ken. TRV
Lord, I would own thy tender care. A Thanksgiving. Jane Taylor. ThGo
Lord, I'm just a little boy. A Child's Christmas Song. T. A. Daly. BiCB
Lord in the Wind, The. James Picot. PoAu-2
Lord Is Good to All, The. Psalms, CXLV: 9, Bible, *O.T.* TRV
Lord Is My Shepherd, The. Sir H. W. Baker. ThGo
Lord Is My Shepherd, The. Psalms, XXIII, Bible, *O.T.* CBEP; PoLF; RePo; TRV
(Lord's My Shepherd, The, *Scottish Psalter.*) TRV
(Twenty-third Psalm.) PoPl; PoPo
Lord Jesus! with what sweetness and delights. Ascension-Day. Henry Vaughan. MeP
Lord, look upon a little child. Jane Taylor. ThGo
Lord, Lord—these miracles, the streets, all say. Stone Too Can Pray. Conrad Aiken. EaLo; MoRP
Lord Lord . . . they have stabbed my reason, so that I write. "Jesse Thoor." *Fr.* Speeches and Invocations. MGP
Lord Lovel (A *and* D *vers., with music;* B *vers.*). *Unknown.* BSO
(Lord Lovel and Lady Nança Bell, *with music.*) BFSS
(Lord Lovell, C *and* E *vers., with music.*) BSO
(Nancy Bell and Lord Lover, F *vers.*) BSO
Lord Lover was down at his old castle gate. Nancy Bell and Lord Lover. *Unknown.* BSO
Lord, make me an instrument of Your [*or* Thy] peace. Prayer of St. Francis of Assisi for Peace [*or* St. Francis' Prayer]. St. Francis of Assisi. PoLF; PoPl; TRV
Lord, my first fruits present themselves to thee. The Dedication. George Herbert. MeP
Lord never grant me what I ask for. The Unforeseen. Conrado Nale Roxlo. MoRP
Lord of all being! throned afar. A Sun-Day Hymn. Oliver Wendell Holmes. TRV
Lord of All Pots and Pans and Things. *Unknown, ad. fr.* Cecily Hallack. TRV. *See also* Divine Office of the Kitchen, The.
(Home Prayer. A.) STF
Lord of all, who reigned supreme, The. Adon 'Olam. *Unknown.* EaLo

Lord of comfort, hope, and love. Give My Heart a Song. Anna M. Gilleland. STF
Lord of My Heart's Elation. Bliss Carman. OBCV
Lord of the bow. In the Gorge. W. S. Merwin. AmPC
Lord of the grass and hill. Veni Creator. Bliss Carman. MoRP
Lord of the pots and pipkins, since I have no time to be. The Divine Office of the Kitchen. Cecily Hallack. PoLF
Lord of Thyself and me, through the sore grief. George Macdonald. *Fr.* Within and Without. TRV
Lord Randal. *Unknown.* CABA; CBEP; DiPo; ILP; PoIE; PoPo; SIV; StP
(Henry, My Son, B *and* C *vers., with music.*) BSO
(Jimmy Randal, D *vers.*) BSO
(Jimmy Random, My Son, I *st., with music.*) BFSS
(Lord Ronald, A *vers., with music.*) BSO
(My Ramboling Son, *with music.*) BFSS
Lord, speak to me that I may speak. A Teacher's Prayer. Frances Ridley Havergal. TRV
Lord, the newness of this day. Prayer. Henry van Dyke. TRV
Lord, the Roman hyacinths are blooming in bowls and. A Song for Simeon. T. S. Eliot. EaLo
Lord—Thine the Day. Dag Hammerskjöld, *tr. fr. Swedish by* Leif Sjöberg *and* W. H. Auden. EaLo
Lord, this humble house we'd keep. Edgar A. Guest. *Fr.* Prayer for the Home. TRV
Lord Thomas and Fair Annet (B, C, *and* D *vers.*). *Unknown.* BSO
(Lord Thomas, B *vers., with music.*) BSNS
Lord Thomas and Fair Ellen, A *vers., with music.*) BSO
(Lord Thomas and Fair Ellinor, A *vers.*) BSNS
(Lord Thomas and the Brown Girl, *with music.*) BFSS
Lord, Thou Hast Been Our Dwelling Place. Psalms, XC, Bible, *O.T.* EaLo
Lord, Thou hast given me a cell. A Thanksgiving to God for His House. Robert Herrick. BoC; SeCP
Lord, Thou hast made this world below the shadow of a dream. McAndrew's Hymn. Kipling. CABL; HaSV
Lord, Thou Hast Suffered. Amy Carmichael. TRV
Lord, thus I sin, repent, and sin again. A Sinner's Lament. Lord Herbert of Cherbury. SeCP
Lord 'Tis Said That from the World. Mechthild von Magdeburg, *tr. fr. German by* Mabel Cotterell. AnML
Lord Ullin's Daughter. Thomas Campbell. GTBS-P; RoGo
Lord Vanover, *with music. Unknown.* BSO
Lord, we thank Thee for affliction. Thank Thee, Lord. Georgia B. Adams. STF
Lord! what a busie, restles thing. The Pursuite. Henry Vaughan. SeCP
Lord, what a change within us one short hour. Prayer. Richard Chenevix Trench. TRV
Lord, what is man? why should he cost you. Charitas Nimia; or, The Deare Bargain. Richard Crashaw. MeP
Lord, when on my bed I lie. Whirring Wheels. John Oxenham. TRV
Lord, when Thou seest that my work is done. After Work. John Oxenham. TRV
Lord, who createdst man in wealth and store. Easter Wings. George Herbert. CABA; MeP; PoSa; PP; SeCP; StP; VaPo
Lord will happiness divine, The. The Contrite Heart. William Cowper. EiCP
Lord William and Lord Douglas, *with music. Unknown.* BFSS
Lord, with what bounty and rare clemency. Ungratefulness. George Herbert. FoBA
Lord, with what glorie wast thou serv'd of old. Sion. George Herbert. MeP
Lordly and Isolate Satyrs, The. Charles Olson. CABL
Lords, knights, and squires, the numerous band. To a Child of Quality, Five Years Old, the Author Then Forty. Matthew Prior. CBEP; EiCP; VaPo
Lord's My Shepherd, The. Psalms, XXIII, Bible, *O.T. See* Lord Is My Shepherd, The.
Lord's Name Be Praised, The! *Unknown.* ThGo
Lords of Creation, The. *Unknown.* PoLF
Lord's Prayer, The. St. Matthew, VI: 9-13, Bible, *N.T.* EaLo; PoLF; TRV
"Lordynges," quod he, "in chirches whan I preche." The Pardoner's Prologue and Tale. Chaucer. *Fr.* The Canterbury Tales. CABL
Lorena, *with music.* H. D. L. Webster. BFSS
Lose This Day Loitering. Goethe, *tr. fr. German by* John Anster. *Fr.* Faust: Prologue. PoLF
(Prologue: "Lose this day loitering, 'twill be the same story.") TRV
Loss falls from the air as the tables turn. Complaint. Joseph Bennett. StP
Loss of gold is much, The. Lines from a Sampler. *Unknown.* ThGo
Loss of the *Central America, with music.* John A. Stone. SGR
Loss of the *Eurydice,* The. Gerard Manley Hopkins. FoBA; VP

Loss of the *Royal George,* The. William Cowper. *See* On the Loss of the *Royal George.*
Lost. Carl Sandburg. PoPl; PoPo; RePo
Lost, The. Jones Very. PoIE
Lost and Found. George Macdonald. TRV
Lost and Found. Edwin Muir. PoDB
Lost and Given Over. E. J. Brady. PoAu-1
Lost Cities, The. Lawrence Durrell. ToPo
Lost Doll, The. Charles Kingsley. *Fr.* The Water Babies. SoPo
Lost Ingredient, The. Anne Sexton. CoPo
Lost Lady Found, The. *Unknown.* BSNS
Lost Language, The. Irving Feldman. AmPC
Lost Leader, The. Robert Browning. FaPL
Lost Love. Robert Graves. ILP
Lost Love, The. Wordsworth. *See* She Dwelt among the Untrodden Ways.
Lost Mistress, The. Robert Browning. CBEP; OBNC
Lost Month. W. S. Merwin. AmPC
Lost Son, The. Theodore Roethke. AP
Lost Voice on This Hill. Burnham Eaton. FiSC
Lost Willie. *Unknown. See* Sweet William ("Weary are the hours of a sailor boy").
Lost Youth. Longfellow. *See* My Lost Youth.
Lotos-Eaters, The. Tennyson. DiPo; FoBA; OnMSP; OnP; PoIE; VP
Choric Song: "There is sweet music here that softer falls," *sel.* OBNC
(There Is Sweet Music Here.) FaBV
"Hateful is the dark-blue sky," I *st.* HaSV
Lottie Mae ("Lottie was a skinny child"). Stanley McNail. FiSC
Lotus-flower is frightened, The. Heine, *tr. fr. German by* D. G. Wright. AGP
Lotus Leaves. Mitsukuni, *tr. fr. Japanese by* Miyamori Asataro. SiGo
Lotuses. Witter Bynner. MoLP
Loud roared the dreadful thunder. The Bay of Biscay. Andrew Cherry. HaSV
Louisa she doth mourn for her loved one departed. Lonely Louisa. *Unknown.* BSO
Louisburg. *Unknown.* ThLM
Lousy Miner, The, *with music.* John A. Stone. SGR
Love. Attilio Bertolucci, *tr. fr. Italian by* Carlo L. Golino. CoIP
Love. First Corinthians, XIII, Bible, *N.T.* TRV
Love. Rupert Brooke. MoLP
Love ("All love at first, like generous wine"). Samuel Butler. CBEP
Love ("Lovers, like wrestlers"). Samuel Butler. ErPo
Love. Samuel Taylor Coleridge. GTBS-P
Love. Tom Dent. NNP
Love ("Immortall Heat, O let thy greater flame"). George Herbert. MeP
Love ("Immortall Love, authour of this great frame"). George Herbert. MeP
Love ("Love bade me welcome, yet my soul drew back"). George Herbert. CABA; FaBV; FoBA; MeP; OnP; PoLF; SeCP; StP
(Christ Our Lord.) BoC
Love. Juan Ramón Jiménez, *tr. fr. Spanish by* Angel Flores. AnSP
Love. Ben Jonson. UnTE
Love. Toyohiko Kagawa. TRV
Love. William Langland, *mod. by* Nevill Coghill. *Fr.* The Vision of Piers Plowman. BoC
Love. "Hugh MacDiarmid." PoIE
Love. Nicholas Moore. ErPo
Love. Henry David Thoreau. CBEP
Love. Ludwig Tieck, *tr. fr. German by* Herman Salinger. SiGo
Love ("I love you"). *Unknown.* TRV
Love ("Love was before the light began"). *Unknown, tr. fr. Arabic by* E. Powys Mathers. *Fr.* The Thousand and One Nights. SiGo
Love. Jones Very. AP
Love among the Manichees. William Dickey. PoCh
Love among the Ruins. Robert Browning. FaBV; VP
Love and a Question. Robert Frost. MoBS
Love and Age. Thomas Love Peacock. *Fr.* Gryll Grange. OBNC
Love and Death. Ben Jonson. *See* Though I Am Young.
Love and forgetting might have carried them. Two Look at Two. Robert Frost. AP; OnP
Love and Hope. Dante Gabriel Rossetti. The House of Life, XLIII. VP
Love and Life. Earl of Rochester. ELP
Love and Marriage. Ray Mathew. PoAu-2
Love and My Lady, Too. Adam de la Halle, *tr. fr. French by* Irma Brandeis. AnML
Love and Sleep. Swinburne. UnTE
Love and Wine. Thomas Shadwell. UnTE
Love at Large. Coventry Patmore. *Fr.* The Angel in the House. StP
Love at the lips was touch. To Earthward. Robert Frost. AP; CABA; PoIE

Love bade me welcome; yet my soul drew back. Love [or Christ Our Lord]. George Herbert. BoC; CABA; FaBV; FoBA; MeP; OnP; PoLF; SeCP; TRV
Love Beleaguered. Katherine Garrison Chapin. MoLP
Love Bit, The. Joel Oppenheimer. CoPo
Love Breathing Thanks and Praise, sel. Richard Baxter. "I preached as never sure to preach again." TRV
Love Calls Us to the Things of This World. Richard Wilbur. PoDB; ToPo
Love Comes Quietly. Robert Creeley. BoLP
Love Continual. John Heywood. CBEP
Love-Death Story, A. Charles Edward Eaton. PoNC
Love Dislikes Nothing. Robert Herrick. CBEP
Love, do not count your labor lost. Sullen Moods. Robert Graves. StP
Love Elegy. Tobias George Smollett. WaPE
Love Enthroned. Dante Gabriel Rossetti. The House of Life, I. OBNC; VP
Love ere he bleeds, an eagle in high skies. Modern Love, XXVI. George Meredith. VP
Love Ever Green. King Henry VIII(?). MeEL
Love Feast, The. W. H. Auden. ErPo
Love feeds, like Intellect, his lamp with truth. William Baylebridge. Fr. Love Redeemed. PoAu-1
Love for a Beautiful Lady. Unknown. MeEL
Love for a Hand. Karl Shapiro. MoLP; ToPo
Love for a Hare. Melvin Walker La Follette. NePoEA-2
Love for Love, sel. Congreve. Nymph and a Swain, A. UnTE
Love for Love's Sake. Henry Carey. WaPE
Love from a source admired. Song from the Gulf. Rolfe Humphries. MoLP
Love, from the awful throne of patient power. The Cross. Shelley. BoC
Love has crept out of her sealèd heart. Flapper. D. H. Lawrence. BoLP
Love has given Him from paradise. Jean de la Ceppède. Fr. Théorèmes Spirituels. RBL
Love has its morn, its noon, its eve, and night. Too Late. Philip Bourke Marston. OBNC
Love he tomorrow, who loved never. The Vigil of Venus. Unknown. UnTE
Love heeds no more the sighing of the wind. The Garden of Shadow. Ernest Dowson. OBNC
Love Henry. Unknown. See Young Hunting.
Love, I am guilty of listening to hot rods. Confession. Ralph Pomeroy. CoPo
Love in a Cottage. J. A. R. McKellar. Fr. Fourth Napoleon. PoAu-2
Love in a Life. Robert Browning. CBEP; OBNC
Love in Exile, sel. Mathilde Blind. "Dost thou remember ever, for my sake." OBNC
Love in Fantastic Triumph. Aphra Behn. Fr. Abdelazer. CBEP
Love in Her Eyes. John Gay. Fr. Acis and Galatea. ELP
Love in her sunny eyes does basking play. The Change. Abraham Cowley. SeCP
Love in May. Jean Passerat, tr. fr. French by Andrew Lang. SiGo
Love in Moonlight. Bhartrihari, tr. fr. Sanskrit by Paul Elmer More. SiGo
Love in my bosom like a bee. Rosalind's Madrigal. Thomas Lodge. Rosalynde; or, Euphues' Golden Legacy. EnRePo; PoIE; UnTE
Love in Reason. Luis de Góngora, tr. fr. Spanish by Edward Churton. RBL
Love in the Valley. George Meredith. VaPo; VP "Under yonder beech-tree single on the greensward," sel. ErPo, 3 sts.; UnTE, 4 sts.
Love in the Winds. Richard Hovey. BoLP
Love Indestructible. Robert Southey. Fr. The Curse of Kehama. OBNC
Love Is a Babel. Unknown. CBEP
Love is a breach in the walls, a broken gate. Love. Rupert Brooke. MoLP
Love Is a Bullet. Frank Borden Hanes. PoNC
Love is a hungry hobo. Old Man's Fancy. Thad Stem, Jr. PoNC
Love Is a Refiner's Fire. Michelangelo, tr. fr. Italian by John Addington Symonds. RBL
Love Is a Sickness. Samuel Daniel. Fr. Hymen's Triumph. CBEP; ELP; PoIE
Love Is a Subtle Spirit That Can Slay. Cino da Pistoia, tr. fr. Italian by Daniel J. Donno. AnML
Love is a torment, there's no question. Love's Torment. Unknown. UnTE
Love is and was my Lord and King. In Memoriam A. H. H., CXXVI. Tennyson. OBNC; VP
Love Is Enough. William Morris. BoLP; FaBV; WePo
Love Is like a Dizziness. James Hogg. LV
Love is like a lamb, and love is like a lion. Thomas Middleton. Fr. Blurt, Master Constable. BoLP
Love Is like the Wild Rose-Briar. Emily Brontë. ELP
Love is not all: it is not meat nor drink. Sonnet XXX. Edna St. Vincent Millay. AmLP; BoLP; MoLP

Love is not love which altereth. Under All Change. Josephine W. Johnson. MoRP
Love is not true: mathematicians know. Dogma. Babette Deutsch. MoLP
Love Is of God. Horatius Bonar. TRV
Love is our argument of joy. News of the World. Anne Ridler. MoLP
Love is the soul of all things, the desire. Tasso, tr. fr. Italian by Romilda Rendel. RBL
Love is too young to know what conscience is. Sonnets, CLI. Shakespeare. CBEP
Love Laughs at Winter. Unknown, tr. fr. Latin by George F. Whicher. UnTE
Love-Lesson, A. Clément Marot, tr. fr. French by Leigh Hunt. RBL
Love-Letter, The. Dante Gabriel Rossetti. The House of Life, XI. VP
Love Letter, A. Unknown. MeEL
Love Lies Bleeding. Christina Rossetti. FaPL
Love Life (and Death) of a Moose, The. Richard Armour. LV
Love Lifted Me. Paris Leary. CoPo
Love Lifts to God. Michelangelo, tr. fr. Italian by John Addington Symonds. RBL
Love lives beyond/ The tomb. John Clare. OBNC
Love, love, a lily's my care. Words for the Wind. Theodore Roethke. AnMoPo; AP; PoCh
Love Made in the First Age. Richard Lovelace. SeCP
Love making all things else his foes. Against Love. Sir John Denham. CBEP
Love-making, The: His and Hers. Eve Merriam. UnTE
"Love me, for I love you"—and answer me. Monna Innominata, VII. Christina Rossetti. VP
Love Me Little, Love Me Long. Unknown. CBEP
Love me, not with smiles, or with flutes, or with the plaited flowers. The Despairing Embrace. Pierre Louÿs. Fr. The Songs of Bilitis. UnTE
Love Me Still. Unknown. See Love Not Me for Comely Grace.
Love, Meet Me in the Green Glen. John Clare. ELP
Love-Moon, The. Dante Gabriel Rossetti. The House of Life, XXXVII. VP
Love must think in music sweetly. Love. Ludwig Tieck. SiGo
Love Not Me for Comely Grace. Unknown. ELP; GTBS-P; PoLF (Love Me Still.) WePo
Love, oh love, oh careless love. Careless Love. Unknown. BFSS; UnTE
Love of field and coppice, The. My Country. Dorothea Mackellar. PoAu-1
Love, of this clearest, frailest glass. In a Glass-Window for Inconstancy. Lord Herbert of Cherbury. SeCP
Love Often Agitates My Heart to Thought. Enzo, King of Sardinia, tr. fr. Italian by James J. Wilhelm. AnML
Love on the Farm. D. H. Lawrence. ErPo; FaBV
Love on the Mountain. Thomas Boyd. BoLP
Love Once, Love Ever. Girolamo Preti, tr. fr. Italian by Sir Edward Sherburne. RBL
Love Perfumes All Parts. Robert Herrick. UnTE
Love Play. William Cavendish, Duke of Newcastle. ErPo
Love Poem: "It is the same if I lie on the left or the right side." Karl Krolow, tr. fr. German by Marianne Leibholz. MGP
Love Poem: "Oh, your thighs." Judson Crews. UnTE
Love Poem: "There is a white mare that my love keeps." Alex Comfort. ErPo
Love Poem: "When we are in love, we love the grass." Robert Bly. BoLP
Love Poem: "Written under Capricorn, a land." Chris Wallace-Crabbe. PoAu-2
Love Poem to Helen. René Guy Cadou, tr. fr. French by Edmund Keely. COFP
Love Redeemed, sels. William Baylebridge. PoAu-1 "As fire, unfound ere pole approaches pole," LXXXVIII. "Love feeds, like Intellect, his lamp with truth," XXXII. "Who questions if the punctual sun unbars," LXXXII.
"Love seeketh not itself to please." The Clod and the Pebble. Blake. Fr. Songs of Experience. CABA; CBEP; FaBV; OBNC
Love set you going like a fat gold watch. Morning Song. Sylvia Plath. AnMoPo
Love, should I fear death most for you or me? Cloud and Wind. Dante Gabriel Rossetti. The House of Life, XLIV. VP
Love Song. Samuel Allen. NNP
Love Song, A. W. F. Hawley. OBCV
Love Song. Harriet Monroe. AmLP
Love Song. Rainer Maria Rilke, tr. fr. German. SiGo, tr. by Kate Flores; TwGP, tr. by Walter Kaufmann
Love Song: I and Thou. Alan Dugan. AP
Love Song of J. Alfred Prufrock, The. T. S. Eliot. AP; CABA; CaFP; CBEP; DiPo; FoBA; ILP; MP; PoIE "Yellow fog that rubs its back upon the window-panes, The," sel. PoPo

Love Song of J. Alfred Prufrock, The *(continued)*
(Yellow Fog.) LOW
Love Sonnets, VIII. Charles Harpur. PoAu-1
Love-Sweetness. Dante Gabriel Rossetti. The House of Life,
XXI. VP
Love That Doth Reign. Petrarch, *tr. by* the Earl of Surrey.
See Love That Liveth and Reigneth in My Thought.
"Love that I hae chosen, I'll therewith be content, The." The
Lawlands o' Holland. *Unknown.* HaSV
Love, that is dead and buried, yesterday. Love Lies Bleeding.
Christina Rossetti. FaPL
Love That Liveth and Reigneth in My Thought. Petrarch, *tr.
fr. Italian by* the Earl of Surrey. Sonnets to Laura: To
Laura in Life, CIX. StP
(Complaint of a Lover Rebuked.) CABA
(Love That Doth Reign.) ILP
Love that rose on stronger wings, The. In Memoriam
A. H. H., CXXVIII. Tennyson. VP
Love thou art absolute sole Lord. Hymn to St. Teresa [*or* In
Memory of the Vertuous and Learned Lady Madre de
Teresa]. Richard Crashaw. CABL; MeP
Love, through your spirit and mine what summer eve. Last
Fire. Dante Gabriel Rossetti. The House of Life, XXX.
VP
Love Thy Country. George Bubb, Baron Melcombe Dodington.
CBEP
Love to his singer held a glistening leaf. Love's Last Gift.
Dante Gabriel Rossetti. The House of Life, LIX. VP
Love to the gentle heart will hasten straight. The Gentle
Heart. Guido Guinicelli. AnML
Love Unknown. Samuel Crossman. BoC
Love Unlike Love. *Unknown.* MeEL
Love walked alone. The Black Riders, XLI. Stephen Crane.
AP
Love was before the light began. Love. *Unknown. Fr.* The
Thousand and One Nights. SiGo
Love, We Attend the Vision of the Rose. Petrarch, *tr. fr.
Italian by* Peter Russell. Sonnets to Laura: To Laura in
Life, CLIX. AnML
Love which is the most difficult mystery. Psyche with the
Candle. Archibald MacLeish. MoLP
Love, why have you led me here. The Young Cordwainer.
Robert Graves. MoBS
Love Will Find Out the Way. *Unknown.* CBEP; WiR
(Great Adventurer, The.) GTBS-P
Love without Hope. Robert Graves. BoLP; GTBS-P
Lovebirds. William Jay Smith. ErPo
Loveliest girl in all our country-side, The. Romance. Luis de
Góngora. RBL
Loveliest of Trees. A. E. Housman. A Shropshire Lad, II.
CaFP; DiPo; ELP; FaBV; ILP; LV; PoLF; RePo
("Loveliest of trees, the cherry now.") VP
Lovelight. Georgia Douglas Johnson. AmNP
Loveliness of Love, The. George Darley. GTBS-P
(Song, A: "It is not Beauty I demand.") OBNC
Lovely as a Flower. Heine, *tr. fr. German by* Kate Flores.
SiGo
Lovely Banks of Boyne, The, *with music. Unknown.* BSNS
Lovely body of the dead, The. Lament for Glasgerion. Elinor
Wylie. AmLP
Lovely hill-torrents are. Song. W. J. Turner. GoJo
Lovely lass o' Inverness, The. Lament for Culloden. Burns.
CBEP; GTBS-P
Lovely lass to a friar came, A. The Lass and the Friar.
Burns. UnTE
Lovely ter of lovely eiye. Christ's Tear Breaks My Heart.
Unknown. MeEL
Lovemaker, The. Robert Mezey. CABA; NePoEA-2
Lovemusic. Carolyn Kizer. ErPo
Lover and the Nightingale, The. *Unknown, tr. fr. Latin by*
John Addington Symonds. UnTE
Lover and the Sculptor, The. Michelangelo, *tr. fr. Italian by*
John Addington Symonds. RBL
Lover, as God May Comfort Me. Agnes de Navarre-Cham-
pagne, *tr. fr. French by* Jacques LeClercq. AnML
Lover Compareth His State to a Ship in Perilous Storm Tossed
on the Sea, The. Sir Thomas Wyatt. *See* My Galley.
Lover Complayneth the Unkindness of His Love, The. Sir
Thomas Wyatt. *See* My Lute, Awake.
Lover Exhorteth His Lady to Take Time, While Time Is, The.
George Turberville. EnRePo
Lover for Shamefastness Hideth His Desire within His Faith-
ful Heart, The. Sir Thomas Wyatt. *See* Long Love
That in My Thought Doth Harbor, The.
Lover Forsaken, The. Sir Thomas Wyatt. *See* They Flee
from Me.
Lover Freed from the Gallows, The, *with music. Unknown.*
BFSS
Lover Left Alone, A. *Unknown.* MeEL
Lover, lover, as God my comfort me. Lover, as God May
Comfort Me. Agnes de Navarre-Champagne. AnML
Lover of swamps. To the Snipe. John Clare. OBNC
Lover of the moorland bare, A. To K[atharine] de M[attos].
Robert Louis Stevenson. OBNC

Lover Praises His Lady's Bright Beauty, The. Shaemas
O'Sheel. BoLP
Lover Showeth How He Is Forsaken of Such as He Sometime
Enjoyed, The. Sir Thomas Wyatt. *See* They Flee from
Me.
Lover to His Lady, The. George Turberville. CTC
Lovers, The. Conrad Aiken. AP
Lovers. Mary Fullerton. PoAu-1
Lovers, The. W. R. Rodgers. WePo
Lovers and madmen have such seething brains. Shakespeare.
Fr. A Midsummer Night's Dream, V, i. PP
Lover's Anger, A. Matthew Prior. ErPo; UnTE
Lover's Appeal, The. Sir Thomas Wyatt. *See* And Wilt Thou
Leave Me Thus?
Lovers, Beware the Dart That Flies. Charles d'Orléans, *tr. fr.
French by* Muriel Kittel. AnML
Lovers, fast in their longing, The. March. William Everson.
ErPo
Lover's Ghost, The. Louis Simpson. FiSC
Lovers in the act dispense. The Thieves. Robert Graves.
GTBS-P
Lovers Infinitenesse. John Donne. MeP; SeCP
Lover's Lament, A ("My little breath, under the willows by the
water-side"). *Unknown, tr. fr. Tewa Indian by* H. J.
Spinden. SiGo
Lover's Lament, The ("Once I courted a fair beauty bride").
Unknown. See Fair Young Miss, The.
Lovers, like wrestlers, when they do not lay. Love. Samuel
Butler. ErPo
Lovers Relentlessly. Stanley Kunitz. UnTE
Lovers' Tasks. *Unknown.* CBEP
Lovers' Walk, The. Dante Gabriel Rossetti. The House of
Life, XII. VP
Lovers who must say farewell. Archibald MacLeish. *Fr.*
What Must. MoLP
Lover's Words, A. Vernon Watkins. DTC
Love's Alchemy [*or* Alchymie]. John Donne. CABA; SeCP
Love's Baubles. Dantel Gabriel Rossetti. The House of Life,
XXIII. VP
Love's Coming. John Shaw Neilson. PoAu-1
Love's Consolation, *sel.* Richard Watson Dixon.
"All who have loved, be sure of this from me." OBNC
Love's Courtship. Thomas Carew. UnTE
Love's Deity [*or* Deitie]. John Donne. DiPo; EnRePo;
FoBA; ILP; SeCP
Love's Diet. John Donne. ILP
Love's Emblems. John Fletcher. *See* Now the Lusty Spring.
Loves End. Lord Herbert of Cherbury. SeCP
Love's Ending. Paul Bartlett. PoNC
Love's Epitaph. William Cavendish, Duke of Newcastle.
CBEP
Love's Eschatology. Vassar Miller. ToPo
Love's Fancy. Dryden. *See* After the Pangs.
Love's Farewell. Michael Drayton. *See* Idea: "Since there's
no help . . ."
Love's Fatality. Dante Gabriel Rossetti. The House of Life,
LIV. VP
Love's Growth. John Donne. FoBA; MeP
Love's Justification. Michelangelo, *tr. fr. Italian by* John
Addington Symonds. RBL
Love's Labour's Lost, *sels.* Shakespeare.
"But love, first learnèd in a lady's eyes," *fr.* IV, iii. PP
If She Be Made of White and Red, *fr.* I, ii. CTC
Love's Perjuries, *fr.* IV, iii. GTBS-P
When Daisies Pied, *fr.* V, ii. CBEP; EnRePo
(Dialogue in Praise of the Owl and the Cuckoo.) DiPo
(Song: "When daisies pied and violets blue.") VaPo
(Spring.) BoC; FoBA; ILP; PoIE
When Icicles Hang by the Wall, *fr.* V, ii. CaFP; CBEP;
GoJo; PoSa; PoSC; RoGo
(Merry Note, A.) WiR
(Song.) OnP
(Winter.) BoC; FoBA; GTBS-P; ILP; PoIE; PoPo
Love's Last Gift. Dante Gabriel Rossetti. The House of Life,
LIX. VP
Love's Longing. *Unknown, tr. fr. Latin by* John Addington
Symonds. UnTE
Love's Lovers. Dante Gabriel Rossetti. The House of Life,
VIII. VP
Love's mariner am I. Cervantes. *Fr.* Don Quixote. RBL
Loves of the Puppets. Richard Wilbur. CoPo
Love's Omnipresence. Joshua Sylvester. GTBS-P
Love's Perjuries. Shakespeare. *Fr.* Love's Labour's Lost, IV,
iii. GTBS-P
Love's Philosophy. Shelley. BoLP; FaBV; GTBS-P; PoIE;
UnTE; WePo
Love's Secret. Blake. *See* Never Seek to Tell Thy Love.
Love's Testament. Dante Gabriel Rossetti. The House of Life,
III. VP
Love's Torment ("Lady, why doth love torment you?"). *Un-
known.* UnTE
Love's Torment ("Love is a torment, there's no question").
Unknown, tr. fr. German by Louis Untermeyer. UnTE

Love's Triumph. Ben Jonson. EnRePo
Love's Usury. John Donne. FoBA
Lovesick. *Unknown, tr. fr. Greek by* Louis Untermeyer. UnTE
Lovesight. Dante Gabriel Rossetti. The House of Life, IV. GTBS-P; OBNC; VP
Loving in truth, and fain in verse my love to show. Astrophel and Stella, I. Sir Philip Sidney. CABA; CBEP; ILP; PoIE; PP
Loving Jesus, gentle Lamb. Charles Wesley. ThGo
Loving Shepherd of thy sheep. A Hymn. Jane E. Leeson. ThGo
Low-anchored cloud. Mist. Henry David Thoreau. AmLP
Low Barometer. Robert Bridges. PoIE
Low beating of the tom-toms, The. African Dance. Langston Hughes. RePo
Low Tide on Grand Pré. Bliss Carman. OBCV
Lowell. James Russell Lowell. *Fr.* A Fable for Critics. AP
Lower, radiant god—the leas are thirsting. Evening. Schiller. TwGP
Lowery Cot. L. A. G. Strong. DaDu
Lowest Trees Have Tops, The. Sir Edward Dyer. CBEP; EnRePo
  (Modest Love, A.) BoLP
Lucasta's World. Richard Lovelace. SeCP
Lucifer. Maxwell Anderson. MoRP
Lucifer in Starlight. George Meredith. CABA; CaFP; CBEP; ILP; OBNC; PoIE; PoPo; PoSa; VP
Lucifer in the Train. Adrienne Cecile Rich. EaLo; NePoEA-2
Lucinda Matlock. Edgar Lee Masters. *Fr.* Spoon River Anthology. FaBV; ILP; PoPo
Luck. W. W. Gibson. HaSV
Luck. Langston Hughes. MoLP
Luckless Collins. William Collins. Three Fragments, 1. WaPF
Lucky Marriage, The. Thomas Blackburn. GTBS-P
Lucky Thing, A. Dorothy Aldis. RePo
Lucy, *complete in 5 parts.* Wordsworth. OBNC
  Sels.
  "I traveled among unknown men." CBEP; FaBV; GTBS-P; ILP; OBNC
  "She dwelt among the untrodden ways." CABA; CBEP; DiPo; ELP; ILP; OBNC; PoPo
  (Lost Love, The.) GTBS-P; PoPo
  (Lucy.) FaBV
  "Slumber did my spirit seal, A." CABA; CaFP; CBEP; DiPo; ELP; FoBA; GTBS-P; ILP; OBNC; OnP; PoIE; WePo
  "Strange fits of passion have I known." CBEP; ILP; OBNC
  "Three years she grew in sun and shower." CBEP; ILP; OBNC; PoIE
  (Education of Nature, The.) GTBS-P
Lucy Gray; or, Solitude. Wordsworth. FoBA
Lucy Lavender. Ivy O. Eastwick. BiCB
Lucy McLockett. Phyllis McGinley. BiCB
Luke 11. Richard Crashaw. CABA
Luke Havergal. E. A. Robinson. AP; CaFP; ILP; PoDB; PoIE
Lullaby: "Beloved, may your sleep be sound." W. B. Yeats. AnMoPo
Lullaby: "Hush, lullay." Léonie Adams. AmLP
Lullaby: "Long canoe, The." Robert Hillyer. LOW
Lullaby: "Sweet and low, sweet and low." Tennyson. *See* Sweet and Low.
Lullaby: "With lights for eyes, our city turns." Dom Moraes. NePoEA-2
Lullaby for Peregrine. Robert P. Tristram Coffin. RePo
Lullaby of a Lover, The. George Gascoigne. *See* Gascoigne's Lullaby.
Lullaby of the Iroquois. Pauline Johnson. ACV
Lullaby of the Nativity, A. *Unknown. See* Lullay My Liking.
Lullay, lullay, la, lullay. Jesus Reassures His Mother. *Unknown.* MeEL
Lullay, Lullay, like a Child. John Skelton. PoIE
  (My Darling Dear, My Daisy Flower.) EnRePo
  (Sleeper Hood-winked, The.) MeEL
Lullay My Liking. *Unknown.* ELP
  (Lullaby of the Nativity.) MeEL
Lulled by La Belle Dame sans Merci he lies. The Enchanted Knight. Edwin Muir. DaDu
Lully, lulla, thou little tiny child. Coventry Carol. *Unknown.* ELP; MeEL
Lully, Lullay [*or* Lulley]. *Unknown.* CBEP; DiPo; ILP
  (Corpus Christi Carol, The.) MeEL
  (Falcon, The.) OnP; StP
  (Lully, Lullay, Lully, Lullay.) PoIE
Lumberman's Life, The. *Unknown.* BSNS
Lunae Custodiens. Lin Carter. FiSC
Lunatic, the Lover, and the Poet, The. Shakespeare. *Fr.* A Midsummer Night's Dream, V, i. DiPo
  ("Lovers and madmen have such seething brains," *sl. longer sel.*) PP

Lunch on Omaha Beach. Bink Noll. StP; ToPo
Lupercalia. Ted Hughes. ToPo
Lupin. Humbert Wolfe. ThGo
Lupus in Fabula. Malcolm Lowry. OBCV
Lure me with lovers. Monogramania. Eve Merriam. UnTE
Lured by my style and tendency. Vademecum-Vadetecum. Nietzsche. TwGP
Lutea Allison. Sir John Suckling. ErPo
Luvin wumman is a licht, A. Love. "Hugh MacDiarmid." PoIE
Luxurious man, to bring his vice in use. The Mower against Gardens. Andrew Marvell. ILP; PP
Lycias. Earl of Rochester. ErPo
Lycidas. Milton. CABA; CaFP; DiPo; FoBA; GTBS-P; ILP; OnP; PoIE; StP; VaPo
  Sels.
  "And call the Vales, and bid them hither cast." WePo
  "Weep no more, woful Shepherds weep no more." BoC
Lycidus, *sel.* Aphra Behn.
  O What Pleasure 'Tis to Find. UnTE
Lydia Is Gone This Many a Year. Lizette Woodworth Reese. GoJo
Lying apart now, each in a separate bed. One Flesh. Elizabeth Jennings. AnMoPo
Lying asleep between the strokes of night. Love and Sleep. Swinburne. UnTE
Lying here quietly beside you. Quietly. Kenneth Rexroth. ErPo
Lying in bed in the dark, I hear the bray. Weather Ear. Norman Nicholson. DaDu
Lyke as a huntsman after weary chace. *See* Like as a huntsman after weary chase.
Lyke as a ship that through the ocean wyde. *See* Like as a ship . . .
Lyke-Wake Dirge, A. *Unknown.* BuBa; CBEP; EaLo; EvOK
Lynceus the Warden. Goethe, *tr. fr. German by* Alexander Gode. AGP
Lyre-Bird, The. Roland Robinson. PoAu-2
Lyrebird by the damp track, frozen, The. The Makers. Nan McDonald. ACV
Lyrebirds. Judith Wright. GoJo
Lyric: "Angora anger who art in heaven." Gil Orlovitz. ToPo
Lyric: "Thrush of wind sang thru the air, A." "Will Inman." PoNC
Lyric: "When I am gone and green." Gil Orlovitz. ToPo
Lyric from a Play, A. *Unknown.* MeEL
Lyric of Doubt. Donald Wandrei. FiSC
Lyrics, *sels.* James Agee. PoP1
  "I loitered weeping with my bride for gladness."
  "No doubt left. Enough deceiving."
  "Not met and marred with the year's whole turn of grief."

M

M., Singing. Louise Bogan. GoJo
Mab. Ben Jonson. *Fr.* The Satyr. WiR
Macadam, gun-grey as the tunny's belt. Van Winkle. Hart Crane. *Fr.* The Bridge. FaBV
McAfee's Confession. *Unknown.* BSO
McAndrew's Hymn. Kipling. CABL
  "Lord, Thou hast made this world below the shadow of a dream," *sel.* HaSV
Macavity; the Mystery Cat. T. S. Eliot. RePo
Macbeth, *sels.* Shakespeare.
  "Canst thou not minister to a mind diseas'd," *fr.* V, iii. TRV
  To-morrow, and To-morrow, *fr.* V, v. DiPo
  ("Tomorrow, and tomorrow, and tomorrow.") PoP1; TRV
McDonogh Day in New Orleans. Marcus B. Christian. AmNP
MacFlecknoe; or, A Satire upon the True-Blue-Protestant Poet T. S. Dryden. CABA; CABL; DiPo; StP; PoIE; PP
Machinery is enough for a scientist. James Oppenheim. *Fr.* Night. TRV
McLellan's Son. *Unknown.* BSNS
Macquarie Place. Robert D. Fitzgerald. PoAu-2
Macrobius Mingling with Nature. Rochelle Owens. CoPo
Mad as the Mist and Snow. W. B. Yeats. AnMoPo
Mad Gardener's Song, The. "Lewis Carroll." *See* Gardener's Song, The.
Mad girl with the staring eyes and long white fingers, The. Cassandra. Robinson Jeffers. VaPo
Mad Lover, The. Alexander Brome. CBEP
Mad Maid's Song, The. Robert Herrick. WiR
Mad Maid's Whim. Randolph Stow. ACV
Mad Marjory. Hugh McCrae. PoAu-1
Mad-Merry Pranks of Robin Good-Fellow, The. *Unknown.* CBEP

Mad Song. Blake. CBEP; ILP
Mad Yak, The. Gregory Corso. CoPo
"Madam, I have come a-courting." The Quaker's Wooing. *Unknown.* BFSS; BSNS
Madam Life's a Piece in Bloom. W. E. Henley. CABA
Madam Mouse Trots. Edith Sitwell. *See* Madame Mouse Trots.
Madam, no more! The time has come to eat. The Elegy. A. D. Hope. ErPo
"Madam, oh, madam, I'll give you a paper of pins." The Keys of Heaven (D *vers.*). *Unknown.* BSO
Madam [*or* Madame], withouten Many Words. Sir Thomas Wyatt. CABA; CBEP; EnRePo
Madam would speak with me. So, now it comes. Modern Love, XXXIV. George Meredith. VP
Madam, ye ben of all beauty shrine. *See* Madame, ye been of all beaute shrine.
Madame. Eleanor Ross Taylor. PoNC
Madame D'Albert's Laugh. Clément Marot, tr. fr. *French by* Leigh Hunt. RBL
Madame, for your newefangelnesse. A Ballade against Woman Inconstant. Chaucer. CABA
Madame [*or* Madam] Mouse Trots. Edith Sitwell. Fr. Façade. DaDu; LOW
Madame, withouten Many Words. Sir Thomas Wyatt. *See* Madam, withouten Many Words.
Madame [*or* Madam], ye been [*or* ben] of all[e] beaute[e] shrine. To Rosemond [*or* Ballade to Rosamund]. Chaucer. CABA; CBEP; MeEL
Madge Wildfire Sings. Sir Walter Scott. *See* Proud Maisie.
Madhouse. Calvin C. Hernton. NNP
Madly Singing in the Mountains. Po Chü-i, tr. fr. *Chinese by* Arthur Waley. CBEP
Madman, The. Constance Urdang. PoP1
Madman's Song, The. John Masefield. Fr. Good Friday. ACV
("Wild duck, stringing through the sky, The.") BoC
Madman's Song. Elinor Wylie. LOW
Madness One Monday Evening. Julia Fields. NNP
Madonna of the Evening Flowers. Amy Lowell. AmLP
Madrigal, A: "Crabbed age and youth." Shakespeare. *See* Crabbed Age and Youth.
Madrigal: Eyes of Clear Serenity. Gutierre de Cetina, tr. fr. *Spanish by* Kate Flores. AnSP
Madrigal: "How should I love my best?" Lord Herbert of Cherbury. SeCP
Madrigal: "Like the Idalian queen." William Drummond of Hawthornden. ELP
Madrigal: "My thoughts hold mortal strife." William Drummond of Hawthornden. *See* My Thoughts Hold Mortal Strife.
Madrigal: "Ravished by all that to the eyes is fair." Michelangelo, tr. fr. *Italian by* George Santayana. RBL
Madrigal: "Receive, oh Nymph adorable." Charles de Sainte-Maure, Duc de Montausier, tr. fr. *French by* Harold M. Priest. Fr. Guirlande de Julie. RBL
Madrigal: "Take, O take those lips away." Shakespeare. *See* Take, I Take Those Lips Away.
Madrigal: "Tell me where is Fancy bred." Shakespeare. *See* Tell Me Where Is Fancy Bred.
Madrigal I: "This life, which seems so fair." Giovanni Battista Guarini, tr. fr. *Italian by* William Drummond of Hawthornden. RBL
("This life, which seems so fair.") GTBS-P
Madrigal de Verano. Federico García Lorca, tr. fr. *Spanish by* Paul Blackburn. ErPo
Maesia's Song. Robert Greene. Fr. Farewell to Folly. CTC
Magdalene. Boris Pasternak, tr. fr. *Russian by* Bernard Guilbert Guerney. MoRP
Maggie and Milly and Molly and May. E. E. Cummings. LOW
(Poem.) PoSC
Maggie and Willie, *with music.* *Unknown.* BSO
Magi, The. W. B. Yeats. CaFP; FoBA; PoDB; PoIE; StP
Magic. Thomas Wolfe. PoP1
Magic Casements. Keats. Fr. Ode to a Nightingale. FaBV
Magic Landscape, A. Afanasy Fet, tr. fr. *Russian by* Babette Deutsch. SiGo
Magic Spells, *sels.* *Unknown, tr. fr. German by* Ruth Yorck *and* Kenward Elmslie. AnML
Go Out, Worm, with Nine Little Worms.
Phol and Wotan Were Riding in the Forest.
Magical Mouse, The. Kenneth Patchen. LOW
Magician and the Baron's Daughter, The. *Unknown.* MeEL
Magna Est Veritas. Coventry Patmore. Fr. The Unknown Eros. GTBS-P; OBNC
Magnet hung in a hardware shop, A. The Fable of the Magnet and the Churn. W. S. Gilbert. Fr. Patience. OnMSP; RePo
Magnetic Mountain, The, *sels.* C. Day Lewis.
"Nearing again the legendary isle," VI. HaSV
Tempt Me No More [for I], XXIV. PoDB; PoP1
Third Enemy Speaks, XXI. EaLo
Magnificat. Arthur Symons. UnTE

Magnolia Belt, The. Helen Bevington. PoNC
Magnolia Tree in Summer. Sacheverell Sitwell. BoC
Magpies in Picardy. T. P. Cameron Wilson. MMA
Mahadeva, great god Siva. The God and the Bayadeer. Goethe. AGP
Maharani of midnight tresses, The. In the Seraglio. David R. Slavitt. ErPo
Mahony's Mountain. Douglas Stewart. PoAu-2
Maid Freed from the Gallows, The (B *vers.*). *Unknown.* BSO
(Gallent Tree, The, A *vers.*) BSO
Maid, I dare not tell her name, A. The Nameless Maiden. *Unknown.* ErPo
Maid Marian, *sel.* Thomas Love Peacock.
Friar, The. SD
Maid of Amsterdam, The. *Unknown.* HaSV
Maid of Athens. Byron. FaBV; FaPL
Maid of Neidpath, The. Thomas Campbell. GTBS-P
Maid of Neidpath, The. Sir Walter Scott. GTBS-P
Maid of the Mountain Brow, The. *Unknown.* BSNS
Maid was walking in her garden, A. The Single Sailor (B *vers.*). *Unknown.* BSNS
Maid, where's my lawrel? Oh my rageing soul! The Enchantment. Theocritus. Fr. Idylls. CTC
Maiden caught me in the Wild, The. The Crystal Cabinet. Blake. DiPo; OBNC
Maiden caught stealing a dahlia, A. Thief. *Unknown.* BBGG
Maiden from the Bosphorus, with eyes as bright as phosphorus, A. How the Helpmate of Blue-Beard Made Free with a Door. Guy Wetmore Carryl. SIV
Maiden in the Moor. *Unknown.* BuBa
(Maiden Lay in the Wilds, The.) MeEL
Maiden Name. Philip Larkin. GTBS-P; ToPo
Maiden sat in an apple-tree, A. The Apple-Tree. Brian Vrepont. PoAu-2
Maidens Came, The. *Unknown.* CBEP
(Lily and the Rose, The.) DTC; StP
Maiden's Denial, A. *Unknown.* ErPo
(Reluctant Lady, The.) UnTE
Maid's Complaint, A. Thomas Campion. UnTE
Maid's Husband, The. Henry Carey. Two Songs, 2. WaPE
Maid's Lament, The. Walter Savage Landor. Fr. The Citation and Examination of William Shakespeare. OBNC
Maid's Thought, The. Robinson Jeffers. BoLP; ErPo
Maids to bed and cover coal. The Bellman's Song. *Unknown.* DiPo
Maid's Tragedy, The, *sels.* Beaumont *and* Fletcher.
Hold Back Thy Hours [Dark Night], fr. I, ii. ILP; UnTE
(Bridal Song.) ErPo
"Lay a garland on my hearse," fr. II, i. ILP
To Bed, to Bed, fr. I, ii. UnTE
Maimed and enormous in the air. The Feast. David Wagoner. NePoEA-2
Maimed Debauchee, The. Earl of Rochester. CABA; CBEP
Main-Deep, The. James Stephens. HaSV; PoPo
Main-Truck, The; or, A Leap for Life. George P. Morris. PoLF
Majesty of horns sweeps in the stagtide. In a Crumbling. Kenneth Patchen. ToPo
Major alterations, The. Something Makes Itself Known. Albert Arnold Scholl. MGP
Major André, *with music.* *Unknown.* BFSS
(Major Andrews' Execution.) BSO
Major's Son, The. *Unknown.* *See* Springfield Mountain.
Make a joyful noise unto the Lord, all ye lands. Psalm C, Bible, *O.T.* LV; RePo; StP
Make Believe. Harry Behn. RePo
Make Friends. Ali Ben Abu Taleb. TRV
Make me a captive, Lord. Christ's Bondservant. George Matheson. STF; TRV
Make me an Intercessor. An Intercessor. *Unknown.* STF
Make me, O Lord, thy spinning wheel[e] complete [*or* of use for thee]. Housewifery [*or* Huswifery]. Edward Taylor. AP; DiPo; EaLo; FaBV; ILP; StP
Make no mistake: if He rose at all. Seven Stanzas at Easter. John Undike. EaLo
Make us Thy mountaineers. The Last Defile. Amy Carmichael. TRV
Make way for the beast with chrome teeth. The Beast with Chrome Teeth. Thurmond Snyder. NNP
Make we mery bothe more and lasse. Now Is the Time of Christmas. *Unknown.* MeEL
Make we mirth. Sing We Yule. *Unknown.* MeEL
Makers, The. Nan McDonald. ACV
Making. Phyllis Webb. PoCh
Malachi. Earl Marlatt. MoRP
Maladies, assembled all, The. On Dr. Crank's Victory over the Gout. Sneyd Davies. WaPE
Malady, Death and Resurrection of Saint Lazarus. *Unknown, tr. fr. French by* Daisy Aldan. AnML
Malcolm's Katie, *sels.* Isabella Valancy Crawford. OBCV
"Bite deep and wide, O Axe, the tree."
"South Wind laid his moccasins aside, The."

Maldive Shark, The. Herman Melville. AP; CBEP
Male & Female Loves in Beulah. Blake. *Fr.* Jerusalem. OBNC
Male Torso. Christopher Middleton. NePoEA-2
Malefic Surgeon, The. Gerrit Lansing. CoPo
Mallee in October. Flexmore Hudson. PoAu-2
Malvern Hill. Herman Melville. AP
Malvolio. Walter Savage Landor. Par
Malzah's Song. Charles Heavysege. *Fr.* Saul. OBCV
Mama told me she found me a feller. Old Beard a-Shakin'. *Unknown.* BFSS
Mamba the Bright-eyed, *sel.* George Gordon McCrae. "Day had fled, the moon arose, The." PoAu-1
Mamble. John Drinkwater. WePo
Mammon Marriage. George Macdonald. CBEP
Man. George Herbert. CABA; MeP; SeCP
Man. Henry Vaughan. CBEP; MeP
Man, A/ And I'm that man. The Shadow. Pierre Reverdy. CoFP
Man adrift on a slim spar, A. Three Poems, 1. Stephen Crane. AP
Man against the Sky, The. E. A. Robinson. AP
Man and a Maid, A, *with music. Unknown.* BFSS
Man and Cows. Andrew Young. DaDu
Man and Woman Walk through the Cancer Ward. Gottfried Benn, *tr. fr. German by* Walter Kaufmann. TwGP
Man-apes. Between the Karim Shahir. Rochelle Owens. CoPo
Man as He Shall Be. Rochelle Owens. CoPo
Man be ware ere thou be woe. Pride Is Out. *Unknown.* CBEP
Man Carrying Thing. Wallace Stevens. PoIE
Man Christ, The. Therese Lindsey. TRV
Man divided into animal, A. Sun of the Center. Robert Kelly. CoPo
Man, dream no more of curious mysteries. Caelica, LXXXVIII. Fulke Greville. EnRePo
Man Exalted. *Unknown.* MeEL
Man Frail, and God Eternal. Isaac Watts. *See* O God Our Help in Ages Past.
Man from Inversnaid, The. Robert Fuller Murray. SD
Man from Ironbark, The. A. B. Paterson. Po-Au-1
Man from Porlock, The. Helen Bevington. EvOK
Man from Snowy River, The. A. B. Paterson. PoAu-1; WePo
Man from the Crowd, The. Sam Walter Foss. PoLF
Man from the Top of the Mind, The. David Wagoner. NePoEA-2
Man had died on the cross, The. The Sepulcher. Annie Johnson Flint. STF
Man Has No Smokestack. *Unknown.* STF
Man He Killed, The. Thomas Hardy. ILP; LV; PoIE; PoPl; PoPo; VP
Man he was to all the country dear, A. The Parson. Goldsmith. *Fr.* The Deserted Village. WePo
Man, hef in mind and mend thy mis. Remember the Last Things. *Unknown.* MeEL
Man Hunt, The. Madison Cawein. SIV
Man I Met, The. Joseph Payne Brennan. FiSC
Man, I suck me tooth when I hear. Parang. Derek Walcott. ToPo
Man in Harmony with Nature. Jones Very. AP
Man in the Manmade Moon, The. X. J. Kennedy. StP
Man in the Moon, The. Mother Goose. SoPo
Man in the Moon, The. *Unknown.* MeEL
Man in the moon looked down on the field, The. Jack o'Lantern. Anna Chandler Ayre. SoPo
Man Is for Woman Made. Peter Anthony Motteux. UnTE
Man Is God's Nature. Richard Eberhart. EaLo; MoRP
Man is gone on a Friday, The. Before the Sabbath. David Ignatow. OPP
Man is the world, and death th' ocean. Elegy on the Lady Marckham. John Donne. FoBA
Man knocked strongly at the door, The. The Man from Porlock. Helen Bevington. EvOK
Man looking into the sea. A Grave. Marianne Moore. CABA; PoIE
Man-made World, A. Stephen Spender. MoRP
Man, Man, Man. *Unknown.* ErPo
Man Meeting Himself. Howard Sergeant. *Fr.* The Leaves of Europe. ToPo
Man-Moth, The. Elizabeth Bishop. PoCh
Man of himself's a little world, but join'd. The Microcosm. Giovanni Battista Guarini. RBL
Man of Life Upright, The. Thomas Campion. EnRePo; PoSa
(Integer Vitae.) CBEP
Man of My Dreams, The. George Cuomo. OPP
Man of My Time. Salvatore Quasimodo, *tr. fr. Italian by* Allen Mandelbaum. PoPl
Man of the World. Michael Hamburger. NePoEA-2
Man of Thessaly, A. *Unknown.* CBEP
Man of Valour to His Fair Lady, The. William Dunbar. MeEL
Man of Words, A. *Unknown.* CBEP

Man once left his wife, A—I'll tell you all about it. Don Pitas Payas. Juan Ruiz, Archpriest of Hita. *Fr.* The Book of True Love. AnML
Man Raking Leaves. Thad Stem, Jr. PoNC
Man said to the universe, A. Stephen Crane. War Is Kind, XXI. AP
Man Saw a Ball of Gold in the Sky, A. Stephen Crane. The Black Riders, XXXV. EvOK; PoPl; PoPo
Man sits in the cellar, The. Of the Man Who Sits in the Cellar. Hans Werner Cohn. MGP
Man so various, that he seemed to be, A. George Villiers, Duke of Buckingham. Dryden. *Fr.* Absalom and Achitophel. PoSa
Man-Test. Edwin Markham. MoRP
Man, that with me trod, The. Tennyson. *Fr.* In Memoriam A. H. H., Epilogue. TRV
Man upon mold, whatsoever thou be. Money Is What Matters. *Unknown.* MeEL
Man Walking and Singing, A. Wendell Berry. AP
"Man wants but little here below." The Wants of Man. John Quincy Adams. PoLF
Man was called Methuselah I remember, The. Methuselah. Rosemary Dobson. *Fr.* The Devil and the Angel. PoAu-2
Man Was Made to Mourn; a Dirge. Burns. PoIE
Man was sitting underneath a tree, A. Seumas Beg. James Stephens. EvOK; RoGo
Man went before a strange God, A. The Black Riders, LI. Stephen Crane. AP
Man Who Finds That His Son Has Become a Thief, The. Raymond Souster. OBCV
Man Who Had Fallen among Thieves, A. E. E. Cummings. AP
Man Who Married Magdalene, The: Variation on a Theme by Louis Simpson. Anthony Hecht. CoPo
Man who never saw our land, The. He Ought to Know! John A. Stone. SGR
Man who sold his lawn to Standard Oil, The. The War against the Trees. Stanley Kunitz. AP
Man Who Thinks He Can, The. Walter D. Wintle. PoLF
Man who was about to hang himself, A. Circumstance. Shelley. CBEP
Man, who with undaunted toils, The. Fable X: The Elephant and the Bookseller. John Gay. EiCP
Man whom God will show true favor, The. The Joyful Traveller. Josef von Eichendorff. AGP
Man whose name was Johnnie Sands, A. Johnnie Sands. *Unknown.* BSO
Man with a marvelous mug, A. A Ballad in "G." Eugene Fitch Ware. PoLF
Man with a scythe: the torrent of his swing. Gardens No Emblems. Donald Davie. NePoEA-2
Man with One Small Hand. P. K. Page. OBCV
Man with the Hoe, The. Edwin Markham. AmLP; EaLo; FaPL; PoPo; TRV
Man with the Rake, The. Christopher Morley. *Fr.* Translations from the Chinese. EvOK
Man without Faith, The. Richard Church. MoRP; WePo
"Man, you too, aren't you, one of these rough followers of the criminal?" In the Servants' Quarters. Thomas Hardy. MoRP
Manchouli. William Empson. AnMoPo
Mandalay. Kipling. FaBV
Manet: The Execution of Emperor Maximilian. W. D. Snodgrass. AmPC
Mangers. W. H. Davies. MoRP
Manhattan Lullaby. Rachel Field. BiCB
Manhattan Skyline. Eugene M. Kayden. LV
Manhole Covers. Karl Shapiro. GoJo
Manhood. Oliver Wendell Holmes. *Fr.* Wind-Clouds and Star-Drifts. AP
Manhood. Sir Thomas More. *Fr.* The Pageants of Thomas More. EnRePo
Manifesto. Paris Leary. CoPo
Manila! City of wounds! George Hitchcock. *Fr.* The Indestructible. PtTo
Mankend I cale. Christ Calls Man Home. *Unknown.* MeEL
Manlet, The. "Lewis Carroll." Par
Manly Heart, The. George Wither. *See* Shall I, Wasting in Despair.
Manner of a Poet's Germination, The. José Garcia Villa. PP
Manoeuvre, The. William Carlos Williams. LOW
Man's a Bubble. Robert Dodsley. CBEP
Man's a Man for A' That, A. Burns. *See* For A' That an' A' That.
Mans Fall, and Recovery. Henry Vaughan. MeP
Man's Going Hence. Samuel Rogers. *Fr.* Human Life. OBNC
Man's no bigger than the way he treats his fellow man, The. Measuring a Man. *Unknown.* STF
Man's soul/ Is like the water. Song of the Spirits over the Waters. Goethe. AGP
Man's Woman, A. Mary Carolyn Davies. PoLF
Mansion, string of cottages, a farm, A. The Inherited Estate. Thom Gunn. ToPo

Manuscripts of God, The. Longfellow. TRV
Many a green isle needs must be. Written in the Euganean Hills, North Italy. Shelley. GTBS-P
Many a Man Has Been Bewitched by an Elf. Heinrich von Morungen, *tr. fr. German by* Gillian Barker *and* Kenneth Gee. AnML
Many a Mickle. Walter de la Mare. FaBV
Many a phrase has the English language. Emily Dickinson. DiPo
Many a time your arms 'round me would cling. The Teasing Lovers. Horace. Odes, III, 9. UnTE
Many are the joys. Intimations of Sublimity. Wordsworth. *Fr.* The Prelude. OBNC
Many Birds. Blake. *Fr.* Auguries of Innocence. ThGo
Many hundred years ago. Noah's Carpenters. *Unknown.* STF
Many in aftertimes will say of you. Monna Innominata, XI. Christina Rossetti. OBNC; VP
Many liberals don't just. Respectabilities. Jon Silkin. NePoEA-2
Many love music but for music's sake. On Music. Walter Savage Landor. GoJo
Many narrow alleys that cut across, The. Small Town. Ernst Stadler. MGP
Many poems may be composed upon the same theme. Praising the Poets of That Country. Howard Nemerov. PP
Many red devils ran from my heart. The Black Riders, XLVI. Stephen Crane. AP
Many trees can stand unshaded. Trees and Cattle. James Dickey. NePoEA-2
Many with ears/ That hear not yet, shall have ears given them. Out of Wisdom Has Come Love. E. A. Robinson. *Fr.* The Three Taverns. MoRP
Many workmen. The Black Riders, XXXI. Stephen Crane. PoPo
Many years from now. To the Children. "Gabriela Mistral." AnSP
Map, The. Elizabeth Bishop. RePo
Map, The. G. C. Oden. AmNP; NNP
Map of the Western Part of the County of Essex in England, A. Denise Levertov. ToPo
Map of the world is on the wall, A: its lying. Y.M.C.A. Writing Room. Roy Fuller. ToPo
Map shows me where it is you are, The. A Private Letter to Brazil. G. C. Oden. AmNP; NNP
Maple Feast. Frances Frost. RePo
Maple Leaves. Shiko, *tr. fr. Japanese by* Harold G. Henderson. SiGo; SoPo
Mappemounde. Earle Birney. OBCV
Marble-Top. E. B. White. LV
Marble, weepe, for thou dost cover. On Margaret Ratcliffe. Ben Jonson. SeCP
March. William Everson. ErPo
March, The. J. C. Squire. PoSC
March into Virginia, The. Herman Melville. AP; PoIE
March shakes the pussy willows out. Spring Families. Frances Frost. RePo
March Winds. Mother Goose. SoPo
Marcus, the sluggard, dreamed he ran a race. The Sluggard. Lucilius. SD
Mares of the Camargue, The. Frédéric Mistral, *tr. fr. Provençal by* George Meredith. *Fr.* Mirèio. PoPl
Margaret. Charles Cotton. *Fr.* Resolution in Four Sonnets . . . Concerning Four Rural Sisters. UnTE
Margaret, are you grieving. Spring and Fall: To a Young Child. Gerard Manley Hopkins. CaFP; DiPo; ELP; FoBA; GoJo; GTBS-P; ILP; PoIE; PoPl; PoSa
Margaret Love Peacock for Her Tombstone, 1826. Thomas Love Peacock. OBNC
Margaret mentioned Indians. Indians. John Fandel. RePo
Margaret of humbler stature by the head. Margaret. Charles Cotton. *Fr.* Resolution in Four Sonnets . . . Concerning Four Rural Sisters. UnTE
Margaritae Sorori [I.M.]. W. E. Henley. Echoes, XXXV. CBEP; OBNC; PoPo
(I.M. Margaritae Sorori.) PoSa
(Some Late Lark Singing.) TRV
Marguerite. Rubén Darío, *tr. fr. Spanish by* Anita Volland. AnSP
Maria. G. A. Stevens. UnTE
Maria Bewell. *Unknown.* BSO
Maria Jane. Alfred Scott-Gatty. BBGG
Maria, when you were only one. For Maria at Four. John Becker. BiCB
Mariana. Tennyson. CABA; CBEP; OBNC; VaPo; VP; WiR
Marie, arise, my indolent sweet saint! Pierre de Ronsard. *Fr.* Amours de Marie. RBL
Marie Magdalene. George Herbert. MeP
Marie Magdalens Complaint at Christs Death. Robert Southwell. MeP
Marigold. Louise Townsend Nicholl. RePo
Marigold, The. George Wither. CBEP
Marina. T. S. Eliot. GTBS-P; PoIE

Mariner, The. Robert Southey. HaSV
Mariners' Carol. W. S. Merwin. EaLo; PoDB
Mariner's Ideal Epitaph. Juan Ramón Jiménez, *tr. fr. Spanish by* Kate Flores. AnSP
Marionettes, The. Walter de la Mare. MMA
Mark Anderson. W. W. Gibson. MMA
Mark Antony [*or* Anthony]. John Cleveland. SeCP
(Whenas the Nightingale.) UnTE
"Mystical grammar of amorous glances," *sel.* DiPo
Mark [*or* Marke] but this flea, and mark[e] in this. The Flea. John Donne. CABA; CBEP; FoBA; SeCP
Mark how the bashful morn in vain. Boldness In Love. Thomas Carew. ErPo; UnTE
Mark where the pressing wind shoots javelin-like. Modern Love, XLIII. George Meredith. FaPL; ILP; OBNC; VP
Mark you the floore? that square & speckled stone. The Church-Floore. George Herbert. MeP
Marke but this flea, and marke in this. *See* Mark but this flea, and mark in this.
Marke, when the evenings cooler wings. To Amoret. Henry Vaughan. SeCP
Market, The. Gary Snyder. *Fr.* Mts. & Rivers. CoPo
Marlowe. Arthur Bayldon. PoAu-1
Marmion, *sels.* Sir Walter Scott.
"But as they left the dark'ning heath," *fr.* VI. ELP
Lochinvar, *fr.* V. EvOK; FABV; OBNC; PoPo; RoGo; SIV
"Where shall the lover rest," *fr.* III. GTBS-P
Marooned. Rachel Field. RePo
Marot to the Queen of Navarre. Clément Marot, *tr. fr. French by* Henry Carrington. RBL
Marriage. Austin Clarke. GTBS-P
Marriage. Gregory Corso. CABA
Marriage. Mark Van Doren. MoLP
Marriage a-la-Mode, *sels.* Dryden.
Whilst Alexis Lay Prest, *fr.* IV, ii. ErPo; UnTE
Why Should a Foolish Marriage Vow? *fr.* I, i. CBEP
(Song: "Why should a foolish marriage vow.") ILP
Marriage of a Virgin, The. Dylan Thomas. ErPo
Marriage of Earth and Heaven, The. Jay Macpherson. OBCV
Marriage: To K. Donald Hall. MoLP
Marrie dear. When in Rome. Mari E. Evans. AmNP
Married Lover, The. Coventry Patmore. The Angel in the House, II, xii, 1. FaPL
Married twice now, I've had two. Mothers-in-Law. Robert Sward. CoPo
Marrying left your maiden name disused. Maiden Name. Philip Larkin. GTBS-P; ToPo
Marsh, The. W. D. Snodgrass. ToPo
Marsh bank, lotus rank. Confucius. *Fr.* The Classic Anthology: Songs of Ch'en. CTC
Marshes of Glynn, The. Sidney Lanier. AP; PoIE
"Ye marshes, how," *sel.* TRV
Martial, the Things for to Attain. Martial, *tr. fr. Latin by* the Earl of Surrey. PoIE
(Means to Attain Happy Life, The.) EnRePo
(My Friend, the Things That Do Attain.) CABA
Martin. Joyce Kilmer. LV
Martin Buber in the Pub. Max Harris. PoAu-2
Martin sat young upon his bed. St. Martin and the Beggar. Thom Gunn. AnMoPo; MoBS
Martyr, The. Herman Melville. LiPo; PoIE
Martyrdom of Bishop Farrar, The. Ted Hughes. PoDB
Martyrdom of Brébeuf and Lalemant, 16 March 1649, The. E. J. Pratt. *Fr.* Brébeuf and His Brethren. OBCV
Marvel No More. Sir Thomas Wyatt. CBEP
Marveling he stands on the cathedral's. Adam. Rainer Maria Rilke. MoRP
Marvell's Garden. Phyllis Webb. OBCV
Mary and Martha. Annie Johnson Flint. STF
Mary Ann. Joseph Tabrar. BoLP
Mary Ann/ Bought a box. Present. Miriam Clark Potter. BiCB
Mary Complains to Other Mothers. *Unknown.* MeEL
Mary had a little lamb. Mary's Lamb. Sarah Josepha Hale. SoPo
Mary Hamilton. *Unknown.* CBEP
Mary! I want a lyre with other strings. To Mary Unwin. William Cowper. GTBS-P
Mary is a gentle name. Gentle Name. Selma Robinson. BiCB; LV
Mary Is with Child. *Unknown.* MeEL
Mary Jane, the Milkmaid, *with music. Unknown.* BFSS
Mary Magdalene, that easy woman. Lent. W. R. Rodgers. DTC
Mary Magdalene's Song. *Unknown, tr. fr. German by* Ruth Yorck *and* Kenward Elmslie. AnML
Mary Morison. Burns. GTBS-P
Mary of the Wild Moor, *with music. Unknown.* BFSS; BSO
Mary on the Silvery Tide. *Unknown.* BSNS
(Out on the Silvery Tide, *with music.*) BSO
Mary, Queen of Heaven. *Unknown.* MeEL

Mary Riley. *Unknown.* BSNS
Mary sat musing on the lamp-flame at the table. The Death of the Hired Man. Robert Frost. FoBA
Mary Suffers with Her Son. *Unknown.* MeEL
Mary Tired. Marjorie Pickthall. ACV
Mary was busy and hurried. Mary and Martha. Annie Johnson Flint. STF
Mary Winslow. Robert Lowell. ILP
Marye, maide, milde and fre. A Song to Mary. William of Shoreham(?). MeEL
Mary's Dream. *Unknown.* BSO
Mary's eyes are blue as azure. Shel Silverstein. BoLP
Mary's Girlhood. Dante Gabriel Rossetti. VP
Mary's Lamb. Sarah Josepha Hale. SoPo
Mary's Song. Eleanor Farjeon. ThGo
Mask, The. Elizabeth Barrett Browning. CBEP; OBNC
Mask of Anarchy, The. Shelley. CABL
Masque of Reason, A, *sel.* Robert Frost. God's Thanks to Job. MoRP
Masque of the Inner Temple and Gray's Inne, *sel.* Francis Beaumont. Shake Off Your Heavy Trance. CBEP
Mass of Love. *Unknown, tr. fr. Spanish by* Anna Pursche. PoPl
Massacre of the Innocents, The. William Jay Smith. EaLo
Master, The. E. A. Robinson. LiPo
Master, The. Schiller, *tr. fr. German by* Walter Kaufmann. TwGP
Master and the Leaves, The. Thomas Hardy. PoIE
Master and the slave go hand in hand, The. Sonnet. E. A. Robinson. PP
Master, destined to be. A Small Thought Speaks for the Flesh. Carleton Drewry. MoRP
Master of human destinies am I. Opportunity. John James Ingalls. PoLF
Master paints a portrait, small but fine, The. After a Dutch Master. Conrad Ferdinand Meyer. AGP
Master-Player, The. Paul Laurence Dunbar. TRV
Master Weaver, The. *Unknown.* STF
Masterindex: 23. Gil Orlovitz. ToPo
Masterpiece of the taxidermist's art, A. Phar Lap in the Melbourne Museum. Peter Porter. PoAu-2
Masters. Kingsley Amis. PoPl
Masters are known in all other fields by what they express. The Master. Schiller. TwGP
Master's Call, The. Oswald J. Smith. STF
Master's in the Garden Again. John Crowe Ransom. AP
Match, The. Francis Ponge, *tr. fr. French by* Clark Blaise. CoFP
Match, A. Swinburne. ELP
Match, The. Henry Vaughan. MeP
Match at Football, A, *sel.* Matthew Concanen. Heaps on Heaps. SD
Match-bark of the younger dog sets fire to, The. Table-Birds. Kenneth Mackenzie. PoAu-2
"*Mater dulcissima,* now the mists descend." Letter to My Mother. Salvatore Quasimodo. CoIP
Materia Nupcial. "Pablo Neruda," *tr. fr. Spanish by* Clayton Eshleman. ErPo
Mathematics. Joel Oppenheimer. CoPo
Mathematics of Encounter. Isabella Gardner. ErPo
Mathematics of Love. Michael Hamburger. NePoEA-2
Matilda. Hilaire Belloc. OnMSP; SIV
Matilda ("Matilda got her stockings wet"). F. Gwynne Evans. BBGG
Matilda Jane, you never look. Doll Song. "Lewis Carroll." SoPo
Matilda told such dreadful lies. Matilda. Hilaire Belloc. OnMSP; SIV
Matins. Denise Levertov. CoPo; ToPo
"Authentic, The! I said," *sel.* PtTo
Mattens. George Herbert. MeP
Matter of Life and Death, A. Anne Ridler. MP
"I did not see the iris move," *sel.* MoLP
Matter of Taste. *Unknown, tr. fr. Greek by* Louis Untermeyer. UnTE
Matthew left his place of toil. Discipleship. C. O. Bales. STF
Matthew, Mark, Luke and John. The White Paternoster [*or* Four Corners to My Bed]. *Unknown.* CBEP; ThGo
Matthew met Richard; when or where. Matthew Prior. *Fr.* Alma; or, The Progress of the Mind. EiCP
Maud. Tennyson. VP
Sels.
Come into the Garden, Maud. BoLP; CBEP; FaBV; PoIE
"I have led her home, my love, my only friend." ELP
O That 'Twere Possible. CBEP
Sleeping House, The. OBNC
There Is None like Her. OBNC
Maud Muller. Whittier. FaPL; PoLF; SIV
Maud Muller all that summer day. Mrs. Judge Jenkins, *parody.* Bret Harte. CABA
Mausoleum. Rainer Maria Rilke, *tr. fr. German by* Christopher Middleton. MGP

Maximus, from Dogtown, I. Charles Olson. CoPo
Maxwelton braes are bonnie. Annie Laurie. William Douglas. FaBV
May. William Barnes. PoSC
May. John Shaw Neilson. PoAu-1
May. Christina Rossetti. VP
May Colvin. *Unknown.* BuBa
May-Day. Aaron Hill. WaPE
May Day. James Reeves. DaDu
May Day. Sara Teasdale. PoSC
May Day Carol, A. *Unknown.* PoSC
May Day Demonstrators. Maurice Lindsay. ACV
Mayday on Holderness. Ted Hughes. ToPo
May he have new life like the fall. John Coltrane—an Impartial Review. Alfred B. Spellman. NNP
May I Feel Said He. E. E. Cummings. ErPo; UnTE
May I for my own self song's truth reckon. The Seafarer. *Unknown, tr. by* Ezra Pound. AP; CTC; OnP; StP
May I Sing to You? *Unknown, tr. fr. French by* Muriel Kittel. AnML
May is Mary's month, and I. The May Magnificat. Gerard Manley Hopkins. VP
May–June, 1940. Robinson Jeffers. StP
May Magnificat, The. Gerard Manley Hopkins. VP
May Margaret sits in her bower door. Hynd Etin. *Unknown.* BuBa
May Moon. Olive Driver. RePo
May My Heart Always Be Open. E. E. Cummings. MoRP
May nothing evil cross this door. Prayer for This House. Louis Untermeyer. PoLF
May others fear, fly, and traduce thy name. To the Learned Critic. Ben Jonson. PP
May she be granted beauty and yet not. For My Daughter. W. B. Yeats. *Fr.* Prayer for My Daughter. MoRP
May Song. Wendell Berry. AP
May Song. Lope de Vega, *tr. fr. Spanish by* Kate Flores. AnSP
May the Ambitious Ever Find. Charles Sackville. UnTE
May the blessing of light be on you. An Old Irish Blessing. *Unknown.* TRV
May the grace of Christ our Saviour. In Sweet Communion. John Newton. TRV
May these delights be yours in the new year. New Year Wishes. May Sarton. MoRP
May they stumble, stage by stage. Traveller's Curse after Misdirection. Robert Graves. DTC
May Thirtieth. *Unknown.* PoSC
May we and all who bear thy name. By Gentle Love. *Unknown.* TRV
Maybe it is true we have to return. Obsessions. Denise Levertov. NePoEA-2
Maybe the men on little northern farms. Lonely Lover. Robert P. Tristram Coffin. MoLP
Mayflower. Conrad Aiken. MP
Maypole, A. Swift. CBEP
May-Pole Dance. *Unknown.* WePo
Me. Walter de la Mare. BiCB; ThGo
Me and My Dog. *Unknown.* PoAu-1
Me clairvoyant. Variations of an Air: After Walt Whitman. G. K. Chesterton. Par
Me happy, night, night full of brightness. Ezra Pound. *Fr.* Homage to Sextus Propertius. ErPo
Me, I'm the man that dug the Murray for Sturt to sail down. They'll Tell You about Me. Ian Mudie. PoAu-2
Me needeth not to boast; I am Eternity. Eternity. Sir Thomas More. *Fr.* The Pageants of Thomas More. EnRePo
Meadow, The. John Wieners. CoPo
Meadow-Field, The. Charles Sangster. *Fr.* Pleasant Memories. OBCV
Meadowsweet. William Allingham. OBNC
Meandering Wye. Robert Bloomfield. *Fr.* The Banks of Wye. OBNC
Meaning, The. Ralph Gustafson. OBCV
Meaning of the Look, The. Elizabeth Barrett Browning. TRV
Means Massacre, The. Robert P. Tristram Coffin. SIV
Means to Attain Happy Life, The. Martial, *tr. by* the Earl of Surrey. *See* Martial, the Things for to Attain.
Meanwhile Achilles, plung'd. Homer. *Fr.* The Iliad, I. PoPl
Meanwhile the woman, from her strawberry lips. Metamorphoses of the Vampire. Baudelaire. ErPo
Measure for Measure, *sel.* Shakespeare. Take, O Take Those Lips Away, *fr.* IV, i (*also given, with add. st., in* The Bloody Brother, *by* John Fletcher, *and others*). CBEP; DiPo; ELP; EnRePo; FaBV; FoBA; ILP; PoIE
(Madrigal.) GTBS-P
Measure Me, Sky. Leonora Speyer. BiCB
Measure of a Man, The. *Unknown.* PoLF; STF
Measure of Success. *Unknown.* STF
Measurement. A. M. Sullivan. RePo
Measuring a Man. *Unknown.* STF

Meddlesome Matty. Ann Taylor. OnMSP
Medea, *sel.* Euripides, *tr. fr. Greek by* Frederic Prokosch. Chorus: "When love has passed its limits." SiGo
Medieval Christ Speaks on a Spanish Sculpture of Himself. Rochelle Owens. CoPo
Mediocrity in Love Rejected. Thomas Carew. *See* Give Me More Love.
Meditatio. Ezra Pound. LOW (Meditation.) WePo
Meditation. Toyohiko Kagawa. TRV
Meditation. Can. 1.2. Thy Love Is Better than Wine. Edward Taylor. *Fr.* Preparatory Meditations, Second Series. MeP
Meditation. Cant. 2.1. The Lilly of the Vallies. Edward Taylor. *Fr.* Preparatory Meditations, First Series. MeP
Meditation. Cant. 5.1. Eate Oh Friendes and Drink Yea Drink Abundantly Oh Beloved. Edward Taylor. *Fr.* Preparatory Meditations, Second Series. MeP
Meditation. Can. 6.11. To See the Fruits of the Vally. Edward Taylor. *Fr.* Preparatory Meditations, Second Series. MeP
Meditation. Col. 1.18. He Is the Head of the Body. Edward Taylor. *Fr.* Preparatory Meditations, Second Series. MeP
Meditation Eight ("I kenning through astronomy divine"). Edward Taylor. *Fr.* Preparatory Meditations, First Series. AP; StP
Meditation. 1 Cor. 3.21.22. All Things Are Yours. Edward Taylor. *Fr.* Preparatory Meditations, First Series. MeP
Meditation. 1 Cor. 3.22 Death Is Yours. Edward Taylor. *Fr.* Preparatory Meditations, First Series. MeP
Meditation. 1 Cor. 3.22. Life Is Youres. Edward Taylor. *Fr.* Preparatory Meditations, First Series. MeP
Meditation. 1 Cor. 3.22. Whether Paul or Apollos, or Cephas. Edward Taylor. *Fr.* Preparatory Meditations, First Series. MeP
Meditation. 1 Cor. 3.23. You Are Christ's. Edward Taylor. *Fr.* Preparatory Meditations, First Series. MeP
Meditation for His Mistresse, A. Robert Herrick. SeCP
Meditation Forty ("Still I complain: I am complaining still"). Edward Taylor. *Fr.* Preparatory Meditations, First Series. AP
(Meditation. 1 Joh. 2.2. He Is a Propitiation for Our Sin.) MeP
Meditation. from 1 Joh. 2.1. If Any Man Sin, We Have an Advocate. Edward Taylor. *Fr.* Preparatory Meditations, First Series. MeP
Meditation. Joh. 15.13. Greater Love Hath No Man than This That a Man Lay Down His Life for His Friends. Edward Taylor. *Fr.* Preparatory Meditations, Second Series. MeP
Meditation on Can. 1.3. Thy Name Is an Ointment Poured Out. Edward Taylor. *Fr.* Preparatory Meditations, First Series. MeP
Meditation on John Constable, A. Charles Tomlinson. NePoEA-2
Meditation on the BMT. Paul Blackburn. CoPo
Meditation One ("What love is this of thine, that cannot bee"). Edward Taylor. *Fr.* Preparatory Meditations, First Series. AP; MeP
Meditation. Rev. 1.8. The Almighty. Edward Taylor. *Fr.* Preparatory Meditations, Second Series. MeP
Meditation Seven ("Thy humane frame, my glorious Lord, I spy"). Edward Taylor. *Fr.* Preparatory Meditations, First Series. VaPo
Meditation Six ("Am I thy gold? Or purse, Lord, for thy wealth"). Edward Taylor. *Fr.* Preparatory Meditations, First Series. AmLP; AP
(Another Meditation at the Same Time.) MeP
Meditation Sixty-eight A ("Methinks I spy Almighty holding in"). Edward Taylor. *Fr.* Preparatory Meditations, Second Series. AP
Meditation Thirty-eight ("Oh! What a thing is man? Lord, who am I?"). Edward Taylor. *Fr.* Preparatory Meditations, First Series. AP
Meditation Twenty ("View, all ye eyes above, this sight which flings"). Edward Taylor. *Fr.* Preparatory Meditations, First Series. AP
Meditation Twenty-nine ("My shattred phancy stole away from mee"). Edward Taylor. *Fr.* Preparatory Meditations, First Series. AP
Meditation under Stars. George Meredith. VP
Meditation upon the Toothache, A. Laurence Lerner. NePoEA-2
Meditations in Time of Civil War. W. B. Yeats. CABL
Meditations of an Old Woman, *sel.* Theodore Roethke. First Meditation. AP; PoDB
Mediterranean, The. Allen Tate. AP; PoCh; VaPo
Meet me my love, meet my love. The Juniper Tree. Wilfred Watson. BoLP
Meet women with tender bearing. The Voice of Experience. Goethe. ErPo; TwGP
Meet your Saviour in the morning. Keeping Victory. Walter E. Isenhour. STF

Meeting. Matthew Arnold. Switzerland, I. ELP; VP (Lake, The.) CBEP
Meeting, A. Daniel Hoffman. CoPo
Meeting a monster of mourning wherever I go. Epistle I. George Barker. PoIE
Meeting and Passing. Robert Frost. FoBA
Meeting at Night. Robert Browning. BoLP; CBEP; DiPo; ELP; FaBV; HaSV; OBNC; PoPl; PoPo; WePo (Meeting at Night—Parting at Morning.) CaFP
Meeting Mary. Eleanor Farjeon. BiCB
Meeting Myself. Edward Lucie-Smith. NePoEA-2
Meeting Point. Louis MacNeice. WePo
Meeting the Easter Bunny. Rowena Bennett. SoPo
Meeting Together of Poles & Latitudes: In Prospect. Margaret Avison. OBCV
Meeting when all the world was in the bud. Loves of the Puppets. Richard Wilbur. CoPo
Meg Merrilies [*or* Merrilees]. Keats. CBEP; ELP; PoPo
Megalometropolitan Carnival, *sel.* David Gascoyne. "When Night has been announced as theme, will it not cause surprise." ACV
Mehitabel Tries Marriage. Don Marquis. *Fr.* Archys Life of Mehitabel. WePo
Melampus. George Meredith. BoC
Melancholy. Rubén Darío, *tr. fr. Spanish by* Anita Volland. AnSP
Melancholy. John Fletcher *and* (at.) Thomas Middleton. *Fr.* The Nice Valour. GTBS-P
Melancholy. August Stramm, *tr. fr. German by* Michael Hamburger. MGP
Melancholy days are come, the saddest of the year, The. The Death of the Flowers. Bryant. PoLF
Melancholy desire of ancient things, A. On an Air of Rameau. Arthur Symons. OBNC
Melchior Vulpius. Marianne Moore. AP
Meleager. Ovid, *tr. fr. Latin by* Arthur Golding. *Fr.* Metamorphoses, VIII. CTC
Melhill Feast. William Barnes. CBEP; OBNC
Melincourt, *sel.* Thomas Love Peacock. Sun-Dial, The. OBNC
Melissa. *Unknown, tr. fr. Greek by* Louis Untermeyer. UnTE
Melita, Rhodopis, and young Rhodocleia. Embarrassed Judge. *Unknown.* UnTE
Mellifluous as bees, these brittle men. On First Looking in on Blodgett's Keats's "Chapman's Homer." George Starbuck. PP
Mellow the moonlight to shine is beginning. A Spinning-Wheel Song. John Francis Waller. BoLP
Mellow year is hasting to its close, The. Sonnet: November. Hartley Coleridge. OBNC
Melodies of Time, The. Thomas Hood. *Fr.* The Plea of the Midsummer Fairies. OBNC
Melton Mowbray Pork Pie, A. Richard Le Gallienne. Par
Memento. Rudolf Hagelstange, *tr. fr. German by* Babette Deutsch. MGP
Mementos, I ("Sorting out letters and piles of my old"). W. D. Snodgrass. NePoEA-2
Mementos, II ("I found them there today"). W. D. Snodgrass. AmPC; NePoEA-2
Memorabilia. Robert Browning. ACV; CABA; CBEP; ILP; OBNC; PP
Memorial. Clark Ashton Smith. FiSC
Memorial Day. Theodosia Garrison. PoSC
Memorial for President Kennedy, A. Robert G. Tucker. OPP
Memorial Service for the Invasion Beach Where the Vacation in the Flesh Is Over. Alan Dugan. MP
Memorial to the Great Big Beautiful Self-sacrificing Advertisers. Frederick Ebright. ThLM
Memorial Verses. Matthew Arnold. CABA; PP
Memorial Wreath. Dudley Randall. NNP
Memories. Whittier. AP
Memories of West Street and Lepke. Robert Lowell. ToPo
Memories of Whitman and Lincoln. James Oppenheim. LiPo
Memory. Thomas Bailey Aldrich. AmLP; PoLF
Memory. Helen Hoyt. PoLF
Memory. Abraham Lincoln. LV
Memory ("I have a room whereinto no one enters"). Christina Rossetti. OBNC
Memory ("I nursed it in my bosom while it lived"). Christina Rossetti. OBNC
Memory. Dante Gabriel Rossetti. CBEP
Memory, A. L. A. G. Strong. DaDu; PoPl
Memory as Memorial in the Last. Edward Marshall. CoPo
Men. Dorothy Parker. BoLP; LV
Men, brother men, that after us yet live. The Epitaph in Form of a Ballad. Villon. CTC
Men don't believe in a devil now. The Devil. *Unknown.* StF
Men have left God not for other gods, they say, but for no god. T. S. Eliot. *Fr.* The Rock. TRV
Men, if you love us, play no more. In the Person of Woman Kind. Ben Jonson. SeCP

Men in Green. David Campbell. PoAu-2
Men Marry What They Need. I Marry You. John Ciardi. MoLP
Men may leave all games. The Sailing of the Pilgrims. *Unknown.* HaSV
Men meet and part. Words Made of Water. Burns Singer. NePoEA-2
Men moving in a trench, in the clear noon. These Men. Leon Gellert. PoAu-1
Men of England, wherefore plough. Song to the Men of England. Shelley. ILP; PoPo
Men of the Alamo, The. James Jeffrey Roche. ThLM
Men of the High North. Robert Service. ACV
Men Only Pretend. *Unknown.* MeEL
Men rent me on rode. Jesus Bids Man Remember. *Unknown.* MeEL
Men saw no portents on that winter night. Young Lincoln. Edwin Markham. LiPo
Men say it was there where Exmoor ends in air. A Winter Legend. Geoffrey Johnson. FiSC
Men Say They Know Many Things. Henry David Thoreau. PoPl
Men seem as alike as the leaves on the trees. The Man from the Crowd. Sam Walter Foss. PoLF
Men that worked for England, The. Elegy in a Country Churchyard. G. K. Chesterton. EvOK; MMA
Men were connected with animals. The Shock. Larry Eigner. CoPo
Men Who March Away. Thomas Hardy. MMA
Menagerie, The. William Vaughn Moody. AP
Menalcas and Enoisa. Philip Wharton. WaPE
Menaphon, *sel.* Robert Greene.
    Sephestia's Song to Her Child. ELP; EnRePo; PoIE
    (Weep Not My Wanton.) CBEP
Mending Wall. Robert Frost. AP; CaFP; DiPo; FaRV; FoBA; ILP; PoPo; PoSa; RePo
Men's Applause. Friedrich Hölderlin, *tr. fr. German by* Walter Kaufmann. TwGP
    (Crowd's Acclaim, The, *tr. by* Martin Zwart.) AGP
Mental Cases. Wilfred Owen. MMA
Mental Traveller, The. Blake. DiPo
Merchant of Venice, The, *sels.* Shakespeare.
    All That Glisters Is Not Gold, *fr.* II, vii. CTC
    Fire Seven Times Tried This, The, *fr.* II, ix. CTC
    "How sweet the moonlight sleeps upon the bank!" *fr.* V, i. BoC
    "Quality of mercy is not strain'd, The," *fr.* IV, i. TRV
    Tell Me Where Is Fancy Bred, *fr.* III, ii. DiPo; ELP; EnRePo; FoBA; ILP
        (Madrigal.) GTBS-P
        (Song.) CTC
        (Where Is Fancy Bred?) WePo
Merchant, to secure his treasure, The. An Ode. Matthew Prior. CABA; CBEP; EiCP; GTBS-P
Merchant not credit you, The. Couldn't Stand the Press. Mart Taylor. SGR
Merchants have their ups and downs. Business. Arthur Guiterman. LV
Merchant's Tale, The, *abr.* Chaucer, *mod. vers. by* Frank Ernest Hill. *Fr.* The Canterbury Tales. UnTE
Mercies and Blessings. *Unknown.* STF
Merciful God, who readst my inmost mind. Prayer. Willem Bilderijk. SiGo
Merciles Beaute. Chaucer. CTC; StP
    (Merciless Beauty.) CBEP
    (Three Roundels of Love Unreturned.) MeEL
Mercy and Love. Robert Herrick. PoPo
Mercy, Lover Mine! *Unknown, tr. fr. Spanish by* William M. Davis. AnML
Merlin. Emerson. AP
Merlin. Edwin Muir. CBEP
Merlin and the Gleam. Tennyson. FoBA; VP
Merlin and Vivien, *sel.* Tennyson. *Fr.* Idylls of the King.
    Vivien's Song. OBNC
Mermaid, The. *Unknown.* HaSV; SIV, *with music*
Mermaid, Dragon, Fiend. Robert Graves. AnMoPo
Mermaid Tavern, The. Keats. *See* Lines on the Mermaid Tavern.
Mermaiden's Vesper Hymn, The. George Darley. *Fr.* Syren Songs. HaSV; OBNC
Mermaids. Kenneth Slessor. *Fr.* The Atlas. PoAu-2
Mermaid's not a human thing, A. Lost and Given Over. E. J. Brady. PoAu-1
Merrie world did on a day, The. *See* Merry world did on a day, The.
Merritt Parkway. Denise Levertov. ToPo
Merry cuckow, messenger of spring, The. Amoretti, XIX. Spenser. ILP
Merry-go-round. Dorothy Baruch. SoPo
Merry Hay-Makers, The; or, Pleasant Pastime between the Young-Men and Maids, in the Pleasant Meadows. *Unknown.* ErPo
Merry it is in the good greenwood. Alice Brand. Sir Walter Scott. *Fr.* The Lady of the Lake. OnMSP

Merry it was in the green forest. Adam Bell, Clym of the Clough, and William of Cloudesley. *Unknown.* BuBa
Merry Little Maid and Wicked Little Monk, The. *Unknown.* ErPo
Merry Margaret. To Mistress Margaret Hussey. John Skelton. *Fr.* The Garlande of Laurell. CBEP; DiPo; GoJo; PoIE; PoSa
Merry, merry Sparrow. The Blossom. Blake. *Fr.* Songs of Innocence. CBEP; FoBA; GoJo
Merry Miner, The. Constance Rourke. RePo
Merry Month of March, The. Wordsworth. EvOK; SoPo
    (Written in March.) GoJo
Merry Note, A. Shakespeare. *See* When Icicles Hang by the Wall.
Merry the green, the green hill shall be merry. Another Song. Donald Justice. NePoEA-2
Merry [or Merrie] world did on a day, The. The Quip. George Herbert. CBEP; ILP; SeCP
Meseemeth I heard cry and groan. The Complaint of the Fair Armoress [or Armouress]. Villon. CTC; UnTE
Mesopotamia. Kipling. MMA
Message from her set his brain aflame, A. Modern Love, V. George Meredith. VP
Message Hidden in an Empty Wine Bottle That I Threw into a Gulley of Maple Trees One Night at an Indecent Hour, A. James Wright. AmPC
Message of the March Wind, The. William Morris. OBNC; WiR
Messages of the Rain. Günter Eich, *tr. fr. German by* Michael Hamburger. MGP
Messmates. Sir Henry Newbolt. HaSV
Metamorphoses, *sels.* Ovid. *tr. fr. Latin by* Arthur Golding. CTC
    Acteon, *fr.* III.
    Conclusion: "Now have I brought a woork too end which neither Joves fierce wrath," *fr.* XV.
    Cyclops, *fr.* XIII.
    Daedalus, *fr.* VIII.
    King Midas, *fr.* XI.
    Meleager, *fr.* VIII.
    Philemon and Baucis, *fr.* VIII.
Metamorphoses of M. John Peale Bishop. ErPo
Metamorphoses of the Vampire. Baudelaire, *tr. fr. French by* Jackson Mathews. ErPo
Metamorphosis. Eli Mandel. ACV
Metaphor. Clark Ashton Smith. FiSC
Methinks Death like one laughing lyes. Epitaph. Cæcil. Boulstr. Lord Herbert of Cherbury. SeCP
Methinks I spy Almighty holding in. Meditation Sixty-eight A. Edward Taylor. *Fr.* Preparatory Meditations, Second Series. AP
Methinks 'tis pretty sport to hear a child. On a Child Beginning to Talk. Thomas Bastard. CBEP
Methodist bell's got the croup, The. Church Bell—Winter Time. Thad Stem, Jr. PoNC
Methought I saw/ Life swiftly treading. The Sea of Death. Thomas Hood. OBNC
Methought I saw a thousand fearful wrecks. Shakespeare. King Richard III, *fr.* I, iv. HaSV
Methought I saw, as I did dream in bed. The Vision [or The Second Vision]. Robert Herrick. CBEP; UnTE
Methought I Saw My Late Espoused Saint. Milton. CABA; FoBA; ILP
    (On His Deceased Wife.) CBEP; DiPo; OnP; StP
    (Sonnet.) VaPo
Methought I Saw the Grave Where Laura Lay. Sir Walter Ralegh. ILP
Methought I stood where trees of every clime. A Dream. Keats. *Fr.* The Fall of Hyperion. OBNC
Methuselah. Rosemary Dobson. *Fr.* The Devil and the Angel. PoAu-2
Methuselah! Song of a Thousand Years. Don Marquis. WePo
Metre Columbia, The. *Unknown.* Par
Mexican Serenade. Arthur Guiterman. BoLP; LV
Mexico Trail, The, *with music. Unknown.* BFSS
Mezzo Cammin. Longfellow. CBEP; ILP
Mia Carlotta. T. A. Daly. WePo
Micah, *sels.* Bible, O.T.
    Neither Shall They Learn War Any More, IV: 1–4. TRV
    Wherewith Shall I Come before the Lord? VI: 6–8. TRV
Mice. Rose Fyleman. EvOK; SoPo
Michael. Wordsworth. DiPo
Micky Thumps. *Unknown.* WePo
Microcosm, The. Giovanni Battista Guarini, *tr. fr. Italian by* Sir Edward Sherburne. RBL
Mid pleasures and palaces though we may roam. Home, Sweet Home. John Howard Payne. FaPL; LV
Mid-Rapture. Dante Gabriel Rossetti. The House of Life, XXVI. VP
'Mid roaring brooks and dark moss-vales. On the Death of a Recluse. George Darley. CBEP
'Mid sunshine, cloud or stormy days. In Every Thing Give Thanks. *Unknown.* STF

Midas, *sel.* John Lyly.
  Pan's Syrinx. ELP
Midas watched the golden crust. The Ungrateful Garden.
  Carolyn Kizer. NePoEA-2
Midcentury Love Letter. Phyllis McGinley. MoLP
Middle-aged, The. Adrienne Rich. NePoEA-2
Middle-aged Child. Inez Hogan. BiCB
Middle-aged life is merry, and I love to lead it. Peekaboo, I
  Almost See You. Ogden Nash. PoLF
Middle Passage. O. B. Hardison, Jr. PoNC
Middle Passage. Robert Hayden. AmNP
  "Deponent further sayeth The Bella J," *sel.* PtTo
Middle-Time, The. Lona M. Fowler. TRV
Midnight. Archibald Lampman. OBCV
Midnight. James Stephens. DTC
Midnight. Henry Vaughan. MeP
Midnight black with clouds is in the sky, A. Earth. Bryant.
  AP
Midnight Interior, A. Siegfried Sasson. MoRP
Midnight is no time for/ Poetry. No Time for Poetry. Julia
  Fields. AmNP
Midnight Skaters, The. Edmund Blunden. GoJo; GTBS-P;
  WePo
Midnight Special, The, *with music. Unknown.* BFSS
Midsummer. James Scully. MP
Midsummer Fantasy. Newman Levy. PoSC
Midsummer Night's Dream, A, *sels.* Shakespeare.
  Asleep, My Love? *fr.* V, i. CTC
  Bottom's Song, *fr.* III, i. CTC
  Flower of This Purple Dye, *fr.* III, ii. CTC
  Lunatic, the Lover, and the Poet, The, *fr.* V, i. DiPo
  ("Lovers and madmen have such seething brains," *sl.
  longer sel.*) PP
  Now the Hungry Lion Roars, *fr.* V, ii. CTC; EnRePo
  (Lion of Winter, The.) WiR
  Through the Forest Have I Gone, *fr.* II, ii. CTC
  Through the House, *fr.* V, ii. CTC
  Up and Down, *fr.* III, ii. CTC
  Violet Bank, A, *fr.* II, i. RePo
  Yet but Three? *fr.* III, ii. CTC
Midsummer Noon in the Australian Forest, A. Charles Har-
  pur. PoAu-1
Midsummer Pause. Fred Lape. PoSC
Midway. Naomi Long Madgett. NNP
Midways of a walled garden. Golden Wings. William Morris.
  OBNC
Midwest. John Frederick Nims. PoP1
Midwinter spring is its own season. Little Gidding. T. S.
  Eliot. *Fr.* Four Quartets. GTBS-P; PoIE
Mighty Fortress Is Our God, A. Martin Luther, *tr. fr. Ger-
  man by* F. H. Hedge. EaLo
  (Feste Burg ist unser Gott, Ein, *tr. by* M. Woolsey
  Stryker.) CTC
Mighty Hunter, The. Mrs. J. B. Worley. PoLF
Mighty Lord Is Money, A. Francisco de Quevedo, *tr. fr.
  Spanish by* William M. Davis. AnSP
Mighty Runner, A. E. A. Robinson. SD
Mighty Thoughts of an Old World, The. Thomas Lovell
  Beddoes. *Fr.* The Ivory Gate. GoJo
Mignon ("Bid me not speak, bid me be still"). Goethe, *tr. fr.
  German by* Walter Kaufmann. TwGP
Mignon ("Knowest thou the land"). Goethe, *tr. fr. German.
  Fr.* Wilhelm Meister. PoP1, *tr. by* Edgar A. Bowring;
  SiGo, *tr. by* James Elroy Flecker
Migod, a picture window. The One-Night Stand: An Ap-
  proach to the Bridge. Paul Blackburn. ErPo
Mikado, The, *sel.* W. S. Gilbert.
  Ko-Ko's Song. LV
Milady, by departure. Song of Parting. João Roiz de Castelo-
  Branco. AnML
Milady, Comely, Candid, Worldly-wise. Guillaume de Ma-
  chaut, *tr. fr. French by* Norman R. Shapiro. AnML
Mild Is the Parting Year. Walter Savage Landor. CBEP
  ("Mild is the parting year, and sweet.") EiCP
Mild offspring of a dark and sullen sire! To an Early Prim-
  rose. Henry Kirke White. OBNC
Mile and mile and mile; but no one would gather. The Sea.
  Francis Webb. PoAu-2
Mile behind is Gloucester town, A. Gloucester Moors. Wil-
  liam Vaughn Moody. AP; FaPL
Miles of pram in the wind and Pam in the gorse track. Pot
  Pourri from a Surrey Garden. John Betjeman. DTC;
  PoCh
Milk-glass bowl hanging by three chains, A. The Corpse-
  Plant. Adrienne Rich. CoPo
Milking before Dawn. Ruth Dallas. ACV
Milking Time. Elizabeth Madox Roberts. GoJo
Milkman, The. Jane W. Krows. SoPo
Milkman's Horse, The. *Unknown.* SoPo
Mill, The. E. A. Robinson. PoIE; PoSa
Miller, The. Chaucer, *mod. vers. by* Nevill Coghill. *Fr.* The
  Canterbury Tales: Prologue. WePo
  (Ten of Chaucer's People: A Stout Miller.) PoSa
Miller That Made His Will, The, *with music. Unknown.*
  BFSS

(Miller's Song, The, *with music, shorter vers.*) BSO
Miller's Daughter, The. Tennyson. CBEP; UnTE
Miller's daughter, The. Spinning Song. Edith Sitwell.
  DaDu
Miller's Song, The. *Unknown. See* Miller That Made His
  Will, The.
Miller's wife had waited long, The. The Mill. E. A. Robin-
  son. PoIE; PoSa
Millions Are Learning How. James Agee. PoP1
Milton, *sels.* Blake.
  And Did Those Feet in Ancient Time, *fr.* Preface. CABA;
  CaFP; CBEP; FaBV; PoSa
  (Jerusalem.) EaLo; EvOK
  (Preface.) ILP; PoIE
  (Prelude.) OBNC
  Lark's Song, The, *fr.* II. WiR
  (Vision of the Lamentation of Beulah over Ololon, A,
  longer sel.) OBNC
  Wild Thyme, The, *fr.* II. WiR
Milton. Longfellow. AmLP; AP; StP
Milton! thou shouldst be living at this hour. London, 1802
  [*or* The Same]. Wordsworth. CABA; DiPo; FaBV;
  FoBA; GTBS-P; ILP; OBNC; PoIE; PoPo; StP
Milton's Prayer for Patience. Elizabeth Lloyd Howell. TRV
Mima. Walter de la Mare. BiCB
Mimi, do you remember. Biftek aux Champignons. Henry
  Augustin Beers. AmLP
Mind. Richard Wilbur. PoIE; PoSa
Mind and humble and more than a thousand. To Cino da
  Pistoia. Onesto da Bologna. AnML
Mind has shown itself at times, The. For the Marriage of
  Faustus and Helen. Hart Crane. AP
Mind Is an Enchanting Thing, The. Marianne Moore. AP
Mine be a cot beside the hill. A Wish. Samuel Rogers.
  GTBS-P
Mine by the right of the white election! Emily Dickinson.
  FaPL
Mine eyes beheld the blessed pity spring. Sonnet. Dante.
  La Vita Nuova, XXIII. PoP1
Mine Eyes Have Seen the Glory. Julia Ward Howe. *See*
  Battle Hymn of the Republic.
Mine, yet no longer mine. Nativity. Ruth Gilbert. *Fr.* The
  Blossom of the Branches. ACV
Mineral Kingdom, The. Jacques Dupin, *tr. fr. French by*
  William Brown. CoFP
Miner's Dream, The, *with music.* John A. Stone. SGR
Miner's Farewell, The, *with music.* Mart Taylor. SGR
Miner's Lament, The, III ("I've just come down from the
  mines"). David G. Robinson. SGR
Miner's Lament, The, II ("Vainly I strive to make a live at
  mining"). *Unknown.* SGR
Miner's Lament, The, I ("When the gold fever raged, I was
  doing very well"), *with music.* John A. Stone. SGR
Miners' Meeting, A, *with music.* John A. Stone. SGR
Mingo's Discourse. Juan del Encina, *tr. fr. Spanish by*
  Beatrice Gilman Proske. RBL
Miniver Cheevy. E. A. Robinson. AP; CaFP; CBEP;
  FaBV; PoLF; PoP1; PoPo; PoSa; StP; VaPo
Minnie and Mattie. Christina Rossetti. *Fr.* Sing-Song.
  GoJo
Minor Bird, A. Robert Frost. LOW
Minor Prophet, A, *sel.* "George Eliot."
  Tide of Faith, The. TRV
Minotaur Poems, *sels.* E. W. Mandel. OBCV
  "It has been hours in these rooms," I.
  "My father was always out in the garage," II.
  Orpheus, VI.
Minstrel, The; or, The Progress of Genuis, *sel.* James Beattie.
  "Ah! who can tell how hard it is to climb," I, *abr.* EnPE
Minstrel and genuis, to whose songs or sighs. Autumnal Ode.
  Aubrey Thomas De Vere. OBNC
Minstrel Boy, The. Thomas Moore. RoGo
Minstrel Responds to Flattery, The. Sir Walter Scott. *Fr.*
  The Lay of the Last Minstrel. OBNC
Minstrel's Song. Thomas Chatterton. *Fr.* Aella. DiPo
  (My Love Is Dead.) WiR
Miracle, The. Allan Dowling. ErPo
Miracle, The. Elsie Melchert Fowler. BiCB
Miracle for Breakfast, A. Elizabeth Bishop. StP
Miracle of Spring, The. Bahar, *tr. fr. Persian by* A. J. Ar-
  berry. SiGo
Miracles. Walt Whitman. MoRP; RePo
Miraculous Place of Love, The. André Frénaud, *tr. fr. French
  by* Paulène Aspel. CoFP
Miraculously, through prayer to Saint Anthony. Robert Fitz-
  gerald. *Fr.* Adulescentia. SD
Miramichi Lightning. Alfred Goldsworthy Bailey. OBCV
Mirandum, *sel.* Vincent Ferrini.
  Sea, The. PtTo
Mirèio, *sels.* Frédéric Mistral, *tr. fr. Provençal.*
  Cocooning, The, *tr. by* Harriet Waters Preston. PoP1
  Mares of the Camargue, The, *tr. by* George Meredith. PoP1
Mirie it is, while sumer ilast. How Long This Night Is. *Un-
  known.* MeEL
Mirror. James Merrill. NePoEA-2

Mirror in February. Thomas Kinsella. GTBS-P
Mirror Perilous, The. Alan Dugan. MP
Mirth. Christopher Smart. *Fr.* Hymns for the Amusement of Children. EiCP
Mirth, with Thee I Mean to Live. Milton. *Fr.* L'Allegro. FaBV
Mirthful Lunacy. Thomas Stoddart. *Fr.* The Death-Wake; or, Lunacy. OBNC
Mis' Smith. Albert Bigelow Paine. PoLF
Misconceptions. Robert Browning. CBEP
Miser pain, delay your gift. Sunken Oboe. Salvatore Quasimodo. CoIP
Miserere. William Pillin. PtTo
Miser's mind thou hast, A. Of a Rich Miser. George Turberville. EnRePo
Misery is greater, as I live, The! Modern Love, XXIV. George Meredith. VP
Misfit, The—1939–1945. C. Day Lewis. BoC
Misfortunes of Elphin, The, *sels.* Thomas Love Peacock.
Song of the Four Winds, The. WiR
War-Song of Dinas Vawr, The, *fr. ch.* 11. CABA; EvOK; OnMSP; StP; WiR
Misgivings. Herman Melville. AP; CBEP
Miss Ella she is twenty-nine. California Bloomer. John A. Stone. SGR
Miss Esther Williams. Penny Wise and Found Poolish. W. W. Watt. PoPo
Miss Flo. Edith Earnshaw. PoNC
Miss Flora McFlimsey, of Madison Square. Nothing to Wear. William Allen Butler. PoLF
Miss Flora unfolded red, work-roughened hands. Miss Flo. Edith Earnshaw. PoNC
Miss Helen Slingsby was my maiden aunt. Aunt Helen. T. S. Eliot. FoBA; PoSa
Miss J. Hunter Dunn, Miss J. Hunter Dunn. A Subaltern's Love-Song. John Betjeman. EvOK; MP
Miss Mary was sitting one fine summer day. The Journeyman Tailor. *Unknown.* BFSS
Miss M.'s a nightingale. 'Tis well. On a Poetess. Gerard Manley Hopkins. PP
Miss Nancy Ellicott. Cousin Nancy. T. S. Eliot. FoBA; PoSa
Miss Rafferty wore taffeta. The Private Dining Room. Ogden Nash. CaFP; PoCh; VaPo
Miss Sallie's Chowchow. Edith Earnshaw. PoNC
Miss T. Walter de la Mare. GoJo; SoPo
Miss Thompson Goes Shopping. Martin Armstrong. WePo
Miss Twye. Gavin Ewart. ErPo
Missing. John Pudney. WePo
Missing all, prevented me, The. Emily Dickinson. AP
Missing Dates. William Empson. AnMoPo; PoIE
Missing My Daughter. Stephen Spender. BoC; GTBS-P
Missions. *Unknown.* STF
Mississippi Girls, *with music. Unknown.* BFSS
Missouri Rhapsody. James Daugherty. RePo
Mist. Henry David Thoreau. AmLP
Mist and All, The. Dixie Willson. SoPo
Mistake, The. Theodore Roethke. UnTE
Mistaken Fair. Earl of Chesterfield. CBEP
Mistakes. George W. Swarberg. STF
Mister Beers. Hugh Lofting. RePo
Mr. Bleaney. Philip Larkin. NePoEA-2; PoIE
Mr. Edwards and the Spider. Robert Lowell. AP; CABA; ILP; MP; ToPo
Mr. Flood's Party. E. A. Robinson. AP; CABA; CaFP; EvOK; FaPL; ILP; OnP; PoPl; PoPo; PoSa
Mr. Frog Went A-Courting. *Unknown. See* Frog and the Mouse, The.
Mr. Frost Goes South to Boston. Firman Houghton. Par
Mr. Kennedy Proposes to Pacify the Caribbeans. George Hitchcock. OPP
Mr. Lerner. Joseph Joel Keith. FiSC
Mr. Mandragon, the Millionaire, he wouldn't have wine or wife. The Good Rich Man. G. K. Chesterton. DTC
Mr. Moon. Bliss Carman. RePo
Mr. Pope. Allen Tate. AP; CABA; MP
Mr. Ripley Parodies Mr. Nash—or Vice Versa. Julian Brown. FiSC
Mister Thomas Jones. Bringing Him Up. Lord Dunsany. BBGG
Mr. Walter de la Mare Makes the Little Ones Dizzy. Samuel Hoffenstein. Par
Mistral wind, you rain cloud leaper. To the Mistral. Nietzsche. TwGP
Mistress, The, *sel.* Abraham Cowley.
Wish, The. BoC; FaPL
Mrs. Alfred Uruguay. Wallace Stevens. AP; MP
Mistress Anne. To Mistress Anne. John Skelton. EnRePo
Mrs. Frances Harris's Petition. Swift. *See* To Their Excellencies the Lords Justices of Ireland, the Humble Petition of Frances Harris.
Mrs. George Reece. Edgar Lee Masters. *Fr.* Spoon River Anthology. LV
Mrs. Hobart-Constantine awakens. Two Ladies Bidding Us "Good Morning." James P. Vaughn. NNP

Mrs. Huff is up a miff tree. Let Your Pastor Know. *Unknown.* STF
Mrs. Judge Jenkins, *parody.* Bret Harte. CABA
Mrs. Lombardi's month-old son is dead. Italian Extravaganza. Gregory Corso. CoPo
Mistress Mary. Mother Goose. SoPo
Mrs. Mouse/ Come out of your house. Cat Asks Mouse Out. Stevie Smith. DaDu
Mistress of Bernal Francés, The. *Unknown, tr. fr. Spanish by* William M. Davis. AnML
Mrs. Peck-Pigeon. Eleanor Farjeon. SoPo
Mrs. Santa Claus' Christmas Present. Alice S. Morris. PoSC
Mrs. Snipkin and Mrs. Wobblechin. Laura E. Richards. SoPo
Mrs. Squirrel/ In a tree. Squirrel. James S. Tippett. RePo
Mrs. Swartz. Don Marquis. ThLM
Mistress without Compare, A. Charles d'Orléans(?). MeEL
Misty mornin' doon the shore wi a hushed and caller air, A. The Smoky Smirr o' Rain. George Campbell Hay. ACV
Mitayo, The. Manuel González Prada, *tr. fr. Spanish by* Kate Flores. AnSP
Mither's Lament, The. Sydney Goodsir Smith. ACV
Mithraic Emblems, *sel.* Roy Campbell.
To the Sun. FaLo
Mithridates. Emerson. AP
Mitten Song, The. Marie Louise Allen. SoPo
Mix a Pancake. Christina Rossetti. *Fr.* Sing-Song. SoPo
Mixed Emotions. Vernon Ward. PoNC
Mobile, immaculate and austere. A Pastoral. Geoffrey Hill. NePoEA-2
Moby Dick, *sel.* Herman Melville.
Ribs and Terrors in the Whale, The, *fr. ch.* 9. EaLo
(Whale, The.) PoPl
Mock Medicine. *Unknown.* MeEL
Mock On, Mock On, Voltaire, Rousseau. Blake. CABA; ILP; OBNC; PoIE
Mockery murders love, they say, and she. Foolish Proverb. *Unknown.* UnTE
Modern Declaration. Edna St. Vincent Millay. MoLP
Modern Dragon, A. Rowena Bennett. SoPo
Modern Hiawatha, The, *parody.* George A. Strong. *Fr.* The Song of Milkanwatha. LV; Par
Modern Love. Keats. CBEP; OBNC
Modern Love. George Meredith. VP
Sels.
"Am I failing? For no longer can I cast," XXIX. CABA; FaPL
"At dinner, she is hostess, I am host," XVII. ILP
"By this he knew she wept with waking eyes," I. ILP; StP
"I play for seasons; not eternities," XIII. OBNC; PoIE
"Mark where the pressing wind shoots javelin-like," XLIII. FaPL; ILP; OBNC
"Thus piteously Love closed what he begat," L. CaFP; FaPL; GTBS-P; ILP; OBNC; PoIE
"We saw the swallows gathering in the sky," XLVII. GTBS-P; OBNC
(We Saw the Swallows.) ELP
Modern Romance, A. Paul Engle. PoPl
Modest and needy is my destiny in thy world, O God! Kibbutz Sabbath. Levi Ben Amittai. EaLo
Modest Love, A. Sir Edward Dyer. *See* Lowest Trees Have Tops, The.
Modest rose puts forth a thorn, The. The Lilly. Blake. *Fr.* Songs of Experience. FoBA
Mohini Chatterjee. W. B. Yeats. MoRP
Moldering Hulk, The. Antonio Machado, *tr. fr. Spanish by* Kate Flores. AnSP; SiGo
Mole. William Jay Smith. MoRP
Molly Bond, *with music. Unknown.* BFSS
Molly Means. Margaret Walker. AmNP
Molly Pitcher. Laura E. Richards. ThLM
Molly Pitcher. Kate Brownlee Sherwood. SIV
Moment. Howard Nemerov. PoDB
Moment after the moment of love, The. King's X. Hollis Summers. StP
Moment before Conception, The. Eve Merriam. UnTE
Moment Eternal, The. Robert Browning. *See* Now.
Moment of silence, first, then there it is, A. The Dial Tone. Howard Nemerov. ToPo
Moment of Vision, The. Richard Eberhart. MoRP
Moment Please, A. Samuel Allen. AmNP
Moment's patience, gentle Mistress Anne, A. William Shakespeare to Mrs. Anne, Regular Servant to the Rev. Mr. Precentor of York. Thomas Gray. ILP
Mon in the mone stond and strit. The Man in the Moon. *Unknown.* MeEL
Monastery, The, *sel.* Sir Walter Scott.
Bible, The, *fr. ch.* 12. TRV
Monday's Child Is Fair of Face. Mother Goose. BiCB
(Birthdays.) CBEP
(Week of Birthdays, A.) SoPo
Money. Richard Armour. LV; PoPl; PoPo
Money Is What Matters. *Unknown.* MeEL
Money, thou bane of bliss, and source of woe. Avarice. George Herbert. FoBA

Monkey, The. Vladislav Khodasevich, *tr. fr. Russian by* Babette Deutsch. PoPo
Monkey Monkey Moo. So Many Monkeys. Marion Edey *and* Dorothy Grider. SoPo
Monkeys and the Crocodile, The. Laura E. Richards. SoPo
Monkey's Raincoat, The. Basho, *tr. fr. Japanese by* Harold G. Henderson. SoPo
Monna Innominata. Christina Rossetti. VP
Sels.
"Many in aftertimes will say of you," XI. OBNC
"Youth gone, and beauty gone if ever there," XIV. OBNC
Monna Lisa. James Russell Lowell. AmLP
Monody. Herman Melville. AP; PoIE
Monody, then the cacophony, The. Courthouse Bell. Thad Stem, Jr. PoNC
Monogramania. Eve Merriam. UnTE
Monologue of a Deaf Man. David Wright. MP
Monster, The. Dorothy Quick. FiSC
Mont Blanc. Shelley. PP
Montana Pastoral. J. V. Cunningham. PoIE
Monterey. Charles Fenno Hoffman. ThLM
Month of roses. And my rhymes. Spring. Rubén Darío. AnSP
Month of the drowned dog, The. After long rain the land. November. Ted Hughes. GTBS-P; NePoEA-2
Months, The. Sara Coleridge. RePo
Months, The. Christina Rossetti. *Fr.* Sing-Song. LV
Montreal. A. M. Klein. OBCV
Monument, The. Elizabeth Bishop. PoIE; PP
Moo cow is a mammal not, The. The Pleasant Cow. Grace Taber Hallock. RePo
Moods, The. W. B. Yeats. CTC
Moon, The. Bhasa, *tr. fr. Sanskrit by* A. Berriedale Keith. SiGo
Moon, The. Elizabeth J. Coatsworth. RePo
Moon. Yvan Goll, *tr. fr. German by* Christopher Middleton. MGP
Moon, The. Ryuho, *tr. fr. Japanese.* SoPo
Moon,/ milk spider of the women. Denunciation. Wolfdietrich Schnurre. MGP
Moon and Fog. August Derleth. FiSC
Moon, as if a dead thing. Occident. Georg Trakl. MGP
Moon at the full. Europe has burst its banks. The Inundation. Howard Sergeant. *Fr.* The Leaves of Europe. ToPo
Moon Compasses. Robert Frost. DiPo
Moon crowned by daisies, The. Love. Attilio Bertolucci. CoIP
Moon Door. Mary Kennedy. BoLP
Moon, grown full now over the sea, The. Looking at the Moon and Thinking of One Far Away. Chang Chiu-ling. SiGo
Moon has climbed the highest hill, The. Mary's Dream. *Unknown.* BSO
Moon in September, The. Kashiprosad Ghose. ACV
Moon in the Mountains, The. Chen Shan-min, *tr. fr. Chinese by* E. D. Edwards. SiGo
Moon in the Water, The. Ryota, *tr. fr. Japanese.* SoPo
Moon is but a golden skull, The. What the Hyena Said. Vachel Lindsay. LV
Moon is distant from the sea, The. Emily Dickinson. DiPo
Moon is gone, The. Night. Sappho. SiGo
Moon like a winter animal licks the salt of your hands, The. The Salt Lake. Yvan Goll. MGP
Moon nails a long horn, The. Second Anniversary. Federico García Lorca. AnSP
Moon-Night. Josef von Eichendorff. *See* Moonlit Night.
Moon on the one hand, The. Early Dawn. Hilaire Belloc. ThGo
Moon Rainbow, A. Robert Browning. BoC
Moon shall be a darkness, The. Valentine Promise. *Unknown.* PoSC
Moon shines bright, The. Greeting. *Unknown.* ThGo
Moon shines bright, the stars give a light, The. A May Day Carol. *Unknown.* PoSC
Moon was full that night in Aragon, The. For My Dead Brother. Alvah Bessie. PtTo
Moon Was Gilding the River, The. Juan Ramón Jiménez, *tr. fr. Spanish by* Eloise Roach. AnSP
Moon with dewy lustre bright, The. Lament for Tintoretta. William Collins. Three Fragments, 3. WaPE
Moonless Darkness Stands Between. Gerard Manley Hopkins. WePo
Moonlight Night, The, *with music. Unknown.* BSO
Moonless night—a friendly one, A. Running the Batteries. Herman Melville. ThLM
Moonlight and music and the sound of waves. The Sleepers. Louis Untermeyer. MoLP
Moonlight in such places alters faces. Moon and Fog. August Derleth. FiSC
Moonlight Night on the Port. Sidney Keyes. DTC
Moonlight . . . Scattered Clouds. Robert Bloomfield. *Fr.* The Farmer's Boy. OBNC
Moonlit Night. Josef von Eichendorff, *tr. fr. German by* D. G. Wright. AGP

(Moon-Night, *tr.* by Mabel Cotterell.) SiGo
Moonmoth and grasshopper that flee our page. A Name for All. Hart Crane. PP
Moon's the North Wind's Cooky, The. Vachel Lindsay. EvOK; SoPo
Moonstar, The. Dante Gabriel Rossetti. The House of Life, XXIX. VP
Mopoke. Louis Lavater. PoAu-1
Moral Essays, *sels.* Pope.
Of the Characters of Women, *fr.* Epistle II.
"Yet Cloe sure was form'd without a spot." ErPo
Of the Use of Riches, Epistle IV. CABL
Moral massacre, the murder, the rape of religion, The. The Child. Reginald Massey. ACV
Moral Proverbs, *sels.* Sem Tob, *tr. fr. Spanish by* Norman T. Di Giovanni. AnML
Some I've Seen So Crudely.
There's No Day without Night.
There's No Finer Treasure.
Whether Long or Sparing, *tr. by* William M. Davis.
Moral Song. John Farrar. RePo
Moral Taxi Ride, The. Erich Kästner, *tr. fr. German by* Jerome Rothenberg. ErPo
Morality of Poetry, The. James Wright. PP
Morals. James Thurber. *Fr.* Further Fables for Our Times. FaBV
Mordent for a Melody. Margaret Avison. ACV
More beautiful and soft than any moth. The Landscape near an Aerodrome. Stephen Spender. StP
More brilliant there the star of passion. Wine and Ocher. Mario Luzi. CoIP
More Foreign Cities. Charles Tomlinson. NePoEA-2
"More Light! More Light!" Anthony Hecht. NePoEA-2
More luck to honest poverty. For A' That and A' That, *parody.* Shirley Brooks. Par
More Nudes for Florence. Harold Witt. ErPo
More Prayer. *Unknown.* STF
More precious than Alladin's jewels. Treasure. Elizabeth-Ellen Long. BiCB
More secure is no one ever. Security. Lina Sandell. STF
"More ships!" some cry; "more guns!" More Prayer. *Unknown.* STF
More than most fair, full of the living fire. Amoretti, VIII. Spenser. CABA
"More than my brothers are to me." In Memoriam A. H. H., LXXIX. Tennyson. VP
More Truth and Light. John Robinson. TRV
More we live, more brief appear, The. The River of Life [*or* A Thought Suggested by the New Year]. Thomas Campbell. GTBS-P; OBNC
More White than Whitest Lilies. Robert Herrick. UnTE
More whyght thou art then primrose leaf my Lady Galatee. Cyclops. Ovid. *Fr.* Metamorphoses. CTC
Morgan. Edward Harrington. PoAu-1
Moriana's Poison. *Unknown, tr. fr. Spanish by* William M. Davis. AnML
Morgiana Dances. William Rose Benét. SIV
Morgue, *sels.* Gottfried Benn, *tr. fr. German by* Walter Kaufmann. TwGP
Beautiful Childhood.
Cycle.
Negro Bride.
Morituri Salutamus, *sel.* Longfellow.
It Is Too Late! PoLF
Mormon Trail, The. Daniel Henderson. SIV
Morning. Emily Dickinson. SoPo
Morning. Alfred Lichtenstein, *tr. fr. German by* Michael Hamburger. MGP
Morning After, The. Heine, *tr. fr. German by* Louis Untermeyer. ErPo; UnTE
Morning after Death, The. Emily Dickinson. *See* Bustle in the house, The.
Morning and evening. Goblin Market. Christina Rossetti. VP
Morning at the Window. T. S. Eliot. CABA; WePo
Morning comes, and thickening clouds prevail, The. The Clouded Morning. Jones Very. WePo
Morning comes, The; not slow, with reddening gold. Sonnets, Part I, XXII. Frederick Goddard Tuckerman. AP
Morning comes to consciousness, The. T. S. Eliot. *Fr.* Preludes. PoPo
Morning Express. Siegfried Sassoon. WePo
Morning Glory, The. Confucius, *tr. fr. Chinese by* Helen Waddell. SiGo
Morning has broken. A Morning Song. Eleanor Farjeon. WePo
Morning haze. Haze. Buson. RePo
Morning Hours, The. *Unknown, tr. fr. Arabic by* Mohammed Marmaduke Pickthall. PoP1
Morning, if this late withered light can claim. The Zonnebeke Road. Edmund Blunden. MMA
Morning is a little lass. Small Song. Frances Frost. RePo
Morning Light the Dew-Drier. Effie Lee Newsome. AmNP
'Morning, Morning. Ray Mathew. PoAu-2

Morning on the Lièvre. Archibald Lampman. SD
Morning Prayer. Nissim Ezekiel. ACV
Morning Prayer, A. Betty Perpetuo. STF
Morning sits outside afraid, The. Night and Morning. Dorothy Aldis. PoSC
Morning Song, A. Eleanor Farjeon. WePo
Morning Song. Sylvia Plath. AnMoPo
Morning Song for a Lover. Howard Sergeant. ToPo
Morning Star. Plato, *tr. fr. Greek by* Shelley. SiGo
Morning Sun. Louis MacNeice. MP
Morning that the world began, The. Why Nobody Pets the Lion at the Zoo. John Ciardi. RePo
Morning; the slow rising of a cold sun. November 22, 1963. Charles Wright. OPP
Morning Watch, The. Henry Vaughan. BoC; MeP
Morning Window. Olive Tilford Dargan. PoNC
Morning Workout. Babette Deutsch. SD
Morning's work went quickly done, The. That Familiar Stranger. Felix Stefanile. FiSC
Morns are meeker than they were, The. Autumn. Emily Dickinson. PoP1
Morrissey and the Black. *Unknown.* BSNS
Morrissey and the Russian. *Unknown.* BSNS
Morrow's Message, The. Dante Gabriel Rossetti. The House of Life, XXXVIII. VP
Mortality. James Devaney. PoAu-1
Mortality. Naomi Long Madgett. NNP
Mortality. *Unknown.* CBEP
Mortality, behold and fear. On the Tombs in Westminster Abbey [or The Tombs in Westminster]. *At. to* Francis Beaumont, *also to* William Basse. GTBS-P; WePo
Morte d'Arthur. Tennyson. ILP; VP
"Old order changeth, yielding place to new, The," *sel.* TRV
Mortgaged to sorrow is this day. Sorrow's Day. Zoe Kincaid Brockman. PoNC
Mortification. George Herbert. FoBA; MeP; SeCP
Mortifying Mistake, A. Anna Maria Pratt. RePo
Mortmain. Robert Penn Warren. PoCh
Morvin. John Fuller. NePoEA-2
Moss-gathering. Theodore Roethke. ILP
Most Foolish Fools, Oh Foolish Mortal Men. Alain Chartier, *tr. fr. French by* Muriel Kittel. AnML
Most Gladly Would I Die of Love. Mechthild von Magdeburg, *tr. fr. German by* R. G. L. Barrett. AnML
Most glorious Lord of life, that on this day. Amoretti, LXVIII [or Easter Morning]. Spenser. BoC; CABA; EnRePo; TRV
Most Hateful Is It to My Eyes. Gace Brulé, *tr. fr. French by* Patricia Terry. AnML
Most High, almighty, good Lord God. The Canticle of the Creatures. St. Francis of Assisi, *tr. by* William M. Davis. AnML
Most high Lord. Cantico del Sole. St. Francis of Assisi, *tr. by* Ezra Pound. CTC
Most like an Arch This Marriage. John Ciardi. MoLP; PoP1
Most Lovely Shade. Edith Sitwell. GTBS-P
Most modern wits, such monstrous fools have shown. Sir Fopling Flutter. Dryden. DiPo
Most near, most dear, most loved and most far. To [or Sonnet to] My Mother. George Barker. BoC; DTC; MP; VaPo
Most of It, The. Robert Frost. CABA; CaFP; PoIE; PoSa
Most-sacred Mountain, The. Eunice Tietjens. MoRP
Most Sovereign Lady. *Unknown.* MeEL
Most sweet it is with unuplifted eyes. The Inner Vision. Wordsworth. GTBS-P
Most Wanted. Robert Watson. PoNC
Most worthye she is in towne, The. In Praise of Ivy. *Unknown.* MeEL
Most wounds can Time repair. At Ease. Walter de la Mare. GTBS-P
Mother, The. S. S. Gardons. NePoEA-2
Mother, The. Nettie Palmer. PoAu-1
Mother. Margaret Widdemer. STF
Mother and Her Son on the Cross, The. *Unknown.* MeEL
Mother and son. Bedtime Tales. Joseph Joel Keith. FiSC
Mother bore this infant in the white moon. Sebastian in Dream. Georg Trakl. MGP
Mother by the Cradle, The. Matthias Claudius, *tr. fr. German by* D. G. Wright. AGP
Mother Goose. *Unknown.* SoPo
Mother Goose Rhyme. Kenneth Rexroth. ErPo
Mother, I Cannot Mind My Wheel. Walter Savage Landor. CABA; StP
Mother I longs to get married. Whistle Daughter Whistle. *Unknown.* ErPo
Mother, I Shall Not Sleep. *Unknown, tr. fr. Spanish by* William M. Davis. AnML
Mother Is a Sun, A. Peggy Bennett. PoSC
Mother likes the frocks and hats. Shop Windows. Rose Fyleman. SoPo
Mother Marie Therese. Robert Lowell. CoPo
Mother, Mother, Make My Bed. *Unknown.* ELP
"Mother, mother, now I'm married." Bill the Weaver. *Unknown.* BSNS

Mother, my Mary Gray. The Division of Parts. Anne Sexton. NePoEA-2
Mother needs Thee, Lord, A. A Mother's Prayer. Jeanette Saxton Coon. STF
Mother o' Mine. Kipling. TRV
"Mother of heaven, regina of the clouds." Le Monocle de Mon Oncle. Wallace Stevens. AP
Mother, oh mother, come shake out your cloth! Song for a Fifth Child. Ruth H. Hamilton. LV
Mother says. Counting Sheep. Eileen Fisher. SoPo
Mother says I'm six. Hard Lines. Tom Robinson. BiCB
Mother, See My Love! *Unknown, tr. fr. Spanish by* William M. Davis. AnML
Mother to Son. Langston Hughes. AmNP; BiCB; LV
Mother took/ Some milk and flour. The Miracle. Elsie Melchert Fowler. BiCB
Mother who owns Christ as Lord, The. God's Ideal Mother. Cora M. Pinkham. STF
Mother will not turn, who thinks she hears, The. Broken Music. Dante Gabriel Rossetti. The House of Life, XLVII. VP
Mothers-in-Law. Robert Sward. CoPo
Mother's Party. Aileen Fisher. BiCB
Mother's Prayer, A. Jeanette Saxton Coon. STF
Mother's Soliloquy, A. Hetty Wright. WaPE
Mother's Tale, The. Eleanor Farjeon. BiCB
Mothers who raise. Double Duty. W. E. Farbstein. PoP1
Moth's kiss, first, The. Robert Browning. *Fr.* In a Gondola. UnTE
Motive for Metaphor, The. Wallace Stevens. AP
Motives of Rhythm, The. Robert Conquest. PP
Motley. Walter de la Mare. MMA
Motor Cars. Rowena Bennett. SoPo
Motto, The. Abraham Cowley. SeCP
Motto to the Songs of Innocence and of Experience. Blake. FoBA
Mounsier Mingo. *Unknown.* CBEP
Mt. Lykaion. Trumbull Stickney. AmLP
Mount of Olives. Henry Vaughan. MeP
Mountain, The. Robert Frost. FaBV
Mountain and the Squirrel, The. Emerson. *See* Fable: "Mountain and the squirrel, The."
Mountain Cottage, The, *with music.* John A. Stone. SGR
Mountain held the town as in a shadow, The. The Mountain. Robert Frost. FaBV
Mountain over Aberdare, The. Alun Lewis. ACV
Mountain road climbed round a cliff, The. Far Bugles. Olive Tilford Dargan. PoNC
Mountain sat upon the plain, The. Emily Dickinson. FaBV
Mountain sheep are sweeter, The. The War-Song of Dinas Vawr. Thomas Love Peacock. *Fr.* The Misfortunes of Elphin. CABA; EvOK; OnMSP; StP; WiR
Mountain Song of Finojosa. Marqués de Santillana, *tr. fr. Spanish by* Martin Nozick. AnML
Mountain stream, A. The Little Valley in Spring. Onitsura. SiGo
Mountain Whippoorwill, The. Stephen Vincent Benét. SIV
Mts. & Rivers, *sel.* Gary Snyder.
Market, The. CoPo
Mountains in the Desert, The ("The mountains blue now"). Robert Creeley. CoPo
Mountaineers, The. Dannie Abse. PP
Mountains. Zoe Kincaid Brockman. *Fr.* Three Cinquains. PoNC
Mountains, The. Walker Gibson. SD
Mountains and plains. Winter. Joso. SiGo
Mountains Are a Lonely Folk, The. Hamlin Garland. RePo
Mountains are moving, rivers. The Redwoods. Louis Simpson. PP
Mountains, The? Rising from some wet ravine. The Mountains. Walker Gibson. SD
Mountains they are silent folk, The. The Mountains Are a Lonely Folk. Hamlin Garland. RePo
Mournful muse of two despairing swains, The. The Eighth Pastoral of Virgil. Vergil. *Fr.* Eclogues. EiCP
Mourning. Andrew Marvell. CABA; SeCP
Mourning. Josephine Van Fossan. STF
Mourning of the Mother of Lorenzo Dávalos. Juan de Mena, *tr. fr. Spanish by* William M. Davis. AnML
Mouse, The. Elizabeth J. Coatsworth. SoPo
Mouse, The. Hilda Conkling. SoPo
Mouse, The. Jean Garrigue. MP
Mouse, The. Hugh McCrae. PoAu-1
Mouse like halting clockwork, in the light, The. Little Fable. Roy Fuller. DaDu
Mouse That Gnawed the Oak-Tree Down, The. Vachel Lindsay. ILP; LOW
Mouse Whose Name Is Time, The. Robert Francis. LOW
Mousemeal. Howard Nemerov. MP
Mouth of a girl who had lain long in the reeds, The. Beautiful Childhood. Gottfried Benn. *Fr.* Morgue. TwGP
Mouth of the Hudson, The. Robert Lowell. CoPo
Mouth to mouth joined we lie, her naked breasts. Tantalos. Paulus Silentiarius. ErPo

Move him into the sun. Futility. Wilfred Owen. CBEP; GTBS-P; MMA
Moved by the miracles of saints. The Raising of the Dead. Rosemary Dobson. PoAu-2
Movie Queen. James P. Vaughn. NNP
Movies for the Home. Howard Moss. NePoEA-2
Mower against Gardens, The. Andrew Marvell. ILP; PP
Mower to the Glow-Worms, The. Andrew Marvell. BoC; CBEP; ELP; SeCP
Mower's Song, The. Andrew Marvell. SeCP
Mowing. Robert Frost. DiPo
Mowing, The. Sir Charles G. D. Roberts. OBCV
Moyst with one drop of thy blood, my dry soule. Resurrection. John Donne. MeP
Much Ado about Nothing, sels. Shakespeare.
    Epitaph: "Done to death by slanderous tongues," fr. V, iii. CTC
    Sigh No More [Ladies], fr. II, iii. BoLP; CBEP; CTC; DiPo; ELP
    Song: "Pardon, goddess of the night," fr. V, iii. CTC
Much had passed/ Since last we parted. Byron Recollected at Bologna. Samuel Rogers. Fr. Italy. OBNC
Much have I travell'd [or travelled] in the realms of gold. On First Looking into Chapman's Homer. Keats. CABA; CaFP; CBEP; DiPo; FaBV; FaPL; FoBA; GTBS-P; ILP; OBNC; PoIE; RoGo; StP
Much madness is divinest sense. Emily Dickinson. AP; CBEP; DiPo; ILP
Mud ("Mud is very nice to feel"). Polly Chase Boyden. FaBV; SoPo
Mud put. The House. Robert Creeley. CoPo
Mud Turtles. Grace Taber Hallock. RePo
Muffled drum's sad roll has beat, The. The Bivouac of the Dead. Theodore O'Hara. FaPL
Muiopotmos, sel. Spenser.
    Butterfly, The. BoC
Muirland Meg. Burns. ErPo
    (She'll Do It.) UnTE
Mulberry Garden, The, sel. Sir Charles Sedley.
    Child and Maiden, fr. III, ii. GTBS-P
Mullabinda. David Rowbotham. PoAu-2
Mullion. A. P. Herbert. SD
Multi-colored hosts drift down the sky, The. Two Leaves. Jesse Stuart. FiSC
Mumps. Elizabeth Madox Roberts. SoPo
Municipal Gallery Revisited, The. W. B. Yeats. GTBS-P
Murder House. Elizabeth J. Coastworth. FiSC
Murder in the Cathedral, sel. T. S. Eliot.
    Forgive Us, O Lord. EaLo
Murder of Moses, The. Karl Shapiro. EaLo
Murdered Girl, The (C vers.). Unknown. BSO
Murmur, A; and your house grows dim. Under the Rain. Eugenio Montale. CoIP
Murmur of a bee, The. Mysteries. Emily Dickinson. TRV
Muse, disgusted at an age and clime, The. On the Prospect of Planting Arts and Learning in America. George Berkeley. PP
Muse-haunted. Hugh McCrae. PoAu-1
Muse, The/ in her dark habit. The Well. Denise Levertov. AP
Muse of Water, A. Carolyn Kizer. AnMoPo
Muse should be sprightly, The. A Skeltoniad. Michael Drayton. PP
Musée des Beaux Arts. W. H. Auden. CABA; CaFP; DiPo; GTBS-P; MP; PoIE; PoSa; StP
Muses' Elysium, The, sel. Michael Drayton.
    Poet's Paradise, The. WiR
Muse's fairest light in no dark time, The. On Ben Jonson. Sidney Godolphin. CBEP
Museum Piece. Richard Wilbur. PoIE; PoPl
Mushroom Gatherers, The. Donald Davie. NePoEA-2
Mushroom is the elf of plants, The. Emily Dickinson. DiPo
Mushrooms. Sylvia Plath. AnMoPo; NePoEA-2
Music. Conrad Aiken. AP
Music. Baudelaire, tr. fr. French by Robert Fitzgerald. SiGo
Music. George Du Maurier, after the French of Sully-Pru-dhomme. CBEP
Music. Emerson. FaBV
Music and Drum. Archibald MacLeish. MoRP
Music I heard with you was more than music. Discordants. Conrad Aiken. BoLP; PoPo
Music in the Air. Ronald McCuaig. ErPo
Music Makers, The. Arthur O'Shaughnessy. FaBV
Music of Colours: The Blossom Scattered. Vernon Watkins. ACV
Music, When Soft Voices Die. Shelley. FaBV; GTBS-P; PoSa
    (To ———.) ILP; OBNC; PoPo
Musical Instrument, A. Elizabeth Barrett Browning. OnMSP
    (Great God Pan, The.) WiR
Musician. Louise Bogan. GoJo
Musicks Duell. Richard Crashaw. SeCP
Musings. William Barnes. OBNC
Musing by a River. Moses Browne. WaPE

Musings of an Insomniac. Edith Ogutsch. FiSC
Musk-ox smells, The. The Long River. Donald Hall. NePoEA-2
Musketaquid. Emerson. AP
Musophilus, sel. Samuel Daniel.
    "How many thousands never heard the name." PP
Must morning always come again? "Novalis." Fr. Hymns to the Night, II. TwGP
Mustang Gray, The, with music. Unknown. BFSS
Mustapha, sel. Fulke Greville.
    O Wearisome Condition. CBEP
Mutability. Shelley. CBEP; OBNC; PoPo
Mutability. Wordsworth. CABA; FoBA; StP
Mutterings over the Crib of a Deaf Child. James Wright. PoPl; StP
Muzak played its groceries. The Assassination. Marvin Solomon. OPP
My Absent God. Cecil Hemley. PoDB
My aged friend, Miss Wilkinson. The Bards. Walter de la Mare. DTC
My Ain Countree. Mary Demarest. TRV
My Airedale Dog. W. L. Mason. SoPo
My America. Oliver La Grone. NNP
My ancestor was called on to go out. The Wind at Your Door. Robert D. Fitzgerald. PoAu-2
My Anna! though thine earthly steps are done. Sonnets, Part II, XXXIV. Frederick Goddard Tuckerman. AP
My Anna! When for her my head was bowed. Sonnets, Part II, XXXI. Frederick Goddard Tuckerman. AP
My annals have it so. Emus. Mary Fullerton. PoAu-1
My aspens dear, whose airy cages quelled. Binsey Poplars, Felled 1879. Gerard Manley Hopkins. AnMoPo; ELP; PoPo; VP
"My author and disposer, what thou biddest." Thus Eve to Adam. Milton. Fr. Paradise Lost. FaBV
My ball is in a bunch of fern. Mullion. A. P. Herbert. SD
My beautiful love, keep bound me. Heine, tr. fr. German by Meno Spann. AGP
My Bed. Lucy Sprague Mitchell. SoPo
My bed is so empty that I keep on waking up. Winter Night. Unknown. WePo
My Bible and I. Unknown. STF
My birthday is coming and I will be six. The Birthday Bus. Mary Ann Hoberman. BiCB
My birthday is coming tomorrow. Growing Up. Unknown. BiCB
My Birthday's in Winter. Zhenya Gay. BiCB
My blessed Lord, art thou a lilly flower? Meditation. Cant. 2.1. The Lilly of the Vallies. Edward Taylor. Fr. Pre-paratory Meditations, First Series. MeP
My Boat Swings Out and Back. Laurence Binyon. WePo
My body being dead, my lims unknown. The Preparative. Thomas Traherne. MeP
My Body in the Walls. Sir Walter Ralegh. CBEP
My body leaves you drop by drop. Absence. "Gabriela Mistral." AnSP
My Bonnie Highland Laddie. Burns. UnTE
My Book of Life. Frances Humphrey. STF
My Books I'd Fain Cast Off, I Cannot Read. Henry David Thoreau. AP
My Brother. Dorothy Aldis. SoPo
My Brother Bert. Ted Hughes. BBGG
My brother Cain, the wounded, liked to sit. Abel. Demetrios Capetanakis. GTBS-P
My brother is inside the sheet. My Brother. Dorothy Aldis. SoPo
My brother Jack was nine in May. The Baby's Debut. James Smith. Par
My Burial Place. Robinson Jeffers. AP
My Cabinets Are Oyster-Shells. Margaret Cavendish, Duchess of Newcastle. ELP
My candle burns at both ends. First Fig [or Figs from Thistles]. Edna St. Vincent Millay. FaBV; PoLF
My cares draw on mine everlasting night. To Delia, XXX. Samuel Daniel. PoIE
My cat. Cat. Dorothy Baruch. SoPo
My Cat Jeoffry. Christopher Smart. See For I Will Consider My Cat Jeoffry.
My cat, washing her tail's tip, is a whorl. Cat on Couch. Barbara Howes. PoSa
My child, my sister, dream. Invitation to the Voyage. Baude-laire. SiGo
My childhood are remembrances of a court in Seville. Portrait. Antonio Machado. AnSP
My childhood is a sphere. The Review. Thomas Traherne. CBEP
My childhood's home I see again. Memory. Abraham Lincoln. LV
My Ciociara Night. Libero de Libero, tr. fr. Italian by Carlo L. Golino. CoIP
My clear-cut heart, my tender soul. Jules Laforgue. Fr. Asides from the Clowns. PoPl
My Cleo's blush is tender, slow. Tender, Slow. Unknown. ErPo
My Companion. Charles Wesley. STF

My Company. Sir Herbert Read. MMA
My Country. Dorothea Mackellar. PoAu-1
My country, 'tis of thee. America. Samuel Francis Smith. PoLF
My country, 'tis to thee and all thy ways. Star-spangled Ode. Phyllis McGinley. ThLM
My cousins, lean hunters. Love Lifted Me. Paris Leary. CoPo
My creditors, whcse hearts no poem stirs. Marot to the Queen of Navarre. Clément Marot. RBL
My Creed. Howard Arnold Walter. See I Would Be True.
My Daily Creed. Unknown. See Creed, A.
My Daily Prayer. Eva Gray. STF
My Dancing Day. Unknown. CBEP
My dark-headed Käthchen, my spit-kitten darling. Song. John Manifold. BoLP; DTC
My darkling child the stars have obeyed. George Barker. Fr. To My Son. MP
My Darling Dear, My Daisy Flower. John Skelton. See Lullay, Lullay, Like a Child.
My daughter cries, and I. Child Crying. Anthony Thwaite. NePoEA-2
My day was filled with many things. Crowded Out. Florence White Willett. STF
My days among the dead are passed. The Scholar. Robert Southey. GTBS-P
My days are in the yellow leaf. Byron. Fr. On This Day I Complete My Thirty-sixth year. TRV
My Days of Love Are Over. Byron. Fr. Don Juan. OBNC
My dead father speaks to me. Death Mask of a Fisherman. George Bruce. ACV
My dear—:/ I do thank you. Letter for Melville 1951. Charles Olson. CoPo
My dear and only love, I pray. I'll Never Love Thee More. James Graham, Marquess of Montrose. CBEP
My dear Daddie bought a mansion. The Little Bird. Walter de la Mare. BiCB
My dear, darkened in sleep, turned from the moon. To Judith Asleep. John Ciardi. MoLP; ToPo
My dear, dumb friend, low lying there. To My Dog "Blanco." Josiah Gilbert Holland. BiCB
My dear, when you. For Vicki at Seven. Sydney King Russell. BiCB
My deare, deare, Lord I do thee Saviour call. Meditation on Can. 1.3. Thy Name Is an Ointment Poured Out. Edward Taylor. Fr. Preparatory Meditations, First Series. MeP
My Dearest Mistress. Unknown. EnRePo
My Death. A. J. M. Smith. OBCV
"My deth I love, my lif ich hate." A Cleric Courts His Lady. Unknown. MeEL
My Didyma is dark, but I aspire. Didyma. Unknown. UnTE
My dishes went unwashed today. Labor Not in Vain. Unknown. STF
My Dog. Marchette Chute. SoPo
My Dog. Tom Robinson. SoPo
My dog lay dead five days without a grave. The Pardon. Richard Wilbur. ToPo
My dog listens when I talk. My Dog. Tom Robinson. SoPo
My dog's so furry I've not seen. The Hairy Dog. Herbert Asquith. SoPo
My duchess was the werst she laffed she bitte. Sonnet. Ernest Walsh. ErPo
My Early Home. John Clare. PoLF
My eighth spring in England I walk among. This Landscape, These People. Zulfikar Ghose. ACV
My enemies came to get me. A Form of Adaptation. Robert Creeley. AmPC
My enemy had bidden me as guest. The Compassionate Fool. Norman Cameron. CBEP; GTBS-P
My epitaph write on your heart. Love's Epitaph. William Cavendish, Duke of Newcastle. CBEP
My eye cannot turn toward you. The First of May. Barbara Guest. AmPC
My eyes are filmed, my beard is grey. The Time of the Barmacides. James Clarence Mangan. RoGo
My Face. Anthony Euwer. PoLF
My face is wet with rain. Walking at Night. Amory Hare. PoLF
My faint spirit was sitting in the light. From the Arabic, an Imitation. Shelley. CBEP
My Fair Lady. Unknown. See Who Shall Have My Fair Lady?
My fairest child, I have no song to give you. A Farewell. Charles Kingsley. LV
My Faith. Schiller, tr. fr. German by Walter Kaufmann. TwGP
My father bequeathed me no wide estates. Heirloom. A. M. Klein. OBCV
My father could go down a mountain faster than I. That Dark Other Mountain. Robert Francis. SD
My father died in nineteen thirty-four. Sonnet for John-John. Marvin Solomon. OPP
My father died when I was all too young. Sestina of Youth and Age. Gelett Burgess. LV

My father has a pair of shoes. Shoes. Tom Robinson. SoPo
My Father in the Night Commanding No. Louis Simpson. MP; NePoEA-2
My father is a quiet man. Fruit of the Flower. Countee Cullen. PoLF
My Father Loved the Jumping-off Place. Robert P. Tristram Coffin. RePo
My Father Moved through Dooms of Love. E. E. Cummings. AnMoPo; AP; CaFP; PoCh; PoIE; VaPo
My father played the melodion. Patrick Kavanagh. Fr. A Christmas Childhood. DTC
My father used to say. Silence. Marianne Moore. PoIE; PoPo; PoSa
My father was a pioneer. My Father Loved the Jumping-off Place. Robert P. Tristram Coffin. RePo
My father was a wealthy merchant. No, Sir. Unknown. BSO
My father was always out in the garage. E. W. Mandel. Fr. Minotaur Poems. OBCV
My father was born with a spade in his hand and traded it. Elegy. John Ciardi. ToPo
My father, what thou lackst thou givest me. Transcendence Wouldn't Do. Jacques Audiberti. CoFP
My Father's Servant Boy. Unknown. BSNS
My Father's way may twist and turn. He Maketh No Mistake. A. M. Overton. STF
My favorite café—so I dreamed recently. Dangerous Establishment. Erich Kästner. MGP
My favorite dress. Her Favorites. Mattie Lee Hausgen. PoPl
My feet live here in a small house. Roommates. James Larkin Pearson. PoNC
My feet took a walk in heavenly grass. Heavenly Grass. Tennessee Williams. PoPl
My, Fellowship, with, God. José Garcia Villa. EaLo
My fingers are but stragglers at the rear. Stragglers. Pietro Aretino. ErPo
My first thought was, he lied in every word. "Childe Roland to the Dark Tower Came." Robert Browning. VP
My folk, now answere me. Jesus Reproaches His People. Unknown. MeEL
My fortitude is all awry. She Sees Another Door Opening. Firman Houghton. Par
My Friend. Marjorie Lorene Buster. STF
My friend from Asia has powers and magic, he plucks a blue leaf from the young blue-gum. Credo. Robinson Jeffers. PoPl
My Friend Is Going, Mother. Pero Meogo, tr. fr. Portuguese by William M. Davis. AnML
My Friend, the Things That Do Attain. Martial, tr. by the Earl of Surrey. See Martial, the Things for to Attain.
My friend told me about kids in a coffee house. On Not Writing an Elegy. Richard Frost. OPP
My friends are borne to one another. Martin Buber in the Pub. Max Harris. PoAu-2
My Galley [Charged with Forgetfulness]. Petrarch, tr. fr. Italian by Sir Thomas Wyatt. Sonnets to Laura: To Laura in Life, CLVI. CABA; CBEP; DiPo; ILP; RBL (Lover Compareth His State to a Ship in Perilous Storm Tossed on the Sea, The.) StP
My Garden. Thomas Edward Brown. FaBV; PoLF; TRV
My Ghostly Father. Charles d'Orléans. CBEP (Confession of a Stolen Kiss.) MeEL
My girl is thin, yet that is why. True Love. Unknown. UnTE
My girl, thou gazest much. The Lover to His Lady. George Turberville. CTC
My girl's tall with hard long eyes. E. E. Cummings. Fr. Sonnets—Realities. UnTE
My God, how gracious art thou! I had slipt. The Relapse. Henry Vaughan. MeP
My God, I heard this day. Man. George Herbert. CABA; MeP; SeCP
My God, if writings may. Obedience. George Herbert. MeP
My God, is any hour so sweet. The Hour of Prayer. Charlotte Elliott. STF
My God is Love. Love. Toyohiko Kagawa. TRV
My God, my God, what queer corner am I in? In the Deep Museum. Anne Sexton. ToPo
My God, thou that didst dye for me. The Dedication. Henry Vaughan. MeP
My God, when I walke in those groves. Religion. Henry Vaughan. MeP
My God, whose law is that ancient heat towards thee. Sonnet [or Untitled]. George Herbert. LV; MeP
My God, whose law I believe in, and have signed to serve in my best. Prayer on the Night before Easter. John Holmes. MoRP
"My golden spurs now bring to me." James Russell Lowell. Fr. The Vision of Sir Launfal. SIV
My Good Old Man, with music. Unknown. BFSS
My grandmother lived on yonder little green. Little Johnny Green [or Grandma's Song]. Unknown. BSNS; BSO
My Grandmother said, "Now isn't it queer." Wonders of Nature. Unknown. ThGo

My Grandmother's Funeral. Jascha Kessler. AmPC
My granny saw the devil walk at twilight. Top Hat and Tales. Lorna Beers. FiSC
My Grave. Thomas Osborne Davis. ACV
My grey-barked trees wave me in. I Stroll. Peter Redgrove. NePoEA-2
My Grief on the Sea. *Unknown, tr. fr. Modern Irish by* Douglas Hyde. HaSV; SiGo
My guest! I have not led you thro'. Interlude. Walter Savage Landor. GTBS-P
My hair is gray [or grey], but not with years. The Prisoner of Chillon. Byron. CABL; PoLF
My hand is left but one. The Prisoner. Rainer Maria Rilke. TwGP
My happy days are past. The Unhappy Miner. *Unknown.* SGR
My head is bald, my breath is bad. Late-flowering Lust. John Betjeman. ErPo
My heart aches, and a drowsy numbness pains. Ode to a Nightingale. Keats. CABA; CaFP; DiPo; FaPL; FoBA; GTBS-P; ILP; OBNC; OnP; PoIE; PoPo; StP; VaPo
My Heart and Body Wish to Take Their Leave. Friedrich von Hausen, *tr. fr. German by* Gillian Barker *and* Kenneth Gee. AnML
My heart dissolved to see Thee bleed. At the Cross. *Unknown.* STF
My heart, I cannot still it. Auspex. James Russell Lowell. AmLP; AP
My heart is a dark forest where no voice is heard. Solitudes. John Hall Wheelock. MoLP
My Heart Is Captive to Gray, Laughing Eyes. Christine de Pisan, *tr. fr. French by* James Edward Tobin. AnML
My heart is empty. All the fountains that should run. Aridity. C. S. Lewis. BoC
My Heart Is Heich Abufe. *Unknown, at. to* Alexander Scott. ErPo
My heart is like a singing bird. A Birthday. Christina Rossetti. BoLP; FaPL; VP; WiR
My heart is sore—I dare not tell. For the Sake of Somebody. Burns. WePo
My Heart Leaps Up [When I Behold]. Wordsworth. BiCB; CABA; CaFP; DiPo; FaBV; FoBA; GTBS-P; ILP; LV; OBNC; PoPl; PoPo; PoSa; SoPo; TRV (Rainbow, The.) CBEP; RoGo
My heart less out of tune with all it loved. Rediscovered Country. André Frénaud. CoFP
My Heart, My Heart Is Mournful. Heine, *tr. fr. German by* James Thomson. PoPl
My heart—the wretched thing—is today. With Its Quiet Tongue. Kamala Das. ACV
My Heart Was Wandering in the Sands. Christopher Brennan. *Fr.* The Twilight of Disquietude. PoAu-1
My Heart's Desire. *Unknown.* STF
My Heart's in the Highlands. Burns. PoPl; SD
My Hiding Place. Kathryn T. Bowsher. STF
My hopes retire; my wishes as before. Walter Savage Landor. *Fr.* Ianthe. OBNC
My Horses. Jean Jaszi. SoPo
My horse's feet beside the lake. A Farewell. Matthew Arnold. Switzerland, III. VP
My House. Jane W. Krows. SoPo
My House. Robert Pack. PoDB
My House. Robert Louis Stevenson. ILP
My hut in spring! Spring in My Hut. Sodo. RePo
My Influence. *Unknown.* STF
My Joy, My Jockey, My Gabriel. George Barker. *Fr.* First Cycle of Love Poems. DaDu; ErPo
My kitty has a little song. Song for a Child. Helen B. Davis. SoPo
My lady carries love within her eyes. Within Her Eyes. Dante. *Fr.* La Vita Nuova. SiGo
My Lady, if you'd have me whole. Heinrich von Morungen, *tr. fr. German by* R. F. Trimble. AGP
My Lady unto Madam makes her bow. Modern Love, XXXVI. George Meredith. VP
My lady was found mutilated. Ballad. Leonard Cohen. OBCV
My lady woke upon a morning fair. On His Lady's Waking. Pierre de Ronsard. RBL
My Lady's face it is they worship there. Sonetto XXXV: To Guido Orlando. Guido Calvalcanti. CTC
My Last Duchess. Robert Browning. CABA; CaFP; CBEP; DiPo; GTBS-P; ILP; OBNC; OnP; PoIE; PoLF; PoPo; PoSa; StP; VaPo; VP
My lefe is faren in a lond. The One I Love Is Gone Away. *Unknown.* MeEL
My life closed twice before its close. Emily Dickinson. AP; DiPo; FoBA; ILP; PoPl (Parting.) CBEP
My life had stood—a loaded gun. Emily Dickinson. AP
My Life Is like the Summer Rose. Richard Henry Wilde. FaPL
My Life, My Death. Hans Egon Holthusen, *tr. fr. German by* Marianne Leibholz. MGP

My life shall touch a dozen lives. My Influence. *Unknown.* STF
My light thou art, without thy glorious sight. To His Mistress. Earl of Rochester. BoLP
My limbs are wasted with a flame. La Bella Donna della Mia Mente. Oscar Wilde. UnTE
My Limbs I Will Fling. William Strode. CBEP
My limbs were weary, and my head oppressed. The Nightingale. *Unknown.* StP
My little bird, how canst thou sit. Of the Child with the Bird at the Bush. Bunyan. CBEP
My little boy, with pale, round cheeks. The Shadows. George Macdonald. TRV
My little breath, under the willows by the water-side we used to sit. A Lover's Lament. *Unknown.* SiGo
My Little Girl Went to the Sea. Federico García Lorca, *tr. fr. Spanish by* Rachel Benson *and* Robert O'Brien. AnSP
My little son, who look'd from thoughtful eyes. The Toys. Coventry Patmore. *Fr.* The Unknown Eros. BoC; CBEP; FaPL; TRV
My little stone. Notes Found near a Suicide. Frank Horne. AmNP
My Log Cabin Home, *with music.* John A. Stone. SGR
My long two-pointed ladder's sticking through a tree. After Apple-picking. Robert Frost. AP; CaFP; DiPo; FoBA; RoGo; StP
My Lord, Although I Strum and Sing. Colin Muset, *tr. fr. French by* Norman R. Shapiro. AnML
My Lord Dragoman, If I Had a Good Steed. Peire Vidal, *tr. fr. Provençal by* Maurice Valency. AnML
My Lord I fain would praise thee well but finde. Meditation. 1 Cor. 3.22. Death Is Yours. Edward Taylor. *Fr.* Preparatory Meditations, First Series. MeP
My Lord Ibrahim. *Unknown, tr. fr. Spanish by* William M. Davis. AnML
My Lord my Life, can envy ever bee. Meditation. 1 Cor. 3.22. Life Is Youres. Edward Taylor. *Fr.* Preparatory Meditations, First Series. MeP
My Lords, I Pray You Now, Give Ear. Raimbaut d'Aurenga, *tr. fr. Provençal by* Maurice Valency. AnML
My lord's young daughter in the earth finds rest. The Step Mother. Helen Adam. FiSC
My Lost Youth. Longfellow. AP; FaBV; GoJo; OnP; PoLF; RoGo; StP (Lost Youth.) HaSV
My Love. E. E. Cummings. ErPo
My Love. James Russell Lowell. FaPL
My love/ Is like the grasses. Ono no Yoshiki. *Fr. Kokin Shu.* SiGo
My love and I we took a walk. On the Banks of the Old Peedee. *Unknown.* BSO
My Love behind Walls. Heather Spears. OBCV
My Love bound me with a kiss. Kisses Make Men Loath to Go. *Unknown.* UnTE
My love came up from Barnegat. The Puritan's Ballad. Elinor Wylie. BoLP
My love comes down from the mountain. Love on the Mountain. Thomas Boyd. BoLP
"My love for you has faded"—thus the Bad. Versions of Love. Roy Fuller. ToPo
My love has talk'd with rocks and trees. In Memoriam A. H. H., XCVII. Tennyson. StP
My love hath vowed he will forsake me. A Maid's Complaint. Thomas Campion. UnTE
My love, he built me a bonny bower. Lament of a Border Widow. *Unknown.* BFSS
My love in her attire doth show her wit. Beauty Self. *Unknown.* GTBS-P; UnTE
My love is as a fever, longing still. Sonnets, CXLVII. Shakespeare. CBEP; DiPo; FoBA
My Love Is Dead. Thomas Chatterton. *See* Minstrel's Song.
My Love Is in a Light Attire. James Joyce. Chamber Music, VII. LOW; StP
My Love is like to ice, and I to fire. Amoretti, XXX. Spenser. ErPo
My Love Is Near. Goethe, *tr. fr. German by* Francis Owen. AGP (Nearness of Her Lover, *tr. by* Walter Kaufmann.) TwGP
My Love Is neither Young nor Old. *Unknown.* EnRePo
My love is o' comely height an' straight. White an' Blue. William Barnes. GTBS-P
My love is of a birth so rare. The Definition of Love. Andrew Marvell. CBEP; DiPo; PoIE; SeCP; StP; VaPo
My Love Is Sleeping. Kenneth Leslie. OBCV
My Love is the voice of a song. David McKee Wright. *Fr.* Dark Rosaleen. PoAu-1
My love lies in the gates of foam. The Churchyard on the Sands. Lord De Tabley. OBNC
My love, my lord. Verses Expressing the Feelings of a Lover. Sister Juana Inés de la Cruz. AnSP
My love, my love, thus spoke my love to me. Thus Spoke My Love. Pieter Corneliszoon Hooft. SiGo

My love, this is the bitterest, that thou. Any Wife to Any Husband. Robert Browning. OBNC

My love within a forest walked alone. Love in Moonlight. Bhartrihari. SiGo

My loved, my honored, much respected friend. The Cotter's Saturday Night. Burns. EiCP

My love's manners in bed. The Way. Robert Creeley. AP

My Lute and I. Sir Thomas Wyatt. MeEL

My Lute, Awake. Sir Thomas Wyatt. CABA; CaFP; CBEP; ELP; EnRePo; ILP
(Lover Complayneth the Unkindness of His Love, The.) StP

My lute, be as thou wert when thou didst grow. To His Lute. William Drummond of Hawthornden. GTBS-P

My Luve's [or Luve is] like a Red, Red Rose. See Red Red Rose, A.

My Mall, I mark that when you mean to prove me. The Author to His Wife, of a Woman's Eloquence. Sir John Harington. ErPo

My mammy she told me to give him a stool. An Old Man Who Came over the Moor (D vers.). Unknown. BSO

My Master Was So Very Poor. Harry Lee. TRV

My masters twain made me a bed. The Canoe. Isabella Valancy Crawford. OBCV

My Mate Bill. G. H. Gibson. PoAu-1

My merry mates! to Neptune's praise. A Dialogue. John Dowland. HaSV

My mind has thunderstorms. Thunderstorms. W. H. Davies. LV

My mind lets go a thousand things. Memory. Thomas Bailey Aldrich. AmLP; PoLF

My Mind to Me a Kingdom Is. Sir Edward Dyer. EnRePo; PoIE; PoSa

My mind was once the true survey. The Mower's Song. Andrew Marvell. ScCP

My mistress' eyes are nothing like the sun. Sonnets, CXXX. Shakespeare. BoLP; CABA; CaFP; CBEP; DiPo; FoBA; ILP; PoIE; PP; StP

My Mistress Makes Music ("My mistress is in music passing skillfull"). Unknown. UnTE

My misunderstandings: for years I thought "muso bello" meant "Bell Muse." Taking a Walk with You. Kenneth Koch. AmPC

My Morning Song. George Macdonald. TRV

My Mother. Unknown. STF

My Mother Bids Me Bind My Hair. Anne Hunter. CBEP

My mother bore me in the southern wild. The Little Black Boy. Blake. Fr. Songs of Innocence. BoC; CABA; CaFP; CBEP; DiPo; EnPE; FoBA; ILP; OBNC; PoIE

My mother groaned, my father wept. Infant Sorrow. Blake. Fr. Songs of Experience. CBEP; DiPo; FoBA; OBNC

My mother made me a cambric shirt. The Cambric Shirt (B vers.). Unknown. BFSS

My mother—preferring the strange to the tame. The Intruder. Carolyn Kizer. NePoEA-2

My mother said that I never should. Gypsies in the Wood. Unknown. DTC

My mother she told me to light him to bed. An Old Man Who Came over the Moor (B vers.). Unknown. BSO

My mother, when young, scrubbed laundry in a tub. In an Iridescent Time. Ruth Stone. PoPl

My mother whistled softly. The Little Whistler. Frances Frost. SoPo

My mother's form was spare and keen. Generations. Robert Clark. PoAu-2

My Mother's Love. Unknown. STF

My name engraved herein. A Valediction: Of My Name in the Window. John Donne. EnRePo

My name is Bill. Bill. J. S. Salzburg. BiCB

My name is Duncan Campbell from the town of Argyle. Duncan Campbell. Unknown. BSNS

My name is George Mann. Story of George Mann. Unknown. BSO

My name is Gustave Ohr. Story of Gustave Ohr. Unknown. BSO

My name is Jack Shepherd; I come from Nashville town. The State of Arkansas. Unknown. BFSS

My name is James A. Wright, and I was born. At the Executed Murderer's Grave. James Wright. AmPC

My name is Jew. The Permanent Delegate. Yuri Suhl. PtTo

My name is [or it is] Joe Bowers. Joe Bowers. Unknown, at. to John Woodward. BFSS; SGR

My name is Mr. Worth. Crinolines and Bloomers. Unknown. ThLM

My name is old Jack Palmer. The Old Keg of Rum. Unknown. PoAu-1

My name is Peter Ambelay. Peter Ambelay. Unknown. BSNS

My name it is Robert Anderson, I'll have you understand. The Flying Cloud. Unknown. BSNS

My name it is Joe Bowers. See My name is Joe Bowers.

My namesake, Little Boots, Caligula. Caligula. Robert Lowell. CoPo

My Need. Unknown. STF

My neighbour moves less and less, attempts less. Dark Women. Ted Hughes. ToPo

My New Year Prayer. Unknown. STF

My New Year's drink is mulled tonight. Ancestors. Robert Graves. AnMoPo

My noble, lovely, little Peggy. A Letter to the Honorable Lady Miss Margaret-Cavendish-Holles-Harley. Matthew Prior. EiCP

My November Guest. Robert Frost. PoLF

My Old Beaver Cap, with music. Unknown. BFSS

My Old Bible. Unknown. STF

My Old Black Billy. Edward Harrington. PoAu-1

My old daddy's gone to France. Putman's Hill (A vers.). Unknown. BSO

My Old Kentucky Home. Stephen Foster. FaBV; FaPL; PoLF

My Old Man. Edith Earnshaw. PoNC

My old man's a white old man. Cross. Langston Hughes. AmNP; PoLF

My only need—you ask me, and I tell you. Sonnet XXXIII. Mark Van Doren. MoLP

My only son, more God's than mine. Jesus and His Mother. Thom Gunn. AnMoPo; CaFP; EaLo

My Other Chinee Cook. Brunton Stephens. PoAu-1

My own dim life should teach me this. In Memoriam A. H. H., XXXIV. Tennyson. VP

My Own Heart Let Me Have More Pity On. Gerard Manley Hopkins. PoDB
("My own heart let me more have pity on; let.") BoC; VP

My Papa's Waltz. Theodore Roethke. CaFP; ILP; PoIE; PoSa

My Parents Kept Me from Children Who Were Rough. Stephen Spender. DaDu

My pathway lies through worse than death. Conquest. Georgia Douglas Johnson. AmNP

"My Peace," the peace of the Lord Most High. Peace. Margaret E. Sangster. TRV

My Pen, Take Pain [a Little Space]. Sir Thomas Wyatt. CBEP; PP

My People. Else Lasker-Schüler, tr. fr. German by Michael Hamburger. MGP

My period had come for prayer. Emily Dickinson. EaLo; PoIE

My Picture Left in Scotland. Ben Jonson. EnRePo; SeCP

My pig-faced kingdom with tongues of wrong. Secular Elegies. George Barker. ToPo

My plaid away, my plaid away. The Elfin-Knight. Unknown. BuBa

My Plan. Marchette Chute. BiCB

My Playmate. Whittier. AP

My Policeman. Rose Fyleman. SoPo

My poor old bones—I've only two. The Lonely Scarecrow. James Kirkup. DaDu

My Prayer. Henry David Thoreau. See Great God, I Ask Thee for No Meaner Pelf.

My Prayer. Unknown. STF

My Pretty Colinn. Unknown. See Lady Isabel and the Elf-Knight.

My Pretty Little Miss, with music. Unknown. BFSS

My Pretty Rose-Tree. Blake. Fr. Songs of Experience. FoBA

My prime of youth is but a frost of cares. Elegy [or His Elegy or Lines before Execution]. Chidiock Tichborne. CBEP; PoIE; PoSa

My puppy likes. Puppy. Aileen Fisher. SoPo

My Rambling Son. Unknown. See Lord Randal.

My red horse has his stable. My Horses. Jean Jaszi. SoPo

My rug is red. My couch, whereon I deal. The Map. G. C. Oden. AmNP; NNP

My Sad Captains. Thom Gunn. NePoEA-2; PoCh; ToPo

My Sailor of Seven. Gerald Brenan. BiCB

My sange es in sihting. A Song of Love for Jesus. Richard Rolle. MeEL

My secrets cry aloud. Open House. Theodore Roethke. AP

My sexual feats. Fred Apollus at Fava's. Nicholas Moore. ErPo

My Shadow. Robert Louis Stevenson. FaBV; SoPo

My shattred phancy stole away from mee. Meditation Twenty-nine. Edward Taylor. Fr. Preparatory Meditations, First Series. AP

My ship moves slowly, vast is its age. Beyond the Horizon. Oskar Loerke. MGP

My Ships. Ella Wheeler Wilcox. PoLF

My shoes fall on the house-top that is so far beneath me. Climb. Winifred Welles. BiCB

My Silks and Fine Array. Blake. CBEP; ELP
(Song.) FoBA; OBNC; PoPo

My sin! my sin, My God, these cursed dregs. Meditation. from I Joh. 2.1. If Any Man Sin, We Have an Advocate. Edward Taylor. Fr. Preparatory Meditations, First Series. MeP

My sister and I. Plans. Helen Morgan Brooks. NNP

My sisters played beyond the doorway. Detail from an Annunciation by Crivelli. Rosemary Dobson. PoAu-2

My smallest fault is jealousy. Wilhelm Busch, *tr. fr. German by* Francis Owen. AGP

My Son, Come Tell It to Me, *with music. Unknown.* BFSS

My son, if thou come to serve the Lord, prepare thy soul for temptation. Ecclesiasticus, Bible, Apocrypha. BoC

My son invites me to witness with him. Mousemeal. Howard Nemerov. MP

My song is love unknown. Love Unknown. Samuel Crossman. BoC

My sorrow, when she's here with me. My November Guest. Robert Frost. PoLF

My Sort o' Man. Paul Laurence Dunbar. AmNP

My soul, be not disturbed. Address to My Soul. Elinor Wylie. AmLP; MoRP

My soul is like the oar that momently. Struggle. Sidney Lanier. CBEP

My soul is sad and much dismayed. The Valley of the Shadow of Death. William Cowper. EiCP

My Soul Is Weary of My Life. Job, X: 1-22, Bible, *O.T.* EaLo

My soul stands at the window of my room. Nostalgia. Karl Shapiro. AP; MP

My soul, there is a country. Peace [*or* The Peace of Heaven]. Henry Vaughan. BoC; CBEP; EaLo; ELP; MeP; WePo

My soul thy sacrifice! I choose thee out. Poems of the Arabic. *Unknown. Fr.* The Thousand and One Nights. ErPo

My soule a world is by contraccion. Sonnet. William Alabaster. MeP

My soule is like a bird; my flesh, the cage. Francis Quarles. *Fr.* Emblems. MeP

My soule, Lord, quailes to thinke that I should bee. Meditation. 1 Cor. 3.23. You Are Christ's. Edward Taylor. *Fr.* Preparatory Meditations, First Series. MeP

My Spectre around Me. Blake. CBEP

My spirit is too weak—mortality. On Seeing the Elgin Marbles. Keats. CABA; DiPo; FoBA; PoIE

My Spirit Longeth for Thee. Byron. BoC

My spirit to yours, dear brother. To Him That Was Crucified. Walt Whitman. MoRP

My Spirit Will Not Haunt the Mound. Thomas Hardy. OBNC

My Star. Robert Browning. EvOK

My street goes nowhere. A longwinded street. A Street in North Carolina. Helen Bevington. PoNC

My Sweet Little Honey. *Unknown.* BSO

My Sweet Old Etcetera. *Fr.* Is 5. E. E. Cummings. CABA; PoP1

My Sweetest Lesbia. Thomas Campion, *after the Latin of* Catullus. CABA; CBEP; EnRePo; UnTE (Vivamus, Mea Lesbia.) StP

My Temper. *Unknown.* STF

My tender parents brought me up. The Murdered Girl (C vers.). *Unknown.* BSO

My thoughts are as a garden-plot, that knows. Thy Garden. Mu'tamid, King of Seville. SiGo

My thoughts are perfumed when toward you they turn. Autumn Verses. Rubén Darío. AnSP

My Thoughts Do Harbour. Shakespeare. *Fr.* The Two Gentlemen of Verona, III, i. CTC

My Thoughts Hold Mortal Strife. William Drummond of Hawthornden. CBEP (Madrigal.) GTBS-P

My True Love. Sir Philip Sidney. *See* My True Love Hath My Heart.

My True Love Has Gone to France. *Unknown. See* Putman's Hill.

My True Love Hath My Heart. Sir Philip Sidney. *Fr.* Arcadia. CBEP; DiPo; ILP (Ditty, A: "My true-love hath my heart, and I have his.") GTBS-P (My True Love.) WePo

My True Sailor Boy. *Unknown. See* Sweet William ("Weary are the hours of a sailor boy").

My two white rabbits. Rabbits. Dorothy Baruch. SoPo

My Valentine. Kitty Parsons. SoPo

My very strict Aunt Matilda can't. Aunt Matilda. Barbara Euphan Todd. BoC

My victorious King receives his vestments from mocking. Jean de la Ceppède. *Fr.* Théorèmes Spirituels. RBL

My Wife. Robert Louis Stevenson. WePo (Husband to a Wife, A.) BoC (To My Wife.) TRV

My wife and I lived all alone. Ballad of the Despairing Husband. Robert Creeley. AmPC; ToPo

My wife asleep, her soft face turned from me. Sonnet: The Window. Carl Bode. ToPo

My wife's new pink slippers. The Thinker. William Carlos Williams. MoLP

My Willie's rare, my Willie's fair. Yarrow. *Unknown.* BSO

My window opens out into the trees. Solace. Clarissa Scott Delany. AmNP

My Wish. Patience Strong. RePo

My Woman. Catullus, *tr. fr. Latin by* Gilbert Highet. PoP1

My words and thoughts do both express this notion. Colossians III: 3: Our Life Is Hid with Christ in God. George Herbert. FoBA

My world was full of wonder until men. The Hero. Geoffrey Drake. HaSV

My worthy Lord, I pray you wonder not. Gascoigne's Woodmanship. George Gascoigne. EnRePo

Myall in Prison, The. Mary Gilmore. PoAu-1

Myra. Fulke Greville. *See* I, with Whose Colors.

Myrtle bush grew shady, The. Jealousy. Mary Elizabeth Coleridge. OBNC

Myself standing in the margin of the text. In the Margin of the Text. Gene Frumkin. PtTo

Myself When Young Did Eagerly Frequent. Omar Khayyám, *tr. fr. Persian by* Edward Fitzgerald. *Fr.* The Rubáiyát. EaLo

Myselves/ The grievers. Ceremony after a Fire Raid. Dylan Thomas. PoDB

Mysteries. Emily Dickinson. TRV

Mysterious Cat, The. Vachel Lindsay. GoJo; SoPo

Mysterious in light of day. Sayings. Goethe. AGP

Mysterious Night! when our first parent knew. To Night [*or* Night]. Joseph Blanco White. BoC; CBEP; RoGo

Mysterious Way, The. William Cowper. *See* Light Shining Out of Darkness.

Mystical grammar of amorous glances. John Cleveland. *Fr.* Mark Antony. DiPo

Mythical Journey, The. Edwin Muir. ILP

Mythological Episode. Robert H. Barlow. FiSC

Mythological Sonnets, *sels.* Roy Fuller. "How startling to find the portraits of the gods," XVI. ErPo "Suns in a skein, the uncut stones of night," VIII. GTBS-P

Mythology. Lawrence Durrell. DTC

Myths. Wieland Schmied, *tr. fr. German by* Eva Hesse. MGP

N

Nae heathen name shall I prefix. To Miss Ferrier. Burns. CBEP

Naiad, hid beneath the bank. A Dirge. William Johnson Cory. OBNC

Naked and breast to breast we lie. Tormenting Virgin. *Unknown.* UnTE

Naked and hungry come we into this world. *Unknown.* ThGo

Naked and knowing my heart my love had left on. The Jewels. Baudelaire. ErPo

Naked before the glass she said. Young Woman. Howard Nemerov. ErPo

Naked earth is warm with Spring, The. Into Battle. Julian Grenfell. MMA

Naked Love did to thine eye. Ice and Fire. Giambattista Marino. RBL

Naked she lay, clasped in my longing arms. The Imperfect Enjoyment. Earl of Rochester. ErPo; UnTE

Naked to earth was I brought—naked to earth I descend. Vanity of Vanities. Palladas. TRV

Naked woman and a dead dwarf, A. Three Poems, 3. Stephen Crane. AP

Namaqualand after Rain. William Plomer. ACV

Namby-Pamby. Henry Carey. Par

Name, The. Robert Creeley. CoPo; ToPo

Name for All, A. Hart Crane. PP

Name in block letters. *None that signified.* A Form of Epitaph. Laurence Whistler. GTBS-P

Name is immortal but only the name, for the rest, The. Jew. Karl Shapiro. ToPo

Name of Jesus, The. John Newton. STF

Nameless, he crept from the hutch of creation. Love for a Hare. Melvin Walker La Follette. NePoEA-2

Nameless Maiden, The. *Unknown.* ErPo

Naming of Cats, The. T. S. Eliot. RePo

Naming of Parts. Henry Reed. *Fr.* Lessons of the War. CaFP; DTC; GoJo; ILP; MP; PoP1; StP; WePo

Naming the Baby. May Richstone. BiCB

Nancy Bell and Lord Lover. *Unknown.* See Lord Lovel.

Nancy Hanks. Rosemary Benét. FaBV; LiPo; PoP1; RePo

Nancy Hanks. Harriet Monroe. LiPo

Nancy Hanks, Mother of Abraham Lincoln. Vachel Lindsay. LiPo; ThLM

Narcisse, Le. Charles de Saint-Maure, Duc de Montausier, *tr. fr. French by* Harold M. Priest. *Fr.* Guirlande de Julie. RBL

Narcissus. Donald Petersen. NePoEA-2

Narcissus. John Press. UnTE

Narcissus and Some Tadpoles. Victor J. Daley. PoAu-1
Narcissus, Come Kiss Us! *Unknown.* ErPo
Narrow fellow in the grass, A. Emily Dickinson. AmLP; AP; CABA; CBEP; DiPo; FoBA; GoJo; ILP; LV; PoIE; PoLF
(Snake, The.) PoPo; VaPo
Narrow glade unfolded, such as Spring, A. An Interview near Florence. Samuel Rogers. *Fr.* Italy. OBNC
Narrow River is salty blue. Marooned. Rachel Field. RePo
Narrow, thorny path he trod, The. The Ascetic. Victor J. Daley. PoAu-1
Naso, you are many men's man; and yet. To Naso. Catullus. ErPo
Nathan Hale. Francis Miles Finch. ThLM
Nathan Hale. *Unknown.* SIV
Nation of hayricks spotting the green solace, A. The Airman Who Flew over Shakespeare's England. Hyam Plutzik. PoP1
Nation of trees, drab green and desolate grey, A. Australia. A. D. Hope. ACV
Nation spoke to a nation, A. Our Lady of the Snows. Kipling. ACV
National Cold Storage Company. Harvey Shapiro. OPP
National Miner, The, *with music.* John A. Stone. SGR
National Winter Garden. Hart Crane. *Fr.* The Bridge. ErPo
Nationality. Mary Gilmore. PoAu-1
Nation's Strength, A. Emerson. TRV
Native, The. W. S. Merwin. NePoEA-2
Native Born. Eve Langley. PoAu-2
Nativitie. John Donne. MeP
Nativitie of Christ, The. Robert Southwell. MeP
Nativity. Ruth Gilbert. *Fr.* The Blossom of the Branches. ACV
Nativity, The. *Unknown.* MeEL
Nativity of Christ, The. Luis de Góngora, *tr. fr. Spanish by* Longfellow. RBL
Nativity of Our Lord and Savior Jesus Christ, The. Christopher Smart. *Fr.* Hymns and Spiritual Songs. EiCP
Natural Law. Babette Deutsch. MoLP
Naturally it is night. Air. W. S. Merwin. AmPC; CoPo
Nature. John Clare. CBEP
Nature ("The rounded world is fair to see"). Emerson. ILP
Nature ("A subtle chain of countless rings"). Emerson. AmLP; ILP
Nature. Longfellow. AP; PoLF; TRV
Nature. Jones Very. AP
Nature and Life. George Meredith. PoIE; VP
Nature and the Poet. Wordsworth. *See* Elegiac Stanzas.
Nature at Three. Bettye Breeser. BiCB
Nature Be Damned. Anne Wilkinson. OBCV
Nature doth have her dawn each day. Stanzas. Henry David Thoreau. AmLP
Nature had made them hide in crevices. New Hampshire, February. Richard Eberhart. MP
Nature, it seems, must always clash with Art. Goethe, *tr. fr. German by* Michael Hamburger. AGP
Nature of an Action, The. Thom Gunn. ACV
Nature of Love, The. James Kirkup. EaLo
Nature of Love, The. Lucretius, *tr. fr. Latin by* Dryden. *Fr.* De Rerum Natura. UnTE
Nature one hour appears a thing unsexed. Francis Thompson. *Fr.* Contemplation. OBNC
Nature selects the longest way. A Northern Suburb. John Davidson. OBNC
Nature, That Gave the Bee. Sir Thomas Wyatt. CBEP
Nature, That Washed Her Hands in Milk. Sir Walter Ralegh. CABA; EnRePo
Nature's first green is gold. Nothing Gold Can Stay. Robert Frost. ILP; PoPo; StP
Natures lay Ideot, I taught thee to love. Elegie VII. John Donne. *Fr.* Elegies. SeCP
Nature's Questioning. Thomas Hardy. PoDB; PoIE
Naughty Boy. Robert Creeley. AmPC
Naughty Preposition, The. Morris Bishop. LV
Nausicäa. Irving Layton. ErPo
Nautical Ballad, A. Charles Edward Carryl. RePo
Nautilus Island's hermit. Skunk Hour. Robert Lowell. AP; PoIE
Nay but you, who do not love her. Song. Robert Browning. BoLP
Nay, and visit me, sweet friend. Invitation to a Mistress. *Unknown.* UnTE
Nay, Ivy, Nay. *Unknown.* CBEP
(Holly and Ivy.) MeEL
Nay! nay! Ivy. Holly against Ivy. *Unknown.* MeEL
Nay, pish; nay, phew! faith and will you? fie! A Maiden's Denial [*or* The Reluctant Lady]. *Unknown.* ErPo; UnTE
Nay, tempt me not to love again. Thomas Moore. *Fr.* Odes to Nea. OBNC
Neaera's Kisses. Johannes Secundus, *tr. fr. Latin by* John Nott. *Fr.* Basia. UnTE
Near Avalon. William Morris. CBEP

Near Perigord. Ezra Pound. CABL
Near to the silver Trent. Sirena. Michael Drayton. *Fr.* The Shepherd's Sirena. CBEP
Near Tablada. Hill Song. Juan Ruiz, Archpriest of Hita. *Fr.* The Book of True Love. AnML
Near yonder copse, where once the garden smiled. Goldsmith. *Fr.* The Deserted Village. TRV
Nearer, My God To Thee. Sarah Flower Adams. FaPL
(Nearer to Thee.) PoLF
Nearing again the legendary isle. C. Day Lewis. *Fr.* The Magnetic Mountain. HaSV
Nearness of Her Lover. Goethe. *See* My Love Is Near.
Neat little packet from Hobart set sail, A. The *Waterwitch.* *Unknown.* PoAu-1
Nebraska. Jon Swan. PoPo
Necessity. Harry Graham. WePo
Necks. Rowena Bennett. RePo
Necromancers, The. John Frederick Nims. PoCh
Ned Bratts. Robert Browning. CABL
Need. Babette Deutsch. MoLP
Need of Being Versed in Country Things, The. Robert Frost. PoSa
"Needy Knife-grinder! whither are you going." The Friend of Humanity and the Knife-Grinder. George Canning *and* John Hookham Frere. Par
Negatives, The. Philip Levine. NePoEA-2
Negro Bride. Gottfried Benn, *tr. fr. German by* Walter Kaufmann. *Fr.* Morgue. TwGP
Negro Judge, A. Frederick Seidel. CoPo
Negro Peddler's Song, A. Fenton Johnson. AmNP
Negro Speaks of Rivers, The. Langston Hughes. AmNP
Negro Woman, A. William Carlos Williams. PoIE
Neither Hook nor Line. Bunyan. SD
Neither love, the subtlety of refinement. The Presence. William Everson. ErPo
Neither on horseback nor seated. Walt Whitman at Bear Mountain. Louis Simpson. NePoEA-2; PoCh; PP
Neither Out Far nor in Deep. Robert Frost. AP; CABA; DiPo
Neither Shall They Learn War Any More. Micah, IV: 1-4, Bible, *O.T.* TRV
Neither Spirit nor Bird. *Unknown, tr. fr. Shoshone Indian by* Mary Austin. SiGo
Neither via Belsen, nor as a maid of all work. Kafka in England. Franz Baermann Steiner. MGP
Nekros. Richard O'Connell. OPP
Nell. Raymond Knister. *Fr.* A Row of Stalls. OBCV
Nell scolded in so loud a din. A Quiet Life and a Good Name. Swift. CBEP
Nellie Rakerfield. Nell. Raymond Knister. *Fr.* A Row of Stalls. OBCV
Nelly Trim. Sylvia Townsend Warner. ErPo
Nelson's Victory. *Unknown.* BSNS
Nelson's Victory at Trafalgar. *Unknown.* BSNS
Nemea. Lawrence Durrell. AnMoPo; GTBS-P
Nemean Odes. Pindar. *See* Odes.
Nemesis. Emerson. PoIE
Nenia. Schiller, *tr. fr. German by* Alexander Gode. AGP
Neon glitter of night. Beale Street, Memphis. Thurmond Snyder. NNP
Nepenthe, *sels.* George Darley.
  Hoopoe. OBNC
  In Dreamy Swoon. OBNC
  Onward to Far Ida. OBNC
  Phoenix, The. CBEP; WiR
  (Hundred-sunned Phenix.) OBNC
  Unicorn, The. OBNC
Nephelidia. Swinburne. Par; VP
Neptune and Mars in Council sate. Louisburg. *Unknown.* ThLM
Nesting Ground, The. David Wagoner. PoCh
Nesting Time. Douglas Stewart. PoAu-2
Nestus Gurley. Randall Jarrell. MP
Net, The. W. R. Rodgers. ErPo
Net Menders, The. Brian Vrepont. PoAu-2
Net to Snare the Moonlight, A. Vachel Lindsay. PoLF
Neurotic, The. C. Day Lewis. ACV
Neutral Tones. Thomas Hardy. CABA; ILP; VP
Never Admit the Pain. Mary Gilmore. PoAu-1
Never Another. Mark Van Doren. MoRP
Never, being damned, see paradise. Those Not Elect. Léonie Adams. PoDB
Never forget who brings the rain. Turn of the Moon. Robert Graves. BoC
Never Give All the Heart. W. B. Yeats. MoLP
Never in all my days. An Amorous Thorn. Franco Sacchetti. AnML
Never May the Fruit Be Plucked. Edna St. Vincent Millay. MoLP
Never mind avarice; the hills. Thinking of Hölderlin. Christopher Middleton. NePoEA-2
Never mind the day we left, or the way the women clung to us. The Klondike. E. A. Robinson. ThLM
Never More, Sailor. Walter de la Mare. HaSV

Never More Will the Wind. Hilda Doolittle ("H. D."). CTC
Never, never may the fruit be plucked from the bough. Never May the Fruit Be Plucked. Edna St. Vincent Millay. MoLP
Never Seek to Tell Thy Love. Blake. BoLP; CBEP; ELP; FaBV; OBNC; StP
(Love's Secret.) PoSa
"Never shall a young man." For Anne Gregory. W. B. Yeats. DiPo; DTC; PoSa
Never the Summer Seemed to Me. *Unknown, tr. fr. German by* Elizabeth Closs. AnML
Never the Time and the Place. Robert Browning. CaFP; VP
Never to see ghosts? Then to be. Ghosts. Alastair Reid. FiSC
Never Too Late, *sels.* Robert Greene.
Palmer's Ode, The. CTC; EnRePo
Never until the mankind making. A Refusal to Mourn the Death, by Fire, of a Child in London. Dylan Thomas. AnMoPo; CABA; DiPo; GTBS-P; MP; PoDB; PoIE; PoPl; StP; ToPo; VaPo
Never Weather-beaten Sail. Thomas Campion. BoC; CBEP
New Adam, The. Frank Belknap Long. FiSC
New and the Old, The. Shiki, *tr. fr. Japanese by* Harold G. Henderson. SiGo
New Baby Calf, The. Edith Newlin Chase. SoPo
New Ballad, A. Mary Leapor. WaPE
New Being, The. Kenneth Patchen. ToPo
New Birth, The. Jones Very. AP
New Bundling Song, A. *Unknown.* ErPo
New Church Organ, The. Will Carleton. PoLF
New Colossus, The. Emma Lazarus. FaBV; FaPL; PoLF; PoPl; TRV
New Corn. T'ao Ch'ien, *tr. fr. Chinese by* Arthur Waley. SiGo
New Day, The, *sel.* Richard Watson Gilder.
Prelude: "Night was dark, though sometimes a faint star, The." PoLF
New England. E. A. Robinson. CABA; VaPo
New England was tall clippers. Citizens in the Round. Robert P. Tristram Coffin. RePo
New Every Morning. *Unknown.* STF
New Faces, The. W. B. Yeats. GTBS-P
New feet within my garden go. Emily Dickinson. DiPo
New Garden, The. Reginald Arkell. RePo
New Generation, The. Schiller, *tr. fr. German by* Walter Kaufmann. TwGP
New Guinea. James McAuley. PoAu-2
New Hampshire. T. S. Eliot. Landscapes, I. GTBS-P; LOW; PoSa
New Hampshire. Donald Hall. NePoEA-2
New Hampshire, February. Richard Eberhart. MP
New Heaven, New Warre. Robert Southwell. MeP
New Icarus, The. Vassar Miller. ToPo
New Leaf, The. *Unknown.* STF
New Leaves. Juan Ramón Jiménez, *tr. fr. Spanish by* H. R. Hays. PoPl
New Letter Writer, The. Helen Bevington. PoNC
New Man, The. Jones Very. AP
New Moon in January. Ted Hughes. ToPo
New Neighbor, The. Rose Fyleman. SoPo
New neighbors came to the corner house at Congress and Green Streets. Clean Curtains. Carl Sandburg. LV
New Pastoral, The, *sel.* Thomas Buchanan Read.
Blennerhassett's Island. ThLM
New Prince, New Pomp. Robert Southwell. ELP; MeP
New Ring, The. Karl Shapiro. MoLP
New River Shore, The. *Unknown.* BSNS
"New Shirt, A!" Why? Paul Grano. PoAu-2
New Shoes. Marjorie S. Watts. SoPo
New shoes, now shoes. Choosing Shoes. ffrida Wolfe. SoPo
New Song of Mary, A. *Unknown.* MeEL
New Song to Sing about Jonathan Bing, A. Beatrice Curtis Brown. SoPo
New Strain. George Starbuck. MP
New Sun, The. John Wain. NePoEA-2
New Technique. Richard Armour. PoPo
New ties, fifteen each, ten. Ties. Raymond Souster. OBCV
New Vintage, The. Douglas Le Pan. OBCV
New World, The. Jones Very. AP
New Year, The. *Unknown.* STF
New Year Carol, A. *Unknown.* PoSC
New Year Idyl, A, *sel.* Eugene Field.
"Upon this happy New Year night." PoSC
New Year Wishes. May Sarton. MoRP
New yeares, expect new gifts: Sister, your harpe. Ben Jonson. SeCP
New-Yeares-Gift Sung to King Charles, 1635, A. Ben Jonson. SeCP
New Year's Day. Rachel Field. SoPo
New Year's Day. Robert Lowell. CABA
New Year's Eve. D. H. Lawrence. ErPo
New Year's Eve in Troy. Adrienne Rich. NePoEA-2

New Year's Gift to Phyllis, The. Matthew Prior. CBEP
New Year's Poem. Margaret Avison. OBCV
New Year's Wishes. Frances Ridley Havergal. STF
New York–Albany. Lawrence Ferlinghetti. PoCh
New York Trader, The. *Unknown.* BSNS
Newark Abbey. Thomas Love Peacock. OBNC
Newcomer's Wife, The. Thomas Hardy. VP
Newer Vainglory, The. Alice Meynell. MoRP
Newfoundland. *Unknown.* BSNS
Newlyweds, The. Cloyd Mann Criswell. PoLF
News, The. "Sec." TRV
News from Amiata. Eugenio Montale, *tr. fr. Italian by* Carlo L. Golino. CoIP
News from a forrein country came. On News. Thomas Traherne. *Fr.* The Third Century. MeP
News from Norwood. Christopher Middleton. NePoEA-2
News from Plymouth, *sel.* Sir William Davenant.
O Thou That Sleep'st. CBEP
News from the Court. David Wagoner. NePoEA-2
News Has Been Spread in France Concerning Me. Charles d'Orléans, *tr. fr. French by* Jacques LeClercq. AnML
News intended for me. Messages of the Rain. Günter Eich. MGP
News of My Friends. Grant Code. FiSC
News of the World. Anne Ridler. MoLP
News of the World II. George Barker. DTC
News Report. David Ignatow. ErPo
Newspaper. Aileen Fisher. SoPo
Newspaper is a collection of half-injustices, A. War Is Kind, XII. Stephen Crane. AP
Newsreel. C. Day Lewis. ILP
Newsvendor with his hut and crutch, The. The Imprisoned. Robert Fitzgerald. MP
Next comes the dull disciple of thy school. Byron. *Fr.* English Bards and Scotch Reviewers. PP
Next Day. Rachel Field. *Fr.* A Circus Garland. SoPo
Next died the Lady, who yon Hall possess'd. The Lady of the Manor. George Crabbe. *Fr.* The Parish Register. OBNC
Next died the Widow Goe, an active dame. George Crabbe. *Fr.* The Parish Register. EnPE
Next, Please. Philip Larkin. EiCP; PoIE
Next to of Course our God [America I]. E. E. Cummings. AP; CABA; PoIE; PoPo; ThLM
Next War, The. Sir Osbert Sitwell. MMA
Niagara. Lydia Huntley Sigourney. AmLP
Nice Valour, The, *sel.* John Fletcher *and* (*at.*) Thomas Middleton.
Melancholy, *fr.* III, iii. GTBS-P
Nice young ma-wa-wan [*or* ma-wan-wan], A. The Rattlesnake Song. *Unknown.* BFSS; RePo
Nietzsche. Stefan George, *tr. fr. German by* Walter Kaufmann. TwGP
Night. S. Baring-Gould. ThGo
Night. Blake. *Fr.* Songs of Innocence. CBEP; PoLF; WiR (Guardian Angels of the Creatures.) BoC
Night, *sel.* Victor J. Daley.
"Suns, planets, stars, in glorious array." PoAu-1
Night. Josef von Eichendorff, *tr. fr. German by* Isabel S. MacInnes. AGP
Night. Charles Heavysege. OBCV
Night. Friedrich Hebbel, *tr. fr. German by* Paul F. Guenther. AGP
Night. Robinson Jeffers. AP
Night, *sel.* James Oppenheim.
"Machinery is enough for a scientist." TRV
Night. Henri de Régnier, *tr. fr. French by* Seumas O'Sullivan. SiGo
Night. Sappho, *tr. fr. Greek by* J. M. Edmonds. SiGo
Night. Shelley. *See* To Night.
Night. Sara Teasdale. SoPo
Night ("Dear night! this world's defeat"). Henry Vaughan. BoC
Night, The ("Through that pure Virgin-shrine"). Henry Vaughan. MeP; VaPo
Night. Joseph Blanco White. *See* To Night.
Night:/ And the taut. Night Music. Chester Kallman. PoPl
Night,/ And the yellow pleasure of candlelight. Song of the Rain. Hugh McCrae. PoAu-1
Night after night forever the dolls lay stiff. The Dolls. John Ciardi. ToPo
Night after night I always come to you. Reunion. John Gould Fletcher. MoLP
Night and Morning. Dorothy Aldis. PoSC
Night, and the down by the sea. At Dieppe: Rain on the Down. Arthur Symons. OBNC
Night and the Pines. Duncan Campbell Scott. OBCV
Night appeared to authorise it, The. Jason and Medea. Alun Lewis. CBEP
Night Café. Gottfried Benn, *tr. fr. German by* Michael Hamburger. MGP
Night Clouds. Amy Lowell. PoPl; PoPo; RePo
Night departs, a black bull, The. Vigil. Juan Ramón Jiménez. AnSP

Night Encampment outside Troy. Homer, *tr. fr. Greek by* Tennyson. *Fr.* The Iliad, VIII. RoGo

Night Fiesta on the River. Qadi ben Lubbal, *tr. fr. Arabic by* Lysander Kemp. AnML

Night goes, the fog lifts, there. Foreign Summer. W. S. Merwin. AmPC

Night grows dark, and weird, and cold, The; and thick drops patter on the pane. The Rain Comes Sobbing to the Door. Henry Kendall. ACV

Night Has a Thousand Eyes, The. Francis William Bourdillon. LV; PoPo; WePo

Night he died, earth's images all came, The. The Planted Skull. Peter Viereck. PP

Night Herding Song. Harry Stephens. RePo

Night herons cry. By the Fire. Elizabeth J. Coatsworth. RePo

Night hides our thefts; all faults then pardoned be. In the Dark None Dainty. Robert Herrick. CBEP

Night Hunt, The. Thomas MacDonagh. RoGo

Night Hymns on Lake Nipigon. Duncan Campbell Scott. OBCV

Night in June, A. James Larkin Pearson. PoNC

Night in June, A. Duncan Campbell Scott. OBCV

Night in May. Ludwig Christoph Hölty, *tr. fr. German by* Helen Sebba. AGP

Night is a pattern of arc-lamps and the rearlights of cars. Combination XI. Helmut Heissenbüttel. MGP

Night is darkening round me, The. Emily Brontë. OBNC

Night is like a silent sea. Night. Josef von Eichendorff. AGP

Night is o'er England, and the winds are still. Peace. Walter de la Mare. MMA

Night it was a holy night, The. Godly Girzie. Burns. ErPo; UnTE

Night knows nothing of the chants of night, The. Re-Statement of Romance. Wallace Stevens. MoLP

Night, light and the night, light. That It That Thing Light. Robert Sward. *Fr.* Five Poems for J. F. K. OPP

Night Mail. W. H. Auden. PoSa; WePo

Night Music. Chester Kallman. PoPl

Night my father got me, The. The Culprit. A. E. Housman. Last Poems, XIV. VP

Night Nurse Goes Her Round, The. John Gray. OBNC

Night of Spring. Thomas Westwood. CBEP

Night of the Full Moon, The. Lloyd Frankenberg. BoLP

Night of the President's Funeral. Richard Barker. OPP

Night of Trafalgar, The. Thomas Hardy. *Fr.* The Dynasts. HaSV

Night on the Prairies. Walt Whitman. MoRP

Night Out. R. A. Simpson. PoAu-2

Night Peril. Sydney King Russell. FiSC

Night Picture of Pownal, A. Barbara Howes. OPP

Night-Piece, A; or, Modern Philosophy. Christopher Smart. VaPo

Night-Piece, A. Wordsworth. FoBA

Night Piece, to Julia, The. Robert Herrick. ELP; FaPL; ILP; PoIE; SeCP; VaPo

  (Night-Piece, The.) UnTE

Night Refuses a Dreamer, The. Grant Code. FiSC

Night Ride. Sir Herbert Read. BoLP; WePo

Night sank upon the dusky beach, and on the purple sea. Macaulay. *Fr.* Lays of Ancient Rome: The Armada. OBNC

Night, say all, was made for rest, The. Upon Visiting His Lady by Moonlight. "A. W." CTC

Nightsong. Philip Booth. MoLP

Night Songs. Thomas Kinsella. ACV

Night Sowing. David Campbell. PoAu-2

Night that has no star lit up by God, The. The New World. Jones Very. AP

Night, that thou seest in so sweet attitude. On Buonarroti's Statue of Night. Giovanni Strozzi. RBL

Night, the starless night of passion, the. The. Sonnet. William Alabaster. MeP

Night Things Are Soft and Loud. Zhenya Gay. RePo

Night Thoughts. Goethe, *tr. fr. German by* Alexander Gode. AGP

  (Thoughts by Night, *tr. by* Walter Kaufmann.) TwGP

Night Thoughts. Edward Young. *See* Complaint, The.

Night Thoughts in Age. John Hall Wheelock. PoDB

Night Thoughts over a Sick Child. Philip Levine. NePoEA-2

Night Train. Robert Francis. LOW

Night was coming very fast, The. The Hens. Elizabeth Madox Roberts. GoJo; SoPo

Night was creeping on the ground, The. Check. James Stephens. LOW

Night was dark, though sometimes a faint star, The. Prelude. Richard Watson Gilder. *Fr.* The New Day. PoLF

Night Will Never Stay, The. Eleanor Farjeon. SoPo

Night-Wind, The. Emily Brontë. PoSa; RoGo

Night with a Holy-Water Clerk, A. *Unknown.* MeEL

Nightfall. The Coolness of My Watered Garden. Juan Ramón Jiménez, *tr. fr. Spanish by* Eloise Roach. AnSP

  (Nightfall.) SiGo

Nightingale, The. Richard Barnfield. *Fr.* The Passionate Pilgrim. GTBS-P

Nightingale, The. Petrarch, *tr. fr. Italian by* Thomas LeMesurier. Sonnets to Laura: To Laura in Death, XLIII. PoPl

Nightingale, The ("My limbs were weary, and my head oppressed"). *Unknown.* StP

Nightingale, The ("One morning, one morning, one morning in May"). *Unknown. See* One Morning in May.

Nightingale and the Glowworm, The. William Cowper. OnMSP

Nightingale, as Soon as April Bringeth, The. Sir Philip Sidney. EnRePo; StP

Nightingale that so forlornly weeps, The. Petrarch. Sonnets to Laura: To Laura in Death, XLIII. RBL

Nightingale Weather. Andrew Lang. ACV

Nightingale Whose Ardent, Soft Despair, The. Petrarch, *tr. fr. Italian by* Dwight Durling. Sonnets to Laura: To Laura in Death, XLIII. AnML

Nightingales. Robert Bridges. OBNC; PoPl

Nightingales warbled without. In the Garden at Swainston. Tennyson. OBNC

Nightlong, Daylong, as the Sweet. *Unknown, tr. fr. Provençal by* Jacques LeClercq. AnML

Nightly tormented by returning doubt. The Struggle. SullyPrudhomme. PoPl

Nightmare. Joseph Payne Brennan. FiSC

Nightmare. R. H. Grenville. FiSC

Nightmare, The. Jascha Kessler. AmPC

Nightmare. Anne Marx. FiSC

Nightmare Abbey, *sels.* Thomas Love Peacock.

  Seamen Three, *fr. ch.* 11. WiR

  Song by Mr. Cypress, *fr. ch.* 11. OBNC; Par

Nightmare in Morganza. Joseph Joel Keith. FiSC

Nightmare Number Four. Robert Bloch. FiSC

Nile, The. Leigh Hunt. OBNC

Nimble as dolphins to. Gimboling. Isabella Gardner. ErPo

Nimbus. Douglas Le Pan. OBCV

Nina loved compromising. Three Women. Alan Dienstag. ErPo

Nina's cross: her alphabet. Cubes. Mary Fullerton. PoAu-1

Nine adulteries, 12 liaisons, 64 fornications and something approaching a rape. The Temperaments. Ezra Pound. ErPo

Nine Inch Will Please a Lady. Burns. ErPo

Nine times the space that measures day and night. Fallen Angels. Milton. *Fr.* Paradise Lost. DiPo

Nine white chickens come. A Black November Turkey. Richard Wilbur. AmLP

1956. Daniel G. Hoffman. PoCh

1914, *sels.* Rupert Brooke.

  Dead, The ("Blow out, you bugles"), III. FaPL

  Dead, The ("These hearts were woven"), IV. MMA

  Peace, I. MMA

  Soldier, The, V. FaBV; FaPL; LV; PoLF; PoPl; PoPo

    (Soldier, The, 1914-1918.) BoC

Nineteen Han Poems, *sel. Unknown, tr. fr. Chinese.*

  Rare Tree, A. SiGo

1916 Seen from 1921. Edmund Blunden. MMA

1967. Thomas Hardy. VP

1934. Donald Hall. PoPl

Nineteen years now. Anniversary. R. S. Thomas. ToPo

90 North. Randall Jarrell. AP; ILP

Nino, the Wonder Dog. Roy Fuller. DaDu

Ninth Moon. Li Ho, *tr. fr. Chinese by* Ho Chih-yuan. SiGo

Niplets. *Unknown, tr. fr. Greek by* Wallace Rice. ErPo

Nipping Pussy's Feet in Fun. Stevie Smith. DaDu

'Nita, Juanita. Elegy for Helen Trent. Paris Leary. CoPo

No boy chooses war. Sailors on Leave. Owen Dodson. AmNP

No city primness train'd my feet. Rustic Childhood. William Barnes. OBNC

No Coming to God without Christ. Robert Herrick. TRV

No Country You Remember. Robert Mezey. AmPC; ToPo

No Coward Soul Is Mine. Emily Brontë. *See* Last Lines.

No distant Lord have I. Companionship. Maltbie D. Babcock. STF

No Doubt. Helen Baker Adams. STF

No Doubt At All, I'll Take Him On as Critic. Marcabru, *tr. fr. Provençal by* Paul Blackburn. AnML

No doubt left. Enough deceiving. James Agee. *Fr.* Lyrics. PoPl

No early buds of laughing spring. Valentine. "C. W. T." RePo

No East or West. John Oxenham. TRV

  (In Christ.) STP

No Escape. Lilith Lorraine. FiSC

No flowers now to wear at/ Sunset. The Waning of the Harvest Moon. John Wieners. CoPo

No form of human framing. One in Christ. Henry van Dyke. TRV

No Greater Love. *Unknown.* STF

No hand has been allowed to touch. Inscription on a Chemise. *Unknown. Fr.* The Thousand and One Nights. ErPo

No hope have I to live a deathless name. Poietes Apoietes. Hartley Coleridge. OBNC
No house of stone. The Elements. H. Davies. RePo
No, I had set no prohibitive sign. Trespass. Robert Frost. FaBV
No—I'll endure ten thousand deaths. Chaste Florimel. Matthew Prior. ErPo
No Images. Waring Cuney. AmNP
No! Indeed. Sir Thomas Wyatt. MeEL
No Joy without Love. Mimnermus, *tr. fr. Greek by* G. Lowes Dickinson. SiGo
No, Little Sweetheart, No. *Unknown, tr. fr. Spanish by* William M. Davis. AnML
No longer ask me, gentle friends. Luckless Collins. William Collins. Three Fragment, 1. WaPE
No longer, Lord, thy sons shall sow. Pax Nobiscum. Earl Marlatt. MoRP
No longer mourn for me when I am dead. Sonnets, LXXI. Shakespeare. CBEP; EnRePo; GTBS-P; ILP; PoIE
No longer now do perfumed swains and merry wanton youths. The Passing of Lydia. Horace. Odes, I, 25. UnTE
No longer torn by what she knows. The Poor Relation. E. A. Robinson. PoIE
No lovelier lass have I seen. Mountain Song of Finojosa. Marqués de Santillana. AnML
No Man an Island. Lucy Smith. PtTo
No man is born into the world whose work. Work. James Russell Lowell. PoSC
No more be grieved at that which thou hast done. Sonnets, XXXV. Shakespeare. CABA; CBEP
No more, my Dear, no more these counsels try. Astrophel and Stella, LXIV. Sir Philip Sidney. FaPL
No more—no more—Oh! never more on me. My Days of Love Are Over. Byron. *Fr.* Don Juan. OBNC
No More Shall I Take Comfort. Rinaldo d'Aquino, *tr. fr. Italian by* Daniel J. Donno. AnML
No More the Slow Stream. Floris Clark McLaren. OBCV
No more wine? then we'll push back chairs and talk. Bishop Blougram's Apology. Robert Browning. OBNC
No more with overflowing light. For a Dead Lady. E. A. Robinson. AmLP; AP; VaPo
No! never such a draught was poured. A Ballad of the Boston Tea-Party. Oliver Wendell Holmes. ThLM
No, Never Think. Pushkin, *tr. fr. Russian by* Babette Deutsch. ErPo
No night could be darker than this night. Twelfth Night. Laurie Lee. BoC
"No, no, dear mother, when we were thine." The Cruel Mother. *Unknown.* BSO
No, No, Fair Heretic. Sir John Suckling. *Fr.* Aglaura. CBEP
(Song: "No, no, fair heretic, it needs must be.") CABA; PoIE
No, no; for my virginity. A True Maid. Matthew Prior. ErPo
No, no! Go from me. I have left her lately. A Virginal. Ezra Pound. AP; ILP
No, no, go not to Lethe, neither twist. Ode on Melancholy. Keats. CABA; CaFP; CBEP; DiPo; FoBA; ILP; OBNC; PoIE; StP; VaPo
No, No, Nigella. *Unknown.* EnRePo
No, no, this bitterness is no new thing. Northwind. Gene Baro. NePoEA-2
No! not for those of women born. From a Hint in the Minor Poets. Samuel Wesley. CBEP
No not this old whalehall can whelm us. Mappemounde. Earle Birney. OBCV
No one can communicate to you. Face of Poverty. Lucy Smith. NNP
No one was in the fields. Tom's Angel. Walter de la Mare. BoC
No paraphrase does. English A. John Ciardi. ToPo
No Platonic Love. William Cartwright. CABA; ErPo; ILP
No Pleasure without Some Pain. Thomas, Lord Vaux. EnRePo
No poet, sure, can be so stupid. An Explanatory Epistle. John Banks. WaPE
No Question. George Dillon. AmLP
No quirt—right?—nor spur. To My Mouse-colored Mare. Tristan Corbière. ErPo
No Retreat. Reed Whittemore. OPP
No Return. Vassar Miller. CoPo; ToPo
No rock along the road but knows. Poet. Donald Jeffrey Hayes. AmNP
No Room. Dorothy Conant Stroud. STF
No season. Outlook Uncertain. Alastair Reid. NePoEA-2
No Second Troy. W. B. Yeats. GTBS-P; PoIE; PoSa
No shepherds now, in smooth alternate verse. George Crabbe. *Fr.* The Village. PP
No shop does the bird use. Elizabeth J. Coatsworth. ThGo
No show of bolts and bars. Love. Henry David Thoreau. CBEP
No single hour can stand for naught. John Clare. OBNC

No, Sir, *with music. Unknown.* BSO
No Sky at All. Hashin. *See* Loneliness.
No sleep! I rise and burn the night away. The Protagonist. Peter Hopegood. PoAu-2
No sleep. The sultriness pervades the air. The House-Top. Herman Melville. AP
No sound of any storm that shakes. Hillcrest. E. A. Robinson. AP; PoIE
No sound—yet my room fills up with thunder. The Peeper. Peter Davison. ErPo
No spring, nor summer beauty hath such grace. Elegy IX: The Autumnal. John Donne. *Fr.* Elegies. DiPo
No state is enviable. To the luck alone. Modern Love, XIX. George Meredith. VP
No storehouse nor barn have we. The Birds of the Air. Hollis Freeman. STF
No sudden thing of glory and fear. Advent Meditation. Alice Meynell. MoRP
No Swan So Fine. Marianne Moore. AmLP; AP
No Thyng Ys to Man So Dere. Robert Mannyng. BoC
No Time for God. *Unknown.* STF
No Time for Poetry. Julia Fields. AmNP
No Time to Hate. Emily Dickinson. PoLF
No time to read, no time to pray. Stop a Minute! *Unknown.* STF
No visible scars. At Thirty Years. Heinz Piontek. MGP
No wandering any more where the feet stumble. Marriage. Mark Van Doren. MoLP
"No water so still as the/ dead fountains of Versailles." No Swan So Fine. Marianne Moore. AmLP; AP
No weather can unbrother brothers. Tour in Rain. Raymond Roseliep. FiSC
No wind of life may strike within. Dutch Seacoast. Kenneth Slessor. *Fr.* The Atlas. PoAu-2
No wonder that Oxford and Cambridge profound. Epigram. *Unknown.* WaPE
No world but this for your eye. Requiem for an Abstract Artist. Jascha Kessler. AmPC
No, worlding, no, 'tis not thy gold. The Second Rapture. Thomas Carew. UnTE
No Worst, There Is None. Gerard Manley Hopkins. AnMoPo; CABA; CBEP; DiPo; FoBA; PoIE; StP
("No worst, there is none. Pitched past pitch of grief.") GTBS-P; VP
(Sonnet.) OBNC
Noah. Hermann Hagedorn. MoRP
Noah an' Jonah an' Cap'n John Smith. Don Marquis. PoLF
Noah's Carpenters. *Unknown.* STF
Noah's Raven. W. S. Merwin. AmPC
Noah's Song. Evan Jones. PoAu-2
Noble is he who falls in front of battle. How Can Man Die Better. Tyrtaeus. SiGo
Noble Nature, The. Ben Jonson. *See* It Is Not Growing like a Tree.
Noblest bodies are but gilded clay. Of Death. Samuel Harding. CBEP
Noblest Charis, you that are. His Discourse with Cupid. Ben Jonson. *Fr.* A Celebration of Charis. SeCP
Nobly, nobly Cape Saint Vincent to the Northwest died away. Home-Thoughts, from the Sea. Robert Browning. CaFP; CBEP; HaSV; ILP
Nobody comes to the graveyard on the hill. The Hill above the Mine. Malcolm Cowley. PoPl
Nobody heard him, the dead man. Not Waving, but Drowning. Stevie Smith. GTBS-P
Nobody Loses All the Time. E. E. Cummings. MP
Nobody stays here long. Not in the Guide-Books. Elizabeth Jennings. MP
Nobody wanted this infant born. Burial. Mark Van Doren. MoBS
Nobody wants to stay on the beach now. The Fisherman. Douglas Stewart. ACV
Nocturnal Landscape. Anton Schnack, *tr. fr. German by* Christopher Middleton. MGP
Nocturnal upon Saint Lucy's Day [Being the Shortest Day], A.) MeP; SeCP
(Nocturnall upon S. Lucies Day, Being the Shortest Day, A.) MeP; SeCP
Nocturne: "I wander through the silent night." Joseph von Eichendorff, *tr. fr. German by* Herman Salinger. SiGo
Nocturne: "Those who give ear to the heart of the night." Rubén Darío, *tr. fr. Spanish by* Kate Flores. AnSP
Nocturne, The: "Why the hell do you use all that black." Carl Bode. PoPl
Nocturne at Bethesda. Arna Bontemps. AmNP
Noël Tragique. Ramon Guthrie. ErPo
Noise of hammers once I heard. The Hammers. Ralph Hodgson. GoJo; PoIE
Noiseless Patient Spider, A. Walt Whitman. AP; CABA; DiPo; EvOK; MoRP; PoIE; PoSa; PP; TRV; WiR
(Spider, The.)
Noises new to the sea and land. The Big Tent under the Roof. Ogden Nash. RePo

Non Sum Qualis Eram Bonae sub Regno Cynarae. Ernest Dowson. BoLP; CABA; FaPL; GTBS-P; OBNC; PoPl (Cynara.) UnTE
Non Sum Qualis Eram in Bona Urbe Nordica Illa. John Hollander. ErPo
Nona Domenica Garnaro sits in the sun. John Ciardi. Fr. Fragments from Italy. ToPo
Nona poured oil on the water and saw the eye. The Evil Eye. John Ciardi. MoBS
None but a Muse in love, can tell. On Fruition. Sir Charles Sedley. ErPo
None Other Lamb. Christina Rossetti. TRV
None should equal the other, but each should equal the highest. Task. Schiller. TwGP
Nonetheless Ali Baba had no richer cave. Quebec Liquor Commission Store. A. M. Klein. ACV; OBCV
Nonpareil's Grave, The. M. J. McMahon. SD
Nonsense Alphabet, A. Edward Lear. SoPo
Noon is the outsider. Eugène Guillevic. Fr. Elegies. CoFP
Noonday April Sun, The. George Love. NNP
Nooses of double meanings swing. Conversation Piece. Arthur Freeman. ErPo
Noosing of the Sun-God, The. Jessie Mackay. ACV
Nor looks that backward life so bare to me. Sonnets, Part I, IV. Frederick Goddard Tuckerman. PoIE
Nor skin nor hide nor fleece. Lethe. Hilda Doolittle ("H. D."). AmLP
Nor when the youthful pair more closely join. Concerning the Nature of Love. Lucretius. Fr. De Rerum Natura. ErPo
Norfolk spring thee, Lambeth holds thee dead. An Epitaph on Clere. Earl of Surrey. CBEP
North. Philip Booth. PoPl
North Country Collier, The. Unknown. HaSV
North Infinity Street. Conrad Aiken. AP
North is weather, Winter, and change. North. Philip Booth. PoPl
North Shore. Peter Davison. CoPo
North, south, east, west, the settlers scatter wide. Alex Wilmot. Fr. The Landing of the British Settlers of 1820. ACV
Northwind. Gene Baro. NePoEA-2
North wind doth blow, The. Poor Robin. Mother Goose. SoPo
North winds send hail, south winds bring rain. The Winds. Thomas Tusser. WiR
Northern Spring, A. Gene Baro. NePoEA-2
Northern Suburb, A. John Davidson. OBNC
Nosce Teipsum, sel. Sir John Davies.
  Soul and the Body, The. CTC
Nosegay for Laura, A. Francis Fawkes. WaPE
Nostalgia. Karl Shapiro. AP; MP
Not a drum was heard, not a funeral note. The Burial of Sir John Moore after [or at] Corunna. Charles Wolfe. CBEP; FaPL; GTBS-P; RoGo
Not a sign of life we rouse. Battery Moving Up to a New Position from Rest Camp: Dawn. Robert Nichols. MMA
Not a sound disturbs the air. A Midsummer Noon in the Australian Forest. Charles Harpur. PoAu-1
Not all of them must suffer. Saints. George Garrett. EaLo
Not All Sweet Nightingales. Luis de Góngora, tr. fr. Spanish by Sir John Bowring. RBL
Not always were you alone with me; often you watched. Woman in Pisa. Mario Luzi. CoIP
Not another bite, not another cigarette. Search. Raymond Souster. OBCV
Not as all other women are. My Love. James Russell Lowell. FaPL
Not as Black Douglas, bannered, trumpeted. Two Wise Generals. Ted Hughes. MoBS
Not as the songs of other lands. An Australian Symphony. George Essex Evans. ACV
Not as the word death. Pavane for the White Queen. Carol Bergé. OPP
Not as when some great Captain falls. Abraham Lincoln; an Horatian Ode. Richard Henry Stoddard. LiPo
Not because of their beauty—though they are slender. The Twins. Judith Wright. PoAu-2
Not black (for darkness is silk like the bride undressed). The Color of Cold. André Pieyre de Mandiargues. CoFP
Not by Bread Alone. James Terry White. PoLF
Not by lost killers stranded. The Biggest Killing. Edward Dorn. CoPo
Not by one measure mayst thou mete our love. Equal Troth. Dante Gabriel Rossetti. The House of Life, XXXII. VP
Not caring to observe the Wind. Of Loving at First Sight. Edmund Waller. SeCP
Not, Celia, that I juster am. Sir Charles Sedley. GTBS-P
Not Changed, but Glorified. Unknown. STF
Not "common speech." Denise Levertov. Fr. A Common Ground. PP
Not every man has gentians in his house. Bavarian Gentians.

D. H. Lawrence. DiPo; GoJo; GTBS-P; PoIE; PoSa
Not far from Cambridge, close to Trumpington. The Reeve's Tale. Chaucer. Fr. The Canterbury Tales. UnTE
Not fifty summers yet have passed thy clime. Oliver Goldsmith, the Younger. Fr. The Rising Village. OBCV
Not for me a giantress. Requirements. Nicarchus. ErPo
Not for one single day. The Day—the Way. John Oxenham. TRV
Not for the fishermen's sake. Backwater Pond: The Canoeists. W. S. Merwin. PoPl
Not forgetting Ko-jen, that. More Foreign Cities. Charles Tomlinson. NePoEA-2
Not furred nor wet, the pointing words yet make. Beaver Pond. Anne Marriott. ACV
Not—"How did he die?" But—"How did he live?" The Measure of a Man. Unknown. PoLF; STF
Not I. Robert Louis Stevenson. WePo
Not I, but God. Annie Johnson Flint. STF
Not I myself know all my love for thee. The Dark Glass. Dante Gabriel Rossetti. The House of Life, XXXIV. VP
Not I, not I, but the wind that blows through me! Song of a Man Who Has Come Through. D. H. Lawrence. GTBS-P; PoIE
Not, I'll not, carrion comfort, Despair, not feast on thee. Carrion Comfort [or Sonnet]. Gerard Manley Hopkins. BoC; CABA; FoBA; OBNC; PoDB; PoIE; VaPo; VP
Not in rich furniture, or fine aray. The H. Communion. George Herbert. MeP
Not in the Guide-Books. Elizabeth Jennings. MP
Not in the world of light alone. The Living Temple. Oliver Wendell Holmes. AP
Not in thy body is thy life at all. Live-in-Love. Dante Gabriel Rossetti. The House of Life, XXXVI. VP
Not in those climes where I have late been straying. Dedication: To Ianthe. Byron. Fr. Childe Harold's Pilgrimage. OBNC
Not in works or vain endeavors. The God in Whom We Trust. Unknown. STF
Not just folklore. Fast Ball. Jonathan Williams. PoNC
Not Knowing, sel. Mary Gardiner Brainard.
  "I know not what shall befall me: God hangs a mist o'er my eyes." TRV
Not knowing where he was or how he got there. A Bewilderment at the Entrance of the Fat Boy into Eden. Daryl Hine. OBCV
Not less because in purple I descended. Tea at the Palaz of Hoon. Wallace Stevens. CBEP
Not like the brazen giant of Greek fame. The New Colossus. Emma Lazarus. FaBV; FaPL; PoPl; TRV
Not long will you thirst. The Sun Sinks. Nietzsche. TwGP
Not Lotte. Katherine Hoskins. ErPo
"Not Marble nor the Gilded Monuments." Archibald MacLeish. AP; ILP; MP
Not marble, nor the gilded monuments. Sonnets, LV. Shakespeare. CABA; CBEP; CTC; DiPo; EnRePo; FoBA; ILP; PoPo; PoSa; PP; VaPo
Not mine own fears, nor the prophetic soul. Sonnets, CVII. Shakespeare. CABA; CBEP; CTC; DiPo; PoIE
Not on our golden fortunes builded high. The Forgotten Man. Edwin Markham. PoLF
Not on Sunday Night. Unknown. STF
Not One Is Turned Away from God. Dorothy Conant Stroud. STF
Not only how far away, but the way that you say it. Judging Distances. Henry Reed. Lessons of the War, II. GTBS-P
Not so in haste, my heart. Be Still, My Heart. Unknown. STF
Not solely that the future she destroys. Modern Love, XII. George Meredith. VP
Not That Hurried Grief. Lorenzo Thomas. OPP
Not that we are weary. In the Trenches. Richard Aldington. MMA
Not the dead calm. To My Friends. Else Lasker-Schüler. MGP
Not There. Unknown. STF
Not through the rational mind. The Recapitulation. Richard Eberhart. MoRP
Not to Die. Simonides, tr. fr. Greek by John Herman Merivale. SiGo
Not to forget not to ever forget. Chant for All the People on Earth. Leslie Woolf Hedley. PtTo
Not to know vice at all, and keepe true state. Epode. Ben Jonson. SeCP
Not Tonight, Josephine. Colin Curzon. ErPo
Not to You I Sighed. Stephen Spender. WePo
Not too chary, not too fast. Requirements. Rufinus. ErPo
Not too lean, and not too fat. Requirements. Rufinus. ErPo
Not too old, and not too young. Requirements. Honestus. ErPo
Not too pallid, as if bleacht. Requirements. Xenos Palaestes. ErPo

Not Waving but Drowning. Stevie Smith. GTBS-P
Not Wholly Lost. Raymond Souster. OBCV
Not with a club, the heart is broken. Emily Dickinson. AP
Not with my hands. Benediction. Donald Jeffrey Hayes. AmNP
Not with the thunder. Breath on a Piece of Broken Glass. Wolfdietrich Schnurre. MGP
Not without Hope Pulsing My Breast. St. John of the Cross, *tr. fr. Spanish by* James Edward Tobin. AnSP
Not writ in water nor in mist. For John Keats, Apostle of Beauty. Countee Cullen. Four Epitaphs, 2. AmNP
Not wrongly moved by this dismaying scene. Sonnet. William Empson. ToPo
Not yet five, and the light. After Hours. Robert Mezey. AmPC; ToPo
Not yet will those measureless fields be green again. The Cenotaph. Charlotte Mew. MMA
Note in Lieu of a Suicide. Donald Finkel. CoPo
Note on Intellectuals. W. H. Auden. PoPl
Note on Local Flora. William Empson. ToPo
Notes for a Movie Script. M. Carl Holman. AmNP
Notes for a Speech. LeRoi Jones. CoPo
Notes for an Autobiography. Charles Edward Eaton. PoNC
Notes Found near a Suicide. Frank Horne. AmNP
Notes from a Slave Ship. Edward Field. PP
Notes on a Certain Terribly Critical Piece. Reed Whittemore. PP
Notes on a Child's Coloring Book. Robert Patrick Dana. PoPl
Notes on a Girl. Peter Kane Default. ErPo
Notes on a Track Meet. David McCord. SD
Nothing before, nothing behind. Faith. Whittier. TRV
Nothing Better. *Unknown.* STF
Nothing could make me sooner to confesse. Of the Progresse of the Soule: The Second Anniversary. John Donne. MeP; SeCP
Nothing, either great or small. What Must I Do to Be Saved? *Unknown.* STF
Nothing Gold Can Stay. Robert Frost. ILP; PoPo; StP
Nothing if not utterly in death. So? James P. Vaughn. AmNP
Nothing in this bright region melts or shifts. From the Highest Camp. Thom Gunn. MP
Nothing is so beautiful as spring. Spring. Gerard Manley Hopkins. ACV; CaFP; DiPo; FaBV; FoBA; ILP; OBNC; PoDB; StP; VP
Nothing is plumb, level or square. Love Song: I and Thou. Alan Dugan. AP
Nothing now to mark the spot. Next Day. Rachel Field. *Fr.* A Circus Garland. SoPo
Nothing remained: Nothing, the wanton name. The Annihilation of Nothing. Thom Gunn. NePoEA-2
Nothing sacred here: no hysterical woman chewing. Verse. Richmond Lattimore. PP
Nothing so sharply reminds a man he is mortal. Departure in the Dark. C. Day Lewis. MP
Nothing to Do? Shelley Silverstein. BBGG
Nothing to do but work. The Pessimist [*or* The Sum of Life]. Benjamin Franklin King, Jr. CTC; WePo
Nothing to Fear. Kingsley Amis. ErPo
Nothing to Wear. William Allen Butler. PoLF
Nothing Will Ever Seem to Me More Cruel. Dante, *tr. fr. Italian by* Judith Goode. AnML
Nothing's announced more softly. Snow at Advent. Christine Busta. MGP
Notice. David McCord. SoPo
Noting in slow sequence by waterclock of rain. The Walk in the Garden. Conrad Aiken. PoCh
Nought loves another as itself. A Little Boy Lost. Blake. *Fr.* Songs of Experience. CBEP; PoIE
Novel, The. Denise Levertov. AP
November. Robert Bridges. OBNC
November. Ted Hughes. GTBS-P; NePoEA-2
November. "Aldo Palazzeschi," *tr. fr. Italian by* Carlo L. Golino. CoIP
November. James Reaney. *Fr.* A Suit of Nettles. OBCV
November Morning. Edmund Blunden. WePo
November Night. Adelaide Crapsey. WePo
November rain's down-pouring all night long. The Gone. Jesse Stuart. FiSC
November 25, 1963. William Butler. OPP
November 25, 1963. Thomas Whitbread. OPP
November 22, 1963. Robert M. Chute. OPP
November 22, 1963. Robert Hollander. OPP
November 22, 1963. Donald L. Jones. OPP
November 22, 1963. Lewis Turco. OPP
November 22, 1963. Charles Wright. OPP
November 26, 1963. Wendell Berry. AP
November's Come. Joseph C. Lincoln. RePo
Novice, The. Edward Davison. ErPo
Now. Robert Browning. CBEP
(Moment Eternal, The.) UnTE
Now/ Shall I pause to speak? Of Violets. Vernon Ward. PoNC

Now again the world is shaken. Foundations. Henry van Dyke. TRV
Now all of the grain stalks stir. Before the Harvest. "Martin Greif." AGP
Now all the truth is out. To a Friend Whose Work Has Come to Nothing. W. B. Yeats. AnMoPo; BoC; DiPo; FoBA
Now and Afterwards. Dinah Maria Mulock Craik. PoLF
Now and Then. Margaret E. Sangster. TRV
Now are you a marsupial? Are You a Marsupial? John Becker. RePo
Now as at all times I can see in the mind's eye. The Magi. W. B. Yeats. CaFP; FoBA; PoDB; PoIE; StP
Now as before do you not hear their voices. Holderlin. Delmore Schwartz. MoRP
Now as I was young and easy under the apple boughs. Fern Hill [*or* Under the Apple Boughs]. Dylan Thomas. BoC; CABA; DiPo; EvOK; FaBV; GoJo; GTBS-P; MP; PoLF; PoPl; RoGo; ToPo; WePo
Now as the river fills with ice. Crew Cut. David McCord. SD
Now as these slaughtered seven hundreds hear. On the *Struma* Massacre. Ralph Gustafson. OBCV
Now, before I sleep. Night Songs. Thomas Kinsella. ACV
Now came still evening on, and twilight gray. Milton. *Fr.* Paradise Lost, IV. PoIE
Now can you see the monument? It is of wood. The Monument. Elizabeth Bishop. PoIE; PP
Not met and marred with the year's whole turn of grief. James Agee. *Fr.* Lyrics. PoPl
Now Charito is sixty. But her hair. Ageless. *Unknown.* UnTE
Now Close the Windows. Robert Frost. LOW; WePo
"Now come, my friend, let's make a bargain." Lord Bateman. *Unknown.* BSO
Now, come on, you good people, and listen while I tell. Leoma Wise. *Unknown.* BSO
Now Does Our World Descend. E. E. Cummings. AP
Now Every Child. Eleanor Farjeon. BiCB
Now, except that he had two heads, Mr. Dooley was in most ways a perfectly normal human being. Mr. Ripley Parodies Mr. Nash—or Vice Versa. Julian Brown. FiSC
Now fades the last long streak of snow. In Memoriam A. H. H., CXV. Tennyson. BoC; GTBS-P; OBNC; PoSa; VP
Now faith is the substance of things hoped for. The Evidence. Hebrews, Bible, *N.T.* TRV
Now far and near on field and hill. So This Is Autumn. W. W. Watt. PoPl
Now fie upon that everlasting Life, I Dye! Valiant Love. Richard Lovelace. SeCP
Now, flaming up the heavens, the potent sun. Summer. James Thomson. *Fr.* The Seasons. StP
Now gentle sleep hath closed up those eyes. The Kiss. George Wither. UnTE
Now glory to the Lord of Hosts, from whom all glories are! Ivry. Macaulay. FaBV
Now go I quietly. Song III. Garcilaso de la Vega. RBL
Now, God be thanked Who has matched us with His hour. Peace. Rupert Brooke. *Fr.* 1914. MMA
Now Goeth Sun under Wood. *Unknown.* CBEP
(Pity for Mary.) MeEL
Now good night. Good Night! Eleanor Farjeon. ThGo
Now, good night, my friends so dear. Farewell. Heinrich Albert. AGP
Now Great and Awesome in My Heart. Francisco de Quevedo, *tr. fr. Spanish by* William M. Davis. AnSP
Now grimy April comes again. For City Spring. Stephen Vincent Benét. PoPl
Now hand in hand, you little maidens, walk. Spring. André Spire. BoLP
Now hardly here and there an hackney-coach. A Description of the Morning. Swift. CABA; CaFP; EiCP; ILP; PoIE; StP
Now Has Come the Gracious Month of May. Christine de Pisan, *tr. fr. French by* Muriel Kittel. AnML
Now hath my life across a stormy sea. On the Brink of Death. Michelangelo. RBL
Now have I brought a woork too end which neither Joves fierce wrath. Conclusion. Ovid. *Fr.* Metamorphoses. CTC
Now he has seen the gray Hsiang-Hsiang. Chinese Ballad. William Empson. ToPo
Now high and low, where leaves renew. Autet e bas. Arnaut Daniel. CTC
Now his nose's bridge is broken, one eye. On Hurricane Jackson. Alan Dugan. SD
Now I am growing lonely. The princes are all dead. Hagen's Dying Song. Felix Dahn. TwGP
Now I am six and going on seven. Growing Up. Arthur Guiterman. BiCB
Now I can be sure of my sleep. On the Hill below the Lighthouse. James Dickey. NePoEA-2
Now I find thy looks were feigned. Ode. Thomas Lodge. *Fr.* Phyllis. EnRePo
Now I have found thee, I will ever more. Sonnet. William Alabaster. MeP

Now I Lay Me. *Unknown.* SoPo
Now I lay me down to dreams. Nursery Rhymes for Surrealists. Grant Code. FiSC
Now I lay me down to sleep. Now I Lay Me. *Unknown.* SoPo
Now I Went Down to the Ringside and Little Henry Armstrong Was There. Kenneth Patchen. ToPo
Now I will tell you an adventure. The Laustic. Marie de France. AnML
Now I'll tell you of my history since eighteen forty seven. Poker Jim. *Unknown.* SGR
Now in midsummer come and all fools slaughtered. Credences of Summer. Wallace Stevens. AP
Now in my middle years I glean. Serene Words. "Gabriela Mistral." AnSP
"Now—in the hour that melts with homesick yearning." Dante's Angels. Dante. *Fr.* Divina Commedia: Purgatorio. BoC
Now in the suburbs and the falling light. Father and Son. Stanley Kunitz. MP
Now in this while gan Daedalus a wearinesse to take. Daedalus. Ovid. *Fr.* Metamorphoses. CTC
Now, innocent, within the deep. M., Singing. Louis Bogan. GoJo
Now is mon hol and soint. When Death Comes. *Unknown.* MeEL
Now Is the Air Made of Chiming Balls. Richard Eberhart. ToPo
Now is the earth a place of desolation. A Wreath for One Lost. Harold Vinal. FiSC
Now is the time for mirth. To Live Merrily, and to Trust to Good Verses. Robert Herrick. PP; SeCP
Now is the time for the burning of the leaves. The Burning of the Leaves. Laurence Binyon. DTC; GTBS-P
Now Is the Time of Christmas. *Unknown.* MeEL
Now it is autumn and the falling fruit. The Ship of Death. D. H. Lawrence. GTBS-P
Now it is here, the summer's richness, poised like a wave. The Waves. Charles Edward Eaton. PoNC
Now it is night, now in the brilliant room. De Anima. Howard Nemerov. ToPo
Now it seems an old forgotten fable. H.M.S. *Glory* at Sydney. Charles Causley. HaSV
Now it was in the county of Wicklow lived Larry McGee. Larry McGee. *Unknown.* BSNS
Now leave the check-reins slack. To the Man after the Harrow. Patrick Kavanagh. GTBS-P
Now let me alone, though I know you won't. Barney O'Hea. Samuel Lover. SIV
Now let us honor with violin and flute. Song. May Sarton. MoRP
Now light the candles; one; two; there's a moth. Repression of War Experience. Siegfried Sassoon. MMA
Now lighted windows climb the dark. Manhattan Lullaby. Rachel Field. BiCB
Now like Another's Child. *Unknown, tr. fr. Spanish by* William M. Davis. AnML
Now listen you landsmen unto me, to tell you the truth I'm bound. The Crocodile. *Unknown.* CBEP
Now lived the youth in freedom, but debarred. Peter Grimes. George Crabbe. *Fr.* The Borough. WePo
Now, Lord, send them summer, some manner of joy. Prayer for Rich and Poor. William Langland. *Fr.* The Vision of Piers Plowman. BoC
Now love be prais'd! that cruel fair. The Bracelet. Tristan l'Hermite. RBL
Now me name is Bull Morgan McCarthy from Thrim. Bull Morgan McCarthy. *Unknown.* BSNS
Now miners, if you'll listen, I'll tell you quite a tale. Coming around the Horn. John A. Stone. SGR
Now must all satisfaction. Certain Mercies. Robert Graves. GTBS-P
Now must I disown poesy. His Repentance. Rutebeuf. AnML
Now, My Bonny, Bonny Boy, *with music. Unknown.* BSO
Now my charms are all o'erthrown. Epilogue. Shakespeare. *Fr.* The Tempest. CTC
Now night walks down the garden path. Ghosts. Winifred Adams Burr. FiSC
Now of that long pursuit. Our God Finds Us. Francis Thompson. *Fr.* The Hound of Heaven. BoC
Now once again the gloomy scene explore. The Pauper's Funeral. George Crabbe. *Fr.* The Village. OBNC
Now one and all, you roses. A Wood Song. Ralph Hodgson. GoJo
Now put aside the flute; sing no sweet air. Consummation. *Unknown.* UnTE
Now quietly falls the night whose crimson dawn. Sailor's Warning. Michael Fitzgerald Page. HaSV
Now ripened berries fill. July. Lyudmila Tatyanicheva. SiGo
Now, royal bride, begins that season keen. To Her Grace the Duchess of Ferrara. Tasso. RBL
Now she burnes as well as I. Song: To Her Againe, She Burning in a Feaver. Thomas Carew. SeCP

Now she will lean away to fold. A Girl in a Window. James Wright. ErPo
Now Skies and Earth Are Stilled and Winds Are Dead. Petrarch, *tr. fr. Italian by* Dwight Durling. Sonnets to Laura: To Laura in Life, CXXXI. AnML
Now skrinketh rose and lilye-flour. The Penitent Hopes in Mary. *Unknown.* MeEL
Now Sleeps the Crimson Petal [Now the White]. Tennyson. *Fr.* The Princess. CABA; CaFP; CBEP; DiPo; ELP; GTBS-P; ILP; OBNC; PoIE; StP; UnTE (Summer Night.) WePo
Now, sometimes in my sorrow shut. In Memoriam A. H. H., XXIII. Tennyson. VP
Now Spring brings back the tepid breeze. Spring. Catullus. PoPl
Now springes the spray. The Singing Maid. *Unknown.* MeEL
Now, starflake frozen on the windowpane. Moment. Howard Nemerov. PoDB
Now swarthy Summer, by rude health embrowned. Summer Images. John Clare. OBNC
Now, Sym was a Glug; and 'tis mentioned so. The Growth of Sym. C. J. Dennis. ACV
Now that a letter gives me ground at last. The Beach Head. Thom Gunn. ToPo
Now that I am dressed I'll go. Peadar Og Goes Courting. James Stephens. BoLP
Now that I have your face by heart, I look. Song for the Last Act. Louise Bogan. AmLP
Now that I, tying thy glass-mask tightly. The Laboratory. Robert Browning. SIV
Now that our love has drifted. Finis. Waring Cuney. AmNP
Now that the day. The Loneliest One. Nietzsche. TwGP
Now that the evening gathers up the day. These Images Remain. May Sarton. MoLP
Now that the flesh is gone, there but remains. The Dream Is Not Enough. Zoe Kincaid Brockman. PoNC
Now that the hearth is crowned with smiling fire. Another Birthday. Ben Jonson. WiR
Now that the midd day heate doth scorch my shame. Sonnet. William Alabaster. MeP
Now that the red glare of thy fall is blown. Francis Thompson. *Fr.* Ode to the Setting Sun. OBNC
Now That the Sunset of Hope. Rosalía de Castro, *tr. fr. Spanish by* Kate Flores. AnSP
Now That the Winter's Gone. Thomas Carew. PoSC (Spring, The.) PoIE; PoSa; WiR
Now that these wings to speed my wish ascend. The Philosophic Flight. Luigi Tansillo. RBL
Now that we're almost settled in our house. In Memory of Major Robert Gregory. W. B. Yeats. DiPo
Now that you have changed the manner. To Guido Guinizelli: Now That You Have Changed the Manner. Bonagiunta Orbicciani. AnML
Now that your nebula, O noble Count, sheds. Dedication: To the Count of Niebla. Luis de Góngora. *Fr.* Fable of Polyphemus and Galatea. AnSP
Now the bright crocus flames, and now. In the Spring. Meleager. SiGo
Now the bright morning star, day's harbinger. Song: On May Morning [*or* Song of May Morning]. Milton. FoBA; PoPl
Now the day is over. Night. S. Baring-Gould. ThGo
Now the frontiers are all closed. Ultimatum. Peggy Pond Church. TRV
Now the golden Morn aloft. Ode on the Pleasure Arising from Vicissitude. Thomas Gray. EiCP; GTBS-P
Now the heart sings with all its thousand voices. The Gateway. A. D. Hope. ErPo; UnTE
Now the Hungry Lion Roars. Shakespeare. *Fr.* A Midsummer Night's Dream, V, ii. CTC; EnRePo (Lion of Winter, The.) WiR
Now the last day of many days. The Recollection [*or* To Jane]. Shelley. GTBS-P; OBNC
Now the Leaves Are Falling Fast. W. H. Auden. StP
Now the Lusty Spring. John Fletcher. *Fr.* The Tragedy of Valentinian. ELP; ErPo (Love's Emblems.) UnTE
Now the moon is rising. Song. Antonio Machado. AnSP
Now the Most High Is Born. James Ryman. MeEL
Now the old barns limber. Autumn Morning. Frances Frost. RePo
Now the parade is coming! Triumphal March. Rubén Darío. AnSP
Now the rich cherry, whose sleek wood. Country Summer. Léonie Adams. GoJo
Now the silvery moon peeps through the arch of leaves. Night in May. Ludwig Christoph Hölty. AGP
Now the stock have started dying, for the Lord has sent a drought. Song of the Artesian Water. A. B. Paterson. ACV
Now the storm begins to lower. The Fatal Sisters. Thomas Gray. EiCP; EnPE
Now the sudden shower's done. Thunder Pools. Robert P. Tristram Coffin. LOW

Now the sweet-voiced nightingale. The Beginning of Day. Euripides. SiGo
Now the white-buskined lamb. At Bungendore. James McAuley. PoAu-2
Now the wild bees that hive in the rocks. The Brown Bear. Mary Austin. PoSC
Now the year's let loose; it skips like a feckless child. April Day: Binsey. Michael Hamburger. DaDu
Now Thebes stood in good estate, now Cadmus might thou say. Acteon. Ovid. *Fr.* Metamorphoses. CTC
Now think on't, Nell the glover fair. Ballade of the Fair Helm-Maker. Villon. UnTE
. . . Now too nigh/ Th' archangel stood. Milton. *Fr.* Paradise Lost, XII. PoIE
Now touch the air softly. A Pavane for the Nursery. William Jay Smith. BoLP; GoJo; PoSC
Now turne again my theme, thou jolly swayne. The Tale of Calidore. Spenser. *Fr.* The Faerie Queene. StP
Now upon this piteous year. The Stranger. Jean Garrigue. MP
Now Venus is an evening star. Waiting. Hilary Corke. ErPo
Now Welcome Summer. Chaucer. *See* Welcome, Summer.
Now westward Sol had spent the richest beames. Musicks Duell. Richard Crashaw. SeCP
Now what in the world shall we dioux. The Sioux. Eugene Field. GoJo
Now What Is Love. Sir Walter Ralegh. *See* Description of Love, A.
Now when the blackboard has explained. The Child's Power of Wonder. P. K. Saha. ACV
Now, when the smoking ruins smoulder low. To J. S. Bach. Michael Thwaites. MoRP
Now, whether it were by peculiar grace. Wordsworth. *Fr.* Resolution and Independence. Par
Now while the wind is up, I hear. Ghostly Reaper. Harold Vinal. FiSC
Now winter downs the dying of the year. Year's End. Richard Wilbur. PoIE
Now Winter Nights [Enlarge]. Thomas Campion. ELP; EnRePo
(Winter Nights.) CBEP
Now wintry blasts have come again. Love Laughs at Winter. *Unknown.* UnTE
Now with drums. Light. Hermann Hagedorn. MoRP
Now with the bells through the apple bloom. Wantage Bells. John Betjeman. WePo
Now wolde I faine sum merey make. A Song in His Lady's Absence. *Unknown.* MeEL
Now you are nearer than my heart. Morning Song for a Lover. Howard Sergeant. ToPo
Now You Shall Speak. Conrad Ferdinand Meyer, *tr. fr. German by* Frances Stillman. AGP
Now your hills beneath a tender moon. Before the Statue of Ilaria del Caretto. Salvatore Quasimodo. CoIP
Nowe welcome, somor, with sonne softe. Welcome, Summer. Chaucer. *Fr.* The Parlement of Foules. MeEL
Nowel! nowel! nowel!/ Nowel! nowel! nowel! Man Exalted. *Unknown.* MeEL
Nowel! nowel! nowel!/ Sing we with mirth. Mary Is with Child. *Unknown.* MeEL
Nowhere are we safe. Hymn Written after Jeremiah Preached to Me in a Dream. Owen Dodson. AmNP
Nowhere So Clearly Have My Inward Eyes. Petrarch, *tr. fr. Italian by* Dwight Durling. Sonnets to Laura: To Laura in Death, XII. AnML
Now's the time for mirth and play. For Saturday [*or* Hymn for Saturday]. Christopher Smart. *Fr.* Hymns for the Amusement of Children. CBEP; EiCP
Nude. Harold Witt. ErPo
Nude Descending a Staircase. X. J. Kennedy. NePoEA-2
Nude Kneeling in Sand. John Logan. ErPo
Nudities. André Spire, *tr. fr. French by* Jethro Bithell. ErPo
Numb, stiff, broken by no sleep. Night Thoughts over a Sick Child. Philip Levine. NePoEA-2
Number 77: "I am a little church (no great cathedral)." E. E. Cummings. *See* I Am a Little Church (No Great Cathedral).
Numbers, The. Joel Oppenheimer. CoPo
Numerella Shore, The. "Cockatoo Jack." PoAu-1
Numbers, *sel.* Bible, *O.T.*
Blessing, A, VI: 24-26. ThGo
Nun, The. Edward Moore. WaPE
Nunc Scio, Quid Sit Amor. L. A. MacKay. OBCV
Nuns at Eve. John Malcolm Brinnin. MP
Nuns' Drinking Song. *Unknown, tr. fr. German by* Ruth Yorck *and* Kenward Elmslie. AnML
Nuns Fret Not at Their Convent's Narrow Room. Wordsworth. PoPo; PP
(Nuns Fret Not.) CABA; ILP
Nuns kept to their garden all night long, The. Legend of the Bewitched Nunnery. Max Herrmann-Neisse. MGP
Nun's Priest's Tale, The. Chaucer. *Fr.* The Canterbury Tales. CABL; StP

Nuptial Eve, A. Sydney Dobell. OBNC
Nuptial Sleep. Dante Gabriel Rossetti. The House of Life, VI (A). VP
Nuptial Song. Lord De Tabley. GTBS-P
Nuptiall Song, or Epithalamie, on Sir Clipseby Crew and His Lady, A. Robert Herrick. SeCP
Nurse. Frances Cornford. LV
Nurse-life wheat, within his green husk growing, The. Caelica, XL. Fulke Greville. EnRePo
Nurse No Long Grief. Mary Gilmore. PoAu-1
Nurse Pinched the Baby, The, *with music. Unknown.* BSO
Nursery, The. Conrad Aiken. *Fr.* The Coming Forth by Day of Osiris Jones. LOW
Nursery Rhyme of Innocence and Experience. Charles Causley. DaDu; GoJo; WePo
Nursery Rhymes for Surrealists. Grant Code. FiSC
Epitaph for a Wooden Soldier.
Nos Moraturi Te Salutamus.
Prayer in Blackout.
Nurse's Song ("When the voices of children are heard on the green/ And laughing"). Blake. *Fr.* Songs of Innocence. CBEP; FoBA
Nurse's Song ("When the voices of children are heard on the green/ And whisp'rings"). Blake. *Fr.* Songs of Experience. FoBA
Nut Tree, The. Mother Goose. *See* I Had a Little Nut Tree.
Nutcrackers and the Sugar-Tongs, The. Edward Lear. PoLF
Nut-gathering Lass, The. Burns. UnTE
Nuts an' May. *Unknown.* EvOK
Nutting. Wordsworth. CBEP
Nymph and a Swain, A. Congreve. *Fr.* Love for Love. UnTE
Nymph Complaining for the Death of Her Faun [*or* Fawn], The. Andrew Marvell. CBEP; SeCP
Nymph, nymph, what are your beads? Overheard on a Salt-marsh. Harold Monro. GoJo
Nymphs, The, *sel.* Leigh Hunt.
"There are the fair-limbed nymphs o' the woods, (look ye)." OBNC
Nymphs and Shepherds, Dance No More. Milton. *Fr.* Arcades. CBEP
(Nymphs and Shepherds.) ELP
Nymph's Reply to the Shepherd, The. Sir Walter Ralegh. CABA; CaFP; CTC; DiPo; ILP; PoPo; PoSa; StP
(Her Reply.) CBEP

O

O. Richard Wilbur. StP
O a lumberman's life is a wearisome life. The Lumberman's Life. *Unknown.* BSNS
O African mother, so full of fear. To Whom Shall They Go? *Unknown.* STF
O Alison Gross that lives in yon tower. Alison Gross. *Unknown.* BuBa
O Autumn, laden with fruit, and stained. To Autumn. Blake. FoBA; WiR
Oh, Barney O'Lean, say what do you mean. Barney O'Lean. *Unknown.* BSO
Oh Beach Love Blossom. Judson Crews. UnTE
O beautiful for spacious skies. America the Beautiful. Katherine Lee Bates. EaLo; FaBV; FaPL; LV
O beautiful forever! I Saw Eternity. Louise Bogan. StP
O bitter sea, tumultuous sea. Song of the Argonauts. William Morris. *Fr.* The Life and Death of Jason. HaSV
O Black and Unknown Bards. James Weldon Johnson. AmNP
O Blackbird, what a boy you are! Vesper. Thomas Edward Brown. BoC
O blessed bodie! Whither art thou thrown? Sepulchre. George Herbert. MeP
Oh Blessed Mary. "Novalis," *tr. fr. German by* D. G. Wright. AGP
O blest unfabled Incense Tree. The Phoenix [*or* Hundred-sunned Phenix]. George Darley. *Fr.* Nepenthe. CBEP; OBNC; WiR
O blithe new-comer! I have heard. To the Cuckoo. Wordsworth. CBEP; ELP; GTBS-P; PoLF
O blush not so! O blush not so! Sharing Eve's Apple. Keats. ErPo
Oh Book! infinite sweetnesse! let my heart. The H. Scriptures, I. George Herbert. MeP
O Bottom/ With the ass's head. Find Out Moonshine. Helen Bevington. PoNC
O Boundless, Boundless Evening. Georg Heym, *tr. fr. German by* Christopher Middleton. MGP
O Boy God, Muse of Poets. Ode to Fidel Castro. Edward Field. CoPo; PtTo
O Boys! O Boys! Oliver St. John Gogarty. DTC
Oh! Breathe Not His Name. Thomas Moore. FaPL

Oh Bright Oh Black Singbeast Lovebeast Catkin Sleek. Michael McClure. CoPo
O Brignall banks are wild and fair. The Outlaw. Sir Walter Scott. *Fr.* Rokeby, III. GTBS-P
Oh, Brother Green, do come to me. Brother Green [*or* The Song of Brother Green]. *Unknown.* BFSS; BSO
O brother in the restless rest of God! Zora Cross. *Fr.* Elegy on an Australian Schoolboy. PoAu-1
O Brother Man. Whittier. TRV
"Oh, bury me not on the Chickamauga!" Bury Me Not on the Chickamauga. *Unknown.* BFSS
"Oh, bury me not on the lone prairie." The Dying Cowboy [*or* Bury Me Not on the Lone Prairie]. *Unknown.* BFSS; FaBV
O, but how white is white, white from shadows come. Music of Colours: The Blossom Scattered. Vernon Watkins. ACV
O! California, *with music.* Isaac W. Baker. SGR
Oh, California, *with music.* John Nichols. SGR
Oh, California, land of gold. California over the Left. "Jack the Grumbler." SGR
O can you love little? O can you love long? The New River Shore. *Unknown.* BSNS
O Captain! My Captain! Walt Whitman. AP; FaBV; LiPo; LV; PoLF; PoPl; RoGo; ThLM
O Carib Isle! Hart Crane. AP
O cat of churlish kind. A Curse on the Cat. John Skelton. *Fr.* Phyllyp Sparowe. EvOK
O Christ who holds the open gate. John Masefield. *Fr.* The Everlasting Mercy. TRV
O city metropole, isle riverain. Montreal. A. M. Klein. OBCV
O clock, your long and solemn tones. The Horologe. Clark Ashton Smith. FiSC
Oh clouds, my children, is your will to roam? The Song of the Sea. Conrad Ferdinand Meyer. AGP
Oh, come all ye good people, it's now I have come to view. James Munks's Confession. *Unknown.* BSO
O come all ye men of learning, and rambling boys beware! Van Dieman's Land. *Unknown.* BSNS
Oh Come, Little Children. Phyllis McGinley. FaBV
O cool in the summer is salad. Salad: After Swinburne. Mortimer Collins. Par
Oh could I tell, ye surely would believe it! St. Paul Speaks. F. W. H. Myers. *Fr.* Saint Paul. BoC
Oh come, my joy, my soldier boy. Ballad. Henry Treece. DaDu
O come with me into this moonlight world. The Night of the Full Moon. Lloyd Frankenberg. BoLP
Oh, could my "was" an "is" become. Cervantes. *Fr.* Don Quixote. RBL
Oh, could we keep the Christmas thrill. The Whole Year Christmas. Angela Morgan. TRV
Oh, could we weep. Nurse No Long Grief. Mary Gilmore. PoAu-1
O Country People. John Hewitt. ACV
O Courtesy, O Harborage Most Sweet! Luis de León, *tr. fr. Spanish by* Brenda M. Sackett. AnSP
O cricket, from your cheery cry. Three Haiku. Basho. PoPo
O Cross, the old horror and fear of you are gone. Jean de la Ceppède. *Fr.* Théorèmes Spirituels. RBL
"O cruel Death, give three things back." Three Things. W. B. Yeats. DTC
O days and hours, your work is this. In Memoriam A. H. H., CXVII. Tennyson. VP
Oh, de boll weevil am a little black bug. De Boll Weevil. *Unknown.* SIV
O Dear Life, When Shall It Be. Sir Philip Sidney. Astrophel and Stella: Tenth Song. EnRePo
O Dear O. *Unknown.* ErPo
O Death, Rock Me Asleep. *Unknown.* CBEP
O depth of wealth, and knowledge in God! To Him Be Glory. Romans, Bible, *N.T.* TRV
O Desolate Eves. Christopher Brennan. *Fr.* The Wanderer. PoAu-1
Oh Did You Hear? Shelley Silverstein. PoSC
Oh, did you once see Shelley plain. Memorabilia. Robert Browning. CBEP
O did you see a troop go by. The Camp within the West. Roderic Quinn. PoAu-1
Oh do not die, for I shall hate. A Fever. John Donne. DiPo
"Oh Doctor, oh Doctor, I have come, come, come." The Dumb Maid. *Unknown.* BFSS
Oh doe not wanton with those eyes. A Song. Ben Jonson. SeCP
Oh don't you remember Bill Walker, the great. The Sonora Fillibusters. John A. Stone. SGR
Oh! don't you remember black Alice, Sam Holt. A Ballad of Queensland (Sam Holt). G. H. Gibson. PoAu-1
Oh, don't you remember sweet Betsey from Pike. Sweet Betsey from Pike. John A. Stone. SGR
Oh, don't you remember the shady old camp. The Shady Old Camp. John A. Stone. SGR
O dream, digestion of my soul! Hymn. "Jakob van Hoddis." MGP

O Dreams, O Destinations, *sel.* C. Day Lewis. "To travel like a bird, lightly to view." GTBS-P
O early one morning I walked out like Agag. The Streets of Laredo. Louis MacNeice. MoBS
O earth, lie heavily upon her eyes. Rest. Christina Rossetti. OBNC; VP
O Earth! thou hast not any wind that blows. The Word. Richard Realf. AmLP; TRV
Oh Ease Oh Body-Strain Oh Love Oh Ease Me Not! Wound-Bore. Michael McClure. CoPo
Oh, East is East, and West is West, and never the twain shall meet. The Ballad of East and West. Kipling. FaBV; PoPo; SIV; TRV
Oh, England! England. *Unknown.* CBEP
Oh England is a pleasant place for them that's rich and high. The Last Buccaneer [*or* The Old Buccaneer]. Charles Kingsley. EvOK; HaSV
O Englishwoman on the Pincian. Thomas Edward Brown. *Fr.* Roman Women. OBNC
Oh, everything is far. Lament. Rainer Maria Rilke. PoPl
O, Fairest of the Rural Maids! Bryant. AmLP; AP; FaPL
O, Falmouth is a fine town with ships in the bay. Home. W. E. Henley. PoLF
O far withdrawn into the lonely West. To K. H. Thomas Edward Brown. OBNC
O father, answer me. Dialogue. Howard Nemerov. PoPl
O Father, bless me good or bad. *Unknown.* ThGo
"Oh, father, father [*or* Oh, Father! oh, Father!] go build me a boat." Sweet William [*or* My True Sailor Boy]. *Unknown.* BFSS; BSO
O Father give me grace and sense. *Unknown.* ThGo
O Father, keep me through this day. My Daily Prayer. Eva Gray. STF
O Flame of Living Love. St. John of the Cross, *tr. fr. Spanish by* Arthur Symons. RBL
(O Living Flame of Love, *tr. by* Stephen Stepanchev.) AnSP
O Flowers, O Flowering Green Pine. Dinis, King of Portugal, *tr. fr. Portuguese by* William M. Davis. AnML
O for a Booke. *Unknown.* PoSC
Oh! for a closer walk with God. Walking with God. William Cowper. EiCP; EnPE; TRV; VaPo
O for a heart of calm repose. Peace. *Unknown.* STF
Oh, for a heart that weeps o'er souls. A Heart That Weeps. Oswald J. Smith. STF
Oh for a poet—for a beacon bright. Sonnet. E. A. Robinson. ILP; PP
O for a sculptor's hand. Balaam. John Keble. OBNC
O for Some Honest Lover's Ghost. Sir John Suckling. CBEP; Par
(Sonnet III.) SeCP
Oh for the face and footstep!—Woods and shores! Sonnets, Part II, XXXII. Frederick Goddard Tuckerman. AP
O for the perfumes that arise. Non Sum Qualis Eram in Bona Urbe Nordica Illa. John Hollander. ErPo
O for the Wings of a Dove. Euripides, *tr. fr. Greek by* Gilbert Murray. *Fr.* Hippolytus. SiGo
O friend! I know not which way I must look. In London, September, 1802 [*or* London, MDCCCII]. Wordsworth. GTBS-P; PoPo
Oh, Galuppi, Baldassaro, this is very sad to find! A Toccata of Galuppi's. Robert Browning. CBEP; GTBS-P; VP
O Gentle Breeze. Vauquelin de la Fresnaye, *tr. fr. French by* William Frederic Giese. RBL
O gentle, gentle land. Night Sowing. David Campbell. PoAu-2
O gentle sleep, that teachest man to die. To Sleep. Jan Kochanowski. SiGo
O gie the lass her fairin', lad. Gie the Lass Her Fairin'. Burns. ErPo
Oh, give me, Lord, Thy love for souls. The Soul Winner's Prayer. Eugene M. Harrison. STF
Oh, give us pleasure in the flowers to-day. A Prayer in Spring. Robert Frost. MoRP; WcPo
O God, early in the morning do I cry unto Thee. Dietrich Bonhoeffer, Awaiting Execution in a Concentration Camp, Prays for His Fellow Prisoners. Dietrich Bonhoeffer. BoC
Oh God! have mercy in this dreadful hour. The Mariner. Robert Southey. HaSV
Oh God, I offer Thee my heart. Consecration. *Unknown.* TRV
O God, make it rain! Prayer for Rain. Herbert Palmer. WePo
O God! O Montreal! Samuel Butler. *See* Psalm of Montreal, A.
O God, O Venus, O Mercury, patron of thieves. The Lake Isle. Ezra Pound. CABA
O God, Our Help in Ages Past. Isaac Watts. EaLo; LV (Man Frail, and God Eternal.) CBEP
O God that art the sole hope of the world. The Venerable Bede, *tr. fr. Latin by* Helen Waddell. BoC
O God, unknown, invisible, secure. John Addington Symonds. *Fr.* An Invocation. TRV
O God we thank Thee for everything. One Thousandth Psalm. Edward Everett Hale. TRV

O Goddess! hear these tuneless numbers, wrung. Ode to Psyche. Keats. CABA; CaFP; CBEP; DiPo; OBNC; PP; StP

O Goddess of the gloomy scene. Ode to Horror. *Unknown.* WaPE

O Golden Fleece she is where she lies tonight. Secular Elegy V. George Barker. ErPo

O Golden Love, what life, what joy but thine? No Joy without Love. Mimnermus. SiGo

O golden-tongued Romance, with serene lute. On Sitting Down to Read *King Lear* Once Again. Keats. DiPo; FoBA

O Great Spirit! *Unknown, tr. fr. Chippewa Indian.* TRV

Oh, grim and gloomy. Grim and Gloomy. James Reeves. RePo

O hame came our goodman at e'en. Our Goodman. *Unknown.* BSNS

"Oh Hangman, oh Hangman, oh Hangman hold your rope." The Hangman Tree. *Unknown.* BFSS

O happy dames! that may embrace. Complaint of the Absence of Her Lover Being upon the Sea. Earl of Surrey. ELP

Oh, happy, happy maid. A Nuptial Eve. Sydney Dobell. OBNC

Oh happy shades! to me unblest. The Shrubbery. William Cowper. CBEP; PoIE; StP

Oh hard is the bed they have made him. Illic Jacet. A. E. Housman. Last Poems, IV. VP

Oh, hark the dogs are barking, love. The Banks of the Condamine. *Unknown.* PoAu-1

O have you heard the latest news? Santy Anna. *Unknown.* BSNS

O heard ye not of the silly blind Harper. The Lochmabyn Harper. *Unknown.* BuBa

O hearken and hear the while I will tell. The Friar and the Fair Maid. *Unknown.* UnTE

O heart, be lifted up; O heart be gay. Good Friday. *Unknown.* BoC

O heart of hearts, the chalice of love's fire. Cor Cordium. Swinburne. VP

O helpless few in my country. The Rest. Ezra Pound. AnMoPo; PP

O holy virgin! clad in purest white. To Morning. Blake. FoBA

O' How deep is thy love says/ the Hymnal. Sept. 1957. Edward Marshall. CoPo

Oh, how I love Humanity. The World State. G. K. Chesterton. PoPo

O How I Love Thy Law. Isaac Watts. STF

Oh, how I love to skip alone. Skipping Along Alone. Winnifred Welles. SoPo

Oh I wish the sun was bright in the sky. The Terrible Robber Men. Padraic Colum. LOW

O how my mind/ Is gravell'd. Confusion. Christopher Hervey. Par

Oh how oft I wake and find. To My God. George Macdonald. TRV

O hurry where by water among trees. The Ragged Wood. W. B. Yeats. BoC; PoPo

O hushed October morning mild. October. Robert Frost. GoJo

O Hymen! O Hymenee! Walt Whitman. ErPo

O I am a poor hard-working man. The Poor Hard-working Man. *Unknown.* BSNS

Oh, I can hear you, God, above the cry. Wind in the Pine. Lew Sarett. TRV

"O I forbid you maidens a' [or all]." Tam Lin [or Tamlane]. *Unknown.* BuBa; CABL

O I hae come from far away. The Witch's Ballad. William Bell Scott. EvOK

O, I ha'nt got no home, nor nothing else, I s'pose. Life in California. David G. Robinson. SGR

Oh, I have slipped the surly bonds of earth. High Flight. John Gillespie Magee, Jr. LV; TRV

O I see flashing that this America is only you and me. Walt Whitman. *Fr.* By Blue Ontario's Shore. PoIE

Oh, I should love to be like one of those. The Youth Dreams. Rainer Maria Rilke. SiGo

"O I thought more of my greasy pots and pans." The *Royal George. Unknown.* BSNS

O if I had a dog I would call him Hunter. Rolling River. *Unknown.* BSNS

O if thou knew'st how thou thyself dost harm. To Aurora. Earl of Stirling. Aurora, Sonnet XXXIII. GTBS-P

Oh, I'm a good old rebel, that's what I am. The Rebel. Innes Randolph. ThLM

Oh I'm in love with the janitor's boy. The Janitor's Boy. Nathalia Crane. PoLF

O, into the earth. Song for the Virgin Mary. *Unknown.* AnML

Oh, is it, then, Utopian. De Profundis. Dorothy Parker. ErPo

Oh, it *is* life! to see a proud. Gallantly within the Ring. John Hamilton Reynolds. SD

Oh, it is up in the Highlands. Bonnie James Campbell. *Unknown.* BFSS

O, it was out by Donnycarney. James Joyce. Chamber Music, XXXI. WePo

Oh, it's now I'm on the Lone Star Trail until I get too old. The Lone Star Trail. *Unknown.* BFSS

"Oh, Jane, do be careful!" Jane, Do Be Careful. Irene Page. BBGG

O Jealous Night. *Unknown.* UnTE

O Jesus, keep my candle burning bright. *Unknown.* ThGo

O Johnny came over the other day. Rio Grande (A *vers.*). *Unknown.* BSNS

Oh, Johnny Fife and Johnny's wife. Johnny Fife and Johnny's Wife. Mildred Plew Merryman. SoPo

Oh, Johnny O Dutchman rode out in the frost. Johnny O Dutchman. *Unknown.* BFSS

Oh, Johnny sailed to sea. The Green Bed. *Unknown.* BSO

O Jonathan Bing, O Bingathon Jon. A New Song to Sing about Jonathan Bing. Beatrice Curtis Brown. SoPo

O joy of creation. What the Bullet Sang. Bret Harte. CBEP

O joys [or joyes]! Infinite sweetness! with what flowers [or flowres]. The Morning Watch. Henry Vaughan. BoC; MeP

Oh King of grief! (a title strange, yet true). The Thanksgiving. George Herbert. MeP

O kingdom of Christ, you and He are one. Jean de la Ceppède. *Fr.* Théorèmes Spirituels. RBL

O kiss me yet again, O kiss me over. Sonnet XVIII. Louise Labé. RBL

O knit me, that am crumpled dust! the heape. Distraction. Henry Vaughan. SeCP

O Lady Mine, Caught You No Glimpse of Him. Guido Cavalcanti, *tr. fr. Italian by* Irma Brandeis. AnML

Oh lady, oh lady, oh lady of Flower. Lady Flower. *Unknown.* BFSS

Oh, land of Castile, you do raise me up. Castile. Miguel de Unamuno. PoP1

O leafy yellowness you create for me. October. Patrick Kavanagh. GTBS-P

O, Let Me Kiss. Karl Gjellerup, *tr. fr. Danish by* Charles Wharton Stork. PoP1

Oh let your shining orb grow dim. To the Sun. Roy Campbell. *Fr.* Mithraic Emblems. EaLo

O Light Invisible, We Praise Thee. T. S. Eliot. *Fr.* The Rock. MoRP

O Light serene! present in one who breathes. Ideal Beauty. Fernando de Herrera. RBL

O, listen for a moment lads, and hear me tell my tale. Jim Jones. *Unknown.* PoAu-1

O listen, listen, ladies gay. Rosabelle. Sir Walter Scott. *Fr.* The Lay of the Last Minstrel, VI. GTBS-P

Oh, little body, do not die. A Child Ill. John Betjeman. DTC

Oh little town of Bethlehem, how still we see thee lie. Carol with Variations. Phyllis McGinley. PoPo

O Living Flame of Love. St. John of the Cross. *See* O Flame of Living Love.

O living will that shalt endure. In Memoriam A. H. H., CXXXI. Tennyson. DiPo; FoBA; VP

O lonely bay of Trinity. The Cable Hymn. Whittier. ThLM

O Lord, at Joseph's humble bench. The Carpenter. George Macdonald. TRV

O Lord, it is not hard to love. Prayer for Neighborhood Evangelism. Annette Jansen. STF

O Lord my sinne doth over-charge thy brest. Sinnes Heavie Loade. Robert Southwell. MeP

O Lord of all compassionate control. The Portrait. Dante Gabriel Rossetti. The House of Life, X. VP

O Lord of life, Thy quickening voice awakes my morning song. My Morning Song. George Macdonald. TRV

O Lord, our God, They mighty hand. Peace Hymn of the Republic. Henry van Dyke. TRV

O Lord our Lord. Psalm VIII, Bible, *O.T.* SiGo

O Lord, support us all the day long. Until the Shadows Lengthen. John Henry Newman. TRV

O Lord, thou hast searched me, and known me. Psalm CXXXIX, Bible, *O.T.* BoC

"O Lord, why grievest Thou?" By the Earth's Corpse. Thomas Hardy. PoDB

O Love, All Love Above. Jacopone da Todi, *tr. fr. Italian by* John Gray. AnML

"O love, art thou a silver fish?" Isabella Valancy Crawford. *Fr.* The Canoe. ACV

O love, be fed with apples while you may. Sick Love. Robert Graves. GTBS-P

"Oh love is fair, and love is rare"; my dear one she said. There's Wisdom in Women. Rupert Brooke. BoLP

O Love, Love, Love! O withering might! Fatima. Tennyson. UnTE

Oh Love! no habitant of earth thou art. The Fatal Spell. Byron. *Fr.* Childe Harold's Pilgrimage. OBNC

O Love, O Love, What Wouldst Thou Make of Me? Jean Froissart, *tr. fr. French by* Jacques LeClercq. AnML

O love of God, God's love, love that alone. For All Sorts and Conditions. Norman Nicholson. EaLo

O Love That Wilt Not Let Me Go. George Matheson. TRV

O love, thou Judas of the martyred soul! Amor Aeternalis. Clark Ashton Smith. FiSC
O love triumphant over guilt and sin. L'Envoi. Frederick I. Knowles. TRV
O love, turn from the unchanging sea, and gaze. October. William Morris. *Fr.* The Earthly Paradise. OBNC
O love, what hours were thine and mine. The Daisy. Tennyson. OBNC
O Love! what shall be said of thee? Fragoletta. Swinburne. UnTE
O lovely age of gold! The Golden Age. Tasso. *Fr.* Aminta. RBL
O lovely Bellerie. To a Fountain. Pierre de Ronsard. RBL
O lovely Galatea, sweeter than. Polyphemus' Love Song. Luis de Góngora. AnSP
O lovely little bird, I watch you fly. Petrarch. *Fr.* Sonnets to Laura: To Laura in Death. RBL
O Lovely Mountain Shepherd Lasses. Franco Sacchetti, tr. fr. *Italian by* Maurice Valency. AnML
O lovers' eyes are sharp to see. The Maid of Neidpath. Sir Walter Scott. GTBS-P
O ludicrous and pensive trinity. Romeo and Juliet. H. Phelps Putnam. ErPo
O luely, luely, cam she in. The Tryst. William Soutar. ErPo
O! maistres mine, till you I me commend. O! Mistress Mine. *Unknown.* MeEL
O Maker of the Mighty Deep. Voyagers. Henry van Dyke. TRV
O man of my own people, I alone. The Jew to Jesus. Florence Kiper Frank. TRV
O! Mankinde. See! Here, My Heart. *Unknown.* MeEL
O Mary, at thy window be. Mary Morison. Burns. GTBS-P
"O Mary, go and call the cattle home." The Sands of Dee. Charles Kingsley. HaSV; SIV
O Master, let me walk with Thee. Service. Washington Gladden. TRV
O Master-Workman of the Race. Jay T. Stocking. TRV
O May I Join the Choir Invisible. "George Eliot." OBNC; TRV
O me! what eyes hath love put in my head. Blind Love. Shakespeare. Sonnets, CXLVIII. GTBS-P
O meeting is a pleasure, but parting is grief. The Cuckoo. *Unknown.* CBEP
"O 'Melia, my dear, this does everything crown." The Ruined Maid. Thomas Hardy. CABA; ErPo
Oh men, give heed! Song of Rapture. Nietzsche. AGP
O merciful Father, my hope is in thee. Prayer before Her Execution. Mary Queen of Scots. TRV
O Merlin in your crystal cave. Merlin. Edwin Muir. CBEP
O! mestress, why. Distant as the Duchess of Savoy. *Unknown.* MeEL
O might those sighes and teares returne againe. Holy Sonnets, III. John Donne. MeP
Oh Mr. Pussy-Cat. Nipping Pussy's Feet in Fun. Stevie Smith. DaDu
O Mistress Mine. Shakespeare. *Fr.* Twelfth Night, II, iii. BoLP; CBEP; CTC; DiPo; ELP; EnRePo; FaBV; FoBA; PoPo; WePo
(Carpe Diem.) GTBS-P
(Song: "O mistress mine, where are you roaming?") GoJo; OnP
O! Mistress Mine. *Unknown.* MeEL
"Oh Molly, pretty Molly, come go with me." Pretty Molly. *Unknown.* BFSS
O mongrel land! My America. Oliver La Grone. NNP
"O monstrous, dead, unprofitable world." Written in Emerson's Essays. Matthew Arnold. ILP
O Moon, Mr. Moon. Mr. Moon. Bliss Carman. RePo
O mortal folk, you may behold and see. An Epitaph. Stephen Hawes. CBEP
O mortal man, who livest here by toil. James Thomson. *Fr.* The Castle of Indolence. EiCP
O [or Oh], most high, almighty, good Lord God. Canticle of the Sun [or The Song of the Creatures]. St. Francis of Assisi. BoC; SiGo
O most unconscious daisy! To a School-Girl. John Shaw Neilson. PoAu-1
O mother, lay your hand on my brow! The Sick Child. Robert Louis Stevenson. PoSC
"Oh, Mother, oh, Mother, come listen to me." Lord Thomas and the Brown Girl. *Unknown.* BFSS
Oh Mother of a Mighty Race. Bryant. AP
Oh my blacke soule! now thou art summoned. Holy Sonnets, IV. John Donne. MeP
O my body! I dare not desert the likes of you in other men and women. Walt Whitman. *Fr.* I Sing the Body Electric. ErPo
O my brothers of the wilderness. Charm for Going a-Hunting. Mary Austin. RePo
O my chief good. Good Friday. George Herbert. FoBA
O my chief good! The Passion. Henry Vaughan. MeP
Oh My Darling Clementine, *with music.* Percy Montrose. SGR

"Oh, my dearest Polly." The Bold Privateer. *Unknown.* BSO
Oh my dearie. Song. Eleanor Ross Taylor. PoNC
O my deir hert, young Jesus sweit. Cradle Song. *Unknown.* EaLo
O my heart's heart, and you who are to me. Monna Innominata, V. Christina Rossetti. VP
O My Luve's like a Red, Red Rose. Burns. *See* Red, Red Rose, A.
Oh, my name is Bob the Swagman, before you all I stand. The Old Bark Hut. *Unknown.* PoAu-1
O my own Italy! though words are vain. Canzone. Petrarch. RBL
Oh, my sweet mother, 'tis in vain. On My Sweet Mother. Sappho. PoP1
O my sweet nightingales, why are you dumb again? For Autumn. Eleanor Farjeon. ThGo
O my true love's a smuggler and sails upon the sea. The Smuggler. *Unknown.* HaSV
Oh never in this hard world was such an absurd. Nesting Time. Douglas Stewart. PoAu-2
O never say that I was false of heart. The Unchangeable. Shakespeare. Sonnets, CIX. GTBS-P
Oh Night. Gaspara Stampa, tr. fr. *Italian by* Harold M. Priest. RBL
O night, more shining and clear, sweeter, gladder. Capitolo VIII. Ariosto. RBL
O Night, O jealous Night, repugnant to my measures! O Jealous Night. *Unknown.* UnTE
O Night O Trembling Night. Stephen Spender. ErPo
O night, to me brighter and more blest. Oh Night. Gaspara Stampa. RBL
O Nightingale, That on Yon Bloomy Spray. Milton. FoBA
(To the Nightingale.) DiPo
Oh No. Robert Creeley. AmPC
Oh, No! Mary Mapes Dodge. BBGG
O No, John! *Unknown.* ErPo; UnTE
Oh, No More, No More! John Ford. *Fr.* The Broken Heart. ELP
O Noble and Most High in Beauty, Thou. Luis de Góngora, tr. fr. *Spanish by* Iain Fletcher. AnSP
O noon that with hot hay reduce. Icarus. Gottfried Benn. MGP
O! Nothing earthly save the ray. Al Aaraaf. Poe. AP
O nothing, in this corporal earth of man. Correlated Greatness. Francis Thompson. *Fr.* The Heart. GTBS-P
O Now the Drenched Land Wakes. Kenneth Patchen. ToPo
O often have I prayed, and thought. Oblique. Archibald Rutledge. TRV
Oh, once I had a fair true lover. The Lover Freed from the Gallows. *Unknown.* BFSS
Oh! once I was a "right smart" lad. The Pike County Miner. Mart Taylor. SGR
"O Paddy dear, and did ye hear the news that's goin' round?" The Wearin' of the Green. *Unknown.* PoSC
"O paleys, whylom croune of houses alle." The Complaint of Troilus. Chaucer. *Fr.* Troilus and Criseyde. DiPo
O parent of each lovely muse. Ode to Fancy. Joseph Warton. EnPE; WaPE
O Phoenix, cherished bird of Arabia. Jean de la Ceppède. *Fr.* Théorèmes Spirituels. RBL
Oh, pleasant eventide! Twilight Calm. Christina Rossetti. OBNC
O poet of the future! The Future. George Frederick Cameron. OBCV
O Polly, love, O Polly, the rout has just begun. High Germany. *Unknown.* CBEP
O poor old Reuben Ranzo. Reuben Ranzo. *Unknown.* BSNS
O potent Earth, and Heaven god-built. Earth and Sky. Euripides. EaLo
O Poverty! thou source of human art. A Hymn to Poverty. Edward Moore. WaPE
O precious codex, volume, tome. To a Thesaurus. Franklin P. Adams. PoP1
Oh precious treasures, which to my grief I found. Sonnet X: On Finding Some Keepsakes of His Dead Mistress. Garcilaso de la Vega. RBL
O Queen, awake to thy renown. Honor and Desert. Coventry Patmore. *Fr.* The Angel in the House. FaPL
O quick quick quick, quick hear the song-sparrow. Cape Ann. T. S. Eliot. *Fr.* Landscapes. DaDu; EvOK; GoJo
O radiant luminary of light interminable. A Prayer to the Father of Heaven. John Skelton. PoIE
O raging seas and mighty Neptune's reign. Coming Homeward Out of Spain. Barnabe Googe. EnRePo
O reverend Chaucere, rose of rethoris all. William Dunbar. *Fr.* The Goldyn Targe. PP
O Rose, Thou Art Sick! Blake. *See* Sick Rose, The.
Oh Roses for the Flush of Youth. Christina Rossetti. ELP
(Song.) GTBS-P; VP
O Ruddier than the Cherry. John Gay. *Fr.* Acis and Galatea. ELP
O Russian faced, woman on the grass. Allen Ginsberg. *Fr.* Kaddish. PtTo

O saw ye bonnie [*or* bonny] Lesley? Bonnie Lesley [*or* Saw Ye Bonny Lesley?]. Burns. CBEP; CTC; GTBS-P; PoIE

Oh, say, can you see, by the dawn's early light. The Star-spangled Banner. Francis Scott Key. FaPL; ThLM

O say what is that thing call'd Light. The Blind Boy. Colley Cibber. GTBS-P; RoGo

O sea,/ Hear my testament. Testament. Attwood Robson. HaSV

O See How Thick the Goldcup Flowers. A. E. Housman. A Shropshire Lad, V. BoLP; FaBV

O seeded grass, you army of little men. John Gould Fletcher. *Fr.* Irradiations. PoPo

O! sely anker, that in thy celle. Go Sad Complaint. Charles d'Orléans(?). MeEL

O Shadow. Shadow Dance. Ivy O. Eastwick. SoPo

O! shairly ye hae seen my love. Ballad. William Soutar. WePo

O She Is as Lovely-Often. Kenneth Patchen. ToPo

Oh, she walked unaware of her own increasing beauty. She Walked Unaware. Patrick MacDonogh. BoLP; ErPo

O ship incoming from the sea. Off Rivière du Loup. Duncan Campbell Scott. OBCV

Oh! sigh no more, no longer paint the air. Sonnet. George Henry Boker. *Fr.* Sonnets. AmLP

Oh, silver tree. Jazzonia. Langston Hughes. AmNP

O simple as the rhymes that tell. Lincoln—the Boy. James Whitcomb Riley. LiPo

O simple Nature, how I do delight. Nature. John Clare. CBEP

O sing unto my roundelay. Minstrel's Song [*or* My Love Is Dead]. Thomas Chatterton. *Fr.* Aella. DiPo; WiR

O Sing unto the Lord a New Song. Psalms, XCVIII, Bible, *O.T.* EaLo

O Singer of Persephone! Theocritus; a Villanelle. Oscar Wilde. StP

"Oh, sister, these are midnight dreams." The Braes o' Yarrow (A *and* B *vers.*). *Unknown.* BFSS

O! sisters too. The Coventry Carol. *Unknown.* MeEL

O, sixteen hundred and ninety one. The Two Witches. Robert Graves. DaDu

Oh Sky, you look so drear! Earth and Sky. Eleanor Farjeon. PoSC

"Oh, slacken the rope, oh, slacken the rope." The Gallent Tree. *Unknown.* BSO

O Sleep! I bring thee this long-cellared wine. Invocation. Philippe Desportes. RBL

O sleep, my babe, hear not the rippling wave. Sara Coleridge. *Fr.* Phantasmion. OBNC

O Sleep, O tranquil son of noiseless Night. To Sleep. Giovanni della Casa. RBL

Oh, slow to smite and swift to spare. Abraham Lincoln [*or* The Death of Lincoln]. Bryant. AP; LiPo; PoPo

Oh, slow up, dogies, quit your roving round. Night Herding Song. Harry Stephens. RePo

O snatch'd away in beauty's bloom! Elegy. Byron. GTBS-P

Oh, so cool. Moral Song. John Farrar. RePo

O soft embalmer of the still midnight! To Sleep [*or* The World of Sleep]. Keats. BoC; FoBA

O solitary pine, how many. Solitary Pine. Prince Ichihara. SiGo

Oh some have killed in angry love. A Rope for Harry Fat. James K. Baxter. MoBS

O Son of God, Afflicted. *Unknown, tr. fr. Greek by* John Brownlee. STF

Oh, sons of sorrow, listen to me. James Bird. *Unknown.* BFSS

O! sop of sorrow, sonkin into cair. Cresseid's Complaint against Fortune. Robert Henryson. *Fr.* The Testament of Cresseid. MeEL

O Sorrow, cruel fellowship. In Memoriam A. H. H., III. Tennyson. VP

O Sorrow, wilt thou live with me. In Memoriam A. H. H., LIX. Tennyson. VP

O Soul, canst thou not understand. Aridity. "Michael Field." BoC; TRV

O sovereign power of love! O grief! O balm. Keats. *Fr.* Endymion. OBNC

O spring has set off her green fuses. The Seasons in North Cornwall. Charles Causley. ACV

Oh spring that hides the wrinkled earth in green. Sonnet. George Henry Boker. *Fr.* Sonnets. AmLP

O Spring the long-desired. *Unknown. Fr.* Carmina Burana. SiGo

O star of morning and of liberty! Sonnets on the Divina Commedia, VI. Longfellow. AP; ILP

O Star (the fairest one in sight). Choose Something like a Star. Robert Frost. PoCh

O starry temple of unvalted space. Sonnet. William Alabaster. MeP

O statue, stand still! Hans Christian Andersen in Central Park. Hy Sobiloff. PoPl

Oh stupid miracle of my own devising. Eastertide. Carl Bode. *Fr.* The Sacred Seasons. ToPo

O suitably-attired-in-leather-boots. Fragment of a Greek Tragedy. A. E. Housman. Par

O sun and skies and clouds of June. October's Bright Blue Weather. Helen Hunt Jackson. PoSC

O Sun, when I stand in my green leaves. To the Sun. Guido Gezelle. SiGo

O sunstruck spray, where change and changeless meet. Some Refrains at the Charles River. Peter Viereck. PoCh

O Sweet Spontaneous. E. E. Cummings. AP

O sweet to-morrow! Song of Hope. Thomas Hardy. VP

O sweete, and bitter monuments of paine. Sonnet. William Alabaster. MeP

O talk not to me of a name great in glory [*or* story]. All for Love. Byron. GTBS-P; PoPo

Oh, tell me, children who have seen. Christmas. Mary Mapes Dodge. BiCB

Oh, thanks for all since the days long past. Synnöve's Song. Björnstjerne Björnson. PoPl

O that frog or flower that stealthily. Mythological Episode. Robert H. Barlow. FiSC

Oh that I could suavely pass. Otherwhere. Frances Angevine Gray. FiSC

O that joy so soon should waste! The Kiss. Ben Jonson. *Fr.* Cynthia's Revels. UnTE

Oh! that my young life were a lasting dream. Dreams. Poe. CBEP

Oh! that the desert were my dwelling-place. By the Deep Sea. Byron. *Fr.* Childe Harold's Pilgrimage. ILP; OBNC

"O that this too solid flesh would melt." On a Young Lady's Going into a Shower Bath. Francis Scott Key. UnTE

Oh that those lips had language! Life has passed. On the Receipt at the Charles River. Peter Viereck. PoCh Receipt of My Mother's Picture Out of Norfolk. William Cowper. EnPE; PoIE

O That 'Twere Possible. Tennyson. *Fr.* Maud. CBEP

Oh, the anguish of Mary! Not There. *Unknown.* STF

Oh, the bitter shame and sorrow. Christ Alone. Theodore Monod. STF

O the black angel who softly stepped from the heart of the tree. To One Who Died Young. Georg Trakl. MGP

O the bonny Christ Church Bells. Christ Church Bells. Henry Aldrich. CBEP

Oh, the broom, the bonny, bonny broom. The Bonny Broom. *Unknown.* BFSS

Oh, the Funniest Thing. *Unknown.* EvOK

O the green light, the mornings of those years. Retrospective Sketch. Gottfried Benn. MGP

Oh, the joy of looking forward. He Is Coming. Gladys M. Gearhart. STF

Oh, the little birds sang east, and the little birds sang west. Round Our Restlessness. Elizabeth Barrett Browning. TRV

Oh the Miller, the dusty, musty Miller. A Ballad of All [the] Trades. *Unknown.* ErPo; UnTE

Oh, the nurse pinched the baby just to tease it. The Nurse Pinched the Baby. *Unknown.* BSO

O the opal and the sapphire of that wandering western sea. Beeny Cliff. Thomas Hardy. OBNC

Oh! the shearing is all over. The Old Bullock Dray. *Unknown.* PoAu-1

Oh the sheer joy of it! Sheer Joy. Ralph Spaulding Cushman. TRV

O the spraying of gardens, to encourage green! On Watering the Garden. Bertolt Brecht. MGP

Oh, the wild joys of living! the leaping from rock up to rock. David's Song. *Fr.* Saul. Robert Browning. FaBV

O, then, I see Queen Mab hath been with you. Queen Mab. Shakespeare. *Fr.* Romeo and Juliet, I, iv. BoC

Oh! there are spirits of the air. To Coleridge. Shelley. CBEP

O there is a little artist. The Fairy Artist. Nellie M. Garabrant. PoPl

O, there once was a Puffin. There *Once* Was a Puffin. Florence Page Jaques. SoPo

Oh, there was a jolly boatman. Jolly Boatman. *Unknown.* BSO

O there was a woman, and she was a widow. Flowers in the Valley. *Unknown.* OnMSP

Oh, there were fifteen men in green. Men in Green. David Campbell. PoAu-2

Oh, these spring days! On the Road to Nara. Matsuo Basho. SiGo

Oh, Think Not I Am Faithful to a Vow! Edna St. Vincent Millay. FaBV

O thorn-crowned brow. Behold the Man! *Unknown.* STF

O thou above who in thy bed. Cervantes. *Fr.* Don Quixote. RBL

O thou all-eloquent, whose mighty mind. Man's Going Hence. Samuel Rogers. *Fr.* Human Life. OBNC

O thou by Nature taught. Ode to Simplicity. William Collins. EiCP

O Thou great mystery. Indian Prayer. Chief Joseph Strongwolf. TRV

O Thou my monster, Thou my guide. Prayer in Mid-Passage. Louis MacNeice. EaLo

O Thou of soul and sense and breath. In Memory of Abraham Lincoln. Oliver Wendell Holmes. LiPo
O thou that achest, pulse o' the unwed vast. Adam to Lilith. Christopher Brennan. *Fr.* Lilith. PoAu-1
O thou that after toil and storm. In Memoriam A. H. H., XXXIII. Tennyson. VP
O thou that lovest a pure, and whitend soul! Dressing. Henry Vaughan. MeP
O thou, that sit'st upon a throne. A Song to David. Christopher Smart. EiCP; EnPE
O Thou That Sleep'st. Sir William Davenant. *Fr.* News from Plymouth. CBEP
O thou, the friend of man, assigned. Ode to Pity. William Collins. EiCP; EnPE
O Thou transcendent! Passage to More than India. Walt Whitman. *Fr.* Passage to India. MoRP
O Thou, wha in the Heavens dost dwell. Holy Willie's Prayer. Burns. EnPE; VaPo
O thou! whatever title suit thee. Address to the Deil. Burns. EiCP; EnPE
O thou who at Love's hour ecstatically. Love's Testament. Dante Gabriel Rossetti. The House of Life, III. VP
Oh Thou, Who Man of Baser Earth Didst Make. Omar Khayyám, tr. fr. Persian by Edward Fitzgerald. *Fr.* The Rubáiyát. EaLo
O thou, who passest thro' our valleys in. To Summer. Blake. FoBA; WiR
O thou, who plumed with strong desire. The Two Spirits. Shelley. WiR
O thou who sitt'st a smiling bride. Ode to Mercy. William Collins. EiCP
O thou whose face hath felt the Winter's Wind. What the Thrush Said. Keats. DiPo
O thou with dewy locks, who lookest down. To Spring. Blake. BoC; CBEP; FoBA; PoLF; WiR
O to Be a Dragon. Marianne Moore. CTC; PoP1
Oh, to be in England. Home-Thoughts, from Abroad. Robert Browning. CBEP; DiPo; FaBV; ILP; LV; OBNC; PoIE; PoLF; PoPo; VP
"Oh! to be in England." Home Truths from Abroad. *Unknown.* Par
Oh, to be there to-night! Ada Cambridge. *Fr.* On Australian Hills. PoAu-1
O to Be Up and Doing. Robert Louis Stevenson. TRV
O to go home at last. Over Shining Shingle. Else Lasker-Schüler. MGP
Oh! to Have a Birthday. Lois Lenski. BiCB
O, to have a little house! An Old Woman of the Roads. Padraic Colum. BoC; RePo
O to sail in a ship! Walt Whitman. *Fr.* A Song of Joys. HaSV
Oh, to vex me, contraryes meet in one. Holy Sonnets, XIX. John Donne. MeP
"O Trade! O Trade! would thou wert dead!" The Symphony. Sidney Lanier. AP; PoPo
O Trivia Goddess, leave these low abodes. Of Walking the Streets by Night. John Gay. *Fr.* Trivia. EiCP
O true and tried, so well and long. In Memoriam A. H. H., Epilogue. Tennyson. VP
Oh, Uncle Noah built him an ark. Old Uncle Noah. *Unknown.* BSO
Oh, Uncle Rat ran up the wall. The Opossum (B *vers.*). *Unknown.* BSO
Oh Venice! Venice! when thy marble walls. Ode on Venice. Byron. CABL
O, very gloomy is the House of Woe. The Haunted House. Thomas Hood. WePo
"Oh, wait a minute! I see my father coming." The Raspel Pole. *Unknown.* BFSS
O Waly, Waly. *Unknown.* ELP
(Forsaken Bride, The.) GTBS-P
Oh wandering is a miller's joy. The Journeyman's Song. Wilhelm Müller. AGP
Oh, wast thou with me, dearest, then. In Memoriam A. H. H., CXXII. Tennyson. VP
O waters running pure and crystal clear. Garcilaso de la Vega. *Fr.* Eclogue I. AnSP
O Waves of the Sea of Vigo. Martín Códax, tr. fr. Portuguese by William M. Davis. AnML
Oh, we started down from Roto when the sheds had all cut out. On the Road to Gundagai. *Unknown.* PoAu-1
O Wearisome Condition. Fulke Greville. *Fr.* Mustapha. CBEP
"O well is [or well's] me, my gay goshawk [or goss-hawk]." The Gay Goshawk. *Unknown.* BuBa; CABL
Oh were I faint with love upon the breast. Sonnet XIII. Louise Labé. RBL
O, were you on the mountain, or say you my love? Were You on the Mountain? *Unknown.* BoLP
Oh Wert Thou in the Cauld Blast. Burns. ELP; EnPE
O Western Wind. *Unknown.* UnTE
O Wha's the Bride? "Hugh MacDiarmid." ErPo; GTBS-P; PoIE
"Oh, what a ball it will be!" they said. Grand Finale. Sara King Carleton. FiSC

O what a cunning guest. Confession. George Herbert. FoBA; MeP
O what a happy soul am I! Blind but Happy. Fanny Crosby. TRV
O! what a thing is love? who can define. Meditation. Joh. 15.13. Greater Love Hath No Man than This That a Man Lay Down His Life for His Friends. Edward Taylor. *Fr.* Preparatory Meditations, Second Series. MeP
Oh! What a thing is man? Lord, who am I? Meditation Thirty-eight. Edward Taylor. *Fr.* Preparatory Meditations, First Series. AP
O! What a thing is might right mannag'd? Meditation. Rev. 1.8. The Almighty. Edward Taylor. *Fr.* Preparatory Meditations, Second Series. MeP
O, what a war of looks was then between them! Shakespeare. *Fr.* Venus and Adonis. UnTE
Oh, what a world of flummery—there's nothing but deceit in it. The Ragged Coat. John Woodward. SGR
Oh, what amiss may I forgive in Thee. Sidney Lanier. *Fr.* The Crystal. TRV
O what are heroes, prophets, men. Pan. Emerson. ILP
"O [or Ah,] what can ail thee, knight-at-arms [or wretched wight]." La Belle Dame sans Merci. Keats. CABA; CBEP; DiPo; ELP; FoBA; GoJo; GTBS-P; ILP; OBNC; OnP; PoIE; PoPo; PoSa; StP; VaPo; WePo
O what can you give me? Idris Davies. *Fr.* Gwalia Deserta. DTC
O what could be more nice? Light Listened. Theodore Roethke. ToPo; UnTE
"Oh! what is that comes gliding in." Sally Simpkin's Lament. Thomas Hood. HaSV
O What Is That Sound Which So Thrills the Ear? W. H. Auden. DaDu
(Ballad) PoPo
Oh, what is the name of King Ringang's daughter? Fair Rohtraut. Eduard Möricke. AGP
"Oh, what is your name, my pretty little maid," he said. The Little Maid. *Unknown.* BSO
O what must it have cost the angels. Birth of Mary. Rainer Maria Rilke. MoRP
O What Pleasure 'Tis to Find. Aphra Behn. *Fr.* Lycidus. UnTE
Oh, what precious peace I find. The Hour of Prayer. Georgia B. Adams. STF
Oh, what sound of gold going. Sunset. Juan Ramón Jiménez. AnSP
Oh! what's the matter? what's the matter? Wordsworth. *Fr.* Goody Blake and Harry Gill. Par
O When I Take My Love Out Walking. Kenneth Patchen. ToPo
Oh, when I was a great big lad. My Old Beaver Cap. *Unknown.* BFSS
Oh, When I Was in Love. A. E. Housman. A Shropshire Lad, XVIII. FaBV
("Oh, when I was in love with you.") WePo
Oh, When I Was Single. *Unknown. See* When I Was a Young Man.
Oh when the early morning at the seaside. East Anglian Bathe. John Betjeman. SD
O when the saints go marchin' in. When the Saints Go Marchin' In. *Unknown.* EaLo
O Where Are You Going? W. H. Auden. *Fr.* The Orators. PoIE; VaPo
"O where are you going?" The False Knight upon the Road. *Unknown.* BuBa; CBEP
"Oh, where are you going, Billy boy, Billy boy." Billy Boy (D *vers.*). *Unknown.* BSO
"Oh, where are you going, my dear kind husband." The Best Old Feller in the World. *Unknown.* BFSS
"O where are you going, my pretty fair maid?" I'm Bound for the Rio Grande. *Unknown.* BSNS
O where are you going? says Milder to Malder. The Cutty Wren. *Unknown.* CBEP; WiR
"Oh where are you going to, all you Big Steamers." Big Steamers. Kipling. Par
"O where hae ye [or have you] been, Lord Randal, my son?" Lord Randal. *Unknown.* CABA; CBEP; DiPo; ILP; PoIE; PoPo; SIV; StP
O Where Have They Vanished All My Years! Walther von der Vogelweide, tr. fr. German by Gillian Barker and Kenneth Gee. AnML
"Oh, where have you been, Billy Boy, Billy Boy." Billy Boy (A and B *vers.*). *Unknown.* BSO
"Oh, where have you been, Jimmy Randal, my son." Jimmy Randal. *Unknown.* BSO
"O where have you been, my long, long [or long-lost] love." The Demon [or Daemon] Lover. *Unknown.* BuBa; CABA; CBEP; PoPo
"O where have you been, Lord Randal, my son?" *See* "O where hae ye been, Lord Randal, my son?"
"Oh, where was I last Christmas night." Oh, Who Will Shoe Your Bonney Feet? *Unknown.* BFSS
O Whisky is the life of man. Whisky Johnny (A *vers.*). *Unknown.* BSNS

O, Whistle and I'll Come to You [or Ye], My Lad. Burns. See Whistle and I'll Come to You, My Lad.
O white clay, O fine clay of the earth cold. Fine Clay. Winifred Shaw. PoAu-1
O White Mistress. Don Johnson. NNP
O, whither sail you, Sir John Franklin? A Ballad of Sir John Franklin. George Henry Boker. OnMSP
Oh who is/ so cosy with. The End of the Day. Robert Creeley. AmPC
"O who is at my bedroom window." Who Is at My Bedroom Window? Unknown. BSNS
Oh Who Is That Young Sinner? A. E. Housman. CBEP
O who rides by night thro' the woodland so wild? The Erlking. Goethe. SIV
O who shall, from this Dungeon, raise. A Dialogue between the Soul and Body. Andrew Marvell. MeP; SeCP
"O who shoe my bonny foot." Annie of Lochroyan. Unknown. BuBa
Oh, Who Will Shoe Your Bonney Feet? with music. Unknown. BFSS
O who will show me those delights on high? Heaven. George Herbert. MeP; SeCP
O who would wish the wind to blow. Brown Adam. Unknown. BuBa
O why do you walk through the fields in gloves. To a Fat Lady Seen from the Train. Frances Cornford. GoJo; WePo
Oh why is heaven built so far. De Profundis. Christina Rossetti. VP
O wild West Wind, thou breath of Autumn's being. Ode to the West Wind. Shelley. CABA; CaFP; CBEP; DiPo; FaBV; FaPL; GTBS-P; ILP; OBNC; OnP; PoIE; PoLF; PoPo; PoSa; StP; VaPo
O Willie's large of limb and bone. The Birth of Robin Hood. Unknown. BuBa
Oh, wilt thou have my hand, Dear, to lie along in thine? Inclusions. Elizabeth Barrett Browning. UnTE
O wind, rend open the heat. Heat. Hilda Doolittle ("H. D."). AP; PoIE; PoPo
O Winter! bar thine adamantine doors. To Winter. Blake. FoBA; WiR
O woman, shapely as the swan. "I Shall Not Die for Thee." Padraic Colum. CTC
O wonderful nonsense of lotions of Lucky Tiger. Haircut. Karl Shapiro. MP
O Woodland Cool. Clemens Brentano, tr. fr. German by Mabel Cotterell. SiGo
O Word of God Incarnate. William Walsham How. TRV
"O words are lightly spoken." The Rose Tree. W. B. Yeats. DiPo; ELP
O World. George Santayana. PoLF; TRV
    (Sonnet: O World.) AmLP
O world, I cannot hold thee close enough! God's World. Edna St. Vincent Millay. FaBV; LV; MoRP; PoPl; PoSC; RePo
O world invisible, we view thee. The Kingdom of God [or In No Strange Land]. Francis Thompson. CaFP; EaLo; GTBS-P; PoIE; PoPo
O world! O life! O time! A Lament. Shelley. GTBS-P; PoPo
O world, thou choosest not the better part. O World [or Sonnet]. George Santayana. AmLP; PoLF; TRV
O world watched over by the cold moon and the mindless stars. Invocation. Carleton Drewry. MoRP
Oh World, Why Do You Thus Pursue Me? Sister Juana Inés de la Cruz, tr. fr. Spanish by Muriel Kittel. AnSP
Oh would I could subdue the flesh. Senex. John Betjeman. DTC
Oh would you know why Henry sleeps. Inhuman Henry; or, Cruelty to Fabulous Animals. A. E. Housman. BBGG
Oh, Yankee Doodle beats the world. City Council. David G. Robinson. SGR
"O ye, all ye that walk in Willowwood." Willowwood, 3. Dante Gabriel Rossetti. The House of Life, LI. VP
O ye wha are sae guid yoursel. Address to the Unco Guid, or the Rigidly Righteous. Burns. EnPE
O years, O months, weeks, days and hours. Maurice Scève. Fr. Délie. RBL
Oh yet we trust that somehow good. In Memoriam A. H. H., LIV. Tennyson. DiPo; EaLo; FaPL; OBNC; PoIE; TRV; VP
O you. Carrefour. Amy Lowell. MoLP
O you dear trees, you have learned so much of beauty. This Way Only. Lesbia Harford. PoAu-1
O You Whom I Often and Silently Come. Walt Whitman. FoBA
O Young and Fearless Prophet. S. Ralph Harlow. TRV
O, young Lochinvar is come out of the west. Lochinvar. Sir Walter Scott. Fr. Marmion. EvOK; FaBV; OBNC; PoPo; RoGo; SIV
O young Mariner. Merlin and the Gleam. Tennyson. FoBA; VP
Oh, your sweetness, softness, smoothness! Lassitude. Paul Verlaine. ErPo

Oh, your thighs. Love Poem. Judson Crews. UnTE
O zummer clote! when the brook's a-sliden. The Clote. William Barnes. ELP
Oak, The. Tennyson. PoPl
Oak-Tree, The. Unknown. CBEP
Oakdale Angel. H. A. Sieber. PoNC
Oaks, how subtle and marine, The. Bearded Oaks. Robert Penn Warren. MP; VaPo
Oars of the Galley, The. Ali ben Hariq, tr. fr. Arabic by Lysander Kemp. AnML
Oars Pulled Up. Conrad Ferdinand Meyer, tr. fr. German by Walter Kaufmann. TwGP
Oatmeal was in their blood and in their names. The Gathering. E. J. Pratt. Fr. Towards the Last Spike. OBCV
Obedience. George Herbert. MeP
Obedience. George Macdonald. TRV
Obey your swine which do exist. Contravention. René Char. CoFP
Obituary. "Max Adeler." DTC
Obituary columns of our paper, The. Synchronized. Larry Rubin. FiSC
Object among dreams, you sit here with your shoes off, An. A Girl in a Library. Randall Jarrell. PoNC
Oblation. Swinburne. BoLP
Obligations. Jane Cooper. AmPC; NePoEA-2
Oblique. Archibald Rutledge. TRV
Obscure Night of the Soul, The. St. John of the Cross. See Dark Night of the Soul, The.
Obscurely yet most surely called to praise. Praise in Summer. Richard Wilbur. PP
Obscurest night involved the sky. The Castaway. William Cowper. CABA; CBEP; EiCP; ELP; EnPE; PoSa
Observation of Facts. Charles Tomlinson. NePoEA-2
Observe God in His works: here fountains flow. Henry Vaughan. Fr. Rules and Lessons. TRV
Observe the Cat upon this page. The Cat. Oliver Herford. FaBV
Observe the Whooping Crane. The Whooping Crane. Vassar Miller. ToPo
Observe this man, he is an engineer. Revelation. Nancy Keesing. PoAu-2
Obsessions. Denise Levertov. NePoEA-2
Obsessions governing an art, The. Aids to Composition. Robert Conquest. PP
Occident. Georg Trakl, tr. fr. German by Michael Hamburger. MGP
Ocean, The. Byron. Fr. Childe Harold's Pilgrimage, IV. FaBV
    ("There is a pleasure in the pathless woods.") HaSV; PoIE
Ocean. Robinson Jeffers. AP
Ocean too has winter-views serene, The. Winter Views Serene. George Crabbe. Fr. The Borough. OBNC
Ocean Wave, The. Unknown. See Lady Isabel and the Elf-Knight.
Ocean Wood, The. Lord De Tabley. CBEP
Octaves, sels. E. A. Robinson. ILP
    "Here by the windy docks I stand alone," XXIII.
    "Like a white wall whereon forever breaks," XVIII.
    "Prophet of dead words defeats himself, The," XX.
October. Robert Frost. GoJo
October. Rose Fyleman. RePo
October. Patrick Kavanagh. GTBS-P
October. William Morris. Fr. The Earthly Paradise. OBNC
October. H. A. Sieber. PoNC
October Days. James Larkin Pearson. PoNC
October Eclogue. Spenser. Fr. The Shepheardes Calender. PP
October Flies. Jascha Kessler. AmPC
October gave a party. October's Party. George Cooper. PoLF; RePo
October is a breakfast food. A Bowl of October. Helen Bevington. PoNC; RePo
October Journey. Margaret Walker. AmNP
October Maples, Portland. Richard Wilbur. CoPo
October Night. Attilio Bertolucci, tr. fr. Italian by Carlo L. Golino. CoIP
October's Bright Blue Weather. Helen Hunt Jackson. PoSC
October's Party. George Cooper. PoLF; RePo
October's Song. Eleanor Farjeon. PoSC
Octopus. A. C. Hilton. Par
Octopus, The. Ogden Nash. SoPo; WePo
Octopussycat. Kenyon Cox. SoPo
Odcomb's Complaint, sel. John Taylor.
    Sonnet: Mackado, Fustian and Motley. CBEP
Ode: Autumn. Thomas Hood. ILP; OBNC
Ode: "Before me, where a raven croaks." Théophile de Viau, tr. fr. French by John R. Galt. RBL
Ode: "God save the Rights of Man!" Philip Freneau. AP
Ode: "How sleep the brave who sink to rest." William Collins. See How Sleep the Brave.
Ode: Inscribed to W. H. Channing. Emerson. AP; ILP
Ode: Intimations of Immortality from Recollections of Early Childhood. Wordsworth. CABA; CaFP; DiPo; FoBA; ILP; OBNC; PoIE; StP

(Ode on Intimations of Immortality from Recollections of Early Childhood.) GTBS-P; VaPo
Sels.
"Our birth is but a sleep and a forgetting." BiCB; EaLo; FaBV; PoSa; TRV
"There was a time when meadow, grove, and stream." BoC
Ode, An: "Merchant, to secure his treasure, The." Matthew Prior. CABA; CBEP; EiCP
("Merchant, to secure his treasure, The.") GTBS-P
Ode: "Now I find thy looks were feigned." Thomas Lodge. *Fr. Phyllis.* EnRePo
Ode: Of Wit. Abraham Cowley. SeCP
Ode: On Intimations of Immortality from Recollections of Early Childhood. Wordsworth. *See* Ode: Intimations of Immortality. . .
Ode: On the Death of William Butler Yeats. A. J. M. Smith. OBCV
Ode, An: Secundum Artem. William Cowper. PP
Ode: "Sleep sweetly in your humble graves." Henry Timrod. LV; StP
(Ode Sung on the Occasion of Decorating the Graves of the Confederate Dead.) AP
Ode: "Spacious firmament on high, The." Addison. *See* Spacious Firmament on High, The.
Ode: Spirit Wooed, The. Richard Watson Dixon. OBNC
Ode, An: To Himselfe. Ben Jonson. *See* Ode to Himself.
Ode: Written in the Beginning of the Year 1746. William Collins. *See* How Sleep the Brave.
Ode for Ben Jonson, An. Robert Herrick. DiPo; PoSa; SeCP
Ode for the American Dead in Korea. Thomas McGrath. PoPl
Ode in Time of Hesitation, An. William Vaughn Moody. AP
Ode on a Distant Prospect of Clapham Academy. Thomas Hood. CBEP
Ode on a Distant Prospect of Eton College. Thomas Gray. CABA; EiCP; EnPE; GTBS-P; StP
Ode on a Grecian Urn. Keats. BoC; CABA; CaFP; CBEP; DiPo; FaPL; FoBA; ILP; OBNC; OnP; PoIE; PoPo; PoSa; StP
Ode on Contemplating Clapham Junction. Christopher Middleton. *Fr. Herman Moon's Hourbook.* NePoEA-2
Ode on Indolence. Keats. OBNC
Ode on Intimations of Immortality from Recollections of Early Childhood. Wordsworth. *See* Ode: Intimations of Immortality . . .
Ode on Melancholy. Keats. CABA; CaFP; CBEP; DiPo; FoBA; ILP; OBNC; PoIE; StP; VaPo
Ode on Solitude. Pope. DiPo; OnP; PoIE; PoPl
(Quiet Life, The.) GTBS-P; PoPo
(Solitude.) CBEP
Ode on the Death of a Favourite Cat [Drowned in a Tub of Gold Fishes]. Thomas Gray. CBEP; EiCP; VaPo
(Cat and the Fish, The.) WiR
(On a Favourite Cat, Drowned in a Tub of Gold Fishes.) GTBS-P
(On the Death of a Favourite Cat, Drowned in a Tub of Gold Fishes.) PoLF
Ode on the Death of [Mr.] Thomson. William Collins. CBEP; EiCP
Ode on the Death of the Duke of Wellington, *sel.* Tennyson. "People's voice, A! we are a people yet." ACV
Ode on the Despoilers of Learning in an American University (1947), An. Yvor Winters. StP
Ode on the Morning of Christ's Nativity. Milton. *See* On the Morning of Christs Nativity.
Ode on the Pleasure Arising from Vicissitude. Thomas Gray. EiCP; GTBS-P
Ode on the Poetical Character. William Collins. EiCP; EnPE; StP
Ode on the Poets. Keats. GTBS-P
Ode on the Popular Superstitions of the Highlands of Scotland, An. William Collins. EiCP; EnPE
Ode on the Spring. Thomas Gray. EiCP; GTBS-P
Ode on Venice. Byron. CABL
Ode Recited at the Harvard Commemoration. James Russell Lowell. AP
"Life may be given in many ways," *sel., fr.* V and VI. LiPo
Ode Sung on the Occasion of Decorating the Graves of the Confederate Dead. Henry Timrod. *See* Ode: "Sleep sweetly in your humble graves."
Ode to a Model. Vladimir Nabokov. PoPl
Ode to a Nightingale. Keats. CABA; CaFP; DiPo; FaPL; FoBA; GTBS-P; ILP; OBNC; OnP; PoIE; PoPo; StP; VaPo
Magic Casements, *sel.* FaBV
Ode to an Æolus's Harp. William Mason. WaPE
Ode to Arnold Schoenberg. Charles Tomlinson. NePoEA-2
Ode to Autumn. Keats. *See* To Autumn.
Ode to Beauty. Emerson. AP
Ode to Duty. Wordsworth. GTBS-P; LV; TRV
Ode to Evening. William Collins. CABA; CaFP; CBEP; EiCP; EnPE; OnP; StP

(To Evening.) GTBS-P
Ode to Evening. Joseph Warton. WaPE
Ode to Fancy. Joseph Warton. EnPE; WaPE
Ode to Fear. William Collins. EiCP; EnPE
Ode to Felipe Ruiz. Luis de León, *tr. fr. Spanish by* Aubrey F. G. Bell. RBL
Ode to Fidel Castro. Edward Field. CoPo
"O Boy-God, Muse of Poets," *sel.* PtTo
Ode to Francisco Salinas. Luis de León, *tr. fr. Spanish by* Edwin Morgan. AnSP
Ode to Himselfe ("Come leave the loathed stage"). Ben Jonson. SeCP
Ode to Himself[e], An ("Where do'st thou careless lie"). Ben Jonson. EnRePo; SeCP
Ode to Horror. *Unknown.* WaPE
Ode to Mercy. William Collins. EiCP
Ode to Mirth. Tobias George Smollett. WaPE
Ode to Morning. William Mason. WaPE
Ode to Nobody. Hans Magnus Enzensberger, *tr. fr. German by* Christopher Middleton. MGP
Ode to Pity. William Collins. EiCP; EnPE
Ode to Psyche. Keats. CABA; CaFP; CBEP; DiPo; OBNC; PP; StP
Ode to Simplicity. William Collins. EiCP
Ode to Sleep. Tobias George Smollett. WaPE
Ode to the Confederate Dead. Allen Tate. AnMoPo; AP; CABA; PoIE
Ode to the Hon. Miss Carteret. Ambrose Philips. WaPE
Ode to the Setting Sun, *sel.* Francis Thompson.
"Now that the red glare of thy fall is blown." OBNC
Ode to the West Wind. Shelley. CABA; CaFP; CBEP; DiPo; FaBV; FaPL; GTBS-P; ILP; OBNC; OnP; PoIE; PoLF; PoPo; PoSa; StP; VaPo
Ode to Winter. Thomas Campbell. GTBS-P
Ode, An, upon a Question Moved, Whether Love Should Continue for Ever? Lord Herbert of Cherbury. SeCP
Ode upon Dr. Harvey, *sel.* Abraham Cowley.
"Coy Nature (which remain'd, though aged grown)." Par
Ode Which Was Prefixed to a Prayer Booke Given to a Young Gentlewoman, An. Richard Crashaw. MeP
Ode Written in MDCCXLVI. William Collins. *See* How Sleep the Brave.
Odes, *sels.* Horace, *tr. fr. Latin.*
I, 5. To a Girl ("Quis multa gracilis"), *tr. by* Milton. WiR
(Another to the Same, *tr. by* William Browne.) WiR
I, 11. Ask Not Ungainly ("Tu ne quaesieris"), *tr. by* Ezra Pound. CTC
I, 23. Time to Choose a Lover ("Vitas hinnuleo"), *tr. by* Patrick Branwell Brontë. UnTE
I, 25. Young Men Come Less Often, The—Isn't It So? ("Parcius iunctas quatiunt fenestras"), *tr. by* Robert Fitzgerald. ErPo
(Passing of Lydia, The, *tr. by* Louis Untermeyer.) UnTE
I, 31. By the Flat Cup ("Quid dedicatum"), *tr. by* Ezra Pound. CTC
I, 33. It Always Happens ("Albi, ne doleas"), *tr. by* Thomas Charles Baring. UnTE
II, 5. Too Young for Love ("Nondum subacta"), *tr. by* Louis Untermeyer. UnTE
II, 8. Barine, the Incorrigible ("Ulla si iuris"), *tr. by* Louis Untermeyer. UnTE
II, 10. Golden Mean, The ("Rectius vives"), *tr. by* Margaret M. Fitzgerald. SiGo
III, 2. Call to Youth ("Angustam amice"), *tr. by* Hugh Vibart MacNaghten. SiGo
III, 9. Teasing Lovers, The ("Donec gratus eram"), *tr. by* Louis Untermeyer. UnTE
III, 29. Ode to Maecenas ("Tyrrhena regum progenies"), *par. by* Dryden. SiGo, 8 *ll.*
III, 30. This Monument Will Outlast ("Exegi monumentum aere perennius"), *tr. by* Ezra Pound. CTC
Odes, *sel.* Pindar, *tr. fr. Greek.*
Nemean Odes.
I Bless This Man, *fr.* XI, *tr. by* Richmond Lattimore. SD
Odes, *sel.* Pierre de Ronsard, *tr. fr. French by* Alan Conder.
IV, 4. On the Choice of His Sepulchre. RBL
Odes to Nea, *sels.* Thomas Moore. OBNC
"I pray you, let us roam no more."
"Nay, tempt me not to love again."
Odi et Amo. Catullus, *tr. fr. Latin by* Ezra Pound. CTC
(To Lesbia, *tr. by* Abraham Cowley.) PoPl
Odorous shade lingers the fair day's ghost, An. Night. Henri de Régnier. SiGo
Odour, The. George Herbert. MeP
Odysseus heard the sirens; they were singing. The Sirens. John Manifold. VaPo
Odysseus' Song to Calypso. Peter Kane Dufault. ErPo
Odyssey, The, *sels.* Homer, *tr. fr. Greek by* George Chapman. CTC
"Downe to the king's most bright-kept baths they went," *fr.* IV.
"For my part, I'le not meddle with the cause," *fr.* XIV.
"From her bed's high and odoriferous roome," *fr.* IV.
"Twelve herds of oxen, no lesse flockes of sheepe," *fr.* XIV.

Odyssey, The, *sels.* (*continued*)
"Where neither king nor shepheard want comes neare," *fr.*
IV.
Odyssey,The. Andrew Lang. OBNC; PoLF
Oedipus, *sel.* Dryden.
Spell, A, *fr.* III, i. WiR
Oedipus at Colonus, *sels.* Sophocles, *tr. fr. Greek.*
"Endure what life God gives and ask no longer span," *tr.* by
W. B. Yeats. DTC
Old Age, *tr.* by A. E. Housman. SiGo
Oedipus at San Francisco. Donald Finkel. CoPo
Oenone. Tennyson. VP
O'er all the hill-tops. Wanderer's Night Song. Longfellow.
PoPl
O'er the snow, through the air, to the mountain. Alpine
Spirit's Song. Thomas Lovell Beddoes. OBNC
O'er the wild gannet's bath. Runilda's Chant. George Darley.
Fr. Ethelstan. HaSV
Of a Bee. Tasso, *tr. fr. Italian by* William Drummond of
Hawthornden. RBL
Of a Contented Mind. Thomas, Lord Vaux. EnRePo
Of a great heroine I mean to tell. Earl of Rochester. *Fr.* A
Panegyric on Nelly. UnTE
Of a pendulum's mildness, with her feet up. A Timepiece.
James Merrill. NePoEA-2
Of a Rich Miser. George Turberville. EnRePo
Of A' the Airts. Burns. EiCP; FaPL
    (I Love My Jean.) ILP
    (Jean.) GTBS-P; WePo
Of a wild colonial boy, Jack Davis was his name. The Wild
Colonial Boy. *Unknown.* BSNS
Of Adam's first wife, Lilith, it is told. Body's Beauty. Dante
Gabriel Rossetti. The House of Life, LXXVIII. ILP
Of all creatures women be best. What Women Are Not. *Un-*
known. MeEL
Of All Known Flowers, Men Hold the Rose Most Rare.
Jean Froissart, *tr. fr. French by* Jacques LeClercq. AnML
Of all the burthens man must bear. Fable XIII: Plutus,
Cupid and Time. John Gay. EiCP
Of all the causes which conspire to blind. Pope. *Fr.* An Essay
on Criticism, Pt. II. ILP; PoIE
Of all the girls that are so smart. Sally in Our Alley. Henry
Carey. CBEP; FaPL; GTBS-P; PoSC
Of all the girls that e'er were seen. Ballad. John Gay. ErPo
Of All the Idiots That Abound. Samuel Hoffenstein. RePo
Of all the northern Scottish chiefs. Sir James the Rose (B
vers.). *Unknown.* BSNS
Of all the race of silver-wingèd flies. The Butterfly. Spenser.
Fr. Muiopotmos. BoC
Of all the rides since the birth of time. Skipper Ireson's
Ride. Whittier. AP; PoLF; PoPo; SIV; ThLM
Of all the Scottish northern chiefs. Sir James the Rose (A
vers.). *Unknown.* BSNS
Of all the ships upon the blue. Captain Reece. W. S. Gilbert.
EvOK
Of all the souls that stand create. Emily Dickinson. AP;
DiPo; FaPL
Of all the thoughts of God that are. The Sleep. Elizabeth
Barrett Browning. TRV
Of all the Tipsham lazybones. Lazybones. Robert P. Tris-
tram Coffin. SIV
Of all the toasts that Britain boasts. Polly Peachum. Henry
Carey. WaPE
Of all the various lots around the ball. The Poet; a Rhapsody.
Mark Akenside. PoPl
Of all wemen that ever were borne. Mary Complains to Other
Mothers. *Unknown.* MeEL
Of an Heroical Answer of a Great Roman Lady to Her Hus-
band. Sir John Harington. ErPo
Of an old King in a story. Variations of an Air: After W. B.
Yeats. G. K. Chesterton. Par
Of asphodel, that greeny flower. William Carlos Williams.
Fr. Asphodel, That Greeny Flower. PP
Of bronze—and blaze. Emily Dickinson. AP
Of Certain Irish Fairies. Arthur Guiterman. PoLF
Of Commerce and Society. Geoffrey Hill. NePoEA-2
Of Constance holy legends tell. The Nun. Edward Moore.
WaPE
Of cool sweet dew and radiance mild. Simples. James Joyce.
PoPl
Of course—I prayed. Emily Dickinson. AP
Of courtesy it is much less. Courtesy. Hilaire Belloc. BoC
Of Death. Samuel Harding. CBEP
Of Dust and Stars. Vernon Ward. PoNC
Of English Verse. Edmund Waller. PP; SeCP
Of fields with dead bestrewed around. Upon the Feast of
St. Simon and St. Jude. Samuel Johnson. EiCP
Of God we ask one favor. Emily Dickinson. EaLo; FoBA
Of Heaven or Hell I have no power to sing. An Apology.
William Morris. *Fr.* The Earthly Paradise. OBNC;
PoIE
Of His Cynthia. Fulke Greville. *See* Away with These Self-
loving Lads.
Of His Lady's Old Age. Pierre de Ronsard, *tr. fr. French by*
Andrew Lang. *Fr.* Sonnets pour Hélène. CTC

("When you are very old, at evening.") RBL
Of living creatures most I prize. Butterfly. William Jay
Smith. GoJo; RePo
Of Love. Kahlil Gibran. *Fr.* The Prophet. PoLF
Of Loving at First Sight. Edmund Waller. SeCP
Of man's first disobedience, and the fruit. Invocation. Mil-
ton. *Fr.* Paradise Lost, I. DiPo
Of Mary. A New Song of Mary. *Unknown.* MeEL
Of Mistress D. S. Barnabe Googe. EnRePo
Of Modern Poetry. Wallace Stevens. PP
Of Money. Barnabe Googe. EnRePo
Of Motion. O. B. Hardison, Jr. PoNC
Of my lady well me rejoise I may! A Description of His
Ugly Lady. Thomas Hoccleve. MeEL
Of Nelson and the North. The Battle of the Baltic. Thomas
Campbell. CBEP; GTBS-P; HaSV; RoGo
Of Neptune's empire let us sing. In Praise of Neptune.
Thomas Campion. CBEP; WiR
Of on that is so fair and bright. A Hymn to Mary. *Unknown.*
MeEL
Of Poor B. B. Bertolt Brecht, *tr. fr. German by* Michael
Hamburger. MGP
Of Seals and Arms. John Taylor. CBEP
Of Swimming in Lakes and Rivers. Bertolt Brecht, *tr. fr.*
German by H. R. Hays. SD
Of That Same. Tasso, *tr. fr. Italian by* William Drummond
of Hawthornden. RBL
Of the birds that fly in the farthest sea. The Flying Fish, II.
John Gray. OBNC
Of the Characteristics of Small Women. Juan Ruiz, Arch-
priest of Hita, *tr. fr. Spanish by* William M. Davis. *Fr.*
The Book of True Love. AnML
Of the Characters of Women, *sel.* Pope. *Fr.* Moral Essays,
Epistle II.
"Yet Cloe sure was form'd without a spot." ErPo
Of the Child with the Bird at the Bush. Bunyan. CBEP
Of the Clock and the Cock. George Turberville. EnRePo
Of the dark past. Ecce Puer. James Joyce. PoIE; PoPl;
StP
Of the filth and order of the world. A Series 5.8. John
Wieners. CoPo
Of the honorable young gentlemen who this year. August-
Advertisement. Theodor Storm. AGP
Of the Implements for Walking the Streets, and Signs of the
Weather. John Gay. *Fr.* Trivia. EiCP
Of the Incomparable Treasure of the Scripture. *Unknown.*
TRV
Of the Last Verses in the Book. Edmund Waller. SeCP
Of the Man Who Sits in the Cellar. Hans Werner Cohn, *tr.*
fr. German by Christopher Middleton. MGP
Of the Months: Twelve Sonnets. Folgore da San Geminiano.
See Sonnets of the Months.
Of the myriad afflictions that beset Hellas. The Breed of
Athletes. Euripides. SD
Of the Progresse of the Soule: The Second Anniversary. John
Donne. SeCP
(Second Anniversarie, The: Of the Progres of the Soule.)
MeP
Of the Unscathing Fire. Anne Ridler. MoLP
Of the Use of Riches. Pope. Moral Essays, Epistle IV.
CABL
Of thee kind boy I ask no red and white. Sonnet II [*or* To
Cupid]. Sir John Suckling. CBEP; StP
Of thes four letters purpose I. A New Song of Mary. *Un-*
known. MeEL
Of thes Frer Minours me thenkes moch wonder. Friars'
Enormities. *Unknown.* MeEL
Of this fair volume which we world do name. The Book of
the World [*or* The Lessons of Nature]. Giambattista
Marino, *tr.* by William Drummond of Hawthornden.
GTBS-P; RBL
Of Violets. Vernon Ward. PoNC
Of Walking the Streets by Night. John Gay. *Fr.* Trivia.
EiCP
Of Women. *Unknown, tr. fr. Arabic by* E. Powys Mathers.
Fr. The Thousand and One Nights. ErPo
Of yore, as now, aringing. The Spinstress' Song. Clemens
Brentano. AGP
Of Young Woman Bent Back among the Flowers. Salvatore
Quasimodo, *tr. fr. Italian by* Allen Mandelbaum. CoIP
Of your trouble, Ben, to ease me. Her Man Described by Her
Owne Dictamen. Ben Jonson. *Fr.* A Celebration of
Charis. SeCP
Off Rivière du Loup. Duncan Campbell Scott. OBCV
Off Saguenay. A. G. Bailey. ACV
Off Spectacle Island. Richard Eberhart. ToPo
Off to the War. Stephen Vincent Benét. *Fr.* John Brown's
Body. SIV
Off Viareggio. Kenneth Pitchford. CoPo
Off wtih sleep, love, up from bed. Love in May. Jean
Passerat. SiGo
Offender, The. Denise Levertov. NePoEA-2
Offering. Thomas MacDonagh. ACV
Office feels like a sealed glass case today, The. What
Grandma Knew. Edward Field. CoPo

Offshore. Philip Booth. SD
Oft Have I Mused. Sir Philip Sidney. EnRePo
Oft have I seen at some cathedral door. Divina Commedia, I. Longfellow. AP; ILP
Oft have I seen, when that renewing breath. Resurrection and Immortality. Henry Vaughan. MeP
Oft I had heard of Lucy Gray. Lucy Gray; or, Solitude. Wordsworth. FoBA
Oft in the Stilly Night. Thomas Moore. CBEP; OBNC (Light of Other Days, The.) GTBS-P; WePo
Oft Thou Hast with Greedy Ear. *Unknown.* EnRePo
Oft-told Tale, An. *Unknown.* SGR
Often beneath the wave, wide from this ledge. At Melville's Tomb. Hart Crane. AmLP; AP; PoIE
Often had I found her fair. Chorale. A. D. Hope. ErPo;UnTE
Often, half-way to sleep. In Procession. Robert Graves. MP
Often I have thought: is this. Margherita Guidacci. *Fr.* All Saints' Day. CoIP
Often I think of the beautiful town. My Lost Youth. Longfellow. AP; FaBV; GoJo; HaSV; OnP; PoLF; RoGo; StP
Often Rebuked. *At.* to Charlotte Brontë *and to* Emily Brontë. PoIE
(Stanzas: "Often rebuked, yet always back returning.") OBNC
Often the evening is red. High Place. André Pieyre de Mandiargues. CoFP
Oftener seen, the more I lust, The. Out of Sight, Out of Mind. Barnabe Googe. EnRePo; PoIE
O'Grady's Goat ("O'Grady lived in Shanty row"). Will S. Hays. PoLF
Ogres and Pygmies. Robert Graves. CABA
Ohio, *with music. Unknown.* BSO
Okay a nightingale, Robin Blaser. *Fr.* The Faerie Queene. CoPo
Old Adam. Thomas Lovell Beddoes. *Fr.* Death's Jest Book. ELP
(Carrion Crow, The.) WiR
(Wolfram's Song.) CBEP
Old Age. Sophocles, *tr. fr. Greek by* A. E. Housman. Oedipus at Colonus. SiGo
Old Age. Edmund Waller. BoC
Old Age am I, with lockes thin and hoar. Age. Sir Thomas More. *Fr.* The Pageants of Thomas More. EnRePo
Old Age Home, The. Theodore Holmes. CoPo
Old age is. To Waken an Old Lady. William Carlos Williams. PoIE
Old Anchor Chanty. Herbert Trench. HaSV
Old, and abandoned by each venal friend. Impromptu [*or* Lord Holland's Seat near M——e, Kent]. Thomas Gray. CABA; EiCP
Old and New Year Ditties, *sel.* Christina Rossetti. "Passing away, saith the World, passing away," III. OBNC
Old and the New, The. "Q. B. M." SoPo
Old Andy never went to school. Here Is Wisdom. James Larkin Pearson. PoNC
Old Arrowhead Thoughts of a Late War. Frank Borden Hanes. PoNC
Old Astronomer, The, *sel.* Sarah Williams. "Though my soul may set in darkness, it will rise in perfect light." TRV
Old Bachelor, The. *Unknown.* BSNS
Old Bangum, *with music. Unknown.* BFSS
Old Bark Hut, The. *Unknown.* PoAu-1
Old battlefield, fresh with Spring flowers again. Three Haiku. Basho. *Fr.* Seven Poems. PoPo; SiGo
Old Beard a-Shakin', *with music. Unknown.* BFSS
Old Bill the Whaler said to me. Bill the Whaler. Will Lawson. PoAu-1
Old Blue. *Unknown.* SD
Old Botany Bay. Mary Gilmore. PoAu-1
Old Bridge, The. Hilda Conkling. PoPo
Old brown thorn trees break in two over Cumner Strand, The. Red Hanrahan's Song about Ireland. W. B. Yeats. ACV
Old Buccaneer, The. Charles Kingsley. *See* Last Buccaneer, The.
Old Bullock Dray, The. *Unknown.* PoAu-1
Old Burying-Ground, The. Whittier. AP
Old Cabin, The. Paul Lawrence Dunbar. PoLF
Old Chimney. Edith Earnshaw. PoNC
Old Chisholm Trail, The, *with music. Unknown.* BFSS
Old Christmas. Roy Helton. SIV
Old Churchyard of Bonchurch, The. Philip Bourke Marston. OBNC
Old Cloak, The. *Unknown.* BuBa
Old Closet. Selma Robinson. LV
Old Countryside. Louise Bogan. AmLP
Old Crabbed Men. James Reeves. ErPo
Old Crumbly Crust, *with music. Unknown.* BFSS
Old Cumberland Beggar, The. Wordsworth. CABL
Old Dan'l. L. A. G. Strong. PoSC
Old Dick Johnson, gentleman adventurer. The Dick Johnson Reel. "Jake Falstaff." EvOK
Old dog barks backward without getting up, The. The Span of Life. Robert Frost. DiPo

Old Eben Flood, climbing alone one night. Mr. Flood's Party. E. A. Robinson. AP; CABA; CaFP; EvOK; FaPL; ILP; OnP; PoPl; PoPo; PoSa
Old Egyptians hid their wit. On Mr. Nash's Picture. Jane Brereton. WaPE
Old England is eaten by knaves. Song. Alexander McLachlan. *Fr.* The Emigrant. OBCV
Old Euclid drew a circle. Euclid. Vachel Lindsay. PoPo
Old Familiar Faces, The. Charles Lamb. CBEP; GTBS-P; PoPl; PoSa
Old Farmer Alone. Robert P. Tristram Coffin. MoLP
Old Father Grimes, that good old man. Roll, Johnny Booger. *Unknown.* BFSS
Old Fellow. Ernest Walsh. ErPo
Old Feminist, The. Phyllis McGinley. ThLM
Old Forty-nine. Mart Taylor. SGR
Old friend, your place is empty now. No more. To Scott. Winifred Letts. PoLF
Old Fritz, on this rotating bed. A Flat One. W. D. Snodgrass. AmPC; AP; NePoEA-2; PoCh
Old Ghost, The. Thomas Lovell Beddoes. WiR
Old Gods, The. Edwin Muir. EaLo
Old Granddaddy's Dead (A *vers., with music*). *Unknown.* BSO
Old Grey Hearse goes rolling by, The. The Hearse Song. *Unknown.* DTC
Old Grumble, *with music. Unknown.* BSO
Old horse dies slow, The. When Structure Fails Rhyme Attempts to Come to the Rescue. William Carlos Williams. PP
Old House waits for no one, The. The House on Maple Hill. Stanley McNail. FiSC
Old Houses of Flanders, The. Ford Madox Ford. CTC
Old Hunter. Guy Owen. PoNC
Old Hup. Thad Stem, Jr. PoNC
Old Inmate, An. Kenneth Mackenzie. PoAu-2
Old Irish Blessing, An. *Unknown.* TRV
Old Ironsides. Oliver Wendell Holmes. AmLP; AP; FaPL; LV; PoPl; ThLM
Old Ironsides at anchor lay. The Main-Truck; or, A Leap for Life. George P. Morris. PoLF
Old Joe Finley had a wee pig. Old Sam Fanny (B *vers.*). *Unknown.* BSO
Old John Bax. Charles H. Souter. PoAu-1
Old Jumpety-Bumpety-Hop-and-Go-One. The Kangaroo. *Unknown.* SoPo
Old Keg of Rum, The. *Unknown.* PoAu-1
Old King Cole. Mother Goose. SoPo
Old King James made a vow. King William and King James. *Unknown.* BFSS
Old Knight, The. George Peele. *See* His Golden Locks.
Old lady writes me in a spidery style, An. A Letter from Brooklyn. Derek Walcott. ToPo
Old Log House. James S. Tippett. RePo
Old, mad, blind, despised, and dying king, An. England in 1819 [*or* Sonnet]. Shelley. CABA; CBEP; StP
Old Man. Elizabeth Jennings. NePoEA-2
Old man asked the girl what she wanted for supper, The. An Old Man's Courtship. *Unknown.* BFSS
Old man bending I come among new faces, An. The Wound-Dresser. Walt Whitman. AP
Old man called for Johnny, The. Johnny and the Highwayman. *Unknown.* BFSS
Old man dozed, The. The hospital quietened. Burns Singer. *Fr.* Sonnets for a Dying Man. NePoEA-2
Old Man Dreams, The. Oliver Wendell Holmes. PoLF
Old man going [*or* traveling] a lone highway, An. The Bridge Builder [*or* Building the Bridge for Him]. Will Allen Dromgoole. STF; TRV
Old man in a lodge within a park, An. Chaucer. Longfellow. AmLP; AP; CBEP; DiPo; PP
Old man leading his jacknife horse, An. Crisis. Thad Stem, Jr. PoNC
Old man leaning on a gate, An. From My Window. Mary Elizabeth Coleridge. OBNC
Old Man Playing with Children. John Crowe Ransom. AnMoPo
Old Man Rain. Madison Cawein. PoSC
Old Man Sat in a Waterfall, An. Norman Nicholson. DaDu
Old Man, traveling a lone highway, An. *See* Old man going a lone highway, An.
Old Man Who Came Over the Moor, An (B *and* D *vers., with music*). *Unknown.* BSO
Old man whose black face, An. The Rainwalkers. Denise Levertov. NePoEA-2
Old man, write your poem. I tell you this, your son. Poetry Revival. Frank Borden Hanes. PoNC
Old Man's Comforts and How He Gained Them, The. Robert Southey. Par
Old Man's Courtship, An. *Unknown.* BFSS
Old Man's Fancy. Thad Stem, Jr. PoNC
Old man's fleet that wounded the Pacific, The. A Memorial for President Kennedy. Robert G. Tucker. OPP
Old man's words, The (something has skittered the cattle). The Panther Possible. William D. Barney. FiSC

Old Marrieds, The. Gwendolyn Brooks. AmNP
Old mayor climbed the belfry tower, The. The High Tide on the Coast of Lincolnshire (1571). Jean Ingelow. OnMSP
Old Meg of Kitrann. Joseph Joel Keith. FiSC
Old Meg she was a gipsy [or gypsy]. Meg Merrilies [or Merrilees]. Keats. CBEP; ELP; PoPo
Old Men, The. Irving Feldman. MP
Old Men. Ogden Nash. EvOK
Old Men Admiring Themselves in the Water, The. W. B. Yeats. GoJo
Old men, white-haired, beside the ancestral graves. Three Haiku. Basho. PoPo
Old Menalcas on a day. The Palmer's Ode. Robert Greene. Fr. Never Too Late. CTC; EnRePo
Old Mr. Hobson's gone to Florida. Post Card. Thad Stem, Jr. PoNC
Old Molly Means was a hag and a witch. Molly Means. Margaret Walker. AmNP
Old moon is tarnished, The. Sea Lullaby. Elinor Wylie. SIV
Old moon my eyes are new moon with human footprint. Poem Rocket. Allen Ginsberg. CoPo
Old Mother Earth woke up from her sleep. A Spring Song. Unknown. PoLF
Old Mother Goose, when. Mother Goose. Unknown. SoPo
Old Mother Hubbard. Mother Goose. OnMSP; SoPo
Old Mother Shuttle. Unknown. EvOK
Old Mother Slipper Slapper jumped out o' bed. The Moonlight Night. Unknown. BSO
Old Mother Twitchet had but one eye. Riddle. Mother Goose. SoPo
Old Nick in Sorel ("Old Nick took a fancy, as many men tell"). Standish O'Grady. OBCV
Old Oaken Bucket, The. Samuel Woodworth. LV
Old One, lie down. Up the Hill, down the Hill. Eleanor Farjeon. PoSC
Old Ones, The. Frances Bellerby. DaDu
Old orange hollow head, eyes aflame. Halloween: A Poem for Children. Robert Watson. PoNC
Old order changeth, yielding place to new, The. Tennyson. Fr. Morte d'Arthur. TRV
Old Paint, with music. Unknown. BFSS
Old Peasant in the Billiard Saloon, The. Huw Menai. ACV
Old Peter Grimes made fishing his employ. Peter Grimes. George Crabbe. Fr. The Borough. EnPE
Old poets fostered under friendlier skies. Poets and Their Bibliographies. Tennyson. PP
Old Pond, The. Basho. See Haiku: "Ancient pond, The."
Old Pope Is Comforted by the Thought of the Young Pompilia, The. Robert Browning. Fr. The Ring and the Book, X. BoC
Old priest Peter Gilligan, The. The Ballad of Father Gilligan. W. B. Yeats. EaLo; PoPo; SIV; WePo
Old Prison, The. Judith Wright. PoAu-2
Old Quin Queeribus. Nancy Byrd Turner. EvOK; SoPo
Old Ramillies, The. Unknown. BSNS
Old Repair Man, The. Fenton Johnson. AmNP
Old Room. Erich Fried, tr. fr. German by Michael Hamburger. MGP
Old rude church, with bare, bald tower, is here, The. Wordsworth's Grave. Sir William Watson. OBNC
Old Sam Fanny (B vers., with music). Unknown. BSO
Old Sam Smith. The Shepherd. Mary Gilmore. ACV; PoAu-1
Old Shepherd's Prayer. Charlotte Mew. EaLo
Old Ships, The. James Elroy Flecker. EvOK; HaSV; RoGo
Old Silver church in a forest, An. Poet to His Love. Maxwell Bodenheim. BoLP; PoPl
Old sisters at our Maris Stella House. Mother Marie Therese. Robert Lowell. CoPo
Old Socrates, whose wisdom did excel. To Master Edward Cobham. Barnabe Googe. EnRePo
Old Song. Louis Dudek. ACV
Old Song, The. Charles Kingsley. See Young and Old.
Old Song, An. "Yehoash," tr. fr. Yiddish by Marie Syrkin. SiGo
Old Song Re-sung, An. John Masefield. EvOK
Old South Boston Aquarium stands, The. For the Union Dead. Robert Lowell. MP
Old Squire, The. Wilfrid Scawen Blunt. SD
Old Stoic, The. Emily Brontë. FaPL; OBNC; PoLF; PoPl; PoPo
Old Summerhouse, The. Walter de la Mare. GTBS-P
Old Swimmer, The. Christopher Morley. LV; SD
Old Taffyham, with music. Unknown. BSO
Old Tennis Player. Gwendolyn Brooks. SD
Old, the mad, the blind have fairest daughters, The. The Beauty of Job's Daughters. Jay Macpherson. ACV; PoCh
Old thorn tree in a stony place, An. Ode: On the Death of William Butler Yeats. A. J. M. Smith. OBCV
Old-Time Sea-Fight, An. Walt Whitman. Fr. Song of Myself. OnMSP
Old Tippecanoe. Unknown. ThLM

Old Toast. Unknown. WePo
Old Tobcy. Guy Owen. PoNC
Old Tree, The. Andrew Young. GoJo
Old Uncle Noah. Unknown. BSO
Old Vicarage, Grantchester, The. Rupert Brooke. FaBV; WePo
Old Virginny. James A. Bland. FaBV
Old warder of these buried bones. In Memoriam A. H. H., XXXIX. Tennyson. FoBA; VP
Old West, The, the old time. Spanish Johnny. Willa Cather. RePo
Old Wharves, The. Rachel Field. SoPo
Old wheel ruts deep still mark the trace. Wheel Ruts. James Daugherty. RePo
Old Whom God Loves, The. Robert Browning. Fr. A Death in the Desert. BoC
Old Wife's Song. Eleanor Farjeon. RePo
Old Winter. Thomas Noel. PoSC
Old Wives' Tale, The, sels. George Peele.
  Gently Dip. ELP
  Voice from the Well, A. CBEP
  Whenas the Rye. CBEP; ELP
Old Woman, The. Joseph Campbell. ACV
Old Woman, The. "Gertrud Kolmar," tr. fr. German by Christopher Middleton. MGP
Old Woman, The. Beatrix Potter. GoJo
Old Woman. Iain Crichton Smith. NePoEA-2
Old Woman Laments the Days of Her Youth, The. Villon. See Complaint of the Fair Amouress, The.
Old Woman of Slapsadam, The. Unknown. BSO
Old Woman of the Roads, An. Padraic Colum. BoC; RePo
Old Woman, Old Woman. Unknown. BSO
  (Deaf Woman's Courtship, The, with music.) BFSS
Old Woman Speaks of the Moon, An. Ruth Pitter. BoC
Old Woman Who Bought a Pig, The. Unknown. See There Was an Old Woman and She Had a Little Pig.
Old Woman Who Went to Market, The, with music. Unknown. BFSS
Old Women, The. George Mackay Brown. NePoEA-2
Old women say that children asleep are saints, The. The Sleeping Saint. Melvin Walker La Follette. CoPo
Old women say that men don't know. Becoming a Dad. Edgar A. Guest. PoLF
Old, worn harp that had been played, An. The Master-Player. Paul Laurence Dunbar. TRV
Old Yew, which graspest at the stones. In Memoriam A. H. H., II. ELP; FoBA; GTBS-P; OBNC; VP
Olden Love-Making. Nicholas Breton. DiPo
Older Grown. Kate Greenaway. BiCB
Older than Eden's planting, older than elves. The Word of Willow. Leah Bodine Drake. FiSC
Oldest Cemetery. Mark Van Doren. FiSC
Oldest Soldier, The. Robert Graves. DTC
Olive, L', sels. Joachim du Bellay, tr. fr. French.
  "Sleep, of all gifts of Heaven held supreme," XIV, tr. by George Wyndham. RBL
  Sonnet to Heavenly Beauty, A, CXIII, tr. by Andrew Lang. CTC; RBL
Olivia. Elijah Fenton. WaPE
Olympic Girl, The. John Betjeman. SD
Olympicus, don't look into a mirror. The Boxer's Face. Lucilius. SD
Ombre and basset laid aside. The South Sea Bubble. Countess of Winchilsea. CBEP
Omelet of A. MacLeish, The. Edmund Wilson. Par
Omnipresence. Edward Everett Hale. TRV
On a Banck as I Sate a Fishing. Sir Henry Wotton. SeCP
On a bank of flowers, in a summer-day. Blooming Nelly. Burns. UnTE
On a Beautiful Landscape. William Bowles. PoPo
On a bright summer morning, the weather being fair. George Riley. Unknown. BSO
On a Certain Lady at Court. Pope. CBEP
On a Child Beginning to Talk. Thomas Bastard. CBEP
On a Child with a Wooden Leg. Bertram Warr. OBCV
On a Cold Night. J. V. Cunningham. PoIE
On a dark, stormy night. The Wreck of Number Nine. Unknown. BFSS
On a day, alack the day! Love's Perjuries. Shakespeare. Fr. Love's Labour's Lost. GTBS-P
On a day when the breath of roses. The Unwanted. C. Day Lewis. PoPl
On a Dead Child. Robert Bridges. OBNC
On a Dream. Keats. See Dream after Reading Dante's Episode of Paolo and Francesca, A.
On a Drop of Dew. Andrew Marvell. ILP; MeP; SeCP
On a Favourite Cat, Drowned in a Tub of Gold Fishes. Thomas Gray. See Ode on the Death of a Favorite Cat.
On a Fifteenth-Century Flemish Angel. David Ray. NePoEA-2
On a flat road runs the well-train'd runner. The Runner. Walt Whitman. SD
On a Fly Drinking Out of His Cup. William Oldys. LV (Fly, The.) CBEP

On a Gentlewoman Walking in the Snowe. William Strode. *See* On Chloris Walking in the Snow.
On a Girdle. Edmund Waller. CABA; GTBS-P; PoIE; StP; UnTE
On a Halfpenny which a Young Lady Gave a Beggar, and which the Author Redeemed for Half-a-Crown. Henry Fielding. CBEP
On a Hand. Hilaire Belloc. BoLP
On a hill there blooms a palm. Tell Him. Chaim Nachman Bialik. *Fr.* Songs of the People. SiGo
On a Honey Bee. Philip Freneau. AP
On a Lady Throwing Snowballs at Her Lover. Christopher Smart. VaPo
On a little green knoll. Old Log House. James S. Tippett. RePo
On a Mild Winter Afternoon. Carlo Betocchi, *tr. fr. Italian by* Carlo L. Golino. CoIP
On a Mountain Road. Wu Ch'ing-jen, *tr. fr. Chinese by* E. D. Edwards. SiGo
On a night of mist and rain. Phyllis. Sydney King Russell. ErPo
On a Painted Lady. William Pattison. WaPE
On a Painting by Patient B of the Independence State Hospital for the Insane. Donald Justice. NePoEA-2
On a Pair of Garters. Sir John Davies. CBEP
On a Poetess. Gerard Manley Hopkins. PP
On a Poet's Lips I Slept. Shelley. ELP (Poet's Dream, The.) GTBS-P
On a Portrait of Mme. Rimsky-Korsakov. Kingsley Amis. NePoEA-2
On a Prayer Book Sent to Mrs. M. R., *sel.* Richard Crashaw. "Dear soul be strong!" ErPo
On a Ruined House in a Romantic Country. Samuel Taylor Coleridge. Par
On a shining silver morning long ago. David McKee Wright. *Fr.* Dark Rosaleen. PoAu-1
On a silver base, within a shell of gold. During the Bath. Giambattista Marino. RBL
On a small six-acre farm dwelt John Grist the miller. Under the Drooping Willow Tree. *Unknown.* CBEP
On a snug evening I shall watch her fingers. Piano after War. Gwendolyn Brooks. AmNP
On a Soldier Fallen in the Philippines. William Vaughn Moody. AP; ThLM
On a Spider. Edward Littleton. WaPE
On a Squirrel Crossing the Road in Autumn, in New England. Richard Eberhart. PoCh
On a starred night Prince Lucifer uprose. Lucifer in Starlight. George Meredith. CABA; CaFP; CBEP; ILP; OBNC; PoIE; PoPo; PoSa; VP
On a straw-colored day. Dream. Solomon Edwards. NNP
On a throne of new gold the Son of the Sky is sitting among his Mandarins. The Emperor. Tu Fu. SIV
On a time the amorous Silvy. The Amorous Silvy. *Unknown.* UnTE
On a Tired Housewife. *Unknown.* EvOK; WePo
On a tree by a river a little tom-tit. Ko-Ko's Song. W. S. Gilbert. *Fr.* The Mikado. LV
On a Virtuous Young Gentlewoman That Died Suddenly. William Cartwright. CBEP
On a Windy Day. Zhenya Gay. RePo
On a Young Lady's Going into a Shower Bath. Francis Scott Key. UnTE
On alien ground, breathing an alien air. Where a Roman Villa Stood, above Freiburg. Mary Elizabeth Coleridge. OBNC
On all that the Lord laboured He lavished His love. Love. William Langland. *Fr.* The Vision of Piers Plowman. BoC
On an Air of Rameau. Arthur Symons. OBNC
On an East Wind from the Wars. Alan Dugan. AP
On an Engraved Gem of Leander. Keats. CBEP
On an Infant Dying as Soon as Born. Charles Lamb. GTBS-P
On an Old Castle-Hunt. Ferdinand von Saar, *tr. fr. German by* George C. Schoolfield. AGP
On and on. The Sea Bird to the Wave. Padraic Colum. RePo
On an Unsuccessful Attempt to Draw Lord Boyle's Picture. Elizabeth Rowe. WaPE
On Another's Sorrow. Blake. *Fr.* Songs of Innocence. CBEP; FaBV
On Australian Hills, *sel.* Ada Cambridge. "Oh, to be there to-night!" PoAu-1
On Being a Woman. Dorothy Parker. PoLF
On Being Arrived at the Age of Twenty-three. Milton. *See* How Soon Hath Time.
On Being Asked for a War Poem. W. B. Yeats. PP
On Ben Jonson. Sidney Godolphin. PP
On Blenheim House. Abel Evans. CBEP
On Board the Steamer, *with music. Unknown.* SGR
On Buonarroti's Statue of Night. Giovanni Strozzi, *tr. fr. Italian by* Harold M. Priest. RBL
On Catching a Dog-Daisy in the Mower. Peter Redgrove. NePoEA-2

On Censure. Swift. CBEP
On Charles II. Earl of Rochester. PoSa
On Children. Kahlil Gibran. *Fr.* The Prophet. PoP1
On Chloris Walking in the Snow. William Strode. ELP (On a Gentlewoman Walking in the Snowe.) BoC
On Christmas Day I weep. Christmas Mourning. Vassar Miller. CoPo
On Christmas Eve. Edith Lovejoy Pierce. MoRP
On Christmas eve they filled the house, some fifty guests all told. Christmas at Babbitt's. Henry Hallam Tweedy. TRV
On cliffs against the sky. Ship's Bell. Glenn Ward Dresbach. BoC
On Court-Worme. Ben Jonson. SeCP
On Crossing the Rhine Bridge at Cologne by Night. Ernst Stadler, *tr. fr. German by* Michael Hamburger. MGP
On Cummorah Hill. The Mormon Trail. Daniel Henderson. SIV
On Don Juan del Norte, Not Don Juan Tenorio del Sur. Alan Dugan. ErPo
On Donne's Poetry. Samuel Taylor Coleridge. CABA; CaFP; CBEP; PP
On Dr. Crank's Victory over the Gout. Sneyd Davies. WaPE
On Drinking. Abraham Cowley. *See* Drinking.
On Dwelling. Robert Graves. CBEP
On ear and ear two noises too old to end. The Sea and the Skylark. Gerard Manley Hopkins. AnMoPo
On Easter morn at early dawn. Meeting the Easter Bunny. Rowena Bennett. SoPo
On Easter morning two egrets. Two Egrets. John Ciardi. CaFP
On either side the river lie. The Lady of Shalott. Tennyson. CABL; DiPo; SIV; VP; WePo; WiR
On eves of cold, when slow coal fires. Town Owl. Laurie Lee. ToPo
On Falling Asleep to Birdsong. William Meredith. PoCh
On Fame. John Banks. WaPE
On Fame. Keats. CABA; CBEP
On Fanny Godwin. Shelley. OBNC
On First Looking in on Blodgett's Keats's "Chapman's Homer." George Starbuck. PP
On First Looking into Chapman's Homer. Keats. CABA; CaFP; CBEP; DiPo; FaBV; FaPL; FoBA; GTBS-P; ILP; OBNC; PoIE; RoGo; StP
On First Looking into Loeb's Horace. Lawrence Durrell. ToPo
On Friday morn as we set sail. The Mermaid. *Unknown.* HaSV
On Fruition. Sir Charles Sedley. ErPo
On Gaulstown House. Swift. CBEP
On Giving. Kahlil Gibran. *Fr.* The Prophet. PoP1
On Growing Old. John Masefield. MoRP; PoLF
On Growing Old. Srinavas Rayaprol. ACV
On Halloween. Shelley Silverstein. PoSC
On hand is 27. Macrobius Mingling with Nature. Rochelle Owens. CoPo
On Heaven. Ford Madox Ford. CTC
On Hellespont, guilty of true love's blood. Hero and Leander. Christopher Marlowe. CABA
On Her Entering Her Room. Richardson Pack. WaPE
On her fleet little charger. The Gardener. Eduard Möricke. AGP
On Her Pleading Want of Time. George Lyttelton. WaPE
On Her Portrait. Sister Juana Inés de la Cruz, *tr. fr. Spanish by* Kate Flores. AnSP
On Himself[e]. Robert Herrick. SeCP; UnTE
On Himself, on Hearing What Was His Sentence. James Graham, Marquess of Montrose. CBEP
On His Blindness. Milton. BoC; CBEP; DiPo; FaBV; FaPL; GTBS-P; PoIE; PoLF; PoP1; PoPo; TRV (Sonnet: "When I consider how my light is spent.") MeP; VaPo (When I Consider How My Light Is Spent.) CABA; CaFP; FoBA; ILP
On His Books. Hilaire Belloc. PoP1
On His Deafness. Joachim du Bellay, *tr. fr. French by* George Wyndham. *Fr.* Les Amours. RBL
On His Deceased Wife. Milton. *See* Methought I Saw My Late Espoused Saint.
On His 86th Birthday. Thomas Hardy. ACV
On His Having Arrived at the Age of Twenty-three. Milton. *See* How Soon Hath Time.
On His Lady's Waking. Pierre de Ronsard, *tr. fr. French by* Andrew Lang. RBL
On His Mistris, the Queen of Bohemia. Sir Henry Wotton. *See* Elizabeth of Bohemia.
On His Return to Italy. Luigi Alamanni, *tr. fr. Italian by* Lorna de' Lucchi. RBL
On Hurricane Jackson. Alan Dugan. SD
On Lavater's Song of a Christian to Christ. Goethe, *tr. fr. German by* Walter Kaufmann. TwGP
On Leaving Bruges. Dante Gabriel Rossetti. CBEP
On Leaving Prison. Luis de León, *tr. fr. Spanish by* Brenda M. Sackett. AnSP

On Leslie Moore. *Unknown.* LV
On Linden, when the sun was low. Hohenlinden. Thomas Campbell. CBEP; GTBS-P; OBNC; OnMSP; RoGo; WePo
On Looking at Stubbs's Anatomy of the Horse. Edward Lucie-Smith. NePoEA-2
On Looking into Henry Moore. Dorothy Livesay. OBCV
On Lord Holland's Seat Near M——e, Kent. Thomas Gray. *See* Impromptu.
On love's worst ugly day. First Meditation. Theodore Roethke. *Fr.* Meditations of an Old Woman. AP; PoDB
On Lucy, Countess[e] of Bedford. Ben Jonson. EnRePo; SeCP
On Main one night when they sounded the chimes. In Medias Res. William Stafford. StP
On Man. Walter Savage Landor. OBNC
On Margaret Ratcliffe. Ben Jonson. SeCP
On Middleton Edge. Andrew Young. SD
On Minding One's Own Business. James Wright. PoPl
On Mr. George Herberts Booke Intituled the Temple of Sacred Poems, Sent to a Gentle-woman. Richard Crashaw. MeP
On Mr. Milton's *Paradise Lost, sel.* Andrew Marvell. "Well mightst thou scorn thy readers to allure." PP
On Mr. Nash's Picture. Jane Brereton. WaPE
On Music. Walter Savage Landor. GoJo
On music drawn away, a sea-borne mariner. Music. Baudelaire. SiGo
On My First Daughter. Ben Jonson. EnRePo; SeCP
On My First Son [or Sonne]. Ben Jonson. CABA; CaFP; DiPo; EnRePo; PoIE; SeCP; StP
On My Lady Isabella Playing on the Lute. Edmund Waller. SeCP
On my Northwest coast in the midst of the night a fishermen's group stands watching. The Torch. Walt Whitman. FoBA
On My Sweet Mother. Sappho, *tr. fr. Greek by* Thomas Moore. PoPl
On News. Thomas Traherne. *Fr.* The Third Century. MeP
On Not Writing an Elegy. Richard Frost. OPP
On Our Crucified Lord, Naked and Bloody. Richard Crashaw. *See* Upon the Body of Our Blessed Lord, Naked and Bloody.
On Oxford. Keats. Par
On pale afternoons. Autumnal. Rubén Darío. AnSP
On Palladio's rural theme, a farmhouse. Air Tunnel, Monticello. Bink Noll. ToPo
On parent knees, a naked new-born child. Epigram. Sir William Jones. PoPl
On Passing Two Negroes on a Dark Country Road Somewhere in Georgia. Conrad Kent Rivers. NNP
On Poetry; a Rhapsody, *sel.* Swift. "Hobbes clearly proves that every creature." PP
On Professor Drennan's Verse. Roy Campbell. GTBS-P
On Reading a Soviet Novel. Roy Fuller. ToPo
On Receiving a Copy of Mr. Austin Dobson's "Old World Idylls." James Russell Lowell. AP
On Receiving News of the War. Isaac Rosenberg. MMA
On Revisiting Cintra after the Death of Catarina. Luís de Camões, *tr. fr. Spanish by* Richard Garnett. RBL
On Rome in the Pontificate of Julius II. Michelangelo, *tr. fr. Italian by* John Addington Symonds. RBL
On Sailing the Wide Ocean. Luís de Góngora, *tr. fr. Spanish by* Edward Meryon Wilson. *Fr.* The Solitudes. RBL
On St. Martin's evening green. Nuns at Eve. John Malcolm Brinnin. MP
On Saturday Evening, the Week at an End. *Unknown, tr. fr. French by* Patricia Terry. AnML
On Seeing a Hair of Lucretia Borgia. Walter Savage Landor. CABA
On Seeing a Lady's Garter. *Unknown.* ErPo
On Seeing a Lock of Milton's Hair. Keats. PP
On Seeing a Movie Based on an Episode from President Kennedy's Life. David Ray. OPP
On Seeing the Elgin Marbles [for the First Time]. Keats. CABA; DiPo; FoBA; PoIE
On Seven Hills. "Will Inman." PoNC
On Shakespeare. Milton. DiPo; FoBA
On Sir Francis Drake. *Unknown.* CBEP
On Sitting Down to Read *King Lear* Once Again. Keats. DiPo; FoBA
On Snow-Flakes Melting on His Lady's Breast. William Martin Johnson. AmLP
On Some South African Novelists. Roy Campbell. GTBS-P; PoPl
On Some Trees Needlessly Slain. Stanton A. Coblentz. TRV
On Some-thing, That Walkes Some-where. Ben Jonson. SeCP
On Springfield Mountain there did dwell/ A noble youth. The Major's Son. *Unknown.* BSO
On Springfield Mountain there did dwell/ With a riting atu. Springfield Mountain (D *vers.*). *Unknown.* BSO
On Stage, off Stage. Robert Watson. PoNC
On starry heights. The Conflict of Convictions. Herman Melville. AP
On stormy days. Brooms. Dorothy Aldis. SoPo

On Such a Night. Thomas Johnston. HaSV
On summer days a rustling tree. Alike. Dorothy Aldis. RePo
On summer mornings when it's hot. The Milkman's Horse. *Unknown.* SoPo
On Sunday afternoons we ate a big dinner. A Sunday in the Thirties. Barbara Hinchcliffe. PtTo
On Susan Pattison. *Unknown.* CBEP
On Taking a Bachelor's Degree. Christopher Smart. VaPo
On Teaching without Pupils. Bertolt Brecht, *tr. fr. German by* Michael Hamburger. MGP
On Ternissa's Death. Walter Savage Landor. *See* Ternissa.
On Thame's bank, a gentle youth. On Her Pleading Want of Time. George Lyttelton. WaPE
On that last night before we went. In Memoriam A. H. H., CIII. Tennyson. VP
On the Armada Which Battled against England. Luis de Góngora, *tr. fr. Spanish by* Brian Soper *and* Iain Fletcher. AnSP
On the Assumption. Richard Crashaw. MeP
On the Athenian Dead at Ecbatana. Plato, *tr. fr. Greek by* Ralph Gladstone. PoPl
On the Author. Burns. CBEP
On the Banishment of Cicero. Philip Wharton. WaPE
On the Back Veld. Crosbie Garstin. ACV
On the Banks of the Old Peedee, *with music. Unknown.* BSO
On the Birth of His Son. Su T'ung-po, *tr. fr. Chinese by* Arthur Waley. TRV
On the Blessed Virgin's Bashfulness. Richard Crashaw. ILP
On the Brink of Death. Michelangelo, *tr. fr. Italian by* John Addington Symonds. RBL
On the Building of Springfield. Vachel Lindsay. MoRP
On the Calculus. J. V. Cunningham. PoIE
On the Cards and Dice. Sir Walter Ralegh. EnRePo
On the Castle of Chillon. Byron. *See* Sonnet on Chillon.
On the Choice of His Sepulchre. Pierre de Ronsard, *tr. fr. French by* Alan Conder. Odes, IV, 4. RBL
On the Coast of Coromandel. The Courtship of the Yonghy-Bonghy-Bo. Edward Lear. EvOK; OnMSP; WiR
On the Collar of a Dog. Swift. StP
On the Completion of the Pacific Telegraph. Jones Very. AP
On the corner, right angular, facing the park. Block Party. Eve Merriam. PtTo
On the Countess Dowager of Pembroke. William Browne. CABA
(Epitaph on the Countess Dowager of Pembroke.) CBEP
On the crooked arm of Columbus, on his cloak. Pigeons. Alastair Reid. MP
On the Death of a Child. Ludwig Uhland, *tr. fr. German by* Oliver Brown. AGP
On the Death of a Favorite Cat, Drowned in a Tub of Gold Fishes. Thomas Gray. *See* Ode on the Death of a Favorite Cat.
On the Death of a Metaphysician. George Santayana. AmLP
On the Death of a Recluse. George Darley. CBEP
On the Death of an Epicure. Richard Graves. CBEP
On the Death of Benjamin Franklin. Philip Freneau. ThLM
On the Death of Catarina de Attayda. Luís de Camões, *tr. fr. Spanish by* Sir Richard F. Burton. RBL
On the Death of Dr. Robert Levet. Samuel Johnson. EiCP; VaPo
(On the Death of Mr. Robert Levet a Practiser in Physic.) CBEP
On the Death of Dr. Swift. *See* Verses on the Death of Dr. Swift.
On the Death of His Son. Lewis Glyn Cothi, *tr. fr. Welsh by* Gwyn Williams. PoPl
On the Death of Joseph Rodman Drake. Fitz-Greene Halleck. AmLP
(Joseph Rodman Drake.) FaPL
On the Death of Mr. Crashaw. Abraham Cowley. SeCP
On the Death of Mr. Robert Levet a Practiser in Physic. Samuel Johnson. *See* On the Death of Dr. Robert Levet.
On the Death of Mr. William Hervey. Abraham Cowley. CBEP; SeCP
On the Death of Sir Thomas Wyatt. Earl of Surrey. CBEP
On the Departure Platform. Thomas Hardy. OBNC
On the desert. War Is Kind, XI. Stephen Crane. AP
On the Eastern Way at the City of Lo-yang. Song. Sung Tzu-hou. SiGo
On the Eclipse of the Moon of October 1865. Charles Tennyson-Turner. OBNC
On the eighth day of March it was, some people say. The Birth of Saint Patrick. Samuel Lover. PoSC
On the Eighth Day of November, *with music. Unknown.* BSO
On the Extinction of the Venetian Republic. Wordsworth. GTBS-P; OBNC
On the far reef the breakers. The Tide Will Win. Priscilla Leonard. TRV
On the first day good enough father and son. Target Practice. Donald Finkel. NePoEA-2
On the first day of Christmas my true love sent to me a

partridge in a pear tree. The Twelve Days of Christmas. *Unknown.* RePo

On the fourteenth of July once so clear was the sky. The Little Fighting Chance. *Unknown.* BSNS

On the Grasshopper and Cricket. Keats. BoC; CBEP; DiPo; FoBA; ILP; LV; PoIE

(Poetry of Earth, The.) PoPo; WiR

On the Grave of a Young Cavalry Officer Killed in the Valley of Virginia. Herman Melville. AP

On the great streams the ships may go. Robert Louis Stevenson. *Fr.* The Canoe Speaks. SD

On the green banks of Shannon, when Sheelah was nigh. The Harper. Thomas Campbell. CBEP

On the green sheep-track, up the heathy hill. Samuel Taylor Coleridge. *Fr.* Fears in Solitude. OBNC

On the headland's grassed and sheltered side. Storm. Judith Wright. PoAu-2

On the Heath on a Morning. Heinrich von Morungen, *tr. fr. German by* J. B. Leishman. AnML

On the Hill below the Lighthouse. James Dickey. NePoEA-2

On the idle hill of summer. A. E. Housman. A Shropshire Lad, XXXV. OBNC

On the Instability of Youth. Thomas, Lord Vaux. EnRePo

On the Island, finding you naked and pearled. That Summer's Shore. John Ciardi. ErPo

On the jetty, our fingers shading. In the Beginning. Daniel G. Hoffman. PP

On the Ladies' Head-Dresses. James Greenwood. WaPE

On the Late Massacre in Piedmont. Milton. CABA; CBEP; ILP; PoIE

(On the Late Massacre in Piemont.) DiPo; FoBA; GTBS-P; StP

On the Linden Overhead a Bird Was Caroling Its Lay. Dietmar von Aist, *tr. fr. German by* Margaret F. Richey. AnML

(Linden Tree, The, *tr. by* Edgar Taylor.) PoP1

On the Little Bighorn. Ray Smith. PtTo

On the long shore, lit by the moon. The Goose Fish. Howard Nemerov. CaFP

On the Loss of the *Royal George.* William Cowper. HaSV; RoGo

(Loss of the *Royal George,* The.) CBEP; GTBS-P

On the low table by the bed. Mark Anderson. W. W. Gibson. MMA

On the lowlands where the angular shadows. The New Adam. Frank Belknap Long. FiSC

On the Make-up of a Poet. H. A. Sieber. PoNC

On the Memory of Mr. Edward King, Drown'd in the Irish Seas. John Cleveland. SeCP

On the Morning of Christs Nativity. Milton. MeP

(Ode on the Morning of Christ's Nativity.) GTBS-P

"Shepherds on the lawn, The," *sel.* BoC

On the morning of noise. Poem at Thirty. John Woods. CoPo

On the Mountain Pass. Matsuo Basho, *tr. fr. Japanese by* Harold G. Henderson. SiGo

On the Move. Thom Gunn. AnMoPo; MP; NePoEA-2; ToPo

On the Name of Jesus. Richard Crashaw. MeP

On the Nature of Things. Lucretius. *See* De Rerum Natura.

On the New Forces of Conscience under the Long Parliament. Milton. CABA; StP

On the New York Central from Chicago to South Bend. Vendor. Raymond Roseliep. FiSC

On the North Shore a reptile lay asleep. The Precambrian Shield. E. J. Pratt. *Fr.* Towards the Last Spike. OBCV

On the Open Earth. André du Bouchet, *tr. fr. French by* Warren Carrier. CoFP

On the other side of the wide blue sea. The Two Brothers. Isaac Leib Carrey. SIV

On the outer Barcoo where the churches are few. A Bush Christening. A. B. Paterson. PoAu-1

On the Outgoing Train. Alan Swallow. PtTo

On the Painting of the Sistine Chapel. Michelangelo, *tr. fr. Italian by* John Addington Symonds. RBL

On the Poet's Leer. David Ray. NePoEA-2

On the pond, which now reposes. Song of the Rushes, V. Nikolaus Lenau. AGP

On the Prospect of Planting Arts and Learning in America. George Berkeley. PP

On the Receipt of My Mother's Picture Out of Norfolk. William Cowper. EnPE; PoIE

On the Rhine. Matthew Arnold. Faded Leaves, IV. VP

On the road through the hills I thought I heard it. Halfheard. Christopher Koch. PoAu-2

On the Road to Gundagai. *Unknown.* PoAu-1

On the Road to Nara. Matsuo Basho, *tr. fr. Japanese by* Harold G. Henderson. SiGo

On the rock the turtles get. Mud Turtles. Grace Taber Hallock. RePo

On the Sacrament. Elizabeth Rowe. Three Hymns, 2. WaPE

On the school platform, draping the folding seats. Political Meeting. A. M. Klein. OBCV

On the Sea. Keats. CABA; DiPo; FoBA

On the sea and at the Hogue, sixteen hundred ninety-two. Hervé Riel. Robert Browning. OnMSP

On the sea or in the air. God Is with Me. Oswald J. Smith. STF

On the Setting Up of Mr. Butler's Monument in Westminster Abbey. Samuel Wesley. CBEP

On the sheep-cropped summit, under hot sun. Cat and Mouse. Ted Hughes. EaLo

On the shores of Lake Michigan. Children of the Wind. Carl Sandburg. WePo

On the Site of a Mulberry-Tree; Planted by Wm. Shakespeare; Felled by the Rev. F. Gastrell. Dante Gabriel Rossetti. CBEP

On the smooth steep escalator, four storeys'/ Rise. The City Considered as a Tulip Tree. Carl Bode. *Fr.* London Sonnets. ToPo

On the soft cushions of time. The Palatine. "Aldo Palazzeschi." CoIP

On the soft wet sand. Broken Faith. Giambattista Marino. RBL

On the Sonnet. Keats. *See* If by Dull Rhymes Our English Must be Chained.

On the Staircase. Wade Wellman. FiSC

On the stiff twig up there. Black Rook in Rainy Weather. Sylvia Plath. MP; NePoEA-2; PoDB; PP

On the *Struma* Massacre. Ralph Gustafson. OBCV

On the Subject of Poetry. W. S. Merwin. PP

On the tallest day in time the dead came back. V-J Day. John Ciardi. PoP1

On the taut shore, the bald skull. Resurrection. Robert Pack. NePoEA-2

On the temple bell. Spring Scene. Taniguchi Buson. PoP1

On the threshold of heaven, the figures in the street. To an Old Philosopher in Rome. Wallace Stevens. AP

On the third day of May. The Boy and the Mantle. *Unknown.* UnTE

On the Tombs in Westminster Abbey. *At. to* Francis Beaumont, *also to* William Basse. GTBS-P

(Tombs in Westminster, The.) WePo

On the Triumph of Judith. Lope de Vega, *tr. fr. Spanish by* Brian Soper. AnSP

On the Twenty-third Psalm. *Unknown.* TRV

On the Universality and Other Attributes of the God of Nature. Philip Freneau. AP

On the University Carrier. Milton. FoBA

On the up-platform at Morpeth station. The Complaint of the Morpethshire Farmer. Basil Bunting. CTC

On the Vanity of Earthly Greatness. Arthur Guiterman. PoP1; PoPo

On the wall beside the kitchen door. Growing. Frances Frost. BiCB

On the way from Fontenay. Vincent Voiture, *tr. fr. French by* Judith McDowell. RBL

On the way to Kew. W. E. Henley. Echoes, XXXVIII. OBNC

On the Wing. Christina Rossetti. StP; VP

On the Words "Dilectus Meus Mihi." St. Theresa of Avila, *tr. fr Spanish by* Jesse Read Wendell. RBL

On This Day I Complete My Thirty-sixth Year. Byron. CABA; ILP

"My days are in the yellow leaf," *sel.* TRV

On This Island, *sel.* W. H. Auden.

"Judge enforcing the obsolete law, The." TRV

On this sweet bank your head thrice sweet and dear. Youth's Spring-Tribute. Dante Gabriel Rossetti. The House of Life, XIV. VP

On Thomas Carew. *Unknown.* CBEP

On tilted toes he tries to reach. Nature at Three. Bettye Breeser. BiCB

On Time. Milton. BoC; CABA; DiPo; MeP; PoPo; StP; TRV

On Time with God. C. D. Nutter. STF

On Tuesday morn at half-past six o'clock. James Rigg. James Hogg. Par

On Visiting the Graves of Hawthorne and Thoreau. Jones Very. AP

On wan dark night on Lac St. Pierre. The Wreck of the *Julie Plante.* William Henry Drummond. OBCV

On Watering the Garden. Bertolt Brecht, *tr. fr. German by* Michael Hamburger. MGP

On Wenlock Edge [the Wood's in Trouble]. A. E. Housman. A Shropshire Lad, XXXI. CABA; GTBS-P; ILP; OBNC; PoIE; VP

On Westwell Downs. William Strode. CBEP

On what silent feet it comes. The Third Day. Edith Lovejoy Pierce. MoRP

On Willy's birthday, as you see. A Party. Laura E. Richards. BiCB; SoPo

On winter nights the fiddling wind see-saws. "Soft Sell." Lorna Beers. FiSC

On with the Message. Wesley Duewel. STF

On yonder hill there sits a noble knight. The Cambric Shirt (C vers.). *Unknown.* BFSS

On yonder hill there stands a creature. O No, John! *Unknown.* ErPo; UnTE

Onan. Paris Leary. CoPo

Once a dream did weave a shade. A Dream. Blake. *Fr.* Songs of Innocence. CBEP

Once a jolly swagman camped by a billabong. Waltzing Matilda. A. B. Paterson. PoAu-1

Once a Kansas zephyr strayed. Zephyr. Eugene Fitch Ware. PoLF

Once a little boy, Jack, was, oh! ever so good. The Sad Story of a Little Boy That Cried. *Unknown.* BBGG

Once a little satellite. Little Satellite. Jane W. Krows. SoPo

Once again our glad thanksgivings. Thanksgiving. A. B. Simpson. STF

Once again the scurry of feet—those myriads. The Face of the Waters. Robert D. Fitzgerald. PoAu-2

Once, and but once found in thy company. Elegie IV: The Perfume. John Donne. *Fr.* Elegies. SeCP

Once around a daisy counting. Counting on Flowers. John Ciardi. PP

Once as a child I loved to hop. Adam's Footprint. Vassar Miller. ToPo

Once as I travelled through a quiet evening. Egrets. Judith Wright. GoJo

Once as Methought Fortune Me Kissed. Sir Thomas Wyatt. CBEP

Once by the Pacific. Robert Frost. AmLP; FoBA; ILP; PoDB; PoPo

Once came an exile, longing to be free. Blennerhassett's Island. Thomas Buchanan Read. *Fr.* The New Pastoral. ThLM

Once Did My Thoughts. *Unknown.* ELP

Once did she hold the gorgeous East in fee. On the Extinction of the Venetian Republic. Wordsworth. GTBS-P; OBNC

Once git a smell o' musk into a draw. Sunthin' in the Pastoral Line. James Russell Lowell. *Fr.* The Biglow Papers. AP

Once here/ my love. Our Dusk: That West. Jonathan Williams. PoNC

Once hid in a fiery twist. The Scratch. James Dickey. AP

Once I am sure there's nothing going on. Church Going. Philip Larkin. AnMoPo; GTBS-P; ILP; MP; PoDB; PoIE; ToPo

Once I courted a beauty, beauty bright [*or* fair beauty bride]. The Fair Young Miss [*or* The Lover's Lament]. *Unknown.* BFSS; BSO

Once I delighted in a single tree. The Exulting. Theodore Roethke. *Fr.* The Dying Man. PoDB

Once I had a green door. Joan's Door. Eleanor Farjeon. BiCB

Once I Had Plenty of Thyme (A *vers., with music*). *Unknown.* BSO

(Saucy Sailor, The, B *vers.*) BSO

Once I knew a brisk young farmer. William Hall. *Unknown.* BFSS

Once I lost my temper. My Temper. *Unknown.* STF

Once I nearly Touched a Bird. Mary Jane Carr. RePo

Once I Pass'd through a Populous City. Walt Whitman. FoBA

Once I was a serving maid who worked in Drury Lane. Bell-bottomed Trousers. *Unknown.* UnTE

Once in a dream (for once I dreamed of you). On the Wing. Christina Rossetti. StP; VP

Once in a lifetime the white fawn run. Old Wife's Song. Eleanor Farjeon. RePo

Once, in a night as black as ink. How Samson Bore Away the Gates of Gaza. Vachel Lindsay. MoRP

Once, in finesse of fiddles I found ecstasy. The Embankment. T. E. Hulme. GTBS-P

Once in royal David's city. Good Tidings of Great Joy! Mrs. C. F. Alexander. ThGo

Once, in the gathering twilight. Recompense. Loring Williams. FiSC

Once it smiled a silent dell. The Valley of Unrest. Poe. AP

Once, long ago, an aged seer. The Seer. Lewis Turco. FiSC

Once Mermaids mocked your ships. Mermaids. Kenneth Slessor. *Fr.* The Atlas. PoAu-2

Once more around should do it, the man confided. Flight of the Roller-Coaster. Raymond Souster. ACV

Once more before I wander. To the Unknown God. Nietzsche. TwGP

Once more the changed year's turning wheel returns. Barren Spring. Dante Gabriel Rossetti. The House of Life, LXXXIII. OBNC; VaPo

Once more the cuckoo's call I hear. Spring. Aubrey Thomas De Vere. *Fr.* The Year of Sorrow. OBNC

Once more the storm is howling, and half hid. A Prayer for My Daughter. W. B. Yeats. AnMoPo; CABA; PoLF; PoPo; VaPo

Once more this autumn-earth is ripe. The Australian. Arthur H. Adams. PoAu-1

Once More unto the Breach. Shakespeare. King Henry V, *fr.* III, i. FaBV ("Once more unto the breach, dear friends, once more.") PoSa

Once on a Certain Nameless Town. Peire Cardenal, *tr. fr. Provençal by* Thomas G. Bergin. AnML

Once on a silver and green day, rich to remember. Brindabella. Douglas Stewart. PoAu-2

Once on a time a knight of high degree. The Merchant's Tale. Chaucer. *Fr.* The Canterbury Tales. UnTE

Once on a time, all in a town. A New Ballad. Mary Leapor. WaPE

Once on a time, as old stories rehearse. A Ballad to the Tune of "The Cut-Purse." Swift. PP

Once on a time I used to be. Harlot's Catch. Robert Nichols. ErPo

Once on a time, some centuries ago. The Sicilian's Tale. Longfellow. *Fr.* Tales of a Wayside Inn. AP

Once on Saipan at the end of the rains. An Island Galaxy. John Ciardi. ToPo

Once Only. Ato Tobira, *tr. fr. Japanese by* Ishii *and* Obata. SiGo

Once-over, The. Paul Blackburn. ErPo

Once or twice this side of death. Crystal Moment. Robert P. Tristram Coffin. LV

Once over summer streams the ice-crusts harden. No Return. Vassar Miller. CoPo; ToPo

Once quiet meant discord and pain. Witnesses. Cecil Hemley. PoDB

Once there was a fence here. Former Barn Lot. Mark Van Doren. FaBV; LOW; PoPl

Once there was an elephant. Eletelephony. Laura E. Richards. GoJo; SoPo

Once there were two brothers. Two Born Brothers. *Unknown.* BSO

Once this soft turf, this rivulet's sands. The Battle-Field. Bryant. PoLF

Once to every man and nation comes the moment to decide. James Russell Lowell. *Fr.* The Present Crisis. TRV

Once, Twice, Thrice. *Unknown.* ErPo

Once upon a midnight dreary, while I pondered, weak and weary. The Raven. Poe. AP; FaBV; FaPL; GoJo; PoPo; RoGo

Once upon a time, in a little wee house. The Funny Old Man and His Wife. *Unknown.* SoPo

Once upon a time there were three little foxes. The Three Foxes. A. A. Milne. GoJo

Once was a fiddler. Play could he. A Fiddler. Walter de la Mare. LOW

Once was every woman the witch. Witches. Ted Hughes. AnMoPo

Once when the snow of the year was beginning to fall. The Runaway. Robert Frost. GoJo; MP; RePo

Once you said joking slyly, "If I'm killed." The Faithful. Jane Cooper. AmPC; NePoEA-2

Once you were daily pilgrimage to me. Now You Shall Speak. Conrad Ferdinand Meyer. AGP

One and one—are one. Emily Dickinson. PoIE

One Bright Morning. *Unknown.* EvOK

One by one, like leaves from a tree. Leaves. Sara Teasdale. PoPl

One by one they appear in. My Sad Captains. Thom Gunn. NePoEA-2; PoCh; ToPo

One came in. Night Peril. Sydney King Russell. FiSC

One candidate has been nominated. The Election. Robert Pack. CoPo

One Centred System. Joel Barlow. *Fr.* The Columbiad. AP

One Certainty, The. Christina Rossetti. OBNC

One could not want a clearer season, when things age but do not grow. October Flies. Jascha Kessler. AmPC

One cup for my self-hood. The Poets at Tea, 10. Barry Pain. Par

One Day. Rupert Brooke. MoLP

One day as I walked by Crocodile Mansions. The Goole Captain. Leonard Clark. DaDu

One day as I was going. The Dispute of Charlot and the Barber. Rutebeuf. AnML

One day between the Lip and the Heart. The Lip and the Heart. John Quincy Adams. AmLP

One day, by appointment, Maria I met. Maria. G. A. Stevens. UnTE

One Day I Fondled Her on My Knees. Judah Halevi, *tr. fr. Hebrew by* William M. Davis. AnML

One day I looked at myself. Reflection. *Unknown.* STF

One day I saw a downy duck. Good Morning. Muriel Sipe. SoPo

One day I wrote her name upon the strand. Amoretti, LXXV. Spenser. CABA; CBEP; ILP; StP

One day, mamma said: "Conrad dear." The Story of Little Suck-a-Thumb. Heinrich Hoffman. EvOK

One Day of Rain. Joseph Payne Brennan. FiSC

One day on our village in the month of July. Death of an Aircraft. Charles Causley. MoBS

One day the amorous Lysander. The Disappointment. Earl of Rochester. UnTE

One Day the Rats of All Degrees. Eustache Deschamps, *tr. fr. French by* Jacques LeClercq. AnML

One day, through the primeval wood. The Calf-Path. Sam Walter Foss. PoLF

One day when I went visiting. I Held a Lamb. Kim Worthington. SoPo

One Day When We Went Walking. Valine Hobbs. SoPo

One day young Johnny he did go. Springfield Mountain (B *vers.*). *Unknown.* BSO

One Dismal Night. St. John of the Cross. *See* Dark Night of the Soul, The.

One divined the occult season. Of Young Woman Bent Back among the Flowers. Salvatore Quasimodo. CoIP

One Down. Richard Armour. SD

One dreamed and saw a gland write Hamlet, drink. A Dream of Surreal Science. Sri Aurobindo Ghose. ACV

One early morning as I rode over. The Dying Cowboy. *Unknown.* BSNS

One evening as I rambled down by the Clarence dock. We're All Away to Sea. *Unknown.* BSNS

One evening as I rambled two miles below Pomroy. Rinordine. *Unknown.* BSNS; BSO

One evening as I went a walking. Mary Riley. *Unknown.* BSNS

One evenin' as the sun went down. The Big Rock Candy Mountain. *Unknown.* WePo

One ever hangs where shelled roads part. At a Calvary near the Ancre. Wilfred Owen. MoRP

One feather is a bird. The Voice. Theodore Roethke. AmLP

One flame-winged brought a white-winged harp-player. Passion and Worship. Dante Gabriel Rossetti. The House of Life, IX. VP

One Flesh. Elizabeth Jennings. AnMoPo

One Foot in Eden. Edwin Muir. GTBS-P

One-foot waterfall, A. Contentment in Poverty. Issa. RePo

One Friday Morn. *Unknown.* OnMSP

One Furrow, The. R. S. Thomas. AnMoPo

One hand is smaller than the other. Man with One Small Hand. P. K. Page. OBCV

One hundred feet from off the ground. Long-Suffering of God. Christopher Smart. *Fr.* Hymns for the Amusement of Children. EiCP

151st Psalm, The. Karl Shapiro. EaLo

One I Love Is Gone Away, The. *Unknown.* MeEL

One in Christ. Henry van Dyke. TRV

"One is reminded of a certain person." Kite Poem. James Merrill. MP

One-1 lama, The. The Lama. Ogden Nash. RePo

One leaf, I thought, has turned bright red. Cardinal. Zoe Kincaid Brockman. PoNC

One lesson, Nature, let me learn of thee. Quiet Work. Matthew Arnold. PoIE; PoPo

One little Indian boy making a canoe. Ten Little Indian Boys. M. M. Hutchinson. SoPo

One little noise of life remained—I heard. On the Eclipse of the Moon of October 1865. Charles Tennyson-Turner. OBNC

One looks from the train. The Orient Express. Randall Jarrell. AP

One Lore. Stefan George, *tr. fr. German by* Walter Kaufmann. TwGP

One man arose who, sharp as lightning, cracked. Another Poem on Nietzsche. Stefan George. TwGP

One man in a house. To Landrum Guy, Beginning to Write at Sixty. James Dickey. PP

One Man Walking a Deserted Platform. Philip Larkin. ToPo

One Man's Goose; or, Poetry Redefined. George Starbuck. PP

One midnight, deep in starlight still. Bankrupt. Cortlandt W. Sayers. PoLF

One Moment My Hope Rises Up on Wings. Garcilaso de la Vega, *tr. fr. Spanish by* Edwin Morgan. AnSP

One more unfortunate. The Bridge of Sighs. Thomas Hood. GTBS-P

One morn before me were three figures seen. Ode on Indolence. Keats. OBNC

One Morning in May, *with music. Unknown.* BFSS; BSO (Nightingale, The.) UnTE

One morning for recreation as I roamed by the seaside. Janie on the Moor (A *vers.*). *Unknown.* BSNS

One morning for recreation as I strolled the beach seaside. Janie on the Moor (B *vers.*). *Unknown.* BSNS

One morning in spring. Fife Tune. John Manifold. GoJo

One morning very early, in the pleasant month of May. The Banks of Brandywine. *Unknown.* BSNS

One must have a mind of winter. The Snow Man. Wallace Stevens. AP; GoJo; PoIE

One must, to find your tomb. Mariner's Ideal Epitaph. Juan Ramón Jiménez. AnSP

One need not be a chamber—to be haunted. Emily Dickinson. DiPo

One night, all tired with the weary day. The Gnat. Joseph Beaumont. CBEP

One night as the moon shone brightly. The Jealous Lover. *Unknown.* BSO

One night came on a hurricane. The Sailor's Consolation. William Pitt. HaSV

One might i' th' year, my dearest Beauties, come. To His Lovely Mistresses. Robert Herrick. CTC; SeCP

One night on last November. The Last Night of November. *Unknown.* BSO

One-Night Stand, The: An Approach to the Bridge. Paul Blackburn. ErPo

One night when the night it blew cold. Mary of the Wild Moor. *Unknown.* BSO

One of the Sidhe. Mary Kennedy. FiSC

One ought not to have to care. The Hill Wife. Robert Frost. FoBA

One Paddy Doyle lived in Killarney. Paddy Doyle. *Unknown.* BSNS

One pleasant summer evening, 'twas in the month of May. The Mountain Cottage. John A. Stone. SGR

One Poet Visits Another. W. H. Davies. DTC

One road leads to London. Roadways. John Masefield. PoPo; RePo

One she floats as Venice might. The Lost Cities. Lawrence Durrell. ToPo

One ship drives east and another drives west. The Winds of Fate. Ella Wheeler Wilcox. TRV

One simple and effective rhyme. Woodpigeons at Raheny. Donald Davie. PP

One solitary bird melodiously. Evening. Charles Sangster. ACV

One son was a jewel to me. On the Death of His Son. Lewis Glyn Cothi. PoP1

One Spring, the old Philosopher, feeling his bones. The Story of Two Gentlemen and the Gardener. Christopher Logue. CABL

One Star Fell and Another. Conrad Aiken. Preludes for Memnon, LVII. PoPo ("One star fell and another as we walked.") BoLP

One star is Minnesota. The Flag. Shelley Silverstein. PoSC

One still dark night, I sat alone and wrote. Sonnets, Part II, XXXIII. Frederick Goddard Tuckerman. AP

One stormy night, when winds blew wild. And Thus He Spoke. John A. Stone. SGR

One-Talent Man. James Larkin Pearson. PoNC

One the summer road that ran by our front porch. Lizards and Snakes. Anthony Hecht. CoPo

One thing comes and another thing goes. Fair Annet's Song. Elinor Wylie. AmLP

One thing I like less than most things is sitting in a dentist chair with my mouth wide open. This Is Going to Hurt Just a Little Bit. Ogden Nash. LV

One Thing I of the Lord Desire. *Unknown.* STF

One thing in all things have I seen. Unity. "Æ." MoRP

One thing is sure. The Pulse. Mark Van Doren. PoP1

One Thing Needful, The. Vassar Miller. PoCh

One thing that literature would be greatly the better for. Very like a Whale. Ogden Nash. DTC; PoLF

One Thing They Say Displeases Me. Reinmar von Hagenau, *tr. fr. German by* Margaret F. Richey. AnML

One Thousand Fearful Words for Fidel Castro. Lawrence Ferlinghetti. CoPo

One Thousandth Psalm, The. Edward Everett Hale. TRV

One Times One, *sel.* E. E. Cummings. ("Plato told/ him: he couldn't," XIII. CTC; ThLM

One tiny golden upward-pointing flame. Candle and Book. Nina Willis Walter. TRV

One to make ready. The Start. *Unknown.* SD

One, Two, Buckle My Shoe. Mother Goose. SoPo

One, Two, Buckle My Shoe. Ogden Nash. BiCB

One, Two, Three! H. C. Bunner. PoLF

1-2-3 was the number he played but today the number came 3-2-1. Dirge. Kenneth Fearing. CaFP; PoIE; PoSa; ThLM

One ugly trick has often spoiled. Meddlesome Matty. Ann Taylor. OnMSP

One wading a Fall meadow finds on all sides. The Beautiful Changes. Richard Wilbur. ILP

One was kicked in the stomach. Gangrene. Philip Levine. AmPC

One-Way Song, *sels.* Wyndham Lewis. ("I would set all things whatsoever front to back." CTC ("In any medium except that of verse." PP

One, who is not, we see: but one, whom we see not, is. The Higher Pantheism in a Nutshell. Swinburne. Par; VP

One who is opulent offers legions of famishing beggars food. Kant and His Interpreters. Schiller. TwGP

One woman may robe herself in a tunic of white wool. Bilitis. Pierre Louÿs. *Fr.* The Songs of Bilitis. UnTE

One Word Is Too Often Profaned. Shelley. *See* To——: "One word is too often profaned."

One writes, that "Other friends remain." In Memoriam A. H. H., VI. Tennyson. VP

One writes when. Two Poems. Edward Marshall. CoPo
Onely a little more. His Poetrie His Pillar. Robert Herrick. SeCP
One's grand flights, one's Sunday baths. The Sense of the Sleight-of-Hand Man. Wallace Stevens. AP; CABA; MP
One's had enough of/ the snow. Rule. Francis Ponge. CoFP
One's-Self I Sing. Walt Whitman. DiPo; PoPo
Onion Skin, The. Kenneth Pitchford. Fr. Good for Nothing Man. CoPo
Only a Beauty, Only a Power. John Masefield. MoRP
Only a bell, a bird, the stillness break. Immense Hour. Juan Ramón Jiménez. AnSP; SiGo
Only a man harrowing clods. In Time of "The Breaking of Nations." Thomas Hardy. CaFP; ILP; MMA; MoRP; PoPo; PoSa; VP
Only a Smile. Unknown. STF
Only Holy Ghost in Birmingham, The. The Ghost in Birmingham. Ishmael Reed. PtTo
Only Joy, Now Here You Are. Sir Philip Sidney. Astrophel and Stella: Fourth Song. EnRePo; UnTE
(Fourth Song.) FaPl
Only last week, walking the hushed fields. Father and Son. F. R. Higgins. ACV; BoC
Only legal swindle which the people cannot sever, The. The Steam Navigation Thieves. John A. Stone. SGR
Only My Opinion. Monica Shannon. SoPo
Only, O Lord, in Thy dear love. Help Us to Live. John Keble. TRV
Only one, Lida, whom you can love, The. To Lida. Goethe. AGP
Only One Life. Gladys M. Bowman. STF
Only quiet death. Threnody. Waring Cuney. AmNP
Only real airship, The. The Dirigible. Ralph W. Bergengren. SoPo
Only teaching on Tuesdays, book-worming. Memories of West Street and Lepke. Robert Lowell. ToPo
Only the Beards Are Different. Bruce Dawe. PoAu-2
Only Thy Dust. Don Marquis. PoLF
Only two patient eyes to stare. Faded Pictures. William Vaughn Moody. AP
Only yesterday powdered and lustful I walked. Ash Wednesday. Alfred Lichtenstein. MGP
Ons in your grace I knowe I was. What Once I Was. Sir Thomas Wyatt. MeEL
Onset, The. Robert Frost. AP
Onward, Christian Soldiers. Sabine Baring-Gould. FaPL
Onward to Far Ida. George Darley. Fr. Nepenthe. OBNC
Opal heart of afternoon, The. The Bracelet of Grass. William Vaughn Moody. AP
Open Door, The. Grace Coolidge. TRV
Open door says, "Come in," The. Doors. Carl Sandburg. LOW
Open House. Theodore Roethke. AP
Open My Eyes. Betty Scott Stam. STF
Open Wardrobe. Günter Grass, tr. fr. German by Michael Hamburger. MGP
Open Your Eyes, Milady, Run Me Through. Guillaume de Machaut, tr. fr. French by Norman R. Shapiro. AnML
Open your windows. In a Girl's Album. Cedric Dover. WePo
Opening Door. Winifred Adams Burr. FiSC
Operation, The. Robert Creeley. ToPo
Operation, The. W. D. Snodgrass. StP; ToPo
Operation—Souls. Unknown. STF
Ophelia's Song. Shakespeare. Fr. Hamlet, IV, v. UnTE
Opportune Overthrow of Humpty Dumpty, The. Guy Wetmore Carryl. BBGG
Opportunity. Harry Graham. DTC
Opportunity. John James Ingalls. PoLF
Opportunity. Edward Rowland Sill. SIV; StP
Opossum, The (B vers., with music). Unknown. BSO
Opusculum paedagogum. Study of Two Pears. Wallace Stevens. AP
Or His Bestowals There. Alice Maynell. BoC
Or the black centaurs, statuesquely still. Ambuscade. Hugh McCrae. PoAu-1
Oracles, The. A. E. Housman. Last Poems, XXV. RoGo
Oracular Portcullis, The. James Reaney. ErPo
Oral Messages, sel. Lawrence Ferlinghetti.
"Dog trots freely in the street, The." ToPo
Orange County Plague: Scenes. Laurence Lieberman. CoPo
Orange Tree, The. John Shaw Neilson. PoAu-1
Oranges in a wooden bowl. Still-Life. Ronald Perry. NePoEA-2
Orara. Henry Kendall. PoAu-1
Orators, The, sel. W. H. Auden.
O Where Are You Going? PoIE; VaPo
Orchard and the Heath, The. George Meredith. OBNC
Orchestra, sel. Sir John Davies. HaSV
"For lo the sea that fleets about the land."
Order and Disorder. Richard Eberhart. PoDB
Oread. Hilda Doolittle ("H. D."). AP; GoJo; RePo
Organ Grinders' Garden, The. Mildred Plew Merryman. SoPo
Orient Express, The. Randall Jarrell. PoNC
Origin, far side of a lake, The. The Alchemist. Robert Kelly. CoPo

Original Love-Story, An. Unknown. BoLP
Original something, fair maid, you would win me, An. To a Young Lady, Who Asked Me to Write Something Original for Her Album. Thomas Campbell. StP
Orgy, The. Antoine-Girard de Saint-Amant, tr. fr. French by Chris Richards. RBL
Orphan's Song, The. Sydney Dobell. ELP; OBNC
Orpheus. E. W. Mandel. Minotaur Poems, VI. OBCV
Orpheus. W. D. Snodgrass. CABA; ToPo
Orpheus and Eurydice. Robert Browning. CTC
Orpheus and Eurydice. Geoffrey Hill. NePoEA-2; PoIE
Orpheus. Eurydice. Hermes. Rainer Maria Rilke, tr. fr. German by Walter Kaufmann. TwGP
Orpheus in Greenwich Village. Jack Gilbert. PP
Orpheus with His Lute. At. to John Fletcher, also to Shakespeare. King Henry VIII, fr. III, i. CBEP; EnRePo; FoBA
Ossian. Joseph Payne Brennan. FiSC
Ostrich Is a Silly Bird, The. Mary E. Wilkins Freeman. SoPo
Othello, sel. Shakespeare.
Othello and Desdemona, fr. V, ii. BoC
Other Person's Place, The. Donald H. Hover. STF
Other Possibility, The. Erich Kästner, tr. fr. German by Walter Kaufmann. TwGP
Other Side of a Mirror, The. Mary Elizabeth Coleridge. CBEP
Other Stanzas with a Divine Meaning Concerning Christ and the Soul. St. John of the Cross, tr. fr. Spanish by E. Allison Peers. RBL
(Stanzas Concerning Christ and the Soul.) BoC
Other Verses with a Divine Meaning. St. John of the Cross, tr. fr. Spanish by E. Allison Peers RBL
Others. Harry Behn. SoPo
Others. Unknown. STF
Others abide our question. Thou art free. Shakespeare. Matthew Arnold. CABA; CaFP; CBEP; PoIE; PoPo; VP
Others because you did not keep. A Deep-sworn Vow. W. B. Yeats. FoBA; PoPo
Others May Praise What They Like. Walt Whitman. FoBA; Par
Others taunt me with having knelt at well-curbs. For Once, Then, Something. Robert Frost. AP
Otherwhere. Frances Angevine Gray. FiSC
Otherwise. Aileen Fisher. LV; SoPo
Otter, An. Ted Hughes. BoC; DaDu; NePoEA-2
Otto. Theodore Roethke. ToPo
Ouch! Edith Earnshaw. PoNC
Our admiral gave orders on the same day. Kelly the Pirate (C vers.). Unknown. BSNS
Our Andy's gone with cattle now. Andy's Gone with Cattle. Henry Lawson. PoAu-1
Our author, by experience, finds it true. Prologue to "Aureng-Zebe." Dryden. CBEP; PP
Our band is few, but true and tried. Song of Marion's Men. Bryant. ThLM
Our Birth Is but a Sleep [and a Forgetting]. Wordsworth. Fr. Ode: Intimations of Immortality from Recollections of Early Childhood. BiCB; EaLo; FaBV; PoSa; TRV
Our Birthday. Marion Edey. BiCB
Our bodies were sunlit spattered. The Serpent of God. Cerise Farallon. UnTE
Our brains ache, in the merciless iced east winds that knive us. Exposure. Wilfred Owen. MMA
Our brother says that Will was born. Dick and Will. Elizabeth Madox Roberts. BiCB
Our bugles sang truce, for the night-cloud had lowered. The Soldier's Dream. Thomas Campbell. FaPL; GTBS-P; RoGo
Our Burden Bearer. Phillips Brooks. TRV
Our campfires shone bright on the mountains. When Sherman Marched Down to the Sea. Samuel H. M. Byers. BFSS
Our Canoe Idles in the Idling Current. Kenneth Rexroth. ErPo
Our Casuarina Tree. Toru Dutt. ACV
Our Cherries. Unknown. BSO
Our Christ. Harry Webb Farrington. STF; TRV
"Our corporal drums are beating." The Banks of the Nile. Unknown. BSNS
Our Dusk: That West. Jonathan Williams. PoNC
Our earthly homes are simple things. Home. Martha Snell Nicholson. STF
Our families in Thine Arms enfold. In Thine Arms. Oliver Wendell Holmes. TRV
Our Father. Roberta Teale Swartz. MoRP
Our Father which [or who] art in heaven. The Lord's Prayer. St. Matthew, Bible, N.T. EaLo; PoLF; TRV
Our fathers came to search for gold. Australia's on the Wallaby. Unknown. PoAu-1
Our fathers wrung their bread from stocks and stones. Children of Light. Robert Lowell. AP; PoPl; ToPo
Our flesh was a battle-ground. The Litany of the Dark People. Countee Cullen. EaLo; MoRP
Our God Finds Us. Francis Thompson. Fr. The Hound of Heaven. BoC

Our God, our help in ages past. *See* O God Our Help in Ages Past.
Our good King Charles within his youthful prime. The Royal Love Scene. Ernest Dowson. UnTE
Our Goodman. *Unknown.* BSNS; BSO; UnTE
Our guests are about to go. So Soon? Richard Armour. LV
Our Happy Home. *Unknown.* ThGo
Our hearths are gone out, and our hearts are broken. The Raven Days. Sidney Lanier. CBEP
Our Help. Psalms, CXXIX: 8, Bible, *O.T.* TRV
Our images withdraw, the rose returns. Beyond Possession. Elizabeth Jennings. BoC
Our Lady of the Snows. Kipling. ACV
Our Lady of the Waves. George Mackay Brown. NePoEA-2
Our life is twofold: Sleep hath its own world: The Dream. Byron. CABL
Our little Bobby started school today. He Will Make the Grade. Edith Earnshaw. PoNC
Our little systems have their day. Tennyson. *Fr.* in Memoriam A. H. H., Proem. TRV
Our lives are not renewable, yet we seek extinctions. High Summer. Jascha Kessler. AmPC
Our lives are Swiss. Emily Dickinson. AP
Our Master. Whittier. TRV
Our moulting days are in their twilight stage. Garnishing the Aviary. Margaret Danner. Far from Africa: Four Poems, 1. AmNP; NNP
Our passions are most like to floods and streams. To the Queen. Sir Walter Ralegh. CBEP
Our Polite Parents. Carolyn Wells. BBGG
Our Prayer of Thanks, *sel.* Carl Sandburg.
"For the gladness here where the sun is shining at evening." TRV
Our Revels Now Are Ended. Shakespeare. *Fr.* The Tempest, IV, i. DiPo
(Stuff of Dreams, The.) FaBV
Our Rock. Francis Scott Key. STF
Our second Eve puts on her mortall shroude. The Virgine Maries Conception. Robert Southwell. MeP
Our Silly Little Sister. Dorothy Aldis. EvOK
Our storm[e] is past, and that storm's tyrannous rage. The Calm. John Donne. CABL; StP
Our Times Are in His Hands. Mary D. Freeze. STF
Our twelve months go round and round. January 1. Marnie Pomeroy. PoSC
Our uncle called us on the phone. Surprise. Harry Behn. BiCB
Our Village—by a Villager. Thomas Hood. CBEP
Our vales are sweet with fern and rose. The Old Burying-Ground. Whittier. AP
Our walk was far among the ancient trees. To M. H. Wordsworth. EiCP
Our youthful hearts do ofttimes weep. The Sailor Boy. *Unknown.* BSO
Oure kinge went forth to Normandy. A Carol of Agincourt. *Unknown.* MeEL
Out. Nathaniel Burt. MoLP
Out came the captain of the gallant ship. The Ship a-Raging. *Unknown.* BFSS
Out comes the bee. Leaving the House of a Friend. Basho. RePo
Out Fishin'. Edgar A. Guest. PoLF
Out in a world of death, far to the northward lying. The Winter Lakes. Wilfred Campbell. OBCV
Out in the Dark. Edward Thomas. GTBS-P
Out in the dark beyond my gates. New Year's Eve in Troy. Adrienne Rich. NePoEA-2
Out in the dark, over the snow. Out in the Dark. Edward Thomas. GTBS-P
Out in the fields which were green last May. A Child's Thought of Harvest. "Susan Coolidge." PoSC
Out in the Fields with God. *Unknown.* TRV
Out in the sunshine fair and free. Written on the Road. Mary Mapes Dodge. BiCB
Out in the Woods with Father. David McCord. ThGo
Out in the yellow meadows, where the bee. Modern Love, XI. George Meredith. VP
Out of a fired ship, which, by no way. Epigram: A Burnt Ship. John Donne. DiPo
Out of a living stone. Michelangelo, *tr. fr. Italian by* Joseph Tusiani. RBL
Out of a Northern city's bay. The Cruise of the *Monitor.* George Henry Boker. ThLM
Out of Bounds. John Banister Tabb. TRV
Out of his cottage to the sun. Old Dan'l. L. A. G. Strong. PoSC
Out of Love. *Unknown, tr. fr. Spanish by* William M. Davis. AnML
Out of me unworthy and unknown. Anne [*or* Ann] Rutledge. Edgar Lee Masters. *Fr.* Spoon River Anthology. AmLP; ILP; LiPo; PoPl; PoSa; PoSC; ThLM
Out of My Study Window. Reed Whittemore. PoPl
Out of my window late at night I gape. In the Night. Elizabeth Jennings. MP

Out of one's birth. Horoscope. J. V. Cunningham. PoIE
Out of School. Hal Summers. DaDu
Out of Sight, Out of Mind. Barnabe Googe. EnRePo; PoIE
Out of the bosom of the air. Snow-Flakes. Longfellow. AmLP; AP; WiR
Out of the cloud my Lord the Sun. Easter Hymn. Michael Thwaites. MoRP
Out of the Cradle Endlessly Rocking. Walt Whitman. AP; CABA; CaFP; DiPo; FaPL; FoBA; ILP; OnP; StP
Out of the Deep Have I Called unto Thee, O Lord. Christina Rossetti. VP
Out of the deep, my child, out of the deep. De Profundis, I. Tennyson. ILP
Out of the depths have I cried unto thee, O Lord. In Darkness and Aridity. Psalm CXXX, Bible, *O.T.* BoC
Out of the dusk a shadow. Evolution. John Banister Tabb. PoPl
Out of the factory chimney, tall. Smoke Animals. Rowena Bennett. RePo
Out of the fire. Pool. Carl Sandburg. AP
Out of the focal and foremost fire. Little Giffen. Francis Orr Ticknor. FaPL
Out of the fog and the gloom. The True Story of Skipper Ireson. Charles Buxton Going. SIV
Out of the golden remote wild west where the sea without shore is. Hesperia. Swinburne. OBNC
Out of the hills of Habersham. Song of the Chattahoochee. Sidney Lanier. AP; DiPo; FaBV; LV
Out of the icy storms the white hare came. Ecclesiastes. Joseph Langland. PoPl
Out of the land of heaven. Poem for Marc Chagall. Leonard Cohen. OBCV
Out of the living word. The Book of Kells. Howard Nemerov. EaLo
Out of the mud two strangers came. Two Tramps in Mud Time. Robert Frost. AP; FoBA
Out of the night that covers me. Invictus. W. E. Henley. Echoes, IV. FaBV; FaPL; LV; OBNC; PoIE; PoPl; PoPo
Out of the Rolling Ocean the Crowd. Walt Whitman. FoBA
Out of the scabbard of the night. Dawn. Frank Dempster Sherman. TRV
Out of the Sea. Witter Bynner. MoLP
Out of the showering snow itself to build. The Winter House. Norman Cameron. CBEP
Out of the sighs and breath of each small citizen. The City: Midnight. Bruce Dawe. PoAu-2
Out of the sparkling sea. Battle: Hit. W. W. Gibson. PoPo
Out of the Vast. Augustus Wright Bamberger. TRV
Out of the West of Lucky Riders. Myron Levoy. OPP
Out of the wine-pot cried the Fly. The Fly. Francisco de Quevedo y Villegas. RBL
Out of the wood of thoughts that grows by night. Cock Crow. Edward Thomas. GTBS-P
Out of This Life. *Unknown.* STF
Out [*or* Owt] of thise blake wawes for to saile [*or* sayle]. Chaucer. *Fr.* Troilus and Criseyde. ILP; PP
Out of us all. Words. Edward Thomas. WePo
Out of what dark, what light? From a country no man knows. The Quickening. Ruth Gilbert. *Fr.* The Blossom of the Branches. ACV
Out of Wisdom Has Come Love. E. A. Robinson. *Fr.* The Three Taverns. MoRP
Out of Your Hands. Theodore Weiss. CoPo
Out of your slepe arise and wake. Man Exalted. *Unknown.* MeEL
Out of your whole life give but a moment! Now [*or* The Moment Eternal]. Robert Browning. CBEP; UnTE
Out on the board the old shearer stands. Click Go the Shears, Boys. *Unknown.* PoAu-1
Out on the Silvery Tide. *Unknown. See* Mary on the Silvery Tide.
Out on the wastes of the Never Never. Where the Dead Men Lie. Barcroft Boake. PoAu-1
"Out, Out—." Robert Frost. CABA; ILP; PoIE; PoPo; SIV
Out Upon It [I Have Loved]. Sir John Suckling. CABA; ErPo; ILP; PoIE; PoSa
Constant Lover, The. FaBV
("Out upon it, I have loved.") BoLP
(Song.) SeCP
Out walking in the frozen swamp one gray day. The Wood-Pile. Robert Frost. CABA; PoPo
Out walking ties left over from a track Cross Ties. X. J. Kennedy. CoPo
Outa Work Blues. Carlos Cortez. PtTo
Outcast. Claude McKay. AmNP
Outlaw, The. Sir Walter Scott. *Fr.* Rokeby, III. GTBS-P
Outlaws. Robert Graves. AnMoPo
Outlook Uncertain. Alastair Reid. NePoEA-2
Outlook wasn't brilliant for the Mudville nine that day, The. Casey at the Bat. Ernest Lawrence Thayer. PoPl; SD; SIV
Outside Bristol Rovers Football Ground. The Ballad of Billy Rose. Leslie Norris. MoBS

Outside my blind a bird lit in a tree. A Play of Opposites. Gray Burr. CuPo

Outside the Door. Annette Wynne. SoPo

Outside the house an ash-tree hung its terrible whips. Discord in Childhood. D. H. Lawrence. CBEP

Outside the lilacs blurred. Keep Darkness. Leslie Nelson Jennings. FiSC

Outside, the snow on a low. Celebration. Robert Sward. *Fr.* Five Poems for J. F. K. OPP

Outspoken buttocks in pink beads. National Winter Garden. Hart Crane. *Fr.* The Bridge. ErPo

Outward Journey. Karl Wolfskehl, *tr. fr. German by* Peter Dronke. MGP

Outwards. *Unknown.* HaSV

Outwitted. Edwin Markham. LV; PoPo; TRV

Out-worn heart, in a time out-worn. Into the Twilight. W. B. Yeats. PoPo

Oven Bird, The. Robert Frost. AP; FoBA; VaPo

Over a bloomy land untrod. In Dreamy Swoon. George Darley. *Fr.* Nepenthe. OBNC

Over and over, the staring owl remembers not to blink. In the Headlights. Charles Edward Eaton. PoNC

Over and under/ The shaking sky. Iron-Wind Dances. Lew Sarett. *Fr.* Thunderstorms. LV

Over back where they speak of life as staying. The Investment. Robert Frost. LV

Over dead craters, hushed with snows. The Christ of the Andes. Edwin Markham. SIV

Over-Heart, The, *sel.* Whittier.
   "World sits at the feet of Christ, The." TRV

Over his keys the musing organist. June. *Fr.* The Vision of Sir Launfal, Prelude. James Russell Lowell. OnMSP; PoLF

Over in the Meadow. *Unknown.* SoPo

Over marsh and swamp and pond. Peepers. Melville Cane. RePo

Over rock and wrinkled ground. Beagles. W. R. Rodgers. SD

Over Shining Shingle. Else Lasker-Schüler, *tr. fr. German by* Christopher Middleton. MGP

Over Sir John's Hill. Dylan Thomas. CABL; DiPo; VaPo

Over the books of bricks. Landscape near a Steel Mill. Herschel Horn. PtTo

Over the briny wave I go. The Kayak. *Unknown.* RePo

Over the dim blue rim of the sea. Outwards. *Unknown.* HaSV

Over the eye behind the moon's cloud. Raison d'Etre. Oliver Pitcher. AmNP; NNP

Over, the four long years! And now there rings. Oxford. Lionel Johnson. OBNC

Over the Heather the Wet Wind Blows. W. H. Auden. DaDu
   (Roman Soldier on the Wall, A.) WePo
   (Roman Wall Blues.) DTC

Over the hill drift heavy yellow clouds. Nietzsche. Stefan George. TwGP

Over the ice she flies. Skating. Kipling. SD

Over the land freckled with snow half-thawed. Thaw. Edward Thomas. GTBS-P

Over the lotus leaves. Lotus Leaves. Mitsukuni. SiGo

Over the mountains/ And under the waves. Love Will Find Out the Way [*or* The Great Adventurer]. *Unknown.* CBEP; GTBS-P; WiR

Over the mountains/ Over the plains. Trains. James S. Tippett. SoPo

Over the river. Ferry-Boats. James S. Tippett. SoPo

Over the Sea to Skye. Robert Louis Stevenson. HaSV

Over the seagulls and the gull white roofs the music lies like heat. Tabernacles. Gerrit Lansing. CoPo

Over the water an old ghost strode. The Old Ghost. Thomas Lovell Beddoes. WiR

Over the west side of this mountain. Lyrebirds. Judith Wright. GoJo

Over the white pond. Decline [*or* Untergang]. Georg Trakl. MGP; TwGP

Over this hearth—my father's seat. The Returned Volunteer to His Rifle. Herman Melville. ThLM

Over 2000 Illustrations and a Complete Concordance. Elizabeth Bishop. PoDB

Over us stands the broad electric face. Terminal. Karl Shapiro. AmLP

Overheard in an Orchard. Elizabeth Cheney. TRV

Overheard on a Saltmarsh. Harold Monro. GoJo

Overlander, The. *Unknown.* PoAu-1

Overnight; very/ Whitely. Mushrooms. Sylvia Plath. AnMoPo; NePoEA-2

Overshadowed by the sprays. Ancient Chinese Map of the World. Wieland Schmied. MGP

Overtakelessness of those, The. Emily Dickinson. MoRP

Owl, The. Tennyson. CBEP
   (Song: Owl, The.) GoJo

Owl, The. Edward Thomas. DTC; GTBS-P; PoIE; PoSa

Owl and the Eel and the Warming-Pan, The. Laura E. Richards. EvOK

Owl and the Pussy-Cat, The. Edward Lear. CBEP; GoJo; GTBS-P; PoLF; PoPl; PoSa; SoPo; WePo

Owl-Critic, The. J. T. Fields. EvOK

Owl King, The. James Dickey. CoPo
   (Call, The.) NePoEA-2

Owls—they whinny down the night. Outlaws. Robert Graves. AnMoPo

Owt of thise blake wawes for to saylle. *See* Out of thise blake wawes for to saile.

Ox of my childhood, steaming. Far Away and Long Ago. Rubén Darío. AnSP

Ox-Tamer, The. Walt Whitman. CBEP

Oxcarts Are Now on Their Way, The. Juan Ramón Jiménez, *tr. fr. Spanish by* Alice Sternberg. AnSP

Oxen, The. Thomas Hardy. CaFP; MoRP; PoDB; PoIE; PoSa; VP

Oxford. Lionel Johnson. OBNC

Oxford to London, 1884. In a Railway Compartment. John Fuller. NePoEA-2

Oyster, The. Francis Ponge, *tr. fr. French by* Tod Perry. CoFP

Oysters. Swift. ErPo

Ozymandias. Shelley. CABA; CaFP; CBEP; DiPo; ILP; LV; OBNC; OnP; PoIE; PoLF; PoPo; PoSa; RoGo; StP
   (Ozymandias of Egypt.) GTBS-P

P

P. Shut, shut the door, good John! fatigu'd, I said. *See* Shut, shut the door, good John! fatigued, I said.

Pack, clouds, away, and welcome day. Thomas Heywood. *Fr.* The Rape of Lucrece. GTBS-P

Package, The. Aileen Fisher. SoPo

Packed in my mind lie all the clothes. The Inward Morning. Henry David Thoreau. AP

Packed with woodpeckers, my head knocks. Raking Leaves. Robert Pack. CoPo

Pact, A. Ezra Pound. CBEP; PoPl

Paddy Doyle. *Unknown.* BSNS

Paddy the Beaver. Thornton Burgess. RePo

Paddy Whack it is me name. Fragments of Irish Songs. *Unknown.* BSO

Pageant, The. Whittier. AmLP

Pageants of Thomas More, The. Sir Thomas More. EnRePo

Paging Professor Gooseberry. Thad Stem, Jr. PoNC

Paid on Both Sides, *sel.* W. H. Auden.
   Concluding Chorus: "Though he believe it, no man is strong." AnMoPo

Pain has an element of blank. Emily Dickinson. AP; CBEP; DiPo; FoBA

Pain is my familiar, now. To My New Mistress. Beverly Bowie. PoPl

Pain of loving you, The. A Young Wife. D. H. Lawrence. ELP; StP

Painful and brief the act. Eve on the barren shore. Eve in Reflection. Jay Macpherson. OBCV

Pains of Sleep, The. Samuel Taylor Coleridge. CBEP; OBNC

Pains, reading, study, are their just pretense. Pope. *Fr.* Epistle to Dr. Arbuthnot. PP

Painted Head. John Crowe Ransom. AP; PoIE

Painter, by unmatch'd desert. The Picture. Anacreon. UnTE

Pair, A. Karl Gjellerup, *tr. fr. Danish by* Charles Wharton Stork. PoPl

Pairs of Wings, A. Stephen Hawes. MeEL

Paisley Officer, The (B *vers.*). *Unknown.* BSNS
   (Bonny Scotland, A *vers.*) BSNS

Palace of Art, The. Tennyson. VP
   To ——: With the Following Poem, *introd.* VP

Palau. Gottfried Benn, *tr. fr. German by* Michael Hamburger. MGP

Palatine, The. "Aldo Palazzeschi," *tr. fr. Italian by* Carlo L. Golino. CoIP

Palaver's No Prayer. John Ciardi. ToPo

Pale amber sunlight falls across. Autumnal. Ernest Dowson. OBNC

Pale Beauty! and a Smile the Pallor There. Petrarch, *tr. fr. Italian by* Edwin Morgan. Sonnets to Laura: To Laura in Life, XCVIII. AnML

Pale beech and pine-tree blue. In a Wood. Thomas Hardy. *Fr.* The Woodlanders. OBNC; PoPl

Pale Blue Casket, The. Oliver Pitcher. NNP

Pale Cold Moon, The. William Renton. WePo

Pale light tatters the stones beyond the hemlock. Sudden Frost. David Wagoner. PoPl

Pale moon was rising o'er yonder high mountain, The. The Rose of Tralee. *Unknown.* BSNS

Palermo, Mother's Day, 1943. William Belvin. PoPl

Palladium. Matthew Arnold. GTBS-P; OBNC; VP

Pallid Cuckoo. David Campbell. PoAu-2

Pallid cuckoo, The. Late Winter. James McAuley. PoAu-2

Palm-Sunday Hymn, A. William Herebert. MeEL
Palm-Tree, The. Henry Vaughan. MeP
Palmer bent, with locks of silver grey, The. Petrarch. *Fr.* Sonnets to Laura: To Laura in Life. RBL
Palmer's Ode, The. Robert Greene. *Fr.* Never Too Late. CTC; EnRePo
Palmström. Christian Morgenstern, *tr. fr. German by* Walter Kaufmann. TwGP
Palmström sets a bunch of candles. The Dreamer. Christian Morgenstern. MGP
Palmström, standing at a lake. Palmström. Christian Morgenstern. TwGP
Palmström, strolling through the town. The Impossible Fact. Christian Morgenstern. TwGP
Pamela was too gentle to deceive. The Tree in Pamela's Garden. E. A. Robinson. MoLP
Pan. Emerson. ILP
Pan on a tram! in a crooked horn blowing. Spring. Hugh McCrae. ACV
Panchatantra, The, *sels. Unknown, tr. fr. Sanskrit by* Arthur W. Ryder.
  Poverty. SIV
  Serpent and the Mouse, The. SIV
  True Friendship. SiGo
Panda, The. William Jay Smith. RePo
Panegyric on Nelly, A, *sel.* Earl of Rochester.
  "Of a great heroine I mean to tell." UnTE
Paneled in Pine. Marguerite George. FiSC
Pangloss's Song; a Comic-Opera Lyric. Richard Wilbur. AP
Pangolin, The. Marianne Moore. AP
Pangur Bán. *Unknown, tr. fr. Old Irish by* Robin Flower. SiGo
Pan's Syrinx. John Lyly. *Fr.* Midas. ELP
Panther, The. Ogden Nash. SoPo
Panther, The. Rainer Maria Rilke, *tr. fr. German.* PoPl, *tr. by* Paul Engle; TwGP, *tr. by* Walter Kaufmann
Panther and Peacock. Gwen Harwood. PoAu-2
Panther is like a leopard, The. The Panther. Ogden Nash. SoPo
Panther, knowing that his spotted hide, The. Amoretti, LIII. Spenser. EnRePo
Panther Possible, The. William D. Barney. FiSC
Panting for breath, towards their parent brook. Apollo and Daphne. Giambattista Marino. RBL
Paper of Pins, A. *Unknown. See* Keys of Heaven, The.
Papuan Shepherd, A. Francis Webb. *Fr.* A Drum for Ben Boyd. PoAu-2
Parable, A. George L. Kress. STF
Parable. Robert Pack. NePoEA-2
Parade. Rachel Field. *Fr.* A Circus Garland. SoPo
Parade, A. Mary Catherine Rose. SoPo
Paradise. George Herbert. SeCP
Paradise Lost, *sels.* Milton.
  Eden, *Bk.* IV, *ll.* 246-268. DiPo
  Eve's Speech to Adam, *Bk.* IV, *ll.* 449-477. DiPo
  Eve's Temptation and Fall, *Bk.* IX, *ll.* 494-792. DiPo
  Exit from Eden, *Bk.* XII, *ll.* 561-649. DiPo
  Fallen Angels, *Bk.* I, *ll.* 50-67. DiPo
  Hail, Holy Light, *Bk.* III, *ll.* 1-55. OnP; PoIE
  Invocation: "Of man's first disobedience, and the fruit," *Bk.* I, *ll.* 1-26. DiPo
  "Now came still evening on, and twilight gray," *Bk.* IV, *ll.* 598-609, 639-658. PoIE
  ". . . Now too nigh/ Th' archangel stood," *Bk.* XII. *ll.* 624-649. PoIE
  Satan's Metamorphosis, *Bk.* X, *ll.* 504-547. StP
  Satan's Speech, *Bk.* I, *ll.* 249-263. DiPo
  "She, as a veil down to the slender waist," *Bk.* IV, *ll.* 304-311. ErPo
  Thus Eve to Adam, *Bk.* IV, *ll.* 635-658. FaBV
  (With Thee Conversing, *ll.* 639-656.) WiR
  War in Heaven, *Bk.* VI, *ll.* 801-892. DiPo
  What Though the Field Be Lost? *Bk.* I, *ll.* 105-124. EaLo
Paradise on earth is found, A. The Poets' Paradise. Michael Drayton. *Fr.* The Muses' Paradise. WiR
Paradise Regained. Milton. CABL
Paradox, A. Aurelian Townsend. SeCP
Paradox of Time, The. Pierre de Ronsard, *tr. fr. French by* Austin Dobson. RBL
Paradox: That Fruition Destroys Love, *sel.* Henry King.
  "Since lovers' joys then leave so sick a taste." ErPo
Parallel Texts. Robert Kelly. CoPo
Parang. Derek Walcott. ToPo
Parasite lichen. Lichen. Mary Fullerton. PoAu-1
Pardon, The. Richard Wilbur. ToPo
Pardon, goddess of the night. Song. Shakespeare. *Fr.* Much Ado about Nothing, V, iii. CTC
Pardon me, lady, but I wanta ast you. Drug Store. John V. A. Weaver. ThLM
Pardoner's Prologue and Tale, The. Chaucer. *Fr.* The Canterbury Tales. CABL
  "In Flaundres whilom was a compaignye," *sel.* PoIE
Parent of joy! heart-easing mirth. Ode to Mirth. Tobias George Smollett. WaPE
Parental Ode to My Son, A. Thomas Hood. PoLF

Parents are sinful now, for they must whisper. Marriage. Austin Clarke. GTBS-P
Paring the Apple. Charles Tomlinson. NePoEA-2; PoIE
Parish Register, The, *sels.* George Crabbe.
  Ancient Virgin, An, *fr.* Pt. III: Burials. OBNC
  Lady of the Manor, The, *fr.* Pt. III: Burials. OBNC
  "Next died the Widow Goe, an active dame," *fr.* Pt. III: Burials. EnPE
Park, The. Robin Blaser. CoPo
Park is filled with night and fog, The. Spring Night. Sara Teasdale. BoLP
Park Poem. Paul Blackburn. CoPo
Parkinson and the Octopus ("Parkinson broached the octopus"). Norma Farber. FiSC
Parklands, The. Stevie Smith. MoBS
Parlement of Foules, The, *sel.* Chaucer.
  Welcome, Summer. MeEL
  (Now Welcome Summer.) CBEP
  (Roundel: "Now welcom somer, with thy sonne softe.") CTC
Parodie, A: "Souls joy, when thou art gone." George Herbert. MeP
Parrot. William Jay Smith. RePo
Parrots, The. W. W. Gibson. RoGo
Parsnip, The. Ogden Nash. WePo
Parson, The. Goldsmith. *Fr.* The Deserted Village. WePo
Parson of a country town was he, The. Chaucer. *Fr.* The Canterbury Tales: Prologue. TRV
Part of Plenty. Bernard Spencer. ErPo; MoLP
Parted Love. Dante Gabriel Rossetti. The House of Life, XLVI. VP
Parted Souls. Lord Herbert of Cherbury. SeCP
Parthenophil and Parthenophe, *sels.* Barnabe Barnes.
  "I burn, yet am I cold; I am a-cold, yet burn," XXXI. PoIE
  "I wish no rich-refined Arabian gold," XLVIII. (Parthenope.) CBEP
Particularly Effortless He Lay. Walter Höllerer, *tr. fr. German by* Christopher Middleton. MGP
Parting. Matthew Arnold. Switzerland, II. VP
Parting. Buson, *tr. fr. Japanese by* Harold G. Henderson. SiGo
Parting. Emily Dickinson. *See* My life closed twice before its close.
Parting, The. Elizabeth Jennings. NePoEA-2
Parting after a Quarrel. Eunice Tietjens. BoLP
Parting at Morning. Robert Browning. CBEP; DiPo; FaBV; OBNC; WiR
Parting Gift. Elinor Wylie. LOW
Parting Shot, A. C. Day Lewis. DaDu
Parting, without a Sequel. John Crowe Ransom. DTC
Partner, leave that grub. War in Camp. John A. Stone. SGR
Part-Time Tenant. Edna Meudt. FiSC
Party, The. Paul Laurence Dunbar. AmNP
Party, A. Laura E. Richards. BiCB; SoPo
Party Bid. Aletha Humphreys. FiSC
Party Line. Joseph Joel Keith. FiSC
Pass by me, go, and hie thee. Death and the Maiden. Matthias Claudius. AGP
Pass It On! *Unknown.* STF
Passage Steamer. Louis MacNeice. HaSV
Passage to India. Walt Whitman. DiPo; FoBA Sels.
  Passage to More than India. MoRP
  "Sail forth—steer for the deep waters only." TRV
Passenger Train. Edith Newlin Chase. SoPo
Passer, The. George Abbe. SD
Passer-by, A. Robert Bridges. BoC; CaFP; HaSV; OBNC; WiR
Passing and Glassing. Christina Rossetti. OBNC
Passing away, saith the World, passing away. Christina Rossetti. *Fr.* Old and New Year Ditties. OBNC
Passing of Arthur, The. Tennyson. *Fr.* Idylls of the King. OBNC
Passing of Lydia, The. Horace, *tr. fr. Latin by* Louis Untermeyer. Odes, I, 25. UnTE
Passing Out. Philip Levine. AmPC
Passing out of a great city. Initial. Arthur Boyars. NePoEA-2
Passing over a high bridge. Sandro Penna, *tr. fr. Italian by* Carlo L. Golino. CoIP
Passing the Graveyard. Andrew Young. DTC
Passing through huddled and ugly walls. The Harbor. Carl Sandburg. PoPl
Passion, The. Milton. MeP
Passion, The. Henry Vaughan. MeP
Passion and Worship. Dante Gabriel Rossetti. The House of Life, IX. VP
Passion came to me in the form of order, A. Order and Disorder. Richard Eberhart. PoDB
Passion of a Lover, The. George Gascoigne. EnRePo
Passion of Jesus, The. *Unknown.* MeEL
Passionate Man's Pilgrimage, The. Sir Walter Ralegh. CABA; CBEP; EnRePo; FaPL; ILP; PoIE
  (His Pilgrimage.) DTC; WePo

Passionate Man's Pilgrimage, The (*continued*)
"Give me my scallop shell of quiet," *sel.* TRV
Passionate Pilgrim, The, *sels.* Shakespeare, *and others.*
Crabbed Age and Youth, XII. Shakespeare. UnTE
(Madrigal, A.) GTBS-P
Nightingale, The. Richard Barnfield. GTBS-P
Passionate Shepherd, The, *sel.* Nicholas Breton.
Country Lad, The. CBEP
(Pastoral: "Who can live in heart so glad.") ELP
Passionate Shepherd to His Love, The. Christopher Marlowe.
BoLP; CABA; CaFP; CTC; DiPo; ELP;
GTBS-P; ILP; OnP; PoIE; PoLF; PoPo; PoSa; StP;
UnTE; WePo
Passions, The. William Collins. EiCP; GTBS-P
Past and Present. Thomas Hood. *See* I Remember, I Remember.
Past eighty, but never in eighty years. Dick Straightup. Ted
Hughes. ToPo
Past Is the Present, The. Marianne Moore. PP
Past Ruined Ilion [Helen Lives]. Walter Savage Landor. *Fr.*
Ianthe. CBEP; CTC; ELP; OBNC; PoIE; PoSa
Pastime ("Pastime with good company"). Henry VIII, King
of England. CTC
Pastor, The. William C. Summers. STF
Pastoral, A: "By the side of a green stagnate pool." G. A.
Stevens. ErPo
Pastoral: "Enquiring fields, courtesies, The." Allen Tate. AP
Pastoral X: "Grapes are ripe, the frost is near, The." Robert
Hillyer. LOW
Pastoral: "If it were only still!" Edna St. Vincent Millay.
RePo
Pastoral: "Little sparrows, The." William Carlos Williams.
MP
Pastoral, A: "Mobile, immaculate and austere." Geoffrey Hill.
NePoEA-2
Pastoral, A: "There went out in the dawning light." *Un-
known, tr. fr. Latin by* John Addington Symonds. UnTE
Pastoral: "Who can live in heart so glad." Nicholas Breton.
See Country Lad, The.
Pastoral Courtship, A. Earl of Rochester. UnTE
Pastoral Poesy. John Clare. ACV
Pastorall Dialogue, A. Thomas Carew. SeCP
Pastor's Friend, The. *Unknown.* STF
Pastourelle. Donald Jeffrey Hayes. AmNP
Pasture, The. Robert Frost. AmLP; BoC; DiPo; GoJo;
PoPl; SoPo; WePo
Pat Young. Kenneth Mackenzie. PoAu-2
Patent Leather Shoe, The. Alfred Lichtenstein, *tr. fr. Ger-
man by* Michael Hamburger. MGP
Paterson, *sels.* William Carlos Williams.
"Better than flowers." MoLP
Preface: "To make a start." AP
"Without invention nothing is well spaced." PP
"Your lovely hands." MoLP
Path by which we twain did go, The. In Memoriam A. H. H.,
XXII. Tennyson. VP
Path of the Stars, The. Thomas S. Jones, Jr. MoRP
Patience, *sels.* W. S. Gilbert.
Bunthorne's Song. VaPo
Fable of the Magnet and the Churn, The. OnMSP; RePo
Patience. Harry Graham. LV
Patience [Hard Thing!]. Gerard Manley Hopkins. BoC;
FoBA
("Patience, hard thing! the hard thing but to pray.") VP
(Sonnet.) OBNC
Patience of Job is a story old, The. Will God's Patience Hold
Out for You? Edythe Johnson. STF
Patriot, The. Sir Walter Scott. *See* Breathes There the Man.
Patriotism. Sir Walter Scott. *See* Breathes There the Man.
Patrol. Ralph Pomeroy. CoPo
Patrolling Barnegat. Walt Whitman. CBEP
Patterns. Amy Lowell. BoLP; OnMSP
Pauca Mea, *sel.* Christopher Brennan.
I Said, This Misery Must End. PoAu-1
Paul. John Oxenham. TRV
Paul. James Wright. PoPl
Paul Jones (A *and* B *vers.*). *Unknown.* BSNS
Paul Revere's Ride. Longfellow. *Fr.* Tales of a Wayside
Inn: The Landlord's Tale, Pt. I. CaFP; FaBV; RePo;
SIV; ThLM
Paul's Wife. Robert Frost. CABL
Pauper's Funeral, The. George Crabbe. *Fr.* The Village.
OBNC
Pause. Rosa Zagnoni Marinoni. FiSC
Pause of Thought, A. Christina Rossetti. OBNC
Pavane for the Nursery, A. William Jay Smith. BoLP;
GoJo; PoSC
Pavane for the White Queen. Carol Bergé. OPP
Pax Nobiscum. Earl Marlatt. MoRP
Paysage Moralisé. John Hollander. ErPo
Pcheek pcheek pcheek pcheek pcheek. The Avenue Bearing the
Initial of Christ into the New World. Galway Kinnell.
CoPo; NePoEA-2; PoDB
Pea-Fields, The. Sir Charles G. D. Roberts. OBCV

Peace. Bhartrihari, *tr. fr. Sanskrit by* Paul Elmer More.
SiGo
Peace. Rupert Brooke. *Fr.* 1914. MMA
Peace. Walter de la Mare. MMA
Peace. George Herbert. ELP; MeP
Peace. Gerard Manley Hopkins. BoC; ELP; GTBS-P
Peace. Margaret E. Sangster. TRV
Peace ("O for a heart of calm repose"). *Unknown.* STF
Peace ("Pees maketh plente"). *Unknown.* MeEL
Peace. Henry Vaughan. CBEP; EaLo; ELP; MeP; WePo
(Peace of Heaven, The.) BoC
Peace and Joy. Shelley Silverstein. PoSC
Peace and Mercy and Jonathan. First Thanksgiving of All.
Nancy Byrd Turner. RePo
Peace; come away: the song of woe. In Memoriam A. H. H.,
LVII. Tennyson. VP
Peace, deep and rich. Prayer to Peace. Euripides. *Fr.* Creso-
phontes. PoPl
Peace does not mean the end of all our striving. G. A. Stud-
dert-Kennedy. *Fr.* The Christian Soldier. TRV
Peace Hymn of the Republic. Henry van Dyke. TRV
Peace in the sober house of Jonas dwelt. Jonas Kindred's
Household. George Crabbe. *Fr.* The Frank Courtship.
OBNC
Peace in the Welsh Hills. Vernon Watkins. GTBS-P
Peace in the World. John Galsworthy. PoLF
Peace, like a Lamb. Leonard Clark. WePo
Peace of a Good Mind, The. Sir Thomas More. *Fr.* The
Twelve Weapons of Spiritual Battle. EnRePo
Peace of great doors be for you, The. For You. Carl Sand-
burg. MoRP
Peace of Heaven, The. Henry Vaughan. *See* Peace.
Peace on Earth. William Carlos Williams. LOW
Peace, peace! he is not dead, he doth not sleep. An Elegy on
the Death of John Keats. Shelley. *Fr.* Adonais. OBNC
Peace pratler, do not lowre. Conscience. George Herbert.
MeP
Peace shall ever by this tombstone be! At the Grave of My
Father. Matthias Claudius. AGP
Peace, the one-time radiant goddess. The Child of Peace.
Selma Lagerlof. PoPl
Peace, the wild valley streaked with torrents. The Straw.
Robert Graves. AnMoPo
Peace to all such! but were there One whose fires. Atticus.
Pope. *Fr.* Epistle to Dr. Arbuthnot. PoSa
Peaceful life;—just toil and rest, A. Lincoln. James Whit-
comb Riley. LiPo
Peaceful Shepherd, The. Robert Frost. MoRP
Peaceful spot is Piper's Flat, A. The folk that live around.
How McDougal Topped the Score. Thomas E. Spencer.
PoAu-1
Peaceful Western Wind, The. Thomas Campion. EnRePo
Peaches, The. Joel Oppenheimer. CoPo
Peacock and Nightingale. Robert Finch. OBCV
Peacock of Java, The. William Jay Smith. RePo
Peacock That Lived in the Land of King George, The, *with
music.* *Unknown.* BSO
Peacocks' pride, The. The Unicorn. "Gertrud Kolmar."
MGP
Peacocks scream and the pear trees quiver. And the Pear Trees
Shiver. Jocelyn Macy Sloan. FiSC
Peadar Og Goes Courting. James Stephens. BoLP
Peanut butter thickly spread. Study Habits. Richard Ar-
mour. LV
Pear-Tree, The. Mary Gilmore. PoAu-1
Pear Tree. Hilda Doolittle ("H. D."). AP
Pear-Trees by the River ("Pear-trees translucent white"). Su
T'ung-po, *tr. fr. Chinese by* E. D. Edwards. SiGo
Pearl, The. Hans Christian Andersen, *tr. fr. Danish by*
Charles Wharton Stork. SiGo
Pearl, The. George Herbert. MeP; SeCP
Pearl, a Girl, A. Robert Browning. CBEP
Peas. *Unknown.* *See* I Eat My Peas with Honey.
Peasant. A. R. S. Thomas. ToPo
Peasant Declares His Love, The. Emile Roumer, *tr. fr. Span-
ish by* John Peale Bishop. ErPo
Peasant Poet, The. John Clare. OBNC
Pease Porridge Hot. Mother Goose. SoPo
Peau de Chagrin of State Street, The. Oliver Wendell Holmes.
AP
Pebble, The. Elinor Wylie. MoRP
Pebbles. Herman Melville. AP
Peddler, sell me a shade of red. Mary Magdalene's Song.
Unknown. AnML
Peddler's Caravan, The. William Brighty Rands. SoPo
Pedigree of Honey, The. Emily Dickinson. FaBV
Pedlar. Confucius, *tr. fr. Chinese by* Ezra Pound. *Fr.* The
Classic Anthology: Wei Wind. CTC
Pedlar, The. Shakespeare. *Fr.* The Winter's Tale, IV, iii.
WiR
Pedlar, A. *Unknown.* *See* Fine Knacks for Ladies.
Peekaboo, I Almost See You. Ogden Nash. PoLF
Peeper, The. Peter Davison. ErPo
Peepers. Melville Cane. RePo

Peeping Tom. Francis Hope. ErPo
Pees maketh plente. Peace. *Unknown.* MeEL
Peewits on the Hills. Alice V. Stuart. ACV
Peg-Leg's Fiddle. Bill Adams. RePo
Peggy Said Good Morning. John Clare. ELP
Penal Law. Austin Clarke. GTBS-P
Penelope, That Longed for the Sight. *Unknown.* EnRePo
Penitent Hopes in Mary, The. *Unknown.* MeEL
Penitent Nun, The. John Lockman. ErPo; UnTE
Pennines in April. Ted Hughes. WePo
Pennsylvania Station. Langston Hughes. AmNP
Penny for a ball of thread, A. Pop Goes the Weasel. *Unknown.* SoPo
Penny Wise and Found Foolish. W. W. Watt. PoPo
People, The. Tomasso Campanella, *tr. fr. Italian by* John Addington Symonds. RBL
People. Lois Lenski. SoPo
People, The. Elizabeth Madox Roberts. GoJo; SoPo
People all over this time of year. Resolutions?—New and Old. Harvey E. Rolfe. STF
People all were sleeping, The. Ballad of the Fair Melisenda. *Unknown.* AnML
People along the sand, The. Neither Out Far nor in Deep. Robert Frost. AP; CABA; DiPo
People are putting up storm windows now. Storm Windows. Howard Nemerov. PoIE
People Buy a Lot of Things. Annette Wynne. SoPo
People expect old men to die. Old Men. Ogden Nash. EvOK
People Hide Their Love. Emperor Wu Ti, *tr. fr. Chinese by* Arthur Waley. SiGo
People is a beast of muddy brain, The. The People. Tomasso Campanella. RBL
People of Spain think Cervantes, The. Cervantes. E. C. Bentley. EvOK
People of the Phoenix do not say "the Phoenix," The. Conventicle. Gerrit Lansing. CoPo
People on the streets draw up and stare, The. Umbra Vitae. Georg Heym. MGP
People walk upon their heads, The. Topsy-turvy Land. H. E. Wilkinson. SoPo
People wondered what Dan Wholebrook found. Star-Pudding. Robert P. Tristram Coffin. PoPo
People, Yes, The, *sels.* Carl Sandburg.
  Copperfaces, The, *fr.* Sec. 51. RePo
  "Lincoln?/ He was a mystery in smoke and flags," Sec. 57. LiPo
  They Have Yarns, Sec. 45. RePo
People's voice, A! we are a people yet. Tennyson. *Fr.* Ode on the Death of the Duke of Wellington. ACV
Perchance that I might learn what pity is. A Prayer for Purification. Michelangelo. RBL
Perched in a tower of this ancestral Wall. At the Great Wall of China. Edmund Blunden. GTBS-P
Percy out of Northumberland, The. Chevy Chase. *Unknown.* BuBa
Percy Shelley. John Peale Bishop. ErPo
Perdie, I Said It Not. Sir Thomas Wyatt. EnRePo
Père Lalemant. Marjorie Pickthall. OBCV
Perennial Mourner. Sydney King Russell. FiSC
Perfect Husband, The. Ogden Nash. LV
Perfect little body, without fault or stain on thee. On a Dead Child. Robert Bridges. OBNC
Perfect Love. Sana'i, *tr. fr. Persian by* A. J. Arberry. SiGo
Perfect Love ("Perfect love the Father giveth"). *Unknown.* STF
Perfect Peace. Isaiah, XXVI: 3, Bible, *O.T.* TRV
Perfect Reactionary, The. Hughes Mearns. LV
Perfection ever rising to perfection. Invocation. *Unknown.* SiGo
Perforated Spirit, The. Morris Bishop. PoPo
Performance, The. James Dickey. NePoEA-2
Performances, assortments, résumés. The Tunnel. Hart Crane. *Fr.* The Bridge. AP
Performing Seal, The. Rachel Field. *Fr.* A Circus Garland. SoPo
Perfume. *Unknown, tr. fr. Greek by* Louis Untermeyer. UnTE
Perhaps a dream; yet surely truth has beamed. Sonnets, Part I, XXIV. Frederick Goddard Tuckerman. AP
Perhaps He will come at the dawning. When Will He Come? *Unknown.* STF
Perhaps it was being inside of something. The History of the World as Pictures. Nancy Sullivan. CoPo
Perhaps the accident of a bird. An Instance. Alastair Reid. PP
Perhaps Today. *Unknown.* STF
Peri Poietikes. Louis Zukofsky. CoPo
Pericles and Aspasia, *sels.* Walter Savage Landor.
  Behold, O Aspasia! I Send You Verses, *fr.* CXC. OBNC
  Corinna to Tanagra, *fr.* XLIV. OBNC
  Death of Artemidora, The, *fr.* LXXXV. OBNC
  Dirce, *fr.* CCXXX. CBEP; CTC; OBNC; StP
Peri's Lament for Hinda, The. Thomas Moore. *Fr.* Lalla Rookh. OBNC

Permanent Delegate, The. Yuri Suhl, *tr. fr. Yiddish by* Max Rosenfeld *and* Walter Lowenfels. PtTo
Perpetual Infirmity of Hope. Sister Juana Inés de la Cruz, *tr. fr. Spanish by* Muriel Kittel. AnSP
Perplext in faith, but pure in deeds. Tennyson. *Fr.* In Memoriam A. H. H., XCVI. TRV
Perrie, Merrie, Dixi, Domini, *with music. Unknown.* BFSS (Perry Merry Dictum Dominee, *with music.*) BSO
Perseus. Louis MacNeice. StP
Pershing at the Front. Arthur Guiterman. SIV
Persimmon, The, Io! Hokku. Chiyo. LV
Person from Porlock, The. Robert Graves. BoC
Person from Porlock, A. R. S. Thomas. BoC
Person who can do, The. Poem. Alan Dugan. ErPo
Personal. Langston Hughes. AmNP
Personal Letter to the Ephesians. Carl Bode. ToPo
Personal Talk. Wordsworth. CABA; DiPo
Perspective. Margaret Avison. OBCV
Perspectives. Dudley Randall. AmNP
Pert paradox, whose green and summer claws. Praying Mantis. Felix Stefanile. FiSC
Perturbations of Uranus, The. Roy Fuller. ErPo
Pessimist, The. Benjamin Franklin King, Jr. WePo
  (Sum of Life, The, *abr.*) CTC
Pete at the Zoo. Gwendolyn Brooks. LOW
Pete Rousecastle the sailor's son. Rousecastle. David Wright. MoBS
Peter. Earl Marlatt. MoRP
Peter Ambelay. *Unknown.* BSNS
Peter and John. Elinor Wylie. MoBS; MoRP
Peter at some immortal cloth, it seemed. The Death of Peter Esson. George Mackay Brown. NePoEA-2
Peter Bell. John Hamilton Reynolds. OBNC
  "It is the thirty-first of March," *sel.* Par
Peter Grimes. George Crabbe. *Fr.* The Borough. EnPE; OBNC; WePo
Peter, Peter, Pumpkin-Eater. Mother Goose. SoPo
Peter Quince at the Clavier. Wallace Stevens. AP; CABA; ILP; MP; VaPo
Peterhof. Edmund Wilson. GoJo
Petit, the Poet. Edgar Lee Masters. *Fr.* Spoon River Anthology. ILP; PoSa
Petition. W. H. Auden. PoDB; PoIE
Pets are the hobby of my brother Bert. My Brother Bert. Ted Hughes. BBGG
'Petually/ constrained am I. To His Wife. John Skelton. CBEP
Phantasmion, *sel.* Sara Coleridge.
  "O sleep, my babe, hear not the rippling wave." OBNC
Phantom Horsewoman, The. Thomas Hardy. CaFP
Phantom-Wooer, The. Thomas Lovell Beddoes. WiR
Phar Lap in the Melbourne Museum. Peter Porter. PoAu-2
Pharisee murmurs when the woman weeps, conscious of guilt, The. Sequaire. Godeschalk. CTC
Pheasant ("Pheasant sat by a bush"). Zulfikar Ghose. ACV
Phidile. Matthias Claudius, *tr. fr. German by* Alexander Gode. AGP
Philander. Donald Hall. ErPo
Philemon and Baucis. Ovid, *tr. fr. Latin by* Arthur Golding. *Fr.* Metamorphoses, VIII. CTC
Philips, whose touch harmonious could remove. An Epitaph upon the Celebrated Claudy Philips, Musician Who Died Very Poor. Samuel Johnson. CBEP
Phillida and Coridon. Nicholas Breton. *See* In the Merry Month of May.
Phillis ("Phillis at first seemed much afraid"). *Unknown.* UnTE
Phillis is my only joy. To Phillis. Sir Charles Sedley. BoLP
Phillis, why shou'd we delay. To Phillis. Edmund Waller. SeCP
Philomela. Matthew Arnold. ILP; PoIE; VP
Philosophers Have Measured Mountains. George Herbert. *See* Agonie, The.
Philosophic Flight, The. Luigi Tansillo, *sometimes at. to* Giordano Bruno, *tr. fr. Italian by* John Addington Symonds. RBL
Philosophical Conversation. Schiller, *tr. fr. German by* Walter Kaufmann. TwGP
Philosophy. Rubén Darío, *tr. fr. Spanish by* Muna Lee. AnSP
Phizzog. Carl Sandburg. SoPo
Phlebas the Phoenician, a fortnight dead. Death by Water. T. S. Eliot. *Fr.* The Waste Land. DaDu; HaSV
Phoebe's getting old they say. Anniversary in September. Beatrice Curtis Brown. BiCB
Phoebus, arise! Summons to Love. William Drummond of Hawthornden. GTBS-P
Phoenix, The. George Darley. *Fr.* Nepenthe. CBEP; WiR (Hundred-sunned Phenix.) OBNC
Phoenix and the Turtle, The. Shakespeare. CABA; CBEP; EnRePo; StP
Phoenix, phoenix in the blood. Appeal to the Phoenix. Louis Untermeyer. UnTE
Phol and Wotan Were Riding in the Forest. *Unknown, tr. fr. German by* Ruth Yorck *and* Kenward Elmslie. *Fr.* Magic Spells. AnML

Phono, at the Boar's Head. Henri Coulette. *Fr.* The War of the Secret Agents. NePoEA-2
Phosphorescence. Melville Cane. RePo
Phyllis, *sel.* Thomas Lodge.
  Ode: "Now I find thy looks were feigned." EnRePo
Phyllis. Sydney King Russell. ErPo
Phyllis. Swift. EiCP
Phyllis. *Unknown, tr. fr. Latin by* John Addington Symonds. UnTE
Phyllis, why should we delay. A Plea for Promiscuity. Edmund Waller. UnTE
Phyllyp Sparowe, *sel.* John Skelton.
  Vengence on Cats. PoSa
  (Curse on the Cat, A, *shorter sel.*) EvOK
Piano. D. H. Lawrence. CBEP; GTBS-P; PoIE; VaPo
Piano after War. Gwendolyn Brooks. AmNP
Piano into the zoo, The. Prevention of Cruelty to Animals. Günter Grass. MGP
Piano Practice. Ian Serraillier. BBGG
Piazza Piece. John Crowe Ransom. AP; CBEP; ErPo; PoSa
Pibroch. Ted Hughes. NePoEA-2; PoCh; PoDB
Pibroch of Donuil Dhu. Gathering Song of Donald the Black. Sir Walter Scott. GTBS-P
Picador Bit, The. Bink Noll. ToPo
Picasso, who knows everything, will tell you. Cocteau's *Opium:* 2. Donald Finkel. CoPo
Pick Me Up. William Jay Smith. RePo
Pick-up, The. J. V. Cunningham. UnTE
Pickup in Tony's Hashhouse. Kenneth Pitchford. *Fr.* Good for Nothing Man. CoPo; ErPo
Picnic, A. Aileen Fisher. SoPo
Picnic. Hugh Lofting. GoJo
Picnic, The. John Logan. BoLP; NePoEA-2
Picnic Day. Rachel Field. SoPo
Pictor Ignotus. Robert Browing. CTC
Picture, The. Anacreon, *tr. fr. Greek by* Thomas Stanley. UnTE
Picture, The, *sel.* Phillip Massinger.
  Song of Pleasure, A. UnTE
Picture of Autumn. Friedrich Hebbel, *tr. fr. German by* Alexander Gode. AGP
Picture of J. T. in a Prospect of Stone, The. Charles Tomlinson. PoCh
Picture of Little T. C. in a Prospect of Flowers, The. Andrew Marvell. CBEP; MeP; SeCP
Picture of the Nativity in the Church of Krena in Chios. C. A. Trypanis. AnMoPo
Pictures in the Fire. Patience Strong. RePo
Pictures of the Gone World, *sel.* Lawrence Ferlinghetti.
  "Just as I used to say." ToPo
Piece by piece I seem. 33. Adrienne Rich. CoPo
Piecemeal the summer dies. Exeunt. Richard Wilbur. PoLF
Pied Beauty. Gerard Manley Hopkins. CABA; CaFP; DiPo; EaLo; FoBA; GoJo; GTBS-P; ILP; MoRP; OBNC; PoDB; PoPl; PoPo; StP; TRV; VP; WePo
Pied Piper of Hamelin, The. Robert Browning. SIV
Pierrot. Sara Teasdale. BoLP; PoPo
Pietà. James McAuley. PoAu-2
Pig lay on a barrow dead, The. View of a Pig. Ted Hughes. MP
Pig Tale, A. James Reeves. SoPo
Pigeon, The. Richard Church. WePo
Pigeons. Günter Eich, *tr. fr. German by* Michael Hamburger. MGP
Pigeons. Alastair Reid. MP
Pig-Tale, A. "Lewis Carroll." *Fr.* Sylvie and Bruno Concluded. WiR
Pike. John Bruce. SD
Pike. Ted Hughes. NePoEA-2
Pike County Miner, The, *with music.* Mart Taylor. SGR
Pike, three inches long, perfect. Pike. Ted Hughes. NePoEA-2
Pilate. Georg Heym, *tr. fr. German by* Christopher Middleton. MGP
Pile the bodies high at Austerlitz and Waterloo. Grass. Carl Sandburg. FaBV; PoLF; PoPl; PoPo
Pilgrim, The. W. B. Yeats. PoSa
Pilgrim Song, The. Bunyan. *Fr.* The Pilgrim's Progress. CBEP; ELP
  (Pilgrim, The.) EvOK
  (Pilgrim's Song.) WiR
Pilgrimage, The. George Herbert. MeP
Pilgrimage, The. Henry Vaughan. MeP
Pilgrim's Progress, The, *sels.* Bunyan.
  Pilgrim Song, The. CBEP; ELP
    (Pilgrim, The.) EvOK
    (Pilgrim's Song.) WiR
  Shepherd Boy's Song, The. ThGo; TRV
    (He That Is Down.) CBEP
    (Shepherd Boy Sings in the Valley of Humiliation, The.) EaLo
    (Shepherd's Song, The.) BoC
    (Song of Low Degree, A.) STF

Pillar of Fame, The. Robert Herrick. SeCP
Pillar of the Cloud, The. Cardinal Newman. LV; OBNC; TRV
  (Lead, Kindly Light.) FaPL
Pilot, The. *Unknown.* STF
Pindaric Ode, A: To the Immortal Memory and Friendship of That Noble Pair, Sir Lucius Cary and Sir H. Morison. Ben Jonson. StP
  (To the Immortall Memorie, and Friendship of That Noble Paire, Sir Lucius Cary, and Sir H. Morison.) SeCP
  It Is Not Growing like a Tree, *sel.* CABA; DiPo; LV; PoIE
    (Noble Nature, The.) GTBS-P; PoPo
    (Short Measures.) WePo
Pine Bough, The. Richard Aldridge. PoSC
Pine branch is so wholesome and so sweet, A. Christmas Eve. Zoe Kincaid Brockman. PoNC
Pine Gum. W. W. E. Ross. OBCV
Pine-Trees in the Courtyard, The. Po Chü-i, *tr. fr. Chinese by* Arthur Waley. SiGo
Pines and the Sea, The. Christopher Pearse Cranch. AmLP; ILP
Pines were dark on Ramoth hill, The. My Playmate. Whittier. AP
Pining for Love. Francis Beaumont. BoLP
Pink Locust, The. William Carlos Williams. PP
Pink, small and punctual. Emily Dickinson. FaBV
Pin-swin or spine-swine, The. His Shield. Marianne Moore. DTC
Pioneer, The. William B. Ruggles. SIV
Pious Celinda. Congreve. ELP; ErPo
  (Pious Selinda.) UnTE
Pipe, The. Sir John Squire. PoPl
Pipe of Tobacco, A, *sels.* Isaac Hawkins Browne. Par
  "Blest Leaf! whose aromatic gales dispense."
  "Boy! bring an ounce of Freeman's best."
Piping down the Valleys Wild. Blake. *Fr.* Songs of Innocence. CBEP; FaBV
  (Introduction.) DiPo; EnPE; GoJo; ILP; OBNC; PoIE
  (Piper, The.) RoGo
Piping sharp as a reed. The Nesting Ground. David Wagoner. PoCh
Pippa Passes, *sel.* Robert Browning.
  Year's at the Spring, The. FaBV
    (Pippa's Song.) CBEP; GoJo; LV; PoPo; TRV
    (Song: "Year's at the spring, The.") PoPl
Pirate, The, *sel.* Sir Walter Scott.
  Song of the Reim-kennar, The. OBNC
Pirate Don Durk of Dowdee, The. Mildred Plew Merryman. SoPo
Pirates, The, *with music. Unknown.* BSO
Pirithous being over hault of mynde and such a one. Philemon and Baucis. Ovid. *Fr.* Metamorphoses. CTC
Pirouette. Audre Lorde. NNP
Pisan Cantos, *sel.* Ezra Pound.
  Ant's a Centaur, The. PoSa
Pistons, valves and wheels and gears. Engineers. Jimmy Garthwaite. SoPo
Pit, A—but Heaven over it. Emily Dickinson. AP
Pitch here the tent, while the old horse grazes. Juggling Jerry. George Meredith. VP
Pitcher. Robert Francis. CaFP; PP; SD
Pitcher of Mignonette, A. H. C. Bunner. LV
"Pitter patter!" Falls the rain. The Umbrella Brigade. Laura E. Richards. SoPo
Pity. Giuseppe Ungaretti, *tr. fr. Italian by* Lowry Nelson, Jr. CoIP
Pity beyond all telling, A. The Pity of Love. W. B. Yeats. FoBA
Pity for Mary. *Unknown. See* Now Goeth Sun under Wood.
Pity of Love, The. W. B. Yeats. FoBA
Pity This Busy Monster, Manunkind. E. E. Cummings. AP; ILP; StP
Pity this girl. The Stranger. Brother Antoninus. ToPo
Pity would be no more. The Human Abstract. Blake. *Fr.* Songs of Experience. DiPo
Place-Ghost. August Derleth. FiSC
Place of Cupid's Fire, The. Thomas Campion. *See* Beauty, Since You So Much Desire.
Place of Peace, The. Edwin Markham. TRV
Places among the stars. The Black Riders, XXIII. Stephen Crane. AP
Plague of Dead Sharks. Alan Dugan. AP
Plague take all your pedants, say I! Sibrandus Schafnaburgensis. Robert Browning. *Fr.* Garden Fancies. CTC
Plain be the phrase, yet apt the verse. A Utilitarian View of the *Monitor*'s Fight. Herman Melville. AP
Plain Language from Truthful James. Bret Harte. CTC
Plain Man, The. Frank Borden Hanes. PoNC
Plain Song, *sel.* Jean Cocteau, *tr. fr. French by* Wallace Fowlie.
  "I have sung, to deceive the evil-sounding clock of time." PoPl
Plain Tales from the Hills, *sel.* Kipling.

By the Hoof of the Wild Goat. OBNC
Plain was grassy, wild and bare, The. The Dying Swan. Tennyson. WiR
Plains of Waterloo, The (A vers.). *Unknown.* BSNS
  (Wellington and Waterloo, B vers.) BSNS
Plaint of the Camel, The. Charles Edward Carryl. EvOK; SoPo
Planet, The. Carl Bode. ToPo
Planking of the vessel torn apart, The. Sonnet. Luis de Góngora. RBL
Plans. Helen Morgan Brooks. NNP
Plans. Dorothy Brown Thompson. BiCB
Planster's Vision, The. John Betjeman. PoPl
Planted Skull, The. Peter Viereck. PP
Planter's Charm. Fay M. Yauger. SIV
Planting a Tree. Nancy Byrd Turner. RePo
Planting Flowers on the Eastern Embankment. Po Chü-i, tr. fr. Chinese by Arthur Waley. SiGo
Planting of the Apple Tree, The, sel. Bryant.
  "Come, let us plant the apple tree." PoSC
Plants Stand Silent Round Me, The. Johannes Jorgensen, tr. fr. Danish by Robert Hillyer. SiGo
Plato told/ him: he couldn't. E. E. Cummings. *Fr.* One Times One. CTC; ThLM
Platonic Lady, The. Earl of Rochester. UnTE
Play, The. C. J. Dennis. *Fr.* The Sentimental Bloke. PoAu-1
Play About, Do. Basko, tr. fr. Japanese by Harold G. Henderson. SoPo
Play of Opposites, A. Gray Burr. CoPo
Play seems out for an almost infinite run, The. It Bids Pretty Fair. Robert Frost. CaFP
Play the Last March Slowly. Richard Davidson. PtTo
Players Ask for a Blessing on the Psalteries and on Themselves, The. W. B. Yeats. PoDB
Playful monkey frisks with grand, A. Retinue. Paul Verlaine. ErPo
Playground of the Pixie. Grant Code. FiSC
Playing one day with Rhodope at dice. A Game of Dice. *Unknown.* UnTE
Plays. Walter Savage Landor. PoPo
Playwright. John Woods. CoPo
Plaza and the Flaming Orange Trees, The. Antonio Machado, tr. fr. Spanish by Kate Flores. AnSP
Plaza Has a Tower, The. Antonio Machado, tr. fr. Spanish by Angel Flores. AnSP
Plea, The. John Drinkwater. MoRP
Plea. Nikolaus Lenau, tr. fr. German by George C. Schoolfield. AGP
Plea for a Captive. W. S. Merwin. NePoEA-2
Plea for Haste, A. Petronius, tr. fr. Latin by Louis Untermeyer. UnTE
Plea for Postponement, A. Petronius, tr. fr. Latin by Louis Untermeyer. UnTE
Plea for Promiscuity, A. Edmund Waller. UnTE
Plea of the Midsummer Fairies, The, sels. Thomas Hood. OBNC
  Fairy's Reply to Saturn, The.
  Green Dryad's Plea, The.
  Melodies of Time, The.
  Shakespeare: The Fairies' Advocate.
Plea to Boys and Girls, A. Robert Graves. GTBS-P
Plea to Eros. *Unknown, tr. fr. Greek by* Louis Untermeyer. UnTE
Pleasant Comedy of Patient Grissell, The, sels. Thomas Dekker and others.
  Art Thou Poor? fr. I, i. CBEP
    (Happy Heart, The.) GTBS-P
  Golden Slumbers, fr. IV, ii. ELP
Pleasant Cow, The. Grace Taber Hallock. RePo
Pleasant Memories, sel. Charles Sangster.
  Meadow-Field, The. OBCV
Pleasant Sounds. John Clare. CBEP
Pleasantness of life was mine once undiminished, The. Friedrich Hölderlin, tr. fr. German by Meno Spann. AGP
Please, everybody, look at me! Five Years Old. Marie Louise Allen. BiCB
Please God, take care of little things. A Prayer for Little Things. Eleanor Farjeon. ThGo
Pleasing Constraint, The. Aristaenetus, tr. fr. Latin by Sheridan and Nathaniel Brassey Halhed. ErPo
Pleasure ("Pleasure could be carried to"). *Unknown, tr. fr. German by* Louis Untermeyer. UnTE
Pleasure It Is. William Cornish. CBEP; MeEL
  (Gratitude.) CTC
Pleasure me not, for love's pleasure drained me. In the Interstices. Ruth Stone. ErPo
Pleasures. Denise Levertov. AP
Pleasures of Imagination, The, sel. Mark Akenside.
  "With what attractive charms this goodly frame," fr. I. EnPE
Pleasures of Merely Circulating, The. Wallace Stevens. LOW
Plodder Seam, The. *Unknown.* ELP
Plot against Proteus, The. A. J. M. Smith. OBCV

Plot against the Giant, The. Wallace Stevens. CaFP
Plot to Assassinate the Chase Manhattan Bank, The. Carl Larsen. PtTo
Ploughing on Sunday. Wallace Stevens. AmLP; GoJo; PoPl
Ploughland has gone to bent, The. Gin the Goodwife Stint. Basil Bunting. CTC
Ploughman, whose gnarly hand yet kindly wheeled. The Waving of the Corn. Sidney Lanier. AP
Plover, The ("Plover, my lover, how lightly you hover"). *Unknown, tr. fr. Swahili by* Alice Werner. SiGo
Plow, they say, to plow the snow, A. Plowmen. Robert Frost. FoBA
Plowman, The. Burns. UnTE
Plowman, The. Raymond Knister. OBCV
Plowman sits in front of his shaded cot, The. Evening Fancy. Friedrich Hölderlin. AGP
Plowmen. Robert Frost. FoBA
Pluck the fruit and taste the pleasure. Song. Thomas Lodge. Fr. Robert, Second Duke of Normany. EnRePo
Plucking the Rushes. *Unknown, tr. fr. Chinese by* Arthur Waley. SiGo
Plum Blossoms. *Unknown, tr. fr. Japanese.* SoPo
Plunging and labouring on in a tide of visions. In Front of the Landscape. Thomas Hardy. OBNC
Plunging limbers over the shattered track, The. Dead Man's Dump. Isaac Rosenberg. CABL; GTBS-P; MMA
Plymouth Rock. Olive Driver. RePo
Poacher, The. *Unknown.* See Lincolnshire Poacher, The.
Pocahontas. Thackeray. OnMSP; SIV; ThLM
Pockets. Rowena Bennett. RePo
Poe and Longfellow. James Russell Lowell. *Fr.* A Fable for Critics. AP
Poem: "And this digester, this digester of food." Conrad Aiken. *Fr.* Time in the Rock. VaPo
Poem: "As the cat/ climbed over." William Carlos Williams. CABA; LOW
Poem, The: "Coming late, as always." W. S. Merwin. PP
Poem: "He lying spilt like water from a bowl." Alison Boodson. ErPo
Poem: "I met a sad girl in our town." Keith Sinclair. ACV
Poem: "If the drink that satisfied." R. A. K. Mason. ACV
Poem: "Like a deaf man meshed in his endless silence." John Wain. PoCh
Poem: "Little brown boy." Helene Johnson. AmNP
Poem: "Maggie and Milly and Molly and May." E. E. Cummings. See Maggie and Milly and Molly and May.
Poem: "Person who can do, The." Alan Dugan. ErPo
Poem: "Rocks dark, green as leaves, The. Moss clings." Robert Sward. *Fr.* Five Poems for J. F. K. OPP
Poem: "We are such stuff as dreams are made of, and these." Hugo von Hofmannsthal, tr. fr. German by Jethro Bithell. SiGo
Poem: "We used to float the paper boats in spring." Donald D. Olsen. PoPl
Poem, A/ is a conversation. On the Make-up of a Poet. H. A. Sieber. PoNC
Poem at Thirty. John Woods. CoPo
Poem Beginning "The." Louis Zukofsky. CoPo
Poem by the Clock Tower, Sumner. James K. Baxter. ACV
Poem for Easter. Laurie Lee. BoC
Poem for Epiphany. Norman Nicholson. PoPl
Poem for Marc Chagall. Leonard Cohen. OBCV
Poem in October. Dylan Thomas. AnMoPo; BoC; CaFP; DaDu; DiPo; PoIE; PoPl; StP; ToPo; WePo
Poem in Prose. Archibald MacLeish. MoLP; PoPl
Poem in the rock and, The. Epitaph. R. S. Thomas. WePo
Poem must not charm us like a play, The. Against the False Magicians. Thomas McGrath. PP
Poem must resist the intelligence, The. Man Carrying Thing. Wallace Stevens. PoIE
Poem of a Glass Blower. *Unknown, tr. fr. French by* Daisy Aldan. AnML
Poem of the mind in the act of finding, The. Of Modern Poetry. Wallace Stevens. PP
Poem of the Son. "Gabriela Mistral," tr. fr. Spanish by Langston Hughes. PoPl
Poem on His Birthday. Dylan Thomas. DiPo
Poem, or Beauty Hurts Mr. Vinal. E. E. Cummings. PoIE
Poem Rocket. Allen Ginsberg. CoPo
Poem should be palpable and mute, A. Ars Poetica. Archibald MacLeish. AP; CaFP; DiPo; PoPl; PoPo; PP; VaPo
Poem to Delight My Friends Who Laugh at Science-Fiction, A. Edwin Rolfe. ThLM
Poem to the Man on My Fire Escape. Diane Wakoski. CoPo
Poem without a Main Verb. John Wain. NePoEA-2
Poems for One Person. Terence Tiller. AnMoPo
Poems from a First Year in Boston. George Starbuck. NePoEA-2
  "Becalmed in old Back Bay's dead water sulk," IV. PoDB
Poems from the Coalfields. Ian Healy. PoAu-2
  Advice from a Nightwatchman.
  Air Shaft.

Poems in Praise of Practically Nothing, *sel.* Samuel Hoffenstein.
"You take a bath, and sit there bathing." EvOK
Poems of Our Climate, The. Wallace Stevens. MP; PP
Poems of the Arabic, *sel. Unknown, tr. fr. Arabic by* Sir Richard Burton. *Fr.* The Thousand and One Nights.
"My soul thy sacrifice! I choose thee out." ErPo
Poet, The. Bryant. AP; PP
Poet, The. W. H. Davies. DTC
Poet, The, *sel.* Emerson.
"Right upward on the road of fame." PP
Poet, A. Thomas Hardy. VP
Poet, The. Keats. *See* Where's the Poet?
Poet, The. James Kirkup. PP
Poet, The. Pope. CBEP
Poet. Karl Shapiro. ToPo
"Poet." William Jay Smith. RePo
Poet, The. Tennyson. PP
Poet, The; a Rhapsody. Mark Akenside. PP
Poet and gangster reach in the dark. The Escapade. David Ignatow. PP
Poet and Goldsmith. Vernon Watkins. PoCh
Poet and His Book, The. Edna St. Vincent Millay. AmLP
Poet and Peasant. R. H. Long. PoAu-1
Poet and Saint! to thee alone are given. On the Death of Mr. Crashaw. Abraham Cowley. SeCP
Poet and the Dun, The. William Shenstone. PP
Poet and War, The. Albert Ehrenstein, *tr. fr. German by* Christopher Middleton. MGP
Poet, gentle creature as he is, The. Wordsworth. *Fr.* The Prelude. PP
Poet in a golden clime was born, The. The Poet. Tennyson. PP
Poet in his lone yet genial hour, The. Apologia pro Vita Sua. Samuel Taylor Coleridge. PP
Poet Loves a Mistress but Not to Marry, The. Robert Herrick. ErPo
Poet of Nature, thou has wept to know. To Wordsworth. Shelley. PoPo
Poet Speaks, The. Georgia Douglas Johnson. AmNP
Poet thought, The. The Patent Leather Shoe. Alfred Lichtenstein. MGP
Poet to His Beloved, A. W. B. Yeats. MoLP
Poet to His Love. Maxwell Bodenheim. BoLP; PoPl
Poetaster, The, *sel.* Ben Jonson.
Hermogenes' Song, *fr.* II, ii. PoIE
Poetical Philander only thought to love. Philander. Donald Hall. ErPo
Poetry. Justinus Kerner, *tr. fr. German by* Martin Zwart. AGP
Poetry. Marianne Moore. AP; CABA; ILP; PoIE; PoPo; PoSa; PP; StP
Poetry Defined. John Holmes. PP
Poetry drives its lines into her forehead. A Young Highland Girl Studying Poetry. Iain Crichton Smith. NePoEA-2; PP
Poetry for Supper. R. S. Thomas. ToPo
Poetry is deepest aching. Poetry. Justinus Kerner. AGP
Poetry is the supreme fiction, madame. A High-toned Old Christian Woman. Wallace Stevens. AP
Poetry of Departures. Philip Larkin. MP; ToPo
Poetry of Earth, The. Keats. *See* On the Grasshopper and Cricket.
Poetry of tragedy is never dead, The. Am I My Neighbor's Keeper? Richard Eberhart. ToPo
Poetry Revival. Frank Borden Hanes. PoNC
Poets. David Wevill. PP
Poets and Their Bibliographies. Tennyson. PP
Poets at Tea, The. Barry Pain. Par
Poet's daily chore, The. Lens. Anne Wilkinson. OBCV
Poet's Dream, The. Shelley. *See* On a Poet's Lips I Slept.
Poets light but lamps, The. Emily Dickinson. PP
Poet's faults, A: some are his own. The Motives of Rhythm. Robert Conquest. PP
Poets in Africa. Roy Campbell. ACV
Poets, like disputants, when reasons fail. Epilogue. Dryden. *Fr.* All for Love. DiPo
Poets Lose Half the Praise. Edmund Waller. PP
Poets Love Nature. John Clare. CBEP
Poets make pets of pretty, docile words. Pretty Words. Elinor Wylie. RePo
Poets may boast, as safely vain. Of English Verse. Edmund Waller. PP; SeCP
Poets' Paradise, The. Michael Drayton. *Fr.* The Muses' Elysium. WiR
Poet's Progress, A. Michael Hamburger. PP
Poet's Simple Faith, The. Victor Hugo, *tr. fr. French.* TRV
Poet's Song, The. Tennyson. ELP
Poet's thoughts are of the skies, The. Poet and Peasant. R. H. Long. PoAu-1
Poets to Come. Walt Whitman. PoPo
Poet's Welcome to His Illegitimate Child, The. Burns. BoC
Poet's Work, The. Philippe Jaccottet, *tr. fr. French by* Richard G. Stern. CoFP

Poietes Apoietes. Hartley Coleridge. OBNC
Point of No Return. Mari Evans. NNP
Pointed Boots. Christopher Middleton. *Fr.* Herman Moon's Hourbook. NePoEA-2
Pointless Pride of Man, The. *Unknown.* MeEL
Points of View. Amy Lowell. LOW
Poised between going on and back, pulled. The Base Stealer. Robert Francis. GoJo; SD
Poised for the leap, clear in the morning light. The Diver. Theobald Purcell-Buret. HaSV
Poised, relaxed, as a cat that waits. Boxer. Joseph P. Clancy. SD
Poison Tree, A. Blake. *Fr.* Songs of Experience. CABA; CaFP; CBEP; DiPo; FoBA; VaPo
Poisoned, by our own lips! That exchange of eloquences. The Technique of Power. Jascha Kessler. AmPC
Poisoned Man, The. James Dickey. ToPo
Poker Jim, *with music. Unknown.* SGR
Pole Star. Archibald MacLeish. AP
Pole Vault. Shiro Murano, *tr. fr. Japanese by* Satoru Sato *and* Constance Urdang. SD
Poles are flying where the two eyes set, The. Discoveries. Vernon Watkins. PoIE
Poles rode out from Warsaw against the German, The. The Abnormal Is Not Courage. Jack Gilbert. PtTo
Polish Reaper, The. Peter Huchel, *tr. fr. German by* Christopher Middleton. MGP
Polish Rider, The. Derek Walcott. ToPo
Politeness. A. A. Milne. PoPl
Political Doctrine. Schiller, *tr. fr. German by* Walter Kaufmann. TwGP
Political Meeting. A. M. Klein. OBCV
Politics. W. B. Yeats. FoBA; PoPo; StP
Politics of Rich Painters, The. LeRoi Jones. CoPo
Polly Band. *Unknown.* BSO
Polly, Dolly, Kate and Molly. *Unknown.* BBGG
Polly, from me, though now a love-sick youth. To a Young Lady. Richard Savage. CBEP
Polly Oliver. *Unknown.* BSNS
Polly Peachum. Henry Carey. WaPE
Polly Perkins. *Unknown.* BoLP; DTC; ELP
Polly Picklenose ("Polly, Polly, goodness gracious"). Leroy F. Jackson. BBGG
Polo Grounds. Rolfe Humphries. SD
Polonius' Advice to Laertes. Shakespeare. *Fr.* Hamlet, I, iii. PoPl
("This above all: to thine own self be true.") TRV
Polyphemus' Love Song. Luis de Góngora, *tr. fr. Spanish by* Frances Fletcher. *Fr.* Fable of Polyphemus and Galatea. AnSP
Polyhymnia, *sel.* George Peele.
His Golden Locks [Time Hath to Silver Turned]. EnRePo; PoIE; PoSa
(Farewell to Arms, A.) BoC
(Old Knight, The.) CBEP
(Sonnet, A: "His golden locks time hath to silver turn'd.") ELP
Polyolbion, *sels.* Michael Drayton. SD
Hawking.
Wrestlers.
Pomegranate, The. Louis Dudek. OBCV
Pomona. William Morris. WiR
Pond, The. Annette von Droste-Hülshoff, *tr. fr. German by* Herman Salinger. SiGo
Pool, The. Leah Bodine Drake. FiSC
Pool. Carl Sandburg. AP
Poor Can Feed the Birds, The. John Shaw Neilson. PoAu-1
Poor Diggings. Mart Taylor. SGR
Poor flea! then thou didst die. Of That Same. Tasso. RBL
Poor Hard-working Man, The. *Unknown.* BSNS
Poor have little, The. Enough Not One. Benjamin Franklin. TRV
Poor Is the Life That Misses. *Unknown.* UnTE
Poor Jack. Charles Dibdin. HaSV
Poor Jane Higgins. A Pig Tale. James Reeves. SoPo
Poor Kit hath lost her key. Kit Hath Lost Her Key. *Unknown.* UnTE
Poor Me. *Unknown, tr. fr. French by* Richard Beaumont. ErPo
Poor Mortals. Sir Robert Howard *and* John Dryden. *Fr.* The Indian Queen. PoIE
Poor Old Horse. David Holbrook. NePoEA-2
Poor old Jonathan Bing. Jonathan Bing. Beatrice Curtis Brown. OnMSP; SoPo
Poor Old Lady. *Unknown.* SoPo
Poor old Widow in her weeds, A. A Widow's Weeds. Walter de la Mare. FaBV
Poor Relation, The. E. A. Robinson. PoIE
Poor Robin. Mother Goose. SoPo
Poor soul, the centre [or center] of my sinful earth. Sonnets, CXLVI [or Soul and Body]. Shakespeare. CABA; CaFP; CBEP; DiPo; EaLo; EnRePo; FoBA; GTBS-P; OnP; PoIE; StP
Poor tired Tim! It's sad for him. Tired Tim. Walter de la Mare. SoPo

Poor Wayfaring Stranger, *with music. Unknown.* BFSS
Poore wench was sighing, and weeping amaine, A. The Bard. James Shirley. ErPo
Poorest women of Berlin, The. Labor Room. Gottfried Benn. TwGP
Pop Goes the Weasel. *Unknown.* SoPo
Popcorn peanuts clams and gum. Bar-Room Matins. Louis MacNeice. EaLo
Pope. Manuel González Prada, *tr. fr. Spanish by* William M. Davis. AnSP
Pope Clement's Illness. Francesco Berni, *tr. fr. Italian by* Harold M. Priest. RBL
Poplar. Gottfried Benn, *tr. fr. German by* Christopher Middleton. PoPl
Poplar Field, The ("The poplars are felled, farewell to the shade"). William Cowper. CBEP; ELP; GTBS-P; ILP; PoSa; RoGo; WiR
Poplars are standing there still as death. Southern Mansion. Arna Bontemps. AmNP
Popular Rhymes. Blake. ThGo
Popularity. Robert Browning. PP
Porphyria's Lover. Robert Browning. CABA; ILP; VP
Porpoise, The. Ogden Nash. RePo
Port Admiral. Frederick Marryat. HaSV
Port after Stormy Seas. Spenser. *Fr.* The Faerie Queene, I, 9. HaSV
Port of Many Ships. John Masefield. HaSV
Portent, The. Herman Melville. AP; CaFP; CBEP; WiR
Portion, The. Jacques Dupin, *tr. fr. French by* Vincent Stewart. CoFP
Portion of this yew. Transformations. Thomas Hardy. AnMoPo; PoIE
Portrait. Francesco Berni, *tr. fr. Italian by* Harold M. Priest. RBL
Portrait, The. Robert Graves. CABA
Portrait. Antonio Machado, *tr. fr. Spanish by* Doreen Bell. AnSP
Portrait. Sam Ragan. PoNC
Portrait, The ("O Lord of all compassionate control"). Dante Gabriel Rossetti. The House of Life, X. VP
Portrait, The ("This is her picture as she was"). Dante Gabriel Rossetti. VP
Portrait by a Neighbor. Edna St. Vincent Millay. LOW
Portrait d'une Femme. Ezra Pound. AP; CABA; MP
Portrait in the Guards, A. Laurence Whistler. GTBS-P
Portrait of a Girl. Conrad Aiken. *Fr.* Priapus and the Pool. GoJo
Portrait of a Lady. T. S. Eliot. MP
Portrait of a Lady. William Carlos Williams. PoIE
Portrait of Silverio Franconetti. Federico García Lorca, *tr. fr. Spanish by* Rachel Benson *and* Robert O'Brien. AnSP
Possession. Lynne Lawner. ErPo
Possession. *Unknown.* TRV
Possessive Lover, The. Ovid, *tr. fr. Latin by* Christopher Marlowe. *Fr.* Amores. UnTE
Possum lies curled, The. Daydreamers. Norma L. Davis. PoAu-2
Post Card. Thad Stem, Jr. PoNC
Postcard from the Volcano, A. Wallace Stevens. AP
Post Mortem. Shakespeare. *See* Sonnets, XXXII.
Post-Roads. Kenneth Slessor. *Fr.* The Atlas. PoAu-2
Post That Fitted, The. Kipling. OnMSP
Postage Stamp Lesson, The. *Unknown.* StF
Poster with my picture on it, The. Unwanted. Edward Field. CoPo
Postern Gate, The, *sel.* Walter Rauschenbusch. "In the castle of my soul." TRV
Postman, The. Laura E. Richards. SoPo
Postman comes when I am still in bed, The. A Sick Child. Randall Jarrell. PoNC
Postscript. Vernon Watkins. OPP
Postscript for Gweno. Alun Lewis. GTBS-P; WePo
Postship. Christoph Meckel, *tr. fr. German by* Christopher Middleton. MGP
Posture for Next Year, A. H. A. Sieber. PoNC
Pot Pourri from a Surrey Garden. John Betjeman. DTC; PoCh
Potomac, The. Karl Shapiro. AP; ToPo
Potomac Town in February. Carl Sandburg. EvOK
Pour O pour that parting soul in song. Song of the Son. Jean Toomer. AmNP
Pour, varlet, pour the water. The Poets at Tea, 1. Barry Pain. Par
Poure widwe, somdel stape in age, A. *See* Povre wydwe, somdeel stape in age, A.
Poverty. *Unknown, tr. fr. Sanskrit by* Arthur W. Ryder. *Fr.* The Panchatantra. SIV
Poverty and Poetry. Thomas Tickell. WaPE
Povre wydwe, somdeel [*or* Poure widwe, somdel] stape in age, A. The Nun's Priest's Tale. Chaucer. *Fr.* The Canterbury Tales. CABL; StP
Power of Fancy, The. Philip Freneau. AP
Power of Love, The. John Fletcher. *See* Hear, Ye Ladies.

Power of Love, The. *Unknown, tr. fr. Arabic by* E. Powys Mathers. *Fr.* The Thousand and One Nights. SiGo
Power of Time, The. Swift. CBEP
Powers and Times Are Not Gods. W. H. Auden. *Fr.* For the Time Being; a Christmas Oratorio. MoRP
Practical hand at catching fish is necessitous, A. Sea Scape with Parable. Richard Eberhart. PoDB
Practical Program for Monks, A. Thomas Merton. CoPo
Practices silence, the way of wind. As a Possible Lover. LeRoi Jones. AmNP
Prairie child. Nancy Hanks. Harriet Monroe. LiPo
Prairie Graveyard. Anne Marriott. OBCV
Prairie Water Colour, A. Duncan Campbell Scott. OBCV
Prairie Wind. Duncan Campbell Scott. ACV
Prairies, The. Bryant. AP
Praise. Edith Daley. TRV
Praise. George Herbert. MeP
Praise. Henry Vaughan. MeP
Praise Doubt. Mark Van Doren. EaLo; MoRP
Praise for an Urn. Hart Crane. AP
Praise God, who wrought for you and me. Magnificat. Arthur Symons. UnTE
Praise Him who makes us happy. Never Another. Mark Van Doren. MoRP
Praise in Summer. Richard Wilbur. PP
Praise the good angel doubt. Praise Doubt. Mark Van Doren. EaLo; MoRP
Praise the Lord, O My Soul! Psalms, CIV, Bible, *O.T.* ThGo
Praise to the End! Theodore Roethke. ToPo
Praise ye the Lord. Psalm CL, Bible, *O.T.* SiGo; TRV
Praised be Diana's fair and harmless light. Homage to Diana. Sir Walter Ralegh. WiR
Praisers of women in their proud and beautiful poems, The. "Not Marble nor the Gilded Monuments." Archibald MacLeish. AP; ILP; MP
Praises of a Countrie Life, The. Ben Jonson. SeCP
Praising the Poets of That Country. Howard Nemerov. PP
Prattle. John Ciardi. BiCB
Pray! Irene Arnold. STF
Pray! Amos R. Wells. STF
Pray but one prayer for me 'twixt thy closed lips. Summer Dawn. William Morris. CBEP; OBNC
Pray, Christian, Pray! *Unknown.* STF
Pray! for earth has many a need. Pray! Amos R. Wells. STF
Pray for Peace, Oh Gentle Virgin Mary. Charles d'Orléans, *tr. fr. French by* Muriel Kittel. AnML
Pray—Give—Go. Annie Johnson Flint. STF
Pray in the early morning. Pray! Irene Arnold. STF
Pray On! *Unknown.* STF
Pray steal me not, I'm Mrs. Dingley's. On the Collar of a Dog. Swift. StP
Pray where would lamb and lion be. Nature Be Damned. Anne Wilkinson. OBCV
Prayer, A: "Angels, where you soar." Alfred Noyes. PoPl
Prayer, A: "Father, we thank Thee for the night." *Unknown.* SoPo
Prayer, A: "Give us a good Digestion, Lord." *Unknown.* STF
Prayer, A: "God, give me sympathy and sense." Margaret Bailey. TRV
Prayer: "God, though this life is but a wraith." Louis Untermeyer. LV
Prayer: "God who created me." Henry Charles Beeching. SD
Prayer: "Have pity on us, Power just and severe." John Hall Wheelock, *after* St. Theresa of Avila. EaLo
Prayer: "I ask you this." Langston Hughes. EaLo
Prayer: "I had thought of putting an/ altar." Isabella M. Brown. NNP
Prayer: "I know not by what methods rare." *Unknown.* STF
Prayer, A: "If I dare pray for one." Vernon Watkins. MoRP; PoPl
Prayer: "If I must of my senses lose." Theodore Roethke. MP
Prayer, A: "Jesus, Thy life is mine!" *Unknown.* STF
Prayer: "Let us not look upon." Witter Bynner. EaLo
Prayer: "Lord, the newness of this day." Henry van Dyke. TRV
Prayer: "Lord, what a change within us one short hour." Richard Chenevix Trench. TRV
Prayer: "Merciful God, who readst my inmost mind." Wilem Bilderdijk, *tr. fr. Dutch by* A. J. Barnouw. SiGo
Prayer: "Prayer must be grounded on the Word." *Unknown.* STF
Prayer: "Prayer, the church's banquet, angels' age." George Herbert. BoC; CABA; DTC; ELP; MeP; TRV
Prayer, A: "Teach me, Father, how to go." Edwin Markham. TRV
Prayer, A: "Through every minute of this day." John Oxenham. TRV
Prayer—Answer. Ednah D. Cheney. STF
Prayer Answered. *Unknown.* STF

Prayer before Birth. Louis MacNeice. AnMoPo; GTBS-P; MP
Prayer before Her Execution. Mary Queen of Scots. TRV
Prayer for Little Things, A. Eleanor Farjeon. ThGo
Prayer for Messiah. Leonard Cohen. OBCV
Prayer for My Daughter, A. W. B. Yeats. AnMoPo; CABA; PoLF; PoPo; VaPo
  For My Daughter, sel. MoRP
Prayer for Neighborhood Evangelism. Annette Jansen. STF
Prayer for Old Age, A. W. B. Yeats. AnMoPo
Prayer for Purification, A. Michelangelo, tr. fr. Italian by John Addington Symonds. RBL
Prayer for Rain. Herbert Palmer. WePo
Prayer for Rich and Poor. William Langland, mod. by Nevill Coghill. Fr. The Vision of Piers Plowman. BoC
Prayer for Strength. Samuel Johnson. TRV
Prayer for the Home, sel. Edgar A. Guest.
  "Lord, this humble house we'd keep." TRV
Prayer for the Household, A. Robert Louis Stevenson. TRV
Prayer for the Speedy End of Three Great Misfortunes. Tr. fr. Irish by Frank O'Connor. DTC
Prayer for This House. Louis Untermeyer. PoLF
Prayer in Darkness, A. G. K. Chesterton. BoC; PoLF
Prayer in Mid-Passage. Louis MacNeice. EaLo
Prayer in Spring, A. Robert Frost. MoRP; WePo
Prayer is the soul's sincere desire. What Is Prayer? James Montgomery. STF; TRV
Prayer Moves the Hand That Moves the World. John A. Wallace. STF
Prayer must be grounded on the Word. Prayer. Unknown. STF
Prayer of Columbus. Walt Whitman. LV
  "All my emprises have been fill'd with Thee," sel. TRV
Prayer of St. Francis of Assisi [for Peace]. St. Francis of Assisi, tr. fr. Italian. PoLF; PoPl
  (St. Francis' Prayer.) TRV
Prayer of the Little Ducks Who Went into the Ark, The. Carmen Bernos de Gasztold, tr. fr. French by Rumer Godden. ThGo
Prayer on the Night before Easter. John Holmes. MoRP
Prayer, the church's banquet, angels' age. Prayer. George Herbert. BoC; CABA; DTC; ELP; MeP; TRV
Prayer to Go to Paradise with the Donkeys, A. Francis Jammes, tr. fr. French by Richard Wilbur. EaLo; MoRP
Prayer to Peace. Euripides, tr. fr. Greek by Moses Hadas. Fr. Cresophontes. PoPI
Prayer to the Father of Heaven, A. John Skelton. PoIE
Prayer to the Sacrament of the Altar, A. Unknown. MeEL
Prayer to the Trinity, A. Unknown. MeEL
Prayer unsaid and mass unsung. The Sea-Ritual. George Darley. Fr. Syren Songs. OBNC; WiR
Prayers I make will then be sweet indeed, The. To the Supreme Being. Michelangelo. SiGo; TRV
Prayers of Steel. Carl Sandburg. AP
Praying Mantis. Felix Stefanile. FiSC
Preacher does better, The. Stand By. Unknown. STF
Preacher was a strange and lonely man, The. Legend of the Hills. Lilith Lorraine. FiSC
Preacher works from morn till night, The. Soft Job. William C. Summers. STF
Preacher's Prayer, The. George Macdonald. TRV
Preacher's Prayer, A. Unknown. STF
Preacher's Wife, The. Unknown. STF
Precambrain Shield, The. E. J. Pratt. Fr. Towards the Last Spike. OBCV
Precaution. Heine, tr. fr. German by Louis Untermeyer. UnTE
Precious Blood, The. Unknown. STF
Precious—mouldering pleasure—'tis, A. Emily Dickinson. DiPo
Preface: "And did those feet in ancient time." Blake. See And Did Those Feet in Ancient Time.
Preface, The: "Infinity, when all things it beheld." Edward Taylor. Fr. Gods Determinations. AmLP; AP; ILP
Preface: "To make a start." William Carlos Williams. Fr. Paterson, I. AP
Preface to a Twenty Volume Suicide Note. LeRoi Jones. AmNP; NNP
Prehistoric Camp, A. Andrew Young. CBEP
Prehistoric Huntsman, The. Donald Wandrei. FiSC
Prejudice. Georgia Douglas Johnson. AmNP
Preliminary Poem for a Modern City. Harry Kemp. LV
Prelude, The, sels. Wordsworth.
  Conclusion: "It was a Summer's night, a close warm night," fr. XIV. OBNC
  Consummate Happiness, fr. IV. OBNC
  "Fair seed-time had my soul, and I grew up," fr. I. OnP
  (Childhood and School-Time.) OBNC
  Fishing, fr. I. SD
  Imagination, How Impaired and Restored, fr. XII. OBNC
  Intimations of Sublimity, fr. II. OBNC
  "Poet, gentle creature as he is, The," fr. I. PP
  Shepherd, The, fr. VIII. OBNC
  Skating, fr. I. SD
  There Was a Boy, fr. V. FoBA; OBNC

  To Coleridge in Sicily, fr. XI. OBNC
Prelude: "Along the roadside, like the flowers of gold." Whittier. Fr. Among the Hills. AP
Prelude: "And did those feet in ancient time." Blake. See And Did Those Feet in Ancient Time.
Prelude: "England! awake! awake! awake!" Blake. Fr. Jerusalem, IV. OBNC
Prelude: "Fields from Islington to Marybone, The." Blake. Fr. Jerusalem, II. OBNC
Prelude: "Night was dark, though sometimes a faint star, The." Richard Watson Gilder. Fr. The New Day. PoLF
Prelude: "Winter evening settles down, The." T. S. Eliot. Preludes, I. DaDu
  (Preludes.) DiPo; MP; PoPl; PoPo; WePo
Prelude to an Evening. John Crowe Ransom. AP; ILP; PoCh
Preludes (I-IV). T. S. Eliot. DiPo; MP; PoPl; WePo Sels.
  "Morning comes to consciousness, The," II. PoPo
  "Winter evening settles down, The," I. PoPo
  (Prelude.) DaDu
Preludes for Memnon, sels. Conrad Aiken.
  "Despair, that seeking for the Ding-an-sich," V. PoDB
  "One star fell and another as we walked," LVII. BoLP; PoPo
  "Sleep: and between the closed eyelids of sleep," III. Also in Preludes to Attitude. PoDB
  Winter for a Moment Takes the Mind; the Snow, I. Also in Preludes to Attitude, IV. StP
Premonition. Edith Ogutsch. FiSC
Prenatal Fantasy. Walter H. Kerr. FiSC
Prentice Boy, The. Unknown. BNS
Preparations. Unknown. See Guest, The.
Preparative, The. Thomas Traherne. MeP
Preparatory Meditations, First Series, sels. Edward Taylor.
  Meditation. Cant. 2.1. The Lilly of the Vallies. MeP
  Meditation Eight ("I kenning through astronomy divine"). AP; StP
  Meditation. 1 Cor. 3.21.22. All Things Are Yours. MeP
  Meditation. 1 Cor. 3.22. Death Is Yours. MeP
  Meditation. 1 Cor. 3.22. Life Is Youres. MeP
  Meditation. 1 Cor. 3.22. Whether Paul or Apollos, or Cephas. MeP
  Meditation. 1 Cor. 3.23. You Are Christ's. MeP
  Meditation Forty ("Still I complain; I am complaining still"). AP
  (Meditation. 1 Joh. 2.2. He Is a Propitiation for Our Sin.) MeP
  Meditation. from 1 Joh. 2.1. If Any Man Sin, We Have an Advocate. MeP
  Meditation on Can. 1.3. Thy Name Is an Ointment Poured Out. MeP
  Meditation One ("What love is this of thine, that cannot bee"). AP; MeP
  Meditation Seven ("Thy humane frame, my glorious Lord, I spy"). VaPo
  Meditation Six ("Am I thy gold? Or purse, Lord, for thy wealth"). AmLP; AP
  (Another Meditation at the Same Time.) MeP
  Meditation Thirty-eight ("Oh! What a thing is man? Lord, who am I?"). AP
  Meditation Twenty ("View, all ye eyes above, this sight which flings"). AP
  Meditation Twenty-nine ("My shattred phancy stole away from mee"). AP
  Reflexion, The. AP
Preparatory Meditations, Second Series, sels. Edward Taylor. MeP
  Meditation. Can. 1.2. Thy Love Is Better than Wine.
  Meditation. Cant. 5.1. Eate Oh Friendes and Drink Yea Drink Abundantly Oh Beloved.
  Meditation. Can. 6.11. To See the Fruits of the Vally.
  Meditation. Col. 1.18. He Is the Head of the Body.
  Meditation. Joh. 15.13. Greater Love Hath No Man than This That a Man Lay Down His Life for His Friends.
  Meditation. Rev. 1.8. The Almighty.
  Meditation Sixty-eight A ("Methinks I spy Almighty holding in"). AP
Presbyterian Wedding, The. Unknown. ErPo
Presence, The. William Everson. ErPo
Presence, The. Denise Levertov. NePoEA-2
Presence. John Moffit. MoRP
Presence, The. Jones Very. PoIE
Present. Miriam Clark Potter. BiCB
Present Crisis, The, sels. James Russell Lowell.
  "Careless seems the great Avenger; history's pages but record." TRV
  "Once to every man and nation comes the moment to decide." TRV
Present in Absence. Unknown. GTBS-P
Present to a Lady, A. Unknown. ErPo
Presentation, The. Robert Southwell. MeP
Presentiment—is that long shadow—on the lawn. Emily Dickinson. AP; CABA
  (Presentiment.) CBEP

Presently at our touch the teacup stirred. Voices from the Other World. James Merrill. MP
Presents. Marchette Chute. EvOK
Presents of money, furs and pearls. The Right Time. *Unknown.* UnTE
Press-Gang, The. *Unknown.* HaSV
Press me not to take more pleasure. The Rose. George Herbert. PoIE
Press of the Spoon River *Clarion* was wrecked, The. Carl Hamblin. Edgar Lee Masters. *Fr.* Spoon River Anthology. ILP
Pretending. Myra Cohn Livingston. BiCB
Pretty Fair Maid, A, *with music. Unknown.* BSO
Pretty Little Girl, The. *Unknown.* BSO
Pretty Mary, *with music. Unknown.* BFSS
Pretty Molly ("Jump up behind me and away we will ride"), *with music. Unknown.* BFSS
Pretty Molly ("Oh Molly, pretty Molly, come go with me"), *with music. Unknown.* BFSS
Pretty Polly. Byron Herbert Reece. BoLP
Pretty Polly ("Get up, get up, pretty Polly, he says"). *Unknown.* UnTE
Pretty Polly ("Good morning, Pretty Polly, we have met in good time"). *Unknown.* BSO
Pretty Polly ("He followed her up, he followed her down"). *Unknown. See* Lady Isabel and the Elf-Knight.
Pretty Polly ("Pretty Polly lay rolling one night on her bed"), *with music. Unknown.* BFSS
Pretty Polly and Sweet William ("Pretty Polly was standing in her bowery door"). *Unknown.* BSO
"Pretty Polly goes dressed in red." Pretty Polly. Byron Herbert Reece. BoLP
Pretty Thing, A. *Unknown.* UnTE
Pretty Words. Elinor Wylie. RePo
Pretzel Man, The. Rachel Field. SoPo
Prevention of Cruelty to Animals. Günter Grass, *tr. fr. German by* Michael Hamburger. MGP
Prey for us the Prince of Pees. A Song to John, Christ's Friend. *Unknown.* MeEL
Priapus and the Pool, *sels.* Conrad Aiken.
  "Fade, then,—die, depart, and come no more," XVII. AmLP
  Portrait of a Girl, IV. GoJo
  "When trout swim down Great Ormond Street," III. AmLP; CaFP
Pride and Hesitation. Cerise Farallon. UnTE
Pride Is Out. *Unknown.* CBEP
Pride of Glencoe, The. *Unknown.* BSNS
Pride of the Fourth and Liquid Element. Luis de Góngora. *See* Clear Honor of the Liquid Element.
Pride of the height, the clear firmament, the beauty of heaven, The. Sun, Moon and Stars. Ecclesiasticus, Bible, Apocrypha. BoC
Pride of Youth. Dante Gabriel Rossetti. The House of Life, XXIV. OBNC; VP
Pride of Youth, The. Sir Walter Scott. *See* Proud Maisie.
Priest and the Mulberry-Tree, The. Thomas Love Peacock. *Fr.* Crotchet Castle. OnMSP
Priest of Christ, The. Thomas Ken. TRV
Priesthood, The. George Herbert. MeP
Priests Disguise as Shepherds. Peire Cardenal, *tr. fr. Provençal by* William M. Davis. AnML
Primaleon of Greece, *sel.* Anthony Munday.
  Beauty Sat Bathing. CBEP; UnTE
  (Colin.) GTBS-P
Prime. W. H. Auden. *Fr.* Horae Canonicae. PoDB
Primer Lesson. Carl Sandburg. PoPl; RePo
Primeval Words: Orphic. Goethe, *tr. fr. German by* Walter Kaufmann. TwGP
Primitivism. O. B. Hardison, Jr. PoNC
Primrose, The. John Donne. MeP
Prince Absalom and Sir Rotherham Redde. Evening. Edith Sitwell. MoBS
Prince of misconstructions, train my love. The Serpent. René Char. *Fr.* Four Fascinators. CoFP
Princess, The, *sels.* Tennyson.
  As thro' the Land at Eve We Went, *fr.* Pt. I. FoBA
  "Ask me no more: the moon may draw the sea," *fr.* Pt. VI. OBNC
  (Ask Me No More.) FoBA; UnTE
  Come Down, O Maid [from Yonder Mountain Height], *fr.* Pt. VII. CABA; CaFP; CBEP; DiPo; FoBA; GTBS-P; OBNC
  Home They Brought Her Warrior Dead, *fr.* Pt. V. FoBA
  Now Sleeps the Crimson Petal [Now the White], *fr.* Pt. VII. CABA; CaFP; CBEP; DiPo; ELP; GTBS-P; ILP; OBNC; PoIE; StP; UnTE
  (Summer Night.) WePo
  Splendor [*or* Splendour] Falls [on Castle Walls], The, *fr.* Pt. III. CBEP; ELP; FaBV; FoBA; GoJo; GTBS-P; ILP; OBNC; PoIE; RoGo; VP
  (Blow, Bugle, Blow.) WePo; WiR
  (Song: "Splendor falls on castle walls, The.") PoPl
  Sweet and Low, *fr.* Pt. II. FoBA; ILP; LV; PoPl
  (Lullaby: "Sweet and low, sweet and low.") PoLF
  Tears, Idle Tears [I Know Not What They Mean], *fr.* Pt.
  IV. CABA; CaFP; DiPo; FoBA; GTBS-P; OBNC; PoIE; PoPo; WePo
  (Song: "Tears, idle tears, I know not what they mean.") PoPl
Princess is sad, and in anguish reposes, The. Sonatina. Rubén Darío. AnSP
Prisoner, The, *sels.* Emily Brontë.
  "He comes with western winds, with evening's wandering airs." BoC; ELP
  "Still, let my tyrants know, I am not doomed to wear." OBNC
Prisoner, The. Rainer Maria Rilke, *tr. fr. German by* Walter Kaufmann. TwGP
Prisoner, The. *Unknown, tr. fr. Spanish by* Kate Flores. AnML
Prisoner for Life, A, *with music. Unknown.* BFSS
Prisoner of Chillon, The. Byron. CABL; PoLF
  Sonnet on Chillon, *sel.* ILP, PoPo
  ("Eternal Spirit of the Chainless Mind!") PoPl
  (On the Castle of Chillon.) GTBS-P
Prisoners. F. W. Harvey. MMA
Prisoner's Song, The, *with music. Unknown.* BSNS
Prithee, say aye or no. The Resolute Courtier. Thomas Shipman. ErPo
Prithee tell me what a beau is. The Beau. *Unknown.* WaPE
Private. A. Edward Thomas. GTBS-P; MMA
Private Dining Room, The. Ogden Nash. CaFP; PoCh; VaPo
Private Letter to Brazil, A. G. C. Oden. AmNP; NNP
Prizegiving. Gwen Harwood. PoAu-2
Pro Patria Mori. Thomas Moore. GTBS-P
Probes, The. Michael Goldman. OPP
Problem, The. Emerson. AP
Problem, A, hypothetical, in the form of a piercing dilemma. P.S. Jascha Kessler. AmPC
Problem in Morals, A. Howard Moss. ErPo
Problem of the night remains total, The. After the Accident. Henri Michaux. CoFP
Problems of a Writing Teacher, The. David Ray. NePoEA-2
Process, The. Robert Kelly. CoPo
Proclaimed Queene and mother of a God. The Visitation. Robert Southwell. MeP
Proclamation, The. Whittier. ThLM
Prodigal, The. Elizabeth Bishop. MP
Prodigal of loves and barbecues. To the (Supposed) Patron. Geoffrey Hill. NePoEA-2
Prodigy, The. A. P. Herbert. EvOK
Proem: "I love the old melodious lays." Whittier. AP
Proem, The: To Love. Giambattista Marino, *tr. fr. Italian by* Philip Ayres. *Fr.* L'Adone. RBL
Proem, A: "When in my walks I meet some ruddy lad." Samuel Ward. AmLP
Professor Eisenbart, asked to attend. Prizegiving. Gwen Harwood. PoAu-2
Professor Eisenbart, with grim distaste. Panther and Peacock. Gwen Harwood. PoAu-2
Professor Nocturnal. Raymond Roseliep. FiSC
Professor Palamedes darts down Westow Street. News from Norwood. Christopher Middleton. NePoEA-2
Proffered Love Rejected. Sir John Suckling. ErPo
  (Rejected Offer, The.) UnTE
Profound the radiance issuing. Eve. David Gascoyne. GTBS-P
Progress. Samuel Hoffenstein. ThLM
Progress. *Unknown.* STF
Progress of Beauty, The. Swift. CABA
Progress of Evening. Walter Savage Landor. OBNC
Progress of Faust, The. Karl Shapiro. DiPo; MP
Progress of Marriage, The. Swift. EiCP
Progress of Poesy, The. Matthew Arnold. PP
Progress of Poesy, The. Thomas Gray. CBEP; EiCP; EnPE; PP
  (Progress of Poesie, The.) GTBS-P
Progress of Poetry, The. Swift. CABA; CBEP; EiCP
Prohibition. Don Marquis. PoPl
Prohibition agents came, The. Mrs. Swartz. Don Marquis. ThLM
Prohibition makes you. Prohibition. Don Marquis. PoPl
Prologue: "All the animals in my poems go into the ark." Jon Silkin. PoDB
Prologue: "Lord, can a crumb of earth [*or* dust] the earth outweigh." Edward Taylor. AmLP; AP; MeP
Prologue: "Lose this day loitering, 'twill be the same story." Goethe. *See* Lose This Day Loitering.
Prologue: "Our author, by experience, finds it true." Dryden. *See* Prologue to "Aureng-Zebe."
Prologue, The: "To sing of wars, of captains, and of kings." Anne Bradstreet. AP
Prologue: "We who with songs beguile your pilgrimage." James Elroy Flecker. *Fr.* The Golden Journey to Samarkand. GoJo
Prologue: "Whan that Aprille [*or* Aprill] with his shoures soote." Chaucer. *See* Canterbury Tales, The.
Prologue: "What flocks of critics hover here to-day." Dryden. *Fr.* All for Love. DiPo
Prologue: "When learning's triumph o'er her barb'rous foes." Samuel Johnson. EiCP

Prologue for a Bestiary. Ronald Perry. NePoEA-2
Prologue to "Aureng-Zebe." Dryden. PP
 (Prologue: "Our author, by experience, finds it true.")
 CBEP
Prologue to Sir Thopas. Chaucer. *Fr.* The Canterbury Tales.
 Par
Prologue to the Canterbury Tales. Chaucer. *See* Canterbury
 Tales, The.
Prologue to the University of Oxford. Dryden. PP
Prologues are over, The. It is a question now. Asides on the
 Oboe. Wallace Stevens. AP
Prometheus. Byron. VaPo
Prometheus. Goethe, *tr. fr. German by* Walter Kaufmann.
 TwGP
Prometheus Unbound, *sel.* Shelley.
 "This is the day, which down the void abysm." PoIE
Promiscuous lovers/ Pine to have. A Problem in Morals.
 Howard Moss. ErPo
Promise. "Æ." BoC
Promise, The. Mary B. Fowler. STF
Promise in Disturbance, The. George Meredith. *Fr.* Modern
 Love. VP
Promise Me a Rose. Bob Merrill. BoLP
Promise of Peace. Robinson Jeffers. AP
Promised Land, The, *sel.* Giuseppe Ungaretti, *tr. fr. Italian by*
 Lowry Nelson, Jr.
 Choruses Descriptive of Dido's States of Mind. CoIP
Promises of heaven Thou givest me, The. To Christ Crucified.
 Miguel de Guevara. RBL
Promissory Note, The. Bayard Taylor. Par
Proof. Ethel Romig Fuller. STF
Proof, The. Richard Wilbur. EaLo
Proof Positive. Deems Taylor, *tr. fr. French.* UnTE
Proper New Ballad, A, Intituled the Faeryes Farewell; or,
 God-a-Mercy Will. Richard Corbett. *See* Fairies' Fare-
 well, The.
Prophecy, A. Christopher Levenson. ErPo
Prophecy. Alfred Lichtenstein, *tr. fr. German by* Christopher
 Middleton. MGP
Prophecy. Walter Shedlofsky. FiSC
Prophet, The, *sels.* Kahlil Gibran.
 Of Love. PoLF
 On Children. PoPl
 On Giving. PoPl
Prophet, The. Pushkin, *tr. fr. Russian by* Babette Deutsch.
 EaLo
"Prophet, The." Sam Ragan. PoNC
Prophet of dead words defeats himself, The. E. A. Robinson.
 Octaves, XX. ILP
Proposition, The. Paul Blackburn. ErPo
Props. John Oxenham. TRV
Proserpine's Ragout. Mary Leapor. WaPE
Prospect of Death, A. Andrew Young. DTC
Prospecting Dream, *with music.* John A. Stone. SGR
Prosper, Archambault, Gilbert, and Cinema. The War of the
 Secret Agents. Henri Coulette. AmPC
Prospice. Robert Browning. CBEP; DiPo; FaBV; FaPL;
 ILP; PoIE; PoLF; TRV
Protagonist. Edith Henrich. MoRP
Protagonist, The. Peter Hopegood. PoAu-2
Protest. Vassar Miller. ToPo
Protest in the Sixth Year of Ch'ien Fu, A. Ts'ao Sung, *tr. fr.*
 Chinese by Arthur Waley. FaBV
Prothalamion. Spenser. CABA; CaFP; EnRePo; GTBS-P;
 OnP; PoIE; StP; VaPo
 "With that I saw two swannes of goodly hewe," *sel.* BoC
Proud Egyptian queen, her Roman guest, The. And She
 Washed His Feet with Her Tears, and Wiped Them with
 the Hairs of Her Head. Sir Edward Sherburne, *after* Giam-
 battista Marino. CBEP; RBL
Proud inclination of the flesh. Villanelle. Dilys Laing. ErPo
Proud Maisie. Sir Walter Scott. *Fr.* The Heart of Mid-
 lothian. CBEP; ILP; PoPo; StP
 (Madge Wildfire Sings.) OBNC
 (Pride of Youth, The.) GTBS-P
Proud of my music, let me often make. Stéphane Mallarmé.
 Fr. L'Après-midi d'un faune. ErPo
Proud Songsters. Thomas Hardy. PoSa
Proud Toad, The. Grace Taber Hallock. RePo
Proud who never loved, The. Sublimation. Alex Comfort.
 ErPo; UnTE
Provençals Right Well May Versify. Dinis, King of Portugal,
 tr. fr. Portuguese by William M. Davis. AnML
Proverb, A. Unknown, *tr. fr. Turkish by* E. Powys Mathers.
 BoLP
Proverbs, *sels.* Bible, O.T.
 "Doth not wisdom cry? and understanding put forth her
 voice?" VIII: 1, 22-31, 34-36. BoC
 "Strength and honour are her clothing," XXXI: 25-29. PoSC
Virtuous Woman, A. XXXI: 10-12, 27-31. TRV
Provide, Provide. Robert Frost. CABA; MP
Prudence. Don Marquis. *Fr.* Archy and Mehitabel. LV
Pruning Trees. Po Chü-i, *tr. fr. Chinese by* Arthur Waley.
 SiGo

P.S. Jascha Kessler. AmPC
P's the Proud Policeman. Phyllis McGinley. *Fr.* All around
 the Town. SoPo
Psalm: "I proclaim Thee great and wonderful." Murilo
 Mendes, *tr. fr. Spanish by* Dudley Poore. MoRP
Psalm of Life, A. Longfellow. DiPo; FaPL; PoLF; PoPl
Psalm of Montreal, A. Samuel Butler. CBEP
 (O God! O Montreal!) DTC
Psalm of St. Priapus, The. James Broughton. ErPo
Psalm of the West, *sel.* Sidney Lanier.
 Story of Vinland, The. ThLM
Psalm to My Belovèd. Eunice Tietjens. BoLP; ErPo
Psalms, *sels.* Bible, O.T.
 Psalm VIII ("O Lord, our Lord . . ."). SiGo
 Psalm XIX ("The heavens declare the glory of God"). TRV
 Psalm XXIII ("The Lord is my shepherd . . ."). CBEP;
 RePo; TRV
 (Lord Is My Shepherd, The.) PoLF
 (Lord's My Shepherd, The, *Scottish Psalter.*) TRV
 (Twenty-third Psalm.) PoPl; PoPo
 "Though I walk through the valley of the shadow of
 death," 4. BoC
 Psalm XXIV ("The earth is the Lord's . . ."). SiGo
 (Earth Is the Lord's, The.) EaLo
 Psalm XXV ("To thee, O Lord, I lift up my soul . . ."), *sel.*
 "All the paths of the Lord are lovingkindness and truth,"
 10, 15-17; LI: 1-13, 9-12, 17; CIV: 1-4, 8-13. BoC
 Psalm XXIX ("Give unto the Lord . . .").
 (Twenty-fourth Psalm, The [*wr.*].) PoPo
 Psalm XLII ("As the hart panteth . . ."). BoC; TRV (1-5,
 7-8)
 Psalm XLVI ("God is our refuge . . ."). TRV
 Psalm LXXXIV ("How amiable are thy tabernacles . . .").
 TRV
 Psalm XC ("Lord, thou hast been our dwelling place . . .").
 (Lord, Thou Hast Been Our Dwelling Place.) EaLo
 Psalm XCVI ("O sing unto the Lord . . .").
 (O Sing unto the Lord a New Song.) EaLo
 Psalm C ("Make a joyful noise unto the Lord . . ."). LV;
 RePo; TRV
 Psalm CIV ("Bless the Lord, O my soul . . .").
 (Praise the Lord, O My Soul!) ThGo
 Psalm CVII ("O give thanks . . ."), *sel.*
 "They that go down to the sea in ships, that do business in
 great waters," 23-30. HaSV
 Psalm CXXI ("I will lift up mine eyes . . ."). CBEP; LV;
 TRV
 Psalm CXXII ("I was glad when they said unto me . . .").
 TRV
 Psalm CXXIV ("If it had not been the Lord . . ."), *sel.*
 Our Help, 8. TRV
 Psalm CXXVII ("Except the Lord build the house . . .").
 TRV
 Psalm CXXVIII ("Blessed is every one that feareth the
 Lord"). TRV
 Psalm CXXX ("Out of the depths . . .").
 (In Darkness and Aridity.) BoC
 Psalm CXXXIII ("Behold how good and how pleasant it is").
 TRV
 Psalm CXXXIV ("Behold, bless ye the Lord"). TRV
 Psalm CXXXVII ("By the rivers of Babylon . . ."). CaFP
 Psalm CXXXIX ("O Lord, thou hast searched me, and
 known me"). BoC
 Psalm CXLV ("I will extol thee, my God . . ."), *sel.*
 Lord Is Good to All, The, 9. TRV
 Psalm CXLVII ("Praise ye the Lord . . ."), *sel.*
 "Sing unto the Lord with Thanksgiving," 7-9, 12. SoPo
 Psalm CL ("Praise ye the Lord . . ."). SiGo; TRV
Psyche. Jones Very. AP
Psyche to Cupid: Her Ditty. James Broughton. ErPo
Psyche with the Candle. Archibald MacLeish. MoLP
Psychological Prediction. Virginia Braisier. BBGG
Public Garden, The. Robert Lowell. AP
Public Nuisance, A. Reginald Arkell. SD
Puck of Pook's Hill, *sels.* Kipling.
 Cities and Thrones and Powers. GoJo; OBNC
 Harp Song of the Dane Women. OBNC
Puck's Song. FaBV
Puff out your chests, till the wind takes its devious way. The
 School for Tenors. Günter Grass. MGP
Pull down the shades baby neighbors don want to see what you
 do. Crawl Blues. Vincent McHugh. ErPo
Pull my daisy. Song: Fie My Fum. Allen Ginsberg. ErPo
Pull up the bell-flow'rs of the spring. St. Mark. Christopher
 Smart. *Fr.* Hymns and Spiritual Songs. EiCP
Pulled up, resting gently, my oars drip. Oars Pulled Up. Con-
 rad Ferdinand Meyer. TwGP
Pulley, The. George Herbert. CBEP; DiPo; EaLo; FoBA;
 ILP; OnP; PoSa; SeCP; StP
 (Gifts of God, The.) GTBS-P; TRV
Pulse, The. Mark Van Doren. PoPl
Pult'ney, methinks you blame my breach of word. Epistle III.
 John Gay. EiCP
Pumpkin, The. Whittier. PoSC

Punch, Brothers, Punch! *Unknown.* CBEP
Puppet Play, The. Padraic Colum. RoGo
Puppy. Edith Earnshaw. PoNC
Puppy. Aileen Fisher. SoPo
Puppy and I. A. A. Milne. SoPo
Pure Death. Robert Graves. GTBS-P
Pure Poet, The. Roy Fuller. ToPo
Pure products of America, The. To Elsie. William Carlos
    Williams. AP; CABA
Pure Simple Love. Aurelian Townsend. SeCP
Purer in Heart. *Unknown.* STF
Purist, The. Ogden Nash. GoJo
Puritan's Ballad, The. Elinor Wylie. BoLP
Purple Cow, The. Gelett Burgess. PoLF; PoPl; SoPo
Purple sky, the down's long spine, The. The Novice. Edward
    Davison. ErPo
Purse, The—Seine. Paul Blackburn. CoPo
Pursuit. Robert Penn Warren. MP
Pursuit, The. Henry Vaughan. SeCP
Pushcart Row. Rachel Field. SoPo
Puss and the Boots, The, *sel.* H. D. Traill.
    "Put case I circumvent and kill him: good." Par
Pussy-Cat, Pussy-Cat. Mother Goose. PoPl
    (Pussycat, Pussycat.) SoPo
Pussy-Willows. Aileen Fisher. RePo
Put case I circumvent and kill him: good. H. D. Traill. *Fr.*
    The Puss and the Boots. Par
Put your head, darling, darling, darling. Dear Dark Head [*or*
    Cean Dubh Deelish]. *Tr. by* Sir Samuel Ferguson. ACV;
    BoLP; SiGo; UnTE
Put your Key. David Gallatin. PtTo
Putman's Hill (A *and* B *vers., with music;* D *vers.*). *Un-*
    known. BSO
    (My True Love Has Gone to France, C *vers.*) BSO
Putting in the Seed. Robert Frost. ErPo
Puzzled Centipede, The. Mrs. Edward Craster. *See* Centipede
    Was Happy Quite, A.
Puzzled Game-Birds, The. Thomas Hardy. VP
Puzzling Example, A. Virginia Sarah Benjamin. BiCD
Pyramis; or, The House of Ascent. A. D. Hope. PoAu-2
Pyramus and Thisbe. John Godfrey Saxe. OnMSP
Python, The. Hilaire Belloc. EvOK

Q

Qua Cursum Ventus. Arthur Hugh Clough. HaSV; PoIE
"Quack! Quack!" Ducks at Dawn. James S. Tippett. SoPo
Quadroon mermaids, Afro angels, black saints. A Ballad of
    Remembrance. Robert Hayden. AmNP
Quaker Graveyard in Nantucket, The. Robert Lowell. AmLP;
    AnMoPo; AP; CABL; PoIE; ToPo
Quaker's Wooing, The, *with music. Unknown.* BFSS; BSNS;
    BSO
Quality of mercy is not strain'd, The. Shakespeare. *Fr.* The
    Merchant of Venice, IV, i. TRV
Quality of these trees, green height, The; of the sky, shining, of
    water. Shine, Republic. Robinson Jeffers. MoRP
Quarrel, The. Conrad Aiken. MoLP; PoPl
Quarried from chaos. Aran. Rudolf Hagelstange. MGP
Quarry, The. Vassar Miller. NePoEA-2
Quarry Pool, The. Denise Levertov. ToPo
Quartette, The. Walter de la Mare. BoC; CBEP
Quebec. *Unknown. See* Brave Wolfe.
Quebec Liquor Commission Store. A. M. Klein. ACV; OBCV
Queen. Dom Moraes. NePoEA-2
Queen and Huntress. Ben Jonson. *Fr.* Cynthia's Revels, V,
    vi. CABA; CBEP
    (Hymn to Diana.) EnRePo; GTBS-P; SeCP; WiR
    ("Queen and huntress, chaste and fair.") ILP
Queen-Ann's-Lace. William Carlos Williams. AP
Queen Bess was Harry's daughter. Stand forward partners all.
    The Looking-Glass. Kipling. EvOK
Queen Mab. Shakespeare. *Fr.* Romeo and Juliet, I. iv. BoC
Queen went from me while I slept, The. Queen. Dom Moraes.
    NePoEA-2
Queen's Wake, The, *sel.* James Hogg.
    Kilmeny. CABL
Queer are the ways of a man I know. The Phantom Horse-
    woman. Thomas Hardy. CaFP
Queerly walking by a slow and pagan clock. Warning to Snake-
    Killers. Robert H. Barlow. FiSC
Queer's Song. Richard Howard. *Fr.* Gaiety. ErPo
Quentin Durward, *sel.* Sir Walter Scott.
    Serenade, A: "Ah! County Guy, the hour is nigh," *fr. ch.* 4.
    GTBS-P
Query. Edith Earnshaw. PoNC
Quest Eternal, The, *sel.* Brajendranath Seal.
    "I was one with the woods; my body, the earth." ACV
Quest of Silence, The, *sel.* Christopher Brennan.

Fire in the Heavens, and Fire along the Hills. PoAu-1
Question, The. W. W. Gibson. MMA
Question, The. F. T. Prince. GTBS-P
Question, The. Frederick Goddard Tuckerman. AP
Question, A. *Unknown.* CBEP
Question Answer'd, The. Blake. ErPo
Question, lords and ladies, is, The. Percy Shelley. John Peale
    Bishop. ErPo
Questions. Heine, *tr. fr. German by* Vernon Watkins. HaSV
Questions for a Flying Squirrel to Answer. Rachel Field.
    RePo
Questions for the Candidate. John Holmes. PP
Quia Amore Langueo. *Unknown.* CBEP; MeEL
Quick, woman, in your net. The Net. W. R. Rodgers. ErPo
Quickening, The. Ruth Gilbert. *Fr.* The Blossom of the
    Branches. ACV
Quickness. Henry Vaughan. BoC; ELP; SeCP
Quiet. Marjorie Pickthall. OBCV
Quiet. Giuseppe Ungaretti, *tr. Italian by* Allen Mandel-
    baum. PoPl
Quiet deepens, The. You will not persuade. Farewell to Van
    Gogh. Charles Tomlinson. GTBS-P
Quiet Flower, The. Josephine W. Johnson. MoRP
Quiet Glades of Eden, The. Robert Graves. ErPo
Quiet Life, The. Pope. *See* Ode on Solitude.
Quiet Life and a Good Name, A. Swift. CBEP
Quiet Things. Grace Noll Crowell. PoLF
Quiet Work. Matthew Arnold. PoIE; PoPo
Quietly. Kenneth Rexroth. ErPo
Quietly as rosebuds. Love's Coming. John Shaw Neilson.
    PoAu-1
Quietness clings to the air. The Snow Fall. Archibald Mac-
    Leish. LOW; PoPl
Quietude of a soft wind, The. The Creditor. Louis MacNeice.
    EaLo
Quill of the goose is a very slight thing, The. Impromptu.
    Francis Atterbury. WaPE
Quilted/ patches, unlike the smooth slick loveliness. Making.
    Phyllis Webb. PoCh
Quinquireme of Nineveh from distant Ophir. Cargoes. John
    Masefield. DiPo; FaBV; ILP; PoPo; RoGo; WcPo
Quip, The. George Herbert. CBEP; ILP; SeCP
Quite close to the abrupt city. Seal Rocks: San Francisco.
    Robert Conquest. PP
Quite spent with thoughts I left my cell, and lay. Vanity of
    Spirit. Henry Vaughan. MeP
Quite unexpectedly as Vasserot. The End of the World. Arch-
    ibald MacLeish. AP; CaFP; ILP; PoIE; PoPo; PoSa;
    StP
Quivering pine needles, a sun. To His Sister. Carlo Betocchi.
    CoIP
Quo Vadis? Myles Connolly. TRV

R

Rabbi Ben Ezra. Robert Browning. OBNC; VP
    "Grow old along with me!" 6 *ll.* BiCB; FaBV; PoPl; TRV
Rabbi Loew. Rainer Maria Rilke, *tr. fr. German by* Walter
    Kaufmann. TwGP
Rabbit, The. Georgia Roberts Durston. SoPo
Rabbit, The. Edith King. SoPo
Rabbit, The. Elizabeth Madox Roberts. SoPo
Rabbit Cry. Edward Lucie-Smith. NePoEA-2
Rabbit has a habit, The. The Rabbit. Georgia Roberts Durs-
    ton. SoPo
Rabbit thieves in silver suit, The. Clothes. Frances Frost.
    RePo
Rabbits. Dorothy Baruch. SoPo
Racing Eight, A. James L. Cuthbertson. PoAu-1
Radar. A. M. Sullivan. LV
Radiator Lions. Dorothy Aldis. SoPo
Radio that told me about the death of Billy the Kid, The. Billy
    the Kid. Jack Spicer. CoPo
Raftery's Dialogue with the Whiskey. Padraic Fallon. DTC
Ragged brown carpet, vast and bare. To the Veld. Arthur
    Shearly Cripps. ACV
Ragged Coat, The. John Woodward. SGR
Ragged, unheeded, stooping, meanly shod. The Poor Can Feed
    the Birds. John Shaw Neilson. PoAu-1
Ragged Wood, The. W. B. Yeats. PoPo
    ("O hurry where by water among trees.") BoC
Raggle Taggle Gypsies, The. *Unknown. See* Wraggle Taggle
    Gipsies, O!, The.
Ragout Fin de Siècle. Erich Kästner, *tr. fr. German by* Walter
    Kaufmann. ErPo; TwGP
Railroad, The. Henry David Thoreau. *See* What's the Rail-
    road.
Railroad bridge's, De/ A sad song. Homesick Blues. Langston
    Hughes. PoPl

Railroad track is miles away, The. Travel. Edna St. Vincent Millay. LV; RePo
Railroad tracks; a flight of wild geese. The New and the Old. Shiki. SiGo
Railroad tracks; the flight of a rocket. The Old and the New. "Q. B. M." SoPo
Railway Junction, The. Walter de la Mare. CBEP
Railway Train, The. Emily Dickinson. See I like to see it lap the miles.
Rain. Einar Benediktsson, tr. fr. Icelandic by Watson Kirkconnell. SiGo
Rain, The. W. H. Davies. LV
Rain. Christopher Fry. Fr. The Boy with a Cart. BoC
Rain, The. George Herbert. BoC
Rain. Howard Moss. ErPo
Rain. Robert Louis Stevenson. GoJo; SoPo
Rain. William Carlos Williams. AP
Rain and the Rainbow, The. Leo Fredericks. ACV
Rain at Night, The. Tu Fu, tr. fr. Chinese. SiGo
Rain comes in various sizes. Rain Sizes. John Ciardi. SoPo
Rain Comes Sobbing to the Door, The. Henry Kendall. ACV
Rain, do not hurt my flowers, but quickly spread. The Rain. George Herbert. BoC
Rain-Frogs, The. Rogetsu, tr. fr. Japanese by Harold G. Henderson. SiGo
Rain had fallen, the Poet arose, The. The Poet's Song. Tennyson. ELP
Rain has silver sandals, The. Footwear. May Justus. SoPo
Rain in the city. City Rain. Rachel Field. SoPo
Rain is plashing on my sill, The. The Unknown Dead. Henry Timrod. AP
Rain is raining all around, The. Rain. Robert Louis Stevenson. GoJo; SoPo
Rain it raineth on the just, The. Just and Unjust. Lord Bowen. PoPl
Rain, it streams on stone and hillock, The. A. E. Housman. Last Poems, XVIII. VP
Rain on the windows, creaking doors. The Division. Thomas Hardy. VP
Rain Palace, The. Yvan Goll, tr. fr. German by Christopher Middleton. MGP
Rain patters on a sea that tilts and sighs. Absences. Philip Larkin. PoCh
Rain, Rain, Go Away. Unknown. SoPo
Rain Riders. Clinton Scollard. SoPo
Rain set early in to-night, The. Porphyria's Lover. Robert Browning. CABA; ILP; VP
Rain Sizes. John Ciardi. SoPo
Rain to the wind said, The. Lodged. Robert Frost. RePo
Rainbow, The. Genesis, VIII: 13, Bible. O.T. BoC
Rainbow, The. Walter de la Mare. SoPo
Rainbow. Robert Huff. NePoEA-2
Rainbow, The. David McCord. SoPo
Rainbow, The. Coventry Patmore. The Angel in the House, II, iii, 2. GTBS-P
Rainbow, The. Christina Rossetti. Fr. Sing-Song. SoPo
Rainbow, The. Wordsworth. See My Heart Leaps Up.
Rainbow arches in the sky, The. The Rainbow. David McCord. SoPo
Rainbow Willow, with music. Unknown. BFSS
Rain's Already with Us, The. Salvatore Quasimodo, tr. fr. Italian by Allen Mandelbaum. CoIP; PoPl
Rainwalkers, The. Denise Levertov. NePoEA-2
Rainy Day, A. Joseph C. Lincoln. RePo
Rainy Day, The. Longfellow. PoLF; PoPl
Rainy Summer, The. Alice Meynell. GoJo
Raise up your valourous right arm, O Spain. On the Armada Which Battled against England. Luis de Góngora. AnSP
Raising of the Dead, The. Rosemary Dobson. PoAu-2
Raison d'Etre. Oliver Pitcher. AmNP; NNP
Raking Leaves. Robert Pack. CoPo
Raleigh Was Right. William Carlos Williams. PP
Ramble-eer, The. Unknown. PoAu-1
Rambling Cowboy, The, with music. Unknown. BFSS
Range-finding. Robert Frost. AmLP; CABA
Ranger, The (A vers., with music; B vers.). Unknown. BSO
Rank with the flesh of man and beast. The Lido. Edmund Wilson. ErPo
Ranolf and Amohia, sel. Alfred Domett.
"It was a wondrous realm beguiled." ACV
Rape of Lucrece, The, sels. Thomas Heywood.
"Pack, clouds, away, and welcome day." GTBS-P
She That Denies Me, I Would Have. ErPo; UnTE
Rape of the Lock, The. Pope. CABA; CABL; DiPo; ILP; StP; VaPo
Rapid day is gone, The; her banner swings the night. Evening. Andreas Gryphius. AGP
Rapture, A. Thomas Carew. ErPo; SeCP
(I Will Enjoy Thee Now, abr.) UnTE
Rare Tree, A. Unknown, tr. fr Chinese. Fr. Nineteen Han Poems. SiGo
Rarely, Rarely Comest Thou. Shelley. CBEP
(Invocation.) GTBS-P
(Song.) OBNC

Rash author, 'tis a vain presumptuous crime. Nicolas Boileau-Despréaux, tr. by Sir William Soames and John Dryden. Fr. L'Art poétique. PP
Raspel Pole, The, with music. Unknown. BFSS
Rassa Rises, Thrives, and Prospers. Bertran de Born, tr. fr. Provençal by William M. Davis. AnML
Rat, The. Andrew Young. WePo
Rat too has a skin (to tan), A. Sans Equity and sans Poise. Confucius. Fr. The Classic Anthology: Yung Wind. CTC
Rather notice, mon cher. To a Solitary Disciple. William Carlos Williams. PP
Rattlesnake, The. Unknown. RePo
(Rattlesnake Song, The, with music.) BFSS
Rav, The/ of Northern White Russia declined. Illustrious Ancestors. Denise Levertov. ToPo
Ravaged Villa, The. Herman Melville. AP; CTC
Raven, The. Samuel Taylor Coleridge. WiR
Raven, The. Poe. AP; FaBV; FaPL; GoJo; PoPo; RoGo
Raven, The. Adrienne Rich. NePoEA-2
Raven croak'd as she sate at her meal, The. The Witch. Robert Southey. WiR
Raven Days, The. Sidney Lanier. CBEP
Ravings. Thomas Hood, the Younger. Par
Ravished by all that to the eyes is fair. Madrigal. Michelangelo. RBL
Raw ulcers and his aspirin signify. A Death before Killing. Gray Burr. OPP
Razors pain you. Résumé. Dorothy Parker. LV; PoPl; PoPo
Read in my face a volume of despairs. To Delia, XXXIX. Samuel Daniel. EnRePo
Read not this Book, in any case. Of the Incomparable Treasure of the Scriptures. Unknown. TRV
Read the Bible Through. Amos R. Wells. STF
Reader, could his limbs be found. Epitaph on a Bombing Victim. Roy Fuller. ToPo
Reader of this poetry, stay. To Ford, Guggenheim, Rockefeller, etc. O. B. Hardison, Jr. PoNC
Reader, we are getting ready to pull out. Epilogue: Author to Reader. Henri Coulette. Fr. The War of the Secret Agents. NePoEA-2
Reader Writes, The. Carl Crane. PoPl
Reading a Medal. Terence Tiller. GTBS-P
Reading Buber. Robert Sward. Fr. Five Poems for J. F. K. OPP
Reading the Book of Hills and Seas. T'ao Ch'ien, tr. fr. Chinese by Arthur Waley. SiGo
Ready she sat with one hand to turn o'er. Leigh Hunt. Fr. The Story of Rimini. EvOK
Realm of Fancy, The. Keats. GTBS-P
Reaper, The. L. H. Allen. PoAu-1
Reaper, The. Wordsworth. See Solitary Reaper, The.
Rear-Guard, The. Siegfried Sassoon. ACV
Reason. Ralph Hodgson. PoIE
Reason. Josephine Miles. PoCh
Reason for Not Writing Orthodox Nature Poetry. John Wain. MP; PP; ToPo
Reason for the Pelican, The. John Ciardi. PoPl; SoPo
Reason has moons, but moons not hers. Reason. Ralph Hodgson. PoIE
Reasonable Affliction, A. Matthew Prior. See Helen Was Just Slipt into Bed.
Reasons for Attendance. Philip Larkin. ToPo
Rebel, The. Mari E. Evans. AmNP
Rebel, The. Innes Randolph. ThLM
Rebirth. Kipling. OBNC
Recall, The. James Russell Lowell. AP
Recall how with frozen fingers December's clouds outspread. The Miracle of Spring. Bahar. SiGo
Recalling the manicured nails on the mandolin. Mr. Kennedy Proposes to Pacify the Caribbeans. George Hitchcock. OPP
Recalling War. Robert Graves. AnMoPo; MMA
Recapitulation, The. Richard Eberhart. MoRP
Receive, oh Nymph adorable. Madrigal. Charles de Sainte-Maure, Duc de Montausier. Fr. Guirlande de Julie. RBL
Receiving Communion. Vassar Miller. NePoEA-2
Recessional. Kipling. CABA; FaBV; OBNC; TRV
Recipe. Unknown, tr. fr. German by Louis Untermeyer. UnTE
Recitative. Ronald McCuaig. PoAu-2
Recognition of Death. Joseph Payne Brennan. FiSC
Recognition of Eve, The. Karl Shapiro. Fr. Adam and Eve. ToPo
Recollection, The. Shelley. GTBS-P
(To Jane: The Recollection.) OBNC
Recompense. Loring Williams. FiSC
Reconciliation. "Æ." MoRP
Reconciliation. C. Day Lewis. MP
Reconciliation. Walt Whitman. FoBA
Reconnaissance. Arna Bontemps. AmNP
Recovery, The. Edmund Blunden. CBEP

Recovery, The. Thomas Traherne. *Fr.* The Third Century. MeP
Recuerdo. Edna St. Vincent Millay. BoLP; EvOK; ThLM
Red brick monastery in, The. The Semblables. William Carlos Williams. AP
Red-Bud, the Kentucky Tree, The. Christmas at Freelands. James Stephens. ILP
Red Dust. Wolfgang Weyrauch, *tr. fr. German* by Michael Hamburger. MGP
Red flame-flowers bloom and die, The. On the Back Veld. Crosbie Garstin. ACV
Red Geranium and Godly Mignonette. D. H. Lawrence. GTBS-P
Red Hanrahan's Song about Ireland. W. B. Yeats. ACV
Red Jack. Mary Durack. PoAu-1
Red lips are not so red. Greater Love. Wilfred Owen. ACV; GTBS-P
Red o'er the forest glows the setting sun. John Keble. *Fr.* Forest Leaves in Autumn. OBNC
Red of the bushwood fire. Camp Fire. Beatrice Marion Bromley. ACV
Red paths that wander through the gray, and cells. With God Conversing. Gene Derwood. MoRP
Red Peony, The. Buson, *tr. fr. Japanese* by Harold G. Henderson. RePo
Red, Red Rose, A. Burns. BoLP; CABA; CBEP; EiCP; FaBV; ILP; LV; PoIE; PoLF; PoPo; PoSa; WePo
(My Luve's like a Red, Red Rose.) PoSC
(O My Luve's like a Red, Red Rose.) DiPo; ELP; GTBS-P
Red river, red river. Virginia. T. S. Eliot. *Fr.* Landscapes. PoSa
Red River Valley, The, *with music*. Unknown. BFSS
Red rose whispers of passion, The. A White Rose. John Boyle O'Reilly. PoPl
Red Wheelbarrow, The. William Carlos Williams. AmLP; VaPo
(Spring and All.) EvOK
Redeemer, The. Siegfried Sassoon. MMA
Redemption. George Herbert. CABA; EaLo; PoSa; SeCP
Redeployment. Howard Nemerov. ThLM
Rediscovered Country. André Frénaud, *tr. fr. French* by Paulène Aspel. CoFP
Redwoods, The. Louis Simpson. PP
Reeve's Tale, The. Chaucer, *mod. vers.* by Frank Ernest Hill. *Fr.* The Canterbury Tales. UnTE
Refined Man, The. Kipling. *Fr.* Epitaphs of the War. MMA
Reflection. Unknown. STF
Reflection after Empire. James Boyer May. PtTo
Reflection from Rochester. William Empson. ToPo
Reflections. Edna Becker. TRV
Reflections. Carl Gardner. NNP
Reflections Dental. Phyllis McGinley. LV
Reflections on the River. Andrew Young. ACV
Reflections on Water. Kenneth Pitchford. CoPo
Reflections Outside of a Gymnasium. Phyllis McGinley. SD
Reflections upon a Recurrent Suggestion by Civil Defense Authorities That I Build a Bombshelter in My Backyard. Reed Whittemore. PoCh
Reflexion, The. Edward Taylor. *Fr.* Preparatory Meditations, First Series. AP
Refrigerium. John Henry Newman. OBNC
Refrigerium. Frederick Goddard Tuckerman. AP
Refugee Blues. W. H. Auden. WePo
Refusal, A. Barnabe Googe. EnRePo
Refusal to Mourn the Death, by Fire, of a Child in London, A. Dylan Thomas. AnMoPo; CABA; DiPo; GTBS-P; MP; PoDB; PoIE; PoPl; StP; ToPo; VaPo
Refuses/ To refuse the racket. Old Tennis Player. Gwendolyn Brooks. SD
Refusing to fall in love with God, he gave. Didymus. Louis MacNeice. EaLo
Regeneration. Henry Vaughan. CABA; MeP
Regent's Park. Rose Fyleman. SoPo
Region of life and light! The Life of the Blessed. Luis de León. RBL
Regrets, *sels*. Joachim du Bellay, *tr. fr. French*. RBL
  Heureux qui, comme Ulysse, a fait un beau voyage, XXXI, *tr. by* G. K. Chesterton.
  Sonnet: "I hate the money-lending avarice," LXVIII, *tr. by* R. N. Currey.
Rehearsal, The, *sel*. George Villiers, Duke of Buckingham.
  "I have made, too, one of the most delicate, dainty similes." Par
Reilly's Farewell. Unknown. BSNS
Rejected Offer, The. Sir John Suckling. *See* Proffered Love Rejected.
Rejoice in God, O ye tongues; give the glory to the Lord, and the Lamb. Christopher Smart. *Fr.* Jubilate Agno. EiCP
Relapse, The. Henry Vaughan. MeP
Releas'd from the noise of the butcher and baker. Jinny the Just. Matthew Prior. CABL

Relentless, black on white, the cable runs. T-Bar. P. K. Page. OBCV
Relic, The. John Donne. CABA; CBEP; EnRePo; ILP; StP (Relique, The.) SeCP
Relief on Easter Eve, The. Thomas Pestel. CBEP
Relieving Guard. Bret Harte. RoGo
Religion. Henry Vaughan. MeP
Relique, The. John Donne. See Relic, The.
Reluctant Lady, The. Unknown. See Maiden's Denial, A.
Remain, ah not in youth alone. Walter Savage Landor. *Fr.* Ianthe. OBNC
Remember. Christina Rossetti. FaBV; OBNC; PoLF; PoPo; VP; WePo
Remember, America. Joel Oppenheimer. *Fr.* 17-18 April, 1961. PtTo
Remember me when I am gone away. Remember. Christina Rossetti. FaBV; OBNC; PoLF; PoPo; VP; WePo
Remember the Day of Judgment. Unknown. MeEL
Remember the Last Things. Unknown. MeEL
Remember the Source. Richard Eberhart. MoRP
Remember Thy Covenant. Edith Lovejoy Pierce. MoRP
Remembering. "Michael Lewis," *after the Chinese. Fr.* Cherry Blossoms. UnTE
Remembering the Thirties. Donald Davie. PP
Remembrance. Emily Brontë. OBNC; PoIE
Remembrance. Shakespeare. See Sonnets, XXX.
Remembrance. Vasily Zhukovsky, *tr. fr. Russian* by Babette Deutsch. SiGo
Remembrances. John Clare. CBEP
Remind you, that there was darkness in my heart. Canticle of Darkness. Wilfred Watson. ACV
Reminder. Unknown. STF
Reminiscence, *sel*. Padraic Colum.
  "I saw the wind to-day!" GoJo; LOW
(Wind, The.) RoGo
Reminiscence of 1820, A, *sel*. H. H. Dugmore.
  "And this is now their home." ACV
Remorse. Pierre Louÿs, *tr. fr. French* by Horace M. Brown. *Fr.* The Songs of Bilitis. UnTE
Remorse is memory awake. Emily Dickinson. FoBA
Remote from the broad, humming highroad. Old Chimney. Edith Earnshaw. PoNC
Remote, unfriended, melancholy, slow. The Traveller. Goldsmith. EnPE
Rendezvous. Robert Hillyer. MoLP
Rendezvous, The. Bernard Spencer. GTBS-P
Renewal, A. James Merrill. PoPl
Renouncement. Alice Meynell. BoLP; OBNC
Renouncing of Love, A. Sir Thomas Wyatt. StP
Renownèd Spenser, lie a thought more nigh. Elegy on Shakespeare. William Basse. CBEP
Rented Garden, The. Bink Noll. ToPo
Renunciation, A. Edward de Vere, Earl of Oxford. GTBS-P
Report from the Carolinas. Helen Bevington. PoNC
Report on Experience. Edmund Blunden. CBEP; GTBS-P
Repose of Rivers. Hart Crane. AP; PoIE
Repression of War Experience. Siegfried Sassoon. MMA
Reprisall, The. George Herbert. MeP
Reproof. Unknown. STF
Reptilian green the wrinkled throat. Sir Gawaine and the Green Knight. Yvor Winters. PoIE
Requiem. Carl Bode. ToPo
Requiem. Robert Louis Stevenson. FaBV; FaPL; HaSV; ILP; OBNC; PoIE; PoLF; PoPl; PoSa
Requiem for an Abstract Artist. Jascha Kessler. AmPC
Requiem for the Plantagenet Kings. Geoffrey Hill. AnMoPo
Requiescat. Matthew Arnold. ELP; ILP; PoSa; VP
Requiescat. Oscar Wilde. OBNC; WePo
Requirements: "Not for me a giantess." Nicarchus, *tr. fr. Greek* by Wallace Rice. ErPo
Requirements: "Not too chary, not too fast." Rufinus, *tr. fr. Greek* by Wallace Rice. ErPo
Requirements: "Not too lean, and not too fat." Rufinus, *tr. fr. Greek* by Wallace Rice. ErPo
Requirements: "Not too old, and not too young." Honestus, *tr. fr. Greek* by Wallace Rice. ErPo
Requirements: "Not too pallid, as if bleacht." Xenos Palaestes, *tr. fr. Greek* by Wallace Rice. ErPo
Rescue, The. Hal Summers. DaDu
Reserved. Walter de la Mare. GTBS-P
Resignation. Matthew Arnold. VP
Resignation, *sel*. Longfellow.
  "There is no Death. What seems so is transition." TRV
Resistor, transistor, condensers in pairs. Frederick Winsor. *Fr.* The Space Child's Mother Goose. LV
Resolute Courtier, The. Thomas Shipman. ErPo
Resolution, The. Vassar Miller. CoPo
Resolution and Independence. Wordsworth. CABA; CBEP; DiPo; OBNC
  "Now, whether it were by peculiar grace," *sel*. Par
Resolution in Four Sonnets, of a Poetical Question Put to Me by a Friend, Concerning Four Rural Sisters, *sels*. Charles Cotton.
  Alice. UnTE

Resolution in Four Sonnets (*continued*)
Margaret. UnTE
Resolutions?—New and Old. Harvey E. Rolfe. STF
Resolve, The. Henry Vaughan. MeP
Resolved. Ottis Shirk. STF
Resolving Doubts. William Dickey. ErPo
Respectabilities. Jon Silkin. NePoEA-2
Rest, The. Ezra Pound. AnMoPo; PP
Rest. Christina Rossetti. OBNC; VP
Rest and Silence. Georg Trakl, *tr. fr. German by* Walter Kaufmann. TwGP
Rest, Heart of the Tired World. Kenneth Patchen. ToPo
Rest in Peace. Wilfred J. Funk. PoLF
Rest is not quitting. True Rest. Goethe. TRV
Rest upon me, eye of darkness. Plea. Nikolaus Lenau. AGP
Re-Statement of Romance. Wallace Stevens. MoLP
Resting Figure. Denise Levertov. ToPo
Restless and clamoured by unsparing birds. Christmas Dawn. Fleur Adcock. ACV
Restrain your child; you'll soon believe. Fable XX: The Old Hen and the Cock. John Gay. EiCP
Restrained/ with branch and young shoot undisclosed. Poplar. Gottfried Benn. PoPl
Résumé. Dorothy Parker. LV; PoPl; PoPo
Resurgam. Marjorie Pickthall. OBCV
Resurrection, The. Jonathan Brooks. AmNP
Resurrection. John Donne. MeP
Resurrection. Frank Horne. PtTo
Resurrection. Robert Pack. NePoEA-2
Resurrection, The, *sel.* W. B. Yeats.
Two Songs from a Play. CABA; FoBA; ILP; PoDB; PoIE
"I saw a staring virgin stand," I.
"In pity for man's darkening thought," II.
Resurrection—an Easter Sequence, *sel.* W. H. Rodgers.
"It was a deliberate moment, and O." ACV
Resurrection and Immortality. Henry Vaughan. MeP
Resurrection Possible and Probable, The. Robert Herrick. ILP
Retaliation, *sel.* Goldsmith.
David Garrick. CBEP
Retinue. Paul Verlaine, *tr. fr. French by* C. F. MacIntyre. ErPo
Retired Colonel, The. Ted Hughes. NePoEA-2
Retirement. *Unknown, tr. fr. Irish by* Frank O'Connor. ErPo
Retreat, The. Charles Cotton. CBEP
Retreat, The. Henry Vaughan. BoC; CABA; CBEP; GTBS-P; PoIE; StP
(Retreate, The.) MeP; SeCP
Retrospective Sketch. Gottfried Benn, *tr. fr. German by* Michael Hamburger. MGP
Return. Bertolt Brecht, *tr. fr. German by* Christopher Middleton. MGP
Return. C. P. Cavafy, *tr. fr. Modern Greek by* John Mavrogordato. ErPo
Return, The. Edna St. Vincent Millay. PoPl
Return. Vassar Miller. ToPo
Return. Adèle Naudé. ACV
Return, The. Ezra Pound. AP
Return, The. Jon Silkin. NePoEA-2
Return, dear Lord, to those who look. Jesus Return. Henry van Dyke. TRV
Return of the Native, The. Harley Matthews. PoAu-2
Return of the Village Lad. Alfred Lichtenstein, *tr. fr. German by* Michael Hamburger. MGP
Return often and take me. Return. C. P. Cavafy. ErPo
Return to Lane's Island. William H. Matchett. PoPl
Return to the most human, nothing less. Santos: New Mexico. May Sarton. EaLo
Return'd from the opera, as lately I sat. A Bon Mot. *Unknown.* ErPo
Returned to Frisco, 1946. W. D. Snodgrass. AP
Returned Volunteer to His Rifle, The. Herman Melville. ThLM
Returning/ to all the unsaid. The Charge. Denise Levertov. NePoEA-2
Returning after dark, I thought. Traditional Red. Robert Huff. NePoEA-2
Returning from Harvest. Vernon Watkins. StP
Returning, We Hear the Larks. Isaac Rosenberg. MMA
Retyred thoughts enjoy their owne delights. Looke Home. Robert Southwell. MeP
Reuben Bright. E. A. Robinson. PoPo; StP
Reuben Ranzo. *Unknown.* BSNS
Reunion. John Gould Fletcher. MoLP
Reunion. W. S. Merwin. AmPC
Reveal Thy Presence now, O Lord. A Grace. Thomas Tiplady. TRV
Reveille. A. E. Housman. A Shropshire Lad, IV. PoLF; PoPo
Revelation. Robert Frost. FoBA; PoDB
Revelation. Nancy Keesing. PoAu-2
Revelation, The. Coventry Patmore. The Angel in the House, I, viii, 2. GTBS-P; OBNC
Revelation, The. William Carlos Williams. MoLP

Revenge, The; a Ballad of the Fleet. Tennyson. FoBA; OnMSP
Revenge of Hamish, The. Sidney Lanier. AP; SIV
Reverie. Don Marquis. PoLF
Reverie of Poor Susan, The. Wordsworth. CBEP; GTBS-P; WiR
Reversions. Alfred Dorn. FiSC
Review, The. Thomas Traherne. CBEP
Review from Staten Island. G. C. Oden. NNP
Reviewer. Goethe, *tr. fr. German by* Walter Kaufmann. TwGP
Revivalist in Boston, A. Adrienne Cecile Rich. EaLo
Revolution. Lesbia Harford. PoAu-1
Revolution. A. E. Housman. Last Poems, XXXVI. VP
Revolution is the pod. Emily Dickinson. AP
Revolutions. Shakespeare. *See* Sonnets, LX.
Revolving doors compete with sales-day traffic. Shoplifter. Solomon Edwards. NNP
Rhapsody. William Stanley Braithwaite. AmNP
Rhapsody on a Windy Night. T. S. Eliot. ACV
Rhapsody to Milton. Sneyd Davies. WaPE
Rhetoric of a Journey. Roy Fuller. ToPo
Rhinoceros, The. Ogden Nash. RePo
Rhodora, The. Emerson. AmLP; AP; FaBV; ILP; PoIE; TRV
Rhyme, The. Robert Creeley. AmPC
Rhyme from the Confino. Luigi Bartolini, *tr. fr. Italian by* Carlo L. Golino. CoIP
Rhyme of Joyous Garde, The, *sel.* Adam Lindsay Gordon.
"We were glad together in gladsome meads." PoAu-1
Rhyme of the Dream-Maker Man, A. William Allen White. PoLF
Rhyme of the Rails. John Godfrey Saxe. PoLF
Rhyme [*or* Rime], the rack of finest wits. A Fit of Rhyme against Rhyme. Ben Jonson. PP; SeCP
Rhymes of a Rolling Stone, *sel.* Robert W. Service.
"Thank God! there is always a Land of Beyond." TRV
Rhyming Riddles, *sels.* Mary Austin. SoPo
"I come more softly than a bird."
"I have no wings, but yet I fly."
Rhythm, The. Robert Creeley. CoPo
Rhythm of scarlet and white on green-lit tables. Watch Ashore—Seletar. Sydney Middleton Clarke. HaSV
Ribald and unbuttoned air, A. Back Lane. R. D. Murphy. PoAu-2
Ribs and Terrors in the Whale, The. Herman Melville. *Fr.* Moby Dick. EaLo
(Whale, The.) PoPl
Rice Pudding. A. A. Milne. BBGG
Rich arrived in pairs, The. The Garden Party. Hilaire Belloc. DTC
Rich in Love and Beggar to My Heart. Guillaume de Machaut, *tr. fr. French by* William M. Davis. AnML
Rich Interior Life, The. Richard Eberhart. MoRP
Rich Lady from Dublin, The, *with music. Unknown.* BFSS
Richard Cory. E. A. Robinson. CaFP; DiPo; DTC; ILP; PoLF; PoPo
Richard has been sent to bed. Dirge for a Bad Boy. E. V. Rieu. BBGG
Richard II. Shakespeare. *See* King Richard II.
Richard, thah thou be ever trichard. Against the Barons' Enemies. *Unknown.* MeEL
Richard the Second. Shakespeare. *See* King Richard II.
Richard the Third. Shakespeare. *See* King Richard III.
Richer. Aileen Fisher. BiCB
Riches I hold in light esteem. The Old Stoic. Emily Brontë. FaPL; OBNC; PoLF; PoPl; PoPo
Rickety wagon lumbers over the hill, A. Sure Signs. Thad Stem, Jr. PoNC
Riddle: "As I was going to St. Ives." Mother Goose. SoPo
Riddle, The: "Down in a garden sits my dearest Love." *Unknown. See* Down in a Garden.
Riddle: "First it was a pretty flower, dressed in pink and white." Christina Rossetti. SoPo
Riddle, The: "He told himself and he told his wife." Ralph Hodgson. PoPl
Riddle: "Higher than a house." Mother Goose. SoPo
Riddle: "Hill full, a hole full, A." Mother Goose. SoPo
Riddle #14: Horn, A. *Unknown, tr. fr. Anglo-Saxon by* Burton Raffel. DiPo
Riddle: "Little Nancy Etticoat." Mother Goose. SoPo
Riddle: "Lives in winter." Mother Goose. SoPo
Riddle #29: Moon and the Sun, The. *Unknown, tr. fr. Anglo-Saxon by* Burton Raffel. CaFP; GoJo
Riddle: "Old Mother Twitchet had but one eye." Mother Goose. SoPo
Riddle: "Shoemaker makes shoes without leather, A." *Unknown.* SoPo
Riddle: "Thirty white horses." Mother Goose. SoPo
Riddle: "Upon a bed of humble clay." Thomas Parnell. WaPE
Riddle: What Am I? Dorothy Aldis. SoPo
Riddle cum diddle cum dido. Kindness to Animals. Laura E. Richards. SoPo
Riddle of Snow and Sun. *Unknown.* CBEP

Riddle of the World, The. Whittier. TRV
Ride. "Klabund," tr. fr. German by Walter Kaufmann. TwGP
Ride a Cockhorse. Mother Goose. SoPo
Rider, The. Horse & Rider. Wey Robinson. SD
Ridiculous Optimist, The. *Unknown.* STF
Riding the black express from heaven to hell. Lucifer in the Train. Adrienne Cecile Rich. EaLo; NePoEA-2
Riding through Ruwu swamp, about sunrise. Bête Humaine. Francis Brett Young. SIV
Right in the middle of the storm it was. The Storm. Elizabeth Jennings. NePoEA-2
Right Is Right. Frederick W. Faber. TRV
Right Kind of People, The. Edwin Markham. PoPo; SIV
Right-of-Way, A: 1865. William Plomer. DTC
Right Time, The. *Unknown, tr. fr. German* by Louis Untermeyer. UnTE
Right under their noses, the green. The Dusk of Horses. James Dickey. AP; ToPo
Right upward on the road of fame. Emerson. *Fr.* The Poet. PP
Righteous Anger. James Stephens. *See* Glass of Beer, A.
Righteous or not, here comes an angry man. A View of the Burning. James Merrill. NePoEA-2
Rights of Women, The. William Cowper. CBEP
Rigid Body Sings. James Clerk-Maxwell. Par
Rigorists. Marianne Moore. PoIE
Rigs o' Barley, The. Burns. *See* Corn Rigs Are Bonny.
Rima. Gustavo Adolfo Bécquer. *See* Invisible Atoms of the Air, The.
Rime of the Ancient Mariner, The. Samuel Taylor Coleridge. CABA; CABL; CaFP; CBEP; DiPo; FaBV; FaPL; ILP; OBNC; PoSa; RoGo; SIV; StP; VaPo; WePo
Sels.
  "Beyond the shadow of the ship," *fr.* IV. BoC
  "He prayeth best, who loveth best," *fr.* VII. 1 st. TRV
  ("He prayeth well who loveth well," 6 ll.) ThGo
  "Sun now rose upon the right, The," *fr.* II. HaSV
Rime, the rack of finest wits. *See* Rhyme, the rack of finest wits.
Ring and the Book, The, *sels.* Robert Browning.
  Giuseppe Caponsacchi, VI. VP
  Old Pope Is Comforted by the Thought of the Young Pompilia, The, *fr.* X. BoC
Ring-around-a-Rosy. Mother Goose. SoPo
Ring out, wild bells, to the wild sky. In Memoriam A. H. H., CVI. Tennyson. DiPo; FaPL; FoBA; PoIE; TRV; VP; WiR
Ring Out Your Bells. Sir Philip Sidney. CABA; EnRePo
  (Litany, A: "Ring out your bells, let mourning shows be spread.") PoIE
Ring so worn, as you behold. His Wife's [*or* Mother's] Wedding Ring. George Crabbe. CBEP; OBNC
Ring Song, *sel.* Naomi Replansky.
  "When that joy is gone for good." PtTo
Ringely, Ringely. Eliza Lee Follen. BiCB
Rings of stars in sky turns. The Dancing Ploughmen. M. K. Joseph. ACV
Rinordine. *Unknown.* BSNS; BSO
Rio Bo. "Aldo Palazzeschi," *tr. fr. Italian* by Carlo L. Golino. CoIP
Rio Grande (A *and* C *vers., with music). Unknown.* BSNS
  (I'm Bound for the Rio Grande, B *vers.*). BSNS
Ripe Fruit, The. *Unknown, tr. fr. Breton* by Louis Untermeyer. UnTE
Ripeness is all; her in her cooling planet. To an Old Lady. William Empson. AnMoPo; GTBS-P; ToPo
Ripping Trip, A, *with music. Unknown.* SGR
Rise, brothers, rise; the waking signs pray to the morning light. The Coromandel Fishers. Sarojini Naidu. RePo
Rise heart; thy Lord is risen. Sing his praise. Easter. George Herbert. MeP
Rise of Shivaji, The. Zulfikar Ghose. MoBS
Rise up, rise up. The Trumpet. Edward Thomas. MMA
Rise up, rise up, Jack Spratt. And you, his wife. Sonnet XIII. Winfield Townley Scott. ErPo
"Rise up, rise up, now, Lord Douglas," she says. The Douglas Tragedy. *Unknown.* PoPo
"Rise up, rise up, ye seven sleepers." The Seven Sleepers. *Unknown.* BFSS
Rise with the Lamb of Innocence. *Unknown.* MeEL
Risest thou thus, dim dawn, again,/ And howlest, issuing out of night. In Memoriam A. H. H., LXXII. Tennyson. OBNC; VP
Risest thou thus, dim dawn, again,/ So loud with voices of the birds. In Memoriam A. H. H., XCIV. Tennyson. VP
Rising Village, The, *sels.* Oliver Goldsmith, the Younger. OBCV
  "How sweet it is, at first approach of morn."
  "Not fifty summers yet have passed thy clime."
  "What noble courage must their hearts have fired."
Rispetti: On the Death of a Child. Paul Heyse, *tr. fr. German by* E. H. Mueller. PoPl
Risselty Rosselty. *Unknown.* DiPo
Rites for a Demagogue. Anthony Thwaite. NePoEA-2

Ritratto. Ezra Pound. PP
Rivals, The. James Stephens. PoPl
River, The. Matthew Arnold. Faded Leaves, I. CBEP; VP
River, The. Hart Crane. *Fr.* The Bridge. AP
River boat had loitered down its way, The. Gamesters All. Du Bose Heyward. SIV
River brought down, The. How We Heard the Name. Alan Dugan. CaFP
River Duddon, The, *sel.* Wordsworth.
  After-Thought. OBNC
River God, The. John Fletcher. *Fr.* The Faithful Shepherdess, III, i. BoC
River Is a Piece of Sky, The. John Ciardi. PoPl; SoPo
River is within us, the sea is all about us, The. T. S. Eliot. *Fr.* Four Quartets: The Dry Salvages. HaSV
River Map, The, and We're Done. Charles Olson. CoPo
River-Merchant's Wife, The; a Letter. Li Po, *tr. fr. Chinese by* Ezra Pound. BoLP; CABA; DTC; MP; PoIE; PoSa; VaPo
River of Life, The. Thomas Campbell. GTBS-P
  (Thought Suggested by the New Year, A.) OBNC
River of Seville. Seguidillas of the Guadalquiver River. Lope de Vega. AnSP
River of Stars, The. Alfred Noyes. OnMSP
River Skater. Winifred Welles. SD
River that must turn full after I stop dying. A 11. Louis Zukofsky. CoPo
Rivers. Giuseppe Ungaretti, *tr. fr. Italian by* Lowry Nelson, Jr. CoIP
Rivers buck like goats in their tent, The. Black Eggs. Hans Arp. MGP
Rivulet-loving wanderer Abraham, The. Abraham. Edwin Muir. MoRP
Rizpah. Tennyson. CABL; SIV
Roaches, The, are winning, Mr. Exterminator. The Last Warehouse. May Miller. PtTo
Road, The. Conrad Aiken. AP
Road, The. Helene Johnson. AmNP
Road is wide and the stars are out and the breath of the night is sweet, The. Roofs. Joyce Kilmer. PoLF
Road might lead to anywhere, A. Roads. Rachel Field. SoPo
Road Not Taken, The. Robert Frost. AP; DiPo; EvOK; FoBA; ILP; MP; PoLF; PoPl; PoPo
Road of Life, The. William Morris. *Fr.* The Earthly Paradise. OBNC
Road to Nijmegen, The. Earle Birney. OBCV
Road to Vagabondia, The. Dana Burnet. PoLF
Roads. Rachel Field. SoPo
Roadways. John Masefield. PoPo; RePo
Roarers in a Ring. Ted Hughes. NePoEA-2
Roaring company that festive night, A. The Dark and the Fair. Stanley Kunitz. PoCh
Roaring Mad Tom. *Unknown. See* Tom o' Bedlam's Song.
Roaring Wind, soaring Wind. The Wind's Song. Eduard Mörike. SiGo
Robert, Second Duke of Normandy, *sel.* Thomas Lodge.
  Song: "Pluck the fruit and taste the pleasure." EnRePo
Robin, The. *Unknown.* PoPo
Robin and the Wren, The. Popular Rhymes. Blake. ThGo
Robin Hood and Alan a Dale. *Unknown.* BuBa
Robin Hood and Guy of Gisborne. *Unknown.* BuBa
Robin Hood and the Bishop of Hereford. BuBa; SIV
Robin Hood and the Butcher. *Unknown.* BuBa
Robin Hood and the Curtal Friar. *Unknown.* BuBa
Robin Hood and the Two Priests. *Unknown.* BuBa
Robin Hood and the Widow's Three Sons. *Unknown.* BuBa; OnMSP
Robin Hood's Funeral. Anthony Munday *and* Henry Chettle. *See* Dirge for Robin Hood.
Robin is the one, The. Emily Dickinson. FaBV
Robin Redbreast. William Allingham. WePo
Robin redbreast in a cage, A. Many Birds. Blake. *Fr.* Auguries of Innocence. ThGo
Robin's Epitaph, A. Samuel Rogers. CBEP
Robins wait for early worms; bees will find their clover. Birds and Bees. *Unknown.* UnTE
Rock, The, *sels.* T. S. Eliot.
  Chorus: "Son of Man, behold with thine eyes, and hear with thine ears." PoDB
  Chorus: "You have seen the house built, you have seen it adorned." PoDB
  "Endless cycle of idea and action." TRV
  "Men have left God not for other gods, they say, but for not god." TRV
  O Light Invisible, We Praise Thee. MoRP
  There Shall Always Be the Church. TRV
  "Where My Word is unspoken." TRV
  Why Should Men Love the Church? MoRP
  "Word of the Lord came unto me, saying, The." TRV
Rock, The. Wallace Stevens. AP
Rock, Ball, Fiddle. *Unknown.* CBEP
Rock grows brittle, The. My People. Else Lasker-Schüler. MGP
Rock-Lily ("The rock-lily's pale spray"). Roland Robinson. PoAu-2

Rock of Ages. Augustus Montague Toplady. CBEP
Rocking. "Gabriela Mistral," *tr. fr. Spanish by* Muriel Kittel. AnSP
Rocks dark, green as leaves, The. Moss clings. Poem. Robert Sward. *Fr.* Five Poems for J. F. K. OPP
Rocks of Scilly, The. *Unknown.* BSNS
Roc's Brood. Samuel M. Bradley. FiSC
Roistering I'll Chaff. Luis de Góngora, *tr. fr. Spanish by* William M. Davis. AnSP
Rokeby, *sels.* Sir Walter Scott.
　Outlaw, The, *fr.* III. GTBS-P
　Rover, The, *fr.* III. GTBS-P
　(Song: "Weary lot is thine, fair maid, A.") OBNC
Roll, Johnny Booger, *with music. Unknown.* BFSS
Roll on, sad world! Not Mercury or Mars. Sonnets, Part II, XVII. Frederick Goddard Tuckerman. AP
Roll on, thou ball, roll on! To the Terrestrial Globe. W. S. Gilbert. PoPl
Rolled umbrella on my wrist, The. Waterloo Bridge. Christopher Middleton. *Fr.* Herman Moon's Hourbook. NePoEA-2
Rolling English Road, The. G. K. Chesterton. EvOK
Rolling John. *sel.* A. J. Wood.
　"Rolling John and night together." PoAu-2
Rolling River, *with music. Unknown.* BSNS
Rom. Cap. 8. Ver. 19. Henry Vaughan. MeP
Roma. Rutilius, *tr. fr. Latin by* Ezra Pound. CTC
Roman Fountain, The. Conrad Ferdinand Meyer, *tr. fr. German.* AGP, *tr. by* Isabel S. MacInnes; TwGP, *tr. by* Walter Kaufmann
Roman Fountain. Rainer Maria Rilke, *tr. fr. German by* Walter Kaufmann. TwGP
Roman Road, The. Thomas Hardy. GoJo
Roman Soldier on the Wall, A. W. H. Auden. *See* Over the Heather the Wet Wind Blows.
Roman Virgil, thou that singest Ilion's lofty temples robed in fire. To Virgil. Tennyson. GTBS-P; StP
Roman Wall Blues. W. H. Auden. *See* Over the Heather the Wet Wind Blows.
Roman Women, *sel.* Thomas Edward Brown.
　"O Englishwoman on the Pincian." OBNC
Romance. Luis de Góngora, *tr. fr. Spanish by* John Pierrepont Rice. RBL
Romance. Poe. AP; CBEP; ILP
Romance. Robert Louis Stevenson. PoSC
　("I will make you brooches and toys for your delight.") BoLP
Romance. W. J. Turner. BiCB; GoJo; ILP; WePo
Romance of the Rose, *sels.* Guillaume de Lorris *and* Jean de Meun, *tr. fr. French by* Charles Dahlberg. AnML
　"I was aware that it was May." Guillaume de Lorris.
　"In short, all men betray us women." Jean de Meun.
Romance, who loves to nod and sing. Romance. Poe. AP; CBEP; ILP
Romans, *sels.* Bible, *N.T.*
　To Him Be Glory, XII: 33-36. TRV
　"Who shall separate us from the love of Christ?" VIII: 35-39. BoC
Romans, rheumatic, goutly, came. La Condition Botanique. Anthony Hecht. MP
Romantic Episode. Vincent Starrett. FiSC
Rome. Joachim du Bellay, *tr. fr. French by* Yvor Winters. *Fr.* Ruins of Rome. RBL
Romeo and Juliet. H. Phelps Putnam. ErPo
Romeo and Juliet, *sels.* Shakespeare.
　Come Night, Come Romeo, *fr.* III, ii. BoLP
　"He jests at scars that never felt a wound," *fr.* II, ii. BoC
　Queen Mab, *fr.* I, iv. BoC
Romish Lady, The. *Unknown.* BFSS, *with music;* BSO
Romney, The. Harriet Monroe. SIV
Ronald Wyn. Robert Bagg. MP
Rondeau: In Good Plain French. Vincent Voiture, *tr. fr. French by* Wilfrid Thorley. RBL
Rondeau: "Jenny kissed me when we met." Leigh Hunt. *See* Jenny Kissed Me.
Rondeau: "Year his winter cloak lets fall, The." Charles d'Orléans. *See* Spring.
Rondel: "Behold the works of William Morris." *Unknown.* Par
Rondel: Beside the Idle Summer Sea. W. E. Henley. OBNC
Rondelay: "Chloe found Amyntas lying." Dryden. DiPo (Kiss Me, Dear.) UnTE
Rondo: "Did I love thee? I only did desire." George Moore. UnTE
Roofs. Joyce Kilmer. PoLF
Roofs are shining from the rain, The. April. Sara Teasdale. PoSC; SoPo
Room, The. Conrad Aiken. AP; PoDB
Room, The. C. Day Lewis. PoCh
Room, The. Elizabeth Jennings. NePoEA-2
Room, The. Francis Webb. *Fr.* Leichhardt in Theatre. PoAu-2
Room after room. Love in a Life. Robert Browning. CBEP; OBNC

Room for Jesus. Barbara H. Staples. STF
Room in Darkness. Mary Elizabeth Counselman. FiSC
Room is full of gold, The. Jason. Anthony Hecht. CoPo
Room looks strange when moonlight falls, The. Summer Moonlight. Patience Strong. RePo
Room room for a blade of the town. The Bully. Earl of Rochester. CBEP
Room! room to turn around in, to breathe and be free. Kit Carson's Ride. Joaquin Miller. SIV
Room was suddenly rich and the great bay-window was, The. Snow. Louis MacNeice. VaPo
Roommates. James Larkin Pearson. PoNC
Rooster, The. Gil Orlovitz. ToPo
Roosters. Elizabeth Bishop. AmLP
Roots, go deep: wrap your coils; fasten your knots. Wild Horses. Carl Sandburg. RePo
Rope for Harry Fat, A. James K. Baxter. MoBS
"Ropeman, ropeman, hold the rope." The Maid Freed from the Gallows (B *vers.*). *Unknown.* BSO
Ropewalk, The. Longfellow. AP
Rosabelle. Sir Walter Scott. *Fr.* The Lay of the Last Minstrel, VI. GTBS-P
Rosalind, in a negligee. Early Unfinished Sketch. Austin Clarke. ErPo
Rosalynde; or, Euphues' Golden Legacy, *sels.* Thomas Lodge.
　Coridon's Song. UnTE
Rosalind's Madrigal. EnRePo; PoIE; UnTE
Rosaline. GTBS-P; UnTE
　(Rosalind.) PoIE
Rose, The. Robert Creeley. AP; ToPo
Rose, The. George Herbert. PoIE
Rose, The. "Gabriela Mistral," *tr. fr. Spanish by* Kate Flores. AnSP
Rose, The. Tasso, *tr. fr. Italian by* William Drummond of Hawthornden. RBL
Rose amid the Heather. Goethe, *tr. fr. German by* Lynda A. Marvin. AGP
Rose Aylmer. Walter Savage Landor. CABA; CBEP; ELP; FaPL; ILP; OBNC; RoGo
Rose-cheeked Laura [Come]. Thomas Campion. CaFP; EnRePo; PoIE
Rose Family, The. Robert Frost. BoLP
Rose for a young head, A. The Watcher. James Stephens. PoDB
Rose is a rose, The. The Rose Family. Robert Frost. BoLP
Rose kissed me today. The Kiss. Austin Dobson. LV
Rose of Britain's Isle, The. *Unknown.* BSNS
Rose of Fire. Antonio Machado, *tr. fr. Spanish by* Kate Flores. AnSP
Rose of Life, The. Luis de Góngora, *tr. fr. Spanish by* Sir Richard Fanshawe. RBL
Rose of Peace, The. W. B. Yeats. PoDB
Rose of Tralee, The. *Unknown.* BSNS
Rose-petals fall without a touch. Reflections on the River. Andrew Young. ACV
Rose Tree, The. W. B. Yeats. DiPo; ELP
Rose was sick and, smiling, died, The. The Funeral Rites of the Rose. Robert Herrick. CABA; PoSa
Rose, when I remember you. To Rose. Sara Teasdale. BiCB
Roseberry to his lady says. Suppertime. Burns. UnTE
Rosebush, Less Presumption. Francisco de Quevedo, *tr. fr. Spanish by* William M. Davis. AnSP
Rosemary and Thyme. *Unknown. See* Elfin Knight, The.
Rosemary Spray, The. Luis de Góngora, *tr. fr. Spanish by* Edward Churton. RBL
Roses. Pierre de Ronsard, *tr. fr. French by* Andrew Lang. RBL
Roses red and jonquils gold. One, Two, Buckle My Shoe. Ogden Nash. BiCB
Rose's Scent, The. *Unknown. See* All Night by the Rose.
Roses, their sharp spines being gone. Bridal Song. Fletcher *and* Shakespeare. *Fr.* The Two Noble Kinsmen. CBEP
Rotation. Julian Bond. NNP
Rouge Bouquet. Joyce Kilmer. PoPl
Rough Are the Roads. Garcilaso de la Vega, *tr. fr. Spanish by* Edwin Morgan. AnSP
Rough Day, The. Jonathan Williams. PoNC
Rough wind, that moanest loud. A Dirge. Shelley. CABA; DiPo; LV; WiR
Rough Winds Do Shake. Louis Simpson. ErPo
Round and around on the glockenspiel. The Birthday-Cake Glockenspiel. Elizabeth Henley. BiCB
Round and Round. Dorothy Brown Thompson. BiCB
Round Dance, & Canticle. Robert Kelly. CoPo
Round moon hangs like a yellow lantern in the trees. The Ancient Thought. Watson Kerr. TRV
Round Our Restlessness. Elizabeth Barrett Browning. TRV
Round the cape of a sudden came the sea. Parting at Morning. Robert Browning. CBEP; DiPo; FaBV; OBNC; WiR
Rounded world is fair to see, The. Nature. Emerson. ILP
Roundel: "Now welcom somer, with thy sonne softe." Chaucer. *See* Welcome, Summer.
Roundel, The: "Roundel is wrought as a ring or a starbright sphere, A." Swinburne. PoIE

Rousecastle. David Wright. MoBS

Route of evanescence, A. Emily Dickinson. AmLP; AP; CaFP; DiPo

Rover, The, *sel.* Aphra Behn.
  When Damon First Began to Love, *fr.* Pt. I, Act II, sc. i. UnTE

Rover, The. Sir Walter Scott. *Fr.* Rokeby, III. GTBS-P (Song: "Weary lot is thine, fair maid, A.") OBNC

Row after row with strict impunity. Ode to the Confederate Dead. Allen Tate. AnMoPo; AP; CABA; PoIE

Row of Stalls, A, *sel.* Raymond Knister.
  Nell. OBCV

Row, row, row your boat. *Unknown.* SD

Row us out from Desenzano, to your Sirmione row! "Frater Ave atque Vale." Tennyson. FoBA; GTBS-P

Rowdy, The, *with music.* John A. Stone. SGR

Rowers, The. Laura Benét. FiSC

Rows of cells are unroofed, The. The Old Prison. Judith Wright. PoAu-2

Royal feast was done, The; the King. The Fool's Prayer. Edward Rowland Sill. OnMSP; PoLF

Royal George, The. *Unknown.* BSNS

Royal Love Scene, The. Ernest Dowson, *ad. fr.* Voltaire. UnTE

Royal Palm. Hart Crane. AP; PoIE

Royal Way of the Holy Cross, The. Thomas à Kempis, *tr. fr. Latin.* BoC

Rozette, because a little while. Villanelle a Rozette. Philippe Desportes. RBL

Rubáiyát of Omar Khayyám of Naishápúr, The. Omar Khayyám, *tr. fr. Persian by* Edward Fitzgerald. FaPL; *much abr.;* ILP, *abr.;* PoIE, *abr.;* SiGo, *much abr. Sels.*
  "Ah Love! could you and I with Him conspire." PoPl
  "Ah, with the grape my fading life provide." GTBS-P
  "Book of verses underneath the bough, A." DiPo
  "Come, fill the cup, and in the fire of spring." FaBV; LV
  "Dreaming when dawn's left hand was in the sky." PoSa
  "For in and out, above, about, below." TRV
  "Myself when young did eagerly frequent." EaLo
  "Oh Thou, who man of baser earth didst make." EaLo
  "Some for the glories of this world; and some." PoPl
  "Wake! For the sun, who scatter'd into flight." OBNC
  "Why, all the saints and sages who discuss'd." TRV

Rudely blows the winter blast. Flora's Flower. *Unknown.* UnTE

Rudolph Is Tired of the City. Gwendolyn Brooks. RePo

Rugby Chapel [November, 1857]. Matthew Arnold. CBEP; VP

Rugged Pyrrhus, he whose sable arm, The. Shakespeare. *Fr.* Hamlet, II, ii. Par

Ruin, The. Charles Tomlinson. NePoEA-2

"Ruin seize thee, ruthless King." The Bard. Thomas Gray. EiCP; EnPe; GTBS-P; StP

Ruined Maid, The. Thomas Hardy. CABA; ErPo

Ruins of a Great House. Derek Walcott. ToPo

Ruins of Rome, *sel.* Joachim du Bellay, *tr. fr. French by* Yvor Winters.
  Rome, VII. RBL

Ruins of the City of Hay. Randolph Stow. PoAu-2

Rule. Francis Ponge, *tr. fr. French by* Donald Justice. CoFP

Rule, Britannia. James Thomson. *Fr.* Alfred, a Masque, II, v (*by* Thomson *and* David Mallet). EiCP; GTBS-P

Ruler of the Queen's Navee, The. W. S. Gilbert. *See* When I Was a Lad.

Rules and Lessons. Henry Vaughan. MeP
  "Observe God in His works: here fountains flow," *sel.* TRV

Rules for Daily Life. *Unknown. See* Begin the Day with God.

Rules for the Road. Edwin Markham. RePo

Rum Tum Tugger, The. T. S. Eliot. EvOK; FaBV

Rumoresque Senum Severiorum. Marcus Argentarius, *tr. fr. Greek by* Dudley Fitts. ErPo

Rumpled sheet, A/ of brown paper. The Term. William Carlos Williams. PoPo; RePo

Run, Kitty, Run! Jimmy Garthwaite. BBGG

Runaway, The. Robert Frost. GoJo; MP; RePo

Runes. Howard Nemerov. PoCh; ToPo

Runilda's Chant. George Darley. *Fr.* Ethelstan. HaSV

Runnable Stag, A. John Davidson. EvOK; SD; WiR

Runner. W. H. Auden. SD

Runner, The. Alexandra Grilikhes. SD

Runner, The. Walt Whitman. SD

Running the Batteries. Herman Melville. ThLM

Running to Paradise. W. B. Yeats. LOW

Rural Sports, *sel.* John Gay.
  Fly-fishing. SD

Rushing Panic in San Francisco. *Unknown.* SGR

Russia and America circle each other. A Woman Unconscious. Ted Hughes. StP

Rustic Childhood. William Barnes. OBNC

Rustic Festival, A. Luis de Góngora, *tr. fr. Spanish by* Edward Meryon Wilson. *Fr.* The Solitudes. RBL

Rustling of leaves under the feet in woods and under hedges, The. Pleasant Sounds. John Clare. CBEP

Rustling of the silk is discontinued, The. Liu Ch'e. Ezra Pound. AP

Ruth, *sel.* Bible, *O.T.*
  "And Ruth said, Intreat me not to leave," I: 16-18. PoPl
  (Entreat Me Not to Leave Thee, 16-17.) TRV

Ruth. Thomas Hood. OBNC

Ruth had been moved out of her job in an/ Hawaiian school. Honolulu and Back. John Logan. AmPC

Ruth; or, the Influences of Nature. Wordsworth. GTBS-P

Rwose in the Dark, The. William Barnes. CBEP

S

S. S. *Lusitania.* Matthew Arnold. CBEP

S.S.R., Lost at Sea—*The Times.* Ralph Gustafson. OBCV

Sabbat, The. Lin Carter. FiSC

Sabrina Fair. Milton. *Fr.* Comus. CBEP; ELP

Sacco Writes to His Son. Alun Lewis. DTC

Sachem voices cloven out of the hills, The. Miramichi Lightning. Alfred Goldsworthy Bailey. OBCV

Sacrament, The. John Donne. TRV

Sacrament of Sleep, The. John Oxenham. PoLF

Sacrament of the Altar, The. *Unknown.* MeEL

Sacramento Gals, *with music.* John A. Stone. SGR

Sacred ape, now, children, see, The. The Ape. Roland Young. PoPl

Sacred hesitation. Goethe. *Fr.* Lila. TwGP

Sacred Seasons, The, *sels.* Carl Bode. ToPo
  Eastertide.
  Feast of Saint Andrew the Apostle.

Sacrifice, *sel.* Emerson.
  "Though love repine, and reason chafe." TRV

Sad alms/ of old forgotten airs. For Hurdy-Gurdy. Sergio Corazzini. CoIP

Sad Hesper o'er the buried sun. In Memoriam A. H. H., CXXI. Tennyson. VP

Sad Lover, The. George Crabbe. *Fr.* Tales of the Hall: Delay Has Danger. OBNC

Sad Shepherd, The, *sels.* Ben Jonson.
  "Here she was wont to go, and here! and here!" ILP
  "Though I am young and cannot tell." ILP
  (Karolin's Song.) PoIE
  (Love and Death.) CBEP
  (Song: "Though I am young and cannot tell.") EnRePo; SeCP
  (Though I Am Young.) ELP

Sad Shepherd, The. W. B. Yeats. HaSV; PP

Sad soft scars, childbitten, The. A Thanks That Flesh Is Sad. John Ciardi. ToPo

Sad Story of a Little Boy That Cried, The. *Unknown.* BBGG

Sadness. Barbara Guest. AmPC

Safe despair it that raves. Emily Dickinson. AP

Safe in their alabaster chambers. Emily Dickinson. AP; CaFP; CBEP

Safely Home. *Unknown.* STF

"Sage and rabbi, stoop to help us from the ban of our sorrow." Rabbi Loew. Rainer Maria Rilke. TwGP

Sage Speaks, The. Nietzsche, *tr. fr. German by* Walter Kaufmann. TwGP

Said Aristotle unto Plato. Owen Wister. PoPl

Said Day to Night. Day and Night. Lady Anne Lindsay. ThGo

Said Hanrahan. P. J. Hartigan. PoAu-1

Said Judge Jessop, "The hyssop." Hyssop. Walter de la Mare. BoC

Said lady once to lover. The Three Bushes. W. B. Yeats. DTC

Said Old Gentleman Gay, "On Thanksgiving Day." A Good Thanksgiving. Annie Douglas Green Robinson. PoLF

Said Peter the Great to a Great Dane. Peterhof. Edmund Wilson. GoJo

Said, Pull her up a bit will you, Mac, I want to unload there. Reason. Josephine Miles. PoCh

Said Simple Sam: "Does Christmas come?" Simple Sam. Leroy F. Jackson. PoSC

Said the Innkeeper. Myles Connolly. TRV

Said the landlord to his lady. Bow Lamkin. *Unknown.* BFSS

Said the Lion to the Lioness—"When you are amber dust." Heart and Mind. Edith Sitwell. MP

Said the old deaf gardener. Lupin. Humbert Wolfe. ThGo

Said the Robin to the Sparrow:/ "I should really like to know." Overheard in an Orchard. Elizabeth Cheney. TRV

Said the sparrow to the robin,/ "I would surely like to know." Feathered Faith. *Unknown.* STF

Said the table to the chair. The Table and the Chair. Edward Lear. SoPo

Said the Whisky Flask. *Unknown.* STF

Said the Wind to the Moon, "I will blow you out." The Wind and the Moon. George Macdonald. GoJo; OnMSP

Sail, A. Mikhail Lermontov, *tr. fr. Russian by* Babette Deutsch. PoPl
"Sail, A! a sail! Oh, whence away." Heart's Content. *Unknown.* PoLF
Sail-bellyer, exciter of boys, come bang. Autumnal Equinox on Mediterranean Beach. Robert Penn Warren. VaPo
Sail forth—steer for the deep waters only. Walt Whitman. *Fr.* Passage to India. TRV
Sailboat, Your Secret. Robert Francis. SD
Sailing Homeward. Chan Fang-sheng, *tr. fr. Chinese by* Arthur Waley. SiGo
Sailing of the Pilgrims, The. *Unknown.* HaSV
Sailing of the *Sword,* The. William Morris. ILP
Sailing, Sailing. Gray Burr. CoPo
Sailing to Byzantium. W. B. Yeats. CABA; CaFP; CBEP; DiPo; FoBA; GTBS-P; ILP; MoRP; OnP; FoDB; PoIE; PoPo; PP; StP
Sailing upon the River. George Crabbe. *Fr.* The Borough. OBNC
Sailor. P. K. Page. ACV
Sailor and the Shepherdess, The. *Unknown.* BSNS
Sailor Boy, The. Tennyson. HaSV
Sailor Boy, The, *with music. Unknown.* BSO
    (Sailor Lad, The, *diff. vers.*) BSO
Sailor in his sailboat, homeward bound, The. Vacationer. Walker Gibson. SD
Sailor Lad, The. *Unknown. See* Sailor Boy, The.
Sailors come/ To the drum. Hornpipe. Edith Sitwell. *Fr.* Façade. GTBS-P
Sailor's Consolation, The. William Pitt. HaSV
Sailor's Mother, The, *sel.* Wordsworth.
    "And thus continuing, she said." Par
Sailors on Leave. Owen Dodson. AmNP
Sailors there are of gentlest breed. Commemorative of a Naval Victory. Herman Melville. AP
Sailor's trade is a dreary life, A. Sweet William (B *vers.*). *Unknown.* BSO
Sailor's trade is the dreariest life, The. Sweet William (C *vers.*). *Unknown.* BSO
Sailor's Tragedy, The. *Unknown.* BSNS
Sailor's Warning. Michael Fitzgerald Page. HaSV
Sailor's Wife, The. William Julius Mickle. GTBS-P; HaSV
Saint. Robert Graves. AnMoPo
St. Agnes' Eve. Tennyson. ILP
St. Agnes' Eve—Ah, bitter chill it was! The Eve of St. Agnes. Keats. CABA; CABL; CaFP; DiPo; FoBA; ILP; OBNC; PoIE; PoLF; StP
St. Alphonsus Rodriguez. Gerard Manley Hopkins. PoIE
Saint and the Poet, The. H. A. Sieber. PoNC
Saint Antony. R. S. Thomas. ToPo
St. Brigid. Denis A. McCarthy. SIV
Saint Francis. John Peale Bishop. EaLo
Saint Francis and Saint Benedight. *Unknown.* EaLo
St. Francis and the Cloud. Marie de L. Welch. MoRP
St. Francis' Prayer. St. Francis of Assisi. *See* Prayer of St. Francis of Assisi.
Saint George and the Dragon ("Saint George he slew the dragon"). Alfred Noyes. RePo
St. Govan. A. G. Prys-Jones. ACV
St. Isaac's Church, Petrograd. Claude McKay. AmNP
St. John, *sel.* Bible, *N.T.*
    "In the beginning was the Word, and the Word was with God, and the Word was God," I: 1-5. BoC
Saint John. Elizabeth J. Coatsworth. MoRP
Saint John the Baptist. William Drummond of Hawthornden. CBEP; EaLo
    (Saint John Baptist.) GTBS-P
St. Lawrence and the Saguenay, The, *sel.* Charles Sangster. Thousand Islands, The. OBCV
St. Luke, *sels.* Bible, *N.T.*
    "And he said, A certain man had two sons," XV: 11-24. BoC
    "And one of the malefactors which were hanged railed on him," XXIII: 39-43. BoC
    "And when he was twelve years old, they went up after the custom of the feast," II: 42-52. BoC
    Angels of Bethlehem, The, II: 8-16. BoC
    (Christmas Eve, II: 8-14.) BiCB
    (First Christmas, The, II: 8-16.) SoPo
St. Malachy. Thomas Merton. CoPo
St. Mark. Christopher Smart. *Fr.* Hymns and Spiritual Songs.
St. Martin and the Beggar. Thom Gunn. AnMoPo; MoBS
Saint Mary Magdalene, *sel.* Richard Crashaw.
    "And now where're he strayes." Par
Sainte Marye Virgine. A Cry to Mary. St. Godric. MeEL
St. Matthew, *sels.* Bible, *N.T.*
    "And seeing the multitudes, he went up," V: 1-10. PoPl
    "Ask, and it shall be given you; seek, and ye shall find," VII: 7-8. BoC
    Lord's Prayer, The, VI: 9-13. EaLo; PoLF; TRV
St. Matthias. Christopher Smart. *Fr.* Hymns and Spiritual Songs. EiCP
St. Patrick, *sel.* Phyllis Garlick.
    "Christ with me, Christ before me, Christ behind me." TRV

Saint Patrick, slave to Milcho of the herds. The Proclamation. Whittier. ThLM
Saint Patrick's Breastplate, *sel.* St. Patrick, *tr. fr. Old Irish.*
    "I bind unto myself today." TRV
Saint Patrick's day in 'sixty-five from New York we set sail. Newfoundland. *Unknown.* BSNS
Saint Paul, *sels.* F. W. H. Myers.
    "Christ! I am Christ's! and let the name suffice you." TRV
    St. Paul Speaks ("Oh could I tell, ye surely would believe it"). BoC
    Saints, The ("So tho' our Daystar from our sight be taken"). BoC
    "Whoso has felt the Spirit of the Highest." TRV
Saint Peter sat by the celestial gate. The Vision of Judgment. Byron. StP
St. Petersburg Paradox, The. O. B. Hardison, Jr. PoNC
Saint Stephen in San Francisco. Melvin Walker La Follette. CoPo
St. Swithin. Daniel Henderson. SIV
St. Teresa's Book-Mark. St. Theresa of Avila, *tr. fr. Spanish.* BoC, *tr. by* E. Allison Peers; SiGo, *tr. by* Longfellow
    (Bookmark, *tr. by* Longfellow.) CTC
    (God Suffices, *tr. by* Mildred E. Johnson.) RBL
    (Lines Written in Her Breviary, *tr. by* Longfellow.) EaLo; TRV
Saint Valentine's Day. Coventry Patmore. *Fr.* The Unknown Eros. OBNC
Saintly Socrates, why do you favor. Socrates and Alcibiades. Friedrich Hölderlin. AGP
Saints. George Garrett. EaLo
Saints have adored the lofty soul of you. Two Sonnets, 1. Charles Sorley. MMA
Saints, The (St. Paul). F. W. H. Myers. *Fr.* Saint Paul. BoC
Salaam Alaikum. *Unknown.* PoLF
Salad. Mortimer Collins. Par
Salad, A. Sydney Smith. LV
Salem. Robert Lowell. CABA; PoPo; ToPo
Salems of Oppression. Joseph Joel Keith. FiSC
Sallow waiter brings me six huge oysters, A. Storm on Fifth Avenue. Siegfried Sassoon. ILP
Sally Brown (A *and* B *vers.*). *Unknown.* BSNS
Sally Brown had a daughter Nellie. Sally Brown (A *vers.*). *Unknown.* BSNS
Sally, dearest Sally, when I go into town. Fragments of Irish Songs. *Unknown.* BSO
Sally in Our Alley. Henry Carey. CBEP; FaPL; GTBS-P
    "Of all the girls that are so smart," *sel.* PoSC
Sally Simpkin's Lament. Thomas Hood. HaSV
Salmon Drowns Eagle. Malcolm Lowry. OBCV
Salmon-fishing. Robinson Jeffers. SD
Saloon is gone up the creek, The. Hemmed-in Males. William Carlos Williams. PoSa
Salt Lake, The. Yvan Goll, *tr. fr. German by* Michael Hamburger. MGP
Salt sea, sweet sea. Bring Back. Anne Ridler. ACV
Salutation, The. Thomas Traherne. MeP; PoIE; SeCP
Salutation of the Dawn. *Unknown, tr. fr. Sanskrit.* PoLF
Salute the last and everlasting day. Ascension. John Donne. MeP
Salvation to all that will is nigh. Annunciation. John Donne. MeP
Sam. Walter de la Mare. FaBV; OnMSP; PoPo; WePo
Sam Bass, *with music. Unknown.* BFSS
Same, The ("Milton! thou shouldst be living at this hour"). Wordsworth. *See* London, 1802.
Same leaves over and over again, The. In Hardwood Groves. Robert Frost. AmLP
Sampan. *Unknown, tr. fr. Chinese.* WePo
Sampler, The. Rachel Field. BiCB
Sampler, The. Nancy Byrd Turner. BiCB
Samson Agonistes. Milton. ILP
    Sels.
    "All is best, though we oft doubt." BoC
    "This only hope relieves me, that the strife." TRV
Samuel, Samuel Palmer. In a Shoreham Garden. Laurence Lerner. NePoEA-2
Samuel Sewall. Anthony Hecht. MP; PoPl
San Francesco, at Night. Yves Bonnefoy, *tr. fr. French by* W. D. Snodgrass. CoFP
San Francisco Company, The. O! California. Isaac W. Baker. SGR
San Francisco Company, of which I've often told, The. Arrival of the San Francisco. Isaac W. Baker. SGR
Sancho Panza's Heritage ("Sancho Panza, peasant and hero"). Christoph Meckel, *tr. fr. German by* Christopher Middleton. MGP
Sandal and garment of yellow and lotus garlands upon his body of blue. *Fr.* Gita Govinda. Jayadeva. ErPo
Sandgate Girl's Lamentation, The. *Unknown.* ELP
Sands of Dee, The. Charles Kingsley. HaSV; SIV
Sands of Time, The. Robert E. Howard. FiSC
Sang Solomon to Sheba. Solomon to Sheba. W. B. Yeats. ELP
Sans Equity and sans Poise. Confucius, *tr. fr. Chinese by*

Ezra Pound. *Fr.* The Classic Anthology: Yung Wind. CTC
Santa Ana came storming, as a storm might come. The Defence of the Alamo. Joaquin Miller. OnMSP
Santa Claus. *Unknown.* SoPo
Santa Claus comes when you're good. Belsnickel. Arthur Guiterman. BBGG
Santa Fe Trail, The. Effortlessly Democratic Santa Fe Trail. Martha Baird. PoPl
Santa Maria Maggiore, Rome. Elizabeth Jennings. DaDu
Santorin. James Elroy Flecker. GoJo; HaSV
Santos: New Mexico. May Sarton. EaLo
Santy Anna. *Unknown.* BSNS
Saon of Acanthus. Callimachus, tr. fr. *Greek by* John Addington Symonds. TRV
Sap, The. Henry Vaughan. MeP
Sarah Byng Who Could Not Read and Was Tossed into a Thorny Hedge by a Bull. Hilaire Belloc. GoJo
Sarah Cynthia Sylvia Stout. Shelley Silverstein. BBGG
Sarajevo. Lawrence Durrell. GTBS-P
Saris go by me from the embassies, The. The Woman at the Washington Zoo. Randall Jarrell. AP; MP
Sarum Primer, sel. *Unknown.*
    God Be in My Head. BoC; EaLo; TRV
Satan. Michael Madhusudan Dutt. ACV
Satan's Metamorphosis. Milton. *Fr.* Paradise Lost. X. StP
Satan's Speech. Milton. *Fr.* Paradise Lost, I. DiPo
Satire III: "Kinde pitty chokes my spleene; brave scorn forbids." John Donne. *Fr.* Satires. CABL; MeP
    (Satire III: Religion.) CABA
    (Satyre III: On Religion.) SeCP
Satire 3: To Sir Francis Brian. Sir Thomas Wyatt. EnRePo
Satire against Mankind, A. Earl of Rochester. CABL
Satires, *sel.* John Donne.
    Satire III: "Kinde pitty chokes my spleene." CABL; MeP
    (Satire III: Religion.) CABA
    (Satyre III: On Religion.) SeCP
Satires, The, *sels.* Juvenal, tr. fr. *Latin.*
    Against Women, *fr.* VI, tr. by Dryden. UnTE
    "Hear what Claudius suffered: When his wife knew he was asleep," *fr.* VI, tr. by Hubert Creekmore. ErPo
    "We are led on," *fr.* X, tr. by L. R. Lind. PoPl
Satires of Circumstance, *sels.* Thomas Hardy.
    At Tea. VaPo
    At the Draper's. VaPo
    By Her Aunt's Grave. PoPo; VaPo
    In Church. DiPo; DTC; PoDB; VaPo; VP
    In the Study. PoPo
Satiric and Censorious Epistle, *sel.* Francisco de Quevedo, tr. fr. *Spanish by* Denise Levertov.
    "I'll not be silent, though you put your finger." AnSP
Satirical Elegy on the Death of a Late Famous General, A. Swift. CABA
    (Satyrical Elegy on the Death of a Late Famous General, A, 1722.) StP
Saturday Morning. Richard Howard. ErPo
Saturday; or, The Flights. John Gay. *Fr.* The Shepherd's Week. EiCP
Saturday Shopping. Katherine Edelman. SoPo
Saturn. Keats. *Fr.* Hyperion; a Fragment, I. OBNC
Satyr, The, *sel.* Ben Jonson.
    Mab. WiR
Satyre III: On Religion. John Donne. *See* Satire III: "Kinde pitty chokes my spleen."
Satyrical Elegy on the Death of a Late Famous General, A, 1722. Swift. *See* Satirical Elegy on the Death of a Late Famous General, A.
Saucer-valley open oven, A. Hiroshima. Murray Noss. PoPo
Saucy Sailor, The. *Unknown. See* Once I Had Plenty of Thyme.
Saul, *sels.* Robert Browning.
    David's Song. FaBV
    "He who did most, shall bear most; the strongest shall stand the most weak." TRV
    "Saul . . . sat out my singing,—one arm around the tent-prop to raise." BoC
Saul, *sels.* Charles Heavysege. OBCV
    Malzah's Song.
    Zaph Describes the Haunts of Malzah.
Saul . . . sat out my singing,—one arm around the tent-prop to raise. Robert Browning. *Fr.* Saul. BoC
Saved, but—. *Unknown.* STF
Saviour looked on Peter, The. Ay, no word. The Look. Elizabeth Barrett Browning. TRV
Saw a lad a rose one day. Rose amid the Heather. Goethe. AGP
Saw Ye Bonny Lesley? Burns. *See* Bonnie Lesley.
Saw You My True Love John? *with music. Unknown.* BFSS
Saw You the Ladies. Heinrich von Morungen, tr. fr. *German by* Gillian Barker *and* Kenneth Gee. AnML
Saxifrage, owl, milk. Honor to Celery. Hans Magnus Enzensberger. MGP
Say good-by er howdy-do. Good-by er Howdy-do. James Whitcomb Riley. CTC

Say he was sad, for there was none to love him. Epitaph. Robert Nathan. MoLP
Say Not. Arthur Hugh Clough. *See* Say Not, the Struggle Nought Availeth.
Say not of me that weakly I declined. Robert Louis Stevenson. OBNC
Say Not, the Struggle Nought Availeth. Arthur Hugh Clough. CABA; CBEP; EaLo; FaPL; GTBS-P; ILP; OBNC; PoIE; TRV
    (Say Not.) FaBV
Say-so is in a woe of shuddered leaves. Irritable Song. Russell Atkins. AmNP
Say That I Should Say. Nicholas Breton. PoIE
Say the snow drifted down. Santa Maria Maggiore, Rome. Elizabeth Jennings. DaDu
Say this city has ten million souls. Refugee Blues. W. H. Auden. WePo
Say This of Horses. Minnie Hite Moody. PoLF
Say what you will in two. Air: Sentir avec ardeur. Marie-Françoise-Catherine de Beauveau, Marquise de Boufflers. CTC
Say, wilt thou more of scenes so sordid know. A Slum Dwelling. George Crabbe. *Fr.* The Borough. OBNC
Say, "You are lovely!" Second Night, or What You Will. Rolfe Humphries. MoLP
Sayings. Goethe, tr. fr. *German by* Heinz Norden *and* Alexander Gode. AGP
Says the old man to the oak-tree. The Oak Tree. *Unknown.* CBEP
Says Tweed to Till. Two Rivers. *Unknown.* BuBa; CBEP
Scarlet poppy smouldering in the fields, The. Narcissus. John Press. UnTE
Scarlet Tanager, The. Joel Benton. AmLP
Scarlet Woman, The. "Hugh MacDiarmid." ACV
Scarred. *Unknown.* STF
Scarred Girl, The. James Dickey. ToPo
Scars Remaining, The. Samuel Taylor Coleridge. *Fr.* Christabel. OBNC
Scent, A, of beeswax, dust; the empty rooms. Meeting Myself. Edward Lucie-Smith. NePoEA-2
Scented Herbage of My Breast. Walt Whitman. AP
Sceptical of the cult, suspicious of the nation. From a Foreign Land. Roy Fuller. OPP
Scholar, The. Robert Southey. GTBS-P
Scholar and Goethe, The. Christian Morgenstern, tr. fr. *German by* Walter Kaufmann. TwGP
Scholar Complains, The. *Unknown.* MeEL
Scholar-Gipsy, The. Matthew Arnold. CABA; ILP; OBNC; VP
    "And near me on the grass lies Glanvil's book," *sel.* ACV
Scholars, The. W. B. Yeats. CaFP; FoBA
School Days. Thad Stem, Jr. PoNC
School for Scandal, The, *sel.* Sheridan.
    Here's to the Maiden, *fr.* III, iii. ELP
School for Tenors, The. Günter Grass, tr. fr. *German by* Michael Hamburger. MGP
School Is Out. Frances Frost. RePo
School is over. It is too hot. The Lonely Street. William Carlos Williams. MP
Schoolboy, The. Blake. *Fr.* Songs of Experience. CBEP
Schoolboys in Winter. John Clare. CBEP
Schoolgirl on Speech-Day in the Open Air. Iain Crichton Smith. NePoEA-2
Schoolmistress, The. William Shenstone. EnPE
Schools. George Crabbe. The Borough, Letter XXIV. CTC
School's Out. W. H. Davies. BoC
Science Fiction. Kingsley Amis. NePoEA-2
Science for the Young. Wallace Irwin. BBGG
Science of the Night, The. Stanley Kunitz. MP; UnTE
Science! true daughter of Old Time thou art! Sonnet: To Science [or To Science]. Poe. Al Aaraaf: Prologue. AP; CBEP; ILP
Scillaes Metamorphosis, *sel.* Thomas Lodge.
    Earth Late Choked with Showers, The. PoSa
Scintilla. William Stanley Braithwaite. AmNP
Scissors and Paste. Zoe Kincaid Brockman. *Fr.* Three Cinquains. PoNC
Scissors Grinder, The. Raymond Roseliep. FiSC
Scolding Wife, The, *with music. Unknown.* BSO
Scorn Not the Sonnet. Wordsworth. DiPo; PP
Scot in the Desert. Laurie Lee ToPo
"Scotch over ice?" the Wolf said to the Tiger. Wolf and Tiger Dining, A. B. Joseph Joel Keith. FiSC
Scotch Rhapsody. Edith Sitwell. MP
Scots Wha Hae. Burns. CABA; EnPE
Scottish Merchant's Daughter, The, *with music. Unknown.* BFSS
Scourge of Villainy, The, *sel.* John Marston.
    To Everlasting Oblivion. CBEP
Scratch, The. James Dickey. AP
Scribe, The. Walter de la Mare. MoRP
Scrutinie, The. Richard Lovelace. SeCP
    (Why Should You Swear?) ELP
Sculptor, wouldst thou glad my soul. Design for a Bowl. Anacreon. UnTE

Sculpture. *Unknown.* PoLF
Sculptured souvenir of the rose wreath wake! Oakdale Angel. H. A. Sieber. PoNC
Scyros. Karl Shapiro. ILP
Scythe of Dreams, The. Joseph Payne Brennan. FiSC
Sea, The. "Barry Cornwall." LV
Sea, The. W. H. Davies. HaSV
Sea, The. Vincent Ferrini. *Fr.* Mirandum. PtTo
Sea, The. Herman Gorter, *tr. fr. Dutch by* A. J. Barnouw. SiGo
Sea, The. D. H. Lawrence. HaSV
Sea, The. James Reeves. HaSV
Sea, The. Francis Webb. PoAu-2
Sea and the Hills, The. Kipling. FaBV
Sea and the Mirror, The, *sel.* W. H. Auden.
Song of the Master and Boatswain. DTC; HaSV
Sea and the Skylark, The. Gerard Manley Hopkins. AnMoPo
Sea and the Tiger, The. Laurence Collinson. PoAu-2
Sea at evening moves across the sand, The. Soldiers Bathing. F. T. Prince. GTBS-P
Sea awoke at midnight from its sleep, The. The Sound of the Sea. Longfellow. AP; PoPo
Sea begins, far out beyond the light, The. Three Nights of Mourning: John F. Kennedy. H. L. Mountzoures. OPP
Sea Bird to the Wave, The. Padraic Colum. RePo
Sea-born queen, who deigns to smile, The. On the Ladies' Head-Dresses. James Greenwood. WaPe
Sea Calm. Langston Hughes. LOW
Sea Captain, The (A *and* B *vers., with music*). *Unknown.* BSNS
Sea-Change. John Masefield. HaSV
Sea cries with its meaningless voice, The. Pibroch. Ted Hughes. NePoEA-2; PoCh; PoDB
Sea Dirge, A. "Lewis Carroll." HaSV
Sea Dirge. Tom Scott. ACV; HaSV
Sea Dirge, A. Shakespeare. *See* Full Fathom Five.
Sea-Fever. John Masefield. FaBV; HaSV; PoLF; PoPl; PoPo; RePo
Sea Fret. Teresa Hooley. HaSV
Sea, great mercury mirror, The. Symphony in Gray Major. Rubén Darío. AnSP
Sea-Grief. Dowell O'Reilly. PoAu-1
Sea-Gull, The. Ogden Nash. PoPo
Seagulls. John Updike. StP
Sea-gulls whiten and dip, The. Amoris Exsul: In the Bay. Arthur Symons. OBNC
Sea Gypsy, The. Richard Hovey. RePo
Sea Hath Its Pearls, The. Heine, *tr. fr. German by* Longfellow. SiGo
Sea Holly. Conrad Aiken. AP
Sea is a hungry dog, The. The Sea. James Reeves. HaSV
Sea is a lonely thing, The. In Exile. Blanche Edith Baughan. ACV
Sea is calm to-night, The. Dover Beach. Matthew Arnold. BoLP; CABA; CaFP; CBEP; DiPo; DTC; EaLo; FaBV; FaPL; GTBS-P; ILP; HaSV; LV; OBNC; OnP; PoIE; PoPl; PoPo; PoSa; StP; TRV; VaPo; VP; WePo
Sea Is Enormous, The. Juan Ramón Jiménez, *tr. fr. Spanish by* James Wright. AnSP
Sea is flecked with bars of grey, The. Les Silhouettes. Oscar Wilde. HaSV
Sea is mighty, but a mightier sways, The. A Hymn of the Sea. Bryant. HaSV
Sea is never still, The. Young Sea. Carl Sandburg. RePo
Sea is strange, The. Waves. Mary Britton Miller. RePo
Sea is up, The. The Sea. Vincent Ferrini. *Fr.* Mirandum. PtTo
Sea laments, The. Echoes. Walter de la Mare. RePo
Sea-Limits, The. Dante Gabriel Rossetti. HaSV
(Chime of the Sea, The.) BoC
Sea Love. Charlotte Mew. BoLP; HaSV; LV
Sea Lullaby. Elinor Wylie. SIV
Sea of Death, The. Thomas Hood. OBNC
Sea Pieces. Robert Fitzgerald. PoPl
Sea Princess, The. Katharine Pyle. SoPo
Sea retains such images, The. Louis Dudek. *Fr.* Europe. OBCV
Sea-Ritual, The. George Darley. *Fr.* Syren Songs. OBNC; WiR
Sea rocks have a green moss, The. Home Thoughts. Carl Sandburg. MoLP
Sea Scape. *See* Seascape.
Seashell. Rubén Darío, *tr. fr. Spanish by* Anita Volland. AnSP
Sea Shell. Amy Lowell. RePo
Sea sucks in the traveller, The. The Sea and the Tiger. Laurence Collinson. PoAu-2
Sea Surface Full of Clouds. Wallace Stevens. AP
Sea, The! the sea! the open sea! The Sea. "Barry Cornwall." LV
Sea was born of the earth without sweet union of love, The. Maximus, from Dogtown, I. Charles Olson. CoPo
Seafarer, The. *Unknown, tr. fr. Anglo-Saxon by* Ezra Pound. AP; CTC; OnP; StP; HaSV, *tr. by* L. Iddings

Seal Rocks: San Francisco. Robert Conquest. PP
Seals and porpoises present. Off Spectacle Island. Richard Eberhart. ToPo
Seals in Penobscot Bay, The. Daniel Hoffman. MP
Seaman, The. *Unknown.* HaSV
Seamen Three. Thomas Love Peacock. *Fr.* Nighmare Abbey. WiR
Search, The. George Herbert. MeP
Search, The. St. John of the Cross. *See* Spiritual Canticle.
Search, The. James Russell Lowell. TRV
Search. Anne Marriott. TRV
Search. Raymond Souster. OBCV
Search, The. Henry Vaughan. MeP; SeCP
Searching the earth, with exile worn. I Said to the Leaf. Carleton Drewry. MoRP
Seas are quiet when the winds give o'er, The. Old Age. Edmund Waller. BoC
Seas were left behind, The. Taliessin's Return to Logres. Charles Williams. ACV
Seascape. W. H. Auden. GTBS-P
Seascape. Stephen Spender. AnMoPo
Sea Scape with Parable. Richard Eberhart. PoDB
Seaside Golf. John Betjeman. PoPl; SD
Season, The? Not yet Spring. The Place? Beside. Rabbit Cry. Edward Lucie-Smith. NePoEA-2
Season of mists and mellow fruitfulness. To Autumn [*or* Ode to Autumn]. Keats. BoC; CABA; CaFP; CBEP; DiPo; FaBV; FoBA; GTBS-P; ILP; OBNC; OnP; PoIE; PoLF; PoPo; PoSa; RoGo; StP; VaPo; WePo
Seasons, The. Mother Goose. SoPo
Seasons, The, *sels.* James Thomson.
Hymn on the Seasons, A. EiCP
Spring. EiCP
Summer. StP
Winter. CABL
Season's anguish, crashing whirlwind, ice. Winter Garden. David Gascoyne. GTBS-P
Season's Here, The! Neidhart von Reuental, *tr. fr. German by* Margaret F. Richey. AnML
Seasons in North Cornwall, The. Charles Causley. ACV
Season's Lovers, The. Miriam Waddington. OBCV
Seasons of the Soul. Allen Tate. AP
Seated statue of himself he seems, A. Farm Boy after Summer. Robert Francis. PoIE; PoSa
Seaweed. Longfellow. AP
Sebastian. Gene Baro. PoDB
Sebastian in Dream. Georg Trakl, *tr. fr. German by* Michael Hamburger. MGP
Seclusion. Eduard Mörike, *tr. fr. German by* D. G. Wright. AGP
Second Air Force. Randall Jarrell. AP
Second Anniversarie, The: Of the Progres of the Soule. John Donne. *See* Of the Progresse of the Soule: The Second Anniversary.
Second Anniversary. Federico García Lorca, *tr. fr. Spanish by* Rachel Benson *and* Robert O'Brien. AnSP
Second Birthday, A. Albert Kayper-Mensah. ACV
Second Brother, The, *sel.* Thomas Lovell Beddoes.
Song: "Strew not earth with empty stars." CBEP
Second Coming, The. W. B. Yeats. CABA; DiPo; EaLo; FoBA; GTBS-P; ILP; MoRP; OnP; PoDB; PoIE; PoPo; StP
Second Corinthians, *sel.* Bible, *N.T.*
God Was in Christ, V: 18-21. TRV
2nd Dance—Seeing Lines—6 February 1964. Jackson MacLow. CoPo
Second Epitaph, A. *Unknown.* MeEL
Second Half. David McCord. SD
Second Night, or What You Will. Rolfe Humphries. MoLP
Second Rapture, The. Thomas Carew. UnTE
Second Sight. W. S. Merwin. StP
Second Sight. H. S. Neill. FiSC
Second Vision, The. Robert Herrick. UnTE
(Vision, The.) CBEP
Secresie Protested. Thomas Carew. *See* Fear Not, Dear Love.
Secret, The. Ralph Spaulding Cushman. STF; TRV
Secret, The. *Unknown.* SoPo
Secret Cavern, The. Margaret Widdemer. RePo
Secret Heart, The. Robert P. Tristram Coffin. PoSC
Secret Land, The. Robert Graves. BoC
Secret Laughter. Christopher Morley. FaBV
Secret Love. John Clare. CBEP; FaPL; OBNC
(I Hid My Love When Young.) WePo
Secret Love, *sel.* Dryden.
I Feed a Flame Within. PoIE
Secret Love or Two I Must Confess, A. Thomas Campion. ErPo
Secret Muse, The. Roy Campbell. BoC
Secret of Song. Christine White. STF
Secret Parting. Dante Gabriel Rossetti. The House of Life, XLV. VP
Secret Place, The. A. A. Pollard. STF
Secret Place of Prayer, The. Georgia B. Adams. STF
Secret Prayer. John Cross Belle. STF

Secret Sits, The. Robert Frost. LOW; SoPo
Secret Thoughts. Christopher Morley. *Fr.* Translations from the Chinese. EvOK
Secretary. Ted Hughes. ErPo; ToPo
Secrets. Elsie Melchert Fowler. BiCB
Secrets of Cisterns, The. Stanley McNail. FiSC
Secular Elegies. George Barker. ToPo
"O Golden Fleece she is where she lies tonight," V. ErPo
Secular Masque, The. Dryden. DiPo
Sels.
  All, All of a Piece Throughout. CBEP; ELP
  Song of Momus to Mars, The. CBEP
Security. Michael Hamburger. PoCh
Security. Lina Sandell. STF
Seduced Girl. Hedylos, *tr. fr. Greek by* Louis Untermeyer. ErPo
  (To Venus.) UnTE
Seduction of Engadu. *Unknown, tr. fr. Babylonian tablets by* William Ellery Leonard. *Fr.* Gilgamesh. ErPo
See/ Me. A Pair of Wings. Stephen Hawes. MeEL
See, as the prettiest graves will do in time. Fame. Robert Browning. PP
See! Here, My Heart. *Unknown.* MeEL
See, His blood He's shedding. Vertiendo Está Sangre. St. Theresa of Avila. RBL
See how it flashes. In a Wine Cellar. Victor J. Daley. PoAu-1
See how the orient dew. On a Drop of Dew. Andrew Marvell. ILP; MeP; SeCP
See how this trim girl. Artemis. Peter Davison. ErPo
See, in the garden there, it hops and lurches about. On a Child with a Wooden Leg. Bertram Warr. OBCV
See me with all the terrors on my roads. The Face. Edwin Muir. GTBS-P
See on those six high wires how her fingers. Girl with Guitar. O. B. Hardison, Jr. PoNC
See! see! she comes; with graceful ease she treads. On Her Entering Her Room. Richardson Pack. WaPE
See, Sir, here's the grand approach. On Blenheim House. Abel Evans. CBEP
See That One? Robert Bagg. ErPo
See the chariot at hand here of love. The Triumph of Charis [*or* Her Triumph]. Ben Jonson. *Fr.* A Celebration of Charis. CABA; CaFP; CBEP; CTC; ELP; OnP; SeCP
See the far hills white with snow. Winter. Jean Jaszi. SoPo
See the lovely morning rise. An Hymn to the Morning. Mary Leapor. WaPE
See the motley mass of humans. Fads and Fancies. Edith Earnshaw. PoNC
See the pretty snowflakes. Falling Snow. *Unknown.* SoPo
See the scrimmage and the scrabble. Greatest Show on Earth. Felicia Lamport. LV
See the stars, love. In a Boat. D. H. Lawrence. BoLP
See There the Star. Gottfried Keller, *tr. fr. German by* Alexander Gode. AGP
See, they are clearing the sawdust course. The Girl on the Milk-white Horse. Rachel Field. *Fr.* A Circus Garland. SoPo
See, they return; ah, see the tentative. The Return. Ezra Pound. AP
See those cherries how they cover. Our Cherries. *Unknown.* BSO
See What a Lovely Shell. Tennyson. GoJo
See, whilst thou weep'st fair Cloe, see. To Cloe Weeping. Matthew Prior. EiCP
See! Winter comes, to rule the varied Year. Winter. James Thomson. *Fr.* The Seasons. CABL
See with what simplicity. The Picture of Little T. C. in a Prospect of Flowers. Andrew Marvell. CBEP; MeP; SeCP
See you the ferny ride that steals. Puck's Song. Kipling. *Fr.* Puck of Pook's Hill. FaBV
Seed Growing Secretly, The. Henry Vaughan. MeP
Seed the sower is sowing, The. Matthias Claudius, *tr. fr. German by* Dorothea M. Singer. AGP
Seed-Time. George Meredith. VP
Seeds. Walter de la Mare. RePo
Seeds. Thurmond Snyder. NNP
Seeds. Muriel Stuart. BoC
Seeds I sowed, The. Seeds. Walter de la Mare. RePo
Seeds in a dry pod, tick, tick, tick. Petit, the Poet. Edgar Lee Masters. *Fr.* Spoon River Anthology. ILP; PoSa
Seeds of Love, The. *Unknown. See* I Sowed the Seeds of Love.
Seein' Things. Eugene Field. LV
Seeing at last how each thing here beneath. No Question. George Dillon. AmLP
Seeing the Elephant, *with music.* David G. Robinson. SGR
Seeing thou art fair, I bar not thy false playing. Advice to a Fair Wanton. Ovid. *Fr. Amores.* UnTE
Seeke not to know my love, for shee. Song: To One That Desired to Know My Mistris. Thomas Carew. SeCP
Seeming as though. Late Show. Issa. RePo
Seemingly more/ Whistle than boy. Whistling Boy. John Robert Quinn. BiCB

Seems like We Must Be Somewhere Else. Denise Levertov. NePoEA-2
Seen from the Train. C. Day Lewis. BoC
Seer, The. Lewis Turco. FiSC
Seers have no monopoly. Communal. Mary Fullerton. PoAu-1
See-Saw, Margery Daw. Mother Goose. SoPo
Seguidillas of the Guadalquivir River. Lope de Vega, *tr. fr. Spanish by* Denise Levertov. AnSP
Self-Dependence. Matthew Arnold. PoIE
Self-Portrait. Robert Pack. CoPo
Self-Sacrifice. Harry Graham. BBGG
Selfsame toothless voice for death or bridal, The. Bell Speech. Richard Wilbur. AP; CABA
Self-unseeing, The. Thomas Hardy. OBNC; VP
Semblables, The. William Carlos Williams. AP
Semi-Private. Mabel MacDonald Carver. FiSC
Semi-Revolution, A. Robert Frost. FoBA
Send Me. Christina Rossetti. TRV
Send soldiers again to kill you, Garcia. Lines to Garcia Lorca. LeRoi Jones. NNP
Seneca. Thomas Merton. CoPo
Senex. John Betjeman. DTC
Senlin, a Biography, *sel.* Conrad Aiken.
  "It is evening, Senlin says, and in the evening." LOW
Sense of the Sleight-of-Hand Man, The. Wallace Stevens. AP; CABA; MP
Sensible Miner, the, *with music.* John A. Stone. SGR
"Sensual will have its moment, The? The brain." Elder Tree. Conrad Aiken. AP
Sensualists, The. Theodore Roethke. ErPo
  (Sensualist, The.) UnTE
Sentencing goes blithely on its way, The. In a Poem. Robert Frost. PP
Sentimental Bloke, The, *sel.* C. J. Dennis.
  Play, The. PoAu-1
Sentry, The. Alun Lewis. DTC
Sentry, The. Wilfred Owen. MMA
Separate place between the thought and felt, A. The Corridor. Thom Gunn. ToPo
Separation. Matthew Arnold. Faded Leaves, III. VP
Separation, A. William Johnson Cory. OBNC
Separation. W. S. Merwin. AmPC
Separation, A. Stephen Spender. MoLP
Sephestia's Song to Her Child. Robert Greene. *Fr.* Menaphon. ELP; EnRePo; PoIE
  (Weep Not My Wanton.) CBEP
September. Gottfried Benn, *tr. fr. German by* Christopher Middleton. MGP
September. Folgore da San Geminiano, *tr. fr. Italian by* Dante Gabriel Rossetti. *Fr.* Sonnets of the Months. SD
September. Helen Hunt Jackson. GoJo; PoLF
September, 1815. Wordsworth. FoBA
September evenings such as these. Watching the Moon. David McCord. RePo
September 1, 1965. Paris Leary. CoPo
September 1, 1939. W. H. Auden. OnP
September in Australia. Henry Kendall. PoAu-1
September in the Park. W. D. Snodgrass. ToPo
September moon over the dark valley, The. Sandro Penna, *tr. fr. Italian by* Carlo L. Golino. CoIP
Sept. 1957. Edward Marshall. CoPo
September 1913. W. B. Yeats. GTBS-P; PoIE
September six o'clock. Sea Pieces. Robert Fitzgerald. PoP1
September twenty-second, Sir: today. After the Surprising Conversions. Robert Lowell. AP; CABA
September Winds. Helen Bevington. PoNC
Sepulcher, The. Annie Johnson Flint. STF
Sepulchre. George Herbert. MeP
Sequaire. Godeschalk, *tr. fr. Latin by* Ezra Pound. CTC
Sequelula to "The Dynasts," A. Max Beerbohm. Par
Sequence of Saint Eulalia, The. *Unknown, tr. fr. French by* Charles Maxwell Lancaster. AnML
Serenade, A: "Ah! County Guy, the hour is nigh." Sir Walter Scott. *Fr.* Quentin Durward. GTBS-P
Serenade: "Hark, once more the flute's complaining." Clemens Brentano, *tr. fr. German by* Anne Jennings. AGP
  (Serenade: "Harken how the flute complains," *tr. by* Herman Salinger.) SiGo
Serenade, A: "Look out upon the stars, my love." Edward Coote Pinkney. AmLP
Serenade of a Loyal Martyr. George Darley. OBNC
Serenade to a Cornish Fox. Charles Causley. HaSV
Serene I fold my hands and wait. Waiting. John Burroughs. FaPL; TRV
Serene, not as a prize for conflict won. On a Portrait of Mme. Rimsky-Korsakov. Kingsley Amis. NePoEA-2
Serene the silver fishes glide. At the Aquarium. Max Eastman. LV; PoPo
Serene Words. "Gabriela Mistral," *tr. fr. Spanish by* Muriel Kittel. AnSP
Serf, The. Roy Campbell. GTBS-P
Sergeant-Major Money. Robert Graves. MMA
Sergeant's Prayer, A. Hugh Brodie. LV
Series 5.8, A. John Wieners. CoPo

Serious and a Curious Night-Meditation, A. Thomas Traherne. SeCP

Serious over my cereals I broke one breakfast my fast. Breakfast with Gerard Manley Hopkins. Anthony Brode. Par

Serious Poem, A. Ernest Walsh. ErPo

Sermon, The. Richard Hughes. BoC

Sermon in the Hospital, The, sel. Harriet Eleanor Hamilton King.

"But yet one thought has often stayed by me." BoC

Serpent, The. René Char, tr. fr. French by Richard G. Stern. Four Fascinators, III. CoFP

Serpent, The. Joseph Langland. MP

Serpent and the Mouse, The. Unknown, tr. fr. Sanskrit by Arthur W. Ryder. Fr. The Panchatantra. SIV

Serpent is shut out from paradise, The. Stanzas to Edward Williams. Shelley. OBNC

Serpent of God, The. Cerise Farallon. UnTE

Serpent Waits, The. Joseph Payne Brennan. FiSC

Serpents exploded, open balconies. Morvin. John Fuller. NePoEA-2

Service. Washington Gladden. TRV

Service Is No Heritage. Unknown. CBEP

"Service Man, The." Kipling. Par

Service Supreme. Unknown. STF

Sestina. Sir Philip Sidney. Fr. Arcadia. StP

Sestina: Altaforte. Ezra Pound. CaFP; PoIE; StP

Sestina for Khasan Israelov. John Wain. Fr. Wildtrack. ToPo

Sestina of Youth and Age. Gelett Burgess. LV

Set of phrases learn't by rote, A. The Furniture of a Woman's Mind. Swift. CaFP; PoIE

Set Me Whereas the Sun [Doth Parch the Green]. Petrarch, tr. fr. Italian by the Earl of Surrey. Sonnets to Laura: To Laura in Life, CXIII. CBEP; ILP; RBL

Set where the upper streams of Simois flow. Palladium. Matthew Arnold. GTBS-P; OBNC; VP

Settler in the olden times went forth, A. Charles Harpur. Fr. The Creek of the Four Graves. PoAu-1

Settler's Lament, The. Unknown. PoAu-1

Settling Some Old Football Scores. Morris Bishop. SD

Seumas Beg. James Stephens. EvOK; RoGo

Seven Ages of Elf-Hood, The. Rachel Field. BiCB

Seven Ages of Man, The. Shakespeare. See All the World's a Stage.

Seven Brethren, The. Unknown. BSNS

Seven Fiddlers, The. Sebastian Evans. OnMSP

Seven Poems, sel. Matsuo Basho, tr. fr. Japanese by Curtis Hidden Page.

"Old battlefield, fresh with Spring flowers again." SiGo (Three Haiku.) PoPo

Seven Sleepers, The, with music. Unknown. BFSS

Seven South African Poems, sel. David Wright.

"Each time I return to Johannesburg it is summer." ACV

Seven Stanzas at Easter. John Updike. EaLo

Seven Times One. Jean Ingelow. Fr. Songs of Seven. BiCB; OBNC (Birthday Morning.) ThGo

Seven Times One Are Seven. Robert Hillyer. BiCB

Seven Times Three—Love. Jean Ingelow. Fr. Songs of Seven. PoLF

Seven Today. Ivy O. Eastwick. BiCB

Seven Wealthy Towns. Unknown. PP

Seven white peacocks against the castle wall, The. What the Orderly Dog Saw. Ford Madox Ford. CTC

17-18 April, 1961, sel. Joel Oppenheimer.

"Remember, America." PtTo

Seventh Hell, The: Of Smoke, Where Fire-Raisers Try in Vain to Escape from a Shower of Hot Sand Falling from a Cloud. Jerome Rothenberg. CoPo

Seventh Property, The. Sir Thomas More. Fr. The Twelve Properties or Conditions of a Lover. EnRePo

Severed Selves. Dante Gabriel Rossetti. The House of Life, XL. VP

Sext. W. H. Auden. Fr. Horae Canonicae. PoDB

Shab-i-da Ru-dy, with music. Unknown. BSO

Shades of Callimachus, Coan ghosts of Philetas. Ezra Pound. Fr. Homage to Sextus Propertius. AnMoPo; PP

Shades of night were falling fast, The. Excelsior. Longfellow. OnMSP

Shadow, The. Pierre Reverdy, tr. fr. French by Joseph de Roche. CoFP

Shadow Dance. Ivy O. Eastwick. SoPo

Shadow Fading, The. Choruses Descriptive of Dido's States of Mind. Giuseppe Ungaretti. Fr. The Promised Land. CoIP

Shadow gates are swinging, The. The Gates of the Year. John Mervin Hull. STF

Shadow, index of the sun. By Day and by Night. W. S. Merwin. AmPC

Shadow like a liquid lies. August Night. May Swenson. MoLP

Shadowed. Burnham Eaton. FiSC

Shadows, The. George Macdonald. TRV

Shadows are long on Soldiers Field. Second Half. David McCord. SD

Shadows for the Sun. Carl Yeargens. PtTo

Shadows grazing eastwards melt. Last Meeting. Gwen Harwood. PoAu-2

Shadows in the Air. Karl Krolow, tr. fr. German by Christopher Middleton. MGP

Shadows in the Water. Thomas Traherne. SeCP

Shadows of the ships, The. Sketch. Carl Sandburg. AP

Shady Old Camp, The, with music. John A. Stone. SGR

Shake Hands. A. E. Housman. More Poems, XXX. WePo

Shake Off Your Heavy Trance. Francis Beaumont. Fr. Masque of the Inner Temple and Gray's Inne. CBEP

Shakespeare. Matthew Arnold. CABA; CaFP; CBEP; PoIE; PoPo; VP

Shakespeare: The Fairies' Advocate. Thomas Hood. Fr. The Plea of the Midsummer Fairies. OBNC

Shakespearean Bear, The. Arthur Guiterman. EvOK

Shall a Frown. Unknown. EnRePo

Shall Earth No More Inspire Thee? Emily Brontë. ELP

Shall I Be Silent? George Herbert. TRV

Shall I begin with Ah, or Oh? An Ode: Secundum Artem. William Cowper. PP

Shall I Come, Sweet Love. Thomas Campion. EnRePo

Shall I compare thee to a summer's day? Sonnets, XVIII [or To His Love]. Shakespeare. CBEP; CTC; DiPo; FaBV; FoBA; GTBS-P; ILP; PoIE; PoLF; PoPl; PoPo; PoSa; StP; WePo

Shall I hopeless then pursue. Love Once, Love Ever. Girolamo Preti. RBL

Shall I Look. Unknown. EnRePo

Shall I love God for causing me to be? The Proof. Richard Wilbur. EaLo

Shall I love him. A Young Girl's Song. Paul Heyse. PoPl

Shall I sonnet-sing you about myself? House. Robert Browning. DiPo; PP

Shall I spend the days of my youth in pride. God's Call. Unknown. STF

Shall I strew on thee rose or rue or laurel. Ave atque Vale. Swinburne. OBNC; StP; VP

Shall I take thee, the Poet said. Emily Dickinson. DiPo

Shall I, Wasting in Despair. George Wither. Fr. Fair Virtue, the Mistress of Philarete, and also Fidelia. BoLP; PoIE (Manly Heart, The.) FaBV; GTBS-P

Shall one be sorrowful because of love. De Amore. Ernest Dowson. OBNC

Shall Reason rule where Reason hath no right. To His Love, That Sent Him a Ring Wherein Was Graved, "Let Reason Rule." George Turberville. EnRePo

Shall they bury me in the deep. My Grave. Thomas Osborne Davis. ACV

Shall you complain who feed the world? To Labor. Charlotte Perkins Stetson Gilman. PoLF

Shame He suffered left its brand, The. Scarred. Unknown. STF

Shameful Death. William Morris. GTBS-P; SIV

Shameful Impotence. Ovid, tr. fr. Latin by Christopher Marlowe. Fr. Amores. ErPo (Impotent Lover, The.) UnTE

Shanty. David Wright. DaDu

Shao and the South, sels. Confucius, tr. fr. Chinese by Ezra Pound. Fr. The Classic Anthology. CTC

"Chkk! chkk! hopper-grass."

"Three stars, five stars rise over the hill."

Shape like folded light, A: embodied air. Aishah-Schechinah. Robert Stephen Hawker. OBNC

Shape of Fear, The. Sydney King Russell. FiSC

Shapes and Signs. James Clarence Mangan. ACV

Sharing Eve's Apple. Keats. ErPo

Sharp is the night, but stars with frost alive. Winter Heavens. George Meredith. CABA

Sharp smoke drifts, A. Landscape with Figures. Theodore Enslin. CoPo

Shattered water made a misty din, The. Once by the Pacific. Robert Frost. AmLP; FoBA; ILP; PoDB; PoPo

She. Theodore Roethke. BoLP; ErPo

She. Richard Wilbur. CoPo; ToPo

She/ wore/ her flossiest smile. Movie Queen. James P. Vaughn. NNP

She always leaned to watch for us. Mother. Margaret Widdemer. STF

She, as a veil down to the slender waist. Milton. Fr. Paradise Lost, IV. ErPo

She bade me follow to her garden, where. Snap-Dragon. D. H. Lawrence. ErPo

She beat the happy pavement. Gratiana Dancing and Singing. Richard Lovelace. CBEP

She Being Brand. E. E. Cummings. ErPo; UnTE

She bore the goblet in her hand. The Two. Hugo von Hofmannsthal. TwGP

She brought him a bag of her own father's gold. Lady Isabel and the Elf Knight (A vers.). Unknown. BSO

She Came and Went. James Russell Lowell. FaPL

She came across the seas steerage class. My Grandmother's Funeral. Jascha Kessler. AmPC

She came in from the snowing air. Ice. Stephen Spender. GTBS-P

She Came Out of the Frost. Aleksandr Blok, *tr. fr. Russian by* Babette Deutsch. PoPl
She comes, and straight therewith her shining orbs do move. Astrophel and Stella, LXXVI. Sir Philip Sidney. CABA
She died in the upstairs bedroom. Death in Leamington. John Betjeman. ACV; PoPl
She does not know. No Images. Waring Cuney. AmNP
She dreamed death came to her one day in May. Prophecy. Walter Shedlofsky. FiSC
She Dwelt among the Untrodden Ways. Wordsworth. CABA; CBEP; DiPo; ELP; ILP; PoIE
(Lost Love, The.) GTBS-P; PoPo
(Lucy.) FaBV; OBNC
She entered, and passionately, the eyes half closed. Desire. Pierre Louÿs. *Fr.* The Songs of Bilitis. UnTE
She even thinks that up in heaven. *See* She thinks that even up in heaven.
She fears him, and will always ask. Eros Turannos. E. A. Robinson. AmLP; AP; ILP; PoIE
She gave me all that woman can. Monna Lisa. James Russell Lowell. AmLP
She-Goat and Slow-Worm. Christian Morgenstern, *tr. fr. German by* Christopher Middleton. MGP
She got her way by shedding tears. Child Wife. Joseph Joel Keith. FiSC
She had a beautiful, bitter face. Devil Doll. Lisa Grenelle. FiSC
She had corn flowers in her hair. Gypsy Jane. William Brighty Rands. SoPo
She had not held her secret long enough. The Visitation. Elizabeth Jennings. MoBS
She has dusted the ornaments, rubbed down the chairs. Humbert Wolfe. *Fr.* The Uncelestial City. BoC
She has finished and sealed the letter. Parting, without a Sequel. John Crowe Ransom. DTC
She has gone out, she is far from me, but I see her. Absence. Pierre Louÿs. *Fr.* The Songs of Bilitis. UnTE
She has gone,—she has left us in passion and pride. Brother Jonathan's Lament for Sister Caroline. Oliver Wendell Holmes. ThLM
She has not found herself a hard pillow. To Clarissa Scott Delany. Angelina W. Grimké. AmNP
She has put on a silver gown and gone. Mad Maid's Whim. Randolph Stow. ACV
She Has Wounded Me Right through My Heart. Heinrich von Morungen, *tr. fr. German by* Gillian Barker *and* Kenneth Gee. AnML
She in whose lipservice. The Goddess. Denise Levertov. AP; PoCh
She is all so slight. After Two Years. Richard Aldington. PoPl
She is as in a field a silken tent. The Silken Tent. Robert Frost. CABA; MP; OnP; PoDB; PoIE
She is dead; and all which die. The Dissolution. John Donne. ILP
She is devout and plump, but not happy. A Baroque Gravure. Thomas Merton. CoPo
She Is Far from the Land. Thomas Hood. DTC; WiR
She Is Far from the Land. Thomas Moore. FaPL; OBNC
She is gentle and also wise. That Ever I Saw. *Unknown.* CBEP
She Is Not Fair. Hartley Coleridge. FaBV
("She is not fair to outward view.") GTBS-P
She is not of the fireside. Revolution. Lesbia Harford. PoAu-1
She is not yet; but he whose ear. The Dominion of Australia. Brunton Stephens. PoAu-1
She is so young, and never never before. Sonnet. Edward Davison. ErPo
She issues radiant from her dressing-room. Modern Love, VII. George Meredith. VP
She Lay All Naked [in Her Bed]. *Unknown.* ErPo; UnTE
She Looked at Me and Her Eyelids Burned. Solomon Ibn Gabirol, *tr. fr. Hebrew by* William M. Davis. AnML
She looked over his shoulder. The Shield of Achilles. W. H. Auden. GTBS-P; OnP; PoDB
She looked up. Hibakusha. Eileen Egan. PtTo
She Loved Her Husband Dearly. *Unknown. See* Johnnie Sands.
She loves him; for her infinite soul is Love. True Woman: Her Love. Dante Gabriel Rossetti. The House of Life, LVII. VP
She made the skies with eyes like. Antiwarwoman. Curtis Zahn. PtTo
She means it for praise and her motive is pure. Ouch! Edith Earnshaw. PoNC
She met a lion face to face. A Cautionary Tale. Anne Wilkinson. OBCV
She might have chosen cities, but the man. Droving Man. Thea Astley. PoAu-2
She might have stolen from his arms. Solitary Confinement. X. J. Kennedy. NePoEA-2
She only knew the birth and death. At Dawn. Arthur Symons. OBNC
She packs the flower beds with leaves. For Fran. Philip Levine. PoCh

She rises clear to memory's eye. Red Jack. Mary Durack. PoAu-1
She rose to his requirement—dropt. Emily Dickinson. CABA; FoBA
She Said. Walter de la Mare. ELP
She said, "Now give me flesh to eat." Cherry. Gene Baro. ErPo
She sang beyond the genius of the sea. The Idea of Order at Key West. Wallace Stevens. AmLP; AP; ILP; PoIE; PP
She sat down below a thorn. Fine Flowers in the Valley. *Unknown.* CBEP
She Saw Me in Church. *Unknown.* MeEL
She seems to come by wing. 2nd Dance—Seeing Lines— 6 February 1964. Jackson MacLow. CoPo
She Sees Another Door Opening. Firman Houghton. Par
She smiled behind a lawny cloud. Fancy Dress. Dorothea Mackellar. PoAu-1
She speaks always in her own voice. The Portrait. Robert Graves. CABA
"She speaks with the accent of her wild seas." The Stranger. "Gabriela Mistral." AnSP
She spoke of things of long ago. Portrait. Sam Ragan. PoNC
She stands in the dead center like a star. The Mother. S. S. Gardons. NePoEA-2
She stay'd not for her robes, but straight arose. Christopher Marlowe. *Fr.* Hero and Leander. UnTE
She stood breast high amid the corn. Ruth. Thomas Hood. OBNC
She stood for love. First Man on Venus. Robert Watson. PoNC
She Stoops to Conquer, *sel.* Goldsmith.
Three Pigeons, The, *fr.* I, ii. ELP
She suns on grass, my dark, my gifted mistress. Nude. Harold Witt. ErPo
She talks without stopping. Query. Edith Earnshaw. PoNC
She Tells Her Love. Robert Graves. WePo
She That Denies Me [I Would Have]. Thomas Heywood. *Fr.* The Rape of Lucrece. ErPo; UnTE
She thinks that even up in heaven [*or* She even thinks that up in heaven]. For a Lady I Know [*or* A Lady I Know.] Countee Cullen. Four Epitaphs, 4. AmNP; TRV
She took the bone from her arm. The Empress. Diane Wakoski. CoPo
She took the dappled partridge flecked with blood. Sonnet. Tennyson. CABA
She turns the pillow, smoothes the rumpled bed. Rites for a Demagogue. Anthony Thwaite. NePoEA-2
She Used to Let Her Golden Hair Fly Free. Petrarch, *tr. fr. Italian by* Morris Bishop. Sonnets to Laura: To Laura in Life, LXIX. AnML
She Walked Unaware. Patrick MacDonogh. BoLP; ErPo
She walks a beach assaulted by the sea. Thanksgiving 1963. Philip Booth. OPP
She Walks in Beauty. Byron. CABA; CBEP; ELP; ILP; OBNC; PoIE; PoPo; RePo; RoGo; VaPo; WePo
(She Walks in Beauty, like the Night). GTBS-P; StP
She walks in beauty like a lake. The Bed. Robert Creeley. StP
She walks with stately grace. Lyric of Doubt. Donald Wandrei. FiSC
She was a city of patience; of proud name. Ypres. Laurence Binyon. MMA
She Was a Phantom of Delight. Wordsworth. CBEP; FaBV; FaPL; FoBA; GTBS-P; ILP; PoPl; StP
She Was All That You Loved. Halldór Laxness, *tr. fr. Icelandic by* Magnús A. Arnason. PoPl
She was beautiful that evening and so gay. An Escape. Abu Nuwas. ErPo
She was careerish in a gentle way. Domestic: Climax. Merrill Moore. ErPo
She Was Poor but She Was Honest. *Unknown.* ErPo
(It's the Same the Whole World Over.) UnTE
She was skilled in music and the dance. Alas! Poor Queen. Marion Angus. ACV
She was urgent to speak of the moon: she offered delight. An Old Woman Speaks of the Moon. Ruth Pitter. BoC
She Went to Stay. Robert Creeley. ToPo
She Wept, She Railed. Stanley Kunitz. ErPo
She Would if She Could, *sel.* Sir George Etherege.
To Little or No Purpose. UnTE
She wrote from England—that new friend I met. Two Little Houses. Edith Earnshaw. PoNC
She yields: my Lady in her noblest mood. Modern Love, XXXIX. George Meredith. VP
Sheaf-Tosser. Eric Rolls. PoAu-2
Shearer's Song, The. *Unknown.* PoAu-1
Shearer's Wife, The. Louis Esson. PoAu-1
Shearing Grass. Peter Redgrove. NePoEA-2
Sheaves, The. E. A. Robinson. AP; DiPo; FaBV; PoSA
Shed in blue-grey weatherboard with a high, A. Hillside. Alexander Craig. PoAu-2
Sheep. Hal Porter. PoAu-2
Sheep shit and fever gold. Sierra Kid. Philip Levine. AmPC

Sheer Joy. Ralph Spaulding Cushman. TRV
Sheets were frozen hard, and they cut the naked hand, The. Christmas at Sea. Robert Louis Stevenson. FaBV; HaSV
Sheffield Apprentice, The, *with music. Unknown.* BFSS
Shell, The. James Stephens. HaSV; LV
She'll Do It. Burns. *See* Muirland Meg.
Shellbrook. William Barnes. OBNC
Shelley. George Herwegh, *tr. fr. German by* Paul F. Guenther. AGP
Shelley's Skylark. Thomas Hardy. FaBV; VP
Shellpicker, The. Ronald Perry. NePoEA-2
Shells, The. Walter Savage Landor. HaSV
Sheltered garden in a sheltered land, A. Homer in a Garden. James Larkin Pearson. PoNC
Shepheardes Calender, The, *sel.* Spenser.
   October Eclogue. PP
Shepheards, The. Henry Vaughan. MeP
Shepheards boy, The (best knowen by that name). Colin Clout's Come Home Again. Spenser. CABL
Shepheards, that wont, on pipes of oaten reed. Astrophel. Spenser. StP
Shepherd, The. Blake. *Fr.* Songs of Innocence. CBEP
Shepherd, The. Mary Gilmore. ACV; PoAu-1
Shepherd, The. *Unknown.* UnTE
Shepherd, The. Wordsworth. *Fr.* The Prelude. OBNC
Shepherd and the Milkmaid, The. *Unknown.* UnTE
Shepherd and the Nymph, The. Walter Savage Landor. *Fr.* Gebir. OBNC
Shepherd-boy his grief is brooding o'er, A. Other Stanzas with a Divine Meaning Concerning Christ and the Soul [*or* Stanzas concerning Christ and the Soul]. St. John of the Cross. BoC; RBL
Shepherd Boy's Song, The. Bunyan. *Fr.* The Pilgrim's Progress. ThGo; TRV
   (He That Is Down.) CBEP
   (Shepherd Boy Sings in the Valley of Humiliation, The.) EaLo
   (Shepherd's Song, The.) BoC
   (Song of Low Degree, A.) STF
Shepherd Kept Sheep on a Hill So High, A. Thomas D'Urfey. ErPo
Shepherd of souls, Thy sheep behold! Three Hymns, 2. Charles Wesley. WaPE
Shepherd sat 'neath a tree one day, A. The Shepherd. *Unknown.* UnTE
Shepherd upon a Hill, The. *Unknown.* CBEP
Shepherd Who with Your Tender Calls. Lope de Vega, *tr. fr. Spanish by* Kate Flores. AnSP
Shepherd, Young and Mournful, Grieves Alone, A. St. John of the Cross, *tr. fr. Spanish by* James Edward Tobin. AnSP
Shepherdess. Norman Cameron. *Fr.* Three Love Poems. GTBS-P
Shepherdess Well Made, A. Dinis, King of Portugal, *tr. fr. Portuguese by* William M. Davis. AnML
Shepherds buried the sun in the bare forest. Rest and Silence. George Trakl. TwGP
Shepherd's Calendar, The, *sel.* John Clare.
   February. OBNC
Shepherd's Calendar, The. Spenser. *See* Shepheardes Calender, The.
Shepherd's Garland, The, *sel.* Michael Drayton.
   Dowsabel. UnTE
Shepherd's Hut, The. Andrew Young. DaDu; DTC
Shepherd's Hymn, The. Richard Crashaw. *Fr.* In the Holy Nativity of Our Lord God. BoC
Shepherds on the lawn, The. Milton. *Fr.* On the Morning of Christ's Nativity. BoC
Shepherds sing; and shall I silent be, The. Shall I Silent Be? George Herbert. TRV
Shepherd's Sirena, The, *sel.* Michael Drayton.
   Sirena. CBEP
Shepherd's Song, The. Bunyan. *See* Shepherd Boy's Song, The.
Shepherd's Week, The, *sels.* John Gay. EiCP
   Friday; or, The Dirge.
   Saturday; or, The Flights.
   Wednesday; or, The Dumps.
Sheridan's Ride. Thomas Buchanan Read. FaBV
Sherman Cyclone, The, *with music. Unknown.* BFSS
She's funny, she's funny. Un-Birthday Cake. Aileen Fisher. BiCB
She's learned to hold her gladness lightly. A Lesson in Detachment. Vassar Miller. NePoEA-2
Shh! The Professor Is Sleeping. John Morris. CABA
Shibboleth. Paul Celan, *tr. fr. German by* Michael Hamburger. MGP
Shield of Achilles, The. W. H. Auden. GTBS-P; OnP; PoDB
Shifting his position to relieve a cramped limb. Christ. Theodore Holmes. CoPo
Shilling life will give you all the facts, A. Who's Who. W. H. Auden. CABA; PoPo
Shiloh; a Requiem. Herman Melville. AP; CBEP; PoPo; StP; WiR
Shine Just Where You Are. *Unknown.* STF

Shine Out, Fair Sun. *Unknown.* ELP
Shine, Perishing Republic. Robinson Jeffers. AmLP; PoIE
   "And Boys, be in nothing so moderate as in love of man," *sel.* TRV
Shine, Republic. Robinson Jeffers. MoRP
Shine, the bolt, the glow, the bright flame of your eye, The. To Her for a Kiss. August Adolf von Haugwitz. AGP
Shiny. James Reeves. RePo
Ship, The. Oliver St. John Gogarty. HaSV
Ship, The. *Unknown.* PoLF
Ship a-Raging, The, *with music. Unknown.* BFSS
Ship, an Isle, a Sickle Moon, A. James Elroy Flecker. HaSV
Ship-building Emperors Commanded. Peter Levi. NePoEA-2
Ship Burning and a Comet All in One Day, A. Richard Eberhart. ToPo
Ship from Thames. Rex Ingamells. PoAu-2
Ship from Valparaiso came, A. The Ship. Oliver St. John Gogarty. HaSV
Ship I have got in the north country, A. The *Golden Vanity. Unknown.* HaSV
Ship is floating in the harbour now, A. Shelley. *Fr.* Epipsychidion. HaSV
Ship of Death, The. D. H. Lawrence. DTC; GTBS-P
Ship of my body has danced in the dance of the storm, The. The Voyage. Karl Shapiro. MoLP
Ship Rock. Jones Very. PoIE
Ship with shields before the sun, A. Near Avalon. William Morris. CBEP
Shipman, The. Chaucer. *Fr.* The Canterbury Tales: Prologue. HaSV
Ships, *sel.* John Masefield.
   "I cannot tell their wonder nor make known." HaSV
Ships. Nancy Byrd Turner. SoPo
Ship's Bell. Glen Ward Dresbach. BoC
Ships of Yule, The. Bliss Carman. BiCB; RePo
Shipwreck, The, *sel.* William Falconer.
   "As the proud horse, with costly trappings gay." HaSV
Shock, The. Larry Eigner. CoPo
Shock-headed Peter! There he stands. Slovenly Peter. Heinrich Hoffman. BBGG
Shock's face I mourn; poor Shock is now no more. An Elegy on a Lap Dog. John Gay. DiPo
Shoemaker, The. *Unknown.* SoPo
Shoemaker makes shoes without leather, A. Riddle. *Unknown.* SoPo
Shoes. Tom Robinson. SoPo
Shoes are at the bottom, The. Open Wardrobe. Günter Grass. MGP
Shoo-li shoo-li shoo-li-rule. Putman's Hill (B *vers.*). *Unknown.* BSO
Shooter's Hill, *sel.* Robert Bloomfield.
   "Health! I seek thee;—dost thou love." OBNC
Shooting, The. Robert Pack. CoPo
Shooting of Dan McGrew, The. Robert W. Service. PoLF
Shop Windows. Rose Fyleman. SoPo
Shoplifter. Solomon Edwards. NNP
Short Is My Rest. *Unknown.* EnRePo
Short Measures. *See* It Is Not Growing like a Tree.
Short Prayer to Mary, A. *Unknown.* MeEL
Short Song of Congratulation, A. Samuel Johnson. CABA; EiCP; ELP; StP
Shot at Night, A. Idella Purnell. SIV
Shot in the Park, A. William Plomer. MP
Shot rings out upon the dreaming night, A. A Shot at Night. Idella Purnell. SIV
Shot, the horse, The. Kennedy Poem. Neil Myers. OPP
Should auld acquaintance be forgot. Auld Lang Syne. Burns. EiCP; EnPE; PoLF
Should I get married? Should I be good? Marriage. Gregory Corso. CABA
Should no man write, say you, but such as do excel? That No Man Should Write but Such as Do Excel. George Turberville. EnRePo
Should the cold Muscovit, whose furre and stove. To the Right Honourable the Countesse of C. William Habington. SeCP
Should the stroller absentmindedly kick. Jean Follain. *Fr.* Comings and Goings. CoFP
Should the wide world roll away. The Black Riders, X. Stephen Crane. AP
Should Thy Love Die. George Meredith. ELP
Should You Go First. A. K. Rowswell. PoLF
Show is not the show, The. Emily Dickinson. DiPo
Show me again the time. Lines to a Movement in Mozart's E-flat Symphony. Thomas Hardy. BoLP; ELP
Show me, dear [*or* deare] Christ, thy spouse so bright and clear. Holy Sonnets, XVIII. John Donne. ILP; MeP
Show Me Thy Feet. Robert Herrick. UnTE
Showman comes with his box of dolls, The. The Puppet Play. Padraic Colum. RoGo
Showre, The. Henry Vaughan. MeP; SeCP
Shrewd Maiden, The, *with music. Unknown.* BSO
Shrimp, The. Moses Browne. WaPE
Shrine to What Should Be. Mari Evans. NNP

Shropshire Lad, A. John Betjeman. MoBS
Shropshire Lad, A. A. E. Housman. *Poems indexed separately by titles and first lines.*
Shrubbery, The. William Cowper. CBEP; PoIE; StP
Shub-Ad. Robert H. Barlow. FiSC
Shui Shu, *sel. Tr. fr. Japanese by* Arthur Waley.
"If it were not for the voice." Nakatsukasa. SiGo
Shut not so soon; the dull-ey'd night. To Daisies, Not to Shut So Soon. Robert Herrick. ELP
Shut [*or* P. Shut], the door, good John! fatigued, I said. Epistle to Dr. Arbuthnot. Pope. CABA; CABL; PoIE
Shuttles of trains going north, going south, drawing threads of blue. Morning Sun. Louis MacNeice. MP
Shy Geordie. Helen B. Cruickshank. ACV
Shy one, shy one. To an Isle in the Water. W. B. Yeats. ThGo
Shyly the silver-hatted mushrooms make. May. John Shaw Neilson. PoAu-1
Siasconset Song. Philip Booth. CaFP; StP
Siberia. James Clarence Mangan. RoGo
Sibrandus Schafnaburgensis. Robert Browning. Garden Fancies, II. CTC
Sic Vita. Henry King. DiPo; ELP; SeCP
(Like to the Falling of a Star.) PoPo
Sicilian's Tale, The. Longfellow. *Fr.* Tales of a Wayside Inn. AP
Sick Child, A. Randall Jarrell. PoNC
Sick Child, The. Robert Louis Stevenson. PoSC
Sick Love. Robert Graves. GTBS-P
Sick Rose, The. Blake. *Fr.* Songs of Experience. CABA; CaFP; CBEP; DiPo; FoBA; ILP; OBNC; PoIE; PoSa; StP
(O Rose, Thou Art Sick!) ELP
Sick Stockrider, The. Adam Lindsay Gordon. ACV; PoAu-1
Sickle Pears. Owen Dodson. AmNP
Sickness, The. Frederick Seidel. CoPo
Sickness of Adam, The. Karl Shapiro. *Fr.* Adam and Eve. AP
Side by side, their faces blurred. An Arundel Tomb. Philip Larkin. NePoEA-2
Siege, The. Sir John Suckling. SeCP
Siege of Rhodes, The, *sel.* Sir William Davenant.
Jealousy. BoLP
Siege of Silence, A. Brother Antoninus. ToPo
Sierra Kid. Philip Levine. AmPC
Siesta. Antonio Machado, *tr. fr. Spanish by* Kate Flores. AnSP
Siesta, The. *Unknown, tr. fr. Spanish by* Bryant. SiGo
Sigh heart, and break not; rest, lark, and wake not. Nuptial Song. Lord De Tabley. GTBS-P
Sigh No More [Ladies]. Shakespeare. *Fr.* Much Ado about Nothing, II, iii. BoLP; CBEP; CTC; DiPo; ELP
Sighing, her sad heart fraught with fears. Christo Smarrito. Giambattista Marino. RBL
Sighs Are Air, and Go to the Air. Gustavo Adolfo Bécquer, *tr. fr. Spanish by* Kate Flores. AnSP
Sight in Camp [in the Daybreak Gray and Dim], A. Walt Whitman. AP; ILP; PoPo; PoSa; TRV
Sight Unseen. Kingsley Amis. ErPo; NePoEA-2
Sightings I. Jerome Rothenberg. CoPo
Signal Fire, The. Aeschylus, *tr. fr. Greek by* Dallam Simpson. *Fr.* Agamemnon. CTC
Signature. Dorothy Livesay. OBCV
Signpost. Robinson Jeffers. PoPo
Sign-Post, The. Edward Thomas. PoIE
Signs. William Soutar. ACV
Signs of Winter. John Clare. PoSC; WiR
Silence. Samuel Miller Hageman. TRV
Silence. Thomas Hood. CBEP; ILP
(Sonnet: Silence.) OBNC
Silence. Marianne Moore. PoIE; PoPo; PoSa
Silence. Charles Hanson Towne. TRV
Silence. Anna Wickham. BoLP
Silence and solitude may hint. An Uninscribed Monument on One of the Battlefields of the Wilderness. Herman Melville. AmLP
Silence, and stealth of dayes! 'tis now. Henry Vaughan. MeP
Silence augmenteth grief, writing increaseth rage. Elegy on the Death of Sidney. Sir Edward Dyer. EnRePo
Silence, in truth, would speak my sorrow best. Tears at the Grave of Sir Albertus Morton. Sir Henry Wotton. SeCP
Silence that I break was more profound, The. Poems for One Person. Terence Tiller. AnMoPo
Silence. The man defined. The Hand at Callow Hill Farm. Charles Tomlinson. NePoEA-2
Silences. Arthur O'Shaughnessy. OBNC
Silences. E. J. Pratt. OBCV; PoCh
Silent Generation, The. Louis Simpson. ThLM
Silent Is the House. Emily Brontë. *See* Visionary, The.
Silent Night. Joseph Mohr, *tr. fr. German.* FaPL
Silent Noon. Dante Gabriel Rossetti. The House of Life, XIX. ELP; ILP; OBNC; VP
Silent One, The. Ivor Gurney. MMA
Silent, Silent Night. Blake. CBEP
Silent Slain, The. Archibald MacLeish. *See* Too-late Born, The.

Silent, with her eyes. Blind Girl. W. S. Merwin. NePoEA-2
Silent Woman, The. Ben Jonson. *See* Epicoene; or, The Silent Woman.
Silentium. Fyodor Tyutchev, *tr. fr. Russian by* Babette Deutsch. PoP1; SiGo, *sl. diff.*
Silk Merchant's Daughter, The, *with music. Unknown* BFSS
Silken Tent, The. Robert Frost. CABA; MP; OnP; PoDB; PoIE
Silkworms, The. Douglas Stewart. AnMoPo; PoAu-2
Silver. Walter de la Mare. PoP1
Silver Age, The. Thom Gunn. ToPo
Silver bark of beech, and sallow. Counting-out Rhyme. Edna St. Vincent Millay. GoJo
Silver dust. Pear Tree. Hilda Doolittle ("H. D."). AP
Silver Herring Throbbed Thick in My Seine, The. Kenneth Leslie. ErPo; OBCV
Silver poplar, a beauty of local fame, The. A Bad Morning. Bertolt Brecht. MGP
Silver-scaled dragon with jaws flaming red, A. The Toaster. William Jay Smith. SoPo
Silver Swan, The. *Unknown.* DiPo; ELP; EnRePo
Silvering through the window moonflakes fall. Cats. Theodor Däubler. MGP
Similar Cases. Charlotte Perkins Stetson Gilman. PoLF
Simile for Her Smile, A. Richard Wilbur. MoLP
Similes for Two Political Characters of 1819. Shelley. CBEP
Simon Lee the Old Huntsman. Wordsworth. GTBS-P
Simon Legree—a Negro Sermon. Vachel Lindsay. SIV
Simon the Cyrenian Speaks. Countee Cullen. AmNP
Simple child, A/ That lightly draws its breath. We Are Seven. Wordsworth. FaPL
Simple her way of smiling was and coy. Ten of Chaucer's People: A Polite Nun. Chaucer. *Fr.* The Canterbury Tales. PoSa
Simple nosegay, A! was that much to ask? The Troll's Nosegay. Robert Graves. PoCh
Simple ring with a single stone, A. A Pearl, a Girl. Robert Browning. CBEP
Simple Sam. Leroy F. Jackson. PoSC
Simple Simon. Mother Goose. SoPo
(Simple Simon and the Pieman.) PoP1
Simples. James Joyce. PoP1
Simplicity's Song. Robert Wilson. *Fr.* Three Ladies of London. CTC
Simply because the sun does not embrace. Michelangelo, *tr. fr. Italian by* Joseph Tusiani. RBL
Simply she stands on the cathedral's. Eve. Rainer Maria Rilke. MoRP
Simultaneously, as soundlessly. Prime. W. H. Auden. *Fr.* Horae Canonicae. PoDB
Sin!/ O only fatal woe. Thomas Traherne. *Fr.* The Third Century. MeP
Sin and Its Cure. *Unknown.* STF
Sin of Omission, The. Margaret E. Sangster. TRV
Sin of self-love possesseth all mine eye. Sonnets, LXII. Shakespeare. EnRePo
Sin that I have a nounparall maistress. A Mistress without Compare. Charles d'Orléans(?). MeEL
Sin! wilt Thou vanquish me! The Recovery. Thomas Traherne. *Fr.* The Third Century. MeP
Since all our keys are lost or broken. An Art of Poetry. James McAuley. ACV
Since brass, nor stone, nor earth, nor boundless sea. Sonnets, LXV. Shakespeare. CABA; DiPo; EnRePo; GTBS-P; PoIE
Since bundling very much abounds. A New Bundling Song. *Unknown.* ErPo
Since, cruel Thyrsis, you my torments slight. A Sonnet, Written by a Nymph in Her Own Blood. Claudio Achillini. RBL
Since early dawn, through manzanita brush. Buck Fever. Bert Cooksley. SIV
Since First I Saw Your Face. *Unknown.* CBEP; ELP
Since God's eye is on the sparrow. God's Eye Is on the Sparrow. Bertha Meyer. STF
Since his death, nothing removes my fear. The Weasel. Robert Pack. CoPo
Since I am coming to that holy room. Hymn to God My God, in My Sickness. John Donne. BoC; CABA; DiPo; DTC; EnRePo; MeP; PoIE; SeCP
Since I believe in God the Father Almighty. Johannes Milton, Senex. Robert Bridges. PoP1
Since I emerged that day from the labyrinth. The Labyrinth. Edwin Muir. PoIE
Since I have lacked the comfort of that light. Amoretti, LXXXVIII. Spenser. EnRePo
Since I must love your north. To My Mountain. Kathleen Raine. RoP1
Since I No Longer Hope, O My Sweet Song. Guido Cavalcanti, *tr. fr. Italian by* Joseph Tusiani. AnML
Since I noo mwore do zee your feäce. The Wife a-Lost. William Barnes. ELP
Since I was ten I have not been unkind. The Final Word. Dom Moraes. NePoEA-2
Since Just Disdain. *Unknown.* EnRePo

Since lovers' joys then leave so sick a taste. Henry King. *Fr.* Paradox: That Fruition Destroys Love. ErPo

Since loving countenance you still refuse. Song. Clément Marot. RBL

Since men grow diffident at last. Youth Sings a Song of Rosebuds. Countee Cullen. PoLF

Since My Courage Is Clarified. Marcabru, *tr. fr. Povençal by* Paul Blackburn. AnML

Since nothing so vain. Old Song. Louis Dudek. ACV

Since now my Silvia is as kind as fair. The Happy Night. John Sheffield, Duke of Buckingham and Normanby. UnTE

Since, Senora, you torment me. The Challenge. *Unknown.* UnTE

Since sev'n sins from these our eyes. A Confession in Brief. Mathurin Régnier. RBL

Since she whom I lov'd hath paid her last debt. Holy Sonnets, XVII. John Donne. FoBA; MeP

Since there's no help, come, let us kiss and part. Idea, LXI [*or* Love's Farewell]. Michael Drayton. BoLP; CABA; CaFP; CBEP; DiPo; EnRePo; FaPL; GTBS-P; ILP; PoIE; PoSa; StP; WePo

Since thou hast view'd some Gorgon, and art grown. Sonnet: The Double Rock. Henry King. SeCP

Since thou wou'dst needs, bewitch'd with some ill charms. To One Married to an Old Man. Edmund Waller. SeCP

Since We Are Property. Lilith Lorraine. FiSC

Since you must go, and I must bid farewell. An Elegy. Ben Jonson. EnRePo

Sincere Flattery of R. B. J. K. Stephen. Par

Sincere Flattery of W. W. (Americanus). J. K. Stephen. Par

Sing a Song of Juniper. Robert Francis. LOW

Sing a song of picnics. Picnic Day. Rachel Field. SoPo

Sing a Song of Sixpence. Mother Goose. PoPl; SoPo

Sing a song of whisky. A Whisky Song. *Unknown.* STF

Sing! cuccu, nu. Sing! cuccu. Sumer Is Icumen In. *Unknown.* MeEL

Sing Little Bird. Maria Hastings. SoPo

Sing lullaby, as women do. Gascoigne's Lullaby [*or* The Lullaby of a Lover]. George Gascoigne. EnRePo; PoIE

Sing me a song of a lad that is gone. Over the Sea to Skye. Robert Louis Stevenson. HaSV

Sing me the men ere this. Heaven. Digby Mackworth Dolben. BoC

Sing, Muse, of the anger of Haroun the Caliph. The Vizier's Apology. Arthur Guiterman. SIV

Sing unto the Lord with Thanksgiving. Psalm CXLVII, Bible, O.T. SoPo

Sing We and Chant It. *Unknown.* EnRePo

Sing we for love and idleness. An Immorality. Ezra Pound. GoJo; PoPl; PoSa

Sing We Yule. *Unknown.* MeEL

Singing. Robert Louis Stevenson. ThGo

Singing Bush, The. William Soutar. ACV

Singing Cat, The. Stevie Smith. BoC; DaDu

Singing Maid, The. *Unknown.* MeEL

Singing my days. Passage to India. Walt Whitman. DiPo; FoBA

Singing through the forests. Rhyme of the Rails. John Godfrey Saxe. PoLF

Single man stands like a bird-watcher, A. The Mouth of the Hudson. Robert Lowell. CoPo

Single Sailor, The (A *and* B *vers.*). *Unknown.* BSNS

Single sleeper lying here, The. Epitaph for the Poet. George Barker. PoIE

Single summer grant me, great powers, A. To the Parcae. Friedrich Hölderlin, *tr. by* Walter Kaufmann. TwGP

Single summer, A, grant me, ye Mighty Ones! To the Parcae. Friedrich Hölderlin, *tr. by* Alexander Gode. AGP

Sing-Song, *sels.* Christina Rossetti.
　Bread and Milk. CBEP
　Caterpillar, The. GoJo; SoPo
　Color. SoPo
　(What Is Pink?) GoJo
　Ferry Me across the Water. GoJo
　(Ferryman, The.) SoPo
　Horses of the Sea, The. GoJo
　House of Cards, The. PoPl
　Hurt No Living Thing. SoPo; ThGo
　Minnie and Mattie. GoJo
　Mix a Pancake. SoPo
　Months, The. LV
　Rainbow, The. SoPo
　"What are heavy? sea-sand and sorrow." HaSV
　Who Has Seen the Wind? GoJo; PoPl

Sink the world! Can that dismay us? A Pair. Karl Gjellerup. PoPl

Sinner's Lament, A. Lord Herbert of Cherbury. SeCP

Sinnes Heavie Loade. Robert Southwell. MeP

Sion. George Herbert. MeP

Sion lies waste, and thy Jerusalem. Caelica, CIX. Fulke Greville. EnRePo

Sioux, The. Eugene Field. GoJo

Sioux Indians, *with music. Unknown.* BFSS

Sir,/ Our times are much degenerate from those. To His Noble Friend, Mr. Richard Lovelace, upon His Poems. Andrew Marvell. PP

Sir, as your mandate did request. The Inventory. Burns. CABL

Sir, down the precipice by Fortune flung. To Guglielmo Gonzaga, Duca di Mantova. Tasso. RBL

Sir Drake, whom well the world's end knew. On Sir Francis Drake. *Unknown.* CBEP

Sir Eustace Grey, *sel.* George Crabbe.
　"Then those ill-favour'd Ones, whom none." ELP

Sir Fopling Flutter. Dryden. DiPo

Sir Gawaine and the Green Knight. Yvor Winters. PoIE

Sir Geoffrey Chaucer. Robert Greene. *See* Description of Sir Geoffrey Chaucer, The.

Sir Humphrey Gilbert, *sel.* Longfellow.
　"He sat upon the deck." HaSV

Sir, I commend to you the spirit. José Garcia Villa. *Fr.* Divine Poems. MoRP

Sir; I read of late. Four Questions Addressed to His Excellency the Prime Minister. James P. Vaughn. AmNP

Sir James the Rose (A *and* B *vers., with music*). *Unknown.* BSNS

Sir John addressed the Snake-god in his temple. Grotesque. Robert Graves. DTC

Sir John Barleycorn. *Unknown.* CBEP

Sir Launcelot and Queen Guinevere. Tennyson. ACV

Sir Neil and Glengyle, *with music. Unknown.* BSNS

Sir, no man's enemy, forgiving all. Petition. W. W. Auden. PoDB; PoIE

Sir Patrick Spens [*or* Spence]. *Unknown.* BuBa; CABA; CABL; CaFP; CBEP; DiPo; ELP; GoJo; HaSV; ILP; OnP; PoIE; PoPo; PoSa; SIV; StP
　(Ballad of Sir Patrick Spens, The.) RoGo

Sir, say no more. Dramatic Fragment. Trumbull Stickney. CBEP

Sir Thopas. Chaucer. *Fr.* The Canterbury Tales. Par

Sir Walter Raleigh the Night before His Death. Sir Walter Ralegh. *See* Even Such Is Time.

Sir Walter Ralegh to His Son. Sir Walter Ralegh. *See* Wood, the Weed, the Wag, The.

Sir William of Deloraine at the Wizard's Tomb. Sir Walter Scott. *Fr.* The Lay of the Last Minstrel. OBNC

Sire So-and-So. The Ineffertile Lea. Hans Arp. MGP

Siren sang, A, and Europe turned away. To the Western World. Louis Simpson. NePoEA-2; PoPl

Sirena. Michael Drayton. *Fr.* The Shepherd's Sirena. CBEP

Sirens, The. John Manifeld. VaPo

Siren's Song, The. William Browne. *Fr.* The Inner Temple Masque. HaSV

Sister and mother and diviner love. To the One of Fictive Music. Wallace Stevens. AP

Sister, Awake! *Unknown.* PoSC

Sister Lou. Sterling A. Brown. AmNP

Sister Nell. *Unknown.* BBGG

"Sister, sister, go to bed!" Brother and Sister. "Lewis Carroll." BBGG

Sister Songs, *sel.* Francis Thompson.
　We Poets Speak. FaBV

Sisters, The. Roy Campbell. ErPo

Sisters are always drying their hair. Triolet against Sisters. Phyllis McGinley. LV

Sit further, and make room for thine own fame. To His Worthy Friend Doctor Witty upon His Translation of the Popular Errors. Andrew Marvell. PP

Sit on the beat. I'm blind, and three parts shell. A Terre. Wilfred Owen. MMA

Sit under a pine on Christmas Eve. Ballad of the Unmiraculous Miracle. Vassar Miller. ToPo

Sits by a fireplace, the seducer talks. Sonnet. Leonard Wolf. ErPo

Sith fortune favors not and all things backward go. A Refusal. Barnabe Googe. EnRePo

Sith my life from life is parted. Marie Magdalens Complaint at Christs Death. Robert Southwell. MeP

Sitteth alle stille and herkneth to me! Against the Barons' Enemies. *Unknown.* MeEL

Sitting Alone. Robert Herrick. *See* Vision, The.

Sitting down near him in the shade. The Smoker. Robert Huff. NePoEA-2

Sitting here. It's Pleasant to Think. Elizabeth J. Coatsworth. RePo

Sitting in our garden you cannot escape symbols. Of the Unscathing Fire. Anne Ridler. MoLP

Sitting in the disorder of my silence. Fulfillment. Vassar Miller. NePoEA-2

Sitting Pretty. Margaret Fishback. PoLF

Six and Thirty. D. E. Stevenson. BiCB

Six Badgers, The. Robert Graves. GoJo

Six Birthday Candles Shining. Mary Jane Carr. BiCB

Six in June. Mary Carolyn Davies. BiCB

Six month child, The. Slippery. Carl Sandburg. BiCB

Six Nuns in the Snow. Phyllis McGinley. LV

Six of Cups. Diane Wakoski. CoPo
Six Questions, The, *with music. Unknown.* BFSS; BSNS
Six Silver Handles. Sydney King Russell. FiSC
Six Variations. Denise Levertov. CoPo
Six Weeks Old. Christopher Morley. BiCB
"Sixpence a week," says the girl to her lover. By Her Aunt's Grave. Thomas Hardy. *Fr.* Satires of Circumstance. PoPo; VaPo
1643 "Veritas" 1878. Oliver Wendell Holmes. *Fr.* Two Sonnets: Harvard. AP
Sixty-eighth Birthday. James Russell Lowell. StP
Sixty thousand faces go dark on the Strip. Night of the President's Funeral. Richard Barker. OPP
Size of a handy pebble, The. The Oyster. Francis Ponge. CoFP
Skater of Ghost Lake, The. William Rose Benét. PoPo; SIV
Skaters, The. John Gould Fletcher. SD
Skaters, The. John Williams. SD
Skaters upon thin ice. Black Water and Bright Air. Constance Carrier. SD
Skater's Waltz, A. Gray Burr. CoPo
Skating. Herbert Asquith. SoPo
Skating. Kipling. SD
Skating. Wordsworth. *Fr.* The Prelude. SD
Skeleton in Armor, The. Longfellow. AP; PoPo
Skeltoniad, A. Michael Drayton. PP
Skeptic, The. Loring Williams. FiSC
Skerryvore ("For love of lovely words"). Robert Louis Stevenson. ILP
Skerryvore: The Parallel ("Here all is sunny"). Robert Louis Stevenson. ILP
Sketch, A. Christina Rossetti. GTBS-P
Sketch. Carl Sandburg. AP
Sketch from Private Life, A. Byron. OBNC
Sketch of His Own Character. Thomas Gray. EiCP
Sketches of Harlem. David Henderson. NNP
Skier. Robert Francis. SD
Skies are brass and the plains are bare, The. Song of the Darling River. Henry Lawson. ACV
Skies cant keep their secret, The! Emily Dickinson. DiPo
Skies are warm and sober, The. Ulalume—a Ballad. Poe. AP; DiPo; PoIE; PoPo
Skill'd to deceive our ears and eyes. The County Member. Winthrop Mackworth Praed. *Fr.* The County Ball. OBNC
Skimming lightly, wheeling still. Shiloh; a Requiem. Herman Melville. AP; CBEP; PoPo; StP; WiR
Skin-and-Bone Lady, The (A *vers., with music*). *Unknown.* BSO
(There Was an Old Woman.) BFSS; BSO (B *vers.*)
Skinny Mrs. Snipkin. Mrs. Snipkin and Mrs. Wobblechin. Laura E. Richards. SoPo
Skipper Ireson's Ride. Whittier. AP; PoLF; PoPo; SIV; ThLM, *sl. abr.*
Skipping Along Alone. Winifred Welles. SoPo
Skirting the river road, (my forenoon walk, my rest). The Dalliance of the Eagles. Walt Whitman. CABA
Skunk, The. Dorothy Baruch. SoPo
Skunk, The. Alfred Noyes. RePo
Skunk Hour. Robert Lowell. AP; PoIE
Sky had kissed the earth to sleep, The. Moonlit Night. Josef von Eichendorff. AGP
Sky is a blue, coiled serpent, The. Francis Carey Slater. *Fr.* Drought. ACV
Sky is close to me, The. I Say to the Mountain. Zoe Kincaid Brockman. PoNC
Sky is low, the clouds are mean, The. Emily Dickinson. CBEP; DiPo; FaBV
Sky is overcast, The. A Night-Piece. Wordsworth. FoBA
Sky, lazily disdaining to pursue, The. Georgia Dusk. Jean Toomer. AmNP
Sky turned smoky blue, the enfeebled sun, The. An Evening at Sea. John Press. HaSV
Sky unfolding its blankets to free, The. Morning Workout. Babette Deutsch. SD
Skylark's Nest, The. R. H. Long. PoAu-1
Skylight, The. Dino Campana, *tr. fr Italian by* Carlo L. Golino. CoIP
Skyline of New York does not excite me, The. Review from Staten Island. G. C. Oden. NNP
Skyscraper. Carl Sandburg. PoPl
Sky-Writer. Vincent Starrett. LV; PoPo
Slant of Sun, A. Stephen Crane. War Is Kind, XIV. VaPo
Slave, The. Hans Werner Cohn, *tr. fr. German by* Christopher Middleton. MGP
Slave, The. Jones Very. AP
Slave and the Iron Lace, The. Margaret Danner. AmNP
Slaves. James Russell Lowell. TRV
Slave's Dream, The. Longfellow. WePo
Slaves to the World. *Unknown* CBEP
Slaying of multitudes should be mourned with sorrow, The. *Unknown. Fr.* Tao Teh King. TRV
Sleep, The. Elizabeth Barrett Browning. TRV
Sleep, A. Larry Eigner. CoPo

Sleep ("Come sleep! O sleep"). Sir Philip Sidney. *See* Astrophel and Stella: Sonnets, XXXIX.
Sleep: and between the closed eyelids of sleep. Conrad Aiken. Preludes for Memnon, III. PoDB
Sleep and death, the dusky eagles. Lament. Georg Trakl, *tr. by* Michael Hamburger. MGP
Sleep and death, the gloomy eagles. Lament. Georg Trakl, *tr. by* Walter Kaufmann. TwGP
Sleep and Poetry. Keats. PP
Sleep, Angry Beauty. Thomas Campion. EnRePo; ErPo
Sleep, baby, sleep! *Unknown, tr. fr.* German by Francis Owen, AGP
Sleep, calm winter sleep, the rides are woollen. Calm Winter Sleep. Hilary Corke. MP
Sleep, comrades, sleep and rest. Decoration Day. Longfellow. PoSC
Sleep, darling boy, so sweet and mild! The Mother by the Cradle. Matthias Claudius. AGP
Sleep evades me, there's no light. Verses Written during a Sleepless Night. Pushkin. PoPl
Sleep Impression. Carl Sandburg. RePo
Sleep, kinsman thou to death and trance. In Memoriam A. H. H., LXXI. Tennyson. VP
Sleep, my darling, sleep. Cradle Song. Louis MacNeice. PoPl
Sleep, of all gifts of Heaven held supreme. Joachim du Bellay. *Fr.* L'Olive. RBL
Sleep on, and dream of Heaven awhile. The Sleeping Beauty. Samuel Rogers. GTBS-P
Sleep! Sleep! Beauty Bright. Blake. *See* Cradle Song: "Sleep, sleep, beauty bright."
Sleep softly . . . eagle forgotten . . . under the stone. The Eagle That Is Forgotten. Vachel Lindsay. MoRP
Sleep stands off to watch me brood the curse. "All My Pretty Ones? Did You Say All?" Bink Noll. ToPo
Sleep sweetly in your humble graves. Ode Sung on the Occasion of Decorating the Graves of the Confederate Dead. Henry Timrod. AP; LV; StP
Sleep, Wayward Thoughts. *Unknown.* EnRePo
Sleeper, The. Poe. AP; CBEP
Sleeper from the Amazon, A. *Unknown.* RePo
Sleeper Hood-winked, The. John Skelton. *See* Lullay, Lullay, like a Child.
Sleepers, The. F. W. Harvey. MMA
Sleepers, The. Louis Untermeyer. MoLP
Sleepers are mangled by the scythe of dreams. The Scythe of Dreams. Joseph Payne Brennan. FiSC
Sleepest Thou Yet, My Sweeting? Dietmar von Aist, *tr. fr.* German by Margaret R. Richey. AnML
Sleeping at Last. Christina Rossetti. VP
Sleeping Beauty, The. Samuel Rogers. GTBS-P
Sleeping butterfly, A. The Butterfly. Kikaku. SoPo
Sleeping Giant, The. Donald Hall. CaFP; MP
Sleeping House, The. Tennyson. *Fr.* Maud. OBNC
Sleeping in fever, I am unfit. For God While Sleeping. Anne Sexton. CABA; NePoEA-2; PoDB
Sleeping Saint, The. Melvin Walker La Follette. CoPo
Sleeping Village. Harold Vinal. FiSC
Sleepless, by the windowpane I stare. Verses at Night. Dannie Abse. MP
Sleepless Dreams. Dante Gabriel Rossetti. The House of Life, XXXIX. VP
Sleighride. Patrick Anderson. OBCV
Slender beech and the sapling oak, The. Beech and Oak. Thomas Love Peacock. CBEP
Slender goblet wreathed in flame, A. Tulip. William Jay Smith. RePo
Slepynge Long in Great Quiete Is Eek a Greet Norice to Leccherie. John Hollander. AmPC; ErPo
Slip off the husk of gravity to lie. The New Icarus. Vassar Miller. ToPo
Slippery. Carl Sandburg. BiCB
Sliprails and the Spur, The. Henry Lawson. PoAu-1
Sloth, The. Theodore Roethke. PoPo
Slovenly Peter. Heinrich Hoffmann, *tr. fr. German.* BBGG
Slow freight wiggles along the rail, The. The Freight Train. Rowena Bennett. RePo
Slow-hooved across the carrion sea. Bombay Arrival. Laurie Lee. ToPo
Slow, horses, slow. Night of Spring. Thomas Westwood. CBEP
Slow Me Down. *Unknown.* STF
Slow moves the acid breath of noon. Field of Autumn. Laurie Lee. ToPo
Slow sift the sands of Time; the yellowed leaves. The Sands of Time. Robert E. Howard. FiSC
Slow sinks, more lovely ere his race be run. Sunset over the Ægean. Byron. *Fr.* The Corsair. OBNC
Slow, Slow, Fresh Fount. Ben Jonson. *Fr.* Cynthia's Revels, I, ii. ELP
(Echo's Song.) PoIE
("Slow, slow, fresh fount, keep time with my salt tears.") ILP
(Song.) EnRePo; SeCP

Slow-worm sings her bed-time prayers, The. She-Goat and Slow-Worm. Christian Morgenstern. MGP
Slowly England's sun was setting o'er the hilltops far away. Curfew Must Not Ring Tonight. Rose Hartwick Thorpe. SIV
Slowly flutters the snow from ash-coloured heavens in silence. Snowfall. Giosuè Carducci, tr. by G. A. Greene. PoPl
Slowly Nan the widow goes. Planter's Charm. Fay M. Yauger. SIV
Slowly, silently, now the moon. Silver. Walter de la Mare. PoPl
Slowly the flakes come down through the ash-gray skies and the shouting. First Snowfall. Giosuè Carducci, tr. by Asa Hughes. SiGo
Slowly the night blooms, unfurling. Flowers of Darkness. Frank Marshall Davis. AmNP
Slowly the poison on the whole blood stream fills. Missing Dates. William Empson. AnMoPo; PoIE
Slowly thy flowing tide. The Ebb Tide. Robert Southey. OBNC
Slowly ticks the big clock. The Big Clock. Unknown. SoPo
Slug in Woods. Earle Birney. OBCV
Sluggard, The. Lucilius, tr. fr. Greek by Humbert Wolfe. SD
Sluggard, The. Isaac Watts. Par; ThGo
Slum Dwelling, A. George Crabbe. Fr. The Borough. OBNC
Slumber Did My Spirit Seal, A. Wordsworth. CABA; CaFP; CBEP; DiPo; ELP; FoBA; GTBS-P; ILP; OnP; PoIE; WePo
(Lucy.) OBNC
Slumber Song. Clemens Brentano, tr. fr. German by Anne Jennings. AGP
Slumb'ring deep in every thing. Wishing Wand. Josef von Eichendorff. AGP
Small, The. Theodore Roethke. AnMoPo
Small April sobbed. April Fool. Eleanor Hammond. SoPo
Small birds swirl around, The. The Small. Theodore Roethke. AnMoPo
Small boy has thrown a stone at a statue, A. The Statue. Robert Finch. OBCV
Small Celandine, The. Wordsworth. See Lesson, A.
Small Game. Philip Levine. AmPC
Small householder now comes out warily, The. Spring Voices. Louis MacNeice. WePo
Small service is true service while it lasts. Written in the Album of a Child. Wordsworth. OBNC
Small Song. Frances Frost. RePo
Small Thought Speaks for the Flesh, A. Carleton Drewry. MoRP
Small Town. Ernest Stadler, tr. fr. German by Christopher Middleton. MGP
Small type of great ones, that do hum. A Fly Caught in a Cobweb. Richard Lovelace. SeCP
Small Wandering Bird Who Singing Go Your Way. Petrarch, tr. fr. Italian by Peter Russell. Sonnets to Laura: To Laura in Death, XC. AnML
Smear of blue peat smoke, The. The Shepherd's Hut. Andrew Young. DaDu; DTC
Smelling or feeling of the several holes. Dishonor. Edwin Denby. ErPo
Smells. Christopher Morley. LV
Smells. Kathryn Worth. RePo
Smile is quite a funny thing. Growing Smiles. Unknown. PoLF
Smile of grief askance that vanishes, A. Pilate. Georg Heym. MGP
Smiling on his death bed lies. King David. Heine. TwGP
Smithfield Market Fire, The. Fred Dallas. WePo
Smoke. Henry David Thoreau. AmLP; VaPo
(Light-winged Smoke, Icarian Bird.) AP
Smoke and nothing the breath of being. Living and Dying. Manuel González Prada. AnSP
Smoke Animals. Rowena Bennett. RePo
Smoke-blackened Smiths. Unknown. See Blacksmiths.
Smoke color. August. Brother Antoninus. ToPo
Smoke from the train-gulf hid by hoardings blunders upward, the brakes of cars. Birmingham. Louis MacNeice. ILP
Smoker, The. Robert Huff. NePoEA-2
Smoky Smirr o' Rain, The. George Campbell Hay. ACV
Smooth it slides upon its travel. Looking-Glass River. Robert Louis Stevenson. LV
Smudged eyeballs. Breakfast in a Bowling Alley in Utica, New York. Adrienne Rich. CoPo
Smuggler, The. Unknown. HaSV
Snail. John Drinkwater. GoJo; SoPo
Snail. David McCord. RePo
Snail, The. James Reeves. RePo
Snail pushes through a green, The. Considering the Snail. Thom Gunn. MP; NePoEA-2
Snail upon the wall. Snail. John Drinkwater. GoJo; SoPo
Snake, The. Emily Dickinson. See Narrow Fellow in the Grass, A.
Snake, The. Kyoshi, tr. fr. Japanese by Harold G. Henderson. RePo
Snake. D. H. Lawrence. DiPo; PoSa; StP; VaPo

Snake. Theodore Roethke. AnMoPo; PoPl
Snake came to my water-trough, A. Snake. D. H. Lawrence. DiPo; PoSa; StP; VaPo
Snake, A! Though it passes. The Snake. Kyoshi. RePo
Snake Trying, The. W. W. E. Ross. OBCV
Snakecharmer. Sylvia Plath. NePoEA-2; PP
Snakes and Snails. Grace Taber Hallock. RePo
Snap-Dragon. D. H. Lawrence. ErPo
Snap-Dragon will never snap, A. A Lucky Thing. Dorothy Aldis. RePo
Snapshot. John Fuller. NePoEA-2
Snapshot for Miss Bricka Who Lost in the Semi-final Round of the Pennsylvania Lawn Tennis Tournament at Haverford, July, 1960, A. Robert Wallace. SD
Snarleyvow; or, The Dog Fiend, sel. Frederick Marryat. Captain Stood on the Carronade, The. HaSV; RePo
Sneeze on a Monday. Unknown. EvOK
Sneezing. Marie Louise Allen. SoPo
Sneezing. Leigh Hunt. LV
Sniffle, The. Ogden Nash. RePo; WePo
Snore in the foam; the night is vast and blind. Tristan da Cunha. Roy Campbell. RoGo
Snoring. Aileen Fisher. SoPo
Snoring in a Smoker, soot-cratered from Stockport. London Train. Paul Dehn. LV
Snorting his pleasure in the dying sun. Landscape, Deer Season. Barbara Howes. GoJo
Snow. Ecclesiasticus, XLIII: 14-16, 18-24, Bible, Apocrypha. BoC
Snow, The. Robert Creeley. AP
Snow, The. Emily Dickinson. See It sifts from leaden sieves.
Snow, The. Donald Hall. NePoEA-2
Snow. Louis MacNeice. VaPo
Snow, The. Vista. Alfred Kreymborg. BoLP
Snow at Advent. Christine Busta, tr. fr. German by Michael Hamburger. MGP
Snow came down last night like moths, The. First Snow in Alsace. Richard Wilbur. AP
Snow-dust driven over the snow. Winter Noon. Sara Teasdale. RePo
Snow falling and night falling fast, oh, fast. Desert Places. Robert Frost. AP; CABA; DiPo; FoBA; PoIE; PoPo
Snow falls deep; the forest lies alone, The. Gypsies. John Clare. CBEP
Snow falls on the cars in Doctors' Row and hoods the headlights. Doctors' Row. Conrad Aiken. AP; PoPl
Snow fell as for Wenceslas. Roarers in a Ring. Ted Hughes. NePoEA-2
Snow-Gum, The. Douglas Stewart. PoAu-2
Snow had begun in the gloaming, The. James Russell Lowell. Fr. The First Snow-fall. PoSC
Snow had buried Stuyvesant, The. Inauguration Day: January 1953. Robert Lowell. ToPo
Snow has left the cottage top, The. February. John Clare. Fr. The Shepherd's Calendar. OBNC
Snow-hills all about. Ice-Skaters. Elder Olson. SD
Snow in the Suburbs. Thomas Hardy. GoJo; VP; WePo
Snow is a strange white word. On Receiving News of the War. Isaac Rosenberg. MMA
Snow is falling from the mouth of this cannon. The Library Is on Fire. René Char. CoFP
Snow is in the oak. The Snow. Donald Hall. NePoEA-2
Snow-Leopard, The. Randall Jarrell. MP
Snow Lies Sprinkled, The. Robert Bridges. HaSV
Snow makes whiteness where it falls. First Snow. Marie Louise Allen. SoPo
Snow Man. See Snowman.
Snow may come as quietly, A. January. Elizabeth J. Coatsworth. PoSC
Snow was falling soft and slow, The. Winter Night. Boris Pasternak. PoPl
Snow-Bird, The. Frank Dempster Sherman. SoPo
Snow-bound. Whittier. AP; WiR
Storm, The, sel. FaBV
Snow-drop of dogs, with ear of brownest dye. Sonnet: To Tartar, a Terrier Beauty. Thomas Lovell Beddoes. OBNC
Snowfall. Giosuè Carducci, tr. fr. Italian by G. A. Greene. PoPl
(First Snowfall, tr. by Asa Hughes.) SiGo
Snowfall, The. Donald Justice. NePoEA-2
Snow Fall, The. Archibald MacLeish. LOW; PoPl
Snow-Flakes. Longfellow. AmLP; AP; WiR
Snowflakes fast were falling, The. A Soldier's Poor Little Boy. Unknown. BSO
Snow Man, The. Wallace Stevens. AP; GoJo; PoIE
Snowman's Resolution, The. Aileen Fisher. SoPo
Snows of Yester-Year, The. Villon. See Ballad of Dead Ladies, The.
Snowstorm. John Clare. WiR
Snow-Storm, The. Emerson. AP; DiPo; LV; PoLF; PoPo; StP; VaPo; WiR
Snowy Day, A. Dafydd ap Gwilym, tr. fr. Welsh by H. Idris Bell. SiGo
Snowy path for squirrel and fox, A. The Brook in February. Sir Charles G. D. Roberts. OBCV

Snugly upon the equal heights. The Old Feminist. Phyllis McGinley. ThLM

So? James P. Vaughn. AmNP

So all day long the noise of battle roll'd. Morte d'Arthur. Tennyson. ILP; VP

So all men come at last to their Explorer's Tree. Burke and Wills. Ken Barratt. PoAu-2

So as I cluch and cling to the brink I must. I. Karl Wolfskehl. MGP

So brilliant a moonshine. Harvest Moon. Ryota. RePo

"So careful of the type?" but no. In Memoriam A. H. H., LVI. Tennyson. DiPo; OBNC; VP

So Cruel Prison. Earl of Surrey. EnRePo; ILP

So faith is strong. The Tide of Faith. "George Eliot." Fr. A Minor Prophet. TRV

So fallen! so lost! the light withdrawn. Ichabod. Whittier. AP; CBEP; LV

So good luck came, and on my roof did light. The Coming of Good Luck. Robert Herrick. CBEP

So have I seen a silver swan. A Song. Unknown. CBEP

So having said, a while he stood, expecting. Satan's Metamorphosis. Milton. Fr. Paradise Lost, X. StP

So he sits down. His host will play for him. Concert Scene. John Logan. NePoEA-2

So he won't talk to me when we meet? Confucius. Fr. The Classic Anthology: Songs of Cheng. CTC

So Hector spake; the Trojans roar'd applause. Night Encampment outside Troy. Homer. Fr. The Iliad. RoGo

So here I sit behind my nasty desk. Any Man to His Secretary. Hilary Corke. ErPo

So he's got there at last, been received as a partner. Security. Michael Hamburger. PoCh

So huge a burden to support. Ill Luck. Baudelaire. PoPl

So I, who love, with all this outward. The Meaning. Ralph Gustafson. OBCV

So Independently the Cedars Grow. Paul Bartlett. PoNC

So intimately like the one I used to be. The Miraculous Place of Love. André Frénaud. CoFP

So it is, my dear. Even So. Dante Gabriel Rossetti. OBNC

So Late into the Night. Byron. See So We'll Go No More a-Roving.

So late one eve as they sat courting. The Bramble Briar. Unknown. BFSS

So lately one evening as I rambled. Dixie's Green Shore. Unknown. BFSS

So light no one noticed. The Song. Edward Dorn. CoPo

So live, that when thy summons comes to join. Bryant. Fr. Thanatopsis. TRV

So Long Folks, Off to the War. Anthony Ostroff. PoPl

So long you wandered on the dusky plain. To His Friend in Elysium. Joachim du Bellay. RBL

So Look the Mornings. Robert Herrick. ELP

So looks Anthea, when in bed she lyes. To Anthea Lying in Bed. Robert Herrick. SeCP

So Love, emergent out of chaos, brought. Love. Ben Jonson. UnTE

So lucky I was in being born. Yankee Cradle. Robert P. Tristram Coffin. EvOK

So Many Monkeys. Marion Edey and Dorothy Grider. SoPo

So many worlds, so much to do. In Memoriam A. H. H., LXXIII. Tennyson. VP

So Might It Be. John Galsworthy. PoLF

So much depends. The Red Wheelbarrow [or Spring and All]. William Carlos Williams. AmLP; EvOK; VaPo

So much have I forgotten in ten years. Flame-Heart. Claude McKay. AmNP

So much have I received at Dido's hands. Christopher Marlowe and Thomas Nashe. Fr. The Tragedy of Dido. HaSV

So Much Loving, So Much Loving. Unknown, tr. fr. Spanish by William M. Davis. AnML

So much that I would give you hovers out. For a Birthday. Elaine V. Emans. BiCB

So Much the More as I Draw near My Land. Adam de la Halle, tr. fr. French by Irma Brandeis. AnML

So my songs hurt your ears. Dilation. "Will Inman." PoNC

So near to death yourself. For a Very Old Man on the Death of His Wife. Jane Cooper. NePoEA-2

So nigh is grandeur to our dust. Emerson. Fr. Voluntaries, III. TRV

So Not Seeing I Sung. Arthur Hugh Clough. Fr. Amours de Voyage. OBNC

("Tibur is beautiful, too, and the orchard slopes, and the Anio.") GTBS-P

So, now I have confest that he is thine. Sonnets, CXXXIV. Shakespeare. CBEP

So oft as I her beauty do behold. Amoretti, LV. Spenser. PoIE

So often we praise our mothers here and merit all their ways. Dear Old Dad. Eva Gilbert Shaver. STF

So, on the bloody sand, Sohrab lay dead. Matthew Arnold. Fr. Sohrab and Rustum. GTBS-P

So open was his mind, so wide. The Independent. Phyllis McGinley. Fr. Epitaphs for Three Prominent Persons. LV

So prim and proper in its guarded close. Wild Garden. James Larkin Pearson. PoNC

So sang he: and as meeting rose and rose. Willowwood, 4. Dante Gabriel Rossetti. The House of Life, LII. VP

So Separate and Strange. Felix Stefanile. FiSC

So she went into the garden. The Great Panjandrum [Himself]. Samuel Foote. Par; PoLF

So smooth, so sweet, so silv'ry is thy voice. Upon Julia's Voice. Robert Herrick. CABA; SeCP

So, So. William Clerke. ELP

So, so, break [or breake] off this last lamenting kiss [or kisse]. The Expiration. John Donne. CBEP; SeCP

So soft streams meet, so springs with gladder smiles. The Welcome to Sack. Robert Herrick. SeCP

So Soon? Richard Armour. LV

So spake the Enemy of mankind, enclosed. Eve's Temptation and Fall. Milton. Fr. Paradise Lost, IX. DiPo

So still. The Stillness. Basho. RePo

So still the pond in morning's gray. The Pond. Annette von Droste-Hülshoff. SiGo

So still the night swinging. Mariners' Carol. W. S. Merwin. EaLo; PoDB

So Sweet Love Seemed. Robert Bridges. FaBV

So sweet, so golden. Christian Hoffmann von Hoffmannswaldau, tr. fr. German by Alexander Gode. AGP

So sweet the plum trees smell. Plum Blossoms. Unknown. SoPo

So That Even a Lover. Louis Zukofsky. CoPo

So That's Who I Remind Me Of. Ogden Nash. PoLF

So, the All-great, were the All-loving too. Robert Browning. Fr. An Epistle Containing the Strange . . . TRV

So the man spread his blanket on the field. A Tall Man Executes a Jig. Irving Layton. PoCh

"So then you won't fight?" Dooley Is a Traitor. James Michie. NePoEA-2

So there stood Matthew Arnold and this girl. The Dover Bitch. Anthony Hecht. NePoEA-2; PP

So these two faced each other there. A Portrait in the Guards. Laurence Whistler. GTBS-P

So. They and I are back from the outside. Requiem. Carl Bode. ToPo

So think things over, pretty Glover. The Belle Heaulmiere to the Daughters of Joy. Villon. AnML

So This Is Autumn. W. W. Watt. PoPl

So tho' our Daystar from our sight be taken. The Saints (St. Paul). F. W. H. Myers. Fr. Saint Paul. BoC

So through the darkness and the cold we flew. Skating. Wordsworth. Fr. The Prelude. SD

So to the sea we came; the sea? that is. Spenser. Fr. Colin Clout's Come Home Again. HaSV

So We'll Go No More a-Roving. Byron. CaFP; ELP; FaPL; ILP; OnP; PoIE; PoSa
 (So Late into the Night.) WiR
 (Song.) BoLP
 (We'll Go No More a-Roving.) CBEP; DiPo; FaBV; PoLF

So Well I Love Thee. Michael Drayton. EnRePo; FaPL

So what said the others and the sun went down. Mrs. Alfred Uruguay. Wallace Stevens. AP; MP

So what's it like being an American Assassin. Lines Written Nov. 22, 23—1963. Gregory Corso. OPP

So White, So Soft, So Sweet. Ben Jonson. Fr. A Celebration of Charis. UnTE

So ye're runnin' fer Congress, mister? le' me tell ye 'bout my son. Whisperin' Bill. Irving Bacheller. PoLF

So zestfully canst thou sing? The Blinded Bird. Thomas Hardy. EaLo; VP

Soap, the Oppressor. Burges Johnson. PoLF

Soapship went a-rocking, A. The Voyage of Jimmy Poo. James A. Emanuel. AmNP; NNP

Sob, gentian blue! Gentian. "Klabund." MGP

Sob, Heavy World. W. H. Auden. DTC

Sober Quaker, The. with music. Unknown. BSO

Sockeye Salmon. Ronald Hambleton. OBCV

Socrates and Alcibiades. Friedrich Hölderlin, tr. fr. German by Palmer Hilty. AGP

Soeur Maire Emilie. Caryll Houselander. BoC

Sofa, The. William Cowper. Fr. The Task. EiCP

Soft Answers. Robert Bagg. UnTE

Soft crying of the dawn while cockatoos. 'Morning, Morning. Ray Mathew. PoAu-2

Soft is the collied night, and cool. Summer Song II. George Barker. ToPo

Soft Job. William C. Summers. STF

Soft lights, the companionship, the beers, The. The Pick-up. J. V. Cunningham. UnTE

Soft melodies, wafted on winds. Leaf Fall. Heinrich Leuthold. AGP

"Soft Sell." Lorna Beers. FiSC

Soft sleep, profoundly pleasing power. Ode to Sleep. Tobias George Smollett. WaPE

Softë season, that bud and bloom forth brings, The. Spring. Earl of Surrey. CBEP

Softening of her face which comes, The. At Only That Moment. Alan Ross. ErPo

Softly and humbly to the Gulf of Arabs. Beach Burial. Kenneth Slessor. PoAu-2

Softly, Drowsily. Walter de la Mare. SoPo

Softly I closed the book as in a dream. The Book. Winfred Ernest Garrison. TRV

Softly in the dusk, a woman is singing to me. Piano. D. H. Lawrence. CBEP; GTBS-P; PoIE; VaPo

Softly sighs the April air. Bel m'es quan lo vens m'alena. Arnaut Daniel. SiGo

Softly, softly, sing a tune. Slumber Song. Clemens Brentano. AGP

Softly the day dies out behind the pines. Evening Landscape. Pol de Mont. SiGo

Softly through mv spirit flow. Heine, tr. fr. German by Francis Owen. AGP

Sohrab and Rustum. Matthew Arnold. CABL; VP

"So, on the bloody sand, Sohrab lay dead," sel. GTBS-P

Soil now gets a rumpling soft and damp, The. The Strong Are Saying Nothing. Robert Frost. FoBA; PoDB

Soiree. Ezra Pound. DTC

Sojourn in the Whale. Marianne Moore. PoIE

Sol, Bronze Age come first Sol. The Windows of Waltham. John Wieners. CoPo

Solace. Clarissa Scott Delany. AmNP

Soldier, The. Rupert Brooke. 1914, V. FaBV; FaPL; LV; PoLF; PoPl; PoPo

(Soldier, The, 1914-1918.) BoC

Soldier, A. Robert Frost. ILP; PoPo; ThLM

Soldier, A. Unknown. See Earl Brand.

Soldier, a soldier just coming from the plain, A. Earl Brand (B vers.). Unknown. BSO

Soldier and statesman, rarest unison. Washington. James Russell Lowell. RePo

Soldier from Missouri, A, with music. Unknown. BFSS

Soldier, The, 1939-1945. Gerald Kersh. BoC

Soldier, oh soldier, a-coming from the plain. A Soldier. Unknown. BSO

Soldier of Waterloo, The, with music. Unknown. BSO

Soldier, rest! thy warfare o'er. Song. Sir Walter Scott. Fr. The Lady of the Lake. OBNC

Soldier rode from east to west, The. The Soldier's Farewell. Unknown. BFSS

Soldier, Soldier, Won't You Marry Me? (A and B vers., with music). Unknown. BSO

Soldier: Twentieth Century. Isaac Rosenberg. MMA

Soldier Walks under the Trees of the University, The. Randall Jarrell. PoPl

Soldiers Bathing. F. T. Prince. GTBS-P

Soldier's Dream, The. Thomas Campbell. FaPL; GTBS-P; RoGo

Soldier's Farewell, The, with music. Unknown. BFSS

Soldiers' Friend, The. George Canning and John Hookham Frere. Par

Soldiers fuzz the city in khaki confusion. Habana. Julian Bond. NNP

Soldier's Poor Little Boy, A. Unknown. BSO

Soldier's Song. Tobias Hume. WiR

Soldier's Wife, The. George Canning and John Hookham Frere. Par

Solemn Hour. Rainer Maria Rilke, tr. fr. German by C. F. MacIntyre. PoPl

Solid ocean and the liquid land, The. The Planet. Carl Bode. ToPo

Soliloquy of the Spanish Cloister. Robert Browning. CABA; CaFP; DiPo; ILP; PoIE; VP

Soliloquy 2. Richard Aldington. MMA

Solitary Confinement. X. J. Kennedy. NePoEA-2

Solitary egret, left behind, a. The White Egret. Li Po. SiGo

Solitary Horseman, The. Guy Owen. PoNC

Solitary Pine. Prince Ichihara, tr. fr. Japanese by Ishii and Obata. SiGo

Solitary pines along the desolate, The. Sandro Penna, tr. fr. Italian by Carlo L. Golino. CoIP

Solitary Reaper, The. Wordsworth. CABA; CaFP; CBEP; DiPo; FoBA; ILP; OBNC; OnP; PoIE; PoSa; RoGo; StP

(Reaper, The.) GTBS-P

Solitary wayfarer! Hoopoe. George Darley. Fr. Nepenthe. OBNC

Solitary Woodsman, The. Sir Charles G. D. Roberts. OBCV

Solitude. Archibald Lampman. CBEP; OBCV

Solitude, A. Denise Levertov. NePoEA-2

Solitude. Pope. See Ode on Solitude.

Solitude. Ella Wheeler Wilcox. PoLF

Solitude of Alexander Selkirk, The. William Cowper. GTBS-P; RoGo

(Verses: "I am monarch of all I survey.") PoIE

(Verses Supposed to Be Written by Alexander Selkirk during His Solitary Abode on the Island of Juan Fernandez.) PoLF

Solitudes, The, sels. Luis de Góngora, tr. fr. Spanish by Edward Meryon Wilson.

Idyllic Scene, An. RBL

"It was the flowery season of the year." AnSP; RBL

On Sailing the Wide Ocean. RBL

Rustic Festival, A. RBL

Wedding Hymn. AnSP; RBL

Solitudes. John Hall Wheelock. MoLP

Solo for Bent Spoon. Donald Finkel. NePoEA-2

Solomon Grundy. Birthday Rhyme. Unknown. BiCB

Solomon on the Vanity of the World, sel. Matthew Prior. "Ye sons of men, with just regard attend." EiCP

Solomon to Sheba. W. B. Yeats. ELP

Solomon, where is thy throne? It is gone in the wind. Gone in the Wind. James Clarence Mangan. CBEP

Sombre and rich, the skies. By the Statue of King Charles at Charing Cross. Lionel Johnson. BoC; OBNC; RoGo

Sombre the night is. Returning, We Hear the Larks. Isaac Rosenberg. MMA

Some Bird. Unknown. STF

Some candle clear burns somewhere I come by. The Candle Indoors. Gerard Manley Hopkins. AnMoPo; DiPo

Some day I'm going to have a store. General Store. Rachel Field. SoPo

Some day our town will grow old. The Springfield of the Far Future. Vachel Lindsay. MoRP

Some days I go with Daddy for a walk. Six and Thirty. D. E. Stevenson. BiCB

Some days my thoughts are just cocoons—all cold, and dull, and blind. Days. Karle Wilson Baker. RePo

Some delight in telling stories. Maurice Scève. Fr. Délie. RBL

Some Fishy Nonsense. Laura E. Richards. SoPo

Some for the glories of this world; and some. Omar Khayyám, tr. by Edward Fitzgerald. Fr. The Rubáiyát. PoPl

Some Foreign Letters. Anne Sexton. PoCh; ToPo

Some four years ago I made Phillis an offer. Epigramme. Philippe Desportes. RBL

Some gain a universal fame. A Ballade of Lawn Tennis. Franklin P. Adams. SD

Some glory in their birth, some in their skill. Sonnets, XCI. Shakespeare. CBEP

Some I've Seen So Crudely. Sem Tob, tr. fr. Spanish by Norman T. Di Giovanni. Fr. Moral Proverbs. AnML

Some keep the Sabbath going to church. Emily Dickinson. DiPo

Some ladies love the jewels in Love's zone. Love's Lovers. Dante Gabriel Rossetti. Fr. The House of Life, VIII. VP

Some like drink. Not I. Robert Louis Stevenson. WePo

Some lit theirs at both ends. Despair. W. S. Merwin. AmPC

Some Late Lark Singing. W. E. Henley. See Margaritae Sorori.

Some Little Bug. Roy Atwell. PoLF

Some men break your heart in two. Experience. Dorothy Parker. BoLP; PoPl

Some men live for warlike deeds. John James Audubon. Stephen Vincent Benét. ThLM

Some Negatives: X. at the Chateau. James Merrill. NePoEA-2

Some night I think if you should walk with me. The Lover Praises His Lady's Bright Beauty. Shaemas O'Sheel. BoLP

Some of us/ these days. Resurrection. Frank Horne. PtTo

Some one. See Someone.

Some people hang portraits up. A Likeness. Robert Browning. CTC

Some primal termite knocked on wood. The Termite. Ogden Nash. PoPl; PoPo

Some Refrains at the Charles River. Peter Viereck. PoCh

Some say, compared to Bononcini. Epigram on Handel and Bononcini. Byron. CBEP

Some say kissin's ae [or that kissing's a] sin. Kissin' [or Kissing's No Sin]. Unknown. BoLP; UnTE

Some say the world will end by fire. Frostbite. Conrad Aiken. PoPo

Some say the world will end in fire. Fire and Ice. Robert Frost. CABA; CaFP; DiPo; FoBA; ILP; PoDB; PoPl; PoPo; WePo

Some say you dye your hair. But I deny it. To Chloe. Unknown. UnTE

Some take back February. A Way of Looking. Helen Bevington. PoNC

Some talk of Alexander, and some of Hercules. The British Grenadiers. Unknown. CBEP

Some that have deeper digged [or digg'd] love's mine [or myne] than I. Love's Alchemy [or Loves Alchymie]. John Donne. CABA; SeCP

Some, the great Adepts, found it. The Adepts. Lawrence Durrell. ErPo

Some things are very dear to me. Sonnet II. Gwendolyn B. Bennett. AmNP

Some Things That Easter Brings. Elsie Parrish. SoPo

Some Things You Cannot Will to Men. Walter E. Isenhour. STF

Some time. See also Sometime.

Some time ago from Rome, in smart array. The Cudgelled but Contented Cuckold. La Fontaine. UnTE

Some Time at Eve. Elizabeth Clark Hardy. PoLF

Some time now past in the autumnal tide. Contemplations. Anne Bradstreet. AP

Some Verses upon the Burning of Our House, July 10th, 1666. Anne Bradstreet. AP
Some were unlucky. Blown a mile to Shoreward. Moonlight Night on the Port. Sidney Keyes. DTC
Some years ago, ere time and taste. The Vicar. Winthrop Mackworth Praed. OBNC
Some years ago, perhaps a hundred. Jack Sheppard. *Unknown.* BSNS
Some years ago you heard me sing. Sarah Byng Who Could Not Read and Was Tossed into a Thorny Hedge by a Bull. Hilaire Belloc. GoJo
Some young and old men. November. "Aldo Palazzeschi." CoIP
Somebody knocked. Who's There? Frances Frost. RePo
Somebody Prayed. *Unknown.* STF
Somebody said that it couldn't be done. It Couldn't Be Done. *Unknown.* STF
Somebody stole my myths. Song to the Tune of "Somebody Stole My Gal." X. J. Kennedy. CoPo
Somebody's Birthday. Abbie Farwell Brown. BiCB
Someone. John Ciardi. BiCB
Some One ("Some one came knocking"). Walter de la Mare. SoPo
Some one is always sitting there. The Little Green Orchard. Walter de la Mare. EvOK
Someone painted pictures on my. Jack Frost. Helen Bayley Davis. SoPo
Someone put a bullet through his orphan brain. Play the Last March Slowly. Richard Davidson. PtTo
Somersault. Dorothy Aldis. SoPo
Something befell. At the Bottom of the Well. Louis Untermeyer. GoJo
Something forgotten for twenty years: though my fathers. A Map of the Western Part of the County of Essex in England. Denise Levertov. ToPo
Something has ceased to come along with me. Death of a Son. Jon Silkin. GTBS-P
Something has spoken to me in the night. Thomas Wolfe. *Fr.* You Can't Go Home Again. TRV
Something in Common. Richard Church. MoRP
Something inspires the only cow of late. The Cow in Apple Time. Robert Frost. CABA; PoLF
Something lives in this house. Tenant. Frances Angevine Gray. FiSC
Something Makes Itself Known. Albert Arnold Scholl, *tr. fr. German by* Christopher Middleton. MGP
Something More. Thad Stem, Jr. PoNC
Something one day occurr'd about a bill. George Crabbe. *Fr.* Tales of the Hall. Par
Something slithers on the beach. The Monster. Dorothy Quick. FiSC
Something startles me where I thought I was safest. This Compost. Walt Whitman. CABA
Something the West Will Remember. H. A. Sieber. PoNC
Something there is that doesn't love a wall. Mending Wall. Robert Frost. AP; CaFP; DiPo; FaBV; FoBA; ILP; PoPo; PoSa; RePo
Something Told the Wild Geese. Rachel Field. PoSC; SoPo
Something Very Elegant. Aileen Fisher. BiCB
Something You Can Do. *Unknown.* STF
Sometime, Somewhere. *Unknown.* STF
Sometimes. Annie Johnson Flint. STF
Sometimes. Thomas S. Jones, Jr. TRV
Sometimes/ I help my dad. Automobile Mechanics. Dorothy Baruch. SoPo
Sometimes a crumb falls. Luck. Langston Hughes. MoLP
Sometimes a light surprises. Joy and Peace in Believing. William Cowper. TRV
Sometimes he was cool like an eternal. Lester Young. Ted Joans. AmNP
Sometimes I fain would find in thee some fault. The Lamp's Shrine. Dante Gabriel Rossetti. The House of Life, XXXV. VP
Sometimes I feel like I will never stop. To Satch [or American Gothic]. Samuel Allen. AmNP; PtTo; SD
Sometimes I have to cross the road. Bobby Blue. John Drinkwater. SoPo
Sometimes I think the hills. The Hills. Rachel Field. RePo
Sometimes in bonnet that she. Heart-summoned. Jesse Stuart. FiSC
Sometimes she is a child within mine arms. Heart's Haven. Dante Gabriel Rossetti. The House of Life, XXII. VP
Sometimes tears of many colors. Georg Grosz. Else Lasker-Schüler. MGP
Sometimes the birds pause in flight. Gray Horizons. Sam Ragan. PoNC
Sometimes the lions' mouths are shut. Sometimes. Annie Johnson Flint. STF
Sometimes [or Somtyme] this world was so steadfast [or stedfast] and stable. Lack of Steadfastness [or Lak of Stedfastnesse]. Chaucer. CBEP; ILP
Sometimes thou seem'st not as thyself alone. Heart's Compass. Dante Gabriel Rossetti. The House of Life, XXVII. VP
Sometimes waking, sometimes sleeping. Nestus Gurley. Randall Jarrell. MP

Sometimes when I see the bare arms of trees in the evening. The Bare Arms of Trees. John Tagliabue. LV
Sometimes when it is bedtime. The Critic. John Farrar. SoPo
Sometimes, when winding slow by brook and bower. Sonnets, Part I, I. Frederick Goddard Tuckerman. PoIE
Sometimes when you are gone. Suite from Catullus. Vincent McHugh. ErPo
Sometimes with One I Love. Walt Whitman. CBEP
Sometimes you hear, fifth-hand. Poetry of Departures. Philip Larkin. MP; ToPo
Somewhere afield here something lies. Shelley's Skylark. Thomas Hardy. FaBV; VP
Somewhere between Crewkerne. Seen from the Train. C. Day Lewis. BoC
Somewhere I Have Never Travelled, Gladly Beyond. E. E. Cummings. AP; BoLP; MP
Somewhere she waits to make you win, your soul in her firm, white hands. The Woman Who Understands. Everard Jack Appleton. PoLF
Somewhere, somewhen I've seen. The Parrots. W. W. Gibson. RoGo
Somewhere the world has a place for you. Take Your Place. *Unknown.* STF
Somewhere there waiteth in this world of ours. Destiny. Sir Edwin Arnold. PoLF
Somewhere upon a battlefield. In Memory of Two Sons. Russell Stellwagon. STF
Somnambulist Ballad. Federico García Lorca, *tr. fr. Spanish by* Robert O'Brien. AnSP
Somtyme this world was so stedfast and stable. *See* Sometimes this world was so steadfast and stable.
Son, The. Edwin Muir. PoDB
"Son,"/ My father used to say. Out in the Woods with Father. David McCord. ThGo
Son, a son, a son, A! I wanted a son of yours. Poem of the Son. "Gabriela Mistral." PoP1
Son and Father. C. Day Lewis. EaLo
Son-Dayes. Henry Vaughan. SeCP
"Son, I am going: the morning" The Mitayo. Manuel González Prada. AnSP
Son, my son! Lament of a Man for His Son. *Unknown, tr. by* Mary Austin. LV
Son of Man, behold with thine eyes, and hear with thine ears. Chorus. T. S. Eliot. *Fr.* The Rock. PoDB
Sonatina. Rubén Darío, *tr. fr. Spanish by* John Crow. AnSP
Sonetto XXXV: To Guido Orlando. Guido Cavalcanti, *tr. fr. Italian by* Ezra Pound. CTC
Sonetto VII: "Who is she that comes, makyng turn every man's eye." Guido Cavalcanti, *tr. fr. Italian by* Ezra Pound. CTC
(Who's This That Comes, as Each Man Looks at Her, *tr. by* G. S. Fraser.) AnML
Song, A: "Absent from thee I languish still." Earl of Rochester. ELP
Song: "Adieu, farewell earth's bliss." Thomas Nashe. *See* Adieu, Farewell, Earth's Bliss.
Song: "April, April." Sir William Watson. *See* April.
Song, A: "As Chloris [or Cloris] full of harmless thoughts." Earl of Rochester. ErPo; UnTE
Song, A: "Ask me no more where Jove bestows." Thomas Carew. CABA; PoIE; SeCP
(Ask Me No More.) ELP
Song: "Before the barn-door crowing." John Gay. *See* Before the Barn-Door Crowing.
Song: "Blow, blow, thou winter wind." Shakespeare. *See* Blow, Blow, Thou Winter Wind.
Song: "Deftly, admiral, cast your fly." W. H. Auden. GTBS-P
Song: "Dressed up in my melancholy." M. Carl Holman. AmNP
Song: "Fair Sylvia, cease to blame my youth." Francis Atterbury. WaPE
Song: "Fear no more the heat o' th' sun." Shakespeare. *See* Fear No More the Heat o' the Sun.
Song: "Feathers of the willow, The." Richard Watson Dixon. CBEP; GTBS-P; OBNC
Song: Fie My Fum. Allen Ginsberg. ErPo
Song: "First month of his absence, The." Alun Lewis. DTC
Song: "For a shape, and a bloom, and an air, and a mien." Edward Moore. WaPE
Song: Fresh from the Dewy Hill, the Merry Year. Blake. FoBA
Song: "Full fathom five thy father lies." Shakespeare. *See* Full Fathom Five.
Song, A: "Gay Florimel, of generous birth." *Unknown.* WaPE
Song: "Go [or Goe] and catch a falling star [or starre]." John Donne. CABA; CaFP; CBEP; DiPo; ELP; EnRePo; ILP; OnP; PoIE; PoP1; PoSa; SeCP; StP
(Go and Catch a Falling Star.) FaBV
Song: "Go, lovely rose!" Edmund Waller. *See* Go, Lovely Rose.

Song: "Grace and beauty has the maid." Gil Vicente, *tr. fr. Spanish by* Alice Jane McVan. SiGo (Cantiga.) RBL
Song: "Gross sun squats above, The." Dom Moraes. NePoEA-2
Song: "He came unlook'd for, undesir'd." Sara Coleridge. CBEP
Song: "He that will court a wench that is coy." *Unknown.* ErPo
Song: "Heavy hours are almost past, The." George Lyttelton. WaPE
Song: "How sweet I roamed from field to field." Blake. CABA; FoBA; OBNC (How Sweet I Roamed.) CBEP
Song: "I make [made, *wr.*] my shroud but no one knows." Adelaide Crapsey. AmLP; LV
Song, The: "I met a ragged man." Theodore Roethke. AP
Song: "I went to her who loveth me no more." Arthur O'Shaughnessy. OBNC
Song: "If a daughter you have, she's the plague of your life." Sheridan. *Fr.* The Duenna. LV
Song: "If the scorn of your bright eyne." Shakespeare. *Fr.* As You Like It, IV, iii. CTC
Song: "If thou art sleeping, maiden." Gil Vicente, *tr. fr. Spanish by* Longfellow. RBL; SiGo
Song: "If you love God, take your mirror between your hands and look." Mahmud Djellaladin Pasha, *tr. fr. Turkish by* E. Powys Mathers. ErPo
Song, A: "In her fair cheeks two pits do lie." Thomas Carew. UnTE
Song XVIII: "In order to remove us." Alfonso X, King of Castile and Leon, *tr. fr. Portuguese by* John E. Keller. AnML
Song, A: "It is not beauty I demand." George Darley. *See* Loveliness of Love, The.
Song: "It was a lover and his lass." Shakespeare. *See* It Was a Lover and His Lass.
Song: Lift Boy. Robert Graves. DTC
Song: "Linnet in the rocky dells, The." Emily Brontë. OBNC
Song: "Lovely hill-torrents are." W. J. Turner. GoJo
Song: Murdring Beautie. Thomas Carew. SeCP
Song: "My dark-headed Käthchen, my spit-kitten darling." John Manifold. BoLP; DTC
Song: My Silks and Fine Array. Blake. *See* My Silks and Fine Array.
Song: "Nay but you, who do not love her." Robert Browning. BoLP
Song: "No, no, fair heretic, it needs must be." Sir John Suckling. *See* No, No, Fair Heretic.
Song III: "Now go I quietly." Garcilaso de la Vega, *tr. fr. Spanish by* Beatrice Gilman Proske. RBL
Song: "Now let us honor with violin and flute." May Sarton. MoRP
Song: "Now the moon is rising." Antonio Machado, *tr. fr. Spanish by* Kate Flores. AnSP
Song, A: "Oh doe not wanton with those eyes." Ben Jonson. SeCP
Song: "O mistress mine, where are you roaming?" Shakespeare. *See* O Mistress Mine.
Song: "Oh my dearie." Eleanor Ross Taylor. PoNC
Song: "Oh roses for the flush of youth." Christina Rossetti. *See* Oh Roses for the Flush of Youth.
Song: "Old England is eaten by knaves." Alexander McLachlan. *Fr.* The Emigrant. OBCV
Song: On May Morning. Milton. FoBA (Song of May Morning.) PoPl
Song: "On the Eastern Way at the City of Lo-yang." Sung Tzu-hou, *tr. fr. Chinese by* Arthur Waley. SiGo
Song: "Out upon it, I have lov'd." Sir John Suckling. *See* Out Upon It.
Song: Owl, The. Tennyson. *See* Owl, The.
Song: "Pardon, goddess of the night." Shakespeare. *Fr.* Much Ado about Nothing, V, iii. CTC
Song: Perswasions to Enjoy. Thomas Carew. SeCP
Song: "Pluck the fruit and taste the pleasure." Thomas Lodge. *Fr.* Robert, Second Duke of Normandy. EnRePo
Song: "Rarely, rarely, comest thou." Shelley. *See* Rarely, Rarely Comest Thou.
Song: "Slow, slow, fresh fount, keep time with my salt tears." Ben Jonson. *See* Slow, Slow, Fresh Fount.
Song: Since Loving Countenance. Clément Marot, *tr. fr. French by* Henry Carrington. RBL
Song: "So have I seen a silver swan." *Unknown.* CBEP
Song, The: "So light no one noticed." Edward Dorn. CoPo
Song: "So, we'll go no more a-Roving." Byron. *See* So We'll Go No More a-Roving.
Song: "Soldier, rest! thy warfare o'er." Sir Walter Scott. *Fr.* The Lady of the Lake. OBNC
Song: "Soules joy, now I am gone." *At. to* the Earl of Pembroke. MeP
Song: "Spirit haunts the year's last hours, A." Tennyson. GTBS-P; ILP; OBNC
Song: "Splendor falls on castle walls, The." Tennyson. *See* Splendor Falls on Castle Walls, The.

Song: "Stay, Phoebus, stay!" Edmund Waller. ILP; SeCP
Song: "Still to be neat, still to be dressed." Ben Jonson. *See* Still to Be Neat.
Song: "Strew not earth with empty stars." Thomas Lovell Beddoes. *Fr.* The Second Brother. CBEP
Song IV: Sudden Light. Dante Gabriel Rossetti. *See* Sudden Light.
Song: "Sunny shaft did I behold, A." Samuel Taylor Coleridge. *See* Glycine's Song.
Song III: "Surrounded by the gentle sound." Garcilaso de la Vega, *tr. fr. Spanish by* Frances Fletcher. AnSP
Song: "Sweetest love, I do not go [*or* goe]." John Donne. CBEP; ELP; EnRePo; FoBA; SeCP (Sweetest Love, I Do Not Go.) FaPl
Song: "Sylvia the fair, in the bloom of fifteen." Dryden. *See* Sylvia the Fair.
Song: "Tears, idle tears, I know not what they mean." Tennyson. *See* Tears, Idle Tears.
Song, A: "Tell me, where is fancy bred." Shakespeare. *See* Tell Me Where Is Fancy Bred.
Song: That Women Are but Men's Shadows [*or* Shaddowes]. Ben Jonson. PoIE; SeCP (That Women Are but Men's Shadows.) CBEP
Song, A: "Thou art the soul of a summer's day." Paul Laurence Dunbar. AmNP
Song: "Though I am young and cannot tell." Ben Jonson. *See* Though I Am Young.
Song: To Celia ("Come, my Celia, let us prove"). Ben Jonson. *See* Come, My Celia.
Song: To Celia ("Drink to me only with thine eyes"). Ben Jonson. *See* To Celia.
Song: "To fix her—'twere a task as vain." Tobias George Smollett. WaPE
Song: To Her Againe, She Burning in a Feaver. Thomas Carew. SeCP
Song: To My Inconstant Mistris. Thomas Carew. SeCP
Song: To My Mistris, I Burning in Love. Thomas Carew. SeCP
Song: To One That Desired to Know My Mistris. Thomas Carew. SeCP
Song: Under the Bronze Leaves. "St.-J. Perse," *tr. fr. French by* T. S. Eliot. *Fr.* Anabasis. PoP1
Song: "Under the greenwood tree." Shakespeare. *See* Under the Greenwood Tree.
Song: "We break the glass, whose sacred wine." Edward Coote Pinkney. AmLP
Song: "We have bathed, where none have seen us." Thomas Lovell Beddoes. *Fr.* Death's Jest Book, IV, iii. OBNC
Song VII: "We should love Saint Mary." Alfonso X, King of Castile and Leon, *tr. fr Portuguese by* John E. Keller. AnML
Song: "We, who are men, how shall we know?" R. S. Thomas. ToPo
Song: "Weary lot is thine, fair maid, A." Sir Walter Scott. *See* Rover, The.
Song: "What shall he have that kill'd the deer?" Shakespeare. *Fr.* As You Like It, IV, ii. CTC
Song: "When daisies pied and violets blue." Shakespeare. *See* When Daisies Pied.
Song: When Early Morn Walks Forth in Sober Gray. Blake. FoBA
Song: "When I am dead, my dearest." Christina Rossetti. *See* When I Am Dead.
Song: "When icicles hang by the wall." Shakespeare. *See* When Icicles Hang by the Wall.
Song: "When lovely woman stoops to folly. Goldsmith. *Fr.* The Vicar of Wakefield, *ch.* 24. ILP; PoP1; VaPo (Stanzas on Women.) ELP (When Lovely Woman Stoops [to Folly].) CBEP; PoIE; StP ("When lovely woman stoops to folly.") GTBS-P
Song: "When the echo of the last footstep dies." E. W. Mandel. OBCV
Song: "When thy beauty appears." Thomas Parnell. *See* When Thy Beauty Appears.
Song, A: "While in the bower, with beauty blessed." Joseph Warton. WaPE
Song: "Who has robbed the ocean wave." John Shaw. AmLP
Song: "Why should a foolish marriage vow." Dryden. *See* Why Should a Foolish Marriage Vow.
Song: "Why so pale and wan, fond lover?" Sir John Suckling. *See* Why So Pale and Wan?
Song, A: "Widow bird sate mourning for her love, A." Shelley. *See* Widow Bird, A.
Song, A: "With love among the haycocks." Ralph Hodgson. GoJo
Song, A: "World is young today, The." Digby Mackworth Dolben. OBNC
Song: "Year's at the spring, The." Robert Browning. *See* Year's at the Spring, The.
Song: "You whom I don't tell that I lie awake." Rainer Maria Rilke, *tr. fr. German by* Walter Kaufmann. TwGP
Song: "Young Philander woo'd me long." *Unknown.* ErPo
Song about Major Eatherly, A. John Wain. CABL; ToPo
Song about Myself, A. Keats. DiPo, *st.* 4; PP

Song Be Delicate. John Shaw Neilson. PoAu-1
Song before the Battle. Friedrich Hauff, *tr. fr. German by* Francis Owen. AGP
Song by Isbrand. Thomas Lovell Beddoes. *Fr.* Death's Jest Book. OBNC
Song by Mr. Cypress. Thomas Love Peacock. *Fr.* Nightmare Abbey. OBNC; Par
Song for a Child. Helen B. Davis. SoPo
Song for a Fifth Child. Ruth H. Hamilton. LV
Song for a Girl. Dryden. ELP; ErPo
　(Sung by a Young Girl.) UnTE
Song for a Marriage. Vassar Miller. ToPo
Song for a Slight Voice. Louise Bogan. AmLP
Song for All Seas, All Ships. Walt Whitman. HaSV; MoRP
Song for an Allegorical Play. John Ciardi. PoCh
Song for Beauty, A. P. Lal. ACV
Song for St. Cecilia's Day. W. H. Auden. MP
Song for Saint Cecilia's Day, A, November 22, 1687. Dryden. CABA; CBEP; DiPo; GTBS-P; ILP; OnP; PoIE
Instruments, The, *sel.* PoPo
Song for Simeon, A. T. S. Eliot. EaLo
Song for the Last Act. Louise Bogan. AmLP
Song for the Virgin Mary. *Unknown, tr. fr. German by* Ruth Yorck *and* Kenward Elmslie. AnML
Song for Zarathustra. Lawrence Durrell. ToPo
Song from a Country Fair. Léonie Adams. GoJo
Song from Shakespeare's "Cymbeline," A. William Collins. EiCP
　(Dirge in "Cymbeline.") ELP
Song from the Gulf. Rolfe Humphries. MoLP
Song in a Winter Night. Bink Noll. ToPo
Song in His Lady's Absence, A. *Unknown.* MeEL
Song in Humility, A. Carleton Drewry. MoRP
Song in the Songless. George Meredith. ACV
Song in the valley of Nemea, A. Nemea. Lawrence Durrell. AnMoPo; GTBS-P
Song is not singing. Kissing the Dancer. Robert Sward. CoPo
Song-Maker, The. Kingsley Fairbridge. ACV
Song of a Fool. W. B. Yeats. *Fr.* Two Songs of a Fool. PoDB
Song of a Heathen, The. Richard Watson Gilder. TRV
Song of a Man Who Has Come Through. D. H. Lawrence. GTBS-P; PoIE
Song of a Thousand Years. Don Marquis. WePo
Song of a Young Lady to Her Ancient Lover, A. Earl of Rochester. ErPo
Song of an Old Sailor. Trefor Davies. HaSV
Song of Autumn. Paul Verlaine, *tr. fr. French by* Arthur Symons. SiGo
Song of Brother Green, The. *Unknown. See* Brother Green.
Song of Dalliance, A. William Cartwright. ErPo
Song of Greatness, A. *Unknown, tr. fr. Chippewa Indian by* Mary Austin. BiCB; RePo
Song of Hiawatha, The, *sels.* Longfellow.
　"As the bow unto the cord is." TRV
　Hiawatha's Childhood. FaBV; RePo
Song of Hope. Thomas Hardy. VP
Song of January. Gerta Kennedy. PoPl
Song of Joys, A, *sel.* Walt Whitman.
　"O to sail in a ship!" HaSV
Song of Kilvani, The: fairest she. The Law of Death. John Hay. SIV
Song of Love and Death, The. Tennyson. *Fr.* Idylls of the King: Lancelot and Elaine. OBNC
Song of Love for Jesus, A. Richard Rolle. MeEL
Song of Low Degree, A. Bunyan. *See* Shepherd Boy's Song, The.
Song of Marion's Men. Bryant. ThLM
Song of May Morning. Milton. *See* Song: On May Morning.
Song of Milkanwatha, The, *parody, sel.* George A. Strong. Modern Hiawatha. LV; Par
Song of Mr. Toad, The. Kenneth Grahame. *See* World Has Held Great Heroes, The.
Song of Momus to Mars, The. Dryden. *Fr.* The Secular Masque. CBEP
Song of My Heart, A. Robert Bridges. ACV
Song of Myself. Walt Whitman. AP; PoIE, *much abr.*
Sels.
　Animals, XXXII. PoPl
　(Beasts, The.) CBEP
　("I think I could turn and live with animals, they are so placid and self-contained.") BoC
　"I believe a leaf of grass is no less than the journey-work of the stars," XXXI. TRV
　"I celebrate myself, and sing myself," I. PP
　"It is time to explain myself—let us stand up," XLIV. DiPo
　Old-Time Sea-Fight, An, XXXV. OnMSP
　"Spotted hawk swoops and accuses me, The," LII. PP
Song of Panama, A. Damon Runyon. ThLM
Song of Parting. João Roiz de Castelo-Branco, *tr. fr. Portuguese by* William M. Davis. AnML
Song of Pleasure, A. Phillip Massinger. *Fr.* The Picture. UnTE

Song of Quoodle, The. G. K. Chesterton. GoJo; WePo
Song of Rapture. Nietzsche, *tr. fr. German by* Frances Stillman. AGP
Song of Solomon, The. Bible, *O.T.*
　(Song of Songs, The.) UnTE
Sels.
　"Voice of my beloved, The!" II: 8-13. PoPl; SiGo (II: 8-14, 16-17; IV: 16)
　Winter is Past, The, II: 11-12. SoPo
　(Time of the Singing of Birds, The.) ThGo
Song of Songs, The. Heine, *tr. fr. German by* Louis Untermeyer. UnTE
Song of sunshine through the rain, A. An Easter Song. "Susan Coolidge." TRV
Song of the Answerer, *sel.* Walt Whitman.
　"Indications and tally of time, The." PP
Song of the Argonauts. William Morris. *Fr.* The Life and Death of Jason. HaSV
Song of the Argonauts, *with music.* Sam C. Upham. SGR
Song of the Arrow, The. Isabella Valancy Crawford. *Fr.* Gisli, the Chieftain. OBCV
Song of the Artesian Water. A. B. Paterson. ACV
Song of the Captured Woman. James Devaney. PoAu-1
Song of the Chattahoochee. Sidney Lanier. AP; DiPo; FaBV; LV
Song of the Creatures, The. St. Francis of Assisi. *See* Canticle of the Sun.
Song of the Darling River. Henry Lawson. ACV
Song of the Emigrants in Bermuda. Andrew Marvell. *See* Bermudas.
Song of the Exposition, *sel.* Walt Whitman.
　"Come, Muse, migrate from Greece and Ionia." PP
Song of the English, A, *sel.* Kipling.
　"We have fed our sea for a thousand years." HaSV
Song of the Four Seasons, A. Austin Dobson. BoC
Song of the Four Winds, The. Thomas Love Peacock. *Fr.* The Misfortunes of Elphin. WiR
Song of the Galley-Slaves. Kipling. GTBS-P
Song of the Harp Player. Goethe. *See* Harp Player's Song, The.
Song of the Idiot, The. Rainer Maria Rilke, *tr. fr. German by* Walter Kaufmann. TwGP
Song of the Inconstant Hylas. Honoré d'Urfé, *tr. fr. French by* Charles Cotton. RBL
Song of the Mad Prince, The. Walter de la Mare. GoJo
Song of the Master and Boatswain. W. H. Auden. *Fr.* The Sea and the Mirror. DTC; HaSV
Song of the Midnight Rain. John Gould Fletcher. MoLP
Song of the Muses, The. Matthew Arnold. WiR
Song of the Old Mother, The. W. B. Yeats. LOW; PoPo
Song of the Open Road. Ogden Nash. PoPo
Song of the Parcae. Goethe, *tr. fr. German by* Charles E. Passage. AGP
Song of the Rain. Hugh McCrae. PoAu-1
Song of the Reim-Kennar, The. Sir Walter Scott. *Fr.* The Pirate. OBNC
Song of the Rice Bargees. Bertolt Brecht, *tr. fr. German by* Christopher Middleton. MGP
Song of the Rushes (V). Nikolaus Lenau, *tr. fr. German by* Roger C. Norton. AGP
Song of the saw, The. Busy Carpenters. James S. Tippett. SoPo
Song of the Sea, The. Conrad Ferdinand Meyer, *tr. fr. German by* D. G. Wright. AGP
Song of the Shetland Fishers. Sir Walter Scott. HaSV
Song of the Shirt, The. Thomas Hood. CABL; FaPL; PoPo
Song of the Son. Jean Toomer. AmNP
Song of the Spirits over the Waters. Goethe, *tr. fr. German by* R. L. Kahn. AGP
Song of the Thrush, The. T. A. Daly. LV
Song of the Train. David McCord. SoPo
Song of the Vivandiere. Heine, *tr. fr. German by* Louis Untermeyer. UnTE
Song of Wandering Aengus, The. W. B. Yeats. BoLP; DiPo; GoJo; LOW; PoSa
Song of the Western Men, The. Robert Stephen Hawker. CBEP; OBNC; RoGo
　(And Shall Trelawny Die?) EvOK
Song of Winter, A. Emily Davis Pfeiffer. ACV
Song of the Woman-Drawer, The. Mary Gilmore. PoAu-1
Song of the Zambra Dance. Dryden. *See* Beneath a Myrtle Shade.
Song of War, A. Matthias Claudius, *tr. fr. German by* Albert Bloch. AGP
Song-Offering, A. Rabindranath Tagore, *tr. fr. Sanskrit by* Rabindranath Tagore. Gitanjali, LVII. SiGo
Song on the Death of Colonel Crafford, A. *Unknown.* BSO
Song Set by John Farmer. *Unknown.* CTC
Song Set by Nicholas Yonge. *Unknown. See* Brown Is My Love.
Song the Body Dreamed in the Spirit's Mad Behest, The. Brother Antoninus. ErPo
Song to a Fair Young Lady Going Out of [the] Town in the Spring. Dryden. CABA; PoIE

Song to Celia ("Come, my Celia, let us prove"). Ben Jonson. *See* Come, My Celia.
Song, to Celia ("Drink to me only with thine eyes"). Ben Jonson. *See* To Celia.
Song to Cloris, A. Earl of Rochester. ErPo
Song to David, A. Christopher Smart. EiCP; EnPE
Sels.
 Beauteous, Yea Beauteous More than These. EaLo
 "He sang of God—the mighty source." TRV
Song to His Purse for the King, A. Chaucer. *See* Complaint to His Purse.
Song to John, Christ's Friend, A. *Unknown.* MeEL
Song to Mary, A. William of Shoreham(?). MeEL
Song to Steingerd. Cormac Ogmundarson, tr. fr. Old Norse by W. G. Collingwood and Jon Stefansson. SiGo
Song to the Men of England. Shelley. ILP; PoPo
Song to the Tune of "Somebody Stole My Gal." X. J. Kennedy. CoPo
Song under Shadow. William Rose Benét. MoRP
Song Wants to Be Light, The. Federico García Lorca, tr. fr. Spanish by Rachel Benson and Robert O'Brien. AnSP
Song you sang you will not sing again, The. Local Places. Howard Moss. NePoEA-2
Song's Eternity. John Clare. CBEP
Songs in Absence, sel. Arthur Hugh Clough.
 Where Lies the Land [to Which the Ship Would Go]? VII. HaSV; ILP; PoIE
Songs light as these may sound, though deep and strong. Dedication to Christina G. Rossetti. Swinburne. StP
Songs of Bilitis, The, sels. Pierre Louÿs, tr. fr. French by Horace M. Brown. UnTE
 Absence.
 Bilitis.
 Desire.
 Despairing Embrace, The.
 Endearments.
 Kiss, The.
 Little House, The.
 Remorse.
Songs of Ch'en, sels. Confucius, tr. fr. Chinese by Ezra Pound. Fr. The Classic Anthology. CTC
 Aliter.
 "Marsh bank, lotus rank."
Songs of Cheng, sels. Confucius, tr. fr. Chinese by Ezra Pound. Fr. The Classic Anthology. CTC
 "Be kind, good sir, and I'll lift my sark."
 "Hep-Cat Chung, 'ware my town."
 "In chariot like an hibiscus flower at his side."
 "So he won't talk to me when we meet?"
Songs of Creation. Heine, tr. fr. German by Walter Kaufmann. TwGP
Songs of Experience, sels. Blake.
 Ah! Sun-Flower. CABA; CBEP; DiPo; ELP; FoBA; OBNC
 Bard, The. TRV
 Chimney Sweeper, The. CABA; EnPE; FoBA; PoIE
 Clod and the Pebble, The. CABA; CBEP; FaBV; OBNC
 Earth's Answer. CBEP; EnPE
 Fly, The. CBEP; DiPo; PoSa
 Garden of Love, The. CABA; CBEP; DiPo; FaBV; FoBA; PoIE; StP; VaPo
 Holy Thursday. EnPE; ILP; PoIE; StP
 Human Abstract, The. DiPo
 Infant Sorrow. CBEP; DiPo; FoBA; OBNC
 Introduction: "Hear the voice of the Bard!" EnPE
  (Hear the Voice of the Bard.) CBEP; ELP
 Lilly, The. FoBA
 Little Boy Lost, A. CBEP; PoIE
 Little Girl Found, The. CBEP; DiPo
 Little Girl Lost, The. DiPo
 London. CABA; CaFP; CBEP; DiPo; EnPE; FoBA; ILP; OBNC; OnP; PoIE; PoSa; StP
 My Pretty Rose-Tree. FoBA
 Nurse's Song. FoBA
 Poison Tree, A. CABA; CaFP; CBEP; DiPo; FoBA; VaPo
 Schoolboy, The. CBEP
 Sick Rose, The. CABA; CaFP; CBEP; DiPo; FoBA; ILP; OBNC; PoIE; PoSa; StP
  (O Rose, Thou Art Sick!) ELP
 Tiger, The. BoC; CBEP; EnPE; PoLF; PoPl; PoPo; PoSa; RoGo; StP; TRV; VaPo; WePo
  (Tyger, The.) CABA; CaFP; DiPo; EaLo; FaBV; FoBA; ILP; OBNC; OnP; PoIE
Songs of Innocence, sels. Blake.
 Blossom, The. CBEP; FoBA; GoJo
 Chimney Sweeper, The. CaFP; CBEP; DiPo; EnPE; FoBA; ILP; PoIE
 Cradle Song, A: "Sweet dreams form a shade." CBEP
 Divine Image, The. CBEP; EnPE; OBNC; PoIE; TRV
 Dream, A. CBEP
 Echoing [or Ecchoing] Green, The. CaFP; CBEP; DiPo; PoSC; WiR
 Holy Thursday. BoC; CBEP; DiPo; EnPE; FoBA; PoIE; StP
 Infant Joy. BiCB; CBEP; FoBA; GoJo; PoLF
 Lamb, The. CABA; CaFP; CBEP; DiPo; EaLo; EnPE; FoBA; GoJo; ILP; PoIE; PoPl; PoPo; TRV; VaPo
 Laughing Song. CBEP; DiPo; GoJo; PoSC; SoPo
 Little Black Boy, The. BoC; CABA; CaFP; CBEP; DiPo; EnPE; FoBA; ILP; OBNC; PoIE
 Little Boy Found, The. CBEP
 Little Boy Lost. CBEP
 Night. CBEP; PoLF; WiR
  (Guardian Angels of the Creatures.) BoC
 Nurse's Song. CBEP; FoBA
 On Another's Sorrow. CBEP; FaBV
 Piping down the Valleys Wild. CBEP; FaBV
  (Introduction: "Piping down the valleys wild.") DiPo; EnPE; GoJo; ILP; OBNC; PoIE
  (Piper, The.) RoGo
 Shepherd, The. CBEP
 Spring. PoPl
Songs of Seven, sels. Jean Ingelow.
 Seven Times One. BiCB; OBNC
  (Birthday Morning.) ThGo
 Seven Times Three—Love. PoLF
Songs of T'ang, sel. Confucius, tr. fr. Chinese by Ezra Pound. Fr. The Classic Anthology.
 Alba. CTC
Songs of the People, sel. Chaim Nachman Bialik, tr. fr. Hebrew by Maurice Samuel.
 Tell Him. SiGo
Songs of the Sea-Children, sels. Bliss Carman. OBCV
 "I see the golden hunter go," LIV.
 "What is it to remember?" LXVI.
Songs of the Squatters. Robert Lowe. PoAu-1
Songs of Travel, sels. Robert Louis Stevenson. OBNC
 "Bright is the ring of words."
 If This Were Faith.
 To S. R. Crockett.
Sonne, The. George Herbert. SeCP
Sonnet, The ("A sonnet is a moment's monument"). Dante Gabriel Rossetti. The House of Life, introd. ILP; StP; VP
 (Sonnet Is a Moment's Monument, A.) PP
Sonnet: "After dark vapours have oppress'd our plains." Keats. *See* After Dark Vapours.
Sonnet: "Alas, 'tis true I have gone here and there." Shakespeare. Sonnets, CX. CBEP
Sonnet VII: "And so one sees all living matter perish." Louise Labé, tr. fr French by Frederic Prokosch. RBL
Sonnet IX: "As soon as I withdraw to take my rest." Louise Labé, tr. fr. French by Alan Conder. RBL
Sonnet: "Beehould a cluster to itt selfe a vine." William Alabaster. MeP
Sonnet: "Being your slave, what should I do but tend." Shakespeare. *See* Sonnets, LVII.
Sonnet: "Beshrew that heart that makes my heart to groan." Shakespeare. Sonnets, CXXXIII. CBEP
Sonnet: "Bright star! would I were steadfast as thou art." Keats. *See* Bright Star! Would I Were Steadfast as Thou Art.
Sonnet: "But be contented: when that fell arrest." Shakespeare. Sonnets, LXXIV. CBEP
Sonnet VI: "Chasten your fears, I have not been destroyed." Mark Van Doren. MoLP
Sonnet: "Dear Geese, whose haunt is where weak waters flow." Luis de Góngora, tr. fr. Spanish by Edward Churton. RBL
Sonnet: Death Warnings. Francisco de Quevedo y Villegas, tr. fr. Spanish by John Masefield. RBL
Sonnet: "Devouring Time, blunt thou the lion's paw." Shakespeare. *See* Sonnets, XIX.
Sonnet: "Don't worry, it will come! You're drawing near." Phillippe Jaccottet, tr. fr. French by Donald Justice. CoFP
Sonnet: "Dost see how unregarded now." Sir John Suckling. ELP
Sonnet: Double Rock, The. Henry King. SeCP
Sonnet: Dress Your Gold Locks. Philippe Desportes, tr. fr. French by Henry Carrington. RBL
Sonnet: England in 1819. Shelley. *See* England in 1819.
Sonnet: "Expense of spirit in a waste of shame, The." Shakespeare. *See* Sonnets, CXXIX.
Sonnet: "Fair is my love that feeds among the lilies." Bartholomew Griffin. Fr. Fidessa, More Chaste than Kind. ErPo
 (Fair Is My Love.) CBEP
Sonnet: "Fair Naiads of the river, that reside." Garcilaso de la Vega, tr. fr. Spanish by Jeremiah H. Wiffen. RBL
Sonnet: "First time he kissed me, he but only kissed." Elizabeth Barrett Browning. *See* Sonnets from the Portuguese: "First time he kissed . . ."
Sonnet: "Full many a glorious morning have I seen." Shakespeare. *See* Sonnets, XXXIII.
Sonnet: "Haile gracefull morning of eternall daye." William Alabaster. MeP
Sonnet I: "He came in silver armor, trimmed with black." Gwendolyn B. Bennett. AmNP

Sonnet: Head Next to Mine. Carl Bode. ToPo
Sonnet, A: "His golden locks time hath to silver turn'd." George Peele. *See* His Golden Locks.
Sonnet: "Holy, holy, holy Lord unnamed." William Alabaster. MeP
Sonnet: "How like a winter hath my absence been." Shakespeare. *See* Sonnets, XCVII.
Sonnet: "How soon hath Time the suttle theef of youth." Milton. *See* How Soon Hath Time.
Sonnet: "How sweet and lovely dost thou make the shame." Shakespeare. Sonnets, XCV. CBEP
Sonnet XLI: "I, being born a woman and distressed." Edna St. Vincent Millay. ErPo
Sonnet: "I grant thou wert not married to my Muse." Shakespeare. Sonnets, LXXXII. CBEP
Sonnet: "I hate the money-lending avarice." Joachim du Bellay, *tr. French by* R. N. Currey. *Fr.* Regrets. RBL
Sonnet: "I said I splendidly loved you; it's not true." Rupert Brooke. CBEP
Sonnet XIV: "I was confused; I cannot promise more." Mark Van Doren. MoLP
Sonnet: "Idly she yawned, and threw her heavy hair." George Moore. ErPo
Sonnet: "If the dull substance of my flesh were thought." Shakespeare. Sonnets, XLIV. CBEP
Sonnet: "If thou survive my well-contented day." Shakespeare. *See* Sonnets, XXXII.
Sonnet: "In faith, I do not love thee with mine eyes." Shakespeare. Sonnets, CXLI. CBEP
Sonnet: "In the old age black was not counted fair." Shakespeare. *See* Sonnets, CXXVII.
Sonnet: "In vain to me the smiling mornings shine." Thomas Gray. *See* Sonnet on the Death of Mr. Richard West.
Sonnet: "Is there a great green commonwealth of Thought." John Masefield. ILP
Sonnet: "It is not death, that sometime in a sigh." Thomas Hood. OBNC
Sonnet: "It is not to be thought of that the flood." Wordsworth. ACV
Sonnet: "Jesu thie love within mee is soe maine." William Alabaster. MeP
Sonnet: Leaves. William Barnes. OBNC
Sonnet: "Let me confess that we two must be twain." Shakespeare. Sonnets, XXXVI. CBEP
Sonnet: "Let me not to the marriage of true minds." Shakespeare. *See* Sonnets, CXVI.
Sonnet: "Let those who are in favour with their stars." Shakespeare. Sonnets, XXV. CBEP
Sonnet: "Lift not the painted veil which those who live." Shelley. OBNC
Sonnet: "Like as the waves make towards the pebbled shore." Shakespeare. *See* Sonnets, LX.
Sonnet: "Like as, to make our appetites more keen." Shakespeare. *See* Sonnets, CXVIII.
Sonnet: "Lo, as a careful housewife runs to catch." Shakespeare. Sonnets, CXLIII. CBEP
Sonnet: "Long time a child, and still a child, when years." Hartley Coleridge. *See* Long Time a Child.
Sonnet XXX: "Love is not all: it is not meat nor drink." Edna St. Vincent Millay. AmLP; BoLP; MoLP
Sonnet: "Love is too young to know what conscience is." Shakespeare. Sonnets, CLI. CBEP
Sonnet: Mackado, Fustian and Motley. John Taylor. *Fr.* Odcomb's Complaint. CBEP
Sonnet: "Master and the slave go hand in hand, The." E. A. Robinson. PP
Sonnet: "Methought I saw my late espouséd saint." Milton. *See* Methought I Saw My Late Espoused Saint.
Sonnet: "Mine eyes beheld the blessed pity spring." Dante, *tr. Italian by* Dante Gabriel Rossetti. La Vita Nuova, XXIII. PoPl
Sonnet: "My duchess was the werst she laffed she bitte." Ernest Walsh. ErPo
Sonnet: "My God, where is that ancient heat towards thee." George Herbert. MeP
(Untitled.) LV
Sonnet: "My love is as a fever, longing still." Shakespeare. *See* Sonnets, CXLVII.
Sonnet: "My mistress' eyes are nothing like the sun." Shakespeare. *See* Sonnets, CXXX.
Sonnet XXXIII: "My only need—you ask me, and I tell you." Mark Van Doren. MoLP
Sonnet: "My soule a world is by contraccion." William Alabaster. MeP
Sonnet: "Night, the starlesse night of passion, The." William Alabaster. MeP
Sonnet: "No longer mourn for me when I am dead." Shakespeare. *See* Sonnets, LXXI.
Sonnet: "No more be grieved at that which thou hast done." Shakespeare. *See* Sonnets, XXXV.
Sonnet: "No worst, there is none. Pitched past pitch of grief." Gerard Manley Hopkins. *See* No Worst, There Is None.
Sonnet: "Not, I'll not, carrion comfort, Despair, not feast on thee." Gerard Manley Hopkins. *See* Carrion Comfort.

Sonnet: "Not marble, nor the gilded monuments." Shakespeare. *See* Sonnets, LV.
Sonnet: "Not mine own fears, nor the prophetic soul." Shakespeare. *See* Sonnets, CVII.
Sonnet: "Not wrongly moved by this dismaying scene." William Empson. ToPo
Sonnet: November. Hartley Coleridge. OBNC
Sonnet: "Now I have found thee, I will ever more." William Alabaster. MeP
Sonnet: "Now that the midd day heate doth scorch my shame." William Alabaster. MeP
Sonnet: "Oh for a poet—for a beacon bright." E. A. Robinson. ILP; PP
Sonnet III: "Oh! for some honest lovers ghost." Sir John Suckling. *See* O for Some Honest Lover's Ghost.
Sonnet XVIII: "O kiss me yet again, O kiss me over." Louise Labé, *tr. fr. French by* Frederic Prokosch. RBL
Sonnet: "Oh! sigh no more, no longer paint the air." George Henry Boker. Sonnets, LXXIX. AmLP
Sonnet: "Oh spring, that hides the wrinkled earth in green." George Henry Boker. Sonnets, CXV. AmLP
Sonnet: "O starry temple of unvalted space." William Alabaster. MeP
Sonnet: "O sweete, and bitter monuments of paine." William Alabaster. MeP
Sonnet XIII: "Oh were I faint with love upon the breast." Louise Labé, *tr. fr. French by* George Wyndham. RBL
Sonnet: O World. George Santayana. *See* O World.
Sonnet II: "Of thee (kind boy) I ask no red and white." Sir John Suckling. SeCP
(To Cupid.) CBEP
Sonnet X: On Finding Some Keepsakes of His Dead Mistress. Garcilaso de la Vega, *tr. fr. Spanish by* Walter T. Pattison. RBL
Sonnet: On the Death of Richard West. Thomas Gray. *See* Sonnet on the Death of Mr. Richard West.
Sonnet: "Patience, hard thing! the hard thing but to pray." Gerard Manley Hopkins. *See* Patience, Hard Thing!
Sonnet: "Planking of the vessel torn apart, The." Luis de Góngora, *tr. fr. Spanish by* Elisha Kane. RBL
Sonnet: "Poor soul, the centre of my sinful earth." Shakespeare. *See* Sonnets, CXLVI.
Sonnet XIII: "Rise up, rise up, Jack Spratt. And you, his wife." Winfield Townley Scott. ErPo
Sonnet: "Shall I compare thee to a summer's day?" Shakespeare. *See* Sonnets, XVIII.
Sonnet: "She is so young, and never never before." Edward Davison. ErPo
Sonnet: "She took the dappled partridge flecked with blood." Tennyson. CABA
Sonnet: Silence. Thomas Hood. *See* Silence.
Sonnet: Silence. Poe. AP
Sonnet: "Since brass, nor stone, nor earth, nor boundless sea." Shakespeare. *See* Sonnets LXV.
Sonnet: "Sits by a fireplace, the seducer talks." Leonard Wolf. ErPo
Sonnet: "So, now I have confest that he is thine." Shakespeare. Sonnets, CXXXIV. CBEP
Sonnet: "Some glory in their birth, some in their skill." Shakespeare. Sonnets, XCI. CBEP
Sonnet II: "Some things are very dear to me." Gwendolyn B. Bennett. AmNP
Sonnet, The: "Sonnet is a moment's monument, A." Dante Gabriel Rossetti. *See* Sonnet, The ("A sonnet is a moment's monument").
Sonnet: "Sunne begins uppon my heart to shine, The." William Alabaster. MeP
Sonnet: "Sure Lord, there is enough in thee to dry." George Herbert. MeP
Sonnet: "Sweet love, renew thy force; be it not said." Shakespeare. *See* Sonnets, LVI.
Sonnet: "Take all my loves, my love, yea, take them all." Shakespeare. Sonnets, XL. CBEP
Sonnet: "Tell me no more how fair she is." Henry King. SeCP
Sonnet: "That thou hast her, it is not all my grief." Shakespeare. Sonnets, XLII. CBEP
Sonnet: "That time of year thou mayst in me behold." Shakespeare. *See* Sonnets, LXXIII.
Sonnet: "They that have power to hurt and will do none." Shakespeare. *See* Sonnets, XCIV.
Sonnet XV: "This is the way we say it in our time." Winfield Townley Scott. ErPo
Sonnet: "This virgin, beautiful and lively day." Stéphane Mallarmé, *tr. French by* Roger Fry. PoPl
Sonnet: "Those flakes of fire, brilliant sparks of light." Pedro Calderon de la Barca, *tr. fr. Spanish by* Eleanor L. Turnbull. RBL
Sonnet: "Those parts of thee that the world's eye doth view." Shakespeare. Sonnets, LXIX. CBEP
Sonnet: "Those pretty wrongs that liberty commits." Shakespeare. Sonnets, XLI. CBEP
Sonnet: "Thou fair-haired angel of the evening." Blake. *See* To the Evening Star.
Sonnet: "Three seasons only in his calendar." George Henry Boker. Sonnets, CXCIV. AmLP

Sonnet: "Three sortes of teares doe from myne eies distraine." William Alabaster. MeP
Sonnet: "Tired with all these, for restful death I cry." Shakespeare. See Sonnets, LXVI.
Sonnet: "'Tis better to be vile than vile esteemed." Shakespeare. Sonnets, CXXI. CBEP
Sonnet: To a Friend. Hartley Coleridge. See To a Friend.
Sonnet: "To me, fair friend, you never can be old." Sonnets, CIV. See Shakespeare.
Sonnet: To Science. Poe. Al Aaraaf: Prologue. ILP
(Sonnet—to Science.) AP
(To Science.) CBEP
Sonnet: To Tartar, a Terrier Beauty. Thomas Lovell Beddoes. OBNC
Sonnet: "Tonight I walked with the grim Florentine." George Henry Boker. Sonnets, LXVI. AmLP
Sonnet: "Two loves I have of comfort and despair." Shakespeare. See Sonnets, CXLIV.
Sonnet, A: "Two voices are there: one is of the deep." J. K. Stephen. Par
Sonnet: "Unhappy man, as soon as he is born." Giambattista Marino, tr. fr. Italian by Lorna de' Lucchi. RBL
Sonnet V: "Venus, who wander clear among the skies." Louise Labé, tr. fr. French by Frederic Prokosch. RBP
Sonnet XII: "Virgins terrify too many men." Winfield Townley Scott. ErPo
Sonnet: "Was it the proud full sail of this great verse." Shakespeare. Sonnets, LXXXVI. CBEP
Sonnet: "Way feare with thy projectes, noe false fyre, A." William Alabaster. MeP
Sonnet: "What meaneth this, that Christ an hymne did singe." William Alabaster. MeP
Sonnet: "What potions have I drunk of Siren tears." Shakespeare. Sonnets, CXIX. CBEP
Sonnet: "When I consider how my light is spent." Milton. See On His Blindness.
Sonnet: "When I do count the clock that tells the time." Shakespeare. See Sonnets, XII.
Sonnet: "When I have fears that I may cease to be." Keats. See When I Have Fears.
Sonnet: "When I have seen by Time's fell hand defaced." Shakespeare. See Sonnets, LXIV.
Sonnet: "When, in disgrace with fortune and men's eyes." Shakespeare. See Sonnets XXIX.
Sonnet: "When in the chronicle of wasted time." Shakespeare. See Sonnets, CVI.
Sonnet: "When most I wink, then do mine eyes best see." Shakespeare. Sonnets, XLIII. CBEP
Sonnet: "When to the sessions of sweet silent thought." Shakespeare. See Sonnets, XXX.
Sonnet XXVIII: "When we are old and these rejoicing veins." Edna St. Vincent Millay. ErPo
Sonnet: "When without tears I looke on Christ, I see." William Alabaster. MeP
Sonnet: "Where are we to go when this is done?" Alfred A. Duckett. AmNP
Sonnet: Window, The. Carl Bode. ToPo
Sonnet: "Winter deepening, the hay all in, The." Richard Wilbur. PoP1
Sonnet: "Why didst thou promise such a beauteous day." Shakespeare. Sonnets, XXXIV. CBEP
Sonnet: "Woman's face, with Nature's own hand painted, A." Shakespeare. Sonnets, XX.
Sonnet XIV: "Yes, and as long as these poor eyes can bring." Louise Labé, tr. fr. French by Frederic Prokosch. RBL
Sonnet: "Yesterday a human deity, today a bit of dust." Luis de Góngora, tr. fr. Spanish by Elisha Kane. RBL
Sonnet: "You say my love no marvel is to you." George Henry Boker. Sonnets, CLIII. AmLP
Sonnet All of a Sudden, A. Lope de Vega, tr. fr. Spanish by Doreen Bell. AnSP
Sonnet for a Picture. Swinburne. VP
Sonnet for John-John. Marvin Solomon. OPP
Sonnet in Autumn. Donald Petersen. NePoEA-2
Sonnet Is a Moment's Monument, A. Dante Gabriel Rossetti. See Sonnet, The ("A sonnet is a moment's monument").
Sonnet on Chillon. Byron. Fr. The Prisoner of Chillon. CABL; ILP; PoPo
("Eternal Spirit of the Chainless Mind!") PoP1
(On the Castle of Chillon.) GTBS-P
Sonnet on the Death of Mr. Richard West. Thomas Gray. StP
(Sonnet: "In vain to me the smiling mornings shine.") EiCP
(Sonnet: On the Death of Richard West.) EnPE
Sonnet to a Negro in Harlem. Helene Johnson. AmNP
Sonnet to Heavenly Beauty, A. Joachim du Bellay, tr. fr. French by Andrew Lang. Fr. L'Olive. CTC; RBL
Sonnet to My Mother. George Barker. See To My Mother.
Sonnet—to Science. Poe. See Sonnet: To Science.
Sonnet to William Wilberforce, Esq. William Cowper. ILP
Sonnet, Written by a Nymph in Her Own Blood, A. Claudio Achillini, tr. fr. Italian by Philip Ayres. RBL
Sonnets, sels. George Henry Boker. AmLP

"Oh! sigh no more, no longer paint the air," LXXIX.
"Oh spring, that hides the wrinkled earth in green," CXV.
"Three seasons only in his calendar," CXCIV.
"Tonight I walked with the grim Florentine," LXVI.
"You say my love no marvel is to you," CLIII.
Sonnets, sels. Shakespeare.
I. "From fairest creatures we desire increase." CTC
II. "When forty winters shall besige thy brow." FoBA
III. Look in thy glass, and tell the face thou viewest." CABA; EnRePo
XII. "When I do count the clock that tells the time." CBEP; DiPo; EnRePo; FoBA
XV. "When I consider everything that grows." DiPo; FoBA
XVII. "Who will believe my verse in time to come." DiPo
XVIII. "Shall I compare thee to a summer's day?" CBEP; CTC; DiPo; FaBV; FoBA; ILP; PoIE; PoLF; PoP1; PoPo; PoSa; StP
(To His Love.) GTBS-P; WePo
XIX. "Devouring Time, blunt thou the lion's paw." CBEP; DiPo; FoBA
XX. "Woman's face, with Nature's own hand painted, A." CBEP; ErPo
XXV. "Let those who are in favour with their stars." CBEP
XXVII. "Weary with toil, I haste me to my bed." DiPo
XXIX. "When, in disgrace with fortune and men's eyes." BoLP; CBEP; CTC; DiPo; FaBV; FoBA; ILP; LV; PoIE; PoP1; PoPo; PoSa; TRV
(Consolation, A.) GTBS-P
XXX. "When to the sessions of sweet silent thought." CABA; CaFP; CBEP; CTC; DiPo; EnRePo; FaBV; ILP; PoIE; PoLF; PoPo
(Remembrance.) GTBS-P; TRV
XXXII. "If thou survive my well-contented day." CBEP; PP
(Post Mortem.) GTBS-P
XXXIII. "Full many a glorious morning have I seen." CBEP; FoBA; ILP
XXXIV. "Why didst thou promise such a beauteous day." CBEP
XXXV. "No more be grieved at that which thou hast done." CABA; CBEP
XXXVI. "Let me confess that we two must be twain." CBEP
XL. "Take all my loves, my love, yea, take them all." CBEP
XLI. "Those pretty wrongs that liberty commits." CBEP
XLII. "That thou hast her, it is not all my grief." CBEP
XLIII. "When most I wink, then do mine eyes best see." CBEP
XLIV. "If the dull substance of my flesh were thought." CBEP
LIII. "What is your substance, whereof are you made." CTC; EnRePo
LV. "Not marble nor the gilded monuments. CABA; CBEP; CTC; DiPo; EnRePo; FoBA; ILP; PoPo; PoSa; PP; VaPo
LVI. "Sweet love, renew thy force; be it not said." CBEP; PoLF
LVII. "Being your slave, what should I do but tend." BoLP
(Absence.) GTBS-P
LX. "Like as the waves make towards the pebbled shore." CBEP; EnRePo
(Revolutions.) GTBS-P
LXII. "Sin of self-love possessth all mine eye." EnRePo
LXIV. "When I have seen by Time's fell hand defaced." CABA; EnRePo; FoBA; ILP; PoIE; PoPo
(Time and Love.) GTBS-P
LXV. "Since brass, nor stone, nor earth, nor boundless sea." CABA; DiPo; EnRePo; PoIE
(Time and Love.) GTBS-P
LXVI. "Tired with all these, for restful death I cry." CBEP; CTC; PoIE
(World's Way, The.) GTBS-P
LXIX. "Those parts of thee that the world's eye doth view." CBEP
LXXI. "No longer mourn for me when I am dead." CBEP; EnRePo; ILP; PoIE
(Triumph of Death, The.) GTBS-P
LXXIII. "That time of year thou mayst in me behold." CABA; CaFP; CBEP; CTC; DiPo; EnRePo; FaBV; FoBA; GTBS-P; ILP; PoIE; PoPo; PoSa; StP; VaPo
LXXIV. "But be contented: when that fell arrest." CBEP
LXXVI. "Why is my verse so barren of new pride." PP
LXXVII. "Thy glass will show thee how thy beauties wear." EnRePo; FoBA
LXXXII. "I grant thou wert not married to my Muse." CBEP
LXXXVI. "Was it the proud full sail of this great verse." CBEP
LXXXVII. "Farewell! thou art too dear for my possessing." FoBA; GTBS-P; StP

XCI. "Some glory in their birth, some in their skill." CBEP
XCIV. "They that have power to hurt and will do none."
CABA; CBEP; PoIE; PoSa
(Life without Passion, The.) GTBS-P
XCV. "How sweet and lovely dost thou make the shame."
CBEP
XCVII. "How like a winter hath my absence been."
CABA; CBEP; DiPo; EnRePo; GTBS-P; VaPo
XCVIII. "From you I have been absent in the spring."
BoC; DiPo
CIV. "To me, fair friend, you never can be old." EnRePo;
GTBS-P; PoIE
CVI. "When in the chronicle of wasted time." CBEP;
CTC; DiPo; EnRePo; FaBV; PoIE; PoPo; StP
(To His Love.) GTBS-P
CVII. "Not mine own fears, nor the prophetic soul."
CABA; CBEP; CTC; DiPo; PoIE
CIX. "Oh never say that I was false of heart."
(Unchangeable, The.) GTBS-P
CX. "Alas, 'tis true I have gone here and there." CBEP
CXVI. "Let me not to the marriage of true minds." BoC;
CABA; CaFP; CBEP; DiPo; EnRePo; FaBV; FoBA;
ILP; LV; OnP; PoIE; PoPl; PoPo; PoSa; TRV
(Let Me Not.)
(True Love.) GTBS-P
CXVIII. "Like as, to make our appetites more keen."
CABA; CBEP
CXIX. "What potions have I drunk of Siren tears." CBEP
CXXI. " 'Tis better to be vile than vile esteemed." CBEP
CXXIV. "If my dear love were but the child of state."
FoBA
CXXVII. "In the old age black was not counted fair."
CBEP; DiPo
CXXVIII. "How oft, when thou, my music, music play'st."
ILP
CXXIX. "Expense of spirit in a waste of shame, The."
CABA; CaFP; CBEP; DiPo; EnRePo; ErPo; FoBA;
OnP; PoIE; StP; VaPo
CXXX. "My mistress' eyes are nothing like the sun."
BoLP; CABA; CaFP; CBEP; DiPo; FoBA; ILP; PoIE;
PP; StP
CXXXIII. "Beshrew that heart that makes my heart to
groan." CBEP
CXXXIV. "So, now I have confest that he is thine."
CBEP
CXXXVIII. "When my love swears that she is made of
truth." CABA; FoBA
CXLI. "In faith, I do not love thee with mine eyes."
CBEP
CXLIII. "Lo, as a careful housewife runs to catch. CBEP
CXLIV. "Two loves I have of comfort and despair."
CABA; CBEP
CXLVI. "Poor soul, the center of my sinful earth."
CABA; CaFP; CBEP; DiPo; EaLo; EnRePo; FoBA;
OnP; PoIE; StP
(Soul and Body.) GTBS-P
CXLVII. "My love is as a fever, longing still." CBEP;
DiPo; FoBA
CXLVIII. "Oh me! what eyes hath Love put in my head."
(Blind Love.) GTBS-P
CLI. "Love is too young to know what conscience is."
CBEP
Sonnets, sels. Frederick Goddard Tuckerman.
Part I.
"All men,—the preacher saith,—whatee or whence,"
XVII. PoIE
"And so the day drops by; the horizon draws," V. PoIE
"By this low fire I often sit to woo," XXV. AP
"For Nature daily through her grand design," XXVI.
AP
"Morning comes, the; not slow, with reddening gold,"
XXII. AP
"Nor looks that backward life so bare to me," IV. PoIE
"Perhaps a dream; yet surely truth has beamed," XXIV.
AP
"Sometimes, when winding slow by brook and bower," I.
PoIE
Part II.
"Breeze is sharp, the sky is hard and blue, The," XIV.
AP
"But unto him came swift calamity," IX. AP
"Companions were we in the grove and glen!" VIII. AP
"Even as a lover, dreaming, unaware," XIII. AP
"Gertrude and Gulielma, sister-twins," XV. AP
"His heart was in his garden; but his brain," VII. AP
"How most unworthy, echoing in mine ears," XII. AP
"My Anna! though thine earthly steps are done," XXXIV.
AP
"My Anna! When for her my head was bowed," XXXI.
AP
"Oh for the face and footsteps!—Woods and shores!"
XXXII. AP
"One still dark night, I sat alone and wrote," XXXIII.
AP

"Roll on, sad world! Not Mercury or Mars," XVII. AP
"Still pressing through these weeping solitudes," XI. AP
"Thy baby, too, the child that was to be," X. AP
"Under the mountain, as when I first knew," XVI. AP
Sonnets—Actualities, sel. E. E. Cummings.
"I like my body when it is with your." ErPo; UnTE
Sonnets at Christmas. Allen Tate. AP
"Ah, Christ, I love you rings to the wild sky," II. PoDB
Sonnets d'Amour, sels. Jean de Sponde, tr. fr. French by
Robert Nugent. RBL
"Whoever were to stand in the heavens, and lower then his
sight," III.
"Winds groaned in the air, darkest cloud, The," XXVI.
Sonnets de la Mort, sels. Jean de Sponde, tr. fr. French.
RBL
"Alas! count your days; the days which have gone," tr. by
Robert Nugent.
"All swells against me, tempts me and assails," tr. by John
R. Galt.
"For whom so many travails? for yourself? whose breath,"
tr. by Robert Nugent.
"Who, who are these whose fawning hearts, debased," tr. by
John R. Galt.
"Yet we must die, and though proud life might dare," tr. by
John R. Galt.
Sonnets for a Dying Man, sels. Burns Singer. NePoEA-2
"Christ comes to mind and comes across the mind," XXXIX.
"I promise you by the harsh funeral," XLVIII.
"Old man dozed, The. The hospital quietened," XV.
"Those flaming Christians with their hygienic rose," XXXIII.
"To see the petrel cropping in the farmyard," XXX.
Sonnets from the Portuguese, sels. Elizabeth Barrett Brown-
ing.
"Beloved, thou hast brought me many flowers," XLIV. ILP;
OBNC
"Can it be right to give what I can give?" IX. CTC
"Face of all the world is changed, I think, The," VII. CTC
"First time he kissed me, he but only kissed," XXXVIII.
CTC; PoPl
"Go from me. Yet I feel that I shall stand," VI. DiPo
"How do I love thee? Let me count the ways," XLIII.
BoLP; CCT; FaBV; FaPL; ILP; LV; PoLF; PoPl;
PoPo; TRV
(Wife to a Husband, A.) BoC
"I thought once how Theocritus had sung," I. OBNC
"If thou must love me, let it be for naught," XIV. BoLP;
CTC; OBNC; PoPo
"Yet, love, mere love, is beautiful indeed," X. CTC
Sonnets of the Months, sels. Folgore da San Geminiano, tr.
fr. Italian.
August, tr. by Dante Gabriel Rossetti. CTC
Come, January, I Give You These Treats, tr. by Joy Gould.
AnML
For April I Give You the Countryside, tr. by Joy Gould.
AnML
In March, for You a Gift of Fish I Boast, tr. by Joy Gould.
AnML
In October, Figuring Up Your Share, tr. by Joy Gould.
AnML
September, tr. by Dante Gabriel Rossetti. SD
Sonnets on the Divina Commedia. Longfellow. See Divina
Commedia.
Sonnets pour Hélène, sels. Pierre de Ronsard, tr. fr. French.
"When you are very old, at evening," tr. by Andrew Lang.
RBL
(Of His Lady's Old Age.) CTC
" 'Who,' cried the elders on the Trojan wall," tr. by Hum-
bert Wolfe. RBL
Sonnets—Realities, sels. E. E. Cummings.
Cambridge Ladies [Who Live in Furnished Souls], The.
CBEP; PoSa
"My girl's tall with hard long eyes." UnTE
Sonnets to Laura, sels. Petrarch, tr. fr. Italian.
To Laura in Death.
"Alas! that liquid look, that lovely face!" I, tr. by Joseph
Auslander. RBL
"Alas! the lovely face, the eyes that save," I, tr. by Anna
Maria Armi. RBL
"Broken is the tall column and the green laurel," II, tr. by
Harold M. Priest. RBL
"Broken the column and the green bay tree," II, tr. by
Anna Maria Armi. RBL
Death Cannot Sour the Sweetness of Her Face, LXXXI,
tr. by Morris Bishop. AnML
Eyes That Drew from Me Such Fervent Praise, The.
XXIV, tr. by Edwin Morgan. AnML
"Eyes, the face, the limbs of heavenly mould, The," XXIV,
tr. by Lady Dacre. RBL
Go, Grieving Rimes of Mine, to That Hard Stone, LX, tr.
by Morris Bishop. AnML
Great Is My Envy of You, Earth, in Your Greed, XXXII,
tr. by Edwin Morgan. AnML
"I mourn unhappy days that are no more," LXXXVI, tr.
by Romilda Rendel. RBL

Sonnets to Laura, *sels.* (*continued*)
"Life hurries on, a frantic refugee," IV, *tr. by* Morris Bishop. RBL
Nightingale, The, XLIII, *tr. by* Thomas Le Mesurier. PoPI
"Nightingale that so forlornly weeps, The," XLIII, *tr. by* Romilda Rendel. RBL
Nightingale Whose Ardent, Soft Despair, The, XLIII, *tr. by* Dwight Durling. AnML
Nowhere So Clearly Have My Inward Eyes, XII, *tr. by* Dwight Durling. AnML
"O lovely little bird, I watch you fly," XC, *tr. by* Morris Bishop. RBL
Small Wandering Bird Who Singing Go Your Way, XC, *tr. by* Peter Russell. AnML
"Zephyr returns, and scatters everywhere," XLII, *tr. by* Morris Bishop. RBL
To Laura in Life.
Absorbed in One Fond Thought That Makes Me Run, CXXXVI, *tr. by* Dwight Durling. AnML
"Alone and ever weary with dark care," XXVIII, *tr. by* T. G. Bergin. RBL
"Blest be the year, the month, the hour, the day," XLVII, *tr. by* Lady Dacre. RBL
"Fair white hind with golden horns, A," CLVII, *tr. by* Harold M. Priest. RBL
Father in Heaven, after Each Lost Day, XLVIII, *tr. by* Bernard Bergonzi. AnML
"I find no peace, and all my war is done," CIV, *tr. by* Sir Thomas Wyatt. DiPo; PoIE; RBL
"I find no peace yet am not armed for war," CIV, *tr. by* Maurice Valency. AnML
If Life Survives These Years of Bitter Woe, XI, *tr. by* Maurice Valency. AnML
"If no love is, O God, what fele I so?" CII, *tr. by* Chaucer. RBL
"It was the day that the sun's rays," III, *tr. by* Harold M. Priest. RBL
"It was the morning of that blessèd day," III, *tr. by* Joseph Auslander. RBL
Long Love That in My Thought Doth Harbor, The, CIX, *tr. by* Sir Thomas Wyatt. CABA
  (Long Love, The.) ILP
  (Lover for Shamefastness Hideth His Desire within His Faithful Heart, The.) StP
"Loose to the breeze her golden tresses flow'd," LXIX. RBL
Love That Liveth and Reigneth in My Thought, CIX, *tr. by* the Earl of Surrey. StP
  (Complaint of a Lover Rebuked.) CABA
  (Love That Doth Reign.) ILP
Love, We Attend the Vision of the Rose, CLIX, *tr. by* Peter Russell. AnML
My Galley Charged with Forgetfulness, CLVI, *tr. by* Sir Thomas Wyatt. CABA; CBEP; DiPo; ILP; RBL
  (Lover Compareth His State to a Ship in Perilous Storm Tossed on the Sea, The.) StP
Now Skies and Earth Are Stilled and Winds Are Dead, CXXXI, *tr. by* Dwight Durling. AnML
Pale Beauty! and a Smile the Pallor There, XCVIII, *tr. by* Edwin Morgan. AnML
"Palmer bent, with locks of silver grey, The," XIV, *tr. by* Lady Dacre. RBL
"Set me whereas the sun doth parch the green," CXIII, *tr. by* the Earl of Surrey. CBEP; ILP; RBL
She Used to Let Her Golden Hair Fly Free, LXIX, *tr. by* Morris Bishop. AnML
Woods Are Wild and Were Not Made for Man, The, CXLIII, *tr. by* Edwin Morgan. AnML
Songs.
Canzone: "Clear, fresh, and dulcet streams." To Laura in Life, Canzone XIV, *tr. by* Leigh Hunt. RBL
From Thought to Thought, from Mountain Peak to Mountain. To Laura in Life, Canzone XVII, *tr. by* Morris Bishop. AnML
Sonnets to Orpheus, *sels.* Rainer Maria Rilke, *tr. fr. German by* Walter Kaufmann. TwGP
"Choose to be changed. Oh experience the rapture of fire," Pt. II, XII.
"God can do it, A. But how can one follow," Pt. I, III.
"Jubilate not when you judge that no rack is required," Pt. II, IX.
Sonnets—Unrealities, *sel.* E. E. Cummings.
"It may not always be so; and I say," I. MoLP
  (It May Not Always Be So.) FaBV
Sonora Filibusters, The, *with music.* John A. Stone. SGR
Sons of freedom, listen to me. James Bird. *Unknown.* BSO
Sons of the Kings. Joan Agnew. BiCB
Soon/ now it/ will be done. Old Arrowhead. Thoughts of a Late War. Frank Borden Hanes. PoNC
Soon there'll come—the signs are fair. Prophecy. Alfred Lichtenstein. MGP
Soote Season, The. Earl of Surrey. *See* Description of Spring.

Sophia Nichols. Robin Blaser. CoPo
Sophisticate. Barbara Young. BiCB
Sophisticated, worldly-wise. I Found God. Mary Afton Thacker. TRV
Sorceress. Gertrude Claytor. FiSC
Sorely Tried Is Israel, the Hapless Folk. Jacob Bar Juda, Hazak, *tr. fr. French by* William M. Davis. AnML
Sorrow. Aubrey Thomas De Vere. WiR
Sorrow. D. H. Lawrence. GTBS-P
Sorrow/ tempers the heart to a compass point. A Defiant Song. Kay Johnson. PtTo
Sorrow is my own yard. The Widow's Lament in Springtime. William Carlos Williams. AP; MoLP; PoIE
Sorrow Is the Only Faithful One. Owen Dodson. AmNP
Sorrow of Love, The. W. B. Yeats. FoBA
Sorrow's Day. Zoe Kincaid Brockman. PoNC
Sorrows of Werther, The. Thackeray. WePo
Sorry I. A Kind of Libation. James L. Weil. OPP
Sort of a Song, A. William Carlos Williams. PoIE; PP
Sort of girl I like to see, The. The Olympic Girl. John Betjeman. SD
Sorting out letters and piles of my old. Mementos, I. W. D. Snodgrass. NePoEA-2
Soul, The. *Unknown.* STF
Soul and Body. Shakespeare. *See* Sonnets, CXLVI.
Soul and the Body, The. Sir John Davies. *Fr.* Nosce Teipsum. CTC
Soul-Light. Dante Gabriel Rossetti. The House of Life, XXVIII. VP
Soul Longs to Return Whence It Came, The. Richard Eberhart. ToPo
Soul of the muses! and supreme in verse! Rhapsody to Milton. Sneyd Davis. WaPE
Soul selects her own Society, The. Emily Dickinson. AP; CABA; CaFP; DiPo; FoBA; PoIE
Soul-Sickness. Jones Very. AP
Soul Winner's Prayer, The. Eugene M. Harrison. STF
Soules joy, now I am gone. Song. *At.* to the Earl of Pembroke. MeP
Souls joy, when thou art gone. A Parodie. George Herbert. MeP
Souls Lake. Robert Fitzgerald. MP
Souls of Poets dead and gone. Lines on the Mermaid Tavern [*or* The Mermaid Tavern]. Keats. DiPo; GTBS-P; ILP; PP
Souls of the righteous are in the hand of God, and there shall no torment touch them, The. The Wisdom of Solomon, Bible, Apocrypha. BoC
Soul's Springtime, The. Georg Trakl, *tr. fr. German by* David Luke. MGP
Sound as if from bells of silver, A. The Pageant. Whittier. AmLP
Sound Country Lass, The. *Unknown.* ErPo
Sound must seem an echo to the sense, The. Pope. *Fr.* An Essay on Criticism. PoPo
Sound of Breaking. Conrad Aiken. PoDB
Sound of the Sea, The. Longfellow. AP; PoPo
Sound of the wind revives former days, The. Jean Follain. *Fr.* Comings and Goings. CoFP
Sound the flute! Spring. Blake. *Fr.* Songs of Innocence. PoPI
Sound which silence makes all you could hear. Cousin Emily and the Night Visitor. Kendrick Smithyman. ACV
Sound-Noise. Memory as Memorial in the Last. Edward Marshall. CoPo
Sounds of the Trades. *Unknown, tr. fr. French by* Daisy Aldan. AnML
Soup. Carl Sandburg. RePo
Sousa. Edward Dorn. CoPo
South of My Days. Judith Wright. PoAu-2
South Sea Bubble, The. Countess of Winchilsea. CBEP
South Wind, The. Robert Bridges. OBNC
South Wind. Georg Trakl, *tr. fr. German by* David Luke. MGP
South-wind brings, The. Threnody. Emerson. AP; StP
South Wind laid his moccasins aside, The. Isabella Valancy Crawford. *Fr.* Malcolm's Katie. OBCV
South wind rose at dusk of the winter day, The. The South Wind. Robert Bridges. OBNC
South-wind strengthens to a gale, The. Low Barometer. Robert Bridges. PoIE
Southern Mansion. Arna Bontemps. AmNP
Southern Road, The. Dudley Randall. NNP
Soutine the Sour. A Story of Soutine. James Schevill. PoCh
Sow by all waters. Fear Not. J. Bullock. STF
Sower, The. Laurence Binyon. MMA
Sower, The. Sir Charles G. D. Roberts. OBCV
Space. William Hart-Smith. *Fr.* Christopher Columbus. PoAu-2
Space. Inez Hogan. RePo
Space, and the twelve clean winds of heaven. The Most-sacred Mountain. Eunice Tietjens. MoRP
Space Child's Mother Goose, The, *sels.* Frederick Winsor. LV

"Little Jack Horner/ Sits in a corner."
"Resistor, transistor, condensers in pairs."
"This little pig built a spaceship."
Space Travel. Jane W. Krows. SoPo
Spacious circle pleasant centre made, A. A Rustic Festival. Luis de Góngora. Fr. The Solitudes. RBL
Spacious Firmament on High, The. Joseph Addison. EaLo; ELP
(Ode.) PoIE; VaPo
Spades take up leaves. Gathering Leaves. Robert Frost. LOW; RePo
Spain 1937. W. H. Auden. CABL
Spain. The wild dust, the whipped corn. Teresa of Avila. Elizabeth Jennings. NePoEA-2
Span of Life, The. Robert Frost. DiPo
Spanish Armada, The. John Still. HaSV
Spanish Friar, The, sel. Dryden.
Farewell, Ungrateful Traitor, fr. V, i. CBEP; ELP
Spanish Galleons Seen by an Aztec, The. Dryden. Fr. The Indian Emperor, I, ii. HaSV
Spanish Johnny. Willa Cather. RePo
Spanish Ladies. Unknown. BSNS
Spanish Lady. Unknown. BSO
Spanish Waters. John Masefield. OnMSP; SIV
Sparkles from the Wheel. Walt Whitman. AP; DiPo
Sparrow dips in his wheel-rut bath, The. The Five Students. Thomas Hardy. GTBS-P
Sparrow's Skull, The. Ruth Pitter. EaLo
Sparrow's Song, The. Unknown. STF
Sparse mists of moonlight hurt our eyes. Festubert: The Old German Line. Edmund Blunden. MMA
Spate in Winter Midnight. Norman MacCaig. BoC; GTBS-P
Speak Gently. David Bates. Par
Speak gently, Spring, and make no sudden sound. Four Little Foxes. Lew Sarett. LV; PoSC; RePo
Speak low to me, my Saviour, low and sweet. Comfort. Elizabeth Barrett Browning. TRV
Speak Out for Jesus. Unknown. STF
Speak roughly to your little boy. The Dutchess' Lullaby. "Lewis Carroll." Fr. Alice's Adventures in Wonderland. BBGG; Par
"Speak! speak! thou fearful guest!" The Skeleton in Armor. Longfellow. AP; PoPo
Speak Thou and Speed. Sir Thomas Wyatt. EnRePo
Speak to me. Take my hand. What are you now? Effort at Speech between Two People. Muriel Rukeyser. MP
Speak with the Sun. David Campbell. ACV
Speaking of Poetry. John Peale Bishop. PP
Spear, The. Abu Zakariyya, tr. fr. Arabic by Lysander Kemp. AnML
Special Starlight. Carl Sandburg. MoRP
Speck went blowing up against the sky, A. A Visit from Abroad. James Stephens. LOW
Speckled cat and a tame hare, A. Song of a Fool. W. B. Yeats. Fr. Two Songs of a Fool. PoDB
Speckled with glints of star and moonshine. Mr. Walter de la Mare Makes the Little Ones Dizzy. Samuel Hoffenstein. Par
Spectator ab Extra. Arthur Hugh Clough. See As I Sat at the Café.
Spectre. Sydney King Russell. FiSC
Spectre is haunting Europe, with no name, A. Manifesto. Paris Leary. CoPo
Spectre Is on the Move, The. G. Allana. ACV
Speculations. O. B. Hardison, Jr. PoNC
Speech after long silence; it is right. After Long Silence. W. B. Yeats. AnMoPo; DiPo; FoBA; PoPl
Speech by Romelio. John Webster. See All the Flowers of the Spring.
Speech of the Salish Chief. Earle Birney. Fr. Damnation of Vancouver. OBCV
Speeches and Invocations, sels. "Jesse Thoor," tr. fr. German by Michael Hamburger. MGP
"Listen, my friends:—our neighbor is ill!—Oh, our neighbor!"
"Lord Lord . . . they have stabbed my reason, so that I write."
Speed. W. H. Davies. MoRP
Speed, bonny boat, like a bird on the wing. Flora MacDonald and the King. Unknown. BFSS
Spell, A. Dryden. Fr. Oedipus. WiR
Spell before Winter, A. Howard Nemerov. ToPo
Spell Eva backe and Ave shall you finde. The Virgins Salutation. Robert Southwell. MeP
Spell of Creation. Kathleen Raine. PoIE
Spell of the Yukon, The. Robert W. Service. PoPl
Spelt from Sibyl's Leaves. Gerard Manley Hopkins. PoDB; VP
Spending hand that alway poureth out, A. Satire 3: To Sir Francis Brian. Sir Thomas Wyatt. EnRePo
Spendthrift. I. A. Richards. PoPl
Sphinx, The. Emerson. AP; DiPo
Sphinx, The, sel. Oscar Wilde.
"How subtle-secret is your smile!" UnTE

Sphinx is drowsy, The. The Sphinx. Emerson. AP; DiPo
Spider, The. Robert P. Tristram Coffin. LV
Spider. Padraic Colum. RoGo
Spider, The. Richard Eberhart. ToPo
Spider, The. Mary Jones. WaPE
Spider. Richmond Lattimore. PP
Spider, The. Walt Whitman. See Noiseless, Patient Spider, A.
Spider and the Fly, The. Mary Howitt. Par
Spider expects the cold of winter, The. The Spider. Richard Eberhart. ToPo
Spider Head ("The spider glints"). Donald Hall. OPP
Spider in the bath, A. The image noted. The Image. Roy Fuller. GTBS-P; ToPo
Spider, salute the Sun! No rancor show. Philosophy. Rubén Darío. AnSP
Spider, Sir Spider. Spider. Padraic Colum. RoGo
Spin, A. Jonathan Williams. PoNC
"Spin, oh my darling daughter, I'll give you a hat." Spinning Song. Unknown. UnTE
Spined and gullet shaped. Free me. Oh Bright Oh Black Singbeast Lovebeast Catkin Sleek. Michael McClure. CoPo
Spinning Song. Edith Sitwell. DaDu
Spinning Song. Unknown, tr. fr. German by Louis Untermeyer. UnTE
Spinning-Wheel Song, A. John Francis Waller. BoLP
Spinstress' Song, The. Clemens Brentano, tr. fr. German by Alexander Gode. AGP
Spiralwise it spins. Time. Ralph Hodgson. GTBS-P
Spires of Oxford, The. Winifred M. Letts. PoLF
Spirit breathes upon the World, The. William Cowper. Fr. The Light and Glory of the World. TRV
Spirit came in childhood, The. The Four Calls. Lydia Hadley. STF
Spirit from Perfecter Ages, A. Arthur Hugh Clough. Fr. Amours de Voyage. OBNC
Spirit haunts the year's last hours, A. Song. Tennyson. GTBS-P; ILP; OBNC
Spirit-Land, The. Jones Very. AmLP
Spirit of Poetry, The. Longfellow. PP
Spirit of Poetry Speaks, The. Richard Eberhart. OPP
Spirit that breathest through my lattice, thou. The Evening Wind. Bryant. AP
Spiritual Canticle [Songs between the Soul and the Spouse]. St. John of the Cross, tr. fr. Spanish. AnSP, tr. by John Frederick Nims; RBL, tr. by E. Allison Peers.
(Search, The, sl. diff., tr. by E. Allison Peers.) BoC
Spit in My Face You Jews, and Pierce My Side. John Donne. Holy Sonnets, XI. FoBA; MeP
Splashing water. The Herd-Boy's Song. Chen Shan-min. SiGo
Spleen. Ernest Dowson. CBEP
Splendid arc of fishnet cast wide upon the sea, The. Feast of Saint Andrew the Apostle. Carl Bode. ToPo
Splendid Shilling, The. John Philips. Par
Splendour Falls [on Castle Walls], The. Tennyson. Fr. The Princess. CBEP; ELP; FaBV; FoBA; GoJo; GTBS-P; ILP; OBNC; PoIE; RoGo; VP
(Blow, Bugle, Blow.) WePo; WiR
(Song.) PoPl
Splendour recurrent. Fraternitas. Confucius. Fr. The Classic Anthology: Deer Sing. CTC
Splinter. Carl Sandburg. RePo
Splinter, flicked, A. New Moon in January. Ted Hughes. ToPo
Split-Rail Fence. Guy Owen. PoNC
Split the lark—and you'll find the music. Emily Dickinson. AP
Spoils. Robert Graves. MoLP
Spontaneous Man, the Gifted Assassin, The. Michael Goldman. OPP
Spoon River Anthology, sels. Edgar Lee Masters.
Anne [or Ann] Rutledge. AmLP; ILP; LiPo; PoPl; PoSa; PoSC; ThLM
"Butch" Weldy. PoPo
Carl Hamblin. ILP
Edmund Pollard. ErPo
Father Malloy. PoPo
Hannah Armstrong. LiPo
Hill, The. AmLP
James Garber. ILP
Lucinda Matlock. FaBV; ILP; PoPo
Mrs. George Reece. LV
Petit, the Poet. ILP; PoSa
Village Atheist, The. EaLo; PoPo
William H. Herndon. LiPo
Sport, an adventitious sprout, A. Perspective. Margaret Avison. OBCV
Spotted hawk swoops by and accuses me, The. Walt Whitman. Fr. Song of Myself. PP
Sprawled on the crates and sacks in the rear of the truck. Green, Green Is El Aghir. Norman Cameron. MoBS
Sprawling summer. Summertime. "Vincenzo Cardarelli." CoIP

Spread beneath me it lies—lean upland. Flying above California. Thom Gunn. ToPo
Sprig of Lime, The. Robert Nichols. GTBS-P
Sprightly the cockcrowing. A Little Song in Assisi. George Barker. ToPo
Spring. Blake. *Fr.* Songs of Innocence. PoP1
Spring, The. Thomas Carew. *See* Now That the Winter's Gone.
Spring. Catullus, *tr. fr. Latin by* L. R. Lind. PoP1
Spring. Rubén Darío, *tr. fr. Spanish by* Anita Volland. AnSP
Spring. Aubrey Thomas De Vere. *Fr.* The Year of Sorrow. OBNC
Spring. Gerard Manley Hopkins. ACV; CaFP; DiPo; FaBV; FoBA; ILP; OBNC; PoDB; StP; VP
Spring, *sel.* Richard Hovey.
"I said in my heart, 'I am sick of four walls and a ceiling.' " RePo
Spring. Philip Larkin. ACV
Spring. James Russell Lowell. *See* Sunthin' in the Pastoral Line.
Spring. Hugh McCrae. ACV
Spring, *sel.* William Miller.
"Spring comes linking and jinking through the woods, The." PoSC
Spring. Thomas Nashe. *Fr.* Summer's Last Will and Testament. CBEP; GTBS-P; PoIE; WiR
Spring. Charles d'Orléans, *tr. fr. French by* Andrew Lang. CTC
  (Rondeau: "Year his winter cloak lets fall, The," *tr. by* J. G. Legge.) SiGo
  (Weather Has Laid Aside His Cloak, The, *tr. by* Muriel Kittel.) AnML
Spring. Christina Rossetti. OBNC
Spring. Shakespeare. *See* When Daisies Pied.
Spring. André Spire, *tr. fr. French by* Jethro Bithell. BoLP
Spring. Earl of Surrey. *See* Description of Spring.
Spring. James Thomson. *Fr.* The Seasons. EiCP
Spring. Henry Timrod. AP
Spring. Paul Verlaine, *tr. fr. French by* Roland Gant *and* Claude Apcher. ErPo
Spring and All ("By the road to the contagious hospital"). William Carlos Williams. AP; CABA; PoIE; PoSa
  (Contagious Hospital, The.) VaPo
Spring and All ("So much depends"). William Carlos Williams. *See* Red Wheelbarrow, The.
Spring and Fall. Gerard Manley Hopkins. CaFP; DiPo; ELP; FoBA; GoJo; GTBS-P; ILP; PoIE; PoP1; PoSa
Spring and the Fall, The. Edna St. Vincent Millay. BoLP
Spring Breeze. Buson, *tr. fr. Japanese by* Harold G. Henderson. RePo
Spring came round, and still he was not dead, The. The Neurotic. C. Day Lewis. ACV
Spring comes linking and jinking through the woods, The. William Miller. *Fr.* Spring. PoSC
Spring Does Not Flow Now, The. Rosalía de Castro, *tr. fr. Spanish by* Muriel Kittel. AnSP
Spring Families. Frances Frost. RePo
Spring Has Come. Antonio Machado, *tr. fr. Spanish by* Kate Flores. AnSP
Spring Has Come to Town with Love. *Unknown. See* Lenten Is Come with Love to Toune.
Spring in My Hut. Sodo, *tr. fr. Japanese by* Harold G. Henderson. RePo
Spring Is a Looping-free Time. Martin Robbins. SD
Spring Is Hard on Us. *Unknown.* ErPo
Spring is showery, flowery, bowery. The Seasons. Mother Goose. SoPo
Spring-Joy Praising God. Praise of the Sun. Catharina Regina von Greiffenberg, *tr. fr. German by* George C. Schoolfield. AGP
Spring Landscape. Melvin Walker La Follette. NePoEA-2
Spring Morning. D. H. Lawrence. BoLP
Spring morning! Galante Garden, I. Juan Ramón Jiménez. PoP1
Spring Night, A. Robert Beloof. PoP1
Spring Night. "Rana Mukerji." UnTE
Spring Night. Sara Teasdale. BoLP
Spring of Joy Is Dry, The. *Unknown.* EnRePo
Spring Offensive. Wilfred Owen. GTBS-P
Spring Offensive, 1941. Maurice Biggs. PoAu-2
Spring Pools. Robert Frost. DiPo
Spring Quiet. Christina Rossetti. GTBS-P; ThGo
Spring Scene. Taniguchi Buson, *tr. fr. Japanese by* Harold G. Henderson. PoP1
Spring shakes the windows; doors whang to. A Spring Wind. Bernard Spencer. GTBS-P
Spring Song. Hilda Conkling. PoSC
Spring Song. Federico García Lorca, *tr. fr. Spanish by* Rachel Benson *and* Robert O'Brien. AnSP
Spring Song, A. *Unknown.* PoLF
Spring, Spring. Pussy-Willows. Aileen Fisher. RePo
Spring: The Lover and the Birds. William Allingham. OBNC

Spring, the sweet spring, is the year's pleasant king. Spring. Thomas Nashe. *Fr.* Summer's Last Will and Testament. CBEP; GTBS-P; PoIE; WiR
Spring too, very soon! Harbingers. Basho. PoP1; RePo
Spring under a Thorn, The. *Unknown.* MeEL
Spring Voices. Louis MacNeice. WePo
Spring Voices. Jesse Stuart. FiSC
Spring was coming, brimful. Yellow Spring. Juan Ramón Jiménez. AnSP
Spring Wind, A. Bernard Spencer. GTBS-P
Spring, with that nameless pathos in the air. Spring. Henry Timrod. AP
Springfield Mountain (B, C, *and* D *vers., with music*). *Unknown.* BSO
  (Major's Son, The, A *vers.*) BSO
Springfield of the Far Future, The. Vachel Lindsay. MoRP
Springtime storm upset, The. The Ark. Eugenio Montale. CoIP
Sprinters, The. Lee Murchison. SD
Squanderings. Witter Bynner. MoLP
Squats on a toad-stool under a tree. Song by Isbrand. Thomas Lovell Beddoes. *Fr.* Death's Jest Book. OBNC
Squeal. Louis Simpson. Par
Squire, The. Chaucer, *mod. by* Nevill Coghill. *Fr.* The Canterbury Tales: Prologue. WePo
Squirrel. James S. Tippett. RePo
Squirrel, The. *Unknown.* SoPo
Squirrel in the Rain. Frances Frost. RePo
Stable-lamp is lighted, A. A Christmas Hymn. Richard Wilbur. CoPo; MoRP
Stages. Roy Macnab. ACV
Stages on a Journey Westward. James Wright. AmPC
Stair, The ("The stair is curved, the railing high"). Gertrude Claytor. FiSC
Stairs. Oliver Herford. RePo
Stairway is not, The. The Jacob's Ladder. Denise Levertov. CaFP; CoPo; ToPo
Stampede of machine and the avarice of man. Swan Song. Som Parkash Ranchan. ACV
Stance. Theodore Enslin. CoPo
"Stand aside." Sun and Cloud. Melville Cane. PoP1
Stand at attention. For John Kennedy, Jr. Raymond Roseliep. OPP
Stand at my window. Apology for Youth. Sister Mary Madeleva. PoP1
Stand by. *Unknown.* STF
Stand close around, ye Stygian set. Dirce. Walter Savage Landor. *Fr.* Pericles and Aspasia. CBEP; CTC; OBNC; StP
Stand on the highest pavement of the stair. La Figlia Che Piange. T. S. Eliot. PoIE
Stand, Stately Tavie. *Unknown.* ErPo
Stand still, and I will read to thee. A Lecture upon the Shadow. John Donne. CABA; CaFP; DiPo; EnRePo; FoBA; SeCP
"Stand still in bright array ye saints, here stand." War in Heaven. Milton. *Fr.* Paradise Lost. DiPo
Stand still, true poet that you are! Popularity. Robert Browning. PP
Stand straight. Rules for the Road. Edwin Markham. RePo
Standing aloof in giant ignorance. To Homer. Keats. CABA; CBEP
Standing on Tiptoe. George Frederick Cameron. OBCV
Stanza from an Early Poem. Christopher Pearse Cranch. *See* Gnosis.
Stanzas: "How beautiful this hill of fern swells on!" John Clare. *Fr.* Child Harold. OBNC
Stanzas: "In a drear-nighted December." Keats. *See* In a Drear-nighted December.
Stanzas: "Nature doth have her dawn each day." Henry David Thoreau. AmLP
Stanzas: "Often rebuked, yet always back returning." *At. to* Charlotte Brontë *and to* Emily Brontë. *See* Often Rebuked.
Stanzas—April, 1814. Shelley. OBNC
Stanzas concerning Christ and the Soul. St. John of the Cross. *See* Other Stanzas with a Divine Meaning Concerning Christ and the Soul.
Stanzas for Music. Byron. *See* There Be None of Beauty's Daughters.
Stanzas from the Grande Chartreuse. Matthew Arnold. VP
Stanzas on a Visit to Longleat House in Wiltshire, October 1953. George Barker. ToPo
Stanzas on the Death of His Father. Jorge Manrique, *tr. fr. Spanish by* Edwin Morgan. AnML
Stanzas on Woman. Goldsmith. *See* Song: "When lovely woman stoops to folly."
Stanzas to Edward Williams. Shelley. OBNC
Stanzas to the Marquise. Corneille, *tr. fr. French by* Alan Conder. RBL
Stanzas Written in Dejection near Naples. Shelley. CABA; CBEP; FaBV; GTBS-P
Star, The. Jane Taylor. Par, *st.* 1; SoPo, 3 *sts.*
  (Stars at Night, The, 3 *sts.*) ThGo

Star Drill. T. Inglis Moore. PoAu-2
Star Light, Star Bright. *Unknown.* SoPo
Star looks down at me, A. Waiting Both. Thomas Hardy. PoPo
Star Morals. Nietzsche, *tr. fr. German by* Walter Kaufmann. TwGP
Star of the Evening. James M. Sayles. Par
Star of the Nativity. Boris Pasternak, *tr. fr. Russian by* Eugene M. Kayden. PoPl
Star-Pudding. Robert P. Tristram Coffin. PoPo
Star Sirius, The. George Meredith. VP
Star-spangled Banner, The. Francis Scott Key. FaPL; ThLM
Star-spangled Ode. Phyllis McGinley. ThLM
Star-Talk. Robert Graves. GoJo
Star that bringest home the bee. To the Evening Star. Thomas Campbell. GTBS-P; TRV
Star that shone on Bethlehem, shine on London City. A Christmas Carol. Gilbert Thomas. MoRP
Stare at the stars, the stars say. Ego. Norman MacCaig. GTBS-P
Stare's Nest by My Window, The. W. B. Yeats. GTBS-P
Starlight like Intuition Pierced the Twelve. Delmore Schwartz. MoRP; PoCh
(Starlight's Intuitions Pierced the Twelve.) PoDB
Starlight Night, The. Gerard Manley Hopkins. DiPo; GTBS-P; VP
(Starlit Night, The.) BoC
Starlight's Intuitions Pierced the Twelve, The. Delmore Schwartz. *See* Starlight like Intuition Pierced the Twelve.
Starlit Night, The. Gerard Manley Hopkins. *See* Starlight Night, The.
Starre, The. George Herbert. MeP
Starre, The. Henry Vaughan. McP
Starry Night, The. Anne Sexton. ToPo
Stars, The. Robert Hamerling, *tr. fr. German by* D. G. Wright. AGP
Stars. Sara Teasdale. MoRP; PoPo
Stars and atoms have no size. Measurement. A. M. Sullivan. RePo
Stars are everywhere to-night, The. Daisies. Andrew Young. GoJo
Stars are glittering in the frosty sky, The. The Winter Galaxy [*or* Winter Night]. Charles Heavysege. ACV; OBCV
Stars are pale, The. Break of Day. John Shaw Neilson. PoAu-1
Stars at Night, The. Jane Taylor. *See* Star, The.
Stars Have Not Dealt, The. A. E. Housman. Additional Poems, XVII. PoPo
("Stars have not dealt me the worst they could do, The.") GTBS-P
Stars, I have seen them fall. A. E. Housman. More Poems, VII. VP
Stars, I pity you and call you hapless! Night Thoughts. Goethe. AGP
Stars lie broken on a lake. Reflections. Edna Becker. TRV
Stars over snow. Night. Sara Teasdale. SoPo
Start, The. *Unknown.* SD
Start Point and Beachy Head. A Channel Rhyme. Cicely Fox Smith. HaSV
Starved, scarred, lenten, amidst ash of air. The Sugaring. A. M. Klein. OBCV
Starving, savage, I aspire. The Tiger of Desire. Tom MacInnes. OBCV
State of Arkansas, The, *with music. Unknown.* BFSS
State with the prettiest name, The. Florida. Elizabeth Bishop. MP
Stately rainbow came and stood, A. The Rainbow. Coventry Patmore. The Angel in the House, II, iii, 2. GTBS-P
Statesman, The. Phyllis McGinley. *Fr.* Epitaphs for Three Prominent Persons. LV
Stationmaster's Lament, The. Jerome Rothenberg. CoPo
Statue, The. Robert Finch. OBCV
Statue, The. John Fuller. NePoE A-2
Statue and the Bust, The. Robert Browning. VP
Status Symbol. Mari Evans. PtTo
Stay near me. Speak my name. Oh, do not wander. Mid-century Love Letter. Phyllis McGinley. MoLP
Stay, Nymph. *Unknown.* EnRePo
Stay, Phoebus, stay! Song. Edmund Waller. ILP; SeCP
Stay, ship from Thames, with fettered sails. Ship from Thames. Rex Ingamells. PoAu-2
Stay, speedy time; behold, before thou pass. Idea, XVII. Michael Drayton. EnRePo
Stay with me, God. The night is dark. The Soldier, 1939–1945. Gerald Kersh. BoC
Stayed where he was. The Boar. Robert Kelly. CoPo
Stealthy is my love. Sandro Penna, *tr. fr. Italian by* Carlo L. Golino. CoIP
Steam Navigation Thieves, The, *with music.* John A. Stone. SGR
Steam Shovel. Charles Malam. PoPo
Steam Threshing-Machine, The. Charles Tennyson-Turner. OBNC

Steamboat is a slow poke, The. Boats. Rowena Bennett. SoPo
Steddefast Crosse, inmong alle other. A Hymn to the Cross. *Unknown.* MeEL
Steeple-Jack, The. Marianne Moore. AmLP; AP; ILP
Steer hither, steer, your winged pines. The Siren's Song. William Browne. *Fr.* The Inner Temple Masque. HaSV
Stella's Birthday. Swift. ILP; PP
Stenographers, The. P. K. Page. OBCV
Step by Step. Barbara C. Ryberg. STF
Step Mother, The. Helen Adam. FiSC
Stephen is just five years old. Blanket Street. Inez Hogan. BiCB
Stern Daughter of the Voice of God! Ode to Duty. Wordsworth. GTBS-P; LV; TRV
Stern eagle of the far north-west. The Song of the Reim-Kennar. Sir Walter Scott. *Fr.* The Pirate. OBNC
Stern Parent, The. Harry Graham. BBGG
Stethoscope tells what everyone fears, The. Academic. Theodore Roethke. StP
Stetit Puella. *Unknown, tr. fr. German by* Elizabeth Closs. AnML
Stevedore. Leslie M. Collins. AmNP
Stick your patent name on a signboard. The River. Hart Crane. *Fr.* The Bridge. AP
Stiff as her Egyptian counterpart. Young Gazelle. Babette Deutsch. AnMoPo
"Still alive—" the message ran. The Emergency Maker. David Wagoner. NePoEA-2
Still and All. Burns Singer. NePoEA-2
Still as of old. Betrayal. Hester H. Cholmondeley. TRV
Still Barred Thy Doors. Aru Dutt. ACV
Still, Citizen Sparrow. Richard Wilbur. AP; ILP; ToPo
Still Day, A. Joseph Cherwinski. RePo
Still Falls the Rain. Edith Sitwell. DTC; MoRP; MP
Still farther would I fly, my child. An Aboriginal Mother's Lament. Charles Harpur. ACV
Still flowering garden of the past, calm suburb of heaven. The Convent at Fahr. Albin Zollinger. MGP
Still glides the stream, slow drops the boat. The River. Matthew Arnold. Faded Leaves, I. CBEP; VP
Still I complain; I am complaining still. Meditation Forty. Edward Taylor. *Fr.* Preparatory Meditations, First Series. AP; MeP
Still, it is dear defiance now to carry. Flags. Gwendolyn Brooks. AmNP
Still, let my tyrants know, I am not doomed to wear. Emily Brontë. *Fr.* The Prisoner. OBNC
Still-Life. Ronald Perry. NePoEA-2
Still like his Master, known by breaking bread. Epitaph on a Worthy Clergyman. Benjamin Franklin. TRV
Still, no one had paid much tribute to the man. Cocteau's *Opium:* 1. Donald Finkel. CoPo
Still onward winds the dreary way. In Memoriam A. H. H., XXVI. Tennyson. VP
Still poised, as if in prayer. My House. Robert Pack. PoDB
Still pressing through these weeping solitudes. Sonnets, Part II, XI. Frederick Goddard Tuckerman. AP
Still sits the school-house by the road. In School Days. Whittier. PoPl; SIV
Still Small Voice, The. A. M. Klein. OBCV
Still, still my eye will gaze long fixed on thee. The Columbine. Jones Very. AP
Still tell not me, no, my God, and tell me no. Though He Slay Me. Vassar Miller. NePoEA-2
Still to Be Neat [Still to Be Dressed]. Ben Jonson, *tr. fr. the Latin of* Jean Bonnefons. *Fr.* Epicoene; or, The Silent Woman, I, i. CABA; CBEP; PoSa; StP
(Clermont's Song.) PoIE; SeCP; VaPo
(Song.) EnRePo
("Still to be neat, still to be dressed.") ILP
Still Voice of Harlem, The. Conrad Kent Rivers. NNP
Stillborn Love. Dante Gabriel Rossetti. The House of Life, LV. VP
Stillness, The. Basho, *tr. fr. Japanese by* Harold G. Henderson. RePo
Stillness. James Elroy Flecker. GoJo
Stillness and splendour of the night. Canticle. James McAuley. PoAu-1
Sting of Death, The. Frederick George Scott. OBCV
Stir Me. *Unknown.* STF
Stocking Fairy. Winifred Welles. SoPo
"Stond well, moder, under Rode." The Mother and Her Son on the Cross. *Unknown.* MeEL
Stone, The. W. W. Gibson. PoPo; SIV
Stone, The. Walter H. Kerr. FiSC
Stone, a Leaf, a Door, A. Thomas Wolfe. PoPl
Stone Angel. Anne Ridler. EaLo
Stone Gentleman, The. James Reeves. DaDu
Stone goes straight, The. Washington Monument by Night. Carl Sandburg. PoSC
Stone lips to the unspoken cave. Orpheus. W. D. Snodgrass. CABA; ToPo

Stone Path, The, *sel.* Oskar Loerke, *tr. fr. German by* Christopher Middleton.
  "Dream's my burden, leaden frost my foe, A." MGP
Stone Too Can Pray. Conrad Aiken. EaLo; MoRP
Stone Walls. Richard Lovelace. WePo
Stone-cutters fighting time with marble, you fore-defeated. To the Stone-Cutters. Robinson Jeffers. ILP; PoCh; PoPl; PP; VaPo
Stones only, the *disjecta membra* of this Great House. Ruins of a Great House. Derek Walcott. ToPo
Stony Limits. "Hugh MacDiarmid." CABL
Stooped over granite—from southern quarries. Granite. Rainer Brambach. MGP
Stop a Minute! *Unknown.* STF
Stop All the Clocks. W. H. Auden. WePo
Stop!— for thy tread is on an empire's dust! Byron. *Fr.* Childe Harold's Pilgrimage, III. ILP
Stop Look Listen. Crossing. Philip Booth. LV
Stop!—not to me, at this bitter departing. Separation. Matthew Arnold. Faded Leaves, III. VP
Stop playing, poet! May a brother speak? Transcendentalism; a Poem in Twelve Books. Robert Browning. DiPo; PP
Stopped. Allen Polite. NNP
Stopping by Woods on a Snowy Evening. Robert Frost. AmLP; AP; CABA; CaFP; DiPo; FaBV; FoBA; GoJo; ILP; MP; PoPo; PoSa; PoSC; RePo
  "Woods are lovely, dark and deep, The," *sel.* TRV
Stopwatch and an Ordnance Map, A. Stephen Spender. MoBS
Store cattle from Nelanjie! The mob goes feeding past. From the Gulf. Will H. Ogilvie. PoAu-1
Stories of Snow. P. K. Page. OBCV
Storm, The. Ben Suhayd, *tr. fr. Arabic by* Lysander Kemp. AnML
Storm, The. Chora, *tr. fr. Japanese by* Harold G. Henderson. RePo
Storm, The. John Donne. CABL
  "Then like two mighty kings which, dwelling far," *sel.* HaSV
Storm, The. George Herbert. MeP
Storm, The. Elizabeth Jennings. NePoEA-2
Storm, The. Henry Vaughan. CBEP; MeP
Storm, The. Whittier. *Fr.* Snow-bound. FaBV
Storm. Judith Wright. PoAu-2
Storm at Sea. Sir William Davenant. RoGo
Storm-dances of gulls, the barking game of seals, The. Divinely Superfluous Beauty. Robinson Jeffers. MoLP; PoPl
Storm from the East, A. Reed Whittemore. PoPl
Storm is over; the land hushes to rest, The. Robert Bridges. GTBS-P
Storm on Fifth Avenue. Siegfried Sassoon. ILP
Storm-wind blows, A. The Storm. Chora. RePo
Storm Windows. Howard Nemerov. PoIE
Stormcock in Elder. Ruth Pitter. BoC
Story, a story, a story I'll make known, A. Green Beds (C vers.). *Unknown.* BSNS
Story, a story to you I will tell, A. The Female Warrior. *Unknown.* BSO
Story, as now we see, was over-written, The. Thermopylae. Michael Thwaites. PoAu-2
Story from Russian Author. Peter Redgrove. NePoEA-2
Story in the Snow, A. Pearl R. Crouch. SoPo
Story of Augustus, Who Would Not Have Any Soup, The. Heinrich Hoffmann, *tr. fr. German.* BBGG; GoJo
Story of George Mann. *Unknown.* BSO
Story of Gustave Ohr, *with music. Unknown.* BSO
Story of Johnny Head-in-Air, The. Heinrich Hoffmann, *tr. fr. German.* BBGG
Story of Little Suck-a-Thumb, The. Heinrich Hoffmann, *tr. fr. German.* EvOK
Story of Rimini, The, *sel.* Leigh Hunt.
  "Ready she sat with one hand to turn o'er." EvOK
Story of Soutine, A. James Schevill. PoCh
Story of the Flowery Kingdom. James Branch Cabell. OnMSP
Story of Two Gentlemen and the Gardener, The. Christopher Logue. CABL
Story of Vinland, The. Sidney Lanier. *Fr.* Psalm of the West. ThLM
Story-Teller, The. Mark Van Doren. LOW
Stowed away in a Montreal lumber room. A Psalm of Montreal [*or* O God! O Montreal!]. Samuel Butler. CBEP; DTC
Stradivarius, *sel.* "George Eliot."
  Working with God. TRV
Stragglers. Pietro Aretino, *tr. fr. Italian by* Samuel Putnam. ErPo
Strange atoms we unto ourselves. Lovelight. Georgia Douglas Johnson. AmNP
Strange beauty, eight-limbed and eight-handed. Octopus. A. C. Hilton. Par
Strange bed, The, whose recurrent dream we are. Hotel de l'Univers et Portugal. James Merrill. NePoEA-2
Strange, but he cheats his master. Man of the World. Michael Hamburger. NePoEA-2
Strange, fantastic claims abound. Christ Alone. Shel Helsley. STF

Stran_e Fits of Passion Have I Known. Wordsworth. CBEP; ILP; OBNC
Strange Fruit. Randolph Stow. PoAu-2
Strange, how this smooth and supple joint can be. Hands. Louis Untermeyer. MoLP
Strange Meeting. Wilfred Owen. AnMoPo; DTC; FaPL; GTBS-P; ILP; MMA; PoIE
Strange now to think of you, gone without corsets & eyes. Kaddish. Allen Ginsberg. AmPC
Strange Passion of a Lover, A. George Gascoigne. EnRePo
Strange pie that is almost a passion. A Melton Mowbray Pork Pie. Richard Le Gallienne. Par
Strange power, I know not what thou art. To Memory. Mary Elizabeth Coleridge. CBEP
Strange Shepherd, Set My Bellwether Free. Lope de Vega, *tr. fr. Spanish by* W. S. Merwin. AnSP
Strange Story, A. *Unknown.* OnMSP
  (There Was an Old Woman.) PoSC
Strange, strange thing it is to know, A. The Sampler. Rachel Field. BiCB
Strange that you let me come so near. The Rat. Andrew Young. WePo
Strange walkers! See their processional. The Mushroom Gatherers. Donald Davie. NePoEA-2
Strangely/ my mother's sad eyes. X-Ray. David Ray. NePoEA-2
Strangeness of Heart. Siegfried Sassoon. MoRP
Stranger, The. Brother Antoninus. ToPo
Stranger, The. Jean Garrigue. MP
Stranger. Thomas Merton. EaLo
Stranger, The. "Gabriela Mistral," *tr. fr. Spanish by* Kate Flores. AnSP
Stranger, The. Adrienne Rich. CoPo
Stranger, approach this spot with gravity. Epitaph on a Dentist. *Unknown.* LV
Stranger Bride. Jocelyn Macy Sloan. FiSC
Stranger came to the door at eve, A. Love and a Question. Robert Frost. MoBS
Stranger, if thou hast learned a truth which needs. Inscription for the Entrance to a Wood. Bryant. AmLP; AP; ILP
Stranger, may I button-hole you. Something in Common. Richard Church. MoRP
Stranger to Europe. Guy Butler. ACV
Stranger to Love, Whoever Loves Not Thee. Lope de Vega, *tr. fr. Spanish by* Iain Fletcher. AnSP
Stranger to the crowd, yet useful to the crowd, A. The Sage Speaks. Nietzsche. TwGP
Stranger, whoe'er thou art, that stoop'st to taste. The Fountain. Giambattista Marino. RBL
Strangers, The. Jones Very. CBEP
Strangers ask. The Tower. Philip Booth. NePoEA-2
Strapping young stockman lay dying, A. The Dying Stockman. *Unknown.* PoAu-1
Straw, The. Robert Graves. AnMoPo
Strawberries in November. John Shaw Neilson. PoAu-1
Strawberries Mit Cream. Rochelle Owens. CoPo
Straws like tame lightnings lie about the grass. Summer Farm. Norman MacCaig. ACV
Stray Dog. Charlotte Mish. PoLF
Stray Dog, near Ecully, Valley of the Rhône. Margaret Avison. OBCV
Strayed Reveller, The. Matthew Arnold. VP
Streams fall down and through the darkness bear, The. Spate in Winter Midnight. Norman MacCaig. BoC; GTBS-P
Street in April, A. Louis Dudek. OBCV
Street in North Carolina, A. Helen Bevington. PoNC
Street Is Waiting for the Night, The. Juan Ramón Jiménez, *tr. fr. Spanish by* Lysander Kemp. AnSP
Street of Agrigentum. Salvatore Quasimodo, *tr. fr. Italian by* Allen Mandelbaum. CoIP
Street Performers, 1851. Terence Tiller. AnMoPo; GTBS-P
Street Scene. Robert Mezey. ToPo
Streets of Laredo, The. Louis MacNeice. MoBS
Streets of the roaring town. On a Soldier Fallen in the Philippines. William Vaughn Moody. AP; ThLM
Streets that slept all afternoon in sun, The. Camptown. John Ciardi. ThLM
Strength and honour are her clothing. Proverbs, Bible, *O.T.* PoSC
Strengthened to live, strengthened to die for. In Distrust of Merits. Marianne Moore. AP; EaLo
Strephon. John Smyth. UnTE
Strephon kissed me in the spring. The Look. Sara Teasdale. BoLP; WePo
Strephon the brisk and gay. Strephon. John Smyth. UnTE
Stretched out full length, his eighty years too ripe. The Old Peasant in the Billiard Saloon. Huw Menai. ACV
Strew not earth with empty stars. Song. Thomas Lovell Beddoes. *Fr.* The Second Brother. CBEP
Strew on her roses, roses. Requiescat. Matthew Arnold. ELP; ILP; PoSa; VP
Striding striving. Melancholy. August Stramm. MGP
Strike among the Poets, A. *Unknown.* PP
Strike Down My Heart with But a Single Blow. Guillaume

de Machaut, *tr. fr. French by* Norman R. Shapiro. AnML

Striking a Lead, *with music.* John A. Stone. SGR

Strings in the Earth and Air. James Joyce. Chamber Music, I. LOW

Striped blouse in a clearing by Bazille, A. Ceremony. Richard Wilbur. PP

Striking like lightning to the quick of the real world. Duns Scotus. Thomas Merton. CoPo

Strong Are Saying Nothing, The. Robert Frost. FoBA; PoDB

Strong, but with gentleness. Variations on a Medieval Theme. Geoffrey Dutton. PoAu-2

Strong man awhile in his kingdom is lord, The. The Eternal. Esaias Tegnér. SiGo

Strong men keep coming on, The. Upstream. Carl Sandburg. MoRP

Strong-shouldered mole. A Dead Mole. Andrew Young. GTBS-P

Strong sob of the chafing stream, The. Orara. Henry Kendall. PoAu-1

Strong Son of God, immortal Love. In Memoriam A. H. H., Proem. Tennyson. EaLo; FaPL; ILP; PoIE; TRV; VP

Strophe. Wolfdietrich Schnurre, *tr. fr. German by* Michael Hamburger. MGP

Struggle. Sidney Lanier. CBEP

Struggle, The. Sully-Prudhomme, *tr. fr. French by* Arthur O'Shaughnessy. PoP1

Stud Groom. John Glassco. OBCV

Student, The. Marianne Moore. MP

Study Habits. Richard Armour. LV

Study of Two Pears. Wallace Stevens. AP

Stuff of Dreams, The. Shakespeare. *See* Our Revels Now Are Ended.

Stuffed Owl, The. Wordsworth. Par

Stupendous are the works of man! Behold. Finale. Paul Bartlett. PoNC

Stupidity Street. Ralph Hodgson. LOW

Subaltern's Love-Song, A. John Betjeman. EvOK; MP

Subject to All Pain. *Unknown.* MeEL

Sublimation. Alex Comfort. ErPo; UnTE

Sublimer strains, O rustic Muse, prepare. Saturday; or, The Flights. John Gay. *Fr.* The Shepherd's Week. EiCP

Submission. *Unknown, tr. fr. Siamese by* E. Powys Mathers. ErPo

Submission in Affliction. *Unknown.* STF

Subterranean City, A. Thomas Lovell Beddoes. StP

Subtle chain of countless rings, A. Nature. Emerson. AmLP; ILP

Suburban Homecoming. John Ciardi. ToPo

Subversive. William Rose Benét. MoRP

Subway, The. Allen Tate. AP

Subway Train. Gottfried Benn, *tr. fr. German by* Michael Hamburger. MGP

Success. William Empson. ToPo

Success is counted sweetest. Emily Dickinson. AP; CABA; CBEP; DiPo; FoBA; GoJo; PoIE; PoPo; StP

Succession, The. Edwin Muir. PoDB

Succumbing. Paul Eaton Reeve. ErPo

Such fame as I have drops from me in a flash. The Perturbations of Uranus. Roy Fuller. ErPo

Such folly of margins that may retaliate. Gil Orlovitz. *Fr.* Art of the Sonnet. ToPo

Such moving sounds, from such a careless touch. On My Lady Isabella Playing on the Lute. Edmund Waller. SeCP

"Such Stuff as Dreams." Franklin P. Adams. LV

Such, such is death: no triumph: no defeat. Two Sonnets, II. Charles Hamilton Sorley. MMA

Sudden autumn winds, like hounds, The. Mary Gilmore. *Fr.* The Disinherited. PoAu-1

Sudden blow, A: the great wings beating still. Leda and the Swan. W. B. Yeats. CABA; CaFP; DiPo; ErPo; FoBA; GTBS-P; ILP; OnP; PoIE; StP; VaPo

Sudden cry in sleep, A; wind rushes through dark streets. The Soul's Springtime. Georg Trakl. MGP

Sudden Frost. David Wagoner. PoP1

Sudden Light. Dante Gabriel Rossetti. CBEP; ELP; OBNC; PoLF

(Song IV: Sudden Light.) CTC

Sudden Shower. John Clare. CBEP; PoSC

Suddenly Afraid. *Unknown.* CBEP

Suddenly, after the quarrel, while we waited. The Quarrel. Conrad Aiken. MoLP; PoP1

Suddenly I saw the cold and rock-delighting heaven. The Cold Heaven. W. B. Yeats. CTC; GTBS-P

Suddenly in sunlight. Final Procession. Audrey McGaffin. OPP

Suddenly night overtakes us. The Terrace. Vittorio Sereni. CoIP

"Suddenly she slapped me, hard across the face." In Memoriam II: Elizabeth in Italy. Richard Weber. ErPo

Suddenly the cherries were there. Transformation. Günter Grass. MGP

Suddenly with intense. The Runner. Alexandra Grilikhes. SD

Suffering. Jacques Audiberti, *tr. fr. French by* Mark Strand. CoFP

Sugar-Plum Tree, The. Eugene Field. SoPo

Sugaring, The. A. M. Klein. OBCV

Suicide. Louis MacNeice. DTC

Suicide in the Copse, The ("The suicide, far from content"). Robert Graves. AnMoPo

Suicide in the Trenches. Siegfried Sassoon. MMA

Suicide of the night—ah, flotsam. Strange Fruit. Randolph Stow. PoAu-2

Suit of Nettles, A, *sels.* James Reaney. OBCV
    January.
    November.

Suite from Catullus. Vincent McHugh. ErPo

Sulky witch and a surly cat, A. Hallowe'en Indignation Meeting. Margaret Fishback. PoSC

Sullen Moods. Robert Graves. StP

Sultan was vexed by a dream, The. Tact. Arthur Guiterman. SIV

Sum of All Known Reverence, The. Walt Whitman. MoRP

Sum of Life, The. Benjamin Franklin King, Jr. *See* Pessimist, The.

Sumer Is Icumen In. *Unknown.* ILP; MeEL; PoIE

(Summer Is Icumen In.) CBEP

Summa contra Gentiles. Paris Leary. CoPo

Summer. John Clare. CBEP

Summer. Cesare Pavese, *tr. fr. Italian by* Norman T. Di Giovanni. CoIP

Summer. Christina Rosseti. CBEP; ELP

Summer. James Thomson. *Fr.* The Seasons. StP

Summer and autumn had been so wet, The. God's Judgment on a Wicked Bishop. Robert Southey. OnMSP

Summer cloud in summer blue, The. Cloud and Flame. John Berryman. AP

Summer Dawn. William Morris. CBEP; OBNC

Summer Days Are Come Again, The. Samuel Longfellow. TRV

Summer ends now; now, barbarous in beauty, the stooks arise. Hurrahing in Harvest. Gerard Manley Hopkins. BoC; CBEP; PoIE; VP

Summer Excursion: Signs and Portents. Helen Bevington. PoNC

Summer Farm. Norman MacCaig. ACV

Summer Has Sent His Minions On. Charles d'Orléans, *tr. fr. French by* Dwight Durling. AnML

Summer has two beginnings. Emily Dickinson. StP

Summer Image. Friedrich Hebbel, *tr. fr. German by* Gerd Gillhoff. AGP

Summer Images. John Clare. CBEP; OBNC

"Summer is coming, summer is coming." The Throstle. Tennyson. PoPo; PoSC

Summer Is Gone. *Unknown, tr. fr. Old Irish by* Sean O'Faolain. PoP1

Summer Is Icumen In. *Unknown. See* Sumer Is Icumen In.

Summer is over, The. October. Rose Fyleman. RePo

Summer, like a dread disease. Thredbo River. Sydney Jephcott. PoAu-1

Summer Moonlight. Patience Strong. RePo

Summer Morning. John Clare. CBEP; PoSC

Summer Morning, A. Rachel Field. SoPo

Summer Morning. Jean Ingelow. ThGo

Summer mounts/ for war. The Rough Day. Jonathan Williams. PoNC

Summer Night, A. Matthew Arnold. CBEP; VP

Summer Night. Ranko, *tr. fr. Japanese by* Harold G. Henderson. RePo

Summer Night. Shiki, *tr. fr. Japanese by* Harold G. Henderson. SiGo

Summer Night. Tennyson. *See* Now Sleeps the Crimson Petal.

Summer of sixty-three, sir, and Conrad was gone away. Kentucky Belle. Constance Fenimore Woolson. SIV

Summer Rain. Elizabeth J. Coatsworth. RePo

Summer Song. E. Nesbit. PoSC

Summer Song I ("I looked into my heart to write"). George Barker. ToPo

Summer Song II ("Soft is the collied night, and cool"). George Barker. ToPo

Summer Stars. Carl Sandburg. LOW; RePo

Summer Storm. Louis Simpson. ErPo

Summer Storm. Louis Untermeyer. UnTE

Summer Storm (*circa* 1916), and God's Grace. Robert Penn Warren. PoDB

Summer Story, The. John Lehmann. MP

Summer that I was ten, The. The Centaur. May Swenson. MP

Summer, this is our flesh. Seasons of the Soul. Allen Tate. AP

Summer was another country, where the birds. Holiday. Adrienne Cecile Rich. MoLP

Summer Wind. Bryant. AP

Summer Wish, A. Christina Rossetti. OBNC

Summers and summers have come, and gone with the flight of the swallow. The Tantramar Revisited. Sir Charles G. D. Roberts. OBCV

Summer's last surviving rose I saw, The. Summer Image. Friedrich Hebbel. AGP
Summer's Last Will and Testament, *sels.* Thomas Nashe.
 Adieu, Farewell, Earth's Bliss. CaFP; ELP; PoIE; PoSa
 (In Time of Pestilence 1593.) CBEP; DTC
 (In Time of Plague.) EnRePo
 (Litany in Time of Plague, A.) CABA
 (Song.) DiPo; StP
 Autumn Hath All the Summer's Fruitful Treasure. EnRePo Spring. CBEP; GTBS-P; PoIE; WiR
Summer's Night, A. Antonio Machado, *tr. fr. Spanish by* James Duffy. AnSP
Summer's pleasures they are gone like to visions every one. Remembrances. John Clare. CBEP
Summertime. "Vincenzo Cardarelli," *tr. fr. Italian by* Cosimo Corsano. CoIP
Summertime Delights Me, The. Airas Nunes, *tr. fr. Portuguese by* William M. Davis. AnML
Summing-up, The. Stanley Kunitz. PoPl
Summoned by love and heat and God knows what. News from the Court. David Wagoner. NePoEA-2
Summoning artists to participate. For John F. Kennedy His Inauguration. Robert Frost. OPP
Summons to Love. William Drummond of Hawthornden. GTBS-P
Summum Bonum. Robert Browning. BoLP
Sun, The. Hugo Ball, *tr. fr. German by* Christopher Middleton. MGP
Sun, The. John Drinkwater. SoPo
Sun, The. Georg Trakl, *tr. fr. German by* Christopher Middleton. MGP
Sun, The/ Spills thin gold wine. In Winter. Zoe Kincaid Brockman. *Fr.* Three Cinquains. PoNC
Sun and Cloud. Melville Cane. PoPl
Sun and Rain and Dew from Heaven. Adam Lindsay Gordon. *Fr.* Ye Wearie Wayfarer. PoLF
Sun and the Rain, The. Lizette Woodworth Reese. ThGo
Sun became a small round moon, The. Climbing in Glencoe. Andrew Young. SD
Sun Came Out in April, The. C. Day Lewis. MoBS
Sun descending in the west, The. Night [or Guardian Angels of the Creatures]. Blake. *Fr.* Songs of Innocence. BoC; CBEP; PoLF; WiR
Sun does arise, The. The Echoing [or Ecchoing] Green. Blake. *Fr.* Songs of Innocence. CaFP; CBEP; DiPo; PoSC; WiR
Sun, God's eye, The. The Nature of Love. James Kirkup. EaLo
Sun goes down, and over all, The. Low Tide on Grand Pré. Bliss Carman. OBCV
Sun goes lime in a throng of oak. First Reader. Paris Leary. CoPo
Sun had gone down o'er the hills in the west, The. Amanda. *Unknown.* BFSS
Sun had left the western road, The. The Spider. Mary Jones. WaPE
Sun had set behind yon hill, The. To Be a Farmer's Boy. *Unknown.* BFSS
Sun has sucked and beat the encircling hills. In Hospital: Poona (II). Alun Lewis. DTC
Sun is a huntress young, The. An Indian Summer Day on the Prairie. Vachel Lindsay. SoPo
Sun is blue and scarlet on my page, The. Falling Asleep over the Aeneid. Robert Lowell. AP; ToPo
Sun is high, The. Young Saxons shouldering oars. North Shore. Peter Davison. CoPo
Sun is not in love with us, The. The Isles of Greece. Demetrios Capetanakis. GTBS-P
Sun is set, The; the swallows are asleep. Evening: Ponte al Mare, Pisa. Shelley. CBEP
Sun is warm, the sky is clear, The. Stanzas Written in Dejection, near Naples. Shelley. CABA; CBEP; FaBV; GTBS-P
Sun lay down orange on a cloud. A Blown Newspaper. "Will Inman." PoNC
Sun may set and rise, The. Lines from Catullus. Sir Walter Ralegh. EnRePo
Sun, Moon and Stars. Ecclesiasticus, XLIII: 1–11, Bible, Apocrypha. BoC
Sun, moon and stars. *Unknown.* ThGo
Sun now rose upon the right, The. Samuel Taylor Coleridge. *Fr.* The Rime of the Ancient Mariner. HaSV
Sun of the Center. Robert Kelly. CoPo
Sun Path, The. Matsuo Basho, *tr. fr. Japanese by* Harold G. Henderson. SiGo
Sun rises in south east corner of things, The. A Ballad of the Mulberry Road. Ezra Pound. LOW
Sun Rising, The. John Donne. CABA; CBEP; DiPo; EnRePo; ILP; PoIE; UnTE; VaPo
 (Sunne Rising, The.) SeCP
Sun shines, The. Tommies in the Train. D. H. Lawrence. MMA
Sun shines bright in the [or our] old Kentucky home, The. My Old Kentucky Home. Stephen Foster. FaBV; FaPL; PoLF

Sun shines warm on seven old soldiers, The. The Oldest Soldier. Robert Graves. DTC
Sun Sinks, The. Nietzsche, *tr. fr. German by* Walter Kaufmann. TwGP
Sun streaked the coffee urn. The Deaths at Paragon, Indiana. John Woods. CoPo
Sun, stun me, sustain me. On Looking into Henry Moore. Dorothy Livesay. OBCV
Sun that brief December day, The. Snow-bound [or The Storm]. Whittier. AP; FaBV; WiR
Sun, the moon, the stars, the seas, the hills and the plains, The. The Higher Pantheism. Tennyson. TRV; VP
Sun upon the lake is low, The. Datur Hora Quieti. Sir Walter Scott. *Fr.* The Doom of Devorgoil, I. GTBS-P
Sun upon the Weirdlaw Hill, The. The Dreary Change. Sir Walter Scott. OBNC
Sun was black with judgment, The, and the moon. Femina contra Mundum. G. K. Chesterton. MoRP
Sun was shining on the sea, The. The Walrus and the Carpenter. "Lewis Carroll." *Fr.* Through the Looking-Glass. FaBV; SoPo
Sun was sinking in the west, The. The Wisconsin Soldier Boy. *Unknown.* BFSS
Sun was witness when his eyes appeared, The. Glitter of Pebbles. Dom Moraes. ACV
Sun went down with heavy glow, The. Wakeful Night. Annette von Droste-Hülshoff. AGP
Sun which doth the greatest comfort bringe, The. Francis Beaumont's Letter from the Country to Jonson. Ben Jonson. SeCP
Sun-beames in the East are spred, The. Epithalamion Made at Lincolnes Inne. John Donne. SeCP
Sunday afternoon. Veracruz. Robert Hayden. AmNP
Sunday Edition. Joseph Joel Keith. FiSC
Sun-Day Hymn, A. Oliver Wendell Holmes. TRV
Sunday in the Thirties, A. Barbara Hinchcliffe. PtTo
Sunday is the dullest day, treating. Sweeney in Articulo. "Myra Buttle." Par
Sunday Morning. Wallace Stevens. AmLP; AP; CABA; CABL; CaFP; OnP; PoDB; PoIE; StP
Sunday Morning, King's Cambridge. John Betjeman. BoC; EaLo
Sunday: New Guinea. Karl Shapiro. PoPl
Sunday: Outskirts of Knoxville, Tennessee. James Agee. ErPo
Sunday School Teacher Speaks, A. *Unknown.* STF
Sunday shuts down on this twentieth-century evening. Boy with His Hair Cut Short. Muriel Rukeyser. MP; PoPl; RoGo
Sunday strollers along a sewage filled Schuykill. To Some Millions Who Survive Joseph Mander, Sr. Sarah E. Wright. PtTo
Sunder me from my bones, O sword of God. The Sword of Surprise. G. K. Chesterton. MoRP
Sundew, The. Swinburne. ELP; OBNC; WePo
Sundial, The. Jane Cooper. AmPC
Sun-Dial, The. Thomas Love Peacock. *Fr.* Melincourt. OBNC
Sundown. Léonie Adams. AmLP
Sundowner, The. John Shaw Neilson. PoAu-1
Sunflower bends to the west, and day, The. Almost a Madrigal. Salvatore Quasimodo. CoIP
Sung by a Young Girl. Dryden. *See* Song for a Girl.
Sunk earlier in the silence of grey cashmere. Slepynge Long in Greet Quiete Is Eek a Greet Norice to Leccherie. John Hollander. AmPC; ErPo
Sunken Evening. Laurie Lee. ToPo
Sunken Oboe. Salvatore Quasimodo, *tr. fr. Italian by* Allen Mandelbaum. CoIP
Sunlicht still on me, you row'd in clood, The. At My Father's Grave. "Hugh MacDiarmid." GTBS-P; PoIE
Sunlight, moonlight. Dream-Song. Walter de la Mare. RePo
Sunlight on the Garden, The. Louis MacNeice. GTBS-P; MP; PoIE; VaPo
Sunlit Vale, The. Edmund Blunden. CBEP
Sunly the day streams. Evening. Robert Wallace. PoPo
Sunne begins uppon my heart to shine, The. Sonnet. William Alabaster. MeP
Sunne Rising, The. John Donne. *See* Sun Rising, The.
Sunny day, the mild cool, The. For a Wedding Performed on Thanksgiving in the Week of President Kennedy's Death. George T. Wright. OPP
Sunny shaft did I behold, A. Glycine's Song. Samuel Taylor Coleridge. PoPl; PoSC
Sunny South, The. *Unknown.* BSNS
Sunrise. Lizette Woodworth Reese. LV
Sunrise. Margaret E. Sangster. TRV
Sun's Darling, The, *sel.* Thomas Dekker *and* John Ford. Haymakers, Rakers, *fr.* III, i. ELP
Suns in a skein, the uncut stones of night. Roy Fuller. Mythological Sonnets, VIII. GTBS-P
Suns, planets, stars, in glorious array. Victor J. Daley. *Fr.* Night. PoAu-1
Sun's way, The. The Sun Path. Matsuo Basho. SiGo

Sunset. Arthur Bayldon. PoAu-1
Sunset. Juan Ramón Jiménez, *tr. fr. Spanish by* Kate Flores. AnSP
Sunset and evening star. Crossing the Bar. Tennyson. CABA; DiPo; FaBV; FaPL; FoBA; HaSV; ILP; LV; OBNC; PoLF; PoPo; TRV; VP
Sunset at Les Eboulements, A. Archibald Lampman. OBCV
Sunset Horn. Myron O'Higgins. AmNP; PtTo
Sunset over the Ægean. Byron. *Fr.* The Corsair. OBNC
Sunshine let it be or frost. After St. Augustine. Mary Elizabeth Coleridge. TRV
Sunthin' in the Pastoral Line. James Russell Lowell. *Fr.* The Biglow Papers, 2d Series, No. VI. AP
(Spring.) FaBV
Superfluous Saddle, The. La Fontaine. UnTE
Superliminare. George Herbert. MeP; SeCP
Superscription, A. Dante Gabriel Rossetti. The House of Life, XCVII. CBEP; GTBS-P; OBNC
Supper after the Last, The. Galway Kinnell. PoCh
Supper bell was ringing as Neill strode, The. Haying. Ethel Romig Fuller. SIV
Suppertime. Burns. UnTE
Supplication, A. Abraham Cowley. GTBS-P
Supplication, A. Sir Thomas Wyatt. *See* Forget Not Yet.
Suppose he had been tabled at thy teats. Luke II. Richard Crashaw. CABA
Supreme Surrender. Dante Gabriel Rossetti. The House of Life, VII. VP
Sure, deck your lower limbs in pants. What's the Use. Ogden Nash. PoPl
Sure, It was so. Man in those early days. Corruption. Henry Vaughan. MeP; SeCP
Sure Lord, there is enough in thee to dry. Sonnet. George Herbert. MeP
Sure Sign, A. Nancy Byrd Turner. SoPo
Sure Signs. Thad Stem, Jr. PoNC
Sure there are poets which did never dream. Cooper's Hill. Sir John Denham. SeCP
Sure thou didst flourish once! and many Springs. The Timber. Henry Vaughan. SeCP
Surely among a rich man's flowering lawns. Meditations in Time of Civil War. W. B. Yeats. CABL
Surely that is not a man. Acrobat. Rachel Field. *Fr.* A Circus Garland. SoPo
Surgeons must be very careful. Emily Dickinson. CBEP; DiPo; FoBA
Surprise. Harry Behn. BiCB
Surprise, The. *Unknown, tr. fr. Greek by* Louis Untermeyer. UnTE
Surprised by Joy. Wordsworth. CBEP; FoBA
(Desideria.) GTBS-P
(To Catherine Wordsworth 1808-1812.) OBNC
Surprises. Jean Conder Soule. BiCB
Surprises. *Unknown.* STF
Surprises are round. Surprises. Jean Conder Soule. BiCB
Surrender. André du Bouchet, *tr. fr. French by* Dori Katz. CoFP
Surrounded by the gentle sound. Song III. Garcilaso de la Vega. AnSP
Survey of Literature. John Crowe Ransom. MP
Survivors, The. S. S. Gardons. AmPC
Susannah and the Elders. *Unknown.* ErPo
Susie's galoshes. Galoshes. Rhoda W. Bacmeister. SoPo
Suspecting hollow trees, the barn to be. Play-wright. John Woods. CoPo
Swallow leaves her nest, The. Dirge [*or* A Voice from the Waters]. Thomas Lovell Beddoes. *Fr.* Death's Jest Book. CBEP; OBNC
Swallow, my sister, O sister swallow. Itylus. Swinburne. StP; PoFE
Swampstrife and spatterdock. The Marsh. W. D. Snodgrass. ToPo
Swan. Edward Lowbury. GTBS-P
Swan among the shadows is like snow. Leda. Rubén Darío. AnSP
Swan has a neck that is curly and long, The. Necks. Rowena Bennett. RePo
Swan Song. Som Parkash Ranchan. ACV
Swans, The. Rubén Darío, *tr. fr. Spanish by* Doreen Bell. AnSP
Swans, The. Edith Sitwell. ACV
Swans, The. Andrew Young. WePo
Swans at Night, *sel.* Mary Gilmore.
"Within the night, above the dark." PoAu-1
Swans Sing. Samuel Taylor Coleridge. EvOK
Swapping Song, The, *with music. Unknown.* BSO
Swart[e] smeked smithes [*or* Black-smocked smiths], smatered with smoke. Blacksmiths [*or* Smoke-blackened Smiths]. *Unknown.* CABA; MeEL; WiR
Sweeney among the Nightingales. T. S. Eliot. AP; CABA; CaFP; DiPo; FoBA; ILP
Sweeney in Articulo. "Myra Buttle." Par
Sweeping the Sky. *Unknown.* SoPo
(There Was an Old Woman.) EvOK

Sweet, a delicate white mouse, A. The Waltzer in the House. Stanley Kunitz. ErPo
Sweet after showers, ambrosial air. In Memoriam A. H. H., LXXXVI. Tennyson. VP
Sweet Afton. Burns. *See* Afton Water.
Sweet and Low. Tennyson. *Fr.* The Princess, Pt. II. FoBA; ILP; LV; PoPl
(Lullaby.) PoLF
Sweet are the thoughts that savour of content. Maesia's Song. Robert Greene. *Fr.* Farewell to Folly. CTC
Sweet Auburn! loveliest village of the plain. The Deserted Village. Goldsmith. EnPE; ILP
Sweet, be not proud of those two eyes. To Dianeme. Robert Herrick. CBEP; GTBS-P; PoPo
Sweet Betsy from Pike, *with music. Unknown.* BFSS
(Sweet Betsey from Pike, *sl. diff. vers., with music, by* John A. Stone.) SGR
"Sweet boy," she says, "this night I'll waste in sorrow." Shakespeare. *Fr.* Venus and Adonis. ErPo
Sweet Chance, that led my steps abroad. A Great Time. W. H. Davies. WePo
Sweet Cupid, Ripen Her Desire. *Unknown.* EnRePo
Sweet cyder is a great thing. Great Things. Thomas Hardy. GTBS-P
Sweet day, so cool, so calm, so bright. Virtue [*or* Vertue]. George Herbert. CABA; CaFP; CBEP; ELP; FoBA; MeP; PoIE; PoSa; SeCP
Sweet dimness of her loosened hair's downfall. Love-Sweetness. Dante Gabriel Rossetti. The House of Life, XXI. VP
Sweet disorder in the dress, A. Delight in Disorder. Robert Herrick. CABA; CBEP; ErPo; FaBV; GTBS-P; ILP; PoIE; PoSa; PP; SeCP; StP; VaPo
Sweet dreams form a shade. A Cradle Song. Blake. *Fr.* Songs of Innocence. CBEP
Sweet Echo, Sweetest Nymph. Milton. *Fr.* Comus. ELP
(Echo.) CBEP
Sweet, exclude me not, nor be divided. Bar Not the Door. Thomas Campion. UnTE
Sweet Gifts. Garcilaso de la Vega, *tr. fr. Spanish by* Edwin Morgan. AnSP
Sweet girl graduate, lean as a fawn, A. Nancy Hanks, Mother of Abraham Lincoln. Vachel Lindsay. LiPo; ThLM
Sweet, harmles lives! (on whose holy leisure). The Shepheards. Henry Vaughan. MeP
Sweet Highland Girl, a very shower. To a Highland Girl [*or* To the Highland Girl of Inversneyde]. Wordsworth. CABL; GTBS-P
Sweet in goodly fellowship. Wine and Love and Lyre. *Unknown.* UnTE
Sweet in her green cell the flower of beauty slumbers. Serenade of a Loyal Martyr. George Darley. OBNC
Sweet Innisfallen. Thomas Moore. OBNC
Sweet is the rose, but growes upon a brere. Amoretti, XXVI. Spenser. ILP
Sweet is true love tho' given in vain, in vain. The Song of Love and Death. Tennyson. *Fr.* Idylls of the King: Lancelot and Elaine. OBNC
Sweet Lady Fair. Christine de Pisan, *tr. fr. French by* Muriel Kittel. AnML
Sweet, Let Me Go. William Corkine. UnTE
Sweet, let us love enjoy. Love Play. William Cavendish, Duke of Newcastle. ErPo
Sweet lips, there are songs about kisses now. Counting. Carl Sandburg. MoLP
Sweet Love,—but oh! most dread Desire of Love. Love's Fatality. Dante Gabriel Rossetti. The House of Life, LIV. VP
Sweet Love, mine only treasure. Where His Lady Keeps His Heart. "A. W." CTC
Sweet love, renew thy force; be it not said. Sonnets, LVI. Shakespeare. CBEP; PoLF
Sweet Mary, *with music. Unknown.* BSO
Sweet "No, no," A—with a sweet smile beneath. A Love-Lesson. Clément Marot. RBL
Sweet Peace, where dost thou dwell? I humbly crave. Peace. George Herbert. ELP; MeP
Sweet procession, rose-blue. Seems like We Must Be Somewhere Else. Denise Levertov. NePoEA-2
Sweet, Red Rose, The. Mary Mapes Dodge. BiCB
Sweet repose, oh tumult sweet in the grass. In the Grass. Annette von Droste-Hülshoff. AGP
Sweet Rose of Virtue. William Dunbar. MeEL
Sweet semi-circled Cynthia played at maw. Sonnet: Mackado, Fustian and Motley. John Taylor. *Fr.* Odcomb's Complaint. CBEP
Sweet Softness with Which Love Serves Me Often, The. Guilhem de Cabestanh, *tr. fr. Provençal by* Paul Blackburn. AnML
Sweet soul, do with me as thou wilt. In Memoriam A. H. H., LXV. Tennyson. VP
Sweet Spring Is Your. E. E. Cummings. LV
Sweet stream, that winds through yonder glade. To a Young Lady. William Cowper. GTBS-P

Sweet Suffolk Owl. *Unknown.* CBEP; EnRePo
Sweet Teviot! on thy silver tide. A Father's Notes of Woe. Sir Walter Scott. *Fr.* The Lay of the Last Minstrel. OBNC
Sweet Tooth, The. Katharine Pyle. BBGG
Sweet twining hedgeflowers wind-stirred in no wise. The Lovers' Walk. Dante Gabriel Rossetti. The House of Life, XII. VP
Sweet Voice of the Woodland Nightingale, The. Le Chastelain de Coucy, *tr. fr. French by* Patricia Terry. AnML
Sweet warrior when shall I have peace with you? Amoretti, LVII. Spenser. StP
Sweet Was the Song. *Unknown.* PoSC
Sweet were the dayes, when thou didst lodge with Lot. Decay. George Herbert. MeP; SeCP
Sweet William ("Sweet William on a fine summer day"). *Unknown.* See Lady Isabel and the Elf Knight.
Sweet William ("Weary are the hours of a sailor boy") (A, B, and C vers., with music; D and E vers.). *Unknown.* BSO
(Lost Willie, F vers.) BSO
(My True Sailor Boy, with music.) BFSS
Sweet William and Lady Marget. *Unknown.* See Fair Margaret and Sweet William.
Sweet William arose [or rose] one morning bright [or merry May morning]. Fair [or Lady] Margaret and Sweet William. *Unknown.* BFSS; BSO
Sweet William's Ghost. *Unknown.* BuBa
Sweetes' Li'l' Feller. Frank L. Stanton. LV
Sweetest fruits, all freshly picked, The. Adam's Offering. Friedrich Hebbel. AGP
Sweetest Home, The. *Unknown.* STF
Sweetest Lives, The. Elizabeth Barrett Browning. TRV
Sweetest Love, I Do Not Go. John Donne. See Song: "Sweetest love, I do not go."
Sweetest of sweets, I thank you: when displeasure. Church-Musick. George Herbert. MeP
Sweit rois of vertew and of gentilnes. Sweet Rose of Virtue. William Dunbar. MeEL
Swell People. Carl Sandburg. LOW
Swet Jesus/ Is cum to us. Welcome! Our Messiah. *Unknown.* MeEL
Swift had pains in his head. War Poet. Roy Fuller. PP
Swift through some trap mine eyes have never found. The Harlequin of Dreams. Sidney Lanier. AP
Swift to the western bounds of this wide land. On the Completion of the Pacific Telegraph. Jones Very. AP
Swift was sweet on Stella. Us Poets. Franklin P. Adams. PoPl
Swiftly the years, beyond recall. New Corn. T'ao Ch'ien. SiGo
Swiftly walk o'er [or over] the western wave. To Night [or Night or To the Night]. Shelley. BoC; CBEP; GTBS-P; ILP; OBNC; PoIE; PoLF; WiR
Swimmer, The. John Crowe Ransom. SD
Swimmers, The. Allen Tate. AP
Swimmers. Louis Untermeyer. SIV
"Then, the quick plunge into the cool, green dark," *sel.* SD
Swimming Lady, The; or, A Wanton Discovery. *Unknown.* ErPo; UnTE
Swing, The. Robert Louis Stevenson. GoJo; LV; SoPo
Switzerland. Matthew Arnold. VP
Sels.
Absence, VI. CBEP
Meeting, I. ELP; VP
(Lake, The.) CBEP
To Marguerite ("We were apart"), IV. CBEP
To Marguerite ("Yes! in the sea of life enisled"), V. ELP; ILP; OBNC
(To Marguerite—Continued.) CABA; CaFP; GTBS-P; VaPo
Sword of Surprise, The. G. K. Chesterton. MoRP
Sylvia and the Bee. Mary Leapor. WaPE
Sylvia and the Fair. Dryden. CBEP; UnTE
(Song: "Sylvia the fair, in the bloom of fifteen.") ErPo
Sylvie and Bruno, *sel.* "Lewis Carroll."
Gardener's Song, The. EvOK
(Mad Gardener's Song, The.) WiR
Sylvie and Bruno Concluded, *sel.* "Lewis Carroll."
Pig-Tale, A. WiR
Symbolum. Goethe, *tr. fr. German by* Alexander Gode. AGP
Sympathy. Paul Laurence Dunbar. AmNP
Symphony. Frank Horne. AmNP
Symphony, The. Sidney Lanier. AP
"O Trade! O Trade! would thou wert dead!" *sel.* PoPo
Symphony in Gray Major. Rubén Darío, *tr. fr. Spanish by* Denise Levertov. AnSP
Synchronized. Larry Rubin. FiSC
Synnöve's Song. Björnstjerne Björnson, *tr. fr. Norwegian by* Charles Wharton Stork. PoPl
Syren Songs, *sels.* George Darley.
Mermaiden's Vesper Hymn, The. HaSV; OBNC
Sea-Ritual, The. OBNC; WiR
System. Robert Louis Stevenson. LV

T

T-Bar. P. K. Page. OBCV
Tabernacles. Gerrit Lansing. CoPo
Table and the Chair, The. Edward Lear. SoPo
Table-Birds. Kenneth Mackenzie. PoAu-2
Table Manners. Gelett Burgess. BBGG
Table Talk, *sel.* William Cowper.
"I know the mind that feels indeed the fire." PP
Tables Turned, The. Wordsworth. CBEP; DiPo
Taborer beat/ Your little drum. Jig for Sackbuts. Dominic Bevan Wyndham Lewis. ErPo
Tact. Arthur Guiterman. SIV
Taffy. *Unknown.* BBGG
Tagus, Farewell. Sir Thomas Wyatt. CBEP; EnRePo
Tail behind, a trunk in front, A. The Elephant. A. E. Housman. FaBV; PoPo
Tail toddle, tail toddle. Tommie Makes My Tail Toddle. Burns. ErPo
Tailor, The. Thomas Lovell Beddoes. WiR
Tailor and the Crow, The (A vers.). *Unknown.* BSNS
(Carrion Crow, The, B and C vers.) BSNS
Tails. Rowena Bennett. RePo
Take all my loves, my love, yea, take them all. Sonnets, XL. Shakespeare. CBEP
Take as a gift. Giving and Taking. James Kirkup. EaLo
Take Back the Virgin Page. Thomas Moore. OBNC
Take him, earth, for cherishing. Prudentius. *Fr.* Cathemerinon. SiGo
Take it from me kiddo. Poem, or Beauty Hurts Mr. Vinal. E. E. Cummings. PoIE
Take me down from this cross, for now my body is broken. Golgotha. John Hall Wheelock. MoRP
Take My Heart. St. Augustine, *tr. fr. Latin.* TRV
Take, O Take Those Lips Away. Shakespeare. *Fr.* Measure for Measure, IV, i; *also given, with add. st., in* The Bloody Brother (*by* John Fletcher, *and others*), V, ii. CBEP; DiPo; ELP; EnRePo; FaBV; FoBA; ILP; PoIE
(Madrigal.) GTBS-P
Take out of time that moment when you stood. The Sundial. Jane Cooper. AmPC
Take this kiss upon the brow! A Dream within a Dream. Poe. AP; CBEP
Take Time to Talk with God. Helen Frazee-Bower. STF
Take time while time doth last. Song Set by John Farmer. *Unknown.* CTC
Take up the White Man's burden. The White Man's Burden. Kipling. StP
Take wings of fancy, and ascend. In Memoriam A. H. H., LXXVI. Tennyson. VP
Take Your Place. *Unknown.* STF
Take your pleasure, dance and play. Invitation to Youth. *Unknown.* UnTE
Taking a Walk with You. Kenneth Koch. AmPC
Taking Down the Tree. Aileen Fisher. RePo
Taking Leave of a Friend. Li Po, *tr. fr. Chinese by* Ezra Pound. AnMoPo
Taking Off. *Unknown.* SoPo
Talbragar. Henry Lawson. PoAu-1
Tale half told and hardly understood, A. Exodus for Oregon. Joaquin Miller. FaPL
Tale of Calidore, The. Spenser. The Faerie Queene, VI, 9. StP
Tale of Custard the Dragon, The. Ogden Nash. PoPl
(Tale of the Custard Dragon, The.) WePo
Tale of the Skunk and Poor Jez, The. John Becker. RePo
Tale the Hermit Told, The. Alastair Reid. NePoEA-2
Tales from a Family Album. Donald Justice. NePoEA-2
Tales of a Wayside Inn, *sels.* Longfellow.
Birds of Killingworth, The (The Poet's Tale), *fr.* Pt. I. OnMSP
Paul Revere's Ride (The Landlord's Tale), *fr.* Pt. I. CaFP; FaBV; RePo; SIV; ThLM
Saga of King Olaf (The Musician's Tale), *fr.* Pt. I. "Dawn is not distant, The," *fr.* xxii. TRV
Sicilian's Tale, The (The Monk of Casal-Maggiore), *fr.* Pt. III. AP
Tales of the Hall, *sels.* George Crabbe.
Sad Lover, The, *fr.* XIII. OBNC
"Something one day occurr'd about a bill," *fr.* VII. Par
Taliessin's Return to Logres. Charles Williams. ACV
Talisman, A. Marianne Moore. GoJo
Talk is of Johnson and a Congress, the. Dec. '63. Robert Sward. *Fr.* Five Poems for J. F. K. OPP
Talk of Chocolate! Francesco Redi. *Fr.* Bacchus in Tuscany. RBL
Talking to Myself, *sel.* Vincent McHugh.
"I am very fond of the little ribs of women." ErPo
Tall and clothed in samite. A White Iris. Pauline B. Barrington. PoLF
Tall elm, The. The Connecticut Elm. Emma Swan. PoPl

Tall Jane is dark who was burnished bright. For Jane Kane, Whom We Knew in Our Young Marriages. Bink Noll. ToPo
Tall Man Executes a Jig, A. Irving Layton. PoCh
Tall Nettles. Edward Thomas. CBEP
Tall people, short people. People. Lois Lenski. SoPo
Tall pines wave, and the winds loudly roar, The. My Log Cabin Home. John A. Stone. SGR
Tall Tale, A; or, A Moral Song. Phyllis Webb. OBCV
Tall, with tow-hair, the texture of hide. Aubade: Dick, the Donkey-Boy. Sir Osbert Sitwell. DaDu
Tam Lin. *Unknown.* CABL
  (Tamlane.) BuBa
Tam o' Shanter. Burns. CABL
Tame beasts menaced silently, The. Capturing Elephants. Franz Baermann Steiner. MGP
Tame Stag, The. John Gay. *See* Fable XIII: Tame Stag, The.
Tamerlane. Victor J. Daley. PoAu-1
Tamerlane. Poe. AP
Tamlane. *Unknown. See* Tam Lin.
Tanagra! think not I forget. Corinna to Tanagra. Walter Savage Landor. *Fr.* Pericles and Aspasia. OBNC
Tangere. Theodore Enslin. CoPo
Tangle of iron rods and spluttered beams, A. Les Halles d'Ypres. Edmund Blunden. MMA
Tangmalangaloo. P. J. Hartigan. PoAu-1
Tank, The. Roland Robinson. PoAu-2
Tanned blonde, The. The Once-over. Paul Blackburn. ErPo
Tansy for August. Theodore Enslin. CoPo
Tant' Amare. *Unknown, tr. fr. Spanish by* Paul Blackburn. ErPo
Tantalus. Paulus Silentiarius, *tr. fr. Greek by* Dudley Fitts. ErPo
Tantanoola Tiger, The. Max Harris. MoBS; PoAu-2
Tantramar Revisited, The. Sir Charles G. D. Roberts. OBCV
Tao Teh King, *sels. Unknown, tr. fr. Chinese.* TRV
  He Walks at Peace.
  "Slaying of multitudes should be mourned with sorrow, The."
Tapers. Frances Angevine Gray. FiSC
Tapers in the great God's hall, The. By Night. Philip Jerome Cleveland. TRV
Tarantella. Hilaire Belloc. WePo
Tarantula rattling at the lily's foot, The. O Carib Isle! Hart Crane. AP
Tardiness. Gelett Burgess. BBGG
Target Practice. Donald Finkel. NePoEA-2
Tarpauling Jacket. *Unknown.* DTC
"Tarry Ye." *Unknown.* STF
Task, The, *sels.* William Cowper.
  Garden, The, III. EnPE
  "I say the pulpit (in the sober use)," *fr.* II. TRV
  Sofa, The, I. EiCP
  "There is a pleasure in poetic pains," *fr.* II. PP
  Winter Morning Walk, The, V. EiCP
  "Would I describe a preacher, such as Paul," *fr.* II. TRV
Task. Schiller, *tr. fr. German by* Walter Kaufmann. TwGP
Tavern Guitar Playing a *Jota* Today. Antonio Machado, *tr. fr. Spanish by* Charles Guenther. AnSP
Tawny are the leaves turned but they still hold. Antique Harvesters. John Crowe Ransom. AP
Tax not the royal Saint with vain expense. Inside of [or Within] King's College Chapel, Cambridge. Wordsworth. *Fr.* Ecclesiastical Sketches. GTBS-P; OBNC
Taxicabs scuttle by on the wet streets. Whaddaya Do for Action in This Place? George Starbuck. NePoEA-2
Taxis. Rachel Field. SoPo
Tay Bridge Disaster, The. William McGonagall. EvOK
Te Martyrum Candidatus. Lionel Johnson. BoC
Tea at the Palaz of Hoon. Wallace Stevens. CBEP
Tea Shop, The. Ezra Pound. WePo
Teach me, Father, how to go. A Prayer. Edwin Markham. TRV
Teach me, my God and King. The Elixer. George Herbert. MeP; ThGo
Teach me some prayer. For Instruction. Vassar Miller. ToPo
Teach Us to Serve Thee, Lord. St. Ignatius of Loyola, *tr. fr. Latin.* TRV
Teacher Sees a Boy, The. Margaret Morningstar. STF
Teacher's Prayer, A. Frances Ridley Havergal. TRV
Teaching without pupils. On Teaching without Pupils. Bertolt Brecht. MGP
Teak Forest, The, *sel.* "Laurence Hope."
  For This Is Wisdom. PoLF
Teams, The. Henry Lawson. PoAu-1
Teapots and Quails. Edward Lear. GoJo
Tear, The. Byron. Par
  (Hours of Idleness.) EvOK
Teare, The. Richard Crashaw. SeCP
Tears. Edward Thomas. CBEP; GTBS-P
Tears at the Grave of Sir Albertus Morton. Sir Henry Wotton. SeCP

Tears Flow in My Heart. Paul Verlaine, *tr. fr. French by* Muriel Kittel. SiGo
Tears, Flow No More. Lord Herbert of Cherbury. CBEP; SeCP
Tears, Idle Tears [I Know Not What They Mean]. Tennyson. *Fr.* The Princess, Pt. IV. CABA; CaFP; DiPo; ELP; FoBA; GTBS-P; OBNC; PoIE; PoPo; PoSa; StP; WePo
  (Song: "Tears, idle tears, I know not what they mean".) PoPl
Tears of the Fatherland. Andreas Gryphius, *tr. fr. German by* George C. Schoolfield. AGP
Tears of the widower, when he sees. In Memoriam A. H. H., XIII. Tennyson. VP
Teasing Lovers, The. Horace, *tr. fr. Latin by* Louis Untermeyer. Odes, III, 9. UnTE
Technique of Laughter, The. Jascha Kessler. AmPC
Technique of Love, The. Jascha Kessler. AmPC
Technique of Power, The. Jascha Kessler. AmPC
Tecumseh, *sels.* Charles Mair. OBCV
  "There was a time on this fair continent."
  "We left/ The silent forest."
Teddy's Wonderings. John Kendrick Bangs. BiCB
Telegram. William J. Margolis. PtTo
Tele-News Blues. Peter Dufault. LV
Telephone line goes cold, A. The Farm on the Great Plains. William Stafford. PoCh
Tell all the truth but tell it slant. Emily Dickinson. AP; DiPo; PoPo
Tell Him. Chaim Nachman Bialik, *tr. fr. Hebrew by* Maurice Samuel. *Fr.* Songs of the People. SiGo
Tell it no one but the wise. Blissful Longing. Goethe, *tr. by* Albert Bloch. AGP
Tell it none except the wise. Blessed Yearning. Goethe, *tr. by* Walter Kaufmann. TwGP
Tell Jesus. *Unknown.* STF
Tell me, can this unsuspecting infant, staring. Picture of the Nativity in the Church of Krena in Chios. C. A. Trypanis. AnMoPo
Tell Me, Daughter, Pretty Daughter. Pero Meogo, *tr. fr. Portuguese by* William M. Davis. AnML
Tell me (my love) since Hymen ty'de. An Hymeneall Dialogue. Thomas Carew. SeCP
Tell me no more how fair she is. Sonnet. Henry King. SeCP
Tell me no more I am deceived. The Better Bargain. Congreve. UnTE
Tell me no more of minds embracing minds. No Platonic Love. William Cartwright. CABA; ErPo; ILP
Tell Me Not Here, It Needs Not Saying. A. E. Housman. Last Poems, XL. CBEP; ELP; GTBS-P; OBNC
Tell me not, in mournful numbers. A Psalm of Life. Longfellow. DiPo; FaPL; PoLF; PoPl
Tell me not, sweet, I am unkind. To Lucasta, [on] Going to the Wars [or Warres]. Richard Lovelace. CABA; CBEP; ELP; FaBV; FaPL; GTBS-P; PoIE; PoPl; SeCP
Tell me now in what hidden way is. The Ballad of Dead Ladies [or The Snows of Yester-Year]. Villon, *tr. by* Dante Gabriel Rossetti. CTC; WiR
Tell Me, O Love. William Hammond. CBEP
Tell me, O Octopus, I begs. The Octopus. Ogden Nash. SoPo; WePo
Tell me, O tell, what kind of thing is wit. Ode: Of Wit. Abraham Cowley. SeCP
Tell me, Pyrrha, what fine youth. Another to the Same. Horace. Odes, I, 5. WiR
Tell me, tell me everything. Curiosity. Harry Behn. SoPo
Tell me where, in what foreign place. Ballad of the Ladies of Olden Times. Villon. AnML
Tell Me Where Is Fancy Bred. Shakespeare. *Fr.* The Merchant of Venice, III, ii. DiPo; ELP; EnRePo; FoBA; ILP
  (Madrigal: "Tell me where is fancy bred.") GTBS-P
  (Song, A: "Tell me, where is fancy bred.") CTC
  (Where Is Fancy Bred?) WePo
Tell you I chyll. John Skelton. *Fr.* The Tunnyng of Elynour Rummyng. StP
Telling the Bees. Whittier. AP; PoIE
Temagami. Archibald Lampman. OBCV
Temper, The. George Herbert. MeP
Temperaments, The. Ezra Pound. ErPo
Tempest, The, *sels.* Shakespeare.
  Clouds, *fr.* IV, i. BoC
  "Cloud-capp'd towers, the gorgeous palaces, The," 5 *ll.* PoPl
  Come unto These Yellow Sands, *fr.* I, ii. CBEP; PoIE
  (Ariel's Song.) CTC; GoJo
  Epilogue: "Now my charms are all o'erthrown," *fr.* V, i. CTC
  Full Fathom Five [Thy Father Lies], *fr.* I, ii. CABA; CaFP; CBEP; DiPo; ELP; FoBA; ILP; PoIE
  (Ariel's Dirge.) EvOK; GoJo
  (Sea Dirge, A.) GTBS-P; HaSV
  (Song.) OnP

Tempest, The, *sels.* (*continued*)
Our Revels Now Are Ended, *fr.* IV, i. DiPo
  (Stuff of Dreams, The.) FaBV
Where the Bee Sucks [There Suck I], *fr.* V, i. CABA;
  CBEP; CTC; DiPo; EnRePo; FaBV; FoBA; ILP
  (Fairy's Life, A.) PoPl
Tempest, The. Henry Vaughan. MeP
Temple. John Donne. MeP
Temple, The. Josephine W. Johnson. MoRP
Temple by the Sea, The. Geoffrey Dutton. ACV
Temple of Infamy, The, *sel.* Charles Harpur.
  "But hark! What hubbub now is this that comes." PoAu-1
Tempt Me No More [for I]. C. Day Lewis. The Magnetic
  Mountain, XXIV. PoDB; PoPl
Temptation. William Cowper. EiCP
Ten Brothers. *Unknown, ad. by* Louis Untermeyer. RePo
Ten Little Indian Boys. M. M. Hutchinson. SoPo
"Ten little toes, ten little toes." The Ideal Age for a Man.
  Monica Shannon. BiCB
Ten of Chaucer's People. Chaucer. *See* Canterbury Tales,
  The: Prologue.
Ten years!—and to my waking eye. The Terrace at Berne.
  Matthew Arnold. Switzerland, VII. VP
Ten years being enough of copra, he souvenired a/ whalestooth.
  Trader's Return. Sylvia Lawson. PoAu-2
Tenancy, The. Mary Gilmore. PoAu-1
Tenant. Frances Angevine Gray. FiSC
Tenant, The. Philippe Jaccottet, *tr. fr. French by* Harry
  Duncan. CoFP
Tender, Slow. *Unknown, tr. fr. Greek by* Wallace Rice.
  ErPo
Tender softness! infant mild! A Mother's Soliloquy. Hetty
  Wright. WaPE
Tender, the young auburn woman. Spring. Paul Verlaine.
  ErPo
Tender-heartedness. Harry Graham. WePo
Tenderly as a/ barber. For the Barbers. Joel Oppenheimer.
  CoPo
Tenderly as a bee that sips. Escalade. Arthur Symons.
  UnTE
Tenderly, day that I have loved, I close your eyes. Day That I
  Have Loved. Rupert Brooke. PoLF
Tenebrae. Juan Ramón Jiménez, *tr. fr. Spanish by* Alice
  Sternberg. AnSP
Tenebris Interlucentem. James Elroy Flecker. CBEP
Tennis in San Juan. Reuel Denney. SD
Tentative Description of a Dinner [Given] to Promote the
  Impeachment of President Eisenhower. Lawrence Ferlin-
  ghetti. CoPo; PtTo
10th Dance—Coming On as a Horn—20 February 1964. Jack-
  son MacLow. CoPo
Tenzone Sequence. Dante *and* Forese Donati, *tr. fr. Italian by*
  James J. Wilhelm. AnML
Terence, This Is Stupid Stuff. A. E. Housman. A Shropshire
  Lad, LXII. CABA; CaFP; ILP; PP; VP
Teresa of Avila. Elizabeth Jennings. NePoEA-2
Teresa was God's familiar. She often spoke. Conversation in
  Avila. Phyllis McGinley. EaLo; PoPo
Terly Terlow. *Unknown.* CBEP
Term, The. William Carlos Williams. PoPo; RePo
Terminal. Karl Shapiro. AmLP
Terminal Theater. Robert Sward. CoPo
Terminus. Emerson. AP; PoLF
Termite, The. Ogden Nash. PoPl; PoPo
Ternarie of Littles, upon a Pipkin of Jellie Sent to a Lady, A.
  Robert Herrick. GoJo
Ternissa. Walter Savage Landor. *Fr.* The Hellenics. OBNC
  (On Ternissa's Death.) ELP
Terrace, The. Vittorio Sereni, *tr. fr. Italian by* Carlo L.
  Golino. CoIP
Terrace at Berne, The. Matthew Arnold. Switzerland, VII.
  VP
Terraces rise and fall, The. Going to Sleep in the Country.
  Howard Moss. PoCh; StP
Terrible Beauty. Kingsley Amis. ErPo; NePoEA-2
Terrible Robber Men, The. Padraic Colum. LOW
Terrible wrath I say, The. Achilles and the King. John
  Logan. AmPC
Terrifying are the attent sleek thrushes on the lawn. Thrushes.
  Ted Hughes. NePoEA-2; PoIE
Terror of Death, The. Keats. *See* When I Have Fears.
Test, The. Emerson. PP
Testament. John Holmes. MoRP
Testament. Attwood Robson. HaSV
Testament. Sister M. Thérèse. MoRP
Testament of Cresseid, The. Robert Henryson. CABL
Cresseid's Complaint against Fortune, *sel.* MeEL
Testimony. Beverly Connelly. FiSC
Tetélestai. Conrad Aiken. PoDB
Tethys' Festival, *sel.* Samuel Daniel.
  Are They Shadows That We See? PoIE
Texas Rangers, The, *with music. Unknown.* BFSS
Texas Trains and Trails. Mary Austin. SoPo
Thalamos. Peter Kane Dufault. ErPo

Thames nocturne of blue and gold, The. Impression du Matin.
  Oscar Wilde. CABA
Thammuz. William Vaughn Moody. AP
Thanatopsis. Bryant. AmLP; AP; DiPo; FaPL; LV
  "So live, that when thy summons comes to join," *sel.* TRV
Thank God for sleep! The Sacrament of Sleep. John Oxen-
  ham. PoLF
Thank God my brain is not inclined to cut. The Menagerie.
  William Vaughn Moody. AP
Thank God! there is always a Land of Beyond. Robert W.
  Service. *Fr.* Rhymes of a Rolling Stone. TRV
Thank God who seasons thus the year. The Fall of the Leaf.
  Henry David Thoreau. AP
Thank Goodness, the moving is over. "When the World Was
  in Building . . ." Ford Madox Ford. CTC
Thank Heaven! the crisis. For Annie. Poe. AP
Thank Thee, Lord. Georgia B. Adams. STF
Thank Thee, O Giver of Life, O God! Thanksgiving. Angela
  Morgan. TRV
Thank-You, A. William Canton. ThGo
Thank you for the world so sweet. E. Rutter Leatham. ThGo
Thankful Heart. F. W. Davis. STF
Thanks and a Plea to Mary. *Unknown.* MeEL
Thanks for the little and the simpler things. Thanksgiving
  Eve. Grantland Rice. LV
Thanks, I will. Phono, at the Boar's Head. Henri Coulette.
  Fr. The War of the Secret Agents. NePoEA-2
Thanks Just the Same. *Unknown.* PoLF
Thanks That Flesh Is Sad, A. John Ciardi. ToPo
Thanks to God. J. A. Hultman. STF
Thanks to the moon. A Night Picture of Pownal. Barbara
  Howes. OPP
Thanksgiving. Emerson. SoPo
Thanksgiving, The. George Herbert. MeP
Thanksgiving. Arthur Ketchum. STF
Thanksgiving. Angela Morgan. TRV
Thanksgiving. Robert Nichols. MMA
Thanksgiving. Margaret E. Sangster. TRV
Thanksgiving. A. B. Simpson. STF
Thanksgiving, A. Jane Taylor. ThGo
Thanksgiving Eve. Grantland Rice. LV
Thanksgiving 1963. Philip Booth. OPP
Thanksgiving Time. *Unknown.* SoPo
Thanksgiving to God for His House, A. Robert Herrick.
  BoC; SeCP
Thanksgiving Wishes. Arthur Guiterman. PoSC
Thar's More in the Man than Thar Is in the Land. Sidney
  Lanier. AP
That aged woman with the bass voice. The Great-Grandmother.
  Robert Graves. DTC
That All Things Are as They Are Used. George Turberville.
  EnRePo
That Beauty I Ador'd Before. Aphra Behn. UnTE
That boat has killed three people. Unlucky Boat. George
  Mackay Brown. NePoEA-2
That Bright Chimeric Beast. Countee Cullen. AmNP
That bull-necked blotch-faced farmer from Drumlore. Ghosts'
  Stories. Alastair Reid. NePoEA-2
That by which we have lost and still shall lose. Lost and
  Found. Edwin Muir. PoDB
That childish thoughts such joys inspire. Thomas Traherne.
  Fr. The Third Century. MeP
That civilization may not sink. Long-legged Fly. W. B.
  Yeats. AnMoPo; CaFP; PoIE
That corner of earth. Aware Aware. Tram Combs. MP
That Dark Other Mountain. Robert Francis. SD
That day everything went wrong. Poetry Defined. John
  Holmes. PP
That day I oft remember, when from sleep. Eve's Speech to
  Adam. Milton. *Fr.* Paradise Lost, IV. DiPo
That day the sunlight lay on the farms. On Heaven. Ford
  Madox Ford. CTC
That Dying. Alastair Reid. OPP
That each, who seems a separate whole. In Memoriam A. H.
  H., XLVII. Tennyson. VP
That evening all in fond discourse was spent. The Sad Lover.
  George Crabbe. *Fr.* Tales of the Hall: Delay Has Danger.
  OBNC
That Ever I Saw. *Unknown.* CBEP
That Familiar Stranger. Felix Stefanile. FiSC
That first Christmas night of all. First Christmas Night of
  All. Nancy Byrd Turner. BiCB
That girl from the sun is bathing in the creek. The Dosser in
  Springtime. Douglas Stewart. ErPo
That holy night when stars shone bright. A Child Is Born.
  Unknown. STF
That Holy Thing. George Macdonald. TRV
That horse whose rider fears to jump will fall. Masters.
  Kingsley Amis. PoPl
That I did always love. Emily Dickinson. FaPL
"That I might have unto my paramour." Christopher Mar-
  lowe. *Fr.* Dr. Faustus. FaPL
That I should have a joyous life. A Gift of God. *Unknown.*
  STF

That Is Even So! *with music.* John A. Stone. SGR
That is no country for old men. Sailing to Byzantium. W. B. Yeats. CABA; CaFP; CBEP; DiPo; FoBA; GTBS-P; ILP; MoRP; OnP; PoDB; PoIE; PoPo; PP; StP
That is rain on dry ground. We heard it. Rain. Christopher Fry. *Fr.* The Boy with a Cart. BoC
That It That Thing Light. Robert Sward. *Fr.* Five Poems for J. F. K. OPP
"That just reminds me of a yarn," he said. The Jester in the Trench. Leon Gellert. PoAu-1
That (like the man sd) Booth. Charles Olson. *Fr.* Anecdotes of the Late War. LiPo
That lover of a night. Crazy Jane on God. W. B. Yeats. FoBA; PoDB
That Nature Is a Heraclitean Fire and of the Comfort of the Resurrection. Gerard Manley Hopkins. CABA; DiPo; GTBS-P
That night your great guns unawares. Channel Firing. Thomas Hardy. CABA; ILP; PoIE; StP; VP
That nightingale, whose strain so sweetly flows. The Nightingale. Petrarch. Sonnets to Laura: To Laura in Death, XLIII. PoPl
That No Man Should Write but Such as Do Excel. George Turberville. EnRePo
That nose is out of drawing. With a gasp. Sonnet for a Picture. Swinburne. VP
That old man at the farm near Norman's Lane. The Farm near Norman's Lane. Mary Finnin. PoAu-2
That on her lap she casts her humble eye. On the Blessed Virgin's Bashfulness. Richard Crashaw. ILP
That selfsame tongue which first did thee entreat. The Constancy of a Lover. George Gascoigne. EnRePo
That she hath gone to Heaven suddenly. Dante. *Fr.* La Vita Nuova, III. CTC
That son of Cain, let him have no more power. A Wish. Vidal de Nicolas. BoC
That son of Italy who tried to blow. Austerity of Poetry. Matthew Arnold. VP
That story which the bold Sir Bedivere. The Passing of Arthur. Tennyson. *Fr.* Idylls of the King. OBNC
That Summer's Shore. John Ciardi. ErPo
That the glass would melt in heat. The Glass of Water. Wallace Stevens. AP; CABA
That the high sheen of death could blot. Midsummer. James Scully. MP
That thou hast her, it is not all my grief. Sonnets, XLII. Shakespeare. CBEP
That time of year thou mayst in me behold. Sonnets, LXXIII. Shakespeare. CABA; CaFP; CBEP; CTC; DiPo; EnRePo; FaBV; FoBA; GTBS-P; ILP; PoIE; PoPo; PoSa; StP; VaPo
That Tree with Its Leaves Atremble. Diego Hurtado de Mendoza, *tr. fr. Spanish by* Kate Flores. AnML
That trumpet tongue which taught a nation. The Demagogue. Phyllis McGinley. *Fr.* Epitaphs for Three Prominent Persons. LV
That was a shocking day. Beasts. Paul Engle. PoCh
That was her beginning, an apparition. First Love. Laurie Lee. ToPo
That was our country, the Four Winds know it. On the Little Bighorn. Ray Smith. PtTo
That was the chirp of Ariel. Wind on the Lyre. George Meredith. CaFP
That was the day they killed the Son of God. The Killing. Edwin Muir. ACV; MoRP; PoPl
That was the souls' weird mine. Orpheus. Eurydice. Hermes. Rainer Maria Rilke. TwGP
That was the year. A Poem to Delight My Friends Who Laugh at Science-Fiction. Edwin Rolfe. ThLM
That week the fall was opulent. Vendanges. 1956. Daniel G. Hoffman. PoCh
That which her slender waist confined. On a Girdle. Edmund Waller. CABA; GTBS-P; PoIE; StP; UnTE
That which is highest and greatest you seek? The plant can instruct you. The Highest. Schiller. TwGP
That which we dare invoke to bless. In Memoriam A. H. H., CXXIV. Tennyson. VP
That Whitsun, I was late getting away. The Whitsun Weddings. Philip Larkin. NePoEA-2
That winter love spoke and we raised no objection. Jig. C. Day Lewis. WePo
That wolf, shivering by the palisade. Colonial Set. Alfred Goldsworthy Bailey. OBCV
That Women Are but Men's Shadows. Ben Jonson. *See* Song: That Women Are but Men's Shadows.
That's All She Wrote. H. A. Sieber. PoNC
That's Faith. S. N. Leitner. STF
That's his saddle across the tie-beam, an' them's his spurs up there. My Mate Bill. G. H. Gibson. PoAu-1
That's my last Duchess painted on the wall. My Last Duchess. Robert Browning. CABA; CaFP; CBEP; DiPo; GTBS-P; ILP; OBNC; OnP; PoIE; PoLF; PoPo; PoSa; StP; VaPo; VP
That's the Way to Talk It. Mart Taylor. SGR

Thaw. Edward Thomas. GTBS-P
The/ Voice of Jesus I. Poem Beginning "The." Louis Zukofsky. CoPo
Theatre, The. James Smith. Par
Theatre of hilltops, drunken, lime-sown. Apennine. Pier Paolo Pasolini. CoIP
Thee for my recitative. To a Locomotive in Winter. Walt Whitman. AmLP; AP; DiPo; FaBV; ILP; StP
Thee, Thee, Only Thee. Thomas Moore. OBNC
Their belongings were buried side by side. The Drawer. George MacBeth. NePoEA-2
Their cheeks are blotched for shame, their running verse. The Bards. Robert Graves. DTC
Their faces, safe as an interior. The Middle-aged. Adrienne Rich. NePoEA-2
Their house faces east, is protected by trees. A Storm from the East. Reed Whittemore. PoPl
Their Lonely Betters. W. H. Auden. GoJo; LOW
Their noonday never knows. Fame. John Banister Tabb. AmLP
Their sense is with their senses all mixed in. Modern Love, XLVIII. George Meredith. VP
Their time past, pulled down. Burning the Christmas Greens. William Carlos Williams. AP; CABL
Thel's Motto. Blake. *Fr.* The Book of Thel. DiPo
Theme. Carl Spitteler, *tr. fr. German by* Margaret Münsterberg. PoPl
Theme. James Stephens. ACV
Theme in Yellow. Carl Sandburg. RePo
Theme tune occurs again, The. Das Liebesleben. Thom Gunn. ErPo
Themes of love and death I have rehearsed, The. Judges, Judges. Gene Baro. NePoEA-2
Then. Dorothy Aldis. BiCB
Then, bedded upon pillows of dark blood. Negro Bride. Gottfried Benn. *Fr.* Morgue. TwGP
Then comes the Winter, like a hale old man. Winter. James Hurnard. PoSC
Then girls will be coming. Afterward. Erich Fried. MGP
Then he lived among wild lands. Stages. Roy Macnab. ACV
. . . then he saddled his steed. Bessie of Ballington Brae. *Unknown.* BSNS
Then Hurrah for Home! *with music.* John A. Stone. SGR
Then it was dusk in Illinois, the small boy. First Song. Galway Kinnell. GoJo; MP
Then like two mighty kings which, dwelling far. John Donne. *Fr.* The Storm. HaSV
Then Lose in Time Thy Maidenhead. *Unknown.* ErPo
Then next a merry woodsman, clad in green. The Green Dryad's Plea. Thomas Hood. *Fr.* The Plea of the Midsummer Fairies. OBNC
Then pallid death at last will with his icy hand. Beauty's Transitoriness. Christian Hoffmann von Hoffmannswaldau. AGP
Then roll the swag and blanket up. The Golden Gullies of the Palmer. *Unknown.* PoAu-1
Then said Almitra, Speak to us of Love. Of Love. Kahlil Gibran. *Fr.* The Prophet. PoLF
Then saith the timid Fay—"Oh, mighty Time!" The Fairy's Reply to Saturn. Thomas Hood. *Fr.* The Plea of the Midsummer Fairies. OBNC
Then Saturn thus:—"Sweet is the merry lark." The Melodies of Time. Thomas Hood. *Fr.* The Plea of the Midsummer Fairies. OBNC
Then strip, lads, and to it, though sharp be the weather. Football Song. Sir Walter Scott. SD
Then, the quick plunge into the cool, green dark. Louis Untermeyer. *Fr.* Swimmers. SD
Then there is this civilising love of death, by which. Ignorance of Death. William Empson. ToPo
Then those ill-favour'd Ones, whom none. George Crabbe. *Fr.* Sir Eustace Grey. ELP
Then what is the answer?—Not to be deluded by dreams. The Answer. Robinson Jeffers. MoRP
Then, when the child was gone. Empty House. Stephen Spender. WePo
Theocritus; a Villanelle. Oscar Wilde. StP
Theologians. Walter de la Mare. EaLo
Theology. Paul Laurence Dunbar. TRV
Théorèmes Spirituels, sels. Jean de la Ceppède, *tr. fr. French by* Clinton Larson. RBL
   "Great Sun, flame of Christ."
   "Love has given Him from paradise."
   "My victorious King receives his vestments from mocking."
   "O Cross, the old horror and fear of you are gone."
   "O Kingdom of Christ, you and He are one."
   "O Phoenix, cherished bird of Arabia."
Theory of Poetry. Archibald MacLeish. AP
There a wind endures that I recall. Street of Agrigentum. Salvatore Quasimodo. CoIP
There are brightest apples on those trees. The Fertile Muck. Irving Layton. OBCV
There are certain things—as, a spider, a ghost. A Sea Dirge. "Lewis Carroll." HaSV

There are fairies at the bottom of our garden. Fairies. Rose Fyleman. SoPo
There are four vibrators, the world's exactest clocks. Four Quartz Crystal Clocks. Marianne Moore. MP
There are hermit souls that live withdrawn. The House by the Side of the Road. Sam Walter Foss. LV; TRV
There are little eyes upon you, and they're watching night and day. To Any Daddy. *Unknown.* STF
There are lonely hearts to cherish. While the Days Are Going By. *Unknown.* STF
There are lots of queer things that discoverers do. Christopher Columbus. Stephen Vincent Benét. RePo
There are many desert places. Missions. *Unknown.* STF
There are many more Good Fridays. Unkept Good Fridays. Thomas Hardy. MoRP
There are many who go to the Vineyard. The Vineyard. *Unknown.* STF
There are men in the village of Erith. Erith. *Unknown.* CBEP
There are moments a man turns from us. Drowning with Others. James Dickey. CoPo
There Are No Gods. Euripides, *tr. fr. Greek by* John Addington Symonds. *Fr.* Bellerophon. EaLo
There are no red leaves in yellow Oxford. Views of the Oxford Colleges. Paris Leary. CoPo
There are no upper hands in love. After You, Madam. Alex Comfort. ErPo; UnTE
There are only two things now. New Year's Eve. D. H. Lawrence. ErPo
There Are Places. Myra Von Riedemann. OBCV
There are portraits and still-lifes [*or* still-lives]. Paring the Apple. Charles Tomlinson. NePoEA-2; PoIE
There are questions that must be asked. Incidents in Playfair House. Nicholas Moore. ErPo
There are seven hills. The Windy Bishop. Wilfred Watson. OBCV
There Are So Many Ways of Going Places. Leslie Thompson. SoPo
There are some critics say our verse is bad. Your Teeth Are Ivory Towers. William Empson. ToPo
There are some days the happy ocean lies. Seascape. Stephen Spender. AnMoPo
There are some heights in Wessex, shaped as if by a kindly hand. Wessex Heights. Thomas Hardy. OBNC
There are some qualities—some incorporate things. Sonnet: Silence. Poe. AP
There are some who believe the Bible. Believe the Bible. A. B. Simpson. STF
There are some who must. Eugène Guillevic. *Fr.* Elegies. CoFP
There are strange things done in the midnight sun. The Cremation of Sam McGee. Robert W. Service. PoLF; SIV
There are the fair-limbed nymphs o' the woods. Leigh Hunt. *Fr.* The Nymphs. OBNC
There are three green eggs in a small brown pocket. At Little Virgil's Window. Edwin Markham. TRV
There are three valleys where the warm sun lingers. The Long Harbour. Mary Ursula Bethell. ACV
There are too many poems with the word. Testament. John Holmes. MoRP
There are tracks which belong to wheels. In the Lupanar at Pompeii. James Dickey. ToPo
There are twelve months in all the year. Robin Hood and the Widow's Three Sons. *Unknown.* BuBa; OnMSP
There are two different kinds, I believe, of human attraction. Arthur Hugh Clough. *Fr.* Amours de Voyage. GTBS-P
There are two women; one I love, and one. Twins. "Owen Meredith." ErPo
There are veins in the hills where jewels hide. The Best Treasure. John J. Moment. TRV
There are white moon daisies in the mist of the meadow. Summer Song. E. Nesbit. PoSC
There Be None of Beauty's Daughters. Byron. ELP; GTBS-P
(For Music.) CBEP
(Stanzas for Music.) DTC; ILP
There be three things seeking my death. Prayer for the Speedy End of Three Great Misfortunes. *Tr. by* Frank O'Connor. DTC
There breaks on me, burning upon me. Song to Steingerd. Cormac Ogmundarson. SiGo
There by the window in the old house. William H. Herndon. Edgar Lee Masters. *Fr.* Spoon River Anthology. LiPo
There calleth me ever a marvelous horn. Home-Sickness. Justinus Kerner. SiGo
There came a bird out of a bush. Lady Isabel and the Elf-Knight. *Unknown.* SIV
There came a day at summer's full. Emily Dickinson. AP; FaPL
There came a ghost to Margret's door. Sweet William's Ghost. *Unknown.* BuBa
There came a knight from out the west. Clootie. *Unknown.* BuBa

There came a knocking at the front door. A Person from Porlock. R. S. Thomas. BoC
There came a wind like a bugle. Emily Dickinson. ILP; PoIE
There came an image in Life's retinue. Death-in-Love. Dante Gabriel Rossetti. The House of Life, XLVIII. VP
There came from rocky dwelling. The Bold Knight and the Gruesome Dragon. Wilhelm Busch. AGP
There came three gypsies to my door. The Gypsy Laddie (A *vers.*). *Unknown.* BSO
There came three men from out the West. Sir John Barleycorn. *Unknown.* CBEP
There Comes a Ship All Laden. Johannes Tauler, *tr. fr. German by* Mabel Cotterell. AnML
There comes an end to summer. To His Mistress. Ernest Dowson. BoLP
"There comes Emerson first, whose rich words, every one." Emerson. James Russell Lowell. *Fr.* A Fable for Critics. AP; PP
"There comes Poe, with his raven, like Barnaby Rudge." Poe and Longfellow. James Russell Lowell. *Fr.* A Fable for Critics. AP
There died a myriad. Ezra Pound. *Fr.* Hugh Selwyn Mauberley. PoIE
There dwelt a man in faire Westmerland [*or* fair Westmoreland]. Johnie [*or* Johnnie] Armstrong. *Unknown.* PoPo; SIV; VaPo
There fared a mother driven forth. The House of Christmas. G. K. Chesterton. MoRP
There had been years of Passion—scorching, cold. "And There Was a Great Calm." Thomas Hardy. MoRP
There has a question been of late. Up-Tails All. *Unknown.* UnTE
"There he is, woman!" The Seduction of Engadu. *Unknown. Fr.* Gilgamesh. ErPo
There he moved, cropping the grass at the purple canyon's lip. The Horse Thief. William Rose Benét. OnMSP
There he stands. see? Two Jazz Poems. Carl Wendell Hines, Jr. AmNP
There I go, with an inscrutable face. The Killer. Richard Eberhart. OPP
There in a Woodland, to My Thought More Bright. Guido Cavalcanti, *tr. fr. Italian by* G. S. Fraser. AnML
There in the bracken was the ominous spoor mark. The Tantanoola Tiger. Max Harris. MoBS; PoAu-2
There, in the earliest and chary spring, the dogwood flowers. Sunday: Outskirts of Knoxville, Tennessee. James Agee. ErPo
There is/ a heart. Finally a Valentine. Louis Zukofsky. OPP
There is a bright garden between low walls. Summer. Cesare Pavese. CoIP
There is a change—and I am poor. A Complaint. Wordsworth. CBEP
There is a delight in singing, tho' none hear. To Robert Browning. Walter Savage Landor. ILP
There is a desert island of the heart. "What Five Books Would You Pick to Be Marooned with on a Desert Island?" Paris Leary. CoPo
There is a destiny that makes us brothers. A Creed. Edwin Markham. PoPl
There is a fever of the spirit. Song by Mr. Cypress. Thomas Love Peacock. *Fr.* Nightmare Abbey. OBNC; Par
There is a flower, the lesser Celandine. A Lesson [*or* The Small Celandine]. Wordsworth. FoBA; GTBS-P
There Is a Garden in Her Face. Thomas Campion. CABA; DiPo; EnRePo; GoJo; ILP; StP
(Cherry-ripe.) CBEP; GTBS-P; PoIE
There is a general idiom to all rime. Karl Shapiro. *Fr.* Essay on Rime. PP
There is a heaven, for ever, day by day. Theology. Paul Laurence Dunbar. TRV
There is a heigh-ho in these glowing coals. Heigh-ho on a Winter Afternoon. Donald Davie. NePoEA-2
There is a house in Patricia Ciociara. My Ciociara Night. Libero de Libero. CoIP
There Is a Lady [Sweet and Kind]. *Unknown.* BoLP; CBEP; ELP
There Is a Land. Isaac Watts. ELP
There Is a Love. Philip Jerome Cleveland. TRV
There Is a Man on the Cross. Elizabeth Cheney. TRV
There is a manner of growing old. On Growing Old. Srinavas Rayaprol. ACV
There is a moment in midsummer when the earth. Midsummer Pause. Fred Lape. PoSC
There is a myth, a tale men tell. The Pearl. Hans Christian Andersen. SiGo
There is a niche provided. For Every Man. Max I. Reich. STF
There is a part of me. No Man an Island. Lucy Smith. PtTo
There Is a Place. Alma Hoellein. STF
There is a place that some men know. The Cross. Allen Tate. AP; PoDB

There is a place where love begins and a place where love ends. Explanations of Love. Carl Sandburg. MoLP
There is a place where thou canst touch the eyes. The Secret Place. A. A. Pollard. STF
There is a pleasure in poetic pains. William Cowper. *Fr.* The Task. PP
There is a pleasure in the pathless woods. The Ocean. Byron. Childe Harold's Pilgrimage, *fr.* IV. FaBV; HaSV; PoIE
There is a quiet spirit in these woods. The Spirit of Poetry. Longfellow. PP
There is a river clear and fair. Fragment. Catherine Fanshawe. Par
There is a secret laughter. Secret Laughter. Christopher Morley. FaBV
There is a secret that the sober mood. Unison. John Hall Wheelock. MoRP
There is a silence where hath been no sound. Silence [*or* Sonnet: Silence]. Thomas Hood. CBEP; ILP; OBNC
There is a singer everyone has heard. The Oven Bird. Robert Frost. AP; FoBA; VaPo
There is a solitude in seeing you. Lightning. Witter Bynner. MoLP
There is a solitude of space. Emily Dickinson. AP
There is a thing which in the light. A Candle. Sir John Suckling. ErPo
There Is a Tide. Shakespeare. *Fr.* Julius Caesar, IV, ii. PoPl
("There is a tide in the affairs of men.") TRV
There is a time for all things, sweet! Carpe Diem. Pierre de Ronsard. RBL
There is a time, we know not when. The Doomed Man. Joseph Addison Alexander. TRV
There is a treasure. God's Treasure. "A. M. N." STF
There is a tree native in Turkestan. Note on Local Flora. William Empson. ToPo
There is a white mare that my love keeps. Love Poem. Alex Comfort. ErPo
There is a wolf in me . . . fangs pointed for tearing gashes. Wilderness. Carl Sandburg. AP
There is a world deep in the seas of night. Dark Yuggoth. Lin Carter. FiSC
There is a yew tree, pride of Lorton Vale. Yew Trees. Wordsworth. CABA; FoBA
There is an evening coming in. Going. Philip Larkin. ToPo
There is an eye that never sleeps. Prayer Moves the Hand That Moves the World. John A. Wallace. STF
"There is Bryant, as quiet, as cool, as dignified." Bryant. James Russell Lowell. *Fr.* A Fable for Critics. AP
There is great mystery, Simone. Hair. Remy de Gourmot. ErPo
"There is Hawthorne, with genius so shrinking and rare." Hawthorne. James Russell Lowell. *Fr.* A Fable for Critics. AP
"There is Lowell, who's striving Parnassus to climb." Lowell. James Russell Lowell. *Fr.* A Fable for Critics. AP
There is never a day so dreary. Consolation. *Unknown.* STF
There is no chapel on the day. Capital Punishment. Oscar Wilde. *Fr.* The Ballad of Reading Gaol. WePo
There is no Death. What seems so is transition. Longfellow. *Fr.* Resignation. TRV
There is no fitter end than this. In Memoriam, S.C.W., v.c. Charles Sorley. MMA
There is no frigate like a book. Emily Dickinson. GoJo; PoLF; PoPl
There Is No God. Arthur Hugh Clough. *Fr.* Dipsychus. FaPL
There is no great and no small. History. Emerson. AmLP
There is no land upon the earth. You Who Don't Believe It. John A. Stone. SGR
There is no longer a straight line. Eternity at Lourmarin. René Char. ToPo
There is no lover hee or shee. A Paradox. Aurelian Townsend. SeCP
There is no one among men that has not a special failing. Madly Singing in the Mountains. Po Chü-i. CBEP
There is no page or servant, most or least. The Seventh Property. Sir Thomas More. *Fr.* The Twelve Properties or Conditions of a Lover. EnRePo
"There is no place to turn," she said. The Sensualists [*or* The Sensualist]. Theodore Roethke. ErPo; UnTE
There is no point in work. The World of Work, as a Poet Would Like It to Be. D. H. Lawrence. BoC
There Is No Reason Why Not to Look at Death. Robert Sward. CoPo
There is no roof in all the world. Waiting for the Morning. *Unknown.* STF
There is no silence upon the earth or under the earth like the silence under the sea. Silences. E. J. Pratt. OBCV; PoCh
There is no sinning against God, what does God care about sin! God and the Holy Ghost. D. H. Lawrence. MoRP
There is no unbelief. Faith. Elizabeth York Case, *wr. at. to* Edward Bulwer-Lytton. TRV

There Is None like Her. Tennyson. *Fr.* Maud. OBNC
There Is Nothing False in Thee. Kenneth Patchen. PoP1
There is nothing more perky. The Turkey. Ogden Nash. RePo
There is nought for thee by thy haste to gain. The Created. Jones Very. PoIE
There is one story and one story only. To Juan at the Winter Solstice. Robert Graves. ILP; MP; PoIE; PoSa
There is Power in a Union. *Unknown, at. to* Joe Hill. ThLM
There is so much loveliness gone out of the world. The Triumph of Doubt. John Peale Bishop. EaLo
There is something about a Martini. A Drink with Something in It. Ogden Nash. PoP1
There is something in the autumn that is native to my blood. A Vagabond Song. Bliss Carman. LV; PoSC; RePo
There Is Sweet Music Here. Tennyson. *See* Choric Song: "There is sweet music here that softer falls."
There is the sign of/ the flower. The Rhyme. Robert Creeley. AmPC
There is the story of a deserted island. Emperors of the Island. Dannie Abse. DaDu
There is this infinite energy, the power of God forever working. Look, How Beautiful. Robinson Jeffers. MoRP
"There is Whittier, whose swelling and vehement heart." Whittier. James Russell Lowell. *Fr.* A Fable for Critics. AP
There is wisdom in the Bible. The Bible. Dorothy Conant Stroud. STF
There Isn't Time. Eleanor Farjeon. RePo
There it is, a block of leaping marble. Cousin Florence. Richard Eberhart. ToPo
There lies a cold corpse upon the sands. Death Song. Robert Stephen Hawker. OBNC
There lies a lone isle in the tropic seas. Easter Island. Frederick George Scott. OBCV
There lies a vale in Ida, lovelier. Oenone. Tennyson. VP
There! little girl, don't cry! A Life-Lesson. James Whitcomb Riley. PoLF
There lived a king into the east. King Orpheo. *Unknown.* BuBa
There lived a sage in days of yore. A Tragic Story. Adelbert von Chamisso, *tr. by* Thackeray. OnMSP; RePo
There lived a wife at Usher's Well. The Wife of Usher's Well. *Unknown.* BuBa; CBEP; DiPo; ILP; OnMSP; PoIE; StP
There lived a young squire in ten months a year. The Jolly Farmer. *Unknown.* BFSS
There lived a young squire in town worthy here. Dog and Gun (A *vers.*). *Unknown.* BSO
There lived a youth, and a well-beloved youth. The Bailiff's Daughter of Islington. *Unknown.* BFSS
There lived three brothers in fair Scotland. Henry Martyn. *Unknown.* BSNS
There may be agony in furnished rooms. The Room. Francis Webb. *Fr.* Leichhardt in Theatre. PoAu-2
There mounts in squalls a sort of rusty mire. The Exile's Return. Robert Lowell. AP
There must be magic. Otherwise. Aileen Fisher. LV; SoPo
There,—my blessing with you! Polonius' Advice to Laertes. Shakespeare. *Fr.* Hamlet, I, iii. PoP1
There once was a noble ranger. The Mustang Gray. *Unknown.* BFSS
There Once Was a Puffin. Florence Page Jaques. SoPo
There once was a witch of Willowby Wood. The Witch of Willowby Wood. Rowena Bennett. RePo
There once was a woman named Jacqueline Gray. Jacqueline Gray. Kenneth Pitchford. *Fr.* Good for Nothing Man. CoPo
There, pay it, James! 'tis cheaply earned. Vers de Société. H. D. Traill. Par
There rolls the deep where grew the tree. In Memoriam A. H. H., CXXIII. Tennyson. FoBA; VP
There sat an old man on a rock. Too Late. Fitz Hugh Ludlow. PoLF
There sat upon the linden tree. The Linden Tree. Dietmar von Aist. PoP1
There Shall Always Be the Church. T. S. Eliot. *Fr.* The Rock. TRV
There Shall Be No More Sea. Elizabeth Dowden. HaSV
There sprang a green brier out of Lord Thomas' mouth. Bonny Barbara Allen (F *vers.*). *Unknown.* BSO
There the black river, boundary to hell. The Southern Road. Dudley Randall. NNP
There the guard changes. November 22, 1963. Donald L. Jones. OPP
There, there is no mountain within miles. Nebraska. Jon Swan. PoPo
There 'tis the Shepherd's task the winter long. The Shepherd. Wordsworth. *Fr.* The Prelude. OBNC
There was a boy. Tom's Sleeping Song. Mark Van Doren. *Fr.* Jonathan Gentry. LOW
There was a blind beggar, he lost his sight. The Blind Beggar's Daughter of Bednall Green. *Unknown.* BSO
There Was a Boy. Wordsworth. *Fr.* The Prelude, V. FoBA; OBNC

There was a Boy bedded in bracken. Carol. John Short. DTC

There was a boy just one year old. Someone. John Ciardi. BiCB

There was a boy whose name was Jim. Jim, Who Ran Away from His Nurse, and Was Eaten by a Lion. Hilaire Belloc. BBGG; EvOK

There was a boy; ye knew him well, ye cliffs. There Was a Boy. Wordsworth. *Fr.* The Prelude. FoBA; OBNC

There was a bride; she lived abroad. The Three Little Babes. *Unknown.* BFSS

There was a brisk girl both bonny and brown. The Brisk Girl. *Unknown.* UnTE

There was a Child Went Forth. Walt Whitman. BiCB; FoBA; StP

There was a Crooked Man. Mother Goose. CBEP (Crooked Sixpence, The.) SoPo

There was a cruel naughty boy. The Cruel Naughty Boy. *Unknown.* BBGG

There was a devil and his name was I. Malzah's Song. Charles Heavysege. *Fr.* Saul. OBCV

There was a fair maiden who dwelt on the plains. The Fair Lady of the Plains. *Unknown.* BFSS

There was a fair young creature who lived by the seaside. Mary on the Silvery Tide. *Unknown.* BSNS

There was a fair young maiden who lived by the sunny seaside. Out on the Silvery Tide. *Unknown.* BSO

There was a flash frigate, from New York she came. Paul Jones (B *vers.*). *Unknown.* BSNS

There was a frog lived in a brook. The Frog Song. *Unknown.* BSO

There was a giant by the Orchard Wall. In the Orchard. James Stephens. LOW; RoGo

There was a giant in times of old. The Dorchester Giant. Oliver Wendell Holmes. OnMSP

There Was a Girl I Used to Go With. Stephen Vincent Benét. *Fr.* John Brown's Body. LOW

There was a glorious time. He Fears His Good Fortune. Thomas Hardy. VP

There was a great commotion. The Lollypops. Cordia Thomas. SoPo

There was a jovial blade. The Scolding Wife. *Unknown.* BSO

There Was a Knight. *Unknown.* UnTE

There was a Knight, a most distinguished man. Ten of Chaucer's People: A Perfect Knight. Chaucer. *Fr.* The Canterbury Tales. PoSa

There was a knight and a lady bride. A Knight and a Lady Bride. *Unknown.* BFSS

There was a knight and he was young. There Was a Knight. *Unknown.* UnTE

There was a lady came from York. The Greenwood Siding. *Unknown.* BSNS

There was a lady in our town. The Wife of Usher's Well. *Unknown.* BSO

There was a lady lived in a hall. Two Red Roses across the Moon. William Morris. CBEP; PoIE

There Was a Lady Loved a Swine. *Unknown.* StP

There was a land where lived no violets. War Is Kind, XXIII. Stephen Crane. AP

There was a lass and a bonnie lass. The Nut-gathering Lass. Burns. UnTE

There was a little family that lived in Bethany. The Little Family. *Unknown.* BFSS; BSO

There Was a Little Girl. *St.* 1, Mother Goose; *sts.* 2 *and* 3, *unknown, at. to* Longfellow. EvOK (Jemima.) BBGG

There was a little old woman, as I've heard tell. The Old Woman Who Went to Market. *Unknown.* BFSS

There was a little old woman, in London she did dwell. She Loved Her Husband Dearly. *Unknown.* BFSS

There was a little postage stamp. The Postage Stamp Lesson. *Unknown.* STF

There Was a Little Ship, *with music. Unknown.* BFSS

There was a little turtle. The Little Turtle. Vachel Lindsay. GoJo; SoPo

There was a lord in Ambertown,/ He courted a lady gay. Lady Isabel and the Elf-Knight (A *and* B *vers.*). *Unknown.* BSNS

There was a lord in Ambertown/ Courted a lady fair. Pretty Polly. *Unknown.* BSO

There was a maid, and a well-favoured maid. Katherine Johnstone. *Unknown.* BuBa

There was a maid of Edinburgh. Kath'rine Jaffrey. *Unknown.* BFSS

There Was a Man and He was Mad, *with music. Unknown.* BSO

There was a man, now please take note. The Goat. *Unknown.* PoLF

There was a man of Thessaly. A Man of Thessaly. *Unknown.* CBEP

There was a man suspended from a nose. To a Nose. Francisco de Quevedo y Villegas, *tr. by* James Edward Tobin. AnSP

There was a man well fastened to a nose. To a Nose. Francisco de Quevedo y Villegas, *tr. by* Jean Willard Burnham. RBL

There was a man whom Sorrow named his friend. The Sad Shepherd. W. B. Yeats. HaSV; PP

There Was a Mighty King. *Unknown. See* Three Rogues, The.

There was a Monk, a leader of the fashions. Ten of Chaucer's People: A Sporting Monk. Chaucer. *Fr.* The Canterbury Tales. PoSa

There was a naughty boy. A Song about Myself. Keats. DiPo; PP

There was a perfect tree. 229. José Garcia Villa. PoP1

There was a pig that sat alone. A Pig-Tale. "Lewis Carroll." *Fr.* Sylvie and Bruno Concluded. WiR

There was a pond on which we learned to skate. A Skater's Waltz. Gray Burr. CoPo

There was a pretty young lady, so handsome, brave, and bold. Pretty Mary. *Unknown.* BFSS

There was a rich lady, from Dublin she came. The Rich Lady from Dublin. *Unknown.* BFSS

There was a rich old farmer. The Rambling Cowboy. *Unknown.* BFSS

There was a road ran past our house. The Unexplorer. Edna St. Vincent Millay. LOW; RePo

There was a roaring in the wind all night. Resolution and Independence. Wordsworth. CABA; CBEP; DiPo; OBNC

There was a Romish lady, brought up in poverty [*or* Popery]. The Romish Lady. *Unknown.* BFSS; BSO

There was a score o likely girls. Cerelle. Margaret Bell Houston. SIV

There was a sea captain that followed the sea. The Sea Captain (B *vers.*). *Unknown.* BSNS

There was a ship and a ship of fame. Captain Glen. *Unknown.* BSNS

There was a ship came [*or* sailed] from the north country [*or* countree]. The Golden Vanity. *Unknown.* CBEP; WiR

There was a sound of revelry by night. The Eve of Waterloo. Byron. *Fr.* Childe Harold's Pilgrimage. FaBV; OBNC

There Was a Time. Edward Thomas. MMA

There was a time before our time. Clipper Ships and Captains. Stephen Vincent Benét. RePo

There was a time on this fair continent. Charles Mair. *Fr.* Tecumseh. OBCV

There was a time when meadow, grove, and stream. Ode: Intimations of Immortality from Recollections of Early Childhood. Wordsworth. BoC; CABA; CaFP; DiPo; FoBA; GTBS-P; ILP; OBNC; PoIE; StP; VaPo

There was a time when this poor frame was whole. There Was a Time. Edward Thomas. MMA

There was a trampling of horses from Calvary. It Is Finished. John Hall Wheelock. MoRP

There was a wealthy merchant. The Banks of Sweet Dundee. *Unknown.* BSO

There was a wealthy merchant. Jack, the Sailor [*or* Jackie Frazier]. *Unknown.* BFSS; BSO

There was a winter. Alba after Six Years. Christopher Middleton. NePoEA-2

There Was a Wyly Ladde. *Unknown.* ErPo

There was a young girl of Asturias. Limerick. *Unknown.* BBGG

There was a young lady from Del. Limerick. *Unknown.* LV

There was a young lady named Bright. Limerick. *Unknown.* LV

There was a young lady of Firle. Limerick. Edward Lear. RePo

There Was a Young Lady of Niger. *Unknown, at. to* Cosmo Monkhouse. SoPo (Limerick.) LV

There was a young lady of Oakham. Limerick. *Unknown.* BBGG

There Was a Young Lady Whose Chin. Edward Lear. SoPo (Limerick.) RePo

There was a young lady whose eyes. Limerick. Edward Lear. GoJo

There was a young lady whose nose. Limerick. Edward Lear. RePo

There was a young man. Victory. Mary Britton Miller. RePo

There was a young man came from the north lands. The Ocean Wave. *Unknown.* BSO

There was a young man from Japan. Limerick. *Unknown.* LV

There was a young man from Port Jervis. At the Tennis Clinic. I. L. Martin. SD

There was a young man from Trinity. A Limerick. *Unknown.* LV

There was a youth, and a well-beloved youth. The Bailiff's Daughter of Islington. *Unknown.* PoPo; RePo

There was an aged monarch. Heine, *tr. fr.* German by Karl Weimar. AGP

There was an ancient craftsman once, who made. The Leaf-Makers. Harold Stewart. PoAu-2

There was an enchanting young bride. Limerick. *Unknown.* LV

There was an Indian, who had known no change. The Discovery. J. C. Squire. PoSC

There was an old lady. Godmother. Phyllis B. Morden. SoPo

There was an old lady of Chertsey. Limerick. Edward Lear. RePo

There was an old man came over the sea. With His Old Gray Beard a-Hanging. *Unknown.* BSO

There was an old man in a boat. The Floating Old Man. Edward Lear. WiR

There Was an Old Man in a Tree. Edward Lear. SoPo (Limerick.) RePo

There was an old man of Antigua. Limerick. *Unknown.* LV

There was an old man of Corfu. Limerick. Edward Lear. RePo

There was an old man of Hong Kong. Limerick. Edward Lear. RePo

There was an old man of Ibreem. Limerick. Edward Lear. RePo

There was an old man of the Dee. Limerick. Edward Lear. RePo

There was an old man of The Hague. Limerick. Edward Lear. EvOK

There was an old man of Thermopylae. Limerick. Edward Lear. EvOK

There Was an Old Man, on Whose Nose. Edward Lear. SoPo

There was an old man who lived in the woods. Old Grumble. *Unknown.* BSO

There was an old man who said: "How." Limerick. Edward Lear. EvOK

There was an old man who said, "Hush!" Limerick. Edward Lear. GoJo

There was an old man who was very well known. The Miller That Made His Will. *Unknown.* BFSS

There was an old man, who when little. Limerick. Edward Lear. RePo

There Was an Old Man with a Beard. Edward Lear. SoPo (Limerick.) RePo

There was an old man with a gong. Limerick. Edward Lear. GoJo

There was an old miller in Mansfield town. The Dishonest Miller (B *vers.*). *Unknown.* BSO

There was an old miser named Clarence. Fragonard. Ogden Nash. RePo

There was an old person of Diss. Limerick. Edward Lear. GoJo

There was an old person of Fratton. A Limerick. *Unknown.* LV

There was an old person of Hurst. Limerick. Edward Lear. RePo

There was an old person of Ickley. Limerick. Edward Lear. EvOK

There was an old person of Minety. Limerick. Edward Lear. RePo

There was an old person of Stroud. Limerick. Edward Lear. RePo

There Was an Old Person of Ware. Edward Lear. PoPl (Limerick.) RePo

There was an old skinflint of Hitching. Buttons. Walter de la Mare. DTC

There was an old woman/ Lived down in a dell. Was She a Witch? Laura E. Richards. SoPo

There was an old woman all skin and bones. The Skin-and-Bone Lady. *Unknown.* BSO

There Was an Old Woman and She Had a Little Pig, *with music.* *Unknown.* BSO (Old Woman Who Bought a Pig, The, *with music.*) BFSS

There was an old woman, as I've heard tell. A Strange Story [*or* There Was an Old Woman]. *Unknown.* OnMSP; PoSC

There was an old woman lived on the seashore. The Two Sisters. *Unknown.* BFSS

There was an old woman of Slapsadam. The Old Woman of Slapsadam. *Unknown.* BSO

There was an old woman tossed up in a basket. Sweeping the Sky [*or* There Was an Old Woman]. *Unknown.* EvOK; SoPo

There was an old woman who bought a pig, uh-uh-huh! The Old Woman Who Bought a Pig. *Unknown.* BFSS

There was an old woman who lived all alone. There Was an Old Woman. *Unknown.* BFSS

There was, before me. The Black Riders, XXI. Stephen Crane. AP

There was crimson clash of war. The Black Riders, XIV. Stephen Crane. AP

There was movement at the station, for the word had passed around. The Man from Snowy River. A. B. Paterson. PoAu-1; WePo

There was music in the air. Music in the Air. Ronald McCuaig. ErPo

There was never a leaf on bush or tree. James Russell Lowell. *Fr.* The Vision of Sir Launfal. SIV

There was never a sound beside the wood but one. Mowing. Robert Frost. DiPo

There Was Never Nothing More Me Pained. Sir Thomas Wyatt. CBEP

There was no ceremony. Lion. Mary Fullerton. PoAu-1

There was no hunted one. The Baying Hounds. Mary Gilmore. PoAu-1

There was no leaf upon its wood. The Singing Bush. William Soutar. ACV

There was once a little animal. Similar Cases. Charlotte Perkins Stetson Gilman. PoLF

There was once a man who smiled. The Ridiculous Optimist. *Unknown.* STF

There was once a young lady of Ryde. Limerick. *Unknown.* EvOK

There Was One I Met upon the Road. Stephen Crane. EaLo

There was rain without, and lightning stalked into the room. Song of the Midnight Rain. John Gould Fletcher. MoLP

There was such speed in her little body. Bells for John Whiteside's Daughter. John Crowe Ransom. AmLP; AP; CaFP; DTC; ILP; PoIE; PoPo; StP; VaPo

There was the sonne of Ampycus of great forecasting wit. Meleager. Ovid. *Fr.* Metamorphoses. CTC

There was the star of course. Christmas Comes. Earle Birney. ACV

There was this road. The Legs. Robert Graves. PoSa

There was three jolly Frenchmen. Three Jolly Frenchmen. *Unknown.* BSO

There was three travelers, travelers three. The Three Travelers. *Unknown.* UnTE

There was tumult in the city. Independence Bell. *Unknown.* SIV

There was two sisters in a bow'r. The Twa Sisters. *Unknown.* CBEP

There went out in the dawning light. A Pastoral. *Unknown.* UnTE

There were four of us about that bed. Shameful Death. William Morris. GTBS-P; SIV

There were four red apples on the bough. August. Swinburne. WiR

There were hours when life was bitter. Now and Then. Margaret E. Sangster. TRV

There were ladies, they lived in a bower. Mary Hamilton. *Unknown.* CBEP

There were saddened hearts in Mudville for a week or even more. Casey's Revenge. James Wilson. OnMSP

There were three brothers from merry Scotland. Andrew Batan. *Unknown.* BSO

There were three brothers in old Scotland. Andrew Bardeen. *Unknown.* BFSS

There were three gipsies a-come to my door. The Wraggle Taggle Gipsies, O! *Unknown.* EvOK; WiR

There were three jolly hunters, a-hunting all alone. Three Jovial Huntsmen; or, The Owl and the Jay Bush. *Unknown.* BFSS

There were three jovial Welshmen. The Three Huntsmen. *Unknown.* OnMSP

There were three kings cam frae the East. The Kings from the East. Heine, *tr. into Scottish by* Alexander Gray. ACV

There were three ladies lived in a bower. Babylon. *Unknown.* SIV

There were three ravens sat on a tree. The Three Ravens. *Unknown.* CABA; CaFP; PoPo

There were three sailors of Bristol city. Little Billee. Thackeray. HaSV

There were three sisters lived in a bower. The Bonnie Banks of Fordie. *Unknown.* BuBa

There were two birds today. The Two Freedoms. Jon Silkin. PoDB

There were two sisters sat in a bower. Binnorie. *Unknown.* BuBa; SIV

There when the water was not potable. Chloride of Lime and Charcoal. Louis Zukofsky. CoPo

There where the course is. At Galway Races. W. B. Yeats. SD

There, where the sun shines first. The Azalea. Coventry Patmore. ELP

There will always be monkeys and peacocks. Swell People. Carl Sandburg. LOW

There will be the cough before the silence, then. Dictum: For a Masque of Deluge. W. S. Merwin. AP

There you sit. Shelley Silverstein. PoSC

There'd Be an Orchestra. F. Scott Fitzgerald. *Fr.* Thousand-and-First Ship. GoJo

"Therefore Is the Name of It Called Babel." Sir Osbert Sitwell. MMA

Therefore, proud Italy, I, by God's grace. On His Return to Italy. Luigi Alamanni. RBL

There'll Never Be Peace. Burns. CBEP

There's a barrel-organ caroling across a golden street. The Barrel-Organ. Alfred Noyes. FaBV; LV

There's a book. Seven Today. Ivy O. Eastwick. BiCB

There's a Catholic church on the corner. Young Buck's Sunday Blues. Kenneth Pitchford. *Fr.* Good for Nothing Man. CoPo

There's a certain slant of light. Emily Dickinson. AP; CABA; CBEP; DiPo; FoBA; ILP; PoSa

There's a glade in Aghadoe, Aghadoe, Aghadoe. Aghadoe. John Todhunter. BoLP

There's a humming in the sky. Aeroplane. Mary McBride Green. SoPo

There's a Light upon the Mountains. Henry Burton. TRV

There's a little secret. Keep Sweet. *Unknown.* STF

There's a lonely stretch of hillocks. Anzac Cove. Leon Gellert. PoAu-1

There's a nice green little gully on the Numerella shore. The Numerella Shore. "Cockatoo Jack." PoAu-1

There's a north wind faintly calling, as the first dead leaves are falling. A Few Signs. Grantland Rice. LV

There's a package. The Package. Aileen Fisher. SoPo

There's a palace in Florence, the world knows well. The Statue and the Bust. Robert Browning. VP

There's a place the man always say. Where? Kenneth Patchen. ToPo

There's a Song in the Air! J. G. Holland. TRV

There's a sweetness in surrender. The Blessings of Surrender. Mary J. Helphingtine. STF

There's a trade you all know well. The Overlander. *Unknown.* PoAu-1

There's a whisper down the field where the year has shot her yield. The Long Trail. Kipling. FaBV

There's a Wideness in God's Mercy. Frederick W. Faber. *Fr.* God Our Father. TRV (All-embracing, The, *sl. diff.*) TRV

There's a woman like a dew-drop, she's so purer than the purest. Robert Browning. *Fr.* A Blot in the 'Scutcheon. UnTE

There's all of pleasure and all of peace. A Friend or Two. Wilbur D. Nesbit. PoLF

There's ghosts on the road here. Wilderness Road. Martha Keller. FiSC

There's half a god in many a man. Inspiration. Mary Fullerton. PoAu-1

There's much afoot in heaven and earth this year. The Rainy Summer. Alice Meynell. GoJo

There's no arrangement. It is a thicket in little. Bunch of Wild Flowers. Luke Zilles. RePo

There's No Day without Night. Sem Tob, *tr. fr. Spanish by* Norman T. Di Giovanni. *Fr.* Moral Proverbs. AnML

There's no dew left on the daisies and clover. Seven Times One [*or* Birthday Morning]. Jean Ingelow. *Fr.* Songs of Seven. BiCB; OBNC; ThGo

There's No Finer Treasure. Sem Tob, *tr. fr. Spanish by* Norman T. Di Giovanni. *Fr.* Moral Proverbs. AnML

There's no respect for youth or age. California Stage Company. John A. Stone. SGR

There's not a joy in the world can give like that it takes away. Youth and Age. Byron. GTBS-P

There's not a pair of legs so thin, there's not a head so thick. The Job That's Crying to Be Done. Kipling. TRV

There's not a tear that brims thine eye unshed. Faithless. Louis Lavater. PoAu-1

There's Nothing like the Sun. Edward Thomas. FaBV

There's panic in Paris. Bicycalamity. Edmund W. Peters. SD

There's part of the sun in an apple. Out of the Vast. Augustus Wright Bamberger. TRV

There's room on the bus. Jittery Jim. William Jay Smith. BBGG

There's something in a stupid ass. Epilogue. Byron. Par

There's something in the air. The Coming of Spring. Nora Perry. SoPo

There's Wisdom in Women. Rupert Brooke. BoLP

Thermopylae. Michael Thwaites. PoAu-2

These. William Carlos Williams. AP

These are my thoughts on realizing. Anniversary. John Wain. MP; NePoEA-2; ToPo

These are stirring times for the editors of newspapers. Powers and Times Are Not Gods. W. H. Auden. *Fr.* For the Time Being. MoRP

These are the days that come on silent feet. October Days. James Larkin Pearson. PoNC

These are the days when birds come back. Emily Dickinson. AP; CaFP; PoIE

These are the desolate, dark weeks. These. William Carlos Williams. AP

These are the fellows who smell of salt to the prairie. Words Are Never Enough. Charles Bruce. OBCV

These are the fields of light, and laughing air. The Pea-Fields. Sir Charles G. D. Roberts. OBCV

These are the gardens of the desert, these. The Prairies. Byrant. AP

These are the patriot brave, who side by side. Epitaph for Chaeroneia. Aristotle. SiGo

These are the saddest of possible words. Baseball's Sad Lexicon. Franklin P. Adams. SD

These, as they change, Almighty Father, these. A Hymn on the Seasons. James Thomson. *Fr.* The Seasons. EiCP

These be/ Three silent things. Triad. Adelaide Crapsey. LV; PoPl

These buildings are too close to me. Rudolph Is Tired of the City. Gwendolyn Brooks. RePo

These bunched soldiers, just now shooting the emperor. Manet: The Execution of Emperor Maximilian. W. D. Snodgrass. AmPC

These fell miasmic rings of mist. Prejudice. Georgia Douglas Johnson. AmNP

These Fought. Ezra Pound. *Fr.* Hugh Selwyn Mauberley. PoSa ("These fought in any case.") PoIE; ThLM

"These Gothic windows, how they wear me out." The Young Glass-Stainer. Thomas Hardy. CTC

These hearts were woven of human joys and cares. The Dead. Rupert Brooke. *Fr.* 1914. MMA

These hours of spring are jolly. The Lover and the Nightingale. *Unknown.* UnTE

These I have loved. The Great Lover. Rupert Brooke. WePo

These I have loved with passion, loved them long. Quiet Things. Grace Noll Crowell. PoLF

These Images Remain. May Sarton. MoLP

These, in the day when heaven was falling. Epitaph on an Army of Mercenaries. A. E. Housman. MMA; PoIE; StP

These leaves, so deeply and so lately green. Color. Melville Cane. RePo

These lines are a discipline he would avoid. Notes on a Child's Coloring Book. Robert Patrick Dana. PoPl

These little limbs [*or* limmes]. The Salutation. Thomas Traherne. MeP; PoIE; SeCP

These little settlements. On the Outgoing Train. Alan Swallow. PtTo

These London wenches are so stout. The Sound Country Lass. *Unknown.* ErPo

These lovely groves of fountain-trees that shake. Golden Bough. Elinor Wylie. LV

These market-dames, mid-aged, with lips thin-drawn. Former Beauties. Thomas Hardy. *Fr.* At Casterbridge Fair. OBNC

These Men. Leon Gellert. PoAu-1

These morning airs. Spring Breeze. Buson. RePo

These native angles of decay. Deserted Buildings under Shefford Mountain. John Glassco. OBCV

These nights we fear the aspects of the moon. Full Moon: New Guinea. Karl Shapiro. PoPo

These particles of fire which glisten in the snow. The Alpine Winter. Antoine-Girard de Saint-Amant. RBL

These pools that, though in forests, still reflect. Spring Pools. Robert Frost. DiPo

These seven houses have learned to face one another. On a Painting by Patient B of the Independence State Hospital for the Insane. Donald Justice. NePoEA-2

These tenants sleeping under ground. Brief Biography. Marguerite George. FiSC

These Things Shall Be. John Addington Symonds. TRV

These to His Memory—since he held them dear. Dedication. Tennyson. *Fr.* Idylls of the King. CABA

These to their country brought an endless name. Not to Die. Simonides. SiGo

These Trees Stand. W. D. Snodgrass. ToPo

These women all. Women. —— Heath. CTC

Thespians at Thermopylae, The. Norman Cameron. GTBS-P

They all were looking for a king. That Holy Thing. George Macdonald. TRV

They Are All Gone. Henry Vaughan. *See* They Are All Gone into the World of Light.

They are all gone away. The House on the Hill. E. A. Robinson. GoJo; LV; PoSa

They Are All Gone into the World of Light. Henry Vaughan. BoC; MeP; SeCP; StP (Beyond the Veil.) FaPL (They Are All Gone.) PoIE (World of Light, The.) CBEP

They are at rest. Refrigerium. Cardinal Newman. OBNC

They are at their places, straining. The Boat Race. Vergil. *Fr.* The Aeneid. SD

They are bringing him down. Casualty. Robert Nichols. MMA

They are curious things that hide in the woods. Forest Shapes. Donald Wandrei. FiSC

They are cutting down the great plane-trees at the end of the gardens. The Trees Are Down. Charlotte Mew. LV

They are gathered, astounded and disturbed. The Last Supper. Rainer Maria Rilke. MoRP

They are gathering round. Concert Party. Siegfried Sassoon. MMA

They are given to. Knee Lunes. Robert Kelly. CoPo

They are moving inwards, the circle is closing. Man Meeting Himself. Howard Sergeant. *Fr.* The Leaves of Europe. ToPo

They are not all sweet nightingales. Not All Sweet Nightingales. Luis de Góngora. RBL

They are not here. And we, we are the Others. The Absent. Edwin Muir. MoRP
They Are Not Long. Ernest Dowson. *See* Vitae Summa Brevis Spem Nos Vetet Incohare Longam.
They are not those who used to feed us. The Puzzled Game-Birds. Thomas Hardy. VP
They are rattling breakfast plates in basement kitchens. Morning at the Window. T. S. Eliot. CABA; WePo
They are rhymes rudely strung with intent less. A Dedication. Adam Lindsay Gordon. PoAu-1
They are slaves who fear to speak. Slaves. James Russell Lovell. TRV
They argued on till dead of night. Theologians. Walter de la Mare. EaLo
They call streets "boulevards" and build them huge. Big Crash Out West. Peter Viereck. PoP1
"They called it Annandale—and I was there." How Annandale Went Out. E. A. Robinson. AP; ILP
They carried him home in late August. A Country Saga. Sam Ragan. PoNC
They chose me from my brothers. Riddle: What Am I? Dorothy Aldis. SoPo
They Closed Her Eyes. Gustavo Adolfo Bécquer, *tr. fr. Spanish by* Muriel Kittel. AnSP
They Crucified My Lord. *Unknown.* STF
They cut down the old pine tree in Tunisia. Guitar Lament for a Mountain Boy. Carl De Suze. CaFP
They did not know this face. Job. Elizabeth Sewell. EaLo
They do not hinder me. They let me go. The Song of the Idiot. Rainer Maria Rilke. TwGP
They do not live in the world. The Animals. Edwin Muir. AnMoPo; PoDB
They dug a trench, and threw him in a grave. A Young Greek, Killed in the Wars. Richard Eberhart. AnMoPo
They Flee from Me. Sir Thomas Wyatt. CABA; CaFP; CBEP; EnRePo; ILP; OnP; PoIE; VaPo
(Lover Forsaken, The.) UnTE
(Lover Showeth How He Is Forsaken of Such as He Sometime Enjoyed, The.) ELP
They fought south of the ramparts. Fighting South of the Ramparts. *Unknown.* SiGo
They found a taxi. He took her home. The Moral Taxi Ride. Erich Kästner. ErPo
They found him deep within an ancient cave. The Prehistoric Huntsman. Donald Wandrei. FiSC
They get drunk, these Great Sled-Makers. The Great Sled-Makers. Kenneth Patchen. ToPo
They got you last night. Aaron Kurtz. *Fr.* Behold the Sea. PtTo
They grew and charcoal bundle shakes itself. Brothers. Solomon Edwards. NNP
They grew and they grew to the church steeple top. Bonny Barbara Allen (E *vers.*). *Unknown.* BSO
They had a Cook with them who stood alone. Ten of Chaucer's People: A Tasty Cook. Chaucer. *Fr.* The Canterbury Tales. PoSa
They hail you as their morning star. Men. Dorothy Parker. BoLP; LV
They have [*or* They've] left thee naked, Lord; O that they had! Upon the Body of Our Blessed Lord [*or* On Our Crucified Lord], Naked and Bloody. Richard Crashaw. CABA; ILP; SeCP; VaPo
They have no song, the sedges dry. Song in the Songless. George Meredith. ACV
They have said, "too risky." To Words. Ralph Pomeroy. CoPo
They Have Told Me Some News. Afonso Lopes de Baian, *tr. fr. Portuguese by* Lawrence A. Sharpe. AnML
They Have Yarns. Carl Sandburg. *Fr.* The People, Yes. RePo
They haven't got no noses. The Song of Quoodle. G. K. Chesterton. GoJo; WePo
They head the list. Horses. Richard Armour. PoP1
They helped every one his neighbour; and everyone said to his brother. Comfort When Work Seems Difficult. Isaiah, Bible, *O.T.* BoC
They Know. Ryah Tumarkin Goodman. FiSC
They left the vine-wreathed cottage and the mansion on the hill. The Women of the West. G. Essex Evans. PoAu-1
They lie in the sunday street. The Dead. C. Day Lewis. MP
They lived alone. The Romney. Harriet Monroe. SIV
They meet but with unwholesome springs. Against Them Who Lay Unchastity to the Sex of Women. William Habington. *Fr.* Castara. SeCP
They meet over water. 3rd Dance—Making a Structure with a Roof or under a Roof—6-7 February 1964. Jackson MacLow. CoPo
They might not need me; but they might. Emily Dickinson. TRV
They must to keep their certainty accuse. The Leaders of the Crowd. W. B. Yeats. PoPo
They nailed my Saviour to the cross. They Crucified My Lord. *Unknown.* STF
They never credit us. The Critics. Lawrence Durrell. ToPo

They put us far apart. Emily Dickinson. AP
They rise like sudden fiery flowers. Fireworks. James Reeves. PoSC
They Roasted Me Instead. Edith Earnshaw. PoNC
They rode along the road till they come to two stacks of oats. A Man and a Maid. *Unknown.* BFSS
They rolled him up in a nice clean sheet. Finnigan's Wake. *Unknown.* BSO
They said, "The Master is coming." Unawares. Emma A. Lent. PoLF
They sailed away in a gallant bark. Dublin Bay. *Unknown.* BFSS
They sat. They stood about. Of Commerce and Society. Geoffrey Hill. NePoEA-2
They Say My Verse Is Sad. A. E. Housman. More Poems, Introd. WePo
("They say my verse is sad: no wonder.") VP
They say that God lives very high. A Child's Thought of God. Elizabeth Barrett Browning. TRV
They Say That in the Unchanging Place. Hilaire Belloc. *Fr.* Dedicatory Ode. PoLF
They say, that Pity in Love's service dwells. Modern Love, XLIV. George Meredith. VP
They Say That the Plants Do Not Speak. Rosalía de Castro, *tr. fr. Spanish by* Kate Flores. AnSP
They say that "Time assuages." Emily Dickinson. FoBA
They say that when they burned young Shelley's corpse. The Fishes and the Poet's Hands. Frank Yerby. AmNP
They say the most of mothers. My Mother. *Unknown.* STF
They say the sea is cold, but the sea contains. Whales Weep Not! D. H. Lawrence. PoIE
They say the war is over. But water still. Redeployment. Howard Nemerov. ThLM
They say there is a sweeter air. A Carriage from Sweden. Marianne Moore. MP
They send him. Field of Plunder. Charles Humboldt. PtTo
They shall not return to us, the resolute, the young. Mesopotamia. Kipling. MMA
They shouldn't call me "little boy" anymore. When a Fellow's Four. Mary Jane Carr. BiCB
They shut the road through the woods. The Way through the Woods. Kipling. OBNC; PoSa; StP; WePo
They sin who tell us Love can die. Love Indestructible. Robert Southey. *Fr.* The Curse of Kehama. OBNC
They sing their dearest songs. During Wind and Rain. Thomas Hardy. ELP; GTBS-P; PoIE; PoSa
They Sing, They Sing. Theodore Roethke. *Fr.* The Dying Man. PoDB
They squat silhouetted against the hills. Kurdish Shepherds. Alan Ross. DaDu
They step through the moonlight. In the Moonlight. Kenneth Patchen. ToPo
They take their stand, each rising. The Boxing Match. Vergil. *Fr.* The Aeneid. SD
They teeter with an inane care among the skewbald stones. Sheep. Hal Porter. PoAu-2
They that go down to the sea in ships, that do business in great waters. Psalm CVII, Bible, *O.T.* HaSV
They that have power to hurt and will do none. Sonnets, XCIV. Shakespeare. CABA; CBEP; GTBS-P; PoIE; PoSa
They That Wait upon the Lord. Isaiah, XL: 28-31, Bible, *O.T.* TRV
("Hast thou not known? hast thou not heard, that the everlasting God," XL: 28-31; XLIX: 13-16.) BoC
They throw in Drummer Hodge, to rest. Drummer Hodge. Thomas Hardy. AnMoPo; GTBS-P; ILP; VP
They told me first she was a tree. Girl. Dom Moraes. NePoEA-2
They told me, Heraclitus, they told me you were dead. Heraclitus. William Johnson Cory, *after* Callimachus. CBEP; OBNC; SiGo; WePo
They told me you had been to her. Evidence Read at the Trial of the Knave of Hearts. "Lewis Carroll." *Fr.* Alice's Adventures in Wonderland. GTBS-P
They took him out to die. "And When He Had Scourged Jesus, He Delivered Him to Be Crucified." W. H. Rodgers. WePo
They took me from the white sun and they. "A Little Boy Lost." Jerome Rothenberg. CoPo
They tried to evolve a sphere. Succumbing. Paul Eaton Reeve. ErPo
They went to sea in a sieve, they did. The Jumblies. Edward Lear. EvOK; GoJo; OnMSP; SoPo; WiR
They Who Tread the Path of Labor. Henry van Dyke. TRV
They will come no more. I Vecchi. Ezra Pound. PoIE
They will never die on that battlefield. Uccello. Gregory Corso. PtTo
They wrought a pillar from the rock of sacred stone. The High Place at Marib. Grant Code. FiSC
They'd make you believe that your problem is one of sex. The New Being. Kenneth Patchen. ToPo
They'll soon be flying to Mars, I hear. Progress. Samuel Hoffenstein. ThLM

They'll Tell You about Me. Ian Mudie. PoAu-2
They're altogether otherworldly now. Grandparents. Robert Lowell. ToPo
They're out of the dark's ragbag, these two. Blue Moles. Sylvia Plath. NePoEA-2
They've been for ages in our mind. Jackolanterns. Rainer Maria Rilke. MGP
They've got a brand-new organ, Sue. The New Church Organ. Will Carleton. PoLF
They've got some pretty horses up in the long dark mountains. Now I Went Down to the Ringside and Little Henry Armstrong Was There. Kenneth Patchen. ToPo
They've left Thee naked, Lord; O that they had. *See* They have left thee naked, Lord; O that they had!
Thief. *Unknown.* BBGG
Thief, The, in me is running a/ round in circles. Zapata & the Landlord. Alfred B. Spellman. NNP
Thiepval Wood. Edmund Blunden. MMA
Thieves. Perseus Adams. ACV
Thieves, The. Robert Graves. GTBS-P
Thin Potomac scarcely moves, The. The Potomac. Karl Shapiro. AP; ToPo
Thin under the arc lights. Tennis in San Juan. Reuel Denney. SD
Thine be those motions strong and sanative. To Coleridge in Sicily. Wordsworth. *Fr.* The Prelude. OBNC
Thine eyes shall see the light of distant skies. To Cole, the Painter, Departing for Europe. Bryant. AP
Thing could barely stand, The. The Bull Calf. Irving Layton. OBCV
Thing of Beauty, A. Keats. *Fr.* Endymion, I. FaBV; PoPl ("Thing of beauty is a joy for ever, A.") BoC; CTC; ILP; OBNC; TRV
Thing Remembered, A. *Unknown, tr. fr. Arabic by* E. Powys Mathers. ErPo
Things being what they are do not imply necessity. Theodore Enslin. Forms, LXXVII. CoPo
Things to Learn About. John Becker. RePo
Think It Over. *Unknown.* STF
Think, Man of Flesh, and be not proud. Speed. W. H. Davies. MoRP
Think, Marquise! what if my face. Stanzas to the Marquise. Corneille. RBL
Think me not unkind and rude. The Apology. Emerson. AP
Think no evil, have no fear. Phyllis. *Unknown.* UnTE
Think No More Lad. A. E. Housman. A Shropshire Lad, XLIX. CABA
(Laugh, Be Jolly.) WePo
("Think no more, lad; laugh, be jolly.") PoPo
Think not that incense-smoke has had its day. Incense. Vachel Lindsay. MoRP
Think of—/ Stepping on shore, and finding it Heaven! Heaven. *Unknown.* PoLF
Think of all the people. The World's So Big. Aileen Fisher. SoPo
Think of Eight Numbers. Shelley Silverstein. BBGG
Think of It, My Soul. Eduard Möricke, *tr. fr. German by* Charles E. Passage. AGP
Think of This. Günter Eich, *tr. fr. German by* Vernon Watkins. MGP
Think of this loss. Toward Colonos. Dabney Stuart. OPP
Think of this, that man is the enemy of man. Think of This. Günter Eich. MGP
Think thou and act; to-morrow thou shalt die. The Choice, 3. Dante Gabriel Rossetti. The House of Life, LXXIII. GTBS-P
Thinke not cause men flatt'ring say. To A. L.: Perswasions to Love. Thomas Carew. SeCP
Thinker, The. William Carlos Williams. MoLP
Thinking of Hölderlin. Christopher Middleton. NePoEA-2
Thinking of you, and all that was, and all. Monna Innominata, IX. Christina Rossetti. VP
Think't thou that this love can stand. Ametas and Thestylis Making Hay-Ropes. Andrew Marvell. SeCP
Third Avenue in Sunlight. Anthony Hecht. NePoEA-2
Third Century, The, *sels.* Thomas Traherne. MeP
"Life of Sabbaths here beneath, A!"
On News.
Recovery, The.
"Sin!/ O only fatal Woe."
"That childish thoughts such joys inspire."
Third Continent, The. Mary Erulkar. ACV
3rd Dance—Making a Structure with a Roof or under a Roof —6-7 February 1964. Jackson MacLow. CoPo
Third Day, The. Edith Lovejoy Pierce. MoRP
Third Enemy Speaks. C. Day Lewis. *Fr.* The Magnetic Mountain. EaLo
Third-grade angels, two by two, The. Christmas Pageant. Margaret Fishback. PoSC
Thirsty Earth, The. Abraham Cowley. *See* Drinking.
Thirteen men by Ruan Shore. Dolor Oogo. Sir Arthur Quiller-Couch. HaSV
Thirteen Ways of Looking at a Blackbird. Wallace Stevens. AP; CABA; DiPo; PoSa
13th Dance—Matching Parcels—21 February 1964. Jackson MacLow. CoPo

Thirty Bob a Week. John Davidson. CABL; OBNC
Thirty Days Hath September. *Unknown.* SoPo
.38, The. Ted Joans. NNP
37th Dance—Banding—22 March 1964. Jackson MacLow. CoPo
33. Adrienne Rich. CoPo
Thirty-two years since, up against the sun. Zermatt: To the Matterhorn. Thomas Hardy. OBNC
Thirty white horses. Riddle. Mother Goose. SoPo
This:/ That is my straight-flying fury. Witch Hazel. Theodore Enslin. CoPo
This a tale that the coachman told. The Coachman's Yarn. E. J. Brady. PoAu-1
This above All Is Precious and Remarkable. John Wain. ToPo
This above all: to thine own self be true. Shakespeare. *See* Polonius' Advice to Laertes.
This ae night, this ae night. A Lyke-Wake Dirge. *Unknown.* BuBa; CBEP; EaLo; EvOK
This ain't Torquemada. Dialect Quatrain. Marcus B. Christian. AmNP
This autumn day—I have not seen its peer. Picture of Autumn. Friedrich Hebbel. AGP
This autumn day the new cross is set up. The Church. Edwin Muir. MoRP
This bedlam is a cracked platter of cold fried eggs. Blotting Paper. Thad Stem, Jr. PoNC
This blackbird stared at us six feet away. Dead and Gone. Anthony Thwaite. DaDu
This Blatant Beast was finally overcome. Saint. Robert Graves. AnMoPo
This Blessed Christ of Calvary. *Unknown.* STF
This Blessed Plot . . . This England. Shakespeare. King Richard II, *fr.* II, i. FaBV
This blue-washed, old, thatched summerhouse. The Old Summerhouse. Walter de la Mare. GTBS-P
This body of my mother, pierced by me. Epithalamium. Leo Kennedy. OBCV
This Bread I Break. Dylan Thomas. PoIE
This busy, vast, inquiring soul. Insatiableness. Thomas Traherne. VaPo
This California is a humbug state. California Humbugs. Mart Taylor. SGR
This chair I trusted, lass, and I looted the leaves. Aristotle to Phyllis. John Hollander. PoCh
This child reflects the sea in every mood. Heritage. Kathleen Merrick. HaSV
This child that God has given you. A Sunday School Teacher Speaks. *Unknown.* STF
This clearing day. Blue on White. Elizabeth J. Coatsworth. RePo
This Compost. Walt Whitman. CABA
This conduit stream that's tangled here and there. Zillebeke Brook. Edmund Blunden. MMA
This consciousness that is aware. Emily Dickinson. AP
This Corruptible. Elinor Wylie. MoRP
This cursèd jealousy, what is't? Jealousy. Sir William Davenant. *Fr.* The Siege of Rhodes. BoIP
This darksome burn, horseback brown. Inversnaid. Gerard Manley Hopkins. CABA; FoBA; GTBS-P; PoIE
This day a year ago, to me. February Birthday. Nancy Byrd Turner. BiCB
This day day dawes. The Lily-white Rose. *Unknown.* MeEL
This death is timely. The Death of Nearchus. Alan Ansen. OPP
"This Do in Remembrance of Me." *Unknown.* STF
This Dust Was Once the Man. Walt Whitman. LiPo
This Easter, Arthur Winslow, less than dead. Death from Cancer. Robert Lowell. In Memory of Arthur Winslow, I. AP; MP; PoSa
This evening, motherly summer moves in the pond. Mayday on Holderness. Ted Hughes. ToPo
This Evening When I Spoke to You. Sister Juana Inés de la Cruz. *tr. fr. Spanish by* Muriel Kittel. AnSP
This face you got. Phizzog. Carl Sandburg. RePo
This fair maid she grumbled. Fragments of Irish Songs. *Unknown.* BSO
This fat woman in canvas knickers. Tourist Time. F. R. Scott. PoPl
This Fevers Me. Richard Eberhart. MoRP
This figure that thou here seest put. To the Reader. Ben Jonson. EnRePo
This fugue must be hummed, found. Dumb Dick. Leslie A. Fiedler. ErPo
This fullness that is emptiness. Definition. May Sarton. MoLP
This girl gave her heart to me. Conrad Aiken. *Fr.* Improvisations: Light and Snow. BoLP
This gives support to insects. 12th Dance—Getting Leather by Language—21 February 1964. Jackson MacLow. CoPo
This golden head has wit in it. Modern Love, XXXI. George Meredith. VP
This Here Is Hell. Samuel M. Bradley. FiSC
This honorable body is hard to beat. California Legislature. John A. Stone. SGR

This Hour. Oliver La Grone. NNP

This house I know—though never seen before. House of Yesterday. Walter Shedlofsky. FiSC

This huge and purged trust I have. My Love behind Walls. Heather Spears. OBCV

This hungry flesh and bone. The Son. Edwin Muir. PoDB

This I beheld, or dreamed it in a dream. Opportunity. Edward Rowland Sill. SIV; StP

This I Can Do. H. T. Lefevre. STF

This I Know, How Love Begins to Be. Albrecht von Johansdorf, tr. fr. German by Margaret F. Richey. AnML

This is a holy, festive Easter day. Easter Day. Juan Ruiz, Archpriest of Hita. Fr. The Book of True Love. AnML

This is a piece too fair. What Is the World? Dryden. Fr. To My Honor'd Friend Sir Robert Howard. TRV

This is a rune I ravelled in the still. The Cow. Bernard O'Dowd. PoAu-1

This is a spray the bird clung to. Misconceptions. Robert Browning. CBEP

This is a tale for a night of snow. The Fair Young Wife. Helen Adam. FiSC

This is a theme for muted coronets. The Plot against Proteus. A. J. M. Smith. OBCV

This is about the stillness in moving things. Runes. Howard Nemerov. PoCh; ToPo

This Is after All Vacation. Louis Zukofsky. CoPo

This is God's house—the blue sky is the ceiling. In the Woods. Frederick George Scott. ACV

This Is Going to Hurt Just a Little Bit. Ogden Nash. LV

This is her picture as she was. The Portrait. Dante Gabriel Rossetti. VP

This is how the flowers grow. How the Flowers Grow. "Gabriel Setoun." SoPo

This is Independence Day. Stephen Vincent Benét. Fr. Listen to the People: Independence Day, 1941. PoSC

This Is Just to Say. William Carlos Williams. AnMoPo; GoJo; PoIE

This is Mab, the mistress-fairy. Mab. Ben Jonson. Fr. The Satyr. WiR

This is Mister Beers. Mister Beers. Hugh Lofting. RePo

This Is My Beloved, sels. Walter Benton. UnTE

"I saw autumn today . . . incipiently, on the sunset."

"It was like something done in fever, when nothing fits."

"White full moon like a great beautiful whore, The."

This Is My Father's World. Maltbie D. Babcock. TRV

This is my letter to the World. Emily Dickinson. AP; DiPo

This is my playes last scene, here heavens appoint. Holy Sonnets, VI. John Donne. MeP; SeCP

This is my prayer to thee, my lord—strike, strike at the root of penury in my heart. For Strength. Rabindranath Tagore. Fr. Gitanjali. MoRP

This Is My Rock. David McCord. SoPo

This is no place for lovers. Advice from a Nightwatchman. Ian Healy. Poems from the Coalfields, II. PoAu-2

This is not death, immortal Margaret. Tasso, tr. fr. Italian by Lorna de' Lucchi. RBL

This is not sorrow, this is work: I build. The Tomb of Lt. John Learmonth, A.I.F. John Manifold. PoAu-2

This is not the man that women choose. Act of Love. Vernon Scannell. ErPo

This is not the wind in the weeping willow tree. Spring Voices. Jesse Stuart. FiSC

This is that blessed Mary, pre-elect. Mary's Girlhood. Dante Gabriel Rossetti. VP

This is the Arsenal. From floor to ceiling. The Arsenal at Springfield. Longfellow. AP

This is the day His hour of life draws near. Sonnets at Christmas, I. Allen Tate. AP

This is the day the circus comes. Parade. Rachel Field. Fr. A Circus Garland. SoPo

This is the day, which down the void abysm. Shelley. Fr. Prometheus Unbound. PoIE

This is the debt I pay. The Debt. Paul Laurence Dunbar. AnMP; TRV

This is the Fall, which yet will break your heart! Fall. Friedrich Hölderlin. AGP

This is the female form. Walt Whitman. Fr. I Sing the Body Electric. ErPo

This is the football hero's moment of fame. Settling Some Old Football Scores. Morris Bishop. SD

This is the gay cliff of the nineteenth century. Brooklyn Heights. John Wain. ToPo

This is the golden beggars; friend is she. Aphrodite Pandemos. Unknown. UnTE

This is the haunted wood, where no man goes. Warning. Sydney King Russell. FiSC

This is the house that Jack built. The House That Jack Built. Unknown. SoPo

This is the house where Jesse White. Lowery Cot. L. A. G. Strong. DaDu

This is the key of the Kingdom. The Key of the Kingdom. Unknown. CBEP

This is the metre Columbian. The soft-flowing trochees and dactyls. The Metre Columbian. Unknown. Par

This is the month, and this the happy morn. On the Morning [or Ode on the Morning] of Christ's Nativity. Milton. GTBS-P; MeP

This is the myrtle of the South. Crepe Myrtle. Charles Edward Eaton. PoNC

This is the night mail crossing the border. Night Mail. W. H. Auden. PoSa; WePo

"This is the night," the dark-faced stranger leered. The Sabbat. Lin Carter. FiSC

This is the promise that hangs on the tree. Christmas 1945. Al Hine. ThLM

This is the safest prayer to pray. Thy Will Be Done. Annie Johnson Flint. STF

This is the shape of the leaf, and this of the flower. Portrait of a Girl. Conrad Aiken. Fr. Priapus and the Pool. GoJo

This is the ship of pearl, which, poets feign. The Chambered Nautilus. Oliver Wendell Holmes. Fr. The Autocrat of the Breakfast Table. AmLP; AP; DiPo; HaSV; LV; PoLF

This is the sleep that fell just after dinner. Madame. Eleanor Ross Taylor. PoNC

This is the stagnant hour. Drunken Lover. Owen Dodson. AmNP

This is the story the Coxswain told. The Coxswain's Line. H. E. Cressman. RePo

This is the surest death. Mortality. Naomi Long Madgett. NNP

This is the time lean woods shall spend. Sundown. Léonie Adams. AmLP

This is the voice of high midsummer's heat. The Mowing. Sir Charles G. D. Roberts. OBCV

This is the way the ladies are. Cantata for Two Lovers. Helga Sandburg. UnTE

This is the way we say it in our time. Sonnet XV. Winfield Townley Scott. ErPo

This is the weather the cuckoo likes. Weathers. Thomas Hardy. EvOK; FaBV; PoIE; RePo; WePo

This is their image: the desert and the wild. Pyramis; or, The House of Ascent. A. D. Hope. PoAu-2

This is their third parting. Now she goes. The Adventurers. John Thompson. PoAu-2

This is where I have been trying to lead a life. Interior. Philippe Jaccottet. CoFP

This lady, curled like a shell. The Shellpicker. Ronald Perry. NePoEA-2

This Landscape, These People. Zulfikar Ghose. ACV

This Last Pain. William Empson. GTBS-P; ToPo

This Life a Dream and Shadow. Sir Thomas More. Fr. The Twelve Weapons of Spiritual Battle. EnRePo

This Life Is All Chequer'd with Pleasures and Woes. Thomas Moore. ELP

This life, which seems so fair. Madrigal I. Giovanni Battista Guarini, tr. by William Drummond of Hawthornden. GTBS-P; RBL

This Lime-Tree Bower My Prison. Samuel Taylor Coleridge. CBEP; PoIE

This little flickering planet. Housemates. Odell Shepard. MoRP

This little instrument of art. Upon a Needle. William Pattison. WaPE

This little pig built a spaceship. Frederick Winsor. Fr. The Space Child's Mother Goose. LV

This Little Pig Went to Market. Mother Goose. SoPo

This little vault, this narrow roome. An Epitaph on the Lady Mary Villers. Thomas Carew. SeCP

This Little Vigil. Charles G. Bell. MoLP

This Living Hand. Keats. See Lines Supposed to Have Been Addressed to Fanny Brawne.

This lonely hill has always. The Infinite. Giacomo Leopardi. SiGo

This, Lord, was an anxious brother and. Funeral Oration for a Mouse. Alan Dugan. AP

This lovely flower fell to seed. For My Grandmother. Countee Cullen. Four Epitaphs, 1. AmNP

This man likes to dive. Cold Logic. Barney Hutchinson. SD

This man sowed faith wherever he moved. The White-haired Man. May Sarton. MoRP

This mast, new-shaved, through whom I rive the ropes. Choosing a Mast. Roy Campbell. BoC; HaSV

This miracle in me I scan. William Baylebridge. Fr. Life's Testament. PoAu-1

This Moment Yearning and Thoughtful. Walt Whitman. RePo

This Monument Will Outlast. Horace, tr. fr. Latin by Ezra Pound. Odes, III, 30. CTC

This Morning. Jay Wright. NNP

This morning. In a Spring Still Not Written Of. Robert Wallace. PP

This morning, as I walked to school. A Story in the Snow. Pearl R. Crouch. SoPo

This morning I threw the windows. This Morning. Jay Wright. NNP

This morning I was bad. Grandmother's Visit. William Wise. RePo

This morning is haunted. Place-Ghost. August Derleth. FiSC

This morning, there flew up the lane. Lady Lost. John Crowe Ransom. PoSa

This morning, timely rapt with holy fire. On Lucy, Countess of Bedford. Ben Jonson. EnRePo; SeCP

This morning two teacups. Two Teacups. Vernon Ward. PoNC

This mossie bank they prest. That aged Oak. A Pastorall Dialogue. Thomas Carew. SeCP

This much, O heaven—if I should brood or rave. A Prayer in Darkness. G. K. Chesterton. BoC; PoLF

This mud, my genesis. Ascent. Wendell Berry. AP

This never-ended searching for the eyes. Egg-and-Dart. Robert Finch. OBCV

This night of frosty wind and stars. The Wind of Time. Joseph Payne Brennan. FiSC

This, of all fates, would be the saddest end. Tragedy. "Æ." MoRP

This old crabbed man, with his wrinkled, fusty clothes. Old Crabbed Men. James Reeves. ErPo

This Old Man. Unknown. SoPo

This only hope relieves me, that the strife. Milton. Fr. Samson Agonistes. TRV

This Pardoner had hair as yellow as wax. Ten of Chaucer's People: A Girlish Pardoner. Chaucer. Fr. The Canterbury Tales. PoSa

This person in the gaudy clothes. Captain Kidd. Stephen Vincent Benét. ThLM

This pinched face of the moon. September in the Park. W. D. Snodgrass. ToPo

This ploughman dead in battle slept out of doors. A Private. Edward Thomas. GTBS-P; MMA

This poem is for my wife. Poem in Prose. Archibald MacLeish. MoLP; PoPl

This points through place. Canoe. Patrick Anderson. SD

This portrait painter boasted twenty sons. The Artist as Cuckold. Unknown. UnTE

This quiet dust was gentlemen and ladies. Emily Dickinson. AP

This rich marble doth inter. An Epitaph on the Marchioness of Winchester. Milton. FoBA

This road is like a tomb. On Passing Two Negroes on a Dark Country Road Somewhere in Georgia. Conrad Kent Rivers. NNP

This room I know so well becomes. The Room. Elizabeth Jennings. NePoEA-2

This royal throne of kings, this sceptered isle. This Blessed Plot . . . This England. Shakespeare. Fr. King Richard II. FaBV

This sticky trail. Snail. David McCord. RePo

This sunlight shames November where he grieves. Autumn Idleness. Dante Gabriel Rossetti. The House of Life, LXIX. ILP

This the downgoing, this. Downgoing. Gustav Davidson. FiSC

This the last refuge I can give you. Love Beleaguered. Katherine Garrison Chapin. MoLP

This time, I mean it. A Little Tumescence. Jonathan Williams. ErPo

This Too Will Pass Away. Unknown. STF

This torch, still burning in my hand. From the Greek Anthology. Crinagoras. SD

This torment of love. Describes Rationally the Irrational Effects of Love. Sister Juana Inés de la Cruz. AnSP

This tragical tale, which, they say, is a true one. Pyramus and Thisbe. John Godfrey Saxe. OnMSP

This tree, here fall'n, no common birth or death. On the Site of a Mulberry-Tree; Planted by Wm. Shakespeare; Felled by the Rev. F. Gastrell. Dante Gabriel Rossetti. CBEP

This truth came borne with bier and pall. In Memoriam A. H. H., LXXXV. Tennyson. VP

This tuft that thrives on saline nothingness. The Air Plant. Hart Crane. PoIE

This ultimate austerity. Desert Claypan. Frederick T. Macartney. PoAu-1

This urge, wrestle, resurrection of dry sticks. Cuttings, Later. Theodore Roethke. AP; PoIE

This vast web, of Nature's weaving. The Cosmic Fabric. Yakov Polonsky. EaLo

This virgin, beautiful and lively day. Sonnet. Stéphane Mallarmé. PoPl

This wallpaper has lines that rise. Missing My Daughter. Stephen Spender. BoC; GTBS-P

This was a day of fumbling and petty accidents. A Hell of a Day. Tim Reynolds. PtTo

This was a poet—it is that. Emily Dickinson. AP; PP

"This was Mr. Bleaney's room. He stayed." Mr. Bleaney. Philip Larkin. NePoEA-2; PoIE

This was our heritage. An Ode on the Despoilers of Learning in an American University (1947). Yvor Winters. StP

This was the woman; what now of the man? Modern Love, III. George Meredith. VP

This Way Only. Lesbia Harford. PoAu-1

This weather's like my troubled mind and eyes. In Rainy-gloomy Weather. John Davies of Hereford. CBEP

This White and Slender Body. Heine, tr. fr. German by Louis Untermeyer. UnTE

This winter's morning, turning the other way. Turning. Robert Finch. OBCV

This winter's weather it waxeth cold. The Old Cloak. Unknown. BuBa

This World a Hunting Is. William Drummond of Hawthornden. CBEP

This world is not conclusion. Emily Dickinson. EaLo

This worlde is full of variaunce. The Duplicity of Women. John Lydgate. MeEL

This wretched life, the trust and confidence. This Life a Dream and Shadow. Sir Thomas More. Fr. The Twelve Weapons of Spiritual Battle. EnRePo

This year (so I hear). A Year without Seasons. Mance Williams. NNP

Thise olde gentil Britouns in hir dayes. The Franklin's Prologue and Tale. Chaucer. Fr. the Canterbury Tales. CABL

Tho'. See also Though.

Tho' if an eye that's downward cast. In Memoriam A. H. H., LXII. Tennyson. VP

Tho' truths in manhood darkly join. In Memoriam A. H. H., XXXVI. Tennyson. VP

Thomas Gray in Patterdale. Norman Nicholson. ACV

Thomas Jefferson. Stephen Vincent Benét. PoPl; RePo

Thomas More to Them That Seek Fortune. Sir Thomas More. EnRePo

Thomas the Rhymer. Unknown. BuBa; ELP; OnMSP (Thomas Rhymer.) CBEP

Thomas was a little glutton. Little Thomas. F. Gwynne Evans. BBGG

Thorn, The, sels. Wordsworth.

"And they had fixed the wedding day." EvOK

"High on a mountain's highest ridge." Par

Thorn Leaves in March. W. S. Merwin. MP

Thornymoor Fields, with music. Unknown. BSO

Those animals that follow us in dream. Lupus in Fabula. Malcolm Lowry. OBCV

Those charming eyes within whose starry sphere. On the Death of Catarina de Attayda. Luís de Camões. RBL

Those clarities detached us, gave us form. The Tourist and the Town. Adrienne Rich. NePoEA-2

Those—dying then. Emily Dickinson. CABA

Those envied places which do know her well. A Day of Love. Dante Gabriel Rossetti. The House of Life, XVI. VP

Those famous men of old, the Ogres. Ogres and Pygmies. Robert Graves. CABA

Those flakes of fire, brilliant sparks of light. Sonnet. Pedro Calderon de la Barca. RBL

Those flaming Christians with their hygienic rose. Burns Singer. Fr. Sonnets for a Dying Man. NePoEA-2

Those houses haunt in which we leave. Ghosts. Elizabeth Jennings. NePoEA-2

Those Images. W. B. Yeats. PP

Those in the vegetable rain retain. Stories of Snow. P. K. Page. OBCV

Those lathered horses galloping past. The Horsemen. Gene Baro. NePoEA-2

Those make thunder though taking pigs somewhere. 13th Dance —Matching Parcels—21 February 1964. Jackson MacLow. CoPo

Those many giant, grey and scattered stones. You Were Shattered. Giuseppe Ungaretti. CoIP

Those Mountains, Mother. Unknown, tr. fr. Spanish by James Duffy. AnML

Those Not Elect. Léonie Adams. PoDB

Those parts of thee that the world's eye doth view. Sonnets, LXIX. Shakespeare. CBEP

Those pretty wrongs that liberty commits. Sonnets, XLI. Shakespeare. CBEP

Those souls that of His own good life partake. Eternal Life. Henry More. TRV

Those who fling off, toss head. Meeting Together of Poles & Latitudes: In Prospect. Margaret Avison. OBCV

Those who give ear to the heart of the night. Nocturne. Rubén Darío. AnSP

Those Who Love. Sara Teasdale. MoLP

Those who said God is praised. For the New Railway Station in Rome. Richard Wilbur. PoDB

Thou are not, Penshurst, built to envious show. See Thou art not, Penshurst . . .

Thou Art Coming to a King. John Newton. TRV

Thou Art Indeed Just, Lord. Gerard Manley Hopkins. CABA; ILP; PoDB; VaPo (Thou Art Indeed Just, Lord, If I Contend.) CaFP; EaLo; GTBS-P; VP

Thou art King of Israel and of Davides kunne. A Palm-Sunday Hymn. William Herebert. MeEL

Thou Art Mine, I Am Thine. Unknown, tr. fr. German by Elizabeth Closs. AnML

Thou art my Hiding Place. My Hiding Place. Kathryn T. Bowsher. STF

Thou Art Not Fair. Thomas Campion. EnRePo

Thou art [or are] not, Penshurst, built to envious show. To Penhurst. Ben Jonson. CABA; CABL; SeCP

Thou art so fair, and yong withall. Youth and Beauty. Aurelian Townsend. SeCP

Thou art the soul of a summer's day. A Song. Paul Laurence Dunbar. AmNP

Thou art the Way. I Am the Way. Alice Meynell. TRV

Thou art the wind and I the lyre. Wind and Lyre. Edwin Markham. TRV

"Thou art! Thou art!!" Lavater says. On Lavater's Song of a Christian to Christ. Goethe. TwGP

Thou barren waste; unprofitable strand. Winter in Lower Canada. Standish O'Grady. Fr. The Emigrant. OBCV

Thou Blind Man's Mark. Sir Philip Sidney. Sometimes considered Sonnet CIX of Astrophel and Stella; also in Certain Sonnets. CABA; EnRePo; ErPo; PoSa; VaPo

Thou blossom bright with autumn dew. To the Fringed Gentian. Bryant. AP; PoLF; StP

Thou, born to sip the lake or spring. On a Honey Bee. Philip Freneau. AP

Thou comest by. 10th Dance—Coming On as a Horn—20 February 1964. Jackson MacLow. CoPo

Thou comest, mush wept for: such a breeze. In Memoriam A. H. H., XVII. Tennyson. VP

Thou Didst Delight My Eyes. Robert Bridges. ELP

Thou didst, O mighty God, exist. Three Hymns, 1. Elizabeth Rowe. WaPE

Thou Didst Say Me. Miriam Waddington. OBCV

Thou enemy of love, how slow you creep. Dawn. Unknown. UnTE

Thou fair-haired angel of the evening. To the Evening Star [or Sonnet]. Blake. FaBV; FoBA; PoLF; PoPo; WiR

Thou gav'st me leave to kiss. Chop-Cherry. Robert Herrick. CBEP; UnTE

"Thou Ghost," I said, "and is thy name To-day?" The Morrow's Message. Dante Gabriel Rossetti. The House of Life, XXXVIII. VP

Thou happy, happy elf. A Parental Ode to My Song. Thomas Hood. PoLF

Thou hast been very tender to the moon. Malvolio. Walter Savage Landor. Par

Thou hast given so much to me. A Heart to Praise Thee. George Herbert. TRV

Thou hast made me; and shall thy work decay. Holy Sonnets, I. John Donne. EnRePo; MeP; SeCP

Thou Hast Made Us for Thyself. St. Augustine, tr. fr. Latin. TRV

Thou hearest the nightingale begin the song of spring. The Lark's Song [or A Vision of the Lamentation of Beulah over Ololon]. Blake. Fr. Milton, II. OBNC; WiR

Thou ill-formed offspring of my feeble brain. The Author to [or and] Her Book. Anne Bradstreet. AP; StP

Thou little bird, thou dweller by the sea. The Little Beach Bird. Richard Henry Dana. AmLP

Thou lovely and beloved, thou my love. Mid-Rapture. Dante Gabriel Rossetti. The House of Life, XXVI. VP

Thou mastering me. The Wreck of the Deutschland. Gerard Manley Hopkins. BoC; CABL; DiPo; OBNC; VP

Thou mighty gulf, insatiate cormorant. To Everlasting Oblivion. John Marston. Fr. The Scourge of Villainy. CBEP

Thou must be true thyself. Be True. Horatius Bonar. TRV

Thou perceivest the flowers put forth their precious odors. The Wild Thyme. Blake. Fr. Milton, II. WiR

Thou seest this world is but a thoroughfare. Eternal Reward, Eternal Pain. Sir Thomas More. Fr. The Twelve Weapons of Spiritual Battle. EnRePo

Thou shalt have one God only; who. The Latest Decalogue. Arthur Hugh Clough. CABA; CaFP; CBEP; GTBS-P; ILP; OBNC; PoIE; TRV; VaPo

Thou sorrow, venom elf[e]. Upon a Spider Catching a Fly. Edward Taylor. AP; CBEP

Thou still unravish'd bride of quietness. Ode on a Grecian Urn. Keats. BoC; CABA; CaFP; CBEP; DiPo; FaPL; FoBA; ILP; OBNC; OnP; PoIE; PoPo; PoSa; StP

Thou Sweetly-smelling Fresh Red Rose. Cielo d'Alcamo, tr. fr. Italian by Dante Gabriel Rossetti. AnML

Thou that in prayeres hes bene lent. Rise with the Lamb of Innocence. Unknown. MeEL

Thou to whom the world unknown. Ode to Fear. William Collins. EiCP; EnPE

Thou wast that all to me, love. To One in Paradise. Poe. AmLP; AP; PoIE; PoLF; PoPo

Thou wast not born for death, immortal Bird! Magic Casements. Keats. Fr. Ode to a Nightingale. FaBV

Thou wert the morning star among the living. Morning Star. Plato, tr. by Shelley. SiGo

Thou which art I, ('tis nothing to be soe). The Storm. John Donne. CABL

Thou who didst nurture mighty men of old. To Italy. Giovanni Guidiccioni. RBL

Thou Who Taught the Thronging People. Henry S. Minde. TRV

Thou, who wouldst wear the name. The Poet. Bryant. AP; PP

Thou, whom the former precepts have. Superliminare. George Herbert. MeP; SeCP

Thou whose birth on earth. Swinburne. Fr. Christmas Antiphones. TRV

Thou, whose sad heart, and weeping head lyes low. Easter-Day. Henry Vaughan. MeP

Thou, whose sweet youth and early hopes inhance. George Herbert. Fr. The Church-Porch. MeP

Thou, Whose Unmeasured Temple Stands. Bryant. TRV

Thou wilt keep him in perfect peace. Perfect Peace. Isaiah, Bible, O.T. TRV

Thou winst thy wealth by war. To the Roving Pirate. George Turberville. EnRePo

Thou wommon boute fere. The Devout Man Prays to His Relations. William Herebert. MeEL

Though. See also Tho'.

Though All the Fates Should Prove Unkind. Henry David Thoreau. AP

(Lines.) ILP

Though beauty be the mark of praise. An Elegy. Ben Jonson. EnRePo

Though brave your beauty be, and feature passing fair. The Lover Exhorteth His Lady to Take Time, While Time Is. George Turberville. EnRePo

Though buds still speak in hints. Field-Glasses. Andrew Young. CBEP

Though Christ a thousand times. In Thine Own Heart. "Angelus Silesius." TRV

Though clock/ To tell how night draws hence, I've none. His Grange, or Private Wealth. Robert Herrick. GoJo

Though earth and man were gone. Emily Brontë. Fr. Last Lines. TRV

Though grief and fondness in my breast rebel. London. Samuel Johnson. EiCP; EnPE

Though he believe it, no man is strong. Concluding Chorus. W. H. Auden. Fr. Paid on Both Sides. AnMoPo

Though He Slay Me. Vassar Miller. NePoEA-2

Though I Am Young. Ben Jonson. Fr. The Sad Shepherd, I, v. ELP

(Karolin's Song.) PoIE

(Love and Death.) CBEP

(Song: "Though I am young and cannot tell.") EnRePo; SeCP

("Though I am young and cannot tell.") ILP

Though I be foul, ugly, lean, and misshape. Death. Sir Thomas More. Fr. The Pageants of Thomas More. EnRePo

Though I be now a grey, grey friar. The Friar. Thomas Love Peacock. Fr. Maid Marian. SD

Though I be wooden Priapus (as thou see'st). Epigrams on Priapus. Unknown. ErPo

Though I have an admiration for your charming resignation. Not Tonight, Josephine. Colin Curzon. ErPo

Though I, like you, don't crowd the marketplaces. To Stephen George. Rainer Maria Rilke. TwGP

Though I speak with the tongues of men and of angels. Love. First Corinthians, Bible, N.T. TRV

Though I walk through the valley of the shadow of death. Psalm XXIII, Bible, O.T. BoC

Though leaves are many, the root is one. The Coming of Wisdom with Time. W. B. Yeats. DiPo

Though loath to grieve. Ode: Inscribed to W. H. Channing. Emerson. AP; ILP

Though love repine, and reason chafe. Emerson. Fr. Sacrifice. TRV

Though my soul may set in darkness, it will rise in perfect light. Sarah Williams. Fr. The Old Astronomer. TRV

Though no kin to those fine glistening. Christening-Day Wishes for My God-Child, Grace Lane Berkley II. Robert P. Tristram Coffin. BiCB

Though one with all that sense or soul can see. Transcendence. Richard Hovey. TRV

Though pain and care are everywhere. Vita Brevis. Unknown. UnTE

Though the Clerk of the Weather insist. Pebbles. Herman Melville. AP

Though the cover is worn. My Old Bible. Unknown. STF

Though the day be never so long. Evensong. George Tankervil. TRV

Though the evening comes with slow steps and has signalled for all songs to cease. The Bird. Rabindranath Tagore. Fr. The Gardener. PoPl; SiGo

Though the great waters sleep. Emily Dickinson. EaLo

Though the midnight found us weary. Sunrise. Margaret E. Sangster. TRV

Though the times be dark and dreary. Bide a Wee! John Oxenham. TRV

Though there are wild dogs. Orpheus and Eurydice. Geoffrey Hill. NePoEA-2; PoIE

Though there was nothing final then. The Parting. Elizabeth Jennings. NePoEA-2

Though three men dwell on Flannan Isle. Flannan Isle. W. W. Gibson. HaSV; SIV; WePo

Though Ye Suppose. John Skelton. CBEP

Though You Are Young. Thomas Campion. EnRePo
 (Youth and Age.) CBEP
Though you Diana-like have liv'd still chaste. Lutea Allison.
 Sir John Suckling. ErPo
Though you regret it. Out of Your Hands. Theodore Weiss.
 CoPo
Thought, A. A. A. Milne. ThGo
Thought, A. Margaret E. Sangster. TRV
Thought-Fox, The. Ted Hughes. NePoEA-2
Thought is deeper than all speech. Gnosis [or Enosis or Stanza
 from an Early Poem]. Christopher Pearse Cranch.
 AmLP; ILP; PoIE
Thought Suggested by the New Year, A. Thomas Campbell.
 See River of Life, The.
Thought went out of my mind today, A. Emily Dickinson. DiPo
Thoughtful little Willie Frazer. Science for the Young. Wal-
 lace Irwin. BBGG
Thoughts by Night. Goethe. See Night Thoughts.
Thoughts in a [Summer] Garden. Andrew Marvell. See
 Garden, The.
Thoughts of Thomas Hardy. Edmund Blunden. PoCh
Thoughts on the Length of Exile. Bertolt Brecht, tr. fr. Ger-
 man by Christopher Middleton. MGP
Thou's welcome, wean! mishanter fa' me. The Poet's Welcome
 to His Illegitimate Child. Burns. BoC
Thousand-and-First Ship, sel. F. Scott Fitzgerald.
 There'd Be an Orchestra. GoJo
Thousand and One Nights, The, sels. Unknown, tr. fr. Arabic
 by E. Powys Mathers.
 Haroun's Favorite Song. SiGo
 Inscription on a Chemise. ErPo
 Love. SiGo
 "My soul thy sacrifice! I choose thee out," tr. by Sir Richard
 Burton. ErPo
 (Poems of the Arabic.)
 Of Women. ErPo
 Power of Love, The. SiGo
Thousand Islands, The. Charles Sangster. Fr. The St. Law-
 rence and the Saguenay. OBCV
Thousand sounds, and each a joyful sound, A. Omnipresence.
 Edward Everett Hale. TRV
Thousand Things, The. Christopher Middleton. NePoEA-2
Thousand years now had his breed, A. E. J. Pratt. Fr. The
 Cachalot. OBCV
Thousandth Poem for Dylan Thomas, A. John Ciardi. ToPo
Thread of Life, The. Christina Rossetti. OBNC
Threading the dance was one who trod. Legend of Ramapo
 Mountain. Jennie M. Palen. FiSC
Threats of the Witness. Yves Bonnefoy, tr. fr. French by
 William Brown. CoFP
Thredbo River. Sydney Jephcott. PoAu-1
Three, The. Nikolaus Lenau, tr. fr. German by Gerd Gillhoff.
 AGP
Three around the Old Gentleman. John Berryman. AP
Three Bad Ones. Unknown. BBGG
Three Bushes, The. W. B. Yeats. DTC
Three Butchers, The. Unknown. BFSS
Three carrion crows in yonder tree. The Three Crows. Un-
 known. BFSS
Three children dancing around an orange tree. Coins and
 Coffins under My Bed. Diane Wakoski. CoPo
Three Cinquains. Zoe Kincaid Brockman. PoNC
Three counties blacken and vanish. L'Aurore Grelottante.
 Peter Levi. NePoEA-2
Three Crows, The, with music. Unknown. BFSS
Three Dreams. James Michie. NePoEA-2
Three Elements. Stephen Vincent Benét. Fr. John Brown's
 Body. EaLo
Three Fishers, The. Charles Kingsley. OnMSP; PoLF; SIV,
 with music
Three Foxes, The. A. A. Milne. GoJo
Three Fragments. William Collins. WaPE
 Lament for Tintoretta, III.
 Limitations of Human Art, II.
 Luckless Collins, I.
Three Gypsies, The. Nikolaus Lenau, tr. fr. German by Gerd
 Gillhoff. AGP
Three gypsies stood at the castle gate. The Raggle Taggle
 Gypsies. Unknown. CBEP
Three Haiku. Basho, tr. fr. Japanese. PoPo
 "O cricket, from your cheery cry."
 "Old battle field, fresh with Spring flowers again."
 "Old men, white-haired, beside the ancestral graves."
Three Helpers in Battle. Mary Elizabeth Coleridge. EaLo
Three Hermits, The. W. B. Yeats. PoDB
Three hours ago he blundered up the trench. A Working Party.
 Siegfried Sassoon. MMA
Three Huntsmen, The. Unknown. See Three Jovial Hunts-
 men.
Three Hymns. Elizabeth Rowe. WaPE
 On the Sacrament, II.
 "Thou didst, O mighty God, exist," I.
 "Ye pure inhabitants of light," III.
Three Hymns. Charles Wesley. WaPE

For One in Doubt, III.
 "Shepherd of souls, Thy sheep behold!" II.
 " 'Twas thus the subtle foe," I.
Three Jet Planes. May Swenson. PoPo
Three Jolly Frenchmen. Unknown. BSO
Three Jovial Gentlemen. Daniel Hoffman. MoBS
Three Jovial Huntsmen; or, The Owl and the Jay Bush, with
 music. Unknown. BFSS
 (Three Huntsmen, The, diff. vers.) OnMSP
Three Kings, The. OnMSP
Three Kings. James P. Vaughn. NNP
Three Kings Came. Thomas W. Shapcott. PoAu-2
Three Kings came riding from far away. The Three Kings.
 Longfellow. OnMSP
Three Kings stepped out of my body. Poem for Epiphany.
 Norman Nicholson. PoP1
Three kings went down to the soul of the sea. Three Kings.
 James P. Vaughn. NNP
Three Ladies of London, sel. Robert Wilson.
 Simplicity's Song. CTC
Three Landscapes, sel. Jerome Rothenberg.
 "Dark bull quartered in my eye, The." CoPo
Three Little Babes, The, with music. Unknown. BFSS
Three little houses. Rio Bo. "Aldo Palazzeschi." CoIP
Three Little Kittens. Unknown, at. to Eliza Cook. SoPo
Three Love Poems. Norman Cameron. GTBS-P
 From a Woman to a Greedy Lover, I.
 In the Queen's Room, II.
 Shepherdess, III.
Three lovely notes he whistled, too soft to be heard. The Un-
 known Bird. Edward Thomas. ACV; DTC
Three men coming down the winter hill, The. Winter Land-
 scape. John Berryman. AP; MP; PoP1
Three miles from town to town over the snow. E. J. Pratt.
 Fr. Brebeuf and His Brethren. ACV
Three Mirrors, The. Edwin Muir. PoIE
Three Monkeys ("Three monkeys once dining in a cocoanut
 tree"). Unknown. STF
Three Movements, The. Donald Hall. NePoEA-2
Three Nights of Mourning: John F. Kennedy. H. L. Mount-
 zoures. OPP
3/19—"just a day's march." Conquistador. Georgia Lee Mc-
 Elhaney. CoPo
Three old hermits took the air. The Three Hermits. W. B.
 Yeats. PoDB
Three Part Invention. Paul Blackburn. CoPo
Three Pigeons, The. Goldsmith. Fr. She Stoops to Conquer.
 ELP
Three Poems. Stephen Crane. AP
 "Chant you loud of punishments," II.
 "Man adrift on a slim spar, A," I.
 "Naked woman and a dead dwarf, A," III.
Three Prison Portraits, sel. Miriam Waddington.
 Drug Addict, The. ACV
Three Ravens, The. Unknown. CABA; CaFP; PoPo
Three riders after harsh defeat. The Three. Nikolaus Lenau.
 AGP
Three Rogues, The (B vers., with music). Unknown. BSO
 (There Was a Mighty King, A vers., with music.) BSO
Three Roundels of Love Unreturned. Chaucer. See Merciles
 Beaute.
Three seasons only in his calendar. Sonnet. George Henry
 Boker. Fr. Sonnets. AmLP
3 Sit-ins Agin. Jonathan Williams. PoNC
Three sortes of teares doe from myne eies distraine. Sonnet.
 William Alabaster. MeP
Three sorts of serpents do resemble thee. Idea, XXX. Michael
 Drayton. EnRePo
Three stars, five stars rise over the hill. Confucius. Fr. The
 Classic Anthology: Shao and the South. CTC
Three strange men came to the Inn. A Lady Comes to an Inn.
 Elizabeth J. Coatsworth. SIV
Three summers since I chose a maid. The Farmer's Bride.
 Charlotte Mew. ErPo
Three Sweethearts. Heine, tr. fr. German by Louis Unter-
 meyer. UnTE
Three Taverns, The, sel. E. A. Robinson.
 Out of Wisdom Has Come Love. MoRP
Three then came forward out of darkness, one. The Road.
 Conrad Aiken. AP
Three Things. W. B. Yeats. DTC
Three things have chained my heart in love. Tres Cosas.
 Baltasar de Alcázar. RBL
Three Things Jeame Lacks. Unknown. MeEL
Three things the Master hath to do. Pray—Give—Go. Annie
 Johnson Flint. STF
Three things there be that prosper all [or up] apace. The
 Wood, the Weed, the Wag [or To His Son]. Sir Walter
 Ralegh. CBEP; EnRePo; PoIE
Three thousand for my brand new car. A Dollar I Gave. Un-
 known. STF
Three times sitting down to bread. Daily Round. Lizette
 Woodworth Reese. Fr. After. ThGo
Three Travelers, The. Unknown. UnTE

Three weeks gone and the combatants gone. Vergissmeinnicht. Keith Douglas. GTBS-P
Three Women. Alan Dienstag. ErPo
Three women have slept with my books. Conon in Exile. Lawrence Durrell. ToPo
Three Woulds. *Unknown.* LV
Three Years She Grew [in Sun and Shower]. Wordsworth. CBEP; ILP; PoIE
(Education of Nature, The.) GTBS-P
(Lucy.) OBNC
Threes. Carl Sandburg. PoLF
Threnody: "Far away." Thomas Lovell Beddoes. StP
Threnody: "Let happy throats be mute." Donald Jeffrey Hayes. AmNP
Threnody: "Only quiet death." Waring Cuney. AmNP
Threnody: "South-wind brings, The." Emerson. AP; StP
Threnody, A: "What, what, what." George T. Lanigan. CBEP
Thrice, and above, blest (my soules halfe) art thou. A Country Life: To His Brother, M. Tho: Herrick. Robert Herrick. SeCP
Thrice happy maid; supremely blest. The Wedding Night. Johannes Secundus. *Fr.* Epithalamium. UnTE
Throb, throb from the mixer. The Pigeon. Richard Church. WePo
Throstle, The. Tennyson. PoPo; PoSC
Throttled on a String of Pearls. Johannes R. Becher, tr. fr. *German by* Christopher Middleton. *Fr.* Transfiguration. MGP
Through All the Employments of Life. John Gay. *Fr.* The Beggar's Opera, I, i. StP
Through all the frozen winter. Smells. Kathryn Worth. RePo
Through Alpine meadows soft suffused. Stanzas from the Grande Chartreuse. Matthew Arnold. VP
Through and through th' inspired leaves. The Book-Worms. Burns. LV
Through Death to Love. Dante Gabriel Rossetti. The House of Life, XLI. VP
Through every minute of this day. Prayer. John Oxenham. TRV
Through grass, through amber'd cornfields, our slow stream. Meadowsweet. William Allingham. OBNC
Through his iron glades. Winter the Huntsman. Sir Osbert Sitwell. WePo
Through painful God-search, he, the doubly striving. Shelley. Georg Herwegh. AGP
Through storms you reach them and from storms are free. The Enviable Isles. Herman Melville. AmLP
Through that pure Virgin-shrine. The Night. Henry Vaughan. MeP; VaPo
Through that window—all else being extinct. The Room. Conrad Aiken. AP; PoDB
Through the black, rushing smoke-bursts. The Song of the Muses. Matthew Arnold. WiR
Through the Blowing Leaves. Glenn Ward Dresbach. BoC
Through the bound cable strands, the arching path. Atlantis. Hart Crane. *Fr.* The Bridge. AmLP
Through the deep woods, at peep of day. The Canadian Herd-Boy. Susanna Moodie. OBCV
Through the Forest Have I Gone. Shakespeare. *Fr.* A Midsummer Night's Dream, II, ii. CTC
Through the forest the men walk all day long. The Boy and the Flute. Björnstjerne Björnson. PoPI
Through the grasses tall and slim. Snakes and Snails. Grace Taber Hallock. RePo
Through the hill by the Rite Nite Motel. A Water Glass of Whisky. X. J. Kennedy. CoPo
Through the House ("Through the house give glimmering light"). Shakespeare. *Fr.* A Midsummer Night's Dream, V, ii. CTC
Through the long winter. And Fall Shall Sit in Judgment. Audre Lorde. NNP
Through the Looking-Glass, sels. "Lewis Carroll."
Humpty Dumpty's Song, *fr. ch.* 6. GTBS-P; OnMSP
"I'll tell thee everything I can," *fr. ch.* 8. Par
Jabberwocky, *fr. ch.* 1. CABA; CaFP; CBEP; DiPo; FaBV; GoJo; LV; PoIE; PoPI; PoPo; VaPo
"To the Looking-Glass world it was Alice that said," *fr. ch.* 9. Par
Walrus and the Carpenter, The, *fr. ch.* 4. FaBV; SoPo
Through the night thy Angels kept. A Thank-You. William Canton. ThGo
Through the Parklands, through the Parklands. The Parklands. Stevie Smith. MoBS
Through the slits of my eyes a perambulator passes. The Sun. Hugo Ball. MGP
Through the starred Judean night. Mary Tired. Marjorie Pickthall. ACV
Through the straight pass of suffering. Emily Dickinson. MoRP
Through the street as I trot when the weather is hot. Midsummer Fantasy. Newman Levy. PoSC
Through the thick morning steam they took shape. A Papuan Shepherd. Francis Webb. *Fr.* A Drum for Ben Boyd. PoAu-2
Through the trees, with the moon underfoot. The Owl King [or The Call]. James Dickey. CoPo; NePoEA-2
Through the Waters. Annie Johnson Flint. STF
Through these green Parthenons. In the Redwood Forest. Ralph Pomeroy. CoPo
Through throats where many rivers meet, the curlews cry. In the White Giant's Thigh. Dylan Thomas. ToPo
Through waves of gold, the waves which were her hair. While His Lady Combs Her Hair. Giambattista Marino. RBL
Through what fierce incarnations, furled. The Beatific Vision. G. K. Chesterton. MoRP
Through winter streets to steer your course aright. Of the Implements for Walking the Streets, and Signs of the Weather. John Gay. *Fr.* Trivia. EiCP
Through winter-time we call on spring. The Wheel. W. B. Yeats. GTBS-P; PoPo
Throughout the World. Sir Thomas Wyatt. CBEP
Throw away Thy rod. Discipline. George Herbert. PoLF
Thrush in February, The. George Meredith. OBNC
Thrush of wind sang thru the air, A. Lyric. "Will Inman." PoNC
Thrushes. Ted Hughes. NePoEA-2; PoIE
Thrushes sing as the sun is going, The. Proud Songsters. Thomas Hardy. PoSa
Thrush's Nest, The. John Clare. GoJo; PoSa
Thrusting of It, The. Burns. *See* Duncan Gray.
Thu sikest sore. Christ's Tear Breaks My Heart. *Unknown.* MeEL
"Thumbs in the thumb-place." The Mitten Song. Marie Louise Allen. SoPo
Thunder Pools. Robert P. Tristram Coffin. LOW
Thunderer, The. Phyllis McGinley. EaLo
Thunderstorms. W. H. Davies. LV
Thunderstorms, scl. Lew Sarett.
Iron-Wind Dances. LV
Thus by himself compell'd to live each day. Peter Grimes. George Crabbe. *Fr.* The Borough. OBNC
Thus ends my Love, but this doth grieve me most. Loves End. Lord Herbert of Cherbury. SeCP
Thus Eve to Adam. Milton. *Fr.* Paradise Lost, IV. FaBV
Thus far, with rough and all-unable pen. Epilogue. Shakespeare. *Fr.* King Henry V. CTC
Thus have I back againe to thy bright name. An Apologie for the Precedent Hymnes on Teresa. Richard Crashaw. MeP
Thus Lovely Sleep. Richard Leigh. ELP
Thus piteously Love closed what he begat. Modern Love, L. George Meredith. CaFP; FaPL; GTBS-P; ILP; OBNC; PoIE; VP
Thus said the Lord in the Vault above the Cherubim. The Last Chantey. Kipling. HaSV
Thus should have been our travels. Over 2000 Illustrations and a Complete Concordance. Elizabeth Bishop. PoDB
Thus, some tall tree that long hath stood. On the Death of Benjamin Franklin. Philip Freneau. ThLM
Thus Spoke My Love. Pieter Corneliszoon Hooft, tr. fr. *Dutch by* A. J. Barnouw. SiGo
Thus, therefore, he who feels the fiery dart. The Nature of Love. Lucretius. *Fr.* De Rerum Natura. UnTE
Thus was this place/ A happy rural seat of various view. Eden. Milton. *Fr.* Paradise Lost, IV. DiPo
Thus would I have it. Exit. John Gould Fletcher. PoPo
Thy azure robe I did behold. Upon Julia's Petticoat. Robert Herrick. UnTE
Thy baby, too, the child that was to be. Sonnets, Part II, X. Frederick Goddard Tuckerman. AP
Thy Beauty Fades. Jones Very. AP
Thy Blood was shed for me. In My Place. Esther Archibald. STF
Thy braes were bonny, Yarrow stream. The Braes of Yarrow. John Logan. GTBS-P
Thy Brother's Blood. Jones Very. AP
Thy converse drew us with delight. In Memoriam A. H. H., CX. Tennyson. VP
Thy country, Wilberforce, with just disdain. Sonnet to William Wilberforce, Esq. William Cowper. ILP
Thy dawn, O Master of the world, thy dawn. James Elroy Flecker. *Fr.* Hassan. WePo
Thy filed words that from thy mouth did flow. Of Mistress D. S. Barnabe Googe. EnRePo
Thy Garden. Mu'tamid, King of Seville, tr. fr. *Arabic by* Dulcie L. Smith. SiGo
Thy glass will show thee how thy beauties wear. Sonnets, LXXVII. Shakespeare. EnRePo; FoBA
Thy grace, Dear Lord's my golden wrack, I finde. Meditation. 1 Cor. 3.22. Whether Paul or Apollos, or Cephas. Edward Taylor. *Fr.* Preparatory Meditations, First Series. MeP
Thy hue, dear pledge, is pure and bright. To a Lock of Hair. Sir Walter Scott. GTBS-P
Thy humane frame, my glorious Lord, I spy. Meditation Seven. Edward Taylor. *Fr.* Preparatory Meditations, First Series. VaPo

Thy husband to a banquet goes with me. The Possessive Lover. Ovid. *Fr. Amores.* UnTE
Thy kisses dost thou bid me count. To Lesbia. Catullus. UnTE
Thy leopard legs and python thighs. The Zoo of You. Arthur Freeman. ErPo
Thy mouth, whereof the worm was amorous. Memorial. Clark Ashton Smith. FiSC
Thy Nail-pierced Hands. Kathryn Bowsher. STF
Thy need is great. For the Earth God. *Unknown.* EaLo
Thy spirit ere our fatal loss. In Memoriam A. H. H., XLI. Tennyson. VP
Thy summer voice, Musketaquit. Two Rivers. Emerson. AmLP; AP
Thy sword within the scabbard keep. The Song of Momus to Mars. Dryden. *Fr. The Secular Masque.* CBEP
Thy trivial harp will never please. Merlin. Emerson. AP
Thy victory is in the heart. Victoria. Henry van Dyke. TRV
Thy voice is on the rolling air. In Memoriam A. H. H., CXXX. Tennyson. DiPo; FaPL; TRV; VP
Thy Way, Not Mine. Horatius Bonar. TRV
Thy Will Be Done. Annie Johnson Flint. STF
Thy Will Be Done. Albert Simpson Reitz. STF
Thy wisdom and Thy might appear. The Burning Bush. Henry van Dyke. TRV
Thyrsis. Matthew Arnold. ILP; OBNC; StP; VP
Tibur is beautiful, too, and the orchard slopes, and the Anio. So Not Seeing I Sung. Arthur Hugh Clough. *Fr. Amours de Voyage.* GTBS-P; OBNC
Tickle Rhyme, The. Ian Serraillier. SoPo
Tide, The. Longfellow. *See* Tide Rises, the Tide Falls, The.
Tide be runnin' the great world over. Sea Love. Charlotte Mew. BoLP; HaSV; LV
Tide of Faith, The. "George Eliot." *Fr. A Minor Prophet.* TRV
Tide Rises, the Tide Falls, The. Longfellow. AmLP; AP; CBEP
  (Tide, The.) WiR
Tide Will Win, The. Priscilla Leonard. TRV
Tides of Love, The. T. A. Daly. PoPl
Tie the moccasin, bind the pack. Young Washington. Arthur Guiterman. PoSC
Ties. Raymond Souster. OBCV
Tiffany, Tiffany. Captain Kelly Lets His Daughter Go to Be a Nun. Thomas Butler Feeney. PoPl
Tiger, The. Blake. *Fr. Songs of Experience.* BoC; CBEP; EnPE; PoLF; PoPl; PoPo; PoSa; RoGo; StP; TRV; VaPo; WePo
  (Tyger, The.) CABA; CaFP; DiPo; EaLo; FaBV; FoBA; ILP; OBNC; OnP; PoIE
Tiger and the *Lion,* The. *Unknown. See* Bold Dighton.
Tiger-Cat Tim. Edith Newlin Chase. SoPo
Tiger Christ unsheathed his sword. For the One Who Would Take Man's Life in His Hands. Delmore Schwartz. ThLM
Tiger Lily. David McCord. GoJo
Tiger of Desire, The. Tom MacInnes. OBCV
Till now the doubtful dusk reveal'd. Tennyson. *Fr.* In Memoriam A. H. H., XCV. GTBS-P
Tilly. James Joyce. PoIE
Tim, an Irish Terrier. W. M. Letts. BoC
Tim Turpin. Thomas Hood. WiR
Timber, The. Henry Vaughan. SeCP
Timbers heaving to heaven we sailed at seven. Crabbing. Norman Levine. OBCV
Time. Ralph Hodgson. GTBS-P
Time. Sir Thomas More. *Fr.* The Pageants of Thomas More. EnRePo
Time. Shelley. Par; PoLF
Time and Eternity. Bunyan. WiR
Time and Love. Shakespeare. *See* Sonnets, LXIV *and* LXV.
Time and the World, whose magnitude and weight. Epitaph. Robert Southey. OBNC
Time Comes for Those Ascending to Descend. Enzo, King of Sardinia, *tr. fr. Italian by* Daniel J. Donno. AnML
Time Does Not Bring Relief. Edna St. Vincent Millay. FaBV
Time draws near the birth of Christ, The. In Memoriam A. H. H., XXVIII. Tennyson. FoBA; VP
Time draws near the birth of Christ, The. In Memoriam A. H. H., CIV. Tennyson. FoBA; VP
Time drops in decay. The Moods. W. B. Yeats. CTC
Time flies, hope flags, life plies a wearied wing. Monna Innominata, X. Christina Rossetti. VP
Time goes, you say? Ah, no! The Paradox of Time. Pierre de Ronsard. RBL
Time has been that these wild solitudes, The. A Winter Piece. Bryant. AP
Time has come for a wench to wed, The. Ballad of the Double Bed. Eve Merriam. UnTE
Time in the Rock, *sel.* Conrad Aiken.
  Poem: "And this digester, this digester of food." VaPo

Time is, The. Anger. Robert Creeley. CoPo
Time is after dinner, The. The Boarder. Louis Simpson. PoPl
Time is of the essence. This is a highly skilled. Polo Grounds. Rolfe Humphries. SD
Time Is Such That Each Brute Beast, The. Ausiàs March, *tr. fr. Catalan by* William M. Davis. AnML
Time is swiftly rolling on, The. Hick's Farewell. *Unknown.* BFSS
Time I've Lost in Wooing, The. Thomas Moore. BoLP
Time of the Barmacides, The. James Clarence Mangan. RoGo
Time of the Singing of Birds, The. The Song of Solomon, Bible, *O.T. See* Winter Is Past, The.
Time Passing, Beloved ("Time passing, and the memories of love"). Donald Davie. NePoEA-2
Time present and time past. Burnt Norton. T. S. Eliot. *Fr.* Four Quartets. CABL
Time rolls his ceaseless course. The Gathering. Sir Walter Scott. *Fr.* The Lady of the Lake. OBNC
Time smiling on this sundial of a world. Winter in Dumbarton. Robert Lowell. ToPo
Time that is moved by little fidget wheels. Five Bells. Kenneth Slessor. PoAu-2
Time to Choose a Lover. Horace, *tr. fr. Latin by* Patrick Branwell Brontë. Odes, I, 23. UnTE
Time to Get Up. Robert Louis Stevenson. ThGo
Time was away and somewhere else. Meeting Point. Louis MacNeice. WePo
Time was, ere Love play'd tricks with me. The Bachelor's Complaint. Luis de Góngora. RBL
Time was when his half million drew. Bewick Finzer. E. A. Robinson. AP
Time, which does all creatures kill. Epitaph: Time, Which Does All Creatures. François Maynard. RBL
Time you won your town the race, The. To an Athlete Dying Young. A. E. Housman. A Shropshire Lad, XIX. CABA; CaFP; ILP; OnP; PoIE; PoPl; PoPo; PoSa; SD; VaPo; VP
Timely blossom, infant fair. To [Miss] Charlotte Pulteney [in Her Mother's Arms]. Ambrose Philips. ELP; GTBS-P
Timepiece, A. James Merrill. NePoEA-2
Time's Revenges. Robert Browning. VP
Timid child with heart oppressed, A. Buffalo Creek. J. Le Gay Brereton. PoAu-1
Timothy Boon. Ivy O. Eastwick. SoPo
Timothy Tiggs and Tomothy Toggs. Some Fishy Nonsense. Laura E. Richards. SoPo
Timothy Tim was a very small cat. Tiger-Cat Tim. Edith Newlin Chase. SoPo
Timothy Winters. Charles Causley. BoC
Tindari, I know you mild. Wind at Tindari. Salvatore Quasimodo. CoIP
Tintern Abbey. Wordsworth. *See* Lines Composed a Few Miles above Tintern Abbey.
Tiny fleece of my own flesh. Close to Me. "Gabriela Mistral." PoPl
Tiny spill of bird-things in a swirl, A. The Finches. Thomas W. Shapcott. PoAu-2
"Tiraha, Te Ra!" The Noosing of the Sun-God. Jessie Mackay. ACV
Tir'd with all these, for restful death I cry. *See* Tired with all these . . .
Tired. Fenton Johnson. PoLF
Tired air groans as the heavies swing over, the river-hollows boom, The. The Thiepval Wood. Edmund Blunden. MMA
Tired Nature's sweet restorer, balmy Sleep. Edward Young. *Fr.* The Complaint. EnPE
Tired Tim. Walter de la Mare. SoPo
Tired [*or* Tir'd] with all these, for restful death I cry. Sonnets, LXVI. Shakespeare. CBEP; CTC; GTBS-P; PoIE
Tired with dull grief, grown old before my day. 1916 Seen from 1921. Edmund Blunden. MMA
'Tis a lesson you should heed. Try Again. *At. to* William Edward Hickson. RePo
'Tis a new life;—thoughts move not as they did. The New Birth. Jones Very. AP
'Tis a soft rogue, this Lycias. Lycias. Earl of Rochester. ErPo
'Tis a world of silences. I gave a cry. Silences. Arthur O'Shaughnessy. OBNC
'Tis better to be vile than vile esteemed. Sonnets, CXXI. Shakespeare. CBEP
'Tis but a Wanton Trick. *Unknown.* UnTE
'Tis Christmas weather, and a country house. Modern Love, XXIII. George Meredith. VP
'Tis dead night round about: Horrour doth creepe. The Lampe. Henry Vaughan. MeP
'Tis done:—I tow'r to that degree. On Taking a Bachelor's Degree. Christopher Smart. VaPo
'Tis fine to play. A Boy's Summer Song. Paul Laurence Dunbar. RePo
'Tis fine to see the Old World, and travel up an down. America for Me. Henry van Dyke. RePo

'Tis hard to find in life. True Friendship. *Unknown. Fr.* The Panchatantra. SiGo
'Tis hard to say, if greater want of skill. An Essay on Criticism. Pope. CABA; PP
'T is held that sorrow makes us wise. In Memoriam A. H. H., CXIII. Tennyson. VP
'Tis known, at least it should be, that throughout. Beppo. Byron. CABL
'Tis Midnight. *Unknown.* LV
'Tis midnight—and on Olive's brow. Gethsemane. W. B. Tappan. STF
'Tis midnight, and the setting sun. 'Tis Midnight. *Unknown.* LV
'Tis morning; and the sun, with ruddy orb. The Winter Morning Walk. William Cowper. *Fr.* The Task. EiCP
'Tis mute, the word they went to hear on high Dodona mountain. The Oracles. A. E. Housman. RoGo
'Tis not how witty nor how free. Kind and True. Aurelian Townsend. CBEP
'Tis not that dying hurts us so. Emily Dickinson. DiPo
'Tis not that I am weary grown. Upon Leaving His Mistress. Earl of Rochester. UnTE
'Tis now cleare day: I see a rose. The Search. Henry Vaughan. MeP; SeCP
'Tis now since I sate down before. The Siege. Sir John Suckling. SeCP
'Tis of a brisk young farmer, in Derbyshire did dwell. The Frolicsome Farmer. *Unknown.* UnTE
'Tis of a rich old merchant. Jack Monroe. *Unknown.* BSO
'Tis of a wild Colonial boy, Jack Doolan was his name. The Wild Colonial Boy. *Unknown.* PoAu-1
'Tis so old and ugly, and yet so convenient. On Gaulstown House. Swift. CBEP
'Tis solemn darkness; the sublime of shade. Night. Charles Heavysege. OBCV
'Tis spring; come out to ramble. The Lent Lily. A. E. Housman. A Shropshire Lad, XXIX. PoSC
'Tis strange, the miser should his cares employ. Of the Use of Riches. Pope. *Fr.* Moral Essays. CABL
'Tis strange to me, who long have seen no face. From Country to Town. Hartley Coleridge. CBEP
'Tis sweet to view, from half-past five to six. The Theatre. James Smith. Par
'Tis the Arabian bird alone. The Chaste Arabian Bird. Earl of Rochester. ErPo
'Tis the Last Rose of Summer. Thomas Moore. ELP; PoPl
'Tis the voice of the Lobster; I heard him declare. The Voice of the Lobster. "Lewis Carroll." *Fr.* Alice's Adventures in Wonderland. EvOK; Par
'T is the voice of the sluggard, I heard him complain. The Sluggard. Isaac Watts. Par; ThGo
'Tis the White Plum Tree. John Shaw Neilson. PoAu-1
'Tis the year's midnight and it is the day's. A Nocturnal [or Nocturnall] upon Saint Lucy's [or S. Lucies] Day. John Donne. CBEP; EnRePo; FoBA; MeP; SeCP
'Tis these that free the small entangled fly. Shakespeare: The Fairies' Advocate. Thomas Hood. *Fr.* The Plea of the Midsummer Fairies. OBNC
'T is time this heart should be unmoved. On This Day I Complete My Thirty-sixth Year. Byron. CABA; ILP
Tis to yourself I speak; you cannot know. Yourself. Jones Very. AmLP
'Tis true, 'tis day; what though it be? Break [or Breake] of Day. John Donne. CABA; EnRePo; ErPo
'T is well; 't is something; we may stand. In Memoriam A. H. H., XVIII. Tennyson. VP
'Tis you that are the music, not your song. Listening. Amy Lowell. PoPo
Titan! to whose immortal eyes. Prometheus. Byron. VaPo
Tithonus. Tennyson. CABA; CABL; CBEP; DiPo; FoBA; ILP; OBNC; VP
Title divine—is mine! Emily Dickinson. AP
Titurel, *sel.* Wolfram von Eschenbach, *tr. fr. German by* Charles E. Passage.
  I Have These Many Evenings Watched for My Beloved. AnML
Titus and Berenice. John Heath-Stubbs. GTBS-P
To ——: "Music, when soft voices die." Shelley. *See* Music, When Soft Voices Die.
To ——: "One word is too often profaned." Shelley. ELP; FaBV; ILP; OBNC; PoLF
  ("One word is too often profaned.") CBEP; GTBS-P
To ——: "When I loved you, I can't but allow." Thomas Moore. BoLP
To ——: With the Following Poem. Tennyson. *Fr.* The Palace of Art. VP
To a Bird after a Storm. Henry Vaughan. *See* Bird, The.
To a Blue Flower. John Shaw Neilson. PoAu-1
To a Candle. Walter de la Mare. ELP
To a Cat. Keats. BoC
  (To Mrs. Reynolds's Cat.) DiPo
To a Chameleon. Marianne Moore. PoPl
To a Child. S. S. Gardons. NePoEA-2

To a Child. Christopher Morley. BiCB
To a Child of Quality Five Years Old. Matthew Prior. VaPo
  (To a Child of Quality, Five Years Old, the Author [Then] Forty.) CBEP; EiCP
To a Child with Eyes. Mark Van Doren. LOW
To a Distant Friend. Wordsworth. *See* Why Art Thou Silent!
To a Dog Injured in the Street. William Carlos Williams. PP
To a Dutch Landscape. Nikolaus Lenau, *tr. fr. German by* Roger C. Norton. AGP
To a Fat Lady Seen from the Train. Frances Cornford. GoJo; WePo
To a Field Mouse. Burns. *See* To a Mouse.
To a Fish. Leigh Hunt. *See* Fish, the Man, and the Spirit, The.
To a Fountain. Pierre de Ronsard, *tr. fr. French by* R. N. Currey. RBL
To a Friend. Matthew Arnold. VP
To a Friend. Hartley Coleridge. CBEP; PoLF
  (Sonnet: To a Friend.) OBNC
To a Friend. Amy Lowell. PoLF
To a Friend, on Her Examination for the Doctorate in English. J. V. Cunningham. EiCP
To a Friend Whose Work Has Come to Nothing. W. B. Yeats. AnMoPo; BoC; DiPo; FoBA
To a Gentleman in Love with a Negro Woman. Sneyd Davies. WaPE
To a Girl. Horace, *tr. fr. Latin by* Milton. Odes, I, 5. WiR
To a Girl. Edmund Waller. *See* To a Very Young Lady.
To a Gnat. *Unknown, tr. fr. Greek by* Louis Untermeyer. UnTE
To a Golden-haired Girl in a Louisiana Town. Vachel Lindsay. MoLP
To a Highland Girl. Wordsworth. CABL
  (To the Highland Girl of Inversneyde.) GTBS-P
To a History Professor. *Unknown, tr. fr. Greek by* Louis Untermeyer. UnTE
To A. L.; Perswasions to Love. Thomas Carew. SeCP
To a Lady Who Did Sing Excellently. Lord Herbert of Cherbury. SeCP
To a Lady Who Sent Me a Copy of Verses at My Going to Bed. Henry King. PP
To a Lady with a Guitar. Shelley. GTBS-P
To a Linnet in a Cage. Francis Ledwidge. RoGo
To a Little Sister, Aged Ten. Alison Elizabeth Cummings. BiCB
To a Lock of Hair. Sir Walter Scott. GTBS-P
To a Locomotive in Winter. Walt Whitman. AmLP; AP; DiPo; FaBV; ILP; StP
To a lodge that stood. Wordsworth. *Fr.* Vaudracour and Julia. EvOK
To a Louse [on Seeing One on a Lady's Bonnet at Church]. Burns. ILP; OnP; PoPo
To a Mountain Daisy. Burns. PoPo
To a Mouse. Burns. DiPo; EiCP; ILP; PoIE; PoLF
  (To a Field Mouse.) CBEP; GTBS-P
To a New York trader I did belong. The New York Trader. *Unknown.* BSNS
To a Nose. Francisco de Quevedo y Villegas, *tr. fr. Spanish.* AnSP, *tr. by* James Edward Tobin; RBL, *tr. by* Jean Willard Burnham
To a Persistent Phantom. Frank Horne. AmNP
To a Photographer. Berton Braley. LV
To a Poet, Who Would Have Me Praise Certain Bad Poets, Imitators of His and Mine. W. B. Yeats. CTC
To a Post-Office Inkwell. Christopher Morley. PoLF
To a School-Girl. John Shaw Neilson. PoAu-1
To a Seamew, *sel.* Swinburne.
  "When I had wings, my brother." HaSV
To a Severe Nun. Thomas Merton. CoPo
To a shore where ancient brooding woods. The Island. Giuseppe Ungaretti. CoIP
To a Short Day and a Great Ring of Shadow. Dante, *tr. fr. Italian by* Sonia Raiziss *and* Alfredo de Palchi. AnML
To a Skylark. Shelley. DiPo; FaBV; GTBS-P; OBNC; OnP; PoIE; PoLF; RoGo; VaPo
To a Snowflake. Francis Thompson. FaBV; PoPl
To a Solitary Disciple. William Carlos Williams. PP
To a Steam Roller. Marianne Moore. PP
To a "Tenting" Boy. Charles Tennyson-Turner. OBNC
To a Thesaurus. Franklin P. Adams. PoPl
To a Very Young Lady. Edmund Waller. SeCP
  (To a Girl.) WiR
  (To the Younger Lady Lucy Sydney.) CBEP
To a Wanton. William Habington. SeCP
To a Waterfowl. Bryant. AmLP; AP; CBEP; DiPo; FaPL; LV; PoLF; PoPo; TRV
To a Western Bard Still a Whoop and a Holler Away from English Poetry. William Meredith. PP
To a woman that I knew. Her Eyes. John Crowe Ransom. PoPl
To a Young Lady. William Cowper. GTBS-P
To a Young Lady. Richard Savage. CBEP

To a Young Lady on Her Leaving [the] Town after the Coronation. Pope. *See* Epistle to Miss Blount.
To a Young Lady That Told Me My Fortune in the Cards. Thomas Catesby Paget. WaPE
To a Young Lady, Who Asked Me to Write Something Original for Her Album. Thomas Campbell. StP
To a Young Wretch. Robert Frost. PoDB
To Age. Walter Savage Landor. FaPL
To Ailsa Rock. Keats. HaSV; OBNC
To Alexander Neville. Barnabe Googe. EnRePo
To All My Dainty Loves, Goodbye. Adam de la Halle, *tr. fr. French by* Irma Brandeis. AnML
To all the spirits of Love that wander by. Supreme Surrender. Dante Gabriel Rossetti. The House of Life, VII. VP
To All You Ladies Now at Land. Charles Sackville. HaSV
To Althea, from Prison. Richard Lovelace. CABA; CBEP; FaPL; GTBS-P; ILP; LV; PoIE; PoPo; PoSa; SeCP
To Amarantha [That She Would Dishevell Her Haire]. Richard Lovelace. SeCP; UnTE
To Amoret [Gone from Him]. Henry Vaughan. CBEP; SeCP
To an Athlete Dying Young. A. E. Housman. A Shropshire Lad, XIX. CABA; CaFP; ILP; OnP; PoIE; PoPl; PoPo; PoSa; SD; VaPo; VP
To an Early Primrose. Henry Kirke White. OBNC
To an Isle in the Water. W. B. Yeats. ThGo
To an Oak Tree. Sir Walter Scott. *Fr.* Waverley. OBNC
To an Old Gentlewoman Who Painted Her Face. George Turberville. EnRePo
To an Old Lady. William Empson. AnMoPo; GTBS-P; ToPo
To an Old Philosopher in Rome. Wallace Stevens. AP
To an open house in the evening. Home at Last. G. K. Chesterton. TRV
To an Unborn Pauper Child. Thomas Hardy. AnMoPo; GTBS-P
To Anthea Lying in Bed. Robert Herrick. SeCP
To Anthea, Who May Command Him Anything. Robert Herrick. BoC; CBEP; GTBS-P; SeCP
To Any Daddy. *Unknown.* STF
To Apollo Making Love. Thomas Tickell. WaPE
To Archimedes said a youth who desired knowledge. Archimedes and the Student. Schiller. TwGP
To assassinate the Chase Manhattan Bank. The Plot to Assassinate the Chase Manhattan Bank. Carl Larsen. PtTo
To Aurora. Earl of Sterling. Aurora, Sonnet XXXIII. GTBS-P
To Autumn. Blake. FoBA; WiR
To Autumn. Keats. BoC; CaFP; DiPo; FoBA; ILP; OBNC; OnP; PoIE; PoLF; PoPo; PoSa; RoGo; StP; VaPo; WePo
(Ode to Autumn.) CABA; CBEP; FaBV; GTBS-P
To Be a Farmer's Boy, *with music. Unknown.* BFSS
To Be a sweetness more desired than Spring. True Woman: Herself. Dante Gabriel Rossetti. The House of Life, LVI. VP
To be alive in such an age! To-Day. Angela Morgan. TRV
To Be Honest, to Be Kind. Robert Louis Stevenson. *Fr.* A Christmas Sermon. PoLF
To Be, or Not to Be. Shakespeare. *Fr.* Hamlet, III, i. DiPo
("To be, or not to be: that is the question.") PoPl; PoSa
To Be or Not to Be. *Unknown.* WePo
To be redeemed the worlds Redeemer brought. The Presentation. Robert Southwell. MeP
To Be Sung. Peter Viereck. FaBV
To be unloved brings sweet relief. Lovers. Mary Fullerton. PoAu-1
To Be with the Dead. Manuel González Prada, *tr. fr. Spanish by* Kate Flores. AnSP
To Bed, to Bed. Beaumont *and* Fletcher. *Fr.* The Maid's Tragedy. UnTE
To begin with she wouldn't have fallen in. Our Silly Little Sister. Dorothy Aldis. EvOK
To Bill Heikkila, American. Irene Paull. PtTo
To Blossoms. Robert Herrick. GTBS-P; SeCP
To Brooklyn Bridge. Hart Crane. *Fr.* The Bridge. AP; CABA; DiPo; ILP; PoDB; PoIE; PoPl; PoPo
To burn is surely bad, to be. House of Fire. Theodore Weiss. CoPo
To buy, or not to buy; that is the question. Investor's Soliloquy. Kenneth Ward. LV
To Castara: Upon Beautie. William Habington. *Fr.* Castara, II. SeCP
To Catherine Wordsworth 1808-1812. Wordsworth. *See* Surprised by Joy.
To Celia ("Come, my Celia, let us prove"). Ben Jonson. *See* Come, My Celia.
To Celia ("Drink to me only with thine eyes"). Ben Jonson. CBEP; FaBV; GTBS-P; LV; PoIE; PoLF; PoPo
(Song: To Celia.) CABA; DiPo; ELP; EnRePo; ILP; PoPl; PoSa; SeCP
To Celia ("Kiss me, sweet: the wary lover"). Ben Jonson. *See* Kiss Me, Sweet.

To Celia ("When, Celia, I intend to flatter you"). *Unknown.* CBEP
To Charlotte Pulteney. Ambrose Philips. GTBS-P
(To Miss Charlotte Pulteney in Her Mother's Arms.) ELP
To Charlotte von Stein. Goethe, *tr. fr. German by* Walter Kaufmann. TwGP
To Chloe. Earnest Albert Hooton. UnTE
To Chloe. *Unknown, tr. fr. Greek by* Louis Untermeyer. UnTE
To Christ. John Donne. *See* Hymn to God the Father, A.
To Christ Crucified. Miguel de Guevara, *tr. fr. Spanish.* AnSP, *tr. by* Iain Fletcher; RBL, *tr. by* Mildred E. Johnson
To Christ Our Lord. Galway Kinnell. MP
To Christopher North. Tennyson. EvOK
To Cino da Pistoia. Onesto da Bologna, *tr. fr. Italian by* Maurice Valency. AnML
To Clarissa Scott Delany. Angelina W. Grimké. AmNP
To Clio. John Dyer. WaPE
To Cloe Weeping. Matthew Prior. EiCP
To Cole, the Painter, Departing for Europe. Bryant. AP
To Coleridge. Shelley. CBEP
To Coleridge in Sicily. Wordsworth. *Fr.* The Prelude. OBNC
To Come Out Singing. Jon Silkin. PoDB
To Corinna. Théophile de Viau, *tr. fr. French by* William Frederic Giese. RBL
To Corinthus came, from Athens hailing. The Bride of Corinth. Goethe. AGP
To Cupid. Sir John Suckling. *See* Sonnet II: "Of thee (kind boy) I ask no red and white."
To Cyriack Skinner ("Cyriack, whose grandsire, on the royal bench"). Milton. GTBS-P
To Cyriack Skinner, upon His Blindness ("Cyriack, this three years' day"). Milton. PoIE
To Mr. Cyriac[k] Skinner [upon His Blindness].) DiPo; FoBA
To Daffodils [*or* Daffadills]. Robert Herrick. CBEP; ELP; EvOK; GoJo; GTBS-P; OnP; PoIE; PoPo; SeCP; WePo
To Daisies, Not to Shut So Soon. Robert Herrick. ELP
To Deck a Woman, *sel.* Ralph Hodgson.
And Every Sky Was Blue and Rain, II. LOW
To Delia, *sels.* Samuel Daniel.
"Beauty, sweet love, is like the morning dew," XLVII. EnRePo
"Care-charmer Sleep, son of the sable Night," LI. CaFP; CBEP; EnRePo; GTBS-P; PoIE; VaPo
"Fair is my love, and cruel as she's fair," VI. EnRePo
"My cares draw on mine everlasting night," XXX (1592 ed.). PoIE
"Read in my face a volume of despairs," XLIV. EnRePo
"When winter snows upon thy sable hairs," XXXIX. CTC; EnRePo
To Destiny. *Unknown, tr. fr. Dahomean song by* Frances Herskovits. EaLo
To Dianeme. Robert Herrick. CBEP; GTBS-P; PoPo
To Dick, on His Sixth Birthday. Sara Teasdale. BiCB
To die be given us, or attain! Resignation. Matthew Arnold. VP
To die like thirsting larks. Dying. Giuseppe Ungaretti. CoIP
To dive for the nimbus on the sea-floor. Nimbus. Douglas Le Pan. OBCV
To Doctor Bale. Barnabe Googe. EnRePo
To Dr. Delany, *sel.* Swift.
"How oft am I for rhyme to seek?" PP
To Doctor Empirick. Ben Jonson. SeCP
To Don Juan de Austria. Fernando de Herrera, *tr. fr. Spanish by* Edward Churton. RBL
To draw no envy, Shakespeare, on thy name. To the Memory of My Beloved Master [*or* the Author, Mr.] William Shakespeare and What He Hath Left Us. Ben Jonson. CABA; EnRePo; ILP; PoIE; PP; SeCP
To drift with every passion till my soul. Hélas. Oscar Wilde. UnTE
To drive Paul out of any lumber camp. Paul's Wife. Robert Frost. CABL
To drum-beat and heart-beat. Nathan Hale. Francis Miles Finch. ThLM
To Earthward. Robert Frost. AP; CABA; PoIE
To Elsie. William Carlos Williams. AP; CABA
To employ her. Europe. John Ashbery. CoPo
To Evening. William Collins. *See* Ode to Evening.
To Everlasting Oblivion. John Marston. *Fr.* The Scourge of Villainy. CBEP
To every class we have a school assign'd. Schools. George Crabbe. *Fr.* The Borough. CTC
To every man. The Treehouse. James A. Emanuel. AmNP; NNP
To every man there openeth. The Ways. John Oxenham. PoLF; TRV
To every thing there is a season, and a time. Ecclesiastes, Bible, *O.T.* PoPl

To fair Fidele's grassy tomb. A Song from Shakespeare's "Cymbeline" [*or* Dirge in "Cymbeline"]. William Collins. EiCP; ELP

To Fanny. Keats. UnTE

To fight aloud, is very brave. Emily Dickinson. AP; DiPo

To fish for pearls in Lethe. The Great Magicians. C. Day Lewis. EaLo

To fix her—'twere a task as vain. Song. Tobias George Smollett. WaPE

To fling my arms wide. Dream Variation[s]. Langston Hughes. AmNP; PoP1

To Ford, Guggenheim, Rockefeller, etc. O. B. Hardison, Jr. PoNC

To free me from domestic strife. On Susan Pattison. *Unknown.* CBEP

To Giulia Grisi. Nathaniel Parker Willis. AmLP

To God. Robert Herrick. TRV

To God's anointed and his chosen flock. "Christo et Ecclesiae" 1700. Oliver Wendell Holmes. *Fr.* Two Sonnets: Harvard. AP

To Goethe. Nietzsche, *tr. fr. German by* Walter Kaufmann. TwGP

To Guglielmo Gonzaga, Duca di Mantova. Tasso, *tr. fr. Italian by* Ida Fasel. RBL

To Guido Cavalcanti. Dante, *tr. fr. Italian by* Daniel J. Donno. AnML

To Guido Guinizelli: Now That You Have Changed the Manner. Bonagiunta Orbicciani, *tr. fr. Italian by* Maurice Valency. AnML

To Have and Too Old. Richard Armour. LV

To have known him, to have loved him. Monody. Herman Melville. AP; PoIE

To have liv'd eminent in a degree. Upon the Death of My Ever Desired Friend Doctor Donne Dean of Pauls. Henry King. SeCP

To have stepped lightly among European marbles. Hark Back. Richard Eberhart. ToPo

To hear an Oriole sing. Emily Dickinson. AP

To Heaven. Ben Jonson. EnRePo; PoIE; SeCP

To Helen. Poe. AP; BoLP; CABA; CaFP; CBEP; FaBV; FaPL; ILP; OnP; PoIE; PoLF; PoPo; StP; VaPo

To Henry Vaughan. A. J. M. Smith. OBCV

To Her Body, against Time. Robert Kelly. CoPo

To Her Far Away. Nikolaus Lenau, *tr. fr. German by* Alexander Gode. AGP

To Her for a Kiss. August Adolf von Haugwitz, *tr. fr. German by* George C. Schoolfield. AGP

To Her Grace the Duchess of Ferrara. Tasso, *tr. fr. Italian by* Harold M. Priest. RBL

To her who first unmade a poet and gave. Offering. Thomas MacDonagh. ACV

To Him Be Glory. Romans, XII: 33-36, Bible, *N.T.* TRV

To Him That Was Crucified. Walt Whitman. MoRP

To Him Who Ever Thought with Love of Me. Gerard Manley Hopkins. PoIE
(Christ Speaks.) BoC

To him who in an hour must die. Two Poems to Miss Lucy Fortescue. George Lyttelton. WaPE

To him who in the love of Nature holds. Thanatopsis. Bryant. AmLP; AP; DiPo; FaPL; LV

To Himself. Paul Fleming, *tr. fr. German by* George C. Schoolfield. AGP

To His Coy Love. Michael Drayton. ErPo
(I Pray Thee Leave.) ELP

To His Coy Mistress. Andrew Marvell. CABA; CaFP; CBEP; DiPo; ELP; ErPo; FaBV; ILP; MeP; OnP; PoIE; PoLF; PoP1; PoSa; SeCP; StP; UnTE; VaPo

To His Ever-worshipped Will from W. H. "Francis." ErPo

To His Forsaken Mistress. *At.* Sir Robert Ayton. ErPo

To His Friend. George Turberville. CTC

To His Friend ——. Henry Vaughan. PP

To His Friend in Elysium. Joachim du Bellay, *tr. fr. French by* Andrew Lang. RBL

To His Girl. Martial, *tr. fr. Latin by* Louis Untermeyer. UnTE

To His Lady. Henry VIII, King of England. CTC

To His Late Majesty, Concerning the True Form of English Poetry, *sel.* Sir John Beaumont.
"He makes sweet music who, in serious lines." PP

To His Love. Ivor Gurney. MMA

To His Love. Shakespeare. *See* Sonnets, XVIII *and* CVI.

To His Love. *Unknown. See* Come Away, Come, Sweet Love.

To His Love, That Sent Him a Ring Wherein Was Graved, "Let Reason Rule." George Turberville. EnRePo

To His Lovely Mistresses. Robert Herrick. CTC; SeCP

To His Lute. William Drummond of Hawthornden. GTBS-P

To His Mistress. Ernest Dowson. BoLP

To His Mistress. Ovid, *tr.* by Dryden. ErPo

To His Mistress. Earl of Rochester. BoLP

To His Mistress [*or* Mistris] Going to Bed. John Donne. Elegies, XIX. ErPo; UnTE
(Elegie XIX: To His Mistris Going to Bed.) SeCP
(Elegy XIX: Going to Bed.) EnRePo
(Elegy to His Mistress Going to Bed.) FoBA

To His Mistress for Her True Picture. Lord Herbert of Cherbury. SeCP

To His Mistress Objecting to Him Neither Toying or Talking. Robert Herrick. FaBV

To His Mistress, the Queen of Bohemia. Sir Henry Wotton. *See* Elizabeth of Bohemia.

To His Mistresses. Robert Herrick. ErPo; SeCP; UnTE

To His Noble Friend, Mr. Richard Lovelace, upon His Poems. Andrew Marvell. PP

To His Saviour, a Child; a Present, by a Child. Robert Herrick. SeCP

To His Sister. Carlo Betocchi, *tr. fr. Italian by* Carlo L. Golino. CoIP

To His Son. Richard Corbet. *See* To His Son, Vincent Corbet . . .

To His Son. Sir Walter Ralegh. *See* Wood, the Weed, the Wag, The.

To His Son, Vincent Corbet, on His Birth-Day, November 10, 1630, Being Then Three Years Old. Richard Corbet. BoC
(To His Son.) CBEP

To His Soul. Emperor Hadrian, *tr. fr. Latin by* Elinor Wylie. PoPI

To His Wife. John Skelton. CBEP

To His Worthy Friend Doctor Witty upon His Translation of the Popular Errors. Andrew Marvell. PP

To His Young Mistress. Anacreon, *tr. fr. Greek by* Abraham Cowley. UnTE

To His Young Mistress. Pierre de Ronsard, *tr. fr. French by* Andrew Lang. *Fr.* Amours de Marie. RBL

To Hold in a Poem. A. J. M. Smith. ACV

To Hölderlin. Rainer Maria Rilke, *tr. fr. German by* David Luke. MGP

To Homer. Keats. CABA; CBEP

To hope is good, but with such wild applause. Hope. Sir Richard Fanshawe. CBEP

To Houston at Gonzales town, ride, Ranger, for your life. The Men of the Alamo. James Jeffrey Roche. ThLM

To Italy. Vincenzo da Filicaia, *tr. fr. Italian by* Romilda Rendel. RBL

To Italy. Giovanni Guidiccioni, *tr. fr. Italian by* Romilda Rendel. RBL

To J. S. Bach. Michael Thwaites. MoRP

To James. Frank Horne. BiCB; LV

To Jane: The Recollection. Shelley. *See* Recollection, The.

To John Donne. Ben Jonson. SeCP; StP

To Juan at the Winter Solstice. Robert Graves. ILP; MP; PoIE; PoSa

To Judith Asleep. John Ciardi. MoLP; ToPo

To K. H. Thomas Edward Brown. OBNC

To K. M. Walter de la Mare. BoC

To Kate, Skating Better than Her Date. David Daiches. SD

To K[atharine] de M[attos]. Robert Louis Stevenson. OBNC

To Keep a True Lent. Robert Herrick. TRV

To Kiss my Celia's fairer breast. On Snow-Flakes Melting in His Lady's Breast. William Martin Johnson. AmLP

To know just how He suffered—would be dear. Emily Dickinson. DiPo

To Labor. Charlotte Perkins Stetson Gilman. PoLF

To land with the postship. Postship. Christoph Meckel. MGP

To Landrum Guy, Beginning to Write at Sixty. James Dickey. PP

To Laughter, to Leering. Richard Eberhart. ToPo

To Lesbia ("I hate, and yet I love thee too"). Catullus. *See* Odi et Amo.

To Lesbia ("Thy kisses dost thou bid me count"). Catullus, *tr. fr. Latin by* George Lamb. UnTE

To Lesbia. John Godfrey Saxe. UnTE

To Lida. Goethe, *tr. fr. German by* Philip Allan Friedman. AGP

To Little or No Purpose. Sir George Etherege. *Fr.* She Would if She Could. UnTE

To live a life, free from gout, pain, and phthisic. Athletic Employment. *Unknown.* SD

To live illusionless, in the abandoned mineshaft. Double Monologue. Adrienne Rich. NePoEA-2

To Live Merrily, and to Trust to Good Verses. Robert Herrick. PP; SeCP

To Lizbie Browne. Thomas Hardy. DTC; ELP

To loosen with all ten fingers held wide and limber. Moss-gathering. Theodore Roethke. ILP

To Lou Gehrig. John Kieran. SD

To Louis XIII. François de Malherbe, *tr. fr. French by* William Frederic Giese. RBL

To love one woman, or to sit. Woman and Tree. Robert Graves. ErPo

To Lucasta, [on] Going beyond the Seas. Richard Lovelace. GTBS-P; HaSV; ILP; SeCP

To Lucasta, [on] Going to the Wars. Richard Lovelace. CABA; CBEP; ELP; FaBV; FaPL; GTBS-P; PoIE; PoPl; SeCP

To Lucrezia d'Este. Tasso, *tr. fr. Italian by* Lorna de' Lucchi. RBL

To M. H. Wordsworth. EiCP
To Madame Lucrezia d'Este, Duchess of Urbino. Tasso, *tr. fr. Italian* by Harold M. Priest. RBL
To make a final conquest of all me. The Fair Singer. Andrew Marvell. CBEP
To make a prairie it takes a clover and one bee. Emily Dickinson. DiPo; PoP1
To make a start. Preface. William Carlos Williams. *Fr.* Paterson, I. AP
To make this condiment, your poet begs. A Salad. Sydney Smith. LV
To make yourselves a nation, that you hope vainly, O Germans. German National Character. Schiller. TwGP
To Marguerite ("We were apart"). Matthew Arnold. *See* Isolation: To Marguerite.
To Marguerite ("Yes! in the sea of life enisled"). Matthew Arnold. Switzerland, V. ELP; ILP; OBNC
(To Marguerite—Continued.) CABA; CaFP; GTBS-P; VaPo; VP
To Market, to Market. Mother Goose. SoPo
To market, to market. Saturday Shopping. Katherine Edelman. SoPo
To Mary ("The twentieth year is wellnigh past"). William Cowper. CBEP; EiCP
(To Mary Unwin.) FaPL
(To the Same.) GTBS-P
To Mary Unwin ("Mary, I want a lyre with other strings"). William Cowper. GTBS-P
To Master Edward Cobham. Barnabe Googe. EnRePo
To me, fair friend, you never can be old. Sonnets, CIV. Shakespeare. EnRePo; GTBS-P; PoIE
To Meadows. Robert Herrick. CBEP
(To Meddowes.) SeCP
To Meet, or Otherwise. Thomas Hardy. OBNC
To Memory. Mary Elizabeth Coleridge. CBEP
To Mercy, Pity, Peace, and Love. The Divine Image. Blake. *Fr.* Songs of Innocence. CBEP; EnPE; OBNC; PoIE; TRV
To Miss ——. Samuel Johnson. CABA
To Miss Charlotte Pulteney in Her Mother's Arms. Ambrose Philips. *See* To Charlotte Pulteney.
To Miss Ferrier. Burns. CBEP
To Miss Georgiana. Ambrose Philips. WaPE
To Mr. Cyriack Skinner upon His Blindness. Milton. *See* To Cyriack Skinner, upon His Blindness.
To Mr. Henry Lawes [Who Had Then Newly Set a Song of Mine in the Year 1635]. Edmund Waller. CTC; PP; SeCP
To Mr. I. L. John Donne. SeCP
To Mr. Lawrence. Milton. *See* Lawrence, of Virtuous Father Virtuous Son.
To Mr. Rowland Woodward. John Donne. MeP
To Mr. T. W. John Donne. PP
To Mistress Anne. John Skelton. EnRePo
To Mrs. Boteler. Mary Chandler. WaPE
To Mistress Isabel Pennell. John Skelton. *Fr.* The Garlande of Laurell. CBEP; PoIE; StP
To Mistress Margaret Hussey. John Skelton. *Fr.* The Garlande of Laurell. CBEP; DiPo; GoJo; PoIE; PoSa
To Mistress Margaret Tilney. John Skelton. *Fr.* The Garlande of Laurell. MeEL
To Mistress Margery Wentworth. John Skelton. *Fr.* The Garlande of Laurell. CBEP; EnRePo
To Mrs. Reynolds's Cat. Keats. *See* To a Cat.
To Morning. Blake. FoBA
To Music Bent Is My Retired Mind. Thomas Campion. EnRePo
To Musique, to Becalme His Fever. Robert Herrick. GoJo
To My Cousin (C. R.) Marrying My Lady (A.). Thomas Carew. SeCP
To My Daughter. Stephen Spender. BoC
To My Dead Friend Ben: Johnson. Henry King. SeCP
To My Dear and Loving Husband. Anne Bradstreet. AP; CBEP; PoLF
To My Dog "Blanco." Josiah Gilbert Holland. PoLF
To my firstborn land, to the south. The Firstborn Land. Ingeborg Bachmann. MGP
To My Friends. Else Lasker-Schüler, *tr. fr. German* by Christopher Middleton. MGP
To My Friends. Peter Levi. NePoEA-2
To My God. George Macdonald. TRV
To My Honor'd Friend Sir Robert Howard, *sel.* Dryden. What Is the World? TRV
To My Most Dearly Loved Friend, Henry Reynolds, Esq., *sel.* Michael Drayton.
"For from my cradle you must know that I." PP
To My Mother. George Barker. BoC; DTC; MP
(Sonnet to My Mother.) VaPo
To My Mother. Louis Ginsberg. PoSC
To My Mother. Poe. AP; PoPo
To My Mountain. Kathleen Raine. PoP1
To My Mouse-colored Mare. Tristan Corbière, *tr. fr. French* by C. F. MacIntyre. ErPo
To My New Mistress. Beverly Bowie. PoP1
To My Son, *sel.* George Barker.

"My darkling child the stars have obeyed." MP
To My Son. *Unknown.* PoLF
To my true king I offered free from stain. A Jacobite's Epitaph. Macaulay. OBNC
To my twin who lives in a cruel country. The Dual Site. Michael Hamburger. MP; NePoEA-2
To My Valentine. *Unknown.* SoPo
To My Wife. Robert Louis Stevenson. *See* My Wife.
To Naso. Catullus, *tr. fr. Latin* by Jack Lindsay. ErPo
To Ned. Herman Melville. HaSV
To Nietzsche. Christian Morgenstern, *tr. fr. German* by Walter Kaufmann. TwGP
To Night. Michelangelo, *tr. fr. Italian* by Harold M. Priest. RBL
To Night. Shelley. CBEP; ILP; OBNC; PoIE; PoLF; WiR
(Night.) BoC
(To the Night.) GTBS-P
To Night. Joseph Blanco White. CBEP; RoGo
(Night.) BoC
To night, grave sir, both my poore house, and I. *See* Tonight, grave sir, both my poor house and I.
To Nobodaddy. Blake. DiPo
To One in Paradise. Poe. AmLP; AP; PoIE; PoLF; PoPo
To one kneeling down no word came. In a Country Church. R. S. Thomas. ToPo
To One Married to an Old Man. Edmund Waller. SeCP
To One Shortly to Die. Walt Whitman. CBEP
To One That Had Little Wit. George Turberville. EnRePo
To One Who Died Young. Georg Trakl, *tr. fr. German* by Christopher Middleton. MGP
To One Who Has Been Long in City Pent. Keats. CBEP
To onpreise women it were a shame. Women Are Worthy. *Unknown.* MeEL
To Paint a Water Lily. Ted Hughes. PP
To Paths Unknown. Whittier. *See* At Last.
To Patricia on Her Christening Day. Edith Ballinger Price. BiCB
To Penshurst. Ben Jonson. CABA; CABL; SeCP
To Perilla. Robert Herrick. SeCP
To Philip Levine, on the Day of Atonement. Robert Mezey. AmPC
To Phillis. Sir Charles Sedley. BoLP
To Phillis. Edmund Waller. SeCP
To pierce through power. J. F. K. Ralph Gordon. OPP
To Ping-ku, Asleep. Lawrence Durrell. AnMoPo
To plant corn here was a futile whim. Playground of the Pixie. Grant Code. FiSC
To Pledge or Not to Pledge. *Unknown.* STF
To Posterity. Bertolt Brecht, *tr. fr. German* by Michael Hamburger. MGP
To Praise the Gift of Love That Binds My Heart. Uc de la Bacalaria, *tr. fr. Provençal* by Norman R. Shapiro. AnML
To Primroses. Robert Herrick. PoP1
To Promise Is One Thing, to Perform Is Another. La Fontaine. UnTE
To R. B. Gerard Manley Hopkins. CBEP; GTBS-P
To R. K. J. K. Stephen. Par
To Remain. C. P. Cavafy, *tr. fr. Modern Greek* by John Mavrogordato. ErPo
To Remi Belleau. Pierre de Ronsard, *tr. fr. French* by R. N. Currey. RBL
To Richard Wright. Conrad Kent Rivers. AmNP
To Robert Browning. Walter Savage Landor. ILP
To Rome Entombed in Her Ruins. Francisco de Quevedo, *tr. fr. Spanish* by Kate Flores. AnSP
To Rosamund [or Rosemond]. Chaucer. CABA; CBEP
(Ballade to Rosamund.) MeEL
To Rose. Sara Teasdale. BiCB
To Roses in the Bosom[e] of Castara. William Habington. *Fr.* Castara. SeCP; UnTE
To S. R. Crockett. Robert Louis Stevenson. *Fr.* Songs of Travel. OBNC
To Sabidius. Martial, *tr. fr. Latin* by Timothe Kendall. DiPo
To Satch. Samuel Allen. AmNP; SD
(American Gothic.) PtTo
To Science. Poe. *See* Sonnet: To Science.
To Scott. Winifred Letts. PoLF
To Search Our Souls. Jane McKay Lanning. TRV
To see a world in a grain of sand. Auguries of Innocence. Blake. CABA; CABL; DiPo; FaBV; ILP; OBNC; OnP; RePo; TRV
To See the Hours of Fever. Gustavo Adolfo Bécquer, *tr. fr. Spanish* by John Crow. AnSP
To see the Lord the shepherds. We Would See Jesus. *Unknown.* STF
To see the petrel cropping in the farmyard. Burns Singer. *Fr.* Sonnets for a Dying Man. NePoEA-2
To see you standing in the sagging bookstore door. The Visit of the Professor of Aesthetics. Margaret Danner. Far from Africa: Four Poems, 3. AmNP
To Seem the Stranger Lies My Lot, My Life. Gerard Manley Hopkins. FoBA
To Silvia. Shakespeare. *See* Who Is Silvia?

To Sing in Ancient Measures. Walter Bauer, *tr. fr. German by* Christopher Middleton. MGP
To sing of wars, of captains, and of kings. The Prologue. Anne Bradstreet. AP
To Sing with Joy from Out a Sorrowing Heart. Christine de Pisan, *tr. fr. French by* Muriel Kittel. AnML
To Sir Toby. Philip Freneau. AP
To Sleep. Giovanni della Casa, *tr. fr. Italian by* John Addington Symonds. RBL
To Sleep. Keats. FoBA
 (World of Sleep, The.) BoC
To Sleep. Jan Kochanowski, *tr. fr. Polish by* Watson Kirkconnell. SiGo
To Sleep. Wordsworth. GTBS-P
To Sleep I give my powers away. In Memoriam A. H. H., IV. Tennyson. VP
To So-kin of Rakuyo, ancient friend, Chancellor of Gen. Exile's Letter. Li Po. CTC
To Some I Have Talked With by the Fire. W. B. Yeats. PoDB
To Some Millions Who Survive Joseph E. Mander, Sr. Sarah E. Wright. PtTo
To spend uncounted years of pain. Arthur Hugh Clough. OBNC
To Spring. Blake. BoC; CBEP; FoBA; PoLF; WiR
To Stella. Swift. EiCP
To Stephan George. Rainer Maria Rilke, *tr. fr. German by* Walter Kaufmann. TwGP
To Summer. Blake. FoBA; WiR
To talk with God. Wait On! *Unknown.* STF
To the Bridge of Love. Juan Ramón Jiménez, *tr. fr. Spanish by* James Wright. AnSP
To the Canary Bird. Jones Very. AP
To the Children. "Gabriela Mistral," *tr. fr. Spanish by* Kate Flores. AnSP
To the Countess of Salisbury. Aurelian Townsend. SeCP
To the Cuckoo. Wordsworth. CBEP; ELP; GTBS-P; PoLF
To the Daemon Sublimity. Clark Ashton Smith. FiSC
To the Daisy. Wordsworth. GTBS-P
To the Dandelion. James Russell Lowell. AP
To the Eternal Feminine. Tristan Corbière, *tr. fr. French by* C. F. MacIntyre. ErPo
To the Evening Star. Blake. FaBV; FoBA; PoLF; WiR
 (Sonnet: "Thou fair-haired angel of the evening.") PoPo
To the Evening Star. Thomas Campbell. GTBS-P; TRV
 (Caroline, II: To the Evening Star.) OBNC
To the Fair Unknown. William Taylor. WaPE
To the Faithful. Marcos Ana, *tr. fr. Spanish by* Chloe Vulliamy *and* Stephen Sedley. BoC
To the figures bathing at the river. A Bodhisattva Undoes Hell. Jerome Rothenberg. CoPo
To the Fringed Gentian. Bryant. AP; PoLF; StP
To the Garden the World. Walt Whitman. AP
To the Ghost of John Milton. Carl Sandburg. PP
To the ghostly garden, to the silent laurel. Autumn Garden. Dino Campana. CoIP
To the Girls of My Graduating Class. Irving Layton. ErPo
To the God of all mercies let my blessing rise today. Cassandra Southwick. Whittier. PoIE
To the Grasshopper and the Cricket. Leigh Hunt. OBNC
To the Highland Girl of Inversneyde. Wordsworth. *See* To a Highland Girl.
To the Holy Spirit. Yvor Winters. PoIE
To the Honorable Charles Montague, Esq. Matthew Prior. EiCP
To the house on the grassy hill. The Presence. Denise Levertov. NePoEA-2
To the Immortal Memory of the Halibut on Which I Dined This Day. William Cowper. HaSV
To the Immortall Memorie, and Friendship of That Noble Paire, Sir Lucius Cary, and Sir H. Morison. Ben Jonson. *See* Pindaric Ode, A.
To the Ivy. John Clare. CBEP
To the Lady-Bird. Mother Goose. *See* Ladybird, Ladybird.
To the Lady Margaret Ley. Milton. GTBS-P
To the Learned Critic. Ben Jonson. PP
To the Leaven'd Soil They Trod. Walt Whitman. AP
To the Looking-Glass world it was Alice that said. "Lewis Carroll." *Fr.* Through the Looking-Glass. Par
To the Lords of Convention 'twas Claver'se who spoke. Bonnie Dundee. Sir Walter Scott. *Fr.* The Doom of Devorgoil. Par
To the Lost Colony. Zoe Kincaid Brockman. PoNC
To the lucky now who have lovers or friends. Alexandria. Lawrence Durrell. ToPo
To the Maids Not to Walk in the Wind. Oliver St. John Gogarty. ErPo
To the Man after the Harrow. Patrick Kavanagh. GTBS-P
To the man-in-the-street, who, I'm sorry to say. Note on Intellectuals. W. H. Auden. PoPl
To the Marchesana of Pescara. Michelangelo, *tr. fr. Italian by* Wordsworth. CTC
To the Memory of Mr. Oldham. Dryden. CABA; CaFP; DiPo; OnP; PoIE; PP; StP; VaPo
To the Memory of My Beloved Master William Shakespeare and What He Hath Left Us. Ben Jonson. CABA

(To the Memory of My Beloved, the Author Mr. [*or* Master] William Shakespeare [and What He Hath Left Us].) ILP; PoIE; PP; SeCP
(To the Memory of My Beloved William Shakespeare and What He Hath Left Us.) EnRePo
To the Memory of the Brave Americans. Philip Freneau. AP; PoLF
To the Mistral. Nietzsche, *tr. fr. German by* Walter Kaufmann. TwGP
To the Moon. Shelley. GTBS-P; RePo
To the Moon. Wordsworth. CBEP
To the Muses. Blake. CBEP
To the Mutable Fair. Edmund Waller. SeCP
To the Night. Shelley. *See* To Night.
To the Nightingale. Countess of Winchilsea. PoIE
To the Nightingale. Milton. *See* O Nightingale, That on Yon Bloomy Spray.
To the One I Love Most. *Unknown.* MeEL
To the One of Fictive Music. Wallace Stevens. AP
To the palace goes my lover. Dispute of Elena and Maria. *Unknown.* AnML
To the Parcae. Friedrich Hölderlin, *tr. fr. German.* AGP, *tr. by* Alexander Gode; TwGP, *tr. by* Walter Kaufmann
To the Poets of Our Time. Jean de Schélandre, *tr. fr. French by* Henry Carrington. RBL
To the Queen. Sir Walter Ralegh. CBEP
To the Reader. Samuel Daniel. PP
To the Reader. Ben Jonson. EnRePo
To the Reader. Denise Levertov. CoPo
To the Reader of These Sonnets. Michael Drayton. *Fr.* Idea. EnRePo
To the Rev. F. D. Maurice. Tennyson. GTBS-P
To the Right Honourable the Countess of C. William Habington. SeCP
To the Right Worthy Knight Sir Fulke Greville. Samuel Daniel. EnRePo
To the Rose. Robert Herrick. SeCP
To the Roving Pirate. George Turberville. EnRePo
To the Same. William Cowper. *See* To Mary.
To the Same. Ben Jonson. *See* Kiss Me, Sweet.
To the Skylark. Wordsworth. GTBS-P
To the Snake. Denise Levertov. NePoEA-2; PoIE; ToPo
To the Snipe. John Clare. OBNC
To the Soul. Sir Frederick Napier Broome. ACV
To the States. Walt Whitman. CTC
To the Stone-Cutters. Robinson Jeffers. ILP; PoCh; PoPl; PP; VaPo
To the Soure Reader. Robert Herrick. SeCP
To the Sun. Roy Campbell. *Fr.* Mithraic Emblems. EaLo
To the Sun. Guido Gezelle, *tr. fr. Flemish by* Jethro Bithell. SiGo
To the (Supposed) Patron. Geoffrey Hill. NePoEA-2
To the Supreme Being. Michelangelo, *tr. fr. Italian by* Wordsworth. SiGo; TRV
To the Terrestrial Globe. W. S. Gilbert. PoPl
To the Thawing Wind. Robert Frost. LOW
To the tomb they did return in coats of mail all dressed. Lament of the Virgin. Gonzalo de Berceo. AnML
To the Translation of Palingenius. Barnabe Googe. EnRePo
To the Unknown God. Nietzsche, *tr. fr. German by* Walter Kaufmann. TwGP
To the Unknown Warrior. G. K. Chesterton. MMA
To the Veld. Arthur Shearly Cripps. ACV
To the Virgin. Rutebeuf, *tr. fr. French by* James Edward Tobin. AnML
To the Virginian Voyage. Michael Drayton. CBEP; EnRePo; StP; ThLM
To the Virgins, to Make Much of Time. Robert Herrick. CABA; DiPo; ELP; FaBV; ILP; OnP; PoIE; PoPl; SeCP; StP
 (Counsel to Girls.) GTBS-P; WePo
 (Gather Ye Rosebuds [While Ye May].) PoPo; PoSa
 (To the Virgins to Make Much of Their Time.) ErPo
To the Western World. Louis Simpson. NePoEA-2; PoPl
To the World: A Farewell for a Gentlewoman, Virtuous and Noble. Ben Jonson. EnRePo; SeCP
To the Younger Lady Lucy Sydney. Edmund Waller. *See* To a Very Young Lady.
To thee now, Christes dere derling. A Song to John, Christ's Friend. *Unknown.* MeEL
To Their Excellencies the Lords Justices of Ireland, the Humble Petition of Frances Harris [Who Must Starve and Die a Maid if It Miscarries]. Swift. ILP; Par
 (Mrs. Frances Harris's Petition.) CBEP
To these I turn, in these I trust. The Kiss. Siegfried Sassoon. MMA
To these, whom Death again did wed. An Epitaph upon a Young Married Couple Dead and Buried Together. Richard Crashaw. ELP; ILP; SeCP
To think, Belleau, that such a man. To Remi Belleau. Pierre de Ronsard. RBL
To think I once saw grocery shops. Counters. Elizabeth J. Coatsworth. SoPo
To think of them. Until Death Do Us Part. Anselm Hollo. OPP

To Think of Time, *sel.* Walt Whitman.
"To think of time . . . to think through the retrospection."
AP
To think to know the country and not know. A Hillside Thaw.
Robert Frost. DiPo; StP
To this generation I would say. Mrs. George Reece. Edgar
Lee Masters. *Fr.* Spoon River Anthology. LV
To this grove of dying poplars. Autumn. "Gabriela Mistral."
AnSP
To this room—it was somewhere at the palace's. The Room.
C. Day Lewis. PoCh
To Time it never seems that he is brave. I Could Give All to
Time. Robert Frost. MoRP
To Toussaint L'Ouverture. Wordsworth. OBNC; TRV
To travel like a bird, lightly to view. C. Day Lewis. *Fr.* O
Dreams, O Destinations. GTBS-P
To Venus. Hedylos. *See* Seduced Girl.
To view these walls each night I come alone. Complains, Being
Hind'red the Sight of His Nymph. Girolamo Preti. RBL
To Violets. Robert Herrick. SeCP
To Virgil. Tennyson. GTBS-P; StP
To Virgins. Robert Herrick. UnTE
To Vittoria Colonna. Michelangelo, *tr. fr. Italian by* Harold
M. Priest. RBL
To Waken an Old Lady. William Carlos Williams. PoIE
To Walk Abroad. Thomas Traherne. ELP
(Walking.) SD
To Walk on Hills. Robert Graves. SD
To what a cumbersome unwieldiness. Love's Diet. John
Donne. ILP
To what new fates, my country, far. Unmanifest Destiny.
Richard Hovey. TRV
To whom, heart, would you complain? Ever more unfrequented.
Complaint. Rainer Maria Rilke. MGP
To Whom Shall I Tell My Sorrows? *Unknown, tr. fr. Span-
ish by* William M. Davis. AnML
To Whom Shall They Go? *Unknown.* STF
To William Earle of Pembroke. Ben Jonson. SeCP
To win love's chase, I took my way. Other Verses with a
Divine Meaning. St. John of the Cross. RBL
To Winter. Blake. FoBA; WiR
To Words. Ralph Pomeroy. CoPo
To Wordsworth. Shelley. PoPo
To you I'll sing a good old song, made by a Quaker pate. Ye
Ancient Yuba Miner, of the Days of '49. Sam C. Upham.
SGR
To You, Lady Virgin Santa Maria. Ramon Llull, *tr. fr.
Catalan by* William M. Davis. AnML
To you, little girl-child, the fairies do give. To a Little Sister,
Aged Ten. Alison Elizabeth Cummings. BiCB
To you, my purs[e], and to noon other wight. Complaint [*or*
The Compleynt of Chaucer] to His Purse [*or* A Song to
His Purse for the King]. Chaucer. CABA; MeEL; PoIE
To Yvor Winters, 1955. Thom Gunn. GTBS-P
Toad the power mower caught, A. The Death of a Toad.
Richard Wilbur. AP; CABA; CaFP; VaPo
Toast to the Flag, A. John Daly. PoLF
Toaster, The. William Jay Smith. SoPo
Tobacco. Graham Lee Lemminger. PoLF
Tobacconist of Eighth Street, The. Richard Eberhart. ToPo
Toccata of Galuppi's, A. Robert Browning. CBEP; GTBS-P;
VP
Today. Mary Frances Butts. TRV
To-Day. Angela Morgan. TRV
Today a rude brief recitative. Song for All Seas, All Ships.
Walt Whitman. HaSV; MoRP
Today Delight's Fair Ship. Lope de Vega, *tr. fr. Spanish by*
William M. Davis. AnSP
Today from the Aurora's bosom. The Nativity of Christ. Luis
de Góngora. RBL
Today I have a birthday. Birthday Candles. Louise Binder
Scott and J. J. Thompson. BiCB
Today I have been happy. All the day. One Day. Rupert
Brooke. MoLP
Today I saw a picture of the cancer cells. The Cancer Cells.
Richard Eberhart. AnMoPo; ToPo
Today I saw a woman wrapped in rags. At the Slackening of
the Tide. James Wright. AmPC; CABA
Today I found lean winter's. The Coming. Anthony Delius.
ACV
Today I'm ill, only today, tomorrow I'll be well. The Old
Woman. "Gertrud Kolmar." MGP
To day old Janus opens the new yeare. A New-Yeares-Gift
Sung to King Charles, 1635. Ben Jonson. SeCP
Today, should you let fall a glass, it would. Tramontana at
Lerici. Charles Tomlinson. GTBS-P
Today the leaves cry, hanging on branches swept by wind.
The Course of a Particular. Wallace Stevens. PoIE
Today the weather brings us rain. The Young Tree. Umberto
Saba. CoIP
To-day the woods are trembling through and through. Corn.
Sidney Lanier. AP
Today upon a bus, I saw. Forgive Me When I Whine. *Un-
known.* STF
To-day we have naming of parts. Naming of Parts. Henry

Reed. *Fr.* Lessons of the War. CaFP; DTC; GoJo; ILP;
MP; PoPl; StP; WePo
Today we think of that great man. For February Twelfth.
Muriel M. Gessner. RePo
Today, while thousands stared with captured eyes. Sky-Writer.
Vincent Starrett. LV; PoPo
Toe sticking out from under the hem, The. On a Fifteenth-
Century Flemish Angel. David Ray. NePoEA-2
Toe upon toe, a snowing flesh. Nude Descending a Staircase.
X. J. Kennedy. NePoEA-2
Together how many hours. Tant' Amare. *Unknown.* ErPo
Together we looked down. Wedding Procession. James A.
Emanuel. NNP
Together with all my stones. Shibboleth. Paul Celan. MGP
Tolerance. Thomas Hardy. MoRP
Toll for the brave! On the Loss [*or* The Loss] of the *Royal
George.* William Cowper. CBEP; GTBS-P; HaSV;
RoGo
Tolling Bells. Lady Kasa, *tr. fr. Japanese by* Ishii *and* Obata.
SiGo
Tom. Sir Osbert Sitwell. DaDu
Tom Bowling. Charles Dibdin. CBEP
Tom Ducket. Jean Jaszi. RePo
Tom Farley. Colin Thiele. PoAu-2
Tom Fool at Jamaica. Marianne Moore. AP
Tom Hight is my name; an old bachelor I am. Hurrah for
Greer County. *Unknown.* BFSS
Tom Moore has sung of '49. The Good Old Days of '50, '1,
and '2. J. Riley Mains. SGR
Tom o' Bedlam's Song. *Unknown.* CBEP; EvOK; PoSa; StP
(Roaring Mad Tom.) WiR
Tom sang for joy, and Ned sang for joy, and old Sam sang for
joy. The Quartette. Walter de la Mare. BoC; CBEP
Tom tied a kettle to the tail of a cat. Three Bad Ones. *Un-
known.* BBGG
Tomb of Lt. John Learmonth, A.I.F., The. John Manifold.
PoAu-2
Tombs in Westminster, The. *At.* to Francis Beaumont, *also to*
William Basse. *See* On the Tombs in Westminster Abbey.
Tommie Makes My Tail Toddle. Burns. ErPo
Tommies in the Train. D. H. Lawrence. MMA
Tommy. Kipling. CABA; FaBV
"Tommy" you was when it began. "The Service Man." Kip-
ling. Par
Tomorrow. John Collins. GTBS-P
Tomorrow. Della Adams Leitner. STF
Tomorrow. Lope de Vega, *tr. fr. Spanish by* Mildred E. John-
son. RBL
Tomorrow,/ hurry, hurry, do! Hurry Tomorrow. Ivy O.
Eastwick. BiCB
To-Morrow and To-Morrow. Shakespeare. *Fr.* Macbeth, V, v.
DiPo
("Tomorrow, and tomorrow, and tomorrow.") PoPl; TRV
Tomorrow Is Not Yet. Henri Michaux, *tr. fr. French by*
Dori Katz *and* Donald Justice. CoFP
Tomorrow is Saint Valentine's Day. Ophelia's Song. Shake-
speare. *Fr.* Hamlet, IV, v. UnTE
To-morrow shall be my dancing day. My Dancing Day. *Un-
known.* CBEP
Tomorrow, tomorrow's the circus parade. The Circus Parade.
Olive Beaupré Miller. SoPo
Tom's Angel. Walter de la Mare. BoC
Tom's Sleeping Song. Mark Van Doren. *Fr.* Jonathan Gentry.
LOW
Tongues with the speed of light. Radar. A. M. Sullivan. LV
Tonight a blackout. Twenty years ago. Christmas Eve under
Hooker's Statue. Robert Lowell. AP; PoDB; ThLM
Tonight [*or* To night], grave sir, both my poor[e] house and I.
Inviting a Friend to Supper. Ben Jonson. EnRePo;
SeCP
To-night I saw three maidens on the beach. Ibant Obscurae.
Thomas Edward Brown. OBNC
Tonight I walked with the grim Florentine. Sonnet. George
Henry Boker. *Fr.* Sonnets. AmLP
Tonight is the night. Hallowe'en. Harry Behn. PoSC; RePo
To-night the very horses springing by. Winter Evening.
Archibald Lampman. OBCV
To-night the winds begin to rise. In Memoriam A. H. H., XV.
Tennyson. GTBS-P; OBNC; PoSa; VP
To-night ungather'd let us leave. In Memoriam A. H. H., CV.
Tennyson. VP
Tonight we took. On Seeing a Movie Based on an Episode
from President Kennedy's Life. David Ray. OPP
To-night while I was pondering in my chair. A Midnight
Interior. Siegfried Sassoon. MoRP
Too Anxious for Rivers. Robert Frost. CBEP
Too Bad! Wilhelm Busch, *tr. fr. German by* Dagmar Lange.
AGP
Too Bright a Day. Norman MacCaig. GTBS-P
Too Busy ("Too busy this morning"). *Unknown.* STF
Too Busy ("Too busy to read a chapter a day"). *Unknown.*
STF
Too dense to have a door. The Haystack. Andrew Young.
DaDu
Too Late. Matthew Arnold. Faded Leaves, II. VP

Too Late. Fitz Hugh Ludlow. PoLF
Too Late. Philip Bourke Marston. OBNC
Too-late Born, The. Archibald MacLeish. GoJo
    (Silent Slain, The.) CABA
Too Literal Pupil, The. Martial, tr. fr. Latin by Louis Unter-
    meyer. UnTE
Too long a sacrifice. W. B. Yeats. Fr. Easter, 1916. PoPo
Too long has time delayed. If You Are No Longer. Vittorio
    Sereni. CoIP
Too Much Sex. Unknown. MeEL
Too Old to Work. Joe Glazer. ThLM
Too poor for a bribe, and too proud to importune. Sketch of
    His Own Character. Thomas Gray. EiCP
Too Young for Love. Horace, tr. fr. Latin by Louis Unter-
    meyer. Odes, II, 5. UnTE
Top Hat and Tales. Lorna Beers. FiSC
Top of a hill, The. How to Tell the Top of a Hill. John
    Ciardi. SoPo
Topsy-turvy Land. H. E. Wilkinson. SoPo
Tora's Song. Knut Hamsun, tr. fr. Norwegian by Charles
    Wharton Stork. PoPl
Torch, The. Walt Whitman. FoBA
Tormenting Virgin. Unknown, tr. fr. Greek by Louis Unter-
    meyer. UnTE
Torment's curl leaps above his brow. Judas. Georg Heym.
    MGP
Torn Nightgown, The. Joel Oppenheimer. CoPo
Torquato Tasso, sels. Goethe, tr. fr. German by Walter Kauf-
    mann. TwGP
    "Am I indeed as wretched as I seem?" fr. V, v.
    "If I may not reflect and fashion poems," fr. V, ii.
Torrismond, sel. Thomas Lovell Beddoes.
    How Many Times? fr. sc. iii. ELP
Torturing Glimpses and Passions Unruly. Heinrich von
    Morungen, tr. fr. German by J. B. Leishman. AnML
Tossed on a Sea of Trouble. Archilochus, tr. fr. Greek by
    William Hay. PoPl
Tottingham Frolic. Unknown. UnTE
Touch of cold in the Autumn night, A. Autumn. T. E.
    Hulme. LOW
Touch of the Master's Hand, The. Myra Brooks Welch. STF;
    TRV
Tour de Force. Peter Kane Dufault. ErPo
Tour in Rain. Raymond Roseliep. FiSC
Tourist and the Town, The. Adrienne Rich. NePoEA-2
Tourist Time. F. R. Scott. PoPl
Toussaint, the most unhappy man of men! To Toussaint
    L'Ouverture. Wordsworth. OBNC; TRV
Toward Avernus. Harold Vinal. FiSC
Toward Colonos. Dabney Stuart. OPP
Toward sun, the sun flared suddenly red. Summer Storm
    (circa 1916), and God's Grace. Robert Penn Warren.
    PoDB
Towards nightfall when the wind. Winter Mask. Allen Tate.
    AmLP
Towards the Last Spike, sels. E. J. Pratt. OBCV
    Gathering, The.
    Precambrian Shield, The.
Towards the Source, sels. Christopher Brennan. PoAu-1
    I Saw My Life as Whitest Flame.
    Let Us Go Down, the Long Dead Night Is Done.
Tower, The. Philip Booth. NePoEA-2
Tower Hill Memorial. Anthony Michael Morrison. HaSV
Tower of Refuge is our God, A! Ein feste Burg ist unser Gott.
    Martin Luther. CTC
Tower of the Dream, The, sel. Charles Harpur.
    "Yes, wonderful are dreams: and I have known." PoAu-1
Towery city and branchy between towers. Duns Scotus's
    Oxford. Gerard Manley Hopkins. GTBS-P; PoIE; VP
Town, The. David Rowbotham. PoAu-2
Town, The. Theodor Storm, tr. fr. German by R. N. Linn.
    AGP
Town does not exist, The. The Starry Night. Anne Sexton.
    ToPo
Town has opened to the sun, The. Bombardment. D. H.
    Lawrence. MMA
Town Owl. Laurie Lee. ToPo
Towns. Corrado Govoni, tr. fr. Italian by Carlo L. Golino.
    CoIP
Town's fast asleep as a child spent from play, The. Deep
    Summer, after Midnight. Thad Stem, Jr. PoNC
Toys, The. Coventry Patmore. The Unknown Eros, I, x.
    BoC; CBEP; FaPL; TRV
Tracer of wind's contour by line of flight. The Butterfly.
    Gray Burr. CoPo
Tract. William Carlos Williams. AnMoPo; AP; CABL; ILP;
    MP; StP
Tract for Autos, A. Arthur Guiterman. RePo
Traction. Howard Moss. OPP
Trader's Return. Sylvia Lawson. PoAu-2
Traditional Red. Robert Huff. NePoEA-2
Tragedy. "Æ." MoRP
Tragedy of Dido, The, sel. Christopher Marlowe and Thomas
    Nashe.
    "So much have I received at Dido's hands." HaSV

Tragedy of Valentinian, The, sels. John Fletcher.
    Care-charming Sleep, fr. V, ii. ELP
    Hear, Ye Ladies, fr. II, v. ELP
    (Power of Love, The.) UnTE
    Now the Lusty Spring, fr. II, v. ELP; ErPo
    (Love's Emblems.) UnTE
Tragic, said I. Oh, tragicker, says she. Noël Tragique. Ramon
    Guthrie. ErPo
Tragic Story, A. Adelbert von Chamisso, tr. fr. German by
    Thackeray. OnMSP; RePo
Trail All Your Pikes, Dispirit Every Drum. Countess of Win-
    chilsea. StP
Trail Breakers. James Daugherty. RePo
Train, The. Emily Dickinson. See I like to see it lap the miles.
Train has stopped for no apparent reason, The. En Route.
    Duncan Campbell Scott. OBCV
Train is a dragon that roars through the dark, A. A Modern
    Dragon. Rowena Bennett. SoPo
Train takes me away from the northern valleys. Rhetoric of a
    Journey. Roy Fuller. ToPo
Train Window. Robert Finch. OBCV
Trains. James S. Tippett. SoPo
Tramontana at Lerici. Charles Tomlinson. GTBS-P
Trampwoman's Tragedy, A. Thomas Hardy. OBNC
Tranquil Night. Luis de León, tr. fr. Spanish by Edwin
    Morgan. AnSP
Transcendence. Richard Hovey. TRV
Transcendence Wouldn't Do. Jacques Audiberti, tr. fr. French
    by Harry Duncan. CoFP
Transcendentalism; a Poem in Twelve Books. Robert Brown-
    ing. DiPo; PP
Transfiguration, sel. Johannes R. Becher, tr. fr. German by
    Christopher Middleton.
    Throttled on a String of Pearls. MGP
Transformation. Günter Grass, tr. fr. German by Michael
    Hamburger. MGP
Transformations. Thomas Hardy. AnMoPo; PoIE
Transformed. D. Weston Gates. STF
Transient as a Rose. John Lydgate. MeEL
Translation of Lines by Benserade. Samuel Johnson. CABA
Translations from the Chinese, sels. Christopher Morley.
    EvOK
    He Comforts Himself.
    Human Instinct, A.
    Man with the Rake, The.
    Secret Thoughts.
Transmigration. Seth D. Cudjoe. ACV
Trap. Walter H. Kerr. FiSC
Trapped Fly, A. Robert Herrick. WiR
Trappist Abbey, The: Matins. Thomas Merton. PoPl
Travel. Edna St. Vincent Millay. LV; RePo
Travel Bureau. Ruth Comfort Mitchell. LV
Traveller, The. Goldsmith. EnPE
Traveler on a dusty road, A. Little and Great. Charles
    Mackay. PoLF
Traveller take heed for journeys undertaken in the dark of the
    year. October Journey. Margaret Walker. AmNP
Traveller's Curse after Misdirection. Robert Graves, fr. the
    Welsh. DTC
Travelling, a man met a tiger, so. Good Taste. Christopher
    Logue. DaDu
Traveling on My Knees. Sandra Goodwin. STF
Tread lightly here, for here, 'tis said. A Robin's Epitaph.
    Samuel Rogers. CBEP
Tread lightly, she is near. Requiescat. Oscar Wilde. OBNC;
    WePo
Treading a field I saw afar. Death on a Live Wire. Michael
    Baldwin. MoBS
Treading pigeon arcs his wings, The. The Ivory Bed. Win-
    field Townley Scott. ErPo
Treason. Sir John Harington. CBEP
    ("Treason doth never prosper; what's the reason?") DiPo
Treasure, The. Sydney Middleton Clarke. HaSV
Treasure. Elizabeth-Ellen Long. BiCB
Treasures. Mary Dixon Thayer. SoPo
Treasures and Glories of Life, The. Manuel González Prada,
    tr. fr. Spanish by Kate Flores. AnSP
Trebetherick. John Betjeman. EvOK
Tree, The. Björnstjerne Björnson, tr. fr. Norwegian. PoSC
Tree, The. Rainer Brambach, tr. fr. German by Christopher
    Middleton. MGP
Tree, The. Alfred Kreymborg. PoPl
Tree, The. Jones Very. PoSC
Tree at My Window. Robert Frost. PoIE; PoPo
Tree Birthdays. Mary Carolyn Davies. BiCB
Tree frogs sing, The. The Rain-Frogs. Rogetsu. SiGo
Tree has entered my hands, The. A Girl. Ezra Pound. BoLP
Tree in Pamela's Garden, The. E. A. Robinson. MoLP
Tree in the Desert, The. Friedrich Hebbel, tr. fr. German by
    Frances Stillman. AGP
Tree of Silence, The. Vassar Miller. NePoEA-2; PoDB
Tree of Time. K. D. Sethna. ACV
Tree-sleeping. Robert P. Tristram Coffin. LOW
Tree Stands Very Straight and Still, The. Annette Wynne.
    SoPo

Tree still bends over the lake. Winter. Sheila Wingfield. BoLP

Tree, Tree. Federico García Lorca, *tr. fr. Spanish.* PoP1

Tree, whereon the pitying skies. The Dying Eusebio's Address to the Cross. Pedro Calderon de la Barca. RBL

Tree Will Mow Thickets. "Will Inman." PoNC

Treehouse, The. James A. Emanuel. AmNP; NNP

Trees. Harry Behn. SoPo

Trees. Joyce Kilmer. PoPo

Trees, The. Adrienne Rich. CoPo

Trees along this city street, The. City Trees. Edna St. Vincent Millay. RePo

Trees & brown squares. The Clearing. LeRoi Jones. CoPo

Trees and Cattle. James Dickey. NePoEA-2

Trees Are Down, The. Charlotte Mew. LV

Trees are in their autumn beauty, The. The Wild Swans at Coole. W. B. Yeats. ACV; DiPo; ILP; PoIE; PoPo; StP; WePo

Trees are the kindest things I know. Trees. Harry Behn. SoPo

Tree's early leaf-buds were bursting their brown, The. The Tree. Björnstjerne Björnson. PoSC

Trees growing—right in front of my window. Pruning Trees. Po Chü-i. SiGo

Trees in the Garden, The. Stephen Crane. War Is Kind, XXVI. VaPo

Trees in the old days used to stand. Carentan O Carentan. Louis Simpson. MoBS

Trees inside are moving out into the forest, The. The Trees. Adrienne Rich. CoPo

Tremulous distance, A. Stance. Theodore Enslin. CoPo

Tres Cosas. Baltasar de Alcázar, *tr. fr. Spanish by* Wayne Rollins. RBL

Trespass. Robert Frost. FaBV

Triad. Adelaide Crapsey. LV; PoP1

Trial, The. Dannie Abse. ACV

Trial Run, A. Robert Frost. WePo

Trials. Grace E. Troy. STF

Tribes, The. Roy Fuller. ToPo

Tribute, The. Coventry Patmore. The Angel in the House, I, iv, 2. FaPL; OBNC

Tribute to the Founder, A. Kingsley Amis. NePoEA-2

Trifle. Georgia Douglas Johnson. AmNP

Trilby, *sel.* George Du Maurier.
  Little Work, A, *after the French of* Leon van Montenaeken, *fr.* Pt. VIII. PoLF

Trilogy for X, *sel.* Louis MacNeice.
  "When clerks and navvies fondle." ErPo

Triolet: "All women born are so perverse." Robert Bridges. LV

Triolet: "Easy is the triolet." W. E. Henley. LV

Triolet against Sisters. Phyllis McGinley. LV

Triolet on a Dark Day. Margaret Fishback. PoSC

Trip to Four or Five Towns, A. John Logan. AmPC

Trip to Louisiana, some favors to find, A. The Lily of the West. *Unknown.* BFSS

Triple Fool, The. John Donne. DiPo; PP

Tristan da Cunha. Roy Campbell. RoGo

Tristram and Iseult. Matthew Arnold. VP

Triumph of Bacchus and Ariadne. Lorenzo de' Medici, *tr. fr. Italian by* Richard Aldington. *Fr.* Carnival Songs. CTC

Triumph of Beautie Song, The, *sel.* James Shirley.
  "Heigh-ho, what shall a shepheard doe." PoPo

Triumph of Charis, The. Ben Jonson. *Fr.* A Celebration of Charis. CABA; CBEP; ELP; OnP
  (Her Triumph.) CaFP; CTC; SeCP

Triumph of Death, The. Shakespeare. *See* Sonnets, LXXI.

Triumph of Doubt, The. John Peale Bishop. EaLo

Triumph of Time, The. Swinburne. VP
  "I will go back to the great sweet mother," *sel.* FaPL

Triumphal March. Rubén Darío, *tr. fr. Spanish by* Charles Guenther. AnSP

Trivia; or, The Art of Walking the Streets of London, *sels.* John Gay.
  Dangers of Foot-ball, The, *fr.* II. SD
  Of the Implements for Walking the Streets, and Signs of the Weather, I. EiCP
  Of Walking the Streets by Night, III. EiCP

Troilus and Cressida, *sel.* Shakespeare.
  "In the reproof of chance," *fr.* I, iii. HaSV

Troilus and Criseyde, *sels.* Chaucer.
  Complaint of Troilus, The, *fr.* V. DiPo
  "Owt [*or* Out] of thise blake wawes for to saylle," *fr.* II. ILP; PP

Troll's Nosegay, The. Robert Graves. PoCh

Troop home to silent grots and caves! The Mermaiden's Vesper Hymn. George Darley. *Fr.* Syren Songs. HaSV; OBNC

Tropes of One Season. Charles Edward Eaton. FiSC

Tropics in New York, The. Claude McKay. AmNP

Trot Along, Pony. Marion Edey *and* Dorothy Grider. SoPo

Trouble. David Keppel. PoLF

Trouble is, I hardly know, The. The New Letter Writer. Helen Bevington. PoNC

Troubles of the Day. William Barnes. GTBS-P

Trout, The. René Char, *tr. fr. French by* Richard G. Stern. Four Fascinators, II. CoFP

Troy Town. Dante Gabriel Rossetti. VP

Truant, The. E. J. Pratt. OBCV

True Beauty, The. Thomas Carew. *See* Disdain Returned.

True Confession of George Barker, The, *sel.* George Barker.
  "I see the young bride move among." ErPo

True Friendship. *Unknown, tr. fr. Sanskrit by* Arthur W. Ryder. *Fr.* The Panchatantra. SiGo

True Love. Shakespeare. *See* Sonnets, CXVI.

True Love. *Unknown, tr. fr. Greek by* Louis Untermeyer. UnTE

True Love in this differs from gold and clay. Shelley. *Fr.* Epipsychidion. OBNC

True Love Warms My Heart. Cercamon, *tr. fr. Provençal by* Paul Blackburn. AnML

True Maid, A. Matthew Prior. ErPo

True Name. Yves Bonnefoy, *tr. fr. French by* W. D. Snodgrass. CoFP

True Night. René Char, *tr. fr. French by* Jackson Mathews. PoP1

True poesy is not in words. Pastoral Poesy. John Clare. ACV

True Rest. Goethe, *tr. fr. German.* TRV

True Riches. Bessie June Martin. STF

True Story of Skipper Ireson, The. Charles Buxton Going. SIV

True Tar, The. Henry Carey. Two Songs, I. WaPE

True Thomas lay on Huntlie bank. Thomas [the] Rhymer. *Unknown.* BuBa; CBEP; ELP; OnMSP

True to a Dream. Donald Petersen. NePoEA-2

True Wisdom. *Unknown.* STF

True Woman: Her Heaven. Dante Gabriel Rossetti. The House of Life, LVIII. VP

True Woman: Her Love. Dante Gabriel Rossetti. The House of Life, LVII. VP

True Woman: Herself. Dante Gabriel Rossetti. The House of Life, LVI. VP

Truly Great, The. Stephen Spender. *See* I Think Continually of Those Who Were Truly Great.

Truly, my Satan, thou art but a dunce. Epilogue. Blake. *Fr.* The Gates of Paradise. CABA; OBNC

Truly, the age I live in is bleak. To Posterity. Bertolt Brecht. MGP

Truisms, The. Louis MacNeice. PoIE

Trumpet, The. Edward Thomas. MMA

Trumpet's loud clangor, The. The Instruments. Dryden. *Fr.* Song for St. Cecilia's Day. PoPo

Trumpet's voice, loud and authoritative, The. Reasons for Attendance. Philip Larkin. ToPo

Trunk of cherry-tree without bark or flowers. Materia Nupcial. "Pablo Neruda." ErPo

Trust Him. *Unknown.* STF

Trust me, I have not earned your dear rebuke. Monna Innominata, VI. Christina Rossetti. VP

Trust Only Yourself. *Unknown.* MeEL

Trusty, dusky, vivid, true. My Wife [*or* To My Wife *or* A Husband to a Wife]. Robert Louis Stevenson. BoC; TRV; WePo

Truth. Chaucer. *See* Balade de Bon Conseyl.

Truth, crushed to earth, shall rise again. Bryant. *Fr.* The Battle-Field. TRV

"Truth," said a traveller. The Black Riders, XXVIII. Stephen Crane. AP

Truth Shall Set You Free. Chaucer. *See* Balade de Bon Conseyl.

Truth: So the frontlet's older legend ran. 1643 "Veritas" 1878. Oliver Wendell Holmes. *Fr.* Two Sonnets: Harvard. AP

Truth the Dead Know, The. Anne Sexton. NePoEA-2; ToPo

Try Again. *At.* William Edward Hickson. RePo

Trying to chop mother down is like. She Went to Stay. Robert Creeley. ToPo

Trying to open locked doors with a sword, threading. Sojourn in the Whale. Marianne Moore. PoIE

Tryst, The. William Soutar. ErPo

Tucking in yellow curls, she poises, set. The Diver. Leonard E. Nathan. ErPo

Tuft of Flowers, The. Robert Frost. AP; CBEP; PoPo

Tulip. William Jay Smith. RePo

Tulip poplar, The, is not a/ poplar. Davenport Gap. Jonathan Williams. OPP

Tulips now are pushing up, The. April. Eunice Tietjens. SoPo

Tumbling among its stones. The Ladder. Gene Baro. NePoEA-2

Tummy Ache. Aileen Fisher. SoPo

Tumult of images insist, A. For John Kennedy of Harvard. Edward Pols. OPP

Tune, A. Arthur Symons. BoLP; OBNC

Tune Thou My Harp. Amy Carmichael. TRV

Tunnel, The. Hart Crane. *Fr.* The Bridge. AP

Tunnyng of Elynour Rummyng, The, *sel.* John Skelton.
"Tell you I chyll." StP
Turkey, The. Ogden Nash. RePo
Turkish Lady, The (A *and* B *vers.*). *Unknown.* BSNS
Turn Again to Life. Mary Lee Hall. PoLF
Turn Back, O Man. Clifford Bax. TRV
Turn Back, You Wanton Flyer. Thomas Campion. UnTE
Turn in the road was illumined, The. Garden of Gethsemane. Boris Pasternak. MoRP
Turn of the Moon. Robert Graves. BoC
"Turn to me in the darkness." Titus and Berenice. John Heath-Stubbs. GTBS-P
Turn to the Left. Deems Taylor, *tr. fr. French.* UnTE
Turn to the watery world! But who to thee. George Crabbe. *Fr.* East Anglian Seas and Shores. HaSV
Turn, turn, two-headed fortune. Tomorrow Is Not Yet. Henri Michaux. CoFP
"Turn, Willie MacIntosh [*or* Mackintosh]." Willie MacIntosh [*or* Mackintosh]. *Unknown.* BFSS; BuBa; CBEP
Turning. Robert Finch. OBCV
Turning and turning in the widening gyre. The Second Coming. W. B. Yeats. CABA; DiPo; EaLo; FoBA; GTBS-P; ILP; MoRP; OnP; PoDB; PoIE; PoPo; StP
Turning the corner, I. Second Sight. W. S. Merwin. StP
Turning-Point. Rainer Maria Rilke, *tr. fr. German by* Michael Hamburger. MGP
Turnip Seller, The. Samuel Johnson. EvOK
Turtle, clam, and crab as well, The. Covering the Subject. Richard Armour. EvOK
Tusks that clashed in mighty brawls, The. On the Vanity of Earthly Greatness. Arthur Guiterman. PoPl; PoPo
Tut! Bah! We take another case. The Poets at Tea, 5. Barry Pain. Par
Tutivillus, the Devil. *Unknown.* MeEL
Twa Brothers, The (B *vers., with music*). *Unknown.* BSO (Two Born Brothers, A *vers., with music.*) BSO
Twa Corbies, The. *Unknown.* CBEP; ELP; GTBS-P; ILP; OnP; StP
(Two Corbies, The.) BuBa
Twa Dogs, The. Burns. CABL
Twa Sisters, The. *Unknown.* CBEP
(Binnorie.) BuBa; SIV
(Twin Sisters, The, A *vers., with music.*) BFSS
(Two Little Sisters, The, *with music.*) BSO
(Two Sisters, The, B *vers., with music.*) BFSS
Twain that were foes, while Mary lived, are fled. His Lady's Death. Pierre de Ronsard. *Fr.* Amours de Marie. RBL
'Twas a cold winter's night and the tempest was snarly. Barney and Katie. *Unknown.* BSO
'Twas a new feeling—something more. Did Not. Thomas Moore. ErPo
'Twas all on a winter's night. Mary of the Wild Moor. *Unknown.* BFSS
'Twas at the landing-place that's just below Mount Wyse. Port Admiral. Frederick Marryat. HaSV
'Twas at the royal feast for Persia won. Alexander's Feast; or, The Power of Music. Dryden. GTBS-P; StP; WiR
'Twas battered and scarred, and the auctioneer. The Touch of the Master's Hand. Myra Brooks Welch. STF; TRV
'Twas Bedford Special Assize, one daft Midsummer's Day. Ned Bratts. Robert Browning. CABL
'Twas brillig, and the slithy toves. Jabberwocky. "Lewis Carroll." *Fr.* Through the Looking-Glass. CABA; CaFP; CBEP; DiPo; FaBV; GoJo; LV; PoIE; PoPl; PoPo; VaPo
'Twas but a single rose. Upon a Virgin Kissing a Rose. Robert Herrick. SeCP
'Twas early in the month of May. Barbara Allen. *Unknown.* CBEP
'Twas early spring when I was young. The Sailor Lad. *Unknown.* BSO
'Twas evening, though not sun-set, and spring-tide. The Shepherd and the Nymph. Walter Savage Landor. *Fr.* Gebir. OBNC
'Twas Friday morn when we set sail. The Mermaid. *Unknown.* SIV
'Twas hurry and scurry at Monmouth Town. Molly Pitcher. Kate Brownlee Sherwood. SIV
'Twas in a basement tobble d'hote. Reverie. Don Marquis. PoLF
'Twas in one summer season. William and Nancy (A *vers.*). *Unknown.* BSNS
'Twas in that island summer where. He Loves and He Rides Away. Sydney Dobell. OBNC
'Twas in that place o' Scotland's Isle. The Twa Dogs. Burns. CABL
'Twas in the days of the Revolution. Emily Geiger. *Unknown.* PoLF
'Twas just before the last fierce charge. The Last Charge. *Unknown.* BSO
'Twas just this time, last year, I died. Emily Dickinson. DiPo
'Twas like a maelstrom, with a notch. Emily Dickinson. CABA

'Twas midnight—Donna Julia was in bed. Byron. *Fr.* Don Juan. UnTE
'Twas midsummer; cooling breezes all the languid forests fanned. The Death of Jefferson. Hezekiah Butterworth. ThLM
'Twas moonlight in the ripe barley. The Walking of the Moon-Woman. John Shaw Neilson. ACV
'Twas noontide of summer. Evening Star. Poe. AP
'Twas of a beautiful young damsel, as I have heard it told. The Banks of Sweet Dundee. *Unknown.* BSNS
'Twas of a young sailor. Green Beds (B *vers.*). *Unknown.* BSNS
'Twas of a young squire in Yarmouth did dwell. The Golden Glove. *Unknown.* BSNS
'Twas of the *Shannon* frigate in the merry month of May. The *Chesapeake* and the *Shannon*. *Unknown.* BSNS
'Twas on a day, a high holiday. Little Matha Grove. *Unknown.* BSNS
'Twas on a Holy Thursday, their innocent faces clean. Holy Thursday. Blake. *Fr.* Songs of Innocence. BoC; CBEP; DiPo; EnPE; FoBA; PoIE; StP
'Twas on a lofty vase's side. Ode on [*or* On] the Death of a Favourite Cat Drowned in a Tub of Gold Fishes [*or* The Cat and the Fish]. Thomas Gray. CBEP; EiCP; GTBS-P; PoLF; VaPo; WiR
'Twas on a winter evening. The Fatal Snowstorm. *Unknown.* BSNS
'Twas on one Sunday morning. Gerry's Rocks (B *vers.*). *Unknown.* BSNS
'Twas on the ninth day of August in the year ninety-eight. Nelson's Victory. *Unknown.* BSNS
'Twas on the shores that round our coast. The Yarn of the *Nancy Bell*. W. S. Gilbert. EvOK; FaBV; HaSV; OnMSP
"'Twas once in my saddle I used to be tipsy." The Cowboy. *Unknown.* BSO
'Twas one cold winter's night when the winds. The Village Pride. *Unknown.* BSNS
'Twas only a cheerful, radiant smile. Life's Little Things. *Unknown.* STF
'Twas only a ripple and just a puff that stirred our old brown sails. The Wreck of the *Glenaloon*. *Unknown.* BSNS
'Twas so, I saw thy birth: that drowsie lake. The Showre. Henry Vaughan. MeP; SeCP
'Twas sung of old how one Amphion. Poverty and Poetry. Thomas Tickell. WaPE
'Twas the night before Christmas, when all through the house. A Visit from St. Nicholas. Clement Clarke Moore. FaBV; OnMSP; PoPl; RePo
'Twas the spring in the air. Danny's Wooing. David McKee Wright. PoAu-1
'Twas thus the subtle love. Three Hymns, 1. Charles Wesley. WaPE
'Twas warm at first, like us. Emily Dickinson. FoBA
'Twas when bright Cynthia with her silver car. A Night-Piece; or, Modern Philosophy. Christopher Smart. VaPo
'Twas when the seas were roaring. A Ballad. John Gay. *Fr.* The What D'Ye Call It. StP
12th Dance—Getting Leather by Language—21 February 1964. Jackson MacLow. CoPo
Twelfth Night. Laurie Lee. BoC
Twelfth Night, *sels.* Shakespeare.
  Come Away, Come Away, Death, *fr.* II, iv. CBEP; FoBA; ILP
  (Clown's Song, The.) CTC
  (Come Away, Death.) DiPo; ELP
  (Dirge of Love.) GTBS-P
  (Feste's Song.) VaPo
  O Mistress Mine, *fr.* II, iii. BoLP; CBEP; CTC; DiPo; ELP; EnRePo; FaBV; FoBA; PoPo; WePo
  (Carpe Diem.) GTBS-P
  (Song: "O mistress mine, where are you roaming?") GoJo; OnP
  When That I Was [and a Little Tiny Boy], *fr.* V, i. EnRePo; PoIE
  (Epilogue: "When that I was and a little tiny boy.") WePo
  (Feste's Final Song.) VaPo
  (Wind and the Rain, The.) CBEP; DiPo; WiR
Twelve Days of Christmas, The. *Unknown.* LV; RePo
Twelve good friends. Peter and John. Elinor Wylie. MoBS; MoRP
"Twelve herds of oxen, no lesse flockes of sheepe." Homer. *Fr.* The Odyssey, XIV. CTC
Twelve o'clock. Rhapsody on a Windy Night. T. S. Eliot. ACV
Twelve Oxen. *Unknown.* RePo
Twelve Properties or Conditions of a Lover, The, *sels.* Sir Thomas More. EnRePo
  Eleventh Property, The.
  First Property, The.
  Seventh Property, The.
Twelve snails went walking after night. The Haughty Snail-King. Vachel Lindsay. LOW

Twelve Weapons of Spiritual Battle, The, *sels.* Sir Thomas More. EnRePo.
 Eternal Reward, Eternal Pain.
 Peace of a Good Mind, The.
 This Life a Dream and Shadow.
Twentieth year is well-nigh past, The. To Mary [*or* To the Same]. William Cowper. CBEP; EiCP; FaPL; GTBS-P
Twenty brothers of Eynhallow, The. Our Lady of the Waves. George Mackay Brown. NePoEA-2
Twenty-five years! I am old, indeed. Conversations. Guido Gozzano. CoIP
Twenty-four Years. Dylan Thomas. DiPo; PoIE; ToPo
Twenty-fourth Psalm, The [*wr.*]. Psalms, XXIX, Bible, *O.T.* PoPo
29th Dance—Having an Instrument—*22 March 1964.* Jackson MacLow. CoPo
22nd November, 1963. George Dekker. OPP
Twenty-third Psalm. Psalms, XXIII, Bible, *O.T. See* Lord Is My Shepherd, The.
Twenty-third Street Runs into Heaven. Kenneth Patchen. ErPo
Twenty Years Ago, *with music. Unknown.* BFSS
Twice. Christina Rossetti. OBNC
Twice or [*or* and] thrice had I loved thee. Air [*or* Aire] and Angels. John Donne. CBEP; EnRePo; SeCP
Twicknam Garden. John Donne. SeCP
 (Twickenham Garden[s].) CBEP; DiPo
Twilight. Feodor Tyutchev, *tr. fr. Russian by* Babette Deutsch. SiGo
Twilight Calm. Christina Rossetti. OBNC
Twilight glitters on the fragmented glass. Judeebug's Country. Joe Johnson. PtTo
Twilight of Disquietude, The, *sels.* Christopher Brennan. PoAu-1
 My Heart Was Wandering in the Sands.
 Years That Go to Make Me Man, The.
Twilight Song, A. Walt Whitman. FoBA
Twin Sisters, The. *Unknown. See* Two Sisters, The.
Twinkle, twinkle, little bat! "Lewis Carroll." *Fr.* Alice's Adventures in Wonderland. Par
Twinkle, twinkle, little star. The Star [*or* The Stars at Night]. Jane Taylor. Par; SoPo; ThGo
Twinkum, twankum, twirlum, twitch. The Little Creature. Walter de la Mare. EvOK
Twins, The. Dorothy Aldis. BiCB
Twins, The. Kathryn Jackson. BiCB
Twins, The. Henry Sambrooke Leigh. BiCB; PoPl
Twins. "Owen Meredith." ErPo
Twins, The. Elizabeth Madox Roberts. BiCB
Twins, The. Karl Shapiro. PoSa
Twins, The. Judith Wright. PoAu-2
Twirling your blue skirts, traveling the sward. Blue Girls. John Crowe Ransom. PoPo; PoSa
Twist-Rime on Spring. Arthur Guiterman. PoSC
Twist the tinsel. Round and Round. Dorothy Brown Thompson. BiCB
Twist thou and twine! in light and gloom. Featherstone's Doom. Robert Stephen Hawker. OBNC
Twisted apple, with rain and magian fire, The. June Morning. Hugh McCrae. PoAu-1
Twitching the leaves just where the drainpipe clogs. Hedgehog. Anthony Thwaite. DaDu
'Twixt optimist and pessimist. The Difference. *Unknown.* LV
Twm was a dunce at school, and was whipped and shaken. The Airy Tomb. R. S. Thomas. ToPo
Two, The. Hugo von Hofmannsthal, *tr. fr. German by* Walter Kaufmann. TwGP
Two against One. *Unknown, tr. fr. Greek by* Louis Untermeyer. UnTE
Two and two four. Exercise Book. Paul Dehn. WePo
Two April Mornings, The. Wordsworth. GTBS-P; PoIE
Two at a Fireside. Edwin Markham. TRV
Two basins—and, surpassing, one ascends. Roman Fountain. Rainer Maria Rilke. TwGP
Two bells go pealing through my age. Harald, the Agnostic Ale-loving Old Shepherd Enemy of the Whisky-drinking Ploughmen and Harvesters, Walks over the Sabbath Hill to the Shearing. George Mackay Brown. NePoEA-2
Two bodies lie beneath this stone. On Thomas Carew. *Unknown.* CBEP
Two Born Brothers. *Unknown. See* Twa Brothers, The.
Two Boys, The. Mary Lamb. CBEP
Two boys uncoached are tossing a poem together. Catch. Robert Francis. PP
Two Brothers, The. Isaac Leib Peretz, *tr. fr. Yiddish by* Jacob Robbins. SIV
Two Cats Make the World ("Two cats at play in the periwinkle"). Vernon Ward. PoNC
Two Corbies, The. *Unknown. See* Twa Corbies, The.
Two Deep Clear Eyes. Walter de la Mare. ThGo
Two Egrets. John Ciardi. CaFP; PoPl
Two empires by the sea. International Hymn. George Huntington. PoLF

Two evils, monstrous either one apart. Winter Remembered. John Crowe Ransom. AP; CaFP; CBEP
Two Foscari, The, *sel.* Byron.
 "How many a time have I." HaSV
Two Freedoms, The. Jon Silkin. PoDB
Two friends talked of dark politics in light. Night Out. R. A. Simpson. PoAu-2
Two Fusiliers. Robert Graves. MMA
Two gates unto the road of life there are. The Road of Life. William Morris. *Fr.* The Earthly Paradise. OBNC
Two Gentlemen of Verona, The, *sels.* Shakespeare.
 My Thoughts Do Harbour, *fr.* III, i. CTC
 Who Is Silvia? *fr.* IV, ii. BoLP; DiPo; EnRePo; FoBA; PoIE
 (To Silvia.) PoPo
 ("Who is Silvia? What is she.") ILP
Two hands lie still, the hairy and the white. Love for a Hand. Karl Shapiro. MoLP; ToPo
Two hands upon the breast. Now and Afterwards. Dinah Maria Mulock Craik. PoLF
Two Hangovers. James Wright. AmPC
250 Willow Lane. Joseph Joel Keith. FiSC
229. José Garcia Villa. PoPl
Two in Bed. Abram Bunn Ross. SoPo
Two in the Campagna. Robert Browning. ELP; GTBS-P; OBNC
 "How say you? Let us, O my dove," *sel.* BoLP
Two Jazz Poems. Carl Wendell Hines, Jr. *See* Jazz Poem.
Two Ladies Bidding Us "Good Morning." James P. Vaughn. NNP
Two Leaves. Jesse Stuart. FiSC
Two Little Babes. *Unknown. See* Cruel Mother, The.
Two Little Children, *with music. Unknown.* BFSS
Two Little Houses. Edith Earnshaw. PoNC
Two Little Sisters, The. *Unknown. See* Twa Sisters, The.
Two little sisters a-marching down the stream. The Twin Sisters. *Unknown.* BFSS
Two Lives and Others. Winfield Townley Scott. PoPl
Two Look at Two. Robert Frost. AP; OnP
Two loves I have of comfort and despair. Sonnets, CXLIV. Shakespeare. CABA; CBEP
Two Lyrics for S. A. Dino Campana, *tr. fr. Italian by* Carlo L. Golino. CoIP
Two magpies under the cypresses. What Birds Were There. Brother Antoninus. ToPo
Two Maidens Went Milking. *Unknown.* UnTE
Two men went up to pray; and one gave thanks. The Newer Vainglory. Alice Meynell. MoRP
Two 'Mericana Men. T. A. Daly. SIV
Two never-ever-will-be lovers each. Mathematics of Encounter. Isabella Gardner. ErPo
Two Noble Kinsmen, The, *sel.* Fletcher *and* Shakespeare.
 Bridal Song, *fr.* I, i. CBEP
Two of us, two of us climb the stairs. Being Twins. Kathryn Jackson. BiCB
Two Old Crows. Vachel Lindsay. LOW; RePo
Two-ones is the name for it, The. The Twins. Elizabeth Madox Roberts. BiCB
Two People. E. V. Rieu. BBGG
Two people. Fast. John Tagliabue. SD
Two people live in Rosamund. Two People. E. V. Rieu. BBGG
Two Poems. Robert J. Abrams. NNP
 "For my unborn son," II.
 "I do not want to turn away," I.
Two Poems. Edward Marshall. CoPo
Two Poems about President Harding. James Wright. AmPC
 His Death, I.
 His Tomb in Ohio, II.
Two Poems on the Catholic Bavarians. Edgar Bowers. PoCh
 "Fierce and brooding holocaust of faith, The," I.
 "I know a wasted place high in the Alps," II.
Two Poems to Miss Lucy Fortescue. George Lyttelton. WaPE
 On Her Pleading Want of Time, II.
 "To him who in an hour must die," I.
Two Prayers. Andrew Gillies. TRV
Two Puritans. *Unknown.* UnTE
Two Red Roses across the Moon. William Morris. CBEP; PoIE
Two Rivers. Emerson. AmLP; AP
Two Rivers. *Unknown.* BuBa; CBEP
Two roads diverged in a yellow wood. The Road Not Taken. Robert Frost. AP; DiPo; EvOK; FoBA; ILP; MP; PoLF; PoPl; PoPo
Two Sails. Conrad Ferdinand Meyer, *tr. fr. German by* Kurt J. Fickert. AGP
Two separate divided silences. Severed Selves. Dante Gabriel Rossetti. The House of Life, XL. VP
Two Sisters, The. *Unknown. See* Twa Sisters, The.
Two Societies, The. John Hall Wheelock. PoCh
Two Songs. Henry Carey. WaPE
 Maid's Husband, The, II.
 True Tar, The, I.
Two Songs from a Play. W. B. Yeats. *Fr.* The Resurrection. CABA; FoBA; ILP; PoDB; PoIE

"I saw a staring virgin stand," I.
"In pity for man's darkening thought," II.
Two Songs of a Fool, *sel.* W. B. Yeats.
  "Speckled cat and a tame hare, A."
  (Song of a Fool.) PoDB
Two Sonnets. Charles Sorley. MMA
  "Saints have adored the lofty soul of you," I.
  "Such, such is Death: no triumph: no defeat," II.
Two Sonnets: Harvard. Oliver Wendell Holmes. AP
  "Christo et Ecclesiae" 1700.
  1643 "Veritas" 1878.
Two Spirits, The. Shelley. WiR
Two stoplights and the Primitive Baptist Church. The Magnolia Belt. Helen Bevington. PoNC
Two Streams, The. Oliver Wendell Holmes. AP
Two Surprises. R. W. McAlpine. PoLF
Two swimmers wrestled on the spar. Emily Dickinson. FoBA
Two tapsters traded on Thames's side. Ballad of the Two Tapsters. Vernon Watkins. MoBS
Two Teacups. Vernon Ward. PoNC
Two There Are I Wish to Celebrate. Howard McCord. PtTo
2000 A.D. Beverly Connelly. FiSC
Two Tramps in Mud Time. Robert Frost. AP; FoBA
Two voices are there: one is of the deep. A Sonnet. J. K. Stephen. Par
Two voices are there, one is of the sea. England and Switzerland 1802. Wordsworth. GTBS-P
Two Voices in a Meadow. Richard Wilbur. CaFP
Two Went Up to the Temple to Pray. Richard Crashaw. TRV
Two Wise Generals. Ted Hughes. MoBS
Two Witches, *sel.* Robert Frost.
  Witch of Coös, The. AP; DiPo
Two Witches, The. Robert Graves. DaDu
Two Wives, The. Daniel Henderson. SIV
Two Years Later. John Wieners. CoPo
'Twould make our eastern people crave. California Ball. John A. Stone. SGR
'Twould ring the bells of Heaven. The Bells of Heaven. Ralph Hodgson. EaLo; GoJo; PoIE; PoSa
Tyger, The. Blake. *See* Tiger, The.
Type of the antique Rome! Rich reliquary. The Coliseum. Poe. AP
Typical of the presents. Uncle. Eleanor Ross Taylor. *Fr.* Family Bible. PoNC
Tyrannic Love, *sel.* Dryden.
  Ah How Sweet It Is to Love, *fr.* IV, i. PoIE
Tywater. Richard Wilbur. PoSa

U

Ubi Sunt Qui ante Nos Fuerunt? *Unknown.* ILP
Uccello. Gregory Corso. PtTo
Ula Masondo's Dream. William Plomer. MoBS
Ulalume—a Ballad. Poe. AP; DiPo; PoIE; PoPo
Ultima Thule. Longfellow. HaSV
Ultimatum. Peggy Pond Church. TRV
Ultra-Germano-Criticasterism. Leigh Hunt. PP
Ulysses. Umberto Saba, *tr. fr. Italian by* Thomas G. Bergin. CoIP
Ulysses. Tennyson. CABA; CaFP; CBEP; DiPo; FoBA; ILP; PoIE; PoPo; PoSa; StP; VaPo; VP
  "I am a part of all that I have met," *sel.* TRV
Ulysses and the Siren. Samuel Daniel. CABA; EnRePo; HaSV; StP
Umamina. B. W. Vilikazi, *tr. fr. Zulu by* R. M. Mfeka. SiGo
Umbra Vitae. Georg Heym, *tr. fr. German by* Christopher Middleton. MGP
Umbrella Brigade, The. Laura E. Richards. SoPo
Umpire, The. Milton Bracker. SD
Umpire, The. Walker Gibson. SD
Umpire is a lonely man, The. The Umpire. Milton Bracker. SD
Unanswered yet? the prayer your lips have pleaded. Sometime, Somewhere. *Unknown.* STF
Unawares. Emma A. Lent. PoLF
Un-Birthday Cake. Aileen Fisher. BiCB
Uncelestial City, The, *sels.* Humbert Wolfe. BoC
  "It is easier to be angry than to pity."
  "She has dusted the ornaments, rubbed down the chairs."
  "You cannot traffick in peace."
Unchangeable, The. Shakespeare. *See* Sonnets, CIX.
Uncle. Eleanor Ross Taylor. *Fr.* Family Bible. PoNC
Uncle Bing. Vincent Starrett. LV
Uncle Dog: The Poet at 9. Robert Sward. CoPo
Uncouth Knight, The. Hugh McCrae. PoAu-1
Undaunted. Nietzsche, *tr. fr. German by* Walter Kaufmann. TwGP

Under a fleshcolored sun that brightens the eastern sky four breaths after midnight. Four Psalms, II. Bertolt Brecht. MGP
Under a lawne, than skyes more cleare. Upon Roses. Robert Herrick. SeCP
Under a splintered mast. A Talisman. Marianne Moore. GoJo
Under a spreading chestnut-tree. The Village Blacksmith. Longfellow. FaPL; LV; PoPl
Under a Telephone Pole. Carl Sandburg. PoPo
Under a toadstool/ Crept a wee Elf. The Elf and the Dormouse. Oliver Herford. OnMSP; SoPo
Under a tree. Mary Is with Child. *Unknown.* MeEL
Under All Change. Josephine W. Johnson. MoRP
Under broad banners and barbarian. Against the Age. Louis Simpson. NePoEA-2
Under Ground. James Reeves. RePo
Under his careful crown he keeps. King Midas Has Asses' Ears. Donald Finkel. NePoEA-2
Under his helmet, up against his pack. Asleep. Wilfred Owen. MMA; WePo
Under Milk Wood. *sels.* Dylan Thomas.
  Every Morning When I Wake. LOW
  Johnnie Crack and Flossie Snail. DaDu; GoJo; LOW
Under my window-ledge the waters race. Coole Park and Ballylee, 1931. W. B. Yeats. GTBS-P
Under night's silent canopy. The Spectre Is on the Move. G. Allana. ACV
Under no hanging heaven-rooted tree. Stony Limits. "Hugh MacDiarmid." CABL
Under the Apple Boughs. Dylan Thomas. *See* Fern Hill.
Under the bronze crown. A Baroque Wall-Fountain in the Villa Sciarra. Richard Wilbur. MP; PoCh; ToPo
Under the bronze leaves a colt was foaled. Song: Under the Bronze Leaves. "St.-J. Perse." *Fr.* Anabasis. PoPl
Under the Casuarina. Elizabeth Riddell. PoAu-2
Under the Drooping Willow Tree. *Unknown.* CBEP
Under the dying sun. The Reaper. L. H. Allen. PoAu-1
Under the elms, on our city street. Grandfather's Ghost. Joseph Payne Brennan. FiSC
Under the Greenwood Tree. Shakespeare. *Fr.* As You Like It, II, v. CBEP; ELP; EnRePo; GTBS-P; WiR
  (Song.) CTC
Under the light, yet under. Emily Dickinson.
Under the Lime Tree. Walther von der Vogelweide, *tr. fr. German by* Thomas Lovell Beddoes. ErPo; UnTE; AnML, *tr. by* Gillian Barker *and* Kenneth Gee
  (Under the Lindens, *tr. by* Ford Madox Ford.) CTC
Under the long dark boughs, like jewels red. Cherry Robbers. D. H. Lawrence. PoIE
Under the mountain, as when I first knew. Sonnets, Part II, XVI. Frederick Goddard Tuckerman. AP
Under the Pines. Arthur S. Bourinot. OBCV
Under the pink quilted covers. The Fortress. Anne Sexton. ToPo
Under the Rain. Eugenio Montale, *tr. fr. Italian by* Carlo L. Golino. CoIP
Under the Sun I Ride Along. Guillaume de Poitiers, *tr. fr. Provençal by* Thomas G. Bergin. AnML
  (Count William's Escapade, *tr. by* Hubert Creekmore.) ErPo
Under the tulip tree in white. A Love-Death Story. Charles Edward Eaton. PoNC
Under the Waterfall. Thomas Hardy. CTC
Under the wide and starry sky. Requiem. Robert Louis Stevenson. FaBV; FaPL; HaSV; ILP; OBNC; PoIE; PoLF; PoPl; PoSa
Under the Willow Shades. Sir William Davenant. ELP
  (Willow, The.) UnTE
Under this stone lies Gabriel John. Gabriel John. *Unknown.* CBEP
Under this stone there lieth at rest. An Epitaph of Sir Thomas Gravener Knight. Sir Thomas Wyatt. EnRePo
Under yonder beech-tree single on the green-sward. Love in the Valley. George Meredith. ErPo; UnTE; VaPo; VP
Undergraduate. Merrill Moore. ErPo
Underneath an old oak tree. The Raven. Samuel Taylor Coleridge. WiR
Underneath my belt. When I Was Lost. Dorothy Aldis. SoPo
Underneath the boardwalk, way, way back. The Secret Cavern. Margaret Widdemer. RePo
Underneath the growing grass. The Bourne. Christina Rossetti. ELP; OBNC
Underneath this myrtle shade. Another. Abraham Cowley. SeCP
Underneath this sable hearse. On [*or* Epitaph on] the Countess Dowager of Pembroke. William Browne. CABA; CBEP
Undersong. Mark Van Doren. PoCh
Understanding. Pauline E. Soroka. PoLF
Undertaking, The. John Donne. CBEP
Undertaking, The. Gerrit Lansing. CoPo
Undertone. Dorothy Quick. FiSC
Underwater eyes, an eel's. An Otter. Ted Hughes. BoC; DaDu; NePoEA-2

Underwear. Lawrence Ferlinghetti. CoPo
Underwood. Howard Moss. MP; NePoEA-2; PP
Undine. Irving Layton. ErPo
Undo Your Heart. *Unknown.* MeEL
Unexplored, The. Burnham Eaton. FiSC
Unexplorer, The. Edna St. Vincent Millay. LOW; RePo
Unexpressed, The. Walt Whitman. PP
Unfaithful Shepherdess, The. *Unknown.* GTBS-P
Unfathomable Sea! whose waves are years. Time. Shelley. Par; PoLF
Unfold! Unfold! Henry Vaughan. ELP
Unforeseen, The. Conrado Nale Roxlo, *tr. fr. Spanish by* Milton Ben Davis. MoRP
Unfortunate Coincidence. Dorothy Parker. PoPl; PoPo
Unfortunate Lover, The. Andrew Marvell. MeP
Unfortunate Man, The, *with music. Unknown.* BFSS
Unfortunate Miss Bailey. *Unknown.* DTC
Unfortunate Reminder, The. William Pattison. UnTE
Unfriendly Fortune. John Skelton. MeEL
Unfriendly friendly universe. The Child Dying. Edwin Muir. GTBS-P
Ungathered Apples, The. James Wright. ErPo
Ungathered Love. Philip Bourke Marston. OBNC
Ungrateful Garden, The. Carolyn Kizer. NePoEA-2
Ungratefulness. George Herbert. FoBA
Unhappy Bella. *Unknown.* ErPo
Unhappy dreamer, who outwinged in flight. On the Death of a Metaphysician. George Santayana. AmLP
Unhappy He. Rubén Darío, *tr. fr. Spanish by* Muna Lee. AnSP
Unhappy man, as soon as he is born. Sonnet. Giambattista Marino. RBL
Unhappy Miner, The, *with music. Unknown.* SGR
Unicorn, The. George Darley. *Fr.* Nepenthe. OBNC
Unicorn, The. "Gertrud Kolmar," *tr. fr. German by* Christopher Middleton. MGP
Unicorn, The. Ella Young. SoPo
Unicorn to hand, A. Haste to the Wedding. Alex Comfort. ErPo
Unicorns at Harvard ("Unicorns are astray"). Norma Farber. FiSC
Uninscribed Monument on One of the Battlefields of the Wilderness, An. Herman Melville. AmLP
Unison. John Hall Wheelock. MoRP
Unison, A. William Carlos Williams. PoIE
Unity. "Æ." MoRP
Universal Prayer, The. Pope. PoIE; VaPo
University Examinations in Egypt. D. J. Enright. MP
Unkept Good Fridays. Thomas Hardy. MoRP
Unkind fate sent the Porlock person. The Person from Porlock. Robert Graves. BoC
Unkindness Has Killed Me. *Unknown.* MeEL
Unknown Bird, The. Edward Thomas. ACV; DTC
Unknown Citizen, The. W. H. Auden. CABA; MoRP; PoPo
Unknown Dead, The. Henry Timrod. AP
Unknown Eros, The. Coventry Patmore. *Poems indexed separately by titles and first lines.*
Unknown Girl in the Maternity Ward. Anne Sexton. CoPo
Unknown God, The. Henry Francis Lyte. TRV
Unknown to all except a few. A Parable. George L. Kress. STF
Unlucky Boat. George Mackay Brown. NePoEA-2
Unmanifest Destiny. Richard Hovey. TRV
Unmoving core, The. Return. Adèle Naudé. ACV
Unprofitablenes. Henry Vaughan. MeP
Unpurged images of day recede, The. Byzantium. W. B. Yeats. CABA; DiPo; FoBA; ILP; PoIE; StP; VaPo
Unquiet Grave, The. *Unknown.* CBEP; DTC; ELP; PoIE; WePo
Unreal, tall as a myth. The Bear on the Delhi Road. Earle Birney. PoCh
Unrest. Richard Watson Dixon. OBNC
Unseen Power, The. Rumi, *tr. fr. Persian by* R. A. Nicholson. SiGo
Unsettled again and hearing Russian spoken. Hearing Russian Spoken. Donald Davie. GTBS-P; NePoEA-2
Unsettled Motorcyclist's Vision of His Death, The. Thom Gunn. NePoEA-2
Unsexed by the cold sea, prone out of it on the beach. Watch Hill. Winfield Townley Scott. ErPo
Untergang. Georg Trakl. *See* Decline.
Unthrift. Coventry Patmore. The Angel in the House, I, iii, 3. FaPL
Until a man should/ come. Man as He Shall Be. Rochelle Owens. CoPo
Until Death Do Us Part. Anselm Hollo. OPP
Until I learned to trust. Progress. *Unknown.* STF
Until the Shadows Lengthen. Cardinal Newman. TRV
Untiring shade, and ghost of dazzling gloom. Black Are the Stars. Raymond Roseliep. FiSC
Untitled. George Herbert. *See* Sonnet: "My God, where is that ancient heat towards thee."
Unto Us a Son Is Given. Alice Meynell. MoRP

Unto you, most froward, this letter I write. A Grotesque Love-Letter. *Unknown.* MeEL
Unwanted, The. C. Day Lewis. PoPl
Unwanted. Edward Field. CoPo
Unwatch'd, the garden bough shall sway. In Memoriam A. H. H., CI. ELP; GTBS-P; OBNC; OnP; VP
Unwelcome. Mary Elizabeth Coleridge. OBNC
Unwillingly Miranda wakes. A Lady Thinks She Is Thirty. Ogden Nash. PoPl
"Up above those top leaves, what do you see." Magnolia Tree in Summer. Sacheverell Sitwell. BoC
Up and Down. Shakespeare. *Fr.* A Midsummer Night's Dream, III, ii. CTC
Up and down/ she walks. The Rose. Robert Creeley. AP; ToPo
Up and Down the City Road. *Unknown.* EvOK
Up and up, the Incense-burner Peak! Having Climbed to the Topmost Peak of the Incense-Burner Mountain. Po Chü-i. SD
Up at a Villa—Down in the City. Robert Browning. CBEP; GTBS-P
Up from my belly, up from my back. Chopping Fire-Wood. Robert Pack. NePoEA-2
Up from the Bed of the River. James Weldon Johnson. *Fr.* The Creation. EaLo
Up from the meadows rich with corn. Barbara Frietchie. Whittier. AP; CTC; FaBV; FaPL; PoLF; PoSC; ThLM
Up from the South, at break of day. Sheridan's Ride. Thomas Buchanan Read. FaBV
Up-Hill. Christina Rossetti. FaPL; OBNC; VP; WiR
Up in the Air. James S. Tippett. SoPo
Up in the Morning Early. Burns. PoSC
Up in the mountain solitudes. An Oft-Told Tale. *Unknown.* SGR
Up in the mountains, it's lonesome all the time. The Mountain Whippoorwill. Stephen Vincent Benét. SIV
Up in the mountains where the hogs are thin. Off to the War. Stephen Vincent Benét. *Fr.* John Brown's Body. SIV
Up shoots the stream and falling pours. The Roman Fountain. Conrad Ferdinand Meyer, *tr. by* Isabel S. MacInnes. AGP
Up spurts the beam, falls, and bestows. The Roman Fountain. Conrad Ferdinand Meyer, *tr. by* Walter Kaufmann. TwGP
Up-Tails All. *Unknown.* UnTE
Up the airy mountain. The Fairies. William Allingham. CBEP; EvOK; FaBV; OnMSP; RoGo
Up the Barley Rows. Sora, *tr. fr. Japanese by* Harold G. Henderson. SoPo
Up the dusty way from Frisco town. Walk, Damn You, Walk! Whittier. PoLF
Up the Hill, down the Hill. Eleanor Farjeon. PoSC
Up the Noran water. Shy Geordie. Helen B. Cruickshank. ACV
Up the reputable walks of old established trees. The Campus on the Hill. W. D. Snodgrass. AP; MP; ToPo
Up to his shoulder. The Bird Fancier. James Kirkup. PoPo
Up to the bed by the window, where I be lyin'. Old Shepherd's Prayer. Charlotte Mew. EaLo
Up to the ranch rides cowboy Freddy. From the Ballad of Two-Gun Freddy. Walter R. Brooks. SoPo
Up! up! my Friend, and quit your books. The Tables Turned. Wordsworth. CBEP; DiPo
Upon a Child That Died. Robert Herrick StP
Upon a darksome night. St. John of the Cross. *Fr.* The Dark Night of the Soul. ErPo
Upon a Dead Man's Head. John Skelton. EnRePo; PoIE
Upon a bed of humble clay. Riddle. Thomas Parnell. WaPE
Upon A. M. Sir John Suckling. ErPo
Upon a mountain height, far from the sea. The Wanderer. Eugene Field. PoPl
Upon a Needle. William Pattison. WaPE
Upon a night an aungell brigh⁴. Now the Most High Is Born. James Ryman. MeEL
Upon a night like this, long years ago. Hawicks' Crossing. Jane Stuart. FiSC
Upon a simmer Sunday morn. The Holy Fair. Burns. EiCP
Upon a Spider Catching a Fly. Edward Taylor. AP; CBEP
Upon a time, before the faery broods. Lamia. Keats. CABL
Upon a Virgin Kissing a Rose. Robert Herrick. SeCP
Upon a wall of medium height. The Opportune Overthrow of Humpty Dumpty. Guy Wetmore Carryl. BBGG
Upon a Wasp Chilled with Cold. Edward Taylor. CBEP
Upon an Easter Morning. Eleanor Farjeon. PoSC
Upon an obscure night. The Obscure Night of the Soul. St. John of the Cross. BoC
Upon Appleton House, to My Lord Fairfax. Andrew Marvell. SeCP
Upon Combing Her Hair. Lord Herbert of Cherbury. StP
Upon His Picture. Thomas Randolph. CBEP
Upon Julia's Clothes. Robert Herrick. CABA; CaFP; CBEP; FaBV; ILP; OnP; PoIE; SeCP; StP
(Whenas in Silk My Julia Goes.) FaPL; GTBS-P

Upon Julia's Fall. Robert Herrick. UnTE
Upon Julia's Petticoat. Robert Herrick. UnTE
Upon Julia's Voice. Robert Herrick. CABA; SeCP
Upon learning that the mother wrote verses. Soiree. Ezra Pound. DTC
Upon Leaving His Mistress. Earl of Rochester. UnTE
Upon Roses. Robert Herrick. SeCP
Upon the beach are thousands of crabs; they are. Crustaceans. Roy Fuller. ToPo
Upon the Bleeding Crucifix. Richard Crashaw. SeCP
Upon the Body of Our Blessed Lord, Naked and Bloody. Richard Crashaw. ILP; SeCP; VaPo
(On Our Crucified Lord, Naked and Bloody.) CABA
Upon the branches of our silence hang our words. The Tree of Silence. Vassar Miller. NePoEA-2; PoDB
Upon the Circumcision. Milton. MeP
Upon the Death of George Santayana. Anthony Hecht. AmLP; CoPo
Upon the Death of My Ever Desired Friend Doctor Donne Dean of Pauls. Henry King. SeCP
Upon the Death of Sir Albert [or Albertus] Morton's Wife. Sir Henry Wotton. SeCP; WePo
(Epitaph on Sir Albert Morton's Wife.) CBEP
Upon the decks they take beef tea. Passage Steamer. Louis MacNeice. HaSV
Upon the Feast of St. Simon and St. Jude. Samuel Johnson. EiCP
Upon the Hard Crest. "Anna Akhmatova," tr. fr. Russian by Babette Deutsch. SiGo
Upon the hills new grass is seen. Twist-Rime on Spring. Arthur Guiterman. PoSC
Upon the Nipples of Julia's Breast. Robert Herrick. ErPo; UnTE
Upon the road of my life. The Black Riders, LX. Stephen Crane. AP
Upon the Sudden Restraint of the Earl of Somerset, Falling from Favour. Sir Henry Wotton. ELP
(Upon the Sudden Restraint of the Earle of Somerset, Then Falling from Favor.) SeCP
Upon the sunny summer hill. Clover for Breakfast. Frances Frost. RePo
Upon the Works of Ben Jonson, sel. John Oldham.
"Let dull and ignorant pretenders art condemn." PP
Upon this happy New Year night. Eugene Field. Fr. A New Year Idyl. PoSC
Upon this Primrose hill. The Primrose. John Donne. MeP
Upon Venus Putting on Mars His Armes. Richard Crashaw. SeCP
Upon Visiting His Lady by Moonlight. "A. W." CTC
Upon Wedlock and Death of Children. Edward Taylor. AP
Upon Westminster Bridge. Wordsworth. See Composed upon Westminster Bridge, September 3, 1802.
Upon you, adolescent virgin. Adolescent. "Vincenzo Cardarelli." CoIP
Upon your snow-white shoulder. Your Snow-white Shoulder. Heine. UnTE
Uproar, An/ a spruce-green sky, bound in iron. The Butterfly. Margaret Avison. OBCV
Uprose the King of Men with speed. The Descent of Odin. Thomas Gray. EiCP
Upstream. Carl Sandburg. MoRP
Urania. Matthew Arnold. VP
Urania speaks with darken'd brow. In Memoriam A. H. H., XXXVII. Tennyson. VP
Urban Roses. Ted Isaac. PoPl
Urging Her of a Promise. Ben Jonson. Fr. A Celebration of Charis. SeCP
Urging, upsurging night. Night. Friedrich Hebbel. AGP
Uriel. Emerson. AP
Us Poets. Franklin P. Adams. PoPl
Use force and chisel, be lapidary, not. Collages and Compositions. Richmond Lattimore. PP
Use me, God, in Thy great harvest field. Send Me. Christina Rossetti. TRV
Use your money while you're living. Your Money and Mine. Unknown. STF
Usually hateful crow, The. Beauty. Basho. SoPo
Utah Carl, with music. Unknown. BFSS
Utilitarian View of the Monitor's Fight, A. Herman Melville. AP
Utopia of Lord Mayor Howard, The. Randolph Stow. PoAu-2

V

V-J Day. John Ciardi. PoPl
V-Letter. Karl Shapiro. AP; MoLP; ThLM
Vacationer. Walker Gibson. SD
Vacillation. W. B. Yeats. PoDB

Vademecum-Vadetecum. Nietzsche, tr. fr. German by Walter Kaufmann. TwGP
Vagabond, The. Robert Louis Stevenson. PoPo
Vagabond Song, A. Bliss Carman. LV; PoSC; RePo
Vagrant, A. Erik Axel Karlfeldt, tr. fr. Swedish by Charles Wharton Stork. PoPl
Vain and Careless. Robert Graves. DaDu; LOW
Vain and not to trust. Woman. Irving Layton. ErPo
Vain excess of flattering fortune's gifts, The. Gascoigne's Memories, II. George Gascoigne. EnRePo
Vain Hope, Adieu. Unknown. EnRePo
Vain is the effort to forget. On the Rhine. Matthew Arnold. Faded Leaves, IV. VP
Vainly I strive to make a "live" at mining. The Miner's Lament, II. Unknown. SGR
Vala; or, The Four Zoas, sels. Blake. OBNC
Enion Replies from the Caverns of the Grave.
Enitharmon Revives with Los.
Lamentation of Enion, The.
Vale from Carthage. Peter Viereck. PoPo
Vale of Teares, A. Robert Southwell. MeP
Valediction, A. Melvin Walker La Follette. CoPo
Valediction, A: Forbidding Mourning. John Donne. CABA; CaFP; DiPo; EnRePo; FaPL; FoBA; ILP; MeP; PoIE; SeCP; VaPo
Valediction, A: Of My Name in the Window. John Donne. EnRePo
Valediction, A: Of Weeping. John Donne. CABA; CBEP; EnRePo; SeCP
Valentine. Donald Hall. BoLP
Valentine, A. Eleanor Hammond. RePo
Valentine. Shelley Silverstein. PoSC
Valentine. "C. W. T." RePo
Valentine Promise. Unknown. PoSC
Valiant Love. Richard Lovelace. SeCP
Valley of the Shadow of Death, The. William Cowper. EiCP
Valley of Unrest, The. Poe. AP
Vampire. Walter H. Kerr. FiSC
Vampire Bride. Felix Stefanile. FiSC
Van Dieman's Land, with music. Unknown. BSNS
Van Winkle. Hart Crane. Fr. The Bridge. FaBV
Vanbrug's House. Swift. PP
Vane on Hughley steeple, The. Hughley Steeple. A. E. Housman. A Shropshire Lad, LXI. VP
Vanity. Robert Graves. GTBS-P
Vanity of Existence, The. Philip Freneau. AP
Vanity of Human Wishes, The; the Tenth Satire of Juvenal, Imitated. Samuel Johnson. CABA; EiCP; EiPE; VaPo
In Imitation of the Tenth Satire of Juvenal, sel. PoIE
Vanity of Spirit. Henry Vaughan. MeP
Vanity of Vanities. Palladas, tr. fr. Greek by M. Hardinge. TRV
Vanity of vanities, the Preacher saith. The One Certainty. Christina Rossetti. OBNC
Vanity, saith the preacher, vanity! The Bishop Orders His Tomb at Saint Praxed's Church. Robert Browning. CABA; CaFP; DiPo; ILP; OnP; PoIE; VaPo; VP
Variation on a Theme by Dylan Thomas. Carl Bode. ToPo
Variations of an Air. G. K. Chesterton. Par
Variations on a Line from Shakespeare's Fifty-sixth Sonnet. E. L. Mayo. PoCh
Variations on a Medieval Theme. Geoffrey Dutton. PoAu-2
Various Wakings. Vincent Buckley. PoAu-2
Vast mild melancholy splendid. Canberra in April. J. R. Rowland. PoAu-2
Vaudracour and Julia, sel. Wordsworth.
"To a lodge that stood." EvOK
Vegetables. Rachel Field. SoPo
Velvet Shoes. Elinor Wylie. GoJo; PoPl; SoPo
Vendor. Raymond Roseliep. FiSC
Venerable Mother Toothache. A Charm against the Toothache. John Heath-Stubbs. DaDu; MP
Veneta. Mary Elizabeth Coleridge. CBEP
Venetian Epigrams, sel. Goethe, tr. fr. German by Walter Kaufmann.
"How they ring their bells, these priests! How pressing." TwGP
Vengence on Cats. John Skelton. Fr. Phyllyp Sparowe. PoSa
Veni Creator. Bliss Carman. MoRP
Venice. Nietzsche, tr. fr. German by Walter Kaufmann. TwGP
Venus Accoutered as Mars. Unknown, tr. fr. Greek by Louis Untermeyer. UnTE
Venus and Adonis, sels. Shakespeare.
"O, what a war of looks was then between them!" UnTE
"'Sweet boy,' she says, 'this night I'll waste in sorrow.'" ErPo
Venus and Cupide. Sir Thomas More. Fr. The Pageants of Thomas More. EnRePo
Venus, take my votive glass. The Lady Who Offers Her Looking-Glass to Venus. Matthew Prior. CBEP
Venus Victrix. Dante Gabriel Rossetti. The House of Life, XXXIII. VP

Venus, what mood inspires you to don. Venus Accoutered as Mars. *Unknown.* UnTE

Venus, who wander clear among the skies. Sonnet V. Louise Labé. RBL

Veracruz. Robert Hayden. AmNP

Verba in Memoriam. Barbara Guest. OPP

Vergissmeinnicht. Keith Douglas. GTBS-P

Vers de Société. H. D. Traill. Par

Verse. Richmond Lattimore. PP

Verse, a breeze 'mid blossoms straying. Youth and Age. Samuel Taylor Coleridge. GTBS-P; OBNC; PoLF

Verse makes heroic [*or* heroick] virtue live. To Mr. Henry Lawes, Who Had Then Newly Set a Song of Mine in the Year 1635. Edmund Waller. CTC; PP; SeCP

Verses: "Even such is time." Sir Walter Ralegh. *See* Even Such Is Time.

Verses: "I am monarch of all I survey." William Cowper. *See* Solitude of Alexander Selkirk, The.

Verses against the Inconsequence of Men's Taste and Strictures. Sister Juana Inés de la Cruz, *tr. fr. Spanish by* Muriel Kittel. AnSP

Verses at Night. Dannie Abse. MP

Verses Expressing the Feelings of a Lover. Sister Juana Inés de la Cruz, *tr. fr. Spanish by* Samuel Beckett. AnSP

Verses Intended to Go with a Posset Dish to My Dear Little Goddaughter, 1882. James Russell Lowell. AP

Verses on the Death of Dr. Swift. Swift. CABL

(On the Death of Dr. Swift.) EiCP

Verses Supposed to Be Written by Alexander Selkirk during His Solitary Abode on the Island of Juan Fernandez. William Cowper. *See* Solitude of Alexander Selkirk, The.

Verses Written during a Sleepless Night. Pushkin, *tr. fr. Russian by* Babette Deutsch. PoPl

Verses Written during the War, 1756-1763. Thomas Osbert Mordaunt. CBEP

Verses Written upon an Ecstasy of High Contemplation. St. John of the Cross. *See* I Entered Where I Did Not Know.

Versions of Love. Roy Fuller. ToPo

Vertiendo Está Sangre. St. Theresa of Avila, *tr. fr. Spanish by* E. Allison Peers. RBL

Vertue. George Herbert. *See* Virtue.

Very Early. Karla Kuskin. SoPo

Very like a Whale. Ogden Nash. DTC; PoLF

Very Lovely. Rose Fyleman. SoPo

Very Nearly. Queenie Scott-Hopper. SoPo

Very old are the woods. All That's Past. Walter de la Mare. GoJo; StP

Very Phoenix, A. Thomas Lodge. CBEP

Very pitiful lady, very young, A. Dante. *Fr.* La Vita Nuova. CTC

Very Rich Man, The. Dorothy Parker. PoPo

Very Strong Stomach Has Mr. Luke, A. Manuel González Prada, *tr. fr. Spanish by* William M. Davis. AnSP

Vesper. Thomas Edward Brown. BoC

Vesture of the Soul, The. "Æ." ACV

Veteran's Day of Recollection, A. John Beecher. PtTo

Vexation, Enemy of Youth. Jordi de Sant Jordi, *tr. fr. Catalan by* William M. Davis. AnML

Vicar, The. George Crabbe. *Fr.* The Borough. OBNC

Vicar, The. Winthrop Mackworth Praed. OBNC

Vicar of Wakefield, The, *sels.* Goldsmith.

Elegy on the Death of a Mad Dog, *fr. ch.* 17. CBEP; PoPo; PoSa; RoGo

Song: "When lovely woman stoops to folly," *fr. ch.* 24. ILP; PoPl; VaPo

(Stanzas on Woman.) ELP

(When Lovely Woman Stoops [to Folly].) CBEP; PoIE; StP

("When lovely woman stoops to folly.") GTBS-P

Vice. Pope. *Fr.* An Essay on Man. PoPl

Vicissitudes of the Creator. Archibald MacLeish. VaPo

Victoria. Henry van Dyke. TRV

Victoria Markets Recollected in Tranquillity, The, *abr.* Frank Wilmot. PoAu-2

Victorious beauty, though your eyes. To the Countesse of Salisbury. Aurelian Townsend. SeCP

Victorious Men of Earth. James Shirley. *Fr.* Cupid and Death. CBEP

(Last Conqueror, The.) GTBS-P

Victory. Mary Britton Miller. RePo

Victory. *Unknown.* STF

Victory Dance, A. Alfred Noyes. PoLF

Victory in Defeat. Edwin Markham. PoLF; PoPl

View. Josephine Miles. RePo

View, all ye eyes above, this sight which flings. Meditation Twenty. Edward Taylor. *Fr.* Preparatory Meditations, First Series. AP

View from the Window, The. R. S. Thomas. BoC

View of a Pig. Ted Hughes. MP

View of the Burning, A. James Merrill. NePoEA-2

Views of the Oxford Colleges. Paris Leary. CoPo

Vigil. Juan Ramón Jiménez, *tr. fr. Spanish by* Willis Barnstone. AnSP

Vigil, The. Denise Levertov. NePoEA-2

Vigil, The. Theodore Roethke. *Fr.* Four for Sir John Davies. PoDB

Vigil of Venus, The. *Unknown, tr. fr. Latin by* Thomas Stanley. UnTE

Vigil Strange I Kept on the Field One Night. Walt Whitman. FoBA

Vigils, *sel.* Siegfried Sassoon.

Down the Glimmering Staircase. PoLF

Village, The, *sels.* George Crabbe.

"Fled are those times, when, in harmonious strains." PoSa

"No shepherds now, in smooth alternate verse." PP

Pauper's Funeral, The. OBNC

"Village Life, and every care that reigns, The." EnPE

Village Atheist, The. Edgar Lee Masters. *Fr.* Spoon River Anthology. EaLo; PoPo

Village Blacksmith, The. Longfellow. FaPL; LV; PoPl

Village Christmas. Margaret Widdemer. RePo

Village Life, and every care that reigns, The. George Crabbe. *Fr.* The Village. EnPE

Village Pride, The. *Unknown.* BSNS

Village Schoolmaster, The. Goldsmith. *Fr.* The Deserted Village. PoSa

Villanelle. William Empson. PoIE

Villanelle. M. D. Feld. SD

Villanelle. Dilys Laing. ErPo

Villanelle a Rozette. Philippe Desportes, *tr. fr. French by* George Wyndham. RBL

Villanelle: The Psychological Hour. Ezra Pound. CTC

Villon's Epitaph. *See* Epitaph in Form of a Ballad, The.

Vine, The. Robert Herrick. ErPo; UnTE

Vine, my Lord, a noble vine indeed, A. Meditation. Can. 1.2. Thy Love Is Better than Wine. Edward Taylor. *Fr.* Preparatory Meditations, Second Series. MeP

Vines of Lebanon that briskly grew, The. Meditation. Can. 6.11. To See the Fruits of the Valley. Edward Taylor. *Fr.* Preparatory Meditations, Second Series. MeP

Vineyard, The. *Unknown.* STF

Violante has commanded me to write. A Sonnet All of a Sudden. Lope de Vega. AnSP

Violet, The. Goethe, *tr. fr. German by* Alexander Gode. AGP

Violet Bank, A. Shakespeare. *Fr.* A Midsummer Night's Dream, II, i. RePo

Violet bloom of summer's end. Tropes of One Season. Charles Edward Eaton. FiSC

Violet on the lea had grown, A. The Violet. Goethe. AGP

Violette, La. Jean Desmarets de Saint-Sorlin, *tr. fr. French by* Judith McDowell. *Fr.* Guirlande de Julie. RBL

Viper, The. Ruth Pitter. DaDu

Virgin Declares Her Beauties, A. Francesco da Barberini, *tr. fr. Italian by* Dante Gabriel Rossetti. ErPo

Virginal, A. Ezra Pound. AP; ILP

Virgine Maries Conception, The. Robert Southwell. MeP

Virginia. T. S. Eliot. *Fr.* Landscapes. PoSa

Virgins Salutation, The. Robert Southwell. MeP

Virgins terrify too many men. Sonnet XII. Winfield Townley Scott. ErPo

Virile Christ, A. Rex Boundy. TRV

Virtue. Walter de la Mare. MMA

Virtue. George Herbert. CABA; CaFP; CBEP; ELP; FoBA; PoIE; PoSa

(Vertue.) MeP; SeCP

Virtue dwells, so runs the tale. The Climb to Virtue. Simonides. SiGo

Virtuous Fox and the Self-righteous Cat, The. John Cunningham. OnMSP

Virtuous Woman, A. Proverbs, XXXI: 10-12, 27-31, Bible, *O.T.* TRV

Vision, A. John Clare. *See* I Lost the Love of Heaven.

Vision, A. Lord Herbert of Cherbury. SeCP

Vision, The ("I dreamed we were both in bed"). Robert Herrick. *See* Vision to Electra, The.

Vision, The ("Methought I saw as I did dream in bed"). Robert Herrick. *See* Second Vision, The.

Vision, The ("Sitting alone as one forsook"). Robert Herrick. ErPo; SeCP

(Sitting Alone.) UnTE

Vision. Frank Sidgwick. MMA

Vision by Sweetwater. John Crowe Ransom. AP

Vision of a Past Warrior. Peter La Farge. PtTo

Vision of Belshazzar, The. Byron. OnMSP; RoGo

Vision of Judgment, The. Byron. StP

Vision of Piers Plowman, The, *sels.* William Langland(?).

"And I bowed my body and beheld all about," 5 *ll.* CTC

Harrowing of Hell, The, *fr.* Passus XXI (C *text*), *mod. by* Nevill Coghill.

Love, *mod. by* Nevill Coghill. BoC

Prayer for Rich and Poor, *fr.* Passus XIV (B *text*), *mod. by* Nevill Coghill. BoC

Vision of Sir Launfal, The. James Russell Lowell. OnMSP

Sels.

"And what is so rare as a day in June," *fr.* Prelude to Pt. I. AmLP; FaPL

(June.) FaBV

"Holy Supper is kept, indeed, The," *fr.* Pt. II. TRV

June ("Over his keys the musing organist"), *fr.* Prelude to Pt. I. PoLF
"My golden spurs now bring to me," Pt. I. SIV
"There was never a leaf on bush or tree," Pt. II. SIV
Vision of the Lamentation of Beulah over Ololon, A. Blake. *See* Lark's Song, The.
Vision to Electra, The. Robert Herrick. SeCP
(Vision, The.) UnTE
Visionary, The. Emily Brontë. BoC; OBNC
(Silent Is the House.) ELP
Visit, The. Robert Mezey. AmPC
Visit by Water. Floris Clark McLaren. OBCV
Visit from Abroad, A. James Stephens. LOW
Visit from St. Nicholas, A. Clement Clarke Moore. FaBV; OnMSP; PoPl; RePo
Visit of the Beloved, The. Ben Hazm, *tr. fr. Arabic by* Lysander Kemp. AnML
Visit of the Professor of Aesthetics, The. Margaret Danner. *Fr.* Far from Africa. AmNP; NNP
Visit to Van Gogh, A. Charles Causley. PoCh
Visitant, The. Theodore Roethke. PoIE
Visitation, The. Elizabeth Jennings. MoBS
Visitation, The. Robert Southwell. MeP
Visitations: VII, *sel.* Louis MacNeice.
And the Lord Was Not in the Whirlwind. EaLo
Visitor, The. Katharine Pyle. BBGG
Visitors. Harry Behn. SoPo
Vista. Alfred Kreymborg. BoLP
Vita Brevis. *Unknown, tr. fr. German by* Louis Untermeyer. UnTE
Vita Nuova, La, *sels.* Dante, *tr. fr. Italian by* Dante Gabriel Rossetti.
"Beyond the sphere which spreads to widest space," XXIX. CTC
(Beyond the Sphere Which Turns Most Distant, *tr. by* Maurice Valency.) AnML
Sonnet: "Mine eyes beheld the blessed pity spring," XXIII. PoPl
"That she hath gone to Heaven suddenly," III. CTC
"Very pitiful lady, very young, A," XIV. CTC
Within Her Eyes, XII. SiGo
"Ye pilgrim folk advancing pensively," XXVIII. CTC
Vitae Summa Brevis Spem Nos Vetet Incohare Longam. Ernest Dowson. StP
(They Are Not Long.) PoSa
Vital Spark of Heavenly Flame. Pope. PoPo
Vitelli rides west toward Fano, the morning sun. The Death of Vitellozzo Vitelli. Irving Feldman. MP
Vivamus, Mea Lesbia. Thomas Campion. *See* My Sweetest Lesbia.
Vivamus, Mea Lesbia. Catullus, *tr. fr. Latin by* Frank O. Copley. StP
Vivien's Song. Tennyson. *See* In Love, If Love Be Love.
Vizier's Apology, The. Arthur Guiterman. SIV
Vlamertinghe: Passing the Chateau. Edmund Blunden. MMA
Vocal Miner, The, *with music.* John A. Stone. SGR
Vodka. John Ciardi. ToPo
Voice, The. Thomas Hardy. AnMoPo; GTBS-P; OBNC
Voice, The. Theodore Roethke. AmLP
Voice from the Waters, A. Thomas Lovell Beddoes. *See* Dirge: "Swallow leaves her nest, The."
Voice from the Well, A. George Peele. *Fr.* The Old Wives' Tale. CBEP
Voice from under the Table, A. Richard Wilbur. PoCh
Voice, loud in that light, to Lucifer crying, A. The Harrowing of Hell. William Langland. *Fr.* The Vision of Piers Plowman. BoC
Voice of Experience, The. Goethe, *tr. fr. German by* Walter Kaufmann. ErPo; TwGP
Voice of my beloved, The! The Song of Solomon, Bible, *O.T.* PoPl; SiGo
Voice of the last cricket, The. Splinter. Carl Sandburg. RePo
Voice of the Lobster, The. "Lewis Carroll." *Fr.* Alice's Adventures in Wonderland, *ch.* 10. EvOK
(" 'Tis the voice of the Lobster; I heard him declare.") Par
Voice That Beautifies the Land, The. *Tr. fr. Navaho Indian by* Washington Matthews. SiGo
Voices from the Other World. James Merrill. MP
Voices moving about in the quiet house. Falling Asleep. Siegfried Sassoon. ILP
Voices of death are sounding. Death of Antoñito el Camborio. Federico García Lorca. AnSP
Volpone, *sel.* Ben Jonson.
"Come, my Celia, let us prove," *fr.* III, vii. EnRePo
(Come, My Celia.) FaBV
(Song to Celia.) ErPo; SeCP
(To Celia.) UnTE
Volume of Chopin, A. James Picot. PoAu-2
Voluntaries, *sel.* Emerson.
In an Age of Fops and Toys, III. PoLF; PoPo
"So nigh is grandeur to our dust," *last* 4 *ll. of* III. TRV
Voluntarily walled themselves up inside the stone. The Old Age Home. Theodore Holmes. CoPo

Vulture, The. Israel Kafu Hoh. ACV
Volunteer, The. Herbert Asquith. MMA
Vow, The. Anthony Hecht. PoCh
Vow to Cupid, The. *Unknown, tr. fr. Latin by* John Addington Symonds. SiGo
Vox Humana. Thom Gunn. NePoAu-2
Voyage, The. Karl Shapiro. MoLP
Voyage of Jimmy Poo, The. James A. Emanuel. AmNP; NNP
Voyage to Montevideo. Dino Campana, *tr. fr. Italian by* Carlo L. Golino. CoIP
Voyagers. Henry van Dyke. TRV
Voyagers' Prayer. *Unknown, tr. fr. Chippewa Indian.* TRV
Voyages (I-VI). Hart Crane. AP; CABL
Sels.
"Above the fresh ruffles of the surf," I. CABA; HaSV; PoIE
"And yet this great wink of eternity," II. AmLP; DTC; PoDB; PoIE; VaPo
"Infinite consanguinity it bears," III. PoIE
"Where icy and bright dungeons lift," VI. CABA
Voyages of Captain Cock, The. William Jay Smith. ErPo; UnTE
Voyeur. John Edward Hardy. ErPo

W

Wae's me, wae's me. The Wandering Spectre. *Unknown.* CBEP
Waile whit ase whalles bon, A. The White Beauty. *Unknown.* MeEL
Wailing, wailing, wailing, the wind over land and sea. Rizpah. Tennyson. CABL; SIV
Wailing wind doth not enough despair, The. Awake. Mary Elizabeth Coleridge. OBNC
Wailings of a maiden I recite. Wednesday; or, The Dumps. John Gay. *Fr.* The Shepherd's Week. EiCP
Wait, Kate! You skate at such a rate. To Kate, Skating Better than Her Date. David Daiches. SD
Wait On! *Unknown.* STF
Waiting. John Burroughs. FaPL; TRV
Waiting. Hilary Corke. ErPo
Waiting. Ruth Apprich Jacob. BiCB
Waiting Both. Thomas Hardy. PoPo
Waiting for the end, boys, waiting for the end. Just a Smack at Auden. William Empson. ToPo
Waiting for the Morning. *Unknown.* STF
Waiting for when the sun an hour or less. In Santa Maria del Popolo. Thom Gunn. GTBS-P; NePoEA-2; PoIE
Waitress, with eyes so marvellous black. Salad: After Browning. Mortimer Collins. Par
Wake All the Dead. Sir William Davenant. *Fr.* The Law against Lovers. CBEP; ELP
Wake! For the Sun, who scattered into flight. Rubáiyát of Omar Khayyám. *Tr. by* Edward Fitzgerald. FaPL; OBNC; PoIE. *See also* Awake! for Morning in the bowl of Night.
Wake, Sleepy Thyrsis. *Unknown.* EnRePo
Wake! the silver dusk returning. Reveille. A. E. Housman. A Shropshire Lad, IV. PoLF; PoPo
Wake Up! Wake Up! Basho, *tr. fr. Japanese by* Harold G. Henderson. SoPo
Wake Up, You Drowsy Sleepers, *with music. Unknown.* BFSS
Wakeful in the Township. Elizabeth Riddell. PoAu-2
Wakeful Night. Annette von Droste-Hülshoff, *tr. fr. German by* S. G. Flygt. AGP
Wakeful, vagrant, restless thing. The Power of Fancy. Philip Freneau. AP
Waken, lords and ladies gay. Hunting Song. Sir Walter Scott. EvOK; GTBS-P; SD; WiR
Waking, The. Theodore Roethke. AP; MP; PoPl; ToPo
Waking Alone. *Unknown.* MeEL
Waking, Child, While You Slept. Ethel Anderson. *Fr.* Bucolic Eclogues. PoAu-2
Waking outside his Babylonian binge. A Thousandth Poem for Dylan Thomas. John Ciardi. ToPo
Waldeinsamkeit. Emerson. AP
Wales England wed; so I was bred. An Autobiography. Ernest P. Rhys. ACV
Walk, The. W. W. Eustace Ross. SD
Walk, Damn You, Walk! William de Vere. PoLF
Walk in Late Summer, A. Theodore Roethke. PoDB
Walk in the Garden, The. Conrad Aiken. PoCh
Walk on the Beach, The. John Gould Fletcher. BoLP; MoLP
Walk this mile in silence. Pastourelle. Donald Jeffrey Hayes. AmNP
Walk-up. W. S. Merwin. CoPo

Walk with thy fellow-creatures: note the hush. Fragment. Henry Vaughan. TRV

Walker, It Is Your Footsteps. Antonio Machado, *tr. fr. Spanish by* Kate Flores. AnSP

Walking. Grace Ellen Glaubitz. SoPo

Walking. Thomas Traherne. *See* To Walk Abroad.

Walking alone in a multitude of loves when morning's light. The Marriage of a Virgin. Dylan Thomas. ErPo

Walking at Night. Amory Hare. PoLF

Walking docile as you do down the empty street. Abasis. Christopher Middleton. *Fr.* Herman Moon's Hourbook. NePoEA-2

Walking in a Meadowe Greene. *Unknown.* ErPo

Walking of the Moon-Woman, The. John Shaw Neilson. ACV

Walking on Water. James Dickey. NePoEA-2

Walking out in the late March midnight. Thorn Leaves in March. W. S. Merwin. MP

Walking through usual flannels and faces. Aunt Cora. Kenneth Pitchford. CoPo

Walking to the museum. Bone Thoughts on a Dry Day. George Starbuck. MP

Walking with God. William Cowper. EiCP; EnPE; TRV; VaPo

Wall, The. Louis MacNeice. PoIE

Wall, no! I can't tell whar he lives. Jim Bludso, of the *Prairie Belle.* John Hay. PoPo

Wall of China, The. Padraic Colum. RoGo

Wallowing in this bloody sty. The Drunken Fisherman. Robert Lowell. AP

Walls have been shaded for so many years, The. The Soldier Walks under the Trees of the University. Randall Jarrell. PoP1

Walrus and the Carpenter, The. "Lewis Carroll." *Fr.* Through the Looking-Glass. FaBV; SoPo

Walsinghame. *Unknown, at. to* Sir Walter Ralegh. *See* As You Came from the Holy Land.

Walt Whitman at Bear Mountain. Louis Simpson. NePoEA-2; PoCh; PP

Waltz. Ruth Forbes Sherry. FiSC

Waltz in the Afternoon, A. Beth Bentley. BoLP

Waltzer in the House, The. Stanley Kunitz. ErPo

Waltzing Matilda. A. B. Paterson. PoAu-1

Wan, fragile faces of joy! Home-Thoughts from France. Isaac Rosenberg. MMA

Wanderer, The, *sels.* Christopher Brennan. PoAu-1
  Come Out, Come Out, Ye Souls That Serve.
  How Old Is My Heart.
  I Cry to You as I Pass Your Windows.
  "I sorrow for youth—ah, not for its wildness (would that were dead!)." ACV
  Land I Came Thro' Last, The.
  O Desolate Eyes.

Wanderer, The. Eugene Field. PoP1

Wanderer, The. John Masefield. CABL

Wanderer Recalls the Past, The. Wordsworth. *Fr.* The Excursion. OBNC

Wanderer's Night Song. Goethe, *tr. fr. German by* Longfellow. PoP1

Wanderer's Song, A. John Masefield. RePo

Wandering Gadling, The. Sir Thomas Wyatt. CBEP

Wandering Jew, The. Robert Mezey. NePoEA-2

Wandering Jew, The. E. A. Robinson. PoDB

Wandering Moon, The. James Reeves. RePo

Wandering Spectre, The. *Unknown.* CBEP

Waning of the Harvest Moon, The. John Wieners. CoPo

Wanne mine eyhnen misten. How Death Comes. *Unknown.* MeEL

Wantage Bells. John Betjeman. WePo

Wanted. Josiah Gilbert Holland. *See* God, Give Us Men!

Wanted—a Man. Edmund Clarence Stedman. LiPo

Wanting for their young limbs praise. To the Girls of My Graduating Class. Irving Layton. ErPo

Wanton troopers riding by. The Nymph Complaining for the Death of Her Fawn [*or* Faun]. Andrew Marvell. CBEP; SeCP

Wants. Philip Larkin. GTBS-P

Wants of Man, The. John Quincy Adams. PoLF

War. Joseph Langland. MP; PoCh

War against the Trees, The. Stanley Kunitz. AnMoPo

War God, The. Stephen Spender. MoRP

War in Camp. John A. Stone. SGR

War in Heaven. Milton. *Fr.* Paradise Lost, VI. DiPo

War is done mother. GI. Raymond Roseliep. FiSC

War Is Kind, *sels.* Stephen Crane.
  "Chatter of a death-demon from a tree-top, The," XIX. AP
  "I explain the silvered passing of a ship at night," VI. AP
  "I have heard the sunset song of the birches," VII. AP
  "In the night," XVIII. AP
  "Man said to the universe, A," XXI. AP
  "Newspaper is a collection of half-injustices, A," XII. AP
  "On the desert," XI. AP
  Slant of Sun, A, XIV. VaPo
  "There was a land where lived no violets," XXIII. AP

Trees in the Garden, The, XXVI. VaPo

War Is Kind, I (title poem). DiPo; PoPo; StP; ThLM ("Do not weep, maiden, for war is kind.") AP; PoLF

War is not declared any more. Every Day. Ingeborg Bachmann. MGP

War of the Secret Agents, The. Henri Coulette. AmPC *Sels.*
  Cinema, at the Lighthouse. NePoEA-2
  Denise: A Letter Never Sent. NePoEA-2
  Epilogue: Author to Reader. NePoEA-2
  Phono, at the Boar's Head. NePoEA-2

War Poet. Roy Fuller. PP

War Poet. Sidney Keyes. AnMoPo

War screams, so peace becomes a whisper. Sunday Edition. Joseph Joel Keith. FiSC

War Song, A. Bertran de Born. *See* I'm Pleased When Gaudy Eastertime.

War Song. John Davidson. OBNC

War-Song of Dinas Vawr, The. Thomas Love Peacock. *Fr.* The Misfortunes of Elphin. CABA; EvOK; OnMSP; StP; WiR

War Song of the Saracens. James Elroy Flecker. *Fr.* Hassan. FaBV

Waradgery Tribe, The. Mary Gilmore. PoAu-1

Waratah. Roland Robinson. PoAu-2

Ward, and still in bonds, one day, A. Regeneration. Henry Vaughan. CABA; MeP

Warden of the universe who flings, The. Premonition. Edith Ogutsch. FiSC

Waring, *sel.* Robert Browning.
  "When I last saw Waring," Pt. II. HaSV

Warm summer sun shine kindly here. Epitaph. Robert Richardson. PoLF

Warm wine, warm baths, warm women, onetime ladies. The Easiest Way. *Unknown.* UnTE

Warmed by her hand and shadowed by her hair. The Love-Letter. Dante Gabriel Rossetti. The House of Life, XI. VP

Warning. Sydney King Russell. FiSC

Warning to Children. Robert Graves. PoIE

Warning to Cupid. *Unknown, tr. fr. Greek by* Louis Untermeyer. UnTE

Warning to My Love, A. David Wagoner. NePoEA-2

Warning to Skeptics, A. Leah Bodine Drake. FiSC

Warning to Snake-Killers. Robert H. Barlow. FiSC

Warning to Those Who Serve Lords, A. *Unknown.* MeEL

Was a Man. Philip Booth. NePoEA-2

Was it a dream? We sail'd, I thought we sail'd. A Dream. Arthur Hugh Clough. GTBS-P

Was it always as now? I find this a strange generation. The New Generation. Schiller. TwGP

Was it his face that so unsettled him? Narcissus. Donald Petersen. NePoEA-2

Was it the proud full sail of this great verse. Sonnets, LXXXVI. Shakespeare. CBEP

Was never aught by Nature's art. That All Things Are as They Are Used. George Turberville. EnRePo

Was She a Witch? Laura E. Richards. SoPo

Was this the face that launched a thousand ships? The Face of Helen. Christopher Marlowe. *Fr.* Dr. Faustus. FaBV

Washed into the doorway. The Guest. Wendell Berry. AP

Washers of the Shroud, The. James Russell Lowell. AP

Washing between the buildings. Larry Eigner. CoPo

Washing the Dishes. Christopher Morley. PoLF

Washing up the dishes and hold your clattering tongue. Lolly Trudom. *Unknown.* BFSS

Washington. James Russell Lowell. RePo

Washington. Nancy Byrd Turner. SoPo

Washington Monument by Night. Carl Sandburg. PoSC

Wasn't this the site, asked the historian. House and Land. Allen Curnow. ACV

Wassail Song, The. *Unknown.* PoSC

Waste Land, The. T. S. Eliot. AP; CABA
  Death by Water, IV. DaDu; HaSV

Wasted Night. *Unknown, tr. fr. Greek by* Louis Untermeyer. UnTE

Watch, The. Frances Cornford. DTC

Watch and Pray. Charlotte Elliott. STF

Watch Ashore—Seletar. Sydney Middleton Clarke. HaSV

Watch Hill. Winfield Townley Scott. ErPo

Watched and well-known to the police, he walks. Variations on a Line from Shakespeare's Fifty-sixth Sonnet. E. L. Mayo. PoCh

Watcher, The. Stanton A. Coblentz. FiSC

Watcher, The. James Stephens. PoDB

Watcher stood on the brink of time, A. The Watcher. Stanton A. Coblentz. FiSC

Watching Clouds. John Farrar. SoPo

Watching oneself. Poem without a Main Verb. John Wain. NePoEA-2

Watching the Moon. David McCord. RePo

Watchman on the Tower, Watch with Care. Raimbaut de Vaqueiras, *tr. fr. Provençal by* Norman R. Shapiro. AnML

Watchman, What of the Night? Swinburne. WiR
Water. Anne Sexton. CoPo
Water Babies, The, *sels.* Charles Kingsley.
  Lost Doll, The. SoPo
  Young and Old. BiCB; LV; PoLF
  (Old Song, The.) CBEP
Water Glass of Whisky, A. X. J. Kennedy. CoPo
Water Island. Howard Moss. MP; NePoEA-2
Water Ouzel. William H. Matchett. PoCh
Water Sprite. Donald Wandrei. FiSC
Water Wheel, The. Antonio Machado, *tr. fr. Spanish by*
  James Duffy. AnSP
Waterfall, The. Henry Vaughan. ILP; MeP; StP; WiR
Waterford Town. *Unknown.* BSNS
Watergaw, The. "Hugh MacDiarmid." PoIE
Waterloo ("As I walked out on a fine summer's evening").
  Unknown. BSNS
Waterloo ("When battle roused each war-like charm"). *See*
  Drummer Boy of Waterloo, The.
Waterloo Bridge. Christopher Middleton. *Fr. Herman Moon's*
  Hourbook. NePoEA-2
Waters and earth once more are parted. After the Second
  Flood. Wilhelm Lehmann. MGP
Watershed. Margaret Avison. OBCV
Waterspout, The. William Hart-Smith. *Fr.* Christopher
  Columbus. PoAu-2
Waterwitch, The. Unknown. PoAu-1
Wave. Barbara Guest. AmPC
Wave, The. Andrew Charles Wehner. HaSV
Wave that is dark piles white and slips to its death, The.
  Fishing Season. Val Vallis. PoAu-2
Waverley, *sel.* Sir Walter Scott.
  To an Oak Tree, *fr. ch. 29.* OBNC
Waves, The. Charles Edward Eaton. PoNC
Waves. Mary Britton Miller. RcPo
Waves are murmuring, The. Dawn. Tasso. RBL
Waves lap lap. Sampan. *Unknown.* WePo
Waves rattling pebbles rocked me asleep. Recitative. Ronald
  McCuaig. PoAu-2
Waving of the Corn, The. Sidney Lanier. AP
Wax. Winfield Townley Scott. ErPo
Waxford Girl, The, *with music. Unknown.* BSO
Way, The. Robert Creeley. AP
Way, The. Edwin Muir. LOW
Way, The. Henry van Dyke. TRV
Way a child's hands stare through glass, The. The Sickness.
  Frederick Seidel. CoPo
Way a crow, The. Dust of Snow. Robert Frost. WePo
Way a split-rail fence has failed, The. Split-Rail Fence.
  Guy Owen. PoNC
Way Down South. *Unknown.* EvOK; SoPo
Way fare with thy projectes, noe false fyre, A. Sonnet.
  William Alabaster. MeP
Way her breasts meet is hidden from me, The. Old Fellow.
  Ernest Walsh. ErPo
Way I read a letter's this, The. Emily Dickinson. DiPo
Way My Ideas Think Me, The. José Garcia Villa. EaLo
Way of Life, The. Joseph V. B. Danquah. ACV
Way of Looking, A. Helen Bevington. PoNC
Way of Looking, A. Elizabeth Jennings. PP
Way of many ways, A: a god. Doctor Faustus. Geoffrey
  Hill. NePo-2
Way through the Woods, The. Kipling. OBNC; PoSa; StP;
  WePo
Way to the Sea, The. Laurence Lerner. NePoEA-2
Wayfarers, The. Rupert Brooke. MoLP
Wayfaring. Georg Trakl, *tr. fr. German by* Christopher
  Middleton. MGP
Ways, The. John Oxenham. PoLF; TRV
Ways of Trains, The. Elizabeth J. Coatsworth. SoPo
We all look on with anxious eyes. When Father Carves the
  Duck. Ernest Vincent Wright. FaBV; PoLF; PoSC
We all were [*or* were all] passengers in that motorcade. Chan-
  nel U.S.A.—Live. Adrien Stoutenburg. OPP; ThLM
"We are all jugs," the potter said. Earthen Jugs. "Gabriela
  Mistral." AnSP
We are all of us dreamers of dreams. Dreamer of Dreams.
  William Herbert Carruth. PoLF
We are all rushing through the world. Rushing Panic in San
  Francisco. *Unknown.* SGR
We Are All Workmen. Rainer Maria Rilke, *tr. fr. German by*
  Babette Deutsch. EaLo
We are assembled here today. Song of the Argonauts. Sam
  C. Upham. SGR
We are budding, Master, budding. The Master and the Leaves.
  Thomas Hardy. PoIE
We are fishermen in a flat scene. Water. Anne Sexton.
  CoPo
We Are Gathered Together. Estelle Gershgoren. PtTo
We Are God's Chosen Few. Swift. TRV
We are large with pity, slow and awkward. False Country of
  the Zoo. Jean Garrigue. MP
We are led on. Juvenal. *Fr.* The Satires. PoPl
We Are Living, We Are Dwelling. Arthur C. Coxe. TRV

We are not come to wage a strife. The Day-Breakers. Arna
  Bontemps. AmNP
We Are Seven. Wordsworth. FaPL
We are such stuff as dreams are made of, and these. Poem.
  Hugo von Hofmannsthal. SiGo
We are the clouds that veil the midnight moon. Mutability.
  Shelley. CBEP
We are the flute, our music is all Thine. The Unseen Power.
  Rumi. SiGo
We are the hollow men. The Hollow Men. T. S. Eliot.
  AP; DiPo; FoBA; OnP; PoPl
We are the music-makers. The Music Makers. Arthur
  O'Shaughnessy. FaBV
We are they who come faster than fate. War Song of the
  Saracens. James Elroy Flecker. *Fr.* Hassan. FaBV
We are travelling west of Alice Springs, and Sam is at the
  wheel. West of Alice. W. E. Harney. PoAu-1
We are true lovers without hope. By Moonlight. May Sarton.
  MoLP
We are two countries girded for the war. Foreign Affairs.
  Stanley Kunitz. AnMoPo
We Bear the Strain of Earthly Care. Ozora S. Davis. TRV
We break the glass, whose sacred wine. Song. Edward Coote
  Pinkney. AmLP
We came by boat in the late arctic twilight. Visit by Water.
  Floris Clark McLaren. OBCV
We came from the hills where the hot winds blow. In Town.
  David McKee Wright. ACV
We came to the church that was left to wind and rain. Church
  of the Holy Innocents, Dunedin. "Robin Hyde." ACV
We came upon the village of the dead. Sleeping Village.
  Harold Vinal. FiSC
We cannot go to the country. Raleigh Was Right. William
  Carlos Williams. PP
We Cannot Kindle. Matthew Arnold. TRV
We caught the tread of dancing feet. The Harlot's House.
  Oscar Wilde. StP
We come to another place. Mathematics. Joel Oppenheimer.
  CoPo
We Are All a Panning, *with music.* Mart Taylor. SGR
We dance round in a ring and suppose. The Secret Sits.
  Robert Frost. LOW; SoPo
We dead men, we dead men can muster more legions. The
  Chorus of the Dead. Conrad Ferdinand Meyer. AGP
We did not know his high, unheard-of head. Archaic Torso
  of Apollo. Rainer Maria Rilke. TwGP
We Do Lie beneath the Grass. Thomas Lovell Beddoes. *See*
  Dirge: "We do lie beneath the grass."
We do not play on graves. Emily Dickinson. StP
We dreamed of one another. You and I. Friedrich Hebbel.
  AGP
"We dwell in Him,"—oh, everlasting Home. In Him. Annie
  Johnson Flint. TRV
We fall like leaves. The Fall. Walter Kaufmann. OPP
We fear to judge a watermelon. A Comparison. *Unknown.* STF
We feared the incubus, the hex. The Woods Grow Darker.
  Leah Bodine Drake. FiSC
We fight. I am clubbed from behind. Terminal Theater.
  Robert Sward. CoPo
We Fought Like the Divil, *with music. Unknown.* BSO
We Give Thee but Thine Own. William Walsham How. STF
We got ready for the battle. Nelson's Victory at Trafalgar.
  Unknown. BSNS
We had a picnic. A Picnic. Aileen Fisher. SoPo
We had climbed the last steep flight of stairs. The Bead Mat.
  Walter de la Mare. CBEP
We had waffles-with-syrup for breakfast. Birthdays. Marchette
  Chute. BiCB
We have a secret, just we three. The Secret. *Unknown.*
  SoPo
We have ascended to this paradise. The Attic. Henri
  Coulette. NePoEA-2; PoPl
We have bathed, where none have seen us. Song. Thomas
  Lovell Beddoes. *Fr.* Death's Jest Book. OBNC
We Have Been Here Before. Morris Bishop. EvOK
We have been shown. Six Variations. Denise Levertov.
  CoPo
We have fed our sea for a thousand years. Kipling. *Fr.* A
  Song of the English. HaSV
We have heard no nightingales singing. Working Class.
  Bertram Warr. OBCV
We have met late—it is too late to meet. A Denial. Eliza-
  beth Barrett Browning. OBNC
"We have met, we have met, my pretty fair maid." James
  Harris (C *vers.*). *Unknown.* BSO
We have sent him seeds of the melon's core. Ku-Klux. Madi-
  son Cawein. ThLM
We have struck the regions wherein we are keel or reef.
  Zone. Louise Bogan. PoCh
We have the wind under our feet. The Dispersion. Heinz
  Piontek. MGP
We have tomorrow. Youth. Langston Hughes. BiCB
We have walked, looking at the actual trees. Leaves before
  the Wind. May Sarton. MoLP

We hurry on, nor passing note. Digby Mackworth Dolben. OBNC

We kissed at the barrier; and passing through. On the Departure Platform. Thomas Hardy. OBNC

We know the winter earth upon the body of the young President. November 26, 1963. Wendell Berry. AP

We laugh and we are troubled. The Beating Heart. Heine. UnTE

We lay together in the sultry night. Summer Storm. Louis Untermeyer. UnTE

We leave the well-beloved place. In Memoriam A. H. H., CII. Tennyson. VP

We left/ The silent forest. Charles Mair. *Fr.* Tecumseh. OBCV

We live in a house light and high in air. The Tenant. Philippe Jaccottet. CoFP

We Live in a Rickety House. Alexander McLachlan. OBCV

We live in our own world. Children's Song. R. S. Thomas. BoC

We looked, we loved, and therewith instantly. Pure Death. Robert Graves. GTBS-P

We Love the Name of Texas, *with music. Unknown.* BFSS

We make our meek adjustments. Chaplinesque. Hart Crane. AP

We make ourselves a place apart. Revelation. Robert Frost. FoBA; PoDB

We may not abide, even with what is most. To Hölderlin. Rainer Maria Rilke. MGP

We May Not Know. Cecil F. Alexander. TRV

We may not work a miracle. The Higher Calling. W. M. Czamanske. STF

We may stop worrying. I M J F K. Ruth Landshoff Yorck. OPP

We men of Earth have here the stuff. Earth Is Enough. Edwin Markham. TRV

We must not, in our hurried lives. His Life Is Ours. Dorothy Conant Stroud. STF

We Must Not Part. *Unknown.* DiPo

We mustn't get discouraged at the things which people say. Discouraged. Lucille Stanaback. STF

We never know how high we are. Emily Dickinson. AP; TRV

We outgrow love like other things. Emily Dickinson. FoBA

We play at paste. Emily Dickinson. CBEP

We Poets Speak. Francis Thompson. *Fr.* Sister Songs. FaBV

We pulled for you when the wind was against us. Song of the Galley-Slaves. Kipling. GTBS-P

We put more coal on the big red fire. Father's Story. Elizabeth Madox Roberts. PoSC

We Put on the Buffalo. Robert P. Tristram Coffin. RePo

We ranging down this lower track. In Memoriam A. H. H., XLVI. Tennyson. VP

We remember, we do not forget, O Trail Breakers. Trail Breakers. James Daugherty. RePo

We rode out to the west of town. Deer Hunt. Sam Ragan. PoNC

We sat and talked. . . . It was June, and the summer light. To K. M. Walter de la Mare. BoC

We sat together at one summer's end. Adam's Curse. W. B. Yeats. DiPo; PP

We sat within the farm-house old. The Fire of Drift-Wood. Longfellow. AP

"We saw reindeer/ browsing." Rigorists. Marianne Moore. PoIE

We saw the bare feet and the quiet hands sprawled on the street stones. In This Hour. Josephine W. Johnson. MoRP

We Saw the Swallows. George Meredith. Modern Love, XLVII. ELP

("We saw the swallows gathering in the sky.") GTBS-P; OBNC; VP

We saw Thee in Thy balmy nest. The Shepherd's Hymn. Richard Crashaw. *Fr.* In the Holy Nativity of Our Lord God. BoC

We search the world for truth, we cull. The Book Our Mothers Read. Whittier. TRV

"We shall cede with a brotherly embrace." The Rise of Shivaji. Zulfikar Ghose. MoBS

We Shall Overcome. *Unknown.* EaLo; ThLM

We shift and bedeck and bedrape us. Swinburne. *Fr.* Dolores. UnTE

We should love Saint Mary. Song VII. Alfonso X, King of Castile and Leon. AnML

We shouldered like pigs along the rail to try. Returned to Frisco, 1946. W. D. Snodgrass. AP

We stood by a pond that winter day. Neutral Tones. Thomas Hardy. CABA; ILP; VP

We Sunday strode—I in leather. The Rented Garden. Bink Noll. ToPo

We swerve to arousal: the trembling man fanged by a copperhead. Copperhead. Charles Edward Eaton. PoNC

We talk'd with open heart, and tongue. The Fountain. Wordsworth. GTBS-P

We, the Few Who Believe. Harold Vinal. FiSC

We thought it was a joke. Nightmare Number Four. Robert Bloch. FiSC

We three are on the cedar-shadowed lawn. Modern Love, XXI. George Meredith. VP

We too, we too, descending once again. The Too-late Born [or The Silent Slain]. Archibald MacLeish. CABA; GoJo

We took no notes of contemplated light. To My Friends. Peter Levi. NePoEA-2

We used to be ten brothers. Ten Brothers. *Unknown, ad. by* Louis Untermeyer. RePo

We used to float the paper boats in spring. Poem. Donald D. Olsen. PoP1

We used to picnic where the thrift. Trebetherick. John Betjeman. EvOK

We wait our turn, as still as mice. The Hospital Waiting-Room. W. H. Davies. CBEP

We walk'd along, while bright and red. The Two April Mornings. Wordsworth. GTBS-P; PoIE

We walked that night between the piled houses. The Window. Iain Crichton Smith. NePoEA-2

We Watch'd Her Breathing. Thomas Hood. *See* Death Bed, The.

We watched the Condors winging towards the Moon. Condors. Padraic Colum. GoJo

We Wear the Mask. Paul Laurence Dunbar. AmNP

We were a noisy crew; the sun in heaven. Fishing. Wordsworth. *Fr.* The Prelude. SD

We were all passengers in that motorcade. *See* We all were passengers . . .

We were antagonists; we knew that. Reflections on Water. Kenneth Pitchford. CoPo

We were apart; day by day. Isolation: To Marguerite. Matthew Arnold. *Fr.* Switzerland. CBEP; VP

We were born grooms, in stable-straw we sleep still. A Dream of Horses. Ted Hughes. NePoEA-2

We were camped on the plains at the head of the Cimarron. The Zebra Dun. *Unknown.* RePo

We were crowded in the cabin. Ballad of the Tempest. James Thomas Fields. PoLF

We were glad together in gladsome meads. Adam Lindsay Gordon. *Fr.* The Rhyme of Joyous Garde. PoAu-1

We were not many, we who stood. Monterey. Charles Fenno Hoffman. ThLM

We were schooner-rigged and rakish, with a long and lissome hull. A Ballad of John Silver. John Masefield. EvOK

We were very tired, we were very merry. Recuerdo. Edna St. Vincent Millay. BoLP; EvOK; ThLM

We were walking down a narrow street. Sadness. Barbara Guest. AmPC

We were young, we were merry, we were very very wise. Unwelcome. Mary Elizabeth Coleridge. OBNC

We who are left, how shall we look again. A Lament. W. W. Gibson. MMA

We, who are men, how shall we know? Song. R. S. Thomas. ToPo

We Who Do Not Grieve in Silence. Oscar Mandel. OPP

We who must act as handmaidens. A Muse of Water. Carolyn Kizer. AnMoPo

We who must write GM a stinging letter. No Retreat. Reed Whittemore. OPP

We Who Were Born. Eiluned Lewis. BiCB

We who with songs beguile your pilgrimage. Prologue. James Elroy Flecker. *Fr.* The Golden Journey to Samarkand. GoJo

We wondered what might change. The Survivors. S. S. Gardons. AmPC

We would be building; temples still undone. Builders. Purd E. Deitz. TRV

We Would See Jesus. *Unknown.* STF

Weak is the assurance that weak flesh reposeth. By Her That Is Most Assured to Her Self. Spenser. Amoretti, LVIII. EnRePo

Weak-winged is song. Ode Recited at the Harvard Commemoration. James Russell Lowell. AP

Wealth in the deep of the rose, The. The Rose. "Gabriela Mistral." AnSP

Wealthy Merchant, The. *Unknown. See* Jack, the Sailor.

Wealthy young esquire of late, we do hear, A. Dog and Gun (B *vers.*). *Unknown.* BSO

Weapon that you fought with was a word, The. He Knoweth Not That the Dead Are Thine. Mary Elizabeth Coleridge. OBNC

Wearied arm and broken sword. Pocahontas. Thackeray. OnMSP; SIV; ThLM

Wearily, drearily, In Prison. William Morris. CBEP

Wearin' of the Green, The. *Unknown.* PoSC

Wearing his equality like a too-small shoe. The Citizen. Vilma Howard. NNP

Wearisome Sonnetteer, feeble and querulous. The Soldier's Wife. George Canning *and* John Hookham Frere. Par

Weary are the hours of a sailor boy. Sweet William (A *vers.*). *Unknown.* BSO

Weary Blues, The. Langston Hughes. FaBV

Weary in Well-doing. Christina Rossetti. VP
Weary is the brooklet's flow. To a Dutch Landscape. Niko-laus Lenau. AGP
Weary lot is thine, fair maid, A. The Rover [or Song]. Sir Walter Scott. *Fr.* Rokeby. GTBS-P; OBNC
Weary of myself, and sick of asking. Self-Dependence. Matthew Arnold. PoIE
Weary wind is slumbering on the wing, The. Sunset. Arthur Bayldon. PoAu-1
Weary with toil, I haste me to my bed. Sonnets, XXVII. Shakespeare. DiPo
Weasel, The. Robert Pack. CoPo
Weather Ear. Norman Nicholson. DaDu
Weather Has Laid Aside His Cloak, The. Charles d'Orléans. *See* Spring.
Weather was better than you would expect, The. Two There Are I Wish to Celebrate. Howard McCord. PtTo
Weathers. Thomas Hardy. EvOK; FaBV; PoIE; RePo; WePo
Webster was much possessed by death. Whispers of Immor-tality. T. S. Eliot. CTC; FoBA; PoIE
We'd found an old Boche dug-out, and he knew. The Sentry. Wilfred Owen. MMA
We'd gained our first objective hours before. Counter Attack. Siegfried Sassoon. SIV
We'd liberated Naples and the Wops. A Veteran's Day of Recollection. John Beecher. PtTo
Wedding Hymn. Luis de Góngora, *tr. fr. Spanish by* Edward Meryon Wilson. *Fr.* The Solitudes. AnSP; RBL
Wedding Night, The. Johannes Secundus, *tr. fr. Latin by* George Ogle. *Fr.* Epithalamium. UnTE
Wedding of Ballyporeen, The. *Unknown.* BSNS
Wedding Procession. James A. Emanuel. NNP
Wedding-Wind. Philip Larkin. ToPo
Wednesday; or, The Dumps. John Gay. *Fr.* The Shepherd's Week. EiCP
Wee May o' Caledon, The. Lewis Spence. ACV
Wee, modest, crimson-tipped flower. To a Mountain Daisy. Burns. PoLF
Wee, sleekit, cow'rin, tim'rous beastie. To a Mouse [or Field Mouse]. Burns. CBEP; DiPo; EiCP; GTBS-P; ILP; PoIE; PoLF
Wee Wee Man, The. *Unknown.* ELP
(Little Wee Man, The.) BuBa
Wee, wee tailor. The Tailor. Thomas Lovell Beddoes. WiR
Wee Willie Winkie. Mother Goose. SoPo
Week of Birthdays, A. Mother Goose. *See* Monday's Child Is Fair of Face.
Weekday, A. Larry Eigner. CoPo
Weel, gin ye speir, I'm no inclined. The Poets at Tea, 9. Barry Pain. Par
Weep no more, woful Shepherds weep no more. Milton. *Fr.* Lycidas. BoC
Weep Not My Wanton. Robert Greene. *See* Sephestia's Song to Her Child.
Weep, not, weep not. Go Down Death (a Funeral Sermon). James Weldon Johnson. AmNP; TRV
Weep—Those Whose Eyes Are Dry Shall Weep. Alfonso Gatto, *tr. fr. Italian by* John A. Scott. CoIP
Weep, weep, ye woodmen, wail. Dirge for Robin Hood [or Robin Hood's Funeral]. Anthony Munday *and* Henry Chettle. *Fr.* Death of Robert, Earl of Huntingdon. CBEP; CTC; WiR
Weep [or Weepe] with me, all you that read. An Epitaph on S. P. [Salomon *or* Salathiel Pavy], a Child of Q. El. [Queen Elizabeth's] Chapel [or Chappel]. Ben Jonson. CABA; EnRePo; PoSa; SeCP; VaPo
Weep You No More. *Unknown.* ELP
Weepe living thinges, of life the mother dyes. The Death of Our Ladie. Robert Southwell. MeP
Weepe with me all you that read. *See* Weep with me. . .
Weeper, The. Richard Crashaw. MeP; SeCP
Weeping and Singing. César Tiempo, *tr. fr. Spanish by* Don-ald Devenish Walsh. MoRP
Weeping Cherry, The. Robert Herrick. WePo
Weeping, I write this. You are dead. November 22, 1963. Lewis Turco. OPP
Wei Wind, *sel.* Confucius, *tr. fr. Chinese by* Ezra Pound. *Fr.* The Classic Anthology. Pedlar. CTC
Weighing the steadfastness [or stedfastness] and state. Man. Henry Vaughan. CBEP; MeP
Weight distributed. One Down. Richard Armour. SD
Weightless Element, A. Gottfried Benn, *tr. fr. German by* Christopher Middleton. PoPI
Weland, the smith, knew woe upon woe. Deor's Lament. *Un-known.* LV
Welcome. Rose Waldo. SoPo
Welcome! all wonders in one sight. The Coming Child. Rich-ard Crashaw. TRV
Welcome dear book, souls joy, and food! H. Scriptures. Henry Vaughan. MeP
Welcome, dear dawn of summer's rising sway. May-Day. Aaron Hill. WaPE

Welcome Maids of Honour. To Violets. Robert Herrick. SeCP
Welcome, old friend! These many years. To Age. Walter Savage Landor. FaPL
Welcome! Our Messiah. *Unknown.* MeEL
Welcome, Summer. Chaucer. *Fr.* The Parlement of Foules. MeEL
(Now Welcome Summer.) CBEP
(Roundel: "Now welcom somer, with thy sonne softe.") CTC
Welcome sweet and sacred cheer. The Banquet. George Herbert. MeP
Welcome sweet, and sacred feast; welcome life! The Holy Communion. Henry Vaughan. MeP
Welcome to Sack, The. Robert Herrick. SeCP
Welcome to Venice, gentle courteous Knight. A Dialogue between the Lovelorn Sir Hugh and Certain Ladies of Venice. Thomas Deloney. UnTE
Wele, herying and worship be to Christ that dere ous boughte. A Palm-Sunday Hymn. William Herebert. MeEL
Well, The. Denise Levertov. AP
"We'll all be rooned," said Hanrahan. Said Hanrahan. P. J. Hartigan. PoAu-1
Well boiled in acid and then laid on glass. Description of a View. William Empson. ACV
Well boss did it ever strike you. The Hen and the Oriole. Don Marquis. *Fr.* Archy and Mehitabel. EvOK
Well dost thou, Love, thy solemn feast to hold. Saint Valen-tine's Day. Coventry Patmore. *Fr.* The Unknown Eros. OBNC
Well-Finder, The. Harold Vinal. FiSC
We'll Go No More a-Roving. Byron. *See* So We'll Go No More a-Roving.
Well I Remember How You Smiled. Walter Savage Landor. *Fr.* Ianthe. CBEP; OBNC
Well! If the bard was weather-wise, who made. Dejection; an Ode. Samuel Taylor Coleridge. CABA; CBEP; OBNC; PoIE; StP
Well it's a long time on the street. Outa Work Blues. Carlos Cortez. PtTo
Well meaning readers! you that come as friends. The Flaming Heart. Richard Crashaw. MeP
We'll Meet Again. J. Danson Smith. STF
"Well met, well met, my old true love." James Harris (D vers.). *Unknown.* BSO
"Well met, well met, my own true love." The House Car-penter [or James Harris]. *Unknown.* BFSS; BSO (A and E vers.)
Well mightst thou scorn thy readers to allure. Andrew Mar-vell. *Fr.* On Mr. Milton's *Paradise Lost.* PP
We'll Never Know. Alma Hoellein. STF
Well, old spy. Award. Ray Durem. NNP; PtTo
Well Pleased Am I with the Gentle Season. Peire Vidal, *tr. fr. Provençal by* Daisy Aldan. AnML
Well pleaseth me the sweet time of Easter. A War Song. Bertrans de Born. CTC
Well, son, I'll tell you. Mother to Son. Langston Hughes. AmNP; BiCB; LV
Well, that was silly; too near the edge. On Catching a Dog-Daisy in the Mower. Peter Redgrove. NePoEA-2
Well, then, gourds. You can call them gourds. The Gourd-Heads. William D. Barney. FiSC
Well, then, I hate Thee, unrighteous picture. The Black Riders, XII. Stephen Crane. AP
Well then! I now do plainly see. The Wish. Abraham Cowley. *Fr.* The Mistress. BoC; FaPL
Well, they are gone, and here must I remain. This Lime-Tree Bower My Prison. Samuel Taylor Coleridge. CBEP; PoIE
"Well, this is where I go down to the river." Heat. Kenneth Mackenzie. PoAu-2
We'll to the woods and gather may. Alons au Bois le May Cueillir. Charles d'Orléans. SiGo
We'll to the Woods No More. A. E. Housman. LOW
Well water. Eight Sandbars on the Takano River. Gary Snyder. CoPo
Well, World, you have kept faith with me. On His 86th Birthday. Thomas Hardy. ACV
Wellington and Waterloo. *Unknown. See* Plains of Waterloo, The.
Wells of Jesus Wounds, The. *Unknown.* MeEL
Welsh, The. E. V. Lucas. LV
Welsh Incident. Robert Graves. BoC; WePo
Welsh Testament, A. R. S. Thomas. ToPo
Welshman by the pit whose Sabbath voice, The. Orpheus. E. W. Mandel. *Fr.* Minotaur Poems. OBCV
Weltschmerz. Frank Yerby. AmNP
Wench in the Street, The. *Unknown.* CBEP
We're a' Dry wi' the Drinkin' o't. *Unknown.* ErPo
We're All Away to Sea. *Unknown.* BSNS
Were beth they biforen us weren. Ubi Sunt Qui ante Nos Fuerunt? *Unknown.* ILP
Were he and the singing two songs, or one? Questions for the Candidate. John Holmes. PP

We're Homeward Bound. *Unknown.* BSNS
Were I a King. Edward de Vere, Earl of Oxford. DiPo
Were I a rose, and did you dare. The Amorist. *Unknown.* UnTE
Were I as base as is the lowly plain. Love's Omnipresence. Joshua Sylvester. GTBS-P
Were I Laid on Greenland's Coast. John Gay. *Fr.* The Beggar's Opera. CBEP
Were I to leave no more than a good friend. The Departure; an Elegy. Henry King. ScCP
Were I (who to my cost already am). A Satire against Mankind. Earl of Rochester. CABL
We're the Pens, Saddened and Dismayed. Guido Cavalcanti, *tr. fr. Italian by* James J. Wilhelm. AnML
Were there no crowns on earth. The Dead President. Edward Rowland Sill. LiPo
Were this impossible, I know full well. A House and Grounds. Leigh Hunt. CBEP
Were you not enchanted evenings. Poem of a Glass Blower. *Unknown.* AnML
Were You on the Mountain? *Unknown, tr. fr. Irish by* Douglas Hyde. BoLP
Wermland was misery's home for Wayland. Deor. *Unknown.* CaFP
Werther had a love for Charlotte. The Sorrows of Werther. Thackeray. WePo
Wesley in Heaven. Thomas Edward Brown. OBNC
Wessex Guidebook. Louis MacNeice. PoIE
Wessex Heights. Thomas Hardy. OBNC
West and away the wheels of darkness roll. Revolution. A. E. Housman. Last Poems, XXXVI. VP
West London. Matthew Arnold. PoPl
West of Alice. W. E. Harney. PoAu-1
West-running Brook. Robert Frost. AP; DiPo
West Wind, The. John Masefield. PoPl
Western Wind, When Wilt Thou Blow. *Unknown.* CaFP; OnP; StP
  (Western Wind.) CABA; CBEP; CTC; DiPo; ILP; MeEL
  (Westron Winde, When Will Thou Blow.) PoIE
Wet Sheet and a Flowing Sea, A. Allan Cunningham. GTBS-P; HaSV; RoGo
Wet Windy Night on a Pavement. A. S. J. Tessimond. WePo
We've been to the wars together. To Lou Gehrig. John Kieran. SD
We've formed our band and are well mann'd. Ho! for California. Jesse Hutchinson. SGR
We've put a fine addition on the good old church at home. The Ladies' Aid. *Unknown.* PoLF
We've taken the dog for his walk. To a Child. S. S. Gardons. NePoEA-2
We've traveled together through life's rugged way. My Bible and I. *Unknown.* STF
Wha Is That at My Bower-Door? Burns. ErPo; UnTE
Wha kens on whatna Bethlehems. The Innumerable Christ. "Hugh MacDiarmid." EaLo
Whaddaya Do for Action in This Place? George Starbuck. NePoEA-2
Whalan of Waitin' a While. J. W. Gordon. PoAu-1
Whale, The. Buson, *tr. fr. Japanese by* Harold G. Henderson. SoPo
Whale, The. John Donne. PoSa
Whale, The. Herman Melville. *See* Ribs and Terrors in the Whale, The.
Whale butting through scarps of moving marble, The. Explorations. Louis MacNeice. ILP
Whale, improbable as lust, The. A Tall Tale; or, A Moral Song. Phyllis Webb. OBCV
Whales have calves. The Guppy. Ogden Nash. WePo
Whales Weep Not! D. H. Lawrence. PoIE
Wha'll buy caller herrin'? Caller Herrin'. Lady Nairne. HaSV
Whan netilles in winter bere roses rede. Impossible to Trust Women. *Unknown.* MeEL
Whan seyd was al this miracle, every man. Prologue to Sir Thopas. Chaucer. *Fr.* The Canterbury Tales. Par
Whan that Aprille [*or* Aprill] with his shoures soote. Prologue. Chaucer. *Fr.* The Canterbury Tales. CaFP; CTC; DiPo; ILP; OnP; PoIE
Whan ye see a dragon. Signs. William Soutar. ACV
Whanne ic se on Rode. I Ought to Weep. *Unknown.* MeEL
What a man may do for love. All for Love. *Unknown.* UnTE
What a moment, what a doubt! Sneezing. Leigh Hunt. LV
What a night! The wind howls, hisses, and but stops. Snowstorm. John Clare. WiR
What a Piece of Work Is a Man. Sophocles, *tr. fr. Greek by* F. L. Lucas. *Fr.* Antigone. SiGo
What a sweet smell rises. Laying the Dust. Denise Levertov. ToPo
What a wild room. A Man-made World. Stephen Spender. MoRP
What about measure, I learnt. Peri Poietikes. Louis Zukofsky. CoPo

What ails John Winter, that so oft. John Winter. Laurence Binyon. HaSV
"What ails you that you look so pale." A Ballad of Marjorie. Dora Sigerson Shorter. SIV
What am I? nosing here, turning leaves over. Wodwo. Ted Hughes. ToPo
What are heavy? sea-sand and sorrow. Christina Rossetti. *Fr.* Sing-Song. HaSV
"What are the bugles blowin' for?" said Files-on-Parade. Danny Deever. Kipling. CaFP; DiPo; GTBS-P; PoLF; PoPo; VaPo
What are the simples the witches want? Herbs and Simples. Martha Keller. FiSC
What are we first? First, animals; and next. Modern Love, XXX. George Meredith. VP
What are we men indeed? Grim torment's habitation. Human Misery. Andreas Gryphius. AGP
What Are Years? Marianne Moore. AP; EaLo; PoDB
What are you able to build with your blocks? Block City. Robert Louis Stevenson. SoPo
What are you, then, my love, my friend, my father. The Quarry. Vassar Miller. NePoEA-2
What avails it, dear Tom, to be honest and true. Written in 1740. Thomas Catesby Paget. WaPE
"What be you a-lookin' at, Emily Ann?" The Pear Tree. Mary Gilmore. PoAu-1
What beauty would have lovely styled. An Epitaph: On Elizabeth Chute. Ben Jonson. EnRePo
What beck'ning [*or* beckoning] ghost along the moonlight shade. Elegy to the Memory of an Unfortunate Lady. Pope. CBEP; OnP
What Birds Were There. Brother Antoninus. ToPo
What bright soft thing is this? The Teare. Richard Crashaw. SeCP
What bring you, sailor, home from the sea. Luck. W. W. Gibson. HaSV
What Can I Give Him? Christina Rossetti. *See* Christmas Carol, A: "In the bleak mid-winter."
What can I give you? Fifth Birthday Gift. Marjorie Lederer. BiCB
What cant, oh, what hypocrisy. Cant. W. H. Davies. MoRP
What care I for the leagues o' sand. The Mither's Lament. Sydney Goodsir Smith. ACV
What care I who gets the credit? Credit. *Unknown.* STF
What cher? Gud cher, gud cher, gud cher. A Cheerful Welcome. *Unknown.* MeEL
"What come that blood on your shirt sleeve?" My Son, Come Tell It to Me. *Unknown.* BFSS
What comfort by Him do we win. By Him. Ben Jonson. TRV
What could be lovelier than to hear. Summer Rain. Elizabeth J. Coatsworth. RePo
What dawn-pulse at the heart of heaven, or last. Beauty's Pageant. Dante Gabriel Rossetti. The House of Life, XVII. VP
What death means is not this. Canticle. Wendell Berry. AP
What desperate nightmare rapts me to this land. Legacy: My South. Dudley Randall. NNP
What did you want to set out on that table. Threats of the Witness. Yves Bonnefoy. CoFP
What dire offense from am'rous causes springs. The Rape of the Lock. Pope. CABA; CABL; DiPo; ILP; StP; VaPo
What Do I Have, That You Seek Out My Friendship? Lope de Vega, *tr. fr. Spanish by* Kate Flores. AnSP
What do people still expect of me? Four Psalms, IV. Bertolt Brecht. MGP
What do they know of penitence. Praise. Edith Daley. TRV
What do they see. Plymouth Rock. Olive Driver. RePo
What do we need for love—a midnight fire. Need. Babette Deutsch. MoLP
"What do you have for breakfast?" A Little Bird. Aileen Fisher. SoPo
What do you see in the fire tonight? Pictures in the Fire. Patience Strong. RePo
What do you sell, O ye merchants? In the Bazaars of Hyderabad. Sarojini Naidu. RePo
What do you think endures? The Greatest City. Walt Whitman. RePo
What Does This Mean? Sir Thomas Wyatt. MeEL
What doth this noise of thoughts within my heart. The Familie. George Herbert. MeP
What Dreamed I? *Unknown.* CBEP
What D'Ye Call It, The, *sel.* John Gay.
  Ballad, A: " 'Twas when the seas were roaring," *fr.* II, viii. StP
What ever 'tis, whose beauty here below. The Starre. Henry Vaughan. MeP
"What Five Books Would You Pick to Be Marooned with on a Desert Island?" Paris Leary. CoPo
What flocks of critics hover here to-day. Prologue. Dryden. *Fr.* All for Love. DiPo
What gentle ghost, besprent with April deaw. An Elegie on the Lady Jane Pawlet, Marchion: of Winton. Ben Jonson. SeCP

What God Hath Promised. Annie Johnson Flint. STF; TRV
What goes into a birthday cake. The Birthday Cake. Victoria Chase. BiCB
What Grandma Knew. Edward Field. CoPo
What great yoked brutes with briskets low. Crossing the Plains. Joaquin Miller. AmLP
What greater torment ever could have been. Lonely Beauty. Samuel Daniel. Fr. The Complaint of Rosamond. CTC
What Greece, when learning flourished, only knew. Prologue to the University of Oxford. Dryden. PP
What guile is this, that those her golden tresses. Amoretti, XXXVII. Spenser. StP
What happens to a dream deferred? Lenox Avenue Mural. Langston Hughes. AmNP
What Harvest Half So Sweet Is. Thomas Campion. UnTE
What Has This Bugbear Death. Lucretius, tr. fr. Latin by Dryden. Fr. De Rerum Natura. CTC
What has this bugbear Death that's worth our care? Death. William Walsh. CBEP
What have I done for you. England, My England. W. E. Henley. PoLF
"What have you there?" the great Panjandrum said. The Truant. E. J. Pratt. OBCV
What heart could have thought you? To a Snowflake. Francis Thompson. FaBV; PoPl
What heave of grapnels will resurrect the fabric. S.S.R., Lost at Sea—The Times. Ralph Gustafson. OBCV
What heav'n-besieged heart is this. A Letter to the Countess of Denbigh. Richard Crashaw. SeCP
What Hee Suffered. Ben Jonson. Fr. A Celebration of Charis. SeCP
What here you see in deceiving tints. On Her Portrait. Sister Juana Inés de la Cruz. AnSP
What hope is here for modern rhyme. In Memoriam A. H. H., LXXVII. Tennyson. PP; VP
What I Expected [Was]. Stephen Spender. AnMoPo; PoIE
What I know. The Wind Shrieked Loud. Elizabeth J. Coatsworth. FiSC
What I See in Me. Unknown. STF
What I shall leave thee none can tell. To His Son, Vincent Corbet, on His Birth-Day, November 10, 1630, Being Then Three Years Old. Richard Corbet. BoC; CBEP
What I Think of Hiawatha. J. W. Morris. Par
What If a Day. Thomas Campion. EnRePo; PoIE
What If a Much of a Which of a Wind. E. E. Cummings. AP
What if I bade you leave. Those Images. W. B. Yeats. PP
What if Orpheus. Orpheus in Greenwich Village. Jack Gilbert. PP
What if some little pain the passage have. Port after Stormy Seas. Spenser. Fr. The Faerie Queene, I, 9. HaSV
What if this present were the worlds last night? Holy Sonnets, XIII. John Donne. MeP; OnP
What in the World! Edith Earnshaw. PoNC
What is a woman that you forsake her. Harp Song of the Dane Women. Kipling. Fr. Puck of Pook's Hill. OBNC
What is Africa to me. Heritage. Countee Cullen. AmNP; FaBV
What is he buzzing in my ears? Confessions. Robert Browning. ELP; GTBS-P
What is this lordling, that cometh from the fight? The Knight Stained from Battle. William Herebert. MeEL
What is it men in women do require? The Question Answer'd. Blake. ErPo
What is it to remember? Bliss Carman. Fr. Songs of the Sea-Children. OBCV
"What is it you're mumbling, old Father, my Dad?" By the Exeter River. Donald Hall. MoBS
What is left at the end? Fore Thought. May Sarton. MoLP
What Is Life. Unknown. EnRePo
What Is Love? sel. A. P. Herbert.
"'What is Love?' the poets question." BoLP
What is lovelier than the gold. Casual Gold. Maud E. Uschold. SoPo
What is more gentle than a wind in summer? Sleep and Poetry. Keats. PP
What is our innocence. What Are Years? Marianne Moore. AP; EaLo; PoDB
What Is Our Life. Sir Walter Ralegh. EnRePo; ILP
What is—"paradise." Emily Dickinson. DiPo
What Is Pink? Christina Rossetti. See Color.
What Is Prayer? James Montgomery. STF, 4 sts.; TRV
What is so rare as a day in June. See And what is so rare as a day in June.
What is song's eternity. Song's Eternity. John Clare. CBEP
What Is That in Thine Hand? Eva Gray. STF
What is the hardest thing of all? Waiting! Waiting. Ruth Apprich Jacob. BiCB
What is the horn that the dawn holds. The Horn. James Reaney. OBCV
What is the matter with Mary Jane? Rice Pudding. A. A. Milne. BBGG
What is the thing of greatest price. The Soul. Unknown. STF

"What is the thing your eyes hold loveliest?" The Newlyweds. Cloyd Mann Criswell. PoLF
What Is the World? Dryden. Fr. To My Honor'd Friend Sir Robert Howard. TRV
"What is this golden bowl, mother." Ballad of the Golden Bowl. Sara Henderson Hay. OnMSP
What is this life, if, full of care. Leisure. W. H. Davies. LV; RePo; WePo
What is this recompense you'd have from me? From a Woman to a Greedy Lover. Norman Cameron. Fr. Three Love Poems. GTBS-P
What is this reverence in extreme delight. Ecstasy. Arthur Symons. UnTE
What is this strange and uncouth thing? The Crosse. George Herbert. MeP
What Is to Come. W. E. Henley. PoIE
What is your substance, whereof are you made. Sonnets, LIII. Shakespeare. CTC; EnRePo
"What is your tragedy, brother of mine?" A Ballad of Despair. Wade Wellman. FiSC
What It Was. Robert Sward. CoPo
What Kind of Mistress He Would Have. Robert Herrick. UnTE
What Kind of Music? James Reeves. RePo
What know I. The Song of the Arrow. Isabella Valancy Crawford. Fr. Gisli, the Chieftain. OBCV
What large, dark hands are those at the window. Love on the Farm. D. H. Lawrence. ErPo; FaBV
What last resting place awaits me. Where? Heine. AGP
What links are ours with orbs that are. Meditation under Stars. George Meredith. VP
What little throat. The Blackbird by Belfast Lough. Unknown. SiGo
What lively lad most pleased me. A Last Confession. W. B. Yeats. ELP; ErPo; FoBA
What longer need hath she of loveliness. Dirge. Sarojini Naidu. ACV
What love is this of thine, that cannot bee. Meditation One. Edward Taylor. Fr. Preparatory Meditations, First Series. AP; MeP
What lovely names for girls there are! Girls' Names. Eleanor Farjeon. BiCB
What lovely things. The Scribe. Walter de la Mare. MoRP
What makes a nation's pillars high. A Nation's Strength. Emerson. TRV
What makes a plenteous harvest, when to turn. Vergil, tr. by Dryden. Fr. Georgics. EiCP
What makes the ducks in the pond, I wonder, go. Regent's Park. Rose Fyleman. SoPo
What makes us rove that starlit corridor. Science Fiction. Kingsley Amis. NePoEA-2
What man is he that yearneth. Old Age. Sophocles. Fr. Oedipus at Colonus. SiGo
What man of ignorance undefiled. Oh Come, Little Children. Phyllis McGinley. FaBV
What? Mars his sword? faire Cytherea say. Upon Venus Putting on Mars His Armes. Richard Crashaw. SeCP
What matter if my words will be. To My Mother. Louis Ginsberg. PoSC
What may the woman labour to confess? Modern Love, XXII. George Meredith. VP
What may words say, or what may words not say. Astrophel and Stella, XXXV. Sir Philip Sidney. CABA
What meaneth this, that Christ an hymne did singe. Sonnet. William Alabaster. MeP
What menethe this? When I lye alone. What Does This Mean? Sir Thomas Wyatt. MeEL
What Mr. Robinson Thinks. James Russell Lowell. The Biglow Papers, 1st Series, No. III. LV
What mortal, when he saw. Human Life. Matthew Arnold. VP
What mournful news that we did hear. The Girl Who Was Drowned at Onslow. Unknown. BSNS
What Must, sel. Archibald MacLeish.
"Lovers who must say farewell." MoLP
What Must I Do to Be Saved? Unknown. STF
What need you, being come to sense. September 1913. W. B. Yeats. GTBS-P; PoIE
Western wind has blown but a few days, The. The Cranes. Po Chü-i. SiGo
What needs my Shakespeare for his honored bones. On Shakespeare. Milton. DiPo; FoBA
What nibbles at the window. Inbound. Burnham Eaton. FiSC
What no, perdy, ye may be sure! No! Indeed. Sir Thomas Wyatt. MeEL
What noble courage must their hearts have fired. Oliver Goldsmith, the Younger. Fr. The Rising Village. OBCV
What of her glass without her? The black grey. Without Her. Dante Gabriel Rossetti. The House of Life, LIII. CBEP; OBNC; VP
What of the faith and fire within us. Men Who March Away. Thomas Hardy. MMA
What of this fabulous country. Canoe-Trip. Douglas Le Pan. OBCV

What Once I Was. Sir Thomas Wyatt. MeEL
What other woman could be loved like you. Soul-Light. Dante Gabriel Rossetti. The House of Life, XXVIII. VP
What passing-bells for these who die as cattle? Anthem for Doomed Youth. Wilfred Owen. EvOK; GTBS-P; PoPo
What poets feel not, when they make. A Caution to Poets. Matthew Arnold. CBEP
What poets mean by what they mean. The Reader Writes. Carl Crane. PoPl
What potions have I drunk of Siren tears. Sonnets, CXIX. Shakespeare. CBEP
What ran under the rosebush? Could It Have Been a Shadow? Monica Shannon. SoPo
What seas what shores what grey rocks and what islands. Marina. T. S. Eliot. GTBS-P; PoIE
What shall be said of this embattled day. Parted Love. Dante Gabriel Rossetti. The House of Life, XLVI. VP
What shall he have that kill'd the deer? Song. Shakespeare. Fr. As You Like It, IV, ii. CTC
What shall I call? The Christening. A. A. Milne. BiCB
What Shall I Do or What Become of Me? Unknown, tr. fr. Spanish by William M. Davis. AnML
What shall I do to be for ever known. The Motto. Abraham Cowley. SeCP
What shall I give my children? who are poor. Gwendolyn Brooks. Fr. The Children of the Poor. PoCh
What shall I say but, having written for use. Answering a Letter from a Younger Poet. Brewster Ghiselin. PoCh
What shall I wish thee? New Year's Wishes. Frances Ridley Havergal. STF
What Shall We Do for the Striking Seamen? Unknown. ThLM
What shall we do for timber? Kilcash. Tr. by Frank O'Connor. WePo
What shall we say it is to be forgiven? Forgiveness. Elizabeth Sewell. EaLo
What Shame Forbids to Speak. Robert Herrick. UnTE
What she collects is men. The Collector. Raymond Souster. ErPo; OBCV
What should be said of him cannot be said. Dante. Michelangelo. RBL
What Should I Say. Sir Thomas Wyatt. EnRePo
What should one. The Picture of J. T. in a Prospect of Stone. Charles Tomlinson. PoCh
What should we name our baby? The Baby's Name. Tudor Jenks. BiCB
What sign do you make, O Swan, with your curved neck. The Swans. Rubén Darío. AnSP
What slender youth bedewed with liquid odours. To a Girl. Horace, tr. by Milton. Fr. Odes. WiR
What Smouldering Senses. Dante Gabriel Rossetti. See Kiss, The.
What soft-cherubic creatures. Emily Dickinson. AP; CABA
What soul would bargain for a cure that brings. Modern Love, XIV. George Meredith. VP
What sphinx of cement and aluminum bashed open their skulls. Allen Ginsberg. Fr. Howl. PoCh
What splendid names for boys there are! Boys' Names. Eleanor Farjeon. BiCB
What sweeter musick can we bring. A Christmas Caroll, Sung to the King in the Presence at White-Hall. Robert Herrick. GoJo
What the Bullet Sang. Bret Harte. CBEP
What the Grecian Earns. Kenneth Patchen. ToPo
What the Hyena Said. Vachel Lindsay. LV
What the Lord High Chamberlain Said. Virginia Woodward Cloud. BBGG
What the Orderly Dog Saw. Ford Madox Ford. CTC
What the Red-haired Bo'sun Said. Charles H. Souter. PoAu-1
What the Thrush Said. Keats. DiPo
What Then? Unknown. STF
What Then Is Love but Mourning. Thomas Campion. EnRePo
What They Are For. Dorothy Aldis. SoPo
What They Do. Eleanor Farjeon. ThGo
What Thing Is Love. George Peele. Fr. The Hunting of Cupid. ELP; EnRePo; UnTE
What tho' thy home. True Riches. Bessie June Martin. STF
What though my joys and comforts die? Robert Lowry. Fr. How Can I Keep from Singing? TRV
What Though the Field Be Lost? Milton. Fr. Paradise Lost. EaLo
What Tomas Said in a Pub. James Stephens. ILP
What Tongue Can Her Perfections Tell. Sir Philip Sidney. Fr. Arcadia. EnRePo
What travellers of matchlesse Venice say. An Elegie Made by Aurelian Townshend in Remembrance of the Ladie Venetia Digby. Aurelian Townshend. SeCP
What Ulysses Said to Circe on the Beach of Aeaea. Irving Layton. ErPo
What was he doing, the great god Pan. A Musical Instrument

[or The Great God Pan]. Elizabeth Barrett Browning. OnMSP; WiR
What was her beauty in our first estate. She. Richard Wilbur. CoPo; ToPo
What was the blond child building. The Builder of Houses. Jane Cooper. AmPC
What weather of shelters. Walter Lowenfels. Fr. Letter to the President. PtTo
What were that moment over. From Far Shores, from Kingdoms. Gottfried Benn. MGP
What, what, what. A Threnody. George T. Lanigan. CBEP
What Will You Do, God, When I Die? Rainer Maria Rilke, tr. fr. German by Babette Deutsch. EaLo
"What will you have for your birthday?" Birthday Gifts. Herbert Asquith. BiCB
What with the Italian. Portrait of Silverio Franconetti. Federico García Lorca. AnSP
What Women Are Not. Unknown. MeEL
What words are these have fallen from me? In Memoriam A. H. H., XVI. Tennyson. VP
What Would I Give! Christina Rossetti. VP
What You Will Learn about the Brobinyak. John Ciardi. EvOK
Whate'er thy countrymen have done. Written in the Beginning of Mezeray's History of France. Matthew Prior. EiCP
Whate'er we leave to God, God does. Inspiration. Henry David Thoreau. AP
Whatever date you name, I know the text. The Scholar and Goethe. Christian Morgenstern. TwGP
Whatever else be lost among the years. Let Us Keep Christmas. Grace Noll Crowell. TRV
Whatever else withheld, withhold not from us. Belief in Plan of Thee. Walt Whitman. TRV
Whatever I have said or sung. In Memoriam A. H. H., CXXV. Tennyson. VP
Whatever is to be come of me. The Wind. Robert Creeley. AmPC
Whatever it is, it must have. American Poetry. Louis Simpson. PP
Whatever it was she had so fiercely fought. The Recognition of Eve. Karl Shapiro. Fr. Adam and Eve. ToPo
Whatever place is poor and small. The Hut. Ruth Pitter. DaDu
What's Hard. Laurence Lerner. NePoEA-2
What's in the larder? But What's in the Larder? Tennyson. ThGo
What's My Thought Like? Thomas Moore. CBEP
What's that we see from far? the spring of day. A Nuptiall Song, or Epithalamie, on Sir Clipseby Crew and His Lady. Robert Herrick. SeCP
What's the good of a wagon. The Gold-tinted Dragon. Karla Kuskin. SoPo
What's the good of breathing? The Frost Pane. David McCord. RePo
What's the Railroad. Henry David Thoreau. ThLM (Railroad, The.) FaBV
What's the Use. Ogden Nash. PoPl
"What's your age?" Mother's Party. Aileen Fisher. BiCB
What's Your Fancy. Unknown. UnTE
Whatso men sayn. Men Only Pretend. Unknown. MeEL
Whatsoever thing I see. Love Dislikes Nothing. Robert Herrick. CBEP
"Whaur are ye gaun?" said the fause knicht. The Fause Knicht on the Road. Unknown. BFSS
Wheel, The. W. B. Yeats. GTBS-P; PoPo
Wheel Ruts. James Daugherty. RePo
Wheesht, Wheesht. "Hugh MacDiarmid." ErPo
Wheestlin' Barber, Da. T. A. Daly. SIV
When. Dorothy Aldis. RePo
When a Fellow's Four. Mary Jane Carr. BiCB
When a friend starts on a journey of a thousand miles. The End of the Year. Su T'ung-po. PoPl
When a Girl Looks Down. Kay Smith. OBCV
When a Man Has Married a Wife. Blake. ErPo
When a Man Hath No Freedom to Fight For at Home. Byron. PoLF; PoSa
When a misfortune happens me. Wilhelm Busch, tr. fr. German by Francis Owen. AGP
When a people reach the top of a hill. The Blue Battalions. Stephen Crane. AP
When a sighing begins. Song of Autumn. Paul Verlaine. SiGo
When Abraham Lincoln was shoveled into the tombs. Cool Tombs. Carl Sandburg. AP; PoLF; PoPo
When Adam Day by Day. A. E. Housman. PoPl
When Adam delf. The Pointless Pride of Man. Unknown. MeEL
When Adam found his rib was gone. The Lady's-Maid's [or Lady's-Maid] Song. John Hollander. ErPo; MP
When age hath made me what I am not now. Upon His Picture. Thomas Randolph. CBEP
When Alexander Pope strolled in the city. Mr. Pope. Allen Tate. AP; CABA; MP

When all his seas with serpents were aflame. Case History. Lilith Lorraine. FiSC

When All Is Done. Paul Laurence Dunbar. TRV

When all is done and said, in the end thus shall you find. Of a Contented Mind. Thomas, Lord Vaux. EnRePo

When all is over and you march for home. Spoils. Robert Graves. MoLP

When All My Five and Country Senses See. Dylan Thomas. ToPo

When All of Them Ran Off. John Hollander. AmPC

When all that matters shall be written down. All That Matters. Edgar A. Guest. LV

When all the ground with snow is white. The Snow-Bird. Frank Dempster Sherman. SoPo

When all the leaves are off the boughs. Thanksgiving Time. *Unknown.* SoPo

When all the world is young, lad. Young and Old [or The Old Song]. Charles Kingsley. *Fr.* The Water Babies. BiCB; CBEP; LV; PoLF

When all this All doth pass from age to age. Caelica, LXIX. Fulke Greville. EnRePo

When all within is dark. From Thee to Thee. Solomon Ibn Gabirol. EaLo

When an elf is as old as a year and a minute. The Seven Ages of Elf-Hood. Rachel Field. BiCB

When Any Mortal (Even the Most Odd). E. E. Cummings. PoDB; PoPl

When as. *See also* Whenas.

When as in Silks My Julia Goes. Robert Herrick. *See* Upon Julia's Clothes.

When as man's life, the light of human lust. Caelica, LXXXVII. Fulke Greville. PoIE

When as the nightingale chanted her vespers. *See* Whenas the Nightingale.

When at home alone I sit. The Little Land. Robert Louis Stevenson. SoPo

When autumn wounds the bough. Autumnal Spring Song. Vassar Miller. PoSa

When awful darkness and silence reign. The Dong with a Luminous Nose. Edward Lear. CBEP; FaBV; WiR

When battle rous'd each warlike band [or charm]. The Drummer Boy of Waterloo [or Waterloo]. *Unknown.* BFSS; BSO

When beechen buds begin to swell. The Yellow Violet. Bryant. AP; PoLF

When Bethlehem's manger first cradled the King. The Cradle and the Cross. A. S. Reitz. STF

When blessed Marie wip'd her Saviours feet. Marie Magdalene. George Herbert. McP

When breezes are soft and skies are fair. Green River. Bryant. AP

When Britain first, at Heaven's command. Rule, Britannia. James Thomson. *Fr.* Alfred, a Masque (by Thomson and David Mallet). EiCP; GTBS-P

When Brother Francis, rich in birds, arose. Saint Stephen in San Francisco. Melvin Walker La Follette. CoPo

When by thy scorn, O murderess, I am dead. The Apparition. John Donne. CABA; CBEP; SeCP

When cats run home and light is come. The Owl [or Song— the Owl]. Tennyson. CBEP; GoJo

When, Celia, I intend to flatter you. To Celia. *Unknown.* CBEP

When chapman billies leave the street. Tam o' Shanter. Burns. CABL

When chill November's surly blast. Man Was Made to Mourn; a Dirge. Burns. PoIE

When Christ Was Born ("When Christ the Babe was born"). John Banister Tabb. ThGo

When Christ was born in Bethlehem. Ballad of the Epiphany. Charles Dalmon. OnMSP

When Christ with care and pangs of death opprest. Christs Sleeping Friends. Robert Southwell. MeP

When clear October suns unfold. Mallee in October. Flexmore Hudson. PoAu-2

When clerks and navvies fondle. Louis MacNeice. *Fr.* Trilogy for X. ErPo

When contracting, the lash seems not to cause. Michelangelo, *tr. fr. Italian by* Joseph Tusiani. RBL

When Daddy. Walking. Grace Ellen Glaubitz. SoPo

When Daffodils Begin to Peer. Shakespeare. *Fr.* The Winter's Tale, IV, ii. CBEP; UnTE

When Daisies Pied. Shakespeare. *Fr.* Love's Labour's Lost, V, ii. CBEP; EnRePo
(Dialogue in Praise of the Owl and the Cuckoo.) DiPo
(Song: "When daisies pied and violets blue.") VaPo
(Spring.) BoC; FoBA; ILP; PoIE

When Damon First Began to Love. Aphra Behn. *Fr.* The Rover, Pt. I, Act II, sc. i. UnTE

When Daniel Boone goes by at night. Daniel Boone. Stephen Vincent Benét. BiCB

When Days Grow Long in May. Jaufré Rudel, *tr. fr.* Provençal by William M. Davis. AnML

When de Saints Go Ma'chin' Home. Sterling A. Brown. AmNP

When death and hell their right in Herod claime. Christs Returne out of Egypt. Robert Southwell. MeP

When Death Came April Twelve 1945. Carl Sandburg. AP

When Death Comes. *Unknown.* MeEL

When Death, shall part us from these kids. A Dialogue between Thyrsis and Dorinda. Andrew Marvell. SeCP

When Death to Either Shall Come. Robert Bridges. PoPl

When deep within our swelling hearts. Childhood's Trials. Mrs. C. F. Alexander. ThGo

When Delia on the Plain Appears. George Lyttelton. CBEP

When descends on the Atlantic. Seaweed. Longfellow. AP

"When did the world begin and how?" The Answers. Robert Clairmont. SoPo

When do I see thee most, beloved one? Lovesight. Dante Gabriel Rossetti. The House of Life, IV. GTBS-P; OBNC; VP

When Don Luis Was in Cuenca. Luis de Góngora, *tr. fr. Spanish by* Alice Jane McVan. RBL

When Doris Danced. Richard Eberhart. CaFP; ErPo

When early morn walks forth in sober gray. Song. Blake. FoBA

When earth was finished and fashioned well. The Choristers. Bliss Carman. ACV

When Earth's last picture is painted, and the tubes are twisted and dried. L'Envoi. Kipling. PoPl; TRV

When Eubolus the Greek learned. Dionysus. Irving Layton. ErPo

When eyeless fish meet her on. The Goddess. Thom Gunn. ToPo

When Faith and Love Which Parted from Thee Never. Milton. FoBA

When far-spent night persuades each mortal eye. Astrophel and Stella. XCIX. Sir Philip Sidney. CABA

When Father Carves the Duck. Ernest Vincent Wright. FaBV; PoLF; PoSC

When first descending from the moorlands. Extempore Effusion upon the Death of James Hogg. Wordsworth. CBEP

When first Diana leaves her bed. The Progress of Beauty. Swift. CABA

When first from my country, a stranger, curiosity caused me to roam. The Green Mossy Banks of the Lea. *Unknown.* BSNS

When first I came to Louisville. The Lily of the West (A vers.). *Unknown.* BSO

When first I heard the people tell. That Is Even So! John A. Stone. SGR

When first I saw true beauty, and thy Joys. Mount of Olives. Henry Vaughan. McP

When first I went to mining, I was uncommon green. An Honest Miner. John A. Stone. SGR

When first my lines [or verse] of heav'nly joyes made mention. Jordan II. George Herbert. McP; PP; SeCP; VaPo

When first the college rolls receive his name. In Imitation of the Tenth Satire of Juvenal. Samuel Johnson. *Fr.* The Vanity of Human Wishes. PoIE

When first the fiery-mantled Sun. Ode to Winter. Thomas Campbell. GTBS-P

When first the peasant, long inclined to roam. The Young Author. Samuel Johnson. EiCP

When first thou didst entice to thee my heart. Affliction. George Herbert. CABA; McP; SeCP

When first thou on me, Lord, wrough'st thy sweet print. The Ebb and Flow. Edward Taylor. AP

When first thy eies unveil, give thy Soul leave. Rules and Lessons. Henry Vaughan. McP

When first thy sweet and gracious eye. The Glance. George Herbert. McP

When first you look upon her face. Leila. George Hill. AmLP

When fishes flew and forests walked. The Donkey. G. K. Chesterton. BoC; FaBV; LV; PoLF; PoPo

When flighting time is on, I go. The Birdcatcher. Ralph Hodgson. PoIE

When for the thorns with which I long, too long. The Coronet. Andrew Marvell. McP; PP

When formed our band we are all well manned. California. *Unknown.* BSO

When Fortune's blind goddess had fled my abode. Dick Turpin's Ride. *Unknown.* BSNS

When forty winters shall besiege thy brow. Sonnets, II. Shakespeare. FoBA

When foxes eat the last gold grape. Escape. Elinor Wylie. RePo

When Freedom from her mountain height. The American Flag. Joseph Rodman Drake. AmLP

When Friendship or Love our sympathies move. The Tear [or Hours of Idleness]. Byron. EvOK; Par

When from a world of tumult we retreat. Casting All Your Care upon Him. *Unknown.* STF

When from this prison drear. Ode to Filipe Ruiz. Luis de León. RBL

When gadding snow makes hill-sides white. Winter. Charles Mair. OBCV; PoSC

When God at first made man. The Pulley [*or* The Gifts of God]. George Herbert. CBEP; DiPo; EaLo; FoBA; GTBS-P; ILP; OnP; PoIE; PoSa; SeCP; StP; TRV
When God Lets My Body Be. E. E. Cummings. PoDB
When God reveals his plans to men. An Eclipse. Pindar. SiGo
When God wants to drill a man. God Knows What He's About. *Unknown.* STF
When gold was first discovered. The National Miner. John A. Stone. SGR
When gold was found in '48, the people said 'twas gas. The Fools of '49. John A. Stone. SGR
When Goody O'Grumpity baked a cake. Goody O'Grumpity. Carol Ryrie Brink. RePo
When gourds are mellow-yellow on the vine. All Souls. Liboria E. Romano. FiSC
When gray threads mar life's pattern. The Master Weaver. *Unknown.* STF
When great-grandmother was ten years old. The Sampler. Nancy Byrd Turner. BiCB
When Green Buds Hang. A. E. Housman. More Poems, IX. ACV
When guests were present, dear little Mabel. Our Polite Parents. Carolyn Wells. BBGG
When he brings home a whale. Naughty Boy. Robert Creeley. AmPC
When he killed the Mudjokivis. The Modern Hiawatha. George A. Strong. *Fr.* The Song of Milkanwatha. LV; Par
When he married her he said. Thalamos. Peter Kane Dufault. ErPo
When he runs hunting the chipmunk stretches. Chipmunk. Marie de L. Welch. RePo
When He was entering Jerusalem. Evil Days. Boris Pasternak. MoRP
When he who adores thee has left but the name. Pro Patria Mori. Thomas Moore. GTBS-P
When here, Lucinda, first we came. Arno's Vale. Charles Sackville. WaPE
When Hitler was the Devil. The Silent Generation. Louis Simpson. ThLM
When I/ die. The Rebel. Mari E. Evans. AmNP
When I a verse shall make. His Prayer to Ben Jonson. Robert Herrick. ILP; PoSa; PP
When I am a man and can do as I wish. The Conjuror. E. V. Lucas. BiCB
When I Am Big, I Mean to Buy. Mary Mapes Dodge. BiCB
When I Am Dead. Christina Rossetti. BoLP; ELP; WePo
(Song: "When I am dead, my dearest.") CBEP; PoLF; VP
(When I Am Dead, My Dearest.) FaPL; PoSa
When I Am Dead. James Edward Wilson. PoLF
When I am dead, and doctors know not why. The Dampe. John Donne. SeCP
When I am dead and over me bright April. I Shall Not Care. Sara Teasdale. PoPl
When I am dead, I hope it may be said. On His Books. Hilaire Belloc. PoPl
When I am Dead, My Dearest. Christina Rossetti. *See* When I Am Dead.
When I am dead you'll find it hard. He and She. Eugene Fitch Ware. PoLF
When I am gone and green. Lyric. Gil Orlovitz. ToPo
When I am listening to the sweet, tuneful airs of my country. I'r hen Iaith a'i Chanedon. Walter Dowding. ACV
When I Am Not with You. Sara Teasdale. BoLP; MoLP
When I am standing on a mountain crest. Love in the Winds. Richard Hovey. BoLP
When I am tired of earnest men. Martin. Joyce Kilmer. LV
When I am walking down the street. New Shoes. Marjorie S. Watts. SoPo
When I am walking with the children, and a girl. The Father. Donald Finkel. CoPo
When I Awoke. Raymond Patterson. NNP
When I behold the heavens as in their prime. Anne Bradstreet. *Fr.* Contemplations. AmLP
When I Breathe This Air. Peire Vidal, *tr. fr. Provençal by* Maurice Valency. AnML
When I Came from Colchis. W. S. Merwin. AP
When I carefully consider the curious habits of dogs. Meditatio [*or* Meditation]. Ezra Pound. LOW; WePo
When I consider everything that grows. Sonnets, XV. Shakespeare. DiPo; FoBA
When I Consider How My Light Is Spent. Milton. *See* On His Blindness.
When I consider men of golden talents. So That's Who I Remind Me Of. Ogden Nash. PoLF
When I contemplate all alone. In Memoriam A. H. H., LXXXIV. Tennyson. VP
When I do count the clock that tells the time. Sonnets, XII. Shakespeare. CBEP; DiPo; EnRePo; FoBA
When I dyed last, and, deare, I dye. The Legacie. John Donne. SeCP

When I fall asleep, and even during sleep. Baudelaire. Delmore Schwartz. MP
When I gaze at the sun. A Moment Please. Samuel Allen. AmNP
When I go from hence let this be my parting word. Let This Be My Parting Word. Rabindranath Tagore. *Fr.* Gitanjali. MoRP
When I grow old I hope to be. Growing Old. Rose Henderson. BiCB
When I Grow Up. Rupert Sargent Holland. BiCB
When I Grow Up. William Wise. BiCB
When I grow up. Plans. Dorothy Brown Thompson. BiCB
When I grow up I mean to go. When I Grow Up. Rupert Sargent Holland. BiCB
When I had firmly answered "No." The Last Ride Together. J. K. Stephen. Par
When I had wings, my brother. Swinburne. *Fr.* To a Seamew. HaSV
When I have borne in memory what has tamed. Wordsworth. GTBS-P
When I Have Fears [That I May Cease to Be]. Keats. CABA; CBEP; DiPo; FoBA; ILP; LV; PoIE; PoPo; PoSa; StP
(Sonnet: "When I have fears that I may cease to be.") OBNC
(Terror of Death, The.) GTBS-P
When I have lost the power to feel the pang. Strangeness of Heart. Siegfried Sassoon. MoRP
When I have rested dead a thousand years. Erosion. James Larkin Pearson. PoNC
When I have seen by Time's fell hand defaced. Sonnets, LXIV. Shakespeare. CABA; EnRePo; FoBA; GTBS-P; ILP; PoIE; PoPo
When I have seen the sun emerge. Emily Dickinson. AP
When I hear the old men. A Song of Greatness. *Tr. by* Mary Austin. RePo
When I Heard at the Close of the Day. Walt Whitman. AP
When I Heard the Learn'd Astronomer. Walt Whitman. CABA; CaFP; CBEP; DiPo; TRV; VaPo
When I hold you in the night. Turn to the Left. Deems Taylor. UnTE
When I last saw Waring. Robert Browning. *Fr.* Waring. HaSV
When I left old New York, to go hunting after gold. Hunting after Gold. John A. Stone. SGR
When I left the States for gold. Seeing the Elephant. David G. Robinson. SGR
When I lie where shades of darkness. Fare Well. Walter de la Mare. GTBS-P
When I lived down in Devonshire. Autobiographical Fragment. Kingsley Amis. DaDu; NePoEA-2
When I look back and in myself behold. On the Instability of Youth. Thomas, Lord Vaux. EnRePo
When I look forth at dawning, pool. Nature's Questioning. Thomas Hardy. PoDB; PoIE
When I look into the mountain air. Chiliasm. Richard Eberhart. EaLo
When I loved you, I can't but allow. To ——. Thomas Moore. BoLP
When I meet the morning beam. The Immortal Part. A. E. Housman. A Shropshire Lad, XLIII. StP
When I meet you, I greet you with a stare. Silence. Anna Wickham. BoLP
When I must come to you, O my God, I pray. A Prayer to Go to Paradise with the Donkeys. Francis Jammes. EaLo; MoRP
When I Peruse the Conquer'd Fame. Walt Whitman. PoPo
When I play on my fiddle in Dooney. The Fiddler of Dooney. W. B. Yeats. DiPo; PoPo
When I put on my Mother's clothes. Pretending. Myra Cohn Livingston. BiCB
When I rode the zebra past your door. Apparitions Are Not Singular Occurrences. Diane Wakoski. CoPo
When I saw my mother's head on the cold pillow. Keine Lazarovitch. Irving Layton. ACV
When I see birches bend to left and right. Birches. Robert Frost. DiPo; FaBV; FoBA; ILP; LV; PoIE; PoLF; PoPl; StP
When I see buildings in a town together. Mr. Frost Goes South to Boston. Firman Houghton. Par
When I See the Skylark Winging. Bernart de Ventadorn, *tr. fr. Provençal by* Daisy Aldan. AnML
(Lark, The, *shorter vers., tr. by* Ezra Pound.) CTC
When I See the Waves. Roi Fernández, *tr. fr. Portuguese by* William M. Davis. AnML
When I shall be divorced, some ten years hence. Youth's Agitations. Matthew Arnold. CBEP
When I shall be without regret. Epitaph. J. V. Cunningham. PoCh
When I stand at the judgment seat of Christ. His Plan for Me. Martha Snell Nicholson. STF
When I Think of the Hungry People. O-Shi-O, *tr. fr. Japanese.* TRV
When I Thy Parts Run O'er. Robert Herrick. UnTE

When I thy singing next shall heare. Againe. Robert Herrick. SeCP
When I try to skate. Skating. Herbert Asquith. SoPo
When I visited America. He Comforts Himself. Christopher Morley. *Fr.* Translations from the Chinese. EvOK
When I wake in the early mist. Very Early. Karla Kuskin. SoPo
When I was a bachelor, I lived by myself [or all alone *or* batchelor early and young]. Foggy, Foggy Dew [*or* The Foggy Dew]. *Unknown.* DTC; ELP; UnTE (*2 vers.*)
When I was a beggarly boy. Aladdin. James Russell Lowell. RoGo
When I was a child and thought as a child, I put. The Wandering Jew. Robert Mezey. NePoEA-2
When I Was a Lad. W. S. Gilbert. *Fr.* H.M.S. Pinafore. PoPo
(Ruler of the Queen's Navee, The.) DiPo
When I was a little boy, and lived by myself. The Swapping Song. *Unknown.* BSO
When I was a windy boy and a bit. Lament. Dylan Thomas. ErPo
When I Was a Young Man (A *vers., with music*). *Unknown.* BSO
(Oh, When I Was Single, B *vers., with music.*) BSO
When I was a youngster I sailed with the rest. Liverpool Girls. *Unknown.* HaSV
When I was as high as that. A Memory. L. A. G. Strong. DaDu; PoPl
"When I was at the party." Betty at the Party. *Unknown.* BiCB
When I was born on Amman hill. The Collier. Vernon Watkins. DaDu; DTC
When I was bound apprentice, in famous Lincolnshire. The Lincolnshire Poacher [*or* The Poacher]. *Unknown.* OnMSP; SD; WiR
When I was but thirteen or so. Romance. W. J. Turner. BiCB; GoJo; ILP; WePo
When I was Christened. David McCord. BiCB
When I was coming down from the country. The Forgotten City. William Carlos Williams. PoPl
When I Was Fair and Young. Elizabeth I, Queen of England. CBEP; CTC
(Importune Me No More.) UnTE
When I was happy in my youth. I Stand Corrected. Margaret Fishback. PoPl
When I was just a little boy. The Ships of Yule. Bliss Carman. BiCB; RePo
When I was little, oh a very small boy. So Long Folks, Off to the War. Anthony Ostroff. PoPl
When I was Lost. Dorothy Aldis. SoPo
When I was making myself a game. Little Rain. Elizabeth Madox Roberts. SoPo
When I was on Night Line. Ego. Philip Booth. MP
When I Was One. A. A. Milne. ThGo
(End, The.) MP
When I was one. Sophisticate. Barbara Young. BiCB
When I Was One-and-Twenty. A. E. Housman. A Shropshire Lad, XIII. BiCB; BoLP; DiPo; ELP; FaBV; PoLF; PoPl; PoPo; VP
When I was only six years old. When I Was Six. Zora Cross. BiCB
When I was seven. Growing Up. Harry Behn. BiCB; SoPo
When I was sick and lay a-bed. The Land of Counterpane. Robert Louis Stevenson. EvOK; ILP; PoPl; SoPo
When I Was Single. BSNS, *with music;* BSO
(I Wish I was Single Again, *with music.*) BFSS
When I Was Six. Zora Cross. BiCB
When I Was Small. André de Chénier, *tr. fr. French by* Elizabeth Gerteiny. ErPo
When I was small and trees were high. Tree-sleeping. Robert P. Tristram Coffin. LOW
When I was strolling 'way down by Lake Erie. The Dying Cowboy (C *vers.*). *Unknown.* BSO
When I was young and full o' pride. Blow Me Eyes! Wallace Irwin. BoLP
When I was young and full of rhymes. Don't Shake the Bottle, Shake Your Mother-in-Law. Phyllis McGinley. LV
When I was young and in my prime, my age being twenty-one. Erin's Lovely Home. *Unknown.* BSNS
When I was young—and very young. Wisdom. Daniel Whitehead Hicky. BiCB
When I was young, I put on rouge. The Onion Skin. Kenneth Pitchford. *Fr.* Good for Nothing Man. CoPo
When I was young, I said to Sorrow. Sorrow. Aubrey Thomas De Vere. WiR
When I was young I took the sea to wife. Song of an Old Sailor. Trefor Davies. HaSV
When I was young, I went to school. The One Furrow. R. S. Thomas. AnMoPo
When I was young the world was a little pond. Return of the Village Lad. Alfred Lichtenstein. MGP
When I went down past Charing Cross. The Poet. W. H. Davies. DTC

When I Went Off to Prospect, *with music*. John A. Stone. SGR
When I would boast of my log-cabin birth. Birthplace. James Larkin Pearson. PoNC
When Icicles Hang by the Wall. Shakespeare. *Fr.* Love's Labour's Lost, V, ii. CaFP; CBEP; GoJo; PoSa; PoSC; RoGo
(Merry Note, A.) WiR
(Song: "When icicles hang by the wall.") OnP
(Winter.) BoC; FoBA; GTBS-P; ILP; PoIE; PoPo
When I'm a little older. My Plan. Marchette Chute. BiCB
"When I'm alone"—the words tripped off his tongue. Alone. Siegfried Sassoon. WePo
When I'm big I want to be. Space. Inez Hogan. RePo
When, in disgrace with fortune and men's eyes. Sonnets, XXIX. Shakespeare. BoLP; CBEP; CTC; DiPo; FaBV; FoBA; GTBS-P; ILP; LV; PoIE; PoPl; PoPo; PoSa; TRV
When in My Arms. Pushkin, *tr. fr. Russian by* Babette Deutsch. ErPo
When in my walks I meet some ruddy lad. A Proem. Samuel Ward. AmLP
When in Rome. Mari E. Evans. AmNP
When in the bedded dark of night. Marriage: To K. Donald Hall. MoLP
When in the chronicle of wasted time. Sonnets, CVI. Shakespeare. CBEP; CTC; DiPo; EnRePo; FaBV; GTBS-P; PoIE; PoPo; StP
When in the Crowd I Suddenly Behold. Robert Nathan. MoLP
When, in the dawn of love and my desire. The Miracle. Allan Dowling. ErPo
When in the dim beginning of the years. Man-Test. Edwin Markham. MoRP
When in the down I sink my head. In Memoriam A. H. H., LXVIII. Tennyson. VP
When in the sun the hot red acres smoulder. The Zulu Girl. Roy Campbell. AnMoPo; PoPl
When inclined to be discouraged. Have Faith in God. Joe Budzynski. STF
When Isaac watched his father strain back. Abraham's Madness. Bink Noll. ToPo
When Israel was in Egypt's land. Go Down, Moses. *Unknown.* EaLo
When it is finally ours, this freedom, this liberty, this beautiful. Frederick Douglass. Robert Hayden. AmNP
When It Is May, and the Darkness Is Short. *Unknown, tr. fr. French by* Patricia Terry. AnML
When it's just past April. The Flower-Cart Man. Rachel Field. SoPo
When its rays fall on its cheeks the cat licks them, thinking them milk. The Moon. Bhasa. SiGo
When Jacky's a Very Good Boy. Mother Goose. EvOK
When Januar' wind war blawin' cauld. The Lass That Made the Bed for Me. Burns. UnTE
When Jesus came to Golgotha they hanged Him on a tree. Indifference. G. A. Studdert-Kennedy. TRV
When John Henry was a little boy. John Henry. *Unknown.* ThLM
When John was christened, up he reached. It Really Happened. Elizabeth Henley. BiCB
When Johnny Comes Marching Home. Patrick Sarsfield Gilmore. PoSC; ThLM
When Joseph was an old man. Joseph and Mary. *Unknown.* BFSS
When Julius Fabricius, Sub-Prefect of the Weald. The Land. Kipling. OnMSP
When lads have done with labor. Humbert Wolfe. Par
When late I attempted your pity to move. An Expostulation. Isaac Bickerstaffe. BoLP
When Lazarus left his charnel-cave. In Memoriam A. H. H., XXXI. Tennyson. VP
When learning's triumph o'er her barb'rous foes. Prologue. Samuel Johnson. EiCP
When Letty had scarce pass'd her third glad year. Letty's Globe. Charles Tennyson Turner. CBEP
When like wistaria against this wall. A Weightless Element. Gottfried Benn. MGP; PoPl
When Lilacs Last in the Dooryard Bloom'd. Walt Whitman. AP; CABA; DiPo; FoBA; LiPo; PoIE; PoPo; StP; VaPo
Death Carol, *sel.* MoRP
(Carol of the Bird, The.) LV
When Lincoln Came to Springfield. Vachel Lindsay. LiPo
When little boys grown patient at last, weary. Death of Little Boys. Allen Tate. MP
When little Dickie Swope's a man. An Impetuous Resolve. James Whitcomb Riley. BiCB
When love has passed its limits. Chorus. Euripides. *Fr.* Medea. SiGo
When love of us called Him to see. Richard Crashaw. BoC
When love was false and I was full of care. The Constant One. George Dillon. AmLP
When Love with unconfinèd wings. To Althea, from Prison.

When Love with unconfinèd wings (continued)
Richard Lovelace. CABA; CBEP; FaPL; GTBS-P; ILP;
LV; PoIE; PoPo; PoSa; SeCP
When Lovely Woman Stoops to Folly. Goldsmith. See Song:
"When lovely woman stoops to folly."
When Lucy McLockett. Lucy McLockett. Phyllis McGinley.
BiCB
When lyart leaves bestrow the yird. The Jolly Beggars.
Burns. EiCP
When maidens such as Hester die. Hester. Charles Lamb.
GTBS-P
When making for the brook, the falconer doth espy. Hawking.
Michael Drayton. Fr. Polyolbion. SD
When man and woman die, as poets sung. The Difference.
Benjamin Franklin. PoPo
When melancholy Autumn comes to Wembley. Harrow-on-the-
Hill. John Betjeman. DaDu
When men a dangerous disease did scape. To Doctor Empirick.
Ben Jonson. SeCP
When men turn mob. Music and Drum. Archibald MacLeish.
MoRP
When men were all asleep the snow came flying. London Snow.
Robert Bridges. GTBS-P; OBNC; PoIE; PoSa; StP;
WePo; WiR
When midnight comes a host of dogs and men. Badger. John
Clare. CBEP; WiR
When miners get into a row about their mining ground. A
Miners' Meeting. John A. Stone. SGR
When Mrs. Gorm (Aunt Eloise). Opportunity. Harry
Graham. DTC
When Morgan crossed the Murray to Peechelba and doom.
Morgan. Edward Harrington. PoAu-1
When Moses came down from the mountain and the cloud.
John Holmes. Fr. The Eleventh Commandment. MoRP
When Moses, musing in the desert, found. The Burning Bush.
Norman Nicholson. EaLo
When most I wink, then do mine eyes best see. Sonnets,
XLIII. Shakespeare. CBEP
When mothers weep and fathers richly proud. The Confirma-
tion. Karl Shapiro. ErPo
When Music, heav'nly maid, was young. The Passions. Wil-
liam Collins. EiCP; GTBS-P
When my arms wrap you round I press. He Remembers
Forgotten Beauty. W. B. Yeats. CTC
When my brother Tommy. Two in Bed. Abram Bunn Ross.
SoPo
When my devotions could not pierce. Deniall. George Herbert.
MeP
When my eyes filled, by your presence possessed. When You
Enraptured Me. Franz Werfel. TwGP
When my grave is broke up again. The Relic [or Relique].
John Donne. CABA; CBEP; EnRePo; ILP; SeCP; StP
When my love swears that she is made of truth. Sonnets,
CXXXVIII. Shakespeare. CABA; FoBA
When my mother died I was very young. The Chimney
Sweeper. Blake. Fr. Songs of Innocence. CaFP; CBEP;
DiPo; EnPE; FoBA; ILP; PoIE
When my young brother was killed. War. Joseph Langland.
MP; PoCh
When nature made her chief work, Stella's eyes. Astrophel
and Stella, VII. Sir Philip Sidney. CABA
When Nature once in lustful hot undress. Giantess. Baude-
laire. ErPo
When night falls. Japan That Sank under the Sea. Satoru
Sato. PoPl
When Night has been announced as theme, will it not cause
surprise. David Gascoyne. Fr. Megalometropolitan Car-
nival. ACV
When night is almost done. Emily Dickinson. TRV
When no one listens. Stranger. Thomas Merton. EaLo
When Nobody Prays. Merl A. Clapper. STF
When None Shall Rail. David Lewis. CBEP
When ocean-clouds over inland hills. Misgivings. Herman
Melville. AP; CBEP
When o'er the waters' azure trail. Earth and Sea. Pushkin.
SiGo
When Old John Bax drove the mail to Coonabarabran. Old
John Bax. Charles H. Souter. PoAu-1
When 'Omer Smote 'Is Bloomin' Lyre. Kipling. Par
When on my bed the moonlight falls. In Memoriam A. H. H.,
LXVII. Tennyson. VP
When on my day of life the night is falling. At Last [or To
Paths Unknown]. Whittier. AP; TRV
When, on our casual way. The Shakespearean Bear. Arthur
Guiterman. EvOK
When, on the bearing mother, death's. Childbirth. Ted
Hughes. ToPo
When once a chic busts through a egg. Gettin' Born. An-
thony Euwer. PoPl
When once the sunset dyes the west with red. Lunae Custo-
diens. Lin Carter. FiSC
When One Loves Tensely. Don Marquis. BoLP
When one starts crying. The Twins. Dorothy Aldis. BiCB
When our brother Fire was having his dog's day. Brother
Fire. Louis MacNeice. AnMoPo

When our rude & unfashion'd words, that long. To a Lady
Who Did Sing Excellently. Lord Herbert of Cherbury.
SeCP
When out by Shellbrook, round by stile and tree. Shellbrook.
William Barnes. OBNC
When over the flowery, sharp pasture's. Flowers by the Sea.
William Carlos Williams. AmLP; GoJo
When people call this beast to mind. The Elephant. Hilaire
Belloc. SoPo
When President John Quincy. John Quincy Adams. Stephen
Vincent Benét. PoP1
When 'Professor Gooseberry gave up his ghost. Paging Pro-
fessor Gooseberry. Thad Stem, Jr. PoNC
When quiet in my room I sit. My Companion. Charles
Wesley. STF
When Raging Love. Earl of Surrey. EnRePo
When remora to his footsteps was his ear. An Idyllic Scene.
Luis de Góngora. Fr. The Solitudes. RBL
When Robin Hood and Little John. The Death of Robin Hood.
Unknown. BuBa
When rosy plumelets tuft the larch. In Memoriam A. H. H.,
XCI. Tennyson. OBNC; VP
When Ruth was left half desolate. Ruth; or, The Influences
of Nature. Wordsworth. GTBS-P
When Sam goes back in memory. Sam. Walter de la Mare.
FaBV; OnMSP; PoPo; WePo
When Satan Fell. D. H. Lawrence. MoRP
When Senses Fled. John Woods. CoPo
When Serpents Bargain for the Right to Squirm. E. E. Cum-
mings. MP
When shall I see the half-moon sink again. End of Another
Home Holiday. D. H. Lawrence. DTC
When she carries food to the table and stoops down. Part of
Plenty. Bernard Spencer. ErPo; MoLP
When she rises in the morning. Gloire de Dijon. D. H.
Lawrence. ELP; ErPo
When she walks in the field of long grass. Field of Long
Grass. A. J. M. Smith. BoLP
When she was in her garden. Ann and the Fairy Song.
Walter de la Mare. Fr. A Child's Day. FaBV
When she was old, deaf, widowed, my grandmother. Grand-
daughter. Eleanor Ross Taylor. Fr. Family Bible.
PoNC
When Sherman Marched Down to the Sea, with music. Sam-
uel H. M. Byers. BFSS
When silver snow decks Susan's clothes. Blind-Man's Buff.
Blake. WiR
When ski-ing in the Engadine. Patience. Harry Graham.
LV
When smoke stood up from Ludlow. A. E. Housman. A
Shropshire Lad, VII. PoPo; VP
When snow like sheep lay in the fold. In Memory of Jane
Fraser. Geoffrey Hill. DaDu
When snows are gone and skies are clear. The Robin. Un-
known. PoPo
When some great sorrow, like a mighty river. This Too Will
Pass Away. Unknown. STF
When Spring comes laughing. A Song of the Four Seasons.
Austin Dobson. BoC
When Spring is in the fields that stained your wing. To a
Linnet in a Cage. Francis Ledwidge. RoGo
When Stella strikes the tuneful string. To Miss ——. Samuel
Johnson. CABA
When storms arise. Hymn. Paul Laurence Dunbar. TRV
When Structure Fails Rhyme Attempts to Come to the Rescue.
William Carlos Williams. PP
When stubble-lands were greening, you came among the stocks.
The Green Autumn Stubble. Unknown. SiGo
When summer's in the city. The Ice-Cream Man. Rachel
Field. SoPo
When sunset falls upon your day. Measure of Success. Un-
known. STF
When supper time is almost come. Milking Time. Elizabeth
Madox Roberts. GoJo
"When that dead face, bowered in the furthest years." The
Love-Moon. Dante Gabriel Rosetti. The House of Life,
XXXVII. VP
When That I Was [and a Little Tiny Boy]. Shakespeare.
Fr. Twelfth Night, V, i. EnRePo; PoIE
(Epilogue: "When that I was and a little tiny boy.")
WePo
(Feste's Final Song.) VaPo
(Wind and the Rain, The.) CBEP; DiPo; WiR
When that joy is gone for good. Naomi Replansky. Fr. Ring
Song. PtTo
When that rich soule which to her heaven is gone. The First
Anniversary: An Anatomie of the World. John Donne.
MeP
When the Assault Was Intended to the City. Milton.
GTBS-P; RoGo
When the autumn winds go wailing. Ungathered Love. Philip
Bourke Marston. OBNC
When the Battle It Was Won. Unknown. BSNS
When the blessed Saviour calls you. You Will Find a Joy in
Service. Dorothy Conant Stroud. STF

When the church seeks a pastor. Some Bird. *Unknown.* STF
When the city cast out the best. Ibycus. John Heath-Stubbs. PoCh
When the crop is fair in the olive-yard. The Cocooning. Frédéric Mistral. *Fr. Mirèio.* PoPl
When the curtain of night, 'tween the dark and the light. Whistling Boy. Nixon Waterman. PoLF
When the echo of the last footstep dies. Song. E. W. Mandel. OBCV
When the enemy surrounds you. The Precious Blood. *Unknown.* STF
When the fight begins within himself. Robert Browning. *Fr.* Bishop Blougram's Apology. TRV
When the first light came and I saw her brush. The Dawn. Sahl ben Malik. AnML
When the flagmakers heard the news from their man in D.C. The Flagmakers. J. M. Murphy. PtTo
When the flesh of summer piecemeal mars the lawn. Sonnet in Autumn. Donald Petersen. NePoEA-2
When the Frost Is on the Punkin. James Whitcomb Riley. FaBV; PoLF
When the Frosts Cover Them. Rosalía de Castro, *tr. fr. Spanish by* Muriel Kittel. AnSP
When the full fields begin to smell of sunrise. The Trappist Abbey. Thomas Merton. PoPl
When the God entered him, impelled by need. Leda. Rainer Maria Rilke. TwGP
When the gold fever raged, I was doing very well. The Miner's Lament, I. John A. Stone. SGR
When the great, busy plants of our cities. What Then? *Unknown.* STF
When the green woods laugh with the voice of joy. Laughing Song. Blake. *Fr.* Songs of Innocence. CBEP; DiPo; GoJo; PoSC
When the grey lake-water rushes. The Solitary Woodsman. Sir Charles G. D. Roberts. OBCV
When the hawk. Strophe. Wolfdietrich Schnurre. MGP
When the horse has been unharnessed and we've flushed the old machine. Cleaning Up. Edward Dyson. PoAu-1
When the Hounds of Spring. Swinburne. *See* Chorus: "When the hounds of spring are on winter's traces."
When the King of Siam disliked a courtier. In Dispraise of Poetry. Jack Gilbert. PP
When the Lamp Is Shattered. Shelley. *See* Lines: "When the lamp is shattered."
When the last Pullman of the day pulls into the Grand Canyon station. View. Josephine Miles. RePo
When the leaf is tight and gray. Look to the Leaf. *Unknown.* UnTE
When the lean recruit threw a shaky salute. The Man in the Manmade Moon. X. J. Kennedy. StP
When the leaves in autumn wither. Autumnus. Joshua Sylvester. StP
When the little armadillo. Mexican Serenade. Arthur Guiterman. BoLP; LV
When the mice awaken. The Vigil. Denise Levertov. NePoEA-2
When the miller starts to grind. Sounds of the Trades. *Unknown.* AnML
When the miner returns from his labor. The Vocal Miner. John A. Stone. SGR
When the Mint Is in the Liquor. Clarence Ousley. PoLF
When the moon comes peeping through my windowpane at night. My Wish. Patience Strong. RePo
When the morning was waking over the war. Among Those Killed in the Dawn Raid Was a Man Aged a Hundred. Dylan Thomas. AnMoPo
When the mouse died at night. The Mouse. Jean Garrigue. MP
When the mouse died, there was a sort of pity. Death of a Whale. John Blight. PoAu-2
When the Nightingale Sings. *Unknown.* CBEP (Fairest between Lincoln and Lindsay.) MeEL
When the nightingale to his mate. Alba. Ezra Pound. *Fr.* Langue d'Oc. PoIE
When the Norn Mother saw the Whirlwind Hour. Lincoln, the Man of the People. Edwin Markham. LiPo
When the north wind moans thro' the blind creek courses. A Gallop of Fire. Marie E. J. Pitt. PoAu-1
When the old flaming prophet climbed the sky. On a Virtuous Young Gentlewoman That Died Suddenly. William Cartwright. CBEP
When the pods went pop on the broom, green broom. A Runnable Stag. John Davidson. EvOK; SD; WiR
When the prairie schooner sailed. We Put on the Buffalo. Robert P. Tristram Coffin. RePo
When the Present has latched its postern behind my tremulous stay. Afterwards. Thomas Hardy. AnMoPo; CBEP; GTBS-P; OBNC; PoIE
"When the Pulitzers showered on some dope." Words for Hart Crane. Robert Lowell. AP; CABA
When the rattlesnake bit, I lay. The Poisoned Man. James Dickey. ToPo
When the Regime ordered that books with dangerous teachings. The Burning of Books. Bertolt Brecht. PoPl

When the rigors of the world assail you. To Laughter, to Leering. Richard Eberhart. ToPo
When the rose is brightest. To Giulia Grisi. Nathaniel Parker Willis. AmLP
When the Saints Go Marchin' In. *Unknown.* EaLo
When the Saviour has given you a blessing, by paper or a book. Pass It On! *Unknown.* STF
When the sheep are in the fauld, and the kye at hame. Auld Robin Gray. Lady Anne Lindsay. GTBS-P
When the Spent Day Begins to Frail. E. E. Cummings. ErPo
When the spent sun throws up its rays on cloud. Acceptance. Robert Frost. MoRP
When the Star Appears at Daybreak. Ramon Llull, *tr. fr. Catalan by* William M. Davis. AnML
When the storm-tossed mariner Ulysses lay. To Madame Lucrezia d'Este, Duchess of Urbino. Tasso. RBL
When the storm was fiercely raging. "It Is I, Be Not Afraid." A. B. Simpson. STF
When the summer fields are mown. Aftermath. Longfellow. AP
When the sun gets low, in winter. Human Things. Howard Nemerov. StP; ToPo
When the tide was out. A Ship Burning and a Comet All in One Day. Richard Eberhart. ToPo
When the torch is taken. Seneca. Thomas Merton. CoPo
When the unknown shall be known. To the Soul. Sir Frederick Napier Broome. ACV
When the Unnatural Warm Fair October. Chad Walsh. StP
When the voices of children are heard on the green/ And laughing. Nurse's Song. Blake. *Fr.* Songs of Innocence. CBEP; FoBA
When the voices of children are heard on the green/ And whisp'rings. Nurse's Song. Blake. *Fr.* Songs of Experience. FoBA
When the Waters of the Spring. Jaufré Rudel, *tr. fr. Provençal by* Maurice Valency. AnML
When the wind blows, walk not abroad. To the Maids Not to Walk in the Wind. Oliver St. John Gogarty. ErPo
When the words rustle no more. Stillness. James Elroy Flecker. GoJo
When the Work's All Done This Fall, *with music. Unknown.* BFSS
When the World Is Burning. Ebenezer Jones. ACV
"When the World Was in Building. . ." Ford Madox Ford. CTC
When they pull me out. Death by Water. Hans Carl Artmann. MGP
When they said the time to hide was mine. The Rabbit. Elizabeth Madox Roberts. SoPo
When They Told Me I Felt the Cold. Gustavo Adolfo Bécquer, *tr. fr. Spanish by* Doreen Bell. AnSP
When they write an end to war, when they blot away the battle. If We Break Faith. Joseph Auslander. TRV
When Things Go Wrong. *Unknown.* STF
When things go wrong as they sometimes will. Don't Quit. *Unknown.* STF
When this yokel comes maundering. The Plot against the Giant. Wallace Stevens. CaFP
When those renouned noble peers of Greece. Amoretti, XLIV. Spenser. CABA
When Thou Must Home [to Shades of Underground]. Thomas Campion. CABA; CBEP; EnRePo; PoSa; VaPo
When thou passest through the waters. Through the Waters. Annie Johnson Flint. STF
When thou, poore excommunicate. Song: To My Inconstant Mistris. Thomas Carew. SeCP
When thou turn'st away from ill. Approaches. George Macdonald. TRV
When thou wakest in the morning. Tell Jesus. *Unknown.* STF
When through the winding cobbled streets of time. The Noonday April Sun. George Love. NNP
When Thy Beauty Appears. Thomas Parnell. CBEP (Song: "When thy beauty appears.") UnTE
When to Her Lute [Corinna Sings]. Thomas Campion. CABA; EnRePo; ILP; OnP
When to my Eyes. Midnight. Henry Vaughan. MeP
When to the music of Byrd or Tallis. King's College Chapel. Charles Causley. BoC
When to the sessions of sweet silent thought. Sonnets, XXX. Shakespeare. CABA; CaFP; CBEP; CTC; DiPo; EnRePo; FaBV; GTBS-P; ILP; PoIE; PoLF; PoPo; StP; TRV
When trials press and foes increase. Trials. Grace E. Troy. STF
When trouble comes your soul to try. The Friend Who Just Stands By. B. Y. Williams. PoLF
When Trout Swim down Great Ormond Street. Conrad Aiken. *Fr.* Priapus and the Pool. AmLP; CaFP
When Truth Disappeared from the World. Airas Nunes, *tr. fr. Portuguese by* William M. Davis. AnML
When tunes jigged nimbler than the blood. Song from a Country Fair. Léonie Adams. GoJo
When two men meet for the first time in all. Law in the Country of the Cats. Ted Hughes. ToPo

When Two Suns Do Appear. Sir Philip Sidney. *Fr.* Arcadia. EnRePo

When, wanton fair, the snowy orb you throw. On a Lady Throwing Snowballs at Her Lover. Christopher Smart. VaPo

When waves invade the yellowing wheat. Composed While under Arrest. Mikhail Lermontov. SiGo

When we are in love, we love the grass. Love Poem. Robert Bly. BoLP

When we are old and these rejoicing veins. Sonnet XXVIII. Edna St. Vincent Millay. ErPo

When we as strangers sought. At an Inn. Thomas Hardy. VP

When we behold. Dahlias. Padraic Colum. GoJo

When We Court and Kiss. Thomas Campion. *See* I Care Not for These Ladies.

When we for age cou'd neither read nor write. Of the Last Verses in the Book. Edmund Waller. SeCP

When we on simple rations sup. Washing the Dishes. Christopher Morley. PoLF

When We Two Parted. Byron. CBEP; DiPo; FaPL; GTBS-P; OBNC; PoLF; WePo

When we were building Skua Light. The Dancing Seal. W. W. Gibson. OnMSP

When we were idlers with the loitering rills. To a Friend [or Sonnet]. Hartley Coleridge. CBEP; OBNC; PoLF

"When we're walking in the garden." The Scottish Merchant's Daughter. *Unknown.* BFSS

When Wesley died, the Angelic orders. Wesley in Heaven. Thomas Edward Brown. OBNC

When Westwell Downs I 'gan to tread. On Westwell Downs. William Strode. CBEP

When whispering strains do softly steal. In Commendation of Music. William Strode. CBEP

When Will He Come? *Unknown.* STF

When will you ever, Peace, wild wooddove, shy wings shut. Peace. Gerard Manley Hopkins. BoC; ELP; GTBS-P

When William went from home (a trader styled). The Ear-Maker and the Mould-Mender. La Fontaine. UnTE

When Wilt Thou Save the People? Ebenezer Elliott. EaLo; WePo

When winds that move not its calm surface sweep. The Landsman. Moschus. SiGo

When winter closed upon the countryside. Six Silver Handles. Sydney King Russell. FiSC

When Winter scourged the meadow and the hill. Ice. Sir Charles G. D. Roberts. OBCV

When winter snows upon thy sable hairs. To Delia, XXXIX. Samuel Daniel. CTC; EnRePo

When winter-time grows wearying, I lift my eyes on high. Winter Branches. Margaret Widdemer. RePo

When winter winds are piercing chill. Woods in Winter. Longfellow. CBEP

When with a serious musing I behold. The Marigold. George Wither. CBEP

When without tears I looke on Christ, I see. Sonnet. William Alabaster. MeP

When yet I might (as now I may no more). On His Deafness. Joachim du Bellay. *Fr.* Les Amours. RBL

When You Are Old. W. B. Yeats. BoLP; CTC; DiPo; FaBV; FoBA; GoJo; MoLP; PoIE; PoLF; PoPl; PoPo; PoSa; PP; WePo

When you are old and beautiful. At Majority. Adrienne Rich. NePoEA-2

When you are old and grey and full of sleep. When You Are Old. W. B. Yeats. BoLP; CTC; DiPo; FaBV; FoBA; GoJo; MoLP; PoIE; PoLF; PoPl; PoPo; PoSa; PP; WePo

When you are very old, at evening. Of His Lady's Old Age. Pierre de Ronsard. *Fr.* Sonnets pour Hélène. CTC; RBL

When you are walking by yourself. Kick a Little Stone. Dorothy Aldis. SoPo

When you ask God in the morning. Be Thankful. Mark Bullock. STF

When you came to me, it was a little before. The Visit of the Beloved. Ben Hazm. AnML

When you came, you were like red wine and honey. A Decade. Amy Lowell. BoLP; PoPl

When you can catch. Then. Dorothy Aldis. BiCB

When you come, as you soon must, to the streets of our city. Advice to a Prophet. Richard Wilbur. AnMoPo; CoPo; MoRP; MP; ToPo

When You Enraptured Me. Franz Werfel, *tr. fr.* German by Walter Kaufmann. TwGP

When you first rub up against God's own skin. Ars Poetica about Ultimates. Tram Combs. MP

When you get to heaven. Surprises. *Unknown.* STF

"When you go down to yonder town." Rosemary and Thyme. *Unknown.* BSO

When you have bathed in the river. Submission. *Unknown.* ErPo

When you kneel below me. Celebration. Leonard Cohen. ErPo

When you read what he said. The Words of Jesus. William Rose Benét. MoRP

When you ride on a train, a passenger train. Passenger Train. Edith Newlin Chase. SoPo

When You See Millions of the Mouthless Dead. Charles Sorley. MMA

When You Shake Loose Your Hair. Francisco de Quevedo, *tr. fr. Spanish* by Roy Campbell. AnSP

When you stand, dig deep and pry! Undaunted. Nietzsche. TwGP

When you take off your clothes. In Nakedness. Marnie Pomeroy. ErPo

When you the sunburnt pilgrim see. Good Counsel to a Young Maid. Thomas Carew. ErPo

When you watch for. Feather or Fur. John Becker. RePo

When you were a girl. Woman. Umberto Saba. CoIP

When young Eternity was born. God. James Larkin Pearson. PoNC

When young I scribbled, boasting, on my wall. The Summing-up. Stanley Kunitz. PoPl

When Younglings First. *Unknown.* EnRePo

When your belly. The Peaches. Joel Oppenheimer. CoPo

When your Christian duty calls you. God Is There. Walter E. Isenhour. STF

When your grapes formed, you swore to save them. Hoarded Grapes. *Unknown.* UnTE

When You're Away. Samuel Hoffenstein. BoLP

"When you're together with her, and you have a good excuse." Juan Ruiz, Archpriest of Hita. *Fr.* The Book of True Love. ErPo

When Youth Had Led. Earl of Surrey. EnRePo

Whenas in Silks My Julia Goes. Robert Herrick. *See* Upon Julia's Clothes.

Whenas—methinks that is a pretty way. To His Ever-worshipped Will from W. H. "Francis." ErPo

Whenas the Nightingale. John Cleveland. *See* Mark Antony.

Whenas the Rye. George Peele. *Fr.* The Old Wives' Tale. CBEP; ELP

Whence comes the crooked wind. La Tour du Sorcier. Sir Osbert Sitwell. DaDu

Whene'er I come where ladies are. Love at Large. Coventry Patmore. *Fr.* The Angel in the House. StP

Whenever a Little Child Is Born. Agnes Carter Mason. BiCB

"Whenever I plunge my arm, like this." Under the Waterfall. Thomas Hardy. CTC

Whenever I ride on the Texas plains. Texas Trains and Trails. Mary Austin. SoPo

Whenever Richard Cory went down town. Richard Cory. E. A. Robinson. CaFP; DiPo; DTC; ILP; PoLF; PoPo

Whenever the moon and stars are set. Windy Nights. Robert Louis Stevenson. GoJo; LV

Whenever there is silence around me. There Is a Man on the Cross. Elizabeth Cheney. TRV

Whenever we touched, I thought of the Lying-in Hospital. Elegy. Robert Layzer. PoPl

Where? Heine, *tr. fr.* German by Helen Sebba. AGP

Where? Kenneth Patchen. ToPo

Where a Roman Villa Stood, above Freiburg. Mary Elizabeth Coleridge. OBNC

Where all things grow according to their own design. The Meadow. John Wieners. CoPo

Where are Elmer, Herman, Bert, Tom and Charley. The Hill. Edgar Lee Masters. *Fr.* Spoon River Anthology. AmLP

Where are the braves, the faces like autumn fruit. Indian Reservation: Caughnawaga. A. M. Klein. OBCV

Where are the fields of dew? The Alphabet. James Reaney. ACV

Where are the gods? Tell me, where is Aegir? We, the Few Who Believe. Harold Vinal. FiSC

Where are the heroes of yesteryear? Where, O Where? Milton Bracker. SD

Where are the ribbons I tie my hair with? Ballade of Lost Objects. Phyllis McGinley. PoCh

Where are the shattering horns of Nineveh. Being Here. Walter Bauer. MGP

Where are we to go when this is done? Sonnet. Alfred A. Duckett. AmNP

Where are you Carl Schulte, former sharper man for H. Quandt & Son? AWOL. George Bratt. PtTo

Where Are You Going. Eliza Lee Follen. SoPo

Where Are You Going, Maiden? Lope de Vega, *tr. fr. Spanish* by W. S. Merwin. AnSP

"Where are you going, my good old man." My Good Old Man. *Unknown.* BFSS

"Where are you going, my little cat?" Where Are You Going. Eliza Lee Follen. SoPo

"Where are you going, my little dear." Dabbling in the Dew. *Unknown.* UnTE

"Where are you going, my pretty little maid?" I said. Mary Jane, the Milkmaid. *Unknown.* BFSS

"Where are you going, my pretty little miss." My Pretty Little Miss. *Unknown.* BFSS

Where are you going, winsome maid. Arrows of Love. Chauras. SiGo

Where are you going, you little pig? Little Piggy. Thomas Hood. SoPo

Where are you hid from me, belovèd one. Legend. John Hall Wheelock. MoLP

"Where art thou going, sober Quaker." The Sober Quaker. *Unknown.* BSO

Where art thou, my beloved Son. The Affliction of Margaret. Wordsworth. GTBS-P

Where Be You Going, You Devon Maid? Keats. ErPo; UnTE

Where beth they, beforen us weren. Contempt of the World. *Unknown.* MeEL

Where bright waters flood the Spring shore. Wild Geese. Shen Yo. SiGo

Where Covent-Garden's famous temple stands. The Dangers of Football. John Gay. *Fr.* Trivia; or, The Art of Walking the Streets of London. SD

"Where did I come from, Mother, and why?" Christmas Lullaby for a New-born Child. Yvonne Gregory. AmNP

Where did the voice come from? I hunted through the rooms. Bedtime Story for My Son. Peter Redgrove. NePoEA-2

Where did you come from, baby dear? Baby. George Macdonald. BiCB; TRV

Where Didst Thou Find, Young Bard. Keats. CBEP

Where Do I Come From? Gustavo Adolfo Bécquer, *tr. fr. Spanish by* Edward Gahan. AnSP

Where dost thou careless[e] lie. An Ode: To Himself[e]. Ben Jonson. EnRePo; SeCP

Where Europe and America build their arches. The Third Continent. Mary Erulkar. ACV

Where every female delights to give her maiden to her husband. Male & Female Loves in Beulah. Blake. *Fr.* Jerusalem. OBNC

Where five old graves lay circled on a hill. The Graveyard. Jane Cooper. NePoEA-2

Where Fled. John Wieners. CoPo

Where Go the Boats? Robert Louis Stevenson. GoJo; SoPo

Where God had walked. The First Autumn. Marshall Schacht. MoRP

Where had I heard this wind before. Bereft. Robert Frost. FaPL; FoBA; PoDB

"Where hae ye been huntin', Lord Ronald my son." Lord Ronald. *Unknown.* BSO

Where hast thou floated, in what seas pursued. To the Immortal Memory of the Halibut on Which I Dined This Day. William Cowper. HaSV

Where have these hands been. Musician. Louise Bogan. GoJo

"Where have you been all day, Henry, my son." Henry, My Son (B *vers.*). *Unknown.* BSO

"Where have you been, Henry, my son." Henry, My Son (C *vers.*). *Unknown.* BSO

Where have you been my blue eyed son? Hard Rain's a-Gonna Fall. Bob Dylan. PtTo

Where Have You Gone? Mari Evans. NNP

Where have you hidden away? Spiritual Canticle. St. John of the Cross. AnSP

Where hills are hard and bare. Abraham's Knife. George Garrett. PoPl

Where His Lady Keeps His Heart. "A. W." CTC

Where I Took Hold of Life. Robert P. Tristram Coffin. BiCB

Where icy and bright dungeons lift. Hart Crane. *Fr.* Voyages. CABA

Where Is Fancy Bred? Shakespeare. *See* Tell Me Where Is Fancy Bred.

Where Is Heaven? Bliss Carman. TRV

Where is the grave of Sir Arthur O'Kellyn? The Knight's Tomb. Samuel Taylor Coleridge. CBEP

Where Is the Place My Thought May Find Repose? Ausiàs March, *tr. fr. Catalan by* William M. Davis. AnML

Where is the true man's fatherland? The Fatherland. James Russell Lowell. PoPl

Where is the world we roved, Ned Bunn. To Ned. Herman Melville. HaSV

Where is this stupendous stranger. The Nativity of Our Lord and Savior Jesus Christ. Christopher Smart. *Fr.* Hymns and Spiritual Songs. EiCP

Where Lies the Land [to Which the Ship Would Go]? Arthur Hugh Clough. Songs in Absence, VII. HaSV; ILP; PoIE

Where lies the land to which yon ship must go? Wordsworth. OBNC

Where, like a pillow on a bed. The Ecstasy [or The Extasy]. John Donne. CABA; CBEP; DiPo; EnRePo; FoBA; MeP; OnP; PoIE; SeCP; StP; UnTE

Where long the shadows of the wind had rolled. The Sheaves. E. A. Robinson. AP; DiPo; FaBV; PoSa

Where Love, There's Heaven. Mary Jacobs. STF

Where More Is Meant. Christopher Morley. RePo

Where my kindred dwell, there I wander. Dawn Boy's Song. *Unknown, tr. by* Washington Matthews. FaBV

Where My Word is unspoken. T. S. Eliot. *Fr.* The Rock. TRV

Where neither king nor shepheard want comes neare. Homer. *Fr.* The Odyssey, IV. CTC

Where now are all my flattering dreams of joy. Love Elegy. Tobias George Smollett. WaPE

Where, O Where? Milton Bracker. SD

Where once the grey scrub's finches cried with thin. The Tank. Roland Robinson. PoAu-2

Where once we danced, where once we sang. An Ancient to Ancients. Thomas Hardy. GTBS-P

Where once we hunted, white men have built many long-houses. Speech of the Salish Chief. Earle Birney. *Fr.* Damnation of Vancouver. OBCV

Where one meets the other. Korea. Harland Ristau. PtTo

Where Roots Tangle. Raymond Roseliep. FiSC

Where Shall a Sorrow Great. *Unknown.* EnRePo

Where shall I hide my head and my face? Breaking. J. Alex Allan. PoAu-2

Where shall the lover rest. Sir Walter Scott. *Fr.* Marmion, III. GTBS-P

Where Shall We Dance? "Gabriela Mistral," *tr. fr. Spanish by* Alice Stone Blackwell. SiGo

Where shall we go? The Hounded Lovers. William Carlos Williams. MoLP

Where Shall Wisdom Be Found? Euripides, *tr. fr. Greek by* Gilbert Murray. *Fr.* Bacchae. SiGo

Where skies are thunderous, by a cypress walk. Some Negatives: X. at the Chateau. James Merrill. NePoEA-2

Where sunless rivers weep. Dream Land. Christina Rossetti. VP

Where the air in this room warms by the fire like a cat. Protest. Vassar Miller. ToPo

Where the Bee Sucks [There Suck I]. Shakespeare. *Fr.* The Tempest, V, i. CABA; CBEP; CTC; DiPo; EnRePo; FaBV; FoBA; ILP (Fairy's Life, A.) PoPl

Where the city's ceaseless crowd moves on the livelong day. Sparkles from the Wheel. Walt Whitman. AP; DiPo

Where the Dead Men Lie. Barcroft Boake. PoAu-1

Where the Hayfields Were. Archibald MacLeish. LOW

Where the Pelican Builds. Mary Hannay Foott. PoAu-1

Where the pools are bright and deep. A Boy's Song. James Hogg. WiR

Where the quiet-colored end of evening smiles. Love among the Ruins. Robert Browning. FaBV; VP

Where the Rainbow Ends. Robert Lowell. AP

Where the remote Bermudas ride. Bermudas [or Song of the Emigrants in Bermuda]. Andrew Marvell. CABA; CBEP; GTBS-P; HaSV; ILP; MeP; SeCP; ThLM

Where the sea gulls sleep or indeed where they fly. The Ballet of the Fifth Year. Delmore Schwartz. MP

Where the thistle lifts a purple crown. Daisy. Francis Thompson. FaBV; OBNC

Where the trees make evening. Imitation of Joy. Salvatore Quasimodo. CoIP

Where the wheel of light is turned. Pole Star. Archibald MacLeish. AP

Where to Seek Love. Blake. *Fr.* William Bond. TRV

"Where was you last night, my rambling son." My Ramboling Son. *Unknown.* BFSS

Where we walk to school each day. Indian Children. Annette Wynne. SoPo

Where we went in the boat was a long bay. The Mediterranean. Allen Tate. AP; PoCh; VaPo

Where were the greenhouses going. Big Wind. Theodore Roethke. GoJo

Where were we in that afternoon? Anniversary. Richmond Lattimore. PoCh

Where Willow Is a Limber Switch. "Will Inman." PoNC

"Where you coming from, Lomey Carter." Old Christmas. Roy Helton. SIV

Where you tread, forget-me-nots come into flower. You Quiet Attender to My Garden. Max Herrmann-Neisse. MGP

Whereas, on certain boughts and sprays. The Lawyer's Invocation to Spring. Henry Howard Brownell. PoLF

Wherefore I ask that ye faint not at my tribulations for you. Ephesians, Bible, *N.T.* BoC

Wherefore, unlaurelled boy! The Enchanted Lyre. George Darley. OBNC

Where's the Poet? Keats. DiPo (Poet, The.) PP

Where's the Queen of Sheba? Gone. Walter de la Mare. GoJo

Whereto should I express. To His Lady. Henry VIII, King of England. CTC

Wherever Beauty Has Been Quick in Clay. John Masefield. MoRP

Wherever earth is home for men. Let There Be Law. Mark Van Doren. MoRP

Wherever I Am. Dryden. *Fr.* The Conquest of Granada, Pt. I. DiPo

Wherever she is moving now, an air. Carmina. Robert Mezey. ToPo

Wherewith Shall I Come before the Lord? Micah, VI: 6-8, Bible, *O.T.* TRV

Whether Long or Sparing. Sem Tob, *tr. fr. Spanish by* William M. Davis. *Fr.* Moral Proverbs. AnML

Whether Men Do Laugh or Weep. Thomas Campion. EnRePo

Whether on Ida's shady brow. To the Muses. Blake. CBEP

Whether to sally and see thee, girl of my dreams. To Meet, or Otherwise. Thomas Hardy. OBNC

Whether two-backed beast or many-splendoured-thing. Onan. Paris Leary. CoPo

Whether we flee or pursue, we are the same. Leviathan; a Poem in Four Movements. Kenneth Pitchford. CoPo

Whether we mutter a Thank you or not. *Unknown*. ThGo

Which Are You? *Unknown*. PoLF

Which I wish to remark. Plain Language from Truthful James. Bret Harte. CTC

Which is the best to hit your taste. Epigram on Two Ladies. Sophia Burrell. ErPo

Which religion do I profess? Not one of the many. My Faith. Schiller. TwGP

"Which way are you going, my pretty little miss." My Sweet Little Honey. *Unknown*. BSO

Which way can you have traveled? Elevation. Franz Werfel. MGP

Whichever harbours poison between cotton, or goes from breathing to a common form. 29th Dance—Having an Instrument—22 March 1964. Jackson MacLow. CoPo

While Anna's peers and early playmates tread. The Stuffed Owl. Wordsworth. Par

While briers an' woodbines budding green. Epistle to John Lapraik, an Old Scottish Bard. Burns. EnPE

While Butler, needy wretch! was yet alive. On the Setting Up of Mr. Butler's Monument in Westminster Abbey. Samuel Wesley. CBEP

While Delia shines at Hurlothrumbo. The Widow and Virgin Sisters. Thomas Tickell. WaPE

While gentlefolks strut in their silver and satins. Bartleme Fair. George Alexander Stevens. ELP

While going the road to sweet Athy. Johnny, I Hardly Knew Ye. *Unknown*. ELP

While here on earth it may not be. Yes, I Have Been to Calvary. Avis B. Christiansen. STF

While His Lady Combs Her Hair. Giambattista Marino, *tr. fr. Italian by* Frank J. Warnke. RBL

"While I sit at the door." Eve. Christina Rossetti. GTBS-P

While I sleeping lay, The. An Hour before the Day. Eduard Möricke. AGP

While I Was Yet a Boy. Friedrich Hölderlin, *tr. fr. German by* Philip Allan Friedman. AGP

While I wrought out these fitful Danaan rhymes. To Some I Have Talked With by the Fire. W. B. Yeats. PoDB

While in the bower, with beauty blessed. A Song. Joseph Warton. WaPE

While in the convention they were nominating the next. Footnote to Lord Acton. Cynthia Ozick. OPP

While malice, Pope, denies thy page. When None Shall Rail. David Lewis. CBEP

While my hair was still cut straight across my forehead. The River-Merchant's Wife; a Letter. Li Po, *tr. by* Ezra Pound. BoLP; CABA; DTC; MP; PoIE; PoSa; VaPo

While nations, howling like Lucifer, fall from the hallowed height. Remember Thy Covenant. Edith Lovejoy Pierce. MoRP

While not a leaf seems faded; while the fields. September, 1815. Wordsworth. FoBA

While on Those Lovely Looks I Gaze. Earl of Rochester. CBEP

While rain, with eve in partnership. Beyond the Last Lamp. Thomas Hardy. OBNC

While snowy nightwinds, blowing bleak. Burncombe Hollow. William Barnes. OBNC

While some are being flies. 37th Dance—Banding—22 March 1964. Jackson MacLow. CoPo

While standing on the brink of woe. He Gave Himself for Me. *Unknown*. STF

While tenderly around me cast. Neaera's Kisses. Johannes Secundus. *Fr.* Basia. UnTE

While that my soul repairs to her devotion. Church Monuments. George Herbert. CABA; FoBA; MeP; PoIE

While that the sun with his beams hot. The Unfaithful Shepherdess. *Unknown*. GTBS-P

While the Days Are Going By. *Unknown*. STF

While the earth remaineth. After the Flood Went Down, God Said. Genesis, Bible, *O.T.* ThGo

While the fish of fire curves its arc. Siesta. Antonio Machado. AnSP

While the king and his ministers keep such a pother. A Wicked Treasonable Libel. Swift. UnTE

While the water-wagon's ringing showers. In the Isle of Dogs. John Davidson. OBNC

While There Is Still the Color of a Rose. Garcilaso de la Vega, *tr. fr. Spanish by* Edwin Morgan. AnSP

While this America settles in the mold of its vulgarity, heavily thickening to empire. Shine, Perishing Republic. Robinson Jeffers. AmLP; PoIE

While we sail and laugh, joke and fight, comes death. In Memoriam; Ingvald Bjorndal and His Comrade. Malcolm Lowry. OBCV

While We Watch These Flowers Fair. Charles d'Orléans, *tr. fr. French by* Muriel Kittel. AnML

While yet the Morning Star. The Unicorn. Ella Young. SoPo

While you cry Victory! or Surrender! Sunset Horn. Myron O'Higgins. PtTo

While you that in your sorrow disavow. A Christmas Sonnet. E. A. Robinson. EaLo; PoDB

Whilst Alexis Lay Prest. Dryden. *Fr.* Marriage a-la-Mode. ErPo; UnTE

Whilst on Septimius' panting breast. Acme and Septimius. Catullus. UnTE

Whilst some affect the sun and some the shade. Robert Blair. *Fr.* The Grave. EnPE

Whilst what I write I do not see. Written in Juice of Lemmon. Abraham Cowley. SeCP

Whip, The. Robert Creeley. ToPo

Whirl up, sea. Oread. Hilda Doolittle ("H. D."). AP; GoJo; RePo

Whirring Wheels. John Oxenham. TRV

Whisky, frisky. The Squirrel. *Unknown*. SoPo

Whisky Johnny (A *and* B *vers., with music*). *Unknown*. BSNS

Whiskey on your breath, The. My Papa's Waltz. Theodore Roethke. CaFP; ILP; PoIE; PoSa

Whisky Song, A. *Unknown*. STF

Whisperer, The. Mark Van Doren. UnTE

Whisperin' Bill. Irving Bacheller. PoLF

Whispers of Immortality. T. S. Eliot. CTC; FoBA; PoIE

Whispers of little winds low in the leaves. Forest Fire. Edna Davis Romig. SIV

Whist. Eugene Fitch Ware. PoLF

Whistle, and I'll Come [to You, My Lad]. Burns. UnTE; WePo
  (O, Whistle and I'll Come to You [*or* Ye, My Lad].) BoLP; ErPo

Whistle, Daughter ("Whistle, daughter, whistle"), *with music*. *Unknown*. BFSS

Whistle Daughter Whistle ("Mother I longs to get married"). *Unknown*. ErPo

Whistling Boy. John Robert Quinn. BiCB

Whistling Boy. Nixon Waterman. PoLF

White, a shingled path. Icos. Charles Tomlinson. GTBS-P

White an' Blue. William Barnes. GTBS-P

White Beauty, The. *Unknown*. MeEL

White Bird, The. Roy McFadden. ACV

White bird featherless. Riddle of Snow and Sun. *Unknown*. CBEP

White Cliffs, The, *sels*. Alice Duer Miller.
  English Are Frosty, The. PoLF
  I Have Loved England. PoLF

White clouds are in the sky. A Chinese Poem Written B.C. 1121. *Unknown*. WePo

White cock's tail, The. Ploughing on Sunday. Wallace Stevens. AmLP; GoJo; PoPl

White dawn had hardly finished, The. Maurice Scève. *Fr.* Délie. RBL

White Devil, The, *sel*. John Webster.
  Call for the Robin Redbreast [and the Wren], *fr.* V, iv. CaFP; CBEP; StP
  (Cornelia's Song.) PoIE
  (Land Dirge, A.) GTBS-P

White Eagle, The. Nan McDonald. PoAu-2

White Egret, The. Li Po, *tr. fr. Chinese by* E. D. Edwards. SiGo

White Fields. James Stephens. PoSC; SoPo

White founts falling in the Courts of the sun. Lepanto. G. K. Chesterton. FaBV

White full moon like a great beautiful whore, The. Walter Benton. *Fr.* This Is My Beloved. UnTE

White Goat, White Ram. W. S. Merwin. PoDB

White Goddess, The. Robert Graves. PoIE

White gum showing, The. Pine Gum. W. W. E. Ross. OBCV

White-haired Man, The. May Sarton. MoRP

White Horse, The. Abu Salt Umayya, *tr. fr. Arabic by* Lysander Kemp. AnML

White horse came to our house once, A. The White Stallion. Guy Owen. PoNC

White Horses. Winifred Howard. SoPo

White House, The. Claude McKay. AmNP

White in the moon the long road lies. A. E. Housman. A Shropshire Lad, XXXVI. ELP; VP

White Iris, A. Pauline B. Barrington. PoLF

White is the color worn for mourning. In Mourning. Abu-l-Hasan al-Husri. AnML

White Island, The. Robert Herrick. WiR

White Man's Burden, The. Kipling. StP

White mares of the moon rush along the sky, The. Night Clouds. Amy Lowell. PoPl; PoPo; RePo

White Moon, The. Paul Verlaine, *tr. fr. French by* Kate Flores. SiGo

White Motor, *sels*. André du Bouchet, *tr. fr. French by* Dori Katz. CoFP
  "I brake to see the vacant field, the sky above the wall."
  "I walk, reunited with fire, in the uncertain paper blending."

White Paternoster, The. *Unknown.* CBEP
　(Four Corners to My Bed, *longer vers.*) ThGo
White Queen. John Fuller. NePoEA-2
White Rose, A. John Boyle O'Reilly. PoPl
White Sand and Grey Sand. *Unknown.* CBEP
White sheep, white sheep. Clouds. *Unknown.* SoPo
White sheet on the tail-gate of a truck, A. Elegy for a Dead
　Soldier. Karl Shapiro. AP; FaPL; ThLM; ToPo
White Ship, The, *sel.* Dante Gabriel Rossetti.
　"By none but me can the tale be told." HaSV
White sky, over the hemlocks bowed with snow. The Buck in
　the Snow. Edna St. Vincent Millay. AmLP
White Stag, The. Ezra Pound. LOW
White Stallion, The. Guy Owen. PoNC
White Was I. Lope de Vega, tr. fr. *Spanish by* Kate Flores.
　AnSP
Whither hast thou hidden thyself, And hast left me, O Be-
　loved, to my sighing? Spiritual Canticle: Songs between
　the Soul and the Spouse. St. John of the Cross. RBL
Whither hast vanishèd. The Search. St. John of the Cross.
　BoC
Whither, midst falling dew. To a Waterfowl. Bryant.
　AmLP; AP; CBEP; DiPo; FaPL; LV; PoLF; PoPo;
　TRV
Whither, O splendid ship, thy white sails crowding. A Passer-
　by [*or* Passer By]. Robert Bridges. BoC; CaFP; HaSV;
　OBNC; WiR
Whither, O, whither art thou fled. The Search. George Her-
　bert. MeP
Whitsun Weddings, The. Philip Larkin. NePoEA-2
Whittier. James Russell Lowell. *Fr.* A Fable for Critics. AP
Who am I thus Thy friendship to procure? Tomorrow. Lope
　de Vega. RBL
Who are these? Why sit they here in twilight? Mental Cases.
　Wilfred Owen. MMA
Who Are You. Gottfried Benn, tr. fr. *German by* Christopher
　Middleton. MGP
"Who are you and whence do you come?" A Vagrant. Erik
　Axel Karlfeldt. PoPl
Who are you, oh misled child. The Beat Child. Chuck Stod-
　dard. LV
"Who are you, Sea Lady." Santorin. James Elroy Flecker.
　GoJo; HaSV
Who are you that can fly? Questions for a Flying Squirrel to
　Answer. Rachel Field. RePo
Who builds a church within his heart. The Church in the
　Heart. Morris Abel Beer. TRV
Who bury the dead. The Heavenly Tree Grows Downward.
　Gerrit Lansing. CoPo
Who Calls the English Cold? Carl Bode. *Fr.* London Sonnets.
　ToPo
Who can find a virtuous woman? A Virtuous Woman. Prov-
　erbs, Bible, *O.T.* TRV
Who can give answer to your questioning. Interrogative.
　Sister M. Thérèse. MoRP
Who can live in heart so glad. The Country Lad [*or* Pastoral].
　Nicholas Breton. *Fr.* The Passionate Shepherd. CBEP;
　ELP
Who can tell his years, for the winds have stretched? A La-
　bourer. R. S. Thomas. ToPo
Who can tell of such adventure above the bounding main.
　Count Arnaldos. *Unknown.* AnML
Who comes to-night? We ope the doors in vain. Henry James.
　Robert Louis Stevenson. OBNC
Who could believe an ant in theory? Credibility. John Ciardi.
　ToPo
"Who," cried the elders on the Trojan wall. Pierre de Ron-
　sard. *Fr.* Sonnets pour Hélène. RBL
Who died on the wires, and hung there, one of two. The
　Silent One. Ivor Gurney. MMA
Who does God's work will get God's pay. God's Pay. *Un-
　known.* STF
Who ere shee bee. *See* Whoe'er she be.
Who Ever. Stefan George, tr. fr. *German by* Walter Kauf-
　mann. TwGP
Who ever had/ Such a whale of a plan. The Wall of China.
　Padraic Colum. RoGo
Who findeth comfort in the stars and flowers. L'Envoi.
　Thomas Lovell Beddoes. *Fr.* Death's Jest Book. OBNC
Who forced the Muse to this alliance? On Professor Drennan's
　Verse. Roy Campbell. GTBS-P
Who gallops so late through wind and wild? The Elf-King.
　Goethe. PoPo
Who gave thee, O Beauty. Ode to Beauty. Emerson. AP
Who goes there, in the night. Apparitions. Thomas Curtis
　Clark. TRV
Who Goes with Fergus? W. B. Yeats. GoJo; PoIE
Who has a friend she will come one day. White Queen. John
　Fuller. NePoEA-2
Who has not found the heaven below. God's Residence. Emily
　Dickinson. TRV
Who has robbed the ocean wave. Song. John Shaw. AmLP
Who Has Seen the Wind? Christina Rossetti. *Fr.* Sing-Song.
　GoJo; PoPl

Who hath desired the sea?—the sight of salt water unbounded.
　The Sea and the Hills. Kipling. FaBV
Who Hath Heard of Such Cruelty Before. Sir Thomas Wyatt.
　CBEP
Who Hath His Fancy Pleased. Sir Philip Sidney. EnRePo
Who Is at My Bedroom Window? *with music. Unknown.*
　BSNS
　(Drowsy Sleeper, The, A, B, *and* C *vers., with music.*)
　BSO
Who is it runs through the many-storied mansion of myth.
　Dwarf of Disintegration. Oscar Williams. PoCh
Who Is It That This Dark Night. Sir Philip Sidney. *Fr.*
　Astrophel and Stella. EnRePo
Who is she that comes, makyng turn every man's eye. Sonetto
　VII. Guido Cavalcanti. CTC
Who Is Silvia? Shakespeare. *Fr.* The Two Gentlemen of
　Verona, IV, ii. BoLP; DiPo; EnRePo; FoBA; ILP;
　PoIE
　(To Silvia.) PoPo
Who is so proud. The Performing Seal. Rachel Field. *Fr.* A
　Circus Garland. SoPo
Who Is Tapping at My Window. A. G. Deming. SoPo
Who is that pretty fellow. Work and Play. Martial. UnTE
"Who knocks?" "I, who was beautiful." The Ghost. Walter
　de la Mare. ELP
Who Knows If the Moon's. E. E. Cummings. LOW
Who knows it not, who loves it not. A Racing Eight. James
　L. Cuthbertson. PoAu-1
Who knows the name and country now. Mangers. W. H.
　Davies. MoRP
Who knows, when raindrops are descending. Rain. Einar
　Benediktsson. SiGo
Who knows whether the sea heals or corrodes? Plague of Dead
　Sharks. Alan Dugan. AP
Who lived at the top end of our street. The Retired Colonel.
　Ted Hughes. NePoEA-2
Who loves not Knowledge? Who shall rail. In Memoriam
　A. H. H., CXIV. Tennyson. VP
Who, minter of medallions. Reading a Medal. Terence Tiller.
　GTBS-P
Who Misses or Who Wins. Thackeray. SD
Who never ate his bread in tears. Song of the Harp-Player.
　Goethe, *tr. by* Herman Salinger. *Fr.* Wilhelm Meister.
　AGP
Who never ate with tears his bread. The Harp Player's Song.
　Goethe, *tr. by* Walter Kaufmann. *Fr.* Wilhelm Meister.
　TwGP
Who often found their way to pleasant meadows. Elegy for
　Minor Poets. Louis MacNeice. PP
Who Owns What? André Frénaud, *tr. fr. French by* Paulène
　Aspel. CoFP
Who Placed, amidst the Tracts of Ash? Antonio Machado, *tr.
　fr. Spanish by* Kate Flores. AnSP
Who Prayed? *Unknown.* STF
Who prop, thou ask'st, in these bad days, my mind? To a
　Friend. Matthew Arnold. VP
Who put that crease in your soul. Chapel Deacon. R. S.
　Thomas. ACV; ToPo
Who puts back into place a fallen bar. The Father's Business.
　Edwin Markham. TRV
Who questions if the punctual sun unbars. William Bayle-
　bridge. *Fr.* Love Redeemed. PoAu-1
Who raps at my window? Halloween. Marnie Pomeroy.
　PoSC
Who Risks It Where a Poet Lives. René Guy Cadou, *tr. fr.
　French by* William Stafford. CoFP
Who said, "Peacock Pie"? The Song of the Mad Prince.
　Walter de la Mare. GoJo
Who say[e]s that fictions on[e]ly and false hair. Jordan.
　George Herbert. CABA; PP; SeCP; VaPo
Who says that it's by my desire. People Hide Their Love.
　Wu Ti, Emperor of Liang. SiGo
Who seeks for heaven alone to save his soul. The Way.
　Henry van Dyke. TRV
Who seeks the way to win renown. A Ballad in Praise of Sea-
　faring Men. *Unknown.* HaSV
Who shall discern the marvels of the sea. The Wonders of the
　Deep. Jean Parmentier. RBL
Who shall doubt, Donne, where I a poet bee. To John Donne.
　Ben Jonson. SeCP
Who Shall Have My Fair Lady? *Unknown.* CBEP
　(My Fair Lady.) UnTE
Who shall know the way. Flight. Harold Vinal. FiSC
Who shall separate us from the love of Christ? Romans, Bible,
　N.T. BoC
Who Slays the Lion? Who Slays the Giant? Walter von der
　Vogelweide, *tr. fr. German by* Gillian Barker *and* Kenneth
　Gee. AnML
Who smoke-snorts toasts o' My Lady Nicotine. Variations of an
　Air: After Robert Browning. G. K. Chesterton. Par
Who So List to Hunt. Sir Thomas Wyatt. *See* Whoso List to
　Hunt.
Who strolls so late, for mugs a bait. French Lisette; a Ballad
　of Maida Vale. William Plomer. ErPo

"Who stuffed that white owl?" No one spoke in the shop. The Owl-Critic. J. T. Fields. EvOK

Who tames the lion now? Lord Alcohol. Thomas Lovell Beddoes. WiR

Who thinks love is a prize to put away. For Eros II. Audrey Wurdemann. MoLP

Who Thou art I know not. God the Architect. Harry Kemp. TRV

Who Translates a Poet Badly. Manual González Prada, tr. fr. Spanish by William M. Davis. AnSP

Who Wants a Birthday? David McCord. BiCB

Who Was It. Heine, tr. fr. German by Richard Garnett. SiGo

Who weeps now anywhere in the world? Solemn Hour. Rainer Maria Rilke. PoPl

Who, who are these whose fawning hearts, debased. Jean de Sponde. Fr. Sonnets de la Mort. RBL

Who will believe my verse in time to come. Sonnets, XVII. Shakespeare. DiPo

Who will go drive with Fergus now. Who Goes with Fergus? W. B. Yeats. GoJo; PoIE

Who will in fairest book of Nature know. Astrophel and Stella, LXXI. Sir Philip Sidney. CABA

Who Will Shoe Your Feet? with music. Unknown. BFSS

Who would be loved, let him possess. Perfect Love. Sana'i. SiGo

Who Would List. Unknown, tr. fr. French by Andrew Lang. Fr. Aucassin and Nicolette. CTC

Who would not be/ The Laureate bold. The Laureate. William Aytoun. Par

Who would true valour [or valor] see. The Pilgrim Song [or The Pilgrim or Pilgrim's Song]. Bunyan. Fr. The Pilgrim's Progress. CBEP; ELP; EvOK; WiR

Whoe'er she be [or Who ere shee bee]. Wishes to His [or for the] Supposed Mistress[e]. Richard Crashaw. GTBS-P; SeCP

Whoever comes to shroud me, do not harm[e]. The Funeral[l]. John Donne. CABA; CBEP; DiPo; EnRePo; MeP; SeCP

Whoever guesses, thinks, or dreams he knows. The Curse. John Donne. CBEP

Whoever were to stand in the heavens, and lower then his sight. Jean de Sponde. Fr. Sonnets d'Amour. RBL

Whoever You Are Holding Me Now in Hand. Walt Whitman. PoSa

Whoever you are! motion and reflection are especially for you. The Divine Ship Sails the Divine Sea for You. Walt Whitman. MoRP

Whole day long, under the walking sun, The. The Sleeping Giant. Donald Hall. CaFP; MP

Whole Duty of Children, The. Robert Louis Stevenson. EvOK; ThGo

Whole gulfs of red and fleets of red. Emily Dickinson. AmLP

Whole towns shut down. The Late Snow & Lumber Strike of the Summer of Fifty-four. Gary Snyder. PtTo

Whole western sky is lemon yellow, The. Tenebrae. Juan Ramón Jiménez. AnSP

Whole Year Christmas, The. Angela Morgan. TRV

Whom first we love, you know, we seldom wed. Changes. "Owen Meredith." PoLF

Whom the Gods Love. Margaret E. Bruner. PoLF

Whon men beth muriest at her mele. All Turns into Yesterday. Unknown. MeEL

Whoopee High Ogie, with music. Unknown. BFSS

Whooping Crane, The. Vassar Miller. ToPo

Who's that knocking on the window? Innocent's Song. Charles Causley. DaDu; GTBS-P

"Who's that tickling my back?" said the wall. The Tickle Rhyme. Ian Serraillier. SoPo

Who's there? Frances Frost. RePo

Who's There, My Heart?—It is We, Your Eyes. Charles d'Orléans, tr. fr. French by Muriel Kittel. AnML

"Who's this come tapping at my chamber." Maggie and Willie. Unknown. BSO

Who's This That Comes, as Each Man Looks at Her. Guido Cavalcanti. See Sonetto VII: "Who is she that comes, makyng turn every man's eye."

Who's Who. W. H. Auden. CABA; PoPo

Whose little beast? Donkey. Mark Van Doren. EaLo

Whose woods these are I think I know. Stopping by Woods on a Snowy Evening. Robert Frost. AmLP; AP; CABA; CaFP; DiPo; FaBV; FoBA; GoJo; ILP; MP; PoPo; PoSa; PoSC; RePo

Whoso delighteth to proven and assay. Thomas More to Them That Seek Fortune. Sir Thomas More. EnRePo

Whoso Draws Nigh to God. Unknown. TRV

Whoso hath felt the Spirit of the Highest. Frederic W. H. Myers. Fr. Saint Paul. TRV

Whoso in love would bear the bell. Ballade [or Ballad] of Ladies' Love. Villon. ErPo; UnTE

Whoso List to Hunt. Sir Thomas Wyatt, after the Italian of Petrarch. CBEP; EnRePo
     (Who So List to Hunt [or Hount].) CABA; PoIE
     ("Whoso list to hunt, I know where is an hind.") RBL

Whoso, Lord God, Being Bold to Say. Walther von der Vogelweide, tr. fr. German by Margaret F. Richey. AnML

Whoso ne knoweth the strength, power, and might. Venus and Cupide. Sir Thomas More. Fr. The Pageants of Thomas More. EnRePo

"Who've ye got there?"—"Only a dying brother." The Brigade Must Not Know, Sir. Unknown. ThLM

Why, all the Saints and Sages who discuss'd. Omar Khayyám, tr. by Edward Fitzgerald. Fr. The Rubáiyát. TRV

Why are we[e] by all creatures waited on? Holy Sonnets, XII. John Donne. CABA; MeP

"Why are you sad, my darling daughter?" The Ripe Fruit. Unknown. UnTE

Why Art Thou Silent! Wordsworth. CBEP
     (To a Distant Friend.) GTBS-P

Why art thou silent & invisible. To Nobodaddy. Blake. DiPo

Why blush, dear girl, pray tell me why? On Seeing a Lady's Garter. Unknown. ErPo

Why, Caelia, is your spreading waist. Fable: The Poet and His Patron. Edward Moore. WaPE

Why came I so untimely forth. To a Very Young Lady [or To a Girl or To the Younger Lady Lucy Sydney]. Edmund Waller. CBEP; SeCP; WiR

Why cannot the one good. The War God. Stephen Spender. MoRP

Why, Chloe, thus squander your prime. A Logical Song. Unknown. ErPo

Why, Damon, with the forward day. The Dying Man in His Garden. George Sewell. GTBS-P

Why did He choose a garden fair. Thy Will Be Done. Albert Simpson Reitz. STF

Why Did I Choose That Man. C. A. Trypanis. AnMoPo

Why Did I Laugh [To-Night]? Keats. CBEP; DiPo

Why Did Stingy Thomas? Manuel González Prada, tr. fr. Spanish by William M. Davis. AnSP

Why did you give no hint that night. The Going. Thomas Hardy. ELP; FaPL; StP

Why did you grant us the searching glance. To Charlotte von Stein. Goethe. TwGP

Why didst thou promise such a beauteous day. Sonnets, XXXIV. Shakespeare. CBEP

Why do I curse the jazz of this hotel? The Jazz of This Hotel. Vachel Lindsay. PoPl

Why do I languish thus, drooping and dull. Dulnesse. George Herbert. MeP

Why do I sing in the morning. Secret of Song. Christine White. STF

Why Do the Bells of Christmas Ring. Eugene Field. SoPo

Why Do We Let Them Oppress Us? Unknown, tr. fr. French by Daisy Aldan. AnML

Why do ye weep, sweet babes? To Primroses. Robert Herrick. PoPl

Why do you cry out, why do I like to hear you. Sound of Breaking. Conrad Aiken. PoDB

"Why do you look so pale, my son William?" The Image. Sylvia Townsend Warner. SIV

Why do you say to me: poet? Desolation of the Poor Sentimental Poet. Sergio Corazzini. CoIP

Why Do You Visit Me, White Moths, So Often? Georg Heym, tr. fr. German by Christopher Middleton. MGP

"Why do you wear your hair like a man/ Sister Helen?" After Dilettante Concetti. H. D. Traill. Par

Why does he call. Testimony. Beverly Connelly. FiSC

Why does my husband beat me? Poor Me. Unknown. ErPo

Why does the raven cry aloud and no eye pities her? The Lamentation of Enion. Blake. Fr. Vala; or, The Four Zoas. OBNC

Why does the sea moan evermore? By the Sea. Christina Rossetti. HaSV

Why does the thin grey strand. Sorrow. D. H. Lawrence. GTBS-P

"Why does [or dois] your brand [or sword] sae drap [or so drop] wi[th] bluid [or blude or blood]. Edward [or Edward, Edward]. Unknown. BuBa; CABA; CaFP; CBEP; ELP; ILP; OnP; PoIE; PoPo; PoSa; SIV; StP

Why don't we rock the casket here in the moonlight? The Pale Blue Casket. Oliver Pitcher. NNP

Why each is striving, from of old. Destiny. Matthew Arnold. VP

Why, everyone speaks Welsh; the stipple sheen. Variation on a Theme by Dylan Thomas. Carl Bode. ToPo

Why flyest thou away with fear? Ballade: To a Fish of the Brooke. John Wolcot. CBEP

Why, Grubbinol, dost thou so wistful seem? Friday; or, The Dirge. John Gay. Fr. The Shepherd's Week. EiCP

Why hast thou nothing in thy face? Epow (Eros). Robert Bridges. ILP; PoIE

Why have they stripped the grass from the sides of the road. The Interpreters. D. J. Enright. PP

Why have ye no reuthe on my child? Mary Suffers with Her Son. Unknown. MeEL

Why have you come to the shining cliffs. The Knight without a Name. Unknown. WiR

Why, having won her, do I woo? The Married Lover. Coventry Patmore. Fr. The Angel in the House. FaPL

Why, if the span of existence may be completed. Elegy IX. Rainer Maria Rilke. Fr. The Duino Elegies. TwGP

Why is a pump like V-sc-nt C-stl-r-gh? What's My Thought Like? Thomas Moore. CBEP
Why is good taste so rarely encountered together with genius? The Difficult Combination. Schiller. TwGP
Why is it that the poets tell. Smells. Christopher Morley. LV
Why is it, when I am in Rome. On Being a Woman. Dorothy Parker. PoLF
Why is my verse so barren of new pride. Sonnets, LXXVI. Shakespeare. PP
Why is the World beloved, that fals is and vein. Despise the World. Unknown. MeEL
Why listen, even the water is sobbing for something. The Maid's Thought. Robinson Jeffers. BoLP; ErPo
Why lovest thou so this brittle worlde's joy? The Peace of a Good Mind. Sir Thomas More. Fr. The Twelve Weapons of Spiritual Battle. EnRePo
Why Nobody Pets the Lion at the Zoo. John Ciardi. RePo
Why Should a Foolish Marriage Vow? Dryden. Fr. Marriage-a-la-Mode. CBEP
(Song: "Why should a foolish marriage vow.") ILP
Why should I blame her that she filled my days. No Second Troy. W. B. Yeats. GTBS-P; PoIE; PoSa
Why Should I Care for the Men of Thames? Blake. CBEP
Why should I find Him here. Christ in the Clay-Pit. Jack Clemo. GTBS-P
Why should I have returned? Noah's Raven. W. S. Merwin. AmPC
Why should it come so seldom, why so late. Michelangelo, tr. fr. Italian by Joseph Tusiani. RBL
Why Should Men Love the Church? T. S. Eliot. Fr. The Rock. MoRP
Why should my sleepy heart be taught. The Falcon. Elinor Wylie. LOW
Why Should This a Desert Be. Shakespeare. Fr. As You Like It, III, ii. CTC
Why should we praise them, or revere. Against Seasons. Robert Mezey. AmPC
Why Should You Swear? Richard Lovelace. See Scrutinie, The.
Why should you wake, my darling, at this hour. A Fairy Tale. Kenneth Mackenzie. PoAu-2
Why So Pale and Wan? Sir John Suckling. Fr. Aglaura. BoLP; CaFP; CBEP; DiPo; ELP; EvOK; FaBV (Encouragements to a Lover.) GTBS-P
(Song: "Why so pale and wan, fond lover?") CABA; PoIE; PoPl; SeCP
Why stays my fair?—See the thick shades descend. Menalcas and Enosia. Philip Wharton. WaPE
Why the hell do you use all that black. The Nocturne. Carl Bode. ToPo
Why the prophet is dancing the sculptor knew. The Isaiah of Souillac. W. S. Merwin. PoDB
Why then? Why there? Elegy for J. F. K. W. H. Auden. OPP
Why this delay? Why waste the time in kissing? A Plea for Haste. Petronius. UnTE
"Why weep ye by the tide, ladie?" Jock o' [or of] Hazeldean. Sir Walter Scott. GTBS-P; ILP; PoPo; StP
"Why weep ye by the tide, ladye." Jock o' Hazeldean. Unknown. BFSS
Why, whenever she can spy me. Time to Choose a Lover. Horace. Odes, I, 23. UnTE
Why! who makes much of a miracle? Miracles. Walt Whitman. MoRP; RePo
Why will they never speak. After a Line by John Peale Bishop. Donald Justice. PoCh
"Why, William, on that old grey stone." Expostulation and Reply. Wordsworth. CBEP
Wicked Polly, with music. Unknown. BFSS; BSO
Wicked Treasonable Libel, A. Swift. UnTE
Wicker Basket, A. Robert Creeley. AmPC; ToPo
Wide Open Are Thy Loving Hands. Bernard of Clairvaux, tr. fr. Latin by C. P. Krauth. TRV
Wide was his parish, with houses far asunder. Ten of Chaucer's People: A Parson. Chaucer. Fr. The Canterbury Tales. PoSa
Widest prairies have electric fences, The. Wires. Philip Larkin. ToPo
Widow and Virgin Sisters, The. Thomas Tickell. WaPE
Widow Bird [Sate Mourning for Her Love], A. Shelley. Fr. Charles the First. CBEP; ELP; WePo
(Song, A: "Widow bird sate mourning for her love, A.") OBNC
("Widow bird sate mourning for her love, A.") GTBS-P
Widow Wearing White or Saffron, The. Pere March, tr. fr. Catalan by William M. Davis. AnML
Widow's Lament in Springtime, The. William Carlos Williams. AP; MoLP; PoIE
Widow's Weeds, A. Walter de la Mare. FaBV
Wife, The. Robert Creeley. AmPC; AP; ToPo
Wife, The. Denise Levertov. ErPo
Wife a-Lost, The. William Barnes. ELP
Wife of Bath, The. Chaucer, mod. vers. by Nevill Coghill. Fr. The Canterbury Tales. WePo

Wife of Usher's Well, The. Unknown. BSO, with music; BuBa; CBEP; DiPo; ILP; OnMSP; PoIE; StP
Wife to a Husband, A. Elizabeth Barrett Browning. See Sonnets from the Portuguese: "How do I love thee?"
Wild Beasts. Evaleen Stein. SoPo
Wild bird, whose warble, liquid sweet. In Memoriam A. H. H., LXXXVIII. Tennyson. VP
Wild boars and all. The Autumn Storm. Basho. RePo
Wild Colonial Boy, The. Unknown. BSNS; PoAu-1
Wild duck, stringing through the sky, The. The Madman's Song. John Masefield. Fr. Good Friday. ACV; BoC
Wild Flower's Song, The. Blake. CBEP
Wild Garden. James Larkin Pearson. PoNC
Wild Geese. Elinor Chipp. RePo
Wild Geese. Shen Yo, tr. fr. Chinese by Arthur Waley. SiGo
Wild Goose, The, with music. Unknown. BSNS
Wild heart turned white in the wood, The. The Heart. Georg Trakl. MGP
Wild Honeysuckle [or Honey Suckle], The. Philip Freneau. AmLP; AP; CBEP; PoLF
Wild Horses. Carl Sandburg. RePo
Wild man that last night I dreamed, The. The Man of My Dreams. George Cuomo. OPP
Wild nights—Wild nights! Emily Dickinson. AP; FaPL; PoIE; UnTE
Wild Oats. W. H. Davies. ACV
Wild pleasure for Saint John, A. Saint John. Elizabeth J. Coatsworth. MoRP
Wild roses have reclaimed the field. Where I Took Hold of Life. Robert P. Tristram Coffin. BiCB
Wild Swans at Coole, The. W. B. Yeats. ACV; DiPo; ILP; PoIE; PoPo; StP; WePo
Wild Thyme, The. Blake. Fr. Milton. WiR
Wild Wilbur. James Kirkup. DaDu
Wild, wild the storm, and the sea high running. Patrolling Barnegat. Walt Whitman. CBEP
Wild winds weep, The. Mad Song. Blake. CBEP; ILP
Wilderness. Carl Sandburg. AP
Wilderness Road. Martha Keller. FiSC
Wilderness Theme. Ian Mudie. PoAu-2
Wildtrack, sel. John Wain. ToPo
Sestina for Khasan Israelov. ToPo
Wilhelm Meister, sels. Goethe, tr. fr. German.
Harp Player's Song, The, fr. Wilhelm Meister's Apprenticeship, Bk. II, ch. 13, tr. by Walter Kaufmann. ToPo
(Song of the Harp-Player, tr. by Herman Salinger.) AGP
Mignon, fr. Wilhelm Meister's Apprenticeship, Bk. III, ch. 1. PoPl, tr. by Edgar A. Bowring; SiGo, tr. by James Elroy Flecker
Wilhelmina Mergenthaler. Harry P. Taber. BBGG
Will came back from school that day. Dunkirk. Robert Nathan. SIV
Will God's Patience Hold Out for You? Edythe Johnson. STF
Will not the Local Party Secretary? On Reading a Soviet Novel. Roy Fuller. ToPo
Will sprawl, now that the heat of day is best. Caliban upon Setebos; or, Natural Theology in the Island. Robert Browning. VP
Will there never come a season. To R. K. J. K. Stephen. Par
Will there really be a morning. Morning. Emily Dickinson. SoPo
Will they ever come to me, ever again. Where Shall Wisdom Be Found? Euripides. Fr. Bacchae. SiGo
Will they never fade or pass! The Farmer Remembers the Somme. Vance Palmer. PoAu-1
Will to Win. F. R. Scott. OBCV
"Will ye gang to the Hielands, Leezie Lindsay." Leezie Lindsay. Unknown. BFSS
"Will ye gang to the Highlands, my jewel, wi' me?" The Blaeberry Courtship (A vers.). Unknown. BSNS
Will You Come? Edward Thomas. GoJo
Will you lend your eyes to Christ. Operation—Souls. Unknown. STF
Will you never be quiet, you mournfullest voice in Nature. Peewits on the Hills. Alice V. Stuart. ACV
Will You Turn a Deaf Ear. W. H. Auden. AnMoPo
"Will you walk a little faster?" said a whiting to a snail. The Lobster Quadrille. "Lewis Carroll." Fr. Alice's Adventures in Wonderland. Par
"Will you walk into my parlor?" said the Spider to the Fly. The Spider and the Fly. Mary Howitt. Par
William and Margaret. Unknown. BSNS
William and Nancy. Unknown. BSNS
(Banks of the Nile, The, B vers.) BSNS
William Blake. James Thomson. CBEP
William Bond, sel. Blake.
Where to Seek Love. TRV
William Dewey, Tranter Reuben, Farmer Ledlow late at plough. Friends Beyond. Thomas Hardy. GTBS-P
William Gifford. Walter Savage Landor. GTBS-P
William H. Herndon. Edgar Lee Masters. Fr. Spoon River Anthology. LiPo

William Hall, *with music. Unknown.* BFSS
William Lisle Bowles. Byron. *Fr.* English Bards and Scotch Reviewers. OBNC
William of Orange; or, The Battle of Boyne (A *vers., with music*). *Unknown.* BFSS
(King William and King James, B *vers., with music.*) BFSS
William Shakespeare to Mrs. Anne, Regular Servant to the Rev. Mr. Precentor of York. Thomas Gray. ILP
Willie. "Max Adeler." BBGG
(In Memoriam.) DTC
Willie and Johnny, *with music. Unknown.* BFSS
Willie MacIntosh. *Unknown.* BFSS; CBEP
(Willie Mackintosh.) BuBa
Willie Taylor (A *and* B *vers.*). *Unknown.* BSNS
(False Lover, The, *with music.*) BFSS
Willie, with a thirst for gore. Careless Willie. *Unknown.* BBGG
Willing Mistress, The. Aphra Behn. *See* Amyntas Led Me to a Grove.
Willing Suspension, A. John Holmes. PoCh
Willow, The. Sir William Davenant. *See* Under the Willow Shades.
Willow shining, The. The Knowledge of Light. Henry Rago. PoCh
Willows carried a slow sound, The. Repose of Rivers. Hart Crane. AP; PoIE
Willowwood. Dante Gabriel Rossetti. The House of Life, XLIX-LII. VP
Willy Drowned in Yarrow. *Unknown.* GTBS-P
Wilt Thou forgive that sin [*or* sinne] where I begun [*or* begunne]. A Hymn[e] to God the Father [*or* To Christ]. John Donne. BoC; CaFP; DiPo; EaLo; EnRePo; FoBA; MeP; PoIE; PoPo; SeCP
Wilt thou go with me, sweet maid. An Invite to Eternity. John Clare. OBNC
Wilt Thou Lend Me Thy Mare? *Unknown.* CBEP
Wilt thou love God, as he thee! then digest. Holy Sonnets, XV. John Donne. MeP
Wiltshire Downs. Andrew Young. GTBS-P
Wind, The. Padraic Colum. *See* I Saw the Wind Today.
Wind, The. Robert Creeley. AmPC
Wind. Aileen Fisher. RePo
Wind, The. Henri Michaux, *tr. fr. French by* Dori Katz. CoFP
Wind, The. Robert Louis Stevenson. SoPo
Wind, The,/ in the waterless grounds of summer. Surrender. André du Bouchet. CoFP
Wind and Lyre. Edwin Markham. TRV
Wind and the Moon, The. George Macdonald. GoJo; OnMSP
Wind and the Rain, The. Shakespeare. *See* When That I Was.
Wind and waters ring the bells. Veneta. Mary Elizabeth Coleridge. CBEP
Wind at Penistone, The. Donald Davie. NePoEA-2
Wind at the Door, The. William Barnes. CBEP; ELP; GTBS-P
Wind at Tindari. Salvatore Quasimodo, *tr. fr. Italian by* Allen Mandelbaum. CoIP
Wind at Your Door, The. Robert D. Fitzgerald. PoAu-2
Wind begun to knead the grass, The. Emily Dickinson. FoBA
Wind billowing out the seat of my britches, The. Child on Top of a Greenhouse. Theodore Roethke. LOW; PoPl; StP; WePo
Wind blew all my wedding-day, The. Wedding-Wind. Philip Larkin. ToPo
Wind came in for several thousand miles all night, The. On an East Wind from the Wars. Alan Dugan. AP
Wind came up out of the sea, A. Daybreak. Longfellow. PoLF
Wind-Clouds and Star-Drifts, *sel.* Oliver Wendell Holmes. Manhood. AP
Wind doth blow to-day my love, The. The Unquiet Grave. *Unknown.* CBEP; DTC; ELP; PoIE; WePo
Wind flapped loose, the wind was still, The. The Woodspurge. Dante Gabriel Rossetti. CaFP; CBEP; ELP; GTBS-P; OBNC; PoIE
Wind from the north: the young spring day. The Song of the Four Winds. Thomas Love Peacock. *Fr.* The Misfortunes of Elphin. WiR
Wind from the south, hook in the mouth. How They Bite. *Unknown.* SD
Wind, Gentle Evergreen. *Unknown.* CBEP
"Wind has a tongue tonight, The," he said. The Chestnut Roasters. Joseph Payne Brennan. FiSC
Wind has lots of noises, The. Wind. Aileen Fisher. RePo
Wind has scattered my city to the sheep, The. Ruins of the City of Hay. Randolph Stow. PoAu-2
Wind hits and returns. The, it is easy to personify. Sophia Nichols. Robin Blaser. CoPo
Wind in the Grass. Mark Van Doren. FaBV
Wind in the Pine. Lew Sarett. TRV
Wind in the Willows, The, *sels.* Kenneth Grahame.

Duck's [*or* Ducks'] Ditty. GoJo; SoPo
World Has Held Great Heroes, The. RePo
(Song of Mr. Toad, The.) GoJo
Wind Is a Cat. Ethel Romig Fuller. SoPo
Wind is blowing, A. The book being written. The Novel. Denise Levertov. AP
Wind is east, but the hot weather continues, The. American Letter: For Gerald Murphy. Archibald MacLeish. ILP
Wind is piercing chill, The. Battlefield. Richard Aldington. MMA
Wind is ruffling the tawny pelt, A. A Far Cry from Africa. Derek Walcott. ToPo
Wind meets me at Penistone, The. The Wind at Penistone. Donald Davie. NePoEA-2
Wind mutters thinly on the sagging wire. Prairie Graveyard. Anne Marriott. OBCV
Wind o' the East dark with rain. The Efficient Wife's Complaint. Confucius. *Fr.* The Classic Anthology: Airs of Pei. CTC
Wind of Time, The. Joseph Payne Brennan. FiSC
Wind on the Lyre. George Meredith. CaFP
Wind rocks the car. Like This Together. Adrienne Rich. CoPo
Wind Shrieked Loud, The. Elizabeth J. Coatsworth. FiSC
Wind-Song. *Tr. fr. Pima Indian Song by* Natalie Curtis. RePo
Wind sways the pines, A. Dirge in Woods. George Meredith. OBNC; VP; WiR
Wind took up the northern things, The. Emily Dickinson. AmLP
Wind tries to part the waves from the sea, The. The Wind. Henri Michaux. CoFP
Wind was a torrent of darkness among the gusty trees, The. The Highwayman. Alfred Noyes. BoLP; FaBV; PoLF; PoPo; SIV
Windhover, The. Gerard Manley Hopkins. AnMoPo; BoC; CABA; CaFP; DiPo; EaLo; FoBA; GTBS-P; ILP; OBNC; OnP; PoDB; PoIE; PoPl; StP; VaPo; VP
Windless northern surge, the sea-gull's scream, The. The Incarnate One. Edwin Muir. PoDB; PoIE
Window, The. Iain Crichton Smith. NePoEA-2
Window in the Breast, A. *Unknown, tr. fr. Greek by* Walter Headlam. SiGo
Window is wide and lo! beyond its bars, The. Interlude: The Casement. Christopher Brennan. PoAu-1
Window-screen sifts the blue cumulus, The. Garden Puzzle. Gray Burr. CoPo
Windows, The. George Herbert. CABA; ILP; MeP; SeCP
(Church Windows, The.) CBEP
Windows of Waltham, The. John Wieners. CoPo
Winds, The. Thomas Tusser. WiR
Winds are bleak, stars are bright. The Victoria Markets Recollected in Tranquillity. Frank Wilmot. PoAu-2
Winds groaned in the air, darkest cloud, The. Jean de Sponde. *Fr.* Sonnets d'Amour. RBL
Wind's in the heart of me, A, a fire's in my heels. A Wanderer's Song. John Masefield. RePo
Winds of Fate, The. Ella Wheeler Wilcox. TRV
"Wind's on the wold, The." Inscription for an Old Bed. William Morris. WiR
Wind's Song, The. Eduard Mörike, *tr. fr. German by* William R. Hughes. SiGo
Winds thru the olive trees. Long, Long Ago. *Unknown.* PoSC
Winds, whisper gently whilst she sleeps. Laura Sleeping. Charles Cotton. ELP
Wind's word, the Hebrew Hallelujah, A. Hallelujah; a Sestina. Robert Francis. PoCh
Windy Bishop, The. Wilfred Watson. OBCV
Windy Nights. Robert Louis Stevenson. GoJo; LV
Wine and Love and Lyre. *Unknown, tr. fr. Latin by* John Addington Symonds. UnTE
Wine and Ocher. Mario Luzi, *tr. fr. Italian by* Carlo L. Golino. CoIP
Wine Menagerie, The. Hart Crane. AP
Wine of Day, The. André du Bouchet, *tr. fr. French by* Warren Carrier. CoFP
Wine of the new vintage they brought us. The New Vintage. Douglas Le Pan. OBCV
Winged enchantment bore you through the dark. February, 1924. Rainer Maria Rilke. TwGP
Winged Hours. Dante Gabriel Rossetti. The House of Life, XXV. VP
Wings. Victor Hugo, *tr. fr. French.* TRV
Wings and Wheels. Nancy Byrd Turner. SoPo
Wings of Time are black and white, The. Compensation. Emerson. AP
Winter. Attilio Bertolucci, *tr. fr. Italian by* Carlo L. Golino. CoIP
Winter. Burns. EiCP
Winter. James Hurnard. PoSC
Winter. Jean Jaszi. SoPo
Winter. Joso, *tr. fr. Japanese by* Harold G. Henderson. SiGo

Winter. Charles Mair. OBCV; PoSC, *abr.*
Winter. Coventry Patmore. The Unknown Eros, I, iii. OBNC
Winter. Dante Gabriel Rossetti. CBEP
Winter. Shakespeare. *See* When Icicles Hang by the Wall.
Winter. Robert Louis Stevenson. ACV; WePo
Winter. James Thomson. *Fr.* The Seasons. CABL
Winter. Sheila Wingfield. BoLP
Winter again and it is snowing. W. D. Snodgrass. *Fr.* Heart's Needle. AP
Winter Branches. Margaret Widdemer. RePo
Winter comes, The; I walk alone. The Winter's Spring. John Clare. PoIE
Winter days and spring and summer still the yearly round renew. Flute Song. *Unknown.* SiGo
Winter deepening, the hay all in, The. Sonnet. Richard Wilbur. PoPl
Winter Evening. Archibald Lampman. OBCV
Winter evening settles down, The. Preludes, I. T. S. Eliot. DaDu; DiPo; MP; PoPl; PoPo; WePo
Winter, feeble dreams. Winter. Attilio Bertolucci. CoIP
Winter for a Moment Takes the Mind; the Snow. Conrad Aiken. *Fr.* Preludes for Memnon. StP
Winter Galaxy, The. Charles Heavysege. OBCV
   (Winter Night.) ACV
Winter Garden. David Gascoyne. GTBS-P
Winter Goes and Weather Betters. Marcabru, *tr. fr. Provençal by* Paul Blackburn. AnML
Winter has a joy for me. I Will Praise the Lord at All Times. William Cowper. EiCP
Winter Has Done Us Great Harm Everywhere. Walther von der Vogelweide, *tr. fr. German by* Margaret F. Richey. AnML
Winter Heavens. George Meredith. CABA
Winter House, The. Norman Cameron. CBEP
Winter Hymn, A—to the Snow. Ebenezer Jones. OBNC
Winter in Dunbarton. Robert Lowell. ToPo
Winter in East Anglia. Edmund Blunden. WePo
Winter in Lower Canada. Standish O'Grady. *Fr.* The Emigrant. OBCV
Winter is cold-hearted. Summer. Christina Rossetti. CBEP; ELP
Winter Is Icumen In. Bradford Smith. PoSC
Winter is icummen in. Ancient Music. Ezra Pound. Par
Winter Is Past, The. The Song of Solomon, II: 11-12, Bible, O.T. SoPo
   (Time of the Singing of Birds, The.) ThGo
Winter Lakes, The. Wilfred Campbell. OBCV
Winter Landscape. John Berryman. AP; MP; PoPl
Winter Legend, A. Geoffrey Johnson. FiSC
Winter Lovers. Robert Watson. PoNC
Winter Mask. Allen Tate. AmLP
Winter Memories. Henry David Thoreau. AmLP
   (Within the Circuit of This Plodding Life.) AP
Winter Morning Walk, The. William Cowper. *Fr.* The Task. EiCP
Winter Night, A. William Barnes. OBNC
Winter Night. Robert Fitzgerald. PoPl
Winter Night. Charles Heavysege. *See* Winter Galaxy.
Winter Night. Boris Pasternak, *tr. fr. Russian by* Eugene M. Kayden. PoPl
Winter Night. *Unknown, tr. fr. Chinese.* WePo
Winter Nights. Thomas Campion. *See* Now Winter Nights Enlarge.
Winter Noon. Sara Teasdale. RePo
Winter, now thy spite is spent. The Vow to Cupid. *Unknown.* SiGo
Winter Piece, A. Bryant. AP
Winter Rain. Christina Rossetti. WiR
Winter Remembered. John Crowe Ransom. AP; CaFP; CBEP
Winter rose, and in one night fled away. May Day. James Reeves. DaDu
Winter Talent, A. Donald Davie. NePoEA-2
Winter the Huntsman. Sir Osbert Sitwell. WePo
Winter Trees. Conrad Diekmann. SD
Winter Views Serene. George Crabbe. *Fr.* The Borough. OBNC
Winter War. "Klabund," *tr. fr. German by* Walter Kaufmann. TwGP
Winter will be feasts and fires in the shut houses. Fall in Corrales. Richard Wilbur. CoPo; VaPo
Winter Will Follow. Richard Watson Dixon. GTBS-P
Winter will not let go of earth. In Defense of Felons. Robert Mezey. ToPo
Winter, You Are Merely a Churl. Charles d'Orléans, *tr. fr. French by* Muriel Kittel. AnML
Winter's house is cold and white. Just a Mile Beyond. Aileen Fisher. RePo
Winters' Spring, The. John Clare. PoIE
Winter's Tale, The, *sels.* Shakespeare.
   Jog On, Jog On, *fr.* IV, ii. CBEP
   Pedlar, The, *fr.* IV, iii. WiR

When Daffodils Begin to Peer, *fr.* IV, ii. CBEP; UnTE
Winter's Tale. A. Dylan Thomas. OnP
Winter's Walk, The. Samuel Johnson. CBEP; EiCP
Wintertime nighs. In Tenebris, I. Thomas Hardy. PoDB
Wintry west extends his blast, The. Winter. Burns. EiCP
Wires. Philip Larkin. ToPo
Wisconsin Soldier Boy, The, *with music. Unknown.* BFSS
Wisdom. Bible, Apocrypha. *See* Wisdom of Solomon, The.
Wisdom. Daniel Whitehead Hicky. BiCB
Wisdom. Sara Teasdale. AmLP
Wisdom. Frank Yerby. AmNP
Wisdom of Solomon, The, *sels.* Bible, Apocrypha. BoC
   "For the whole world before thee is as a little grain of the balance," XI: 23-27.
   "Souls of the righteous are in the hand of God, and there shall no torment touch them, The," III: 1-9.
   Wisdom, VII: 21-29.
Wise guys, The. Kid Stuff. Frank Horne. AmNP
Wish, The. Abraham Cowley. *Fr.* The Mistress. BoC; FaPL
Wish, A. Vidal de Nicolas, *tr. fr. Spanish by* Chloe Vulliamy *and* Stephen Sedley. BoC
Wish, A. Samuel Rogers. GTBS-P
Wish for the New Year, A. Phillips Brooks. STF
Wish, that of the living whole, The. In Memoriam A. H. H., LV. Tennyson. DiPo; OBNC; VP
Wishes for the Supposed Mistress. Richard Crashaw. GTBS-P
   (Wishes: To His (Supposed) Mistress.) SeCP
Wishing My Death. *Unknown. See* Alone Walking.
Wishing Wand. Josef von Eichendorff, *tr. fr. German by* Alison Turner. AGP
Wit Wonders. *Unknown. See* Divine Paradox, The.
Witch, The. Stanley McNail. FiSC
Witch, The. Robert Southey. WiR
Witch Doctor. Robert Hayden. AmNP
Witch-elms that counterchange the floor. In Memoriam A. H. H., LXXXIX. Tennyson. OBNC; VP
Witch Hazel. Theodore Enslin. CoPo
Witch in every closet. Party Bid. Aletha Humphreys. FiSC
Witch of Coös, The. Robert Frost. *Fr.* Two Witches. AP; DiPo
Witch of Willowby Wood, The. Rowena Bennett. RePo
Witch that came (the withered hag), The. Provide, Provide. Robert Frost. CABA; MP
Witches. The. Leah Bodine Drake. FiSC
Witches. Ted Hughes. AnMoPo
Witching Hour. Norma Farber. FiSC
Witch's Ballad, The. William Bell Scott. EvOK
With a garlande of thornes kene. Christ Complains to Sinners. *Unknown.* MeEL
With a lantern that wouldn't burn. The Draft Horse. Robert Frost. CaFP
With a last roar upon the rails. December 3. Vittorio Sereni. CoIP
With a long heavy heave, my very famous men. Old Anchor Chanty. Herbert Trench. HaSV
With a love a madness for Shelley. I Am 25. Gregory Corso. CoPo
With a stronger wind. True Night. René Char. PoPl
With a sudden sweet surprise. Ship Rock. Jones Very. PoIE
With all my will, but much against my heart. A Farewell. Coventry Patmore. The Unknown Eros, I, xvi. GTBS-P; OBNC
With Annie gone. For Anne. Leonard Cohen. BoLP; PoCh
With back to stars that patch. Dark House in Autumn. Conrad Pendleton. FiSC
With blackest moss the flower-plots. Mariana. Tennyson. CABA; CBEP; OBNC; VaPo; VP; WiR
With collars be they yoked, to prove the arm at length. Wrestlers. Michael Drayton. *Fr.* Polyolbion. SD
With deep affection. The Bells of Shandon. Francis Sylvester Mahony. RoGo
With divine rhythm the ocean. Rocking. "Gabriela Mistral." AnSP
With Donne, whose muse on dromedary trots. On Donne's Poetry. Samuel Taylor Coleridge. CABA; CaFP; CBEP; PP
With Easter banners flaunting in the breeze. Marlowe. Arthur Bayldon. PoAu-1
With Eyes at the Back of Our Heads. Denise Levertov. ToPo
With favouring winds o'er sunlit seas. Ultima Thule. Longfellow. HaSV
With fingers weary and worn. The Song of the Shirt. Thomas Hood. CABL; FaPL; PoPo
With flintlocked guns and polished stocks. In Hardin County, 1809. Lulu E. Thompson. PoSC
With focus sharp as Flemish-painted face. The Dome of Sunday. Karl Shapiro. AP
With God Conversing. Gene Derwood. MoRP
With Him. Julia E. Martin. STF
With his kinde mother who partakes thy woe. Temple. John Donne. MeP
With His Old Gray Beard a-Hanging, *with music. Unknown.* BSO

With his two-fist sword, enscintillant, he cut an apple down. The Uncouth Knight. Hugh McCrae. PoAu-1
With his weapon a shovel. Arawata Bill. Denis Glover. ACV
With honeysuckle, over-sweet, festoon'd. Arbor Vitae. Coventry Patmore. The Unknown Eros, II, iii. OBNC
With How Sad Steps. O Moon, Thou Climbst the Skies. Sir Philip Sidney. Astrophel and Stella, XXXI. CAFP; DiPo; EnRePo; ILP; PoIE; StP
With how sad steps, O Moon, thou climb'st the sky. To the Moon. Wordsworth. CBEP
With its cloud of skirmishers in advance. An Army Corps on the March. Walt Whitman. PoLF
With Its Quiet Tongue. Kamala Das. ACV
With jagged nails she tore her face. Mourning of the Mother of Lorenzo Dávalos. Juan de Mena. AnML
With kisses my lips were wounded by you. Healing the Wound. Heine. UnTE
With Life and Death I walked when Love appeared. Hymn to Colour. George Meredith. OBNC
With lights for eyes, our city turns. Lullaby. Dom Moraes. NePoEA-2
With little here to do or see. To the Daisy. Wordsworth. GTBS-P
With loitering step and quiet eye. In November. Archibald Lampman. OBCV
With Love among the haycocks. A Song. Ralph Hodgson. GoJo
With love exceeding a simple love of the things. Melampus. George Meredith. BoC
With lullay, lullay, like a child[e]. Lullay, Lullay, like a Child [or My Darling Dear, My Daisy Flower or The Sleeper Hood-winked]. John Skelton. EnRePo; MeEL; PoIE
With maidenly and modest sips. The Kiss and the Cup. Unknown. UnTE
With margerain [or marjoram] gentle. To Mistress Margery Wentworth. John Skelton. Fr. The Garlande of Laurell. CBEP; EnRePo
With Mournful Tones My Verses Start. Cercamon, tr. fr. Provençal by Harvey Birenbaum. AnML
With no pretentions, in the grass I hide. La Violette. Jean Desmarets de Saint-Sorlin. Fr. Guirlande de Julie. RBL
With paciens thou hast us fed. Farewell! Advent. James Ryman. MeEL
With porcupine locks. The Katzenjammer Kids. James Reaney. OBCV
With proud thanksgiving, a mother for her children. For the Fallen. Laurence Binyon. WePo
With roses crowned, the nymph that I adore. Evening Beauty. Vincent Voiture. RBL
With rue my heart is laden. A Shropshire Lad, LIV. A. E. Housman. VP
With seven matching calfskin cases for his new suits. Home Leave. Barbara Howes. MP
With sick and famisht eyes. Longing. George Herbert. MeP
With six small diamonds for his eyes. The Spider. Robert P. Tristram Coffin. LV
With snow-white veil and garments as of flame. Sonnets on the Divina Commedia, IV. Longfellow. AP; ILP
With song I seek my fate to cheer. Love's Longing. Unknown. UnTE
With such compelling cause to grieve. In Memoriam A. H. H., XXIX. Tennyson. VP
With such unseemly caution have I taken heed. St. Francis and the Cloud. Marie de L. Welch. MoRP
With Tense Imagination. Clemente Rèbora, tr. fr. Italian by Carlo L. Golino. CoIP
With that I saw two swannes of goodly hewe. Spenser. Fr. Prothalamion. BoC
With the effect as of carving, almost, the hillside. For an Age of Plastics. Plymouth. Donald Davie. NePoEA-2
With the other geese within the goosehouse. January. James Reaney. Fr. A Suit of Nettles. OBCV
With the spring moon's first beams. Spring Night. "Rana Mukerji." UnTE
With Thee. Cora M. Pinkham. STF
With Thee Conversing. Milton. Fr. Paradise Lost, IV. WiR
With their lithe long strong legs. Bullfrog. Ted Hughes. DaDu
With this ambiguous earth. Or His Bestowals There. Alice Meynell. BoC
With this it all began: that with each step. Landscape before Easter. Werner Zemp. MGP
With trembling fingers did we weave. In Memoriam A. H. H., XXX. Tennyson. VP
With Two Fair Girls. Unknown, tr. fr. Greek by Robert G. MacGregor. ErPo
With Usura/ With usura hath no man a house of good stone. Canto XLV. Ezra Pound. AnMoPo; PoIE
With Wavering Feet I Walked. Vladimir Solovyov, tr. fr. Russian by Babette Deutsch. SiGo

With weary steps I loiter on. In Memoriam A. H. H., XXXVIII. Tennyson. VP
With what attractive charms this goodly frame. Mark Akenside. Fr. The Pleasures of Imagination. EnPE
With what deep murmurs through time's silent stealth. The Waterfall [or The Water-Fall]. Henry Vaughan. ILP; MeP; StP; WiR
"With Whom Is No Variableness, neither Shadow of Turning." Arthur Hugh Clough. TRV
With wine and words of love and every [or fervid] vow. Seduced Girl [or To Venus]. Hedylos. ErPo; UnTE
With wringing hands and aching breast. The Drummer Boy of Waterloo. Unknown. BSO
With wrinkled hide and great frayed ears. The Elephant. Rachel Field. Fr. A Circus Garland. SoPo
With yellow pears is hanging. Half of Life. Friedrich Hölderlin. TwGP
With you. Hippocrene. Amy Lowell. MoLP
With your sun-white hair and your smile. Out of the Sea. Witter Bynner. MoLP
Within a basket tucked away. The Serpent and the Mouse. Unknown. Fr. The Panchatantra. SIV
Within a budding grove. Spring: The Lover and the Birds. William Allingham. OBNC
Within a thick and spreading hawthorn bush. The Thrush's Nest. John Clare. GoJo; PoSa
Within an open curled sea of gold. A Vision. Lord Herbert of Cherbury. SeCP
Within and Without, sel. George Macdonald.
"Lord of Thyself and me, through the sore grief." TRV
Within Her Eyes. Dante, tr. fr. Italian by Dante Gabriel Rossetti. La Vita Nuova, XII. SiGo
Within King's College Chapel, Cambridge. Wordsworth. See Inside of King's College Chapel, Cambridge.
Within My Breast. Sir Thomas Wyatt. EnRePo
Within my heart a stab I felt. En las Internas Entrañas. St. Theresa of Avila. RBL
Within the Circuit of This Plodding Life. Henry David Thoreau. See Winter Memories.
Within the city of my death. José Garcia Villa. Divine Poems, 74. MoRP
Within the flower there lies a seed. Spell of Creation. Kathleen Raine. PoIE
Within the gentle heart Love shelters him. Canzone: Of the Gentle Heart. Guido Guinicelli. CTC
Within the introspection of my dying. Parable. Robert Pack. NePoEA-2
Within the night, above the dark. Mary Gilmore. Fr. Swans at Night. PoAu-1
Within the streams, Pausanias saith. The Last Chance. Andrew Lang. SD
Within these walls, Pity will war with Death. A Hospital. Alfred Noyes. PoP1
Within this awful volume lies. The Bible. Sir Walter Scott. Fr. The Monastery. TRV
Within this sober frame expect. Upon Appleton House, to My Lord Fairfax. Andrew Marvell. SeCP
Without Benefit of Declaration. Langston Hughes. AmNP
Without Ceremony. Vassar Miller. CoPo
Without Her. Dante Gabriel Rossetti. The House of Life, LIII. CBEP; OBNC; VP
Without invention nothing is well spaced. William Carlos Williams. Fr. Paterson. PP
Without More Weight. Giuseppe Ungaretti, tr. fr. Italian by Allen Mandelbaum. PoP1
Without My Heart, Love, Thou Shalt Not Depart. Agnes de Navarre-Champagne, tr. fr. French by Jacques LeClercq. AnML
Without Name. Pauli Murray. AmNP
Withouten you. Little Elegy. Elinor Wylie. LOW
Witness, The. Sri Ananda Acharya. ACV
Witness how it comes to pass. Epitaph in Sirmio. David Morton. PoLF
Witnesses. Cecil Hemley. PoDB
Witnesses. W. S. Merwin. AmPC
Wit's-End Corner. Unknown. STF
Wits of the present age, who please and shine. To the Poets of Our Time. Jean de Schélandre. RBL
Wizard, from your misty censer, brew. Evocation. Herman Stowell King. FiSC
Wizard's Funeral, The. Richard Watson Dixon. ELP
Wmffre the Sweep. Rolfe Humphries. EaLo
Wodwo. Ted Hughes. ToPo
Woefully Arrayed. At. to John Skelton. CABA; CBEP; EnRePo
(Wofully Araide.) MeEL
Woe's me, woe's me. The Ghost's Lament. Unknown. BuBa
Wolf and Tiger Dining, A. B. Joseph Joel Keith. FiSC
Wolfram's Song. Thomas Lovell Beddoes. See Old Adam.
Wolves, The. Galway Kinnell. NePoEA-2
Woman. Irving Layton. ErPo
Woman. Umberto Saba, tr. fr. Italian by Thomas G. Bergin. CoIP

Woman. *Unknown, tr. fr. German by* Louis Untermeyer. UnTE
Woman and Tree. Robert Graves. ErPo
Woman at the Washington Zoo, The. Randall Jarrell. AP; MP
Woman at the Window, The. Donald Wandrei. FiSC
Woman from Genoa. Dino Campana, *tr. fr. Italian by* Carlo L. Golino. CoIP
Woman full of wile. Growing Old. *Unknown.* ErPo
Woman-Hater, The, *sel.* Beaumont *and* Fletcher.
    Come, Sleep, *fr.* III, i. ELP
Woman in Pisa. Mario Luzi, *tr. fr. Italian by* Carlo L. Golino. CoIP
Woman Is a Branchy Tree, A. James Stephens. ErPo
Woman much missed, how you call to me, call to me. The Voice. Thomas Hardy. AnMoPo; GTBS-P; OBNC
Woman named Tomorrow, The. Four Preludes on Playthings of the Wind, I. Carl Sandburg. AmLP; AP
Women of the West, The. G. Essex Evans. PoAu-1
Woman one wonderful morning, A. Europa. William Plomer. MoBS
Woman par Excellence. Rochelle Owens. CoPo
Woman Telephoning. Joseph Joel Keith. FiSC
Woman: that is to say. Of Women. *Unknown. Fr.* The Thousand and One Nights. ErPo
Woman to Man. Judith Wright. PoAu-2
Woman Unconscious, A. Ted Hughes. StP
Woman Waits for Me, A. Walt Whitman. ErPo
Woman who lived in Holland, of old, A. Going Too Far. Mildred Howells. OnMSP
Woman Who Understands, The. Everard Jack Appleton. PoLF
Woman with Girdle. Anne Sexton. ErPo
Woman with the caught fox. Plea for a Captive. W. S. Merwin. NePoEA-2
Womanisers. John Press. ErPo
Woman's Arms. Anacreon, *tr. fr. Greek by* Abraham Cowley. UnTE
Woman's face, with Nature's own hand painted. Sonnets, XX. Shakespeare. CBEP; ErPo
Woman's Fate, A. Rainer Maria Rilke, *tr. fr. German by* Walter Kaufmann. TwGP
Woman's Last Word, A. Robert Browning. CBEP; UnTE
Woman's love, April weather. Constancies. *Unknown.* UnTE
Woman's Resolution. *Unknown.* BSO
Woman's white body is a song. The Song of Songs. Heine. UnTE
Women. Louise Bogan. MP
Women. William Cartwright. ErPo
Women. ——— Heath. CTC
Women are dancing around a fire. A Message Hidden in an Empty Wine Bottle That I Threw into a Gulley of Maple Trees One Night at an Indecent Hour. James Wright. AmPC
Women Are Worthy. *Unknown.* MeEL
Women ben full of ragerie. Imitation of Chaucer. Pope. Par
Women have no wilderness in them. Women. Louise Bogan. MP
Women of Trachis, *sel.* Sophocles, *tr. fr. Greek by* Ezra Pound.
    "Kupris bears trophies away." CTC
Women's Eyes. Bhartrihari, *tr. fr. Sanskrit by* Arthur W. Ryder. SiGo
Wonder. Thomas Traherne. CBEP; MeP; PoIE; SeCP; StP
Wonderful way is the King's Highway, A. The King's Highway. John Masefield. TRV
Wonders are many, but there is no wonder. What a Piece of Work Is a Man. Sophocles. *Fr.* Antigone. SiGo
Wonders of Nature. *Unknown.* ThGo
Wonders of the Deep, The. Jean Parmentier, *tr. fr. French by* Henry Carrington. RBL
Wondrous Son of God. Berniece Goertz. STF
Wonga Vine. Judith Wright. PoAu-2
Wood shakes in the breeze, The. The Old Tree. Andrew Young. GoJo
Wood So Wild, The. *Unknown. See* I Must Go Walk the Wood.
Wood Song, A. Ralph Hodgson. GoJo
Wood, the Weed, the Wag, The. Sir Walter Ralegh. CBEP
    (Sir Walter Ralegh to His Son.) EnRePo
    (To His Son.) PoIE
Wood-Thrush. John Hall Wheelock. PoDB
Woodlanders, The, *sel.* Thomas Hardy.
    In a Wood. OBNC; PoPl
Woodman, Spare That Tree. George P. Morris. LV
Woodman's axe renews its hollow stroke, The. The Summer. John Clare. CBEP
Woodpigeons at Raheny. Donald Davie. PP
Wood-Pile, The. Robert Frost. CABA; VaPo
Woods are lovely, dark and deep, The. Robert Frost. *Fr.* Stopping by Woods on a Snowy Evening. TRV
Woods Are Wild and Were Not Made for Man, The. Petrarch, *tr. fr. Italian by* Edwin Morgan. Sonnets to Laura: To Laura in Life, CXLIII. AnML

Woods decay, the woods decay and fall, The. Tithonus. Tennyson. CABA; CABL; CBEP; DiPo; FoBA; ILP; OBNC; VP
Woods Grow Darker, The. Leah Bodine Drake. FiSC
Woods in Winter. Longfellow. CBEP
Woods of Westermain, The. George Meredith. VP
Woods shall not decry the murderous stroke, The. On Some Trees Needlessly Slain. Stanton A. Coblentz. TRV
Woods stretch deep to the mountain-side, The. The Man Hunt. Madison Cawein. SIV
Woods were still and the snow was deep, The. Christmas Eve Legend. Frances Frost. BiCB
Woodspurge, The. Dante Gabriel Rossetti. CaFP; CBEP; ELP; GTBS-P; OBNC; PoIE
Woof of the Sun, Ethereal Gauze. Henry David Thoreau. *See* Haze.
Wooing, The. *Unknown, tr. fr. Latin by* John Addington Symonds. UnTE
Woolworth Philodendron, The. Stephen Sandy. CoPo
Woosel cock so black of hue, The. Bottom's Song. Shakespeare. *Fr.* A Midsummer Night's Dream, III, i. CTC
Word, The. Richard Realf. AmLP; TRV
Word. Stephen Spender. PoPo; PP
Word Comes Down, The. Pierre Reverdy, *tr. fr. French by* Joseph de Roche. CoFP
Word has been abroad, The; is back, with a tanned look. Annunciations. Geoffrey Hill. NePoEA-2
Word of God, The. J. Harold Gwynne. STF
Word of God came unto me, The. In the Garden of the Lord. Helen Keller. LV; TRV
Word of the Lord by night, The. Boston Hymn. Emerson. TRV
Word of Willow, The. Leah Bodine Drake. FiSC
Word over all, beautiful as the sky. Reconciliation. Walt Whitman. FoBA
Word shines still, The. For a Christening. Vernon Watkins. MoRP
Words. Helen Morgan Brooks. NNP
Words. Charles Harpur. PoAu-1
Words. Edward Thomas. WePo
Words. *Unknown.* PoLF
Words are deeds. The words we hear. Words. Charles Harpur. PoAu-1
Words Are Never Enough. Charles Bruce. OBCV
Words cannot utter. Easter Day. Christina Rossetti. VP
Words escape me, I face a loss. Reading Buber. Robert Sward. *Fr.* Five Poems for J. F. K. OPP
Words for a Resurrection. Leo Kennedy. OBCV
Words for Hart Crane. Robert Lowell. AP; CABA
Words for the Raker of Leaves. Léonie Adams. PoCh
Words for the Wind. Theodore Roethke. AnMoPo; AP; PoCh
Words in Time. Archibald MacLeish. PoCh
Words Made of Water. Burns Singer. NePoEA-2
Words of a poem should be glass. Glass. Robert Francis. PP
Words of hymns abruptly plod, The. Hymn. Louise Townsend Nicholl. EaLo
Words of Jesus, The. William Rose Benét. MoRP
Wordsworth's Grave. Sir William Watson. OBNC
Work. James Russell Lowell. PoSC
Work. Henry van Dyke. TRV
Work; a Song of Triumph. Angela Morgan. PoLF
Work and Play. Martial, *tr. fr. Latin by* Louis Untermeyer. UnTE
Work Horses. Edith Newlin Chase. SoPo
Work of a look hourly weakened, The. The Poet's Work. Philippe Jaccottet. CoFP
Work of Happiness, The. May Sarton. MoRP
Work without Hope. Samuel Taylor Coleridge. CABA; ILP
Worke is done, The: young men, and maidens set. On Himselfe. Robert Herrick. SeCP
Workers earn it. Money. Richard Armour. LV; PoPl; PoPo
Working Class. Bertram Warr. OBCV
Working Party, A. Siegfried Sassoon. MMA
Working people long ago, The. Labor Day. Marnie Pomeroy. PoSC
Working with God. "George Eliot." *Fr.* Stradivarius. TRV
Workman plied his clumsy spade, A. Two Surprises. R. W. McAlpine. PoLF
Workshop, The. Aileen Fisher. SoPo
World, The. Christina Rossetti. VP
World, The. Henry Vaughan. CABA; CBEP; DiPo; FaBV; FaPL; ILP; MeP; OnP; PoIE; SeCP; StP
World an Illusion, The. *Unknown.* MeEL
World as Meditation, The. Wallace Stevens. AP
World below the Brine, The. Walt Whitman. AmLP; HaSV
World did say to me, The. The Crazy World. William Gay. PoAu-1
World doesn't crumble apart, The. Watershed. Margaret Avison. OBCV
World Goes Turning, The. George Dillon. AmLP
World Has Held Great Heroes, The. Kenneth Grahame. *Fr.* The Wind in the Willows. RePo

World Has Held Great Heroes, The (*continued*) (Song of Mr. Toad, The.) GoJo
World I Have Not Made. Elizabeth Jennings. ACV
World Is a Mighty Ogre, The. Fenton Johnson. AmNP
World is charged with the grandeur of God, The. God's Grandeur. Gerard Manley Hopkins. BoC; CABA; CaFP; DiPo; FoBA; ILP; MoRP; OBNC; PoDB; PoIE; PoPo; StP; VP
World is cold and gray and wet, The. Young Love. Sara Teasdale. BoLP
World is full of women's eyes, The. Women's Eyes. Bhartrihari. SiGo
World is heated seven times, The. A Night in June. Duncan Campbell Scott. OBCV
World Is Too Much with Us, The. Wordsworth. CABA; CaFP; CBEP; DiPo; FoBA; HaSV; ILP; OnP; PoIE; PoLF; StP ("World is too much with us, The; late and soon.") GTBS-P; OBNC
World is young today, The. A Song. Digby Mackworth Dolben. OBNC
World Narrowed to a Point, The. William Carlos Williams. MoLP
World of dew, The. Haiku. Issa. CaFP
World of Light, A. Elizabeth Jennings. NePoEA-2
World of Light, The. Henry Vaughan. *See* They Are All Gone into the World of Light.
World of Sleep, The. Keats. *See* To Sleep.
World of stars and space being His bauble, The. Receiving Communion. Vassar Miller. NePoEA-2
World of the Lord came unto me saying, The. T. S. Eliot. *Fr.* The Rock. TRV
World of Work, as a Poet Would Like It to Be, The. D. H. Lawrence. BoC
World sits at the feet of Christ, The. Whittier. *Fr.* The Over-Heart. TRV
World State, The. G. K. Chesterton. PoPo
World, that all contains, is ever moving, The. Caelica, VII. Fulke Greville. EnRePo
World turns and its turning wheels, The. The Epistemological Rag. Gray Burr. CoPo
Worldly possessions? 'twas easy to find them. Tora's Song. Knut Hamsun. PoP1
World's a bubble, and the life of man, The. Life [*or* In Vitam Humanam]. Francis Bacon. GTBS-P; PoIE
World's a floore, whose swelling heapes retaine, The. Francis Quarles. *Fr.* Emblems. MeP
World's a garden, The; pleasures are the flowers. The Garden. Joshua Sylvester. CBEP
World's at war, The! O powers above, conspire. A Song of War. Matthias Claudius. AGP
World's Bible, The. Annie Johnson Flint. STF; TRV
World's End, The. G. K. Chettur. ACV
World's End, The. William Empson. ToPo
World's Great Age Begins Anew, The. Shelley. *Fr.* Hellas. PoIE
World's So Big, The. Aileen Fisher. SoPo
World's Way, The. Shakespeare. *See* Sonnets, LXVI.
World's Wonders, The. Robinson Jeffers. PoDB
World's Worst Boxer, The. Lucilius, *tr. fr. Greek by* Humbert Wolfe. SD
Worry. George W. Swarberg. STF
Worship of virtu is the mede. A Carol of St. George. *Unknown.* MeEL
Worship the Lord, the God of wild cold kind. The Lord in the Wind. James Picot. PoAu-2
Worshiper, The. Vassar Miller. NePoEA-2
Worst of all diseases, The. Sin and Its Cure. *Unknown.* STF
Worthy London prentice, A. The London Prentice. *Unknown.* UnTE
Worthy woman from beside Bath city, A. The Wife of Bath. Chaucer. *Fr.* The Canterbury Tales. WePo
"Wot's in a name?" she sez . . . An' then she sighs. The Play. C. J. Dennis. *Fr.* The Sentimental Bloke. PoAu-2
Would God that I might be an ape. Primitivism. O. B. Hardison, Jr. PoNC
Would I Be Called a Christian? Mrs. J. F. Moser. STF
Would I could cast a sail on the water. The Collar-Bone of a Hare. W. B. Yeats. AnMoPo
Would I describe a preacher, such as Paul. William Cowper. *Fr.* The Task. TRV
Would I Might Rouse the Lincoln in You All. Vachel Lindsay. *Fr.* Litany of the Heroes. LiPo; PoSC
Would I might wake St. Francis in you all. Vachel Lindsay. *Fr.* Litany of the Heroes. MoRP
Would that the structure brave, the manifold music I build. Abt Vogler. Robert Browning. DiPo; VP
Would ye have fresh cheese and cream? Fresh Cheese and Cream. Robert Herrick. UnTE
Would you have a young virgin of fifteen years. What's Your Fancy. *Unknown.* UnTE
Would you have Freedom from wage-slavery? There Is Power in a Union. *Unknown, at. to* Joe Hill. ThLM

Would you hear of an old-time sea-fight? An Old-Time Sea-Fight. Walt Whitman. *Fr.* Song of Myself. OnMSP
Would You in Venus' Wars Succeed. *Unknown.* ErPo
Would you like to see a city given over. The City of Golf. Robert Fuller Murray. SD
Would you make blazes. Ultra-Germano-Criticasterism. Leigh Hunt. PP
Wouldn't it be lovely if the rain came down. Very Lovely. Rose Fyleman. SoPo
Wouldst thou hear what man can say. Epitaph on Elizabeth, L. H. Ben Jonson. CABA; ELP; EnRePo; PoIE; SeCP
Wound-Dresser, The. Walt Whitman. AP
Wounded deer leaps highest, A. Emily Dickinson. AP; FoBA
Woven you are of the spring, lovers. Rose of Fire. Antonio Machado. AnSP
Wrack. Irving Feldman. AmPC
Wraggle Taggle Gipsies [O!], The. *Unknown.* EvOK; WiR (Johnie Faa.) BuBa (Raggle Taggle Gypsies, The.) CBEP
Wrapped in his shroud of wax, his swoon of wounds. Poem for Easter. Laurie Lee. BoC
Wrapped up, O Lord, in man's degeneration. Caelica, XCVIII. Fulke Greville. EnRePo
Wreath, A. George Herbert. SeCP
Wreath for One Lost, A. Harold Vinal. FiSC
Wreath of flowers as cold as snow, A. The Birth. Rosemary Dobson. PoAu-2
Wreathed garland of deserved praise, A. A Wreath. George Herbert. SeCP
Wreck of Number Nine, The, *with music. Unknown.* BFSS
Wreck of the *Atlantic,* The. *Unknown.* BSNS
Wreck of the *Deutschland,* The. Gerard Manley Hopkins. CABL; DiPo; OBNC; VP ("Thou mastering me," Pt. I. BoC
Wreck of the *Glenaloon,* The. *Unknown.* BSNS
Wreck of the *Hesperus,* The. Longfellow. FaPL; SIV
Wreck of the *Julie Plante,* The. William Henry Drummond. OBCV
Wreckers heave, and lift and split, on twenty sites, in town. Preliminary Poem for a Modern City. Harry Kemp. LV
Wreckers' Prayer, The. Theodore Goodridge Roberts. OBCV
Wrestler, The. Stefan George, *tr. fr. German by* David Luke. LV
Wrestlers. Michael Drayton. *Fr.* Polyolbion. SD
"Write an article," suggests a letter. The Economical Poet. Christian Morgenstern. TwGP
Written at Oxford: On Stealing the Body of a Girl for Dissection. *Unknown.* StP
Written in Early Spring. Wordsworth. *See* Lines Written in Early Spring.
Written in Emerson's Essays. Matthew Arnold. ILP
Written in Juice of Lemmon. Abraham Cowley. SeCP
Written in March. Wordsworth. *See* Merry Month of May, The.
Written in 1740. Thomas Catesby Paget. WaPE
Written in the Album of a Child. Wordsworth. OBNC
Written in the Beginning of Mezeray's History of France. Matthew Prior. EiCP
Written in the Euganean Hills, North Italy. Shelley. GTBS-P
Written on the Night before His Execution. Sir Walter Ralegh. *See* Even Such Is Time.
Written on the Road. Mary Mapes Dodge. BiCB
Written under Capricorn, a land. Love Poem. Chris Wallace-Crabbe. PoAu-2
Wyandotte's Farewell Song, The, *with music. Unknown.* BSO
Wyatt resteth here that quick could never rest. On the Death of Sir Thomas Wyatt. Earl of Surrey. CBEP
Wynken, Blynken, and Nod. Eugene Field. SoPo (Dutch Lullaby, A.) AmLP; PoP1

X

X Minus X. Kenneth Fearing. AmLP
X-Ray. David Ray. NePoEA-2

Y

Y.M.C.A. Writing Room. Roy Fuller. ToPo
Yachts, The. William Carlos Williams. AP; ILP; OnP; VaPo
Yak, The. Hilaire Belloc. FaBV
Yak. William Jay Smith. RePo
Yankee captains and their wives. The Captains of Small Farms. Robert P. Tristram Coffin. RePo
Yankee Cradle. Robert P. Tristram Coffin. EvOK
Yankee ship going down the river, A. Blow, Boys, Blow! *Unknown.* BSNS

Yardbird's Skull. Owen Dodson. AmNP
Yarn of gold and silk spun. Complaint of the Weavers. Chrétien de Troyes. *Fr.* Yvain. AnML
Yarn of the *Nancy Bell,* The. W. S. Gilbert. EvOK; FaBV; HaSV; OnMSP
Yarrow, *with music. Unknown.* BSO
Yarrow Unvisited. Wordsworth. GTBS-P
Yarrow Visited. Wordsworth. GTBS-P
Ye Alps audacious, thro' the heav'ns that rise. The Hasty-Pudding. Joel Barlow. AP
Ye Ancient Divine Ones. Arthur Hugh Clough. *Fr.* Amours de Voyage. OBNC
Ye Ancient Yuba Miner, of the Days of '49, *with music.* Sam C. Upham. SGR
Ye Banks and Braes [o' Bonnie Doon]. Burns. CBEP; ELP; StP; WePo
  (Banks o' Doon, The.) BoLP
  (Highland Mary.) FaPL; GTBS-P
  ("Ye banks and braes o' bonnie Doon.") GTBS-P
Ye [*or* Yee] blushing virgins happy [*or* happie] are. To Roses in the Bosom[e] of Castara. William Habington. *Fr.* Castara. SeCP; UnTE
Ye cities on the Euphrates! Age. Friedrich Hölderlin. AGP
Ye Clouds! that far above me float and pause. France; an Ode. Samuel Taylor Coleridge. StP
Ye distant spires, ye antique towers. Ode on a Distant Prospect of Eton College. Thomas Gray. CABA; EiCP; EnPE; GTBS-P; StP
Ye elms that wave on Malvern Hill. Malvern Hill. Herman Melville. AP
Ye famed physicians of this place. A Lamentable Case. Sir Charles Hanbury Williams. ErPo; UnTE; WaPE
Ye flaming powers, and winged warriours bright. Upon the Circumcision. Milton. MeP
Ye flippering soule. An Address to the Soul Occasioned by a Rain. Edward Taylor. AP
Ye Flowery Banks. Burns. CABA
Ye galleys of our land. Galleys of Spain. *Unknown.* RBL
Ye genii who in secret state. Limitations of Human Art. William Collins. Three Fragments, 2. WaPE
Ye Gods! of Time I am Weary. Christine de Pisan, *tr. fr. French by* Muriel Kittel. AnML
Ye Gods! the raptures of that night! The Enjoyment. *Unknown.* ErPo
Ye green-robed Dryads, oft at dusky eve. The Enthusiast; or, The Lover of Nature. Joseph Warton. EnPE
Ye have been fresh and green. To Meadows [*or* To Meddowes]. Robert Herrick. EiCP; SeCP
"Ye have robbed," said he, "ye have slaughtered and made an end." He Fell among Thieves. Sir Henry Newbolt. OnMSP
Ye Highlands and ye Lowlands [*or* Lawlands]. The Bonny Earl of Murray [*or* o' Moray]. *Unknown.* BuBa; CBEP; ELP
Ye ladies that live in the city or town. The Link. Robert Lowth. WaPE
Ye learned sisters which have oftentimes. Epithalamion. Spenser. CABL; EnRePo; ILP
Ye living lamps, by whose dear light. The Mower to the Glow-Worms. Andrew Marvell. BoC; CBEP; ELP; SeCP
Ye lords of creation, men you are called. The Lords of Creation. *Unknown.* PoLF
Ye Mariners of England. Thomas Campbell. CBEP; GTBS-P
Ye marshes, how. Sidney Lanier. *Fr.* The Marshes of Glynn. TRV
Ye motions of delight, that through the fields. Imagination, How Impaired and Restored. Wordsworth. *Fr.* The Prelude. OBNC
Ye pilgrim folk advancing pensively. Dante. *Fr.* La Vita Nuova. CTC
Ye powers unseen, to whom the bards of Greece. Inscription. Mark Akenside. CBEP
Ye pure inhabitants of light. Three Hymns, 3. Elizabeth Rowe. WaPE
Ye rambling boys of Erin, ye rambling boys beware. The Banks of Newfoundland. *Unknown.* BSNS
Ye say, they all have passed away. Indian Names. Lydia Huntly Sigourney. PoLF; RePo
Ye Sons of Columbia, *with music. Unknown.* BFSS
Ye sons of men, with just regard attend. Matthew Prior. *Fr.* Solomon on the Vanity of the World. EiCP
Ye sons of North Britain, you that used to range. Donald Munro. *Unknown.* BSNS
Ye sorrowing people! who from bondage fly. The Fugitive Slaves. Jones Very. AP
Ye storm-winds of Autumn! Parting. Matthew Arnold. Switzerland, II. VP
Ye swains who roam from fair to fair. Would You in Venus' Wars Succeed. *Unknown.* ErPo
Ye sylvan Muses, loftier strains recite. The Birth of the Squire. John Gay. EiCP
Ye that pasęn by the weiye. Jesus to Those Who Pass By. *Unknown.* MeEL
Ye, too, marvellous Twain, that erect on the Monte Cavallo.

Ye Ancient Divine Ones. Arthur Hugh Clough. *Fr.* Amours de Voyage. OBNC
Ye trees and shrubs, each plant. Cervantes. *Fr.* Don Quixote. RBL
Ye Wearie Wayfarer, *sel.* Adam Lindsay Gordon.
  Sun and Rain and Dew from Heaven. PoLF
Ye wise, instruct me to endure. On Censure. Swift. CBEP
Ye young debaters over the doctrine. The Village Atheist. Edgar Lee Masters. *Fr.* Spoon River Anthology. EaLo; PoPo
Yea, let me praise my lady whom I love. He Will Praise His Lady. Guido Guinicelli. SiGo
Yeah here am I. Two Jazz Poems [*or* Jazz Poem]. Carl Wendell Hines, Jr. AmNP; PtTo
Year a bird flies against the drum, The. For Now. W. S. Merwin. CoPo
Year ago today, A. Birthday Garden. Ivy O. Eastwick. BiCB
Year ago you came, A. Pietà. James McAuley. PoAu-2
"Year and I are dying out together, The." Lament in Autumn. Harold Stewart. PoAu-2
Year has changed his mantle cold, The. Spring. Charles d'Orléans, *tr. by* Andrew Lang. CTC
Year his winter cloak lets fall, The. Rondeau. Charles d'Orléans, *tr. by* J. G. Legge. SiGo
Year of Sorrow, The, *sel.* Aubrey Thomas De Vere.
  Spring. OBNC
Year without Seasons, A. Mance Williams. NNP
Years. Walter Savage Landor. CBEP
Years ago, at a private school. An Ever-fixed Mark. Kingsley Amis. ErPo
Years are flowers and bloom with, The. God's Garden. Richard Burton. TRV
Year's at the Spring, The. Robert Browning. *Fr.* Pippa Passes. FaBV
  (Pippa's Song.) CBEP; GoJo; LV; PoPo; TRV
  (Song: "Year's at the spring, The.") PoPl
Years Back When We Were Children. "Der Wilde Alexander," *tr. fr. German by* Robert Lowell. AnML
Years creep slowly by, Lorena, The. Lorena. H. D. L. Webster. BFSS
Year's End. Richard Wilbur. PoIE
Years, many parti-colour'd years. Years. Walter Savage Landor. CBEP
Years That Go to Make Me Man, The. Christopher Brennan. *Fr.* The Twilight of Disquietude. PoAu-1
Yeats in Dublin, *sel.* Vernon Watkins.
  "'Young poets, The,' he murmured." PP
Yee blushing virgins happie are. *See* Ye blushing virgins happy are.
Yellow-belly, yellow-belly, come and take a swim. Yes, by Golly. *Unknown.* SD
Yellow butterflies. Korosta Katzina Song. *Unknown.* SiGo
Yellow Cat, The. Leslie Nelson Jennings. FiSC
Yellow Fog. T. S. Eliot. *Fr.* The Love Song of J. Alfred Prufrock. LOW
  ("Yellow fog that rubs its back upon the window-panes, The.") PoPo
Yellow Spring. Juan Ramón Jiménez, *tr. fr. Spanish by* Angel Flores. AnSP
Yellow sun yellow. The Ballad of Red Fox. Melvin Walker La Follette. LOW
Yellow Violet, The. Bryant. AP; PoLF
Yep, that's me. Stranger, ain't yew? Wal, step in. The Brothers. Amy Groesbeck. FiSC
Yes, and as long as these poor eyes can bring. Sonnet XIV. Louise Labé. RBL
Yes, by Golly. *Unknown.* SD
Yes! hope may with my strong desire keep pace. To the Marchesana of Pescara. Michelangelo. CTC
Yes, I Could Love If I Could Find. *Unknown.* ErPo
Yes, I got another Johnny; but he was to Number One. My Other Chinee Cook. Brunton Stephens. PoAu-1
Yes, I Have Been to Calvary. Avis B. Christiansen. STF
Yes! I have seen the ancient oak. Felicia Dorothea Hemans. *Fr.* The Brereton Omen. CTC
Yes, I know from where I came! Ecce Homo. Nietzsche. TwGP
Yes, I remember Adlestrop. Adlestrop. Edward Thomas. GoJo
Yes, I will love thee when the sun. A Love Song. W. F. Hawley. OBCV
Yes: in the sea of life enisled [*or* enisl'd]. To Marguerite—Continued. Matthew Arnold. *Fr.* Switzerland. CABA; CaFP; ELP; GTBS-P; ILP; OBNC; VaPo; VP
Yes, magic lyre! now all complete. Ode to an Æolus's Harp. William Mason. WaPE
Yes Please Gentlemen. A. R. D. Fairburn. ACV
Yes, that fair neck, too beautiful by half. Madame D'Albert's Laugh. Clément Marot. RBL
Yes. The will decided. But how can the heart decide. A Separation. Stephen Spender. MoLP
Yes, there is a holy pleasure in thine eye. Admonition to a Traveller. Wordsworth. GTBS-P

Yes, true, children will take advantage of. The Little Girl. Nicholas Moore. ErPo

Yes when the dark withdrew I suffered light. A World of Light. Elizabeth Jennings. NePoEA-2

Yes, wonderful are dreams: and I have known. Charles Harpur. *Fr.* The Tower of the Dream. PoAu-1

Yes, yours, my love, is the right human face. The Confirmation. Edwin Muir. WePo

Yesterday a human deity, today a bit of dust. Sonnet. Luis de Góngora. RBL

Yesterday all the past. The language of size. Spain 1937. W. H. Auden. CABL

Yesterday rain fell in torrents. You Could Say. Robert Mezey. AmPC; ToPo

Yesterday Rebecca Mason. I Almost Did—Very Nigh—Had Not God Stopped the Lie. Elizabeth Turner. ThGo

Yestreen I had a pint o' wine. Anna [*or* The Gowden Locks of Anna]. Burns. CBEP; UnTE

Yestreen the queen had four Marys. The Four Marys. *Unknown.* BFSS

Yet but Three? Shakespeare. *Fr.* A Midsummer Night's Dream, III, ii. CTC

"Yet Cloe sure was form'd without a spot." Pope. *Fr.* Moral Essays: Of the Characters of Women. ErPo

Yet Do I Marvel. Countee Cullen. AmNP

Yet do not be afraid, yet give no post forlorn. To Himself. Paul Fleming. AGP

Yet how the solitude of man torments. Journey into Misery. Yvan Goll. MGP

Yet I could think, indeed, the perfect call. Arthur Hugh Clough. *Fr.* Dipsychus. OBNC

Yet if His Majesty, our sovereign [*or* soveraign] lord. The Guest [*or* Guests *or* Preparations]. *Unknown.* BoC; CBEP; EaLo; EvOK; WePo

Yet if some voice that man could trust. In Memoriam A. H. H., XXXV. Tennyson. VP

Yet it was plain she struggled, and that salt. Modern Love, VIII. George Meredith. VP

Yet Listen Now. Amy Carmichael. TRV

Yet, love, mere love, is beautiful indeed. Sonnets from the Portuguese, X. Elizabeth Barrett Browning. CTC

Yet love will dream and Faith will trust. Life and Love. Whittier. TRV

Yet often I think the king of that country. The Gospel of Labor. Henry van Dyke. TRV

Yet once more, O ye laurels, and once more. Lycidas. Milton. CABA; CaFP; DiPo; FoBA; GTBS-P; ILP; OnP; PoIE; StP; VaPo

Yet pity for a horse o'er-driven. In Memoriam A. H. H., LXIII. Tennyson. VP

Yet thou, they say, for marriage dost provide. Against Women. Juvenal. *Fr.* Satires. UnTE

Yet to the wondrous St. Peter's, and yet to the solemn Rotonda. Ah, That I Were Far Away. Arthur Hugh Clough. *Fr.* Amours de Voyage. OBNC

Yet we must die, and though proud life might dare. Jean de Sponde. *Fr.* Sonnets de la Mort. RBL

Yet wulde I nat the causer fared amisse. Subject to All Pain. *Unknown.* MeEL

Ye've left the sun an' the can'le licht and the starlight. The Licht Nichts. Violet Jacob. ACV

Yew-Tree, The. Vernon Watkins. EaLo

Yew Trees. Wordsworth. CABA; FoBA

Yield all, my love; but be withal as coy. Upon A. M. Sir John Suckling. ErPo

Yielding clod lulls iron off to sleep. Battlefield. August Stramm. MGP

"Yon doth sit a Spanish lady." Spanish Lady. *Unknown.* BSO

Yon flakes that fret the eastern sky. More Poems, XXV. A. E. Housman. VP

Yonder comes my woman! It's how do you know? The Midnight Special. *Unknown.* BFSS

Yonder School, *with music. Unknown.* BFSS

Yonder See. A. E. Housman. Last Poems, XI. WePo

Yonder, that swarm of things insectual. A Sequelula to "The Dynasts." Max Beerbohm. Par

Yonder, yonder see the fair rainbow. Corn-grinding Song. *Tr. by* Natalie Curtis. RePo

You. John Masefield. MoRP

You and I. Friedrich Hebbel, *tr. fr. German by* Calvin S. Brown. AGP

You and I and Amyas. William Cornish. CBEP

You and the hoary poet. November 22, 1963. Robert Hollander. OPP

You, Andrew Marvell. Archibald MacLeish. AmLP; AP; CaFP; FaBV; MP; PoIE; StP; VaPo

You Are a Part of Me. Frank Yerby. AmNP

You are a sunrise. To a Golden-haired Girl in a Louisiana Town. Vachel Lindsay. MoLP

You are a tulip seen to day. A Meditation for His Mistresse. Robert Herrick. SeCP

You are alone, distanced and shunned, impress this. Outward Journey. Karl Wolfskehl. MGP

You are beautiful. What Ulysses Said to Circe on the Beach of Aeaea. Irving Layton. ErPo

You are coming home at night. Coming Home. Rolfe Humphries. MoRP

You are disdainful and magnificent. Sonnet to a Negro in Harlem. Helene Johnson. AmNP

You are frightened of death? You wish you could live forever? Immortality. Schiller. TwGP

You are loveliness and all desire. Living and Dying. "Michael Lewis." *Fr.* Cherry Blossoms. UnTE

You are not dead, no. Love. Juan Ramón Jiménez. AnSP

"You are old, Father William," the young man cried. The Old Man's Comforts and How He Gained Them. Robert Southey. Par

"You are old, Father William," the young man said. Father William. "Lewis Carroll." *Fr.* Alice's Adventures in Wonderland. BiCB; FaPL; GoJo; Par; PoLF; RePo

You are over there, Father Malloy. Father Malloy. Edgar Lee Masters. *Fr.* Spoon River Anthology. PoPo

You are still the one with the stone and the sling. Man of My Time. Salvatore Quasimodo. PoP1

You are the brave who do not break. In Time of Crisis. Raymond Patterson. PtTo

You are the stately sunset. Metaphor. Clark Ashton Smith. FiSC

You Ask Me How Contempt Who Claims to Sleep. J. V. Cunningham. StP

(Epigram.) ErPo

You Ask Me, Why, though Ill at Ease. Tennyson. CABA

You became. My Company. Sir Herbert Read. MMA

You believe in a live city. News of My Friends. Grant Code. FiSC

You Black Bright Stars. *Unknown.* EnRePo

You brave heroic minds. To the Virginian Voyage. Michael Drayton. CBEP; EnRePo; StP; ThLM

You broke your teeth upon the question Why. The Resolution. Vassar Miller. CoPo

You brought me a cluster of seaweed. Woman form Genoa. Dino Campana. CoIP

You came, you went, a fleeting guest. On the Death of a Child. Ludwig Uhland. AGP

You can fool the hapless public. You Can't Fool God. Grenville Kleiser. STF

"You can talk about yer sheep dorgs," said the man from Allan's Creek. Daley's Dorg Wattle. W. T. Goodge. PoAu-1

You cannot hope. Humbert Wolfe. BoC

You cannot rest behind the plate. Villanelle. M. D. Feld. SD

You cannot traffick in peace. Humbert Wolfe. *Fr.* The Uncelestial City. BoC

You cannot will men your health. Some Things You Cannot Will to Men. Walter E. Isenhour. STF

You Can't Be Wise. Paul Engle. PoP1

You Can't Fool God. Grenville Kleiser. STF

You Can't Go Home Again, *sel.* Thomas Wolfe. TRV

"Something has spoken to me in the night." TRV

You captains brave and bold, hear our cries, hear our cries. Captain Robert Kidd. *Unknown.* BSNS

You Charmed Me Not. Dryden. *Fr.* An Evening's Love, II, i. DiPo

You child, how can you dare complain. Equals. Louis Untermeyer. UnTE

You come and say that it is restful here. From an Old Maid. Vassar Miller. ToPo

You come to fetch me from my work tonight. Putting in the Seed. Robert Frost. ErPo

You could not stop the snow the sky dumped down. Lines for a President. Robert Watson. OPP

You Could Say. Robert Mezey. AmPC; ToPo

You could see him, walking between the rifles. The Crime Was in Granada. Antonio Machado. AnSP

You courtiers scorn us country clowns. Court and Country Love. *Unknown.* UnTE

You did late review my lays. To Christopher North. Tennyson. EvOK

You did not come. A Broken Appointment. Thomas Hardy. CBEP; DTC

You did right, injured husband, to ruin the face. Insufficient Vengeance. Martial. UnTE

You Did Well to Leave, Arthur Rimbaud! René Char, *tr. fr. French by* Rosalind Sherk. CoFP

You do look, my son, in a moved sort. Clouds. Shakespeare. *Fr.* The Tempest. BoC

You don't have to tell how you live each day. It's in Your Face. *Unknown.* PoLF

You don't remember the customs-house. The Customs-House. Eugenio Montale. CoIP

You empress of the stars, the heavens' worthy crown. Spring-Joy Praising God. Praise of the Sun. Catharina Regina von Greiffenberg. AGP

You Eyes, you large and all-inquiring Eyes. For Arvia. E. A. Robinson. BiCB

You Felons on Trial in Courts. Walt Whitman. CBEP

You gave them all the dances, but came home with me. The Technique of Laughter. Jascha Kessler. AmPC
You give but little when you give of your possessions. On Giving. Kahlil Gibran. *Fr.* The Prophet. PoPl
You go aboard of a leaky boat. A Ripping Trip. *Unknown.* SGR
You gote-heard Gods, that love the grassie mountaines. Sestina. Sir Philip Sidney. *Fr.* Arcadia. StP
You grottoes and you fountains. On the Choice of His Sepulchre. Pierre de Ronsard. *Fr.* Odes. RBL
You had been gone so long, and no one knew. To the Lost Colony. Zoe Kincaid Brockman. PoNC
You have a face of carved stone. The Earth and Death. Cesare Pavese. CoIP
You have a face that's sweeter than grape mash. Michelangelo, *tr. fr. Italian by* Harold M. Priest. RBL
You have asked, my little friend, why I'm so sad and still. Utah Carl. *Unknown.* BFSS
You have been good to me, I give you this. Idolatry. Arna Bontemps. AmNP
You have beheld a smiling Rose. The Lilly in a Christal. Robert Herrick. SeCP
You Have Done So Much by Your Great Gentleness. Christine de Pisan, *tr. fr. French by* Muriel Kittel. AnML
You have heaped my hands with rubies. Odysseus' Song to Calypso. Peter Kane Dufault. ErPo
You have heard the cry of the cock in the air. From the Fortress of Upper Bergamo. Salvatore Quasimodo. CoIP
You Have in You the Flowers and the Green Grass. Guido Cavalcanti, *tr. fr. Italian by* G. S. Fraser. AnML
You have seen the house built, you have seen it adorned. Chorus. T. S. Eliot. *Fr.* The Rock. PoDB
You hungry birds, I bring my crumbs. Crumbs. Walter de la Mare. SoPo
You pity, miserable stars. Thoughts by Night. Goethe. TwGP
You know it's April by the falling-off. B Negative. X. J. Kennedy. NePoEA-2
You know the fellow. A Public Nuisance. Reginald Arkell. SD
You know the old woman. The Old Woman. Beatrix Potter. GoJo
You know the way. Lemuel's Blessing. W. S. Merwin. CoPo
You know w'at for ees school keep out? Leetla Giorgio Washeenton. T. A. Daly. PoSC
You know, we French stormed Ratisbon. An Incident of the French Camp. Robert Browning. PoPo; RoGo
You leaning there over the fence with phlox. September. Gottfried Benn. MGP
You learned Lear's *Nonsense Rhymes* by heart, not rote. A Plea to Girls and Boys. Robert Graves. GTBS-P
You leave us: you will see the Rhine. In Memoriam A. H. H., XCVIII. Tennyson. VP
You left me, sweet, two legacies. Emily Dickinson. FaPL
You like it under the trees in autumn. The Motive for Metaphor. Wallace Stevens. AP
You like not that French novel? Tell me why. Modern Love, XXV. George Meredith. VP
You Lingering Sparse Leaves of Me. Walt Whitman. CBEP
You little stars that live in skies. Caelica, IV. Fulke Greville. CBEP
You look for Rome in Rome, O traveler. To Rome Entombed in Her Ruins. Francisco de Quevedo. EnSP
You looked at me with eyes grown bright with pain. Parting after a Quarrel. Eunice Tietjens. BoLP
You, love, and I. Counting the Beats. Robert Graves. DTC; ELP; GTBS-P; PoIE
You love us when we're heroes, home on leave. Glory of Women. Siegfried Sassoon. MMA
You may call, you may call. The Bad Kittens. Elizabeth J. Coatsworth. RePo
You may hear a pygmy talking. No Doubt. Helen Baker Adams. STF
You may not stand in the halls of fame. Be Friendly. Walter E. Isenhour. STF
You may talk o' gin and beer. Gunga Din. Kipling. FaPL; OnMSP; PoPl; PoPo; WePo
You may think it quite an easy task. The Preacher's Wife. *Unknown.* STF
You meaner beauties of the night. Elizabeth of Bohemia [or To His Mistress, the Queen of Bohemia]. Sir Henry Wotton. CBEP; ELP; GTBS-P; SeCP
You might suppose it easy. The Boatman. Jay Macpherson. OBCV
You, my son. The Open Door. Grace Coolidge. TRV
You need a place much more than time. The Invitation. Tom Buchan. ACV
You need not see what someone is doing. Sext. W. H. Auden. *Fr.* Horae Canonicae. PoDB
You needn't always be scrubbing the tiles, Hendrickje. The Evenings of Certain Lives. Gottfried Benn. MGP
You, Neighbor God. Rainer Maria Rilke, *tr. fr. German by* Babette Deutsch. MoRP
You praise the firm restraint with which they write. On Some South African Novelists. Roy Campbell. GTBS-P; PoPl

You probably could put their names to them. ". . . As When Emotion Too Far Exceeds Its Cause." G. C. Oden. AmNP
You Quiet Attender to My Garden. Max Herrmann-Neisse, *tr. fr. German by* Christopher Middleton. MGP
You remember Davies? He died, you know. Death of a Peasant. R. S. Thomas. PoIE
You Rise Up. Paul Eluard, *tr. fr. French by* Wallace Fowlie. PoPl
You roam above in the light. Hyperion's Song of Fate. Friedrich Hölderlin. AGP
You, sad Captain, big-knobbed staff of life. The Voyages of Captain Cock. William Jay Smith. ErPo; UnTE
You said,/ "A man has to change sometime." Heart Path. Vernon Ward. PoNC
You said, "How strange! Among all who have come by." Following the Sun. Jascha Kessler. AmPC
You said that your people. To Richard Wright. Conrad Kent Rivers. AmNP
You said to me: But I will be your comrade. Nudities. André Spire. ErPo
You say, as I have often given tongue. To a Poet, Who Would Have Me Praise Certain Bad Poets, Imitators of His and Mine. W. B. Yeats. CTC
You say, but with no touch of scorn. In Memoriam A. H. H., XCVI. Tennyson. FoBA; VP
You say I love not, 'cause I do not play. To His Mistress Objecting to Him neither Toying or Talking. Robert Herrick. FaBV
You say it will cost much to follow. The Cost. Flora L. Osgood. STF
You say my Love no marvel is to you. Sonnet. George Henry Boker. *Fr.* Sonnets. AmLP
You Say, the Summer Is Here Now. Reinmar von Hagenau, *tr. fr. German by* Gillian Barker *and* Kenneth Gee. AnML
You say there's only evil in this war. Evening Prayer. Amelia Josephine Burr. SIV
You, say, "Where goest thou?" I cannot tell. The Poet's Simple Faith. Victor Hugo. TRV
You say yes and I say yes. Point of No Return. Mari Evans. NNP
You See Me like the Elephant. Richart de Berbezilh, *tr. fr. Provençal by* Harvey Birenbaum. AnML
You see the ways the fisherman doth take. Neither Hook nor Line. Bunyan. SD
You see this dog. It was but yesterday. Flush or Faunus. Elizabeth Barrett Browning. BoC
You see this pebble-stone? It's a thing I bought. The Cock and the Bull. Charles Stuart Calverley. Par
You see, where'er you look, on earth but vainness' hour. All Is Vanity. Andreas Gryphius. AGP
You should see these musical mice. New Strain. George Starbuck. MP
You simple-minded African bird. Autumn Song. Noel Harry Brettell. ACV
You sleeping child asleep, away. To Ping-ku, Asleep. Lawrence Durrell. AnMoPo
You smile a plump uncle smile. Most Wanted. Robert Watson. PoNC
You speak. You say: Today's character is not. As You Leave the Room. Wallace Stevens. AP
You stand near the window as lights wink. Twenty-third Street Runs into Heaven. Kenneth Patchen. ErPo
You strange, astonished-looking, angle-faced. To a Fish. Leigh Hunt. *Fr.* The Fish, the Man, and the Spirit. BoC; HaSV; RoGo
You stupid men, who do accuse. Verses against the Inconsequence of Men's Taste and Strictures. Sister Juana Inés de la Cruz. AnSP
You take a bath, and sit there bathing. Samuel Hoffenstein. *Fr.* Poems in Praise of Practically Nothing. EvOK
You talk about your business. Speak Out for Jesus. *Unknown.* STF
You, that decipher out the fate. Mourning. Andrew Marvell. CABA; SeCP
You that do search for every purling spring. Astrophel and Stella, XV. Sir Philip Sidney. ILP
You that have spent the silent night. Gascoigne's Good Morrow. George Gascoigne. EnRePo
You That in Love Find Luck. Sir Thomas Wyatt. CBEP
You that in merriment delight. Kate and Her Horns. *Unknown.* BSNS
You that seek what life is in death. Caelica, LXXXII. Fulke Greville. EnRePo
You that with allegory's curious frame. Astrophel and Stella, XXVIII. Sir Philip Sidney. ILP
You there, and you, and you. Bacchanal. Irving Layton. OBCV
You think that when a woman yields. In Your Arrogance. Lynne Lawner. ErPo
You thought my heart too far diseased. In Memoriam A. H. H., LXVI. Tennyson. VP
You trill by the treeful! Carolina Wrens. Edith Earnshaw. PoNC

You Went Away. Karl Krolow, *tr. fr. German by* Marianne Leibholz. MGP
You were a witness, lamp, you saw him kneel. All-knowing Lamp. *Unknown.* UnTE
You Were at the Dead River. George Abbe. FiSC
You were only a grainy face in the newspapers. Not That Hurried Grief. Lorenzo Thomas. OPP
You Were Shattered. Giuseppe Ungaretti, *tr. fr. Italian by* Lowry Nelson, Jr. CoIP
You, who behold in wonder Rome and all. Rome. Joachim du Bellay. *Fr.* Ruins of Rome. RBL
You Who Don't Believe It, *with music.* John A. Stone. SGR
You Who Were Made for This Music. Louis Zukofsky. CoPo
You who were the snake hidden under my house. Fire at Murdering Hut. Judith Wright. ACV
You whom I don't tell that I lie awake. Song. Rainer Maria Rilke. TwGP
You! whom the aged brandy does not burn. The Nightmare. Jascha Kessler. AmPC
You whom the kings saluted; who refused not. To the Unknown Soldier. G. K. Chesterton. MMA
You will come one day in a waver of love. Dream Girl. Carl Sandburg. MoLP
You Will Find a Joy in Service. Dorothy Conant Stroud. STF
You work in the factory all of your life. Too Old to Work. Joe Glazer. ThLM
You would think the fury of aerial bombardment. The Fury of Aerial Bombardment. Richard Eberhart. AnMoPo; ILP; MP; PoIE; PoPo; ToPo
You, you are all unloving, loveless, you. The Sea. D. H. Lawrence. HaSV
"You'd be better off dead!" they said. Ghost. R. H. Grenville. FiSC
You'd be surprised, I'm sure, to know. A Little Word. *Unknown.* STF
You'd better be. The Skunk. Dorothy Baruch. SoPo
You'd have men's hearts up from the dust. Near Perigord. Ezra Pound. CABL
You'le aske perhaps wherefore I stay. An Excuse of Absence. Thomas Carew. SeCP
You'll not forget these rocks and what I told you? Dialogue on the Headland. Robert Graves. ACV
Young Africa's Resolve. Dennis Osadebay. ACV
Young and Old. Charles Kingsley. *Fr.* The Water Babies, *ch. 2.* BiCB; LV; PoLF
(Old Song, The.) CBEP
Young Argonauts. Sheila Wingfield. SD
Young Author, The. Samuel Johnson. EiCP
Young Bather, The. *Unknown, tr. fr. Greek by* Louis Untermeyer. UnTE
Young Beichan and Susie Pye. *Unknown.* OnMSP
(Lord Bakeman, *with music.*) BSNS
(Lord Bateman, *with music;* BSO
(Young Bekie.) BuBa
Young Blondes. Gavin Ewart. ErPo
Young boys are stealing my loquats, The. Thieves. Perseus Adams. ACV
Young Bride, A. Sappho, *tr. fr. Greek by* Dante Gabriel Rossetti. SiGo
Young Buck's Sunday Blue. Kenneth Pitchford. *Fr.* Good for Nothing Man. CoPo
Young Charlotte. *Unknown.* BSNS; BSO, *with music*
Young child, Christ, is straight and wise, The. Child. Carl Sandburg. TRV
Young Cordwainer, The. Robert Graves. MoBS
Young Coridon and Phillis. Sir Charles Sedley. ErPo
Young Dandelion, The. Dinah Maria Mulock Craik. RePo
Young Democracy, *sel.* Bernard O'Dowd.
"Hark! Young Democracy from sleep." PoAu-1
Young Edmund. *Unknown.* BSNS
(Young Edmondale, *with music.*) BFSS
Young Endymion sleeps Endymion's sleep, The. Keats. Longfellow. AP
Young Flash the Deer. Thornton Burgess. RePo
Young Gazelle. Babette Deutsch. AnMoPo
Young Girl: Annam. Padraic Colum. LOW
Young girl stood beside me, The. The Orange Tree. John Shaw Neilson. PoAu-1
Young Girl's Song, A. Paul Heyse, *tr. fr. German by* E. H. Mueller. PoPl
Young Glass-Stainer, The. Thomas Hardy. CTC
Young Greek, Killed in the Wars, A. Richard Eberhart. AnMoPo
Young, having risen early, had gone, The. The Guardians. Geoffrey Hill. NePoEA-2
Young Henry came to Mary. The Paisley Officer (B *vers.*). *Unknown.* BSNS
Young Highland Girl Studying Poetry, A. Iain Crichton Smith. NePoEA-2; PP
Young homosexuals and hot girls, The. Lone Gentleman. "Pablo Neruda." ErPo
Young Hunting (B *vers., with music; C vers.*) *Unknown.* BFSS

(Love Henry, A *vers., with music.*) BFSS
Young I am, and yet unskill'd. Song for a Girl [*or* Sung by a Young Girl]. Dryden. ELP; ErPo; UnTE
Young I was who now am old. On Himself. Robert Herrick. UnTE
Young John. *Unknown.* BuBa
Young Johnny, *with music. Unknown.* BFSS
Young Johnny Scott, *with music. Unknown.* BFSS
Young Lincoln. Edwin Markham. LiPo
Young Love. Sara Teasdale. BoLP
Young man, alone, on the high bridge over the Tagus, A. The High Bridge above the Tagus River at Toledo. William Carlos Williams. CTC
Young Man in April, The. Rupert Brooke. BoLP
Young man left his native shores, A. Look Out Below! Charles R. Thatcher. PoAu-1
Young man loves a maiden, A. Heine, *tr. fr. German by* D. G. Wright. AGP
Young Man Who Wouldn't Plow Corn, The, *with music. Unknown.* BFSS
Young May Moon, The. Thomas Moore. ELP
Young Men Come Less Often, The—Isn't It So? Horace, *tr. fr. Latin by* Robert Fitzgerald. Odes, I, *25.* ErPo
Young men leave the country for the town, The. The Way to the Sea. Laurence Lerner. NePoEA-2
Young men riding in the street. Image from D'Orleans. Ezra Pound. LOW
Young people, all attention give and hear what I do say. The Blind Man's Regret. *Unknown.* BFSS
Young people who delight in sin [*or* hear, and I will tell]. Wicked Polly. *Unknown.* BFSS; BSO
Young Philander woo'd me long. Song. *Unknown.* ErPo
"Young poets, The," he murmured. Vernon Watkins. *Fr.* Yeats in Dublin. PP
Young President, The: March 1964. John Tagliabue. OPP
Young Rogers, the Miller, *with music. Unknown.* BSO
Young Sammy Watkins. *Unknown.* BBGG
Young Sea. Carl Sandburg. RePo
Young squirrel's mother, The, said, "Come out!" Squirrel in the Rain. Frances Frost. RePo
Young Strephon and Phillis. *Unknown.* UnTE
Young Tree, The. Umberto Saba, *tr. fr. Italian by* Thomas G. Bergin. CoIP
Young virgins all, I pray draw near. The Turkish Lady. *Unknown.* BSNS
Young Washington. Arthur Guiterman. PoSC
Young Wife, A. D. H. Lawrence. ELP; StP
Young Woman. Howard Nemerov. ErPo
Young women they [*or* they'll] run like hares on the mountain. Hares on the Mountain. *Unknown.* ErPo; UnTE
Your absence has gone through me. Separation. W. S. Merwin. AmPC
Your arms will clasp the gathered grain. The Island. Edwin Muir. PoIE
Your Body Is Stars. Stephen Spender. MoLP
Your body to hold, your perfect breasts. Undine. Irving Layton. ErPo
Your boy's-ambition was to be a Horseman. Stud Groom. John Glassco. OBCV
Your buttonholes for eyes, your solemn face. The Statue. John Fuller. NePoEA-2
Your children are not your children. On Children. Kahlil Gibran. *Fr.* The Prophet. PoPl
Your clear and living voice among the ruins. The Temple. Josephine W. Johnson. MoRP
Your closeness is not near enough. The Distance in Your Touch. "Will Inman." PoNC
Your door is shut against my tightened face. The White House. Claude McKay. AmNP
Your eyen two will slay me suddenly. *See* You yen two wol slee me sodenly.
Your eyes, your flowing hair. Auburn. Paul Verlaine. ErPo
Your face is an Eastern garden of response and gladness. Summa contra Gentiles. Paris Leary. CoPo
Your Face Is Written in My Soul. Garcilaso de la Vega, *tr. fr. Spanish by* Edwin Morgan. AnSP
Your Fair Looks Inflame My Desire. Thomas Campion. UnTE
Your fair looks urge my desire. Be Wise, and Fly Not. Thomas Campion. UnTE
Your flute. The Flute-Players. Jean-Joseph Rabéarivelo. SiGo
Your Footsteps on the Stair ("Your footsteps, light and hastening"). Zoe Kincaid Brockman. PoNC
Your ghost will walk, you lover of trees. "De Gustibus." Robert Browning. VP
Your Hands. Ernest Dowson. UnTE
Your hands lie open in the long fresh grass. Silent Noon. Dante Gabriel Rossetti. The House of Life, XIX. ELP; ILP; OBNC; VP
Your heifer's pretty neck is not yet broke. Too Young for Love. Horace. *Fr.* Odes. UnTE
Your husband will be with us at the treat. To His Mistress. Ovid. ErPo

Your kisses, and the way you curl. Leves Amores. Arthur Symons. UnTE

Your Last Drive. Thomas Hardy. OBNC

Your Lily Eyes Said Yes. Manuel González Prada, *tr. fr. Spanish by* Kate Flores. AnSP

Your Little Hands. Samuel Hoffenstein. BoLP

Your lonely song awoke me. October Night. Attilio Bertolucci. CoIP

Your Looks So Often Cast. Sir Thomas Wyatt. EnRePo

Your lovely hands. William Carlos Williams. *Fr.* Paterson. MoLP

Your midriff sags toward your knees. Woman with Girdle. Anne Sexton. ErPo

Your mind and you are our Sargasso Sea. Portrait d'une Femme. Ezra Pound. AP; CABA; MP

Your Money and Mine. *Unknown.* STF

"Your Need Is Greater than Mine." Theodore Enslin. CoPo

Your parents dislike me. Sweet Mary. *Unknown.* BSO

Your Place. John Oxenham. TRV

Your shadow I have seen you play with often. The Child and the Shadow. Elizabeth Jennings. NePoEA-2

Your smiling, or the hope, the thought of it. A Simile for Her Smile. Richard Wilbur. MoLP

Your smoky heart is witness. Ode to Nobody. Hans Magnus Enzensberger. MGP

Your Snow-white Shoulder. Heine, *tr. fr. German by* Louis Untermeyer. UnTE

Your tall French legs, my V for victory. Will to Win. F. R. Scott. OBCV

Your tear raises the column of song. The Portion. Jacques Dupin. CoFP

Your Teeth Are Ivory Towers. William Empson. ToPo

Your thighs are appletrees. Portrait of a Lady. William Carlos Williams. PoIE

Your thoughts dont have words every day. Emily Dickinson. DiPo

Your train leaves at eleven forty-five and it is now but eleven thirty-nine and a half. Dr. Fell and Points West. Ogden Nash. RePo

Your ugly token. Upon a Dead Man's Head. John Skelton. EnRePo; PoIE

Your voice, with clear location of June days. June Light. Richard Wilbur. CaFP

Your walking smiles across to me. Encounter. August Stramm. MGP

Your wistful eyes searched each one as he passed. Stray Dog. Charlotte Mish. PoLF

Your words, my friend, right healthful caustics, blame. Astrophel and Stella, XXI. Sir Philip Sidney. CABA

Your World. Georgia Douglas Johnson. AmNP

Your yen [*or* eyen] two wol slee me sodenly [*or* will slay me suddenly]. Mercil
es Beaute [*or* Three Roundels of Love Unreturned]. Chaucer. CBEP; CTC; MeEL; StP

You're ravishing and, plain to see. To His Girl. Martial. UnTE

You're starting, my boy, on life's journey. Have Courage, My Boy, to Say, No. *Unknown.* STF

You're through—now walking up and down. The Ageing Athlete. Neil Weiss. SD

Yours. Rabindranath Tagore. MoRP

Yourself. Jones Very. AmLP

Youth. Langston Hughes. BiCB

Youth and Age. Byron. GTBS-P

Youth and Age. Thomas Campion. *See* Though You Are Young.

Youth and Age. Samuel Taylor Coleridge. GTBS-P; OBNC; PoLF

Youth and Age on Beaulieu River, Hants. John Betjeman. MP

Youth and Art. Robert Browning. CTC

Youth and Beauty. Aurelian Townsend. SeCP

Youth cocks his hat and rides up the street. Points of View. Amy Lowell. LOW

Youth Dreams, The. Rainer Maria Rilke, *tr. fr. German by* Ludwig Lewisohn. SiGo

Youth gone, and beauty gone if ever there. Monna Innominata, XIV. OBNC; VP

Youth, greedy for burdens. Happiness. Umberto Saba. CoIP

Youth, I offer you this silver cup. The Fount. Rubén Darío. AnSP

Youth in Arms, *sel.* Harold Monro.
  Carrion. MMA

Youth is conservative. A Human Instinct. Christopher Morley. *Fr.* Translations from the Chinese. EvOK

Youth rambles on life's arid mount. The Progress of Poesy. Matthew Arnold. PP

Youth saluted all with courtesy, The. On Sailing the Wide Ocean. Luis de Góngora. *Fr.* The Solitudes. RBL

Youth Sings a Song of Rosebuds. Countee Cullen. PoLF

Youth's Agitations. Matthew Arnold. CBEP

Youth's Antiphony. Dante Gabriel Rossetti. The House of Life, XIII. VP

Youth's Spring-Tribute. Dante Gabriel Rossetti. The House of Life, XIV. VP

Youth's the Season. John Gay. *Fr.* The Beggar's Opera. WiR

You've Filled My Mind So Full of Grief. Guido Cavalcanti, *tr. fr. Italian by* James J. Wilhelm. AnML

You've lost your religion, the Rabbi said. Debate with the Rabbi. Howard Nemerov. PoPl

Ypres. Laurence Binyon. MMA

Yule-clog sparkled keen with frost, The. Tennyson. *Fr.* In Memoriam A. H. H., LXXVIII. TRV

Yung Wind, *sels.* Confucius, *tr. fr. Chinese by* Ezra Pound. *Fr.* The Classic Anthology. CTC
  Baroness Mu Impeded in Her Wish to Help Famine Victims in Wei.
  Sans Equity and sans Poise.

Yvain, *sel.* Chrétien de Troyes, *tr. fr. French by* Daisy Aldan. Complaint of the Weavers. AnML

Z

Zapata & the Landlord. Alfred B. Spellman. NNP

Zaph Describes the Haunts of Malzah. Charles Heavysege. *Fr.* Saul. OBCV

Zebra. "Isak Dinesen." GoJo

Zebra Dun, The. *Unknown.* RePo

Zechariah. Earl Marlatt. MoRP

Zen Archer, The. James Kirkup. EaLo

Zenith. Juan Ramón Jiménez, *tr. fr. Spanish by* Kate Flores. AnSP

Zephyr. Eugene Fitch Ware. PoLF

Zephyr returns, and scatters everywhere. Petrarch. *Fr.* Sonnets to Laura: To Laura in Death. RBL

Zermatt: To the Matterhorn. Thomas Hardy. OBNC

Zillah (A *vers.*). *Unknown.* BSNS
  (Diamond Ring, The, B *vers.*) BSNS

Zillebeke Brook. Edmund Blunden. MMA

Zobo Bird, The. Frank A. Collymore. GoJo

Zone. Louise Bogan. PoCh

Zonnebeke Road, The. Edmund Blunden. MMA

Zoo of You, The. Arthur Freeman. ErPo

Zooming across the sky. Up in the Air. James S. Tippett. SoPo

Zooming overhead, A . . . and steel-framed birds. Aladdin Throws Away His Lamp. Elias Lieberman. LV

Zulu Girl, The. Roy Campbell. AnMoPo; PoPl

"Zut!" cried the Princess, with a breezy smile. Romantic Episode. Vincent Starrett. FiSC

AUTHOR INDEX

"A., F. P." *See* ADAMS, FRANKLIN
   PIERCE.
"A. E." *See* "Æ."
"A. M. N." *See* "N., A. M."
"A. W." *See* "W., A."
ABBE, GEORGE. Changed, *sel.*
   Clean Gentleman, The.
   Death Is a Little Thing.
   Passer, The.
   You Were at the Dead River.
ABRAMS, ROBERT J. Two Poems
ABSE, DANNIE. Emperors of the Island.
   Letter to Alex Comfort.
   Mountaineers, The.
   Trial, The.
   Verses at Night.
ABU-L-HASAN AL-HUSRI. In Mourning.
ABU-L-HASAN BEN AL-QABTURNUH. In
   Battle.
ABU NUWAS [*or* NUAS]. Escape, An
ABU SALT UMAYYA. White Horse, The.
ABU ZAKARIYYA. Spear, The.
ACHARYA, SRI ANANDA. Witness, The.
ACHILLINI, CLAUDIO. Sonnet, Written
   by a Nymph in Her Own Blood, A.
ADAM DE LA HALLE. All Too Much I
   Long to See.
   Love and My Lady, Too.
   So Much the More as I Draw near My
   Land.
   To All My Dainty Loves, Goodbye.
ADAM, HELEN. Fair Young Wife, The.
   Step Mother, The.
ADAMS, ARTHUR HENRY. Australian, The.
ADAMS, BILL (Bertram Martin Adams).
   Peg-Leg's Fiddle.
ADAMS, FRANKLIN PIERCE ("F. P. A.").
   Ballade of Lawn Tennis, A.
   Baseball Note.
   Baseball's Sad Lexicon.
   "Such Stuff as Dreams."
   To a Thesaurus.
   Us Poets.
ADAMS, GEORGIA B. Family Altar, The.
   Helping Hand, A.
   Hour of Prayer, The.
   Secret Place of Prayer, The.
   Thank Thee, Lord.
ADAMS, HELEN BAKER. No Doubt.
ADAMS, JAMES BARTON. At a Cowboy
   Dance.
   Cowboy's Life, The, *at.*
ADAMS, JOHN QUINCY. Lip and the
   Heart, The.
   Wants of Man, The.
ADAMS, LÉONIE (Mrs. William Troy).
   Bell Tower.
   Country Summer.
   Lullaby: "Hush, lullay."
   Song from a Country Fair.
   Sundown.
   Those Not Elect.
   Words for the Raker of Leaves.
ADAMS, PERSEUS. Thieves.
ADAMS, SARAH FLOWER (Mrs. William
   Bridges Adams). Nearer, My God
   to Thee.
   Nearer to Thee.
ADCOCK, FLEUR. Christmas Dawn.
ADDISON, JOSEPH. Ode: "Spacious firm-
   ament on high, The."
   Spacious Firmament on High, The.
"ADELER, MAX" (Charles Heber Clark).
   In Memoriam.
   Obituary.
   Willie.
"Æ" (George William Russell). Chiv-
   alry.
   Promise.
   Reconciliation.
   Tragedy.

Unity.
Vesture of the Soul, The.
AESCHYLUS. Agamemnon, *sel.*
   Signal Fire, The. *Fr.* Agamemnon.
AGEE, JAMES. Happy Hen, The.
   Lyrics, *sels.*
   Millions Are Learning How.
   Sunday: Outskirts of Knoxville, Ten-
   nessee.
AGNES DE NAVARRE-CHAMPAGNE. Lover,
   as God May Comfort Me.
   Without My Heart, Love, Thou Shalt
   Not Depart.
AGNEW, JOAN. Sons of the Kings.
AIKEN, CONRAD. Coming Forth by Day
   of Osiris Jones, The, *sel.*
   Discordants.
   Doctors' Row.
   Elder Tree.
   Frostbite.
   Goya.
   Improvisations: Light and Snow, *sel.*
   Lovers, The.
   Mayflower.
   Music.
   Music I Heard. *Fr.* Discordants.
   North Infinity Street.
   Nursery, The. *Fr.* The Coming Forth
   by Day of Osiris Jones.
   One Star Fell and Another. *Fr.* Prel-
   udes for Memnon.
   Poem: "And this digester, this digester
   of food." *Fr.* Time in the Rock.
   Portrait of a Girl. *Fr.* Priapus and
   the Pool.
   Preludes for Memnon, *sels.*
   Priapus and the Pool, *sels.*
   Quarrel, The.
   Road, The.
   Room, The.
   Sea Holly.
   Senlin, a Biography, *sel.*
   Sound of Breaking.
   Stone Too Can Pray.
   Tetélestai.
   Time in the Rock, *sel.*
   Walk in the Garden, The.
   When Trout Swim down Great Or-
   mond Street. *Fr.* Priapus and the
   Pool.
   Winter for a Moment Takes the Mind;
   the Snow. *Fr.* Preludes for Memnon.
AIKIN, ANNA LETITIA. *See* BARBAULD,
   ANNA LETITIA.
AIRAS NÚÑEZ [*or* NUNES]. Bailada:
   "Let's dance now, all of us, all of
   us, oh my maidens."
   Let the Three of Us Now Dance, Oh
   Friends.
   Summertime Delights Me, The.
   When Truth Disappeared from the
   World.
AKENSIDE, MARK. Inscription.
   Pleasures of Imagination, The, *sel.*
   Poet, The; a Rhapsody.
"AKHMATOVA, ANNA" (Anna Andreyevna
   Gorenko). Upon the Hard Crest.
ALABASTER, WILLIAM. Sonnet: "Bee-
   hould a cluster to itt selfe a vine."
   Sonnet: "Haile gracefull morning of
   eternall daye."
   Sonnet: "Holy, holy, holy Lord un-
   named."
   Sonnet: "Jesu thie love within mee is
   soe maine."
   Sonnet: "My soule a world is by con-
   traccion."
   Sonnet: "Night, the starless night of
   passion, The."
   Sonnet: "Now I have found thee, I will
   ever more."

Sonnet: "Now that the midd day heate
   doth scorch my shame."
Sonnet: "O starry temple of unvalted
   space."
Sonnet: "O sweete, and bitter monu-
   ments of paine."
Sonnet: "Sunne begins uppon my heart
   to shine, The."
Sonnet: "Three sortes of teares doe
   from myne eies distraine."
Sonnet: "Way feare with thy projectes,
   noe false fyre, A."
Sonnet: "What meaneth this, that
   Christ an hymne did singe."
Sonnet: "When without tears I looke
   on Christ, I see."
ALAMANNI, LUIGI. On His Return to
   Italy.
ALBERT, HEINRICH. Farewell.
ALBRECHT VON JOHANSDORF. I Found
   without a Guard.
   If I Saw One Who Could Say He Was
   Come from Her.
   This I Know, How Love Begins to Be.
ALCAMO, CIULLO D'. *See* CIULLO D'AL-
   CAMO.
ALCÁZAR, BALTASAR DE. Tres Cosas.
ALDINGTON, RICHARD. After Two Years.
   Battlefield.
   Bombardment.
   Carnival Songs, *sel., tr.*
   Lesbia.
   In the Trenches.
   In the Tube.
   Soliloquy 2.
   Triumph of Bacchus and Ariadne, *tr.*
   Fr. Carnival Songs.
ALDIS, DOROTHY. Alike.
   Brooms.
   Clouds.
   First Winter's Day.
   Hiding.
   Hungry Waves, The.
   I Have to Have It.
   In Spring in Warm Weather.
   In the Barnyard.
   Kick a Little Stone.
   Lucky Thing, A.
   My Brother.
   Night and Morning.
   Our Silly Little Sister.
   Radiator Lions.
   Riddle: What Am I?
   Somersault.
   Then.
   Twins, The.
   What They Are For.
   When.
   When I Was Lost
ALDRICH, HENRY. Christ Church Bells.
ALDRICH, THOMAS BAILEY. Memory.
ALDRIDGE, RICHARD. Pine Bough, The.
ALEXANDER, CECIL FRANCES (Mrs. Wil-
   liam Alexander). All Things Bright
   and Beautiful.
   Childhood's Trials.
   Good Tidings of Great Joy!
   We May Not Know.
ALEXANDER, JOSEPH ADDISON. Doomed
   Man, The.
ALEXANDER, SIR WILLIAM. *See* STIR-
   LING, WILLIAM ALEXANDER, EARL
   OF.
ALEXANDER, MRS. WILLIAM. *See* ALEX-
   ANDER, CECIL FRANCES.
ALFONSO X, KING OF CASTILE AND LEON.
   Song XVIII: "In order to remove
   us."
   Song VII: "We should love Saint
   Mary."
ALI BEN ABU TALEB. Make Friends.

ALI BEN HARIQ. Oars of the Galley, The.
ALIGHIERI, DANTE. *See* DANTE ALI-
GHIERI.
ALLAN, EDWIN. Ass, The.
ALLAN, JAMES ALEXANDER. Breaking.
ALLANA, GULAM ALI. Spectre Is on the
Move, The.
ALLEN LESLIE HOLDSWORTH. Reaper,
The.
ALLEN, MARIE LOUISE. First Snow.
Five Years Old.
Mitten Song, The.
Sneezing.
ALLEN, SAMUEL ("Paul Vesey"). Ameri-
can Gothic.
If the Stars Should Fall.
Love Song.
Moment Please, A.
To Satch.
ALLINGHAM, WILLIAM. Abbot of Inis-
falen, The.
Across the Sea.
Amy Margaret.
Earth's Night.
Fairies, The.
Four Ducks on a Pond.
Meadowsweet.
Robin Redbreast.
Spring: The Lover and the Birds.
ALLISON, YOUNG EWING. Derelict.
ALMA-TADEMA, LAURENCE. If No One
Ever Marries Me.
AMIS, KINGSLEY. After Goliath.
Autobiographical Fragment.
Dream of Fair Women, A.
Ever-fixed Mark, An.
Masters.
Nothing to Fear.
On a Portrait of Mme. Rimsky-Korsa-
kov.
Science Fiction.
Sight Unseen.
Terrible Beauty.
Tribute to the Founder, A.
AMMONS, A. R. Belief.
ANA, MARCOS. To the Faithful.
ANACREON. Design for a Bowl.
Heat.
Picture, The.
To His Young Mistress.
Woman's Arms.
"ANGELUS SILESIUS" (Johannes Schef-
fler). In Thine Own Heart.
ANDERSEN, HANS CHRISTIAN. Pearl, The.
ANDERSON, ETHEL LOUISA MASON. Bu-
colic Eclogues, *sel.*
Kunai-mai-pa Mo.
Waking, Child, While You Slept. *Fr.*
Bucolic Eclogues.
ANDERSON, MAXWELL. Lucifer.
ANDERSON, PATRICK. Camp.
Canoe.
Capital Square.
Sleighride.
ANGERMAYER, FRANCES. Conversion.
ANGIOLIERI, CECCO. Despair Herself Re-
gards Me as Her Son.
If I Were Fire, I'd Burn the World
Away.
ANGUS, MARION. Alas! Poor Queen.
ANSEN, ALAN. Death of Nearchus, The.
Fit of Something against Something, A.
ANSTER, JOHN. Faust, *sel., tr.*
Lose This Day Loitering, *tr. Fr.* Faust.
Prologue: "Lose this day loitering,
'twill be the same story," *tr. Fr.*
Faust.
ANTONINUS, BROTHER (William Ever-
son). August.
Canticle to the Christ in the Holy
Eucharist, A.
Canticle to the Waterbirds, A.
Hospice of the Word.
In All These Acts.
Jacob and the Angel.
March.
Presence, The.
Siege of Silence, A.
Song the Body Dreamed in the Spirit's
Mad Behest, The.
Stranger, The.
What Birds Were There.
APPLETON, EVERARD JACK. Woman Who
Understands, The.

ARBERRY, A. J. As Salt Resolved in the
Ocean, *tr.*
At Peace, *tr.*
Miracle of Spring, The, *tr.*
Perfect Love, *tr.*
ARCHIBALD, ESTHER. In My Place.
ARCHILOCHUS. Be Still, My Soul.
Tossed on a Sea of Trouble.
ARETINO, PIETRO. Stragglers.
ARGENTARIUS, MARCUS. Rumoresque
Senum Severiorum.
ARISTAENETUS. Pleasing Constraint, The.
ARIOSTO, LUDOVICO [*or* LODOVICO]. Cap-
itolo VIII.
ARISTOTLE. Epitaph for Chaeroneia.
ARKELL, REGINALD. New Garden, The.
Public Nuisance, A.
ARMATTOE, R. E. G. Deep down the
Blackman's Mind.
ARMOUR, RICHARD. Ant, The.
Covering the Subject.
Good Sportsmanship.
Horses.
Money.
Love Life (and Death) of a Moose,
The.
New Technique.
One Down.
So Soon?
Study Habits.
To Have and Too Old.
ARMSTRONG, JOHN. Imitation of Spen-
ser, An.
ARMSTRONG, MARGARET D. Invocation
for the New Year.
ARMSTRONG, MARTIN. Miss Thompson
Goes Shopping.
ARNOLD, SIR EDWIN. Destiny.
ARNOLD, IRENE (Mrs. Major Arnold).
Pray!
ARNOLD MATTHEW. Absence. *Fr.* Swit-
zerland.
Austerity of Poetry.
Buried Life, The.
Calm Soul of All Things. *Fr.* Lines
Written in Kensington Gardens.
Caution to Poets, A.
Destiny.
Dover Beach.
Dream, A.
Empedocles on Etna, *sel.*
Euphrosyne.
Faded Leaves.
Farewell, A. *Fr.* Switzerland.
Forsaken Merman, The.
Human Life.
In Harmony with Nature.
In Utrumque Paratus.
Isolation: To Marguerite. *Fr.* Swit-
zerland.
Lake, The. *Fr.* Switzerland.
Last Word, The.
Lines Written in Kensington Gardens,
sel.
Longing. *Fr.* Faded Leaves.
Meeting. *Fr.* Switzerland
Memorial Verses.
On the Rhine. *Fr.* Faded Leaves.
Palladium.
Parting. *Fr.* Switzerland.
Philomela.
Progress of Poesy, The.
Quiet Work.
Requiescat.
Resignation.
River, The. *Fr.* Faded Leaves.
Rugby Chapel.
S. S. *Lusitania.*
Scholar-Gipsy, The.
Self-Dependence.
Separation. *Fr.* Faded Leaves.
Shakespeare.
Sohrab and Rustum.
Song of the Creatures, The, *tr.*
Song of the Muses, The.
Stanzas from the Grande Chartreuse.
Strayed Reveller, The.
Summer Night, A.
Switzerland.
Terrace at Berne, The. *Fr.* Switzer-
land.
Thyrsis.
To a Friend.
To Marguerite. *Fr.* Switzerland.

To Marguerite—Continued. *Fr.* Swit-
zerland.
Too Late. *Fr.* Faded Leaves.
Tristram and Iseult.
Urania.
We Cannot Kindle.
West London.
Written in Emerson's Essays.
Youth's Agitations.
ARP, HANS. Baobab.
Black Eggs.
Kaspar Is Dead.
Ineffertile Lea, The.
ARRIETA, RAFAEL ALBERTO. January
Night.
ARTMANN, HANS CARL. Death by Water.
ASBAJE, JUANA DE. *See* JUANA INÉS DE
LA CRUZ, SISTER.
ASHBERY, JOHN. Europe.
"ASMUS." *See* CLAUDIUS, MATTHIAS.
ASQUITH, HERBERT. Birthday Gifts.
Elephant, The.
Hairy Dog, The.
Skating.
Volunteer, The.
ASTLEY, THEA. Droving Man.
ATKINS, RUSSELL. At War.
Irritable Song.
It's Here in the.
ATO TOBIRA. Once Only.
ATTERBURY, FRANCIS. Impromptu.
Song: "Fair Sylvia, cease to blame my
youth."
ATWELL, ROY. Some Little Bug.
AUCHTERLONIE, DOROTHY (Mrs. H. M.
Green). Apopemptic Hymn.
AUDELAY, JOHN. Be True to Your Con-
dition in Life.
In His Utter Wretchedness.
AUDEN, WYSTAN HUGH. As I Walked
Out One Evening.
Atlantis.
Ballad: O What Is That Sound?
Chorus: "Doom is dark and deeper
than any sea-dingle."
Composer, The.
Concluding Chorus: "Though he be-
lieve it, no man is strong." *Fr.*
Paid on Both Sides.
Consider This and in Our Time.
Cultural Presupposition, The.
Elegy for J. F. K.
For the Time Being; a Christmas
Oratorio, *sels.*
He Is the Way. *Fr.* For the Time
Being.
Horae Canonicae, *sels.*
In Memory of W. B. Yeats.
In Praise of Limestone.
In Time of War, *sel.*
James Honeyman.
Law like Love.
Lay Your Sleeping Head, My Love.
Love Feast, The.
Musée des Beaux Arts.
Night Mail.
Note on Intellectuals.
Now the Leaves Are Falling Fast.
O What Is That Sound Which So
Thrills the Ear?
O Where Are You Going? *Fr.* The
Orators.
On This Island, *sel.*
Orators, The, *sel.*
Over the Heather the Wet Wind Blows.
Paid on Both Sides, *sel.*
Petition.
Powers and Times Are Not Gods. *Fr.*
For the Time Being.
Prime. *Fr.* Horae Canonicae.
Refugee Blues.
Roman Soldier on the Wall, A.
Roman Wall Blues.
Runner.
Sea and the Mirror, The, *sel.*
Seascape.
September 1, 1939.
Sext. *Fr.* Horae Canonicae.
Shield of Achilles, The.
Sob, Heavy World.
Song: "Deftly, admiral, cast your fly."
Song for St. Cecilia's Day.
Song of the Master and Boatswain.
Fr. The Sea and the Mirror.

Spain 1937.
Stop All the Clocks.
Their Lonely Betters.
Unknown Citizen, The.
Who's Who.
Will You Turn a Deaf Ear.
AUDEN, WYSTAN HUGH, and LEIF SJÖBERG. Lord—Thine the Day, tr.
AUDIBERTI, JACQUES. Suffering.
Transcendence Wouldn't Do.
AUGUSTINE, SAINT. Take My Heart.
Thou Hast Made Us for Thyself.
"AUNT MARY [or MAY]." See LATHBURY, MARY ARTEMISIA.
AUSLANDER, JOSEPH. Blackbird Suddenly, A.
If We Break Faith.
Sonnets to Laura, sels., tr.
AUSTIN, ALBERT GORDON. Chez-Nous.
AUSTIN, MARY. Brown Bear, The.
Charm for Going a-Hunting.
Grizzly Bear.
Lament of a Man for His Son, tr.
Neither Spirit nor Bird, tr.
Rhyming Riddles, sels.
Song of Greatness, A, tr.
Texas Trains and Trails.
AVISON, MARGARET. Butterfly, The.
Meeting Together of Poles & Latitudes: In Prospect.
Mordent for a Melody.
New Year's Poem.
Perspective.
Stray Dog, near Ecully, Valley of the Rhône.
Watershed.
"AVOND, JAN VAN." See SLATER, FRANCIS CAREY.
AYER, ETHAN. Exceeding Great Army, An.
AYERS, VIVIAN. Instantaneous.
AYRE, ANNA CHANDLER. Jack o'Lantern.
AYRES, PHILIP. Adone, L', sel., tr.
Apollo and Daphne, tr.
Complains, Being Hind'red the Sight of His Nymph, tr.
Cynthia Sporting, tr.
Describes the Place Where Cynthia Is Sporting Herself, tr.
Fly, The, tr.
Proem, The: To Love, tr. Fr. L'Adone.
Sonnet, Written by a Nymph in Her Own Blood, A, tr.
AYSCOUGH, FLORENCE, and AMY LOWELL. See LOWELL, AMY, and FLORENCE AYSCOUGH.
AYTON [or AYTOUN], SIR ROBERT. To His Forsaken Mistress, at.
AYTOUN, WILLIAM EDMONSTOUNE [or EDMONDSTONE]. Execution of Montrose, The.
Laureate, The.

B

"B., C. B." Because You Prayed.
"B. V." ("Bysshe Vanolis"). See THOMSON, JAMES.
BABCOCK, DONALD CAMPBELL. In a Garden.
BABCOCK, MALTBIE DAVENPORT. Be Strong.
Companionship.
"Give Us This Day Our Daily Bread."
This Is My Father's World.
BACHELLER, IRVING. Whisperin' Bill.
BACHMANN, INGEBORG. Every Day.
Firstborn Land, The.
Fog Land.
BACMEISTER, RHODA WARNER. Bridges.
Galoshes.
BACON, FRANCIS. In Vitam Humanan.
Life.
BACON, JOSEPHINE DODGE DASKAM. Brother, Lift Your Flag with Mine.
BAGG, ROBERT. Ronald Wyn.
See That One?
Soft Answers.
BAHAR. Miracle of Spring, The.

BAÏF, JEAN ANTOINE DE. Carpe Diem.
BAILEY, ALFRED GOLDSWORTHY. Algonkian Burial.
Colonial Set.
Miramichi Lightning.
Off Saguenay.
BAILEY, LIBERTY HYDE. Farmer.
BAILEY, MARGARET. Prayer, A: "God, give me sympathy and sense."
BAIRD, MARTHA. Effortlessly Democratic Sante Fe Trail.
BAKER, SIR HENRY WILLIAMS. Lord Is My Shepherd, The.
BAKER, ISAAC W. Arrival of the San Francisco.
O! California.
BAKER, KARLE WILSON ("Charlotte Wilson"). Days.
I Shall Be Loved as Quiet Things.
BALDWIN, MICHAEL. Death on a Live Wire.
BALDWIN, WILLIAM. Christ, My Beloved.
BALES, C. O. Discipleship.
BALL, HUGO. Sun, The.
BAMBERGER, AUGUSTUS WRIGHT. Out of the Vast.
BANGS, JOHN KENDRICK. Little Elf, The.
Little Elfman, The.
Teddy's Wonderings.
BANKS, JOHN. Description of London, A.
Explanatory Epistle, An.
On Fame.
BANNING, LEX. Captain Arthur Phillip and the Birds.
BARBAULD, ANNA LETITIA (Anna Letitia Aikin). Life.
BARBERINI, FRANCESCO DA. Virgin Declares Her Beauties, A.
BARHAM, RICHARD HARRIS. See "INGOLDSBY, THOMAS."
BARING-GOULD, SABINE. Night.
Onward, Christian Soldiers.
BARKER, GEORGE. Channel Crossing.
Epistle I: "Meeting a monster of mourning wherever I go."
Epitaph for the Poet.
Evening Star.
First Cycle of Love Poems, sel.
Little Song in Assisi, A.
My Joy, My Jockey, My Gabriel. Fr. First Cycle of Love Poems.
News of the World II.
Secular Elegies.
Secular Elegy V.
Sonnet to My Mother.
Stanzas on a Visit to Longleat House in Wiltshire, October 1953.
Summer Song I ("I looked into my heart to write").
Summer Song II ("Soft is the collied night, and cool").
To My Mother.
To My Son, sel.
True Confession of George Barker, The, sel.
BARKER, RICHARD. Night of the President's Funeral.
BARLOW, JOEL. Advice to a Raven in Russia December, 1812.
Columbiad, The, sel.
Hasty-Pudding, The.
One Centred System. Fr. The Columbiad.
BARLOW, ROBERT HAYWARD. Edgar Allan Poe.
Mythological Episode.
Shub-Ad.
Warning to Snake-Killers.
BARNARD, LADY ANNE. See LINDSAY, LADY ANNE.
BARNES, BARNABE. Parthenope. Fr. Parthenophil and Parthenophe.
Parthenophil and Parthenophe, sels.
BARNES, WILLIAM. Burncombe Hollow.
Clote, The.
In Church.
May.
Melhill Feast.
Musings.
Rustic Childhood.
Rwose in the Dark, The.
Shellbrook.
Sonnet: Leaves.

Troubles of the Day.
White an' Blue.
Wife a-Lost, The.
Wind at the Door, The.
Winter Night, A.
BARNEY, WILLIAM D. Gourd-Heads, The.
In the Beginninging.
Panther Possible, The.
BARNFIELD [or BARNEFIELD], RICHARD. Epitaph on Drake.
Nightingale, The. Fr. The Passionate Pilgrim.
BARNOUW, ADRIAAN J. For translations from Dutch, see SiGo.
BARO, GENE. Cherry.
Horsemen, The.
Judges, Judges.
Ladder, The.
Lament for Better or Worse.
Northern Spring, A.
Northwind.
Sebastian.
BARR, ALICE M. Guard Thy Tongue.
BARRATT, KEN. Burke and Wills.
BARRINGTON, PAULINE B. White Iris, A.
BARSTOW, HENRY H. If Easter Be Not True.
BARTLETT, PAUL. Apology.
City Rain.
Finale.
Lèse Majesté.
Love's Ending.
So Independently the Cedars Grow.
BARTOLINI, LUIGI. Colors.
Rhyme from the Confino.
BARUCH, DOROTHY WALTER. Automobile Mechanics.
Barber's Clippers.
Cat.
I Would Like to Be—a Bee.
Lawn-Mower.
Merry-go-round.
Rabbits.
Skunk, The.
BASHO (Matsuo Basho). Beauty.
Cicada-Shell.
Haiku: "Ancient pond, The."
Harbingers.
In My New Clothing.
Monkey's Raincoat, The.
Old Pond, The.
On the Mountain Pass.
On the Road to Nara.
Seven Poems, sels.
Sun Path, The.
Three Haiku.
Wake Up! Wake Up!
BASKO. Play About. Do.
BASS, GEORGE HUSTON. Life Cycle in the Delta.
BASSE, WILLIAM. Angler's Song, The, sel.
Elegy on Shakespeare.
On the Tombs in Westminster Abbey, at.
Tombs in Westminster, The, at.
BASTARD, THOMAS. On a Child Beginning to Talk.
BATES, DAVID. Speak Gently.
BATES, KATHARINE LEE. America the Beautiful.
BAUDELAIRE, CHARLES. Cat, The.
Giantess.
Ill Luck.
Invitation to the Voyage.
Jewels, The.
Landscape.
Metamorphoses of the Vampire.
Music.
BAUER, WALTER. Being Here.
To Sing in Ancient Measures.
BAUGHAN, BLANCHE EDITH. In Exile.
BAX, CLIFFORD. Turn Back, O Man.
BAXTER, JAMES KEIR. Poem by the Clock Tower, Sumner.
Rope for Harry Fat, A.
BAXTER, RICHARD. Love Breathing Thanks and Praise, sel.
BAYLDON, ARTHUR ALBERT DAWSON. Marlowe.
Sunset.
BAYLEBRIDGE, WILLIAM (originally Charles William Blocksidge). Life's Testament, sels.
Love Redeemed, sels.

BEATRIZ [*or* BEATRITZ] DE DIA. Estat ai en greu cossirier.
I Dwell in Deep Anxiety.
BEATTIE, JAMES. Minstrel, The; or, The Progress of Genius, *sel.*
BEAUMONT, FRANCIS. Masque of the Inner Temple and Gray's Inne, *sel.*
On the Tombs in Westminster Abbey, *at.*
Pining for Love.
Shake Off Your Heavy Trance. *Fr.* Masque of the Inner Temple and Gray's Inne.
Tombs in Westminster, The, *at.*
BEAUMONT, FRANCIS, *and* JOHN FLETCHER. Bridal Song. *Fr.* The Maid's Tragedy.
Come, Sleep. *Fr.* The Woman-Hater.
Hold Back Thy Hours [Dark Night]. *Fr.* The Maid's Tragedy.
Maid's Tragedy, The, *sels.*
To Bed, to Bed. *Fr.* The Maid's Tragedy.
Woman-Hater, The, *sel.*
BEAUMONT, SIR JOHN. To His Late Majesty, Concerning the True Form of English Poetry, *sel.*
BEAUMONT, JOSEPH. Gnat, The.
BEAVER, BRUCE. Cow Dance.
BECHER, JOHANNES R. Ecstasy Dream Grace, *sel.*
If I Roared. *Fr.* Ecstasy Dream Grace.
Throttled on a String of Pearls. *Fr.* Transfiguration.
Transfiguration, *sel.*
BECHTEL, LOUISE SEAMAN. Grandfather Frog.
BECKER, EDNA. Reflections.
BECKER, JOHN. Are You a Marsupial?
Feather or Fur.
For Maria at Four.
Tale of the Skunk and Poor Jez, The.
Things to Learn About.
BECKETT, SAMUEL. Describes Rationally the Irrational Effects of Love, *tr.*
Verses Expressing the Feelings of a Lover, *tr.*
BÉCQUER, GUSTAVO ADOLFO. Arrow Flying Past, An.
As the Breeze That Cools the Blood.
Dark in a Corner of the Room.
Darkling Swallows Will Come Again, The.
Gentle Breeze with a Whispered Cry, The.
Great Waves Breaking with a Roar.
I Am Ardent, I Am Brunette.
I Lay Awake, Wandering in That Limbo.
Into Her Eyes a Tear Crept.
Invisible Atoms of the Air, The.
It Goes against My Interest to Confess It.
Rima.
Sighs Are Air, and Go to the Air.
They Closed Her Eyes.
To See the Hours of Fever.
When They Told Me I Felt the Cold.
Where Do I Come From?
BEDDOES, THOMAS LOVELL. Alpine Spirit's Song.
Carrion Crow, The. *Fr.* Death's Jest Book.
Death's Jest Book, *sels.*
Dirge: "If thou wilt ease thine heart." *Fr.* Death's Jest Book.
Dirge: "Swallow leaves her nest, The." *Fr.* Death's Jest Book.
Dirge: "We do lie beneath the grass." *Fr.* Death's Jest Book.
Dream-Pedlary.
How Many Times? *Fr.* Torrismond.
Ivory Gate, The, *sel.*
L'Envoi: "Who findeth comfort in the stars and flowers." *Fr.* Death's Jest Book.
Lord Alcohol.
Mighty Thoughts of an Old World, The. *Fr.* The Ivory Gate.
Old Adam. *Fr.* Death's Jest Book.
Old Ghost, The.
Phantom-Wooer, The.
Second Brother, The, *sel.*

Song: "Strew not earth with empty stars." *Fr.* The Second Brother.
Song: "We have bathed, where none have seen us." *Fr.* Death's Jest Book.
Song by Isbrand. *Fr.* Death's Jest Book.
Sonnet: To Tartar, a Terrier Beauty.
Subterranean City, A.
Tailor, The.
Threnody: "Far away."
Torrismond, *sel.*
Under the Lime Tree, *tr.*
Voice from the Waters, A. *Fr.* Death's Jest Book.
We Do Lie beneath the Grass. *Fr.* Death's Jest Book.
Wolfram's Song. *Fr.* Death's Jest Book.
BEDE [*or* BEDA *or* BAEDA], THE VENERABLE. O God that art the sole hope of the world.
BEECHER, JOHN. Veteran's Day of Recollection, A.
BEECHING, HENRY CHARLES. Prayer: "God who created me."
BEER, MORRIS ABEL. Church in the Heart, The.
BEER, PATRICIA. Fifth Sense, The.
BEERBOHM, SIR MAX. Sequelula to "The Dynasts," A.
BEERS, HENRY AUGUSTIN. Biftek aux Champignons.
BEERS, LORNA. "Soft Sell."
Top Hat and Tales.
BEHN, APHRA. Abdelazar, *scl.*
Amyntas Led Me to a Grove. *Fr.* The Dutch Lover.
Beneath a Cool Shade.
Dutch Lover, The, *sel.*
Love in Fantastic Triumph. *Fr.* Abdelazar.
Lycidus, *scl.*
O What Pleasure 'Tis to Find. *Fr.* Lycidus.
Rover, The, *sel.*
That Beauty I Ador'd Before.
When Damon First Began to Love. *Fr.* The Rover.
Willing Mistress, The. *Fr.* The Dutch Lover.
BEHN, HARRY. Christmas Carol, A.
Curiosity.
Follow the Leader.
Gnome, The.
Growing Up.
Hallowe'en.
Invitation.
Kite, The.
Last Leaf, The.
Make Believe.
Others.
Surprise.
Trees.
Visitors.
"BELL, ACTON." *See* BRONTË, ANNE.
BELL, CHARLES G. Banana.
Fire, The.
Girl Walking.
This Little Vigil.
"BELL, CURRER." *See* BRONTË, CHARLOTTE.
"BELL, ELLIS." *See* BRONTË, EMILY.
BELLAMANN, HENRY. Charleston Garden, A.
BELLAY, JOACHIM DU. *See* DU BELLAY, JOACHIM.
BELLE, JOHN CROSS. Secret Prayer.
BELLERBY, FRANCES. Old Ones, The.
BELLI, GIUSEPPE GIOACCHINO. Confessor, The.
BELLOC, HILAIRE. Courtesy.
Dedication on the Gift of a Book to a Child.
Dedicatory Ode, *sel.*
Early Dawn.
Elephant, The.
Frog, The.
Garden Party, The.
Godolphin Horne.
Grandmamma's Birthday.
Henry King.
Hippopotamus, The.

Jim, Who Ran Away from His Nurse, and Was Eaten by a Lion.
Juliet.
Llama, The.
Lord Finchley.
Matilda.
On a Hand.
On His Books.
Python, The.
Sarah Byng Who Could Not Read and Was Tossed into a Thorny Hedge by a Bull.
Tarantella.
They Say That in the Unchanging Place. *Fr.* Dedicatory Ode.
Yak, The.
BELOOF, ROBERT. Spring Night, A.
BELSHAM, R. A. Christ for Everything.
BELVIN, WILLIAM. Palermo, Mother's Day, 1943.
BENEDIKTSSON, EINAR. Rain.
BENÉT, LAURA. Babylon.
Rowers, The.
BENÉT, ROSEMARY (Mrs. Stephen Vincent Benét). Nancy Hanks.
BENÉT, STEPHEN VINCENT. Abraham Lincoln.
Captain Kidd.
Christopher Columbus.
Clipper Ships and Captains.
Cotton Mather.
Daniel Boone.
Dulce Ridentem.
For City Spring.
Jack Ellyat Heard the Guns. *Fr.* John Brown's Body.
John Brown's Body, *sels.*
John James Audubon.
John Quincy Adams.
Lewis and Clark.
Listen to the People: Independence Day, 1941, *sel.*
Mountain Whippoorwill, The.
Off to the War. *Fr.* John Brown's Body.
There Was a Girl I Used to Go With. *Fr.* John Brown's Body.
Thomas Jefferson.
Three Elements. *Fr.* John Brown's Body.
BENÉT, WILLIAM ROSE. Fancy, The.
Horse Thief, The.
Jesse James.
Light in the Temple, The.
Morgiana Dances.
Skater of Ghost Lake, The.
Song under Shadow.
Subversive.
Words of Jesus, The.
BEN HAZM. Visit of the Beloved, The.
BENJAMIN, VIRGINIA SARAH. Puzzling Example, A.
BENN, GOTTFRIED. Beautiful Childhood. *Fr.* Morgue.
Caryatid.
Cycle. *Fr.* Morgue.
Evenings of Certain Lives, The.
From Far Shores, from Kingdoms.
Icarus.
Labor Room.
Man and Woman Walk through the Cancer Ward.
Morgue, *sels.*
Negro Bride. *Fr.* Morgue.
Night Café.
Palau.
Poplar.
Retrospective Sketch.
September.
Subway Train.
Weightless Element, A.
Who Are You.
BENNETT, GWENDOLYN B. Hatred.
Heritage.
Sonnet I: "He came in silvern armor, trimmed with black."
Sonnet II: "Some things are very dear to me."
BENNETT, HENRY HOLCOMB. Flag Goes By, The.
BENNETT, JOSEPH DEERICKS. Complaint.
BENNETT, LERONE, JR. Blues and Bitterness.

BISHOP, MORRIS (continued)
Naughty Preposition, The.
Perforated Spirit, The.
Settling Some Old Football Scores.
Sonnets to Laura, sels., tr.
We Have Been Here Before.
BISHOP, VERNA. Choose.
BITHELL, JETHRO. For translations from Flemish, French, and German, see BoLP; ErPo; SiGo.
BJÖRNSON, BJÖRNSTJERNE. Boy and the Flute, The.
Synnöve's Song.
Tree, The.
BLACKBURN, PAUL. Bañalbufar, a Brazier, Relativity, Cloud Formations & the Kindness & Relentlessness of Time, All Seen through a Window While Keeping the Feet Warm at the Same Time As.
El Camino Verde.
Estat ai en greu cossirier, tr.
Jewels, The, tr.
Letter, The.
Madrigal de Verano, tr.
Meditation on the BMT.
Once-over, The.
One-Night Stand, The: An Approach to the Bridge.
Park Poem.
Proposition, The.
Purse, The—Seine.
Tant' Amare, tr.
Three Part Invention.
For translations from Provençal, see AnML.
BLACKBURN, THOMAS. Ganga.
Hospital for Defectives.
Jonah.
Lucky Marriage, The.
BLADEN, PETER. Coronation Day at Melrose.
BLAIR, ROBERT. Grave, The, sel.
BLAKE, MARIE. Barter.
BLAKE, WILLIAM. Ah! Sun-Flower. Fr. Songs of Experience.
And Did Those Feet in Ancient Time. Fr. Milton.
Auguries of Innocence.
Bard, The. Fr. Songs of Experience.
Blind-Man's Buff.
Blossom, The. Fr. Songs of Innocence.
Book of Thel, The.
Children of a Future Age.
Chimney Sweeper, The. Fr. Songs of Experience.
Chimney Sweeper, The. Fr. Songs of Innocence.
Clod and the Pebble, The. Fr. Songs of Experience.
Cradle Song: "Sleep, sleep, beauty bright."
Cradle Song, A: "Sweet dreams form a shade." Fr. Songs of Innocence.
Crystal Cabinet, The.
Divine Image, A. ("Cruelty has a human heart").
Divine Image, The. ("To Mercy, Pity, Peace, and Love"). Fr. Songs of Innocence.
Dream, A. Fr. Songs of Innocence.
Earth's Answer. Fr. Songs of Experience.
Echoing Green, The. Fr. Songs of Innocence.
Enion Replies from the Caverns of the Grave. Fr. Vala; or, The Four Zoas.
Enitharmon Revives with Los. Fr. Vala; or, The Four Zoas.
Epigraph: "I give you the end of a golden string." Fr. Jerusalem.
Epilogue: "Truly, my Satan, thou art but a dunce." Fr. The Gates of Paradise.
Eternity.
Fair Elenor.
Fly, The. Fr. Songs of Experience.
Garden of Love, The. Fr. Songs of Experience.
Gates of Paradise, The, sel.
Guardian Angels of the Creatures. Fr. Songs of Innocence.

Hear the Voice of the Bard. Fr. Songs of Experience.
Holy Thursday. Fr. Songs of Experience.
Holy Thursday. Fr. Songs of Innocence.
How Sweet I Roamed.
Human Abstract, The. Fr. Songs of Experience.
I Asked a Thief to Steal Me a Peach.
I Heard an Angel Singing.
I Laid Me Down upon a Bank.
I Saw a Chapel All of Gold.
If You Trap the Moment.
Infant Joy. Fr. Songs of Innocence.
Infant Sorrow. Fr. Songs of Experience.
Introduction: "Hear the voice of the Bard!" Fr. Songs of Experience.
Introduction: "Piping down the valleys wild." Fr. Songs of Innocence.
Jerusalem ("And did those feet in ancient time"). Fr. Milton.
Jerusalem, sels.
Lamb, The. Fr. Songs of Innocence.
Lamentation of Enion, The. Fr. Vala; or, The Four Zoas.
Lark's Song, The. Fr. Milton.
Laughing Song. Fr. Songs of Innocence.
Lilly, The. Fr. Songs of Experience.
Little Black Boy, The. Fr. Songs of Innocence.
Little Boy Lost, A. Fr. Songs of Experience.
Little Boy Lost. Fr. Songs of Innocence.
Little Girl Found, The. Fr. Songs of Experience.
Little Girl Lost, The. Fr. Songs of Experience.
Little Vagabond, The.
London. Fr. Songs of Experience.
Love's Secret.
Mad Song.
Male & Female Loves in Beulah. Fr. Jerusalem.
Many Birds. Fr. Auguries of Innocence.
Mental Traveller, The.
Milton, sels.
Mock On, Mock On, Voltaire, Rousseau.
Motto to the Songs of Innocence and of Experience.
My Pretty Rose-Tree. Fr. Songs of Experience.
My Silks and Fine Array.
My Spectre around Me.
Never Seek to Tell Thy Love.
Night. Fr. Songs of Innocence.
Nurse's Song. Fr. Songs of Experience.
Nurse's Song. Fr. Songs of Innocence.
O Rose, Thou Art Sick! Fr. Songs of Experience.
On Another's Sorrow. Fr. Songs of Innocence.
Piper, The. Fr. Songs of Innocence.
Piping down the Valleys Wild. Fr. Songs of Innocence.
Poison Tree, A. Fr. Songs of Experience.
Popular Rhymes.
Prelude: "And did those feet in ancient time." Fr. Milton.
Prelude: "England! awake! awake! awake!" Fr. Jerusalem.
Prelude: "Fields from Islington to Marybone, The." Fr. Jerusalem.
Questions Answer'd, The.
Schoolboy, The. Fr. Songs of Experience.
Shepherd, The. Fr. Songs of Innocence.
Sick Rose, The. Fr. Songs of Experience.
Silent, Silent Night.
Sleep! Sleep! Beauty Bright.
Song: Fresh from the Dewy Hill, the Merry Year.
Song: "How sweet I roamed from field to field."

Song: My Silks and Fine Array.
Song: When Early Morn Walks Forth in Sober Gray.
Songs of Experience, sels.
Songs of Innocence, sels.
Sonnet: "Thou fair-haired angel of the evening."
Spring. Fr. Songs of Innocence.
Thel's Motto. Fr. The Book of Thel.
Tiger [or Tyger], The. Fr. Songs of Experience.
To Autumn.
To Morning.
To Nobodaddy.
To Spring.
To Summer.
To the Evening Star.
To the Muses.
To Winter.
Vala; or, The Four Zoas, sels.
Vision of the Lamentation of Beulah over Ololon, A. Fr. Milton.
When a Man Has Married a Wife.
Why Should I Care for the Men of Thames?
Where to Seek Love. Fr. William Bond.
Wild Flower's Song, The.
Wild Thyme, The. Fr. Milton.
William Bond, sel.
BLAND, EDITH NESBIT. See NESBIT, EDITH.
BLAND, JAMES A. Old Virginny.
BLASER, ROBIN. Faerie Queene, The, sel.
Park, The.
Sophia Nichols.
BLICHER, STEEN STEENSEN. Heather, The.
BLIGHT, JOHN. Becalmed.
Death of a Whale.
BLIND, MATHILDE. After-Glow, The.
Autumn Tints.
Love in Exile, sel.
BLIXEN, KAREN. See "DINESEN, ISAK."
BLOCH, ROBERT. Nightmare Number Four.
BLOCKSIDGE, WILLIAM. See BAYLEBRIDGE, WILLIAM.
BLOK, ALEKSANDR ALEKSANDROVICH. Little Catkins.
She Came Out of the Frost.
BLOOMFIELD, ROBERT. Banks of Wye, The, sels.
Coracle Fishers, The. Fr. The Banks of Wye.
Farmer's Boy, The, sel.
Meandering Wye. Fr. The Banks of Wye.
Moonlight . . . Scattered Clouds. Fr. The Farmer's Boy.
Shooter's Hill, sel.
BLOOMGARDEN [or BLUMGARTEN], SOLOMON. See "YEHOASH."
BLUNDEN, EDMUND. At the Great Wall of China.
Festubert: The Old German Line.
Les Halles d'Ypres.
Midnight Skaters, The.
1916 Seen from 1921.
November Morning.
Recovery, The.
Report on Experience.
Sunlit Vale, The.
Thiepval Wood.
Thoughts of Thomas Hardy.
Vlamertinghe: Passing the Chateau.
Winter in East Anglia.
Zillebeke Brook.
Zonnebeke Road, The.
BLUNT, WILFRID SCAWEN. Esther, sel.
Old Squire, The.
BLY, ROBERT. Love Poem: "When we are in love, we love the grass."
BOAKE, BARCROFT HENRY. Where the Dead Men Lie.
BOCCACCIO, GIOVANNI. Ballata: "I am young and fain to sing." Fr. The Decameron.
Decameron, The, sel.
BODE, CARL. Bad Children, The.
Burial of Terror, The.
City Considered as a Tulip Tree, The. Fr. London Sonnets.

Covent Garden Market. *Fr.* London Sonnets.
Eastertide. *Fr.* The Sacred Seasons.
Feast of Saint Andrew the Apostle. *Fr.* The Sacred Seasons.
London Sonnets, *sels.*
Nocturne, The.
Personal Letter to the Ephesians.
Planet, The.
Requiem.
Sacred Seasons, The, *sels.*
Sonnet: Head Next to Mine.
Sonnet: Window, The.
Variation on a Theme by Dylan Thomas.
Who Calls the English Cold? *Fr.* London Sonnets.
BODENHEIM, MAXWELL. Poet to His Love.
BOETHIUS (Anicius Manlius Severinus Boethius). Consolation of Philosophy, *sel.*
Happy Too Much. *Fr.* Consolation of Philosophy.
BOGAN, LOUISE. Cartography.
Evening in the Sanitarium.
I Saw Eternity.
M., Singing.
Musician.
Old Countryside.
Song for a Slight Voice.
Song for the Last Act.
Women.
Zone.
BOILEAU-DESPRÉAUX, NICOLAS. Art poétique, L', *sel.*
BOKER, GEORGE HENRY. Ballad of Sir John Franklin, The.
Cruise of the *Monitor,* The.
Sonnet: "Oh! sigh no more, no longer paint the air." *Fr.* Sonnets.
Sonnet: "Oh spring, that hides the wrinkled earth in green." *Fr.* Sonnets.
Sonnet: "Three seasons only in his calendar." *Fr.* Sonnets.
Sonnet: "Tonight I walked with the grim Florentine." *Fr.* Sonnets.
Sonnet: "You say my love no marvel is to you." *Fr.* Sonnets.
Sonnets, *sels.*
BONAR, HORATIUS. Be True.
Blessing and Honor.
Love Is of God.
Thy Way, Not Mine.
BOND, HORACE JULIAN. Bishop of Atlanta, The: Ray Charles.
Habana.
Rotation.
BONHOEFFER, DIETRICH. Dietrich Bonhoeffer, Awaiting Execution in a Concentration Camp, Prays for His Fellow Prisoners.
BONNEFOY, YVES. Art of Poetry, The.
San Francesco, at Night.
Threats of the Witness.
True Name.
BONTEMPS, ARNA. Black Man Talks of Reaping, A.
Close Your Eyes!
Day-Breakers, The.
Golgotha Is a Mountain.
Idolatry.
Nocturne at Bethesda.
Reconnaissance.
Southern Mansion.
BOODSON, ALISON. Poem: "He lying spilt like water from a bowl."
BOOTH, PHILIP. Adam.
Crossing.
Ego.
First Lesson.
Great Farm.
Instruction in the Art.
Nightsong.
North.
Offshore.
Siasconset Song.
Thanksgiving 1963.
Tower, The.
Was a Man.
BORIE, LYSBETH BOYD. Five-in-June.
Five Years Old.
Grace Ananne [*or* GraceAnAnne].

BÖTTICHER, HANS. *See* "RINGELNATZ, JOACHIM."
BOTTRALL, RONALD. Icarus.
BOUCHET, ANDRÉ DU. *See* DU BOUCHET, ANDRÉ.
BOUFLERS, MARIE-FRANÇOISE-CATHERINE DE BEAUVEAU, MARQUISE DE. Air: Sentir avec ardeur.
BOUNDY, REX. Virile Christ, A.
BOURDILLON, FRANCIS WILLIAM. Night Has a Thousand Eyes, The.
BOURINOT, ARTHUR STANLEY. Under the Pines.
BOURNE, VINCENT. Cricket, The.
Housekeeper, The.
BOWEN, CHARLES SYNGE CHRISTOPHER BOWEN, BARON. Just and Unjust.
BOWER, HELEN FRAZEE-. *See* FRAZEE-BOWER, HELEN.
BOWERS, EDGAR. Two Poems on the Catholic Bavarians.
BOWIE, BEVERLY. To My New Mistress.
BOWLES, WILLIAM LISLE. On a Beautiful Landscape.
BOWMAN, GLADYS M. Only One Life.
BOWRA, CECIL MAURICE. For translations from Greek, see EaLo; SiGo.
BOWRING, SIR JOHN. Galleys of Spain, *tr.*
Not All Sweet Nightingales, *tr.*
BOWSHER, KATHRYN T. My Hiding Place.
Thy Nail-pierced Hands.
BOYARS, ARTHUR. Initial.
BOYD, MARK ALEXANDER. Fra Bank to Bank.
"BOYD, NANCY." *See* MILLAY, EDNA ST. VINCENT.
BOYD, THOMAS. Love on the Mountain.
BOYDEN, POLLY CHASE. Mud.
BRACKER, MILTON. Umpire, The.
Where, O Where?
BRADBY, GODFREY FOX. In Hoc Signo.
BRADBY, H. C. Comfort for the Sleepless.
BRADFORD, GAMALIEL. God.
BRADLEY, KATHERINE, *and* EDITH COOPER. *See* "FIELD, MICHAEL."
BRADLEY, SAMUEL M. Roc's Brood.
This Here Is Hell.
BRADSTREET, ANNE. Author to [*or* and] Her Book, The.
Contemplations.
Fresh and the Spirit, The.
In Memory of My Dear Grandchild, Elizabeth Bradstreet, Who Deceased August, 1665, Being a Year and a Half Old.
Letter to Her Husband, Absent upon Publick Employment, A.
Prologue, The: "To Sing of wars, of captains, and of kings."
Some Verses upon the Burning of Our House, July 10th, 1666.
To My Dear and Loving Husband.
BRADY, EDWIN JAMES. Coachman's Yarn, The.
Lost and Given Over.
BRAINARD, MARY GARDINER. Not Knowing, *sel.*
BRAITHWAITE, WILLIAM STANLEY. House of Falling Leaves, The, *sel.*
House of Falling Leaves We Entered in, The. *Fr.* The House of Falling Leaves.
Rhapsody.
Scintilla.
BRALEY, BERTON. To a Photographer.
BRAMBACH, RAINER. Granite.
Tree, The.
BRAND, MILLEN. Local Light.
BRASIER, VIRGINIA. Psychological Prediction.
BRATT, GEORGE. AWOL.
BRECHT, BERTOLT. Bad Morning, A.
Burning of Books, The.
Changing the Wheel.
Children's Crusade 1939.
Coal for Mike.
Farmer's Concern, The.
Four Psalms.
General, That Tank.
Iron.
Of Poor B. B.
Of Swimming in Lakes and Rivers.

On Teaching without Pupils.
On Watering the Garden.
Return.
Song of the Rice Bargees.
Thoughts on the Length of Exile.
To Posterity.
BREESER, BETTYE. Nature at Three.
BRENAN, GERALD. My Sailor of Seven.
BRENNAN, CHRISTOPHER JOHN. Adam to Lilith. *Fr.* Lilith.
Anguish'd Doubt Broods over Eden, The. *Fr.* Lilith.
Come Out, Come Out, Ye Souls That Serve. *Fr.* The Wanderer.
Fire in the Heavens, and Fire along the Hills. *Fr.* The Quest of Silence.
How Old Is My Heart. *Fr.* The Wanderer.
I Cry to You as I Pass Your Windows. *Fr.* The Wanderer.
I Said, This Misery Must End. *Fr.* Pauca Mea.
I Saw My Life as Whitest Flame. *Fr.* Towards the Source.
Interlude: The Casement.
Land I Came Thro' Last, The. *Fr.* The Wanderer.
Let Us Go Down, the Long Dead Night Is Done. *Fr.* Towards the Source.
Lilith, *sels.*
Lilith on the Fate of Man. *Fr.* Lilith.
My Heart Was Wandering in the Sands. *Fr.* The Twilight of Disquietude.
O Desolate Eves. *Fr.* The Wanderer.
Pauca Mea, *sel.*
Towards the Source, *sels.*
Twilight of Disquietude, The, *sels.*
Wanderer, The, *sels.*
Years That Go to Make Me Man, The. *Fr.* The Twilight of Disquietude.
BRENNAN, JOSEPH PAYNE. Avery Anameer.
Chestnut Roasters, The.
Ghost-Town Saloon: Winter.
Grandfather's Ghost.
Humming Stair, The.
Last Pagan Mourns for Dark Rosaleen, The.
Man I Met, The.
Nightmare.
One Day of Rain.
Ossian.
Recognition of Death.
Scythe of Dreams, The.
Serpent Waits, The.
Wind of Time, The.
BRENTANO, CLEMENS MARIA. O Woodland Cool.
Serenade: "Hark, once more the flute's complaining."
Serenade: "Harken how the flute complains."
Slumber Song.
Spinstress' Song, The.
BRERETON, JANE. On Mr. Nash's Picture.
BRERETON, JOHN LE GAY. Buffalo Creek.
BRETON, NICHOLAS. Come, Little Babe.
Country Lad, The. *Fr.* The Passionate Shepherd.
Honourable Entertainment Given to the Queen's Majesty in Progress at Elvetham, 1591, The, *sel.*
In the Merry Month of May. *Fr.* The Honourable Entertainment Given to the Queen's Majesty in Progress at Elvetham, 1591.
Olden Love-making.
Passionate Shepherd, The, *sel.*
Pastoral: "Who can live in heart so glad." *Fr.* The Passionate Shepherd.
Phillida and Coridan. *Fr.* The Honourable Entertainment Given to the Queen's Majesty in Progress at Elvetham, 1591.
Say That I Should Say.
BRETTELL, NOEL HARRY. Autumn Song.
BREWSTER, ELIZABETH. In the Library.
BRIDGES, ROBERT. Awake, my heart, to be loved, awake, awake!

BRIDGES, ROBERT (*continued*)
Country Music, *tr.*
Σρως (Eros).
I Have Loved Flowers.
I Heard a Linnet Courting.
I Never Shall Love the Snow Again.
I Will Not Let Thee Go.
Johannes Milton, Senex.
London Snow.
Low Barometer.
Nightingales.
November.
On a Dead Child.
Passer-by, A.
Snow Lies Sprinkled, The.
So Sweet Love Seemed.
Song of My Heart, A.
South Wind, The.
Storm is over, the land hushes to rest, The.
Thou Didst Delight My Eyes.
Triolet: "All women born are so perverse."
When Death to Either Shall Come.
BRINK, CAROL RYRIE. Goody O'Grumpity.
BRINNIN, JOHN MALCOLM. Hotel Paradiso e Commerciale.
Nuns at Eve.
BROCKMAN, ZOE KINCAID. Cardinal.
Christmas Eve.
Cold Wind Blows, A.
Concerning Wings.
Dream Is Not Enough, The.
I Say to the Mountain.
In an Editor's Office.
In Winter. *Fr.* Three Cinquains.
Mountains. *Fr.* Three Cinquains.
Scissors and Paste. *Fr.* Three Cinquains.
Sorrow's Day.
Three Cinquains.
To the Lost Colony.
Your Footsteps on the Stair.
BRODE, ANTHONY. Breakfast with Gerard Manley Hopkins.
BRODIE, HUGH R. Sergeant's Prayer, A.
BROME, ALEXANDER. Mad Lover, The.
BROMLEY, BEATRICE MARION. Camp Fire.
BRONTË, ANNE ("Acton Bell"). He Doeth All Things Well.
BRONTË, CHARLOTTE ("Currer Bell"). Often Rebuked, *at.*
Stanzas: "Often rebuked, yet always back returning," *at.*
BRONTË, EMILY ("Ellis Bell"). Anticipation.
Death.
Fall, Leaves, Fall.
How still, how happy! These are words.
If grief for grief can touch thee.
Last Lines.
Little while, a little while, A.
Love Is Like the Wild Rose-Briar.
Night is darkening round me, The.
Night Wind, The.
No Coward Soul Is Mine.
Often Rebuked, *at.*
Old Stoic, The.
Prisoner, The, *sels.*
Remembrance.
Shall Earth No More Inspire Thee?
Silent Is the House.
Song: "Linnet in the rocky dells, The."
Stanzas: "Often rebuked, yet always back returning," *at.*
Visonary, The.
BRONTË, PATRICK BRANWELL. Time to Choose a Lover, *tr.*
BROOKE, FULKE GREVILLE, 1ST BARON. *See* GREVILLE, FULKE, 1ST BARON BROOKE.
BROOKE, RUPERT. Channel Passage, A.
Clouds.
Day That I Have Loved.
Dead, The ("Blow out, you bugles"). *Fr.* 1914.
Dead, The ("These hearts were woven"). *Fr.* 1914.
Fish, The.
Great Lover, The.
Heaven.
Hill, The.

Love.
1914, *sels.*
Old Vicarage, Grantchester, The.
One Day.
Peace. *Fr.* 1914.
Soldier, The. *Fr.* 1914.
Sonnet: "I said I splendidly loved you; it's not true."
There's Wisdom in Women.
Wayfarers, The.
Young Man in April.
BROOKS, GWENDOLYN. Andre.
Assassination of John F. Kennedy, The.
Chicago *Defender* Sends a Man to Little Rock, Fall, 1957, The.
Children of the Poor, The, *sel.*
Flags.
Old Marrieds, The.
Old Tennis Player.
Pete at the Zoo.
Piano after War.
Rudolph Is Tired of the City.
BROOKS, HELEN MORGAN. Plans.
Words.
BROOKS, JONATHAN HENDERSON. Resurrection, The.
BROOKS, PHILLIPS. Christmas Carol, A: "Everywhere, everywhere, Christmas tonight!"
Our Burden Bearer.
Wish for the New Year, A.
BROOKS, SHIRLEY. For A' That and A' That, *parody.*
BROOKS, WALTER ROLLIN. From the Ballad of Two-Gun Freddy.
BROOME, SIR FREDERICK NAPIER. To the Soul.
BROUGHTON, JAMES RICHARD. Psalm of St. Priapus, The.
Psyche to Cupid: Her Ditty.
BROWN, ABBIE FARWELL. Somebody's Birthday.
BROWN, BEATRICE CURTIS. Anniversary in September.
Jonathan Bing.
New Song to Sing about Jonathan Bing, A.
BROWN, GEORGE MACKAY. Death of Peter Esson, The.
Five Voyages of Arnor, The.
Harald, the Agnostic Ale-loving Old Shepherd Enemy of the Whisky-drinking Ploughmen and Harvesters, Walks over the Sabbath Hill to the Shearing.
Old Women, The.
Our Lady of the Waves.
Unlucky Boat.
BROWN, ISABELLA M. Prayer: "I had thought of putting an/ altar."
BROWN, JULIAN. Mr. Ripley Parodies Mr. Nash—or Vice Versa.
BROWN, KATE LOUISE. Christmas Candle, The.
In the Heart of a Seed.
BROWN, STERLING ALLEN. Sister Lou.
When de Saints Go Ma'chin' Home.
BROWN, THOMAS EDWARD. I Bended unto Me.
Ibant Obscurae.
My Garden.
Roman Women, *sel.*
To K. H.
Vesper.
Wesley in Heaven.
BROWNE, FELICIA DOROTHEA. *See* HEMANS, FELICIA DOROTHEA.
BROWNE, ISAAC HAWKINS. Pipe of Tobacco, A, *sels.*
"BROWNE, MATTHEW." *See* RANDS, WILLIAM BRIGHTY.
BROWNE, MOSES. Barber, The.
Musing by a River.
Shrimp, The.
BROWNE, WILLIAM. Another to the Same, *tr.*
Epitaph on the Countess Dowager of Pembroke.
Inner Temple Masque, The, *sel.*
On the Countess Dowager of Pembroke.
Siren's Song, The. *Fr.* The Inner Temple Masque.
BROWNELL, HENRY HOWARD. Lawyer's Invocation to Spring, The.

BROWNING, ELIZABETH BARRETT. Aurora Leigh, *sel.*
Beloved, thou hast brought me many flowers. *Fr.* Sonnets from the Portuguese.
Bianca among the Nigthingales.
Can it be right to give what I can give? *Fr.* Sonnets from the Portuguese.
Child's Thought of God, A.
Comfort.
Denial, A.
Face of all the world is changed, I think, The. *Fr.* Sonnets from the Portuguese.
First time he kissed me, he but only kissed. *Fr.* Sonnets from the Portuguese.
Flush or Faunus.
Go from me. Yet I feel that I shall stand. *Fr.* Sonnets from the Portuguese.
Great God Pan, The.
Grief.
How do I love thee? Let me count the ways. *Fr.* Sonnets from the Portuguese.
I thought once how Theocritus had sung. *Fr.* Sonnets from the Portuguese.
If thou must love me, let it be for nought. *Fr.* Sonnets from the Portuguese.
Inclusions.
Look, The.
Mask, The.
Musical Instrument, A.
Round Our Restlessness.
Sleep, The.
Sonnets from the Portuguese, *sels.*
Sweetest Lives, The.
Wife to a Husband, A. *Fr.* Sonnets from the Portuguese.
Yet, love, mere love, is beautiful indeed. *Fr.* Sonnets from the Portuguese.
BROWNING, ROBERT. Abt Vogler.
Andrea del Sarto.
Any Wife to Any Husband.
Appearances.
Asolando, *sel.*
Belief and Unbelief. *Fr.* Bishop Blougram's Apology.
Bishop Blougram's Apology.
Bishop Orders His Tomb at Saint Praxed's Church, The.
Blot in the 'Scutcheon, A, *sel.*
Boot and Saddle.
Caliban upon Setebos; or, Natural Theology in the Island.
"Childe Roland to the Dark Tower Came."
Cleon.
Confessions.
David's Song. *Fr.* Saul.
"De Gustibus."
Death in the Desert, A, *sels.*
Epilogue: "At the midnight in the silence of the sleep-time." *Fr.* Asolando.
Epistle, An, Containing the Strange Medical Experience of Karshish, the Arab Physician.
Face, A.
Fame.
Fifine at the Fair, *sel.*
Flower's Name, The. *Fr.* Garden Fancies.
Fra Lippo Lippi.
Garden Fancies, *sels.*
Giuseppe Caponsacchi. *Fr.* The Ring and the Book.
Glove, The.
Grammarian's Funeral, A.
Grow Old Along with Me. *Fr.* Rabbi Ben Ezra.
Hervé Riel.
Home-Thoughts, from Abroad.
Home-Thoughts, from the Sea.
House.
How It Strikes a Contemporary.
How They Brought the Good News from Ghent to Aix.
In a Gondola, *sel.*
Incident of the French Camp, An.

Laboratory, The.
Last Ride Together, The.
Life in a Love.
Likeness, A.
Lost Leader, The.
Lost Mistress, The.
Love among the Ruins.
Love in a Life.
Meeting at Night.
Memorabilia.
Misconceptions.
Moment Eternal, The.
Moon Rainbow, A.
My Last Duchess.
My Star.
Ned Bratts.
Never the Time and the Place.
Now.
Old Pope Is Comforted by the Thought of the Young Pompilia, The. *Fr.* The Ring and the Book.
Old Whom God Loves, The. *Fr.* A Death in the Desert.
Orpheus and Eurydice.
Parting at Morning.
Pearl, a Girl, A.
Pictor Ignotus.
Pied Piper of Hamelin, The.
Pippa Passes, *sel.*
Pippa's Song. *Fr.* Pippa Passes.
Popularity.
Porphyria's Lover.
Prospice.
Rabbi Ben Ezra.
Ring and the Book, The, *sels.*
Saul, *sels.*
Sibrandus Schafnaburgensis. *Fr.* Garden Fancies.
Soliloquy of the Spanish Cloister.
Song: "Nay but you, who do not love her."
Song: "Year's at the spring, The." *Fr.* Pippa Passes.
Statue and the Bust, The.
Summum Bonum.
Time's Revenges.
Toccata of Galuppi's, A.
Transcendentalism; a Poem in Twelve Books.
Two in the Campagna.
Up at a Villa—Down in the City.
Waring, *sel.*
Woman's Last Word, A.
Year's at the Spring, The. *Fr.* Pippa Passes.
Youth and Art.
BRUCE, CHARLES. Words Are Never Enough.
BRUCE, GEORGE. Death Mask of a Fisherman.
BRUCE, JOHN. Pike, The.
BRUNER, MARGARET E. Epitaph for a Cat.
Whom the Gods Love.
BRYANT, WILLIAM CULLEN. Abraham Lincoln.
Achilles' Revenge, *tr. Fr.* The Iliad.
Antiquity of Freedom, The.
Battle-Field, The.
Death of Lincoln, The.
Death of the Flowers, The.
Earth.
Evening Wind, The.
Forest Hymn, A.
Green Mountain Boys, The.
Green River.
Hymn of the Sea, A.
Inscription for the Entrance to a Wood.
Life of the Blessed, The, *tr.*
Oh Fairest of the Rural Maids.
Oh Mother of a Mighty Race.
Planting of the Apple tree, The, *sel.*
Poet, The.
Prairies, The.
Siesta, The, *tr.*
Song of Marion's Men.
Summer Wind.
Thanatopsis.
Thou, Whose Unmeasured Temple Stands.
To a Waterfowl.
To Cole, the Painter, Departing for Europe.

To the Fringed Gentian.
Winter Piece, A.
Yellow Violet, The.
BUCHAN, TOM. Invitation, The.
BUCHMAN, MARION. First-born.
BUCKINGHAM, GEORGE VILLIERS, 2D DUKE OF. Rehearsal, The, *sel.*
BUCKINGHAM AND NORMANBY, DUKE OF. See SHEFFIELD, JOHN, DUKE OF BUCKINGHAM AND NORMANBY.
BUCKLEY, VINCENT. Late Tutorial.
Various Wakings.
BUDZYNSKI, JOE. Have Faith in God.
BUKOWSKI, CHARLES. Day I Kicked a Bankroll Out the Window, The.
BULLOCK, J. Fear Not.
BULLOCK, MARK. Be Thankful.
BULLOCK, MARY. Blessed Nearness.
BULWER-LYTTON, EDWARD ROBERT, 1ST EARL OF LYTTON. See "MEREDITH, OWEN."
BUNNER, HENRY CUYLER. Grandfather Watts's Private Fourth.
One, Two, Three!
Pitcher of Mignonette, A.
BUNTING, BASIL. Complaint of the Morpethshire Farmer, The.
De Rerum Natura, *sel., tr.*
Gin the Goodwife Stint.
BUNYAN, JOHN. He That Is Down. *Fr.* The Pilgrim's Progress.
Lanthorn is to keep the candle light, The.
Neither Hook nor Line.
Of the Child with the Bird at the Bush.
Pilgrim, The. *Fr.* The Pilgrim's Progress.
Pilgrim Song, The. *Fr.* The Pilgrim's Progress.
Pilgrim's Progress, The, *sels.*
Shepherd Boy Sings in the Valley of Humiliation, The. *Fr.* The Pilgrim's Progress.
Shepherd Boy's Song, The. *Fr.* The Pilgrim's Progress.
Song of Low Degree, A. *Fr.* The Pilgrim's Progress.
Time and Eternity.
BUONARROTI. See MICHELANGELO BUONARROTI.
BURET, THEOBALD PURCELL-. See PURCELL-BURET, THEOBALD.
BÜRGER, GOTTFRIED AUGUST. Lenore.
BURGESS, GELETT. Adolphus Elfinstone.
Ah, Yes, I Wrote the "Purple Cow."
Alphabet of Famous Goops, An, *sel.*
Felicia Ropps.
I Wish That My Room Had a Floor.
Purple Cow, The.
Sestina of Youth and Age.
Table Manners.
Tardiness.
BURGESS, THORNTON. Paddy the Beaver.
Young Flash the Deer.
BURLIN, NATALIE CURTIS. See CURTIS, NATALIE.
BURNET, DANA. Road to Vagabondia, The.
BURNETT, OLIVE H. Best for Us, The.
BURNS, ROBERT. Address to the Deil.
Address to the Unco Guid, or the Rigidly Righteous.
Ae Fond Kiss.
Afton Water.
Anna.
Auld Lang Syne.
Banks o' Doon, The.
Bannockburn.
Birks of Aberfeldy, The.
Blooming Nelly.
Bonnie Lesley.
Book-Worms, The.
Comin' thro' the Rye.
Composed in Spring.
Corn Rigs Are Bonny.
Cotter's Saturday Night, The.
Could You Do That?
Duncan Gray ("Can ye play me Duncan Gray").
Duncan Gray ("Duncan Gray cam here to woo").
Epistle to James Smith.
Epistle to John Lapraik, an Old Scottish Bard.

Farewell, A: "Go fetch to me a pint o' wine."
For A' That and A' That.
For the Sake of Somebody.
Gie the Lass Her Fairin'.
Godly Girzie.
Gowden Locks of Anna, The.
Green Grow the Rashes.
Highland Mary.
Holy Fair, The.
Holy Willie's Prayer.
How Can I Keep My Maidenhead?
I Do Confess Thou Art Sae Fair.
I Hae a Wife o' My Ain.
I Love My Jean.
I Murder Hate by Field or Flood.
I Once Was a Maid. *Fr.* The Jolly Beggars.
I'm Owre Young to Marry Yet.
Inventory, The.
Is There for Honest Poverty.
Jean.
John Anderson My Jo.
Jolly Beggars, The.
Lament for Culloden.
Lass and the Friar, The.
Lass That Made the Bed for Me, The.
Man Was Made to Mourn; a Dirge.
Man's a Man for A' That, A.
Mary Morison.
Muirland Meg.
My Bonnie Highland Laddie.
My Heart's in the Highlands.
My Luve's like a Red, Red Rose.
Nine Inch Will Please a Lady.
Nut-gathering Lass, The.
O My Luve's like a Red, Red Rose.
O, Wert Thou in the Cauld Blast.
O, Whistle and I'll Come to You [or Ye, My Lad].
Of A' the Airts.
On the Author.
Plowman, The.
Poet's Welcome to His Illegitimate Child, The.
Red, Red Rose, A.
Rigs o' Barley, The.
Saw Ye Bonny Lesley?
Scots Wha Hae.
She'll Do It.
Suppertime.
Sweet Afton.
Tam o' Shanter.
There'll Never Be Peace.
Thrusting of It, The.
To a Field Mouse.
To a Louse [on Seeing One on a Lady's Bonnet at Church].
To a Mountain Daisy.
To a Mouse.
To Miss Ferrier.
Tommie Makes My Tail Toddle.
Twa Dogs, The.
Up in the Morning Early.
Wha Is That at my Bower-Door?
Whistle, and I'll Come [to You, My Lad].
Winter.
Ye Banks and Braes [o' Bonnie Doon].
Ye Flowery Banks.
BURR, AMELIA JOSEPHINE. Evening Prayer.
BURR, GRAY. Butterfly, The.
Death before Killing, A.
Epistemological Rag, The.
Garden Puzzle.
Glance at the Album, A.
Play of Opposites, A.
Sailing, Sailing.
Skater's Waltz, A.
BURR, WINIFRED ADAMS. Ghosts.
Opening Door.
BURRELL, SOPHIA. Epigram on Two Ladies.
BURROUGHS, JOHN. Waiting.
BURT, NATHANIEL. Out.
BURTON, HENRY. There's a Light upon the Mountains.
BURTON, JOHN. Do I Really Pray?
BURTON, RICHARD. God's Garden.
BURTON, SIR RICHARD FRANCIS. On the Death of Catarina de Attayda, *tr.*
Thousand and One Nights, The, *sel., tr.*

BUSCH, WILHELM. Bold Knight and the Gruesome Dragon, The.
My smallest fault is jealousy.
Too Bad!
When a misfortune happens me.
BUSH, JOCELYN. Little Red Sled, The.
BUSON (Taniguchi Buson). Parting.
Spring Scene.
Whale, The.
BUSTA, CHRISTINE. Snow at Advent.
BUSTER, MARJORIE LORENE. My Friend.
BUTLER, GUY. Stranger to Europe.
BUTLER, SAMUEL (1612-80). Love ("All love at first, like generous wine").
Love ("Lovers, like wrestlers").
BUTLER, SAMUEL (1835-1902). O God! O Montreal!
Psalm of Montreal, A.
BUTLER, WILLIAM. November 25, 1963.
BUTLER, WILLIAM ALLEN. Nothing to Wear.
BUTTERWORTH, HEZEKIAH. Death of Jefferson, The.
"BUTTLE, MYRA" (Victor William Williams Saunders Purcell). Sweeney in Articulo.
BUTTS, MARY FRANCES. Today.
BYERS, SAMUEL H. M. When Sherman Marched Down to the Sea.
BYNNER, WITTER ("Emanuel Morgan"). Dream.
I Need No Sky.
Lightning.
Looking at the Moon and Thinking of One Far Away, tr.
Lotuses.
Out of the Sea.
Prayer: "Let us not look upon."
Squanderings.
BYNNER, WITTER, and KIANG KANG-HU. Green Stream, A, tr.
BYRON, GEORGE GORDAN NOEL BYRON, 6TH BARON. All for Love.
And Angling, Too. Fr. Don Juan.
Beppo.
By the Deep Sea. Fr. Childe Harold's Pilgrimage.
Childe Harold's Farewell to England. Fr. Childe Harold's Pilgrimage.
Childe Harold's Pilgrimage, sels.
Corsair, The, sel.
Darkness.
Dedication: "Bob Southey! You're a poet—Poet-laureate." Fr. Don Juan.
Dedication: To Ianthe. Fr. Childe Harold's Pilgrimage.
Destruction of Sennacherib, The.
Don Juan, sels.
Dream, The.
Elegy: "O snatch'd away in beauty's bloom!"
Elegy on Thyrza.
English Bards and Scotch Reviewers, sels.
Epilogue: "There's something in a stupid ass."
Eve of Waterloo, The. Fr. Childe Harold's Pilgrimage.
Fare Thee Well.
Fatal Spell, The. Fr. Childe Harold's Pilgrimage.
For Music.
Fragment: "I would to heaven that I were so much clay." Fr. Don Juan.
Haidée and Don Juan. Fr. Don Juan.
Hours of Idleness.
I Speak Not, I Trace Not, I Breathe Not Thy Name.
Isles of Greece, The. Fr. Don Juan.
Lake Leman. Fr. Childe Harold's Pilgrimage.
Maid of Athens.
My Days of Love Are Over. Fr. Don Juan.
My Spirit Longeth for Thee.
Ocean, The. Fr. Childe Harold's Pilgrimage.
Ode on Venice.
On the Castle of Chillon. Fr. The Prisoner of Chillon.
On This Day I Complete My Thirty-sixth Year.
Prisoner of Chillon, The.
Prometheus.

She Walks in Beauty [like the Night].
Sketch from Private Life, A.
So Late into the Night.
So We'll Go No More a-Roving.
Song: "So, we'll go no more a-roving."
Sonnet on Chillon. Fr. The Prisoner of Chillon.
Stanzas for Music.
Sunset over the Ægean. Fr. The Corsair.
Tear, The.
There Be None of Beauty's Daughters.
Two Foscari, The, sel.
Vision of Belshazzar, The.
Vision of Judgment, The.
We'll Go No More a-Roving.
When a Man Hath No Freedom to Fight for at Home.
When We Two Parted.
William Lisle Bowles. Fr. English Bards and Scotch Reviewers.
Youth and Age.
BYRON, JOHN. Epigram on Handel and Bononcini.

C

"C. B. B." See "B., C. B."
"C. W. T." See "T., C. W."
CABELL, JAMES BRANCH. Story of the Flowery Kingdom.
CABRAL, OLGA. Empire State, sel.
CADOU, RENÉ GUY. Love Poem to Helen.
Who Risks It Where a Poet Lives.
CALDERÓN DE LA BARCA, PEDRO. Dying Eusebio's Address to the Cross, The.
Sonnet: "Those flakes of fire, brilliant sparks of light."
CALLANAN, JEREMIAH [or JAMES] JOHN [or JOSEPH]. Convict of Clonmel, The, tr.
CALLIMACHUS. Heraclitus.
Saon of Acanthus.
CALVERLEY, CHARLES STUART. Ballad: "Auld wife sat at her ivied door, The."
Cock and the Bull, The.
Countryman's Wooing, A, tr.
CAMBRIDGE, ADA (Mrs. George Frederick Cross). Faith.
On Australian Hills, sel.
CAMERON, GEORGE FREDERICK. Future, The.
Standing on Tiptoe.
CAMERON, NORMAN. Compassionate Fool, The.
Forgive Me, Sire.
From a Woman to a Greedy Lover. Fr. Three Love Poems.
Green, Green Is El Aghir.
In the Queen's Room. Fr. Three Love Poems.
Shepherdess. Fr. Three Love Poems.
Thespians at Thermopylae, The.
Three Love Poems.
Winter House, The.
CAMÕES [or CAMOËNS], LUÍS [or LUIZ] VAZ DE. On Revisiting Cintra after the Death of Catarina.
On the Death of Catarina de Attayda.
CAMPANA, DINO. Autumn Garden.
Chimera, The.
Skylight, The.
Two Lyrics for S. A.
Voyage to Montevideo.
Woman from Genoa.
CAMPANELLA, TOMMASO [or TOMASSO]. People, The.
CAMPBELL, DAVID. Ariel.
Harry Pearce.
Men in Green.
Night Sowing.
Pallid Cuckoo.
Speak with the Sun.
CAMPBELL, JOSEPH ("Seosamh Mac-Cathmhaoil"). Old Woman, The.
CAMPBELL, ROY. Allegory of the Brevity of Things Human, tr.
Autumn.

Cat, The, tr.
Choosing a Mast.
Christ in the Hospital.
Horses on the Camargue.
Ill Luck, tr.
Mithraic Emblems, sel.
On Professor Drennan's Verse.
On Some South African Novelists.
Poets in Africa.
Secret Muse, The.
Serf, The.
Sisters, The.
To the Sun. Fr. Mithraic Emblems.
Tristan da Cunha.
When You Shake Loose Your Hair, tr.
Zulu Girl, The.
CAMPBELL, THOMAS. Battle of the Baltic.
Caroline, II: To the Evening Star.
Freedom and Love.
Harper, The.
Hohenlinden.
Jilted Nymph, The.
Lines on Leaving a Scene in Bavaria.
Lord Ullin's Daughter.
Maid of Neidpath, The.
Ode to Winter.
River of Life, The.
Soldier's Dream, The.
Thought Suggested by the New Year, A.
To a Young Lady, Who Asked Me to Write Something Original for Her Album.
To the Evening Star.
Ye Mariners of England.
CAMPBELL, WILFRED (William Wilfred Campbell). How One Winter Came in the Lake Region.
Indian Summer.
Winter Lakes, The.
CAMPION [or CAMPIAN], THOMAS. Awake, Awake!
Bar Not the Door.
Be Wise, and Fly Not.
Beauty, Since You So Much Desire.
Cherry-ripe.
Come, Follow Me.
Come, You Pretty False-eyed Wanton.
Dido.
Fain Would I Wed a Fair Young Man.
Follow Thy Fair Sun.
Follow Your Saint.
I Care Not for These Ladies.
In Praise of Neptune.
In the Dark What the Day Doth Forbid.
Integer Vitae.
It Fell on a Summer's Day.
Kind Are Her Answers.
Maid's Complaint, A.
Man of Life Upright, The.
My Sweetest Lesbia.
Never Weather-beaten Sail.
Now Winter Nights.
Peaceful Western Wind, The.
Place of Cupid's Fire, The.
Rose-cheeked Laura.
Secret Love or Two I Must Confess, A.
Shall I Come, Sweet Love.
Sleep, Angry Beauty.
There Is a Garden in Her Face.
Thou Art Not Fair.
Though You Are Young.
To Music Bent Is My Retired Mind.
Turn Back, You Wanton Flyer.
Vivamus, Mea Lesbia.
What Harvest Half So Sweet Is.
What If a Day.
What Then Is Love but Mourning.
When Thou Must Home [to Shades of Underground].
When to Her Lute Corinna Sings.
When We Court and Kiss.
Whether Men Do Laugh or Weep.
Winter Nights.
Your Fair Looks Inflame My Desire.
Youth and Age.
CANE, MELVILLE. Alpine View.
Color.
Peepers.
Phosphorescence.
Sun and Cloud.
CANNING, GEORGE, and JOHN HOOKHAM

FRERE. Friend of Humanity and the Knife-Grinder, The.
Inscription: For the Door of the Cell in Newgate Where Mrs. Brownrigg, the 'Prentice-Cide, Was Confined Previous to Her Execution.
Soldiers' Friend, The.
Soldier's Wife, The.
CANTON, WILLIAM. Hold Thou My Hands.
Thank-You, A.
CAPETANAKIS, DEMETRIOS. Abel.
Isles of Greece, The.
CARBELL, E. T. Frogs' Singing-School, The.
"CARDARELLI, VINCENZO" (Nazareno Cardarelli). Adolescent.
Autumn.
Evening of Gavinana.
Liguria.
Summertime.
CARDENAL, PEIRE. I Am an Enemy to Trickery and Pride.
Once on a Certain Nameless Town.
Priests Disguise as Shepherds.
CARDONA-HINE, ALVARO. Bulosan Now.
CARDUCCI, GIOSUÈ. First Snowfall.
Snowfall.
CAREW, THOMAS. Ask Me No More.
Boldness in Love.
Celia Bleeding, to the Surgeon.
Disdain Returned.
Elegy [or Elegie] upon the Death of the Dean[e] of [St.] Paul's, Dr. John Donne, An.
Epitaph on the Lady Mary Villers, An.
Excuse of Absence, An.
Fear Not, Dear Love.
Give Me More Love.
Good Counsel to a Young Maid.
He That Loves a Rosy Cheek.
Hymeneall Dialogue, An.
I Will Enjoy Thee Now.
Ingratefull Beauty Threatned.
Love's Courtship.
Mediocrity in Love Rejected.
Now That the Winter's Gone.
Pastorall Dialogue, A.
Rapture, A.
Second Rapture, The.
Secresie Protested.
Song, A: "Ask me no more where Jove bestows."
Song, A: "In her fair cheeks two pits do lie."
Song: Murdring Beautie.
Song: Perswasions to Enjoy.
Song: To Her Againe, She Burning in a Feaver.
Song: To My Inconstant Mistris.
Song: To My Mistris, I Burning in Love.
Song: To One That Desired to Know My Mistris.
Spring, The.
To A. L.: Perswasions to Love.
To My Cousin (C. R.) Marrying My Lady (A.).
True Beauty, The.
CAREY, HENRY. Love for Love's Sake.
Maid's Husband, The. Fr. Two Songs.
Namby-Pamby.
Polly Peachum.
Sally in Our Alley.
True Tar, The. Fr. Two Songs.
Two Songs.
CARLETON, SARA KING. Grand Finale.
CARLETON, WILL. New Church Organ, The.
CARLYLE, THOMAS. Corn Must Be Sown.
CARMAN, BLISS. Choristers, The.
Christmas Song.
Daphne.
Hem and Haw.
Lord of My Heart's Elation.
Low Tide on Grand Pré.
Mr. Moon.
Ships of Yule, The.
Songs of the Sea-Children, sels.
Vagabond Song, A.
Veni Creator.
Where Is Heaven?
CARMER, CARL. Antique Shop.

CARMICHAEL, AMY. Comforted.
Deliver Me.
Do We Not Hear Thy Footfall?
Evening Star, The.
Flame of God.
For All in Pain.
Have We Not Seen Thy Shining Garments Hem.
Hope.
Last Defile, The.
Lord, Thou Hast Suffered.
Tune Thou My Harp.
Yet Listen Now.
CARPENTER, WILLIAM BOYD. Before Thy Throne.
CARR, MARY JANE. Birthday of the Lord, The.
Once I Nearly Touched a Bird.
Six Birthday Candles Shining.
When a Fellow's Four.
CARRIER, CONSTANCE. Black Water and Bright Air.
CARRINGTON, HENRY. For translations from French, see RBL.
"CARROLL, LEWIS" (Charles Lutwidge Dodgson). Alice's Adventures in Wonderland, sels.
Brother and Sister.
Doll Song.
Dutchess' Lullaby, The. Fr. Alice's Adventures in Wonderland.
Evidence Read at the Trial of the Knave of Hearts. Fr. Alice's Adventures in Wonderland.
Father William. Fr. Alice's Adventures in Wonderland.
Gardener's Song, The. Fr. Sylvie and Bruno.
How Doth the Little Crocodile. Fr. Alice's Adventures in Wonderland.
Humpty Dumpty's Song. Fr. Through the Looking-Glass.
Hunting of the Snark, The.
Jabberwocky. Fr. Through the Looking-Glass.
Lobster Quadrille, The. Fr. Alice's Adventures in Wonderland.
Mad Gardener's Song, The. Fr. Sylvie and Bruno.
Manlet, The.
Pig-Tale, A. Fr. Sylvie and Bruno Concluded.
Sea Dirge, A.
Sylvie and Bruno, sel.
Sylvie and Bruno Concluded, sel.
Through the Looking-Glass, sels.
Voice of the Lobster, The. Fr. Alice's Adventures in Wonderland.
Walrus and the Carpenter, The. Fr. Through the Looking-Glass.
CARRUTH, WILLIAM HERBERT. Dreamer of Dreams.
Each in His Own Tongue.
CARRYL, CHARLES EDWARD. Nautical Ballad, A.
Plaint of the Camel, The.
CARRYL, GUY WETMORE. Ballad, A: "As I was walkin' the jungle round, a-killin' of tigers an' time."
Embarrassing Episode of Little Miss Muffet, The.
How the Helpmate of Blue-Beard Made Free with a Door.
Opportune Overthrow of Humpty Dumpty, The.
CARTER, LIN. Carcosa.
Dark Yuggoth.
Dream-Daemon, The.
Lunae Custodiens.
Sabbat, The.
CARTWRIGHT, WILLIAM. No Platonic Love.
Song of Dalliance, A.
On a Virtuous Young Gentlewoman That Died Suddenly.
Women.
CARVER, MABEL MACDONALD. Addict.
Semi-Private.
CARY, PHOEBE. Legend of the Northland, A.
CASA, GIOVANNI DELLA. To Sleep.
CASE, ELIZABETH YORK. Faith.
CASTRO, ROSALÍA DE. Atmosphere Is Incandescent, The.

Bells, The.
Feeling Her End Would Come with Summer's End.
From the Cadenced Roar of the Waves.
He Who Weeps Goes Not Alone.
Hour after Hour, Day after Day.
I in My Bed of Thistles.
I Know Not What I Seek Eternally.
I Love You . . . Why Do You Hate Me?
Justice of Man! I Go in Search of You.
Now That the Sunset of Hope.
Spring Does Not Flow Now, The.
They Say That the Plants Do Not Speak.
When the Frost Cover Them.
CATER, CATHERINE. Here and Now.
CATHER, WILLA SIBERT. Spanish Johnny.
CATO, NANCY. Independence.
CATULLUS, CAIUS [or GAIUS] VALERIUS. Acme and Septimius.
Catullus Talks to Himself.
Dialogue with a Door.
Flavius, If Your Girl Friend.
Invitation to an Invitation, An.
My Woman.
Odi et Amo.
Spring.
To Lesbia ("I hate, and yet I love thee too").
To Lesbia ("Thy kisses dost thou bid me count").
To Naso.
Vivamus, Mea Lesbia.
CAUSLEY, CHARLES. Cowboy Song.
Death of an Aircraft.
H.M.S. Glory at Sydney.
Innocent's Song.
King's College Chapel.
Nursery Rhyme of Innocence and Experience.
Seasons in North Cornwall, The.
Serenade to a Cornish Fox.
Timothy Winters.
Visit to Van Gogh, A.
CAVAFY, CONSTANTINE P. Return.
To Remain.
CAVALCANTI, GUIDO. Ballata V: "Light do I see within my Lady's eyes."
Beauty of Woman of Noble Heart.
Canzone: Donna Mi Priegha.
Fresh Newborn Rose.
He Compares All Things with His Lady, and Finds Them Wanting.
If Mercy Were a Friend to My Desires.
Lady Begs Me, A.
O Lady Mine, Caught You No Glimpse of Him.
Since I No Longer Hope, O My Sweet Song.
Sonetto XXXV: To Guido Orlando.
Sonetto VII: "Who is she that comes, makyng turn every man's eye."
There in a Woodland, to My Thought More Bright.
We're the Pens, Saddened and Dismayed.
Who's This That Comes, as Each Man Looks at Her.
You've Filled My Mind So Full of Grief.
You Have in You the Flowers and the Green Grass.
CAVENDISH, MARGARET, DUCHESS OF NEWCASTLE. See NEWCASTLE, MARGARET CAVENDISH, DUCHESS OF.
CAVENDISH, WILLIAM, DUKE OF NEWCASTLE. See NEWCASTLE, WILLIAM CAVENDISH, DUKE OF.
CAWEIN, MADISON. Ku-Klux.
Man Hunt, The.
Old Man Rain.
CECCO ANGIOLIERI DA SIENA. See ANGIOLIERI, CECCO.
CELAN, PAUL. Fugue of Death.
In Memoriam Paul Eluard.
Jugs, The.
Shibboleth.
CERCAMON. True Love Warms My Heart.
With Mournful Tones My Verses Start.
"CEIRIOG." See HUGHES, JOHN CEIRIOG.

CERVANTES SAAVEDRA, MIGUEL DE. Don Quixote, sels.
Epitaph: "Below there rests the knight." Fr. Don Quixote.
Epitaph: "Here Dulcinea doth lie." Fr. Don Quixote.
"Love's mariner am I." Fr. Don Quixote.
"Oh, could my 'was' and 'is' become." Fr. Don Quixote.
"O thou above who in thy bed." Fr. Don Quixote.
CETINA, GUTIERRE DE. Happy Hours That Hurry Away.
In What Region, in What Part of the World?
Madrigal: Eyes of Clear Serenity.
CHAFFEE, ELEANOR ALLETTA. Cobbler, The.
Difference, The.
CHAMBERLAIN, ENOLA. After the Dark.
CHAMISSO, ADELBERT [or ALBERT] VON. Tragic Story, A.
CHAN FANG-SHENG. Sailing Homeward.
CHANDLER, MARY. To Mrs. Boteler.
CHANG CHIU-LING. Looking at the Moon and Thinking of One Far Away.
CHAPIN, KATHERINE GARRISON (Mrs. Francis Biddle). Love Beleaguered.
CHAPMAN, GEORGE. Odyssey, The, sels., tr.
CHAR, RENÉ. Antonin Artaud.
Bull, The. Fr. Four Fascinators.
Contravention.
Eternity at Lourmarin.
For Two Children.
Four Fascinators.
Lark, The. Fr. Four Fascinators.
Library Is on Fire, The.
Lightning Victory.
Serpent, The. Fr. Four Fascinators.
Trout, The. Fr. Four Fascinators.
True Night.
You Did Well to Leave, Arthur Rimbaud!
CHARLES D'ORLÉANS. See ORLÉANS, CHARLES, DUC D'.
CHARTIER, ALAIN. Almighty God, Who Made the Noble State.
Most Foolish Fools, Oh Foolish Mortal Men.
CHASE, EDITH NEWLIN. New Baby Calf, The.
Passenger Train.
Tiger-Cat Tim.
Work Horses.
CHASE, VICTORIA. Birthday Cake, The.
CHASSIGNET, JEAN-BAPTISTE. His Scorn of Life and Consolation for Death.
CHASTELAIN DE COUCY, LE. Sweet Voice of the Woodland Nightingale, The.
CHATTERTON, THOMAS. Aella, sel.
Excelente Balade of Charitie, An.
Minstrel's Song. Fr. Aella.
My Love Is Dead. Fr. Aella.
CHATTOPADHYAYA, HARINDRANTH. Imagery.
CHAUCER, GEOFFREY. Balade de Bon Conseyl.
Ballade against Woman Inconstant, A.
Ballade to Rosamund.
Canterbury Tales, The, sels.
Compleynt of Chaucer to His Purse, The.
Complaint of Troilus, The. Fr. Troilus and Criseyde.
Complaint to His Purse.
Franklin's Prologue and Tale, The. Fr. The Canterbury Tales.
Gentilesse.
Hide, Absolon.
Lack of Steadfastness.
Lady without Paragon, A.
Lak of Stedfastnesse.
Merchant's Tale, The. Fr. The Canterbury Tales.
Merciles Beaute [or Merciless Beauty].
Miller, The. Fr. The Canterbury Tales.
Now Welcome Summer.
Nun's Priest's Tale, The. Fr. The Canterbury Tales.
Pardoner's Prologue and Tale, The. Fr. The Canterbury Tales.

Parlement of Foules, The, sel.
Prologue: "Whan that Aprille with his shoures soote." Fr. The Canterbury Tales.
Prologue to Sir Thopas. Fr. The Canterbury Tales.
Reeve's Tale, The. Fr. The Canterbury Tales.
Roundel: "Now welcom somer, with thy sonne softe." Fr. The Parlement of Foules.
Shipman, The. Fr. The Canterbury Tales.
Sir Thopas. Fr. The Canterbury Tales.
Song to His Purse for the King, A.
Sonnets to Laura, sel., tr.
Squire, The. Fr. The Canterbury Tales.
Ten of Chaucer's People. Fr. The Canterbury Tales.
Three Roundels of Love Unreturned.
To Rosamund [or Rosemond].
Troilus and Criseyde, sels.
Truth Shall Set You Free.
Welcome, Summer. Fr. The Parlement of Foules.
Wife of Bath, The. Fr. The Canterbury Tales.
CHAURAS. Arrows of Love.
Black Marigolds, at.
I Love Long Black Eyes, at. Fr. Black Marigolds.
CHENEY, EDNAH DOW. Prayer—Answer.
CHENEY, MRS. ELIZABETH (1859-). Overheard in an Orchard.
CHENEY, ELIZABETH. There Is a Man on the Cross.
CHÉNIER, ANDRÉ MARIE DE. When I Was Small.
CHEN SHAN-MIN. Herd-Boy's Song, The.
Moon in the Mountains, The.
CHERBURY, EDWARD HERBERT, 1ST BARON. See HERBERT OF CHERBURY.
CHERRY, ANDREW. Bay of Biscay, The.
CHERWINSKI, JOSEPH. Still Day, A.
CHESTERFIELD, PHILIP DORMER STANHOPE, 4TH EARL OF. Mistaken Fair.
CHESTERTON, GILBERT KEITH. Beatific Vision, The.
Donkey, The.
Elegy in a Country Churchyard.
Femina contra Mundum.
For a War Memorial.
Good Rich Man, The.
Heureux qui, comme Ulysse, a fait un beau voyage, tr.
Holy of Holies, The.
Home at Last.
House of Christmas, The.
Lepanto.
Prayer in Darkness, A.
Rolling English Road, The.
Song of Quoodle, The.
Sword of Surprise, The.
To the Unknown Warrior.
Variations of an Air.
World State, The.
CHETTLE, HENRY. Damelias' Song to His Diaphenia, at.
Diaphenia, at.
CHETTLE, HENRY, and ANTHONY MUNDAY. See MUNDAY, ANTHONY, and HENRY CHETTLE.
CHETTUR, GOVINDA KRISHNA. World's End.
CHIPP, ELINOR. Wild Geese.
CHISOKU. Dragonfly, The.
CHIYO. Haiku: "I wonder in what fields today."
Hokku: "Persimmon, The, lo!"
CHODZIESNER, GERTRUD. See "KOLMAR, GERTRUD."
CHOLMONDELEY, HESTER H. Betrayal.
CHRÉTIEN DE TROYES. Complaint of the Weavers. Fr. Yvain.
Yvain, sel.
CHRISTIAN, MARCUS B. Dialect Quatrain.
McDonogh Day in New Orleans.
CHRISTIANSEN, AVIS B. Yes, I Have Been to Calvary.
CHRISTINE DE PISAN. See PISAN, CHRISTINE DE.

CHURCH, PEGGY POND. Ultimatum.
CHURCH, RICHARD. Man without Faith, The.
Pigeon, The.
Something in Common.
CHUTE, MARCHETTE GAYLORD. Birthdays.
Cats.
Dandelions.
My Dog.
My Plan.
Presents.
CHUTE, ROBERT M. November 22, 1963.
CIARDI, JOHN. After Sunday Dinner We Uncles Snooze.
Aunt Mary.
Camptown.
Children When They're Very Sweet.
Credibility.
Counting on Flowers.
Dan Dunder.
Dolls, The.
Elegy: "My father was born with a spade in his hand and traded it."
Elegy Just in Case.
English A.
Evil Eye, The.
Fragments from Italy, sel.
Gift, The.
How to Tell the Top of a Hill.
I Took a Bow and Arrow.
In Ego with Us All.
In Place of a Curse.
Island Galaxy, An.
In the Stoneworks.
Men Marry What they Need. I Marry You.
Most like an Arch This Marriage.
Palaver's No Prayer.
Prattle.
Rain Sizes.
Reason for the Pelican, The.
River Is a Piece of Sky, The.
Someone.
Song for an Allegorical Play.
Suburban Homecoming.
Thanks That Flesh Is Sad, A.
That Summer's Shore.
Thousandth Poem for Dylan Thomas, A.
To Judith Asleep.
Two Egrets.
V-J Day.
Vodka.
What You Will Learn about the Brobinyak.
Why Nobody Pets the Lion at the Zoo.
CIBBER, COLLEY. Blind Boy, The.
CINO DA PISTOIA. Ah Me, Alas! Am I So Very Base.
Ah, Woe to Me Alas, for Love Has Bound.
Love Is a Subtle Spirit That Can Slay.
CIULLO [or CIELO] D'ALCAMO. Thou Sweetly-smelling Fresh Red Rose.
CLAIRMONT, ROBERT. Answers, The.
CLANCY, JOSEPH P. Boxer.
CLAPPER, MERL A. When Nobody Prays.
CLAR, CLARENCE E. In His Service.
CLARE, JOHN. Badger.
Bits of Straw.
Break of Day.
Child Harold, sel.
Clock-a-Clay.
Come Hither, My Dear One.
Country Letter.
Crow, The.
Death.
Dying Child, The.
Eternity of Nature.
February. Fr. The Shepherd's Calendar.
Gypsies.
Hares at Play.
Hesperus.
Honey Dew Falls from the Tree.
I Am.
I Hid My Love When Young.
I Lost the Love of Heaven.
I Ne'er Was Struck.
I Pass in Silence.
Invite to Eternity, An.
Language has not the power to speak what love indites.
Little Trotty Wagtail.

Love lives beyond/ The tomb.
Love, Meet Me in the Green Glen.
My Early Home.
Nature.
No single hour can stand for naught.
Pastoral Poesy.
Peasant Poet, The.
Peggy Said Good Morning.
Pleasant Sounds.
Poets Love Nature.
Remembrances.
Schoolboys in Winter.
Secret Love.
Shepherd's Calendar, The, *sel.*
Signs of Winter.
Snowstorm.
Song's Eternity.
Stanzas: "How beautiful this hill of fern swells on!" *Fr. Child Harold.*
Sudden Shower.
Summer.
Summer Images.
Summer Morning.
Thrush's Nest, The.
To the Ivy.
To the Snipe.
Vision, A.
Winter's Spring, The.
CLARK, CHARLES HEBER. *See* "ADELER, MAX."
CLARK, LEONARD. Among Shallows.
Goole Captain, The.
Peace, like a Lamb.
CLARK, ROBERT. Generations.
CLARK, THOMAS CURTIS. Apparitions.
CLARKE, AUSTIN. Early Unfinished Sketch.
Marriage.
Penal Law.
CLARKE, SYDNEY MIDDLETON. Treasure, The.
Watch Ashore—Seletar.
CLAUDIUS, MATTHIAS ("Asmus"). At the Grave of My Father.
Death and the Maiden.
Mother by the Cradle, The.
Phidile.
Seed the sower is sowing, The.
Song of War, A.
CLAYTOR, GERTRUDE. Sorceress.
Stair, The.
CLEANTHES. God Leads the Way.
CLEGHORN, SARAH NORCLIFFE. Golf Links [Lie So Near the Mill], The.
CLEMO, JACK R. Christ in the Clay-Pit.
CLERK-MAXWELL, JAMES. *See* MAXWELL, JAMES CLERK.
CLERKE, WILLIAM. So, So.
CLEVELAND, JOHN. Antiplatonick, The.
Mark Antony [*or* Anthony].
On the Memory of Mr. Edward King, Drown'd in the Irish Seas.
Whenas the Nightingale.
CLEVELAND, PHILIP JEROME. By Night.
I Yield Thee Praise.
There Is a Love.
CLIFFORD, JOHN. God's Word.
CLOUD, VIRGINIA WOODWARD. What the Lord High Chamberlain Said.
CLOUGH, ARTHUR HUGH. Ah, That I Were Far Away. *Fr. Amours de Voyage.*
Amours de Voyage, *sels.*
As I Sat at the Café. *Fr. Dipsychus.*
Columbus.
Dipsychus, *sels.*
Juxtaposition. *Fr. Amours de Voyage.*
Latest Decalogue, The.
Qua Cursum Ventus.
Say Not the Struggle Nought Availeth.
So Not Seeing I Sung. *Fr. Amours de Voyage.*
Songs in Absence, *sel.*
Spectator ab Extra.
Spirit from Perfecter Ages, A. *Fr. Amours de Voyage.*
"There Is No God." *Fr. Dipsychus.*
To spend uncounted years of pain.
Where Lies the Land [to Which the Ship Would Go]? *Fr. Songs in Absence.*
"With Whom Is No Variableness, neither Shadow of Turning."
Ye Ancient Divine Ones. *Fr. Amours de Voyage.*

COATSWORTH, ELIZABETH JANE (Mrs. Henry Beston). April Fool.
Bad Kittens, The.
Barn, The.
Bedtime.
Blue on White.
Bread the Holy.
By the Fire.
Candle and Star.
Counters.
Daniel Webster's Horses.
Down the Rain Falls.
Empty House.
Fragment from Nothing.
Green Woods.
How Gray the Rain.
It's Pleasant to Think.
January.
Lady Comes to an Inn, A.
Moon, The.
Mouse, The.
Murder House.
No shop does the bird use.
Saint John.
Summer Rain.
Ways of Trains, The.
Wind Shrieked Loud, The.
COBLENTZ, CATHERINE CATE. Housewife, The.
COBLENTZ, STANTON ARTHUR. Atlantis.
On Some Trees Needlessly Slain.
Watcher, The.
"COCKATOO JACK." Numerella Shore, The.
COCTEAU, JEAN. Plain Song, *sel.*
CODE, GRANT. Ballad of Two Kings.
Building of Sand.
Foreboding.
High Place at Marib, The.
Highway to Nowhere.
News of My Friends.
Night Refuses a Dreamer, The.
Nursery Rhymes for Surrealists.
Playground of the Pixie.
COFFIN, ROBERT PETER TRISTRAM. Ballad of Cap'n Pye.
Captains of Small Farms, The.
Christening-Day Wishes for My God-Child, Grace Lane Berkley II.
Crystal Moment.
Citizens in the Round.
Hen Overboard.
Lady of the Tomahawk, The.
Lazybones.
Lonely Lover.
Lullaby for Peregrine.
Means Massacre, The.
My Father Loved the Jumping-off Place.
Old Farmer Alone.
Secret Heart, The.
Spider, The.
Star-Pudding.
Thunder Pools.
Tree-sleeping.
We Put on the Buffalo.
Where I Took Hold of Life.
Yankee Cradle.
COGSWELL, FRED. Christmas Carol, A: "Holly wreath that now, The."
COHAN, GEORGE MICHAEL. Life's a Funny Proposition after All.
COHEN, LEONARD. Ballad: "My lady was found mutilated."
Celebration.
For Anne.
If It Were Spring.
Kite Is a Victim, A.
Poem for Marc Chagall.
Prayer for Messiah.
COHN, HANS WERNER. Of the Man Who Says in the Cellar.
Slave, The.
COLE, SAMUEL VALENTINE. Hammer and Anvil.
COLE, WILLIAM. Just Dropped In.
COLERIDGE, DERWENT. And So Men Say, I Love Thee!
COLERIDGE, HARTLEY. From Country to Town.
He Lived amidst th' Untrodden Ways.
Imitation of Wordsworth, An.
Long Time a Child.
Poietes Apoietes.
She Is Not Fair.

Sonnet: "Long time a child, and still a child, when years."
Sonnet: November.
Sonnet: To a Friend.
To a Friend.
COLERIDGE, MARY ELIZABETH. After Reading Certain Books.
After St. Augustine.
Awake.
Blue Bird, The.
From My Window.
Gone.
He Knoweth Not That the Dead Are Thine.
I Saw a Stable.
Jealousy.
Other Side of a Mirror, The.
Three Helpers in Battle.
To Memory.
Unwelcome.
Veneta.
Where a Roman Villa Stood, above Freiburg.
COLERIDGE, SAMUEL TAYLOR. Apologia pro Vita Sua.
Christabel, *sel.*
Dejection; an Ode.
Do You Ask What the Birds Say?
Fears in Solitude, *sel.*
Fragment, A: "Encinctured with a twine of leaves."
France; an Ode.
Frost at Midnight.
Glycine's Song.
I Mix in Life.
Knight's Tomb, The.
Kubla Khan; or, A Vision in a Dream.
Love.
On a Ruined House in a Romantic Country.
On Donne's Poetry.
Pains of Sleep, The.
Raven, The.
Rime of the Ancient Mariner, The.
Scars Remaining, The. *Fr. Christabel.*
Song: "Sunny shaft did I behold, A."
Swans Sing.
This Lime-Tree Bower My Prison.
Work without Hope.
Youth and Age.
COLERIDGE, SARA. Months, The.
Phantasmion, *sel.*
Song: "He came unlook'd for, undesir'd."
COLIN MUSET. My Lord, Although I Strum and Sing.
COLLINS, JOHN. Tomorrow.
COLLINS, LESLIE MORGAN. Stevedore.
COLLINS, MORTIMER. If.
Salad.
COLLINS, WILLIAM. Dirge in "Cymbeline."
How Sleep the Brave.
Lament for Tintoretta. *Fr. Three Fragments.*
Limitations of Human Art. *Fr. Three Fragments.*
Luckless Collins. *Fr. Three Fragments.*
Ode: "How sleep the brave who sink to rest."
Ode: Written in the Beginning of the Year 1746.
Ode on the death of [Mr.] Thomson.
Ode on the Poetical Character.
Ode on the Popular Superstitions of the Highlands of Scotland, An.
Ode to Evening.
Ode to Fear.
Ode to Mercy.
Ode to Pity.
Ode to Simplicity.
Ode Written in MDCCXLVI.
Passions, The.
Song from Shakespeare's "Cymbeline," A.
Three Fragments.
To Evening.
COLLINSON, LAURENCE. Sea and the Tiger, The.
COLLYMORE, FRANK A. Zobo Bird, The.
COLUM, PADRAIC. Asses, *sel.*
Condors.
Dahlias.

COLUM, PADRAIC (*continued*)
I Saw the Wind Today. *Fr.* Reminiscence.
"I Shall Not Die for Thee."
Interior.
Old Woman of the Roads, An.
Puppet Play, The.
Reminiscence, *sel.*
Sea Bird to the Wave, The.
Spider.
Terrible Robber Men, The.
Wall of China, The.
Wind, The. *Fr.* Reminiscence.
Young Girl: Annam.
COMBS, TRAM. Ars Poetica about Ultimates.
Aware Aware.
I Flung Up My Arm Half from Sleep.
Just after Noon with Fierce Shears.
COMFORT, ALEX. After Shakespeare.
After You, Madam.
Haste to the Wedding.
Love Poem: "There is a white mare that my love keeps."
Sublimation.
CONCANEN, MATTHEW. Heaps on Heaps. *Fr.* A Match at Football.
Match at Football, A, *sel.*
CONDER, ALAN. *For translations from French, see* RBL.
CONFUCIUS. Airs of Pei, *sel. Fr.* The Classic Anthology.
Alba. *Fr.* The Classic Anthology: Songs of T'ang.
Aliter. *Fr.* The Classic Anthology: Songs of Ch'en.
Baroness Mu Impeded in Her Wish to Help Famine Victims in Wei. *Fr.* The Classic Anthology: Yung Wind.
Chou and the South, *sel. Fr.* The Classic Anthology.
Classic Anthology, The, *sels.*
Deer Sing, *sel. Fr.* The Classic Anthology.
Efficient Wife's Complaint, The. *Fr.* The Classic Anthology: Airs of Pei.
Fraternitas. *Fr.* The Classic Anthology: Deer Sing.
Morning Glory, The.
Pedlar. *Fr.* The Classic Anthology: Wei Wind.
Sans Equity and sans Poise. *Fr.* The Classic Anthology: Yung Wind.
Shao and the South, *sel. Fr.* The Classic Anthology.
Songs of Ch'en, *sels. Fr.* The Classic Anthology.
Songs of Cheng, *sels. Fr.* The Classic Anthology.
Songs of T'ang, *sel. Fr.* The Classic Anthology.
Wei Wind, *sel. Fr.* The Classic Anthology.
Yung Wind, *sels. Fr.* The Classic Anthology.
CONGREVE, WILLIAM. Better Bargain, The.
False! or Inconstancy.
False Though She Be [to Me].
Love for Love, *sel.*
Nymph and a Swain, A. *Fr.* Love for Love.
Pious Celinda [*or* Selinda].
CONKLIN, GRACE HAZARD. After Sunset.
CONKLING, HILDA. Mouse.
Old Bridge, The.
Spring Song.
CONNELLY, BEVERLY. Testimony.
2000 A.D.
CONNER, J. WALTER. John Chinaman, My Jo.
CONNOLLY, MYLES. Quo Vadis?
Said the Innkeeper.
CONON DE BÉTHUNE. If This Insensate Rage.
CONQUEST, ROBERT. Adriatic.
Aids to Composition.
Motives of Rhythm, The.
Seal Rocks: San Francisco.
CONSTABLE, HENRY. Damelias' Song to His Diaphenia, *at.*
Diaphenia, *at.*
COOK, ELIZA. Three Little Kittens, *at.*

COOKSLEY, BERT. Buck Fever.
COOLIDGE, GRACE *(Mrs. Calvin Coolidge).* Open Door, The.
"COOLIDGE, SUSAN" (Sarah Chauncey Woolsey). Child's Thought of Harvest, A.
Easter Song, An.
COON, JEANETTE SAXTON. Mother's Prayer, A.
COOPER, EDITH, *and* KATHERINE BRADLEY. *See* "FIELD, MICHAEL."
COOPER, GEORGE. October's Party.
COOPER, JANE. Builder of Houses, The.
Faithful, The.
For a Very Old Man on the Death of His Wife.
For Thomas Hardy.
Graveyard, The.
Obligations.
Sundial, The.
COPLEY, FRANK O. Vivamus, Mea Lesbia, *tr.*
CORAZZINI, SERGIO. Desolation of the Poor Sentimental Poet.
For Hurdy-Gurdy.
CORBETT, RICHARD. Certain True Woords Spoken Concerning One Benet Corbett after Her Death.
Fairies' Farewell, The.
Farewell to the Fairies.
Proper New Ballad, A, Intituled The Faeryes Farewell; or, God-A-Mercy Will.
To His Son [Vincent Corbet, on His Birth-Day, November 10, 1630, Being Then Three Years Old].
CORBETT, MRS. E. T. Inventor's Wife, The.
CORBIÈRE, TRISTAN (Edouard Joachim Corbière). To My Mouse-colored Mare.
To the Eternal Feminine.
CORKE, HILARY. Any Man to His Secretary.
Calm Winter Sleep.
Choice, The.
Waiting.
CORKINE, WILLIAM. Sweet, Let Me Go.
CORNEILLE, PIERRE. Stanzas to the Marquise.
CORNFORD, FRANCES (Darwin). Corner of the Field, The.
Dogs. *Fr.* Feri's Dream.
Feri's Dream.
Flowers in a Meadow, The.
Nurse.
To a Fat Lady Seen from the Train.
Watch, The.
CORNISH, WILLIAM. Gratitude.
Pleasure It Is.
You and I and Amyas.
"CORNWALL, BARRY" (Bryan Waller Procter). Sea, The.
CORRINGTON, JOHN WILLIAM. Communique, I, *sel.*
CORSO, GREGORY. But I Do Not Need Kindness.
Dream of a Baseball Star.
I Am 25.
Italian Extravaganza.
Last Warmth of Arnold, The.
Lines Written Nov. 22, 23—1963.
Mad Yak, The.
Marriage.
Uccello.
CORTEZ, CARLOS. Outa Work Blues.
CORY, WILLIAM JOHNSON. Dirge, A: "Naiad, hid beneath the bank."
Eton Boating Song.
Heraclitus, *after* Callimachus.
Separation, A.
COSINS, JOHN. Come, Holy Ghost, our souls inspire, *ad.*
COTTERELL, MABEL. *For translations from German, see* AnML; SiGo.
COTTON, CHARLES. Alice. *Fr.* Resolution in Four Sonnets.
Epigramme: "Some four years ago I made Phillis an offer," *tr.*
Evening.
Laura Sleeping.
Margaret. *Fr.* Resolution in Four Sonnets.
Resolution in Four Sonnets, of a Po-

etical Question Put to Me by a Friend, Concerning Four Rural Sisters, *sels.*
Retreat, The.
Song of the Inconstant Hylas, *tr.*
COULETTE, HENRI. Attic, The.
Cinema, at the Lighthouse. *Fr.* The War of the Secret Agents.
Denise: A Letter Never Sent. *Fr.* The War of the Secret Agents.
Epilogue: Author to Reader. *Fr.* The War of the Secret Agents.
Intaglio.
Phono, at the Boar's Head. *Fr.* The War of the Secret Agents.
War of the Secret Agents, The.
COUNSELMAN, MARY ELIZABETH. Room in Darkness.
COWDERY, CECIL, *and* AVRAHM YARMOLINSKY. *See* YARMOLINSKY, AVRAHM, *and* CECIL COWDERY.
COWLEY, ABRAHAM. Acme and Septimius, *tr.*
Another.
Change, The.
Country Mouse, The.
Drinking.
Epicure, The.
Extasie, The.
Grasshopper, The.
Heat, *tr.*
Mistress, The, *sel.*
Motto, The.
Ode: Of Wit.
Ode upon Dr. Harvey, *sel.*
On Drinking.
On the Death of Mr. Crashaw.
On the Death of Mr. William Hervey.
Supplication, A.
Thirsty Earth, The.
To His Young Mistress, *tr.*
To Lesbia, *tr.*
Wish, The. *Fr.* The Mistress.
Woman's Arms, *tr.*
Written in Juice of Lemmon.
COWLEY, MALCOLM. Hill above the Mine, The.
COWPER, WILLIAM. Castaway, The.
Contrite Heart, The.
Cricket, The, *tr.*
Diverting History of John Gilpin, The.
Epitaph on Johnson.
Garden, The. *Fr.* The Task.
God Moves in a Mysterious Way.
I Will Praise the Lord at All Times.
In His Mental Illness, William Cowper Finds He Is Not Alone.
Jehovah-Rophi.
John Gilpin.
Joy and Peace in Believing.
Light and Glory of the World, The.
Light Shining Out of Darkness.
Lines Written on a Window-Shutter at Weston.
Loss of the *Royal George,* The.
Mysterious Way, The.
Nightingale and the Glowworm, The.
Ode, An: Secundum Artem.
On the Loss of the *Royal George.*
On the Receipt of My Mother's Picture Out of Norfolk.
Poplar Field, The.
Rights of Women, The.
Shrubbery, The.
Sofa, The. *Fr.* The Task.
Solitude of Alexander Selkirk, The.
Sonnet to William Wilberforce, Esq.
Table Talk, *sel.*
Task, The, *sels.*
Temptation.
To a Young Lady.
To Mary.
To Mary Unwin.
To the Immortal Memory of the Halibut on Which I Dined This Day.
To the Same.
Valley of the Shadow of Death, The.
Verses: "I am monarch of all I survey."
Verses Supposed to Be Written by Alexander Selkirk during His Solitary Abode on the Island of Juan Fernandez.
Walking with God.

Winter Morning Walk, The. *Fr.* The Task.
COXE, ARTHUR CLEVELAND. We Are Living, We Are Dwelling.
COX, KENYON. Octopussycat.
CRABBE, CHRIS WALLACE-. *See* WALLACE-CRABBE, CHRIS.
CRABBE, GEORGE. Ancient Virgin, An. *Fr.* The Parish Register.
Borough, The, *sels.*
Critics.
Delay Has Danger, *sel. Fr.* Tales of the Hall.
East Anglian Seas and Shores, *sel.*
Frank Courtship, The, *sel.*
His Wife's [*or* Mother's] Wedding Ring.
Jonas Kindred's Household. *Fr.* The Frank Courtship.
Lady of the Manor, The. *Fr.* The Parish Register.
Parish Register, The. *sels.*
Pauper's Funeral, The. *Fr.* The Village.
Peter Grimes. *Fr.* The Borough.
Sad Lover, The. *Fr.* Tales of the Hall.
Sailing upon the River. *Fr.* The Borough.
Schools. *Fr.* The Borough.
Sir Eustace Grey, *sel.*
Slum Dwelling, A. *Fr.* The Borough.
Tales of the Hall, *sels.*
Vicar, The. *Fr.* The Borough.
Village, The, *sels.*
Winter Views Serene. *Fr.* The Borough.
CRADDLE, W. Egoism.
CRAIG, ALEXANDER. Hillside.
CRAIK, DINAH MARIA MULOCK. Now and Afterwards.
Young Dandelion, The.
CRANCH, CHRISTOPHER PEARSE. Enosis.
Gnosis.
Pines and the Sea, The.
Stanza from an Early Poem.
CRANE, CARL. Reader Writes, The.
CRANE, HART. Above the Fresh Ruffles of the Surf. *Fr.* Voyages.
Air Plant, The.
And yet this great wink of eternity. *Fr.* Voyages.
At Melville's Tomb.
Atlantis. *Fr.* The Bridge.
Ave Maria. *Fr.* The Bridge.
Black Tambourine.
Bridge, The, *sels.*
Broken Tower, The.
Chaplinesque.
For the Marriage of Faustus and Helen.
Hurricane, The.
Legend.
Name for All, A.
National Winter Garden. *Fr.* The Bridge.
O Carib Isle!
Praise for an Urn.
Repose of Rivers.
River, The. *Fr.* The Bridge.
Royal Palm.
To Brooklyn Bridge. *Fr.* The Bridge.
Tunnel, The. *Fr.* The Bridge.
Van Winkle. *Fr.* The Bridge.
Voyages.
Wine Menagerie, The.
CRANE, NATHALIA. Janitor's Boy, The.
CRANE, STEPHEN. Black Riders, The, *sels.*
Blade[s] of Grass, The. *Fr.* The Black Riders.
Blue Battalions, The.
Do Not Weep, Maiden, for War Is Kind. *Fr.* War Is Kind.
I Stood upon a High Place. *Fr.* The Black Riders.
Man Saw a Ball of Gold in the Sky, A. *Fr.* The Black Riders.
Slant of Sun, A. *Fr.* War Is Kind.
There Was One I Met upon the Road.
Three Poems.
Trees in the Garden, The. *Fr.* War Is Kind.
War is Kind, *sels.*

CRANE, WALTER. Crocus, The.
CRAPSEY, ADELAIDE. November Night.
Song: "I make my shroud but no one knows."
Triad.
CRASHAW, RICHARD. Apologie for the Precedent Hymnes on Teresa, An.
Charitas Nimia; or, The Deare Bargain.
Coming Child, The.
Death's Lecture at the Funeral of a Young Gentleman.
Epitaph upon a Young Married Couple [Dead and Buried Together], An.
Flaming Heart, The.
Hymn to St. Teresa.
Hymne for the Epiphanie, A. Sung as by the Three Kings.
Hymne of the Nativity, Sung as by the Shepheards, An.
In Memory of the Vertuous and Learned Lady Madre de Teresa That Sought an Early Martyrdome.
In the Holy Nativity of Our Lord God, a Hymn Sung as by the Shepherds.
Letter to the Countess of Denbigh, A.
Luke 11.
Musicks Duell.
Ode Which Was Prefixed to a Prayer Booke Given to a Young Gentlewoman, An.
On a Prayer Book Sent to Mrs. M. R., *sel.*
On Mr. George Herbert's Booke Intituled the Temple of Sacred Poems, Sent to a Gentle-woman.
On Our Crucified Lord, Naked and Bloody.
On the Assumption.
On the Blessed Virgin's Bashfulness.
On the Name of Jesus.
Saint Mary Magdalene, *scl.*
Shepherd's Hymn, The, *sel.*
Teare, The.
Two Went Up to the Temple to Pray.
Upon the Bleeding Crucifix.
Upon the Body of Our Blessed Lord, Naked and Bloody.
Upon Venus Putting on Mars His Armes.
Weeper, The.
When love of us called Him to see.
Wishes for [*or* to] the [*or* His] Supposed Mistress.
CRASTER, MRS. EDWARD. Centipede Was Happy Quite, A.
Puzzled Centipede, The.
CRAWFORD, DAN. Jesus and I.
CRAWFORD, ISABELLA VALANCY. Canoe, The.
Gisli, the Chieftain, *sel.*
Malcolm's Katie, *sels.*
Song of the Arrow, The. *Fr.* Gisli, the Chieftain.
CREECH, THOMAS. Enchantment, The, *tr. Fr.* Idylls.
Idylls, *sel., tr.*
CREEKMORE, HUBERT. Book of True Love, The, *sel., tr.*
Count William's Escapade, *tr.*
Lament of the Lovely Helmet-Dealer, *tr.*
Satires, The (*of* Juvenal), *sel., tr.*
CREELEY, ROBERT. Anger.
Ballad of the Despairing Husband.
Bed, The.
Death of Venus, The.
Distance.
Door, The.
End of the Day, The.
Form of Adaptation, A.
Form of Women, A.
Hart Crane.
House, The.
I Know a Man.
Immoral Proposition, The.
Invoice, The.
Jack's Blues.
Kore.
Language, The.
Love Comes Quietly.
Mountains in the Desert, The.
Name, The.
Naughty Boy.
Oh No.

Operation, The.
Rhyme, The.
Rhythm, The.
Rose, The.
She Went to Stay.
Snow, The.
Way, The.
Whip, The.
Wicker Basket, A.
Wife, The.
Wind, The.
CRESSMAN, H. E. Coxswain's Line, The.
CREWS, JUDSON. Declaration at Forty.
Love Poem.
Oh Beach Love Blossom.
CRINAGORAS [*or* KRINAGORAS]. From the Greek Anthology.
CRIPPS, ARTHUR SHEARLY. To the Veld.
CRISWELL, CLOYD MANN. Newlyweds, The.
CROSBY, FANNY (Frances Jane Crosby). All the Way My Saviour Leads Me.
Blind but Happy.
CROSS, MRS. GEORGE FREDERICK. *See* CAMBRIDGE, ADA.
CROSS, MARY ANN [*or* MARIAN] EVANS LEWES. *See* "ELIOT, GEORGE."
CROSS, ZORA. Elegy on an Australian Schoolboy, *sel.*
When I Was Six.
CROSSMAN, SAMUEL. Love Unknown.
CROUCH, PEARL RIGGS. Story in the Snow, A.
CROWELL, GRACE NOLL (Mrs. Norman H. Crowell). Let Us Keep Christmas.
Quiet Things.
CROWNE, JOHN. I hate those potent madmen, who keep all.
CRUICKSHANK, HELEN B. Shy Geordie.
CUDJOE, SETH D. Transmigration.
CULLEN, COUNTEE. Any Human to Another.
For a Lady I Know. *Fr.* Four Epitaphs.
For John Keats, Apostle of Beauty. *Fr.* Four Epitaphs.
For My Grandmother. *Fr.* Four Epitaphs.
For Paul Laurence Dunbar. *Fr.* Four Epitaphs.
Four Epitaphs.
Fruit of the Flower.
Heritage.
Judas Iscariot.
Lady I Know, A.
Litany of the Dark People, The.
Simon the Cyrenian Speaks.
That Bright Chimeric Beast.
What Is Africa to Me? *Fr.* Heritage.
Yet Do I Marvel.
Youth Sings a Song of Rosebuds.
CUMMINGS, ALISON ELIZABETH. To a Little Sister, Aged Ten.
CUMMINGS, EDWARD ESTLIN. All in Green Went My Love Riding.
Annie Died the Other Day.
Anyone Lived in a Pretty How Town.
Buffalo Bill's.
Cambridge Ladies [Who Live in Furnished Souls], The. *Fr.* Sonnets—Realities.
Chanson Innocente ("In just-spring").
Chanson Innocente ("Little tree").
Dominic Has a Doll.
Enter No (Silence Is the Blood Whose Flesh).
Four [1].
From Spiralling Ecstatically This.
Her Careful Distinct Sex Whose Sharp Lips Comb.
I Am a Little Church (No Great Cathedral).
I Like My Body When It Is with Your. *Fr.* Sonnets—Actualities.
I Sing of Olaf [Glad and Big].
I Thank You God [for Most This Amazing].
If I Have Made, My Lady.
In Just-Spring.
In Time of Daffodils.
Is 5, *sel.*
It May Not Always Be So.
It's jolly/ odd what pops into.
Little Tree.

CUMMINGS, EDWARD ESTLIN (*cont.*)
Maggie and Milly and Molly and May.
Man Who Had Fallen among Thieves, A.
May I Feel Said He.
May My Heart Always Be Open.
My Father Moved through Dooms of Love.
My Love.
My Sweet Old Etcetera.
Next to of Course God [America I].
Nobody Loses All the Time.
Now Does Our World Descend.
Number 77: "I am a little church (no great cathedral)."
O Sweet Spontaneous.
One Times One, *sel.*
Pity This Busy Monster, Manunkind.
Plato told/ him: he couldn't.
Poem: "Maggie and Milly and Molly and May."
Poem, or Beauty Hurts Mr. Vinal.
She Being Brand.
Somewhere I Have Never Travelled, Gladly Beyond.
Sonnets—Actualities, *sel.*
Sonnets—Realities, *sels.*
Sonnets—Unrealities, *sel.*
Sweet Spring Is Your.
What If a Much of a Which of a Wind.
When Any Mortal (Even the Most Odd).
When God Lets My Body Be.
When Serpents Bargain for the Right to Squirm.
When the Spent Day Begins to Frail.
Who Knows If the Moon's.
CUNEY, WARING. Finis.
No Images.
Threnody: "Only quiet death."
CUNNINGHAM, ALLAN. John Grumlie.
Wet Sheet and a Flowing Sea, A.
CUNNINGHAM, JAMES VINCENT. August Hail.
Elders at Their Services Begin, The.
Epigram: "And now you're ready who while she was here."
Epigram: "You ask me how Contempt who claims to sleep."
Epitaph: "When I shall be without regret."
Five Epigrams.
For My Contemporaries.
Horoscope.
In Whose Will Is Our Peace?
It Was in Vegas.
Lip.
Montana Pastoral.
On a Cold Night.
On the Calculus.
Pick-up, The.
To a Friend, on Her Examination for the Doctorate in English.
You Ask Me How Contempt Who Claims to Sleep.
CUNNINGHAM, JOHN. Virtuous Fox and the Self-righteous Cat, The.
CUNNINGHAME-GRAHAM, ROBERT. *See* GRAHAM, ROBERT.
CUOMO, GEORGE. Man of My Dreams, The.
CURNOW, ALLEN. House and Land.
CURREY, RALPH NIXON. Epitaph on Rabelais, *tr.*
In Memoriam Roy Campbell.
Sonnet: "I hate the money-lending avarice," *tr.*
To a Fountain, *tr.*
To Remi Belleau, *tr.*
CURTIS, NATALIE (Natalie Curtis Burlin). Corn-grinding Song, *tr.*
Korosta Katzina Song, *tr.*
Wind-Song, *tr.*
CURTIS, THELMA. God's Will Is Best.
CURZON, COLIN. Not Tonight, Josephine.
CUSHMAN, RALPH SPAULDING. Secret, The.
Sheer Joy.
CUTHBERTSON, JAMES LISTER. Racing Eight, A.
CZAMANSKE, W. M. Higher Calling, The.

D

"D., H." *See* DOOLITTLE, HILDA.
DAFYDD AP [*or* AB] GWILYM. Snowy Day, A.
DAHN, FELIX. Hagen's Dying Song.
DAICHES, DAVID. To Kate, Skating Better than Her Date.
DALEY, EDITH. Praise.
DALEY, VICTOR JAMES WILLIAM PATRICK. Ascetic, The.
Dreams.
Faith.
In a Wine Cellar.
Narcissus and Some Tadpoles.
Night, *sel.*
Tamerlane.
DALFIN D'ALVERNHE. *See* PEIROL *and* DALFIN D'ALVERNHE.
DALLAS, FRED. Smithfield Market Fire, The.
DALLAS, RUTH. Milking before Dawn.
DALMON, CHARLES. Ballad of the Epiphany.
DALY, JOHN. Toast to the Flag, A.
DALY, THOMAS AUGUSTINE. Child's Christmas Song, A.
Leetla Boy, Da.
Leetla Giorgio Washeenton.
Mia Carlotta.
Song of the Thrush, The.
Tides of Love, The.
Two 'Mericana Men.
Wheestlin' Barber, Da.
DALZIEL, KATHLEEN. He Could Have Found His Way.
DANA, RICHARD HENRY. Little Beach Bird, The.
DANA, ROBERT PATRICK. Notes on a Child's Coloring Book.
DANIEL, ARNAUT. Aura amara, L'.
Autet e bas.
Bel m'es quan lo vens m'alena.
DANIEL, SAMUEL. Are They Shadows That We See? *Fr.* Tethys' Festival.
Beauty, sweet love, is like the morning dew. *Fr.* To Delia.
Care-Charmer Sleep [Son of the Sable Night]. *Fr.* To Delia.
Complaint of Rosamond, The, *sel.*
Delia. *See* To Delia.
Description of Beauty, A, *sel.*
Early Love. *Fr.* Hymen's Triumph.
Enjoy Thy April Now. *Fr.* A Description of Beauty.
Epistle to Henry Wriothesley, Earl of Southampton.
Fair is my love, and cruel as she's fair. *Fr.* To Delia.
First Flame. *Fr.* Hymen's Triumph.
Hymen's Triumph, *sels.*
Lonely Beauty. *Fr.* The Complaint of Rosamond.
Love Is a Sickness. *Fr.* Hymen's Triumph.
Musophilus, *sel.*
My cares draw on mine everlasting night. *Fr.* To Delia.
Read in my face a volume of despairs. *Fr.* To Delia.
Tethys' Festival, *sel.*
To Delia, *sels.*
To the Reader.
To the Right Worthy Knight Sir Fulke Greville.
Ulysses and the Siren.
When winter snows upon thy sable hairs. *Fr.* To Delia.
DANIELLS, ROY. Farewell to Winnipeg.
DANNER, MARGARET. Dance of the Abakweta. *Fr.* Far from Africa.
Elevator Man Adheres to Form, The.
Etta Moten's Attic. *Fr.* Far from Africa.
Far from Africa.
Garnishing the Aviary. *Fr.* Far from Africa.
Slave and the Iron Lace, The.
Visit of the Professor of Aesthetics, The. *Fr.* Far from Africa.

DANQUAH, JOSEPH V. B. Way of Life, The.
DANTE ALIGHIERI. Beyond the sphere which spreads to widest space. *Fr.* La Vita Nuova.
Beyond the Sphere Which Turns Most Distant. *Fr.* La Vita Nuova.
Dante and Beatrice in the Earthly Paradise. *Fr.* Divina Commedia: Purgatorio.
Dante's Angels. *Fr.* Divina Commedia: Purgatorio.
Dante's Heaven. *Fr.* Divina Commedia: Paradiso.
Divina Commedia, *sels.*
I Seek to Make My Speech a Yawp as Bitter.
Nothing Will Ever Seem to Me More Cruel.
Sonnet: "Mine eyes beheld the blessed pity spring." *Fr.* La Vita Nuova.
That she hath gone to Heaven suddenly. *Fr.* La Vita Nuova.
To a Short Day and a Great Ring of Shadow.
To Guido Cavalcanti.
Very pitiful lady, very young, A. *Fr.* La Vita Nuova.
Vita Nuova, La, *sels.*
Within Her Eyes. *Fr.* La Vita Nuova.
Ye pilgrim folk advancing pensively. *Fr.* La Vita Nuova.
DANTE ALIGHIERI *and* FORESE DONATI. Tenzone Sequence.
DARGAN, OLIVE TILFORD. Birth.
Far Bugles.
Guest Room.
Homeward Song.
Morning Window.
DARÍO, RUBÉN (Félix Rubén García Sarmiento). Autumn Verses.
Autumnal.
Doom.
Eheu!
Far Away and Long Ago.
Fount, The.
I Pursue a Form.
Leda.
Marguerite.
Melancholy.
Nocturne: "Those who give ear to the heart of the night."
Philosophy.
Seashell.
Sonatina.
Spring.
Swans, The.
Symphony in Gray Major.
Triumphal March.
Unhappy He.
DARLEY, GEORGE. Dove's Loneliness, The.
Enchanted Lyre, The.
Ethelstan, *sel.*
Hoopoe. *Fr.* Nepenthe.
Hundred-sunned Phenix. *Fr.* Nepenthe.
In Dreamy Swoon. *Fr.* Nepenthe.
Lilian's Song.
Loveliness of Love, The.
Mermaiden's Vesper Hymn, The. *Fr.* Syren Songs.
Nepenthe, *sels.*
On the Death of a Recluse.
Onward to Far Ida. *Fr.* Nepenthe.
Phoenix, The. *Fr.* Nepenthe.
Runilda's Chant. *Fr.* Ethelstan.
Sea-Ritual, The. *Fr.* Syren Songs.
Serenade of a Loyal Martyr.
Song, A: "It is not beauty I demand."
Syren Songs, *sels.*
Unicorn, The. *Fr.* Nepenthe.
DARLING, MARGARET STANION. Country Lane.
DARWIN, FRANCES. *See* CORNFORD, FRANCES.
DAS, KAMALA. With Its Quiet Tongue.
DASWANI, TILOTTAMA. I, Pluto.
DÄUBLER, THEODOR. Cats.
DAUGHERTY, JAMES HENRY. Gates of the Rockies.
Missouri Rhapsody.
Trail Breakers.
Wheel Ruts.

DAVENANT [*or* D'AVENANT], SIR WIL-
LIAM. Christians Reply to the
Philosopher, The, *sel.*
Jealousy. *Fr.* The Siege of Rhodes.
Law against Lovers, The, *sel.*
Life and Death. *Fr.* The Christians
Reply to the Philosopher.
News from Plymouth, *sel.*
O Thou That Sleep'st. *Fr.* News from
Plymouth.
Siege of Rhodes, The, *sel.*
Storm at Sea.
Under the Willow Shades.
Wake All the Dead. *Fr.* The Law
against Lovers.
Willow, The.
DAVIDSOHN, HANS. *See* "HODDIS, JAKOB
VAN."
DAVIDSON, GUSTAV. Ambushed by Angels.
Downgoing.
From Nothing Strange.
DAVIDSON, JOHN. Ballad of a Nun, A.
Ballad of Hell, A.
In Romney Marsh.
In the Isle of Dogs.
London.
Northern Suburb, A.
Runnable Stag, A.
Thirty Bob a Week.
War Song.
DAVIDSON, RICHARD. Play the Last
March Slowly.
DAVIE, DONALD. Corrib: An Emblem.
For an Age of Plastics. Plymouth.
Fountain, The.
Gardens No Emblems.
Hearing Russian Spoken.
Heigh-ho on a Winter Afternoon.
Mushroom Gatherers, The.
Remembering the Thirties.
Time Passing, Beloved.
Wind at Penistone, The.
Winter Talent, A.
Woodpigeons at Raheny.
DAVIES, IDRIS. Gwalia Deserta, *sel.*
Lay Preacher Ponders, The.
DAVIES, JOHN, OF HEREFORD. In Rainy-
gloomy Weather.
DAVIES, SIR JOHN. Nosce Teipsum, *sel.*
On a Pair of Garters.
Orchestra, *sel.*
Soul and the Body, The. *Fr.* Nosce
Teipsum.
DAVIES, MARY CAROLYN. Man's Woman,
A.
Six in June.
Tree Birthdays.
DAVIES, SNEYD. On Dr. Crank's Vic-
tory over the Gout.
Rhapsody to Milton.
To a Gentleman in Love with a Negro
Woman.
DAVIES, TREFOR. Song of an Old Sailor.
DAVIES, WILLIAM HENRY. Cant.
Dreams of the Sea.
Elements, The.
Example, The.
Great Time, A.
Greeting, A.
Hospital Waiting-Room, The
I Am the Poet Davies, William.
Inquest, The.
Leisure.
Mangers.
One Poet Visits Another.
Poet, The.
Rain, The.
School's Out.
Sea, The.
Speed.
Thunderstorms.
Wild Oats.
DAVIS, EMILY. *See* PFEIFFER, EMILY.
DAVIS, F. W. Thankful Heart.
DAVIS, FRANK MARSHALL. Flowers of
Darkness.
Four Glimpses of Night.
DAVIS, HELEN BAYLEY. Jack Frost.
Song for a Child.
DAVIS, KATHERINE. Act II.
DAVIS, NORMA L. Daydreamers.
DAVIS, OZORA STEARNS. We Bear the
Strain of Earthly Care.
DAVIS, THOMAS OSBORNE. My Grave.

DAVISON, EDWARD. Novice, The.
Sonnet: "She is so young, and never
never before."
DAVISON, FRANCIS. Cupid's Pastime.
DAVISON, PETER. Artemis.
Breaking of the Day, The.
Finale: Presto.
North Shore.
Peeper, The.
DAWE, BRUCE. City, The: Midnight.
Only the Beards Are Different.
DAY LEWIS, CECIL. Children look down
upon the morning-grey.
Christmas Eve.
Come, Live with Me and Be My Love.
Dead, The.
Departure in the Dark.
Emily Brontë.
Great Magicians, The.
In the Heart of Contemplation.
In the Shelter.
Jig.
Magnetic Mountain, The, *sels.*
Misfit, The—1939-1945.
Neurotic, The.
Newsreel.
O Dreams, O Destinations, *sel.*
Parting Shot, A.
Reconciliation.
Room, The.
Seen from the Train.
Son and Father.
Sun Came Out in April, The.
Tempt Me No More [for I]. *Fr.* The
Magnetic Mountain.
Third Enemy Speaks. *Fr.* The Mag-
netic Mountain.
Unwanted, The.
DEAMER, DULCIE. Artemis.
DEARMER, GEOFFREY. Giraffe, The.
DEHN, PAUL. Exercise Book.
Game of Consequences, A.
"Jenny Kiss'd Me When We Met."
London Train.
DEI-ANANG, MICHAEL. Africa Speaks.
DEITZ, PURD EUGENE. Builders.
DEKKER, GEORGE. 22nd November, 1963.
DEKKER, THOMAS, *and* JOHN FORD.
Haymakers, Rakers. *Fr.* The Sun's
Darling.
Sun's Darling, The, *sel.*
DEKKER, THOMAS, *and others.* Art
Thou Poor? *Fr.* The Pleasant Com-
edy of Patient Grissell.
Golden Slumbers. *Fr.* The Pleasant
Comedy of Patient Grissell.
Happy Heart, The. *Fr.* The Pleasant
Comedy of Patient Grissell.
Pleasant Comedy of Patient Grissell,
The, *sels.*
DE LA MARE, WALTER ("Walter Ramal").
Afraid.
Alas, Alack.
All but Blind.
All That's Past.
Ann and the Fairy Song. *Fr.* a
Child's Day.
At Ease.
At Home, Alone with the Cat.
At the Keyhole.
Bandog, The.
Barber's, The.
Bards, The.
Bead Mat, The.
Bunches of Grapes.
Buttons.
Child's Day, A, *sel.*
Christening, The.
Corner, The.
Crumbs.
Cupboard, The.
Dream-Song.
Echoes.
False Gods.
Fare Well.
Fiddler, A.
Fly, The.
Ghost, The.
Gone.
Grace.
Horseman, The.
Hyssop.
In the Dying of Daylight.
Listeners, The.

Little Bird, The.
Little Creature, The.
Little Green Orchard, The.
Many a Mickle.
Marionettes, The.
Me.
Mima.
Miss T.
Motley.
Never More, Sailor.
Old Summerhouse, The.
Peace.
Quartette, The.
Railway Junction, The.
Rainbow, The.
Reserved.
Sam.
Scribe, The.
Seeds.
She Said.
Silver.
Softly, Drowsily.
Some One.
Song of the Mad Prince, The.
Theologians.
Tired Tim.
To a Candle.
To K. M.
Tom's Angel.
Two Deep Clear Eyes.
Virtue.
Widow's Weeds, A.
DELANEY, CLARISSA SCOTT. Solace.
DELEGALL, WALT. Elegy for a Lady, *sel.*
DELIUS, ANTHONY. Coming, The.
DELONEY, THOMAS. Dialogue between
the Lovelorn Sir Hugh and Certain
Ladies of Venice, A.
DEMAREST, MARY AUGUSTA. My Ain
Countree.
DEMING, A. G. Who Is Tapping at My
Window.
DENBY, EDWIN. Dishonor.
Girl, A.
DENHAM, SIR JOHN. Against Love.
Cooper's Hill.
DENNEY, REUEL. Tennis in San Juan.
DENNIS, CLARENCE JAMES. Growth of
Sym, The.
Play, The. *Fr.* The Sentimental Bloke.
Sentimental Bloke, The, *sel.*
DENNY, SIR EDWARD. Hope of Our
Hearts.
DENT, THOMAS C. Come Visit My Gar-
den.
Love.
DENWOOD, JONATHAN. Bleeberrying.
DERBY, EDWARD GEORGE GEOFFREY SMITH
STANLEY, 14TH EARL OF. Iliad,
The, *sel., tr.*
DE REGNIERS, BEATRICE SCHENK. Keep
a Poem in Your Pocket.
DERLETH, AUGUST. Moon and Fog.
Place-Ghost.
DEROSIER, LOLA. Last Day, The.
DERWOOD, GENE. In Common.
With God Conversing.
DESCHAMPS, EUSTACHE. Am I, Am I,
Am I Fair?
But Is There No Flower, Perfume or
Violet?
One Day the Rats of All Degrees.
DESMARETS DE SAINT-SORLIN, JEAN.
Guirlande de Julie, *sel.*
Violette, La. *Fr.* Guirlande de Julie.
DESPORTES, PHILIPPE. Epigramme: "Some
four years ago I made Phillis an
offer."
Invocation: "O Sleep! I bring thee this
long-cellared wine."
Sonnet: Dress Your Gold Locks.
Villanelle a Rozette.
DE SUZE, CARL. Guitar Lament for a
Mountain Boy.
DE TABLEY, JOHN BYRNE LEICESTER
WARREN, 3D BARON. Anticipation.
Churchyard on the Sands, The.
Nuptial Song.
Ocean Wood, The.
DEUTSCH, BABETTE (Mrs. Avrahm Yar-
molinsky). After the Second Flood,
tr.
As Ocean Holds the Globe, *tr.*
Black Diamond, *tr.*

DEUTSCH, BABETTE (*continued*)
Dogma.
Fresh Paint, *tr.*
Grapes, *tr.*
Haiku: "Falling flower, The," *tr.*
In the Clear Cold, *tr.*
July, *tr.*
Little Catkins, *tr.*
Magic Landscape, A, *tr.*
Memento, *tr.*
Monkey, The, *tr.*
Morning Workout.
Natural Law.
Need.
No, Never Think, *tr.*
Prophet, The, *tr.*
Remembrance, *tr.*
Sail, A, *tr.*
She Came Out of the Frost, *tr.*
Silentium, *tr.*
Twilight, *tr.*
Upon the Hard Crest, *tr.*
Verses Written during a Sleepless Night, *tr.*
We Are All Workmen, *tr.*
What Will You Do, God, When I Die? *tr.*
When in My Arms, *tr.*
With Wavering Feet I Walked, *tr.*
You, Neighbor God, *tr.*
Young Gazelle.
DEUTSCH, BABETTE, and AVRAHM YARMO-LINSKY. Legend of the Bewitched Nunnery, *tr.*
DEVANEY, JAMES MARTIN. Evening Gleam, The.
Mortality.
Song of the Captured Woman.
DE VERE, AUBREY THOMAS. Autumnal Ode.
Sorrow.
Spring. *Fr.* The Year of Sorrow.
Year of Sorrow, The, *sel.*
DE VERE, EDWARD, 17TH EARL OF OX-FORD. *See* VERE, EDWARD DE.
DE VERE, WILLIAM. Walk, Damn You, Walk!
DE VITO, ETHEL BARNETT. Birthday Gift.
DHINGRA, BALDOON. Day and Night.
DIBDIN, CHARLES. Poor Jack.
Tom Bowling.
DICKEY, JAMES. Beholders, The.
Between Two Prisoners.
Call, The.
Dog Sleeping on My Feet, A.
Drowning with Others.
Dusk of Horses, The.
Heaven of Animals, The.
Hospital Window, The.
In the Lupanar at Pompeii.
In the Tree House at Night.
Lifeguard, The.
On the Hill below the Lighthouse.
Owl King, The.
Performance, The.
Poisoned Man, The.
Scarred Girl, The.
Scratch, The.
To Landrum Guy, Beginning to Write at Sixty.
Trees and Cattle.
Walking on Water.
DICKEY, WILLIAM. Love among the Manichees.
Resolving Doubts.
DICKINSON, EMILY. After great pain, a formal feeling comes.
Ample make this bed.
Apparently with no surprise.
Arcturus is his other name.
As imperceptibly as grief.
At half-past three, a single bird.
At least—to pray—is left—is left.
Auctioneer of parting, The.
Autumn.
Beauty is not caused—it is.
Because I could not stop for Death.
Behind me—dips eternity.
Belshazzar had a letter.
Bird came down the walk, A.
Brain is wider than the sky, The.
Brain, within it's groove, The.
Bring me the sunset in a cup.

Brook of the Heart, The.
Bustle in a house, The.
Chariot, The.
Chartless.
Clock stopped, A—not the mantel's.
Color—caste—denomination.
Come slowly, Eden.
Could mortal lips divine.
Crumbling is not an instant's act.
Death is the supple suitor.
Departed—to the judgment.
Did the harebell loose her girdle.
Elysium is as far as to.
Essential oils are wrung.
Exultation is the going.
Faith is a fine invention.
Farther [*or* Further] in summer than the birds.
Finding is the first act.
Four trees—upon a solitary acre.
God made a little gentian.
God's Residence.
Going to Him! Happy letter!
Grass so little has to do, The.
Have you got a brook in your little heart?
He ate and drank the precious words.
He preached upon "breadth" till it argued him narrow.
Heart asks pleasure first, The.
Heaven has different signs to me.
"Heavenly Father"—take to Thee.
Hope is a subtle glutton.
Hope is the thing with feathers.
How many times these low feet staggered.
I cannot live with you.
I died for Beauty—but was scarce.
I dreaded that first robin so.
I dwell in possibility.
I felt a cleaving in my mind.
I felt a funeral, in my brain.
I gave myself to him.
I had not minded—walls.
I heard a fly buzz—when I died.
I know some lonely houses off the road.
I know that He exists.
I like a look of agony.
I like to see it lap the miles.
I lost a world—the other day!
I never hear the word "escape."
I never lost as much but twice.
I never saw a moor.
I reckon—when I count at all.
I saw no way—the heavens were stitched.
I started early—took my dog.
I stepped from plank to plank.
I taste a liquor never brewed.
I took my power in my hand.
I went to heaven.
I years had been from home.
If I can stop one heart from breaking.
If I shouldn't **be alive.**
If my bark sink.
If you were coming in the fall.
I'll tell you how the sun rose.
I'm nobody! Who are you?
Immortal is an ample word.
In winter, in my room.
It dropped so low—in my regard.
It is an honorable thought.
It makes no difference abroad.
It might be lonelier.
It sifts from leaden sieves.
It was not death, for I stood up.
I've seen a dying eye.
Just lost, when I was saved!
Last night that she lived, The.
Lay this laurel on the one.
Light exists in spring, A.
Lightly stepped a yellow star.
Lightning is a yellow fork, The.
Like rain it sounded till it curved.
Little madness in the spring, A.
Little Tippler, The.
Many a phrase has the English language.
Mine by the right of the white election!
Missing all, prevented me, The.
Moon is distant from the sea, The.
Morning.
Morning after Death, The.
Mountain sat upon the plain, The.

Much madness is divinest sense.
Mushroom is the elf of plants, The.
My life closed twice before its close.
My life had stood—a loaded gun.
My period had come for prayer.
Mysteries.
Narrow fellow in the grass, A.
New feet within my garden go.
No time to hate.
Not with a club, the heart is broken.
Of all the souls that stand create.
Of bronze—and blaze.
Of course—I prayed.
Of God we ask one favor.
One and one—are one.
One need not be a chamber—to be haunted.
Our lives are Swiss.
Overtakelessness of those, The.
Pain has an element of blank.
Parting.
Pedigree of Honey, The.
Pink, small and punctual.
Pit, A—but heaven over it.
Poets light but lamps, The.
Precious—mouldering pleasure—'tis, A.
Presentiment—is that long shadow—on the lawn.
Railway Train, The.
Remorse is memory awake.
Revolution is the pod.
Robin is the one, The.
Route of evanescence, A.
Safe despair it is that raves.
Safe in their alabaster chambers.
Shall I take thee, the poet said.
She rose to his requirement—dropt.
Show is not the show, The.
Skies cant keep their secret, The!
Sky is low, the clouds are mean, The.
Snake, The.
Snow, The.
Some keep the Sabbath going to church.
Soul selects her own society, The.
Split the lark—and you'll find the music.
Success is counted sweetest.
Summer has two beginnings.
Surgeons must be very careful.
Tell all the truth but tell it slant.
That I did always love.
There came a day at summer's full.
There came a wind like a bugle.
There is a solitude of space.
There is no frigate like a book.
There's a certain slant of light.
These are the days when birds come back.
They might not need me; but they might.
They put us far apart.
They say that "time assuages."
This consciousness that is aware.
This is my letter to the world.
This quiet dust was gentlemen and ladies.
This was a poet—it is that.
This world is not conclusion.
Those—dying then.
Though the great waters sleep.
Thought went up my mind today, A
Through the straight pass of suffering.
'Tis not that dying hurts us so.
Title divine—is mine!
To fight aloud, is very brave.
To hear an oriole sing.
To know just how he suffered—would be dear.
To make a prairie it takes a clover and one bee.
Train, The.
'Twas just this time, last year, I died.
'Twas like a maelstrom, with a notch.
'Twas warm at first, like us.
Two swimmers wrestled on the spar.
Under the light, yet under.
Way I read a letter's this, The.
We do not play on graves.
We never know how high we are.
We outgrow love like other things.
We play at paste.
What is—"paradise."
What soft—Cherubic creatures.

When I have seen the sun emerge.
When night is almost done.
Whole gulfs of red and fleets of red.
Wild nights—wild nights.
Wind begun to knead the grass, The.
Wind took up the northern things, The.
Wounded deer leaps highest, A.
You left me, sweet, two legacies.
Your thoughts dont have words every day.
DIEKMANN, CONRAD. Winter Trees.
DIENSTAG, ALAN. Three Women.
DIETMAR VON AIST. Lady Stood Alone, A.
   Linden Tree, The.
   On the Linden Overhead a Bird Was Caroling Its Lay.
   Sleepest Thou Yet, My Sweeting?
DILLON, GEORGE. April's Amazing Meaning.
   Constant One, The.
   Landscape, tr.
   No Question.
   World Goes Turning, The.
"DINESEN, ISAK" (Karen Blixen). Zebra.
DINIS [or DINIZ], KING OF PORTUGAL.
   John Bolo's Acting Grim.
   O Flowers, O Flowering Green Pine.
   Provençals Right Well May Versify.
   Shepherdess Well Made, A.
DIXON, RICHARD WATSON. By the Sea.
   Judgment of the May, The.
   Love's Consolation, sel.
   Ode: Spirit Wooed, The.
   Song: "Feathers of the willow, The."
   Unrest.
   Winter Will Follow.
   Wizard's Funeral, The.
DJELLALADIN PASHA, MAHMUD. Song: "If you love God, take your mirror between your hands and look."
DOBBS, KILDARE. Exequy: To Peter Allt.
DOBELL, SYDNEY THOMPSON. Balder, sel.
   Chanted Calendar, A. Fr. Balder.
   Desolate.
   He Loves and He Rides Away.
   Nuptial Eve, A.
   Orphan's Song, The.
DOBSON, HENRY AUSTIN. Ars Victrix, sel.
   Ballad to Queen Elizabeth, A.
   Fame and Friendship.
   Garden Song, A.
   Kiss, The.
   Little Blue Ribbons.
   Paradox of Time, The, tr.
   Song of the Four Seasons, A.
DOBSON, ROSEMARY DE BRISSAC. Across the Straits.
   Birth, The.
   Detail from an Annunciation by Crivelli.
   Devil and the Angel, The, sels.
   Methuselah. Fr. The Devil and the Angel.
   Raising of the Dead, The.
DODDRIDGE, PHILIP. How Gentle God's Commands.
DODGE, MARY MAPES. Christmas.
   Lazy Lou.
   Oh, No!
   Sweet, Red Rose, The.
   When I Am Big, I Mean to Buy.
   Written on the Road.
DODGSON, CHARLES LUTWIDGE. See "CARROLL, LEWIS."
DODINGTON, GEORGE BUBB, BARON MELCOMBE. Love Thy Country.
DODSLEY, ROBERT. Man's a Bubble.
DODSON, OWEN. Drunken Lover.
   Hymn Written after Jeremiah Preached to Me in a Dream.
   Sailors on Leave.
   Sickle Pears.
   Sorrow Is the Only Faithful One.
   Yardbird's Skull.
DOLBEN, DIGBY MACKWORTH. Heaven.
   Song, A: "World is young today, The."
   We hurry on, nor passing note.
DOMETT, ALFRED. Ranolf and Amohia, sel.
DONAHUE, JACK. Brave Donahue, at.

DONATI, FORESE, and DANTE ALIGHIERI. See DANTE ALIGHIERI and FORESE DONATI.
DONIAN, MITCHELL. If someone asks you.
DONNE, JOHN. Air[e] and Angels.
   Anatomie of the World, An.
   Anniversary [or Anniversarie], The.
   Annunciation.
   Apparition, The.
   As due by many titles I resigne. Fr. Holy Sonnets.
   Ascension.
   At the round earths imagin'd corners, blow. Fr. Holy Sonnets.
   Bait[e], The.
   Batter my heart, three-personed God; for you. Fr. Holy Sonnets.
   Blossom[e], The.
   Break[e] of Day.
   Broken Heart, The.
   Calm, The.
   Canonization, The.
   Comparison, The.
   Computation, The.
   Crucifying.
   Curse, The.
   Dampe, The.
   Death, be not proud, though some have called thee. Fr. Holy Sonnets.
   Dissolution, The.
   Dreame, The.
   Ecstasy, The.
   Elegie VII: "Natures lay Ideot, I taught thee to love." Fr. Elegies.
   Elegie XVI: On His Mistris [or Mistress]. Fr. Elegies.
   Elegie XIX: To His Mistris Going to Bed. Fr. Elegies.
   Elegies, sels.
   Elegy IX: Autumnal, The. Fr. Elegies.
   Elegy XIX: Going to Bed. Fr. Elegies.
   Elegy V: His Picture. Fr. Elegies.
   Elegy X: "Image of her whom I love, more then she." Fr. Elegies.
   Elegie IV: Perfume, The. Fr. Elegies.
   Elegy on His Mistress. Fr. Elegies.
   Elegy on the Lady Marckham. Fr. Elegies.
   Elegy to His Mistress Going to Bed. Fr. Elegies.
   Epigram: Burnt Ship, A.
   Epithalamion Made at Lincolnes Inne.
   Expiration, The.
   Extasie [or Extasy], The.
   Father, part of his double interest. Fr. Holy Sonnets.
   Fever, A.
   First Anniversary, The: An Anatomie of the World.
   Flea, The.
   Funeral[l], The.
   Go and Catch a Falling Star.
   Good Friday, 1613. Riding Westward.
   Good-Morrow, The.
   His Picture.
   Holy Sonnets, sels.
   Hymn [or Hymne] to Christ, at the Author's Last Going into Germany, A.
   Hymn [or Hymne] to God, My God, in My Sickness.
   Hymn [or Hymne] to God the Father, A.
   I am a little world made cunningly. Fr. Holy Sonnets.
   If faithfull soules be alike glorifi'd Fr. Holy Sonnets.
   If poisonous minerals [or poysonous mineralls], and if that tree. Fr. Holy Sonnets.
   Indifferent, The.
   La Corona.
   Lecture upon the Shadow, A.
   Legacie, The.
   Lovers Infinitenesse.
   Love's Alchemy [or Alchymie].
   Love's Deity [or Deitie].
   Love's Diet.
   Love's Growth.
   Love's Usury.
   Nativitie.
   Nocturnal[l] upon St. Lucy's [or S.

Lucies] Day, Being the Shortest Day, A.
   O might those sighes and teares returne againe. Fr. Holy Sonnets.
   Oh my blacke Soule! now thou art summoned. Fr. Holy Sonnets.
   Oh, to vex me, contraryes meet in one. Fr. Holy Sonnets.
   Of the Progresse of the Soule: The Second Anniversary.
   Primrose, The.
   Relic [or Relique], The.
   Resurrection.
   Sacrament, The.
   Satire III: "Kinde pitty chokes my spleen; brave scorn forbids." Fr. Satires.
   Satire III: Religion. Fr. Satires.
   Satires, sel.
   Satyre III: On Religion. Fr. Satires.
   Second Anniversary [or Anniversarie], The: Of the Progresse of the Soule.
   Show me, dear[e] Christ, thy spouse so bright and clear. Fr. Holy Sonnets.
   Since she whom I lov'd hath payd her last debt. Fr. Holy Sonnets.
   Song: "Go and catch a falling star."
   Song: "Sweetest love, I do not go[e]."
   Spit in my face you Jews, and pierce my side. Fr. Holy Sonnets.
   Storm, The.
   Sun [or Sunne] Rising, The.
   Sweetest Love, I Do Not Go.
   Temple.
   This is my playes last scene, here heavens appoint. Fr. Holy Sonnets.
   Thou hast made me; and shall thy work decay? Fr. Holy Sonnets.
   To Christ.
   To His Mistris [or Mistress] Going to Bed.
   To Mr. I. L.
   To Mr. Rowland Woodward.
   To Mr. T. W.
   Triple Fool, The.
   Twicknam [or Twickenham] Garden.
   Undertaking, The.
   Valediction, A: Forbidding Mourning.
   Valediction, A: Of My Name in the Window.
   Valediction, A: Of Weeping.
   Whale, The.
   What if this present were the worlds last night? Fr. Holy Sonnets.
   Why are we by all creatures waited on? Fr. Holy Sonnets.
   Wilt thou love God, as he thee! then digest. Fr. Holy Sonnets.
DOOLITTLE, HILDA ("H. D."). Adonis.
   Erige Cor Tuum ad Me in Caelum.
   From Citron-Bower.
   Heat.
   Lethe.
   Never More Will the Wind.
   Oread.
   Pear Tree.
DORN, ALFRED. Dark Hotel.
   Invisible Painter.
   Reversions.
DORN, EDWARD. Biggest Killing, The.
   From Gloucester Out.
   Song, The: "So light no one noticed."
   Sousa.
DORSET, CHARLES SACKVILLE, 6TH EARL OF. See SACKVILLE, CHARLES, 6TH EARL OF DORSET.
DOUGLAS, GAWIN [or GAVIN]. Aeneid, The, sel., tr.
   Batalis and the Man, The, tr. Fr. The Aeneid.
DOUGLAS, KEITH CASTELLAIN. Vergissmeinnicht.
"DOUGLAS, MARIAN" (Annie Douglas Green Robinson). Good Thanksgiving, A.
DOUGLAS, WILLIAM. Annie Laurie.
DOVER, CEDRIC. In a Girl's Album.
DOWDEN, EDWARD. Autumn Song, An.
DOWDEN, ELIZABETH DICKENSON WEST (Mrs. Edward Dowden). There Shall Be No More Sea.
DOWDING, WALTER. I'r hen Iaith a'i Chanedon.
DOWLAND, JOHN. Dialogue, A.

DOWLING, ALLAN. I Sought with Eager Hand.
Joy of Love, The.
Miracle, The.
DOWSON, ERNEST CHRISTOPHER. Autumnal.
Breton Afternoon.
Cynara.
De Amore.
Garden of Shadow, The.
Let Be at Last.
Non Sum Qualis Eram Bonae sub Regno Cynarae.
Royal Love Scene, The.
Spleen.
They Are Not Long.
To His Mistress.
Vitae Summa Brevis Spem Nos Vetet Incohare Longam.
Your Hands.
DRAKE, GASTON V. Contrary Boy, The.
DRAKE, GEOFFREY. Hero, The.
DRAKE, JOSEPH RODMAN. American Flag, The.
DRAKE, LEAH BODINE. Gods of the Dana, The.
Green Door, The.
Pool, The.
Warning to Skeptics, A.
Witches, The.
Woods Grow Darker, The.
Word of Willow, The.
DRAYTON, MICHAEL. Agincourt.
Ballad of Agincourt, The.
Calling to mind since first my love begun. Fr. Idea.
Cupid, dumb idol, peevish saint of love. Fr. Idea.
Dowsabel. Fr. The Shepherd's Garland.
Hawking. Fr. Polyolbion.
How many paltry, foolish, painted things. Fr. Idea.
I Pray Thee Leave.
Idea, sels.
Like an adventurous seafarer am I. Fr. Idea.
Love's Farewell. Fr. Idea.
Muses' Elysium, The, sel.
Poets' Paradise, The. Fr. The Muses' Elysium.
Polyolbion, sels.
Shepherd's Garland, The, sel.
Shepherd's Sirena, The, sel.
Since there's no help, come let us kiss and part. Fr. Idea.
Sirena. Fr. The Shepherd's Sirena.
Skeltoniad, A.
So Well I Love Thee.
Stay, speedy time; behold, before thou pass. Fr. Idea.
Three sorts of serpents do resemble thee. Fr. Idea.
To His Coy Love.
To My Most Dearly Loved Friend, Henry Reynolds, Esq., sel.
To the Reader of These Sonnets. Fr. Idea.
To the Virginian Voyage.
Wrestlers, The. Fr. Polyolbion.
DRESBACH, GLENN WARD. Ship's Bell.
Through the Blowing Leaves.
DREWRY, CARLETON. I Said to the Leaf.
In This Strange House.
Invocation: "O world watched over by the cold moon and the mindless stars."
Small Thought Speaks for the Flesh, A.
Song in Humility, A.
DRINKWATER, JOHN. Bird's Nest, The.
Bobby Blue.
Foundation of Faith.
Mamble.
Plea, The.
Snail.
Sun, The.
DRISCOLL, LOUISE. Hold Fast Your Dreams.
DRIVER, OLIVE. Lake Winnipesaukee.
May Moon.
Plymouth Rock.
DROMGOOLE, WILL ALLEN. Bridge Builder, The.

Building the Bridge for Him.
DROSTE-HÜLSHOFF, ANNETTE ELIZABETH, BARONESSE VON. In the Grass.
Pond, The.
Wakeful Night.
DRUMMOND, WILLIAM, OF HAWTHORNDEN. Book of the World, The, tr.
Doth then the World go thus, doth all thus move?
Happiness of a Flea, The, tr.
If Crossed with All Mishaps.
In this World's Raging Sea.
Ivory, Coral, Gold, The.
Lessons of Nature, The, tr.
Madrigal: "Like the Idalian queen."
Madrigal: "My thoughts hold mortal strife."
Madrigal I: "This life which seems so fair," tr.
My Thoughts Hold Mortal Strife.
Of a Bee, tr.
Of That Same, tr.
Rose, The, tr.
Saint John the Baptist.
Summons to Love.
This World a Hunting Is.
To His Lute.
DRUMMOND, WILLIAM HENRY. Wreck of the Julie Plante, The.
DRYDEN, JOHN. Absalom and Achitophel, Pt. I.
After the Pangs of a Desperate Lover. Fr. An Evening's Love.
Against Women, tr. Fr. The Satires (of Juvenal).
Ah How Sweet It Is to Love. Fr. Tyrannic Love.
Alexander's Feast; or, The Power of Music.
All, All of a Piece Throughout. Fr. The Secular Masque.
All for Love, sels.
Amphitryon, sel.
Art of Love, sels., tr.
Aureng-Zebe, sel.
Beneath a Myrtle Shade. Fr. The Conquest of Granada.
Calm Was the Even. Fr. An Evening's Love.
Concerning the Nature of Love, tr. Fr. De Rerum Natura.
Conquest of Granada, The, sels.
De Rerum Natura, sels, tr.
Eclogues, sel., tr.
Eighth Pastoral of Virgil, The, tr. Fr. Eclogues.
Epilogue: "Poets, like disputants, when reasons fail." Fr. All for Love.
Evening's Love, An, sels.
Fairest Isle. Fr. King Arthur.
Farewell, Ungrateful Traitor. Fr. The Spanish Friar.
George Villiers, Duke of Buckingham. Fr. Absalom and Achitophel.
Georgics, sel., tr.
Hourly I Die. Fr. Amphitryon.
I Feed a Flame Within. Fr. Secret Love.
Indian Emperor, The, sel.
Instruments, The. Fr. Song for St. Cecilia's Day.
King Arthur, sel.
Kiss Me, Dear.
Love's Fancy. Fr. An Evening's Love.
MacFlecknoe; or, A Satire upon the True-Blue-Protestant Poet, T. S.
Marriage a-la-Mode, sels.
Nature of Love, The, tr. Fr. De Rerum Natura.
Odes (of Horace), sel., tr.
Oedipus, sel.
Prologue: "Our author, by experience, finds it true." Fr. Aureng-Zebe.
Prologue: "What flocks of critics hover here to-day." Fr. All for Love.
Prologue to "Aureng-Zebe."
Prologue to the University of Oxford.
Rondelay: "Chloe found Amyntas lying."
Satires, The (of Juvenal), sel., tr.
Secret Love, sel.
Secular Masque, The.
Sir Fopling Flutter.

Song: "Sylvia the fair, in the bloom of fifteen."
Song: "Why should a foolish marriage vow." Fr. Marriage a-la-Mode.
Song for a Girl.
Song for St. Cecelia's Day, 1687, A.
Song of Momus to Mars, The. Fr. The Secular Masque.
Song of the Zambra Dance. Fr. The Conquest of Granada.
Song to a Fair, Young Lady Going Out of the Town in the Spring.
Spanish Friar, The, sel.
Spanish Galleons Seen by an Aztec, The. Fr. The Indian Emperor.
Spell, A. Fr. Oedipus.
Sung by a Young Girl.
Sylvia, the Fair.
To His Mistress, tr.
To My Honor'd Friend Sir Robert Howard, sel.
To the Memory of Mr. Oldham.
Tyrannic Love, sel.
What Has This Bugbear Death, tr. Fr. De Rerum Natura.
What Is the World? Fr. To My Honor'd Friend Sir Robert Howard.
Wherever I Am. Fr. The Conquest of Granada.
Whilst Alexis Lay Prest. Fr. Marriage a-la-Mode.
Why Should a Foolish Marriage Vow? Fr. Marriage a-la-Mode.
You Charmed Me Not. Fr. An Evening's Love.
DRYDEN, JOHN, and SIR ROBERT HOWARD. See HOWARD, SIR ROBERT, and JOHN DRYDEN.
DRYDEN, JOHN, and SIR WILLIAM SOAMES. See SOAMES, SIR WILLIAM, and JOHN DRYDEN.
DU BELLAY, JOACHIM. Amours, Les, sel.
Heureux qui, comme Ulysse, a fait un beau voyage. Fr. Regrets.
Olive, L', sels.
On His Deafness. Fr. Les Amours.
Regrets, sels.
Rome. Fr. Ruins of Rome.
Ruins of Rome, sel.
Sonnet: "I hate the money-lending avarice." Fr. Regrets.
Sonnet to Heavenly Beauty, A. Fr. L'Olive.
To His Friend in Elysium.
DU BOUCHET, ANDRÉ. On the Open Earth.
Surrender.
White Motor, sels.
Wine of Day, The.
DUCKETT, ALFRED A. Sonnet: "Where are we to go when this is done?"
DUDEK, LOUIS. Air by Sammartini, An.
Europe, sels.
Old Song: "Since nothing so much is."
Pomegranate, The.
Street in April, A.
DUEWEL, WESLEY. On with the Message.
DUFAULT, PETER KANE. Notes on a Girl.
Odysseus' Song to Calypso.
Tele-News Blues.
Thalamos.
Tour de Force.
DUGAN, ALAN. Elegy: "I know but will not tell."
Funeral Oration for a Mouse.
How We Heard the Name.
Love Song: I and Thou.
Memorial Service for the Invasion Beach Where the Vacation in the Flesh Is Over.
Mirror Perilous, The.
On an East Wind from the Wars.
On Don Juan del Norte, Not Don Juan Tenorio del Sur.
On Hurricane Jackson.
Plague of Dead Sharks.
Poem: "Person who can do, The."
DUGGAN, EILEEN. Contrast.
DUGMORE, H. H. Reminiscence of 1820, A, sel.

DU MAURIER, GEORGE LOUIS PALMELLA BUSSON. Little Work, A. *Fr.* Trilby.
Music.
Trilby, *sel.*
DUNBAR, PAUL LAURENCE. Accountability.
Boy's Summer Song, A.
Compensation.
Dawn.
Death Song, A.
Debt, The.
Encouraged.
Get Somebody Else.
Howdy, Honey, Howdy!
Hymn: "When storms arise."
Hymn, A, after Reading "Lead Kindly Light."
Life.
Lincoln.
Master-Player, The.
My Sort o' Man.
Old Cabin, The.
Party, The.
Song, A: "Thou art the soul of a summer's day."
Sympathy.
Theology.
We Wear the Mask.
When All Is Done.
DUNBAR, WILLIAM. Amends to the Tailors and Soutars.
Fear of Death Confounds Me, The.
Goldyn Targe, The, *sel.*
Hymn of the Resurrection, A.
Hymn to Mary, A.
Lament for the Makers [or Makaris, Quhen He Wes Seik].
Man of Valour to His Fair Lady, The.
Sweet Rose of Virtue.
DUNCAN, MARY LUNDIE. Jesus, tender shepherd, hear me.
DUNN, MAXWELL WALTER DUMONT. I Danced before I Had Two Feet.
DUNSANY, EDWARD JOHN MORETON DRAX PLUNKETT, 18TH BARON. Bringing Him Up.
DUPIN, JACQUES. Air.
Fits and Starts, *sel.*
Mineral Kingdom, The.
Portion, The.
DURACK, MARY (Mrs. H. C. Miller). Red Jack.
DUREM, RAY. Award.
D'URFEY [or DURFEY or D'URFÉ], THOMAS. Fool's Preferment, A, *sel.*
I'll Sail upon the Dog-Star. *Fr.* A Fool's Preferment.
Shepherd Kept Sheep on a Hill So High, A.
DURLING, DWIGHT. *For translations from French and Italian, see AnML.*
DURRELL, LAWRENCE. Adepts, The.
Alexandria.
Ballad of the Good Lord Nelson, A.
Conon in Exile.
Critics, The.
Dmitri of Carpathos.
Epitaph: "Here lies Michael of the small bone."
Green Man.
Lost Cities, The.
Mythology.
Nemea.
On First Looking into Loeb's Horace.
Sarajevo.
Song for Zarathustra.
To Ping-ku, Asleep.
DURSTON, GEORGIA ROBERTS. ("George Durston"). Rabbit, The.
DUTT, ARU. Still Barred Thy Doors.
DUTT, MICHAEL MADHUSUDAN. Satan.
DUTT, TORU. Our Casuarina Tree.
DUTTON, GEOFFREY. January.
Temple by the Sea, The.
Variations on a Medieval Theme.
DUVAR, JOHN HUNTER. *See* HUNTER-DUVAR, JOHN.
DYER, SIR EDWARD. Elegy on the Death of Sidney.
Fancy, Farewell.
Lowest Trees Have Tops, The.
Modest Love, A.

My Mind to Me a Kingdom Is.
DYER, JOHN. To Clio.
DYLAN, BOB (*originally* Robert Zimmerman). Hard Rain's a-Gonna Fall.
DYMENT, CLIFFORD. Axe in the Wood, The.
DYSON, EDWARD GEORGE. Cleaning Up.

E

"E." *See* FULLERTON, MARY ELIZABETH.
"EAGLE, SOLOMON." *See* SQUIRE, SIR JOHN COLLINGS.
EARNSHAW, EDITH. Baby-Sitter Blues.
Carolina Wrens.
Fads and Fancies.
He Gave Up Golf.
He Will Make the Grade.
I Felt like Slapping Him.
Just a Breeze!
Miss Flo.
Miss Sallie's Chowchow.
My Old Man.
Old Chimney.
Ouch!
Puppy.
Query.
They Roasted Me Instead.
Two Little Houses.
What in the World!
"EASTAWAY, EDWARD." *See* THOMAS, EDWARD.
EASTMAN, MAX. At the Aquarium.
Composed While under Arrest. *tr.*
EASTWICK, IVY O. Birthday Cake.
Birthday Garden.
Hurry Tomorrow.
I'm Glad My Birthday Comes in May!
Lucy Lavender.
Seven Today.
Shadow Dance.
Timothy Boon.
EATON, BURNHAM. Inbound.
Lost Voice on This Hill.
Shadowed.
Unexplored, The.
EATON, CHARLES EDWARD. Carol: "Here's a wreath of Christmas holly."
Compleat Swimmer, The.
Copperhead.
Crepe Myrtle.
In the Headlights.
Love-Death Story, A.
Notes for an Autobiography.
Tropes of One Season.
Waves, The.
EBERHART, RICHARD. Am I My Neighbor's Keeper?
Attitudes.
Book of Nature, The.
Cancer Cells, The.
Chiliasm.
Cousin Florence.
Fury of Aerial Bombardment, The.
Groundhog, The.
Hark Back.
Horse Chestnut Tree, The.
I Walked Out to the Graveyard to See the Dead.
If I Could Only Live at the Pitch That Is Near Madness.
In After Time.
Incomparable Light.
Killer, The.
Man Is God's Nature.
Moment of Vision, The.
New Hampshire, February.
Now Is the Air Made of Chiming Balls.
Off Spectacle Island.
On a Squirrel Crossing the Road in Autumn, in New England.
Order and Disorder.
Recapitulation, The.
Remember the Source.
Rich Interior Life, The.

Sea Scape with Parable.
Ship Burning and a Comet All in One Day, A.
Soul Longs to Return Whence It Came, The.
Spider, The.
Spirit of Poetry Speaks, The.
This Fevers Me.
To Laughter, to Leering.
Tobacconist of Eighth Street, The.
When Doris Danced.
Young Greek, Killed in the Wars, A.
EBERLING, GEORGIA MOORE. Centuries Are His, The.
EBRIGHT, FREDERICK. Memorial to the Great Big Beautiful Self-sacrificing Advertisers.
EDELMAN, KATHERINE. Saturday Shopping.
EDEY, MARION. Our Birthday.
EDEY, MARION, *and* DOROTHY GRIDER. So Many Monkeys.
Trot Along, Pony.
EDGAR, MARY S. Camp Hymn, The.
EDWARDS [or EDWARDES], RICHARD. In Going to My Naked Bed.
EDWARDS, SOLOMON. Brothers.
Dream.
Shoplifter.
EGAN, EILEEN. Hibakusha.
EHRENSTEIN, ALBERT. Car Journey.
Poet and War, The.
EICH, GÜNTER. Messages of the Rain.
Pigeons.
Think of This.
EICHENDORFF, JOSEPH, BARON VON. Hermit, The.
Joyful Traveller, The.
Moon-Night.
Moonlit Night.
Night.
Nocturne.
Wishing Wand.
EIGNER, LARRY. Bird shadows mounting.
Dog yelped, skunk let fly, The.
I will have an image.
Shock, The.
Sleep, A.
Washing between the Buildings.
Weekday, A.
"ELIOT, GEORGE" (Mary Ann [or Marian] Evans Lewes Cross). At Set of Sun.
Minor Prophet, A, *sel.*
O, May I Join the Choir Invisible.
Stradivarius, *sel.*
Tide of Faith, The. *Fr.* A Minor Prophet.
Working with God. *Fr.* Stradivarius.
ELIOT, THOMAS STEARNS. Anabasis, *sel., tr.*
Ash Wednesday.
Aunt Helen.
Burnt Norton. *Fr.* Four Quartets.
Cape Ann. *Fr.* Landscapes.
Chorus: "Son of Man, behold with thine eyes, and hear with thine ears." *Fr.* The Rock.
Chorus: "You have seen the house built, you have seen it adorned." *Fr.* The Rock.
Cousin Nancy.
Death by Water. *Fr.* The Waste Land.
Dove, The. *Fr.* Four Quartets.
Dry Salvages, The. *Fr.* Four Quartets.
Forgive Us, O Lord. *Fr.* Murder in the Cathedral.
Four Quartets, *sels.*
Gerontion.
Growltiger's Last Stand.
Hippopotamus, The.
Hollow Men, The.
Journey of the Magi.
La Figlia Che Piange.
Landscapes, *sels.*
Lines for Cuscuscaraway and Mirza Murad Ali Beg.
Little Gidding. *Fr.* Four Quartets.
Love Song of J. Alfred Prufrock, The.
Macavity: The Mystery Cat.

ELIOT, THOMAS STEARNS (*cont.*)
Marina.
Morning at the Window.
Murder in the Cathedral, *sel.*
Naming of Cats, The.
New Hampshire. *Fr.* Landscapes.
O Light Invisible, We Praise Thee. *Fr.* The Rock.
Portrait of a Lady.
Prelude: "Winter evening settles down, The." *Fr.* Preludes.
Preludes.
Rhapsody on a Windy Night.
Rock, The, *sels.*
Rum Tum Tugger, The.
Song: Under the Bronze Leaves, *tr.* *Fr.* Anabasis.
Song for Simeon, A.
Sweeney among the Nightingales.
There Shall Always Be the Church. *Fr.* The Rock.
Virginia. *Fr.* Landscapes.
Waste Land, The.
Whispers of Immortality.
Why Should Men Love the Church? *Fr.* The Rock.
Yellow Fog. *Fr.* The Love Song of J. Alfred Prufrock.
ELIZABETH I, QUEEN OF ENGLAND. Consolation of Philosophy, *sel., tr.*
Doubt of Future Foes, The.
Happy Too Much, *tr.* *Fr.* Consolation of Philosophy.
Importune Me No More.
When I Was Fair and Young.
ELLIOT, JANE. Lament for Flodden.
ELLIOTT, CHARLOTTE. Hour of Prayer, The.
Watch and Pray.
ELLIOTT, EBENEZER. When Wilt Thou Save the People?
ELMSLIE, W. G. Hand That Held It, The.
ELUARD, PAUL. You Rise Up.
EMANS, ELAINE V. Birthday.
For a Birthday.
EMANUEL, JAMES A. Get Up, Blues.
Treehouse, The.
Voyage of Jimmy Poo, The.
Wedding Procession.
EMERSON, RALPH WALDO. Alphonso of Castile.
Apology, The.
Bacchus.
Blight.
Boston Hymn.
Brahma.
Compensation.
Concord Hymn.
Days.
Each and All.
Fable: "Mountain and the squirrel, The."
Fragments on the Poet and the Poetic Gift, *sel.*
Give All to Love.
Good-bye.
Hamatreya.
History.
Hymn Sung at the Completion of the Concord Monument April 19, 1836.
In the Age of Fops and Toys. *Fr.* Voluntaries.
Merlin.
Mithridates.
Mountain and the Squirrel, The.
Music.
Musketaquid.
Nation's Strength, A.
Nature ("The rounded world is fair to see").
Nature ("A subtle chain of countless rings").
Nemesis.
Ode: Inscribed to W. H. Channing.
Ode to Beauty.
Pan.
Poet, The, *sel.*
Problem, The.
Rhodora, The.
Sacrifice, *sel.*
Snow-Storm, The.
Sphinx, The.
Terminus.

Test, The.
Thanksgiving.
Threnody: "South-wind brings, The."
Two Rivers.
Uriel.
Voluntaries, *sel.*
Waldeinsamkeit.
EMMONS, DICK. Cold Fact.
EMPSON, WILLIAM. Aubade.
Bacchus.
Camping Out.
Chinese Ballad.
Description of a View.
Doctrinal Point.
Four Legs, Three Legs, Two Legs.
Ignorance of Death.
Just a Smack at Auden.
Legal Fiction.
Let It Go.
Manchouli.
Missing Dates.
Note on Local Flora.
Reflection from Rochester.
Sonnet: "Not wrongly moved by this dismaying scene."
Success.
This Last Pain.
To an Old Lady.
Villanelle.
World's End, The.
Your Teeth Are Ivory Towers.
ENCINA, JUAN DEL. Chorus: "Let us give ourselves to pleasure."
Mingo's Discourse.
ENGLE, PAUL. Beasts.
Cat's Eye.
Eternity at Lourmarin, *tr.*
For Two Children, *tr.*
Modern Romance, A.
Panther, The, *tr.*
You Can't Be Wise.
ENGLISH, THOMAS DUNN. Battle of New Orleans, The.
ENRIGHT, DENNIS JOSEPH. Interpreters, The.
Laughing Hyena, by Hokusai, The.
University Examinations in Egypt.
ENSLIN, THEODORE. Belongings, The.
Forms, *sel.*
Landscape with Figures.
Stance.
Tangere.
Tansy for August.
Witch Hazel.
"Your Need Is Greater Than Mine."
ENZENSBERGER, HANS MAGNUS. For a Senior College Textbook.
Honor to Celery.
Ode to Nobody.
ENZO, KING OF SARDINIA. Love Often Agitates My Heart to Thought.
Time Comes for Those Ascending to Descend.
ERULKAR, MARY. Third Continent, The.
ESCHENBACH, WOLFRAM VON. *See* WOLFRAM VON ESCHENBACH.
ESENIN, SERGEI. *See* YESENIN, SERGEI.
ESSON, LOUIS (Thomas Louis Buvelot Esson). Shearer's Wife, The.
ETHEREGE, SIR GEORGE. She Would if She Could, *sel.*
To Little or No Purpose. *Fr.* She Would if She Could.
EURIPIDES. Bacchae, *sel.*
Beginning of Day, The.
Bellerophon, *sel.*
Breed of Athletes, The.
Chorus: "When love has passed its limits." *Fr.* Medea.
Cresophontes, *sel.*
Earth and Sky.
Hippolytus, *sel.*
Medea, *sel.*
O for the Wings of a Dove. *Fr.* Hippolytus.
Prayer to Peace. *Fr.* Cresophontes.
There Are No Gods. *Fr.* Bellerophon.
Where Shall Wisdom Be Found? *Fr.* Bacchae.
EUWER, ANTHONY. Gettin' Born.
My Face.
EVANS, ABBIE HUSTON. All Those Hymnings up to God.
Fundament Is Shifted, The.

EVANS, ABEL. On Blenheim House.
EVANS, F. GWYNNE. Little Thomas.
Matilda.
EVANS, GEORGE ESSEX. Australian Symphony, An.
Women of the West, The.
EVANS, MARI E. And the Old Women Gathered.
Emancipation of George-Hector, The (a Colored Turtle).
If There Be Sorrow.
Point of No Return.
Rebel, The.
Shrine to What Should Be.
Status Symbol.
When in Rome.
Where Have You Gone?
EVANS, MARY ANN [or MARIAN]. *See* "ELIOT, GEORGE."
EVANS, SEBASTIAN. Seven Fiddlers, The.
EVERAERTS, JAN NICOLAI. *See* JOHANNES SECUNDUS.
EVERSON, WILLIAM. *See* ANTONINUS, BROTHER.
EWART, GAVIN. Miss Twye.
Young Blondes.
EZEKIEL, NISSIM. Enterprise.
Morning Prayer.

F

"F. B. P." *See* "P., F. B."
"F. P. A." *See* ADAMS, FRANKLIN PIERCE.
FABER, FREDERICK WILLIAM. All-embracing, The. *Fr.* God Our Father.
God Our Father, *sel.*
Right Is Right.
There's a Wideness in God's Mercy. *Fr.* God Our Father.
FAERSTEIN, CHANA. Bulletin.
FAIDIT, GAUCELM. Knight Was with His Lady Fondly Lying, A.
FAIDIT, GAUCELM, UC DE LA BACALARIA, and SAVARIC DE MAULEON. Debate, A.
FAIRBRIDGE, KINGSLEY OGILVIE. Song-Maker, The.
FAIRBRIDGE, WOLFE SEYMOUR. Consecration of the House.
FAIRBURN, ARTHUR REX DUGARD. Yes Please Gentlemen.
FALCONER, WILLIAM. Shipwreck, The, *sel.*
FALLON, PADRAIC. Raftery's Dialogue with the Whiskey.
"FALSTAFF, JAKE" (Herman Fetzer). Day in Spring, A.
Dick Johnson Reel, The.
Elfin Wife, The.
FANDEL, JOHN. Indians.
FANSHAWE, CATHERINE MARIA. Fragment: "There is a river clear and fair."
FANSHAWE, SIR RICHARD. Hope.
Rose of Life, The, *tr.*
FARALLON, CERISE. Pride and Hesitation.
Serpent of God, The.
FARBER, NORMA. Parkinson and the Octopus.
Unicorns at Harvard.
Witching Hour.
FARBSTEIN, W. E. Double Duty.
FARJEON, ELEANOR. Bedtime.
Boys' Names.
Cats.
Child's Carol.
City Streets and Country Roads.
Down! Down!
Earth and Sky.
For Autumn.
For Them.
Girls' Names.
Good Bishop Valentine.
Good Night!
Great Discovery, The.
Jim at the Corner.

Joan's Door.
Mary's Song.
Meeting Mary.
Morning Song, A.
Mother's Tale, The.
Mrs. Peck-Pigeon.
Night Will Never Stay, The.
Now Every Child.
October's Song.
Old Wife's Song.
Prayer for Little Things, A.
There Isn't Time.
Up the Hill, down the Hill.
Upon an Easter Morning.
What They Do.
FARRAR, JOHN CHIPMAN. Chanticleer.
Critic, The.
Moral Song.
Watching Clouds.
FARRINGTON, HARRY WEBB. Our Christ.
FAULKS, THEODOSIA. See GARRISON, THEODOSIA PICKERING.
FAWKES, FRANCIS. Brown Jug, The.
Nosegay for Laura, A.
FAZIO DEGLI UBERTI. I Gaze upon Her Light Crisp-curling Hair.
FEARING, KENNETH. Dirge: "1-2-3 was the number he played but today the number came 3-2-1."
King Juke.
X Minus X.
FEENEY, THOMAS BUTLER. Captain Kelly Lets His Daughter Go to Be a Nun.
FELD, M. D. Villanelle.
FELDMAN, IRVING. Ark, The.
Assimilation.
Death of Vitellozzo Vitelli, The.
Flood.
Greenwich Village Saturday Night.
Hand, The.
Lost Language, The.
Old Men, The.
Wrack.
FENTON, ELIJAH. Olivia.
FERGUSON, SIR SAMUEL. Cean Dubh Deelish, tr.
Dear Dark Head, tr.
Fairy Thorn, The.
FERGUSSON, ROBERT. Auld Reikie.
FERLINGHETTI, LAWRENCE. Away Above a Harborful.
Christ Climbed Down.
Coney Island of the Mind, A, sels.
Funny Fantasies Are Never So Real as Oldstyle. Fr. A Coney Island of the Mind.
Great Chinese Dragon, The.
I Am Waiting, sel.
New York—Albany.
One Thousand Fearful Words for Fidel Castro.
Oral Messages, sel.
Pictures of the Gone World, sel.
Tentative Description of a Dinner [Given] to Promote the Impeachment of President Eisenhower.
Underwear.
FERNÁNDEZ, ROI [or ROY]. When I See the Waves.
FERNÁNDEZ TORNEOL [or DE TURNEOL], NUÑO. Arise, Fond Lover, Who Sleeps on Chilly Mornings.
FERRINI, VINCENT. Mirandum, sel.
Sea, The. Fr. Mirandum.
FERRY, DAVID. Johnson on Pope.
Lines for a Dead Poet.
FET [or FOETH], AFANSI AFANASIE-VICH. Magic Landscape, A.
FETZER, HERMAN. See "FALSTAFF, JAKE."
FIEDLER, LESLIE A. Dumb Dick.
I Seek to Make My Speech a Yawp as Bitter, tr.
FIELD, EDWARD. Graffiti.
Notes from a Slave Ship.
Ode to Fidel Castro.
Unwanted.
What Grandma Knew.
FIELD, EUGENE. Duel, The.
Dutch Lullaby, A.
Jest 'fore Christmas.
Leap-Year Episode, A, at.
Little Boy Blue.

New Year Idyl, A, sel.
Seein' Things.
Sioux, The.
Sugar-Plum Tree, The.
Wanderer, The.
Why Do the Bells of Christmas Ring.
Wynken, Blynken, and Nod.
"FIELD, MICHAEL" (Katherine Bradley and Edith Cooper). Aridity.
FIELD, RACHEL LYMAN (Mrs. Arthur Pederson). Acrobat. Fr. A Circus Garland.
Animal Store, The.
Birthday, A.
Circus Garland, A, sels.
City Rain.
Elephant, The. Fr. A Circus Garland.
Flower-Cart Man, The.
General Store.
Girl on the Milk-white Horse, The. Fr. A Circus Garland.
Hills, The.
I Want a Pasture.
Ice-Cream Man, The.
I'd Like to Be a Lighthouse.
In Praise of Dust.
Manhattan Lullaby.
Marooned.
New Year's Day.
Next Day. Fr. A Circus Garland.
Old Wharves, The.
Parade. Fr. A Circus Garland.
Performing Seal, The. Fr. A Circus Garland.
Picnic Day.
Pretzel Man, The.
Pushcart Row.
Questions for a Flying Squirrel to Answer.
Roads.
Sampler, The.
Seven Ages of Elf-Hood, The.
Something Told the Wild Geese.
Summer Morning, A.
Taxis.
Vegetables.
FIELDING, HENRY. Don Quixote in England, sel.
Hunting Song. Fr. Don Quixote in England.
On a Halfpenny Which a Young Lady Gave a Beggar, and Which the Author Redeemed for Half-a-Crown.
FIELDS, JAMES THOMAS. Ballad of the Tempest.
Owl-Critic, The.
FIELDS, JULIA. I Heard a Young Man Saying.
Madness One Monday Evening.
No Time for Poetry.
FILICAJA [or FILICAIA], VINCENZO DA. To Italy.
FINCH, ANNE, COUNTESS OF WINCHIL-SEA. See WINCHILSEA, ANNE FINCH, COUNTESS OF.
FINCH, FRANCIS MILES. Blue and the Gray, The.
Nathan Hale.
FINCH, ROBERT. Effect of Snow, The, sel.
Egg-and-Dart.
Peacock and Nightingale.
Statue, The.
Train Window.
Turning.
FINKEL, DONALD. Bush on Mount Venus, The.
Cocteau's Opium.
Father, The.
Give Way.
Great Wave, The: Hokusai.
Hunting Song.
Imbecile, The.
King Midas Has Asses' Ears.
Note in Lieu of a Suicide.
Oedipus at San Francisco.
Solo for Bent Spoon.
Target Practice.
FINNIN, OLIVE MARY (Mrs. J. J. Con-nellan). Farm near Norman's Lane, The.
FISHBACK, MARGARET. Christmas Pageant.
Complacent Cliff-Dweller, The.

Hallowe'en Indignation Meeting.
I Stand Corrected.
I Take 'Em and Like 'Em.
Kerchoo!
Sitting Pretty.
Triolet on a Dark Day.
FISHER, A. G. Day by Day.
FISHER, AILEEN. All Dressed Up for Easter.
Autumn Rain.
Birthday Cake.
But That Was Yesterday.
Counting Sheep.
Down in the Hollow.
Fireflies.
Hayfield.
Hoppity Toads.
Houses.
Just a Mile Beyond.
Little Bird, A.
Little Brother.
Mother's Party.
Newspaper.
Otherwise.
Package, The.
Picnic, A.
Puppy.
Pussy-Willows.
Richer.
Snoring.
Snowman's Resolution, The.
Something Very Elegant.
Taking Down the Tree.
Tummy Ache.
Un Birthday Cake.
Wind.
Workshop, The.
World's So Big, The.
FITCH, ROBERT. High Brow.
FITTS, DUDLEY. Andante, ma Non Assai, tr.
Rumoresque Senum Severiorum, tr.
Tantalos, tr.
FITZGERALD, EDWARD. Myself When Young Did Eagerly Frequent, tr. Fr. The Rubáiyát of Omar Khay-yám.
Oh Thou, Who Man of Baser Earth Didst Make, tr. Fr. The Rubáiyát of Omar Khayyám.
Rubáiyát of Omar Khayyám, The, sels.
FITZGERALD, FRANCIS SCOTT. There'd Be an Orchestra. Fr. Thousand-and-First Ship.
Thousand-and-First Ship, sel.
FITZGERALD, ROBERT DAVID. Back from the Paved Way.
Face of the Waters, The.
Glad World.
Macquarie Place.
Wind at Your Door, The.
FITZGERALD, ROBERT STUART. Adule-scentia, sel.
Before Harvest.
Cobb Would Have Caught It.
Imprisoned, The.
Music, tr.
Sea Pieces.
Souls Lake.
Winter Night.
Young Men Come Less Often, The—Isn't It So? tr.
FLECKER, JAMES ELROY. Golden Journey to Samarkand, The, sel.
Hassan, sel.
Mignon, tr. Fr. Wilhelm Meister.
Old Ships, The.
Prologue: "We who with songs beguile your pilgrimage." Fr. The Golden Journey to Samarkand.
Santorin.
Ship, an Isle, a Sickle Moon, A.
Stillness.
Tenebris Interlucentem.
War Song of the Saracens. Fr. Hassan.
Wilhelm Meister, sel., tr.
FLEMING, PAUL. To Himself.
FLETCHER, GILES, THE ELDER. In time the strong and stately turrets fall. Fr. Licia.
Licia, sel.
FLETCHER, GILES, THE YOUNGER. Christ's Victory and Triumph, sel.

FLETCHER, GILES, THE YOUNGER (*cont.*)
He Is a Path. *Fr.* Christ's Victory and Triumph.
FLETCHER, IAIN. O Noble and Most High in Beauty, Thou, *tr.*
Stranger to Love, Whoever Loves Not Thee, *tr.*
To Christ Crucified, *tr.*
FLETCHER, IAIN, AND BRIAN SOPER. *See* SOPER, BRIAN, *and* IAIN FLETCHER.
FLETCHER, JOHN. Beauty Clear and Fair. *Fr.* The Elder Brother.
Care-charming Sleep. *Fr.* The Tragedy of Valentinian.
Come Hither, You That Love.
Come, Shepherds, Come. *Fr.* The Faithful Shepherdess.
Do Not Fear. *Fr.* The Faithful Shepherdess.
Elder Brother, The, *sel.*
Faithful Shepherdess, The, *sels.*
Hear, Ye Ladies. *Fr.* The Tragedy of Valentinian.
Love's Emblems. *Fr.* The Tragedy of Valentinian.
Now the Lusty Spring. *Fr.* The Tragedy of Valentinian.
Orpheus with His Lute, *at. Fr.* Shakespeare's "King Henry VIII."
Power of Love, The. *Fr.* The Tragedy of Valentinian.
River God, The. *Fr.* The Faithful Shepherdess.
Tragedy of Valentinian, The, *sels.*
FLETCHER, JOHN, *and* FRANCIS BEAUMONT. *See* BEAUMONT, FRANCIS, *and* JOHN FLETCHER.
FLETCHER, JOHN, *and* (*at.*) THOMAS MIDDLETON. Melancholy. *Fr.* The Nice Valour.
Nice Valour, The, *sel.*
FLETCHER, JOHN, *and* WILLIAM SHAKESPEARE. Bridal Song. *Fr.* The Two Noble Kinsmen.
Two Noble Kinsmen, The, *sel.*
FLETCHER, JOHN GOULD. Exit.
Irradiations, *sel.*
Lincoln.
Reunion.
Skaters, The.
Song of the Midnight Rain.
Walk on the Beach, The.
FLETCHER, PHINEAS. Hymn, A: "Drop, drop, slow tears."
Litany, A: "Drop, drop, slow tears."
FLINT, ANNIE JOHNSON. Answered Prayer, The.
At the Place of the Sea.
Cross and the Tomb, The.
He Giveth More Grace.
In Him.
Mary and Martha.
Not I, but God.
Pray—Give—Go.
Sepulcher, The.
Sometimes.
Through the Waters.
Thy Will Be Done.
What God Hath Promised.
World's Bible, The.
FLORES, ANGEL. *For translations from Spanish, see* AnSP.
FLORES, KATE. Love Song, *tr.*
Lovely as a Flower, *tr.*
Moldering Hulk, The, *tr.*
Prisoner, The, *tr.*
That Tree with Its Leaves Atremble, *tr.*
White Moon, The, *tr.*
For other translations from Spanish, see AnSP.
FLOWER, ROBIN. Pangur Bán, *tr.*
FOETH, AFANASI. *See* FET, AFANASI AFANASIEVICH.
FOLGORE DA SAN GEMINIANO [*or* GEMIGNANO]. August. *Fr.* Sonnets of the Months.
Come, January, I Give You These Treats. *Fr.* Sonnets of the Months.
For April I Give You the Countryside. *Fr.* Sonnets of the Months.
In March, for You a Gift of Fish I Boast. *Fr.* Sonnets of the Months.
In October, Figuring Up Your Share. *Fr.* Sonnets of the Months.

September. *Fr.* Sonnets of the Months.
Sonnets of the Months, *sels.*
FOLLAIN, JEAN. Comings and Goings, *sels.*
Extensions, *sel.*
FOLLANSBEE, MITCHELL D. I Like to Quote.
FOLLEN, ELIZA LEE (Cabot). Ringely, Ringely.
Where Are You Going.
FONTAINE, JEAN DE LA. *See* LA FONTAINE, JEAN DE.
FOOTE, SAMUEL. Great Panjandrum, The.
FOOTT, MARY HANNAY. Where the Pelican Builds.
FORD, FORD MADOX (*formerly* Ford Madox Hueffer). Old Houses of Flanders, The.
On Heaven.
Under the Lindens, *tr.*
What the Orderly Dog Saw.
"When the World Was in Building. . ."
FORD, JOHN. Broken Heart, The, *sels.*
Can You Paint a Thought? *Fr.* The Broken Heart.
Oh, No More, No More! *Fr.* The Broken Heart.
FORD, JOHN, *and* THOMAS DEKKER. *See* DEKKER, THOMAS, *and* JOHN FORD.
FORESE DONATI *and* DANTE ALIGHIERI. *See* DANTE ALIGHIERI *and* FORESE DONATI.
FORSTER, WILLIAM. Devil and the Governor, The, *sel.*
FOSS, SAM WALTER. Calf-Path, The.
House by the Side of the Road, The.
Man from the Crowd, The.
FOSTER, STEPHEN COLLINS. Jeanie with the Light Brown Hair.
My Old Kentucky Home.
FOWLER, ELSIE MELCHERT. If You Never Talked with Fairies.
If You've Never.
Miracle, The.
Secrets.
FOWLER, LONA M. Middle-Time, The.
FOWLER, MARY B. Promise, The.
FOWLIE, WALLACE. Délie, *sels., tr.*
It May Be, *tr.*
Plain Song, *sel., tr.*
You Rise Up, *tr.*
FOX-SMITH, CICELY. *See* SMITH, CICELY FOX.
"FRANCIS." To His Ever-worshipped Will from W. H.
FRANCIS, SAINT. *See* FRANCIS OF ASSISI, SAINT.
FRANCIS, ROBERT. Base Stealer, The.
Catch.
Epitaph: "Believer he and unbeliever both."
Farm Boy after Summer.
Glass.
Hallelujah; a Sestina.
Hide-and-Seek.
High Diver.
Mouse Whose Name Is Time, The.
Night Train.
Pitcher.
Sailboat, Your Secret.
Sing a Song of Juniper.
Skier.
That Dark Other Mountain.
FRANCIS OF ASSISI, SAINT. Canticle of the Creatures.
Canticle of the Sun.
Cantico del Sole.
Prayer of St. Francis of Assisi for Peace.
St. Francis' Prayer.
Song of the Creatures, The.
FRANK, FLORENCE KIPER. Jew to Jesus, The.
FRANKENBERG, LLOYD. Night of the Full Moon, The.
FRANKLIN, BENJAMIN. Difference, The.
Enough Not One.
Epitaph: "Body of, The."
Epitaph on a Worthy Clergyman.
FRASER, GEORGE SUTHERLAND. Instead of an Elegy.
There in a Woodland, to My Thought More Bright, *tr.*

You Have in You the Flowers and the Green Grass, *tr.*
FRAZEE-BOWER, HELEN. Take Time to Talk with God.
FREDERICKS, LEO. Rain and the Rainbow, The.
FREEMAN, ARTHUR. Conversation Piece. Zoo of You, The.
FREEMAN, HOLLIS. Birds of the Air, The.
FREEMAN, JOHN. Armistice Day.
FREEMAN, MARY ELEANOR WILKINS. Ostrich Is a Silly Bird, The.
FREEZE, MARY D. Our Times Are in His Hands.
FRÉNAUD, ANDRÉ. Miraculous Place of Love, The.
Rediscovered Country.
Who Owns What?
FRENEAU, PHILIP. Amanda's Complaint.
Death. *Fr.* The House of Night.
House of Night, The, *sel.*
Hurricane, The.
Indian Burying Ground, The.
Ode: "God save the Rights of Man!"
On a Honey Bee.
On the Death of Benjamin Franklin.
On the Universality and Other Attributes of the God of Nature.
Power of Fancy, The.
To Sir Toby.
To the Memory of the Brave Americans.
Vanity of Existence, The.
Wild Honeysuckle [*or* Honey Suckle], The.
FRERE, JOHN HOOKHAM, *and* GEORGE CANNING. *See* CANNING, GEORGE, *and* JOHN HOOKHAM FRERE.
FREY, HERMANN. *See* "GREIF, MARTIN."
FRIED, ERICH. Afterward.
Blind, The.
Old Room.
FRIEDRICH VON HAUSEN. If I Might Live to See the Day.
In My Dream I Saw a Woman.
My Heart and Body Wish to Take Their Leave.
FRITSCH, H. S. How Old Are You? *at.*
FROISSART, JEAN. Be Gallant, Mannerlie and Pure of Heart.
O Love, O Love, What Wouldst Thou Make of Me?
Of All Known Flowers, Men Hold the Rose Most Rare.
FROST, FRANCES MARY. Autumn Morning.
Blue Smoke.
Christmas Eve Legend.
Clothes.
Clover for Breakfast.
Growing.
Little Whistler, The.
Maple Feast.
School Is Out.
Small Song.
Spring Families.
Squirrel in the Rain.
Who's There?
FROST, RICHARD. On Not Writing an Elegy.
FROST, ROBERT. Acceptance.
Acquainted with the Night.
After Apple-picking.
Aim Was Song, The.
All Revelation.
Axe-Helve, The.
Bearer of Evil Things, The.
Bereft.
Birches.
Brown's Descent; or, The Willy-Nilly Slide.
But God's Own Descent. *Fr.* Kitty Hawk.
Choose Something like A Star.
Come In.
Cow in Apple Time, The.
Death of the Hired Man, The.
Departmental.
Desert Places.
Design.
Directive.
Draft Horse, The.
Dust of Snow.
Egg and the Machine, The.
Fear of God, The.

Fire and Ice.
For John F. Kennedy His Inauguration.
For Once, Then, Something.
Forgive, O Lord, My Little Jokes on Thee.
Gathering Leaves.
Gift Outright, The.
God's Thanks to Job. *Fr.* A Masque of Reason.
Hill Wife, The.
Hillside Thaw, A.
Home. *Fr.* The Death of the Hired Man.
Home Burial.
I Could Give All to Time.
In a Poem.
In Hardwood Groves.
Investment, The.
It Bids Pretty Fair.
Kitty Hawk, *sel.*
Last Word of a Bluebird, The.
Lodged.
Love and a Question.
Masque of Reason, A, *sel.*
Meeting and Passing.
Mending Wall.
Minor Bird, A.
Moon Compasses.
Most of It, The.
Mountain, The.
Mowing.
My November Guest.
Need of Being Versed in Country Things, The.
Neither Out Far nor in Deep.
Nothing Gold Can Stay.
Now Close the Windows.
October.
Once by the Pacific.
Onset, The.
"Out, Out—."
Oven Bird, The.
Pasture, The.
Paul's Wife.
Peaceful Shepherd, The.
Plowmen.
Prayer in Spring, A.
Provide, Provide.
Putting in the Seed.
Range-finding.
Revelation.
Road Not Taken, The.
Rose Family, The.
Runaway, The.
Secret Sits, The.
Semi-Revolution, A.
Silken Tent, The.
Soldier, A.
Span of Life, The.
Spring Pools.
Stopping by Woods on a Snowy Evening.
Strong Are Saying Nothing, The.
To a Young Wretch.
To Earthward.
To the Thawing Wind.
Too Anxious for Rivers.
Tree at My Window.
Trespass.
Trial Run, A.
Tuft of Flowers, The.
Two Look at Two.
Two Tramps in Mud Time.
Two Witches, *sel.*
West-running Brook.
Witch of Coös, The. *Fr.* Two Witches.
Wood-Pile, The.
FRUMKIN, GENE. In the Margin of the Text.
FRY, CHRISTOPHER. Boy with a Cart, The, *sel.*
    Rain. *Fr.* The Boy with a Cart.
FRY, ROGER. Little Air, *tr.*
    Sonnet: "This virgin, beautiful and lively day," *tr.*
FUGUET, DOLLETT. Blithe Mask, The.
FULLER, ETHEL ROMIG. Haying.
    Hope's Forecast.
    Proof.
    Wind Is a Cat.
FULLER, JOHN. Band Music.
    In a Railway Compartment.
    Morvin.
    Snapshot.

Statue, The.
White Queen.
FULLER, ROY. Crustaceans.
    Day, The.
    During a Bombardment by V-Weapons.
    Epitaph on a Bombing Victim.
    From a Foreign Land.
    Ides of March, The.
    Image, The.
    Little Fable.
    Mythological Sonnets, *sels.*
    Nino, the Wonder Dog.
    On Reading a Soviet Novel.
    Perturbations of Uranus, The.
    Pure Poet, The.
    Rhetoric of a Journey.
    Tribes, The.
    Versions of Love.
    War Poet.
    Y.M.C.A. Writing Room.
FULLERTON, MARY ELIZABETH ("E."). Communal.
    Cubes.
    Emus.
    Flesh.
    Inspiration.
    Lichen.
    Lion.
    Lovers.
FUNK, WILFRED JOHN. Rest in Peace.
FYLEMAN, ROSE. Balloon Man, The.
    Best Game the Fairies Play, The.
    Birthday Child, The.
    Dentist, The.
    Fairies.
    Fairy Went a-Marketing, A.
    Have You Watched the Fairies?
    Mice.
    My Policeman.
    New Neighbor, The.
    October.
    Regent's Park.
    Shop Windows.
    Very Lovely.

G

GACE BRULÉ. Most Hateful Is It to My Eyes.
GALE, NORMAN. Bartholomew.
GALLATIN, DAVID. Put Your Key.
GALSWORTHY, JOHN. Peace in the World.
    So Might It Be.
GALT, JOHN. Canadian Boat-Song, *at.*
GARABRANT, NELLIE M. Fairy Artist, The.
GARCÍA LORCA, FEDERICO. Ampara.
    Arrest of Antoñito el Camborio.
    Death of Antoñito el Camborio.
    Faithless Wife, The.
    Guitar, The.
    Madrigal de Verano.
    My Little Girl Went to the Sea.
    Portrait of Silverio Franconetti.
    Second Anniversary.
    Somnambulist Ballad.
    Song Wants to Be Light, The.
    Spring Song.
    Tree, Tree.
GARCILASO [*or* GARCILASSO] DE LA VEGA. Eclogue I, *sel.*
    I Came to a Valley in the Wilderness.
    One Moment My Hope Rises Up on Wings.
    Rough Are the Roads.
    Song III: "Now go I quietly."
    Song III: "Surrounded by the gentle sound."
    Sonnet: "Fair Naiads of the river, that reside."
    Sonnet X: On Finding Some Keepsakes of His Dead Mistress.
    Sweet Gifts.
    While There Is Still the Color of a Rose.
    Your Face is Written in My Soul.
GARDNER, CARL. Reflections.
GARDNER, ISABELLA. Gimboling.
    Mathematics of Encounter.

GARDONS, S. S. Fourth of July.
    Mother, The.
    Survivors, The.
    To a Child.
GARLAND, HAMLIN. Do You Fear the Wind?
    In the Days When the Cattle Ran.
    Mountains Are a Lonely Folk, The.
GARLICK, PHYLLIS L. St. Patrick, *sel.*
GARNETT, RICHARD. On Revisiting Cintra after the Death of Catarina, *tr.*
    Who Was It, *tr.*
GARRETT, GEORGE. Abraham's Knife.
    Saints.
GARRIGUE, JEAN. False Country of the Zoo.
    Mouse, The.
    Stranger, The.
GARRISON, THEODOSIA PICKERING (Mrs. Frederic J. Faulks). Ilicet.
    Memorial Day.
GARRISON, WINFRED ERNEST. Book, The.
GARSTIN, CROSBIE. On the Back Veld.
GARTHWAITE, JIMMY (Wymond Bradbury Garthwaite). Engineers.
    Run, Kitty, Run!
GASCOIGNE, GEORGE. Constancy of a Lover, The.
    Dan Bartholomew's Dolorous Discourses.
    Gascoigne's Good Morrow.
    Gascoigne's Lullaby.
    Gascoigne's Memories, *sels.*
    Gascoigne's Praise of His Mistress.
    Gascoigne's Woodmanship.
    Green Knight's Farewell to Fancy, The.
    In Praise of a Gentlewoman.
    Inscription in a Garden.
    Lullaby of a Lover, The.
    Passion of a Lover, The.
    Strange Passion of a Lover, A.
GASCOYNE, DAVID. Elegy, An: "Friend, whose unnatural early death."
    Eve.
    Ex Nihilo.
    Megalometropolitan Carnival, *sel.*
    Winter Garden.
GASZTOLD, CARMEN BERNOS DE. Prayer of the Little Ducks Who Went into the Ark, The.
GATES, D. WESTON. Transformed.
GATTO, ALFONSO. Dead in the Villages.
    Grass and Milk.
    Weep—Those Whose Eyes Are Dry Shall Weep.
GAY, JOHN. Acis and Galatea, *sels.*
    Ballad: "Of all the girls that e'er were seen."
    Ballad, A: "'Twas when the seas were roaring." *Fr.* The What D'Ye Call It.
    Before the Barn-Door Crowing. *Fr.* The Beggar's Opera.
    Beggar's Opera, The, *sels.*
    Birth of the Squire, The.
    Black-eyed Susan.
    Dangers of Foot-ball, The. *Fr.* Trivia.
    Elegy on a Lap Dog, An.
    Epistle III: "Pult'ney, methinks you blame my breach of word."
    Fable IV: Eagle, and the Assembly of Animals, The.
    Fable X: Elephant and the Bookseller, The.
    Fable L: Hare and Many Friends, The.
    Fable VII: Lion, the Fox, and the Geese, The.
    Fable XX: Old Hen and the Cock, The.
    Fable XIII: Plutus, Cupid and Time.
    Fable XLV: Poet and the Rose, The.
    Fable XIII: Tame Stag, The.
    Fable II: Vulture, the Sparrow, and Other Birds, The.
    Fable V: Wild Boar and the Ram, The.
    Fly-fishing. *Fr.* Rural Sports.
    Friday; or, The Dirge. *Fr.* The Shepherd's Week.
    Go, Rose.
    Highwaymen, The. *Fr.* The Beggar's Opera.
    If the Heart of a Man. *Fr.* The Beggar's Opera.
    Love in Her Eyes. *Fr.* Acis and Galatea.

GAY, JOHN (*continued*)
O' Ruddier than the Cherry. *Fr.* Acis
and Galatea.
Of the Implements for Walking the
Streets, and Signs of the Weather.
Fr. Trivia.
Of Walking the Streets by Night. *Fr.*
Trivia.
Rural Sports, *sel.*
Saturday; or, The Flights. *Fr.* The
Shepherd's Week.
Shepherd's Week, The, *sels.*
Tame Stag, The.
Through All the Employments of Life.
Fr. The Beggar's Opera.
Trivia; or, The Art of Walking the
Streets of London, *sels.*
Wednesday; or, The Dumps. *Fr.* The
Shepherd's Week.
Were I Laid on Greenland's Coast.
Fr. The Beggar's Opera.
What D'Ye Call It, The, *sel.*
Youth's the Season. *Fr.* The Beggar's
Opera.
GAY, WILLIAM. Crazy World, The.
GAY, ZHENYA. Elephant Is an Odd Af-
fair, An.
My Birthday's in Winter.
Night Things Are Soft and Loud.
On a Windy Day.
GEARHART, GLADYS M. He Is Coming.
GELLERT, LEON MAXWELL. Anzac Cove.
In the Trench.
Jester in the Trench, The.
These Men.
GEORGE, MARGUERITE. Brief Biography.
Here I Lie.
Paneled in Pine.
GEORGE, STEFAN. Another Poem on
Nietzsche.
Nietzsche.
One Lore.
Who Ever.
Wrestler, The.
GERARD, EDWIN ("Trooper Gerardy").
Lofty Lane.
GERHARDT, PAUL. Give to the Winds
Thy Fears.
Go out in this dear summertide.
GERSHGOREN, ESTELLE. We Are Gath-
ered Together.
GERSHWIN, IRA. Embraceable You.
GESSNER, MURIEL M. For February
Twelfth.
GEZELLE, GUIDO. To the Sun.
GHISELIN, BREWSTER. Answering a Let-
ter from a Younger Poet.
GHOSE, KASHIPROSAD. Moon in Septem-
ber, The.
GHOSE, MANMOHAN. London.
GHOSE, SRI AUROBINDO. Dream of Sur-
real Science, A.
GHOSE, ZULFIKAR. Pheasant.
Rise of Shivaji, The.
This Landscape, These People.
GIACOMO DA LENTINO. Frightful Basi-
lisk, Most Poisonous, The.
I Have Set My Heart on Serving God.
GIBBS, ELSIE. Four.
GIBRAN, KAHLIL. Of Love. *Fr.* The
Prophet.
On Children. *Fr.* The Prophet.
On Giving. *Fr.* The Prophet.
Prophet, The, *sels.*
GIBSON, EVELYN K. Heartsearch.
GIBSON, GEORGE HERBERT ("Ironbark").
Ballad of Queensland, A (Sam Holt).
My Mate Bill.
GIBSON, WALKER. Athletes.
Epistle to the Reader.
Mountains, The.
Umpire, The.
Vacationer.
GIBSON, WILFRED WILSON. Battle:
Hit.
Dancers, The.
Dancing Seal, The.
Flannan Isle.
Lament, A.
Luck.
Mark Anderson.
Parrots, The.
Question, The.
Stone, The.

GILBERT, ANN TAYLOR. *See* TAYLOR,
ANN.
GILBERT, DOROTHY. At the Brooklyn
Docks.
GILBERT, JACK. Abnormal Is Not Cour-
age, The.
In Dispraise of Poetry.
Orpheus in Greenwich Village.
GILBERT, JAMES STANLEY. Beyond the
Chagres.
GILBERT, RUTH. Annunciation. *Fr.*
The Blossom of the Branches.
Blossom of the Branches, The, *sels.*
Nativity. *Fr.* The Blossom of the
Branches.
Quickening, The. *Fr.* The Blossom of
the Branches.
GILBERT, SIR WILLIAM SCHWENCK.
Bunthorne's Song. *Fr.* Patience.
Captain Reece.
Fable of the Magnet and the Churn,
The. *Fr.* Patience.
Gondoliers, The, *sel.*
Grand Inquisitor's Song, The. *Fr.*
The Gondoliers.
H.M.S. Pinafore, *sel.*
Ko-Ko's Song. *Fr.* The Mikado.
Mikado, The, *sel.*
Patience, *sels.*
Ruler of the Queen's Navee, The. *Fr.*
H.M.S. Pinafore.
To the Terrestrial Globe.
When I Was a Lad. *Fr.* H.M.S.
Pinafore.
Yarn of the *Nancy Bell,* The.
GILDER, RICHARD WATSON. New Day,
The, *sel.*
Prelude: "Night was dark, though
sometimes a faint star, The." *Fr.*
The New Day.
Song of a Heathen, The.
GILLELAND, ANNA M. Give My Heart
a Song.
GILLIES, ANDREW. Two Prayers.
GILLILAN, STRICKLAND. Folks Need a
Lot of Loving.
GILLMAN, FREDERICK J. God Send Us
Men, *sel.*
GILMAN, CHARLOTTE PERKINS STETSON.
Similar Cases.
To Labor.
GILMORE, MARY JEAN. Baying Hounds,
The.
Disinherited, The, *sel.*
Eve-Song.
Myall in Prison, The.
Nationality.
Never Admit the Pain.
Nurse No Long Grief.
Old Botany Bay.
Pear-Tree, The.
Shepherd, The.
Song of the Woman-Drawer, The.
Swans at Night, *sel.*
Tenancy, The.
Waradgery Tribe, The.
GILMORE, PATRICK SARSFIELD ("Louis
Lambert"). When Johnny Comes
Marching Home.
"GINGER." *See* IRWIN, WALLACE.
GINSBERG, ALLEN. Aether.
American Change.
Howl, *sel.*
Journals Nov. 22, '63
Kaddish.
Poem Rocket.
Song: Fie My Fum.
GINSBERG, LOUIS. To My Mother.
GIRAUT DE BORNELH. Heavenly King,
Glorious God of Light.
GIURLANI, ALDO. *See* "PALAZZESCHI,
ALDO."
GJELLERUP, KARL. O, Let Me Kiss.
Pair, A.
GLADDEN, WASHINGTON. Service.
GLASSCO, JOHN. Burden of Junk, The.
Deserted Buildings under Shefford
Mountain.
Stud Groom.
GLAUBITZ, GRACE ELLEN. Christmas
Birthday.
Walking.
GLAZER, JOSEPH. Too Old to Work.
GLOVER, DENIS. Arawata Bill.

GOCH, LLEWELYN. Elegy for Lucy
Lloyd.
GODDEN, RUMER. Prayer of the Little
Ducks Who Went into the Ark, The,
tr.
GODESCHALK. Sequaire.
GODLEY, ELIZABETH. Extremely Naughty
Children.
GODOLPHIN, SIDNEY. On Ben Jonson.
GODOY ALCAYAGA, LUCILA. *See* "MIS-
TRAL, GABRIELA."
GODRIC, SAINT. Cry to Mary, A.
GOECKINGK, LEOPOLD VON. After the
First Nocturnal Visit.
As the First Snow Fell.
GOERTZ, BERNIECE. Wondrous Son of
God.
GOETHE, JOHANN WOLFGANG VON. Ah,
your dewy pinions swinging.
Blessed Yearning.
Blissful Longing.
Bride of Corinth, The.
Elf-King, The.
Erlking, The.
Faust, *sel.*
Ganymed[e].
God and the Bayadeer, The.
Harp Player's Song, The. *Fr.* Wil-
helm Meister.
Lila, *sel.*
Lose This Day Loitering. *Fr.* Faust.
Lynceus the Warden.
Mignon. *Fr.* Wilhelm Meister.
My Love Is Near.
Nature, it seems, must always clash
with Art.
Nearness of Her Lover.
Night Thoughts.
On Lavater's Song of a Christian to
Christ.
Primeval Words: Orphic.
Prometheus.
Reviewer.
Rose amid the Heather.
Sayings.
Song of the Harp-Player. *Fr.* Wil-
helm Meister.
Song of the Parcae.
Song of the Spirits over the Waters.
Symbolum.
Thoughts by Night.
To Charlotte von Stein.
To Lida.
Torquato Tasso, *sels.*
True Rest.
Venetian Epigrams, *sel.*
Violet, The.
Voice of Experience, The.
Wanderer's Night Song.
Wilhelm Meister, *sels.*
GOGARTY, OLIVER ST. JOHN. O Boys!
O Boys!
Ship, The.
To the Maids Not to Walk in the
Wind.
GOING, CHARLES BUXTON. True Story
of Skipper Ireson, The.
GOLDING, ARTHUR. Acteon, *tr. Fr.*
Metamorphoses.
Conclusion: "Now have I brought a
woork too end which neither Joves
fierce wrath," *tr. Fr.* Metamor-
phoses.
Cyclops, *tr. Fr.* Metamorphoses.
Daedalus, *tr. Fr.* Metamorphoses.
King Midas, *tr. Fr.* Metamorphoses.
Meleager, *tr. Fr.* Metamorphoses.
Metamorphoses, *sels., tr.*
Philemon and Baucis, *tr. Fr.* Meta-
morphoses.
GOLDMAN, MICHAEL. Probes, The.
Spontaneous Man, the Gifted Assassin,
The.
GOLDSMITH, OLIVER. David Garrick.
Fr. Retaliation.
Deserted Village, The.
Elegy on That Glory of Her Sex, Mrs.
Mary Blaize, An.
Elegy on the Death of a Mad Dog. *Fr.*
The Vicar of Wakefield.
Parson, The. *Fr.* The Deserted Vil-
lage.
Retaliation, *sel.*
She Stoops to Conquer, *sel.*

Song: "When lovely woman stoops to folly." *Fr.* The Vicar of Wakefield.
Stanzas on Woman. *Fr.* The Vicar of Wakefield.
Three Pigeons, The. *Fr.* She Stoops to Conquer.
Traveller, The.
Vicar of Wakefield, The, *sels.*
Village Schoolmaster, The. *Fr.* The Deserted Village.
When Lovely Woman Stoops [to Folly]. *Fr.* The Vicar of Wakefield.
GOLDSMITH, OLIVER, THE YOUNGER. Rising Village, The, *sels.*
GOLINO, CARLO L. *For translations from Italian, see* CoIP.
GOLL, IWAN [*or* YVAN]. Journey into Misery.
Moon.
Rain Palace, The.
Salt Lake, The.
GOMBAULD, JEAN OGIER DE. Amarante, L'. *Fr.* Guirlande de Julie.
Guirlande de Julie, *sel.*
GÓNGORA Y ARGOTE, LUIS DE. Allegory of the Brevity of Things Human.
Capture of Larache, The.
Clear Honor of the Liquid Element.
Country Bachelor's Complaint, The.
Deceiver Time.
Dedication: To the Count of Niebla. *Fr.* Fable of Polyphemus and Galatea.
Fable of Polyphemus and Galatea, *sels.*
Idyllic Scene, An. *Fr.* The Solitudes.
Let Me Go Warm.
Love in Reason.
Nativity of Christ, The.
Not All Sweet Nightingales.
O Noble and Most High in Beauty, Thou.
On Sailing the Wide Ocean. *Fr.* The Solitudes.
On the Armada Which Battled against England.
Polyphemus' Love Song. *Fr.* Fable of Polyphemus and Galatea.
Pride of the Fourth and Liquid Element.
Roistering I'll Chaff.
Romance.
Rose of Life, The.
Rosemary Spray, The.
Rustic Festival, A. *Fr.* The Solitudes.
Solitudes, The, *sels.*
Sonnet: "Dear Geese, whose haunt is where weak waters flow."
Sonnet: "Planking of the vessel torn apart, The."
Sonnet: "Yesterday a human deity, today a bit of dust."
Wedding Hymn. *Fr.* The Solitudes.
When Don Luis Was in Cuenca.
GONZÁLEZ PRADA, MANUEL. Cosmos Shows His Power, The.
How Old Is Pilar?
If the Tomb Is Not Oblivion.
Inca's Arrows, The.
Into the Hearth They Are Tossing Logs.
Living and Dying.
Mitayo, The.
Pope.
To Be with the Dead.
Treasures and Glories of Life, The.
Very Strong Stomach Has Mr. Luke, A.
Who Translates a Poet Badly.
Why Did Stingy Thomas?
Your Lily Eyes Said Yes.
GOODGE, WILLIAM T. Daley's Dorg Wattle.
GOODMAN, PAUL. Long Lines.
GOODMAN, RYAH TUMARKIN. They Know.
GOODWIN, SANDRA. Traveling on My Knees.
GOOGE, BARNABE. Coming Homeward Out of Spain.
Epitaph of the Death of Nicholas Grimald, An.
Going towards Spain.
Of Mistress D. S.
Of Money.

Out of Sight, Out of Mind.
Refusal, A.
To Alexander Neville.
To Doctor Bale.
To Master Edward Cobham.
To the Translation of Palingenius.
GORDON, ADAM LINDSAY. Dedication, A: "They are rhymes rudely strung with intent less."
Rhyme of Joyous Garde, The, *sel.*
Sick Stockrider, The.
Sun and Rain and Dew from Heaven. *Fr.* Ye Wearie Wayfarer.
Ye Wearie Wayfarer, *sel.*
GORDON, DON. Kimono, The.
GORDON, JAMES WILLIAM ("Jim Grahame"). Whalan of Waitin' a While.
GORDON, RALPH. J. F. K.
GORENKO, ANNA ANDREYEVNA. *See* "AKHMATOVA, ANNA."
GORTER, HERMAN. Sea, The.
GOSSE, SIR EDMUND WILLIAM. Boy and the Flute, The, *tr.*
GOULD, ROBERT. Fair, and Soft, and Gay, and Young.
GOURMONT, REMY DE. Hair.
GOVONI, CORRADO. Beauty.
Little Trumpet, The.
Towns.
GOZZANO, GUIDO. Absence.
Conversations.
Difference, The.
GRAHAM, HARRY ("Col. D. Streamer").
Aunt Eliza.
Children's Don't, A, *sel.*
Necessity.
Opportunity.
Patience.
Self-Sacrifice.
Stern Parent, The.
Tender-heartedness.
GRAHAM, JAMES, MARQUESS OF MONTROSE. I'll Never Love Thee More.
On Himself, on Hearing What Was His Sentence.
GRAHAM, ROBERT (Robert Cunninghame-Graham). If doughty deeds my lady please.
GRAHAM, WILLIAM SYDNEY. Listen. Put on Morning.
"GRAHAME, JIM." *See* GORDON, JAMES WILLIAM.
GRAHAME, KENNETH. Duck's [*or* Ducks'] Ditty. *Fr.* The Wind in the Willows.
Song of Mr. Toad, The. *Fr.* The Wind in the Willows.
Wind in the Willows, The, *sels.*
World Has Held Great Heroes, The. *Fr.* The Wind in the Willows.
GRANO, PAUL LANGTON. "New Shirt, A!" Why?
GRANSDEN, KARL WATTS. Fifth of November.
GRASS, GÜNTER. Open Wardrobe.
Prevention of Cruelty to Animals.
School for Tenors, The.
Transformation.
GRAVES, JOHN WOODCOCK. John Peel.
GRAVES, RICHARD. On the Death of an Epicure.
GRAVES, ROBERT. Allie.
Ancestors.
Apples and Water.
Bards, The.
Blue-Fly, The.
Certain Mercies.
Cool Web, The.
Counting the Beats.
Despite and Still.
Devil's Advice to Story-Tellers, The.
Dialogue on the Headland.
Down, Wanton, Down.
1805.
Escape.
Flying Crooked.
Foreboding, The.
Frosty Night, A.
Great-Grandmother, The.
Grotesque ("Dr. Newman with the crooked pince-nez").
Grotesque ("Sir John addressed the Snake-god in his temple").

Henry and Mary.
I'd Love to Be a Fairy's Child.
In Broken Images.
In Procession.
In the Wilderness.
Last Post, The.
Legs, The.
Lollocks.
Lost Love.
Love without Hope.
Mermaid, Dragon, Fiend.
Ogres and Pygmies.
Oldest Soldier, The.
On Dwelling.
Outlaws.
Person from Porlock, The.
Plea to Boys and Girls, A.
Portrait, The.
Pure Death.
Quiet Glades of Eden, The.
Recalling War.
Saint.
Secret Land, The.
Sergeant-Major Money.
She Tells Her Love.
Sick Love.
Six Badgers, The.
Song: Lift Boy.
Spoils.
Star-Talk.
Straw, The.
Suicide in the Copse, The.
Sullen Moods.
Thieves, The.
To Juan at the Winter Solstice.
To Walk on Hills.
Traveller's Curse after Misdirection.
Troll's Nosegay, The.
Turn of the Moon, The.
Two Fusiliers.
Two Witches, The.
Vain and Careless.
Vanity.
Warning to Children.
Welsh Incident.
White Goddess, The.
Woman and Tree.
Young Cordwainer, The.
GRAY, ALEXANDER. Kings from the East, The, *tr.*
GRAY, EVA. Christ, My Salvation.
It Was for Me.
Light and Love, Hope and Faith.
My Daily Prayer.
What Is That in Thine Hand?
GRAY, FRANCES ANGEVINE. Otherwhere.
Tapers.
Tenant.
GRAY, JOHN. Flying Fish, The, II.
Night Nurse Goes Her Round, The.
GRAY, THOMAS. Bard, The.
Cat and the Fish, The.
Descent of Odin, The.
Elegy Written in a Country Churchyard.
Fatal Sisters, The.
Hymn to Adversity.
Impromptu.
Ode on a Distant Prospect of Eton College.
Ode on the Death of a Favourite Cat [Drowned in a Tub of Goldfishes].
Ode on the Pleasure Arising from Vicissitude.
Ode on the Spring.
On [the Death of] a Favorite Cat, Drowned in a Tub of Gold Fishes.
On Lord Holland's Seat near M——e, Kent.
Progress of Poesy, The.
Sketch of His Own Character.
Sonnet: "In vain to me the smiling mornings shine."
Sonnet on the Death of Mr. Richard West.
William Shakespeare to Mrs. Anne, Regular Servant to the Rev. Mr. Precentor of York.
GREEN, HENRY MACKENZIE. Cicada, The.
GREEN, JUDITH. Bush-Fiddle, The.
GREEN, MARY MCBRIDE. Aeroplane.
GREEN, MATTHEW. Epigram, An: "Gil's history appears to me."

GREENAWAY, KATE. Little Phillis.
Little Wind.
Older Grown.
GREENE, ROBERT. Description of Sir
Geoffrey Chaucer, The. *Fr.* Greene's
Vision.
Farewell to Folly, *sel.*
Greene's Vision, *sel.*
Maesia's Song. *Fr.* Farewell to Folly.
Menaphon, *sel.*
Never Too Late, *sel.*
Palmer's Ode, The. *Fr.* Never Too
Late.
Sephestia's Song to Her Child. *Fr.*
Menaphon.
Sir Geoffrey Chaucer. *Fr.* Greene's
Vision.
Weep Not My Wanton. *Fr.* Men-
aphon.
GREENWOOD, JAMES. On the Ladies'
Head-Dresses.
GREGORY, AUGUSTA GREGORY, LADY.
Donall Oge: Grief of a Girl's Heart,
tr.
GREGORY, HORACE. Flavius, If Your
Girl Friend, *tr.*
Foreigner Comes to Earth on Boston
Common, A.
GREGORY, YVONNE. Christmas Lullaby
for a New-born Child.
"GREIF, MARTIN" (Hermann Frey).
Before the Harvest.
GREIFFENBERG, CATHARINA REGINA VON.
Spring-Joy Praising God. Praise of
the Sun.
GRENELLE, LISA. Devil Doll.
GRENFELL, JULIAN. Into Battle.
GRENVILLE, R. H. Borderline.
Ghost.
Intuition.
Nightmare.
GREVILLE, FULKE, 1ST BARON BROOKE.
Absence, the noble truce. *Fr.* Cae-
lica.
All my senses, like beacon's flame.
Fr. Caelica.
Away with these self-loving lads. *Fr.*
Caelica.
Caelica, *sels.*
Caelica, I overnight was finely used.
Fr. Caelica.
Cupid, thou naughty boy, when thou
wert loathed. *Fr.* Caelica.
Down in the depth of mine iniquity.
Fr. Caelica.
Earth with thunder torn, with fire
blasted, The. *Fr.* Caelica.
Eternal Truth, almighty, infinite. *Fr.*
Caelica.
Faction, that ever dwells. *Fr.* Caelica.
Farewell, sweet boy; complain not of
my truth. *Fr.* Caelica.
Fie, foolish Earth, think you the heaven
wants glory. *Fr.* Caelica.
I, with whose colors Myra dressed her
head. *Fr.* Caelica.
In night, when colors all to black are
cast. *Fr.* Caelica.
Man, dream no more of curious mys-
teries. *Fr.* Caelica.
Mustapha, *sel.*
Myra. *Fr.* Caelica.
Nurse-life wheat, within his green husk
growing, The. *Fr.* Caelica.
O Wearisome Condition. *Fr.* Mus-
tapha.
Of His Cynthia. *Fr.* Caelica.
Sion lies waste, and thy Jerusalem.
Fr. Caelica.
When all this All doth pass from age
to age. *Fr.* Caelica.
World, that all contains, is ever mov-
ing, The. *Fr.* Caelica.
Wrapped up, O Lord, in man's degen-
eration. *Fr.* Caelica.
You Little Stars. *Fr.* Caelica.
You that seek what life is in death.
Fr. Caelica.
GRIDER, DOROTHY, *and* MARION EDEY.
See EDEY, MARION, *and* DOROTHY
GRIDER.
GRIEVE, CHRISTOPHER MURRAY. *See*
"MACDIARMID, HUGH."
GRIFFIN, BARTHOLOMEW. Fair Is My

Love. *Fr.* Fidessa, More Chaste
than Kind.
Fidessa, More Chaste than Kind, *sel.*
Sonnet: "Fair is my Love that feeds
among the lilies." *Fr.* Fidessa, More
Chaste than Kind.
GRILIKHES, ALEXANDRA. Runner, The.
GRIMKÉ, ANGELINA WELD. Black Fin-
ger, The.
To Clarissa Scott Delany.
GROESBECK, AMY. Brothers, The.
GROUP, VERDA. I Know.
GRYPHIUS, ANDREAS. All Is Vanity.
Concerning the Birth of Christ, 1657.
Epitaph for Mariana, His Brother
Paul's Little Daughter.
Evening.
Human Misery.
Tears of the Fatherland.
GUARINI, GIOVANNI BATTISTA. Madrigal
I: "This life, which seems so fair."
Microcosm, The.
GUEST, BARBARA. Belgravia.
"Everything in the Air Is a Bird."
First of May, The.
Hero Leaves His Ship, The.
Les Réalités.
Sadness.
Verba in Memoriam.
Wave.
GUEST, EDGAR ALBERT. All That Mat-
ters.
Becoming a Dad.
Out Fishin'.
Prayer for the Home, *sel.*
GUEVARA, MIGUEL DE. To Christ Cru-
cified.
GUIDACCI, MARGHERITA. All Saints'
Day, *sel.*
GUIDICCIONI, GIOVANNI. To Italy.
GUILHADE, JOAN DE. Alas, Ugly Lady,
You Complained.
For Mr. X I've Only Mischief.
Friend, I Can't Deny.
GUILHEM DE CABESTANH. Sweet Soft-
ness with Which Love Serves Me
Often, The.
GUILLAUME DE LORRIS *and* JEAN DE
MEUN. Romance of the Rose, The,
sels.
GUILLAUME DE MACHAUT [*or* MA-
CHAULT]. Ah! How I Fear, Milady,
Lest I Die.
As Lilies White, More Crimson than
the Rose.
I Curse the Hour, the Moment and the
Day.
If I Must Feel Your Wrath Eternally.
Milady, Comely, Candid, Worldly-wise.
Open Your Eyes, Milady, Run Me
Through.
Rich in Love and Beggar to My Heart.
Strike Down My Heart with But a
Single Blow.
GUILLAUME DE POITIERS (Guillem IX,
Count of Poitou, *or* William IX,
Count of Poitiers). Count Wil-
liam's Escapade.
I'll Make Some Verses Just for Fun.
In the Fair Times of New-born Spring.
Under the Sun I Ride Along.
GUILLEVIC, EUGÈNE. Elegies, *sels.*
GUINICELLI [*or* GUINIZELLI], GUIDO.
Canzone: Of the Gentle Heart.
Gentle Heart, The.
He Will Praise His Lady.
GUIOT DE DIJON. I Will Sing and So
Relieve.
GUITERMAN, ARTHUR. Belsnickel.
Business.
Eight Oars and a Coxswain.
Growing Up.
Habits of the Hippopotamus.
Hills.
Lament for the Alamo.
Mexican Serenade.
Of Certain Irish Fairies.
On the Vanity of Earthly Greatness.
Pershing at the Front.
Shakespearean Bear, The.
Tact.
Thanksgiving Wishes.
Tract for Autos, A.
Twist-Rime on Spring.

Vizier's Apology, The.
Young Washington.
GUITTONE D'AREZZO. Have Mercy,
Love! Give Ear.
GUMILEV [*or* GUMILYOV], NIKOLAI
STEPANOVICH. Black Diamond.
GUNN, THOM. Annihilation of Nothing,
The.
Beach Head, The.
Black Jackets.
Byrnies, The.
Considering the Snail.
Corridor, The.
Das Liebesleben.
Flying above California.
From the Highest Camp.
Goddess, The.
In Santa Maria del Popolo.
Inherited Estate, The.
Innocence.
Jesus and His Mother.
Loot.
My Sad Captains.
Nature of an Action, The.
On the Move.
St. Martin and the Beggar.
Silver Age, The.
To Yvor Winters, 1955.
Unsettled Motorcyclist's Vision of His
Death, The.
Vox Humana.
GÜNTHER, JOHANN CHRISTIAN. Conso-
lation-Aria.
GURNEY, IVOR. Bohemians, The.
Silent One, The.
To His Love.
GUSTAFSON, RALPH. Armorial.
At the Ocean's Verge.
Fish, The.
Meaning, The.
On the *Struma* Massacre.
S.S.R., Lost at Sea—*The Times.*
GUTHRIE, RAMON. Noël Tragique.
GUYON, JEANNE MARIE BOUVIER DE LA
MOTTE. Adoration.
By Thy Life I Live.
GWYNNE, J. HAROLD. Word of God,
The.

H

"H., M. G." He Never Will Forget.
"H. D." *See* DOOLITTLE, HILDA.
"H. H." *See* JACKSON, HELEN HUNT.
HABINGTON, WILLIAM. Against Them
Who Lay Unchastity to the Sex of
Women. *Fr.* Castara.
Castara, *sels.*
To a Wanton.
To Castara: Upon Beautie. *Fr.* Cas-
tara.
To Roses in the Bosom of Castara.
Fr. Castara.
To the Right Honourable the Countesse
of C.
HADLEY, LYDIA. Four Calls, The.
HADRIAN, EMPEROR (Publius Aelius
Hadrianus). To His Soul.
HAGEDORN, HERMANN. Light.
Noah.
HAGELSTANGE, RUDOLF. Aran.
Memento.
HAGEMAN, SAMUEL MILLER. Silence.
HALE, EDWARD EVERETT. Lend a Hand.
Omnipresence.
One Thousandth Psalm, The.
HALE, SARAH JOSEPHA BUELL. Mary's
Lamb.
HALEVI [*or* HA-LEVI], JUDAH [*or* JEHU-
DAH]. Afráh.
Cups without Wine Are Lowly.
Earth, like a Girl, Sipped the Rains,
The.
One Day I Fondled Her on My Knees.
HALHED, NATHANIEL BRASSEY, *and*
RICHARD BRINSLEY SHERIDAN. *See*
SHERIDAN, RICHARD BRINSLEY, *and*
NATHANIEL BRASSEY HALHED.
HALL, DONALD. Airstrip in Essex, An.

Body Politic, The.
By the Exeter River.
Child, The.
In the Old House.
Long River, The.
Marriage: To K.
New Hampshire.
1934.
Philander.
Sleeping Giant, The.
Snow, The.
Spider Head.
Three Movements, The.
Valentine.
HALL, MARGARET S. Life Is So Short.
HALL, MARY LEE. Turn Again to Life.
HALL, RODNEY. Eyewitness.
HALLACK, CECILY. Divine Office of the Kitchen, The.
HALLECK, FITZ-GREENE. Fanny, sel.
Joseph Rodman Drake.
On the Death of Joseph Rodman Drake.
HALLOCK, GRACE TABER. Comfortable Apple Trees, The.
Dog and the Cat, The.
Grasshopper Hop-o-the Grasses.
Mud Turtles.
Pleasant Cow, The.
Proud Toad, The.
Snakes and Snails.
HAMBLETON, RONALD. Sockeye Salmon.
HAMBURGER, MICHAEL. April Day: Binsey.
Blind Man.
Dual Site, The.
Epitaph for a Horseman.
Man of the World.
Mathematics of Love.
Poet's Progress, A.
Security.
For translations from German, see AGP; MGP; MoBS.
HAMERLING, ROBERT. Stars, The.
HAMILTON, RUTH H. Song for a Fifth Child.
HAMMARSKJÖLD, DAG. Lord—Thine the Day.
HAMMOND, ELEANOR. April Fool.
Valentine, A.
HAMMOND, WILLIAM. Tell Me, O Love.
HAMSUN, KNUT. Tora's Song.
HANBURY-WILLIAMS, SIR CHARLES. *See* WILLIAMS, SIR CHARLES HANBURY.
HANES, FRANK BORDEN. Au Beau Milieu.
In Labyrinths.
Love Is a Bullet.
Old Arrowhead Thoughts of a Late War.
Plain Man, The.
Poetry Revival.
HANSEN-BAY, C. Lord Christ, My Darling Is So Dear.
HARDENBERG, GEORG FRIEDRICH PHILIPP VON. *See* "NOVALIS."
HARDING, SAMUEL. Of Death.
HARDISON, OSBORNE BENNETT, JR. Girl with Guitar.
Impressions.
Middle Passage.
Of Motion.
Primitivism.
St. Petersburg Paradox, The.
Speculations.
To Ford, Guggenheim, Rockefeller, etc.
HARDY, ELIZABETH [*or* LIZZIE] CLARK. Some Time at Eve.
HARDY, JOHN EDWARD. Voyeur.
HARDY, THOMAS. Achtung, tr.
After a Journey.
After the Visit.
Afterwards.
Ah, Are You Digging on My Grave?
Ancient to Ancients, An.
"And There Was a Great Calm."
At a Country Fair.
At an Inn.
At Casterbridge Fair, sel.
At Castle Boterel.
At Tea. *Fr.* Satires of Circumstance.
At the Draper's. *Fr.* Satires of Circumstance.
Beeny Cliff.
Beyond the Last Lamp.

Blinded Bird, The.
Broken Appointment, A.
By Her Aunt's Grave. *Fr.* Satires of Circumstance.
By the Earth's Corpse.
Channel Firing.
Choirmaster's Burial, The.
Convergence of the Twain, The.
Curate's Kindness, The.
Dark-eyed Gentleman, The.
Darkling Thrush, The.
Dead and the Living One, The.
Division, The.
Drummer Hodge.
During Wind and Rain.
Dynasts, The, *sel.*
Epitaph on a Pessimist.
Faintheart in a Railway Train.
Five Students, The.
Former Beauties. *Fr.* At Casterbridge Fair.
Friends Beyond.
Garden Seat, The.
God-forgotten.
God's Education.
God's Funeral.
Going, The.
Great Things.
Hap.
He Abjures Love.
He Fears His Good Fortune.
Heredity.
I Look into My Glass.
I Looked Up from My Writing.
I Need Not Go.
I Said to Love.
In a Wood. *Fr.* The Woodlanders.
In Church. *Fr.* Satires of Circumstance.
In Death Divided.
In Front of the Landscape.
In Tenebris, *sel.*
In the Servants' Quarters.
In the Study. *Fr.* Satires of Circumstance.
In Time of "The Breaking of Nations."
Let Me Enjoy.
Lines to a Movement in Mozart's E-flat Symphony.
Man He Killed, The.
Master and the Leaves, The.
Men Who March Away.
My Spirit Will Not Haunt the Mound.
Nature's Questioning.
Neutral Tones.
Newcomer's Wife, The.
Night of Trafalgar, The. *Fr.* The Dynasts.
1967.
On His 86th Birthday.
On the Departure Platform.
Oxen, The.
Phantom Horsewoman, The.
Poet, A.
Proud Songsters.
Puzzled Game-Birds, The.
Roman Road, The.
Ruined Maid, The.
Satires of Circumstance, sels.
Self-unseeing, The.
Shelley's Skylark.
Snow in the Suburbs.
Song of Hope.
To an Unborn Pauper Child.
To Lizbie Browne.
To Meet, or Otherwise.
Tolerance.
Trampwoman's Tragedy, A.
Transformations.
Under the Waterfall.
Unkept Good Fridays.
Voice, The.
Waiting Both.
Weathers.
Wessex Heights.
Woodlanders, The, *sel.*
Young Glass-Stainer, The.
Your Last Drive.
Zermatt: To the Matterhorn.
HARE, AMORY. Walking at Night.
HARFORD, LESBIA VENNER. Beauty and Terror.
Day's End.
Experience.

He Had Served Eighty Masters.
Revolution.
This Way Only.
HARINGTON, SIR JOHN (1561–1612). Author to His Wife, of a Woman's Eloquence, The.
Of an Heroical Answer of a Great Roman Lady to Her Husband.
Treason.
HARLOW, S. RALPH. O Young and Fearless Prophet.
HARNEY, WILLIAM EDWARD. West of Alice.
HARPUR, CHARLES. Aboriginal Mother's Lament, An.
Creek of the Four Graves, The, *sel.*
Love Sonnets, *sel.*
Midsummer Noon in the Australian Forest, A.
Temple of Infamy, The, *sel.*
Tower of the Dream, The, *sel.*
Words.
HARRINGTON, EDWARD PHILLIP. Bushrangers, The.
Morgan.
My Old Black Billy.
HARRIS, HAZEL HARPER. Gifts.
HARRIS, MAX. Martin Buber in the Pub.
Tantanoola Tiger, The.
HARRISON, EUGENE M. Soul Winner's Prayer, The.
HART-SMITH, WILLIAM. Christopher Columbus, *sels.*
Cipangu. *Fr.* Christopher Columbus.
Comes Fog and Mist. *Fr.* Christopher Columbus.
Departure. *Fr.* Christopher Columbus.
Space. *Fr.* Christopher Columbus.
Waterspout, The. *Fr.* Christopher Columbus.
HARTE, BRET (Francis Bret Harte). Chicago.
Her Letter.
Mrs. Judge Jenkins.
Plain Language from Truthful James.
Relieving Guard.
What the Bullet Sang.
HARTIGAN, PATRICK JOSEPH ("John O'Brien"). Said Hanrahan.
Tangmalangaloo.
HARVEY, FREDERICK WILLIAM. Ducks.
Prisoners.
Sleepers, The.
HARVEY, J. E. Forgetting God.
HARWOOD, GWEN. Last Meeting.
Panther and Peacock.
Prizegiving.
"HASHIMURA TOGO." *See* IRWIN, WALLACE.
HASHIN. Loneliness.
No Sky at All.
HASKINS, M. LOUISE. Gate of the Year, The, *sel.*
HASTINGS, MARIA. Farmyard Song, A.
Sing Little Bird.
HAUFF, FRIEDRICH. Song before the Battle.
HAUGWITZ, AUGUST ADOLF VON. To Her for a Kiss.
HAUSGEN, MATTIE LEE. Her Favorites.
HAVERGAL, FRANCES RIDLEY. Another Year.
New Year's Wishes.
Teacher's Prayer, A.
HAWES, STEPHEN. Epitaph, An: "O mortal folk, you may behold and see."
Pair of Wings, A.
HAWKER, ROBERT STEPHEN. Aishah-Schechinah.
And Shall Trelawny Die?
Featherstone's Doom.
Song of the Western Men, The.
HAWKES, HENRY WARBURTON. Amid the Din of Earthly Strife.
HAWLEY, WILLIAM FITZ. Love Song, A.
HAY, GEORGE CAMPBELL. Smoky Smirr o' Rain, The.
HAY, JOHN (1838–1905). Enchanted Shirt, The.
Jim Bludso, of the *Prairie Belle.*
Law of Death, The.

HAY, JOHN (1915—). Amor Mysticus, *tr.*
HAY, SARA HENDERSON. Ballad of the Golden Bowl.
HAYDEN, ROBERT EARL. Ballad of Remembrance, A.
Frederick Douglas.
Middle Passage, *sel.*
Veracruz.
Witch Doctor.
HAYES, DONALD JEFFREY. Alien.
Apoggiatura.
Benediction.
Haven.
Pastourelle.
Poet.
Threnody: "Let happy throats be mute."
"HAYES, EVELYN." *See* BETHELL, MARY URSULA.
HAYS, HOFFMAN REYNOLDS. Burning of Books, The, *tr.*
Coal for Mike, *tr.*
Conclusive Voyage, The, *tr.*
Galante Garden, I, *tr.*
New Leaves, *tr.*
Of Swimming in Lakes and Rivers, *tr.*
HAYS, WILL S. O'Grady's Goat.
HAZEL, ROBERT. Guard of Honor.
HAZO, SAMUEL. Challenge.
HEADLAM, WALTER. In the Spring, *tr.*
Life after Death, *tr.*
Window in the Breast, A, *tr.*
HEALY, IAN. Advice from a Nightwatchman. *Fr.* Poems from the Coalfields.
Air Shaft. *Fr.* Poems from the Coalfields.
Poems from the Coalfields, *sels.*
HEARD, LILLIAN G. Humble Service.
HEATH, ——. Women.
HEATH-STUBBS, JOHN. Beggar's Serenade.
Charm against the Toothache, A.
Hearing the Cuckoo.
History of the Flood, The.
Ibycus.
Lady's Complaint, The.
Titus and Berenice.
HEAVYSEGE, CHARLES. Malzah's Song. *Fr.* Saul.
Night.
Saul, *sels.*
Winter Galaxy, The.
Zaph Describes the Haunts of Malzah. *Fr.* Saul.
HEBBEL, FRIEDRICH. Adam's Offering.
Night.
Picture of Autumn.
Summer Image.
Tree in the Desert, The.
You and I.
HEBER, REGINALD. By Cool Siloam's Shady Rill.
HECHT, ANTHONY. Adam.
Behold the Lilies of the Field.
Birdwatchers of America.
Divination by a Cat.
Dover Bitch, The.
End of the Weekend, The.
Jason.
La Condition Botanique.
Letter, A.
Lizards and Snakes.
Man Who Married Magdalene, The: Variation on a Theme by Louis Simpson.
"More Light! More Light!"
Samuel Sewall.
Third Avenue in Sunlight.
Upon the Death of George Santayana.
Vow, The.
HEDGE, FREDERIC HENRY. Mighty Fortress Is Our God, A, *tr.*
HEDLEY, LESLIE WOOLF. Chant for All the People on Earth.
HEDYLUS [or HEDYLOS]. Seduced Girl.
To Venus.
HEIDENSTAM, VERNER VON. Fellow-Citizens.
Home.
How Easily Men's Cheeks Are Hot.
HEINE, HEINRICH. After Our Wedding Day.

Beating Heart, The.
Bertrand de Born.
Fir Tree, A.
Fir tree standing lonely, A.
Gods of Greece, The.
Healing the Wound.
I Close Her Eyes.
I used to have the fairest fatherland.
Katharine.
King David.
Kings from the East, The.
Lotus-flower is frightened, The.
Lovely as a Flower.
Morning After, The.
My beautiful love, keep bound me.
My Heart, My Heart Is Mournful.
Precaution.
Questions.
Sea Hath Its Pearls, The.
Softly through my spirit flow.
Song of Songs, The.
Song of the Vivandiere.
Songs of Creation.
There was an aged monarch.
This White and Slender Body.
Three Sweethearts.
Where?
Who Was It.
Young man loves a maiden, A.
Your Snow-white Shoulder.
HEINRICH VON MORUNGEN. Ah Me, Shall I No Longer See.
Lady, Wilt Thou Heal My Smart?
Many a Man Has Been Bewitched by an Elf.
My Lady, if you'd have me whole.
On the Heath on a Morning.
Saw You the Ladies.
She Has Wounded Me Right Through the Heart.
Torturing Glimpses and Passions Unruly.
HEISSENBÜTTEL, HELMUT. Combination XI.
Fragment III.
HELPHINGTINE, MARY J. Blessings of Surrender, The.
HELSLEY, SHEL. Christ Alone.
HELTON, ROY ADDISON. Old Christmas.
HEMANS, FELICIA DOROTHEA (Browne). Brereton Omen, The, *sel.*
Hour of Death, The.
Landing of the Pilgrim Fathers, The.
HEMLEY, CECIL. If He Were Anywhere.
My Absent God.
Witnesses.
HENDERSON, DANIEL. Mormon Trail, The.
St. Swithin.
Two Wives, The.
HENDERSON, DAVID. Downtown-Boy Uptown.
Sketches of Harlem.
HENDERSON, HAROLD GOULD. For translations from Japanese, see PoPl; RePo; SiGo; SoPo.
HENDERSON, ROSE. Growing Old.
HENDERSON, RUTH EVELYN. Boy's Day.
HENLEY, ELIZABETH. Birthday-Cake Glockenspiel, The.
It Really Happened.
HENLEY, WILLIAM ERNEST. Alons au bois le may cueillir, *tr.*
And Lightly, like the Flowers, *tr.*
England, My England.
Home.
I Am the Reaper.
I. M. Margaritae Sorori.
Invictus.
Madam Life's a Piece in Bloom.
Margaritae Sorori.
On the Way to Kew.
Out of the night that covers me.
Rondel: Beside the Idle Summer Sea.
Some Late Lark Singing.
Triolet: "Easy is the triolet."
What Is to Come.
HENRICH, EDITH. Protagonist.
HENRY VIII, KING OF ENGLAND. Holly, The.
Love Ever Green.
Pastime.
To His Lady.

HENRYSON, ROBERT. Cresseid's Complaint against Fortune. *Fr.* The Testament of Cresseid.
Testament of Cresseid, The.
HENSCHKE, ALFRED. *See* "KLABUND."
HEPBURN, THOMAS NICOLL. *See* "SETOUN, GABRIEL."
HERBERT, SIR ALAN PATRICK. Beaucourt Revisited.
Mullion.
Prodigy, The.
What Is Love? *sel.*
HERBERT, EDWARD. *See* HERBERT OF CHERBURY, EDWARD HERBERT, 1ST BARON.
HERBERT, GEORGE. Affliction ("Broken in pieces all asunder").
Affliction ("When first thou didst entice to thee my heart").
Agonie, The.
Altar, The.
Ana(Mary Army)gram.
And Now in Age I Bud Again.
Avarice.
Bag, The.
Banquet, The.
Bitter-sweet.
British Church, The.
Bunch of Grapes, The.
Christ Our Lord.
Church-Floore, The.
Church-Lock and Key.
Church-Monuments.
Church-Musick.
Church-Porch, The, *sels.*
Church Windows, The.
Collar, The.
Colossians III: 3: Our Life Is Hid with Christ in God.
Confession.
Conscience.
Crosse, The.
Dawning, The.
Death.
Decay.
Dedication, The: "Lord, my first fruits present themselves to thee."
Deniall.
Discipline.
Dooms-Day.
Dulnesse.
Easter.
Easter Wings.
Elixir, The.
Employment ("He that is weary, let him sit").
Even-Song.
Familie, The.
Flower, The.
Foil, The.
Forerunners, The.
Gifts of God, The.
Glance, The.
Good Friday.
Grieve Not the Holy Spirit, &c.
Heart to Praise Thee, A.
Heaven.
Holdfast, The.
H. Communion, The.
H. Scriptures, The.
I got me flowers to strew Thy way.
Invitation, The.
Jordan ("When first my lines of heav'nly joyes made mention").
Jordan ("Who says that fictions only and false hair").
Judgement.
L'Envoy: "King of glorie, King of peace."
Let all the world in every corner sing.
Life.
Longing.
Love ("Immortall Heat, O let thy greater flame").
Love ("Immortall Love, authour of this great frame").
Love ("Love bade me welcome: yet my soul drew back").
Man.
Marie Magdalene.
Mattens.
Mortification.
Obedience.
Odour, The.

Paradise.
Parodie, A: "Souls joy, when thou art gone."
Peace.
Pearl, The.
Philosophers Have Measured Mountains.
Pilgrimage, The.
Praise.
Prayer: "Prayer the Church's banquet, angels' age."
Priesthood, The.
Pulley, The.
Quip, The.
Rain, The.
Redemption.
Reprisall, The.
Rose, The.
Search, The.
Sepulchre.
Shall I Be Silent?
Sion.
Sonne, The.
Sonnet: "My God, where is that ancient heat towards thee."
Sonnet: "Sure Lord, there is enough in thee to dry."
Starre, The.
Storm, The.
Superliminare.
Teach me, my God and King.
Temper, The.
Thanksgiving, The.
Ungratefulness.
Untitled.
Virtue [or Vertue].
Windows, The.
Wreath, A.
HERBERT, WILLIAM, EARL OF PEMBROKE. See PEMBROKE, WILLIAM HERBERT, EARL OF.
HERBERT OF CHERBURY, EDWARD HERBERT, 1ST BARON. Description, A.
Epitaph. Cæcil. Boulstr.
In a Glass-Window for Inconstancy.
Loves End.
Madrigal: "How should I love my best?"
Ode, An, upon a Question Moved, Whether Love Should Continue for Ever?
Parted Souls.
Sinner's Lament, A.
Tears, Flow No More.
To a Lady Who Did Sing Excellently.
To His Mistress for Her True Picture.
Upon Combing Her Hair.
Vision, A.
HERDER, JOHANN GOTTFRIED VON. "Dream, A—'tis but a dream, our being."
HEREBERT, WILLIAM. Devout Man Prays to His Relations, The.
Knight Stained from Battle, The.
Palm-Sunday Hymn, A.
HERFORD, OLIVER. Cat, The.
Chimpanzee, The.
Dog, The.
Earth.
Elf and the Dormouse, The.
I Heard a Bird Sing.
Stairs.
HERNTON, CALVIN C. Distant Drum, The.
Madhouse.
HERRERA, FERNANDO DE. Ideal Beauty.
To Don Juan de Austria.
HERRICK, ROBERT. Againe.
Another Grace for a Child.
Apparition of His Mistresse Calling Him to Elizium, The.
Argument of His Book, The.
Bad Season Makes the Poet Sad, The.
Bellman, The.
Ceremonies for Candlemas Eve.
Cherry [or Cherrie]-ripe.
Child's Grace, A.
Chop-Cherry.
Christmas Caroll, A, Sung to the King in the Presence at White-Hall.
Clothes Do but Cheat and Cozen Us.
Coming of Good Luck, The.
Corinna's Going a-Maying.

Counsel to Girls.
Country Life, A: To His Brother, M. Tho: Herrick.
Delight in Disorder.
Dew Sat on Julia's Hair.
Four Sweet Months, The.
Fresh Cheese and Cream.
Funeral Rites of the Rose, The.
Gather Ye Rose-Buds [While Ye May].
Hag, The.
Here a little child I stand.
His Age.
His Cavalier.
His Creed.
His Desire.
His Fare-well to Sack.
His Grange, or Private Wealth.
His Litany to the Holy Spirit.
His Poetrie His Pillar.
His Prayer for Absolution.
His Prayer to Ben Jonson.
Hock-Cart, The; or, Harvest Home.
Humility.
I'll Come to Thee.
In the Dark None Dainty.
Lilly in a Christal, The.
Love Dislikes Nothing.
Love Perfumes All Parts.
Mad Maid's Song, The.
Meditation for His Mistresse, A.
Mercy and Love.
More White than Whitest Lilies.
Night-Piece, to Julia, The.
No Coming to God without Christ.
Nuptiall Song, or Epithalamie, on Sir Clipseby Crew and His Lady, A.
Ode for Ben Jonson, An.
On Himself[e].
Pillar of Fame, The.
Poet Loves a Mistress but Not to Marry, The.
Resurrection Possible and Probable, The.
Second Vision, The.
Show Me Thy Feet.
Sitting Alone.
So Look the Mornings.
Sweet disorder in the dress, A.
Ternarie of Littles, upon a Pipkin of Jellie Sent to a Lady, A.
Thanksgiving to God, for His House, A.
To Anthea Lying in Bed.
To Anthea, Who May Command Him Anything.
To Blossoms.
To Daffodils [or Daffadills].
To Daisies, Not to Shut So Soon.
To Dianeme.
To God.
To His Lovely Mistresses.
To His Mistresses.
To His Mistress Objecting to Him neither Toying or Talking.
To His Saviour, a Child; a Present, by a Child.
To Keep a True Lent.
To Live Merrily, and to Trust to Good Verses.
To Meadows [or Meddowes].
To Musique, to Becalme His Fever.
To Perilla.
To Primroses.
To the Rose.
To the Soure Reader.
To the Virgins, to Make Much of Time.
To Violets.
To Virgins.
Trapped Fly, A.
Upon a Child That Died.
Upon a Virgin Kissing a Rose.
Upon Julia's Clothes.
Upon Julia's Fall.
Upon Julia's Petticoat.
Upon Julia's Voice.
Upon Roses.
Upon the Nipples of Julia's Breast.
Vine, The.
Vision, The.
Vision to Electra, The.
Weeping Cherry, The.
Welcome to Sack, The.
What Kind of Mistress He Would Have.

What Shame Forbids to Speak.
When I Thy Parts Run O'er.
Whenas in Silks My Julia Goes.
White Island, The.
HERRMANN-NEISSE, MAX. Legend of the Bewitched Nunnery.
You Quiet Attender to My Garden.
HERSCHELL, WILLIAM M. Kid Has Gone to the Colors, The.
HERVEY, CHRISTOPHER. Confusion.
HERWEGH, GEORG. Shelley.
HESSE, HERMANN. Alone.
HEWITT, JOHN. O Country People.
HEYM, GEORG. And the Horns of Summer Fell Silent.
Judas.
O Boundless, Boundless Evening.
Pilate.
Umbra Vitae.
Why Do You Visit Me, White Moths, So Often?
HEYSE, PAUL. Rispetti: On the Death of a Child.
Young Girl's Song, A.
HEYWARD, DuBOSE. Gamesters All.
HEYWOOD, JOHN. Jack and His Father.
Love Continual.
HEYWOOD, THOMAS. Rape of Lucrece, The, sels.
She That Denies Me [I Would Have]. Fr. The Rape of Lucrece.
HICKSON, WILLIAM EDWARD. Try Again, at.
HICKY, DANIEL WHITEHEAD. Wisdom.
HIGGINS, FREDERICK ROBERT. Father and Son.
HIGHAM, CHARLES. Barnacle Geese.
HIGHAM, THOMAS FARRANT. For translations from Greek, see SiGo.
HIGHET, GILBERT. Homage to Ezra Pound.
My Woman, tr.
HILL, AARON. May-Day.
HILL, GEOFFREY. Annunciations.
Doctor Faustus.
Genesis.
Guardians, The.
In Memory of Jane Fraser.
In Piam Memoriam.
Of Commerce and Society.
Orpheus and Eurydice.
Pastoral, A: "Mobile, immaculate and austere."
Requiem for the Plantagenet Kings.
To the (Supposed) Patron.
HILL, GEORGE. Leila.
HILL, JOE. There Is Power in a Union, at.
HILLYER, ROBERT SILLIMAN. Book of the Dead, sels., tr.
Dead Man Ariseth and Singeth a Hymn to the Sun, The, tr. Fr. Book of the Dead.
He Is like the Lotus, tr. Fr. Book of the Dead.
Lullaby: "Long canoe, The."
Pastoral X: "Grapes are ripe, the frost is near, The."
Plants Stand Silent Round Me, The, tr.
Rendezvous.
Seven Times One Are Seven.
HILTON, ARTHUR CLEMENT. Ding Dong.
Octopus.
HINCHCLIFFE, BARBARA. Sunday in the Thirties, A.
HINE, AL (Alfred Blakelee Hine). Christmas 1945.
HINE, DARYL. Bewilderment at the Entrance of the Fat Boy into Eden, A.
Bluebeard's Wife.
Doppelganger, The.
In Praise of Music in Time of Pestilence.
HINES, CARL WENDELL, JR. Jazz Poem.
Two Jazz Poems.
HINKSON, KATHARINE TYNAN. See TYNAN, KATHARINE.
HITCHCOCK, GEORGE. Indestructible, The, sel.
Mr. Kennedy Proposes to Pacify the Caribbeans.

HOBBS, VALINE. One Day When We Went Walking.
HOBERMAN, MARY ANN. Birthday Bus, The.
Comparison.
HOCCLEVE [or OCCLEVE], THOMAS. Description of His Ugly Lady, A.
"HODDIS, JAKOB VAN" (Hans Davidsohn). End of the World.
Hymn: "O dream, digestion of my soul!"
HODGSON, RALPH. And Every Sky Was Blue and Rain. Fr. To Deck a Woman.
Bells of Heaven, The.
Birdcatcher, The.
Eve.
Great Auk's Ghost, The.
Hammers, The.
Reason.
Riddle, The.
Song, A: "With Love among the haycocks."
Stupidity Street.
Time.
To Deck a Woman, sel.
Wood Song, A.
HOELLEIN, ALMA. There Is a Place.
We'll Never Know.
HOFFENSTEIN, SAMUEL. Breathes There a Man.
Mr. Walter de la Mare Makes the Little Ones Dizzy.
Of All the Idiots That Abound.
Poems in Praise of Practically Nothing, sel.
Progress.
When You're Away.
Your Little Hands.
HOFFMAN, CHARLES FENNO. Monterey.
HOFFMAN, DANIEL GERARD. At the Winter Solstice.
City of Satisfactions, The.
Exploration.
Flushing Meadows, 1939.
In the Beginning.
In the Days of Rin-Tin-Tin.
Letter to Wilbur Frohock, A.
Meeting, A.
1956.
Seals in Penobscot Bay, The.
Three Jovial Gentlemen.
HOFFMANN, HEINRICH. Slovenly Peter.
Story of Augustus Who Would Not Have Any Soup, The.
Story of Johnny Head-in-Air, The.
Story of Little Suck-a-Thumb, The.
HOFFMANN VON HOFFMANNSWALDAU, CHRISTIAN. Beauty's Transitoriness.
So sweet, so golden.
HÖFLER, PETER KARL. See "THOOR, JESSE."
HOFMANNSTHAL, HUGO VON. Ballad of Outer Life.
Poem: "We are such stuff as dreams are made of, and these."
Two, The.
HOGAN, INEZ. Blanket Street.
Middle-aged Child.
Space.
HOGG, JAMES ("The Ettrick Shepherd"). Boy's Song, A.
Flying Tailor, The.
Isabelle.
James Rigg.
Kilmeny. Fr. The Queen's Wake.
Love Is like a Dizziness.
Queen's Wake, The, sel.
HOLBROOK, DAVID. Delivering Children.
HOH, ISRAEL KAFU. Vulture, The.
Fingers in the Door.
Living? Our Supervisors Will Do That for Us!
Poor Old Horse.
HÖLDERLIN [or HOELDERLIN], FRIEDRICH. Age.
Crowd's Acclaim, The.
Death.
Descend, Beautiful Sun.
Evening Fancy.
Fall.
Half of Life.
Hyperion's Song of Fate.
Men's Applause.

Pleasantness of life was mine once undiminished, The.
Socrates and Alcibiades.
To the Parcae.
While I Was Yet a Boy.
HOLLAND, JOSIAH GILBERT. God, Give Us Men!
There's a Song in the Air!
To My Dog Blanco.
Wanted.
HOLLAND, NORAH M. Little Dog-Angel, A.
HOLLAND, RUPERT SARGENT. When I Grow Up.
HOLLANDER, JOHN. Aristotle to Phyllis.
By the Sea.
Digging It Out.
Great Bear, The.
Lady's-Maid's [or Lady's Maid] Song, The.
Lion Named Passion, A.
Non Sum Qualis Eram in Bona Urbe Nordica Illa.
Paysage Moralisé.
Slepynge Long in Greet Quiete Is Eek a Greet Norice to Leccherie.
When All of Them Ran Off.
HOLLANDER, ROBERT. November 22, 1963.
HÖLLERER, WALTER. Face of the Fisherman, The.
Particularly Effortless He Lay.
HOLLO, ANSELM. Until Death Do Us Part.
"HOLM, SAXE." See JACKSON, HELEN HUNT.
HOLMAN, MOSES CARL. And on This Shore.
Letter across Doubt and Distance.
Notes for a Movie Script.
Song: "Dressed up in my melancholy."
HOLMES, GEORGIANA. See "KLINGLE, GEORGE."
HOLMES, JOHN. Eleventh Commandment, The, sel.
Poetry Defined.
Prayer on the Night before Easter.
Questions for the Candidate.
Testament.
Willing Suspension, A.
HOLMES, OLIVER WENDELL. Autocrat of the Breakfast Table, The, sel.
Ballad of the Boston Tea-Party, A.
Ballad of the Oysterman, The.
Brother Jonathan's Lament for Sister Caroline.
Chambered Nautilus, The. Fr. The Autocrat of the Breakfast Table.
"Christo et Ecclesiae" 1700. Fr. Two Sonnets: Harvard.
Contentment.
Deacon's Masterpiece, The; or, The Wonderful "One-Hoss Shay."
Dorchester Giant, The.
Dorothy Q.
Height of the Ridiculous, The.
In Memory of Abraham Lincoln.
In Thine Arms.
Last Leaf, The.
Living Temple, The.
Manhood. Fr. Wind-Clouds and Star-Drifts.
Old Ironsides.
Old Man Dreams, The.
Peau de Chagrin of State Street, The.
1643 "Veritas" 1878. Fr. Two Sonnets: Harvard.
Sun-Day Hymn, A.
Two Sonnets: Harvard.
Two Streams, The.
Wind-Clouds and Star-Drifts, sel.
HOLMES, THEODORE. Buddha.
Christ.
Dysynni Valley, The.
Old Age Home, The.
HOLTHUSEN, HANS EGON. Last Letter.
My Life, My Death.
HÖLTY, LUDWIG HEINRICH CHRISTOPH. Night in May.
HOME, ANNE. See HUNTER, ANNE.
HOMER. Achilles' Revenge. Fr. The Iliad.
Iliad, The, sels.
Night Encampment outside Troy. Fr. The Iliad.

Odyssey, The, sels.
HONESTUS. Requirements: "Not too old, and not too young."
HONIG, EDWIN. For translations from Spanish, see AnML.
HOOD, THOMAS. Bridge of Sighs, The.
Death Bed, The.
Fairy's Reply to Saturn, The. Fr. The Plea of the Midsummer Fairies.
Faithless Nelly [or Nellie] Gray.
False Poets and True.
Good Night.
Green Dryad's Plea, The. Fr. The Plea of the Midsummer Fairies.
Haunted House, The.
I Remember, I Remember.
It Was Not in the Winter.
Little Piggy.
Melodies of Time, The. Fr. The Plea of the Midsummer Fairies.
Ode: Autumn.
Ode on a Distant Prospect of Clapham Academy.
Our Village—by a Villager.
Parental Ode to My Son, A.
Past and Present.
Plea of the Midsummer Fairies, The, sels.
Ruth.
Sally Simpkin's Lament.
Sea of Death, The.
Shakespeare: The Fairies' Advocate. Fr. The Plea of the Midsummer Fairies.
She Is Far from the Land.
Silence.
Song of the Shirt, The.
Sonnet: "It is not death, that sometime in a sigh."
Sonnet: Silence.
Tim Turpin.
We Watch'd Her Breathing.
HOOD, TOM (Thomas Hood, Jr.). Ravings.
HOOFT, PIETER CORNELISZOON. Thus Spoke My Love.
HOOLEY, TERESA. Sea Fret.
HOOTON, EARNEST ALBERT. To Chloe.
HOPE, ALEC DERWENT. Australia.
Chorale: "Often had I found her fair."
Death of the Bird, The.
Elegy, The: "Madam, no more! The time has come to eat."
Epistle, An: "First, last and always dearest, closest, best."
Gateway, The.
Imperial Adam.
Pyramis; or, The House of Ascent.
HOPE, FRANCIS. Peeping Tom.
"HOPE, LAURENCE" (Adela Florence Cory Nicolson). For This Is Wisdom. Fr. The Teak Forest.
Teak Forest, The, sel.
HOPEGOOD, PETER. Dithyramb in Retrospect.
Protagonist, The.
HOPKINS, GERARD MANLEY. As Kingfishers Catch Fire.
At the Wedding March.
Bad I am, but yet thy child.
Binsey Poplars, Felled 1879.
Brothers.
Bugler's First Communion, The.
Caged Skylark, The.
Candle Indoors, The.
Carrion Comfort.
Christ Speaks.
Duns Scotus's Oxford.
Felix Randal.
God's Grandeur.
Habit of Perfection, The.
Harry Ploughman.
Heaven-Haven.
Hurrahing in Harvest.
I Have Desired to Go.
I Wake and Feel the Fell of Dark.
In the Valley of the Elwy.
Inversnaid.
Leaden Echo and the Golden Echo, The.
Loss of the Eurydice, The.
May Magnificat, The.
Moonless Darkness Stands Between.
My Own Heart Let Me Have More Pity On.

No Worst, There Is None.
On a Poetess.
Patience, Hard Thing!
Peace.
Pied Beauty.
St. Alphonsus Rodriguez.
Sea and the Skylark, The.
Sonnet: "No worst, there is none. Pitched past pitch of grief."
Sonnet: "Not, I'll not, carrion comfort, Despair, not feast on thee."
Sonnet: "Patience, hard thing! the hard thing but to pray."
Spelt from Sibyl's Leaves.
Spring.
Spring and Fall.
Starlight Night, The.
That Nature Is a Heraclitean Fire and of the Comfort of the Resurrection.
Thou Art Indeed Just, Lord [If I Contend].
To Him Who Ever Thought with Love of Me.
To R. B.
To Seem the Stranger Lies My Lot, My Life.
Windhover, The.
Wreck of the *Deutschland,* The.
HOPKINS, KENNETH. Bubble, The.
HOPPER, QUEENIE SCOTT-. *See* SCOTT-HOPPER, QUEENIE.
HORACE (Quintus Horatius Flaccus).
Another to the Same. *Fr. Odes.*
Ask Not Ungainly. *Fr. Odes.*
Barine, the Incorrigible. *Fr. Odes.*
By the Flat Cup. *Fr. Odes.*
Call to Youth. *Fr. Odes.*
Golden Mean, The. *Fr. Odes.*
It Always Happens. *Fr. Odes.*
Odes, *sels.*
Passing of Lydia, The. *Fr. Odes.*
Teasing Lovers, The. *Fr. Odes.*
This Monument Will Outlast. *Fr. Odes.*
Time to Choose a Lover. *Fr. Odes.*
To a Girl. *Fr. Odes.*
Too Young for Love. *Fr. Odes.*
Young Men Come Less Often, The—Isn't It So? *Fr. Odes.*
HORN, EDWARD NEWMAN. Darling, If You Only Knew.
HORN, HERSCHEL. Landscape near a Steel Mill.
HORNE, FRANK. Kid Stuff.
Notes Found near a Suicide.
Resurrection.
Symphony.
To a Persistent Phantom.
To James.
HOSKINS, KATHERINE. Bee and the Petunia, The.
Not Lotte.
HOUGHTON, FIRMAN. Mr. Frost Goes South to Boston.
She Sees Another Door Opening.
HOUSELANDER, CARYLL. Soeur Marie Emilie.
HOUSMAN, ALFRED EDWARD. Along the Field as We Came By.
Be still, my soul, be still; the arms you bear are brittle.
Because I Liked You.
Bredon Hill.
Carpenter's Son, The.
Chestnut casts his flambeaux, and the flowers, The.
Crossing alone the nighted ferry.
Culprit, The.
Delight it is in youth and May.
Easter Hymn.
Eight o'Clock.
Elephant, The.
Epitaph on an Army of Mercenaries.
Farewell to Barn and Stack and Tree.
Fragment of a Greek Tragedy.
He Would Not Stay for Me.
Her Strong Enchantments Failing.
Here Dead Lie We.
Hughley Steeple.
I did not lose my heart in summer's even.
I hoed and trenched and weeded.
I to My Perils.
Illic Jacet.
Immortal Part, The.

In the Morning.
Infant Innocence.
Inhuman Henry; or, Cruelty to Fabulous Animals.
Into My Heart.
Is My Team Ploughing.
Lads in their hundreds to Ludlow come in for the fair, The.
Laugh, Be Jolly.
Lent Lily, The.
Loveliest of Trees.
Oh, See How Thick the Goldcup Flowers.
Oh, When I Was in Love.
Oh Who Is That Young Sinner?
Oedipus at Colonus, *sel., tr.*
Old Age, *tr. Fr.* Oedipus at Colonus.
On the idle hill of summer.
On Wenlock Edge the Wood's in Trouble.
Oracles, The.
Rain, it streams on stone and hillock, The.
Reveille.
Revolution.
Shake Hands.
Stars Have Not Dealt, The.
Stars, I have seen them fall.
Tell Me Not Here, It Needs Not Saying.
Terence, This Is Stupid Stuff.
They Say My Verse Is Sad.
Think No More Lad.
To an Athlete Dying Young.
We'll to the Woods No More.
When Adam Day by Day.
When Green Buds Hang.
When I Was One-and-twenty.
When smoke stood up from Ludlow.
White in the Moon.
With rue my heart is laden.
Yon flakes that fret the eastern sky.
Yonder See.
HOUSTON, MARGARET BELL. Cerelle.
HOVER, DONALD H. Other Person's Place, The.
HOVEY, RICHARD. Immanence.
Love in the Winds.
Sea Gypsy, The.
Spring, *sel.*
Transcendence.
Unmanifest Destiny.
HOW, WILLIAM WILSHAM. O Word of God Incarnate.
We Give Thee but Thine Own.
HOWARD, DOROTHY S. Birkett's Eagle.
HOWARD, HENRY. *See* SURREY, HENRY HOWARD, EARL OF.
HOWARD, RICHARD. Gaiety, *sel.*
Queer's Song. *Fr.* Gaiety.
Saturday Morning.
HOWARD, SIR ROBERT, *and* JOHN DRYDEN. Indian Queen, The, *sel.*
Poor Mortals. *Fr.* The Indian Queen.
HOWARD, ROBERT ERVIN. Earth-born.
Sands of Time, The.
HOWARD, VILMA. Citizen, The.
HOWARD, WINIFRED. White Horses.
HOWE, JULIA WARD. Battle Hymn of the Republic.
Mine Eyes Have Seen the Glory.
HOWELL, ELIZABETH LLOYD. Milton's Prayer for Patience.
HOWELLS, MILDRED. Going Too Far.
HOWES, BARBARA (Mrs. William Jay Smith). Cat on Couch.
Chimera.
Early Supper.
Home Leave.
Landscape, Deer Season.
L'Ile du Levant: The Nudist Colony.
Night Picture of Pownal, A.
HOWITT, MARY. Spider and the Fly, The.
HOYT, HELEN (Mrs. William W. Lyman). At Daybreak.
Memory.
HUCHEL, PETER. Coin from Bir el Abbas.
Polish Reaper, The.
HUDSON, FLEXMORE. Mallee in October.
HUEFFER, FORD MADOX. *See* FORD, FORD MADOX.
HUFF, ROBERT. Getting Drunk with Daughter.

Rainbow.
Smoker, The.
Traditional Red.
HUGHES, JOHN CEIRIOG ("Ceiriog").
Alun Mabon's Song.
HUGHES, LANGSTON. African Dance.
Border Line.
Bound No'th Blues.
Close to Me, *tr.*
Cross.
Dream Variation.
Dreams.
Homesick Blues.
I Dream a World.
I, Too [Sing America].
In Time of Silver Rain.
Jazzonia.
Lenox Avenue Mural.
Let America Be America Again.
Luck.
Mother to Son.
Negro Speaks of Rivers, The.
Pennsylvania Station.
Personal.
Poem of the Son, *tr.*
Prayer: "I ask you this."
Sea Calm.
Weary Blues, The.
Without Benefit of Declaration.
Youth.
HUGHES, RICHARD. Sermon, The.
HUGHES, TED. Bullfrog.
Cat and Mouse.
Childbirth.
Complaint.
Crag Jack's Apostasy.
Dark Women.
Dick Straightup.
Dream of Horses, A.
Encounter.
Foxgloves.
Gog.
Hawk in the Rain, The.
Hawk Roosting.
Jaguar, The.
Law in the Country of the Cats.
Lupercalia.
Martyrdom of Bishop Farrar, The.
Mayday on Holderness.
My Brother Bert.
New Moon in January.
November.
Otter, An.
Pennines in April.
Pibroch.
Pike.
Retired Colonel, The.
Roarers in a Ring.
Secretary.
Thought-Fox, The.
Thrushes.
To Paint a Water Lily.
Two Wise Generals.
View of a Pig.
Witches.
Wodwo.
Woman Unconscious, A.
HUGO, RICHARD F. Kennedy Ucciso.
HUGO, VICTOR. Be like the Bird.
Good Night.
House and Home.
Poet's Simple Faith, The.
Wings.
HULL, JOHN MERVIN. Gates of the Year, The.
HULME, THOMAS ERNEST. Above the Dock.
Autumn.
Embankment, The.
HULTMAN, J. A. Thanks to God.
HUMBOLDT, CHARLES. Field of Plunder.
HUME, TOBIAS. Fain Would I Change That Note, *at.*
Soldier's Song.
HUMPHREY, FRANCES. My Book of Life.
HUMPHREYS, ALETHA. Arachnida, Female.
Party Bid.
HUMPHRIES, ROLFE. Aeneid, The, *sels., tr.*
Aeolus.
Autumnal.
Boat Race, The, *tr. Fr.* The Aeneid.
Boxing Match, The, *tr. Fr.* The Aeneid.

HUMPHRIES, ROLFE (*continued*)
Coming Home.
Looking Up at Airplanes, Always.
Polo Grounds.
Second Night, or What You Will.
Song from the Gulf.
Wmffre the Sweep.
HUNOLD, CHRISTIAN FRIEDRICH. Concerning Time.
HUNT, LEIGH (James Henry Leigh Hunt). Abou Ben Adhem.
Aminta, *sel., tr.*
Bacchus in Tuscany, *sel., tr.*
Canzone: "Clear, fresh, and dulcet streams," *tr. Fr.* Sonnets to Laura.
Fish Answers, A. *Fr.* The Fish, the Man, and the Spirit.
Fish, the Man, and the Spirit, The, *sel.*
Glove and the Lions, The.
Golden Age, The, *tr. Fr.* Aminta.
House and Grounds, A.
Jenny Kissed Me.
Love-Lesson, A, *tr.*
Madame D'Albert's Laugh, *tr.*
Nile, The.
Nymphs, The, *sel.*
To the Grasshopper and the Cricket.
Rondeau: "Jenny kissed me when we met."
Sneezing.
Sonnets to Laura, *sel., tr.*
Story of Rimini, The, *sel.*
To a Fish. *Fr.* The Fish, the Man, and the Spirit.
Ultra-Germano-Criticasterism.
HUNTER, ANNE (Home). My Mother Bids Me Bind My Hair.
HUNTER, JOHN. Dear Master, In Whose Life I See.
HUNTER-DUVAR, JOHN. De Roberval, *sel.*
La Belle Sauvage. *Fr.* De Roberval.
HUNTINGTON, GEORGE. International Hymn.
HURLEY, MARY RITA. Beach House.
HURNARD, JAMES. Winter.
HURTADO DE MENDOZA, DIEGO. That Tree with Its Leaves Atremble.
HUTCHINSON, BARNEY. Cold Logic.
HUTCHINSON, JESSE. Ho! for California!
HUTCHINSON, M. M. Ten Little Indian Boys.
HUXLEY, ALDOUS. Après-midi d'un faune, L', *sel., tr.*
HYDE, DOUGLAS. My Grief on the Sea, *tr.*
Were You on the Mountain? *tr.*
"HYDE, ROBIN" (Iris Guiver Wilkinson). Church of the Holy Innocents, Dunedin.

I

IBN AL-TALLA. Artichoke, The.
IBN GABIROL, SOLOMON. Behold the Lovely Maid!
From Thee to Thee.
I Have Sough Thee Daily.
She Looked at Me and Her Eyelids Burned.
IBYCUS. In the Spring.
ICHIHARA, PRINCE. Solitary Pine.
IGNATIUS LOYOLA, SAINT. Teach Us to Serve Thee, Lord.
IGNATOW, DAVID. Before the Sabbath.
Escapade, The.
News Report.
INGALLS, JOHN JAMES. Opportunity.
INGAMELLS, REX. Golden Bird, The.
Ship from Thames.
INGELOW, JEAN. Birthday Morning. *Fr.* Songs of Seven.
Calling the Cows Home. *Fr.* The High Tide on the Coast of Lincolnshire (1571).
Divided, *sel.*
High Tide on the Coast of Lincolnshire, The (1571).
Seven Times One. *Fr.* Songs of Seven.
Seven Times Three. *Fr.* Songs of Seven.
Songs of Seven, *sels.*
Summer Morning.
"INGOLDSBY, THOMAS" (Richard Harris Barham). Ingoldsby Legends, The, *sel.*
Jackdaw of Rheims, The. *Fr.* The Ingoldsby Legends.
"INMAN, WILL" (William A. McGirt, Jr). Be.
Blown Newspaper, A.
Dilation.
Distance in Your Touch, The.
Jacqueline.
Lyric: "Thrush of wind sang thru the air, A."
On Seven Hills.
Tree Will Mow Thickets.
Where Willow Is a Limber Switch.
IQBAL, MUHAMMAD. Invocation, An, *sel.*
"IRONBARK." *See* GIBSON, GEORGE HERBERT.
"IRONQUILL." *See* WARE, EUGENE FITCH.
IRVIN, ERIC. Christmas 1942.
IRVIN, MARGARET. Chanticleer.
IRWIN, WALLACE ("Ginger"; "Hashimura Togo"). Blow Me Eyes!
Science for the Young.
ISAAC, TED. Urban Roses.
ISENHOUR, WALTER E. Be Friendly.
Down-Pullers, The.
Give Us Sober Men.
God Is There.
Going Home with Jesus.
Happiness.
If You're the Man You Ought to Be.
It's Wonderful.
Jesus Never Fails.
Keeping Victory.
Some Things You Cannot Will to Men.
ISHII *and* OBATA. For translations from *Japanese, see* SiGo.
ISSA. Haiku: "World of dew, The."

J

JACCOTTET, PHILIPPE. Crossing, The.
Interior.
Poet's Work, The.
Sonnet: "Don't worry, it will come! You're drawing near."
Tenant, The.
"JACK THE GRUMBLER." California over the Left.
JACKSON, HELEN HUNT ("H. H."; "Saxe Holm"). Last Prayer, A.
October's Bright Blue Weather.
September.
JACKSON, KATHRYN. Being Twins.
Brown Bear's Honey Song.
Twins, The.
JACKSON, LEROY F. I've Got a New Book from My Grandfather Hyde.
Jelly Jake and Butter Bill.
Polly Picklenose.
Simple Sam.
JACKSON, SARA. Lily McQueen.
JACOB, MAX. It May Be.
JACOB, RUTH APPRICH. Waiting.
JACOB, VIOLET. Licht Nichts, The.
JACOB BAR JUDA, HAZAK. Sorely Tried Is Israel, the Hapless Folk.
JACOBS, MARY. Where Love, There's Heaven.
JACOPONE DA TODI. O Love, All Love Above.
JAHIER, PIERO. Evening Party.
JAMMES, FRANCIS. Prayer to Go to Paradise with the Donkeys, A.
JANSEN, ANNETTE. Prayer for Neighborhood Evangelism.
JAQUES, FLORENCE PAGE. There Once Was a Puffin.
JARRELL, RANDALL. Camp in the Prussian Forest, A.
Death of the Ball Turret Gunner, The.
Eighth Air Force.
Girl in a Library, A.
Jonah.
Nestus Gurley.
90 North.
Orient Express, The.
Second Air Force.
Sick Child, A.
Soldier Walks under the Trees of the University, The.
Snow-Leopard, The.
Woman at the Washington Zoo, The.
JASZI, JEAN. Clock, The.
Clouds.
Fight.
My Horses.
Tom Ducket.
Winter.
JAYADEVA. Gita Govinda, *sel.*
JEAN DE MEUN *and* GUILLAUME DE LORRIS. *See* GUILLAUME DE LORRIS *and* JEAN DE MEUN.
JEFFERS, ROBINSON. Answer, The.
Apology for Bad Dreams.
Birds.
Bloody Sire, The.
But I Am Growing Old and Indolent.
Cassandra.
Continent's End.
Credo.
Divinely Superfluous Beauty.
Excesses of God, The.
Eye, The.
Hurt Hawks.
Let Them Alone.
Look, How Beautiful.
Maid's Thought, The.
May–June, 1940.
My Burial Place.
Night.
Ocean.
Promise of Peace.
Salmon-fishing.
Shine, Perishing Republic.
Shine, Republic.
Signpost.
To the Stone-Cutters.
World's Wonders, The.
JENKS, TUDOR. Baby's Name, The.
JENNINGS, ELIZABETH. Answers.
Beyond Possession.
Child and the Shadow, The.
Disguises.
Fountain.
Ghosts.
Harvest and Consecration.
In the Night.
Not in the Guide-Books.
Old Man.
One Flesh.
Parting, The.
Room, The.
Santa Maria Maggiore, Rome.
Storm, The.
Teresa of Avila.
Visitation, The.
Way of Looking, A.
World I Have Not Made.
World of Light, A.
JENNINGS, LESLIE NELSON. Keep Darkness.
Yellow Cat, The.
JENSEN, JOHANNES V. Bathing Girl, A.
JEPHCOTT, SYDNEY WHEELER. Thredbo River.
JIMÉNEZ, JUAN RAMÓN. Conclusive Voyage, The.
Countryside Sleeps, Trembling, The.
Dawn Brings with It, The.
Definitive Journey, The.
Faster, Earth, Faster.
Galante Garden, I.
Immense Hour.
Love.
New Leaves.
Mariner's Ideal Epitaph.
Moon Was Gilding the River, The.
Nightfall. The Coolness of My Watered Garden.
Oxcarts Are Now on Their Way, The.
Sea Is Enormous, The.
Street Is Waiting for the Night, The.
Sunset.

Tenebrae.
To the Bridge of Love.
Vigil.
Yellow Spring.
Zenith.
JOANS, TED. It Is Time.
Lester Young.
.38, The.
JOHANNES SECUNDUS (Jan Nicolai Everaerts). Basia, *sels.*
Epithalamium, *sel.*
Insatiate, The. *Fr.* Basia.
Neaera's Kisses. *Fr.* Basia.
Wedding Night, The. *Fr.* Epithalamium.
JOHN OF THE CROSS, SAINT. Dark Night of the Soul, The.
I Entered Where I Did Not Know.
I Know Full Well the Water's Flowing Power.
I Live and Do Not Live in Myself.
Not without Hope Pulsing My Breast.
O Flame of Living Love.
O Living Flame of Love.
Obscure Night of the Soul, The.
One Dismal Night.
Other Stanzas with a Divine Meaning Concerning Christ and the Soul.
Other Verses with a Divine Meaning.
Search, The.
Shepherd, Young and Mournful, Grieves Alone, A.
Spiritual Canticle: Songs between the Soul and the Spouse.
Stanzas concerning Christ and the Soul.
Verses Written upon an Ecstasy of High Contemplation.
JOHNSON, BURGES. Soap, the Oppressor.
JOHNSON, DON ALLEN ("Mustafa"). O White Mistress.
JOHNSON, EDYTHE. Will God's Patience Hold Out for You?
JOHNSON, EMILY PAULINE ("Tekahionwake"). Lullaby of the Iroquois.
JOHNSON, FENTON. Counting.
Daily Grind, The.
Negro Peddler's Song, A.
Old Repair Man, The.
Tired.
World Is a Mighty Ogre, The.
JOHNSON, GEOFFREY. Winter Legend, A.
JOHNSON, GEORGIA DOUGLAS. Common Dust.
Conquest.
Heart of a Woman, The.
I Want to Die While You Love Me.
Lovelight.
Poet Speaks, The.
Prejudice.
Trifle.
Your World.
JOHNSON, HELENE. Invocation: "Let me be buried in the rain."
Poem: "Little brown boy."
Road, The.
Sonnet to a Negro in Harlem.
JOHNSON, JAMES WELDON. Creation, The.
Go Down Death (a Funeral Sermon).
Lift Every Voice and Sing.
O Black and Unknown Bards.
Up from the Bed of the River. *Fr.* The Creation.
JOHNSON, JOE. Judeebug's Country.
JOHNSON, JOSEPHINE WINSLOW. Betrayal, The.
In This Hour.
Quiet Flower, The.
Temple, The.
Under All Change.
JOHNSON, KAY. Defiant Song, A.
JOHNSON, LIONEL PIGOT. By the Statue of King Charles at Charing Cross.
Dark Angel, The.
Dead.
In Memory, *sel.*
Oxford.
Te Martyrum Candidatus.
JOHNSON, LOUIS. Adversaries.
JOHNSON, PAULINE. *See* JOHNSON, EMILY PAULINE.
JOHNSON, SAMUEL (1709–84). Epitaph

upon the Celebrated Claudy Philips, Musician Who Died Very Poor, An.
I Put My Hat upon My Head.
In Imitation of the Tenth Satire of Juvenal. *Fr.* The Vanity of Human Wishes.
London; a Poem in Imitation of the Third Satire of Juvenal.
On the Death of Mr. [*or* Dr.] Robert Levet [a Practiser in Physic].
Prologue: "When Learning's triumph o'er her barb'rous foes."
Short Song of Congratulation, A.
To Miss ——.
Translation of Lines by Benserade.
Turnip Seller, The.
Upon the Feast of St. Simon and St. Jude.
Vanity of Human Wishes, The; the Tenth Satire of Juvenal, Imitated.
Winter's Walk, The.
Young Author, The.
JOHNSON, SAMUEL (1822–82). City of God.
Prayer for Strength.
JOHNSON, WILLIAM MARTIN. On Snow-Flakes Melting on His Lady's Breast.
JOHNSTON, GEORGE. Beside the Sea.
JOHNSTON, THOMAS. On Such a Night.
JONES, ARTHUR GLYN PRYS-. *See* PRYS-JONES, ARTHUR GLYN.
JONES, DONALD L. November 22, 1963.
JONES, EBENEZER. Development of Idiotcy, A.
When the World Is Burning.
Winter Hymn, A—to the Snow.
JONES, EVAN. Noah's Song.
JONES, GLYN. Esyllt.
JONES, JESSIE ORTON. I Can Climb Our Apple Tree.
JONES, LEROI. As a Possible Lover.
Clearing, The.
Contract.
Dance, The.
Death of Nick Charles, The.
Each Morning. *Fr.* Hymn for Lanie Poo.
End of Man Is His Beauty, The.
Epistrophe.
Hegel.
Hymn for Lanie Poo, *sel.*
Insidious Dr. Fu Man Chu, The.
Invention of Comics, The.
Lines to Garcia Lorca.
Notes for a Speech.
Politics of Rich Painters, The.
Preface to a Twenty Volume Suicide Note.
JONES, MARY. Spider, The.
JONES, T. GWYNN. Grave, The.
JONES, THOMAS SAMUEL, JR. As in a Rose-Jar.
Path of the Stars, The.
Sometimes.
JONES, SIR WILLIAM. Epigram: "On parent knees, a naked new-born child."
JONSON, BEN. Against Consummation, *tr.*
Another Birthday.
Another. In Defence of Their Inconstancie.
Another Ladyes Exception Present at the Hearing. *Fr.* A Celebration of Charis.
Ask Not to Know This Man.
Begging Another Kiss. *Fr.* A Celebration of Charis.
Begging Another, on Colour of Mending the Former. *Fr.* A Celebration of Charis.
By Him.
Celebration of Charis, A, *sels.*
Clayming a Second Kisse by Desert. *Fr.* A Celebration of Charis.
Clerimont's Song. *Fr.* Epicoene.
Come, My Celia. *Fr.* Volpone.
Cynthia's Revels, *sels.*
Doing a Filthy Pleasure Is [and Short], *tr.*
Echo's Song. *Fr.* Cynthia's Revels.
Elegie, An: "Let me be what I am, as Virgil cold."

Elegie on the Lady Jane Pawlet, Marchion: of Winton, An.
Elegy, An: "Since you must go, and I must bid farewell."
Elegy, An: "Though beauty be the mark of praise."
Epicoene; or, The Silent Woman, *sel.*
Epitaph, An: On Elizabeth Chute.
Epitaph on Elizabeth, L. H.
Epitaph on S. P. [Salomon *or* Salathiel Pavy], a Child of Q. El. [Queen Elizabeth's] Chapel [*or* Chappel], An.
Epode.
Execration upon Vulcan, An.
Fit of Rime against Rime [*or* Rhyme against Rhyme], A.
For Love's Sake. *Fr.* A Celebration of Charis.
Francis Beaumont's Letter from the Country to Jonson.
Her Man Described by Her Owne Dictamen. *Fr.* A Celebration of Charis.
Her Triumph. *Fr.* A Celebration of Charis.
Hermogenes's Song. *Fr.* The Poetaster.
His Discourse with Cupid. *Fr.* A Celebration of Charis.
His Excuse for Loving. *Fr.* A Celebration of Charis.
Hour-Glass [*or* Houre-Glasse], The.
How He Saw Her. *Fr.* A Celebration of Charis.
Humble Petition of Poor Ben to the Best of Monarchs, Masters, Men, King Charles, The.
Hymn to Diana. *Fr.* Cynthia's Revels.
Hymne to God the Father, A.
In the Person of Woman Kind.
Inviting a Friend to Supper.
It Is Not Growing like a Tree. *Fr.* A Pindaric Ode.
Karolin's Song. *Fr.* The Sad Shepherd.
Kiss, The. *Fr.* Cynthia's Revels.
Kiss Me, Sweet.
Little Shrub Growing By, A.
Love.
Love and Death.
Love's Triumph.
Mab. *Fr.* The Satyr.
My Picture Left in Scotland.
New yeares, expect new gifts: sister, your harpe.
New-Yeares-Gift Sung to King Charles, 1635, A.
Noble Nature, The. *Fr.* A Pindaric Ode.
Ode to Himselfe ("Come leave the loathed stage").
Ode to Himself[e], An ("Where do'st thou careless lie").
On Court-Worme.
On Lucy, Countess[e] of Bedford.
On Margaret Ratcliffe.
On My First Daughter.
On My First Son [*or* Sonne].
On Some-thing, That Walkes Some-where.
Pindaric Ode, A.
Poetaster, The, *sel.*
Praises of a Countrie Life, The.
Queen and Huntress. *Fr.* Cynthia's Revels.
Sad Shepherd, The, *sels.*
Satyr, The, *sel.*
Short Measures. *Fr.* A Pindaric Ode.
Silent Woman, The, *sel.*
Slow, Slow, Fresh Fount. *Fr.* Cynthia's Revels.
So White, So Soft, So Sweet. *Fr.* A Celebration of Charis.
Song, A: "Oh doe not wanton with those eyes."
Song: "Slow, slow, fresh fount, keepe time with my salt teares." *Fr.* Cynthia's Revels.
Song: "Still to be neat, still to be dressed." *Fr.* Epicoene.
Song: That Women Are but Mens Shadows [*or* Shaddowes].
Song: "Though I am young and cannot tell." *Fr.* The Sad Shepherd.

JONSON, BEN (*continued*)
Song to Celia ("Come, my Celia, let us prove"). *Fr.* Volpone.
Song to Celia ("Drink to me only with thine eyes").
Still to Be Neat [Still to Be Dressed]. *Fr.* Epicoene.
That Women Are but Men's Shadows.
Though I Am Young. *Fr.* The Sad Shepherd.
To Celia ("Come, my Celia, let us prove"). *Fr.* Volpone.
To Celia ("Drink to me only with thine eyes").
To Celia ("Kiss me, sweet").
To Doctor Empirick.
To Heaven.
To John Donne.
To Penshurst.
To the Immortall Memorie, and Friendship of That Noble Paire, Sir Lucius Cary, and Sir H. Morison.
To the Learned Critic.
To the Memory of My Beloved Master [or the Author, Mr.] William Shakespeare, and What He Hath Left Us.
To the Reader.
To the Same.
To the World: A Farewell for a Gentlewoman, Virtuous and Noble.
To William Earle of Pembroke.
Triumph of Charis, The. *Fr.* A Celebration of Charis.
Urging Her of a Promise. *Fr.* A Celebration of Charis.
Volpone, *sel.*
What Hee Suffered. *Fr.* A Celebration of Charis.
JØRGENSEN, JOHANNES. Plants Stand Silent Round Me, The.
JOSEPH, MICHAEL KENNEDY. Dancing Ploughmen, The.
JOSO. Little Duck, The.
Winter.
JOYCE, JAMES. Chamber Music, *sels.*
Ecce Puer.
Flower Given to My Daughter, A.
Goldenhair. *Fr.* Chamber Music.
Lean Out of the Window. *Fr.* Chamber Music.
My Love Is in a Light Attire. *Fr.* Chamber Music.
Simples.
Strings in the Earth and Air. *Fr.* Chamber Music.
Tilly.
JUANA INÉZ DE LA CRUZ, SISTER (*originally* Juana de Asbaje). Describes Rationally the Irrational Effects of Love.
Elusive Shadow of My Substance, Stay.
Hope.
I Can neither Hold You nor Let You Go.
In Acknowledgment of the Praises of European Writers.
Oh World, Why Do You Thus Pursue Me?
On Her Portrait.
Perpetual Infirmity of Hope.
This Evening When I Spoke to You.
Verses against the Inconsequence of Men's Taste and Strictures.
Verses Expressing the Feelings of a Lover.
JUDSON, ADONIRAM. In Spite of Sorrow.
JUNGE, CARL S. Dinosaur, The.
JUSTICE, DONALD. After a Line by John Peale Bishop.
Anonymous Drawing.
Another Song.
Beyond the Hunting Woods.
But That Is Another Story.
Color of Cold, The, *tr.*
Crossing, The, *tr.*
High Place, *tr.*
In Bertram's Garden.
On a Painting by Patient B of the Independence State Hospital for the Insane.
Rule, *tr.*
Sonnet: "Don't worry, it will come! You're drawing near," *tr.*

Snowfall, The.
Tales from a Family Album.
JUSTICE, DONALD, *and* DORI KATZ. Lightning Victory, *tr.*
Tomorrow Is Not Yet, *tr.*
JUSTUS, MAY. Footwear.
JUVENAL. Against Women. *Fr.* The Satires.
Satires, The, *sels.*

K

KAGAWA, TOYOHIKO. Love.
Meditation.
KAIKINI, P. R. Donkey, The.
KALLMAN, CHESTER. Night Music.
KARLFELDT, ERIK AXEL. Imagined Happiness.
Vagrant, A.
KASA, LADY. Tolling Bells.
KÄSTNER, ERICH. Dangerous Establishment.
Legend, Not Quite Housebroken.
Moral Taxi Ride, The.
Other Possibility, The.
Ragout Fin de Siècle.
KATZ, DORI, *and* DONALD JUSTICE. *See* JUSTICE, DONALD, *and* DORI KATZ.
KAUFMANN, WALTER. Fall, The.
For translations from German, see ErPo; TwGP.
KAVANAGH, PATRICK. Christmas Childhood, A, *sel.*
Important Statement.
October.
To the Man after the Harrow.
KAYDEN, EUGENE M. Caucasus, The, *tr.*
Manhattan Skyline.
Star of the Nativity, *tr.*
Winter Night, *tr.*
KAYPER-MENSAH, ALBERT. Second Birthday, A.
KEATS, JOHN. Addressed to Haydon.
After Dark Vapours.
Bright Star [Would I Were Steadfast as Thou Art].
Bruised Titans, The. *Fr.* Hyperion.
Dedication: To Leigh Hunt, Esq.
Dream, A. *Fr.* The Fall of Hyperion.
Dream, A, after Reading Dante's Episode of Paolo and Francesca.
Endymion, *sels.*
Epistle to John Hamilton Reynolds.
Eve of St. Agnes, The.
Fall of Hyperion, The, *sel.*
God of the Meridian.
Happy Insensibility.
Human Seasons, The.
Hyperion; a Fragment, *sels.*
If by Dull Rhymes Our English Must Be Chained.
In a Drear-nighted December.
Keen, Fitful Gusts Are Whispering Here and There.
La Belle Dame sans Merci.
Lamia.
Lines on the Mermaid Tavern.
Lines Supposed to Have Been Addressed to Fanny Brawne.
Magic Casements. *Fr.* Ode to a Nightingale.
Meg Merrilies.
Mermaid Tavern, The.
Modern Love.
Ode on a Grecian Urn.
Ode on Indolence.
Ode on Melancholy.
Ode on the Poets.
Ode to a Nightingale.
Ode to Autumn.
Ode to Psyche.
On a Dream.
On an Engraved Gem of Leander.
On Fame.
On First Looking into Chapman's Homer.
On Oxford.
On Seeing a Lock of Milton's Hair.
On Seeing the Elgin Marbles [for the First Time].

On Sitting Down to Read *King Lear* Once Again.
On the Grasshopper and [the] Cricket.
On the Sea.
On the Sonnet.
Poet, The.
Poetry of Earth, The.
Realm of Fancy, The.
Saturn. *Fr.* Hyperion.
Sharing Eve's Apple.
Sleep and Poetry.
Song about Myself, A.
Sonnet: "After dark vapours have oppress'd our plains."
Sonnet: "Bright star! would I were steadfast as thou art."
Sonnet: "When I have fears that I may cease to be."
Stanzas: "In a drear-nighted December."
Terror of Death, The.
Thing of Beauty, A. *Fr.* Endymion.
This Living Hand.
To a Cat.
To Ailsa Rock.
To Autumn.
To Fanny.
To Homer.
To Mrs. Reynolds's Cat.
To One Who Has Been Long in City Pent.
To Sleep.
What the Thrush Said.
When I Have Fears [That I May Cease to Be].
Where Be You Going, You Devon Maid.
Where Didst Thou Find, Young Bard.
Where's the Poet?
Why Did I Laugh [To-Night]?
World of Sleep, The.
KEBLE, JOHN. Balaam.
Forest Leaves in Autumn, *sel.*
Help Us to Live.
KEESING, NANCY. Bread.
Revelation.
KEITH, JOSEPH JOEL. Bedtime Tales.
Child Wife.
Flogged Child.
Mr. Lerner.
Nightmare in Morganza.
Old Meg of Kitrann.
Party Line.
Salems of Oppression.
Sunday Edition.
250 Willow Lane.
Wolf and Tiger Dining, A.
Woman Telephoning.
KELLER, GOTTFRIED. Character Assassins, The.
Evening Song.
See There the Star.
KELLER, HELEN. In the Garden of the Lord.
KELLER, MARTHA. Herbs and Simples.
Wilderness Road.
KELLY, ROBERT. Alchemist, The.
Boar, The.
Boat, The.
Exchanges II, The.
Going.
Knee Lunes.
Parallel Texts.
Process, The.
Round Dance, & Canticle.
Sun of the Center.
To Her Body, against Time.
KELLY, THOMAS. Head That Once Was Crowned with Thorns, The.
KELLY, WALT. Boston Charlie.
KEMP, HARRY. God the Architect.
Preliminary Poem for a Modern City.
KEMPIS, THOMAS À. *See* THOMAS À KEMPIS.
KEN, THOMAS. Direct This Day.
Priest of Christ, The.
KENDALL, HENRY CLARENCE. Bell-Birds.
Beyond Kerguelen.
Jim the Splitter.
Last of His Tribe, The.
Orara.
Rain Comes Sobbing to the Door, The.
September in Australia.
KENDALL, TIMOTHE. To Sabidius, *tr.*

KENNEDY, GEOFFREY ANKETELL STUD-
DERT-. *See* STUDDERT-KENNEDY,
GEOFFREY ANKETELL.
KENNEDY, GERTA. At the Nadir.
Christmas Songs.
Song of January.
KENNEDY, LEO. Epithalamium.
Words for a Resurrection.
KENNEDY, MARY. Moon Door.
One of the Sidhe.
KENNEDY, X. J. Ars Poetica.
B Negative.
Cross Ties.
Down in Dallas.
Faces from a Bestiary.
First Confession.
Hearthside Story.
In a Prominent Bar in Secaucus.
Lilith.
Little Elegy.
Man in the Manmade Moon, The.
Nude Descending a Staircase.
Solitary Confinement.
Song to the Tune of "Somebody Stole
My Gal."
Water Glass of Whisky, A.
KEPPEL, DAVID. Trouble.
KERNAHAN, COULSON. Cricket Triolet, A.
KERNER, JUSTINUS. Home-Sickness.
Poetry.
KERR, WALTER H. Hanged Thing, The.
Prenatal Fantasy.
Stone, The.
Trap.
Vampire.
KERR, WATSON. Ancient Thought, The.
KERSH, GERALD. Soldier, The, 1939–
1945.
KESSLER, JASCHA. Following the Sun.
Gardener at Thirty, The.
High Summer.
My Grandmother's Funeral.
Nightmare, The.
October Flies.
P.S.
Requiem for an Abstract Artist.
Technique of Laughter, The.
Technique of Love, The.
Technique of Power, The.
KETCHUM, ANNIE CHAMBERS. Bonnie
Blue Flag, The.
KETCHUM, ARTHUR. Thanksgiving.
KEY, FRANCIS SCOTT. On a Young
Lady's Going into a Shower Bath.
Our Rock.
Star-spangled Banner, The.
KEYES, SIDNEY. Moonlight Night on
the Port.
War Poet.
KHAYYÁM, OMAR. *See* OMAR KHAYYÁM.
KHODASEVICH, VLADISLAV FELITSYANO-
VICH. Monkey, The.
KIANG KANG-HU *and* WITTER BYNNER.
See BYNNER, WITTER, *and* KIANG
KANG-HU.
KIERAN, JOHN. To Lou Gehrig.
KIKAKU. Butterfly, The.
Cock Again, The.
KILMER, ALINE (Mrs. Joyce Kilmer).
Experience.
KILMER, JOYCE. Easter.
Martin.
Roofs.
Rouge Bouquet.
Trees.
KING, BEN (Benjamin Franklin King,
Jr.). If I Should Die To-Night.
Pessimist, The.
Sum of Life, The.
KING, EDITH. Rabbit, The.
KING, HARRIET ELEANOR HAMILTON.
Sermon in the Hospital, The, *sel.*
KING, HENRY, BISHOP OF CHICHESTER.
Contemplation upon Flowers, A.
Departure, The; an Elegy.
Exequy, The.
Like to the Falling of a Star.
Paradox: That Fruition Destroys Love,
sel.
Sic Vita.
Sonnet: Double Rock, The.
Sonnet: "Tell me no more how fair she
is."
To a Lady Who Sent Me a Copy of
Verses at My Going to Bed.

To My Dead Friend Ben: Johnson.
Upon the Death of My Ever Desired
Friend Doctor Donne Dean of Pauls.
KING, HERMAN STOWELL. Evocation.
KINGSLEY, CHARLES. Farewell, A: "My
fairest child, I have no song to give
you."
Last Buccaneer, The.
Lost Doll, The. *Fr.* The Water
Babies.
Old Buccaneer, The.
Old Song, The. *Fr.* The Water
Babies.
Sands of Dee, The.
Three Fishers, The.
Water Babies, The, *sels.*
Young and Old. *Fr.* The Water
Babies.
KINNELL, GALWAY. Avenue Bearing the
Initial of Christ into the New World,
The.
Duck-chasing.
First Song.
For Robert Frost, *sel.*
Supper after the Last, The.
To Christ Our Lord.
Wolves, The.
KINSELLA, THOMAS. Another Septem-
ber.
Mirror in February.
Night Songs.
KIPLING, RUDYARD. Ballad of East and
West, The.
Batteries Out of Ammunition. *Fr.*
Epitaphs of the War.
Big Steamers.
By the Hoof of the Wild Goat. *Fr.*
Plain Tales from the Hills.
Camel's Hump, The. *Fr.* Just-so
Stories.
Cities and Thrones and Powers. *Fr.*
Puck of Pook's Hill.
Cold Iron.
Danny Deever.
Drifter off Tarentum, A. *Fr.* Epitaphs
of the War.
Epitaphs of the War, 1914–18, *sels.*
Gunga Din.
Harp Song of the Dane Women. *Fr.*
Puck of Pook's Hill.
If.
Jane's Marriage.
Job That's Crying to Be Done, The.
Just-so Stories, *sel.*
King, The.
Land, The.
Last Chantey, The.
L'Envoi: "When earth's last picture
is painted, and the tubes are twisted
and dried."
Liner She's a Lady, The.
Long Trail, The.
Looking-Glass, The.
Mandalay.
McAndrew's Hymn.
Mesopotamia.
Mother o' Mine.
Our Lady of the Snows.
Plain Tales from the Hills, *sel.*
Post That Fitted, The.
Puck of Pook's Hill, *sels.*
Puck's Song. *Fr.* Puck of Pook's Hill.
Rebirth.
Recessional.
Refined Man, The. *Fr.* Epitaphs of
the War.
Sea and the Hills, The.
"Service Man, The."
Skating.
Song of the English, A, *sel.*
Song of the Galley-Slaves.
Tommy.
Way through the Woods, The.
When 'Omer Smote 'Is Bloomin'
Lyre.
White Man's Burden, The.
KIRKCONNELL, WATSON. Rain, *tr.*
To Sleep, *tr.*
KIRKUP, JAMES. Bird Fancier, The.
Eve of Christmas, The.
Giving and Taking.
Lonely Scarecrow, The.
Nature of Love, The.
Poet, The.
Wild Wilbur.

Zen Archer, The.
KIZER, CAROLYN. Great Blue Heron,
The.
Intruder, The.
Lovemusic.
Muse of Water, A.
Ungrateful Garden, The.
"KLABUND" (Alfred Henschke). After
Tsui-tao.
All That Comes to Be.
Gentian.
Ride.
Winter War.
KLEIN, ABRAHAM MOSES. Bestiary.
Heirloom.
Indian Reservation: Caughnawaga.
Montreal.
Political Meeting.
Quebec Liquor Commission Store.
Still Small Voice, The.
Sugaring, The.
KLEISER, GRENVILLE. You Can't Fool
God.
KLINE, BETSY W. Be Still.
"KLINGLE, GEORGE" (Georgiana Klingle
Holmes). As Thy Days So Shall
Thy Strength Be.
KNICKMAN, LESTER. Could You Spare
Some Time for Jesus?
KNIGHT, JOHN. Father to the Man.
KNISTER, RAYMOND. Change.
Feed.
Hawk, The.
Nell. *Fr.* A Row of Stalls.
Plowman, The.
Row of Stalls, A, *sel.*
KNOWLES, FREDERIC LAWRENCE. L'En-
voi: "O love triumphant over guilt
and sin."
KOCH, CHRISTOPHER. Half-heard.
KOCH, KENNETH. Artist, The.
Aus einer Kindheit.
Departure from Hydra, The.
Fresh Air.
Geography.
Taking a Walk with You.
KOCHANOWSKI, JAN. To Sleep.
KOEHLER, G. STANLEY. In Arlington
Cemetery.
"KOLMAR, GERTRUD" (Gertrud Chodzies-
ner). Old Woman, The.
Unicorn, The.
KONRICK, VERA BISHOP. Erda.
KRAMER, ARTHUR. Adventures.
KRESS, GEORGE L. Parable, A.
KREYMBORG, ALFRED. Epigram: "Isn't
it."
Tree, The.
Vista.
KRINAGORAS. *See* CRINAGORAS.
KROLOW, KARL. Love Poem: "It is the
same if I lie on the left or the right
side."
Shadows in the Air.
You Went Away.
KRONTHAL, JOSEPH. Be Careful What
You Say.
KROWS, JANE W. Lesson, The.
Little Satellite.
Milkman, The.
My House.
Space Travel.
KUMIN, MAXINE W. 400-Meter Free-
style.
KUNITZ, STANLEY JASSPON. Benediction.
Dark and the Fair, The.
End of Summer.
Father and Son.
Foreign Affairs.
Lovers Relentlessly.
Science of the Night, The.
She Wept, She Railed.
Summing-up, The.
Waltzer in the House.
War against the Trees, The.
"KURENBERG, THE KNIGHT OF." Fal-
con, The.
I reared me a falcon longer than one
year.
I Stood on a Battlement the Late Eve
Darkened.
KURTZ, AARON. Behold the Sea, *sel.*
KUSKIN, KARLA. Gold-tinted Dragon,
The.
Very Early.

L

LABÉ, LOUISE. Sonnet VII: "And so
one sees all living matter perish."
Sonnet IX: "As soon as I withdraw to
take my rest."
Sonnet XVIII: "O kiss me yet again,
O kiss me over."
Sonnet XIII: "Oh were I faint with
love upon the breast."
Sonnet V: "Venus, who wander clear
among the skies."
Sonnet XIV: "Yes, and as long as
these poor eyes can bring."
LA CEPPÈDE, JEAN DE. Théorèmes
Spirituels, sels.
LA FARGE, PETER. Vision of a Past
Warrior.
LA FOLLETTE, MELVIN WALKER. Arriv-
als and Departures.
Ballad of Red Fox, The.
I Knew a Boy with Hair like Gold.
Love for a Hare.
Saint Stephen in San Francisco.
Sleeping Saint, The.
Spring Landscape.
Valediction, A.
LA FONTAINE, JEAN DE. Cudgelled but
Contented Cuckold, The.
Ear-Maker and the Mould-Mender, The.
Fair Exchange, A.
Gascon Punished, The.
Superfluous Saddle, The.
To Promise Is One Thing, to Perform
Is Another.
LAFORGUE, JULES. Asides from the
Clowns, sel.
For the Book of Love.
LAGERKVIST, PÄR. Beauty Is Most at
Twilight's Close.
LAGERLÖF, SELMA. Child of Peace, The.
LA GRONE, OLIVER. Bathed Is My
Blood.
My America.
This Hour.
LAIGHT, FREDERICK E. Drought.
LAING, DILYS. Villanelle.
LAL, P. Song for Beauty, A.
LAMB, CHARLES. Hester.
Housekeeper, The, The.
In My Own Album.
Old Familiar Faces, The.
On an Infant Dying as Soon as Born.
LAMB, CHARLES, and MARY LAMB.
Anger in its time and place.
LAMB, MARY. Two Boys, The.
"LAMBERT, LOUIS." See GILMORE, PAT-
RICK SARSFIELD.
LAMPMAN, ARCHIBALD. City of the End
of Things, The.
Heat.
In November.
January Morning, A.
Midnight.
Morning on the Lièvre.
Solitude.
Sunset at Les Eboulements, A.
Temagami.
Winter Evening.
LAMPORT, FELICIA. Greatest Show on
Earth.
LANDOR, WALTER SAVAGE. According
to eternal laws.
Alas! 'tis very sad to hear.
Behold, O Aspasia! I Send You Verses.
Fr. Pericles and Aspasia.
Citation and Examination of William
Shakespeare, The, sel.
Corinna to Tanagra. Fr. Pericles and
Aspasia.
Death.
Death of Artemidora, The. Fr. Peri-
cles and Aspasia.
Dirce. Fr. Pericles and Aspasia.
Dying Speech of an Old Philosopher.
Fr. The Last Fruit off an Old Tree.
For an Epitaph at Fiesole.
Gebir, sel.
Hellenics, The, sel.
I Strove with None. Fr. The Last
Fruit off an Old Tree.

Ianthe, sels.
Interlude.
Ireland.
Last Fruit off an Old Tree, The, sel.
Lately Our Poets.
Leaf after Leaf.
Lines to a Dragon Fly.
Maid's Lament, The. Fr. The Cita-
tion and Examination of William
Shakespeare.
Malvolio.
Mild Is the Parting Year.
Mother, I Cannot Mind My Wheel.
On Man.
On Music.
On Seeing a Hair of Lucretia Borgia.
On Ternissa's Death. Fr. The Hel-
lenics.
Past Ruined Ilion [Helen Lives].
Pericles and Aspasia, sels.
Plays.
Progress of Evening.
Rose Aylmer.
Shells, The.
Shepherd and the Nymph, The. Fr.
Gebir.
Ternissa. Fr. The Hellenics.
To Age.
To Robert Browning.
Well I Remember How You Smiled.
Fr. Ianthe.
William Gifford.
Years.
LANG, ANDREW. Aucassin and Nicolette,
sel., tr.
Deadly Kisses, tr.
His Lady's Death, tr.
His Lady's Tomb, tr.
In the Spring, tr.
Last Chance, The.
Love in May, tr.
Nightingale Weather.
Odyssey, The.
Of His Lady's Old Age, tr.
On His Lady's Waking, tr.
Roses, tr.
Sonnet to Heavenly Beauty, A, tr.
Spring, tr.
To His Friend in Elysium, tr.
To His Young Mistress, tr.
When you are very old, at evening, tr.
Who Would List, tr. Fr. Aucassin
and Nicolette.
LANGLAND, JOSEPH. Ecclesiastes.
Serpent, The.
War.
LANGLAND, WILLIAM. Harrowing of
Hell, The. Fr. The Vision of Piers
Plowman.
Love. Fr. The Vision of Piers Plow-
man.
Prayer for Rich and Poor. Fr. The
Vision of Piers Plowman.
Vision of Piers Plowman, The, sels.
LANGLEY, EVE. Native Born.
LANIER, SIDNEY. Ballad of Trees and
the Master, A.
Corn.
Crystal, The, sel.
Evening Song.
Harlequin of Dreams, The.
Marshes of Glynn, The.
Psalm of the West, sel.
Raven Days, The.
Revenge of Hamish, The.
Song of the Chattahoochee.
Story of Vinland, The. Fr. Psalm of
the West.
Struggle.
Symphony, The.
Thar's More in the Man than Thar
Is in the Land.
Waving of the Corn, The.
LANIGAN, GEORGE THOMAS. Threnody,
A: "What, what, what."
LANNING, JANE MCKAY. To Search Our
Souls.
LANSING, GERRIT. Conventicle.
Ghazel of Absence, A.
Heavenly Tree Grows Downward, The.
Malefic Surgeon, The.
Tabernacles.
Undertaking, The.
LAPE, FRED. From This the Struggle.

Midsummer Pause.
LARCOM, LUCY. Hal's Birthday.
LARKIN, PHILIP. Absences.
Arundel Tomb, An.
At Grass.
Church Going.
Deceptions.
Going.
Heaviest of Flowers, the Head.
I Remember, I Remember.
If, My Darling.
Lines on a Young Lady's Photograph
Album.
Maiden Name.
Mr. Bleaney.
Next Please.
One Man Walking a Deserted Plat-
form.
Poetry of Departures.
Reasons for Attendance.
Spring.
Wants.
Wedding-Wind.
Whitsun Weddings.
Wires.
LARSEN, CARL. Plot to Assassinate the
Chase Manhattan Bank, The.
LASKER-SCHÜLER, ELSE. Georg Grosz.
My People.
Over Shining Shingle.
To My Friends.
LATHBURY, MARY ARTEMISIA ("Aunt
Mary"). Bread of Life, The.
Break Thou the Bread of Life.
Day Is Dying in the West.
LATHROP, WALTER. Here Is a Toast
That I Want to Drink.
LATTIMORE, RICHMOND. Anniversary.
Cleobulus' Epitaph, tr.
Collages and Compositions.
I Bless This Man, tr. Fr. Odes (of
Pindar).
It.
Odes (of Pindar), sel., tr.
Spider.
Verse.
LAUGHLIN, JAMES. Eclogues (of Ver-
gil), sel., tr.
LAUREN, JOSEPH. Butterfly and the
Caterpillar, The.
LAVANT, CHRISTINE. Don't Dare Be
Larger than a Sparrow's Head.
Jesus Christ, I Pray with All My
Might.
LAVATER, LOUIS. Faithless.
Mopoke.
LAWNER, LYNNE. In Your Arrogance.
Possession.
LAWRENCE, DAVID HERBERT. Bat.
Bavarian Gentians.
Bombardment.
Cherry Robbers.
Discord in Childhood.
Elephant Is Slow to Mate, The.
End of Another Home Holiday.
Evil Is Homeless.
Flapper.
Gloire de Dijon.
God and the Holy Ghost.
Hands of God, The.
How Beastly the Bourgeois Is.
In a Boat.
In the Cities.
Lightning.
Love on the Farm.
New Year's Eve.
Piano.
Red Geranium and Godly Mignonette.
Sea, The.
Ship of Death, The.
Snake.
Snap-Dragon.
Song of a Man Who Has Come
Through.
Sorrow.
Spring Morning.
Tommies in the Train.
Whales Weep Not!
When Satan Fell.
World of Work, as a Poet Would Like
It to Be, The.
Young Wife, A.
LAWSON, HENRY. Andy's Gone with
Cattle.

Ballad of the Drover.
Sliprails and the Spur, The.
Song of the Darling River.
Talbragar.
Teams, The.
LAWSON, SYLVIA. Trader's Return.
LAWSON, WILLIAM. Bill the Whaler.
LAXNESS, HALLDÓR. She Was All That You Loved.
LAYTON, IRVING. Bacchanal.
Birth of Tragedy, The.
Boys in October.
Bull Calf, The.
Cold Green Element, The.
Dionysus.
Fertile Muck, The.
Golfers.
Keine Lazarovitch.
Nausicäa.
Tall Man Executes a Jig, A.
To the Girls of My Graduating Class.
Undine.
What Ulysses Said to Circe on the Beach of Aeaea.
Woman.
LAYTON, JAMES SEXTON. Actor, The.
Crime and Punishment.
Line of Life, The.
LAYZER, ROBERT. Elegy: "Whenever we touched, I thought of the Lying-in Hospital."
LAZARUS, EMMA. New Colossus, The.
LEAPOR, MARY. Hymn to the Morning, An.
New Ballad, A.
Proserpine's Ragout.
Sylvia and the Bee.
LEAR, EDWARD. By Way of Preface.
Calico Pie.
Cold Are the Crabs.
Courtship of the Yonghy-Bonghy-Bo, The.
Dong with a Luminous Nose, The.
Floating Old Man, The.
How Pleasant to Know Mr. Lear.
Jumblies, The.
Limerick: "There was a young lady of Firle."
Limerick: "There was a young lady whose chin."
Limerick: "There was a young lady whose eyes."
Limerick: "There was a young lady whose nose."
Limerick: "There was an old lady of Chertsey."
Limerick: "There was an old man in a tree."
Limerick: "There was an old man of Corfu."
Limerick: "There was an old man of Hong Kong."
Limerick: "There was an old man of Ibreem."
Limerick: "There was an old man of the Dee."
Limerick: "There was an old man of The Hague."
Limerick: "There was an old man of Thermopylae."
Limerick: "There was an old man who said: 'How.'"
Limerick: "There was an old man who said, 'Hush!'"
Limerick: "There was an old man who when little."
Limerick: "There was an old man with a beard."
Limerick: "There was an old man with a gong."
Limerick: "There was an old person of Diss."
Limerick: "There was an old person of Hurst."
Limerick: "There was an old person of Ickley."
Limerick: "There was an old person of Minety."
Limerick: "There was an old person of Stroud."
Limerick: "There was an old person of Ware."
Nonsense Alphabet, A.
Nutcrackers and the Sugar-Tongs, The.

Owl and the Pussy Cat, The.
Table and the Chair, The.
Teapots and Quails.
There Was a Young Lady Whose Chin.
There Was an Old Man in a Tree.
There Was an Old Man, on Whose Nose.
There Was an Old Man with a Beard.
There Was an Old Person of Ware.
LEARY, PARIS. Elegy for Helen Trent.
First Reader.
Love Lifted Me.
Manifesto.
Onan.
September 1, 1965.
Summa contra Gentiles.
Views of the Oxford Colleges.
"What Five Books Would You Pick to Be Marooned with on a Desert Island?"
LEATHAM, E. RUTTER. Thank you for the world so sweet.
LeCRON, HELEN COWLES. Little Charlie Chipmunk.
LEDERER, MARJORIE. Fifth Birthday Gift.
LEDWIDGE, FRANCIS. To a Linnet in a Cage.
LEE, HARRY. My Master Was So Very Poor.
LEE, LAURIE. Apples.
April Rise.
Autumn Apples.
Bombay Arrival.
Edge of Day, The.
Field of Autumn.
First Love.
Home from Abroad.
Long Summer.
Long Way, The.
Poem for Easter.
Scot in the Desert.
Sunken Evening.
Town Owl.
Twelfth Night.
LEE, MUNA. January Night, tr.
Philosophy, tr.
Unhappy He, tr.
LEE, WALTER M. Father, Teach Me.
LEESON, JANE ELIZA. Hymn, A: "Loving Shepherd of thy sheep."
LEFEVRE, H. T. This I Can Do.
LE GALLIENNE, RICHARD. Ballade-Catalogue of Lovely Things, A.
Called Away.
Melton Mowbray Pork Pie, A.
LÉGER, ALEXIS SAINT-LÉGER. See "PERSE, ST.-J."
LEHMANN, GEOFFREY. Last Campaign, The.
LEHMANN, JOHN. Ballad of Banners (1944), The.
Summer Story, The.
LEHMANN, WILHELM. After the Second Flood.
February Moon.
LEIGH, HENRY SAMBROOKE. Twins, The.
LEIGH, RICHARD. Thus Lovely Sleep.
LEITNER, DELLA ADAMS. Forbearance.
Tomorrow.
LEITNER, S. N. That's Faith.
LEMMINGER, GRAHAM LEE. Tobacco.
LEMONT, JESSIE. Autumn, tr.
LENAU, NIKOLAUS. Plea.
Song of the Rushes, sel.
Three, The.
Three Gypsies, The.
To a Dutch Landscape.
To Her Far Away.
LENSKI, LOIS. Oh! to Have a Birthday.
People.
LENT, EMMA A. Unawares.
LEÓN, LUIS PONCE DE (Fray Luis de León). At the Ascension.
Life of the Blessed, The.
Life Withdrawn, The.
O Courtesy, O Harborage Most Sweet!
Ode to Felipe Ruiz.
Ode to Francisco Salinas.
On Leaving Prison.
Tranquil Night.
LEONARD, PRISCILLA. Tide Will Win, The.

LEONARD, WILLIAM ELLERY. Gilgamesh, sel., tr.
Seduction of Engadu, The, tr. Fr. Gilgamesh.
LEOPARDI, GIACOMO. Infinite, The.
LE PAN, DOUGLAS. Canoe-Trip.
Incident, An.
Lion, Leopard, Lady.
New Vintage, The.
Nimbus.
LERMONTOV, MIKHAIL YUREVICH. Composed While under Arrest.
Sail, A.
LERNER, LAURENCE DAVID. In a Shoreham Garden.
Meditation upon the Toothache, A.
Way to the Sea, The.
What's Hard.
LESLIE, KENNETH. Easter Song.
From Soil Somehow the Poet's Word.
My Love Is Sleeping.
Silver Herring Throbbed Thick in My Seine, The.
LETTS, WINIFRED M. (Mrs. W. H. Foster Verschoyle). Spires of Oxford, The.
Tim, an Irish Terrier.
To Scott.
LEUTHOLD, HEINRICH. Leaf Fall.
LEVENSON, CHRISTOPHER. Prophecy, A.
LEVERTOV [or LEVERTOFF], DENISE. Charge, The.
Come into Animal Presence.
Common Ground, A, sel.
Far Away and Long Ago, tr.
Goddess, The.
Gypsy's Window, The.
House of Alvargonzález, The, tr.
Illustrious Ancestors.
Jacob's Ladder, The.
Laying the Dust.
Little Carol of the Virgin, A, tr.
Map of the Western Part of the County of Essex in England, A.
Matins.
Merritt Parkway.
Novel, The.
Obsessions.
Offender, The.
Pleasures.
Presence, The.
Quarry Pool, The.
Rainwalkers, The.
Resting Figure.
Satiric and Censorious Epistle, sel., tr.
Seems like We Must Be Somewhere Else.
Seguidillas of the Guadalquiver River, tr.
Six Variations.
Solitude, The.
Symphony in Gray Major, tr.
To the Reader.
To the Snake.
Vigil, The.
Well, The.
Wife, The.
With Eyes at the Back of Our Heads.
LEVI, PETER. Fox-coloured Pheasant Enjoyed His Peace, The.
He Met Her at the Green Horse.
In a Corner of Eden.
L'Aurore Grelottante.
Ship-building Emperors Commanded.
To My Friends.
LEVI BEN AMITTAI. Kibbutz Sabbath.
LEVI ISAAC OF BERDITSHEV. Invocation: "Good morning to you, Lord of the world!"
LEVINE, NORMAN. Crabbing.
LEVINE, PHILIP. Drunkard, The.
For Fran.
Gangrene.
Negatives, The.
Night Thoughts over a Sick Child.
Passing Out.
Sierra Kid.
Small Game.
LEVOY, MYRON. Out of the West of Lucky Riders.
LEVY, AMY. London Plane-Tree, A.
LEVY, NEWMAN. Midsummer Fantasy.
LEWIS, ALUN. All Day It Has Rained.
In Hospital: Poona (I).

LEWIS, ALUN (continued)
In Hospital: Poona (II).
Jason and Medea.
Mountain over Aberdare, The.
Postscript for Gweno.
Sacco Writes to His Son.
Sentry, The.
Song: "First month of his absence, The."
LEWIS, CECIL DAY. See DAY LEWIS, CECIL.
LEWIS, CLIVE STAPLES. Aridity.
LEWIS, DAVID. Dark Night of the Soul, tr.
When None Shall Rail.
LEWIS, DOMINIC BEVAN WYNDHAM ("Timothy Shy"). Jig for Sackbuts.
LEWIS, EILUNED. We Who Were Born.
LEWIS, GARDNER E. Invitation to an Invitation, An, tr.
"LEWIS, MICHAEL." Broken Monologue.
Cherry Blossoms, sels.
Cursing and Blessing. Fr. Cherry Blossoms.
Leaving. Fr. Cherry Blossoms.
Living and Dying. Fr. Cherry Blossoms.
Longing. Fr. Cherry Blossoms.
Remembering. Fr. Cherry Blossoms.
LEWIS, WYNDHAM. One-Way Song, sel.
LEWIS GLYN COTHI. On the Death of His Son.
LEWISOHN, LUDWIG. Youth Dreams, The, tr.
L'HERMITE, TRISTAN. See TRISTAN L'HERMITE.
LIBERO, LIBERO DE. My Ciociara Night.
LICHTENSTEIN, ALFRED. Ash Wednesday.
Galoshes, The.
Morning.
Patent Leather Shoe, The.
Prophecy.
Return of the Village Lad.
LIEBERMAN, ELIAS. Aladdin Throws Away His Lamp.
I Am an American.
LIEBERMAN, LAURENCE. Orange County Plague: Scenes.
LI HO. Ninth Moon.
LILIENCRON, DETLEV, FREIHERR VON. Band Marches, The.
LINCOLN, ABRAHAM. Faith of Abraham Lincoln, The.
I Am Not Bound to Win.
Memory.
LINCOLN, JOSEPH CROSBY. November's Come.
Rainy Day, A.
LIND, LEVI ROBERT. Satires, The (of Juvenal), sel., tr.
Spring, tr.
LINDEMAN, JACK. Lament for the Frontiers of the Empire.
LINDSAY, LADY ANNE (Lady Anne Lindsay Barnard). Auld Robin Gray.
Day and Night.
LINDSAY, FORBES. Ball and the Club, The.
LINDSAY, JACK. Budding Spring.
To Naso, tr.
LINDSAY, MAURICE. May Day Demonstrators.
LINDSAY, VACHEL. Abraham Lincoln Walks at Midnight.
Babylon, Babylon, Babylon the Great.
Broncho That Would Not Be Broken, The.
Congo, The.
Daniel.
Daniel Jazz, The.
Eagle That Is Forgotten, The.
Euclid.
Explanation of the Grasshopper, An.
Factory Windows Are Always Broken.
Flower-fed Buffaloes, The.
General William Booth Enters Heaven.
Ghosts [or Ghost] of the Buffaloes, The.
Haughty Snail-King, The.
How Samson Bore Away the Gates of Gaza.

In the Congo. Fr. The Congo.
Incense.
Indian Summer Day on the Prairie, An.
Jazz of This Hotel, The.
Johnny Appleseed's Hymn to the Sun.
Leaden-eyed, The.
Lion, The.
Litany of the Heroes, sels.
Little Turtle, The.
Moon's the North Wind's Cooky, The.
Mouse That Gnawed the Oak-Tree Down, The.
Mysterious Cat, The.
Nancy Hanks, Mother of Abraham Lincoln.
Net to Snare the Moonlight, A.
On the Building of Springfield.
Simon Legree—a Negro Sermon.
Springfield of the Far Future, The.
To a Golden-haired Girl in a Louisiana Town.
Two Old Crows.
What the Hyena Said.
When Lincoln Came to Springfield.
Would I Might Rouse the Lincoln in You All. Fr. Litany of the Heroes.
LINDSEY, THERESE KAYSER. Man Christ, The.
LINK, LENORE M. Holding Hands.
LI PO [or LI TAI PO or in Japanese RIHAKU]. Clearing at Dawn.
Conversation in the Mountains.
Exile's Letter.
In the Mountains on a Summer Day.
Lament of the Frontier Guard.
River-Merchant's Wife, The; a Letter.
Taking Leave of a Friend.
White Egret, The.
LISTER, RICHARD PERCIVAL. I Sometimes Think.
LI TAI PO. See LI PO.
LITTLETON, EDWARD. On a Spider.
LIVESAY, DOROTHY. Fantasia.
Improvisation on an Old Theme.
On Looking into Henry Moore.
Signature.
LIVINGSTON, MYRA COHN. Pretending.
LLULL, RAMON. See LULL, RAMON.
"LLYWELYN" (Beryl Llywelyn Lucas). Birds.
LOCKMAN, JOHN. Penitent Nun, The.
LODGE, THOMAS. Coridon's Song. Fr. Rosalynde.
Earth Late Choked with Showers, The. Fr. Scillaes Metamorphosis.
Ode: "Now I find thy looks were feigned." Fr. Phyllis.
Phyllis, sel.
Robert, Second Duke of Normandy, sel.
Rosalind. Fr. Rosalynde.
Rosalind's Madrigal. Fr. Rosalynde.
Rosaline. Fr. Rosalynde.
Rosalynde; or, Euphues' Golden Legacy, sels.
Scillaes Metamorphosis, sel.
Song: "Pluck the fruit and taste the pleasure." Fr. Robert, Second Duke of Normandy.
Very Phoenix, A.
LOERKE, OSKAR. Beyond the Horizon.
Bird Causeways, The.
Stone Path, The, sel.
LOFTING, HUGH. Betwixt and Between.
Mister Beers.
Picnic.
LOGAN, JOHN (1748–88). Braes of Yarrow, The.
LOGAN, JOHN (1923–). Achilles and the King.
Concert Scene.
Honolulu and Back.
Lines to His Son on Reaching Adolescence.
Nude Kneeling in Sand.
Picnic, The.
Trip to Four or Five Towns, A.
LOGUE, CHRISTOPHER. Good Taste.
Story of Two Gentlemen and the Gardener, The.
LONG, ELIZABETH-ELLEN. Treasure.
LONG, FRANK BELKNAP. Adjuration.
It Is Not Only the Dead.

New Adam, The.
LONG, RICHARD HOOPELL. Poet and Peasant.
Skylark's Nest, The.
LONGFELLOW, HENRY WADSWORTH. Aftermath.
Arrow and the Song, The.
Arsenal at Springfield, The.
Belisarius.
Birds of Killingworth, The. Fr. Tales of a Wayside Inn.
Bookmark, tr.
Bridge, The.
Building of the Ship, The, sel.
Challenge, The.
Chamber over the Gate, The.
Chaucer.
Children's Hour, The.
Christmas Bells.
Clear Honor of the Liquid Element, tr.
Cross of Snow, The.
Dante, tr.
Day Is Done, The.
Daybreak.
Decoration Day.
Divina Commedia (poems introductory to the translation).
Excelsior.
Fire of Drift-Wood, The.
God of the Earth, the Sky, the Sea.
Harvest Moon, The.
Hawthorne—May 23 1864.
Hiawatha's Childhood. Fr. The Song of Hiawatha.
Him Evermore I Behold.
How strange the sculptures that adorn these towers! Fr. Divina Commedia.
Hymn to the Night.
I enter, and I see thee in the gloom. Fr. Divina Commedia.
I Heard the Bells on Christmas Day.
I lift mine eyes, and all the windows blaze. Fr. Divina Commedia.
Ideal Beauty, tr.
In the Churchyard at Cambridge.
It Is Too Late! Fr. Morituri Salutamus.
Jemima, at.
Jewish Cemetery at Newport, The.
Jugurtha.
Keats.
Killed at the Ford.
Let Me Go Warm, tr.
Lines Written in Her Breviary, tr.
Lost Youth.
Manuscripts of God, The.
Mezzo Cammin.
Milton.
Morituri Salutamus, sel.
My Lost Youth.
Nativity of Christ, The, tr.
Nature.
O star of morning and of liberty. Fr. Divina Commedia.
Oft have I seen at some cathedral door. Fr. Divina Commedia.
Paul Revere's Ride. Fr. Tales of a Wayside Inn.
Psalm of Life, A.
Rainy Day, The.
Resignation, sel.
Ropewalk, The.
St. Teresa's Book-Mark, tr.
Sea Hath Its Pearls, The, tr.
Seaweed.
Sicilian's Tale, The. Fr. Tales of a Wayside Inn.
Sir Humphrey Gilbert, sel.
Skeleton in Armor, The.
Slave's Dream, The.
Snow-Flakes.
Song: "If thou art sleeping, maiden," tr.
Song of Hiawatha, The, sel.
Sound of the Sea, The.
Spirit of Poetry, The.
Summer Days Are Come Again, The.
Tales of a Wayside Inn, sels.
There Was a Little Girl, at.
Three Kings, The.
Tide, The.
Tide Rises, the Tide Falls, The.
Ultima Thule.

Village Blacksmith, The.
Wanderer's Night Song, *tr.*
With snow-white veil and garments as of flame. *Fr.* Divina Commedia.
Woods in Winter.
Wreck of the *Hesperus,* The.
LOPE DE VEGA CARPIO, FÉLIX. At Dawn the Virgin Is Born.
Christmas Cradlesong, A.
Ice and Fires Contend with My Child.
If her forehead was not snow.
If You Leave at Daybreak.
Little Carol of the Virgin, A.
May Song.
On the Triumph of Judith.
Seguidillas of the Guadalquiver River.
Shepherd Who with Your Tender Calls.
Sonnet All of a Sudden, A.
Strange Shepherd, Set My Bellwether Free.
Stranger to Love, Whoever Loves Not Thee.
Today Delight's Fair Ship.
Tomorrow.
What Do I Have, That You Seek Out My Friendship?
Where Are You Going, Maiden?
White Was I.
LOPES DE BAIAN, AFONSO. They Have Told Me Some News.
LORDE, AUDRE. And Fall Shall Sit in Judgment.
Pirouette.
LORENZO, JUAN. Book of Alexander, The, *sel.*
LORRAINE, LILITH. Case History.
It May Be like This.
Legend of the Hills.
No Escape.
Since We Are Property.
LORRIS, GUILLAUME DE, *and* JEAN DE MEUN. *See* GUILLAUME DE LORRIS *and* JEAN DE MEUN.
LOUŸS, PIERRE. Absence. *Fr.* The Songs of Bilitis.
Bilitis. *Fr.* The Songs of Bilitis.
Desire. *Fr.* The Songs of Bilitis.
Despairing Embrace, The. *Fr.* The Songs of Bilitis.
Endearments. *Fr.* The Songs of Bilitis.
Kiss, The. *Fr.* The Songs of Bilitis.
Little House, The. *Fr.* The Songs of Bilitis.
Remorse. *Fr.* The Songs of Bilitis.
Songs of Bilitis, The, *sels.*
LOVE, GEORGE. Noonday April Sun, The.
LOVELACE, RICHARD. Another.
Black Patch on Lucasta's Face, A.
Fly Caught in a Cobweb, A.
Gratiana Dancing and Singing.
La Bella Bona Roba.
Love Made in the First Age.
Lucasta's World.
Scrutinie, The.
Stone Walls.
To Althea from Prison.
To Amarantha [That She Would Dishevell Her Haire].
To Lucasta, [on] Going beyond the Seas.
To Lucasta, [on] Going to the Wars.
Valiant Love.
Why Should You Swear?
LOVER, SAMUEL. Barney O'Hea.
Birth of Saint Patrick, The.
Lanty Leary.
LOWBURY, EDWARD. Swan.
LOWE, ROBERT, VISCOUNT SHERBROOKE. Songs of the Squatters.
LOWELL, AMY. Carrefour.
Decade, A.
Hippocrene.
Listening.
Madonna of the Evening Flowers.
Night Clouds.
Patterns.
Points of View.
Sea Shell.
To a Friend.
LOWELL, AMY, *and* FLORENCE AYSCOUGH. Excursion, The.
LOWELL, JAMES RUSSELL. Aladdin.

Auspex.
Biglow Papers, The, *sels.*
Bryant. *Fr.* A Fable for Critics.
Cooper. *Fr.* A Fable for Critics.
Courtin', The. *Fr.* The Biglow Papers.
Emerson. *Fr.* A Fable for Critics.
Fable for Critics, A, *sels.*
Fatherland, The.
First Snow-fall, The, *sel.*
Hawthorne. *Fr.* A Fable for Critics.
June. *Fr.* The Vision of Sir Launfal.
Lowell. *Fr.* A Fable for Critics.
Monna Lisa.
My Love.
Ode Recited at the Harvard Commemoration.
On Receiving a Copy of Mr. Austin Dobson's "Old World Idylls."
Poe and Longfellow. *Fr.* A Fable for Critics.
Present Crisis, The, *sels.*
Recall, The.
Search, The.
She Came and Went.
Sixty-eighth Birthday.
Slaves.
Spring. *Fr.* The Biglow Papers.
Sunthin' in the Pastoral Line. *Fr.* The Biglow Papers.
To the Dandelion.
Verses Intended to Go with a Posset Dish to My Dear Little Goddaughter, 1882.
Vision of Sir Launfal, The, *sels.*
Washers of the Shroud, The.
Washington.
What Mr. Robinson Thinks. *Fr.* The Biglow Papers.
Whittier. *Fr.* A Fable for Critics.
Work.
LOWELL, ROBERT (Traill Spence), JR. After the Surprising Conversions.
As a Plane Tree by the Water.
Caligula.
Children of Light.
Christmas Eve under Hooker's Statue.
Christmas in Black Rock.
Colloquy in Black Rock.
Dead in Europe, The.
Death from Cancer. *Fr.* In Memory of Arthur Winslow.
Drunken Fisherman, The.
Exile's Return, The.
Falling Asleep over the Aeneid.
For the Union Dead.
Ford Madox Ford.
Grandparents.
Holy Innocents, The.
In Memory of Arthur Winslow.
Inauguration Day: January 1953.
Mary Winslow.
Memories of West Street and Lepke.
Mr. Edwards and the Spider.
Mother Marie Therese.
Mouth of the Hudson, The.
New Year's Day.
Public Garden, The.
Quaker Graveyard in Nantucket, The.
Salem.
Skunk Hour.
Where the Rainbow Ends.
Winter in Dunbarton.
Words for Hart Crane.
Years Back When We Were Children, *tr.*
LOWENFELS, WALTER. Letter to the President, *sel.*
LOWENFELS, WALTER, *and* MAX ROSENFELD. Permanent Delegate, The, *tr.*
LOWRY, MALCOLM. Cain Shall Not Slay Abel Today on Our Good Ground.
In Memoriam; Ingvald Bjorndal and His Comrade.
Lupus in Fabula.
Salmon Drowns Eagle.
LOWRY, ROBERT. How Can I Keep from Singing? *sel.*
LOWTH, ROBERT. Link, The.
LUCAS, BERYL LLYWELYN. *See* "LLYWELYN."
LUCAS, EDWARD VERRALL. Conjuror, The.
Welsh, The.

LUCAS, FRANK LAURENCE. Antigone, *sel., tr.*
What a Piece of Work Is a Man, *tr. Fr.* Antigone.
LUCCHI, LORNA DE'. For translations from Italian, *see* RBL.
LUCIE-SMITH, EDWARD. At the Roman Baths, Bath.
Fault, The.
Meeting Myself.
On Looking at Stubbs's Anatomy of the Horse.
Rabbit Cry.
LUCILLIUS [*or* LUCILIUS]. Boxer's Face, The.
Sluggard, The.
World's Worst Boxer, The.
LUCRETIUS (Titus Lucretius Carus). Concerning the Nature of Love. *Fr.* De Rerum Natura.
De Rerum Natura, *sels.*
Nature of Love, The. *Fr.* De Rerum Natura.
What Has This Bugbear Death. *Fr.* De Rerum Natura.
LUDLOW, FITZ HUGH [*or* FITZHUGH]. Too Late.
LUFF, W. I Buried the Year.
LULL [*or* LLULL], RAMON. To You, Lady Virgin Santa Maria.
When the Star Appears at Daybreak.
LUTHER, MARTIN. Away in a Manger.
Cradle Hymn.
Feste Burg ist unser Gott, Ein.
Mighty Fortress Is Our God, A.
LUZI, MARIO. Ivory.
Wine and Ocher.
Woman in Pisa.
LYDGATE, JOHN. Duplicity of Women, The.
Transient as a Rose.
LYLY, JOHN. Alexander and Campaspe, *sel.*
Cupid and [My] Campaspe. *Fr.* Alexander and Campaspe.
Midas, *sel.*
Pan's Syrinx. *Fr.* Midas.
LYONS, RICHARD. Goodbye the Office.
LYTE, HENRY FRANCIS. Abide with Me.
Unknown God, The.
LYTTELTON, GEORGE, BARON LYTTELTON. On Her Pleading Want of Time.
Song: "Heavy hours are almost past, The."
Two Poems to Miss Lucy Fortescue.
When Delia on the Plain Appears.
LYTTON, EDWARD ROBERT BULWERLYTTON, 1ST EARL OF. *See* "MEREDITH, OWEN."

M

"M., Q. B." Old and the New, The.
"M. G. H." *See* "H., M. G."
MACAINSH, NOEL. Kangaroo by Nightfall.
McALPINE, R. W. Two Surprises.
MACARTNEY, FREDERICK THOMAS BENNETT. Desert Claypan.
MACAULAY, THOMAS BABINGTON MACAULAY, 1ST BARON. Armada, The, *sel. Fr.* Lays of Ancient Rome.
Horatius. *Fr.* Lays of Ancient Rome.
Ivry.
Jacobite's Epitaph, A.
Lays of Ancient Rome, *sels.*
McAULEY, JAMES PHILLIP. Art of Poetry, An.
At Bungendore.
Canticle.
Late Winter.
New Guinea.
Pietà.
MacBETH, GEORGE. Bedtime Story.
Compasses, The.
Drawer, The.
McBURNEY, WILLIAM B. ("Carroll Malone"). Croppy Boy, The.
MacCAIG, NORMAN. Ego.
Laggandoan, Harris.

MacCaig, Norman (continued)
  Spate in Winter Midnight.
  Summer Farm.
  Too Bright a Day.
McCarrell, Stuart. Assassinations
  1963, The.
McCarthy, Denis Aloysius. St.
  Brigid.
M'Carthy [or McCarthy], Justin
  Huntly. If I Were King, sel.
"MacCathmhaoil, Seosamh." See
  Campbell, Joseph.
McClure, Michael. Aelf-scin, the
  Shining Scimmer the Gleam, the
  Shining, The.
  Fidelio.
  Oh Bright Oh Black Singbeast Love-
  beast Catkin Sleek.
  Oh Ease Oh Body-Strain Oh Love O
  Ease Me Not! Wound-Bore.
McCord, David. Cocoon.
  Crew Cut.
  Dog in a Car.
  Epitaph on a Waiter.
  Every Time I Climb a Tree.
  Frost Pane, The.
  Notes on a Track Meet.
  Notice.
  Out in the Woods with Father.
  Rainbow, The.
  Second Half.
  Snail.
  Song of the Train.
  This Is My Rock.
  Tiger Lily.
  Watching the Moon.
  When I Was Christened.
  Who Wants a Birthday?
McCord, Howard. Two There Are I
  Wish to Celebrate.
McCrae, George Gordon. Mamba the
  Bright-eyed, sel.
McCrae, Hugh Raymond. Ambuscade.
  Camden Magpie.
  Colombine.
  Enigma.
  Evening.
  I Blow My Pipes.
  Joan of Arc.
  June Morning.
  Mad Marjory.
  Mouse, The.
  Muse-haunted.
  Song of the Rain.
  Spring.
  Uncouth Knight, The.
McCrae, John. In Flanders Fields.
McCuaig, Ronald. Au Tombeau de
  Mon Père.
  L'Après Midi d'une Fille aux Cheveux
  de Lin.
  Music in the Air.
  Recitative.
"MacDiarmid [or McDiarmid], Hugh"
  (Christopher Murray Grieve). At
  My Father's Grave.
  I Heard Christ Sing.
  Innumerable Christ, The.
  Love.
  O Wha's the Bride?
  Scarlet Woman, The.
  Stony Limits.
  Watergaw, The.
  Wheesht, Wheesht.
MacDonagh, Thomas. Night Hunt,
  The.
  Offering.
Macdonald [or MacDonald], George.
  Approaches.
  Baby.
  Carpenter, The.
  Lost and Found.
  Mammon Marriage.
  My Morning Song.
  Obedience.
  Preacher's Prayer, The.
  Shadows, The.
  That Holy Thing.
  To My God.
  Wind and the Moon, The.
  Within and Without, sel.
MacDonald, James Edward Hervey.
  Hanging, The.
McDonald, L. A. It's You.

McDonald, Nan. Hatters, The.
  Makers, The.
  White Eagle, The.
MacDonald, Wilson Pugsley. John
  Graydon.
MacDonogh, Patrick. Flowering Cur-
  rant.
  She Walked Unaware.
Macdougall, Arthur R., Jr. Captain
  of the Years.
McElhaney, Georgia Lee. Conquista-
  dor.
  Dervish.
  Effigy.
McFadden, Roy. White Bird, The.
McGaffey, Ernest. Geronimo.
McGaffin, Audrey R. Final Proces-
  sion.
McGinley, Phyllis. All around the
  Town, sels.
  Ballade of Lost Objects.
  B's the Bus. Fr. All around the
  Town.
  C Is for the Circus. Fr. All around
  the Town.
  Carol with Variations.
  Conversation in Avila.
  Country Club Sunday.
  Daniel at Breakfast.
  Demagogue, The. Fr. Epitaphs for
  Three Prominent Persons.
  Don't Shake the Bottle, Shake Your
  Mother-in-Law.
  Enigma for Christmas Shoppers.
  Epitaphs for Three Prominent Persons.
  Independent, The. Fr. Epitaphs for
  Three Prominent Persons.
  Lucy McLockett.
  Midcentury Love Letter.
  Oh Come, Little Children.
  Old Feminist, The.
  P's the Proud Policeman. Fr. All
  Around the Town.
  Reflections Dental.
  Reflections Outside of a Gymnasium.
  Six Nuns in the Snow.
  Star-spangled Ode.
  Statesman, The. Fr. Epitaphs for
  Three Prominent Persons.
  Thunderer, The.
  Triolet against Sisters.
McGirt, William A., Jr. See "Inman,
  Will."
McGonagall, William. Death of
  Prince Leopold, The.
  Tay Bridge Disaster, The.
McGrath, Thomas. Against the False
  Magicians.
  Letter to an Imaginary Friend, sel.
  Ode for the American Dead in Korea.
MacGregor, Robert Guthrie. With
  Two Fair Girls, tr.
Machado, Antonio. Autumn Dawn.
  Breeze Tells Me, Loved One, The.
  Crime Was in Granada, The.
  Deep Song.
  Denuded Is the Earth.
  Eye You See Isn't, The.
  Good Thing Is, We Know, The.
  Her Street Is Dark.
  House of Alvargonzález, The.
  Moldering Hulk, The.
  Plaza and the Flaming Orange Trees,
  The.
  Plaza Has a Tower, The.
  Portrait.
  Rose of Fire.
  Siesta.
  Song: "Now the moon is rising."
  Spring Has Come.
  Summer's Night, A.
  Tavern Guitar Playing a Jota Today.
  Walker, It Is Your Footsteps.
  Water Wheel, The.
  Who Placed, amidst the Tracts of Ash?
Machaut, Guillaume de. See Guil-
  laume de Machaut.
McHugh, Vincent. Crawl Blues.
  Deposition by John Wilmot, A.
  Suite from Catullus.
  Talking to Myself, sel.
Macías Ó Namorado. I Went in Quest
  of Measure.
MacInnes, Tom. Tiger of Desire, The.

MacIntyre, Carlyle Ferren. Lament:
  "Oh, everything is far," tr.
  Retinue, tr.
  Solemn Hour, tr.
  To My Mouse-colored Mare, tr.
  To the Eternal Feminine, tr.
Mackay, Charles. Little and Great.
McKay, Claude. Flame-Heart.
  If We Must Die.
  Outcast.
  St. Isaac's Church, Petrograd.
  Tropics in New York, The.
  White House, The.
Mackay, Jessie. Noosing of the Sun-
  God, The.
Mackay, Louis Alexander ("John
  Smalacombe"). Admonition for
  Spring.
  Battle Hymn of the Spanish Rebellion.
  Ill-tempered Lover, The, sel.
  Nunc Scio, Quid Sit Amor.
Mackellar, Dorothea. Dusk in the
  Domain.
  Fancy Dress.
  My Country.
McKellar, John Alexander Ross.
  Fourth Napoleon, sel.
  Love in a Cottage. Fr. Fourth Napo-
  leon.
Mackenzie, Kenneth. Fairy Tale, A.
  Heat.
  Legerdemain.
  Old Inmate, An.
  Pat Young.
  Table-Birds.
MacLachlan, Alexander. Emigrant,
  The, sel.
  Song: "Old England is eaten by
  knaves." Fr. The Emigrant.
  We Live in a Rickety House.
McLaren, Floris Clark. No More the
  Slow Stream.
  Visit by Water.
MacLeish, Archibald. American Let-
  ter: For Gerald Murphy.
  Ars Poetica.
  Conquistador, sel.
  Curse God and Die, You Said to Me.
  Fr. J. B.
  End of the World, The.
  Immortal Autumn.
  J. B., sel.
  L'An Trentiesme de Mon Eage.
  Music and Drum.
  "Not Marble nor the Gilded Monu-
  ments."
  Poem in Prose.
  Pole Star.
  Psyche with the Candle.
  Silent Slain, The.
  Snow Fall, The.
  Theory of Poetry.
  Too-late Born, The.
  Vicissitudes of the Creator.
  What Must, sel.
  Where the Hayfields Were.
  Words in Time.
  You, Andrew Marvell.
"Macleod, Fiona" (William Sharp).
  Autumnal Evening, An.
McLeod, Irene Rutherford (Mrs.
  Aubrey de Sélincourt). Lone Dog.
MacLow, Jackson. 1st Dance—Making
  Things New—6 February 1964.
  2nd Dance—Seeing Lines—6 February
  1964.
  10th Dance—Coming On as a Horn—
  20 February 1964.
  3rd Dance—Making a Structure with
  a Roof or under a Roof—6-7 Febru-
  ary 1964.
  13th Dance—Matching Parcels—21
  February 1964.
  37th Dance—Banding—22 March 1964.
  12th Dance—Getting Leather by Language—21 February 1964.
  29th Dance—Having an Instrument—
  22 March 1964.
McMahon, M. J. Nonpareil's Grave,
  The.
Macnab, Roy. Stages.
McNail, Stanley. Elsie's House.
  House on Maple Hill, The.
  Lottie Mae.

Secrets of Cisterns, The.
Witch, The.
MacNeice, Louis. And the Lord Was Not in the Whirlwind. *Fr.* Visitations.
Bagpipe Music.
Bar-Room Matins.
Birmingham.
Brother Fire.
Clowns.
Conscript, The.
Cradle Song.
Creditor, The.
Didymus.
Dublin.
Eclogue for Christmas, An.
Elegy for Minor Poets.
Explorations.
Glass Falling.
Hands and Eyes.
Holes in the Sky, *sel.*
Horses.
Libertine, The.
Meeting Point.
Morning Sun.
Passage Steamer.
Perseus.
Prayer before Birth.
Prayer in Mid-Passage.
Snow.
Spring Voices.
Streets of Laredo, The.
Suicide.
Sunlight on the Garden, The.
Trilogy for X, *sel.*
Truisms, The.
Visitations, *sel.*
Wall, The.
Wessex Guidebook.
Macomber, W. Christ Is Coming.
Macpherson, James ("Ossian"). Carthon, *sel.*
MacPherson, Jay. Beauty of Job's Daughters, The.
Boatman, The.
Eurynome.
Eve in Reflection.
Go Take the World.
Innocents, The.
Marriage of Earth and Heaven, The.
Madeleva, Sister Mary. Apology for Youth.
Madgett, Naomi Long. Midway.
Mortality.
Madison, Dolley. La Fayette.
Maeterlinck, Maurice. Last Words, The.
Magee, John Gillespie, Jr. High Flight.
Mahony, Francis Sylvester ("Father Prout"). Bells of Shandon, The.
Mains, J. Riley. Good Old Days of '50, '1, and '2, The.
Mair, Charles. Fireflies, The, *sel.*
Tecumseh, *sels.*
Winter.
Major, Clarence. Celebrated Return.
Malam, Charles. Steam Shovel.
Malherbe, François de. Consolation to M. du Périer.
To Louis XIII.
Mallarmé, Stéphane. Après-midi d'un faune, L', *sel.*
Little Air.
Sonnet: "This virgin, beautiful and lively day."
Mallet, David, *and* James Thomson. *See* Thomson, James, *and* David Mallet.
Malleville, Claude de. Couronne Impériale, La. *Fr.* Guirlande de Julie.
Guirlande de Julie, *sel.*
Malloch, Douglas. If Easter Eggs Would Hatch.
"Malone, Carroll." *See* McBurney, William B.
Malouf, David. At My Grandmother's.
Mandel, Eli W. Fire Place, The.
Metamorphosis.
Minotaur Poems, *sels.*
Orpheus. *Fr.* Minotaur Poems.
Song: "When the echo of the last footstep dies."
Mandel, Oscar. We Who Do Not Grieve in Silence.

Mandiargues, André Pieyre de. *See* Pieyre de Mandiargues, André.
Mangan, James Clarence. Gone in the Wind.
Homesickness, *tr.*
Shapes and Signs.
Siberia.
Time of the Barmacides, The.
Manifold, John Streeter. Bunyip and the Whistling Kettle, The.
Fife Tune.
Griesly Wife, The.
Sirens, The.
Song: "My dark-haired Käthchen, my spit-kitten darling."
Tomb of Lt. John Learmonth, A.I.F., The.
Mannyng [*or* Manning], Robert. No Thyng Ys to Man So Dere.
Manrique, Jorge. Stanzas on the Death of His Father.
Marcabru [*or* Marcabrun]. I'll Tell You in My Own Way.
In April around Easter the Streams Grow Clear.
No Doubt at All, I'll Take Him On as Critic.
Since My Courage Is Clarified.
Winter Goes and Weather Betters.
Marcela de Carpio de San Felix, Sister. Amor Mysticus.
March, Auziàs [*or* Ausiàs]. Time Is Such That Each Brute Beast, The.
Where Is the Place My Thought May Find Repose?
March, Pere. Ladies I Like Well Dressed.
Widow Wearing White or Saffron, The.
Marcus Argentarius. *See* Argentarius, Marcus.
Margolis, William J. Telegram.
Marguerite de Navarre. Dizain to Clément Marot.
Marie de France. Laustic, The.
Marino, Giambattista [*or* Giovanni Battista]. Adone, L', *sel.*
Apollo and Daphne.
Book of the World, The.
Broken Faith.
Chloris' Eyes and Breasts.
Christo Smarrito.
Conscience.
Cynthia Sporting.
During the Bath.
Fountain, The.
Ice and Fire.
Lessons of Nature, The.
Proem, The: To Love. *Fr.* L'Adone.
Sonnet: "Unhappy man, as soon as he is born."
While His Lady Combs Her Hair.
Marinoni, Rosa Zagnoni. Pause.
Markham, Edwin. At Little Virgil's Window.
Christ of the Andes, The.
Creed, A.
Earth Is Enough.
Father's Business, The.
Forgotten Man, The.
Free Nation, A.
How the Great Guest Came.
Lincoln Slain.
Lincoln, the Man of the People.
Lincoln Triumphant.
Man-Test.
Man with the Hoe, The.
Outwitted.
Place of Peace. The.
Prayer, A: "Teach me, Father, how to go."
Right Kind of People, The.
Rules for the Road.
Two at a Fireside.
Victory in Defeat.
Wind and Lyre.
Young Lincoln.
Marlatt, Earl Bowman. Malachi.
Pax Nobiscum.
Peter.
Zechariah.
Marlowe, Christopher. Advice to a Fair Wanton, *tr. Fr.* Amores.
Amores, *sels., tr.*
Apology for Loose Behavior, *tr. Fr.* Amores.

Dr. Faustus, *sel.*
Elegies, *sel., tr.*
Elegy to His Mistress, *tr.*
Face of Helen, The. *Fr.* Dr. Faustus.
Fragment, A.
Hero and Leander.
Impotent Lover, The, *tr. Fr.* Amores.
In Summer's Heat, *tr. Fr.* Amores.
Passionate Shepherd to His Love, The.
Possessive Lover, The, *tr. Fr.* Amores.
Shameful Impotence, *tr. Fr.* Elegies.
Marlowe, Christopher, *and* Thomas Nashe. Tragedy of Dido, The, *sel.*
Marot, Clément. Aux bon vieulx temps.
Epitaph on Jean Veau.
Love-Lesson, A.
Madame D'Albert's Laugh.
Marot to the Queen of Navarre.
Song: Since Loving Countenance.
Marquis, Don (Donald Robert Marquis).
Archy and Mehitabel, *sels.*
Archy Confesses. *Fr.* Archy and Mehitabel.
Archy Does His Part, *sel.*
Fate Is Unfair. *Fr.* Archy Does His Part.
Hen and the Oriole, The. *Fr.* Archy and Mehitabel.
Honey Bee, The.
Hot-Weather Song, A.
Mehitabel Tries Marriage. *Fr.* Archys Life of Mehitabel.
Mrs. Swartz.
Noah an' Jonah an' Cap'n John Smith.
Only Thy Dust.
Prohibition.
Prudence. *Fr.* Archy and Mehitabel.
Reverie.
Song of a Thousand Years.
When One Loves Tensely.
Marriott, Anne. Beaver Pond.
Prairie Graveyard.
Search.
Marryat, Frederick. Captain Stood on the Carronade, The. *Fr.* Snarleyvow; or, The Dog Fiend.
Port Admiral.
Snarleyvow; or, The Dog Fiend, *sel.*
Marshall, Edward. Memory as Memorial in the Last.
Sept. 1957.
Two Poems.
Marshall, Jack. Elegy for the New Year.
Marston, John. Delicious Beauty.
Scourge of Villainy, The, *sel.*
To Everlasting Oblivion. *Fr.* The Scourge of Villainy.
Marston, Philip Bourke. Old Churchyard of Bonchurch, The.
Too Late.
Ungathered Love.
Martial (Marcus Valerius Martialis).
Abnegation.
Advantages of Learning, The.
Bad Joke, A.
Familiarity Breeds Indifference.
Incentive, The.
Insufficient Vengeance.
Martial, the Things for to Attain.
Means to Attain Happy Life, The.
My Friend, the Things That Do Attain.
To His Girl.
To Sabidius.
Too Literal Pupil, The.
Work and Play.
Martin, Bessie June. Let Me Look at Me.
True Riches.
Martin, David. Gordon Childe.
Martin, I. L. At the Tennis Clinic.
Dark Eyes at Forest Hills.
Martin, John. God's Dark.
Martin, Julia E. With Him.
Martin, Philip. In March.
Martín Códax. Ah, Waves, I Come to See.
O Waves of the Sea of Vigo.
Martindale, Cyril Charlie. God Leads the Way, *tr.*
Marvell, Andrew. Ametas and Thestylis Making Hay-Ropes.
Bermudas.

MARVELL, ANDREW (continued)
Character of Holland, The.
Clorinda and Damon.
Coronet, The.
Definition of Love, The.
Dialogue between the Resolved Soul, and Created Pleasure, A.
Dialogue between the Soul and Body, A.
Dialogue between Thyrsis and Dorinda, A.
Eyes and Tears.
Fair Singer, The.
Garden, The.
Horatian Ode upon Cromwell's Return from Ireland, An.
Mourning.
Mower against Gardens, The.
Mower to the Glow-Worms, The.
Mower's Song, The.
Nymph Complaining for the Death of Her Fawn [or Faun], The.
On a Drop of Dew.
On Mr. Milton's *Paradise Lost, sel.*
Picture of Little T. C. in a Prospect of Flowers, The.
Song of the Emigrants in Bermuda.
Thoughts in a [Summer] Garden.
To His Coy Mistress.
To His Noble Friend, Mr. Richard Lovelace, upon His Poems.
To His Worthy Friend Doctor Witty upon His Translation of the Popular Errors.
Unfortunate Lover, The.
Upon Appleton House, to My Lord Fairfax.
MARX, ANNE. Nightmare.
MARY QUEEN OF SCOTS. Prayer before Her Execution.
MASEFIELD, JOHN. Ballad of John Silver, A.
Cargoes.
Creed, A.
Dead Knight, The.
Drop Me the Seed.
Everlasting Mercy, The, *sels.*
Good Friday, *sel.*
King's Highway, The.
Laugh and Be Merry.
Madman's Song, The. *Fr.* Good Friday.
Old Song Re-sung, An.
On Growing Old.
Only a Beauty, Only a Power.
Port of Many Ships.
Roadways.
Sea-Change.
Sea Fever.
Ships, *sel.*
Sonnet: Death Warnings, *tr.*
Sonnet: "Is there a great green commonwealth of Thought."
Spanish Waters.
Wanderer, The.
Wanderer's Song, A.
West Wind, The.
Wherever Beauty Has Been Quick in Clay.
You.
MASON, AGNES LOUISA CARTER. Whenever a Little Child Is Born.
MASON, RONALD ALLISON KELLS. Poem: "If the drink that satisfied."
MASON, W. L. My Airedale Dog.
MASON, WALT. Football.
MASON, WILLIAM. Ode to an Æolus's Harp.
Ode to Morning.
MASSEY, REGINALD. Child, The.
MASSINGER, PHILIP. Picture, The, *sel.*
Song of Pleasure, A. *Fr.* The Picture.
MASTERS, EDGAR LEE. Anne Rutledge. *Fr.* Spoon River Anthology.
"Butch" Weldy. *Fr.* Spoon River Anthology.
Carl Hamblin. *Fr.* Spoon River Anthology.
Edmund Pollard. *Fr.* Spoon River Anthology.
Father Malloy. *Fr.* Spoon River Anthology.
Hannah Armstrong. *Fr.* Spoon River Anthology.

Hill, The. *Fr.* Spoon River Anthology.
James Garber. *Fr.* Spoon River Anthology.
Lucinda Matlock. *Fr.* Spoon River Anthology.
Mrs. George Reece. *Fr.* Spoon River Anthology.
Petit, the Poet. *Fr.* Spoon River Anthology.
Spoon River Anthology, *sels.*
Village Atheist, The. *Fr.* Spoon River Anthology.
William H. Herndon. *Fr.* Spoon River Anthology.
MASTIN, FLORENCE RIPLEY. Eight-Cylinder Man.
MATCHETT, WILLIAM H. Return to Lane's Island.
Water Ouzel.
MATHERS, EDWARD POWYS. Arrows of Love, *tr.*
Black Marigolds, *tr.*
Emperor, The, *tr.*
Escape, An, *tr.*
Garden of Bamboos, The, *tr.*
Haroun's Favorite Song, *tr. Fr.* The Thousand and One Nights.
I Love Long Black Eyes, *tr.*
Inscription on a Chemise, *tr. Fr.* The Thousand and One Nights.
Love, *tr. Fr.* The Thousand and One Nights.
Of Women, *tr. Fr.* The Thousand and One Nights.
Power of Love, The, *tr. Fr.* The Thousand and One Nights.
Proverb, A, *tr.*
Song: "If you love God, take your mirror between your hands and look," *tr.*
Submission, *tr.*
Thing Remembered, A, *tr.*
Thousand and One Nights, The, *sels., tr.*
MATHESON, GEORGE. Christ's Bondservant.
O Love That Wilt Not Let Me Go.
MATHEW, RAY. At a Time.
Love and Marriage.
'Morning, Morning.
MATTHEWS, HARLEY. Return of the Native, The.
MATTHEWS, WASHINGTON. Dawn Boy's Song, *tr.*
Voice That Beautifies the Land, The, *tr.*
"MAURICE, FURNLEY." *See* WILMOT, FRANK.
MAXWELL, JAMES CLERK. Rigid Body Sings.
MAY, JAMES BOYER. Reflection after Empire.
MAYNARD, DON. Athlete.
MAYNARD, FRANÇOIS. Armand! I lose my vital heat.
Epitaph: Time, Which Does All Creatures.
MAYO, EDWARD LESLIE. Variations on a Line from Shakespeare's Fifty-sixth Sonnet.
MEARNS, HUGHES. Antigonish.
Little Man Who Wasn't There, The.
Perfect Reactionary, The.
MECHTHILD VON MAGDEBURG. Ails a Human Heart.
Dearest Love of God, I Pray Thee, Evermore Enfold My Soul.
Lord 'Tis Said That from the World.
Most Gladly Would I Die of Love.
MECKEL, CHRISTOPH. Postship.
Sancho Panza's Heritage.
MEDICI, LORENZO DE'. Canzone: "Into a little close of mine I went."
Carnival Songs, *sel.*
Triumph of Bacchus and Ariadne. *Fr.* Carnival Songs.
MEIGS, MILDRED PLEW. *See* MERRYMAN, MILDRED PLEW.
MELCOMBE, BARON. *See* DODINGTON, GEORGE BUBB, BARON MELCOMBE.
MELEAGER. Gusts of Winter Are Gone, The.
I'll Twine White Violets.

In the Spring.
MELVILLE, HERMAN. Aeolian Harp, The.
After the Pleasure Party.
Art.
Berg, The.
Billy Budd, *sel.*
Billy in the Darbies. *Fr.* Billy Budd.
Clarel, *sel.*
Commemorative of a Naval Victory.
Conflict of Convictions, The.
Dirge for McPherson, A.
Enviable Isles, The.
Epilogue: "If Luther's day expand to Darwin's year." *Fr.* Clarel.
House-Top, The.
Maldive Shark, The.
Malvern Hill.
March into Virginia, The.
Martyr, The.
Misgivings.
Moby Dick, *sel.*
Monody.
On the Grave of a Young Cavalry Officer Killed in the Valley of Virginia.
Pebbles.
Portent, The.
Ravaged Villa, The.
Returned Volunteer to His Rifle, The.
Ribs and Terrors in the Whale, The. *Fr.* Moby Dick.
Running the Batteries.
Shiloh; a Requiem.
To Ned.
Uninscribed Monument on One of the Battlefields of the Wilderness, An.
Utilitarian View of the *Monitor's* Fight, A.
Whale, The. *Fr.* Moby Dick.
MENA, JUAN DE. Mourning of the Mother of Lorenzo Dávalos.
MENAI, HUW (Hugh Menai Williams). Old Peasant in the Billiard Saloon, The.
MENDES, MURILO. Psalm: "I proclaim Thee great and wonderful."
MENSAH, ALBERT KAYPER-. *See* KAYPER-MENSAH, ALBERT.
MEOGO, PERO. In the Green Grass.
My Friend Is Going, Mother.
Tell Me, Daughter, Pretty Daughter.
MEREDITH, GEORGE. Am I failing? For no longer can I cast. *Fr.* Modern Love.
At dinner she is hostess, I am host. *Fr.* Modern Love.
By this he knew she wept with waking eyes. *Fr.* Modern Love.
Dirge in Woods.
Hymn to Colour.
I play for Seasons; not Eternities. *Fr.* Modern Love.
It ended, and the morrow brought the task. *Fr.* Modern Love.
Juggling Jerry.
Lark Ascending, The.
Love in the Valley.
Lucifer in Starlight.
Mares of the Camargue, The, *tr. Fr.* Mirèio.
Mark where the pressing wind shoots javelin-like. *Fr.* Modern Love.
Meditation under Stars.
Melampus.
Modern Love.
Nature and Life.
Orchard and the Heath, The.
Promise in Disturbance, The. *Fr.* Modern Love.
Seed-Time.
Should Thy Love Die.
Song in the Songless.
Star Sirius, The.
Thrush in February, The.
Thus piteously Love closed what he begat. *Fr.* Modern Love.
We saw the swallows gathering in the sky. *Fr.* Modern Love.
Wind on the Lyre.
Winter Heavens.
Woods of Westermain, The.
"MEREDITH, OWEN (Edward Robert Bulwer-Lytton, 1st Earl of Lytton).
Changes.

Going Back Again.
Twins.
MEREDITH, WILLIAM. On Falling Asleep to Birdsong.
To a Western Bard Still a Whoop and a Holler Away from English Poetry.
MEREDITH, WILLIAM TUCKEY. Farragut.
MERIVALE, JOHN HERMAN. Not to Die, *tr.*
MERRIAM, EVE. Ballad of the Double Bed.
Block Party.
Direct Song.
Love-making, The: His and Hers.
Moment before Conception, The.
Monogramania.
MERRICK, KATHLEEN. Heritage.
MERRILL, BOB. Promise Me a Rose.
MERRILL, JAMES. Country of a Thousand Years of Peace, The.
Drowning Poet, The.
Hotel de l'Univers et Portugal.
Kite Poem.
Laboratory Poem.
Mirror.
Renewal, A.
Some Negatives: X. at the Chateau.
Timepiece, A.
View of the Burning, A.
Voices from the Other World.
MERRYMAN, MILDRED PLEW (Mrs. Carl Merryman; formerly Mildred Plew Meigs). Johnny Fife and Johnny's Wife.
Organ Grinders' Garden, The.
Pirate Don Durk of Dowdes, The.
MERTON, THOMAS. Baroque Gravure, A.
Duns Scotus.
Elegy for the Monastery Barn.
Practical Program for Monks, A.
St. Malachy.
Seneca.
Stranger.
To a Severe Nun.
Trappist Abbey, The: Matins.
MERWIN, WILLIAM STANLEY. Air.
Annunciation, The.
At Dawn the Virgin Is Born, *tr.*
Backwater Pond: The Canoeists.
Blind Girl.
Bones, The.
By Day and by Night.
Defeated, The.
Despair.
Dictum: For a Masque of Deluge.
Drunk in the Furnace, The.
For Now.
Foreign Summer.
Grandmother and Grandson.
Ice and Fires Contend with My Child, *tr.*
Iceberg, The.
In the Gorge.
In the Night Fields.
Isaiah of Souillac, The.
John Otto.
Lemuel's Blessing.
Lost Month.
Mariners' Carol.
Native, The.
Noah's Raven.
On the Subject of Poetry.
Plea for a Captive.
Poem, The.
Reunion.
Second Sight.
Separation.
Strange Shepherd, Set My Bellwether Free, *tr.*
Thorn Leaves in March.
Walk-up.
When I Came from Colchis.
Where Are You Going, Maiden? *tr.*
White Goat, White Ram.
Witnesses.
METASTASIO, PIETRO. Age of Gold.
MEUDT, EDNA. Part-Time Tenant.
MEUN, JEAN DE, *and* GUILLAUME DE LORRIS. *See* GUILLAUME DE LORRIS *and* JEAN DE MEUN.
MEW, CHARLOTTE. Cenotaph, The.
Farmer's Bride, The.
Old Shepherd's Prayer.

Sea Love.
Trees Are Down, The.
MEYER, BERTHA. God's Eye Is on the Sparrow.
MEYER, CONRAD FERDINAND. Abundance.
After a Dutch Master.
At the Gate of Heaven.
Chorus of the Dead, The.
Feet in the Fire, The.
In the Sistina.
Now You Shall Speak.
Oars Pulled Up.
Roman Fountain, The.
Song of the Sea, The.
Two Sails.
MEYER, LUCY R. He Was Not Willing.
MEYERSTEIN, EDWARD HARRY WILLIAM. Chameleon, The.
MEYNELL, ALICE (Mrs. Wilfrid Meynell). Advent Meditation.
I Am the Way.
Newer Vainglory, The.
Or His Bestowals There.
Rainy Summer, The.
Renouncement.
Unto Us a Son Is Given.
MEZEY, ROBERT. After Hours.
Against Seasons.
Carmina.
Coffee-House Lecture, A.
Corinna in Vendome, *tr.*
Funeral Home, The.
In Defense of Felons.
Lovemaker, The.
No Country You Remember.
Street Scene.
To Philip Levine, on the Day of Atonement.
Visit, The.
Wandering Jew, The.
You Could Say.
MEZQUIDA, ANNA BLAKE. Hope.
MICHAUX, HENRI. After the Accident.
Tomorrow Is Not Yet.
Wind, The.
MICHELANGELO BUONARROTI. Artist and His Work, The.
Beauty and the Artist.
Danger of loss eternal.
Dante.
David.
Heart-Coldness.
If my rough hammer gives a human face.
I know not if from uncreated spheres.
Just as an empty form.
Just as a silkworm with much selfless pain.
Light and Darkness.
Love Is a Refiner's Fire.
Love Lifts to God.
Lover and the Sculptor, The.
Love's Justification.
Madrigal: "Ravished by all that to the eyes is fair."
On Rome in the Pontificate of Julius II.
On the Brink of Death.
On the Painting of the Sistine Chapel.
Out of a living stone.
Prayer for Purification, A.
Simply because the sun does not embrace.
To Night.
To the Marchesana of Pescara.
To the Supreme Being.
To Vittoria Colonna.
When contracting, the lash seems not to cause.
Why should it come so seldom, why so late.
You have a face that's sweeter than grape mash.
MICHIE, JAMES. Closing Time.
Dooley Is a Traitor.
Three Dreams.
MICKLE, WILLIAM JULIUS. Sailor's Wife, The.
MIDDLETON, CHRISTOPHER. Abasis. *Fr.* Herman Moon's Hourbook.
Alba after Six Years.
Ant Sun, The. *Fr.* Herman Moon's Hourbook.

Forenoon, The. *Fr.* Herman Moon's Hourbook.
Herman Moon's Hourbook, *sels.*
Male Torso.
News from Norwood.
Ode on Contemplating Clapham Junction. *Fr.* Herman Moon's Hourbook.
Pointed Boots. *Fr.* Herman Moon's Hourbook.
Thinking of Hölderlin.
Thousand Things, The.
Waterloo Bridge. *Fr.* Herman Moon's Hourbook.
For translations from German, see MGP; PoP1.
MIDDLETON, THOMAS. Blurt, Master Constable, *sel.*
MIDDLETON, THOMAS (*at.*), *and* JOHN FLETCHER. *See* FLETCHER, JOHN, *and* (*at.*) THOMAS MIDDLETON.
MILES, JOSEPHINE. Frontier.
In Identity.
Reason.
View.
MILLAY, EDNA ST. VINCENT ("Nancy Boyd"). Afternoon on a Hill.
And You as Well Must Die, Beloved Dust.
Buck in the Snow, The.
City Trees.
Counting-out Rhyme.
Dirge without Music.
Elegy: "Let them bury your big eyes."
Euclid Alone.
Figs from Thistles.
First Fig.
God's World.
Lament: "Listen, children:/ Your father is dead."
Look, Edwin!
Modern Declaration.
Never May the Fruit Be Plucked.
Oh, Think Not I Am Faithful to a Vow!
Pastoral: "If it were only still!"
Poet and His Book, The.
Portrait by a Neighbor.
Recuerdo.
Return, The.
Sonnet XLI: "I, being born a woman and distressed."
Sonnet XXX: "Love is not all: it is not meat nor drink."
Sonnet XXVIII: "When we are old and these rejoicing veins."
Spring and the Fall, The.
Time Does Not Bring Relief.
Travel.
Unexplorer, The.
MILLER, ALICE DUER. English Are Frosty, The. *Fr.* The White Cliffs.
I Have Loved England. *Fr.* The White Cliffs.
White Cliffs, The, *sels.*
MILLER, JOAQUIN (Cincinnatus Heine [*or* Hiner] Miller). Alaska.
Byron, *sel.*
Columbus.
Crossing the Plains.
Cuba Libre.
Defence of the Alamo, The.
Exodus for Oregon.
In Men Whom Men Condemn as Ill. *Fr.* Byron.
Kit Carson's Ride.
MILLER, MARY BRITTON. Cat.
Victory.
Waves.
MILLER, MAY. Last Warehouse, The.
MILLER, MERLIN G. Just to Be Glad.
MILLER, OLIVE BEAUPRÉ. Circus Parade, The.
MILLER, VASSAR. Adam's Footprint.
At a Child's Baptism.
Autumnal Spring Song.
Ballad of the Unmiraculous Miracle.
Bout with Burning.
Christmas Mourning.
Faintly and from Far Away.
Fantasy on the Resurrection.
Final Hunger, The.
For Instruction.
From an Old Maid.

MILLER, VASSAR (*continued*)
Fulfillment.
How Far?
In Consolation.
Joyful Prophecy.
Lesson in Detachment, A.
Love's Eschatology.
New Icarus, The.
No Return.
One Thing Needful, The.
Protest.
Quarry, The.
Receiving Communion.
Resolution, The.
Return.
Song for a Marriage.
Though He Slay Me.
Tree of Silence, The.
Whooping Crane, The.
Without Ceremony.
Worshiper, The.
MILLER, WILLIAM. Spring, *sel.*
MILLIKIN, RICHARD ALFRED. Groves of Blarney, The.
MILNE, ALAN ALEXANDER. Binker.
Christening, The.
End, The.
Engineer, The.
Forgiven.
Furry Bear.
Good Little Girl, The.
Growing Up.
Happiness.
Hoppity.
If I Were King.
In the Fashion.
Politeness.
Puppy and I.
Rice Pudding.
Thought, A.
Three Foxes, The.
When I Was One.
MILTON, JOHN. Another on the University Carrier.
Arcades, *sel.*
At a Solemn Music [or Musick].
At a Vacation Exercise in the College, Part Latin, Part English, *sel.*
Comus, *sels.*
Cromwell, Our Chief of Men.
Echo. *Fr.* Comus.
Eden. *Fr.* Paradise Lost.
Epitaph on the Marchioness of Winchester, An.
Eve's Speech to Adam. *Fr.* Paradise Lost.
Eve's Temptation and Fall. *Fr.* Paradise Lost.
Exit from Eden. *Fr.* Paradise Lost.
Fallen Angels. *Fr.* Paradise Lost.
Hail, Holy Light. *Fr.* Paradise Lost.
How Soon Hath Time [the Subtle Thief of Youth].
Il Penseroso.
Invocation: "Of man's first disobedience, and the fruit." *Fr.* Paradise Lost.
Lady, That in the Prime of Earliest Youth.
L'Allegro.
Lawrence, of Virtuous Father Virtuous Son.
Let Us with a Gladsome Mind.
Lycidas.
Methought I Saw My Late Espoused Saint.
Mirth, with Thee I Mean to Live. *Fr.* L'Allegro.
Nymphs and Shepherds [Dance No More]. *Fr.* Arcades.
O Nightingale, That on Yon Bloomy Spray.
Ode on the Morning of Christ's Nativity.
On Being Arrived at the Age of Twenty-three.
On His Blindness.
On His Deceased Wife.
On His Having Arrived at the Age of Twenty-three.
On Shakespeare.
On the Late Massacre in Piedmont [or Piemont].
On the Morning of Christs Nativity.

On the New Forcers of Conscience under the Long Parliament.
On the University Carrier.
On Time.
Paradise Lost, *sels.*
Paradise Regained.
Passion, The.
Sabrina Fair. *Fr.* Comus.
Samson Agonistes.
Satan's Metamorphosis. *Fr.* Paradise Lost.
Satan's Speech. *Fr.* Paradise Lost.
Song: On May Morning.
Sonnet VII: "How soon hath Time the subtle thief of youth."
Sonnet: "Methought I saw my late espoused saint."
Sonnet: "When I consider how my light is spent."
Sweet Echo, Sweetest Nymph. *Fr.* Comus.
Thus Eve to Adam. *Fr.* Paradise Lost.
To a Girl, *tr.*
To Cyriack Skinner ("Cyriack, whose grandsire, on the royal bench").
To [Mr.] Cyriack Skinner, upon His Blindness.
To Mr. Cyriac Skinner ("Cyriac, this three years' day").
To Mr. Lawrence.
To the Lady Margaret Ley.
To the Nightingale.
Upon the Circumcision.
War in Heaven. *Fr.* Paradise Lost.
What Though the Field Be Lost? *Fr.* Paradise Lost.
When Faith and Love Which Parted from Thee Never.
When I Consider How My Light Is Spent.
When the Assault Was Intended to the City.
With Thee Conversing. *Fr.* Paradise Lost.
MIMNERMUS. No Joy without Love.
MINDE, HENRY S. Thou Who Taught the Thronging People.
MIR, MARJORIE. Four Days in November.
MISH, CHARLOTTE. Stray Dog.
MISTRAL, FRÉDÉRIC. Cocooning, The.
Mares of the Camargue, The. *Fr.* Mirèio.
Mirèio, *sel.*
"MISTRAL, GABRIELA" (Lucila Godoy Alcayaga). Absence.
Autumn.
Ballad: "He went by with another."
Close to Me.
Earthen Jugs.
Intimate.
Poem of the Son.
Rocking.
Rose, The.
Serene Words.
Stranger, The.
To the Children.
Where Shall We Dance?
MITCHELL, LUCY SPRAGUE. House of the Mouse, The.
It Is Raining.
My Bed.
MITCHELL, RUTH COMFORT (Mrs. William Sanborn Young). Travel Bureau, The.
MITSUKUNI. Lotus Leaves.
MOFFIT, JOHN. Closing Cadence.
Presence.
MOHR, JOSEPH. Silent Night.
MOLL, ERNEST G. Eagles over the Lambing Paddock.
Gnarled Riverina Gum-Tree, A.
MOMADAY, N. SCOTT. Earth and I Gave You Turquoise.
MOMENT, JOHN J. Best Treasure, The.
MONK OF MONTAUDON [or MONTAUDUN]. I Like Gayety and Horsing Around.
I Much Dislike, I Dare Avow It.
MONKHOUSE, COSMO. Limerick: "There was a young lady of Niger," *at.*
There Was a Young Lady of Niger, *at.*
MONOD, THEODORE. Christ Alone.

MONRO, HAROLD. At Home, Alone with the Dog.
Carrion. *Fr.* Youth in Arms.
Overheard on a Saltmarsh.
Youth in Arms, *sel.*
MONROE, HARRIET. Lincoln.
Love Song.
Nancy Hanks.
Romney, The.
MONT, POL DE. Evening Landscape.
MONTALE, EUGENIO. Ark, The.
Customs-House, The.
Day and Night.
Dora Markus.
Eastbourne.
Eel, The.
Falsetto.
News from Amiata.
Under the Rain.
MONTAUSIER, CHARLES DE SAINTE-MAURE, DUC DE. Guirlande de Julie, *sels.*
Madrigal: "Receive, oh Nymph adorable." *Fr.* Guirlande de Julie.
Narcisse, Le. *Fr.* Guirlande de Julie.
MONTGOMERY, CARRIE JUDD. Discerning the Lord's Body.
MONTGOMERY, JAMES. What Is Prayer?
MONTROSS [or MONTROSE], PERCY. Oh My Darling Clementine.
MOODIE, SUSANNA STRICKLAND (Mrs. John Wedderburn Dunbar Moodie). Canadian Herd-Boy, The.
MOODY, MINNIE HITE. Say This of Horses.
MOODY, WILLIAM VAUGHN. Bracelet of Grass, The.
Faded Pictures.
Gloucester Moors.
Menagerie, The.
Ode in Time of Hesitation, An.
On a Soldier Fallen in the Philippines.
Thammuz.
MOORE, CLEMENT CLARKE. Visit from St. Nicholas, A.
MOORE, EDWARD. Fable: Poet and His Patron, The.
Hymn to Poverty, A.
Nun, The.
Song: "For a shape, and a bloom, and an air, and a mien."
MOORE, GEORGE. Rondo: "Did I love thee? I only did desire."
Sonnet: "Idly she yawned, and threw her heavy hair."
MOORE, JOHN TRAVERS. Last Flower, The.
MOORE, JULIA A. Ashtabula Disaster, The.
MOORE, MARIANNE. Armour's Undermining Modesty.
Carriage from Sweden, A.
Face, A.
Four Quartz Crystal Clocks.
Grave, A.
His Shield.
I May, I Might, I Must.
In Distrust of Merits.
Melchior Vulpius.
Mind Is an Enchanting Thing, The.
No Swan So Fine.
O to Be a Dragon.
Pangolin, The.
Past Is the Present, The.
Poetry.
Rigorists.
Silence.
Sojourn in the Whale.
Steeple-Jack, The.
Student, The.
Talisman, A.
To a Chameleon.
To a Steam Roller.
Tom Fool at Jamaica.
What Are Years?
MOORE, MAURICE. Easter, Day of Christ Eternal.
MOORE, MERRILL. Domestic: Climax.
Undergraduate.
MOORE, NICHOLAS. Fred Apollus at Fava's.
Incidents in Playfair House.
Little Girl, The.
Love.

MOORE, THOMAS. Abnegation, *tr.*
At the Mid Hour of Night.
Believe Me, If All Those Endearing Young Charms.
Design for a Bowl, *tr.*
Did Not.
Echo[es].
Epitaph on Robert Southey.
Go Where Glory Waits Thee.
Golden Hour, The. *Fr.* Lalla Rookh.
Harp That Once through Tara's Halls, The.
I Saw from the Beach.
Journey Onwards, The.
Kiss, The.
Lalla Rookh, *sels.*
Light of Other Days, The.
Minstrel Boy, The.
Oh! Breathe Not His Name.
Odes to Nea, *sels.*
Oft in the Stilly Night.
On My Sweet Mother, *tr.*
Peri's Lament for Hinda, The. *Fr.* Lalla Rookh.
Pro Patria Mori.
She Is Far from the Land.
Sweet Innisfallen.
Take Back the Virgin Page.
Thee, Thee, Only Thee.
This Life Is All Chequer'd with Pleasures and Woes.
Time I've Lost in Wooing, The.
'Tis the Last Rose of Summer.
To ——: "When I loved you, I can't but allow."
What's My Thought Like?
Young May Moon, The.
MOORE, TOM INGLIS. Comrade in Arms.
Star Drill.
MORAES, DOM. Final Word, The.
Glitter of Pebbles.
Girl.
Lullaby: "With lights for eyes, our city turns."
Queen.
Song: "Gross sun squats above, The."
MORDAUNT, THOMAS OSBERT. Verses Written during the War, 1756–1763.
MORDEN, PHYLLIS B. Godmother.
MORE, HANNAH. Book, A.
MORE, HENRY. Eternal Life.
MORE, PAUL ELMER. Love in Moonlight, *tr.*
Peace, *tr.*
MORE, SIR THOMAS (Saint Thomas More). Age. *Fr.* The Pageants of Thomas More.
Childhood. *Fr.* The Pageants of Thomas More.
Davy, the Dicer.
Death. *Fr.* The Pageants of Thomas More.
Eleventh Property, The. *Fr.* The Twelve Properties or Conditions of a Lover.
Eternal Reward, Eternal Pain. *Fr.* The Twelve Weapons of Spiritual Battle.
Eternity. *Fr.* The Pageants of Thomas More.
Fame. *Fr.* The Pageants of Thomas More.
First Property, The. *Fr.* The Twelve Properties or Conditions of a Lover.
Manhood. *Fr.* The Pageants of Thomas More.
Pageants of Thomas More, The.
Peace of a Good Mind, The. *Fr.* The Twelve Weapons of Spiritual Battle.
Seventh Property, The. *Fr.* The Twelve Properties or Conditions of a Lover.
This Life a Dream and Shadow. *Fr.* The Twelve Weapons of Spiritual Battle.
Thomas More to Them That Seek Fortune.
Time. *Fr.* The Pageants of Thomas More.
Twelve Properties or Conditions of a Lover, The, *sels.*
Twelve Weapons of Spiritual Battle, The, *sels.*

Venus and Cupide. *Fr.* The Pageants of Thomas More.
MORELAND, JOHN RICHARD. His Hands.
MORGAN, ANGELA. Choice.
God Does Do Such Wonderful Things.
Thanksgiving.
To-Day.
Whole Year Christmas, The.
Work; a Song of Triumph.
MORGAN, EDWIN. Fain Would I Live in Safest Freedom, *tr.*
For translations from Italian, see AnML.
For translations from Spanish, see AnML; AnSP.
"MORGAN, EMANUEL." *See* BYNNER, WITTER.
MORGENSTERN, CHRISTIAN. Ant-ology.
Dreamer, The.
Economical Poet, The.
Glasses, The.
Impossible Fact, The.
L'Art pour l'Art.
Palmström.
Scholar and Goethe, The.
She-Goat and Slow-Worm.
To Nietzsche.
MÖRIKE [*or* MÖRICKE], EDUARD FRIE-DRICH. Fair Rohtraut.
Gardener, The.
Hour before the Day, An.
In Spring.
Seclusion.
Think of It, My Soul.
Wind's Song, The.
MORITAKE, ARAKIDA. Haiku: "Falling flower, The."
MORLEY, CHRISTOPHER. Animal Crackers.
Crib, The.
He Comforts Himself. *Fr.* Translations from the Chinese.
Human Instinct, A. *Fr.* Translations from the Chinese.
Man with the Rake, The. *Fr.* Translations from the Chinese.
Old Swimmer, The.
Secret Laughter.
Secret Thoughts. *Fr.* Translations from the Chinese.
Six Weeks Old.
Smells.
To a Child.
To a Post-Office Inkwell.
Translations from the Chinese, *sels.*
Washing the Dishes.
Where More Is Meant.
MORNINGSTAR, MARGARET. Teacher Sees a Boy, The.
MORRIS, ALICE S. Mrs. Santa Claus' Christmas Present.
MORRIS, FRANCIS ST. VINCENT. Eleventh Hour, The.
MORRIS, GEORGE POPE. Main-Truck, The; or, A Leap for Life.
Woodman, Spare That Tree.
MORRIS, JOHN. Letter from a Friend, A.
Shh! The Professor Is Sleeping.
MORRIS, J. W. What I Think of Hiawatha.
MORRIS, WILLIAM. Apology, An: "Of Heaven or Hell I have no power to sing." *Fr.* The Earthly Paradise.
Defence of Guenevere, The.
Earthly Paradise, The, *sels.*
Garden by the Sea, A.
Golden Wings.
Haystack in the Floods, The.
In Prison.
Inscription for an Old Bed.
Life and Death of Jason, The, *sel.*
Love Is Enough.
Message of the March Wind, The.
Near Avalon.
October. *Fr.* The Earthly Paradise.
Pomona.
Road of Life, The. *Fr.* The Earthly Paradise.
Sailing of the *Sword,* The.
Shameful Death.
Song of the Argonauts. *Fr.* The Life and Death of Jason.
Summer Dawn.

Two Red Roses across the Moon.
MORRISON, ANTHONY MICHAEL. Tower Hill Memorial.
MORRISON, MARGARET. I'm the Police Cop Man, I Am.
MORRISSETT, ANN. Here I Am.
MORTON, DAVID. Epitaph in Sirmio.
MOSCHUS. Landsman, The.
MOSEN, JULIUS. Dreaming Lake, The.
MOSER, MRS. J. F. Would I Be Called a Christian?
MOSS, HOWARD. Gift to Be Simple, The.
Going to Sleep in the Country.
Horror Movie.
Local Places.
Movies for the Home.
Problem in Morals, A.
Rain.
Traction.
Underwood.
Water Island.
MOTTEUX, PETER ANTHONY [*or* PIERRE ANTOINE]. Man Is for Woman Made.
MOUNTZOURES, H. L. Three Nights of Mourning: John F. Kennedy.
MUDIE, IAN. They'll Tell You about Me.
Wilderness Theme.
MUIR, EDWIN. Abraham.
Absent, The.
Animals, The.
Antichrist.
Ballad of the Flood.
Brothers, The.
Castle, The.
Child Dying, The.
Church, The.
Confirmation, The.
Day, The.
Enchanted Knight, The.
Face, The.
For Ann Scott-Moncrieff.
Good Man in Hell, The.
Horses, The.
Incarnate One, The.
Island, The.
Killing, The.
Labyrinth, The.
Lost and Found.
Merlin.
Mythical Journey, The.
Old Gods, The.
One Foot in Eden.
Son, The.
Succession, The.
Three Mirrors, The.
Way, The.
"MUKERJI, RANA." Spring Night.
MULGAN, ALAN. Golden Wedding, *sel.*
MÜLLER, WILHELM. At the Fountain by the Gateway.
Journeyman's Song, The.
MULLINS, HELENE (Helen Gallagher Mullins). Even in the Darkness.
MUNDAY, ANTHONY. Beauty Sat Bathing. *Fr.* Primaleon of Greece.
Colin. *Fr.* Primaleon of Greece.
Fidele and Fortunio, *sel.*
Fidele's Song. *Fr.* Fidele and Fortunio.
Primaleon of Greece, *sel.*
MUNDAY, ANTHONY, *and* HENRY CHET-TLE. Death of Robert, Earl of Huntington, *sel.*
Dirge: "Weep, weep, ye woodmen, wail." *Fr.* Death of Robert, Earl of Huntington.
Dirge for Robin Hood. *Fr.* Death of Robert, Earl of Huntingdon.
Robin Hood's Funeral. *Fr.* Death of Robert, Earl of Huntingdon.
MÜNSTERBERG, MARGARETE. Theme, *tr.*
MURANO, SHIRO. Pole Vault.
MURCHISON, LEE. In the Beginning Was the.
Sprinters, The.
MURPHY, JAMES M. Flagmakers, The.
MURPHY, R. D. Back Lane.
MURRAY, GILBERT. *For translations from Greek, see* SiGo.
MURRAY, PAULI. Dark Testament.
Without Name.

MURRAY, ROBERT FULLER. City of Gulf, The.
Man from Inversnaid, The.
MUSET, COLIN. See COLIN MUSET.
"MUSTAFA." See JOHNSON, DON ALLEN.
MU'TAMID, KING OF SEVILLE. Thy Garden.
MYERS, FREDERIC WILLIAM HENRY. Saint Paul, sels.
St. Paul Speaks. Fr. Saint Paul.
Saints, The (St. Paul). Fr. Saint Paul.
MYERS, NEIL. Kennedy Poem.

N

"N., A. M." God's Treasure.
NABOKOV, VLADIMIR. Ode to a Model.
NAIDU, SAROJINI. Coromandel Fishers, The.
Dirge: "What longer need hath she of loveliness."
In the Bazaars of Hyderabad.
NAIRNE, CAROLINA OLIPHANT, BARONESS. Caller Herrin'.
Land o' the Leal, The.
NAKATSUKASA. Shui Shu, sel.
NALÉ ROXLO, CONRADO. Unforeseen, The.
NASH, OGDEN. Adventures of Isabel.
Ant, The.
Big Tent under the Roof, The.
Boy Who Laughed at Santa Claus, The.
Camel, The.
Carol for Children, A.
Celery.
Decline and Fall of a Roman Umpire.
Dr. Fell and Points West.
Drink with Something in It, A.
Eel, The.
Firefly, The.
Fragonard.
Guppy, The.
Hippopotamus, The.
Hunter, The.
I Never Even Suggested It.
Kindly Unhitch That Star, Buddy.
Lady Thinks She Is Thirty, A.
Lama, The.
Lather as You Go.
Line-up for Yesterday.
Octopus, The.
Old Men.
One, Two, Buckle My Shoe.
Panther, The.
Parsnip, The.
Peekaboo, I Almost See You.
Perfect Husband, The.
Porpoise, The.
Private Dining Room, The.
Purist, The.
Rhinoceros, The.
Sea-Gull, The.
Sniffle, The.
So That's Who I Remind Me Of.
Song of the Open Road.
Tale of Custard the Dragon [or the Custard Dragon], The.
Termite, The.
This Is Going to Hurt Just a Little Bit.
Turkey, The.
Very like a Whale.
What's the Use.
NASHE, THOMAS. Adieu, Farewell, Earth's Bliss. Fr. Summer's Last Will and Testament.
Autumn Hath All the Summer's Fruitful Treasure. Fr. Summer's Last Will and Testament.
In Time of Plague [or Pestilence], 1593. Fr. Summer's Last Will and Testament.
Litany in Time of Plague, A. Fr. Summer's Last Will and Testament.
Song: "Adieu, farewell earth's bliss." Fr. Summer's Last Will and Testament.

Spring. Fr. Summer's Last Will and Testament.
Summer's Last Will and Testament, sels.
NASHE, THOMAS, and CHRISTOPHER MARLOWE. See MARLOWE, CHRISTOPHER, and THOMAS NASHE.
NATHAN, LEONARD E. Diver, The.
NATHAN, ROBERT. Dunkirk.
Epitaph: "Say he was sad, for there was none to love him."
When in the Crowd I Suddenly Behold.
NAUDÉ, ADÈLE. Return.
NEALE, JOHN MASON. Good King Wenceslas, tr.
NEIDHART VON REUENTAL. And If Some Place I Have a Home.
I Never Saw the Field.
Season's Here, The!
NEILL, H. S. Second Sight.
NEILSON, JOHN SHAW. Beauty Imposes.
Break of Day.
Cool, Cool Country, The.
Crane Is My Neighbour, The.
Love's Coming.
May.
Orange Tree, The.
Poor Can Feed the Birds, The.
Song Be Delicate.
Strawberries in November.
Sundowner, The.
'Tis the White Plum Tree.
To a Blue Flower.
To a School-Girl.
Walking of the Moon-Woman, The.
NEISSE, MAX HERRMANN-. See HERRMANN-NEISSE, MAX.
NEMEROV, HOWARD. Book of Kells, The.
Boom!
Brainstorm.
De Anima.
Debate with the Rabbi.
Dial Tone, The.
Dialogue.
Elegy for a Nature Poet.
Goose Fish, The.
History of a Literary Movement.
Human Things.
Lion & Honeycomb.
Moment.
Mousemeal.
Praising the Poets of That Country.
Redeployment.
Runes.
Spell before Winter, A.
Storm Windows.
Young Woman.
"NERUDA, PABLO" (Neftalí Ricardo Reyes Basualto). Lone Gentleman.
Materia Nupcial.
NESBIT, EDITH (Edith Nesbit Bland). Summer Song.
NESBIT, WILBUR DICK. Friend or Two, A.
NEWBOLT, SIR HENRY. Drake's Drum.
He Fell among Thieves.
Messmates.
NEWCASTLE, MARGARET CAVENDISH, DUCHESS OF. My Cabinets Are Oyster-Shells.
NEWCASTLE, WILLIAM CAVENDISH, DUKE OF. Love Play.
Love's Epitaph.
NEWMAN, JOHN HENRY, CARDINAL. Lead, Kindly Light.
Pillar of the Cloud, The.
Refrigerium.
Until the Shadows Lengthen.
NEWMAN, JOSEPH S. Baby Toodles.
NEWSOME, MARY EFFIE LEE. Morning Light the Dew-Drier.
NEWTON, JOHN. In Sweet Communion.
Name of Jesus, The.
Thou Art Coming to a King.
NICARCHUS. Requirements: "Not for me a giantess."
NICHOLL, LOUISE TOWNSEND. Hymn: "Words of hymns abruptly plod, The."
Marigold.
NICHOLS, JOHN. Oh, California.
NICHOLS, ROBERT. Battery Moving Up to a New Position from Rest Camp: Dawn.

By the Wood.
Casualty.
Day's March, The.
Harlot's Catch.
Sprig of Lime, The.
Thanksgiving.
NICHOLSON, MARTHA SNELL. His Plan for Me.
Home.
NICHOLSON, NORMAN. Burning Bush, The.
For All Sorts and Conditions.
For the Bicentenary of Isaac Watts.
Old Man Sat in a Waterfall, An.
Poem for Epiphany.
Thomas Gray in Patterdale.
Weather Ear.
NICHOLSON, REYNOLD ALLEYNE. Unseen Power, The, tr.
NICOL, ABIOSEH. Continent That Lies within Us, The.
NICOLAS, VIDAL DE. Wish, A.
NICOLSON, ADELA FLORENCE CORY. See "HOPE, LAURENCE."
NIETZSCHE, FRIEDRICH WILHELM. Ecce Homo.
Loneliest One, The.
Sage Speaks, The.
Song of Rapture.
Star Morals.
Sun Sinks, The.
To Goethe.
To the Mistral.
To the Unknown God.
Undaunted.
Vademecum-Vadetecum.
Venice.
NIMS, JOHN FREDERICK. Midwest.
Necromancers, The.
Spiritual Canticle, tr.
NOEL, HENRY. Gaze Not on Swans.
NOEL, THOMAS. Old Winter.
NOLL, BINK. Abraham's Madness.
Afternoon for a Small Boy.
Air Tunnel, Monticello.
"All My Pretty Ones? Did You Say All?"
For Jane Kane, Whom We Knew in Our Young Marriages.
Lunch on Omaha Beach.
Picador Bit, The.
Rented Garden, The.
Song in a Winter Night.
NORRIS, LESLIE. Ballad of Billy Rose, The.
NORSE, HAROLD. Confessor, The, tr.
NORTH, JESSICA NELSON (Mrs. Reed Inness MacDonald). Balloon Man.
NORTON, CAROLINE ELIZABETH SARAH SHERIDAN (afterwards Lady Stirling-Maxwell). I Do Not Love Thee.
NOSS, MURRAY. Hiroshima.
"NOVALIS" (Georg Friedrich Philipp von Hardenberg). Hymns to the Night, sel.
Oh Blessed Mary.
NOWLAN, ALDEN A. Aunt Jane.
NOYES, ALFRED. Barrel-Organ, The.
Betsy Jane's Sixth Birthday.
Blinded Soldier to His Love, The.
Butterflies.
Daddy Fell into the Pond.
Forty Singing Seamen.
Highwayman, The.
Hospital, A.
Prayer, A: "Angels, where you soar."
River of Stars, The.
Saint George and the Dragon.
Skunk, The.
Victory Dance, A.
NUTTER, C. D. On Time with God.

O

OBATA and ISHII. See ISHII and OBATA.
"O'BRIEN, JOHN." See HARTIGAN, PATRICK JOSEPH.
OCCLEVE, THOMAS. See HOCCLEVE, THOMAS.

O'CONNELL, RICHARD. Nekros.
O'CONNOR, FRANK (*originally* Michael O'Donovan). Autumn, *tr.*
Blackbird by Belfast Lough, The, *tr.*
Growing Old, *tr.*
Hermit's Song, The, *tr.*
Kilcash, *tr.*
Prayer for the Speedy End of Three Great Misfortunes, *tr.*
Retirement, *tr.*
O'CONOR, NORREYS JEPHSON. In the Moonlight.
O'CURRY, EUGENE. Do You Remember That Night? *tr.*
ODEN, GLORIA CATHERINE. ". . . As When Emotion Too Far Exceeds Its Cause."
Carousel, The.
Map, The.
Private Letter to Brazil, A.
Review from Staten Island.
O'DOWD, BERNARD PATRICK. Alma Venus, *sel.*
Australia.
Bush, The, *sel.*
Cow, The.
Young Democracy, *sel.*
O'FAOLÁIN, SEÁN. Summer Is Gone, *tr.*
OGILVIE, WILLIAM HENRY. Death of Ben Hall, The.
From the Gulf.
How the Fire Queen Crossed the Swamp.
OGLE, GEORGE. Epithalamium, *sel., tr.*
Wedding Night, The, *tr. Fr.* Epithalamium.
OGMUNDARSON, CORMAC. Song to Steingerd.
O'GORMAN, NED. Childhood.
O'GRADY, STANDISH. Emigrant, The, *sel.*
Old Nick in Sorel.
Winter in Lower Canada. *Fr.* The Emigrant.
OGUTSCH, EDITH. Musings of an Insomniac.
Premonition.
O'HARA, FRANK. Biotherm.
O'HARA, THEODORE. Bivouac of the Dead, The.
O'HIGGINS, MYRON. Sunset Horn.
O'KEEFE, JOHN. Amo Amas.
OKOPENKO, ANDREAS. Green Melody.
OLDHAM, JOHN. Letter from the Country to a Friend in Town, A.
Upon the Works of Ben Jonson, *sel.*
OLDMIXON, JOHN. I Lately Vowed.
OLDYS, WILLIAM. Fly, The.
On a Fly Drinking Out of His Cup.
OLIPHANT, CAROLINA. *See* NAIRNE, CAROLINA OLIPHANT, BARONESS.
OLSEN, DONALD D. Poem: "We used to float the paper boats in spring."
OLSON, CHARLES. Anecdotes of the Late War, *sel.*
Letter for Melville 1951.
Letter 27.
Librarian, The.
Lordly and Isolate Satyrs, The.
Maximus, from Dogtown, I.
River Map, The, and We're Done.
OLSON, ELDER. Crucifix.
Essay on Deity.
Ice-Skaters.
OMAR KHAYYÁM. Myself When Young Did Eagerly Frequent. *Fr.* The Rubáiyát.
Oh Thou, Who Man of Baser Earth Didst Make. *Fr.* The Rubáiyát.
Rubáiyát, The, *sels., tr. by* Fitzgerald.
ONESTO DA BOLOGNA. To Cino da Pistoia.
ONITSURA. Coolness.
Directions.
Little Valley in Spring, The.
ONO NO YOSHIKI. Kokin Shu, *sel.*
OPPENHEIM, JAMES. Memories of Whitman and Lincoln.
Night, *sel.*
OPPENHEIMER, JOEL. Cartography.
Couple, The.
For the Barbers.
Leave It to Me Blues.

Love Bit, The.
Mathematics.
Numbers, The.
Peaches, The.
17–18 April, 1961, *sel.*
Torn Nightgown, The.
ORBICCIANI, BONAGIUNTA. To Guido Guinizelli: Now That You Have Changed the Manner.
O'REILLY, DOWELL PHILIP. Sea-Grief.
O'REILLY, JOHN BOYLE. Builder's Lesson, A.
White Rose, A.
ORLÉANS, CHARLES, DUC D'. Ah, God, Who Made Her Good to See.
Alons au bois le may cueillir.
Away with You! Begone! Begone!
Come, Death—My Lady Is Dead.
Come, Let Us Taste Delight.
Confession of a Stolen Kiss.
Go Sad Complaint.
I Love Him Who Loves Me, Otherwise None.
In the Book of My Thought.
Lovers, Beware the Dart That Flies.
Mistress without Compare, A.
My Ghostly Father.
News Has Been Spread in France Concerning Me.
Pray for Peace, Oh Gentle Virgin Mary.
Rondeau: "Year his winter cloak lets fall, The."
Spring.
Summer Has Sent His Minions On.
Weather Has Laid Aside His Cloak, The.
While We Watch These Flowers Fair.
Who's There, My Heart?—It Is We, Your Eyes.
Winter, You Are Merely a Churl.
ORLOVITZ, GIL. Art of the Sonnet, *sels.*
Homage to Charles Laughton.
Index (8).
Lyric: "Angora anger who art in heaven."
Lyric: "When I am gone and green."
Masterindex: 23.
Rooster, The.
OSADEBAY, DENNIS. Young Africa's Resolve.
OSGOOD, FLORA L. Come unto Me.
Cost, The.
O'SHAUGHNESSY, ARTHUR WILLIAM EDGAR. Music Makers, The.
Silences.
Song: "I went to her who loveth me no more."
Struggle, The, *tr.*
O'SHEEL, SHAEMAS. He Whom a Dream Hath Possessed.
Lover Praises His Lady's Bright Beauty, The.
O-SHI-O. When I Think of the Hungry People.
"OSSIAN." *See* MACPHERSON, JAMES.
OSTRIKER, ALICIA. Hybris, Nemesis, One, Two, Three.
OSTROFF, ANTHONY. Intimate Party in Guadalajara, Dec. 1963.
So Long Folks, Off to the War.
"O'SULLIVAN, SEUMAS" (James Starkey). Night, *tr.*
OUSLEY, CLARENCE. When the Mint Is in the Liquor.
OVERTON, A. M. He Maketh No Mistake.
OVID (Publius Ovidius Naso). Acteon. *Fr.* Metamorphoses.
Advice to a Fair Wanton. *Fr.* Amores.
Amores, *sels.*
Apology for Loose Behavior. *Fr.* Amores.
Art of Love, The, *sels.*
Conclusion: "Now have I brought a woork too end which neither Joves fierce wrath." *Fr.* Metamorphoses.
Cyclops. *Fr.* Metamorphoses.
Daedalus. *Fr.* Metamorphoses.
Elegy to His Mistress.
Impotent Lover, The. *Fr.* Amores.
In Summer's Heat. *Fr.* Amores.
King Midas. *Fr.* Metamorphoses.
Meleager. *Fr.* Metamorphoses.

Metamorphoses, *sels.*
Philemon and Baucis. *Fr.* Metamorphoses.
Possessive Lover, The. *Fr.* Amores.
Shameful Impotence. *Fr.* Amores.
To His Mistress.
OWEN, GUY. Aunt Ella.
Conspiracy, The.
Deserted Farm.
Hawk.
It Is Not the Sea.
Old Hunter.
Old Tobey.
Solitary Horseman, The.
Split-Rail Fence.
White Stallion, The.
OWEN, WILFRED. A Terre.
Anthem for Doomed Youth.
Arms and the Boy.
Asleep.
At a Calvary near the Ancre.
Chances, The.
Conscious.
Disabled.
Dulce et Decorum Est.
End, The.
Exposure.
Futility.
Greater Love.
Hospital Barge at Cérisy.
Insensibility.
Mental Cases.
Sentry, The.
Spring Offensive.
Strange Meeting.
OWENS, ROCHELLE. Between the Karim Shahir.
Chugachimute I Love the Name.
Evolution.
Macrobius Mingling with Nature.
Man as He Shall Be.
Medieval Christ Speaks on a Spanish Sculpture of Himself.
Strawberries Mit Cream.
Woman par Excellence.
OXENHAM, JOHN (*originally* William Arthur Dunkerley). After Work.
Bide a Wee!
Christ, The.
Day, The—the Way.
In Christ.
Influence.
Judgment Day.
Life's Chequer-Board.
Little Poem of Life, The.
Little Te Deum of the Commonplace, A, *sel.*
No East or West.
Paul.
Prayer, A: "Through every minute of this day."
Props.
Sacrament of Sleep, The.
Your Place.
Ways, The.
Whirring Wheels.
OXFORD, EARL OF. *See* VERE, EDWARD DE, EARL OF OXFORD.
OZICK, CYNTHIA. Footnote to Lord Acton.

P

"P., F. B." Hierusalem, *at.*
Jerusalem, My Happy Home, *at.*
PACK, RICHARDSON. On Her Entering Her Room.
PACK, ROBERT. Adam on His Way Home.
Boat, The.
Chopping Fire-Wood.
Descending.
Don't Sit under the Apple Tree with Anyone Else but Me.
Election, The.
Father.
In a Field.
My House.
Parable.

PACK, ROBERT (continued)
Raking Leaves.
Resurrection.
Self-Portrait.
Shooting, The.
Weasel, The.
PAGE, CURTIS HIDDEN. Carpe Diem, tr.
Haiku: "I wonder in what fields to-day," tr.
Hokku: "Persimmon, The, lo!" tr.
Marie, arise, my indolent sweet saint! tr.
Seven Poems, sel., tr.
PAGE, IRENE. Jane, Do Be Careful.
PAGE, MICHAEL FITZGERALD. Sailor's Warning.
PAGE, PATRICIA K. Adolescence.
Arras.
Man with One Small Hand.
Sailor.
Stenographers, The.
Stories of Snow.
T-Bar.
PAGET, THOMAS CATESBY. To a Young Lady That Told Me My Fortune in the Cards.
Written in 1740.
PAIN, BARRY. Poets at Tea, The.
PAINE, ALBERT BIGELOW. Mis' Smith.
"PALAZZESCHI, ALDO" (Aldo Giurlani).
Ailing Fountain, The.
Ara Mara Amara.
November.
Palatine, The.
Rio Bo.
PALEN, JENNIE M. Legend of Ramapo Mountain.
PALLADAS. Vanity of Vanities.
PALMER, HERBERT EDWARD. Prayer for Rain.
PALMER, NETTIE. Mother, The.
PALMER, VANCE (Edward Vance Palmer).
Farmer Remembers the Somme, The.
PAPINI, GIOVANNI. Eighth Poem.
PARKER, DOROTHY. Actress, The.
Choice, The.
De Profundis.
Experience.
Inscription for the Ceiling of a Bedroom.
Inventory.
Men.
On Being a Woman.
Résumé.
Unfortunate Coincidence.
Very Rich Man, The.
PARKES, FRANK. African Heaven.
PARMENTIER, JEAN. Wonders of the Deep, The.
PARNELL, THOMAS. Riddle: "Upon a bed of humble clay."
Song: "When thy beauty appears."
When Thy Beauty Appears.
PARRISH, ELSIE. Some Things That Easter Brings.
PARSONS, KITTY. My Valentine.
PARTRIDGE, SYBIL F. (Sister Mary Xavier). Just for Today.
PASOLINI, PIER PAOLO. Appennine.
PASSERAT, JEAN. Love in May.
PASTERNAK, BORIS LEONIDOVICH. Caucasus, The.
Evil Days.
Fresh Paint.
Garden of Gethsemane.
Magdalene.
Star of the Nativity.
Winter Night.
PATCHEN, KENNETH. As We Are So Wonderfully Done with Each Other.
At the New Year.
Because He Liked to Be at Home.
Because My Hands Hear the Flowers Thinking.
Carts of the Wee Blind Lass, The.
Christ! Christ! Christ! That the World.
Do I Not Deal with Angels.
Easy Decision, An.
For Miriam.
Great Sled-Makers, The.
I Went to the City.
In a Crumbling.
In the Moonlight.

Land of the Never-ending Heart.
Little Green Blackbird, The.
Magical Mouse, The.
New Being, The.
Now I Went Down to the Ringside and Little Henry Armstrong Was There.
O Now the Drenched Land Wakes.
O She Is as Lovely-Often.
O When I Take My Love Out Walking.
Rest, Heart of the Tired World.
There Is Nothing False in Thee.
Twenty-third Street Runs into Heaven.
What the Grecian Earns.
Where?
PATERSON, ANDREW BARTON. Bush Christening, A.
Bushman's Song, A.
Clancy of the Overflow.
Man from Ironbark, The.
Man from Snowy River, The.
Song of the Artesian Water.
Waltzing Matilda.
PATMORE, COVENTRY KERSEY DIGHTON.
Angel in the House, The, sels.
Arbor Vitae.
Azalea, The.
Departure.
Farewell, A: "With all my will, but much against my heart."
Honor and Desert. Fr. The Angel in the House.
Love at Large. Fr. The Angel in the House.
Magna Est Veritas.
Married Lover, The. Fr. The Angel in the House.
Rainbow, The. Fr. The Angel in the House.
Revelation, The. Fr. The Angel in the House.
Saint Valentine's Day.
Toys, The.
Tribute, The. Fr. The Angel in the House.
Unthrift. Fr. The Angel in the House.
Winter.
PATRICK, SAINT. Saint Patrick's Breastplate, sel.
PATTERSON, RAYMOND. In Time of Crisis.
When I Awoke.
PATTISON, WILLIAM. On a Painted Lady.
Unfortunate Reminder, The.
Upon a Needle.
PAUL THE SILENTIARY. See PAULUS SILENTIARIUS.
PAULL, IRENE. To Bill Heikkila, American.
PAULUS SILENTIARIUS [or PAUL THE SILENTIARY]. Earth and Death, The.
PAVESE, CESARE. Earth and Death, The.
Summer.
PAYNE, JOHN. Ballad [or Ballade] of Ladies' Love, tr.
Ballade of the Fair Helm-Maker, tr.
Ballade of Villon and Fat Margot, tr.
PAYNE, JOHN HOWARD. Home, Sweet Home.
PEACOCK, THOMAS LOVE. Beech and Oak.
Crotchet Castle, sel.
Fate of a Broom, The—an Anticipation.
Friar, The. Fr. Maid Marian.
Gryll Grange, sel.
Indignation of Taliesin, The.
Love and Age. Fr. Gryll Grange.
Maid Marian, sel.
Margaret Love Peacock for Her Tombstone, 1826.
Melincourt, sel.
Misfortune of Elphin, The, sels.
Newark Abbey.
Nightmare Abbey, sels.
Priest and the Mulberry-Tree, The. Fr. Crotchet Castle.
Seamen Three. Fr. Nightmare Abbey.
Song by Mr. Cypress. Fr. Nightmare Abbey.
Song of the Four Winds. Fr. The Misfortunes of Elphin.
Sun-Dial, The. Fr. Melincourt.

War-Song of Dinas Vawr, The. Fr. The Misfortunes of Elphin.
PEARSON, JAMES LARKIN. Birthplace.
Erosion.
Fifty Acres.
God.
Here Is Wisdom.
Homer in a Garden.
I Ain't No Candidate.
Night in June, A.
October Days.
One-Talent Man.
Roommates.
Wild Garden.
PEELE, GEORGE. And Who Has Seen a Fair Alluring Face.
Bethsabe's Song. Fr. David and Bethsabe.
David and Bethsabe, sel.
Farewell to Arms, A. Fr. Polyhymnia.
Gently Dip. Fr. The Old Wives' Tale.
His Golden Locks Time Hath to Silver Turned. Fr. Polyhymnia.
Hunting of Cupid, The, sel.
Old Knight, The. Fr. Polyhymnia.
Old Wives' Tale, The, sels.
Polyhymnia, sel.
Sonnet, A: "His golden locks time hath to silver turn'd." Fr. Polyhymnia.
Voice from the Well, A. Fr. The Old Wives' Tale.
What Thing Is Love? Fr. The Hunting of Cupid.
Whenas the Rye. Fr. The Old Wives' Tale.
PEIFER, MRS. ROY L. Crucifixion.
PEIROL and DALFIN D'ALVERNHE. Dalfin, a Target for Your Bow.
PEMBROKE, WILLIAM HERBERT, EARL OF. Song: "Soules joy, now I am gone," at.
PENDLETON, CONRAD. Dark House in Autumn.
PENNA, SANDRO. Little Venetian square, The.
Passing over a high bridge.
Solitary pines along the desolate, The.
September moon over the dark valley, The.
Stealthy is my love.
PERCIVAL, JAMES GATES. Coral Grove, The.
PERETZ, ISAAC LEIB [or YITZCHOK LEIBUSH]. Two Brothers, The.
PERPETUO, BETTY. Morning Prayer, A.
PERRY, NORA. Coming of Spring, The.
PERRY, RONALD. Prologue for a Bestiary.
Shellpicker, The.
Still-Life.
"PERSE, ST.-J." (Alexis Saint-Léger Léger). Anabasis, sel.
Song: Under the Bronze Leaves. Fr. Anabasis.
PESTEL, THOMAS. Relief on Easter Eve, The.
PETERS, ANNE. Kevin O'Culihain, Zorro Tio of the Andes, Exile, sel.
PETERS, EDMUND W. Bicycalamity.
PETERSEN, DONALD. Narcissus.
Sonnet in Autumn.
True to a Dream.
PETERSEN, M. Kitchen Prayer, A.
PETERSHAM, MAUD, and MISKA PETERSHAM. Lazy Mary, Will You Get Up?
PETRARCH (Francesco Petrarca). Absorbed in One Fond Thought That Makes Me Run. Fr. Sonnets to Laura.
Alas! that liquid look, that lovely face! Fr. Sonnets to Laura.
Alas! that lovely face, the eyes that save. Fr. Sonnets to Laura.
Alone and ever weary with dark care. Fr. Sonnets to Laura.
Blest be the year, the month, the hour, the day. Fr. Sonnets to Laura.
Broken is the tall column and the green laurel. Fr. Sonnets to Laura.
Broken the column and the green bay tree. Fr. Sonnets to Laura.
Canzone: "Clear, fresh, and dulcet streams." Fr. Sonnets to Laura.

Canzone: "O my own Italy! though words are vain."
Complaint of a Lover Rebuked. *Fr.* Sonnets to Laura.
Death Cannot Sour the Sweetness of Her Face. *Fr.* Sonnets to Laura.
Eyes That Drew from Me Such Fervent Praise, The. *Fr.* Sonnets to Laura.
Eyes, the face, the limbs of heavenly mould, The. *Fr.* Sonnets to Laura.
Fair white hind with golden horns, A. *Fr.* Sonnets to Laura.
Father in Heaven, after Each Lost Day. *Fr.* Sonnets to Laura.
From Thought to Thought, from Mountain Peak to Mountain. *Fr.* Sonnets to Laura.
Go, Grieving Rimes of Mine, to That Hard Stone. *Fr.* Sonnets to Laura.
Great Is My Envy of You, Earth, in Your Greed. *Fr.* Sonnets to Laura.
I find no peace, and all my war is done. *Fr.* Sonnets to Laura.
I Find No Peace, yet Am Not Armed for War. *Fr.* Sonnets to Laura.
I mourn unhappy days that are no more. *Fr.* Sonnets to Laura.
If Life Survives These Years of Bitter Woe. *Fr.* Sonnets to Laura.
If no love is, O God, what fele I so? *Fr.* Sonnets to Laura.
It Is the Evening Hour; the Rapid Sky.
It was the day that the sun's rays. *Fr.* Sonnets to Laura.
It was the morning of that blessed day. *Fr.* Sonnets to Laura.
Life hurries on, a frantic refugee. *Fr.* Sonnets to Laura.
Long Love That in My Thought Doth Harbor, The. *Fr.* Sonnets to Laura.
Loose to the breeze her golden tresses flow'd. *Fr.* Sonnets to Laura.
Love That Doth Reign. *Fr.* Sonnets to Laura.
Love That Liveth and Reigneth in My Thought. *Fr.* Sonnets to Laura.
Love, We Attend the Vision of the Rose. *Fr.* Sonnets to Laura.
Lover Compareth His State to a Ship in Perilous Storm Tossed on the Sea, The. *Fr.* Sonnets to Laura.
Lover for Shamefastness Hideth His Desire within His Faithful Heart, The. *Fr.* Sonnets to Laura.
My Galley [Charged with Forgetfulness]. *Fr.* Sonnets to Laura.
Nightingale, The. *Fr.* Sonnets to Laura.
Nightingale that so forlornly weeps, The. *Fr.* Sonnets to Laura.
Nightingale Whose Ardent, Soft Despair, The. *Fr.* Sonnets to Laura.
Now Skies and Earth Are Stilled and Winds Are Dead. *Fr.* Sonnets to Laura.
Nowhere So Clearly Have My Inward Eyes. *Fr.* Sonnets to Laura.
O lovely little bird, I watch you fly. *Fr.* Sonnets to Laura.
Pale Beauty! and a Smile the Pallor There. *Fr.* Sonnets to Laura.
Palmer bent, with locks of silver grey, The. *Fr.* Sonnets to Laura.
Set Me Whereas the Sun [Doth Parch the Green]. *Fr.* Sonnets to Laura.
She Used to Let Her Golden Hair Fly Free. *Fr.* Sonnets to Laura.
Small Wandering Bird Who Singing Go Your Way. *Fr.* Sonnets to Laura.
Sonnets to Laura, *sels.*
Woods Are Wild and Were Not Made for Man, The. *Fr.* Sonnets to Laura.
Zephyr returns, and scatters everywhere. *Fr.* Sonnets to Laura.
PETRONIUS ARBITER (Caius Petronius Arbiter). Against Consummation.
Doing a Filthy Pleasure Is, and Short.
Good God, What a Night That Was.
Plea for Haste, A.
Plea for Postponement, A.

PFEIFFER, EMILY (Davis). Song of Winter, A.
PHELPS, ELIZABETH STUART. *See* WARD, ELIZABETH STUART PHELPS.
PHILIPS, AMBROSE. Ode to the Hon. Miss Carteret.
To [Miss] Charlotte Pulteney [in Her Mother's Arms].
To Miss Georgiana.
PHILIPS, JOHN. Splendid Shilling, The.
PHILLIPPS, THOMAS. I Love a Flower.
PICKARD, CYNTHIA. Cinderella.
PICKERING, THEODOSIA. *See* GARRISON, THEODOSIA PICKERING.
PICKTHALL, MARJORIE LOWRY CHRISTIE. Mary Tired.
Père Lalemant.
Quiet.
Resurgam.
PICOT, JAMES. Lord in the Wind, The.
Volume of Chopin, A.
PIERCE, DOROTHY MASON. John Plans.
PIERCE, EDITH LOVEJOY. Apocalypse.
On Christmas Eve.
Remember Thy Covenant.
Third Day, The.
PIEYRE DE MANDIARGUES, ANDRÉ. Big Theater, The.
Color of Cold, The.
High Place.
PILLIN, WILLIAM. Miserere.
PINDAR. Eclipse, An.
I Bless This Man. *Fr.* Nemean Odes.
Life after Death.
Nemean Odes, *sel.*
"PINDAR, PETER" (John Wolcot). Ballade: To a Fish of the Brooke.
PINKHAM, CORA M. God's Ideal Mother.
With Thee.
PINKNEY, EDWARD COOTE. Health, A.
Serenade, A: "Look out upon the stars, my love."
Song: "We break the glass, whose sacred wine."
PIONTEK, HEINZ. At Thirty Years.
Blacksmith's Daughter, The.
Dispersion, The.
PISAN, CHRISTINE DE. Ah Moon, You Shine Too Long.
Alone Am I, Alone I Wish to Be.
Alone in Martyrdom I Have Been Left.
Gods and Goddesses, Those Great, The.
I Will No Longer Serve You.
If Frequently to Mass.
If I'm in Church More Often Now.
My Heart Is Captive to Gray, Laughing Eyes.
Now Has Come the Gracious Month of May.
Sweet Lady Fair.
To Sing with Joy from Out a Sorrowing Heart.
Ye Gods! of Time I Am Weary.
You Have Done So Much by Your Great Gentleness.
PITCHER, OLIVER. Pale Blue Casket, The.
Raison d'Etre.
PITCHFORD, KENNETH. Aunt Cora.
Blizzard Ape, The.
Blues Ballad. *Fr.* Good for Nothing Man.
Death Swoops.
Good for Nothing Man, *sels.*
Jacqueline Gray. *Fr.* Good for Nothing Man.
Leviathan; a Poem in Four Movements.
Off Viareggio.
Onion Skin, The. *Fr.* Good for Nothing Man.
Pickup in Tony's Hashhouse. *Fr.* Good for Nothing Man.
Reflections on Water.
Young Buck's Sunday Blues. *Fr.* Good for Nothing Man.
PITT, MARIE ELIZABETH JOSEPHINE. Gallop of Fire, A.
PITT, WILLIAM. Sailor's Consolation, The.
PITTER, RUTH. Bat, The.
Close, Mortal Eyes.
Fishers, The.
For Sleep or Death.

Herding Lambs.
Hut, The.
If You Came.
Old Woman Speaks of the Moon, An.
Sparrow's Skull, The.
Stormcock in Elder.
Viper, The.
PLANZ, ALAN. Conjecture for a Short Mechanic.
PLATEN, AUGUST, GRAF VON. Fain Would I Live in Safest Freedom.
PLATH, SYLVIA (Mrs. Ted Hughes). Black Rook in Rainy Weather.
Blue Moles.
Colossus, The.
Ghost's Leavetaking, The.
Kindness.
Morning Song.
Mushrooms.
Snakecharmer.
PLATO. Country Music.
Inner Man, The.
Morning Star.
On the Athenian Dead at Ecbatana.
PLOMER, WILLIAM. Dorking Thigh, The.
Europa.
Flying Bum, The: 1944.
French Lisette; a Ballad of Maida Vale.
Namaqualand after Rain.
Right-of-Way, A: 1865.
Shot in the Park, A.
Ula Masondo's Dream.
PLUNKETT, EDWARD JOHN MORETON DRAX. *See* DUNSANY.
PLUNKETT, JOSEPH MARY. I See His Blood upon the Rose.
PLUTZIK, HYAM. Airman Who Flew over Shakespeare's England, The.
Importance of Poetry, or the Coming Forth from Eternity into Time, The.
Jim Desterland.
PO CHÜ-I. Cranes, The.
Dreaming That I Went with Li and Yü to Visit Yüan Chen.
Having Climbed to the Topmost Peak of the Incense-Burner Mountain.
Madly Singing in the Mountains.
Pine-Trees in the Courtyard, The.
Planting Flowers on the Eastern Embankment.
Pruning Trees.
POE, EDGAR ALLAN. Al Aaraaf.
Alone.
Annabel Lee.
Bells, The.
City in the Sea, The.
Coliseum, The.
Conqueror Worm, The.
Dream-Land.
Dream within a Dream, A.
Dreams.
Eldorado [or El Dorado].
Eulalie.
Evening Star.
For Annie.
Haunted Palace, The.
Israfel.
Lenore.
Raven, The.
Romance.
Sleeper, The.
Sonnet: Silence.
Sonnet: To Science. *Fr.* Al Aaraaf.
Tamerlane.
To Helen.
To My Mother.
To One in Paradise.
To Science. *Fr.* Al Aaraaf.
Ulalume—a Ballad.
Valley of Unrest, The.
POITIERS, GUILLAUME DE. *See* GUILLAUME DE POITIERS.
POLITE, ALLEN. Am Driven Mad.
Stopped.
POLIZIANO, ANGELO. Ballata: "I found myself one day all, all alone."
POLLARD, A. A. Secret Place, The.
POLONSKY, YAKOV PETROVICH. Cosmic Fabric, The.
POLS, EDWARD. For John Kennedy of Harvard.
POMEROY, MARNIE. April Fools' Day.

POMEROY, MARNIE (*continued*)
Ground Hog Day.
Halloween.
In Nakedness.
January 1.
Labor Day.
POMEROY, RALPH. Confession.
Corner.
In Hotels Public and Private.
In the Redwood Forest.
Islands.
Letter to Pasternak.
Patrol.
To Words.
POMEROY, WILLIAM J. Beyond Barriers.
PONGE, FRANCIS. Match, The.
Oyster, The.
Rule.
POORE, DUDLEY. Psalm: "I proclaim Thee great and wonderful," *tr.*
POOTS, TOM. Black Spirit.
POPE, ALEXANDER. Atticus. *Fr.* Epistle to Dr. Arbuthnot.
Elegy to the Memory of an Unfortunate Lady.
Engraved on the Collar of a Dog [Which I Gave to His Royal Highness].
Epigram: Engraved on the Collar of a Dog Which I Gave to His Royal Highness.
Epigram: "I am His Highness' dog at Kew."
Epistle to Dr. Arbuthnot.
Epistle to Miss Blount.
Essay on Criticism, An.
Essay on Man, An, *sels.*
Farewell to London, A.
Imitation of Chaucer.
Know Then Thyself. *Fr.* An Essay on Man.
Little Learning Is a Dangerous Thing, A. *Fr.* An Essay on Criticism.
Moral Essays, *sels.*
Ode on [*or* to] Solitude.
Of the Characters of Women, *sel. Fr.* Moral Essays.
Of the Use of Riches. *Fr.* Moral Essays.
On a Certain Lady at Court.
Poet, The.
Quiet Life, The.
Rape of the Lock, The.
Solitude.
To a Young Lady on Her Leaving Town after the Coronation.
Universal Prayer, The.
Vice. *Fr.* An Essay on Man.
Vital Spark of Heavenly Flame.
POPHAM, IVOR. Child, The.
PORTER, HAL. Adam—the First Kiss.
Lalique.
Sheep.
PORTER, PETER. Phar Lap in the Melbourne Museum.
POTEAT, EDWIN MCNEILL. Grace at Evening.
POTTER, BEATRIX. Old Woman, The.
POTTER, MIRIAM CLARK. Cake.
Present.
POUND, EZRA. A Perigord pres del muralh, *tr.*
Age of Gold, *tr.*
Air: Sentir avec ardeur, *tr.*
Airs of Pei, *sel., tr. Fr.* The Classic Anthology.
Alba. *Fr.* Langue d'Oc.
Alba, *tr. Fr.* The Classic Anthology: Songs of T'ang.
Aliter, *tr. Fr.* The Classic Anthology: Songs of Ch'en.
Ancient Music.
And Thus in Nineveh.
Ant's a Centaur, The. *Fr.* The Pisan Cantos.
Ask Not Ungainly, *tr. Fr.* Odes (*of* Horace).
Aura amara, L', *tr.*
Autet e bas, *tr.*
Ballad of the Goodly Fere.
Ballad of the Mulberry Road, A.
Ballata V: "Light do I see within my Lady's eyes," *tr.*

Baroness Mu Impeded in Her Wish to Help Famine Victims in Wei, *tr. Fr.* The Classic Anthology: Yung Wind.
By the Flat Cup, *tr. Fr.* Odes (*of* Horace).
Cantico del Sole, *tr.*
Canto I: "And then went down to the ship."
Canto II: "Hang it all, Robert Browning."
Canto XLV: "With Usura/ With usura hath no man a house of good stone."
Canzone: Donna Mi Priegha, *tr.*
Chou and the South, *sel., tr. Fr.* The Classic Anthology.
Clara.
Classic Anthology, The, *sels., tr.*
Commission.
Conversations in Courtship, *sel., tr.*
Dance Figure.
Deer Sing, *sel., tr. Fr.* The Classic Anthology.
Δωρια (Doria).
E. P. Ode pour l'Election de Son Sepulcre. *Fr.* Hugh Selwyn Mauberley.
Efficient Wife's Complaint, The, *tr. Fr.* The Classic Anthology: Airs of Pei.
Envoi (1919). *Fr.* Hugh Selwyn Mauberley.
Exile's Letter, *tr.*
For E. McC.
Fraternitas, *tr. Fr.* The Classic Anthology: Deer Sing.
Further Instructions.
Garden, The.
Garret, The.
Girl, A.
Homage to Sextus Propertius, *sels.*
Hugh Selwyn Mauberley.
I Vecchi.
Image from D'Orleans.
Immorality, An.
In a Station of the Metro.
Ité.
Lake Isle, The.
Lament of the Frontier Guard, *tr.*
Langue d'Oc, *sel.*
Lark, The, *tr.*
Liu Ch'e.
Meditatio[n].
Near Perigord.
Odes (*of* Horace), *sels., tr.*
Odi et Amo, *tr.*
Pact, A.
Pedlar, *tr. Fr.* The Classic Anthology: Wei Wind.
Pisan Cantos, The, *sel.*
Portrait d'une Femme.
Rest, The.
Return, The.
Ritratto.
River-Merchant's Wife, The; a Letter, *tr.*
Roma, *tr.*
Sans Equity and sans Poise, *tr. Fr.* The Classic Anthology: Yung Wind.
Seafarer, The, *tr.*
Sequaire, *tr.*
Sestina: Altaforte.
Shao and the South, *sels., tr. Fr.* The Classic Anthology.
Soiree.
Songs of Ch'en, *sels., tr. Fr.* The Classic Anthology.
Sonetto XXXV: To Guido Orlando, *tr.*
Sonetto VII: "Who is she that comes, makyng turn every man's eye," *tr.*
Songs of Ch'en, *sels., tr. Fr.* The Classic Anthology.
Songs of T'ang, *sel., tr. Fr.* The Classic Anthology.
Taking Leave of a Friend, *tr.*
Tea Shop, The.
Temperaments, The.
These Fought. *Fr.* Hugh Selwyn Mauberley.
This Monument Will Outlast, *tr. Fr.* Odes (*of* Horace).

Villanelle: The Psychological Hour.
Virginal, A.
War Song, A, *tr.*
White Stag, The.
Women of Trachis, *sel., tr.*
Yung Wind, *sels., tr. Fr.* The Classic Anthology.
POWELL, FREDERICK YORK. Last Words, The, *tr.*
PRAED, WINTHROP MACKWORTH. County Ball, The, *sel.*
County Member, The. *Fr.* The County Ball.
Good-Night to the Season.
Vicar, The.
PRATT, ANNA MARIA. Mortifying Mistake, A.
PRATT, EDWIN JOHN. Brébeuf and His Brethren, *sels.*
Cachalot, The, *sel.*
Dying Eagle, The.
Gathering, The. *Fr.* Towards the Last Spike.
Martyrdom of Brébeuf and Lalemant, 16 March 1649, The. *Fr.* Brébeuf and His Brethren.
Precambrian Shield, The. *Fr.* Towards the Last Spike.
Silences.
Towards the Last Spike, *sels.*
Truant, The.
PRESS, JOHN. African Christmas.
Evening at Sea, An.
Narcissus.
Womanisers.
PRESTON, KEITH. Awful Responsibility, An.
Humorist, The.
PRESTON, MARGARET JUNKIN. First Thanksgiving Day, The.
PRETI, GIROLAMO. Complains, Being Hind'red the Sight of His Nymph.
Describes the Place Where Cynthia Is Sporting Herself.
Love Once, Love Ever.
PRICE, EDITH BALLINGER. To Patricia on Her Christening Day.
PRICE, HERBERT. Buffalo, The.
PRINCE, FRANK TEMPLETON. Babiantje, The.
Question, The.
Soldiers Bathing.
PRINGLE, THOMAS. Caffer Commando, The, *sel.*
PRIOR, MATTHEW. Against Modesty in Love.
Alma; or, The Progress of the Mind, *sel.*
Better Answer, A.
Chaste Florimel.
Cupid Mistaken.
Dutch Proverb, A.
Epitaph, An: "Interr'd beneath this marble stone."
For My Own Monument.
Helen Was Just Slipped into Bed.
Jinny the Just.
Lady Who Offers Her Looking-Glass to Venus, The.
Letter to the Honorable Lady Miss Margaret-Cavendish-Holles-Harley, A.
Lover's Anger, A.
New Year's Gift to Phyllis, The.
Ode, An: "Merchant, to secure his treasure, The."
Reasonable Affliction, A.
Solomon on the Vanity of the World, *sel.*
To a Child of Quality, Five Years Old [the Author Then Forty].
To Cloe Weeping.
To the Honorable Charles Montague, Esq.
True Maid, A.
Written in the Beginning of Mezeray's History of France.
PROCTER, BRYAN WALLER. See "CORNWALL, BARRY."
PROKOSCH, FREDERIC. Chorus: "When love has passed its limits," *tr.*
Medea, *sel., tr.*
Sonnet VII: "And so one sees all living matter perish," *tr.*

Sonnet XVIII: "O kiss me yet again, O kiss me over," *tr.*
Sonnet V: "Venus, who wander clear among the skies," *tr.*
Sonnet XIV: "Yes, and as long as these poor eyes can bring," *tr.*
"PROUT, FATHER." *See* MAHONY, FRANCIS SYLVESTER.
PRUDENTIUS (Aurelius Clemens Prudentius). Cathemerinon, *sels.*
PRUDHOMME, SULLY-. *See* SULLY-PRUDHOMME.
PRYS-JONES, ARTHUR GLYN. St. Govan.
PUDNEY, JOHN. For Johnny.
Missing.
PURCELL, VICTOR WILLIAM WILLIAMS SAUNDERS. *See* "BUTTLE, MYRA."
PURCELL-BURET, THEOBALD. Diver, The.
PURNELL, IDELLA. Shot at Night, A.
PUSHKIN, ALEKSANDR SERGEYEVICH. Earth and Sea.
Grapes.
I Loved You Once.
No, Never Think.
Prophet, The.
Verses Written during a Sleepless Night.
When in My Arms.
PUTNAM, HOWARD PHELPS. Romeo and Juliet.
PYLE, KATHARINE. Sea Princess, The.
Sweet Tooth, The.
Visitor, The.

Q

"Q." *See* QUILLER-COUCH, SIR ARTHUR THOMAS.
"Q. B. M." *See* "M., Q. B."
QADI BEN LUBBAL. Night Fiesta on the River.
QUARLES, FRANCIS. Compass Needle, A.
Emblems, *sels.*
QUASIMODO, SALVATORE. Almost a Madrigal.
Ancient Winter.
And Suddenly It's Evening.
Before the Statue of Ilaria del Caretto.
From the Fortress of Upper Bergamo.
Gentle Hill, The.
Imitation of Joy.
Letter to My Mother.
Man of My Time.
Of Young Woman Bent Back among the Flowers.
Rain's Already with Us, The.
Street of Agrigentum.
Sunken Oboe.
Wind at Tindari.
QUEVEDO Y VILLEGAS, FRANCISCO GÓMEZ DE. Ah, What of Life! Does No One Answer Me?
Birds Are in the Air at Ease.
Everything Is Swept Away by the Brief Year.
Fly, The.
From the White Day to Take Me.
Happy and Contented in Your Hut.
I Gazed upon My Country's Walls.
Mighty Lord Is Money, A.
Now Great and Awesome in My Heart.
Rosebush, Less Presumption.
Satiric and Censorious Epistle, *sel.*
Sonnet: Death Warnings.
To a Nose.
To Rome Entombed in Her Ruins.
When You Shake Loose Your Hair.
QUICK, DOROTHY. Forest, The.
House of Life.
Monster, The.
Undertone.
QUILLER-COUCH, SIR ARTHUR THOMAS ("Q"). Dolor Oogo.
QUINN, JOHN ROBERT. Whistling Boy.
QUINN, RODERIC JOSEPH. Camp within the West, The.
Fisher, The.

R

RABÉARIVELO, JEAN-JOSEPH. Flute-Players, The.
RAGAN, SAM. Country Saga, A.
Deer Hunt.
Deserted House.
Gray Horizons.
Hidden Scars.
Hunger and Rain.
Portrait.
Prophet, The.
RAGO, HENRY. Knowledge of Light, The.
RAIMBAUT D'AURENGA. Full Well I Know How to Speak of Love.
My Lords, I Pray You Now, Give Ear.
RAIMBAUT DE VAQUEIRAS. High Waves That Ride the Sea.
Watchman on the Tower, Watch with Care.
RAINE, KATHLEEN JESSIE. Spell of Creation.
To My Mountain.
RALEGH, SIR WALTER. Affection and Desire.
As You Came from the Holy Land, *at.*
Author's Epitaph, Made by Himselfe, The.
Come to Me Soon.
Conceit Begotten by the Eyes.
Conclusion, The.
Description of Love, A.
Epitaph: "Even such is Time, which takes in trust."
Epitaph on the Earl of Leicester.
Even Such Is Time.
False Love.
Farewell to the Court.
Her Reply.
His Pilgrimage.
Homage to Diana.
Lie, The.
Lines from Catullus.
Methought I Saw the Grave Where Laura Lay.
My Body in the Walls.
Nature, That Washed Her Hands in Milk.
Now What Is Love.
Nymph's Reply to the Shepherd, The.
On the Cards and Dice.
Passionate Man's Pilgrimage, The.
Sir Walter Ralegh to His Son.
Sir Walter Raleigh the Night before His Death.
To His Son.
To the Queen.
Verses: "Even such is time, that takes in trust."
Walsinghame, *at.*
What Is Our Life?
Wood, the Weed, the Wag, The.
Written on the Night before His Execution.
"RAMAL, WALTER." *See* DE LA MARE, WALTER.
RAMSAUR, HUGH WILGUS. Epitaph, Found Somewhere in Space.
RANCHAN, SOM PARKASH. Swan Song.
RANDALL, DUDLEY. I Loved You Once, *tr.*
Legacy: My South.
Memorial Wreath.
Perspectives.
Southern Road, The.
RANDOLPH, INNES. Rebel, The.
RANDOLPH, THOMAS. Upon His Picture.
RANDS, WILLIAM BRIGHTY ("Matthew Browne"). Godfrey Gordon Gustavus Gore.
Gypsy Jane.
Peddler's Caravan, The.
RANSOM, JOHN CROWE. Antique Harvesters.
Bells for John Whiteside's Daughter.
Blue Girls.
Captain Carpenter.
Dead Boy.

Equilibrists, The.
Her Eyes.
Here Lies a Lady.
Janet Waking.
Judith of Bethulia.
Lady Lost.
Master's in the Garden Again.
Old Man Playing with Children.
Painted Head.
Parting, without a Sequel.
Piazza Piece.
Prelude to an Evening.
Survey of Literature.
Swimmer, The.
Vision by Sweetwater.
Winter Remembered.
RAO, K. RAGHAVENDRA. Journey to Golgotha, The.
RAUSCHENBUSCH, WALTER. Postern Gate, The, *sel.*
RAY, DAVID. On a Fifteenth-Century Flemish Angel.
On Seeing a Movie Based on an Episode from President Kennedy's Life.
On the Poet's Leer.
Problems of a Writing Teacher, The.
X-Ray.
RAYAPROL, SRINAVAS. On Growing Old.
RAYMOND, ROSSITER WORTHINGTON. Concerning Them That Are Asleep.
READ, SIR HERBERT EDWARD. Boy in the Barn, The.
Cradle Song: "Hush, honey, hush."
Early Astir.
Happy Warrior, The.
My Company.
Night Ride.
READ, THOMAS BUCHANAN. Blennerhassett's Island. *Fr.* The New Pastoral.
New Pastoral, The, *sel.*
Sheridan's Ride.
REALF, RICHARD. Word, The.
REANEY, JAMES. Alphabet, The.
Chough, The.
Horn, The.
January. *Fr.* A Suit of Nettles.
Katzenjammer Kids, The.
November. *Fr.* A Suit of Nettles.
Oracular Portcullis, The.
Suit of Nettles, A, *sels.*
RÈBORA, CLEMENTE. Lombardy Bell.
With Tense Imagination.
REDGROVE, PETER. Bedtime Story for My Son.
Corposant.
Early Morning Feed.
Ghostly Father, The.
I Stroll.
On Catching a Dog-Daisy in the Mower.
Shearing Grass.
Story from Russian Author.
REDI, FRANCESCO. Bacchus in Tuscany, *sels.*
REECE, BYRON HERBERT. Pretty Polly.
REED, HENRY. Chard Whitlow.
Judging Distances. *Fr.* Lessons of the War.
Lessons of the War, *sels.*
Naming of Parts. *Fr.* Lessons of the War.
REED, ISHMAEL. Ghost in Birmingham, The.
REESE, LIZETTE WOODWORTH. After, *sel.*
Christmas Folk-Song, A.
Daily Round. *Fr.* After.
Lydia Is Gone This Many a Year.
Sun and the Rain, The.
Sunrise.
REEVE, PAUL EATON. Succumbing.
REEVES, CLAUDE. Down on Roberts' Farm.
REEVES, JAMES. Beech Leaves.
Catullus to Lesbia.
Cows.
Fireworks.
Grim and Gloomy.
Little Brother, The.
May Day.
Old Crabbed Men.
Pig Tale, A.
Sea, The.

REEVES, JAMES *(continued)*
Shiny.
Snail, The.
Stone Gentleman, The.
Under Ground.
Wandering Moon, The.
What Kind of Music?
REEVES, KATHERINE. Enigma.
REEVES, WILLIAM PEMBER. Colonist in
His Garden, A.
REGENSBURG, DER BURGGRAVE VON.
All Winter I Lay Alone until a Lady
Brought Me Solace.
RÉGNIER, HENRI DE. Night.
RÉGNIER, MATHURIN. Confession in
Brief, A.
Epitaph: "I lived my life from day
to day."
REICH, MAX ISAAC. For Every Man.
REID, ALASTAIR. Figures on the Frieze,
The.
For Her Sake.
Game of Glass, A.
Ghosts.
Ghosts' Stories.
In Memory of My Uncle Timothy.
Instance, An.
Outlook Uncertain.
Pigeons.
Tale the Hermit Told, The.
That Dying.
REINMAR VON HAGENAU. Day on Which
I Took the Cross, The.
I Think That Love Will Come My
Way.
One Thing They Say Displeases Me.
You Say, the Summer Is Here Now.
REITZ, ALBERT SIMPSON. Cradle and
the Cross, The.
Thy Will Be Done.
RENTON, WILLIAM. Fisher, The.
Pale Cold Moon, The.
REPLANSKY, NAOMI. Ring Song, *sel.*
REVERDY, PIERRE. Features of the Sky.
Shadow, The.
Word Comes Down, The.
REXROTH, KENNETH. About the Cool
Water.
Advantages of Learning, The, *tr.*
Clear after Rain, *tr.*
End of the Year, The, *tr.*
For Mary.
From the Greek Anthology, *tr.*
Good God, What a Night That Was,
tr.
Infinite, The, *tr.*
Letter to William Carlos Williams, A.
Mother Goose Rhyme.
Our Canoe Idles in the Idling Current.
Quietly.
REYES BASUALTO, NEFTALÍ RICARDO.
See "NERUDA, PABLO."
REYNOLDS, ELIZABETH GARDNER. Little
Black Dog, The.
REYNOLDS, JOHN HAMILTON. Gallantly
within the Ring.
Peter Bell; a Lyrical Ballad.
REYNOLDS, TIM. Hell of a Day, A.
RHODES, CHARLEY (Charles Bensell).
Days of '49, The.
RHYS, ERNEST P. Autobiography, An.
Elegy for Lucy Lloyd, *tr.*
Grave, The, *tr.*
RICE, GRANTLAND. Alumnus Football.
Few Signs, A.
Thanksgiving Eve.
RICE, WALLACE. Niplets, *tr.*
Requirements, *tr.*
Tender, Slow, *tr.*
RICH, ADRIENNE CECILE. At Majority.
Breakfast in a Bowling Alley in Utica,
New York.
Corpse-Plant, The.
Double Monologue.
Holiday.
Like This Together.
Lucifer in the Train.
Middle-aged, The.
New Year's Eve in Troy.
Raven, The.
Revivalist in Boston, A.
Stranger, The.
33.
Tourist and the Town, The.

Trees, The.
RICHARD CŒUR DE LION (Richard Lion-
Heart). In No Way Can a Pris-
oner Reveal.
RICHARD OF CAISTRE. Hymn to Jesus,
A.
RICHARDS, IVOR ARMSTRONG. Spend-
thrift.
RICHARDS, LAURA ELIZABETH (Mrs.
Henry Richards). Antonio.
Ballad of China, A.
Eletelephony.
Gregory Griggs.
High Barbaree, The.
Jippy and Jimmy.
Kindness to Animals.
Little John Bottlejohn.
Mrs. Snipkin and Mrs. Wobblechin.
Molly Pitcher.
Monkeys and the Crocodile, The.
Owl and the Eel and the Warming-
Pan, The.
Party, A.
Postman, The.
Some Fishy Nonsense.
Umbrella Brigade, The.
Was She a Witch?
RICHARDSON, ROBERT. Epitaph: "Warm
summer sun shine kindly here."
RICHART DE BERBEZILH. You See Me
like the Elephant.
RICHSTONE, MAY. Naming the Baby.
RICHTER, MARGARET R. Fir tree stand-
ing lonely, A, *tr.*
RIDDELL, ELIZABETH. Under the Casua-
rina.
Wakeful in the Township.
RIDLER, ANNE. Bring Back.
Matter of Life and Death, A.
News of the World.
Of the Unscathing Fire.
Stone Angel.
RIEDEMANN, MYRA VON. Horses.
Last Will of the Drunk.
There Are Places.
RIEU, EMILE VICTOR. Dirge for a Bad
Boy.
Two People.
RIHAKU. *See* LI PO.
RILEY, JAMES WHITCOMB. Away.
Good-by er Howdy-do.
Impetuous Resolve, An.
Life-Lesson, A.
Lincoln.
Lincoln—the Boy.
Little Orphant Annie.
When the Frost Is on the Punkin.
RILKE, RAINER MARIA. Adam.
Archaic Torso of Apollo.
Autumn.
Birth of Christ.
Birth of Mary.
Buddha.
Buddha in the Glory.
Complaint.
Dedication of 1924, A.
Dove that remained outside, outside
the dovecote.
Duino Elegies, The, *sel.*
Elegy IX: "Why, if the span of exist-
ence may be completed." *Fr.* The
Duino Elegies.
Eve.
February, 1924.
Garden of Olives, The.
Jackolanterns.
Joseph's Suspicion.
Lament: "Oh, everything is far."
Last Supper, The.
Leda.
Love Song: "How am I to withhold
my soul."
Love Song: "How could I keep my
soul so that it might."
Mausoleum.
Orpheus. Eurydice. Hermes.
Panther, The.
Prisoner, The.
Rabbi Loew.
Roman Fountain.
Solemn Hour.
Song: "You whom I don't tell that I
lie awake."
Song of the Idiot, The.

Sonnets to Orpheus, *sels.*
To Hölderlin.
To Stephan George.
Turning-Point.
We Are All Workmen.
What Will You Do, God, When I Die?
Woman's Fate, A.
You, Neighbor God.
Youth Dreams, The.
RIMBAUD, ARTHUR. Childhood, *sel.*
Fr. Illuminations.
Illuminations, *sel.*
RINALDO D'AQUINO. No More Shall I
Take Comfort.
"RINGELNATZ, JOACHIM" (Hans Bötti-
cher). Ambition.
Cassel (Carps at Wilhelmstrasse 15).
RIST, JOHANN VON. Eternity to Come.
RISTAU, HARLAND. Korea.
RIVERS, CONRAD KENT. Four Sheets to
the Wind and a One-Way Ticket to
France.
On Passing Two Negroes on a Dark
Country Road Somewhere in Georgia.
Still Voice of Harlem, The.
To Richard Wright.
ROBBINS, MARTIN. Spring Is a Loop-
ing-free Time.
ROBERTS, SIR CHARLES GEORGE
DOUGLAS. Brook in February, The.
Ice.
Logs, The.
Mowing, The.
Pea-Fields, The.
Solitary Woodsman, The.
Sower, The.
Tantramar Revisited, The.
ROBERTS, DANIEL CRANE. God of Our
Fathers.
ROBERTS, ELIZABETH MADOX. Butter-
bean Tent, The.
Christmas Morning.
Circus, The.
Cornfield, The.
Dick and Will.
Father's Story.
Firefly.
Hens, The.
Horse.
Little Rain.
Milking Time.
Mumps.
People, The.
Rabbit, The.
Twins, The.
ROBERTS, THEODORE GOODRIDGE. Blue
Heron, The.
Wreckers' Prayer, The.
ROBINSON, ANNIE DOUGLAS GREEN.
See "DOUGLAS, MARIAN."
ROBINSON, DAVID G. City Council.
Life in California.
Miner's Lament, The, III.
Seeing the Elephant.
ROBINSON, EDWIN ARLINGTON. Altar,
The.
Bewick Finzer.
Calvary.
Clerks, The.
Christmas Sonnet, A.
Cliff Klingenhagen.
Credo.
Dark Hills, The.
Demos.
Eros Turannos.
For a Dead Lady.
For Arvia.
George Crabbe.
Gift of God, The.
Glass Houses.
Hillcrest.
House on the Hill, The.
How Annandale Went Out.
Karma.
Klondike, The.
Luke Havergal.
Man against the Sky, The.
Master, The.
Mighty Runner, A.
Mill, The.
Miniver Cheevy.
Mr. Flood's Party.
New England.
Octaves, *sels.*

Out of Wisdom Has Come Love. *Fr.*
The Three Taverns.
Poor Relation, The.
Reuben Bright.
Richard Cory.
Sheaves, The.
Sonnet: "Master and the slave go hand in hand, The."
Sonnet: "Oh for a poet—for a beacon bright."
Three Taverns, The, *sel.*
Tree in Pamela's Garden, The.
Wandering Jew, The.
ROBINSON, JOHN. More Truth and Light.
ROBINSON, ROLAND EDWARD. Dancers, The.
Lyre-Bird, The.
Rock-Lily.
Tank, The.
Waratah.
ROBINSON, SELMA. Ballad of the Huntsman.
Ferry Ride.
Gentle Name.
Old Closet.
ROBINSON, TOM (Thomas Pendleton Robinson). Hard Lines.
My Dog.
Shoes.
ROBINSON, WEY. Horse & Rider.
ROBSON, ATTWOOD. Testament.
ROCHE, JAMES JEFFREY. Men of the Alamo, The.
ROCHESTER, JOHN WILMOT, 2D EARL OF. Bully, The.
Chaste Arabian Bird, The.
Et Cetera.
Disappointment, The.
Description of Maidenhead, A.
Fall, The.
Imperfect Enjoyment, The.
Love and Life.
Lycias.
Maimed Debauchee, The.
On Charles II.
Panegyric on Nelly, A, *sel.*
Pastoral Courtship, A.
Platonic Lady, The.
Satire against Mankind, A.
Song, A: "Absent from thee I languish still."
Song, A: "As Chloris full of harmless thoughts."
Song of a Young Lady to Her Ancient Lover, A.
Song to Cloris, A.
To His Mistress.
Upon Leaving His Mistress.
While on Those Lovely Looks I Gaze.
RODGERS, WILLIAM ROBERT. And There Was Mary Magdalene and the Other Mary, Sitting Over against the Sepulchre.
"And When He Had Scourged Jesus, He Delivered Him to Be Crucified."
Apollo and Daphne.
Beagles.
Carol: "Deep in the fading leaves of night."
Lent.
Life's Circumnavigators.
Lovers, The.
Net, The.
Resurrection—an Easter Sequence, *sel.*
ROETHKE, THEODORE. Academic.
Bat, The.
Beast, The.
Big Wind.
Child on Top of a Greenhouse.
Cuttings, Later.
Cycle, The.
Dolor.
Dying Man, The, *sels.*
Elegy for Jane.
Exulting, The. *Fr.* The Dying Man.
Far Field, The.
Field of Light, A.
First Meditation. *Fr.* Meditations of an Old Woman.
Four for Sir John Davies.
I Knew a Woman [Lovely in Her Bones].
In a Dark Time.

Lady and the Bear, The.
Light Listened.
Lost Son, The.
Meditations of an Old Woman, *sel.*
Mistake, The.
Moss-gathering.
My Papa's Waltz.
Open House.
Otto.
Praise to the End!
Prayer: "If I must of my senses lose."
Sensualists [*or* Sensualist], The.
She.
Sloth, The.
Small, The.
Snake.
Song, The: "I met a ragged man."
They Sing, They Sing. *Fr.* The Dying Man.
Vigil, The. *Fr.* Four for Sir John Davies.
Visitant, The.
Voice, The.
Waking, The.
Walk in Late Summer, A.
Words for the Wind.
ROGERS, SAMUEL. Another and the Same. *Fr.* Human Life.
Byron Recollected at Bologna. *Fr.* Italy.
Captivity.
Ginevra.
Human Life, *sels.*
Interview near Florence, An. *Fr.* Italy.
Italy, *sels.*
Man's Going Hence. *Fr.* Human Life.
Robin's Epitaph, A.
Sleeping Beauty, The.
Wish, A.
ROGETSU. Rain-Frogs, The.
ROIZ DE CASTELO-BRANCO, JOÃO. Song of Parting.
ROLFE, EDWIN. Poem to Delight My Friends Who Laugh at Science-Fiction, A.
ROLFE, HARVEY E. Resolutions?—New and Old.
ROLLE OF HAMPOLE, RICHARD. Song of Love for Jesus, A.
ROLLS, ERIC. Little Sticks.
Sheaf-Tosser.
ROMANO, LIBORIA E. All Souls.
ROMIG, EDNA DAVIS. Forest Fire.
RONSARD, PIERRE DE. Amours de Marie, *sels.*
And Lightly, like the Flowers.
Carpe Diem.
Corinna in Vendome.
Deadly Kisses.
Epitaph on Rabelais.
His Lady's Death. *Fr.* Amours de Marie.
His Lady's Tomb. *Fr.* Amours de Marie.
Let me decease within thine arms, my Dear.
Marie, arise, my indolent sweet saint! *Fr.* Amours de Marie.
Odes, *sel.*
Of His Lady's Old Age. *Fr.* Sonnets pour Hélène.
On His Lady's Waking.
On the Choice of His Sepulchre. *Fr.* Odes.
Paradox of Time, The.
Roses.
Sonnets pour Hélène, *sels.*
To a Fountain.
To His Young Mistress. *Fr.* Amours de Marie.
To Remi Belleau.
"Who," cried the elders on the Trojan wall. *Fr.* Sonnets pour Hélène.
When you are very old, at evening. *Fr.* Sonnets pour Hélène.
ROSE, MARY CATHERINE. Clown, The.
Parade, A.
ROSELIEP, RAYMOND FRANCIS. Alan.
Black Are the Stars.
For John Kennedy, Jr.
GI.
In Time of Darkness.
Professor Nocturnal.

Scissors Grinder, The.
Tour in Rain.
Vendor.
Where Roots Tangle.
ROSENBERG, ISAAC. Break of Day in the Trenches.
Dead Man's Dump.
Girl to Soldier on Leave.
Home-Thoughts from France.
Immortals, The.
On Receiving News of the War.
Returning, We Hear the Larks.
Soldier: Twentieth Century.
ROSENFELD, MAX, *and* WALTER LOWENFELS. *See* LOWENFELS, WALTER, *and* MAX ROSENFELD.
ROSENPLÜT, HANS. He Who Scrubs a Raven White.
ROSS, ABRAM BUNN. Two in Bed.
ROSS, ALAN. At Only That Moment.
Kurdish Shepherds.
Les Saintes-Maries-de-la-Mer.
ROSS, W. W. EUSTACE. Creek, The.
Diver, The.
If Ice.
Pine Gum.
Snake Trying, The.
Walk, The.
ROSSETTI, CHRISTINA GEORGINA. After Death.
Another Spring.
Apple Gathering, An.
Battle Within, The.
Before the Paling of the Stars.
Better Resurrection, A.
Birds of Paradise.
Birthday, A.
Bourne, The.
Bread and Milk. *Fr.* Sing-Song.
By the Sea.
Caterpillar, The. *Fr.* Sing-Song.
Christmas Carol, A: "Before the paling of the stars."
Christmas Carol, A: "In the bleak midwinter," *sel.*
Color. *Fr.* Sing-Song.
Consider.
De Profundis.
Dream Land.
Easter Day.
Echo.
Eve.
Ferry Me across the Water. *Fr.* Sing-Song.
Ferryman, The. *Fr.* Sing-Song.
First Spring Day, The.
Goblin Market.
Good Friday.
Horses of the Sea, The. *Fr.* Sing-Song.
House of Cards, The. *Fr.* Sing-Song.
Hurt No Living Thing. *Fr.* Sing-Song.
In the Bleak Mid-Winter.
Love Lies Bleeding.
Many in aftertimes will say of you. *Fr.* Monna Innominata.
May.
Memory ("I have a room whereinto no one enters").
Memory ("I nursed it in my bosom while it lived").
Minnie and Mattie. *Fr.* Sing-Song.
Mix a Pancake. *Fr.* Sing-Song.
Monna Innominata.
Months, The. *Fr.* Sing-Song.
None Other Lamb.
Oh Roses for the Flush of Youth.
Old and New Year Ditties, *sel.*
On the Wing.
One Certainty, The.
Out of the Deep Have I Called unto Thee, O Lord.
Passing and Glassing.
Pause of Thought, A.
Rainbow, The. *Fr.* Sing-Song.
Remember.
Rest.
Riddle: "First it was a pretty flower, dressed in pink and white."
Send Me.
Sing-Song, *sels.*
Sketch, A.
Sleeping at Last.

ROSSETTI, CHRISTINA GEORGINA (cont.)
Song: "Oh roses for the flush of youth."
Song: "When I am dead, my dearest."
Spring.
Spring Quiet.
Summer.
Summer Wish, A.
Thread of Life, The.
Twice.
Twilight Calm.
Up-Hill.
Weary in Well-doing.
What Can I Give Him?
What Is Pink? Fr. Sing-Song.
What Would I Give!
When I am Dead [My Dearest].
Who Has Seen the Wind? Fr. Sing-Song.
Winter Rain.
World, The.
Youth gone, and beauty gone if ever there. Fr. Monna Innominata.
ROSSETTI, DANTE GABRIEL. August, tr. Fr. Sonnets of the Months.
Autumn Idleness. Fr. The House of Life.
Ballad of Dead Ladies, The, tr.
Barren Spring. Fr. The House of Life.
Beauty's Pageant. Fr. The House of Life.
Birth-Bond, The. Fr. The House of Life.
Beyond the sphere which spreads to widest space, tr. Fr. La Vita Nuova.
Blessed Damozel, The.
Body's Beauty. Fr. The House of Life.
Bridal Birth. Fr. The House of Life.
Broken Music. Fr. The House of Life.
Canzone: Of the Gentle Heart, tr.
Chime of the Sea, The.
Chimes.
Choice, The. Fr. The House of Life.
Cloud and Wind. Fr. The House of Life.
Dark Glass, The. Fr. The House of Life.
Day of Love, A. Fr. The House of Life.
Death-in-Love. Fr. The House of Life.
Equal Troth. Fr. The House of Life.
Even So.
Genius in Beauty. Fr. The House of Life.
Gracious Moonlight. Fr. The House of Life.
He Compares All Things with His Lady, and Finds Them Wanting, tr.
He Will Praise His Lady, tr.
Heart's Compass. Fr. The House of Life.
Heart's Haven. Fr. The House of Life.
Heart's Hope. Fr. The House of Life.
Her Gifts. Fr. The House of Life.
His Mother's Service to Our Lady, tr.
Honeysuckle, The.
Hope Overtaken. Fr. The House of Life.
House of Life, The, sels.
Jenny.
Kiss, The. Fr. The House of Life.
Lamp's Shrine, The. Fr. The House of Life.
Last Fire. Fr. The House of Life.
Life-in-Love. Fr. The House of Life.
Love and Hope. Fr. The House of Life.
Love Enthroned. Fr. The House of Life.
Love-Letter, The. Fr. The House of Life.
Love-Moon, The. Fr. The House of Life.
Love-Sweetness. Fr. The House of Life.
Lovers' Walk, The. Fr. The House of Life.
Love's Baubles. Fr. The House of Life.

Love's Fatality. Fr. The House of Life.
Love's Last Gift. Fr. The House of Life.
Love's Lovers. Fr. The House of Life.
Love's Testament. Fr. The House of Life.
Lovesight. Fr. The House of Life.
Mary's Girlhood.
Memory.
Mid-Rapture. Fr. The House of Life.
Moonstar, The. Fr. The House of Life.
Morrow's Message, The. Fr. The House of Life.
Nuptial Sleep. Fr. The House of Life.
On Leaving Bruges.
On the Site of a Mulberry-Tree; Planted by Wm. Shakespeare; Felled by the Rev. F. Gastrell.
Parted Love. Fr. The House of Life.
Passion and Worship. Fr. The House of Life.
Portrait, The. Fr. The House of Life.
Pride of Youth. Fr. The House of Life.
Sea Limits, The.
Secret Parting. Fr. The House of Life.
September, tr. Fr. Sonnets of the Months.
Severed Selves. Fr. The House of Life.
Silent Noon. Fr. The House of Life.
Sleepless Dreams. Fr. The House of Life.
Snows of Yester-Year, The, tr.
Song IV: Sudden Light.
Sonnet, The ("A sonnet is a moment's monument"). Fr. The House of Life.
Sonnet: "Mine eyes beheld the blessed pity spring," tr. Fr. La Vita Nuova.
Sonnets of the Months, sels., tr.
Soul-Light. Fr. The House of Life.
Stillborn Love. Fr. The House of Life.
Sudden Light.
Superscription, A. Fr. The House of Life.
Supreme Surrender. Fr. The House of Life.
That she hath gone to Heaven suddenly, tr. Fr. La Vita Nuova.
Thou Sweetly-smelling Fresh Red Rose, tr.
Through Death to Love. Fr. The House of Life.
Troy Town.
True Woman: Her Heaven. Fr. The House of Life.
True Woman: Her Love. Fr. The House of Life.
True Woman: Herself. Fr. The House of Life.
Venus Victrix. Fr. The House of Life.
Very pitiful lady, very young, A, tr. Fr. La Vita Nuova.
Virgin Declares Her Beauties, A, tr.
Vita Nuova, La, sels., tr.
What Smouldering Senses. Fr. The House of Life.
White Ship, The, sel.
Willowwood. Fr. The House of Life.
Winged Hours. Fr. The House of Life.
Winter.
Within Her Eyes, tr. Fr. La Vita Nuova.
Without Her. Fr. The House of Life.
Woodspurge, The.
Ye pilgrim folk advancing pensively, tr. Fr. La Vita Nuova.
Young Bride, A, tr.
Youth's Antiphony. Fr. The House of Life.
Youth's Spring-Tribute. Fr. The House of Life.
ROTHENBERG, JEROME DENNIS. Bodhisattva Undoes Hell, A.
"Little Boy Lost, A."

Moral Taxi Ride, The, tr.
Seventh Hell, The: Of Smoke, Where Fire-Raisers Try in Vain to Escape from a Shower of Hot Sand Falling from a Cloud.
Sightings I.
Stationmaster's Lament, The.
Three Landscapes, sel.
ROTHENBERG, JEROME G. Cortège.
ROUMER, EMILE. Peasant Declares His Love, The.
ROURKE, CONSTANCE. Merry Miner, The.
ROWBOTHAM, DAVID. Mullabinda.
Town, The.
ROWE, ELIZABETH. On an Unsuccessful Attempt to Draw Lord Boyle's Picture.
On the Sacrament. Fr. Three Hymns.
Three Hymns.
ROWLAND, J. R. Canberra in April.
ROWSE, ALFRED LESLIE. Death-Bed.
How Many Miles to Mylor?
ROWSWELL, ALBERT K. Should You Go First.
RUBIN, LARRY. Druggist, The.
For a Poetry Reading to Which No One Came.
Synchronized.
RUDEL, JAUFRÉ. He Has Not Sung Who's Made No Sound.
When Days Grow Long in May.
When the Waters of the Spring.
RUFINUS DOMESTICUS. Andante, ma Non Assai.
Faint Heart.
Requirements: "Not too chary, not too fast."
Requirements: "Not too lean, and not too fat."
RUGGLES, WILLIAM B. Pioneer, The.
RUIZ, JUAN [or JEAN], ARCHPRIEST OF HITA. Book of True Love, The, sels.
Don Pitas Payas. Fr. The Book of True Love.
Easter Day. Fr. The Book of True Love.
Encounter of the Archpriest with Ferrand García. Fr. The Book of True Love.
Hill Song. Fr. The Book of True Love.
Of the Characteristics of Small Women. Fr. The Book of True Love.
RUKEYSER, MURIEL. Are You Born?
Boy with His Hair Cut Short.
Effort at Speech between Two People.
RUMI, JALAL [or JELAL] ED-DIN [or DSCHELLALEDDIN]. As Salt Resolved in the Ocean.
At Peace.
Unseen Power, The.
RUNYON, DAMON (Alfred Damon Runyon). Song of Panama, A.
RUSSELL, GEORGE WILLIAM. See "Æ."
RUSSELL, SYDNEY KING. For Vicki at Seven.
Forecast.
Night Peril.
Perennial Mourner.
Phyllis.
Shape of Fear, The.
Six Silver Handles.
Spectre.
Warning.
RUTEBEUF. Dispute of Charlot and the Barber, The.
His Poverty.
His Repentance.
To the Virgin.
RUTILIUS. Roma.
RUTLEDGE, ARCHIBALD. Oblique.
RYAN, ABRAM JOSEPH (Father Ryan). Conquered Banner, The.
RYBERG, BARBARA C. Step by Step.
RYDER, ARTHUR WILLIAM. Panchatantra, The, sels., tr.
Poverty, tr. Fr. The Panchatantra.
Serpent and the Mouse, The, tr. Fr. The Panchatantra.
True Friendship, tr. Fr. The Panchatantra.
Women's Eyes, tr.

RYMAN, JAMES. Farewell! Advent.
Now the Most High Is Born.
RYOTA. Moon in the Water, The.
RYUHO. Moon, The.

S

SAADI. *See* SADI.
SAAR, FERDINAND VON. On an Old
Castle-Park.
SABA, UMBERTO. Ashes.
Broken Glass, The.
Fruit and Greens.
Goat, The.
Happiness.
Ulysses.
Woman.
Young Tree, The.
SABIN, EDWIN LEGRAND. Easter.
SACCHETTI, FRANCO. Amorous Thorn,
An.
O Lovely Mountain Shepherd Lasses.
SACKVILLE, CHARLES, 6TH EARL OF
DORSET. Arno's Vale.
Fire of Love, The.
May the Ambitious Ever Find.
To All You Ladies Now at Land.
SADAIYE. Blossoms and Storm.
SADI [*or* SAADI] (Muslih-ud-Din). Gul-
istan, The, *sel.*
Hyacinths to Feed Thy Soul. *Fr.* The
Gulistan.
SAHA, P. K. Child's Power of Wonder,
The.
SAHL BEN MALIK. Dawn, The.
SAINT. *See under names of individual
saints.*
SAINT-AMANT, ANTOINE-GIRARD DE. Al-
pine Winter, The.
Enjoyment, The.
Orgy, The.
SAINTE-MAURE, CHARLES DE, DUC DE
MONTAUSIER. *See* MONTAUSIER,
CHARLES DE SAINTE-MAURE, DUC
DE.
SALINGER, HERMAN. *For translations
from German, see* AGP; AnML;
SiGo.
SALWAY, OWEN C. He Cares.
SALZBURG, J. L. Bill.
SAN GEMINIANO [*or* GEMIGNANO], FOL-
GORE DA. *See* FOLGORE DA SAN
GEMINIANO.
SANA'I. Perfect Love.
SÁNCHEZ CALAVERA, FERRÁN. By God,
My Lords, Let Us Lift the Veil.
SANDBURG, CARL. Arithmetic.
At a Window.
Boxes and Bags.
Broken-Face Gargoyles.
Chicago.
Child.
Children of the Wind.
Clean Curtains.
Cool Tombs.
Copperfaces, The. *Fr.* The People,
Yes.
Counting.
Doors.
Dream Girl.
Explanations of Love.
Faith of Abraham Lincoln, The, *arr.*
Fog.
For You.
Four Preludes on Playthings of the
Wind.
Grass.
Great Hunt, The.
Hammer, The.
Handfuls.
Harbor, The.
Hits and Runs.
Home Thoughts.
Horses and Men in the Rain.
I Am the People, the Mob.
Jazz Fantasia.
Long Shadow of Lincoln, The.
Lost.
Our Prayer of Thanks, *sel.*

People, Yes, The, *sels.*
Phizzog.
Pool.
Potomac Town in February.
Prayers of Steel.
Primer Lesson.
Sketch.
Skyscraper.
Sleep Impression.
Slippery.
Soup.
Special Starlight.
Splinter.
Summer Stars.
Swell People.
Theme in Yellow.
They Have Yarns. *Fr.* The People,
Yes.
Threes.
To the Ghost of John Milton.
Under a Telephone Pole.
Upstream.
Washington Monument by Night.
When Death Came April Twelve 1945.
Wild Horses.
Wilderness.
Young Sea.
SANDBURG, HELGA. Cantata for Two
Lovers.
SANDELL, LINA. Security.
SANDY, STEPHEN. Destruction of Bul-
finch's House, The.
Hiawatha.
Woolworth Philodendron, The.
SANGSTER, CHARLES. Evening.
Meadow-Field, The. *Fr.* Pleasant
Memories.
Pleasant Memories, *sel.*
St. Lawrence and the Saguenay, The,
sel.
Thousand Islands, The. *Fr.* The St.
Lawrence and the Saguenay.
SANGSTER, MARGARET ELIZABETH (Mun-
son) (1838–1912). Bit of the Book,
A.
Faith.
If Christ Were Here To-Night.
Now and Then.
Peace.
Sin of Omission, The.
Sunrise.
Thanksgiving.
Thought, A.
SANNAZARO, JACOPO (Actius Sincerus
Sannazarius). Like to These Un-
measurable Mountains.
SANT JORDI, JORDI DE. Below the Brow
I Bear Your Lovely Countenance.
I Have No Liking for One Who in All
Things Is Not.
Vexation, Enemy of Youth.
SANTAYANA, GEORGE. I know not if
from uncreated spheres, *tr.*
Madrigal: "Ravished by all that to the
eyes is fair," *tr.*
O World.
On the Death of a Metaphysician.
Sonnet: O World.
SANTILLANA, IÑIGO LÓPEZ DE MENDOZA,
MARQUÉS DE. Far from You and
Close to Care.
Mountain Song of Finojosa.
SAPPHO. Achtung.
Garden, A.
Night.
On My Sweet Mother.
Young Bride, A.
SARETT, LEW. Angus McGregor.
Four Little Foxes.
God Is at the Anvil.
Iron-Wind Dances. *Fr.* Thunder-
storms.
Thunderstorms, *sel.*
Wind in the Pine.
SARTON, MAY. By Moonlight.
Definition.
Fore Thought.
In Time like Air.
Leaves before the Wind.
Light Left On, A.
New Year Wishes.
Santos: New Mexico.
Song: "Now let us honor with violin
and flute."

These Images Remain.
White-haired Man, The.
Work of Happiness, The.
SASSOON, SIEGFRIED. Absolution.
All-Souls' Day.
Alone.
Asking for It.
At the Grave of Henry Vaughan.
Babylon.
Base Details.
"Blighters."
Brevities.
Concert-Interpretation.
Concert Party.
Counter-Attack.
Death-Bed, The.
December Stillness.
Does It Matter?
Down the Glimmering Staircase. *Fr.*
Vigils.
Everyone Sang.
Falling Asleep.
General, The.
Glory of Women.
Kiss, The.
Litany of the Lost.
Midnight Interior, A.
Morning Express.
Rear-Guard, The.
Redeemer, The.
Repression of War Experience.
Storm on Fifth Avenue.
Strangeness of Heart.
Suicide in the Trenches.
Vigils, *sel.*
Working Party, A.
SATO, SATORU. Japan That Sank under
the Sea.
SATO, SATORU, *and* CONSTANCE URDANG.
See URDANG, CONSTANCE, *and* SATORU
SATO.
SAVAGE, RICHARD. Bastard's Lot, The.
To a Young Lady.
SAVARIC DE MAULEON, GAUCELM FAIDIT,
and UC DE LA BACALARIA. *See*
FAIDIT, GAUCELM, UC DE LA BACA-
LARIA, *and* SAVARIC DE MAULEON.
SAXE, JOHN GODFREY. Blind Men and
the Elephant, The.
Early Rising.
How Cyrus Laid the Cable.
Pyramus and Thisbe.
Rhyme of the Rails.
To Lesbia.
SAYERS, DOROTHY LEIGH. Dante and
Beatrice in the Earthly Paradise, *tr.*
Fr. Divina Commedia.
Dante's Angels, *tr. Fr.* Divina Com-
media.
Dante's Heaven, *tr. Fr.* Divina Com-
media.
Divina Commedia, *sels., tr.*
Just Vengeance, The, *sel.*
SAYLES, JAMES M. Star of the Evening.
SAYRES, CORTLANDT W. Bankrupt.
SBARBARO, CAMILLO. Be Still My Soul,
Weary of Pleasure.
SCANNELL, VERNON. Act of Love.
Jealous Wife, The.
SCÈVE, MAURICE. Délie, *sels.*
SCHACHT, MARSHALL. First Autumn,
The.
SCHEFFLER, JOHANNES. *See* "ANGELUS
SILESIUS."
SCHÉLANDRE, JEAN DE. To the Poets of
Our Time.
SCHEVILL, JAMES. Story of Soutine, A.
SCHILLER, JOHANN CHRISTOPH FRIE-
DRICH VON. Archimedes and the
Student.
Class Distinction.
Deutsches Reich.
Difficult Combination, The.
Evening.
German National Character.
Gifts of Fortune, The.
Highest, The.
Immortality.
Kant and His Interpreters.
Key, The.
Master, The.
My Faith.
Nenia.
New Generation, The.
Philosophical Conversation.

SCHILLER, JOHANN CHRISTOPH FRIE-
DRICH VON (*continued*)
Political Doctrine.
Task.
SCHLEGEL, KATHARINA VON. Be Still,
My Soul.
SCHMIED, WIELAND. Ancient Chinese
Map of the World.
Myths.
SCHNACK, ANTON. Nocturnal Landscape.
SCHNURRE, WOLFDIETRICH. Breath on a
Piece of Broken Glass.
Denunciation.
Strophe.
SCHOLL, ALBERT ARNOLD. Something
Makes Itself Known.
SCHULZ, DALE. His Presence.
SCHWAB, ANTONIA Y. Danse Macabre.
SCHWARTZ, DELMORE. Aria.
At a Solemn Musick.
Ballet of the Fifth Year, The.
Baudelaire.
For the One Who Would Take Man's
Life in His Hands.
Heavy Bear Who Goes with Me, The.
Holderlin.
How Strange Love Is, in Every State
of Consciousness.
I Wakened to a Calling.
In the Naked Bed, in Plato's Cave.
Starlight like Intuition [*or* Starlight's
Intuitions] Pierced the Twelve.
SCOLLARD, CLINTON. Rain Riders.
SCOTT, ALEXANDER. My Heart Is Heich
Abufe, *at.*
SCOTT, DUNCAN CAMPBELL. At Gull
Lake: August, 1810.
En Route.
Night and the Pines.
Night Hymns on Lake Nipigon.
Night in June, A.
Off Rivière du Loup.
Prairie Water Colour, A.
Prairie Wind.
SCOTT, FRANCIS REGINALD. Bangkok.
Bonne Entente.
Canadian Authors Meet, The.
Lakeshore.
Laurentian Shield.
Tourist Time.
Will to Win.
SCOTT, FREDERICK GEORGE. Dawn.
Easter Island.
In the Woods.
Sting of Death, The.
SCOTT, JOHN, OF AMWELL. Drum, The.
SCOTT, LOUISE BINDER, *and* J. J.
THOMPSON. Birthday Candles.
Birthday Gifts.
SCOTT, TOM. Sea Dirge.
SCOTT, SIR WALTER. Alice Brand. *Fr.*
The Lady of the Lake.
Bible, The. *Fr.* The Monastery.
Bonnie Dundee. *Fr.* The Doom of
Devorgoil.
Breathes There the Man. *Fr.* The
Lay of the Last Minstrel.
Bride of Lammermoor, The, *sel.*
Coronach. *Fr.* The Lady of the Lake.
Datur Hora Quieti. *Fr.* The Doom of
Devorgoil.
Doom of Devorgoil, The, *sels.*
Dreary Change, The.
Erlking, The, *tr.*
Farewell, Thou Minstrel Harp. *Fr.*
The Lady of the Lake.
Father's Notes of Woe, A. *Fr.* The
Lay of the Last Minstrel.
Football Song.
Gathering, The. *Fr.* The Lady of the
Lake.
Gathering Song of Donald the Black.
Harp of the North. *Fr.* The Lady of
the Lake.
Heart of Midlothian, The, *sel.*
Hunting Song.
Jock of [*or* o'] Hazeldean.
Lady of the Lake, The, *sels.*
Lay of the Last Minstrel, The, *sels.*
Lochinvar. *Fr.* Marmion.
Look Not Thou. *Fr.* The Bride of
Lammermoor.
Madge Wildfire Sings. *Fr.* The Heart
of Midlothian.

Maid of Neidpath, The.
Marmion, *sels.*
Minstrel Responds to Flattery, The.
Fr. The Lay of the Last Minstrel.
Monastery, The, *sel.*
Outlaw, The. *Fr.* Rokeby.
Patriot, The. *Fr.* The Lay of the Last
Minstrel.
Patriotism. *Fr.* The Lay of the Last
Minstrel.
Pirate, The, *sel.*
Pride of Youth, The. *Fr.* The Heart
of Midlothian.
Proud Maisie. *Fr.* The Heart of Mid-
lothian.
Quentin Durward, *sel.*
Rokeby, *sels.*
Rosabelle. *Fr.* The Lay of the Last
Minstrel.
Rover, The. *Fr.* Rokeby.
Serenade, A: "Ah! County Guy, the
hour is nigh." *Fr.* Quentin Dur-
ward.
Sir William of Deloraine at the Wiz-
ard's Tomb. *Fr.* The Lay of the
Last Minstrel.
Song: "Soldier, rest! thy warfare
o'er." *Fr.* The Lady of the Lake.
Song: "Weary lot is thine, fair maid,
A." *Fr.* Rokeby.
Song of the Reim-kennar, The. *Fr.*
The Pirate.
Song of the Shetland Fishers.
To a Lock of Hair.
To an Oak Tree. *Fr.* Waverley.
Waverley, *sel.*
SCOTT, WILLIAM BELL. Witch's Ballad,
The.
SCOTT, WINFIELD TOWNLEY. Biography
for Traman, *sel.*
Blue Sleigh.
Come Green Again.
Double Tree, The.
Fish Sonata, The.
Ivory Bed, The.
Landscape as Metal and Flowers.
Sonnet XIII: "Rise up, rise up, Jack
Spratt. And you, his wife."
Sonnet XV: "This is the way we say
it in our time."
Sonnet XII: "Virgins terrify too
many men."
Two Lives and Others.
Watch Hill.
Wax.
SCOTT-GATTY, SIR ALFRED SCOTT.
Maria Jane.
SCOTT-HOPPER, QUEENIE. Very Nearly.
SCULLY, JAMES. Glass Blower, The.
Midsummer.
SEAL, BRAJENDRANATH. Quest Eternal,
The, *sel.*
"SEC." News, The.
SEDLEY, SIR CHARLES. Child and
Maiden. *Fr.* The Mulberry Garden.
Get You Gone.
Mulberry Garden, The, *sel.*
Not, Celia, that I juster am.
On Fruition.
To Phillis.
Young Coridon and Phillis.
SEEGER, ALAN. I Have a Rendezvous
with Death.
SEIDEL, FREDERICK. Dayley Island.
Negro Judge, A.
Sickness, The.
SELJOUK, MEHDI ALI. Like the Prime
Mover.
SELLAR, WALTER CARRUTHERS, *and*
ROBERT JULIAN YEATMAN. *See*
YEATMAN, ROBERT JULIAN, *and*
WALTER CARRUTHERS SELLAR.
SEM TOB. Moral Proverbs, *sels.*
Some I've Seen So Crudely. *Fr.*
Moral Proverbs.
There's No Day without Night. *Fr.*
Moral Proverbs.
There's No Finer Treasure. *Fr.* Moral
Proverbs.
Whether Long or Sparing. *Fr.* Moral
Proverbs.
SEN, PRADIP. And Then the Sun.
SERENI, VITTORIO. December 3.
If You Are No Longer.

Terrace, The.
SERGEANT, HOWARD. High Kingdom.
Inland Sea, The.
Inundation, The. *Fr.* The Leaves of
Europe.
Leaves of Europe, The, *sels.*
Man Meeting Himself. *Fr.* The
Leaves of Europe.
Morning Song for a Lover.
SERRAILLIER, IAN. After Ever Happily;
or, The Princess and the Woodcutter.
Headless Gardener, The.
Piano Practice.
Tickle Rhyme, The.
SERVICE, ROBERT WILLIAM. Cremation
of Sam McGee, The.
Men of the High North.
Rhymes of a Rolling Stone, *sel.*
Shooting of Dan McGrew, The.
Spell of the Yukon, The.
SETHNA, K. D. Tree of Time.
"SETOUN, GABRIEL" (Thomas Nicoll
Hepburn). Fairy Ship, The.
How the Flowers Grow.
SEWELL, ELIZABETH. Forgiveness.
Job.
SEWELL, GEORGE. Dying Man in His
Garden, The.
SEXTON, ANNE. All My Pretty Ones.
Division of Parts, The.
Farmer's Wife, The.
For God While Sleeping.
Fortress, The.
Her Kind.
In the Deep Museum.
Letter Written on a Ferry Crossing
Long Island Sound.
Lost Ingredient, The.
Some Foreign Letters.
Starry Night, The.
Truth the Dead Know, The.
Unknown Girl in the Maternity Ward.
Water.
Woman with Girdle.
SHADWELL, THOMAS. Love and Wine.
SHAKESPEARE, WILLIAM. Absence. Son-
nets, LVII.
Alas, 'tis true I have gone here and
there. Sonnets, CX.
All That Glisters Is Not Gold. *Fr.*
The Merchant of Venice.
All the World's a Stage. *Fr.* As You
Like It.
Antony and Cleopatra, *sel.*
Antony's Oration. *Fr.* Julius Caesar.
Ariel's Dirge. *Fr.* The Tempest.
Ariel's Song. *Fr.* The Tempest.
As You Like It, *sels.*
Asleep, My Love? *Fr.* A Mid-
summer Night's Dream.
Being your slave, what should I do but
tend. Sonnets, LVII.
Beshrew that heart that makes my
heart to groan. Sonnets, CXXXIII.
Blind Love. Sonnets, CXLVIII.
Blow, Blow, Thou Winter Wind. *Fr.*
As You Like It.
Bottom's Song. *Fr.* A Midsummer
Night's Dream.
But be contented: when that fell arrest.
Sonnets, LXXIV.
Carpe Diem. *Fr.* Twelfth Night.
Cleopatra: The Barge She Sat In.
Fr. Antony and Cleopatra.
Clouds. *Fr.* The Tempest.
Clown's Song, The. *Fr.* Twelfth
Night.
Come Away, Come Away, Death. *Fr.*
Twelfth Night.
Come Night, Come Romeo. *Fr.* Romeo
and Juliet.
Come unto These Yellow Sands. *Fr.*
The Tempest.
Consolation, A. Sonnets, XXIX.
Crabbed Age and Youth. *Fr.* The
Passionate Pilgrim.
Cymbeline, *sels.*
Devouring Time, blunt thou the lion's
paws. Sonnets, XIX.
Dialogue in Praise of the Owl and the
Cuckoo. *Fr.* Love's Labour's Lost.
Dirge of Love. *Fr.* Twelfth Night.
Epilogue: "Now my charms are all
o'erthrown." *Fr.* The Tempest.

Epilogue: "Thus far, with rough and all-unable pen." *Fr.* King Henry V.
Epilogue: "When that I was and a little tiny boy." *Fr.* Twelfth Night.
Epitaph: "Done to death by slanderous tongues." *Fr.* Much Ado about Nothing.
Expense of spirit in a waste of shame, The. Sonnets, CXXIX.
Fairy's Life, A. *Fr.* The Tempest.
Farewell! thou art too dear for my possessing. Sonnets, LXXXVII.
Fear No More [the Heat o' the Sun]. *Fr.* Cymbeline.
Feste's Final Song. *Fr.* Twelfth Night.
Feste's Song. *Fr.* Twelfth Night.
Fidele. *Fr.* Cymbeline.
Fidele's Dirge. *Fr.* Cymbeline.
Fire Seven Times Tried This, The. *Fr.* The Merchant of Venice.
Flower of This Purple Dye. *Fr.* A Midsummer Night's Dream.
From fairest creatures we desire increase. Sonnets, I.
From you have I been absent in the spring. Sonnets, XCVIII.
Full Fathom Five [Thy Father Lies]. *Fr.* The Tempest.
Full many a glorious morning have I seen. Sonnets, XXXIII.
Hamlet, *sels.*
Hark, Hark! the Lark. *Fr.* Cymbeline.
How like a winter hath my absence been. Sonnets, XCVII.
How oft, when thou, my music, music play'st. Sonnets, CXXVIII.
How sweet and lovely dost thou make the shame. Sonnets, XCV.
I grant thou were not married to my Muse. Sonnets, LXXXIV.
If my dear love were but the child of state. Sonnets, CXXIV.
If She Be Made of White and Red. *Fr.* Love's Labour's Lost.
If the dull substance of my flesh were thought. Sonnets, XLIV.
If thou survive my well-contented day. Sonnets, XXXII.
In faith, I do not love thee with mine eyes. Sonnets, CXLI.
In the old age black was not counted fair. Sonnets, CXXVII.
It Was a Lover [and His Lass]. *Fr.* As You Like It.
Jog On, Jog On. *Fr.* The Winter's Tale.
Julius Caesar, *sels.*
King Henry V, *sels.*
King Henry VIII, *sel.*
King Richard II, *sels.*
King Richard III, *sel.*
Let me confess that we two must be twain. Sonnets, XXXVI.
Let me not to the marriage of true minds. Sonnets, CXVI.
Let those who are in favour with their stars. Sonnets, XXV.
Let's Talk of Graves. *Fr.* King Richard II.
Life without Passion, The. Sonnets, XCIV.
Like as the waves make towards the pebbled shore. Sonnets, LX.
Like as, to make our appetites more keen. Sonnets, CXVIII.
Lion of Winter, The. *Fr.* A Midsummer Night's Dream.
Lo, as a careful housewife runs to catch. Sonnets, CXLIII.
Look in thy glass, and tell the face thou viewest. Sonnets, III.
Love is too young to know what conscience is. Sonnets, CLI.
Love's Labour's Lost, *sels.*
Love's Perjuries. *Fr.* Love's Labour's Lost.
Lunatic, the Lover, and the Poet, The. *Fr.* A Midsummer Night's Dream.
Macbeth, *sels.*
Madrigal, A: "Crabbed age and youth." *Fr.* The Passionate Pilgrim.
Madrigal: "Take, O take those lips away." *Fr.* Measure for Measure.

Madrigal: "Tell me where is Fancy bred." *Fr.* The Merchant of Venice.
Measure for Measure, *sel.*
Merchant of Venice, The, *sels.*
Merry Note, A. *Fr.* Love's Labour's Lost.
Midsummer Night's Dream, A, *sels.*
Much Ado about Nothing, *sels.*
My love is as a fever, longing still. Sonnets, CXLVII.
My mistress' eyes are nothing like the sun. Sonnets, CXXX.
My Thoughts Do Harbour. *Fr.* The Two Gentlemen of Verona.
No longer mourn for me when I am dead. Sonnets, LXXI.
No more be grieved at that which thou hast done. Sonnets, XXXV.
Not marble, nor the gilded monuments. Sonnets, LV.
Not mine own fears, nor the prophetic soul. Sonnets, CVII.
Now the Hungry Lion Roars. *Fr.* A Midsummer Night's Dream.
O Mistress Mine. *Fr.* Twelfth Night.
Once More unto the Breach. *Fr.* King Henry V.
Ophelia's Song. *Fr.* Hamlet.
Orpheus with His Lute, *at. also to* Fletcher. *Fr.* King Henry VIII.
Othello, *sel.*
Othello and Desdemona. *Fr.* Othello.
Our Revels Now Are Ended. *Fr.* The Tempest.
Pedlar, The. *Fr.* The Winter's Tale.
Phoenix and the Turtle, The.
Polonius' Advice to Laertes. *Fr.* Hamlet.
Poor soul, the centre of my sinful earth. Sonnets, CXLVI.
Post Mortem. Sonnets, XXXII.
Queen Mab. *Fr.* Romeo and Juliet.
Remembrance. Sonnets, XXX.
Revolutions. Sonnets, LX.
Romeo and Juliet, *sels.*
Sea Dirge, A. *Fr.* The Tempest.
Seven Ages of Man, The. *Fr.* As You Like It.
Shall I compare thee to a summer's day? Sonnets, XVIII.
Sigh No More, Ladies. *Fr.* Much Ado about Nothing.
Sin of Self-Love. Sonnets, LXII.
Since brass, nor stone, nor earth, nor boundless sea. Sonnets, LXV.
So, now I have confest that he is thine. Sonnets, CXXXIV.
Some glory in their birth, some in their skill. Sonnets, XCI.
Song: "Blow, blow, thou winter wind." *Fr.* As You Like It.
Song: "Fear no more the heat o' th' sun." *Fr.* Cymbeline.
Song: "Full fathom five thy father lies." *Fr.* The Tempest.
Song: "If the scorn of your bright eyne." *Fr.* As You Like It.
Song: "It was a lover and his lass." *Fr.* As You Like It.
Song: "O mistress mine, where are you roaming?" *Fr.* Twelfth Night.
Song: "Pardon, goddess of the night." *Fr.* Much Ado about Nothing.
Song, A: "Tell me, where is fancy bred." *Fr.* The Merchant of Venice.
Song: "Under the greenwood tree." *Fr.* As You Like It.
Song: "What shall he have that kill'd the deer?" *Fr.* As You Like It.
Song: "When daisies pied and violets blue." *Fr.* Love's Labour's Lost.
Song: "When icicles hang by the wall." *Fr.* Love's Labour's Lost.
Sonnet: "Alas, 'tis true I have gone here and there." Sonnets, CX.
Sonnet: "Being your slave, what should I do but tend." Sonnets, LVII.
Sonnet: "Beshrew that heart that makes my heart to groan." Sonnets, CXXXIII.
Sonnet: "But be contented: when that fell arrest." Sonnets, LXXIV.
Sonnet: "Devouring Time, blunt thou the lion's paw." Sonnets, XIX.

Sonnet: "Expense of spirit in a waste of shame, The." Sonnets, CXXIX.
Sonnet: "Full many a glorious morning have I seen." Sonnets, XXIII.
Sonnet: "How like a winter hath my absence been." Sonnets, XCVII.
Sonnet: "How sweet and lovely dost thou make the shame." Sonnets, XCV.
Sonnet: "I grant thou wert not married to my Muse." Sonnets, LXXXII.
Sonnet: "If the dull substance of my flesh were thought." Sonnets, XLIV.
Sonnet: "If thou survive my well-contented day." Sonnets, XXXII.
Sonnet: "In faith, I do not love thee with mine eyes." Sonnets, CXLI.
Sonnet: "In the old age black was not counted fair." Sonnets, CXXVII.
Sonnet: "Let me confess that we two must be twain." Sonnets, XXXVI.
Sonnet: "Let me not to the marriage of true minds." Sonnets, CXVI.
Sonnet: "Let those who are in favour with their stars." Sonnets, XXV.
Sonnet: "Like as the waves make towards the pebbled shore." Sonnets, LX.
Sonnet: "Like as, to make our appetites more keen." Sonnets, CXVIII.
Sonnet: "Lo, as a careful housewife runs to catch." Sonnets, CXLIII.
Sonnet: "Love is too young to know what conscience is." Sonnets, CLI.
Sonnet: "My love is as a fever, longing still." Sonnets, CXLVII.
Sonnet: "My mistress' eyes are nothing like the sun." Sonnets, CXXX.
Sonnet: "No longer mourn for me when I am dead." Sonnets, LXXI.
Sonnet: "No more be grieved at that which thou hast done." Sonnets, XXXV.
Sonnet: "Not marble, nor the gilded monuments." Sonnets, LV.
Sonnet: "Not mine own fears, nor the prophetic soul." Sonnets, CVII.
Sonnet: "Poor soul, the centre of my sinful earth." Sonnets, CXLVI.
Sonnet: "Shall I compare thee to a summer's day?" Sonnets, XVIII.
Sonnet: "Since brass, nor stone, nor earth, nor boundless sea." Sonnets, LXV.
Sonnet: "So, now I have confest that he is thine." Sonnets, CXXXIV.
Sonnet: "Some glory in their birth, some in their skill." Sonnets, XCI.
Sonnet: "Sweet love, renew thy force; be it not said." Sonnets, LVI.
Sonnet: "Take all my loves, my love, yea, take them all." Sonnets, XL.
Sonnet: "That thou hast her, it is not all my grief." Sonnets, XLII.
Sonnet: "That time of year thou may'st in me behold." Sonnets, LXXIII.
Sonnet: "They that have power to hurt and will do none." Sonnets, XCIV.
Sonnet: "Those parts of thee that the world's eye doth view." Sonnets, LXIX.
Sonnet: "Those pretty wrongs that liberty commits." Sonnets, XLI.
Sonnet: "Tired with all these, for restful death I cry." Sonnets, LXVI.
Sonnet: " 'Tis better to be vile than vile esteemed." Sonnets, CXXI.
Sonnet: "To me, fair friend, you never can be old." Sonnets, CIV.
Sonnet: "Two loves I have of comfort and despair." Sonnets, CXLIV.
Sonnet: "Was it the proud full sail of this great verse." Sonnets, LXXXVI.
Sonnet: "What potions have I drunk of Siren tears." Sonnets, CXIX.
Sonnet: "When I do count the clock that tells the time." Sonnets, XII.
Sonnet: "When I have seen by Time's fell hand defaced." Sonnets, LXIV.
Sonnet: "When, in disgrace with for-

SHAKESPEARE, WILLIAM (*continued*)
tune and men's eyes." Sonnets, XXIX.
Sonnet: "When in the chronicle of wasted time." Sonnets, CVI.
Sonnet: "When most I wink, then do mine eyes best see." Sonnets, XLIII.
Sonnet: "When to the sessions of sweet silent thought." Sonnets, XXX.
Sonnet: "Why didst thou promise such a beauteous day." Sonnets, XXXIV.
Sonnet: "Woman's face with Nature's own hand painted, A." Sonnets, XX.
Sonnets, *sels.*
Soul and Body. Sonnets, CXLVI.
Spring. *Fr.* Love's Labour's Lost.
Stuff of Dreams, The. *Fr.* The Tempest.
Sweet love, renew thy force; be it not said. Sonnets, LVI.
Take all my loves, my love, yea, take them all. Sonnets, XL.
Take, O Take Those Lips Away. *Fr.* Measure for Measure.
Tell Me Where Is Fancy Bred. *Fr.* The Merchant of Venice.
Tempest, The, *sels.*
That thou hast her, it is not all my grief. Sonnets, XLII.
That time of year thou may'st in me behold. Sonnets, LXXIII.
There Is a Tide. *Fr.* Julius Caesar.
They that have power to hurt and will do none. Sonnets, XCIV.
This Blessed Plot . . . This England. *Fr.* King Richard II.
Those parts of thee that the world's eye doth view. Sonnets, LXIX.
Those pretty wrongs that liberty commits. Sonnets, XLI.
Through the Forest Have I Gone. *Fr.* A Midsummer Night's Dream.
Through the House. *Fr.* A Midsummer Night's Dream.
Thy glass will show thee how thy beauties wear. Sonnets, LXXVII.
Time and Love ("Since brass, nor stone, nor earth, nor boundless sea"). Sonnets, LXV.
Time and Love ("When I have seen by Time's fell hand defaced"). Sonnets, LXIV.
Tired with all these, for restful death I cry. Sonnets, LXVI.
'Tis better to be vile than vile esteemed. Sonnets, CXXI.
To Be, or Not to Be. *Fr.* Hamlet.
To His Love ("Shall I compare thee to a summer's day?"). Sonnets, XVIII.
To His Love ("When in the chronicle of wasted time"). Sonnets, CVI.
To me, fair friend, you never can be old. Sonnets, CIV.
To Silvia. *Fr.* The Two Gentlemen of Verona.
To-Morrow, and To-Morrow. *Fr.* Macbeth.
Triumph of Death, The. Sonnets, LXXI.
Troilus and Cressida, *sel.*
True Love. Sonnets, CXVI.
Twelfth Night, *sels.*
Two Gentlemen of Verona, The, *sels.*
Two loves I have of comfort and despair. Sonnets, CXLIV.
Unchangeable, The. Sonnets, CIX.
Under the Greenwood Tree. *Fr.* As You Like It.
Up and Down. *Fr.* A Midsummer Night's Dream.
Venus and Adonis, *sels.*
Violet Bank, A. *Fr.* A Midsummer Night's Dream.
Was it the proud full sail of this great verse. Sonnets, LXXXVI.
Weary with toil, I haste me to my bed. Sonnets, XXVII.
What is your substance, whereof are

you made. Sonnets, LIII.
What potions have I drunk of Siren tears. Sonnets, CXIX.
When Daffodils Begin to Peer. *Fr.* The Winter's Tale.
When Daisies Pied. *Fr.* Love's Labour's Lost.
When forty winters shall besiege thy brow. Sonnets, II.
When I consider everything that grows. Sonnets, XV.
When I do count the clock that tells the time. Sonnets, XII.
When I have seen by Time's fell hand defaced. Sonnets, LXIV.
When Icicles Hang by the Wall. *Fr.* Love's Labour's Lost.
When, in disgrace with fortune and men's eyes. Sonnets, XXIX.
When in the chronicle of wasted time. Sonnets, CVI.
When most I wink, then do mine eyes best see. Sonnets, XLIII.
When my love swears that she is made of truth. Sonnets, CXXXVIII.
When That I Was and a Little Tiny Boy. *Fr.* Twelfth Night.
When to the sessions of sweet silent thought. Sonnets, XXX.
Where Is Fancy Bred? *Fr.* The Merchant of Venice.
Where the Bee Sucks [There Suck I]. *Fr.* The Tempest.
Who Is Silvia? *Fr.* Two Gentlemen of Verona.
Who will believe my verse in time to come. Sonnets, XVII.
Why didst thou promise such a beauteous day. Sonnets, XXXIV.
Why is my verse so barren of new pride. Sonnets, LXXVI.
Why Should This a Desert Be. *Fr.* As You Like It.
Wind and the Rain, The. *Fr.* Twelfth Night.
Winter. *Fr.* Love's Labour's Lost.
Winter's Tale, The, *sels.*
Woman's face, with Nature's own hand painted, A. Sonnets, XX.
World's Way, The. Sonnets, LXVI.
Yet but Three? *Fr.* A Midsummer Night's Dream.
SHAKESPEARE, WILLIAM, *and* JOHN FLETCHER. *See* FLETCHER, JOHN, *and* WILLIAM SHAKESPEARE.
SHAKESPEARE, WILLIAM, *and others.* Passionate Pilgrim, The, *sel.*
SHANNON, MONICA. Could It Have Been a Shadow?
Ideal Age for a Man, The.
Only My Opinion.
SHAPCOTT, THOMAS WILLIAM. Finches, The.
Three Kings Came.
SHAPIRO, HARVEY. National Cold Storage Company.
SHAPIRO, KARL. Adam and Eve, *sels.*
Alphabet, The.
As You Say; an Anti-Poem. *Fr.* The Bourgeois Poet.
August Saturday Night on the Negro Street.
Auto Wreck.
Bourgeois Poet, The, *sels.*
Buick.
Confirmation, The.
Dirty Word, The.
Dome of Sunday, The.
Drug Store.
Elegy for a Dead Soldier.
Essay on Rime, *sels.*
First Time, The.
Full Moon: New Guinea.
Garden in Chicago, A.
Giantess, *tr.*
Glass Poem.
Haircut.
Jew.
Love for a Hand.
Manhole Covers.
Murder of Moses, The.
New Ring, The.
Nostalgia.

151st Psalm, The.
Poet.
Potomac, The.
Progress of Faust, The.
Recognition of Eve, The. *Fr.* Adam and Eve.
Scyros.
Sickness of Adam, The. *Fr.* Adam and Eve.
Sunday: New Guinea.
Terminal.
Twins, The.
V-Letter.
Voyage, The.
SHARP, WILLIAM. *See* "MACLEOD, FIONA."
SHARPLESS, STANLEY J. In Praise of Cocoa, Cupid's Nightcap.
SHAVER, EVA GILBERT. Dear Old Dad.
SHAW, JOHN. Song: "Who has robbed the ocean wave."
SHAW, WINIFRED MAITLAND. Fine Clay.
SHEDLOFSKY, WALTER. House of Yesterday.
Prophecy.
SHEFFIELD, JOHN, DUKE OF BUCKINGHAM AND NORMANBY. Happy Night, The.
SHELLEY, PERCY BYSSHE. Adonais.
Alastor; or, The Spirit of Solitude.
Arethusa.
Aziola, The.
Charles the First, *sel.*
Circumstance.
Cloud, The.
Cross, The.
Death.
Dirge, A: "Rough wind, that moanest loud."
Dream of the Unknown, A.
Elegy on the Death of John Keats, An. *Fr.* Adonais.
England in 1819.
Epipsychidion, *sels.*
Evening: Ponte al Mare, Pisa.
Flight of Love, The.
From the Arabic; an Imitation.
Hellas, *sel.*
Hymn of Pan.
Hymn to Intellectual Beauty.
Hymn to the Spirit of Nature.
I fear thy kisses, gentle maiden.
Indian Serenade, The.
Invitation, The.
Invocation: "Rarely, rarely, comest thou."
Lament, A: "O world! O life! O time!"
Landsman, The, *tr.*
Lines: "When the lamp is shattered."
Lines to a Critic.
Lines to an Indian Air.
Love's Philosophy.
Mask of Anarchy, The.
Mont Blanc.
Morning Star, *tr.*
Music, When Soft Voices Die.
Mutability.
Night.
Ode to the West Wind.
On a Poet's Lips I Slept.
On Fanny Godwin.
One Word Is Too Often Profaned.
Ozymandias [of Egypt].
Poet's Dream, The.
Prometheus Unbound, *sel.*
Rarely, Rarely, Comest Thou.
Recollection, The.
Similes for Two Political Characters of 1819.
Song: "Rarely, rarely, comest thou."
Song, A: "Widow bird sate mourning for her love, A."
Song to the Men of England.
Sonnet: England in 1819.
Sonnet: "Lift not the painted veil which those who live."
Stanzas—April, 1814.
Stanzas to Edward Williams.
Stanzas Written in Dejection near Naples.
Time.

To ——: "Music, when soft voices die."
To ——: "One word is too often profaned."
To a Lady, with a Guitar.
To a Skylark.
To Coleridge.
To Jane: The Recollection.
To Night.
To the Moon.
To the Night.
To Wordsworth.
Two Spirits, The.
When the Lamp Is Shattered.
Widow Bird [Sate Mourning for Her Love], A. *Fr.* Charles the First.
World's Great Age Begins Anew, The. *Fr.* Hellas.
Written in the Euganean Hills, North Italy.
SHEN YO. Wild Geese.
SHENSTONE, WILLIAM. Landskip, The.
Poet and the Dun, The.
Schoolmistress, The.
SHEPARD, ODELL. Housemates.
SHERBROOKE, VISCOUNT. *See* LOWE, ROBERT, VISCOUNT SHERBROOKE.
SHERBURNE, SIR EDWARD. And She Washed His Feet with Her Tears, and Wiped Them with the Hairs of Her Head, *tr.*
Chloris' Eyes and Breasts, *tr.*
Christo Smarrito, *tr.*
Conscience, *tr.*
Fountain, The, *tr.*
Ice and Fire, *tr.*
Love Once, Love Ever, *tr.*
Microcosm, The, *tr.*
SHERIDAN, RICHARD BRINSLEY. Duenna, The, *sel.*
Geranium, The.
Here's to the Maiden. *Fr.* The School for Scandal.
School for Scandal, The, *sel.*
Song: "If a daughter you have, she's the plague of your life." *Fr.* The Duenna.
SHERIDAN, RICHARD BRINSLEY, *and* NATHANIEL BRASSEY HALHED. Pleasing Constraint, The, *tr.*
SHERMAN, FRANK DEMPSTER. Dawn.
Snow-Bird, The.
SHERRY, RUTH FORBES. Waltz.
SHERWOOD, KATE BROWNLEE. Molly Pitcher.
SHIKI. At Matsushima.
New and the Old, The.
Summer Night.
SHIKO. Maple Leaves.
SHIPMAN, THOMAS. Epitaph on His Grandfather, An.
Resolute Courtier, The.
SHIRK, OTTIS. Resolved.
SHIRLEY, JAMES. Bard, The.
Contention of Ajax and Ulysses, The, *sel.*
Cupid and Death, *sel.*
Cupids Call.
Death the Leveller. *Fr.* The Contention of Ajax and Ulysses.
Glories of Our Blood and State, The. *Fr.* The Contention of Ajax and Ulysses.
Last Conqueror, The. *Fr.* Cupid and Death.
Triumph of Beautie Song, The, *sel.*
Victorious Men of Earth. *Fr.* Cupid and Death.
SHOREY, GEORGE H. Bubbles.
SHORT, JOHN. Carol: "There was a Boy bedded in bracken."
SHORTER, DORA SIGERSON. Ballad of Marjorie, A.
SHOVE, FREDEGOND. Farmer, The.
SHULER, CHESTER E. Faithful Few, The.
"SHY, TIMOTHY." *See* LEWIS, DOMINIC BEVAN WYNDHAM.
SIDGWICK, FRANK. Vision.
SIDNEY, SIR PHILIP. Arcadia, *sels.*
Astrophel and Stella, *sels.*
Come Sleep [O Sleep, the Certain Knot of Peace]. *Fr.* Astrophel and Stella.

Ditty, A: "My true-love hath my heart, and I have his." *Fr.* Arcadia.
Fourth Song: "Only joy, now here you are." *Fr.* Astrophel and Stella.
Having this day my horse, my hand, my lance. *Fr.* Astrophel and Stella.
He That Loves.
Highway, since you my chief Parnassus be. *Fr.* Astrophel and Stella.
His Being Was in Her Alone.
I never drank of Aganippe well. *Fr.* Astrophel and Stella.
In Wonted Walks.
Leave Me, O Love. *Fr.* Astrophel and Stella.
Litany, A: "Ring out your bells, let mourning shows be spread."
Loving in truth, and fain in verse my love to show. *Fr.* Astrophel and Stella.
My True Love Hath My Heart. *Fr.* Arcadia.
Nightingale, as Soon as April Bringeth, The.
No More, My Love. *Fr.* Astrophel and Stella.
O Dear Life, When Shall It Be. *Fr.* Astrophel and Stella.
Oft Have I Mused.
Only Joy! Now Here You Are. *Fr.* Astrophel and Stella.
Ring Out Your Bells.
Sestina. *Fr.* Arcadia.
She comes, and straight therewith her shining orbs do move. *Fr.* Astrophel and Stella.
Sleep. *Fr.* Astrophel and Stella.
Thou Blind-Man's Mark. *Fr.* Astrophel and Stella.
What may words say, or what may words not say. *Fr.* Astrophel and Stella.
What Tongue Can Her Perfections Tell. *Fr.* Arcadia.
When far-spent night persuades each mortal eye. *Fr.* Astrophel and Stella.
When Nature made her chief work, Stella's eyes. *Fr.* Astrophel and Stella.
When Two Suns Do Appear. *Fr.* Arcadia.
Who Hath His Fancy Pleased.
Who Is It That This Dark Night. *Fr.* Astrophel and Stella.
Who will in fairest book of Nature know. *Fr.* Astrophel and Stella.
With How Sad Steps, O Moon, Thou Climbst the Skies. *Fr.* Astrophel and Stella.
You that do search for every purling spring. *Fr.* Astrophel and Stella.
You that with allegory's curious frame. *Fr.* Astrophel and Stella.
Your words, my friend, right healthful caustics, blame. *Fr.* Astrophel and Stella.
SIEBER, HERMAN ALEXANDER. Blue Ridge Parkway.
From the Alembic.
H-Bomb Evening Down, An.
Oakdale Angel.
October.
On the Make-up of a Poet.
Posture for Next Year, A.
Saint and the Poet, The.
Something the West Will Remember.
That's All She Wrote.
SIGERSON, DORA. *See* SHORTER, DORA SIGERSON.
SIGOURNEY, LYDIA HUNTLEY. Indian Names.
Niagara.
SIKELIANOS, ANGELOS [*or* ANGHELOS]. Doric.
"SILESIUS, ANGELUS." *See* "ANGELUS SILESIUS."
SILKIN, JON. And I Turned from the Inner Heart.
Death of a Bird.
Death of a Son.
Deeply Gone.

Epilogue: "All the people in my poems walk into the dark."
First It Was Singing.
Furnished Lives.
Prologue: "All the animals in my poems go into the ark."
Respectabilities.
Return, The.
To Come Out Singing.
Two Freedoms, The.
SILL, EDWARD ROWLAND. Dead President, The.
Fool's Prayer, The.
Life.
Opportunity.
SILVERSTEIN, SHELLEY. Flag, The.
George Washington.
I must remember.
If I Had a Firecracker.
Mary's eyes are blue as azure.
Nothing to Do?
Oh Did You Hear?
Peace and Joy.
Sarah Cynthia Sylvia Stout.
There you sit.
Think of Eight Numbers.
Valentine.
SIMMONDS, J. Johnnie Sands, *at.*
She Loved Her Husband Dearly, *at.*
SIMONIDES (of Ceos). Cleobulus' Epitaph.
Climb to Virtue, The.
Greek Dead at Thermopylae, The.
Not to Die.
SIMPSON, ALBERT BENJAMIN. Abiding.
Believe the Bible.
It Is I, Be Not Afraid.
Thanksgiving.
SIMPSON, LOUIS. Against the Age.
American Poetry.
As Birds Are Fitted to the Boughs.
Bird, The.
Boarder, The.
Carentan O Carentan.
Dream of Governors, A.
Early in the Morning.
Green Shepherd, The.
Hot Night on Water Street.
Lover's Ghost, The.
My Father in the Night Commanding No.
Redwoods, The.
Rough Winds Do Shake.
Silent Generation, The.
Squeal.
Summer Storm.
To the Western World.
Walt Whitman at Bear Mountain.
SIMPSON, R. A. Night Out.
SINCLAIR, JOHN. Johnnie Sands, *at.*
She Loved Her Husband Dearly, *at.*
SINCLAIR, KEITH. Poem: "I met a sad girl in our town."
SINGER, BURNS. Sonnets for a Dying Man, *sels.*
Still and All.
Words Made of Water.
SIPE, MURIEL. Good Morning.
SITWELL, EDITH. Aubade.
Dirge for the New Sunrise. *Fr.* Three Poems of the Atomic Age.
Evening.
Façade, *sel.*
Heart and Mind.
Hornpipe. *Fr.* Façade.
How Many Heavens.
Kitchen Song.
Madame [*or* Madam] Mouse Trots. *Fr.* Façade.
Most Lovely Shade.
Scotch Rhapsody.
Spinning Song.
Still Falls the Rain.
Swans, The.
Three Poems of the Atomic Age, *sel.*
SITWELL, SIR OSBERT. Aubade: Dick, the Donkey-Boy.
La Tour du Sorcier.
Next War, The.
"Therefore Is the Name of It Called Babel."
Tom.
Winter the Huntsman.

SITWELL, SACHEVERELL. Lime Avenue, The.
Magnolia Tree in Summer.
SJÖBERG, LEIF, and WYSTAN HUGH AUDEN. See AUDEN, WYSTAN HUGH, and LEIF SJÖBERG.
SKEAT, WALTER WILLIAM. Clerk Ther Was of Cauntebrigge Also, A.
SKELTON, JOHN. Curse on the Cat, A. Fr. Phyllyp Sparowe.
Garlande of Laurell, The, sels.
L'Envoy: To His Book.
Lullay, Lullay, like a Child.
My Darling Dear, My Daisy Flower.
Phyllyp Sparowe, sels.
Prayer to the Father of Heaven, A.
Sleeper Hood-winked, The.
Though Ye Suppose.
To His Wife.
To Mistress Anne.
To Mistress Isabell Pennell. Fr. The Garlande of Laurell.
To Mistress Margaret Hussey. Fr. The Garlande of Laurell.
To Mistress Margaret Tilney. Fr. The Garlande of Laurell.
To Mistress Margery Wentworth. Fr. The Garlande of Laurell.
Tunnyng of Elynour Rummyng, The, sel.
Unfriendly Fortune.
Upon a Dead Man's Head.
Vengence on Cats. Fr. Phyllyp Sparowe.
Woefully Arrayed, at.
SKELTON, ROBIN. Ballad of a Mine, A.
History.
SLATER, FRANCIS CAREY ("Jan van Avond"). Drought, sel.
SLAVITT, DAVID R. In the Seraglio.
SLESSOR, KENNETH. Atlas, The, sels.
Beach Burial.
Country Towns.
Dutch Seacoast. Fr. The Atlas.
Five Bells.
Five Visions of Captain Cook, sel.
Gulliver.
King of Cuckooz, The. Fr. The Atlas.
Mermaids. Fr. The Atlas.
Post-Roads. Fr. The Atlas.
SLOAN, JOCELYN MACY. And the Pear Trees Shiver.
Invaders, The.
Stranger Bride.
"SMALACOMBE, JOHN." See MACKAY, LOUIS ALEXANDER.
SMART, CHRISTOPHER. All the Scenes of Nature Quicken.
Beauteous, Yea Beauteous More than These. Fr. A Song to David.
Flowers in a Garden.
For I Will Consider My Cat Jeoffry. Fr. Jubilate Agno.
For Saturday. Fr. Hymns for the Amusement of Children.
Gratitude. Fr. Hymns for the Amusement of Children.
Hymn for Saturday. Fr. Hymns for the Amusement of Children.
Hymns and Spiritual Songs, sels.
Hymns for the Amusement of Children, sels.
Instruments, The.
Jubilate Agno, sels.
Long-Suffering of God. Fr. Hymns for the Amusement of Children.
Mirth. Fr. Hymns for the Amusement of Children.
My Cat Jeoffry. Fr. Jubilate Agno.
Nativity of Our Lord and Savior Jesus Christ, The. Fr. Hymns and Spiritual Songs.
Night-Piece, A; or, Modern Philosophy.
On a Lady Throwing Snowballs at Her Lover.
On Taking a Bachelor's Degree.
St. Mark. Fr. Hymns and Spiritual Songs.
St. Matthias. Fr. Hymns and Spiritual Songs.
Song to David, A.

SMITH, ARTHUR JAMES MARSHALL. Archer, The.
Field of Long Grass.
Like an Old Proud King in a Parable.
My Death.
Ode: On the Death of William Butler Yeats.
Plot against Proteus, The.
To Henry Vaughan.
To Hold in a Poem.
SMITH, BRADFORD. Winter Is Icumen In.
SMITH, CICELY FOX. Channel Rhyme, A.
SMITH, CLARK ASHTON. Amor Aeternalis.
Horologe, The.
Incubus of Time, The.
Memorial.
Metaphor.
To the Daemon Sublimity.
SMITH, EDWARD LUCIE-. See LUCIE-SMITH, EDWARD.
SMITH, FLORENCE MARGARET. See SMITH, STEVIE.
SMITH, GOLDWIN. I'll Twine White Violets, tr.
SMITH, HILDA WORTHINGTON. Carpenter of Galilee, The.
SMITH, HORACE [or HORATIO]. Address to a Mummy.
SMITH, HORACE [or HORATIO], and JAMES SMITH. Baby's Debut, The.
Theatre, The.
SMITH, IAIN CRICHTON. End of the Season on a Stormy Day—Oban.
Old Woman.
Schoolgirl on Speech-Day in the Open Air.
Window, The.
Young Highland Girl Studying Poetry, A.
SMITH, J. DANSON. We'll Meet Again.
SMITH, JAMES, and HORACE SMITH. See SMITH, HORACE, and JAMES SMITH.
SMITH [or SMYTH], JOHN (1662–1717). Strephon.
SMITH, KAY. Eye of Humility, The.
When a Girl Looks Down.
SMITH, LUCY. Face of Poverty.
No Man an Island.
SMITH, OSWALD J. Another Year.
God Is with Me.
God's Presence Makes My Heaven.
Heart That Weeps, A.
I Turn to Jesus.
Master's Call, The.
SMITH, RAY. On the Little Bighorn.
SMITH, SAMUEL FRANCIS. America.
SMITH, SIDNEY GOODSIR. See SMITH, SYDNEY GOODSIR.
SMITH, STEVIE (Florence Margaret Smith). Cat Asks Mouse Out.
Nipping Pussy's Feet in Fun.
Not Waving but Drowning.
Parklands, The.
Singing Cat, The.
SMITH, SYDNEY. Salad, A.
SMITH, SYDNEY GOODSIR. For My Newborn Son.
Mither's Lament, The.
SMITH, VIVIAN. Bedlam Hills.
Last Summer, The.
SMITH, WILLIAM HART-. See HART-SMITH, WILLIAM.
SMITH, WILLIAM JAY. American Primitive.
Asides from the Clowns, sel., tr.
Autumn.
Butterfly.
Closing of the Rodeo, The.
Dog.
Fish.
Galileo Galilei.
Green Place, A.
Independence Day.
Jittery Jim.
Laughing Time.
Lovebirds.
Massacre of the Innocents, The.
Mole.
Panda, The.
Parrot.
Pavane for the Nursery, A.

Peacock of Java, The.
Pick Me Up.
Poet.
Toaster, The.
Tulip.
Voyages of Captain Cock, The.
Yak.
SMITHYMAN, KENDRICK. Cousin Emily and the Night Visitor.
SMOLLETT, TOBIAS GEORGE. Ode to Mirth.
Ode to Sleep.
Song: "To fix her—'twere a task as vain."
SMYTH, JOHN. See SMITH, JOHN (1662–1717).
SNELLING, LOIS. Know It Is Christmas.
SNODGRASS, WILLIAM DEWITT. April Inventory.
Campus on the Hill, The.
Cardinal, A.
Flat One, A.
Heart's Needle.
Home Town.
Leaving Ithaca.
Manet: The Execution of Emperor Maximilian.
Marsh, The.
Mementos, I ("Sorting out letters and piles of my old").
Mementos, II ("I found them there today").
Operation, The.
Orpheus.
Returned to Frisco, 1946.
September in the Park.
These Trees Stand.
True Name, tr.
San Francesco, at Night, tr.
SNYDER, GARY. Eight Sandbars on the Takano River.
Foxtail Pine.
Hunting.
Late Snow & Lumber Strike of the Summer of Fifty-four, The.
Market, The. Fr. Mts. & Rivers.
Mts. & Rivers, sels.
SNYDER, THURMOND. Beale Street, Memphis.
Beast with Chrome Teeth, The.
Seeds.
SOAMES, SIR WILLIAM, and JOHN DRYDEN. Art poétique, L', sel., tr.
SOBILOFF, HY. Hans Christian Andersen in Central Park.
SOLOMON, MARVIN. Assassination, The.
Sonnet for John-John.
SOLOVIEV [or SOLOVYOV], VLADIMIR SERGEYEVICH. With Wavering Feet I Walked.
SOPER, BRIAN. On the Triumph of Judith, tr.
SOPER, BRIAN, and IAIN FLETCHER. On the Armada Which Battled against England, tr.
SOPHOCLES. Antigone, sel.
Oedipus at Colonus, sels.
Old Age. Fr. Oedipus at Colonus.
What a Piece of Work Is a Man. Fr. Antigone.
Women of Trachis, sel.
SORA. Up the Barley Rows.
SORLEY, CHARLES HAMILTON. All the Hills and Vales Along.
In Memoriam, S.C.W., V. C.
Two Sonnets.
When You See Millions of the Mouthless Dead.
SOROKA, PAULINE E. Understanding.
SOULE, JEAN CONDER. Surprises.
SOUSTER, RAYMOND. Bed without a Woman, A.
Collector, The.
Flight of the Roller-Coaster.
Man Who Finds That His Son Has Become a Thief, The.
Not Wholly Lost.
Search.
Ties.
SOUTAR, CHARLES HENRY. After Johnson's Dance.
Irish Lords.
Old John Bax.
What the Red-haired Bo'sun Said.

SOUTAR, WILLIAM. Ballad: "O! shairly ye hae seen my love."
Signs.
Singing Bush, The.
Tryst, The.
SOUTHEY, ROBERT. After Blenheim.
Battle of Blenheim, The.
Curse of Kehama, The, *sels.*
Ebb Tide, The.
Epitaph: "Time and the World, whose magnitude and weight."
God's Judgment on a Wicked Bishop.
How the Waters Come Down at Lodore.
Kehama's Curse. *Fr.* The Curse of Kehama.
Love Indestructible. *Fr.* The Curse of Kehama.
Mariner, The.
Old Man's Comforts and How He Gained Them, The.
Scholar, The.
Witch, The.
SOUTHWELL, ROBERT. At Home in Heaven.
Burning Babe, The.
Christs Returne out of Egypt.
Christs Sleeping Friends.
Death of Our Ladie, The.
Flight into Egypt, The.
Her Nativity.
Looke Home.
Marie Magdalens Complaint at Christs Death.
Nativitie of Christ, The.
New Heaven, New Warre.
New Prince, New Pomp[e].
Presentation, The.
Sinnes Heavie Loade.
Vale of Teares, A.
Virgine Maries Conception, The.
Virgins Salutation, The.
Visitation, The.
SPACKS, BARRY. By This to Remember.
SPEARS, HEATHER. My Love behind Walls.
SPELLMAN, ALFRED B. John Coltrane— an Impartial Review.
Zapata & the Landlord.
SPENCE, LEWIS. Wee May o' Caledon, The.
SPENCER, ANNE. For Jim, Easter Eve.
Letter to My Sister.
Lines to a Nasturtium (a Lover Muses).
SPENCER, BERNARD. Part of Plenty.
Rendezvous, The.
Spring Wind, A.
SPENCER, THEODORE. Day, The.
SPENCER, THOMAS EDWARD. How Mc-Dougal Topped the Score.
SPENDER, STEPHEN. Almond Blossom in Wartime.
Daybreak.
Elementary School Classroom in a Slum, An.
Empty House.
Express, The.
Generous Years, The.
I Think Continually of Those [Who Were Truly Great].
Ice.
Immortal Spirit, The.
Landscape near an Aerodrome, The.
Man-made World, A.
Missing My Daughter.
My Parents Kept Me from Children Who Were Rough.
Not to You I Sighed.
O Night O Trembling Night.
Port Bou.
Seascape.
Separation, A.
Stopwatch and an Ordnance Map, A.
To My Daughter.
Truly Great, The.
War God, The.
What I Expected [Was].
Word.
Your Body Is Stars.
SPENSER, EDMUND. Amoretti, *sels.*
And Is There Care in Heaven? *Fr.* The Faerie Queene.
Astrophel.

Butterfly, The. *Fr.* Muiopotmos.
By Her That Is Most Assured to Her Self. *Fr.* Amoretti.
Colin Clout's Come Home Again.
Easter Morning. *Fr.* Amoretti.
Epithalamion.
Faerie Queene, The, *sels.*
Fresh Spring, the herald of love's mighty king. *Fr.* Amoretti.
Guardian Angels of Men. *Fr.* The Faerie Queene.
How long shall this like dying life endure. *Fr.* Amoretti.
Laurel leaf, which you this day do wear, The. *Fr.* Amoretti.
Lyke as a huntsman after weary chace. *Fr.* Amoretti.
Lyke as a ship that through the ocean wyde. *Fr.* Amoretti.
Merry cuckow, messenger of spring, The. *Fr.* Amoretti.
More than most fair, full of the living fire. *Fr.* Amoretti.
Most glorious Lord of life, that on this day. *Fr.* Amoretti.
Muiopotmos, *sel.*
My love is like to ice, and I to fire. *Fr.* Amoretti.
October Eclogue. *Fr.* The Shepheardes Calender.
One day I wrote her name upon the strand. *Fr.* Amoretti.
Panther, knowing that his spotted hide, The. *Fr.* Amoretti.
Port after Stormy Seas. *Fr.* The Faerie Queene.
Prothalamion.
Shepheardes [or Shepherd's] Calender, The, *sel.*
Since I have lacked the comfort of that light. *Fr.* Amoretti.
Sweet is the rose, but growes upon a brere. *Fr.* Amoretti.
Sweet warrior when shall I have peace with you? *Fr.* Amoretti.
Tale of Calidore, The. *Fr.* The Faerie Queene.
What guile is this, that those her golden tresses. *Fr.* Amoretti.
When those renowned noble peers of Greece. *Fr.* Amoretti.
"SPERVOGEL." Do You Know What the Hedgehog Said?
He Who Asks a Wolf to Dine Soon Has Cause to Wail.
SPEYER, LEONORA. Measure Me, Sky.
SPICER, JACK. Billy the Kid.
Book of Merlin, The.
Book of Percival, The.
SPINDEN, HERBERT JOSEPH. Lover's Lament, A, *tr.*
SPIRE, ANDRÉ. Nudities.
Spring.
SPITTELER, CARL. Theme.
SPONDE, JEAN DE. Sonnets d'Amour, *sels.*
Sonnets de la Mort, *sels.*
SQUIRE, SIR JOHN COLLINGS ("Solomon Eagle"). Discovery, The.
March, The.
Pipe, The.
STADLER, ERNST. On Crossing the Rhine Bridge at Cologne by Night.
Small Town.
STAFFORD, WILLIAM. Farm on the Great Plains, The.
For the Grave of Daniel Boone.
In Medias Res.
Who Risks It Where a Poet Lives, *tr.*
STAM, BETTY SCOTT. Open My Eyes.
STAMPA, GASPARA. Deeply repentant of my sinful ways.
I am now so weary with waiting.
Ladies, who of my lord would fain be told.
Oh Night.
STANABACK, LUCILLE. Discouraged.
STANHOPE, PHILIP DORMER. *See* CHESTERFIELD, PHILIP DORMER STANHOPE, 4TH EARL OF.
STANLEY, EDWARD GEORGE GEOFFREY SMITH, 14TH EARL OF DERBY. *See* DERBY, EARL OF.
STANLEY, THOMAS. Bracelet, The, *tr.*

Enjoyment, The, *tr.*
Picture, The, *tr.*
Vigil of Venus, The, *tr.*
STANTON, FRANK LEBBY. Sweetes' Li'l' Feller.
STAPLES, BARBARA H. Room for Jesus.
STARBUCK, GEORGE. Bone Thoughts on a Dry Day.
Fable for Blackboard.
New Strain.
On First Looking in on Blodgett's Keats's "Chapman's Homer."
One Man's Goose; or, Poetry Redefined.
Poems from a First Year in Boston.
Whaddaya Do for Action in This Place?
STARKEY, JAMES. *See* "O'SULLIVAN, SEUMAS."
STARRETT, VINCENT. Death of Santa Claus, The.
Femme Fatale.
Romantic Episode.
Sky-Writer.
Uncle Bing.
STEDMAN, EDMUND CLARENCE. Abraham Lincoln.
Hand of Lincoln, The.
How Old Brown Took Harper's Ferry.
Wanted—a Man.
STEFANILE, FELIX. Little Night Music, A.
Praying Mantis.
So Separate and Strange.
That Familiar Stranger.
Vampire Bride.
STEIN, EVALEEN. Wild Beasts.
STEIN, GERTRUDE. Afterwards, *sel.*
STEINER, FRANZ BAERMANN. Capturing Elephants.
8th May 1945.
Kafka in England.
STELLWAGON, RUSSELL. In Memory of Two Sons.
STEM, THAD, JR. Blotting Paper.
Boy on the Back of a Wagon.
Church Bell—Winter Time.
Courthouse Bell.
Crisis.
Deep Summer, after Midnight.
Little Saucers, Big Saucers.
Man Raking Leaves.
Old Hup.
Old Man's Fancy.
Paging Professor Gooseberry.
Post Card.
School Days.
Something More.
Sure Signs.
STEPANCHEV, STEPHEN [or STEPAN]. I Live and Do Not Live in Myself, *tr.*
O Living Flame of Love, *tr.*
STEPHEN, JAMES KENNETH. Grievance, A.
Last Ride Together, The.
Sincere Flattery of R. B.
Sincere Flattery of W. W. (Americanus).
Sonnet, A: "Two voices are there: one is of the deep."
To R. K.
STEPHENS, BRUNTON (James Brunton Stephens). Dominion of Australia, The.
My Other Chinee Cook.
STEPHENS, HARRY. Night Herding Song.
STEPHENS, JAMES. Check.
Christmas at Freelands.
Danny Murphy.
Egan O Rahilly, *tr.*
Glass of Beer, A.
Goat Paths, The.
In the College of Surgeons.
In the Orchard.
In Waste Places.
Little Things.
Main-Deep, The.
Midnight.
Peadar Og Goes Courting.
Righteous Anger.
Rivals, The.
Seumas Beg.
Shell, The.

STEPHENS, JAMES (continued)
Theme: "Golden eve is all astir, The."
Visit from Abroad, A.
Watcher, The.
What Tomas Said in a Pub.
White Fields.
Woman Is a Branchy Tree, A.
STEPHENS, JAMES, and WAI-LIM YIP.
Fits and Starts, tr.
STEPHENS, JAMES BRUNTON. See
STEPHENS, BRUNTON.
STERLING, GEORGE. Black Vulture, The.
STEVENS, GEORGE ALEXANDER. Bartleme Fair.
Maria.
Pastoral, A: "By the side of a green
stagnate pool."
STEVENS, MAXINE. How Can You?
STEVENS, WALLACE. Anecdote of the
Jar.
Anglais Mort à Florence.
Arrival at the Waldorf.
As You Leave the Room.
Asides on the Oboe.
Connoisseur of Chaos.
Course of a Particular, The.
Credences of Summer.
Disillusionment of Ten o'Clock.
Domination of Black.
Dry Loaf.
Earthy Anecdote.
Emperor of Ice-Cream, The.
Esthétique du Mal.
Final Soliloquy of the Interior Paramour.
Glass of Water, The.
High-toned Old Christian Woman, A.
Idea of Order at Key West, The.
Le Monocle de Mon Oncle.
Life Is Motion.
Man Carrying Thing.
Mrs. Alfred Uruguay.
Motive for Metaphor, The.
Of Modern Poetry.
Peter Quince at the Clavier.
Pleasures of Merely Circulating, The.
Plot against the Giant, The.
Ploughing on Sunday.
Poems of Our Climate, The.
Postcard from the Volcano, A.
Re-Statement of Romance.
Rock, The.
Sea Surface Full of Clouds.
Sense of the Sleight-of-Hand Man,
The.
Snow Man, The.
Study of Two Pears.
Sunday Morning.
Tea at the Palaz of Hoon.
Thirteen Ways of Looking at a Blackbird.
To an Old Philosopher in Rome.
To the One of Fictive Music.
World as Meditation, The.
STEVENSON, DOROTHY EMILY. Six and
Thirty.
STEVENSON, ROBERT LOUIS. Away with
Funeral Music.
Bed in Summer.
Block City.
Bright is the ring of words. Fr.
Songs of Travel.
Canoe Speaks, The, sel.
Careful Angler, The.
Celestial Surgeon, The.
Christmas at Sea.
Christmas Sermon, A, sel.
Cow, The.
Day Returns, The.
Evensong.
Foreign Children.
Good and Bad Children.
Henry James.
Husband to a Wife, A.
I will make you brooches and toys for
your delight.
If This Were Faith. Fr. Songs of
Travel.
In the Highlands.
It is very nice to think.
Land of Counterpane, The.
Land of Story-Books, The.
Little Land, The.

Looking-Glass River.
My House.
My Shadow.
My Wife.
Not I.
O to Be Up and Doing.
Over the Sea to Skye.
Prayer for the Household, A.
Rain.
Requiem.
Romance.
Say not of me that weakly I declined.
Sick Child, The.
Singing.
Skerryvore: The Parallel.
Songs of Travel, sels.
Swing, The.
System.
Time to Get Up.
To Be Honest, to Be Kind. Fr. A
Christmas Sermon.
To K[atharine]. de M[attos].
To My Wife.
To S. R. Crockett. Fr. Songs of
Travel.
Vagabond, The.
Where Go the Boats?
Whole Duty of Children, The.
Wind, The.
Windy Nights.
Winter.
STEVENSON, WILLIAM. Drinking Song,
at. Fr. Gammer Gurton's Needle.
Gammer Gurton's Needle, sel., at.
STEWART, DOUGLAS. Brindabella.
Dosser in Springtime, The.
Fisherman, The.
Garden of Ships, The.
Mahony's Mountain.
Nesting Time.
Silkworms, The.
Snow-Gum, The.
STEWART, HAROLD. Lament in Autumn.
Leaf-Makers, The.
STICKNEY, TRUMBULL. Be Still. The
Hanging Gardens Were a Dream.
Dramatic Fragment.
Live Blindly.
Mt. Lykaion.
STIDGER, WILLIAM LEROY. I Saw God
Wash the World.
STILL, JOHN. Drinking Song, at. Fr.
Gammer Gurton's Needle.
Gammer Gurton's Needle, sel., at.
Spanish Armada, The.
STIRLING, WILLIAM ALEXANDER, EARL
OF. Aurora, sel.
To Aurora. Fr. Aurora.
STIRLING-MAXWELL, LADY. See NORTON, CAROLINE ELIZABETH SARAH.
STOCKING, JAY THOMAS. O MasterWorkman of the Race.
STODDARD, CHUCK. Beat Child, The.
STODDARD, RICHARD HENRY. Abraham
Lincoln; an Horatian Ode.
STODDART, THOMAS TOD. Death-Wake,
The; or, Lunacy, sel.
Her, a Statue.
Mirthful Lunacy. Fr. The DeathWake; or, Lunacy.
STONE, JOHN A. And Thus He Spoke.
Arrival of the Greenhorn.
Australia and the Amazon.
Away Up on the Yuba.
California as It Is and Was.
California Ball.
California Bank Robbers.
California Bloomer.
California Legislature.
California Stage Company.
Coming around the Horn.
Crossing the Plains.
Emigrant from Pike.
Fools of '49, The.
Gambler, The.
Gold Lake and Gold Bluff.
Hangtown Gals.
Happy Miner, The.
He Ought to Know!
He's the Man for Me.
Honest John and William Relief.
Honest Miner, An.
Humbug Steamship Companies.

Hunting after Gold.
I Often Think of Writing Home.
I'm Sad and Lonely Here.
Joaquin the Horse-Thief.
Last Good-bye, The.
Life by the Cabin Fire, A.
Loss of the Central America.
Lousy Miner, The.
Miner's Dream, The.
Miner's Lament, The, I ("When the
gold fever raged, I was doing very
well").
Miners' Meeting, A.
Mountain Cottage, The.
My Log Cabin Home.
National Miner, The.
Prospecting Dream.
Rowdy, The.
Sacramento Gals.
Sensible Miner, The.
Shady Old Camp, The.
Sonora Filibusters, The.
Steam Navigation Thieves, The.
Striking a Lead.
Sweet Betsey from Pike.
That Is Even So!
Then Hurrah for Home!
Vocal Miner, The.
War in Camp.
When I Went Off to Prospect.
You Who Don't Believe It.
STONE, RUTH. In an Iridescent Time.
In the Interstices.
STONE, WALTER. Compelled to Love.
STORK, CHARLES WHARTON. For translations from Danish, Norwegian, and
Swedish, see PoPl; SiGo.
STORM, THEODOR. August-Advertisement.
Both my eyes, my dearest, close.
Consolation.
July.
Town, The.
STOUTENBURG, ADRIEN. Channel U.S.A.
—Live.
STOW, RANDOLPH. Dust.
Mad Maid's Whim.
Ruins of the City of Hay.
Strange Fruit.
Utopia of Lord Mayor Howard, The.
STRAMM, AUGUST. Battlefield.
Encounter.
Melancholy.
"STREAMER, COL. D." See GRAHAM,
HARRY.
STROBEL, MARION (Mrs. James Herbert
Mitchell). Another Song.
Captive.
STRODE, WILLIAM. In Commendation
of Music.
My Limbs I Will Fling.
On a Gentlewoman Walking in the
Snowe.
On Chloris Walking in the Snow.
On Westwell Downs.
STRONG, GEORGE A. Modern Hiawatha,
The. Fr. The Song of Milkanwatha.
Song of Milkanwatha, The, sel.
STRONG, LEONARD ALFRED GEORGE.
Brewer's Man, The.
By the Firelight.
Lowery Cot.
Memory, A.
Old Dan'l.
STRONG, PATIENCE. My Wish.
Pictures in the Fire.
Summer Moonlight.
STRONGWOLF, CHIEF JOSEPH. Indian
Prayer.
STROUD, DOROTHY CONANT. Bible, The.
He Lives! He Lives to Bless!
His Life Is Ours.
No Room.
Not One Is Turned Away from God.
You Will Find a Joy in Service.
STROZZI, GIOVANNI. On Buonarroti's
Statue of Night.
STRYKER, MELANCTHON WOOLSEY. Feste
Burg ist unser Gott, Ein, tr.
STUART, ALICE V. Peewits on the Hills.
STUART, DABNEY. Toward Colonos.
STUART, JANE. Hawicks' Crossing.
STUART, JESSE. Extended Invitation.

Gone, The.
Heart-summoned.
Spring Voices.
Two Leaves.
STUART, JOHN. Come unto Me.
STUART, MURIEL. In the Orchard.
Seeds.
STUBBS, JOHN HEATH-. *See* HEATH-STUBBS, JOHN.
STUDDERT-KENNEDY, GEOFFREY ANKETELL ("Woodbine Willie"). Awake, Awake to Love and Work.
Christian Soldier, The, *sel.*
Indifference.
SUCKLING, SIR JOHN. Against Fruition.
Aglaura, *sels.*
Answer to Some Verses Made in His Praise, An.
Ballad upon a Wedding, A.
Candle, A.
Constant Lover, The. *Fr.* Aglaura.
Deformed Mistress, The.
Encouragements to a Lover. *Fr.* Aglaura.
Lutea Allison.
No, No, Fair Heretic. *Fr.* Aglaura.
O for Some Honest Lover's Ghost.
Out upon It [I Have Loved].
Proffered Love Rejected.
Rejected Offer, The.
Siege, The.
Song: "No, no, fair heretic, it needs must be." *Fr.* Aglaura.
Song: "Out upon it, I have lov'd."
Song: "Why so pale and wan, fond lover?" *Fr.* Aglaura.
Sonnet: "Dost see how unregarded now."
Sonnet III: "Oh! for some honest Lovers ghost."
Sonnet II: "Of thee (kind boy) I ask no red and white."
To Cupid.
Upon A. M.
Why So Pale and Wan. *Fr.* Aglaura.
SUHL, YURI. Permanent Delegate, The.
SULLIVAN, ALOYSIUS MICHAEL. Measurement.
Radar.
SULLIVAN, NANCY. History of the World as Pictures, The.
SULLY-PRUDHOMME, RENÉ FRANÇOIS ARMAND. Struggle, The.
SUMMERS, HAL. April Fool.
Out of School.
Rescue, The.
SUMMERS, HOLLIS SPURGEON. Concerning Unnatural Nature: An Inverted Form.
King's X.
SUMMERS, WILLIAM C. Pastor, The.
Soft Job.
SUNG-TZU-HOU. Song: "On the Eastern Way at the City of Lo-yang."
SURREY, HENRY HOWARD, EARL OF. Alas, So All Things Now.
Complaint of a Lover Rebuked, *tr. Fr.* Sonnets to Laura.
Complaint of the Absence of Her Lover Being upon the Sea.
Complaint That His Ladie after She Knew of His Love Kept Her Face Alway Hidden from Him.
Description of Spring.
Epitaph on Clere, An.
Frailty and Hurtfulness of Beauty, The.
Give Place, Ye Lovers.
Laid in My Quiet Bed.
Love That Doth Reign, *tr. Fr.* Sonnets to Laura.
Love That Liveth and Reigneth in My Thought, *tr. Fr.* Sonnets to Laura.
Martial, the Things for to Attain. *tr.*
Means to Attain Happy Life, The, *tr.*
My Friend, the Things That Do Attain, *tr.*
On the Death of Sir Thomas Wyatt.
Set Me Whereas the Sun [Doth Parch the Green], *tr. Fr.* Sonnets to Laura.
So Cruel Prison.
Sonnets to Laura, *sels., tr.*
Soote Season, The.

Spring.
When Raging Love.
When Youth Had Led.
SUTHERLAND, EFUA. It Happened.
SU T'UNG-PO. End of the Year, The.
On the Birth of His Son.
Pear-Trees by the Fence.
SWALLOW, ALAN. On the Outgoing Train.
SWAN, EMMA. Connecticut Elm, The.
SWAN, JON. Nebraska.
SWARBERG, GEORGE W. Mistakes.
Worry.
SWARD, ROBERT. Celebration. *Fr.* Five Poems for J.F.K.
Dec. '63. *Fr.* Five Poems for J.F.K.
Five Poems for J.F.K.
Kissing the Dancer.
Mothers-in-Law.
Poem: "Rocks dark, green as leaves, The. Moss clings." *Fr.* Five Poems for J.F.K.
Reading Buber. *Fr.* Five Poems for J.F.K.
Terminal Theater.
That It That Thing Light. *Fr.* Five Poems for J.F.K.
There Is No Reason Why Not to Look at Death.
Uncle Dog: The Poet at 9.
What It Was.
SWARTZ, ROBERTA TEALE. Our Father.
SWENSON, MAY. August Night.
Café Tableau.
Cause & Effect.
Centaur, The.
Garden at St. John's, The.
Three Jet Planes.
SWIFT, JONATHAN. Ballad to the Tune of "The Cut-Purse," A.
Baucis and Philemon.
Beautiful Young Nymph Going to Bed, A.
Catullus de Lesbia.
Description of a City Shower, A.
Description of the Morning, A.
Epigram: "As Thomas was cudgelled one day by his wife."
Furniture of a Woman's Mind, The.
Half Your Book.
Lady's Dressing Room, The.
Maypole, A.
Mrs. Frances Harris's Petition.
On Censure.
On Gaulstown House.
On Poetry; a Rhapsody, *sel.*
On the Collar of a Dog.
On the Death of Dr. Swift.
Oysters.
Phyllis.
Power of Time, The.
Progress of Beauty, The.
Progress of Marriage, The.
Progress of Poetry, The.
Satirical [*or* Satyrical] Elegy on the Death of a Late Famous General, A.
Stella's Birthday.
To Dr. Delany, *tr.*
To Stella.
To Their Excellencies the Lords Justices of Ireland, the Humble Petition of Frances Harris [Who Must Starve and Die a Maid if It Miscarries].
Vanbrug's House.
Verses on the Death of Dr. Swift.
We Are God's Chosen Few.
Wicked Treasonable Libel, A.
SWINBURNE, ALGERNON CHARLES. Atalanta in Calydon, *sels.*
August.
Ave atque Vale.
Ballad of Dreamland, A.
Ballade of the Women of Paris, *tr.*
Before Sunset.
Before the Beginning of Years. *Fr.* Atalanta in Calydon.
Child's Laughter, A.
Chorus: "Before the beginning of years." *Fr.* Atalanta in Calydon.
Chorus: "When the hounds of spring are on winter's traces." *Fr.* Atalanta in Calydon.
Christmas Antiphones, *sel.*
Complaint of the Fair Armoress [*or* Armouress], The, *tr.*

Cor Cordium.
Dedication to Christina G. Rossetti.
Dolores.
Envoi: "Fly, white butterflies, out to sea."
Epitaph in Form of a Ballad, The, *tr.*
Faustine.
Forsaken Garden, A.
Fragment on Death, A, *tr.*
Fragoletta.
Garden of Proserpine, The.
Hertha.
Hesperia.
Higher Pantheism in a Nutshell, The.
Hounds of Spring, The. *Fr.* Atalanta in Calydon.
Hymn to Proserpine.
In the Orchard, *tr.*
Itylus.
Leave-taking, A.
Love and Sleep.
Match, A.
Nephelidia.
Oblation.
Roundel, The: "Roundel is wrought as a ring or a starbright sphere, A."
Sonnet for a Picture.
Sundew, The.
To a Seamew, *sel.*
Triumph of Time, The.
Watchman, What of the Night?
When the Hounds of Spring. *Fr.* Atalanta in Calydon.
SYLVESTER, JOSHUA. Autumnus.
Garden, The.
Go, Silly Worm.
Love's Omnipresence.
SYMONDS, JOHN ADDINGTON. Artist and His Work, The, *tr.*
Ballata: "I found myself one day all, all alone," *tr.*
Beauty and the Artist, *tr.*
Bellerophon, *sel., tr.*
Canzone: "Into a little close of mine I went," *tr.*
Flora's Flower, *tr.*
Heart-Coldness, *tr.*
Invitation to the Dance, *tr.*
Invitation to Youth, *tr.*
Invocation, An: "To God, the everlasting, who abides," *sel.*
Light and Darkness, *tr.*
Love Is a Refiner's Fire, *tr.*
Love Lifts to God, *tr.*
Lover and the Nightingale, The, *tr.*
Lover and the Sculptor, The, *tr.*
Love's Justification, *tr.*
Love's Longing, *tr.*
On Rome in the Pontificate of Julius II, *tr.*
On the Brink of Death, *tr.*
On the Painting of the Sistine Chapel, *tr.*
Pastoral, A: "There went out in the dawning light," *tr.*
People, The, *tr.*
Philosophic Flight, The, *tr.*
Phyllis, *tr.*
Prayer for Purification, A, *tr.*
Saon of Acanthus, *tr.*
There Are No Gods, *tr. Fr.* Bellerophon.
These Things Shall Be.
To Sleep, *tr.*
Vow to Cupid, The, *tr.*
Wine and Love and Lyre, *tr.*
Wooing, The, *tr.*
SYMONS, ARTHUR. Amoris Exsul: In the Bay.
At Dawn.
At Dieppe: Rain on the Down.
Bianca.
Ecstasy.
Emmy.
Envoi: "All that remains for me."
Escalade.
Fairy Wood, The.
In Ireland: By the Pool at the Third Rosses.
Let Mine Eyes See Thee, *tr.*
Leves Amores.
Magnificat.
O Flame of Living Love, *tr.*

SYMONS, ARTHUR (*continued*)
Obscure Night of the Soul, The, *tr.*
On an Air of Rameau.
Song of Autumn, *tr.*
Tune, A.

T

"T., C. W." Valentine.
TABB, JOHN BANISTER. Evolution.
Faith.
Fame.
Good Night!
Out of Bounds.
When Christ Was Born.
TABER, HARRY PERSONS. Wilhelmina Mergenthaler.
TABLEY, LORD DE. *See* DE TABLEY, JOHN BYRNE LEICESTER WARREN, 3D BARON.
TABRAR, JOSEPH. Mary Ann.
TAGLIABUE, JOHN. Bare Arms of Trees, The.
Fast.
Young President, The: March 1964.
TAGORE, RABINDRANATH. Bird, The. *Fr.* The Gardener.
For Strength. *Fr.* Gitanjali.
Gardener, The, *sel.*
Gitanjali, *sels.*
Home, The.
I Have Got My Leave. *Fr.* Gitanjali.
If It Is Not My Portion. *Fr.* Gitanjali.
Krishnakali.
Let This Be My Parting Word. *Fr.* Gitanjali.
Song-Offering, A. *Fr.* Gitanjali.
Yours.
TALBOT, ETHEL. Crab-Apple.
TANKERVIL, GEORGE. Evensong.
TANSILLO, LUIGI. Philosophic Flight, The.
T'AO CH'IEN. *See* TAO YUAN-MING.
TAO YUAN-MING [*or* T'AO CH'IEN]. I Built My Hut.
New Corn.
Reading the Book of Hills and Seas.
TAPPAN, WILLIAM BINGHAM. Gethsemane.
TASSO, TORQUATO. Aminta, *sel.*
Ancient, winged god, thou who didst first draw breath.
Dawn.
From the mantle of night.
Golden Age, The. *Fr.* Aminta.
Love is the soul of all things, the desire.
Of a Bee.
Of That Same.
Rose, The.
This is not death, immortal Margaret.
To Guglielmo Gonzaga, Duca di Mantova.
To Her Grace the Duchess of Ferrara.
To [Madame] Lucrezia d'Este [Duchess of Urbino].
TATE, ALLEN. Aeneas at Washington.
Cross, The.
Death of Little Boys.
Mediterranean, The.
Mr. Pope.
Ode to the Confederate Dead.
Pastoral: "Enquiring fields, courtesies, The."
Seasons of the Soul.
Sonnets at Christmas.
Subway, The.
Swimmers, The.
Winter Mask.
TATYANICHEVA, LUDMILA [*or* LYUDMILA]. July.
TAULER, JOHANNES. There Comes a Ship All Laden.
TAYLOR, ANN (Ann Taylor Gilbert). Meddlesome Matty.
TAYLOR, BAYARD. Angelo Orders His Dinner.
Bedouin Song.
Camerados.
Promissory Note, The.

TAYLOR, DEEMS. Concerning Mme. Robert, *tr.*
Hors d'Oeuvre, *tr.*
Proof Positive, *tr.*
Turn to the Left, *tr.*
TAYLOR, EDWARD. Address to the Soul Occasioned by a Rain, An.
Another Meditation at the Same Time. *Fr.* Preparatory Meditations, First Series.
Ebb and Flow, The.
Glory of and Grace in the Church Set Out, The. *Fr.* Gods Determinations.
Gods Determinations Touching His Elect, *sels.*
Housewifery [*or* Huswifery].
Joy of Church Fellowship Rightly Attended, The. *Fr.* Gods Determinations.
Meditation. Can. 1.2. Thy Love Is Better than Wine. *Fr.* Preparatory Meditations, Second Series.
Meditation. Cant. 2.1. The Lilly of the Vallies. *Fr.* Preparatory Meditations, First Series.
Meditation. Cant. 5.1. Eate Oh Friendes and Drink Yea Drink Abundantly Oh Beloved. *Fr.* Preparatory Meditations, Second Series.
Meditation. Can. 6.11. To See the Fruits of the Vally. *Fr.* Preparatory Meditations, Second Series.
Meditation. Col. 1.18. He Is the Head of the Body. *Fr.* Preparatory Meditations, Second Series.
Meditation Eight ("I kenning through astronomy divine"). *Fr.* Preparatory Meditations, First Series.
Meditation. 1 Cor. 3.21.22. All Things Are Yours. *Fr.* Preparatory Meditations, First Series.
Meditation. 1 Cor. 3.22. Death Is Yours. *Fr.* Preparatory Meditations, First Series.
Meditation. 1 Cor. 3.22. Life Is Youres. *Fr.* Preparatory Meditations, First Series.
Meditation. 1 Cor. 3.22. Whether Paul or Apollos, or Cephas. *Fr.* Preparatory Meditations, First Series.
Meditation. 1 Cor. 3.23. You Are Christ's. *Fr.* Preparatory Meditations, First Series.
Meditation. 1 Joh. 2.2. He Is a Propitiation for Our Sin. *Fr.* Preparatory Meditations, First Series.
Meditation Forty ("Still I complain; I am complaining still"). *Fr.* Preparatory Meditations, First Series.
Meditation from 1 Joh. 2.1. If Any Man Sin, We Have an Advocate. *Fr.* Preparatory Meditations, First Series.
Meditation. Joh. 15.13. Greater Love Hath No Man than This That a Man Lay Down His Life for His Friends. *Fr.* Preparatory Meditations, Second Series.
Meditation on Can. 1.3. Thy Name Is an Ointment Poured Out. *Fr.* Preparatory Meditations, First Series.
Meditation One ("What love is this of thine, that cannot bee"). *Fr.* Preparatory Meditations, First Series.
Meditation. Rev. 1.8. The Almighty. *Fr.* Preparatory Meditations, Second Series.
Meditation Seven ("Thy humane frame, my glorious Lord, I spy"). *Fr.* Preparatory Meditations, First Series.
Meditation Six ("Am I thy gold? Or purse, Lord, for thy wealth"). *Fr.* Preparatory Meditations, First Series.
Meditation Sixty-eight A ("Methinks I spy Almighty holding in"). *Fr.* Preparatory Meditations, Second Series.
Meditation Thirty-eight ("Oh! What a thing is Man?"). *Fr.* Preparatory Meditations, First Series.
Meditation Twenty ("View, all ye eyes above"). *Fr.* Preparatory Meditations, First Series.

Meditation Twenty-nine ("My shattred Phancy stole away from mee"). *Fr.* Preparatory Meditations, First Series.
Preface, The: "Infinity, when all things it beheld." *Fr.* Gods Determinations.
Preparatory Meditations, First Series, *sels.*
Preparatory Meditations, Second Series, *sels.*
Prologue: "Lord, can a crumb of earth [*or* dust] the earth outweigh."
Reflexion, The. *Fr.* Preparatory Meditations, First Series.
Upon a Spider Catching a Fly.
Upon a Wasp Chilled with Cold.
Upon Wedlock and Death of Children.
TAYLOR, ELEANOR ROSS. Buck Duke and Mamma.
Family Bible, *sels.*
Granddaughter. *Fr.* Family Bible.
In the Churchyard.
Madame.
Song: "Oh my dearie."
Uncle. *Fr.* Family Bible.
TAYLOR, JANE. I Love Little Pussy.
Lord, look upon a little child.
Star, The.
Stars at Night, The.
Thanksgiving, A.
TAYLOR, JEFFREYS. Lion and the Mouse, The.
TAYLOR, JOHN. Odcomb's Complaint, *sel.*
Of Seals and Arms.
Sonnet: Mackado, Fustian and Motley. *Fr.* Odcomb's Complaint.
TAYLOR, MART. California Humbugs.
Couldn't Stand the Press.
Do They Miss Me at Home? A Parody.
John Chinaman's Appeal.
Miner's Farewell, The.
Old Forty-nine.
Pike County Miner, The.
Poor Diggings.
That's the Way to Talk It.
We Are All a Panning.
TAYLOR, WILLIAM. Brewer's Coachman, The.
To the Fair Unknown.
TEASDALE, SARA. All That Was Mortal.
April.
Barter.
Coin, The.
Falling Star, The.
February Twilight.
Flight, The.
From the Sea.
Grace before Sleep.
I Shall Not Care.
I Stood upon a Star.
Lamp, The.
Late October.
Leaves.
Long Hill, The.
Look, The.
May Day.
Night.
Pierrot.
Spring Night.
Stars.
Those Who Love.
To Dick, on His Sixth Birthday.
To Rose.
When I Am Not with You.
Winter Noon.
Wisdom.
Young Love.
TEGNÉR, ESAIAS. Eternal, The.
"TEKAHIONWAKE." *See* JOHNSON, EMILY PAULINE.
TENNYSON, ALFRED TENNYSON, 1ST BARON. All in All.
As thro' the Land at Eve We Went. *Fr.* The Princess.
Ask Me No More. *Fr.* The Princess.
Balloon, The.
Be near me when my light is low. *Fr.* In Memoriam.
Beggar Maid, The.
Blow, Bugle, Blow. *Fr.* The Princess.
Break, Break, Break.
Brook, The.
But What's in the Larder?

Calm is the morn without a sound. *Fr.* In Memoriam.
Charge of the Light Brigade, The.
Choric Song: "There is sweet music here that softer falls." *Fr.* The Lotos-Eaters.
Come Down, O Maid [from Yonder Mountain Height]. *Fr.* The Princess.
Come into the Garden, Maud. *Fr.* Maud.
Crossing the Bar.
Daisy, The.
Danube to the Severn gave, The. *Fr.* In Memoriam.
Dark house, by which once more I stand. *Fr.* In Memoriam.
De Profundis, *sel.*
Death of the Old Year, The, *sel.*
Dedication: "These to His Memory— since he held them dear." *Fr.* Idylls of the King.
Doors, where my heart was used to beat. *Fr.* In Memoriam.
Dying Swan, The.
Eagle, The.
Enoch Arden, *sel.*
Fatima.
Flower in the Crannied Wall.
For I Dipped into the Future. *Fr.* Locksley Hall.
"Frater Ave atque Vale."
Go By.
Guinevere, *sel. Fr.* Idylls of the King.
Higher Pantheism, The.
Home They Brought Her Warrior Dead. *Fr.* The Princess.
I climb the hill: from end to end. *Fr.* In Memoriam.
I held it truth, with him who sings. *Fr.* In Memoriam.
Idylls of the King, *sels.*
If Sleep and Death be truly one. *Fr.* In Memoriam.
Iliad, The, *sel., tr.*
In Love, if Love Be Love. *Fr.* Idylls of the King.
In Memoriam A. H. H.
In the Garden at Swainston.
Is it, then, regret for buried time. *Fr.* In Memoriam.
Kraken, The.
Lady Clare.
Lady of Shalott, The.
Lancelot and Elaine, *sel. Fr.* Idylls of the King.
Lines: "Here often, when a child I lay reclined."
Locksley Hall.
Lotos-Eaters, The.
Lullaby: "Sweet and low, sweet and low." *Fr.* The Princess.
Mariana.
Maud.
Merlin and the Gleam.
Merlin and Vivien, *sel. Fr.* Idylls of the King.
Miller's Daughter, The.
Morte d'Arthur.
Night Encampment outside Troy, *tr. Fr.* The Iliad.
Now fades the last long streak of snow. *Fr.* In Memoriam.
Now Sleeps the Crimson Petal. *Fr.* The Princess.
O living will that shalt endure. *Fr.* In Memoriam.
O That 'Twere Possible. *Fr.* Maud.
Oh yet we trust that somehow good. *Fr.* In Memoriam.
Oak, The.
Ode on the Death of the Duke of Wellington, *sel.*
Oenone.
Old warder of these buried bones. *Fr.* In Memoriam.
Old Yew, which graspest at the stones. *Fr.* In Memoriam.
Owl, The.
Palace of Art, The.
Passing of Arthur, The. *Fr.* Idylls of the King.
Poet, The.
Poets and Their Bibliographies.

Poet's Song, The.
Princess, The, *sels.*
Revenge, The; a Ballad of the Fleet.
Ring out, wild bells, to the wild sky. *Fr.* In Memoriam.
Rizpah.
Sailor, Boy, The.
St. Agnes' Eve.
See What a Lovely Shell.
Sir Launcelot and Queen Guinevere.
Sleeping House, The. *Fr.* Maud.
"So careful of the type?" but no. *Fr.* In Memoriam.
Song: Owl, The.
Song: "Spirit haunts the year's last hours, A."
Song: "Splendor falls on castle walls, The." *Fr.* The Princess.
Song: "Tears, idle tears, I know not what they mean." *Fr.* The Princess.
Song of Love and Death. *Fr.* Idylls of the King.
Sonnet: "She took the dappled partridge flecked with blood."
Splendour Falls [on Castle Walls], The. *Fr.* The Princess.
Strong Son of God, immortal Love. *Fr.* In Memoriam.
Summer Night. *Fr.* The Princess.
Sweet and Low. *Fr.* The Princess.
Tears, Idle Tears. *Fr.* The Princess.
There Is None like Her. *Fr.* Maud.
There Is Sweet Music Here. *Fr.* The Lotos-Eaters.
There rolls the deep where grew the tree. *Fr.* In Memoriam.
Throstle, The.
Thy voice is on the rolling air. *Fr.* In Memoriam.
Till now the doubtful dusk reveal'd. *Fr.* In Memoriam.
Time draws near the birth of Christ, The. *Fr.* In Memoriam.
Tithonus.
To ——: With the Following Poem. *Fr.* The Palace of Art.
To Christopher North.
To the Rev. F. D. Maurice.
To Virgil.
To-night the winds begin to rise. *Fr.* In Memoriam.
Ulysses.
Unwatch'd, the garden bough shall sway. *Fr.* In Memoriam.
Vivien's Song. *Fr.* Idylls of the King.
Wish, that of the living whole, The. *Fr.* In Memoriam.
You Ask Me, Why, though Ill at Ease.
You say, but with no touch of scorn. *Fr.* In Memoriam.

TENNYSON, CHARLES. *See* TURNER, CHARLES TENNYSON.
TENNYSON, FREDERICK. Glory of Nature, The.
TERESA, SAINT, OF AVILA. *See* THERESA, SAINT, OF AVILA.
TERESA, SANTA, DE JESÚS. *See* THERESA, SAINT, OF AVILA.
TESSIMOND, ARTHUR SEYMOUR JOHN. Wet Windy Night on a Pavement.
THACKER, MARY AFTON. I Found God.
THACKERAY, WILLIAM MAKEPEACE. Little Billee.
Pocahontas.
Sorrows of Werther, The.
Tragic Story, A, *tr.*
Who Misses or Who Wins.
THATCHER, CHARLES ROBERT. Look Out Below!
THAYER, ERNEST LAWRENCE. Casey at the Bat.
THAYER, MARY DIXON (Mrs. Maurice Fremont-Smith). Treasures.
THEOCRITUS. Countryman's Wooing, A. *Fr.* Idylls.
Enchantment, The. *Fr.* Idylls.
Idylls, *sels.*
THERESA [or TERESA], SAINT, OF AVILA. Bookmark.
En las Internas Entrañas.
God Suffices.
Let Mine Eyes See Thee.
Lines Born of the Fire of Love for God.

Lines Written in Her Breviary.
On the Words "Dilectus Meus Mihi."
St. Teresa's Book-Mark.
Vertiendo Está Sangre.
THÉRÈSE, SISTER MARY. Contemplative, The.
For Simone Weil.
Interrogative.
Testament.
THIELE, COLIN. Aircraft, Landing.
Bert Schultz.
Tom Farley.
THOMAS, CORDIA. Lollypops, The.
THOMAS, DYLAN. After the Funeral.
Altarwise by Owl-Light.
Among Those Killed in the Dawn Raid Was a Man Aged a Hundred.
And Death Shall Have No Dominion.
Ceremony after a Fire Raid.
Conversation of Prayer, The.
Do Not Go Gentle into That Good Night.
Do You Not Father Me.
Especially When the October Wind.
Every Morning When I Wake. *Fr.* Under Milk Wood.
Fern Hill.
Force That through the Green Fuse Drives the Flower, The.
Hand That Signed the Paper, The.
Hunchback in the Park, The.
In My Craft or Sullen Art.
In the Beginning.
In the White Giant's Thigh.
Incarnate Devil.
Johnnie Crack and Flossie Snail. *Fr.* Under Milk Wood.
Lament: "When I was a windy boy and a bit."
Light Breaks Where No Sun Shines.
Marriage of a Virgin, The.
Over Sir John's Hill.
Poem in October.
Poem on His Birthday.
Refusal to Mourn the Death, by Fire, of a Child in London, A.
This Bread I Break.
Twenty-four Years.
Under Milk Wood, *sels.*
Under the Apple Boughs.
When All My Five and Country Senses See.
Winter's Tale, A.
THOMAS, EDITH MATILDA. Babushka.
THOMAS, EDWARD. ("Edward Eastaway"). Adlestrop.
As the Team's Head-Brass.
Cock Crow.
Combe, The.
If I Should Ever by Chance.
In Memoriam: Easter 1915.
Lights Out.
Long Small Room, The.
Out in the Dark.
Owl, The.
Private, A.
Sign-Post, The.
Tall Nettles.
Tears.
Thaw.
There Was a Time.
There's Nothing like the Sun.
Trumpet, The.
Unknown Bird, The.
Will You Come?
Words.
THOMAS, GILBERT. Christmas Carol, A: "Star that shone on Bethlehem, shine on London city."
THOMAS, LORENZO. Not That Hurried Grief.
THOMAS, RONALD STUART. Age.
Airy Tomb, The.
Anniversary.
Blackbird Singing, A.
Bread.
Chapel Deacon.
Children's Song.
Country Clergy, The.
Cynddylan on a Tractor [in Spring].
Day in Autumn, A.
Death of a Peasant.
Epitaph: "Poem in the rock and, The."
Farm Child.

But unto him came swift calamity. *Fr.* Sonnets.
By this low fire I often sit to woo. *Fr.* Sonnets.
Companions were we in the grove and glen. *Fr.* Sonnets.
Even as a lover, dreaming, unaware. *Fr.* Sonnets.
For Nature daily through her grand design. *Fr.* Sonnets.
Gertrude and Gulielma, sister-twins. *Fr.* Sonnets.
His heart was in his garden; but his brain. *Fr.* Sonnets.
How most unworthy, echoing in mine ears. *Fr.* Sonnets.
Morning comes; not slow, with reddening gold, The. *Fr.* Sonnets.
My Anna! though thine earthly steps are done. *Fr.* Sonnets.
My Anna! When for her my head was bowed. *Fr.* Sonnets.
Oh for the face and footstep!—Woods and shores! *Fr.* Sonnets.
One still dark night, I sat alone and wrote. *Fr.* Sonnets.
Perhaps a dream; yet surely truth has beamed. *Fr.* Sonnets.
Question, The.
Refrigerium.
Roll on, sad world! Not Mercury or Mars. *Fr.* Sonnets.
Sonnets, *sels.*
Still pressing through these weeping solitudes. *Fr.* Sonnets.
Thy baby, too, the child that was to be. *Fr.* Sonnets.
Under the mountain, as when I first knew. *Fr.* Sonnets.
Tu Fu. Clear after Rain.
Emperor, The.
Excursion, The.
Rain at Night, The.
TURBERVILE [*or* TURBERVILE], GEORGE.
Lover Exhorteth His Lady to Take Time, While Time Is, The.
Lover to His Lady, The.
Of a Rich Miser.
Of the Clock and the Cock.
That All Things Are as They Are Used.
That No Man Should Write but Such as Do Excel.
To an Old Gentlewoman Who Painted Her Face.
To His Friend.
To His Love, That Sent Him a Ring Wherein Was Graved, "Let Reason Rule."
To One That Had Little Wit.
To the Roving Pirate.
TURCO, LEWIS. Gather These Bones.
House and Shutter.
November 22, 1963.
Seer, The.
TURNBULL, ELEANOR L. Castile, *tr.*
Sonnet: "Those flakes of fire, brilliant sparks of light," *tr.*
TURNER, CHARLES TENNYSON. Artist on Penmaenmawr, The.
Letty's Globe.
On the Eclipse of the Moon of October 1865.
Steam Threshing-Machine, The.
To a "Tenting" Boy.
TURNER, ELIZABETH. I Almost Did—Very Nigh—Had Not God Stopped the Lie.
TURNER, NANCY BYRD. Black and Gold.
Down a Sunny Easter Meadow.
February Birthday.
First Christmas Night of All.
First Thanksgiving of All.
Old Quin Queeribus.
Planting a Tree.
Sampler, The.
Ships.
Sure Sign, A.
Washington.
Wings and Wheels.
TURNER, WALTER JAMES. In Time like Glass.
Romance.

Song: "Lovely hill-torrents are."
TUSIANI, JOSEPH. *For translations from Italian, see* AnML; RBL.
TUSSER, THOMAS. Winds, The.
TWEEDY, HENRY HALLAM. Christmas at Babbitt's.
TYCHBORN, CHIDIOCK. *See* TICHBORNE, CHIDIOCK.
TYLER, ROYALL. Epigram: "How many drag the marriage chain."
TYNAN, KATHARINE (Katharine Tynan Hinkson). All in the April Morning.
Childless Woman in Heaven, The.
TYRTAEUS. How Can Man Die Better.
TYUTCHEV, FEODOR [*or* FYODOR] IVANOVICH. As Ocean Holds the Globe.
Silentium.
Twilight.

U

UBERTI, FAZIO DEGLI. *See* FAZIO DEGLI UBERTI.
UC DE LA BACALARIA. To Praise the Gift of Love That Binds My Heart.
UC DE LA BACALARIA, GAUCELM FAIDIT, *and* SAVARIC DE MAULEON. *See* FAIDIT, GAUCELM, UC DE LA BACALARIA, *and* SAVARIC DE MAULEON.
UHLAND, LUDWIG (Johann Ludwig Uhland). Bertran de Born.
Hope in Springtime.
Lad of the Mountain, The.
On the Death of a Child.
ULRICH VON LICHTENSTEIN [*or* LIECHTENSTEIN]. Among Sweet Tones in Forest Bowers.
UNAMUNO, MIGUEL DE. Castile.
UNDERHILL, EVELYN (Mrs. Stuart Moore). Holy Spirit, The.
UNGARETTI, GIUSEPPE. Choruses Descriptive of Dido's States of Mind. *Fr.* The Promised Land.
Dying.
I Am a Creature.
In Memoriam.
Island, The.
Pity.
Promised Land, The, *sel.*
Quiet.
Rivers.
Without More Weight.
You Were Shattered.
UNTERMEYER, LOUIS. Advice to Bachelors, *tr.*
Advice to Country Girls, *tr.*
Age and Youth, *tr.*
All for Love, *tr.*
Appeal to the Phoenix.
At the Bottom of the Well.
Bad Joke, A, *tr.*
Barine, the Incorrigible, *tr.*
Beating Heart, The, *tr.*
Birds and Bees, *tr.*
Boastful Husbandman, *tr.*
Burning Bush.
By Moonlight, *tr.*
Caliban in the Coal Mines.
Catullus Talks to Himself, *tr.*
Caution, *tr.*
Challenge, The, *tr.*
Confessional, The, *tr.*
Constancies, *tr.*
Dark Chamber, The.
Edgar A. Guest Considers "The Good Old Woman Who Lived in a Shoe" and the Good Old Truths Simultaneously.
Equals.
Familiarity Breeds Indifference, *tr.*
Fool of Love, The, *tr.*
Hair-dressing.
Hands.
Healing the Wound, *tr.*
Heaven, *par.*
I Close Her Eyes, *tr.*
I Hate to See You Clad, *tr.*

Incentive, The, *tr.*
Insufficient Venegeance, *tr.*
Interrupted Romance, *tr.*
Katharine, *tr.*
Look to the Leaf, *tr.*
Love's Torment, *tr.*
Morning After, The, *tr.*
Passing of Lydia, The, *tr.*
Plea for Haste, A, *tr.*
Plea for Postponement, A, *tr.*
Pleasure, *tr.*
Prayer: "God, though this life is but a wraith."
Prayer for This House.
Precaution, *tr.*
Recipe, *tr.*
Right Time, The, *tr.*
Ripe Fruit, The, *tr.*
Seduced Girl, *tr.*
Sleepers, The.
Song of Songs, The, *tr.*
Song of the Vivandiere, *tr.*
Spinning Song, *tr.*
Summer Storm.
Swimmers.
Teasing Lovers, The, *tr.*
This White and Slender Body, *tr.*
Three Sweethearts, *tr.*
To His Girl, *tr.*
Too Literal Pupil, The, *tr.*
Too Young for Love, *tr.*
Vita Brevis, *tr.*
Woman, *tr.*
Work and Play, *tr.*
Your Snow-white Shoulder, *tr.*
For translations from Greek, see UnTE.
UPDIKE, JOHN. Seagulls.
Seven Stanzas at Easter.
UPHAM, SAM C. Song of the Argonauts.
Ye Ancient Yuba Miner, of the Days of '49.
URDANG, CONSTANCE. In Acknowledgment of the Praises of European Writers, *tr.*
Madman, The.
URDANG, CONSTANCE, *and* SATORU SATO. Pole Vault, *tr.*
URFÉ, HONORÉ D'. Song of the Inconstant Hylas.
USCHOLD, MAUD E. Casual Gold.

V

VALLE, ADRIANO DEL. Cradle Song of the Elephants.
VALLIS, VAL. Fishing Season.
VANADA, LILLIAN SCHULZ. Fuzzy Wuzzy, Creepy Crawly.
"VAN AVOND, JAN." *See* SLATER, FRANCIS CAREY.
VANBRUGH, SIR JOHN. Aesop, *sel.*
In the Sprightly Month of May. *Fr.* Aesop.
VAN DOREN, MARK. Burial.
Donkey.
Eternity's Low Voice.
Former Barn Lot.
God of Galaxies, The.
He's Coming.
Inconsistent.
Jonathan Gentry, *sel.*
Let There Be Law.
Marriage.
Never Another.
Oldest Cemetery.
Praise Doubt.
Pulse, The.
Sonnet VI: "Chasten your fears, I have not been destroyed."
Sonnet XIV: "I was confused; I cannot promise more."
Sonnet XXXIII: "My only need—you ask me, and I tell you."
Story-Teller, The.
To a Child with Eyes.
Tom's Sleeping Song. *Fr.* Jonathan Gentry.

VAN DOREN, MARK (*continued*)
Undersong.
Whisperer, The.
Wind in the Grass.
VAN DYKE, HENRY. America for Me.
Burning Bush, The.
Children in the Market-Place.
Foundations.
Four Things.
Gospel of Labor, The.
Home.
Hymn of Joy.
Hymn of Labor.
Jesus Return.
One in Christ.
Peace Hymn of the Republic.
Prayer: "Lord, the newness of this day."
They Who Tread the Path of Labor.
Victoria.
Voyagers.
Way, The.
Work.
VAN FOSSAN, JOSEPHINE. Mourning.
"VANOLIS, BYSSHE." *See* THOMSON, JAMES (1834–1882).
VAUGHAN, HENRY. Admission.
After the Storm.
As time one day by me did pass.
Ascension-Day.
Ascension-Hymn.
Begging.
Beyond the Veil.
Bird, The.
Brittish Church, The.
Christs Nativity.
Cock-crowing.
Come, come, what doe I here?
Corruption.
Dedication, The: "My God, thou that didst dye for me."
Distraction.
Dressing.
Easter-Day.
Easter Hymn.
Evening-Watch, The.
Fragment: "Walk with thy fellow-creatures: note the hush."
God's Saints.
H. Scriptures.
Holy Communion, The.
I Walked the Other Day.
Joy of My Life.
Lampe, The.
Man.
Mans Fall, and Recovery.
Match, The.
Midnight.
Morning Watch, The.
Mount of Olives.
Night ("Dear night! this world's defeat").
Night, The ("Through that pure Virgin-shrine").
Palm-Tree, The.
Passion, The.
Peace.
Peace of Heaven, The.
Pilgrimage, The.
Praise.
Pursuite, The.
Quickness.
Regeneration.
Relapse, The.
Religion.
Resolve, The.
Resurrection and Immortality.
Retreat[e], The.
Rom. Cap. 8. Ver. 19.
Rules and Lessons.
Sap, The.
Search, The.
Seed Growing Secretly, The.
Shepheards, The.
Showre, The.
Silence, and stealth of dayes! 'tis now.
Son-Dayes.
Starre, The.
Storm, The.
Tempest, The.
They Are All Gone [into the World of Light].
Timber, The.

To a Bird after a Storm.
To Amoret [Gone from Him].
To His Friend ——.
Unfold! Unfold!
Unprofitablenes.
Vanity of Spirit.
Waterfall, The.
World, The.
World of Light, The.
VAUGHN, JAMES P. Four Questions Addressed to His Excellency the Prime Minister.
Movie Queen.
So?
Three Kings.
Two Ladies Bidding Us "Good Morning."
VAUQUELIN DE LA FRESNAYE, JEAN. O Gentle Breeze.
VAUX, THOMAS, 2D BARON VAUX OF HARROWDEN. Aged Lover Renounceth Love, The.
He Renounceth All the Effects of Love.
No Pleasure without Some Pain.
Of a Contented Mind.
On the Instability of Youth.
VEGA, GARCILASO DE LA. *See* GARCILASO DE LA VEGA.
VENABLE, WILLIAM HENRY. Founders of Ohio, The.
VERE, EDWARD DE, 17TH EARL OF OXFORD. Renunciation, A.
Were I a King.
VERGIL [*or* VIRGIL] (Publius Vergilius Maro). Aeneid, The, *sels.*
Batalis and the Man, The. *Fr.* The Aeneid.
Boat Race, The. *Fr.* The Aeneid.
Boxing Match, The. *Fr.* The Aeneid.
Chariot Race, The. *Fr.* Georgics.
Eclogues, *sels.*
Eighth Pastoral of Virgil, The. *Fr.* Eclogues.
Georgics, *sels.*
VERLAINE, PAUL. Auburn.
I Hate to See You Clad.
Lassitude.
Retinue.
Song of Autumn.
Spring.
Tears Flow in My Heart.
White Moon, The.
VERY, JONES. Abdolonymus the Sidonian.
April Snow, The.
Barberry-Bush, The.
Broken Bowl, The.
Clouded Morning, The.
Columbine, The.
Created, The.
Dead, The.
Fugitive Slaves, The.
Garden, The.
Hand and Foot, The.
Life.
Lost, The.
Love.
Man in Harmony with Nature.
Nature.
New Birth, The.
New Man, The.
New World, The.
On the Completion of the Pacific Telegraph.
On Visiting the Graves of Hawthorne and Thoreau.
Presence, The.
Psyche.
Ship Rock.
Slave, The.
Soul-Sickness.
Spirit-Land, The.
Strangers, The.
Thy Beauty Fades.
Thy Brother's Blood.
To the Canary Bird.
Tree, The.
Yourself.
"VESEY, PAUL." *See* ALLEN, SAMUEL.
VIAU, THÉOPHILE DE. Ode: "Before me, where a raven croaks."
To Corinna.
VICENTE, GIL. Ballad of Flérida.

Cantiga: "Grace and beauty has the maid."
Song: "Grace and beauty has the maid."
Song: "If thou art sleeping, maiden."
VICTOR, FLORENCE. Berlin Crisis.
Contest.
VIDAL, PEIRE. I Put an End to Singing.
It'll Be a Long Time Again before My Friends.
My Lord Dragoman, If I Had a Good Steed.
Well Pleased Am I with the Gentle Season.
When I Breathe This Air.
VIERECK, PETER. Big Crash Out West.
Kilroy.
Planted Skull, The.
Some Refrains at the Charles River.
To Be Sung.
Vale from Carthage.
VILIKAZI, B. W. Umamina.
VILLA, JOSÉ GARCIA. Divine Poems, *sels.*
God, Is, like, Scissors.
Manner of a Poet's Germination, The.
My, Fellowship, with, God.
229.
Way My Ideas Think Me, The.
VILLIERS, GEORGE, 2D DUKE OF BUCKINGHAM. *See* BUCKINGHAM, GEORGE VILLIERS, 2D DUKE OF.
VILLON, FRANÇOIS. Ballad for Fat Margot.
Ballad of Dead Ladies, The.
Ballad [*or* Ballade] of Ladies' Love.
Ballad of the Ladies of Olden Times.
Ballade of the Fair Helm-Maker.
Ballade of the Women of Paris.
Ballade of Villon and Fat Margot.
Belle Heaulmiere to the Daughters of Joy, The.
Complaint of the Fair Armoress [*or* Armouress].
Epitaph in Form of a Ballad, The.
Fragment on Death, A.
His Mother's Service to Our Lady.
I Am François, to My Dismay.
Lament of the Lovely Helmet-Dealer.
Old Woman Laments the Days of Her Youth, The.
Snows of Yester-Year, The.
Villon's Epitaph.
VINAL, HAROLD. Flight.
Gentleman in Oils.
Ghostly Reaper.
Heimdall.
Sleeping Village.
Toward Avernus.
We, the Few Who Believe.
Well-Finder, The.
Wreath for One Lost, A.
VIRGIL. *See* VERGIL.
VOGELWEIDE, WALTHER, VON DER. *See* WALTHER VON DER VOGELWEIDE.
VOITURE, VINCENT. Evening Beauty.
On the way from Fontenay.
Rondeau: In Good Plain French.
VREPONT, BRIAN. Apple-Tree, The.
Net Menders, The.

W

"W., A." In Praise of the Sun.
Upon Visiting His Lady by Moonlight.
Where His Lady Keeps His Heart.
WADDELL, HELEN. Carmina Burana, *sel.*, *tr.*
Cathemerinon, *sels.*, *tr.*
In the Woods Alone, *tr.*
Morning Glory, The, *tr.*
O God that art the sole hope of the world, *tr.*
WADDINGTON, MIRIAM. Catalpa Tree.
Drug Addict, The. *Fr.* Three Prison Portraits.
Season's Lovers, The.

Thou Didst Say Me.
Three Prison Portraits, *sel.*
WAGNER, CHRISTIAN. Lilacs.
WAGONER, DAVID. Emergency Maker, The.
Feast, The.
Man from the Top of the Mind, The.
Nesting Ground, The.
News from the Court.
Sudden Frost.
Warning to My Love, A.
WAGONER, GLENN E. I Never Knew.
WAGSTAFF, BLANCHE SHOEMAKER. Earth Trembles Waiting.
WAI-LIM YIP *and* JAMES STEPHENS. *See* STEPHENS, JAMES, *and* WAI-LIM YIP.
WAIN, JOHN. Anniversary.
Apology for Understatement.
Au Jardin des Plantes.
Boisterous Poem about Poetry, A, *sel.*
Brooklyn Heights.
Confusions of the Alphabet.
New Sun, The.
Poem: "Like a deaf man meshed in his endless silence."
Poem without a Main Verb.
Reason for Not Writing Orthodox Nature Poetry.
Sestina for Khasan Israelov. *Fr.* Wildtrack.
Song about Major Eatherly, A.
This above All Is Precious and Remarkable.
Wildtrack, *sel.*
WAITE, ARTHUR EDWARD. At the End of Things, *sel.*
WAKOSKI, DIANE. Apparitions Are Not Singular Occurrences.
Coins and Coffins under My Bed.
Empress, The.
Justice Is Reason Enough.
Poem to the Man on My Fire Escape.
Six of Cups.
WALCOTT, DEREK. Alba.
Bronze.
Far Cry from Africa, A.
Letter from Brooklyn, A.
Parang.
Polish Rider, The.
Ruins of a Great House.
WALDO, ROSE. Welcome.
WALEY, ARTHUR. Clearing at Dawn, *tr.*
Cranes, The, *tr.*
Crossing the River, *tr.*
Dreaming That I Went with Li and Yü to Visit Yüan Chen, *tr.*
Fighting South of the Ramparts, *tr.*
Having Climbed to the Topmost Peak of the Incense-Burner Mountain, *tr.*
I Built My Hut, *tr.*
In the Mountains on a Summer Day, *tr.*
Kokin Shu, *sel., tr.*
Madly Singing in the Mountains, *tr.*
New Corn, *tr.*
On the Birth of His Son, *tr.*
People Hide Their Love, *tr.*
Pine-Trees in the Courtyard, The, *tr.*
Planting Flowers on the Eastern Embankment, *tr.*
Plucking the Rushes, *tr.*
Protest in the Sixth Year of Ch'ien Fu, A, *tr.*
Pruning Trees, *tr.*
Reading the Book of Hills and Seas, *tr.*
Sailing Homeward, *tr.*
Shui Shu, *sel., tr.*
Song: "On the Eastern Way at the City of Lo-yang," *tr.*
Wild Geese, *tr.*
WALKER, MARGARET. For My People.
Molly Means.
October Journey.
WALLACE, EDNA KINGSLEY. Growing Up.
WALLACE, JOHN AIKMAN. Prayer Moves the Hand That Moves the World.
WALLACE, ROBERT. Double Play, The.
Evening.
In a Spring Still Not Written Of.
Snapshot for Miss Bricka Who Lost

in the Semi-final Round of the Pennsylvania Lawn Tennis Tournament at Haverford, July, 1960, A.
WALLACE, WILLIAM ROSS. Hand That Rocks the Cradle Is the Hand That Rules the World, The.
WALLACE-CRABBE, CHRIS. Ancient Historian.
Love Poem.
WALLER, EDMUND. Go, Lovely Rose.
Of English Verse.
Of Loving at First Sight.
Of the Last Verses in the Book.
Old Age.
On a Girdle.
On My Lady Isabella Playing on the Lute.
Plea for Promiscuity, A.
Poets Lose Half the Praise.
Song: "Go, lovely Rose."
Song: "Stay Phoebus, stay."
To a Girl.
To a Very Young Lady.
To Mr. Henry Lawes [Who Had Then Newly Set a Song of Mine in the Year 1635].
To One Married to an Old Man.
To Phillis.
To the Mutable Fair.
To the Younger Lady Lucy Sydney.
WALLER, JOHN FRANCIS. Spinning-Wheel Song, A.
WALSH, CHAD. When the Unnatural Warm Fair October.
WALSH, DONALD DEVENISH. Weeping and Singing, *tr.*
WALSH, ERNEST. I Played on the Grass with Mary.
Old Fellow.
Serious Poem, A.
Sonnet: "My duchess was the werst she laffed she bitte."
WALSH, WILLIAM (1663–1708). Death.
Despairing Lover, The.
WALSH, WILLIAM (20th century). Letter: The Japanese, to Her Husband at War.
WALTER, HOWARD ARNOLD. I Would Be True.
My Creed.
WALTER, NINA WILLIS. Candle and Book.
WALTHER VON DER VOGELWEIDE. Alas, whereto have vanished all my years!
Children Won't Do What They Ought.
I Sat Cross-legged upon a Stone.
Lady World, You Tell the Devil.
O Where Have They Vanished All My Years!
Under the Lime Tree.
Under the Lindens.
Who Slays the Lion? Who Slays the Giant?
Whoso, Lord God, Being Bold to Say.
Winter Has Done Us Great Harm Everywhere.
WANDREI, DONALD. Challenger, The.
Forest Shapes.
Lyric of Doubt.
Prehistoric Huntsman, The.
Water Sprite.
Woman at the Window, The.
WANG WEI. Green Stream, A.
WARD, ELIZABETH STUART PHELPS. Eternal Christmas.
WARD, KENNETH. Investor's Soliloquy.
WARD, SAMUEL. Proem, A: "When in my walks I meet some ruddy lad."
WARD, VERNON. As You Are, My Friend.
Heart Path.
Mixed Emotions.
Of Dust and Stars.
Of Violets.
Two Cats Make the World.
Two Teacups.
WARE, EUGENE FITCH ("Ironquill"). Ballad in "G," A.
He and She.
Whist.
Zephyr.
WARNER, SUSAN B. Candle Burning in the Night, A.

WARNER, SYLVIA TOWNSEND. Image, The.
Nelly Trim.
WARR, BERTRAM J. Deviator, The.
On a Child with a Wooden Leg.
Working Class.
WARREN, JOHN BYRNE LEICESTER, BARON DE TABLEY. *See* DE TABLEY, JOHN BYRNE LEICESTER WARREN, BARON.
WARREN, ROBERT PENN. Autumnal Equinox on Mediterranean Beach.
Bearded Oaks.
Dark Woods, *sel.*
Dogwood, The. *Fr.* Dark Woods.
Flower, The.
Mortmain.
Pursuit.
Summer Storm (*circa* 1916), and God's Grace.
WARTON, JOSEPH. Enthusiast, The; or, The Lover of Nature.
Ode to Evening.
Ode to Fancy.
Song, A: "While in the bower, with beauty blessed."
WATERMAN, NIXON. Johnny's History Lesson.
Whistling Boy.
WATKINS, EDWARD. Figures of Authority.
WATKINS, VERNON. Ballad of the Trial of Sodom.
Ballad of the Two Tapsters.
Collier, The.
Discoveries.
For a Christening.
Heron, The.
In Spring, *tr.*
Lady with the Unicorn, The.
Lover's Words, A.
Music of Colours: The Blossom Scattered.
Peace in the Welsh Hills.
Poet and Goldsmith.
Postscript.
Prayer, A: "If I dare pray for one."
Questions, *tr.*
Returning from Harvest.
Think of This, *tr.*
Yeats in Dublin, *sel.*
Yew-Tree, The.
WATSON, ROBERT. First Man on Venus.
Halloween, a Poem for Children.
Lines for a President.
Most Wanted.
On Stage, off Stage.
Winter Lovers.
WATSON, SARA RUTH. Bouncing Ball.
WATSON, WILFRED. Canticle of Darkness.
Emily Carr.
Juniper Tree, The.
Windy Bishop, The.
WATSON, SIR WILLIAM. April.
Song: "April, April."
Wordsworth's Grave.
WATT, LAUCHLAN MACLEAN. I Bind My Heart.
WATT, W. W. Penny Wise and Found Poolish.
So This Is Autumn.
WATTS, ALARIC ALEXANDER. Austrian Army, An.
WATTS, ISAAC. Against Idleness and Mischief.
Cradle Hymn.
Cradle Song: "Hush! my dear, lie still and slumber."
From All That Dwell below the Skies.
I Sing the Mighty Power of God.
Let Dogs Delight.
Little Busy Bee.
Man Frail, and God Eternal.
O God Our Help in Ages Past.
O How I Love Thy Law.
Sluggard, The.
There Is a Land.
WATTS, MARJORIE SEYMOUR. New Shoes.
WEAVER, JOHN VAN ALSTYN. Concerning the Economic Independence of Women.

WEAVER, JOHN VAN ALSTYN (*cont.*)
Drug Store.
WEBB, FRANCIS. Captain of the *Oberon,*
The. *Fr.* A Drum for Ben Boyd.
Drum for Ben Boyd, A, *sels.*
Five Days Old.
Idyll.
Leichhardt in Theatre, *sel.*
Papuan Shepherd, A. *Fr.* A Drum
for Ben Boyd.
Room, The. *Fr.* Leichhardt in Thea-
tre.
Sea, The.
WEBB, PHYLLIS. Making.
Marvell's Garden.
Tall Tale, A; or, A Moral Song.
WEBER, RICHARD. In Memoriam I:
Elizabeth at Twenty.
In Memoriam II: Elizabeth in Italy.
WEBSTER, H. D. L. Lorena.
WEBSTER, JOHN. All the Flowers of the
Spring. *Fr.* The Devil's Law Case.
Call for the Robin Redbreast [and the
Wren]. *Fr.* The White Devil.
Cornelia's Song. *Fr.* The White
Devil.
Devil's Law Case, The, *sels.*
Dirge, A: "Hark, now everything is
still." *Fr.* The Duchess of Malfi.
Duchess of Malfi, The, *sel.*
Land Dirge, A. *Fr.* The White Devil.
Speech by Romelio. *Fr.* The Devil's
Law Case.
White Devil, The, *sel.*
WEEVER, ROBERT. See WEVER, ROB-
ERT.
WEHNER, ANDREW CHARLES. Wave,
The.
WEIL, JAMES L. Fancy Fishing.
Kind of Libation, A.
WEISBURD, MEL. Between Chicago and
St. Paul.
WEISS, NEIL. Ageing Athlete, The.
Hike, The.
WEISS, THEODORE. Dance Called David,
The.
Egyptian Passage, An.
Fire at Alexandria, The.
House of Fire.
Out of Your Hands.
WELCH, MARIE DE L. Chipmunk.
St. Francis and the Cloud.
WELCH, MYRA BROOKS. Touch of the
Master's Hand, The.
WELHAVEN [or WELLHAVEN], JOHAN
SEBASTIAN CAMMERMEYER. Like an
April Day.
WELLES, WINIFRED. Climb.
River Skater.
Skipping Along Alone.
Stocking Fairy.
WELLESLEY, DOROTHY, DUCHESS OF
WELLINGTON. Buried Child, The.
Fr. Deserted House.
Deserted House, *sel.*
Fishing.
WELLHAVEN, JOHAN SEBASTIAN CAMMER-
MEYER. See WELHAVEN, JOHAN SE-
BASTIAN CAMMERMEYER.
WELLINGTON, DOROTHY WELLESLEY,
DUCHESS OF. See WELLESLEY,
DOROTHY.
WELLMAN, WADE. Ballad of Despair,
A.
On the Staircase.
WELLS, AMOS RUSSEL. Pray!
Read the Bible Through.
WELLS, CAROLYN. How to Tell the Wild
Animals.
Our Polite Parents.
WELLS, JAMES. Golden Rule, The.
WENTWORTH, WILLIAM CHARLES. Aus-
tralasia, *sel.*
WERFEL, FRANZ. Elevation.
When You Enraptured Me.
WERNER, ALICE. Plover, The, *tr.*
WESLEY, CHARLES. Christ, Whose Glory
Fills the Skies.
Easter Hymn.
Ever-living Church, The.
Father, How Wide Thy Glories Shine.
For One in Doubt. *Fr.* Three Hymns.
Loving Jesus, gentle Lamb.
My Companion.

Three Hymns.
WESLEY, JOHN. Give to the Wind Thy
Fears, *tr.*
To the Supreme Being, *tr.*
WESLEY, SAMUEL (1691–1739). From a
Hint in the Minor Poets.
On the Setting Up of Mr. Butler's
Monument in Westminster Abbey.
WEST, ARTHUR GRAEME. God, How I
Hate You.
WEST, ELIZABETH DICKINSON. See
DOWDEN, ELIZABETH DICKINSON
WEST.
WESTLAKE, NANCY. Celle Qui Meurt.
WESTON, MILDRED. Father.
WESTWOOD, THOMAS. Night of Spring.
WEVER, ROBERT. In an Arbour Green.
In Youth Is Pleasure.
WEVILL, DAVID. Poets, The.
WEYRAUCH, WOLFGANG. Everest of
Tears.
Red Dust.
WHARTON, PHILIP. Menalcas and
Enosia.
On the Banishment of Cicero.
WHEELER, CHARLES ENOCH. Adjura-
tion.
WHEELOCK, JOHN HALL. Earth.
Golgotha.
Holy Earth, The, *sel.*
I Sought You.
In the Immense Cathedral. *Fr.* The
Holy Earth.
It Is Finished.
Legend.
Lift your arms to the stars.
Night Thoughts in Age.
Prayer: "Have pity on us, Power just
and severe."
Solitudes.
Two Societies, The.
Unison.
Wood-Thrush.
WHICHER, GEORGE FRISBIE. Invitation
to a Mistress, *tr.*
Juliana, *tr.*
Love Laughs at Winter, *tr.*
WHISTLER, LAURENCE. Flight.
Form of Epitaph, A.
Portrait in the Guards, A.
WHITBREAD, THOMAS. Civilities.
November 25, 1963.
WHITE, BLANCO. See WHITE, JOSEPH
BLANCO.
WHITE, CHRISTINE. Secret of Song.
WHITE, ELWYN BROOKS. Classic Waits
for Me, A.
Marble-Top.
WHITE, GEORGE. I Came to Jesus.
WHITE, HENRY KIRKE. Clifton Grove,
sel.
To an Early Primrose.
WHITE, JAMES TERRY. Not by Bread
Alone.
WHITE, JOSEPH BLANCO. Black Is a
Soul.
Night.
To Night.
WHITE, STEWART EDWARD. Bung Yer
Eye.
WHITE, WILLIAM ALLEN. Rhyme of the
Dream-Maker Man, A.
WHITMAN, WALT. After the Dazzle of
Day.
After the Sea-Ship.
Ages and Ages Returning at Intervals.
Ah, Poverties, Wincings, and Sulky
Retreats.
Animals. *Fr.* Song of Myself.
Army Corps on the March, An.
As Adam Early in the Morning.
Beasts, The. *Fr.* Song of Myself.
Beat! Beat! Drums!
Beginning My Studies.
Belief in Plan of Thee.
Bivouac on a Mountain Side.
By Blue Ontario's Shore, *sel.*
By the Bivouac's Fitful Flame.
Carol of the Bird, The. *Fr.* When
Lilacs Last in the Dooryard Bloom'd.
Cavalry Crossing a Ford.
Centenarian's Story, The.
Chanting the Square Deific.
City Dead-House, The.

Come Up from the Fields Father.
Crossing Brooklyn Ferry.
Dalliance of the Eagles, The.
Darest Thou Now O Soul.
Death Carol. *Fr.* When Lilacs Last
in the Dooryard Bloom'd.
Dismantled Ship, The.
Divine Ship Sails the Divine Sea for
You, The.
From Pent-up Aching Rivers.
Good-bye My Fancy!
Greatest City, The.
Had I the Choice.
Hand-Mirror, A.
Hast Never Come to Thee an Hour.
Here the Frailest Leaves of Me.
Hush'd be the Camps To-Day.
I Dream'd in a Dream.
I Hear America Singing.
I Hear and Behold God in Every Ob-
ject.
I Hear It Was Charged against Me.
I Heard You Solemn-sweet Pipes of
the Organ.
I Saw in Louisiana a Live-Oak Grow-
ing.
I Sing the Body Electric.
I Sit and Look Out.
In Cabined Ships at Sea.
In Paths Untrodden.
Last Invocation, The.
Lo, Victress on the Peaks.
Look Down Fair Moon.
Long, Too Long America.
Miracles.
Night on the Prairies.
Noiseless Patient Spider, A.
O Captain! My Captain!
O Hymen! O Hymenee!
O You Whom I Often and Silently
Come.
Old-Time Sea-Fight, An. *Fr.* Song of
Myself.
Once I Pass'd through a Populous City.
One's-Self I Sing.
Others May Praise What They Like.
Out of the Cradle Endlessly Rocking.
Out of the Rolling Ocean the Crowd.
Ox-Tamer, The.
Passage to India.
Passage to More than India. *Fr.*
Passage to India.
Patrolling Barnegat.
Poets to Come.
Prayer of Columbus.
Reconciliation.
Runner, The.
Scented Herbage of My Breast.
Sight in Camp [in the Daybreak Gray
and Dim], A.
Sometimes with One I Love.
Song for All Seas, All Ships.
Song of Joys, A, *sel.*
Song of Myself.
Song of the Answerer, *sel.*
Song of the Exposition, *sel.*
Sparkles from the Wheel.
Spider, The.
Sum of All Known Reverence, The.
There Was a Child Went Forth.
This Compost.
This Dust Was Once the Man.
This Moment Yearning and Thought-
ful.
To a Locomotive in Winter.
To Him That Was Crucified.
To One Shortly to Die.
To the Garden the World.
To the Leaven'd Soil They Trod.
To the States.
To Think of Time, *sel.*
Torch, The.
Twilight Song, A.
Unexpressed, The.
Virgil Strange I Kept on the Field
One Night.
When I Heard at the Close of the Day.
When I Heard the Learn'd Astronomer.
When I Peruse the Conquer'd Fame.
When Lilacs Last in the Dooryard
Bloom'd.
Whoever You Are Holding Me Now
in Hand.
Woman Waits for Me, A.

World below the Brine, The.
Wound-Dresser, The.
You Felons on Trial in Courts.
You Lingering Sparse Leaves of Me.
WHITNEY, F. B. God Knows the Answer.
WHITTAKER, FREDERICK. Custer's Last Charge.
WHITTEMORE, REED. Alfred Lord Tennyson.
No Retreat.
Notes on a Certain Terribly Critical Piece.
Out of My Study Window.
Reflections upon a Recurrent Suggestion by Civil Defense Authorities That I Build a Bombshelter in My Backyard.
Storm from the East, A.
WHITTIER, JOHN GREENLEAF. Abraham Davenport.
All's Well.
Among the Hills, sel.
Andrew Rykman's Prayer, sel.
At Last.
Barbara Frietchie.
Barefoot Boy, The.
Bartholdi Statue, The.
Book Our Mothers Read, The.
Brewing of Soma, The, sel.
Brown of Ossawatomie.
Cable Hymn, The.
Cassandra Southwick.
Dear Lord and Father of Mankind. Fr. The Brewing of Soma.
Emancipation Group, The.
Eternal Goodness, The, sel.
Faith.
Ichabod.
In Earthen Vessels.
In School-Days.
Laus Deo!
Life and Love.
Maud Muller.
Memories.
My Playmate.
O Brother Man.
Old Burying-Ground, The.
Our Master.
Over-Heart, The, sel.
Pageant, The.
Prelude: "Along the roadside, like the flowers of gold." Fr. Among the Hills.
Proclamation, The.
Proem: "I love the old melodious lays."
Pumpkin, The.
Riddle of the World, The.
Skipper Ireson's Ride.
Snow-bound.
Storm, The. Fr. Snow-bound.
Telling the Bees.
To Paths Unknown.
WICKHAM, ANNA (Mrs. Patrick Hepburn). Silence.
WIDDEMER, MARGARET. Companions.
Ghost to Come.
Mother.
Secret Cavern, The.
Village Christmas.
Winter Branches.
WIENERS, JOHN. Acts of Youth, The.
For Jan.
In the Half Light of Holding and Giving.
Meadow, The.
Series 5.8, A.
Two Years Later.
Waning of the Harvest Moon, The.
Where Fled.
Windows of Waltham, The.
WILBUR, RICHARD. Advice to a Prophet.
Baroque Wall-Fountain in the Villa Sciarra, A.
Beasts.
Beautiful Changes, The.
Bell Speech.
Black November Turkey, A.
Ceremony.
Christmas Hymn, A.
Death of a Toad, The.
Digging for China.
Exeunt.
Fall in Corrales.

First Snow in Alsace.
For the New Railway Station in Rome.
In the Smoking-Car.
Invitation to the Voyage, tr.
Juggler.
June Light.
Junk.
Lamarck Elaborated.
Love Calls Us to the Things of This World.
Loves of the Puppets.
Mind.
Museum Piece.
O.
October Maples, Portland.
Pangloss's Song; a Comic-Opera Lyric.
Pardon, The.
Praise in Summer.
Prayer to Go to Paradise with the Donkeys, A, tr.
Proof, The.
She.
Simile for Her Smile, A.
Sonnet: "Winter deepening, the hay all in, The."
Still, Citizen Sparrow.
Two Voices in a Meadow.
Tywater.
Voice from under the Table, A.
Year's End.
WILCOX, ELLA WHEELER. Faith.
My Ships.
Solitude.
Winds of Fate, The.
WILD [or WILDE], ROBERT. Epitaph for a Godly Man's Tomb, An.
WILDE, OSCAR. Ballad of Reading Gaol, The.
Capital Punishment. Fr. The Ballad of Reading Gaol.
E Tenebris.
Harlot's House, The.
Hélas.
Impression du Matin.
La Bella Donna della Mia Mente.
Les Silhouettes.
Requiescat.
Sphinx, The, sel.
Theocritus; a Villanelle.
WILDE, RICHARD HENRY. My Life Is like the Summer Rose.
WILDE, ROBERT. See WILD, ROBERT.
"WILDE ALEXANDER, DER." Years Back When We Were Children.
WILKINS, ALICE. Elephant's Trunk, The.
WILKINSON, ANNE. Carol: "I was a lover of turkey and holly."
Cautionary Tale, A.
Falconry.
Lens.
Nature Be Damned.
WILKINSON, H. E. Topsy-turvy Land.
WILKINSON, IRIS GUIVER. See "HYDE, ROBIN."
WILKINSON, MARGUERITE OGDEN BIGELOW. Guilty.
WILLETT, FLORENCE WHITE. Crowded Out.
WILLIAM IX, COUNT OF POITIERS. See GUILLAUME DE POITIERS.
WILLIAM OF SHOREHAM. Song to Mary, A.
WILLIAMS, BERTYE YOUNG. Friend Who Just Stands By, The.
WILLIAMS, CHARLES. Taliessin's Return to Logres.
WILLIAMS, SIR CHARLES HANBURY. Come, Chloe, and Give Me Sweet Kisses.
Lamentable Case, A.
WILLIAMS, GWYN. On the Death of His Son, tr.
WILLIAMS, JOHN. Skaters, The.
WILLIAMS, JONATHAN. Cobwebbery.
Credo.
Davenport Gap.
Empire Finals at Verona, The, sel.
Fast Ball.
Flower-Hunter in the Fields, The.
In England's Green & (a Garland and a Clyster).
Little Tumescence, A.
Our Dusk: That West.

Rough Day, The.
Spin, A.
3 Sit-ins Agin.
WILLIAMS, LORING. Recompense.
Skeptic, The.
WILLIAMS, MANCE. For Lover Man, and All the Other Young Men Who Failed to Return from World War II.
Year without Seasons, A.
WILLIAMS, OSCAR. Chant.
Dwarf of Disintegration.
Edgar Guest.
Last Supper, The.
Little Steamboat.
WILLIAMS, ROGER. God Makes a Path.
WILLIAMS, SARAH. Old Astronomer, The, sel.
WILLIAMS, TENNESSEE. Heavenly Grass.
WILLIAMS, WILLIAM CARLOS. Asphodel, That Greeny Flower, sel.
Bull, The.
Burning the Christmas Greens.
Contagious Hospital, The.
Dance, The.
Dawn.
Descent, The.
El Hombre.
Flowers by the Sea.
Forgotten City, The.
Garden, The.
Gift, The.
Hemmed-in Males.
High Bridge above the Tagus River at Toledo, The.
Hounded Lovers, The.
Injury, The.
Jungle, The.
Lighthearted William.
Lonely Street, The.
Manoeuvre, The.
Negro Woman, A.
Pastoral: "Little sparrows, The."
Paterson, sels.
Peace on Earth.
Pink Locust, The.
Poem: "As the cat."
Portrait of a Lady.
Preface: "To make a start." Fr. Paterson.
Queen-Ann's-Lace.
Rain.
Raleigh Was Right.
Red Wheelbarrow, The.
Revelation, The.
Semblables, The.
Sort of a Song, A.
Spring and All.
Term, The.
These.
Thinker, The.
This Is Just to Say.
To a Dog Injured in the Street.
To a Solitary Disciple.
To Elsie.
To Waken an Old Lady.
Tract.
Unison, A.
When Structure Fails Rhyme Attempts to Come to the Rescue.
Widow's Lament in Springtime, The.
World Narrowed to a Point, The.
Yachts, The.
WILLIS, NATHANIEL PARKER. To Giulia Grisi.
WILLSON, DIXIE. Mist and All, The.
WILMOT, ALEX. Landing of the British Settlers of 1820, The, sel.
WILMOT, FRANK ("Furnley Maurice"). Victoria Markets Recollected in Tranquillity, The.
WILMOT, JOHN, EARL OF ROCHESTER. See ROCHESTER, JOHN WILMOT, 2D EARL OF.
"WILSON, CHARLOTTE." See BAKER, KARLE WILSON.
WILSON, EDMUND. Lido, The.
Omelet of A. MacLeish, The.
Peterhof.
WILSON, JAMES. Casey's Revenge.
WILSON, JAMES EDWARD. When I Am Dead.
WILSON, ROBERT. Simplicity's Song. Fr. Three Ladies of London.

WILSON, ROBERT (*continued*)
Three Ladies of London, *sel.*
WILSON, ROBERT BURNS. It Is in Winter That We Dream of Spring.
WILSON, T. P. CAMERON ("Tipcuca").
Magpies in Picardy.
WINCHILSEA, ANNE FINCH, COUNTESS OF. South Sea Bubble, The.
To the Nightingale.
Trail All Your Pikes, Dispirit Every Drum.
WINGFIELD, SHEILA. Winter.
Young Argonauts.
WINSOR, FREDERICK. Space Child's Mother Goose, The, *sels.*
WINTERS, YVOR. Fragment, A: "I cannot find my way to Nazareth."
John Day, Frontiersman.
John Sutter.
Ode on the Despoilers of Learning in an American University (1947), An.
Rome, *tr.*
Sir Gawaine and the Green Knight.
To the Holy Spirit.
WINTLE, WALTER D. Man Who Thinks He Can, The.
WINWARD, STEPHEN F. Day by Day.
WISE, WILLIAM. Grandmother's Visit.
When I Grow Up.
WISTER, OWEN. Said Aristotle unto Plato.
WITHER, GEORGE. Fair Virtue, the Mistress of Philarete, *sel.*
Fidelia, *sel.*
I Loved a Lass.
Kiss, The.
Manly Heart, The. *Fr.* Fair Virtue, *and also in* Fidelia.
Marigold, The.
Shall I, Wasting in Despair. *Fr.* Fair Virtue, *and also in* Fidelia.
WITT, HAROLD. More Nudes for Florence.
Nude.
WODEHOUSE, E. A. Afforestation.
WOLCOT, JOHN. See "PINDAR, PETER."
WOLF, LEONARD. Sonnet: "Sits by a fireplace, the seducer talks."
WOLFE, CHARLES. Burial of Sir John Moore after [or at] Corunna, The.
WOLFE, FFRIDA. Choosing Shoes.
Four and Eight.
WOLFE, HUMBERT. Autumn.
Blackbird, The.
Boxer's Face, The, *tr.*
Gray Squirrel, The.
In the City.
Lupin.
Sluggard, The, *tr.*
Sonnets pour Hélène, *sel., tr.*
Uncelestial City, The, *sels.*
When lads have done with labor.
"Who," cried the elders on the Trojan wall, *tr. Fr.* Sonnets pour Hélène.
World's Worst Boxer, The, *tr.*
You cannot hope.
WOLFE, THOMAS. Magic.
Stone, a Leaf, a Door, A.
You Can't Go Home Again, *sel.*
WOLFRAM VON ESCHENBACH. Bursting Leaves, Flowers Opening.
I Have These Many Evenings Watched for My Beloved. *Fr.* Titurel.
It Has Thrust Its Talons through the Morning Clouds.
Lady at the Watchman's Song Perceived, A.
Lament for the Love of Heroes, The. Titurel, *sel.*
WOLFSKEHL, KARL. I.
Outward Journey.
WOOD, A. J. Rolling John, *sel.*
WOOD, WILLIAM. A Deux.
WOODBERRY, GEORGE EDWARD. Ideal Passion, *sel.*
Immortal Love. *Fr.* Ideal Passion.
"WOODBINE WILLIE." See STUDDERT-KENNEDY, GEOFFREY ANKETELL.
WOODDESON, RICHARD. Lass of Isleworth Mill, The.
WOODGATE, M. V. Fire.
WOODS, JOHN. Deaths at Paragon, Indiana, The.
Playwright.

Poem at Thirty.
When Senses Fled.
WOODS, MARGARET LOUISA. I've heard, I've heard.
WOODWARD, JOHN. Joe Bowers, *at.*
Ragged Coat, The.
WOODWORTH, SAMUEL. Old Oaken Bucket, The.
WOOLSEY, SARAH CHAUNCEY. See "COOLIDGE, SUSAN."
WOOLSON, CONSTANCE FENIMORE. Kentucky Belle.
WORDSWORTH, WILLIAM. Address to My Infant Daughter.
Admonition to a Traveller.
Affliction of Margaret, The.
After-Thought. *Fr.* The River Duddon.
By the Sea.
Childhood and School-Time. *Fr.* The Prelude.
Complaint, A.
Composed at Neidpath Castle, the Property of Lord Queensbury 1803.
Composed upon Westminster Bridge, September 3, 1802.
Conclusion: "It was a summer's night, a close warm night." *Fr.* The Prelude.
Consummate Happiness. *Fr.* The Prelude.
Daffodils [The].
Desideria.
Ecclesiastical Sketches, *sel.*
Education of Nature, The.
Elegiac Stanzas.
England and Switzerland 1802.
Evening Walk, An, *sel.*
Excursion, The, *sel.*
Expostulation and Reply.
Extempore Effusion upon the Death of James Hogg.
Fishing. *Fr.* The Prelude.
Fountain, The.
Goody Blake and Harry Gill, *sel.*
Green Linnet, The.
I Traveled among Unknown Men.
I Wandered Lonely as a Cloud.
Imagination, How Impaired and Restored. *Fr.* The Prelude.
In London, September, 1802.
In These Fair Vales.
Inner Vision, The.
Inside of King's College Chapel, Cambridge. *Fr.* Ecclesiastical Sketches.
Intimations of Sublimity. *Fr.* The Prelude.
It Is a Beauteous Evening, Calm and Free.
Lesson, A.
Liberty, *sel.*
Lines Composed a Few Miles above Tintern Abbey.
Lines Written in Early Spring.
London, 1802.
Lost Love, The.
Lucy: "I travell'd among unknown men."
Lucy: "She dwelt among th' untrodden ways."
Lucy: "Slumber did my spirit seal, A."
Lucy: "Strange fits of passion have I known."
Lucy: "Three years she grew in sun and shower."
Lucy Gray; or, Solitude.
Merry Month of March, The.
Michael.
Mutability.
My Heart Leaps Up [When I Behold].
Nature and the Poet.
Night-Piece, A.
Nuns Fret Not [at Their Convent's Narrow Room].
Nutting.
Ode: Intimations of Immortality from Recollections of Early Childhood.
Ode on Intimations of Immortality from Recollections of Early Childhood.
Ode to Duty.
Old Cumberland Beggar, The.
On the Extinction of the Venetian Republic.

Our Birth Is but a Sleep [and a Forgetting]. *Fr.* Ode: Intimations of Immortality from Recollections of Early Childhood.
Personal Talk.
Prelude, The, *sels.*
Rainbow, The.
Reaper, The.
Resolution and Independence.
Reverie of Poor Susan, The.
River Duddon, The, *sel.*
Ruth; or, The Influences of Nature.
Sailor's Mother, The, *sel.*
Same, The ("Milton! thou shouldst be living at this hour").
Scorn Not the Sonnet.
September, 1815.
She Dwelt among the Untrodden Ways.
She Was a Phantom of Delight.
Shepherd, The. *Fr.* The Prelude.
Simon Lee the Old Huntsman.
Skating. *Fr.* The Prelude.
Slumber Did My Spirit Seal, A.
Small Celandine, The.
Solitary Reaper, The.
Sonnet: "It is not to be thought of that the flood."
Strange Fits of Passion Have I Known.
Stuffed Owl, The.
Surprised by Joy.
Tables Turned, The.
There Was a Boy. *Fr.* The Prelude.
Thorn, The, *sels.*
Three Years She Grew in Sun and Shower.
Tintern Abbey.
To a Distant Friend.
To a Highland Girl.
To Catherine Wordsworth 1808–1812.
To Coleridge in Sicily. *Fr.* The Prelude.
To M. H.
To Sleep.
To the Cuckoo.
To the Daisy.
To the Highland Girl of Inversneyde.
To the Marchesana of Pescara, *tr.*
To the Moon.
To the Skylark.
To the Supreme Being, *tr.*
To Toussaint L'Ouverture.
Two April Mornings, The.
Upon Westminster Bridge.
Vaudracour and Julia, *sel.*
Wanderer Recalls the Past, The. *Fr.* The Excursion.
We Are Seven.
When I have borne in memory what has tamed.
Where lies the land to which yon ship must go?
Why Art Thou Silent!
Within King's College Chapel, Cambridge. *Fr.* Ecclesiastical Sketches.
World Is Too Much with Us, The.
Written in Early Spring.
Written in March.
Written in the Album of a Child.
Yarrow Unvisited.
Yarrow Visited.
Yew-Trees.
WORLEY, MRS. J. B. Mighty Hunter, The.
WORTH, KATHRYN. Smells.
WORTHINGTON, KIM. I Held a Lamb.
WOTTON, SIR HENRY. Character of a Happy Life, The.
Elizabeth of Bohemia.
Epitaph on Sir Albert Morton's Wife.
On a Banck as I Sate a Fishing.
On His Mistris, the Queen of Bohemia.
Tears at the Grave of Sir Albertus Morton.
To His Mistress, the Queen of Bohemia.
Upon the Death of Sir Albert [or Albertus] Morton's Wife.
Upon the Sudden Restraint of the Earl[e] of Somerset, [Then] Falling from Favor.
WRIGHT, BRUCE McM. African Affair, The.
WRIGHT, CHARLES. November 22, 1963.

WRIGHT, DAVID. Funeral Oration, A.
Monologue of a Deaf Man.
Rousecastle.
Seven South African Poems, sel.
Shanty.
WRIGHT, DAVID McKEE. Danny's
Wooing.
Dark Rosaleen, sels.
In Town.
WRIGHT, ERNEST VINCENT. When
Father Carves the Duck.
WRIGHT, FREDERICK ADAM. Faint
Heart, tr.
WRIGHT, GEORGE T. For a Wedding
Performed on Thanksgiving in the
Week of President Kennedy's Death.
WRIGHT, HETTY. Disappointed Wife,
The.
Epitaph on Herself, An.
Mother's Soliloquy, A.
WRIGHT, JAMES. Accusation, The.
At the Executed Murderer's Grave.
At the Slackening of the Tide.
Blessing, The.
Breath of Air, A.
Cold Divinities, The.
Dawn Brings with It, The, tr.
Ghost, The.
Girl in a Window, A.
Message Hidden in an Empty Wine
Bottle That I Threw into a Gulley of
Maple Trees One Night at an In-
decent Hour, A.
Morality of Poetry, The.
Mutterings over the Crib of a Deaf
Child.
On Minding One's Own Business.
Paul.
Sea Is Enormous, The, tr.
Stages on a Journey Westward.
To the Bridge of Love, tr.
Two Hangovers.
Two Poems about President Harding.
Ungathered Apples, The.
WRIGHT, JAY. This Morning.
WRIGHT, JUDITH. Bull, The.
Bullocky.
Egrets.
Fire at Murdering Hut.
Hawthorne Hedge, The.
Lyrebirds.
Old Prison, The.
South of My Days.
Storm.
Twins, The.
Woman to Man.
Wonga Vine.
WRIGHT, RICHARD. Between the World
and Me.
Hokku Poems.
WRIGHT, SARAH E. To Some Millions
Who Survive Joseph Mander, Sr.
WU CH'ING-JEN. On a Mountain Road.
WURDEMANN, AUDREY. For Eros II.
WU TI, EMPEROR OF LIANG. People
Hide Their Love.
WYATT, SIR THOMAS. And Wilt Thou
Leave Me Thus?
Blame Not My Lute.
Disdain Me Not.
Enemy of Life, The.
Epigram: "Face that should content
me wonders well, A."
Epitaph of Sir Thomas Gravener
Knight, An.
Forget Not Yet.
Hate Whom Ye List.
He Is Not Dead.
I Am as I Am.
I Find No Peace, tr. Fr. Sonnets to
Laura.
I Have Sought Long.
If Thou Wilt Mighty Be.
In Faith Methinks It Is No Right.
Is It Possible?
It May Be Good.
It Was My Choice.
Like to These Unmeasurable Moun-
tains, tr.
Long Love That in My Thought Doth
Harbor, The, tr. Fr. Sonnets to
Laura.
Lover Compareth His State to a Ship
in Perilous Storm Tossed on the
Sea, The, tr. Fr. Sonnets to Laura.

Lover Complayneth the Unkindness of
His Love, The.
Lover for Shamefastness Hideth His
Desire within His Faithful Heart,
The, tr. Fr. Sonnets to Laura.
Lover Forsaken, The.
Lover Showeth How He Is Forsaken
of Such as He Sometime Enjoyed,
The.
Lover's Appeal, The.
Madam, withouten Many Words.
Marvel No More.
My Galley [Charged with Forgetful-
ness], tr. Fr. Sonnets to Laura.
My Lute and I.
My Lute Awake.
My Pen, Take Pain [a Little Space].
Nature, That Gave the Bee.
No! Indeed.
Once as Methought Fortune Me
Kissed.
Perdie, I Said It Not.
Renouncing of Love, A.
Satire 3: To Sir Francis Brian.
Sonnets to Laura, sels., tr.
Speak Thou and Speed.
Supplication, A.
Tagus, Farewell.
There Was Never Nothing More Me
Pained.
They Flee from Me.
Throughout the World.
Wandering Gadling, The.
What Does This Mean?
What Once I Was.
What Should I Say.
Who Hath Heard of Such Cruelty
Before.
Whoso List to Hunt.
Within My Breast.
You That in Love Find Luck.
Your Looks So Often Cast.
WYLIE, ELINOR. Address to My Soul.
Atavism.
Eagle and the Mole, The.
Escape.
Fair Annet's Song.
Falcon, The.
Golden Bough.
Hymn to Earth.
Lament for Glasgerion.
Little Elegy.
Lodging for the Night, A.
Madman's Song.
Parting Gift.
Pebble, The.
Peter and John.
Pretty Words.
Puritan's Ballad, The.
Sea Lullaby.
This Corruptible.
To His Soul, tr.
Velvet Shoes.
WYNNE, ANNETTE. I Keep Three
Wishes Ready.
Indian Children.
Leaves Do Not Mind at All, The.
Outside the Door.
People Buy a Lot of Things.
Tree Stands Very Straight and Still,
The.

X

XAVIER, SISTER MARY. See PARTRIDGE,
SYBIL F.
XENOS PALAESTES. Requirements: "Not
too pallid, as if bleacht."

Y

YARMOLINSKY, AVRAHM, and CECIL
COWDERY. Cosmic Fabric, The, tr.
YARMOLINSKY, AVRAHM, and BABETTE
DEUTSCH. See DEUTSCH, BABETTE,
and AVRAHM YARMOLINSKY.
YAUGER, FAY McCORMICK. Planter's
Charm.

YEARGENS, CARL. Shadows for the Sun.
YEATMAN, ROBERT JULIAN, and WALTER
CARRUTHERS SELLAR. How I
Brought the Good News from Aix
to Ghent (or Vice Versa).
YEATS, WILLIAM BUTLER. Adam's
Curse.
After Long Silence.
Among School Children.
At Galway Races.
Ballad of Father Gilligan, The.
Before the World Was Made.
Brown Penny.
Byzantium.
Cap and Bells, The.
Cat and the Moon, The.
Chambermaid's Second Song, The.
Circus Animals' Desertion, The.
Cold Heaven, The.
Collar-Bone of a Hare, The.
Coming of Wisdom with Time, The.
Coole Park and Ballylee, 1931.
Cradle Song, A: "Angels are stooping,
The."
Crazy Jane and Jack the Journeyman.
Crazy Jane on God.
Crazy Jane Talks with the Bishop.
Deep-sworn Vow, A.
Dialogue of Self and Soul, A.
Dolls, The.
Down by the Salley Gardens.
Dream of Death, A.
Easter 1916.
Falling of the Leaves, The.
Fiddler of Dooney, The.
First Confession, A.
Fisherman, The.
For Anne Gregory.
For My Daughter. Fr. Prayer for My
Daughter.
Four Ages of Man, The.
Gyres, The.
He Remembers Forgotten Beauty.
He Thinks of His Past Greatness
When a Part of the Constellations of
Heaven.
He Thinks of Those Who Have Spoken
Evil of His Beloved.
In Memory of Eva Gore-Booth and
Con Markiewicz.
In Memory of Major Robert Gregory.
Into the Twilight.
Irish Airman Foresees His Death, An.
John Kinsella's Lament for Mrs. Mary
Moore.
Lake Isle of Innisfree, The.
Lamentation of the Old Pensioner, The.
Lapis Lazuli.
Last Confession, A.
Leaders of the Crowd, The.
Leda and the Swan.
Long-legged Fly.
Lullaby: "Beloved, may your sleep be
sound."
Mad as the Mist and Snow.
Magi, The.
Meditations in Time of Civil War.
Mohini Chatterjee.
Moods, The.
Municipal Gallery Revisited, The.
Never Give All the Heart.
New Faces, The.
No Second Troy.
O hurry where by water among trees.
Oedipus at Colonus, sel., tr.
Old Men Admiring Themselves in the
Water, The.
On Being Asked for a War Poem.
Pilgrim, The.
Pity of Love, The.
Players Ask for a Blessing on the
Psalteries and on Themselves, The.
Poet to His Beloved, A.
Politics.
Prayer for My Daughter, A.
Prayer for Old Age, A.
Ragged Wood, The.
Red Hanrahan's Song about Ireland.
Resurrection, The, sel.
Rose of Peace, The.
Rose Tree, The.
Running to Paradise.
Sad Shepherd, The.
Sailing to Byzantium.
Scholars, The.

YEATS, WILLIAM BUTLER (*cont.*)
Second Coming, The.
September 1913.
Solomon to Sheba.
Song of a Fool. *Fr.* Two Songs of a Fool.
Song of the Old Mother, The.
Song of Wandering Aengus, The.
Sorrow of Love, The.
Stare's Nest by My Window, The.
Three Bushes, The.
Three Hermits, The.
Three Things.
Those Images.
To a Friend Whose Work Has Come to Nothing.
To a Poet, Who Would Have Me Praise Certain Bad Poets, Imitators of His and Mine.
To an Isle in the Water.
To Some I Have Talked With by the Fire.
Two Songs from a Play. *Fr.* The Resurrection.
Two Songs of a Fool, *sel.*
Vacillation.
Wheel, The.
When You Are Old.
Who Goes with Fergus?
Wild Swans at Coole, The.
"YEHOASH" (Solomon Bloomgarden [*or* Blumgarten]). Old Song, An.
YERBY, FRANK. Calm after Storm.
Fishes and the Poet's Hands, The.
Weltschmerz.
Wisdom.
You Are a Part of Me.

YESENIN [*or* ESENIN], SERGEI ALEKSANDROVICH. In the Clear Cold.
YORCK, RUTH LANDSHOFF. I M J F K.
YOUNG, ANDREW. Christmas Day.
Climbing in Glencoe.
Culbin Sands.
Daisies.
Dead Mole, A.
Eagle, The.
Field-Glasses.
Haystack, The.
Hymn: "Lord, by whose breath all souls and seeds are living."
Man and Cows.
Old Tree, The.
On Middleton Edge.
Passing the Graveyard.
Prehistoric Camp, A.
Prospect of Death, A.
Rat, The.
Reflections on the River.
Shepherd's Hut, The.
Swans, The.
Wiltshire Downs.
YOUNG, BARBARA. Being Gypsy.
Sophisticate.
YOUNG, EDITH LILLIAN. Disappointment.
YOUNG, EDWARD. Complaint, The; or, Night Thoughts on Life, Death and Immortality, *sel.*
YOUNG, EDWIN. Have I Done My Best for Jesus?
YOUNG, ELLA. Unicorn, The.
YOUNG, FRANCIS BRETT. Bête Humaine.
YOUNG, ROLAND. Ape, The.
Flea, The.

Z

ZAHN, CURTIS. Antiwarwoman.
ZANGWILL, ISRAEL. Angels Came a-Mustering, The, *tr.*
At the Worst, *sel.*
I Have Sought Thee Daily, *tr.*
ZEITLIN, ISRAEL. *See* TIEMPO, CÉSAR.
ZEMP, WERNER. Landscape before Easter.
ZESEN, PHILIP VON. Evening Song.
ZHUKOVSKY, VASILY ANDREYEVICH. Remembrance.
ZILLES, LUKE. Bunch of Wild Flowers.
Details.
ZOLLINGER, ALBIN. Convent at Fahr, The.
ZORRO, JOAN. Along the River Shore.
Hair, My Pretty Hair.
In Lisbon by the Sea.
Let's Dance, Let's Dance, Us Pretties.
ZUKOFSKY, LOUIS. A II.
Chloride of Lime and Charcoal.
Finally a Valentine.
Green Leaf, The.
Guests, The.
Peri Poietikes.
Poem Beginning "The."
So That Even a Lover.
This Is after All Vacation.
You Who Were Made for This Music.

SUBJECT INDEX

ABERDARE, WALES. Mountain over Aberdare, The. Alun Lewis.
ABRAHAM
  Abraham. Edwin Muir.
  Abraham's Madness. Noll.
ACHILLES
  Achilles and the King. John Logan.
  Achilles' Revenge. *Fr.* The Iliad. Homer, *tr. fr. Greek by*
    Bryant.
ACTAEON. Acteon. *Fr.* Metamorphoses. Ovid, *tr. fr. Latin*
  by Golding.
ACTING AND ACTORS
  David Garrick. *Fr.* Retaliation. Goldsmith.
  Thespians at Thermopylae, The. Norman Cameron.
ADAM
  Adam. Rilke, *tr. fr. German by* Norton.
  Adam Lay Ibounden. *Unknown.*
  Adam—the First Kiss. Hal Porter.
  Imperial Adam. A. D. Hope.
  Lady's-Maid's Song, The. Hollander.
  Lilith. X. J. Kennedy.
  Recognition of Eve, The. *Fr.* Adam and Eve. Karl Shapiro.
  Sickness of Adam, The. *Fr.* Adam and Eve. Karl Shapiro.
  229. Villa.
ADAMS, JOHN QUINCY. John Quincy Adams. S. V. Benét.
ADDISON, JOSEPH. Atticus. *Fr.* Epistle to Dr. Arbuthnot. Pope.
ADLESTROP, ENGLAND. Adlestrop. Edward Thomas.
ADONIS
  Adonis. Doolittle ("H. D.").
  Venus and Adonis, *sels.* Shakespeare.
ADVENT
  Advent Meditation. Alice Meynell.
  Farewell! Advent. Ryman.
ADVERTISING
  Memorial to the Great Big Beautiful Self-sacrificing Adver-
    tisers. Ebright.
  Nightmare Number Four. Robert Bloch.
  Sky-Writer. Starrett.
AEGEAN SEA. Santorin. Flecker.
AENEAS
  Dido. Thomas Campion.
  Tragedy of Dido, The, *sel.* Marlowe *and* Nashe.
AENEID, THE (Vergil). Falling Asleep over the Aeneid. Rob-
  ert Lowell.
ÆNGUS. Song of Wandering Ængus, The. Yeats.
ÆOLIAN HARPS. Ode to an Æolus's Harp. William Mason.
AFRICA
  Africa Speaks. Dei-Anang.
  African Dance. Langston Hughes.
  African Heaven. Frank Parkes.
  Congo, The. Vachel Lindsay.
  Continent That Lies within Us, The. Abioseh Nicol.
  Deep Down the Blackman's Mind. Armattoe.
  Far Cry from Africa, A. Walcott.
  Far from Africa. Danner.
  Song-Maker, The. Kingsley Fairbridge.
  Stages. Macnab.
  Tribes, The. Roy Fuller.
  What Is Africa to Me? *Fr.* Heritage. Countee Cullen.
  Young Africa's Resolve. Osadebay.
AFRICA, SOUTH. *See* SOUTH AFRICA
AFTERNOON. Afternoon for a Small Boy. Noll.
AFTON (river), SCOTLAND. Afton Water. Burns.
AFZAL KHAN. Rise of Shivaji, The. Ghose.
AGE. *See* OLD AGE; YOUTH
AGINCOURT, BATTLE OF
  Agincourt. Drayton.
  Carol of Agincourt, A. *Unknown.*
AIR PLANTS. Air Plant, The. Hart Crane.
AIR RAIDS
  Among Those Killed in the Dawn Raid Was a Man Aged a
    Hundred. Dylan Thomas.
  Bombardment. D. H. Lawrence.
  Ceremony after a Fire Raid. Dylan Thomas.
  Dead in Europe, The. Robert Lowell.
  Erige Cor Tuum ad Me in Caelum. Doolittle ("H. D.").
  In the Shelter. Day Lewis.
  Refusal to Mourn the Death, by Fire, of a Child in London,
    A. Dylan Thomas.
  Still Falls the Rain. Edith Sitwell.
AIR WARFARE
  Death of the Ball Turret Gunner, The. Jarrell.

Fury of Aerial Bombardment, The. Eberhart.
Irish Airman Foresees His Death, An. Yeats.
Second Air Force. Jarrell.
AIRPLANES
  Aeroplane. M. M. Green.
  Landscape near an Aerodrome, The. Spender.
  Looking Up at Airplanes, Always. Humphries.
  Taking Off. *Unknown.*
  Three Jet Planes. May Swenson.
  Up in the Air. Tippett.
ALAMO
  Defence of the Alamo, The. Joaquin Miller.
  Lament for the Alamo. Arthur Guiterman.
  Men of the Alamo, The. Roche.
ALASKA. Alaska. Joaquin Miller.
ALE. Bring Us in Good Ale. *Unknown.*
ALEXANDER THE GREAT. Book of Alexander, The, *sel.* Lorenzo.
ALFONSO X, KING OF CASTILE AND LEON. Alphonso of Castile.
  Emerson.
ALL FOOLS' DAY. *See* APRIL FOOLS' DAY
ALL-SOULS' DAY. All-Souls' Day. Sassoon.
ALMOND TREES. Almond Blossom in Wartime. Spender.
ALPHONSUS RODRIGUEZ, SAINT. St. Alphonsus Rodriguez.
  G. M. Hopkins.
ALSACE, FRANCE. First Snow in Alsace. Wilbur.
ALTARS. Altar, The. George Herbert.
ALTGELD, JOHN PETER. Eagle That Is Forgotten, The. Vachel
  Lindsay.
AMERICA (United States of). *See* UNITED STATES
AMERICAN REVOLUTION
  Centenarian's Story, The. Walt Whitman.
  Concord Hymn. Emerson.
  Emily Geiger. *Unknown.*
  Green Mountain Boys, The. Bryant.
  Independence Bell. *Unknown.*
  Major André. *Unknown.*
  Molly Pitcher. L. E. Richards.
  Molly Pitcher. K. B. Sherwood.
  Nathan Hale. F. M. Finch.
  Nathan Hale. *Unknown.*
  Paul Revere's Ride. *Fr.* Tales of a Wayside Inn. Long-
    fellow.
  To the Memory of the Brave Americans. Freneau.
AMERICANS
  I Am an American. Lieberman.
  I Hear America Singing. Walt Whitman.
  I, Too, Sing America. Langston Hughes.
  See also UNITED STATES
ANCESTORS AND ANCESTRY
  Ancestors. Robert Graves.
  Children of Light. Robert Lowell.
ANDERSEN, HANS CHRISTIAN. Hans Christian Andersen in
  Central Park. Sobiloff.
ANDRÉ, JOHN. Major André. *Unknown.*
ANGELS
  On a Fifteenth-Century Flemish Angel. David Ray.
  Tom's Angels. De la Mare.
ANGER
  Anger. Creeley.
  Anger in Its Time and Place. Charles *and* Mary Lamb.
  Poison Tree, A. *Fr.* Songs of Experience. Blake.
ANIMALS
  See also names of classes of the animal kingdom (e.g., Birds)
    and names of animals (e.g., Dogs)
  Animal Store, The. Rachel Field.
  Animals, The. Edwin Muir.
  Animals. *Fr.* Song of Myself. Walt Whitman.
  Come into Animal Presence. Levertov.
  Daydreamers. N. L. Davis.
  Familiar Friends. Tippett.
  Farmyard Song, A. Maria Hastings.
  Heaven of Animals, The. Dickey.
  How to Tell the Wild Animals. Carolyn Wells.
  In the Wilderness. Robert Graves.
  It's Pleasant to Think. Coatsworth.
  Jump or Jingle. Beyer.
  Kindness to Animals. *Unknown.*
  Over in the Meadow. *Unknown.*
ANNUNCIATION OF THE VIRGIN. *See* MARY, THE VIRGIN
ANTEATERS. Pangolin, The. Marianne Moore.
ANTHONY, SAINT. Saint Antony. R. S. Thomas.

ANTONY (Marc Antony)
Early in the Morning. Louis Simpson.
Mark Anthony. John Cleveland.
ANTONY, SAINT. *See* ANTHONY, SAINT
ANTS
Ant, The. Armour.
Ant, The. Ogden Nash.
Ant-ology. Morgenstern, *tr. fr. German by* Hull.
Departmental. Robert Frost.
APENNINES (mountains). Evening of Gavinana. "Vincenzo Cardarelli," *tr. fr. Italian by* Corsano.
APES. Ape, The. Roland Young.
APHRODITE
Aphrodite Pandemos. *Unknown.*
See also VENUS
APOLLO
Apollo and Daphne. Marino, *tr. fr. Italian by* Ayres.
Archaic Torso of Apollo. Rilke.
APOSTLES
Peter and John. Wylie.
Starlight like Intuition Pierced the Twelve. Schwartz.
Te Martyrum Candidatus. Lionel Johnson.
APPLE TREES
Comfortable Apple Trees, The. Hallock.
Planting of the Apple Tree, The, *sel.* Bryant.
APPLES
After Apple-picking. Robert Frost.
Apple Gathering, An. C. G. Rossetti.
Apples. Laurie Lee.
Autumn Apples. Laurie Lee.
APRIL
See also April *in* TITLE AND FIRST LINE INDEX
All in the April Morning. Katharine Tynan.
April's Amazing Meaning. George Dillon.
For April I Give You the Countryside. *Fr.* Sonnets of the Months. Folgore da San Geminiano, *tr. fr. Italian by* Gould.
For City Spring. S. V. Benét.
Great Farm. Philip Booth.
Home Thoughts from Abroad. Robert Browning.
Like an April Day. J. S. C. Welhaven, *tr. fr. Norwegian by* Stork.
Peepers. Melville Cane.
Song: "April, April." William Watson.
Spring Song. García Lorca, *tr. fr. Spanish by* Benson *and* O'Brien.
Street in April, A. Dudek.
This Fevers Me. Eberhart.
APRIL FOOLS' DAY
All Fools' Day. *Unknown.*
April Fool. Coatsworth.
April Fool. Eleanor Hammond.
April Fools' Day. Marnie Pomeroy.
Oh Did You Hear? Silverstein.
ARAN ISLANDS, IRELAND. Aran. Hagelstange, *tr. fr. German by* Hamburger.
ARBOR DAY. Arbor Day Tree, An. *Unknown.*
ARBORVITAE. Arbor Vitae. *Fr.* The Unknown Eros. Coventry Patmore.
ARBUTUS. Pink, small and punctual. Emily Dickinson.
ARCHIMEDES. Archimedes and the Student. Schiller.
ARES. *See* MARS
ARITHMETIC. *See* MATHEMATICS
ARKANSAS. State of Arkansas, The. *Unknown.*
ARLINGTON NATIONAL CEMETERY. Potomac, The. Karl Shapiro.
ARMADA. *See* SPANISH ARMADA
ARMISTICE DAY. Everyone Sang. Sassoon.
ARMSTRONG, JOHN OR JOHNNIE. Johnnie Armstrong. *Unknown.*
ARNOLD, THOMAS. Rugby Chapel. Matthew Arnold.
ART
See also PAINTING AND PAINTERS; PORTRAITS; SCULPTURE AND SCULPTORS
Ars Victrix, *sel.* Gautier, *tr. fr. French by* Dobson.
Art. Melville.
Artist, The. Kenneth Koch.
Leaf-Makers, The. Harold Stewart.
Palace of Art, The. Tennyson.
ARTEMIS
Artemis. Deamer.
See also DIANA
ARTHURIAN LEGEND
Defence of Guenevere, The. William Morris.
Lady of Shalott, The. Tennyson.
Merlin and the Gleam. Tennyson.
Morte d'Arthur. Tennyson.
Near Avalon. William Morris.
Passing of Arthur, The. *Fr.* Idylls of the King. Tennyson.
Sir Launcelot and Queen Guinevere. Tennyson.
Vision of Sir Launfal, *sel.* J. R. Lowell.
ARTICHOKES. Artichoke, The. Ibn al-Talla, *tr. fr. Arabic by* Davis.
ASCENSION DAY
Ascension-Day. Henry Vaughan.
Ascension-Hymn. Henry Vaughan.

At the Ascension. León, *tr. fr. Spanish by* Tobin.
ASH WEDNESDAY. Ash Wednesday. T. S. Eliot.
ASSES. *See* DONKEYS
ASTRONOMERS AND ASTRONOMY. When I Heard the Learn'd Astronomer. Walt Whitman.
ATHENS, GREECE. Spring Wind, A. Bernard Spencer.
ATHLETES
Ageing Athlete, The. Neil Weiss.
Athletes. Walker Gibson.
Breed of Athletes, The. Euripides, *tr. fr. Greek by* Hadas.
To an Athlete Dying Young. *Fr.* A Shropshire Lad. A. E. Housman.
ATLANTIC (ship). Wreck of the *Atlantic,* The. *Unknown.*
ATLANTIS
Atlantis. S. A. Coblentz.
Atlantis. *Fr.* The Bridge. Hart Crane.
ATOMIC BOMB
Seventh Hell, The: Of Smoke, Where Fire-Raisers Try in Vain to Escape from a Shower of Hot Sand Falling from a Cloud. Rothenberg.
See also HIROSHIMA
AUDEN, WYSTAN HUGH. Just a Smack at Auden. Empson.
AUDUBON, JOHN JAMES. John James Audubon. S. V. Benét.
AUGUST
See also August *in* TITLE AND FIRST LINE INDEX
Tansy for August. Enslin.
AUSTEN, JANE. Jane's Marriage. Kipling.
AUSTRALIA
Aboriginal Mother's Lament, An. Harpur.
Australian Symphony, An. G. E. Evans.
Song of the Darling River. Henry Lawson.
Temple by the Sea, The. Dutton.
Poetry in Australia. *Volume I: From the Ballads to Brennan* (PoAu-1). T. I. Moore, comp.
Poetry in Australia. *Volume II: Modern Australian Verse* (PoAu-2). Douglas Stewart, comp.
AUTHORS AND AUTHORSHIP
Author and Her Book, The. Bradstreet.
Canadian Authors Meet, The. F. R. Scott.
Devil's Advice to Story-Tellers, The. Robert Graves.
Fable X: Elephant and the Bookseller, The. John Gay.
Novel, The. Levertov.
On His Books. Hilaire Belloc.
On Teaching without Pupils. Brecht, *tr. fr. German by* Hamburger.
Squeal. Louis Simpson.
Young Author, The. Samuel Johnson.
AUTOMATION. New Letter Writer, The. Bevington.
AUTOMOBILES
Auto Wreck. Karl Shapiro.
Automobile Mechanics. Baruch.
Buick. Karl Shapiro.
Car Journey. Ehrenstein, *tr. fr. German by* Middleton.
Driver's Prayer, A. *Unknown.*
Eight-Cylinder Man. Mastin.
Lather as You Go. Ogden Nash.
Merritt Parkway. Levertov.
Motor Cars. Rowena Bennett.
Tract for Autos, A. Guiterman.
AUTUMN
See also Autumn *and* Autumnal *in* TITLE AND FIRST LINE INDEX
Abundance. C. F. Meyer, *tr. fr. German by* Sebba.
And the Horns of Summer Fell Silent. Heym, *tr. fr. German by* Hamburger.
Autumnus. Joshua Sylvester.
Beech Leaves. James Reeves.
Burning of the Leaves, The. Binyon.
Child's Thought of Harvest, A. "Susan Coolidge."
Clear after Rain. Tu Fu, *tr. fr. Chinese by* Rexroth.
Cranes, The. Po Chü-i, *tr. fr. Chinese by* Waley.
Day in Autumn, A. R. S. Thomas.
Down! Down! Farjeon.
End of Summer, The. Basho, *tr. fr. Japanese by* Henderson.
End of Summer. Kunitz.
Fall. Hölderlin, *tr. fr. German by* Hellmann.
Fall in Corrales. Wilbur.
Fall, Leaves, Fall. Emily Brontë.
Field of Autumn. Laurie Lee.
Fall of the Leaf, The. Thoreau.
Few Signs, A. Grantland Rice.
For Autumn. Farjeon.
God's World. E. S. Millay.
Golden Bough. Wylie.
How One Winter Came in the Lake Region. Wilfred Campbell.
Hurrahing in Harvest. G. M. Hopkins.
Immortal Autumn. MacLeish.
In the Clear Cold. Yesenin, *tr. fr. Russian by* Deutsch.
Lament in Autumn. Harold Stewart.
Last Flower, The. J. T. Moore.
Leaves Do Not Mind at All, The. Annette Wynne.
Leaves of Europe, The, *sel.* ("Autumn again, the leopard-like and burning"). Sergeant.
Marigold. Nicholl.

Mist and All, The. Dixie Willson.
New York—Albany. Ferlinghetti.
Ninth Moon. Li Ho, *tr. fr. Chinese by* Ho Chih-yuan.
October Maples, Portland. Wilbur.
Ode: Autumn. Thomas Hood.
Pastoral X: "Grapes are ripe, the frost is near, The." R. S. Hillyer.
Picture of Autumn. Hebbel, *tr. fr. German by* Gode.
School Days. Stem.
Seed-Time. George Meredith.
So This Is Autumn. W. W. Watt.
Something Told the Wild Geese. Rachel Field.
Song: "Feathers of the willow, The." R. W. Dixon.
Song: "Spirit haunts the year's last hours, A." Tennyson.
Song of Autumn. Verlaine, *tr. fr. French by* Symons.
Sonnet in Autumn. Donald Petersen.
Spell before Winter, A. Nemerov.
Summer Is Gone. *Unknown, tr. fr. Old Irish by* O'Faolain.
Tell Me Not Here. A. E. Housman.
To Autumn. Blake.
To Autumn. Keats.
Tropes of One Season. C. E. Eaton.
Vagabond Song, A. Bliss Carman.
Weather Ear. Norman Nicholson.
When the Frost Is on the Punkin. J. W. Riley.
Words for the Raker of Leaves. Léonie Adams.
See also SEPTEMBER; OCTOBER; NOVEMBER
AVIATION AND AVIATORS
Aircraft, Landing. Colin Thiele.
Airman Who Flew over Shakespeare's England, The. Plutzik.
Ego. Philip Booth.
Europe. John Ashbery.
High Flight. Magee.
See also AIR WARFARE
AVON (river). Ebb Tide, The. Robert Southey.

B

BABIES
Anniversary in September. B. C. Brown.
Baby. George Macdonald.
Child Crying. Thwaite.
Cradle Song: "Sleep, sleep, beauty bright." Blake.
Cradle Song, A: "Sweet dreams from a shade." *Fr.* Songs of Innocence. Blake.
Five Days Old. Francis Webb.
For Two Children. Char, *tr. fr. French by* Engle.
I Found God. Thacker.
Infant Joy. *Fr.* Songs of Innocence. Blake.
Infant Sorrow. *Fr.* Songs of Experience. Blake.
Mother by the Cradle, The. Matthias Claudius, *tr. fr. German by* Wright.
Mother's Soliloquy, A. Hetty Wright.
Phantasmion, *sel.* ("O sleep, my babe, hear not the rippling wave"). S. T. Coleridge.
Ringely, Ringely. Follen.
Six Weeks Old. Christopher Morley.
Slippery. Sandburg.
Sweetes' Li'l Feller. F. L. Stanton.
To Miss Charlotte Pulteney in Her Mother's Arms. Ambrose Philips.
To Rose. Teasdale.
Unknown Girl in the Maternity Ward. Sexton.
BABYLON
Babylon. Laura Benét.
Babylon. Sassoon.
BACH, JOHANN SEBASTIAN
All Those Hymnings up to God. A. H. Evans.
To J. S. Bach. Thwaites.
BADGERS. Six Badgers, The. Robert Graves.
BALAAM (Bible). Balaam. Keble.
BALACLAVA, CRIMEA. Charge of the Light Brigade, The. Tennyson.
BALE, JOHN. To Doctor Bale. Googe.
BALLADS AND FOLK SONGS
Ballads and Folk Songs of the Southwest (BFSS). Ethel and Chauncey O. Moore, comps.
Ballads and Sea Songs from Nova Scotia (BSNS). W. Roy Mackenzie, comp.
Ballads and Songs from Ohio (BSO). Mary O. Eddy, comp.
Bundle of Ballads, A (BuBa). Ruth Manning-Sanders, comp.
Songs of the Gold Rush, The (SGR). Richard A. Dwyer and Richard E. Lingenfelter, eds.
BALLOONS
Balloon Man, The. Fyleman.
Balloon Man. J. N. North.
BALTIC, BATTLE OF. Battle of the Baltic, The. Thomas Campbell.
BANANAS. Banana. C. G. Bell.

BANDS. Band Marches, The. Liliencron, *tr. fr. German by* Brown.
BANNOCKBURN, BATTLE OF. Scots Wha Hae. Burns.
BARBERRIES. Barberry-Bush, The. Very.
BARBERS
Barber, The. Moses Browne.
Barber's, The. De la Mare.
Barber's Clippers. Baruch.
For the Barbers. Oppenheimer.
Haircut. Karl Shapiro.
BARNS. Human Things. Nemerov.
BARNYARDS. In the Barnyard. Dorothy Aldis.
BARONS' WAR. Against the Baron's Enemies. *Unknown.*
BARREL ORGANS. *See* HURDY-GURDIES
BASEBALL
Base Stealer, The. Robert Francis.
Baseball Note. F. P. Adams.
Baseball's Sad Lexicon. F. P. Adams.
Casey at the Bat. E. L. Thayer.
Casey's Revenge. James Wilson.
Cobb Would Have Caught It. Robert Fitzgerald.
Decline and Fall of a Roman Umpire. Ogden Nash.
Double-Play, The. Robert Wallace.
Dream of a Baseball Star. Corso.
Hits and Runs. Sandburg.
Line-up for Yesterday. Ogden Nash.
Pitcher. Robert Francis.
Polo Grounds. Humphries.
Umpire, The. Bracker.
Umpire, The. Walker Gibson.
Villanelle. Feld.
Where, O Where? Bracker.
BASS, SAM. Sam Bass. *Unknown.*
BATH, ENGLAND. At the Roman Baths, Bath. Lucie-Smith.
BATHS AND BATHING. Soap, the Oppressor. Burges Johnson.
BATS
See also Bat *in* TITLE AND FIRST LINE INDEX
Intruder, The. Kizer.
"Twinkle, twinkle, little bat!" *Fr.* Alice's Adventures in Wonderland. "Lewis Carroll."
BAUDELAIRE, CHARLES. Ave atque Vale. Swinburne.
BAVARIA. Lines on Leaving a Scene in Bavaria. Thomas Campbell.
BEACHES
Fads and Fancies. Earnshaw.
Gray Horizons. Ragan.
BEARS
Bear on the Delhi Road, The. Birney.
Brown Bear, The. Mary Austin.
Furry Bear. A. A. Milne.
Grizzly Bear. Mary Austin.
Tails. Rowena Bennett.
BEAUMONT, SIR GEORGE. Elegiac Stanzas. Wordsworth.
BEAUTY
See also Beauty *in* TITLE AND FIRST LINE INDEX
Beauty's Transitoriness. Hoffmann von Hoffmannswaldau, *tr. fr. German by* Schoolfield.
Behold, O Aspasia! I Send You Verses. *Fr.* Pericles and Aspasia. W. S. Landor.
Description of Beauty, A, *sel.* Samuel Daniel.
Do Not, Oh Do Not Prize. *Unknown.*
Each and All. Emerson.
Endymion, *sel.* ("A thing of beauty is a joy forever"). Keats.
Frailty and Hurtfulness of Beauty, The. Earl of Surrey.
Hen and the Oriole, The. *Fr.* Archy and Mehitabel. Marquis.
Hymn to Intellectual Beauty. Shelley.
I died for beauty—but was scarce. Emily Dickinson.
Ideal Beauty. Herrera, *tr. fr. Spanish by* Longfellow.
Independence Day. W. J. Smith.
Inner Man, The. Plato, *tr. fr. Greek.*
Ladies, You See Time Flieth. *Unknown.*
Lonely Beauty. *Fr.* The Complaint of Rosamond. Samuel Daniel.
Oh World, Why Do You Thus Pursue Me? Sister Juana Inés de la Cruz, *tr. fr. Spanish by* Kittell.
Ode on a Grecian Urn. Keats.
Ode to Beauty. Emerson.
Pied Beauty. G. M. Hopkins.
Something More. Stem.
Song, A: "It is not Beauty I demand." Darley.
Song for Beauty, A. Lal.
Sonnet to Heavenly Beauty, A. Du Bellay, *tr. fr. French by* Lang.
Spring Night. Teasdale.
To His Friend. Turberville.
Wherever Beauty Has Been Quick in Clay. Masefield.
BEAVERS
Beaver Pond. Anne Marriott.
Paddy the Beaver. Thornton Burgess.
BEER. Glass of Beer, A. James Stephens.
BEES
Honey Bee, The. Marquis.
I Would Like to Be—a Bee. Baruch.

BEES (*continued*)
Little Busy Bee. Isaac Watts.
Of a Bee. Tasso, *tr. fr. Italian by* Drummond of Hawthornden.
On a Honey Bee. Freneau.
Pedigree of Honey, The. Emily Dickinson.
Telling the Bees. Whittier.
BEETLES. World's End. Chettur.
BEGGING AND BEGGARS
Jolly Beggar, The. *Unknown.*
Jolly Beggars, The. Burns.
Old Cumberland Beggar, The. Wordsworth.
Tom o' Bedlam's Song. *Unknown.*
BELIEF, RELIGIOUS. *See* FAITH
BELISARIUS. Belisarius. Longfellow.
BELLBIRDS. Bell-Birds. Henry Kendall.
BELLEAU, REMI. To Remi Belleau. Ronsard, *tr. fr. French by* Currey.
BELLS
See also Bell *and* Bells *in* TITLE AND FIRST LINE INDEX
Christ Church Bells. Henry Aldrich.
Christmas Bells. Longfellow.
Church Bell—Winter Time. Stem.
Courthouse Bell. Stem.
Wantage Bells. Betjeman.
BELSHAZZAR
Belshazzar had a letter. Emily Dickinson.
Vision of Belshazzar, The. Byron.
BERKELEY, GEORGE. Fountain, The. Davie.
BERMUDA. Bermudas. Marvell.
BERTRAND DE BORN
Bertran de Born. Uhland, *tr. fr. German by* Kaufmann.
Bertrand de Born. Heine, *tr. fr. German by* Kaufmann.
Near Perigord. Pound.
BIBLE
Anvil of God's Word, The. *Unknown.*
Believe the Bible. A. B. Simpson.
Bible, The. Stroud.
Bit of the Book, A. M. E. Sangster.
Book, The. W. E. Garrison.
Book Our Mothers Read, The. Whittier.
God's Treasure. "A. M. N."
H. Scriptures, The. George Herbert.
H. Scriptures. Henry Vaughan.
Light and Glory of the World, The, *sel.* ("The Spirit breathes upon the World"). Cowper.
My Bible and I. *Unknown.*
My Companion. Charles Wesley.
My Old Bible. *Unknown.*
Of the Incomparable Treasure of the Scriptures. *Unknown.*
Read the Bible Through. A. R. Wells.
Word of God, The. Gwynne.
BICYCLES AND BICYCLING. Bicycalamity. E. W. Peters.
BILLBOARDS. Summer Excursion: Signs and Portents. Bevington.
BILLY THE KID. Billy the Kid. *Unknown.*
BINSEY, ENGLAND. April Day: Binsey. Hamburger.
BIRCH TREES. Birches. Robert Frost.
BIRDS
See also Bird *and* Birds *in* TITLE AND FIRST LINE INDEX
After the Storm. Henry Vaughan.
". . . As When Emotion Too Far Exceeds Its Cause." Oden.
Auspex. J. R. Lowell.
Ballata: "I found myself one day all, all alone." Poliziano, *tr. fr. Italian by* Symonds.
Be like the Bird. Hugo, *tr. fr. French.*
Blinded Birds, The. Hardy.
Canticle to the Waterbirds, A. Brother Antoninus.
Cape Ann. *Fr.* Landscapes. T. S. Eliot.
Chaste Arabian Bird, The. Earl of Rochester.
Children of the Wind. Sandburg.
Choristers, The. Bliss Carman.
Death of the Bird, The. A. D. Hope.
Do You Ask What the Birds Say? S. T. Coleridge.
Flight. Laurence Whistler.
Flying Fish, The. John Gray.
Invitation. Harry Behn.
Lady Lost. Ransom.
Lark's Song, The. *Fr.* Milton. Blake.
Little Beach Bird, The. R. H. Dana.
Many Birds. *Fr.* Auguries of Innocence. Blake.
Nesting Time. Douglas Stewart.
No shop does the bird use. Coatsworth.
Of the Child with the Bird at the Bush. Bunyan.
Once I Nearly Touched a Bird. M. J. Carr.
Over Sir John's Hill. Dylan Thomas.
People Buy a Lot of Things. Annette Wynne.
Popular Rhymes. Blake.
Proud Songsters. Thomas Hardy.
Puzzled Game-Birds, The. Thomas Hardy.
Sea-Change. Masefield.
Sing Little Bird. Maria Hastings.
Spring: The Lover and the Birds. Allingham.
To a Waterfowl. Bryant.

Tom's Sleeping Song. *Fr.* Jonathan Genry. Van Doren.
Unknown Bird, The. Edward Thomas.
Wings. Victor Hugo, *tr. fr. French.*
See also names of birds (e.g., CANARIES*)*
BIRDS' NESTS. Bird's Nest, The. Drinkwater.
BIRDS OF PARADISE. Birds of Paradise, The. J. P. Bishop.
BIRMINGHAM, ALABAMA. Ghost in Birmingham, The. Ishmael Reed.
BIRMINGHAM, ENGLAND. Birmingham. MacNeice.
BIRTH
Arrivals and Departures. La Follette.
At Birth. Thwaite.
Birth. O. T. Dargan.
Childbirth. Ted Hughes.
Labor Room. Benn, *tr. fr. German by* Kaufmann.
Morning Song. Plath.
Prayer before Birth. MacNeice.
BIRTHDAYS
Another Birthday. Jonson.
Birthdays. *Unknown.*
Poem in October. Dylan Thomas.
Poem on His Birthday. Dylan Thomas.
Seven Times One. *Fr.* Songs of Seven. Ingelow.
Birthday Candles Burning Bright (BiCB). Sara *and* John E. Brewton, eds.
BISHOPS. *See* CLERGY
BLACKBIRDS
See also Blackbird *in* TITLE AND FIRST LINE INDEX
Dead and Gone. Thwaite.
Death of a Bird. Silkin.
Thirteen Ways of Looking at a Blackbird. Wallace Stevens.
Vesper. T. E. Brown.
BLACKSMITHS
Blacksmiths. *Unknown.*
Blacksmith's Daughter, The. Piontek, *tr. fr. German by* Hamburger.
Village Blacksmith, The. Longfellow.
BLAKE, WILLIAM. William Blake. James Thomson.
BLARNEY, IRELAND. Groves of Blarney, The. Millikin.
BLENHEIM, BATTLE OF. Battle of Blenheim, The. Robert Southey.
BLENHEIM PARK, ENGLAND. On Blenheim House. Abel Evans.
BLENNERHASSETT ISLAND, WEST VIRGINIA. Blennerhassett's Island. *Fr.* The New Pastoral. T. B. Read.
BLINDNESS
All but Blind. De la Mare.
At a Country Fair. Thomas Hardy.
Blind, The. Fried, *tr. fr. German by* Middleton.
Blind Boy, The. Cibber.
Blind but Happy. Fanny Crosby.
Blind Man. Hamburger.
Blind Man's Regret, The. *Unknown.*
Blinded Bird, The. Thomas Hardy.
Blinded Soldier to His Love, The. Noyes.
Hibakusha. Eileen Egan.
In the Garden of the Lord. Helen Keller.
Mock Medicine. *Unknown.*
On His Blindness. Milton.
Samson Agonistes. Milton.
Smoker, The. Robert Huff.
Solitude, A. Levertov.
To Cyriack Skinner, upon His Blindness. Milton.
BLOOMER, AMELIA JENKS. Crinolines and Bloomers. *Unknown.*
BLUE JAYS. Blue on White. Coatsworth.
BLUE RIDGE MOUNTAINS. Blue Ridge Parkway. Sieber.
BLUEBIRDS
Blue Bird, The. M. E. Coleridge.
Last Word of a Bluebird, The. Robert Frost.
BOATS
Boats. R. B. Bennett.
Eton Boating Song. W. J. Cory.
Excursion, The. Tu Fu, *tr. fr. Chinese by* Lowell *and* Ayscough.
Little Steamboat. Oscar Williams.
Ship Burning and a Comet All in One Day, A. Eberhart.
Where Go the Boats. R. L. Stevenson.
BOER WAR. Drummer Hodge. Thomas Hardy.
BOLL WEEVILS
Ballad of the Boll Weevil, The. *Unknown.*
De Boll Weevil. *Unknown.*
BOMBAY, INDIA. Bombay Arrival. Laurie Lee.
BOMBS AND BOMBING. *See* AIR RAIDS.
BONES. Bone Thoughts on a Dry Day. George Starbuck.
BONHOMME RICHARD (ship). Paul Jones. *Unknown.*
BONNIVARD, FRANÇOIS DE. Prisoner of Chillon, The. Byron.
BONONCINI, GIOVANNI BATTISTA. Epigram on Handel and Bononcini. Byron.
BOOKS
Book, A. Hannah More.
Book-Worms, The. Burns.
Burning of Books, The. Brecht, *tr. fr. German by* Hays.
Classic Waits for Me, A. E. B. White.
Dedication on the Gift of a Book to a Child. Hilaire Belloc.
Fire at Alexandria, The. Theodore Weiss.

First Reader. Paris Leary.
Half Your Book. Swift.
If someone asks you. Donian.
O for a Booke. *Unknown.*
Precious—mouldering pleasure—'tis, A. Emily Dickinson.
Sibrandus Schafnaburgensis. *Fr.* Garden Fancies. Robert Browning.
Tables Turned, The. Wordsworth.
There is no frigate like a book. Emily Dickinson.
"What Five Books Would You Pick to Be Marooned with on a Desert Island?" Paris Leary.
BOONE, DANIEL
   Daniel Boone. S. V. Benét.
   For the Grave of Daniel Boone. William Stafford.
BOOTH, WILLIAM. General William Booth Enters into Heaven. Vachel Lindsay.
BORGIA, LUCREZIA. On Seeing a Hair of Lucretia Borgia. W. S. Landor.
BORN, BERTRAND DE. *See* BERTRAND DE BORN
BOSTON, MASSACHUSETTS
   Poems from a First Year in Boston. Starbuck.
   Whaddaya Do for Action in This Place? Starbuck.
   Where the Rainbow Ends. Robert Lowell.
BOSTON TEA PARTY. Ballad of the Boston Tea-Party, A. O. W. Holmes.
BOURGEOISIE. How Beastly the Bourgeois Is. D. H. Lawrence.
BOWLES, WILLIAM LISLE. William Lisle Bowles. *Fr.* English Bards and Scotch Reviewers. Byron.
BOXING AND BOXERS
   Boxer. J. P. Clancy.
   Boxer's Face, The. Lucilius, *tr. fr. Greek by* Wolfe.
   Boxing Match, The. *Fr.* The Aeneid. Vergil, *tr. fr. Latin by* Humphries.
   Fancy, The. W. R. Benét.
   Gallantly within the Ring. J. H. Reynolds.
   Morrissey and the Black. *Unknown.*
   Morrissey and the Russian. *Unknown.*
   Nonpareil's Grave, The. M. J. McMahon.
   On Hurricane Jackson. Alan Dugan.
   World's Worst Boxer, The. Lucilius, *tr. fr. Greek by* Wolfe.
BOYNE, BATTLE OF THE
   King William and King James. *Unknown.*
   William of Orange; or, The Battle of Boyne. *Unknown.*
BOYS. *See* CHILDHOOD AND CHILDREN; YOUTH
BRADDOCK, EDWARD. Braddock's Fate, with an Incitement to Revenge. Tilden.
BRAHMA. Brahma. Emerson.
BREAD. Bread. Keesing.
BREBEUF, JEAN DE. Brebeuf and His Brethren, *sels.* E. J. Pratt.
BRIDES. *See* MARRIAGE
BRIDGES
   Bridge, The. Longfellow.
   Bridges. Bacmeister.
   Old Bridge, The. Hilda Conkling.
BRIDGET, SAINT. St. Brigid. D. A. McCarthy.
BRONTË, EMILY. Emily Brontë. Day Lewis.
BROOKLYN, NEW YORK
   Brooklyn Heights. Wain.
   Crossing Brooklyn Ferry. Walt Whitman.
   Meditation on the BMT. Paul Blackburn.
BROOKLYN BRIDGE. To Brooklyn Bridge. *Fr.* The Bridge. Hart Crane.
BROOKS
   Brook, The. Tennyson.
   Brook in February, The. C. G. D. Roberts.
   Inversnaid. G. M. Hopkins.
   Ladder, The. Baro.
   Orara. H. C. Kendall.
   West-running Brook. Robert Frost.
BROTHERHOOD
   Any Human to Another. Countee Cullen.
   Ballad of East and West. Kipling.
   Fellow-Citizens. Heidenstam, *tr. fr. Swedish by* Stork.
   Fraternitas. *Fr.* The Classic Anthology: Deer Sing. Confucius, *tr. fr. Chinese by* Pound.
   I Sought My Soul. *Unknown.*
   Indian Prayer. Strongwolf.
   Little Black Boy, The. *Fr.* Songs of Innocence. Blake.
   No East or West. Oxenham.
   Resurrection. Frank Horne.
   Something in Common. Richard Church.
   These Things Shall Be. Symonds.
   This Moment Yearning and Thoughtful. Walt Whitman.
   To Him That Was Crucified. Walt Whitman.
   We Bear the Strain of Earthly Care. O. S. Davis.
   We Shall Overcome. *Unknown.*
   World State, The. G. K. Chesterton.
BROWN, JOHN
   Brown of Ossawatomie. Whittier.
   Glory Hallelujah! or, John Brown's Body. *Unknown.*
   How Old Brown Took Harper's Ferry. E. C. Stedman.
   Portent, The. Melville.

BROWNING, ROBERT. To Robert Browning. W. S. Landor.
BRYANT, WILLIAM CULLEN. Bryant. *Fr.* A Fable for Critics. J. R. Lowell.
BUCKINGHAM, GEORGE VILLIERS, 2D DUKE OF. George Villiers, Duke of Buckingham. *Fr.* Absalom and Achitophel. Dryden.
BUDDHA
   Buddha. Theodore Holmes.
   Buddha. Rilke, *tr. fr. German by* Kaufmann.
   Buddha in the Glory. Rilke, *tr. fr. German by* Kaufmann.
BUFFALOES, AFRICAN. Buffalo, The. Herbert Price.
BUFFALOES, AMERICAN
   Buffalo Skinners, The. *Unknown.*
   Flower-fed Buffaloes, The. Vachel Lindsay.
   Ghosts of the Buffaloes, The. Vachel Lindsay.
   We Put on the Buffalo. R. P. T. Coffin.
BUGLES. Splendor Falls, The. *Fr.* The Princess. Tennyson.
BULLFIGHTS AND BULLFIGHTERS. Picador Bit, The. Noll.
BULLS. *See* Bull *in* TITLE AND FIRST LINE INDEX
BUSES. B's the Bus. *Fr.* All around the Town. McGinley.
BUTLER, SAMUEL. On the Setting Up of Mr. Butler's Monument in Westminster Abbey. Samuel Wesley.
BUTTERFLIES
   See also Butterflies *and* Butterfly *in* TITLE AND FIRST LINE INDEX
   Concerning Wings. Brockman.
   Envoi: "Fly, white butterflies, out to sea." Swinburne.
   Example, The. W. H. Davies.
   Flying Crooked. Robert Graves.
   Haiku: "Falling flower, The." Moritake, *tr. fr. Japanese by* Deutsch.
BYRON, GEORGE GORDON NOEL BRYON, 6TH BARON
   Byron Recollected at Bologna. *Fr.* Italy. Samuel Rogers.
   Memorial Verses. Matthew Arnold.
BYZANTIUM
   Byzantium. Yeats.
   Sailing to Byzantium. Yeats.

C

CABOT, RICHARD. White-haired Man, The. Sarton.
CAESAR, JULIUS
   Antony's Oration. *Fr.* Julius Caesar. Shakespeare.
   Early in the Morning. Louis Simpson.
CALIBAN. Caliban upon Setebos. Robert Browning.
CALIFORNIA
   California. *Unknown.*
   Flying above California. Thom Gunn.
   Orange County Plague: Scenes. Lieberman.
CALIGULA. Caligula. Robert Lowell.
CALVARY. *See* CRUCIFIXION, THE
CALVES
   Bull Calf, The. Layton.
   New Baby Calf, The. E. N. Chase.
CAMARGUE, FRANCE. Horses on the Camargue. Roy Campbell.
CAMBRIDGE UNIVERSITY
   Inside of King's College Chapel, Cambridge. *Fr.* Ecclesiastical Sketches. Wordsworth.
   King's College Chapel. Causley.
   Sunday Morning, King's Cambridge. Betjeman.
CAMELLIAS. Camellia, The. Basho, *tr. fr. Japanese by* Henderson.
CAMELS
   Camel, The. Ogden Nash.
   Plaint of the Camel, The. C. E. Carryl.
CAMPBELL, ROY. In Memoriam Roy Campbell. Currey.
CAMPING
   Camping Out. Empson.
   Few Signs, A. Grantland Rice.
CANADA. Oxford Book of Canadian Verse, The (OBCV). A. J. M. Smith, ed.
CANARIES. To the Canary Bird. Very.
CANBERRA, AUSTRALIA. Canberra in April. J. R. Rowland.
CANCER
   Cancer Cells, The. Eberhart.
   Death from Cancer. *Fr.* In Memory of Arthur Winslow. Robert Lowell.
   Man and Woman Walk through the Cancer Ward. Benn.
CANDLEMAS
   Ceremonies for Candlemas Eve. Herrick.
   Ground Hog Day. Marnie Pomeroy.
   If Candlemas Day be fair and bright. *Unknown.*
   If Candlemas Day be dry and fair. *Unknown.*
CANDLES. Dreamer, The. Morgenstern, *tr. fr. German by* Hull.
CANOES AND CANOEING
   Backwater Pond: The Canoeists. Merwin.
   Canoe. Patrick Anderson.

CANOES AND CANOEING (*continued*)
Canoe, The. I. V. Crawford.
Canoe Speaks, The, *sel.* R. L. Stevenson.
Lullaby: "Long canoe, The." Robert Hillyer.
CAPITALISM
Latest Decalogue, The. Clough.
Symphony, The. Sidney Lanier.
CARDINALS (birds)
Cardinal. Brockman.
Morning Window. O. T. Dargan.
CARP. Cassel (Carps at Wilhelmstrasse 15). "Joachim Ringelnatz," *tr. fr. German by* Middleton.
CARPENTERS. Busy Carpenters. Tippett.
CARS. *See* AUTOMOBILES
CARSON, KIT. Kit Carson's Ride. Joaquin Miller.
CARY, SIR LUCIUS. To the Immortall Memorie, and Friendship of That Noble Paire, Sir Lucius Cary, and Sir H. Morison. Jonson.
CASTILE, SPAIN. Castile. Unamuno, *tr. fr. Spanish.*
CASTRO, FIDEL
Ode to Fidel Castro. Edward Field.
One Thousand Fearful Words for Fidel Castro. Ferlinghetti.
CASUARINA TREES. Our Casuarina Tree. Toru Dutt.
CATALPA TREES. Catalpa Tree. Miriam Waddington.
CATERPILLARS
Butterfly and the Caterpillar, The. Lauren.
Caterpillar, The. *Fr.* Sing-Song. C. G. Rossetti.
Cocoon. McCord.
Fuzzy Wuzzy, Creepy Crawly. Vanada.
Only My Opinion. Monica Shannon.
Tickle Rhyme, The. Serraillier.
CATS
See also Cat *and* Cats *in* TITLE AND FIRST LINE INDEX
Bad Kittens, The. Coatsworth.
Bird Fancier, The. Kirkup.
Brothers. Solomon Edwards.
Cat's Conscience, A. *Unknown.*
Divination by a Cat. Hecht.
Dog and the Cat, The. Hallock.
Epitaph for a Cat. Bruner.
Fight. Jaszi.
My Cat Jeoffry. *Fr.* Jubilate Agno. Christopher Smart.
Growltiger's Last Stand. T. S. Eliot.
I Love Little Pussy. Jane Taylor.
Love for a Hare. La Follette.
Macavity: The Mystery Cat. T. S. Eliot.
Mysterious Cat, The. Vachel Lindsay.
Naming of Cats, The. T. S. Eliot.
Nipping Pussy's Feet in Fun. Stevie Smith.
Ode on the Death of a Favourite Cat Drowned in a Tub of Gold Fishes. Thomas Gray.
Owl and the Pussy-Cat, The. Edward Lear.
Pangur Bán. *Unknown, tr. fr. Irish by* Flower.
Poem: "As the cat/ climbed over." W. C. Williams.
Rescue, The. Hal Summers.
Rum Tum Tugger, The. T. S. Eliot.
Run, Kitty, Run! Garthwaite.
Singing Cat, The. Stevie Smith.
Song for a Child. H. B. Davis.
Three Little Kittens. Eliza Cook.
Tiger-Cat Tim. E. N. Chase.
To a Cat. Keats.
Two Cats Make the World. Vernon Ward.
Vengence on Cats. *Fr.* Phyllyp Sparowe. John Skelton.
Yellow Cat, The. L. N. Jennings.
CATTLE
From the Gulf. Ogilvie.
Wires. Philip Larkin.
See also BULLS; CALVES; COWS; OXEN
CATULLUS (Caius Valerius Catullus). "Frater Ave atque Vale." Tennyson.
CAUCASUS. Caucasus, The. Pasternak, *tr. fr. Russian by* Kayden.
CAVALRY. Cavalry Crossing a Ford. Walt Whitman.
CECILIA, SAINT
Song for St. Cecilia's Day. Auden.
Song for Saint Cecilia's Day, 1687. Dryden.
CEDAR GROVE (ship). *Cedar Grove, The. Unknown.*
CEDAR TREES. So Independently the Cedars Grow. Paul Bartlett.
CELANDINE. Small Celandine, The. Wordsworth.
CELERY. Celery. Ogden Nash.
CEMETERIES
Hughley Steeple. *Fr.* A Shropshire Lad. A. E. Housman.
Jewish Cemetery at Newport, The. Longfellow.
Old Burying-Ground, The. Whittier.
Old Churchyard of Bonchurch, The. P. B. Marston.
Oldest Cemetery. Van Doren.
Part-Time Tenant. Meudt.
Prairie Graveyard. Anne Marriott.
Sleeping Village. Vinal.
Soul Longs to Return Whence It Came, The. Eberhart.
See also GRAVES
CENTAURS. Ambuscade. Hugh McCrae.

CENTIPEDES. Centipede Was Happy Quite, A. Craster.
CHAGALL, MARC. Poem for Marc Chagall. Leonard Cohen.
CHAMELEONS
Chameleon, The. Meyerstein.
To a Chameleon. Marianne Moore.
CHANCE. *See* FORTUNE
CHANGE
Answering a Letter from a Younger Poet. Ghiselin.
Beautiful Changes, The. Wilbur.
Change. Knister.
Disguises. Elizabeth Jennings.
Fair Annet's Song. Wylie.
Fault, The. Lucie-Smith.
Matter of Life and Death, A. Ridler.
Mutability. Shelley.
New Sun, The. Wain.
Van Winkle. *Fr.* The Bridge. Hart Crane.
World, that all contains, is ever moving, The. *Fr.* Caelica. Fulke Greville.
CHANTICLEER. *See* COCKS
CHAPMAN, GEORGE. On First Looking into Chapman's Homer. Keats.
CHAGRES RIVER, PANAMA. Beyond the Chagres. J. S. Gilbert.
CHANNING, WILLIAM HENRY. Ode: Inscribed to W. H. Channing. Emerson.
CHARIOT RACING. Chariot Race, The. *Fr.* Georgics. Vergil, *tr. fr. Latin by* Bovie.
CHARLES I, KING OF ENGLAND. By the Statue of King Charles at Charing Cross. Lionel Johnson.
CHARLES II, KING OF ENGLAND. On Charles II. Earl of Rochester.
CHARLES, RAY. Bishop of Atlanta, The: Ray Charles. H. J. Bond.
CHARLES RIVER, MASSACHUSETTS. Some Refrains at the Charles River. Peter Viereck.
CHARLESTON, SOUTH CAROLINA. Charleston. Timrod.
CHATTAHOOCHEE RIVER, GEORGIA. Song of the Chattahoochee. Sidney Lanier.
CHAUCER, GEOFFREY
Chaucer. Longfellow.
Description of Sir Geoffrey Chaucer, The. *Fr.* Greene's Vision. Robert Greene.
Goldyn Targe, The, *sel.* ("O reverend Chaucere, rose of rethoris all"). William Dunbar.
CHERRY TREES. Loveliest of Trees, the Cherry Now. *Fr.* A Shropshire Lad. A. E. Housman.
CHESAPEAKE (ship). *Chesapeake and the Shannon, The. Unknown.*
CHEVY CHASE, BATTLE OF. *See* OTTERBOURNE [*or* OTTERBURN], BATTLE OF
CHICAGO, ILLINOIS. Chicago. Sandburg.
CHICKAMAUGA, BATTLE OF. Bury Me Not on the Chickamauga. *Unknown.*
CHICKENS. Gettin' Born. Euwer.
CHILDHOOD AND CHILDREN
See also Child; Childhood; *and* Children *in* TITLE AND FIRST LINE INDEX
Adventures. Arthur Kramer.
Barefoot Boy, The. Whittier.
Beat Child, The. Chuck Stoddard.
Boy's Day. R. E. Henderson.
Builder of Houses, The. Jane Cooper.
Centaur, The. May Swenson.
Children's Hour, The. Longfellow.
Child's Laughter, A. Swinburne.
Child's Power of Wonder, The. Saha.
Conjuror, The. E. V. Lucas.
Fern Hill. Dylan Thomas.
First Song. Kinnell.
For Vicki at Seven. S. K. Russell.
Four. Elise Gibbs.
Good and Bad Children. R. L. Stevenson.
Growing Up. Harry Behn.
Growing Up. A. A. Milne.
Growing Up. E. K. Wallace.
Holy Thursday. *Fr.* Songs of Experience. Blake.
Holy Thursday. *Fr.* Songs of Innocence. Blake.
I Remember, I Remember. Thomas Hood.
If I Could Only Live at the Pitch That Is near Madness. Eberhart.
Impetuous Resolve, An. J. W. Riley.
Jest 'fore Christmas. Eugene Field.
John Plans. D. M. Pierce.
Life-Lesson, A. J. W. Riley.
Little Boy Blue. Eugene Field.
Middle-aged Child. Inez Hogan.
Monday's Child Is Fair of Face. *Unknown.*
My Parents Kept Me from Children Who Were Rough. Spender.
My Plan. Chute.
Nurse's Song. *Fr.* Songs of Innocence. Blake.
Ode: Intimations of Immortality from Recollections of Early Childhood. Wordsworth.
Oh Come, Little Children. McGinley.

Old Oaken Bucket, The. Samuel Woodworth.
On a Child Beginning to Talk. Bastard.
On Children. *Fr.* The Prophet. Gibran.
Past and Present. Thomas Hood.
Plans. D. B. Thompson.
Plaza and the Flaming Orange Trees, The. Machado, *tr. fr.*
  Spanish by Flores.
Poem by the Clock Tower, Sumner. J. K. Baxter.
Reserved. De la Mare.
Retreat, The. Henry Vaughan.
Return of the Village Lad. Lichtenstein, *tr. fr. German by*
  Hamburger.
Review, The. Traherne.
Rustic Childhood. William Barnes.
Seein' Things. Eugene Field.
Six of Cups. Wakoski.
So Long Folks, Off to the War. Ostroff.
Speak Gently. David Bates.
Speak Roughly to Your Little Boy. *Fr.* Alice's Adventures
  in Wonderland. "Lewis Carroll."
System. R. L. Stevenson.
Tamerlane. V. J. Daley.
There Was a Boy. *Fr.* The Prelude. Wordsworth.
There Was a Child Went Forth. Walt Whitman.
To a Child. Gardons.
To a Child. Christopher Morley.
Toys, The. *Fr.* The Unknown Eros. Coventry Patmore.
Twenty Years Ago. *Unknown.*
Two Deep Clear Eyes. De la Mare.
Under the Apple Boughs. Dylan Thomas.
What in the World! Earnshaw.
When I Grow Up. R. S. Holland.
When I Grow Up. Wise.
Whole Duty of Children, The. R. L. Stevenson.
Years Back When We Were Children. "Der Wilde
  Alexander," *tr. fr. German by* Lowell.
See also BABIES; YOUTH
CHILDREN'S VERSE
  Beastly Boys and Ghastly Girls (BBGG). William Cole, ed.
  Dawn and Dusk (DaDu). Charles Causley, ed.
  Reading of Poetry, The (RePo). William D. Sheldon,
    Nellie Lyons, *and* Polly Rouault, eds.
  Sound of Poetry, The (SoPo). Mary C. Austin *and* Queenie
    B. Mills, eds.
CHILLON CASTLE, SWITZERLAND
  Prisoner of Chillon, The. Byron.
  Sonnet on Chillon. *Fr.* The Prisoner of Chillon. Byron.
CHIMNEY SWEEPS
  Chimney Sweeper, The. *Fr.* Songs of Experience. Blake.
  Chimney Sweeper, The. *Fr.* Songs of Innocence. Blake.
  Wmffre the Sweep. Humphries.
CHIMPANZEES. Chimpanzee, The. Oliver Herford.
CHINA, GREAT WALL OF
  At the Great Wall of China. Blunden.
  Wall of China, The. Padraic Colum.
CHIPMUNKS
  Chipmunk. M. de L. Welch.
  Little Charlie Chipmunk. LeCron.
CHISHOLM TRAIL. Old Chisholm Trail, The. *Unknown.*
CHRIST. *See* JESUS CHRIST
CHRISTENINGS
  Christening, The. De la Mare.
  Christening-Day Wishes for My God-Child, Grace Lane
    Berkley II. R. P. T. Coffin.
  For a Christening. Vernon Watkins.
  Gifts. H. H. Harris.
  It Really Happened. Elizabeth Henley.
  To Patricia on Her Christening Day. E. B. Price.
  When I Was Christened. McCord.
CHRISTMAS
  See also Christmas *in* TITLE AND FIRST LINE INDEX
  African Christmas. Press.
  As I Went Out on Christmas Day. *Unknown.*
  Babushka. E. M. Thomas.
  Ballad of the Unmiraculous Miracle. Vassar Miller.
  Barn, The. Coatsworth.
  Before the Paling of the Stars. C. G. Rossetti.
  Bethlehem of Judea. *Unknown.*
  Birth of Christ. Rilke, *tr. fr. German by* Norton.
  Birthday of the Lord, The. M. J. Carr.
  Burning Babe, The. Southwell.
  Burning the Christmas Greens. W. C. Williams.
  Candle and Star. Coatsworth.
  Cause for Wonder, A. *Unknown.*
  Carol: "Here's a wreath of Christmas holly." C. E. Eaton.
  Carol for Children, A. Ogden Nash.
  Chanson Innocente ("Little tree"). E. E. Cummings.
  Cherry-Tree Carol, The. *Unknown.*
  Child Is Born, A. *Unknown.*
  Child's Carol. Farjeon.
  Child's Christmas Song, A. T. A. Daly.
  Christ Climbed Down. Ferlinghetti.
  Concerning the Birth of Christ, 1657. Gryphius, *tr. fr. Ger-*
    man by Schoolfield.

Contrast. Duggan.
Cradle and Throne. *Unknown.*
Cradle Hymn. Martin Luther.
Cradle Hymn. Isaac Watts.
Dear Son, Leave Thy Weeping. *Unknown.*
Earth and Sky. Farjeon.
Eclogue for Christmas, An. MacNeice.
Eternal Christmas. E. S. Phelps.
Eve of Christmas, The. Kirkup.
Far Trumpets Blowing. L. F. Benson.
First Christmas, The. St. Luke, Bible, *N.T.*
First Christmas Night of All. N. B. Turner.
Friendly Beasts, The. *Unknown.*
Good King Wenceslas. *Unknown, tr. fr. Latin by* Neale.
Good Tidings of Great Joy! C. F. Alexander.
His Name at the Top. *Unknown.*
House of Christmas, The. G. K. Chesterton.
I Saw a Stable. M. E. Coleridge.
I Saw Three Ships. *Unknown.*
In Honour of Christmas. *Unknown.*
In the Holy Nativity of Our Lord God. Crashaw.
Jest 'fore Christmas. Eugene Field.
Joy to the World. *Unknown.*
Karma. E. A. Robinson.
Kid Stuff. Frank Horne.
Know It Is Christmas. Snelling.
Let Us Keep Christmas. G. N. Crowell.
Light Now Shineth, The. *Unknown.*
Little Tree. E. E. Cummings.
Long, Long Ago. *Unknown.*
Lullaby of the Nativity, A. *Unknown.*
Man Exalted. *Unknown.*
Mangers. W. H. Davies.
Mary Tired. Pickthall.
Mary's Song. Farjeon.
Mrs. Santa Claus' Christmas Present. A. S. Morris.
Mother's Tale, The. Farjeon.
Nativity, The. *Unknown.*
Nativity of Christ, The. Góngora, *tr. fr. Spanish by* Long-
  fellow.
Nativitie of Christ, The. Southwell.
Nativity of Our Lord and Savior Jesus Christ, The. *Fr.*
  Hymns and Spiritual Songs. Christopher Smart.
New Prince, New Pomp. Southwell.
Now Every Child. Farjeon.
Now Is the Time of Christmas. *Unknown.*
Now the Most High Is Born. Ryman.
On the Morning of Christ's Nativity. Milton.
On Christmas Eve. E. L. Pierce.
Oxen, The. Thomas Hardy.
Round and Round. D. B. Thompson.
Shepheards, The. Henry Vaughan.
Shepherd upon a Hill, The. *Unknown.*
Silent Night. Mohr, *tr. fr. German.*
Simple Sam. L. F. Jackson.
Sing We Yule. *Unknown.*
Sonnets at Christmas. Allen Tate.
Special Starlight. Sandburg.
Star of the Nativity. Pasternak, *tr. fr. Russian by* Kayden.
Sweet Was the Song. *Unknown.*
Taking Down the Tree. Aileen Fisher.
Terly Terlow. *Unknown.*
There's a Song in the Air! J. G. Holland.
Time draws near the birth of Christ, The. *Fr.* In Memoriam.
  Tennyson.
To Christ Our Lord. Kinnell.
Twelve Days of Christmas, The. *Unknown.*
Unto Us a Son Is Given. Alice Meynell.
Village Christmas. Widdemer.
Visit from St. Nicholas, A. C. C. Moore.
What Can I Give Him? C. G. Rossetti.
When Christ Was Born. Tabb.
Whole Year Christmas, The. Angela Morgan.
Why Do the Bells of Christmas Ring? Eugene Field.
See also MAGI; TWELFTH NIGHT
CHURCHES
  Church, The. Edwin Muir.
  Church Going. Philip Larkin.
  Church of the Holy Innocents, Dunedin. "Robin Hyde."
  Great Churches. *Unknown.*
  I Am a Little Church (No Great Cathedral). E. E. Cum-
    mings.
  In Church. William Barnes.
  In Santa Maria del Popolo. Thom Gunn.
  Ladies' Aid, The. *Unknown.*
  St. Isaac's Church, Petrograd. Claude McKay.
  Santa Maria Maggiore, Rome. Elizabeth Jennings.
  Sunday Morning, King's Cambridge. Betjeman.
CICADAS
  Cicada, The. H. M. Green.
  Cicada-Shell. Basho, *tr. fr. Japanese.*
CICERO (Marcus Tullius Cicero). On the Banishment of
  Cicero. Philip Wharton.
CINDERELLA. Cinderella. Pickard.

Cino da Pistoia. To Cino da Pistoia. Onesto da Bologna, tr. fr. Italian by Valency.
Circe. Strayed Reveller, The. Matthew Arnold.
Circuses
  See also Circus in Title and First Line Index
  Big Tent under the Roof, The. Ogden Nash.
  C Is for the Circus. Fr. All around the Town. McGinley.
  Horses. MacNeice.
Cisterns. Secrets of Cisterns, The. McNail.
Cities
  Across the Straits. R. de B. Dobson.
  Block Party. Eve Merriam.
  City Considered as a Tulip Tree, The. Fr. London Sonnets. Carl Bode.
  City Streets and Country Roads. Farjeon.
  Complacent Cliff-Dweller, The. Fishback.
  Country Mouse, The. Abraham Cowley.
  "Everything in the Air Is a Bird." Barbara Guest.
  Greatest City, The. Walt Whitman.
  I Went to the City. Patchen.
  In the Cities. D. H. Lawrence.
  Lion Named Passion, A. Hollander.
  More Foreign Cities. Tomlinson.
  Mr. Frost Goes South to Boston. Firman Houghton.
  Preliminary Poem for a Modern City. Kemp.
  Preludes. T. S. Eliot.
  Town, The. Storm, tr. fr. German by Linn.
  Up at a Villa—Down in the City. Robert Browning.
Civil Rights. We Shall Overcome. Unknown.
Civil War, American
  Alphabet, The. Unknown.
  Barbara Frietchie. Whittier.
  Battle-Hymn of the Republic. J. W. Howe.
  Blue and the Gray, The. F. M. Finch.
  Brigade Must Not Know, Sir, The. Unknown.
  Brother Green. Unknown.
  Brother Jonathan's Lament for Sister Caroline. O. W. Holmes.
  By the Bivouac's Fitful Flame. Walt Whitman.
  Cavalry Crossing a Ford. Walt Whitman.
  Charleston. Timrod.
  Cruise of the Monitor, The. Boker.
  Farragut. W. T. Meredith.
  For the Union Dead. Robert Lowell.
  John Brown's Body, sels. S. V. Benét.
  Kentucky Belle. Woolson.
  Little Giffen. Ticknor.
  Malvern Hill. Melville.
  March into Virginia, The. Melville.
  Memorial Wreath. Dudley Randall.
  Ode: "Sleep sweetly in your humble graves." Timrod.
  Ode to the Confederate Dead. Allen Tate.
  Portent, The. Melville.
  Rebel, The. Innes Randolph.
  Running the Batteries. Melville.
  Sheridan's Ride. T. B. Read.
  Shiloh—a Requiem. Melville.
  Sight in Camp, A. Walt Whitman.
  Soldier from Missouri, A. Unknown.
  Twilight Song. Walt Whitman.
  Unknown Dead, The. Timrod.
  Utilitarian View of the Monitor's Fight, A. Melville.
  Vigil Strange I Kept on the Field One Night. Walt Whitman.
  When Johnny Comes Marching Home. P. S. Gilmore.
  When Sherman Marched Down to the Sea. S. H. M. Byers.
  Whisperin' Bill. Irving Bacheller.
Civil War, Spanish
  Battle Hymn of the Spanish Rebellion. L. A. MacKay.
  For My Dead Brother. Bessie.
  Port Bou. Spender.
  Spain 1937. Auden.
Clark, William. Lewis and Clark. S. V. Benét.
Cleopatra
  Cleopatra: The Barge She Sat In. Fr. Antony and Cleopatra. Shakespeare.
  In Praise of a Gentlewoman. Gascoigne.
Clergy
  Bishop Orders His Tomb at Saint Praxed's Church, The. Robert Browning.
  Collar, The. George Herbert.
  Country Clergy, The. R. S. Thomas.
  Deserted Village, The, sel. ("Near yonder copse, where once the garden smiled"). Goldsmith.
  Epitaph on a Worthy Clergyman. Benjamin Franklin.
  In Church. Thomas Hardy.
  Lay Preacher Ponders, The. Idris Davies.
  Parson, The. Fr. The Deserted Village. Goldsmith.
  Pastor, The. W. C. Summers.
  Preacher's Prayer, The. George Macdonald.
  Priest of Christ, The. Ken.
  Priesthood, The. George Herbert.
  Priests Disguise as Shepherds. Cardenal, tr. fr. Provençal by Davis.

Problem, The. Emerson.
Prologue, sel. ("The parson of a country town was he"). Fr. The Canterbury Tales. Chaucer.
Sermon, The. Richard Hughes.
Soft Job. W. C. Summers.
Some Bird. Unknown.
Task, The, sel. ("I say the pulpit (in the sober use)"). Cowper.
Task, The, sel. ("Would I describe a preacher, such as Paul"). Cowper.
Vicar, The. Fr. The Borough. Crabbe.
Vicar, The. Praed.
Clerks. Dolor. Roethke.
Clocks
  Big Clock, The. Unknown.
  Clock, The. Jaszi.
  Four Quartz Crystal Clocks. Marianne Moore.
  Sun-Dial, The. Fr. Melincourt. Peacock.
  Watch, The. Frances Cornford.
Clothing
  Clothes. Frances Frost.
  Cold Fact. Emmons.
  Crinolines and Bloomers. Unknown.
  Delight in Disorder. Herrick.
  Her Favorites. Hausgen.
  My love in her attire doth show her wit. Unknown.
  Nothing to Wear. W. A. Butler.
  Open Wardrobe. Grass, tr. fr. Germn by Hamburger.
  Underwear. Ferlinghetti.
  Upon Julia's Clothes. Herrick.
Clouds
  See also Cloud and Clouds in Title and First Line Index
  Clouded Morning, The. Very.
  Night Clouds. Amy Lowell.
  Watching Clouds. J. C. Farrar.
Clough, Arthur Hugh. Thyrsis. Matthew Arnold.
Clowns
  Clown, The. M. C. Rose.
  Clowns. MacNeice.
Coal Mining and Miners
  Avondale Mine Disaster, The. Unknown.
  Ballad of a Mine, A. Robin Skelton.
  Caliban in the Coal Mines. Louis Untermeyer.
  Collier, The. Vernon Watkins.
  Hills above the Mine, The. Malcolm Cowley.
  Plodder Seam, The. Unknown.
  Poems from the Coalfields. Ian Healy.
Cobblers. See Shoemakers
Cobham, Edward. To Master Edward Cobham. Googe.
Cockroaches. Last Warehouse, The. May Miller.
Cocks
  Before the Barn-Door Crowing. Fr. The Beggar's Opera. John Gay.
  Chanticleer. J. C. Farrar.
  Chanticleer. Margaret Irvin.
  Cock Again, The. Kikaku, tr. fr. Japanese by Henderson.
  I Have a Gentle Cock. Unknown.
  Roosters. Elizabeth Bishop.
  To Be or Not to Be. Unknown.
  What They Do. Farjeon.
Cocoa. In Praise of Cocoa, Cupid's Nightcap. S. J. Sharpless.
Cold
  Bañalbufar, a Brazier, Relativity, Cloud Formations & the Kindness & Relentlessness of Time, All Seen through a Window While Keeping the Feet Warm at the Same Time As. Paul Blackburn.
  Color of Cold, The. Pieyre de Mandiargues, tr. fr. French by Justice.
  Tramontana at Lerici. Tomlinson.
Cole, Thomas. To Cole, the Painter, Departing for Europe. Bryant.
Coleridge, Samuel Taylor
  Bards, The. De la Mare.
  English Bards and Scotch Reviewers, sel. ("Next comes the dull disciple of thy school"). Byron.
  Man from Porlock, The. Bevington.
  Person from Porlock, The. Robert Graves.
  Person from Porlock, A. R. S. Thomas.
  To Coleridge. Shelley.
  To Coleridge in Sicily. Fr. The Prelude. Wordsworth.
Coliseum. See Colosseum
Colleges and Universities
  Epigram: "No wonder that Oxford and Cambridge profound." Unknown.
  Schools. Fr. The Borough. Crabbe.
  Student, The. Marianne Moore.
Cologne, Germany. On Crossing the Rhine Bridge at Cologne by Night. Stadler, tr. fr. German by Hamburger.
Colors
  Color. Fr. Sing-Song. C. G. Rossetti.
  Colors. Bartolini, tr. fr. Italian by Golino.
  What Is Pink? Fr. Sing-Song. C. G. Rossetti.
Colosseum. Coliseum, The. Poe.

COLUMBUS, CHRISTOPHER
Ave Maria. *Fr.* The Bridge. Hart Crane.
Christopher Columbus. S. V. Benét.
Columbus. Clough.
Columbus. Joaquin Miller.
Discovery, The. Squire.
Great Discovery, The. Farjeon.
Prayer of Columbus. Walt Whitman.
COMMUNION. *See* EUCHARIST
CONCENTRATION CAMPS
Bird, The. Louis Simpson.
Camp in the Prussian Forest, A. Jarrell.
Chant for All the People on Earth. Hedley.
Fugue of Death. Celan, *tr. fr. German by* Middleton.
Gift, The. Ciardi.
CONCORD, MASSACHUSETTS. Concord Hymn. Emerson.
CONDORS. Condors. Padraic Colum.
CONFEDERACY
Bonnie Blue Flag, The. A. C. Ketchum.
Conquered Banner, The. A. J. Ryan.
Ode: "Sleep sweetly in your humble graves." Timrod.
Ode to the Confederate Dead. Allen Tate.
CONQUISTADORS
Conquistador. McElhaney.
Conquistador, *sel.* Archibald MacLeish.
Inca's Arrows, The. González Prada, *tr. fr. Spanish by* Flores.
CONSTABLE, JOHN. Meditation on John Constable, A. Tomlinson.
CONSTITUTION (ship). Old Ironsides. O. W. Holmes.
CONTENTMENT
See also Contentment *in* TITLE AND FIRST LINE INDEX
Character of a Happy Life. Henry Wotton.
Ode on Solitude. Pope.
Of a Contented Mind. Vaux.
Quiet Life, The. Pope.
COOK, JAMES. Five Visions of Captain Cook, *sel.* ("Flowers turned to stone! Not all the botany"). Slessor.
COOLE, IRELAND. Coole Park and Ballylee, 1931. Yeats.
COOPER, JAMES FENIMORE. Cooper. *Fr.* A Fable for Critics. J. R. Lowell.
COPENHAGEN, DENMARK. Non Sum Qualis Eram in Bona Urbe Nordica Illa. Hollander.
COPPERHEADS. Copperhead. C. E. Eaton.
CORK, IRELAND. Bells of Shandon, The. Mahony.
CORN
Corn. Sidney Lanier.
Corn Must Be Sown. Thomas Carlyle.
Corn-grinding Song. *Tr. fr. Zuni Indian by* Curtis.
Korosta Katzina Song. *Tr. fr. Hopi Indian by* Curtis.
Waving of the Corn, The. Sidney Lanier.
CORNWALL, ENGLAND
Ballad of a Mine, A. Robin Skelton.
Harrow-on-the-Hill. Betjeman.
Seasons in North Cornwall, The. Causley.
Song of the Western Men, The. Hawker.
COUNTRY CLUBS. Country Club Sunday. McGinley.
COUNTRY LIFE
See also Country *in* TITLE AND FIRST LINE INDEX
City Streets and Country Roads. Farjeon.
Deserted Village, The. Goldsmith.
Elegy Written in a Country Churchyard. Thomas Gray.
Epistle to Miss Blount. Pope.
Francis Beaumont's Letter from the Country to Jonson. Jonson.
Georgics, *sel.* ("What makes a plenteous harvest, when to turn"). Vergil, *tr. fr. Latin by* Dryden.
Grass and Milk. Gatto, *tr. fr. Italian by* Scott.
On Westwell Downs. William Strode.
Our Village—by a Villager. Thomas Hood.
Pastoral: "Who can live in heart so glad." *Fr.* The Passionate Shepherd. Nicholas Breton.
Philemon and Baucis. *Fr.* Metamorphoses. Ovid, *tr. fr. Latin by* Golding.
Praises of a Countrie Life, The. Jonson.
Rudolph Is Tired of the City. Gwendolyn Brooks.
Up at a Villa—Down in the City. Robert Browning.
Village, The, *sels.* Crabbe.
COURAGE
Abnormal Is Not Courage, The. Jack Gilbert.
Invictus. W. E. Henley.
To fight aloud is very brave. Emily Dickinson.
COVENTRY, ENGLAND. I Remember, I Remember. Philip Larkin.
COWBOYS
At a Cowboy Dance. J. B. Adams.
Closing of the Rodeo, The. W. J. Smith.
Cowboy Song. Causley.
Cowboy's Dream, The. *Unknown.*
Cowboy's Lament, The. *Unknown.*
Cowboy's Life, The. *At. to* J. B. Adams.
Dying Cowboy, The ("Oh bury me not on the lone prairie"). *Unknown.*

From the Ballad of Two-Gun Freddy. W. R. Brooks.
Old Chisholm Trail, The. *Unknown.*
When the Work's All Done This Fall. *Unknown.*
Whoopee High Ogie. *Unknown.*
See also STOCKMEN
COWS
See also Cow *and* Cows *in* TITLE AND FIRST LINE INDEX
Calling the Cows Home. *Fr.* The High Tide on the Coast of Lincolnshire, 1571. Ingelow.
Canadian Herd-Boy, The. Moodie.
Cattle. *Unknown.*
Colly, My Cow. *Unknown.*
Man and Cows. Andrew Young.
Midsummer. Scully.
Milking Time. E. M. Roberts.
Pleasant Cow, The. Hallock.
Trees and Cattle. Dickey.
CRABBE, GEORGE. George Crabbe. E. A. Robinson.
CRABS AND CRABBING
Crabbing. Levine.
Crustaceans. Roy Fuller.
CRADLE SONGS. *See* LULLABIES
CRANE, HART
Hart Crane. Creeley.
Words for Hart Crane. Robert Lowell.
CRANES
Crane Is My Neighbour, The. J. S. Neilson.
Whooping Crane, The. Vassar Miller.
CRASHAW, RICHARD. On the Death of Mr. Crashaw. Abraham Cowley.
CREATION
All Things Bright and Beautiful. C. F. Alexander.
Creation. Bhushan.
Creation, The. J. W. Johnson.
Genesis. Geoffrey Hill.
Pulley, The. George Herbert.
Songs of Creation. Heine, *tr. fr. German by* Kaufmann.
Spacious Firmament on High, The. Addison.
Tiger, The. *Fr.* Songs of Experience. Blake.
What Is the World? *Fr.* To My Honor'd Friend Sir Robert Howard. Dryden.
CREDO. *See* FAITH
CREPE MYRTLE. Crepe Myrtle. C. E. Eaton.
CREW RACING
Boat Race, The. *Fr.* The Aeneid. Vergil, *tr. fr. Latin by* Humphries.
Crew Cut. McCord.
Eight Oars and a Coxswain. Guiterman.
Racing Eight, A. Cuthbertson.
CRICKET (game)
Cricket Triolet, A. Kernahan.
How McDougal Topped the Score. T. E. Spencer.
CRICKETS
Cricket, The. Vincent Bourne, *tr. fr. Latin by* Cowper.
Little Night Music, A. Stefanile.
On the Grasshopper and Cricket. Keats.
Splinter. Sandburg.
To the Grasshopper and the Cricket. Leigh Hunt.
CRIMEAN WAR
Charge of the Light Brigade, The. Tennyson.
Heights of Alma, The. *Unknown.*
CRITICISM AND CRITICS
Critics. Crabbe.
Critics, The. Durrell.
English Bards and Scotch Reviewers, *sels.* Byron.
Epistle to Dr. Arbuthnot, *sel.* ("Pains, reading, study, are their just pretense"). Pope.
Essay on Criticism, An. Pope.
In Acknowledgment of the Praises of European Writers. Sister Juana Inés de la Cruz, *tr. fr. Spanish by* Urdang.
Interpreters, The. Enright.
Lines to a Critic. Shelley.
Narcissus and Some Tadpoles. V. J. Daley.
Notes on a Certain Terribly Critical Piece. Reed Whittemore.
On First Looking in on Blodgett's Keats's "Chapman's Homer." George Starbuck.
Poets, The. Wevill.
To a Steam Roller. Marianne Moore.
To His Noble Friend, Mr. Richard Lovelace, upon His Poems. Marvell.
To the Learned Critic. Jonson.
Ultra-Germano-Criticasterism. Leigh Hunt.
CROCKETT, SAMUEL RUTHERFORD. To S. R. Crockett. *Fr.* Songs of Travel. R. L. Stevenson.
CROCODILES
Crocodile, The. *Unknown.*
How Doth the Little Crocodile. *Fr.* Alice's Adventures in Wonderland. "Lewis Carroll."
If You Should Meet a Crocodile. *Unknown.*
CROCUSES. Crocus, The. Walter Crane.
CROMWELL, OLIVER
Cromwell, Our Chief of Men. Milton.

CROMWELL, OLIVER (*continued*)
Horatian Ode upon Cromwell's Return from Ireland, An. Marvell.
CROSS, THE
A. B. C. of Devotion, An. *Unknown*.
Above the Hills of Time. Tiplady.
Crucifix. Elder Olson.
Dying Eusebio's Address to the Cross, The. Calderon de la Barca, *tr. fr. Spanish by* McCarthy.
Hymn to the Cross, A. *Unknown*.
In Thine Own Heart. "Angelus Silesius," *tr. fr. German*.
Royal Way of the Holy Cross, The. Thomas à Kempis, *tr. fr. Latin*.
Thought, A. M. E. Sangster.
CROWS
Crow, The. John Clare.
Three Crows, The. *Unknown*.
To Be or Not to Be. *Unknown*.
CRUCIFIXION
"And When He Had Scourged Jesus, He Delivered Him to Be Crucified." Rodgers.
At the Cross. *Unknown*.
Behold the Man! *Unknown*.
Calvary. E. A. Robinson.
Crucifix. Elder Olson.
Crucifixion. Peifer.
Crucifixion, The. *Unknown*.
Golgotha. Wheelock.
Good Friday. C. G. Rossetti.
He Gave Himself for Me. *Unknown*.
Hours of the Passion, The. *Unknown*.
I Saw One Hanging. *Unknown*.
In Memory of Two Sons. Stellwagon.
In My Place. Archibald.
Indifference. Studdert-Kennedy.
It Is Finished. Wheelock.
Killing, The. Edwin Muir.
Last Day, The. Derosier.
Passion of Jesus, The. *Unknown*.
Resurrection—an Easter Sequence, *sel.* ("It was a deliberate moment, and O"). Rodgers.
Scarred. *Unknown*.
Still Falls the Rain. Edith Sitwell.
There Is a Man on the Cross. Cheney.
They Crucified My Lord. *Unknown*.
Thy Nail-pierced Hands. Bowsher.
We May Not Know. C. F. Alexander.
We'll Never Know. Hoellein.
Yes, I Have Been to Calvary. A. B. Christiansen.
Yet Listen Now. Amy Carmichael.
CRUSADES
I Will Sing and So Relieve. Guiot de Dijon, *tr. fr. French by* Terry.
Lepanto. G. K. Chesterton.
CUBA
Cuba Libre. Joaquin Miller.
In the Margin of the Text. Frumkin.
CUCKOOS
Cuckoo, The. *Unknown*.
Hearing the Cuckoo. Heath-Stubbs.
Late Winter. McAuley.
Pallid Cuckoo. David Campbell.
Sumer Is Icumen In. *Unknown*.
To the Cuckoo. Wordsworth.
When Daisies Pied. *Fr.* Love's Labour's Lost. Shakespeare.
CULLODEN, BATTLE OF. Lament for Culloden. Burns.
CUPID
Eros. Robert Bridges.
Plea to Eros. *Unknown*.
Warning to Cupid. *Unknown*.
CUSTER, GEORGE ARMSTRONG
Custer's Last Charge. Whittacker.
Custer's Last Fierce Charge. *Unknown*.
CYCLONES. Sherman Cyclone, The. *Unknown*.
CYCLOPS. Cyclops. *Fr.* Metamorphoses. Ovid, *tr. fr. Latin by* Golding.

D

DAEDALUS. Daedalus. *Fr.* Metamorphoses. Ovid, *tr. fr. Latin by* Golding.
DAFFODILS
Daffodils. *Unknown, tr. fr. Japanese*.
I Wandered Lonely as a Cloud. Wordsworth.
To Daffodils. Herrick.
DAHLIAS. Dahlias. Padraic Colum.
DAISIES
To a Mountain Daisy. Burns.

To the Daisy ("With little here to do or see"). Wordsworth.
DANCING AND DANCERS
Bailada. Airas Núñez, *tr. fr. Portuguese by* Thornton.
Dance, The. W. C. Williams.
Dance of the Abakweta. *Fr.* Far from Africa. Danner.
Reasons for Attendance. Philip Larkin.
Waltz in the Afternoon, A. Beth Bentley.
DANDELIONS
Casual Gold. Uschold.
Lucky Thing, A. Dorothy Aldis.
To the Dandelion. J. R. Lowell.
Young Dandelion, The. Craik.
DANIEL. Daniel. Vachel Lindsay.
DANTE ALIGHIERI
Dante. Michelangelo, *tr. fr. Italian by* Longfellow.
Sonnets on the Divina Commedia. Longfellow.
DANUBE (river). Song III: "Surrounded by the gentle sound." Garcilaso de la Vega, *tr. fr. Spanish by* Fletcher.
DAPHNE
Apollo and Daphne. Marino, *tr. fr. Italian by* Ayres.
Daphne. Bliss Carman.
DAVENPORT, ABRAHAM. Abraham Davenport. Whittier.
DAVID (Bible)
King David. Heine, *tr. fr. German by* Kaufmann.
Song to David, A. Christopher Smart.
DAVIES, SIR JOHN. Four for Sir John Davies. Roethke.
DAVIES, WILLIAM. I Am the Poet Davies, William. W. H. Davies.
DAWN
See also Dawn *in* TITLE AND FIRST LINE INDEX
Alba. Walcott.
At Dawn. Arthur Symons.
Aubade. Edith Sitwell.
Break of Day. John Clare.
Break of Day. J. S. Neilson.
Cock Crow. Edward Thomas.
Clearing at Dawn. Li T'ai-po, *tr. fr. Chinese by* Waley.
Daybreak. Longfellow.
Early Dawn. Hilaire Belloc.
Edge of Day, The. Laurie Lee.
Hark, Hark! the Lark. *Fr.* Cymbeline. Shakespeare.
In the Naked Bed, in Plato's Cave. Schwartz.
Moon Was Gilding the River, The. Jiménez, *tr. fr. Spanish by* Roach.
Prelude: "Night was dark, though sometimes a faint star, The." *Fr.* The New Day. R. W. Gilder.
Salutation of the Dawn, The. *Unknown, tr. fr. Sanskrit*.
Spectre Is on the Move, The. Allana.
Summer Dawn. William Morris.
Thy dawn, O Master of the world, thy dawn. *Fr.* Hassan. Flecker.
See also MORNING; SUNRISE
DAY
Day and Night. Dhingra.
Day and Night. Anne Lindsay.
Revolution. A. E. Housman.
Vigil. Jiménez, *tr. fr. Spanish by* Barnstone.
DAYBREAK. *See* DAWN
DEAFNESS
Monologue of a Deaf Man. David Wright.
Mutterings over the Crib of a Deaf Child. James Wright.
On His Deafness. Du Bellay, *tr. fr. French by* Wyndham.
DEATH
See also Death *in* TITLE AND FIRST LINE INDEX
Absent, The. Edwin Muir.
Acceptance. Robert Frost.
Adieu, Farewell, Earth's Bliss. Nashe. *Fr.* Summer's Last Will and Testament.
After Death. C. G. Rossetti.
After Sunset. G. H. Conkling.
After Work. Oxenham.
Afterwards. Thomas Hardy.
Algonkian Burial. A. G. Bailey.
All the Hills and Vales Along. Sorley.
Alone in Martyrdom I Have Been Left. Christine de Pisan, *tr. fr. French by* Kittel.
And Death Shall Have No Dominion. Dylan Thomas.
And You as Well Must Die, Beloved Dust. E. S. Millay.
Archer, The. A. J. M. Smith.
Asleep. Wilfred Owen.
Epilogue: "At the midnight in the silence of the sleep-time." *Fr.* Asolando. Robert Browning.
At Last. Whittier.
Aunt Mary. Ciardi.
Auto Wreck. Karl Shapiro.
Autumnal. Humphries.
Away. J. W. Riley.
Because I could not stop for death. Emily Dickinson.
Bourne, The. C. G. Rossetti.
Bridge of Sighs, The. Thomas Hood.
Buck in the Snow, The. E. S. Millay.
Bustle in a house, The. Emily Dickinson.
By God, My Lords, Let Us Lift the Veil. Sánchez Calavera, *tr. fr. Spanish by* Davis.

Canticle. Wendell Berry.
Child Dying, The. Edwin Muir.
Child Ill, A. Betjeman.
Choric Song, *sel.* ("Hateful is the dark-blue sky"). Tennyson.
City Dead-House, The. Walt Whitman.
Cold Green Element, The. Irving Layton.
Come Away, Come Away, Death. *Fr.* Twelfth Night. Shakespeare.
Conqueror Worm, The. Poe.
Consolation to M. Du Périer. Malherbe, *tr. fr. French by* Carrington.
Cool Tombs. Sandburg.
Coronach. *Fr.* The Lady of the Lake. Walter Scott.
Crossing the Bar. Tennyson.
Dark Hotel. Alfred Dorn.
Dead, The ("Blow out, you bugles"). *Fr.* 1914. Rupert Brooke.
Dead, The ("These hearts were woven"). *Fr.* 1914. Rupert Brooke.
Dead Man's Dump. Isaac Rosenberg.
Death-Bed. Rowse.
Death-Bed, The. Sassoon.
Deaths at Paragon, Indiana, The. John Woods.
Departure. *Fr.* The Unknown Eros. Coventry Patmore.
Dirge: "Swallow leaves her nest, The." *Fr.* Death's Jest Book. Beddoes.
Dirge: "What longer need hath she of loveliness." Naidu.
Dirge in Woods. George Meredith.
Dirge without Music. E. S. Millay.
Divine Poems, *sel.* ("Within the city of my death"). Villa.
Do Not Go Gentle into That Good Night. Dylan Thomas.
Downgoing. Gustav Davidson.
Dying Californian, The. *Unknown.*
Earth out of Earth. *Unknown.*
Emperor of Ice-Cream, The. Wallace Stevens.
Empty House. Spender.
End, The. Wilfred Owen.
Epitaph: "I lived my life from day to day." Mathurin Régnier, *tr. fr. French by* Fasel.
Epitaph. Cæcil. Boulstr. Herbert of Cherbury.
Epitaph on S. P., a Child of Q. El. Chapel, An. Jonson.
Escape. Robert Graves.
Exequy: To Peter Allt. Dobbs.
Exit. J. G. Fletcher.
Extended Invitation. Jesse Stuart.
Fear No More the Heat o' the Sun. *Fr.* Cymbeline. Shakespeare.
Fear of Death Confounds Me, The. William Dunbar.
Fearful Death. *Unknown.*
Feeling Her End Would Come with Summer's End. Castro, *tr. fr. Spanish by* Flores.
Finale: Presto. Peter Davison.
Flat One, A. W. D. Snodgrass.
For a Dead Lady. E. A. Robinson.
For E. McC. Pound.
For Johnny. Pudney.
Foreboding, The. Robert Graves.
Fragment on Death, A. Villon, *tr. fr. French by* Swinburne.
Funeral, The. Donne.
Funeral Hymn. *Unknown, tr. fr. Sanskrit by* Macdonell.
Garden of Proserpine, The. Swinburne.
Ghostly Reaper. Vinal.
Go Down, Death. J. W. Johnson.
Grave, The, *sel.* Robert Blair.
Guitar Lament for a Mountain Boy. De Suze.
Here Dead Lie We. A. E. Housman.
Here Lies a Lady. Ransom.
Hide-and-Seek. Robert Francis.
His Lady's Death. Ronsard, *tr. fr. French by* Lang.
His Scorn of Life and Consolation for Death. Chassignet, *tr. fr. French by* Galt.
Hour of Death, The. Hemans.
House of Falling Leaves We Entered in, The. *Fr.* The House of Falling Leaves. W. S. Braithwaite.
How Death Comes. *Unknown.*
I felt a funeral in my brain. Emily Dickinson.
I Gazed upon My Country's Walls. Quevedo, *tr. fr. Spanish by* Flores.
I Have a Rendezvous with Death. Seeger.
I Have Got My Leave. *Fr.* Gitanjali. Tagore.
I heard a fly buzz when I died. Emily Dickinson.
Ignorance of Death. Empson.
Improvisation on an Old Theme. Dorothy Livesay.
In the Trench. Leon Gellert.
I've seen a dying eye. Emily Dickinson.
Lament: "Listen, children." E. S. Millay.
Lament: "Sleep and death, the dusky eagles." Trakl, *tr. fr. German by* Hamburger.
Lament for the Makaris, Quhen He Wes Seik. William Dunbar.
Lament of a Man for His Son. *Tr. fr. Paiute Indian by* Austin.

Land o' the Leal, The. Nairne.
Last Invocation, The. Walt Whitman.
Last Lines. Emily Brontë.
Last night that she lived, The. Emily Dickinson.
Last night while I was dreaming. *Unknown, tr. fr. German by* Wright.
Law of Death, The. John Hay.
Leaf after Leaf. W. S. Landor.
L'Envoi: "Who findeth comfort in the stars and flowers." *Fr.* Death's Jest Book. Beddoes.
Let me decease with thine arms, my dear. Ronsard, *tr. fr. French by* Wyndham.
Let's Talk of Graves. *Fr.* Richard II. Shakespeare.
Life and Death. *Fr.* The Christians Reply to the Philosopher. Davenant.
Living and Dying. González Prada, *tr. fr. Spanish by* Flores.
Malefic Surgeon, The. Lansing.
Man Walking and Singing, A. Wendell Berry.
Margaritae Sorori. W. E. Henley.
Missing. Pudney.
Mither's Lament, The. S. G. Smith.
Mortality. Devaney.
Mortification. George Herbert.
Mourning of the Mother of Lorenzo Dávalos. Mena, *tr. fr. Spanish by* Davis.
My Death. A. J. M. Smith.
My life closed twice before its close. Emily Dickinson.
My Life Is like the Summer Rose. R. H. Wilde.
My Life, My Death. Holthusen, *tr. fr. German by* Leibholz.
Nature. Longfellow.
Next, Please. Philip Larkin.
Never More Will the Wind. *Fr.* Hymen. Doolittle ("H. D.").
Now Great and Awesome in My Heart. Quevedo, *tr. fr. Spanish by* Davis.
O Death, Rock Me Asleep. *Unknown.*
Ode to the Confederate Dead. Allen Tate.
Of Death. Samuel Harding.
Of the Progresse of the Soule: The Second Anniversary. Donne.
Oh, could my "was" an "is" become. *Fr.* Don Quixote. Cervantes, *tr. fr. Spanish by* Putnam.
Old man dozed, The. The hospital quietened. *Fr.* Sonnets for a Dying Man. Burns Singer.
On a Dead Child. Robert Bridges.
On an Infant Dying as Soon as Born. Charles Lamb.
On the Death of His Son. Lewis Glyn Cothi, *tr. fr. Welsh by* Williams.
Out of the Cradle Endlessly Rocking. Walt Whitman.
Over Sir John's Hill. Dylan Thomas.
Overtakelessness of those, The. Emily Dickinson.
Parted Souls. Herbert of Cherbury.
Philosophic Flight, The. Luigi Tansillo, *tr. fr. Italian by* Symonds.
Pietà. McAuley.
Poor Wayfaring Stranger. *Unknown.*
Prospice. Robert Browning.
Pure Death. Robert Graves.
Reconciliation. Day Lewis.
Remembrance. Zhukovsky, *tr. fr. Russian by* Deutsch.
Requiescat. Matthew Arnold.
Requiescat. Oscar Wilde.
Rest. C. G. Rossetti.
Rose of Life, The. Góngora, *tr. fr. Spanish by* Fanshawe.
Resurgam. Pickthall.
Rites for a Demagogue. Thwaite.
Rough Are the Roads. Garcilaso de la Vega, *tr. fr. Spanish by* Morgan.
Sea of Death, The. Thomas Hood.
Seed the sower is sowing, The. Matthias Claudius, *tr. fr. German by* Singer.
Serious and a Curious Night-Meditation, A. Traherne.
Ship, The. *Unknown.*
Ship of Death. D. H. Lawrence.
Should You Go First. Rowswell.
Sleeping at Last. C. G. Rossetti.
So Might It Be. Galsworthy.
Soliloquy 2. Aldington.
Some Late Lark Singing. W. E. Henley.
Some Time at Eve. E. C. Hardy.
Song III: "Now go I quietly." Garcilaso de la Vega, *tr. fr. Spanish by* Proske.
Song: "Spirit haunts the year's last hours, A." Tennyson.
Song: "When I am dead, my dearest." C. G. Rossetti.
Sonnet: Death Warnings. Quevedo, *tr. fr. Spanish by* Masefield.
Sonnet I: "He came in silvern armor, trimmed with black." G. B. Bennett.
Sonnet: "It is not death." Thomas Hood.
Sonnet XIII: "Oh were I faint with love upon the breast." Labé, *tr. fr. French by* Wyndham.
Sonnet: "Yesterday a human deity." Góngora, *tr. fr. Spanish by* Kane.

DEATH (*continued*)
Sonnet: "Poor soul, the center of my sinful earth." Sonnets, CXLVI. Shakespeare.
Sonnets de la Mort, *sels.* Sponde, *tr. fr. French by* Nugent.
Sonnets to Laura: To Laura in Death, *sel.* ("Life hurries on, a frantic refugee"). Petrarch, *tr. fr. Italian by* Bishop.
Sonnets to Laura: To Laura in Death, *sel.* ("The nightingale that so forlornly weeps"). Petrarch, *tr. fr. Italian by* Rendel.
Speed. W. H. Davies.
Stop All the Clocks. Auden.
Strangeness of Heart. Sassoon.
Sunlight on the Garden, The. MacNeice.
Tenancy, The. Mary Gilmore.
Testament. John Holmes.
Thanatopsis. Bryant.
That Familiar Stranger. Stefanile.
There Is No Reason Why Not to Look at Death. Sward.
They Are All Gone. Henry Vaughan.
This is my playes last scene, here heavens appoint. *Fr.* Holy Sonnets. Donne.
Though I Am Young. *Fr.* The Sad Shepherd. Jonson.
Threnody: "Only quiet death." Cuney.
'Tis not that dying hurts us so. Emily Dickinson.
To an Athlete Dying Young. A. E. Housman.
To Be or Not to Be. *Fr.* Hamlet. Shakespeare.
To Daffodils. Herrick.
To Giulia Grisi. N. P. Willis.
To His Mistress for Her True Picture. Herbert of Cherbury.
To One Who Died Young. Trakl, *tr. fr. German by* Middleton.
To See the Hours of Fever. Bécquer, *tr. fr. Spanish by* Crow.
To Think of Time, *sel.* ("To think of time . . . to think through the retrospection"). Walt Whitman.
Transmigration. Cudjoe.
Twa Corbies, The. *Unknown.*
'Twas just this time, last year, I died. Emily Dickinson.
'Twas warm at first like us. Emily Dickinson.
Two Societies, The. Wheelock.
Two Sonnets. Sorley.
Upon a Dead Man's Head. John Skelton.
Victorious Men of Earth. *Fr.* Cupid and Death. James Shirley.
Vital Spark of Heavenly Flame. Pope.
Wake All the Dead. *Fr.* The Law against Lovers. Davenant.
We Are Seven. Wordsworth.
What Has This Bugbear Death. *Fr.* De Rerum Natura. Lucretius, *tr. fr. Latin by* Dryden.
When Death Comes. *Unknown.*
When Death to Either Shall Come. Robert Bridges.
When I Am Dead. J. E. Wilson.
When I Have Fears. Keats.
When Lilacs Last in the Dooryard Bloom'd. Walt Whitman.
When You See Millions of the Mouthless Dead. Sorley.
Why Do You Visit Me, White Moths, So Often? Heym, *tr. fr. German by* Middleton.
Zenith. Jiménez, *tr. fr. Spanish by* Flores.
DECEMBER
December Stillness. Sassoon.
I Heard a Bird Sing. Oliver Herford.
Stanzas: "In a drear-nighted December." Keats.
DECORATION DAY. *See* MEMORIAL DAY
DEER
Buck Fever. Cooksley.
Buck in the Snow, The. E. S. Millay.
Deer Hunt. Ragan.
Landscape, Deer Season. Barbara Howes.
Like as a huntsman. *Fr.* Amoretti. Spenser.
Nymph Complaining for the Death of Her Fawn, The. Marvell.
Runnable Stag, A. John Davidson.
Tame Stag, The. John Gay.
Young Flash the Deer. Thornton Burgess.
DEGAS, EDGAR. Museum Piece. Wilbur.
DEMOCRACY. Young Democracy, *sel.* ("Hark! Young Democracy from sleep"). O'Dowd.
DEMPSEY, JACK ("Nonpareil"). Nonpareil's Grave, The. M. J. McMahon.
DENTISTS
Dentist, The. Fyleman.
Epitaph on a Dentist. *Unknown.*
This Is Going to Hurt Just a Little Bit. Ogden Nash.
DESERTS. Scot in the Desert. Laurie Lee.
DESPAIR
Carrion Comfort. G. M. Hopkins.
Castaway, The. Cowper.
Circumstance. Shelley.
City of Dreadful Night, The. James Thomson.
Darkling Thrush, The. Thomas Hardy.
Despair. Merwin.
In Tenebris, *sel.* ("Wintertime nighs"). Thomas Hardy.
Leaden Echo and the Golden Echo, The. G. M. Hopkins.
DESTINY. *See* FATE
DEUTSCHLAND (ship). Wreck of the *Deutschland,* The. G. M. Hopkins.

DEVIL. *See* SATAN
DEW
Haiku: "World of dew, The." Issa, *tr. fr. Japanese by* Keene.
On a Drop of Dew. Marvell.
DIANA (goddess)
Homage to Diana. Ralegh.
Hymn to Diana. *Fr.* Cynthia's Revels. Jonson.
DIDO. *See* AENEAS
DIES IRAE. *See* JUDGMENT DAY
DIGBY, LADY VENETIA. Elegie Made by Mr. Aurelian Townshend in Remembrance of the Ladie Venetia Digby, An. Aurelian Townsend.
DINAS VAWR. War Song of Dinas Vawr, The. *Fr.* The Misfortune of Elphin. Peacock.
DINOSAURS. Dinosaur, The. Junge.
DIRIGIBLES. Dirigible, The. Bergengren.
DIVING AND DIVERS
Cold Logic. Barney Hutchinson.
Diver, The. W. W. E. Ross.
Fantasia. Dorothy Livesay.
High Diver. Robert Francis.
DOBSON, AUSTIN. On Receiving a Copy of Mr. Austin Dobson's "Old World Idylls." J. R. Lowell.
DOGS
See also Dog *and* Dogs *in* TITLE AND FIRST LINE INDEX
Bandog, The. De la Mare.
Daley's Dorg Wattle. Goodge.
Elegy on a Lap Dog, An. John Gay.
Elegy on the Death of a Mad Dog. Goldsmith.
Feri's Dream. Frances Cornford.
Flush or Faunus. E. B. Browning.
Hairy Dog, The. Herbert Asquith.
Harper, The. Thomas Campbell.
I Came to a Valley in the Wilderness. Garcilaso de la Vega, *tr. fr. Spanish by* Morgan.
Little Black Dog, The. E. G. Reynolds.
Little Dog-Angel, A. N. M. Holland.
Little Dog under the Wagon, The. *Unknown.*
Lone Dog. I. R. McLeod.
My Airedale Dog. W. L. Mason.
My Dog. Chute.
My Dog. Tom Robinson.
Nino, the Wonder Dog. Roy Fuller.
Old Blue. *Unknown.*
Oral Messages, *sel.* ("The dog trots freely in the street"). Ferlinghetti.
Puppy. Earnshaw.
Puppy. Aileen Fisher.
Rest in Peace. Funk.
Sonnet: To Tartar, a Terrier Beauty. Beddoes.
Stray Dog. Mish.
Stray Dog, near Ecully, Valley of the Rhône. Avison.
Tim, an Irish Terrier. Letts.
To My Dog "Blanco." J. G. Holland.
To Scott. Letts.
Uncle Dog: The Poet at 9. Sward.
DOLLS
Doll Song. "Lewis Carroll."
Dolls, The. Ciardi.
Lost Doll, The. *Fr.* The Water Babies. Charles Kingsley.
DOLPHINS. Porpoise, The. Ogden Nash.
DON JUAN. Haidée and Don Juan. *Fr.* Don Juan. Byron.
DON QUIXOTE. Don Quixote, *sels.* Cervantes, *tr. fr. Spanish by* Putnam.
DONKEYS
See also Donkey *in* TITLE AND FIRST LINE INDEX
Ass, The. Edwin Allan.
Prayer to Go to Paradise with the Donkeys, A. Jammes, *tr. fr. French by* Wilbur.
DONNE, JOHN
Elegie upon the Death of the Deane of Pauls, Dr. John Donne, An. Thomas Carew.
On Donne's Poetry. S. T. Coleridge.
To John Donne. Jonson.
Upon the Death of My Ever Desired Friend Doctor Donne Dean of Pauls. Henry King.
DOUGLASS, FREDERICK. Frederick Douglass. R. E. Hayden.
DOVER, ENGLAND. Dover Beach. Matthew Arnold.
DOVES
Dove's Loneliness, The. Darley.
Far Away and Long Ago. Dario, *tr. fr. Spanish by* Levertov.
DRAGONFLIES
Dragonfly, The. Chisoku, *tr. fr. Japanese by* Henderson.
Lines to a Dragon Fly. W. S. Landor.
DRAGONS
Gold-tinted Dragon, The. Kuskin.
O to Be a Dragon. Marianne Moore.
Tale of Custard the Dragon, The. Ogden Nash.
DRAKE, SIR FRANCIS
Drake's Drum. Newbolt.
Epitaph on Drake. Barnfield.
On Sir Francis Drake. *Unknown.*
DRAKE, JOSEPH RODMAN. On the Death of Joseph Rodman Drake. Halleck.

DREAMING AND DREAMS
 See also Dream; Dreamer; Dreaming; *and* Dreams *in* TITLE AND FIRST LINE INDEX
 As Ocean Holds the Globe. Tyutchev, *tr. fr. Russian by* Deutsch.
 Chimera. Barbara Howes.
 Eye of Humility, The. Kay Smith.
 He Whom a Dream Hath Possessed. O'Sheel.
 Hold Fast Your Dreams. Louise Driscoll.
 Ivory, Coral, Gold, The. William Drummond.
 Epistle to John Hamilton Reynolds. Keats.
 Harlequin of Dreams, The. Sidney Lanier.
 Hymn: "O dream, digestion of my soul!" "Jakob van Hoddis," *tr. fr. German by* Middleton.
 Kubla Khan. S. T. Coleridge.
 Nightmare. J. P. Brennan.
 Nightmare. Grenville.
 Nightmare. Anne Marx.
 Poem: "We are such stuff as dreams are made of, and these." Hofmannsthal, *tr. fr. German by* Bithell.
 Prelude to an Evening. Ransom.
 Rhyme of the Dream-Maker Man, A. W. A. White.
 Scythe of Dreams, The. J. P. Brennan.
 Sleeping Saint, The. La Follette.
 Tower of the Dream, The, *sel.* Harpur.
 True to a Dream. Donald Petersen.
DRESS. *See* CLOTHING
DRINKING
 Bar, The. *Unknown.*
 Brewer's Coachman, The. William Taylor.
 Drink with Something in It, A. Ogden Nash.
 Drinking. Abraham Cowley, *after the Greek of* Anacreon.
 Drinking Song. *Fr.* Gammer Gurton's Needle. *At. to* William Stevenson *and* John Still.
 Fill the Bowl, Butler! *Unknown.*
 Good Thing Is, We Know, The. Machado, *tr. fr. Spanish by* Davis.
 Lord Alcohol. Beddoes.
 Old Keg of Rum, The. *Unknown.*
 Quebec Liquor Commission Store. A. M. Klein.
 Said the Whisky Flask. *Unknown.*
 Sir John Barleycorn. *Unknown.*
 Three Pigeons, The. Goldsmith.
 Whisky Song, A. *Unknown.*
 See also DRUNKARDS
DROUGHT
 Drought. Laight.
 Drought, *sel.* F. C. Slater.
 Said Hanrahan. Hartigan.
DRUG ADDICTION
 Cocteau's *Opium:* 1. Finkel.
 Drug Addict, The. *Fr.* Three Prison Portraits. Miriam Waddington.
 Solo for Bent Spoon. Finkel.
 Success. Empson.
DRUG STORES
 Drug Store. Karl Shapiro.
 Drug Store. J. V. Weaver.
 Les Réalités. Barbara Guest.
DRUMS. Drum, The. John Scott.
DRUNKARDS
 Closing Time. Michie.
 Drunk in the Furnace, The. Merwin.
 Drunkard, The. Philip Levine.
 Drunkard's Doom, The. *Unknown.*
 Drunkard's Dream, The. *Unknown.*
 Two Hangovers. James Wright.
DUBLIN, IRELAND. Dublin. MacNeice.
DUCKS
 Duck-chasing. Kinnell.
 Ducks. F. W. Harvey.
 Ducks at Dawn. Tippett.
 Duck's Ditty. *Fr.* The Wind in the Willows. Kenneth Grahame.
 Little Duck, The. Joso, *tr. fr. Japanese by* Henderson.
 Prayer of the Little Ducks Who Went into the Ark, The. Gasztold, *tr. fr. Spanish by* Godden.
 Regent's Park. Fyleman.
DULLES, JOHN FOSTER. Just Dropped In. William Cole.
DUNBAR, PAUL LAURENCE. For Paul Laurence Dunbar. Countee Cullen.
DUNDEE, JOHN GRAHAM OF CLAVERHOUSE, 1ST VISCOUNT (Bonnie Dundee). Bonnie Dundee. *Fr.* The Doom of Devorgoil. Walter Scott.
DUNKIRK, FRANCE. Dunkirk. Nathan.
DUNS SCOTUS, JOHN
 Duns Scotus. Merton.
 Duns Scotus's Oxford. G. M. Hopkins.
DUNWICH, ENGLAND. At Dunwich. Thwaite.
DUSK
 Dusk of Horses, The. Dickey.
 Georgia Dusk. Toomer.
 Sundown. Léonie Adams.
 See also EVENING; SUNSET; TWILIGHT
DUST. In Praise of Dust. Rachel Field.

DUSTIN, HANNAH. Lady of the Tomahawk, The. R. P. T. Coffin.
DUTY
 Ode to Duty. Wordsworth.
 Voluntaries. Emerson.

E

EAGLES
 Dalliance of the Eagles, The. Walt Whitman.
 Dying Eagle, The. E. J. Pratt.
 Eagle, The. Tennyson.
 Eagle, The. Andrew Young.
 Eagle and the Mole, The. Wylie.
 Salmon Drowns Eagle. Malcolm Lowry.
 White Eagle, The. Nan McDonald.
EARTH
 See also Earth *and* World *in* TITLE AND FIRST LINE INDEX
 Book of the World, The. Marino, *tr. fr. Italian by* William Drummond.
 Hamatreya. Emerson.
 Hymn to Earth. Wylie.
 In the Immense Cathedral. *Fr.* The Holy Earth. Wheelock.
 Landsman, The. Moschus, *tr. fr. Greek by* Shelley.
 O Sweet Spontaneous. E. E. Cummings.
 Wonder. Traherne.
 Word, The. Realf.
EASTER
 See also Easter *in* TITLE AND FIRST LINE INDEX
 All Dressed Up for Easter. Aileen Fisher.
 Alleluia! Alleluia! Let the Holy Anthem Rise. *Unknown.*
 Blessing and Honor. Bonar.
 Cross and the Tomb, The. A. J. Flint.
 Down a Sunny Easter Meadow. N. B. Turner.
 Harrowing of Hell, The. *Fr.* The Vision of Piers Plowman. William Langland, *mod. by* Coghill.
 He Lives! He Lives to Bless! Stroud.
 His Life Is Ours. Stroud.
 Hymn of the Resurrection, A. William Dunbar.
 If Easter Be Not True. H. H. Barstow.
 If Easter Eggs Would Hatch. Malloch.
 Landscape before Easter. Zemp, *tr. fr. German by* Middleton.
 Lent Lily, The. A. E. Housman.
 Meeting the Easter Bunny. R. B. Bennett.
 Most glorious Lord of life, that on this day. *Fr.* Amoretti. Spenser.
 Not There. *Unknown.*
 Poem for Easter. Laurie Lee.
 Resurrection, The. J. H. Brooks.
 Sepulcher, The. A. J. Flint.
 Seven Stanzas at Easter. Updike.
 Some Things That Easter Brings. Elsie Parrish.
 Third Day, The. E. L. Pierce.
 Upon an Easter Morning. Farjeon.
 Words for a Resurrection. Leo Kennedy.
EASTER ISLAND. Easter Island. F. G. Scott.
EATHERLY, CLAUDE R. Song about Major Eatherly, A. Wain.
EATING. *See* FOOD
ECHO. *See* Echo *in* TITLE AND FIRST LINE INDEX
ECHO (nymph). Echo. *Fr.* Comus. Milton.
EDINBURGH, SCOTLAND. Auld Reikie. Robert Fergusson.
EDUCATION. *See* COLLEGES AND UNIVERSITIES; SCHOLARS AND SCHOLARSHIP; SCHOOLS
EDWARD I, KING OF ENGLAND
 Bard, The. Thomas Gray.
 Death of King Edward I, The. *Unknown.*
EDWARDS, JONATHAN
 Mr. Edwards and the Spider. Robert Lowell.
 Poems from a First Year in Boston, *sel.* ("Becalmed in old Back Bay's dead water sulk"). George Starbuck.
EELS
 Eel, The. Montale, *tr. fr. Italian by* Golino.
 Eel, The. Ogden Nash.
EGRETS
 Egrets. Judith Wright.
 Two Egrets. Ciardi.
 White Egret, The. Li Po, *tr. fr. Chinese by* Edwards.
EINSTEIN, ALBERT. Gift to Be Simple, The. Howard Moss.
EISENHOWER, DWIGHT DAVID
 Inauguration Day: January 1953. Robert Lowell.
 Tentative Description of a Dinner to Promote the Impeachment of President Eisenhower. Ferlinghetti.
ELEPHANTS
 See also Elephant *in* TITLE AND FIRST LINE INDEX
 Capturing Elephants. Steiner, *tr. fr. German by* Middleton.
 Cradle Song of the Elephants. Valle, *tr. fr. Spanish by* Malkus.
 Elephant's Trunk, The. Alice Wilkins.
 Holding Hands. L. M. Link.
ELGIN MARBLES. On Seeing the Elgin Marbles. Keats.
ELIZABETH, QUEEN OF BOHEMIA. Elizabeth of Bohemia. Henry Wotton.

ELIZABETH I, QUEEN OF ENGLAND
Looking-Glass, The. Kipling.
To the Queen. Ralegh.
ELM TREES. Connecticut Elm, The. Emma Swan.
ELUARD, PAUL. In Memoriam Paul Eluard. Celan, *tr. fr. German by* Hamburger.
ELVES. *See* FAIRIES
EMANCIPATION PROCLAMATION (1863). Proclamation, The. Whittier.
EMERSON, RALPH WALDO. Emerson. *Fr.* A Fable for Critics. J. R. Lowell.
EMMET, ROBERT
Oh! Breathe Not His Name. Thomas Moore.
She Is Far from the Land. Thomas Moore.
EMUS. Emus. M. E. Fullerton.
ENGINEERS. Engineers. Garthwaite.
ENGLAND
See also England *in* TITLE AND FIRST LINE INDEX
Airman Who Flew over Shakespeare's England, The. Plutzik.
Ancient Music. Pound.
And Did Those Feet in Ancient Time. *Fr.* Milton. Blake.
Channel Crossing. George Barker.
"De Gustibus." Robert Browning.
Elegy in a Country Churchyard. G. K. Chesterton.
Home Thoughts, from Abroad. Robert Browning.
Home Thoughts, from the Sea. Robert Browning.
Home Truths from Abroad. *Unknown.*
I Have Loved England. *Fr.* The White Cliffs. A. D. Miller.
I Traveled among Unknown Men. *Fr.* Lucy. Wordsworth.
International Hymn. George Huntington.
Letty's Globe. C. T. Turner.
London, 1802. Wordsworth.
Mask of Anarchy, The. Shelley.
Old Vicarage, Grantchester, The. Rupert Brooke.
On Wenlock Edge. A. E. Housman.
Pennines in April. Ted Hughes.
Puck's Song. *Fr.* Puck of Pook's Hill. Kipling.
Return, The. Silkin.
Ruins of a Great House. Walcott.
Rule, Britannia. James Thomson.
Soldier, The. *Fr.* 1914. Rupert Brooke.
Song: "Old England is eaten by knaves." *Fr.* The Emigrant. Alexander McLachlan.
Song to the Men of England. Shelley.
This Blessed Plot . . . This England. *Fr.* King Richard II. Shakespeare.
This Landscape, These People. Zulfikar Ghose.
You Ask Me, Why, though Ill at Ease. Tennyson.
ENGLAND, CHURCH OF. Hippopotamus, The. T. S. Eliot.
ENGLISH, THE
English Are Frosty, The. *Fr.* The White Cliffs. A. D. Miller.
It Is Not to Be Thought of. Wordsworth.
Song of the English, A, *sel.* ("We have fed our sea for a thousand years"). Kipling.
Who Calls the English Cold? *Fr.* London Sonnets. Carl Bode.
ENGLISH CHANNEL
Channel Crossing. George Barker.
Channel Passage, A. Rupert Brooke.
Channel Rhyme, A. C. F. Smith.
ENGLISH LANGUAGE. *See* LANGUAGE
EPIPHANY. *See* TWELFTH NIGHT
ERIE, LAKE, BATTLE OF. James Bird. *Unknown.*
ERIE CANAL. Erie Canal, The. *Unknown.*
EROS. *See* CUPID
ESKIMOS. Kayak, The. *Unknown.*
ESSEX, ENGLAND. Map of the Western Part of the County of Essex in England, A. Levertov.
ESTHER (Bible). Monna Innominata, *sel.* ("I, if I perish, perish'—Esther spake"). C. G. Rossetti.
ETERNITY
Dream, A—'tis but a dream, our being. Herder, *tr. fr. German by* Gode.
Eternity to Come. Rist, *tr. fr. German by* Kramer.
Face of the Waters, The. R. D. Fitzgerald.
I Saw Eternity. Bogan.
World, The. Henry Vaughan.
ETON COLLEGE. Ode on a Distant Prospect of Eton College. Thomas Gray.
EUCHARIST
Bread of Life, The. Lathbury.
Canticle to the Christ in the Holy Eucharist, A. Brother Antoninus.
Dressing. Henry Vaughan.
H. Communion, The. George Herbert.
On the Sacrament. Elizabeth Rowe.
Receiving Communion. Vassar Miller.
Sacrament, The. Donne.
Sacrament of the Altar, The. *Unknown.*
"This Do in Remembrance of Me." *Unknown.*
EUCLID
Euclid. Vachel Lindsay.
Euclid Alone. E. S. Millay.
EULALIA, SAINT. Sequence of Saint Eulalia, The. *Unknown, tr. fr. French by* Lancaster.

EURYDICE (ship). Loss of the *Eurydice*, The. G. M. Hopkins.
EUROPE. Of Commerce and Society. Geoffrey Hill.
EVE
See also Eve *in* TITLE AND FIRST LINE INDEX
Imperial Adam. A. D. Hope.
Lady's-Maid's Song, The. Hollander.
Recognition of Eve, The. *Fr.* Adam and Eve. Karl Shapiro.
She. Wilbur.
229. Villa.
EVENING
See also Evening *in* TITLE AND FIRST LINE INDEX
And Suddenly It's Evening. Quasimodo, *tr. fr. Italian by* Mandelbaum.
Autumnal Evening, An. Sharp ("Fiona Macleod").
It Is a Beauteous Evening, Calm and Free. Wordsworth.
Nightfall. Jiménez, *tr. fr. Spanish by* Roach.
O Boundless, Boundless Evening. Heym, *tr. fr. German by* Middleton.
Ode to Evening. William Collins.
Ode to Evening. Joseph Warton.
Prelude: "Winter evening settles down, The." *Fr.* Preludes. T. S. Eliot.
Progress of Evening. W. S. Landor.
Small Song. Frances Frost.
Sunken Evening. Laurie Lee.
Winter Evening. Lampman.
Word Comes Down, The. Reverdy, *tr. fr. French by* Roche.
See also DUSK; TWILIGHT; SUNSET
EVENING STAR
Evening Star. George Barker.
Evening Star. Poe.
Star of the Evening. Sayles.
To the Evening Star. Blake.
To the Evening Star ("Gem of the crimson-colour'd even"). Thomas Campbell.
To the Evening Star ("Star that bringest home the bee"). Thomas Campbell.
EVEREST (mountain). Victory. M. B. Miller.
EXECUTIONS
Crime and Punishment. J. S. Layton.
Eight o'Clock. A. E. Housman.
What Birds Were There. Brother Antoninus.
See also HANGING
EXILE
Canadian Boat Song, The. *Unknown, at. to* Galt.
Thoughts on the Length of Exile. Brecht, *tr. fr. German by* Middleton.
EYES
Eye You See Isn't, The. Machado, *tr. fr. Spanish by* Davis.
Who's There, My Heart?—It Is We, Your Eyes. Charles d'Orléans, *tr. fr. French by* Kittel.

F

FACTORIES. Factory Windows Are Always Broken. Vachel Lindsay.
FAIRIES
See also Fairies *and* Fairy *in* TITLE AND FIRST LINE INDEX
Ann and the Fairy Song. *Fr.* A Child's Day. De la Mare.
Best Game the Fairies Play, The. Fyleman.
Bubbles. G. H. Shorey.
Could It Have Been a Shadow? Monica Shannon.
Crab-Apple. Ethel Talbot.
Dusk in the Domain. Dorothy Mackellar.
Elf and the Dormouse, The. Oliver Herford.
Elfin Wife, The. "Jake Falstaff."
Farewell to the Fairies. Corbet.
Goblin Market. C. G. Rossetti.
Godmother. Morden.
Have You Watched the Fairies? Fyleman.
How to Treat Elves. Morris Bishop.
I'd Love to Be a Fairy's Child. Robert Graves.
If You Never. E. M. Fowler.
In the Moonlight. O'Conor.
Little Elfman, The. J. K. Bangs.
Mab. *Fr.* The Satyr. Jonson.
Of Certain Irish Fairies. Guiterman.
One of the Sidhe. Mary Kennedy.
Queen Mab. *Fr.* Romeo and Juliet. Shakespeare.
Sea Princess, The. Katharine Pyle.
Seven Ages of Elf-Hood, The. Rachel Field.
Shakespeare. *Fr.* The Plea of the Midsummer Fairies. Thomas Hood.
Stocking Fairy. Welles.
Thomas the Rhymer. *Unknown.*
Tree Stands Very Straight and Still, The. Annette Wynne.
Very Nearly. Scott-Hopper.
Water Sprite. Wandrei.
Wee Wee Man, The. *Unknown.*
When I Was Six. Zora Cross.

Where the Bee Sucks, There Suck I. *Fr.* The Tempest. Shakespeare.
White Horses. Winifred Howard.
FAITH
See also Credo *and* Faith *in* TITLE AND FIRST LINE INDEX
Bishop Blougram's Apology. Robert Browning.
Candle and Book. N. W. Walter.
Captain of the Years. A. R. Macdougall.
Creed, A. Masefield.
Disappointment. E. L. Young.
Dover Beach. Matthew Arnold.
Evensong. R. L. Stevenson.
Feathered Faith. *Unknown.*
Foundation of Faith. Drinkwater.
God in Whom We Trust, The. *Unknown.*
Have Faith in God. Budzynski.
His Creed. Herrick.
I never saw a moor. Emily Dickinson.
If This Were Faith. *Fr.* Songs of Travel. R. L. Stevenson.
Joy and Peace in Believing. Cowper.
Last Lines. Emily Brontë.
Light Shining Out of Darkness. Cowper.
Man without Faith, The. Richard Church.
Not Knowing, *sel.* M. G. Brainard.
O World. Santayana.
Obedience. George Macdonald.
Poet's Simple Faith, The. Hugo, *tr. fr. French.*
Possession. *Unknown.*
Riddle of the World, The. Whittier.
Say Not. Clough.
Silence. C. H. Towne.
That's Faith. Leitner.
Thy Way, Not Mine. Bonar.
Tide of Faith, The. *Fr.* A Minor Prophet. "George Eliot."
Trust Him. *Unknown.*
Voyagers. Henry van Dyke.
Wit Wonders. *Unknown.*
FALCONS
Ah Me Poor Wretch, Who Loved a Falcon. *Unknown, tr. fr. Italian by* Raiziss *and* Palchi.
Falcon, The. "The Knight of Kürenberg," *tr. fr. German.*
Hawking. *Fr.* Polyolbion. Drayton.
Windhover, The. G. M. Hopkins.
FALL. *See* AUTUMN
FALMOUTH, ENGLAND. Home. W. E. Henley.
FAME
See also Fame *in* TITLE AND FIRST LINE INDEX
I'm nobody! Who are you? Emily Dickinson.
On Fame. John Banks.
On Fame. Keats.
Provide Provide. Robert Frost.
To an Athlete Dying Young. A. E. Housman.
FAMILY LIFE
Concerning the Eoconomic Independence of Women. J. V. Weaver.
Cotter's Saturday Night, The. Burns.
Family. *Unknown.*
FANCY. *See* IMAGINATION
FANTASY. *Fire and Sleet and Candlelight* (FiSC). August Derleth, ed.
FARMING AND FARMERS
By the Sweat of My Brow I Toiled. *Unknown, tr. fr. French by* Aldan.
Cynddylan on a Tractor. R. S. Thomas.
Farm near Norman's Lane, The. Mary Finnin.
Farmer. L. H. Bailey.
Farmer's Concern, The. Brecht, *tr. fr. German by* Hamburger.
Haying. E. R. Fuller.
Hill Farmer Speaks, The. R. S. Thomas.
Hock-Cart, The. Herrick.
Milking before Dawn. Ruth Dallas.
Mowing, The. C. G. D. Roberts.
Ploughing on Sunday. Wallace Stevens.
Sower, The. C. G. D. Roberts.
Strong Are Saying Nothing, The. Robert Frost.
Summer Farm. MacCaig.
Young Man Who Wouldn't Plow Corn, The. *Unknown.*
See also FIELDS AND PASTURES
FARRAGUT, DAVID GLASGOW. Farragut. W. T. Meredith.
FATE
Destiny. Edwin Arnold.
Doom. Darío, *tr. fr. Spanish by* Flores.
Hap. Thomas Hardy.
Nemesis. Emerson.
To Himself. Paul Fleming, *tr. fr. German by* Schoolfield.
Winds of Fate, The. E. W. Wilcox.
Woman's Fate, A. Rilke, *tr. fr. German by* Kaufmann.
See also FORTUNE
FATHERS
See also Father *in* TITLE AND FIRST LINE INDEX
Abraham's Madness. Noll.
All My Pretty Ones. Sexton.
American Primitive. W. J. Smith.
At My Father's Grave. "Hugh MacDiarmid."

At the Grave of My Father. Matthias Claudius, *tr. fr. German by* Singer.
Au Tombeau de Mon Père. McCuaig.
Dear Old Dad. Shaver.
Does Daddy Go? *Unknown.*
Early Morning Feed. Redgrove.
Elegy: "My father was born with a spade in his hand and traded it." Ciardi.
Father's Story. E. M. Roberts.
Figures of Authority. Edward Watkins.
Hallelujah; a Sestina. Robert Francis.
If I could rise and see my father young. *Fr.* Art of the Sonnet. Orlovitz.
Lines to His Son on Reaching Adolescence. John Logan.
My Father Moved through Dooms of Love. E. E. Cummings.
My Papa's Waltz. Roethke.
Secret Heart, The. R. P. T. Coffin.
Sestina of Youth and Age. Gelett Burgess.
Sohrab and Rustum. Matthew Arnold.
Stanzas on the Death of His Father. Jorge Manrique, *tr. fr. Spanish by* Morgan.
To Any Daddy. *Unknown.*
When Father Carves the Duck. E. V. Wright.
FAUST
Dr. Faustus, *sel.* ("That I might have unto my paramour"). Marlowe.
Progress of Faust, The. Karl Shapiro.
FEAR
Fairy Tale, A. Kenneth Mackenzie.
Fragment from Nothing. Coatsworth.
News, The. "Sec."
Ode to Fear. William Collins.
Shape of Fear, The. S. K. Russell.
Woods Grow Darker, The. L. B. Drake.
FEBRUARY
At the Nadir. Gerta Kennedy.
Brook in February, The. C. G. D. Roberts.
February. *Fr.* The Shepherd's Calendar. John Clare.
February Twilight. Teasdale.
Mirror in February. Kinsella.
Way of Looking, A. Bevington.
When. Dorothy Aldis.
FENCES. Split-Rail Fence. Guy Owen.
FENCING. For E. McC. Pound.
FERRY BOATS
Ferry-Boats. Tippett.
Ferry Ride. Selma Robinson.
Ferryman, The. C. G. Rossetti.
Letter Written on a Ferry Crossing Long Island Sound. Sexton.
FIDDLES AND FIDDLERS
Fiddler of Dooney, The. Yeats.
Mountain Whippoorwill, The. S. V. Benét.
Paging Professor Gooseberry. Stem.
Seven Fiddlers, The. Sebastian Evans.
FIELD, CYRUS. How Cyrus Laid the Cable. Saxe.
FIELD ATHLETICS
Challenge. Hazo.
Pole Vault. Murano, *tr. fr. Japanese by* Sato *and* Urdang.
FIELDS AND PASTURES
Cornfield, The. E. M. Roberts.
Meadow-Field, The. *Fr.* Pleasant Memories. Charles Sangster.
Mower's Song, The. Marvell.
Pastoral: "If it were only still!" E. S. Millay.
Pasture, The. Robert Frost.
To Meadows. Herrick.
See also FARMING AND FARMERS
FIFTH OF NOVEMBER. *See* GUY FAWKES DAY
FINCHES. Finches, The. Shapcott.
FIR TREES. Fir Tree, A. Heine, *tr. fr. German by* Kaufmann.
FIRE
Execration upon Vulcan, An. Jonson.
Fire and Ice. Robert Frost.
Fire at Alexandria, The. Theodore Weiss.
Love Is a Refiner's Fire. Michelangelo, *tr. fr. Italian by* Symonds.
Smithfield Market Fire, The. Fred Dallas.
Some Verses upon the Burning of Our House, July 10th, 1666. Bradstreet.
FIREFLIES
See also Fireflies *and* Firefly *in* TITLE AND FIRST LINE INDEX
Phosphorescence. Cane.
FIREWORKS. Fireworks. James Reeves.
FISH
See also Fish *in* TITLE AND FIRST LINE INDEX
At the Aquarium. Max Eastman.
Ballade: To a Fish of the Brooke. Wolcot.
Flying Fish, The. John Gray.
Pike. Ted Hughes.
To the Immortal Memory of the Halibut on Which I Dined This Day. Cowper.
FISHING AND FISHERMEN
See also Fisher; Fishermen; Fishers; *and* Fishing *in* TITLE AND FIRST LINE INDEX

FISHING AND FISHERMEN (continued)
And Angling, Too. Fr. Don Juan. Byron.
Angler's Song, The, sel. ("As inward love breeds outward talk"). Basse.
Careful Angler, The. R. L. Stevenson.
Coromandel Fishers, The. Naidu.
Feast of Saint Andrew the Apostle. Fr. The Sacred Seasons. Carl Bode.
Caller Herrin'. Nairne.
Coracle Fishers, The. Fr. The Banks of Wye. Bloomfield.
Drunken Fisherman, The. Robert Lowell.
Fly-fishing. Fr. Rural Sports. John Gay.
Green Stream, A. Wang Wei, tr. fr. Chinese by Bynner and Kiang Kang-hu.
How They Bite. Unknown.
Instruction in the Art. Philip Booth.
Last Chance, The. Andrew Lang.
Neither Hook nor Line. Bunyan.
Net Menders, The. Vrepont.
Out Fishin'. E. A. Guest.
Pike, The. John Bruce.
Salmon-fishing. Jeffers.
Sea Scape with Parable. Eberhart.
Silver Herring Throbbed Thick in My Seine, The. Kenneth Leslie.
Sockeye Salmon. Hambleton.
Song of the Shetland Fishers. Walter Scott.
Three Fishers, The. Charles Kingsley.
Torch, The. Walt Whitman.
Words are Never Enough. Charles Bruce.
FLAGS, CONFEDERACY
Bonnie Blue Flag, The. A. C. Ketcham.
Conquered Banner, The. A. J. Ryan.
FLAGS, UNITED STATES
American Flag, The. J. R. Drake.
Brother, Lift Your Flag with Mine. J. D. Bacon.
Flag, The. Silverstein.
Flag Goes By, The. H. H. Bennett.
Flagmakers, The. J. M. Murphy.
Star-spangled Banner, The. Key.
Toast to the Flag, A. John Daly.
FLANDERS, BELGIUM
In Flanders Fields. John McCrae.
Into Battle. Julian Grenfell.
Old Houses of Flanders, The. F. M. Ford.
FLEAS
Flea, The. Donne.
Flea, The. Roland Young.
Happiness of a Flea, The. Tasso, tr. fr. Italian by William Drummond.
Of That Same. Tasso, tr. fr. Italian by William Drummond.
FLEUR-DE-LIS. See IRIS
FLIES
See also Fly in TITLE AND FIRST LINE INDEX
Blue-Fly, The. Robert Graves.
October Flies. Kessler.
On a Fly Drinking out of His Cup. Oldys.
Spider and the Fly, The. Mary Howitt.
FLODDEN FIELD, ENGLAND
But as they left the dart'ning heath. Fr. Marmion. Walter Scott.
Lament for Flodden. Jane Elliot.
FLORIDA. Florida. Elizabeth Bishop.
FLOODS
Flood. Feldman.
No More the Slow Stream. F. C. McLaren.
FLOWERS
See also Flower and Flowers in TITLE AND FIRST LINE INDEX
Allegory of the Brevity of Things Human. Góngora, tr. fr. Spanish by Campbell.
Blossom, The. Donne.
Bunch of Wild Flowers. Zilles.
Chanted Calendar, A. Fr. Balder. Sydney Dobell.
Contemplation upon Flowers, A. Henry King.
Flower's Name, The. Fr. Garden Fancies. Robert Browning.
For the doubling of flowers is the improvement of the gard'ner's talent. Fr. Jubilate Agno. Christopher Smart.
Funeral Home, The. Mezey.
How the Flowers Grow. "Gabriel Setoun."
I'll Twine White Violets. Meleager, tr. fr. Greek by Smith.
Lark's Song, The. Fr. Milton. Blake.
Matter of Life and Death, A. Ridler.
Of All Known Flowers, Men Hold the Rose Most Rare. Froissart, tr. fr. French by LeClercq.
Planting Flowers on the Eastern Embankment. Po Chü-i, tr. fr. Chinese by Waley.
Tapers. F. A. Gray.
To Blossoms. Herrick.
Trees in the Garden, The. Stephen Crane.
Troll's Nosegay, The. Robert Graves.
While We Watch These Flowers Fair. Charles d'Orléans, tr. fr. French by Kittel.
Wonga Vine. Judith Wright.

See also names of flowers (e.g., DAFFODILS)
FLUTES
Amateur Flute, The. Unknown.
Flute-Players, The. Rabéarivelo, tr. fr. French by Blair.
FOG
Fog. Sandburg.
Yellow fog that rubs its back upon the window-panes, The. Fr. The Love Song of J. Alfred Prufrock. T. S. Eliot.
See also HAZE; MIST
FOOD
Beautiful soup, so rich and green. Fr. Alice's Adventures in Wonderland. "Lewis Carroll."
Goody O'Grumpity. Brink.
Hasty-Pudding, The. Joel Barlow.
Inviting a Friend to Supper. Jonson.
Marble-Top. E. B. White.
Melton Mowbray Pork Pie, A. Le Gallienne.
My Other Chinee Cook. Brunton Stephens.
Salad. Mortimer Collins.
Salad, A. Sydney Smith.
Tres Cosas. Alcázar, tr. fr. Spanish by Rollins.
Welsh, The. E. V. Lucas.
When in Rome. M. E. Evans.
FOOLS. Fool's Prayer, The. E. R. Sill.
FOOTBALL
Football. Walt Mason.
In the Beginning Was the. Murchison.
Passer, The. Abbe.
Second Half. McCord.
Settling Some Old Football Scores. Morris Bishop.
See also SOCCER
FORD, FORD MADOX. Ford Madox Ford. Robert Lowell.
FOREST FIRES. Forest Fire. Romig.
FORESTS
Dirge in Woods. George Meredith.
Dogwood, The. Fr. Dark Woods. R. P. Warren.
Forest Hymn, A. Bryant.
Forest Shapes. Wandrei.
Hidden Scars. Ragan.
In November. Lampman.
In the Redwood Forest. Ralph Pomeroy.
In the Woods. F. G. Scott.
Inscription for the Entrance to a Wood. Bryant.
Now You Shall Speak. C. F. Meyer, tr. fr. German by Stillman.
Plants Stand Silent Round Me, The. Jørgensen, tr. fr. Danish by Hillyer.
Solitary Woodsman, The. C. G. D. Roberts.
Stopping by Woods on a Snowy Evening. Robert Frost.
Waldeinsamkeit. Emerson.
Walk, The. W. W. E. Ross.
Way through the Woods, The. Kipling.
Woods of Westermain, The. George Meredith.
Woods in Winter. Longfellow.
FORTUNE
Coming of Good Luck, The. Herrick.
Gifts of Fortune, The. Schiller, tr. fr. German by Gode.
Most Foolish Fools, Oh Foolish Mortal Men. Chartier, tr. fr. French by Kittel.
Thomas More to Them That Seek Fortune. Thomas More.
See also FATE
FORTY-NINERS. Songs of the Gold Rush, The (SGR). Richard A. Dwyer and Richard E. Lingenfelter, eds.
FOUNTAINS
See also Fountain in TITLE AND FIRST LINE INDEX
Ailing Fountain, The. "Aldo Palazzeschi," tr. fr. Italian by Golino.
Baroque Wall-Fountain in the Villa Sciarra, A. Wilbur.
Roman Fountain, The. C. F. Meyer, tr. fr. German by Kaufmann.
Roman Fountain. Rilke, tr. fr. German by Kaufmann.
To a Fountain. Ronsard, tr. fr. French by Currey.
FOURTH OF JULY
Fireworks. James Reeves.
Grandfather Watts's Private Fourth. H. C. Bunner.
If I Had a Firecracker. Silverstein.
Independence Bell. Unknown.
Listen to the People: Independence Day, 1941, sel. S. V. Benét.
FOXES
Ballad of Red Fox, The. La Follette.
Four Little Foxes. Sarett.
Fox Walked Out, The. Unknown.
FOXGLOVE. Foxgloves. Ted Hughes.
FRANCE
Four Sheets to the Wind and a One-Way Ticket to France, 1933. Rivers.
France; an Ode. S. T. Coleridge.
Contemporary French Poetry (CoFP). Alexander Aspel and Donald Justice, eds.
Renaissance and Baroque Lyrics (RBL). Harold Martin Priest, ed.
FRANCESCA DA RIMINI. Story of Rimini, The, sel. ("Ready she sat with one hand to turn o'er"). Leigh Hunt.

FRANCIS OF ASSISI, SAINT
Little Song in Assisi, A. George Barker.
Saint Francis. J. P. Bishop.
St. Francis and the Cloud. M. de L. Welch.
FRANCIS I, KING OF FRANCE. Glove and the Lions, The.
Leigh Hunt.
FRANCK, CÉSAR. All Those Hymnings Up to God. A. H.
Evans.
FRANKLIN, BENJAMIN. On the Death of Benjamin Franklin.
Freneau.
FRANKLIN, SIR JOHN. Ballad of Sir John Franklin, A. Boker.
FREEDOM
Antiquity of Freedom, The. Bryant.
Fain Would I Live in Safest Freedom. Platen, tr. fr. German by Morgan.
France; an Ode. S. T. Coleridge.
Free Nation, A. Edwin Markham.
Harp That Once through Tara's Halls, The. Thomas Moore.
Ode: "God save the Rights of Man!" Freneau.
Proem: "I love the old melodious lays." Whittier.
Shine, Republic. Jeffers.
To Althea from Prison. Lovelace.
When a Man Hath No Freedom to Fight for at Home. Byron.
FREDERICKSBURG, BATTLE OF. Battle of Fredericksburg, The.
Unknown.
FRENCH, THE
Epistle III: "Pult'ney, methinks you blame my breach of
word." John Gay.
Letter to Wilbur Frohock, A. Daniel Hoffman.
FRENCH AND INDIAN WARS. Means Massacre, The. R. P. T.
Coffin.
FRENCH REVOLUTION. France; an Ode. S. T. Coleridge.
FRIARS
Friar Complains, A. Unknown.
Friars' Enormities. Unknown
FRIENDSHIP
Around the Corner. C. H. Towne.
Arrow and the Song, The. Longfellow.
Auld Lang Syne. Burns.
Be. "Will Inman."
Best Treasure, The. Moment.
Fame and Friendship. II. A. Dobson.
Friend Who Just Stands By, The. B. Y. Williams.
Friend or Two, A. W. D. Nesbit.
Gone. M. E. Coleridge.
In Memory of Major Robert Gregory. Yeats.
Letter to a Friend. John Thompson.
Make Friends. Ali ben Abu Taleb.
To a Friend. Hartley Coleridge.
To a Friend. Amy Lowell.
They Say That in the Unchanging Place. Fr. Dedicatory
Ode. Hilaire Belloc.
True Friendship. Fr. The Panchatantra. Unknown, tr. fr.
Sanskrit by Ryder.
Under All Change. J. W. Johnson.
When to the sessions of sweet silent thought. Sonnets, XXX.
Shakespeare.
Why Art Thou Silent. Wordsworth.
Window in the Breast, A. Unknown, tr. fr. Greek by
Headlam.
Written in the Album of the Child. Wordsworth.
FRIETCHIE, BARBARA. Barbara Frietchie. Whittier.
FROGS
Bullfrog. Ted Hughes.
Frog, The. Hilaire Belloc.
Frogs' Singing-School, The. E. T. Carbell.
Grandfather Frog. L. S. Bechtel.
Moral Song. J. C. Farrar.
Peepers. Cane.
FRONTIERS. Lullaby for Peregrine. R. P. T. Coffin.
FROST
Apparently with no surprise. Emily Dickinson.
Fairy Artist, The. Garabrant.
Frost at Midnight. S. T. Coleridge.
Frost Pane, The. McCord.
Jack Frost. H. B. Davis.
Little Jack Frost. Unknown.
Pageant, The. Whittier.
Sudden Frost. Wagoner.
FROST, ROBERT. Three around the Old Gentleman. Berryman.
FUNERALS
After the Funeral. Dylan Thomas.
Attitudes. Eberhart.
Choirmaster's Burial, The. Thomas Hardy.
Dirge for McPherson, A. Melville.
Funeral, The. Donne.
Italian Extravaganza. Corso.
Lovers, The. Conrad Aiken.
My Grandmother's Funeral. Kessler.
Paging Professor Gooseberry. Stem.
Pauper's Funeral, The. Fr. The Village. Crabbe.
Sea-Ritual, The. Fr. Syren Songs. Darley.
They Closed Her Eyes. Bécquer, tr. fr. Spanish by Kittel.
Tract. W. C. Williams.

G

GALATEA. Fable of Polyphemus and Galatea, sels. Góngora,
tr. fr. Spanish by Fletcher.
GALILEO. Galileo Galilei. W. J. Smith.
GALOSHES
Galoshes. Bacmeister.
Galoshes, The. Lichtenstein, tr. fr. German by Hamburger.
GALUPPI, BALDASSARO. Toccata of Galuppi's, A. Robert
Browning.
GAMBLING
Gambler, The. J. A. Stone.
Gamesters All. DuBose Heyward.
GAMES. See SPORTS AND GAMES
GANYMEDE. Ganymede. Goethe, tr. fr. German by Kaufmann.
GARCÍA LORCA, FEDERICO. Crime Was in Granada, The.
Machado, tr. fr. Spanish by Flores.
GARDENS
See also Garden in TITLE AND FIRST LINE INDEX
Charleston Garden, A. Bellamann.
Flowers in a Garden. Christopher Smart.
For Jim, Easter Eve. Anne Spencer.
Flower's Name, The. Fr. Garden Fancies. Robert Browning.
Forsaken Garden, A. Swinburne.
Just after Noon with Fierce Shears. Tram Combs.
Mower against Gardens, The. Marvell.
My Garden. T. E. Brown.
New Garden, The. Arkell.
Old Quin Queeribus. N. B. Turner.
On Watering the Garden. Brecht, tr. fr. German by Ham-
burger.
Rented Garden, The. Noll.
Their Lonely Betters. Auden.
To Mrs. Boteler. Mary Chandler.
Widow's Weeds, A. De la Mare.
Wild Garden. Pearson.
GARFIELD, JAMES ABRAM. Garfield's Murder. Unknown.
GARRICK, DAVID. David Garrick. Fr. Retaliation. Goldsmith.
GEESE
Barnacle Geese. Charles Higham.
Difference, The. Gozzano, tr. fr. Italian by Golino.
Wild Geese. Chipp.
Wild Geese. Shen Yo, tr. fr. Chinese by Waley.
GEHRIG, HENRY LOUIS (Lou). To Lou Gehrig. Kieran.
GENTIANS
Bavarian Gentians. D. H. Lawrence.
God made a little gentian. Emily Dickinson.
GEORGE, SAINT. Carol of St. George, A. Unknown.
GEORGE III, KING OF ENGLAND. Vision of Judgment, The.
Byron.
GEORGE, STEFAN. To Stephan George. Rilke, tr. fr. German
by Kaufmann.
GEORGIA. Georgia Dusk. Toomer.
GERANIUMS. Red Geranium and Godly Mignonette. D. H.
Lawrence.
GERMANS, THE. German National Character. Schiller, tr. fr.
German by Kaufmann.
GERMANY
Anthology of German Poetry (AGP). Alexander Gode and
Frederick Ungar, eds.
Modern German Poetry: 1910–1960 (MGP). Michael Ham-
burger and Christopher Middleton, eds.
Twenty German Poets (TwGP). Walter Kaufmann, ed.
GERONIMO. Geronimo. McGaffey.
GETHSEMANE
Garden of Gethsemane. Pasternak, tr. fr. Russian by Guerney.
Garden of Olives, The. Rilke, tr. fr. German by Norton.
Gethsemane. Tappan.
GHOST TOWNS
Ghost-Town Saloon: Winter. J. P. Brennan.
News of My Friends. Code.
GHOSTS
See also Ghost and Ghosts in TITLE AND FIRST LINE INDEX
Companions. Widdemer.
Gone, The. Jesse Stuart.
Grandfather's Ghost. J. P. Brennan.
Old Ghost, The. Beddoes.
Place-Ghost. Derleth.
Shadowed. Burnham Eaton.
Shepherd's Hut, The. Andrew Young.
Spring Voices. Jesse Stuart.
Tenant. F. A. Gray.
Tom. Osbert Sitwell.
Two Wives, The. Daniel Henderson.
Wilderness Road. Martha Keller.
GIRAFFES. Giraffe, The. Geoffrey Dearmer.
GIRLS. See CHILDHOOD AND CHILDREN; YOUTH
GLASS BLOWERS
Glass Blower, The. Scully.

GLASS BLOWERS (*continued*)
Poem of a Glass Blower. *Unknown, tr. fr. French by* Aldan.
GLOUCESTER, MASSACHUSETTS. Gloucester Moors. W. V. Moody.
GLOWWORMS. Mower to the Glow-Worms, The. Marvell.
GNATS. Gnat, The. Joseph Beaumont.
GOATS. *See* Goat *in* TITLE AND FIRST LINE INDEX
GOD
Adon 'Olam. *Unknown, tr. fr. Hebrew by* Mendes.
Almighty God, Who Made the Noble State. Chartier, *tr. fr. French by* Tobin.
At a Solemn Musick. Schwartz.
Belief in Plan of Thee. Walt Whitman.
Best for Us, The. Burnett.
Caliban upon Setebos. Robert Browning.
Child's Thought of God, A. E. B. Browning.
Cosmos Shows His Power, The. González Prada, *tr. fr. Spanish by* Davis.
Divine Image, The. *Fr.* Songs of Innocence. Blake.
Down in the Depth of Mine Iniquity. *Fr.* Caelica. Fulke Greville.
Each in His Own Tongue. W. H. Carruth.
Eclipse, An. Pindar, *tr. fr. Greek by* Bowra.
Essay on Deity. Elder Olson.
Even-Song. George Herbert.
Excesses of God, The. Jeffers.
Eyewitness. Rodney Hall.
First Autumn, The. Schacht.
God. Pearson.
God Does Do Such Wonderful Things. Angela Morgan.
God Doeth All Things Well. *Unknown.*
God-forgotten. Thomas Hardy.
God Is at the Anvil. Sarett.
God, Is, like, Scissors. Villa.
God Is There. Isenhour.
God Is with Me. O. J. Smith.
God Knows What He's About. *Unknown.*
God Makes a Path. Roger Williams.
God of Galaxies, The. Van Doren.
God of Our Fathers. D. C. Roberts.
God of the Earth, the Sky, the Sea. Samuel Longfellow.
God the Architect. Kemp.
God's Grandeur. G. M. Hopkins.
God's Will Is Best. Thelma Curtis.
Higher Pantheism, The. Tennyson.
His Plan. *Unknown.*
Holy of Holies, The. G. K. Chesterton.
Hound of Heaven, The. Francis Thompson.
How Many Heavens. Edith Sitwell.
Hymn of Joy. Henry van Dyke.
Hymn to God the Father, A. Donne.
I am the Reaper. W. E. Henley.
I Have Sought Thee Daily. Ibn Gabirol, *tr. fr. Hebrew by* Zangwill.
I See God. *Unknown.*
I Sing the Mighty Power of God. Isaac Watts.
If He Were Anywhere. Hemley.
Imagery. Chattopadhyaya.
Immanence. Hovey.
Instantaneous. Ayers.
Invocation: "Perfection ever rising to perfection." *Unknown, tr. fr. Sotho by* Franz.
Invocation, An: "To God, the everlasting, who abides," *sel.* Symonds.
Kingdom of God, The. Francis Thompson.
Let Us with a Gladsome Mind. Milton.
Light Shining Out of Darkness. Cowper.
Livid lightnings flashed in the clouds, The. *Fr.* The Black Riders. Stephen Crane.
Look, How Beautiful. Jeffers.
Lord Is My Shepherd, The. H. W. Baker.
Man went before a strange God, A. *Fr.* The Black Riders. Stephen Crane.
Master Weaver, The. *Unknown.*
Meditation Six ("Am I thy gold? Or purse, Lord, for thy wealth.") *Fr.* Preparatory Meditations, First Series. Edward Taylor.
Mighty Fortress Is Our God, A. Luther, *tr. fr. German by* Hedge.
Moon is distant from the sea, The. Emily Dickinson.
Morning Hours, The. *Unknown, tr. fr. Arabic by* Pickthall.
My Absent God. Hemley.
My Hiding Place. Bowsher.
O God, Our Help in Ages Past. Isaac Watts.
Old Repair Man, The. Fenton Johnson.
Our Rock. Key.
On the Universality and Other Attributes of the God of Nature. Freneau.
Our Father. Swartz.
Peace. Henry Vaughan.
Pillar of the Cloud, The. J. H. Newman.
Postern Gate, The, *sel.* ("In the castle of my soul"). Rauschenbusch.
Prayer to the Father of Heaven, A. John Skelton.

Preface, The. *Fr.* Gods Determinations. Edward Taylor.
Presence, The. Very.
Psalm: "I proclaim Thee great and wonderful." Murilo Mendes, *tr. fr. Spanish by* Poore.
Secret, The. R. S. Cushman.
Security. Sandell.
Send Me. C. G. Rossetti.
Shadows, The. George Macdonald.
Siesta. Machado, *tr. fr. Spanish by* Flores.
Song of the Creatures, The. St. Francis of Assisi, *tr. fr. Italian by* Arnold.
Sonnet: "My God, where is that ancient heat towards Thee." George Herbert.
Spacious Firmament on High, The. Joseph Addison.
Sun-Day Hymn, A. O. W. Holmes.
There Is No God. *Fr.* Dipsychus. Clough.
There Is Nothing False in Thee. Patchen.
There's a Wideness in God's Mercy. Faber.
Third Enemy Speaks. *Fr.* The Magnetic Mountain. Day Lewis.
This Is My Father's World. M. D. Babcock.
Three Hymns, I ("Thou didst, O mighty God, exist"). Elizabeth Rowe.
To the Unknown God. Nietzsche, *tr. fr. German by* Kaufmann.
Transcendence. Hovey.
Unseen Power, The. Rumi, *tr. fr. Persian by* Nicholson.
Veni Creator. Bliss Carman.
What Tomas Said in a Pub. James Stephens.
With Thee. Pinkham.
You. John Masefield.
Yours. Tagore.
GOETHE, JOHANN WOLFGANG VON
Memorial Verses. Matthew Arnold.
Scholar and Goethe, The. Christian Morgenstern, *tr. fr. German by* Kaufmann.
Sorrows of Werther, The. Thackeray.
To Goethe. Nietzsche, *tr. fr. German by* Kaufmann.
GOGH, VINCENT VAN
Farewell to Van Gogh. Tomlinson.
Visit to Van Gogh, A. Causley.
GOLD MINING AND MINERS
Arawata Bill. Denis Glover.
Broken-down Digger, The. *Unknown.*
Cleaning Up. Edward Dyson.
Golden Gullies of the Palmer, The. *Unknown.*
Look Out Below! Thatcher.
Songs of the Gold Rush, The (SGR). Richard A. Dwyer and Richard E. Lingenfelter, eds.
GOLD RUSH, THE. *See* FORTY-NINERS
GOLF
Afforestation. E. A. Wodehouse.
Ball and the Club, The. Forbes Lindsay.
City of Golf, The. R. F. Murray.
Golfers. Layton.
He Gave Up Golf. Earnshaw.
Mullion. A. P. Herbert.
One Down. Armour.
Public Nuisance, A. Arkell.
Seaside Golf. Betjeman.
GOLGOTHA. *See* CRUCIFIXION, THE
GOOD FRIDAY
See also Good Friday *in* TITLE AND FIRST LINE INDEX
Unkept Good Fridays. Thomas Hardy.
See also CRUCIFIXION, THE
GORE-BOOTH, EVE. In Memory of Eva Gore-Booth and Con Markiewicz. Yeats.
GORSE. Song of Winter, A. E. D. Pfeiffer.
GOSPEL SINGERS. And the Old Women Gathered. Mari Evans.
GOVAN, SAINT. St. Govan. Prys-Jones.
GOYA, LUCIENTES, FRANCISCO JOSÉ DE. Goya. Conrad Aiken.
GRANADA, SPAIN. Crime Was in Granada, The. Machado, *tr. fr. Spanish by* Flores.
GRAND PRÉ, NOVA SCOTIA. Low Tide on Grand Pré. Bliss Carman.
GRANDFATHERS
Epitaph on His Grandfather, An. Shipman.
Grandparents. Robert Lowell.
Old Man Playing with Children. Ransom.
GRANDMOTHERS
At My Grandmother's. Malouf.
Grandmamma's Birthday. Hilaire Belloc.
For my Grandmother. *Fr.* Four Epitaphs. Countee Cullen.
Grandmother and Grandson. Merwin.
Grandmother's Visit. Wise.
Grandparents. Robert Lowell.
My Grandmother's Funeral. Kessler.
GRANTCHESTER, ENGLAND. Old Vicarage, Grantchester, The. Rupert Brooke.
GRAPES. Grapes. Pushkin, *tr. fr. Russian by* Yarmolinsky.
GRASS
Blade [*or* Blades] of Grass. *Fr.* The Black Riders. Stephen Crane.
Former Barn Lot. Van Doren.

Grass. Sandburg.
Grass so little has to do, The. Emily Dickinson.
Shearing Grass. Redgrove.
GRASSHOPPERS
Explanation of the Grasshopper, An. Vachel Lindsay.
Grasshopper, The. Abraham Cowley.
Grasshopper Green. *Unknown.*
Grasshopper Hop-o-the-Grasses. Hallock.
On the Grasshopper and Cricket. Keats.
To the Grasshopper and the Cricket. Leigh Hunt.
GRAVES
Ah, Are You Digging on My Grave? Thomas Hardy.
Ample make this bed. Emily Dickinson.
Beach Burial. Slessor.
Brief Biography. Marguerite George.
Call for the Robin Redbreast. *Fr.* The White Devil. John Webster.
Dirge: "We do lie beneath the grass." *Fr.* Death's Jest Book. Beddoes.
Grave, The. T. G. Jones, *tr. fr. Welsh by* Rhys.
Graveyard, The. Jane Cooper.
Hide-and-Seek. Robert Graves.
Invocation: "Let me be buried in the rain." Helene Johnson.
My Burial Place. Jeffers.
My Grave. T. O. Davis.
On the Choice of His Sepulchre. *Fr.* Odes. Ronsard, *tr. fr. French by* Conder.
Unknown Dead, The. Timrod.
Where? Heine, *tr. fr. German by* Sebba.
See also CEMETERIES
GRAY, THOMAS. Sketch of His Own Character. Thomas Gray.
GREATNESS
I Think Continually of Those Who Were Truly Great. Spender.
Song of Greatness, A. *Tr. fr. Chippewa Indian by* Austin.
Stop!—for thy tread is on an Empire's dust! *Fr.* Childe Harold's Pilgrimage. Byron.
GREECE
Fair Greece! sad relic of departed worth! *Fr.* Childe Harold's Pilgrimage. Byron.
Isles of Greece, The. *Fr. Don Juan.* Byron.
Isles of Greece, The. Capetanakis.
Nemea. Durrell.
GREEK GODS. Gods of Greece, The. Heine, *tr. fr. German by* Kaufmann.
GREENE, NATHANAEL. To the Memory of the Brave Americans. Freneau.
GREGORY, ROBERT. In Memory of Major Robert Gregory. Yeats.
GRENVILLE, SIR RICHARD. *Revenge,* The. Tennyson.
GRIEF
After great pain, a formal feeling comes. Emily Dickinson.
Break, Break, Break. Tennyson.
Carousel, The. Oden.
Chamber over the Gate, The. Longfellow.
Dirge, A: "Rough wind, that moanest loud." Shelley.
Farewell to the Court. Ralegh.
Great Waves Breaking with a Roar. Bécquer, *tr. fr. Spanish by* Haines.
Grief. E. B. Browning.
He Who Weeps Goes Not Alone. Castro, *tr. fr. Spanish by* Flores.
Iliad, The, *sel.* ("Meanwhile Achilles, plung'd"). Homer, *tr. fr. Greek by* Derby.
In Mourning. Abu-l-Hasan al-Husri, *tr. fr. Arabic by* Kemp.
Lost Love. Robert Graves.
Mourning. Marvell.
No Worst, There Is None. G. M. Hopkins.
On Another's Sorrow. *Fr.* Songs of Innocence. Blake.
Nurse No Long Grief. Mary Gilmore.
On My First Son [*or* Sonne]. Jonson.
Raven Days, The. Sidney Lanier.
Sad Shepherd, The. Yeats.
Safe despair it is that raves. Emily Dickinson.
Shrubbery, The. Cowper.
Sonnet: "In vain to me the smiling mornings shine." Thomas Gray.
Sonnets, Part II, *sel.* ("But unto him came swift calamity"). F. G. Tuckerman.
Sonnets, Part II, *sel.* ("How most unworthy, echoing in mine ears"). F. G. Tuckerman.
Sonnets, Part II, *sel.* ("One still dark night, I sat alone and wrote"). F. G. Tuckerman.
Sonnets to Laura: To Laura in Death, *sel.* ("O lovely little bird, I watch you fly"). Petrarch, *tr. fr. Italian by* Bishop.
Sorrow. A. T. de Vere.
Sorrow. D. H. Lawrence.
Sorrow Is the Only Faithful One. Dodson.
Sorrow's Day. Brockman.
Tears Flow in My Heart. Verlaine, *tr. fr. French by* Kittel.
To Sing with Joy from out a Sorrowing Heart. Christine de Pisan, *tr. fr. French by* Kittel.

Victory in Defeat. Edwin Markham.
When They Told Me I Felt the Cold. Bécquer, *tr. fr. Spanish by* Bell.
Widow's Lament in Springtime, The. W. C. Williams.
You've Filled My Mind So Full of Grief. Cavalcanti, *tr. fr. Italian by* Wilhelm.
GRIMALD [*or* GRIMALDE *or* GRIMOALD], NICHOLAS. Epitaph of the Death of Nicholas Grimald, An. Googe.
GROSZ, GEORG. Georg Grosz. Lasker-Schüler, *tr. fr. German by* Middleton.
GROUND-HOG DAY. *See* CANDLEMAS
GROUNDHOGS. Groundhog, The. Eberhart.
GUEST, EDGAR ALBERT
Edgar A. Guest Considers "The Good Old Woman Who Lived in a Shoe" and the Good Old Truths Simultaneously. Louis Untermeyer.
Edgar Guest. Oscar Williams.
GUILT
Guilty. Marguerite Wilkinson.
Just Vengeance, The, *sel.* ("I have sinned; I have betrayed the innocent blood"). D. L. Sayers.
Pursuit. R. P. Warren.
Rime of the Ancient Mariner, The. S. T. Coleridge.
Think of This. Eich, *tr. fr. German by* Watkins.
GUINIZELLI, GUIDO. To Guido Guinizelli: Now That You Have Changed the Manner. Orbicciani, *tr. fr. Italian by* Valency.
GUITARS
Girl with Guitar. Hardison.
Guitar, The. García Lorca, *tr. fr. Spanish by* Benson and O'Brien.
Tavern Guitar Playing a *Jota* Today. Machado, *tr. fr. Spanish by* Guenther.
GUITEAU, CHARLES. Charles Guiteau. *Unknown.*
GULL LAKE, CANADA. At Gull Lake: August, 1810. D. C. Scott.
GULLS
Ballet of the Fifth Year, The. Schwartz.
From This the Strength. Lape.
Gray Horizons. Ragan.
Sea-Gull, The. Ogden Nash.
Seagulls. Updike.
To a Seamew, *sel.* ("When I had wings, my brother"). Swinburne.
GUM TREES
Gnarled Riverina Gum-Tree, A. Moll.
Snow-Gum, The. Douglas Stewart.
GUNS. Shooting, The. Robert Pack.
GUY FAWKES DAY. Fifth of November. Gransden.
GYPSIES
Being Gypsy. Barbara Young.
Gypsies. John Clare.
Gypsy Laddie, The. *Unknown.*
Gypsy's Window, The. Levertov.
Meg Merrilies. Keats.
Scholar-Gipsy, The. Matthew Arnold.
Three Gypsies, The. Lenau, *tr. fr. German by* Gillhoff.
Wraggle Taggle Gipsies [O!], The. *Unknown.*

H

HAIR
Hair, My Pretty Hair. Zorro, *tr. fr. Portuguese by* Davis.
On the Ladies' Head-Dresses. James Greenwood.
HAIRCUTS. Haircut. Karl Shapiro.
HALE, NATHAN
Nathan Hale. F. M. Finch.
Nathan Hale. *Unknown.*
HALLAM, ARTHUR HENRY. In Memoriam A. H. H. Tennyson.
HALLOWEEN
See also Halloween *in* TITLE AND FIRST LINE INDEX
Black and Gold. N. B. Turner.
Ghoulies and Ghosties. *Unknown.*
If You've Never. E. M. Fowler.
Jack o'Lantern. Ayre.
On Halloween. Silverstein.
Riddle: What Am I? Dorothy Aldis.
Theme in Yellow. Sandburg.
HANDEL, GEORGE FRIDERIC. Epigram on Handel and Bononcini. Byron.
HANGING
Hanging, The. J. E. H. MacDonald.
HANKS, NANCY
Nancy Hanks. R. C. Benét.
Nancy Hanks. Harriet Monroe.
Nancy Hanks, Mother of Abraham Lincoln. Vachel Lindsay.
HAPPINESS
Character of a Happy Life. Henry Wotton.
Happiness. Isenhour.
Of God we ask one favor. Emily Dickinson.

HAPPINESS (*continued*)
Wish, The. *Fr.* The Mistress. Abraham Cowley.
Work of Happiness, The. Sarton.
HARBORS. Harbor, The. Sandburg.
HARDING, WARREN GAMALIEL. Two Poems about President Harding. James Wright.
HARDY, THOMAS
For Thomas Hardy. Jane Cooper.
Thoughts of Thomas Hardy. Blunden.
HARES
Ecclesiastes. Joseph Langland.
Hares at Play. John Clare.
HARLEM, NEW YORK CITY
Lenox Avenue Mural. Langston Hughes.
Sketches of Harlem. David Henderson.
Still Voice of Harlem, The. C. K. Rivers.
HARPERS FERRY, WEST VIRGINIA. How Old Brown Took Harper's Ferry. Stedman.
HARPS
Dark in a Corner of the Room. Bécquer, *tr. fr. Spanish by* Flores
Harp That Once through Tara's Halls, The. Thomas Moore.
HARRISON, WILLIAM HENRY. Old Tippecanoe. *Unknown.*
HARVARD UNIVERSITY. Unicorns at Harvard. Farber.
HARVEST
Antique Harvesters. Ransom.
Before the Harvest. Grief, *tr. fr. German by* Stillman.
Harvest and Consecration. Elizabeth Jennings.
Hock-Cart, The. Herrick.
Hurrahing in Harvest. G. M. Hopkins.
Reaper, The. L. H. Allen.
Returning from Harvest. Vernon Watkins.
Solitary Reaper, The. Wordsworth.
HARVEY, WILLIAM. Ode upon Dr. Harvey, *sel.* Abraham Cowley.
HATE
Fragment from Nothing. Coatsworth.
Hatred. G. B. Bennett.
Law in the Country of the Cats. Ted Hughes.
Song about Major Eatherly, A. Wain.
Sonnet: "I hate the money-lending avarice." Du Bellay, *tr. fr. French by* Currey.
Tragedy. "Æ."
HAUSER, KASPAR. Caspar Hauser Song. Trakl, *tr. fr. German by* Luke.
HAVANA, CUBA. Habana. Julian Bond.
HAWAII. Honolulu and Back. John Logan.
HAWKS
See also Hawk *in* TITLE AND FIRST LINE INDEX
Hawk in the Rain, The. Ted Hughes.
Hurt Hawks. Jeffers.
Over Sir John's Hill. Dylan Thomas.
HAWTHORN
Hawthorn Hedge, The. Judith Wright.
I Bended unto Me. T. E. Brown.
HAWTHORNE, NATHANIEL
Hawthorne. *Fr.* A Fable for Critics. J. R. Lowell.
Hawthorne—May 23 1864. Longfellow.
Monody. Melville.
On Visiting the Graves of Hawthorne and Thoreau. Very.
HAY. Hayfield. Aileen Fisher.
HAYDON, BENJAMIN ROBERT. Addressed to Haydon. Keats.
HAZE
Haze. Thoreau.
See also FOG; MIST
HEAT. *See* Heat *in* TITLE AND FIRST LINE INDEX
HEATHER. Heather, The. Blicher, *tr. fr. Danish by* Stork.
HEAVEN
See also Heaven *in* TITLE AND FIRST LINE INDEX
At Last. Whittier.
Childless Woman in Heaven, The. Katharine Tynan.
Cold Heaven, The. Yeats.
General William Booth Enters into Heaven. Vachel Lindsay.
God's Residence. Emily Dickinson.
Going Home with Jesus. Isenhour.
Heaven has different signs to me. Emily Dickinson.
Home at Last. G. K. Chesterton.
I never saw a moor. Emily Dickinson.
I went to heaven. Emily Dickinson.
In Him. A. J. Flint.
Lady I Know, A. Countee Cullen.
Let Us Go Down, the Long Dead Night Is Done. *Fr.* Towards the Source. Christopher Brennan.
Letter from Brooklyn, A. Walcott.
Life after Death. Pindar, *tr. fr. Greek by* Headlam.
Life of the Blessed, The. León, *tr. fr. Spanish by* Bryant.
My Ain Countree. Demarest.
Ode to Felipe Ruiz. León, *tr. fr. Spanish by* Bell.
One Centred System. *Fr.* The Columbiad. Joel Barlow.
Peace. Henry Vaughan.
Port of Many Ships. Masefield.
Promise. "Æ."
Safely Home. *Unknown.*

Sister Lou. S. A. Brown.
Surprises. *Unknown.*
Theology. P. L. Dunbar.
There Is a Land. Isaac Watts.
To His Friend in Elysium. Du Bellay, *tr. fr. French by* Lang.
Uncelestial City, The, *sel.* ("You cannot traffick in peace"). Humbert Wolfe.
We Are God's Chosen Few. Swift.
We'll Meet Again. J. D. Smith.
What is—"paradise." Emily Dickinson.
Where Is Heaven? Bliss Carman.
World, The. Henry Vaughan.
See also PARADISE
HEDGEHOGS. Hedgehog. Thwaite.
HEIDELBERG, GERMANY. Thinking of Hölderlin. Christopher Middleton.
HEIKKILA, BILL. To Bill Heikkila, American. Irene Paull.
HEIMDALL. Heimdall. Vinal.
HELEN OF TROY
Face of Helen, The. *Fr.* Dr. Faustus. Marlowe.
Past ruin'd Ilion Helen lives. *Fr.* Ianthe. W. S. Landor.
To Helen. Poe.
Troy Town. D. G. Rossetti.
White Queen. John Fuller.
"Who," cried the elders on the Trojan wall. *Fr.* Sonnets pour Hélène. Ronsard, *tr. fr. French by* Wolfe.
HELL
Ballad of Hell, A. John Davidson.
Good Man in Hell, The. Edwin Muir.
Satan's Speech. *Fr.* Paradise Lost. Milton.
Song about Major Eatherly, A. Wain.
Theology. P. L. Dunbar.
HENRY II, KING OF ENGLAND. If All the Grief and Sorrow, the Strife. Bertrand de Born, *tr. fr. Provençal by* Wilhelm.
HENRY V, KING OF ENGLAND. King Henry the Fifth, *sel.* ("Once more unto the breach, dear friends, once more"). Shakespeare.
HENS
Hen Overboard. R. P. T. Coffin.
Hens, The. E. M. Roberts.
What They Do. Farjeon.
HERACLITUS. Heraclitus. W. J. Cory.
HERBERT, GEORGE. On Mr. George Herberts Booke Intituled the Temple of Sacred Poems, Sent to a Gentlewoman. Crashaw.
HERMITS. Hermit, The. Eichendorff, *tr. fr. German.*
HERO AND LEANDER
Hero and Leander, *sels.* Marlowe.
On an Engraved Gem of Leander. Keats.
HEROD THE GREAT
Ballad of Two Kings. Code.
Flight into Egypt, The. Southwell.
Innocents, The. Jay Macpherson.
Innocent's Song. Causley.
HEROES
How Sleep the Brave. William Collins.
I Think Continually of Those Who Were Truly Great. Spender.
Litany of the Heroes, *sels.* Vachel Lindsay.
Man from the Crowd, The. S. W. Foss.
Upstream. Sandburg.
HERONS
Blue Heron, The. T. G. Roberts.
Great Blue Heron, The. Kizer.
Heron, The. Vernon Watkins.
HERVEY, WILLIAM. On the Death of Mr. William Hervey. Abraham Cowley.
HIAWATHA
Modern Hiawatha, The. *Fr.* The Story of Milkanwatha. G. A. Strong.
What I Think of Hiawatha. J. W. Morris.
HIGHLANDS OF SCOTLAND
Canadian Boat-Song. *Unknown, at. to* Galt.
In the Highlands. R. L. Stevenson.
My Heart's in the Highlands. Burns.
HILLS AND MOUNTAINS
See also Hill; Hills; Mountain; *and* Mountains *in* TITLE AND FIRST LINE INDEX
Alpine Spirit's Song. Beddoes.
Climbing in Glencoe. Andrew Young.
Golgotha Is a Mountain. Bontemps.
Having Climbed to the Topmost Peak of the Incense-Burner Mountain. Po Chü-i, *tr. fr. Chinese by* Waley.
Hike, The. Neil Weiss.
In the Mountains on a Summer Day. Li Po, *tr. fr. Chinese by* Waley.
Lad of the Mountain, The. Uhland, *tr. fr. German by* Owen.
On Middleton Edge. Andrew Young.
Sleeping Giant, The. Donald Hall.
That Dark Other Mountain. Robert Francis.
To My Mountain. Raine.
To Walk on Hills. Robert Graves.

HIPPOPOTAMUSES
Habits of the Hippopotamus. Guiterman.
Hippopotamus, The. Hilaire Belloc.
Hippopotamus, The. Ogden Nash.
HIROSHIMA, JAPAN
Dirge for the New Sunrise. *Fr.* Three Poems of the Atomic Age. Edith Sitwell.
Hell of a Day, A. Tim Reynolds.
Hibakusha. Eileen Egan.
Hiroshima. Noss.
Kimono, The. Don Gordon.
Two There Are I Wish to Celebrate. McCord.
HISTORY AND HISTORIANS. Ancient Historian. Wallace-Crabbe.
HOGG, JAMES. Extempore Effusion upon the Death of James Hogg. Wordsworth.
HOHENLINDEN, BATTLE OF. Hohenlinden. Thomas Campbell.
HOKUSAI, KATSUSHIKA
Camden Magpie. Hugh McCrae.
Great Wave, The: Hokusai. Finkel.
HOLBEIN, HANS. Fancy Dress. Dorothea Mackellar.
HÖLDERLIN, JOHANN CHRISTIAN FRIEDRICH
Hölderlin. Schwartz.
To Hölderlin. Rilke, *tr. fr. German by* Luke.
HOLIDAY, BILLIE
Blues and Bitterness. Lerone Bennett.
Elegy for a Lady, *sel.* Delegall.
HOLIDAYS. *Poems for Seasons and Celebrations* (PoSC). William Cole, ed.
HOLLAND. *See* NETHERLANDS
HOLLY
Holly against Ivy. *Unknown.*
Holly and Ivy ("Holly and ivy made a great party"). *Unknown.*
Holly and the Ivy, The ("The holly and the ivy/ When they are both full grown"). *Unknown.*
Nay, Ivy, Nay. *Unknown.*
HOLY GRAIL. Vision of Sir Launfal, The. J. R. Lowell.
HOME
See also Home *in* TITLE AND FIRST LINE INDEX
And If Some Place I Have a Home. Neidhart von Reuental, *tr. fr. German by* Richey.
At Home, Alone with the Cat. De la Mare.
At Home, Alone with the Dog. Monro.
Do You Know What the Hedgehog Said? "Spervogel," *tr. fr. German by* Yorck *and* Elmslie.
Fifty Acres. Pearson.
Good-bye. R. W. Emerson.
Heart's Content. *Unknown.*
Heureux qui, comme Ulysse, a fait un beau voyage. *Fr.* Regrets. Du Bellay, *tr. fr. French by* Chesterton.
Home from Abroad. Laurie Lee.
Home, Sweet Home. J. H. Payne.
My Early Home. John Clare.
Old Woman of the Roads, An. Padraic Colum.
Poetry of Departures. Philip Larkin.
Prayer for This House. Louis Untermeyer.
Prayer for the Household, A. R. L. Stevenson.
Return of the Native, The. Harley Matthews.
Roofs. Joyce Kilmer.
Search. Anne Marriott.
Sweetest Home, The. *Unknown.*
Thanksgiving to God for His House, A. Herrick.
True Riches. B. J. Martin.
Wish, The. Abraham Cowley.
HOMER
Homer in a Garden. Pearson.
On First Looking into Chapman's Homer. Keats.
Seven Wealthy Towns. *Unknown.*
To Homer. Keats.
HOMESICKNESS. Homesick Blues. Langston Hughes.
HOMESTEADERS
Hurrah for Greer County. *Unknown.*
Little Old Sod Shanty. *Unknown.*
HONEY. Brown Bear's Honey Song. Kathryn Jackson.
HONEYSUCKLE
Honeysuckle, The. D. G. Rossetti.
Wild Honeysuckle, The. Freneau.
HOOPOES. Hoopoe. *Fr.* Nepenthe. Darley.
HOPE
See also Hope *in* TITLE AND FIRST LINE INDEX
Anticipation. Emily Brontë.
Circumstance. Shelley.
Darkling Thrush, The. Thomas Hardy.
Hope is a subtle glutton. Emily Dickinson.
Hope is the thing with feathers. Emily Dickinson.
I dwell in possibility. Emily Dickinson.
Leaden Echo and the Golden Echo, The. G. M. Hopkins.
Message of the March Wind, The. William Morris.
New Every Morning. *Unknown.*
Pause of Thought, A. C. G. Rossetti.
Perpetual Infirmity of Hope. Sister Juana Inés de la Cruz, *tr. fr. Spanish by* Kittel.
Say Not the Struggle Nought Availeth. Clough.

Song of Hope. Thomas Hardy.
HORACE. On First Looking into Loeb's Horace. Durrell.
HORATIUS. Horatius. *Fr.* Lays of Ancient Rome. Macaulay.
HORNS (musical instruments). Riddle #14: A Horn. *Unknown, tr. fr. Anglo-Saxon by* Raffel.
HORSE CHESTNUT TREES. Horse Chestnut Tree, The. Eberhart.
HORSE RACING
At Galway Races. Yeats.
At Grass. Philip Larkin.
Galway Races. *Unknown.*
Morning Workout. Deutsch.
Tom Fool at Jamaica. Marianne Moore.
HORSES
See also Horse *and* Horses *in* TITLE AND FIRST LINE INDEX
At Grass. Philip Larkin.
Blessing, A [*or* The]. James Wright.
Broncho That Would Not Be Broken, The. Vachel Lindsay.
Dream of Horses, A. Ted Hughes.
Dusk of Horses, The. James Dickey.
Gallop of Fire, A. M. E. J. Pitt.
Horsemen, The. Baro.
Horses on the Camargue. Roy Campbell.
Hunter Trials. Betjeman.
Kentucky Belle. Woolson.
Man from Snowy River, The. Paterson.
Mares of the Camargue, The. *Fr.* Mirèio. Frédéric Mistral, *tr. fr. Provençal by* Meredith.
Milkman's Horse, The. *Unknown.*
My Horses. Jaszi.
Nell. *Fr.* A Row of Stalls. Knister.
Phar Lap in the Melbourne Museum. Peter Porter.
Runaway, The. Robert Frost.
Say This of Horses. M. H. Moody.
Tom Fool at Jamaica. Marianne Moore.
White Horse, The. Abu Salt Umayya, *tr. fr. Arabic by* Kemp.
Wild Horses. Sandburg.
Work Horses. E. N. Chase.
HOSPITALS
Evening in the Sanitarium. Bogan.
Hospital, A. Noyes.
Hospital Waiting-Room, The. W. H. Davies.
In Hospital: Poona (II). Alun Lewis.
Operation, The. W. D. Snodgrass.
HOTTENTOTS. Midsummer Fantasy. Newman Levy.
HOUSEKEEPING. On a Tired Housewife. *Unknown.*
HOUSES
See also House *and* Houses *in* TITLE AND FIRST LINE INDEX
Bless This House. *Unknown.*
Consecration of the House. W. S. Fairbridge.
Destruction of Bulfinch's House, The. Sandy.
Directive. Robert Frost.
Golden Wedding, *sel.* ("Breaking a line of pines, a wide white gate"). Mulgan.
I know some lonely houses off the road. Emily Dickinson.
My House. Krows.
My House. R. L. Stevenson.
Old Houses of Flanders, The. F. M. Ford.
Old Log House. Tippett.
On Gaulstown House. Swift.
Ruin, The. Tomlinson.
Two Little Houses. Earnshaw.
See also HOME
HUDSON RIVER
Egyptian Passage, An. Theodore Weiss.
Mouth of the Hudson, The. Robert Lowell.
HUNDRED YEARS WAR. Ballad of Banners (1944), The. John Lehmann.
HUNGER
Hunger and Rain. Ragan.
When I Think of the Hungry People. O-Shi-O, *tr. fr. Japanese.*
HUNTING AND HUNTERS
All in Green Went My Love Riding. E. E. Cummings.
Badger. John Clare.
Beagles. Rodgers.
Charm for Going a-Hunting. Mary Austin.
Crystal Moment. R. P. T. Coffin.
Deer Hunt. Ragan.
Haymakers, Rakers. *Fr.* The Sun's Darling. Dekker.
Horse & Rider. Wey Robinson.
Hunter, The. Ogden Nash.
Hunting Song. *Fr.* Don Quixote in England. Fielding.
Hunting Song. Finkel.
Hunting Song. Walter Scott.
John Peel. J. W. Graves.
Mighty Hunter, The. Worley.
Old Hunter. Guy Owen.
Old Squire, The. W. S. Blunt.
Rainbow. Robert Huff.
Runnable Stag, A. John Davidson.
September. *Fr.* Sonnets of the Months. Folgore da San Geminiano, *tr. fr. Italian by* Rossetti.

HUNTING AND HUNTERS (*continued*)
  Small Game. Philip Levine.
  Target Practice. Finkel.
  Three Huntsmen, The. *Unknown.*
HURDY-GURDIES
  Barrel Organ, The. Noyes.
  For Hurdy-Gurdy. Corazzini, *tr. fr. Italian by* Farrar.
  Organ Grinders' Garden, The. M. P. Merryman.
HURRICANES
  Hurricane, The. Hart Crane.
  Hurricane, The. Freneau.
HYANCINTHS. Babiaantje, The. Prince.
HYDERABAD, INDIA. In the Bazaars of Hyderbad. Naidu.

I

I.W.W. *See* INDUSTRIAL WORKERS OF THE WORLD
IBN EZRA, ABRAHAM BEN MEIR. Rabbi Ben Ezra. Robert Browning.
IBYCUS. Ibycus. Heath-Stubbs.
ICARUS
  Daedalus. *Fr.* Metamorphoses. Ovid, *tr. fr. Latin by* Golding.
  Icarus. Benn, *tr. fr. German by* Hamburger.
  Icarus. Bottrall.
  Musée des Beaux Arts. Auden.
  New Icarus, The. Vassar Miller.
ICE. Fire and Ice. Robert Frost.
ICE CREAM. Ice-Cream Man, The. Rachel Field.
ICE-SKATING. *See* SKATING AND SKATES
ICEBERGS
  Berg, The. Melville.
  Iceberg, The. Merwin.
ILLNESS
  Bout with Burning. Vassar Miller.
  Dark Women. Ted Hughes.
  Don't Shake the Bottle, Shake Your Mother-in-Law. McGinley.
  Flat One, A. W. D. Snodgrass.
  In Praise of Music in Time of Pestilence. Hine.
  Land of Counterpane, The. R. L. Stevenson.
  Lion, Leopard, Lady. Le Pan.
  Night Nurse Goes Her Round, The. John Gray.
  Passing Out. Philip Levine.
  Ye Gods! of Time I Am Weary. Christine de Pisan, *tr. fr. French by* Kittel.
IMAGINATION
  Attic, The. Coulette.
  Blanket Street. Inez Hogan.
  Block City. R. L. Stevenson.
  Falcon, The. Wylie.
  Land of Counterpane, The. R. L. Stevenson.
  Land of Story-Books, The. R. L. Stevenson.
  Little Land, The. R. L. Stevenson.
  Lunatic, the Lover, and the Poet, The. *Fr.* A Midsummer Night's Dream. Shakespeare.
  Make Believe. Harry Behn.
  Mrs. Alfred Uruguay. Wallace Stevens.
  Ode to Fancy. Joseph Warton.
  One Day When We Went Walking. Hobbs.
  Pictures in the Fire. Patience Strong.
  Pleasures of Imagination, The, *sel.* Akenside.
  Power of Fancy, The. Freneau.
  Realm of Fancy, The. Keats.
  Secret Land, The. Robert Graves.
  Seein' Things. Eugene Field.
  Ships of Yule, The. Bliss Carman.
  Tell Me, Where Is Fancy Bred. *Fr.* The Merchant of Venice. Shakespeare.
  Underwood. Howard Moss.
IMMORTALITY
  Adonais, *sel.* ("He has outsoared the shadow of our night"). Shelley.
  All That Was Mortal. Teasdale.
  Complaint, The; or, Night Thoughts on Life, Death and Immortality, *sel.* Edward Young.
  Death, Be Not Proud. *Fr.* Holy Sonnets. Donne.
  I Lost the Love of Heaven. John Clare.
  If my bark sink. Emily Dickinson.
  Immortal Spirit, The. Spender.
  Immortality. Schiller, *tr. fr. German by* Kaufmann.
  In After Time. Eberhart.
  Invite to Eternity, An. John Clare.
  It is an honorable thought. Emily Dickinson.
  New Birth, The. Very.
  Not to Die. Simonides, *tr. fr. Greek by* Merivale.

  O May I Join the Choir Invisible. "George Eliot."
  Ode: Intimations of Immortality from Recollections of Early Childhood. Wordsworth.
  Of the Progresse of the Soule: The Second Anniversary. Donne.
  Recapitulation, The. Eberhart.
  Resignation, *sel.* ("There is no Death. What seems so is transition"). Longfellow.
  Resurrection and Immortality. Henry Vaughan.
  Sailing to Byzantium. Yeats.
  Saon of Acanthus. Callimachus, *tr. fr. Greek by* Symonds.
  Sudden Light. D. G. Rossetti.
  They Are All Gone into the World of Light. Henry Vaughan.
  Village Atheist, The. *Fr.* Spoon River Anthology. E. L. Masters.
INDEPENDENCE DAY. *See* FOURTH OF JULY
INDIA
  Child, The. Reginald Massey.
  In Hospital: Poona (II). Alun Lewis.
  Passage to India. Walt Whitman.
  Third Continent, The. Erulkar.
  This Landscape, These People. Zulfikar Ghose.
INDIAN SUMMER. Indian Summer. Wilfred Campbell.
INDIANA. Midwest. Nims.
INDIANS, AMERICAN
  Copperfaces, The. *Fr.* The People, Yes. Sandburg.
  Ghosts of the Buffaloes, The. Vachel Lindsay.
  Hiawatha. Sandy.
  Hiawatha's Childhood. *Fr.* The Song of Hiawatha. Longfellow.
  Indian Burying Ground, The. Freneau.
  Indian Children. Annette Wynne.
  Indian Names. Sigourney.
  Indian Reservation: Caughnawaga. A. M. Klein.
  Indians. John Fandel.
  Lullaby of the Iroquois. Pauline Johnson.
  Song on the Death of Colonel Crafford, A. *Unknown.*
  Speech of the Salish Chief. *Fr.* Damnation of Vancouver. Birney.
  Vision of a Past Warrior. Peter La Farge.
INDUSTRIAL WORKERS OF THE WORLD. There Is Power in a Union. *Unknown, at. to* Joe Hill.
INFANTS. *See* BABIES
INKWELLS. To a Post-Office Inkwell. Christopher Morley.
INNISFREE, IRELAND. Lake Isle of Innisfree, The. Yeats.
INNOCENTS, SLAUGHTER OF THE. *See* HEROD THE GREAT
INSANITY. *See* MADNESS
INSECTS. *See names of insects (e.g.,* ANTS)
INTELLECT
  Alma; or, The Progress of the Mind, *sel.* Prior.
  Brain is wider than the sky, The. Emily Dickinson.
  Cleon. Robert Browning.
  Details. Zilles.
  In This Strange House. Drewry.
  Mind. Wilbur.
  Mind Is an Enchanting Thing, The. Marianne Moore.
  My Mind to Me a Kingdom Is. Edward Dyer.
  Of a Contented Mind. Vaux.
  One Lore. Stefan George, *tr. fr. German by* Kaufmann.
  Solomon on the Vanity of the World, *sel.* ("Ye sons of men, with just regard attend"). Prior.
  Thunderstorms. W. H. Davies.
INVENTORS. Inventor's Wife, The. Mrs. E. T. Corbett.
IRELAND
  Colin Clout's Come Home Again. Spenser.
  Corrib. An Emblem. Davie.
  Easter 1916. Yeats.
  Gods of the Dana, The. L. B. Drake.
  Harp That Once through Tara's Halls, The. Thomas Moore.
  I Am of Ireland. *Unknown.*
  In Ireland: By the Pool at the Third Rosses. Arthur Symons.
  Ireland. W. S. Landor.
  Ireland with Emily. Betjeman.
  Minstrel Boy, The. Thomas Moore.
  Red Hanrahan's Song about Ireland. Yeats.
  Rose Tree, The. Yeats.
  September 1913. Yeats.
  Sweet Innisfallen. Thomas Moore.
IRIS (flower). White Iris, A. P. B. Barrington.
IRISH, THE. Boys of Wexford, The. *Unknown.*
IRONSIDES (ship). *See* CONSTITUTION
ISAIAH. Isaiah of Souillac, The. Merwin.
ISLANDS
  Enviable Isles, The. Melville.
  Islands. Ralph Pomeroy.
ISRAELOV, KHASAN. Sestina for Khasan Israelov. *Fr.* Wildtrack. Wain.
ITALY
  Canzone: "O my own Italy! though words are vain." Petrarch, *tr. fr. Italian by* Lady Dacre.
  Daisy, The. Tennyson.
  "De Gustibus." Robert Browning.
  Fragments from Italy, *sel.* Ciardi.

Hotel Paradiso e Commerciale. Brinnin.
Italy, *sels.* Samuel Rogers.
On His Return to Italy. Alamanni, *tr. fr. Italian by* Lucchi.
To Italy. Filicaja, *tr. fr. Italian by* Rendel.
To Italy. Guidiccioni, *tr. fr. Italian by* Rendel.
Written in the Euganean Hills, North Italy. Shelley.
Contemporary Italian Poetry (CoIP). Carlo L. Golino, ed.
Renaissance and Baroque Lyrics (RBL). Harold Martin Priest, ed.
IVRY-LA-BATAILLE, FRANCE. Ivry. Macaulay.
IVY
Holly against Ivy. *Unknown.*
Holly and Ivy ("Holly and ivy made a great party"). *Unknown.*
Holly and the Ivy, The ("The holly and the ivy/ When they are both full grown"). *Unknown.*
In Praise of Ivy. *Unknown.*
Nay, Ivy, Nay. *Unknown.*
To the Ivy. John Clare.

J

JACKSON, THOMAS JONATHAN (Stonewall Jackson). Brigade Must Not Know, Sir, The. *Unknown.*
JACOB. Jacob and the Angel. Brother Antoninus.
JAGUARS. Jaguar, The. Ted Hughes.
JAMES, HENRY. Henry James. R. L. Stevenson.
JAMES, JESSE
Jesse James. W. R. Benét.
Jesse James ("Jesse James was a man who killed many a man"). *Unknown.*
Jesse James ("It was on a Wednesday night, the moon was shining bright"). *Unknown.*
JANUARY
Come, January, I Give You These Treats. *Fr.* Sonnets of the Months. Folgore da San Geminiano, *tr. fr. Italian by* Gould.
January Morning, A. Lampman.
Song of January. Gerta Kennedy.
JAPAN. Japan That Sank under the Sea. Satoru Sato.
JAZZ
Jazz Fantasia. Sandburg.
Jazz of This Hotel, The. Vachel Lindsay.
Jazz Poem. C. W. Hines.
Jazzonia. Langston Hughes.
JEALOUSY. Jealousy. *Fr.* The Siege of Rhodes. Davenant.
JEANNE D'ARC. *See* JOAN OF ARC
JEFFERSON, THOMAS
Air Tunnel, Monticello. Noll.
Death of Jefferson, The. Butterworth.
Thomas Jefferson. S. V. Benét.
JEROME, SAINT. Thunderer, The. McGinley.
JERUSALEM
Jerusalem. *Fr.* Milton. Blake.
Jerusalem, My Happy Home. *Unknown.*
JESUS CHRIST
Agonie, The. George Herbert.
All in the Morning. *Unknown.*
Amid the Din of Earthly Strife. H. W. Hawkes.
And Did Those Feet in Ancient Time. *Fr.* Milton. Blake.
Approaches. George Macdonald.
Attraction. *Unknown.*
Bag, The. George Herbert.
Ballad of the Golden Bowl. S. H. Hay.
Ballad of the Goodly Fere. Pound.
Ballad of Trees and the Master, A. Sidney Lanier.
Because He Was Tempted. *Unknown.*
Birthplace. Pearson.
Bitter Withy, The. *Unknown.*
Blessing and Honor. Bonar.
Burning Babe, The. Southwell.
By Him. Jonson.
Carpenter of Galilee, The. H. W. Smith.
Charitas Nimia; or, The Deare Bargain. Crashaw.
Cherry-Tree Carol, The. *Unknown.*
Child. Sandburg.
Christ. Theodore Holmes.
Christ, The. Oxenham.
Christ Complains to Sinners. *Unknown.*
Christ for Everything. Belsham.
Christ in the Clay-Pit. Clemo.
Christ Is Coming. Macomber.
Christ of the Andes, The. Edwin Markham.
Christ with me, Christ before me, Christ behind me. *Fr.* St. Patrick. Garlick.
Christmas Folk-Song, A. L. W. Reese.
Christo Smarrito. Marino, *tr. fr. Italian by* Sherburne.

Christs Nativity. Henry Vaughan.
Christs Returne out of Egypt. Southwell.
Christ's Tear Breaks My Heart. *Unknown.*
Circumcision of Our Lord, The. *Unknown, tr. fr. French by* Aldan.
Coming Child, The. Crashaw.
Companionship. M. D. Babcock.
Cradle and the Cross, The. Reitz.
Crow and the Crane, The. *Unknown.*
Devout Prayer of the Passion, A. *Unknown.*
Discerning the Lord's Body. C. J. Montgomery.
Do We Not Hear Thy Footfall? Amy Carmichael.
Eve of Christmas, The. Kirkup.
Evil Days. Pasternak, *tr. fr. Russian by* Guerney.
Fairest Lord Jesus. *Unknown.*
Father to the Man. John Knight.
Guest, The. *Unknown.*
He Knows the Way. *Unknown.*
He Is a Path. *Fr.* Christ's Victory and Triumph. Giles Fletcher.
He Never Will Forget. "M. G. H."
He Was Not Willing. L. R. Meyer.
Head That Once Was Crowned with Thorns, The. Thomas Kelly.
Him Evermore I Behold. Longfellow.
His Hands. J. R. Moreland.
Hymn of Labor. Henry van Dyke.
Hymn of the Incarnation, A. *Unknown.*
I Heard Christ Sing. "Hugh MacDiarmid."
I Met the Master. *Unknown.*
I See His Blood upon the Rose. J. M. Plunkett.
I Turn to Jesus. O. J. Smith.
I Wonder as I Wander. *Unknown, arr. by* J. J. Niles.
If Christ Were Here To-Night. M. E. Sangster.
In the Wilderness. Robert Graves.
It Was for Me. Eva Gray.
Jesus and His Mother. Thom Gunn.
Jesus Bids Man Remember. *Unknown.*
Jesus Contrasts Man and Himself. *Unknown.*
Jesus, My Sweet Lover. *Unknown.*
Jesus Reassures His Mother. *Unknown.*
Jesus Reproaches His People. *Unknown.*
Jesus to Those Who Pass By. *Unknown.*
Journey to Golotha, The. Rao.
Killing, The. Edwin Muir.
La Corona. Donne.
Light in the Temple, The. W. R. Benét.
Little Family, The. *Unknown.*
Little Jesus. Francis Thompson.
Love Unknown. Samuel Crossman.
Love Unlike Love. *Unknown.*
Man Christ, The. Therese Lindsey.
Middle-Time, The. L. M. Fowler.
Mighty Fortress Is Our God, A. Luther, *tr. fr. German.*
Mother and Her Son on the Cross, The. *Unknown.*
Mount of Olives. Henry Vaughan.
My Dancing Day. *Unknown.*
My Friend. Buster.
My Master Was So Very Poor. Harry Lee.
Night, The ("Through that pure Virgin-shrine"). Henry Vaughan.
No East or West. Oxenham.
O Master-Workman of the Race. Stocking.
O Son of God, Afflicted. *Unknown, tr. fr. Greek by* Brownles.
O Young and Fearless Prophet. Harlow.
On Lavater's Song of a Christian to Christ. Goethe, *tr. fr. German by* Kaufmann.
One in Christ. Henry van Dyke.
Our Christ. Farrington.
Our Master. Whittier.
Out of Bounds. Tabb.
Pair of Wings, A. Stephen Hawes.
Palm-Sunday Hymn, A. Herebert.
Protagonist, The. Peter Hopegood.
Search, The. J. R. Lowell.
Search, The. Henry Vaughan.
Simon the Cyrenian Speaks. Countee Cullen.
Son, The. Edwin Muir.
Song of a Heathen, The. R. W. Gilder.
Song of Love for Jesus, A. Rolle.
Still Falls the Rain. Edith Sitwell.
Subversive. W. R. Benét.
That Holy Thing. George Macdonald.
Théorèmes Spirituels, *sels.* La Ceppède, *tr. fr. French by* Larson.
This Blessed Christ of Calvary. *Unknown.*
Thou Who Taught the Thronging People. Minde.
To Christ Crucified. Guevara, *tr. fr. Spanish by* Fletcher.
Upon the Bleeding Crucifix. Crashaw.
Upon the Body of Our Blessed Lord, Naked and Bloody. Crashaw.
Virile Christ, A. Boundy.
We Bear the Strain of Earthly Care. O. S. Davis.

JESUS CHRIST *(continued)*
  We Would See Jesus. *Unknown.*
  What Do I Have That You Seek Out My Friendship? Lope de Vega, *tr. fr. Spanish by* Flores.
  When love of us called Him to see. Crashaw.
  When Will He Come? *Unknown.*
  Windhover, The. G. M. Hopkins.
  Woefully Arrayed. *At. to* John Skelton.
  Wondrous Son of God. Goertz.
  Words of Jesus, The. W. R. Benét.
JEWS
  Alphabet, The. Karl Shapiro.
  Ark, The. Feldman.
  Breaking of the Day, The. Peter Davison.
  Chant for All the People on Earth. Hedley.
  Debate with the Rabbi. Nemerov.
  Heirloom. A. M. Klein.
  Jew. Karl Shapiro.
  Jew to Jesus, The. F. K. Frank.
  Jewish Cemetery at Newport, The. Longfellow.
  Memento. Hagelstange, *tr. fr. German by* Deutsch.
  Miserere. Pillin.
  Note in Lieu of a Suicide. Finkel.
  151st Psalm, The. Karl Shapiro.
  Permanent Delegate, The. Suhl.
  Sorely Tried Is Israel, the Hapless Folk. Jacob Bar Juda, Hazak, *tr. fr. French by* Davis.
  Still Small Voice, The. A. M. Klein.
  Summa contra Gentiles. Paris Leary.
  To Philip Levine, on the Day of Atonement. Mezey.
  Wandering Jew, The. Mezey.
  Wandering Jew, The. E. A. Robinson.
  Weeping and Singing. Tiempo, *tr. fr. Spanish by* Walsh.
  Wrack. Feldman.
JOAN OF ARC. Joan of Arc. Hugh McCrae.
JOB (Bible)
  God's Thanks to Job. *Fr.* A Masque of Reason. Robert Frost.
  Job. Elizabeth Sewell.
JOHANNESBURG, SOUTH AFRICA. Seven South African Poems, *sel.* ("Each time I return to Johannesburg it is summer"). David Wright.
JOHN, SAINT
  Peter and John. Wylie.
  Song to John, Christ's Friend, A. *Unknown.*
JOHN THE BAPTIST, SAINT
  Saint John. Coatsworth.
  Saint John the Baptist. William Drummond.
JOHNSON, SAMUEL. Epitaph on Johnson. Cowper.
JONAH
  Jonah. Thomas Blackburn.
  Jonah. Jarrell.
  Noah an' Jonah an' Cap'n John Smith. Marquis.
JONES, JOHN PAUL. Paul Jones. *Unknown.*
JONSON, BEN
  His Prayer to Ben Jonson. Herrick.
  Humble Petition of Poor Ben to the Best of Monarchs, Masters, Men, King Charles, The. Jonson.
  Ode for Ben Jonson, An. Herrick.
  Ode to Himselfe ("Come leave the loathed stage"). Jonson.
  Ode to Himselfe, An ("Where do'st thou carelesse lie"). Jonson.
  On Ben Jonson. Godolphin.
  To My Dead Friend Ben: Johnson. Henry King.
  Upon the Works of Ben Jonson, *sel.* John Oldham.
JOSEPH, SAINT
  Eve of Christmas, The. Kirkup.
  Joseph's Suspicion. Rilke, *tr. fr. German by* Norton.
JUDAS ISCARIOT
  Betrayal. Cholmondeley.
  Judas. Heym, *tr. fr. German by* Middleton.
  Judas Iscariot. Countee Cullen.
  Judas Sells His Lord. *Unknown.*
JUDGMENT DAY
  Apocalypse. E. L. Pierce.
  Judgement. George Herbert.
  Judgment Day. Oxenham.
  Remember the Day of Judgment. *Unknown.*
JUDITH (Apochrypha). On the Triumph of Judith. Lope de Vega, *tr. fr. Spanish by* Soper.
JUGGLERS
  Juggler. Wilbur.
  Juggling Jerry. George Meredith.
JUKE BOXES. King Juke. Fearing.
JULY
  July. Storm, *tr. fr. German by* Gode.
  July. Lyudmila Tatyanicheva, *tr. fr. Russian by* Deutsch.
JUNE
  And what is so rare as a day in June. *Fr.* The Vision of Sir Launfal. J. R. Lowell.
  June Morning. Hugh McCrae.
  Night in June, A. Pearson.
  Night in June, A. D. C. Scott.
JUNIPER. Sing a Song of Juniper. Robert Francis.

K

KAFKA, FRANZ. Kafka in England. Steiner, *tr. fr. German by* Hamburger.
KANGAROOS
  Kangaroo, The. *Unknown.*
  Kangaroo by Nightfall. Macainsh.
  Native Born. Langley.
  Pockets. Rowena Bennett.
  Tails. Rowena Bennett.
KANT, IMMANUEL. Kant and His Interpreters. Schiller, *tr. fr. German by* Kaufmann.
KATZENJAMMER KIDS. Katzenjammer Kids, The. Reaney.
KAYAKS. Kayak, The. *Unknown.*
KEATS, JOHN
  Adonais. Shelley.
  For John Keats, Apostle of Beauty. *Fr.* Four Epitaphs. Countee Cullen.
  Keats. Longfellow.
KENNEDY, JOHN FITZGERALD
  Assassinations 1963, The. McCarrell.
  Channel U.S.A.—Live. Stoutenburg.
  Down in Dallas. X. J. Kennedy.
  November 26, 1963. Wendell Berry.
  Of Poetry and Power (OPP). Erwin A. Glikes *and* Paul Schwaber, eds.
KENTUCKY. My Old Kentucky Home. Stephen Foster.
KIDD, WILLIAM
  Captain Kidd. S. V. Benét.
  Captain Robert Kidd. *Unknown.*
KILCASH, IRELAND. Kilcash. *Unknown, tr. fr. Irish by* O'Connor.
KILLDEERS. Nesting Ground, The. Wagoner.
KING, EDWARD
  Lycidas. Milton.
  On the Memory of Mr. Edward King, Drown'd in the Irish Seas. John Cleveland.
KIPLING, RUDYARD
  Ballad, A: "As I was walkin' the jungle round, a-killin' of tigers an' time." G. W. Carryl.
  To R. K. J. K. Stephen.
KITES
  Kite, The. Harry Behn.
  Kite, A. *Unknown.*
  Kite Is a Victim, A. Leonard Cohen.
KLONDIKE. Klondike, The. E. A. Robinson.
KNIFE-GRINDERS. Sparkles from the Wheel. Walt Whitman.
KNIGHTHOOD AND KNIGHTS
  Knight Stained from Battle, The. Herebert.
  My Lord Dragoman, If I Had a Good Steed. Vidal, *tr. fr. Provençal by* Valency.
  Old Knight, The. *Fr.* Polyhymnia. George Peele.
KOLLWITZ, KAETHE. Death Swoops. Pitchford.
KOREA
  Korea. Ristau.
  Ode for the American Dead in Korea. Thomas McGrath.
KRAKEN. Kraken, The. Tennyson.
KU KLUX KLAN. Ku-Klux. Cawein.

L

LABOR AND LABORING CLASSES
  See also Work *in* TITLE AND FIRST LINE INDEX
  Business. Guiterman.
  Daniel at Breakfast. McGinley.
  Dignity of Labor, The. Bersohn.
  Forgotten Man, The. Edwin Markham.
  Gospel of Labor, The. Henry van Dyke.
  Hymn of Labor. Henry van Dyke.
  I Hear America Singing. Walt Whitman.
  Labor Day. Pomeroy.
  Labourer, A. R. S. Thomas.
  Man with the Hoe, The. Edwin Markham.
  Quiet Work. Matthew Arnold.
  Song of the Rice Bargees. Brecht, *tr. fr. German by* Middleton.
  Song of the Shirt, The. Thomas Hood.
  Testament. Sister M. Thérèse.
  There you sit. Silverstein.
  They Who Tread the Path of Labor. Henry van Dyke.
  To Labor. C. P. S. Gilman.
  Too Old to Work. Glazer.
  Two Tramps in Mud Time. Robert Frost.
  Working Class. Warr.
  World of Work, as a Poet Would Like It to Be, The. D. H. Lawrence.

LADYBIRDS. Ladybird, Ladybird. Mother Goose.
LA FAYETTE, MARIE JOSEPH, MARQUIS DE. La Fayette. Madison.
LAKES AND PONDS
Dreaming Lake, The. Mosen, *tr. fr. German by* Jennings.
Pond, The. Droste-Hülshoff, *tr. fr. German by* Salinger.
Young Argonauts. Wingfield.
LALEMANT, GABRIEL
Martyrdom of Brébeuf and Lalemant, 16 March 1649, The. *Fr.* Brébeuf and His Brethren. E. J. Pratt.
Père Lalemant. Pickthall.
LAMB, CHARLES. This Lime-Tree Bower My Prison. S. T. Coleridge.
LAMBS
All in the April Morning. Katharine Tynan.
I Held a Lamb. Worthington.
Lamb, The. *Fr.* Songs of Innocence. Blake.
Pallid Cuckoo. David Campbell.
LANGUAGE
At a Vacation Exercise in the College, Part Latin, Part English, *sel.* Milton.
Bonne Entente. F. R. Scott.
Dirty Word, The. Karl Shapiro.
English A. Ciardi.
Hearing Russian Spoken. Davie.
Language, The. Creeley.
Language has not the power to speak what love indites. John Clare.
Many a phrase has the English language. Emily Dickinson.
Naughty Preposition, The. Morris Bishop.
Primer Lesson. Sandburg.
To a Thesaurus. F. P. Adams.
Tree of Silence, The. Vassar Miller.
Very like a Whale. Ogden Nash.
Word. Spender.
Words. Harpur.
Words. *Unknown.*
LAPRAIK, JOHN. Epistle to John Lapraik, an Old Scottish Bard. Burns.
LARACHE, MOROCCO. Capture of Larache, The. Góngora, *tr. fr. Spanish by* Fletcher.
LARKS
Caged Skylark, The. G. M. Hopkins.
For Saturday. *Fr.* Hymns for the Amusement of Children. Christopher Smart.
Lark Ascending, The. George Meredith.
Larks, The. *Fr.* Four Fascinators. Char, *tr. fr. French by* Stern.
Lark's Song, The. *Fr.* Milton. Blake.
Sea and the Skylark, The. G. M. Hopkins.
Shelley's Skylark. Thomas Hardy.
Skylark's Nest, The. R. H. Long.
To a Skylark. Shelley.
LAST SUPPER
Last Supper, The. Rilke, *tr. fr. German by* Norton.
Last Supper, The. Oscar Williams.
LATIMER, HUGH. Latimer's Light. *Unknown.*
LAUGHTER
Early Supper. Barbara Howes.
Laughing Song. *Fr.* Songs of Innocence. Blake.
Technique of Laughter, The. Kessler.
To Laughter, to Leering. Eberhart.
Why Did I Laugh. Keats.
LAURENTIAN MOUNTAINS, CANADA. Laurentian Shield. F. R. Scott.
LAWES, HENRY. To Mr. Henry Lawes. Edmund Waller.
LAWRENCE, EDWARD. To Mr. Lawrence. Milton.
LAWYERS AND LAW
Law like Love. Auden.
Legal Fiction. Empson.
LAZARUS
Dives and Lazarus. *Unknown.*
Epistle, An, Containing the Strange Medical Experience of Karshish, the Arab Physician. Robert Browning.
Malady, Death and Resurrection of Saint Lazarus. *Unknown, tr. fr. French by* Aldan.
Raising of the Dead, The. Dobson.
LEADERSHIP. Masters. Amis.
LEANDER. *See* HERO AND LEANDER
LEAR, KING. On Sitting Down to Read *King Lear* Once Again. Keats.
LEAR, EDWARD. How Pleasant to Know Mr. Lear. Lear.
LEARNING. Little Learning Is a Dangerous Thing, A. *Fr.* Essay on Criticism. Pope.
LEAVES
Beech Leaves. James Reeves.
Blue Smoke. Frances Frost.
Burning of the Leaves, The. Binyon.
Color. Cane.
Forest Leaves in Autumn, *sel.* Keble.
Gathering Leaves. Robert Frost.
Golden Bough. Wylie.
In the College of Surgeons. James Stephens.
Last Leaf, The. Harry Behn.
Leaf Fall. Leuthold, *tr. fr. German by* Wright.

Leaves. Teasdale.
Leaves Do Not Mind at All, The. Annette Wynne.
Man Raking Leaves. Stem.
Maple Leaves. Shiko, *tr. fr. Japanese by* Henderson.
Master and the Leaves, The. Thomas Hardy.
New York—Albany. Ferlinghetti.
October. Sieber.
So This Is Autumn. W. W. Watt.
Sonnet: Leaves. William Barnes.
LEDA
Leda. Darío, *tr. fr. Spanish by* Bell.
Leda. Rilke, *tr. fr. German by* Kaufmann.
Leda and the Swan. Yeats.
LEGREE, SIMON. Simon Legree—a Negro Sermon. Vachel Lindsay.
LEICESTER, ROBERT DUDLEY, EARL OF. Epitaph on the Earl of Leicester. Ralegh.
LEIF ERICSSON. Story of Vinland, The. *Fr.* Psalm of the West. Sidney Lanier.
LEISURE. Leisure. W. H. Davies.
LENT
To Keep a True Lent. Herrick.
To Search Our Souls. Lanning.
LEOPARDS. Snow-Leopard, The. Jarrell.
LEOPOLD, DUKE OF ALBANY. Death of Prince Leopold, The. McGonagall.
LEPANTO, BATTLE OF
Lepanto. G. K. Chesterton.
To Don Juan de Austria. Herrera, *tr. fr. Spanish by* Churton.
LETTERS
Going to him! Happy letter! Emily Dickinson.
Night Mail. Auden.
Way I read a letter's—this, The. Emily Dickinson.
LEVETT [*or* LEVET], ROBERT. On the Death of Dr. Robert Levet. Samuel Johnson.
LEWIS, MERIWETHER. Lewis and Clark. S. V. Benét.
LIBERTY. *See* FREEDOM
LIBERTY, STATUE OF
Bartholdi Statue, The. Whittier.
New Colossus, The. Emma Lazarus.
LICE
Immortals, The. Isaac Rosenberg.
To a Louse. Burns.
LIÈVRE RIVER, QUEBEC. Morning on the Lièvre. Lampman.
LIFE
See also Life *in* TITLE AND FIRST LINE INDEX
Ah, What of Life! Does No One Answer Me? Quevedo, *tr. fr. Spanish by* Davis.
All the World's a Stage. *Fr.* As You Like It. Shakespeare.
Alumnus Football. Grantland Rice.
Anniversary. Wain.
Bankrupt. Sayres.
Behind me—dips eternity. Emily Dickinson.
Glad World. R. D. Fitzgerald.
Human Life. Matthew Arnold.
Human Life, *sels.* Samuel Rogers.
It's in Your Face. *Unknown.*
Life. Francis Bacon.
Life's a Funny Proposition After All. G. M. Cohan.
Life's Chequer-Board. Oxenham.
Life's Lessons. *Unknown.*
Living and Dying. González Prada, *tr. fr. Spanish by* Flores.
Long Hill, The. Teasdale.
Madrigal I: "This life, which seems so fair." Guarini, *tr. fr. Italian by* Drummond of Hawthornden.
Matter of Life and Death, A. Ridler.
Nature and Life. George Meredith.
Psalm of Life, A. Longfellow.
Quickness. Henry Vaughan.
Rainy Day, The. Longfellow.
Sum of Life, The, *sel.* B. F. King.
This Life Is All Chequer'd with Pleasures and Woes. Thomas Moore.
'Tis not that dying hurts us so. Emily Dickinson.
Tomorrow, and Tomorrow. *Fr.* Macbeth. Shakespeare.
We hurry on, nor passing note. Dolben.
What Is Our Life. Ralegh.
Whist. E. F. Ware.
Willing Suspension, A. John Holmes.
LIGHT
Light. Herman Hagedorn.
Song-Offering, A. *Fr.* Gitanjali. Tagore, *tr. fr. Sanskrit by* Tagore.
LIGHTHOUSES
Flannan Isle. W. W. Gibson.
I'd Like to Be a Lighthouse. Rachel Field.
Skerryvore ("For love of lovely words"). R. L. Stevenson.
Skerryvore: The Parallel ("Here all is sunny"). R. L. Stevenson.
LIGHTNING
Lightning is a yellow fork, The. Emily Dickinson.
Local Light. Brand.
Miramichi Lightning. A. G. Bailey.

LIGURIA, ITALY. Liguria. "Vincenzo Cardarelli," *tr. fr. Italian by* Corsano.
LILACS. Lilacs. Christian Wagner, *tr. fr. German by* Singer.
LILIES
  Lilly, The. *Fr.* Songs of Experience. Blake.
  Tiger Lily. McCord.
LILITH. Body's Beauty. *Fr.* The House of Life. D. G. Rossetti.
LINCOLN, ABRAHAM
  Abraham Lincoln. S. V. Benét.
  Abraham Lincoln. Bryant.
  Abraham Lincoln Walks at Midnight. Vachel Lindsay.
  Anne Rutledge. *Fr.* Spoon River Anthology. E. L. Masters.
  For February Twelfth. M. M. Gessner.
  In Hardin County, 1809. L. E. Thompson.
  Lincoln and the Poets. W. W. Betts.
  Martyr, The. Melville.
  Nancy Hanks. Rosemary Benét.
  O Captain! My Captain! Walt Whitman.
  When Lilacs Last in the Dooryard Bloom'd. Walt Whitman.
  Would I Might Rouse the Lincoln in You All. *Fr.* Litany of the Heroes. Vachel Lindsay.
LINCOLNSHIRE, ENGLAND. High Tide on the Coast of Lincolnshire (1571), The. Ingelow.
LINNETS
  Green Linnet, The. Wordsworth.
  I Heard a Linnet Courting. Robert Bridges.
  To a Linnet in a Cage. Ledwidge.
LIONS
  Lion, The. Vachel Lindsay.
  Lion and the Mouse, The. Jeffreys Taylor.
  Why Nobody Pets the Lion at the Zoo. Ciardi.
LIPPO LIPPI, FRA. Fra Lippo Lippi. Robert Browning.
LITTLE ROCK, ARKANSAS. Chicago *Defender* Sends a Man to Little Rock, Fall, 1957, The. Gwendolyn Brooks.
LLAMAS. Llama, The. Hilaire Belloc.
LOCOMOTIVES. To a Locomotive in Winter. Walt Whitman.
LOCUSTS. Locust, The. *Tr. fr. Zuni Indian by* Cushing.
LODORE, ENGLAND. How the Waters Come Down at Lodore. Southey.
LONDON, ENGLAND
  See also London *in* TITLE AND FIRST LINE INDEX
  Barrel-Organ, The. Noyes.
  Bells of London, The. *Unknown.*
  Composed upon Westminster Bridge. Wordsworth.
  Description of a View. Empson.
  Description of London, A. John Banks.
  Farewell to London, A. Pope.
  Important Statement. Patrick Kavanagh.
  London Snow. Robert Bridges.
  Simplicity's Song. Robert Wilson.
  West London. Matthew Arnold.
  Who Calls the English Cold? *Fr.* London Sonnets. Bode.
LONELINESS
  Alone. Sassoon.
  Bare Arms of Trees, The. Tagliabue.
  Bereft. Robert Frost.
  Blown Newspaper, A. "Will Inman."
  Desert Places. Robert Frost.
  Desolate. Sydney Dobell.
  Dove's Loneliness, The. Darley.
  I explain the silvered passing of a ship at night. *Fr.* War Is Kind. Stephen Crane.
  Loneliness. Hashin, *tr. fr. Japanese by* Henderson.
  Search. Souster.
  To Marguerite. *Fr.* Switzerland. Matthew Arnold.
LONGFELLOW, HENRY WADSWORTH. Poe and Longfellow. *Fr.* A Fable for Critics. J. R. Lowell.
LONGLEAT HOUSE. Stanzas on a Visit to Longleat House in Wiltshire, October 1953. George Barker.
LORD'S SUPPER. *See* EUCHARIST
LOTUS
  He is like the Lotus. *Fr.* Book of the Dead. *Unknown, tr. fr. Egyptian by* Hillyer.
  Lotus-Eaters, The. Tennyson.
  Lotus-flower is frightened, The. Heine, *tr. fr. German by* Wright.
LOUIS XIII, KING OF FRANCE. To Louis XIII. Malherbe, *tr. fr. French by* Giese.
LOUISBURG, NOVA SCOTIA. Louisburg. *Unknown.*
LOUSE. *See* LICE
LOVE
  Book of Love Poems, A (BoLP). William Cole, ed.
  Erotic Poetry (ErPo). William Cole, ed.
  Modern Love Poems (MoLP). D. J. Klemer, ed.
  Uninhibited Treasury of Erotic Poetry (UnTE). Louis Untermeyer, ed.
LOWELL, JAMES RUSSELL. Lowell. *Fr.* A Fable for Critics. J. R. Lowell.
LUCIFER. *See* SATAN
LULLABIES
  See also Cradle Song *and* Lullaby *in* TITLE AND FIRST LINE INDEX
  Christmas Cradlesong, A. Lope de Vega, *tr. fr. Spanish by* Ticknor.
  Dutch Lullaby, A. Eugene Field.
  Mother by the Cradle, The. Matthias Claudius, *tr. fr. German by* Wright.
  Phantasmion, *sel.* ("O sleep, my babe, hear not the rippling wave"). S. T. Coleridge.
  Sleep, baby, sleep. *Unknown, tr. fr. German by* Owen.
  Slumber Song. Brentano, *tr. fr. German by* Jennings.
  Sweet and Low. *Fr.* The Princess. Tennyson.
LUMBERING AND LUMBERMEN
  Jam at Gerry's Rocks, The. *Unknown.*
  Jim the Splitter. Henry Kendall.
  Logs, The. C. G. D. Roberts.
  Lumberman's Life, The. *Unknown.*
  Paul's Wife. Robert Frost.
  Peter Ambelay. *Unknown.*
LUPIN. Lupin. Humbert Wolfe.
LUSITANIA (ship). S.S. Lusitania. Matthew Arnold.
LUTES. To His Lute. William Drummond.
LYNCHING
  Between the World and Me. Richard Wright.
  Man Hunt, The. Cawein.
  Swimmers, The. Allen Tate.
LYRES
  Enchanted Lyre, The. Darley.
  Supplication, A. Cowley.
LYREBIRDS
  Lyre-Bird, The. Roland Robinson.
  Lyrebirds. Judith Wright.

M

MACHADO, ANTONIO. Portrait. Machado, *tr. fr. Spanish by* Bell.
MACHINERY
  Egg and the Machine, The. Robert Frost.
  Steam Shovel. Malam.
  Steam Threshing-Machine, The. Tennyson-Turner.
  Trial Run, A. Robert Frost.
MADNESS
  Brain, within it's groove, The. Emily Dickinson.
  Hatters, The. Nan McDonald.
  Mad Maid's Whim. Stow.
  Madman, The. Urdang.
  Mental Cases. Wilfred Owen.
  Much madness is divinest sense. Emily Dickinson.
  On a Painting by Patient B of the Independence State Hospital for the Insane. Justice.
  Once on a Certain Nameless Town. Cardenal, *tr. fr. Provençal by* Bergin.
  Tom o' Bedlam's Song. *Unknown.*
MAGI
  Gift, The. W. C. Williams.
  Hymne for the Epiphanie, A. Sung as by the Three Kings. Crashaw.
  Journey of the Magi. T. S. Eliot.
  Kings from the East, The. Heine, *tr. fr. German into Scottish by* Gray.
  Magi, The. W. B. Yeats.
  Poem for Epiphany. Norman Nicholson.
  Three Kings, The. Longfellow.
MAGIC
  Fairy Story. B. E. Todd.
  La Belle Dame sans Merci. Keats.
MAGNOLIAS. Magnolia Tree in Summer. Sacheverell Sitwell.
MAGPIES. Camden Magpie. Hugh McCrae.
MALACHI. Malachi. Marlatt.
MALACHY, SAINT. St. Malachy. Merton.
MAN
  All the Flowers of the Spring. *Fr.* The Devil's Law Case. John Webster.
  All the World's a Stage. *Fr.* As You Like It. Shakespeare.
  Before the Beginning of Years. *Fr.* Atalanta in Calydon. Swinburne.
  Birds Are in the Air at East. Quevedo, *tr. fr. Spanish by* Davis.
  Cant. W. H. Davies.
  Cantata for Two Lovers. Helga Sandburg.
  Contemplations. Bradstreet.
  Divine Ship Sails the Divine Sea for You, The. Walt Whitman.
  Essay on Man, *sels.* Pope.
  Fish, the Man, and the Spirit, The, *sels.* Leigh Hunt.
  For A' That and A' That. Burns.
  Human Seasons, The. Keats.
  Hymn to Earth. Wylie.
  I Sing the Body Electric. Walt Whitman.

Invocation: "O world watched over by the cold moon and the mindless stars." Drewry.
It Is Not Growing like a Tree. *Fr.* A Pindaric Ode. Jonson.
Like as the Damask Rose You See. *Unknown.*
Like Flowers We Spring. *Unknown.*
Man. George Herbert.
Man. Henry Vaughan.
Man, Man, Man. *Unknown.*
Man Meeting Himself. *Fr.* The Leaves of Europe. Sergeant.
Man Was Made to Mourn; a Dirge. Burns.
Manhood. *Fr.* The Pageants of Thomas More. Thomas More.
Man's a Bubble. Dodsley.
Measure of a Man. *Unknown.*
Measuring a Man. *Unknown.*
Meditatio. Pound.
Men. Dorothy Parker.
Microcosm, The. Guarini, *tr. fr. Italian by* Sherburne.
New Being, The. Patchen.
Of Dust and Stars. Vernon Ward.
On Man. W. S. Landor.
One's-Self I Sing. Walt Whitman.
Our birth is but a sleep and a forgetting. *Fr.* Ode: Intimations of Immortality from Recollections of Early Childhood. Wordsworth.
Pity This Busy Monster, Manunkind. E. E. Cummings.
Poem: "And this digester, this digester of food." *Fr.* Time in the Rock. Conrad Aiken.
Salutation, The. Traherne.
Sans Equity and sans Poise. *Fr.* The Classic Anthology: Yung Wind. Confucius, *tr. fr. Chinese by* Pound.
Satire against Mankind, A. Earl of Rochester.
Sic Vita. Henry King.
Sonnet: "Unhappy man, as soon as he is born." Marino, *tr. fr. Italian by* Lucchi.
Truant, The. E. J. Pratt.
Up from the Bed of the River. *Fr.* The Creation. J. W. Johnson.
What a Piece of Work Is a Man. *Fr.* Antigone. Sophocles, *tr. fr. Greek by* Lucas.
Words Made of Water. Burns Singer.
MANTIS
Don't Sit under the Apple Tree with Anyone Else but Me. Robert Pack.
Praying Mantis. Stefanile.
MAPLE SYRUP
Maple Feast. Frances Frost.
Sugaring, The. A. M. Klein.
MAPS
Ancient Chinese Map of the World. Schmied, *tr. fr. German by* Middleton.
Map, The. Elizabeth Bishop.
Map, The. Oden.
Mappemounde. Birney.
Mermaids. *Fr.* The Atlas. Slessor.
Private Letter to Brazil, A. Oden.
MARC ANTONY *See* ANTONY
MARCH
In March. Philip Martin.
In March, for You a Gift of Fish I Boast. *Fr.* Sonnets of the Months. Folgore da San Geminiano, *tr. fr. Italian by* Gould.
Merry Month of March, The. Wordsworth.
Thorn Leaves in March. Merwin.
MARCKHAM, LADY BRIDGET. Elegy on the Lady Marckham. Donne.
MARGARET OF NAVARRE. Marot to the Queen of Navarre. Marot, *tr. fr. French by* Carrington.
MARIB, YEMEN. High Place at Marib, The. Code.
MARIGOLDS. Marigold, The. Wither.
MARION, FRANCIS. Song of Marion's Men. Bryant.
MARKETING. Miss Thompson Goes Shopping. Martin Armstrong.
MARKIEWICZ, CONSTANCE GEORGINE, COUNTESS. In Memory of Eva Gore-Booth and Con Markiewicz. Yeats.
MARLBOROUGH, JOHN CHURCHILL, 1ST DUKE OF. Satirical Elegy on the Death of a Late Famous General, A. Swift.
MARLOWE, CHRISTOPHER. Marlowe. Bayldon.
MAROT, CLÉMENT. Dizain to Clement Marot. Margaret of Navarre, *tr. fr. French by* Thorley.
MARRIAGE
See also Marriage *and* Wedding *in* TITLE AND FIRST LINE INDEX
Adversaries. Louis Johnson.
After Our Wedding Day. Heine, *tr. fr. German by* Kaufmann.
Anniversary. R. S. Thomas.
Any Wife to Any Husband. Robert Browning.
At the Wedding March. G. M. Hopkins.
Ballad of the Despairing Husband. Creeley.
Balad upon a Wedding, A. Suckling.
But That Is Another Story. Justice.
Curate's Kindness, The. Thomas Hardy.

Disappointed Wife, The. Hetty Wright.
Epigram: "How many drag the marriage chain." Royall Tyler.
Epitaph upon a Young Married Couple Dead and Buried Together, An. Crashaw.
Epithalamion. Spenser.
Epithalamion Made at Lincolnes Inne. Donne.
Eurynome. Jay Macpherson.
His Mother's [*or* Wife's] Wedding Ring. Crabbe.
Hokku: "Persimmon, The, lo!" Chiyo, *tr. fr. Japanese by* Page.
Investment, The. Robert Frost.
Jealous Wife, The. Scannell.
Love and Marriage. Mathew.
Lucky Marriage, The. Thomas Blackburn.
Mehitabel Tries Marriage. *Fr.* Archys Life of Mehitabel. Marquis.
Men Marry What They Need. I Marry You. Ciardi.
Most like an Arch This Marriage. Ciardi.
My Wife. R. L. Stevenson.
New Ring, The. Karl Shapiro.
Newlyweds, The. Criswell.
Nuptiall Song, or Epithalamie, on Sir Clipseby Crew and His Lady, A. Herrick.
Our Happy Home. *Unknown.*
Perfect Husband, The. Ogden Nash.
Poem in Prose. MacLeish.
Progress of Marriage, The. Swift.
Prothalamion. Spenser.
Sandgate Girl's Lamentation, The. *Unknown.*
Song for a Marriage. Vassar Miller.
Thinker, The. W. C. Williams.
To Have and Too Old. Armour.
To My Dear and Loving Husband. Bradstreet.
Unthrift. *Fr.* The Angel in the House. Coventry Patmore.
Upon the Death of Sir Albertus Morton's Wife. Henry Wotton.
Washing the Dishes. Christopher Morley.
Why Should a Foolish Marriage Vow. *Fr.* Marriage a-la-Mode. Dryden.
Wife, The. Creeley.
Young Wife, A. D. H. Lawrence.
MARS (god). Song of Momus to Mars, The. *Fr.* The Secular Masque. Dryden.
MARSHES
Laggandoan, Harris. MacCaig.
Marsh, The. W. D. Snodgrass.
Marshes of Glynn, The. Sidney Lanier.
MARSUPIALS. Are You a Marsupial? John Becker.
MARTIN, SAINT. St. Martin and the Beggar. Thom Gunn.
MARTYRS
Martyrdom of Bishop Farrar, The. Ted Hughes.
On the Late Massacre in Piedmont. Milton.
Sebastian. Baro.
Through the straight pass of suffering. Emily Dickinson.
MARY, THE VIRGIN
Aishah-Schechinah. Hawker.
Annunciation, The. Merwin.
Annunciation, The. *Unknown.*
At Dawn the Virgin Is Born. Lope de Vega, *tr. fr. Spanish by* Merwin.
Birth of Mary. Rilke, *tr. fr. German by* Norton.
Cherry-Tree Carol, The. *Unknown.*
Christo Smarrito. Marino, *tr. fr. Italian by* Sherburne.
Death of Our Ladie, The. Southwell.
Devout Man Prays to His Relations, The. Herebert.
Five Joys of Mary, The. *Unknown.*
Her Nativity. Southwell.
Hymn to Mary, A. William Dunbar.
Hymn to Mary, A. *Unknown.*
I Sing of a Maiden. *Unknown.*
In Praise of Mary. *Unknown.*
Jesus and His Mother. Thom Gunn.
Jesus Comforts His Mother. *Unknown.*
Jesus Reassures His Mother. *Unknown.*
Little Hymn to Mary, A. *Unknown.*
Lullay My Liking. *Unknown.*
Mary Complains to Other Mothers. *Unknown.*
Mary Is with Child. *Unknown.*
Mary, Queen of Heaven. *Unknown.*
Mary Tired. Pickthall.
Mary's Girlhood. D. G. Rossetti.
May Magnificat, The. G. M. Hopkins.
Mother and Her Son on the Cross, The. *Unknown.*
New Song of Mary, A. *Unknown.*
On the Assumption. Crashaw.
On the Blessed Virgin's Bashfulness. Crashaw.
Penitent Hopes in Mary, The. *Unknown.*
Quia Amore Langueo. *Unknown.*
Sonetto XXXV: To Guido Orlando. Cavalcanti, *tr. fr. Italian by* Pound.
Song XVIII: "In order to remove us." Alfonso X, *tr. fr. Portuguese by* Keller.

MARY, THE VIRGIN (continued)
Song VII: "We should love Saint Mary." Alfonso X, tr. fr. Portuguese by Keller.
Song for the Virgin Mary. Unknown, tr. fr. German by Yorck and Elmslie.
Song to Mary, A. William of Shoreham(?).
Sweet Was the Song. Unknown.
To the Virgin. Rutebeuf, tr. fr. French by Tobin.
Virgine Maries Conception, The. Southwell.
Visitation, The. Elizabeth Jennings.
Visitation, The. Southwell.
Where Are You Going, Maiden? Lope de Vega, tr. fr. Spanish by Merwin.
MARY, QUEEN OF SCOTS. Alas! Poor Queen. Angus.
MARY MAGDALEN
And She Washed His Feet with Her Tears, and Wiped Them with the Hairs of Her Head. Sherburne, after the Italian of Marino.
Lent. Rodgers.
Magdalene. Pasternak, tr. fr. Russian by Guerney.
Marie Magdalene. George Herbert.
Marie Magdalens Complaint at Christs Death. Southwell.
Mary Magdalene's Song. Unknown, tr. fr. German by Yorck and Elmslie.
Weeper, The. Crashaw.
MATCHES. Match, The. Ponge, tr. fr. French by Blaise.
MATHEMATICS. Arithmetic. Sandburg.
MATHER, COTTON. Cotton Mather. S. V. Benét.
MATTERHORN
High Brow. Fitch.
Zermatt: To the Matterhorn. Thomas Hardy.
MAXIMILIAN, EMPEROR OF MEXICO. Manet: The Execution of Emperor Maximilian. W. D. Snodgrass.
MAY
See also May and May Day in TITLE AND FIRST LINE INDEX
Among Sweet Tones in Forest Bowers. Ulrich von Lichtenstein, tr. fr. German by Oliver.
Corinna's Going a Maying. Herrick.
Glycine's Song. S. T. Coleridge.
Home-Thoughts from Abroad. Robert Browning.
I Never Saw the Field. Neidhart von Reuental, tr. fr. German by Richey.
Judgment of the May, The. R. W. Dixon.
Love in May. Passerat, tr. fr. French by Lang.
May Magnificat, The. G. M. Hopkins.
May Song. Lope de Vega, tr. fr. Spanish by Flores.
Now Has Come the Gracious Month of May. Christine de Pisan, tr. fr. French by Kittel.
Season's Here, The! Neidhart von Reuental, tr. fr. German by Richey.
Song: On May Morning. Milton.
Vow to Cupid, The. Unknown, tr. fr. Latin by Symonds.
MEADOWSWEET. Meadowsweet. Allingham.
MEDICI, FERDINAND DE'. Statue and the Bust, The. Robert Browning.
MEDITERRANEAN SEA. Mediterranean, The. Allen Tate.
MELAMPUS. Melampus. George Meredith.
MELANCHOLY
See also Melancholy in TITLE AND FIRST LINE INDEX
Il Penseroso. Milton.
Ode on Melancholy. Keats.
MELEAGER. Meleager. Fr. Metamorphoses. Ovid, tr. fr. Latin by Golding.
MELVILLE, HERMAN
At Melville's Tomb. Hart Crane.
Letter for Melville 1951. Charles Olson.
MEMORIAL DAY
Decoration Day. Longfellow.
March, The. Squire.
May Thirtieth. Unknown.
Memorial Day. Theodosia Garrison.
MEMORY
See also Memory in TITLE AND FIRST LINE INDEX
Ballade-Catalogue of Lovely Things, A. Le Gallienne.
Coin, The. Teasdale.
I Remember, I Remember. Thomas Hood.
Memories. Whittier.
Memory as Memorial in the Last. Edward Marshall.
Oft in the Stilly Night. Thomas Moore.
Old Familiar Faces, The. Charles Lamb.
Remember. C. G. Rossetti.
Remembrances. John Clare.
Song of My Heart, A. Robert Bridges.
To Memory. M. E. Coleridge.
Tune, A. Arthur Symons.
When to the sessions of sweet silent thought. Sonnets, XXX. Shakespeare.
MEMPHIS, TENNESSEE. Beale Street, Memphis. Thurmond Snyder.
MEN. See MAN
MERCY
Ode to Mercy. William Collins.
Quality of mercy is not strain'd, The. Fr. The Merchant of Venice. Shakespeare.

Song for an Allegorical Play. Ciardi.
MERLIN. See Merlin in TITLE AND FIRST LINE INDEX
MERMAID TAVERN. Lines on the Mermaid Tavern. Keats.
MERMAIDS AND MERMEN
Forsaken Merman, The. Matthew Arnold.
Mermaid, The. Unknown.
Mermaiden's Vesper Hymn, The. Fr. Syren Songs. Darley.
Mermaids. Fr. The Atlas. Slessor.
My Cabinets Are Oyster-Shells. Duchess of Newcastle.
Sam. De la Mare.
Santorin. Flecker.
METHUSELAH. Methuselah. Fr. The Devil and the Angel. R. de B. Dobson.
MEXICAN WAR
Bivouac of the Dead, The. Theodore O'Hara.
Monterey. C. F. Hoffman.
Santy Anna. Unknown.
What Mr. Robinson Thinks. Fr. The Biglow Papers. J. R. Lowell.
MEZERAY, FRANÇOIS EUDES DE. Written in the Beginning of Mezeray's History of France. Prior.
MICE
See also Mouse in TITLE AND FIRST LINE INDEX
Diary of a Church Mouse. Betjeman.
Four III. E. E. Cummings.
Funeral Oration for a Mouse. Alan Dugan.
House of the Mouse, The. L. S. Mitchell.
Lion and the Mouse, The. Jeffreys Taylor.
Little Fable. Roy Fuller.
Madam Mouse Trots. Edith Sitwell.
Mice. Fyleman.
New Strain. George Starbuck.
To a Mouse. Burns.
MICHELANGELO
David. Michelangelo, tr. fr. Italian by Priest.
In the Sistina. C. F. Meyer, tr. fr. German by Kaufmann.
On Buonarroti's Statue of Night. Strozzi, tr. fr. Italian by Priest.
On the Painting of the Sistine Chapel. Michelangelo, tr. fr. Italian by Symonds.
To Vittoria Colonna. Michelangelo, tr. fr. Italian by Priest.
MIDAS
King Midas. Fr. Metamorphoses. Ovid, tr. fr. Latin by Golding.
Ungrateful Garden, The. Kizer.
MIDDLE AGE
At Thirty Years. Piontek, tr. fr. German by Hamburger.
Middle-aged, The. Adrienne Rich.
MIGNONETTE
Pitcher of Mignonette, A. H. C. Bunner.
Red Geranium and Godly Mignonette. D. H. Lawrence.
MILKMEN. Milkman, The. Krows.
MILKWEED. Two Voices in a Meadow. Wilbur.
MILLS AND MILLERS
Journeyman's Song, The. Wilhelm Müller, tr. fr. German by Owen.
Miller's Song, The. Unknown.
MILTON, JOHN
Johannes Milton, Senex. Robert Bridges.
London, 1802. Wordsworth.
Milton, sel. Blake.
Milton. Longfellow.
Milton's Prayer for Patience. E. L. Howell.
On Mr. Milton's Paradise Lost, sel. Marvell.
On Seeing a Lock of Milton's Hair. Keats.
Rhapsody to Milton. Sneyd Davies.
To the Ghost of John Milton. Sandburg.
MIND. See INTELLECT
MINING AND MINERS. See COAL MINING AND MINERS; GOLD MINING AND MINERS
MINISTERS OF THE GOSPEL. See CLERGY
MIRACLES
Higher Calling, The. Czamanske.
Miracle for Breakfast, A. Elizabeth Bishop.
Miracles. Walt Whitman.
MIRRORS. Hand-Mirror, A. Walt Whitman.
MISSISSIPPI RIVER. River, The. Fr. The Bridge. Hart Crane.
MISSOURI (state). Missouri Rhapsody. James Daugherty.
MISSOURI RIVER. Others May Praise What They Like. Walt Whitman.
MIST
Mist. Thoreau.
See also FOG; HAZE
MITHRIDATES THE GREAT. Mithridates. Emerson.
MOLES
Dead Mole, A. Andrew Young.
Eagle and the Mole, The. Wylie.
Mole. W. J. Smith.
MONASTERIES
Trappist Abbey, The: Matins. Merton.
Semblables, The. W. C. Williams.
MONEY
American Change. Allen Ginsberg.

As I Sat at the Café. A. H. Clough.
Avarice. George Herbert.
Dialogue. Nemerov.
Mighty Lord Is Money, A. Quevedo, *tr. fr. Spanish by* Davis.
Money. Armour.
Money Is What Matters. *Unknown.*
Of Money. Googe.
Song to His Purse for the King, A. Chaucer.
Spectator ab Extra. Clough.
Wilt Thou Lend Me Thy Mare? *Unknown.*
Your Money and Mine. *Unknown.*
MONITOR (ship)
Cruise of the *Monitor,* The. Boker.
Utilitarian View of the *Monitor*'s Fight, A. Melville.
MONKEYS
Monkey, The. Khodasevich, *tr. fr. Russian by* Deutsch.
So Many Monkeys. Edey *and* Grider.
Tails. Rowena Bennett.
Three Monkeys. *Unknown.*
MONKS
Elegy for the Monastery Barn. Merton.
Practical Program for Monks. Merton.
Soliloquy of the Spanish Cloister. Robert Browning.
Stanzas from the Grande Chartreuse. Matthew Arnold.
MONMOUTH, BATTLE OF. Molly Pitcher. L. E. Richards.
MONT BLANC. Mont Blanc. Shelley.
MONTERREY, MEXICO. Monterey. C. F. Hoffman.
MONTHS
Months, The. Sara Coleridge.
Months, The. C. G. Rossetti.
Thirty Days Hath September. *Unknown.*
MONTICELLO, VIRGINIA. Air Tunnel, Monticello. Noll.
MONTREAL, CANADA
Montreal. A. M. Klein.
Psalm of Montreal, A. Samuel Butler.
MONTROSE, JAMES GRAHAM, 5TH EARL OF. Execution of Montrose, The. Aytoun.
MOON
See also MOON *in* TITLE AND FIRST LINE INDEX
Above the Dock. Hulme.
Ah Moon, You Shine Too Long. Christine de Pisan, *tr. fr. French by* Kittel.
Cat and the Moon, The. Yeats.
Denunciation. Schnurre, *tr. fr. German by* Hamburger.
Encounter. Ted Hughes.
February Moon. Wilhelm Lehmann, *tr. fr. German by* Hamburger.
Golden Bird, The. Ingamells.
Harvest Moon, The. Longfellow.
Harvest Moon. Ryota, *tr. fr. Japanese by* Henderson.
Horseman, The. De la Mare.
In the Moonlight. Patchen.
Look Down Fair Moon. Walt Whitman.
Lunae Custodiens. Lin Carter.
Man in the Moon, The. *Unknown.*
May Moon. Driver.
Mr. Moon. Bliss Carman.
Moon and Fog. Derleth.
Moon in September, The. Kashiprosad Ghose.
Moon in the Mountains, The. Chen Shan-min, *tr. fr. Chinese by* Edwards.
Moon in the Water, The. Ryota, *tr. fr. Japanese.*
Moon is distant from the sea, The. Emily Dickinson.
Moon's the North Wind's Cooky, The. Vachel Lindsay.
My Wish. Patience Strong.
Myths. Schmied, *tr. fr. German by* Hesse.
New Moon in January. Ted Hughes.
On the Eclipse of the Moon of October 1865. Tennyson-Turner.
Pale Cold Moon, The. Renton.
Plain Man, The. F. B. Hanes.
Riddle #29: The Moon and the Sun. *Unknown, tr. fr. Anglo-Saxon by* Raffel.
Shiny. James Reeves.
Silver. De la Mare.
Summer Moonlight. Patience Strong.
To the Moon. Shelley.
To the Moon. Wordsworth.
Turn of the Moon. Robert Graves.
Wandering Moon, The. James Reeves.
Watching the Moon. McCord.
White in the moon the long road lies. *Fr.* A Shropshire Lad. A. E. Housman.
White Moon, The. Verlaine, *tr. fr. French by* Flores.
Wind and the Moon, The. George Macdonald.
With How Sad Steps, O Moon! Thou Climb'st the Skies. *Fr.* Astrophel and Stella. Philip Sidney.
MOORE, SIR JOHN. Burial of Sir John Moore at Corunna, The. Charles Wolfe.
MOOSE. Love Life (and Death) of a Moose, The. Armour.
MOPOKES. Mopoke. Lavater.
MORISON, SIR HENRY. To the Immortall Memorie, and Friendship of That Noble Paire, Sir Lucius Cary, and Sir H. Morison. Jonson.

MORNING
Beginning of Day, The. Euripides, *tr. fr. Greek.*
Description of the Morning, A. Swift.
Early Astir. H. E. Read.
Early Rising. Saxe.
Field of Light, A. Roethke.
Full many a glorious morning have I seen. Sonnets, XXXIII. Shakespeare.
Haze. Buson, *tr. fr. Japanese by* Henderson.
Hymn to the Morning, An. Leapor.
Impression du Matin. Oscar Wilde.
January Morning, A. Lampman.
June Morning. Hugh McCrae.
Matins. Levertov.
Morning. Emily Dickinson.
Morning at the Window. T. S. Eliot.
Morning comes to the consciousness, The. *Fr.* Preludes. T. S. Eliot.
'Morning, Morning. Mathew.
Morning Song, A. Farjeon.
Morning Sun. MacNeice.
No Time for Poetry. Julia Fields.
Ode to Morning. William Mason.
Reveille. A. E. Housman.
Small Song. Frances Frost.
Softly, Drowsily. De la Mare.
Summer Morning. John Clare.
Summer Morning, A. Rachel Field.
To Morning. Blake.
Turning. Robert Finch.
Very Early. Kuskin.
See also DAWN; SUNRISE
MORRIS, WILLIAM. Rondel: "Behold the works of William Morris." *Unknown.*
MORTON, SIR ALBERTUS. Tears at the Grave of Sir Albertus Morton. Henry Wotton.
MOSES
Angels Came a-Mustering, The. *Unknown, tr. fr. Hebrew by* Zangwill.
Eleventh Commandment, The, *sel.* ("When Moses came down from the mountain and the cloud"). John Holmes.
Go Down, Moses. *Unknown.*
Murder of Moses, The. Karl Shapiro.
MOTHER
See also Mother *in* TITLE AND FIRST LINE INDEX
Are All the Children In? *Unknown.*
At My Mother's Knee. *Unknown.*
Certain True Woords Spoken Concerning One Benet Corbett after Her Death. Richard Corbett.
Childless Woman in Heaven, The. Katharine Tynan.
Division of Parts, The. Sexton.
God's Ideal Mother. Pinkham.
Keine Lazarovitch. Layton.
Lord Christ, My Darling Is So Dear. Hansen-Bay.
Mary Complains to Other Mothers. *Unknown.*
Mother is a Sun, A. Peggy Bennett.
Mother o' Mine. Kipling.
My Mother. *Unknown.*
My Mother's Love. *Unknown.*
Night and Morning. Dorothy Aldis.
Oedipus at San Francisco. Finkel.
On the Receipt of My Mother's Picture Out of Norfolk. Cowper.
Piano. D. H. Lawrence.
Sick Child, The. R. L. Stevenson.
Song for a Fifth Child. R. H. Hamilton.
Song of the Old Mother. Yeats.
To My Mother. George Barker.
To My Mother. Louis Ginsberg.
To My Mother. Poe.
To Whom Shall They Go? *Unknown.*
When a Girl Looks Down. Kay Smith.
MOTHS. Where More Is Meant. Christopher Morley.
MOTION PICTURES. Horror Movie. Howard Moss.
MOTORCYCLES AND MOTORCYCLING
Lordly and Isolate Satyrs, The. Charles Olson.
On the Move. Thom Gunn.
Unsettled Motorcyclist's Vision of His Death, The. Thom Gunn.
MOUNTAINS. *See* HILLS AND MOUNTAINS
MOUSE. *See* MICE
MOVIES. *See* MOTION PICTURES
MUD
Colloquy in Black Rock. Robert Lowell.
Mud. Boyden.
MULES. Water Wheel, The. Machado, *tr. fr. Spanish by* Duffy.
MUMPS. Mumps. E. M. Roberts.
MUSEUMS
Municipal Gallery Revisited, The. Yeats.
Museum Piece. Wilbur.
MUSHROOMS
Mushroom is the elf of plants, The. Emily Dickinson.
Mushrooms. Plath.

N

NEVILLE, ALEXANDER. To Alexander Neville. Googe.
NEW ENGLAND
  Citizens in the Round. R. P. T. Coffin.
  Mayflower. Conrad Aiken.
  New England. E. A. Robinson.
NEW GUINEA. New Guinea. McAuley.
NEW HAMPSHIRE
  New Hampshire. *Fr.* Landscapes. T. S. Eliot.
  New Hampshire. Donald Hall.
NEW ORLEANS, BATTLE OF. Battle of New Orleans, The.
  T. D. English.
NEW YEAR
  Another Year. Havergal.
  Another Year. O. J. Smith.
  At the New Year. Patchen.
  Cheerful Welcome, A. *Unknown.*
  Death of the Old Year, The, *sel.* Tennyson.
  End of the Year, The. Su T'ung-po, *tr. fr. Chinese by*
    Rexroth.
  Gates of the Year, The. J. M. Hull.
  Happy New Year! Happy New Year! *Unknown.*
  I Buried the Year. Luff.
  Invocation for the New Year. M. D. Armstrong.
  January 1. Marnie Pomeroy.
  New Year, The. *Unknown.*
  New Year Carol, A. *Unknown.*
  New Year Idyl, A, *sel.* Eugene Field.
  New Year Wishes. Sarton.
  New yeares, expect new gifts: Sister, your harpe. Jonson.
  New Year's Day. Rachel Field.
  New Year's Day. Robert Lowell.
  New Year's Poem. Avison.
  New Year's Wishes. Havergal.
  Parable, A. Kress.
  Resolutions?—New and Old. H. E. Rolfe.
  Ring out, wild bells, to the wild sky. *Fr.* In Memoriam
    A.H.H. Tennyson.
  Secular Masque, The. Dryden.
  Up the Hill, down the Hill. Farjeon.
  Wassail Song, The. *Unknown.*
  Wish for the New Year, A. Phillips Brooks.
  Year's End. Wilbur.
NEW YORK (city)
  Avenue Bearing the Initial of Christ into the New World,
    The. Kinnell.
  B Negative. X. J. Kennedy.
  Ferry Ride. Selma Robinson.
  Greenwich Village Saturday Night. Feldman.
  Imprisoned, The. Robert Fitzgerald.
  Letter to N. Y. Elizabeth Bishop.
  Manhatten Skyline. Kayden.
  Storm on Fifth Avenue. Sassoon.
NEW ZEALAND
  Colonist in His Garden, A. W. P. Reeves.
  In Town. D. M. Wright.
  It was a wondrous realm beguiled. *Fr.* Ranolf and Amohia.
    Domett.
  Long Harbour, The. Bethell.
NEWSPAPERS
  Newspaper is a collection of half-injustices, A. *Fr.* War Is
    Kind. Stephen Crane.
  Sunday Edition. J. J. Keith.
NEWSREELS. Newsreel. Day Lewis.
NEWTON, SIR ISAAC. On Mr. Nash's Picture. Jane Brereton.
NIAGARA FALLS. Niagara. Sigourney.
NIBELUNGEN LEGENDS. Hagen's Dying Song. Dahn, *tr. fr.*
  German by Kaufmann.
NIETZSCHE, FRIEDRICH WILHELM
  Another Poem on Nietzsche. Stefan George, *tr. fr. German*
    by Kaufmann.
  Nietzsche. Stefan George, *tr. fr. German by* Kaufmann.
  To Nietzsche. Morgenstern, *tr. fr. German by* Kaufmann.
NIGHT
  See also Night *in* TITLE AND FIRST LINE INDEX
  Acquainted with the Night. Robert Frost.
  By the Fire. Coatsworth.
  Check. James Stephens.
  City, The: Midnight. Dawe.
  Countryside Sleeps, Trembling, The. Jiménez, *tr. fr. Span-*
    ish by Roach.
  Day and Night. Dhingra.
  Day and Night. Anne Lindsay.
  Day Is Done, The. Longfellow.
  Deep Summer, after Midnight. Stem.
  Domination of Black. Wallace Stevens.
  End of the Day, The. Creeley.
  Four Glimpses of Night. F. M. Davis.
  God's Dark. John Martin.
  Going to Sleep in the Country. Howard Moss.
  How sweet the moonlight sleeps upon this bank! *Fr.* The
    Merchant of Venice. Shakespeare.
  Hymn to the Night. Longfellow.
  Impressions. Hardison.
  Midnight. Lampman.

  Moonlit Night. Eichendorff, *tr. fr. German.*
  Night and the Pines. D. C. Scott.
  Night Hymns on Lake Nipigon. D. C. Scott.
  Night in June, A. Pearson.
  Night in June, A. D. C. Scott.
  Night of Spring. Thomas Westwood.
  Night-Piece, A. Wordsworth.
  Night Things Are Soft and Loud. Zhenya Gay.
  Night Will Never Stay, The. Farjeon.
  Nocturne. Eichendorff, *tr. fr. German by* Salinger.
  Oh Night. Stampa, *tr. fr. Italian by* Priest.
  Revolution. A. E. Housman.
  Scissors and Paste. *Fr.* Three Cinquains. Brockman.
  Simply because the sun does not embrace. Michelangelo, *tr.*
    fr. Italian by Tusiani.
  Starlit Night, The. G. M. Hopkins.
  Starry Night, The. Sexton.
  Summer Moonlight. Patience Strong.
  Summer Night, A. Matthew Arnold.
  Terrace, The. Sereni, *tr. fr. Italian by* Golino.
  To Night. Shelley.
  To Night. J. B. White.
  Untergang. Trakl, *tr. fr. German by* Kaufmann.
  Vigil. Jiménez, *tr. fr. Spanish by* Barnstone.
  Wakeful Night. Droste-Hülshoff, *tr. fr. German by* Flygt.
  Walking at Night. Amory Hare.
  Watchman, What of the Night? Swinburne.
  Wet Windy Night on a Pavement. Tessimond.
  When night has been announced as theme, will it not cause
    surprise. *Fr.* Megalometropolitan Carnival. Gascoyne.
  Winter Night. Robert Fitzgerald.
  Winter Nights. Thomas Campion.
  See also EVENING; SUNSET
NIGHTINGALES
  See also Nightingale *in* TITLE AND FIRST LINE INDEX
  Bianca among the Nightingales. E. B. Browning.
  If it were not for the voice. *Fr.* Shui Shu. Nakatsukasa,
    tr. fr. Japanese by Waley.
  Nightingale Weather. Andrew Lang.
  Nightingales. Robert Bridges.
  O Nightingale, That on Yon Bloomy Spray. Milton.
  Ode to a Nightingale. Keats.
  Philomela. Matthew Arnold.
  To the Nightingale. Countess of Winchilsea.
NIJMEGEN, NETHERLANDS. Road to Nijmegen, The. Birney.
NILE (river). Nile, The. Leigh Hunt.
NILE, BATTLE OF THE. Nelson's Victory. *Unknown.*
NIPIGON LAKE, CANADA. Night Hymns on Lake Nipigon.
  D. C. Scott.
NOAH
  Ballad of the Flood. Edwin Muir.
  History of the Flood, The. Heath-Stubbs.
  Noah. Hagedorn.
  Noah an' Jonah an' Cap'n John Smith. Marquis.
  Noah's Carpenters. *Unknown.*
  Noah's Song. Evan Jones.
  Old Uncle Noah. *Unknown.*
NORTH, CHRISTOPHER. To Christopher North. Tennyson.
NORTH CAROLINA. *Poets of North Carolina* (PoNC). Richard
  Walser, ed.
NORTH WIND
  Northwind. Baro.
  Snow-Storm, The. Emerson.
NOSES. To a Nose. Quevedo, *tr. fr. Spanish by* Tobin.
NOVA SCOTIA. *Ballads and Sea Songs from Nova Scotia*
  (BSNS). W. Roy Mackenzie, comp.
NOVEMBER
  In November. Lampman.
  My November Guest. Robert Frost.
  November. Robert Bridges.
  November. Ted Hughes.
  November Morning. Blunden.
  November Night. Crapsey.
  Sonnet: November. Hartley Coleridge.
NUCLEAR WAR
  Advice to a Prophet. Wilbur.
  H-Bomb Evening Down, An. Sieber.
  In a twinkling/ of a flash-boom. *Fr.* The Empire Finals at
    Verona. J. C. Williams.
  Letter to the President, *sel.* ("What weather of shelters").
    Lowenfels.
NUDISTS. L'Ile du Levant: The Nudist Colony. Barbara
  Howes.
NUNS
  Alas! If I Had Married. *Unknown, tr. fr. Catalan by*
    Davis.
  Ballad of a Nun, A. John Davidson.
  Convent at Fahr, The. Zollinger, *tr. fr. German by* Middleton.
  Heaven-Haven. G. M. Hopkins.
  Legend of the Bewitched Nunnery. Herrmann-Neisse, *tr. fr.*
    German by Deutsch *and* Yarmolinsky.
  Mother Marie Therese. Robert Lowell.
  Nun, The. Edward Moore.
  Nuns at Eve. Brinnin.

NUNS (continued)
Nuns' Drinking Song. Unknown, tr. fr. German by Yorck
    and Elmslie.
Six Nuns in the Snow. McGinley.
Soeur Marie Emilie. Houselander.
Street Scene. Mezey.
To a Severe Nun. Merton.
NURSES
Night Nurse Goes Her Round, The. John Gray.
Nurse. Frances Cornford.
NYMPHS. Nymphs, The, sel. ("There are the fair-limbed
    Nymphs o' the Woods"). Leigh Hunt.

O

OAK TREES
Bearded Oaks. R. P. Warren.
Oak, The. Tennyson.
To an Oak Tree. Fr. Waverley. Walter Scott.
OBAN, SCOTLAND. End of the Season on a Stormy Day—Oban.
    I. C. Smith.
OCEAN. See SEA
OCTOBER
See also October in TITLE AND FIRST LINE INDEX
Bowl of October, A. Bevington.
Boys in October. Layton.
Especially When the October Wind. Dylan Thomas.
In October, Figuring Up Your Share. Fr. Sonnets of the
    Months. Folgore da San Geminiano, tr. fr. Italian by
    Gould.
Late October. Teasdale.
Mallee in October. Flexmore Hudson.
October Days. Pearson.
October Journey. Margaret Walker.
October's Bright Blue Weather. H. H. Jackson.
October's Party. George Cooper.
October's Song. Farjeon.
Poem in October. Dylan Thomas.
Vagabond Song, A. Bliss Carman.
OCTOPUSES
Octopus. A. C. Hilton.
Octopus, The. Ogden Nash.
Parkinson and the Octopus. Farber.
ODYSSEUS. See ULYSSES
ODYSSEY. Odyssey, The. Andrew Lang.
OHIO (state). Founders of Ohio, The. Venable.
OLD AGE
See also Age and Old Age in TITLE AND FIRST LINE INDEX
Academic. Roethke.
After a Line by John Peale Bishop. Justice.
Aged Lover Renounceth Love, The. Vaux.
Ah How I Like to See Great Power Pass. Bertrand de
    Born, tr. fr. Provençal by Wilhelm.
Ancient to Ancients, An. Thomas Hardy.
April Inventory. Snodgrass.
Autumn. Humbert Wolfe.
Beyond the Horizon. Loerke, tr. fr. German by Middleton.
Birthday. Emans.
Chough, The. Reaney.
Complaint of the Fair Armoress. Villon, tr. fr. French by
    Swinburne.
Conversations. Gozzano, tr. fr. Italian by Golino.
Corner, The. De la Mare.
Covent Garden Market. Fr. London Sonnets.
Curate's Kindness, The. Thomas Hardy.
Crabbed Age and Youth. Fr. The Passionate Pilgrim.
    Shakespeare.
Danny Murphy. James Stephens.
Do Not Go Gentle into That Good Night. Dylan Thomas.
Ever On. Unknown.
Father William. Fr. Alice's Adventures in Wonderland.
    "Lewis Carroll."
Gerontion. T. S. Eliot.
Great-Grandmother, The. Robert Graves.
Growing Old. Rose Henderson.
His Age. Herrick.
His Golden Locks Time Hath to Silver Turned. Fr. Poly-
    hymnia. George Peele.
How Old Are You? At. to Edward Tuck and to H. S.
    Fritsch.
How Old Is Pilar? González Prada, tr. fr. Spanish by Davis.
I Look into My Glass. Thomas Hardy.
If You Never. E. M. Fowler.
It Is Too Late! Fr. Morituri Salutamus. Longfellow.
Laid in My Quiet Bed. Earl of Surrey.
Lamentation of the Old Pensioner, The. Yeats.
Last Leaf, The. O. W. Holmes.
Leaden Echo and the Golden Echo, The. G. M. Hopkins.

Long Hill, The. Teasdale.
Long Time a Child. Hartley Coleridge.
Love Is like the Wild Rose-Briar. Emily Brontë.
Man's Going Hence. Fr. Human Life. Samuel Rogers.
Meditations of an Old Woman. Roethke.
New Generation, The. Schiller, tr. fr. German by Kaufmann.
November. "Aldo Palazzeschi," tr. fr. Italian by Golino.
Old Age Home, The. Theodore Holmes.
Old Man. Elizabeth Jennings.
Old Man Dreams, The. O. W. Holmes.
Old Man's Comforts and How He Gained Them, The.
    Southey.
Old Men, The. Feldman.
Old Men. Ogden Nash.
Old Men Admiring Themselves in the Water, The. Yeats.
Old Ones, The. Bellerby.
Old Peasant in the Billiard Saloon, The. Menai.
Old Woman, The. Joseph Campbell.
Old Woman, The. "Gertrud Kolmar," tr. fr. German by
    Middleton.
Old Woman. I. C. Smith.
Old Woman Laments the Days of Her Youth, The. Villon,
    tr. fr. French by Kittel.
On Falling Asleep to Birdsong. William Meredith.
On Growing Old. Masefield.
On Growing Old. Rayaprol.
Peekaboo, I Almost See You. Ogden Nash.
Pictures of the Gone World, sel. ("Just as I used to say").
    Ferlinghetti.
Pleasantness of life was mine once undiminished, The.
    Hölderlin, tr. fr. German by Spann.
Points of View. Amy Lowell.
Poor Relation, The. E. A. Robinson.
Prayer for Old Age, A. Yeats.
Promise of Peace. Jeffers.
Provide, Provide. Robert Frost.
Rabbi Ben Ezra. Robert Browning.
Retirement. Unknown.
Sailing to Byzantium. Yeats.
Sixty-eighth Birthday. J. R. Lowell.
Song from a Country Fair. Léonie Adams.
Song of the Old Mother, The. Yeats.
Span of Life, The. Robert Frost.
Stanzas to the Marquise. Corneille, tr. fr. French by Conder.
Terminus. Emerson.
That time of year thou may'st in me behold. Sonnets,
    LXXIII. Shakespeare.
Though You Are Young. Thomas Campion.
To Age. W. S. Landor.
To an Old Lady. Empson.
Too Late. F. H. Ludlow.
Too Old to Work. Glazer.
Twenty Years Ago. Unknown.
Upon His Picture. Thomas Randolph.
When You Are Old. Yeats.
Whom the Gods Love. Bruner.
Young and Old. Fr. The Water Babies. Charles Kingsley.
Youth and Age. Byron.
Youth and Age. S. T. Coleridge.
Youth and Age on Beaulieu River, Hants. Betjeman.
OLDHAM, JOHN. To the Memory of Mr. Oldham. Dryden.
OPPORTUNITY. Opportunity. J. J. Ingalls.
OPTIMISM. Difference, The. Unknown.
ORCHARDS. Little Green Orchard, The. De la Mare.
ORGAN-GRINDERS. See HURDY-GURDIES
ORPHEUS
Orpheus. W. D. Snodgrass.
Orpheus and Eurydice. Robert Browning.
Orpheus. Eurydice. Hermes. Rilke, tr. fr. German by Kaufmann.
Orpheus with His Lute. Fr. King Henry VIII. At. to
    Shakespeare and to Fletcher.
Sonnets to Orpheus, sels. Rilke, tr. fr. German by Kaufmann.
OSTRICHES. Ostrich Is a Silly Bird, The. M. E. W. Freeman.
OTTERBOURNE [or OTTERBURN], BATTLE OF
Battle of Otterburn, The. Unknown.
Chevy Chase. Unknown.
OTTERS. Otter, An. Ted Hughes.
OUSE (river), ENGLAND. Reflections on the River. Andrew
    Young.
OUTLAWS. See ROBBERS AND OUTLAWS
OVENBIRDS. Oven Bird, The. Robert Frost.
OWLS
In the Headlights. C. E. Eaton.
Owl, The. Edward Thomas.
Owl and the Pussy-Cat, The. Edward Lear.
Owl-Critic, The. J. T. Fields.
Song: Owl, The. Tennyson.
Sweet Suffolk Owl. Unknown.
Town Owl. Laurie Lee.
OXEN
Crossing the Plains. Joaquin Miller.

Far Away and Long Ago. Darío, *tr. fr. Spanish* by Lever-
tov.
Herd-Boy's Song, The. Chen Shan-min, *tr. fr. Chinese* by
Edwards.
Ox-Tamer, The. Walt Whitman.
Oxcarts Are Now on Their Way, The. Jiménez, *tr. fr.
Spanish* by Sternberg.
Oxen, The. Thomas Hardy.
Twelve Oxen. *Unknown.*
OXFORD, ENGLAND
Duns Scotus's Oxford. G. M. Hopkins.
On Oxford. Keats.
Oxford. Lionel Johnson.
Prologue to the University of Oxford. Dryden.
Spires of Oxford, The. Letts.
Views of the Oxford Colleges. Paris Leary.
OYSTERS
Oyster, The. Ponge, *tr. fr. French* by Perry.
Oysters. Swift.

P

PACIFIC OCEAN
Eye, The. Jeffers.
Once by the Pacific. Robert Frost.
PACIFISM AND PACIFISTS
Dooley Is a Traitor. Michie.
I Sing of Olaf. E. E. Cummings.
PAGE, SATCHELL. To Satch. Samuel Allen.
PAIN
After great pain, a formal feeling comes. Emily Dickinson.
For All in Pain. Amy Carmichael.
Never Admit the Pain. Mary Gilmore.
90 North. Jarrell.
No Pleasure without Some Pain. Vaux.
Pain has an element of blank. Emily Dickinson.
To My New Mistress. Beverly Bowie.
PAINTING AND PAINTERS
After a Dutch Master. C. F. Meyer, *tr. fr. German* by
Coogan.
Andrea del Sarto. Robert Browning.
Anonymous Drawing. Justice.
Dance, The. W. C. Williams.
Detail from an Annunciation by Crivelli. Rosemary Dobson.
Elegiac Stanzas. Wordsworth.
Face, A. Robert Browning.
Fra Lippo Lippi. Robert Browning.
Georg Grosz. Lasker-Schüler, *tr. fr. German* by Middleton.
Great Wave, The: Hokusai. Finkel.
History of the World as Pictures, The. Nancy Sullivan.
In Santa Maria del Popolo. Thom Gunn.
Limitations of Human Art. *Fr.* Three Fragments. Wil-
liam Collins.
Meditation on John Constable, A. Tomlinson.
Musée des Beaux Arts. Auden.
Nocturne, The. Bode.
On a Fifteenth-Century Flemish Angel. David Ray.
On an Unsuccessful Attempt to Draw Lord Boyle's Picture.
Elizabeth Rowe.
Painted Head. Ransom.
Pictor Ignotus. Robert Browning.
Picture of the Nativity in the Church of Krena in Chios.
Trypanis.
Politics of Rich Painters, The. LeRoi Jones.
Requiem for an Abstract Artist. Kessler.
Romney, The. Harriet Moore.
Sonnet for a Picture. Swinburne.
Story of Soutine, A. Schevill.
Winter Landscape. Berryman.
PALAU (island). Palau. Benn, *tr. fr. German* by Hamburger.
PALM TREES
Fir Tree, A. Heine, *tr. fr. German* by Kaufmann.
Royal Palm. Hart Crane.
PAN (god)
Great God Pan, The. E. B. Browning.
Hymn of Pan. Shelley.
Musical Instrument, A. E. B. Browning.
PANAMA CANAL. Song of Panama, A. Runyon.
PANGOLINS. *See* ANTEATERS
PANTHERS
Panther, The. Ogden Nash.
Panther, The. Rilke, *tr. fr. German.*
PARADES
Parade, A. M. C. Rose.
Triumphal March. Darío, *tr. fr. Spanish* by Guenther.
PARADISE
Paradise Regained. Milton.
See also HEAVEN

PARENTHOOD
Adam. Hecht.
Andre. Gwendolyn Brooks.
Becoming a Dad. E. A. Guest.
Culprit, The. A. E. Housman.
Dad's Greatest Job. *Unknown.*
Father, The. Finkel.
For My Newborn Son. S. G. Smith.
Fruit of the Flower. Countee Cullen.
Heart's Needle. W. D. Snodgrass.
Joyful Prophecy. Vassar Miller.
Name, The. Creeley.
Nativity. *Fr.* The Blossom of the Branches. Ruth Gilbert.
On My First Daughter. Jonson.
On My First Son [*or Sonne*]. Jonson.
On the Birth of His Son. Su T'ung-po, *tr. fr. Chinese* by
Waley.
Parental Ode to My Son, A. Thomas Hood.
Poet's Welcome to His Illegitimate Child, The. Burns.
Prayer for My Daughter, A. Yeats.
Service Supreme. *Unknown.*
Song: "If a daughter you have, she's the plague of your
life." *Fr.* The Duenna. Sheridan.
To His Son, Vincent Corbet. Corbet.
Upon Wedlock and Death of Children. Edward Taylor.
See also FATHERS; MOTHER
PARIS, FRANCE. Four Sheets to the Wind and a One-Way
Ticket to France. Rivers.
PARKER, CHARLIE. Yardbird's Skull. Dodson.
PARKS. Public Garden, The. Robert Lowell.
PARLIAMENT (Great Britain). On the New Forcers of Con-
science under the Long Parliament. Milton.
PARODIES. *Parodies: An Anthology from Chaucer to Beer-
bohm—and After* (Par). Dwight Macdonald, ed.
PARROTS
Parrot. W. J. Smith.
Parrots, The. W. W. Gibson.
PARSNIPS. Parsnip, The. Ogden Nash.
PASSOVER. Still Small Voice, The. A. M. Klein.
PASTERNAK, BORIS LEONIDOVICH. Letter to Pasternak. Ralph
Pomeroy.
PASTORS. *See* CLERGY
PASTURES. *See* FIELDS AND PASTURES
PATIENCE
Patience [Hard Thing!]. G. M. Hopkins.
St. Teresa's Book-Mark. St. Theresa of Avila, *tr. fr.
Spanish* by Peers.
PATRICK, SAINT
Birth of Saint Patrick, The. Lover.
Wearin' of the Green, The. *Unknown.*
PATRIOTIC SONGS, AMERICAN
America. S. F. Smith.
America for Me. Henry van Dyke.
America the Beautiful. K. L. Bates.
Battle Hymn of the Republic. J. W. Howe.
Star-spangled Banner, The. Key.
PATRIOTIC SONGS, ENGLISH. Rule, Britannia. *Fr.* Alfred,
a Masque. James Thomson.
PATRIOTISM
Barbara Frietchie. Whittier.
Breathes There the Man. *Fr.* The Lay of the Last Minstrel.
Walter Scott.
Dulce et Decorum Est. Wilfred Owen.
I Am an American. Lieberman.
I Hear America Singing. Walt Whitman.
Kid Has Gone to the Colors, The. Herschell.
Pro Patria Mori. Thomas Moore.
Scots Wha Hae. Burns.
PAUL, SAINT
Paul. Oxenham.
Saint Paul, *sels.* F. W. H. Myers.
PAWLET, LADY JANE, MARCHIONESS OF WINTON. Elegie on
the Lady Jane Pawlet, Marchion: of Winton, An. Jonson.
PEACE
See also Peace in TITLE AND FIRST LINE INDEX
At Peace. Rumi, *tr. fr. Persian* by Arberry.
Child of Peace, The. Lagerlöf, *tr. fr. Swedish* by Stork.
Christian Soldier, The, *sel.* Studdert-Kennedy.
Dear Lord and Father of Mankind. *Fr.* The Brewing of
Soma. Whittier.
Evening Star, The. Amy Carmichael.
He Walks at Peace. *Fr.* Tao Teh King. *Unknown, tr. fr.
Chinese.*
Hope's Forecast. E. R. Fuller.
O Brother Man. Whittier.
Peace, like a Lamb. Leonard Clark.
Pray for Peace, O Gentle Virgin Mary. Charles d'Orléans,
tr. fr. French by Kittel.
Prayer to Peace. *Fr.* Cresophontes. Euripides, *tr. fr. Greek*
by Hadas.
Rose of Peace, The. Yeats.
Uncelestial City, The, *sel.* ("You cannot traffick in peace").
Humbert Wolfe.

PEACHES. Peaches, The. Oppenheimer.
PEACOCK, MARGARET LOVE. Margaret Love Peacock for Her Tombstone, 1826. Peacock.
PEACOCKS
  Peacock and Nightingale. Robert Finch.
  Peacock of Java, The. W. J. Smith.
PEAR TREES. Pear Tree. Doolittle ("H. D.").
PEARS. Study of Two Pears. Wallace Stevens.
PEAS. I Eat My Peas with Honey. *Unknown.*
PEASANTS. Peasant, A. R. S. Thomas.
PEDDLERS AND PEDDLING
  Peddler's Caravan, The. Rands.
  Pedlar, The. *Fr.* The Winter's Tale. Shakespeare.
PEELE CASTLE, ENGLAND. Elegiac Stanzas. Wordsworth.
PEEWEES. *See* PEWEES
PELICANS. Reason for the Pelican, The. Ciardi.
PEMBROKE, MARY SIDNEY HERBERT, COUNTESS OF. On the Countess Dowager of Pembroke. William Browne.
PEMBROKE, WILLIAM, EARL OF. To William Earle of Pembroke. Jonson.
PENSHURST, ENGLAND. To Penshurst. Jonson.
PEONIES. Red Peony, The. Buson, *tr. fr. Japanese by* Henderson.
PERSEPHONE
  Garden of Proserpine, The. Swinburne.
  Goddess, The. Thom Gunn.
  Hymn to Proserpine. Swinburne.
PERSEUS. Perseus. MacNeice.
PERSHING, JOHN JOSEPH. Pershing at the Front. Guiterman.
PESSIMISM. Difference, The. *Unknown.*
PETER, SAINT
  In the Servants' Quarters. Thomas Hardy.
  Look, The. E. B. Browning.
  Meaning of the Look, The. E. B. Browning.
  Peter. Marlatt.
  Peter and John. Wylie.
PETRELS. To see the petrel cropping in the farmyard. *Fr.* Sonnets for a Dying Man. Burns Singer.
PEWEES. Peewits on the Hills. A. V. Stuart.
PHEASANTS. Pheasant. Zulfikar Ghose.
PHILIPPINE ISLANDS. Indestructible, The, *sel.* ("Manila! City of wounds!"). Hitchcock.
PHILODENDRON. Woolworth Philodendron, The. Sandy.
PHILOSOPHY AND PHILOSOPHERS
  On the Death of a Metaphysician. Santayana.
  Story of Two Gentlemen and the Gardener, The. Logue.
  To an Old Philosopher in Rome. Wallace Stevens.
PHOENIX. Phoenix, The. *Fr.* Nepenthe. Darley.
PHOTOGRAPHS
  Glance at the Album, A. Gray Burr.
  Lines on a Young Lady's Photograph Album. Philip Larkin.
  To a Photographer. Berton Braley.
PHYSICIANS
  Epistle, An, Containing the Strange Medical Experience of Karshish, the Arab Physician. Robert Browning.
  On Dr. Crank's Victory over the Gout. Sneyd Davies.
  Surgeons must be very careful. Emily Dickinson.
PICNICS
  Picnic, A. Aileen Fisher.
  Picnic. Lofting.
  Picnic Day. Rachel Field.
PIGEONS
  Country Rhyme. *Unknown.*
  Mrs. Peck-Pigeon. Farjeon.
  Pigeon, The. Richard Church.
  Pigeons. Eich, *tr. fr. German by* Hamburger.
  Pigeons. Alastair Reid.
PIGS
  Boar, The. Robert Kelly.
  Feed. Knister.
  Little Piggy. Thomas Hood.
  Pig-Tale, A. *Fr.* Sylvie and Bruno Concluded. "Lewis Carroll."
  View of a Pig. Ted Hughes.
PIKE. Pike, The. John Bruce.
PILATE. *See* PONTIUS PILATE
PILGRIM FATHERS
  Boston Hymn. Emerson.
  Children of Light. Robert Lowell.
  If I Were a Pilgrim Child. Rowena Bennett.
  Landing of the Pilgrim Fathers, The. Hemans.
  Passionate Man's Pilgrimage. Ralegh.
  Pilgrim Song, The. *Fr.* The Pilgrim's Progress. Bunyan.
PINE TREES
  Choosing a Mast. Roy Campbell.
  Foxtail Pine. Gary Snyder.
  Pine Bough, The. Aldridge.
  Pine Gum. W. W. E. Ross.
  Pine-Trees in the Courtyard, The. Po Chü-i, *tr. fr. Chinese by* Waley.
  Pines and the Sea, The. Cranch.
  Solitary Pine. Prince Ichihara, *tr. fr. Japanese by* Ishii *and* Obata.

PIONEERS
  Camp within the West, The. Roderic Quinn.
  Creek of the Four Graves, The, *sel.* ("A settler in the olden times went forth"). Harpur.
  Exodus for Oregon. Joaquin Miller.
  Founders of Ohio, The. Venable.
  Missouri Rhapsody. Daugherty.
  My Father Loved the Jumping-off Place. R. P. T. Coffin.
  Pioneer, The. Ruggles.
  Trail Breakers. Daugherty.
  Wheel Ruts. Daugherty.
  Where the Pelican Builds. Foott.
  Wilderness Theme. Mudie.
  Women of the West, The. G. E. Evans.
PIRATES AND PIRACY
  Andrew Batan. *Unknown.*
  Ballad of Cap'n Pye. R. P. T. Coffin.
  Ballad of John Silver, A. Masefield.
  Captain Robert Kidd. *Unknown.*
  Derelict. Y. E. Allison.
  Flying Cloud, The. *Unknown.*
  Kelly the Pirate. *Unknown.*
  Last Buccaneer, The. Charles Kingsley.
  Pirate Don Durk of Dowdee, The. Merryman.
  Pirates, The. *Unknown.*
  Spanish Waters. Masefield.
  To the Roving Pirate. Turberville.
PISA, ITALY. Evening: Ponte al Mare, Pisa. Shelley.
PITCHER, MOLLY
  Molly Pitcher. L. E. Richards.
  Molly Pitcher. K. B. Sherwood.
PITY. Ode to Pity. William Collins.
PLAGUE. In Time of Plague [*or* Pestilence], 1593. *Fr.* Summer's Last Will and Testament. Nashe.
PLANE TREES. London Plane-Tree, A. Amy Levy.
PLOVERS. Plover, The. *Unknown, tr. fr. Swahili by* Werner.
PLOWING
  Harry Ploughman. G. M. Hopkins.
  Ploughing on Sunday. Wallace Stevens.
  Plowman, The. Knister.
  Plowmen. Robert Frost.
  Song: "We, who are men, how shall we know?" R. S. Thomas.
  When smoke stood up from Ludlow. *Fr.* A Shropshire Lad. A. E. Housman.
PLUM TREES. 'Tis the White Plum Tree. J. S. Neilson.
PLYMOUTH, ENGLAND. For an Age of Plastics. Plymouth. Davie.
PLYMOUTH ROCK. Plymouth Rock. Driver.
POACHING AND POACHERS. Lincolnshire Poacher, The. *Unknown.*
POCAHONTAS. Pocahontas. Thackeray.
POE, EDGAR ALLAN
  Edgar Allan Poe. R. H. Barlow.
  Poe and Longfellow. *Fr.* A Fable for Critics. J. R. Lowell.
POETRY AND POETS
  See also Poet *and* Poetry *in* TITLE AND FIRST LINE INDEX
  Adam's Curse. Yeats.
  Alma; or, The Progress of the Mind, *sel.* ("Matthew met Richard; when or where"). Prior.
  Argument of His Book, The. Herrick.
  Ars Poetica. MacLeish.
  Ars Poetica about Ultimates. Combs.
  Art of Poetry. Bonnefoy, *tr. fr. French by* Stewart.
  Art of Poetry, An. McAuley.
  As You Say; an Anti-Poem. Karl Shapiro.
  Austerity of Poetry. Matthew Arnold.
  Baudelaire. Schwartz.
  Birth of Tragedy, The. Layton.
  But I Am Growing Old and Indolent. Jeffers.
  Canadian Authors Meet, The. F. R. Scott.
  Caution to Poets, A. Matthew Arnold.
  Coffee-House Lecture, A. Mezey.
  Coney Island of the Mind, A, *sel.* ("Constantly risking absurdity"). Ferlinghetti.
  Day Is Done, The. Longfellow.
  Dedication: "Bob Southey! You're a poet—Poet-laureate." *Fr.* Don Juan. Byron.
  Dedication, A: "They are rhymes rudely strung with intent less." A. L. Gordon.
  Desolation of the Poor Sentimental Poet. Corazzini, *tr. fr. Italian by* Farrar.
  Distant Drum, The. Hernton.
  E. P. Ode pour l'Election de Son Sepulcre. *Fr.* Hugh Selwyn Mauberley. Pound.
  Economical Poet, The. Morgenstern, *tr. fr. German by* Kaufmann.
  Epilogue: "Poets, like disputants, when reasons fail." *Fr.* All for Love. Dryden.
  Epistle to Dr. Arbuthnot, An. Pope.
  Epistle to James Smith. Burns.
  Essay on Criticism, An, *sels.* Pope.
  Experience. Harford.

Explanatory Epistle, An. John Banks.
Fable: Poet and His Patron, The. Edward Moore.
Fable XLV: Poet and the Rose, The. John Gay.
Fishes and the Poet's Hands, The. Yerby.
Fit of Rime against Rime, A. Jonson.
For My Contemporaries. J. V. Cunningham.
His Poetrie His Pillar. Herrick.
Honor to Celery. Enzensberger, tr. fr. German by Middleton.
House. Robert Browning.
How It Strikes a Contemporary. Robert Browning.
I Am 25. Corso.
I Like to Quote. Follansbee.
I Never Drank of Aganippe Well. Fr. Astrophel and Stella. Philip Sidney.
In My Craft or Sullen Art. Dylan Thomas.
It Goes against My Interest to Confess It. Bécquer, tr. fr. Spanish by Bell.
Jordan ("When first my lines of heav'nly joys made mention"). George Herbert.
Jordan ("Who says that fictions only and false hair"). George Herbert.
Jugurtha. Longfellow.
Lake Isle, The. Pound.
Landscape. Baudelaire, tr. fr. French by Dillon.
Late Tutorial. Buckley.
Lately Our Poets. W. S. Landor.
Laureate, The. Aytoun.
Lens. Anne Wilkinson.
Let Them Alone. Jeffers.
Library Is on Fire, The. Char, tr. fr. French by Freedman, Justice, and Aspel.
Lost Language, The. Feldman.
Madly Singing in the Mountains. Po Chü-i, tr. fr. Chinese by Waley.
Makers, The. Nan McDonald.
Man with the Rake, The. Fr. Translations from the Chinese. Christopher Morley.
Merlin. Emerson.
Metre Columbian, The. Unknown.
Namby-Pamby. Henry Carey.
New Technique. Armour.
Not marble nor the gilded monuments. Sonnets, LV. Shakespeare.
Not mine own fears, nor the prophetic soul. Sonnets, CVII. Shakespeare.
Ode on the Poetical Character. William Collins.
Ode on the Poets. Keats.
Of English Verse. Edmund Waller.
On a Spider. Littleton.
On the Make-up of a Poet. Sieber.
On the Sonnet. Keats.
Onan. Paris Leary.
One Poet Visits Another. W. H. Davies.
One-Talent Man. Pearson.
Past Ruin'd Ilion Helen Lives. W. S. Landor.
Pastoral Poesy. John Clare.
Peasant Poet, The. John Clare.
Peri Poietikes. Zukofsky.
Person from Porlock, The. Robert Graves.
Person from Porlock, A. R. S. Thomas.
Piping down the Valleys Wild. Fr. Songs of Innocence. Blake.
Plea to Boys and Girls, A. Robert Graves.
Poem: "If the drink that satisfied." R. A. K. Mason.
Poet and His Book, The. E. S. Millay.
Poet and War, The. Ehrenstein, tr. fr. German by Middleton.
Poetry for Supper. R. S. Thomas.
Poetry Revival. Hanes.
Poet's Dream, The. Shelley.
Poets in Africa. Roy Campbell.
Poets Love Nature. John Clare.
Poet's Song, The. Tennyson.
Poet's Work, The. Jaccottet, tr. fr. French by Stern.
Poietes Apoietes. Hartley Coleridge.
Poverty and Poetry. Tickell.
Proem: "I love the old melodious lays." Whittier.
Progress of Poesy, The. Thomas Gray.
Progress of Poetry, The. Swift.
Prologue: "Our author, by experience, finds it true." Fr. Aureng-Zebe. Dryden.
Prologue, The: "To sing of wars, of captains, and of kings." Bradstreet.
Prologue: "What flocks of critics hover here to-day." Fr. All for Love. Dryden.
Pure Poet, The. Roy Fuller.
Reader Writes, The. Carl Crane.
Reason for Not Writing Orthodox Nature Poetry. Wain.
Roundel, The: "Roundel is wrought as a ring or a starbright sphere, A." Swinburne.
Seaweed. Longfellow.
Shall I take thee, the poet said. Emily Dickinson.
So That's Who I Remind Me Of. Ogden Nash.

Sonnet, The ("A sonnet is a moment's monument"). Fr. The House of Life. D. G. Rossetti.
Sonnet: "Oh for a poet—for a beacon bright." E. A. Robinson.
Sonnet All of a Sudden, A. Lope de Vega, tr. fr. Spanish by Bell.
Survey of Literature. Ransom.
Terence, this is stupid stuff. Fr. A Shropshire Lad. A. E. Housman.
Theory of Poetry. MacLeish.
There is no frigate like a book. Emily Dickinson.
This was a poet—it is that. Emily Dickinson.
Thought-Fox, The. Ted Hughes.
To a Poet, Who Would Have Me Praise Certain Bad Poets, Imitators of His and Mine. Hardison.
To Ford, Guggenheim, Rockefeller, etc. Hardison.
To Hold in a Poem. A. J. M. Smith.
To My Friends. Peter Levi.
To Stella. Swift.
To the Nightingale. Countess of Winchilsea.
To the Parcae. Hölderlin, tr. fr. German by Kaufmann.
To the Poets of Our Time. Schélandre, tr. fr. French by Carrington.
To the Stone-Cutters. Jeffers.
Transcendentalism; a Poem in Twelve Books. Robert Browning.
Us Poets. F. P. Adams.
Versions of Love. Roy Fuller.
War Poet. Sidney Keyes.
We Poets Speak. Fr. Sister Songs. Francis Thompson.
Weltschmerz. Yerby.
When I Have Fears That I May Cease to Be. Keats.
Where's the Poet? Keats.
Who Risks It Where a Poet Lives. Cadou, tr. fr. French by Stafford.
Who Translates a Poet Badly. González Prada, tr. fr. Spanish by Davis.
Who will believe my verse in time to come. Sonnets, XVII. Shakespeare.
Words. Edward Thomas.
Poems on Poetry (PP). Robert Wallace and James G. Taaffe, eds.
POLICEMEN
Bobby Blue. Drinkwater.
Corner. Ralph Pomeroy.
I'm the Police Cop Man, I Am. Margaret Morrison.
My Policeman. Fyleman.
P's the Proud Policeman. Fr. All Around the Town. McGinley.
POLITICS AND POLITICIANS
Election, The. Robert Pack.
Epitaphs for Three Prominent Persons. McGinley.
Greatest Show on Earth. Lamport.
I Ain't No Candidate. Pearson.
Political Meeting. A. M. Klein.
Similes for Two Political Characters of 1819. Shelley.
POLLOCK, JACKSON. Requiem for an Abstract Artist. Kessler.
POMEGRANATES. Pomegranate, The. Dudek.
PONDS. See LAKES AND PONDS.
PONTIUS PILATE. Pilate. Heym, tr. fr. German by Middleton.
POOL (game). Rotation. Julian Bond.
POPE, ALEXANDER
Johnson on Pope. Ferry.
Mr. Pope. Allen Tate.
On Mr. Nash's Picture. Jane Brereton.
When None Shall Rail. David Lewis.
POPLAR TREES
Binsey Poplars, Felled 1879. G. M. Hopkins.
Poplar. Benn, tr. fr. German by Middleton.
Poplar Field, The. Cowper.
POPOCATAPETL (volcano), MEXICO. Romance. W. J. Turner.
PORPOISES
Off Spectacle Island. Eberhart.
Porpoise, The. Ogden Nash.
PORTRAITS
Dorothy Q. O. W. Holmes.
Faded Pictures. W. V. Moody.
Likeness, A. Robert Browning.
On Her Portrait. Sister Juana Inés de la Cruz, tr. fr. Spanish by Flores.
POSTMEN. Postman, The. L. E. Richards.
POTOMAC (river). Potomac, The. Karl Shapiro.
POUND, EZRA. Homage to Ezra Pound. Highet.
POVERTY
Baudelaire. Schwartz.
Challenge, The. Longfellow.
Children of the Poor, The, sel. Gwendolyn Brooks.
Come, Live with Me and Be My Love. Day Lewis.
Contentment in Poverty. Issa, tr. fr. Japanese by Henderson.
Elementary School Class Room in a Slum, An. Spender.
Epistle I: "Meeting a monster of mourning wherever I go." George Barker.

POVERTY (*continued*)
Face of Poverty. Lucy Smith.
Furnished Lives. Silkin.
His Poverty. Rutebeuf, *tr. fr. French by* Tobin.
Holy Thursday. *Fr.* Songs of Experience. Blake.
Hymn to Poverty, A. Edward Moore.
Is There for Honest Poverty. Burns.
Poverty. *Fr.* The Panchatantra. *Unknown, tr. fr. Sanskrit by* Ryder.
Poverty and Poetry. Tickell.
Said the Innkeeper. Myles Connolly.
Slum Dwelling, A. *Fr.* The Borough. Crabbe.
Thirty Bob a Week. John Davidson.
Timothy Winters. Causley.
We Live in a Rickety House. Alexander McLachlan.
Wench in the Street, The. *Unknown.*
PRAIRIES
In the Days When the Cattle Ran. Garland.
Kit Carson's Ride. Joaquin Miller.
Night on the Prairies. Walt Whitman.
Prairie Graveyard. Anne Marriott.
Prairie Water Colour, A. D. C. Scott.
Prairie Wind. D. C. Scott.
Prairies, The. Bryant.
To make a prairie it takes a clover and one bee. Emily Dickinson.
PRAYER
Do I Really Pray? John Burton.
Hour of Prayer, The. Charlotte Elliott.
More Prayer. *Unknown.*
Pray! Irene Arnold.
Pray! A. R. Wells.
Pray, Christian, Pray! *Unknown.*
Pray On! *Unknown.*
Prayer: "Prayer must be grounded on the Word." *Unknown.*
Prayer: "Prayer the churches banquet, angels age." George Herbert.
Prayer Moves the Hand That Moves the World. J. A. Wallace.
Secret Place, The. A. A. Pollard.
Secret Place of Prayer, The. G. B. Adams.
Somebody Prayed. *Unknown.*
Thy Will Be Done. A. J. Flint.
Two Went Up to the Temple to Pray. Crashaw.
What Is Prayer? James Montgomery.
Whirring Wheels. Oxenham.
Who Prayed? *Unknown.*
PRAYING MANTIS. *See* MANTIS
PREACHERS. *See* CLERGY
PRECEDENT. Calf-Path, The. Foss.
PRETZELS. Pretzel Man, The. Rachel Field.
PRIDE
Godolphin Horne. Belloc.
Pointless Pride of Man, The. *Unknown.*
Pride Is Out. *Unknown.*
Primer Lesson. Sandburg.
PRIESTS. *See* CLERGY
PRIMROSES
To an Early Primrose. H. K. White.
To Primroses. Herrick.
PRIOR, MATTHEW. For My Own Monument. Prior.
PRISONS AND PRISONERS
Ballad of Reading Gaol, The. Oscar Wilde.
Captivity. Samuel Rogers.
Certain Mercies. Robert Graves.
Convict of Clonmel, The. *Unknown, tr. fr. Irish by* Callanan.
For a Convict's Wife, *sel.* Trumbo.
In Prison. William Morris.
Kirtle Gaol. *Unknown.*
Memories of West Street and Lepke. Robert Lowell.
Old Prison, The. Judith Wright.
On Leaving Prison. León, *tr. fr. Spanish by* Sackett.
Prisoner, The, *sel.* Emily Brontë.
Prisoner, The. Rilke, *tr. fr. German by* Kaufmann.
Prisoner, The. *Unknown, tr. fr. Spanish by* Flores.
Prisoner for Life, A. *Unknown.*
Prisoner of Chillon, The. Byron.
Prisoner's Song, The. *Unknown.*
To Althea from Prison. Lovelace.
Wind at Your Door, The. R. D. Fitzgerald.
PROMETHEUS. Prometheus. Byron.
PROPERTIUS, SEXTUS. Homage to Sextus Propertius, *sel.* Pound.
PROSERPINA *or* PROSERPINE. *See* PERSEPHONE
PROSPECTORS. *See* GOLD MINING AND MINERS
PROVENCE, FRANCE
Cocooning, The. *Fr.* Mirèio. Frédéric Mistral, *tr. fr. Provençal by* Preston.
Visit to Van Gogh, A. Causley.
When I Breathe This Air. Vidal, *tr. fr. Provençal by* Valency.
PSYCHE. Ode to Psyche. Keats.

PUPPETS
Puppet Play, The. Padraic Colum.
Street Performers, 1851. Tiller.
PUSSY WILLOWS
Little Gray Pussy. *Unknown.*
Pussy-Willows. Aileen Fisher.
PYRAMIDS. Pyramis; or, The House of Ascent. A. D. Hope.
PYTHONS. Python, The. Belloc.

Q

QUADALQUIVER (river), SPAIN. Seguidillas of the Guadalquiver River. Lope de Vega, *tr. fr. Spanish by* Levertov.
QUEEN ANNE'S LACE (flower). Lèse Majesté. Paul Bartlett.

R

RABBITS
See also Rabbit *in* TITLE AND FIRST LINE INDEX
Love for a Hare. La Follette.
Rabbit Cry. Lucie-Smith.
Rabbits. D. W. Baruch.
Story in the Snow, A. Crouch.
RABELAIS, FRANÇOIS. Epitaph on Rabelais. Ronsard, *tr. fr. French by* Currey.
RADAR. Radar. A. M. Sullivan.
RADIO. Elegy for Helen Trent. Paris Leary.
RAILROAD TRAINS. *See* TRAINS
RAILROADS
Casey Jones. *Unknown.*
Dr. Fell and Points West. Ogden Nash.
Georgie Allen. *Unknown.*
Railway Junction, The. De la Mare.
Terminal. Karl Shapiro.
What's the Railroad. Thoreau.
Wreck of Number Nine, The. *Unknown.*
RAIN
See also Rain *in* TITLE AND FIRST LINE INDEX
At Dieppe: Rain on the Down. Arthur Symons.
Autumn Rain. Aileen Fisher.
City Rain. Paul Bartlett.
City Rain. Rachel Field.
Cycle, The. Roethke.
Description of a City Shower, A. Swift.
Down the Rain Falls. Coatsworth.
Footwear. Justus.
Glass Falling. MacNeice.
How Gray the Rain. Coatsworth.
I Saw God Wash the World. Stidger.
In Time of Silver Rain. Langston Hughes.
It Is Raining. L. S. Mitchell.
Lime Avenue, The. Sacheverell Sitwell.
Little Rain. E. M. Roberts.
Messages of the Rain. Eich, *tr. fr. German by* Hamburger.
Ode on Contemplating Clapham Junction. *Fr.* Herman Moon's Hourbook. Christopher Middleton.
Old Man Rain. Cawein.
Others. Harry Behn.
Prayer for Rain. H. E. Palmer.
Rain and the Rainbow, The. Fredericks.
Rain at Night, The. Tu Fu, *tr. fr. Chinese.*
Rain Comes Sobbing to the Door, The. Henry Kendall.
Rain-Frogs, The. Rogetsu, *tr. fr. Japanese by* Henderson.
Rain, Rain, Go Away. *Unknown.*
Rain Riders. Scollard.
Rain Sizes. Ciardi.
Rainy Day, A. J. C. Lincoln.
Smoky Smirr o' Rain, The. G. C. Hay.
Song of the Rain. Hugh McCrae.
Sudden Shower. John Clare.
Summer Rain. Coatsworth.
Thunder Pools. R. P. T. Coffin.
Turn of the Moon. Robert Graves.
Umbrella Brigade, The. L. E. Richards.
Very Lovely. Fyleman.
Who Is Tapping at My Window. Deming.
Winter Rain. C. G. Rossetti.
RAINBOWS
See also Rainbow *in* TITLE AND FIRST LINE INDEX
Moon Rainbow, A. Robert Browning.
My Heart Leaps Up. Wordsworth.
RAMEAU, JEAN PHILIPPE. On an Air of Rameau. Arthur Symons.
RAMILLIES (ship). Old *Ramillies,* The. *Unknown.*
RATS. Rat, The. Andrew Young.
RATTLESNAKES. Rattlesnake, The. *Unknown.*

RAVENS
  See also RAVEN *in* TITLE AND FIRST LINE INDEX
  Advice to a Raven in Russia, December, 1812. Joel Barlow.
REASON
  Credibility. Ciardi.
  Reason. Ralph Hodgson.
  See also INTELLECT
REDWOOD TREES. Redwoods, The. Louis Simpson.
REFUGEES
  Disperson, The. Piontek, *tr. fr. German by* Middleton.
  Refugee Blues. Auden.
REINDEER. Rigorists. Marianne Moore.
RELIGION
  Bangkok. F. R. Scott.
  Boom! Nemerov.
  Garden of Love, The. *Fr.* Songs of Experience. Blake.
  Love Lifted Me. Paris Leary.
  Religion. Henry Vaughan.
  Satire III: "Kinde pitty chokes my spleene; brave scorn
    forbids." *Fr.* Satires. Donne.
  Sunday Morning. Wallace Stevens.
RELIGIOUS VERSE
  Book of Comfort, A (BoC). Elizabeth Goudge, ed.
  Earth Is the Lord's, The (EaLo). Helen Plotz, comp.
  Meditative Poem, The (MeP). Louis L. Martz, ed.
  Modern Religious Poems (MoRP). Jacob Trapp, ed.
  Poems of Doubt and Belief (PoDB). Tom F. Driver *and*
    Robert Pack, eds.
  Speaker's Treasury of 400 Quotable Poems, The (STF).
    Croft M. Pentz, comp.
  Treasury of Religious Verse, The (TRV). Donald T. Kauff-
    man, comp.
RESURRECTION, THE. *See* EASTER
REVENGE (ship). *Revenge,* The. Tennyson.
REVERE, PAUL. Paul Revere's Ride. *Fr.* Tales of a Wayside
  Inn. Longfellow.
REVOLUTION. Semi-Revolution, A. Robert Frost.
REYNOLDS, HENRY. To My Most Dearly Loved Friend, Henry
  Reynolds, Esq., *sel.* ("For from my cradle you must
  know that I"). Drayton.
RHINE (river). On Crossing the Rhine Bridge at Cologne by
  Night. Stadler, *tr. fr. German by* Hamburger.
RHINOCEROSES. Rhinoceros, The. Ogden Nash.
RHODORA. Rhodora, The. Emerson.
RICHARD I, KING OF ENGLAND (Richard Coeur de Lion). In
  No Way Can a Prisoner Reveal. Richard I, King of
  England, *tr. fr. French by* Terry.
RICHES. *See* WEALTH.
RIMBAUD, ARTHUR. You Did Well to Leave, Arthur Rimbaud!
  Char, *tr. fr. French by* Sherk.
RIVERS
  Along the River Shore. Zorro, *tr. fr. Portuguese by* Davis.
  Green River. Bryant.
  Looking-Glass River. R. L. Stevenson.
  Musing by a River. Moses Browne.
  Negro Speaks of Rivers, The. Langston Hughes.
  River God, The. *Fr.* The Faithful Shepherdess. John
    Fletcher.
  River Is a Piece of Sky, The. Ciardi.
  Sailing upon the River. *Fr.* The Borough. Crabbe.
  Two Rivers. Emerson.
  Two Streams, The. O. W. Holmes.
  Way to the Sea, The. Laurence Lerner.
ROADS
  Conspiracy, The. Guy Owen.
  Merritt Parkway. Levertov.
  Post-Roads. *Fr.* The Atlas. Slessor.
  Road, The. Helene Johnson.
  Road Not Taken, The. Robert Frost.
  Roads. Rachel Field.
  Roadways. Masefield.
  Rolling English Road, The. G. K. Chesterton.
  Walker, It Is Your Footsteps. Machado, *tr. fr. Spanish by*
    Flores.
ROBBERS AND OUTLAWS
  Brennan on the Moor. *Unknown.*
  Bushrangers, The. E. P. Harrington.
  Cole Younger. *Unknown.*
  Death of Ben Hall, The. W. H. Ogilvie.
  Jack Donahue. *Unknown.*
  Jack Sheppard. *Unknown.*
  Morgan. E. P. Harrington.
  Sam Bass. *Unknown.*
  Wild Colonial Boy, The. *Unknown.*
ROBIN GOODFELLOW. Mad-Merry Pranks of Robin Good-
  Fellow, The. *Unknown.*
ROBIN HOOD
  Birth of Robin Hood, The. *Unknown.*
  Death of Robin Hood, The. *Unknown.*
  Dirge for Robin Hood. *Fr.* Death of Robert, Earl of
    Huntington. Munday *and* Chettle.
  Robin Hood and Alan a Dale. *Unknown.*
  Robin Hood and Guy of Gisborne. *Unknown.*
  Robin Hood and the Bishop of Hereford. *Unknown.*

  Robin Hood and the Butcher. *Unknown.*
  Robin Hood and the Curtal Friar. *Unknown.*
  Robin Hood and the Two Priests. *Unknown.*
  Robin Hood and the Widow's Three Sons. *Unknown.*
ROBINS
  Robin, The. *Unknown.*
  Robin Redbreast. Allingham.
  Robin is the one, The. Emily Dickinson.
  Robin's Epitaph, A. Samuel Rogers.
  Secret, The. *Unknown.*
ROBOTS. Man from the Top of the Mind, The. Wagoner.
ROCK LILIES. Rock-Lily. R. E. Robinson.
ROCKS. *See* STONES AND ROCKS
ROLLER-COASTERS. Flight of the Roller-coaster. Souster.
ROME, ITALY
  For the New Railway Station in Rome. Wilbur.
  Roma. Rutilius, *tr. fr. Latin by* Pound.
  Rome. Du Bellay, *tr. fr. French by* Winters.
  Tibur is beautiful, too, and the orchard slopes, and the Anio.
    Fr. Amours de Voyage. Clough.
  To Rome Entombed in Her Ruins. Quevedo, *tr. fr. Spanish
    by* Flores.
ROMEO AND JULIET. Play, The. *Fr.* The Sentimental Bloke.
  Dennis.
ROOSEVELT, FRANKLIN DELANO. When Death Came April
  Twelve 1945. Sandburg.
ROOSTERS. *See* COCKS
ROPE. Ropewalk, The. Longfellow.
ROSES
  Fable XLV: Poet and the Rose, The. John Gay.
  Landscape as Metal and Flowers. W. T. Scott.
  Rose, The. "Gabriela Mistral," *tr. fr. Spanish by* Flores.
  Rose, The. Tasso, *tr. fr. Italian by* Drummond.
  Rose amid the Heather. Goethe, *tr. fr. German by* Marvin.
  Rose Family, The. Robert Frost.
  Rosebush, Less Presumption. Quevedo, *tr. fr. Spanish by*
    Davis.
  Sick Rose, The. *Fr.* Songs of Experience. Blake.
  Summer Image. Hebbel, *tr. fr. German by* Gillhoff.
  'Tis the Last Rose of Summer. Thomas Moore.
  To the Rose. Herrick.
  White Rose, A. J. B. O'Reilly.
ROUSSEAU, JEAN JACQUES. Mock On, Mock On, Voltaire,
  Rousseau. Blake.
ROYAL GEORGE (ship). Loss of the *Royal George,* The.
  Cowper.
RUSSELL, LUCY, COUNTESS OF BEDFORD. On Lucy Countesse
  of Bedford. Jonson.
RUSSIA
  On Reading a Soviet Novel. Roy Fuller.
  Sestina for Khasan Israelov. *Fr.* Wildtrack. Wain.
RUTLEDGE, ANN. Anne Rutledge. *Fr.* Spoon River Anthology.
  E. L. Masters.

S

SABBATH
  Attending Church. *Unknown.*
  Not on Sunday Night. *Unknown.*
  Some keep the Sabbath going to church. Emily Dickinson.
  Son-Dayes. Henry Vaughan.
  Sunday Morning. Wallace Stevens.
SACCO-VANZETTI CASE. Sacco Writes to His Son. Alun Lewis.
SACRAMENT, THE. *See* EUCHARIST
SAILING AND SAILORS
  Becalmed. Blight.
  Forty Singing Seamen. Noyes.
  Jolly Sailors Bold. *Unknown.*
  Long Trail, The. Kipling.
  Off Rivière du Loup. D. C. Scott.
  Offshore. Philip Booth.
  Old Song Re-sung, An. Masefield.
  Peg-Leg's Fiddle. Bill Adams.
  Rime of the Ancient Mariner, The. S. T. Coleridge.
  Sailboat, Your Secret. Robert Francis.
  Sailing, Sailing. Gray Burr.
  Sailor. P. K. Page.
  Sea Gypsy, The. Hovey.
  Seafarer, The. *Unknown, tr. fr. Anglo-Saxon by* Pound.
  Song for All Seas, All Ships. Walt Whitman.
  Storm at Sea. Davenant.
  Two Sails. C. F. Meyer, *tr. fr. German by* Fickert.
  Vacationer. Walker Gibson.
  Wet Sheet and a Flowing Sea, A. Allan Cunningham.
  What the Red-Haired Bo'sun Said. Souster.
  Where Lies the Land. Clough.
  Ye Mariners of England. Thomas Campbell.
  Harrap Book of Sea Verse, The (HaSV). Ronald Hope, ed.
  See also SEA CHANTEYS

SAINT AGNES'S EVE
Eve of Saint Agnes, The. Keats.
St. Agnes' Eve. Tennyson.
SAINT VALENTINE'S DAY. *See* VALENTINE'S DAY
SAINTS. Saints. George Garrett.
SALEM, MASSACHUSETTS
Salem. Robert Lowell.
Salems of Oppression. J. J. Keith.
SALINAS, FRANCISCO. Ode to Francisco Salinas. León, *tr. fr. Spanish by* Morgan.
SALMON
Salmon Drowns Eagle. Malcolm Lowry.
Sockeye Salmon. Hambleton.
SALVATION ARMY. General William Booth Enters into Heaven. Vachel Lindsay.
SAMSON (Bible)
How Samson Bore Away the Gates of Gaza. Vachel Lindsay.
Samson Agonistes. Milton.
SAN FRANCISCO, CALIFORNIA
Great Chinese Dragon, The. Ferlinghetti.
Returned to Frisco, 1946. W. D. Snodgrass.
Seal Rocks: San Francisco. Conquest.
SANCHO PANZA. Sancho Panza's Heritage. Meckel, *tr. fr. German by* Middleton.
SAND
Culbin Sands. Andrew Young.
White Sand and Grey Sand. *Unknown.*
SANDUCAR DE BARRAMEDA, SPAIN. Summer's Night, A. Machado, *tr. fr. Spanish by* Duffy.
SANTA CLAUS
Boy Who Laughed at Santa Claus, The. Ogden Nash.
Death of Santa Claus, The. Starrett.
Mrs. Santa Claus' Christmas Present. A. S. Morris.
Santa Claus. *Unknown.*
Visit from St. Nicholas, A. C. C. Moore.
SANTE FÉ TRAIL. Effortlessly Democratic Santa Fe Trail. Martha Baird.
SANTAYANA, GEORGE. Upon the Death of George Santayana. Hecht.
SARACENS. War Song of the Saracens. *Fr.* Hassan. Flecker.
SARAJEVO, YUGOSLAVIA. Sarajevo. Durrell.
SARTO, ANDREA DEL. Andrea del Sarto. Robert Browning.
SATAN
Address to the Deil. Burns.
Dark Angel, The. Lionel Johnson.
Devil, The. *Unknown.*
Epilogue: "Truly, my Satan, thou art but a dunce." *Fr.* The Gates of Paradise. Blake.
Fallen Angels. *Fr.* Paradise Lost. Milton.
Lucifer. Maxwell Anderson.
Lucifer in Starlight. George Meredith.
Lucifer in the Train. A. C. Rich.
Sir, I commend you to the spirit. *Fr.* Divine Poems. Villa.
Top Hat and Tales. Lorna Beers.
When Satan Fell. D. H. Lawrence.
SATELLITES. Little Satellite. Krows.
SATIRIC VERSE
Absalom and Achitophel, Pt. I. Dryden.
Bagpipe Music. MacNeice.
Battle of Blenheim, The. Southey.
Beau, The. *Unknown.*
Beautiful Young Nymph Going to Bed, A. Swift.
Beppo. Byron.
Blind Men and the Elephant, The. Saxe.
Boom! Nemerov.
Bunthorne's Song. *Fr.* Patience. W. S. Gilbert.
Cambridge Ladies. *Fr.* Sonnets—Realities. E. E. Cummings.
Canadian Authors Meet, The. F. R. Scott.
Carol with Variations. McGinley.
Country Club Sunday. McGinley.
Country Mouse, The. Cowley.
Dirge: "1-2-3 was the number he played but today the number came 3-2-1." Fearing.
Does It Matter? Sassoon.
Don't Shake the Bottle, Shake Your Mother-in-Law. McGinley.
Elegy on a Lap Dog, An. John Gay.
Epistle III: "Pult'ney, methinks you blame my breach of word." John Gay.
Epistle to Dr. Arbuthnot, An. Pope.
Epistle to Miss Blount. Pope.
Epitaph, An: "Interred beneath this marble stone." Prior.
Epitaphs for Three Prominent Persons. McGinley.
Fable: "Mountain and the squirrel, The." Emerson.
Furniture of a Woman's Mind, The. Swift.
Godolphin Horne. Belloc.
Golf Links, The. Cleghorn.
Good Rich Man, The. G. K. Chesterton.
Gray Squirrel, The. Humbert Wolfe.
Greatest Show on Earth. Lamport.
Here Lies a Lady. Ransom.
Higher Pantheism in a Nutshell, The. Swinburne.
Hybris, Nemesis, One, Two, Three. Ostriker.

Impossible Fact, The. Morgenstern, *tr. fr. German by* Kaufmann.
In Church. Thomas Hardy.
In Westminster Abbey. Betjeman.
Lady's Dressing Room, The. Swift.
Latest Decalogue, The. Clough.
London. Samuel Johnson.
Lovers, The. Conrad Aiken.
MacFlecknoe. Dryden.
Miniver Cheevy. E. A. Robinson.
Mrs. Frances Harris's Petition. Swift.
Mouse That Gnawed the Oak-Tree Down, The. Vachel Lindsay.
Next to of Course God. E. E. Cummings.
Nightmare Number Four. Robert Bloch.
Oh Come, Little Children. McGinley.
Of the Characters of Women, *sel. Fr.* Moral Essays. Pope.
Of the Use of Riches. *Fr.* Moral Essays. Pope.
On Charles II. Rochester.
Ozymandias. Shelley.
Pity This Busy Monster, Manunkind. E. E. Cummings.
Plato told/ him: he couldn't. E. E. Cummings.
Plot to Assassinate the Chase Manhattan Bank, The. Larsen.
Poem, or Beauty Hurts Mr. Vinal. E. E. Cummings.
Pope Clement's Illness. Berni, *tr. fr. Italian by* Priest.
Progress. Hoffenstein.
Progress of Beauty, The. Swift.
Progress of Marriage, The. Swift.
Progress of Poetry, The. Swift.
Rape of the Lock, The. Pope.
Reasonable Affliction, A. Prior.
Reflections Dental. McGinley.
Résumé. Dorothy Parker.
Richard Cory. E. A. Robinson.
Rooster, The. Orlovitz.
Satire III: "Kinde pitty chokes my spleene; brave scorn forbids." *Fr.* Satires. Donne.
Satires, *sels.* Juvenal, *tr. fr. Latin.*
Satires of Circumstance, *sels.* Thomas Hardy.
Satirical Elegy on the Death of a Late Famous General, A. Swift.
Short Song of Congratulation, A. Samuel Johnson.
Sonnet: "Dear Geese, whose haunt is where weak waters flow." Góngora, *tr. fr. Spanish by* Churton.
Temple of Infamy, The, *sel.* ("But hark! What hubbub now is this that comes"). Harpur.
To a Louse [on Seeing One on a Lady's Bonnet at Church]. Burns.
To a Nose. Quevedo, *tr. fr. Spanish by* Burnham.
Treason. Sir John Harington.
Tunnyng of Elynour Rummyng, The, *sel.* Skelton.
Vanity of Human Wishes, The. Samuel Johnson.
Verses on the Death of Dr. Swift. Swift.
Victory Dance, A. Noyes.
Virtuous Fox and the Self-righteous Cat, The. John Cunningham.
Vision of Judgment, The. Byron.
War Is Kind. Stephen Crane.
Were I a King. Vere.
What Mr. Robinson Thinks. *Fr.* The Biglow Papers. J. R. Lowell.
When a Man Hath No Freedom to Fight for at Home. Byron.
Wicked Treasonable Libel, A. Swift.
World State, The. G. K. Chesterton.
SAUL (Bible). Saul, *sel.* Robert Browning.
SCARECROWS. Lonely Scarecrow, The. Kirkup.
SCHOENBERG, ARNOLD. Ode to Arnold Schoenberg. Tomlinson.
SCHOLARS AND SCHOLARSHIP
Clerk Ther Was of Caunterbrigge Also, A. Skeat.
Grammarian's Funeral, A. Robert Browning.
Ode on the Despoilers of Learning in an American University (1947), An. Yvor Winters.
On Taking a Bachelor's Degree. Christopher Smart.
Scholar, The. Southey.
Scholar Complains, The. *Unknown.*
Scholar-Gipsy, The. Matthew Arnold.
Scholars, The. Yeats.
Schools. *Fr.* The Borough. Crabbe.
To a Friend, on Her Examination for the Doctorate in English. J. V. Cunningham.
SCHOOLS
Elementary School Classroom in a Slum, An. Spender.
Exercise Book. Dehn.
Farm Boy after Summer. Robert Francis.
He Will Make the Grade. Earnshaw.
In School-Days. Whittier.
Ode on a Distant Prospect of Clapham Academy. Thomas Hood.
School Is Out. Frances Frost.
Schoolboy, The. *Fr.* Songs of Experience. Blake.
Schools. *Fr.* The Borough. Crabbe.
SCHOOLMASTERS. *See* TEACHING AND TEACHERS

SCIENCE
Coy nature (which remain'd, though aged grown). *Fr.* Ode upon Dr. Harvey. Abraham Cowley.
Laboratory Poem. James Merrill.
Letter to Alex Comfort. Abse.
Revelation. Keesing.
Sonnet: To Science. *Fr.* Al Aaraaf. Poe.
SCIENCE FICTION. Science Fiction. Amis.
SCOTLAND
Bagpipe Music. MacNeice.
Cotter's Saturday Night, The. Burns.
Ode on the Popular Superstitions of the Highlands of Scotland, An. William Collins.
Patriot, The. *Fr.* The Lay of the Last Minstrel. Walter Scott.
Scots Wha Hae. Burns.
SCOTS, THE. Gathering, The. *Fr.* Towards the Last Spike. E. J. Pratt.
SCRIPTURES, HOLY. *See* BIBLE
SCULPTURE AND SCULPTORS
Archaic Torso of Apollo. Rilke, *tr. fr. German by* Kaufmann.
Artist and His Work, The. Michelangelo, *tr. fr. Italian by* Symonds.
Arundel Tomb, An. Philip Larkin.
Caryatid. Benn, *tr. fr. German by* Hamburger.
Hans Christian Andersen in Central Park. Sobiloff.
Lover and the Sculptor, The. Michelangelo, *tr. fr. Italian by* Symonds.
On Seeing the Elgin Marbles. Keats.
Proem, A: "When in my walks I meet some ruddy lad." Samuel Ward.
Statue, The. John Fuller.
SEA
See also Sea *in* TITLE AND FIRST LINE INDEX
Absences. Philip Larkin.
Amoris Exsul: In the Bay. Arthur Symons.
At Melville's Tomb. Hart Crane.
At the Slackening of the Tide. James Wright.
Break, Break, Break. Tennyson.
By the Sea. R. W. Dixon.
By the Sea. Hollander.
Calm, The. Donne.
Chime of the Sea. D. G. Rossetti.
Cold Divinities, The. James Wright.
Coral Grove, The. Percival.
Dover Beach. Matthew Arnold.
Earth and Sea. Pushkin, *tr. fr. Russian by* Kisch.
East Anglian Bathe. Betjeman.
Grave, A. Marianne Moore.
Grim and Gloomy. James Reeves.
I started early, took my dog. Emily Dickinson.
Kraken, The. Tennyson.
Landsman, The. Moschus. *tr. fr. Greek by* Shelley.
Main-Deep, The. James Stephens.
Moldering Hulk, The. Machado, *tr. fr. Spanish by* Flores.
Moon is distant from the sea, The. Emily Dickinson.
Morality of Poetry, The. James Wright.
Neither Out Far nor in Deep. Robert Frost.
Ocean, The. *Fr.* Childe Harold's Pilgrimage. Byron.
Ocean. Jeffers.
Ocean Wood, The. De Tabley.
Off Saguenay. A. G. Bailey.
On the Sea. Keats.
Oread. Doolittle ("H. D.").
Out of the Cradle Endlessly Rocking. Walt Whitman.
Patrolling Barnegat. Walt Whitman.
Pebbles. Melville.
Pines and the Sea, The. Cranch.
Plague of Dead Sharks. Alan Dugan.
Purse, The—Seine. Paul Blackburn.
Quaker Graveyard in Nantucket, The. Robert Lowell.
Sea and the Hills, The. Kipling.
Sea and the Skylark, The. G. M. Hopkins.
Sea Fever. Masefield.
Sea-Grief. Dowell O'Reilly.
Sea Lullaby. Wylie.
Sea Pieces. Robert Fitzgerald.
Sea retains such images, The. *Fr.* Europe. Dudek.
Sea Surface Full of Clouds. Wallace Stevens.
Seascape. Auden.
Seascape. Spender.
Seashell. Darío, *tr. fr. Spanish by* Volland.
Shell, The. James Stephens.
Silences. E. J. Pratt.
Sketch. Sandburg.
Song of the Sea, The. C. F. Meyer, *tr. fr. German by* Wright.
Sonnets, Part II, *sel.* ("The breeze is sharp, the sky is hard and blue"). F. G. Tuckerman.
Sound of the Sea, The. Longfellow.
Symphony in Gray Major. Darío, *tr. fr. Spanish by* Levertov.
Tide, The. Longfellow.

Triumph of Time, The, *sel.* Swinburne.
Wanderer's Song, A. Masefield.
Wave. Barbara Guest.
Winter Views Serene. *Fr.* The Borough. Crabbe.
Wonders of the Deep, The. Parmentier.
World below the Brine, The. Walt Whitman.
Young Sea. Sandburg.
Harrap Book of Sea Verse, The (HaSV). Ronald Hope, ed.
SEA CHANTEYS
Old Anchor Chanty. Herbert Trench.
Ballads and Sea Songs from Nova Scotia (BSNS). W. Roy Mackenzie, comp.
SEA GULLS. *See* GULLS
SEA SHELLS. *See* SHELLS
SEA VOYAGES. *See* VOYAGES
SEALS
Dancing Seal, The. W. W. Gibson.
Off Spectacle Island. Eberhart.
Seals in Penobscot Bay, The. Daniel Hoffman.
SEASONS
Against Seasons. Mezey.
Human Seasons, The. Keats.
Hymn on the Seasons, A. *Fr.* The Seasons. James Thomson.
Love Song, A. W. F. Hawley.
Seasons of the Soul. Allen Tate.
Solace. Delany.
Song of the Four Seasons, A. Austin Dobson.
Wheel, The. Yeats.
Winter Will Follow. R. W. Dixon.
SECOND WORLD WAR. *See* WORLD WAR II
SECRETARIES. Secretary. Ted Hughes.
SEED
In the Heart of a Seed. K. L. Brown.
Seeds. De la Mare.
Seeds. Muriel Stuart.
SELKIRK, ALEXANDER. Verses Supposed to Be Written by Alexander Selkirk. Cowper.
SENECA. Seneca. Merton.
SENNACHERIB, KING OF ASSYRIA. Destruction of Sennacherib, The. Byron.
SEPARATION
Division, The. Thomas Hardy.
Farewell. Heinrich Albert, *tr. fr. German by* Zwart.
Farewell, A. *Fr.* The Unknown Eros. Coventry Patmore.
Parting after a Quarrel. Tietjens.
Separation, A. W. J. Cory.
Separation. Merwin.
Taking Leave of a Friend. Li Po, *tr. fr. Chinese by* Pound.
When We Two Parted. Byron.
You Went Away. Krolow, *tr. fr. German by* Leibholz.
SEPTEMBER
Another September. Kinsella.
September. Benn, *tr. fr. German by* Middleton.
September. H. H. Jackson.
September in Australia. Henry Kendall.
September in the Park. W. D. Snodgrass.
September Winds. Bevington.
Tell Me Not Here, It Needs Not Saying. A. E. Housman.
SERFS. *See* SLAVERY
SEWALL, SAMUEL. Samuel Sewall. Hecht.
SHADOWS
Child and the Shadow, The. Elizabeth Jennings.
Lecture upon the Shadow, A. Donne.
My Shadow. R. L. Stevenson.
Shadow Dance. Eastwick.
Shadows in the Air. Krolow, *tr. fr. German by* Middleton.
SHADWELL, THOMAS. MacFlecknoe. Dryden.
SHAFTESBURY, ANTHONY ASHLEY COOPER, 1ST EARL OF. Absalom and Achitophel, *sel.* Dryden.
SHAKESPEARE, WILLIAM
Elegy on Shakespeare. Basse.
On Shakespeare. Milton.
On Sitting Down to Read *King Lear* Once Again. Keats.
On the Site of a Mulberry-Tree; Planted by Wm. Shakespeare; Felled by the Rev. F. Gastrell. D. G. Rossetti.
Shakespeare. Matthew Arnold.
To the Memory of My Beloved Master William Shakespeare. Jonson.
To the Reader. Jonson.
William Shakespeare to Mrs. Anne, Regular Servant to the Rev. Mr. Precentor of York. Thomas Gray.
SHANNON (ship)
Chesapeake and the *Shannon,* The ("The *Chesapeake* so bold"). *Unknown.*
Chesapeake and the *Shannon,* The (" 'Twas of the Shannon frigate in the merry month of May"). *Unknown.*
SHARECROPPERS. Down on Roberts' Farm. Claude Reeves.
SHARKS. Maldive Shark, The. Melville.
SHAW, ROBERT GOULD. Ode in Time of Hesitation, An. W. V. Moody.
SHEEP
Ariel. David Campbell.
Darby Ram, The. *Unknown.*

SHEEP (*continued*)
  Happy Sheep, The. Thorley.
  Sheep. Hal Porter.
SHEEPHERDERS
  Tom Farley. Colin Thiele.
  Shepherd, The. Mary Gilmore.
  See also SHEPHERDS AND SHEPHERDESSES
SHEEPSHEARING
  Click Go the Shears, Boys. *Unknown.*
  Flash Jack from Gundagai. *Unknown.*
  Shearer's Song, The. *Unknown.*
SHELLEY, PERCY BYSSHE
  Cor Cordium. Swinburne.
  Fishes and the Poet's Hands, The. Yerby.
  Memorabilia. Robert Browning.
  Percy Shelley. J. P. Bishop.
  Shelley. Herwegh, *tr. fr. German by* Guenther.
  Shelley's Skylark. Thomas Hardy.
SHELLS
  Chambered Nautilus, The. *Fr.* The Autocrat of the Break-
    fast Table. O. W. Holmes.
  Seashell. Darío, *tr. fr. Spanish by* Volland.
  Sea Shell. Amy Lowell.
  See What a Lovely Shell. Tennyson.
  Shell, The. James Stephens.
  Shells, The. W. S. Landor.
  Wanderer, The. Eugene Field.
SHENANDOAH VALLEY, VIRGINIA. Portent, The. Melville.
SHEPHERDS AND SHEPHERDESSES
  Herding Lambs. Pitter.
  Kurdish Shepherds. Alan Ross.
  Moonlight . . . Scattered Clouds. *Fr.* The Farmer's Boy.
    Bloomfield.
  Nymph's Reply to the Shepherd, The. Ralegh.
  O Lovely Mountain Shepherd Lasses. Sacchetti, *tr. fr.
    Italian by* Valency.
  Passionate Shepherd to His Love, The. Marlowe.
  Shepherd, The. *Fr.* Songs of Innocence. Blake.
  Shepherd, The. *Fr.* The Prelude. Wordsworth.
  See also SHEEPHERDERS
SHERIDAN, PHILIP HENRY. Sheridan's Ride. T. B. Read.
SHERMAN, WILLIAM TECUMSEH. When Sherman Marched
  Down to the Sea. Byers.
SHILOH, BATTLE OF. Shiloh. Melville.
SHIPS
  After the Sea-Ship. Walt Whitman.
  As the proud horse, with costly trappings gay. *Fr.* The
    Shipwreck. William Falconer.
  Big Steamers. Kipling.
  Building of the Ship, The, *sel.* Longfellow.
  Cargoes. Masefield.
  Choosing a Mast. Roy Campbell.
  Clipper Ships and Captains. S. V. Benét.
  Dismantled Ship, The. Walt Whitman.
  Garden of Ships, The. Douglas Stewart.
  Leave Her, Johnny. *Unknown.*
  Liner She's a Lady, The. Kipling.
  Marooned. Rachel Field.
  O to sail in a ship! *Fr.* A Song of Joys. Walt Whitman.
  Old Ships, The. Flecker.
  Outwards. *Unknown.*
  Passer-by, A. Robert Bridges.
  She Is Far from the Land. Thomas Hood.
  Ship, The. Gogarty.
  Ships, *sel.* Masefield.
  Ships. N. B. Turner.
  Ship's Bell. Dresbach.
  Ships of Yule, The. Bliss Carman.
  Song for All Seas, All Ships. Walt Whitman.
  Spanish Galleons Seen by an Aztec, The. *Fr.* The Indian
    Emperor. Dryden.
  Wanderer, The. Masefield.
  Where Lies the Land to Which Yon Ship Must Go? Words-
    worth.
  See also BOATS; YACHTS
SHIPWRECKS
  Aeolian Harp, The. Melville.
  Berg, The—a Dream. Melville.
  Cedar Grove, The. *Unknown.*
  Convergence of the Twain, The. Thomas Hardy.
  Loss of the *Eurydice,* The. G. M. Hopkins.
  Old *Ramillies,* The. *Unknown.*
  On the Loss of the *Royal George.* Cowper.
  Skipper Ireson's Ride. Whittier.
  Wreck of the *Atlantic,* The. *Unknown.*
  Wreck of the *Deutschland,* The. G. M. Hopkins.
  Wreck of the *Glenaloon,* The. *Unknown.*
  Wreck of the *Hesperus,* The. Longfellow.
  Wreck of the *Julie Plante,* The. W. H. Drummond.
SHIVAJI. Rise of Shivaji, The. Zulfikar Ghose.
SHOEMAKERS
  Amends to the Tailors and Soutars. William Dunbar.
  Cobbler, The. Chaffee.
  Shoemaker, The. *Unknown.*

SHOES
  Choosing Shoes. ffrida Wolfe.
  New Shoes. M. S. Watts.
  Shoes. Tom Robinson.
SHOPPING AND SHOPS
  Counters. Coatsworth.
  General Store. Rachel Field.
  Market, The. *Fr. Mts. & Rivers.* Snyder.
  Pushcart Row. Rachel Field.
  Saturday Shopping. Edelman.
  Shop Windows. Fyleman.
  Victoria Markets Recollected in Tranquillity, The, *sel.* Wil-
    mot.
SHRIMPS. Shrimp, The. Moses Browne.
SIBERIA. Siberia. Mangan.
SICKNESS. *See* ILLNESS
SIDNEY, SIR PHILIP. Elegy on the Death of Sidney. Edward
  Dyer.
SILENCE
  See also Silence *in* TITLE AND FIRST LINE INDEX
  After the Dazzle of Day. Walt Whitman.
  Burke and Wills. Barratt.
  Pastourelle. D. J. Hayes.
  Rest and Silence. Trakl, *tr. fr. German by* Kaufmann.
  Silences. E. J. Pratt.
  Silentium. Tyutchev, *tr. fr. Russian by* Deutsch.
  Sonnet: Silence. Poe.
  Stillness, The. Basho, *tr. fr. Japanese by* Henderson.
  Triad. Crapsey.
  Witnesses. Hemley.
SILKWORMS
  Psyche. Very.
  Silkworms, The. Douglas Stewart.
SIMEON (Bible). Light in the Temple, The. W. R. Benét.
SIMHATH TORAH. Hand, The. Feldman.
SIMON, SAINT, AND SAINT JUDE. Upon the Feast of St.
  Simon and St. Jude. Samuel Johnson.
SIMPLICITY. Ode to Simplicity. William Collins.
SIN
  Christ Complains to Sinners. *Unknown.*
  Confession in Brief, A. Régnier, *tr. fr. French by* Thorley.
  I stood upon a high place. *Fr.* The Black Riders. Stephen
    Crane.
  Sin and Its Cure. *Unknown.*
  Sinnes Heavie Loade. Southwell.
  Sting of Death, The. F. G. Scott.
SINGING AND SINGERS
  At a Solemn Musick. Milton.
  Everyone Sang. Sassoon.
  M., Singing. Bogan.
  Quartette, The. De la Mare.
  School for Tenors, The. Grass, *tr. fr. German by* Ham-
    burger.
  Singing. R. L. Stevenson.
  Solitary Reaper, The. Wordsworth.
  To a Lady Who Did Sing Excellently. Herbert of Cher-
    bury.
  Swans Sing. S. T. Coleridge.
SIOUX INDIANS
  On the Little Bighorn. Ray Smith.
  Sioux, The. Eugene Field.
  Sioux Indians. *Unknown.*
SKATING AND SKATES
  See also Skating *in* TITLE AND FIRST LINE INDEX
  Black Water and Bright Air. Carrier.
  Fast. Tagliabue.
  Ice-Skaters. Elder Olson.
  River Skater. Welles.
  Skaters, The. J. G. Fletcher.
  Skaters, The. John Williams.
  Skater's Waltz, A. Gray Burr.
  To Kate, Skating Better than Her Date. Daiches.
SKIING
  Skier. Robert Francis.
  T-Bar. P. K. Page.
SKUNKS
  See also Skunk *in* TITLE AND FIRST LINE INDEX
  Tale of the Skunk and Poor Jez, The. John Becker.
SKY
  Features of the Sky. Reverdy, *tr. fr. French by* Roche.
  Winter Heavens. George Meredith.
SKYLARKS. *See* LARKS
SKYSCRAPERS. Skyscraper. Sandburg.
SKYWRITING. Sky-Writer. Starrett.
SLAUGHTER OF THE INNOCENTS. *See* HEROD THE GREAT
SLAVERY
  Fugitive Slaves, The. Very.
  Middle Passage. Robert Hayden.
  Old Cabin, The. P. L. Dunbar.
  Serf, The. Roy Campbell.
  Slaves. J. R. Lowell.
  Slave's Dream, The. Longfellow.
  Song of the Galley-Slaves. Kipling.
  Sympathy. P. L. Dunbar.

To Sir Toby. Freneau.
SLEDS
Little Red Sled, The. Bush.
Winter Lovers. Robert Watson.
SLEEP
Care-Charmer Sleep. *Fr.* To Delia. Samuel Daniel.
Care-charming Sleep. *Fr.* The Tragedy of Valentinian. John Fletcher.
Come, Sleep! O Sleep, the certain knot of peace. *Fr.* Astrophel and Stella. Philip Sidney.
Falling Asleep. Sassoon.
Final Hunger, The. Vassar Miller.
Hymns to the Night, *sel.* "Novalis," *tr. fr. German by* Kaufmann.
Invocation: "O Sleep! I bring thee this long-cellared wine." Desportes, *tr. fr. French by* Giese.
Lullaby: "Beloved, may your sleep be sound." Yeats.
Ode to Sleep. Smollett.
Sacrament of Sleep, The. Oxenham.
Siesta, The. *Unknown, tr. fr. Spanish by* Bryant.
Sleep, The. E. B. Browning.
Sleep and Poetry. Keats.
Sleep, of all gifts of Heaven held supreme. *Fr.* L'Olive. Du Bellay.
To Sleep. Casa, *tr. fr. Italian by* Symonds.
To Sleep. Keats.
To Sleep. Kochanowski, *tr. fr. Polish by* Kirkconnell.
To Sleep. Wordsworth.
SLEIGHS
Blue Sleigh. W. T. Scott.
Sleighride. Patrick Anderson.
SLOTHS. Sloth, The. Roethke.
SLUGS. Slug in Woods. Birney.
SMILES
Growing Smiles. *Unknown.*
Little Things. *Unknown.*
Mask, The. E. B. Browning.
Only a Smile. *Unknown.*
They might not need me; but they might. *Fr.* Emily Dickinson.
SMITH, JOHN. Noah an' Jonah an' Cap'n John Smith. Marquis.
SMOKE
Smoke. Thoreau.
Smoke Animals. Rowena Bennett.
SMUGGLERS. Smuggler, The. *Unknown.*
SNAILS
See also Snail *in* TITLE AND FIRST LINE INDEX
Considering the Snail. Thom Gunn.
Housekeeper, The. Vincent Bourne, *tr. fr. Lat. in by* Lamb.
Snakes and Snails. Hallock.
SNAKES
See also Snake *in* TITLE AND FIRST LINE INDEX
In a Garden. D. C. Babcock.
Narrow fellow in the grass, A. Emily Dickinson.
Serpent, The. *Fr.* Four Fascinators. Char, *tr. fr. French by* Stern.
Serpent, The. Joseph Langland.
Snake Trying, The. W. W. E. Ross.
Snakecharmer. Plath.
Snakes and Snails. Hallock.
To the Snake. Levertov.
Viper, The. Pitter.
SNAPDRAGONS. Lucky Thing, A. Dorothy Aldis.
SNEEZES. Sneezing. Leigh Hunt.
SNIPES. To the Snipe. John Clare.
SNOW
See also Snow *in* TITLE AND FIRST LINE INDEX
April Snow, The. Very.
As the First Snow Fell. Goeckingk, *tr. fr. German by* Schoolfield.
Brindabella. Douglas Stewart.
Digging It Out. Hollander.
Effect of Snow, The. Robert Finch.
Falling Snow. *Unknown.*
First Snow. M. L. Allen.
First Snow in Alsace. Wilbur.
First Snow-fall, The, *sel.* J. R. Lowell.
First Winter's Day. Dorothy Aldis.
It sifts from leaden sieves. Emily Dickinson.
January. Coatsworth.
Late Show. Issa, *tr. fr. Japanese by* Henderson.
London Snow. Robert Bridges.
Magic Landscape, A. Fet, *tr. fr. Russian by* Deutsch.
Onset, The. Robert Frost.
Outside the Door. Annette Wynne.
Snow at Advent. Busta, *tr. fr. German by* Hamburger.
Snow in the Suburbs. Thomas Hardy.
Snow Man, The. Wallace Stevens.
Snow-bound. Whittier.
Snowfall. Carducci, *tr. fr. Italian.*
Snowfall, The. Justice.
Snow Fall, The. MacLeish.
Snow-Flakes. Longfellow.
Snowstorm. John Clare.

Snow Storm, The. Emerson.
Snowy Day, A. Dafydd ap Gwilym, *tr. fr. Welsh by* Bell.
Stopping by Woods on a Snowy Evening. Robert Frost.
Stories of Snow. P. K. Page.
To a Snowflake. Francis Thompson.
Velvet Shoes. Wylie.
White Fields. James Stephens.
Winter. Joso, *tr. fr. Japanese by* Henderson.
Winter Noon. Teasdale.
Winter Hymn, A—to the Snow. Ebenezer Jones.
SNOWBIRDS. Snow-Bird, The. F. D. Sherman.
SOCCER
Dangers of Foot-ball, The. *Fr.* Trivia. John Gay.
Football Song. Walter Scott.
Heaps on Heaps. *Fr.* A Match at Football. Concanen.
Man from Inversnaid, The. R. F. Murray.
SOCRATES. Socrates and Alcibiades. Hölderlin, *tr. fr. German by* Hilty.
SODOM. Ballad of the Trial of Sodom. Vernon Watkins.
SOHRAB. Sohrab and Rustum. Matthew Arnold.
SOLDIERS
See also Soldier *in* TITLE AND FIRST LINE INDEX
A Terre. Wilfred Owen.
All Day It Has Rained. Alun Lewis.
Anthem for Doomed Youth. Wilfred Owen.
Apples and Water. Robert Graves.
Army Corps on the March, An. Walt Whitman.
Bivouac of the Dead, The. Theodore O'Hara.
British Grenadiers, The. *Unknown.*
By the Bivouac's Fitful Flame. Walt Whitman.
Cavalry Crossing a Ford. Walt Whitman.
Conscript, The. MacNeice.
Danny Deever. Kipling.
Disabled. Wilfred Owen.
Dulce et Decorum Est. Wilfred Owen.
Elegy for a Dead Soldier. Karl Shapiro.
Epitaph for Chaeroneia. Aristotle, *tr. fr. Greek by* Kennedy.
Epitaph on an Army of Mercenaries. A. E. Housman.
Faithless Nelly Gray. Thomas Hood.
Fighting South of the Ramparts. *Unknown, tr. fr. Chinese by* Waley.
For the Fallen. Binyon.
General, The. Sassoon.
Gunga Din. Kipling.
Happy Warrior, The. Herbert Read.
How Can Man Die Better. Tyrtaeus, *tr. fr. Greek by* Higham.
Hugh Selwyn Mauberley, *sel.* ("These fought in any case"). Pound.
In an Age of Fops and Toys. *Fr.* Voluntaries. Emerson.
Jester in the Trench, The. Leon Gellert.
Johnny, I Hardly Knew Ye. *Unknown.*
Kid Has Gone to the Colors, The. Herschell.
Kilroy. Peter Viereck.
Lofty Lane. Gerard.
Man He Killed, The. Thomas Hardy.
Men in Green. David Campbell.
Men Who March Away. Thomas Hardy.
Misfit, The—1939-1945. Day Lewis.
Naming of Parts. *Fr.* Lessons of the War. Henry Reed.
Nostalgia. Karl Shapiro.
O What Is That Sound Which So Thrills the Ear? Auden.
Oldest Soldier, The. Robert Graves.
On a Soldier Fallen in the Philippines. W. V. Moody.
Over the Heather the Wet Wind Blows. Auden.
Pershing at the Front. Guiterman.
Portrait in the Guards, A. Laurence Whistler.
Rear-Guard, The. Sassoon.
Returned Volunteer to His Rifle, The. Melville.
Sentry, The. Alun Lewis.
Sergeant-Major Money. Robert Graves.
"Service Man, The." Kipling.
Old battlefield, fresh with spring flowers again. *Fr.* Seven Poems. Basho, *tr. fr. Japanese by* Page.
Sight in Camp in the Daybreak Gray and Dim, A. Walt Whitman.
Soldier, Rest! *Fr.* The Lady of the Lake. Walter Scott.
Soldier: Twentieth Century. Isaac Rosenberg.
Soldiers Bathing. Prince.
Soldier's Dream, The. Thomas Campbell.
Soldier's Song. Tobias Hume.
Strange Meeting. Wilfred Owen.
Three, The. Lenau, *tr. fr. German by* Gillhoff.
Tomb of Lt. John Learmonth, A.I.F., The. Manifold.
Tommy. Kipling.
Vergissmeinnicht. Keith Douglas.
Volunteer, The. Herbert Asquith.
Whisperin' Bill. Bacheller.
Wound-Dresser, The. Walt Whitman.
SOLITUDE
See also Solitude *in* TITLE AND FIRST LINE INDEX
Alastor; or, The Spirit of Solitude. Shelley.
Deviator, The. Warr.
Eighth Poem. Papini, *tr. fr. Italian by* Golino.

SOLITUDE (*continued*)
Immense Hour. Jiménez, *tr. fr. Spanish by* Gahan.
In the Woods Alone. *Unknown, tr. fr. Latin by* Waddell.
Journey into Misery. Goll, *tr. fr. German by* Middleton.
Ode on Solitude. Pope.
On Looking into Henry Moore. Livesay.
Peace. Bhartrihari, *tr. fr. Sanskrit by* More.
Quarry Pool, The. Levertov.
Quiet. Pickthall.
Reading the Book of Hills and Seas. T'ao Ch'ien, *tr. fr. Chinese by* Waley.
Room, The. Day Lewis.
Seclusion. Möricke, *tr. fr. German by* Wright.
Solitudes. Wheelock.
Sonnets to Laura: To Laura in Life, *sel.* ("Alone and ever weary with dark care"). Petrarch, *tr. fr. Italian by* Bergin.
There is a solitude of space. Emily Dickinson.
Wants. Philip Larkin.
SOLOMON
Building of Solomon's Temple, The. *Unknown.*
Solomon on the Vanity of the World, *sel.* Matthew Prior.
Solomon to Sheba. Yeats.
SOMERSET, ROBERT CARR, EARL OF. Upon the Sudden Restraint of the Earl of Sommerset, Falling from Favour. Henry Wotton.
SOPHOCLES. Wind, Gentle Evergreen. *Unknown.*
SOREL, CANADA. Old Nick in Sorel. Standish O'Grady.
SORROW. *See* GRIEF
SOUSA, JOHN PHILIP. Sousa. Edward Dorn.
SOUTH, THE. When the Mint Is in the Liquor. Ousley.
SOUTH AFRICA
Autumn Song. Brettell.
Caffer Commando, The, *sel.* Pringle.
Camp Fire. B. M. Bromley.
Coming, The. Delius.
Landing of the British Settlers of 1820, The, *sel.* Alex Wilmot.
Namaqualand after Rain. Plomer.
On Some South African Novelists. Roy Campbell.
On the Back Veld. Garstin.
Poets in Africa. Roy Campbell.
Reminiscence of 1820, A, *sel.* Dugmore.
To the Veld. Cripps.
SOUTH WIND. South Wind, The. Robert Bridges.
SOUTHEY, ROBERT
Dedication: "Bob Southey! You're a poet—Poet-laureate." *Fr. Don Juan.* Byron.
Epitaph on Robert Southey. Thomas Moore.
SOUTINE, CHAIM. Story of Soutine, A. Schevill.
SPACE (outer space)
Space. Inez Hogan.
Space Travel. Krows.
SPAIN
Spain 1937. Auden.
Anthology of Spanish Poetry, An (AnSP). Angel Flores, ed.
Renaissance and Baroque Lyrics (RBL). Harold Martin Priest, ed.
SPANISH AMERICAN WAR
Ode in Time of Hesitation, An. W. V. Moody.
On a Soldier Fallen in the Philippines. W. V. Moody.
SPANISH ARMADA
Armada, The, *sel. Fr. Lays of Ancient Rome.* T. B. Macaulay.
Ballad to Queen Elizabeth, A. Austin Dobson.
On the Armada Which Battled against England. Góngora, *tr. fr. Spanish by* Soper *and* Fletcher.
Spanish Armada, The. Still.
SPANISH CIVIL WAR. *See* CIVIL WAR, SPANISH
SPARROWS
House and Shutter. Turco.
Sparrow's Song, The. *Unknown.*
SPHINX
Sphinx, The. Emerson.
Sphinx, The, *sel.* Oscar Wilde.
SPIDERS
See also Spider *in* TITLE AND FIRST LINE INDEX
Arachnida, Female. Aletha Humphreys.
Design. Robert Frost.
Mr. Edwards and the Spider. Robert Lowell.
Noiseless Patient Spider, A. Walt Whitman.
On a Spider. Littleton.
Spider and the Fly, The. Mary Howitt.
Upon a Spider Catching a Fly. Edward Taylor.
SPORTS AND GAMES
Good Sportsmanship. Armour.
Sprints and Distances (SD). Lillian Morrison, comp.
SPRING
See also Spring *in* TITLE AND FIRST LINE INDEX
Admonition for Spring. L. A. MacKay.
Alons au bois le may cueillir. Charles d'Orléans, *tr. fr. French by* Henley.
Another Spring. C. G. Rossetti.
Barren Spring. *Fr. The House of Life.* D. G. Rossetti.

Budding Spring. Jack Lindsay.
Chorus: "When the hounds of spring are on winter's traces." *Fr. Atalanta in Calydon.* Swinburne.
Cold Spring, A. Elizabeth Bishop.
Coming of Spring, The. Nora Perry.
Composed in Spring. Burns.
Day in Spring, A. "Jake Falstaff."
Echoing Green, The. *Fr. Songs of Innocence.* Blake.
First Spring Day, The. C. G. Rossetti.
Four Sweet Months, The. Herrick.
Gusts of Winter Are Gone, The. Meleager, *tr. fr. Greek by* Chamberlayne.
Harbingers. Basho, *tr. fr. Japanese by* Henderson.
Home Thoughts, from Abroad. Robert Browning.
Home Truths from Abroad. *Unknown.*
Hope in Springtime. Uhland, *tr. fr. German by* Zwart.
I dreaded that first robin, so. Emily Dickinson.
If Ice. W. W. E. Ross.
If it were not for the voice. *Fr. Shui Shu.* Nakatsukasa, *tr. fr. Japanese by* Waley.
In Just-Spring. E. E. Cummings.
In Spring. Mörike, *tr. fr. German by* Watkins.
In Spring in Warm Weather. Dorothy Aldis.
In the Spring. Ibycus, *tr. fr. Greek by* Headlam.
In the Spring. Meleager, *tr. fr. Greek by* Lang.
Just a Mile Beyond. Aileen Fisher.
Kerchoo! Fishback.
Lawyer's Invocation to Spring, The. H. H. Brownell.
Lenten Is Come with Love to Toune. *Unknown.*
Light exists in spring, A. Emily Dickinson.
Lines Written in Early Spring. Wordsworth.
Little madness in the spring, A. Emily Dickinson.
Little Valley in Spring, The. Onitsura, *tr. fr. Japanese by* Henderson.
Love's Emblems. *Fr. The Tragedy of Valentinian.* John Fletcher.
Mayflower. Conrad Aiken.
Miracle of Spring, The. Bahar, *tr. fr. Persian by* Arberry.
New Corn. T'ao Ch'ien, *tr. fr. Chinese by* Waley.
New feet within my garden go. Emily Dickinson.
Night of Spring. Thomas Westwood.
Northern Spring, A. Baro.
Now fades the last long streak of snow. *Fr. In Memoriam A. H. H.* Tennyson.
Now That the Winter's Gone. Thomas Carew.
O Spring the long-desired. *Fr. Carmina Burana. Unknown, tr. fr. Latin by* Waddell.
Ode on the Spring. Thomas Gray.
On a Banck as I Sate a Fishing. Wotton.
On the Road to Nara. Basho, *tr. fr. Japanese by* Henderson.
Peaceful Western Wind, The. Thomas Campion.
Prayer in Spring, A. Robert Frost.
Rondeau: "Year his winter cloak lets fall, The." Charles d'Orléans, *tr. fr. French by* Legge.
Smells. Kathryn Worth.
Sonnet: "Oh spring that hides the wrinkled earth in green." Boker.
Spring and All. W. C. Williams.
Spring Families. Frances Frost.
Spring Has Come. Machado, *tr. fr. Spanish by* Flores.
Spring in My Hut. Sodo, *tr. fr. Japanese by* Henderson.
Spring Is a Looping-free Time. Martin Robbins.
Spring Landscape. La Follette.
Spring Morning. D. H. Lawrence.
Spring Pools. Robert Frost.
Spring Quiet. C. G. Rossetti.
Spring Song. Hilda Conkling.
Spring Song, A. *Unknown.*
Spring: The Lover and the Birds. Allingham.
Spring Voices. MacNeice.
Sweet Spring Is Your. E. E. Cummings.
To Spring. Blake.
Twist-Rime on Spring. Guiterman.
When Daffodils Begin to Peer. *Fr. The Winter's Tale.* Shakespeare.
Written in Early Spring. Wordsworth.
Year's at the Spring, The. *Fr. Pippa Passes.* Robert Browning.
Yellow Spring. Jiménez, *tr. fr. Spanish by* Flores.
See also MARCH; APRIL; MAY
SPRINGFIELD, ILLINOIS
Abraham Lincoln Walks at Midnight. Vachel Lindsay.
On the Building of Springfield. Vachel Lindsay.
Springfield of the Far Future, The. Vachel Lindsay.
SQUASH (sport). Civilities. Whitbread.
SQUIRRELS
Fable: "Mountain and the squirrel, The." Emerson.
Gray Squirrel, The. Humbert Wolfe.
Of All the Idiots That Abound. Hoffenstein.
On a Squirrel Crossing the Road in Autumn, in New England. Eberhart.
Questions for a Flying Squirrel to Answer. Rachel Field.
Squirrel. Tippett.

Squirrel, The. *Unknown.*
Squirrel in the Rain. Frances Frost.
STAIRS. Stairs. Oliver Herford.
STARS
After the Dazzle of Day. Walt Whitman.
Choose Something like a Star. Robert Frost.
Daisies. Andrew Young.
Falling Star, The. Teasdale.
Great Bear, The. Hollander.
I see the golden hunter go. *Fr.* Songs of the Sea-Children. Bliss Carman.
Meditation under Stars. George Meredith.
My Star. Robert Browning.
See There the Star. Gottfried Keller, *tr. fr. German by* Gode.
Sonnet: "Those flakes of fire, brilliant sparks of light." Calderon de la Barca, *tr. fr. Spanish by* Turnbull.
Star Drill. T. I. Moore.
Star Morals. Nietzsche, *tr. fr. German by* Kaufmann.
Star Sirius, The. George Meredith.
Star-Talk. Robert Graves.
Starlight Night, The. G. M. Hopkins.
Starry Night, The. Sexton.
Stars, The. Hamerling, *tr. fr. German by* Wright.
Stars. Teasdale.
Summer Stars. Sandburg.
Suns in a skein, the uncut stones of night. *Fr.* Mythological Sonnets. Roy Fuller.
Thoughts by Night. Goethe, *tr. fr. German by* Kaufmann.
Twinkle, twinkle, little star. Jane Taylor.
Winter Galaxy, The. Heavysege.
You Black Bright Stars. *Unknown.*
STEEL. Prayers of Steel. Sandburg.
STEEPLES. Steeple Jack, The. Marianne Moore.
STENOGRAPHERS. Stenographers, The. P. K. Page.
STEVEDORES. Stevedore. L. M. Collins.
STOCK MARKET. Investor's Soliloquy. Kenneth Ward.
STOCKMEN
Andy's Gone with Cattle. Henry Lawson.
Ballad of the Drover. Henry Lawson.
Dying Stockman, The. *Unknown.*
Harry Pearce. David Campbell.
Man from Snowy River, The. A. B. Paterson.
My Mate Bill. G. H. Gibson.
Sick Stockrider, The. A. L. Gordon.
See also COWBOYS
STOICISM. Old Stoic, The. Emily Brontë.
STONECUTTERS. To the Stone-Cutters. Jeffers.
STONES AND ROCKS
Granite. Brambach, *tr. fr. German by* Middleton.
To Ailsa Rock. Keats.
Two Voices in a Meadow. Wilbur.
STORMCOCKS. Stormcock in Elder. Pitter.
STORMS
See also Storm *in* TITLE AND FIRST LINE INDEX
Ballad of the Tempest. J. T. Fields.
Bay of Biscay, The. Cherry.
Blossoms and Storm. Sadaiye, *tr. fr. Japanese by* Henderson.
By the Lightning We Lost Our Sight. *Unknown.*
Upon a Wasp Chilled with Cold. Edward Taylor.
Clear was the course of the cold floods. *Fr.* The Destruction of Troy. *Unknown.*
End of the World. "Jakob van Hoddis," *tr. fr. German by* Middleton.
Golden Hour, The. *Fr.* Lalla Rookh. Thomas Moore.
Misgivings. Melville.
Myths. Schmied, *tr. fr. German by* Hesse.
Now Is the Air Made of Chiming Balls. Eberhart.
Patrolling Barnegat. Walt Whitman.
Storm at Sea. Davenant.
Storm from the East, A. Whittemore.
Storm on Fifth Avenue. Sassoon.
Storm Is Over, The. Robert Bridges.
Summer Storm (*circa* 1916), and God's Grace. R. P. Warren.
STORY POEMS
Modern Ballads and Story Poems (MoBS). Charles Causley, ed.
100 More Story Poems (OnMSP). Elinor Parker, comp.
STRADIVARI, ANTONIO. Working with God. *Fr.* Stradivarius. "George Eliot."
STRAVINSKY, IGOR. Concert-Interpretation. Sassoon.
STRAWBERRIES. Strawberries in November. J. S. Neilson.
STREETS
Bedford Avenue. Berger.
Street in North Carolina, A. Bevington.
Street Is Waiting for the Night, The. Jiménez, *tr. fr. Spanish by* Kemp.
STRIKES AND STRIKERS
Late Snow & Lumber Strike of the Summer of Fifty-four, The. Snyder.
What Shall We Do for the Striking Seamen? *Unknown.*
STUBBS, GEORGE. On Looking at Stubbs's Anatomy of the Horse. Lucie-Smith.

STUDENTS
For a Senior College Textbook. Enzensberger, *tr. fr. German by* Hesse.
Student, The. Marianne Moore.
Study Habits. Armour.
SUBURBS
Northern Suburb, A. John Davidson.
Suburban Homecoming. Ciardi.
SUBWAYS
Graffiti. Edward Field.
In a Station of the Metro. Pound.
In the Tube. Richard Aldington.
Subway, The. Allen Tate.
Tunnel, The. *Fr.* The Bridge. Hart Crane.
SUCCESS
Kindly Unhitch That Star, Buddy. Ogden Nash.
Measure of Success. *Unknown.*
Success is counted sweetest. Emily Dickinson.
SUICIDE
Actor, The. J. S. Layton.
Justice Is Reason Enough. Wakoski.
Last Letter. Holthusen, *tr. fr. German by* Leibholz.
Mill, The. E. A. Robinson.
Résumé. Dorothy Parker.
Richard Cory. E. A. Robinson.
Suicide. MacNeice.
Suicide in the Copse, The. Robert Graves.
Suicide in the Trenches. Sassoon.
To be, or not to be: that is the question. *Fr.* Hamlet. Shakespeare.
SUMMER
See also Summer *and* Summer Morning *in* TITLE AND FIRST LINE INDEX
Alike. Dorothy Aldis.
As imperceptibly as grief. Emily Dickinson.
Atmosphere Is Incandescent, The. Castro, *tr. fr. Spanish by* Morgan.
Bed in Summer. R. L. Stevenson.
Boy's Summer Song, A. P. L. Dunbar.
Coolness in Summer. Ryusui, *tr. fr. Japanese by* Henderson.
Country Summer. Léonie Adams.
Credences of Summer. Wallace Stevens.
Deep Summer, after Midnight. Stem.
Exeunt. Wilbur.
Farm Boy after Summer. Robert Francis.
Go out in this dear summertide. Gerhardt, *tr. fr. German by* Schoolfield.
Haymakers, Rakers. *Fr.* The Sun's Darling. Dekker.
Long Summer. Laurie Lee.
Midsummer Noon in the Australian Forest, A. Harpur.
Midsummer Pause. Lape.
Musings. William Barnes.
Never the Summer Seemed to Me. *Unknown, tr. fr. German by* Closs.
Rainy Summer, The. Alice Meynell.
Rough Day, The. Jonathan Williams.
School Is Out. Frances Frost.
Sumer Is Icumen In. *Unknown.*
Summer Dawn. William Morris.
Summer Days Are Come Again, The. Samuel Longfellow.
Summer Has Sent His Minions on. Charles d'Orléans, *tr. fr. French by* Durling.
Summer Images. John Clare.
Summer Night. Ranko, *tr. fr. Japanese by* Henderson.
Summer Song. Edith Nesbit.
Summer Wind. Bryant.
Summertime. "Vincenzo Cardarelli," *tr. fr. Italian by* Corsano.
Summertime Delights Me, The. Airas Nunes, *tr. fr. Portuguese by* Davis.
These are the days when birds come back. Emily Dickinson.
Throstle, The. Tennyson.
To Summer. Blake.
Walk in Late Summer, A. Roethke.
Waves, The. C. E. Eaton.
Welcome, Summer. *Fr.* The Parlement of Foules. Chaucer.
See also JUNE; JULY; AUGUST
SUN
See also Sun *in* TITLE AND FIRST LINE INDEX
Dead Man Ariseth and Singeth a Hymn to the Sun, The. *Fr.* Book of the Dead. *Unknown, tr. fr. Egyptian by* Hillyer.
Descend, Beautiful Sun. Hölderlin, *tr. fr. German by* Friedman.
Full many a glorious morning have I seen. Sonnets, XXXIII. Shakespeare.
I'll tell you how the sun rose. Emily Dickinson.
In Praise of the Sun. "A. W."
Indian Summer Day on the Prairie, An. Vachel Lindsay.
Johnny Appleseed's Hymn to the Sun. Vachel Lindsay.
Morning Sun. MacNeice.
Riddle #29: The Moon and the Sun. *Unknown, tr. fr. Anglo-Saxon by* Raffel.
Shine Out, Fair Sun. *Unknown.*

SUN (*continued*)
　Spring-Joy Praising God. Praise of the Sun. Greiffenberg, *tr. fr. German by* Schoolfield.
　Sun Path, The. Basho, *tr. fr. Japanese by* Henderson.
　Sun Rising, The. Donne.
　There's Nothing like the Sun. Edward Thomas.
　To the Sun. *Fr.* Mithraic Emblems. Roy Campbell.
　To the Sun. Gezelle, *tr. fr. Flemish by* Bithell.
SUNDAY. *See* SABBATH
SUNDEW. Sundew, The. Swinburne.
SUNFLOWERS. Ah! Sun-Flower. *Fr.* Songs of Experience. Blake.
SUNRISE
　See also Sunrise *in* TITLE AND FIRST LINE INDEX
　Ant Sun, The. *Fr.* Herman Moon's Hourbook. Christopher Middleton.
　I'll tell you how the sun rose. Emily Dickinson.
　Sun Rising, The. Donne.
　See also DAWN; MORNING
SUNSET
　See also Sunset *in* TITLE AND FIRST LINE INDEX
　Datur Hora Quieti. *Fr.* The Doom of Devorgoil. Walter Scott.
　Denuded Is the Earth. Machado, *tr. fr. Spanish by* Gahan.
　Myths. Schmied, *tr. fr. German by* Hesse.
　Sunset at Les Eboulements, A. Lampman.
　Sunset over the Ægean. *Fr.* The Corsair. Byron.
　Tenebrae. Jiménez, *tr. fr. Spanish by* Sternberg.
　Whole gulfs of red and fleets of red. Emily Dickinson.
　See also DUSK; EVENING; TWILIGHT
SUPERNATURAL. *Fire and Sleet and Candlelight* (FiSC). August Derleth, ed.
SURREY, ENGLAND. Pot-Pourri from a Surrey Garden. Betjeman.
SUSANNA (Bible)
　Peter Quince at the Clavier. Wallace Stevens.
　Susannah and the Elders. *Unknown.*
SUTTER, JOHN. John Sutter. Yvor Williams.
SWANS
　See also Swans *in* TITLE AND FIRST LINE INDEX
　Dying Swan, The. Tennyson.
　Sitting Pretty. Fishback.
　Swan. Lowbury.
　Swans at Night, *sel.* Mary Gilmore.
　Wild Swans at Coole, The. Yeats.
　With that I saw two swannes of goodly hewe. *Fr.* Prothalamion. Spenser.
SWEDEN. Carriage from Sweden, A. Marianne Moore.
SWIFT, JONATHAN. Verses on the Death of Dr. Swift. Swift.
SWIMMERS
　See also Swimmers *in* TITLE AND FIRST LINE INDEX
　Black Water and Bright Air. Carrier.
　Come on In. *Unknown.*
　Compleat Swimmer, The. C. E. Eaton.
　Diver, The. Purcell-Buret.
　First Lesson. Philip Booth.
　400-Meter Freestyle. Kumin.
　Lesson, The. Krows.
　Of Swimming in Lakes and Rivers. Brecht, *tr. fr. German by* Hays.
　Old Swimmer, The. Christopher Morley.
　Swimmer, The. Ransom.
　Two Foscari, The, *sel.* Byron.
　Yes, by Golly. *Unknown.*
SWINGS. Swing, The. R. L. Stevenson.
SWITHIN, SAINT. St. Swithin. Daniel Henderson.
SWITZERLAND. England and Switzerland 1802. Wordsworth.
SYDNEY, AUSTRALIA. H.M.S. *Glory* at Sydney. Causley.
SYNGE, JOHN MILLINGTON. Memory, A. L. A. G. Strong.

T

TAI, CHINA. Most-sacred Mountain, The. Tietjens.
TAILORS
　Amends to the Tailors and Soutars. William Dunbar.
　Flying Tailor, The. Hogg.
TALIESIN. Taliessin's Return to Logres. Charles Williams.
TAMERLANE. Tamerlane. Poe.
TANAGERS. Scarlet Tanager, The. Joel Benton.
TAXIS. Taxis. Rachel Field.
TEA. Poets at Tea, The. Pain.
TEACHING AND TEACHERS
　Late Tutorial. Buckley.
　Schoolmistress, The. Shenstone.
　Village Schoolmaster, The. *Fr.* The Deserted Village. Goldsmith.
TEAMSTERS. How the Fire Queen Crossed the Swamp. Ogilvie.
TEARS
　Eyes and Tears. Marvell.

Flow Not So Fast. *Unknown.*
　Hymn, A: "Drop, drop, slow tears." Phineas Fletcher.
　Sonnet: "Three sortes of teares doe from myne eies distraine." Alabaster.
　Tear, The. Byron.
　Teare, The. Crashaw.
　Tears, Flow No More. Herbert of Cherbury.
　Tears, Idle Tears. *Fr.* The Princess. Tennyson.
　Valediction, A: Of Weeping. Donne.
　Weeper, The. Crashaw.
TEETH. Reflections Dental. McGinley.
TELEGRAPH. On the Completion of the Pacific Telegraph. Very.
TELEPHONES. Under a Telephone Pole. Sandburg.
TELETYPE. Tele-News Blues. Dufault.
TELEVISION. Mousemeal. Nemerov.
TEMAGAMI. *See* TIMAGAMI LAKE, CANADA
TENNIS
　At the Tennis Clinic. I. L. Martin.
　Ballade of Lawn Tennis, A. F. P. Adams.
　Dark Eyes at Forest Hills. I. L. Martin.
　Miraculously, through prayer to Saint Anthony. *Fr.* Adulescentia. Robert Fitzgerald.
　Old Tennis Player. Gwendolyn Brooks.
　Olympic Girl, The. Betjeman.
　Snapshot for Miss Bricka Who Lost in the Semi-final Round of the Pennsylvania Lawn Tennis Tournament at Haverford, July, 1960, A. Robert Wallace.
　Tennis in San Juan. Denney.
TENNYSON, ALFRED TENNYSON, 1ST BARON. Alfred Lord Tennyson. Whittemore.
TERMITES. Termite, The. Ogden Nash.
TEXAS
　Disheartened Ranger, The. *Unknown.*
　Mississippi Girls. *Unknown.*
　Mustang Gray, The. *Unknown.*
　Texas Rangers, The. *Unknown.*
　Texas Trains and Trails. Mary Austin.
　We Love the Name of Texas. *Unknown.*
　Wisconsin Soldier Boy, The. *Unknown.*
THAMES (river), ENGLAND. Bab-Lock-Hythe. Binyon.
THANKSGIVING
　See also Thanksgiving *in* TITLE AND FIRST LINE INDEX
　Another Grace for a Child. Herrick.
　Are We Thankful? *Unknown.*
　Be Thankful. Bullock.
　Grace. De la Mare.
　Grace at Evening. Poteat.
　Grace before Sleep. Teasdale.
　Hymn: "Lord, by whose breath all souls and seeds are living." Andrew Young.
　I Thank You God for Most This Amazing. E. E. Cummings.
　In Every Thing Give Thanks. *Unknown.*
　Little Te Deum of the Commonplace, A, *sel.* ("For all Thy ministries"). Oxenham.
　Little Te Deum of the Commonplace, A, *sel.* ("For maiden sweetness, and for strength of men"). Oxenham.
　One Thousandth Psalm, The. E. E. Hale.
　Our Prayer of Thanks, *sel.* Sandburg.
　Thank-You, A. William Canton.
　Thank you for the world so sweet. Leatham.
　Thankful Heart. F. W. Davis.
　Thanks to God. Hultman.
　Thanksgiving Eve. Grantland Rice.
　Thanksgiving to God for His House, A. Herrick.
　Whether we mutter a thank you or not. *Unknown.*
THANKSGIVING DAY
　First Thanksgiving Day, The. M. J. Preston.
　First Thanksgiving of All. N. B. Turner.
　Good Thanksgiving, A. A. D. G. Robinson.
　Pumpkin, The. Whittier.
　Thanksgiving Time. *Unknown.*
　Thanksgiving Wishes. Guiterman.
THEATER
　Big Theater, The. Pieyre de Mandiargues, *tr. fr. French by* Wright.
　Prologue: "When learning's triumph o'er her barb'rous foes." Samuel Johnson.
　Theatre, The. James Smith.
THEOCRITUS. Theocritus; a Villanelle. Oscar Wilde.
THERESA, SAINT, OF AVILA
　Apologie for the Precedent Hymnes on Teresa, An. Crashaw.
　Conversation in Avila. McGinley.
　Flaming Heart, The. Crashaw.
　In Memory of the Vertuous and Learned Lady Madre de Teresa That Sought an Early Martyrdome. Crashaw.
　Teresa of Avila. Elizabeth Jennings.
THERMOPYLAE, BATTLE OF
　Greek Dead at Thermopylae, The. Simonides, *tr. fr. Greek by* Higham.
　Thermopylae. Thwaites.
THOMAS, DYLAN. Thousandth Poem for Dylan Thomas, A. Ciardi.
THOMSON, JAMES. Ode on the Death of Mr. Thomson. William Collins.

THOREAU, HENRY DAVID. On Visiting the Graves of Hawthorne and Thoreau. Very.
THOUSAND ISLANDS, NEW YORK and ONTARIO. Thousand Islands, The. Fr. The St. Lawrence and the Saguenay. Charles Sangster.
THIRTY YEARS WAR. Tears of the Fatherland. Gryphius, tr. fr. German by Schoolfield.
THREE KINGS. See MAGI
THRUSHES
Come In. Robert Frost.
Darkling Thrush, The. Thomas Hardy.
Song of the Thrush, The. T. A. Daly.
Thrushes. Ted Hughes.
Thrush's Nest, The. John Clare.
What the Thrush Said. Keats.
TIDE
Tide Rises, the Tide Falls, The. Longfellow.
Tide Will Win, The. Priscilla Leonard.
TIGERS. Tiger, The. Fr. Songs of Experience. Blake.
TILL (river), ENGLAND. Two Rivers. Unknown.
TIMAGAMI LAKE, CANADA. Temagami. Lampman.
TIME
See also Time in TITLE AND FIRST LINE INDEX
All That's Past. De la Mare.
Ancient, winged god, thou who didst first draw breath. Tasso, tr. fr. Italian by Lucchi.
And Lightly, like the Flowers. Ronsard, tr. fr. French by Henley.
As I Walked Out One Evening. Auden.
Burnt Norton. Fr. Four Quartets. T. S. Eliot.
But Is There No Flower, Perfume or Violet? Deschamps, tr. fr. French by Kittel.
Canzone: "Into a little close of mine I went." Lorenzo de' Medici, tr. fr. Italian by Symonds.
Carpe Diem. Ronsard, tr. fr. French by Page.
Cities and Thrones and Powers. Fr. Puck of Pook's Hill. Kipling.
Concerning Time. Hunold, tr. fr. German by Schoolfield.
Day, The. Theodore Spencer.
Days. R. W. Emerson.
Deceiver Time. Góngora, tr. fr. Spanish by Tobin.
Devouring Time, blunt thou the lion's paw. Sonnets, XIX. Shakespeare.
Dialogue betwixt Time and a Pilgrime, A. Aurelian Townsend.
Epitaph: "Even such is Time, which takes in trust." Ralegh.
Fable XIII: Plutus, Cupid and Time. John Gay.
Four Quartz Crystal Clocks. Marianne Moore.
Hour after Hour, Day after Day. Castro, tr. fr. Spanish by Kittel.
I Could Give All to Time. Robert Frost.
In a Prominent Bar in Secaucus One Day. X. J. Kennedy.
Ladies, You See Time Flieth. Unknown.
Like as the waves make towards the pebbled shore. Sonnets, LC. Shakespeare.
Moods, The. Yeats.
Mouse Whose Name Is Time, The. Robert Francis.
Nature, That Washed Her Hands in Milk. Ralegh.
North Infinity Street. Conrad Aiken.
On Time. Milton.
Paradox of Time, The. Ronsard, tr. fr. French by Dobson.
Plays. W. S. Landor.
Power of Time, The. Swift.
River of Life, The. Thomas Campbell.
Roses. Ronsard, tr. fr. French by Lang.
Sands of Time, The. R. E. Howard.
Since brass, nor stone, nor earth, nor boundless sea. Sonnets, LXV. Shakespeare.
So, So. Clerke.
Song Set by John Farmer. Unknown.
Sun-Dial, The. Fr. Melincourt. Peacock.
They say that "time assuages." Emily Dickinson.
Thought Suggested by the New Year, A. Thomas Campbell.
Thy Beauty Fades. Very.
Time and Eternity. Bunyan.
To His Coy Mistress. Marvell.
To the Virgins, to Make Much of Time. Herrick.
To Think of Time, sel. Walt Whitman.
When I consider everything that grows. Sonnets, XV. Shakespeare.
When I do count the clock that tells the time. Sonnets, XII. Shakespeare.
When I have seen by Time's fell hand defaced. Sonnets, LXIV. Shakespeare.
Who Was It. Heine, tr. fr. German by Garnett.
Words in Time. MacLeish.
You, Andrew Marvell. MacLeish.
TINTORETTO. Lament for Tintoretta. Fr. Three Fragments. William Collins.
TITANIC (ship). Convergence of the Twain, The. Thomas Hardy.
TITUS (Roman emperor). Titus and Berenice. Heath-Stubbs.
TOADS
Death of a Toad, The. Wilbur.
Hoppity Toads. Aileen Fisher.
Proud Toad, The. Hallock.
TOBACCO
Man Has No Smokestack. Unknown.
Pipe of Tobacco, A, sels. I. H. Browne.
Said the Whisky Flask. Unknown.
Tobacco. Hemminger.
TOLEDO, SPAIN. High Bridge above the Tagus River at Toledo, The. W. C. Williams.
TOOTHACHE
Charm against the Tooth-Ache, A. Heath-Stubbs.
Meditation upon the Toothache, A. Laurence Lerner.
TOURISTS. Tourist and the Town, The. Adrienne Rich.
TOUSSAINT L'OUVERTURE, FRANÇOIS DOMINQUE. To Toussaint L'Ouverture. Wordsworth.
TOYS
Land of Counterpane, The. R. L. Stevenson.
Little Boy Blue. Eugene Field.
Toys, The. Fr. The Unknown Eros. Coventry Patmore.
TRACK ATHLETICS
From the Greek Anthology. Crinagoras, tr. fr. Greek by Rexroth.
Mighty Runner, A. E. A. Robinson.
Notes on a Track Meet. McCord.
Runner. Auden.
Runner, The. Walt Whitman.
Sluggard, The. Lucilius, tr. fr. Greek by Wolfe.
Sprinters, The. Murchison.
To James. Frank Horne.
TRAFALGAR, BATTLE OF
Nelson's Victory at Trafalgar. Unknown.
Night of Trafalgar, The. Fr. The Dynasts. Thomas Hardy.
TRAINS
Crossing. Philip Booth.
Engine. Tippett.
Engineer, The. A. A. Milne.
Express, The. Spender.
Freight Train, The. Rowena Bennett.
I like to see it lap the miles. Emily Dickinson.
London Train. Dehn.
Modern Dragon, A. Rowena Bennett.
Morning Express. Sassoon.
Night Mail. Auden.
Night Train. Robert Francis.
Orient Express, The. Jarrell.
Passenger Train. E. N. Chase.
Rhyme of the Rails. Saxe.
Song of the Train. McCord.
To a Locomotive in Winter. Walt Whitman.
Trains. Tippett.
Travel. E. S. Millay.
View. Josephine Miles.
Ways of Trains, The. Coatsworth.
TRASH
From This the Strength. Lape.
Junk. Wilbur.
TRAVEL
Home Leave. Barbara Howes.
Movies for the Home. Howard Moss.
Over 2000 Illustrations and a Complete Concordance. Elizabeth Bishop.
Travel. E. S. Millay.
Travel Bureau, The. R. C. Mitchell.
TREASON. Treason. Sir John Harington.
TREES
See also Tree and Trees in TITLE AND FIRST LINE INDEX
Autumnal Spring Song. Vassar Miller.
Axe in the Wood, The. Dyment.
Bare Arms of Trees, The. Tagliabue.
Bedtime. Coatsworth.
Brooms. Aldis.
City Trees. E. S. Millay.
Double Tree, The. W. T. Scott.
Every Time I Climb a Tree. McCord.
Four trees—upon a solitary acre. Emily Dickinson.
In a Wood. Fr. The Woodlanders. Thomas Hardy.
Note on Local Flora. Empson.
Old Tree, The. Andrew Young.
Planting a Tree. N. B. Turner.
Pruning Trees. Po Chü-i, tr. fr. Chinese by Waley.
That Tree with Its Leaves Atremble. Hurtado de Mendoza, tr. fr. Spanish by Flores.
This Way Only. Harford.
Tree at My Window. Robert Frost.
Tree Birthdays. M. C. Davies.
Tree in the Desert, The. Hebbel, tr. fr. German by Stillman.
Tree Will Mow Thickets. "Will Inman."
Trees and Cattle. James Dickey.
Trees Are Down, The. Mew.
War against the Trees, The. Kunitz.
Winter Branches. Widdemer.
Woodman, Spare That Tree. G. P. Morris.

TREES (continued)
Yes! I have seen the ancient oak. Fr. The Brereton Omen. F. D. Hemans.
See also names of trees (e.g., OAK TREES)
TRELAWNY, SIR JONATHAN. Song of the Western Men, The. R. S. Hawker.
TRENT (river), ENGLAND. Sirena. Fr. The Shepherd's Sirena. Drayton.
TRISTRAM. Tristram and Iseult. Matthew Arnold.
TRISTAN DA CUNHA (islands). Tristan da Cunha. Roy Campbell.
TROILUS AND CRESSIDA
Testament of Cresseid, The. Henryson.
Troilus and Criseyde, sels. Chaucer.
TROJAN WAR. Night Encampment outside Troy. Fr. The Iliad. Homer, tr. fr. Greek by Tennyson.
TROUT. Trout, The. Fr. Four Fascinators. Char, tr. fr. French by Stern.
TROY. Palladium. Matthew Arnold.
TRUTH
Be True. Bonar.
Cassandra. Jeffers.
Coming of Wisdom with Time, The. Yeats.
Eternal, The. Tegnér, tr. fr. Swedish by Stork.
Goddess, The. Levertov.
I Am an Enemy to Trickery and Pride. Cardenal, tr. fr. Provençal by Birenbaum.
I died for beauty. Emily Dickinson.
Lie, The. Ralegh.
Magna Est Veritas. Fr. The Unknown Eros. Coventry Patmore.
1643 "Veritas" 1878. Fr. Two Sonnets: Harvard. O. W. Holmes.
Standing on Tiptoe. G. F. Cameron.
Tell all the truth but tell it slant. Emily Dickinson.
Truth, crushed to earth, shall rise again. Fr. The Battle-field. Bryant.
"Truth," said a traveller. Fr. The Black Riders. Stephen Crane.
When Truth Disappeared from the World. Airas Nunes, tr. fr. Portuguese by Davis.
TULIPS. Tulip. W. J. Smith.
TURKEYS
Black November Turkey, A. Wilbur.
November's Come. J. C. Lincoln.
Table-Birds. Kenneth Mackenzie.
Turkey, The. Ogden Nash.
TURPIN, RICHARD (Dick Turpin)
Dick Turpin and the Lawyer. Unknown.
Dick Turpin's Ride. Unknown.
TURTLES
Little Turtle, The. Vachel Lindsay.
Mud Turtles. Hallock.
TWEED (river), SCOTLAND and ENGLAND. Two Rivers. Unknown.
TWELFTH NIGHT
Ballad of the Epiphany. Dalmon.
Old Christmas. Helton.
Poem for Epiphany. Norman Nicholson.
Twelfth Night. Laurie Lee.
Twelve Days of Christmas, The. Unknown.
TWILIGHT
Beauty Is Most at Twilight's Close. Lagerkvist, tr. fr. Swedish by Laycock.
Street Is Waiting for the Night, The. Jiménez, tr. fr. Spanish by Kemp.
Twilight. Tyutchev, tr. fr. Russian by Deutsch.
Twilight Calm. C. G. Rossetti.
See also DUSK; EVENING; SUNSET
TWINS
See also Twins in TITLE AND FIRST LINE INDEX
Being Twins. Kathryn Jackson.
Betwixt and Between. Lofting.
Dick and Will. E. M. Roberts.
Grace Ananne. Borie.

U

UCCELLO, PAOLO. Uccello. Corso.
ULYSSES
Strayed Reveller, The. Matthew Arnold.
Ulysses. Saba, tr. fr. Italian by Bergin.
Ulysses. Tennyson.
Ulysses and the Siren. Samuel Daniel.
World as Meditation, The. Wallace Stevens.
UMBRELLAS. Elf and the Dormouse, The. Oliver Herford.
UNEMPLOYMENT. Outa Work Blues. Cortez.
UNICORNS
See also Unicorn in TITLE AND FIRST LINE INDEX

Inhuman Henry; or, Cruelty to Fabulous Animals. A. E. Housman.
Unicorns at Harvard. Farber.
UNIONS, LABOR. There Is Power in a Union. Unknown, at. to Joe Hill.
UNITED STATES
America. S. F. Smith.
America for Me. Henry van Dyke.
America the Beautiful. K. L. Bates.
American Letter: For Gerald Murphy. MacLeish.
Brown River, Smile. Toomer.
By Blue Ontario's Shore, sel. Walt Whitman.
Gift Outright, The. Robert Frost.
I Hear America Singing. Walt Whitman.
International Hymn. George Huntington.
It Is Time. Joans.
Let America Be America Again. Langston Hughes.
Long, Too Long America. Walt Whitman.
Millions Are Learning How. Agee.
My America. La Grone.
New Colossus, The. Emma Lazarus.
Next to of Course God. E. E. Cummings.
Oh Mother of a Mighty Race. Bryant.
Ode Recited at the Harvard Commemoration. J. R. Lowell.
Passage to India. Walt Whitman.
Peace Hymn of the Republic. Henry van Dyke.
Rooster, The. Orlovitz.
17-18 April, 1961, sel. Oppenheimer.
Shine, Perishing Republic. Jeffers.
Shine, Republic. Jeffers.
Star-spangled Banner, The. Key.
Star Spangled Ode. McGinley.
To the States. Walt Whitman.
To the Western World. Louis Simpson.
This Land Is Mine (ThLM). Al Hine, ed.
UNIVERSITIES. See COLLEGES AND UNIVERSITIES
UNWIN, MARY
To Mary Unwin. Cowper.
To the Same. Cowper.
URIEL. Uriel. Emerson.

V

VACATION. Movies for the Home. Howard Moss.
VAGABONDS
Big Rock Candy Mountain, The. Unknown.
Hunchback in the Park, The. Dylan Thomas.
November. Ted Hughes.
Road to Vagabondia, The. Dana Burnet.
VALENCIA, SPAIN. Song: "Now the moon is rising." Machado, tr. fr. Spanish by Flores.
VALENTINE'S DAY
See also Valentine in TITLE AND FIRST LINE INDEX
Good Bishop Valentine. Farjeon.
Mary's eyes are blue as azure. Silverstein.
My Valentine. Kitty Parsons.
Saint Valentine's Day. Fr. The Unknown Eros. Coventry Patmore.
Sure Sign, A. N. B. Turner.
Valentine Promise. Unknown.
VALKYRIES. Fatal Sisters, The. Thomas Gray, after the Icelandic.
VAMPIRES
Vampire. W. H. Kerr.
Vampire Bride. Stefanile.
VAN GOGH, VINCENT. See GOGH, VINCENT VAN
VANBRUGH, SIR JOHN. Vanbrug's House. Swift.
VAUGHAN, HENRY
At the Grave of Henry Vaughan. Sassoon.
To Henry Vaughan. A. J. M. Smith.
VEGETABLES. Vegetables. Rachel Field.
VEGETARIANS. Flying Bum, The: 1944. Plomer.
VENICE, ITALY
Ode on Venice. Byron.
On the Extinction of the Venetian Republic. Wordsworth.
Toccata of Galuppi's, A. Robert Browning.
Venice. Nietzsche, tr. fr. German by Kaufmann.
VENUS (goddess)
Darling of God and Men, beneath the gliding stars. Fr. De Rerum Natura. Lucretius, tr. fr. Latin by Bunting.
Death of Venus, The. Creeley.
Venus Accoutered as Mars. Unknown.
Venus and Adonis, sels. Shakespeare.
VENUS (planet). Hesperus. John Clare.
VERACRUZ, MEXICO. Veracruz. Robert Hayden.
VERGIL. To Virgil. Tennyson.
VERSAILLES, FRANCE. No Swan So Fine. Marianne Moore.
VIAREGGIO, ITALY. Off Viareggio. Pitchford.
VILLON, FRANÇOIS. I Am François, to My Dismay. Villon, tr. fr. French by Birenbaum.

VINLAND. Story of Vinland, The. *Fr.* Psalm of the West. Sidney Lanier.

VIOLETS
Of Violets. Vernon Ward.
On the Mountain Pass. Basho, *tr. fr. Japanese* by Henderson.
To Violets. Herrick.
Violet, The. Goethe, *tr. fr. German* by Gode.
Yellow Violets, The. Bryant.

VIRGIL. *See* VERGIL.

VIRGIN MARY. *See* MARY, THE VIRGIN

VIRGINIA
Old Virginny. Bland.
To the Virginian Voyage. Drayton.
Virginia. *Fr.* Landscapes. T. S. Eliot.

VODKA. Vodka. Ciardi.

VOGLER, GEORG JOSEPH. Abt Vogler. Robert Browning.

VOITURE, VINCENT. On the way from Fontenay. Voiture, *tr. fr. French* by McDowell.

VOLTAIRE. Mock On, Mock On, Voltaire, Rousseau. Blake.

VOYAGES
On Sailing the Wide Ocean. *Fr.* The Solitudes. Góngora, *tr. fr. Spanish* by Wilson.
Passage to India. Walt Whitman.
To the Virginian Voyage. Drayton.
Voyages. Hart Crane.
Where Lies the Land to Which the Ship Would Go? Clough.

VULPIUS, MELCHIOR. Melchior Vulpius. Marianne Moore.

VULTURES
Black Vulture, The. George Sterling.
Still, Citizen Sparrow. Wilbur.
Vulture, The. Hoh.

W

WAGTAILS. Little Trotty Wagtail. John Clare.

WAITERS. Epitaph on a Waiter. McCord.

WALES
Bard, The. Thomas Gray.
Dysynni Valley, The. Theodore Holmes.
Gwalia Deserta, *sel.* Idris Davies.
In Hospital: Poona (I). Alun Lewis.
In the Valley of the Elwy. G. M. Hopkins.
I'r hen Iaith a'i Chanedon. Dowding.
Peace in the Welsh Hills. Vernon Watkins.

WALLS. Mending Wall. Robert Frost.

WALSINGHAM, ENGLAND
Lament for Walsingham. *Unknown.*
Walsinghame. Ralegh.

WANDERER (ship). *Wanderer,* The. Masefield.

WANDERLUST
Vagabond, The. R. L. Stevenson.
Wakeful in the Township. Elizabeth Riddell.
Wanderer, The, *sels.* Christopher Brennan.

WAR
Absolution. Sassoon.
After Tsui-tao. "Klabund," *tr. fr. German* by Kaufmann.
Against the Age. Louis Simpson.
Anthem for Doomed Youth. Wilfred Owen.
Apparitions. T. C. Clark.
Arms and the Boy. Wilfred Owen.
Arsenal at Springfield, The. Longfellow.
Asking for It. Sassoon.
Battle-Field, The. Bryant.
Battlefield. Stramm, *tr. fr. German* by Hamburger.
Beat! Beat! Drums! Walt Whitman.
Between Two Prisoners. James Dickey.
Bloody Sire, The. Jeffers.
Celle Qui Meurt. Westlake.
Channel Firing. Thomas Hardy.
Christmas Eve under Hooker's Statue. Robert Lowell.
Communique, I, *sel.* Corrington.
Does It Matter? Sassoon.
Drum, The. John Scott.
Dulce et Decorum Est. Wilfred Owen.
Eleventh Hour, The. F. S. Morris.
Every Day. Bachmann, *tr. fr. German* by Middleton.
Fury of Aerial Bombardment, The. Eberhart.
Greater Love. Wilfred Owen.
Housemates. Odell Shepard.
I'm Pleased When Gaudy Eastertime. Bertrand de Born, *tr. fr. Provençal.*
In Time of "The Breaking of Nations." Thomas Hardy.
Iron-Wind Dances. *Fr.* Thunderstorms. Sarett.
Judging Distances. *Fr.* Lessons of the War. Henry Reed.
Long War, The. Laurie Lee.
Man He Killed, The. Thomas Hardy.
Man-made World, A. Spender.
Nocturnal Landscape. Schnack, *tr. fr. German* by Middleton.

Old battlefield, fresh with spring flowers again. *Fr.* Seven Poems. Basho, *tr. fr. Japanese* by Page.
On the idle hill of summer. A. E. Housman.
Peaceful Shepherd, The. Robert Frost.
Play the Last March Slowly. Richard Davidson.
Protest in the Sixth Year of Ch'ien Fu, A. Ts'ao Sung, *tr. fr. Chinese* by Waley.
Rear-Guard, The. Sassoon.
Recalling War. Robert Graves.
Return. Brecht, *tr. fr. German* by Middleton.
Rhyme of Joyous Garde, The, *sel.* A. L. Gordon.
Sergeant's Prayer, A. Brodie.
Sestina: Altaforte. Pound.
Silent Slain, The. MacLeish.
Song before the Battle. Hauff, *tr. fr. German* by Owen.
Song of War, A. Claudius, *tr. fr. German* by Bloch.
Spires of Oxford, The. Letts.
Strange Meeting. Wilfred Owen.
Sunset Horn. Myron O'Higgins.
Triumphal March. Darío, *tr. fr. Spanish* by Guenther.
There was crimson clash of war. *Fr.* The Black Riders. Stephen Crane.
Trail All Your Pikes, Dispirit Every Drum. Countess of Winchilsea.
Vale from Carthage. Peter Viereck.
War Is Kind. Stephen Crane.
War Song. John Davidson.
War-Song of Dinas Vawr, The. *Fr.* The Misfortunes of Elphin. Peacock.
What the Orderly Dog Saw. F. M. Ford.
Winter War. "Klabund," *tr. fr. German* by Kaufmann.
Y.M.C.A. Writing Room. Roy Fuller.

WASHINGTON, GEORGE
George Washington. Silverstein.
George Washington. Tippett.
Leetla Giorgio Washeenton. T. A. Daly.
Washington. J. R. Lowell.
Washington. N. B. Turner.
Young Washington. Guiterman.

WASHINGTON, D.C.
Aeneas at Washington. Allen Tate.
Effigy. McElhaney.

WASHINGTON MONUMENT. Washington Monument by Night. Sandburg.

WASPS
New Hampshire, February. Eberhart.
Upon a Wasp Chilled with Cold. Edward Taylor.

WATER
Muse of Water, A. Kizer.
Reflections on Water. Pitchford.
Song of the Artesian Water. A. B. Paterson.
Water. Sexton.
Water Wheel, The. Machado, *tr. fr. Spanish* by Duffy.
Well, The. Levertov.

WATER LILIES
Clote, The. William Barnes.
To Paint a Water Lily. Ted Hughes.

WATER OUZELS. Water Ouzel. Matchett.

WATERFALLS. Waterfall, The. Henry Vaughan.

WATERFOWL. To a Waterfowl. Bryant.

WATERLOO, BATTLE OF
Drummer Boy of Waterloo, The. *Unknown.*
Eve of Waterloo, The. *Fr.* Childe Harold's Pilgrimage. Byron.
Plains of Waterloo, The. *Unknown.*
Soldier of Waterloo, The. *Unknown.*
Wellington and Waterloo. *Unknown.*

WATTS, ISAAC. For the Bicentenary of Isaac Watts. Norman Nicholson.

WAVES
Hungry Waves, The. Aldis.
Sea Bird to the Wave, The. Padraic Colum.
Waves. M. B. Miller.
When I See the Waves. Fernandez, *tr. fr. Portuguese* by Davis.

WEALTH
Of the Use of Riches. *Fr.* Moral Essays. Pope.
Very Rich Man, The. Dorothy Parker.

WEATHER
Weather Has Laid Aside His Cloak, The. Charles d'Orléans, *tr. fr. French* by Kittel.
Weathers. Thomas Hardy.

WEAVERS. Complaint of the Weavers. *Fr.* Yvain. Chrétien de Troyes, *tr. fr. French* by Aldan.

WEBSTER, DANIEL
Daniel Webster's Horses. Coatsworth.
Ichabod. Whittier.

WEDDINGS. *See* MARRIAGE

WEIL, SIMONE. For Simone Weil. Sister M. Thérèse.

WELLINGTON, ARTHUR WELLESLEY, 1ST DUKE OF. Ode on the Death of the Duke of Wellington, *sel.* Tennyson.

WELSH, THE
Variation on a Theme by Dylan Thomas. Bode.
Welsh Testament, A. R. S. Thomas.

WENCESLAS, SAINT. Good King Wenceslas. *Unknown, tr. fr. Latin by* Neale.
WESLEY, CHARLES. Wesley in Heaven. T. E. Brown.
WESSEX, ENGLAND. Wessex Guidebook. MacNeice.
WEST, RICHARD. Sonnet: On the Death of Richard West. Thomas Gray.
WEST (United States). How Cyrus Laid the Cable. Saxe.
WEST WIND
  Ode to the West Wind. Shelley.
  West Wind, The. Masefield.
WESTMINSTER ABBEY. On the Tombs in Westminster Abbey. *At. to* Beaumont, *also to* Basse.
WHALES AND WHALING
  Bill the Whaler. Will Lawson.
  Cachalot, The, *sel.* E. J. Pratt.
  Greenland Fishery, The. *Unknown.*
  Leviathan; a Poem in Four Movements. Pitchford.
  Quaker Graveyard in Nantucket, The. Robert Lowell.
  Waterwitch, The. *Unknown.*
  Whale, The. Buson, *tr. fr. Japanese by* Henderson.
  Whale, The. Donne.
  Whales Weep Not! D. H. Lawrence.
WHARVES. Old Wharves, The. Rachel Field.
WHEAT
  Bread the Holy. Coatsworth.
  Sheaves, The. E. A. Robinson.
WHISKY
  Raftery's Dialogue with the Whiskey. Padraic Fallon.
  Whisky Johnny. *Unknown.*
WHITMAN, WALT
  Memories of Whitman and Lincoln. Oppenheim.
  Pact, A. Pound.
  Song of Myself. Walt Whitman.
  Walt Whitman at Bear Mountain. Louis Simpson.
WHITTIER, JOHN GREENLEAF. Whittier. *Fr.* A Fable for Critics. J. R. Lowell.
WILBERFORCE, WILLIAM. Sonnet to William Wilberforce, Esq. Cowper.
WILDE, OSCAR. Arrest of Oscar Wilde at the Cadogan Hotel, The. Betjeman.
WILLIAM III, KING OF ENGLAND (William of Orange)
  King William and King James. *Unknown.*
  William of Orange; or, The Battle of Boyne. *Unknown.*
WILLIAM X, COUNT OF POITOU. With Mournful Tones My Verses Start. Cercamon, *tr. fr. Provençal by* Birenbaum.
WILLIAMS, THEODORE SAMUEL (Ted). Dream of a Baseball Star. Corso.
WILLIAMS, WILLIAM CARLOS
  Letter to William Carlos Williams, A. Rexroth.
  Out of Your Hands. Theodore Weiss.
WILLOW TREES
  Where Willow Is a Limber Switch. "Will Inman."
  Word of Willow, The. L. B. Drake.
WINCHESTER, JANE SAVAGE, MARCHIONESS OF. Epitaph on the Marchioness of Winchester, An. Milton.
WIND
  See also Wind *in* TITLE AND FIRST LINE INDEX
  Aeolus. Humphries.
  Another Ode to the North-East Wind. *Unknown.*
  Autumnal Equinox on Mediterranean Beach. R. P. Warren.
  Autumn Storm, The. Basho, *tr. fr. Japanese by* Henderson.
  Big Wind. Roethke.
  Evening Wind, The. Bryant.
  I saw the wind today. *Fr.* Reminiscence. Padraic Colum.
  Like rain it sounded till it curved. Emily Dickinson.
  Little Wind. Greenaway.
  Moon's the North Wind's Cooky, The. Vachel Lindsay.
  Now Close the Windows. Robert Frost.
  On a Windy Day. Zhenya Gay.
  On Wenlock Edge the wood's in trouble. *Fr.* A Shropshire Lad. A. E. Housman.
  Prairie Wind. D. C. Scott.
  School Days. Stem.
  September Winds. Bevington.
  Song of the Four Winds, The. *Fr.* The Misfortunes of Elphin. Peacock.
  South Wind laid his moccasins aside, The. *Fr.* Malcolm's Katie. I. V. Crawford.
  Storm, The. Chora, *tr. fr. Japanese by* Henderson.
  Summer Wind. Bryant.
  To the Mistral. Nietzsche, *tr. fr. German by* Kaufmann.
  To the Thawing Wind. Robert Frost.
  Who Has Seen the Wind? *Fr.* Sing-Song. C. G. Rossetti.
  Wind and the Moon, The. George Macdonald.
  Wind at Penistone, The. Davie.
  Wind in the Grass. Van Doren.
  Wind Is a Cat. E. R. Fuller.
  Wind-Song. *Tr. fr. Pima Indian by* Curtis.
  Wind took up the northern things, The. Emily Dickinson.
  Winds, The. Tusser.
  Wind's Song, The. Mörike, *tr. fr. German by* Hughes.
  Windy Nights. R. L. Stevenson.
  See also NORTH WIND; SOUTH WIND; WEST WIND

WINDHOVERS. *See* FALCONS
WINE
  Bacchus. Emerson.
  Bacchus in Tuscany, *sel.* Redi, *tr. fr. Italian by* Lucchi.
  Cups without Wine Are Lowly. Halevi, *tr. fr. Hebrew by* Davis.
  Fly, The. Quevedo, *tr. fr. Spanish by* Ayres.
  His Fare-well to Sack. Herrick.
  In a Wine Cellar. V. J. Daley.
  Love and Wine. Shadwell.
  Orgy, The. Saint-Amant, *tr. fr. French by* Richards.
  Welcome to Sack, The. Herrick.
WINNIPEG, CANADA. Farewell to Winnipeg. Daniells.
WINNIPESAUKEE, LAKE, NEW HAMPSHIRE. Lake Winnipesaukee. Driver.
WINTER
  See also Winter *and* Winter Night *in* TITLE AND FIRST LINE INDEX
  Alpine Winter, The. Saint-Amant, *tr. fr. French by* Burckhardt.
  Ancient Music. Pound.
  At the Winter Solstice. D. G. Hoffman.
  Autumn Hath All the Summer's Fruitful Treasure. *Fr.* Summer's Last Will and Testament. Nashe.
  Blow, Blow, Thou Winter Wind. *Fr.* As You Like It. Shakespeare.
  Calm Winter Sleep. Corke.
  Colonial Set. A. G. Bailey.
  Crumbs. De la Mare.
  Dead of Winter. Towne.
  How One Winter Came in the Lake Region. Wilfred Campbell.
  Human Things. Nemerov.
  Ice. C. G. D. Roberts.
  In Defense of Felons. Mezey.
  In Winter. *Fr.* Three Cinquains. Brockman.
  It Is in Winter That We Dream of Spring. R. B. Wilson.
  Just a Mile Beyond. Aileen Fisher.
  Lalique. Hal Porter.
  Midnight. Lampman.
  Now Winter Nights Enlarge. Thomas Campion.
  Ode to Winter. Thomas Campbell.
  Old Winter. Thomas Noel.
  Out of My Study Window. Whittemore.
  Prelude: "Winter evening settles down, The." *Fr.* Preludes. T. S. Eliot.
  Schoolboys in Winter. John Clare.
  Shine Out, Fair Sun. *Unknown.*
  Signs of Winter. John Clare.
  Snow Man, The. Wallace Stevens.
  Song: "Lovely hill-torrents are." W. J. Turner.
  Song in a Winter Night. Noll.
  Sonnet: "Winter deepening, the hay all in, The." Wilbur.
  Spate in Winter Midnight. MacCaig.
  Still Day, A. Cherwinski.
  Stone Path, The, *sel.* Loerke, *tr. fr. German by* Middleton.
  Stopping by Woods on a Snowy Evening. Robert Frost.
  Storm, The. *Fr.* Snow-bound. Whittier.
  Thaw. Edward Thomas.
  There's a certain slant of light. Emily Dickinson.
  To Winter. Blake.
  Triolet on a Dark Day. Fishback.
  Turning. Robert Finch.
  Up in the Morning Early. Burns.
  Visit, The. Mezey.
  When Icicles Hang by the Wall. *Fr.* Love's Labour's Lost. Shakespeare.
  Widow Bird Sate Mourning for Her Love, A. *Fr.* Charles the First. Shelley.
  Winter Evening. Lampman.
  Winter for a Moment Takes the Mind. *Fr.* Preludes for Memnon. Conrad Aiken.
  Winter Has Done Us Great Harm Everywhere. Walther von der Vogelweide, *tr. fr. German by* Richey.
  Winter Hymn, A—to the Snow. Ebenezer Jones.
  Winter in Dunbarton. Robert Lowell.
  Winter in East Anglia. Blunden.
  Winter in Lower Canada. *Fr.* The Emigrant. Standish O'Grady.
  Winter Is Icumen In. Bradford Smith.
  Winter Lakes, The. Wilfred Campbell.
  Winter Landscape. Berryman.
  Winter Memories. Thoreau.
  Winter Nights. Thomas Campion.
  Winter Piece, A. Bryant.
  Winter Remembered. Ransom.
  Winter the Huntsman. Osbert Sitwell.
  Winter, You Are Merely a Churl. Charles d'Orléans, *tr. fr. French by* Kittel.
  Winter's Spring, The. John Clare.
  Winter's Tale, A. Dylan Thomas.
  Woods in Winter. Longfellow.
  Year's End. Wilbur.

You Could Say. Mezey.
See also December; January; February
Winters, Yvor. To Yvor Winters, 1955. Thom Gunn.
Wishes. I Keep Three Wishes Ready. Annette Wynne.
Wit. Ode: Of Wit. Cowley.
Witchcraft
See also Witch *and* Witches *in* Title and First Line Index
Hag, The. Herrick.
Herbs and Simples. Martha Keller.
La Tour du Sorcier. Osbert Sitwell.
Little Creature, The. De la Mare.
Molly Means. Margaret Walker.
Spell, A. *Fr.* Oedipus. Dryden.
Tailor, The. Beddoes.
Two Witches, The. Robert Graves.
Witch of Coos, The. Robert Frost.
Witch of Willowby Wood, The. Rowena Bennett.
Witch's Ballad, The. W. B. Scott.
Witching Hour. Farber.
Wolfe, James. Brave Wolfe. *Unknown.*
Women
See also Woman *and* Women *in* Title and First Line Index
Against Women. *Unknown.*
And There Was Mary Magdalene and the Other Mary, Sitting Over against the Sepulchre. Rodgers.
Another. In Defence of Their Inconstancie. Jonson.
Ballade of the Women of Paris. Villon, *tr. fr. French by* Swinburne.
Cantata for Two Lovers. Helga Sandburg.
Changes. "Owen Meredith."
Divine Office of the Kitchen, The. Hallack.
Duplicity of Women, The. Lydgate.
Furniture of a Woman's Mind, The. Swift.
Hand That Rocks the Cradle Is the Hand That Rules the World, The. W. R. Wallace.
Hares on the Mountain. *Unknown.*
Heart of a Woman, The. G. D. Johnson.
Here's to the Maiden. *Fr.* The School for Scandal. Sheridan.
I Never Even Suggested It. Ogden Nash.
I Sing the Body Electric. Walt Whitman.
Impossible to Trust Women. *Unknown.*
In her first passion woman loves her lover. *Fr.* Don Juan. Byron.
In short, all men betray us women. *Fr.* The Romance of the Rose. Jean de Meun, *tr. fr. French by* Dahlberg.
Lords of Creation, The. *Unknown.*
Lost and Given Over. E. J. Brady.
Man, Man, Man. *Unknown.*
Man's Woman, A. M. C. Davies.
No Thyng Ys to Man So Dere. Mannyng.
Of the Characteristics of Small Women. *Fr.* The Book of True Love. Ruiz, *tr. fr. Spanish by* Davis.
Of the Characters of Women, *sel. Fr.* Moral Essays. Pope.
Of Women. *Fr.* The Thousand and One Nights. *Unknown, tr. fr. Arabic by* Mathers.
Renunciation, A. Vere.
She. Wilbur.
She Was a Phantom of Delight. Wordsworth.
Song: That Women Are but Mens Shadows. Jonson.
Song: "When lovely woman stoops to folly." *Fr.* The Vicar of Wakefield. Goldsmith.
Song of Songs, The. Heine, *tr. fr. German by* Untermeyer.
To the Eternal Feminine. Corbière, *tr. fr. French by* MacIntyre.
Tribute, The. *Fr.* The Angel in the House. Coventry Patmore.
What Women Are Not. *Unknown.*
Woman Is a Branchy Tree, A. James Stephens.
Woman Waits for Me, A. Walt Whitman.
Woman Who Understands, The. Appleton.
Woman's Arms. Anacreon, *tr. fr. Greek by* Cowley.
Women Are Worthy. *Unknown.*
Woodchucks. Clover for Breakfast. Frances Frost.
Woodpeckers
Legend of the Northland, A. Phoebe Cary.
Who's There? Frances Frost.
Woods *See* Forests
Words. *See* Language
Wordsworth, Catherine. To Catherine Wordsworth 1808–1812. Wordsworth.
Wordsworth, William
Bards, The. De la Mare.
Epilogue: "There's something in a stupid ass." Byron.
He Lived amidst th' Untrodden Ways. Hartley Coleridge.
Lost Leader, The. Robert Browning.
Memorial Verses. Matthew Arnold.
Next comes the dull disciple of thy school. *Fr.* English Bards and Scotch Reviewers. Byron.
Sonnet, A: "Two voices are there: one is of the deep." J. K. Stephen.
To Wordsworth. Shelley.
Wordsworth's Grave. William Watson.

Work. *See* Labor and Laboring Classes
World. *See* Earth
World War I
"And There Was a Great Calm." Thomas Hardy.
Anzac Cove. Leon Gellert.
Break of Day in the Trenches. Isaac Rosenberg.
Counter-Attack. Sassoon.
Dead Man's Dump. Isaac Rosenberg.
Dulce et Decorum Est. Wilfred Owen.
Evening Prayer. A. J. Burr.
Farmer Remembers the Somme, The. Vance Palmer.
In Flanders Fields. John McCrae.
In Memoriam: Easter 1915. Edward Thomas.
It's jolly/ odd what pops into. E. E. Cummings.
Other Possibility, The. Kästner, *tr. fr. German by* Kaufmann.
Private, A. Edward Thomas.
Rouge Bouquet. Joyce Kilmer.
Spring Offensive. Wilfred Owen.
Strange Meeting. Wilfred Owen.
These Fought. *Fr.* Hugh Selwyn Mauberley. Pound.
These Men. Leon Gellert.
Men Who March Away: Poems of the First World War (MMA). I. M. Parsons, ed.
World War II
Ballad of Banners (1944), The. John Lehmann.
Beach Burial. Slessor.
Bird, The. Louis Simpson.
Breaking. J. A. Allan.
Carentan O Carentan. Louis Simpson.
Carol with Variations. McGinley.
Chez-Nous. A. G. Austin.
Children's Crusade 1939. Brecht, *tr. fr. German by* Hamburger.
Christmas 1942. Irvin.
Death of an Aircraft. Causley.
Death of the Ball Turret Gunner, The. Jarrell.
Dunkirk. Nathan.
Eighth Air Force. Jarrell.
For Lover Man, and All the Other Young Men Who Failed to Return from World War II. Mance Williams.
Full Moon: New Guinea. Karl Shapiro.
Hero, The. Geoffrey Drake.
In Distrust of Merits. Marianne Moore.
In Westminster Abbey. Betjeman.
Kilroy. Peter Viereck.
Lunch on Omaha Beach. Noll.
May–June, 1940. Jeffers.
Memorial to the Great Big Beautiful Self-sacrificing Advertisers. Ebright.
Notes for a Movie Script. Holman.
Palermo, Mother's Day, 1943.
Scyros. Karl Shapiro.
Second Air Force. Jarrell.
September 1, 1939. Auden.
Silent Generation, The. Louis Simpson.
Spring Offensive, 1941. Biggs.
Sunday: New Guinea. Karl Shapiro.
V–J Day. Ciardi.
V–Letter. Karl Shapiro.
Veteran's Day of Recollection, A. Beecher.
War. Joseph Langland.
World's Fair, 1939. Flushing Meadows, 1939. Daniel Hoffman.
Worth, Charles Frederick. Crinolines and Bloomers. *Unknown.*
Wrens. Country Rhyme. *Unknown.*
Wrestling and Wrestlers
Wrestler, The. Stefan George, *tr. fr. German by* Luke.
Wrestlers. *Fr.* Polyolbion. Drayton.
Wyatt, Sir Thomas. On the Death of Sir Thomas Wyatt. Earl of Surrey.
Wye (river), Wales *and* England
Lines Composed a Few Miles above Tintern Abbey, on Revisiting the Banks of the Wye during a Tour, July 13, 1798. Wordsworth.
Meandering Wye. *Fr.* The Banks of Wye. Bloomfield.

Y

Yachts. Yachts, The. W. C. Williams.
Yaks
See also Yak *in* Title and First Line Index
Mad Yak, The. Corso.
Yarrow *or* Yarrow Water, Scotland
Braes of Yarrow, The. John Logan.
Yarrow Unvisited. Wordsworth.
Yarrow Visited. Wordsworth.

YEATS, WILLIAM BUTLER
 In Memory of W. B. Yeats. Auden.
 Ode: On the Death of William Butler Yeats. A. J. M.
 Smith.
 Winter Mask. Allen Tate.
 Yeats in Dublin, *sel.* Vernon Watkins.
YEW TREES
 Old Warder of These Buried Bones. *Fr.* In Memoriam
 A. H. H. Tennyson.
 Old Yew, Which Graspest at the Stones. *Fr.* In Memoriam
 A. H. H. Tennyson.
 Yew-Trees. Wordsworth.
YOUNG, BRIGHAM. Mormon Trail, The. Daniel Henderson.
YOUNG, LESTER. Lester Young. Joans.
YOUNGER, COLE. Cole Younger. *Unknown.*
YOUTH
 See also Youth *and* Youth and Age *in* TITLE AND FIRST LINE
 INDEX
 Adolescent. "Vincenzo Cardarelli," *tr. fr. Italian by* Cor-
 sano.
 Ah How I Like to See Great Power Pass. Betrand de Born,
 tr. fr. Provençal by Wilhelm.
 Apology for Youth. Sister Mary Madeleva.
 At Majority. Adrienne Rich.
 Ballade of Lost Objects. McGinley.
 Barefoot Boy, The. Whittier.
 Boy's Song, A. Hogg.
 Chestnut casts his flambeaux, and the flowers, The. A. E.
 Housman.
 Conversations. Gozzano, *tr. fr. Italian by* Golino.
 Crabbed Age and Youth. *Fr.* The Passionate Pilgrim.
 Shakespeare.
 Fern Hill. Dylan Thomas.
 Generous Years, The. Spender.
 How Soon Hath Time, the Subtle Thief of Youth. Milton.
 In a Spring Still Not Written Of. Robert Wallace.
 In an Age of Fops and Toys. *Fr.* Voluntaries. Emerson.
 Intimations of Sublimity. *Fr.* The Prelude. Wordsworth.

 Laid in My Quiet Bed. Earl of Surrey.
 My Lost Youth. Longfellow.
 New Generation, The. Schiller, *tr. fr. German by* Kaufmann.
 On the Instability of Youth. Vaux.
 Points of View. Amy Lowell.
 Sestina of Youth and Age. Gelett Burgess.
 Short Song of Congratulation, A. Samuel Johnson.
 Thieves. Perseus Adams.
 When I Was One-and-twenty. *Fr.* A Shropshire Lad.
 A. E. Housman.
 Wisdom. Hicky.
 Youth and Age on Beaulieu River, Hants. Betjeman.
 Youth Sings a Song of Rosebuds. Countee Cullen.
 Youth's Agitations. Matthew Arnold.
 Youth's the Season. *Fr.* The Beggar's Opera. John Gay.
 Young and Old. *Fr.* The Water Babies. Charles Kingsley.
YUKON TERRITORY
 Men of the High North. Service.
 Spell of the Yukon, The. Service.

Z

ZEBRAS. Zebra. "Isak Dinesen."
ZECHARIAH. Zechariah. Marlatt.
ZEUS
 Europa. Plomer.
 Leda. Rilke, *tr. fr. German by* Kaufmann.
 Leda and the Swan. Yeats.
ZOOS
 False Country of the Zoo. Garrigue.
 Jaguar, The. Ted Hughes.
 Woman at the Washington Zoo, The. Jarrell.
ZULU. Zulu Girl, The. Roy Campbell.